DATE DUE

DEMCO 38-296

THE CQ Researcher

formerly Editorial Research Reports

JANUARY — DECEMBER 1992

The right to make direct use of material contained in The CQ Researcher is strictly reserved to newspaper, magazine, radio and television clients of the service. Others wishing to quote from the reports for other than academic purposes must first obtain written permission.

Elements of The CQ Researcher

(formerly Editorial Research Reports)

Subscribers to *The CQ Researcher* receive 48 reports per year. Each report provides background on a current topic of widespread interest. Designed as a starting place for research, the reports define the issues and include a chronology and extensive bibliographies. A feature called "At Issue," which quotes opposing viewpoints from two experts, also is a part of each report.

The publication is available in various formats.

THE REPORT

The report, about 12,000 words in length, is issued on Friday four times a month. Each report treats a subject that is in the news or likely to be in the news in the near future.

BOUND REPORTS

The weekly reports are bound into quarterly paperback editions and an annual hardbound cumulation.

INDEX

A subject index to the reports is published each quarter and cumulated annually. The latest index may be found (in the blue pages) at the back of this volume.

For more information call Congressional Quarterly, 800-432-2250 or 202-887-8500.

CITATION

Recommended format for citing these reports in a bibliography, based on The Modern Language Association of America's *Handbook for Writers of Research Papers,* 3rd edition, follows.

Clark, Charles S. "The Obscenity Debate." *The CQ Researcher* 20 Dec. 1991: 969-992.

THE CQ Researcher

formerly Editorial Research Reports

CONTENTS   1992

T
H
E

CQ Researcher ®

PUBLISHED BY CONGRESSIONAL QUARTERLY INC., IN CONJUNCTION WITH EBSCO PUBLISHING

Term Limits

Will a recent setback derail the term-limit movement?

S ETTING TERM LIMITS FOR MEMBERS OF CONGRESS
has long been talked about, but proposals drew little
attention. In the last three years, however, a national
term-limit movement has suddenly grown up,
building on Americans' longstanding distrust of professional
politicians and recent complaints of abuses by members of
Congress. But term limits face a seemingly insurmountable
obstacle: Congress itself, which is unlikely to approve a
constitutional amendment restricting congressional tenure. To
circumvent Congress, term-limit supporters are trying a legally
uncertain strategy: initiatives to limit terms of congressional
delegations in individual states. Colorado voters approved a
12-year limit in 1990, but Washington state rejected a more
stringent measure in November. Now, efforts are under way to
place initiatives on the ballot in at least a dozen states.

 January 10, 1992 • Volume 2, No. 1 • 1-24

Formerly Editorial Research Reports

COVER ART: BARBARA SASSA-DANIELS

CQ Researcher

January 10, 1992
Volume 2, No. 1

EDITOR
Sandra Stencel

MANAGING EDITOR
Thomas J. Colin

ASSOCIATE EDITOR
Richard L. Worsnop

STAFF WRITERS
Charles S. Clark
Mary H. Cooper
Rodman D. Griffin

PRODUCTION EDITOR
Laurie De Maris

EDITORIAL ASSISTANT
Thomas H. Moore

GRAPHICS
Jack Auldridge

PUBLISHED BY
Congressional Quarterly Inc.

CHAIRMAN
Andrew Barnes

VICE CHAIRMAN
Andrew P. Corty

EDITOR AND PUBLISHER
Neil Skene

EXECUTIVE EDITOR
Robert W. Merry

PUBLICATIONS MARKETING/SALES
Robert Smith

EDITOR, EBSCO PUBLISHING
Melissa Kummerer

The CQ Researcher (ISSN 1056-2036). Formerly Editorial Research Reports. Published weekly (48 times per year, not printed the first Friday of any month with five Fridays) by Congressional Quarterly Inc., 1414 22nd St., N.W., Washington, D.C. 20037. Rates are furnished upon request. Second-class postage paid at Washington, D.C. POSTMASTER: Send address changes to The CQ Researcher, 1414 22nd St., N.W., Washington, D.C. 20037.

Term Limits

By Kenneth Jost

The Issues

Stop the average voter on the street and ask what he thinks about Congress, and the answer will be predictable: indecisive, overly partisan, beholden to special interests and oblivious to the problems of Americans who live outside the Washington Beltway. But ask the same person how he feels about his own representative in Congress, and you get a different answer: does a good job, stays in touch, helps the district and takes care of constituents' problems.

This public ambivalence toward Congress helps explain why federal lawmakers have been serving longer and winning re-election more consistently at the same time that Congress as a whole has been getting lower and lower ratings in the polls. To critics of Congress, however, the paradox proves that there is something wrong with the system. And many of these Congress bashers are now pushing a drastic political remedy: a fixed limit — as short as six years in the House — on how long any individual senator or representative can serve in Washington.

The idea of term limits for members of Congress has been popular for many years, but proposals drew little attention or debate until recently. In the last three years, however, the notion has grown into a national movement that, for a moment, seemed poised to sweep the country and perhaps force the biggest turnover on Capitol Hill in a century.

The idea's popularity stems from the longstanding American distrust of professional politicians and from a litany of complaints about abuses by members of Congress: pork-barrel politics, wasteful spending, junket-

eering and so forth. And to many Republicans, term limits seem to offer a way to toss out entrenched Democratic incumbents and weaken or end the Democrats' virtual 37-year congressional reign.

Advocates of term limits, however, faced a seemingly insuperable obstacle: Congress itself. Term limits, it was assumed, could be enacted only through a constitutional amendment that would have to be approved by two-thirds majorities in the House and Senate before being submitted to state legislatures for ratification. No one thought members of Congress would be the least bit inclined to approve an amendment to cut short their own political careers.

After inserting an endorsement of term limits in the 1988 Republican Party platform, however, supporters of the idea hit upon a creative way to circumvent the likely congressional roadblock. An individual state, they argued, had the right to restrict the tenure of its own congressional delegation without a constitutional amendment. Hence the strategy: Pro-

posals would be placed directly on statewide ballots to limit terms for both the state's legislators and members of Congress.

In November 1990 Colorado became the first state to vote on such a proposal — and it passed overwhelmingly. That vote, combined with approval of term limits for state legislators in California and Oklahoma, helped spark similar movements in more than a dozen states. Emboldened leaders of national term-limit organizations forecast a rapid succession of state votes for congressional term limits that would bring pressure on Congress to approve an amendment setting tenure limits for all its members.

Opponents, including many current and former members of Congress and a host of established political organizations and observers, contend that term limits would deprive Congress of many of its most capable members, shift power to the president and limit the right of voters to choose whoever they want to represent them in Washington. And they argue that, in any event, the change could come about only through a constitutional amendment, not by state law or initiative.

For most of 1991, however, opponents only presented their case against term limits in the media, doing little to defeat them or to deflect the growing public support for the idea. Polls recorded 70 percent approval of term limits and showed that support to be fairly consistent among Republicans and Democrats as well as different racial groups and diverse income and educational levels. And Congress sank even lower in public esteem in the fall when an audit showed that House members had been routinely bouncing checks at their own private bank.

So, as Washington state voters prepared to hold an off-year election on term limits for the state's congressional delegation, virtually everyone expected another landslide victory for the concept. But opponents — led by Speaker of the House Thomas S. Foley, a Democrat who stood to lose the eastern Washington congressional seat he had held since 1965 — mounted a well-financed campaign against the proposal in the last two weeks before the November vote.

They based their campaign on political realities rather than political theory. The state had benefited from the congressional delegation's seniority, they argued, but stood to lose political clout — and federal dollars — to bigger states like California if most of the delegation's members were barred from re-election beginning in 1994. The campaign worked: The state's voters rejected the term-limit proposal, Initiative 553, by 120,000 votes.

Term-limit supporters, however, professed to be encouraged by the closeness of the vote. Moreover, in future campaigns they planned to avoid the mistakes that they recognized in hindsight — chiefly, the initiative's retroactive provision, which affected current members of the delegation like Foley. After regrouping in Washington, D.C., they began strengthening a national network to push term-limit proposals at the local level. The plan was to support groups trying to put initiatives on the ballots in a dozen or more states in 1992 and 1994.

As term-limit supporters work to put their plans before the voters, here are some of the major issues that they, and opponents of term limits, face:

Are term limits needed to increase competitiveness in congressional elections?

Supporters of term limits say a restriction on congressional tenure is the only way to break the virtual

lock that incumbents have on their positions. As proof, they cite these stark statistics: The re-election rate for House incumbents has been above 90 percent for all but four election years since 1950 and exceeded 95 percent in the last four elections. Senate incumbents are more susceptible to changing political fortunes, but they have averaged 75 percent re-election rates since World War II.

Critics of Congress say that the lawmakers rack up these phenomenal job retention rates by milking every possible political advantage from their office — at the expense of the national good. They describe Congress as "a perpetual re-election machine" in which lawmakers exploit their free mailing privilege to send out self-serving propaganda, use committee positions to amass intimidating campaign war chests and employ office staff to store up political debts with constituent favors.

The only way to give voters a true choice at the polls, proponents of term limits say, is to force incumbents out of office at periodic intervals. "Voters are deciding," *Wall Street Journal* editorial writer John H. Fund explains, "that the only way they can ensure a real choice at the ballot box is to democratically guarantee that no one has a lifetime hold on an office."[1]

Political scientists and observers agree on the increasing power of congressional incumbency. "Nowadays, it is nearly impossible to topple a House incumbent, short of a major scandal or misstep," note political scientists Roger H. Davidson, a professor of government at the University of Maryland, and Walter J. Oleszek, a senior specialist in national government at the Congressional Research Service.[2]

But Democratic congressional leaders and other term-limit opponents say the re-election rates give a misleading picture about turnover in

office. Mainly, they note that incumbent members of Congress who seek re-election have always fared well. For example, the re-election rate for House incumbents has fallen below 70 percent only seven times in U.S. history. And the rate for Senate incumbents since World War II is only slightly higher than the figures for the three previous decades following ratification of the 17th Amendment, providing for direct popular election of senators.

What has changed, term-limit opponents note, is the percentage of lawmakers who seek re-election. Up to the Civil War, one-third or so of House members stepped down from their posts at each biennial election. Since World War I, however, the number of House members seeking re-election has been a fairly constant 90 percent. The percentage of senators seeking re-election has shown greater variability but has generally been above 80 percent for most of the 20th century.[3] Opponents of term limits say this increase in congressional careerism is the main reason behind declining congressional turnover rather than the claimed abuses of office that critics of Congress emphasize.

Despite the increasing congressional careerism, term-limit opponents make the second point that there is still substantial turnover in congressional membership over time because of resignations, retirements or deaths. As House Speaker Foley noted repeatedly prior to the vote in Washington state, House turnover was more than 60 percent during President Reagan's two terms in office and about 75-80 percent going back to the Watergate years in the mid-1970s. "There is this turnover," Foley said Oct. 27 on the NBC program "Meet the Press," "but people don't understand that."

Opponents' broadest point, however, is that term limits would restrict voters' rights to keep their represen-

Low Turnover Rate Sparks Term-Limit Drive

Supporters say term limits are necessary to break the virtual lock congressional incumbents have on their positions. They point out that the re-election rate for House incumbents (indicated by the solid line in the graph below) has averaged more than 90 percent since 1950. Others note that incumbents have always fared well; the re-election rate for incumbents has fallen below 70 percent only seven times in U.S. history. What has changed is the percentage of lawmakers who seek re-election. Up to the Civil War, many House members left office after one or two terms, which meant there was substantial turnover every two years. Since the late 19th century, more and more House members have made a career out of serving in Congress, leading to a significant increase in the overall House return rate (indicated as a dotted line in the graph).

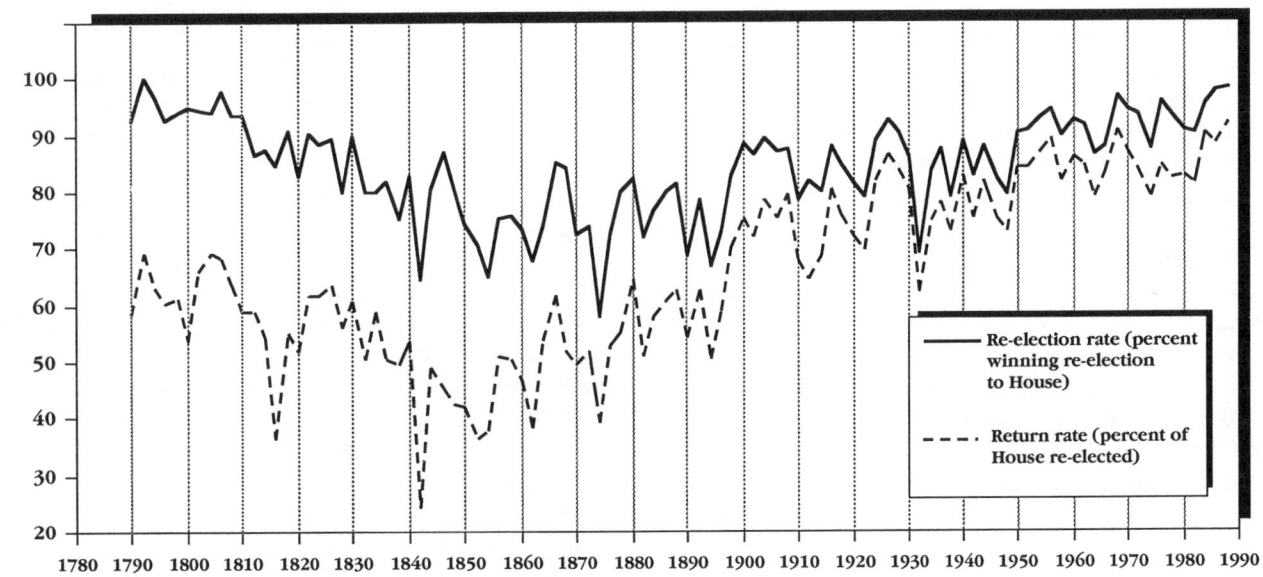

Re-election rate (percent winning re-election to House)

- - - Return rate (percent of House re-elected)

Source: Congressional Research Service, Re-election Rates of House Incumbents: 1790-1988, 1989

tative or senator in office if they want. "Restrictions on the freedom of citizens to run for office and to vote for candidates they favor — and to do so as often as they care to — betray two basic democratic principles: popular consent and majority rule," Victor Kamber, a Democratic political consultant, wrote in an anti-term-limit tract in the fall.[4]

Term limits are not needed to get incumbents out of office, Kamber continued. "Citizens who dislike their incumbents," he wrote, "already have the only tool needed to boot them out of office — the vote." In any event, he argued, term limits would not of themselves make congressional elections more competitive between the two parties. That goal, he

said, would require the redrawing of most congressional districts, more active recruitment of candidates by both parties and campaign finance reforms.

Many other opponents of term limits have also pointed to campaign finance reforms — especially the use of public campaign financing — as the key to improving challengers' chances in House and Senate races. But the political conservatives who dominate the term-limit movement strongly oppose public financing, especially when tied to spending limits. One group, Citizens for Congressional Reform, describes public financing as "irresponsible" and spending limits as "only a good deal for the incumbent."[5]

Would term limits improve the performance of members of Congress?

Term-limit supporters argue that restricting congressional tenure would produce a new breed of "citizen legislators" who would be more in tune with the day-to-day concerns of the public at large, less beholden to special interests and less susceptible to what editorial writer John Fund terms the "culture of ruling." At the same time, they say that these non-professional lawmakers would be less concerned about cultivating popular approval and more inclined to risk their constituents' disapproval to vote for what is really in the national interest.

"[T]he longer a legislator is in office, the greater the number of special interests he or she becomes associated with," Fund wrote in 1990. "[T]he longer a legislator works in Washington, D.C., or in a state capital, the more self-important that person becomes."

Unlimited congressional tenure is responsible, term-limit supporters argue, for an explosion in congressional staff — a fourfold increase between 1960 and 1980 alone[6] — and the preoccupation with constituent service and funneling federal dollars into a member's district or state. It leads lawmakers as well to devote more and more time to amassing large campaign treasuries that will scare off any potential challengers. In short, term-limit supporters argue, politically focused activities take members' attention away from substantive legislative work and lead them to substitute parochial interests for the greater national good.

While political conservatives and Republicans voice these views most frequently, they are shared by some on the opposite side of the political spectrum. "When you put people in Congress who don't have long-term ambitions, they may be much more likely to be courageous," says Mark P. Petracca, a liberal Democrat and a professor of political science at the University of California at Irvine. Hendrik Hertzberg, a senior editor of *The New Republic,* similarly envisions "a cohort of comparatively disinterested legislators, relieved from re-election pressures and free to consult their consciences as well as their pollsters and contributors."[7]

Opponents make several responses. Most broadly, they argue that term limits would force out of office some of the most respected lawmakers of both parties, depriving Congress of "the experience, institutional memory, wisdom and judgment needed to govern effectively."[8] Term-limit opponents point to congressional statesmen of previous eras

— John C. Calhoun, Henry Clay and Daniel Webster in the 19th century, and Arthur H. Vandenberg, Hubert H. Humphrey and Sam Ervin in the 20th century — as examples of lawmakers whose careers would have been cut short by term limits.

Opponents also contend that term limits would bring relatively few changes in lawmakers' behavior and that any changes that did occur would be more negative than positive. Lawmakers limited to 12 years in office — or six or eight years, as the term-limit movement is now advocating — would still probably be career politicians, not citizen legislators, the opponents contend. Lawmakers would still be politically motivated, but instead of focusing on their current position, they would be looking to move on — perhaps to the other body of Congress or to an elective position in state or local government.

Lawmakers who did leave government, the opponents argue, would gravitate toward lobbying or other government-related jobs that would force them to curry favor with special interests in their final years in office. "Instead of fresh-faced citizen legislators, we'd end up with men and women who knew that after 12 years they had to seek a new line of work, most probably with the very interests that are lobbying them," *Wall Street Journal* Washington Bureau Chief Albert R. Hunt notes in a column opposing term limits.[9]

As for the parochialism deplored by critics of Congress, term-limit opponents argue that lawmakers inevitably will give priority to the interests of their respective districts or states. In a term-limit world, Victor Kamber argued, legislators would still "do whatever is necessary and as often as necessary to protect their positions, just as they do today."

This natural tendency, the opponents contend, fits precisely with lawmakers' responsibility under the

Constitution to represent their constituents. As historian Arthur Schlesinger Jr. argues, the term-limit movement is "profoundly anti-democratic" in suggesting that legislators "will better serve the national interest when they ignore the wishes of their constituents."[10]

Less partisan analysts see the effects of term limits as more subtle and less certain than the pro or con forces. For example, Michael Malbin, a former Republican congressional staffer and now director of the Center for Legislative Studies at the State University of New York in Albany, argues that term-limited legislators will work to make a name for themselves beyond their present constituencies. That would mean playing to the press more, he says, while giving less attention to "unpublicized chores" that are needed to keep the institution running.

Mark Petracca somewhat agrees on the point, but views things more positively. He believes term limits would result in "a greater emphasis on accomplishing a smaller number of things," forcing "issue entrepreneurs" to build coalitions on an issue-by-issue basis.

The effect on party leadership is sharply disputed. Malbin foresees "much more wide-open fights for party leadership" that would operate to weaken the influence of party leaders. Hertzberg, on the other hand, argues that party leadership would actually be strengthened by undermining the "totally personal power bases" of long-serving senators and representatives and increasing the number of elections fought on truly national issues."

For his part, Petracca thinks change would be healthy. "Every time we've had a leadership turnover," he says, "we've had policy innovation. During those time periods, you shake the institution up, and they're able to get things done for a while that they couldn't before."

All these arguments are necessarily speculative, however, since prior to 1990, legislative term limits had not been on the books anywhere in the United States for 200 years. David Broder, *The Washington Post's* influential political reporter and columnist, cited that uncertainty — and the likelihood of unintended consequences — as a key reason for opposing term limits. "Conservatives, of all people, should be cautious about promoting such fundamental change without looking at the consequences," he wrote recently.[11]

Would term limits cause Congress to lose power to the president, lobbyists or its own staff?

Opposing sides in the debate agree on one likely effect of restricting congressional tenure: a reduction in the power of Congress compared with the power of the president and the executive branch. But they differ on the desirability of such a shift in power.

Term-limit supporters, especially the movement's conservative Republican core, view congressional "micromanagement" as a major cause of wasteful spending and government inefficiency. Senior lawmakers earmark appropriations bills to force expenditures on wasteful pork-barrel projects or mandate programs that the administration wants to cut. Thus powerful committee leaders — like House Appropriations Committee Chairman Jamie L. Whitten, a Mississippi Democrat now in his 26th two-year term — use their positions to impose their will on government agencies.

But opponents, many of whom regard the president as already too powerful, say an inexperienced Congress will be hampered in carrying out its legitimate responsibilities as an equal branch of government. "It is hard to imagine a greater boon for the Imperial Presidency," historian

The Value of Incumbency

The vast majority of House members seeking re-election in 1990 were either unopposed or faced challengers who did not have enough funds to mount effective campaigns.

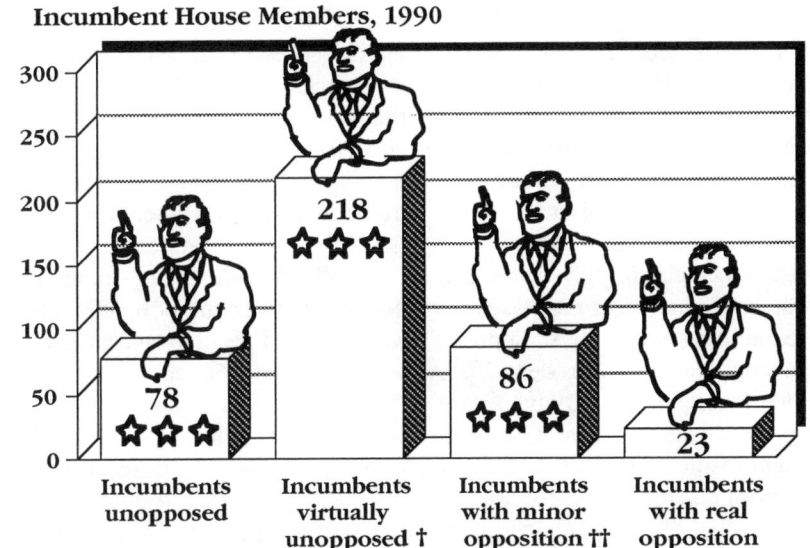

Incumbent House Members, 1990

Incumbents unopposed	Incumbents virtually unopposed †	Incumbents with minor opposition ††	Incumbents with real opposition
78	218	86	23

† *Challengers in these races raised less than $25,000.*
†† *Challengers in these races raised more than $25,000 but less than half the amounts the incumbents raised.*

Source: Common Cause

Schlesinger wrote, "than to purge Congress of experienced legislators who are specialists in issues, who know the workings of government and who remember where bodies are buried. What president would not prefer a revolving-door Congress filled with amateurs learning the ropes from scratch and condemned to vanish when they have gained the experience to be effective?"

The pulling and tugging between Congress and the White House has gone on throughout U.S. history, of course, with Congress in the ascendancy for most of the 19th century and the president gaining greater power for most of the 20th. Many Democrats viewed the increase in presidential power favorably when Franklin D. Roosevelt, Harry S Truman and John F. Kennedy were pushing liberal domestic policies. But they became disenchanted with pres-

idential power when Lyndon B. Johnson circumvented Congress to wage war in Vietnam. Meanwhile, Republicans shifted positions, too, endorsing expanded presidential power during the current era of divided government with Republicans in control of the White House and Democrats holding Capitol Hill.

Term-limit opponents argue that the Republicans' political impasse is the real driving force behind the term-limit movement. They note that the Republican Party endorsed term limits in its 1988 platform; that the first term-limit organization — Americans to Limit Congressional Terms (ALCT) — was founded by a Republican consultant, Eddie Mahe Jr.; and that the major spokesmen and financial contributors to the national movement have been Republicans. The motive, opponents say, is clear: to force out incumbent Democrats and gain the control of Congress that they have been unable to win at the polls.

Term-limit supporters respond by pointing to the Democrats within the movement, such as former Oklahoma state legislator Cleta Mitchell Detheridge, who chaired ALCT, and Washington state activist Sheryl Bockwinkel, who headed the campaign for Initiative 553. They also note that term limits would affect senior lawmakers of both parties. But their professions of bipartisanship seem a bit strained, especially in light of the pro term-limit statements in the past year by the nation's two highest Republican officeholders — President Bush and Vice President Dan Quayle.

Opponents also believe that term limits will result in unhealthy shifts of power from elected members of Congress to lobbyists and unelected congressional staff. They say that less experienced members of Congress would depend on staff and lobbyists for information and expertise and that change would run counter to the term-limit movement's stated goal of enhancing democracy and political accountability.

But term-limit supporters argue the effects would be precisely the opposite. Congressional staff members would turn over more frequently, they reason, and thus have less time or ability to take on political power. And, for the same reason, career lobbyists would have less time to forge the kind of personal ties with long-serving members of Congress that often accounts for their special access or influence.

Are state-imposed term limits for members of Congress constitutional?

Term-limit opponents vigorously insist that states have no power to restrict the tenure of members of Congress, and they have the weight of expert historical and legal opinion on their side. *(See stories, pp. 11, 15.)*

Historically, the opponents note that the Articles of Confederation restricted the tenure of members of Congress, but that tenure restrictions were dropped when the new Constitution was written in 1787. "Given that we have evidence that the framers did consider and did in fact reject term limits, it is much harder to make the case that term limits would be constitutional without an amendment," says Robert Katzmann, a visiting fellow in governmental studies at the Brookings Institution.[12]

Legally, term-limit opponents point out that the Constitution sets age, citizenship and residency requirements for House and Senate members and then goes on to state: "Each House shall be the judge of the elections, returns, and qualifications of its own members." As House legal counsel Steven Ross puts it, those provisions together show that no state can add a substantive qualification for election to Congress. And he and other term-limit opponents note that the Supreme Court upheld that interpretation in a 1969 case — *Powell v. McCormack* — upsetting an effort by the House of Representatives itself to bar Adam Clayton Powell from taking his office after the New York Demo-

crat's re-election to his congressional seat.[13]

Term-limit supporters contend the history and law are less clear. Historically, they minimize the Founding Fathers' rejection of tenure restrictions by noting that the Constitutional Convention dropped the proposal without any discussion as "entering into too much detail for general propositions."[14] They continue by saying that the Founding Fathers probably expected members of Congress to serve for fairly short periods and that congressional tenure was in fact much shorter in early U.S. history than it now is.

Legally, supporters of limits rely on a constitutional provision that gives the states authority to set the "times, places and manner of holding elections" for members of Congress. They contend that term limits fall within that definition and analogize to a number of Supreme Court and lower federal court decisions upholding other kinds of laws regulating congressional elections. Opponents say those decisions have nothing to do with term limits, and supporters acknowledge that the legality of state-mandated term limits is at best uncertain and sure to be challenged. ∎

BACKGROUND

Changes in Congress

Today's Congress would be virtually unrecognizable to its early members. Many of the changes are readily visible, of course. Washington is much bigger than it was when the city became the nation's capital in 1801. The federal government is much bigger, too, its powers greater and its role in international affairs vastly enlarged. Congress itself has grown. Since 1790, the House has ex-

panded from 65 members to 435, the Senate from 26 members to 100. And congressional staff, who numbered fewer than 200 as late as 1890, now total more than 18,000 serving the offices of members and committees.[15]

Less visibly, members' attitudes toward service in Congress have profoundly changed as well. In the early years, members viewed their time in the primitive capital as "splendid misery" — a thankless and temporary civic duty rather than an attractive or long-term career.[16] House members customarily served no more than four years, senators no more than six.

Continued on p. 10

Chronology

1700s *"Rotation in office" is supported by many political thinkers in England and America. The Articles of Confederation limit tenure of members of the Continental Congress, but the idea is dropped in the Constitution.*

1776
Pennsylvania Constitution, in effect from 1776 to 1790, limits tenure of state legislators.

1781
Articles of Confederation limit delegates to Continental Congress to three years' service over a six-year period.

1787
Constitution provides for two-year terms for House members and six-year terms for senators. Provision for unspecified restrictions on tenure of members of Congress is rejected by Constitutional Convention without debate.

1797
President George Washington leaves office after declining to seek election to a third term. The two-term tradition for presidents continues until Franklin D. Roosevelt runs for third term in White House in 1940.

———— • ————

1800s *Congressional service is widely viewed as unattractive duty for much of the century, and turnover in House is high. House members typically serve only one or two terms until after the Civil War, when longevity gradually increases.*

1846
Abraham Lincoln elected to House of Representatives after winning Whig Party nomination from incumbent with argument that "turnabout is fair play."

———— • ————

1900-1950 *Congress begins to assume its modern shape with the "institutionalization" of party rules and committee structures in the House and popular election of senators. Longer service by members of Congress is widely viewed as desirable.*

1913
States ratify 17th Amendment providing for direct election of senators.

1947
Congress approves 22nd Amendment to limit president to two four-year terms; states complete ratification in 1951.

———— • ————

1950-1989 *Interest in limiting congressional tenure increases, but no action is taken.*

1951
President Harry Truman proposes 12-year limit on congressional tenure, but proposal goes nowhere.

1978
Senate Judiciary subcommittee holds hearing on limiting lawmakers' terms, but no further action is taken.

1988
Republican Party platform endorses limits on congressional tenure.

1989
President Bush and Vice President Dan Quayle endorse term limits for Congress.

———— • ————

1990s *Term-limit movement wins approval of three state initiatives limiting state legislators' tenure — including one containing restrictions on congressional tenure.*

Sept. 18, 1990
Oklahoma voters overwhelmingly approve 12-year term limit for state legislators.

Nov. 6, 1990
Colorado voters overwhelmingly approve 12-year limit for members of state's congressional delegation along with limits for state legislators. Congressional limits, described by many as unconstitutional, would take effect in 2002. California approves limits for state legislators on same day.

Oct. 10, 1991
California Supreme Court finds no state or federal constitutional bar to limiting terms of state legislators and other state officials.

Nov. 5, 1991
Washington state voters unexpectedly reject Initiative 553, which would have retroactively limited terms of the state's congressional delegation. Term-limit supporters vow to get more initiatives on ballot in 1992 and 1994.

Continued from p. 8

And turnover in House membership was high. As Mark Petracca notes, it was rare throughout the 1800s for the percentage of first-term members serving in the House to be less than 40-45 percent.[17]

Petracca, a supporter of term limits, cites these data to show the wide acceptance of the notion of "rotation in office" during early U.S. history. As he explained to a conference on term limits at the State University of New York in Albany in October, many of America's revolutionary thinkers endorsed rotation in office as a way to give more people an opportunity to serve in government and as a "check on tyranny and the unbridled usurpation of political power."

The Articles of Confederation adopted by the 13 original states in 1781 included a limit on congressional tenure, but the limits were dropped when the new Constitution was written in 1787. Nevertheless, Petracca concludes that the frequent turnover in House membership over the next century demonstrates that rotation in office "remained a popular principle ... a principle with considerable practical effect, albeit much of it voluntary."

In her compilation of proposals to limit congressional tenure, Sula Richardson, an analyst with the Congressional Research Service, similarly points to the prevalence of the idea up to the Civil War. She notes that one House member introduced a proposal in the First Congress to limit representatives to six years' service during an eight-year period and to restrict senators to five one-year terms during a six-year period. But the House never voted on the proposal. Indeed, no term-limit proposal ever came to a vote in Congress until 1947.

Length of Service Increases

Congressional longevity began increasing after the Civil War. The average length of service doubled from four years to eight between the mid-1860s and the early 20th century. Congress had become an attractive career, and politicians and political thinkers alike encouraged the change in attitude. By World War I, Petracca acknowledges, support for rotation in office had declined to the point that the idea was hardly discussed, much less advocated.

Petracca attributes the change in attitude to the abuses of the spoils system — the practice of political patronage President Andrew Jackson created by extending the principle of rotation in office to administrative posts. "The corruption and intrigue associated with the spoils system at all levels of government eventually rubbed off on rotation," he writes. Congressional careerism was also encouraged by other factors, including the growth of the federal government, the emphasis of the reform-minded progressive movement on taking politics out of government administration and the development of what Petracca calls "the culture and norms of professionalism."

In addition, both Petracca and Richardson say that organizational changes described by political scientist Nelson W. Polsby as "the institutionalization" of the House of Representatives made longer service in Congress more attractive. Standing committees were established, party rules were written that limited the Speaker's discretion in making committee assignments and seniority was given greater importance in the selection of committee chairmen.

Meanwhile, reformers won ratification of the 17th Amendment in 1913 to provide for direct election of senators rather than selection by state legislatures, as the Constitution had originally provided. The campaign for direct election of senators spanned three decades and succeeded only after populists and progressives effectively forced the Senate to accede to popular will through the use of the newly created initiative process. Beginning at the turn of the century, a number of states passed initiatives establishing direct party primaries to nominate candidates for the Senate and, in some cases, binding state legislators to vote for the nominees. By 1912 — when senatorial primaries were in use in 29 states — the Senate bowed to the pressure and approved the amendment that was ratified by the states the next year.

Implications for Today

Today, term-limit supporters cite that history as a model of how to force Congress to approve tenure restrictions. Citizens for Congressional Reform envisions enacting term-limit plans like Colorado's in most of the 23 states that permit voter initiatives. Collectively, those states account for 46 of 100 senators and more than 40 percent of the House membership.

"As soon as half of the Congress is subject to short-term limits ...," the group's brochure states, "the attitude at the Capitol is likely to change." The combined pressure from the public and from members already subject to term limits would lead Congress either to pass a law limiting terms (by a simple majority) or to approve a constitutional amendment (by a two-thirds majority).

Opponents respond to this scenario by sticking to their position that binding term limits can be enacted only by constitutional amendment, not by state initiative or even by a congressional statute. As for the supporters' political strategy, opponents point to the defeat of the Washington state initiative to argue that the voters are likely to be turned around on the issue after a full-scale campaign.

Approval of the 17th Amendment may have contributed to increased turnover in Senate seats over the next several decades. The overall re-election rates for senators between

Continued on p. 12

Founding Fathers Wrestled With Term Limits

Thomas Jefferson favored limiting the time an individual could serve in Congress. In fact, term limits were contained in the nation's first charter — the Articles of Confederation — but dropped from the new Constitution. And the opponents of term limits, among them Alexander Hamilton and James Madison, made the same arguments in 1787 and 1788 that are being heard today.

The Articles of Confederation, adopted in 1781 after the American victory in the Revolutionary War, provided that "delegates" to the new Continental Congress would be elected by their respective state legislatures for one-year terms and be limited to three-years' service over a six-year period.

Three years later, controversy erupted when one delegate from Massachusetts, two from Delaware and two from Rhode Island "reached the end of their public service in Congress," according to historian Mark P. Petracca.† The Massachusetts and Delaware delegates retired quietly, but the Rhode Islanders fought to keep their seats. Fearing that the dispute would interfere with other business, delegates simply dropped the matter.

Petracca says support for rotation in office began to wane as the weakness of the Confederation became apparent and because of the forced retirement of six "popular and effective executives" in states with charters containing rotation provisions. But the idea had enough support that it was included in the so-called Virginia Plan presented by Edmund Randolph to the Constitutional Convention in 1787.

However, the convention spent more time debating the length of terms than the issue of tenure restrictions. The final decision — two-year terms — for the popularly elected House members reflected a compromise between one-year terms and three-year terms; senators, still to be chosen by state legislatures, were given six-year terms. As for tenure restrictions, they were dropped without debate along with other parts of the Virginia Plan that the delegates viewed "as entering into too much detail for general propositions." ††

Thomas Jefferson, serving as ambassador to France during the convention, wrote back to complain: "I ... greatly dislike ... the abandonment in every instance of the principle of rotation in office, and most particularly in the case of the President." ‡ And Anti-Federalists used the issue as one of many in arguing against the proposed Constitution during the 10-month ratification debate in September 1787 and August 1788.

In New York, the Anti-Federalist commentator who signed himself as Brutus wrote that rotation in office "would give opportunity to bring forward a greater number of men to serve their country" and would give those who had served "the advantage of becoming better acquainted with the condition and politics of their constituents." In Virginia, Richard Henry Lee warned, "Even good men in office, in time imperceptibly lose sight of the people, and gradually fall into measures prejudicial to them."

The arguments persuaded some states to propose amending the Constitution to include rotation for the presidency. But the Federalist forces sharply challenged rotation as interfering with the people's right to choose their officials, depriving the new government of experienced officials and reducing the incentives for political accountability.

"The people are the best judge of who ought to represent them," said New York's delegate, Robert Livingston, who said rotation would "take away the strongest stimulus to public virtue — the hopes of honors and rewards."

James Madison, perhaps the most influential figure in the convention, sharply stated the argument against limits in one of the *Federalist Papers,* the series of tracts he, Hamilton and John Adams wrote to support ratification of the Constitution: "A few of the members [of Congress] ... will possess superior talents; will by frequent re-elections, become members of long standing; will be thoroughly masters of the public business, and perhaps not unwilling to avail themselves of those advantages. The greater the proportion of new members ... the more apt they be to fall into the snares that may be laid for them." ‡‡

The arguments against rotation in office fit in with the Federalists' general view that a stronger national government was needed after the chaotic days of the Confederation. Their arguments carried the day, and President George Washington and the new Congress took office in 1789 with no tenure restrictions written into the Constitution. But Petracca and others argue that the idea remained popular — and point to Washington as proof.

His decision to retire after two terms set a precedent that was followed until President Franklin D. Roosevelt sought a third term in 1940. And Washington had anticipated his action as early as 1792. In a letter to Madison, Washington wrote: "The spirit of the government may render a rotation in the elected officers of it most congenial with the ideas [the people have] of liberty and safety."

---

† Mark P. Petracca, "Rotation in Office: The History of an Idea," paper presented at *Term Limits: A National Conference,* State University of New York at Albany, Oct. 11-12, 1991, p. 15.

†† *Constitutional Convention, The Debates in the Federal Convention of 1787,* p. 34, cited in Sula P. Richardson, "Congressional Tenure: A Review of Efforts to Limit House and Senate Service," Congressional Research Service, Sept. 13, 1989.

‡ This and other quotations that follow are from Petracca, *op. cit.,* pp. 19-24.

‡‡ *Federalist No. 53,* cited in Victor Kamber, "Modern Day Snake Oil: Term Limitations and Why They Must Be Defeated," p. 15.

Long Have They Served

Most of Congress' elder statesmen — members whose longevity has helped them win influential committee chairmanships and other leadership positions — are Democrats.

REPRESENTATIVES	YEAR ELECTED
Jamie Whitten (D., Miss.)	1941
Charles Bennett (D., Fla.)	1948
Jack Brooks (D., Texas)	1952
William Natcher (D., Ky.)	1953
Dante Fascell (D., Fla.)	1954
John Dingell (D., Mich.)	1955
William Broomfield (R., Mich.)	1956
Bob Michel (R., Ill.)	1958
Dan Rostenkowski (D., Ill.)	1958
Neal Smith (D., Iowa)	1958

SENATORS	YEAR ELECTED
Strom Thurmond (R., S.C.)	1956
Robert Byrd (D., W.Va.)	1958
Quentin Burdick (D., N.D.)	1960
Claiborne Pell (D., R.I.)	1960
Edward Kennedy (D., Mass.)	1962
Daniel Inouye (D., Hawaii)	1962

Source: Congressional Quarterly

Continued from p. 10
1790 and 1912 was 75 percent, but the rate fell below that figure in 16 of the next 20 biennial elections. Beginning in 1955, however, Senate elections became less volatile, with re-election rates above 80 percent in 10 of the next 19 election years.[18]

Meanwhile, House membership was becoming much more stable. Since 1916, about nine out of 10 House members have sought re-election in each biennial election. Re-election rates were typically in the 80 percent range over the next three decades and, beginning in 1950, have stayed almost uniformly above 90 percent.[19]

As Richardson points out, far from being controversial, this increase in congressional careerism was generally welcomed at first. "[P]ublic and congressional sentiment leaned toward encouraging rather than discouraging longevity in Congress," she writes. Eventually, the congressional seniority system would bring renewed attention to term-limit proposals, but not before a controversy over presidential terms.

Presidential Term Limits

In 1940, President Franklin Roosevelt broke the two-term precedent established by George Washington and ran — successfully — for a third four-year term. Roosevelt won again in 1944 but died just three months into his fourth term. In 1946, Republicans captured control of Congress and began working their revenge on Roosevelt by pushing a constitutional amendment to limit presidents to two terms as a matter of law, not just custom.

When the Senate was considering the proposed 22nd Amendment in 1947, Sen. W. Lee O'Daniel, D-Texas, offered a substitute to limit all elected officials, including members of Congress, to a single term of six years. The proposal was defeated by a vote of 82-1, with O'Daniel casting the only vote for it. Congress went on to approve the 22nd Amendment by comfortable majorities, and despite its partisan origins the amendment had broad backing as it gained ratification by three-fourths of the states by 1951.

The same year, Harry Truman became the first president to formally urge restrictions on congressional tenure: a 12-year limit on service in each house of Congress. As Richardson writes, the plan was viewed as an attack on the congressional seniority system. At the time — and through the 1960s — many congressional committees were chaired by long-serving Democrats from the one-party South who were more conservative than the national Democratic Party. Truman's proposal "stirred much controversy," says Richardson, but no action.

Implications for Republicans

For Republicans, the presidential term limitation has had an ironic effect. The only presidents to be affected by the two-term limit have been Republicans: Dwight D. Eisenhower, Richard M. Nixon and Ronald Reagan. And, as Democratic consultant Victor Kamber argues in his anti-term-limit tract, their lame-duck status limited their power while in office: "Since the adoption of the 22nd Amendment, no president — be it Eisenhower, Nixon or Reagan — has been as effective, purposeful, productive and as much in command during his second and final term as he was in his first term."

The woes of Republican presidents have been accentuated by changes in Congress. Even though the GOP has won seven out of the last 10 presidential elections, the Democratic Party has established unprecedented dominance on Capitol Hill. Democrats have controlled the House since 1955 and lost control of the Senate for only six years — 1981-1987 — during the same period.

Meanwhile, congressional careerism increased, along with incumbent re-election rates. As a result, Republican presidents have confronted a Democratic-controlled Congress whose many long-serving members have the experience and political ability to challenge administration policies.

Public Support Grows

Public support for congressional term limits increased during this period of divided government, but the issue received little attention until 1988. Gallup polls registered 49 percent approval of limiting congressional tenure in 1964 and 59 percent approval in 1977 and 1981.[20] More than 60 term-limit proposals were introduced between 1975 and 1988, but none was ever voted on in committee or on the House or Senate floor. And, as Professor Petracca notes, the issue was not mentioned in any of a number of major discussions of constitutional reform during the 1980s.[21]

In Congress, the number of proposals to alter congressional terms or tenure increased during the 1970s, reflecting what Sula Richardson calls "heightened interest in ... increasing the effectiveness and accountability of Congress." Many people in and out of Congress were advocating four-year House terms to reduce the time demands and political pressures resulting from the need to stand for re-election every two years. As Richardson's compilation shows, of the 70 congressional tenure proposals introduced in Congress from 1975 through 1980, 17 called for longer terms, another 23 included longer terms with tenure limits and 30 proposed tenure restrictions alone.

Key 1978 Hearing

The mixed motives for reconsidering congressional terms and tenure were reflected in a hearing held by the Senate Judiciary Subcommittee on the Constitution in March 1978 — the only congressional hearings ever held on tenure-restriction proposals. The Senate sponsors of term-limit proposals — Democrat Dennis DeConcini of Arizona and Republican John C. Danforth of Missouri — both argued that Congress would become more representative if its members were citizen legislators rather than professional politicians. But Rep. Berkeley Bedell of Iowa, a second-term House Democrat who was sponsoring a proposal combining a four-year House term with tenure restrictions for House and Senate members, emphasized the goals of sparing House members from frequent electioneering and reforming the seniority system as well as encouraging greater turnover in Congress.[22]

The panel of political scientists called as witnesses, however, unanimously opposed the term-limit proposals, saying they would reduce congressional authority and infringe on voters' freedom to choose their own representatives in Washington. Norman J. Ornstein, then a professor of political science at Catholic University and now a prominent Congress-watcher with the American Enterprise Institute, acknowledged the decreasing turnover in Congress to be "a worrisome problem" but said it should be solved "through the electoral marketplace" rather than by a constitutional amendment.

The subcommittee's chairman, Democrat Birch Bayh of Indiana, allowed DeConcini to preside over the hearing, but only after opening the session himself with the disclaimer that he had "serious reservations" about the idea. No further action was taken on any of the proposals.

Proposals to lengthen House terms to four years also went nowhere after being aired by the same Senate subcommittee in 1979.[23] Over the next decade, tenure-restriction proposals came to outnumber proposals for longer House terms, but none got as far as a hearing — much less a floor vote — in either the House or Senate.

In 1988, the Republican Party did endorse congressional tenure limits in its national platform. "We favor a constitutional amendment," the platform read, "which would place some restriction on the number of consecutive terms a man or woman may serve in the U.S. House of Representatives or the U.S. Senate." The provision, which was part of a package of congressional-reform proposals introduced by Rep. Thomas F. Hartnett, R.-S.C., received little attention, however, either at the party's convention or in the presidential campaign.[24] ∎

CURRENT SITUATION

A Hot Issue

The term-limit issue caught fire in 1989 and 1990, ignited by a core of Republican operatives and conservative activists in Washington and fed by growing public disenchantment with Congress and incumbents generally. Polls found more than 60 percent of the public in favor of term limits for Congress. In November 1990, Oklahoma, California and Colorado became the first states to set tenure limits for state legislators since Pennsylvania changed its Constitution 200 years earlier. Colorado's voter-approved initiative also included a provision to limit its two U.S. senators and six U.S. representatives to 12 years' consecutive service in either house.*

The fire's spread was slowed in 1991, however, when Washington state voters rejected a stronger, retroactive congressional term-limit provision that would have forced more than half of the state's delegation to retire after 1994. The result showed that voters could be persuaded by arguments on the practical advantages of congressional seniority — at least if they were strongly pushed by someone as prominent as House Speaker Foley.

But the opposing sides in the debate agreed that the voting signaled no broad change in public attitudes toward Congress. The vote also indicated that the results of a planned new round of term-limit initiatives in the 1992 and 1994 elections would depend on the course of campaigning state by state.

Supporters Organize

The organized term-limit movement can be traced to Republican political consultants Eddie Mahe Jr. and LaDonna Lee. They began to look at the issue in early 1989 and established Americans to Limit Congressional Terms (ALCT) that summer. As described by political newsletter editor Stuart Rothenberg, Mahe and Lee brought some Democrats into the organization's hierarchy to establish it as a bipartisan organization and then concentrated on serving as a national information clearinghouse on the issue rather than creating local chapters.[25]

A second Washington-based term-limit group, Citizens for Congressional Reform (CCR), was begun in November 1990 as a project of the free-market, anti-tax group Citizens for a Sound Economy and then spun off as a separate organization in Feb-

ruary 1991. Rothenberg says that it, too, concentrated on advocacy and clearinghouse functions but also worked more directly with state organizations on initiative campaigns, developing new proposals, gathering signatures to qualify them for the ballot and raising campaign funds. The group's effectiveness came into question during the Washington state campaign, however, after opponents attacked its heavy spending in that race and its financial backing from two billionaire oil executives with libertarian views, Charles G. and David H. Koch of Wichita, Kan.[26]

The strategy of using state initiatives, necessitated by Congress' evident unwillingness to approve a constitutional amendment restricting members' service, put the term-limit movement in the hands of state activists. It also meant that state legislators would be caught up in the debate. Despite their similar results, the three 1990 campaigns showed that the issue would take different courses in different states.

Action in the States

Oklahoma, the first state to vote on a term-limit proposal, had the simplest plan and the simplest campaign. The initiative was developed, promoted and largely financed by a wealthy Republican businessman, Lloyd Noble II. It provided for a lifetime limit of 12 years in the state Legislature — with service in either house counting toward the limit. Sitting members were grandfathered, and political custom limited the initiative's impact even further: Few Oklahoma legislators served as long as 12 years.

The initiative gained only limited attention before the election. Within the state, campaigning over a school-financing issue was more intense. Term-limit opponents waged a poor-

ly financed campaign only at the last minute. Nationally, the limited coverage of the issue was eclipsed by the budget battles on Capitol Hill and Iraq's invasion of Kuwait. But when Oklahoma voters approved the initiative with 67 percent of the vote, it ensured that greater attention would be given to initiatives on the ballots in California and Colorado.

Colorado's proposal was developed by state Sen. Terry Considine, a Republican who had unsuccessfully sought his party's nomination for the U.S. Senate in 1986. Considine established an organization he named Coloradans Back in Charge in the winter of 1989-90 to sponsor an initiative to amend the state's Constitution to limit state legislators and executive officers to eight years' service and members of Congress to 12 years.

Campaigning within the state was somewhat more active than in Oklahoma, though there was again little organized opposition. The state's congressional delegation divided evenly on the plan, with three Republicans and one Democrat (Rep. Ben Nighthorse Campbell) supporting it while three Democrats and one Republican (Rep. Joel Hefley) opposed it. National attention was focused on the campaign, and the constitutionality of the congressional limits was questioned in many quarters. But Colorado voters were undeterred and approved the initiative with 71 percent of the vote on Nov. 6, 1990.

Intense Fight in California

A more intense campaign took place in California over two competing proposals. One initiative, written by Democratic Attorney General John van de Kamp as part of what proved to be an unsuccessful gubernatorial campaign, included public financing of campaigns, contribution limits and ethics provisions along with a 12-year limit on service in the state Leg-

Continued on p. 16

---

*The 12-year limit, if upheld by the courts, would not affect the state's current congressional delegation until 2002.

Constitution Holds Key to Term-Limit Debate

If a state can prohibit an incumbent state officeholder or a recently declared "independent" candidate from running for Congress, why can't it set a term limit for its own U.S. representatives and senators?

That's what term-limit supporters ask when their opponents insist that the Constitution absolutely prohibits any state from limiting how long a member of Congress can serve.

But most experts say term limits flunk the constitutional test. House Speaker Thomas S. Foley, D-Wash., says state-imposed term limits are "patently, clearly unconstitutional applied to Congress." Conservative constitutional law expert Walter Berns, a professor at Georgetown Law School, agrees: "It would take a constitutional amendment to do it. I think that's abundantly clear." †

The arguments against state-imposed term limits come straight from the Constitution. Article I defines the qualifications — age, residency and citizenship — for serving in the House or Senate and then says each house "shall be the judge of the elections, returns and qualifications of its own members." As House legal counsel Steven Ross argues, these provisions make clear that states cannot add a substantive legal qualification for election to Congress.

The arguments on the other side have been set forth by two conservative Washington lawyers, Stephen Glazier and William H. Mellor, and by *Wall Street Journal* editorial writer John H. Fund.†† They insist that term limits are not an additional "qualification" for Congress but a permissible regulation under a separate constitutional provision that gives states authority to prescribe the "time, place and manner" of holding congressional elections. And they point to two U.S. Supreme Court decisions that have been used to uphold state election laws limiting who can and cannot run for Congress.

The first decision — *Storer v. Brown* in 1974 — upheld a California law that prohibited independent candidates in congressional races who had changed to independent status from a party affiliation within 11 months of the election. Glazier notes that a federal district court relied on the decision in the same year to bar an incumbent Pennsylvania congressman from running as an independent after having been defeated for renomination in a party primary.

The second Supreme Court ruling — *Clements v. Fashing* in 1982 — upheld a Texas law that prohibited incumbents in certain state offices from running for other state offices. The justices found the law to be a valid regulation of the conduct of state officeholders and rejected arguments that it infringed on the political rights of the officeholder or the voters. Glazier points out that the federal appeals court for Arizona cited the decision the next year in upholding the state's law that no incumbent state

officeholder could run for Congress.

House counsel Ross derides these arguments. He maintains that the Supreme Court's 1969 decision in *Powell v. McCormack* — barring the House's attempt to unseat Rep. Adam Clayton Powell Jr., D-N.Y. — clearly held that even the House and Senate have no authority to expand on the three qualifications for Congress set out in the Constitution.

Whether a state can impose term limits on its congressional representatives has not been ruled on by any court. Colorado voters approved a term-limit provision in 1990, but the 12-year limit will not affect the state's current congressional delegation until 2002. Washington state voters in November defeated a term-limit initiative that would have taken effect after the 1994 elections.

One prospect for an immediate ruling on the issue had been in Florida, where an eight-year congressional term limit is contained in an initiative being pushed for the November ballot. Florida law provides that initiatives can be reviewed by the state Supreme Court before going on the ballot. Opponents used this clearance procedure to urge the justices to bar the initiative on several grounds, including the federal constitutional issue. But just after Christmas, the justices declined to decide the question in advance of a vote.

Term-limit initiatives for state lawmakers also face an array of legal issues under state laws. In Florida, for example, the initiative being pushed for November was also challenged as a violation of the state's so-called single-subject rule because it combines limits for state legislators and Cabinet members, as well as members of Congress. In Washington, an old advisory opinion by the state's attorney general had concluded that the initiative process could not be used to alter legislative terms. The defeat of the initiative left the issue unresolved.

Term-limit proponents were encouraged by a California Supreme Court ruling in October upholding a term-limit measure approved by the state's voters in 1990. The 6-1 decision in *Legislature v. Eu* upheld Proposition 140 against a variety of state and federal constitutional arguments, including a claim that it infringed on voters' and officeholders' political rights. Supporters hope the lengthy opinion will be influential on courts in other states.

---

† Foley and Berns were quoted in "National Drive to Limit Terms Casts Shadow Over Congress," *Congressional Quarterly Weekly Report,* Oct. 26, 1991, pp. 3101-3105.

†† Stephen Glazier, "Each State Can Limit Re-Election to Congress," *The Wall Street Journal,* June 19, 1990, p. A20; William H. Mellor, "Term Limits Are Constitutional," *The Wall Street Journal,* Oct. 31, 1991, p. A22; John H. Fund, "Term Limitation: An Idea Whose Time Has Come," *Cato Institute Policy Analysis No. 141,* Oct. 30, 1990, pp. 10-13.

Continued from p. 14

islature. The other initiative — crafted by a Republican Los Angeles County supervisor, Pete Schabarum — was a much blunter attack on the Democratic-controlled Legislature. Appearing on the ballot as Proposition 140, it called for six-year limits on legislators' tenure, a 40 percent reduction in the Legislature's operating budget and elimination of the legislative retirement system.

The campaign became a bitter partisan fight. The state's Democratic Assembly Speaker, Willie Brown, raised $5 million to fight both initiatives. Brown and a fellow Democrat, state Senate President David Roberti, came under fierce attack from Proposition 140's backers, most of them from the Republican Party's right wing. Liberal interest groups lined up against Proposition 140, though some — including the state's chapter of Common Cause — backed the other term-limit measure, Proposition 131. When the campaigning was over, Proposition 131 was defeated, but the more stringent Proposition 140 won approval with 52 percent of the vote.[27]

Initiative 553

Term-limit proponents moved to capitalize on their three consecutive victories. They convened a national conference in Washington, D.C., to draw more media attention to the movement and a conference in San Jose, Calif., to bring together activists on the issue from around the country. About 150 persons from more than a dozen states attended the San Jose session, which was co-sponsored by Citizens for Congressional Reform and Considine's renamed group, Americans Back in Charge. Stuart Rothenberg calls the session "the most significant national event" in the movement because of the advice and encouragement pro-

vided to local pro-term-limit activists.

Among the people attending the San Jose conference was Sheryl Bockwinkel, a liberal Democratic activist from Washington state who had been involved in an unsuccessful 1990 challenge to one of the state's senior representatives in Congress, Democrat Norm Dicks. Dicks had the incumbent's normal advantages in the race: He outspent challenger Mike Collier 16 to 1 and refused to debate him. When Collier gained only 28 percent of the vote, Bockwinkel turned her frustration into a broad assault on incumbents. "There are only two parties left — the incumbents and the rest of us," she remarked later.[28]

The day after the 1990 election, Bockwinkel read about the Oklahoma term-limit initiative and, with an associate, formed a state organization — Legislative Initiative Mandating Incumbent Terms (LIMIT) — to get an even stronger measure on Washington's 1991 ballot. The proposal (eventually designated as Initiative 553) called for six- or eight-year limits for state legislators, two six-year terms for U.S. senators and three two-year terms for U.S. House members. Most significantly, the initiative would take effect immediately, with incumbents already over the limits required to step down after completing one more term. That would have meant that Speaker Tom Foley and five of the state's other seven representatives would have been required to leave office after 1994.

Bockwinkel used the contacts she made with national term-limit groups to consolidate her organization and to bring other state groups around to supporting her initiative. But by April, the petition drive had only $20,000 and nowhere near the 150,001 signatures needed to get on the ballot. At that point, Citizens for Congressional Reform stepped in with financial help — $177,000 over the next three months — and also

brought in a professional signature-gathering firm from California. With that help, the initiative gained the needed signatures by July and went on to survive a legal effort by opponents to block it from the ballot.

Organized opposition to the initiative was slow to develop. Leaders of "No on 553" traveled to Washington, D.C., in September to try to interest the state's congressional delegation in helping finance a $1.7 million campaign against the measure. "The delegation sent them packing," says David Olson, a political scientist at the University of Washington who followed the campaign. But "No on 553" did succeed in raising $300,000 from diverse sources that included the Philip Morris tobacco company, Kaiser Aluminum and the National Rifle Association along with labor, environmental and good-government groups within the state.

Media Blitz Warns Voters

The money financed a clever media blitz that warned voters that losing the seniority of the state's representatives would leave the state at the mercy of California's giant congressional delegation on the most vital of Western regional issues: water. "Term limits would give congressmen from Los Angeles the power to divert our water to California," one radio ad warned.[29] For his part, Foley noted the benefits that Washington had gained from such long-serving members as the late Sens. Warren G. Magnunson and Henry M. Jackson and warned of becoming subservient to California without the protection of such seniority.

A spokesman for Initiative 553 acknowledged before the election that the tactic was working, but outside the state virtually no one anticipated the final result. Voters rejected Initiative 553 by a 120,000-vote margin: 811,686 to 690,828. As David Gergen, editor at large at *U.S. News & World*

Continued on p. 18

At Issue:

Are term limits a bad idea?

GEORGE F. WILL

Syndicated columnist
FROM *THE WASHINGTON POST,* JAN. 7, 1990

mandatory rotation of members of Congress was required in the Continental Congress. ... The 1988 Republican platform endorsed the idea of limits on terms but flinched from specifying them. This year a dozen bills propose limits....

In the first House election after George Washington was elected president, 40 percent of incumbents were defeated, allaying anxieties about an entrenched "government of strangers." In the 19th century, 40 to 50 percent of House seats changed hands at each election, often through voluntary retirements: 19th-century travel and life in Washington boardinghouses were experiences easy to forsake. After the turmoil of the early 1860s, House seniority began to rise. Establishment of standing committees made seniority matter, and the expanding role of Washington made Congress matter more. But not until the turn of the 20th century did the average House seniority even reach five years.

What has changed since 1945 is the number of incumbents seeking reelection, ranging from a low of 382 (1978) to 411 (1956, 1966). Still, during Reagan's presidency, 55 percent of the House turned over; since 1974, 81 percent, since Speaker Tom Foley was elected in 1964, 93 percent. Average seniority in the House in 1971 was six terms; today it is 5.8. In today's Senate, the mean years of service is 9.8. A two-term limit would eliminate 20 senators....

Limits on terms would indeed prune much deadwood, but also would chop down the tall cotton: All great careers are long. [Some believe] the ratio of mediocrity (or worse) to excellence is too high to protect the former for the sake of the latter. Could be, but so could this: Limits on terms might confirm the axiom that all improvements make matters worse....

The idea of limiting terms recurs because there is deep in America's soul a streak of Jeffersonian sentimentality unsuited to today's Hamiltonian realities. Ideologically, Americans favor citizen-legislators because Americans like to think they favor a small central government comprehensible by amateurs who could not do much damage anyway. Practically, however, Americans are remorseless Hamiltonians, demanding an immense government ... and career legislators looking after their constituency interests.

Incumbents win because Americans despise Congress but love their particular congressman, who toils tirelessly to deliver services. Incumbents are entrenched by democratic choices, and Americans have a constitutional right to democracy, not good government.

GEORGE F. WILL

Syndicated columnist
FROM *THE ORLANDO SENTINEL,* OCT. 3, 1991

i have changed my mind.

Myriad forms of evidence have driven me to the conclusion that my opposition to limitations on the number of terms legislators — local, state and national — can serve is mistaken....

Colorado's enactment of limits last year rebutted the assertion that limits are merely a partisan ploy by Republicans who are unable to beat Democrats.... Colorado's senators and six members of Congress are evenly divided between the parties, and its legislature has Republican majorities in both chambers. Also, in Washington state, liberal Democrats are prominent in the drive [defeated in November] to enact limits more stringent than Colorado's: retroactive limits. Furthermore, 70 percent of Americans favor term limits.

Of course, an even higher percentage of legislators oppose them — even though the president and a majority of governors live with limits.

True, many great careers are long, and long legislative careers would become impossible. However, more talent is excluded from public service by clogging the system with immovable incumbents ... than would be lost by term limits.

It is said that interest groups will have magnified influence if "rookies" replace "experienced professionals" in legislatures. But why then, in 1990, did so many California interest groups fight so fiercely against the term limits passed by initiative? Because those interests have the incumbents (of both parties, who get the lion's share of campaign contributions) wired....

Increasingly, Congress creates problems its members then rush forth to "solve." Congress creates programs, which entail bureaucracies; then members act as ombudsmen, intervening on behalf of grateful constituents....

To govern is to choose. A legislature's primary duty is to budget. Careerism has rendered the professional political class unwilling to make hard choices — the only important kind....

There are many questions about term limits. How many terms are appropriate? Can states constitutionally limit the terms of their congressional delegations? If not, how can the political class be brought to heel?.... What will be the sociology of legislatures when service in them cannot be a career, only a leave of absence from real life? What kind of person, at what point in life, will run?

Consider this column fair warning: I shall often [return] to the case for term limits.

Continued from p. 16

Report, remarked the next day, "a wheel has come off the wagon of the term-limit movement."[30]

After the election, term-limit supporters tried to put the best face on the defeat. "As close as this one was, it has to be encouraging," ALCT founder Eddie Mahe told *USA Today.* Mary Ann Best, executive director of Citizens for Congressional Reform, told Congressional Quarterly: "We are not discouraged. I think it's going to spread like wildfire." But Speaker Foley countered: "I think the prairie fire went out, clearly in the state of Washington, and went out dramatically."[31]

Campaign Mistakes Identified

The mistakes made by the term-limit campaign were evident in hindsight. "The campaign was ineptly run," says Ed Crane, a major advocate for the issue at the Cato Institute. Supporters were outspent on media despite a 2-to-1 overall financial advantage, "acted as though the campaign was over a week before the election" and never responded to the California issue. (In fact, in the closing days of the campaign two prominent Californians were brought in to campaign for term limits: Republican Schabarum and former Democratic Gov. Edmund G. "Jerry" Brown Jr.)

Crane also believes the provision to apply the new term limits retroactively struck many people as unfair. "You don't want to make it retroactive because that's unfair to people in office," he says.

Opponents, however, contend that the same type of campaign that worked in Washington could be repeated in other states. "The campaign struck themes that, although they were state-specific, can be presented to voters across the country," says Rick Scott, political action director for the American Federation of State, County and Municipal Employees (AFSCME). AFSCME's state affiliate played a major role in putting together the "No on 553" campaign.

Scott identifies three issues as key to the defeat of the initiative: the term-limit movement's funding by "two right-wing billionaires ... who were, coincidentally, associated with an industry that wants offshore drilling," the restriction on voters' right to pick a candidate of their own choice and the seniority issue. While Foley may have been especially effective as a symbol of the costs of term limits, Scott says, "if you go across the country, you're going to find a lot of popular congressmen ... [and] you're going to have seasoned members of Congress in other states who have served states' interests well." ∎

OUTLOOK

New Initiatives Planned

Term-limit supporters say they hope to get initiatives to restrict state legislative and congressional tenure on the ballot in a dozen or more states in 1992 and 1994. Opponents have only a meager national organization. But the campaign in Washington shows that it is harder to get an initiative on the ballot and easier to defeat one than is commonly understood. And the initiative strategy is made more difficult because of its limited availability — only 23 states permit initiatives — and the strong doubts about the constitutionality of limiting congressional tenure.

After the defeat of Initiative 553, the two original national term-limit organizations — Americans to Limit Congressional Terms and Citizens for Congressional Reform — assumed lower profiles and allowed the Colorado-based group, Americans Back in Charge, to take the lead role in coordinating the state-by-state campaigning. Paul Ogle, the group's chairman, lists 10 states as among the most likely to have term-limit initiatives in 1992 or 1994 — Arizona, Arkansas, Florida, Massachusetts, Michigan, Missouri, Ohio, Oregon, South Dakota and Wyoming — and says efforts are under way but not as far along in Idaho, Maine and Montana.

The only national group established to oppose the term-limit movement was a skeletal clearinghouse and speakers bureau that took the double name Americans for Ballot Freedom: Let the People Decide. According to its executive director, Linda Rogers Kingsbury, the group was formally set up in May 1991 and raised about $100,000 — $30,000 of it from AFSCME. When fundraising failed to progress, the group scaled back and then virtually disbanded on Oct. 1.

Kingsbury, who now fields media calls from her home, says anti-term-limit forces are organized in some states and not in others. "It's a 'Catch-22' for the opponents," she explains. "There's really no reason to start expending money until you're dealing with something real." But, as the voting in Washington showed, opponents can exploit that situation by concentrating their spending in the final weeks of the campaign after supporters have depleted their resources. The Washington campaign also showed that state interest groups can be mobilized to fight term-limit measures and that the power of incumbency can bring in money at the national level as well.

Florida Next?

At the end of 1991, Florida was the state to watch. A group financed by an Orlando-area business executive and Republican Party activist, Phil Handy, was moving to qualify an eight-year term-limit initiative for state legislators, Cabinet members and members of Congress for the upcoming November ballot. Opponents, using a pre-election clearance procedure, asked the Florida Supreme Court to bar the measure from the ballot. They contended that the combination of offices covered by the measure violated the state's "single-subject rule" for initiatives. And they also asked the justices to rule that congressional term limits would violate the U.S. Constitution. Just before Christmas, however, the justices refused to block the initiative. They also refused to rule on the constitutional question unless the measure passed.

The constitutional issue remains a major question mark for term-limit proponents' effort to restrict congressional tenure. Most political and legal experts believe that the states have no power to limit congressional terms. Acknowledging the doubts, supporters have now begun discussing alternative mechanisms to achieve the goal, such as state laws to allow incumbents who have served past fixed limits to run only as write-in candidates or to require candidates to submit ballot statements on whether they will abide by term limits if elected.

With the defeat of the retroactive Washington state measure, however, no definitive legal ruling will emerge before a new round of state initiative drives. Supporters believe they can reach the ballot in many states and win most, if not all, of the contests. Opponents, however, say that the Washington vote means that the term-limit movement will not sweep to victory unopposed and that voters in other states will look at the opposing arguments more carefully than in the first round of campaigns in 1990.

Term limits have clearly become a volatile issue, though, and the movement seems unlikely to yield in the near future short of a decisive string of defeats at the polls.

Kenneth Jost is a free-lance writer in Washington, D.C.

Notes

[1] John H. Fund, "Term Limitation: An Idea Whose Time Has Come," *Cato Institute Policy Analysis No. 141,* Oct. 30, 1990, p. 8.

[2] Roger H. Davidson and Walter J. Oleszek, *Congress and Its Members,* 3rd ed. (1990), p. 59.

[3] David C. Huckabee, "Re-election Rates of House Incumbents: 1790-1988," Congressional Research Service, March 16, 1989, pp. 2, 5-13; "Re-election Rates of Senate Incumbents: 1790-1988," Congressional Research Service, May 15, 1990, pp. 7-12.

[4] The Kamber Group, *Modern Day Snake Oil: Term Limitations and Why They Must Be Defeated,* 1991, p. 8.

[5] Trudy Pearce, *Cleaning Up Congress,* Citizens for Congressional Reform Foundation, 1991, p. 94.

[6] Mark P. Petracca, "The Poison of Professional Politics," *Cato Institute Policy Analysis No. 151,* May 10, 1991, p. 3.

[7] Hendrik Hertzberg, "Twelve Is Enough," *The New Republic,* May 14, 1990, p. 26.

[8] Kamber, *op. cit.,* p. 21.

[9] Albert R. Hunt, "Congress's Terms: Just Fine As They Are," *The Wall Street Journal,* April 24, 1990, p. A18.

[10] Arthur Schlesinger Jr., "A Bad Idea, Whose Time Has Come," *The Wall Street Journal,* Oct. 29, 1991, p. A22.

[11] David S. Broder, "A Heavy Hitter Joins the Term-Limits Team," *The Washington Post,* Oct. 16, 1991, p. A27.

[12] Quoted in *Congressional Quarterly Weekly Report,* Oct. 26, 1991, p. 3102.

[13] Powell, who had represented Harlem for 22 years beginning in World War II, was a flamboyant and controversial figure, repeatedly prosecuted for tax evasion and other alleged offenses and held in contempt of court. He was also criticized for lavish travel at government expense and for various abuses of power.

[14] Pearce, *op. cit.,* p. 12. The quoted description comes from the Constitutional Convention's contemporary account, *The Debates in the Federal Convention of 1787,* p. 34, and is cited in Sula P. Richardson, "Congressional Tenure: A Review of Efforts to Limit House and Senate Service," Congressional Research Service, Sept. 13, 1989, p. 3.

[15] Davidson and Oleszek, *op. cit.,* p. 27. Mark Petracca says congressional staff totaled more than 25,000 as of 1985 — a figure that apparently includes related congressional agencies such as the Library of Congress and the General Accounting Office. See Petracca, *loc. cit.*

[16] The quoted phrase is from James Sterling Young, *The Washington Community: 1800-1828* (1966).

[17] Mark P. Petracca, "Rotation in Office: The History of an Idea," paper presented at *Term Limits: A National Conference,* State University of New York at Albany, Oct. 11-12, 1991 [the Albany Conference], p. 26.

[18] Huckabee, *Senate Re-election Rates,* pp. 2, 10-12.

[19] Huckabee, *House Re-election Rates,* pp. 10-13.

[20] Cited in Gary W. Copeland, "Term Limitations and Political Careers: Up, Down, In, or Out," paper presented at the Albany Conference, p. 6.

[21] Petracca, "Rotation in Office," p. 35 and accompanying footnote.

[22] U.S. Senate, Committee on the Judiciary, Subcommittee on the Constitution, "Congressional Tenure," Hearings, 95th Congress, 2nd session, March 14 and 16, 1978. All three proposals were in the form of proposed constitutional amendments. DeConcini's called for 12-year limits for senators and 14-year limits for House members; Danforth's called for 12-year limits for House and Senate members alike. Bedell's would have permitted three four-year terms for House members and three six-year terms for senators.

[23] U.S. Senate, Committee on the Judiciary, Subcommittee on the Constitution, "Four-Year U.S. House of Representatives Terms," Hearing, 96th Congress, 1st session, 1979.

[24] *1990 Congressional Quarterly Almanac,* p. 13.

[25] Stuart Rothenberg, "How Term Limits Became a National Phenomenon," *State Legislatures,* January 1992, p. 23. Rothenberg's article is an updated version of his paper, "Transplanting Term Limits: Political Mobilization and Grass Roots Politics," presented at the Albany Conference.

[26] *Ibid.,* pp. 24-25. See also *The* (Tacoma, Washington) *Morning News Tribune,* Oct. 13, 1991, p. A1.

[27] See Copeland, *op. cit.;* Charles M. Price, "Term Limit Politics in California," paper presented at the Albany Conference, pp. 2-6.

[28] See David J. Olson, "Term Limits Politics in Washington: The 1991 Battleground," paper presented at the Albany Conference. The quotation is from the *Seattle Post-Intelligencer,* July 18, 1991, p. A1.

[29] Quoted in the *Los Angeles Times,* Nov. 5, 1991, p. A24.

[30] Remarks made on PBS' "MacNeil-Lehrer NewsHour."

[31] *USA Today,* Nov. 7, 1991, p. A1; *Congressional Quarterly Weekly Report,* Nov. 9, 1991, p. 3262.

Bibliography

Selected Sources Used

Books

Davidson, Roger H., and Oleszek, Walter J., *Congress and Its Members,* 3rd edition, Congressional Quarterly, 1990.

This one-volume overview of the inner workings of Congress highlights the interrelationship between lawmaking and electoral politics. Although written before the 1990 and '91 votes on term-limit proposals, the book provides useful context and statistics for examining the opposing arguments on the issue.

Articles

Corwin, Erik H., "Limits on Legislative Terms: Legal and Policy Implications," *Harvard Journal on Legislation,* June 1991.

This student-written law review article critically evaluates the legal and policy arguments for term limits. The footnotes include valuable citations to political science literature as well as to the key court decisions in the debate over limiting congressional terms without a constitutional amendment.

Elving, Ronald D., "Foley Helps Put the Brakes on Drive for Term Limits," *Congressional Quarterly Weekly Report,* Nov. 9, 1991.

The article examines the reasons for the upset defeat of the Washington state term-limit initiative. CQ's earlier coverage of the issue can be found in the *Weekly Reports* of Feb. 24, 1990, Sept. 9, 1990, and Oct. 26, 1991, and in the *1990 Congressional Quarterly Almanac,* p. 14.

Fund, John H., "Term Limitation: An Idea Whose Time Has Come," *Cato Institute Policy Analysis No. 141,* Oct. 30, 1990.

Fund, a *Wall Street Journal* editorial writer, sets out the arguments in favor of congressional term limits in this report written for the libertarian Cato Institute.

Petracca, Mark, "The Poison of Professional Politics," *Cato Institute Policy Analysis No. 151,* May 10, 1991.

Petracca, an assistant professor of politics and society at the University of California at Irvine, uses history and current events to argue that term limits are needed to reduce "the professionalism and careerism that dominates American politics."

Rothenberg, Stuart, "How Term Limits Became a National Phenomenon," *State Legislatures,* January 1992.

Rothenberg, editor and publisher of *The Rothenberg Political Report,* describes the organizations in the term-limit movement and briefly notes the lack of organized national opposition. Rothenberg also wrote a general survey on the issue in advance of the Washington state vote (see *Nation's Business,* November 1991).

Reports and Studies

Congressional Research Service, *Congressional Tenure: A Review of Efforts to Limit House and Senate Service,* Sept. 13, 1989.

This 16-page report summarizes the history of proposals to limit the tenure of members of Congress from the American Revolution to the present and outlines opposing arguments. Two other Research Service reports provide valuable background on the issue: *Re-election Rates of House Incumbents, 1790-1988* (March 16, 1989) and *Re-election Rates of Senate Incumbents, 1790-1988* (May 15, 1990).

The Kamber Group, *Modern Day Snake Oil: Term Limitations and Why They Must Be Defeated,* 1991.

This 60-page advocacy tract by a Washington-based political consulting firm organizes the major issues in the debate over term limits, giving substantially more space and weight to arguments against limits.

Pearce, Trudy, *Term Limitation: The Return to a Citizen Legislature,* Citizens for Congressional Reform Foundation, 1990.

This 28-page advocacy tract was written by the public-information director for the pro-term-limits organization Citizens for Congressional Reform. Pearce also wrote a longer report, *Cleaning Up Congress: A Citizen's Guide to Congressional Reform,* detailing the current critique of Congress on issues ranging from political perks to congressional micromanagement of executive branch policy.

The Next Step

Additional Articles from Current Periodicals from EBSCO Publishing's Database

Addresses & essays

"Make it easier to throw the bums out," *Business Week,* **Nov. 19, 1990, p. 190.**

Editorial. Covers how the U.S. political system offers the voters little real choice when voting. Why incumbents nearly always win; the idea of term-limitation; carrying campaign funds to the next election.

Becker, G.S., "Reforming Congress: Why limiting terms won't work," *Business Week,* **Aug. 6, 1990, p. 18.**

Describes how only an unrealistic view of human nature could presume that taking away the right to continue at a job will improve performance. More likely, congressmen will take less interest in their work and will spend their time arranging future careers. Learning the ropes; political favors.

Borger, G., "Can term limits do the job?" *U.S. News & World Report,* **Nov. 11, 1991, p. 34.**

Discusses the debate over limiting congressional terms and highlights the more drastic measure that is needed for the current disorder in Congress. The example of voters in Washington state this week; the benefits of term limits; the idea of putting an end to imperial Congress; welcoming citizen legislatures; political scholar Mark Petracca's research on term limits; voters want change; the elimination of special interests.

Bremer, K. and Ciardiello, J., "Paul Wellstone," *Progressive,* **March 1991, p. 34.**

Presents an interview with U.S. Senator Paul Wellstone (D.-Minn.). Mandatory limits on terms in the Senate; ideas for campaign reform; evaluation of the president's energy proposal; perception of a new world disorder; more.

Buckley, W.F. Jr., "Send that congressman home," *National Review,* **Nov. 19, 1990, p. 60.**

Editorial. Analyzes a current trend toward limiting terms for state and congressional representatives. Why term limitation is gaining popularity; questionable constitutionality of the concept; recommendation that House terms be limited, with no restrictions on tenure in the Senate.

Clift, E., "Term limits won't work," *Newsweek,* **Nov. 11, 1991, p. 30.**

Opinion. Argues that despite their visceral appeal, term limits will not work. Probability that they are unconstitutional; support for term limits from wealthy conservatives who want to overturn the Democratic domination of Capitol Hill; why legislators would still by dependent on political-action committee (PAC) money, even if term limitation succeeds; comment of Michael Waldman of Public Citizen; more.

Crane, E.H., "Term limits for a citizen legislature," *Vital Speeches,* **Dec. 15, 1990, p. 147.**

Presents a speech by Edward H. Crane, president of the Cato Institute, delivered at the Conference on Term Limits, which deals with the need for legislative term limitation.

Epps, G., "Will power," *Nation,* **Nov. 18, 1991, p. 612.**

Comments on the change of heart of *Washington Post* columnist George F. Will who, after originally opposing limits on political terms of office, now agrees that there should be a limit on the number of terms members of Congress can serve. States that the treatment of Will's shift suggests that he and his fellow pundits have amassed too much political power. Outlook; column limits as a possible solution to the problem.

Evans, R. and Novak, R., "The best way to clean up Congress," *Reader's Digest,* **March 1991, p. 112.**

Argues in favor of limiting the number of terms lawmakers can serve in office as a way of cutting power and making Congress work better and more efficiently. Gives examples of abuse of power; cites public opinion poll results on term limitation. INSET: New faces needed (in Congress).

Greenfield, M., "Everyone vs. Congress," *Newsweek,* **Nov. 11, 1991, p. 80.**

Opinion. Argues that legislators still retain a negative image despite past reforms and questions whether term limits really can change anything. Three broad phases of Congress during the author's lifetime; the phoniness on view during the Clarence Thomas hearings; more.

Hertzberg, H., "Twelve is enough," *New Republic,* **May 14, 1990, p. 22.**

Examines a current proposal to institute a 12-year limit for members of Congress. Factors to consider; arguments in favor of the term limit; criticisms of the proposal; why the author believes the limit should be approved.

Kramer, M., "Congress: Twelve is enough," *Time,* **May 7, 1990, p. 34.**

Comments that bills masquerading as campaign reform are little more than incumbent protection acts. At least a third of the states are actively considering a constitutional amendment limiting service in the House or Senate to 12 years because Congress has developed into a "House of Lords, a ruling elite insulated from accountability to all but the interests who spend lavishly to win its attention."

Will, G.F., "A case for term limits," *Newsweek,* **Oct. 21, 1991, p. 76.**

States that being elected to Congress is regarded as being sent on a looting raid for one's friends. The argument about consolidating 3,000 Washington-area Central Intelligence Agency (CIA) jobs in Sen. Robert Byrd's West Virginia; Byrd's background; his rise to his current eminence through poverty; cost of truncating the careers of great legislators.

Debates & issues

"Dateline: Washington," *Nation's Business,* **February 1991, p. 9.**

Presents a series of brief articles about political news of interest to small business owners, including efforts of groups to limit congressional terms.

"How to make Congress more representative," *Congressional Quarterly Weekly Report,* **Oct. 26, 1991, p. 3166.**

Opinion. Discusses that most U.S. citizens feel the personality of Congress has little in common with the average American, and offers some examples for a more representative Congress. A study by the author of a sampling of public sentiment through a nationwide survey on radio talk shows; the variety of issue interests; the term-limit movement; percentage comparison between the average citizen and Congress on age, gender and race; details.

"Swift reply," *Broadcasting,* **March 11, 1991, p. 6.**

Announces that Tele-Communications Inc.'s video editorial endorsing 12-year limits on congressional terms caught the attention of Democrat Al Swift of Washington, a senior member of the House Energy and Commerce Committee. Swift sent a letter to TCI President John Malone characterizing the video as "ill informed" and "sloppy."

"Voter, heal thyself," *Economist,* **Sept. 29, 1990, p. 24.**

Explores the growing support among voters for several movements aimed at limiting the terms that state and federal representatives may serve. Reasons for the support; Americans for Term Limitation, the main pressure group behind the idea; call for a constitutional amendment limiting terms; who stands to lose from such an amendment; statistics on Congress; conclusions.

Barnes, F., "So you want to reform Congress?" *American Spectator,* **September 1989, p. 14.**

Lists the reforms the author feels are necessary to make Congress more representative of their states and districts, including eliminating PACs; raising the individual contribution limit from $1,000 to $5,000, or eliminating it altogether; free television airtime for candidates, some of it during prime time; a requirement that candidates spend campaign money on their campaigns, or lose it; and a limitation on congressional terms.

Barone, M. and Gergen, D., "The term-limit express," *U.S. News & World Report,* **Oct. 29, 1990, p. 30.**

Comments that the campaign to limit the number of years a politician can stay in office has received a major boost from the budget debacle in Washington and is heading toward possible victory this November in two states. Inflated war chests and weak challengers; tapping voter rage; California referendums; existing term limits on the president and 22 governors' offices; constitutional amendment.

Cook, R., "Incumbents hear rumblings of discontent at home," *Congressional Quarterly Weekly Report,* **Sept. 22, 1990, p. 3032.**

Stresses that although 1990 has forecast a "status quo" political year, in 1992 offices from president to dogcatcher will be on the ballot, and Democrats' control of the Senate and possibly the House will be at risk. Heat felt by incumbents for 1990 elections; Charles H. Keating Jr. affair; major poll shows voter dissatisfaction; time limits on legislative terms; ramifications for congressional voting in November.

Dwyer, P. and Jones, D., "Term limits: Popular revolt or extremist crusade?" *Business Week,* **Nov. 11, 1991, p. 40.**

Examines the term-limit referendum and whether or not voters disillusioned by political corruption are likely to approve the limiting of office terms for Congress. Cites Washington state as the stiffest in provisions; the movement's big money comes from rich, far-right individuals; Citizens for Congressional Reform (CCR); where does the money come from; Democrats' belief that the movement is a Republican plot; polls that show nationwide support for limits.

Dwyer, P. and Wildstrom, S.H., "'Incumbent' could be a four-letter word next year," *Business Week,* **Oct. 21, 1991, p. 45.**

Suggests that this has been a miserable year for Congress, and odds are rising that incumbents will face retribution, either by defeat at the polls or from a burgeoning crop of state initiatives to limit legislative terms. A series of scandals; painful retirements may come next year if voters turn on incumbents; the term-limitation movement; downside.

Kinsley, M., "Voters in chains," *New Republic,* **April**

2, 1990, p. 4.

Examines a proposed Constitutional amendment that would restrict U.S. representatives and senators to 12 years of service. Reasons for the suggested limit; opponents' response; key issues in the debate; author's argument against a term limit.

Montgomery, P., "Should congressional terms be limited?" *Common Cause*, July/August 1990, p. 31.

Discusses the pros and cons of limiting members of Congress to 12 years in office. Includes excerpts of comments on the issue of limiting congressional terms, from newspapers and a member of Congress.

Mukenge, M. and Johnson, C., "Out with the old?" *U.S. News & World Report*, Jan. 14, 1991, p. 62.

Presents a chart listing the most senior members of Congress who would be out of a job if a law were enacted limiting terms to 12 years.

Oreskes, M., "Bush backs move for limiting terms of U.S. lawmakers," *The New York Times*, Dec. 12, 1990, p. A1.

Says that President Bush has decided to push for a constitutional amendment to limit the number of terms for members of Congress. This idea is widely popular among voters but widely unpopular among members of Congress.

Payne, J.L., "Limiting government by limiting congressional terms," *Public Interest*, spring 1991, p. 106.

Argues that there is a strong case for limiting congressional terms and debates Nelson W. Polsby's assessment that term limitation is "destructive." Poll on how many people favor limiting terms; the issue of experience; competence; the Federal Election Campaign Act of 1971 and the creation of the Federal Election Commission in 1975; the National Taxpayers Union (NTU); more.

Salholz, E., Clift, E., et al., "There's got to be a better way," *Newsweek*, Oct. 22, 1990, p. 24.

Criticizes the current political system which all but ensures members of Congress lifetime tenure. Americans hate Congress but love their congressmen. Limiting the number of terms congressmen can serve; influence lobbyists wield in the current system; past attempts at reform and continued hope for reform.

Siegel, F., "Divided, we stand ... still," *Commonweal*, Jan. 11, 1991, p. 12.

Examines the struggle for national power between the executive and legislative branches as well as the Republican and Democratic parties. The demise of party government in America; term limitations on Congress.

State initiatives

" 'It's a slap of reality,' " *Time*, Feb. 18, 1991, p. 44.

Describes the effects on the California Legislature of Proposition 140, which mandated the cut of nearly 40 percent in the legislative operating budget and limits the terms of assemblymen (six years) and senators (eight years). Layoffs announced; predicted brain-drain; suffering constitutionally when rotating legislators will be unable to manage the checks-and-balances system; lawsuits vs. a slap of reality; legislative Speaker Willie Brown and his campaign against the ballot initiative.

"Out you go," *Economist*, Nov. 24, 1990, p. 22.

Reports that California voters approved Proposition 140, which sets strict limits on the number of years any statewide officeholder can serve. Voter anger; impact on politicians; Democrats are hardest hit; the Voting Rights Act; other consequences of the move; details; outlook.

Angelo, B., "An ethical guru monitors morality," *Time*, June 3, 1991, p. 9.

Interviews former Congresswoman Barbara C. Jordan, who is currently trying to clean up Texas government. Considers such subjects as, among others, how did your job come into being; don't most people think, cynically, that politics is a crooked business; would the proposed term limitation for Congress raise political standards.

Egan, T., "Campaign on term limits breeds unusual alliances," *The New York Times*, Oct. 31, 1991, p. A1.

Discusses the term-limit proposal on the Nov. 5 ballot in Washington state. Provisions of the proposal; backers on both sides of the campaign; grass-roots beginning.

Egan, T., "Building on mistrust of officials, voters in West try to limit terms," *The New York Times*, Sept. 23, 1991, p. A1.

Discusses the term-limit measure proposed in Washington state. If put on the ballot this November, it would throw out the entire congressional delegation three years after the vote. There are also backers for statewide referendums in 1992 or later in other Western states.

Elving, R.D., "National drive to limit terms casts shadow over Congress," *Congressional Quarterly Weekly Report*, Oct. 26, 1991, p. 3101.

Considers the term-limit movement that has swept the U.S. in 1991 with 45 states' introduction of term limits in various forms, according to the National Council of State Legislatures. The California Supreme Court's Oct. 10 upholding of that state's 1990 election law, which limits the length of state legislators' careers; Washington state's expected approval of Initiative 553 on Nov. 5; more. INSETS: A good idea?; *Powell v. McCormack* (1969).

Back Issues

Great Research on Current Issues Starts Right Here... Recent topics covered by The CQ Researcher are listed below. Issues dated before May 10, 1991, were published under the name of Editorial Research Reports.

Back issues are available for $4.00 (subscribers) or $7.00 (non-subscribers). Quantity discounts apply to orders over ten. To order, call Congressional Quarterly 1-800-432-2250.

Future Topics

▶ *Oil Spills*

▶ *Should Hunting Be Banned?*

▶ *America's Threatened Coastlines*

PUBLISHED BY CONGRESSIONAL QUARTERLY INC., IN CONJUNCTION WITH EBSCO PUBLISHING

Oil Spills

Increasing U.S. dependence on oil imports heightens risks to environment

C ALAMITOUS OIL SPILLS IN RECENT YEARS HAVE focused attention on the devastation the world's leading energy source can wreak on the environment. In Alaska, the 1989 grounding of the supertanker *Exxon Valdez* in Prince William Sound caused the worst U.S. oil spill ever and prompted Congress to pass stringent oil-pollution legislation. In the Persian Gulf, "eco-terrorism" committed by Iraqi forces during the gulf war left hundreds of wells burning and oil free-flowing out of Kuwait's refineries and oil-shipping terminals. With the United States and much of the global community increasingly dependent on petroleum moved by supertankers, oil spills will continue to threaten the environment for the foreseeable future.

  January 17, 1992 • Volume 2, No. 2 • 25-48

Formerly Editorial Research Reports

COVER ART: BARBARA SASSA-DANIELS

The CQ Researcher

January 17, 1992
Volume 2, No. 2

EDITOR
Sandra Stencel

MANAGING EDITOR
Thomas J. Colin

ASSOCIATE EDITOR
Richard L. Worsnop

STAFF WRITERS
Charles S. Clark
Mary H. Cooper
Rodman D. Griffin

PRODUCTION EDITOR
Laurie De Maris

EDITORIAL ASSISTANT
Thomas H. Moore

GRAPHICS
Jack Auldridge

PUBLISHED BY
Congressional Quarterly Inc.

CHAIRMAN
Andrew Barnes

VICE CHAIRMAN
Andrew P. Corty

EDITOR AND PUBLISHER
Neil Skene

EXECUTIVE EDITOR
Robert W. Merry

PUBLICATIONS MARKETING/SALES
Robert Smith

EDITOR, EBSCO PUBLISHING
Melissa Kummerer

The CQ Researcher (ISSN 1056-2036). Formerly Editorial Research Reports. Published weekly (48 times per year, not printed the first Friday of any month with five Fridays) by Congressional Quar-terly Inc., 1414 22nd St., N.W., Washington, D.C. 20037. Rates are furnished upon request. Second-class postage paid at Washington, D.C. POSTMAS-TER: Send address changes to The CQ Researcher, 1414 22nd St., N.W., Washington, D.C. 20037.

Oil Spills

By Mary H. Cooper

The Issues

A year ago, the world watched appalled and helpless as crude oil poured into the Persian Gulf, creating the worst oil spill in history. Its cause was also without precedent: not an accident but rather a purposeful act of wartime vengeance. Iraqi forces occupying oil-rich Kuwait opened the tiny kingdom's refineries and oil-loading terminals, dumping 250 million gallons of crude into the water. They also torched more than 700 Kuwaiti oil wells, releasing hundreds of tons of smoke and toxic chemicals into the air.

The gulf oil debacle must have seemed painfully ironic on Capitol Hill, coming as it did just months after Congress passed the Oil Pollution Act of 1990, the most sweeping U.S. statute ever to address the issue of preventing and cleaning up oil spills.

As the world's biggest consumer of oil, the United States had suffered many big spills. But none had caused the public outcry unleashed after the supertanker *Exxon Valdez* — its captain drunk and below decks, an uncertified third mate at the helm — ran aground in Alaska's pristine Prince William Sound. In the days that followed the March 24, 1989, incident, 11 million gallons of crude poured from the tanker's broken hull, causing the biggest spill in U.S. history.

Shocked by the television images of dying, oil-soaked birds and sea otters and by the confused and delayed cleanup, Americans pressed Congress to act. Among other things, the powerful new law it created makes tanker operators more directly liable for spills and outlines procedures to shorten the cleanup response time.

When it comes to U.S. oil pollution, however, the *Exxon Valdez* actually represents only a drop in the bucket. An estimated 80 million to 91 million gallons of oil spilled into U.S. waters from 1980 to 1986, mostly from tankers and oil barges. Since 1976 there have been eight "catastrophic" oil spills (involving a minimum of 1 million gallons) in U.S. waters resulting from tanker accidents, while an average of 18 "major" spills (involving the release of more than 10,000 gallons each) have occurred every year between 1978 and 1990.

But the toll could have been worse, considering the nation's tanker accident rate: From 1980 to 1988, tankers in U.S. waters were involved in 468 groundings, 371 collisions, 97 rammings, 55 fires and explosions and 95 deaths.[1]

Even after the *Exxon Valdez* spill had heightened awareness of the need for faster response to spills and better design and operation of tankers, the accidents continued to occur. In January 1990, an Exxon tanker ran aground off Staten Island, in New York. Neither the company nor the Coast Guard had sufficient equipment to contain the spill, and before suitable supplies reached the site from Alabama, more than 500,000 gallons of heating oil had contaminated the surrounding wetlands.

The following month, the *American Trader*, moored outside Los Angeles harbor, apparently sailed over its own anchor, puncturing the hull and spilling 400,000 gallons of crude. In June, fire broke out aboard the *Mega Borg*, a Norwegian tanker, as it transferred oil to a tanker off the Texas coast. Environmental disaster was avoided only because most of the cargo burned or evaporated.

No one knows exactly how much oil enters the world's oceans and waterways from all sources. The National Research Council puts the annual total at 3.2 million metric tons (986 million gallons) but concedes that other estimates range from 1.7 million to 8.8 million metric tons (524 million to 2.7 billion gallons).

Surprisingly, the available statistics show that oil spills resulting from accidents are far less significant than the oil that is released in small amounts each year from maritime shippers dumping bilge water, other oil-contaminated wastes such as refinery wastewater and municipal and industrial runoff. (See table, p. 34.)

Further, scientists generally agree that the release of carbon dioxide and other "greenhouse gases" through combustion of oil and the other fossil fuels — coal and, to a lesser degree, natural gas — causes far more damage to the environment than oil spills.* "Oil pollution tends to be a

---

*The Worldwatch Institute, a Washington environmental organization, estimates that global emissions of greenhouse gases have nearly quadrupled since 1950.

Trouble on the Tanker Routes

Serious oil spills caused by supertanker accidents generally occur along the main tanker routes (shown by the solid line in the map below). Accidents tend to occur most frequently on the routes serving North America and Western Europe, where industrialized nations are heavy oil users, and in the Persian Gulf region, source of much of the world's petroleum.

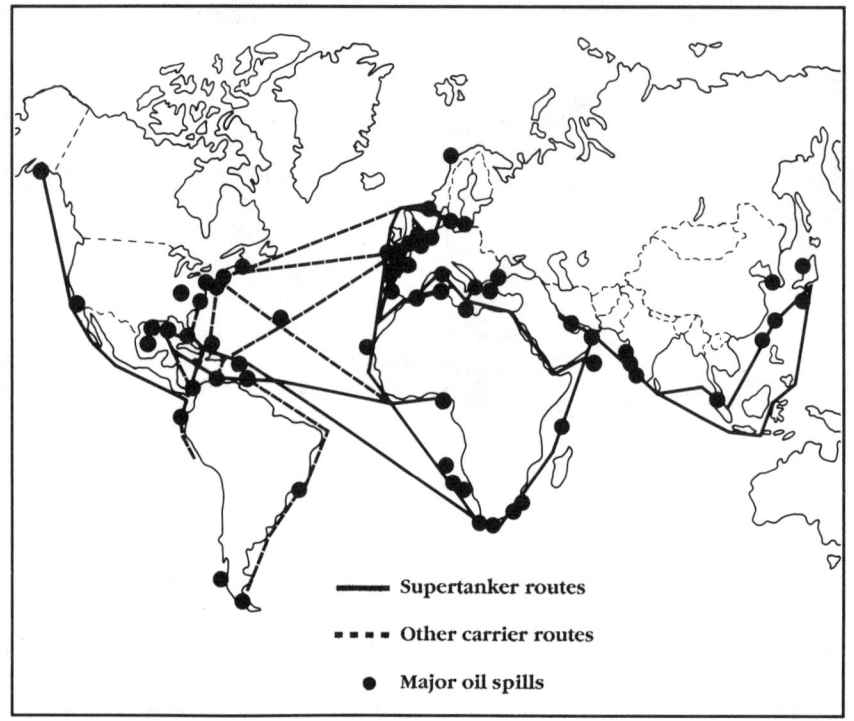

— Supertanker routes

- - - - Other carrier routes

● Major oil spills

Source: World Resources Institute

highly dramatic type of pollution and is highly visible and unfortunately photogenic," says Richard S. Golob, publisher of *Golob's Oil Pollution Bulletin,* a newsletter that monitors oil spills around the world. "The reality is that the major concerns related to oil use are not oil spills."

By their magnitude and impact on public opinion, however, the *Exxon Valdez* and the Persian Gulf disasters have provided the opportunity for scientists to better determine the environmental effects of oil spills and for policy-makers to come up with better ways to prevent them. As experts assess the problem, here are some of the key questions they are asking:

Do oil spills cause long-term harm to the environment?

When crude oil spills on land, much of it can be contained and recovered before it causes irreparable harm to the environment. But when it seeps into ground water and rivers, the oil spreads farther away from the site of the spill or leak, making it harder to remove from the environment and exposing plant and animal life to greater risk from pollution.

The greatest danger from inland oil spills and leaks is pollution of drinking water. Leaks from underground storage facilities are especially dangerous because they can pollute ground water for some time

before they are detected. While they are more quickly detected, spills into rivers pose a special problem both because the currents spread the oil quickly downstream and because communities often depend upon rivers for their water supplies.

Spills in the open seas often have little evident impact because the oil is quickly dispersed over vast areas. Oil contains volatile hydrocarbons such as benzene and toluene, which quickly evaporate, removing part of the spill from the water. The worst environmental consequences arise when oil spills occur in open water near coastlines. There, the oil disperses as quickly as it does at sea, making it hard to contain and remove, while at the same time it can come aground and contaminate beaches, marshes and inlets.

In such spills, the first obvious victims are birds and other aquatic wildlife that live along the shoreline. Birds cannot distinguish between clean water and an oil slick. When ducks, geese and other water birds land on oil-polluted water, their feathers become blanketed with oil, removing the air pockets that provide buoyancy and keep them afloat. Birds that do not drown often die after ingesting the toxic substance as they try to clean their feathers.

Spills can decimate bird populations if they occur along seasonal migration flyways, as occurred in the Persian Gulf. Despite efforts to clean birds following that spill, an estimated 20,000 to 30,000 cormorants, grebes and other waterfowl perished.[2] More than 36,000 dead birds were found after the *Exxon Valdez* spill, and those were thought to account for no more than 10 percent of the total. A similar fate befell otters, seals and other aquatic mammals. More than 1,000 dead sea otters were found in Alaska.[3]

Birds and mammals that survive the initial contact with spilled oil often starve because organisms further down the food chain perish upon contact with the oil, among them fish, shellfish, aquatic plants, coral reefs and grasses. The *Amoco Cadiz* spill off the coast of France in 1978 annihilated the region's oyster beds. Crabs and mollusks along hundreds of miles of Mexico's coastline in the Gulf of Mexico were killed following the 1979 blowout of *Ixtoc I,* an offshore oil well.[4]

Plants and animals that are already endangered are at high risk from spills. Because of their fragile wetland habitat, mangroves throughout the world have been depleted by pollution as well as deforestation. The Persian Gulf spill destroyed rare mangrove swamps on Karan Island off the coast of Saudi Arabia.

Why aren't current oil clean-up methods more effective?

There have been few breakthroughs in oil-spill technology in recent years. Even under the right conditions today's equipment is only partially able to clean up spills. Typically, floating booms are used to contain the spilled oil, while barges equipped with salvage pumps known as skimmers recover oil from the water's surface.

The amount of oil that skimmers can retrieve varies according to the oil's viscosity and weather conditions. They are more successful with small spills in ports and harbors than in the open sea.

According to the Office of Technology Assessment, however: "Even under ideal conditions, with equipment and trained personnel nearby and good weather, it is not realistic to expect to recover more than 30 percent of the oil from a major spill. Probably less than half that amount is more likely."[5]

But conditions are rarely ideal.

Many accidents occur when high winds and choppy seas make containment and removal all but impossible. Ice further complicates recovery. One of the biggest inland spills in the United States occurred in January 1988 when a storage tank near Pittsburgh collapsed, pouring 1 million gallons of diesel fuel into the Monongahela River. Because the river was frozen, most of the oil flowed downstream under the surface ice. Cleanup crews were able to string booms across the river downstream from the spill to contain part of the fuel and suction it off the surface into tanker trucks.

Under certain conditions, chemical dispersants, or detergents, can be effective in breaking up the slick before it reaches the shore. First used extensively in 1967 to clean up the 36-million-gallon spill from the *Torrey Canyon* off the southwestern coast of England, dispersants break up the oil into small droplets, which then sink to the bottom.

Unfortunately, the agents used in 1967 proved toxic, exterminating shellfish and algae over a large area. Since then, less harmful agents have

> **Even under ideal conditions, the Office of Technology Assessment notes, it is unrealistic to expect to recover more than 30 percent of the oil from a major spill. Probably less than half that amount is more likely.**

been applied, most effectively under foul weather conditions, which enhance their effectiveness in breaking up oil slicks.

Burning also removes spilled oil from water, sometimes cleaning up 90 percent of a spill. But because it pollutes the air with napthalenes and other heavy hydrocarbons, burning is only acceptable far at sea. It has been most frequently employed in the Arctic, where heavy ice rules out other cleanup methods.[6]

Time is of the essence in oil-spill cleanup procedures, especially in the marine environment. Just how fast a spill can spread depends on the strength and direction of water currents.

If the oil cannot be removed from the water quickly — often within hours — the cleanup effort may have to move to the shoreline. By that stage, however, plant and animal life is already jeopardized, and there are few effective ways to remove the sticky sludge.

The latest in shoreline cleanup technology was put to the test on the shores of Prince William Sound in 1989. One of the most promising techniques was bioremediation, the use of naturally occurring microbes to literally gobble up the contaminants. The technique was later used in the Gulf of Mexico following the 1990 *Mega Borg* spill.

The action of these oil-eating microorganisms, which under normal conditions act with sunlight to slowly break down petroleum hydrocarbons, can be accelerated by adding nutrients such as nitrogen and phosphorus to the contaminated surface. Exxon Corp. and the Environmental Protection Agency (EPA) spread nutrients along more than 150 miles of Prince William Sound shoreline. But the results of the effort are in dispute.

Oil Spills for the Record Books

Oil spills occur for mostly understandable reasons: fires, explosions, groundings, earthquakes, collisions and tank ruptures. Although the 11-million gallon Exxon Valdez spill was the biggest in U.S. history, it ranks just 36th on the international scene.

No.	Date	Spill	Location	Millions of gallons
1	1991	Kuwait Oil Terminals/Sabotage	Persian Gulf	252
2	1979-1980	*Ixtoc I*, Well Blowout	Mexico	139-428†
3	1983	Nowruz Oil Field, Well Blowout(s)	Persian Gulf	80-185
4	1983	*Castillo de Bellver*/Broke, Fire	South Africa	50-80†
5	1978	*Amoco Cadiz*/Grounding	France	67-76
6	1979	*Aegan Caption/Atlantic Empress*	off Tobago	49†
7	1980-1981	D-103 Libya, Well Blowout	Libya	42
8	1979	*Atlantic Empress*/Fire	Barbados	41.5†
9	1967	*Torrey Canyon*/Grounding	England	35.7-38.6†
10	1980	*Irene's Serenade*/Fire	Greece	12.3-36.6†
11	1972	*Sea Star*/Collision, Fire	Gulf of Oman	35.3†
12	1981	Kuwait National Petroleum Tank	Kuwait	31.2
13	1976	*Urquiola*/Grounding	Spain	27-30.7†
14	1970	*Othello*/Collision	Sweden	18.4-30.7
15	1977	*Hawaiian Patriot*/Fire	N Pacific	30.4†
16	1979	*Independenta*	Turkey	28.9
17	1978	No. 126 Well/Pipe	Iran	28
18	1975	*Jakob Maersk*	Portugal	25†
19	1985	BP Storage Tank	Nigeria	23.9
20	1985	*Nova*/Collision	Iran	21.4
21	1978	BP, Shell Fuel Dept.	Zimbabwe	20
22	1971	*Wafra*	South Africa	19.6†
23	1989	*Kharg 5*, Explosion	Morocco	19
24	1974	*Metula*/Grounding	Chile	16
25	1983	*Assimi*/Fire	off Oman	15.8†
26	1970	*Polycommander*	Spain	3-15.3
27	1978	Tohoku Storage Tanks, Earthquake	Japan	15
28	1978	*Andros Patria*	Spain	14.6
29	1983	*Pericles GC*	Qatar	14
30	1985	Ranger, TX, Well Blowout	Texas	6.3-13.7
31	1968	*World Glory*/Hull Failure	South Africa	13.5
32	1970	*Ennerdale*/Struck Granite	Seychelles	12.6
33	1974	Mizushima Refinery, Tank Rupture	Japan	11.3
34	1973	*Napier*	SE Pacific	11†
35	1980	*Juan A. Lavalleja*	Algeria	11
36	1989	*Exxon Valdez*/Grounding	Alaska	10.8
37	1978	Turkish Petroleum Corporation	Turkey	10.7
38	1979	*Burmah Agate*/Collision, Fire	Texas	1.3-10.7†
39	1971	Texaco Oklahoma, 120 miles offshore	North Carolina	9.2-10.7
40	1972	*Trader*	Mediterranean	10.4
41	1976	*St. Peter*	SE Pacific	10.4
42	1977	*Irene's Challenge*	Pacific	10.4
43	1972	*Golden Drake*	NW Atlantic	9.5
44	1970	*Chryssi*	NW Atlantic	9.5
45	1969	*Pacocean*/Broke in two	NW Pacific	9.2
46	1977	*Caribbean Sea*	E Pacific	9.2
47	1976	*Grand Zenith*/Disappearance	NW Atlantic	8.9
48	1976	*Cretan Star*	Indian Ocean	8.9
49	1969	*Keo*/Hull failure	Massachusetts	8.8
50	1969	Storage Tank	New Jersey	8.4

† *Fire burned part of spill.*
Sources: Office of Technology Assessment and news sources

Exxon claimed that bioremediation greatly sped up the natural cleaning process, but some scientists said it did little more than introduce more toxic materials to an already damaged environment.[7]

Although he agrees that the technique's effectiveness in Alaska is open to question, Richard Golob calls bioremediation "an excellent technique for degrading hydrocarbons" and "a very useful tool in the spill-control arsenal" once methods for applying and formulating the nutrients are improved.

The Alaska cleanup effort cast even more doubt on the effectiveness of another modern technique for removing spilled oil: pressurized hot-water cleansing of oil-covered sand and rocks. Blasting with 140-degree water proved effective in removing the oil, but two years after the cleanup operation, scientists found that the treated rocks were still devoid of plant and animal life, while rocks that were left to recover naturally hosted algae, limpets and hermit crabs.[8]

Despite the lack of notable progress in spill technology, there have been advances in coordinating responses to oil spills. Since the *Exxon Valdez* spill, when confusion and delays at the scene impaired the cleanup effort, the oil industry has created a regional response plan that it controls through the Marine Spill Response Corp. (MSRC), set up in December 1990.

But the new system is not yet ready to grapple with the major spills it was designed to handle. An MSRC office has been set up in Washington, says Bill Taylor, a spokesman for the American Petroleum Institute, which represents the U.S. oil industry. But it could take another two or three years, Taylor adds, before the corporation reaches its "full operational capability, based on ordering, supplying and getting the equipment in place." ∎

BACKGROUND

Tanker Development

Ever since "black gold" was first discovered to possess superior qualities as a fuel for lighting, heating and transportation, it has posed daunting shipping and storage problems. Because both crude oil and its refined products are liquid, oil spills have gone hand in hand with petroleum use.

Beginning in the 1850s, oil's main value was as a lighting fuel. Refined into kerosene, oil was to radically alter life in the United States and Europe. Even before Thomas Edison's invention of the incandescent light bulb three decades later, kerosene lighting allowed industrial production to continue in spite of darkness for the first time. But kerosene is highly volatile, and it often exploded during transportation and use.

Crude oil was less dangerous to ship than kerosene, but it nevertheless presented problems for early shippers, especially after major oil fields were discovered in Russia, the Middle East and East Asia in the late 19th century. Because the greatest demand for oil was in the industrial countries of Europe and in the United States, oil producers had to overcome many obstacles in shipping their product to market.

At first, crude oil from the Russian fields at Baku near the Caspian Sea was shipped in wooden barrels on boats, barges and railroad cars to markets in Europe, and onto ships bound for North America. But the land around the Baku fields was virtually barren, and there was little wood available for making barrels. Besides, the cost of transporting the oil barrels from the fields to market was high.[9] Wooden and metal barrels also were dangerous because they could split or fall over in rough seas,

often causing fires and explosions on board.

Ludwig Nobel, the Swedish developer of the Russian oil fields, designed the first oil tanker as a way to reduce transport costs by shipping oil in bulk. His initial efforts met with ballast problems, as the oil's movements inside the ship pitched it off balance in rough seas. Stability was improved by dividing the cargo bay into several tanks, and in 1878 Nobel's first bulk tanker began operating successfully in the Caspian Sea.[10]

By the mid-1880s, tankers carrying almost a million gallons of oil were crossing the Atlantic. In 1892, the first oil tanker passed through the Suez Canal bringing crude from the Royal Dutch Co.'s fields in the Dutch East Indies to markets in Europe. Completed in 1869, the canal, controlled by British and French interests, provided a vital passage between the Red Sea and the Mediterranean for oil bound from the Persian Gulf region and East Asia to the West.

From the beginning, oil tankers lost their cargo in storms at sea, by running aground and in collisions. Untold quantities of crude spilled into the sea during both world wars, when tankers became strategic targets for submarines out to disrupt fuel deliveries. During their siege of the U.S. Atlantic coast, German U-boats sank four times as many oil tankers as could be built during the first three months of 1942. The high losses prompted U.S. oil-transport companies in 1943 to build the Big Inch, the longest oil pipeline ever constructed, from the Texas oil fields to the East Coast.[11]

A Historic Change

In 1947, the United States crossed a historic threshold when it imported more oil than it exported. Ever since then, the country has depended on the safe transport of oil from overseas to meet its energy needs. In-

creasingly, oil fields in the Persian Gulf region became the world's primary source of fuel.

But less than a decade later, the United States and Western Europe were to discover their vulnerability to interruptions in foreign oil supplies. In November 1956 Egyptian President Gamal Abdel Nasser closed the Suez Canal to tanker traffic in an attempt to wrest control of the waterway from the British and French and expel the colonial powers from the Middle East.

Although the Suez crisis was resolved within a few months, and tanker traffic restored by the spring of 1957, this first major world oil crisis prompted the oil companies to seek alternative routes. This meant shipping crude around the Cape of Good Hope, adding thousands of miles to the trip from the oil fields to market. Tankers then in operation, little changed since Nobel's prototypes, couldn't hold enough oil to make the longer route economically feasible. Typically, they had a carrying capacity of 10,000 to 15,000 tons of cargo and supplies, contained in multiple storage compartments.

Although most industry analysts thought that significantly bigger ships would cost too much to build and operate, Japanese shipbuilders used efficient diesel engines and light, high-strength steel to produce the first supertankers. In the 1960s these behemoths, about five times the size of the older tankers, came to dominate the oil shipping business.[12] By 1975, the largest tankers — at some 400 meters long the largest moving objects ever made — could carry more than 500,000 tons of cargo and supplies.

Such enormous capacity enabled supertankers to slash shipping costs, encouraging the world's growing dependence on oil. And when the next oil crises did occur, in 1967, 1973 and 1979-80, transportation was no longer the issue, but rather pricing and availability.*

Supertankers and Spills

The development of supertankers brought about more than a revolution in oil transport. It also ushered in an age of unprecedented oil spills. Before the supertankers appeared, spills rarely caused measurable environmental damage, mainly because the small, early ships had less on board to spill. They also tended to carry refined petroleum products, such as gasoline and heating oil. Because these products are lighter and less viscous than crude, they tend to evaporate more completely. Much of the crude oil spilled from a supertanker does not evaporate but moves with the water currents, often reaching the coastline, where it causes the greatest environmental damage.

Some of the very technological advances that made it possible to transport large quantities of oil aboard a single vessel made that vessel more vulnerable to adverse weather or traffic conditions. A key to reducing transport costs is lowering the ship's weight. According to a study of tanker design by the National Research Council (NRC), efforts to reduce the weight of supertankers left "less margin to tolerate construction or maintenance errors or unusual operational events."[13]

One way shipbuilders reduced tankers' structural weight was to reduce the number of storage compartments. Although this change has not resulted in stability problems like those experienced with Nobel's early design, it does mean that a single

---

*The Organization of Petroleum Exporting Countries (OPEC) precipitated the crises, in 1967 and 1973 by imposing an embargo on the sale of their oil to the West, and in 1979-80 by cutting production, which caused oil prices to triple.

rupture in the supertanker's hull is likely to produce a much bigger spill than in an older tanker with smaller, multiple storage compartments.[14] On the other hand, concentrating large quantities of oil in fewer ships reduces the risk of collision.

There are about 6,000 oil tankers of all sizes currently in operation, about half of which are at sea at the same time. About a third of this global tanker traffic — carrying 1.7 billion tons (524 billion gallons) of crude oil and refined products each year — passes through U.S. waters. The busiest oil ports are Houston, which handles an average of five tankers a day, and New York, which receives an average of four tankers daily. Almost 100 million tons (31 billion gallons) of crude leave the port of Valdez, Alaska, the only major U.S. port for loading crude, each year. About the same amount of crude and refined products is received at New York, the U.S. port that handles the biggest volume of oil cargo.[15]

Much of the U.S. tanker traffic involves imported oil, which accounts for almost half the oil consumed in the United States. About a third of the imports come from the Middle East, a quarter from the Caribbean and a fifth from West Africa. The remainder is shipped from Northern Europe and Southeast Asia.[16] The heavy dependence of the United States on foreign oil means that most of the tankers that visit U.S. ports — 80 percent of the 1,500 different vessels in 1989, according to the National Research Council — are foreign. The exception to this trend is Valdez, where U.S.-flag ships dominate the oil trade by law.

Transfer Problems

Once a supertanker reaches its destination, the oil is pumped through on-board pipes to an onshore pipeline linked to storage tanks. However, because of their deep draft, supertankers often are

unable to enter harbors and unload their cargo directly at oil-storage facilities. Instead, they transfer all or part of their cargo to sturdy barges built to withstand impact against piers and tugboats, a process known as lightering.

Once enough cargo has been removed, the ships are often able to enter the port safely. Lightering is common in many U.S. coastal areas, including the Gulf of Mexico, San Francisco Bay and the lower Delaware Bay. Lightering is also required in many foreign oil destinations, where the water is too shallow for big tankers, including the Mediterranean, the English Channel, Argentina, the Middle East and East Asia.[17]

A more recent alternative to lightering is the deepwater port, an oil loading or offloading facility built away from shallow waters. Oil is transferred between onshore facilities and tankers through underwater pipelines. The only such facility in the United States is the 10-year-old Louisiana OffShore Oil Port (LOOP), 18 miles off the coast of Louisiana. Plans to build another deepwater facility in the gulf, 27 miles off Freeport, Texas, were recently put on hold because of high construction costs. If built, TexPort could receive almost a third of the 100 million tons (31 billion gallons) of foreign oil currently imported each year by the United States. The oil companies involved in the plan estimated at one point that it would take five years to complete the project at a cost of up to $1.3 billion.[18]

Causes of Spills

Early in the history of oil development, gushers accounted for much of the oil spilled into the environment. When a drill reaches oil far underground, tremendous pressure

Continued on p. 34

Chronology

1860s-1880s
Oil production spreads from the United States to other countries, including Russia and East Asia, spurring the development of oil tankers.

1861
The first transatlantic shipment of oil moves from Philadelphia to London, carried in wooden barrels aboard the 224-ton *Elizabeth Watts,* a square-rigged sailing vessel.

1878
Ludwig Nobel, "the Oil King of Baku," launches the world's first bulk-oil tanker, the *Zoroaster,* which carries Russian oil through the Caspian Sea and on to markets in Western Europe.

———— • ————

1960s
The era of large oil spills begins as supertankers enter into service, carrying bigger loads of crude oil than the smaller vessels that once dominated oil shipping.

1966
Japanese shipbuilders launch the world's first supertanker, the 210,000-ton *Idemitsu Maru.*

1967
The *Torrey Canyon* spills 36 million gallons of oil into the English Channel and onto coastal beaches. Detergents used to break up the oil slick prove toxic and decimate algae and shellfish.

1969
An oil well blows out in Santa Barbara Channel, polluting the beaches of Southern California and bringing the problem of oil pollution to public attention.

1970s-1980s
Despite the opening of new fields in Alaska, America continues to depend on foreign oil, increasing tanker traffic in U.S. waters.

1977
The 800-mile-long Trans-Alaska Pipeline links the Prudhoe Bay oil fields to Valdez, which becomes the country's leading oil-loading port.

1978
The *Amoco Cadiz* spills 68 million gallons of crude oil off France's Brittany coast.

1979
About 140 million gallons of crude, a world record for the time, spill into Mexican waters off the Yucatan Peninsula after an offshore well, *Ixtoc 1,* blows out.

1988
The Iran-Iraq War ends after eight years of fighting, during which 80 million gallons of oil spill into the Persian Gulf.

January 1988
One of the worst inland spills in U.S. history occurs when an oil-storage tank collapses near Pittsburgh, pouring a million gallons of diesel fuel into the Monongahela River.

March 24, 1989
The supertanker *Exxon Valdez* runs aground off the coast of Alaska and spills about 11 million gallons of oil into Prince William Sound, causing the worst oil spill in U.S. waters.

1990s
The **Exxon Valdez** *disaster focuses public attention on spill prevention and triggers passage of stricter legislation to improve the safety of tanker transportation.*

June 1990
President Bush announces a moratorium on offshore oil drilling for the Georges Bank, the Florida Keys, Oregon, Washington state and most of California until the year 2000. The same month, an explosion aboard the Norwegian tanker *Mega Borg* spills 4 million gallons of oil into the Gulf of Mexico off the Texas coast. Catastrophe is avoided when fire consumes most of the oil.

Aug. 4, 1990
Congress passes the Oil Pollution Act, the most sweeping U.S. law ever to address the problem of preventing and cleaning up oil spills. President Bush signs the bill into law Aug. 18.

December 1990
The oil industry creates the Marine Spill Response Corp. to improve the industry's handling of spills in U.S. waters.

January 1991
Iraqi troops begin sabotaging Kuwaiti refineries and oil-loading terminals, acts of "ecoterrorism" that spill 250 million gallons of crude into the Persian Gulf. The world's biggest oil spill devastates the coast of Saudi Arabia.

Sept. 30, 1991
Alaska Gov. Walter J. Hickel signs a $1 billion agreement settling federal and state claims against Exxon Corp. stemming from the *Exxon Valdez* spill.

Petroleum Sources of Marine Pollution

The biggest sources of marine petroleum pollution are municipal wastes and tanker operations, which each dump an estimated 216 million gallons per year into the water. Accidents involving tankers account for an estimated 123 million gallons of spilled petroleum.

Source	Million gallons per year
Natural sources	
Marine seeps	62
Sediment erosion	15
TOTAL	77 (7.8%)
Offshore production	15 (1.5%)
Transportation	
Tanker operations	216
Dry-docking	9
Marine terminals	6
Bilge and fuel oils	92
Tanker accidents	123
Nontanker accidents	6
TOTAL	453 (45.9%)
Atmosphere	92 (9.3%)
Municipal and industrial wastes and runoff	
Municipal wastes	216
Refineries	31
Nonrefining industrial wastes	62
Urban runoff	37
River runoff	12
Ocean dumping	6
TOTAL	363 (36.8%)
TOTAL, ALL SOURCES	986

Note: Percent totals are inexact due to rounding.
Source: National Research Council

Continued from p. 32

forces the oil up to the surface. Before the development of equipment to close off the drill passage, oil spewed into the air until the pressure fell and pumps took over the job of extracting the rest. Spills also occurred during transport to market, as wooden barrels often broke during rail or barge accidents.

The discovery of vast oil reserves in Russia, the Middle East and East Asia inevitably meant more spills at sea, as new tankers carried the oil to Western industrial nations and later to developing countries. By the 1970s and '80s, about 3.2 million tons (986 million gallons) of oil and refined products were entering the marine environment every year, according to a National Research Council study.[19]

Maritime transportation of oil accounted for almost half of this spillage, more than any other cause. *(See table above.)* Most of these spills, however, were not the result of tanker accidents but rather the intentional dumping of oil-contaminated water into harbors and open waters. For many years, tanker operators would clean out some of their emptied oil tanks in port before refilling them with ballast water for the return trip.

By 1985, improvements in tanker design and the development of international safety regulations had significantly reduced marine oil spills from tanker accidents to 0.4 million tons of oil and refined products, or only 13 percent of the 3.2 million tons polluting the marine environment each year. Larger amounts of oil continued to be released through municipal and industrial runoff and intentional dumping of petroleum-contaminated waste during maritime shipping operations.[20]

Offshore Platforms

But oil spills at sea continue to pose the greatest risk of accidental release of petroleum into the environment. In addition to tanker and barge accidents, offshore oil platforms have contributed to the pollution problem as the search for new sources of oil has extended into the open seas.

The biggest oil spill in history, before the Persian Gulf spill of 1991 claimed the record, occurred in 1979 at the site of the Mexican national oil company's 170-foot-deep exploratory well, *Ixtoc I,* in the Gulf of Mexico. A blowout, or underwater gusher, sent 140 million gallons of crude into the water, and some of it onto Texas beaches, before the well could be capped 295 days later.

Although blowouts and other accidents can be extremely hard to correct at extreme depth, offshore platforms operating in U.S. waters have been responsible for relatively few spills, none of them catastrophic. In response to the *Exxon Valdez* spill, however, President Bush in June 1990 suspended offshore drilling rights off the coasts of Oregon, Washington and most of California as well as the Florida Keys and the Georges Bank fishing grounds off the New England coast until the year 2000 to allow for further study of the environmental impact of offshore oil development.

Pipeline Leaks

Accidents at the wellhead, along pipelines and at storage tanks on land generally pose much less of a threat because they are more easily detected, and the oil does not spread far from the accident site unless it occurs near a river or other body of water. That's what happened in 1988 when a storage tank collapsed in western Pennsylvania, sending a million gallons of diesel fuel into the frozen Monongahela River. Impeded by the ice, cleanup crews couldn't prevent the fuel from flowing far downstream, where it contaminated the drinking water of several communities before it was brought under control.

Leaks from pipelines, both above and below ground, can be quickly detected by the fall in pressure they cause. The above-ground Trans-Alaska Pipeline, which carries about 1.5 million gallons of crude each day from the oil fields of Prudhoe Bay 800 miles to the port of Valdez, has suffered 14 leaks since it went into operation in 1977. None have been considered disastrous to the environment.

But locating the source of leaks in underground pipelines can be time-consuming. In December, for example, more than 400,000 gallons of fuel oil spilled from an underground pipeline that runs from Houston to New York City before the leak was found near Greenville, S.C. Two communities had to use alternative sources of drinking water for several weeks during the cleanup.

Underground storage tanks containing crude oil, gasoline and heating oil pose a special risk of serious spills because slow leaks can go undetected for long periods, tainting the groundwater for miles around. Although there are no firm figures, says Richard Golob, "There are about 1.5 million underground storage tanks in the United States, of which about 100,000 are leaking or start leaking each year."

Such leaks can have a lasting impact on affected communities. More than a year after a 250,000-gallon leak from an underground jet-fuel tank farm was detected in Fairfax County, Va., a Washington suburb, homeowners are still negotiating settlements with the Texaco affiliate that operates the facility. They are seeking compensation for the resulting loss in property values.

New Tanker Designs

Cleanup technology has made little progress in recent years, even after the high-profile disasters in Alaska and the Persian Gulf. Greater progress has been made in finding ways to keep oil spills from happening in the first place.

The main focus of preventive technology has been in the field of tanker design. Like the *Exxon Valdez,* the vast majority of supertankers and smaller oil barges now in operation have single-layer hulls; that is, only one layer of steel separates the oil from the water. If the force of impact from grounding or colliding with another vessel is great enough to breach the hull, oil from the cargo tank that is ruptured in the accident will spill into the water.

By surrounding the tanker's bottom or sides with a second skin and leaving an air space between the two, shipbuilders can greatly reduce the likelihood that an accidental rupture of the vessel's outer hull will release oil. Tankers carrying hazardous chemicals in U.S. waters are required to have double hulls, but oil tankers and barges have been exempt from this safeguard.

Double hulls and double bottoms are not ideal for oil tankers, however. For one thing, they cannot prevent all spills resulting from impact: It is unlikely, for example, that Prince William Sound would have been spared

had the *Exxon Valdez* been fitted with a double hull because of the high force of impact when the tanker ran aground. Oil companies resist double-hulled vessels because they can't carry as much as a single-hulled vessel of the same weight, and thus are more expensive to operate. Finally, double hulls present a safety risk. Crude oil and refined products contain volatile hydrocarbons such as toluene and benzene, which could collect in the space between the outer hull and the containment tanks. If ignited, these substances could cause an explosion resulting in loss of human life as well as the release of the ship's entire oil cargo.

Another preventive measure focuses on loading. Normally, tankers are filled to capacity. But this raises the pressure of the oil inside the cargo tank higher than the pressure exerted by the seawater that is displaced by the tanker. As a result, when a rupture occurs, the oil spills out until the pressure inside the tank falls below that of the surrounding water. If shippers were to fill tankers only to the point where the pressure exerted by the oil is slightly less than the pressure exerted by the surrounding water against the tanker's hull, a process known as hydrostatic loading, the oil would remain inside the tank even if it were ruptured.[21]

The Coast Guard and the National Academy of Sciences are currently studying design changes that would permit hydrostatic loading, double hulls and several other techniques aimed at preventing spills.

Proper Maintenance Crucial

Design changes notwithstanding, preventing oil spills will largely depend on proper maintenance. In the United States, monitoring the maintenance and operation of oil tankers and barges falls to the Coast Guard. According to Bruce Novak, manager of public affairs at the Guard's special staff office, created to write regu-

Europe's Cooperative Approach to Cleanups

All the world knows that Iraqi forces unleashed the biggest oil disaster in history when they sabotaged Kuwait's oil wells and loading terminals. Most Americans would probably rank the *Exxon Valdez* spill right near the Persian Gulf disaster in the list of all-time big spills. But they'd be wrong.

There have been many bigger oil spills in the world's oceans and harbors. In fact, the 11-million-gallon spill in Alaska ranks only 36th in the global rankings. *(See list, p. 30.)*

At least eight accidents have caused spills bigger than the Alaskan disaster in waters belonging to European countries, which, like the United States, depend on imported oil for most of their energy needs. When the *Amoco Cadiz* went aground off the coast of France in 1978, it released as much as 76 million gallons, which polluted vast sections of the Brittany coast. England suffered a similar calamity when the *Torrey Canyon* spilled 36 million gallons into its coastal waters in 1967.

These earlier accidents prompted several European countries to devise joint oil-spill response plans, which the congressional Office of Technology Assessment (OTA) sees as superior to the U.S. ability to cope with major spills.†

Like the United States, European countries hold the owners and operators responsible for cleaning up spills from land-based facilities, such as pipelines, storage tanks and offshore platforms. They must have plans and equipment on hand to cope with emergencies on their own. The government will intervene only when the owners and operators are overwhelmed by the magnitude of the spill. But virtually all European governments assume full responsibility for cleaning up oil spills from tankers and other seagoing vessels. The unlucky vessel's owner and insurer pay for the cleanup.

European governments also determine responsibility for marine-spill cleanups according to the location of the pollution. Shoreline cleanups normally are handled by local governments. Central government personnel and equipment come into play in offshore accidents and contribute to onshore efforts when the spill is too big for local authorities to handle.

France and Norway were found to be far better equipped and organized to respond to oil spills that threaten their coastlines than is the United States. France improved its response after the *Amoco Cadiz* accident, while Norway has developed elaborate plans for dealing with offshore oil fields in the turbulent North Sea.

> **To coordinate their cleanup efforts, Britain, Norway and six other countries maintain a regional spill-response team.**

Because of the large number of countries lining Europe's waterways, major oil spills often threaten more than one country. To coordinate their cleanup efforts, Britain, Norway and six other countries maintain a regional spill-response team. And the 12-member European Community (EC) keeps an inventory of all spill equipment in the community that could be deployed in a major disaster.

"On the whole," concludes the OTA study, "European countries are better organized than the United States, have more resources on which to draw and conduct more frequent training exercises."

---

† Office of Technology Assessment, *Coping with an Oiled Sea*, March 1990.

lations required by the 1990 Oil Pollution Act, the Guard requires the use of certain technical devices and construction methods to minimize the risk of spills. Among these are segregated ballast tanks that are to be filled only with seawater and not oil, in an effort to reduce wastewater pollution. In vessel operation, the Guard monitors the navigational equipment and attempts to enforce rules limiting the number of hours the crew can work.

"Any vessel that's built to operate under a U.S. flag has to have its plans approved by us," Novak says. "And foreign-flag vessels operating in U.S. waters must also conform to our requirements." This mandate over foreign vessels is significant because of the 6,609 oil tankers afloat today, only about 4 percent are registered in the United States. Further, about half these tankers have passed the normal 15-year retirement age. The General Accounting Office (GAO) cites evidence that these older tankers are disproportionately involved in accidents resulting in oil spills.[22]

In addition to monitoring tanker maintenance and operations in U.S. waters, the Coast Guard, through its 48 port offices around the country, inspects the facilities where tankers unload. Slightly more than half the spills in U.S. waters occur during the transfer of oil, usually through pipelines, into waterfront storage tanks. The Coast Guard has been unable to significantly reduce the frequency of these accidents. In 1988 alone, the amount of oil that was spilled at waterfront facilities totaled more than twice the amount that poured out of the 3-year-old *Exxon Valdez* the following year.

The GAO blames the Coast Guard for part of the accident problem. "Although the Coast Guard's responsibility to regulate and inspect waterfront facilities is adequately defined, the agency was not inspecting pipes between the dock and storage area," GAO reported in October. "These pipes pose a significant pollution risk because of their short distance from the water and their age. At one port we visited, for example, their average age was 30 years."[23]

Response Delays

One of the critical factors that transformed the *Exxon Valdez* accident from a containable spill to a catastrophe was the long time that elapsed between the tanker's grounding and the arrival of oil-containment and cleanup equipment. Once it arrived, 36 hours after the accident, disagreement over responsibilities among the myriad government agencies and private salvage firms at the scene added further chaos to the cleanup effort. Meanwhile, oil continued to pour into the sound, carried far from the ship by the strong currents and churned by the rough seas into a brown froth that covered the beaches. The slick eventually polluted 1,300 square miles of water and coastline.

Similarly, when the *Mega Borg*, a Norwegian supertanker, was rocked

by an explosion that set the vessel afire in the Gulf of Mexico in June 1990, the delayed response threatened to turn a containable release of oil into a bad spill. The fire broke out following an explosion of volatile hydrocarbons in the pump room while the tanker, too big to come to port, was unloading its cargo onto a barge. The vessel's owners lost precious time when they called on the U.S. subsidiary of a European cleanup firm, which imported firefighting equipment from the Netherlands, rather than using equipment that was available in nearby Houston. Booms to contain the spill had to be brought in from California, wasting further time.

Despite the heavy tanker traffic through the gulf, the oil-containment equipment that was available locally was inadequate for such a big spill.[24] Fortunately, less than 4 million gallons of the *Mega Borg's* 38-million-gallon cargo spilled into the water because most of the oil burned during the weeklong fire. Much of the spilled oil evaporated in the summer heat.

Fallout from Exxon Valdez
The *Exxon Valdez* disaster demonstrated the need for an industrywide system to quickly respond to oil spills. Until that accident, there was little interest in oil-spill policy because the system, which left the industry responsible for cleanup activities, had proved adequate for most of the numerous but relatively minor spills that had occurred in U.S. waters.

When a spill occurs, an on-scene coordinator from the Coast Guard determines whether the polluter is able to contain it. If the coordinator concludes that government help is needed, however, the responsibilities are less clear. Several federal agencies then have to agree on how to assign tasks, a time-consuming process that, as in the case of the *Exxon Valdez*,

can allow the spill to spread beyond anyone's ability to contain it.

When the on-site coordinator determines that government help is required, the Coast Guard must respond from one of only two "national strike team" bases, one in San Francisco, the other in Mobile, Ala. A third team is now being set up at Fort Dix, N.J., to serve the Eastern Seaboard.

By the time it was over, the cleanup operation following the 1989 accident cost Exxon some $2.5 billion.* To avoid future problems, the major oil companies set up the Petroleum Industry Response Organization in June 1989, based on five regional response teams that were to be equipped to contain and clean up major spills. Each team was to have at its disposal a full array of equipment as well as barges to receive the salvaged oil at the site, all at a five-year start-up cost to the industry of an estimated $400 million.

Oil Pollution Act

When the *Exxon Valdez* ran aground in March 1989, Congress had yet to pass legislation aimed at preventing oil spills and apportioning the financial liability for spills in U.S. waters. For 16 years lawmakers had been considering a measure to pre-empt the individual liability rules in force in the states. The negative publicity surrounding the Alaska spill, the delays in cleanup operations and the lack of adequate monitoring of tanker operations in Valdez pushed Congress to act. On Aug. 4, 1990, lawmakers

---

*Exxon Corp. also faced fines for its role in the spill. Under a settlement reached Sept. 30, 1991, Exxon agreed to pay civil and criminal penalties of just over $1 billion. The settlement was denounced as, in the words of Rep. George Miller, D-Calif., "not a sufficient punishment for one of the worst environmental tragedies in this nation's history." *(See At Issue, p. 41.)*

passed the Oil Pollution Act, which President Bush signed Aug. 18.

The act increases the financial liabilities of companies that handle and transport oil. The law holds liable only the owners and operators of vessels, pipelines and storage facilities, not the owner of the oil that is being transported. Depending on the nature of the facility responsible for the spill, tanker or storage owners and operators can be held liable for between $2 million (the liability cap for vessels weighing 3,000 gross tons or less) and $350 million (the maximum liability for onshore facilities and deepwater ports). The money is used to pay for the cleanup costs and the economic damages suffered by local inhabitants or other injured parties. Cleanup costs that exceed the spiller's ability to pay are to be covered by a $1 billion oil-industry fund.

When spills are the result of negligence, the responsible party must cover all the costs. The financial cost to spillers can be higher, however, as the new law allows states to determine their own liability levels as well as civil and criminal fines and penalties for violating state oil pollution laws. The Oil Pollution Act also increases some federal fines and penalties for negligence, endangerment and intentional violations.

But the act goes far beyond the liability issue and includes many provisions aimed at preventing spills from occurring. Responding to public outrage over the fact that the captain of the *Exxon Valdez* was intoxicated at the time of the accident, lawmakers included tough penalties against reckless, drunken or drugged seamen and set new rules limiting the number of hours tanker crews can work. They required changes in vessel construction, notably the use of double hulls or bottoms on all oil-carrying vessels within 25 years.

Also under the act, new oil-spill response procedures will go into effect as soon as the Coast Guard

writes the regulations. The law requires all oil tankers and barges to carry enough equipment to start cleanup operations at the first sign of a spill. Further, each tanker must have a response plan to deal with accidents.

The law calls for a National Response System, headquartered in Elizabeth City, N.C., to administer the Coast Guard's strike teams, provide logistical support to spill emergencies and keep a national inventory of all government and private response equipment. It calls for about $15 mil-

lion in new Coast Guard equipment to be permanently deployed in 19 sites around the country. *(See map, p. 39.)*

To avoid the confusion that delayed the cleanup effort in Prince William Sound, the law more clearly defines the responsibilities and authority of the Coast Guard's on-scene coordinator and requires the owners and operators of oil vessels and storage facilities — the potential spillers — to develop "worst-case" spill plans and submit them for approval to the Coast Guard. ∎

CURRENT SITUATION

The Oil Industry Acts

As lawmakers were drawing up the strict regulations required by the Oil Pollution Act, the oil industry concluded that earlier efforts to improve its own response to oil spills was inadequate. Hence it expanded on the Petroleum Industry Response Organization to include not only oil companies but also the shippers and pipeline operators that fall under the new law's liability provisions.

Renamed the Marine Spill Response Corporation (MSRC), the private, nonprofit group was set up in December 1990. The Washington-based corporation was given the task of coordinating future spill cleanup efforts through five regional oil-spill response centers, each designed to make a "best-effort" response to very large spills.

The industry decided to concentrate its efforts on catastrophic spills, defined as one the size of the *Exxon Valdez* or any other spill that local response teams are unable to handle.

"The other spills are being handled in a relatively satisfactory manner," says Steve Duca, an MSRC vice president. The industry response group is also limiting its focus to the maritime environment.

"We're not going to be in the river systems, and we're not going to be in the Great Lakes," Duca says. Nor, he adds, will MSRC set up operations in Alaska. "Alaska has the equivalent of our regional capability out of Valdez."

From the oil and shipping industry's viewpoint, the Oil Pollution Act is revolutionizing the way oil cargo is treated in the United States. The requirement that all tankers as well as onshore and offshore facilities have a plan to deal with worst-case spills is the key to the new law's thrust.

"The message is that the polluter will pay," Duca says. "It comes from a general thesis that if conditions are stringent enough and the penalties are harsh enough, that is an extremely good way to ensure that there will not be a lax performance" by oil shippers and handlers. "It also supports another truism, that those who derive profit from the enterprise have an obligation to assure that any costs associated with their operations from a spill are borne by them."

Coast Guard and Industry Gear Up to Battle Spills

Spurred by the Exxon Valdez *spill, the oil industry created the Marine Spill Response Corp. Its response teams and equipment sites will be operational in about three years. Under the Oil Pollution Act of 1990, a National Response System will be headquartered in Elizabeth City, N.C., to administer the Coast Guard's strike force teams and to keep a national inventory of all government and private response equipment. The law also calls for the maintenance of 19 Coast Guard spill-equipment sites around the country.*

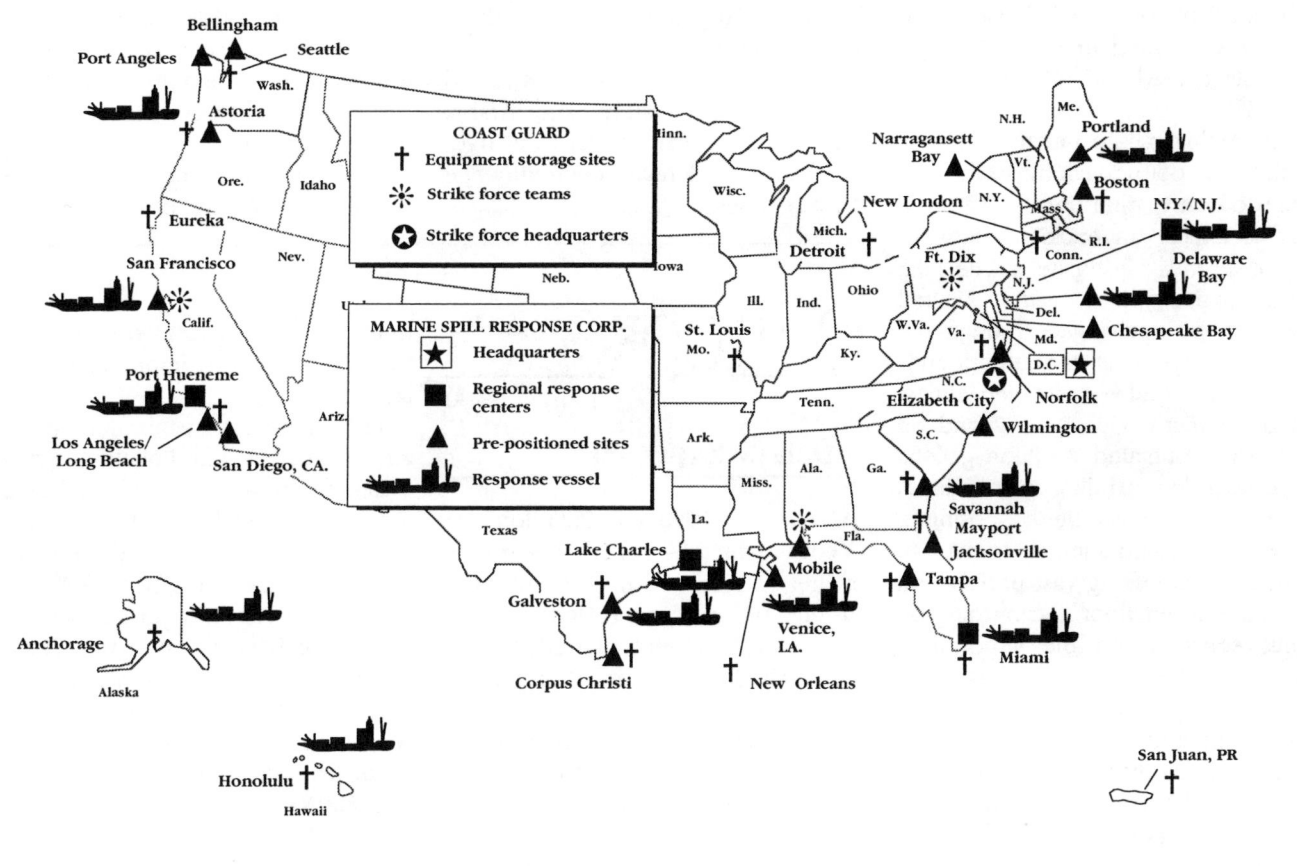

Sources: U.S. Coast Guard, Marine Spill Response Corp.

The MSRC won't come cheap. The initial estimates of $400 million to set up and run the five regional centers and their branch offices during the first five years of operation have mounted to $1 billion. Most of the funding will come from the big oil companies, among them Exxon and Chevron, which also own and operate tankers and other facilities that fall under the Oil Pollution Act's jurisdiction.

Persian Gulf Spill

While the government and industry have taken steps to prevent oil spills and limit pollution when they occur within 200 miles of U.S. territory, much remains to be done on the international level. Several European countries have developed model spill-response systems. *(See box, p. 36.)* But the "ecoterrorism" that dev-

astated the Persian Gulf during hostilities last year demonstrated the need for far greater international coordination to respond to major spills in international waters.

The Persian Gulf disaster posed a number of unique problems. Iraqi forces intentionally ruptured oil tanks, opened the shut-off valves at Kuwait's Sea Island terminal in the gulf, dumped oil from several Iraqi tankers and opened the valves at the

Mina Al-Bakr offshore terminal. These acts released an estimated 250 million gallons of oil into a body of water that had already sustained heavy pollution during the Iran-Iraq War of 1980-88.

The gulf spill has produced what newsletter publisher Richard Golob calls an "environmental disaster" that is "unprecedented in world history." Currents spread the oil along more than 350 miles of coastline, mostly in Saudi Arabia, while much of the oil sank to the bottom, taking an incalculable toll on marine life. Because the gulf is almost an enclosed body of water, scientists estimate it will take three to five years for the polluted water to be exchanged through the Straits of Hormuz at its southern end.

Iraqi forces also sabotaged almost all of Kuwait's 858 active inland oil wells. An estimated 7 billion gallons have been left standing in "oil lakes" throughout the oil fields, posing a long-term environmental threat. In addition to releasing vast pools of oil onto the desert floor, the burning oil wells spewed into the atmosphere hundreds of tons of toxic gases, including sulfur dioxide, carbon dioxide, ozone and carbon monoxide. As the soot and oily particles from these oil fires fell from their 800-mile-long plume, acid rain contributed further to the environmental damage.

International Response

The Persian Gulf spill found the region's governments ill-equipped to deal with the emergency. Saudi Arabia, whose water supply was threatened as the slick moved down the coast, appealed for help in cleaning up the spill, an effort the Saudi government estimates will cost more than $450 million. In response, the International Maritime Organization (IMO), a United Nations agency, set up the Gulf Oil Pollution Disaster Fund to facilitate the transfer of cleanup equipment to the most endangered areas. But the IMO was able to collect only

$5 million for the fund.

The lack of funds, together with the apparent insensitivity of local governments to the environmental consequences of such a vast oil spill, has resulted in long delays in the cleanup effort. The U.N. Security Council issued a resolution holding Iraq financially responsible for damages caused by its occupation of Kuwait. But before any of the affected governments — mainly Saudi Arabia and Kuwait — can collect from Iraq, they must undertake environmental damage assessments.

Many environmental groups, however, blame the cleanup delay on a lack of interest by the United States and other members of the coalition that drove Saddam Hussein out of Kuwait last year. "The coalition members had the necessary resources and funding to mobilize rapidly to wage the gulf war, but they have sadly not organized a concerted response to the war's environmental aftermath," Golob testified recently before a congressional panel. "That aftermath is not merely a local or regional issue. It is an international problem."[25] ∎

OUTLOOK

Delays Expected

While the 1990 Oil Pollution Act was generally hailed as a means of greatly reducing the risk of catastrophic oil spills in the United States, its provisions cannot take effect until the Coast Guard writes more than 40 safety regulations to conform to the act's provisions. The law calls on the Coast Guard to finish this job in two years. "The reality is that we'll probably get a good start on it in two years but that our charter will have to be renewed next January," says Bruce Novak.

Complicating the Coast Guard's rule-making task is the opposition by industry and environmental groups to some of the act's provisions. One complaint voiced by shipbuilders and tanker operators concerns the requirement that all oil-carrying vessels have double hulls by 2015. This would add to the cost of shipping oil because it would reduce carrying capacity — by 28 percent in the case of 35,000-ton tankers, which frequently call at U.S. ports.[26] While the Coast Guard is writing the regulation requiring double hulls, studies are cur-

rently under way to assess the effectiveness of other improvements in tanker design.

Environmental organizations generally hailed the Oil Pollution Act as a significant advance in their quest for environmental protection and perhaps the one positive outcome of the *Exxon Valdez* spill. "It would obviously never have happened but for the *Exxon Valdez*," says Sarah Chasis, senior attorney for the Natural Resources Defense Council (NRDC) in New York. The law falls short, however, of many environmentalists' wishes. The NRDC, for example, was disappointed that it does not hold the owners of spilled oil cargo liable for damages.

Chasis also expresses frustration over the law's implementation. "Our concern right now is focused on the double-hull provision, the requirements that will be set for existing tankers and the slowness with which the act is being implemented," she says.

Among the more vocal critics of the new law are international protection and indemnity groups, known as P&I clubs, which include tanker owners who pool funds in order to indemnify each other against lawsuits. P&I clubs are responsible for insuring most of the world's shipped cargo, including

Continued on p. 42

At Issue:

Is $1 billion sufficient payment for the Exxon Corp.'s role in the Exxon Valdez oil spill?

CHARLES E. COLE

Attorney General for the state of Alaska
FROM A STATEMENT BEFORE THE HOUSE BUDGET COMMITTEE'S TASK FORCE ON URGENT FISCAL ISSUES, OCT. 31, 1991.

*t*he Task Force seems to be of the view that the Exxon criminal plea agreement and civil consent decree ... approved by the United States District Court [in October 1991] are inadequate because they do not impose sufficient financial punishment on Exxon. The state [of Alaska] does not agree with this view.

The state of Alaska was, in every sense of the word, the victim of the *Exxon Valdez* oil spill. The oil fouled our beaches and our tidelands; it injured and killed our fish, our birds and our marine mammals — birds, fish and mammals upon which our citizens depend. Several paths were available to the state in its approach to the litigation following the spill. One was a policy of revenge and punishment. That is, an effort to exact the highest financial toll possible on Exxon, with the primary goal of punishing it financially, regardless of whether this approach yielded the greatest benefit to the damaged Alaska environment. The state did not choose this path. Rather, since the inception of its legal efforts, the state of Alaska focused its resources on maximizing the amount of money which could be made available at the earliest opportunity for healing of the damaged Alaska environment. In my view these settlement agreements accomplish this objective. ...

The reason for this support lies in the shared belief of most Alaskans that what is most important is not simply the amount of punishment inflicted upon Exxon, but the degree to which the injured Alaska environment can be restored as a result of the settlement agreements. ...

While Exxon has voluntarily expended in excess of $2 billion on the actual physical cleanup, government "response costs" have amounted to far less. While I am uncertain about the amount of response costs expended by the United States, the total unreimbursed response costs to date for the state are approximately $39 million. Large cleanup expenditures in the future are not likely since both the state of Alaska and the Coast Guard are of the view that very little additional cleanup activities would be environmentally fruitful. Any future projects will be readily covered by the settlement funds. Even the inclusion of unreimbursed injury assessment costs incurred by the state would only add an additional $29 million to the amount of state out-of-pocket costs. Thus, the actual cost of the cleanup to the state is well-covered by the civil settlement.

DAVID C. CAMPBELL

Resource economist for the National Wildlife Federation
FROM STATEMENT BEFORE THE HOUSE BUDGET COMMITTEE'S TASK FORCE ON URGENT FISCAL ISSUES, OCT. 31, 1991.

*m*arine biologist Sylvia Earle best expressed the difficulty of ever compensating fully for damage from the *Exxon Valdez* spill as she left oil-soaked Prince William Sound in April 1989:

"How do you weigh the forever cost of this catastrophe? ... I could go on, but what may be of most concern, ultimately, is those things that are not obvious and often not visible. It's not just the otters, or the birds, or the herring, or the magical beauty of Prince William Sound. It's the countless invertebrates that live in the ocean and on the shores; it's the diatoms, the phytoplankton and zooplankton, the amphipods, the mollusks and crustaceans, the little fish, the bigger fish that eat them, and on and on through the food chain. It's the system."

We believe that the economic value of the settlement ... is insufficient compensation for the public natural resources damage caused by the spill. ... Compensation should include all the costs of cleaning up damaged sites, the costs of either restoring or replacing the damaged resource and the value of any residual damage for lost services of the resource. ...

The language in the settlement and associated statements to the press would have the public believe that Exxon will incur total costs in excess of $3 billion. ... Staff from our Alaska office and Dr. Jay Hair, the federation's president, surveyed Exxon's "cleaned-up sites" and found that many measures did little for the resource and that a large portion of the $2.1 billion spent was not cost effective. Therefore, the value of the compensation to the public resources from Exxon's unplanned cleanup is much less than $2.1 billion.

The economic value of the civil settlement is approximately $475 million as compared to the advertised amount of $1 billion. The economic value is less than the nominal value for two reasons: The payment of the settlement is stretched out over 10 years until September 1, 2000, and because Exxon will be able to deduct the civil payments from its federal and state tax liability. ... Thus, the effective value of the settlement is less than one-half of the advertised $1 billion. ...

In summary, the settlement will cost Exxon only $434 million and cost the American taxpayer $250 million in lost revenues. And that does not take into account the enormous, irreplaceable loss of the public's natural resources.

Continued from p. 40

oil. Currently, the clubs provide at least $500 million in oil-spill coverage to individual shippers, which meets Oil Pollution Act financial-responsibility requirements for tankers passing through U.S. waters. However, the new law also requires that P&I clubs agree to be sued directly for spill costs and waive all the conditions they can now apply to defend themselves from suits, such as failure by a ship owner to pay premiums on time.

So far, the P&I clubs have refused to agree to either of these conditions. If no compromise is reached, the impasse could jeopardize the supply of foreign oil to the United States."Unless the various sectors of the international maritime community, the Congress and the Coast Guard can find effective solutions to this impending crisis, we seem likely to witness a marked decline in the quality and volume of tanker service to the United States," reads a statement to Congress by Intertanko, the international association of independent tanker owners based in Oslo, Norway. "Such a decline will have supply and monetary effects that every American will feel at the gas pump and in his utility bills."[27]

For its part, the Coast Guard is going ahead and writing the new regulation requiring all oil tankers in U.S. waters to have a certificate of financial responsibility. "The showdown will come," Novak says, "if the P&I clubs refuse to issue the certificates, and oil imports come to a halt, or Congress blinks" and amends the Oil Pollution Act before that happens.

Reducing Oil Imports

Few industry analysts expect that oil tankers will cease operations in the world's biggest oil market anytime soon; rather, they think a compromise will be reached to avert a cutback in oil supplies to the United States. However, the issues raised by the new law may add pressure to

Congress to approve legislation that seeks to reduce the country's dependence on foreign oil.

A key provision of this controversial legislation, which the Senate refused to consider before it recessed last November, would allow drilling in Alaska's Arctic National Wildlife Refuge (ANWR). If Congress does approve the legislation this year, the risks of environmental degradation from oil spills may shift somewhat from the open water to the land, port facilities and offshore platforms and ports where pipelines are used to transport crude and refined products.

Already, aging pipelines, such as the 15-year-old Trans-Alaska Pipeline, are subject to greater numbers of spills. "It is a significant issue and will probably become increasingly so as these pipelines age," says the NRDC's Chasis.

Over the longer term, tanker accidents, too, no doubt will continue spilling oil into U.S. waters, especially since the country will likely depend even more on imports to satisfy its thirst for oil. (The most optimistic scientists concede that the oil reserves that may lie under the ANWR would give only a temporary boost to domestic oil supplies.)

Once the world's biggest oil exporter, the United States has, since the late 1940s, imported more oil than it has sold to foreign nations. And despite the push for alternative energy sources and energy conservation, the country's dependence on oil imports is rising because domestic reserves are drying up.By 1990 the United States was importing 42 percent of the oil it consumed, or 7.1 million barrels a day out of total daily consumption of 16.9 million barrels. By 2010, imports will likely satisfy almost three-quarters of the country's oil needs.[28]

That means more tanker traffic in U.S. ports and coastal waters. And with increased tanker traffic will come greater risks of accidents and oil spills. ∎

Notes

[1] Natural Resources Defense Council, *No Safe Harbor,* 1990.

[2] See John Horgan, "The Muddled Cleanup in the Persian Gulf," *Scientific American,* October 1991.

[3] Alaska Department of Environmental Conservation, *Oil Spill Chronicle,* Vol. I, No. 17, 1989.

[4] See World Resources Institute, *World Resources 1990-91.*

[5] Office of Technology Assessment, *Coping with an Oiled Sea,* March 1990, p. 16.

[6] See Marguerite Holloway, "Soiled Shores," *Scientific American,* October 1991.

[7] *Ibid.*

[8] *Ibid.*

[9] Daniel Yergin, *The Prize: The Epic Quest for Oil, Money, and Power* (1991), p. 59.

[10] *Ibid.*

[11] *Ibid.,* p. 375.

[12] *Ibid.,* p. 557.

[13] National Research Council, *Tanker Spills: Prevention by Design* (1991), p. 30.

[14] *Ibid.,* p. 32.

[15] *Ibid.,* pp. 2, 38.

[16] *Ibid.,* p. 4.

[17] *Ibid.,* p. 35.

[18] *Ibid.,* p. 36.

[19] National Research Council, *Oil in the Sea: Inputs, Fates, and Effects* (1985).

[20] *Ibid.*

[21] See Holloway, *op. cit.,* p. 114.

[22] General Accounting Office, *Coast Guard: Inspection Program Improvements Are Under Way to Help Detect Unsafe Tankers,* October 1991.

[23] General Accounting Office, *Coast Guard: Oil Spills Continue Despite Waterfront Facility Inspection Program,* Oct. 24, 1991, p. 2.

[24] See Mark Ivey and Vicky Cahan, "How Congress and Big Oil Can Clean up Their Cleanup Act," *Business Week,* June 25, 1990.

[25] Golob testified Oct. 17, 1991, before three subcommittees of the House Merchant Marine and Fisheries Committee in a hearing on the Persian Gulf oil spill.

[26] National Research Council, *Tanker Spills, op. cit.*

[27] Intertanko presented its statement to the House Merchant Marine and Fisheries Coast Guard Subcommittee on Nov. 6, 1991.

[28] Office of Technology Assessment, "U.S. Oil Import Vulnerability: The Technical Replacement Capability," OTA Report Brief, October 1991. Also see Mary H. Cooper, "Oil Imports," *The CQ Researcher,* Aug. 23, 1991, pp. 585-608.

Bibliography

Selected Sources Used

Books

Davidson, Art, *In the Wake of the* Exxon Valdez: *The Devastating Impact of the Alaska Oil Spill,* Sierra Club Books, 1990.

The author retraces the events following the 1989 grounding of the *Exxon Valdez* off the coast of Alaska, which caused the biggest oil spill in U.S. history. Through extensive interviews, he also provides a firsthand view of the spill's impact on the local population.

National Research Council, *Tanker Spills: Prevention by Design,* National Academy Press, 1991.

"Wherever tank vessels travel, laden with crude oil or petroleum products, the threat of pollution exists." This is the premise of the National Research Council's study of global tanker spills and construction changes that could reduce their frequency. The researchers found that most tanker accidents do not result in oil spills and that most spills in U.S. waters occur as a result of groundings, as in the *Exxon Valdez* spill of 1989. The authors call on the U.S. government to conduct further research into double hulls and other structural changes to improve tanker safety.

Sullivan, George, *Supertanker! The Story of the World's Biggest Ships,* Dodd, Mead & Co., 1978.

This well-illustrated volume describes the evolution of oil tankers into the biggest ships ever to sail. It illustrates the materials and work that go into building these behemoths, as well as their major ports of call. One chapter on oil pollution describes the technology available to clean up major spills at the time the book was written. Most of that equipment is still used today.

Yergin, Daniel, *The Prize: The Epic Quest for Oil, Money and Power,* Simon & Schuster, 1991.

Yergin, author of *Energy Future,* which described energy alternatives in the wake of the energy crises of the 1970s, presents a comprehensive history of the oil industry. The volume includes much information about the early days of oil exploitation and the personalities involved in its expansion into a global industry.

Articles

Holloway, Marguerite, "Soiled Shores," *Scientific American,* October 1991.

This widely cited article reports findings that some of the cleanup technologies used to remove oil from Alaska's shoreline after the *Exxon Valdez* spill may have done more harm than good. Rocks and sandy areas that were scoured with pressurized hot water, for example, were devoid of plant and animal life two years after the cleanup, while living organisms had returned to adjacent areas that had been left untreated.

Openchowski, Charles, "Federal Implementation of the Oil Pollution Act of 1990," *Environmental Law Reporter,* October 1991.

The author explains how authority for federal oil-spill response is divided among several executive branch agencies under the 1990 Oil Pollution Act. That law, the most sweeping oil-pollution statute ever passed, gives the federal government a bigger policing role, increases the liability limits for polluters and creates a $1 billion, industry-financed damage-compensation fund.

Reports and Studies

Natural Resources Defense Council, *No Safe Harbor: Tanker Safety in America's Ports,* 1990.

This study points out, dramatically, that an oil spill the size of the one released by the *Exxon Valdez* would stretch from Boston to the Outer Banks of North Carolina on the East Coast and from Mendocino to San Diego along the coast of California. It examines the vulnerability of three major U.S. oil-receiving ports — San Francisco Bay, New York harbor and Los Angeles harbor — to tanker spills and prescribes measures to prevent tanker accidents in those waters.

Office of Technology Assessment, U.S. Congress, *Bioremediation for Marine Oil Spills,* May 1991.

Following the *Exxon Valdez* spill, vast stretches of oil-covered beaches were treated with nutrients to stimulate the action of naturally occurring microbes that break down oil molecules. This oil-spill technique, called bioremediation, accelerates the cleanup process. But scientists dispute its effectiveness in many environments, such as salt marshes, where it may have toxic effects that outweigh its efficacy in removing oil.

Office of Technology Assessment, U.S. Congress, *Coping with an Oiled Sea,* March 1990.

This report examines the array of options available for combating oil spills at sea. Conducted in the wake of the *Exxon Valdez* spill, the study focuses on issues that came up during the cleanup operation in Alaska, such as the division of responsibilities in a major spill and the choice of technology to be used under varying environmental conditions. It concludes with a review of European spill-response techniques and practices.

The Next Step

Additional Articles from Current Periodicals from EBSCO Publishing's Database

Alaska

"Evidence of Valdez damage released," *National Parks,* **July/August 1991, p. 13.**

Discusses the findings of a once-secret federal study that reveals far more serious ongoing damage to Alaska's coastal waters from the 1989 *Exxon Valdez* oil spill (Prince William Sound) than was previously known. National parks affected; 26 archaeological sites; disruption of the traditional Native Alaskan lifestyle; murres and sea otters killed; pink salmon eggs; current status of litigation.

"Exxon case ends, but not effects of spill," *National Parks,* **May/June 1991, p. 16.**

Discusses the terms of the legal settlement between the federal government, the state of Alaska, and Exxon Corp. as compensation for the 1989 *Exxon Valdez* oil spill in Prince William Sound. Scientific findings leaked to the press; damage to bird and fish populations, especially to the murres, large black-and-white diving birds.

Laycock, G., "The disaster that won't go away," *Audubon,* **September 1990, p. 106.**

Examines the continuing environmental, social, and economic impact of the *Exxon Valdez* oil spill in Prince William Sound, Alaska. Comments by local residents, commercial fishermen, and state environmental officials; power of the oil industry; potential long-range impact on wildlife; Alaska Oil Spill Commission's report and recommendations. INSET: Full speed ahead (Alaska oil exploration).

Books & reading

"Booklist: Nonfiction," *Horn Book Magazine,* **November/December 1990, p. 762.**

Reviews the book "Sea Otter Rescue: The Aftermath of an Oil Spill," by Roland Smith.

Clarke, L., "Reviews: Population, ecology, and urban and community studies," *Contemporary Sociology,* **September 1991, p. 737.**

Reviews the books "In the Wake of the *Exxon Valdez*: The Devastating Impact of the Alaska Oil Spill," by Art Davidson and "Oil Age Eskimos," by Joseph G. Jorgensen.

Davidson, A., "In the wake of the *Exxon Valdez*," *Alaska,* **May 1990, p. 28.**

Excerpt from "In the Wake of the *Exxon Valdez*," Part I. Recounts hindrances to cleaning birds following the *Exxon*

Valdez spill. Problems with authority and responsibility; finding birds instead of cleaning them; conflict with the Fish and Wildlife Service; International Bird Rescue Research Center.

Davidson, A., "In the wake of the *Exxon Valdez*," *Alaska,* **June 1990, p. 36.**

Excerpt from "In the Wake of the *Exxon Valdez*," Part II. Describes how Jay Holcomb of the International Bird Rescue Center set up another bird rescue center in Seward. Following the oil out of Prince William Sound; dealing with angry fishermen; struggles with Exxon Corp.

Davidson, A., "Valdez reflections," *Sierra,* **May/June 1990, p. 42.**

Reflects on the impact and implications of the *Exxon Valdez* oil spill. Ecological and social impact; Exxon Corp.'s responsibility; inadequacy of current technology to efficiently clean up spills; proposal for a national energy policy; the importance of energy conservation.

Egan, T., "Goo galore," *The New York Times Book Review,* **May 28, 1991, p. 23.**

Reviews the book "Out of the Channel: The *Exxon Valdez* Oil Spill in Prince William Sound," which recounts the events of the cleanup effort that took place after the *Exxon Valdez* ran aground, by John Keeble.

Nickum, M.J., "Book reviews: Science & technology," *Library Journal,* **June 15, 1990, p. 130.**

Reviews the book "White Silk and Black Tar: A Journal of the Alaska Oil Spill," by Page Spencer.

Cleanup

Aldhous, P., "Big test for bioremediation," *Nature,* **Feb. 7, 1991, p. 447.**

States that the oil slick in the Persian Gulf may have its slow recovery accelerated by a new technique called bioremediation. This technique adds nutrients to supplement the natural process of biodegradation.

Crawford, M., "Bacteria effective in Alaska cleanup," *Science,* **March 30, 1990, p. 1537.**

Describes the experimental technique used effectively on oil-soaked beaches after the *Exxon Valdez* spilled its oil in Prince William Sound in March 1989, which involved spraying the beaches with a fertilizer called Inipol, raising the level of oil-degrading bacteria. Oil degradation below the surface; toxic effects; problems with technique.

Dane, A. and Mangiat, J., "Oil slick buster," *Popular Mechanics,* May 1990, p. 58.

Reports on SeaClean, a mammoth oil-skimming rig that is based on an already built mobile offshore drilling platform. Rising 12 stories above the waterline, SeaClean will be used to battle oil spills in rough seas.

Kerr, R.A., "A lesson learned, again, at Valdez," *Science,* May 19, 1991, p. 371.

Reports on a National Oceanic and Atmospheric Administration (NOAA) announcement that said the use of powerful streams of hot seawater to clean up the oil spilled in Prince William Sound after the *Exxon Valdez* oil spill was more damaging than leaving the oil in place. Damage to animal and plant species; comparisons of beaches with and without treatment.

Mangan, K.S., "U. of Texas microbiologist seeks to persuade skeptical colleagues that bacteria could be useful...," *The Chronicle of Higher Education,* Sept. 19, 1990, p. A5.

Describes the oil-eating microorganisms of Carl H. Oppenheimer, University of Texas at Austin, which were used when two separate oil spills in the Gulf of Mexico threatened the Texas coastline. Breaking oil into harmless fatty acids that sea life can then eat; process holds promise; success overseas; frustrating reticence.

Parker, P.A., "Dispersants gain ground," *Environmental Action,* March/April 1991, p. 10.

Examines the use of dispersants in cleaning up oil spills. Impact of environmental effects; EPA adjusting regulations implementing the Federal Oil Pollution Act of 1990.

Debates & issues

"Another crude year," *Discover,* January 1991, p. 70.

Maps the numerous oil spills of at least 10,000 gallons that occurred around the world in 1990. Lists the date, location, volume, and cause of each spill.

"Are oil spills an environmental hazard?" *Consumers' Research Magazine,* January 1991, p. 14.

Argues that oil spills in the ocean are not a major environmental catastrophe. Life cycle of an oil spill; environmental effects; resilient oceans. The article is excerpted from "Oil in the Ocean: The Short- and Long-Term Impacts of a Spill," by the Congressional Research Service of the Library of Congress. INSET: Damages due to cleanup.

Busch, L., "Science under wraps in Prince William Sound," *Science,* May 10, 1991, p. 772.

Discusses the restrictions imposed on environmental scientists trying to collect data on environmental damage from the *Exxon Valdez* oil spill in Prince William Sound, Alaska. Gag order from Alaska attorney general; collapse of $1 billion deal between Exxon Corp., Alaska, and U.S. government; questions about research scientists' loyalty; comments on pros and cons of gag order; impact on cleanup strategies decisions; example of fish stream cleanup problems.

Byrnes, P., "The price of addiction," *Wilderness,* summer 1990, p. 3.

Summarizes the Wilderness Society's report, "A Hundred Spills, A Thousand Excuses," on the 100 worst oil spills since March 1989. Necessary legislation; society recommendations; most significant spills.

Turner, M.H., "Oil spill: Legal strategies block ecology communications," *Bioscience,* April 1990, p. 238.

Addresses the lack of published biological data due to the legal aftermath of the oil spill of the *Exxon Valdez* tanker in Prince William Sound. Tight-lipped science; disappointing scope; million-dollar research; lawyers block research publications; body-count biology; educated guesses; cleanup cooperation; migration of biologists; reservations.

Wheelwright, J., "Muzzling science," *Newsweek,* May 22, 1991, p. 10.

Opinion. Asserts that the investigation of the *Exxon Valdez* oil spill of March 1989 has been a nightmare for scientists. Reports issued by the U.S. that just aggravated the confusion and controversy; explanation of the confusion; gag order making treason of scientists' scholarly chats; more.

Wills, J., "Europe's answer to oil spills," *New Scientist,* May 18, 1991, p. 36.

Asserts that, according to a study by Alaskan marine biologist Frederika Ott, if the U.S. had the same environmental safeguards as Scotland and Norway, the *Exxon Valdez* disaster might not have happened. Ott's study of the oil industry of Alaska, Shetland and Norway; Ott's qualifications; state of Alaska's pollution watchdog Dan Lawn's visit to Norway's Sture terminal and Sullom Voe in October 1989; division of responsibilities in Valdez.

Economic aspects

Begley, S., Cohn, B., et al., "One deal that was too good for Exxon," *Newsweek,* May 6, 1991, p. 54.

Considers Judge H. Russel Holland's rejection of the settlement Exxon Corp. agreed to pay to settle criminal misdemeanor charges arising out of the gigantic oil spill in Alaska's Prince William Sound. Exxon Corp.'s chairman, Lawrence Rawl, showed no remorse; Exxon Corp.'s out-of-pocket costs with the settlement would have been very small; dissatisfaction with how dirty the sound remains; 30 days for Exxon Corp. to decide whether to renegotiate.

Holusha, J., "Warning by big oil," *The New York Times,* Jan. 29, 1990, p. D1.

Reports on the larger bites in profits expected because of the need to meet environmental regulations in the wake of the *Exxon Valdez* oil spill. Some analysts speculate that a continued strengthening of environmental requirements could pinch oil companies' profits, drive smaller companies out of business and increase pressure on consumer prices.

Environmental aspects

"Waging war on the earth," *Environmental Action,* March/April 1991, p. 20.

Presents excerpts from interviews with four scientists by the Arms Control Network concerning the environmental consequences of the Persian Gulf War. Members of U.S. House of Representatives and scientists urging investigation by the United Nation's Environment Programme; Dr. John Cox, David Ferguson, J.L. Cloudsley-Thompson, and Matthew Meselson are interviewed; consequences of oil spills including burning fields, bombing of nuclear and chemical facilities.

Drew, L., "Truth and consequences along oiled shores," *National Wildlife,* June/July 1990, p. 34.

Reports on the negative impact of the *Exxon Valdez* spill on the environment and wildlife in Alaska. Relaxed regulations and enforcement; effective cleanup work of locals; formation of the Oil Reform Alliance; effect on birds, sea otters, seals, sea lions and pink salmon fry. INSET: Seeking justice after the spill.

Farb, N. and Egan, T., "One year later," *The New York Times Magazine,* May 15, 1990, p. 34.

Discusses the environmental impact one year later of the March 24, 1989 *Exxon Valdez* oil spill at Prince William Sound in Alaska. Worst toll on wildlife of any industrial accident; biologists' opinions divided on long-term effects of the spill.

Gulf of Mexico

Adler, J., Annin, P., et al., "More oil on the waters," *Newsweek,* June 25, 1990, p. 60.

Reports the explosion on board the oil tanker *Mega Borg* in the Gulf of Mexico, which had the potential to release 38 million gallons of oil in the gulf, three times as much as the *Exxon Valdez.* American oil industry to establish five "response centers" around the country; Petroleum Industry Response Organization; need for legislation regarding oil spills; adequate handling of the fire and cleanup. INSET: Bills and spills.

Law & legislation

"The oil complex," *Sierra,* January/February 1991, p. 134.

Suggests that the passage of the 1990 Oil Spill Liability Act was only the beginning step in making oil transport safer. Alaskan oil spills; conservationists will continue protection work.

Kuntz, P., "Oil-spill conferees near end with deal on double hulls," *Congressional Quarterly Weekly Report,* July 14, 1990, p. 2215.

Declares that almost all U.S. oil tankers would be required to have double hulls by the year 2010 under a compromise approved July 12 by House and Senate oil-spill conferees. Host of secondary issues; phase out 45 percent of the nation's single-hulled fleet's oil capacity; approved without public discussion; concessions made; more.

Pyne, J.H., "New oil spill law will affect all Americans," *Vital Speeches,* Dec. 15, 1990, p. 149.

Presents a speech by J.H. Pyne, President of Dixie Carriers Inc., delivered before the Propeller Club's 1990 American Merchant Marine and Maritime Industry Conference, which deals with flaws in the new U.S. oil spill legislation.

Persian Gulf

Begley, S., Manegold, C.S., et al., "Saddam's ecoterror," *Newsweek,* Feb. 4, 1991, p. 36.

Details how Saddam Hussein ordered a massive attack against the Persian Gulf last week by opening oil pumps at Sea Island Terminal. The Iraqi oil flood has created environmental hazards and military obstacles. Impact on the gulf ecosystem; how the spill could hamper the Saudi economy; environmentalists' worst fears; how the floating oil emulsifies and becomes more hazardous. INSETS: Iraq's crude weapon; how to clean up a spill.

Elmer-DeWitt, P., Dowell, W., et al., "A man-made hell on earth," *Time,* March 18, 1991, p. 36.

Comments that up close, the ecological damage inflicted on Kuwait is worse than anyone dared imagine. Virtually all the oil wells were wrecked, 600 or so are still ablaze; poisonous fumes dangerous to the very young and very old; oil spills off Kuwait; acid rain, respiratory problems and carcinogens; oil slicks, burning wells, and unexploded mines; making ecoterrorism a war crime.

Jenish, D., "War's dark tide," *Maclean's,* March 4, 1991, p. 48.

Discusses Canada's efforts to help Bahrain and Qatar fight the oil spills in the Persian Gulf. Ecology of the gulf; dangers to desalination plants; shorebirds, fisheries, etc.; allied bombing.

Lemonick, M.D., Gup, T., et al., "Dead sea in the making," *Time*, Feb. 11, 1991, p. 40.

Details the expected results of Saddam Hussein's engineered oil slick estimated at 50 miles long and 12 miles wide that is breaking into pieces as it moves down the Persian Gulf. Probable projected target — the desalination plants in Saudi Arabia; great danger; protecting key areas; extraordinary sensitivity of this particular stretch of the planet; coral reefs, commercially important fish, sea mammals.

Pearce, F., MacKenzie, D., et al., "Wildlife choked by the world's worst oil slick," *New Scientist*, Feb. 2, 1991, p. 24.

Comments on the effects of the massive oil spill in the Persian Gulf on the ecology of the region. What caused the slick; allied bombing to stop the flow; possibility of manually opening the valves; making a mess of Kuwait; frequency of oil spills in the area; species at risk; coral reefs and pearl oyster beds; more.

Sheppard, C. and Price, A., "Will marine life survive the gulf war?" *New Scientist*, March 9, 1991, p. 36.

Comments on the possible impact of the oil pollution in the Gulf on marine life. Difficulty in assessing the damage to the ecosystem; threat of damage to oxygen producing plants and algae; possible damage to the gulf's fisheries; impact of extreme climate on the gulf's marine life.

Petroleum industry

Clarke, L. and Siebold, J.O., "Oil-spill fantasies," *Atlantic*, November 1990, p. 65.

Criticizes the oil industry's procedures for responding to an oil spill. *Exxon Valdez* spill in Alaska a classic example; truth about ability to contain or recover spilled oil; other spills; alternative cleanup and containment methods.

Wolff, C., "Federal agents condemn Exxon's monitoring in S.I. Spill," *The New York Times*, Jan. 20, 1990, p. 27.

Reports that officials of the EPA say that Exxon Corp. was negligent and irresponsible for failing for 12 years to fix the leak-detection system on a pipeline that ruptured Jan. 1, spilling several hundred thousand gallons of oil into the Arthur Kill. Damage to wetlands on Staten Island.

Prevention

Buderi, R. and Templeton, F., "New tanker technology may block that leaky oil," *Business Week*, Sept. 30, 1991, p. 82.

Reports that through efforts to minimize the environmental damage from future oil spills, Energy Transportation Group Inc. has unveiled a system that it claims will stem the flow of oil from ruptured tankers.

Cook, W.J., "An easy way out of this mess," *U.S. News & World Report*, June 25, 1990, p. 14.

Discusses oil spills in American waters and suggests that the solution is to change the way we think about oil tankers. Notoriously fragile and poorly maintained; enter the double hull; operating under the flags of nations with lax standards; the government doesn't help much.

Wald, M., "Tighter ships," *The New York Times*, June 17, 1990, Section 4, p. 1.

Discusses redesigning oil tankers in order to protect against oil spills. Debate over double-hull construction of tankers; filling tankers to only 80 percent capacity as a possible solution; costs to shipping companies; reference to *Exxon Valdez*.

Research

Dane, A., "Learning from disaster," *Popular Mechanics*, September 1991, p. 94.

Follows up on some of the research that was undertaken after the *Exxon Valdez* spilled 11 million gallons of oil into Alaska's Prince William Sound in 1989. How the catastrophe presented a unique opportunity to learn.

Stone, R., "Icy inferno: Researchers plan oil blaze in Arctic," *Science*, Sept. 13, 1991, p. 1203.

Examines plans by researchers to deliberately spill and set afire thousands of gallons of crude oil in the Beaufort Sea in order to determine how an oil spill can be handled in Arctic waters. Special hazards; tests of alternative cleanup technologies; approval from local environmental officials and residents; need for EPA approval.

Wiley, J.P. Jr., "Phenomena, comment and notes," *Smithsonian*, August 1991, p. 24.

Reports that five years after the disastrous oil spill off the coast of Panama near the Smithsonian's Galeta Marine Laboratory, scientists' findings contradict what we thought we knew of oil's effects. Brian Keller, manager of the oil spill project; consideration of the plausibility of using so much oil for our automobiles.

Technological aspects

Buderi, R., "Oil spills: Figuring out whodunit," *Business Week*, March 25, 1991, p. 89.

Reports that, thanks to a novel application of mass spectrometry from BP America Inc., some tar balls, which occasionally wash up on beaches for no reason, can now be tracked to their source. Oil from different regions often have unique characteristics, which show up as ratios between carbon isotopes, so on a mass spectrometer oils from different regions will register differently. Uses in exploration; where analysis can be performed.

Back Issues

Great Research on Current Issues Starts Right Here... Recent topics covered by The CQ Researcher are listed below. Issues dated before May 10, 1991, were published under the name of Editorial Research Reports.

Back issues are available for $4.00 (subscribers) or $7.00 (non-subscribers). Quantity discounts apply to orders over ten. To order, call Congressional Quarterly 1-800-432-2250.

Future Topics

▶ *Should Hunting Be Banned?*

▶ *America's Threatened Coastlines*

▶ *Alternative Medicine*

Hunting Controversy

Friends and foes of hunting are locked in a bitter public debate

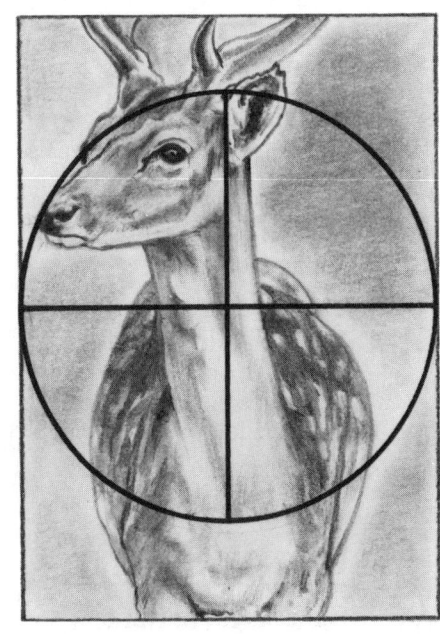

A LL ACROSS THE COUNTRY, HUNTERS ARE UNDER assault by animal-rights groups and environmentalists who condemn the killing of animals by sportsmen as inhumane. Initially caught off balance by the attacks, hunters have mounted a counter-offensive. Hunting, they claim, is not only a cherished American tradition and a spiritually enriching activity but also an effective wildlife-management tool. As they trade charges, both sides hope to sway the thinking of the vast non-hunting majority of the American public. The stakes are high: Opponents of hunting aim for nothing less than legislation abolishing sport hunting. But even if the nation's 18 million hunters win the battle of words, continuing population growth and shrinking wildlife habitat seem sure to change their sport in ways not to their liking.

 January 24, 1992 • Volume 2, No. 3 • 49-72

Formerly Editorial Research Reports

COVER ART: BARBARA SASSA-DANIELS

THE CQ Researcher

January 24, 1992
Volume 2, No. 3

EDITOR
Sandra Stencel

MANAGING EDITOR
Thomas J. Colin

ASSOCIATE EDITOR
Richard L. Worsnop

STAFF WRITERS
Charles S. Clark
Mary H. Cooper
Rodman D. Griffin

PRODUCTION EDITOR
Laurie De Maris

EDITORIAL ASSISTANT
Thomas H. Moore

GRAPHICS
Jack Auldridge

PUBLISHED BY
Congressional Quarterly Inc.

CHAIRMAN
Andrew Barnes

VICE CHAIRMAN
Andrew P. Corty

EDITOR AND PUBLISHER
Neil Skene

EXECUTIVE EDITOR
Robert W. Merry

PUBLICATIONS MARKETING/SALES
Robert Smith

EDITOR, EBSCO PUBLISHING
Melissa Kummerer

The CQ Researcher (ISSN 1056-2036). Formerly
Editorial Research Reports. Published weekly (48
times per year, not printed the first Friday of any
month with five Fridays) by Congressional Quarterly Inc., 1414 22nd St., N.W., Washington, D.C.
20037. Rates are furnished upon request. Second-
class postage paid at Washington, D.C. POSTMAS-
TER: Send address changes to The CQ Researcher,
1414 22nd St., N.W., Washington, D.C. 20037.

Hunting Controversy

BY RICHARD L. WORSNOP

THE ISSUES

In much of the country, the start of the hunting season also marks the start of the anti-hunting season. As hunters head for woods and wetlands, militant opponents of hunting show up to rail against "blood sport." Confrontations between the groups sometimes turn ugly.

Consider recent events at Mason Neck National Wildlife Refuge in Fairfax County, Va., near Washington. In 1990, shouting protesters tried to block hunters from entering the 1,000-acre refuge along the Potomac River for a six-day deer hunt. To dramatize their cause, the protesters encased their feet in cement at the refuge's entrance. Ten were arrested.

Protesters turned up the heat last year, when about 30 chanting, sign-waving demonstrators disrupted the opening of the refuge's deer season. One of their tactics was to park a van and automobile, with bumpers interlocked, on a narrow stretch of roadway leading to the refuge. Wildlife officials delayed the hunt for 45 minutes while tow trucks removed the vehicles. The illegal parkers, members of the Fund for Animals, an animal-rights group, were arrested on charges of obstructing the free passage of others. Two other protesters were charged with violating the terms of their demonstration permit, which relegated demonstrators to a roped-off area near the refuge entrance.

Similar showdowns have occurred in other parts of the country, particularly the Northeast and California. All the while, a war of words rages in pro- and anti-hunting publications and also in general-interest magazines and newspapers. The rhetoric

can be passionate, as in a much-discussed article by short-story writer Joy Williams in the October 1990 *Esquire*.

"Hunters kill for play, for entertainment," Williams wrote. "They kill for the thrill of it, to make an animal 'theirs.'... The animal becomes the property of the hunter by its death. Alive, the beast belongs only to itself. This is unacceptable to the hunter." After much more in this vein, Williams concluded by asserting, "It's preposterous that every year less than 7 percent of the population turns the skies into shooting galleries and the woods and fields into abattoirs. It's time to stop actively supporting and passively allowing hunting, and time to stigmatize it." [1]

Hunters fired back in a number of pro-hunting journals. *Field & Stream* Conservation Editor George Reiger, who had been blasted by Williams, wrote that opponents of hunting "have produced what amounts to a literature of loathing, the likes of which hasn't been seen since the anti-Semitic tirades of the 1930s." He

called hunting foes "rudderless people who would sabotage family tradition, common sense and the confidence derived from the hunting experience in a vain effort to achieve the myth of the Peaceable Kingdom." [2]

Meanwhile, big guns in the pro-hunting movement like the 3-million-member National Rifle Association (NRA) and the million-member Wildlife Legislative Fund of America (WLFA) maintain the pressure on elected officials. Since 1981, for example, the WLFA has helped persuade 44 state legislatures to pass laws against harassment of hunters in the field.

Pro- and anti-hunting forces alike portray themselves as underdogs in a high-stakes showdown with an implacable foe. *Outdoor Life* Associate Editor Ralph P. Stuart noted that "anti-hunting groups are well-organized, well-oiled machines that live to unload on ragtag groups of hunters who stand up to defend themselves." [3] For their part, hunting opponents charge that hunters hold the upper hand because state game and wildlife agencies are staffed overwhelmingly by hunting advocates.

Despite the unyielding tone of public statements issued by both sides, there are signs that some private soul-searching is under way — at least on the part of hunters. *Field & Stream* Executive Editor David E. Petzal wrote last spring that ethical sport hunters should confront the "slob hunter" problem head-on. "As we come under increasing attack," Petzal wrote, "we can deny until we are blue in the face that ... yahoos who chase game in pickups" and shoot in the direction of sounds they hear in the woods are not truly hunters. "But in the court of public opinion where our case is being tried,

A Good Year for Hunters

Hunters in the U.S. bagged a staggering variety and quantity of game animals during the 1988-1989 season, including 50 million mourning doves, 4 million whitetail deer, 12,000 moose, 1,100 brown and grizzly bears and 90 musk ox. Hunters say they aid wildlife management by culling herds that outgrow their habitat. Groups against sport hunting say there is no excuse for killing animals not needed for food.

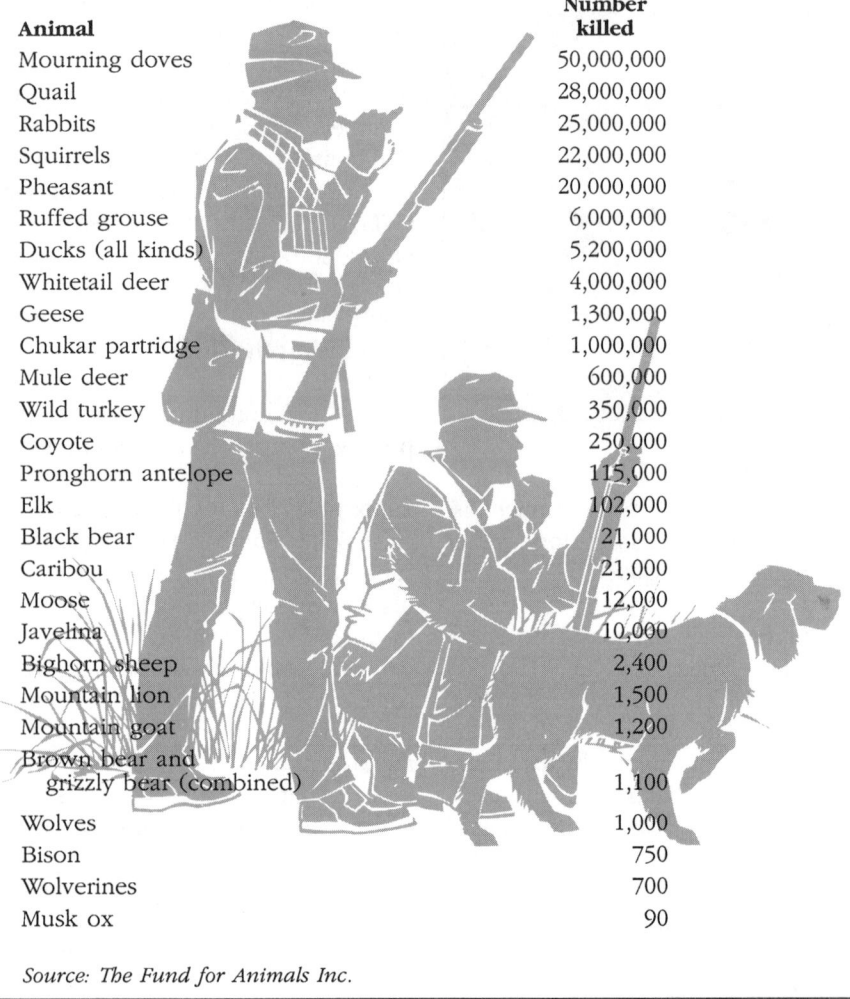

Animal	Number killed
Mourning doves	50,000,000
Quail	28,000,000
Rabbits	25,000,000
Squirrels	22,000,000
Pheasant	20,000,000
Ruffed grouse	6,000,000
Ducks (all kinds)	5,200,000
Whitetail deer	4,000,000
Geese	1,300,000
Chukar partridge	1,000,000
Mule deer	600,000
Wild turkey	350,000
Coyote	250,000
Pronghorn antelope	115,000
Elk	102,000
Black bear	21,000
Caribou	21,000
Moose	12,000
Javelina	10,000
Bighorn sheep	2,400
Mountain lion	1,500
Mountain goat	1,200
Brown bear and grizzly bear (combined)	1,100
Wolves	1,000
Bison	750
Wolverines	700
Musk ox	90

Source: The Fund for Animals Inc.

they are, and we stand accountable for them."[4]

In Petzal's opinion, poachers and other game-law violators can never be eliminated entirely. But hunters have an obligation, he says, to see to it that everyone who kills animals for sport possesses a basic set of skills, including the ability to track wounded game. Failure to adopt a skills-testing program, which would be funded by hunters themselves, could lead to the demise of sport hunting.

"We are seeing the end of free and easy access to hunting land," Petzal continued. "That is now a relic of the past. Cheap licenses and minimal competence requirements are another relic. We can mourn the former if we like, but we had better do away with the latter ... and soon."

Thomas Heberlein, chairman of the University of Wisconsin's department of rural sociology, voices similar sentiments. "There is a growing public demand that hunters be trained and certified to shoot well, to understand animals and their ecosystems and to be proficient in effective ways of hunting," he says. "There is a desperate need to know something of the dynamics of the human hunter. We are trying to manage a joint human and biological system but have scientific data on only one side of the equation."[5]

As pro- and anti-hunting forces continue to trade barbs, the underlying issues that divide them sometimes are lost. Here are questions that surface repeatedly in the hunting debate:

Why has anti-hunting sentiment increased in recent years?

Until sometime between 1910 and 1920, the United States was a predominantly rural society. Hunting was a deeply ingrained tradition in the towns and farms where most people lived, places where hunters hunted to put meat on the family table. Today, in contrast, the U.S. is overwhelmingly urban, and relatively few Americans know much about hunting. In fact, anecdotal evidence strongly suggests that urban Americans are more likely than others to embrace anti-hunting arguments.

Throughout history, hunters have regarded the pursuit of game as a rite of passage to manhood, transmitted from father to son. Since World War II, however, an increasing number of households have been fatherless families where hunting lore is not passed on. And once a family hunting tradition dies out, it may be impossible to resurrect. Today there are about 18 million American hunters, but many believe the number is lower than it has been in previous years.

Some people oppose hunting because it endangers the lives of hunters and non-hunters alike. According to the National Safety Council, 138 persons died in firearm-related hunting accidents in 1989, the last year for which complete data are available.

In a widely publicized incident in Maine on Nov. 15, 1988, Karen Wood, the mother of twin girls, was fatally shot in the chest by a deer hunter. The tragedy initially attracted attention because it had occurred while Wood was standing in her own back yard in a suburb of Bangor. Interest was rekindled when a grand jury declined to indict the hunter for manslaughter. However, a second panel indicted him, and he went to trial in October 1990. He was found not guilty.

The verdict seemed to show that hunters receive the benefit of the doubt in areas where the hunting ethic is well-established, as in Maine. Some observers speculated that the verdict may also have been influenced by differences between Maine natives and newcomers and between rural and urban lifestyles. The Wood family had moved to Maine from Iowa only four months before the shooting, and their home was in a new subdivision that had been carved out of deer-hunting territory.

While some anti-hunting advocates cite such tragic accidents as reason enough to ban hunting, animal-rights groups have joined the fray on another level: to prevent harm to animals. Over the past decade, they have become key players in the campaign to curb or outlaw sport hunting. The 200,000-member Fund for Animals and the million-member Humane Society of the United States have been especially active in the fight.

The fund aims for nothing less than the abolition of hunting in the United States. "Our goal is to get sport hunting in the same category as cock fighting and dog fighting," says National Director Wayne Pacelle. "Our opponents say that hunting is an American tradition. We say traditions can change."[6]

In pursuit of its objective, the group has staged numerous protests at hunting grounds across the country. Last Sept. 2, about 1,000 members of the fund and other groups converged on Hegins, Pa., in an attempt to disrupt the town's annual Labor Day pigeon shoot. Protesters managed to release a few birds before the shooting started. But such protests are of secondary importance, says Pacelle, because "it's the lawsuits that get hunts stopped."

Pacelle's remark came during a tour of Montana in early October, shortly after a Fund for Animals suit temporarily halted Montana's fall grizzly bear hunting season. Earlier, the organization took legal action against the state's bison hunt, which the Legislature subsequently voted to abolish. *(See story, p. 60.)*

Saving the bison was a sweet victory, but the cancellation of California's 1989 bear-hunting season probably represents the most significant anti-hunting triumph yet. The state acted in response to a lawsuit against the Department of Fish and Game filed by the Fund for Animals, the Animal Legal Defense Fund and the Wildlife Conservancy of California. The three groups claimed that holding the hunt would put the department in violation of the California Environmental Quality Act, which requires full public disclosure of possible environmental effects of projects or regulatory actions under state or local government jurisdiction. In effect, the plaintiffs alleged that the state's procedures for setting bear-hunting regulations were inadequate and should be replaced by a full environmental-impact report.

Ruling in their favor, Sacramento County Superior Court Judge Cecily Bond said California game officials henceforth "must consider on a yearly basis whether to establish, continue, repeal or amend regulations relating to the hunting seasons for black bears." She called continuing the hunts without a full study of the bear population a "prescription for extinction."

Animal-rights groups oppose hunting from what they describe as the philosophical/ethical position that animals have inherent legal and human rights, just as humans do. According to this viewpoint, humans do not have the right to use animals for any reason, including research, recreation and food — or sport hunting.[7]

This belief is not embraced by all anti-hunting activists, however. Luke A. Dommer, chairman of the Committee to Abolish Sport Hunting (CASH), describes his organization as "a nature-preservation group dedicated to the preservation of biological diversity. We feel that hunting as it stands now and the management of wildlife for that purpose contribute to the loss of biological diversity. And on top of that, we don't believe in recreational killing."

Not surprisingly, Dommer finds the animal-rights movement's opposition to hunting overly rigid. "As much as I'm against recreational killing, I don't say that every hunter is a bad or unethical person," he says. "Hunters grow up in an environment where it's all right, it's ethical, to go hunting. So who can pass judgment on hunters' morals?"

Echoing an argument often made by supporters of hunting, Dommer says animal-rights advocates generally display a lack of knowledge about how nature works. "We have to come to grips with the reality that all life on Earth subsists on other life, from the highest to the lowest forms," he says. "That's the way it has always been. But we as human beings have the capacity to eliminate as much unnecessary suffering and unnecessary killing [of animals] as we possibly can."

CASH takes the position that wildlife is "a national treasure" that

Pondering the Mystique of Hunting

Why do hunters hunt? Cynics say it is because they take pleasure in killing helpless wild creatures. Hunters insist that the pursuit and taking of game is spiritually rewarding in ways that non-hunters will never comprehend. Hunting, wrote the Spanish philosopher and essayist José Ortega y Gasset, is nothing less than "a deep and permanent yearning in the human condition."

In a much-quoted passage, Ortega went on to assert:

"To the sportsman the death of the game is not what interests him; that is not his purpose. What interests him is everything that he had to do to achieve that death — that is, the hunt. Therefore what was before only a means to an end is now an end in itself. Death is essential because without it there is no authentic hunting: the killing of the animal is the natural ... goal of hunting itself, not of the hunter. The hunter seeks this death because it is no less than the sign of reality for the whole hunting process. To sum up, one does not hunt in order to kill; on the contrary, one kills in order to have hunted." †

Ortega's long essay, penned in 1942, influenced other writers who have sought to explain the mystique of hunting. George Reiger, the conservation editor of *Field & Stream* magazine, declared in March 1990 that killing "one's first whitetail, buck or doe, is an occasion of mingled elation and solemnity. It should be treated with the reverence due any other milestone in a person's life. Deer hunting is a ritual understood only by those who've been there." ††

Poet Sydney Lea was moved to ponder why he hunts after spotting an automobile bumper sticker that read, "Animals Are Little People in Fur Coats." The animal-rights message offended Lea's sense of esteem for the animals he stalks. "I have respect precisely for the animal's nonhumanity," he recently wrote. "To deny the animal its nonhumanity is to patronize. Animals are not people, little or big. (The bumper sticker's very stress on the diminutive shows the patronizing touch; is a bull elk a little anything, for God's sake?) It's the otherness of wild animals — both the hunters and the hunted — that introduces wonder into my psychic life." ‡

John Baird Callicott, a University of Wisconsin philosophy professor who once taught a course on environmental ethics, subscribes to the hunting credo even though he himself is a non-hunter. "If the effect of hunting upon the hunter is to achieve a psychic return to a primeval human estate in which man lived harmoniously within the biosphere ... hunting can be one of the greatest goods available to modern man," he wrote.

But Callicott added this caveat: "If, on the other hand, hunting serves only to brutalize the hunter, to nurture his blood lust and to intensify his hostility to nature and hatred of godforsaken, untamed beasts, then sport hunting should be condemned as an abomination." ‡‡

---

† José Ortega y Gasset, *Meditations on Hunting* [translated from the Spanish by Howard B. Wescott] (1972), pp. 110-111.

†† George Reiger, "How Should We Manage Our Deer?" *Field & Stream*, March 1990, p. 25.

‡ Sydney Lea, "The Death of a Hunting Dog," *Sports Illustrated*, Dec. 2, 1991, p. 12.

‡‡ John Baird Callicott, "Remarks on Hunting," *Hunting: Sport or Sin?* (anthology published by the College of Natural Resources, University of Wisconsin — Stevens Point), 1974.

"should not be controlled by any special-interest group ... without regard for the rights of the vast majority of people for whom that treasure is held in trust." Consequently, one of the group's chief aims is to increase the representation of non-hunters and hunting opponents on government agencies charged with management of fish and game resources.

What do hunters say in defense of their sport?

When opponents of hunting began their fight in the 1980s, they caught hunters off guard at first with their legal initiatives and skill at influencing popular opinion. But pro-hunting groups soon mounted their own public relations campaign. As one wildlife writer put it, "It's time for us to convince the silent majority that we are the friends of wildlife in this country." [8]

Sport hunters claim much of the credit for reversing the depletion of North American wildlife in the 19th century. "It was the American sportsman who stepped in to give wildlife a second chance," the WLFA claims. "American sportsmen called for federal and state wildlife conservation programs ... for parks and refuges to conserve wildlife ... and for laws to stop the dangerous practice of market hunting. Sportsmen worked to improve wildlife habitat and to establish wildlife conservation laws and programs." [9]

Nonetheless, some hunting advocates feel uncomfortable defending an activity they believe needs no justification. "Hunters have a hard time articulating the reasons they hunt ... probably because our language is a little shy of the right words to express these very personal feelings," says Gary Anderson, the NRA's executive director of general operations. "And on top of that, our public image is vulnerable. The media define hunting as a blood sport, then ... [publish] photographs of bloody carcasses and grinning hunters. In essence, this hides the true meaning of a hunt, and depicts hunters as less than what they truly are — responsible participants in nature." *(See "At Issue," p. 65.)*

To buttress that claim, American hunters point out that they contribute more than $1 billion a year to wildlife conservation programs. The money comes from federal excise taxes on hunting equipment and ammunition, fishing boats and supplies, as well as from state hunting and fishing license fees and federal and state "duck stamps." *(See p. 61.)* In addition, the WLFA estimates that local, state and national sportsmen's organizations contribute $50 million a year to wildlife conservation projects.

The 550,000 pro-hunting members of Ducks Unlimited, for example, raise money to protect wetlands in Canada and the United States used by migratory waterfowl as well as by numerous animal species. (Other bird species have friends among the hunters too, among them Pheasants Forever and the Ruffed Grouse Society.)

Pro-hunting groups also take pride in their education programs. An NRA testing program for students from the United States and Canada focuses on knowledge of the rifle, shotgun, archery, wildlife identification and other areas. A principal goal of the NRA youth program is to make hunters aware of their role in conservation.

A more difficult task, hunters have found, is showing non-hunters the positive aspects of stalking game for sport. Hunters and many wildlife biologists say, for example, that hunting prevents the prolific whitetail deer from multiplying beyond the capacity of its habitat to sustain the species. Some experts think that without hunting the whitetail population might even "crash," transforming a robust wildlife species into a threat-

ened or endangered one.

In like manner, hunters argue that hunting and trapping of predators is sometimes justified to protect other wild creatures. "Wildlife refuges must trap coyote, fox, raccoon and other predators, which can otherwise wipe out the concentrated nests of waterfowl and shorebirds," asserted nature writer Richard Conniff. "On the Louisiana coast, landowners ... must trap simply to keep the marshes from being nibbled bare of grass by muskrat and nutria and washed out to sea."[10]

Similar considerations led the Santa Catalina Island Conservancy to hire four hunters in January 1990 to kill some 2,000 wild goats on the island south of Los Angeles. Eliminating the voracious animals was seen as the only way to give native grasses, shrubs and animals a chance to flourish. Prior to the hunt, the goats had stripped much of the island's vegetation.

But Cleveland Amory, the founder and president of the Fund for Animals, bitterly condemned the members of the conservancy for not relocating the animals and for visiting "this kind of unnecessary cruelty on goats, which are much more worthy inhabitants of the island than they'll ever be."[11]

To burnish their image among non-hunters, hunters have been helping to shape legislation to promote hunter ethics and competency. This approach bore fruit last year with the passage of New Jersey's Sportsman's Responsibility Bill. The measure requires game-law violators to pay the state for loss of wildlife ($200 per deer, for instance, plus possible criminal penalties). The law also makes hunters responsible for the careless handling of a weapon, regardless of whether it caused any damage; mandates the loss of a hunting license for two years for repeat violations; and requires game-law violators to take a remedial hunter-education course. "Tough stuff," commented *Field &*

Stream Contributing Editor Lionel Atwill, "but necessary."[12]

Another image-enhancing venture involves giving surplus game meat to the poor and homeless. Individual hunters traditionally have shared their bounty with the needy, but now they are doing it on a coordinated basis — and attracting favorable media attention. One such program, Sportsmen Against Hunger, is run by Safari Club International, which promotes its hunting trips as helpful to wildlife management. Last year, three Colorado chapters of the club distributed 100,000 pounds of deer, elk and antelope meat to hungry Coloradans.

"Some hunters criticize this program, saying it allows hunters to kill more game to donate to the needy," says Bob Young, chairman of Sportsmen Against Hunger. "But that's not the case. We are adamant about having hunters share only their surplus harvest with less-fortunate people. If every hunter would donate just 5 pounds from a deer or 10 pounds from an elk to this program, there would be enough meat to feed the needy everywhere. This program has the potential to provide millions of pounds of high-protein meat to hungry people nationwide."[13]

Do deer and duck hunting support wildlife management and conservation?

Popular opinion about hunting often hinges on the identity of the prey. Hunters and non-hunters alike agree that rare species like the whooping crane and bald eagle should be off-limits. Protective feelings also run high over grizzly bears and desert bighorn sheep. But when it comes to deer, the positions of pro- and anti-hunting groups may be more polarized than on any other subject.

Hunters take credit for helping the decimated U.S. whitetail deer population begin its recovery at the start of the 20th century. Hunters fund the

A Nation of Hunters

Across the U.S. some 16 million† hunters bought hunting licenses in 1990, from 1.2 million in Pennsylvania to just 12,782 in Rhode Island. The states with the most hunters tend to be in the less populous regions, such as the South and Midwest. California tallied a relatively low 390,665 hunters, reflecting increasing urbanization and stricter laws against hunting.

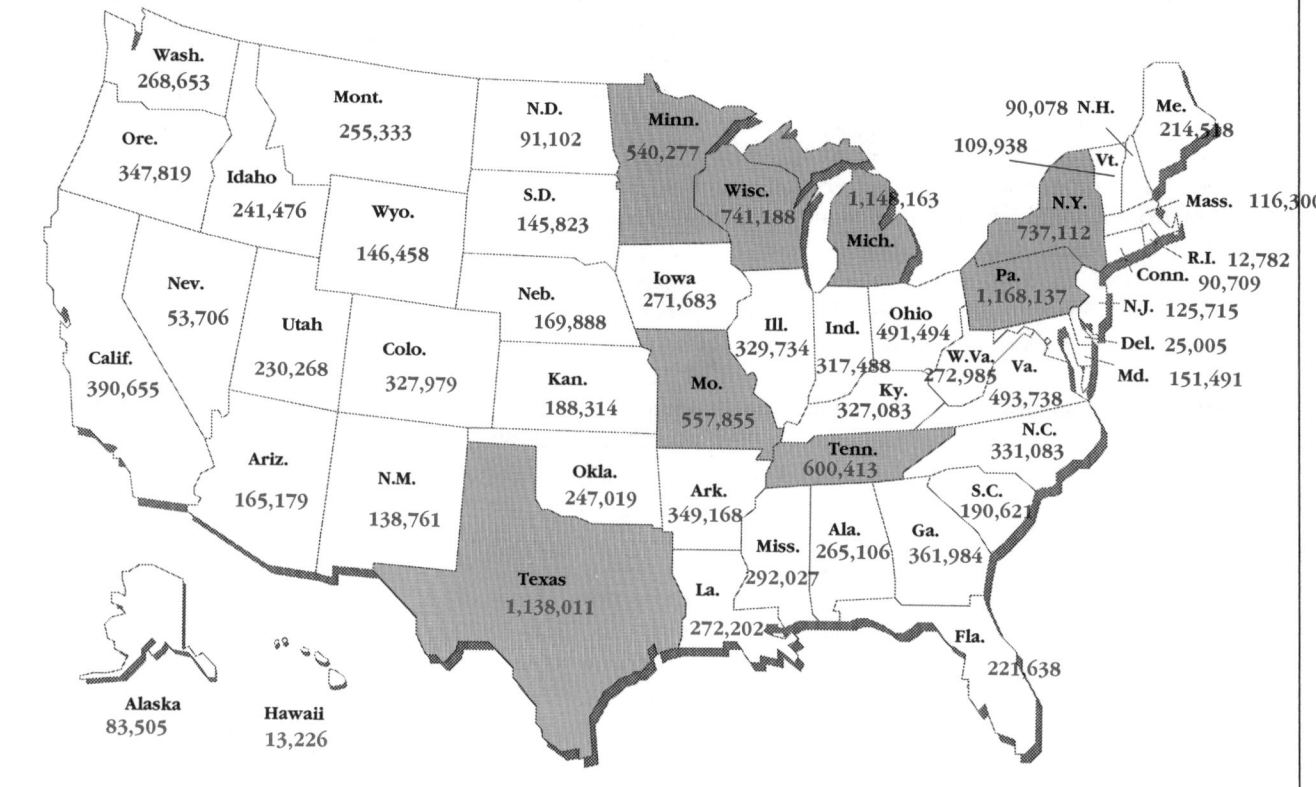

Wash. 268,653
Mont. 255,333
N.D. 91,102
Minn. 540,277
N.H. 90,078
109,938
Me. 214,548
Ore. 347,819
Idaho 241,476
Wyo. 146,458
S.D. 145,823
Wisc. 741,188
1,148,163
Mich.
Vt.
N.Y. 737,112
Mass. 116,300
Nev. 53,706
Utah 230,268
Colo. 327,979
Neb. 169,888
Iowa 271,683
Ill. 329,734
Ind. 317,488
Ohio 491,494
Pa. 1,168,137
R.I. 12,782
Conn. 90,709
N.J. 125,715
Calif. 390,665
Kan. 188,314
Mo. 557,855
Ky. 327,083
W.Va. 272,985
Va. 493,738
Del. 25,005
Md. 151,491
Ariz. 165,179
N.M. 138,761
Okla. 247,019
Ark. 349,168
Tenn. 600,413
N.C. 331,083
Texas 1,138,011
Miss. 292,027
Ala. 265,106
Ga. 361,984
S.C. 190,621
La. 272,202
Fla. 221,638
Alaska 83,505
Hawaii 13,226

† This total is lower than the Census Bureau tally used in this report, which includes hunters who don't have licenses.
Source: U.S. Fish and Wildlife Service

acquisition and maintenance of deer habitat, they say, and keep deer herds at an optimum size by harvesting surplus animals.

Opponents beg to differ. They insist whitetails are thriving because the shy critters have moved into habitat niches vacated by once-abundant species. Above all, the opponents say, state game commissions increase the size of deer herds by deliberately manipulating the animals' sex ratio.

If deer are left undisturbed, they give birth to roughly equal numbers of male and female fawns. But game commissions required for years that hunters take only adult males during hunting season. "By killing off the bucks, they establish ratios anywhere from 2 to 15 females to each male," says Luke Dommer, of the Committee to Abolish Sport Hunting. "This maximizes the birthrate because ... one male can impregnate any number of females."[14]

The result in some parts of the country has been a deer explosion. During winter months, deer wander into residential gardens in outlying suburbs and nibble on ornamental shrubs and trees. They also become serious traffic hazards. The National Safety Council estimates that motor vehicles nationwide kill more than 350,000 deer — and about 100 drivers and passengers — each year.

Such statistics have prompted game commissions to revisit their buck-biased policies. According to Susan Hagood, a wildlife-issues specialist at the Humane Society, "The vast majority of states have now established doe-only seasons, or either-sex seasons, or antlerless [females and immature males] seasons ... to prevent further population increases." Still, because of their antlers, bucks are likely to remain the trophy of choice.

Similarly, officials have had to rethink hunting policies concerning migratory waterfowl.* Duck hunting aroused relatively little comment until a decade ago. But the population — once estimated at 100 million birds — plummeted to about 62 million during the 1980s, prompting the U.S. Fish and Wildlife Service to reduce bag limits and hunting days.

Sport hunting, however, had little to do with the duck population crash. An extended drought had settled over Canada and the United States in the middle of the decade. This dried up swamps, ponds and other prairie wetlands needed by migratory waterfowl for resting, breeding, nesting and feeding. The same thing had happened during the Dust Bowl years of the Great Depression. But in the 1930s, the wetlands eventually filled with water after the drought lifted, and the duck population rebounded.

That failed to happen this time, mainly because farmers had drained, filled and put into cultivation many of the dried-up wetlands on their property. Other wetlands were stripped of critical surrounding vegetation and cover, making them less suitable as breeding and nesting sites. Now, even though normal rainfall patterns seem to be resuming in the stricken region, recovery of the duck population seems doubtful. In addition, notes Patricia Yoxall, director of information and education for Ducks Unlimited, "the population of people continues to grow, too," further diminishing wildlife habitat.

Poaching also is a problem, though its severity is hard to assess. Some wildlife experts say the illegal kill of ducks equals the legal take. Other estimates put the poaching toll much higher. Even so, Ducks Unlimited biologist Mike Johnson calls habitat loss "a far greater problem" than poaching.

---

*"Migratory waterfowl" refers to the 10 major bird species that hunters refer to collectively as ducks, among them mallards, widgeons, canvasbacks and northern pintails.

One thing is certain: Wildlife officials realized in the 1980s that ducks needed help. In May 1986, the U.S. and Canada agreed to establish a joint North American Waterfowl Management Plan. The 15-year project aims to restore enough wetland habitat in the two countries to support a breeding population of 62 million and a fall flight of 100 million ducks. Conservation and pro-hunting organizations supporting the plan include Ducks Unlimited, the Audubon Society, the National Wildlife Federation, and the Wildlife Management Institute.

The task is complicated by poisoning from lead shot, a decades-old hazard. By some estimates, 2 or 3 percent of the nation's waterfowl die from lead poisoning each year. When ducks dive for food on lake or stream bottoms, they often ingest lead pellets from hunters' shotgun shells. Concern over lead poisoning has grown with evidence that endangered bald eagles, picking up pellets themselves or eating waterfowl killed or crippled by toxic lead levels, have been dying in growing numbers. Even if all duck hunters in the U.S. switched overnight to less toxic steel ammunition, lead shot already on the ground will threaten future generations of waterfowl.*

What types of hunting are the most controversial?

Hunting opponents often reserve their sharpest criticism for bowhunting. To many non-hunters, the bow and arrow would seem to make for a more equal contest between stalker and prey than pursuit with a firearm. Experienced hunters dismiss the notion as sentimental claptrap. "Man is the most skilled predator the Earth has ever known, and hunting is simply no contest between him and animals," Thomas McIntyre, hunting editor of *Sports Afield,* wrote in a

---

*Federal law now makes it illegal to take migratory waterfowl with lead shot.

1988 book on the art and spirit of hunting. "There isn't even a referee. Whatever rules do exist in hunting, beyond government-imposed game laws, are those the hunter imposes on himself, and abides by." [15]

To enthusiasts, bowhunting appeals on several levels. Bowhunting seasons are longer, earlier in the year and quieter and less crowded than firearms seasons. Moreover, game animals are more plentiful and approachable before the firearms start blasting away.

But hunting opponents see a fundamental flaw with bowhunting: the inherent difficulty of shooting arrows accurately, even with the most advanced equipment. Because of the pronounced "rainbow" trajectory of an arrow, the bowhunter must estimate his distance from the prey and adjust his shot to compensate for the arc.

The opponents claim that for every animal hit by an arrow and retrieved by a hunter, at least one other animal is hit and not retrieved. Most of the wounded animals, they say, die from septic infection, peritonitis, blood loss or other painful complications. Moreover, opponents contend, the most skillful bowhunters wound more game than the least skillful. "While novice archers usually miss animals entirely, better shooters connect more often, wounding a high percentage of them with random hits," wrote Wayne Pacelle. [16]

To project a more positive view of their sport — and to defeat state and local efforts to outlaw it — bowhunters formed the Bowhunter Defense Coalition. Like hunters who use firearms, bowhunters argue that they help prevent game animals from overpopulating and thus contribute to sound wildlife management. And they insist that most animals recover quickly from arrow wounds.

The bowhunters' lobbying really hit the bull's eye in New Jersey, where every year half a dozen townships prohibit the shooting of bows or shotguns, effectively barring hunting. A particularly ominous development emerged in 1985 in the form of a proposed statewide ban on broadheads, a lethal arrow widely used by bowhunters that employs a flat, triangle-shaped steel tip with sharp edges. The United Bowhunters of New Jersey mounted a successful drive against the bill and increased its membership from about 750 to more than 4,000 in the process. Hunters regard the campaign as especially significant because New Jersey is the nation's most densely populated state and a bastion of anti-hunting sentiment.

There is one form of hunting, however, that supporters and opponents of the sport condemn with almost equal fervor: "canned" hunts of animals that are released into small enclosures to be gunned down by trophy hunters. Prices are pegged to the rarity of the species, many of which are not native to North America, among them exotic "big cats" obtained from breeders, dealers and zoos.

In October 1990, state fish and game agents raided a preserve in Oklahoma where hunters paid up to $4,000 to kill bears and cougars in a fenced area the size of a football field. The owner of the preserve was fined and sentenced to prison, but not for any hunting violations. He pleaded guilty to two cruelty charges based on the "deplorable state" of the preserve's animal pens.

In a similar case last year, a California couple were sentenced to a total of 180 days in jail and $42,000 in fines after being convicted of violating state laws by permitting exotic-cat hunts at their ranch. For $3,500 hunters got to kill tigers, leopards and jaguars, pose for photographs with the dead animals and take home the stuffed skins. California law does not prohibit the killing of animals not native to the state, but it does bar the possession of body parts, including hides, of animals protected under the 1973 federal Endangered Species Act.[17] ■

remains is protected in sanctuaries or game parks, where limited hunting is permitted to cull surplus animals.

U.S. and Canadian hunting traditions have radically different origins from Europe's. When European settlers arrived in North America, they were stunned by the abundance of animals and birds. Even as late as 1877, a Shakopee, Minn., hunter identifying himself only as "Rusticus" wrote in a letter of his amazement at seeing a skyful of ducks early on an October evening: "Thousands of birds are on the wing ... and later, as the daylight begins to fade into the grey of the evening, one would think from the terrific flights that the birds were aiming at the hunters' heads, for often we have to 'duck' our heads to escape being knocked over."[18]

Ironically, systematic extermination of wildlife was reaching epic dimensions in the United States just as Rusticus was penning his rhapsodic account. As early as Colonial times, laws had been passed to conserve wildlife, principally by restrictions on hunting, but they were rarely enforced. Since wild game was plentiful, it was taken for granted that any man good with a gun could have his larder full most of the year. The pioneer's notion that wildlife represented meat for the table led in time to fur trapping and commercial hunting. So insatiable was the demand for fur hats and other clothing that the beaver at one point was in danger of extinction.

The Bison's Fate

The bison suffered more than any other native animal from the depredations of white hunters. When European explorers first arrived in America, bison herds probably constituted the biggest aggregation of land animals anywhere in the world. It has been estimated that well into the 19th century there were at least 40 million of them.

Every spring and autumn this huge

Continued on p. 60

BACKGROUND

Evolving Attitudes

Humans have always hunted, but not for quite the same reasons that they do today. In prehistoric times, men stalked animals and birds for sheer survival. Freshly killed wildlife provided not only food but also fur, feathers, bones and teeth, all put to use as clothing, shelter, tools or adornment.

The greatest change in hunting has been the shift from hunting for survival to hunting for sport. As animals were domesticated and agriculture took root, the need to pursue wild animals for nourishment gradually waned. Though game meat still was prized by many, wild animals came

to be regarded as trophies to be displayed as badges of status.

This change coincided, in Europe at least, with increasing social stratification. Even now, the guiding assumption in Western Europe is that game belongs to the landowner, who is responsible for preserving it. Hunting is for a privileged few rather than open to all, and laws are strict. To hunt, a sportsman generally must be the guest of a landowner or of a resort that has leased hunting property. In England, fox hunting has evolved into a complex social ritual of the aristocracy and landed gentry.

European hunting attitudes and practices also have been shaped by demography. As the density of the continent's human population rose, the number of wild animals — especially big-game species — declined because of habitat loss. Most of what

Chronology

19th Century

Early European settlers are awed by the abundance of wildlife in North America. But relentless hunting of some seemingly inexhaustible species exacts a heavy toll.

1840
Herds of bison west of the Mississippi River are estimated to number as many as 40 million animals.

1860s-70s
Building of the transcontinental railroads and introduction of the Winchester repeating rifle lead to the slaughter of millions of bison.

1883
The last sizable buffalo herd in the wild, comprising some 10,000 animals in North Dakota, is systematically exterminated between September and November 1883. By 1889, the world population of American bison is down to about 1,000.

1895
Heavy hunting reduces the number of whitetail deer in the United States from a million animals to an estimated 350,000.

— • —

1900-1929
Though hunting remains largely unregulated, game animals benefit from growing public concern about conserving natural resources.

1900
The Lacey Act outlaws interstate transportation of wildlife harvested or possessed in violation of the laws of the state from which or to which it is transported. The immediate objective was to save the bison from extinction by poaching in Yellowstone National Park. By reducing the profitability of market hunting, the act sharply reduced in the illegal killing of wildlife.

September 1914
Martha, the world's last surviving passenger pigeon, dies at age 29 in the Cincinnati Zoo. Her frozen carcass is shipped to the Smithsonian Institution for display. Passenger pigeons, thought to be the most numerous bird species that ever existed, were hunted to extinction by the end of the 19th century.

1929
Thanks to conservation efforts begun around the turn of the century, world stocks of American bison rise to 18,494, mostly in Canada.

1929
The Migratory Bird Conservation Act authorizes the purchase of land for federal waterfowl refuges.

— • —

1930s
The federal government assumes an increasingly prominent role in wildlife management.

1934
Under the Migratory Bird Hunting Stamp Act, hunters over age 16 must buy a $1 federal waterfowl stamp (known as a "duck stamp") before taking migratory waterfowl anywhere in the country. Proceeds from the stamps are earmarked for new waterfowl refuge areas.

1937
The Federal Aid in Wildlife Restoration Act, also known as the Pittman-Robertson Act, directs that proceeds from an 11 percent excise tax on sporting arms and ammunition be used for grants to the states to cover 75 percent of state costs for cooperative programs in wildlife research, management and development.

1970s-1990s
Responding to rising public concern about the survival of wildlife, the government takes additional steps to control hunting.

1971
Congress enacts legislation making it a federal crime to shoot, harass or hunt any bird, fish or animal from an airplane. Violators face up to $5,000 in fines and a year in prison.

1973
The Endangered Species Act makes it a federal offense to hunt, trap or capture animals, birds or fish from a wildlife species designated as endangered or threatened. In addition, the law prohibits the purchase, sale or transport of articles made from such creatures.

May 1986
The United States and Canada sign an agreement calling on public and private groups in both countries to join forces to save wetlands and the migratory waterfowl that rely on them as breeding grounds. The goal of the 15-year North American Waterfowl Management Plan is "the restoration of enough habitat across the two countries to hold a breeding population of 62 million and a fall flight of 100 million ducks."

Oct. 17, 1990
A jury in Bangor, Maine, finds deer hunter Donald Rogerson not guilty of manslaughter. Two years earlier, Rogerson had fatally shot Karen Wood, the mother of two children, as she stood in her back yard one afternoon during hunting season.

Montana Bison Hunt Stirs Passions

For historical reasons, the hunting of bison (also called buffalo) arouses strong emotions even among people with little interest in wildlife issues. Nearly every American knows that the great herds of buffalo that once roamed the Western Plains were hunted nearly to extinction in the 19th century. Bison encountered today in a zoo, wrote a recent contributor to *The New Republic* magazine, "awaken a dim yet powerful public memory, a potent stirring of nobility and guilt. They are a caged myth. An American unicorn." † This being so, legalized hunting of buffalo often stirs strong opposition.

Opposition certainly materialized when 569 bison were killed after they wandered out of Yellowstone National Park into Montana in the winter of 1988-89. In 1985, the Montana Legislature had declared bison a big-game animal and authorized licensed hunters called by the state Department of Fish, Wildlife and Parks to shoot bison that left the park. The hunt was justified as a means of controlling the size of the park's bison herd. Also, Montana ranchers wanted to prevent Yellowstone bison from infecting their animals with brucellosis, a disease that can cause domestic cattle to abort their calves.

The 1988-89 Montana bison hunt drew nationwide media coverage because of the unusually large number of animals killed and because the Fund for Animals staged angry protests at the scene. Fund members stood between bison hunters and their prey, smeared blood on at least one hunter and poked another with a ski pole.

Controversy continued to simmer even after the 1988-89 hunt ended. On April 8, 1991, Judge George H. Rever-comb of U.S. District Court in Washington, D.C., issued a temporary restraining order halting plans to kill 25 bison for the purpose of determining the extent of brucellosis contagion in the Yellowstone herd.†† Two days later, the National Park Service announced it was abandoning the project for good. The Fund for Animals hailed the decision as a major victory.

Meanwhile, Montana bowed to the inevitable as Republican Gov. Stan Stephens on April 9 signed into law a bill ending the bison-hunting program. Although the measure directed the National Park Service and the state Livestock Department to devise a new bison-culling program, Montana law gives the department no authority to kill wild animals for control purposes.

The bill reportedly was passed out of concern that adverse publicity from the bison hunt could discourage tourism. Jim Glass, president of the Wildlife Legislative Fund of America, tried without success to counter that argument by asking legislators, "But what about the hunter-tourist? What message will [the bill] send them — other than STAY HOME?" ‡

---

† David Montgomery, "Buffalophobia," *The New Republic,* Dec. 23 & 30, 1991, p. 13. Montgomery is a reporter for *The Buffalo* (N.Y.) *News.*

†† Three bison already had been killed when Revercomb issued his decision.

‡ From a February 1991 letter to members of the Montana House of Representatives and Senate.

Continued from p. 58
population migrated, and the sight of the vast herds on the move made a deep impression on contemporary observers. "Towards evening, on the rise of a hill, we were suddenly greeted by a sight which seemed to astonish even the oldest among us," an account written in 1832 stated. "The whole plain, as far as the eye could see, was covered by one enormous mass of buffalo." [19]

Systematic hunting of bison by white men became an activity of some consequence around 1825, and from 1850 on it grew with each passing year. The slaughter had a twofold purpose: to provide Eastern markets with tongues (considered a great delicacy at the time), hides, robes and even bones, and to starve the Plains Indians into submission by eliminating their principal source of food. The Indians themselves aided in the killing; they exchanged bison skins for such articles as knives, firearms, tobacco and whiskey.

Construction of the Union Pacific Railroad in the 1860s was the event that really doomed the bison. Great armies of workers had to be fed, and the easiest way to do this was to shoot the docile and ever-present buffalo. Beginning in 1867, butchery on an unprecedented scale all but exterminated the huge herds in little more than 15 years; from 1870 to 1875, at least 2 million of the animals were killed every year.

By 1883, only one large bison herd, consisting of around 10,000 animals, was left in the United States. And it, too, was exterminated. Cree Indians and white hunters moved into North Dakota in September 1883. They guarded potholes and built fires along river banks to keep the beasts from water. In about two months the herd was wiped out.

In 1888, the landscape artist Albert Bierstadt painted "The Last of the Buffalo," an elegiac canvas suggesting that what had long seemed impossible might soon come true. A census taken the following year showed a total bison population of 541, made up of several small groups of animals.

But the bison herds of yore have left a valuable and lasting heritage in the deep wallows they formed across the Great Plains. "A hundred years after the wild buffalo's demise," wrote historian Charles F. Waterman, "the old wallows remain as prairie potholes and serve as gathering spots for nesting mallards. And among the old wallows were similar pits that once were the caves of ancient hunters."[20]

End of Passenger Pigeons

The classic case of wildlife extinction through hunting was the passenger pigeon, probably the most plentiful bird the world has ever known. Accounts of the immense pigeon flocks over North America in the early 19th century strain the imagination. The famed wildlife painter John James Audubon estimated that one such flight contained well over a billion pigeons. The birds passed over him for hours on end and in such concentration that sunlight was almost blotted out. In all directions as far as the eye could see the sky was filled with pigeons, layer upon layer, and all flying at speeds approaching 60 mph. By way of comparison, the total bird population of the British Isles is thought to be about 200 million; the single flock observed by Audubon may have contained five times that number.

As with the bison, the coming of white settlers and the railroads amounted to a death sentence for the savory passenger pigeon. Professional hunters in the 1860s and '70s amassed huge profits from pigeons sent by rail to major towns and cities. Taking them was easy. Firing at a flock on the wing with both barrels of a shotgun often brought down more than 100 birds, and as many as 3,000 roosting pigeons could be trapped in a skillfully laid net. Sometime the flocks flew so low that large numbers could be knocked down with a pole.

Even so prolific a bird as the passenger pigeon could not withstand an annual slaughter in the tens of millions. By the 1880s it was clear that unless immediate preventive measures were taken, the passenger pigeon would be annihilated. Nothing was done. By the early 1900s the few remaining wild specimens had disappeared. Hunting ceased, but it hardly mattered. "When the killing, stopped the remnants never recovered," Waterman wrote, "for their way of life was based on their numbers."[21]

The Cincinnati Zoological Gardens had foreseen the fate of the passenger pigeon. Accordingly, the zoo bought a few pairs of birds in 1879 in the hope of keeping the species alive if it became extinct in the wild. But the pigeons did not thrive in captivity. One by one, the few that were hatched and reared died until only Martha, hatched in 1885, remained. Martha died in September 1914, and her frozen carcass was shipped for display to the Smithsonian Institution in Washington, D.C.

By the time of Martha's death, America's lackadaisical approach to wildlife management and hunting was undergoing fundamental change. The country's seemingly inexhaustible stock of animals and birds clearly was in jeopardy. Indiscriminate hunting had reduced the nationwide population of whitetail deer — once one of the most prolific big-game species — from a million animals to an estimated 350,000 in 1895.*

Early Wildlife Laws

Agitation against large-scale commercial hunting first found expression in the 1900 Lacey Act, named

---

*Today, the U.S. population of whitetails is estimated at up to 20 million.

for Rep. John F. Lacey, R-Iowa. It outlawed the interstate transportation of wildlife harvested or possessed in violation of the laws of the state from which or to which it was sent. One goal was to save the bison — an easy target for poachers in Yellowstone National Park — from extinction. Another was to curb the slaughter of adult nesting egrets for their plumage, then widely used to trim women's hats. Though some illegal plume selling continued after the law took effect, fashion came to the rescue as milliners shifted from feathers to artificial flowers.

Migratory bird treaties negotiated in 1916 with Britain and in 1936 with Mexico also affected hunting, although indirectly. The pacts provided for the conservation and protection of wild birds moving back and forth between the three countries. The implementing Migratory Bird Treaty Act of 1918, along with related legislation enacted later, forbade any hunting or injury to such birds.

Congress provided additional safeguards in the Migratory Bird Conservation Act of 1929, which authorized the purchase of new areas for waterfowl refuges. Five years later, Congress passed the landmark Migratory Bird Hunting Stamp Act. Under this law, hunters over age 16 were required to purchase a $1 federal waterfowl stamp (a "duck stamp") before hunting migratory waterfowl anywhere in the country. Proceeds from the stamps were earmarked for the purchase of waterfowl refuge areas as authorized by the 1929 Migratory Bird Conservation Act. Most states have since enacted legislation mimicking the federal duck stamp law. Over the years, the price of a federal duck stamp has increased to $15.

The Pittman-Robertson Act

The key federal statute on hunting is the 1937 Federal Aid in Wildlife Restoration Act, known as the Pittman-Robertson Act for its two

Presidents Who Hunt: A Breed Apart

George Bush is the latest addition to the short list of U.S. presidents who have hunted for recreation. The others were Benjamin Harrison, Theodore Roosevelt, Dwight D. Eisenhower and Lyndon B. Johnson.

President Richard M. Nixon, a non-hunter, knew that Soviet leader Leonid I. Brezhnev was fond of the sport. Thus, when Brezhnev visited the United States in 1973, Nixon presented him with a custom-made hunting rifle, its stock decorated with an American eagle and Russian bear of inlaid gold. The gift was accompanied by a plaque that read: "To His Excellency, Leonid Brezhnev, From the Sportsmen of America," and, below that, "From Sportsman to Sportsman."

Theodore Roosevelt was the nation's No. 1 Hunter-in-Chief, bar none. Legendary in their day, TR's exploits in the Far West, Africa and South America live on in the eight books he wrote, among them *Hunting Trip of a Ranchman* (1885), and *Through the Brazilian Wilderness* (1914).

Author Mark Twain took to the lecture platform to denounce Roosevelt's hunting trips, but he isn't alone. Fund for Animals founder Cleveland Amory also castigated the rough-riding Roosevelt in his 1974 book, *Man Kind? Our Incredible War on Wildlife.* Both writers expressed particular distaste for Roosevelt's pursuit of large game animals.

Now President Bush is catching flak for shooting quail, which he has done for the past quarter-century on annual trips to the Texas ranch of businessman William S. Farish III. The protests began in 1988, when Bush was the president-elect. Confronted by animal-rights activists, Bush said: "These aren't animals — these are wild quail. You've got to eat. Our forefathers ate by harvesting game." But he expressed reservations about whether he could bring himself to kill an animal like a deer.

Bush's words failed to mollify hunting opponents such as Dana Forbes, a regional representative of the Fund for Animals. In a letter sent to the president shortly before this year's hunt at the Farish ranch, she said: "We are asking that you take a step toward the vision of a kinder, gentler world that you have offered us by choosing to spare the lives of the birds."

She told reporters in Beeville, Texas, near the hunting site, that Bush "doesn't need to kill animals in order to eat, so we feel his hunting is very inappropriate."†

---

† Quoted in *The Washington Times,* Dec. 28, 1991.

chief sponsors, Sen. Key Pittman, D-Nev., and Rep. A. Willis Robertson, D-Va. Today the Pittman-Robertson (P-R) program is financed by an 11 percent excise tax on rifles, shotguns, ammunition and archery equipment and a 10 percent tax on handguns. After the tax receipts are transferred by the Treasury Department to the U.S. Fish and Wildlife Service, the money is distributed to the states according to a formula based on the state's area, population and number of licensed hunters. The funds are used for wildlife conservation, hunter education and shooting-range construction.

States must contribute $1 to the P-R program for every $3 of federal money received, thus increasing overall funding by 25 percent. The state contribution comes mainly from the sale of hunting licenses. The Pittman-Robertson Act also autho-rizes the use of some tax receipts for administrative costs, a provision that makes the program self-supporting. Hunters are proud of the fact that no general Treasury funds go to support P-R. Anti-hunting groups, they note, have no comparable program funded by members' tax dollars.

Prodded by mounting popular interest in environmental issues, Congress in the early 1970s began displaying renewed interest in wildlife and hunting issues. A 1971 law, for example, made it a federal crime to shoot, harass or hunt any bird, fish or animal from an airplane.*

Violators were made subject to as much as $5,000 in fines and up to one year in prison. A Wyoming pi-lot testifying before a Senate subcommittee in August 1971 stated that sheep ranchers had killed about 500 bald and golden eagles from aircraft.

The Endangered Species Act

A far more significant law, the Endangered Species Act, followed in 1973. The measure extended federal protection to species "threatened" with extinction as well as "endangered" — those in immediate danger of becoming extinct. A threatened species list was added to the endangered species list that had been kept by the Fish and Wildlife Service since 1967.

The 1973 law increased penalties for violations of existing legal restrictions on foreign trade and interstate commerce in listed species, and imposed new curbs on the hunting or trapping of listed species. Native

---

*Exceptions, however, were often permitted for employees or agents of the federal or state governments or holders of federal or state permits to protect land, water, animals, people or crops.

Alaskans engaged in activities necessary for subsistence were exempted from the prohibitions, and special permits to engage in prohibited acts, such as collecting live animals, could be issued for scientific study or to ensure the survival of a species.

During his 1988 presidential election campaign, George Bush said there would be "no net loss" of wetlands during his administration. As president, he helped fulfill that promise a year later when he signed a bill to increase North America's dwindling waterfowl by preserving its wetlands habitat. The measure carried out both the North American Waterfowl Management Plan, a 1986 treaty between the United States and Canada, and a 1988 agreement that included Mexico.

The proposed National Biological Diversity Conservation Act, which failed to clear Congress in 1991, could be a harbinger of future battles between pro- and anti-hunting groups. Described as "a bill to conserve the diversity of fish, wildlife and biological systems in the U.S.," the legislation might seem unobjectionable on its face. But hunters and hunting opponents hold sharply opposing views about it.

According to CASH's Luke Dommer, "We shouldn't be contributing to the loss of biological diversity in the name of hunting. U.S. wildlife should be managed to preserve biological diversity, not to manipulate it for the benefit of a small minority of the population that wants trophy animals to hunt."

In contrast, Al Wolter, director of national affairs at the WLFA, opposes the biological diversity bill on the grounds that it has a hidden purpose — the abolition of sport hunting. "Biodiversity is a catchword that is going to spell a lot of problems for foresters and wildlife managers," he says. "First, the term has yet to be defined; second, even if it were defined, no systematic way of applying it has ever been devised." ∎

— all except Alabama, Hawaii, Massachusetts, Nebraska, New Jersey and New Mexico. Wolter predicts that the six holdouts will fall into line soon.

Hunting opponents were heartened in 1987 when the state Supreme Court overturned Connecticut's harassment law as "unconstitutionally vague." However, the Connecticut Legislature in 1990 passed a second version that is still on the statute books.

"There have been several arrests made under state hunter-harassment laws," Wolter says, "but we detect a certain shyness on some states' part to enforce the laws. We encourage them to be more assertive, because if the law is flawed we'd like to know about it so we can strengthen it, as Connecticut did."

Most harassment incidents involve hunters of deer and other large game. According to Patricia Yoxall of Ducks Unlimited, waterfowl hunters generally have been left alone. "Americans still perceive ducks as something you can eat," she says, "so they can understand a harvest of ducks much more readily than a harvest of deer, even though deer hunters frequently eat their kill as well. Duck hunting just seems more of a practical kind of sport. Also, people tend to react more to the taking of mammals."

Federal Anti-Harassment Bill Stalls

Efforts to enact a federal law protecting hunters from protesters have not gotten far. Anti-harassment bills were introduced in Congress in 1990 and 1991 but didn't reach the floor of the House or Senate. Hunting organizations say a federal ban is needed because it is not clear whether state anti-harassment laws apply to hunters stalking game on federally owned land.

In fact, an unrelated bill introduced in Congress last year (HR 330)

Current Situation

Harassment of Hunters

Today, harassment of hunters in the field sharply divides both sides in the hunting debate. Opponents insist the First Amendment guarantee of free speech protects their right to protest vocally when hunters go out to stalk game. Testifying before a congressional subcommittee in 1990, the Fund for Animals' Wayne Pacelle said: "There is no reason to suggest that the possession of a hunting license entitles a person to first claim on a living animal. Legally speaking ... it is as fair to shout at an animal as it is to shoot an animal."

Pacelle went on to argue that "no court has ever determined that there was 'a right to hunt.' It's a recreational activity that the state licenses and regulates. And the state can prohibit the activity for a variety of reasons, whether they be ethical, ecological or safety concerns." [22]

Though he opposes sport hunting, Luke Dommer scorns hunter harassment as mere sensationalism. "The press loves to pick up on this kind of stuff," he says. "But as a viable means to stop hunting, it has no value whatsoever. And it is dangerous. I'm quite afraid there are going to be people killed and hurt while doing this."

Hunters have been successful in pressing for state legislation to outlaw harassment. Since 1981, such laws have been enacted by 44 states

Wildlife Refuges in Name Only

The National Wildlife Refuge System, which began to take shape early this century, was envisioned as a network of "inviolate sanctuaries" off-limits to sport hunting. But the policy didn't last long.

When the Upper Mississippi River Wildlife and Fish Refuge opened in 1924, hunting and fishing were permitted. Then, in 1948, Congress enacted a law authorizing the purchase of California cropland for the cultivation of food for migratory waterfowl. The purpose was to keep ducks from feeding on commercial crops. The law also opened the duck-food acreage to public waterfowl hunting.

Revisions of the 1934 Migratory Bird Hunting Stamp Act in 1949 and 1958 gave hunters additional access to lands originally set aside for wildlife protection. The 1949 law authorized the secretary of the Interior to allow public hunting on up to 25 percent of any waterfowl sanctuary that had been purchased with "duck stamp" revenue. The 1958 law permitted hunting on up to 40 percent of such sanctuaries. In the 1960s, moreover, hunters even won the right to hunt numerous species of game animals in selected wildlife refuges.

According to a survey by the Humane Society of the United States, hunting is allowed in 262 of the nation's 466 wildlife refuges. The society estimated that hunters killed at least 305,000 animals and birds on refuges in

Hunting in National Wildlife Refuges	
Number of refuges	466
Refuges allowing hunting	262
Annual hunter visits to refuges	737,433
Migratory bird hunting (ducks, geese, swans, doves, cranes and others)	303,497
Upland game hunting (rabbit, hare, squirrel, opossum, fox, raccoon, bobcat, turkey, quail, partridge, pheasant and others)	201,209
Big game hunting (deer, moose, elk, caribou, bear, antelope, mountain goat, coyote and others)	232,727
Animals killed (minimum)	305,097†
Animals wounded and not retrieved (minimum)	11,288†

† Figures for 1983; other figures are for 1989-90.
Source: The Humane Society of the United States

1983, the most recent year for which complete statistics are available. Hunters, who regularly account for about 5 percent of annual visits to the National Wildlife Refuge System, logged 737,433 visits in 1989-90.

The Advisory Board on Wildlife Management, a citizen group appointed by Interior Secretary Stewart L. Udall, called for a new look at refuge hunting policies as long ago as 1968. "If all possible surplus [wildlife] populations are hunted," the board stated, "the refuge becomes little different from the rest of the countryside." Accordingly, the board urged that refuges be developed as "showplaces for all kinds of wildlife." To this end, it urged that "all forms of disturbance, including hunting ... be so regulated in areas of visitor concentration as to favor an optimal display of wild birds and mammals, gentle enough to be easily seen by the visiting public."

Nothing came of that recommendation at the time, but it was not forgotten. It resurfaced in 1989 as the proposed Refuge Wildlife Protection Act. The chief aim of the bill, introduced by Rep. Bill Green, R-N.Y., was to prohibit the killing of wildlife for sport, recreational or commercial purposes throughout the National Wildlife Refuge system. The measure remained bottled up in committee during the 101st Congress. Green reintroduced it Jan. 3, 1991, the first day of the 102nd Congress, but again it never reached the House floor.

would have banned hunting in all federally protected wilderness areas. The Humane Society and other anti-hunting groups strongly support the legislation.

"Of all the abuses in the National Wildlife Refuge System — and there are a lot of them — hunting and trapping are the most egregious in terms of violating the principles for which the refuges were established," says wildlife-issues special-

ist Susan Hagood.

In urging passage of the bill last April, Rep. Frank Annunzio, D-Ill., described it as "another safeguard to protect the natural diversity of animal life in all our wilderness areas." The measure was still gathering dust in the House Merchant Marine and Fisheries Committee when Congress adjourned in November. But it may well be heard from again this year.

Hunting Accidents

Meanwhile, accidents like the fatal shooting of Karen Wood in Maine continue to bolster hunting opponents' case for tighter hunting controls. The tragedy initially attracted attention because Wood was standing in her own back yard when she was shot by Donald Rogerson, a

Continued on p. 66

At Issue:

Does hunting contribute to sound wildlife-management policies?

GARY ANDERSON

Executive Director of General Operations, National Rifle Association (NRA). **FROM** *ARE HUNTERS HEADED FOR EXTINCTION?* **(1990 NRA POLICY STATEMENT).**

yes

hunters have a hard time articulating the reasons they hunt, probably because our language is a little shy of the right words to express these very personal feelings. And on top of that, our public image is vulnerable. The media defines hunting as a blood sport, then glamorizes its position by printing photographs of bloody carcasses and grinning hunters. In essence, this hides the true meaning of a hunt and depicts hunters as less than what they truly are — responsible participants in nature....

We're justified in arguing that we pay our own way — and for everyone else, too. The truth is, hunting has underwritten the bulk of America's wildlife conservation effort — game species, non-game species, even backyard songbirds have directly benefited. But nobody's going to believe it unless they actually physically hunt. The sheer emotion and silliness flowing from the other side has an ace in the hole we hunters can't compete with. They're crusading for live animals (eternal life, to hear them tell it) while portraying us as crusaders for dead ones ... when just the opposite is true....

Some 16 million Americans purchased hunting licenses ... [in 1989], contributing approximately $500 million to the wildlife-conservation effort. Hunting licenses, combined with taxes on sporting arms and ammunition, have furnished nearly $6 billion — that's with a "b" — to benefit wildlife.

Now, the other side doesn't contribute one red cent. Yet they get good press, and they get free access to some 4 million acres of wildlife habitat provided by hunters' dollars. Once there, they harass us while posing for TV cameras, and the end result is that a few million more Americans are duped into thinking all hunters are bloodthirsty. In return we rant and we seethe, which is just what the anti-hunting crowd wants us to do.

Anger is not going to turn back this tide of anti-hunting propaganda. Right now we need to recall the intelligence and the vision responsible for our thriving herds of deer, elk, and flocks of wild turkey. We pulled together and worked hard to make these species and others success stories. Now something else is endangered, and it is us. Let's police our ranks, promote education and promote hunting's positive image.

LUKE A. DOMMER

Chairman, Committee to Abolish Sport Hunting (CASH). **FROM** *A HUNTER'S DELUSIONS* **(CASH BROCHURE).**

no

deer store up critical fat reserves designed to help them survive through the winter. They move about infrequently and conservatively so that this energy is not expended prematurely. Then come the sport hunters. Shotgun and rifle season. Muzzleloader season. Bow and arrow season. Special season. And for weeks ... [the deer] are spooked, harassed and pursued. Their fat reserves are depleted [in] eluding the hunters, and this is a death sentence for many deer who are lucky enough to escape the bullets and arrows ... [only to die from] starvation caused by sports hunters....

It is almost incredible that [wildlife] management [officials] and hunters have virtually annihilated such natural predators as the wolf in the lower 48 states. Unbelievably, these paranoid killers of animals are at it again in Alaska, the last stronghold of the wolf. Trapping, shooting and poisoning have reduced the wolf from 15,000 a decade ago to a mere 4,000 animals ... and for what? So that sport hunters can bag more moose and caribou heads to mount on the walls of their trophy dens.

Natural predators are essential to the ecosystem of wildlife because they cull (remove the unfit) and promote the long-term survival potential of herbivorous species. Hunters, on the other hand, are unnatural predators, with their fluorescent caps, heating pads, electric socks, freeze-dried doe droppings and camouflage toilet paper to keep them from being mistaken for a whitetail deer. These arrogant nincompoops of the underbrush would have us believe that highly evolved terrestrial vertebrates are crops to be harvested like corn or potatoes and that bullet holes improve the health of the animals.

They have also succumbed to the myopic delirium that wildlife is a guaranteed "renewable resource." Alas, they cannot tell that to the Labrador duck, because the last one was blasted away in 1911 by Sporty Goodfellow.

In fact, hunters work against nature and contrary to the process of natural selection by exterminating natural predators and constantly removing prime male ungulates from the herds. This has nothing whatsoever to do with culling. The vast majority of bucks are killed by sport hunters before they reach adulthood. This, coupled with the trophy hunting of mature bucks, causes a shortage of prime males, leaving more inferior animals to reproduce.

Hunting Anyone? It's (Almost) as Popular as Tennis

Swimming, with some 70 million fans, far outdistances hunting as the country's most popular sport. But hunting, with nearly 18 million adherents, is more than three times as popular as cross-country skiing and twice as popular as racquetball. Hunting even edges out baseball, though tennis beats it by a whisker.

Activity	All persons	Men	Women	Activity	All persons	Men	Women
	(numbers in thousands)				*(numbers in thousands)*		
Swimming	70,489	33,213	37,277	Softball	22,092	13,437	8,655
Exercise walking	66,558	23,680	42,879	Tennis	18,844	10,420	8,424
Bicycle riding	59,641	28,354	28,587	Hunting with firearms	17,715	16,129	1,586
Camping (vacation/				Baseball	15,406	12,132	3,273
overnight)	46,514	24,577	21,936	Calisthenics	15,141	6,816	8,325
Fishing — fresh water	41,005	27,902	13,104	Football	14,287	12,779	1,949
Bowling	40,810	21,252	19,556	Target shooting	12,607	10,039	2,569
Exercising with				Backpacking/			
equipment	31,476	16,477	14,998	wilderness camping	11,357	7,269	4,088
Basketball	26,182	19,091	7,091	Fishing — salt water	11,326	8,311	3,015
Aerobic exercising	25,108	4,173	20,935	Soccer	11,168	7,450	3,718
Volleyball	25,071	12,972	12,098	Skiing — alpine/			
Running/jogging	24,803	14,485	10,318	downhill	11,034	6,886	4,148
Hiking	23,516	12,606	10,910	Racquetball	8,244	6,151	2,093
Golf	23,156	17,411	5,745	Skiing — cross country	4,906	2,359	2,547

Note: Data are for 1989
Source: U.S. Census Bureau, Statistical Abstract of the United States: 1991, *1991.*

Continued from p. 64
supermarket produce manager.

Rogerson testified that he had been deer hunting in woods behind the Wood house and fired one shot after spotting a deer in his rifle scope. He said he fired a second shot after sighting what he thought was the white underside of a deer's tail. But investigators found no telltale hoofmarks near Wood's body. They did note, however, that she had been wearing white mittens.

After a trial, Rogerson was found not guilty. Rather than resolving anything, the verdict seemed to reopen the debate about hunting. According to one school of thought, Wood was partly responsible for her death. Besides the white mittens, she was wearing a dark blue coat instead of the brightly colored outerwear that many Maine residents habitually don during hunting season.* If Wood had

*The Maine Legislature enacted a law this year requiring hunters to wear blaze-orange clothing.

been properly attired, the reasoning went, she might never have been shot.

A year later, in 1990, another hunting accident captured headlines nationwide. As was their annual custom, truck driver Gene W. Bulak and his 18-year-old son, Michael, set out with friends one November day to stalk deer in upstate New York. Both Bulaks had on green-and-black checked jackets and wore no brightly colored accessories such as caps or scarves.* Soon after the two hunters split up in an attempt to locate deer they had spotted earlier, Gene Bulak fired once from his shotgun, mortally wounding his son in the head. When he discovered what he had done, Bulak committed suicide with his son's shotgun.

---

*New York state does not have a law requiring hunters to wear blaze-orange clothing.   ∎

OUTLOOK

Shared Goals

Though hunters and their opponents seem to have only a deep disdain for each other, some observers discern some shared goals: acquiring and maintaining wildlife habitat; eliminating poaching and other forms of illegal hunting and preservation of genetically strong wildlife populations. By joining forces, it is said, the two sides might be able to accomplish more than either could by acting alone.

John F. Turner, director of the U.S. Fish and Wildlife Service, is among those who believe that environmental issues could give friends and foes of hunting a way to resolve their differences. "The real tragedy [for wildlife] is pollution, pesticides, urbanization, deforestation, hazardous waste, lack of water and wetland destruction," Turner said in a 1990 magazine interview. "I get tears in my eyes when I see this self-destructive waste of energy by the anti-hunting groups. Let's focus our main energies on mutual interests and arm-wrestle on the others." [23]

Cooperation between hunting supporters and animal-rights groups seems unlikely in the foreseeable future, mostly because of the groups' ultimate goal: eliminating all forms of hunting. "The trouble with the animal-rights movement is that they don't have any flexibility," says CASH's Luke Dommer. "As much as I'm against recreational killing, and the management of wildlife for that purpose, I don't say that every hunter is a bad person per se."

Wolter says he wouldn't rule out joint action by friends and foes of hunting — at least in theory. But he agrees with Dommer that a rapprochement with animal-rights purists is highly unlikely, adding that stopping all consumer uses of animals is unrealistic. "The only message they understand is defeat."

Susan Hagood of the Humane Society says her organization occasionally has joined coalitions including pro-hunting groups to press for such things as renewal of endangered-species legislation or adoption of rules against driftnet fishing. She acknowledges, though, that fundamental disagreement on hunting issues usually bars more extensive cooperation.

In the end, forces beyond the control of either side could determine the outcome of the hunting debate. Historian Charles Waterman predicted nearly 20 years ago that "There will be more and more hunters using less and less land. Already in the United States, parallels to the European concept are surfacing, in which game is owned privately and harvested by a privileged few.... Those hunters imbued with the independent spirit of the frontiersman will be unhappy to find themselves subject to increasingly restrictive regulations." [24]

While that's hardly a happy prospect for America's rugged individualists, Dommer warns that the real problem hunters face is not bureaucracy but the ticking "human time bomb" and "the loss of numerous plant and animal species because of this overpopulation."

"It's kind of ludicrous to talk about saving hunting and wildlife," he says, "unless you also start talking about how world population growth can be controlled." ∎

Notes

[1] Joy Williams, "The Killing Game," *Esquire,* October 1990, pp. 114, 128.

[2] George Reiger, "Our Achilles Heel," *Field & Stream,* January 1991, p. 8.

[3] Ralph P. Stuart, "A Case Against Hunting," *Outdoor Life,* March 1990, p. 1.

[4] David E. Petzal, "One of Us," *Field & Stream,* May 1991, p. 14. The standing title of Petzal's hunting column is "Endangered Tradition."

[5] Quoted by Bill Stokes, "The Guns of Autumn," *Chicago Tribune Magazine,* Oct. 13, 1991, p. 27.

[6] Quoted in the *Bozeman* (Mont.) *Daily Chronicle,* Oct. 8, 1991.

[7] For background, see "Animal Rights," *The CQ Researcher,* May 24, 1991, pp. 301-324.

[8] Duncan Barnes, "Up Front," *Field & Stream,* October 1990, p. 5.

[9] Wildlife Legislative Fund of America, "America's Wildlife is Thriving" (1986 brochure).

[10] Richard Conniff, "Fuzzy-Wuzzy Thinking About Animal Rights," *Audubon,* November 1990, p. 132.

[11] Quoted in the *Los Angeles Times,* Feb. 1, 1990, p. A3.

[12] Lionel Atwill, "What Is the UBNJ?" *Field & Stream,* November 1991, p. 97.

[13] Quoted by Bob McNally, "Hunters Helping the Hungry," *Outdoor Life,* December 1991, p. 72.

[14] Quoted by Wayne Pacelle, "An Interview With Luke Dommer," *The Animals' Agenda,* January 1989, p. 7.

[15] Thomas McIntyre, *The Way of the Hunter: The Art and Spirit of Modern Hunting* (1988), p. 61.

[16] Wayne Pacelle, "Bowhunting: A Most Primitive Sport," *The Animals' Agenda,* May 1990, p. 17.

[17] For background, see "Endangered Species," *The CQ Researcher,* June 21, 1991, pp. 393-416.

[18] Quoted by Rep. James L. Oberstar, D-Minn., during a Sept. 22, 1988, hearing of the U.S. House Subcommittee of Fisheries and Wildlife Conservation and the Environment on "Waterfowl Decline in the Mississippi Flyway."

[19] Quoted by Philip Street, *Vanishing Animals* (1961), p. 158.

[20] Charles F. Waterman, *Hunting in America* (1973), p. 48.

[21] *Ibid.,* p. 139.

[22] Testimony before Subcommittee on Forests, Family Farms and Energy of the House Agriculture Committee, March 14, 1990.

[23] Michael Satchell (with Joannie M. Schrof), "The American Hunter Under Fire," *U.S. News & World Report,* Feb. 5, 1990, p. 35.

[24] Waterman, *op. cit.,* p. 239.

Bibliography

Selected Sources Used

Books

Amory, Cleveland, *Man Kind? Our Incredible War on Wildlife,* Harper & Row, 1974.

Amory, the founder of the Fund for Animals, sets forth the animal-rights view of hunting, tersely summarized in the slogan, "Support Your Right to Arm Bears."

Hobusch, Erich, *Fair Game: A History of Hunting, Shooting and Animal Conservation,* Arco Publishing Co., 1980.

Hobusch traces the history of hunting from prehistoric to modern times. His approach is episodic, with separate chapters devoted to ancient Egypt, the near-extinction of bison on the American Great Plains in the 19th century and the elaborate hunting rituals of the British Isles.

Ortega y Gasset, José, *Meditations on Hunting* (translated from the Spanish by Howard B. Wescott), Charles Scribner's Sons, 1972.

The noted Spanish essayist and philosopher ponders the reasons why men continue to hunt animals in the modern era, long after the passing of prehistoric hunter-gatherer societies.

Thomas, Richard H., *The Politics of Hunting,* Gower Publishing Company Ltd., 1983.

Thomas examines the evolution of hunting in Britain, the rise of anti-hunting and pro-hunting lobbies there and the emergence of hunting as an issue in national politics.

Waterman, Charles F., *Hunting in America,* Holt, Rinehart and Winston, 1973.

In this historical survey of North American hunting, Waterman goes from 12,000 years ago to the present day and then offers some informed guesses about what the future holds for hunting in the New World.

Articles

Barrett, Todd, "Oh, Deer!" *National Wildlife,* October-November 1991.

Why have whitetail deer herds in the United States grown to unprecedented size, and what — if anything — should be done about it? Barrett looks at the sharply different approaches favored by hunters and hunting opponents.

Conniff, Richard, "Fuzzy-Wuzzy Thinking About Animal Rights," *Audubon,* November 1990.

Conniff, a prolific writer on outdoor sports and nature issues, dissects the animal-rights case against hunting and finds it wanting.

Famularo, Thom, "Is Duck Hunting Still Worth It?" *Outdoor Life,* November 1991.

Famularo, a duck-hunting enthusiast, answers with a resounding "Yes!" and then goes on to examine the reasons why the question was worth asking in the first place.

McNally, Bob, "Hunters Helping the Hungry," *Outdoor Life,* December 1991.

According to McNally, hunters reap good will by sharing their game with needy people.

Pacelle, Wayne, "Wildlife Mismanagement," *The Animals' Agenda,* September 1991.

Pacelle, national director of the Fund for Animals, sets forth his organization's case against sport hunting. "Despite pretenses to the contrary, hunters maim and kill animals for recreation," he argues. "At worst, they not only inflict suffering, but imperil species."

Rudner, Ruth, "Fenced In ... Or Finished," *Field & Stream,* November 1991.

An in-depth look at the controversy over Montana's program (now abolished) for permitting the hunting of bison that wander into the state from their refuge in Yellowstone National Park.

Reports and Studies

U.S. House Subcommittee on Forests, Family Farms and Energy, Committee on Agriculture, National Forest Hunter Safety and Protection Act of 1989 (published proceedings of hearing held March 14, 1990).

Witnesses debate whether a federal law is needed to protect hunters in the field from harassment by hunting opponents.

U.S. House Subcommittee on Fisheries and Wildlife Conservation and the Environment, Committee on Merchant Marine and Fisheries, Waterfowl Decline in the Mississippi Flyway (published proceedings of hearing held Sept. 22, 1988).

Wildlife experts and members of Congress offer reasons for the sharp decline of migratory waterfowl populations during the 1980s and discuss possible ways of undoing the damage.

The Next Step

Additional Articles from Current Periodicals from EBSCO Publishing's Database

Addresses & essays

Howard, W.E., "Animal rights vs. hunters," *Outdoor Life,* **April 1991, p. 110.**
Opinion. Argues that those who call themselves "animal rightists" have forgotten that nature doesn't care about rights. Suggests that wildlife must be protected from nature, not just man.

Magnuson, J., "Reflections of an Oregon bow hunter," *Christian Century,* **March 13, 1991, p. 292.**
Recounts the author's experiences and feelings about bowhunting in an age when the sport is being decried as ecological irresponsibility. The struggle for survival among North America's indigenous peoples is also discussed.

Williams, J., "The killing game," *Esquire,* **October 1990, p. 112.**
Discusses why the American hunter is insatiable, overequipped and grossly incompetent. Why hunters hunt; the problem of the hunter's lack of skill; how they view themselves. INSET: Why I hunt, by R. Bass.

Williamson, L., "Know thy enemy," *Outdoor Life,* **February 1991, p. 49.**
Opinion. Condemns the animal-rights movement, which foils hunters, biomedical research, farmers, poultry processors and a variety of other people who use animals for fun, food or profit. Presents demographic and attitudinal behavioral data about animal-rightists.

Case studies

Conley, C., "The tag game," *Outdoor Life,* **November 1990, p. 71.**
Examines a furor that erupted in August when anti-hunting hang tags were found on H. Cotler Co. clothing in a J.C. Penney store in Savage, Md. Reaction to incident; comments by Cotler and J.C. Penney management. INSET: Interior secretary views harassment, by M. Lujan.

Gross, K. and Sawicki, S., "A tragic hunting accident in Maine kills a mother in her own backyard," *People,* **Nov. 5, 1990, p. 75.**
Covers the 1988 hunting accident in which Donald Rogerson, now 47, killed Karen Wood, 37, when she was in her back yard. Rogerson was acquitted on a manslaughter charge.

Lowry, T., "The little boy with a gun," *Ladies' Home Journal,* **April 1991, p. 124.**
Relates the true story of Cameron Kocher, 9, who took a hunting rifle and shot his 7-year-old playmate, Jessica Carr, to death. Soon Kocher may stand trial as an adult — the youngest person in this century to do so. Living with the gun; legal loopholes.

Debates & issues

"Cut to the chase," *Economist,* **Nov. 10, 1990, p. 33.**
Examines the growing anti-blood-sports lobby in America. Videos of kills; Wayne Pacell, director of the Fund for Animals; increase in protesters of hunting; what the issue involves; details.

Coner, B. and Leahy, J., "Hunter harassment: Plaguing our American heritage," *Outdoor Life,* **October 1990, p. 82.**
Reports on a growing anti-hunting movement in America. INSETS: Hunter-harassment laws; protect what's right; Oh no, there they are! (anti-hunter tactics); philosophical chameleons (contradictory beliefs of most animal-rightists); hunter harassment: Case histories; a fight against innuendoes and half-truths; a letter of extremes; suits and legislation; stand up and be counted; terrorists tactics; current hunting-related bills in Congress; how to counteract the trend.

Gaddis, M., "Taking a life," *Audubon,* **November 1990, p. 108.**
Examines the ethics of sport hunting. As the author enters middle age and becomes more introspective, he wonders if a time will come when he quits hunting. Respect for the life of the prey and self-respect; anti-hunting faction; author's philosophy concerning the emotional lives of wild creatures; turkey hunt; encounter with a whitetail buck that the author decided not to shoot.

Hammond, J., "Caught in a cross-fire," *Alaska,* **September 1990, p. 72.**
Examines the hunting-guide controversy in Alaska. Tarnished public image; abolition of residency requirements; creation of master-guide licensing; problem of aerial outfitters.

Knox, M.L., "In the heat of the hunt," *Sierra,* **November/December 1990, p. 48.**
Studies the debate between hunters and animal lovers

while discussing a Montana bison hunt where hunters were physically attacked by protesters; hunters as conservationists and the Pittman-Robertson Fund; animal-rights advocates call for humane methods to control wildlife populations. INSETS: Why I hunt, by D. Sisson; Why I don't hunt, by S. Rugger; Why we hunt, by H. Fontova; Iguana hunt, by D. Sobel.

Mitchell, E., Shocket, K., et al., "Shooting leopards in a barrel," *Time,* June 10, 1991, p. 61.

Describes "canned hunts," slaughter, not sport, where well-to-do hunters in the U.S. are paying thousands of dollars to shoot defenseless exotic animals at point-blank range. Floyd Lester Patterson III: rancher in Monterey County, Calif., charged with 27 misdemeanors involving illegal possession and transportation of animals on the endangered-species list; Charles B. Bartholomew: Bryan County, Okla., plea bargained to six months in jail; legal pressure.

Pattison, S., "When animal rightists have their way," *Consumer Alert,* March/April 1991, p. 8.

Contends that hunting is necessary to solve Princeton, N.J.'s, problems caused by deer overpopulation. Car accidents; Lyme disease; Fish, Game and Wildlife department vs. animal-rights groups.

Petzal, D.E., "Joy Williams hates you!" *Field & Stream,* December 1990, p. 16.

Examines an article written by Joy Williams in the October issue of *Esquire* accusing hunters of being "bloodthirsty, piggish and grossly incompetent." Questions where she got her information; defends hunters.

Petzal, D.E. and Tanenbaum, R., "One of us," *Field & Stream,* May 1991, p. 14.

Opinion. Comments on the public opinion of hunters, and how accidents perpetrated by non-professional and non-caring people with guns are negatively forming public opinion. Calls for the nation's fish and game departments to require demonstration of skills and knowledge prior to giving out hunting licenses.

Reiger, G., "Our Achilles' heel," *Field & Stream,* January 1991, p. 8.

Discusses why hunters must be more diligent than ever about their responsibilities as sportsmen. The growing anti-hunting sentiment; how the author helped develop "outdoor ethics"; what these rules are.

Reiger, G., "The untold story," *Field & Stream,* June 1990, p. 16.

Examines how editors of *The Rotarian* and *U.S. News & World Report* softened the author's pro-hunting message. Toned down or eliminated important points in his arguments; urges hunters to employ passive resistance.

Shedd, W., "The giant stirs," *Outdoor Life,* October 1991, p. 80.

Examines how sportsmen around the country have banded together and are successfully fighting off the threat from anti-hunting groups. Specific examples of how sportsmen are fighting back and winning battles in a number of states. INSET: Hunter-harassment laws, by S. Golin.

Turbak, G., "The cougar makes a comeback," *Field & Stream,* January 1991, p. 34.

Reports on the increase in attacks by cougars in the Western states. Description of several incidents; why cougar incidents are on the rise; estimated number of these animals in California; false premises employed by the anti-hunters to ban the hunting of cougars.

Williamson, L., "The subsistence sham," *Outdoor Life,* March 1991, p. 32.

Opinion. Discusses controversy over Alaska subsistence laws regarding hunting and fishing. Specifics of various legislation; arguments by sportsmen; possible solutions.

Law & legislation

Matthews, J., "The domino effect," *Outdoor Life,* March 1991, p. 61.

Gives details on the 1990 assault on hunting, fishing and wildlife resources in California. How anti-hunting activists won in the courts, at the polls and in the Legislature; importance of hunters and fisherman getting involved so further battles will not be lost in other states.

Petzal, D.E., "2 modest proposals," *Field & Stream,* July 1990, p. 26.

Recommends proposals for safer hunting. Prison sentences for hunters who accidentally shoot other hunters; national hunter marksmanship test; Wisconsin law for blind hunters.

Reynolds, J., "Sportsmen responsibility bill," *Field & Stream,* February 1991, p. 56.

Summarizes New Jersey's 1990 Sportsmen Responsibility Bill, which deals with the ethical and responsible behavior of hunters, fishermen and trappers, and penalties for violating regulations.

Study & teaching

Atwill, L., "Anti-hunting 101," *Field & Stream,* August 1991, p. 46.

Examines the West Virginia University course "Wildlife Attitudes," known facetiously as "Anti-Hunting 101." Professor David Samuel, Ph.D. in wildlife biology, began the course in 1975. It looks at public attitudes and perceptions of hunters, hunting and wildlife in America.

Reynolds, J., "Hunting confrontations," *Field & Stream,* May 1991, p. 59.

Announces the availability of the National Rifle Association (NRA) brochure, "Hunting's future? ... It's Up To You." It offers tips on handling anti-hunter confrontations and on protecting hunting's future.

Wildlife conservation

Egan, T., "An outcry over hunt of endangered grizzly," *The New York Times,* Sept. 22, 1991, p. 1.

Reports that several conservation groups are trying to stop the annual grizzly bear hunt in Montana. The grizzly is classified by the federal government as a species threatened with extinction. Montana official's argument that the hunt actually helps the grizzlies; estimation of the number of bears in the northern Rockies; possible lawsuit by conservation groups; more.

Pettis, M., "The bear facts," *Progressive,* June 1991, p. 12.

Reports on efforts of the Utah Wilderness Association and the Utah Audubon Society to get bear hunting banned in Utah. Bear baiting; Utah Wildlife Board meetings.

Rennicke, J., "The killing line," *Backpacker,* April 1991, p. 114.

Examines the controversy over the hunting of buffalo that stray out of Yellowstone National Park (Wyoming, Idaho, Montana) into Montana during the winter. History of buffalo hunting; Buffalo's comeback; ranchers and animal-rights groups; "Bucella abortus" bacteria; Montana's policy; National Park Service.

For More Information

Committee to Abolish Sport Hunting, Box 43, White Plains, N.Y. 10605, (914) 428-7523.

Founded in 1976, CASH works to abolish all forms of recreational hunting through public education and lobbying. It also seeks to reshape government wildlife-management programs, arguing that existing policies are designed primarily to offer recreational opportunities for hunters at taxpayer expense.

Ducks Unlimited, One Waterfowl Way, Long Grove, Ill. 60047, (708) 438-4300.

One of the nation's oldest wildlife-conservation groups, the pro-hunting group strives to create or restore wetlands used by migratory waterfowl in Canada, the United States and Mexico.

Fund for Animals, 850 Sligo Ave., Suite LL2, Silver Spring, Md. 20910, (301) 585-2595.

Organized in 1967, the fund opposes sport hunting from an animal-rights perspective. Its motto: "We Speak for Those Who Can't." Its anti-hunting activities, which often receive extensive media coverage, include demonstrations aimed at alerting animals to the presence of hunters.

Humane Society of the United States, 2100 L St. N.W., Washington, D.C. 20037, (202) 452-1100.

The society is a membership group whose chief concern is to ease the suffering of animals used in medical research; the group also opposes legalized sport hunting in federal wildlife refuges.

National Rifle Association, 1600 Rhode Island Ave. N.W., Washington, D.C. 20036, (202) 828-6000.

Long noted as one of the most sophisticated and powerful lobbying groups in Washington, the NRA promotes the interests of hunters and users of firearms. Among other activities, it sponsors programs designed to hone the skills of novice hunters.

Natural Resources Defense Council, 40 20th St., New York, N.Y. 10011, (212) 727-2700.

Combining scientific and legal approaches to the problems of the environment, the council conducts studies, brings legal actions and informs the public.

North American Hunting Club, 12301 Whitewater Dr., P.O. Box 3401, Minnetonka, Minn. 55343, (612) 936-9333.

The club seeks to improve the hunting skills of its members and promote enjoyment of the sport. It leases hunting lands for the use of its members and furnishes information about hunting outfitters.

Professional Bowhunters Society, P.O. Box 20066, Charlotte, N.C. 28202, (704) 536-6009.

An affiliate of the American Archery Council, the society seeks to upgrade the sport of bowhunting. It seeks to ensure the taking of game in a humane and sportsmanlike manner and to provide training in safety, shooting skills and hunting techniques.

Wildlife Legislative Fund of America, 801 Kingsmill Parkway, Columbus, Ohio 43229-1137, (614) 888-4868.

Founded in 1978, the fund has a wide-ranging membership including sportsmen and sportsmen's groups, lobbyists, legal specialists and media experts. It works to protect the sportsman's legal right to hunt, fish and trap and promotes sound wildlife-management practices. It is in the forefront of efforts to combat the arguments and activities of anti-hunting and animal-rights organizations.

Back Issues

Great Research on Current Issues Starts Right Here... Recent topics covered by The CQ Researcher are listed below. Issues dated before May 10, 1991, were published under the name of Editorial Research Reports.

JULY 1990
Do Americans Still Love Marriage?
Death Penalty Debate
Decline of Rural America
United Nations in the 1990s

AUGUST 1990
Democracy in the Philippines
Initiatives: True Democracy?
Hard Times at Newspapers
Teens Balance School & Jobs

SEPTEMBER 1990
Dangers of Alcohol
Western Alliance After the Cold War
Tobacco Industry
Right to Die

OCTOBER 1990
Organ Transplants
Energy Policy Options
Search for Arab Unity
Child Support

NOVEMBER 1990
Lotteries and Gambling
Post-Cold War Choices
Setting Limits on Medical Care
Multicultural Education

DECEMBER 1990
Cable TV Regulation
Americans' Search for Their Roots
Is Insurance System a Failure?
Why Schools Still Have Tracking

JANUARY 1991
Growing Influence of Boycotts
Should the U.S. Reinstate the Draft?
America's Archaeological Past
Peace Corps' Challenges in '90s

FEBRUARY 1991
Regional Impact of Recession
Puerto Rico's Status
Redistricting: Mapping Power
Nuclear Power

MARCH 1991
Acid Rain
Cost of the Gulf War
Reassessing Gun Laws
Future for Man in Space

APRIL 1991
Social Security
Canadian Crisis Over Quebec
California Drought
Electromagnetic Radiation

MAY 1991
School Choice
Racial Quotas
Animal Rights
U.S. and Japan

JUNE 1991
Children and Divorce
Teenage Suicide
Endangered Species
Europe 1992

JULY 1991
Teenagers and Abortion
Soviet Republics Rebel
Mexico's Emergence
Athletes and Drugs

AUGUST 1991
Sexual Harassment
Fetal Tissue Research
Oil Imports
The Palestinians

SEPTEMBER 1991
Police Brutality
Advertising Under Attack
Saving the Forests
Foster Care Crisis

OCTOBER 1991
Pay-Per-View TV
Youth Gangs
Gene Therapy
World Hunger

NOVEMBER 1991
Fast-Food Shake-Up
The Greening of Eastern Europe
Business' Role in Education
Cuba In Crisis

DECEMBER 1991
Retiree Health Benefits
Asian Americans
The Obscenity Debate
The Disabilities Act

JANUARY 1992
Term Limits
Oil Spills

Back issues are available for $4.00 (subscribers) or $7.00 (non-subscribers). Quantity discounts apply to orders over ten. To order, call Congressional Quarterly 1-800-432-2250.

Future Topics

▶ *Alternative Medicine*

▶ *America's Threatened Coastlines*

▶ *New Era in Asia*

The CQ Researcher

PUBLISHED BY CONGRESSIONAL QUARTERLY INC., IN CONJUNCTION WITH EBSCO PUBLISHING

Alternative Medicine

Unproven treatments gain followers, draw warnings of quackery

I T'S NOT WHAT THE DOCTOR ORDERED, BUT
millions of Americans are exploring medical treatments
that have not been approved by mainstream authorities.
Ranging from age-old acupuncture and chiropractic to
strange new crystal therapies and psychic surgery, the
treatments attract everyone from terminal cancer and AIDS
patients to those left cold by the crisis-oriented, "impersonal"
approach of conventional doctors. Organizations that work to
expose health fraud warn against profiteers who prey on a
gullible public. But that hasn't stopped enthusiasts of the
alternative treatments from setting up networks to fight for
respectability, which, in turn, might bring research funding,
licensing and recognition from medical peers.

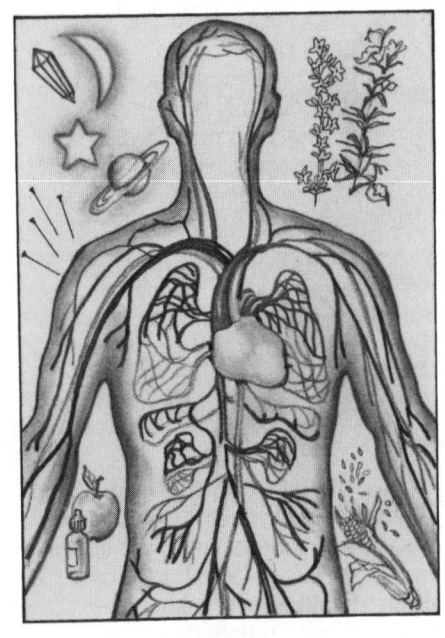

THIS ISSUE

CQ **January 31, 1992 • Volume 2, No. 4 • 73 - 96**

Formerly Editorial Research Reports

COVER ART: BARBARA SASSA-DANIELS

THE CQ Researcher

January 31, 1992
Volume 2, No. 4

EDITOR
Sandra Stencel

MANAGING EDITOR
Thomas J. Colin

ASSOCIATE EDITOR
Richard L. Worsnop

STAFF WRITERS
Charles S. Clark
Mary H. Cooper
Rodman D. Griffin

PRODUCTION EDITOR
Laurie De Maris

EDITORIAL ASSISTANT
Thomas H. Moore

GRAPHICS
Jack Auldridge

PUBLISHED BY
Congressional Quarterly Inc.

CHAIRMAN
Andrew Barnes

VICE CHAIRMAN
Andrew P. Corty

EDITOR AND PUBLISHER
Neil Skene

EXECUTIVE EDITOR
Robert W. Merry

PUBLICATIONS MARKETING/SALES
Robert Smith

EDITOR, EBSCO PUBLISHING
Melissa Kummerer

The CQ Researcher (ISSN 1056-2036). Formerly Editorial Research Reports. Published weekly (48 times per year, not printed the first Friday of any month with five Fridays) by Congressional Quarterly Inc., 1414 22nd St., N.W., Washington, D.C. 20037. Rates are furnished upon request. Second-class postage paid at Washington, D.C. POSTMASTER: Send address changes to The CQ Researcher, 1414 22nd St., N.W., Washington, D.C. 20037.

Alternative Medicine

BY CHARLES S. CLARK

THE ISSUES

In 1987, Berkley Bedell learned he was one of the 1 million Americans a year who are diagnosed with cancer. The retired fishing tackle manufacturer underwent conventional surgery to have his prostate gland removed and followed up with a series of radiation treatments. But later blood tests showed that his malignancy had not been arrested. So Bedell joined the growing number of Americans who are turning to the chancy world of alternative medicine. Today, he credits his return to good health to his subsequent treatments with the compound 714-X, an unproven camphor-derived injection developed by a controversial Quebec doctor named Gaston Naessens.

Unlike the average cancer survivor, however, Berkley Bedell is a former member of Congress. The Iowa Democrat (1975-86) spent much of last year lobbying Capitol Hill for an amendment sponsored by his friend Sen. Tom Harkin, D-Iowa, a current presidential candidate, to create a federal Office of Alternative Medicine. In November, President Bush signed the measure into law, and the $2 million office is being set up at the National Institutes of Health.*

Though just a drop in the bucket by federal budget standards, the office is a symbol of the new visibility being won by medical treatments that have not gained mainstream approval. There are other signs.

Since 1990 New York state has allowed recovering drug addicts with low incomes to receive reimburse-

*The measure was included in the fiscal 1992 appropriations bill for the Labor, Education and Health and Human Services departments.

ment from the federal-state Medicaid program when they undergo acupuncture, the ancient Chinese system of planting needles at key points on the body. Over the past decade there has been a 21 percent increase in weekly visits to chiropractors, according to that industry's trade group, though the spinal manipulation technique is still scorned by many doctors for its claims of success in treating ailments other than back pain. There's also been a notable revival of the 200-year-old discipline of homeopathy, whose unorthodox array of natural remedies has attracted numerous celebrity adherents, including Queen Elizabeth II and rock star Tina Turner.

The public at large has taken notice. Nearly 30 percent of those responding to a recent poll by Yankelovich Clancy Shulman said they had tried some form of unconventional therapy, half within the past year.[1] The top magazine of the natural health field, *East West Natural Health,*[2] reports that its circulation has grown from 100,000 to 150,000 in the past

year. Medical authorities estimate that as many as 1,000 American doctors have abandoned conventional practices to take up alternative medicine.

The reasons for the growing fascination with medicine's fringe are many. With the baby-boom generation now at an age when health is a conversation topic, observers say the boomers' legendary self-absorption is producing new demands for attention. "Most people see a doctor for all of 10 minutes and walk out with a bunch of prescriptions, but the baby boomers want more from doctors," says Dr. Deepak Chopra, author of several currently popular books on the ancient Indian system of Ayurvedic medicine *(see p. 83).*[3]

William Jarvis, a professor at the University of Loma Linda in California and a prominent critic of alternative medicine, traces the current interest in alternative treatments to "a general alienation from technology that found its fruition during the Vietnam War," when environmental concerns were raised about such issues as the use of the crop defoliant Agent Orange. "As life expectancy approaches human lifespan," Jarvis adds, "the limitations of science become apparent. And since longevity research is not finding a youth pill, the new attitude is, 'What has basic science done for us lately?'"

Others see the movement as a class conflict, a reaction against the image of doctors as rich, arrogant and privileged among average people who are seeking "empowerment" and a democratization of health care. Indeed, many of the activists who champion the so-called "health freedom movement" speak of a conspiracy by the profit-driven "medical-industrial complex" to keep workable cancer cures from coming to fruition.

If there is a unifying theme to the

January 31, 1992   75

alternative medicine movement, it comes under the label "holistic," a school of medical thought that seeks to treat the whole person, on the assumption that we are more than just the sum of our body parts. As described by the American Holistic Medicine Association, holistic healers go beyond the "treatment only" perspective to create a system of interaction and growth that emphasizes personal responsibility and integration of body, mind, emotions and spirit.

On a practical level, that means establishing a partnership between healer and patient (or "client," as some prefer) that permits a long-term examination of the quality of the person's life. "I'm talking about fatigue, chronic pain, backaches, digestive upsets, bronchitis and a general sense of not being well," says James S. Gordon, a psychiatrist and professor at Georgetown University School of Medicine and author of several books on holistic medicine.[4]

The therapies offered for such chronic but not life-threatening ailments can include everything from massage to fruit diets to the application of electrical devices to measure the body's "energy force." A patient's interest in one unconventional treatment frequently leads to another, as information is spread through word of mouth at such places as health food stores.

Inquirers find themselves drawn into ancient Eastern views of the relationship between mind and body. "The notion of the energy field in the body doesn't jibe with Western thinking," says a Washington, D.C., writer who has spent years visiting chiropractors, experimenting with faith healing and using a treatment known as Bach's flower remedies (see glossary, p. 84) to deal with stress. "But once you buy that, you can buy lots of things."

For practitioners, alternative medicine can mean a career estranged from the accepted thinking of "allo-pathic" medicine, the term alternative practitioners use for conventional medicine.* Holistic dentists, for example, often shun silver or mercury fillings and advise against the use of fluoride for fear of introducing "toxins" into the body.

Few insurance companies will reimburse patients who use unproven treatments, though that is changing. Alternative practitioners often face sanctions from health regulators — an estimated 1,500 of them are currently under attack by state disciplinary boards.[5] And they must undergo heavy doses of criticism from self-described "quack-buster" organizations, the most prominent of which is Jarvis' National Council Against Health Fraud.

To Jarvis and his network of hundreds of experts, "Alternative medicine is merely a marketing term for what is unscientific." They point to estimates that Americans spend as much as $27 billion a year on unproven treatments, all of which, they argue, can muster only anecdotal testimony as to their worth. The true scientific method, health-fraud activists remind the public, requires that potential treatments show results in controlled laboratory experiments. The tests must be "double blind," meaning that neither the patients nor the research doctors know which patients are getting the treatment and which are getting only a useless placebo for comparison.

To seekers of alternative approaches, of course, the medical establishment is too categorical in its dismissal of new treatments that might fill some unmet needs or provide a miracle cure. "[Conventional] medicine is very good at managing trauma, acute bacterial infections, medical and surgical

emergencies and other crises," argues Dr. Andrew Weil in one of several books he has written advocating alternative medicine. "It is very bad at managing viral infections, chronic degenerative disease, allergy and auto-immunity, many of the serious kinds of cancer, mental illness ... and all those conditions in which the mind plays an active role in creating susceptibility to the disease."[6]

As the debate over alternative medicine continues, here are some key issues on which the outcome will turn:

Is the interest in alternative medicine a sign that conventional medicine is failing?

When Gay Marshall, a Silver Spring, Md., mother of two, began experiencing chronic fatigue last year, she sought treatment from an acupuncturist. Her conventional doctor, she recalls, was not giving her any "direct eye contact." When she would enter the office, "he would sigh, as if to say, 'Oh, God, another patient.' I could sense that."

As modern medicine has become preoccupied with new technologies, doctors have become increasingly specialized, permitting themselves less and less time with patients and less familiarity with their patients' personal lives. According to a study reported in American Medical News, practitioners of unproven medicines spend an average of eight times longer with patients than conventional doctors do, taking psychosomatic complaints seriously, asking about jobs, families and hobbies.[7]

Clearly, the driving force behind much of alternative medicine is the efforts of patients to increase the demands they make on doctors. Feminist health groups, for example, are now offering seminars to medical students on how to handle patients sensitively and communicate in a nonsexist manner during pelvic exams.

And there remain some patients whom conventional doctors may sim-

---

*Allopathic medicine is the system of treating disease with remedies that produce effects different from or opposite to those produced by the disease. It is the opposite of homeopathy, which uses agents that produce effects like the disease. For more details, see p. 80.

ply be unsuited to treat. In Hawaii, for example, native healers called "kahunas" are still using herbs and a philosophy of self-empowerment to treat hundreds of the island state's minorities who might otherwise go without health care. But there are also many average middle-class Americans who are longing for a type of medicine that is simpler, more personalized and open to their own participation. "There is a growing sense [among all Americans] that regular medicine gives drugs too readily, is too expensive and too dangerous," says Dr. Weil.[8]

Many of those who are attracted to alternative medicine are understandably disappointed with the lack of progress in finding cures for many serious diseases. "The reality is that if you get AIDS or cancer, conventional medicine is not going to cure you," says former Rep. Bedell. Moreover, many cancer victims who seek solace in natural herbs or macrobiotic diets do so because they are appalled at the side effects — nausea and hair loss, for example — associated with conventional treatments such as radiation and chemotherapy.

The experiences described in a recent article by a recovered cancer victim are typical of many who have turned to alternative medicine. Bonnie J. Randolph, a Philadelphia nurse and aspiring clinical psychologist, was diagnosed with ovarian cancer in 1985. Surgery and other conventional treatments (mostly chemotherapy) produced only discomfort. She writes of how her life was saved by an alternative method known as metabolic treatment, involving massive doses of enzymes, a special diet and coffee enemas.

"I was thrilled to be with this man," she says of her doctor, Nicholas Gonzalez, a prominent but controversial practitioner in New York City. Her alternative treatment cost 10-20 percent of what conventional treatment costs but it still is not accepted by most members of the med-

---

Looking for Alternatives

Nearly 30 percent of those responding to a recent poll said they had tried some form of alternative medicine. The vast majority would do so again.

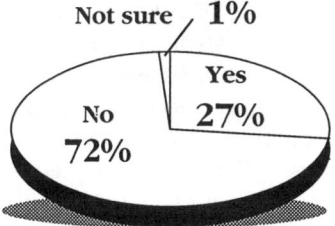

Have you personally ever sought medical help from a practitioner of alternative medicine?

Not sure 1%
Yes 27%
No 72%

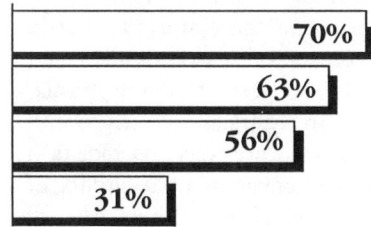

Why did you decide to try an alternative medical approach? †
Was it because:

You were interested in a new approach to treatment — 70%

Someone recommended it to you — 63%

Conventional medical treatment was unsuccessful — 56%

The proposed conventional treatment was unsatisfactory because it involved surgery or drugs — 31%

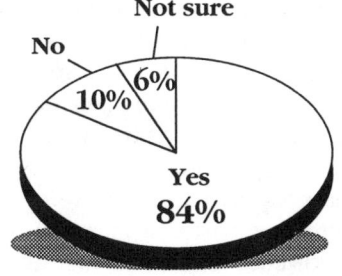

Would you go back to an alternative doctor again or recommend going to others? †

Not sure 6%
No 10%
Yes 84%

† *Among those who have sought help from a practitioner of alternative medicine.*
Source: Poll conducted Oct. 23, 1991, for Time/CNN *by Yankelovich Clancy Shulman*

---

ical community. Six years after her diagnosis, Randolph is alive and free of pain. "It is tragic," she writes, "that such a simple, non-invasive program that doesn't even require hospitalization has been ignored for 25 years, when there have been millions of cancer patients who have died that could have been helped."[9]

There is enough anecdotal and word-of-mouth testimony to kindle hopes about alternative cures and create a sense of defiance toward conventional authorities who attack them. A 1986 Harris poll on alterna-

tive medicine conducted for the Department of Health and Human Services (HHS) found that only one in 10 respondents who had used an unproven cure reported that it wasn't effective at all. In the more recent Yankelovich poll, 84 percent of those who had used an unproven cure said they would use it again.

In response to such testimonials, mainstream medical authorities stick to their arguments about the need to wait for proffered cures to be scientifically proven. Prominent among these authorities is Stephen Barrett, an Allentown, Pa., psychiatrist and author of numerous books about health fraud, including an aggressive attack on quackery and alternative medicine called *Health Schemes, Scams and Frauds.* Barrett denies that the interest in alternative medicine reflects a failure of conventional medicine. "It's like saying that the success of astrology rests on the failure of astronomy," he says. "There are some needs that can't be met by medicine." [10]

More narrowly, medical authorities rebut the claim that alternative cures are more humane to patients. The *New England Journal of Medicine* reported last April on a study by Barrie R. Cassileth, a professor of medicine at the University of Pennsylvania, who compared cancer patients receiving traditional care such as radiation and chemotherapy with a group of patients who received their care at the Livingston-Wheeler clinic in San Diego, which offers an alternative treatment relying primarily on a vegetarian diet, coffee enemas and a special vaccine. After asking the patients about their degree of pain, nausea and physical well-being, she found that the patients undergoing conventional treatment reported a more satisfactory existence. "Alternatives to conventional care are not free of side effects," Cassileth said, "and we should treat with suspicion statements that they are free of toxicities." [11]

Jarvis of the National Council Against Health Fraud acknowledges that many mainstream doctors now admit there is a need for more emotional involvement with their patients. But he rejects the notion that alternative care-givers automatically have better personal relations with patients. "Quacks are confident," he says. "They're more arrogant than empathetic. They're conspiratorial."

Are there risks to using alternative medical treatments?

"One of the pluses of alternative medicine," says the Washington writer who has sampled several types, "is that when it is not invasive, the worst it can do is not work."

To crusaders against health fraud, such thinking is known as "the gambler's fallacy." It ignores the multiple risks presented by unproven treatments, they say, risks that range from psychological turmoil to costly delays in seeking conventional treatment to, in some reported cases, unnecessary death.

In the 1986 Harris poll, only 2.5 percent of those who had used an alternative treatment said it had been harmful. (Extrapolated to the whole population, however, that would total 1 million people.) Still, the informal — even underground — ways in which alternative treatments are circulated raise concerns about dangerous misinformation.

Surveys have shown that sales staff in natural food stores, despite limited medical training, are often willing to offer advice and referrals. Word-of-mouth advice can be contradictory. Gay Marshall recalls hearing that a diet of natural juices had been highly recommended by some alternative practitioners, even as a cancer remedy, but a San Francisco macrobiologist waved her away from it, saying it was "too much yin, too cold for the body." *

Natural herbs, in particular, though used for centuries in teas, ointments and suppositories, have been known to contain contaminants. Confusion is common because herbs are known by multiple names, and because people who insist on picking their own can easily mistake a deadly plant for a therapeutic one. Experts also warn that using herbal remedies without a doctor's supervision leaves a patient vulnerable to side effects. The fox-

---

*"Yin" in this context refers to the human organs involved with absorption and discharge, such as the stomach and bladder. Holistic practitioners often apply the ancient Chinese concept of yin and yang, which, more generally, refers to the positive and negative forces that healthy individuals keep in balance.

glove plant, for example, is said to help control heart rhythm, but an overdose can be fatal. Similarly, peppermint can help digestion but may cause small children to choke. [12]

Mainstream medical authorities also express concern about the safety of folk medicine. In 1989, a Northern Arizona University anthropologist who had studied folk remedies used by 31 Mexican-American communities in Texas reported that as many as 10 percent of the local children had gotten lead poisoning. [13] (Lead remedies are advocated in some Hispanic communities for common ailments such as constipation, and in parts of Asia, Africa and the Middle East to aid teething babies or to prevent umbilical-cord infections.)

On the psychological level, critics are concerned that the desire for "empowerment" common in holistic health thinking causes patients to blame themselves for their illnesses. Michio Kushi, the guiding force behind the macrobiotic diet, may sound harsh when he maintains "that cancer, heart disease and other chronic illnesses are caused by personal lifestyle choices and not by outside agents such as bacteria or viruses." [14] Similarly, a holistic health counselor treating a patient who was distressed over having genital herpes writes of how she counseled the patient that the herpes was "a higher self-intervention, an obstacle that is meant to cause us to stop long enough to re-evaluate what we are creating for ourselves as well as the consequences of our choices." [15]

Telling patients that psycho-social factors will affect their disease can make them feel responsible if the disease worsens. "It's a dilemma," says Malin Dollinger, an oncologist at the University of Southern California at Los Angeles. "If you believe that you can help to fight your own cancer, it's easy to conclude that, if you don't get better, it's your fault." [16]

Continued on p. 80

AIDS Remedies: All Views Are 'Subjective'

The rapid spread of the AIDS virus in the past decade† has spawned some of the most militant alternative medicine activists. Gay and alternative health groups have organized protests of government and private health authorities they believe are suppressing possible cures. They also have been operating underground "buyers clubs," which trade and smuggle unproven products and information kits involving such proposed AIDS remedies as Chinese herbs, vitamins and doses of garlic.

The Food and Drug Administration (FDA) has issued warnings about the alternative treatments. "AIDS is a quack's dream come true, an incurable fatal disease surrounded by fear and ignorance," says one agency publication.†† It describes a Honduran herbalist operating in Brooklyn, N.Y., in 1986 who was charging $500 for an "AIDS cure." The "cure" consisted of the same regimen of special food and herbs that he had been prescribing for all ailments.

The array of items the FDA frowns upon includes laetrile, snake venom and a photography chemical called DNCB, which is said to clear up lesions. The agency also tells AIDS patients to be skeptical of "natural therapies, vitamins, minerals and special diets, special lights, acupuncture, guided imagery and bottled T-cells (critical immune cells that are depleted by the AIDS virus) as well as advertisements for 'anti-AIDS pills.'" It also advises victims not to waste their time — or money — on such psychic treatments as channeling, crystal therapy and yoga.

Other critics such as Dr. John Renner of the National Council Against Health Fraud have warned AIDS victims away from "pond scum," a blue-green algae that is sold for $20 a bottle. He cites instances of AIDS quacks telling people to stop taking their medicine and go to Brazil to take water, air and raw vegetables or go to Switzerland to receive herbal remedies and "ozone therapy," which involves drawing blood and heating it or injecting it with ozone. Renner says the main thing AIDS victims should steer clear of are therapies whose contents are kept secret.

At present, there is no official list of discredited AIDS remedies. In 1990, the National Institute of Allergies and Infectious Diseases, whose director is Anthony S. Fauci, the top U.S. AIDS researcher, was considering a grant to a Washington, D.C., company called Emprise to compile a computer database giving scientific critiques of unproven AIDS remedies. It was presented as similar to a database on unproven cancer therapies that the company had prepared for use by doctors in counseling patients.

AIDS activist groups as well as cancer-cure activists protested the proposal, saying it would amount to a "blacklist" that threatened the rights of people with AIDS to experiment with diverse treatments. The application was subsequently withdrawn because, in the words of Grace Powers Monaco, who ran Emprise, "the alternative cancer people misrepresented it to the AIDS people."

Currently, the National AIDS Information Clearinghouse, a part of the federal Centers for Disease Control in Atlanta, keeps an informal list of unproven remedies but does not critique them. The FDA keeps an import-alert list to help customs and postal officials keep out unpermitted products offered as AIDS remedies.

AIDS victims who seek medical evaluations of purported treatments can call a telephone hotline run by the San Francisco-based Project Inform, which works closely with the National Institutes of Health, or subscribe to publications such as *AIDS Treatment News,* also in San Francisco. Information kits on potential alternative cures are available from such groups as People with AIDS Health Group and the Health-Education AIDS Liaison (HEAL), both in New York City. The Health Group publishes a newsletter on AIDS remedies, while HEAL offers a 500-page compendium on holistic approaches to AIDS and other illnesses.

Many AIDS activists argue that a majority of people with AIDS around the world do not have access to Western medicine and are being treated with remedies indigenous to their traditional cultures, such as herbs and hyperthermia. They say such remedies have not been given adequate study in the United States.

But the self-described quack-busters find the cure-seekers too indiscriminate. "Many homosexual groups are already alienated from society," says William Jarvis of the National Council Against Health Fraud. "They speak of the CIA and a conspiracy to eliminate gays. For their cures, there is no such thing as bad publicity. There's a waiting market if they're simply mentioned." But Jarvis also notes that the FDA has become more tolerant of alternative treatments in recent years and says he hopes that users of unproven remedies will keep careful records so that experts can study their results.

Derek Hodel, executive director of the People With AIDS Health Group, says the underground buyers clubs have been influential in pressuring the FDA to permit Americans access to certain traditional drugs that may be useful in fighting AIDS and that are sold only overseas.

"There *are* fraudulent therapies out there for AIDS and cancer," Hodel says. "But sometimes regulators, in cracking down on fraud, interfere with people's right to choose. No one knows whether [blue-green] algae is effective, so the question is whether people should have the right to eat the stuff. A subjective view is the best you're going to get in this ballgame."

---

† According to the federal Centers for Disease Control, 133,232 people died from AIDS in the U.S. in the past decade.

†† *FDA Consumer,* October 1987.

Continued from p. 78

The American Cancer Society warns that "methods that require that patients accept the idea that their emotions contributed to their cancer are not innocuous. The patient who already feels guilty for delaying seeking treatment, or who is vulnerable to self-doubt and depression, may become more upset.... Coupled with high fees and lack of follow-up, these treatments constitute a greater psychological hazard than is usually recognized."[17]

Jarvis adds that people who learn they are terminally ill go through several well-known phases — denial, anger, bargaining, depression and acceptance. "They get their priorities right," he says. "They spend their lives doing what's important.... But the quack ties people up in a roller coaster of hope and despair, and the patients find themselves in psychological upheaval instead of moving on to acceptance."[18]

Health-fraud activists point out that many who work under the rubric of alternative health care oppose immunization, fluoridation, pasteurization and other scientifically proven health measures. Where they present the most danger, Jarvis says, is with treatable diseases such as diabetes, intestinal blockage and meningitis.

Religious healers cause Jarvis the most concern, as the age-old practice of faith healing has by no means disappeared from modern society. *(See story, p. 87.)* The hope that many people place in faith healing is in many cases fueled by television evangelists claiming to perform miracle cures. "Quack-busters" are cracking down. James "The Amazing" Randi, a popular magician, has appeared on NBC's "The Tonight Show" to duplicate the sleight of hand he says is used in psychic surgery and evangelistic faith healing. He has also written a book exposing religious health fraud.[19]

Reports of actual physical harm from alternative treatments can be found in medical literature. The water and coffee enemas recommended by many of the "metabolic treatments" of cancer have been linked to several deaths, though the victims reportedly took the enemas more often than the recommended frequency.[20] The newsletter of the National Council Against Health Fraud described the 1988 death from Hodgkin's disease of 17-year-old Sonja Boden. Her parents had gone to court and won the right to have her treated by macrobiotic diet, acupuncture, massage and "positive thinking" at the Perfect Health Institute in Detroit. The judges agreed, as long as her disease remained in remission. When the disease worsened, the parents finally sought chemotherapy, and their daughter's tumors shrank 40 percent before she died. Her doctors said her odds of survival had dropped from 85 percent to 50 percent because of the delays in care.[21]

Alternative medicine proponents are quick to point out that few among them advocate the complete abandonment of conventional medicine. "I realize a need for doctors in cases of accidents or a diagnosis," says Joseph M. Kadans, a lawyer and author of two books on natural herbs who operates a holistic medicine adult education center in Van Nuys, Calif. "All naturopaths need doctors. Our main idea is not to diagnose or treat but to get people to turn back to a simple life." ∎

BACKGROUND

Every Man a Doctor

Part of the allure of alternative medicine is the fact that many of its exotic theories and remedies have come down through the centuries from ancient China, India and Greece. Holistic health enthusiasts see a spiritual ancestor in Galen, a 2nd-century Greek physician to Roman Emperor Marcus Aurelius who encountered opposition from rival theorists when he sought to unite mind and body.

The current alternative medicine movement descends more directly, however, from a peculiarly American historical figure, an early-19th-century New Hampshire farmer named Samuel Thompson. A self-taught botanist, Thompson rode to national fame during the era of Jacksonian democracy with his philosophy of "every man his own doctor."

The prevailing medical thought at the time — best represented by Dr. Benjamin Rush, one of the signers of the Declaration of Independence — relied heavily on what were called "heroic" measures, which treated most ailments with painful bleeding and purging. Thompson believed common sense was more valuable than elite medicine. He wrote that physicians had learned nothing about the true nature of the medicines they prescribed except "how much poison [could] be given without causing death."[22]

Thompson asserted that all disease was caused by cold. The remedy, therefore, was heat, in the form of grueling steam baths in scalding water mixed with various natural herbs. He traveled the country promoting his methods to thousands of followers. By the time of his death in 1843, Thompson's once-popular methods were falling out of favor.

Homeopathic Medicine

In 1825, Americans were introduced to another alternative discipline, known as homeopathy. Brought over from Europe by disciples of its founder, German physician Samuel Hahnemann, homeopathy was based on the "Law of Similars,"

Continued on p. 82

Chronology

1800s
Homeopathy comes to United States from Germany. Rise of naturopathy as a reaction against drugs. Development of "mechanistic" treatments such as chiropractic and osteopathy.

1920s
Practitioners offer such cancer "cures" as treatments with radio waves or colored lights. Edward Cayce introduces psychic diagnoses and treatments.

1930s
Birth of modern consumer movement.

1938
Federal Food, Drug and Cosmetic Act gives Food and Drug Administration (FDA) authority to police fraudulent health products, though not health practices.

1950s
Diverse alternative cancer cures draw crackdown from FDA and the American Medical Association (AMA).

1960s
Rise of counterculture, back-to-nature movement, skepticism of medical establishment. Interest in Zen and other Eastern philosophies presages holistic medicine movement.

1962
AMA establishes Committee on Quackery.

1970s
Holistic health movement gathers steam; health food stores proliferate; backers of alternative cancer therapies spark controversy over laetrile.

1972
Ancient Chinese practice of acupuncture gains new exposure in U.S. after Nixon administration's diplomatic opening to China.

1975
Faced with lawsuits from newly licensed chiropractors, the AMA abolishes its Committee on Quackery.

April 12, 1976
Congress passes amendment to Food, Drug and Cosmetic Act to restrict FDA enforcement powers and ease marketing of new food supplements.

1977
Four chiropractors bring antitrust suit against the AMA, accusing it of trying to destroy the chiropractic profession.

1978
American Holistic Medical Association is founded. AMA annual meeting devotes special section to holistic medicine.

1980s
Arrival of AIDS prompts new experimentation with unproven remedies. Federal government toughens stance against health fraud.

May 31, 1984
House Select Aging Committee's Subcommittee on Health and Long-Term Care releases report on its four-year study on "Medical Quackery: A $10 Billion Scandal." FDA responds by launching health-fraud initiative.

1990s
New respectability for acupuncture and chiropractic.

Nov. 22, 1991
Congress passes bill creating Office of Alternative Medicine at National Institutes of Health.

Jan. 13, 1992
Complying with a court ruling that ended 15 years of litigation, the AMA publishes a statement reversing its longstanding policy and acknowledging that it is ethical for doctors to refer patients to chiropractors. But the statement specifies that neither professional ethics, the law nor the court's injunction require such referrals.

Continued from p. 80

the notion that "like cures like." Practitioners would arrive with a kit containing a couple of hundred vials of herbs and minerals and administer to a patient suffering from, say, nausea, the very substance that causes nausea in healthy individuals.

A second principle of homeopathy was that the smallest dose of a remedy is always best, the theory being that the body needs only a small dose to restore its natural self-healing abilities and that large doses bring toxic side-effects. In practice, that meant that many of the remedies were heavily diluted with water or other harmless substances.

Homeopathy became highly influential by the mid-19th century and several homeopathic colleges flourished. (The American Medical Association was formed in 1846 partly to counter the influence of this rival discipline.) In the following decades, homeopathy continued to be taught in major medical schools, and its remedies were accorded legal status in the 1938 Federal Food, Drug and Cosmetic Act. Academic and popular interest, however, had waned by this time, and would not revive until the holistic health movement emerged in the 1970s.

Today, there are an estimated 1,000-3,000 homeopathic doctors and more than 70 homeopathic self-care study groups in the country, according to the National Center for Homeopathy in Alexandria, Va. An estimated $2.5 billion in non-prescription homeopathic drugs were sold worldwide in 1988, according to the Food and Drug Administration (FDA).

Current followers of homeopathy cite numerous personal testimonials to its effectiveness and an increasing number of scientific studies. In 1986, the respected British medical journal *The Lancet* reported on an experiment in which hay fever patients did better with homeopathic remedies than a control group. But health-fraud activists continue to voice skepticism. Says psychiatrist Stephen Barrett, "It's no better than taking a drink of tap water."[23]

The FDA in recent years has become concerned about homeopathic remedies being used to treat serious illnesses. In 1988 the agency issued guidelines to help manufacturers and homeopathic pharmacists determine which remedies could be sold without a prescription. One sign of the growth of homeopathy is that a few remedies are now being advertised on television.

Mind-Body Connection

One of the central tenets of alternative medicine is its notion that the mind can have tremendous influence over the health of the body. It was in the 17th century that French philosopher René Descartes sparked an intellectual revolution when he posited a strict division between the mind and body in medicine. Before Descartes, the two were very much integrated, as holistic health adherents have noted. After Descartes, one writes, doctors began to "concentrate on the body machine and to neglect psychological, social and environmental aspects of illness."[24]

As happened often throughout history, however, individuals came forth with thinking that went against the grain. In the late 19th century, the notion of interplay between the mind and body was resurrected by a French apothecary named Émile Coué (1857-1926). After witnessing a patient's recovery from a serious illness after being given only a harmless placebo, Coué devised a self-healing technique he called autosuggestion, which simply instructed the patient to repeat a positive phrase about himself. Autosuggestion won followers around the world.

The mind-body riddle was further complicated in the 1920s with the emergence of paranormal activist Edgar Cayce (1877-1945), the author and "prophet" who offered widely publicized psychic diagnoses and treatments from his headquarters in Virginia Beach, Va. Cayce became known as the "sleeping prophet" because he would put himself into a trance and diagnose patients' ailments, prescribe remedies and, according to anecdotal evidence, heal the sick. He was prosecuted several times for fortune telling, drug law violations and even suspected murder, but he always escaped conviction. Though no scientific proof of Cayce's psychic healing powers was ever presented, he won thousands of adherents, and his foundation and affiliated clinics remain active today.

By the 1940s and '50s, the study of psychosomatic medicine — the notion that some illnesses were caused by mental processes — had achieved recognized status among scientific researchers. In 1975 Herbert Benson, a Harvard cardiologist, published the influential book *The Relaxation Response,* which outlined a system of stress reduction and better health through meditation. (Benson is active today promoting "mind-body clinics" that seek to integrate meditation into daily medical practice.)

On the popular level, few holistic thinkers have matched the influence of the late Norman Cousins, longtime editor of *The Saturday Review.* His 1979 book, *Anatomy of an Illness as Perceived by the Patient,* told of his recovery in the mid-1960s from what doctors had said was an irreversible collagen illness (a disease of the connective tissue). Cousins attributed his recovery largely to his self-designed laughter therapy program. With the approval of his doctor, he subjected himself to large amounts of intravenous vitamins while he read anthologies of American humor essays and watched Marx Brothers movies and old episodes of "Candid Camera." His recovery was considered miraculous and he went on to become a medical lecturer. (Cousins died Nov. 30, 1990, at age 75 after suffering a heart attack.)

The late 1970s also gave prominence to one of holistic medicine's best-known spokesmen, New Haven, Conn., surgeon and cancer specialist Bernie S. Siegel. As he explains in his 1986 best-seller, *Love, Medicine and Miracles,* Siegel applies a highly personalized, spiritual approach to working with what he calls "exceptional cancer patients," those who have survived the terminal illness much longer than expected. In a method he calls "carefrontation," Siegel encourages doctors to closely identify with patients to inspire them to use will power and a positive attitude to conquer disease. "We must revise physician education and create caring compassionate physicians, not technicians," he writes.[25] He believes that many of these patients have "the ability to throw statistics aside" and beat the survival odds to a degree that is scientifically significant.

Siegel draws his share of criticism. Physician Melvin Konner has said that Siegel's results can be attributed to the "placebo effect," * and the fact that some cancers simply go into remission for no apparent reason.[26] Siegel tells patients what they want to hear, Konner says.

According to Konner, Siegel also conveys to patients what may be a disturbing message that it was certain decisions they made in their lives that brought on the cancer. Siegel is known to ask his patients, for example, "Why did you need this illness?"

While many conventional practitioners remain skeptical, some mind-over-body claims are difficult to dis-

---

*The "placebo effect" refers to a beneficial effect of a medical technology that cannot be attributed to properties of the technology itself. Often considered psychologically engendered well-being or improvement in a condition brought on by the belief of the patient that the technology itself is beneficial.

miss. In October 1989, for example, the medical world took notice of a report in *The Lancet* about a Stanford University Medical School study of cancer patients who had received psychosocial support (what Siegel might call "carefrontation") and a control group of patients. Women who had received the emotional support survived 36.6 months, compared with only 18.9 months for the control group.[27]

Transcendental Medication

Perhaps the most radical application of mind-over-body medicine is the ancient Indian Ayurvedic medicine promoted by guru Maharishi Mahesh Yogi, founder of Transcendental Meditation (TM). "The fundamental premise of Ayurveda is that consciousness is primary, matter is secondary," says Deepak Chopra, the method's main spokesman.[28] Ayurvedic (the word is Hindu for the "science of life") posits a central "life force," or energy field, called "prana." Its methods of Yoga, massage and aromatherapy applied to individuals after an evaluation of their "body type" combines ancient healing traditions with modern research. It has won increasingly serious study in medical journals in recent years.

Ayurvedic's efforts to unite the body with the mind lead its spokesmen to make some eyebrow-raising remarks. "Although everyone falls prey to the aging process, no one has ever proved that it is necessary," Chopra has written.[29] Practitioners of Ayurvedic medicine have been criticized by the National Council Against Health Fraud for charging as much as $11,000 for treatments that can consist of 216 types of enemas made from such materials as testicles of peacocks, swans and turtles, and ritualistic sacrifices to gods. Ayurvedic, the council says, is "a marketing term for a variety of health products and services of limited, questionable or unproved value."[30]

'Fringe' Technologies

Though much of alternative medicine is a reaction against high technology, maverick health researchers have come up with their share of technological solutions that have riled the medical establishment. One of the earliest was Indian-born scientist Dinshah Ghadiali, the inventor of spectro-chrome therapy.

Introduced in New York City in 1920, his method involved the exposure of body parts to colors projected by filters over the light bulb of a machine similar to a slide projector. He claimed success in treating ailments as diverse as headaches, burns, suppression of urine and varicose veins. The FDA found that his technique had no curative effects and in 1947 forced Ghadiali to quit selling his machines. He died penniless in 1966. His disciples, however, continue to promote spectro-chrome therapy. It was severely denounced during a congressional probe of quackery in the early 1980s.

Perhaps the most famous of alternative medicine's machine-makers was Wilhelm Reich, the Austrian psychoanalyst and disciple of Sigmund Freud who came to the United States in the 1940s. Reich developed a theory that human sexual energy was a cosmic force that was the key to health. He called that energy "orgone," a combination of orgasm and hormone. To tap into it, Reich invented the "orgone box," a refrigerator-sized apparatus in which patients would sit to have their energy funneled to certain bodily areas in the hope of curing everything from impotence to cancer.

Reich was imprisoned for fraud by federal authorities in 1957 and died the same year. Some of his theories were adopted by physician Alexander Lowen, the author of several books on energy and the body who runs the International Institute for Bioener-

A Glossary of Alternative Treatments...

Acupuncture: Use of needles, heat and massage applied to key points and "pathways" on the body to balance circulation of energy. Used for physical, psychological and emotional ailments. Originated in China 3,000 years ago; used in the United States since the 1930s.

Alexander technique: Training to alter a patient's posture to "re-educate the muscular system" and ease pain. Originated in late 19th century by Australian stage actor Matthias Alexander.

Aromatherapy: Use of oils from jasmine, sage, lavender and other plants to treat such ailments as colds, menstrual cramps and skin diseases. Can be swallowed, inhaled or rubbed into the skin. Originated in the 1920s by French chemist René Maurice Gattefosse.

Ayurvedic medicine: Use of "natural" diet, herbs, exercise and "rejuvenation" therapies (such as massage and aromatic scents) as preventive health care tailored to each patient's "body type." Originated in India 5,000 years ago. Promoted since 1985 by Maharishi Mahesh Yogi, founder of Transcendental Meditation.

Bach's flower remedies: Oral use of 38 flower and alcohol-based formulas manufactured in Wallingford, England, to cure everything from shyness to fear to drug dependency. Originated in the 1930s by British physician Edward Bach.

Bioenergetic analysis: Muscle-relaxing therapy for emotional complaints based on Wilhelm Reich's concept of the centrality of the sexual organism in health. Assumption is that what goes on in the body reflects what goes on in the mind and vice versa. Pioneered in the 1950s by Dr. Alexander Lowen of New York City.

Biofeedback: Use of sensor equipment to monitor involuntary functions such as temperature, sweat, brain wave patterns and blood flow. Patients suffering from headaches, insomnia, high blood pressure or anxiety watch monitors and try to will their way to normal functioning. Developed by various scientists in Europe, with progress in the United States beginning in the 1960s.

Chelation therapy: Intravenous doses of a synthetic amino acid used to treat heart disease and other serious ailments. The acid (called EDTA) was developed to cure lead poisoning in the 1930s by Detroit cardiologist Norman E. Clarke.

Chiropractic: Manipulation of the spinal column and other areas to relieve lower back pain by correcting "misalignments" of vertebrae. Practitioners also use manipulation of the spinal column to treat internal ailments, stress, poor nutrition and emotional complaints. Originated by David Daniel Palmer in Iowa in 1895.

Crystal healing: Use of stones such as quartz, amazonite and aventurine to restore wellness and treat ailments as serious as leukemia, bursitis, Parkinson's disease and blindness. Movement spread across the United States in mid-1980s. Crystal Academy of Advanced Healing Arts is located in Taos, N.M.

Guided imagery therapy: Patients are instructed to mentally visualize their immune systems fighting diseases such as cancer. Introduced in the United States by oncologist O. Carl Simonton and psychologist Stephanie Matthews in the 1970s.

Herbalism: Intake of potions derived from the roots, stems, leaves and seeds of plants to treat a variety of ail-

---

gic Analysis in New York City.

Another unorthodox technology that is still making waves today is the notion of a powerful microscope that can isolate disease-causing microorganisms that go undetected by mainstream science. The pioneer in this field was a medical researcher from San Diego named Royal Raymond Rife, who claimed in the early 1930s to have found a cure for cancer.

Rife created a microscope that relied on an unusual method of lighting that he said allowed him to isolate the cancer-causing virus and electronically destroy it. He set up a network of clinics to apply the treat-

ment and claimed some success. His work was attacked as quackery, and medical journals ceased to publish his writings. Beginning in the 1970s, New Age health enthusiasts began publicizing Rife's life and work, and recent writings mention his treatment as a possible cure for AIDS.[31]

A modern counterpart to Rife is Gaston Naessens, a Quebec scientist who was prosecuted for criminal negligence and fraud (and acquitted in 1989). Naessens developed a powerful microscope he says can isolate subcellular organisms in human blood that he calls somatids. The examination of these organisms,

he argues, allows researchers to predict the advent of a degenerative disease as much as 18 months before conventional symptoms develop.[32]

Naessens' related treatment, the compound 714-X, is said to have restored the health of 750 out of 1,000 cancer victims and has reported some success against AIDS. Compound 714-X is what former Rep. Bedell credits with bringing on a remission of his cancer. Bedell has escorted medical researchers from the National Institutes of Health on a visit to Naessens' lab. He hopes that Naessens will be awarded a U.S. government grant to build a better microscope.

... From Acupuncture to Shiatsu Massage

ments and improve general health. Recorded use by ancient cultures as early as 2,500 B.C. Continued through the Renaissance until discredited in the 19th century. Modern interest resumed in Great Britain in late 1940s.

Homeopathy: Use of drugs from homeopathic pharmacies to expose the body to more of the substance that has caused an ailment, using the principle of "let like cure like." Originated around 1800 by German physician Samuel Hahnemann.

Hypnotherapy: Use of hypnosis to put patients in a suggestible trance as an aid in treating migraines, arthritis and nicotine addiction, and to help ease pain of chemotherapy. Orginated in late 18th century by Austrian physician Franz Anton Mesmer.

Iridology: Examination of the eye, particularly the iris, to diagnose mental and physical ailments all over the body. Originated independently in Hungary and Sweden in late 19th century. Introduced in United States in 1904 by Dr. Henry Lahn.

Kirlian photography: Use of special cameras by faith healers to produce an image of an energy force called an "aura" around the body. They study the aura for clues to physical and emotional ailments. Introduced in the late 1950s by Soviet scientists Semyon and Valentina Kirlian.

Macrobiotics: A preventive health diet based on natural whole grains and cooked vegetables that has been touted as a cancer cure. Followers are also concerned with ecology, respect for ancestors and world peace. Popularized in the United States by Japanese businessman Michio Kushi of Brookline, Mass., beginning in 1978.

Naturopathy: Use of fasting, water immersion, massage, body building and psychotherapy to eliminate the body's "toxic waste material," said to be the cause of all disease. Administered by a private naturopath or at a health spa. Popularized in a 1936 book by Harry Benjamin.

Psychic surgery: Opening an incision in the body allegedly without using a knife and healing the incision "spiritually" after surgery. (Skeptics say the process involves sleight of hand.) Originated by "shamans" in traditional cultures in the Philippines and Brazil. Some use in Britain and the United States. Brazilian practitioners use knives but no stitches.

Osteopathy: Manipulation of the spine to treat muscle spasms, pain or bone disease as well as ailments all over the body said to be caused by spinal "lesions" or imbalances. Originated in 19th century by American doctor Andrew Taylor Still. Unlike students of chiropractic, osteopathic students receive training similar to that of medical students.

Reflexology: Manipulation of the feet to clear "pathways" to ease ailments as headaches or stomachaches. Divides the foot into "zones" of energy. Originated in 1920s by American nose and throat doctor William H. Fitzgerald.

Rolfing: High-pressure massage and manipulation of the spine to align vertebrae with gravity as if straightening a "pile of bricks." Said to free the mind and emotions. Originated in 1940s by American chemist Ida Rolf.

Shiatsu: Massage from therapist's fingers, elbows or feet to bear down on body's energy points to treat ailments from migraines to diarrhea. Originated in Japan 1,000 years ago. (Shiatsu means "finger pressure.")

Cancer Wars

Since cancer emerged in the 20th century as a leading cause of death, the medical world has been offered a steady diet of diverse and contradictory cancer "cures." The sense of desperation exhibited, understandably, by victims and their loved ones has made the debate over cancer treatments considerably more passionate than any casual health food store discussion of crystal therapy or oriental massage.

Two decades after President Richard M. Nixon launched the federal war on cancer, significant progress has been made only on cancers affecting children, such as leukemia. The resulting frustration has bitterly divided adherents of mainstream medicine from their tightly organized opponents in the alternative camp.

"In the 'war over cancer therapies,'" writes one observer, "both sides often describe the opposition as a malevolent monolith. Thus the cancer establishment has characterized the alternative and adjunctive cancer therapies as the work of quacks preying on desperate and credulous cancer victims, while the proponents of alternative therapies have depicted established therapies as the 'cut, burn and poison therapies' of a cynical and profit-driven conspiracy."[33]

The earliest proffered cancer cures are largely forgotten today. "Chamlee's Cancer Specific Purifies-the-Blood Cure" became known in the early part of the century, followed in the 1920s and '30s by cures based on radio waves and readings from electronic microscopes *(see above)*, followed by Koch's glyoxylide (distilled water) cure in the '40s, which was sold in $25 ampules to at least 3,000 health practitioners.

A more famous cure from the first

half of the century featured the herbs and inorganic compounds promoted by clinician Harry Hoxsey, who said his concoction was invented by his great-grandfather. Hoxsey sold a lifetime supply of his medicines to more than 10,000 people at $400 per patient. Hoxsey wouldn't release his formulas, so the *Journal of the American Medical Association (JAMA)* labeled him a charlatan, prompting a libel suit that Hoxsey won. After a decade in court, the FDA finally shut him down in the late 1950s, though a form of the Hoxsey treatment is still offered at clinics across the U.S. border in Tijuana, Mexico.

By the 1950s, *JAMA* had compiled a sizable record of crusading against quackery in cancer treatments. In 1954, the American Cancer Society began releasing its continually updated list of unproven treatments, which provides detailed scientific statements about all major unproven cancer cures.

The 1970s brought what perhaps was the cancer war's most highly publicized battle — the controversy over the substance known as laetrile, derived from a chemical found in apricots and other fruits. It was developed by a California father-and-son team, both named Ernst Krebs, in the early 1950s. Informally called Vitamin B-17, laetrile was tested by the National Cancer Institute five times from 1957-75, with no report of success as a cancer cure. But when practitioners touted it (a Mexican doctor named Ernesto Contreras claimed he had used it successfully on 16,000 cancer patients), word spread like wildfire around the United States. An estimated 70,000 people tried it for pain control and cancer treatment or prevention.

When Contreras, by request, submitted 12 successful case reports to the FDA, however, the agency found that six of the patients had died, one still had cancer, three could not be located and two had gotten orthodox therapy.[34] Critics also began publicizing the risks of laetrile — the fact that it contains cyanide, for example.

The FDA refused to approve laetrile, but by 1982 it was legalized by legislation or court order in all states. One of the legacies of the laetrile flap was the formation in 1973 of the Committee for Freedom of Choice in Medicine, now in Chula Vista, Calif. At its peak it had 30,000 members in all 50 states. It remains active today, promoting alternative treatments in Mexico, publishing a magazine and fighting what it calls "health fascism" at the FDA.

Flare-Up at OTA

Most recently, the cancer war was waged over a controversial first-of-its-kind report on unconventional cancer treatments by the normally staid congressional Office of Technology Assessment (OTA). The project originated in 1986 at the instigation of then-Rep. Guy Molinari, R-N.Y., whose constituents included many enthusiasts of immuno-augmentative-therapy (IAT), a cancer treatment developed by a zoologist named Lawrence Burton and dispensed in a clinic in the Bahamas.

When interest had heightened and some 40 members of Congress were requesting the report, OTA expanded its research to cover all the major unproven cancer treatments, among them the Vitamin C therapy of Nobel Prize-winning chemist Linus Pauling; the enzyme, coffee-enema and diet-oriented "metabolic" treatments known as the Gerson and Kelley methods; and the "antineoplastons" method, a treatment using synthesized chemicals that "reprogram misdirected cells" developed by Stanislaw R. Burzynski, a Stafford, Texas, doctor.

In early 1990, early drafts of the report began circulating. Its major conclusion was that there were no effective unproven cancer cures that were undeservedly being shut out by medical authorities. Cancer-cure activists across the country then barraged their members of Congress with letters, and some of them called for the removal of the OTA project director, Hellen Gelband.

Representatives from groups such as Project Cure, People Against Cancer, the Foundation for the Advancement of Innovative Medicine and the National Health Federation converged on Washington in March 1990 demanding that OTA soften the report. (Capitol Hill security forces were beefed up for fear of violence.) And alternative cancer publications such as *The Cancer Chronicles* published stinging critiques, one calling the report "a comprehensive devaluation, presenting mainly derogatory statements and innuendoes concerning the therapies, larded with puffery for the agencies that repress them." (Ironically, the OTA report also drew flak from the quack-buster camp and from the National Cancer Institute, which argued that it wasn't hard enough on promoters of unproven treatments.)

Despite the controversy, Gelband believes the final report filled an unmet need and "corrected a gap in the system." The National Cancer Institute subsequently issued a clear set of guidelines intended to help promoters of unproven cancer treatments navigate the technical obstacles to winning scientific testing of their methods.

Chiropractors' Victory

The alternative treatment that has traveled the farthest toward mainstream acceptance is most likely chiropractic. The number of its practitioners has climbed from 32,000 in the 1970s to 50,000 today, according to the American Chiropractic Association. One in 20 Americans now uses the spinal manipulations to remedy supposed misalignments of vertebrae (chiropractors call them "subluxations") to treat back pain and other ailments whose relationship with the spine is less accepted.

Faith Healers and Freedom of Religion

In the summer of 1986, 7-year-old Amy Hermanson of Sarasota, Fla., developed a sore throat. Within weeks she had slipped into a coma. Soon she was dead of what an autopsy determined was juvenile diabetes. Because her parents are Christian Scientists, they had chosen to confront her illness with prayer instead of taking her to a doctor. In April 1989, a Florida court convicted the couple of "willful or culpable negligence" — criminal child abuse.

Such cases have become increasingly common over the past decade. Since 1982, U.S. courts have ruled on 24 cases involving parents who relied on faith healing rather than medicine for their children. Seven of the cases involved Christian Scientists; the others involved Jehovah's Witnesses and followers of such charismatic sects as Faith Assembly, End Time Ministries and Christ Miracle Healing Center. Most of the defendants were convicted, though many, like the Hermansons, were given suspended sentences.

Groups that practice faith healing worry health-fraud activists far more than proponents of New Age alternative treatments. "Most of these alternative-medicine types are smart enough to have their patients continue to use regular doctors and limit themselves to the areas in which they're licensed," says Rita Swan, a former Christian Scientist who now runs an advocacy group called Children's Healthcare is a Legal Duty (CHILD) in Sioux City, Iowa. "Religious healers can't be licensed by the state and don't limit themselves to what they're capable of doing."

Swan's group, along with professional organizations such as the American Academy of Pediatrics and the American Medical Association, lobby states to change laws and publicize efforts of prosecutors and social workers who crack down on parents who deny their children health care.

But they're up against a major obstacle: First Amendment rights to freedom of religion. According to Swan, 43 states have exemptions for religious healers in their child-abuse laws, and six others have an exemption for "non-medical remedial treatment." † (Only South Dakota has no religious exemptions, having repealed them in 1990.) Such laws, Swan says, are primarily the result of lobbying by the Christian Science Church.

David N. Williams, one of the church's Washington representatives, says such a view overstates Christian Science's influence. But the church does have representatives in state capitals, and its publications point to some 300 state and federal laws and regulations that accommodate the spiritual-healing tenets of Christian Science.

The church's principles, which go back to the 1870s writings of church founder Mary Baker Eddy, were articulated in a 1986 statement the church submitted to the federal Centers for Disease Control: "From a larger, spiritual perspective, disease is ultimately the result of living within a radically limited view of God and the nature of man. Healing in Christian Science is accomplished through drawing closer to God." ††

More than 7,100 testimonials of physical healings from 1969 to 1988 were recorded in Christian Science journals, including cases of cancer, polio, meningitis and broken bones, some of which were reportedly healed in a day. Church officials also argue that Christian Scientists do not lose disproportionate numbers of children to illness when compared with other groups. "Christian Scientists," Williams has written, "feel that a greater number of children would, in effect, have been 'martyred' to medical technology if their parents hadn't had the freedom to turn in a wholly different spiritual direction for healing." ‡

Christian Scientists say they differ from fundamentalists in that they have their own nurses and health facilities, and have a long history of cooperation with health officials, reporting communicable diseases and complying with mandatory immunizations. Church members are not compelled to practice faith healing, Williams says, and many people who become Christian Scientists do so after they've personally experienced a healing through prayer. Church morale has not suffered from the spate of court cases, he adds. "On the contrary, members have rallied. Their loyalty and solidarity have been confirmed."

† This January, the Supreme Court affirmed a Minnesota court decision refusing to allow criminal prosecution of a Christian Science couple who relied only on prayer healing until their 11-year-old son died of diabetes.
†† Quoted in *Freedom and Responsibility: Christian Science Healing for Children, First Church of Christ Scientist* (1989), p. 3.
‡ *Ibid.,* p. 66.

Recent studies by the RAND Corp., a think tank in Santa Monica, Calif., and others have found that chiropractors can do more for back pain than traditional medical treatment. And 90 percent of those responding to a 1991 Gallup poll commissioned by the chiropractors said they found the treatment effective.

Chiropractors recently won a legal victory that its spokesmen regard as a turning point in winning respectability and cooperation from doctors. This January, the American Medical Association (AMA), long the nemesis of the chiropractic profession, complied with a court order and published a statement reversing its long-standing policy and acknowledging that it is ethical for doctors to refer patients to chiropractors.[35]

The statement was the result of a 15-year lawsuit brought against the 270,000-member AMA, charging the doctors with antitrust violations and a conspiracy to destroy the chiropractic profession by boycotting their services since the 1960s. It was in 1977 that Chester Wilk and three other chiropractors filed the suit, saying they wanted "fair treatment by tax-supported institutions, hospitals, insurance plans, HMOs and other groups that have burdened those patients with anticompetitive barriers."[36]

In September 1987, a district court ruled in favor of the chiropractors, and that ruling was upheld by an appeals court in February 1990. After the Supreme Court declined to hear the AMA's further appeal, the doctors group published the new statement. Though acknowledging that it is ethical for doctors to refer patients to chiropractors, the statement specifies that neither professional ethics, the law nor the court's injunction require such referrals.

Many doctors today still voice skepticism about the qualifications and claims of chiropractors, charging them with aggressively recruiting patients on the basis of still unproven theories. As Barrett puts it: "Despite the dangers of unscientific treatments, chiropractors enjoy wider latitude in their scope of practice than any other health practitioners except physicians. By comparison, other independent health care providers must practice within far stricter limits. Dentists don't treat stomach ulcers. Psychologists don't order medication for a heart condition. Optometrists don't treat epilepsy. But chiropractors may get away with 'treating' all three diseases by claiming they are related to spinal problems."[37]

Barrett and Jarvis of the National Council Against Health Fraud have been implored by the chiropractors to show more tolerance. David Shingler, director of communications for the chiropractors' association, says Barrett and Jarvis represent "elements of the medical community that are held hostage to the past. They're not progressive. Dr. Jarvis is not representative of mainstream medicine. I don't think the public is well-served by an extremist." ∎

and bladder-kidney problems. The acupuncturists' president, Peter Marinakis, says he hopes the new office will help persuade the FDA to reclassify acupuncture as safe and effective and that his group will be asked to participate in its work.

The Office of Alternative Medicine is also welcomed by Jarvis of the National Council Against Health Fraud, though for different reasons. He predicts that the work of the office will deprive the "quacks" of "the Galileo ploy," their excuse that fresh-thinking scientists are being persecuted like the famous 16th-century astronomer.

Alternative Insurance

Few insurance companies are willing to reimburse policy holders for medical treatments that have not been approved by government and professional authorities. (A notable exception is acupuncture, which is covered by more than 70 percent of insurers, according to Marinakis.) Indeed, many practitioners who dabble in alternatives are "blacklisted" by insurance companies, according to Monica Miller, a lobbyist for the Foundation for the Advancement of Innovative Medicine in Kinderhook, N.Y. New regulations expected soon from the Health Care Financing Administration, which determines what treatments get covered by the federal Medicare and Medicaid programs, are not expected to soften a longtime policy against covering alternative treatments.

The gap created by this situation is being filled in part by Alternative Health Insurance Services, a new program run by a Calabasas, Calif., couple who got their start in alternative medicine by running a health food store. As described by founder Steve Gorman, Alternative Health Insurance Services offers coverage to patients who seek such treatments as

CURRENT SITUATION

NIH's New Office

The new federal Office of Alternative Medicine is still in the planning stages, according to the National Institutes of Health. But it is envisioned as a vehicle for matching the proponents of the most promising unproven cures with government research money and exposure to the public. Bedell says he hopes the office's highest priorities will be cures for cancer, AIDS and multiple sclero-

sis. Frank Wiewel, the founder of People Against Cancer who lobbied hard for the new office, says the unproven cancer treatments he hopes will be given immediate attention are Burton's immune augmentative therapy, Burzynski's "antineoplastons" method and the metabolic approaches of Gerson and Kelley (see p. 86).

Another group that is excited about the office is the Washington-based American Association of Acupuncture and Oriental Medicine. Though acupuncture is now legal in 23 states and boasts 6,000 licensed practitioners, the FDA continues to keep it on its list of treatments under investigation, resisting its claims to treat ailments as diverse as infertility, sciatica, skin disorders, tendonitis, poor eyesight

Continued on p. 90

At Issue:

Can alternative medicine coexist with conventional medicine?

DR. C. NORMAN SHEALY AND CAROLINE M. MYSS

*Shealy is a neurosurgeon and the founder
of the American Holistic Medical Association;
Myss is a "human consciousness" lecturer*
FROM *THE CREATION OF HEALTH: MERGING TRADI-
TIONAL MEDICINE WITH INTUITIVE DIAGNOSIS,* 1988.

DR. STEPHEN BARRETT

*Psychiatrist and health educator affiliated
with* Consumer Reports
FROM *HEALTH SCHEMES, SCAMS AND FRAUDS,* 1990.

traditional and holistic practitioners have much to learn from one another. The holistic world is not a fad; it marks a major turning point in the evolution of our understanding.... Indeed, this unified concept is much more scientific, even though we do not yet have all the facts to support the interrelationships. Bringing in intuitive influence leads one to accept that there is a capacity to perceive electromagnetic influence of consciousness. That "energy" has to be considered along with data from the physical and chemical planes....

In fact, once science acknowledges adequately the crucial nature of intuition as the basis for discovery, it will become possible to include, in medical school, courses in development of intuitive skills. Physicians will benefit from the expansion of personal ability, and the quality of medical practice will take a quantum leap forward....

As we move toward a medical paradigm for the 21st century, physicians and other health care professionals will work as teams. The days of the solo practitioners are passing, as is the extraordinary awe and blind faith accorded physicians. No one person can integrate all the facts. Patients will be recognized as part of the healing team.

Manipulation of the spine ... will be an integral part of evolution and treatment, as well as massage. Acupuncture and various forms of electrical and electromagnetic therapy will be coupled with the use of music and sound to assist in balancing the electromagnetic energy system. Nutrition and a healthy lifestyle will be taught and exemplified by all the team members. Relaxation techniques will be essential components, as will a comprehensive exercise program, including aerobic exercise and hatha yoga. The concepts of naturopathy will become a standard part of medicine.

The subtle energy benefits of homeopathy will be discovered to be of use especially in individuals who are choosing a healthy lifestyle. And I suspect that empirical research will ultimately reveal the power of crystals to magnify consciousness and balance subtle energy....

Spiritual healing will provide the ... framework for all the related physical, chemical and behavioral approaches. Therapeutic touch and other forms of "laying on of hands" will be as accepted as aspirin. Drugs and surgery will remain as adjuncts, to be used as giant Band-Aids in acute situations, to tide patients over until they can develop the strength to enter consciously the path to their own spiritual transformation, to express fully the light of the Soul.

perhaps the main difference between science and pseudoscience is the rigidity of the latter. Science is self-correcting and expands or revises its belief as new evidence arises. If a new concept doesn't fit with accepted scientific beliefs, the scientific community will determine whether the concept is flawed or current beliefs must be altered. But quack beliefs — no matter how illogical they are or how often they are refuted — are rarely abandoned by promoters as long as they are marketable.

The procedures described above have enabled medical science to make remarkable progress. But some unscientific practitioners ... view things differently. They suggest that the disease has one basic cause — a failure of the body to protect itself — which can be corrected by whatever they happen to believe. Fringe medical practitioners, for example, typically allege that allergies or metabolic imbalances are the underlying cause of innumerable symptoms. "Natural health" advocates claim that the main causes of ill health are "pollution" and faulty living habits. When health fails, they say, the way to restore it is to conform to "nature's laws" through diet, exercise and various measures to "detoxify" the body. Taking conventional drugs merely exposes the body to further pollution.

Some unscientific approaches are based on the magical idea that an object of enchantment can be "mapped" onto an accessible place and manipulated to control one's destiny. Thus, while chiropractors concentrate on the spine, acupuncturists needle the skin, reflexologists massage the hands or feet and iridologists focus on the eyes. The effects they claim may not be demonstrable by scientific tests, but so what? Since satisfied customers attest to the correctness of their approach, further proof is unnecessary.

Unscientific practitioners often claim that they are "too busy helping sick people get well" to demonstrate the efficacy of their treatment by performing research acceptable to the scientific community. This is a ploy. It is neither time-consuming nor expensive to conduct a simple follow-up study in which the condition of patients before and after treatment is carefully documented. In fact, most of the data needed for such a study should be recorded as part of ordinary medical practice. If an unproven treatment for a serious disease really shows promise, independent researchers will be eager to evaluate it.

Continued from p. 88

acupuncture, chiropractic, homeopathy and naturopathy as well as conventional treatments. "You get more for your money," he says.

His policies are reinsured by Lloyd's of London and are marketed through a network of 2,000 independent agents and by professional groups such as massage therapists. It recently won new credibility, he says, when he signed up the Amalgamated Clothing and Textile Workers union to offer the service nationwide.

"We don't recommend one treatment over another," Gorman says, and the service will not cover some of the "fringier" treatments, such as crystal therapy or psychic healing. It is open to innovative approaches, however, and doesn't exclude treatments simply because the AMA hasn't approved them. "We try to communicate to consumers that we are partners," Gorman says.

Governmental Tolerance

The tolerance for practitioners of alternative medicine varies widely from state to state. According to Pam Brinegan, executive director of a licensing enforcement body affiliated with the Council of State Governments in Lexington, Ky., there are more than 1,000 professions regulated by the states, but only 50-60 of them are regulated by all states the same way. "What's quackery in one state isn't in another," she says.

It's a "schizophrenic situation," says Miller of the innovative medicine foundation. She says the states that are most tolerant are Alaska, Washington, and Maryland. Alaska enacted a law in 1990 saying that a doctor could not be found guilty of incompetence simply because his methods were unconventional unless infliction of harm had been demonstrated. Washington state followed with a sim-

ilar law, and Maryland is considering a package that would emulate Alaska's law, set up an alternative health board and also require that the state physicians' board include at least one alternative practitioner.

According to Miller, the states that have cracked down the hardest on alternative practitioners are North Carolina, Nevada and West Virginia. North Carolina has an unusual law under which a practitioner can be guilty of misconduct if there is "deviation from prevailing medical practice," Miller says. "The implication is that science can't advance in North Carolina."Homeopathy enthusiasts as well as the American Civil Liberties Union recently have rallied to the cause of homeopathist George Guess, who is fighting an attempt by North Carolina authorities to revoke his license.

On the federal level, many backers of alternative treatments express hope that the FDA's drug approval process can be accelerated, particularly when it comes to cooperating with governments of countries that permit certain drugs that are banned in the United States.

Miller's group is supporting the Access to Life-Saving Therapies Act introduced by Sen. Alphonse M. D'Amato, R-N.Y., and Rep. Tom Campbell, R-Calif. It would alter FDA procedures on approving drugs and change the concept of "efficacy" of treatments so as to concentrate more on safety, leaving the question of effectiveness to trial consumers at an earlier stage in the approval process. The current definition "is inhumane," Miller says, because it prevents terminally ill people from trying treatments they want to try. ∎

OUTLOOK

Increasing Acceptance

The lifestyles of many alternative medicine enthusiasts make them easy targets of ridicule. The "oddball West Hollywood-San Francisco-Santa Fe-UFO watchers," in Jarvis' words, often oversell the promise of their treatments or assume too much baggage from the cornucopia of vague New Age culture. (The dust jacket of a popular holistic health book describes the author as "an administrator with the Berkeley Holistic Health Center ... [a] masseuse, flamenco dancer and metaphysical practitioner [who] is currently completing a program to become a professional prayer therapist through the Teaching of the Inner Christ, a nonsectarian metaphysical fellowship."[38])

Critics such as Jarvis are also alarmed by the movement's notions of "freedom" of health. "Providing

health care is not a right but a privilege," he says. "Like a pilot on an airplane, you hold the life of strangers in your hands. So you have to meet certain standards."

Few can deny, however, that some alternative disciplines merit investigation, and that several of them appear to work, even if scientists aren't sure exactly why. Hypnotherapy, for example, is now used by some 15,000 health professionals, according to the American Society of Clinical Hypnosis, to help patients kick the smoking habit or ease the pain of chemotherapy, among other things. The AMA has called for more research into it.

What's more, advocates of alternative medicine can point to increasing evidence of mainstream acceptance. This September, for example, the University of Maryland Medical Center announced a first-of-its-kind effort to expand its pain clinic to offer "fringe" treatments such as acupuncture, herbs and electrical stimulation to "bridge the gap between conventional methods and those less-understood methods."[39]

To health-fraud activists, testimonials from level-headed citizens about the success of mysterious cures can be explained in various ways. Says Stephen Barrett, "Most single episodes of disease recover simply with the passage of time, and most chronic ailments have symptom-free periods."[40] He and others cite the placebo effect and point out that a condition is sometimes misdiagnosed, so that a quack takes credit for curing a condition that never existed. Some patients take conventional treatment at the same time they use an alternative treatment, so no one can say for sure which worked.

"Legitimate science may try something for a while but will eventually abandon it when it's found to be ineffective," adds Dr. John Renner of the National Council Against Health Fraud. "But quackery never gives up. It keeps using ineffective remedies even when they are known to be ineffective."[41]

Cold skepticism, of course, is of little comfort to disillusioned consumers of modern health care and to the terminally ill with little to lose. "I haven't found anything sure-fire," says Berkley Bedell of his explorations of alternative science. "But I have a real problem with those people who say you shouldn't [explore unproven cures.] Yes, some will be taken in by the fraudulent, but it's worth taking a little chance."

That many patients are coming to this conclusion has not been lost on today's doctors. Cancer expert Cassileth advises doctors who discover that their patients are branching out to unproven methods to avoid conveying a lack of concern or respect for the patient's decision. "Don't become angry or condescending," she suggests. "Don't convey that you consider the patient foolish.... Don't say, 'You're throwing your money away.' Don't say, 'That's the silliest thing I've ever heard,' or 'That's completely unscientific.'" Such be-

havior shuts down the lines of communication, she adds. "The best way to prevent a patient from getting involved [in an ineffective cure] is to establish a good relationship ahead of time."[42]

On the personal level, if not yet on the level of epidemiology, alternative medicine has provoked new ways of thinking about health and living that are likely to continue. As Gay Marshall said of her decision to turn to unconventional healers: "I'm almost glad I came down with chronic fatigue. It opened up new windows. It's been a change of path." ∎

Notes

[1] The poll was conducted on Oct. 23, 1991, for *Time*/CNN. See "Why New Age Medicine Is Catching On," *Time*, Nov. 4, 1991, p. 68.

[2] The magazine's former title was *East West*.

[3] Quoted in *Time, op. cit.,* p. 69.

[4] Quoted in Carol Stevens, "Miracle Medicine?" *The Washingtonian*, November 1990, p. 165.

[5] Jack Anderson and Dale Van Atta, "They're Not Quacks," *The Washington Post*, March 17, 1991.

[6] Andrew Weil, Natural Health, *Natural Medicine: A Comprehensive Manual for Wellness and Self-Care* (1990), p. viii.

[7] *American Medical News*, Nov. 17, 1989, p. 47. The newspaper is published by the American Medical Association.

[8] Quoted in *Newsweek*, special issue, summer 1991, p. 31.

[9] *East West*, November-December 1991, p. 52.

[10] Quoted in *American Medical News*, Nov. 17, 1989, p. 47.

[11] Quoted in *The New York Times*, April 25, 1991.

[12] Information cited in *The New York Times*, Feb. 15, 1990, by health columnist Jane E. Brody, quoting such books as David Spoerke Jr., *Herbal Medications* (1980) and Varro E. Tyler, *The New Honest Herbal* (1987).

[13] See *Science News*, Jan. 28, 1989, p. 135.

[14] Michio Kushi, *The Macrobiotic Approach to Cancer* (1991), p. 18.

[15] C. Norman Shealy and Caroline M. Myss, *The Creation of Health: Merging Traditional Medicine with Intuitive Diagnosis* (1988), p. 206.

[16] Quoted in *American Medical News*, June 17, 1991, p. 29.

[17] Jimmie C. Holland, M.D., "Why Patients Seek Unproven Cancer Remedies: A Psychological Perspective," American Cancer Society, 1982.

[18] Quoted in *American Medical News*, Nov. 10, 1989, p. 49.

[19] James Randi, *The Faith Healers* (1989).

[20] Office of Technology Assessment, *Unconventional Cancer Treatments*, September 1990, p. 47.

[21] *NCAHF Newsletter*, January-February 1989.

[22] Quoted in James Harvey Young, *The Toadstool Millionaires: A Social History of Patent Medicines in America Before Federal Regulation* (1961), p. 44.

[23] Quoted in *Newsweek, op. cit.,* p. 31.

[24] F. Capra, *The Turning Point* (1982), quoted in Kristine Beyerman Alster, *The Holistic Health Movement* (1989), p. 11.

[25] Bernie Siegel, *Love Medicine and Miracles* (1986), p. vi.

[26] Writing in *The New York Times Magazine*, April 13, 1988.

[27] *American Medical News*, June 17, 1991, p. 29.

[28] Quoted in *Harvard Magazine*, September-October 1989, p. 24.

[29] Deepak Chopra, *Perfect Health: The Complete Mind/Body Guide* (1991), p. 171.

[30] *NCAHF Newsletter*, July-August 1991.

[31] Rife's story is told in Barry Lynes, *The Cancer Cure that Worked!: Fifty Years of Suppression* (1987).

[32] Naessens' story is told in Christopher Bird, *The Persecution and Trial of Gaston Naessens* (1991).

[33] A June 1987 conference paper written by M. Lerner, quoted in *Unconventional Cancer Treatments*, Office of Technology Assessment, 1990, p. 5.

[34] See Stephen Barrett, *Health Schemes, Scams and Frauds* (1990), p. 104.

[35] Published in *American Medical News*, Jan. 13, 1992, p. 4.

[36] Quoted in *The New York Times*, Feb. 9, 1990.

[37] Barrett, *op. cit.,* p. 181.

[38] See Alster, *op. cit.,* p. 156.

[39] Reported in the *Baltimore Evening Sun*, Sept. 19, 1991.

[40] Quoted in *American Medical News*, Nov. 19, 1989, p. 49.

[41] Quoted in *The New York Times*, June 9, 1988.

[42] Barrie R. Cassileth and Helene Brown, *CA — A Cancer Journal for Clinicians*, cited in *American Medical News*, Nov. 17, 1989, p. 47.

Bibliography

Selected Sources Used

Books

Alster, Kristine Beyerman, *The Holistic Health Movement,* University of Alabama Press, 1989.

Alster's dissertation, written at Boston University, offers an authoritative overview of the history and theory behind the holistic health movement, which has gathered momentum in the United States over the past two decades.

Barrett, Stephen and the Editors of *Consumer Reports, Health Schemes, Scams and Frauds,* Consumers Union, 1990.

One of the country's top "quack-busters" produced this aggressive exposé of certain members of the alternative health movement. It offers consumers advice on such "fringe" treatments as homeopathy and chiropractic and analyzes questionable products such as expensive vitamin programs, weight-loss regimens and "cures" for arthritis.

Bird, Christopher, *The Persecution and Trial of Gaston Naessens: The True Story of the Efforts to Suppress an Alternative Treatment for Cancer, AIDS, and Other Immunologically Based Diseases,* H.J. Kramer Inc., 1991.

A California journalist and alternative health enthusiast recounts the career and trial on fraud charges of a controversial Quebec doctor, Gaston Naessens, who claims to have invented a new microscope and related method of killing microorganisms that cause disease, including cancer.

Chopra, Deepak, M.D., *Perfect Health: The Complete Mind/Body Guide,* Harmony Books, 1991.

This survey by the best-selling author and foremost American advocate for the ancient Indian discipline known as Ayurvedic medicine explains the philosophy and methods of the treatment promoted by proponents of Transcendental Meditation.

Cousins, Norman, *Anatomy of an Illness As Perceived by the Patient,* W.W. Norton and Co, 1979.

The late editor of *The Saturday Review* tells of his experience with holistic medicine, including his famous self-designed laughter treatment, which he believes healed his deadly disease.

Editors of Time Life Books, *Powers of Healing,* Time-Life Books, 1989.

Part of a series entitled *Mysteries of the Unknown,* this illustrated survey of ancient and current alternative medical disciplines offers colorful details of the personalities and controversies that have shaped this field.

Inglis, Brian and West, Ruth, *The Alternative Health Guide,* Dorling Kindersley Ltd., 1983.

Inglis, an Irish medical journalist, and West, a British education professor, have compiled a comprehensive encyclopedia of unconventional medical disciplines, describing their origins, techniques and legal status.

Shealy, C. Norman and Myss, Caroline M., *The Creation of Health: Merging Traditional Medicine with Intuitive Diagnosis,* Stillpoint Publishing, 1988.

A neurosurgeon who founded the American Holistic Medical Association teamed up with a "human consciousness" lecturer to produce this treatise in favor of "intuitive" healing applied alongside conventional medicine. Numerous case studies of patients are described.

Siegel, Bernie S., M.D., *Love, Medicine & Miracles,* Harper and Row, 1986.

A New Haven, Conn., surgeon and well-known advocate of holistic medicine recounts his experiences working with "exceptional cancer patients," who used emotional support and will power to overcome the disease.

Weil, Andrew, *Health and Healing,* Houghton Mifflin, 1988.

A Harvard medical school graduate who now runs a holistic clinic in Tucson, Ariz., has written some of the best-received expert evaluations of alternative medical techniques and philosophy. This volume deals with the interplay between conventional and alternative treatments.

Reports and Studies

Office of Technology Assessment, *Unconventional Cancer Treatments,* U.S. Government Printing Office, September 1990.

Congress' scientific advisory arm prepared this thorough report on the methods and status of unproven cancer treatments. Heated debate and outside pressure on the agency from advocates of alternative cancer cures made this the most controversial project in OTA's history.

The Next Step

Additional Articles from Current Periodicals from EBSCO Publishing's Database

Books & reading

Baker, R., "Book reviews," *New England Journal of Medicine,* June 27, 1991, p. 1901.

Reviews two books, "The Encyclopedia of Alternative Health Care," by Kristin Gottschalk Olsen, and "Health Schemes, Scams and Frauds," by Stephen Barrett and the editors of *Consumer Reports.*

Clarke, A.E., "Reviews," *Contemporary Sociology,* September 1990, p. 742.

Reviews the book "Caring and Responsibility: The Crossroads of Holistic Practice and Traditional Medicine," by June S. Lowenberg.

Conrad, P., "Reviews," *Contemporary Sociology,* July 1991, p. 621.

Reviews the book "Holistic Health and Biomedical Medicine: A Countersystem Analysis," by Stephen Lyng.

Kupferberg, N., "Book reviews: Reference," *Library Journal,* May 1, 1991, p. 72.

Reviews the book "An Encyclopedia of Natural Medicine," by Michael T. Murray and Joseph E. Pizzorno.

McQuade, M., "Forecasts: How-to," *Publishers Weekly,* Aug. 23, 1991, p. 60.

Reviews the book "The Family Guide to Homeopathy: Symptoms and Natural Solutions," by Andrew Lockie.

Nutton, V., "The hillbilly herbalist," *TLS,* Jan. 11, 1991, p. 21.

Reviews two volumes on alternative medicine: "Herbal Medicine Past and Present. Volume One: Trying to Give Ease." "Volume Two: A Reference Guide to Medicinal Plants," by John K. Crellin and Jane Philpott, who provide an unusual approach to one of the oldest of all therapies, herbs. An important contribution to the sociology of medical thinking, a work distilled from eight years of studying the healing practices of a modern herbalist in Alabama.

Ullman, D., Thompson, K., et al., "Summer reading," *Utne Reader,* July/August 1991, p. 138.

Reviews several books suggested for summer reading: "The Healing Herbs," by Michael Castleman; "Encyclopedia of Natural Medicine," by Michael Murray and Joseph Pizzorno; "Between Heaven and Earth: A Guide to Chinese Medicine," by Harriet Beinfield and Efrem Korngold; nine other titles.

Warner, J.H., "Reviews of books: United States," *American Historical Review,* December 1990, p. 1644.

Reviews the book "Alternative Medicine and American Religious Life," by Robert C. Fuller.

Debates & issues

"New doctor roles for 21st century," *USA Today,* August 1989, p. 11.

Offers predictions on the changing role of physicians in the 21st century. Alternative health-care givers; impact of medical technology.

"Psychosocial intervention and the natural history of cancer," *The Lancet,* Oct. 14, 1989, p. 901.

Advises physicians to pursue an intellectually honest approach to the psychosocial management of cancer. Related research; alternative medicine approaches.

Dean, M., "Cancer, Lancet, and the media," *The Lancet,* Sept. 22, 1990, p. 735.

Comments on the extensive media coverage of the latest development in cancer treatment in the British press. The role of holistic medicine in the treatment of cancer was published previously in *The Lancet.*

Grossman, W., "Ask a Mars question, get a Mars answer," *New Scientist,* Oct. 19, 1991, p. 53.

Examines the skeptical movement in Europe. Recent third annual Euroskeptics conference held in Amsterdam; explanation of skeptics; the question of alternative medicine; skeptical movement in the United States; concerns of individual countries.

Madden, K., "The MDs vs. the healers," *Harper's Bazaar,* November 1990, p. 180.

Explores the renewed popularity of alternative healing methods. Historical perspective of humans' attraction to healing arts that stand on the outside of traditional medicine; examples of old and new forms of alternate therapy; drawing the line between quacks and honest medicine.

Health self-care

Conlin, D.W., "Future health care" *Futurist,* May/June 1988, p. 13.

Discusses future health care, which will emphasize self-responsibility, self-care, prevention and alternative health-care methods. These alternative methods will be seen as complements to traditional medical techniques. Health-care trends; financial incentives for innovation.

Graham, B., "Bridging the gap," *Health*, February 1991, p. 62.

Explains some ways in which patients can incorporate both conventional and alternative medicine in their health-care decisions. Trend toward more acceptance of non-traditional treatments; role of communication with physicians; finding a doctor open to alternative treatments; examples. INSET: Exploring alternatives.

Ponce De Leon, J., "Taking charge of your health," *Publishers Weekly*, May 3, 1991, p. 19.

Contends that consumers are turning to books for more information on alternative healing, self-care, and traditional medical facts. J. I. Rodale, founder of the organic movement in this country; holistic approaches; combining East/West traditions; concern over cancer; redefining the female perspective; concern for children. INSET: Helping children cope, by D. Maryles.

Holistic medicine

Reuben, C., "On the cuspid," *Ms.*, June 1989, p. 16.

Discusses holistic dentistry. Several holistic dentists discuss their methods of treating patients. Psychoneuroimmunology; Holistic Dental Association; Chinese medicine; effect of food and nutrition; office design; acupuncture; nutritional therapy; controversy over silver amalgam fillings; opposition of the American Dental Association.

Villarosa, L., "New age rage," *Essence*, January 1990, p. 25.

Discusses the growing trend of blacks to practice a holistic form of health care that integrates ancient African ideas. Illnesses of body, mind and spirit; tips for holistic lifestyle techniques.

Homeopathy

"The water that lost its memory," *Time*, Aug. 8, 1988, p. 73.

Discusses a report in the British science journal *Nature*, now rejected, on a phenomenon that defies the laws of physics and molecular biology. The debunked theory contended that water retained a "memory" of some molecules it once contained in solution. Impact on theories of homeopathy; critics; reaction. J. Langone.

Begley, S., Wright, L., et al., "Can water 'remember'?" *Newsweek*, July 25, 1988, p. 66.

Report on homeopathy, a school of medicine that says "microdoses" of compounds that would otherwise cause symptoms of a disease can actually cure it, that is now on

the verge of a renaissance. Recent research says water may hold the "memory" of a substance it once contained. Research; history; examples.

Castleman, M., "The healing powers of homeopathic medicines," *Redbook*, March 1991, p. 44.

Covers the controversy over homeopathic medicine, which is an alternative form of healing that involves administering minute doses of natural substances. Recounts how a physician overcame his feelings of disbelief after homeopathy cured his son's chronic bronchitis.

Denworth, L., Glick, D., et al., "Doctoring without drugs," *Newsweek*, summer 1991, p. 30.

Considers alternative medicine that is based on the theory that the body has a natural healing ability. Homeopathic remedies; Dr. Ifeoma Ikenze, a Marin County, Calif., pediatrician who uses homeopathy in her practice; what conventional doctors want; naturopaths and other practitioners claim to treat the cause of disease, not the symptoms.

Frey, N., "The French approach," *Harper's Bazaar*, November 1990, p. 181.

Examines the popularity of homeopathy in France. Brief history of homeopathy as a healing science based on the premise that like cures like; basic techniques that are the backbone of modern homeopathy; mixed views on the process among the medical community.

Gould, D., "A little of what you don't fancy," *New Scientist*, June 22, 1991, p. 54.

Reveals that the Royal London Homoeopathic Hospital wants to become a self-governing trust. The Bloomsbury and Islington Health Authority; the unnatural entanglement between the National Health Service and a branch of alternative medicine; Samuel Hahnemann and the invention of homeopathy; homeopathy in Britain; more.

Revkin, A. C., "Dilutions of grandeur," *Discover*, January 1989, p. 74.

Discusses the investigation into French researcher Jacques Benveniste's study on homeopathic theory and the conclusions of *Nature* magazine's investigative team. Defines homeopathy; Benveniste's report published by *Nature* on June 30; experiments performed.

Ullman, D., "Homeopathy: medicine for the 21st century," *Futurist*, July/August 1988, p. 43.

Explains homeopathy, or alternative natural medicine. Predicts that homeopathy will be combined with conventional medicine in the 21st century. Natural drugs; diseases of the 21st century; "High-touch" medicine (acupuncture, massage, etc); healing as an art.

Overviews

Burton, J. L., "Herbal remedies — an alternative," *The Lancet,* Dec. 22, 1990 and Dec. 29, 1990, p. 1565.

Explores five remedies derived from animal products taken from the "Four Books of that Learned and Renowned Doctor Lazarus Riverius" of 1678. Cholic pain; hysterical epilepsy; cancer; cough and catarrh in an infant; small pox.

Cullerton, B., "Ready to go holistic?" *Harper's Bazaar,* November 1990, p. 180.

Presents a quiz to determine latent holistic tendencies. Includes an analysis of results.

Findlay, S., Podolsky, D., et al., "Wonder cures from the fringe," *U.S. News & World Report,* Sept. 23, 1991, p. 68.

Discusses how unconventional medicine, long dismissed by mainstream doctors, is getting a closer look. Highlights the following approaches that offer power over pain: acupuncture, hypnosis and biofeedback; how each approach works; stress-reduction programs as a supplement to drugs, dietary changes and exercise. INSETS: Under the needles (one man's report on acupuncture), by D.P. Wiener; overdosing on stress, and on the 101 ways to relieve it.

McCarthy, L. F., "Healing's alternate paths," *Harper's Bazaar,* November 1990, p. 182.

Presents an overview of current alternative medicines, from psychology to reflexology, herbal healing to traditional medical science. Focuses on how they would treat several common, everyday ailments, such as headaches, backaches and mild depression.

Nickles, L., "Psychic schmooze," *Harper's Bazaar,* November 1990, p. 182.

Presents a skeptic's survey of New Age healing methods. Tarot readings; astrology; psychics; palm reading.

Podolsky, D., "Big claims, no proof," *U.S. News & World Report,* Sept. 23, 1991, p. 77.

Presents a guide to six alternative healing treatments, cures for illnesses that are intriguing, if largely unproven. Treatments include: homeopathy, herbalism, naturopathy, aromatherapy, Maharishi Ayur-Veda and reflexology. Highlights for each treatment, what the treatment entails, the claim of its effectiveness and the evidence behind its effectiveness.

Wallis, C., Horowitz, J. M., et al., "Why new age medicine is catching on," *Time,* Nov. 4, 1991, p. 68.

Investigates an array of alternative therapies that are substituting for surgery, drugs and quick fixes from the doctor. Among the more accepted: acupuncture, biofeedback, hypnosis, guided imagery, chiropractic; therapists as cross-fertilizers; chief danger of alternative medicine; translating the workings of alternative medicine into something doctors can understand. INSETS: Alternative medicine; my excellent alternative adventure, by E. Linden.

Research

Howard, B., "Ape apothecary: Self-prescribing chimps lead researchers to nature's medicine cabinet," *Omni,* February 1991, p. 30.

Reports on research that apparently shows that chimpanzees medicate themselves with medicinal plants. One example is the Gombe chimpanzee and the young leaves of the aspilia plant, which has antibiotic properties. Signs of intelligence; potential use of aspilia compound in cancer therapy; use of natural medicines in their home countries.

Pool, R., "Unbelievable results spark a controversy," *Science,* July 22, 1988, p. 407.

Discussion of a decision by the British journal *Nature* to publish results of an immunological experiment. Details and what seem to be unbelievable results; two-year hold on publication and then recently replicated; homeopathic tie-in and controversy raised; other issues.

Back Issues

Great Research on Current Issues Starts Right Here… Recent topics covered by The CQ Researcher are listed below. Issues dated before May 10, 1991, were published under the name of Editorial Research Reports.

JULY 1990
Do Americans Still Love Marriage?
Death Penalty Debate
Decline of Rural America
United Nations in the 1990s

AUGUST 1990
Democracy in the Philippines
Initiatives: True Democracy?
Hard Times at Newspapers
Teens Balance School & Jobs

SEPTEMBER 1990
Dangers of Alcohol
Western Alliance After the Cold War
Tobacco Industry
Right to Die

OCTOBER 1990
Organ Transplants
Energy Policy Options
Search for Arab Unity
Child Support

NOVEMBER 1990
Lotteries and Gambling
Post-Cold War Choices
Setting Limits on Medical Care
Multicultural Education

Back issues are available for $4.00 (subscribers) or $7.00 (non-subscribers). Quantity discounts apply to orders over ten. To order, call Congressional Quarterly 1-800-432-2250.

DECEMBER 1990
Cable TV Regulation
Americans' Search for Their Roots
Is Insurance System a Failure?
Why Schools Still Have Tracking

JANUARY 1991
Growing Influence of Boycotts
Should the U.S. Reinstate the Draft?
America's Archaeological Past
Peace Corps' Challenges in '90s

FEBRUARY 1991
Regional Impact of Recession
Puerto Rico's Status
Redistricting: Mapping Power
Nuclear Power

MARCH 1991
Acid Rain
Cost of the Gulf War
Reassessing Gun Laws
Future for Man in Space

APRIL 1991
Social Security
Canadian Crisis Over Quebec
California Drought
Electromagnetic Radiation

MAY 1991
School Choice
Racial Quotas
Animal Rights
U.S. and Japan

JUNE 1991
Children and Divorce
Teenage Suicide
Endangered Species
Europe 1992

JULY 1991
Teenagers and Abortion
Soviet Republics Rebel
Mexico's Emergence
Athletes and Drugs

AUGUST 1991
Sexual Harassment
Fetal Tissue Research
Oil Imports
The Palestinians

SEPTEMBER 1991
Police Brutality
Advertising Under Attack
Saving the Forests
Foster Care Crisis

OCTOBER 1991
Pay-Per-View TV
Youth Gangs
Gene Therapy
World Hunger

NOVEMBER 1991
Fast-Food Shake-Up
The Greening of Eastern Europe
Business' Role in Education
Cuba In Crisis

DECEMBER 1991
Retiree Health Benefits
Asian Americans
The Obscenity Debate
The Disabilities Act

JANUARY 1992
Term Limits
Oil Spills
Hunting Controversy

Future Topics

▶ *America's Threatened Coastlines*

▶ *New Era in Asia*

▶ *Assisted Suicide*

THE CQ Researcher

PUBLISHED BY CONGRESSIONAL QUARTERLY INC., IN CONJUNCTION WITH EBSCO PUBLISHING

Threatened Coastlines

Development is taking a toll on America's fragile shores

L IVING BY THE SEA IS THE DREAM OF MANY
Americans. But it is also a modern hazard, as Hurricane
Hugo so vividly demonstrated in 1989 when it battered
South Carolina and caused 21 deaths and $7 billion
in damage. Every year America's coasts on average erode 1 to
2 feet, putting lives and property at risk. But coastal geologists
say the real problem is not erosion but man's penchant for
building at the water's edge, interfering with the sea's natural
cycle of ebb and flow. While many states have enacted laws
to regulate rampant development along fragile shorelines,
they have encountered fierce opposition from private property
advocates and homeowners who cherish their piece of the
beach — no matter how tenuous it may be.

 February 7, 1992 • Volume 2, No. 5 • 97 - 120

Formerly Editorial Research Reports

COVER PHOTO: NORMAN MARTIN, TEXAS SEA GRANT PROGRAM

The CQ Researcher

February 7, 1992
Volume 2, No. 5

EDITOR
Sandra Stencel

MANAGING EDITOR
Thomas J. Colin

ASSOCIATE EDITOR
Richard L. Worsnop

STAFF WRITERS
Charles S. Clark
Mary H. Cooper
Rodman D. Griffin

PRODUCTION EDITOR
Laurie De Maris

EDITORIAL ASSISTANT
Thomas H. Moore

GRAPHICS
Jack Auldridge

PUBLISHED BY
Congressional Quarterly Inc.

CHAIRMAN
Andrew Barnes

VICE CHAIRMAN
Andrew P. Corty

EDITOR AND PUBLISHER
Neil Skene

EXECUTIVE EDITOR
Robert W. Merry

PUBLICATIONS MARKETING/SALES
Robert Smith

EDITOR, EBSCO PUBLISHING
Melissa Kummerer

The CQ Researcher (ISSN 1056-2036). Formerly Editorial Research Reports. Published weekly (48 times per year, not printed the first Friday of any month with five Fridays) by Congressional Quarterly Inc., 1414 22nd St., N.W., Washington, D.C. 20037. Rates are furnished upon request. Second-class postage paid at Washington, D.C. POSTMASTER: Send address changes to The CQ Researcher, 1414 22nd St., N.W., Washington, D.C. 20037.

Threatened Coastlines

BY RODMAN D. GRIFFIN

THE ISSUES

The two-story beach house stands — though just barely — a few feet from the water's edge, tilting precariously on wooden pilings toward the Atlantic Ocean. Rocked by the storm that slammed into the mid-Atlantic Coast in early January, it is a quarter-million dollars on stilts — ready to topple into the sea, seemingly at any moment.

About 50 other once-coveted houses on Delaware's South Bethany Beach share the same fate. The winter storm, the worst to hit the area in more than a decade, erased 50 to 75 feet of beach, severed sewer lines and sent water gushing down streets. It also demolished more than half of neighboring Rehoboth Beach's boardwalk.

Nearby Ocean City, Md., fared better, buffered by 6 million cubic yards of sand (an amount equal to 600,000 dump truck loads) pumped onto the beach as part of a major beach nourishment project. Completed in August 1991, the three-year undertaking has cost the city — and federal taxpayers — about $40 million. But the storm wiped out 80-90 percent of the manmade dunes, which act as protective barriers and were supposed to last a hundred years. The U.S. Army Corps of Engineers estimates it will cost $12 million to replace them.

The scourge of coastal erosion is not unique to mid-Atlantic beaches. From Maine to Texas, billions of dollars worth of property is being laid open to the whims of the ocean and gulf as shores retreat at frightening speed. In North Carolina, parts of the Outer Banks are losing 15 feet yearly, leaving the renowned candy-striped Cape Hatteras lighthouse in imminent peril. If it doesn't fall down first, it's

likely to end up like Morris Island lighthouse, near Charleston, S.C. Once on solid land, it now stands a quarter of a mile offshore.

In California, some 86 percent of the state's 1,100 miles of exposed Pacific shoreline is receding at an average rate of between 6 inches and 2 feet a year. The worst case, by far, is the Louisiana coast, which is losing 30 to 60 feet of coastal wetlands a year. *(See story, page 109.)*

"It's no secret any more what's happening on the coast," says Stephen Leatherman, director of the Laboratory for Coastal Research at the University of Maryland. "Ten years ago we didn't have good data on erosion rates. Now we do, and we know about 90 percent of the coast is eroding."

The threat has driven many communities to seek refuge behind sea walls and jetties, only to find that these costly engineering projects often make the erosion worse, either for them or for neighbors down the coast. Other seaside resorts, like Ocean City, Atlantic City, N.J., and Myrtle Beach, S.C., have spent vast

sums of mostly federal money to pump new sand onto their beaches, only to see the sand disappear again within a few years.

And if things weren't bad enough, the National Academy of Sciences warns of worse to come. Over the next century, the academy reported in 1987, the sea level in the U.S. will creep up between two and five feet, more than double the rate over the last 200 years.[1] The likely cause, scientists believe, is the so-called "greenhouse effect," a global atmospheric warming trend spurred by pollution.* Such a rise could inundate many low-lying islands and eventually threaten such areas as the New York City borough of Manhattan and Miami Beach. "If the sea level rises one foot, all the [nation's] recreational beaches will erode in about 40 years," warns Jim Titus, a coastal expert at the Environmental Protection Agency (EPA).

For all the danger, people are still clamoring to own seafront property. At present, half of the American population lives within 50 miles of a coastal beach or one of the five Great Lakes. In the years ahead, experts project, more than 75 percent of all Americans will live in these areas.

But with more people comes more development, more erosion — and more hazard. "If we had a Category 5 hurricane** hit the Miami-Palm Beach area head-on, it could cause $50 billion to $60 billion in damage," warns Jerry Jarrell, deputy director at the National Hurricane Center in Cor-

---

*The greenhouse effect occurs when fossil-fuel gases collect above the Earth and hold in radiated heat, causing the polar ice caps to melt.

**A Category 5 hurricane has winds greater than 155 mph or a storm surge greater than 18 feet above normal. The last to hit the United States was Hurricane Camille in 1969, which slammed into Louisiana and Mississippi, causing $5.1 billion in damage. *(See table, p. 102.)*

al Gables, Fla. "We've been building in high-hazard areas as if the danger didn't exist."

Recreational property — not to mention life and limb — is not all that is at risk. According to some experts, land-based development contributes 70-80 percent of the pollution that fouls coastal waters, endangers wild-life and threatens commercial and recreational fisheries.

The lands and waters of the coasts are immensely valuable, and not only to real estate developers and sun worshipers. Barrier islands, spits and beaches shelter inland areas from storm and wind damage, erosion, flooding and rising seas. Dunes act as sand warehouses, replacing what is eroded from the shore. The coasts also provide essential habitat for many bird and wildlife species. Wetlands serve as nurseries and spawning grounds for commercial fish species and are home to one-third of all endangered species.

Yet for all their value, coastal wetlands, shorelines and waters are being contaminated by pollution, much of it attributable to shoreline development. Every year, coastal development dumps roughly 2.3 trillion gallons of partially treated sewage wastes directly into coastal waters.[2] Runoff from city streets and parking lots, along with pesticides and fertilizers that leach off farmlands, add an additional burden of pollution. As a result, environmentalists say the very things that attract people to the coasts are being jeopardized.

There is a pressing national interest in reversing the decline of America's coastal areas. A 1986 report by the Federal Emergency Management Agency (FEMA), which administers disaster relief programs, stressed that "unless an effective solution is found, by the year 2000 the sum of the individual decisions to exploit the coastal commons could add up to a series of unparalleled national disasters."[3]

Invariably, the demands for more

coastal development butt up against the demands for more public access and the needs for protecting our fragile coasts. As this year's spate of winter storms wreaks its havoc, here are some of the questions being asked:

Are beach protection techniques effective?

Until recently, the preferred method of combating the sea's inland march was to construct massive structures, such as sea walls, bulkheads and jetties. When properly designed and built, they can at least protect the property behind them. But many scientists now say that such structures accelerate the erosion of sand on the beaches in front of them.

"Sea walls destroy beaches; it's a proven fact," declares Orrin H. Pilkey Jr., a Duke University geologist. In a recent study of scores of sites on the Atlantic Coast, Pilkey and his colleagues found that beach width on "stabilized" beaches was dramatically lower than on beaches with no sea walls. Many of the stabilized shorelines had no beach at all.[4]

Other forms of armoring, such as groins, short piers of stone extending from the beach directly out into the water, can slow erosion by trapping sand carried by crosscurrents. But further down the beach, the lack of drifting sand can worsen erosion. "It's like robbing Peter to pay Paul," says Stephen Leatherman.

Jetties can cause beach larceny on an even grander scale. Long concrete or rock structures, they jut far out into the water to keep inlets and harbors navigable by keeping sand and silt from drifting in. Like groin fields, jetties can keep sand from replenishing beaches down current. The construction of a jetty 50 years ago at the southern end of Ocean City has caused neighboring Assateague Island, a national seashore, to lose 2,500 to 3,000 feet. Experts say the

northern end of the island may disappear in 20 to 30 years. On Florida's Atlantic Coast, the U.S. Army Corps of Engineers estimates that about 85 percent of the beach erosion is caused by the maintenance of 19 inlets, all but one of them made or modified by man to link the open ocean and inland waterways.

More recently, the trend has been away from "hardening" the shoreline. In fact, five states — Maine, North Carolina, South Carolina, New Jersey and Massachusetts — now prohibit or severely limit the use of sea walls, groins and other erosion-prevention structures.

"Beach nourishment is the alternative of choice as far as the Army Corps of Engineers is concerned," says John Housley, a coastal engineer at the corps. When done correctly, Housley says beach replenishment can be a cost-effective way to protect a community and provide needed recreational facilities, especially in resort towns dependent on income from tourism. The country's most successful example is Miami Beach. Between 1977 and 1982, a 10-mile stretch of its anemic shoreline was rejuvenated with a brand new 300-foot-wide beach — at a cost of $51 million. Ninety percent of that beach is still intact, after only minor, periodic replenishments.

Beach nourishment, however, is expensive — and often temporary — as the Ocean City case indicates. In a study of 90 replenished beaches on the East Coast, researchers led by Orrin Pilkey concluded that none north of Florida lasted more than five years. On the Gulf of Mexico, only 10 percent lasted more than five years. One of the more notorious flops took place in 1981 at Wrightsville Beach, N.C., when the Corps of Engineers widened the dwindling beach by 200 feet. Price tag: $4.4 million. Since then, the beach has been swept away and replenished by the corps several times.

"Beach replenishment is a fine way to go, except that it is out of the question in terms of cost," says Pilkey. "We're dealing with $1 million per mile for a beach that will last for two to four years." Pilkey estimates that it will cost New Jersey $10 billion over the next decade to keep its beaches replenished.

Unfortunately, for many highly developed seaside communities, there are no palatable alternatives. Losing the beach would trigger a devastating erosion of tax base. "When development is at stake, the choices are narrow — and expensive, regardless of which way you go," says Hans Neuhauser, senior vice president of the Georgia Conservancy, a nonprofit environmental group that promotes a balance between conservation and economic growth. "You either lose your buildings and possibly your tax base — or you nourish the beach. The real issue has to do with . . . who pays for it."

Does the federal government "subsidize" coastal development in high-risk areas?

For years, projects to save shorelines went on without much criticism. But recently, scientists and government officials have begun to question such expenditures of public funds, which, they say, too often go to protect second homes and investment property or help maintain residences in constantly flooded areas where development should not take place. "The medium-income person, as a taxpayer, is subsidizing the second home of the rich," complains EPA's Jim Titus. "It turns out that's what a lot of this erosion control really is."

Even more objectionable, critics say, are the federal subsidies for coastal infrastructure. "If we didn't build the infrastructure — the roads, sewers and schools — there wouldn't be the pressure to develop in harm's way," says Rebecca Hughes, legislative representative of the Association

of State Flood Plain Managers. "As soon as the government makes the decision to build infrastructure, it's a green light to developers."

Another chief target of critics is the National Flood Insurance Program (NFIP), established in 1968 to provide insurance for property in flood-prone areas.* The program was designed to defray the billions of dollars the fed-

---

*Under the Flood Insurance Act, shoreline structures can be insured against storms and flood up to a maximum value of $185,000.

---

eral government was paying out annually to inland and shore communities overcome by flooding. The areas were of such high risk that no private insurance companies would offer coverage.

In exchange for offering subsidized insurance, the program requires tougher building standards that would limit flood damage to homes, such as elevating structures to above the 100-year flood level and installing breakaway walls. But opponents of the program charge that it

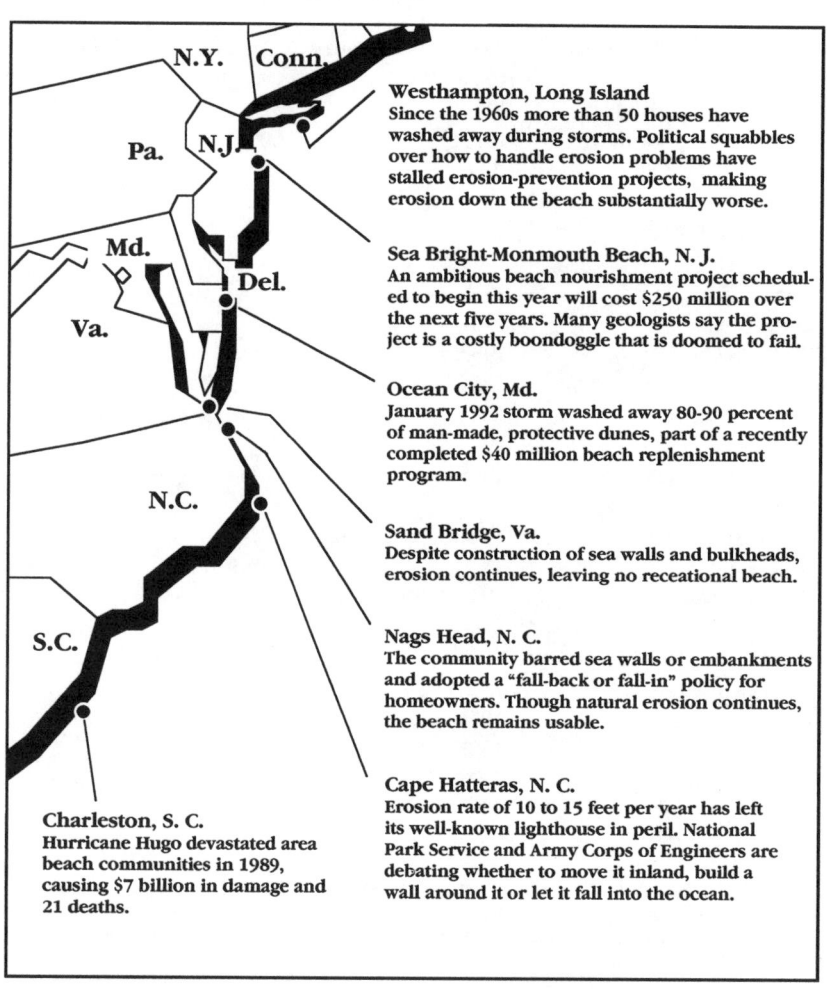

Turning Back the Tide

Attempts by coastal areas to cope with beach erosion have met with mixed results. Here are some examples along the Atlantic Coast:

Westhampton, Long Island
Since the 1960s more than 50 houses have washed away during storms. Political squabbles over how to handle erosion problems have stalled erosion-prevention projects, making erosion down the beach substantially worse.

Sea Bright-Monmouth Beach, N. J.
An ambitious beach nourishment project scheduled to begin this year will cost $250 million over the next five years. Many geologists say the project is a costly boondoggle that is doomed to fail.

Ocean City, Md.
January 1992 storm washed away 80-90 percent of man-made, protective dunes, part of a recently completed $40 million beach replenishment program.

Sand Bridge, Va.
Despite construction of sea walls and bulkheads, erosion continues, leaving no recreational beach.

Nags Head, N. C.
The community barred sea walls or embankments and adopted a "fall-back or fall-in" policy for homeowners. Though natural erosion continues, the beach remains usable.

Cape Hatteras, N. C.
Erosion rate of 10 to 15 feet per year has left its well-known lighthouse in peril. National Park Service and Army Corps of Engineers are debating whether to move it inland, build a wall around it or let it fall into the ocean.

Charleston, S. C.
Hurricane Hugo devastated area beach communities in 1989, causing $7 billion in damage and 21 deaths.

Hurricane Hall of Fame

The most intense, deadliest and costliest hurricanes to affect the United States from 1900 to 1991.

Hurricane	Year	Category	Deaths	Damage ($ billion)
Florida Keys	1935	5	408	
Camille (La., Miss.)	1969	5	256	$5.1
Florida Keys, south Texas	1919	4	600-900	
Florida, Lake Okeechobee	1928	4	1,836	
Donna (Florida, east U.S.)	1960	4	50	1.8
Galveston, Texas	1900	4	6,000	.7
Grand Isle, La.	1909	4	350	
New Orleans, La.	1915	4	275	
Carla (Texas)	1961	4	46	1.9
Hugo (S.C.)	1989	4	21	7.0
Miami, Fla.	1926	4	243	1.3
Hazel (S.C., N.C.)	1954	4	95	1.4
Audery (La., Texas)	1957	4	390	.7
Galveston, Texas	1915	4	275	1.5
Celia (south Texas)	1970	3		1.5
Allen (south Texas)	1980	3		.4
New England	1938	3	600	3.5
Frederic (Ala., Miss.)	1979	3		3.4
Northeast U.S.	1944	3	390	.9
Betsy (Fla., La.)	1965	3	75	6.3
Diana (N.C.)	1984	3	184	4.1
Carol (northeast U.S.)	1954	3	60	2.3
Alicia (north Texas)	1983	3		2.3
Agnes (northeast U.S.)	1972	2	122	6.3
Bob (northeast U.S.)	1991	2	18	1.5
Diane (N.C.)	1955	1		4.1

Note: A Category 5 hurricane has winds greater than 155 mph or storm surge greater than 18 feet above normal. A Category 4 hurricane has winds 131-155 mph or storm surge 13-18 feet above normal; Category 3 has winds 111-130 mph or storm surge 9-12 feet above normal; Category 2 has winds 96-110 mph or storm surge 6-8 feet above normal and Category 1 has winds 74-95 mph or storm surge 4-5 feet above normal.

Source: National Oceanic and Atmospheric Administration

has encouraged people to build in hazardous areas. "The whole reason for the flood insurance program was to reduce danger. Instead, it has increased it," says Gary Magnuson, vice president of the Center for Marine Conservation in Washington. "There is a sense that 'If locals let me build it, it must be safe.' Unfortunately, that isn't the case."

"The flood insurance program is doing more than anything else — private or public — to threaten Ameri-

ca's coastlines," adds Wesly Ward, director of land conservation for The Trustees of Reservations, a Massachusetts-based land trust that manages several coastal properties. "It acts as an incentive to build — and rebuild — in hazardous coastal areas."

Officials at the Corps of Engineers tell story after story of damaged or destroyed homes that are rebuilt with flood insurance payments, only to be battered again in the next storm. Repeat claims involve only 2 percent of

the insured properties but account for roughly one-third, more than $1 billion, of the total losses.[5]

"The [flood insurance] program has turned into another bailout disaster waiting to happen," writes Beth Millemann, executive director of the Coast Alliance, a national group of coastal activists. "The Federal Emergency Management Agency (FEMA), which implements it, estimates that a single catastrophic storm year would cost $3.5 billion to $4 billion in flood insurance claims against a meager [$400 million] in the fund at present."[6]

Even without a catastrophe, program losses outran income by $657 million from 1978 to 1987, a deficit made up by the taxpayers. FEMA officials are quick to point out that the program has been self-sufficient for the last four years, and that insurance premiums on new policies reflect the actual risks involved. More important, they argue that without the improved building standards brought about by the flood insurance program, damage and loss of life from coastal storms would be significantly greater.

As to the argument that shoreline construction is encouraged by the availability of federal flood insurance,* FEMA officials assert that the picture is more complex than that. "The program takes more of a hit than it deserves," says Frank Thomas, assistant administrator of the program at FEMA. "I'd like to point out that Miami Beach was there a long time before federal flood insurance came along."

Does the lack of coordination at the federal, state and local levels worsen coastal development problems?

A major problem in the battle against coastal erosion — and pollu-

---

*The average annual premium for a policy on a house in a high-hazard area is $469, compared with $272 for all policies. Legislation to reform the flood insurance program and make rates more actuarial is currently pending in the Senate (see p. 112).

tion — is the lack of governmental coordination. Says Dick McCarthy, a former member of the California Coastal Commission: "We have a series of fractionalized local efforts that has each community involved in its own projects, often without taking into account the effects its protective measures may have on adjacent areas."

For example, the Corps of Engineers began putting in a series of groins along posh Westhampton Beach on Long Island in the mid-1960s to prevent erosion. When state and local governments backed off due to the lack of financing and differences of opinion over methodology, the project was put on hold, two-thirds completed. The result has been drastically worse erosion along vast stretches of the beach — and one of the longest-running shorefront development disputes in New York state.* "It's 90 percent politics and 10 percent science," explains Leatherman.

In a separate case involving pollution, New York City's 60-year-old practice of dumping municipal sludge and other waste material 12 miles off the Atlantic Coast has seriously damaged the commercial fishing industries in New York and New Jersey. "The coastal environment is a shared ecosystem," says the Coast Alliance's Beth Millemann. "The national coast cannot sustain fragmented management. The intent of the Coastal Zone Management Act of 1972 was to help states to coordinate their policies based on federal guidelines."

One problem with getting the federal government involved in coastal management is that there is no single responsible government agency. The Corps of Engineers comes closest, but it is often compromised by its dual mission: protect vulnerable wetlands and keep waterways navigable.

---

*During last Halloween's nor'easter, 16 houses were washed away, bringing the total to more than 50 since the project was undertaken. A federal lawsuit is pending.

"There is no independent means of monitoring the effectiveness and environmental impact of their projects," complains Leatherman. "It's like having the fox guard the henhouse."

Currently, 12 federal agencies administer at least 21 programs affecting the coastal water environment. The wide variety of federal, state and local regulations make coastal issues confusing from a management perspective. Coastal zone management is handled primarily on a state-by-state basis with federal guidelines; the corps operates federally with little state role; and the flood insurance program is usually run by local governments.

Congressional jurisdictions are no clearer: In the House, flood insurance is handled by the Banking Committee, coastal zone management by the Merchant Marine Committee and the Clean Water Act by the Public Works

Committee. "Anything that affects three different committees is bound to be hamstrung," says Gary Magnuson. "Even if federal agencies talk, you still need local and state cooperation to link things together."

And if that isn't enough, Magnuson adds, "the long-term planning and foresight needed to manage coastal resources smacks up against the political process. Politicians focus on the quick fix to stay in office." Compounding that problem, there is little political incentive for legislators in Maine to vote money to address coastal problems in Louisiana. As it is, funding for coastal zone management programs is extremely scarce. This year's budget for coastal management, covering some 95,000 miles of U.S. shoreline (including inlets), is $40 million, less than the cost of many individual beach nourishment projects. ∎

BACKGROUND

Sea-Level Rise

Coastal erosion is one of the natural processes that have altered the world's shorelines ever since the oceans formed some 3 billion years ago.

Over geologic time, the daily scouring action of waves and the pounding of storms, as well as the rise and fall of ocean levels, have changed coastlines dramatically. "Sandy beaches are dynamic," says Orrin Pilkey at Duke. "They are meant to erode."

The melting of the great glaciers, which began 20,000 years ago, caused global sea levels to rise 400 feet. Some low-lying areas were simply flooded — or turned into islands. Roughly 12,000 years ago, an area about 70 miles off Cape Cod —

now the prolific Georges Bank fishing grounds — was covered with forest. The barrier islands off the Carolinas and Georgia, once covered with high dunes, were gradually surrounded by sea, and now they're basically flat.

Scientists say sea-level fluctuations are part of a natural cycle. But the process is exacerbated by less well understood — and perhaps more ominous — factors. Over the past 100 years, the ocean has risen more than a foot, a rate faster than at any time in the past millennium. Most scientists believe the rise in sea level — and resulting acceleration in coastal erosion — is magnified by a fundamental change in world climate caused by the greenhouse effect.

Since the Industrial Revolution, people have been burning greater quantities of fossil fuels, such as coal, oil and gas. One byproduct is carbon dioxide, which locks in the excess heat that would normally radiate

State Coastal Management Programs

The 1972 Coastal Zone Management Act provided federal guidelines for developing coastal management programs but made participation voluntary. Over the past two decades, the federal government has approved programs in 24 of the 30 coastal states, which includes those bordering the Great Lakes.

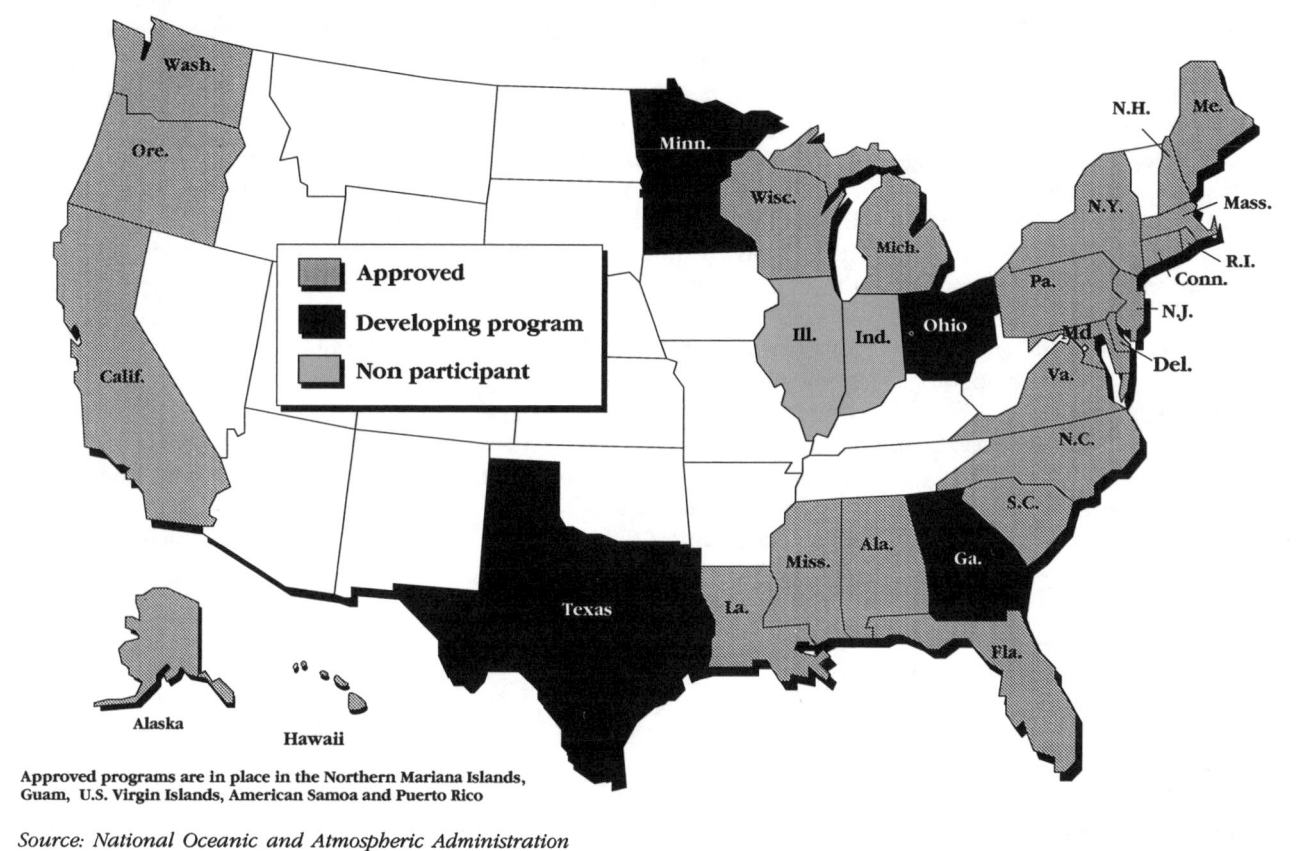

Approved programs are in place in the Northern Mariana Islands, Guam, U.S. Virgin Islands, American Samoa and Puerto Rico

Source: National Oceanic and Atmospheric Administration

back out into space. As a result, the atmosphere is gradually growing warmer, thus melting the polar ice caps and raising sea levels. Scientists know the process is accelerating; sea levels are expected to rise at least a foot in just another half-century.

Meanwhile, as the oceans rise, some coastal land is actually sinking. Much of the East Coast, for example, is made up of silt deposited from rivers, bays and inlets over the past 5,000 to 8,000 years. As the sediments gradually compress under their own weight, the surface sinks. On the Gulf Coast, a process called subsidence, caused in part by the extraction of ground water and pe-

troleum from subterranean layers of sand and clay, has caused the land, already virtually at sea level, to drop at a rate of 3 feet a century. *(See story, p. 109.)*

Development Pressures

None of this, of course, would be so critical if development hadn't concentrated on the coasts. In fact, some geologists dispute the contention that coastlines are threatened. "The only things threatened are the property and the buildings we have foolishly put in harm's way," Pilkey

says. "Beach, shoreline and coasts simply retreat. When houses fall into the sea, it is not some kind of natural disaster; it's a purely man-made problem."

That may be true. Nonetheless, development along coastlines today reflects patterns of settlement begun during the earliest days of civilization. Since ancient times, the oceans and resources of coastal areas have been used by man for transportation, food, recreation and waste disposal.

Realizing that development in hazardous areas costs the Treasury money, the federal government more than 50 years ago adopted the 1936 Flood

Continued on p. 106

Chronology

1900s-1950s
As coastal communities grow, there is little land-use regulation, and management is left mainly to local jurisdictions.

Sept. 8, 1900
Category 5 hurricane hits Galveston, Texas, killing 6,000 people.

1922
To protect its famous amusement park, New York's Coney Island undertakes the first recorded beach nourishment project in the United States.

1936
Federal government passes the Flood Control Act, intended to reduce high cost of flood damage.

1960s
Public becomes more aware of the risks of coastal development and the need for environmental legislation.

1968
Congress enacts the National Flood Insurance Act to limit increasing expenditures for flood control and disaster relief.

1969
Santa Barbara oil spill awakens the nation to dangers of coastal pollution; blue-ribbon panel releases the "Stratton Report," declaring the need for greater environmental protection.

1970s
Government officially acknowledges need for coordinated environmental policy and adopts a more active role in managing coastal resources.

Oct. 12, 1972
Coastal Zone Management Act (CZMA) is passed by Congress, establishing national program for the management, protection and development of U.S. coastal areas.

April 27, 1979
North Carolina passes oceanfront setback regulations, setting the standard for other states to follow.

1980s
Efforts to regulate coastal development are hampered by lack of government funding and boom in construction activity along coastlines.

Oct. 1, 1982
Congress passes the Coastal Barrier Resources Act of 1982, banning federal subsidies for development on 186 undeveloped coastal barrier islands, spits and beaches along the Atlantic and Gulf coasts.

1987
National Academy of Sciences releases report predicting that the sea level in the U.S. will rise at unprecedented rate, endangering many coastal areas.

Feb. 5, 1988
Upton-Jones Amendment to the National Flood Insurance Act provides incentive to raze or relocate structures in imminent hazard from coastal erosion.

Sept. 22, 1989
Hurricane Hugo rips apart South Carolina coast, causing 21 deaths and $7 billion in damage.

1990s
Federal agencies attempt to coordinate programs and shift focus from land-use planning to water quality issues.

Nov. 5, 1990
The CZMA is reauthorized, adding new emphasis on dealing with coastal pollution problems.

Nov. 16, 1990
Congress passes the Coastal Barrier Improvement Act of 1990, extending the barrier island system to include 31,000 acres along the Great Lakes, plus 788,000 new acres along the Atlantic and Gulf coasts.

May 1, 1991
By a vote of 318-18, the House adopts the Flood Insurance, Mitigation, and Erosion Management Act, which would reform the federal flood insurance program.

Nov. 11, 1991
The U.S. Supreme Court agrees to take on *Lucas v. South Carolina Coastal Council,* a case that could have profound impact on state coastal zone management laws.

Barrier Islands in Motion

Using computerized measuring techniques, scientists are tracking with new precision the erosion that is eating away 90 percent of the nation's coasts. Their findings are bad news, especially for the 295 barrier islands that lie like beads on a necklace along the coast from New England to Texas. Lying just offshore, these long sandy strips of land are home to many of the nation's most picturesque resorts and coastal towns.

Barrier islands are at once the most vulnerable and the most resilient parts of the coastline.† Formed and nourished by sand carried on currents, they are constantly in motion, rising, falling and migrating.

Over time, winds, waves and storms move sand from the oceanside to the landward side of the barrier. As the oceanside of the island erodes, the landward side builds up. This process can be sudden, as when great surges of water from hurricanes break across a barrier and deposit large amounts of sand on the backside. Or it can be gradual, as when waves striking a beach at an angle create a kind of sand conveyor that moves sand down the beach.

"What happens on the beaches," Duke University geologist Orrin Pilkey explains, "is a complex interaction that varies according to frequency, size, duration and intensity of the waves, particularly in storms." On barrier island beaches, this is further complicated by the orientation of the island geographically — whether it lies parallel or crosswise to the prevailing winds.

"Both the beaches and the entire island interact with oceanic waves that contain enormous power," Pilkey continues. "In a hour, during a major storm, the waves can change the shape of millions of cubic yards of sand.

During one storm, Oregon Inlet in North Carolina was widened from a half-mile to two miles in just hours, a mind-boggling event." Much of this action, he notes, occurs where beachgoers can't see it, because beaches extend into the water to depths of 30 to 40 feet.

Though beaches are constantly changing shape, each beach has an equilibrium slope, determined by the size of waves that strike it and the sand grains that form it. Like a person shifting to find a comfortable position in a chair, the beach shifts to restore its equilibrium.

The same beach typically has one profile in summer and another in winter. The waves whipped by winter storms tend to erode the beaches, making them narrower and steeper. Winter storms deposit enormous amounts of sand offshore, where it awaits gentler summer waves that will push it back to the beach. This explains why the summertime beach typically is broader and less steep.

As the sea level rises, geologists say the beach slope may stay the same but the beach itself will move inland. As storm overwash chews the dunes, a new dune line eventually forms on what was once the back of the barrier island, or even the lagoon or bay behind it. Over the course of millennia, many sandy barrier islands have retreated up the gentle coastal plain. Barrier islands in the Gulf of Mexico have retreated 80 miles, for instance. And if given a chance, these and other sandy coastal barriers will continue to retreat by continually rolling over on themselves.

---

† For background, see Stephen P. Leatherman, *Barrier Island Handbook* (1988).

Continued from p. 104

Control Act. The law brought the federal government into flood damage reduction by requiring federal investment in projects to prevent wholesale, destructive flooding and the vast accompanying property losses.[7]

The costs of flooding in storm-prone coastal areas had devastated several U.S. cities well before the Flood Control Act passed. Between 1900 and 1935, 27 hurricanes hit the United States, killing more than 10,000 people and causing billions of dollars in damage. Miami Beach lost 243 people and most of its buildings when a hurricane struck in

1926, shortly after the area was landfilled and turned into a resort. Reconstruction in the hurricane's wake cost an estimated $1.3 billion. And two years after the act was passed, another hurricane killed 600 people in New England and Long Island, causing $3.5 billion in damage.

These calamities have done little to discourage people from putting up more buildings along the ocean. "Ocean storms often sweep the slate clean," says Gary Magnuson, "but there seems to be a frontier attitude of helping people rebuild rather than learning from our mistakes."

With increasing population and affluence after World War II, Americans began settling coastal barriers — strips of sand dune, marsh and sometimes forest — in greater and greater numbers. Before the war, less than 10 percent of the country's coastal barriers were developed at all. By 1980, half of the 295 barriers along the Atlantic and Gulf coasts had been at least partially developed, and more than 70 were heavily developed, most with large government subsidies — for roads, bridges, sewers, fire departments, flood insurance, etc.[8] Atlantic City, N.J., Virginia Beach, Va., and Hilton

Head, N.C., among others, were all built on barrier islands.

Between 1950 and 1980, the exodus to the coasts swelled the coastal population by more than 30 million people. The development craze, which peaked in the 1980s, often followed a predictable pattern: Most older coastal structures were vacation homes built with septic systems. When those communities expanded, and seasonal bungalows were transformed into permanent homes, septic fields were no longer adequate because of stricter environmental laws. So the community usually opted to put in sewer lines and electricity. "All the land that was undeveloped was suddenly golden," says Rebecca Hughes. "It may have been in a wetland, an erosion zone or a flood plain, but that didn't stop the developers." This process has been repeated in myriad coastal communities.

Environmental Impact

As property owners began to buy up seaside property and erect multimillion-dollar houses, condominiums, hotels and resorts on the shifting sand, the natural process of erosion began to matter to growing numbers of Americans. Along with the roads, parking lots, airfields and commercial interests that serve them, development projects not only put more people and property in harm's way but also unwittingly accelerated the damage to U.S. coastal areas.

On the West Coast, houses that perch atop cliffs create new runoff patterns for rainfall and irrigation; combined with seepage from septic systems, the drainage weakens the land itself. In addition, massive dams on rivers have deprived West Coast beaches of their main source of replacement sand, causing severe beach erosion.

On the East and Gulf coasts, the major problem is destruction of beaches and sand dunes that normally check the ocean's force. It is mainly the dunes that keep coastal areas, including barrier islands, intact, explains environmentalist Wesly Ward. "The natural process is for dunes to roll over on themselves," he says. When the ocean breaks through, "what was once the secondary dune becomes the primary dune. When you have houses on the beach, there's no place for the dunes to move."

Sand dunes can also be destroyed in subtler ways. For a dune to form in the first place, sand must somehow be trapped, much as a snow fence traps drifting snow. In this case, the trap is dune grass. After the dunes form, the roots anchor the sand in place. "Dune grass is pretty hardy stuff," explains Stephen Leatherman. "It can take salt spray and high winds. But it just never evolved to take heavy pedestrian traffic or dune buggies." Since the plants depend on chlorophyll in their green leafy parts to convert sunlight into food, he says, and since there is only so much food reserve in the roots, "a couple of weekends with a few hundred people walking back and forth to the beach, or a single pass from an off-road vehicle, kills off the dune grass."

Pollution Threat

A more insidious form of damage to coastal areas is caused by pollution. In 10 coastal states surveyed by the Natural Resources Defense Council, there were at least 1,400 beach closings and pollution advisories during 1990 because of high bacterial counts or the threat of high bacterial counts, which were caused largely by sewage or other microbiological contamination.[9]

Part of the cause of coastal pollution is the multitude of pollutants discharged directly or indirectly into the coastal zone, either on land or in the water. For example, sewage treatment plants and industrial operations in New England discharge 575 billion gallons of contaminated wastewater directly into the sea every year. And another 700 billion gallons of polluted storm water flows annually into the sea from the region's urban areas.[10]

The cost of the resulting contamination is high. A recent five-year study by the University of Georgia concluded that parts of the Florida Keys coral reef, the continent's only living barrier reef, are dying at a rate of 10 percent a year. The likely reason: pollution, mainly in the form of nutrients from human sewage and agricultural runoff, which stimulates algae growth that overwhelms parts of the reef.[11]

Experts say the combination of sewage pollution, industrial discharges and agricultural runoff is largely responsible for the closure of 53 percent of the productive shellfish beds on the Atlantic and Pacific coasts and 58 percent in the Gulf of Mexico.

"Let's face it, development along the coasts is not the same as development in the Great Plains," comments David Owens, an associate professor of government at the University of North Carolina. With water and air, it is much simpler to set national standards. When it comes to coastal areas, "the management system is more complex," adds Owens. "You have to balance development and tourism with open space and traditional fisheries. The issues are more complex than in any other traditional natural resource program."

Coastal Management

As the nation started becoming more aware of the environment in the late 1960s, the inadequacy of state and federal policies on coastal development drew more attention.* Debate in Congress centered on the growing and often conflicting pressures on the nation's coasts — pressures for more recreation areas, increased commercial, industrial and residential development, as well as pressures to preserve existing coastal wilderness areas and critical fish and wildlife habitats.

In 1972, the same year Congress passed landmark clean water legislation, it passed the Coastal Zone Management Act (CZMA). The act declared that it was in the national interest to have wise management of the nation's 12,383 miles of oceanside — 88,633 miles if the entire tidal shoreline of bays, estuaries and other inlets are included, plus 4,530 miles of coastline along the Great Lakes. The act provided federal guidelines for developing coastal management programs but made participation voluntary.

"The coast is a lot better off than it was before the CZMA was passed," says Gary Magnuson at the Center for Marine Conservation. "It was the first national land-use legislation in this country."

Basically, the CZMA offered planning grants to states to develop their own programs for resolving conflicts over land and water uses in coastal areas. The 35 states and territories bordering the Atlantic, Gulf, Pacific and Great Lakes had two powerful incentives for participating: The act provided two-thirds of the cost of developing a coastal management program, and it guaranteed that federal activities must be consistent with state plans "to the maximum extent practicable."

However, funding for the program has been meager — and several times during the Reagan years attempts were made to scrap the program entirely. Nevertheless, since 1972, 24 of the 30 coastal states have established

*An oil spill in 1969 off the coast of Santa Barbara, Calif., focused attention on the need for more environmental protection.

federally approved coastal management programs.[12] (See map, p. 104.)

States Retain Flexibility

Some states have aggressively used the law to protect their resources. Under the CZMA, federal activity must be consistent with state coastal management programs. Thus, California, Florida and Massachusetts have used the "consistency provision" to block sale of federal oil exploration leases, in effect restricting oil drilling off their shores. Similarly, the CZMA lets states challenge EPA projects involving ocean dumping as well as Corps of Engineers dredging projects.

"One of the principal benefits of the CZMA has been that it enables states to retain flexibility," says David Owens. While beach access is a top priority in California, development in coastal hazard zones is of greater concern in North Carolina. And while coastal water quality is extremely important for Maryland's Chesapeake Bay, it is less of an issue in Minnesota. "The coastal program has allowed managers to focus on relevant issues pressing in their own setting," says Owens.

At the same time, however, flexibility has permitted many states, such as Maryland, Georgia and Mississippi, to adopt a laissez-faire attitude toward building in sensitive coastal zones. "During the go-go years of the 1970s and 1980s," says Stephen Leatherman, "many communities

placed no limits on where you could develop. The feeling was that if you had a deed, you had a God-given right to develop."

The cause for coastal preservation received a boost in 1982 with passage of the Coastal Barrier Resources Act (CBRA), which protected 186 undeveloped islands, spits and beaches along the Atlantic and Gulf coasts where federal spending for roads, bridges and flood insurance is prohibited. The act does not prevent landowners from building on their land, but shifts costs and risks from the federal government to the private sector.* A 1989 analysis of the law found that since CBRA was enacted, major development of 10 or more structures had occurred on fewer than 5 percent of the protected areas.[13]

The Tax Reform Act of 1986 also had a powerful, though unintended, impact on coastal development. The law eliminated several key provisions of the Internal Revenue Code that had encouraged property development, including the investment tax credit, accelerated depreciation for real property and preferential taxation of capital gains. Although not specifically directed toward environmental concerns, these changes tended to inhibit development of coastal areas.

*In 1990 the CBRA was amended to include additional coastal barriers — including low-lying islands along the Great Lakes as well as the Atlantic and Gulf coasts. ∎

CURRENT SITUATION

Stemming the Tide

"If we had known 30 years ago what we know now, New Jersey and much of the rest of the country

would be in better shape," then Gov. Thomas H. Kean said in 1987. "We wouldn't have built in those areas."[14]

Even now, however, billions of dollars' worth of coastal development — some would say runaway overdevelopment — cannot simply be abandoned. Meanwhile, America's love affair with the coast continues unabated. Previously untouched coastal areas are being developed for

Continued on p. 110

Louisiana's Vanishing Wetlands

While coastal erosion is a problem for most coastal states, it is a veritable crisis for Louisiana. Along a broad expanse of southern Louisiana, between the Atchafalaya and Mississippi rivers, a million acres of coastal wetlands have disappeared since 1900. Scientists now estimate that an additional 40 to 60 square miles are vanishing every year — a rate that could double by 1995.[†] Within a decade many Louisiana parishes, or counties, could be engulfed by the sea.[††]

"It's a catastrophe that's happening to the wetlands. You're looking at the genocide of an entire ecosystem," says Oliver Houck, an environmental lawyer and professor at Tulane University. Indeed, the loss of the state's marshes affects more than just local residents: The area provides almost 30 percent of the nation's fish harvest and 40 percent of the fur catch, and is a winter habitat for two-thirds of the migratory birds in the Mississippi flyway.

Financed by industry grants, federal appropriations and a state trust fund fueled by oil and gas royalties, scientists and engineers are struggling to save this critical resource.[‡] But they are only beginning to understand the host of influences that are combining to destroy it. In 1990 experts at the United States Geological Survey and the Argonne National Laboratory in Illinois began a five-year effort to classify and map sources of wetland loss.

Scientists believe the principal culprit is subsidence, partly the result of man's tinkering with nature's plumbing along the southern Mississippi River. The land is made of sediment laid down over centuries by the ever-shifting waterway. In the past, the river would have made up for subsidence by adding new sediment in its spring floods. But by the 1950s, the dams built on its tributaries had sharply reduced the load of sediment. And the river itself has been walled off from the marshes by miles of levees.

"In contrast to most erosion problems elsewhere, Louisiana's problems are largely man-made," says Jim Titus, a coastal expert at the Environmental Protection Agency (EPA). In bayou country, where channels deep enough for barges have been cut through marshes, the dredging process, coupled with waves caused by ship and boat traffic, has also helped accelerate the normal process of shoreline loss. What is more, saltwater from the Gulf of Mexico has flowed into the marshes, killing marsh grass and endangering local fisheries.

Federal and state agencies, including the Army Corps of Engineers, EPA and the Louisiana Department of Natural Resources, are currently working together on a comprehensive plan to address Louisiana's crisis. Many landowners are pinning their hopes on marsh management. Some have built levees and other structures that limit saltwater intrusion and scouring by tides, while others are experimenting with spraying a thin layer of sedi-

ment from bays and bayous over marshland. The state is currently spending $40 million annually on more than a dozen such projects, but the results so far have been mixed.

A recent study by researchers at Louisiana State University (LSU) concluded that marsh management was not consistently effective in preventing wetland loss. Half of the managed areas were no better off than the unmanaged controls, and only five of the 16 sites studied showed improvement.[‡‡]

A different approach to arresting wetland loss relies on putting the river back into the marshland, rather than keeping the ocean out. The idea is to use a flood of fresh water to push back saltwater and prevent it from poisoning the plants whose roots hold the marsh together. Under this scenario, enormous diversion structures carry Mississippi River water through canals or spillways to the marsh behind the levees. The corps has designed a $76 million diversion project at Bonnet Carré and a $41 million project at Davis Pond, both upriver from New Orleans.

While engineers and public officials debate the merits of a range of mitigation efforts, scientists are continuing their basic research into the geology and ecology of the delta. David Soileau, head of Louisiana's Wetland Conservation and Restoration Task Force, says these efforts could eventually create ways to replace or restore marshland as quickly as it is lost. "I predict — perhaps even in 20 years — we will have reached a static relationship between wetlands lost and wetland gain in Louisiana," he says.

But for most other scientists and engineers, the notion of "no net loss" is an impossible dream. The most they hope is to slow the rate at which their state is disappearing. "If you look at the numbers — sediment in the river and the techniques and costs of getting that sediment out — the achievement of 'no net loss' is not attainable," says Shea Penland, associate director of the Louisiana Geological Survey. "The river of today is not the river of yesterday that built the delta."

Meanwhile, until scientists find a better way to resolve the crisis, every hour another four acres of Louisiana wetlands succumb to the Gulf of Mexico.

[†] Most U.S. wetlands — 95 percent — are freshwater areas found inland, usually on or adjacent to agricultural property. Coastal wetlands, on the other hand, are saltwater or brackish enclaves subject to fluctuation with ocean tides. Louisiana contains 40 percent of the nation's coastal wetlands.

[††] New Orleans is 1-3 feet below sea level.

[‡] The oil industry has a particularly keen interest in saving the wetlands: If they become submerged, mineral rights could revert to the state.

[‡‡] Cited in *The New York Times,* Nov. 20, 1990.

Continued from p. 108

the first time, and already developed areas are being redeveloped. There are more hotels, condominiums and cottages for beach visitors than ever before, and many of our shorefront communities now have sizable and growing year-round populations.

The value of coastal real estate has engendered a special interest in keeping shorelines from moving — and generated a host of makeshift solutions to erosion. On Galveston Bay, for example, desperate ranchers have positioned junked cars on the shore to prevent the waters from washing away roads. In Louisiana, shrimpers use wire mesh and old tires to keep the bay waters from chewing away at their bluffs. On Long Island, beach residents shore up dunes with driftwood and old tires. And innovative Carlsbad, Calif., does everything from planting plastic kelp to laying a sausagelike tube along the beach in order to trap sand normally washed away during high tide.

Although geologists say that nothing can stop the sea's inexorable movement inland, few beach communities are prepared to let themselves fall into the ocean block by block. The real estate is just too valuable. Ocean City, for example, generates roughly one-third of Maryland's tourism revenue, and its beachfront property has been valued at $2.5 billion. To protect that investment, the city got approval from Congress and the state for its $40 million beach nourishment program, begun in 1988. Explains Mayor Fish Powell: "Without our beaches, we don't have anything. That's the reason people come here."

Counting on Beach Nourishment

There are dozens of communities like Ocean City up and down the nation's shorelines, largely summer tourist playgrounds and investment havens that are looking to beach nourishment for their salvation: South

Padre Island in Texas; Sea Bright and Cape May in New Jersey; Dauphine Island in Alabama; Hunting Island and Hilton Head in South Carolina.

One problem with beach replenishment programs, says Stephen Leatherman, is that "beaches are like icebergs — only 10 percent of the active part of the beach is above water." Moreover, once a beach has been replenished it must receive regular infusions of sand if it is to survive the assaults that diminished it in the first place. And although significant advances in the planning, monitoring and maintenance of beach nourishment projects have been made, the scientific theory for designing these projects remains relatively untested.

"In many cases beach nourishment is a reasonable, though temporary, solution," says Norbert Psuty, director of the Center for Coastal and Environment Studies at Rutgers University. "Because most barrier islands are sufficiently large, broad and high, beach nourishment can buy time, support the local infrastructure and economy and do so in an economically viable way. The bottom line is that it shouldn't be more costly than the value derived."

The high cost of beach nourishment makes it financially impractical for all but the most densely developed beaches. Environmental concerns are also a limiting factor in many places. Finding an environmentally acceptable source of suitable sand and transporting it to the beach site is a difficult and costly task.

Furthermore, the congressional approval process for beach nourishment projects generally takes at least eight years and more typically 15 to 20 years. This has led some communities to adopt projects on their own. For instance, every day in spring convoys of dump trucks unload sand onto Virginia Beach, costing the city roughly $800,000 each year. The project dates back to the 1960s,

when the city imposed a 0.5 percent "sand tax" on hotels. It's now financed out of general funds.

Setback Laws

Other states and local communities are taking a different tack. So far, more than one-third of coastal states have established minimum oceanfront setbacks for new construction. Rather than trying to control the location of the shoreline, they accept its dynamic nature and are trying to manage adjacent development in order to minimize the loss of property that would otherwise occur when the shoreline moves.

Michigan and North Carolina, for example, require that any new single-family houses be built at least 30 times the erosion rate from the dune line and that multi-family units like apartment buildings and hotels be located 60 times the erosion rate. No efforts can be made to build permanent structures to hold back the sea because that further erodes the beach. When houses fall into the ocean, they can only be rebuilt according to the setback rules, a policy irreverently referred to as "fall back or fall in."

While virtually everybody agrees that setbacks make sense, they have serious consequences for property owners, developers and beach cities. For individual property owners and developers, they reduce the available land for construction. For cities, they reduce the amount of high-priced development that could dramatically expand their tax bases. Town officials and homeowners' groups say private property rights are sacred and should not be compromised. *(See story, page 111.)*

"Regulation goes beyond what is necessary to accomplish goals of environmental concern," says Don

Continued on p. 112

The Lucas Case: Private Property vs. Public Interest

Most people agree that managing fragile coastal resources is a good thing. But what happens when private property rights — among the most sacred of rights granted by the U.S. Constitution — are trampled in the process? Does that constitute what's known in legal language as a "taking," and therefore require compensation? The U.S. Supreme Court will deliberate the issue early next month in *Lucas v. South Carolina Coastal Council*. The outcome has broad implications for state efforts to regulate land use, not just for beachfront property but for wetlands and other wilderness areas as well.

"The Supreme Court turns down 19 of 20 cases," says Rutherford Platt, a professor of geography and planning law at the University of Massachusetts. "By accepting this one they are setting it up as a test case on the taking issue. If the court chooses to overturn the state, it could be the *Roe v. Wade* of land-use regulation."

The case involves developer David Lucas, who paid $975,000 for two beachfront lots on the Isle of Palms in South Carolina in 1986. But before he could put up houses, the state passed a beach-management law intended to preserve the coastline and to prevent "unwise development." The law forbade Lucas from building on the lots because the property was in an "inlet erosion zone."

Lucas sued South Carolina, contending that he was no better off than if the state had simply taken the land away — in which case the Constitution would have required that he be paid for his loss. The Fifth Amendment prohibits the taking of private property by the government without just compensation.

Siding with Lucas, a state trial court awarded him $1.2 million in compensation to cover the market value of the properties, plus interest and legal costs. But the South Carolina Supreme Court, on a 3-2 vote, reversed the decision, declaring, "The legislation here is necessary to prevent serious injury to the community." † Lucas appealed to the nation's highest court.

"When I bought the lots, I was in total compliance with all rules and regulations," he says. "I had satisfied myself from the ecological and hydrological studies I had done that in the long run this was a pretty safe investment of money as far as Mother Nature goes." ††

The state of South Carolina as well as numerous other states and environmental groups say they are sympathetic to Lucas' plight, but they argue that the greater public good is at stake. "The nub of the issue is whether the government can regulate property to prevent a public harm without giving rise to a compensation claim," says John Echeverria, chief counsel for the National Audubon Society. "I do not know that we can pay for every eco-nomic knock that people suffer."

Indeed, environmental laws that protect the public interest, such as pollution laws, often entail costs to individual companies, but that doesn't mean the government should compensate polluters. Similarly, land-use zoning changes almost always give rise to changes in property values. The circumstances in the Lucas saga are often reversed: A zoning change will add to the value of some property. Yet there is no constitutional mechanism for society to recoup that value.

Despite a long list of precedents favoring the state's case, proponents of strong coastal zone management laws have reason for concern. Four years ago, the Supreme Court gave property owners two tentative victories in Southern California cases. In one case, the court said the California Coastal Commission could not force the owner of a Ventura beachfront home to give the public right of way to walk on his beach without compensation. In the second case, the court said Los Angeles County officials could be forced to pay compensation if they denied a church a permit to build on a mountain campsite.

These victories, plus the court's new conservative bent, have led many to fear what the *Lucas* case could portend. "An adverse decision in this case could make it impossible for federal regulators to protect citizens' property and the environment in endangered coastal regions," says Thomas Campbell, general counsel at the National Oceanographic and Atmospheric Administration.

Orrin Pilkey Jr., a Duke geologist and one of the country's top experts on beach erosion, goes even further. "If Lucas wins, we can kiss our beaches goodbye," he says. "This will lead to increased pressure for sea walls."

The case is not nearly as absolute as it seems. For one thing, under a 1990 amendment to South Carolina's Beach Management Act, Lucas has the right to apply for a variance to build a 3,200 square-foot structure on each of the properties. Taking that into account, it is possible that the court will bounce the case back to the state.

The question still remains, however, whether the Supreme Court will choose to ignore those particulars and, as Rutherford Platt suggests, make a sweeping judgment on the taking issue. Either way, says Kerry Kehoe, legislative counsel at the Washington-based Coastal States Organization, "The danger of *Lucas* is that people will read the decision more broadly than they should. It could have a chilling effect on efforts to manage the coasts."

---

† Quoted in the *Los Angeles Times,* Nov. 19, 1991.

†† Quoted in *The Washington Post,* Jan. 4, 1992.

Continued from p. 110
Kirkman, executive director of the Carteret County Economic Development Council in North Carolina. "There is an increasing tendency toward mandating low-density, large-lot development, preserving beach access for the very rich. This has resulted in coastal areas being less competitive vis-à-vis upland areas."

Some states, under pressure from affected developers and property owners, have simply drawn lines in the sand that will continue to be overtopped by floods and eaten away by erosion. Others, such as Georgia and Mississippi, haven't developed setbacks at all.

"There is definitely going to be pressure to develop an area that is susceptible to flooding," says Jeff Blanchard, chief planner with the San Francisco Bay Conservation and Development Commission. "That's where the crunch comes. Scientists can give all the facts and opinions ... but, eventually, it will boil down to politics."

One example of that pressure is in South Carolina. In 1988, the state adopted the Beachfront Management Act, which established a so-called "dead zone" 20 feet landward of the dune line; within the zone, existing structures "damaged beyond repair" could not be reconstructed. The law also increased the setbacks for new construction. Then in 1990, the state amended the law, eliminating the dead zone and granting Folly Beach, near Charleston, a complete exemption, despite the fact that the beachfront property suffered immense damage during Hurricane Hugo and is eroding at a rate of 4 feet a year.[15]

Similarly, although a 1981 law permits New York state to redesignate coastal areas "not for development" after major storm damage, a 1985 amendment requires a 12-month delay before redesignation, leaving ample time for rebuilding.

Setback laws are intended to assure that buildings have a modest "safety zone" to buffer them from storm damage and to allow them to enjoy a reasonable life span before being threatened by erosion. But what happens when erosion does catch up to the structures, as is happening now to older developments — and as will almost certainly happen to many new shorefront developments 10 or 20 years from now?

North Carolina officials estimate that some 5,000 existing structures in that state alone may be lost to ocean erosion over the next 60 years. Michigan officials estimate that nearly 1,000 structures on the Lake Michigan shoreline were at risk during the high lake levels in the mid-1980s.

Encouraging Relocation

One possible solution that is getting increasingly serious attention is relocation of threatened structures. "We have been relocating structures since the Victorian Age," says Beth Millemann at the Coast Alliance. "Relocation is mechanically feasible. For lightly developed areas — even moderately developed areas — it will make more sense over the long run to move rather than spend $50 million to $60 million on beach nourishment programs with a life span of two to five years maximum."

New programs are being developed to encourage and assist relocation efforts. For example, in 1985 Michigan began providing low-interest loans to relocate structures threatened by high lake levels. And on the national level, Congress amended the federal flood insurance program in 1987 to provide coverage for the costs of relocating imminently endangered structures, rather than waiting for them to fall in the ocean, triggering far more expensive total-loss claims.*

---

*Under the Upton-Jones amendment, FEMA will pay up to 40 percent of the insured value of the house to move it to a site away from a flood hazard area. The amendment also allows payments of up to 110 percent of the value of the policy to owners who raze their houses entirely and restore the beach.

Because it is completely voluntary, and people are reluctant — or unable — to move structures back, the amendment has failed to achieve its primary goal. "We expected a larger number of claims, but people have an emotional attachment to their beach houses," says Frank Thomas at FEMA. "They haven't taken advantage of relocation." Besides, the program still guarantees insurance no matter how many times the property is damaged by flood or storm, and with no increase in rates.

Flood Insurance Reform

There is widespread feeling, even among FEMA officials, that the flood insurance program is in need of reform. "FEMA has done a good job at elevating houses and improving building standards, but it doesn't take into account the hazards of erosion over time," says Stephen Leatherman. "That's like ignoring the fact that a cancer patient smokes four packs of cigarettes a day."

Last May, in an effort to address these concerns, the House adopted the Flood Insurance, Mitigation, and Erosion Management Act by a sweeping 318-18 vote. The proposed law has three main components. First, communities that receive federally guaranteed flood insurance would be required to determine their rates of shoreline erosion so that development within those areas can be restricted accordingly, using a formula modeled after the North Carolina setback law. Second, the bill would strengthen enforcement provisions mandating that lenders require property owners in flood-prone areas to obtain flood insurance. And third, it would set up a mitigation assistance program, funded by a $5 surcharge on insurance premiums, to help communities reduce repeat-loss claims.

Continued on p. 114

At Issue:

Can coastal areas stand more growth and still maintain their ecosystems?

LAWRENCE R. ZUCCHINO

President of Paton/Zucchino and Associates, a landscape architecture firm in Raleigh, N.C.
FROM *EPA JOURNAL*, SEPTEMBER/OCTOBER 1989.

yes

We can expect continued development in our coastal areas and increasing pressure on the ability of our coastal areas to sustain their ecological integrity.

If we are to deal with these pressures more effectively, we must begin to restructure our traditional view of the problem. There is no question of the need to maintain viable coastal ecosystems. However, we must take a hard look at the notion that our coastal areas must remain sparsely developed agrarian and resource-extractive areas. The simple inertia of current development will take us well past that point during the next decade.

Our coastal areas and their people deserve a dynamic and diversified economy. We need not squander a viable tax base on the waterfront by restricting development that need not harm the environment but may simply offend some people's notion of a rural aesthetic.

Much of the debate about the ability of our coastal ecosystems to withstand further growth has centered on land-based residential development and its associated impacts. In our East Coast estuaries, water quality degradation and wetlands loss have been attributed to this growth. . . .

However, coastal water quality is much more impacted by nutrient overloading from agricultural activity than from development. Considerably more wetland loss results from the timber industry than from development activity. This is not to point the finger elsewhere. It is to say that we need to avoid attacking the most convenient target and instead begin to direct an intelligent effort toward managing true impacts on our coastal ecosystems.

We can begin by restructuring our thinking about regulatory controls on land development, which often promote the ineffective use of land. For instance, we hear continually about the "problem" of high-density development. It is folly to say that high density in and of itself causes environmental degradation. Poorly conceived and implemented regulation and development cause environmental degradation. Alternately, increased development densities can provide the economic basis for protecting critical habitats and improving water quality. . . .

We cannot solve the problem with the simplistic solution of no growth. Growth in our coastal areas is going to occur. Our coastal areas must maintain their ecological integrity. Success in managing this growth will be measured in the next decade by how creatively we deal with these competing visions.

VIVIAN D. NEWMAN

Chair of the Sierra Club's National Coastal Committee
FROM *EPA JOURNAL*, SEPTEMBER/OCTOBER 1989.

no

We can have more coastal development — and ecosystems, too!

Just one thing, though. First bring back Peter the Great to carry out the environmental controls. He was the Russian tsar under whose reign the penalty for cutting down a single tree in the tsar's forest (which today might read ecosystems or public trust) was summary execution, with no exceptions made. You might say he was the last leader of any nation to have truly grasped the exigencies of environmental law and order.

Of course, such methods have gone out of style in today's age of negotiated conflict resolution and the Executive Order on Takings (which requires federal agencies to assess the economic impacts of federal actions on private landowners). Our modern leaders and lawmakers have embraced risk assessment and growth management, flaccid concepts dreamt up in some office charged with making discomfiting choices. We live in the heyday of legalistic wheeler-dealers hired for princely sums to cajole the professional equivocators into settling for zoning variances, permit modifications and mitigation projects.

Daily compromises have assured a steady flow of toxic discharges, sediment, nutrients and floatables into our waters. Obeisance to the false idols of convenience and greed all too often is behind the ridicule of waste reduction at the source and organic no-till farming and energy conservation as laughable, possibly dangerous notions. Befouled beaches and polluted shellfish beds attest to the efficacy of today's tyranny of small-minded decision-makers who have replaced the tyranny of an energetic despot like Peter the Great.

Coasts and wetlands represent only a tiny fraction of our total land mass, but their incomparable riches are not found elsewhere. The life they have supported for centuries — so miraculously diverse and abundant — has been a source of wonder and self-replenishing usefulness to human beings. But "live simply, so that others may simply live" is a rarely heard credo today, especially when it comes to the habitat of humbler creatures; overriding "public benefit" has altered if not obliterated most of these ecologically vital areas.

Let's face facts — it's simply too late now even for Peter the Great (harsh, draconian, un-American as he may be remembered) to restore what was. But we must borrow at least some of his governing style if we wish to avert or postpone the collapse of our coastal ecosystems.

Continued from p. 112

Under the bill, communities wouldn't have to participate in the program, but if they didn't, new construction and buildings that have seen major renovations would be ineligible for federal insurance. Opponents of the legislation, such as the National Association of Realtors, allege that it infringes upon property rights and will result in a wholesale retreat from the coast.

"That's a clear misreading of the bill's intent," responds Rebecca Hughes of the Flood Plain Managers Association. "Homeowners wouldn't lose their mortgages and wouldn't be forced to do anything. Why should the government be required to bail people out of their own poor decisions?" Owners of existing insured structures situated in areas of imminent risk would have two years to take advantage of demolition or relocation benefits before losing full insurance coverage.

The Senate is expected to take up a companion version of the House bill sometime this spring. Although lobbies representing real estate interests and shorefront homeowners' groups have mounted loud opposition, the administration generally supports the bill, and backers are confident it will pass. "The issues of coastal zone management and flood insurance were never married," says Gary Magnuson at the Center for Marine Conservation. "The proposed legislation is an attempt to bring them into sync."

Non-Point-Source Pollution

The 1990 reauthorization of the Coastal Zone Management Act takes the notion of coordinating coastal policies one step further. "Before 1990, the CZMA dealt mainly with land-use planning," says Jeff Zinn, a coastal expert at the Congressional Research Service. "Now, other things have been mixed in, giving it more of a water quality focus."

The CZMA reauthorization legislation requires that EPA establish uniform national guidelines for controlling non-point-source pollution — runoff from city streets, mining operations and farms. The measure also requires states to establish non-point-source pollution control programs, or run the risk of losing CZMA funding.

Experts agree, however, that addressing this problem will be one of their most daunting challenges. Recent data indicate that as much as 40 percent of coastal pollution can be attributed to non-point sources. "It is much more difficult to deal with non-point-source pollution than pollution that comes out of the ends of pipes," says Hans Neuhauser at the Georgia Conservancy. ∎

OUTLOOK

'Strategic Retreat'

"We're moving closer to the sea and the sea is moving closer to us. We're on a collision course," warns Stephen Leatherman. The National Oceanic and Atmospheric Administration (NOAA) predicts that by the year 2000, 8 million more people will live near the nation's coasts, and the average property losses from major storms could reach $5 billion each year.[16]

As recent events have shown, anti-erosion measures that might be expected to last for years can be wiped out by a single big storm. Experts point out that the Eastern United States has enjoyed the relative peace of a "low-storm phase" for the past 25 years.* Many believe the lull cannot last. "Because of continued development in high-hazard areas," warns Norbert Psuty of Rutgers, "the longer this phase continues, the worse the damage will be when a big storm finally hits."

Unfortunately, for most people who live in hurricane zones, hurricanes mean nothing until they mean everything. Like death, a hurricane is a looming abstraction. "We're putting

---

*Between 1830 and 1964, 25 hurricanes hit the Florida coast. Since 1972, not one has hit Florida.

a lot more valuable property in a vulnerable position," observes Jerry Jarrell at the National Hurricane Center. Three-quarters of the damage from hurricanes this century occurred in the last 20 years, even though there hasn't been a Category 5 hurricane since 1969.

More worrisome, says Jarrell, is the fact that construction of roads has not kept up with rampant development. This poses a particular risk on island chains, such as the Florida Keys, where access is limited. "In the event of a major hurricane, our concern is that people wouldn't be able to evacuate," says Jarrell. The National Weather Service recommends a 12-hour evacuation time for hurricane-prone regions. But in the Keys — the most vulnerable area in the United States — evacuation time is an estimated 27 hours. The potential for disaster is palpable.

But even without a catastrophic event, nature's gradual grinding of the coast will take its toll. Given the foreboding predictions of global warming and the accompanying sea-level rise, some coastal experts are advocating a "strategic retreat" from development in high-hazard zones. In all, the coastline of the Northeastern United States may recede an average of 200 feet in the next 50 years; in some parts of Florida, where the land is flatter, the sea might move in as much as 500 feet.[17]

"It's my feeling," says Leatherman, "that [these high-risk areas] should not be inhabited. It's really a matter of whether your capital expenditures are worth the recreational return. These people who bought have enjoyed the location. But when one considers that indeed the shoreline is moving, that enjoyment has to be finite."

Adds Duke geologist Pilkey: "We face economic and environmental realities that leave us two choices. One, plan a strategic retreat now, or two, undertake a vastly expensive program of armoring the coastline and, as required, retreating through a series of unpredictable disasters. By acting now we can hold down the cost and preserve the beach for future generations."

Obviously, in some communities, particularly those that rely on their beaches as tourist attractions, retreat will remain an untenable option. For them, the issue is how to pay for continuous shore protection programs. Taxpayers who never visit the coasts may not be willing to help foot the bill forever. Indeed, in the future we are likely to see more communities forced to pay for beach nourishment projects out of their own pockets.

Some states already have begun planning for the future by requiring strict setback regulations, encouraging research into new, non-destructive beach management technologies and disallowing the use of "hard" structures that damage the shoreline.

At the same time, nonprofit groups, such as the Washington-based Nature Conservancy, have accelerated their efforts to protect coastlines and provide more public access. The conservancy has sheltered more than 700,000 acres from development in 13 states, including 13 barrier islands off the coast of Virginia.

"To date, successes have been more by accident than by strategic plan," says Hans Neuhauser. "I feel confident that good management of beach areas will head us in the right direction. There ought to be some segments where there is intensive use, where people can drive up close to the beach, and others where there is heavily restricted access. Sophisticated management on a regional basis could get us away from uniform degradation of the entire coastline."

"What we need is some sort of national agenda for the coasts," adds the University of North Carolina's David Owens. Most coastal experts agree that efforts to coordinate policies are likely to become more common in the 1990s. The effectiveness of this approach will be tested later this year when reauthorization of the clean water act is taken up by Congress. Says Owens: "We've spent 10 to 15 years building institutions. Now we need some results."

Ultimately, whether the U.S. is successful at protecting its coasts — and regulating destructive development — will depend on several factors. At a minimum, it will require greater policy coordination among regulatory agencies and a psychological change that takes into account human limits in controlling the sea — as well as the coasts' limits for absorbing human pollution. "The coastline is a precious resource that should not be squandered," says conservationist Gary Magnuson. "We know enough to understand what needs to be done. All we need is the political will to act." ∎

Notes

[1] National Research Council, National Academy of Sciences, *Responding to Changes in Sea Level: Engineering Implications* (1987).

[2] See Natural Resources Defense Council, *Ebb Tide for Pollution: Actions for Cleaning Up Coastal Waters,* August 1989.

[3] Cited by Beth Millemann in *The Washington Post,* Aug. 4, 1991.

[4] See Orrin H. Pilkey Jr. and Howard L. Wright III, "Sea Walls Versus Beaches," *Journal of Coastal Research,* autumn 1988, p. 41.

[5] Malcolm Simmons, "National Flood Insurance Program Issues," *Congressional Research Service Issue Brief,* Dec. 16, 1991, p. 8. According to the General Accounting Office, $555 million of these losses were for properties in coastal communities.

[6] Millemann, *op. cit.*

[7] Beth Millemann, *And Two if By Sea: Fighting the Attack on America's Coasts* (1986), p. 2.

[8] See Michael Weber, "Using Common Sense to Protect the Coasts," *Coast Alliance,* August 1990, p. 18.

[9] Natural Resources Defense Council, "Testing the Waters: A Study of Beach Closings in Ten Coastal States," August 1991, p. 5.

[10] *And Two if By Sea, op. cit.,* p. 22.

[11] *The Washington Post,* Dec. 29, 1991. See also Philip Caputo, "The Lost Keys," *The New York Times Sunday Magazine,* Dec. 15, 1991, p. 55.

[12] For a detailed analysis, see The Center for Urban and Regional Studies, The University of North Carolina at Chapel Hill, "Evaluation of the National Coastal Zone Management Program," February 1991, p. 9.

[13] Study by H. Crane Miller cited by Weber, *op. cit.,* p. 15.

[14] Quoted in *Time,* Aug. 10, 1987, p. 41.

[15] During the hurricane, 86 structures on Folly Beach were more than 50 percent damaged. For a detailed account, see Rutherford Platt, et. al., "The Folly at Folly Beach and Other Failings of U.S. Coastal Erosion Policy," *Environment,* November 1991, p. 7.

[16] See National Oceanic and Atmospheric Administration, *Population Change along the Nation's Coasts: 1960-2010* (1990), p. 4.

[17] See National Research Council, *Managing Coastal Erosion* (1990), p. 27.

Bibliography

Selected Sources Used

Books

Leatherman, Stephen P., *Barrier Island Handbook,* The University of Maryland, 1988.

This book describes the geology of barrier islands and how they are being affected by erosion and steadily rising sea levels.

Millemann, Beth, *And Two if by Sea,* Coast Alliance Inc., 1988.

In this guide to coastal management, the author has compiled a wealth of detailed facts and figures on coastal pollution and the hazards of overdevelopment. The book highlights states with model legislation in specific areas, such as ocean dumping and coastal zone management, and is extensively footnoted.

National Research Council, *Managing Coastal Erosion,* National Academy Press, 1990.

Written in response to a request from the Federal Emergency Management Agency, this book is an authoritative guide on coastal erosion and has been relied upon by federal officials and policy-makers, particularly with respect to proposed reforms in the federal flood insurance program. The authors are among the leading experts on coastal geology.

Articles

Environmental Protection Agency, "Can Our Coasts Survive More Growth?" *EPA Journal,* September/October 1989.

The EPA devoted an entire issue of *EPA Journal* to the subject of environmental protection of U.S. coastlines. The articles provide a useful survey of the salient issues.

Pilkey, Orrin H., and Howard L. Wright III, "Sea Walls Versus Beaches," *Journal of Coastal Research,* autumn 1988.

Pilkey and Wright take a thorough look at the pros and cons of beach stabilization techniques, based on field studies of numerous coastal sites.

Platt, Rutherford H., et al., "The Folly at Folly Beach and Other Failings of U.S. Coastal Erosion Policy," *Environment,* November 1991.

The authors provide a fascinating glimpse at the politics behind coastal erosion policy, as played out in the wake of Hurricane Hugo. The article also gives instructive background on South Carolina coastal management policy.

Reports and Studies

Brower, David J., et al., *Evaluation of the National Coastal Zone Management Program,* The Center for Urban and Regional Studies, University of North Carolina, February 1991.

This 215-page examination of the national coastal management program serves as excellent background, particularly with respect to issues faced by planning experts. It also contains a detailed summary of individual state programs.

Davison, A. Todd, et al., *Beach Nourishment as a Coastal Management Tool,* unpublished paper, 1992.

This is a well-documented assessment of the state-of-the-art of beach nourishment. The paper also surveys important projects and studies under way.

Natural Resources Defense Council, *Ebb Tide for Pollution: Actions for Cleaning Up Coastal Waters,* August 1989.

The NRDC has compiled a useful and very readable report on the principal pollution problems that confront policy-makers, including suggestions for change.

Natural Resources Defense Council, *Testing the Waters: A Study of Beach Closings in Ten Coastal States,* August 1991.

As the title suggests, this study examines the specific causes for beach closings and explores how those problems can be remedied.

Simmons, Malcolm, *National Flood Insurance Program Issues,* Congressional Research Service Issue Brief, Dec. 16, 1991.

Simmons gives a brief summary of the evolution and current debate over the federal flood insurance program.

U.S. Army Corps of Engineers, *Shoreline Erosion Control Demonstration Program Revisited,* 1989.

The corps describes various beach stabilization techniques at specific sites. Overall, this report is an interesting look at the federal approach to dealing with erosion.

The Next Step

Additional Articles from Current Periodicals from EBSCO Publishing's Database

Case studies

"Hatteras Lighthouse stays put for now," *National Parks,* **July/August 1990, p. 11.**

Discusses the National Park Service's decision to let the endangered Cape Hatteras Lighthouse (N.C.) remain where it is for now. Erosion of North Carolina's Outer Banks; sandbag revetment; National Academy of Sciences' 1988 study.

"Largest marina in U.S. built on Great Lakes," *Civil Engineering,* **November 1990, p. 27.**

Describes a new marina offering 1,500 slips to Lake Michigan boaters that was carved out of raw land. According to the International Marina Institute, the North Point Marina, on the Illinois-Wisconsin border, is the largest freshwater basin in the U.S. Concerns including shoreline erosion; environmental assessments of the project.

"Steel seawall fights beach erosion in Virginia," *Civil Engineering,* **September 1990, p. 12.**

Notes the construction of an 8-foot-high steel sea wall in Virginia to protect remaining beach and homes. Joint investment of homeowners; details of the wall's structure.

Applebome, P., "After Hugo, a storm over beach development," *The New York Times,* **Sept. 24, 1989, p. A1.**

Examines the aftermath of Hurricane Hugo in South Carolina. Conflict created by a current law restricting building and repairs on beachfront property, originally designed to curb overdevelopment and beach erosion; property owners' and real estate professionals' objection to enforcement of the law.

Dean, C., "Beach loss: Outer Banks are offering a test case," *The New York Times,* **July 9, 1991, p. C1.**

Describes how the sea is washing away the sand of the Outer Banks of North Carolina. When the lighthouse was built in 1870, 1,500 feet of dunes and beach guarded it from the waves, but today that is down to 300 feet. The $87 million plan proposed by the Army Corps of Engineers.

Lyall, S., "Man vs. nature in L.I. beach restoration," *The New York Times,* **May 10, 1991, p. B1.**

Discusses the erosion along Dune Road in Westhampton Beach, L.I., the direct result of a plan to preserve the beach by capturing drifting sand in a series of jetties. The plan was cut short with just half the jetties built, thus saving the eastern end of the beach while starving the western end of sand.

Ninivaggi, D., "Managing New York's mosquito coast," *Conservationist,* **July/August 1989, p. 26.**

Talks about the importance of New York's tidal wetlands and how they have been damaged by humans over the years. Discusses methods of mosquito control in marshes and their side effects, and how the open marsh water management program makes mosquito control and habitat restoration compatible goals on Long Island.

Schmitt, E., "Back-to-nature plan pits islanders vs. 'mainlanders,'" *The New York Times,* **Dec. 12, 1989, p. B1.**

Reports on a Long Island planning agency recommendation that nearly 5,000 residents and businesses on Fire Island, vulnerable to erosion, be gradually eliminated and the island returned to nature. Incorporation of elements of the plan into a revision of Islip's townwide master plan; barrier island protects mainland from the Atlantic; property taxes; islanders and mainlanders have little in common.

Schmitt, E., "Return L.I.'s Barrier Islands to nature, a panel urges," *The New York Times,* **Dec. 8, 1989, p. B1.**

Reports that a Long Island planning agency recommended that almost 5,000 houses and businesses on Fire Island and in other shore resort areas threatened by erosion be gradually eliminated and that the barrier islands they stand on be returned to nature. The proposal, by the Long Island Regional Planning Board, comes only a few months after Hurricane Hugo devastated the developed barrier islands off South Carolina and at a time of concern that global warming is raising sea levels.

Udall, J.R., "A wild, swinging river," *Sierra,* **May/June 1990, p. 22.**

Reports on the negative effects irregular flows from the Glen Canyon Dam are having on the Colorado River and Grand Canyon National Park. Erosion of beaches; endangered species; disturbance of raft trips; environmental impact statement ordered; irregular flows used to meet peak power demands.

Debates & issues

Lowenstein, F., "The rising tide," *Technology Review,* **July 1988, p. 17.**

Discusses beach erosion near the Cape Hatteras Lighthouse in North Carolina. "Responding to Changes in Sea Level: Engineering Implications," a report from the National Research Council (NRC) on beach erosion in other areas of the U.S.; impact of rising sea levels; NRC recommendations.

Phillips, J., "The circle of soil erosion," *Focus,* spring 1991, p. 24.

Studies soil erosion problems in North America. Belief of many environmentalists that soil conservation has come full circle since the 1930s and that the high erosion rates of the dust bowl era are coming back; highlights of research on the issue conducted by physical geographer John Wilson of Montana State University.

Schueler, D.G. and Gould, P., "Losing Louisiana," *Audubon,* July 1990, p. 78.

Examines the reasons why Louisiana's coastal marshlands, including the Mississippi River Delta, are in danger of complete destruction. Wetland habitat; fisheries; damage caused by the U.S. Army Corps of Engineers and the oil and gas industry; proposals by the Coalition to Restore Coastal Louisiana.

Shacochis, B., "Written in the big wind," *Harper's Magazine,* September 1991, p. 45.

Describes how hurricanes form, the destruction caused by several big ones along the Atlantic Coast and discusses insistence of developers to continue to build along the coast. What a hurricane leaves behind; pro-development commissioners reluctant to call for evacuations; learning from hurricanes.

Williams, T., "Tires, trees, terns, terrapins," *Audubon,* May 1989, p. 26.

The author discusses the environmental community and certain federal agencies' opposition to beach buggy organizations and their attempts to alleviate beach erosion by planting dead Christmas trees and beachgrass. Author's membership in the Massachusetts Beach Buggy Association (MBBA); endangered piping plovers and diamondback terrapins; National Park Service; Soil Conservation Service.

Natural causes

"Bob," *Economist,* Aug. 24, 1991, p. 26.

Reports on Hurricane Bob, which inflicted damage on the East Coast of the United States in August 1991. Damage to New England, particularly the islands of Martha's Vineyard and Nantucket; assessment of damage to Massachusetts as reported by Governor William Weld; details.

"Charleston after Hugo," *Southern Living,* February 1990, p. 29.

Discusses the damage to and restoration of Charleston,

S.C., and coastal area north of the city after Hurricane Hugo struck the city in September 1989. Trees; buildings. INSET: How the rest of South Carolina's coast fared.

"The brutal lesson of Hurricane Hugo," *U.S. News & World Report,* Oct. 2, 1989, p. 13.

Discusses Hurricane Hugo, which rampaged through a dozen Caribbean islands and struck the South Carolina coast with 135-mph winds. Covers devastation in South Carolina beach resorts and on barrier islands.

"What is prognosis for Carolina beaches?" *Earth Science,* winter 1989, p. 8.

Reports that coastal geologists believe it may take years for coastal South Carolina to recover from the devastating Category 4 Hurricane Hugo, and some areas submerged by the storm may never resurface.

Magnuson, E., "Winds of chaos," *Time,* Oct. 2, 1989, p. 16.

Recounts the track and destruction, through the Caribbean to the Carolinas, left by Hurricane Hugo, the fiercest storm to strike the U.S. East Coast since 1979. Cost of damage; path of the storm.

Nemeth, M., "The winds of fury," *Maclean's,* Oct. 2, 1989, p. 34.

Describes the destruction caused by Hurricane Hugo as it crossed the Caribbean and the U.S. Carolina coast. Damage in Puerto Rico, the U.S. Virgin Islands, South Carolina; other islands; Canadian aid.

Schmitt, E., "Big what if: How a Hugo might hit L.I.," *The New York Times,* Feb. 6, 1990, p. B1.

Examines what the effect might be if a hurricane made landfall on Long Island. Efforts to hold back erosion of beaches and shifting of barrier islands; catastrophic destruction and loss of life; scientific methods of determining the forecast.

Smothers, R., "Heavy rains delay the vast cleanup in the South," *The New York Times,* Sept. 26, 1989, p. A1.

Reports that driving winds and rain are hampering cleanup efforts from Hurricane Hugo on the coast from Georgia to North Carolina. Statistics on damage from hurricane; citizen reactions.

Preservation

"Submerging the spirit," *Time,* Jan. 9, 1989, p. 29.

Discusses how discarded Christmas trees in New Orleans, La., are being submerged in marshes along Lake Pontchartrain to form an underwater dike to stop coastal erosion.

Clark, J. R., "Management of coastal barrier biosphere reserves," *Bioscience,* May 1991, p. 331.

Proposes working concepts for UNESCO's Man and the Biosphere program that can be used to conserve the natural resources of Atlantic coastal barrier ecosystems. Management needs; management status; two examples of coastal barrier conservation; role of biosphere reserves and research programs; the science opportunity; potential of biosphere reserves; concepts and objectives.

Dyer, M. I. and Holland, M. M., "The biosphere-reserve concept: Needs for a network design," *Bioscience,* May 1991, p. 319.

Focuses on new programmatic developments in coastal-marine environments along part of the Atlantic seaboard of North America. Biosphere-reserve concept; common needs of landscape ecology and biosphere reserves; networks; relationships among research and conservation sites; constraints.

Joyner, L., "The Southern seacoast," *Southern Living,* June 1991, p. 70.

Describes the natural instability of coastal beaches, particularly in the South, and gives advice for protecting the beaches from natural and man-made problems. Natural flow of sand; erosion; building directly on beaches; sand replacement; preventing development; retreating from the sea; regulations for beachfront owners. INSETS: Beach basics; help protect our beaches.

Monastersky, R., "Sea wall's seal of approval," *Science News,* Dec. 17, 1988, p. 398.

Describes a study of sea walls' effects on beaches, which concluded that any erosion caused was only temporary. Composition of the walls.

Mullins, G. W. and Neuhauser, H., "Public education for protecting coastal barriers," *Bioscience,* May 1991, p. 326.

Urges public participation in making a successful biosphere-reserve program. Public education; techniques and incentives; strategies for action.

Ray, G. C. and Gregg, W. P. Jr., "Establishing biosphere reserves for coastal barrier ecosystems," *Bioscience,* May 1991, p. 301.

Suggests the application of the biosphere-reserve concept to the problems of coastal barriers. Coastal-zone concept; policy and protection of U.S. East Coast barriers; evolution of the concept; challenges and opportunities. INSET: Workshop on coastal barrier biosphere reserves.

Ruben, B., "Preserving Louisiana's vanishing wetlands," *Environmental Action,* January/February 1991, p. 26.

Describes efforts by the Louisiana Coastal Wetlands Interfaith Stewardship Plan and the Coalition to Restore Coastal Louisiana to preserve the state's eroding wetlands. Rate of erosion; Sarah Schoeffler and Paul Kemp; work involved.

Sedimentary deposits

Marcus, W. A. and Kearney, M. S., "Upland and coastal sediment sources in a Chesapeake estuary," *Annals of the Association of American Geographers,* September 1991, p. 408.

Suggests that coastal erosion may be the dominant process driving sediment inputs along the entire length of many tributary estuaries of the Chesapeake over the past several centuries. The new data comes from the South River, Md., and from reexamination of existing literature. Previous research; study area; methods; results; coastal erosion; sediment budgets; human impacts; European settlement; conclusions.

Monastersky, R., "Sand's incredible journey," *Science News,* Nov. 12, 1988, p. 318.

Describes how sand from East Coast U.S. beaches slowly moves south over millions of years.

Research

Collier, B. L., "Crusader on the beach," *The New York Times Magazine,* Dec. 4, 1988, p. 64.

Profile of Orrin H. Pilkey Jr., professor of marine geology at Duke University in North Carolina. His interest in saving the beaches of the world; stand against oceanfront development; critics of his views; how he teaches students.

Kerr, R. C., "Erosion of a stable density gradient by sedimentation-driven convection," *Nature,* Oct. 3, 1991, p. 423.

Presents experimental results that under certain circumstances the density gradient of ocean and lake sedimentation is eroded in a number of cycles of decreasing intensity and increasing duration. Also develops a physical model of this phenomenon; methods; results; discussion.

Back Issues

Great Research on Current Issues Starts Right Here... Recent topics covered by The CQ Researcher are listed below. Issues dated before May 10, 1991, were published under the name of Editorial Research Reports.

JULY 1990
Do Americans Still Love Marriage?
Death Penalty Debate
Decline of Rural America
United Nations in the 1990s

AUGUST 1990
Democracy in the Philippines
Initiatives: True Democracy?
Hard Times at Newspapers
Teens Balance School & Jobs

SEPTEMBER 1990
Dangers of Alcohol
Western Alliance After the Cold War
Tobacco Industry
Right to Die

OCTOBER 1990
Organ Transplants
Energy Policy Options
Search for Arab Unity
Child Support

NOVEMBER 1990
Lotteries and Gambling
Post-Cold War Choices
Setting Limits on Medical Care
Multicultural Education

DECEMBER 1990
Cable TV Regulation
Americans' Search for Their Roots
Is Insurance System a Failure?
Why Schools Still Have Tracking

JANUARY 1991
Growing Influence of Boycotts
Should the U.S. Reinstate the Draft?
America's Archaeological Past
Peace Corps' Challenges in '90s

FEBRUARY 1991
Regional Impact of Recession
Puerto Rico's Status
Redistricting: Mapping Power
Nuclear Power

MARCH 1991
Acid Rain
Cost of the Gulf War
Reassessing Gun Laws
Future for Man in Space

APRIL 1991
Social Security
Canadian Crisis Over Quebec
California Drought
Electromagnetic Radiation

MAY 1991
School Choice
Racial Quotas
Animal Rights
U.S. and Japan

JUNE 1991
Children and Divorce
Teenage Suicide
Endangered Species
Europe 1992

JULY 1991
Teenagers and Abortion
Soviet Republics Rebel
Mexico's Emergence
Athletes and Drugs

AUGUST 1991
Sexual Harassment
Fetal Tissue Research
Oil Imports
The Palestinians

SEPTEMBER 1991
Police Brutality
Advertising Under Attack
Saving the Forests
Foster Care Crisis

OCTOBER 1991
Pay-Per-View TV
Youth Gangs
Gene Therapy
World Hunger

NOVEMBER 1991
Fast-Food Shake-Up
The Greening of Eastern Europe
Business' Role in Education
Cuba In Crisis

DECEMBER 1991
Retiree Health Benefits
Asian Americans
The Obscenity Debate
The Disabilities Act

JANUARY 1992
Term Limits
Oil Spills
Hunting Controversy
Alternative Medicine

Back issues are available for $4.00 (subscribers) or $7.00 (non-subscribers). Quantity discounts apply to orders over ten. To order, call Congressional Quarterly 1-800-432-2250.

Future Topics

▶ *New Era in Asia*

▶ *Assisted Suicide*

▶ *Future of the Job Market*

PUBLISHED BY CONGRESSIONAL QUARTERLY INC., IN CONJUNCTION WITH EBSCO PUBLISHING

New Era in Asia

The Cold War's end forces changes in U.S. policies

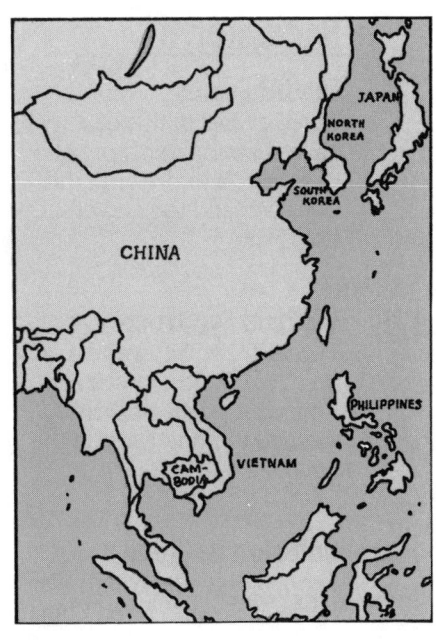

W ITH THE END OF THE COLD WAR, American foreign policy is entering a period of sweeping readjustment. And nowhere is the need for new policies clearer than in East Asia. Long held together by their opposition to the Soviet Union, the United States and its Asian allies are now finding that their most crucial interests in the strategic region — especially concerning trade — are frequently in conflict. The United States is currently re-evaluating its longstanding economic embargo against Vietnam, for example, and there is the continuing trade dispute with Japan. From a strategic standpoint, potential hot spots still remain — particularly in unpredictable North Korea and in newly hard-line China — that could escalate if the rancorous trade disputes can't be resolved.

 February 14, 1992 • Volume 2, No. 6 • 121-144

Formerly Editorial Research Reports

COVER ART: BARBARA SASSA-DANIELS

February 14, 1992
Volume 2, No. 6

EDITOR
Sandra Stencel

MANAGING EDITOR
Thomas J. Colin

ASSOCIATE EDITOR
Richard L. Worsnop

STAFF WRITERS
Charles S. Clark
Mary H. Cooper
Rodman D. Griffin

PRODUCTION EDITOR
Laurie De Maris

EDITORIAL ASSISTANT
Thomas H. Moore

GRAPHICS
Jack Auldridge

PUBLISHED BY
Congressional Quarterly Inc.

CHAIRMAN
Andrew Barnes

VICE CHAIRMAN
Andrew P. Corty

EDITOR AND PUBLISHER
Neil Skene

EXECUTIVE EDITOR
Robert W. Merry

PUBLICATIONS MARKETING/SALES
Robert Smith

EDITOR, EBSCO PUBLISHING
Melissa Kummerer

The CQ Researcher (ISSN 1056-2036). Formerly Editorial Research Reports. Published weekly (48 times per year, not printed the first Friday of any month with five Fridays) by Congressional Quarterly Inc., 1414 22nd St., N.W., Washington, D.C. 20037. Rates are furnished upon request. Second-class postage paid at Washington, D.C. POSTMASTER: Send address changes to The CQ Researcher, 1414 22nd St., N.W., Washington, D.C. 20037.

New Era in Asia

By Patrick G. Marshall

The Issues

Nearly 20 years after the last U.S. troops withdrew from Vietnam, the United States has finally begun talks on reviving relations with the Southeast Asian country. Why the abrupt policy change? The reason is simple: U.S. relations with Asia are at a historic turning point.

With the Cold War officially over, the United States faces serious new problems in the strategic region — from a shaky settlement of Cambodia's civil war to an unpredictable North Korea building a nuclear bomb, from China's crackdown on dissidents to ongoing trade disputes with affluent Japan.

Just how the United States will adapt to post-Cold War Asia is still uncertain. But it is likely that a U.S.-Vietnam rapprochement may be a bellwether for America's future role in the region.

For more than 40 years after World War II, the Cold War with the communist countries — primarily China and the former Soviet Union — was the axis on which American foreign policy in Europe and Asia turned. It was, for example, because of communist expansionism that the United States fought in Korea in the early 1950s, defended China's government-in-exile in Taiwan from the communist regime of mainland China and, finally, went to war in Vietnam in the early 1960s.

Indeed, the threat from the Soviet Union and China served as a sort of glue holding the United States and its Asian allies together. With security interests in mind, the United States for years overlooked trade disputes with Japan. And South Korea, needing American protection, welcomed U.S.

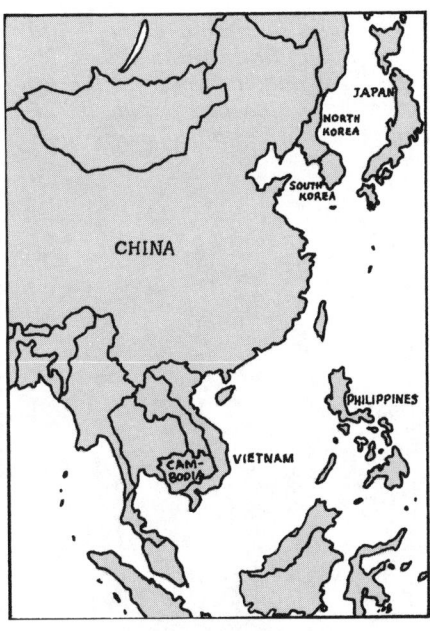

troops and responded quickly to requests from the United States for trade reforms. Similarly, the Philippines, incapable of guarding its own borders, leased vast bases to the U.S. Navy and Air Force.

The dramatic collapse of the Soviet Union, combined with China's turning inward, has unsettled the balance of power and interests that stabilized the Pacific Rim for decades. Suddenly, U.S. policy-makers are faced with challenges — and opportunities — on every front.

As Secretary of State James A. Baker III noted in a recent issue of *Foreign Affairs,* President Bush's January trip to Asia marked "a point in time when disparate historical lines are intersecting: the commemoration of the 50th anniversary of the attack on Pearl Harbor; the end of the U.S.-Soviet confrontation; and the prospect of laying to rest the Vietnam War era." Baker predicted "a new chapter of U.S. engagement in the region as we approach the 21st century." [1]

Three issues in particular will face American policy-makers in 1992:

What conditions should the U.S. put on re-establishing relations with Vietnam?

After the United States pulled out of South Vietnam in 1975, it treated newly unified Vietnam as an enemy. In addition to showing no interest in establishing diplomatic relations with the new country, the United States continued the economic embargo and other sanctions — such as prohibiting telecommunications between the two countries — that had been invoked against North Vietnam during the war. Finally, the United States used its influence to block Vietnam from obtaining aid from the World Bank, the International Monetary Fund and the Asian Development Bank.

But in April 1991 Secretary of State Baker signaled a major course change, laying out a "road map" for the renewal of relations between the United States and Vietnam. Baker's overture was driven by the need for Vietnamese help in settling Cambodia's civil war and by pressure from U.S. companies interested in doing business in Vietnam.

The main U.S. conditions — spelled out to the Vietnamese at the United Nations on April 9 — called for Vietnam to cooperate on the Cambodian peace effort and to account for 2,273 American soldiers listed as missing in action or prisoners of war during the Vietnam War.

The current debate in the United States over relations with Vietnam is not over whether they should be re-established, but whether the U.S. conditions must be met first.

A key condition has, in fact, already been fulfilled. Vietnam was instrumental in obtaining the peace agreement now in place in Cambodia. Some in the United States have charged, however, that Vietnam has not fulfilled the second condition.

U.S. Trade Deficits Highest in Asia

Of the five countries that ran the highest surpluses in trade with the United States in 1990, the first three were in Asia: Japan, Taiwan and China. Incomplete figures from 1991 show that the three nations remained the top surplus countries, the only difference being that China had displaced Taiwan from the No. 2 spot. Japan's surplus, however, remained many times that of any other U.S. trading partner.

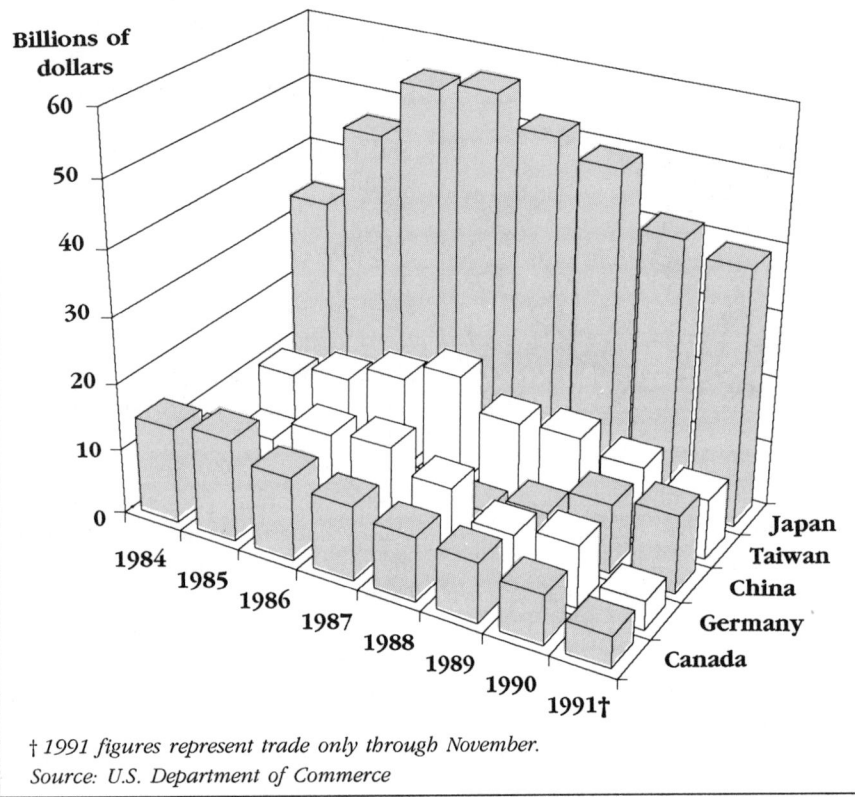

† 1991 figures represent trade only through November.
Source: U.S. Department of Commerce

"The Vietnamese could resolve hundreds of cases of missing Americans immediately if they made the political decision to do so," says Ann Mills Griffiths, executive director of the National League of Families of American Prisoners and Missing in Southeast Asia.

She contends that Vietnam has repeatedly demonstrated that it cannot be trusted, and she says that the conditions spelled out by Baker must be fulfilled before any concessions — such as modifying the embargo — are made. "Once you lift the embargo," says Griffiths, "there is no holding back on the international financial institution loans, which is the primary objective of Vietnam."

Others argue that relations between the United States and Vietnam should have been re-established long ago. "We ought to have [done it] six months or 10 years ago," says Thomas Robinson, an analyst at the American Enterprise Institute, a conservative think tank in Washington, D.C. "The sooner we do it, the better off we're going to be."

Rep. Sam Gejdenson, D-Conn., agrees, noting that business interests would be a primary beneficiary of a thaw. "Just about the only industrialized country that is not doing any business at all in Vietnam is the United States," he noted during congressional hearings on the embargo last June. "U.S. policy is to deny Vietnam hard currency. But since no one else pays any attention to the embargo, we are not succeeding in denying Vietnam anything except contact with the United States. ... As a result, American businesses are losing out once again to Japan and the [European Community]." [2]

Should the U.S. reduce its military presence in East Asia?

The Soviet threat was the primary justification for maintaining a U.S. Pacific fleet of 190 ships in the region, as well as nearly 400,000 personnel and more than 800 combat aircraft. With the breakup of the Soviet Union, however, many have called for a significant drawing down of those forces.

"At this point, with the Soviet Union gone, there's absolutely no question that we will and should reduce the size of American forces in the Pacific," says Thomas McNaugher, a senior scholar at the Brookings Institution, a think tank in Washington. "If the Navy we had there in 1989 was capable of taking on the Russians, and the Russians aren't there, then I don't think we need quite that big a Navy."

In fact, even before the complete collapse of the Soviet Union, the Bush administration had committed itself to a gradual reduction. In February 1990, Defense Secretary Dick Cheney announced the withdrawal of 12,000 of the more than 90,000 U.S. troops stationed in Japan and South Korea. [3]

Since the breakup, some members of Congress have suggested still greater reductions. But there is general agreement that the United States should not entirely abandon its military role in the Pacific — with or without a Soviet threat. After all, the Soviet Union was not the only military threat in the region. Military strategists cannot overlook such potential adversaries as North Korea, Vietnam and China.

Indeed, the very absence of the Soviet threat has increased the region's instability, leaving the Chinese and North Korean governments feeling defensive and no doubt contributing to China's recent clampdown on internal dissent. Smaller countries, too, worry that without the Soviets to deal with the United States may withdraw, leaving them to deal on their own with the two Asian superpowers — China and Japan.

At present, the prospect of facing a resurgent Japan is probably the most worrisome for the majority of Asian countries. Many of them — including China, South Korea and the Philippines — suffered under a notoriously brutal Japanese occupation during World War II. And Japan's continuing reputation as a xenophobic, inwardly turned nation has not eased the fears, particularly when combined with Japan's overwhelming economic predominance.

McNaugher believes the United States could significantly reduce its forces under one condition: "Asian countries would accept a reduction provided that the U.S.-Japan relationship remains steady. If you get the U.S. and northeast Asia stabilized, everything becomes easier."

Robinson at the American Enterprise Institute disagrees. He argues that, while the forces could be shifted around, "We ought to maintain our forces, and probably at more or less the same levels. We don't have a major threat from the Soviet Union. But we may well have a problem with China someday. And troops will] keep the Korean situation from going critical."

How should the U.S. deal with its trade deficits in Asia?

The nagging recession in the United States, coupled with the onset of a presidential campaign year, has given trade issues heightened importance in recent months. And, since the worst of America's trade deficits are with Asian countries, the most intense focus has been across the Pacific.

The country running the largest surplus in trade with the United States is, of course, Japan. Many officials and analysts say that's because the Japanese unfairly protect their home markets, shutting out exports from the United States and other trade partners. At $41 billion, Japan's 1990 surplus* with the United States is nearly four times that of the country with the next-largest surplus, Taiwan.

President Bush's recent trip to Japan, though not originally planned as a trade mission, quickly became one as voters' increasing concern about the recession became clear. Though administration officials have played up the trip as a success, many nongovernment analysts consider that it was a bust.

On the surface, Bush seemed to have produced results, including a Japanese pledge to increase purchases of U.S. auto parts from about $9 billion this year to approximately $19 billion in two years. The Japanese also promised to increase the U.S. share of several Japanese markets, including paper, glass, construction and government purchases of computers; to change tax codes to make foreign investments less costly; and to encourage car dealers in Japan to also carry American cars.

But critics noted that most of the promises were old news. The Japanese government had, for example, already agreed to increase its annual purchases of U.S. auto parts to $18 billion before Bush's trip.

"It's a fig leaf," says James Clad, a specialist on Asia at the Carnegie Endowment for International Peace. The concessions by Japan "simply in-

_____

*Preliminary figures indicate that Japan's 1991 surplus will surpass the 1990 surplus by about $2 billion.

volve the foreign ministry trick of basically taking what's out there anyway, dressing it up and saying, 'This is what we're going to do for you.' But it's simply an accretion of things that have been announced already."

Another problem with the Japanese concessions, Clad notes, is that they are just that — concessions. Agreements to increase America's share of Japan's markets by specified amounts do not actually open those markets, he says. They merely invite future disputes over market shares as well as complaints by other trade partners that they are not getting the same treatment.

But many in the United States — including the Bush administration, if the recent agreements are an indication — have reluctantly concluded that market-sharing agreements are the only way to deal effectively with Japan.

"We've been having this negotiation for 30 years, and it's been the same negotiation, but we change the name," says Clyde Prestowitz, director of the Economic Strategy Institute in Washington and a former U.S. trade negotiator. "We used to call it textiles, then we called it television, then we called it steel, then we called it semiconductors and now we're calling it autos."

Prestowitz faults the president's recent trip for several reasons. "First of all," he says, "I would not take 21 business executives with me, and secondly, I would not even mention the word 'trade' in public." Instead, says Prestowitz, "I would go to Japan on a nice state visit, sign a nice declaration, and quietly in the back room with [Prime Minister Kiichi] Miyazawa and some of the key Japanese leaders, say in the most forceful terms possible, 'Gentlemen, we cannot keep on going this way. We're allies, and we've got to stay that way. But the only way we'll be able to do that is if we address the structural and policy asymmetries between our two systems. We'll only be able to do that by managing the trade.'"

Other ways to correct the trade imbalance have been proposed. In late December, just before Bush's trip, House Majority Leader Richard A. Gephardt, D-Mo., introduced legislation mandating cuts in Japanese car imports unless Japan wipes out its U.S. trade surplus within five years.

That's not the solution favored by C. Fred Bergsten, director of the Institute for International Economics. He has long argued that the answer to America's trade deficits is neither market-sharing deals nor protectionist measures but American fiscal policy. Bergsten, a former assistant Treasury secretary, links most of the trade imbalance to currency fluctuations, which he blames on U.S. budget deficits.

Bergsten argued last December that two steps are urgently required. "First," he wrote, "the value of the yen should be raised substantially. In addition, the Japanese must be encouraged to end the recent stagnation in their domestic spending, which has led to renewed reliance on exports."[4]

But James Clad warns that the United States should not focus narrowly on repairing the trade deficit with Japan, simply because several other countries in the region also run big surpluses, among them Taiwan and China. "We are on firmer ground talking about generic difficulties," says Clad. "That may in the end point to Japan as a prime offender, but this is equally applicable to sweatshop industries in Thailand and elsewhere. It's a matter that has to be approached in trade relations globally." ■

BACKGROUND

Fateful Events

Three defining events have shaped the history of East Asia during this century: World War II, the Cold War and the ending of the Cold War.

World War II saw the rise and subsequent fall of Japanese suzerainty over much of the region, followed by U.S. occupation of Japan and overwhelming American influence over most of East Asia.

The Cold War with the Soviet Union, and to a lesser degree with China, shaped American policies in the region for nearly four decades following the war. It was the perceived need to block the advance of communism that drove America's decision to rebuild Japan, to isolate China and protect the exiled Chinese government in Taiwan, to go to war in Korea and, later, to shoulder France's role in Vietnam.

It was also Cold War-driven security concerns that caused the United States to unilaterally open its markets, not only to Japan but also to Hong Kong, Singapore, Thailand, South Korea and many other Asian countries in an attempt to strengthen friendly regimes.

The end of the Cold War is quickly proving to be no less of a watershed event than the Cold War itself, involving as it does the withdrawal of the Soviet threat and the uncertainty of a changed relationship — both economic and military — between the United States and East Asia.

That new relationship, of course, cannot be explained solely in terms of World War II and the Cold War. Four countries in particular have

Vietnam	
Type of government:	Communist
Head of government:	Prime Minister Vo Van Kiet
Population:	68,488,000 (1990 est.)
Area:	128,401 sq. miles (the size of New Mexico)
Capital:	Hanoi
GNP:	$12.6 billion (1987)
Per capita income:	$180 (1987)
Literacy rate:	78%
Defense spending:	19.4% GNP (1986)

been of special concern to the United States over the past 50 years: Vietnam, China, Korea and Japan.

Vietnam Syndrome

The Vietnam War was both the longest war in American history and the only one American forces didn't win. From the day in February 1955 when the first U.S. military advisers arrived to train South Vietnamese forces, to April 29, 1975, when the last U.S. troops pulled out of Saigon, an estimated 1.5 million people died in the conflict, more than 56,000 of them Americans.

It was a war few U.S. policy-makers at the time understood. Most seemed to believe they were fighting communist expansionism, when in fact they were fighting a host of other forces, including nationalism, resentment born of decades of foreign occupation and fear of South Vietnam's corrupt government.

Gen. Maxwell Taylor, a former ambassador to Saigon, later observed: "First, we didn't know ourselves. We thought we were going into another Korean War, but this was a different country. Secondly, we didn't know our South Vietnamese allies. We never understood them.... And we knew even less about North Vietnam. Who was Ho Chi Minh? Nobody really knew. So, until we know the enemy and know our allies and know ourselves, we'd better keep out of this dirty kind of business. It's very dangerous."[5]

The United States did not get to know Vietnam any better after the

Continued on p. 128

Chronology

1940s-1950s
With the defeat of Japan during World War II — and the rise to prominence of the United States and the Soviet Union — Asia, like Europe, is divided politically by the Cold War.

1949
Japan, under U.S. occupation, enacts the Foreign Exchange and Foreign Trade Control Law, which requires government licenses for all imports.

December 1949
Nationalist forces flee China's mainland to Taiwan as Communists led by Mao Tse-tung take over the government.

June 25, 1950
North Korea invades South Korea. U.N. forces, primarily U.S. troops, counterattack.

November 1950
China enters the Korean War on the side of North Korea.

July 21, 1954
Cease-fire agreement between Vietnamese communists and the French divides Vietnam into North and South.

February 1955
First U.S. military advisers arrive in South Vietnam.

1970s
Decade marked by the end of the U.S. war with Vietnam, an American-Chinese rapprochement and Japan's rise to economic pre-eminence.

April 1971
Chinese Premier Chou En-lai invites a U.S. pingpong team to Beijing, signaling a new era in U.S.-China relations.

February 1972
President Richard M. Nixon visits China.

April 29, 1975
United States pulls the last of its troops from South Vietnam.

Dec. 25, 1978
Vietnam invades Cambodia and overthrows the Khmer Rouge government.

1980s
Trade issues take the spotlight, with the United States running huge trade deficits worldwide, and especially with Japan, Taiwan and Hong Kong.

October 1983
South Korea's president escapes death when his motorcade is delayed on the way to welcoming ceremonies in Rangoon, Burma, but 21 people are killed, including four Cabinet members, when a bomb planted by North Korean agents explodes.

1987
Japan's trade surplus with the United States reaches an all-time high of $56.3 billion.

June 3, 1989
Chinese troops attack demonstrators in Tiananmen Square in Beijing, killing possibly as many as 5,000 people.

September 1989
Vietnam pulls the last of its troops from Cambodia.

1990s
Asia struggles to find a new balance after the end of the Cold War between the United States and the Soviet Union.

February 1990
Defense Secretary Dick Cheney announces that, as a result of the ending of the Cold War, the United States will gradually withdraw 12,000 troops from Japan and South Korea.

July 1990
Secretary of State James A. Baker III announces that the United States will no longer support Cambodia's U.N. seat, being held by a coalition including the Khmer Rouge. The U.S. move is interpreted as a signal to the other coalition partners to negotiate with the Vietnamese-backed Hun Sen government.

October 1990
China and South Korea open trade bureaus in each other's capitals, a sign of closer political relations.

April 1991
Secretary of State Baker spells out conditions for re-establishing relations with Vietnam, including Vietnamese cooperation in attaining a peace agreement in Cambodia and in determining the fate of unaccounted for U.S. servicemen from the Vietnam War.

Nov. 27, 1991
U.S. and Vietnamese negotiators begin talks in New York aimed at re-establishing diplomatic relations.

January 1992
President Bush travels to Australia, Singapore, Korea and Japan on a trip billed primarily as a trade mission to Tokyo. The trip draws mixed reviews from analysts in the United States.

Winds of Change in Asia

The end of the Cold War is forcing sweeping readjustments of U.S. trade and defense policies in Asia.

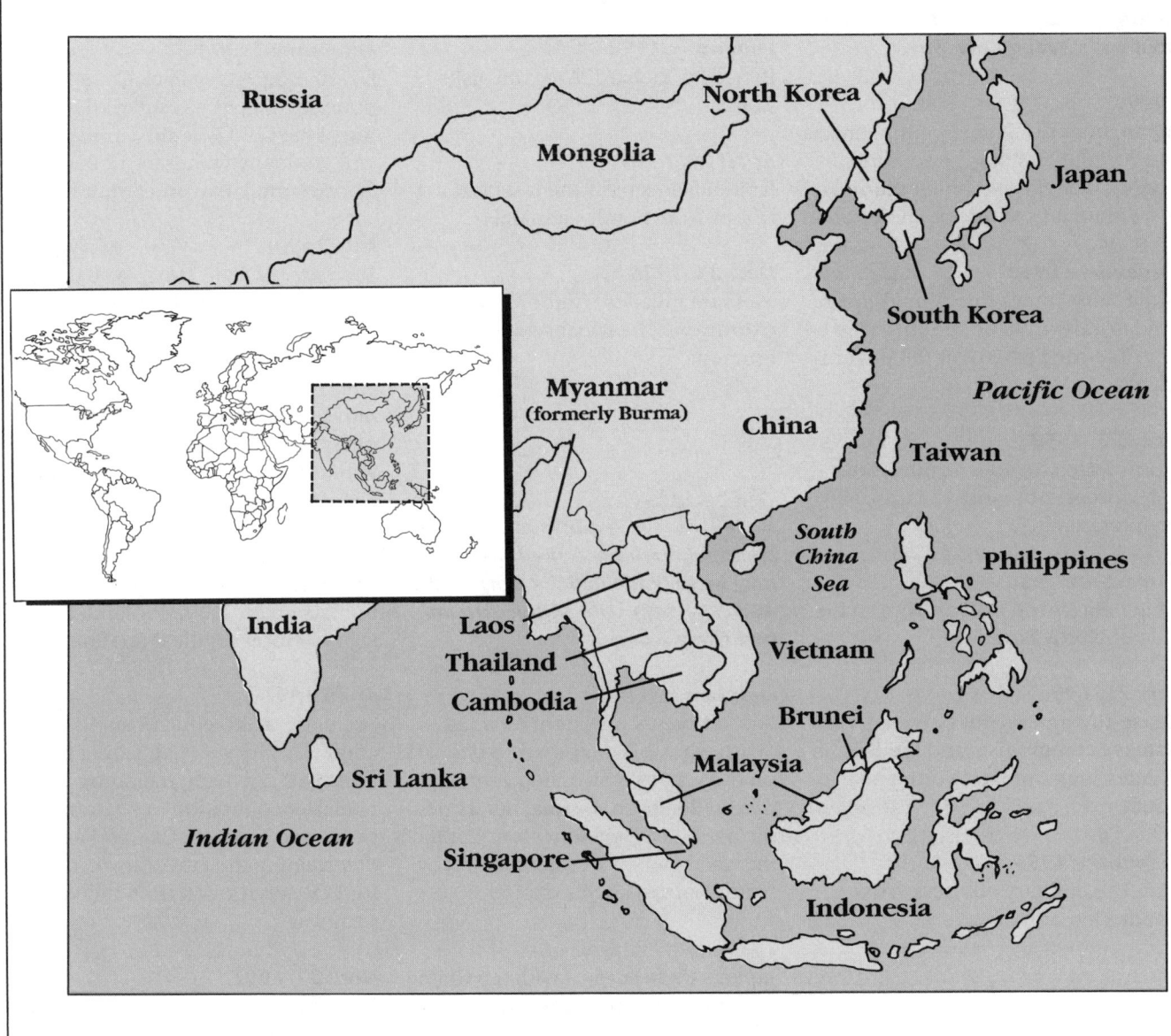

Continued from p. 126
war. Though many countries soon recognized the newly unified Vietnam, the United States did not, maintaining the trade embargo that had been imposed during the war. The United States even prevented Vietnam from obtaining aid from interna-

tional financial institutions, including the World Bank and International Monetary Fund.*

Though the American refusal to

---

*Some $4.7 billion in aid was promised to Hanoi by President Richard M. Nixon in a secret letter during the Paris peace talks.

deal with Vietnam was at least in part a case of sour grapes, it was also spurred by Hanoi's treatment of Vietnamese in the south. Thousands of former soldiers and employees of the Americans were sent to harsh "re-education" camps. Farms were collectivized, businesses shut down and gold and other valuables confiscated.

U.S. opposition to Vietnam hardened further when, on Christmas Day 1978, Vietnam invaded Cambodia. The United States immediately made Vietnamese withdrawal a prerequisite for any steps toward normalization.

Vietnam's costly occupation of Cambodia — combined with U.S. economic sanctions and the devastation brought by years of warfare — turned the country into one of the poorest in the world. By 1988, after three years of crop failures, 3 million Vietnamese were living "on the edge of starvation," according to normally tight-lipped Vietnamese officials, and the economy was in a shambles.[6]

It was more than even Vietnam's hard-line leadership could withstand. In 1986, 11 years after the war, the government began a process of reform on many fronts — most of them aimed at encouraging foreign investment and at ending the U.S.-led embargo on international aid. The first step was the resignation of three top party leaders and the election of Nguyen Van Lihn as a reform premier. Lihn quickly abandoned the country's disastrous centralized planning of the economy, disbanded many of the inefficient agricultural cooperatives and introduced incentives to stimulate modest private enterprise.

Vietnam Takes Conciliatory Steps

Over the next two years, while continuing its policy of single-party rule and suppression of political dissent, Vietnam's government — to the surprise of many Western skeptics — undertook several conciliatory steps, including:

■ Implementing a new law on foreign investment, described by some analysts as the most liberal foreign-investment law in a communist country.

■ Announcing plans to withdraw its troops from Cambodia by the end of 1989.

■ Allowing U.S. military experts to search for the remains of missing American servicemen, and promising to help excavate crash sites.

■ Agreeing to the voluntary return of Vietnamese refugees turned away from Hong Kong as "economic refugees" and increasing the number of Vietnamese allowed to emigrate legally, including political prisoners.

■ Revising the Constitution to excise language accusing China, France, Japan and the United States of aggression and imperialism.

What's more, Vietnam lived up to its promise to withdraw from Cambodia, pulling out the last of its troops in September 1989.

The Bush administration — responding to Vietnam's overtures, as well as to pressure from Congress to lift the embargo — soon altered its Vietnam policy dramatically. In July 1990, Secretary of State Baker announced the United States would no longer support the holding of Cambodia's U.N. seat by a coalition that included the Khmer Rouge. That was an unmistakable sign to other coalition members that it was time to talk to the Vietnamese-backed Hun Sen government.

In December, the United States announced that it was prepared to start formal talks with Vietnam on normalizing relations as soon as a peace agreement was ratified in Cambodia. Assistant Secretary of State Richard H. Solomon predicted that full diplomatic relations could be achieved within two years, provided that Vietnam also made satisfactory steps toward resolving the fate of the 2,300 missing American servicemen. On Nov. 21, 1991, State Department and Vietnamese officials began talks in New York City on re-establishing relations between the two countries.

China	
Type of government:	Communist
Head of government:	Premier Li Peng
Population:	1,130,065,000 (1990 est.)
Area:	3,705,390 sq. miles (slightly larger than the United States)
Capital:	Beijing
GNP:	$350 billion (1988)
Per capita income:	$258 (1986)
Literacy rate:	70%
Defense spending:	4.4% GNP (1987)

Collision in China

One historian has described relations between the United States and China as "a tale of how Americans, preoccupied with the affairs of Europe, thought they could use China, subordinating its needs and interests to the realization of weightier objectives elsewhere."[7]

Indeed, the United States "used" China as an ally in World War II against Japan and showed relatively little concern for China afterwards. And, when the communist regime of Mao Tse-tung won the civil war in China after World War II, the U.S. continually sought to play the Chinese off against the Soviet Union. For most of the 30 years following the war, in fact, U.S. policy-makers considered China as an enemy, first as a close enemy, when China entered the Korean War on the side of the North in November 1950, and then as somewhat more distant enemy who threatened to spread communism in Asia.

In addition to Korea, U.S. and Chinese interests collided directly in Taiwan and Vietnam. In December 1949, the defeated Nationalist government of Chiang Kai Shek fled to Taiwan, 90 miles off the coast of China. Nearly a year later, when it looked like China might be planning an invasion of Taiwan while the United States was tied down in Korea, President Harry S Truman sent the U.S. Seventh Fleet to guard the Taiwan Straits.

During the Vietnam War, U.S. troops did not directly face Chinese forces, but Chinese aid to North Vietnam angered the United States.

Nonetheless, throughout the 1960s another trend was emerging that would bring the United States and China closer: the deteriorating relationship between China and the Soviet Union. In 1969, border disputes actually led to skirmishing.

Nixon Opens the Door

Even before he was elected president in 1968, Richard M. Nixon had written that China could be an ally against the Soviet Union, and when as president he was searching for a way out of Vietnam, Nixon reasoned that China might value U.S. support against the Soviet Union enough to help pressure the Vietnamese into a settlement acceptable to the United States.

According to Georgetown University history Professor Nancy Bernkopf Tucker, "Progress toward reconciliation accelerated after Chinese hardliners, worried about security, ideology and Westernization, lost out to more pragmatic leadership."[8] In April 1971, "pingpong diplomacy" became a byword when Premier Chou En-lai invited a team of American players to China.

Nixon responded to China's signal that October by agreeing to let China take Taiwan's seat in the United Nations, a move the United States had previously blocked. The opening to China was finally capped in February 1972 when Nixon visited Beijing at the invitation of Chou En-lai.

The end of the Vietnam War in 1975, combined with worsening U.S.-Soviet relations, particularly after the Russian invasion of Afghanistan in 1979, ensured a period of relative amity between the United States and China. That era of good relations began to wind down, not coincidentally, just as relations between the United States and Soviet Union started to improve with the coming to power of then-Soviet President Mikhail S. Gorbachev.

At the same time that China's leaders worried about warming U.S.-Soviet relations, they saw new threats to their own leadership within China. Economic reforms begun in the 1980s encouraged many Chinese to press for political reforms as well. When Gorbachev arrived in Beijing on May 15, 1989, for the first Sino-Soviet summit in 30 years, more than a million Chinese marched to demand the resignation of Premier Deng Xiaoping. Similar demonstrations occurred in more than a dozen other cities. Western media flocked to the events, describing a Chinese counterpart to the Soviet *perestroika,* or political opening.

On June 3, however, Chinese troops closed the brief political opening. They marched on Tiananmen Square in Beijing, the center of the protest. Though casualty figures are uncertain, estimates of the deaths range up to 5,000, with as many as 10,000 injured and hundreds arrested. The newly hard-line leadership launched manhunts for the protest leaders, followed by trials and long jail sentences.

Most of the industrialized countries, including the United States, reacted to the crackdown by imposing trade and diplomatic sanctions on Beijing. Many Western observers feared a resurgence of hard-line communism in the wake of Tiananmen — if not civil war. But the reality was somewhat more complex. While the government did, indeed, clamp down on political expression, it continued on its course of economic reforms. In fact, over the past two years, the Chinese government has taken several additional steps toward a market economy, from forming crude stock markets in early 1991 to encouraging people to buy their formerly "rented" homes.

Reforms Energize Chinese Economy

China's economy has responded vigorously to the reforms, growing by as much as 6 percent a year. Un-fortunately for the United States, the boom is largely based on a growing trade surplus with the U.S. As a matter of fact, China has become the United States' second-largest surplus-trade partner, behind Japan. *(See graph, p. 124.)* And many in Congress blamed the gap on unfair trade practices by China, including use of prison labor for manufacturing exports.

In earlier times, the United States might have overlooked such trade disputes — and perhaps even the political oppression and human rights violations that followed Tiananmen Square. But the recession made many in Congress less flexible.

Despite these problems, President Bush decided to patch things up with the Chinese. Within hours of the lifting of martial law in Beijing on Jan. 10, 1990, for example, the United States lifted its opposition to loans to China from the World Bank. And a bare six months after the massacre at Tiananmen Square, Bush waived a congressional ban on loans to U.S. companies doing business with China, at the same time approving the sale of three communications satellites to China. Bush also used veto threats to prevent Congress from passing economic sanctions in late 1990, and in May 1991 he overrode heavy congressional opposition to renewing China's most-favored-nation trade status.

"We want to promote positive change in the world through the force of our example, not simply profess our purity," Bush said in a commencement address at Yale University on May 27, 1991. "We want to advance the cause of freedom, not just snub nations that aren't yet wholly free."

Despite criticism from Congress, Bush met with Chinese Prime Minister Li Peng at the United Nations on Jan. 31, 1992 — their first meeting since the 1989 crackdown at Tiananmen Square.

South Korea's Dilemma

South Korea has historically been a country caught between a rock and hard places. The rock is North Korea. The three hard places are China, the Soviet Union and Japan.

Occupied by Japan before and during World War II, South Korea at war's end was occupied by the Soviet Union in the North and U.S. forces in the South. The Soviets blocked Korean efforts at reunifying the country, and in 1948 the Democratic People's Republic of Korea (DPRK), or North Korea, was officially formed under Kim Il Sung, who still holds power. The South responded by forming the Republic of Korea, with Syngman Rhee as the elected president.

On June 25, 1950, North Korea, armed primarily by the Soviet Union, invaded the South. Backed by the United Nations Security Council, U.S. troops counterattacked and by the end of October had driven North Korea back almost to the Chinese border. At that point, China sent its troops across the Yalu River to support the North Koreans, eventually forcing a stalemate in the war with the country divided along its present border.

The conflict did have one beneficial side effect, particularly for South Korea and Japan: The dollars spent by the large U.S. military contingent that stayed behind helped to energize their economies — as did generous aid from America and preferential access to U.S. markets.

In the 40 years since the Korean War, South Korea has become one of the world's leading industrialized countries. It has also run a relatively healthy trade surplus with the United States in recent years, though it has proven more cooperative than Japan in adopting measures to reduce the gap.

But while South Korea has prospered, it has also faced an ongoing military threat from North Korea. The degree of militarization in North Korea can be hard for Americans to grasp. "North Korea still devotes between 15 percent and 20 percent of its meager GNP* to the military," writes political scientist Lawrence E. Grinter of the University of California at Santa Cruz. "Its approximately 840,000-man standing army is comprised of 13 percent of all North Korean males of military age (17 to 49) [including] 100,000 commandos, the largest commando force in the world.... By the mid-1980s, the DPRK was fielding over 2,600 tanks and 4,000 to 5,000 artillery guns and howitzers, perhaps three-fourths as many as the U.S. Army has worldwide."[9]

And the North is not all threat. It is, as South Korean and U.S. policymakers continually point out, unpredictable and capable of almost anything. In October 1983, for example, North Korean agents planted a bomb at welcoming ceremonies in Rangoon, Burma, in an attempt to assassinate then-President Chun Doo Hwan of South Korea. Chun was not there; his motorcade was delayed. But 21 people died, including four Cabinet ministers. In November 1987, North Korean agents took a far higher toll when they blew up a South Korean airliner, killing 115. Even more ominously, there is evidence that the North may be building a nuclear bomb, a longtime concern of the United States.

North Korea Loses Its Allies

But just as the ending of the Cold War has dramatically affected other countries in Asia, so, too, has North Korea faced fundamental changes, among them the defection of its two staunchest, and most generous, allies — the Soviet Union and China.

Even before the Soviet Union's breakup, it had cut its aid to North Korea and established ties with the South. A June 1990 meeting between Mikhail Gorbachev and South Korean President Roh Tae Woo in California resulted in $2.3 billion in loans for the Soviets, while the South Koreans walked away with a new sense of political legitimacy. The following September, the Soviet Union and South Korea established formal diplomatic relations.

The North has also watched as China began in the late 1980s to improve relations with South Korea. Indirect trade between the two countries, which had been a paltry $500 million in 1987, suddenly jumped to more than $3 billion in 1988. In October 1990, the two countries underscored the importance of their trade relationship by opening

South Korea	
Type of government:	Republic
Head of government:	President Roh Tae Woo
Population:	43,919,000 (1990 est.)
Area:	38,025 sq. miles (slightly larger than Indiana)
Capital:	Seoul
GNP:	$171 billion (1988)
Per capita income:	$2,180 (1986)
Literacy rate:	92%
Defense spending:	5.8% GNP (1987)

North Korea	
Type of government:	Communist state
Head of government:	President Kim Il-Sung
Population:	23,059,000 (1990 est.)
Area:	46,540 sq. miles (slightly smaller than Mississippi)
Capital:	Pyongyang
GNP:	$20 billion (1988)
Per capita income:	Not available
Literacy rate:	99%
Defense spending:	24% GNP (1988)

*By comparison, the U.S. spends between 6-7 percent of its GNP on the military.

Making Peace With Vietnam…

Renewing relations with Vietnam presents great opportunities for both the United States and Vietnam — and perhaps some risk for the U.S. One thing is certain: Because the war remains such a powerful memory for many Americans, it is among the most delicate issues in the region.

On the plus side for the United States, rapprochement would mean continuing Vietnamese cooperation with the recent peace treaty in Cambodia. Vietnam helped fashion the agreement, no doubt in hope the U.S. would lift its economic embargo. But Vietnam is still well-positioned to create trouble. According to one possible scenario, if conditions in Vietnam worsened or failed to improve, Vietnam might use the threat of aggression in Cambodia as leverage to obtain economic concessions from the United States.

Lifting the embargo would bring more tangible benefits to the United States, namely new business opportunities. Drawn by Vietnam's reputation for low wages and hard workers, and encouraged by new foreign investment laws that are among the most liberal in the region, companies from many other industrialized countries have begun investing in Vietnam.

According to the U.S.-Vietnam Trade Council, the top 10 foreign investors (as of October 1990) were France, Britain, Hong Kong, Australia, the Netherlands, Canada, Japan, the former Soviet Union, Taiwan and Sweden.

Oil is one of the biggest attractions in Vietnam. The country has large proven reserves, and estimates of potential reserves range from 1 billion to 10 billion barrels. Japan is buying about 90 percent of Vietnam's current output, and one of Japan's largest oil companies reportedly will sign a contract with Vietnam this month to develop a new oil field. Royal Dutch/Shell and British Petroleum also have exploration and production agreements.

U.S. firms — and oil companies in particular — are anxious to gain access to Vietnam before the best opportunities are grabbed up. "Japan will soon be Vietnam's No. 1 trading partner," said Virginia Foote, director of the Trade Council. "The Japanese are ahead of the pack." †

The gains that rapprochement could mean for Vietnam are even more substantial. With the collapse of the Soviet Union, Vietnam lost one of its largest aid donors, a damaging blow to its struggling economy. The unemployment rate is reportedly 20 percent, and inflation is a staggering 7 percent a month.

Even more urgently needed by Vietnam than trade and investment are loans from international banks — loans that have been blocked by the United States since the end of the Vietnam War. Without them, Vietnam will have trouble upgrading its basic infrastructure — roads, bridges, utilities — enough to continue attracting foreign companies.

Given such troubles, some observers say that before lifting the trade and aid embargo, the United States should insist on Vietnam fulfilling every condition laid out by the Bush administration last year. Or, they warn, Vietnam may never do so.

The one major condition that is unfulfilled, contends Ann Mills Griffiths, executive director of the National League of Families of American Prisoners and Missing in Southeast Asia, is accounting for missing American servicemen.

It's far from certain, however, that Vietnam is hiding much. Despite occasional reports of American prisoners still alive in Vietnam, few knowledgeable observers take

semi-diplomatic "trade bureaus" in each other's capitals. And, in November 1991, for the first time, a Chinese foreign minister met with a South Korean president in Seoul.

With both China and the Soviet Union's newly independent nations courting South Korea, the handwriting would appear to be on the wall for North Korea. The basic choices facing Kim Il-Sung are to hold to his past course and face increasing isolation and poverty, or open up to the outside world.

Given North Korea's unpredict-ability, analysts are unwilling to theorize about the future, but there are signs that the country may be moving toward the latter course.

In September 1990, North Korean officials held talks with representatives of Japan's ruling Liberal Democratic Party (LDP) and 10 Japanese government officials. In return for the LDP asking the Japanese government to apologize for its treatment of Korea during World War II and to pay compensation, the North in October released two Japanese merchant seamen who had been charged with spying.

Also, in early 1991 the State Department announced that North Korea had turned over the remains of five U.S. servicemen from the Korean War and offered to return more in the near future. More recently, and most promisingly — though many analysts remain distrustful of North Korea — the North signed a draft agreement with South Korea on Dec. 31, 1991, that commits both countries to forsaking nuclear weapons and allowing on-site inspections.

...Advantages for Everyone?

such reports seriously. In fact, according to H. Bruce Franklin, a professor of American studies at Rutgers University, of the more than 2,273 Americans once listed as missing, "Today only one man is still officially listed as either missing in action or a prisoner of war."

Franklin argues that the issue of missing servicemen has been kept alive solely for political reasons and that the number of bodies supposedly unaccounted for in Vietnam is relatively small. "For the Second World War, after which the United States was free to explore every battlefield, the 78,750 still unaccounted for represent 19.4 percent of the total 405,399 killed," Franklin writes. "For the Korean War, more than 15 percent of the dead are still unaccounted for. In contrast, the unaccounted for from the Vietnam War constitute less than 4 percent of the 58,152 killed." ††

However, Maj. Gen. Oleg Kalugin, a former top official of Soviet counterintelligence, reiterated before a Senate panel on Jan. 21 his assertion that Soviet agents had interrogated U.S. prisoners of war in Vietnam as late as 1978, nearly five years after the war ended.‡

Apart from the question of missing servicemen, some observers have argued that the United States should withhold concessions until Vietnam matches its economic reforms with political reforms.

"If we are to make peace with a former enemy," James Webb, a former secretary of the Navy, said last June, "and to bring the weight of our national strength to bear in a manner that will preserve the present government, it is our duty as a nation to demand specific guarantees from the communists that those who stood with us will have the same chance as every other Vietnamese to benefit from our new relations." ⫫

Actually, the Vietnamese government has somewhat improved its human rights record. At the end of 1991, according to the *Far Eastern Economic Review,* Vietnam released 16 of the remaining 106 prisoners in re-education camps and promised that the rest would be out by June of this year.⧻† Also released in recent months were four prominent political prisoners accused of disseminating anti-communist propaganda. The government also agreed to allow the International Red Cross to visit the only remaining re-education camp.

At the same time, however, Vietnam has shown no interest in permitting open political dissent, much less direct challenges to the party's leadership. Last November, for example, the government sentenced Dr. Nguyen Dan Que, Vietnam's first member of Amnesty International, to 20 years in prison for alleged subversive activities.

But others argue convincingly that the United States cannot afford to make democratic elections and high human-rights standards a prerequisite to improved relations. "The isolation of Vietnam has not served our purposes thus far," noted Sen. Frank H. Murkowski, R-Alaska. "The free flow of Western ideas, people and goods may." ⧻††

---

† Foote testified at a joint hearing of the House Subcommittee on International Economic Policy and Trade and the House Asian and Pacific Affairs Subcommittee, June 21, 1991.

†† Quoted in Franklin, Bruce H., "The POW/MIA Myth: How The White House and Hollywood Combines to Foster a National Fantasy," *The Atlantic,* December 1991, p. 47.

‡ *Congressional Quarterly Weekly Report,* Jan. 25, 1991, p. 181.

⫫ Webb testified at the June 21, 1991, hearing.

⧻† *Far Eastern Economic Review,* Jan. 9, 1992.

⧻†† Murkowski testified at the June 21, 1991, hearing.

Rebirth of Japan

The roots of today's ambiguous and increasingly contentious U.S.-Japan relationship can be clearly traced to three Truman administration policy decisions following World War II:

■ Including a clause in Japan's post-war Constitution, written under the direction of the occupying Americans, forbidding Japan's use of force except in defense of the Japanese islands. This meant that the United States would provide for Japan's security, thus giving the U.S. key bases in the North Pacific while freeing Japan's economy from maintaining a large military force.*

■ Leaving the bureaucracy of Japan's government-industrial complex largely intact to aid in reconstruction. The darkening Cold War with the Soviet Union and the closeness of Communist China convinced U.S. policymakers that aiding Japan's recovery

---

*After the war, the Allies permitted Japan to maintain a small self-defense force.

---

was essential. Occupation authorities did break up the huge *zaibatsu* — large groups of companies owned by a small number of families — that were blamed in part for Japan's role in the war. But with the same industrial leaders and government bureaucrats left in place, the breakup was not thorough enough to prevent the return of *zaibatsu* as soon as the occupation ended in 1951.

■ Giving Japan and a few other Asian countries virtually free access to U.S. markets, without demanding the same right in return. Japan quickly took full advantage of the situation. In 1949, the country erected strong tariff and quota barriers — even as the world's industrial powers were negotiating to dismantle tariffs and quotas. The same year, Japan's parliament, the Diet, passed a foreign-trade control law that required all imports to have government licenses.

The effect of these new policies on U.S. companies doing business in Japan was dramatic. In 1951, about half of all cars sold in Japan were American-made. By 1955, the entire foreign share of Japan's auto sales was 8 percent; it had fallen to just 0.4 percent by 1959.

As long as the United States was running overall trade surpluses, U.S. administrations accepted the Japanese trade gap as the price for its security arrangements with Japan. But when the United States started to show overall trade deficits in the mid-1970s, concern began to grow. By 1987, the U.S. deficit had mushroomed to $174 billion from about $35 billion in 1980 — making it clear to Congress and the White House that action was necessary. Japan, it was noted, accounted for $56 billion of that increase all by itself.

U.S. Tries to Crack Japanese Markets

In the early 1980s, the United States began a decade of intense — and largely fruitless — trade negotiations with Japan. Failing to achieve real opening of Japan's markets, the Reagan administration adopted a strategy of negotiating for greater market access in specified sectors — a "laundry-list strategy," in the words of one analyst. Deals were reached on semiconductors, telecommunications equipment and autos.

When George Bush moved into the White House in 1989, the United States was still running an annual trade deficit with Japan of nearly $52 billion, down only about $4 billion from the high point of 1987. President Bush, an even stronger advocate of free trade than Ronald Reagan, launched a new round of talks with Japan. The focus was on "structural impediments" to bilateral trade — government regulations, business practices, lax antitrust laws and so forth.

The effectiveness of those efforts can perhaps best be measured by the stubbornness of Japan's trade surpluses. While South Korea's surplus with the United States was cut by more than half from 1987 to 1991, for example, Japan's has dropped by only about 25 percent during the same period.

The souring of economic relations between the United States and Japan has been accompanied by increasing stress on their security relationship. Noting that U.S. protection was saving Japan billions on defense, many in Congress have called for Japan to assume a larger share of the burden.

As early as 1981, for example, Sen. Jesse Helms, R-N.C., proposed an amendment — quickly tabled — to renegotiate the U.S.-Japan security treaty and make it reciprocal. It was followed quickly in the House by a bill introduced by Rep. Stephen L. Neal, D-N.C., calling for Japan to pay a "security tax" of 2 percent of the country's GNP. Later in 1981, 68 congressmen signed a letter urging Japan to give up on the 1 percent cap the government had placed on defense expenditures in 1976.

Japan	
Type of government:	Parliamentary democracy
Head of government:	Prime Minister Kiichi Miyazawa
Population:	123,778,000 (1990 est.)
Area:	145,856 sq. miles (slightly smaller than California)
Capital:	Tokyo
GNP:	$1.8 trillion (1989)
Per capita income:	$15,030 (1989)
Literacy rate:	99%
Defense spending:	1% GNP (1987)

Defense Spending

Pressure from the White House met with some success in May 1981, when Reagan pressed visiting Japanese Prime Minister Zenko Suzuki to increase defense spending.

Though the country's defense outlays have yet to reach 2 percent of GNP — compared to the roughly 3 percent spent by NATO allies and the 5-6 percent spent by the United States — actual outlays have been about $30 billion for the past several years because of the immense growth of Japan's GNP. That makes Japan the world's third-biggest spender on defense, behind only the United States and the former Soviet Union.

But though the U.S. government pressed Japan throughout the 1980s to increase its defense capabilities, under President Bush there has been a clear change in policy. One major reason for the change: The perceived receding of the Soviet threat has given other states reservations about Japanese rearmament.

As a result, the United States has pressed Japan to pick up more of the cost for stationing U.S. forces in Japan. At the end of the 1980s, Japan was already paying about 40 percent of the $7.5 billion annual tab. But that wasn't enough for many in Congress. In 1989, for example, Rep. Patricia Schroeder, D-Colo., recommended a "defense protection fee" on all Japanese imports, to make the connection between our protection and their prosperity as explicit as possible.

In December 1990, Japan tried to placate the United States by agreeing to increase its share of defense costs to about 50 percent of the total. But Japan angered many Americans by refusing to send personnel to aid the allies during the Persian Gulf War — even though Japan depends heavily on gulf oil. Even more upsetting was Japan's reluctance to help fund the war. Only after much wrangling did the Japanese Diet approve $13 billion for the effort. ∎

CURRENT SITUATION

End of the Cold War

If the Cold War was the glue that held together the American alliance in the Pacific, its demise means the loosening of that alliance, at least for now. Without the threat of the Soviet Union, economic interests that were submerged in the interest of maintaining an alliance are surfacing, as are new trade conflicts — and not only between Japan and the United States. The end of the Cold War is also causing many countries in the region to rethink their security needs.

Unsettling as the changes in East Asia may be, the current instability carries at least as much opportunity as it does risk. Most analysts — American and Asian alike — agree that the United States must maintain a significant military presence in Asia for some time to come. The disappearance of the Soviet threat has left something of a power vacuum, and until some new security arrangement is developed most countries in East Asia are wary of suggestions that the United States might pull out.

"Our presence there now in the western Pacific is reassuring to an awful lot of people in that part of the world," Defense Secretary Cheney said last November. "If we were to withdraw, there would be pressures on other governments to try to fill that vacuum."[10]

Many fear that Japan might be the one to try. "Wartime antagonisms do still run high in some of these countries," writes *New York Times* reporter David Sanger, "especially in places like Singapore, where 130,000 Chinese were killed as Japanese forces swept down the Malay Peninsula and captured the city in the winter of 1941-42. In Korea, a Japanese colony for 40 years and today Japan's biggest Asian manufacturing rival, enmity for the Japanese often bobbles to the surface in conversations, especially when the subject turns to how Japan has cut South Korea off from new

> Without the threat of the Soviet Union, economic interests that were submerged in the interest of maintaining the Pacific alliance are surfacing, as are new trade conflicts.

Japanese-developed technology."[11]

The fear is not so much that Japan would again invade its neighbors, says Thomas McNaugher of the Brookings Institution. "The real problem is that if Japan were to move to a much more independent strategic position, everybody's defense budgets would go up to hedge," he explains. "And everybody would become more suspicious and worried."

New Strategic Concerns

But Japan is not the only reason for a U.S. military presence in the region. Both the United States and Japan worry about North Korea, which has by some estimates the world's fifth-largest conventional army, making it quite capable of causing trouble even if it keeps its promise to forsake nuclear weapons.

Ironically, if North Korea's recent overtures to the South turn out to be sincere and the two countries reunite, a regional arms race could result. "The real concern [for Japan] is a unified Korea that has this huge army and is increasingly an economic competitor," says McNaugher. "They, in fact, have more resources than Japan. The resources are mostly in the North, and most of the industry is in the South. If you put that together, that tweaks the Japanese concern on the economic side."

Some strategists see other potential security problems. "We may well have a problem with China someday," says Thomas Robinson of the American Enterprise Institute. "And most important, [we need to maintain a strong presence] for purposes of leading Asia in construction of a new Asian security system. We're the only ones that can do that, and we have to have the wherewithal to do that in terms of actual forces. Without us, the situation could well fall apart."

While there is general agreement that the United States should remain in the Pacific, a host of tactical problems remains. The major one is repositioning American air and naval forces no longer welcome in the Philippines.

In fact, it was recently announced that part of the force will move to Singapore, though details have yet to be worked out. Negotiations are also under way with Malaysia and Thailand for access to suitable ports. And there have even been some suggestions from Vietnam about using the facilities at Cam Rahn Bay, built by the United States during the Vietnam War.

A potentially greater problem than finding new bases in the region may be pressure in Congress for cuts in U.S. forces overseas. "Every dollar that we spend on a troop in Japan — that is not spent on educating our children, on building our infrastructure or improving the health of our citizens or improving the kind of factories that we have — is one dollar lost in our economic battle to stay No. 1," Rep. Charles E. Schumer (D-N.Y.) told the House last year.[12]

In light of the almost certain increase in pressure for further defense budget cuts, those in Congress who want to maintain forces in Asia are pushing for Asian countries, especially Japan, to pay a larger share of the costs. Japan and South Korea agreed recently to increase their payments for the cost of maintaining U.S. troops, but many see the contributions as still insufficient. Though Japan agreed in late 1990 to increase its share of the $7.5 billion annual cost from 40 to 50 percent, that fell far short of a congressional demand in a joint resolution that Japan pay the entire bill or American troops would be withdrawn.

Trade Deficits

The toughest issue for U.S. policymakers to deal with in East Asia is American trade deficits. And there is no question that Japan is the key country to deal with — and the most difficult.[13] Japan's surpluses, which reached $56 billion in 1987 before falling to $41 billion in 1990, are now on the rise again. And despite years and years of pestering from the United States to open its markets, the most important sectors* are still hard for foreigners — not just Americans — to crack.

The fact is that while some of Japan's trade barriers are blatant — such as tax policies and statutes governing, say, insurance companies —

_____

*Americans complain that the Japanese markets for such key products as cars, financial services (including insurance) and agricultural products are largely closed.

the most serious and wide-ranging barriers are more subtle. Many of Japan's markets are closed simply because Japanese companies like doing business with each other, and because Japanese consumers like doing business with Japanese companies. That is the type of behavior that, though it may violate the spirit of free trade, is very difficult to legislate against.

That's why many trade analysts, including Clyde Prestowitz, believe the only way the United States can deal with the Japanese is by market-sharing agreements, under which Japan grants the United States a set share of a given market.

While other trade experts question the need for market-sharing pacts, there seems to be general agreement that President Bush's recent trip to Japan was the wrong approach. Advocates of free trade were discouraged to find that none of the measures agreed to by Japan would actually drop trade barriers. Instead, Japan simply agreed to increase U.S. sales by a specified amount. And, except in the one rather narrow category of computer purchases by the Japanese government, the market-sharing deals that were cut didn't satisfy the American business executives accompanying Bush.

Meanwhile, the United States has other trade problems in the region. Of the 16 countries with the largest U.S. trade surpluses in 1990, seven are from East Asia, including the top three: Japan, China and Taiwan.

China is a particular problem. The United States and China narrowly averted a trade war in January over alleged Chinese pirating of U.S. computer software, music and pharmaceuticals. U.S. sanctions, which China promised to retaliate against if imposed, were avoided at the last minute when China agreed to adopt international standards for protecting such intellectual property.

Even if China follows through on that commitment, other disputes wait in the wings. U.S. companies have charged China with dumping textiles on the U.S. market. And last October, the Commerce Department began an investigation into China's barriers to imports.

Finally, Congress will have to vote on renewing China's most-favored-nation (MFN) trade status later this year. The Bush administration barely won last year's approval of MFN status for China, and only after being warned by Congress that renewal would hinge on a "significant improvement" in China's human rights and trade policies.

Over the past few months, however, reports of China's use of prison labor to manufacture goods for export have attracted increasing criticism from many in Congress, who have called for economic sanctions against China. Even if the Bush administration avoids sanctions, it can expect a harder time winning a vote on MFN status unless conditions change soon in China. ∎

_____

OUTLOOK

The U.S. and Japan

Two reliable generalizations can be made about East Asia: One, it is a region in flux, and two, analysts are reluctant to go out on a limb as to

where the volatile region is headed. They are, however, quick to point to emerging trends that, if they are extended, could be particularly worrisome.

The most disturbing possibility — from both a strategic and a trade standpoint — would be a rupture in the U.S.-Japan relationship. And ana-

Continued on p. 138

At Issue:

Does the U.S. auto industry deserve protection from Japanese imports?

LEE A. IACOCCA

Chairman, Chrysler Corp.
FROM *THE DETROIT FREE PRESS,* JUNE 17, 1991.

*i*t looked for a while as if we'd finally solved the mystery of the Bermuda Triangle, but it's still with us. And so is an even bigger mystery that takes place somewhere in the middle of the Pacific Ocean.

Picture two ships, both loaded with trucks, one sailing west from America to Japan, and the other heading this way. The one going west is loaded with Jeep Cherokees, and the one coming this way is carrying Toyota minivans. The Cherokee carries a manufacturer's suggested retail price in the United States of $22,300. The Toyota minivan has almost the identical price in its home market of Japan — $22,200.

Then something strange happens. Somehow as these two ships pass in the night, the price tags on all the American trucks go up and those from Japan all go down.

For example, that $22,300 Cherokee gets marked up $12,000 to $34,400 while the price tag on the Japanese minivan goes down $7,000 to $15,200. The two trucks that started their boat rides at almost exactly the same price are $19,200 apart by the time one lands in Long Beach, Calif., and the other one hits the docks at Yokohama, Japan.

The price of the Cherokee goes up because of Japanese non-tariff trade barriers designed to protect that market from foreign competition, and the price of the Toyota goes down because they're being illegally "dumped" in this market to grab market share from American auto companies.

When a product is sold in this country for less than it costs to make or less than consumers in the home market pay for it, that's dumping. And it's against the law. It's illegal because common sense tells you that the foreign producer isn't doing that because he's got a soft spot in his heart for the American consumer. He wants to control the market so one day he can dictate prices....

That's why General Motors, Ford and Chrysler filed a formal complaint with the federal government [last June] accusing Japanese companies of dumping minivans into the American market. The dumping action is long overdue. You can bet that the hordes of Japanese lobbyists will be working overtime to defeat it. But American taxpayers, American auto companies and their workers, and ultimately American consumers are all at risk when foreign companies can manipulate the American market the way Japan has done for years.

Maybe this will be the beginning of the end. Maybe we can start taking some of the mystery out of our auto trade with Japan and start putting some fairness in.

JAMES BOVARD

Associate Policy Analyst, Cato Institute
FROM *THE NEW YORK TIMES,* JAN. 7, 1992.

*w*hen the Japanese don't buy sufficient numbers of relatively low-quality American cars, the U.S. government responds by making it more difficult for American citizens to buy relatively high-quality Japanese cars. Rep. Richard Gephardt, D-Mo., introduced legislation [last December] to penalize Japan for its trade deficit with the United States. Michigan congressmen are licking their chops over the prospect of new restrictions on Japanese auto imports.

The assault on these imports is also being fueled by the Commerce Department's recent preliminary finding that Toyota and Mazda have been selling their minivans at unfairly low prices, "dumping" them in the United States.

Sen. Donald Riegle, D-Mich., declared that the minivan case "is an illustration of the systematic pattern of trade cheating by Japan that must be stopped."

But the findings prove only the absurdity and unfairness of the U.S. dumping law. The Commerce Department found Toyota guilty of selling its minivans for roughly 1 percent less than the department approved.... Mazda was found guilty of a 7.19 percent dumping margin largely because the government arbitrarily compared the price of 470 vans sold under special circumstances in Japan with the price of 30,000 vans sold by Mazda dealers in the U.S.

The Japanese were not selling their minivans at a loss or for less than they sold for in Japan. If American companies had done what the Japanese companies did, they would never have been penalized. The dumping laws make a mockery of U.S. demands for a level playing field.

Japanese auto exports to the United States have been restricted by quotas since 1981, when President Ronald Reagan pressured the Japanese into reducing their exports. A 1987 International Monetary Fund study estimated that the subsequent artificial shortage of cars for sale in the U.S. cost American consumers $17 billion between 1981 and 1984, resulting in an average increase of $1,650 for new car prices (domestic and import) in 1984....

The Japanese government last month reportedly ordered a further reduction in the number of cars exported to the United States. Tokyo has successfully pressured companies to buy more American auto parts, even if those parts are of lower quality.

The U.S. auto industry is not a victim of unfair play but rather of its own incompetence. If 10 years of protection did not close the U.S.-Japan auto quality gap, further protection will simply be extortion of American consumers.

U.S. Complaints About Japanese Trade Barriers

Though the United States has whittled down its trade deficits with many countries over the past 10 years, the trade gap with Japan has stubbornly remained above $40 billion a year. Many in the U.S. charge that Japan's persistent surpluses are a result of unfair trade practices. In fact, Japan's overt trade barriers — tariffs, quotas and other government-imposed policies — are only slightly higher than those in the U.S. But many claim the Japanese gain trade advantages by using many more subtle methods, including failure to enforce patent laws and lax oversight of possible antitrust violations.

Among the 17 pages of complaints cited in the 1991 U.S. Trade Representative's report on foreign trade barriers — and Japan has the longest entry of any country in the report — are the following:

- **High tariffs on several categories of manufactured products, including petrochemicals, aluminum products and paper.**

- **High tariffs on certain agricultural products, including beef, fruit juices, sugar, oranges and forest products.**

- **Restrictions, implemented through a tariff/quota system, on foreign leather goods.**

- **Government subsidies to Japanese lumber companies.**

- **Collusive behavior in Japan's paper industry.**

- **A total prohibition on imports of foreign rice.**

- **Import quotas on fish products.**

- **Lack of adequate intellectual property protection, especially protection for U.S.-owned patents.**

- **Japan's copyright protection for sound recordings extends for only 30 years, compared with 40 years in the United States.**

- **Registering trademarks takes 4 years in Japan compared to 13 months in the United States, and there is no penalty for infringement during those 4 years.**

- **Inadequate foreign access to Japan's engineering and construction markets.**

- **Licensing requirements hinder the efforts of foreign insurance companies to compete in Japan.**

- **Unwarranted regulation of foreign investments in several sectors, including aircraft, agriculture, oil, mining, leather and tobacco.**

- **Restricted access of U.S. auto companies to Japanese distributors.**

- **Restricted access of foreign auto-parts makers to Japanese markets.**

- **Restricted access of U.S. computer makers to Japanese government.**

Source: Office of the U.S. Trade Representative, 1991 National Trade Estimate Report on Foreign Trade Barriers, *March 1991*

Continued from p. 136

lysts are generally agreed that if such a rupture were to occur, it would begin with a dispute over trade issues.

The most likely "doomsday" scenario begins with Japan failing to open its markets, or at least to deliver greater market share to foreigners. The United States and other countries then respond with stronger protectionist measures, beginning a full trade war. Nervous about Japan's military intentions, as well as those of their neighbors, area countries launch an arms race.

In fact, with the perception of a lessened U.S. commitment to the region, arms sales have been on the rise, particularly in Southeast Asia. What's more, protectionist legislation is introduced every year in Congress, and during a presidential campaign year it may be hard to resist. And, as the world saw in the 1920s, protectionist measures tend to beget more protectionist measures, leading to a breakdown of the international trading system.

To some extent, many analysts already see a partial breakdown in the deadlock over the current round of talks on the General Agreement on Tariffs and Trade (GATT), the international pact that governs trade. Another sign is the gradual emergence of regional trading blocs.

Regional Trade Blocs

"During the past two years," *Forbes* reporter Edwin A. Finn Jr. wrote in 1989, "the broad outlines of these blocs have started to emerge.... The trend is most pronounced with Europe, where regional integration is most advanced. Inside the European Community (EC), trade jumped nearly 15 percent since 1985, while EC trade with non-member countries actually fell by an estimated 10 percent."[14]

The trend has continued with the establishment of a free-trade pact between the United States and Canada in 1988, and current negotiations to add Mexico to the group, which would create an immense North American trade bloc.[15]

Many American policy-makers are concerned that a similar, and potentially more ominous, bloc may be forming in Asia. As Finn notes, Japan has already "virtually recolonized Asia, building factories throughout the region."[16]

Some analysts think that the United States may not fully appreciate the risks of increasing this fragmentation into trading blocs, especially as far as Asia is concerned. "In the United States," warn Ayako Doi and Kim Willenson, editor and publisher of *Japan Digest,* "the issue is still largely how to get Japan to play by the economic rules that govern the rest of the industrial world. In Japan, the thoughts of opinion leaders have turned in a startlingly different direction: There is now open talk of re-creating *Dai Toa Kyoei-ken* (the Greater East Asia Co-Prosperity Sphere), a phrase once used to justify Japan's 'anti-colonial' assault on Asia."[17]

Asia specialist James Clad agrees that Japan's growing economic influence could have unwanted political effects. "I can't help but see the kind of nascent possibilities for political influence that are there — given the tremendous preponderance of Japanese influence in Southeast Asia — not being translated more and more into more overt forms of political pressure," he says.

Many states in the region would echo the sentiments in a recent editorial in the respected British magazine *The Economist:* "Only America can ensure that Japan is not tempted, because of Western neglect and hauteur, to build an economic and perhaps military zone of its own in Asia." The U.S.-Japan partnership, the editorial argued, is "indispensable for the stability of Asia and the Pacific. A strong Japan linked to the United States is something Asia can welcome. A strong Japan severed from America would be intolerable to Asians and Russians alike."[18]

But while Japan may be the most important country to deal with in Asia now, some analysts warn that China will inevitably become an increasingly important player in the near future. "If Japan is the strategic problem for the next 10 years, probably China is the next question," says Thomas McNaugher, who advocates planning for China's emergence now rather than later. "As long as the U.S. and Japan agree on China," he says, "China will remain more or less concerned about its own internal development."

Thomas Robinson of the American Enterprise Institute agrees. "Now we have ad hoc agreements that are left over from the Cold War. In the long run I think we ought to be building with all the Asian countries but particularly with the major powers — China, Japan and Russia, and possibly with India — a system of Asian security."

As for China, Robinson says, "If we and the Japanese stick together, and we and the Russians move as we are doing to reconcile our differences and draw down our forces and cooperate, that makes three already. The Chinese don't want to stay outside. I think they'll come in." ∎

Notes

1 James A. Baker III, "America in Asia: Emerging Architecture for a Pacific Community, *Foreign Affairs,* winter, 1991-92, p. 1.

2 Testimony at a joint hearing before the Subcommittee on International Economic Policy and Trade and the Subcommittee on Asian and Pacific Affairs of the House Foreign Affairs Committee, June 21, 1991.

3 For background, see "Should the U.S. Reduce Its Pacific Forces?" *Editorial Research Reports,* April 20, 1990, pp. 221-236.

4 Writing in *The New York Times,* Dec. 28, 1991.

5 Quoted in Stanley Karnow, *Vietnam: A History* (1983), p. 19.

6 *Far Eastern Economic Review,* May 26, 1988.

7 Nancy Bernkopf Tucker, "China and America: 1941-1991," *Foreign Affairs,* winter 1991/92, p. 75.

8 *Ibid.*

9 Lawrence E. Grinter, "Policy of the United States Toward East Asia: Tough Adjustments," in *Security, Strategy and Policy Responses in the Pacific Rim,* edited by Young Whan Kihl and Lawrence E. Grinter (1989), p. 38.

10 Quoted in *The Washington Post,* Nov. 23, 1991.

11 *The New York Times,* Dec. 5, 1991.

12 Quoted in *Congressional Quarterly Weekly Report,* May 25, 1991, p. 1385.

13 For background, see "The U.S. and Japan," *The CQ Researcher,* May 31, 1991, pp. 325-348.

14 Edwin A. Finn Jr., "Sons of Smoot-Hawley," *Forbes,* Feb. 6, 1989, p. 38.

15 For background see "North America Trade Pact: A Good Idea?" *Editorial Research Reports,* Dec. 8, 1989, pp. 682-696; and "Mexico's Emergence," *The CQ Researcher,* July 19, 1991, pp. 489-512.

16 Finn, *op. cit.*

17 Doi and Willenson were quoted in *The Washington Post,* Aug. 11, 1991.

18 *The Economist,* Feb. 24, 1990, p. 11.

Patrick G. Marshall is a free-lance writer in the Washington, D.C., area and managing editor of the National Security Syndicate, *which supplies opinion-page articles to newspapers.*

Bibliography

Selected Sources Used

Books

Besher, Alexander, *The Pacific Rim Almanac*, Harper-Perrenial, 1991.

A fascinating compendium of information on countries of the Pacific Rim, this 824-page tome offers a grab bag of factoids, reprinted articles and a wealth of statistical information. The only real shortcoming: the book frequently fails to cite the source of statistical data.

Clad, James, *Behind the Myth: Business, Money and Power in Southeast Asia*, Grafton, 1989.

Written by a longtime correspondent for the *Far Eastern Economic Review,* this book fills a major gap in the literature on business and politics in Southeast Asia. Clad turns a journalist's eye on the booming opportunities and pitfalls of ventures in such underreported places as Malaysia, Thailand and Indonesia.

Johnson, Chalmers; Tyson, Laura D'Andrea; and Zysman, John, eds., *Politics and Productivity: How Japan's Development Strategy Works*, Ballinger, 1989.

This book offers sophisticated analyses of Japan's industrial policy and what it implies for the United States. The authors argue that U.S. may well have to adopt a different form of capitalism, one directed at fostering industrial growth.

Karnow, Stanley, *Vietnam: A History*, Viking, 1983.

Arguably the best single-volume history of the Vietnam War, this detailed, credible account reads like a novel.

Kotkin, Joel, and Yoriko Kishimoto, *The Third Century: America's Resurgence in the Asian Era*, Crown, 1988.

Not everyone thinks the United States is losing the battle with Japan. Kotkin and Kishimoto argue that Japanese industrial policy discourages innovation and that the Japanese economy is already losing steam. They warn that the United States should not change its economy to compete with Japan.

Lincoln, Edward J., *Japan's Unequal Trade*, Brookings, 1990.

As this book demonstrates, the economists have begun to move beyond the anecdotal in discussing Japan's trade practices, now that an increasing amount of data is available. Lincoln reviews the arguments on both sides and comes to the conclusion that Japan's trade practices are, indeed, unfair but that the United States should not abandon its own commitment to free trade in order to counter Japan.

Prestowitz, Clyde V., *Trading Places: How We Allowed Japan to Take the Lead*, Basic Books, 1988.

When it first appeared, this book attracted a lot of attention because it was the most convincing argument to date that the Japanese systematically practiced unfair trading practices. Today, most of Prestowitz's arguments are almost taken for granted.

Articles

Franklin, Bruce H., "The POW/MIA Myth: How the White House and Hollywood Combined to Foster A National Fantasy," *The Atlantic,* December 1991.

Franklin fairly well demolishes the arguments of those who claim that American prisoners of war are still being held in Southeast Asia. But more important, the article describes how certain parties twisted the POW issue for their own interests, with the American public being the dupes.

Ito, Kan, "Trans-Pacific Anger," *Foreign Policy,* spring 1990.

Ito, a Japanese journalist, says U.S. policy-makers had better wake up to the fact that Japan can no longer be treated as a dependent vassal state. The only way the U.S.-Japan relationship can be maintained, Ito argues, is if the United States willingly gives Japan a larger strategic role.

Tucker, Nancy Bernkopf, "China and America: 1941-1991," *Foreign Affairs,* winter 1991/92.

Tucker does a very creditable job of summarizing U.S.-Chinese relations since World War II. She makes no startling arguments and provides no fresh insights, but for a way to get up to speed quickly on the basics, this is an excellent place to start.

Van Wolferen, Karel, "The Japan Problem Revisited," *Foreign Affairs,* fall 1990.

Wolferen is convinced that Japanese policy-makers "are simply not ready to discuss with the outside world how their economy and informal power system interact." Accordingly, the United States will have to apply more pressure than it has in the past to achieve change in Japan. If both countries don't deal with the situation maturely, Wolferen says, it could mean the end of the international trading system.

The Next Step

Additional Articles from Current Periodicals from EBSCO Publishing's Database

Asia

"Feeling wind from the west," *The Economist,* **Aug. 24, 1991, p. 31.**

Examines how the consequences of the attempted coup in the Soviet Union could be bigger for Asia — especially Communist Asia — than those elsewhere. Asian reaction to the attempting ousting of Soviet President Mikhail Gorbachev; impact of the Soviet reforms on the communist trio of China, Vietnam and North Korea; strategy taken by China's Deng Xiaoping; details; outlook.

Labate, J., "Snapshot of the Pac Rim," *Fortune,* **Oct. 7, 1991, p. 128.**

Presents a chart for each of 11 Pacific Rim countries, whose economies entered a new phase of double-digit growth during the past decade. Includes gross national product, population, trade balance, inflation rate, stock market capitalization and foreign access to stock market.

Lee, D., "Asia, the next era of growth," *Business Week,* **Nov. 11, 1991, p. 56.**

Explores how Asian economies will flourish as commerce triumphs over ideology. Asia's map is quietly realigning in ways as significant as Europe's; Japan's expansion of its economic, diplomatic, and perhaps even military mandate throughout the region; shock waves as the U.S. redefines its role in the region; President Bush's upcoming Asian visit; some Asian anti-American rhetoric; can Asians achieve the standard of industrialization set by the West and Japan; Asian desire.

Balance of trade

"Gist: U.S.-Japan trade," *Dispatch,* **Aug. 5, 1991, p. 567.**

Focuses on trade between the United States and Japan, the world's two largest economies, with a combined gross national product estimated at $8.5 trillion in 1990, almost 40 percent of the world GNP. Macroeconomic factors; structural factors; market access. INSET: U.S. policy.

Javetski, B. and T. Aritake, "Why Washington likes its dollar weak," *Business Week,* **Oct. 21, 1991, p. 31.**

Explores the fact that a stronger Japanese yen will probably reverse the growing trade deficit. Annual meeting of the International Monetary Fund and World Bank; U.S. currency's plunge is beneficial to the economy — and politically helpful to the Bush administration; Wall Streeters are bullish on the greenback longer-term; optimism of bounce back of the dollar by analysts; the yen's pressure on the dollar; hope that a weaker dollar will defuse trade tension.

Books & reading

Myint, H., "Reviews," *Economic Development & Cultural Change,* **October 1991, p. 233.**

Reviews the book "Global Adjustment and the Future of Asia-Pacific Economy: Papers and Proceedings of the Conference on Global Adjustment and the Future of Asian-Pacific Economy Held on May 11-13, 1988 in Tokyo," edited by Miyohei Shinohara and Fu-Chen Lo.

China

"A biggish stick," *The Economist,* **Oct. 19, 1991, p. 26.**

Considers American trade policy regarding China. Allegations that Chinese prisons are really factories; division over Chinese trade policy within the administration of President Bush; actions of Carla A. Hills, the U.S. trade representative.

"Recent action in the Congress," *Congressional Digest,* **October 1991, p. 231.**

Presents summaries of recent action in Congress concerning U.S. trade relations with China. Background to the actions; introduction of S. 1367 by Sen. George J. Mitchell, D-Maine, on June 25, 1991; introduction of HR 2211 by Rep. Nancy Pelosi, D-Calif., on May 2, 1991; action on the House floor; action on the Senate floor; details.

"United States-China Act of 1991," *Congressional Digest,* **October 1991, p. 225.**

Discusses how the crackdown by the Chinese government on the student uprising in Tiananmen Square in June 1989 altered American attitudes toward China's leaders and changed China's trade status into a moral, rather than simply an economic, question. The legislation now under consideration places stringent conditions relating to human rights and fair trading practices on the renewal of China's most-favored-nation (MFN) status. Supporters; opposers; President Bush's intentions to veto.

Buckley, W. F. Jr., "Most unfavored nation," *National Review,* **June 24, 1991, p. 54.**

Editorial. Contemplates President Bush's recommendation to continue to grant most-favored-nation trade status to China. Why both the U.S. and China appear to benefit from the policy; historical background of the MFN status; pros and cons of linking human rights to trade.

Cloud, D.S., "China MFN vote falls short of veto-proof margin," *Congressional Quarterly Weekly Report,* **July 27, 1991, p. 2053.**

Details how Senate Majority Leader George J. Mitchell's, D-Maine, summer-long drive to wrest control of China policy from President George Bush fell 12 votes short of overriding a veto. White House opposes anything but unconditional renewal of most-favored-nation (MFN) trade status for China; Congress wanted to punish China for several things; legislation stalled in the Senate; Mitchell's bill; the opposition. INSETS: George vs. George, by C. Alston; MFN datelines.

Cloud, D.S., "GOP loyalty to Bush may be key in fight over China status," *Congressional Quarterly Weekly Report,* **June 29, 1991, p. 1737.**

Examines the debate ensuing in Congress over whether or not to renew China's most-favored-nation (MFN) trade status, with President Bush pushing for unconditional renewal while several committees are demanding some sweeping changes first. Retaliation for Tiananmen Square massacre; Senate Majority Leader George J. Mitchell's legislation; signs of trouble; some of the conditions. INSETS: Decision on China's MFN trade status no easy call for Washington senators; Pelosi vs. Mitchell.

Nelan, B.W., J.A. FlorCruz, et al., "Getting China wrong," *Time,* **June 10, 1991, p. 35.**

Suggests Washington is getting it wrong about China, a police state controlled by a Communist Party dictatorship and dedicated to socialist central planning with a few market mechanisms. Putting China in a special category; overestimation of China's importance; no great military or economic power; movement toward a more open society.

Worthy, F.S. and Langan, P.A., "Making it in China," *Fortune,* **June 17, 1991, p. 103.**

Describes what the loss of their most-favored-nation status would mean for China and its exports. President Bush's May 1991 announcement that he would renew China's status triggered a sharp response from Senate Democrats who had been wanting to punish China since the Tiananmen Square massacre two years ago. Outlook if China were to be stripped of its most-favored-nation status; who MFN status is given to and why.

"Go east, American business — to Asia," *Business Week,* **Nov. 11, 1991, p. 190.**

Editorial. States that Americans need to pay more attention to booming East Asia. The U.S. is confronted by the need for a revolutionary shift in priorities; preoccupation with Europe; the risk of being left behind economically; U.S. must continue to use its bargaining leverage; a prime

market for East Asia's products; industrial prowess seems certain to become the basis for political as well as economic influence.

Krugman, P.R., "America's reduced role," *U.S. News & World Report,* **Sept. 30, 1991, p. 75.**

Reports that America's ability to influence world trade negotiations has declined because of its diminished role in the world economy. Why Japan is still viewed suspiciously by its trade partners; the current disarray in the world marketplace has begun to stimulate regional trade activity between neighboring nations.

Powell, B. and P. McKillop, "Sayonara, America," *Newsweek,* **Aug. 19, 1991, p. 32.**

Considers Japan's growing economic power and America's decline. Tokyo's direct investment in its neighbors that has created jobs and lifted living standards; American loss showing up on the corporate bottom line; how broader consequences of Japan's economic dominance in East Asia are beginning to register in Washington; how the balance of power is changing as a result; past Japanese investments that are now paying off; more.

Investments, Japanese — United States

"Should we fear Japanese buyouts?" *USA Today,* **August 1991, p. 10.**

Examines the American public's hostility toward the wave of Japanese buyouts of United States industries and property purchases. Why these investments are actually good for the country; negative effects of the irrational attitudes toward Japan.

Powell, B., J. Gordon, et al., "What Japan will buy next," *Newsweek,* **Nov. 11, 1991, p. 48.**

Asserts that the Japanese will move out of the U.S. real estate market in the 1990s and target small U.S. high-tech firms for acquisition. The Toray Industries acquisition as a model for Japanese direct investment in the 1990s; mistakes they made in real estate investments; how the economic sobriety which has seized the U.S. also stretches across the Pacific; problems for Japanese auto parts suppliers that moved to America. INSET: Out (bad Japanese investments).

Japan

"Left to rot in Japan," *The Economist,* **Sept. 14, 1991, p. 35.**

Examines the repercussions of the collapse of the Soviet Union for Japan. The Japanese Communist Party; history of communism in Japan; leftist violence on the decline; Kenji Miyamoto, leader of the Communist Party in Japan; fragmentation of the ultra-left parties; the Japanese Red Army, led by Fusako Shigenobu; details.

Impoco, J., "Behind diplomatic smiles," *U.S. News & World Report,* Nov. 11, 1991, p. 51.

Details how America and Japan may be growing apart, even though they are still friends and allies. The rapid shift in the two nations' relative economic power, chronic trade wrangles and the declining Soviet threat; each are potential threats to their economic security; Japan's trade surplus with the U.S. has dropped 25 percent in 1990; how the end of the Cold War is adding to the economic strains; more.

Neff, R., B. Javetski, et al., "The Japan that can say 'get lost,'" *Business Week,* Oct. 14, 1991, p. 58.

Explores the economic friction that is coming to the fore, threatening the vaunted New World Order in which Japan underwrites America's vision of global stability. Tokyo's lessening concern in trying to please the U.S.; the strength of Japan's economic growth; the Bush administration's attempt to breathe new life into the "global partnership"; lists U.S.-Japanese points of friction; the continuing slide of U.S. opinion of Japan at the grass-roots level; more.

Korea

"U.S.-South Korean relations," *Dispatch,* July 8, 1991, p. 484.

Presents remarks by President Bush and President Roh Tae Woo of South Korea, Secretary of State James A. Baker III and Richard H. Solomon, Assistant Secretary for East Asian and Pacific Affairs, at the White House, July 1991, concerning Korea's economic success and thriving democracy. New opening to the Soviet Union; lasting peace in Korea; world change over the past two years; new world order in Korea; overview of the discussions of the two presidents.

Harrison, S.S., "A chance for detente in Korea," *World Policy Journal,* fall 1991, p. 599.

Looks at how North and South Korea remain locked in a costly military confrontation that undermines their economic and political stability and paralyzes progress toward reunification. North Korea's pursuit of conciliatory policies toward South Korea, the United States, and Japan; U.S. policy's contribution to the stalemate; Kim Dae Jung's rule of South Korea; the most sensitive issues; growing polarization of South Korean politics; more.

Military

"A base idea," *The Economist,* Sept. 7, 1991, p. 34.

Looks at the debate in the Philippines over whether the United States should be allowed to keep two military bases (Clark Air Base and Subic Bay Naval Station) there. Damage to Clark Air Base by the eruption of Mount Pinatubo; theories of why the U.S. wants to keep the bases operating; sentiment of the Philippine people; upcoming vote in the Philippine Senate; details.

Borrus, A., P. Engardio, et al., "Carving out a place in the Pacific century," *Business Week,* Nov. 11, 1991, p. 64.

States that the military pullback in East Asia means the U.S. must seek influence based on strong economic ties. The changing U.S./Asia relationship; the U.S. government's demand for fairer trading terms and access to Asian markets; President Bush's goal when he visits Asia; small and midsize U.S. companies are on thin ground in Asia; linking the U.S. economy to East Asia's dynamism.

Taiwan

"Most highly favoured nations," *The Economist,* July 27, 1991, p. 22.

Reports on why America has always opposed Taiwan's wish to join the General Agreement on Tariffs and Trade (GATT), to which it applied 18 months ago, and discusses President Bush's reasoning for changing his mind to support Taiwan's application. Bush's decision to renew most-favoured-nation (MFN) trading status for China; the administration's gesture of support to Taiwan for its membership of the GATT.

Weinberger, C.W. "Taiwan's rosy future," *Forbes,* Oct. 28, 1991, p. 33.

Commentary. Presents the opinion of *Forbes* publisher Casper W. Weinberger concerning Taiwan's promising future and the serious policy error made by the U.S. 12 years ago when it cut formal ties with Taiwan in order to establish diplomatic relations with mainland China. The USA-ROC Economic Council engaged in active trade discussions and supported the interests of Americans seeking to do business in Taiwan; rules that forbade upper-level government participation; a closer U.S. relationship.

Vietnam

"Obstacle course," *The Economist,* Aug. 3, 1991, p. 32.

Comments on the efforts of Vietnam to normalize relations with both the United States and China. Hard memories; the search for a solution in Cambodia; hopes for demilitarization; the 2,273 American servicemen listed as missing in action after the Vietnam War; the MIA lobby in America.

"Weighing up Vietnam," *The Economist,* Oct. 19, 1991, p. 35.

Asserts that one day Vietnam may overcome the consequences of having won its war against America. American trade policies that discriminate against Vietnam; Vietnamese government policies; problems with China.

Back Issues

Great Research on Current Issues Starts Right Here... Recent topics covered by The CQ Researcher are listed below. Issues dated before May 10, 1991, were published under the name of Editorial Research Reports.

Back issues are available for $4.00 (subscribers) or $7.00 (non-subscribers). Quantity discounts apply to orders over ten. To order, call Congressional Quarterly 1-800-432-2250.

Future Topics

▶ *Assisted Suicide*

▶ *Future of the Job Market*

▶ *Women and Sports*

Assisted Suicide

Should doctors help hopelessly ill patients take their lives?

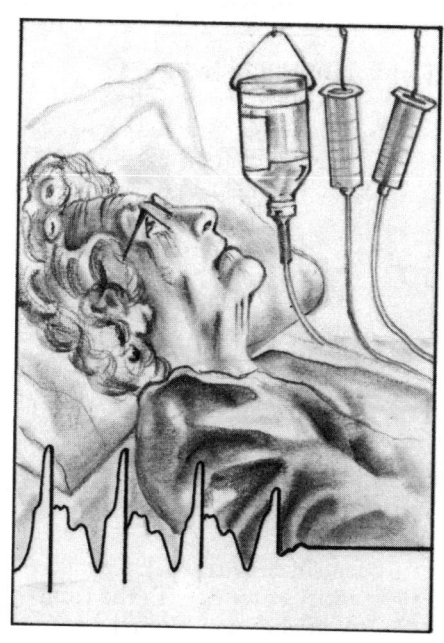

MERICAN DOCTORS, LONG ACCUSTOMED TO
preserving lives, are coming under increasing
pressure to help patients end their lives. Sometimes
the demand is for "assisted suicide," in which the
physician supplies a hopelessly ill patient with the means to
commit suicide. There also are calls for "active euthanasia,"
when the physician ends the person's life. Proponents of "aid
in dying" say a person who is suffering from a painful or
terminal illness has the right to medical help in cutting life
short. Opponents say the practice poses ethical problems.
They say that legalizing voluntary euthanasia and assisted
suicide could, among other things, lead to policies that
sanction involuntary killing of the aged and infirm.

 February 21, 1992 • Volume 2, No. 7 • 145-168

Formerly Editorial Research Reports

COVER ART: BARBARA SASSA-DANIELS

CQ Researcher

February 21, 1992
Volume 2, No. 7

EDITOR
Sandra Stencel

MANAGING EDITOR
Thomas J. Colin

ASSOCIATE EDITOR
Richard L. Worsnop

STAFF WRITERS
Charles S. Clark
Mary H. Cooper
Rodman D. Griffin

PRODUCTION EDITOR
Laurie De Maris

EDITORIAL ASSISTANT
Thomas H. Moore

GRAPHICS
Jack Auldridge

PUBLISHED BY
Congressional Quarterly Inc.

CHAIRMAN
Andrew Barnes

VICE CHAIRMAN
Andrew P. Corty

EDITOR AND PUBLISHER
Neil Skene

EXECUTIVE EDITOR
Robert W. Merry

PUBLICATIONS MARKETING/SALES
Robert Smith

EDITOR, EBSCO PUBLISHING
Melissa Kummerer

The CQ Researcher (ISSN 1056-2036). Formerly Editorial Research Reports. Published weekly (48 times per year, not printed the first Friday of any month with five Fridays) by Congressional Quarterly Inc., 1414 22nd St., N.W., Washington, D.C. 20037. Rates are furnished upon request. Second-class postage paid at Washington, D.C. POSTMASTER: Send address changes to The CQ Researcher, 1414 22nd St., N.W., Washington, D.C. 20037.

Assisted Suicide

BY RICHARD L. WORSNOP

THE ISSUES

In the 1970s, Americans began demanding "death with dignity" — the right to refuse life-sustaining treatment in the event of terminal illness or injury.[1] Now a thornier issue is coming to the fore as health-care professionals and their patients debate the merits of terminating life by suicide, possibly with the aid of a doctor.

The idea seems to enjoy broad acceptance. Fifty-eight percent of those responding to a January 1991 Gallup Poll said a person has "the moral right" to end his or her life when the person "has a disease that is incurable." Moreover, 66 percent of those queried said a person had the same moral right when suffering "great pain" with "no hope of improvement." And 65 percent said yes to this question: "When a person has a disease that cannot be cured, do you think doctors should be allowed by law to end the patient's life by some painless means if the patient and his family request it?"

Trained as they are to preserve life, most doctors are troubled by the thought of helping patients end their lives. Nonetheless, the issue is receiving considerable attention in medical publications, and some of the commentary is sympathetic. Writing in *The New England Journal of Medicine,* Drs. Christine K. Cassel and Diane E. Meier asserted: "The rigid view that physicians should never assist in suicide denies the complexity of the personal meanings life can have in favor of a single-minded devotion to its maximal duration."[2]

Most doctors hesitate to endorse assisted suicide on legal grounds. Although taking one's life is no crime, helping someone else commit suicide

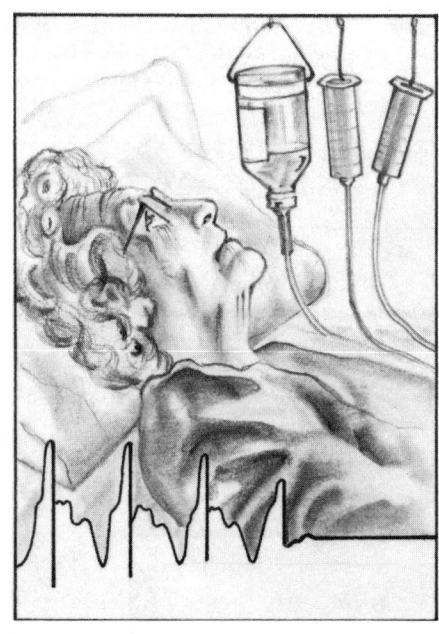

often is. According to Choice in Dying, a right-to-die group in New York City, 27 states have statutes that make assisted suicide a crime.[3] *(See map, p. 150.)*

Some right-to-die proponents are working to eliminate criminal sanctions against assisted suicide — and occasionally against active euthanasia as well. There is a crucial difference between the two. An assisted suicide is one in which a second party, usually a doctor, furnishes drugs and instructions to the person planning to take his or her life. With active euthanasia, it is the doctor who administers the lethal drug dose. Since it is tantamount to homicide, active euthanasia is illegal in every state. But few U.S. doctors who perform it have been brought to trial, and none has ever been convicted and imprisoned. *(See story, p. 154.)*

As awareness of "aid in dying" spreads, the concept is emerging as a political issue. Last November, Washington state voters rejected a ballot proposal to make it legal for mentally competent persons with fewer than

six months to live to enlist a doctor's assistance with suicide. It was the first time the question had been put before the electorate in any state, but it probably will not be the last. Signatures are now being gathered for a similar ballot initiative in California, and an Oregon initiative campaign is tentatively scheduled for 1994.

At the federal level, the focus has been on the "death-with-dignity" issue. The Supreme Court, in the 1990 case *Cruzan v. Missouri,* recognized the principle that a person has a constitutionally protected right to refuse unwanted medical treatment.* The Cruzan decision sparked fresh interest in "living wills," written instructions that spell out what an individual wants in such circumstances or that designate a family member or friend as a proxy to make such decisions. Congress kept the ball rolling by passing the Patient Self-Determination Act. The 1990 law requires all federally and state-funded providers of health care to inform patients of their rights to refuse medical or surgical treatment and to formulate an advance directive to that effect.

It is too soon to evaluate the impact of the law, which took effect Dec. 1, 1991. But Choice in Dying, which distributes living-will forms,

---

*Nancy Beth Cruzan, 25, lapsed into an apparently irreversible coma after a 1983 auto accident. Before the accident, she had said several times that if she were faced with life as a "vegetable," she would not want to live. Her parents went to court in 1987 to force the hospital to remove the tube by which she was being given nutrition and water. The Missouri Supreme Court refused to allow the life support to be withdrawn, saying there was no "clear and convincing" evidence Nancy Cruzan wanted that done. The U.S. Supreme Court agreed, but it also held that a person whose wishes were clearly known had a constitutional right to refuse life-sustaining medical treatment. A probate court judge in Jasper County, Mo., ruled Dec. 14, 1990, that Cruzan's parents had the right to remove their daughter's feeding tube, which they immediately proceeded to do. Nancy Cruzan died Dec. 26, 1990.

How the Public Views Suicide

A majority of those responding to a January 1991 Gallup Poll agree that a person has the right to end his or her own life if he or she is terminally ill or is suffering great pain and has no hope of improvement. But few Americans condone the suicide of a healthy person.

Do you think a person has the moral right to end his or her life under these circumstances?

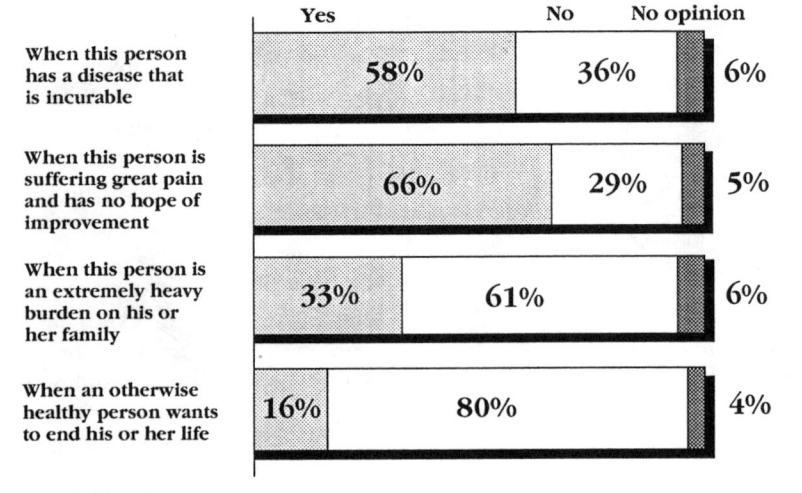

	Yes	No	No opinion
When this person has a disease that is incurable	58%	36%	6%
When this person is suffering great pain and has no hope of improvement	66%	29%	5%
When this person is an extremely heavy burden on his or her family	33%	61%	6%
When an otherwise healthy person wants to end his or her life	16%	80%	4%

Source: Gallup Organization

reports a "big increase" in the number of institutions requesting the documents. "We're doing a lot more bulk orders," says spokesman Joel Roselin. "And media coverage of the new law has prompted more individuals to contact us for living wills."

Though media coverage of right-to-die issues is growing, some terms tossed about in the debate are confusing to laymen. Consider the word euthanasia, which in ancient Greece meant simply a "good death." "By the end of the 19th century," one observer noted, "it referred to the ... taking of life in order to end suffering. By the end of World War II it had come to mean the taking of life without permission."[4]

Today, medical ethicists draw a sharp line between "passive euthanasia" and "active euthanasia." The passive form involves withholding or removing life-sustaining treatment from a terminally stricken patient. Active euthanasia, in which a doctor partici-

pates in a patient's suicide, typically entails heavy sedation followed by a lethal injection. This is how patients who opt for active euthanasia in the Netherlands are put to death. The practice technically is illegal there, but Dutch courts have set forth conditions in which doctors may end terminally ill patients' lives without risk of prosecution. *(See story, p. 158.)*

Doctors play a key role — but only an indirect one — in assisted suicide. In the usual scenario, a sympathetic physician prescribes enough drugs to kill a seriously ill patient if the pills are taken all at once. Jack Kevorkian, a Michigan physician, carries assisted suicide a step further. In the past two years, he has helped three women take their lives while hooked up to "suicide machines" he built. (Kevorkian calls the machines "Mercitrons.") A Michigan judge will rule Feb. 28 on whether Kevorkian will be tried on murder charges in connection with the two most recent

of those deaths *(see p. 157)*.

Euthanasia is quite literally a life-or-death question, stirring passionate feelings on all sides. Because discussions of the issue can generate more heat than light, some key points tend to get overlooked. Here are some questions experts feel should be examined thoroughly before any binding policy decisions are made:

Does rising interest in euthanasia and assisted suicide reflect concern about the high cost of medical care?

To a great but partly unspoken extent, interest in euthanasia stems from concern about the high cost of medical care for those least able to afford it — the aged and poverty-stricken. Some experts on right-to-die issues say this consideration provided the main impetus for the Patient Self-Determination Act.

Julie A. Grimstad, executive director of the Center for the Rights of the Terminally Ill in Hurst, Texas, says the new law is "purely and simply a cost-containment measure" because it will encourage the spread of living wills instructing doctors to cease life-sustaining treatment in certain conditions. "If you have a dead patient," says Grimstad, "it doesn't cost you anything in medical care."

The notion of promoting living wills as a health-care cost-containment tool is hardly new, Grimstad points out. She cites a memo prepared in 1977 by Robert A. Derzon, then head of the U.S. Health Care Financing Administration. He wrote it a year after California enacted the nation's first living-will statute. The "cost-saving from a nationwide push toward 'living wills' is likely to be enormous," Derzon argued, since the savings would accrue also "to Medicaid and the V.A. [Veterans Administration] and Defense Department health programs."

Thomas H. Murray, director of the Center for Biomedical Ethics at Case Western Reserve University in Cleveland, agrees that "assisted dying" could help control health-care spending, but he worries about its misuse. "There's a good chance of inequality in assisted dying," he says, "with it being offered most readily to those least able to pay for regular medical care or long-term care."

If the cost of providing the elderly with health care seems onerous now, the situation promises to become critical in the near future. According to the U.S. Census Bureau, the number of very old Americans (85 or older) increased from 580,000 in 1950 to 3.1 million in 1990. The total is projected to reach 5.3 million by 2005.

The American way of death has been growing more costly in other ways as well. As recently as 50 years ago, most old people died at home. Today, the vast majority spend their final days in a nursing home or hospital, often at considerable expense. Relatively few perish from pneumonia, once known as the "old man's friend" because it brought a peaceful release to many elderly people at the brink of death. Most strains of the disease are now easily treatable with antibiotics.

A dwindling supply of volunteers to care for the frail elderly poses additional problems. The trend is attributed to the movement of housewives into the full-time work force and to the decline of religious orders.

Old people with fixed incomes need no reminders about the soaring cost of health care. Despairing of their ability of pay for treatment of a serious illness or injury, they may lapse into a deep depression and begin to entertain notions of suicide. They may also grow despondent over the prospect of becoming a financial and emotional burden on their children.

Whether morbid thoughts of this nature drive elderly people to take their lives — with or without a physician's aid — is impossible to ascertain. But a study issued in September 1991 by a researcher for the federal

Centers for Disease Control in Atlanta reported that the incidence of suicide among people ages 65 and older had risen substantially since 1980. Dr. Richard Sattin found that the suicide rate for Americans ages 65 or older increased by 21 percent from 1980 to 1986. Between 1950 to 1980, the suicide rate for this age group had drifted steadily downward.

More recent data show a continuation of the post-1980 pattern. According to federal figures for 1990, the suicide rate was 4 percent higher than in 1986 for people ages 75 to 84 and 6 percent higher for those 85 and older. On the other hand, the 1990 figures showed an 8 percent drop in the suicide rate for people in the 65-74 bracket.

Sattin declined to speculate on why the 30-year decline in suicide rates for the elderly suddenly stopped and reversed direction. "All we can say is that there is an increasing trend," he said.[5] Dr. Kevorkian, however, pointed to loneliness as a potential trigger of suicidal behavior in old people. "When their health starts breaking down, they're terrified," he said. "They don't know

where to turn."[6]

In this state of mind, elderly Americans may fall prey to the arguments of those who say people of advanced age should end their lives for the good of society. Then-Colorado Gov. Richard D. Lamm drew the ire of groups representing the aged when he said in 1984 that elderly persons who are terminally ill have a "duty to die and get out of the way. Let the other society, our kids, build a reasonable life."[7]

Margaret P. Battin, an associate professor of philosophy at the University of Utah, elaborated on Lamm's suggestion in a 1987 article in the quarterly journal *Ethics*. "It is not at all difficult to imagine the development of social expectations around the notion that there is a time to die, or indeed, that it is a matter of virtue or obligation to choose to die," she wrote. "To be effective, these expectations would presumably be coupled with supportive social practices — for instance, pre-death counseling, physician assistance in providing the actual means of inducing death or ceremonial recognition from such institutions as churches."[8]

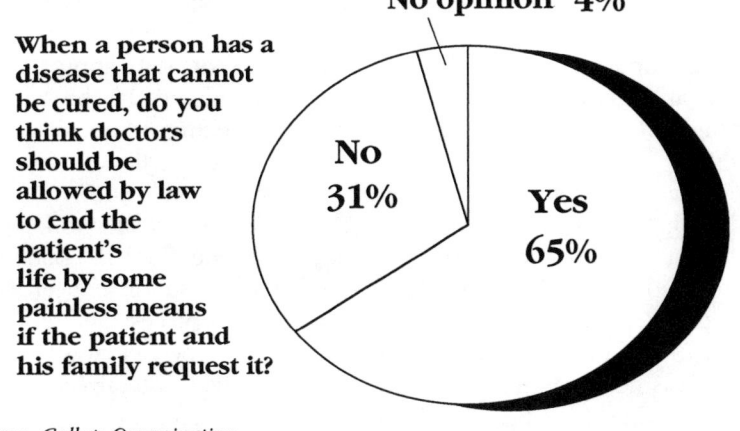

How the Public Views Physician-Assisted Suicide

Nearly two-thirds of those responding to a January 1991 Gallup Poll support physician-assisted suicide if the patient and his family request it.

When a person has a disease that cannot be cured, do you think doctors should be allowed by law to end the patient's life by some painless means if the patient and his family request it?

No opinion 4%

No 31%

Yes 65%

Source: Gallup Organization

Assisted Suicide Is a Crime in Some States

The 27 states that are shaded gray on the map below have statutes that make assisted suicide a crime, according to a recent survey by Choice in Dying, a right-to-die group in New York City. In some of those states, assisted suicide is considered a form of manslaughter; in others it is a separately defined crime.

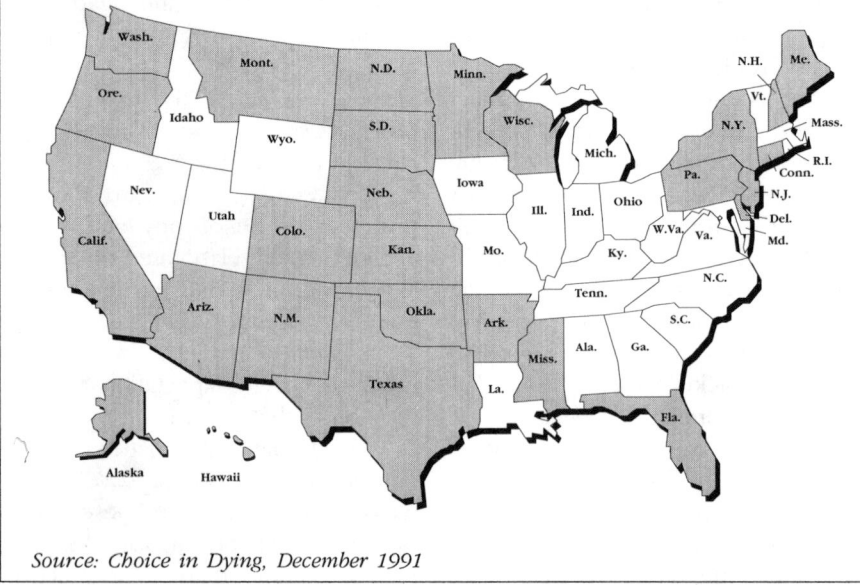

Source: Choice in Dying, December 1991

Are assisted suicide and active euthanasia morally justified?

Though cost issues will continue to spice the debate on assisted suicide and active euthanasia, the key question is whether a person has the moral right to take his or her own life before death occurs naturally. The Stoics of ancient Rome believed the answer was yes. As they saw it, "He is at liberty to die who does not wish to live." But the Stoics looked askance at impulsive suicide. The act was justifiable, they thought, only after sifting carefully through the pros and cons.

Judeo-Christian tradition, on the other hand, holds that a person has no inherent right to commit suicide. Summing up the traditional Christian view, *Commonweal* magazine declared in an editorial last fall that human life is not "merely the possession of the one who bears it. It is an inherited gift, and as such, has

meaning not only for oneself but for those who bestowed it, those who have shared it and those who will follow."[9]

Terminating life through euthanasia or assisted suicide complicates matters by involving persons other than the one targeted for death. *Commonweal* takes the position that "letting die" by disconnecting a terminally ill patient's life-support systems "is totally different from euthanasia or state-approved physician aid-in-dying. In the latter case, society is being asked to approve a form of state-sanctioned murder."[10]

Many medical ethicists feel the same way. Susan M. Wolf, a lawyer and researcher for the Hastings Center, an organization concerned with medical and professional ethics, says there are "no circumstances" in which active euthanasia or physician-assisted suicide are justifiable.

Leon R. Kass, a physician and bio-

chemist who writes frequently on right-to-die issues, says "it is precisely the setting of fixed limits on violating human life that makes possible our efforts at dignified relations with our fellow men, especially when their neediness and disability try our patience. We will never be able to relate ... decently to people if we are entitled always to consider that one option before us is to make them dead."[11]

Thomas Murray at Case Western Reserve University would not go that far. "It's pretty clear that there are cases when active euthanasia almost certainly can be morally justified," he says. "One is on the field of combat, when someone is mortally wounded and suffering horribly. Obviously, he is going to die in a few hours in any event. Before that happens, he may fall into the hands of the enemy and be tortured. So, the option is either to kill him yourself now or allow him to suffer and die anyway. It's a terrible thing, but euthanasia is probably justified under these circumstances."

Some euthanasia foes rest their case on the premise that the Hippocratic oath requires doctors to oppose any act that might endanger a patient's life. Attributed to Hippocrates, the ancient Greek physician regarded as the father of modern medicine, the oath is administered to many (but by no means all) medical school graduates. It states in part that "you will exercise your art solely for the cure of your patients and will give no drug, perform no operation, for a criminal purpose, even if asked, far less suggest it."

For their part, advocates of euthanasia and assisted suicide say a person has the right to seek help in ending his life, provided it is a "rational" decision. A key consideration is the suicidal person's state of mind, argue the authors of a widely discussed article about hopelessly ill patients in *The New England Journal of Medicine*. "The physician who considers helping a patient who requests assistance with suicide must determine first that the patient is indeed beyond all help and not merely suffering from a treatable depression of the sort common in people with terminal illnesses. Such a depression requires therapeutic intervention." Taking that and other factors into account, 10 of the 12 co-authors concluded that "it is not immoral for a physician to assist in the rational suicide of a terminally ill person."[12]

The "rational decision" argument doesn't impress Leon Kass. "Verbal 'requests' made under duress rarely reveal the whole story," he says. "Often a demand for euthanasia is, in fact, an angry or anxious plea for help, born of fear of rejection or abandonment, or made in ignorance of available alternatives that could alleviate pain and suffering."[13]

Murray discerns irony in the situation, noting that the very advances in medical technology that led to longer lives have now produced demands for more technology to end life. Americans today have a horror of "prolonged institutionalized dying," he says. They are repelled by the thought of "dying completely out of control, tethered to machines, perhaps in a lot of pain, perhaps in a kind of dazed twilight. They want to avoid that at all costs. And it looks as if active euthanasia or assisted suicide is the way to avoid that."

Anecdotal evidence suggests that assisted suicide is seen as a desirable option by many victims of Alzheimer's disease and acquired immune deficiency syndrome (AIDS). Janet Adkins, 54, the first person to die with the aid of one of Dr. Kevorkian's suicide machines, had been diagnosed with Alzheimer's. She decided to take her life before the disease ran its likely course, leaving her mentally and physically helpless. Adkins was a member of the Hemlock Society, which advocates the right of terminally ill people to end their lives

through assisted suicide.

Derek Humphry, a co-founder of the Hemlock Society, reports that the group's membership has become "a lot younger" since the AIDS scare began to gather momentum around 1983. "Also, it's a lot more male than it was," Humphry says.[14]

Some AIDS victims choose suicide rather than endure the disorder's painful and humiliating final stages, which can include blindness, dementia and emaciation. David Lewis, an AIDS counselor in Vancouver, British Columbia, disclosed in July 1990 that he had helped eight AIDS-infected male friends take lethal doses of drugs after doctors prescribed the medication. Defending his actions, Lewis said: "People at that terminal phase in their life should be able to say, 'It is enough. I don't want to suffer anymore. I want to die.' To refuse to help them would be criminal."[15]

Opponents of assisted suicide respond by saying, in effect, "Miracles can happen." They point to the many documented cases of people who regained consciousness after comas lasting months or even years. Moreover, they insist it is always possible that new drugs will be found to combat diseases now regarded as invariably fatal or disabling.

Above all, foes of assisted suicide warn that legalization will lead to abuses. The Dutch experience is often cited in this connection. In the Netherlands, says Susan Wolf, "the practice [of euthanasia] is seeping beyond the guidelines that are meant to confine it. Euthanasia usually is not reported to the authorities, although it is supposed to be under Dutch law. Evidently the process is not workable. We have yet to see a process that *is* workable."

Murray, who supports assisted suicide in certain cases, has reservations about elevating the practice to a fixed social policy. Pointing to the situation in the Netherlands, he says: "There is some evidence that doctors are deciding on behalf of patients when it is time for them to go. That's always what people who have qualms about active euthanasia and assisted suicide worry about." He therefore opposes legalization of euthanasia, "not because I think people always are morally wrong when they do it but because I fear that, once legalized, it would become so open for errors as well as potential abuses." ∎

BACKGROUND

Movement's Roots

Proposals to legalize voluntary euthanasia for the incurably ill became a focal point of public-policy debate in several countries toward the end of the 19th century. In 1906, a bill to that end was introduced in the Ohio legislature, sparking heated controversy. Opponents said the measure would invite abuse by fortune-hunters seeking a shortcut to an inheritance, families wishing to unload burdensome relatives and in-

competent doctors looking for a way to cover up their mistakes. Although the Ohio bill went down to defeat, the idea that inspired it lived on.

A euthanasia movement emerged in Britain in 1935 with the founding of the Voluntary Euthanasia Society. The following year, Parliament voted down legislation sponsored by the society allowing terminally ill persons to seek euthanasia. The author G.K. Chesterton observed in 1937 that "Some are proposing what is called euthanasia; at present only a proposal for killing those who are a nuisance to themselves; but soon to be applied to those who are a nuisance to other people."

State Laws Governing Living Wills

All states except Nebraska have some kind of living-will law. Some of the laws provide for the appointment of a health-care proxy to make decisions on a patient's behalf. The specifics of living will and health-care agent legislation vary greatly from state to state.

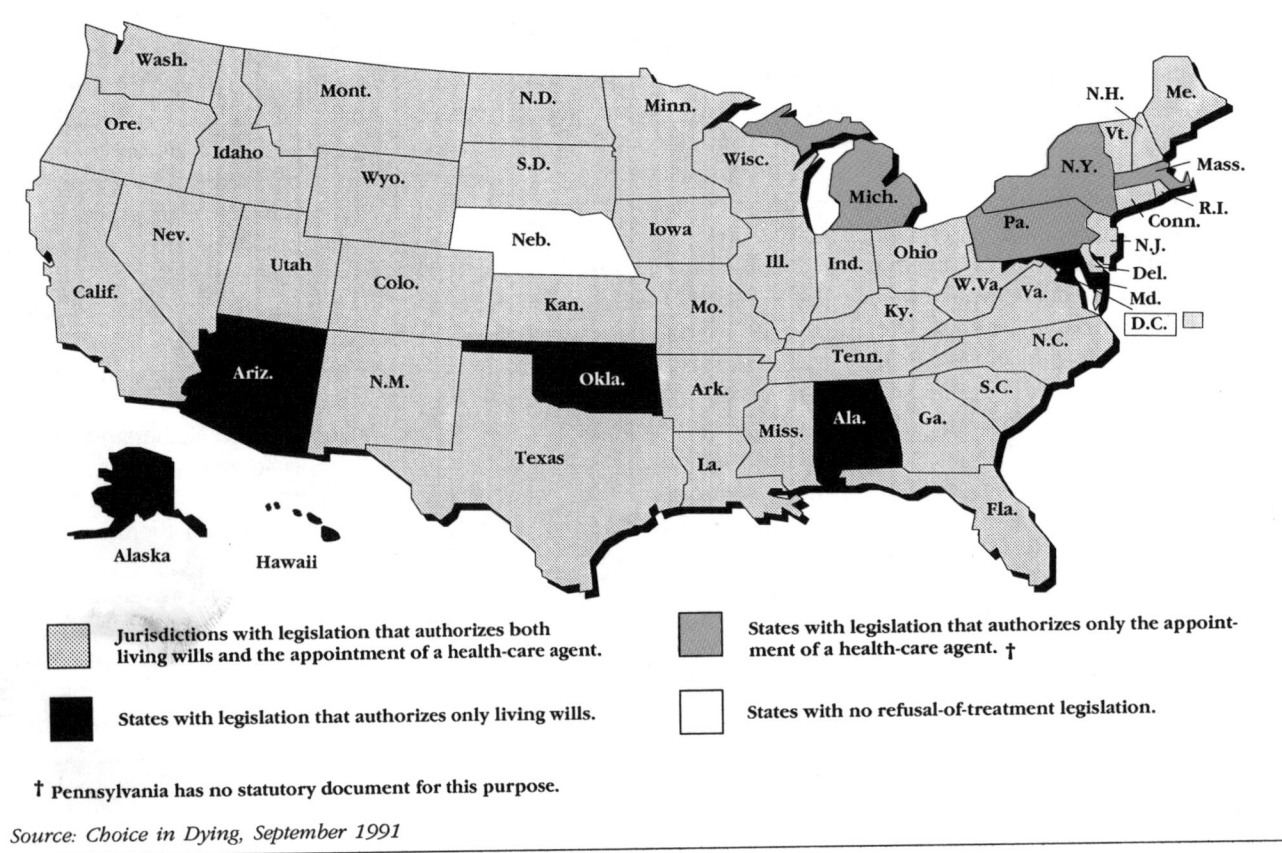

Jurisdictions with legislation that authorizes both living wills and the appointment of a health-care agent.

States with legislation that authorizes only living wills.

States with legislation that authorizes only the appointment of a health-care agent. †

States with no refusal-of-treatment legislation.

† **Pennsylvania has no statutory document for this purpose.**

Source: Choice in Dying, September 1991

Chesterton's prophecy came to pass not in his native land but in Germany, where euthanasia was scrutinized more closely than perhaps anywhere else in the world. German interest in the issue was ignited by a book published in 1920, *The Permission to Destroy Life Unworthy of Life*. Co-authors Alfred Hoche, a psychiatry professor, and Karl Binding, a law professor, wrote that patients who asked for "death assistance" should be able to obtain doctors' help in ending their lives, provided safeguards were part of the package. These included review of all death requests by a three-member panel, acknowledgment of the right

to withdraw a death request at any time and grants of legal immunity to physicians who perform euthanasia.

Seeking to defuse objections to their program, Hoche and Binding asserted that killing was consistent with medical ethics in certain instances. People suffering from brain damage, mental retardation and severe psychiatric illness were "mentally dead," they argued, hence terminating their lives was not homicide but rather "an allowable, useful act."

Nazi Atrocities

When the Nazis took power in Germany in 1933, they bent the ideas articulated by Hoche and Binding in-

to sinister new shapes. One of the first laws they enacted provided for compulsory sterilization of people with hereditary illnesses. This accorded with the Nazi belief that the first obligation of medical science was attending to the health of the German nation's "folk body" (*Volkskörper*), not the health of individual patients. The Nazis then proceeded to identify entire groups of people perceived as threats to the "folk body" — criminals, the physically and mentally handicapped, homosexuals and "inferior" races. Adoption of a policy calling for mass extermination of undesirables was the next step.

Continued on p. 155

Chronology

1920s-1930s
Whether it is morally defensible to terminate lives considered "useless" becomes a subject of academic and popular debate. Nazi Germany's mass exterminations during World War II bring the idea into disrepute.

1920
In their book *The Permission to Destroy Life Unworthy of Life,* German Professors Alfred Hoche and Karl Binding argue that patients who request "death assistance" should, under carefully controlled conditions, be able to obtain the help of physicians in terminating their lives.

Jan. 17, 1937
Conducting its first nationwide survey on euthanasia, the Gallup Poll asks, "Do you favor mercy deaths under government supervision for hopeless invalids?" Forty-six percent of those interviewed say yes and 54 percent say no. But the proportion of yes answers exceeds 50 percent in the Middle Atlantic, Mountain and Pacific states.

1938
A German child known only as "Baby Knauer" is put to death by physicians in the first recorded case of destruction of a life deemed "empty and meaningless." The child's father had written to Adolf Hitler seeking permission for the euthanasia. Authorization was granted after doctors found that Baby Knauer was blind, retarded and missing an arm and a leg.

1970s
With memories of the Nazi Holocaust receding, interest in voluntary euthanasia revives.

1973
In a provisional policy statement, the Royal Dutch Medical Association declares: "[L]egally euthanasia should remain a crime, but . . . if a physician, after having considered all the aspects of the case, shortens the life of a patient who is incurably ill and in the process of dying, the court will have to judge whether there was a conflict of duties which could justify the act of the physician." The statement sparks a decade-long debate in the Netherlands on the morality of euthanasia.

1978
In *Jean's Way,* English journalist Derek Humphry describes how he assisted in the death of his wife, who had been suffering from bone cancer, by supplying her with a cup of coffee laced with Secobarbital and codeine.

1980s
Euthanasia supporters become more outspoken in demanding the right of terminally ill individuals to end their lives at a time of their choosing.

1980
The Hemlock Society is founded by Derek Humphry and his second wife, Ann Wickett Humphry, to support the option of voluntary euthanasia for the advanced terminally ill and the incurably ill.

March 27, 1984
Colorado Democratic Gov. Richard D. Lamm comes under fire from groups representing the elderly when he tells the Colorado Health Lawyers Association that terminally ill people have a "duty to die and get out of the way."

1990s
Several widely publicized cases of assisted suicide underscore the growing urgency of the issue.

June 4, 1990
Janet Adkins, an Oregon woman in the early stages of Alzheimer's disease, kills herself with the aid of a "suicide machine" devised by Dr. Jack Kevorkian. Adkins was a member of the Hemlock Society.

Jan. 6, 1991
In the most recent Gallup Poll on euthanasia, 58 percent of the respondents say a person has a "moral right to end his or her life" when suffering from incurable disease; 66 percent say a person has that right when "suffering great pain" with "no hope of improvement."

Aug. 18, 1991
Final Exit, a suicide manual by Hemlock Society co-founder Derek Humphry, vaults to the No. 1 spot on *The New York Times'* list of best-selling "advice" hardcover books.

Oct. 23, 1991
Sherry Miller and Margery Wantz, Michigan women suffering from serious physical disorders, commit suicide with the help of two new devices designed by Dr. Kevorkian.

Nov. 5, 1991
By a margin of 54 percent to 46 percent, Washington state voters reject a ballot proposal to legalize euthanasia for terminally ill persons.

Jan. 12, 1992
The ABC television network shows "Last Wish," a dramatization of an actual assisted suicide.

Feb. 3, 1992
A Michigan grand jury indicts Dr. Kevorkian for murder in the deaths of Miller and Wantz.

Physician-Assisted Suicide: Mercy or Murder?

Only 11 U.S. physicians have been charged with killing a terminally ill patient or family member. None has ever been convicted and imprisoned.

1935 Harold Blazer of Montevista, Colo., was accused of murdering his 30-year-old-daughter, Hazel, a victim of cerebral spinal meningitis. The doctor, his wife and another daughter had cared for Hazel her entire life. One day Blazer placed a handkerchief soaked in chloroform over Hazel's nose and mouth and kept it there until she died. He was acquitted at his trial.

1950 Hermann N. Sander of Manchester, N.H., was charged with murdering Abbie C. Borroto, a terminally ill patient. At the request of Borroto's husband, Sander injected Borroto with 40 cc of air. She died within 10 minutes. When he logged the fatal injection into hospital records, Sander was reported to authorities. After a three-week trial, the jury returned a verdict of innocent.

1972 Vincent Montemarano, the chief surgical resident at Nassau County (N.Y.) Medical Center, was indicted for murdering Eugene Bauer, 59. Bauer, suffering from terminal throat cancer, died five minutes after Montemarano gave him a shot of potassium chloride. At the trial, the defense argued that the state had not proved Bauer was alive before receiving the injection. The jury returned a not-guilty verdict.

1982 Robert J. Nejdl and Neil L. Barber of Los Angeles County, Calif., were charged with murder for removing life-support equipment in 1981 from Clarence Herbert, 55. Herbert had suffered a heart attack after surgery and remained in a coma for three days before his condition was declared hopeless. Nejdl and Barber disconnected Herbert's life supports at his family's request. He died six days later. In 1983, an appeals court dismissed the charges against the doctors.

1985 John Kraai of Fairport, N.Y., was charged with murdering his friend and patient, Frederick Wagner, who suffered from Alzheimer's disease. On the day Wagner died, Kraai gave him three shots of insulin. Three weeks after his arrest, the doctor killed himself by lethal injection.

1986 Joseph Hassman of Berlin, N.J., was charged with murdering his mother-in-law, Esther Davis, a victim of Alzheimer's. At the family's request, Hassman gave Davis a lethal injection of Demerol. He was found guilty at his trial

and was sentenced to two years' probation, fined $10,000 and ordered to perform 400 hours of community service.

1987 Peter Rosier of Fort Myers, Fla., was acquitted of murder charges in the death of his wife, Patricia, who was a terminal cancer patient. Mrs. Rosier tried to take her life with an overdose of Seconal, but when the powerful sedative failed to take hold her husband injected her with morphine. That didn't work either. Acting without Peter Rosier's knowledge, Patricia's stepfather, Vincent Delman, ended her life by smothering her. Delman's role came to light only after he was granted immunity from prosecution in exchange for his testimony in Peter Rosier's trial.

1989 Donald Caraccio of Troy, Mich., was charged with murdering a female hospital patient who was terminally ill and comatose. Caraccio gave the patient a shot of potassium chloride in the presence of other medical staff. Accepting Caraccio's guilty plea at the subsequent trial, the judge sentenced him to five years' probation combined with community service.

1990 Richard Schaeffer of Redondo Beach, Calif., was arrested on suspicion of having caused the death of a patient who was suffering from the effects of a stroke and other ailments. The dead man's wife was also arrested. Both were released pending further investigation. One year later, charges against the two suspects were dismissed.

1990 Jack Kevorkian of Royal Oak, Mich., was charged in Demember with murdering Hemlock Society member Janet Adkins the previous June 4. An Alzheimer's victim, Adkins had flown from her home in Oregon to Michigan, where Kevorkian connected her to a "suicide machine" in the back of his parked van. Adkins pressed the button that caused lethal drugs to flow into her body. The charge against Kevorkian was dismissed on Dec. 13.

1992 Kevorkian became the first American physician to face more than one murder charge in connection with assisted suicide. A grand jury in Oakland County, Mich., indicted him Feb. 3 on two murder counts in the 1991 deaths of Sherry Miller and Marjorie Wantz. A Michigan judge is scheduled to rule Feb. 28 on whether there is enough evidence to warrant a trial in Oakland County Circuit Court.

Source: The Hemlock Society.

Continued from p. 152

"Prior to Auschwitz and the other death camps," psychiatrist Robert J. Lifton has written, "the Nazis established a policy of direct medical killing: that is, killing arranged within medical channels, by means of medical decisions, and carried out by doctors and their assistants."[16] This program, which the Nazis called "euthanasia," progressed from coercive sterilizations to the killing of "impaired" children in hospitals, "impaired" adults from mental hospitals and "impaired" inmates of concentration camps to, finally, mass killings, mostly of Jews, in extermination camps.

Dr. Leo Alexander, a medical adviser to the prosecution at the Nuremberg trials of Nazi war criminals, said the German doctors' crimes had their beginnings in "the [physicians'] acceptance of the attitude, basic in the euthanasia movement, that there is such a thing as life not worthy to be lived" — the notion popularized years earlier by Hoche and Binding.

Writing just a few years after the fall of the Third Reich, Alexander expressed concern that the same basic attitude was taking root in the United States as medicine became more scientific. American physicians, he wrote, were "getting dangerously close" to regarding themselves as "mere technicians of rehabilitation." As such, they were drawing distinctions between acute and chronic diseases, with the chronically ill patient carrying "an obvious stigma as the one less likely to be fully rehabilitable for social usefulness. In an increasingly utilitarian society these patients are being [increasingly] looked down upon ... as unwanted ballast."[17]

In fact, a euthanasia movement already existed in the United States at the time Alexander wrote. The Euthanasia Society of America, founded early in 1938, initially advocated only the legalization of voluntary euthanasia. The group's lawyer, Charles E.

Nixdorff, explained that U.S. public opinion was "not yet ready to accept the broader principle." He added, however, that the euthanasia society "hoped eventually to legalize the putting to death of non-volunteers beyond the help of medical science."[18]

Death With Dignity

At the time Nixdorff spoke, few people could have imagined the atrocities that the Nazis would commit during World War II. Liberation of the death camps in 1945 revealed the full truth about the Holocaust for the first time. For at least a generation after that, the idea of medically aided euthanasia sank into general disrepute.

Then, as memories of the World War II era faded, interest in "assisted death" began to revive. The initial stress was on "death with dignity," a shorthand term for the right of a terminally ill person to refuse life-sustaining medical treatment. In the mid-1970s, the tragic case of Karen Ann Quinlan brought the issue into sharp focus.

Quinlan, a 21-year-old New Jersey resident, collapsed during a party in April 1975 after taking a mixture of tranquilizer pills and alcohol. Her breathing ceased for at least two 15-minute periods. Quinlan's condition deteriorated further after hospitalization, with all examining physicians concluding that she had suffered irreversible damage and was in a "persistent vegetative state." They said she had no chance of recovering.

Quinlan's parents eventually consulted a Roman Catholic priest, who told them that church teachings held there was no moral obligation to continue extraordinary means to sustain life when there was no realistic hope of recovery. The parents decided Karen should be taken off the respirator. But her physicians and the

hospital turned down the request.

The Quinlans then went to court with a petition asking that their daughter be allowed to die "with grace and dignity." The trial court judge refused to authorize disconnection of the respirator. However, in March 1976 the New Jersey Supreme Court reversed the lower court decision, arguing that Karen had a right to refuse treatment on the basis of her constitutionally protected right of privacy. Since she was incompetent, the court said, the "only practical way" her right could be exercised was to allow her guardian and family to decide "whether she would exercise it in these circumstances."

While the state did have an interest in the preservation of life, the court said, the state's interest "weakens and the individual's right to privacy grows as the degree of bodily invasion increases and the prognosis dims." In the Quinlan case, the court said, the state's interest had to yield. And so, about a year after she had fallen into a coma, and in the expectation that she would die soon thereafter, the respirator was removed. To everyone's surprise, Karen Quinlan then began breathing on her own and lived another nine years.

Living Wills

Significant as it was in its own right, the New Jersey Supreme Court's landmark decision also spurred interest in living wills — advance directives about the use and removal of artificial life supports. All states except Nebraska have some kind of living-will law. (See map, p. 152.) Some of the laws provide for the appointment of a health-care proxy to make decisions on a patient's behalf, often through a "durable power of attorney." All the laws grant doctors immunity from prosecution for any actions taken in carrying out the provisions of a living will.

Congress gave the living-will movement a push when it approved the

Patient Self-Determination Act at the end of 1990. The law, which took effect Dec. 1, 1991, requires hospitals and other health-care facilities that receive Medicare or Medicaid payments to inform patients about their ability to make out advance directives. Sen. John C. Danforth, R-Mo., one of the chief sponsors of the measure, said it "encourages people to at least start thinking about planning ahead."

Expert opinion about the law is mixed. Thomas Murray of Case Western Reserve University regards it as "a responsible piece of legislation" that already has helped educate the public and the medical profession about "control over dying." He notes that "hospitals have had to reconstruct their admissions policies to make sure that these questions get posed to people.... It's a step in the right direction."

Julie Grimstad of the Center for the Rights of the Terminally Ill thinks otherwise. "Do you want to be hit with a living will to sign when you enter a hospital through the emergency room?" she asks. "No. You just want to get into a hospital bed." In Grimstad's view, "It makes about as much sense for somebody to make out a property will on admission to a hospital as it does to make out a living will. You don't have enough time to give the matter due consideration."

Grimstad also objects to the fact that the Patient Self-Determination Act addresses only living wills and similar legal arrangements. She would give prospective patients the option of signing a Protective Medical Decisions Document (PMDD), a legal instrument developed by the International Anti-Euthanasia Task Force. The PMDD directs that food and water be provided "unless death is inevitable and truly imminent so that the effort to sustain my life is futile or unless I am unable to assimilate food and fluids." It also calls for continuation of ordinary nursing and medical care and pain relief appro-

priate to the condition "even in the face of death."

The Hemlock Society

Derek Humphry of the Hemlock Society applauds the Patient Self-Determination Act, calling it "the final rung that needed to be reached. It's no good having living wills unless hospitals and doctors are going to cooperate with having them filled out." He also agrees with part of what Grimstad advocates: "We're great believers in filling out a living will saying, 'I want to be kept on life-support systems,' if that's what people want."

Humphry, 61, founded the Hemlock Society in 1980 with his second wife, Ann Wickett,* and two other persons. The organization's aim was to promote "voluntary euthanasia for the terminally ill through assisted suicide." But not in every case. "We do

not encourage any form of suicide for mental-health or emotional reasons," Humphry says. "We certainly do not believe in giving up the minute a person is informed that he or she has a terminal illness, which is a common misconception of our critics." [19]

Humphry's beliefs about assisted suicide spring from personal experience. In 1975 he helped his first wife, who was suffering from incurable bone cancer, to take her life by supplying her with a cup of coffee laced with a lethal mixture of secobarbital and codeine. He wrote a book about the experience, *Jean's Way,* in 1978 and emigrated to the United States from his native England the same year.

---

*Ann Wickett Humphry, 49, who had been diagnosed with breast cancer, committed suicide in October 1991. She and Derek Humphry were divorced in 1990. ∎

CURRENT SITUATION

'Final Exit'

In recent years, Humphry has become a familiar figure on national and local television. The Hemlock Society has flourished, too. It now has about 47,000 members, Humphry says, including "several hundred" doctors. "Plenty of doctors now feel they can be open about their views on this," he says, "even though they dare not practice what they preach."

Humphry estimates that Hemlock Society membership has grown by about 20 percent since his most recent book, *Final Exit,* was published last spring. In August 1991 it vaulted to the No. 1 spot on *The New York Times'* list of best-selling "advice,

how-to and miscellaneous" hardcover books. Sales to date total just over 500,000 copies, Humphry reports, adding that a paperback edition is scheduled for publication in August.

Less than 200 pages long and printed in extra-large type for the benefit of readers with poor eyesight, *Final Exit* recapitulates the arguments and advice Humphry has been dispensing for years. As a basic strategy, he recommends an overdose of any one of a number of prescription drugs. To guard against failure, he also urges that a plastic bag be slipped over the head and fastened securely about the neck.* A four-page table lists recommended drugs by generic and trade names, along with information on what constitutes a lethal dose and how many tablets of standard size must be ingested to

---

*The psychoanalyst Bruno Bettelheim, a Hemlock Society member, committed suicide in 1990 by using the drug overdose-plastic bag combination.

produce death.

Humphry surmises that some people have bought *Final Exit* mainly out of curiosity about its contents. "But I really think it's a book that people probably skim and then put away as a reference work, along with their dictionaries and health guidebooks," he says. "It is definitely a book that you store away for possible need later on."

Some people have likened the debate on active euthanasia and assisted suicide to the abortion controversy, but Humphry says the comparison is inexact. "Ours is a bigger debate, in the sense that everybody is going to die," he says. "On the other hand, relatively few people have abortions or need to have abortions. I'm in favor of abortion, but as little of it as possible. With abortion, people are moralizing about other people's lives to a large extent. But in the death-with-dignity movement, we're talking about your own life. Therefore, we are addressing a much more universal issue."

'Doctor Death'

The Hemlock Society is the only national organization that promotes active voluntary euthanasia for the terminally ill. However, individuals not affiliated with the society are pursuing similar goals on their own. Prominent among them is Jack Kevorkian, the Michigan physician who gained notoriety by helping three women end their lives with suicide machines of his design. All three women were seriously though not terminally ill.

The first woman to die with Kevorkian's assistance was Janet Adkins, 54, a Hemlock Society member from Portland, Ore., who was diagnosed with Alzheimer's disease in 1989. When the illness started to affect her mind, she resolved to end

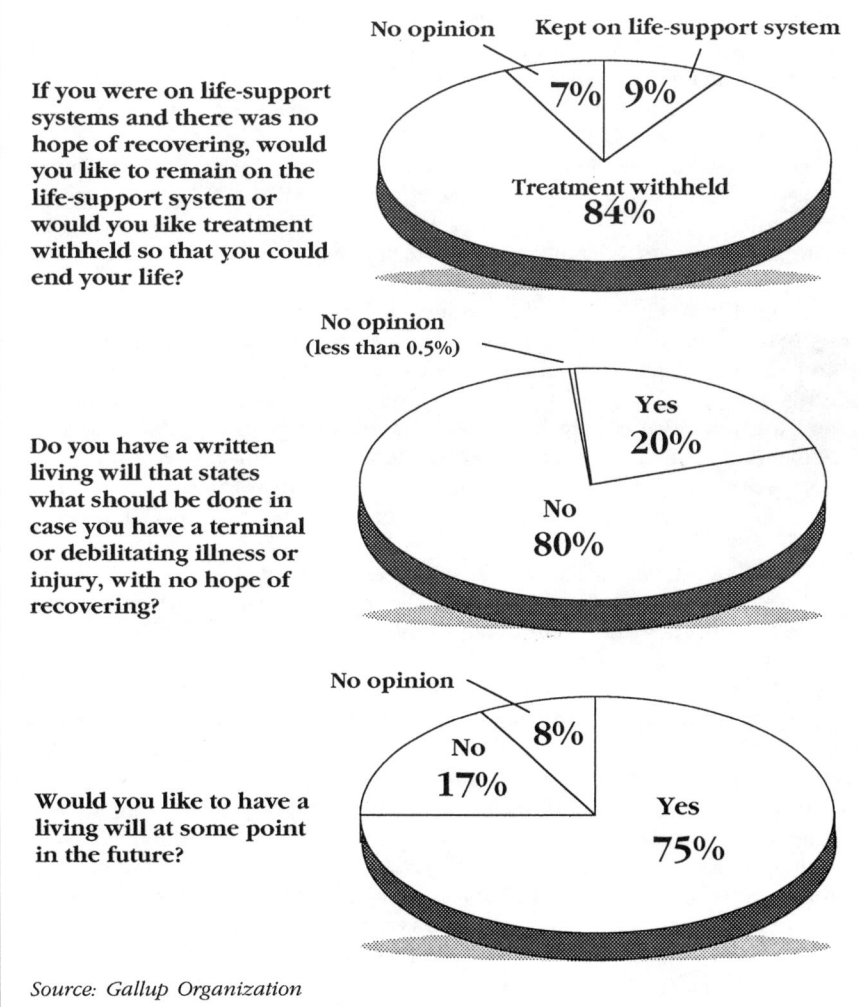

Living Wills: Popular But Unused

The vast majority of those responding to a January 1991 Gallup Poll said they would refuse life-sustaining treatment in the event of terminal illness or injury. But only 20 percent of the respondents had prepared a living will stating what they wanted done in such circumstances. The idea of a living will had strong appeal, however: 75 percent of the respondents said they would like to have one at some point in the future.

If you were on life-support systems and there was no hope of recovering, would you like to remain on the life-support system or would you like treatment withheld so that you could end your life?

No opinion 7% Kept on life-support system 9% Treatment withheld 84%

Do you have a written living will that states what should be done in case you have a terminal or debilitating illness or injury, with no hope of recovering?

No opinion (less than 0.5%) Yes 20% No 80%

Would you like to have a living will at some point in the future?

No opinion 8% No 17% Yes 75%

Source: Gallup Organization

her life before reaching a state of helplessness. She got in touch with Kevorkian, whom she had read about and seen on television. He, in turn, told her to contact him again when she was ready to carry out her plan.

Adkins and her husband flew to Royal Oak, Mich., on June 3, 1990, for an interview with Kevorkian. On

the basis of that one face-to-face encounter, the doctor concluded that Adkins' euthanasia request was rational. The following day, as her husband waited in a nearby motel, Adkins was hooked up intravenously to an inverted bottle of saline solution hanging from a metal frame in the back of Kevorkian's parked van. Two other bottles also were suspend-

How the Netherlands Handles Euthanasia

Sooner or later, discussions about active euthanasia and assisted suicide in the United States turn to the situation in the Netherlands. Although euthanasia still is a criminal offense there, punishable by up to 12 years in prison, it is increasingly tolerated in practice. Dutch physicians who put hopelessly ill patients to death after being asked to do so are not prosecuted if they follow certain guidelines formulated by the courts.

In a series of Dutch court cases decided between 1973 and 1984, two conditions were deemed essential for legitimizing euthanasia. First, the patient must make the request at his own initiative, repeatedly and explicitly expressing his wish to die. Second, the patient must be suffering from severe physical or mental pain, with no prospect of recovery.

Since 1984, Dutch courts have added a third condition — that a physician intending to perform euthanasia first consult a colleague to confirm the accuracy of the diagnosis, verify the planned means of bringing about death and ascertain that all legal requirements are being met. Some court cases have also cited as requirements the presence of an incurable disease or a demand that death by euthanasia not inflict unnecessary suffering on others.

Typically, a Dutch euthanasia patient is first given a shot of barbiturates, which causes unconsciousness within three to five seconds. A follow-up shot of curare produces death in 10 to 20 minutes by paralyzing the respiratory system.

A Dutch doctor who performs euthanasia is not permitted to attribute death to "natural causes" on the death certificate. Rather, he or the coroner must inform the police that a medically aided death has occurred. The police, in turn, report to the district attorney, who decides whether to prosecute.

In practice, few Dutch doctors bother to notify the authorities about deaths from euthanasia. Only about a dozen cases a year impel prosecutors even to make preliminary inquiries. Guilty verdicts have occasionally been returned in the few cases that went to trial, but in each instance the conviction was overturned by a higher court on the ground that the doctor acted out of "higher necessity."

Consequently, the extent of euthanasia in the Netherlands is largely a matter of informed conjecture. Estimates range all the way from 2,000 to 10,000 or even 20,000 cases a year. Most acts of euthanasia are performed by physicians not in hospitals or nursing facilities but in patients' homes. Surveys show, in addition, that about 80 percent of all Dutch patients requesting euthanasia are terminal cancer cases.

American opponents of euthanasia are bothered by anecdotal evidence that increasing numbers of aged Dutch patients are being put to death without having requested it. Such reports are hard to document for obvious reasons, but they are widely accepted by U.S. experts. Julie A. Grimstad, executive director of the Center for the Rights of the Terminally Ill in Hurst, Texas, estimates that "about a third of all active-euthanasia deaths in the Netherlands are involuntary. And that doesn't include the deaths that were brought about by stopping medical treatment or stopping food and water."

Critics point to other signs that Dutch policy on euthanasia may be skidding down an ethical "slippery slope." In 1987, for example, a committee of the Royal Dutch Medical Association suggested that minors be allowed to obtain euthanasia over the objections of their parents. "Sometimes a 15-year-old child can have a mature judgment," a report by the committee stated, and "sometimes parents can have immature judgment." No such cases have come before Dutch courts thus far.

Now that a euthanasia movement seems to be gathering strength in the United States, many people are wondering if the Netherlands experience will be replicated on this side of the Atlantic. According to Rita L. Marker, executive director of the International Anti-Euthanasia Task Force in Steubenville, Ohio, "It not only *could* happen here, but it *will* happen if we're not very, very careful."

---

ed from the frame. One contained sodium pentothal (a sedative) and the other a solution of potassium chloride and succinylcholine (a muscle relaxant).

Acting on Kevorkian's instructions, Adkins pressed a button that shut off the flow of saline solution and opened the line of sodium pentothal, causing her to lose consciousness. After one minute, an automatic timer closed the pentothal line and released the contents of the third bottle. Adkins' heart stopped beating within six minutes.

The Hemlock Society approved of what Kevorkian and Adkins did because, Humphry wrote, "it knew at first hand that she had been contemplating this for at least six months, had been refused help by other doctors and her family was in psychological counseling." Moreover, the fact that Adkins had to travel 2,000 miles to fulfill her final wish showed that "We need to change the law so that this sort of compassionate help by a doctor can happen at home or in the hospital."[20]

Murder Indictment

The furor aroused by Adkins' death had barely subsided when it became known that Kevorkian had helped two other women kill themselves in similar fashion. Sherry Miller, 43, a multiple-sclerosis victim, and Margery Wantz, 58, suffering from a severe but unspecified pelvic disorder, died within an hour of each other on Oct. 23, 1991, while connected to suicide machines in a secluded cabin about 40 miles north of Detroit. The women, who knew each other only through Kevorkian, had asked to die on a balmy day just after sunset.

News accounts of the Miller and Wantz deaths solidified Kevorkian's reputation as "Dr. Death." The double assisted suicide also led to calls for disciplinary action. Acting at the behest of Michigan Attorney General Frank Kelley, the state Board of Medicine on Nov. 20, 1991, voted 8-0 to suspend Kevorkian's medical license. The doctor has appealed the decision. A grand jury in Oakland County, Mich., where Miller and Wantz died, indicted Kevorkian Feb. 3, 1992, on two counts of murder and one count of delivery of a controlled substance in connection with their deaths. A murder charge brought against him in the Adkins case was dismissed in December 1990 on the ground that Michigan has no law prohibiting assisted suicide.

Adkins' death had been ruled a suicide. However, an Oakland County medical examiner recorded the cause of Wantz's and Miller's deaths as homicide, triggering the grand jury probe. District Judge James P. Sheehy has said he will rule Feb. 28 on what, if any, charges Kevorkian will face at trial.

Kevorkian is not letting the controversy (and legal troubles) keep him from working.* Speaking by telephone Nov. 2 to participants in a conference on secular humanism in Kansas City, Mo., he called euthana-

_____
*The *Detroit Free Press* reported Feb. 12 that Kevorkian advised a cancer-stricken dentist in Los Angeles by telephone and by mail on how to kill himself with a suicide machine, and the man later did so.

sia the "last civil right" and criticized doctors for not defending it. He went further in an article in the February 1992 issue of the *American Journal of Forensic Psychiatry,* a quarterly publication for psychiatrists who serve as expert witnesses in legal cases. Kevorkian recommended the formation of panels of suicide specialists ("obitiatrists"), who would review requests from people wishing to take their lives. He said in a subsequent interview that "You can't let it be done by every doctor or it certainly would be abused." [21]

Some of Kevorkian's opponents have accused him of employing methods used by the doctors who helped implement Nazi Germany's euthanasia program. He angrily rejects the charge. "First of all, the Nazis never bothered about consent, informed or not," he wrote in a 1991 book on "planned death." He added that "many, if not most of the [Nazi] 'experiments' were for rather frivolous aims" and were, in addition, "*wartime* atrocities beyond any hope of civilized control." [22]

Washington Initiative

Though he presumably did not plan it that way, Kevorkian seems to have influenced the fate of the nation's first ballot proposal to legalize voluntary euthanasia. Initiative 119, which appeared on the Washington ballot Nov. 5, 1991, sought to amend the state's 1979 Natural Death Act to permit "physician aid in dying," defined as "a medical service provided in person by a physician that will end the life of a conscious and mentally competent qualified person in a dignified, painless and humane manner, when requested voluntarily by the patient through a written directive executed at the time the service is desired."

The wording of Initiative 119 gave

no details about the precise form that a physician's aid in dying would take. However, literature distributed by Washington Citizens for Death With Dignity, the group sponsoring the measure, indicated it would mean a lethal dose of oral or intravenous medication.

The proposed law provided that a request for a doctor's assistance in dying must be made in writing by the terminally ill patient in the presence of two independent witnesses. Furthermore, two examining physicians had to certify in writing that the patient suffered from a terminal illness likely to result in death within six months. Unlike a 1988 measure that failed to qualify for the California ballot, Initiative 119 did not allow incompetent patients to receive euthanasia on the basis of previously executed advance directives.

At first, Initiative 119 seemed headed for a decisive victory. A statewide poll in early October found that 61 percent of likely voters favored the measure, while 27 percent opposed it and 12 percent were undecided. On Election Day, though, Washington voters rejected Initiative 119 by a margin of 54 to 46 percent.

What happened? Julie Grimstad credits opponents with educating voters about the proposal's flaws, such as the provision on terminal illness. "How do you define a terminal illness?" she asks. "And what doctor in his right mind is going to tell a patient he has only six months to live? Most doctors know that if you've got 'six months to live,' you might actually live a year, or two years, or three — or you might die tomorrow. Writing a specific death expectancy into law is ludicrous, because medicine doesn't operate that way. Besides, does 'will die in six months' mean *without* treatment? Or *with* treatment?"

Rita L. Marker, executive director of the International Anti-Euthanasia Task Force in Steubenville, Ohio, and

Suicide and the Elderly

After declining steadily for 30 years, the incidence of suicide among Americans 65 and older rose sharply from 1980 to 1986. Suicide rates are highest among those ages 75-84. This group contains a large proportion of people who have just lost spouses or are seriously ill.

Deaths per 100,000 population

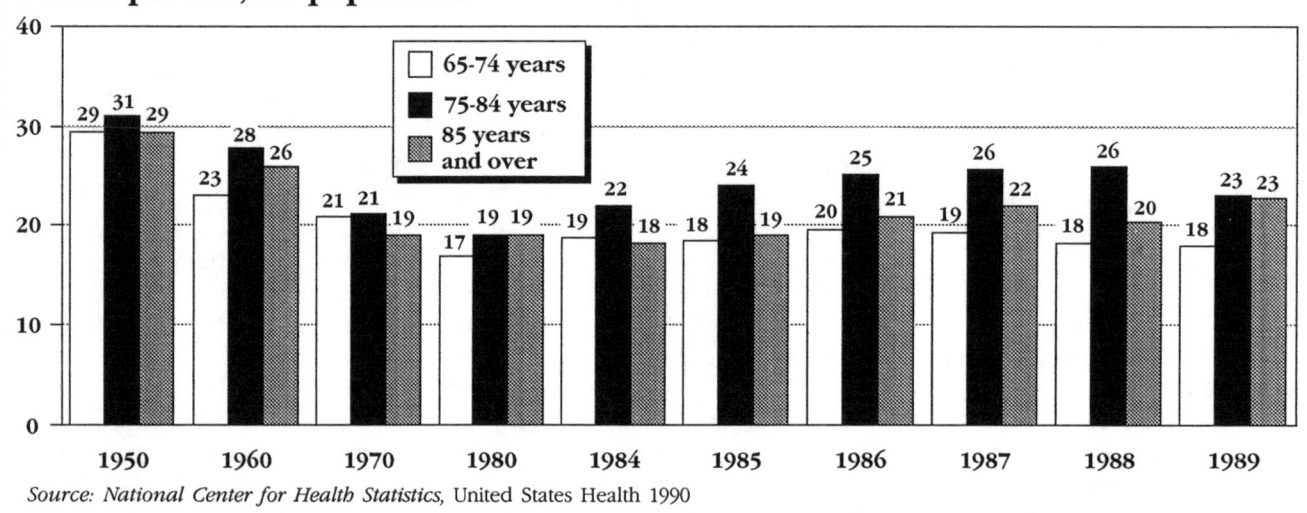

Source: *National Center for Health Statistics*, United States Health 1990

a Washington native, visited the state twice during the initiative campaign. "If the vote had been held two weeks later," she says, "Initiative 119 probably would have been defeated by an even greater margin, because people were becoming aware of just exactly what it meant." Marker surmises that many Washingtonians flinched at the prospect of living in a "euthanasia tourism" mecca. "There's no question that euthanasia clinics would have opened close to the airport," she says. "They also would have served people who live in Washington — particularly older people who could be easily persuaded that aid in dying is one of the options they could choose."

Humphry attributes the defeat of Initiative 119 to two factors: semantics and a perceived lack of safeguards. He says proponents erred in stressing "aid in dying," a term that can mean "anything from a physician's lethal injection ... to holding hands with the dying patient and saying, 'I love you.'" This allowed

opponents to score points with voters by using the words "suicide" and "euthanasia." Failing to draft detailed guidelines on how euthanasia would be carried out was another blunder, Humphry feels. The public, he says, "did not want euthanasia laws on the books without built-in safeguards — a sign of the general distrust of the medical and legal professions." [23]

Many commentators suggested that the two most recent suicides arranged by Kevorkian, coming as they did just two weeks before the Washington vote, played a key role in sinking Initiative 119. Humphry disagrees, saying the suicides "may have marginally affected the result but not significantly." [24] In Marker's opinion, "It was not so much what Kevorkian did as that people reflected on what could be done in Washington if Initiative 119 passed." When Kevorkian "jumped back onto the front pages," she says, "people thought, 'Wait a minute. Is Initiative 119 about this, too?' In fact, that's exactly what it was about."

California Campaign

Even as the Initiative 119 returns were being tallied, a similar campaign was getting under way in California. In October 1991, the California attorney general's office authorized Californians Against Human Suffering (CAHS), an affiliate of Americans Against Human Suffering Inc., to gather signatures for the purpose of placing a proposed death-with-dignity law on the Nov. 3, 1992, ballot. The group has until March 5 to collect the required 387,000 valid signatures.

Jack Nicholl, the director of CAHS, has set a goal of 570,000 signatures to provide a cushion against error. "We're probably in the mid-300,000s now," he says. "It's not in the bag, but we've got a real good shot at it."

The California initiative differs from the Washington proposal in that a request for aid in dying must be "enduring" — that is, made on more

Continued on p. 162

At Issue:

Should doctors take part in planned suicides?

Timothy J. Lace

*Student, Texas A&M University
College of Medicine*
FROM *JOURNAL OF THE AMERICAN MEDICAL
ASSOCIATION,* DEC. 1, 1989.

i believe ... that physicians can play a positive role in the active euthanasia of mentally competent, terminally ill people who request assistance in ending their own lives. It is crucial that physicians who choose to help dying patients in this way should be free to do so without the fear of criminal prosecution.

There are those who will say that active euthanasia is not part of the physician's role and never has been. Historical evidence, however, indicates that it was common practice for Grecian and Roman physicians to assist in suicide. The Hippocratic Oath, which forbids that the physician give a "deadly drug to anybody, not even if asked for it, nor will I make a suggestion to this effect," is inconsistent with values expressed by many historical sources and atypical of the realities of ancient medical practice.

Platonists, cynics, stoics and other classical philosophers considered suicide an honorable alternative to hopeless illness.... Thus, there does exist a classical foundation for this practice — a practice that continues today but now carries with it the risk of criminal prosecution....

The desire to cure is admirable, and only in approaching disease in this way can cures be effected. However, because we view ourselves as healers, the death of a patient often becomes very difficult to accept. Let us not forget that in addition to the vital task of healing, physicians perform other functions. We ameliorate human suffering when cure is not possible, and we provide structure for people in times of chaos. When we recognize the importance of these latter roles in which we spend a great deal of time, we will more easily accept death as an inescapable fate that is not always the foe. We need not view this inevitable part of the life cycle as evil....

There is a growing trend among 20th-century physicians to accept the death of patients without a sense of failure. This trend is illustrated by the growing acceptance of living wills and do-not-resuscitate orders, concepts unheard of only a few years ago. Given that death is fated for all, are there not instances in which it is perhaps more humane to help people with terminal illness end their own lives if they so desire?

I believe there are such instances. We must not let our personal need to cure take precedence over the right of patients to determine for themselves the course of their lives — it may be all the control they have left.

Samuel F. Hunter

*Student, University of Texas Medical
School at Galveston*
FROM *JOURNAL OF THE AMERICAN MEDICAL
ASSOCIATION,* DEC. 1, 1989.

t he patient's perspective on his own illness — a perspective the physician helps create — crucially affects his quality of life. Our role as physicians should be to maximize the potential for a long and rich life, even though death is inevitable....

Instead of promoting active euthanasia, we can best serve our patients by accurate prognosis and skillful management of complications and pain. Along with social workers and the clergy, we can bolster emotional strength. When we no longer heal, we palliate and comfort. This has been the time-honored tradition of medicine. Adding death-on-demand to our armamentarium would subvert society's faith in us.... If society demands the right to euthanasia, it does not need physicians to supply or encourage that choice. Condemned murderers are executed by injection without our help; should we not also shun unnatural death by active euthanasia?

In contrast to this kind of killing, permitting death from a terminal illness without intervening (passive or voluntary euthanasia) offers fewer obstacles, and the legal system can help us decide when it is appropriate. The avoidance of unnecessary distress and expense has always been part of our ministry to the patient. We are therefore obliged to protect the terminally ill patient's option to end life-prolonging treatment.

When the patient is not fully cognizant and has not expressed his or her wishes in a legal document, many interests can compete. Institutions and medical providers welcome paying customers, while insurers benefit from withholding treatment. Families may hope to prolong or shorten the patient's life according to their own benefit. Our own emotions can also provoke self-conflict. We lack the time and training to evaluate properly a patient's familial, social and financial environment. The objectivity, neutrality, and oversight of a judge can equitably deal with these conflicting concerns. Physicians should therefore resist laws that abrogate the role of the court in order to streamline "death with dignity."

Maintaining the emotional well-being and self-image of our patients should be a major goal, but active euthanasia violates our fundamental precepts of healing and disrupts important social, emotional and spiritual processes. To procure death with honor for our patients, let us not be the angels of death, but ministers of healing ... and hope.

Continued from p. 160

than one occasion. In addition, the California measure establishes a separate set of safeguards for nursing-home residents, bars intimidation of patients and tampering with advance directives, suggests psychiatric or psychological consultation if a doctor is unsure whether a patient is competent and requires that fees be "fair and reasonable."

Several features of the 1988 Humane and Dignified Death Act, which failed to qualify for the 1988 California ballot, have been incorporated into the new legislation. These include requirements that (1) a request for aid in dying be made voluntarily, in writing and in the presence of two disinterested persons; (2) two physicians who have examined the patient must agree that a terminal condition exists; (3) physicians who do not wish to render aid in dying may freely refuse to do so; (4) insurance policies remain unaffected by an aid-in-dying decision; and (5) physicians who provide aid in dying receive immunity from criminal, civil or administrative action.

Mindful of Kevorkian's purported influence on the Initiative 119 balloting, CAHS addressed an open letter to him on Nov. 21. "Please, Dr. Kevorkian, stop what you are doing," the letter read. "The California initiative provides the next opportunity for society to consider allowing new choices at life's end. Let men and women decide the issue by examining their own conscience free of the fears you invoke with your unaccountable actions. You cast too dark a shadow on what so many see as a ray of hope."

ABA Rejects Assisted-Suicide Proposal

The American Bar Association (ABA) may have cast a shadow on the California campaign when it voted down a resolution endorsing laws that allow doctors to help terminally ill patients commit suicide. The resolution, sponsored by the Beverly Hills (Calif.) Bar Association, was rejected Feb. 3 by the ABA's House of Delegates at its midwinter meeting in Dallas.

Television journalist Betty Rollin, the author of *Last Wish,* a book about how she helped her cancer-stricken mother commit suicide, pleaded with the lawyers to adopt the resolution. "You have to rescue these people," she said. "This is an emergency." But the delegates sided with the arguments of John Pickering, head of the ABA's Commission on Legal Problems of the Elderly. "The law has gone as far as it should," he said. "There is a line between refusing medical treatment and deliberate killing."

Although Rollin failed to sway the attorneys, she has done much to increase awareness of euthanasia in recent years. For one thing, she wrote the foreword to Humphry's *Final Exit.* And on Jan. 12, a dramatization of her own book was shown on national television, with Patty Duke as Betty Rollin and Maureen Stapleton as Rollin's mother. The TV movie received favorable reviews.

Humphry, too, has earned stage credits. "Is This the Day?" a play based on his 1978 book, *Jean's Way,* had its American premiere at the Soreng Theater in Eugene, Ore., Jan. 31-Feb. 2. At present, there are no plans for any future productions in the United States.

It hardly matters, because active euthanasia and assisted suicide are now staple fare on television news-magazine and interview shows. "Face the Nation," "60 Minutes," "Donahue," "Nightline," "Good Morning, America," "The MacNeil-Lehrer News-Hour," "CBS Nightwatch" and "CNN Crossfire," among others, have examined the issue. Kevorkian's most recent appearance on "Donahue" was Jan. 31; he was interviewed by Barbara Walters on ABC's "20/20" Feb. 14.

TV discussions about euthanasia and assisted suicide are becoming more forthright. Rita Marker, who has appeared as a panelist on numerous talk shows, says "The kill-and-tell story has become increasingly prevalent just in the last six or eight months." As recently as two years ago, she says, people who appeared on television to explain how they helped a spouse commit suicide routinely used pseudonyms or disguised themselves. Now they use their own names, knowing there is little chance they will be prosecuted for the acts they describe.

"My concern is not so much that the people who have done these things be prosecuted," says Marker. "I worry because these kinds of stories grab at the emotions and because people are no longer shocked. [Euthanasia] is starting to take on the aura of, if not respectability, at least acceptability." ∎

OUTLOOK

Battle Continues

Most combatants in the conflict over legalizing active euthanasia and assisted suicide say the struggle is still in its early stages. Washington's Initiative 119 "was only one battle in a war that has just started," says Marker. "This is the beginning of a very long conflict, and we're going to see battle after battle in state after state."

Marker thinks skirmishes will continue to occur on "three or four fronts." There will be action "in the legislatures and the initiative process, and probably something on the court level. We'll also see more situations like those involving Kevorkian, where someone will test the limits of the law and say, 'Now see what you can do — see whether you can catch me.'"

Derek Humphry envisions a much shorter contest. Reviewing developments to date, he says: "We first had a stab at it in California in 1988, but we didn't qualify [for the ballot]. We just weren't strong enough. But we made a lot of noise, and we got the subject aired and our legislation critiqued. Then we had a narrow defeat in Washington. Now we've moved ... down to California. Oregon is next. In 1994, [the] Hemlock [Society] of Oregon will be going for [euthanasia] legislation."

Humphry notes also that euthanasia bills have been introduced in the Maine, New Hampshire, Iowa and Michigan. "We think it's extremely significant that the Hemlock Society had nothing do do with any of these bills," he says. "It shows that politicians are waking up to the public interest in this subject."

In Humphry's opinion, the euthanasia movement is certain to prevail within the next few years. "By the end of the century, this subject will be a closed book," he says. "We will have legislated to the extent that is necessary, and society will have moved on to other major problems."

Though she offers no predictions, Julie Grimstad voices hope that people will weigh the consequences of legalized euthanasia before reaching a final decision. "It's not like abortion, which doesn't affect you personally because you are not the fetus," she says. "Euthanasia occurs at the other end of life's spectrum, and we're all going to get there. So I think people should be vitally interested in what is happening and do some soul-searching. Are we promoting something that we're going to be sorry for when we're 80 years old? We know from demographics that 80-year-olds in the year 2010 are not going to be very welcome, because we will not be able to support them.

"So, are we laying the groundwork

for our children to eliminate us, just as we have eliminated unborn lives by abortion? We have taught our children a hefty lesson in that regard: If you're inconvenient, if you interfere with our jobs, if you cost too much, we will kill you before you are born. Now, are our children going to look at us when we're senile and say, 'Well, Mom, it's time to go'? If the law says they can do it, they will."

Thomas Murray feels it is possible the euthanasia debate will end not in triumph for one side or the other but in reconsideration of the American approach to dying. "I would like to see the federal government provide much greater support for alternative ways of dying," he says. "I'm thinking in particular of hospice care, which doesn't have to be given in an institution. In fact, the care site usually is the home. There are home-nursing visits, but the day-to-day caregivers tend to be members of the family."

"'Return dying to the home' might be an appropriate theme for the 1990s," Murray continues. "Home birth became popular in the 1980s, so why not home death? That's where most people used to die. People should have the opportunity to die in a setting where they can retain a sense of their own humanity." ■

Notes

[1] For background, see "Right to Die: Medical, Legal and Moral Issues," *Editorial Research Reports*, Sept. 28, 1990, pp. 553-567.

[2] Christine K. Cassel and Diane E. Meier, "Morals and Moralism in the Debate Over Euthanasia and Assisted Suicide," *The New England Journal of Medicine*, Sept. 13, 1990, p. 751.

[3] Choice in Dying is the new name for two organizations that have merged. Their former names were Concern for Dying and Society for the Right to Die.

[4] George Howe Colt, *The Enigma of Suicide* (1991), p. 358.

[5] Quoted in *The New York Times*, Sept. 19, 1991.

[6] Quoted in *USA Today*, Sept. 16, 1991.

[7] Address before Colorado Health Lawyers Association, Denver, March 28, 1984.

[8] Margaret P. Battin, "Age Rationing and the Just Distribution of Health Care: Is There a Duty to Die?" *Ethics*, January 1987, pp. 335-36.

[9] "Not Before Time," *Commonweal*, Oct. 11, 1991, p. 564.

[10] *Ibid.*

[11] Leon R. Kass, "Death With Dignity and the Sanctity of Life," *The Human Life Review*, spring 1990, pp. 37-38.

[12] Sidney H. Wanzer, et al., "The Physician's Responsibility Toward Hopelessly Ill Patients: A Second Look," *The New England Journal of Medicine*, March 30, 1989, p. 848.

[13] Leon R. Kass, "Why Doctors Must Not Kill," *Commonweal*, Aug. 9, 1991, p. 473.

[14] Quoted in E. Robert Sinnett, et al., "Voluntary Euthanasia and the Right to Die: A Dialogue With Derek Humphry," *Journal of Counseling and Development*, June 1989, p. 570.

[15] Quoted in *Maclean's*, July 16, 1990, p. 14.

[16] Robert J. Lifton, *The Nazi Doctors: Medical Killing and the Psychology of Genocide* (1986), p. 21.

[17] Leo Alexander, "Medical Science Under Dictatorship," in Dennis J. Horan and David Mall, eds., *Death, Dying and Euthanasia* (1980), pp. 584, 587. Alexander's article originally appeared in *The New England Journal of Medicine* in 1949.

[18] *The New York Times*, Jan. 27, 1939, cited in Rita L. Marker, et al., "Euthanasia: A Historical Overview," *Maryland Journal of Contemporary Legal Issues*, summer 1991, p. 276.

[19] Remarks in a debate, "Can There Be Rational Suicide?" sponsored by the Center for Applied Biomedical Ethics, Denver, June 25-27, 1986.

[20] Derek Humphry, *Final Exit* (1991), p. 139.

[21] Quoted in *USA Today*, Jan. 24, 1992.

[22] Jack Kevorkian, *Prescription: Medicide — The Goodness of Planned Death* (1991), p. 37.

[23] Derek Humphry, "Why Were They Beaten in Washington?" *Hemlock Quarterly*, January 1992, p. 4.

[24] *Ibid.*

Bibliography

Selected Sources Used

Books

Baird, Robert M., and Stuart E. Rosenbaum, *Euthanasia: The Moral Issues,* Prometheus Books, 1989.

This anthology comprises some of the most widely discussed articles about active and passive euthanasia published in recent years.

Colt, George Howe, *The Enigma of Suicide,* Summit Books, 1991.

Colt, a staff writer for *Life* magazine, starts by exploring the reasons for adolescent suicide and then provides a broad historical overview of the practice by people of all ages. The book also examines the right-to-die movement.

Humphry, Derek, *Final Exit: The Practicalities of Self-Deliverance and Assisted Suicide for the Dying,* The Hemlock Society, 1991.

Some reviewers said they were put off by the matter-of-fact tone of Humphry's book, but that may be just the approach that its readers were looking for. Humphry offers numerous tips on the most effective and least painful ways to commit suicide and indicates how far an individual can legally go in helping another one take his life.

Kevorkian, Jack, *Prescription: Medicide — The Goodness of Planned Death,* Prometheus Books, 1991.

Kevorkian, known as "Dr. Death" because of his espousal of physician-assisted suicide, devotes much of this book to another of his pet causes. He calls for allowing condemned criminals to choose death by irreversible anesthesia, with the proviso that their bodies could then be used for organ donation or medical experimentation.

Osgood, Nancy J., *Suicide in the Elderly: A Practitioner's Guide to Diagnosis and Mental Health Intervention,* Aspen Systems Corp., 1985.

"[O]ld people in America kill themselves because old age has nothing worthwhile to offer them," says Osgood. She adds: "As long as we view the aged as useless, nonproductive people to be pitied and feared — perhaps because we see them as living portraits of what we will become if we live long enough — the elderly suicide rate will remain high."

Articles

Burleigh, Michael, "Euthanasia and the Third Reich," *History Today,* February 1990.

Burleigh describes how the Nazis' euthanasia policy operated during the prewar years when it was directed at the German people themselves. Of particular interest is his account of how Nazi propagandists manipulated popular opinion on euthanasia through motion pictures.

Kass, Leon R., "Death With Dignity & the Sanctity of Life," *The Human Life Review,* spring 1990.

Kass dismisses the notion that there is a "right to die." "In the name of choice people claim the right to choose to cease to be choosing beings," he writes. "From such a right to refuse not only treatment but life itself — from a right to become dead — it is then a small step to the right to be made dead: From my right to die will follow your duty to assist me in dying, i.e., to become the agent of my death, if I am not able, or do not wish, to kill myself."

Marker, Rita L.; Joseph R. Stanton; Mark E. Recznik; and Keith A. Fournier, "Euthanasia: A Historical Overview," *Maryland Journal of Contemporary Legal Issues,* summer 1991.

Marker and her co-authors survey the history of euthanasia in modern times from the perspective of those who firmly oppose the practice. They conclude: "Anyone who thinks that the intentional and deliberate killing of patients, once unleashed, can be strictly controlled should drink deeply from the well of history before the nation further embraces such a course."

Quill, Timothy E., "Death and Dignity — A Case of Individualized Decision Making," *The New England Journal of Medicine,* March 7, 1991.

Quill, a physician from Rochester, N.Y., describes how he agonized over what to do when his patient (identified only as "Diane") rejected the arduous treatment that would have given her only a one-in-four chance of survival, and how he helped her when she said she wanted to end her life. (Quill was neither prosecuted nor professionally disciplined for what he did.)

Singer, Peter A., and Mark Siegler, "Euthanasia — A Critique," *The New England Journal of Medicine,* June 28, 1990.

Singer and Siegler summarize key developments in the right-to-die movement as well as the pros and cons of euthanasia. They conclude that euthanasia is "unacceptable" as public policy "because of the likelihood, or even the inevitability, of involuntary euthanasia — persons being euthanized without their consent or against their wishes."

The Next Step

Additional Articles from Current Periodicals from EBSCO Publishing's Database

Addresses & essays

"Dial 119 for murder," *Commonweal,* Aug. 9, 1991, p. 452.

Editorial. Considers the implications of Washington state's Initiative 119, which would allow physicians to consciously end the lives of competent terminal patients who request relief from their sufferings. Why the practice seems to be gaining public approval; the dignity of life; Jewish and Christian traditions and the care of the dying; more.

"The last consumer item," *National Review,* Dec. 31, 1990, p. 14.

Questions why society has been quick to condemn Dr. Jack Kevorkian, maker of a homemade "suicide machine." Argues that Kevorkian's invention is a natural outcome of America's increasingly secular society, which no longer attaches intrinsic value to human life.

Conwell, Y. and E. D. Caine, "Rational suicide and the right to die," *The New England Journal of Medicine,* Oct. 10, 1991, p. 1100.

Presents a commentary on the growing attention given to the right to die, rational suicide and physician-assisted suicide. Case of Janet Adkins and her doctor Jack Kevorkian. Statistics in the United States; suicide in the elderly; views of the psychiatric profession; role of physicians like Timothy Quill who support assisted suicide.

Goodwin, J. S., "Mercy killing: Mercy for whom?" *Journal of the American Medical Association,* Jan. 16, 1991, p. 326.

Argues against the mercy killing of Alzheimer patients. Comments that mercy killing is the ultimate selfish act.

Jonsen, A. R., "Initiative 119: What is at stake?" *Commonweal,* Aug. 9, 1991, Supplement p. 2.

Opposes Washington state's Initiative 119 which would allow a competent, terminally ill patient to request of his or her physician "aid-in-dying." History of Washington's public policy about death and dying; why it may be the first state to legalize active euthanasia; public and medical opinion on the proposal; cataclysmic implications if the bill is passed.

Mallison, M. B., "The sorrow and the pity of 'Final Exit,'" *American Journal of Nursing,* September 1991, p. 7.

Editorial. Contends that the popularity of Derek Humphry's book "Final Exit" is largely a response to inadequate health resources, and that few people would choose voluntary euthanasia if they had access to appropriate care. Depression; fear of suffering; fear of impoverishment from illness; World Health Organization recommends that governments attend to pain relief first; view of American Geriatrics Society.

May, W. F., "Rising to the occasion of our death," *Christian Century,* July 11, 1990 and July 18, 1990, p. 662.

Editorial. Argues against regularized mercy killing. Passive vs. active euthanasia; responsibility to care for the aging and ill; Jack Kevorkian case study.

Books & reading

Mattingly, S. S., "Book reviews," *The New England Journal of Medicine,* Aug. 1, 1991, p. 367.

Reviews two books "Euthanasia: Toward an Ethical Social Policy," by David C. Thomasma and Glenn C. Graber, and "Drawing the Line: Life, Death, and Ethical Choices in an American Hospital," by Samuel Gorovitz.

Case studies

Angell, M., "The case of Helga Wanglie," *The New England Journal of Medicine,* Aug. 15, 1991, p. 511.

Editorial. Discusses the "right to die" case of Helga Wanglie in which the family wanted to continue life-sustaining treatment and the doctors wanted her to be removed from the respirator. Court decision supporting Wanglie's family.

Borger, G., "The odd odyssey of 'Dr. Death,'" *U.S. News & World Report,* Aug. 27, 1990 and Sept. 3, 1990, p. 27.

Profiles Jack Kevorkian, a doctor who has been ostracized by the medical community for helping Alzheimer's patient Janet Adkins kill herself last June. No doubts about helping Adkins die; controversy over euthanasia.

Borger, G., "The shadows lurking behind Dr. Death," *U.S. News & World Report,* Dec. 17, 1990, p. 30.

Reports that Dr. Jack Kevorkian has been charged with the murder of Janet Adkins, 54, a woman who used his suicide machine to choose death over life. While courts and legislatures wrangle with the legal complexities governing death, the doctors cannot wait: patients need answers.

Busalacchi, P., "How can they?" *Hastings Center Report,* September/October 1990, p. 6.

Relates the personal story of a man whose daughter, like Nancy Cruzan, is in a persistent vegetative state. His reaction to Supreme Court ruling; opinion of former Surgeon General Dr. C. Everett Koop.

Goode, E.E., "Defending the right to die," *U.S. News & World Report,* Sept. 30, 1991, p. 38.

Discusses the best-selling guide to suicide, "Final Exit," by Derek Humphry, and addresses why the author has placed himself at the center of a highly emotional moral debate over voluntary euthanasia and the right to die. Humphry's own personal tragedy of aiding in his wife's death; what dying involves, according to Humphry; his critics' argument; his troubled childhood; the purpose of the National Hemlock Society; the process of dying.

Taylor, G.W., D. Wolff, et al., "AIDS 'mercy killings,'" *Maclean's,* July 16, 1990, p. 14.

Examines the controversy surrounding Vancouver-based AIDS counselor David Lewis' recent claim that he has helped eight AIDS-infected friends end their own lives. Debate over the legal and moral implications of euthanasia; comments by AIDS activists and counselors on both sides of the debate.

Debates & issues

"Should the doctor ever help?" *Harvard Health Letter,* August 1991, p. 4.

Considers the question "Should doctors help their patients to die?" A controversial decision by a doctor to give a large dose of morphine to a terminal cancer patient; discussion of an article in the March, 1990 issue of *The New England Journal of Medicine,* which maintained that "it is not immoral for a physician to assist in the rationale suicide of a terminally ill person"; an interview with Daniel D. Federman; how is suicide determined to be "rational?"; more.

Ames, K., L. Wilson, et al., "Last rights," *Newsweek,* Aug. 26, 1991, p. 40.

Reports that when dying is all that awaits them, more and more people are choosing certain death now rather than uncertain life on medical support systems. More individuals confronting their own mortality; how medicine has changed people's views on dying; popularity of Derek Humphry's book "Final Exit"; what can help in ensuring a dignified, humane death; living will; health-care proxy; durable power of attorney for health care.

Carton, R.W., "The road to euthanasia," *Journal of the American Medical Association,* April 25, 1990, p. 2221.

Editorial. Discusses the trends toward active euthanasia, and reports attempts to try to set standards of behavior somewhere between active euthanasia and support of biologic life always, and at all costs.

Jenish, D., "Death defined," *Maclean's,* Aug. 26, 1991, p. 40.

Examines the debate in North America about euthanasia and the rights of the terminally ill. Success of the suicide manual "Final Exit," by Derek Humphry, founder of the Hemlock Society (Eugene, Ore.); debate over doctor-assisted suicide; Detroit, Mich., patient Marjorie Wantz, 58, who suffers from chronic, severe pelvic pain; role of Dr. Jack Kevorkian in the suicide of Janet Adkins, 54, of Portland, Ore.; similar cases; euthanasia legislation in the United States and Canada.

Kass, L.R., "Why doctors must not kill," *Commonweal,* Aug. 9, 1991, Supplement p. 8.

Asserts that doctors should not be licensed to kill. Why the current taboo against doctors killing patients (even on request) is the very embodiment of reason and wisdom; projected impact of legalized euthanasia on the doctor-patient relationship; psychological dangers of the practice; ethical conflicts; medical and technological advances; analysis in light of Washington state's euthanasia proposal, Initiative 119.

Leo, J., "Cozy little homicides," *U.S. News & World Report,* Nov. 11, 1991, p. 28.

Presents a commentary on the issue of euthanasia. Reviews "Regulating Death," a very sobering book about euthanasia in the Netherlands, by Carlos Gomez; why Dutch doctors have been allowed to kill patients for almost two decades, even though mercy killing is illegal in that country; details how some cases of euthanasia are considered homicide; Gomez's reaction to Initiative 119, the euthanasia proposition on the ballot this week in Washington state; more.

Selzer, R., "A question of mercy," *The New York Times Magazine,* Sept. 22, 1991, p. 32.

Considers the problematic issues connected with physician-aided euthanasia. The author's comments about a case of euthanasia he was confronted with; what eventually happened to the patient seeking euthanasia assistance from the author.

Spritz, N., "Speeding the dying," *Hastings Center Report,* July/August 1991, p. 4.

Comments on a panel at the 72nd annual meeting of the American College of Physicians entitled "Should Physicians Help Seriously Ill People Die?" Issue of possible loss of trust in physicians; comments against the legal or moral acceptance of physician assisted suicide; panelists; meaning of the word "euthanasia"; more.

Sprung, C. L. and R. C. Bone, "Changing attitudes and practices in forgoing life-sustaining treatments," *Journal of the American Medical Association,* April 25, 1990, p. 2211.

Reviews changes over the past 20 years in the practice of medicine in life-sustaining situations, from the medical and legal viewpoints. Quinlan case; other examples; discrimination against vegetative and aged patients; active euthanasia laws worldwide; conclusion.

Law & legislation

Campbell, C. S., "To die in Wa," *Hastings Center Report,* March/April 1991, p. 3.

Discusses Initiative 119 in Washington state, which is a referendum question on assisted suicide and euthanasia. Citizens for Death with Dignity; renaming Washington's Natural Death Act; opponents of Initiative 119; lethal injections; more.

Case, T. W., "Dying made easy," *National Review,* Nov. 4, 1991, p. 25.

Reports on Initiative 119, a measure still to be publicly voted on that would make Washington state the only place in the world where active euthanasia was sanctioned by law. Support by the Washington Citizens for Death with Dignity and the Hemlock Society; opposition from a political action committee called 119 Vote No!, represented by the state branch of the American Medical Association, the state hospital association, and the state Catholic Conference; medical ethics; more.

Egan, T., "Washington voters weigh if there is a right to die," *The New York Times,* Oct. 14, 1991, p. A1.

Discusses Washington state's Death With Dignity proposal, Initiative 119, which will appear on the Nov. 5 ballot, at which time voters will decide if doctors should be allowed to kill terminally ill patients who have asked to die. More than 223,000 signatures were gathered by people who believe that the timing of one's death is a basic right.

Robinson, A. B., "Death with dignity in Washington state," *Christian Century,* Oct. 30, 1991, p. 988.

Editorial. Outlines the measure known as Initiative 119, "Death with Dignity," which will be voted on by the people of Washington state on November 5, 1991, and if passed will legally sanction suicide and euthanasia. Amendments and revisions to the 1979 Washington Natural Death Act; Washington as the first jurisdiction in the world to legalize physician-assisted death; opponents of the measure; the relation of individual rights and community responsibility; more.

Moral & religious aspects

"Assisted death," *The Lancet,* Sept. 8, 1990, p. 610.

Investigates and reports on the ethics of prolonging life and assisting death. Compiled by the Institute of Medical Ethics Working Party on the Ethics of Prolonging Life and Assisting Death. Objections to assisting death; killing and letting die in principle; relief of suffering; prolonging life; justification for assisting death; when a doctor may assist death.

"House calls," *National Review,* July 9, 1990, p. 15.

Argues that in light of Dr. Jack Kevorkian's suicide machine and the way he took the life of his 54-year-old patient, life had no intrinsic value so why should the end of life come with any grace. Dying with "dignity" in the back of a camper; Kevorkian's "playing God."

Kass, L. R. "Death with dignity and the sanctity of life," *Commentary,* March 1990, p. 33.

Reports on the confrontation between those who believe in death with dignity and those who uphold the sanctity of life. Euthanasia and termination of medical treatment; Judeo-Christian tradition; taboo against murder; death as intrinsically undignified.

Netherlands

Fumento, M., "The dying Dutchman: Coming soon to a nursing home near you," *American Spectator,* October 1991, p. 18.

Discusses the widespread practice of euthanasia in the Netherlands and the vulnerability of the United States to the practice. An ever-expanding definition of what is allowable; the arguments over whether it is ever really voluntary; down the slippery slope of demographic management; medical costs in the United States and the predictions of an increase in the elderly population.

Nowak, R., "Dutch doctors call for legal euthanasia," *New Scientist,* Oct. 12, 1991, p. 17.

Reports on the wide use of euthanasia in the Netherlands. Who uses euthanasia; officially it counts as murder in the country but is not prosecuted; doctor support for euthanasia.

van der Maas, P. J., J. J. M. van Delden, et al., "Euthanasia and other medical decisions concerning the end of life," *The Lancet,* Sept. 14, 1991, p. 669.

Presents the first results of the Dutch nationwide study on euthanasia and other medical decisions concerning the end of life (MDEL). The study was done at the request of the Dutch government in preparation for a discussion about legislation on euthanasia. Methods; results; discussion.

Back Issues

Great Research on Current Issues Starts Right Here... Recent topics covered by The CQ Researcher are listed below. Issues dated before May 10, 1991, were published under the name of Editorial Research Reports.

AUGUST 1990
Democracy in the Philippines
Initiatives: True Democracy?
Hard Times at Newspapers
Teens Balance School & Jobs

SEPTEMBER 1990
Dangers of Alcohol
Western Alliance After the Cold War
Tobacco Industry
Right to Die

OCTOBER 1990
Organ Transplants
Energy Policy Options
Search for Arab Unity
Child Support

NOVEMBER 1990
Lotteries and Gambling
Post-Cold War Choices
Setting Limits on Medical Care
Multicultural Education

DECEMBER 1990
Cable TV Regulation
Americans' Search for Their Roots
Is Insurance System a Failure?
Why Schools Still Have Tracking

Back issues are available for $4.00 (subscribers) or $7.00 (non-subscribers). Quantity discounts apply to orders over ten. To order, call Congressional Quarterly 1-800-432-2250.

JANUARY 1991
Growing Influence of Boycotts
Should the U.S. Reinstate the Draft?
America's Archaeological Past
Peace Corps' Challenges in '90s

FEBRUARY 1991
Regional Impact of Recession
Puerto Rico's Status
Redistricting: Mapping Power
Nuclear Power

MARCH 1991
Acid Rain
Cost of the Gulf War
Reassessing Gun Laws
Future for Man in Space

APRIL 1991
Social Security
Canadian Crisis Over Quebec
California Drought
Electromagnetic Radiation

MAY 1991
School Choice
Racial Quotas
Animal Rights
U.S. and Japan

JUNE 1991
Children and Divorce
Teenage Suicide
Endangered Species
Europe 1992

JULY 1991
Teenagers and Abortion
Soviet Republics Rebel
Mexico's Emergence
Athletes and Drugs

AUGUST 1991
Sexual Harassment
Fetal Tissue Research
Oil Imports
The Palestinians

SEPTEMBER 1991
Police Brutality
Advertising Under Attack
Saving the Forests
Foster Care Crisis

OCTOBER 1991
Pay-Per-View TV
Youth Gangs
Gene Therapy
World Hunger

NOVEMBER 1991
Fast-Food Shake-Up
The Greening of Eastern Europe
Business' Role in Education
Cuba In Crisis

DECEMBER 1991
Retiree Health Benefits
Asian Americans
The Obscenity Debate
The Disabilities Act

JANUARY 1992
Term Limits
Oil Spills
Hunting Controversy
Alternative Medicine

FEBRUARY 1992
Threatened Coastlines
New Era in Asia

Future Topics

▶ *Future of the Job Market*

▶ *Women and Sports*

▶ *Teenage Drinking*

Jobs in the '90s

What will it take to succeed in the years ahead?

U NLIKE PREVIOUS RECESSIONS, IN WHICH
blue-collar workers bore the brunt of
unemployment, the current downturn has left
white-collar workers out in the cold as well. Large
corporations, once the guarantors of job security, are
eliminating jobs at all levels in an effort to raise productivity.
While corporate restructuring may enable U.S. firms to better
compete in the global marketplace, it also foreshadows a
fundamental change in employer-employee relations:
Growing numbers of Americans will be forced into part-time
work with low pay, no job security and few benefits. The keys
to success in this less-predictable workplace will be
education, training and a willingness to alter career goals.
Above all, experts caution, employees should not expect
lifelong employment with a single company.

 February 28, 1992 • Volume 2, No. 8 • 169-192

Formerly Editorial Research Reports

COVER ART: BARBARA SASSA-DANIELS

THE CQ Researcher

February 28, 1992
Volume 2, No. 8

EDITOR
Sandra Stencel

MANAGING EDITOR
Thomas J. Colin

ASSOCIATE EDITOR
Richard L. Worsnop

STAFF WRITERS
Charles S. Clark
Mary H. Cooper
Rodman D. Griffin

PRODUCTION EDITOR
Laurie De Maris

EDITORIAL ASSISTANT
Thomas H. Moore

GRAPHICS
Jack Auldridge

PUBLISHED BY
Congressional Quarterly Inc.

CHAIRMAN
Andrew Barnes

VICE CHAIRMAN
Andrew P. Corty

EDITOR AND PUBLISHER
Neil Skene

EXECUTIVE EDITOR
Robert W. Merry

PUBLICATIONS MARKETING/SALES
Robert Smith

EDITOR, EBSCO PUBLISHING
Melissa Kummerer

The CQ Researcher (ISSN 1056-2036). Formerly Editorial Research Reports. Published weekly (48 times per year, not printed the first Friday of any month with five Fridays) by Congressional Quarterly Inc., 1414 22nd St., N.W., Washington, D.C. 20037. Rates are furnished upon request. Second-class postage paid at Washington, D.C. POSTMASTER: Send address changes to The CQ Researcher, 1414 22nd St., N.W., Washington, D.C. 20037.

Jobs in the '90s

BY MARY H. COOPER

THE ISSUES

Last August, a 49-year-old man appeared at the Joliet office of the Illinois Department of Employee Security. He had just lost his $37,000-a-year job at a local cleaning-equipment firm after 17 years with the company. Although he belonged to a union, the blue-collar worker lost his job to automation after the firm installed packaging machines that enabled one person to do the job of 10. After six months of unemployment and retraining through the Illinois Dislocated Workers Assistance Center, he landed a new job — with a 40 percent pay cut — in the area's expanding petrochemical industry.

A 42-year-old mortgage banker who filed her claim for unemployment compensation at the same office a month earlier has not been so lucky. Although she has a degree in finance and earned $65,000 a year processing mortgages at a now-defunct savings and loan institution in nearby Chicago, she is still unemployed and will soon run out of unemployment benefits. Her husband also is unemployed. They have one child in high school and two in college to support.

These are just two casualties of the current recession. Nearly 9 million Americans are now out of work. That's some 2 million more unemployed since the current recession began in July 1990. Unemployment, which stood at 7.1 percent of the work force in January, is at its highest level since the summer of 1986. More than 25 million workers — one in five of the total work force* —

*The workforce is defined as the number of people with jobs and the number looking for jobs.

were out of work at some time during 1991. What's more, the jobless are requiring more time to find new employment. A third of those unemployed Americans were out of work for more than nine months, prompting the Bush administration to reverse course and support an extension of unemployment compensation.

Today's jobless statistics, as troubling as they are, actually hint at forces far more devastating — forces that are forever changing the American workplace. For this recession is unlike the typical recession in a fundamental — and frightening — way: In many cases, the jobs that have been lost will not come back when the economy picks up again. That means that today's unemployed will have to look elsewhere for jobs. For many, that means changing not only employers but also industries, or moving to other parts of the country. Still others will have to undergo retraining in an effort to move into new occupations altogether.

And for a growing number of American workers, the very essence of employment will change. For

them, the permanent, full-time job with a single employer will be a thing of the past. These workers will join the ranks of the so-called "contingent work force," a growing group that includes part-time and self-employed workers. This new, detached relationship with employers may appeal to some professionals and technical workers, who look forward to the freedom and challenge it offers them. But for many more, the change means lower pay and fewer or no benefits — and greater job insecurity.

As gloomy as the future may be, today's unemployed have a more immediate concern: Where should they look for work? "In the next six to eight months," offers Tom Nardone, an economist at the Bureau of Labor Statistics (BLS), "it will depend on the business cycle, and that's very unpredictable."

Over the longer term, however, the job picture is clearer. BLS predicts that the changing U.S. economy will create 18 million new jobs during the 1990s. "If you look at what has gone on over the past decade," says Nardone, "it's apparent that the new jobs are going to be mainly white collar. Over the long term, there will be a lot of technical jobs, and jobs in the health field."

These new jobs will require more training than most jobs have required since the end of World War II, when America's factories paid relatively low-skilled workers high enough wages to enable an entire generation of blue-collar workers to enjoy a middle-class standard of living. That was then.

This is now: "The problem in the future is that young people coming out of high school will not be able to get the jobs that were available to them in the decades gone past," says Douglas Fraser, former head of the United Auto Workers union (UAW) and now a professor of labor studies

Fastest-Growing Occupations, 1990-2005

The Bureau of Labor Statistics projects that U.S. businesses will add nearly 25 million new jobs between 1990 and 2005. In general, the highest rates of job growth — that is, the percentage increases — will occur in occupations that require higher levels of education and training. A substantial number of those jobs will be in health-services industries. Many slower-growing occupations are expected to add significant numbers of new jobs, primarily because of their large employment bases. (See table, p. 173.)

Occupation	Employment 1990	2005	Numerical change	% change
	(numbers in thousands)			
Home health aides	287	550	263	91.7
Paralegals	90	167	77	85.2
Systems analysts and computer scientists	463	829	366	78.9
Personal and home-care aides	103	183	79	76.7
Physical therapists	88	155	67	76.0
Medical assistants	165	287	122	73.9
Operations-research analysts	57	100	42	73.2
Human-services workers	145	249	103	71.2
Radiologic technologists and technicians	149	252	103	69.5
Medical secretaries	232	390	158	68.3
Physical and corrective therapy assistants and aides	45	74	29	64.0
Psychologists	125	204	79	63.6
Travel agents	132	214	82	62.3
Correction officers	230	372	142	61.4
Data-processing equipment repairers	84	134	50	60.0
Flight attendants	101	159	59	58.5
Computer programmers	565	882	317	56.1
Occupational therapists	36	56	20	55.2
Surgical technologists	38	59	21	55.2
Medical-records technicians	52	80	28	54.3
Management analysts	151	230	79	52.3
Respiratory therapists	60	91	31	52.1
Child-care workers	725	1,078	353	48.8
Marketing, advertising and public relations managers	427	630	203	47.4
Legal secretaries	281	413	133	47.4
Receptionists and information clerks	900	1,322	422	46.9
Registered nurses	1,727	2,494	767	44.4
Nursing aides, orderlies and attendants	1,274	1,826	552	43.4
Licensed practical nurses	644	913	269	41.9
Cooks, restaurant	615	872	257	41.8

Source: Monthly Labor Review, November 1991

at Wayne State University in Detroit. "This is a big difference. Blue-collar workers are going to be a shrinking part of our economy."

As more and more of America's assembly lines shut down, new kinds of jobs will become available. According to Robert Reich, a professor of public policy at Harvard University's John F. Kennedy School of Government, "Any job that requires a degree of conceptual skill — identifying and solving problems — is likely to be a job that will re-emerge, maybe not in its exact present form, but in some form. These jobs are in greater and greater demand as the global economy shifts to products and services that are premised on the need for problem-solving."

As experts analyze the employment outlook, these are some of the key questions being asked:

Are the job losses of the current recession permanent?

Unemployment rises with any economic downturn. When employers anticipate or begin to experience falling demand for the goods and services they produce, they trim their payrolls to cut costs and avoid accumulating excessive inventory. When business picks up, idled employees are called back to their jobs. Many workers furloughed during this recession can also expect to be called back when the economy recovers.

But for many U.S. workers, this traditional cycle of layoff and re-employment has been broken. Countless large U.S. corporations, which for most of the postwar era have offered a virtual guarantee of job security, are announcing plans to eliminate thousands of jobs. In the past few months alone, General Motors Corp. announced it would ax 74,000 jobs; International Business Machines Corp., 20,000; Pan American World Airways Inc., 7,500; McDonnell Douglas, 3,800.

According to Dan Lacey, editor of the newsletter *Workplace Trends,* U.S. corporations announced more than half a million permanent staff cuts in 1991. "Right now, we're running at about 2,700 permanent staff cuts per business day," Lacey says.

To distinguish between seasonal layoffs and permanent job cuts, Lacey counts only those reductions that publicly held corporations are required by the Securities and Exchange Commission to announce in advance (because they may affect stock prices). Initially, eliminating jobs costs companies big money, typically about $100,000 per employee, Lacey estimates, for such expenses as severance pay, outplacement services and the cost of terminating leases for space that is no longer needed.

Some companies hasten to correct the notion that they are turning thousands of workers out onto the streets. "We've had people leave the company through voluntary incentive programs, but we've never had a layoff in more than 42 years," says IBM spokeswoman Kathleen Ryan. Even now, she says, the company intends to reach its goal of 20,000 job cuts through "voluntary attrition."

Similarly, Sears, Roebuck & Co., which announced in January that it would cut 7,000 positions, says it does not plan any layoffs. "Because of the heavy [personnel] turnover in retailing," says Gordon Jones, a Sears spokesman, "we hope to be able to transfer most of those people to new positions. The jobs have been eliminated, but the people have not been laid off necessarily."

What kinds of jobs are being eliminated?

Just as the corporations that are eliminating jobs cut across the spectrum of American industry, the jobs that are disappearing affect employees at virtually every occupational level. Blue-collar jobs have been the target of restructuring efforts since the early 1970s, when U.S. companies stepped up efforts to automate production lines and began setting up assembly plants in countries where wages were lower. "The shedding of blue-collar jobs was accelerated a little bit because of this recession," says Harvard's Reich, "but many of those blue-collar jobs were already on the chopping block."

Occupations With Largest Job Growth

Retail sales leads the list of occupations the Bureau of Labor Statistics projects will have the largest numerical job increases between 1990 and 2005. Jobs in health and educational services and in the rapidly expanding food and beverage industry also are well-represented.

Occupation	Employment 1990	2005	Numerical change	% change
	(numbers in thousands)			
Salespersons, retail	3,619	4,506	887	24.5
Registered nurses	1,727	2,494	767	44.4
Cashiers	2,633	3,318	685	26.0
General office clerks	2,737	3,407	670	24.5
Truck drivers, light and heavy	2,362	2,979	617	26.1
General managers and top executives	3,086	3,684	598	19.4
Janitors and clerks, including maids and housekeeping cleaners	3,007	3,562	555	18.5
Nursing aides, orderlies and attendants	1,274	1,826	552	43.4
Food counter, fountain and related workers	1,607	2,158	550	34.2
Waiters and waitresses	1,747	2,196	449	25.7
Teachers, secondary school	1,280	1,717	437	34.2
Receptionists and information clerks	900	1,322	422	46.9
Systems analysts and computer scientists	463	829	366	78.9
Food-preparation workers	1,156	1,521	365	31.6
Child-care workers	725	1,078	353	48.8
Gardeners and groundskeepers, except farm	874	1,222	348	39.8
Accountants and auditors	985	1,325	340	34.5
Computer programmers	565	882	317	56.1
Teachers, elementary	1,362	1,675	313	23.0
Guards	883	1,181	298	33.7
Teacher aides and educational assistants	808	1,086	278	34.4
Licensed practical nurses	644	913	269	41.9
Clerical supervisors and managers	1,218	1,481	263	21.6
Home health aides	287	550	263	91.7
Cooks, restaurant	615	872	257	41.8
Maintenance repairers, general utility	1,128	1,379	251	22.2
Secretaries, except legal and medical	3,064	3,312	248	8.1
Cooks, short-order and fast-food	743	989	246	33.0
Stock clerks, sales floor	1,242	1,451	209	16.8
Lawyers	587	793	206	35.1

Source: Monthly Labor Review, *November 1991*

Today, however, many white-collar jobs are following blue-collar jobs into oblivion. Among these are low-level managers, from foremen to division chiefs, who were hired to oversee production workers. Middle-management positions are also disappearing, Reich says, following the discovery by many corporations that they had grown too big and inflexible and could operate more efficiently by removing entire layers of

Declining Occupations, 1990-2005

The Bureau of Labor Statistics projects that jobs in the manufacturing sector will decline by nearly 600,000 by the year 2005. The decline in manufacturing jobs means it will be more difficult for those without a college education to obtain higher-paying jobs. Other occupations expected to lose large numbers of jobs are farming, bookkeeping and word processing.

Occupation	Employment 1990	2005	Numerical change	% change
		(numbers in thousands)		
Farmers	1,074	850	-224	-20.9
Bookkeeping, accounting and auditing clerks	2,276	2,143	-133	-5.8
Child-care workers, private household	314	190	-124	-39.5
Sewing machine operators, garment	585	469	-116	-19.8
Electrical and electronic assemblers	232	128	-105	-45.1
Typists and word processors	972	869	-103	-10.6
Cleaners and servants, private household	411	310	-101	-24.5
Farm workers	837	745	-92	-11.0
Electrical and electronic-equipment assemblers, precision	171	90	-81	-47.5
Textile draw-out and winding-machine operators and tenders	199	138	-61	-30.6
Switchboard operators	246	189	-57	-23.2
Machine-forming operators and tenders, metal and plastic	174	131	-43	-24.5
Machine tool cutting operators and tenders, metal and plastic	145	104	-42	-28.6
Telephone and cable TV line installers and repairers	133	92	-40	-30.4
Central office and PBX installers and repairers	80	46	-34	-42.5
Central office operators	53	22	-31	-59.2
Statistical clerks	85	54	-31	-36.1
Packaging and filling machine operators and tenders	324	297	-27	-8.3
Station installers and repairers, telephone	47	21	-26	-55.0
Bank tellers	517	492	-25	-4.8
Lathe and turning machine tool setters and set-up operators, metal and plastic	80	61	-20	-24.4
Grinders and polishers, hand	84	65	-19	-22.5
Electromechanical equipment assemblers, precision	49	31	-18	-36.5
Grinding machine setters and set-up operators, metal and plastic	72	54	-18	-25.1
Service station attendants	246	229	-17	-7.1
Directory assistance operators	26	11	-16	-59.4
Butchers and meat cutters	234	220	-14	-5.9
Chemical equipment controllers, operators and tenders	75	61	-14	-19.1
Drilling and boring machine tool setters and set-up operators, metal and plastic	52	39	-13	-25.6
Meter readers, utilities	50	37	-12	-24.8

Source: Monthly Labor Review, November 1991

management that stood between the top brass and production workers.

In addition to corporate America's ongoing restructuring efforts, several unrelated events have increased the recession's impact on jobs. The collapse of the commercial real estate market, for example, has eliminated jobs in that sector and in such related fields as finance, law and sales. "Most of the jobs that were lost are not coming back because commercial real estate got wildly out of balance," Reich says.

The crisis in the savings and loan and the commercial banking industries has also taken its toll, primarily among white-collar workers. Finally, the end of the Cold War has prompted cancellations of Pentagon contracts for weapons that are no longer needed. "Many aerospace jobs that were caught up in the big military binge of the 1980s are not coming back," Reich says. *(See story, p. 183.)*

Do corporate restructuring efforts that entail job reductions improve productivity and competitiveness?

Enhancing productivity and competitiveness, of course, is the aim of corporate restructuring efforts. As foreign competitors have made inroads into some of this country's biggest markets, such as automobiles and computer technology, many companies have jettisoned whole divisions in order to concentrate on producing what they do best.

By eliminating redundant or unnecessary jobs, companies can reduce payroll costs as well as the ever-mounting expense of health-care benefits. Last year, in the wake of continued layoffs, U.S. productivity rose by 0.2 percent, marking the first annual gain in three years. And the nation's exports have risen in recent months, bringing the trade deficit down last year to around $65 billion, its lowest level since 1983.

"Clearly, there are more companies now that are saying, 'We've restructured our operations and tried to decentralize decision-making; there are too many layers of management,'" says Thomas Kochan, a professor of management and human resources at the Massachusetts Institute of Technology's Sloan School of Management.

The danger, Kochan worries, is that corporations may not be taking the right steps now to further improve their competitive positions. "Instead of taking a positive approach to adjustment," he says, "they are deciding to just lay off a lot more managers. The real question is whether corporations are using this as an opportunity to fundamentally restructure by reallocating influence and decentralizing decision-making powers." That, Kochan says, means "empowering workers at lower levels to make more of a contribution to managing the firm, not just reducing jobs. I think it is probably wishful thinking to say that companies are doing this in any kind of thoughtful way."

The move toward contingent workers is merely another step corporations are taking to become leaner and more efficient. Experts are of two minds, however, over the ways productivity will be affected by the change. Much depends on how corporations go about it. Contracting out for certain tasks can improve productivity all around, says Reich, "if these jobs are filled by smaller businesses that pay a lot, in which the employees work in teams and their jobs involve a great deal of creativity."

Corporations that fill jobs in this way, he says, "may be giving the economy a great shot in the arm in terms of entrepreneurism." But companies that hire workers on a contingent basis merely because they don't want to pay them fringe benefits may pay a heavy price in low morale, lack of commitment and absenteeism. "This can be quite dangerous," Reich says, "because in the emerging economy so much depends on the initiative and creativity of workers."

Some labor analysts say the shift toward contingency workers, no matter how companies go about it, is a positive step. "The increase in transiency benefits the economy more than it damages the economy because it makes us more adaptive and it cuts costs," says Audrey Freedman, a labor economist at The Conference Board, a business research organization in New York. Moreover, she adds, contingency workers "enable even large, old-line corporations to spring about with light feet." Without this change, she says, big U.S. firms could "drown in their own fat."

Do the structural changes in the U.S. economy foreshadow a permanent fall in living standards?

Recessions always take their toll on the living conditions of workers — even those who only face temporary layoffs. And the current downturn, as it drags on beyond most economists' earlier forecasts, is spreading the pain to more and more Americans. According to The Conference Board's January Consumer Confidence Survey, almost one in four households experienced unemployment at some time over the past year, and the family member who was out of work took an average of six months to find a new job. But fully a third of the jobless took nine months or more to become re-employed.

For most people, however, finding a new job does not end the hardship. Confirming widespread anecdotal evidence, The Conference Board reports that 45 percent of its respondents who found new employment over the past 12 months were earning less money in their new jobs; only a fifth reported that they made more.

"Basically, what we're seeing is downward mobility," says newsletter editor Dan Lacey. "The truth is, the average American is barely keeping

his head above water. It used to take the labor of one human being to support the average middle-class family. Now it takes two."

Many studies of family income over the past decade confirm Lacey's observation. One of the more recent studies, released last month by the Joint Economic Committee of Congress, found that 80 percent of two-parent families with children had seen no improvement in their standard of living over the past decade, even though they were working longer hours. "Fully 80 percent of these families are on a treadmill — they saw their net family income decline over the past decade or grow by a smaller percentage than did their hours of work," said Sen. Paul S. Sarbanes, D-Md., the committee chairman.

"To merely maintain their standard of living, or to avoid falling even further behind, they have had to increase their hours of work at the expense of their time with family and community," Sarbanes continued. "Only the very top fifth of these families enjoyed clear gains in their standard of living." [1]

Not only do more family members have to work to stay even, but the jobs they can find often are not as well-paying as those held down by the lone family breadwinner of the past. "The auto industry offers well-paying jobs," notes Douglas Fraser. "Auto workers become homeowners, and many of them are the first generation in their families to send their kids to college. Right now there are those who are earning up to $35,000 a year plus rich fringe benefits.

"Literally thousands used to go into the auto plants from the neighborhoods in which the auto plants are located. But those jobs are no longer available to today's youth. In an urban center, like here in Detroit, I don't know what these kids do. I suppose they go into the service industries."

Indeed, the American economy,

once dominated by the manufacturing of autos and other durable goods, has been shifting to the production of services for more than a decade. Jobs in the service sector, a vast category that includes health care, insurance, banks, restaurants and business services, generally pay lower wages — often $5 or $6 an hour — than manufacturing jobs, which in the steel and auto industries commonly fetch $14 an hour.

As a result, the shift to services has lowered living standards for most workers. "The blue-collar middle class is a vanishing breed," says Donald Ratajczak, director of Georgia State University's economic forecasting center in Atlanta. "When people talk about the middle class that's suffering today, that's the part of the middle class that's dying. And I don't see anything bringing it back."

Restructuring is causing hardship among all occupational categories. The most recent wave of layoffs is hurting even highly skilled workers. According to the American Management Association, middle managers account for no more than 8 percent of the work force but represent 17 percent of all workers who have been laid off in the past three years. "A typical middle-management job will pay anywhere from $30,000 to $100,000," says MIT's Kochan. "Those people will have considerable difficulty because the higher the salary, the more likely they are to have difficulty replicating that salary."

White-collar workers in general may find it harder to make ends meet in the 1990s. Even after the recession ends, predicts economist Richard S. Belous, "many white-collar jobs will become ... contingent. This has serious implications for the American social-welfare system and economy."[2]

As always, education is one of the strongest safety nets today's workers have to prevent a fall in living standards. "If you're not college educated, you're seeing your real income

stagnate or even decline," says Robert Reich. "If you are college educated, your income is growing. The gap between the two is widening."

Living standards fall even further for workers who move from full-time, permanent employment to contingent work. Not only do part-timers usually make lower hourly earnings than full-timers, but they typically

also have none of their valuable fringe benefits, such as health insurance, pension plans and paid vacations. "To the extent that contingent workers are overwhelmingly non-college educated," Reich says, "the trend toward contingent work simply aggravates a situation that was already causing problems and is potentially quite dangerous for society." ∎

BACKGROUND

Postwar Economic Boom

The "American dream" — complete with home ownership, a new car in the driveway, consumer goods and college for the children — is largely a postwar phenomenon. With Europe and much of East Asia in ruins, the United States alone among the combatants of World War II emerged with its factories, railroads and other infrastructure intact. The end of the war in 1945 marked the beginning of an unprecedented boom in the U.S. economy that continued almost unabated for more than two decades, as American factories satisfied growing demands for goods not only at home but throughout the world.

American production workers benefited directly from the expansion of basic industries centered in the Midwest. High school graduates could go directly to work in the steel mills or auto factories and enjoy good earnings that rose steadily, offering them a place in the coveted middle class. "Prior to World War II, people who were employees were not middle-class," says *Workplace Trends* Editor Lacey. "The paycheck-based middle class is a postwar creation."

As corporations vied for workers to meet the growing demand for their products, employees, often

through labor unions, won new fringe benefits as a condition of employment. Defined-benefit pensions, assuring workers of adequate retirement income, health insurance for themselves and their families and paid vacations became commonplace during this period. Some large corporations, such as IBM, even promised job security for non-union employees, who were mostly white-collar and managerial workers. The notion of corporate loyalty, described in William H. Whyte Jr.'s 1957 best-seller, *The Organization Man,* emerged in which hard-working employees who stayed with the firm were rewarded with job security, rising incomes and a comfortable retirement.

The steady rise in American workers' earnings stopped abruptly in 1973. That was the year of the first oil crisis, unleashed when the Organization of Petroleum Exporting Countries (OPEC) imposed an embargo on its oil exports, upon which the United States, Europe and Japan were heavily dependent. Oil prices quadrupled within the year, causing double-digit inflation that undermined the purchasing power of Americans' paychecks. Demand for U.S. products faltered both at home and abroad, causing economic stagnation. By the end of the decade, another oil crisis had further dampened economic growth, and unemployment — spurred by factory layoffs — had grown to 7.8 percent.

Continued on p. 178

Chronology

_1940s-1960s_ _The postwar economic boom establishes the model for middle-class Americans' expectations of ever-rising earnings and job security._

1956
William H. Whyte Jr. describes the emerging ethos of the corporate employee in his best-selling book, _The Organization Man._ According to an often-unspoken pledge of reciprocal loyalty, the company offered job security, rising earnings and generous fringe benefits in return for the employee's commitment to stay with the firm for his entire career.

_1970s_ _Rising labor costs and growing competition from overseas suppliers prompt U.S. corporations to step up automation and set up plants in low-cost countries._

1973
The steady rise in workers' earnings that has marked the postwar period comes to a halt after the first of a series of oil crises sparks inflation and slows economic growth.

1979
In the first phase of corporate restructuring, manufacturers begin cutting production jobs. General Motors, Ford and Chrysler will eliminate 350,000 jobs over the next decade.

_1980s_ _Corporations eliminate millions of blue-collar jobs in an attempt to "restructure" their operations to become more competitive with foreign producers._

1981-82
The worst recession since the Great Depression of the 1930s takes its greatest toll on the manufacturing industries of the Midwest, pushing unemployment among blue-collar workers to double-digit levels.

1985
IBM — hurt by mounting competition from foreign computer makers — begins cutting its work force.

1989
A wave of bank consolidations and closures begins, resulting in the loss of more than 100,000 jobs in that sector to date.

_1990s_ _Restructuring begins to cut into white-collar employment as corporations eliminate many middle-management positions._

July 1990
Recession begins, accelerating the pace of layoffs. While blue-collar workers continue to bear the brunt of unemployment, companies are for the first time cutting out entire layers of middle management to reduce labor costs and make their operations more flexible to changing economic conditions. As a result, white-collar unemployment spreads throughout U.S. industry.

August 1990
Sears, the nation's third-largest retailer, begins a cost-reduction program that will cut about 33,000 positions by the end of 1991.

1991
Restructuring accelerates. U.S. corporations announce more than a half million permanent staff cuts affecting both production and white-collar workers.

Nov. 26, 1991
IBM announces it will cut 20,000 jobs next year.

Dec. 18, 1991
General Motors says it will close 21 of its 125 North American plants and pare 74,000 positions, or 18 percent of its work force, over the next four years.

Jan. 7, 1992
Sears announces it will eliminate an additional 7,000 positions by automating customer-service tasks.

Jan. 21, 1992
United Technologies Corp. announces it will cut 13,900 jobs in its defense and civilian industries.

Feb. 4, 1992
Congress approves legislation providing an additional 13 weeks of unemployment compensation. President Bush, who blocked or vetoed two similar measures in 1991, signs the bill into law Feb. 7.

Feb. 24, 1992
General Motors names the first 12 of 21 plants to be closed in the U.S. and Canada. GM also posts a $4.45 billion loss for 1991 — the largest in American corporate history.

_2000s_ _The global marketplace continues to transform American employment patterns._

2005
According to the Labor Department, most of the 24.6 million new jobs that will be added to the U.S. economy over the 15-year period ending in 2005 will be high-skill positions requiring more training than most of the jobs they will replace.

Continued from p. 176

Impact of the 1981 Recession

But the worst was yet to come: In 1981 the most crushing recession since the Great Depression of the 1930s hit the country, causing massive layoffs and turning the once-booming industrial Midwest into the "Rust Belt." By December 1982, nearly 11 million American workers were unemployed.

Throughout the 1970s, U.S. industries had watched as their competitors in Japan and Western Europe made steady inroads into the markets they had dominated for a quarter-century. By the early 1980s, the United States' share of the world's manufactured exports had fallen from more than 25 percent to less than 17 percent.[3] Indeed, flourishing Japan enjoyed a $10 billion annual trade surplus with the United States by 1980, selling the U.S. steel, autos and other products that they could produce more efficiently than their American counterparts due to lower labor costs, greater automation and better quality control.

The current round of permanent job cuts is merely the continuation of a trend that began during the 1981-82 recession, when 5.1 million workers were displaced due to permanent plant closings. Although the pace of permanent job losses slowed during the subsequent economic expansion that stretched over most of the decade, an additional 4.3 million workers were displaced due to plant closings or job reductions from 1985 through 1989.[4]

This phase of corporate restructuring started in the steel industry and later spread to many goods-producing industries as well, as manufacturers automated their production lines and set up assembly plants from Taiwan to Mexico, where labor costs are lower. Although 22 million new jobs were created during the expansion of the 1980s, most were low-paying positions in service industries.

White-Collar Layoffs

The current recession, like its predecessors, has been accompanied by rising unemployment and seasonal layoffs by manufacturers, such as the Big Three automakers. Of the 1.7 million jobs that have been lost since the recession began, says economic forecaster Donald Ratajczak, 800,000 are manufacturing jobs and almost 500,000 are in construction. "That means that more than half the job losses are traditional," he says. But this recession is also different in some ways that suggest changes that are yet to come in the labor market.

In the first place, this recession has been broader than the last downturn. In 1981-82, service industries — wholesale and retail trade, communications, food services, business services, health care and the sector that comprises finance, insurance and real estate — continued to grow, though slowly. This time almost all these industries are losing jobs.

Job losses are "not highly concentrated, as during most recessions, among the production workers in manufacturing," says Audrey Freedman of The Conference Board, "which would mean highly concentrated in the Rust Belt." This time "everybody's being affected." While the percentage of unemployed today is overwhelmingly blue-collar, the number of white-collar unemployed — about 3 million — is about the same as that of blue-collar workers.[5]

That marks a clear departure from previous recessions. "We've seen reductions in blue-collar staffs in the past without equivalent reductions in white-collar workers," says Thomas Kochan of MIT. "It seems to me that this is the first phase of dealing with problems of white-collar productivity that companies are going through."

Some of the large corporations that have announced massive job cuts illustrate Kochan's point. IBM, the nation's fourth-largest corporation and the employer of 186,600 people in the United States, announced last year that it would eliminate 20,000 jobs in 1992, bringing the total number of job reductions by "Big Blue" since 1985 to 35,000.[6] Although the company says it doesn't intend to lay off any workers, it hopes to lure current workers into early retirement with its "individual transition option," a package of financial incentives.

According to IBM spokeswoman Kathleen Ryan, almost 19,000 company employees opted for early retirement in 1991 alone; the program expires July 31. Ryan says jobs at all levels are included in the current cutback, which is part of IBM's effort to decentralize its mammoth operation in order to respond more quickly to the volatile market for computer technology.

Some service industries are cutting payrolls through automation, just as manufacturers have been doing for years. Sears, the country's third-largest retailer, announced last August it would cut 33,000 jobs in the United States and Canada, mostly clerical and support positions, by the end of 1991. In January, Sears put an additional 7,000 jobs on the chopping block. The new cuts will follow the installation of computer terminals and telephone kiosks throughout Sears' 868 stores. The new equipment will let customers check their credit balances, order from catalogs and buy gift certificates automatically.

"The new terminals can perform a lot of the functions that used to be performed in our customer-service areas," says company spokesman Gordon Jones. He adds that the job cuts will affect all levels of employees "because we are restructuring the organization literally from top to bottom." Sears' efforts appear to be paying off. At a time when retailers are reeling from the recession, Sears last year opened 25 new stores and several new distribution centers.

Who Says American Workers Are Lazy?

Yoshio Sakurauchi, a prominent Japanese politician, caused an outcry in the United States last month when he blamed America's enduring trade deficit with Japan and other industrial powers on the laziness of American workers. The nation's economic woes, he said, stem from the "deterioration in quality of U.S. workers," who "want high pay without working for it."

The heated reaction to Sakurauchi's remarks, which were widely reported by the U.S. media, stems from more than Americans' longstanding resentment of Japanese trade practices. The fact is, American workers do work hard. According to Harvard University economist Juliet B. Schor, "people report their leisure time has declined by as much as one-third since the early 1970s."

In her newly published study, *The Overworked American,* Schor writes: "Predictably, [Americans] are spending less time on the basics, like sleeping and eating. Parents are devoting less attention to their children. Stress is on the rise, partly owing to the 'balancing act' of reconciling the demands of work and family life."†

Schor's findings are confirmed by numerous other studies. One study, recently prepared for the Joint Economic Committee of Congress, found that income gains among two-parent families during the 1980s came from more hours of work, not from increases in hourly pay. Most of the extra work was performed by wives, whose paid labor increased by 32 percent over the decade.††

Forty years ago, it was commonly held that automation would gradually reduce the need for human labor. Labor experts were predicting four-day weeks, a six-month work year and retirement before age 40. So what went wrong? Schor points to the capitalist system itself, which can only flourish if people consume increasing quantities of goods and services to keep up with the Joneses. The Joneses, of course, have to do the same to stay ahead, setting up a pattern of behavior that Schor calls an "insidious cycle of work and spend."

Schor advises American workers to get out of the "squirrel cage" altogether by trading some income for more leisure time. For most workers, that means quitting their full-time jobs and working part time. Given the plight of contingent workers today — lower incomes, fewer fringe benefits and little job security — few American workers are likely to make that trade-off voluntarily.

Fewer still would embrace Sakurauchi's solution: emulating Japanese workers by working even harder. After all, Japan is plagued by an outbreak of a new disease called *karoshi* — death by overwork.

---

† Juliet B. Schor, *The Overworked American: The Unexpected Decline of Leisure* (1991), p. 5.

†† Joint Economic Committee, *Families on a Treadmill: Work and Income in the 1980s,* January 1992.

Cuts in Defense and Financial Jobs

Competitive pressures are not the only forces behind the corporate drive to restructure. The end of the Cold War has reduced, if not eliminated, the need for many big-ticket weapons systems designed specifically to counter the perceived military threat from the now-defunct Soviet Union. Although the defense budget remains huge — at an estimated $270 billion this year — the Bush administration has called for cuts in Pentagon spending of $50 billion over the next five years, most of it from the weapons procurement budget, which now stands at just over $64 billion a year.

As weapons contracts are scaled back or eliminated, defense contractors are closing plants and cutting staff. Most of the layoffs, says Ratajczak, will affect "production workers, the people who put missiles and airplanes together. But a lot of people who coordinate with the Pentagon, employees involved in weapons design and marketing," also will lose their jobs, he says. *(See story, p. 183.)* United Technologies Corp., for example, announced in January that it would cut 13,900 jobs by 1995, including 12 percent at the executive level.

In addition to defense, several other industries are eliminating jobs for reasons seemingly unrelated to the recession. The financial services sector has been rocked by a series of crises, beginning with the savings and loan debacle of the mid-1980s, followed by the collapse of several large brokerage houses in the wake of the corporate takeover boom and, most recently, a wave of failures among commercial banks. As a result, many financial institutions are being bought out by their rivals, resulting in widespread consolidation and job losses.

The banking industry alone has lost more than 100,000 jobs in the rash of mergers that accelerated in 1989. BankAmerica's buyout of Security Pacific, for example, is expected to eliminate 10,000 white-collar jobs on the West Coast. "It's not as though the bank down the street is the only one consolidating and laying off people," Ratajczak explains. "That bank is laying off thousands, and the bank in the next big city is laying off thousands, and so there's no place for these people to go." ∎

CURRENT SITUATION

Contingent Work Force

Despite the many jobs disappearing across the spectrum of American industry, the unemployment rate measures a surprisingly low 7.1 percent of the labor force. That's high compared with normal economic conditions but by no means as dramatic as the reports of permanent job losses would suggest. During the 1981-82 recession, for example, unemployment peaked at more than 11 percent.

One reason for the relatively low jobless figure is that many unemployed people have simply stopped looking for work. The Labor Department estimates that these "discouraged workers," who are not included in the unemployment figures, number 1.1 million.

Also left out of the statistics are 6.7 million people doing part-time work because they couldn't find acceptable full-time positions. "What we've got is large numbers of people cobbling together an income by doing less than a full week of work," says The Conference Board's Freedman. She calls this approach to the job market "the contingent way of piecing together a living."

The actual number of people who have joined the contingent work force is unknown. That's because the Labor Department has no measure for this group of workers. Some analysts, including newsletter editor Dan Lacey and economist Richard Belous, who have studied the matter in some detail, estimate that contingent workers make up as much as a third of the total U.S. work force.[7]

But BLS economist Tom Nardone is skeptical, especially since the total may include not only poorly paid temporary and fast-food workers but also well-heeled consultants as well as doctors and lawyers who are self-employed. "It all comes down to a question of job security, and that is very hard to measure," he says. "The point is, how many lousy jobs are there? We don't have a measure for that."

Whatever the number of workers involved, everyone agrees that there is a marked shift toward contingent workers, and that the change makes sense for business. For one thing, the shift can save employers a lot on fringe benefits, especially health insurance, whose costs are rising faster than any other employer-provided benefit. "If you look at who gets health insurance from their employers, it's much less frequent among part-time workers than among full-time workers," says Nardone, who adds that only 67 percent of full-timers have health coverage.

Reducing the in-house payroll may also help companies become more competitive, says Freedman, enabling them to quickly change their products, their marketing techniques, even their factory or retail locations in response to new business conditions. "The rapidity with which they can adapt is very much affected by whether they have a long-term, stable kind of work force or whether they can pick and choose, in effect, by going to the supermarket and picking up a new crop of people to handle something that may not last more than three months," she says.

According to Freedman, many companies turned to the contingent labor market in the 1980s. IBM is typical. As the company pared its permanent, full-time work force, it brought in outside firms to handle certain operations; it currently has contracts with 1,400 vendors and suppliers and employs about 33,000 contingent workers. "The trend is definitely to contract out to vendors the support-type services we need," says company spokeswoman Ryan.

For example, Marriott Corp., the hotel and food service chain, operates some of IBM's cafeterias, while Manpower Inc., a temporary-help agency, provides clerical and secretarial services as well as more highly skilled workers.

Sears also contracts out for many former in-house functions, including maintenance, typesetting, advertising and transportation. "To be competitive today," says spokesman Gordon Jones, "we have to have the cost structure that our competitors do, and one of the ways our competitors keep their costs down is by having outside companies do the work." While Sears offers health and other benefits to some of its permanent part-time workers, so-called "part-time regulars" who put in 30 hours a week, Jones acknowledges that many of the contingent workers do not receive benefits from the subcontractors.

"If those outside companies provide minimal benefits, it's probably going to be one of the ways they hold their costs down when we go to them," he says. "In terms of the social impact on the country, I'm sure our senior executives are concerned, but at the same time there's the need to be competitive."

Core vs. Contingent Workers

As more and more companies hire contingent workers, some experts say serious morale problems could arise between these lower-paid employees and the better-paid permanent, or "core," workers they often work with. Former UAW President Fraser cites the problems that arose in the early 1980s, when airlines and other troubled industries tried to cut personnel costs by introducing the "two-tier" wage scale, which gave much lower pay to new hires — even when they had better skills than the older workers.

"People lived with it for awhile," Fraser says, "but [the system caused]

Continued on p. 182

How Students View the Job Market

Twenty-five years ago, college graduates were virtually assured of getting jobs upon graduation. "You stood on the street corner and waved your degree and people came along and offered you a job," says Tom Johnson, director of career advising and placement for liberal arts majors at the University of Wisconsin-Madison. Today, as many of those graduates' children near the end of their own college days and prepare to enter the job market, their view is decidedly more pessimistic.

"I was thinking about becoming a teacher when I get out of school, but it was scary thinking of going out [into the job market] because there are so many people graduating with the economy the way it is," says Elizabeth Bright, a history major at the University of Virginia who expects to graduate this May. Like many of her contemporaries, Bright is deferring her plunge into the job market until the recession ends. She's applying to veterinary school.

"People always have animals that are sick, so once you're a vet there's pretty much always a demand for your services," she says. Bright's decision is not purely pragmatic — she had dreamed of becoming a vet before considering a teaching career. But, she says, "If I had come out of school and found the job I wanted, I might not have been so apt to change my mind."

Mark Beemer, a journalism major at Wisconsin, is also changing his career plans. As photo editor of *The Daily Cardinal,* a school newspaper, Beemer will offer prospective employers solid experience and academic credentials when he graduates in May. But, he figures, "The market is pretty bleak in every field, especially journalism. A lot of big papers are going to 'stringers' rather than hiring staffers." To broaden his career choices, Beemer is also considering graduate school and a degree in studio photography.

Graduate school is not fail-safe, however, especially for students seeking a master's degree in business administration. In great demand during the expansionary 1980s, MBAs today are finding that recent corporate restructuring efforts have eliminated entire layers of management. Law school graduates are also encountering an unfriendly job market, though long-term job prospects for lawyers are good.

Medicine appears to be fairly immune to labor market fluctuations. "There are ample job opportunities in all the fields I have an interest in," says Steven Blash, a first-year medical student at the University of Maryland at Baltimore who is planning a career in pediatrics or family practice. Blash adds, however, that "a lot of the reduced

pressure I feel comes from the knowledge that I will be in school for another four years."

Graduate school isn't for everyone, of course, and some college seniors are coming up with ingenious inroads into the job market. Anna Maria O'Brien, who expects to graduate this spring from Georgetown University's School of Foreign Service, decided some time ago to defer long-term career plans. Like many liberal arts majors, she says, "I don't know what I want to do, only what I don't want to do."

Instead of taking the Foreign Service exam and entering directly into government employment, a typical career path for the school's graduates, O'Brien has gotten a job teaching English at a local Berlitz Language Center. But she hopes to transfer to a Berlitz center overseas after graduation. For now, O'Brien says, "There's too much that I want to do outside the career course." Following her stint abroad, she says, "I'll come back to look seriously."

Looking seriously is what it will take, especially for liberal arts majors without postgraduate degrees. "There are jobs available," says Tom Johnson, "but they require a great deal of work to find, especially for the liberal arts graduates," who are not fully trained for any specific occupation. "One of my great concerns is that students see a difficult job market, make the quantum leap to the assumption that there are no jobs available and stop searching. That's a tragic, tragic mistake."

Johnson advises students to start looking as early as possible. Even as freshmen, he says, students can take steps to improve their job prospects by taking courses that will hone certain skills, such as computer literacy and writing and speaking effectively. No matter what jobs they are offering, Johnson says, employers today want candidates with good problem-solving skills, which can be improved by obtaining an understanding of basic mathematics and statistics.

When considering career choices, Johnson advises students to "identify their skills and values." Then, by doing a little research, they can find job opportunities in virtually any industry in the country, even in such troubled businesses as retailing and banking. "To make a gross generalization that any particular industry is down the chute is a tactical, if not a strategic, error," he says.

Above all, Johnson says, "Job applicants can no longer afford to be passive in the job market. We can no longer say that 'because I have a degree I am entitled to a job, and all I have to do is sit by the telephone and wait for someone to make me an offer.'"

> **Students can take steps to improve their job prospects by taking courses that will hone certain skills, such as writing and speaking effectively.**

Continued from p. 180
such friction that the companies that had two-tier just threw up their hands in despair. You rarely see it anymore."

Two-tier wage scales may be on the wane, but some of the same problems afflict contingent work. "There's a big question about who's taking whose job away, and why somebody working side by side on the same job is earning half as much, with no security, no benefits and in most cases no union," says Thomas Kochan of MIT.

For their part, Kochan adds, the permanent workers "feel that the company has an incentive to give all the work to these cheap folks and take their jobs away." He cites studies showing how resentment between core and contingent workers may even pose physical threats in certain industries, such as oil and chemical manufacturing, where safety risks already abound.[8]

Safety aside, Kochan says contingent work may do more long-term harm than good, even to the companies that promote it to improve productivity. "I don't think this employment relationship is good for the economy," he says. "You've got to have solid personal relationships to get along and solve problems in groups. You have to understand the culture and the setting because that's all part of what an organization is about."

If contingent work becomes entrenched in the labor market, Kochan predicts, "quality and productivity will go down."

Contingent Work Spreads

Once typified by the "Kelly Girl" and other low-level white-collar temporaries, contingent workers are no longer confined to low-wage occupations. "Contingent work is creeping up and becoming much more high-level white collar," Belous says, as corporations begin to subcontract for accountants and providers of other financial services.

But contingent work has also moved much more into blue-collar occupations, particularly through "leasing" of employees for specific tasks. Leasing allows corporations to delegate a task to an agency that assumes all responsibility for the personnel who do the work. Although some leasing agencies provide benefits to their workers, Belous says they are usually less generous than benefits the corporation would normally provide full-time workers. He adds, "It's not unusual to read about some unscrupulous leasing operation that told its employees they had benefits but just pocketed the money."

Contingent workers have fewer defenses against such abuses than full-time workers. "Unions have their collective backs to the wall," says Reich of Harvard, citing the fall in union membership to a mere 13 percent of the work force today. "In most industries, the unions are only a pale reflection of their former selves," he says. "It's very difficult for the unions to put contingent workers at the top of an agenda that's already crowded with the demands by unionized workers for protection from other corporate incursions."

The move to contingent work is not bad for everyone, of course, especially among professional, managerial and technical workers. They can sell their special skills more easily to a number of clients than, say, a laborer or an assembler. "Contingent workers don't necessarily make less," says Dan Lacey. "Some who are consultants make a lot of money. So contingent working is not necessarily downward mobility, but it is certainly less predictable than the paycheck."

Belous agrees that contingent work can prove beneficial for some workers. "Many workers view it as a way to gain increased freedom, and that's what they want. And let's face it, a lot of corporations would be out of business without contingent workers. It's not an unmitigated evil."

Consumers Retrench

Although the changes being brought about by corporate America's efforts to restructure may produce better times ahead, most working Americans appear unconvinced. Recent surveys indicate a pervasive loss of confidence among U.S. workers. Perhaps the most closely followed sounding of opinion on prevailing business conditions, The Conference Board's monthly Consumer Confidence Survey, plummeted last fall and fell again in January. Almost half the respondents said jobs were "hard to get," and those predicting fewer available jobs six months from now outnumbered those forecasting a resurgence in new job opportunities by about 2 to 1.

The survey showed that it isn't only the unemployed who are pulling the purse strings tight. "When people who are employed are concerned about the security of their jobs," says Conference Board economist Freedman, "they're not going to undertake major spending," such as a new car or a house.

In fact, citing the weak economy, 40 percent of the survey respondents said they were deferring major purchases — no surprise to retailers. "Where we have been hurt by the recession," says Sears spokesman Gordon Jones, "has been the lack of consumer confidence and willingness to make major purchases or replace — on other than a need basis — washers and dryers, or furniture."

Sears is not alone. Retail sales grew by less than 1 percent last year, the lowest level in 30 years, according to the Commerce Department. As sales stagnated at most stores, retailers laid off more workers, perpetuating what Freedman calls the "snowball effect" of recessionary layoffs and falling consumer spending.

Just how much the fall in consum-
Continued on p. 184

What's Next for Defense Industry Workers?

When it comes to corporate restructuring, the defense industry has not been spared. But unlike most industries that are cutting jobs and making other changes to better compete in an increasingly global economy, the defense industry is largely dependent on a single customer — the Pentagon.

With the Cold War's demise, that customer is tightening the purse strings. The result is growing joblessness in a sector that only a few years ago was booming. Since the Berlin Wall fell in 1989, more than 160,000 U.S. defense industry jobs have been lost, according to the Bureau of Labor Statistics.

In his January budget request, President Bush asked Congress to trim $50 billion from the defense budget over the next five years. According to Senate Armed Services Committee Chairman Sam Nunn, D-Ga., these cuts alone will trigger the loss of up to 2 million defense jobs.

Job losses will be felt the most by workers in some of the major programs set up during the arms buildup of the early- to mid-1980s, such as the B-2 "stealth" bomber and the *Seawolf*-class nuclear submarine. The overriding purpose of these weapons — deterring a nuclear exchange with the Soviet Union — largely evaporated with the Soviet Union's collapse. General Dynamics Corp., chief contractor on the *Seawolf* project, has announced layoffs of up to 4,000 workers by the end of this year at its Electric Boat division's shipyard in Groton, Conn.†

When the Pentagon cuts back a program that is already in production, like the B-2, blue-collar workers often bear the brunt of the cuts. But when a program in the research-and-development stage is eliminated, the impact is also felt among white-collar workers. For example, when the Pentagon recently canceled the A-12 program, aimed at producing the next generation of Navy fighter-attack bombers, McDonnell Douglas, the main contractor, laid off 5,000 workers. "A lot of engineers and white-collar management people lost their jobs then," says Conrad Schmidt, an economic policy analyst at the Defense Budget Project in Washington.

Employees of defense contractors are especially vulnerable to sudden job loss. Unlike employers in the civilian sector, who are required to notify employees before they close a plant, defense contractors can shut down operations as soon as the Pentagon decides to cancel or cut back a weapons program. "When workers have had prenotification of plant closures," Schmidt says, "they have had a much higher rate of successful job generation after that. A-12 workers had no notice, and those folks had a lot longer time without a job."

Communities that depend on defense contractors for jobs are in a bind. Absent any federal plans for converting idled defense facilities to civilian use, local governments are left with the task of helping jobless defense workers adjust to the post-Cold War era. At a time of severe budgetary strain, however, most localities have limited resources for this service. Some turn to business to help the unemployed find alternative work. Joe Cartwright, a specialist at the Pentagon's office of economic adjustment, says business and local government in St. Louis, Mo., "have done a good job in promoting worker adjustment and creating new business opportunities."

St. Louis has had to cope recently with two major layoffs from McDonnell Douglas, one of the nation's biggest defense contractors and a major area employer. In August 1990 the company laid off 5,000 workers, and six months later laid off an additional 5,000 employees on the A-12 project. After determining that about 10 percent of the former employees — mostly skilled computer technicians and engineers — were interested in starting their own businesses, the St. Louis County Economic Council organized classes on business start-ups. The council also convinced McDonnell Douglas to turn over some of the office space it no longer needed for use as "small-business incubators" to help the prospective entrepreneurs get started.

The borrowed facilities, says Dave Alexander, the council's marketing director, have helped people "who had an idea to take to market but lacked the money to rent space, hire secretaries and buy copy machines and computers."

The local government's efforts, combined with McDonnell Douglas' outplacement services, have helped ease the adjustment process. "Fifteen percent of the people laid off from McDonnell Douglas increased their wages," Cartwright says. But even in St. Louis, Cartwright adds, success stories "are far outweighed by the people who are still going through a dislocation and an adjustment — in most cases — to a lower wage."

A survey by the Economic Council of almost 2,000 former McDonnell Douglas employees illustrates a recurrent theme of corporate restructuring — the need for workers to abandon the notion of identifying a career with work for a single employer. "Many of the longtime McDonnell Douglas employees noted that their job-seeking skills were rusty and that they had developed a specialization that was only well-suited to the defense industry," the survey found. "More recent employees ... on the other hand, tended to treat the layoff as just another modest bump on the road."††

---

† See Helen Dewar, "With Cold War Won, Jobs Are Being Lost," *The Washington Post*, Feb. 14, 1992.

†† E. Terrance Jones, *The Layoffs at McDonnell Douglas: A Survey Analysis*, September 1991.

er confidence is due to normal retrenching during a recessionary period or to concern over the long-term conditions of the U.S. economy is uncertain. But some analysts see a disturbing pattern in which the spread of contingent work feeds concerns over job security, causing consumers to cut back on spending. While few will dispute the benefits of more prudent personal consumption after the debt-ridden 1980s, the sudden pullback in consumer spending is prolonging the recession.

"What we're looking at is the disappearance of the overwhelming predictability of income that supports our consumer economy," says newsletter editor Dan Lacey. "Middle-class living in America requires this kind of predictable, obedient behavior. As that becomes less available, consumer confidence drops."

Restructuring Threatens Benefits

Another long-term trend that appears to be contributing to consumers' malaise is the threat to benefits posed by restructuring efforts. As health-care costs continue to rise, even full-time employees are suffering an erosion of insurance coverage. In an effort to reduce their own exposure to health-care inflation, employers are forcing workers to pay higher premiums or switch to plans offering fewer services.

Changes in pension coverage add further uncertainty to workers' lives. Defined-benefit pensions, which assure employees of a predictable income upon retirement, were once the most common type of employer-provided retirement plan. But many employers no longer offer them. Increasingly, employers that provide pensions at all are opting for defined-contribution plans, such as tax-deferred savings plans. These cost the employer less and require contributions from employees who choose to participate. The amount of retirement income these plans produce,

however, depends on how well the investment fund is managed.

"Fringe benefits are another aspect of low consumer confidence," says Robert Reich. "Some economists find it a tremendous mystery that consumer confidence is so low during this recession. I don't think there is any mystery at all." In addition to the steady erosion of benefits among the full-time employed, Reich says, "obviously, people are not going to spend very much money when they are already highly indebted and scared to death that they may be next in line to lose their jobs."

Bush Administration Responds

Until recently, the Bush administration has downplayed the seriousness of the recession and the mounting joblessness that is going hand in hand with corporate restructuring. Twice last year, President Bush blocked or vetoed congressional measures to extend unemployment compensation to the long-term unemployed. But after his approval rating plummeted in the polls as unemployment continued to rise, the president signed into law a third extension measure that Congress approved Feb. 4. The $2.7 billion emergency program would provide an additional 13 weeks of benefits for the unemployed who exhaust their 26 weeks of state benefits and then exhaust the 13 to 26 weeks of extended federal benefits enacted last year. Altogether, jobless workers could receive either 52 or 59 weeks of benefits, depending upon the severity of the unemployment in their state.

Jobs were also the centerpiece of the economic program contained in Bush's budget proposal for fiscal 1993, sent to Congress on Jan. 29. In addition to several tax credits aimed at short-term stimulation of the economy, Bush called for "job-creating investments," including a cut in the capital gains tax, a 15 percent invest-

ment tax allowance and a moratorium on federal business regulations.

Many economists — as well as Bush's Democratic opponents in this presidential election year — criticized his economic proposals as insufficient, given the long-term nature of unemployment today and the likelihood of far-reaching changes in the domestic job market as U.S. corporations compete in the global economy. "I'm not super-thrilled by the economics that I heard," says Georgia State University forecaster Ratajczak of Bush's Jan. 28 State of the Union address, in which the president outlined his budget proposals. "If you're scared about the economy and you don't know what the other guy will do, you may vote for this guy," he says. "If someone gets re-elected because of fear, you have to wonder where things are going."

Investing in People

Many economists applaud Bush's decision to go along with the extension of unemployment benefits. Kochan of MIT says, however, that incentives are needed to encourage the jobless to use their idle time to get training for new employment. "In the short term," he says, "the most positive step would be to allow people on unemployment to use some of the time to enroll in training and retraining programs."

Over the longer term, Kochan adds, government and business alike need to "rethink our whole policy on investing in people. If we're going to be serious about having tax incentives for research and development and for investment in hardware, plants and equipment, then it's time to learn the lessons of the last 10 years and match that with equivalent incentives for investment in training, retraining and education."

Continued on p. 186

At Issue:

Do the economic benefits of contingent work outweigh the hardship it imposes on workers?

MARVIN H. KOSTERS

Director of economic policy studies at the American Enterprise Institute
FROM TESTIMONY BEFORE THE JOINT ECONOMIC COMMITTEE, JAN. 10, 1992.

yes

Changes in the characteristics of jobs and in the legal and regulatory environment have contributed to the emergence of new types of employment arrangements, sometimes called contingent employment. The trend toward white-collar employment has meant that the typical job-seeker is now more likely to prepare a résumé to facilitate matching a worker's skills with an employer's needs than to go to a firm's employment office and fill out an application for a job that might be available. The process for matching workers' occupational skills with specific job requirements is probably more complex in professional and technical job markets than for traditional blue-collar production worker jobs.

In addition, offering a worker a more-or-less permanent position entails a larger commitment, a bigger investment, than in the past.... Some type of temporary employment arrangement can help to avoid the possibility of the potentially costly mistake of bringing a worker directly on the payroll whose services might be needed only temporarily....

Contingent employment is often criticized for the absence of job security it entails and because compensation is often paid primarily in wages, with few non-wage benefits. Avoiding the costs of some of these benefits, of course, particularly for workers who may not value them highly, is one of the reasons why these employment arrangements have become more prevalent. Although lack of health plan coverage is often associated with temporary employment arrangements, encouraging the purchase of health insurance by such workers by providing for them the same tax-advantaged terms as for workers covered by employer-paid health plans makes more sense than discouraging this type of employment.

The growth of contingent employment arrangements has sometimes been viewed as an undesirable development because it is seen as supplanting traditional wage and salary employment. This is a seriously incomplete and misleading view. It seems to be much more appropriate to view at least some forms of contingent employment as a constructive supplement to traditional wage and salary jobs that sometimes helps to facilitate entry into such jobs. Employment of this kind can be expected to result in more jobs than would otherwise be available, because it is in part a response to changes in the character of job-matching and to legal and regulatory aspects of the labor market.

DAN LACEY

Editor of Workplace Trends, a newsletter
FROM TESTIMONY BEFORE THE JOINT ECONOMIC COMMITTEE, JAN. 10, 1992.

no

Although most of Corporate America is hesitant to admit it because of potential political liabilities, the hard truth is that it is becoming standard management practice in U.S. corporations to cut permanent staff to the absolute minimum number of persons required to continue profitable operations — while utilizing a variety of innovative, non-permanent employment relationships to cope efficiently with fluctuating workloads. This strategy is most often referred to in management circles as the "core-staff concept."

The adoption of the core-staff concept affects employees at virtually all levels of the typical corporate structure. For example, both blue-collar and white-collar workers typically suffer income and benefit cuts when they move from employment in a big company to a small one, or to self-employment or another non-traditional work relationship. So the public debates that have been conducted in recent months over whether the recession that we have been experiencing is a "blue-collar" or a "white-collar" one are moot, at best.

The shift by large corporations to core staffing and its derivatives is putting to death the comfortable employment relationship that the typical big-corporation employee — no matter what color the collar of the shirt, blouse or uniform they wear to work — enjoyed during the postwar boom decades.

Put most succinctly, the expectation of long-term, steady employment at ever-rising wages, with full company-paid benefits has become obsolete. Yet nearly all the components of contemporary middle-class living in America — such postwar consumer institutions as 30-year mortgages, five-year car loans and revolving consumer credit — are based upon those obsolete, boom-era workplace expectations.

Obviously, the process of moving from the boom-style employment standard to the post-boom model is a very traumatic one for middle-class Americans. Most members of this traumatized group still have jobs and are not represented in the unemployment statistics. But a rapidly growing number are no longer employed in the secure, consistent, predictable fashion that middle-class living in the United States demands. Is there really any wonder, then, why consumer confidence has been so low? Boom-style employment is dying a very painful death, and the entire U.S. economy is suffering as a result.

Educational Requirements for Growth Jobs

The table below indicates the level of education required for the jobs the Bureau of Labor Statistics projects will grow most rapidly or have the largest numerical increases by the year 2005.

Group I: *Occupations generally requiring a bachelor's degree or more education*
System analysts and
  computer scientists
Physical therapists
Operations-research analysts
Psychologists
Computer programmers
Occupational therapists
Management analysts
Marketing, advertising and
  public relations managers
General managers and top executives
Teachers, secondary school
Teachers, elementary school
Accountants and auditors
Lawyers

Group II: *Occupations generally requiring some post-secondary training or extensive employer training*
Paralegals
Radiologic technologists and
  technicians
Medical assistants
Physical and corrective therapy
  assistants and aides
Data-processing equipment repairers
Medical-records technicians
Surgical technicians
Cooks, restaurant
Respiratory therapists
Licensed practical nurses
Maintenance repairers, general utility
Teacher aides and
  educational assistants
Registered nurses
Legal secretaries
Medical secretaries

Group III: *Occupations generally requiring high school graduation or less education*
Home health aides
Human services workers
Personal and home-care aides
Correction officers
Travel agents
Flight attendants
Salespersons, retail
General office clerks
Cashiers
Food counter, fountain and
  related workers
Truck drivers, light and heavy
Nursing aides, orderlies and attendants
Janitors and cleaners, including maids
  and housekeepers
Waiters and waitresses
Food-preparation workers
Receptionists and information clerks
Gardeners and groundskeepers,
  except farm
Guards
Child-care workers
Secretaries, except legal and medical
Cooks, short-order and fast-food
Clerical supervisors and managers
Stock clerks, sales floor

Source: Monthly Labor Review, *November 1991*

Continued from 184

Martin Weitzman, an economics professor at Harvard, suggests a different approach to job security. Rather than paying full wages to workers and then laying off the more expendable employees during recessions, he suggests making part of the wage contingent on company profits. Instead of laying off marginal workers at the beginning of a recession, he says, companies could simply reduce the profit-sharing component of all employees' wages while keeping its work force intact.

Although he sees "no miracle cures for long-term structural problems," Weitzman says that profit-sharing could reduce general unemployment by giving employers "somewhat more incentives to take on workers in good times and less incentive to lay them off in bad times." ∎

OUTLOOK

Blue-Collar Blues

The good news for today's unemployed workers is that recessions don't last forever. Even the current downturn, which has outlived economists' forecasts, is deemed likely by most experts to end sometime in the next few months. With the recovery, expected to be modest by historical standards, will come new employment opportunities.

The bad news is that many job seekers will be unable to find the same kinds of jobs they lost during the recession. Corporate restructuring and continued automation of the workplace are now taking their toll on many white-collar occupations

once considered recession-proof. In an effort to streamline operations, big companies have eliminated many middle-management jobs. Lower-level white-collar workers, such as clerical and office-support staff, may also find their jobs gone for good. Even when business picks up again, their former employers may well turn to lower-cost contingent workers.

Blue-collar workers, more accustomed to seasonal layoffs than their white-collar counterparts, may have the toughest time of all. "That kind of job simply won't be there," says Audrey Freedman of The Conference Board. "You're still going to have your engineers, the people who design, finance and market the stuff, but you're not going to have that middle-class blue-collar worker."

As the economy picks up, the want ads will reflect the ongoing restructuring of the labor market. The Bureau of Labor Statistics predicts that between 1990 and 2005, U.S. businesses will add 24.6 million new jobs, increasing total employment by 20 percent over the current level.

But many currently unemployed workers, especially those with few skills, will have trouble finding a job. "In general, the projections show faster rates of employment growth for occupations that require higher levels of education or training and slower rates of growth for those requiring less formal education or training," conclude the authors of a BLS study on employment trends.[9]

Three broad occupational groups — professionals, technicians and executive, administrative and managerial workers — will grow from just over a quarter of the work force today to 41 percent by 2005, the BLS predicts. Virtually all the fastest-growing occupations examined by the BLS are in the service sector. As the number of elderly people increases, many employment opportunities will be found in health care, while advances in telecommunications and computer technology hold promise for technically skilled workers.

In most cases, these occupations require a college education or extensive technical training. For today's unemployed, or even current workers who are considering new fields, this poses a problem: Few can turn to their employers for help. "Will employers continue to do as much training as they have been doing, which isn't a lot?" Freedman asks. "My guess is they won't. Firms mostly spent their training dollars on managerial people anyway. But to the extent that they did training, it was with the idea that the trained employee — say, a production worker — would stay with them for a long time and therefore it would be worth it to spend a week or so training them."

As corporations seek contingent workers to perform more and more

of their jobs, however, they are less likely to make that kind of long-term investment. Instead, employers will simply depend on their subcontractors for training. In this way, Freedman says, "it's not only moving out the final function or job, it's moving out the human resource investment costs to the subcontractor."

Stay in School

For young people who have yet to enter the labor market, the experts are unanimous on one point: Stay in school long enough to gain a marketable skill. That means finishing high school at the very least. The BLS predicts that the job prospects for high school dropouts, already poor, are only going to get worse in coming years. High school graduates are more than twice as likely as dropouts to land a job in the fastest-growing occupations.

Today, however, the job market is still tight for graduates of college and even postgraduate degree programs in business, law and other professional disciplines. "The whole market is down," says Thomas Kochan of MIT. "Clearly, the market is as bad as we've seen it for MBAs for a long time. A significant number of people who come out of business schools without strong technical backgrounds are going to have a very difficult time. Now, more than in the past, education and skills really matter in the labor market in a very significant way."

If education is the key to a job seeker's success, flexibility comes in a close second. Economist Richard Belous advises blue-collar and white-collar workers alike to take advantage of community college courses to hone their skills; to stay aware of changes in their industry that may foreshadow a downsizing that could cost them their jobs; and to form a network of contacts who might help them when the time comes to change jobs.

Above all, Belous warns, "Don't think you're going to enter into one

corporate womb and be nurtured there for the rest of your life. That's just not the case anymore." ∎

Notes

[1] Sarbanes spoke Jan. 17, 1992, upon releasing the study, *Families on a Treadmill: Work and Income in the 1980s,* which was prepared by the Joint Economic Committee's Democratic staff.

[2] Belous, vice president and senior economist for the National Planning Association in Washington, testified Jan. 10, 1992, before the Joint Economic Committee.

[3] See Barry Bluestone and Bennett Harrison, *The Deindustrialization of America* (1982), p. 5.

[4] See Diane E. Herz, "Worker Displacement Still Common in the Late 1980s," *Monthly Labor Review,* May 1991, pp. 3-9.

[5] From data presented Jan. 10, 1992, by William G. Barron Jr., deputy commissioner of the Bureau of Labor Statistics, to the Joint Economic Committee.

[6] See John Greenwald, "Permanent Pink Slips," *Time,* Sept. 9, 1991, pp. 54-56.

[7] See, for example, Richard S. Belous, *The Contingent Economy: The Growth of the Temporary, Part-Time and Subcontracted Workforce,* National Planning Association, 1989.

[8] See Thomas A. Kochan, John C. Wells and Michal Smith, "The Consequences of a Failed Industrial Relations System: Contract Workers in the Petrochemical Industry," a draft study; and Lamar University's John Gray Institute, *Managing Workplace Safety and Health: The Case of Contract Labor in the U.S. Petrochemical Industry,* July 1991.

[9] George Silvestri and John Lukasiewicz, "Occupational Employment Projections," *Monthly Labor Review,* November 1991, p. 64.

Bibliography

Selected Sources Used

Books

Bluestone, Barry, and Bennett Harrison, *The Deindustrialization of America: Plant Closings, Community Abandonment, and the Dismantling of Basic Industry*, Basic Books, 1982.

The authors examine the early stages of corporate restructuring, which began in earnest during the last recession, in 1981-82. As manufacturers beefed up automation of assembly lines and exported many of the remaining production jobs to countries with lower labor costs, restructuring was felt mainly among blue-collar workers. Today the impact has spread to virtually all occupations.

Kanter, Rosabeth Moss, *When Giants Learn to Dance*, Simon & Schuster, 1989.

The Harvard Business Review's editor takes a look at the impact of corporate restructuring on the workplace. Managers and professionals are seeing their once-secure jobs disappear, a trend Kanter says marks the end of the "corpocratic" career, in which highly trained personnel sought to advance through the ranks of a single corporation.

Whyte, William H. Jr., *The Organization Man*, Simon & Schuster, 1956.

This best-seller of the 1950s describes the career path that was then becoming the norm for mid- to upper-level management in large U.S. corporations. Unlike today's employees, organization men were encouraged to identify with one employer and look to that company for all future advancement.

Articles

Cutler, David M., and Lawrence F. Katz, "Untouched by the Rising Tide," *The Brookings Review*, winter 1992, pp. 40-45.

Two Harvard economists present evidence of a growing gap in wages between workers with the highest and the lowest earnings during the 1980s. As education and training have become increasingly important determinants of workers' income, young male college graduates saw their weekly earning grow 30 percent more than did young men with a high school education or less over the decade.

Reports and Studies

Belous, Richard S., *The Contingent Economy: The Growth of the Temporary, Part-Time and Subcontracted Work Force*, National Planning Association, 1989.

Contingent work is becoming more widespread, replacing much full-time, permanent employment, the author reports. Use of contingent workers helps employers reduce their labor costs and gives them greater flexibility in responding to changing market conditions. Some contingent workers like the arrangement because it gives them more time for other work or activities. But contingent work also frequently means less job security and lower earnings than full-time employment.

Bureau of National Affairs, *Downsizing: Creative Approaches to Corporate Change*, 1991.

Corporate restructuring and layoffs, called "rightsizing" by some business consultants, is occurring in virtually every U.S. industry. Increasingly, firms are permanently eliminating staff positions and hiring part-time and temporary workers in their place. Even among workers who do not lose their jobs, the process is causing morale problems, as employees often find their workloads increased and fear for their own jobs.

Congressional Budget Office, *Family Incomes of Unemployment Insurance Recipients and the Implications for Extending Benefits*, February 1990.

Unemployment compensation has been available for jobless Americans for the past half century. Although it is two years old, this study provides useful background information on proposals to extend unemployment compensation for the long-term unemployed. One such measure was enacted earlier this year.

Johnston, William B., and Arnold H. Packer, *Workforce 2000: Work and Workers for the 21st Century*, Hudson Institute, June 1987.

Prepared for the Reagan administration, this study gained widespread recognition for the emphasis it gave to the need for better training and education of future workers. The authors predicted that service industries would replace manufacturing industries as the nation's chief employers by the turn of the century and that service industry jobs would require more highly skilled workers than many current positions.

Kathryn Troy, *Rethinking Employment Security*, The Conference Board, Research Bulletin No. 244, 1990.

The 1980s marked the end of employers' "paternalistic" relations with their employees, the author writes in assessing the growing loss of job security and fringe benefits as companies try to reduce their labor costs. She predicts that employers will use less costly lures, such as flexible hours, to attract qualified workers in the 1990s.

The Next Step

Additional Articles from Current Periodicals from EBSCO Publishing's Database

Case studies

"Allied-Signal posts $880 million writeoff, slashes 8,000 jobs in restructuring," *Aviation Week,* **Oct. 14, 1991, p. 74.**

Outlines reductions being taken at Allied-Signal following implementation of new Chief Executive Officer Lawrence A. Bossidy's plan to remove layers of management. Several years of weak earnings and two years of negative cash flow triggered the major restructuring of the aerospace, automotive and materials company. Actions being taken; current work force; sales; savings.

"Apple cuts back to get more," *Cadence,* **August 1991, p. 28.**

Reports that Apple Computer Inc. will be restructuring parts of the company to reduce operating expenses. Work force reduction; relocating, consolidating functions; reducing management-level positions; change of business strategy.

Barron, J., "With cogs laid off, wheels of justice are grinding," *The New York Times,* **Oct. 3, 1991, p. B1.**

Comments on the way the budget cuts and layoffs that began last week in New York City are leaving the courts shorthanded and are delaying cases. New York Gov. Mario M. Cuomo was sued in order to force him to spend more money on the court system. Effects of the cuts.

Carmody, D., "Layoffs at Time Inc.'s magazines," *The New York Times,* **Aug. 20, 1991, p. D1.**

States that Time-Warner Inc. will lay off 105 editorial employees at six of its magazines, bringing the total number of layoffs to about 10 percent of the 6,000 staff positions at *Fortune, Life, Money, People, Sports Illustrated* and *Time.*

Holusha, J., "Another blow to Westinghouse," *The New York Times,* **Oct. 8, 1991, p. D1.**

Takes a look at Westinghouse Electric Corp. The Pittsburgh-based company has taken a major write-off for the second time this year as a result of real estate problems in its financial-services subsidiary. Net loss of $1.48 billion in third quarter; elimination of 4,000 jobs; efforts to raise cash; other troubled sectors.

Mallory, M., "'How can we be laid off if we own the company?'" *Business Week,* **Sept. 9, 1991, p. 66.**

Looks at the problems at Weirton Steel Corp., the main-

stay of Weirton, W.Va., which has eliminated 1,000 of its 8,200 jobs with more still to go, despite the fact that the company is owned by its employees. Workers protesting the use of outside employees while union members lose jobs; employee stock-ownership plan (ESOP); other companies with the same problem; sacrifices the employees have made to make the company work; details; prospects.

Markoff, J., "Executives are shifted by IBM," *The New York Times,* **Aug. 2, 1991, p. D1.**

Details International Business Machines Corp.'s (IBM's) efforts to compete more aggressively by streamlining its top management. Realignment of top executives, thereby eliminating a layer of management; high-growth areas to be emphasized.

Shapiro, E., "Cost cuts at Frito-Lay to include 1,800 jobs," *The New York Times,* **Sept. 17, 1991, p. D1.**

Discusses Frito-Lay Inc.'s big changes that are planned to lower its cost of doing business. The company's battles with Borden Inc. and Eagle Snacks Inc. that have lowered the profits of all major makers of salty snacks.

Wilgus, A.L., "Forging change in spite of adversity," *Personnel Journal,* **September 1991, p. 60.**

Examines the restructuring of East Chicago, Ind.-based Inland Steel Bar Co. amid problems such as failing profits, job loss and labor unrest. The inclusion of the union in the organizational redesign effort; results; background information; obstacles. INSETS: A vision of the future; shifting responsibility to employees through education; lessons learned from applying for the Baldridge Award.

Colleges & universities

Grassmuck, K., "Colleges discover the human toll as they struggle to cut work forces," *The Chronicle of Higher Education,* **July 10, 1991, p. A1.**

Details how rising costs and dwindling resources have spurred dozens of colleges to lay off scores of workers, many of them long-time employees, and considers their struggle to find the proper way to reduce their work forces. Scope of the layoffs; officials are cautious; Middlebury College, Dartmouth, San Diego State, Northeastern University. INSET: Layoffs in academe: careful planning advised.

Mack, T., "Slow learners," *Forbes,* **July 22, 1991, p. 56.**

Discusses how many universities are starting to feel

some of the same pressures to improve efficiency that businesses consider an everyday experience. Tells how many are dealing with layoffs, dropping budgets, and department closings. Revenue sources drying up; costs of research rising sharply; eliminating the weakest parts; examples of cuts being made; whether or not research will suffer.

Weiss, S., "The hard times roll on Syracuse campus," *The New York Times,* Oct. 29, 1991, p. B1.

Says that Syracuse University, after the good years of the 1980s, is now retrenching. Budget cuts includes a salary freeze for all employees and could eliminate major academic programs over the next several years. Drop in undergraduate enrollment; similar troubles at other universities.

Economic recovery

"Business leaders expect more layoffs," *U.S. News & World Report,* Oct. 28, 1991, p. 20.

Reports that President George Bush's chief economic adviser, Michael J. Boskin, told business leaders at a closed-door session of the Business Council that the economy is improving, and discussed ways of bolstering the economy. More layoffs anticipated, especially in the service sector; Citicorp last week reported $885 million in losses; results of a survey of 7,000 business owners across the country; the Republicans' benefits-extension bill.

Cooper, J. C. and K. Madigan, "Recovery-room report: The patient is still feeling weak," *Business Week,* Sept. 23, 1991, p. 31.

Examines the signs of economic recovery that are starting to appear, but warns that job growth is barely sufficient to support the pace of income and spending necessary to guarantee the recovery's survival. Lack of recovery in service employment; decline of services other than health care to lowest level since January 1990; restructuring of operations to cut costs and improve profits; consumer debt; sharp decline in capital spending; lack of consumer optimism.

Cooper, J. C. and K. Madigan, "The pall over the recovery? Blame it on pink slips," *Business Week,* Nov. 18, 1991, p. 33.

Presents a business outlook that reports that the latest data on the recovery offers few clues that point to a growing economy. Continued layoffs; the leading indicators index hasn't risen since July; job growth is almost non-existent; employment is especially slack in the goods-producing side of the economy; a shrinking money supply; negative signals; any answer will have to include faster job growth; the recovery remains invisible to most consumers.

Forecasting

"Where the new jobs are," *Fortune,* Nov. 4, 1991, p. 13.

States that, despite the ongoing layoffs in many sectors and an unyielding 6.7 percent national unemployment rate, new job growth is spurting at high-tech companies with fewer than 1,000 employees. Manufacturers of biotech products, computer software, and environmental equipment leading the way; examples; beneficiaries of the boom; outlook.

Brownstein, V., J. Spiers, et al., "Though some jobs are gone for good, employment will rise again," *Fortune,* Nov. 18, 1991, p. 29.

Details how the recovering economy has affected the job market, and shows how the market seems to be strengthening only haltingly. What is holding employment down; job eliminations continuing; traditional job market indicators; inventories staying low; what type of companies are providing most of the new jobs.

Recession's Impact

"Blacks are hit hardest by job loss: Labor study," *Jet,* Sept. 16, 1991, p. 5.

Presents the results of a study which shows that blacks suffer more than whites when they try to find new jobs after losing old jobs.

Hicks, J. P., "Blacks see bias trend in job cuts," *The New York Times,* Sept. 23, 1991, p. D1.

Says that black professionals are becoming more concerned that they are being disproportionately hurt by widening layoffs and that their opportunities for advancement are becoming severely crippled. Concerns expressed by the National Black MBA Association; reasons for the bias trend.

Kilborn, P. T., "For forlorn millions, the recession goes on," *The New York Times,* July 28, 1991, p. 1.

Contends that, despite experts' beliefs that the economy is growing after a year in recession, millions of people are still out of work and looking for jobs. Fewer jobs, worse jobs; three theaters of despair; example of one man's hardship.

Krugman, P. R., "Why the unemployment rate is surprisingly low," *U.S. News & World Report,* Oct. 14, 1991, p. 62.

Reports that last week's figures confirm that unemployment remains a major economic problem in America, but the reported numbers are low — well below the 7.4 percent average unemployment rate in 1984. Reason why the unemployment rate doesn't look as bad as other economic statistics; what the smaller than expected rise in unemployment during the current downturn suggests; some jobs eliminated during this recession will never be restored; future economic growth impeded.

Mandel, M.J., "The slump struck some states more than once," *Business Week*, Aug. 5, 1991, p. 16.

Looks at the uneven toll the recession took on manufacturing jobs. Lists five states which lost and gained jobs during this time.

Mandel, M.J., "When the going gets tough, the tough get self-employed," *Business Week*, July 22, 1991, p. 14.

Looks at the recent increase in the levels of self-employment during the last year and tells how the increase has mostly been involuntary. How the downturn hit managers and professionals hard; why many of the new ventures may be short-lived; financial rewards may even be meager for successful startups; how self-employment is likely to keep rising, at least into 1992.

Mandel, M.J., R. King, et al., "White-collar America is still in a lot of pain," *Business Week*, Sept. 30, 1991, p. 22.

Examines the recession's effect on middle class, college-educated, white-collar workers who have previously been the bedrock of past recoveries. Less consumer spending; continued layoffs which span the entire economy; hopes that interest rate cuts will revive business.

May, T. Jr. and J. Spiers, "Slowdown in services," *Fortune*, Oct. 21, 1991, p. 24.

Contemplates the reversion to the old pattern of a gain in jobs in private services during a recession. This change in pattern suggests that the three-decade boom in private service hiring may have played out. Other findings about service sector jobs; more.

Scott, M.S., "Is your job on the line?" *Black Enterprise*, August 1991, p. 107.

Presents highlights of a *Black Enterprise* survey on readers' attitudes about work, career advancement and job security. Characteristics of the typical survey respondent; concerns about the recession; areas of dissatisfaction; positive aspects of their lives.

Restructuring

Fisher, A.B. and T. Welsh, "Morale crisis," *Fortune*, Nov. 18, 1991, p. 70.

Gives tips to companies in need of some new strategies to keep middle managers — who are angry and fearful of losing their jobs — consistent and happy. Gives examples of how some companies are coping; with fewer managerial bodies around, those left often end up working harder and

longer, for the same pay; effects of restructuring; how to prevent middle managers from leaving; hiring management consultants; more.

Nussbaum, B., "I'm worried about my job!" *Business Week*, Oct. 7, 1991, p. 94.

Comments on the demise of the once-solid foundation of the corporate career. Examines how the forces of fierce global competition and industrial consolidation are compelling corporations to cut entire layers of middle managers and whole categories of professional staffs making way for the migrant manager and free-lance professional of the 1990s. The new career path; presents several career success stories; more.

Tetzeli, R., "Whose jobs will disappear next?" *Fortune*, Oct. 7, 1991, p. 12.

Looks at the dismal employment figures from the Labor Department for the service industry. Tells how there's going to be a lot more restructuring to make companies strong enough to compete in the world market. Shows the difference between commercial and industrial construction in the years 1980, 1986, 1990 and 1991.

Vocational guidance

"Too many," *Economist*, Aug. 24, 1991, p. 25.

Examines why university students in America who graduated this year face the worst job market since the 1981-82 economic slump. How the recession is making things worse; which degrees are faring better and worse; healthcare industry; mathematics and engineering; details; outlook.

Dunn, D., "That's outplacement, not job placement," *Business Week*, Oct. 28, 1991, p. 146.

Reports on the difficulties faced by laid-off workers when attempting to find new employment, and their misconceptions of outplacement services. A survey of 1,800 companies found that 20 percent expect layoffs; outplacement counselor Marshall Stellfox; advice; outplacement fees.

Filipowski, D., "Welcome to the cold, cruel world," *Personnel Journal*, July 1991, p. 18.

Reports that according to a recruiting trends survey conducted by Michigan State University there were almost 10 percent fewer job openings for college graduates in 1991. Decrease for 1990 was 13.3 percent; most serious drop in job openings since the 1982-83 recession; forcing students to accept positions with smaller companies.

Back Issues

Great Research on Current Issues Starts Right Here... Recent topics covered by The CQ Researcher are listed below. Issues dated before May 10, 1991, were published under the name of Editorial Research Reports.

AUGUST 1990
Democracy in the Philippines
Initiatives: True Democracy?
Hard Times at Newspapers
Teens Balance School & Jobs

SEPTEMBER 1990
Dangers of Alcohol
Western Alliance After the Cold War
Tobacco Industry
Right to Die

OCTOBER 1990
Organ Transplants
Energy Policy Options
Search for Arab Unity
Child Support

NOVEMBER 1990
Lotteries and Gambling
Post-Cold War Choices
Setting Limits on Medical Care
Multicultural Education

DECEMBER 1990
Cable TV Regulation
Americans' Search for Their Roots
Is Insurance System a Failure?
Why Schools Still Have Tracking

Back issues are available for $4.00 (subscribers) or $7.00 (non-subscribers). Quantity discounts apply to orders over ten. To order, call Congressional Quarterly 1-800-432-2250.

JANUARY 1991
Growing Influence of Boycotts
Should the U.S. Reinstate the Draft?
America's Archaeological Past
Peace Corps' Challenges in '90s

FEBRUARY 1991
Regional Impact of Recession
Puerto Rico's Status
Redistricting: Mapping Power
Nuclear Power

MARCH 1991
Acid Rain
Cost of the Gulf War
Reassessing Gun Laws
Future for Man in Space

APRIL 1991
Social Security
Canadian Crisis Over Quebec
California Drought
Electromagnetic Radiation

MAY 1991
School Choice
Racial Quotas
Animal Rights
U.S. and Japan

JUNE 1991
Children and Divorce
Teenage Suicide
Endangered Species
Europe 1992

JULY 1991
Teenagers and Abortion
Soviet Republics Rebel
Mexico's Emergence
Athletes and Drugs

AUGUST 1991
Sexual Harassment
Fetal Tissue Research
Oil Imports
The Palestinians

SEPTEMBER 1991
Police Brutality
Advertising Under Attack
Saving the Forests
Foster Care Crisis

OCTOBER 1991
Pay-Per-View TV
Youth Gangs
Gene Therapy
World Hunger

NOVEMBER 1991
Fast-Food Shake-Up
The Greening of Eastern Europe
Business' Role in Education
Cuba In Crisis

DECEMBER 1991
Retiree Health Benefits
Asian Americans
The Obscenity Debate
The Disabilities Act

JANUARY 1992
Term Limits
Oil Spills
Hunting Controversy
Alternative Medicine

FEBRUARY 1992
Threatened Coastlines
New Era in Asia
Assisted Suicide

Future Topics

▶ *Women and Sports*

▶ *Teenage Drinking*

▶ *Solid Waste Crisis*

PUBLISHED BY CONGRESSIONAL QUARTERLY INC., IN CONJUNCTION WITH EBSCO PUBLISHING

Women and Sports

Will women catch up with men in the race for opportunities?

THE LAST TWO DECADES HAVE SEEN GREAT GAINS for girls and women in sports. As participation in fitness training and competition has soared, performance has improved so much that two researchers recently predicted that top women runners may someday overtake men. But the male-dominated world of athletics doesn't yet offer a level playing field. Female athletes still face discrimination as amateurs, and at the professional level struggling teams have to scramble for sponsors and fans. A study by the National Collegiate Athletic Association, due this spring, may help gauge inequities in college funding and other opportunities. Meanwhile, Title IX, a 20-year-old law that was supposed to end discrimination in sports, is today being blamed for drastically shrinking the ranks of female coaches and administrators.

I N S I D E THIS ISSUE

 March 6, 1992 • Volume 2, No. 9 • 193-216

Formerly Editorial Research Reports

COVER ART: BARBARA SASSA-DANIELS

THE CQ Researcher

March 6, 1992
Volume 2, No. 9

EDITOR
Sandra Stencel

MANAGING EDITOR
Thomas J. Colin

ASSOCIATE EDITOR
Richard L. Worsnop

STAFF WRITERS
Charles S. Clark
Mary H. Cooper
Rodman D. Griffin

PRODUCTION EDITOR
Laurie De Maris

EDITORIAL ASSISTANT
Thomas H. Moore

GRAPHICS
Jack Auldridge

PUBLISHED BY
Congressional Quarterly Inc.

CHAIRMAN
Andrew Barnes

VICE CHAIRMAN
Andrew P. Corty

EDITOR AND PUBLISHER
Neil Skene

EXECUTIVE EDITOR
Robert W. Merry

PUBLICATIONS MARKETING/SALES
Robert Smith

EDITOR, EBSCO PUBLISHING
Melissa Kummerer

The CQ Researcher (ISSN 1056-2036). Formerly Editorial Research Reports. Published weekly (48 times per year, not printed the first Friday of any month with five Fridays) by Congressional Quarterly Inc., 1414 22nd St., N.W., Washington, D.C. 20037. Rates are furnished upon request. Second-class postage paid at Washington, D.C. POSTMASTER: Send address changes to The CQ Researcher, 1414 22nd St., N.W., Washington, D.C. 20037.

Women and Sports

By Susan L. Morse

The Issues

Publicly challenging the natural superiority of men in sports is asking for a fight. Two researchers at the University of California at Los Angeles got one earlier this year when they baldly predicted women could outrun men by the middle of the next century, if current trends continue.

Researchers Brian J. Whipp and Susan A. Ward reached their conclusion by plotting the average running speeds of Olympic record-setters over the past century and comparing rates of improvement. The women's rate was twice as high as men's. "This is not me talking," protested Whipp to a skeptical *New York Times* reporter. "It's the data." [1]

But not many were buying it. *USA Today* found the conclusions "open to debate." [2] Fred Lebow, president of the New York Road Runners Club, was quoted as saying: "Women will never pass men. Never, never." [3] And the bible of men's athletics, *Sports Illustrated,* said the study "flies in the face of earlier, more intelligent research." [4]

Could it be? Men on the defensive about sports? Twenty years ago people would have laughed at the very notion. But 20 years ago sports was a whole different ballgame.

In 1971 only 294,000 girls played high school sports, compared with nearly 2 million today. "Don't worry," parents of tomboys consoled one another. "They'll grow out of it." Most did. They had to. At colleges like the University of Michigan, the budget for women's sports was zero, and would-be athletes raised funds by selling apples at football games. [5] Coeds' coaches — nearly all women — were unpaid, the equipment make-do and

the practice time catch as catch can. Both in school, where gym classes were sex-segregated, and out, competition with boys was discouraged: Girls were routinely banned from Little League and other playing fields.

But the social revolution that was transforming the workplace, the family and education quickly spread to the gym, spurred by a new fitness craze and a potent federal law. Title IX of the Education Amendments of 1972 outlawed discrimination by sex in all schools receiving federal funds. The floodgates opened, and a new era in sports began.

Women today are roughly a third of all college athletes. They make up the majority of new participants in weight training, running, cycling and basketball. And more females than males swim, exercise aerobically and ride bicycles. Even such physically grueling contests as triathlons have seen jumps in female participation, from 1,200 women in 1982 to 72,000 in 1990. [6]

More girls are exposed to sports at a young age, encouraged by a major shift in social attitudes: Nearly 90

percent of the 1,000 parents interviewed in a 1988 study viewed sports participation as important for their daughters as for their sons. [7]

Female athletes' visibility and credibility have increased, too. While at annual sports rites like the Super Bowl women still appear only as nubile distractions, other audiences are learning that talented female players provide just as good entertainment as the men.

College basketball is a case in point. Last season, some 4 million fans attended women's games, more than double the attendance in 1981-82. CBS cameras followed the thrilling National Collegiate Athletic Association (NCAA) championship game on March 31, 1991, in which Tennessee squeaked past Virginia in triple overtime, 70-67.* And just last month No. 2-ranked Virginia stole first place from Maryland before 14,500 fans — the fourth-largest regular season crowd in women's basketball history. *(See table, p. 197.)*

And talk about a steal. American women ran away with the gold this year at the Winter Olympics in Albertville, France, scooping up all five of the American team's first-place medals and nine of 11 U.S. medals overall.

But despite such gains, women's access still is severely limited: The playing field is far from level. "Sports in our society," says Donna Lopiano, director of intercollegiate athletics for women at the University of Texas at Austin, "is still a right for little boys and a privilege for little girls." [8]

At the university level, equity in sports is regarded as something of a joke. Nationwide, female college athletes routinely get a third of the team spots, less than a third of the scholarship dollars and a mere fifth of the

---

*This year's NCAA women's basketball finals will be held April 4-5 in the Los Angeles Sports Arena.

March 6, 1992   195

Money for College Sports: Who Gets It

Since 1981, the amount of money spent for both men's and women's athletics has increased significantly. While women's programs have grown at a much faster rate, they continue to receive far less money than men's programs. The exception is at schools without football, where spending on women's programs is much closer to the men's level, though still lagging.

NCAA Division	Average Expenses Per School			% of 1989 total expenses
	1981	**1985**	**1989**	
	(dollar amounts in thousands)			
Division I-A				
Men's program	$4,308	$6,153	$7,882	82%
Women's program	502	799	1,805	18
Division I-AA				
Men's program	1,189	1,990	2,421	76
Women's program	176	367	785	24
Division I-AAA				
Men's program	631	878	1,296	68
Women's program	188	206	618	32
II with football				
Men's program	392	719	854	72
Women's program	101	155	325	28
II-no football				
Men's program	232	418	523	63
Women's program	72	148	296	37
III with football				
Men's program	249	339	351	68
Women's program	48	65	168	32
III-no football				
Men's program	144	154	179	54
Women's program	37	37	133	46

Source: National Collegiate Athletic Association, "Revenues and expenses of intercollegiate athletics programs," 1990

total athletic budget.[9]

At the Olympic level, opportunities also are limited. Women's water polo, weightlifting, ice hockey, wrestling, soccer and pentathlon all have world championships — but no Olympic status, in most cases because the sports can't meet required participation levels. Men compete in all 33 Olympics sports categories, while women only compete in 24 of them. One-third of all events are for men only.[10]

Fewer than ever female student athletes enter careers in physical education, and leadership ranks are shrinking. In 1972 women coached more than 90 percent of college women's sports

teams and headed nearly all women's college athletic programs. Female coaches today head less than a quarter of all teams. Female athletic directors, at 16 percent, are practically an endangered species.[11] *(See story, p. 204.)*

The fight for women's sports is ultimately a fight for greater social access. "Sports has traditionally been used to train males for the competitive world of corporate games," says Lopiano. Sports, she says, teaches "loyalty, playing as a team, playing a role" — all with direct application in business. "When you remove sports from the training of women, you make them less competitive in other

activities, including the work world."

As researchers examine women's status in sports, here are some of the questions being asked:

Why do men's and women's sports programs still get unequal treatment?

The overwhelmingly male sports establishment is often seen as indifferent to women's second-class status. Athletic directors, 84 percent male, generally endorse athletic opportunity for women. But in practice, says Ellen Vargyas, senior counsel at the National Women's Law Center in Washington, they often resist adding women's teams, which are seen as a drain on resources and practice time. "We don't have this model of 'Let's see who's interested, and we'll accommodate them,'" says Vargyas. "Instead, institutions fight tooth and nail when girls and women make efforts to form a new team."

Too often, when women's teams *do* come first is when schools face a budget squeeze. "Institutions ... in financial trouble are, for the first time in history, treating sports equally — when it comes to cuts," says Christine Grant, women's athletic director at the University of Iowa. "The problem is the women's sports were never equal in the first place, so when you cut equally, you're cutting women disproportionately."[12]

In early 1990 the University of Oklahoma announced plans to ax women's intercollegiate basketball, then reinstated the program after players threatened suit. The College of William and Mary in Virginia cut two women's teams — basketball and swimming — in February 1991, then did an about-face when female team members threatened to press sex-discrimination charges. Princeton, Yale and other Ivy League schools also considered cutting women's sports but backed off. As financial pressures on colleges increase, observers expect to see more women's teams threatened.

Public support, meanwhile, has lagged, fed by misconceptions about what federal law requires. Kelly Sahner, a graduate student in education at the State University of New York at Buffalo, says she once asked a fellow student what he knew about Title IX. "'Oh,' he replied, 'that's when I was growing up and they took money away from us and gave it to the girls.'" A corollary is that women's sports bleed dollars from "revenue producers" like football. But despite its label, football eats up far more revenue at most schools — in scholarships, coaches, travel and equipment — than it produces.

When money isn't at issue, there are other ways to deny women equal access to sports. In Texas, female student athletes and their families have lobbied the state for years to sanction fast-pitch softball as an interscholastic league sport. Not enough interest, they've been told. As a result, Michael Anne Brothers' varsity team in Alvin, Texas, can't advance to playoffs. "The bottom line," says her mother, "is that our girls don't get the benefits and the exposure to colleges ... that [boys' sports] get through a playoff situation. We're not going to have any college coaches come down here ... just to watch Alvin High School play ball."

Refusals to establish teams or leagues on the grounds that "We don't have any women good enough to play," infuriate Margaret Dunkle, a senior fellow with the American Council on Education. Schools don't have trained female athletes, Dunkle says, because they haven't trained them.

The subtleness of much of today's discrimination also makes it harder to fight. Almost no one claims publicly anymore, as former NCAA Executive Director Walter Byers did in 1974, that women don't deserve equal treatment. "Discrimination has gone underground," says Peggy Kellers, director of the National Association for Girls and Women in Sport. "No one's talking about it, no one's raising questions." [13]

Women's Basketball Brings Out the Crowds

The popularity of women's college basketball is growing by leaps and bounds. Some 4 million fans attended games last season, more than double the number in 1981-82. Last month, a standing-room-only crowd of 14,500 in College Park, Md., watched No. 2 Virginia dethrone top-ranked Maryland.

Teams, site	Attendance	Date
Texas at Tennessee	23,912	Dec. 9, 1987
Stanford vs. Auburn†	20,023	April 1, 1990
Auburn vs. Louisiana Tech, Virginia vs. Stanford††	19,467	March 30, 1990
Louisiana Tech vs. Texas, Tennessee vs. Long Beach State‡	15,615	March 29, 1987
Ohio State at Iowa	15,500	Jan. 31, 1988
Ohio State at Iowa	14,821	Feb. 3, 1985
Virginia at Maryland	14,500	Feb. 11, 1992
Purdue at Iowa	13,498	Feb. 11, 1990
Iowa at Ohio State	13,320	Feb. 26, 1988
Old Dominion at Western Kentucky	12,951	Feb. 12, 1986

† *NCAA final in Knoxville, Tenn.*
†† *NCAA semifinal in Knoxville, Tenn.*
‡ *NCAA semifinal in Austin, Texas*

Source: The Washington Post, *Feb. 13, 1992*   **Photo: University of Maryland**

Sometimes the enemy isn't policy, but ingrained cultural behavior. Take the case of Julie Croteau, the first woman to play college baseball. First-baseman Croteau won the acceptance of her teammates at St. Mary's College in Maryland. She played hard, traded quips with fellow players and let occasional jibes from the stands roll off her thick skin. For three seasons. Then last spring she hung up her glove, at age 20.

"I'm miserable," she conceded. "I've spent more time fighting and being emotionally destroyed by baseball than enjoying the game." What finished her, she said, was her own team's barrage of sexually degrading comments about women. Knowing the comments weren't aimed at her personally made them no less upsetting. "What they're doing is just the tip of what most teams must be doing," she said. "It's scary." [14]

Boys vs. Girls: Adding Up the Totals

Far more high school boys participate in sports than girls, but girls have made great strides since 1971. After an initial surge in the 1970s, however, participation figures for girls leveled off. Today, nearly twice as many high school boys participate in athletics as girls.

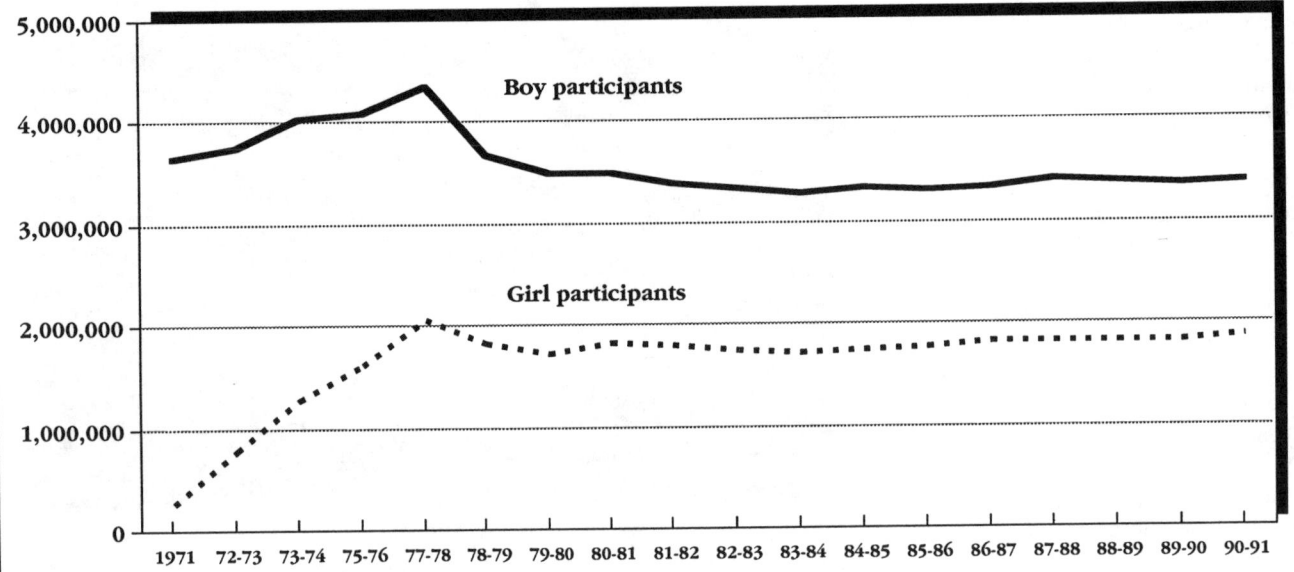

Note: Data was not collected for school years 1974-75 and 1976-77.
Source: National Federation of State High School Associations

Has the government done enough to ensure equality?

Women's explosive entry into sports was well under way before the ink was dry on Title IX, the federal law widely credited with prompting it. "In 1970," says Helen Upton, assistant director of the National Federation of State High School Associations, "during the hearings on legislation that would become Title IX, there were fewer than 300,000 female participants in high school sports. Two years later we saw half a million more. This was in 1972, when there was still no indication Title IX would apply to high school athletics. In 1974 we saw another half million.... The peaking of girls' participation occurred in 1976-78."

Since then, growth has plateaued. *(See graph, above.)* The number of girls who took part in high school interscholastic sports in 1990-91 — 1.9 million — was virtually unchanged from the late 1970s.

"Has progress stalled?" asks Kathryn Reith, advocacy director of the Women's Sports Foundation in New York City. "I would argue forcefully that it has.... Within the first six years of Title IX, we came a long way, but not far enough. We're sort of stuck at the level of discrimination they [the educational institutions] are comfortable with."

There are two main reasons the law hasn't done more: First, it was so vaguely written that the courts and Congress took 16 years to define its impact. Second, it hasn't been widely enforced. This especially angers women's sports advocates.

Vargyas at the Women's Law Center calls the Education Department's Office for Civil Rights (OCR), which is charged with Title IX enforcement, "a black hole. Nothing comes out." Protests haven't helped. "It's like punching Jell-O. You can't make them do anything," she says.

"From my perspective," says Arthur Bryant, executive director of the Trial Lawyers for Public Justice, "virtually every major educational institution ... is in violation of Title IX. The problem is that the government is not enforcing the law.... Most universities recognize this. That's why they remain in violation."

The OCR has been repeatedly criticized by Congress for not doing its job. In a 1988 blast, the majority staff of the House Committee on Education and Labor said: "In its failure to enforce the civil rights laws entrusted to it, the Office for Civil Rights has caused harm to those whom it was established to protect, has shown contempt for the federal courts and has defied the Congress."[15]

Over the last 10 years, OCR has logged 611 athletics complaints, including 36 in 1991. In only 71 of these (about 12 percent) did the OCR formally spell out the violations needing correction. The 1991 ratio was slightly higher: about 16 percent.[16] The agency has never terminated federal funding to an institution for violation of Title IX.

Assistant Secretary for Civil Rights Michael Williams won't comment on his office's performance before he took over in mid-1990. Of the 1991 record, he says, "We have no control over the merit of an individual's complaint. If you conclude from [the numbers] that the department hasn't been vigilant in investigating them, that's an incorrect assumption."

The OCR cites a February finding against Brooklyn College of the City University of New York as proof of Williams' vow to make Title IX enforcement a top priority. The finding in the closely watched case acknowledged many of the athletic department violations alleged by two physical education professors in 1990 (see p. 207).

Longstanding conflict over the scope of Title IX hasn't helped enforcement. In 1984 the Supreme Court in *Grove City College v. Bell* in effect exempted athletics from Title IX by ruling the law applied only to programs that directly received federal funds. The OCR immediately dismissed 64 discrimination complaints. With the Civil Rights Restoration Act of 1988, Congress made *all* programs liable, whether they or their parent institution received federal funds.

The biggest question remaining is whether the law bases equity on total institutional enrollment, fairly equally balanced between men and women, or on athletics representation, more skewed in favor of males. "The law is pretty clear," insists NCAA Executive Director Dick Schultz. "The law describes equity as based on the number of participants" — a position that lets him represent the typical college athletic department's 70-30 split of resources as in compliance.

But that's not equity as Donna Lopiano sees it. "Title IX requires scholarship opportunities to be proportional to participation and athletics participation to have the same gender mix as the general student population," she says.[17]

While calling both positions "somewhat simplistic," Michael Williams seems to lean more to Lopiano's view. In a school where women participate at a rate much smaller than their enrollment ratio, he says, neither number can be considered alone "because participation rates may be down because of discrimination."

Why has sexuality remained such a troublesome question?

Since 1968, women who compete in international athletic contests have had to submit to a chromosomal "sex test" that is known to be flawed. The first year it was given, Olympic swimmer Debbie Meyer, who had not yet menstruated at age 16, was so panicked about the test she paid to take it privately in advance.[18]

In 1985 Spanish hurdler Maria Patino was less fortunate. The day before the World University Games in Kobe, Japan, the athlete learned that, according to her genes, she was not a woman. She lost her right to compete and her scholarship and flew home in disgrace. The test was later proven wrong.[19]*

American sports psychologist Thomas Tutko thinks the underlying message of such tests is clear: "It's a way of saying, 'If you're this good at sport, you can't be a real woman.'"[20] American girls get the message early. After puberty, their participation in sports falls. Those who persevere learn either to ignore the sexual putdowns or avoid them by exaggerating their sexuality.

Some wear jewelry and makeup, pose for photos with boyfriends, play

---

*In February 1992 a committee of the International Amateur Athletic Federation, the world's leading track and field group, urged that the genetic tests be dropped.

in tight-fitting clothes. Florence Griffith-Joyner and Jackie Joyner-Kersee both excelled at the last Olympics, but because "Flo Jo" flaunted her sexuality, hers is the more lasting image. The media willingly conspire in the sex stereotyping of female athletes. Regulation volleyball doesn't excite many viewers, but there's no problem getting network coverage for beach volleyball played by women in bikinis.

What everyone is afraid of, say women's sports advocates, is the "L" word. That's "L" as in "lesbian." Homophobia is one more weapon used to keep girls and women out of sports or trivialize their athletic achievements.

According to Bruce Ogilvie, a sports psychologist and former consultant to the U.S. Olympic team, "I receive more questions about the potential danger to a daughter's sexuality than anything else. Parents want to know, 'How can I protect my daughter from succumbing to the seduction of athletes?'"[21] Author Mariah Burton Nelson and others say a far bigger (and rarely discussed) problem is seduction of female athletes by male coaches.

There *are* lesbians in sports, just as there are gay men in sports, but the fact that the term is applied indiscriminately to female athletes in general suggests it has a different meaning.

"When someone shouts from the stands to the playing field, 'Oh, you big dyke,' they have no idea what your sexual orientation is," asserts Mary Jo Kane, who teaches on women and sports at the University of Minnesota. Sexual orientation is not at issue, she says; intimidation and control are. "Women are terrified of that label, so to that extent, it works.... It keeps us all fighting among ourselves and blaming lesbians for the problem."

Sexuality profoundly defines almost every aspect of women's sports,

Female Sports Reporters: Ready for Prime Time?

Who doesn't remember Lisa Olson? In September 1990 the *Boston Herald* sports reporter headed into the locker room of the National Football League's New England Patriots for an interview and touched off a furor in the media and sports. After investigating her charges that several team members exposed themselves to her, that one propositioned her and that the team owner called her an obscene name, the NFL slapped the team with a $72,500 fine.†

If the incident symbolized the hostility women still face in sports, it was an even more pointed reminder of their outsider status in the privileged arena of sports reporting.

"When the whole Lisa Olson incident broke, I heard a very powerful statement from one of the women in my class," recalls Mary Jo Kane, who teaches a course on women and sports at the University of Minnesota. "She said, and her voice was quavering, 'It sure makes me think twice about whether I want to go into sports journalism if this is the type of treatment I'm going to receive.'... The message was very clear: If you're going to be a female sportswriter, you will suffer extreme consequences."

That's somewhat of an overstatement. Female sports reporters may be used to harassment, but Olson's was an extreme case — one that occurred, incidentally, 13 years after a federal judge upheld female reporters' right to enter the "sanctum sanctorum." Since the Olson incident, most teams have opted for towels rather than a second test of the NFL's seriousness, and reporters and athletes are both going about their jobs.

A harder problem for women to solve is access to the elite club of sports reporters in the first place. Some doors have been pushed open. These days almost every major daily newspaper has a woman covering sports, though female editors are relatively rare. But at the higher strata, particularly in broadcast journalism, women are more noticeable for their absence. The implicit message here, many women say, is that just as in college and pro coaching and administration, women are just not ready for the big time.

There are a few notable exceptions: Sherry Ross broke precedent in January by becoming an analyst for the National Hockey League's New Jersey Devils radio broadcasts. "No one wanted to be an astronaut until we saw people in space," Ross told *USA Today*. "Maybe other women will now see this profession exists for them." ††

On TV, familiar women include CBS's Lesley Visser, who interviewed Redskins Coach Joe Gibbs after his team won the Super Bowl; NBC's Gayle Gardner, the first female sports anchor to appear weekly on a major network; and Paula Zahn, who co-hosted CBS' coverage of the 1992 Winter Olympics. Tennis commentator Mary Carillo, who appears on CBS and cable's ESPN, is the only woman in the booth covering a championship-level men's sport. No woman does play-by-play. Few if any women get equal pay. And no hordes of women are crowding in behind the pioneers.

Financially troubled sports divisions aren't falling over themselves to promote any of the estimated 50 female sportscasters who work at the 630 network affiliates nationwide. Phyllis George, who exploded the male-only sportscasting tradition by appearing on CBS's *The NFL Today* from 1975 to 1984, says she thought she'd see women pouring into the studio by now. "I'm still watching," she told *Sports Illustrated* last year. "And where are all the women?" ‡

---

† In February 1992 Olson reached an out-of-court settlement of her sexual harassment suit against the Patriots.

†† *USA Today*, Jan 15, 1992, p. 2C.

‡ Quoted in Sally Jenkins, "Who Let Them In?" *Sports Illustrated*, June 17, 1991, p. 78.

---

from their ranking to their coverage. "I do not think it's a coincidence," says Kane, "that golf and tennis are the only two sports that have caught on at a professional level.... They're the only two you can play and still look like a lady."

TV and the print media go to great lengths to underscore female athletes' sexuality. "When Chris Evert announced she was retiring from tennis," recalls Kane, "her photo appeared on the cover of *Sports Illustrated* — and women are almost never on the cover." But the photos inside showed her with the various men in her life. "You have to ask, 'Why don't you want to talk ... about her as an athlete?'"

Job screening for coaches and administrators reportedly includes speculation about a female candidate's sexual orientation. *(See story p. 204.)* A gay label is costly. Pat Griffin, an associate professor of education and former coach at the University of Massachusetts at Amherst, talks about a rumored "list that tells which coaches in Division I are straight and which are gay. It doesn't matter if it's true or not. Just the rumor that there is such a list terrifies coaches."

Some gay women in sports, usually those with secure status, have openly addressed their homosexuality. Griffin, a tenured professor who conducts homophobia workshops around the country, is one of them. "I think that invisibility is one of the biggest problems with women and sport," she says. "In that climate of silence and invisibility, all the stereotypes thrive." She and other activists have denounced Penn State's women's basketball coach Rene Portland for publicly stating she wants no lesbians on her team.[22]

Homosexuality is less of an issue for men in sports. Homosexual or not, "male athletes fit the image of what we expect men to be in this culture," says Griffin. "People usually don't think the quarterback on the college football team is gay because he fits their gender image, but that's the first thing they think about the center on the women's basketball team."

Must women's sports follow the male model?

One measure of how much women are catching up with men is disconcerting: As money and prestige have grown, so has the incidence of cheating, injury and health abuse.

Eastern Kentucky University lost two women's basketball scholarships in 1990-91 for giving cash and other improper benefits to two players; Florida A & M University was put on two years' probation and prohibited from postseason play for improper recruiting and giving illegal benefits to female tennis players. Other colleges have been penalized for infractions that seem to coaches and players to be growing in number.

"Women's basketball has come a long way," said Nancy Mayer, a University of Virginia player in 1986. "It is much more competitive, and some teams and coaches want to do whatever they have to to win."[23]

Olympic silver medalist and basketball whiz Nancy Lieberman recalls one coach's words back in the '70s when colleges were wooing the then-high school senior with illegal gifts, including a car and an apartment. "This is called equality," he told her. "The men have been cheating for years."[24]

Injuries, likewise, are approaching men's levels. A study of men's and women's varsity teams found comparable injury rates: 42 percent for men vs. 39 percent for women.[25]

And while drugs and steroids aren't considered the problems they are in

As money and prestige have grown, so has the incidence of cheating, injury and health abuse.

men's sports, women's sports have their own health abuses, among them anorexia and bulimia. About 20 percent of female college athletes are reported to have eating disorders. One study of female athletes claimed that 74 percent of gymnasts, 47 percent of distance runners and 25 percent of softball, track and tennis athletes had "practiced eating disorder behaviors daily for at least one month."[26]

Other ethical questions are plaguing women's sports lately, too. Many women now agonize over the sponsorship of women's tennis by tobacco giant Philip Morris Co. "Blood money," Health and Human Services Secretary Louis W. Sullivan calls it.[27]

The trends are giving new urgency to a question of self-definition that has haunted the women's sports movement for decades: Just whose game are they playing? "We're at a crossroads," says Nelson, "where we could play as the men play — we could follow in their sneaker steps. We seem to be choosing not to, but I'm an optimist."

"When Title IX was in its conception stage," Nelson adds, "the women who we regarded as the 'old school' P.E. teachers were saying, 'We don't

want what men have' — because men always played sports in an arena beset by politics and scandal. But young feminists like me were saying, 'We *do* want what they have. We want the scholarships, we want the opportunities.' Now when you see what a mess men's sports are in — with rampant cheating, steroid use, unnecessary injuries — you realize women need to choose: Are we going to remember the spirit of the game or are we going to let greed distort our vision?"

In her talks around the country, Burton advocates a different framework for women's competition. "It's only because the media focus on men's football, baseball and basketball that we think sports are about humiliation and slaughter and putting other people down," she says. "I really don't think sports are about that for most people. They're about physical fitness and fun and play." (See "At Issue," p. 209.)

They weren't that for her when she played center on the women's basketball team at Stanford University. "I played until my knees were irreparably damaged. I was taught to ignore the pain, or to do things to lessen it ... but nobody ever suggested I do something else." She'd like to see a more caring model.

"I see it in Jackie Joyner-Kersee, who befriended her top German rival, Heike Drechsler," she says. "I see it in a lot of the top women's softball and volleyball teams, where women rotate the coaching position and the top starting position and talk about the play after the game."

And she sees it in Jack Giles, the swim coach at Arcadia High School in Phoenix, which has a no-cut policy. "Boys and girls are in the pool together. They've won the state championship for the last two years, so he knows what he's doing. But he's not focused exclusively on winning. He's also interested in developing people." ∎

BACKGROUND

Overcoming Stereotypes

The ancient Greeks didn't just exclude women from Olympic competition. They barred them from even viewing the games on pain of death. According to legend, those caught disobeying were hurled off the cliffs. But some plucky women established their own counterpart — the all-female Herean Games at Olympia, held a month before the Olympics. Females in Sparta, another macho Greek society, were encouraged to train from girlhood in running, jumping and javelin throwing, on the theory that athletics built better breeders.

It would be many grim centuries later before large numbers of women would experience such freedom again. In 19th-century America, the well-to-do insisted on women's frailty, even while poor women lived lives of backbreaking toil. The modern concept of sports that formed by the end of the century excluded women. Popular leaders including Teddy Roosevelt glorified men's athleticism to combat what they saw as the "feminizing" effects of a more sedentary, post-industrial way of life. Sports, they said, built character, perseverance, strength and respect for authority — traits considered irrelevant for women.

But not all women thought so. Such women's colleges as Vassar began incorporating physical education into their curricula. And though critics warned physical exertion would damage women's reproductive capabilities and leave them too tired to fulfill their "womanly duties," students appeared to benefit. Other women followed suit, shedding tight corsets to gain freedom of movement.

For decades, the emphasis in women's gym classes was on play rather than competitive sport. Claiming

women were more susceptible than men to heart strain, fatigue and other injury, educators changed game rules to restrict movement and vigorously opposed women's participation in Olympic games and tournaments. Athletic scholarships were rejected as potentially exploitative. "A game for every girl and a girl for every game," proclaimed the motto of the women's division of the National Amateur Athletic Federation in the 1930s. Women physical educators brandished the popular slogan to reassure women that all females would have an opportunity in sports, albeit not at a highly competitive level.[28] The philosophy prevailed well into the 1960s.

Passage of Title IX

But the reactionary voices couldn't stay the changes under way in women's attitudes, an outgrowth of the civil rights movement of the 1960s and the feminist revolution. In the early 1970s girls poured into the gyms. By 1972 they had a law — Title IX of the Education Amendments — guaranteeing their right to be there. Under the law, gym classes went coed and schools had a choice: Provide equal sports teams for girls or let girls try out along with the guys.*

The athletic establishment stormed while the government labored to draw up implementation guidelines. The NCAA tried to exempt athletics from Title IX and failed. Next it tried to exclude "revenue sports," meaning men's football and basketball. The law, said then-Executive Director Walter Byers, would mean the doom of intercollegiate sports.[29] But in 1978, the year schools were first required to be in compliance, a federal judge dismissed an NCAA suit seek-

---

*Schools were not required to sponsor coed teams in contact sports like football and basketball.

ing to have Title IX overturned as a threat to men's sports.

Meanwhile, female sports figures suddenly soared in stature. In 1971 tennis superstar Billie Jean King became the first athlete of her sex to win $100,000. Two years later she endeared herself to millions of American women with her resounding defeat of the legendary Bobby Riggs in a much ballyhooed "Battle of the Sexes" match, played before a national TV audience in the Houston Astrodome. Others making headlines included the spritely Romanian gymnast Nadia Comaneci, earning three gold medals at the 1976 Olympics, and marathon swimmer Diana Nyad, who in August 1979 made an unprecedented 60-mile swim from the Bahamas to Florida.

In 1972 women launched a short-lived experiment in self-governance by forming the Association for Intercollegiate Athletics for Women (AIAW), supporting top-level competition for women. The organization lasted 11 years before it was broken by its old enemy. In 1983 the bigger, more powerful NCAA forced the group out of existence after wooing away members and scheduling championships to conflict with AIAW contests.

Some of the biggest victories in the 1970s were won by youngsters like 12-year-old Maria Pepe of Hoboken, N.J., who went to court with her parents in 1972 to fight for her right to play on her local Little League team. Battered by bad publicity and the prospect of countless other lawsuits, the national Little League organization reluctantly admitted girls in 1974.

Across the country, girls asked the courts to back their right to try out for previously all-boys' ice hockey, football and soccer teams. Often, what they won was the right to be rejected by derisive coaches after a pro forma tryout or subjected to the cruelty of fellow players if they made the team.

Continued on p. 204

Chronology

1900-1920s

Society slowly throws off the Victorian ideal of the frail woman and grows more tolerant of women's physical activity. But physical education instructors strenuously oppose competition for women.

1900
The first women compete in the Olympics, in Paris.

1914
The American Olympic Committee formally opposes women's Olympic participation except in floor exercises, where they wear long skirts.

1919
Suzanne Lenglen debuts at Wimbledon, scandalizing spectators with her short, uncorseted tennis dress.

1920
Female swimmers become the first American women to win full Olympic status.

1930s-1950s

Female sports greats make waves as social rules for women relax.

1927-32
Tennis champ Helen Wills Moody wins eight times at Wimbledon.

1932
Mildred Didrikson, who became a celebrated golfer in the 1940s under the name Babe Didrikson Zaharias, takes three track and field medals in the Los Angeles Olympics.

1950
Althea Gibson breaks the color bar in American tennis, advancing to the U.S. Lawn Tennis Association playoffs.

1960s-1970s

Civil-rights activism and a new feminist movement spark a revolution in girls and women's sports.

1968
Sex tests are given for the first time to women in international competition.

1972
Congress passes Title IX of the Education Amendments, outlawing sex discrimination by all recipients of federal funds.

Sept. 20, 1973
Billie Jean King defeats Bobby Riggs in the nationally televised "Battle of the Sexes" tennis match.

1974
Little League baseball admits girls.

May 20, 1974
The Tower amendment, excluding revenue sports from Title IX requirements, dies in a House-Senate conference committee.

July 21, 1975
Title IX goes into effect.

1980s

Supreme Court weakens Title IX.

1982-83
With membership dwindling, the AIAW folds, leaving the National Collegiate Athletic Association (NCAA) as the major group representing women in sports.

Feb. 28, 1984
The U.S. Supreme Court, in *Grove City College v. Bell*, narrows the scope of Title IX by ruling that the law applies only to programs that directly receive federal aid.

1987
Washington state's Supreme Court finds that Washington State University treated women unfairly in its sports programs.

1988
Ending an eight-year federal court fight, Temple University in Philadelphia agrees to boost women's sports after a judge blasts its preferential treatment of men's football and basketball.

March 22, 1988
Congress enacts the Civil Rights Restoration Act over President Ronald Reagan's veto. The act overturns *Grove City* and prohibits sex discrimination throughout educational institutions receiving federal funds.

1990s

Efforts accelerate by cash-strapped colleges to drop women's sports teams. Title IX gets a boost from the Supreme Court.

1990 and 1991
The University of Oklahoma and the College of William and Mary drop plans to cut women's basketball after players threaten legal action.

January 1992
The NCAA delays imposing a 10 percent cut in athletic scholarships for women until the release of its gender-equity study.

Feb. 26, 1992
In a unanimous ruling seen as a major boost to the power of Title IX, the U.S. Supreme Court permits students to sue for monetary damages for sexual harassment and other forms of sex discrimination at schools and colleges.

Where Have All the Women Gone?

For one group of women, the federal sex-equity law known as Title IX backfired. While it helped thousands of female athletes onto the field and into the gym, it cost many women their jobs as coaches and administrators. Women's poor representation in leadership today prevents them from reordering athletic priorities or serving as role models for students.

The decline in influence stemmed from the merging of most men's and women's college athletic departments in the years following passage of the law in 1972. Despite warnings from the Education Department's Office for Civil Rights that mergers could hurt women, most colleges brought operations under one roof to maximize efficiency and cost savings. Suddenly women who had budgeted and run their own departments lost those responsibilities to men who became their bosses.

Figures compiled by two Brooklyn College professors, R. Vivian Acosta and Linda Jean Carpenter, paint a startling picture of the setbacks. (See graph at right.)

Female coaches also lost ground in the wake of Title IX. As women's sports mushroomed, more coaching slots opened than could be filled by available female candidates with expe-

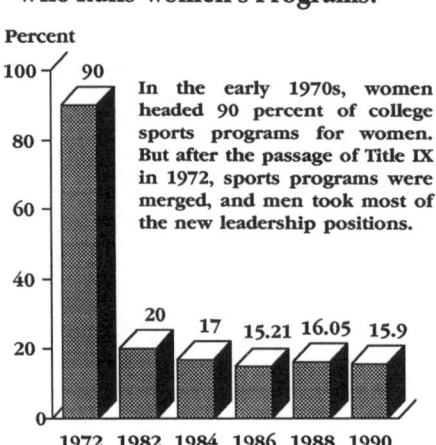

Who Runs Women's Programs?

Percent

In the early 1970s, women headed 90 percent of college sports programs for women. But after the passage of Title IX in 1972, sports programs were merged, and men took most of the new leadership positions.

| 1972 | 1982 | 1984 | 1986 | 1988 | 1990 |
| 90 | 20 | 17 | 15.21 | 16.05 | 15.9 |

Source: R. Vivian Acosta and Linda Jean Carpenter, "Women in Intercollegiate Sports," 1990

rience. As salaries grew, more and more male coaches began muscling in, edging out female rivals by impressing male administrators with their greater qualifications.

In 1972, according to Acosta and Carpenter, more than 90 percent of women's team coaches were female; today that figure is 47 percent. In high school, the picture is reportedly similar. "The lack of leaders," says Carpenter, "is a pretty heavy price to pay for the good things Title IX has done."†

Discrimination in hiring reportedly keeps women's leadership figures low. Donna Lopiano, women's athletic director at the University of Texas, one of the few schools with separate men's and women's sports administrations, says female candidates hear: "'If you are young, you are going to have childbearing problems; if you are a parent, there is no way you can handle the time and recruiting demands of this job; if you do not have children, you are a homosex-

ual; and if you get to 40, you are too old because you are going to have all those hot flashes and everything.'"††

In 1988 Charlotte West, acting athletic director at Southern Illinois University, made news when she was passed over for the top job despite her 30 years in the school's sports administration. Selected in her place was

---

Continued from p. 202

Grove City Ruling

In 1984 the U.S. Supreme Court dealt Title IX a crushing blow in *Grove City College v. Bell.* The court ruled that only those specific college *departments* that receive federal money must follow the law. Title IX complaints plummeted. In March 1988 Congress overturned the ruling. The Civil Rights Restoration Act of 1988, passed over President Ronald Reagan's veto, outlawed sex discrimination *throughout* educational institutions receiving federal funds.

Elsewhere, courts were providing encouragement. In 1988 Philadel-

phia's Temple University conceded a long federal court battle by agreeing to overhaul its women's athletics program. Earlier, the judge in *Haffer v. Temple University* had ruled the university could not justify spending some $2,100 more per male athlete than female athlete in order to support "revenue-producing" sports like men's football and basketball. In fact, the term was a misnomer: In 1985-86, Temple's football team lost $622,137, and its men's basketball team lost $200,000. In any case, the judge held that "financial concerns cannot justify gender discrimination."[30]

However, because relatively few Ti-

tle IX cases have been brought to a ruling, the federal courts have not yet resolved important differences in interpretation. One of the most influential recent legal victories for women's sports came in a state rather than a federal court case. In 1987 Washington state's highest court found the state university guilty of pervasive sex discrimination in its athletics program. The ruling in *Blair et al. v. Washington State University* criticized the college for failing to include men's football in computations comparing men's and women's sports.

The court said that women's athletic funding was expected to reflect

---

... To Programs Headed by Men

former St. Louis Cardinal quarterback Jim Hart, who came virtually without administrative experience. "These jobs can be learned," Southern Illinois President John Guyon said in Hart's defense.‡

Disparities in pay compound disparities in status. The median salary of a female athletic director is $10,783 less than a male A.D.'s, says Lopiano. For every dollar earned by male coaches of men's basketball, she says female coaches of women's basketball make 39 cents.

Connie Phorngren, an assistant professor of physical education at Boise State University in Idaho, cataloged women coaches' complaints from personal interviews: High on the list were second-class status, isolation and measurement against a higher standard. "With a male coach," Phorngren says, "it's assumed they're capable until they prove they're not. With women, they have to prove they're capable. Women feel they can't make mistakes."

Female students are only too aware of their women coaches' frustrations. Only 5 percent of female student athletes surveyed by the NCAA in 1988-89 said they planned a career in college athletics.‡‡

Some don't scare so easily. Kelly Sahner, 24, who is studying for a master's in education at the State University of New York at Buffalo, plans on being an athletic director, despite the discrimination she's witnessed as an athlete and school sports information director. The discouraging numbers, she says, "fuel my fire."

Role models, though scarce, also offer hope. Judith Sweet, for example, longtime athletic director at the University of California-San Diego, is now midway through her two-year term as the NCAA's first woman president. *Atlanta Constitution* columnist Furman Bisher greeted her election with these words: "Dr. Judith Sweet is no doubt quite a competent person, but this is mainly a male organization, and I consider her ascension as pure tokenism. Like having a debutante as head of the National Muleskinners Association."‡‡‡

Women's sports advocates say affirmative action may be needed to stem the leadership drain in women's sports. A statewide recruitment campaign in Colorado, for example, is credited with raising the level of women coaching high school girls' teams from 38 percent to 41 percent. Programs to promote the hiring of women as assistant coaches on men's as well as women's college teams, say others, could give women the experience they need to match men's credentials.

Meanwhile, women like Barbara Hedges continue to break barriers. Last summer Hedges became the University of Washington's athletics director. This made her the first woman to head a sports program at the toughest competitive level of college athletics — Division I-A.

† R. Vivian Acosta and Linda Jean Carpenter, *Women in Intercollegiate Sport,* 1990, p. 1.

†† Quoted in *The Dallas Morning News,* April 28, 1991, p. 4J.

‡ Quoted in Matthew Goodman, "Where the Boys Are," *Washington Monthly,* April 1989, p. 18-20.

‡‡ NCAA Study on Women in Intercollegiate Athletics, June 6, 1991, p. 9.

‡‡‡ Quoted in Debbie Becker, "Sweet's Job Surpasses Her Dreams," *USA Today,* Jan 14, 1992, p. 1.

women's enrollment, *not* lower athletic participation figures. The ruling prompted a statewide overhaul of intercollegiate athletics, with unprecedented support from the state Legislature. Because the complaint was filed under a state law, however, members of the athletic establishment minimized its impact.

The recession of the early 1990s produced a new threat, as cash-strapped colleges sought to cut women's teams added in the 1970s and '80s. Under the threat of Title IX lawsuits, some backed off, but as financial pressures increase, it's likely other schools will consider cuts. ■

CURRENT SITUATION

Prospects Improving

By inches, progress continues. Some women's college teams have hit on new ways to generate publicity and revenue. Attendance has skyrocketed since 1983, when the University of Iowa began selling a season pass to women's athletics called the Hawkeye "Goal Card." The University of Missouri boosts income by inviting other women's teams to compete in the annual "Purina Cat Classic," sponsored by Ralston Purina Co. Minnesota sports boosters papered the Twin Cities with images of female athletes after the state Legislature agreed in 1985 to provide full funding for university women's athletics. And in 1990 the Sara Lee Corp. signed on as the first national corporate sponsor of NCAA women's sports programs, promising to spend at least $6 million over three years.[31]

Awareness is growing at the high school level, too. A Florida state

Continued on p. 207

Minority Women and Sports

Sports doesn't lead society; it reflects it, says former U.S. Olympic rowing champion Anita DeFrantz, now president of the Amateur Athletic Foundation of Los Angeles. So it follows, she says, that racism — like sexism — is an integral part of the American sports system.

The well-publicized achievements of a few talented individuals like track stars Florence Griffith-Joyner and Jackie Joyner-Kersee obscure the fact, DeFrantz and others argue, that black and minority women are the real underclass in sports.

Data is scarce because the subject has drawn so little attention in the past. But that is changing. The National Collegiate Athletic Association (NCAA), the Women's Sports Foundation and independent researchers are among those now examining how race affects women's participation in sports. Still, there is enough material to suggest DeFrantz may be right.

For minority women, money poses perhaps the greatest barrier. "For too long," complains DeFrantz, "sports has been the province of the wealthy." Schools and communities have traditionally helped fund sports programs for boys and men; girls and women, in contrast, have had to pay for their own transportation, equipment, coaches and training. "I do know of kids," says DeFrantz, "who desperately wanted the opportunity to take part in sports, and there was nothing. I was one of them."

Until the mid-1970s, girls from low-income families couldn't turn their athletic talents into a free ticket to college; there were virtually no athletic scholarships for women.[†]

The money hurdle, says DeFrantz, looms large as ever "especially these days when we're seeing so many cutbacks in the public schools. Often the first thing that goes is what is called extracurricular activities.... I've seen no studies that this is having a disproportionate impact on minorities, but common sense leads you to that result."

Minority girls must clear bigger social hurdles, too, to take part in sports. A 1988 study found that black girls were more likely than white girls to feel that "boys make fun of girls who play sports" and to have parents who feel sports are more important to boys than to girls.[††]

Sports doesn't provide an equal payback to minority girls who manage to clear those hurdles. A 1989 study of more than 13,000 high school students funded by Miller Lite beer showed that Hispanic girls in high school sports

were more likely to finish school and get good jobs. But black female athletes who entered the work force right after high school fared worse in their careers than nonathletes.[‡]

Within sports, observers say, minority women often face limited opportunities. "Black females are encouraged to go into certain sports," says Kathryn Reith, director of advocacy at the Women's Sports Foundation. "You don't see women outside of basketball and track" — what Olympic silver medalist and track star Willye White calls the "poverty sports" — "and for women in those sports, there's heavy emphasis on appearance.... [They] spend a lot of time being beautiful. I think there's a heavy cultural influence there."

Gains appear to have been made in at least one area: college participation. A 1976-77 study showed that minorities constituted 16 percent of female undergraduates but only 8 percent of female athletes. Minority women were half as likely as white women to play on a college sports team.[‡‡] But according to one study, participation caught up 10 years later. Figures compiled in 1986-87 by R. Vivian Acosta and Linda Jean Carpenter of Brooklyn College show that black women made up 10.3 percent of intercollegiate athletes, just over their enrollment rate.

In sports leadership, minority women are particularly scarce. Only an estimated 5 percent of college coaches and administrators are minority women. In a piece DeFrantz authored for *Sports Illustrated,* she noted:

■ Of 106 Division I schools that field women's basketball teams, only 11 are coached by black women.

■ None of the executive directors of the 50 governing bodies for U.S. Olympic sports are black women.

■ A black woman has never served on any U.S. Olympic basketball coaching staff.[‡‡†]

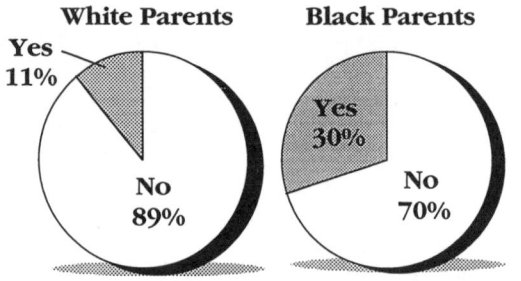

**What Parents Think:
Do You Believe Sports Are More
Important for Boys Than for Girls?**

White Parents

Yes 11%

No 89%

Black Parents

Yes 30%

No 70%

Source: The Wilson Report, *1988*

---

† Margaret Dunkle, "Minority Women and Intercollegiate Athletics," part of an unpublished manuscript, p. 7.

†† "The Wilson Report: Moms, Dads, Daughters and Sports."

‡ "The Women's Sports Foundation Report: Minorities in Sports."

‡‡ Research by Alpha Alexander cited in Margaret Dunkle, "Minority and Low-Income Girls and Young Women in Athletics," *Equal Play,* spring/summer 1985, p. 1.

‡‡† "We've Got to Be Strong," *Sports Illustrated,* Aug. 12, 1991.

Continued from p. 205

commission is investigating why twice as many boys as girls take part in high school athletics and why male coaches outnumber women nearly 4 to 1. In the wake of a class-action lawsuit, the Montana association governing interscholastic sports reminds member schools regularly about gender-equity requirements; in five years the gap between Montana boys and girls in high school sports has shrunken from 9,000 to 2,100. In Washington state, the Office of Equity Education makes on-site inspections, paying special attention to the salaries of male and female coaches and to the caliber of sports facilities used by men's and women's teams.[32]

Brooklyn College Cited

But where enforcement muscle is still wanting is at the top. The Office for Civil Rights sent a signal of hope with its February finding that the Brooklyn College athletic department violated Title IX by giving women fewer athletic opportunities and shortchanging them in several areas, including equipment; the scheduling of game and practice times; coaching assignments and pay; and publicity and recruitment. The college has promised to correct the violations and add women's teams, if necessary, starting this fall. Still to be seen is whether the OCR will monitor corrections more aggressively than it has in the past, in keeping with new priorities set by Assistant Secretary for Civil Rights Michael Williams.

The Brooklyn College case has attracted wide attention because of the extent of the abuses claimed and their documentation. Linda Jean Carpenter and R. Vivian Acosta, the two tenured physical education professors who filed the 1990 complaint against the school, say the whole thing grew out of some worn-out gym shoes. Each year, members of the women's basketball team re-

ceived one new pair, supposed to last the season. While male players received two and three pairs a season, the women reportedly were keeping their soles together with Krazy Glue. Other violations confirmed by the OCR included:

- Female students (56 percent of the student body) outnumber male students at the college but have a much lower participation rate (30 percent) in sports. Although female students have expressed interest in fencing, soccer and gymnastics, these sports are not offered.
- Two men's teams (football and wrestling) have exclusive use of a locker room, a privilege enjoyed by no women's team; the women's access to an alternate, shared locker room is limited.
- Coaches for two of the three women's teams have no experience in those sports; men's team coaches all have several years of experience.[33]

In discussing OCR's finding, Williams described Brooklyn's situation as "fairly unique" and cautioned against using the case as a basis for drawing assumptions about the treatment of women on other campuses.

Many women, however, remain critical of OCR's manner of investigating complaints. "They'll ask the athletic director, 'Do you have groups of women coming to you to organize?' The athletic director will say 'No,' and the inspector will say 'OK,'" charges Mariah Burton Nelson. Asking such questions of athletic directors, says Reith of the Women's Sports Foundation, is like "asking the fox if any hens have been eaten lately."[34]

And in too many cases, researchers say, only the most blatant discrimination tends to be reported. Those student athletes who know their rights under the law — by most estimates, not many — fear retaliation if they complain. In some states, particularly in the South, there is no one to complain to; Title IX compliance officers have not been designat-

ed, in violation of federal law.[35]

There's one area where female college athletes as a rule outpace male jocks: in academics. The women have to do better. Professional opportunities are extremely limited. Only tennis and golf have sizable followings and relatively hefty purses. Professional leagues in most other sports — including basketball, volleyball and softball — have failed, for want of fans, sponsors, coverage or some combination of the three.

Gender-Equity Study

Women's sports advocates are hopeful that the findings of an NCAA gender-equity study, expected out shortly, may focus attention on continuing inequities. Results, sure to get wide press attention, could help persuade the NCAA not to impose 10 percent cuts on women's athletic scholarships. The cuts were approved by the NCAA a year ago but implementation was delayed pending the release of the study.* Women argue the cuts are unfair because they receive fewer scholarships to begin with.

NCAA Executive Director Schultz told the Knight Commission** in January that he had seen the study: It would show the majority of schools in compliance with Title IX, he said, but still point to a serious gender-equity problem.

The study, according to Merrily Dean Baker, associate executive director of the NCAA, compares average spending on men's and women's athletic programs, scholarship num-

---

*The NCAA is going ahead with plans to cut men's scholarships by 10 percent. The cuts will be phased in over two to three years beginning in the 1992-93 academic year.

**The privately funded Knight Foundation Commission on Intercollegiate Athletics was chartered in 1989 to propose a reform agenda for college sports.

bers and amounts and recruiting. In all, 860 colleges were polled; some 700 responded. (No colleges will be named in the study.) "I don't think there's been anything this comprehensive before," she says. "Hopefully, it will catalyze some action over the next couple of years."

How much of that action will involve the NCAA is unclear. "We don't have the ability to mandate what members do in those particular areas," says Schultz. "If the survey showed dramatic inequities, the Presidents' Commission* would probably draw up legislation, though it's difficult for us to legislate that."

Women have expressed wide distrust of the survey, in view of the NCAA's history as a staunch Title IX opponent. "The NCAA and gender equity are sort of an oxymoron," says Vargyas at the National Women's Law Center. Many also complained the study lacked credibility because those polled were almost exclusively male.

"Let me caution you about their data," says Linda Jean Carpenter. "The senior women administrators at almost all of the colleges never saw [the study]. I'm appalled at that. At all the speaking engagements I have, I ask, 'How many of you have seen the study?' Only one or two raise their hands. So you kind of wonder."

At the University of Iowa, Women's Athletic Director Christine Grant shares similar views: "If you ask a male athletic director if his school is in compliance, he'll say, 'Yes, it is.' You ask women, and they say, 'Are you kidding?' No one wants to collect this data. Women do it under threat of their jobs.... This is one of the huge obstacles that's prevented more progress in women's sports. If they open their mouths, they're gone."

The NCAA's Baker acknowledges she's heard complaints from female administrators and coaches that they

*The NCAA's Presidents' Commission is made up of 44 college presidents.

were not consulted. But that, she says, doesn't mean the study is biased. "That's speculation," she says. "The responses had to be signed by the president of each institution. If the president signs off on it, we have to accept it as valid data." She also denies persistent rumors that some senior women administrators had seen and disputed data from their colleges. "We haven't released figures to anyone," she says. ∎

OUTLOOK

Surprises Possible

A slow economy and institutional intransigence make a quick turnaround for women's sports unlikely. But some upcoming events hold the potential for surprise. The 1992 presidential election and growing demands for college athletic reform could quicken the pace. And a recent Supreme Court decision on sexual discrimination could bring a flood of Title IX suits. But more likely, say observers, is a continued slow accumulation of incremental gains.

Recession-year politicking has concentrated on bread-and-butter issues, but a high court decision on abortion this session could move women's rights toward the top of the agenda. Already, the OCR shows signs of coming to life in an election year. Enforcement could become a higher priority in a Democratic administration.

The Supreme Court provided an important new enforcement weapon with its Feb. 26 decision in *Franklin v. Gwinnett County Public Schools*. The court's 9-0 ruling permits students to sue for damages for sexual harassment and other forms of sex discrimination. "This is a major win that opens up Title IX dramatically," said Marcia Greenberger, director of the National Women's Law Center. "Having a real remedy will give an enormous push for equity" in schools and colleges.[36]

The case, heard in December, concerns Christine Franklin, a high school student in suburban Atlanta, Ga., who charged that a teacher harassed her and forced her to have sex with him and that school officials failed to take adequate action on her complaint. Both a lower court and the Court of Appeals ruled she was not entitled to monetary damages. But in another recent Title IX case, the Appeals Court ruled monetary damages were available.

Ellen Vargyas calls the unanimous decision a breakthrough. "Kids and coaches now have something to compensate for the extraordinary disincentives to coming forward [with a complaint], the biggest of which is being scared to death kids will lose their spots, coaches will lose their jobs." The number of Title IX lawsuits will probably jump. Colleges will stop discriminating, says Vargyas, if it becomes expensive for them to discriminate.

Reform Proposals

Another source of possible help — or harm — is a growing movement to call colleges to task for the excesses of runaway athletic programs. Pressure for reform, from without and within the academic world, could reap a dividend for female athletes tired of paying involuntary tribute to football. Or it could make them pay, along with the men, for abuses that are not their fault.

Some say the cap on scholarships passed last year by the NCAA but not yet implemented is an example of

Continued on p. 210

At Issue:

Does athletic competition in the U.S. go too far?

ALFIE KOHN

Author of No Contest: The Case Against Competition
FROM *WOMEN'S SPORTS & FITNESS MAGAZINE*,
JULY/AUGUST 1990

yes

i learned my first game at a birthday party. You remember it: X players scramble for X-minus-one chairs each time the music stops. In every round a child is eliminated until at the end only one is left triumphantly seated while everyone else is standing on the sidelines, excluded from play, unhappy ... losers.

This is how we learn to have a good time in America.

Several years ago I wrote a book called *No Contest*, which, based on the findings of several hundred studies, argued that competition undermines self-esteem, poisons relationships and holds us back from doing our best. I was mostly interested in the win/lose arrangement that defines our workplaces and classrooms, but I found myself nagged by the following question: If competition is so destructive and counterproductive during the week, why do we take for granted that it suddenly becomes benign and even desirable on the weekend?

This is a particularly unsettling line of inquiry for athletes or parents. Most of us, after all, assume that competitive sports teach all sorts of useful lessons and, indeed, that games by definition must produce a winner and a loser. But I've come to believe that recreation at its best does not require people to try to triumph over others....

The underlying theory is simple: All games involve achieving a goal despite the presence of an obstacle, but nowhere is it written that the obstacle has to be someone else. The idea can be for each person on the field to make a specified contribution to the goal ... or for everyone to work with her partners against a time limit.

Note the significance of an "opponent" becoming a "partner." The entire dynamic of the game shifts, and one's attitude toward the other players changes with it....

No matter how many bad feelings erupt during competition, we have a marvelous talent for blaming the individuals rather than focusing on the structure of the game itself — a structure that makes my success depend on your failure. Cheating may just represent the logical conclusion of this arrangement rather than an aberration.

As radical or surprising as it may sound, the problem isn't just that we compete the wrong way or that we push winning on our children too early. The problem is competition itself. What we need to be teaching our daughters and sons is that it's possible to have a good time — a better time — without turning the playing field into a battlefield.

MARIAH BURTON NELSON

Author of Good Sports: Women's Way of Playing
FROM *WOMEN'S SPORTS & FITNESS MAGAZINE*,
JULY/AUGUST 1990

no

competition can damage self-esteem, create anxiety and lead to cheating and hurt feelings. But so can romantic love. No one suggests we do away with love; rather, we must perfect our understanding of what love means.

So too with competition. "To compete" is derived from the Latin *competere,* meaning "to seek together." Women seem to understand this. Maybe it's because we sat on the sidelines for so long, watching. Maybe it's because we were raised to be kind and nurturing. I'm not sure why it is. But I've noticed that it's not women who greet each other with a ritualistic "Who won?"; not women who memorize scores and statistics; not women who pride themselves on "killer instincts." Passionate though we are, women don't take competition that seriously.

We understand that trying to win is not tantamount to trying to belittle; that winning is not wonderful if the process of play is not challenging, fair, or fun; and that losing, though at times disappointing, does not connote failure. For women, if sports are power plays, they're not about power over (power as dominance) but power to (power as competence). Sports are not about domination and defeat but caring and cooperation....

I think it's the responsibility of these women — and the men who remain unblinded by the seductive glow of victory — to share this vision with young players. Children, it seems to me, naturally enjoy comparing their skills: "How far can you throw the ball? Farther than I can? How did you do it? Will you show me?" It's only when adults ascribe undue importance to victory that losing becomes devastating and children get hurt.

Adults must show children that what matters is how one plays the game. It's important that we not just parrot that cliché, but demonstrate out commitment to fair, participatory competition by paying equal attention to skilled and unskilled children; by allowing all children to participate fully in games, regardless of the score; and by caring more about the process than results.

Some of my best friends are the women and men who share a court or pool or field with me. Together we take risks, make mistakes, laugh, push ourselves and revel in the grace and beauty of sports. Who wins? Who cares? ... At its best, competition is not divisive but unifying, not hateful but loving. Like other expressions of love, it should not be avoided simply because it has been misunderstood.

The 10 Most Popular Girls' Sports

Basketball is easily the most popular sport among American high school girls, with 387,802 players, followed by track and field (320,763 participants) and volleyball (300,810).

Sport	Number of participants
Basketball	387,802
Track and field (outdoor)	320,763
Volleyball	300,810
Softball (fast-pitch)	219,464
Tennis	132,607
Soccer	121,722
Cross-country	106,514
Swimming and diving	88,122
Field hockey	48,384
Golf	41,410

Source: National Federation of State High School Associations, 1990-91 Sports Participation Survey

Continued from p. 208
such a penalty. Another NCAA reform also on hold would limit hires in entry-level coaching positions, the most likely place for women and minorities. "They are punishing the daughters for the sons they couldn't control," says Chris Voelz, women's athletic director at the University of Minnesota.[37]

Donna Lopiano at the University of Texas is pushing an alternative reform proposal. In heretical fashion, it proposes that the NCAA:

■ Limit the number of reserve players in football. Setting a uniform squad limit of, say 85 players (down from the 125 to 150 standard for top-ranked Division I-A schools), she says, would not compromise quality or competitiveness.

■ Cap the number of football scholarships. Savings here and from a reduced squad size would be enough

to add three or four new women's sports, she says, without dropping a single men's sports program.

■ Increase the number of scholarships in large-squad women's sports such as swimming, track and field and softball. This, Lopiano argues, would be less expensive than adding many new women's sports, each with their own coaches.

■ Establish several new NCAA championships in large-squad women's sports like water polo and crew, and set high scholarship limits for those sports.[38]

NCAA Executive Director Schultz acknowledges the proposal could get more serious consideration if the NCAA's forthcoming gender-equity study shows wide inequities. What chance would he give it? He chuckles. "Whether the membership would pass that kind of legislation is another thing." Further, he warns such a

proposal could backfire. "If you reduce spending by $500,000, that doesn't automatically mean that money would go to the women's program.... You have to be careful you don't do something that will end up hurting women."

While gender equity is not the reform movement's central issue, there have been some noises in that direction. On Capitol Hill, one of the loudest voices for change belongs to Rep. Tom McMillen, D-Md., a former University of Maryland and National Basketball Association (NBA) player, who introduced a bill last fall called "The Collegiate Athletic Reform Act." Complying with Title IX is among the bill's specific goals. Schools that don't adhere to policies stipulated would, under the bill, incur a tax penalty.[39]

How much the reform movement will be able to accomplish is still under question. Within the NCAA, the Presidents' Commission has been talking reform since the mid-1980s without having instituted major changes. Donna Lopiano says college presidents are "being held hostage by winning coaches, alumni and members of university governing boards.... The average tenure of Division I football and basketball coaches is higher than the tenure of their college presidents."[40]

Tight Economy Could Have Impact

To the extent that the reform movement is fueled by a need to cut costs, a tight economy could spur action. "As financial pressures increase, colleges are going to be put to the test of re-evaluating what the significance really is of football and basketball, and whether they're interested in providing them as aspects of education," says Arthur Bryant, executive director of the Trial Lawyers for Public Justice. But the money crunch will continue to hurt women, too.

"I think the financial pressures on colleges are going to increase, particularly with the NCAA putting pressure on universities to cut costs," says Bryant. "That's often going to mean trying to cut costs by short-changing women, even more than they currently are. Ultimately, what will be necessary to change is either the OCR jumping in and saying, 'You can't do this,' or people whose rights are being violated protesting and filing suit to stop it."

Vargyas takes a similar view: "Until and unless we get some leadership on this issue, advocates for women's equity in sports are going to continue to have to fight rear-guard actions and keep slugging away. The leadership has to come either from the federal government, from OCR and the Department of Education, or from the university community, which has not been demonstrated. Or we could look for leadership from the NCAA, which I'm not exactly holding my breath for.... I don't see anything emerging. In the absence of that, we're looking at continued incremental improvements over the long haul."

Says Vargyas, the mother of an 8-year-old girl, "It's a long fight. I'm absolutely convinced we will win this. I just hope we win it in time for my daughter." ∎

_____

Susan L. Morse is a free-lance writer in the Washington, D.C., area who edited a recent major study on gender equity in education.

Notes

1 Quoted in Natalie Angier, "2 Experts Say Women Who Run May Overtake Men," *The New York Times,* Jan. 7, 1992, p. C3.

2 Quoted in Tim Friend and Anita Manning, "Women Gain Ground on Men in Sport," *USA Today,* Jan. 2, 1992, p. 1.

3 Angier, *op. cit.*

4 Kenny Moore, "Missing the Mark," *Sports Illustrated,* Jan. 20, 1992, p. 9.

5 "Out of the Tunnel Into History," *Time,* Aug. 20, 1984, p. 73.

6 See Mariah Burton Nelson, Are We Winning Yet? (1991), p. 28; "Working-Out Girls," *Mademoiselle,* November 1990, p. 118; and Elizabeth Frank, "Women Are Giving Triathlons a Run," *The New York Times,* July 23, 1990, p. C10.

7 Wilson Sporting Goods Co., in cooperation with the Women's Sports Foundation, "The Wilson Report: Moms, Dads, Daughters and Sports," June 7, 1988.

8 Donna Lopiano, "Attracting Women to the Coaching Profession: Recruiting, Education and Retention," speech to U.S. Olympic Committee Conference on Certification of Coaches, Colorado Springs, Colo., Sept. 27, 1991, p. 3.

9 Donna Lopiano, "Subtle Gender Discrimination: The New Immorality in Sport," paper submitted March 1991 to Institute for International Sport, p. 1.

10 Figures from the U.S. Olympic Committee for the 1992 games.

11 Lopiano, "Subtle Gender Discrimination," *op. cit.,* p. 1.

12 Quoted in Alison Muscatine, "Women's Sports Making Gains but Still Struggling for Equality," *The Washington Post,* April 1, 1991, p. C8.

13 Quoted in Jay P. Goldman, "Leveling the Playing Field for Female Athletes," *The School Administrator,* December 1991, p. 21.

14 Quoted in Mariah Burton Nelson, "Field of Nightmares," *Women's SportsPages,* September/October 1991, p. 4.

15 Quoted in Doug Bedell, "Title IX Case Could Set Precedent," third in series titled "Title IX: Equality at a Standstill," *Dallas Morning News,* Sept. 3, 1991, p. 10B.

16 U.S. Department of Education, Office for Civil Rights, Planning Analysis and Systems Services Division.

17 Donna Lopiano, "Critical Problems Involved in Achieving Title IX Compliance," unpublished manuscript, Oct. 21, 1991, p. 1.

18 Adrianne Blue, *Grace Under Pressure: The Emergence of Women in Sport* (1987), p. 145.

19 Christopher Anderson, "Tests on Athletes Can't Always Find Line Between Males and Females," *The Washington Post,* Jan. 6, 1992, p. A3.

20 Quoted in Blue, *op. cit.,* p. 144.

21 Quoted in *Are We Winning Yet?, op. cit.,* p. 142.

22 Douglas Lederman, "Penn State Coach's Comments About Lesbian Athletes May Be Used to Test University's New Policy on Bias," *The Chronicle of Higher Education,* June 5, 1991, p. A27.

23 Quoted in Charles Farrell, "Big Jump in Money and Prestige Spurs Cheating in Women's Basketball, Coaches and Players Say," *The Chronicle of Higher Education,* Jan. 29, 1986, p. 25.

24 Quoted in Janice Kaplan, *Women and Sports* (1979), p. 166-167.

25 Richard R. Lanese et al., "Injury and Disability in Matched Men's and Women's Intercollegiate Sports," *American Journal of Public Health,* December 1990, p. 1459.

26 1991 informational brochure, National Association for Girls & Women in Sport, p. 4.

27 Quoted in "Health Chief Asks Athletes to Shun Tobacco Company 'Blood Money,'" *The New York Times,* Feb. 24, 1990, p. 12.

28 Stephanie L. Twin, *Out of the Bleachers: Writings on Women and Sport* (1979), pp. xxii-xxiii, xxxii.

29 B. Barnes and N. Scannell, "No Sporting Chance: The girls in the locker room," *The Washington Post,* May 12, 1974, p. A14.

30 Quoted in TLPJ Newsletter, published by Trial Lawyers for Public Justice, December 1987, p. 5.

31 "Athletics Notes," *The Chronicle of Higher Education,* Sept. 26, 1990, p. A48.

32 Goldman, *op. cit.,* p. 25.

33 Letter of Finding in Brooklyn College case, U.S. Department of Education, Feb. 14, 1992.

34 Quoted in Laura Mansnerus, "Women Take to the Field," *The New York Times,* Jan. 5, 1992, section 4A, p. 40.

35 Study in progress by Katherine Hanson, associate director, Center for Equity and Cultural Diversity, Education Development Center, Newton, Mass.

36 Quoted in *The New York Times,* Feb. 27, 1992, p. A1.

37 Quoted in Jeannie Roberts, "The Road to Reform?" *Women's SportsPages,* February 1991, p. 6.

38 Donna Lopiano, "Critical Problems," *op. cit.,* p. 3.

39 Ken Denlinger, "McMillen Urges Congress to Attack NCAA's Evils at Root: Money," *The Washington Post,* Oct. 17, 1991, p. B3.

40 Statement before the House Subcommittee on Postsecondary Education, Committee on Education and Labor, May 18, 1969, p. 9.

Bibliography

Selected Sources Used

Books

Blue, Adrianne, *Grace Under Pressure: The Emergence of Women in Sport*, Sidgwick & Jackson, 1987.

A British sportswriter measures female athletes' gains worldwide against the inequalities they still face. Chapters cover sex testing, drug abuse, eating disorders and homophobia, among other subjects.

Guttman, Allan, *Women's Sports: A History*, Columbia University Press, 1991.

An Amherst College teacher and author of several books on sports traces the social history of women's sports from the ancient Greeks to the present. He touches briefly on controversies regarding sexuality and women's performance relative to men's.

Nelson, Mariah Burton, *Are We Winning Yet? How Women Are Changing Sports and Sports Are Changing Women*, Random House, 1991.

Nelson, a former college and pro basketball player and a widely published sportswriter and lecturer, offers the case histories and views of prominent female athletes in support of her positions on equity, women's performance vis-à-vis men's, homophobia and the "partnership" model of women's sports.

Twin, Stephanie L., *Out of the Bleachers: Writings on Women and Sport*, The Feminist Press, 1979.

This anthology includes historic arguments for and against women's participation in athletics as well as pieces by contemporary athletes and writers about social pressures, especially the pressure to conform to a gender stereotype.

Articles

Goldman, Jay, "Leveling the Playing Field for Female Athletes," *The School Administrator*, December 1991, p. 20.

The managing editor of *The School Administrator* assesses the gains and failures of the past 20 years in high school sports.

Goodman, Matthew, "Where the Boys Are," *Washington Monthly*, April 1989, p. 18.

Goodman describes the purge of women administrators from college sports and the barriers blocking the further advance of the few women who remain.

Jenkins, Sally, "Who Let Them In?" *Sports Illustrated*, June 17, 1991, p. 78.

Jenkins profiles the handful of leading female sportscasters and describes the obstacles still facing them and their lower-profile female colleagues.

Rounds, Kate, "Why Men Fear Women's Teams," *Ms.*, January/February 1991, p. 43.

A writer and sports enthusiast discusses the part homophobia has played in the failures of several women's pro sports teams.

Swift, E.M., "Women of Mettle," *Sports Illustrated*, March 2, 1992, pp. 38-39.

American women ran away with the gold this year at the Winter Olympics in Albertville, France, winning all five of the American team's first-place medals and nine of 11 U.S. medals overall.

Reports and Studies

Lopiano, Donna, *Subtle Gender Discrimination: The New Immorality in Sport*, paper submitted March 1991 to the Institute for International Sport in conjunction with National Sportsmanship Day Program on April 24, 1991.

Lopiano describes how merged athletic budgets can hide inequities between men's and women's athletic programs and gives examples. She also discusses the bias toward "revenue" sports and what she calls the "insufficient-interest loophole," used to deny women access to team sports. Excerpts from her paper were published in *USA Today* on April 23, 1991.

***The Wilson Report: Moms, Dads, Daughters and Sports*, Wilson Sporting Goods Co. in cooperation with the Women's Sports Foundation, June 7, 1988.**

A study of 1,000 parents and 500 of their daughters focuses on attitudes toward girls' and boys' participation in sports.

Women's Sports Foundation, *The Women's Sports Foundation Report: Minorities in Sports*, 1989.

A study funded by Miller Lite beer compares the effects of athletic participation on black, white and Hispanic high school students.

The Next Step

Additional Articles from Current Periodicals from EBSCO Publishing's Database

Books & reading

Levin, S., "Women's ways of winning," *Women's Sports & Fitness*, May/June 1991, p. 17.

Reviews the book "Are We Winning Yet?" by Mariah Burton Nelson. Examines women's involvement and opportunities in sports.

Careers

Jenkins, S., "Who let them in," *Sports Illustrated*, June 17, 1991, p. 78.

Discusses the increasing number of women sportscasters on television and comments on the progress they have made as well as the obstacles they still face. Problem of smaller salaries and less airtime then their male counterparts; Gayle Gardner of NBC; Robin Roberts and other women at ESPN; Lesley Visser and Mary Carillo; groundbreaking reporting of Phyllis George; difficulties of their jobs; more.

Munnings, F., "Sidelined," *Women's Sports & Fitness*, September 1990, p. 40.

Explores why the percentage of women in coaching is half what it was 20 years ago. Includes a conversation with three coaches that gives insight into the possibilities and problems facing women coaches today. Ann Koger, coach of tennis and volleyball at Haverford College; Debbie Meyer-Reyes, swim coach at California State University at Sacramento; Tara VanDerveer, women's basketball coach at Stanford University. INSETS: Players up, coaches down; getting started.

Reith, K., "Playing the career field," *Women's Sports & Fitness*, September 1991, p. 64.

Discusses professional opportunities for women athletes who want to turn their sports skills into a job. Sports careers for women; competition; coaching; master's degree programs in sports administration. INSET: Help yourself (resources for women).

Colleges & universities

Becker, D., "Making the cut," *Women's Sports & Fitness*, May/June 1991, p. 70.

Looks at recent budget cuts considered at the National Collegiate Athletic Association (NCAA) convention in January, which reduced women's scholarships and the number of coaching slots for women.

Levin, S., "Intercollegiate athletics," *Women's Sports & Fitness*, September 1991, p. 60.

Presents a list of colleges and universities that have dominated championships in women's sports. Offers a list of milestones in women's college sports. INSETS: Name that team (short list of women's sports teams); tractor-pull, tiddlywinks and other varsity sports (list of schools that offer unusual sports); 19 good reasons to move north of the border (women's sports at Canadian universities).

Palmason, D. and M. McCloy, "Playing to learn," *Women's Sports & Fitness*, September 1991, p. 52.

Introduces a special section on the challenges and possibilities that college sports presents for women.

Debates & issues

"Are men taking over women's sports?" *Glamour*, September 1991, p. 119.

Editorial. Argues that since more money has flowed to women's sports, men have increasingly taken over women's coaching jobs. Calls for women to take action to help increase the number of women coaches.

Anderson, C., "Olympic row over sex testing," *Nature*, Oct. 31, 1991, p. 784.

Reveals that Xavier Estivill of the Cancer Research Institute at the Turan Reinals Hospital in Barcelona, Spain, has turned down a request by the International Olympic Committee to conduct a trial sex test on women athletes who will participate in the 1992 Olympic Games. The test based on the polymerase chain reaction (PCR) analysis may lead to increased misdiagnosis of women athletes as men.

Carlson, A. and P. Freed, "When is a woman not a woman?" *Women's Sports & Fitness*, March 1991, p. 24.

Describes the sex testing policy adopted in 1968 by the International Olympic Committee which requires all women athletes to be tested, and its impact on Maria Jose Martinez Patino of Spain, who failed the test. Background and details; Patino's protest of the ruling; the buccal smear; reversal of the sex test ruling.

Cohen, S., "Smoke screen," *Women's Sports & Fitness*, May/June 1991, p. 54.

Examines the growing controversy over the link between cigarettes and tennis. Pressure to withdraw from sponsorship of cigarette firms; Virginia Slims' sponsorship;

Philip Morris' contribution to women's tennis. INSET: Under fire (cigarette sponsorship).

DeFrantz, A., "We've got to be strong," Sports Illustrated, Aug. 12, 1991, p. 77.

Opinion. Considers how the obstacles facing black women in sports have scarcely diminished with time. Stresses the importance of acknowledging that you are the target of racism or sexism and calling people on it. Offers personal accounts of racism and sexism in the United States.

Greising, D., "Whap! Ace. Point. You call this tennis?" Business Week, Sept. 9, 1991, p. 71.

Questions whether the new, high-tech tennis rackets being produced today are hurting the game more than helping it. Widebody design makes the racket board-stiff and gives players uncommon power; used by virtually all women players; power vs. finesse; wide rackets dominate sales since 1987; what the racket consists of; how the racket makes matches shorter; different gimmicks for each manufacturer; high-tech infiltrating other sports as well.

Heldman, G.M., "It's 'Slims' or none," World Tennis, August 1990, p. 88.

Opinion. Argues that opponents of Virginia Slims-sponsored women's tennis are misguided and should spend their energy trying to get sponsors to pay women as much as men and give women as many tournaments as men.

Ingram, K., "Covering the bases," Women's Sports & Fitness, September 1991, p. 62.

Presents a roundtable discussion with four women who are college athletes in different sports, as well as divisions. Challenges they face, depending on the sport they play and the division they are in; issues facing female athletes.

Kort, M., "Carrying a torch," Women's Sports & Fitness, July/August 1991, p. 68.

Discusses the difficulty women's sports have had in obtaining Olympic status. Requirements set by the International Olympic Committee for an event to make the Olympic program; poor representation of women on the national governing bodies of their sports.

Noden, M. and R. Demak, "The worst of times," Sports Illustrated, Oct. 7, 1991, following p. 2.

Notes that the 1991 track season was the second straight in which no women's world record was set. Thoughts as to the causes of the failure to break records; focus on reduced drug use; comparison with performance in men's track.

Rounds, K., "Why men fear women's teams," Ms., January/February 1991, p. 43.

Examines the reasons why women's team sports don't get corporate sponsors, television coverage, fan support, etc. Looks at women's softball, basketball, volleyball, and baseball. Looks and image; fear of lesbians; outlook for women of color; promoter Bill Byrne's Women's Pro Basketball League Inc. (WPBL); tennis star Billie Jean King's Team Tennis; businesswomen's lack of support; World War II-vintage All-American Girl's Professional Baseball League (AAGPBL).

Ruffini, G., "The Super Bowl's real score," Ms., November/December 1991, p. 93.

Examines evidence supporting the possible link between sports spectating and the battering of women. Battering on Super Bowl Sunday; why men resort to battering after watching sports on television; criticism of current evidence; comments by Anne Menard, director of the Connecticut Coalition Against Domestic Violence, and other experts.

White, D. and J. Morgan, "In her own image," Skiing, December 1991, p. 172.

Presents an exclusive survey by Skiing magazine which asks women skiers what they have on their mind as they remake the face of this male-oriented sport. Alpine feminism; Rick Vetromile's, education vice president for PSIA-Rocky Mountain, regional symposium on women and skiing this January at Telluride; the growth of women-only instructional programs; more. INSET: And the survey says.... (results of the Skiing survey).

Yates, B., "Real men don't hold hands," Car & Driver, September 1991, p. 16.

Opinion. Argues that race-car drivers shouldn't hold hands at the track with their wives or girlfriends because it's against the sport's image. Contends that very few women can compete on the track with men, and women should not be on the track or in the pits.

Economic aspects

Walzer, E., "Trimming the field," Women's Sports & Fitness, September 1991, p. 78.

Discusses the reasons why field hockey is being cut from college budgets. Cutbacks in athletic programs; replacement by soccer at Loyola College; collegiate women's sports programs; concerns.

Law & legislation

Monaghan, P., "NAIA delegates vote against increasing athletes' eligibility to 5 years," The Chronicle of Higher Education, Oct. 16, 1991, p. A49.

Recaps the recent annual convention of the National Association of Intercollegiate Athletics, which defeated a proposal to allow students to compete in sports programs for five years instead of the current four and voted down several proposals aimed at hastening the growth of women's sports programs. Proposals dealing with sex equity; comments from delegates.

Mass-media coverage

Palmason, D., "Wide world of women's sports," *Women's Sports & Fitness,* September 1991, p. 15.

Reports on the success of "Sports Journal," the first televised sports show to focus on women's college athletics. Description of the series; how to order a videotape of the series.

Physical aspects

Lanese, R.R., R.H. Strauss, et al., "Injury and disability in matched men's and women's intercollegiate sports," *American Journal of Public Health,* December 1990, p. 1459.

Studies eight matched men's and women's intercollegiate varsity teams prospectively for one academic year to determine the incidence of athletic injury and resulting disability. Sports in which both men and women participated in a comparable manner included: basketball, fencing, gymnastics, swimming, tennis, indoor track, outdoor track, and volleyball. Methods and results.

Neporent, L., "In it for the long run," *Women's Sports & Fitness,* October 1991, p. 10.

Looks at the possibility that women may be more suited than men for long-distance running, or ultrarunning. Women's attributes that may contribute to their success in superendurance events.

Williams, K., "Deadly dieting," *Women's Sports & Fitness,* December 1991, p. 22.

Examines the prevalence of eating disorders among female athletes. The issue of body weight; how many of the disorders are developed; how stress of competition affects the athlete; the 'high' experienced from a release of both adrenaline and beta-endorphins; spotting eating disorders; lists several eating disorder organizations.

Profiles

Kaufmann, E. and B. Wald, "Ascent of woman," *Women's Sports & Fitness,* July/August 1991, p. 32.

Profiles Lynn Hill, 30, the world's top female rock climber. Hill has a goal of being the first woman to climb the 5.14b-rated "Maginot Ligne" in southern France. Personal background; career highlights; product endorsements; views on training and mental attitude.

Kort, M., "Making waves," *Women's Sports & Fitness,* April 1991, p. 56.

Profiles Anita DeFrantz, 38, a lifetime member of the International Olympic Committee, and the most powerful woman in amateur sports in the U.S. DeFrantz's career in sports; personal background; views on women's equity in sports. INSET: Women's sports in the media.

McCloy, M., "Heli heaven," *Women's Sports & Fitness,* December 1991, p. 24.

Reports on the excitement of heli-skiing, a sport in which less than 5 percent of the participants are women. What heli-skiing is; how to take part.

Nelson, M.B., "Julie Croteau," *Women's Sports & Fitness,* September 1991, p. 54.

Profiles Julie Croteau, a student at St. Mary's College in Maryland, who is the first woman to play college baseball. Account of Croteau's efforts to break into an all-male sport. INSET: Editor's note (Croteau's decision to quit playing baseball).

Stratte-McClure, J., "Up on her high horse," *People,* Oct. 28, 1991, p. 103.

Focuses on Marie Sara Bourseiller of France who is a horseback bullfighter and the only woman to join these ranks. The key to being so successful; when she decided to go into the sport; her training; how she feels about the controversial sport.

Sex discrimination

Lederman, D., "Advocates for women's sports await Supreme Court ruling on sex-discrimination case," *The Chronicle of Higher Education,* Oct. 23, 1991, p. A38.

Outlines the case *Franklin v. Gwinnett County Public Schools,* which is considered by advocates of women's sports as a potent new weapon in the fight for sex equity in college athletic programs. Details of the lawsuit, discrimination under Title IX of the Education Amendments of 1972; question if victims of Title IX discrimination should be eligible for damages beyond compensatory rewards; using punitive damages to prod colleges toward equity.

MacLean, P.A., "Tee'd off," *Women's Sports & Fitness,* April 1991, p. 40.

Examines how private golf clubs discriminate against women with unequal tee times, restricted access to club rooms and restricted voting rights. All-male golf clubs; subtle discrimination; economic pressures to change club policy; sex (gender) discrimination; anti-discrimination policies. INSETS: Tee for two (two-tee system for both men and women), by J. Nelson; what you can do (against discrimination).

Back Issues

Great Research on Current Issues Starts Right Here... Recent topics covered by The CQ Researcher are listed below. Issues dated before May 10, 1991, were published under the name of Editorial Research Reports.

AUGUST 1990
Democracy in the Philippines
Initiatives: True Democracy?
Hard Times at Newspapers
Teens Balance School & Jobs

SEPTEMBER 1990
Dangers of Alcohol
Western Alliance After the Cold War
Tobacco Industry
Right to Die

OCTOBER 1990
Organ Transplants
Energy Policy Options
Search for Arab Unity
Child Support

NOVEMBER 1990
Lotteries and Gambling
Post-Cold War Choices
Setting Limits on Medical Care
Multicultural Education

DECEMBER 1990
Cable TV Regulation
Americans' Search for Their Roots
Is Insurance System a Failure?
Why Schools Still Have Tracking

Back issues are available for $4.00 (subscribers) or $7.00 (non-subscribers). Quantity discounts apply to orders over ten. To order, call Congressional Quarterly 1-800-432-2250.

JANUARY 1991
Growing Influence of Boycotts
Should the U.S. Reinstate the Draft?
America's Archaeological Past
Peace Corps' Challenges in '90s

FEBRUARY 1991
Regional Impact of Recession
Puerto Rico's Status
Redistricting: Mapping Power
Nuclear Power

MARCH 1991
Acid Rain
Cost of the Gulf War
Reassessing Gun Laws
Future for Man in Space

APRIL 1991
Social Security
Canadian Crisis Over Quebec
California Drought
Electromagnetic Radiation

MAY 1991
School Choice
Racial Quotas
Animal Rights
U.S. and Japan

JUNE 1991
Children and Divorce
Teenage Suicide
Endangered Species
Europe 1992

JULY 1991
Teenagers and Abortion
Soviet Republics Rebel
Mexico's Emergence
Athletes and Drugs

AUGUST 1991
Sexual Harassment
Fetal Tissue Research
Oil Imports
The Palestinians

SEPTEMBER 1991
Police Brutality
Advertising Under Attack
Saving the Forests
Foster Care Crisis

OCTOBER 1991
Pay-Per-View TV
Youth Gangs
Gene Therapy
World Hunger

NOVEMBER 1991
Fast-Food Shake-Up
The Greening of Eastern Europe
Business' Role in Education
Cuba In Crisis

DECEMBER 1991
Retiree Health Benefits
Asian Americans
The Obscenity Debate
The Disabilities Act

JANUARY 1992
Term Limits
Oil Spills
Hunting Controversy
Alternative Medicine

FEBRUARY 1992
Threatened Coastlines
New Era in Asia
Assisted Suicide
Jobs in the '90s

Future Topics

▶ *Teenage Drinking*

▶ *Solid Waste Crisis*

▶ *The Mafia*

THE CQ Researcher

PUBLISHED BY CONGRESSIONAL QUARTERLY INC., IN CONJUNCTION WITH EBSCO PUBLISHING

Underage Drinking

Is the government using the right tactics in its crackdown?

ILLEGAL ALCOHOL USE IS EASING OFF AT SCHOOLS and colleges, but drips of progress toward temperance may not be enough. Concerned federal officials blame underage drinking for disturbing levels of campus violence and emotional problems, as well as a large proportion of traffic deaths. Just two months ago, the White House Office of National Drug Control Policy addressed alcohol for the first time in its strategy to combat illegal drugs. The issue is also being confronted by the alcoholic beverage industry, which is spending unprecedented sums on advertising to remind Americans that they must be 21 to drink. Though most everyone agrees on a need for multiple solutions — including beefed-up law enforcement, education campaigns and improved family communication — there is little consensus on how tough is too tough.

 March 13, 1992 • Volume 2, No. 10 • 217-240

Formerly Editorial Research Reports

COVER ART: BARBARA SASSA-DANIELS

March 13, 1992
Volume 2, No. 10

EDITOR
Sandra Stencel

MANAGING EDITOR
Thomas J. Colin

ASSOCIATE EDITOR
Richard L. Worsnop

STAFF WRITERS
Charles S. Clark
Mary H. Cooper
Rodman D. Griffin

PRODUCTION EDITOR
Laurie De Maris

EDITORIAL ASSISTANT
Thomas H. Moore

GRAPHICS
Jack Auldridge

PUBLISHED BY
Congressional Quarterly Inc.

CHAIRMAN
Andrew Barnes

VICE CHAIRMAN
Andrew P. Corty

EDITOR AND PUBLISHER
Neil Skene

EXECUTIVE EDITOR
Robert W. Merry

PUBLICATIONS MARKETING/SALES
Robert Smith

EDITOR, EBSCO PUBLISHING
Melissa Kummerer

The CQ Researcher (ISSN 1056-2036). Formerly Editorial Research Reports. Published weekly (48 times per year, not printed the first Friday of any month with five Fridays) by Congressional Quarterly Inc., 1414 22nd St., N.W., Washington, D.C. 20037. Rates are furnished upon request. Second-class postage paid at Washington, D.C. POSTMASTER: Send address changes to The CQ Researcher, 1414 22nd St., N.W., Washington, D.C. 20037.

Underage Drinking

BY CHARLES S. CLARK

THE ISSUES

The extracurricular frolic known as spring break has for years been associated with carefree volleyball and chug-a-lug contests, played out on party-packed beaches emblazoned with banners promoting brands of beer.

Nowadays, though, the college-crowd revelry in fabled spots like Florida's Daytona Beach has turned a bit tame. The "Party 'til you puke" T-shirts have been upstaged by posters cautioning students to "Party Smart" and to remember that "Good beer is aged. You should be, too." Wristbands and handstamps certifying that the bearer is of legal age* are required at Daytona's hotels and nightclubs. Thousands of arriving students are handed copies of the city's rules for conduct, and fraternity members are even signing "Safe Spring Break" pledges.

Daytona police report a marked drop in arrests and deaths among inebriated youths who fall from condo or hotel balconies.** "In the past three years, the beer companies' presence has been minimal and almost apologetic," says nightclub owner Walter Curtis, who heads the city's "responsible vendor" campaign against alcohol abuse. "You're lucky if you can get a beer T-shirt."

Spring break's new look comes at a time when the country's ongoing efforts against youthful alcohol abuse have produced notable signs of progress. Traffic deaths from drunken driving have fallen steadily, with

those involving teenagers 16 to 19 declining by 39.1 percent from 1982 to 1990, according to the National Highway Traffic Safety Administration (NHTSA). Alcohol consumption has also dropped in the past 10 years, among high school students by 18 percent and among college students by 7 percent, according to the latest survey conducted for the federal government by the University of Michigan's Institute of Social Research. *(See graph, p. 229.)*

The new temperance, however, has not produced complacency among alcohol-abuse authorities. Quite the contrary. For the past year, Surgeon General Antonia Novello has been unveiling a series of reports dramatizing the extent to which underage Americans drink. She has proposed ways to toughen enforcement of the drinking-age laws and called for curbs on beer, wine and liquor advertising that glamorizes drinking in the eyes of young people.

Sharing Novello's concern, the Office of Substance Abuse Prevention (OSAP) at the Department of Health and Human Services (HHS) has launched a "Put on the Brakes" campaign to publicize the harm that alcohol inflicts on youth. Since 1989 the Education Department has been helping colleges and universities set up anti-alcohol-abuse programs so that they may continue to qualify for federal funds. And just two months ago, the White House Office of National Drug Control Policy, addressing alcohol for the first time in its strategy to combat illegal drugs, announced a campaign against underage drinking.

To these agencies and allied private groups, the proverbial glass is still half-empty, despite the recent signs of progress. They note that traffic fatalities remain the No. 1 killer of youths ages 16 to 24, with alcohol involved in half the 3,361 teen highway fatalities in 1990. More than half the nation's junior and senior high school students — 10.6 million youngsters — have consumed alcohol in the past year, HHS estimates. According to the University of Michigan survey, 30 percent of high school students and 43 percent of college students have indulged in "binge drinking," consuming five to six drinks at a sitting.

"What seems different today," says OSAP spokesman Lewis D. Eigen, "is that we're getting reports from all over that kids are getting drunk not just inadvertently at a party, but as a result of intentionally downing the greater and greater amounts of alcohol that are needed to get that effect."

The damage visited upon young drinkers by alcohol abuse has been voluminously documented.[1] Alcohol is involved in 70 percent of the cases of campus violence, 64 to 68 percent of the campus property damage and 40 percent of the academic failures, according to The College Alcohol Survey, a 1991 study of 400 colleges.[2]

---

*The legal drinking age in all 50 states and the District of Columbia is 21.

**In 1989, Daytona police reported eight falls from balconies, resulting in three serious injuries and one death. In 1991, no falls were reported.

Why Do Young People Start Drinking?

Common wisdom often blames advertising for starting teenagers on alcoholic beverages. But only 8 percent of the youths responding to a recent poll named advertising as the main cause of young people starting to drink. By a wide margin, peer pressure and parents were seen as the most influential factors.

Which one or two of the things on this list do you think have the most to do with causing young people to start drinking alcoholic beverages such as beer, liquor and wine?

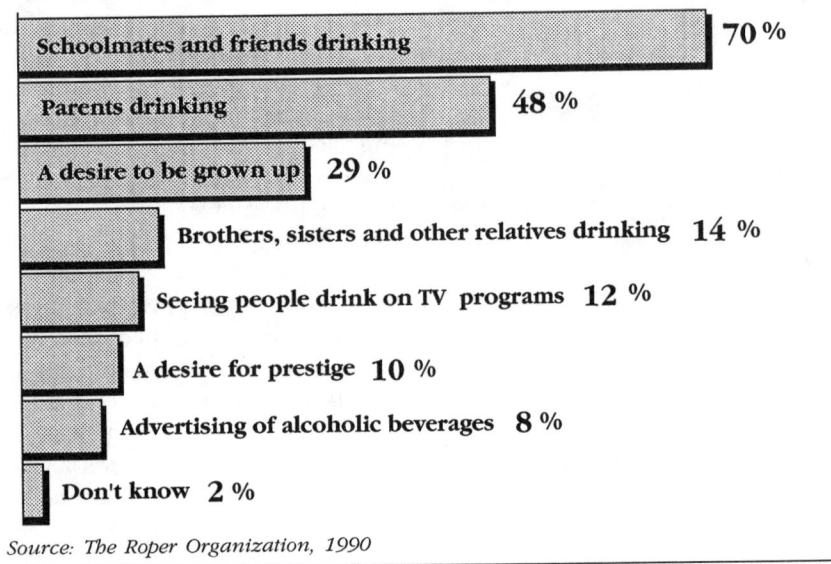

Schoolmates and friends drinking **70 %**

Parents drinking **48 %**

A desire to be grown up **29 %**

Brothers, sisters and other relatives drinking **14 %**

Seeing people drink on TV programs **12 %**

A desire for prestige **10 %**

Advertising of alcoholic beverages **8 %**

Don't know **2 %**

Source: The Roper Organization, 1990

Alcohol is also a factor in as many as 58 percent of the sexual assaults on college campuses, according to a 1990 survey conducted by the Campus Violence Prevention Center in Towson, Md. Alcohol is involved in more than half of all youth suicides and in 90 percent of campus hazing deaths, according to the OSAP. *(See box, p. 222.)*

No area of a young person's life, it seems, is immune from the substance that has long been society's lubricant. That's why there's no simple bumper-sticker slogan that offers a solution to underage drinking. What on the surface might seem a straightforward problem of law enforcement in reality is a puzzle surrounded by issues that adult society has yet to come to grips with. No one doubts, for example, that the failed experiment of Prohibition (1920-33) looms over today's thinking on youth and alcohol.

Indeed, many on the front lines of the alcohol-abuse problem agree with Edward H. Hammond, president of Fort Hays State University in Kansas, who calls the state laws setting the drinking age at 21 "a dismal social failure."[3] Similarly, parents and public officials who remember their own youthful initiations into alcohol can be reluctant to clamp down harshly on a youth crime that is clearly mainstream behavior.

"The 'Just say no' approach, to most people on campus, is not terribly realistic," says Sheldon E. Steinbach, general counsel of the American Council on Education, who advises college administrators on alcohol policies. "Kids arrive on campus with a drinking habit and as such present a problem that needs to be dealt with in an intelligent manner,

not [through a policy regulation] designed to make people feel good but one that accomplishes something."

The spate of youth alcohol policies being tested across the country has produced a split along lines similar to the debate over adult alcohol abuse. Some campuses are attempting a strict "no-use" policy, one advocated by many health professionals to emphasize up front that alcohol is a drug that is potentially lethal. Other campuses are trying a "responsible-use" policy, one that concedes a certain level of underage alcohol use, but which expresses its concern in efforts such as the "Think Before You Drink" campaign promoted by the alcohol industry.

Add to this brew the adolescent's struggle with authority during that painful phase between childhood and adulthood, and you have in underage drinking a vast, perhaps permanent, public problem. "College students like to be treated as adults," says Paul McDonald, a junior at Princeton University. "And when they are treated as children, it's bound to create a backlash."[4]

As the current campaign against underage drinking unfolds, here are some of the issues that will affect the outcome:

Is the government overreacting in its campaign against underage drinking?

At the end of 1991, having spent the year touring the country warning that "We are losing the war on underage drinking," Surgeon General Novello met with beer, wine and liquor executives. The parley produced a joint statement calling for cooperation between the industry and the government and intensified efforts to reduce underage drinking.

Outside such face-to-face meetings, however, the spirit is not always so cooperative. "With the numbers going down [for drunken driving and teen consumption]," says Jeff Becker, a spokesman for the Beer Institute, the beer industry's Washington lobby, "there should be some recognition for programs that are working. The surgeon general's reports lack any comment like 'Hey, young people, you've done a better job than the rest of country.'"

Novello came in for particularly scathing criticism from Ruth Engs, a professor of applied health at Indiana University whose research is cited frequently by the alcoholic beverage industry. "I think the surgeon general is getting a bit hysterical," she said. "Heavy drinking among students has been a tradition for 1,000 years. It's always been part of student life." [5] (See "At Issue," p. 233.)

Many in the industry question the timing of the government's campaign, viewing it as a cynical attempt to capitalize on a pressing social issue and thus magnify the problem so that federal agencies can maintain large budgets. "The 'right thing' today is doing things for young people," says Becker. "As society gets older, it gets more protective of youth, and baby-boomer parents are now saying, 'You won't be able to do the same crazy things we did.'"

Others in the industry blast the surgeon general and HHS officials for working with private "neo-prohibitionist" groups. Rick Guldan, director of public affairs for the National Beer Wholesalers Association, says that the agency maintains "a damn-near incestuous relationship with [private] anti-alcohol people funded with our tax dollars."

A spokeswoman for Novello says the surgeon general was mindful of recent progress in combating underage drinking but felt that progress on alcohol wasn't as great as progress on abuse of illicit drugs. "We were worried that the nation would congratulate itself and go home, instead of recognizing that this is pervasive and hasn't gone away," the spokeswoman said. She added that "HHS

has a goal of reducing America's alcohol intake by 20 percent by the year 2000, which is not a goal of the alcoholic beverage industry."

Whatever the reasons for its timing, the campaign against underage drinking has substantial backing. The nation's college and university presidents identified "substance abuse, primarily alcohol," as their most serious campus problem in a 1989 survey.[6] In a recent survey taken by the National Association of Student Councils, 46 percent of the students polled called alcohol the most serious problem in their schools. And according to a 1990 poll, 75 percent of Americans believe the teen drinking problem has worsened in the past five years.[7]

"I don't think it's hysterical to worry about 8,000 to 10,000 kids dying a year from alcohol," says OSAP spokesman Eigen. "This isn't a class where you get 'A' for effort. If we could wave a magic wand and reduce teen drinkers by a third tomorrow, it would still mean we have a tremendous health problem."

Is alcohol advertising to blame for underage drinking?

In November, the surgeon general unloaded her most controversial barrage in the campaign against underage drinking: an indictment of the alcoholic beverage industry's $2 billion annual advertising effort for sending a "mixed message" to the nation's youth. Novello's move carried the campaign into a complicated legal mine field that raises issues of advertisers' rights to free speech.[8]

But Novello's initiative pleased health activists who argue that advertising is a part of the social environment that must change if drinking is to be reduced. Novello singled out TV beer and wine ads that show bikini-clad women and athletic men playing sports. "The ads [would] have youth believing that instead of getting up early, exercising, going to school,

playing a sport, all they have to do to fit in is learn to drink the right alcoholic beverage," Novello said.[9]

Notwithstanding their condemnations of underage drinking, Novello argued, the alcohol companies are clearly targeting young drinkers in their ads. Examples include such campaigns as Budweiser's hip (and now retired) Spuds McKenzie and its comic-strip character Budman, as well as Halloween-oriented promotions for Coors' ("Elvira, Mistress of the Dark") and Miller's ("Scream for Miller"). The most egregious ad cited was the TV spot for St. Ides Malt Liquor, which features rap star Ice Cube chanting, "In a black can, why don't ya grab a six-pack and get your girl in the mood quicker ... with St. Ides Malt Liquor."

The question of whether advertising actually lures youth into alcohol consumption has been bandied about for decades. By the time teenagers reach driving age, according to the Center for Science in the Public Interest, they will have been exposed to 75,000 ads for alcoholic beverages.

A 1986 study commissioned by the federal Bureau of Alcohol, Tobacco and Firearms surveyed 665 teens in four states and found a "strongly positive" relationship between exposure to alcohol ads and a tendency to drink.[10]

More recently, a 1990 study based on interviews with 468 11- and 12-year-olds found that 88 percent could identify Spuds McKenzie with Budweiser, nine times the number who could identify a Coca-Cola slogan.[11] It concluded that children who are exposed to alcohol ads "are likely to have beliefs about beer consumption that are more in line with a commercial reality (e.g. fun and good times) than a public health reality (e.g. caution and risk)."

Critics of alcohol ads also point to the powerful cultural influences of ads that subtly teach youthful drinkers about alcohol etiquette. New

When Minors Drink: Case Studies in Tragedy

Since embarking on its "Put on the Brakes" campaign against alcohol abuse in 1991, the Health and Human Services Department's Office of Substance Abuse Prevention has been publishing a compendium of serious alcohol-related incidents reported among college students and other underage drinkers. The following is a sampling from December 1991:

College Drinkers

• The father of an intoxicated 20-year-old killed in a fall from a window of the Alpha Tau Omega fraternity at Clemson University is suing the university, the fraternity and two downtown bars.

• A 22-year-old tennis player from Sweden who was a student at Franklin and Marshall College was found unconscious in his dormitory room. He died in the emergency room of respiratory arrest with a blood-alcohol content of .40 percent, four times the legal limit.

• A University of New Haven student was charged with vehicular manslaughter while intoxicated after his car struck a tree, killing one passenger and injuring two others.

• At the University of Idaho, five students died last fall in alcohol-related incidents, and the emergency room at the university medical center reported that 80 percent of its cases are alcohol-related.

• A California Polytechnic State University fraternity member from San Luis Obispo, Calif., suffered an acute alcohol overdose after a drinking game. He had a usually fatal blood alcohol level of .57 percent.

• Charges of rape against a University of Richmond student were dismissed when the victim testified that she was too drunk to know she was being sexually assaulted, and the defendant testified that he was so drunk that he did not realize at first that she was not consenting. The two were among a group drinking beer and grain alcohol in a dorm room.

• Undercover policemen arrested 63 underage drinkers at a party given by New Hampshire Technical Institute students in Bow, N.H.

• Four students at the University of Tennessee were killed in an alcohol-related automobile crash after a birthday celebration. The driver, a 20-year-old sophomore,

survived, being the only one wearing a seat belt. He has been charged with four counts of vehicular homicide.

Underage Drinkers in General

• A physician and his wife from Mount Vernon, Ill., were hospitalized after a 19-year-old driver crossed the center line and struck their vehicle head-on. The youth was also hospitalized and charged with driving under the influence, illegal transportation of alcohol, illegal consumption of alcohol and improper lane use.

• An intoxicated high school senior from Orange, N.C., died of a severe head injury after being hit by a train.

• A 17-year-old honor student at a Trenton, N.J., private school drowned in a river after drinking heavily and smoking marijuana with her boyfriend.

• Three Waverly, Ill., teenagers were hospitalized after driving into a moving train; they were ticketed for illegal possession and consumption of alcohol by a minor.

• In West Bend, Wis., a 12-year-old and a 14-year-old were found lying unconscious in a snowbank with blood alcohol levels exceeding .23 percent.

• A 16-year-old Durham, N.C., boy has been accused of killing a woman by dropping a boulder from an overpass onto her car after drinking.

• In New Lenox, Ill., hosts were found liable for serving drinks to a 15-year-old girl, who was drunk when she hit a tree and killed a passenger.

• An intoxicated 17-year-old boy from Fayetteville, N.C., died when he crashed his car. The boy's aunt, who gave him four bottles of wine, has been sued.

• A 16-year-old Wausau, Wis., boy who got drunk on beer has been charged with arson that caused more than $400,000 in damages to a rural elementary school.

• A 17-year-old girl from Louisville, Ky., whose hand was run over by a drunken date after a party, is suing her date, the country club where the party was held and the party sponsor for not controlling the drinking.

• An 81-year-old man from Patrick Springs, Va., was convicted of selling whiskey to an 18-year-old boy who later died when he crashed his car.

• A former bartender from Woolstock, Iowa, was arrested for supplying alcohol to a 20-year-old cocktail waitress who died from alcohol poisoning.

York University media Professor Neil Postman cites the comical Bud Lite commercials in which a drinker in a bar who orders a "Lite" is handed a silly object such as a floor lamp. "The fully initiated drinker knows his beers and orders by brand," Postman writes. "Knowing exactly what he wants is an important characteristic of adulthood and masculinity." [12]

Such ads are a major part of the social environment, notes George Hacker of the Advocacy Institute in Washington. As director of the institute's Alcohol Advocacy Resource Center, Hacker aims to change the environment. "There's a connection between the environment and peer pressure," he says. "Ads tell you where to do it, who to do it with, how to do it. There are so many other messages that are positive, like health clubs. If it weren't for the massive onslaught of competing messages, we would have less inebriation."

The alcoholic beverage industry vigorously denies that it targets youths. "You do not target your marketing resources to audiences who can't buy your products," says the Beer Institute's Becker.

The reason alcohol ads use sexy models was explained at a November hearing of the House Select Committee on Children, Youth and Families. "Faced with ... the necessity of gaining consumer attention amid overwhelming media 'clutter,'" said Boston University marketing Professor John E. Calfee, "alcohol advertising adopts the same techniques that are used in numerous other mature markets, such as those for automobiles, cosmetics, soap, clothing.... Prominent among these is the use of attractive settings in which youthful and vigorous models indulge in activities that are enjoyed by most segments of society."

Possible links between advertising and alcohol consumption, industry spokesmen point out, have been rejected by the Federal Trade Commission and Health and Human Services Secretary Louis W. Sullivan. "It's an issue that is clearly settled," says Becker, "yet federal taxpayer dollars are being spent on it."

Industry officials cite academic papers that criticize the studies that purport to show a link, and they point to numerous peer-reviewed studies that they say prove there is no correlation. A Canadian study, for example, conducted after the lifting of a 58-year alcohol-advertising ban in Saskatchewan, used sales data from 1981 to 1987 to show that total alcohol sales actually decreased when advertising resumed (the exception was sales of beer, which rose slightly).[13]

Advertising's impact was also dismissed in a 1990 Roper poll that asked youths where they got their ideas about, among other things, drinking alcoholic beverages. Seventy percent named their schoolmates and friends, 48 percent said their parents, 12 percent said seeing people drink on TV programs and only 8 percent said advertising.

Nevertheless, the alcohol industry has clearly responded to public criticism of its advertising. Viewers of this year's Super Bowl were exposed to as many industry-sponsored ads for "responsible drinking" as they were to conventional beer ads featuring alluring women or humor. And the voluntary advertising code adopted by the industry's Century Council was modified in 1990 (in response to a poll) to discourage advertising that targets youth; shows people drinking while engaging in activities that require alertness, such as driving cars and boats; links alcohol to personal performance, popularity, success or to a sports celebrity; or promotes alcohol at any event youths are likely to attend.

In the Century Council poll, 73 percent of the respondents agreed "strongly" or "somewhat" that alcohol advertising is a "major contributor to underage drinking." Only 7 percent, however, thought that eliminating alcohol ads would solve the teen drinking problem.

Should alcohol abuse be approached in tandem with illegal drug abuse?

In January, on the day the White House announced that its war on drugs was expanding to take on underage drinking, the "NBC Nightly News" ran a feature on teen alcohol abuse. In a letter to anchorman Tom

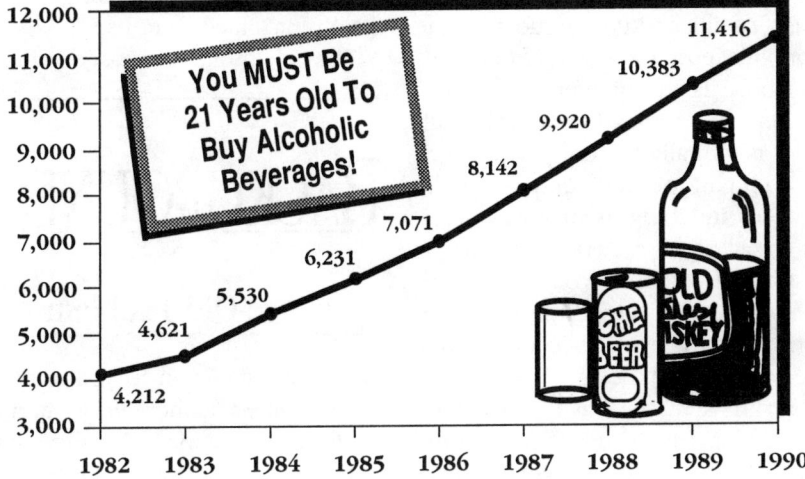

Raising Drinking Age To Save Lives

Traffic fatalities involving young drivers have been reduced 13 percent since 1975, when states began setting the minimum drinking age at 21. Backers credit these laws — in force in all states and the District of Columbia — with having saved more than 11,000 lives.

Cumulative Lives Saved

You MUST Be 21 Years Old To Buy Alcoholic Beverages!

4,212 · 4,621 · 5,530 · 6,231 · 7,071 · 8,142 · 9,920 · 10,383 · 11,416

1982 1983 1984 1985 1986 1987 1988 1989 1990

Source: National Highway Transportation Safety Administration

Brokaw, Fred Meister, president of the Distilled Spirits Council of the United States (DISCUS), called the segment "exclusionary, biased and misrepresentative." He said NBC failed to mention the recent declines in underage drinking and exaggerated the importance of the crackdown on alcohol compared with the much larger effort against illicit drugs.

The publicity gained for alcohol issues through the link with the drug war was welcomed, by contrast, by such groups as Mothers Against Drunk Driving (MADD) and the National Council on Alcoholism and Drug Dependence, both of which had spent years lobbying for such a linkup. (Critics complained, however, that the new drug strategy calls for no new funds to fight alcohol abuse. It promises enhanced coordination with other agencies and calls on parents to promote abstinence.)

The new alcohol stance taken by "drug czar" Bob Martinez is a departure from that of his predecessor, William J. Bennett, who considered concerns about alcohol abuse a "distraction" from the anti-drug agenda. "They are not morally equivalent," Bennett said in 1986. "When one buys into drugs, one is first of all supporting a widespread criminal conspiracy."[14]

Those who link alcohol use with abuse of illicit drugs argue that the economic cost to society from alcohol abuse is the greater of the two. Furthermore, writes Lewis Eigen, "alcohol is virtually the only drug which a small part of our culture actually practices imbibing as much as possible in as short a period of time as possible. Even the worst crack addicts do not try to ingest as much cocaine as they possibly can within a fixed period of time."[15]

Health activists have long been bothered that anti-drug officials use the term "substance abuse" without making it clear that legal alcohol is part of the problem along with the "more glamorous" challenges of criminal

drug use and trafficking. To Pat Taylor, a lobbyist on alcohol issues for the Center for Science in the Public Interest, "There are tremendous economic forces at work in our society promoting alcohol as a necessary ingredient to a successful and glamorous life. The failure to even include the word alcohol in federal alcohol and other drug legislation is a clear message to Americans about the federal government's perception of alcohol's contribution to the drug problem."[16]

Many professionals who treat substance abuse favor a combined effort because most treatment centers handle both drug and alcohol abuse. Indeed, activists against alcohol abuse increasingly argue that alcohol is a "gateway drug" that leads to harder drugs: first to marijuana then to cocaine, crack or heroin.

Commonly cited evidence for the gateway theory comes from a series of surveys of 7th- to 12th-graders in New York. "While all drinkers do not necessarily go on to use illicit substances," notes a summary, "nearly all extensive users of hard drugs have used alcohol regularly before initiating their drug use.... Policy implications are that prevention efforts to delay the onset of drinking by young people will have the added effect of delaying (or blocking) the initiation into illicit drug use."[17]

The alcoholic beverage industry

bristles at the alcohol/drug comparison. The Distilled Spirits Council has blasted the gateway theory, dismissing as "pseudo-science" any biomedical notion that alcohol activates a pleasure center in the brain that gradually requires ever more powerful stimulants. "The vast majority of youth who have experimented with alcohol for decades," it argues, "do so without ever going to illegal drug use."

Anheuser-Busch Inc., in a letter to shareholders on the drug issue, argued that unlike alcohol, crack cocaine and heroin cannot be used responsibly, and pointed to the tax revenues that alcohol provides the government in contrast to illegal drugs. Wine Institute President John De Luca says that fighting alcohol as part of the war on drugs "is going to confuse kids by loading up the vehicle with too many issues. They're savvy and hip enough to know they can go into a restaurant and see a glass of wine. A glass of chardonnay is not a stick of crack cocaine."

Two months before leaving his drug czar post, William Bennett appeared to change his thinking on the alcohol/drug question. As co-chair of the National Commission on Drug-Free Schools, he released a report in September 1990 calling for higher alcohol excise taxes to deter use by youth. The report calls alcohol a gateway drug. ∎

BACKGROUND

An Age-Old Problem

Alcohol's attraction to young people has rattled authorities around the world for centuries. In the United States in the 1820s, author Nathaniel Hawthorne recalled his classmates at Bowdoin College drinking fluid from their alcohol lamps to skirt campus

prohibitions. Decades later, anti-saloon activists helped to pass Prohibition in 1919 by circulating pictures of children sneaking alcohol out of taverns.

Early surveys showed that teen drinking in the United States began a rapid rise after World War II, when most of American society was drinking more as well. During the years 1941-50, only 29 percent of teenagers were drinkers, but from 1951 to 1965 the percentage rose to 63 percent.[18]

Continued on p. 226

Chronology

1960s
Rise of illicit drug use increases teen rebelliousness. Local laws loosened to permit more retailers to sell alcohol.

1966
Beginning of a rise in the average number of teens reporting having been drunk once in their life and the average number getting drunk monthly.

1970s
States lower their drinking ages. Youth alcohol consumption rises.

1971
National Institute of Alcohol Abuse and Alcoholism is established.

July 5, 1971
Amendment giving 18-year-olds the right to vote becomes law, prompting many states to lower the legal drinking age.

1980s
Alcohol consumption drops with trend toward health consciousness. Anti-alcohol-abuse movement gathers momentum with formation of pressure groups against drunken driving and student alcohol abuse.

1981
Inter-Association Task Force on Alcohol and Other Substance Issues is created by a number of colleges to study campus alcohol marketing.

1982
President Ronald Reagan appoints National Commission Against Drunk Driving.

July 17, 1984
President Reagan signs highway bill containing National Minimum Drinking Age Act.

October 1984
Annual National Collegiate Alcohol Awareness Week is launched.

Sept. 25, 1986
Congress passes Higher Education Act Amendments requiring all colleges and universities receiving federal financial aid to have drug abuse prevention programs for officers, employees and students.

Oct. 27, 1986
President Reagan signs anti-drug bill containing Drug-Free Schools and Communities Act establishing and expanding campus drug abuse and prevention programs.

Nov. 18, 1988
President Reagan signs omnibus anti-drug bill creating White House drug czar, requiring drug-free workplace policies and requiring health labels on alcoholic beverage containers.

Dec. 14-16, 1988
Surgeon General C. Everett Koop holds workshop on drunken driving; his office releases recommendations for curbing drunken driving five months later.

Dec. 11, 1989
President Bush proclaims Drunk Driving Awareness Week.

Dec. 12, 1989
President Bush signs Drug-Free Schools and Communities Act Amendments requiring educational institutions receiving federal money to adopt anti-drug and alcohol abuse programs.

1990s
The federal government and alcoholic beverage companies wage campaign against underage drinking.

Sept. 15, 1990
National Commission on Drug-Free Schools releases report calling alcohol and tobacco the most misused drugs and criticizing the alcohol and tobacco industries for targeting youth.

March 5, 1991
Surgeon General Antonia Novello calls news conference asking alcohol companies to tone down spring break promotions.

June 22, 1991
Surgeon General Novello releases survey of 7th- to 12th-graders estimating that half of the nation's 20.7 million youths drink.

Sept. 11, 1991
Surgeon general releases report citing lax state enforcement of drinking-age laws, calling enforcement a "myth."

Nov. 4, 1991
Surgeon general releases report criticizing alcoholic beverage advertisers for targeting youth.

Jan. 27, 1992
White House Drug Office releases anti-drug strategy that for the first time includes campaign against underage drinking.

How Intoxication Is Measured

The standard measure of intoxication is the blood alcohol concentration, or BAC. It reflects the percentage of alcohol found in the blood. A 140-pound person who has had two drinks will have a BAC reading of .05 percent, which means that there are .05 grams of pure alcohol per 100 milliliters of blood. Most jurisdictions consider a person legally intoxicated at BACs of .08 to .10 percent. Above .30 percent, a person can die due to respiratory depression or inhaling vomit while unconscious.

Number of drinks	Body weight in pounds							
	100	120	140	160	180	200	220	240
1	.04	.03	.03	.02	.02	.02	.02	.02
2	.08	.06	.05	.05	.04	.04	.03	.03
3	.11	.09	.08	.07	.06	.06	.05	.05
4	.15	.12	.11	.09	.08	.08	.07	.06
5	.19	.16	.13	.12	.11	.09	.09	.08
6	.23	.19	.16	.14	.13	.11	.10	.09
7	.26	.22	.19	.16	.15	.13	.12	.11
8	.30	.25	.21	.19	.17	.15	.14	.13
9	.34	.28	.24	.21	.19	.17	.15	.14
10	.38	.31	.27	.23	.21	.19	.17	.16

Source: American Council on Alcoholism

Continued from p. 224

From 1966 to 1975 the total rose to 70 percent, the increase probably slowing, analysts noted, because of the growing popularity of marijuana and hard drugs.

Still, the percentage of teens getting intoxicated greatly increased in the late 1960s and '70s. Before 1966, the average number who got drunk monthly was reported at 9.89 percent; after 1966 and into the 1970s, it shot up to 18.6 percent. Also in the postwar period, the average age of initiation into alcohol has been falling. In the 1940s and '50s, teens began experimenting with alcohol at ages 13 or 14. By the 1980s, the average age was 12. (In 1987, a *Weekly Reader* survey found that 34 percent of 4th-graders felt some pressure to drink wine coolers.)

Why Teens Drink

There used to be a stereotype among observers of adolescents that young drinkers were from troubled homes on "the wrong side of the tracks." Nowadays, it is largely accepted that teenagers are just as likely to drink if they come from well-to-do families and are active in school clubs.

In a survey conducted for the surgeon general's office last year, 41 percent of the young people polled said they drank when they were upset, 25 percent drank because they were bored and 25 percent drank to feel high. "When you've had several drinks at a party," said an Alexandria, Va., high school senior, "there is this great feeling of escape — from parents, college applications, SATs.... You may feel ugly during the week, but at the party you feel attractive, all the self-doubt is gone." [19]

Kids drink for essentially the same reasons as adults, except that among teens there is the added pressure to emulate older kids, to taste the forbidden fruit and to impress one's peers. "Everyone's talking about what they did, how drunk someone got," said a high school senior from Leesburg, Va. "Or, if they drive drunk and they make it from one point to another, they'll brag about that." [20]

Among students in rural areas, or in car-dependent suburbs that lack movie theaters or teen centers, drinking often springs from boredom. With six-packs of beer nearly as cheap as soft drinks, it's an inexpensive way to pass leisure time. Some adolescents and young adults treat drinking as a game. In bars, some compete to "drink the wall" — ordering every drink listed on the bar's menu board. College dorms host "around the world" parties, where each room serves a different type of alcohol, and partygoers go from one room to the next. Also popular is the "beer bong," a device fashioned from a funnel and tube purchased from a hardware store that enables a drinker to consume as much as two six-packs in an hour. [21]

Among college students as well as adults, drinking is often used as a conversational lubricant. "For most students [and non-students, too]," writes Eigen, "it is a lot easier to say to a friend, 'Let's go to Benny's and hoist a few,' than it is to say, 'I'm worried about some personal problems and would like to share this with you and get some advice and sympathy.'"

Another motive is the normal adolescent rebelliousness that gets expressed in alcohol, drugs or sex. "It's experimentation to establish moral values," notes Pamela Beer, who heads the Washington Regional Alcohol Program, a coalition working to reduce problem drinking. "That's how kids leave home. It's a breaking-away process."

That such rebelliousness has risen in recent decades is borne out, according to Fort Hays University President Hammond, by a decline in "key life skills" — including self-discipline, motivation, judgment and maturity — as measured in an annual survey of high school seniors.

It is a common belief — among adults as well as teenagers — that al-

Special Problems of the Teen Alcoholic

Few adolescents have been drinking long enough to develop the physical signs of the classic adult alcoholic — cirrhosis of the liver or withdrawal symptoms such as sweating, tremors and hallucinations. But an estimated 4.6 million Americans ages 14 to 17 are "problem drinkers," according to the National Institute of Alcohol Abuse and Alcoholism. This means they have suffered negative consequences from alcohol such as arrest, involvement in an accident, poor job performance or a health impairment such as alcohol addiction.

The roots of alcoholism are often observable early on. Eighty percent of the alcoholics in a study done at the School of Medicine at the University of Missouri-Columbia began drinking regularly before the age of 19.† (The average age was 13, but many were 11 or 9.)

Minors are more likely than adults to drink in secret, and they are more likely than adults to need approval from peers. Adolescents who are problem drinkers are also more likely to resist treatment efforts, usually because they fear "misunderstanding, restriction, punishment, rejection or abandonment," according to youth specialist George Beschner of the National Institute of Drug Abuse.††

"Everyone with this disease denies it," says Leota Lind, a counselor at the Fountain Center Adolescent Treatment Unit in Albert Lea, Minn. "But with teens, it's more difficult to break through the denial because they haven't experienced the significant losses and consequences such as divorce, job loss and loss of their children. They experience dropping out or bad family relations, but these are not viewed as consequences."

Once a teen navigates the psychological and practical obstacles to getting treatment (for the young, finding transportation to a clinic can be an obstacle), counselors must focus on "habilitation, not rehabilitation," Lind says. "While adult abusers have learned social skills and already have problem-solving abilities, adolescent substance abuse interferes with the ability to learn those skills."

The alcohol abuse must remain the chief focus of treatment, she says, but in order to achieve recovery, teen alcoholics must also learn the skills needed to handle education, family, social relationships and employment.

---

† Reported in *USA Weekend* magazine, February 1988.
†† George Beschner, "The Problem of Adolescent Drug Abuse: An Introduction to Intervention Strategies," *Treatment Services for Adolescent Substance Abusers*, Health and Human Services Department, 1985, p. 1.

---

cohol is an aphrodisiac. Physiologically, experts note, drinking has the opposite effect, though psychologically it clearly helps loosen inhibitions. Surveys of the young show that both males and females believe that a woman who drinks alcohol on a date comes across as a more-willing sex partner.[23] The risks, as counselors stress, are hurried, impersonal sex that is later regretted, greater chance of pregnancy and disease (an estimated 16 percent of teens who drink use condoms less often after drinking) and date rape.

Perhaps the most potent influence on teenagers' decisions to drink may be their parents. A 1978 study by North Carolina's Research Triangle Institute showed that 59 percent of all students with at least one parent who they believed drank regularly were themselves heavy drinkers. Moreover, teens whose parents approved of teen drinking were twice as likely to drink heavily as those whose parents disapproved.

Poor communication with parents also has been shown to be a predictor of youth alcohol use. A recent study based on in-depth interviews with 37 New England students showed that students who had at least one "open" parental figure were less likely to abuse drugs or alcohol.[22]

Attitudes of Parents

Parents are as divided as society itself on the issue of teen drinking. For every mom or dad working to organize a crackdown, there are others who criticize police for arresting juvenile offenders, go to court to prevent revocation of their child's driver's license or deny that their inebriated child has a drinking problem. In the upstate New York town of East Aurora last year, the entire community was split when a father sued the school board after it suspended his son, the high school quarterback, for drinking a beer at a fire department picnic.[24]

Recalling their own youthful experiments with drinking, many parents pass it off as a stage, resent it when teachers get involved and are unwilling to spend time smelling their kids' breath, searching their rooms or imposing a curfew. "A lot of parents are grateful if their kids aren't smoking pot or snorting cocaine," said Hanne Lille-Schulsted, a Lawrence, Kan., drug-abuse specialist.[25]

When tragedy strikes right at home, parents, understandably, often become energized. Last year, when a University of Florida junior died of asphyxiation after chugging 23 shots of liquor in a barroom drink-off, his parents started a campaign to toughen Florida laws concerning barroom liability.

A source of tension among parents is their dependence on each other for group supervision. Steinbach of the American Council on Education made waves when he permitted his 12th-grade daughter to host a very wet New Year's Eve party. Students were required to bring sleeping bags and had to deposit their car keys with Steinbach, who monitored the drinking games periodically to be sure everybody was still breathing. "The alternative is an unchaperoned house, parking lot or field somewhere," he says. "I'm concerned about safety."

John Hagan, principal of Bowie High School in Bowie, Md., said, "I don't want to see a parent condoning drinking. But I would rather see enough communication between parent and child so that a kid can call up and say, 'Hey, I'm drunk. Come and get me, Dad.'"[26]

Kids themselves, ironically, often say parents should get tougher. When a Michigan State University survey asked students what would reduce their alcohol consumption, 70 to 90 percent named such parental actions as supervising parties, keeping closer control over home alcohol supplies and making a greater effort to discuss kids' weekend activities.[27]

Drinking-Age Debate

The age limit for drinking has differed from state to state for so long that it has remained a continuous topic of debate. In the modern era, the story begins in the early 1970s with the successful movement to give 18-year-olds the right to vote. The Vietnam war was raging, and a

central argument was that someone old enough to die for his country should be old enough to vote. The same logic was applied to the drinking age, and by 1973 24 states had lowered their drinking age.

By the mid-1970s, however, rising highway deaths prompted many states to hike the drinking age to 21. By the early 1980s, the drunken-driving problem had prompted formation of several activist organizations, and the Gallup Poll was showing 77 percent of Americans favoring a higher drinking age.

Interest in a tougher drinking law culminated in 1984 with passage of a major highway bill containing the National Minimum Drinking Age Act, which required states that had not already done so to raise the drinking age to 21 if they wanted to continue receiving federal highway funds.* It took three years for all the states to comply.

The reasoning behind the law, the National Highway Transportation Safety Administration points out, is that teenagers cause a high percentage of alcohol-related deaths in proportion to the number of miles they drive. And a teenager who has had three drinks is 20 times more likely than an adult to have an accident. The NHTSA estimates that laws setting the drinking age at 21 have reduced traffic fatalities by 13 percent, or 11,000 lives, since 1975. (See graph, p. 223.)

This view is not universally accepted, however. The drop in deaths from drunk driving stems from better education, not the drinking age, contends university President Hammond. Many college presidents say the law has simply driven drinking underground, where it is harder to super-

---

*The federal law makes several exceptions to the 21 age limit, including possession of alcohol for an established religious purpose and use by servicemen and women under 21 on military bases.

vise in a community that is split between a large undergraduate population that's under 21 and a surprising number of older students. The College Alcohol Survey showed that 45 percent of college administrators prefer a legal drinking age below 21.

In today's "dry" climate, however, few lawmakers — and fewer lobbyists for the alcoholic beverage industry — are pressing to lower the drinking age. An exception is the National Licensed Beverage Association (NLBA), which represents the owners of bars, taverns and restaurants. "The quick fix didn't work, and cars became bars," says NLBA lobbyist John Chwat. "We've created an underclass of 18-to-21-year-olds." His group would rather see students drink in a supervised environment where servers have been trained to recognize drunkenness.

Lax Enforcement Criticized

More prominent on today's agenda is the call for better enforcement of the drinking-age law. In the Gallup Youth Poll, 8 in 10 teen drinkers in 1990 said obtaining alcohol is very easy or fairly easy, up from 69 percent in 1988. The laxity of many drinking establishments and retailers was demonstrated in a 1991 experiment by the Insurance Institute for Highway Safety, which sent underage purchasers into stores in the District of Columbia and New York state. In the District, 97 percent of the stores sold alcohol to the minors; in upscale Westchester County, the rate was 80 percent.

A recent report from the surgeon general complains about loopholes in state drinking-age laws, noting that six states don't expressly prohibit minors from purchasing alcohol and that 21 states do not specifically prohibit consumption by minors. It also complained that courts are lenient and that penalties for youths who use alcohol are not sufficient, set in some states as low as $15.[28]

State officials say that the reasons for weak enforcement are budget and staff cuts, the lack of jurisdiction of alcoholic beverage control boards and the fact that police are more interested in illicit drugs.

Anti-Abuse Efforts

What stands out about today's alcohol-abuse debate is the degree to which the beer, wine and spirits companies are working to combat the problem. That's partly because during the late 1980s public acceptance of measures to curb alcohol abuse — among them sobriety checkpoints and harsher penalties for drunken driving — rose dramatically.

Anheuser-Busch has spent more than $100 million in the past decade on "responsible-drinking" advertising and community-outreach programs. Similar ads have been produced by the Advertising Council and the nonprofit National Council on Alcoholism and Drug Dependence.

The Beer Institute has distributed more than 2 million point-of-sale posters and fliers to retailers to help prevent underage purchases, and the Licensed Beverage Information Council funds a phone-referral service for teens with alcohol and drug problems and distributes educational brochures for class use. The Wine Institute also contributes to education efforts and alcohol research programs, among them a drunken-driving intervention program at UCLA.

The Distilled Spirits Council is working with government, industry and advocacy groups supporting the Washington Area Regional Alcohol Program, which is attempting to design a model community program that, according to DISCUS President Meister, "could write the book on how to address teen drinking ... for years to come."

Beyond pressure from the current trend toward temperance, colleges and universities have additional mo-

Trends in High School Drinking

In the past decade, monthly alcohol use among high school seniors has gradually declined, from 72 percent in 1980 to 54 percent in 1991. Occasional heavy drinking, however, remains widespread. In 1991, 30 percent of seniors polled reported having five drinks in a row in the prior two-week period, compared with 41 percent in 1980.

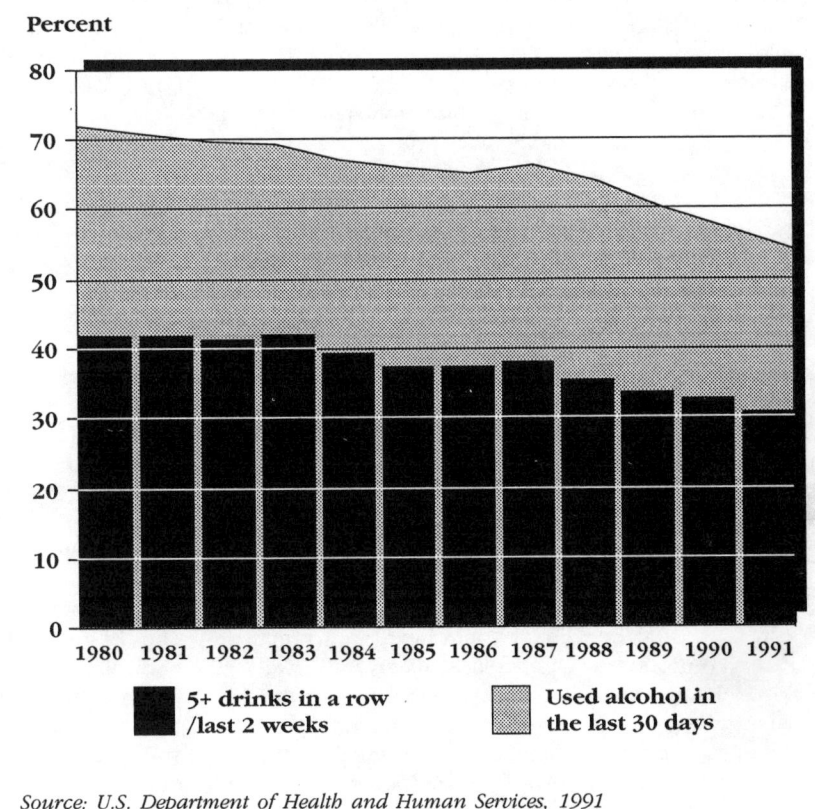

Percent

■ 5+ drinks in a row /last 2 weeks

▨ Used alcohol in the last 30 days

Source: U.S. Department of Health and Human Services, 1991

tives for action: spiraling insurance costs (due to colleges' recently expanded liability for campus drinking incidents), and a federal law that conditions government education funding on the implementation of programs to curb alcohol abuse. The Education Department's network of such programs has spread to 3,300 colleges. The College Alcohol Survey in 1991 found that 90 percent of the schools had increased their alcohol-education efforts since 1988.

Students Tackle the Problem

On the student level, the Interfraternity Council, made up of 61 cam-

pus men's groups at schools nationwide, is taking a "businesslike risk-management stance toward loose chapters," according to Drew Hunter, executive director of the campus group BACCHUS (Boost Alcohol Consciousness Concerning the Health of University Students), "and many are being closed down."

In addition, campuses are experimenting with such measures as the University of Texas' "dry rush week," the University of Maryland's ban on weeknight parties and the "sober dorms," or wellness wings, set up at Rutgers University in New Jersey and

Continued on p. 231

Fake IDs Are Familiar Teen Accoutrements

An unintended result of raising the drinking age has been a flood of false identification cards, which on many school campuses are as familiar as cheerleader pompoms. "At least 75 percent of all college students own a fake ID, and at the bars, they hardly check them," Camile Jones, a 19-year-old student at Champlain College in Burlington, Vt., told a reporter in 1989.†

A bartender or a sales clerk in a hurry to make a sale can pass over the most flagrantly phony driver's licenses or state liquor board cards. "The vendor asked for ID," a state official recalled in a recent federal report on enforcement of drinking-age laws. "The 16-year-old boy — who looked 16 — presented the ID of a 5-foot, 4-inch female, except he had taped his picture on it. He was a 6-foot, 5-inch male. Nonetheless, the clerk sold the beer to him." ††

A streetwise teenager bent on buying alcohol has several venues for procuring fake IDs. Manhattan's Times Square hosts numerous storefronts offering "Photo-identification," where for as little as $10 adolescents can buy documents of all types, including student IDs for nearly every college in the country. There is sizable underground traffic in stolen blank license forms and in mail-order "personal ID cards." Fake IDs can even be obtained on some college campuses. An 18-year-old Vermont College student arrested in 1988 was found to have earned $20,000 selling fake ID cards. He'd taken a liquor control card to a printer in Florida who produced stacks of facsimiles.

Bill Holden, an alcohol policy specialist with the National Highway Traffic Safety Administration (NHTSA), says that counterfeiting identification documents has been made easier in recent years by color photocopying and other high-tech machines. Stolen or borrowed driver's licenses can be stripped of their lamination, pasted over with a different photograph and then photocopied and relaminated to disguise the extra layer.

Applying for licenses is surprisingly easy, Holden says. "All you need in some states is a baptismal certificate to get one by mail." Florida issues a million duplicate licenses a year to people who say they lost theirs, many of whom may be impostors who have their pictures mounted with an older person's data.

NHTSA offers a videotaped course to train state officials in detecting identity documents that have been fabricated, altered or transferred to another individual. Amateurish efforts to alter licenses — changes in the type done by hand, for example — are easiest to detect, Holden says.

The best ID forgers start from scratch by falsifying "breeder documents" — birth certificates, Social Security cards and baptismal certificates that are used to apply for the all-important driver's license. Motor vehicle officials are taught to watch for poorly printed birth certificates, particularly if the name of a locality has been typed in rather than pre-printed. Other common forgery giveaways include less-than-official-looking government seals (fabricators often use a notary seal or an irrelevant corporate seal) and code numbers that don't match official numbers assigned to each region.

Help in thwarting the use of fake IDs is increasingly being offered by bartenders and retail clerks, though courts have ruled that they are not subject to prosecution if they accept a fake ID that appears proper.‡ Advice on proper checking is provided in a pamphlet by the alcoholic beverage industry's Century Council, and a booklet illustrating the authentic driver's licenses for all 50 states is distributed by Anheuser-Busch Inc. A Milwaukee club uses video equipment to enlarge and project the ID image on a screen, rendering invalid ones more apparent and serving as a deterrent. Other bars offer their bouncers a bounty payment for confiscating fake IDs.

Though 46 states have laws against misrepresenting one's age, groups campaigning against underage drinking say they are unevenly enforced. Holders of fake IDs in Wisconsin, for example, have their drivers's licenses suspended for 30 to 90 days, plus they pay $50 and perform community service. In Vermont, by contrast, the student who earned $20,000 selling hundreds of fake IDs was charged only with using a fake ID and fined a mere $50. The 1991 College Alcohol Survey showed that only 58 percent of colleges and universities impose a fine or institutional probation for users of fake IDs.

MADD favors new legislation to discourage fake IDs, among them bills to require more tamper-proof licenses. A federal law on the books, the 1982 False Identification Crime Control Act, is regarded by many as too weak. It affects only abusers who carry at least five false documents and applies only when the criminal crosses state lines.

"We'd like a federal law with teeth," says John Chwat, chief lobbyist for the National Licensed Beverage Association, "so that the Postal Service can prosecute mailing of fake IDs and the Justice Department could go after manufacturers." The bar, tavern and restaurant owners in the association also want new state laws and more responsibility assumed by parents in policing against fake IDs. They are less pleased with state efforts to boost penalties for vendors who serve underage drinkers.

"My clients are fed up," Chwat says. "You can't hold an entire retail industry accountable as an enforcement arm."

---

† *Burlington [Vt.] Free Press,* April 16, 1989.

†† Inspector General Richard P. Kusserow, "Youth and Alcohol: Laws and Enforcement," Health and Human Services Department, 1991, p. 11.

‡ See *Brannigan v. Raybuck,* Arizona Supreme Court, 1983.

Continued from p. 229

other campuses for students who need to be shielded from alcohol.

Before partying at Willamette College in Salem, Ore., fraternities and other groups must first bring in a qualified speaker on alcohol education or other drugs. Chico State University in California has eliminated the sale of beer mugs and shot glasses at campus stores. Princeton has banned kegs, calling them "a symbol of the free and easy availability of alcohol." (Rutgers took the opposite view, banning individual cans and bottles on the assumption that kegs are easier to count and monitor.)

Overall, according to The College Alcohol Survey, 75 percent of campuses still permit beer for those old enough to drink, and 67 percent permit hard liquor. But increases are reported in the number of schools that prohibit alcohol advertising on campus radio (58 percent), bulletin boards (55 percent) and student newspapers (21 percent.)

Designated Drivers

One of the best-known ways to combat alcohol-related tragedies is appointing a designated driver in each group of drinkers. The idea swept into public consciousness (it's now in the dictionary) after it was imported from Scandinavia in the mid-1980s by the Alcohol Project at Harvard University's School of Public Health. A 1991 Roper poll showed that 93 percent of Americans think the designated driver is a good idea, while 78 percent, according to a recent Gallup Poll, would forgo drinking and be the designated driver.

Jay Winsten, director of the Harvard program, in recent years has tested a public-service campaign using billboards that read, "The Designated Driver is the Life of the Party." The program has demonstrated some progress in boosting young people's awareness and reducing drunken driving arrests on Martha's Vineyard.

Winsten persuaded the Writers Guild of America to pass a resolution urging writers in Hollywood to weave designated drivers into their scripts. In the past few years, the effort has made its mark on more than 100 episodes of such shows as "L.A. Law," "Dallas" and "Cheers."

Winsten emphasizes that designated drivers by his definition should not drink *any* alcohol during an event. In reality, some critics note, the designated driver is often merely the least drunk person in the group.

The designated-driver program is actively supported by the alcoholic beverage industry, one reason why critics also attack it for sending a message, as Edward Hammond puts it, "that it's OK to get plastered if someone else is driving." The designated-driver idea lets people off the hook, agrees alcohol-policy researcher David S. Anderson of George Mason University in Fairfax, Va. "Young people are myopic," he says. "They say, 'Oh, we have a drunk-driving problem, I won't drive,' and they don't think of the health consequences. The health damage from alcohol may be higher now that the perception of danger is removed."

Awareness Groups

Underage drinking has stirred action by private citizens in addition to government and industry. One of the best known is MADD, which was launched in 1980 by Candy Lightner, of Sacramento, Calif., whose daughter was killed by a drunken driver. The Dallas-based group, with 3 million members and supporters, counsels bereaved families and holds candlelight rallies commemorating victims of drunken drivers. Its national staff lobbies for tougher enforcement of drinking-age laws.

A similar but more "grass-roots-oriented" group is RID (Remove Intoxicated Drivers), which was founded in 1978 by former talk show host Doris Aiken, whose friends lost a child.

Based in Schenectedy, N.Y., it has a decentralized network of local chapters (155 in 40 states) that appear in court on behalf of victims of drunk drivers. Its newsletter calls for higher alcohol taxes and restrictions on alcohol ads.

At the college level, the best-known alcohol-awareness group is Denver, Colo.-based BACCHUS. Founded in 1975 at the University of Florida, BACCHUS has 500 campus chapters nationwide and a growing number overseas. It works on the principle that "young people can play a uniquely effective role, unmatched by professional educators, in encouraging their peers to reflect on, talk honestly about and develop responsible habits and attitudes toward beverage alcohol use or non-use."

BACCHUS strives for a non-preachy communication approach, reflected in such brochures as "Sex Under the Influence," and "The BACCHUS Guide to a Successful Party," which acknowledge the temptations and prevalence of alcohol. "Groups like BACCHUS survive all trends in prevention because we don't choose whether alcohol is good or bad," says Drew Hunter. "We look at impaired driving, how to change the environment and such."

BACCHUS has been criticized for not describing alcohol as a drug and for accepting funding from the alcohol industry. "BACCHUS' philosophical posture is governed by funding from beer companies," charges Christine Lubinski, director of public policy at the National Council on Alcoholism and Drug Dependence. "They support policies that don't challenge limits on drinkers."

Not setting limits is also a fundamental tenet at Marlboro, Mass.-based SADD (Students Against Driving Drunk). It was founded in 1981 by high school teacher Robert Anastas, who lost two students to alcohol-related car accidents. With chapters now in 17,000 high schools,

8,000 middle schools and 1,500 colleges (in the United States and abroad), SADD has been the subject of a book and a made-for-TV movie.

"If the problems of drinking and driving, underage drinking and drug abuse are yours, then the solutions to those problems lie with you," goes the SADD philosophy.

SADD's key tool is getting students and parents to sign its "Contract for Life," which permits the signer who has had too much to drink or whose friends are drunk to come to parents for a taxi or a ride — no questions asked. "I have discussed with you and fully understand your attitude toward any involvement with underage drinking or the use of illegal drugs," the students' pledge reads.

SADD helps organize alcohol-free proms and parties and publicizes its message using buttons, posters, T-shirts, manuals and tote bags. For years, SADD accepted funding from the alcohol industry. It stopped in 1989 because the "public perception was that we shouldn't," said Executive Director William Cullinane.

The best way to appeal to a broad range of students and avoid the "goody-two-shoes image," according to SADD National Representative Rob Aptaker, is "don't hide your light under a bushel. Kids who don't drink are real quiet. Those who abuse alcohol become high-profile." Aptaker says a typical SADD approach is "to have a student get on the school P.A. system and say, 'Hey, I'm Scotty. I'm captain of the wrestling team and I'm drug- and alcohol-free, and here's why.' He doesn't say, 'You should be, too,' or 'Everyone who drinks is a jerk.' " ∎

CURRENT SITUATION

State Crackdowns

Concrete action against underage drinking often comes attached to efforts against alcohol abuse in society as a whole. Currently, many states are considering alcohol legislation to meet demands of last year's federal highway reauthorization bill. After lobbying battles between such groups as MADD and the National Restaurant Association, a compromise in that bill set up a new $20 billion grant program that rewards states that adopt alcohol and drug-impaired driving enforcement programs.

To receive federal funds, states must meet four out of five requirements:

∎ Revoke drunken drivers' licenses;
∎ Set up sobriety checkpoints;
∎ Set a 0.10 blood-alcohol content standard for drunken driving (reduced to 0.08 after three years);
∎ Step up enforcement of the legal drinking age;
∎ Establish laws preventing drunken driving.

Grants are given only to states that make it unlawful to possess open containers of alcohol in a moving motor vehicle and that revoke the license plates and registrations of repeat drunken drivers.

In January, Utah passed a "Not-a-Drop" law that will suspend for 90 days the driver's licenses of any underage person caught with alcohol in the bloodstream. Some 30 other states currently permit a police officer to confiscate — on the spot — the license of anyone charged with drunken driving. So-called administrative license revocation is being pushed by a citizens' movement led by the National Coalition to Prevent Impaired Driving.

The procedure, supporters say, deters both potential drunken drivers and repeat offenses by those who've been caught. Offenders are also encouraged to seek treatment for their drinking problems. Under many such laws, a police officer who confiscates a license may issue a temporary license and provide legal notification of the offender's right to a hearing.

Opponents of administrative revocation say it violates constitutional rights to due process. Nine states have recently considered such laws.

Action in Congress

Many health activists concerned with youth drinking have long favored a bill to require alcohol ads to include health warnings. Building on a 1988 federal law requiring health warning labels on alcoholic beverage containers, a proposal by Rep. Joseph P. Kennedy II, D-Mass., and Sen. Strom Thurmond, R-S.C., would require TV and print ads to carry warnings that alcohol can cause mental retardation and birth defects, can impair one's ability to drive, may be hazardous if used with other drugs, may be addictive and is illegal for those under 21.

"Alcohol advertising," Thurmond said in introducing the bill in March 1991, "is the greatest single source of alcohol education for Americans, and rarely does it encourage them to consider the consequences of drinking."

The labeling bill has the backing of the National Parent-Teacher's Association, the American Medical Association, MADD and the Center for Science in the Public Interest, among others. It is opposed by the alcoholic beverage industry and the National Association of Broadcasters, which say that time-consuming health warnings would prompt the alcohol industry to drop its 15-second TV ads — at considerable revenue loss for the networks.

Industry officials say the bill un-

Continued on p. 234

At Issue:

Should the surgeon general crack down on underage drinking?

ANTONIA NOVELLO

Surgeon General of the United States
FROM *SAN FRANCISCO CHRONICLE,* SEPT. 5, 1991

Some maintain underage drinking is a rite of passage, but I say it is a passage to madness not maturity. Underage drinking leads to disaster on the highway, on the job, in school and at home. Contra Costa County and Salisbury, Md., are a continent apart, but recently they were linked in tragedy. Eight teenagers in California, after an early morning drinking spree, died after they were thrown like rag dolls from their pickup truck in a gruesome head-on collision. In Maryland, a 15-year-old boy died after consuming 26 shots of vodka at an unsupervised teen party that advertised: "All you can drink — $3."

Alcohol is an equal-opportunity destroyer. A recent report from the Health and Human Services inspector general discloses: There are almost 21 million students attending grades 7-12 nationwide, 10.6 million of whom drink!

The good news is that about half our teens do not drink. But at least 8 million use alcohol every week, and almost half a million go on weekly binges.

They have a common story — lack of parental supervision, missed opportunities, poor scholastic performance, lawbreaking, runaway, sexually transmitted diseases, wrecked physical health, violence, accidents, depression and suicide. Most take their first drink when they are 13.

Several reasons are given for underage drinking: to get high, boredom, being upset and being alone. I also offer these: lack of information, peer pressure, curiosity, no direction in life, a rejection of community values and, yes, addiction. Two out of three teenagers cannot distinguish alcohol from non-alcoholic beverages because they look the same in stores; almost 2 million do not know that a law for minimum age to purchase alcohol exists; a third do not understand the intoxicating effects of alcohol.

Many of those who drink drive. Although 92 percent of teenagers surveyed said a person should never drink and drive, almost a third of those who drink admitted they frequently ride with a friend who has been drinking.

It is obvious something is wrong. At the very least, we are not properly educating our young people about alcohol's harmful effects.

Our laws must be enforced, and advertisers, the hired guns of the alcohol industry, must be given a clear message that we will not tolerate clever promotions aimed at our youth. Each of us has a role to play in educating teens about risks associated with alcohol consumption. It is time we all are part of the solution or surely we will be part of the problem.

ROBERT RENO

Columnist
FROM *NEWSDAY,* Nov. 6, 1991

Is it possible that the surgeon general of the United States hasn't heard that there is a serious AIDS epidemic, that infant mortality rates in many parts of America are a medical and political disgrace, that there is a crisis in health-care affordability, that cardiovascular disorders and gangrenous gall bladders are killing unnecessary millions of Americans.

Someone must tell her. Because Antonia Novello has got this thing about teenage drinking that borders on the obsessive. Just wait until she discovers warts.

Now all of us deplore excessive teenage drinking. If we see a dipsomaniacal adolescent doing something piggy on our front lawn, we are careful to express our disapproval. We have gone so far as to criminalize teenage drinking in most states, so it is not as if the problem hasn't been recognized and addressed with severity....

Only a few months ago Novella went national with her concern about college drinking on spring break, citing the example of the inebriated celebrants who performed consensual sex in a hot tub at a Texas resort. Now I say as long as the little wretches weren't out driving, pulling up shrubbery, harassing senior citizens or blowing their tuition checks, the surgeon general should go back to curing cancer.... But no, now she's sounding the alarm about advertising, claiming that it tends to glamorize drinking among the young.

The people in beer ads are too attractive, their portrayed life-styles too inviting, she says. Assuming this indefatigable fussbudget is not proposing the repeal of the First Amendment or re-enactment of the 18th — and nothing in her ravings to date suggest this — we can just imagine the sort of beer commercial that would be allowed under whatever new industry code she has in mind. It might approve, for instance, a pitiful old lady lying helplessly on the floor of her living room strewn with beer cans screaming in a grating voice: "I've fallen and I can't get up! Will some jerk please bring me a Coors."

A humorless, moralizing surgeon general can do more to encourage teenage drinking than any beer ad. What she does, essentially, to these young minds is to give them a role model of the sort of abstemious, authoritarian adult they desperately do not want to be. [If].... she has time on her hands, a good informational crusade on better care for AIDS patients, excessive surgical fees, even teenage pregnancy — and not for heaven's sake with a "nice girls don't do that" approach — might suggest itself to her.

Continued from p. 232
constitutionally infringes on advertisers' free-speech rights, and they rebut the notion that ads represent the main source of alcohol education. According to a 1990 Gallup Poll for *Advertising Age* magazine, 74 percent of the public wants warning labels in TV alcohol ads. Neither the House nor Senate version has emerged from committee.

Restructuring Federal Agencies

A bill that on the surface seems an inside-Washington bureaucratic struggle is nonetheless being watched carefully by many in the alcohol-abuse debate. The ADAMHA Reorganization Act, introduced by Sens. Edward M. Kennedy, D-Mass., and Orrin G. Hatch, R-Utah, would reconfigure several alcohol policy offices within the HHS's vast Alcohol, Drug Abuse and Mental Health Administration. The goal is to separate research from treatment in the hope of raising the prestige of both. The issue, Kennedy told fellow senators, is "whether it's useful to ask a single agency to research the causes and cures of a disease at the same time that it provides services to those suffering from the disease."

To "eliminate competition, confusion and overlap," the Kennedy-Hatch bill — which is backed by HHS Secretary Sullivan — would move the National Institute of Drug Abuse, the National Institute of Alcoholism and Alcohol Abuse and the National Institute of Mental Health out of ADAMHA and place them under the umbrella of the research-oriented National Institutes of Health. This, backers say, would affirm the status of mental illness and substance abuse as diseases and, in the words of a lobbyist for the Center for Science in the Public Interest, provide an "opportunity to reassess the low priority alcohol and the prevention of alcohol-related problems have received under the present structure."

The Wine Institute has expressed concern that the reorganization would result in new funding for OSAP, which it fears would launch a new communications effort directed against alcoholic beverage consumption. House members with jurisdiction on the subject have called the restructuring unnecessary, and the bill, which is attached to a larger measure dealing with mental health grants to the states, is heading toward a House-Senate conference with an uncertain future. ∎

hol's risks. The two goals do not appear compatible. According to RID founder Doris Aiken, if society actually eliminated youth drinking and adult binge drinking, the alcohol companies "would lose half their income."

MADD President Kirk notes that the industry continues to use catchy slogans such as "Know when to say when," or "Think when you drink," which, she says, fail to educate about the dangers of alcohol. To achieve its goal of reducing alcohol-related traffic fatalities by 20 percent by the year 2000, MADD favors stronger state enforcement measures, such as a legal limit of zero blood-alcohol content for people under 21. "It will also take a great deal of networking and education of young people," Kirk says, warning that such efforts are currently endangered by nationwide budget cuts in school health curricula and driver-education programs.

Youthful ignorance about alcohol is a common concern. The surgeon general's survey estimated that 5.6 million junior and senior high school students are unaware that the drinking age is 21, and that more than 2.6 million students do not know that a person can die from alcohol abuse. Nearly a third of high school seniors in the University of Michigan survey believed there's no great risk in having four or five drinks almost every day.

More encouraging, however, is the Gallup Youth Poll, which showed that 78 percent of young people believe drinking is having a serious effect on society. Educational materials from alcohol industry, government and advocacy groups are getting more sophisticated. An OSAP alcohol-education manual, for example, notes that teens "do not want to look stupid or lose control in front of their peers." It recommends that alcohol educators emulate commercial advertisers with materials that state and then solve a problem, and use humor

OUTLOOK

Sobering Problems

The magic potion that banishes all youthful alcohol abuse is clearly not soon to hit the market. As new generations of teenagers gaze upon life's temptations, the issue is likely to remain a major battleground in the larger war over alcohol in society. The alcohol industry's "responsible drinking" ads and its lowered promotional profile among college students has not satisfied critics. "They may pos-

ture toward altruism," says Paul Gillette, a Los Angeles beverage industry consultant, "but if they're so conscientious, how come they were not so conscientious 10 years ago when everybody was sponsoring wet T-shirt contests at spring break? They've all gotten religion now that the neo-prohibitionists are breathing down their necks."[29]

A corporation's need to remain profitable bodes for a fighting stance by the alcohol industry, and the $2 billion a year the industry spends advertising alcoholic beverages is likely to continue dwarfing the scant millions allocated to warn about alco-

and slice-of-life enactments in which a doubter is converted.

How Tough Should Enforcement Be?

The sleeper political issue, in the view of OSAP spokesman Lewis Eigen, is the question of whether the drinking-age laws should be stringently enforced or just left as "moral pronunciamentos." It's the $64,000 question. Despite the newly invigorated campus alcohol policies, nearly 75 percent of college officials reported no improvement in alcohol-related problems in 1991, with 30 percent saying problems had increased, according to The College Alcohol Survey. "If they make the rules harder, kids will try harder to break them," said Lara Deming, a 19-year-old student at Virginia Tech, in Blacksburg. "I don't think they can do anything to keep kids from drinking." [30]

"Courts have said that in order to monitor the personal lives of students, you would have to impair the ability of students to mature," says Steinbach of the American Council on Education. "It would be virtually impossible without turning the campus into a police state."

Some administrators have suggested that before alcohol policies are implemented a reality check is needed, so that authorities aren't left with a grim choice between expelling half the student body and presiding over a set of rules that are dismissed as a joke. Eigen suggests it might be better to start with an education campaign and then ease into lesser penalties that could be toughened later.

Others warn that students will not respond to what they see as hypocrisy among adults. "We're giving conflicting messages," says George Mason University's Anderson. "We as individuals need to come to grips with it: At the Kiwanis Club, at church, do we have our holiday bash?"

"The forbidden fruit and fire-and-brimstone approach is not working,"

says the Wine Institute's De Luca. He says he learns from his college-age children, who feel less of a need for the "rite of passage of tying one on" because they were exposed to wine early on. Like others in the industry, De Luca believes education in moderate drinking is what works. "I tell the alcohol activists that they can't accomplish in this field what we can accomplish on our own."

Dealing with youth alcohol abuse appears to require less idealism and more realism. As Eigen writes, it is useful to view the problem "as an 'eternal struggle,' such as that between good and evil, truth and falsehood, freedom, ignorance and other problems which we can commit our resources and skills to improve the situation, but never really eliminate." [31] ■

Notes

[1] For more on alcohol as a health issue, see "Dealing with the Dangers of Alcohol," Editorial Research Reports, Sept. 7, 1990, pp. 510-523.

[2] David S. Anderson and Angelo F. Gadaleto, "The College Alcohol Survey," George Mason University and West Chester University, 1991.

[3] For background, see "America's New Temperance Movement," Editorial Research Reports, Dec. 21, 1984, pp. 937-956; and "Teenage Drinking," Editorial Research Reports, May 15, 1981, pp. 349-368.

[4] Quoted in The New York Times, Oct. 8, 1991.

[5] Quoted in The Wall Street Journal, March 13, 1991.

[6] Carnegie Foundation for the Advancement of Teaching, Campus Life: In Search of Community, 1989.

[7] The poll was commissioned by the alcoholic beverage industry's Century Council, which was established in 1991 to combat alcohol abuse.

[8] See "Advertising Under Attack," The CQ Researcher, Sept. 13, 1991, pp. 657-80.

[9] Quoted in The Washington Post, Nov. 5, 1991.

[10] Chuck Atkin, John Hocking and Martin Block, "Teenage Drinking: Does Advertising Make a Difference?" published in Youth and Alcohol Abuse: Readings and Resources (1986), p. 63.

[11] Lawrence Wallack, et al., "TV Beer Commercials and Children: Exposure, Attention, Beliefs, and Expectations About Drinking as an Adult," AAA Foundation for Traffic Safety, 1990.

[12] Neil Postman, et al., "Myths, Men and Beer: An Analysis of Beer Commercials on Broadcast Television, 1987," AAA Foundation for Traffic Safety, p. 19.

[13] See Cheryl R. Makowsky and Paul C. Whitehead, "Advertising and Alcohol Sales: A Legal Impact Study," Journal of Studies on Alcohol, Vol. 52, No. 6, 1991, pp. 555-567.

[14] Quoted in The Washington Times, Sept. 16, 1986.

[15] Lewis D. Eigen, "Alcohol Practices, Policies and Potentials of American Colleges and Universities," OSAP White Paper, Health and Human Services Department, September 1991.

[16] Letter to Sen. Orrin G. Hatch, R-Utah, ranking Republican member of the Labor and Human Resources Committee, July 11, 1991.

[17] Results are summarized in a newsletter, The Problem Drinker Project, New York State Division of Alcoholism and Alcohol Abuse, November 1990.

[18] Joan Sieber, "Socialization of Alcohol Use, Abuse and Abstinence in Adolescents," unpublished paper, California State University-Hayward, 1988.

[19] Quoted in Patrick Welsh, "Kids and Booze," The Washington Post, Dec. 31, 1990.

[20] Quoted in The Washington Post, Feb. 19, 1992.

[21] Welch, op cit.

[22] Randy R. Kafka and Perry London, "Communication in Relationships and Adolescent Substance Use: The Influence of Parents and Friends," Adolescence, Vol. 26, No. 103, fall 1991, p. 587.

[23] Antonia Abbey, "Acquaintance Rape and Alcohol Consumption on College Campuses: How are They Linked?" Journal of American College Health, January 1991, p. 165.

[24] The New York Times, Sept. 30, 1991.

[25] Quoted in Time, Feb. 13, 1988, p. 94.

[26] Ibid.

[27] "Youth Driving Without Impairment: A Community Challenge," National Commission Against Drunk Driving, October 1989.

[28] Inspector General Richard P. Kusserow, "Youth and Alcohol: Laws and Enforcement," Health and Human Services Department, 1991, p. 10.

[29] Quoted in the Los Angeles Times, Oct. 15, 1991.

[30] Quoted in The New York Times, Dec. 31, 1991.

[31] Eigen, op. cit.

Bibliography

Selected Sources Used

Books

Bartimole, Carmella R. and John E. Bartimole, *Teenage Alcoholism and Substance Abuse: Causes, Consequences and Cures,* Frederick Fell Publishers Inc., 1987.

A survey of the effects of alcohol and illicit drug abuse, with commentary on why teens use drugs and what parents can do about it.

Cohen, Susan and Daniel Cohen, *A Six-Pack and a Fake I.D.: Teens Look at the Drinking Question,* M. Evans and Co., 1986.

Two writers of books for adolescents offer a peer-level view of the teen drinking scene and its role in the social, academic and sexual lives of today's youth. The book also discusses policy issues such as the legal drinking age.

Felsted, Carla Martindell, ed., *Youth and Alcohol Abuse: Readings and Resources,* Oryx Press, 1986.

An anthology of articles by academics and government experts on underage drinking, alcoholism and treatment and policy issues such as the debate over the influence of advertising.

Lang, Alan R., *Alcohol: Teenage Drinking (The Encyclopedia of Psychoanalytic Drugs),* Chelsea House Publishers, 1985.

A Florida State University psychology professor discusses the history, motivations and policy issues raised by underage drinking. The book contains a list of state alcohol agencies.

Olson, Steve, with Dean R. Gerstein, *Alcohol in America: Taking Action to Prevent Abuse,* National Academy Press, 1985.

Papers condensed from a conference held by the National Institute of Alcoholism and Alcohol Abuse form a narrative of alcohol policy issues including consumption trends, tax levels, underage drinking and enforcement efforts against drunk driving. The forward was written by former Secretary of Labor Elizabeth H. Dole.

Reports and Studies

Anheuser-Busch Cos., *Family Talk About Drinking,* 1989.

A three-part booklet from a major brewer gives specific suggestions for teaching children about responsible alcohol use. The most teachable years, it says, are ages 9 to 11.

Eigen, Lewis D., *Alcohol Practices, Policies, and Potentials of American Colleges and Universities: An OSAP White Paper,* Health and Human Services Department, September 1991.

The author, an educational psychologist and former director of the National Clearinghouse for Alcohol and Drug Information, uses a wealth of anecdotes and facts to analyze the issues raised in the search for a solution to campus alcohol abuse.

National Institute on Drug Abuse, *Drug Use Among American High School Seniors, College Students and Young Adults, 1975-1990,* Health and Human Services Department, 1991.

Data tables and analysis of long-term rates of alcohol and drug use among youth, as measured in the annual surveys by the University of Michigan Institute for Social Research.

Office of Substance Abuse Prevention, *Young Teens: Who They Are and How to Communicate with Them About Alcohol and Other Drugs,* Health and Human Services Department, February 1991.

An overview of the psychological, sociological and educational aspects of teen drug and alcohol use, giving specific recommendations for prevention programs that bring in all community elements.

Wallack, Lawrence, et al., *TV Beer Commercials and Children: Exposure, Attention, Beliefs and Expectations About Drinking as an Adult,* AAA Foundation for Traffic Safety, fall 1990.

Academic research funded by an affiliate of the American Automobile Association uses survey data to argue for a strong relationship between exposure to alcoholic beverage advertisements and young people's tendency to drink.

Wine and Spirits Wholesalers of America, *Let's Talk About Drinking: A Guide for Families,* 1991.

A booklet of advice in question-and-answer format to educate parents and children on problems of teen drinking and the responsible use of alcohol.

The Next Step

Additional Articles from Current Periodicals from EBSCO Publishing's Database

Advertising

Colford, S. W., "FTC may crash beer promos' campus party," *Advertising Age,* **March 25, 1991, p. 3.**

Announces that the Federal Trade Commission's staff is drafting voluntary guidelines to cover alcohol marketing practices, particularly beer promotion on college campuses and during spring break. Questions of the guidelines' approval; Judith Wilkenfeld, assistant director of advertising practices at the FTC; ongoing investigation into youth-directed advertising; issues addressed by the guidelines.

Hardy, J. E., "This ad's for you," *Scholastic Update,* **Nov. 16, 1990, p. 18.**

Explores the impact of alcohol advertising on teen alcohol consumption. Arguments against such advertising; response from beer and wine companies; why alcohol companies advertise during sports events; mixed messages sent to teenagers.

Siler, J. F., "It isn't Miller time yet, and this Bud's not for you," *Business Week,* **June 24, 1991, p. 52.**

Reports how, faced with growing public concern about drunken driving, fetal alcohol syndrome, and other possible effects of alcohol abuse, the nation's brewers have stepped up their own campaigns to promote responsible drinking and curb teenage consumption. Plans from Anheuser-Busch Cos. and Philip Morris' Miller Brewing Co.; spring break; use and abuse.

Case studies

Glaberson, W., "Quarterback's beer focuses town on drinking rule," *The New York Times,* **Sept. 30, 1991, p. B1.**

Discusses the reaction in East Aurora, N.Y., to the suspension of Matthew J. Plauman, a 17-year-old quarterback, from the high school's athletic teams for an entire season because he was seen drinking beer at a fire department picnic. Others also suspended; criticism.

Karlsberg, E., "Alcoholic teens: their sobering story," *Teen Magazine,* **June 1991, p. 20.**

Gives first-person accounts of two teenage girls' battles with alcoholism. Both girls say that one can stop drinking only if one chooses to do so for oneself. How they started drinking; example of an alcoholic father; the compulsive-addictive personality; treatment programs such as New Beginnings and Alcoholics Anonymous. INSETS: Untitled

(statistics on alcohol-related traffic deaths involving teenagers); Untitled (Where to contact Alcoholics Anonymous).

LeBlanc, A. N. and D. Seltzer, "Drinking in America," *Seventeen,* **March 1990, p. 179.**

Part 1 of 2. Presents a special report on teenage alcoholism. Examines the drinking problems of a teenage girl. Her background; how she was introduced to drugs and alcohol; her parents' reaction; how her problem became worse; how bad it got. INSET: A nation under the influence, by S. Nelson.

LeBlanc, A. N. and D. Seltzer, "Drinking in America," *Seventeen,* **April 1990, p. 77.**

Part 2 of 2. Presents a special report on teenage alcoholism. Looks at the recovery of a 16-year-old alcoholic. How she was helped; her progress.

Colleges & universities

Dodge, S., "Use of beer kegs banned by some colleges and national fraternities," *The Chronicle of Higher Education,* **June 12, 1991, p. A27.**

Details the current move by 34 of the 62 national fraternities that have approved a "risk management" policy that bans beer kegs from chapter houses. Work of the Fraternity Insurance Purchasing Group that helps fraternities take steps to make them more attractive to insurance companies; federal law concerning alcohol and drug policies; national fraternity officials strictly enforcing the ban; recent actions at schools.

Debates & issues

"Alcohol-related traffic fatalities among youth and young adults — United States, 1982-1989," *Journal of the American Medical Association,* **Arpil 17, 1991, p. 1930.**

Summarizes data from the National Highway Traffic Safety Administration's (NHTSA) Fatal Accident Reporting System on trends in alcohol-related traffic fatalities (ARTFs) in the U.S. from 1982 through 1989. Contributing factors to the reduction in ARTFs and impaired driving among young persons; current NHTSA efforts to reduce alcohol-impaired driving among youth and young adults.

Barringer, F., "With teens and alcohol, it's just say when," *The New York Times,* **June 23, 1991, Section 4 p. 1.**

Reports that alcohol, with its staying power as the intoxicant of choice among the young, has become the nation's most persistent problem drug. Children of alcohol, whose numbers have waxed and waned over the centuries; public officials, in recent days and months, have had more and more to say about the dangers of alcohol use by young people.

Bates, M. E. and J. I. Tracey, "Cognitive functioning in young 'social drinkers': Is there impairment to detect?" *Journal of Abnormal Psychology*, August 1990, p. 242.

Presents results of a study to determine whether alcohol intake patterns affect cognitive skills during adolescence. Results show little direct relation between drinking behaviors and cognitive performance in young non-clinical males and females. Need for longitudinal data; subjects; cognitive measures, alcohol and drug measures; more.

DeRanleau, M. and S. Brodner, "Bennett butts out," *Mother Jones*, March/April 1991, p. 20.

Criticizes former drug czar William J. Bennett for not releasing the National Commission on Drug-Free Schools report that concluded alcohol and tobacco are a greater threat than illicit drugs. Bennett's support of Sen. Jesse Helms, R-N.C., who accepted contributions from Philip Morris.

Ellickson, P. L. and R. D. Hays, "Antecedents of drinking among young adolescents with different alcohol use histories," *Journal of Studies on Alcohol*, September 1991, p. 398.

Tests separate path analytic models for seventh-grade users and non-users to assess the impact of cognitive, social influence and behavioral antecedents on adolescent drinking 3 and 12 months later. Method; participants; results; discussion; implications for prevention.

Elson, J., A. Blackman, et al., "Drink until you finally drop," *Time*, Dec. 16, 1991, p. 64.

Focuses on alcohol consumption by America's minors, and a study from the office of Surgeon General Antonia Novello, which found that 8 million of the nation's 20.7 million youths in grades seven through 12 drink every week. Alcohol abuse is not only the No. 1 health problem among young people, it is also the leading cause of death among teenagers. Houses without parents and illegal clubs; boredom, peer pressure and psychological pain.

Foderaro, L. W., "Despite crack, liquor can still hold its teen-agers," *The New York Times*, Oct. 7, 1989, p. 25.

Reports that national surveys show that despite the use of cocaine dominating public concern about drug abuse in teenagers, drinking remains more prevalent among high school seniors than among adults, as the drug of choice. Society as a whole, has to some extent given up the battle to get students not to drink; complacency growing as people become more intolerant of deadlier drugs; Students Against Driving Drunk; anti-drinking campaigns.

Krantz, P., "Is your child hooked on drugs or alcohol?" *Better Homes & Gardens*, February 1990, p. 41.

Discusses the use of drugs and alcohol among 12- to 17-year-olds. How drugs harm; danger signs of use or abuse in teens; why kids use drugs; for parents who suspect use; when to hospitalize; stopping abuse before it starts; how to find help.

McClellan, M. C., "The problem of teenage drinking," *Phi Delta Kappan*, June 1990, p. 810.

Interviews Rosemary Rehak, dean of students at Bloomington (Ind.) High School South; William Bailey, director of the Alcohol-Drug Information Center, Indiana University, Bloomington; and Sigurd Zielke, regional director of clinical education for the Koala Centers, on teenage alcohol consumption. Changes in alcohol use patterns; media messages; adult models; role of public school; education.

Schwartz, S., "Decision factors and program preferences of drug-using and non-using students," *Journal of Drug Issues*, summer 1991, p. 527.

Examines factors considered by high school youth when deciding whether to use alcohol and marijuana along with student perceptions of various drug prevention initiatives. Methods, results, and conclusions; endorsement of interventive strategies; concern about injuring another person; endorsement of information about the consequences of substance abuse; importance of subgroup analyses with reference to drug program design and evaluation.

Wallace, J. M. Jr. and J. G. Bachman, "Explaining racial/ethnic differences in adolescent drug use," *Social Problems*, August 1991, p. 333.

Studies whether the often large racial/ethnic differences in cigarette, alcohol, marijuana and cocaine use are attributable to racial/ethnic differences in background or important lifestyle factors. Results that indicate that controlling for background alone does not account for most racial/ethnic differences in drug use; drug use among Native American youth; more.

Prevention programs

Elkind, D., "Teens and alcohol," *Parents*, January 1991, p. 122.

Looks at alcohol abuse among teenagers and how it develops. Gives parents advice on helping children avoid substance abuse and helping children already addicted.

Hansen, W. B., J. W. Graham, et al., "Program integrity as a moderator of prevention program effectiveness," *Journal of Studies on Alcohol,* November 1991, p. 568.

Reports the results of a test of the quality of program delivery (program integrity) as a variable that may moderate the effectiveness of alcohol prevention programs. Tests the two theory-based programs, Resistance Training and Normative Education, on fifth-grade students. Measurements of program integrity; method; results.

Reports

"Current tobacco, alcohol, marijuana, cocaine use," *Journal of the American Medical Association,* Oct. 16, 1991, p. 2061.

Presents selected data on current use of tobacco, alcohol, marijuana and cocaine use among ninth- to 12th-grade students from two components of the Youth Risk Behavior Surveillance System. Includes an editorial note from the Centers for Disease Control (CDC).

Crowley, J. E., "Educational status and drinking patterns: How representative are college students?" *Journal of Studies on Alcohol,* January 1991, p. 10.

Reports that, using data from a large nationally representative sample, multiple regressions using sex, ethnicity, age, and educational status showed that drinking patterns of college students differed significantly from those of dropouts, high school graduates and former college students. Method; results; discussion.

Kilty, K. M., "Drinking styles of adolescents and young adults," *Journal of Studies on Alcohol,* November 1990, p. 556.

Uses a model that had been applied to "normal" drinking behaviors of adults to study drinking among adolescents and young adults. A typology of drinking behavior has special relevance for this group, since the adolescent years and young adult years are formative in the development of drinking habits. Includes method, results, and discussion; references.

Kreutter, K. J., H. Gewirtz, et al., "Drug and alcohol prevention project for sixth-graders: First-year findings," *Adolescence,* summer 1991, p. 287.

Presents data of the first-year results of a three-year program evaluation for a drug and alcohol prevention project. One hundred fifty-two sixth-graders made up the target group, which received instruction using Botvin's life skills training curriculum. Method; results; discussion.

Social aspects

Chassin, L., F. Rogosch, et al., "Substance use and symptomatology among adolescent children of alcoholics," *Journal of Abnormal Psychology,* November 1991, p. 449.

Assesses the magnitude and specificity of parental alcoholism as a risk factor for internalizing symptomatology, externalizing symptomatology, and alcohol and drug use in adolescence. Method; results; discussion.

Kafka, R. R. and P. London, "Communication in relationships and adolescent substance use: The influence of parents and friends," *Adolescence,* fall 1991, p. 587.

Presents a study that focuses on the openness of communication in teenagers' relationships with mother, father (or parental figure), and closest friend, and its correlation with teenagers' use of cigarettes, alcohol, marijuana, and other drugs. The predictive value for substance use of perceived pressure from friends, friends' substance use, and parents' substance use was also analyzed. Method; results; discussion.

Martin, M. J. and M. E. Pritchard, "Factors associated with alcohol use in later adolescence," *Journal of Studies on Alcohol,* January 1991, p. 5.

Assesses the relative influence of a number of family and individual characteristics on the frequency and intensity of alcohol use in a group of older adolescents. Logistic regression analyses; method; results; discussion.

Traux, S., "To drink?" *Current Health 2,* October 1990, p. 12.

Discusses factors influencing teen drinking of alcohol and what a teenager should consider before making a decision. Peer pressure; influence of advertisements; Spuds McKenzie, part of an extensive campaign directed at young drinkers; family attitude toward alcohol use; choosing not to drink.

Treatment programs

Pardeck, J. T., "Using books to prevent and treat adolescent chemical dependency," *Adolescence,* spring 1991, p. 201.

Presents strategies for using the bibliotherapeutic process to prevent and treat adolescent alcohol and drug abuse. Overviews definitions, goals, and principles of bibliotherapy; presents synopses of several useful books that focus on chemical dependency.

Warner, J. and A. Dunkin, "Helping a teen who just can't say no," *Business Week,* July 15, 1991, p. 149.

Looks at how the treatment for drug- or alcohol-addicted teens has become increasingly sophisticated and gives tips on what to do if your child is at risk. Employee-assistance programs from your company; costs for detoxification and rehabilitation; responsible programs to get involved with.

Back Issues

Great Research on Current Issues Starts Right Here... Recent topics covered by The CQ Researcher are listed below. Issues dated before May 10, 1991, were published under the name of Editorial Research Reports.

SEPTEMBER 1990
Dangers of Alcohol
Western Alliance After the Cold War
Tobacco Industry
Right to Die

OCTOBER 1990
Organ Transplants
Energy Policy Options
Search for Arab Unity
Child Support

NOVEMBER 1990
Lotteries and Gambling
Post-Cold War Choices
Setting Limits on Medical Care
Multicultural Education

DECEMBER 1990
Cable TV Regulation
Americans' Search for Their Roots
Is Insurance System a Failure?
Why Schools Still Have Tracking

JANUARY 1991
Growing Influence of Boycotts
Should the U.S. Reinstate the Draft?
America's Archaeological Past
Peace Corps' Challenges in '90s

Back issues are available for $4.00 (subscribers) or $7.00 (non-subscribers). Quantity discounts apply to orders over ten. To order, call Congressional Quarterly 1-800-432-2250.

FEBRUARY 1991
Regional Impact of Recession
Puerto Rico's Status
Redistricting: Mapping Power
Nuclear Power

MARCH 1991
Acid Rain
Cost of the Gulf War
Reassessing Gun Laws
Future for Man in Space

APRIL 1991
Social Security
Canadian Crisis Over Quebec
California Drought
Electromagnetic Radiation

MAY 1991
School Choice
Racial Quotas
Animal Rights
U.S. and Japan

JUNE 1991
Children and Divorce
Teenage Suicide
Endangered Species
Europe 1992

JULY 1991
Teenagers and Abortion
Soviet Republics Rebel
Mexico's Emergence
Athletes and Drugs

AUGUST 1991
Sexual Harassment
Fetal Tissue Research
Oil Imports
The Palestinians

SEPTEMBER 1991
Police Brutality
Advertising Under Attack
Saving the Forests
Foster Care Crisis

OCTOBER 1991
Pay-Per-View TV
Youth Gangs
Gene Therapy
World Hunger

NOVEMBER 1991
Fast-Food Shake-Up
The Greening of Eastern Europe
Business' Role in Education
Cuba In Crisis

DECEMBER 1991
Retiree Health Benefits
Asian Americans
The Obscenity Debate
The Disabilities Act

JANUARY 1992
Term Limits
Oil Spills
Hunting Controversy
Alternative Medicine

FEBRUARY 1992
Threatened Coastlines
New Era in Asia
Assisted Suicide
Jobs in the '90s

MARCH 1992
Women and Sports

Future Topics

▶ *Solid Waste Crisis*

▶ *The Mafia*

▶ *Welfare Reform*

THE CQ Researcher

PUBLISHED BY CONGRESSIONAL QUARTERLY INC., IN CONJUNCTION WITH EBSCO PUBLISHING

Garbage Crisis

Can a nation of "waste makers" deal with the garbage glut?

THE RECESSION MAY HAVE BANKRUPTED businesses and idled factories, but it has not stopped Americans from producing record amounts of trash. Americans annually toss out enough to fill a bumper-to-bumper convoy of garbage trucks halfway to the moon. But while Americans are discarding more waste, the nation's disposal options seem to be narrowing. Faced with diminishing landfill space, increasing political opposition to landfills and incinerators and lack of markets for recycled materials, communities are at a crossroads. Many seem incapable or unwilling to plan for the future, even as waste-management costs are skyrocketing. Unless government and business leaders can work together with consumers to alleviate the crisis, experts say garbage will not only pose a hazard to the environment but also to the economy.

 March 20, 1992 • Volume 2, No. 11 • 241-264

Formerly Editorial Research Reports

COVER ART: BARBARA SASSA-DANIELS

March 20, 1992
Volume 2, No. 11

EDITOR
Sandra Stencel

MANAGING EDITOR
Thomas J. Colin

ASSOCIATE EDITOR
Richard L. Worsnop

STAFF WRITERS
Charles S. Clark
Mary H. Cooper
Rodman D. Griffin

PRODUCTION EDITOR
Laurie De Maris

EDITORIAL ASSISTANT
Thomas H. Moore

GRAPHICS
Jack Auldridge

PUBLISHED BY
Congressional Quarterly Inc.

CHAIRMAN
Andrew Barnes

VICE CHAIRMAN
Andrew P. Corty

EDITOR AND PUBLISHER
Neil Skene

EXECUTIVE EDITOR
Robert W. Merry

PUBLICATIONS MARKETING/SALES
Robert Smith

EDITOR, EBSCO PUBLISHING
Melissa Kummerer

The CQ Researcher (ISSN 1056-2036). Formerly Editorial Research Reports. Published weekly (48 times per year, not printed the first Friday of any month with five Fridays) by Congressional Quarterly Inc., 1414 22nd St., N.W., Washington, D.C. 20037. Rates are furnished upon request. Second-class postage paid at Washington, D.C. POSTMASTER: Send address changes to The CQ Researcher, 1414 22nd St., N.W., Washington, D.C. 20037.

Garbage Crisis

BY RODMAN D. GRIFFIN

THE ISSUES

The mine-scarred countryside on either side of Interstate 80 in eastern Pennsylvania has the unflattering nickname "Garbage Alley." In the past two years, waste-management companies have built or proposed more than 30 disposal sites — landfills, garbage incinerators, auto-upholstery dumps and hazardous-waste treatment facilities — in a 50-mile radius of the tiny town of Clearfield, north of Allentown.

Ten years ago in this hardscrabble coal country, bumper stickers advised: "If you're hungry and out of work, eat an environmentalist." Today, the strip-mine battles of the 1980s have given way to the fight over trash. Local conservationists, trying to shield their state from truckloads of East Coast garbage, are facing off against the backers of regional landfills. "It's close to a war out here," growls Hillary Bida, a Pennsylvania farmer and environmental activist.

A similar story is told in Center Point, Ind., where citizens resorted to staking out the local landfill and photographing caravans of garbage trucks to prove to state and local officials that the dump had become a destination for out-of-state refuse. During the first three months of last year, about three-quarters of the trash pouring into the Center Point landfill came from New York, New Jersey and the Philadelphia area.[1]

The garbage crisis struck first and hardest in the densely populated Northeast, but it is really a national problem. From Maine to Mississippi, from Maryland to Montana, communities are groping for solutions. The conundrum is obvious: an oversupply of rubbish and an undersupply of

places to put it. The mismatch has sent garbage disposal costs skyrocketing. Landfilling costs, commonly referred to as tipping fees, in some areas of the country now exceed $120 per ton, compared with less than $10 per ton just a few years ago.[2]

As environmental standards become stricter and the siting of new landfills and incinerators encounters increasingly vocal opposition — the "Not In My Back Yard" syndrome, or NIMBY[3] — the stopgap solution for many East Coast localities has been to export the problem. Some 40,000 tons of garbage travel the nation's highways each day — nearly one-tenth of the total waste stream. "It's easier to pay a large premium to ship [garbage] out of state than to pay the political price to expand capacity at home," says Allen Moore, president of the National Solid Wastes Management Association (NSWMA).

Realizing that East Coast waste threatens to overwhelm the Midwest's landfill capacity, many states, including Indiana and Pennsylvania, are legislating roadblocks to slow the influx of garbage. But the Supreme Court has ruled that such laws violate the interstate commerce clause of the Constitution.

"This whole furor over the interstate transportation of garbage is dealing with a symptom of the problem," says Daniel J. Weiss, the Sierra Club's Washington director of environmental quality. "The real disease is that we're running out of space to put our solid waste. We have to find ways of reducing the amount of waste we produce."

Indeed, our wasteful ways are catching up with us. In 1960 Americans discarded 2.7 pounds of trash apiece each day. This figure now stands at 4 pounds a day — almost three-quarters of a ton per year for every man, woman and child, roughly twice the amount generated in Japan and Germany.

"Solid waste generation per capita is going up every year," says Joel Hirschhorn, a solid waste consultant in Washington. "Making waste disposal easier or more economical ultimately is a disservice. It brings us to the 'out-of-sight, out-of-mind' mentality Americans have seized upon."

The garbage crisis didn't appear overnight, of course. Environmentalists warned of it in the 1970s, and some citizens conscientiously toted cans, bottles and paper to recycling centers. But there were scant markets for the recycled material, and enthusiasm faded like last year's newsprint. The urgency seemed to wane as well: Garbage, after all, isn't as frightening as toxic waste. But America's options are narrowing. Federal law prohibits dumping trash into the ocean. Incineration is under attack on economic and environmental grounds. Recycling is gaining popularity, but currently only 13 percent of U.S. solid waste lives again as something else.

In the future, Americans will sim-

What's In Our Garbage?

Paper products are the biggest components of municipal waste, followed by grass clippings and other yard wastes.

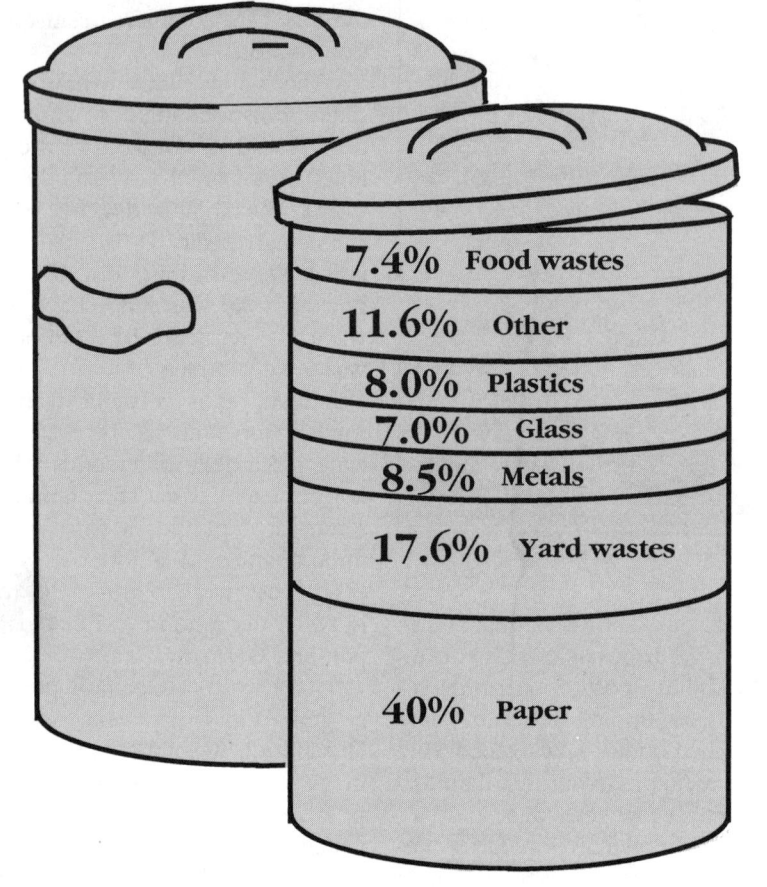

7.4% Food wastes

11.6% Other

8.0% Plastics

7.0% Glass

8.5% Metals

17.6% Yard wastes

40% Paper

Source: U.S. Environmental Protection Agency, Office of Solid Waste

ply not be able to put the more than 180 million tons of solid waste they generate each year into landfills, where 70 percent of it now goes. The Environmental Protection Agency (EPA) estimates that some 18,500 municipal landfills were operating in this country in 1979. Today that number has dwindled to less than 5,000 — and experts project that EPA regulations announced last fall will force the closure of an additional 2,000 dumps over the next three years. *(See story, p. 247.)* By the end of the decade, three-quarters of the nation's existing landfill space will be exhausted or closed.

Garbage woes are hard to cure in a society that annually tosses out 240 million tires, 1.6 billion pens, 2 billion razors and blades and 16 billion disposable diapers. While opinions differ about the severity of the problem and the range of safe and realistic options available to address it, most experts agree that the waste-management challenge is not conducive to quick-fix solutions. Resolving it, they say, will require a long-term, cooperative effort by government policy-makers, industry leaders and consumers. Here are some of the issues that will have to be addressed:

Should recycling programs be mandatory?

Recycling is often depicted as a panacea capable of managing most of the municipal solid waste. Barry Commoner, a noted environmentalist and director of the Center for the Biology of Natural Systems at Queens College in New York, contends that 80 to 90 percent of the waste stream is recyclable.

Most experts, however, say even a 50 percent recycling rate would be extremely ambitious, despite the broad public support recycling enjoys. A 1991 public opinion poll[4] indicated that 86 percent of Americans support mandatory recycling; presently, 40 percent of U.S. recycling programs are mandatory.

Over the past three years, as more states have adopted or expanded recycling laws, the number of curbside collection programs has grown to 3,500 from 600, reaching 15 million households and thousands of office buildings. Even in sparsely populated states with plenty of landfill space, communities see recycling as a way to participate in a nationwide response to pollution from an overflowing waste stream.

The question remains, however, whether mandatory recycling makes prudent policy. "Recycling pursued according to current practices in the United States often results in everyone losing — not only government, business and local communities but also the environment," Professors George C. Lodge and Jeffrey F. Rayport of the Harvard Business School wrote recently. "And the problem is only getting worse."[5]

According to some estimates, the cost of waste collection has quadrupled in New York, and air pollution has worsened in Los Angeles because of the approach to recycling taken in those communities. To introduce recycling collection in Los Angeles, the city had to add 600 diesel trucks to the 1,000-truck fleet already in operation. "Recycling is not cost-free environmentally," notes Washington consultant Hirschhorn. "It involves basic industrial procedures that cause waste and pollution."

Other critics argue that mandatory recycling policies put an extra burden on municipal finances at a time when budgets are strained. "Recycling programs are efficient when they are able to turn a profit," says Jerry Taylor, director of natural resource studies at the Cato Institute, a conservative think tank in Washington. "But most of these mandatory curbside programs aren't profitable. They're simply subsidizing the collection and processing of materials that probably should be buried or burned."

To compare recycling with other waste management methods, experts say, communities must take into account the economic and environmental cost of collection, transportation and reprocessing. A recent report by the Tellus Institute, a public-interest environmental research group in Boston, has done just that. The study looked at the so-called "full life-cycle" costs of recycling, including transport and reprocessing, and compared those with the cost of landfilling or incinerating the same waste, and the cost of making new products out of "virgin" materials. The institute concluded that recycling wins out for aluminum, glass, paper, cardboard and most other recyclable wastes.[6] A possible exception is plastics, which are relatively cheap to make and expensive to recycle. (See story, p. 253.)

For most communities, however, the bottom line is out-of-pocket cost: If it costs $100 a ton to dump garbage in a landfill, recycling a portion of it at $130 a ton actually costs only $30 more than burying it. The recycling system might even break even, because recycling saves expensive landfill space. But at traditional dumping fees of only $25 a ton or less, the same recycling system be-comes a $105-a-ton option — one politically much more difficult to sustain over time.

"Recycling is getting a bad rap in the media," says Naomi Friedman, an analyst at the Institute for Local Self-Reliance in Washington. "It is not seen as an integrated part of the waste-disposal system, but as an add-on cost." In fact, recycling programs have enabled some communities like Naperville, Ill., south of Chicago, and Takoma Park, Md., a suburb of Washington, to cut back on garbage collection days — and thereby save money.

Success stories notwithstanding, recycling programs face a bumpy future. Recycling's biggest problem is lack of markets. "It's always been a chicken-and-egg problem," says the Sierra Club's Weiss. "Companies are reluctant to buy recycled products because of unsteady supply — and communities are reluctant to collect because of the uncertainty of buyers."

What this has meant in the real world is that collection centers in many cities and towns are buried in old newspapers, green wine and beer bottles* and plastic milk jugs that nobody wants. Whereas four years ago New York received $60 a ton for its old newspapers, the city now pays $40 a ton to have them carted away.

Even when markets exist, recycling efforts can be frustrated by a temporary surplus, a shortage of railroad cars or a drop in demand as economically pressed factories cut back production. Newsprint shipments to Europe fell off 18 months ago, for example, when the military commandeered almost all available ocean-shipping containers during the Persian Gulf War buildup.

---

*Recycled glass must be separated by color to meet end-product quality requirements. Since two-thirds of the glass made in the U.S. is clear and only one-tenth is green, there are few markets for green glass.

William D. Ruckelshaus, chief executive of Browning-Ferris Industries Inc. (BFI) and former head of the EPA, sees such disruptions as "temporary and understandable." But he warns that "nothing will kill recycling faster than overreaction" to the problems. "The big danger is that people will get turned off and discouraged," he says. "Unless there is consistent public demand for recycling to continue, the politicians will lose interest in a hurry."[7]

To help absorb the newsprint glut, about 40 newspaper de-inking plants are being planned and built in the United States and Canada. In Pennsylvania, companies are buying old newspapers for insulation and dairy-cow bedding. Minnesota hopes to attract companies that turn old newspapers into such molded products as egg cartons.

"Over time the equation will shift toward recycling," says Ellen Harrison, associate director of the Waste Management Program at Cornell University, "especially if it becomes more efficient in transport and creating markets." But even once markets adjust, recycling 50 percent of the solid waste stream by the year 2000 would still leave some 100 million tons of garbage to be disposed of annually.

"Recycling certainly has its place," says Robert Gould, editor of the *Resource Recovery Yearbook*. "But a lot of people naively think that if they recycle everything, they won't need landfills and [incinerators] anymore. That's clearly not the case anywhere in the world. Even Japan, which is much further along as far as recycling goes, still incinerates 50 percent of its refuse."

Why are incinerators and landfills so difficult to site?

Ensuring adequate garbage disposal ranks third — behind improving public education and providing affordable housing — on the public's list of "extremely serious" local concerns. This was the finding of a poll conducted for the NSWMA by Cambridge Associates Inc. in 1989. But when the 1,500 adults included in the poll were asked whether they favored constructing new landfills or incinerators in their communities, most responded with a resounding no.

"In most of the country there is plenty of land for landfills," says Randy Johnson, county commissioner in Hennepin County, Minn. "What is lacking is the political will to site them." Landfills are still highly controversial, adds the NSWMA's Allen Moore. "Many people think they are unsafe or just don't want them near them."

The fact is that badly constructed and poorly operated landfills have been linked to serious surface-water and ground-water pollution and to dangerous gas emissions. According to the EPA, some 200 municipal landfills have been designated "superfund" sites requiring immediate attention because they pose a serious threat to the environment. The clean-up costs that result from inappropriate landfilling can be enormous, in some instances exceeding $50 million per site. Even today, only about one-quarter of existing landfills are monitored for contamination of ground water, the source of a significant part of the drinking water consumed by Americans.[8]

People object to incinerators for similar reasons: They emit dioxins into the air, and the toxic ash they produce poses additional disposal problems. These days, however, newly built landfills and incinerators are much safer than their predecessors, especially given new guidelines for landfills issued by the EPA last fall. *(See story, p. 247.)* Nevertheless, they still suffer the same perception problem. "Every major community has defeated a waste-disposal project, some fairly, some unfairly," says Cornell's Harrison. "The issue has more to do with public mistrust of private developers and the government than it

does with the technology."

Whether the NIMBY phenomenon is justified or not, it is a reality. And it has been joined by the other acrimonious acronyms: LULU (Locally Undesirable Land Use), MINE (Money is Never Enough) and NIMEY (Not in My Election Year). "It's a lot easier to get a politician to snip a ribbon opening a recycling facility than a landfill," explains Robert Davis, vice president of recycling for BFI, which both hauls garbage and recycles it.[9] Of course, for some communities recycling centers and composting plants aren't welcome either. Though politically correct, they create smells and road traffic that are unacceptable to local residents.

Even if every ounce of garbage could find a home — albeit in some cases more than a thousand miles away — the NIMBY syndrome has confounded the waste-management process. "NIMBY has led to prolonged legal struggles to get landfills and incinerators sited," says Robert Ham, an environmental engineer at the University of Wisconsin. "And that means substantial tax dollars are being wasted." Not to mention time. Already, siting a new waste-disposal facility can take five years or more, and an additional two to three years to obtain a permit and construct the facility.[10]

Part of the problem, according to William Ruckelshaus, is that state governments have been extremely reluctant to exercise their authority: State officials don't want to seem like a Goliath beating down some rural David over garbage disposal. But in Ruckelshaus' view, inaction at the state level has enabled the crisis to fester. In effect, he says, states have delegated responsibility to localities without providing the incentives to make waste management possible.

A notable exception to the trend is Wisconsin, which is siting enough landfill and incinerator capacity to keep up with its needs. Since 1982

the state has legally required municipal and county governments to establish local negotiating committees to respond to applications for landfills. The committees, which include a prescribed number of private citizens as well as elected officials, are empowered to negotiate the financial and other contractual relations between the landfill owner and local governments.

The state's Department of Natural Resources must first approve the environmental and health aspects of a landfill. Then the proposal goes to a siting board, a negotiating forum for the landfill developer and local citizens and, if necessary, the arbitrator of last resort. Of the 33 landfills sited since 1984, only three have gone to arbitration.[11]

Should one state be forced to accept another state's garbage?

Hauling trash over state lines is nothing new. The practice has gone on so quietly and for so long that most states don't even know how much garbage is coming in. What they do know is that their landfills are filling up.

With only seven years of landfill capacity left in Indiana, Hoosier state officials are fighting mad. "We're sick and tired of accepting other people's garbage," Indiana Democratic Gov. Evan Bayh fumed last year.[12] In 1990 Sen. Daniel R. Coats, R-Ind., introduced legislation that would have enabled states to seal their borders to imported trash. The bill passed in the Senate by a 67-18 vote, but it was later killed in conference committee, and has since become entangled in a slow-moving congressional effort to amend the 1976 Resource Conservation and Recovery Act (RCRA), which governs waste treatment and handling.*

_____

*Sen. Coats plans to reintroduce his bill next month if there is no action on RCRA reauthorization before then.

Say Goodbye to the Town Dump

Ever since the 1970s the prevailing thought within the environmental movement has been that small is somehow always better. These days, however, that common wisdom has been turned on its head. At least when it comes to landfills, the slogan of the 1990s is "big is beautiful."

Last September, the Environmental Protection Agency (EPA) announced new regulations that during the next few years may force the closure of half the nation's 5,000 landfills — particularly smaller, "open" landfills. Such dumps often create uncontrolled, explosive methane gas and leach hazardous fluids into surface and ground water. Perhaps half of all U.S. wells are still being contaminated by poor waste-management practices, environmentalists say.

The new standards will require virtually all landfills to monitor adjacent ground water for the presence of 45 organic chemicals and 25 metals that could be leached from the municipal garbage. The rules also require new and expanded landfills to use double liners made of flexible materials, to install pipes to collect tainted water that leaches through the trash and to continue environmental management of the sites for 30 years after their closure.

To bring the remaining landfills up to code will cost at least $330 million, and possibly more, according to the EPA. With costs so huge, the big winners will be the large waste companies, since only they can afford the new landfill technologies. Modern landfills — with their liners and gas and liquid drainage systems — cost $400,000 to $700,000 an acre, not counting the land itself.

Economies of scale and the expense of finding sites where the locals are friendly also encourage these companies to gather garbage on a regional basis. "With the cost of construction you need a pretty decent-sized volume to offset your fixed costs," says Kevin J. Sullivan of Waste Management Inc. "And you'd rather have one site instead of 10 or 20 — it's just easier to manage ... and to site."

Although they are wary of their waste-management bedfellows, many national environmental leaders say the firms' enlightened role is a price worth paying for better ground-water protection. "We can't be asking for very strict, environmentally protective design features at landfills or incinerators or recycling facilities without expecting big money to have to be involved," says Allen Hershkowitz, senior scientist at the Natural Resources Defense Council. "And big money is usually accompanied by big companies."

"I'm not saying I'm necessarily pleased with this," Hershkowitz continues, "but the record right now is that the larger facilities tend to be better operated in large part because they are run by better-capitalized companies that are more vulnerable to regulatory enforcement."

For the most part, the controversy pits rich industrialized states against their poorer rural neighbors. Landfill capacity in 22 states — mainly in the highly populated regions of the Northeast and Midwest and in Florida — is expected to be exhausted in less than 10 years.* Lawmakers from these areas oppose legislation that would make it more expensive, or impossible, to get rid of their trash.

For one thing, argues Sen. Bill Bradley, D-N.J., today's trash importers may be tomorrow's trash exporters. New Jersey, which now exports half its garbage and is the focus of other states' ire, was a net garbage importer just a decade ago. Ironically, it is a 1978 Supreme Court decision preventing New Jersey from banning out-of-state trash that now impedes other states from blockading New Jersey's waste. In applying the interstate commerce clause of the U.S. Constitution, the court declared that garbage is a commodity to be treated no differently from any other item of commerce.[13]

Besides, opponents of interstate garbage bans argue, many communities welcome trash imports as a way to bolster their local economies. Gilliam County, Ore., for example, wanted Seattle's garbage so badly it fought Oregon state legislators' attempts to tax out-of-state garbage coming into Oregon. Seattle's decision to use the Gilliam County landfill generated $1 million in 1991 for the community, money that was used to improve schools, roads and other community facilities. That's not small change for a community with only 1,800 inhabitants.

"Communities are entering into private contracts," says Taylor of the Cato Institute. "They are fully responsible for environmental hazards. If they choose to accept the trash, why is it anyone else's business?"

Legislators whose states have been targeted for waste exports, however, don't always buy that logic. They see themselves as victims of the other states' excesses. "Interstate garbage

*The National Solid Wastes Management Association is compiling data on state landfill capacity. The association is scheduled to release its findings in May.

What Happens to Our Garbage?

Currently only 13 percent of the nation's waste is recycled. Most of the rest is put in landfills.

Milions of tons per year

Note: Percentages may not add due to rounding.
Source: National Solid Wastes Management Association

haulers promise prosperity to depressed rural areas," Sen. Nancy Landon Kassebaum, R-Kan., noted at a hearing last June. "But these firms are not philanthropists concerned about rural America — big money is involved. Garbage is a byproduct of prosperity, not a precondition for it."[14]

Indeed, the nation's largest waste management companies, such as Waste Management Inc. and BFI, have expended large sums on public relations campaigns to convince rural communities of the merits of garbage — and have profited handsomely from their efforts.[15]

Ultimately, most people in the waste-disposal industry agree that it's ludicrous to send garbage rolling hundreds of miles. Trucking trash — or sending it by rail[16] — at best is a short-term fix. At worst, it's a waste of millions of dollars. New Jersey alone spends more than $100 million a year unloading its refuse.

But as long as the marketplace — and the courts* — favor garbage exports, the practice is likely to continue. Ironically, many of the states crying foul, including Indiana and Pennsylvania, are sending millions of

---

*A Michigan case involving the export of solid waste will be taken up by the Supreme Court this June.

tons of their own trash on the road. All but 12 states are garbage importers *and* exporters. Experts say the challenge is to shorten the distance by fostering regional cooperation — neighboring states working together to solve the universal problem of garbage disposal.

"This is not really an environmental issue as much as it is a political issue," says Allen Hershkowitz, senior scientist at the Natural Resources Defense Council (NRDC). "The issue is not how far [the garbage] goes, but what kind of facility it ends up in. Half the material sent is recyclable and shouldn't be part of the waste stream to begin with." ∎

BACKGROUND

Problems Pile Up

Over 2,500 years ago, government officials in the Greek city-state of Athens opened the world's first recorded municipal landfill, decreeing that wastes were to be transported at least one mile beyond the city gates. Like many Greek innovations, however, the practice of waste removal was lost in medieval Europe, where urban dwellers continued to toss their trash out the window until the 14th century.

During Colonial times, America's waste-management techniques were hardly more sophisticated. Believing that the supply of land and natural resources was boundless, the colonists simply dumped their waste in a convenient spot or burned it as a source of fuel. It wasn't until the mid-19th century that several cities established boards of health and passed ordinances against indiscriminate dumping of refuse.[17]

As the population grew and the country urbanized, the volume of discarded solid waste increased. Yet Americans continued to depend on rather primitive dumping practices. By the late 1800s, New York City's street cleaning commissioner reported that garbage "defiled the beaches in an intolerable degree." In cities across the country, trash sometimes accumulated into chest-high piles of kitchen slops, cinders, pots, boots and manure. Rain turned it to slime; dry, it was dusty. As Rudyard Kipling said of Chicago: "I desire urgently never to see it again. Its air is dirt."[18]

Although municipalities felt little pressure to develop alternatives to open dumping, garbage posed sanitary and aesthetic problems that required a different method of disposal. But early waste-reduction schemes, such as converting garbage to fertilizer and grease to soap, produced foul odors and proved to be economically inviable.

In response, the first American garbage incinerator was constructed on Governor's Island, New York, in 1895. By 1920 there were incinerators in 12 American cities, and on the eve of World War II some 700 incinerators were in operation. Then, rather abruptly, incinerators fell into a period of decline. The advantages were plain (they burned garbage up), but so were the disadvantages (they discharged foul odors, noxious gases and gritty smoke). Aesthetic concerns, combined with high construction costs and poor operating practices, ultimately led municipalities to begin shutting down their incinerators in the 1950s.

By then, America had turned from open dumping to the sanitary landfill as the preferred method for waste disposal.* But still, little consideration was given to the potential environmental consequences. Disposal sites were often located on wetlands, marshes, quarries and gravel pits — the most convenient places to discard waste. World War II brought about a resurgence in recycling and reclamation of glass, paper and metals, but the patriotic obligation ended with the war. Although the secondary-materials industries continued to function, the recycling ethic was virtually discarded by the emerging consumer society.

Packaging of goods took on new significance. One of the reasons was the rise of self-service merchandising through supermarkets and other consumer outlets. This new direction in marketing required packages that would help sell the product or reduce theft or damage of products

---

*Early "sanitary landfills" differed from open dumps in that they were layered: 12 inches of garbage were covered with 18 to 24 inches of ashes or street sweepings; then another layer of garbage. Chemicals were sometimes sprayed on the fill to retard putrefaction.

(packaging now makes up one-third of all waste). For the sake of convenience, non-returnable bottles and cans replaced returnables — a practice heavily promoted by the powerful liquor and soft-drink lobbies.

Government Takes Notice

As the amount of waste mounted, so did the costs of collecting and disposing of it. In 1940, local governments had spent only $300 million on the task; by the early 1960s, the figure had risen to about $1 billion. The federal Solid Waste Disposal Act of 1965 recognized that the problem had become a national one and declared that federal leadership and assistance were required to find better methods of disposal.

Nevertheless, until the environmental movement gained popular support in the late 1960s and early '70s, few municipalities implemented stringent landfill operating procedures to protect the environment. Waste managers did not always recognize the potential dangers posed by badly polluted wastewater leaching from landfills into surrounding aquifers and surface waters. In addition, no efforts were undertaken to control highly explosive methane gas, which is naturally produced in landfills during the decomposition process.

A series of federal actions — beginning with passage of the Resource Conservation and Recovery Act in 1976 — called upon the EPA to monitor state management of dumps and to pressure officials to close those that leak toxic liquids or gases. The 1976 law launched the nation's hazardous-waste management program and focused attention on conserving energy and other resources, but it said very little about the critical questions of garbage and recycling. In practice the RCRA covers less than 9 percent of the nation's waste.

Although some states, such as Oregon and Vermont, passed bottle bills and other recycling legislation on

The Problem With Problem Wastes

When most people think of garbage, they think of discarded newspapers, plastic packaging, used soup cans, food wastes, etc. But while such items contribute to the nation's garbage crisis, they are not as difficult to dispose of as the items listed below.

Motor oil: About 180 million gallons of used motor oil and 390 million gallons of oil from businesses are thrown into the trash or poured down sewers each year (an amount 57 times greater than the *Exxon Valdez* spill). Cheap oil prices have resulted in only a 10 percent recycling rate for used motor oil in recent years.

Tires: Only 14 percent of the 240 million tires discarded each year are recycled or incinerated with energy recovery. An additional 44.5 million tires are reused. The remainder, about 200 million tires a year, are thrown in stockpiles, joining the estimated 2 bil-

lion to 3 billion tires already there. Such stockpiles are a fire hazard and can be breeding grounds for disease-carrying mosquitoes.

Batteries: Even though about 90 percent of the lead-acid batteries sold in the United States are recycled each year, a recent EPA report found that the discarded ones are still a major source of lead in municipal waste. New laws aim to capture the remaining 10 percent for recycling.

Appliances: Only 7 percent of the 3 million tons of major appliances — stoves, washing machines and refrigerators — discarded each year are recycled. Scrap dealers are often reluctant to accept appliances because some older models contain PCBs (polychlorinated biphenyls), which make them too expensive to handle.

Source: National Solid Wastes Management Association

---

their own, markets faltered and recycling failed to capture significant portions of the waste stream. Meanwhile, 300 to 400 new municipal landfills were being built each year.

Thus the stage was set for the serious solid-waste management dilemma facing America today. Most municipalities in the U.S. became heavily dependent on landfilling for disposing of waste and were, in most instances, unaware of the construction technology and operating procedures necessary to avoid the serious environmental and safety hazards. These problems led to strict federal and state guidelines that have since forced the closing of thousands of landfill sites throughout the country.

A few notorious cases of groundwater pollution at industrial dumps, such as at Love Canal in upstate New York, and many less spectacular cases involving city garbage dumps made the public sensitive to any de-

cision involving landfills. When the EPA undertook a survey in 1986, it found that there were still 1,000 open pits in use and that 5 percent of the municipal landfills had never been inspected.

Foreign Comparisons

Higher population densities forced Japan and a number of countries in Western Europe to face the environmental faults of landfills long before the United States had to. Those nations experienced shortages of dumping space and rising landfill costs much sooner. Their lower waste-generation rates, higher levels of recycling and greater reliance on incineration reflect this earlier awakening to landfill problems.

Japan, for instance, burns 43 to 53 percent of its garbage and recycles another 26 to 39 percent. West Germany, when it was a separate nation, incinerated 27 percent of its solid

waste and planned to increase that number to 50 percent by 1995. Its citizens recycled about one-third of their paper, aluminum and glass. Several Western European nations, including Denmark, France, Sweden and Switzerland, throw half or less of their waste into landfills.[19] In contrast, the United States landfilled more than 80 percent of its waste until the late 1980s, and still buries nearly three-quarters of it.

Remember the *Mobro*

If the garbage glut seemed abstract to Americans, it became ominously real in the summer of 1987. It was then that an ill-fated scow called the *Mobro* left Islip, Long Island, carrying some 3,000 tons of garbage and sailed into America's collective con-

Continued on p. 252

Chronology

1800s-1930s
Open dumping is the waste-disposal method of choice, but as sanitation conditions worsen, communities begin to consider other alternatives.

1885
The nation's first garbage incinerator is built on Governor's Island in New York.

1898
Col. George E. Waring, New York City's street cleaning commissioner, organizes the first rubbish-sorting plant for recycling in the U.S.

1930
New York City and Fresno, Calif., become the first U.S. cities to experiment with sanitary landfill technology.

1940s-1960s
The consumer society generates larger volumes of waste. The country continues to rely almost exclusively on sanitary landfills for disposal.

1959
American Society of Civil Engineers publishes the standard guide to sanitary landfilling. To guard against rodents and odors, the guide suggests compacting the refuse and covering it with a layer of soil each day.

1965
The first federal solid-waste management law, the Solid Waste Disposal Act, authorizes research and provides for state grants.

1970s
Environmental awareness peaks, and legislators respond by passing laws to clean up toxic dump sites and to encourage voluntary recycling.

1970
Nation celebrates first Earth Day. The 1970 Resource Recovery Act amends the Solid Waste Disposal Act and requires the federal government to issue waste-disposal guidelines.

1971
Oregon passes the nation's first bottle bill.

1973
The Arab oil embargo engenders new interest in waste-to-energy incinerators.

September 1976
Congress passes the Resource Conservation and Recovery Act, creating the first significant role for the federal government in waste management. The law emphasizes energy conservation and launches the nation's hazardous-waste management program.

1978
U.S. Supreme Court strikes down — as an infringement of federal power to regulate commerce — a New Jersey law forbidding the importation of solid or liquid waste originated or collected out of state. In applying the commerce clause of the U.S. Constitution, the court declares that garbage is a commodity to be treated no differently from any other item of commerce.

1980s
As the garbage crisis hits home, the federal government sets new waste-disposal guidelines and states begin to experiment with mandatory recycling legislation.

1986
Rhode Island enacts the nation's first statewide mandatory recycling law. Citizens and businesses must separate recyclables from their trash.

1987
The *Mobro,* the Islip, N.Y., garbage barge, is turned away by six states and three countries, drawing public attention to the landfill capacity shortage in the Northeast.

Sept. 22, 1988
Environmental Protection Agency (EPA) sets waste management priorities, favoring source reduction, followed by recycling, incineration and landfilling.

1990s
Communities and business rally behind recycling but markets falter, leading the government to contemplate more intervention.

April 16, 1991
McDonald's Corp. announces plan that aims to reduce waste in its 8,500 U.S. restaurants by 80 percent.

Sept. 9, 1991
EPA announces tougher standards for landfills, such as requirements for double liners, special collection systems to protect ground water and 30-year monitoring of sites after they close.

Continued from p. 250

science. The barge was looking for a place to get rid of its cargo. North Carolina turned it away. So did five other states, including Florida and Louisiana, as well as Belize, the Bahamas and Mexico. After 57 forlorn days on the high seas, the *Mobro* returned to New York, still bearing its by now infamous load. Three and a half months later, the trash was burned and finally buried back home in Islip.

The plight of the *Mobro* captured the public's attention — and shocked policy-makers. Practically every locality was united in the need to reduce the amount of garbage going to the landfill. The question was how to do it in the most economic, least divisive and most environmentally benign way.

One frequently used, but increasingly controversial alternative is burning trash to boil water, creating steam for generating electricity. Amid skyrocketing fuel costs and a fear of resource shortages in the late 1970s, incinerators had experienced a rebirth. They were modified and renamed "waste-to-energy" plants. Also referred to as "resource-recovery" plants, these newfangled facilities promised to provide steam and electricity while simultaneously reducing trash volume by 90 percent.

The United States currently has some 130 such waste-to-energy plants in operation, and another 20 or so are under construction, according to NSWMA. But more than 60 others have been blocked, canceled or delayed. What once seemed an innovative solution to two problems encountered serious operational problems as well as public opposition.[20] *(See story, p. 255.)*

Waste Management Hierarchy

In 1988 the EPA set up what is now commonly referred to as the "waste management hierarchy" to minimize dependence on landfills.

While most communities will clearly need to rely on an integrated approach to waste management, incorporating a combination of disposal methods, the EPA concluded that waste reduction should be the first priority, followed by recycling, waste-to-energy incineration and, finally, landfilling.

Widely accepted by environmentalists and industrialists, EPA's plan set ambitious goals to be reached by the end of 1992:

■ Reduce the amount of waste created by 25 percent through such means as reduced packaging.

■ Boost the overall recycling rate to 25 percent.

■ Incinerate 20 percent of the remaining garbage in waste-to-energy plants.

■ Reserve landfills for materials that cannot be burned or recycled, as well as for the often-toxic ash that results from incineration.

It's already clear that the country will fall far short of EPA's 1992 targets, but many experts credit the

plan with prompting action at the state and local level.

One of the best examples of an integrated approach to waste management is none other than Islip, N.Y., once a national symbol for America's reluctance to clean up after itself. Embarrassed by the *Mobro* affair into taking stronger action, the community made recycling of glass, metal cans and paper mandatory. It also provided for separate collection of grass clippings and other yard wastes, the biggest components of municipal waste after paper. *(See chart, p. 244.)* Ninety-five percent of Islip households are participating in the recycling program, and the community now has one of the largest municipal composting facilities in the country. But while recycling is an important disposal strategy, Islip Supervisor Frank Jones says that 50 percent of the town's waste stream is disposed of in its new waste-to-energy facility. "It's dangerous for a community to put all its solid-waste eggs in one basket," he says.   ■

CURRENT SITUATION

Heaps of Trouble

"Historians may allude to this as the Throwaway Age," social critic Vance Packard wrote in his 1960 classic, *The Waste Makers*. Three decades later, his description of the second half of the 20th century is still apt. In fact, in the United States the throwaway society has grown ever more disposable, substituting squeezable plastic ketchup bottles for glass, generating more than 12 billion glossy mail-order catalogs each year and annually burying

some 1 billion individual foil-lined boxes of fruit juice, complete with shrink wrapping and a plastic-encased straw on the side.

America's garbage glut is epitomized by the crisis in New York City, which by itself generates some 27,000 tons of garbage daily, with half of that being exported to Pennsylvania and the Midwest. The forced closure of dumps has left New York's 7 million people with just one landfill, Fresh Kills, the world's largest, sprawling over 4,950 acres on Staten Island. Within the next decade, when this monument to the throwaway society reaches a height nearly twice that of the Statue of Liberty, it will be closed.

At that point, New York will either pay more to send its garbage else-

Continued on p. 254

Legacy of the Plastics Revolution

They are everywhere: coffee cups and burger boxes, trash and grocery bags, diapers and margarine tubs and containers for everything from milk to anti-freeze — billions of pieces of trash, all made of seemingly indestructible plastic.

The statistics of the Plastics Revolution are mindboggling: The United States produces 60 billion pounds of plastic resins annually, and sales of plastic products exceed $150 billion a year. Demand is so intense that companies like Dow Chemical are operating plants at full tilt. Every hour of every day, Americans use 2.5 million plastic bottles.

But whether they have thought about it or not, the people who purchase all this plastic are also buying into a Faustian bargain: Sooner or later plastic turns into garbage, and the stuff degrades so slowly that mankind may spend eternity with the computer keyboards and microwave trays people buy so eagerly today. Roughly a third of all plastic is sold as disposable products with useful lives measured in days or sometimes minutes.

As part of the landfill problem, plastics are relatively benign — they don't cause serious leaching problems, for example. But they do take up space. Plastics constitute only 8 percent of municipal solid waste by weight, but 18 percent by volume. Moreover, based on industry predictions that worldwide consumption of plastics will grow 50 percent during the 1990s, it is likely that their weight and volume proportion in the waste stream will grow.

Rumblings from U.S. voters — an overwhelming majority of whom see plastics as the cause of the solid-waste crisis — are setting off an avalanche of legislation that business leaders fear could bury the plastics industry. In 1990 alone, more than 500 laws were proposed by state and local governments regulating the use of plastics, through packaging taxes, degradability requirements and other restrictions that could significantly raise the cost of making products with plastic.

To fight such efforts, plastics companies began promoting the use of "biodegradable" plastics. But biodegradable plastics have a problem: Their decomposition is dependent on exposure to sun and water — two things that landfills are specifically designed to lack. Even naturally biodegradable materials like paper and food do not break down in many landfills because of lack of mois-

ture, oxygen or warmth, as "garbologist" William Rathje of the University of Arizona has shown. He dug up newspapers from the 1950s that were readable and mummified hot dogs that were intact, if not exactly edible.

"The word 'biodegradable' has been abused by the plastics industry," says Joel Hirschhorn, a consultant in Washington. "Biodegradable plastics are 80 to 90 percent conventional plastics. When they finally do decompose, they leave residues of powder that could be more dangerous than the original product."

More important, if biodegradable plastics ever became more commonplace, they would complicate plastics recycling, now seen as the more likely practice in the future. Certain types of plastics have relatively high recycling rates *(see box)*, but overall, only 1 percent of plastics are recycled.

"People don't realize just how cheap plastics are to manufacture," says Hirschhorn. "Unless taxes are put on virgin material, [recycling] may never be economically practical." Though recycled plastics can fetch $200 per ton, it takes a lot of plastic shopping bags to tip the scales.

There are other limitations as well. The Food and Drug Administration will not permit recycled plastic to be used to serve or store food, since it cannot be decontaminated. Furthermore, different plastics have different chemical makeup, which complicates sorting them. And some products — like squeezable ketchup bottles — are made of up to six layers of polymers, making them virtually useless for reprocessing.

Between the collection problems and the sorting problems, experts doubt anyone will get rich recycling plastic anytime soon. But increasingly, secondary uses are being found for what is euphemistically called post-consumer plastic: Plastics are being reborn as park benches, flower pots and filler for ski jackets.

"The future of plastics recycling is still a total mystery," says Robert Ham, an environmental engineer at the University of Wisconsin. "We can't build an effective plastics recycling program by churning out boutique products." Indeed, it would take 98 million four-foot park benches to use up the 6 million tons of plastic packaging produced in this country each year. Then again, plastics recycling is still in its infancy. Phase II of the Plastics Revolution may be just around the corner.

Giving New Life to Plastics

Some plastics are easier to recycle than others:

PET: polyethylene terephthalate (vegetable-oil and soda bottles); 5 percent recycled as carpet, paint containers, auto parts, tennis balls, shower curtains.

HDPE: high-density polyethylene (milk and detergent jugs, dull grocery bags); 32 percent recycled as detergent and engine-oil bottles, plastic lumber, recycling bins, soft-drink base cups, combs.

PVC: polyvinyl chloride (vegetable-oil bottles, food wrap); 10 percent recycled as tile, drainage pipe.

LDPE: low-density polyethylene (glossy grocery bags, bread bags); 34 percent recycled as garbage bags, recycling bins.

PP: polypropylene (jar lids, tubs and syrup bottles); 10 percent recycled as grocery-basket handles, auto batteries.

PS: polystyrene (foamed fast-food ware, clear flatware and salad boxes); 9 percent recycled as desk accessories, trays, insulation, packing "peanuts," VCR cassettes.

Source: R.W. Beck and Associates

Continued from p. 252

where, or rely on another alternative to trash disposal. Already, tipping fees at Fresh Kills have jumped from roughly $55 per ton in 1988 to more than $120 per ton today.

"The polarization between recycling and incineration has been so extreme," says Marian Chertow, director of the Program on Solid Waste Policy at Yale University, "that the city has been immobilized. Some government leaders favor incineration, environmentalists want only recycling and composting and communities want none of the above, at least not in their back yard." The result: New York has no waste-to-energy incinerators, one leaf composting plant and just one government recycling center in East Harlem.

In 1989 the city started curbside recycling — reaching 1.8 million households — but the program hasn't exactly turned trash into cash. Recycling cost New York roughly $127 million in 1991, and Mayor David N. Dinkins proposed suspending the program for one year to alleviate the city's budget crisis. "On top of the political problems, New York's recycling program has been hampered by a host of structural problems," says Chertow, "including an old fleet of trucks, a unionized work force and an entrenched bureaucracy."

The mounting crisis has inspired the city to prepare a 20-year solid-waste management plan, its first integrated waste plan ever. Taking up 600 pages of text and some 12,000 pages of appendixes, the plan is scheduled to be released in early April. However, surmounting New York's problems will not be easy. "We have a problem-plagued recycling program," concedes Jim Meyer, deputy director for policy planning at New York's Office of Waste Management. "But we are confident we can redirect it and make it cost-effective. But it will take a few years — and some innovations."

Seattle Digs Out

Many other American cities, particularly older ones, share the same political inertia as New York. One exception is Seattle, which has taken a different — and more successful — approach to dealing with waste. When faced with the task of cleaning up two superfund landfill sites in the early 1980s, at a cost of $78 million, the city initially sought to build an incinerator. But in 1988, after years of contentious hearings, the city changed its strategy.

"There was just too much citizen opposition" to the incinerator, recalls Deputy Mayor William Stafford. "When it became clear that it would be very difficult to site the facility, the energy went elsewhere."[21] Instead Seattle adopted an ambitious waste reduction, recycling and composting plan.

The program has four main components that distinguish it from programs in most other cities. First, the city set up a separate solid waste utility, ensuring greater accountability and efficiency. Second, the city contracted out recycling collection on a competitive basis, reducing bureaucracy and cost. Third, it established a "pay-as-you-throw" program, whereby households pay for disposal by the can, creating incentives for reducing waste. And finally, the city invested heavily in the program, spending a fair amount of money publicizing it.

The results are impressive. The city boosted its recycling rate from 22 percent in 1985 to 33 percent in 1990. Seattle also composts 7 percent of its municipal waste. Together the two programs have reduced the amount of waste requiring disposal by 40 percent. Seattle hopes to bring that figure up to 60 percent by 1998.

Recycling Mania

With amazing speed, recycling has shed its tie-dyed image, attracted investment from big business and inspired political passion. Over the course of just a few years it has evolved into a $14 billion industry. According to the Institute for Self-Reliance, at least 10 cities boast recycling rates greater than 25 percent.[22] Yet the national rate is still just 13 percent (one of the lowest recycling rates of any industrialized country).

"A common myth is that all you have to do is collect the stuff and someone will buy it," says William Ferretti, an official of the New York State Department of Economic Development. "Recycling is a market-based activity." Indeed, until those commodities are taken somewhere else and used again, the recycling loop is incomplete.

Successful recycling on a larger scale will depend on finding markets for recycled products. What follows is a status report on the potential markets for recyclable materials:

Aluminum: Turning bauxite into new aluminum is 10 times more expensive than reprocessing used cans. That's one key reason some 55 percent of all aluminum beverage cans are recycled today. Even so, Americans still toss out enough aluminum every three months to rebuild the nation's entire airline fleet.

Glass: Reusing old glass also costs less than forging virgin materials. To date only 13 percent of it is recycled, but markets are growing steadily. Several states have passed laws requiring the use of crushed glass in "glassphalt" (a combination of glass and asphalt) to pave roads.

Paper: Industry officials like to boast that nearly 30 percent of all paper products consumed in this country are recycled, turning up in cereal boxes, toilet paper, even bedding for farm animals. Still, that leaves more than 50 million tons clogging landfills and going up smokestacks annually.

Yard Waste: Composting leaves and grass clippings could eliminate nearly one-fifth of the nation's waste,

Continued on p. 256

Are Incineration and Recycling Compatible?

Twenty years ago, even some environmentalists thought the United States could burn its way out of the garbage mess. The Arab oil embargo of the early 1970s generated support for new waste-to-energy plants, in which garbage is burned to produce steam for generating electricity. But that enthusiasm quickly dissipated as many of the first waste-to-energy plants belched toxic fumes into the atmosphere — when they worked at all.

Baltimore's experiment with incineration was typical. The city, as part of an Environmental Protection Agency (EPA) plan to demonstrate waste-conversion technology, spent $25 million to build a waste-to-energy plant. But that facility, operated by Monsanto Co., had constant problems with its shredders, combustion temperature and air-pollution controls. Two years later, Monsanto walked away from the project, leaving behind a smelly fiasco. The plant closed in 1981 — five years after it opened.

The problem with many early plants was that they were based on European technology. Builders discovered that European garbage was not like the home-grown variety. For one thing, U.S. waste is full of plastics, which produce high temperatures and corrosive gases. And Americans throw out everything from old refrigerators to used motor oil. So standard mass-burn plants that had been used successfully in Switzerland, Germany and Denmark since the 1950s couldn't handle American trash.

Supporters of waste-to-energy plants insist that initial operating problems have largely been overcome. "Over the last decade," says Richard Magee, director of the Hazardous Substances Management Research Center at the New Jersey Institute of Technology, "the levels of dioxins coming from incineration have been reduced a thousandfold."

Newer plants are equipped with high-temperature furnaces, scrubbers and other state-of-the-art pollution-abatement systems. And instead of shoveling garbage into a furnace wholesale, some modern plants sort it and convert it into so-called "refuse-derived fuel" before incineration. But critics say the plants cost on average $400 million to $500 million and still produce a toxic residue that has to be landfilled.

The big stink over incineration has as much to do with politics as it does with pollution. "Because most city trash can be burned or recycled, but not both, construction of incinerators would block the expansion of recycling and reduce its economic advantages," argues environmentalist Barry Commoner.† Incinerators and large-scale recycling programs compete for paper, plastic and other recyclables with high heating value to fuel boilers for peak burning. As reduction and recycling programs mature, they pull tons of material out of the waste stream — materials that otherwise go to incinerators.

Already some communities that are recycling much of their own waste are scrambling to find others' waste to feed their garbage burners. Newark, N.J.'s, incinerator was guaranteed by Essex Country officials to receive 1,800 tons of garbage a day. The county can deliver only half that amount, because the population is down and recycling is up (to 39 percent). The shortfall has left officials scouting other counties to get more trash to burn. The reason: Essex County has a "put-or-pay" contract with the incinerator operator to deliver enough trash or give up more cash (in penalties).

Essex County's dilemma defines the real world problem for solid-waste managers: Efficient recycling of high-energy-yielding garbage undercuts revenue for incineration. A few years ago, New Jersey, which has had mandatory recycling for five years, planned to build 22 new incinerators; now officials say they need just two.

In most cases, however, when these two waste-management options clash, incineration wins. In 1989, for example, Babylon, N.Y., could not meet the 225,000 tons a year requirement for its incinerator and had to burn half of the newspapers it had collected for recycling. Few civic-minded officials are willing to turn their backs on a half-billion-dollar capital investment.

Although recycling holds the edge in creating new jobs, protecting the environment and conserving natural resources, many government officials still favor incinerators. There is always demand for the energy they produce, whereas recycling markets are still very much in flux. A 1987 survey by *New York Newsday* found that state governments had spent 39 times as much money on incineration as on recycling programs.

"The old burn vs. recycle debate is outdated," says Jim Meyer, deputy director for policy planning at New York City's Office of Waste Management. "We have to look at integrated waste management, a concept that hasn't entered into the public conscience. If we are to get out of this mess we will need both incineration and recycling."

Allen Hershkowitz, senior scientist at the Natural Resources Defense Council, agrees that the two waste-management techniques can be compatible — but only if incineration practices are made more efficient. "At present, 60 to 70 percent of what goes into incinerators is recyclable, non-combustible or compostable," he says. "Before we build more incinerators, we should give more environmentally benign strategies a chance."

---

†Op-ed article in *The New York Times*, May 29, 1991. Although recycling programs can be more expensive to operate, capital costs for incineration are roughly three times those for recycling facilities capable of handling the same amount of trash.

Continued from p. 254

but composting programs divert less than 2 percent of yard waste and are just now beginning to gain attention. The EPA estimates that the amount of composted yard waste will rise from 500,000 tons in 1988 to 9.5 million tons in 1995.

Plastics: The U.S. produces 62 billion pounds of plastic resins annually, and sales of plastic products exceed $150 billion a year. Yet only 1 percent of plastics is recaptured. Manufacturers are scrambling to find new uses, from plastic park benches to filler for ski jackets, but serious technological and environmental problems are hindering the effort. (See story, p. 253.)

"We see garbage not as a problem but as a resource, an opportunity for business," says recycling expert Naomi Friedman. "Beyond being environmentally benign, recycling can create economic growth. We're used to exporting waste paper to Asia, then importing it as finished products. That's absurd. Why not do the reprocessing here?"

Corporations Join the Bandwagon

Though slow to respond — and some say reacting out of fear rather than conviction — many major players in the business community have jumped on the recycling bandwagon. International Business Machines Corp. now recycles its computer housings. By 1994, AT&T plans to cut paper use by 15 percent and to recycle at least 35 percent of its waste. Last March, the plastics industry, led by E. I. Du Pont de Nemours & Co. and Procter & Gamble Co., announced a program to extend plastics recycling to 5,000 communities and to ensure that by 1995, 25 percent of all plastic bottles and containers used in the United States will be recycled (from about 6 percent in 1991). In fact, Procter & Gamble has already switched to 100 percent recycled plastics for all of its Spic & Span bottles

and has reached 25 percent recycled material in its other laundry and cleaning products and packaging.

As laudable as the proposal is, however, some experts say it is bound to be insufficient for two reasons. First, the problem is too serious for only a few industry players to solve on their own. And second, even industrial powerhouses like Du Pont and Procter & Gamble will fail to reach their targets unless a recycling infrastructure is designed and managed regionally and nationally.

Today, for instance, Procter & Gamble has difficulty obtaining enough high-quality recyclable material. It needs milk and water jugs (high density polyethylene or HDPE) to package Spic & Span. But in the late 1980s, some 99 percent of the 2.7 billion pounds of HDPE produced went into the nation's landfills. "It went there despite the fact that demand for it exists," write Harvard Business School Professors Lodge and Rayport. "And clearly there is the supply. Missing are the critical elements of a system to connect the supply and demand in a predictable, credible manner."[23]

In a different situation, McDonald's Corp. had to back off its plan to recycle its polystyrene hamburger clamshells due to sorting problems and supply shortages.[24] With 60 to 70 percent of McDonald's customers taking their food away from the restaurants, there simply would not be enough polystyrene waste to make the program work.* If McDonald's, which serves 22 million customers a day, cannot generate a sufficient stream of recyclable materials, many experts wonder who can.

Government's Role

Historically, the American marketplace has been driven by demand for products, not supply of raw materi-

als. But some lawmakers — and business leaders — have concluded that the free market needs adjusting if recycling is to make a significant dent in the nation's garbage piles.

Advocates of this approach say governments have considerably more power than private companies to create demand for recycled products. For one thing, governments at all levels consume one-fifth of the country's gross national product. By giving preference to recycled goods through their procurement codes, public agencies can use their buying power to create an almost immediate demand that expands total markets. Governments can also generate demand for recycling by banning certain products from landfills, including yard waste and recyclable paper, as both Wisconsin and Massachusetts have done.[25]

A dozen states now offer low-interest loans, grants or tax credits to companies that make products from recycled materials. And at least 38 states have adopted purchasing programs designed to lift demand for products with recycled content.* For example, in 1989 Connecticut approved a state law requiring newspapers to use an increasing amount of recycled newsprint. Six other states now also require publishers to use a specified percentage of recycled newsprint. Connecticut and Rhode Island require that telephone books be printed on recycled paper. And Wisconsin now sets recycled content standards for plastic containers.

It may take years, however, for such policies to have an impact. In many parts of the country, the cost of recycled paper products is still sharply

Continued on p. 258

---

*Instead, McDonald's has opted to use a lighter-weight plastic-paper wrap, which will be landfilled.

---

*Some simply set goals, but 20 states allow agencies to pay premium prices for recycled materials. One of the more ambitious recycled-content laws was enacted in California in 1989. It requires that all glass containers manufactured in the state be made from 15 percent cullet, or crushed glass, with the percentage rising to 65 percent by 2005.

At Issue:

Is the United States running out of environmentally safe landfill space?

Peter L. Grogan

*President of the National Recycling Coalition,
and a partner in the national consulting
engineering firm of R. W. Beck and Associates*
FROM *IN BUSINESS*, JANUARY/FEBRUARY 1992

yes

Some economists argue that most of the country is not — as conventional wisdom has it — running out of landfill space. Many of us would like to see the geographical data for all 50 states ... backing up those assertions.

We *are* running out of landfill space. More important, is the issue really "available space" or is it a question of our right to dig a hole whenever we feel the need to bury our garbage because it seems easier than the role of responsible stewardship?

Those who argue that landfills can solve the garbage crisis focus their criticism on the economics of recycling. In a myopic sense, large-scale recycling could be seen as leaving taxpayers and users of solid waste disposal services paying a larger bill, as some critics say. But following the same logic, we would be best (most cheaply, that is) served by simply throwing our trash in the street. It's even cheaper than landfilling, unless you consider the public-health angle. . . .

Landfill proponents also claim that recyclables collection is too expensive for rural areas. However, rural communities provide garbage collection, fire protection and mail service economically; it's a fallacy to argue that they can't provide recycling services. In fact, there are trucks on the market right now that are specifically designed to provide combined recycling and trash collection for rural areas. . . .

If we base our decisions solely on economics, which is a mistake to begin with, why isn't the "anti-recycling" group considering the long-term economics: the economics of resources? Visit the countries in Europe and Asia that will be the economic powers of the next century, and you'll find higher solid waste recovery rates, and consequently better resource usage, than we have in the U.S.

When recycling opponents question the economics of recycling, it makes me wonder if they have thought about the effects of removing potentially productive real estate from future uses. And I wonder if creating environmental and safety hazards just to support an unhealthy national consumption pattern makes sense to them. In a nation whose economy is faltering and whose trade deficit is beyond recovery, does it make sense to encourage the international community to take advantage of recovering the resources in our waste stream? Healthy economies overseas are that way partially because they manage their limited resources better than we do.

Clark Wiseman

*Professor of economics at Gonzaga University
in Spokane, Wash.*
**FROM *THE WALL STREET JOURNAL*,
JULY 18, 1991.**

no

The frenzied national push for recycling is largely the result of grossly mistaken beliefs about landfilling and the magnitude of the disposal problem, together with a seriously flawed decision-making process in the siting of landfills.

What most people don't know about landfills could fill a landfill. At the current rate, if all the nation's solid waste for the next 500 years were piled or buried in a single landfill to a depth of 100 yards, this "national landfill" would require a square site less than 20 miles on a side. . . .

Most people also don't know that the amount of solid waste generated nationally has grown at only a 2 percent average rate over the past 30 years, considerably less than the growth of GNP. This means that our "throwaway society" is actually throwing out a progressively smaller share of its output. There are indications that this rate of growth is declining as the economy becomes more service-oriented.

The view is widely held that landfilling should be minimized because of the great environmental risks. But landfills are constantly becoming less obnoxious. New federal and state performance standards are comprehensive and stringent, with environmental considerations entering into all relevant aspects of landfill construction and operation. . . .

If our landfills are to be environmental Cadillacs, the issue then becomes one of sticker price. As might be expected, this will vary according to differences in land prices. A new landfill can cost up to five times as much as a standard 1975 landfill. Even so, landfill costs account for only about 25 cents of the cost of disposing of the garbage in a standard 32-gallon can. . . .

The solid waste problem is not one of space, economy or even cost. The problem is a political one — that of siting new landfills. Anticipating the loss of amenities or property values, potentially affected property owners unite into a group capable of bending government to its will. The special-interest nature of the resulting policies is not different in nature from farm subsidies, protective tariffs and unnecessary military installations, all of which confer losses upon citizens at large. . . .

The choking off of a viable alternative like low cost and environmentally sound landfills is wasteful of society's resources. Before continuing to run headlong toward politically popular but costlier alternatives — including recycling — it would be wise to give increased attention to the real cause of the so-called solid waste "crisis."

Continued from p. 256

higher than that of virgin stock, as the Internal Revenue Service found out when it sought bids for recycled paper for tax forms in 1990.[26] And sometimes the policies have backfired. When Minneapolis banned all plastic food packaging that won't degrade or can't be recycled, city officials not only found they lacked the economic infrastructure to process recyclables but also saw food distributors threatening to pull everything off the shelves. City officials have since deferred the program a year and have begun working with the Council for Solid Waste Solution, a lobby group for the plastics industry, to find a compromise.

Push for a National Program

"We are at a critical juncture," Steven Polan, former commissioner of the New York City Sanitation Department, told a congressional committee last April. "Will recycling succeed or will it be the fad of the '90s? The federal government will make the difference."[27] Although solid-waste management traditionally has been a state or local responsibility, many experts now believe only a national recycling and waste reduction program can establish the necessary infrastructure to end the garbage crisis, reduce pollution and save energy.

Last November, Rep. Gerry Sikorski, D-Minn., introduced legislation designed to stimulate the demand side of the recycling equation. Part of Sikorski's bill is modeled after recent laws in eight states that require a minimum percentage of recycled content in certain products, including newsprint, aluminum and glass packaging, tissue and other paper goods.[28]

"We need federal recycling legislation to balance supply and demand," says the NRDC's Hershkowitz. Opponents of the legislation decry it as excessive regulation that will hurt business and cost taxpayers. "What the government is trying to do is mandate recycling at a national level that

doesn't make sense," says Taylor of the Cato Institute. "The costs will be reflected in product prices. In the final analysis, the goal of saving resources won't be accomplished. In fact, it will expend more resources than it saves."

OUTLOOK

Waste Not, Want Not

Experts agree that easing the nation's garbage glut will require a blend of cures: a change in the nation's convenience-oriented, buy-and-dispose-of mentality; less waste built in at the factory; more recycling; cleaner trash-incineration plants; and more and better landfills. "As a society, we don't seem able to decide how to decide on these issues," says Dick Schuler, director of the Cornell Waste Management Institute.[29] He says people will only start paying attention when trash removal begins costing the average household $1,000 a year. In many parts of the country, that time may not be far off.

"It used to be so easy," says Cornell's Harrison. "All you had to do was put your garbage on the curb, and someone picked it up. It was like one-stop shopping. Now communities are overwhelmed by what they have to think about to get rid of garbage."

Most experts agree that the waste-management hierarchy — reducing and recycling as much trash as possible, then burning or burying the rest — is the wisest, and perhaps only, long-term solution. Some environmentalists still bitterly oppose incineration, but organizations from the Natural Resources Defense Fund to the congressional Office of Technology Assessment say that the nation will need a judicious mix of all four methods to handle its trash in the future.

That may be debatable. But in any case, warns Weiss of the Sierra Club, "Without a national law, we'll be left with a checkerboard approach. That would be bad news for us — and for the packaging industry. Instead of one law to comply with, there'd be 50." ∎

"Time and again, source reduction is at the top of the waste hierarchy, but few people do anything about it," says Harrison. "Whereas recycling is something you can see, source reduction is invisible — it's hard to get a handle on it." Moreover, it is difficult for people to believe in the reality of the problem when the garbage is picked up every day and fees are a relatively small fraction of the average person's income.

Even with the changes that will result from new state recycling laws, it's hard to imagine the national trash heap shrinking as long as the consuming public wants throwaway options in everything from diapers to cameras. "A major cause of the solid-waste crisis is that the costs of solid-waste disposal are largely hidden from American consumers," contends Peter S. Menell, a University of California law professor. "For most Americans, the cost of throwing away an additional item of refuse has been zero."[30] But the price of convenience is getting higher all the time. And as more cities adopt pay-as-you-throw schemes like the one in Seattle,* Americans may finally get the message.

Europe's Vision

Although some U.S. cities are creatively managing their waste problems, most experts look to Europe and Japan for guidance. "In general,

---

*In 1990, one year after Seattle's plan went into effect (see p. 254), the amount of waste hauled to landfills dropped by 22 percent.

other countries use less packaging than the U.S., recycle more of it and are considering policy measures stronger than measures being considered in the U.S.," concludes a recent report on recycling.[31]

Europe's answer to the source reduction issue has been to place greater responsibility at the doorstep of industry — which produces much of the waste to begin with and is probably better able to handle it. For example, in Germany product distributors must take back and recycle packaging containers or otherwise face stiff fines.

The rationale goes like this: If industry collects the materials, and must pay to do so, there is an incentive for industry to reduce waste generation, whether through the use of thinner and lighter materials, or by introducing reusable packaging. If government provides collection and marketing, as is the case in the United States, there is less incentive.

In fact, in the United States the incentives usually run the other way. Americans value attractive packaging and the convenience of products such as disposable diapers. They show this at the checkout counter, which is a powerful incentive for the people who supply such products. Disposal costs are rarely, if ever, included in product costs. Instead, those costs are borne by the government — in other words, the taxpayer.

Moreover, in terms of recycling efficiency, industry is more likely than government to have a clear understanding of the demands of the market with regard to quality. If industry must find markets, it will be more sensitive to the need to eliminate contaminants from the recycling waste stream, by designing packaging that is more easily recycled.

There are, of course, many critics of this approach. The opponents point out that packaging makes up one-third of the waste stream, meaning that two-thirds is generated by others.

If only those industries involved in packaging are forced to bear the burden of financing or managing the collection of recycling, one group of waste generators would be burdened while others remained free. Many argue, too, that markets are already providing appropriate signals to the industries involved. Industry will reduce packaging and will utilize recycled products if the marketplace will reward it for doing so.[32] To suggest that government should override the decisions of the marketplace could invite inefficiency and create distortions.

Despite concerns, most experts agree that without greater government intervention, the war against waste will be lost. "We have to get waste management out of the taxpayer's budget," says Hershkowitz of the NRDC. "Last year we spent $12 billion getting rid of garbage. Money was taken from schools, drug-treatment programs and fire and police budgets. It's an absurd social priority." According to the NRDC and other environmental groups, the European model makes sense.

But is it too radical for the United States? "This is about as radical as fuel efficiency standards were in the late 1970s," responds Hershkowitz. "The U.S. paper and plastics industries are where the auto industry was 20 years ago. Today, Germany and Japan are producing products from recycled materials — and for the most part Americans aren't. If we don't respond here, we'll lose competitiveness to Japan and Germany in yet another industrial sector." ∎

Notes

[1] See *The Wall Street Journal*, April 26, 1991.
[2] Annual surveys of 72 municipal landfills by the National Solid Wastes Management Association show that between 1982 and 1988, the average cost to dump wastes more than doubled — from $10.80 per ton of delivered garbage to $26.93.
[3] For background, see "Not In My Back Yard!" *Editorial Research Reports*, June 9, 1989, pp. 305-320.
[4] ICR Survey Research Group for The Associated Press, April 12-16, 1991.
[5] George C. Lodge and Jeffrey F. Rayport, "Knee-deep and Rising; America's Recycling Crisis," *Harvard Business Review*, September/October 1991, p. 132.
[6] *Tellus Institute Packaging Study,* Tellus Institute, 1992.
[7] Quoted in *The Wall Street Journal*, Jan. 17, 1992.
[8] See the *Los Angeles Times*, Sept. 12, 1991.
[9] Quoted in *Forbes*, Oct. 14, 1991, p. 40.
[10] See Office of Technology Assessment, *Facing America's Trash*, 1989, p. 16.
[11] See *Forbes, op. cit.*, p. 41.
[12] Quoted in *The Wall Street Journal*, April 26, 1991.
[13] *Philadelphia v. New Jersey*, 437 U.S. 617 at 622 (1978).
[14] Quoted in *National Journal*, Oct. 19, 1991, p. 2542.
[15] See *Business Week*, May 20, 1991, p. 116, and March 5, 1990, p. 48.
[16] Although only 5 percent is presently sent by rail, it is becoming much more common. See Randy Woods, "The Railroad: In the Long Run," *Waste Age*, December 1991, p. 35.
[17] Martin V. Melosi, *Garbage in the Cities* (1981), p. 14.
[18] Quoted in *Smithsonian*, April 1990, p. 150.
[19] John E. Young, "Discarding the Throwaway Society," *Worldwatch Paper 101*, January 1991, p. 16.
[20] According to the Office of Technology Assessment, waste-to-energy plants generate just 0.2 percent of the nation's electricity.
[21] Quoted in "Recycling," *Governing*, August 1990, p. 8A.
[22] See Institute for Local Self-Reliance, *Beyond 40 Percent* (1990).
[23] Lodge and Rayport, *op. cit.*, p. 133.
[24] See "The Growing Influence of Boycotts," *Editorial Research Reports*, Jan. 4, 1991, pp. 1-16; and "Fast-Food Shake-Up," *The CQ Researcher*, Nov. 8, 1991, pp. 825-848.
[25] See National Solid Wastes Management Association, *Recycling in the States: 1990 Review*, and "America Turns to Recycling," *Editorial Research Reports*, Nov. 17, 1989, pp. 649-664.
[26] See *The Wall Street Journal*, Jan. 27, 1992.
[27] Polan testified before the House Energy and Commerce Subcommittee on Transportation and Hazardous Materials, April 24, 1991.
[28] There is also a movement afoot to pass a national bottle bill. However, critics say a national bill would reduce recycling revenues by taking bottles and aluminum cans, the most valuable component of the waste stream, out of curbside bins. See "Bottle Bills: Headed for a Collision at Curbside?" *Garbage*, January/February 1992, p. 45.
[29] Quoted in *Smithsonian, op. cit.*, p. 154.
[30] Quoted in *Governing*, February 1992, p. 40.
[31] James E. McCarthy, *Recycling and Reducing Packaging Waste: How the United States Compares to Other Countries*, CRS [Congressional Research Service] Report for Congress, Nov. 8, 1991, p. 2.
[32] *Ibid.*, p. 90.

Bibliography

Selected Sources Used

Books

Chertow, Marian R., *Garbage Solutions: A Public Official's Guide to Recycling and Alternative Solid Waste Management Technologies,* National Resource Recovery Association, U.S. Conference of Mayors, 1989.

This 74-page book is a primer on the roles source reduction, recycling and composting can play in a community's solid-waste management strategy. The author is director of the Program on Solid Waste Policy at Yale University.

Melosi, Martin V., *Garbage in the Cities: Refuse, Reform and the Environment, 1880-1980,* Texas A & M University Press, 1981.

In this widely respected history of waste management, the author traces in extensive detail how Europe and the United States have dealt with garbage over the last century. The study is particularly illuminating in its chapters dealing with the early history of waste management.

Articles

Arrandale, Tom, "Recycling: Getting Down to Business," *Governing,* August 1991, p. 35.

Arrandale takes a close look at how recycling programs are faring, with a focus on the problem of finding markets for recycled goods. The survey contains useful information on different state approaches to recycling.

Environmental Protection Agency, "The Garbage Crisis: Understanding It — Finding Answers," *EPA Journal,* March/April 1989.

Although a bit dated, this issue of *EPA Journal* is devoted entirely to the garbage crisis. There are a number of interesting interviews and articles on a broad spectrum of issues, including incineration, source reduction and medical waste. The issue also contains a number of case studies.

Lodge, George C., and Jeffrey F. Rayport, "Knee-deep and Rising: America's Recycling Crisis," *Harvard Business Review,* September/October 1991.

Two Harvard Business School professors present a provocative and compelling argument for why recycling's success will depend on greater coordination between industry and government. The authors use two case studies, McDonald's Corp. and the city of Minneapolis, as the foundation for their prescriptions.

O'Leary, Philip R., et al., "Managing Solid Waste," *Scientific American,* December 1988.

This straightforward article serves as an excellent over-view of the solid-waste crisis and the various technologies that are now viewed as mainstream alternatives to landfills.

Reports and Studies

***Characterization of Municipal Solid Waste in the United States: 1990 Update,* Office of Solid Waste and Emergency Response, Environmental Protection Agency, June 1990.**

Many of the statistics commonly cited in the garbage debate come from this exhaustive report, an update of a 1988 study. The report projects that by 1995, 20 to 28 percent of the waste stream will be recycled, up from 13 percent today.

Levenson, Howard, et al., *Facing America's Trash: What Next for Municipal Solid Waste?* U.S. Congress Office of Technology Assessment, October 1989.

This comprehensive, detailed examination of the municipal solid-waste problem and the various ways it can be addressed is the single most important work on the subject. Actions taken by local communities or others regarding solid waste are likely to be more effective, the report concludes, if they are drawn up in the context of a coherent national policy.

McCarthy, James E., *Recycling and Reducing Packaging Waste: How the United States Compares to Other Countries,* CRS Report for Congress, Congressional Research Service, Nov. 8, 1991.

McCarthy surveys how other industrialized countries are attempting to reduce solid-waste generation, notably through packaging, and compares those efforts with current U.S. practices.

Platt, Brenda, et al., *Beyond 40 Percent: Record-Setting Recycling and Composting Programs,* Institute for Local Self-Reliance, 1990.

This book-length study, published by Island Press, takes a detailed look at recycling/composting programs in 17 localities. Programs are compared using rigorous methodology to ensure fairness. This is a particularly useful guide for understanding which approaches to resource recovery have been successful to date.

Young, John E., *Discarding the Throwaway Society,* Worldwatch Institute, January 1991.

The author takes a critical look at how industrialized nations encourage overconsumption and examines alternatives to landfilling. The report concludes that changing behavioral patterns is essential and that recycling is more cost-effective than incineration.

The Next Step

Additional Articles from Current Periodicals from EBSCO Publishing's Database

Addresses & essays

Patterson, W. C., "Are we throwing away the planet's future?" *New Scientist,* Nov. 16, 1991, p. 8.

Opinion. Contends that we have been grappling with the wrong end of the problem of finite resources. He asserts that "the legacy of past excesses will take decades and untold sums to rectify."

Ruckelshaus, W. D., "Solid waste in America," *Vital Speeches,* Oct. 1, 1991, p. 765.

Presents a speech by William D. Ruckelshaus delivered before The Cleveland City Club in Cleveland, Ohio, on June 21, 1991, dealing with the solid-waste crisis.

Case studies

Lyall, S., "As L. I.'s garbage mounts, its taxes do, too," *The New York Times,* Nov. 14, 1990, p. B1.

Discusses the problem of trash disposal on Long Island. Nine of the 10 towns in Suffolk County proposed tax increases in their 1991 budgets largely because of the spiraling cost of collecting and disposing of garbage. Scarcity of incinerators and recycling plants; sensitive underground water supply.

Simmons, J. D., "Triana, Alabama: Dumping the dump," *Ms.,* September/October 1991, p. 86.

Tells how activists in Triana, Ala., successfully prevented Alabama's Solid Waste Disposal Authority (SWDA) from establishing a landfill within the town.

Consumer education

Foderaro, L. W., "Trying to hold down the garbage pipe," *The New York Times,* Nov. 30, 1990, p. B1.

Explains pre-cycling — being conscious of buying habits and their effect on the amount of trash going to ever-shrinking landfill space. Buying in bulk to avoid extravagantly packaged products; choosing recyclable containers; shunning disposable or poorly made goods; "environmental shopping" tours; labeling programs.

Debates & issues

"Throwing things away," *Economist,* Oct. 5, 1991, p. 13.

Editorial. Argues that waste treatment is becoming more and more expensive. Assertion that the problem is largely

man-made; need for governments to tackle the root causes of the municipal-rubbish mountain; perceiving waste sites as sources of income.

DiChristina, M., "How we can win the war against garbage," *Popular Science,* October 1990, p. 57.

With 80 percent of U.S. landfills closing in just 20 years, Americans are in danger of drowning in trash. How new technologies that degrade, recycle or burn garbage more efficiently are offering a lifeline. INSETS: Shredding and burning trash for energy; perishable plastics; no longer the town dump; the disposable-diaper debate.

Dimino, R., "Problem materials," *Environmental Action,* March/April 1991, p. 26.

Deals with the problem of materials used in packaging. "Corrugated" materials represent about 29 percent of all packaging waste; packaging includes aseptic drink boxes; concern over toxic impact of production and use.

Hager, M., B. Harlan, et al., "'Dances with garbage,'" *Newsweek,* April 29, 1991, p. 36.

Considers how engineers are beginning to use Indian reservations as toxic dumping grounds. How the Sioux and other Native Americans have saved land from the ravages of white men; why some impoverished American Indian tribes are leasing reservation property for landfills; doing business with the Indians can mean less red tape and lower taxes; Cabazon reservation near Palm Springs, Calif.; Mississippi's Choctaws negotiating a contract.

Hunter, B. T, "Plastic food and beverage packaging," *Consumers' Research Magazine,* August 1990, p. 8.

Discusses conservation problems connected with plastic packaging of foods and beverages. Difficult to recycle; landfill problems.

Kemper, V., "Dump patrol," *Common Cause,* May/June 1991, p. 7.

Discusses the practice of transporting trash and garbage from one state to landfills in another state. Legislative attempts to block outside waste; environmentalists say the answer lies in recycling and composting programs in every state.

Lyons, J., "The garbage war between the states," *Forbes,* Oct. 15, 1990, p. 92.

Debates whether or not it would be unconstitutional for states containing toxic-waste dumps to close their doors to out-of-state garbage. How this law could violate the commerce clause of the U.S. Constitution; case in Alabama; details of the commerce clause; comments from both sides of the heated controversy; the most sensible approach to the problem.

Passell, P., "The garbage problem: It may be politics, not nature," *The New York Times*, Feb. 26, 1991, p. C1.

Comments on the garbage problem. Public alarm over air and water quality; transporting garbage; recycling; incinerating.

Shaw, J.S., "Some big reasons NOT to recycle," *Advertising Age*, Aug. 12, 1991, p. 24.

Opinion. Challenges the pressure put on publishers to use recycled paper for several reasons. Lower demand for land for growing trees; pollution capabilities; misuse of human resources; economic considerations.

International aspects

"Doing it their way," *Canadian Geographic*, August/September 1991, p. 12.

Discusses how residents of Canadian communities plagued by garbage crises can follow the example of Hornby Island, British Columbia. Old landfill closed; islanders set up their own recycling depot; cost-efficiency; financed through property taxes.

Corelli, R., "Trans-Canada trash," *Maclean's*, Sept. 17, 1990, p. 88.

Examines some of the ways Canada's cities and towns are dealing with garbage. Recycling is becoming more popular. Need for more landfill sites; reduction in packaging; Pollution Probe's Canadian Green Consumer Guide.

Johnson, J., "Waste that no one wants," *New Scientist*, Sept. 8, 1990, p. 50.

Investigates the problems of the disposal of domestic refuse in Britain as transport costs rise and landfill sites fill up. Alternative refuse-derived fuel (RDF) plants and compost; problems of leachate and landfill gas. Recycling refuse and the market. INSET: The biggest compost heaps in the world.

Katsumi, Y., "Tokyo's serious waste problem," *Japan Quarterly*, fall 1990, p. 328.

Asserts that in just a few years, central Tokyo will be overwhelmed by the gigantic volume of solid waste generated by its 8 million inhabitants and discusses the extent of this problem concentrating on the city's 23 wards, independent bodies within the city. Five hundred million tons of rubbish in 1989; never-ending problem; use of incinerators despite pollution they cause; wards' garbage disposal un-

der Tokyo metropolitan government; incinerator capacity; what can be done.

Landfills

"Smokies landfill threatens black bears," *National Parks*, July/August 1991, p. 10.

Reports that officials in Haywood, County, N.C., have decided to locate the White Oak landfill on a site between Great Smoky Mountains National Park (N.C., Tenn.) and the Pisgah National Forest (N.C.). The National Parks and Conservation Association, the National Park Service, and other conservation organizations oppose the project because the garbage dump will be an unhealthy attraction for the Smokies' black bear population. Various dangers to the bears; where readers can write.

Rathje, W.L. and L. Psihoyos, "Once and future landfills," *National Geographic*, May 1991, p. 116.

Reports how researchers are digging deep into garbage, seeking to solve the problem of mounting waste. How they have uncovered surprising facts about what's in America's landfills and how long it lasts. INSETS: Trash technology digs deep; It's 1991: do you know what your trash is?; New York's great pile; pop-top field guide; anatomy of a landfill.

Simon, R., "Yes, in my backyard," *Forbes*, Sept. 3, 1990, p. 72.

Reports that while lots of people are fighting to keep regional dumps out of their towns, a few municipalities are more than happy to take other people's garbage — for the right price. Accepting environmentally safe landfills into communities; benefits of having a landfill in your town; little opposition; host fees.

Wolkomir, R. and J. Wolkomir, "Landfills," *Good Housekeeping*, April 1991, p. 84.

Investigates landfills, America's chief garbage repositories. How much garbage is generated each day by the average American; how the new landfills are constructed; how the problem of landfills can be helped.

Law & legislation

Davis, P.A., "Senate acts to force cleanup by government polluters," *Congressional Quarterly Weekly Report*, Oct. 26, 1991, p. 3121.

Discusses the overwhelming Senate vote in October 1991 to pass a bill (S 596) that would not only end the claimed immunity of executive branch polluters to penalties levied under the nation's solid waste laws but also give federal and state regulators more power to hasten the cleanup of hazardous wastes on government land. The Bush administration and Republican senators's approval of the bill; similar House-passed bills; federal government pollution; more.

Proposals

Andrews, B.H., J. Ecker, et al., "Composting: Computing the right recipe," *Civil Engineering,* June 1991, p. 55.

Considers how modern, efficient composting facilities could alleviate regional waste-disposal problems during the composting process. Effect of tight environmental restrictions on landfills and other disposal options in New England; Maine Department of Environmental Protection (MDEP); decomposition at the Hawk Ridge facility in Maine; details.

Burke, L.M. and A.E. Haubert, "Burying by the bale," *Civil Engineering,* August 1991, p. 58.

Reports on the Gallatin National Balefill, now under construction in Illinois, which represents the next generation of engineering solutions to the growing solid-waste disposal crisis. What the system consists of; located in the village of Fairview; to open in 1992; developer, Gallatin National Co. and its designer, STS Consultants, Ltd.; design features; quality assurance; more. INSET: The legal side.

Dickman, S., "Car-eating bacteria," *Nature,* April 11, 1991, p. 453.

Reveals a solution to the solid-waste disposal problem for 2 million unwanted East German Trabant cars. Chemists are working on isolating strains of bacteria that will be able to digest the resins that make up the car's body.

Farmanfarmaian, R., "Saving the environment," *McCall's,* January 1991, p. 65.

Looks at possible solutions to America's garbage crisis, including a proposal to use garbage recycling to create jobs. Economic benefits of recycling; need for public commitment to recycling; refusal to buy overpackaged products; confusion over recycling; need for federal government's involvement; call for secretary of the Environment. INSETS: Readers take action; get the message to Bush; about the survey.

Loupe, D.E., "To rot or not," *Science News,* Oct. 6, 1990, p. 218.

Examines the work being done to redesign landfills so that buried waste rots. Landfills should be wet and should swirl moisture and bacteria around garbage so it can decay quickly. INSET: Prospectors mine landfills for profit.

Recycling

"Paper recycling: Fact from fiction," *Home Mechanix,* October 1991, p. 15.

Discusses Times Mirror magazines' policy regarding the use of recycled paper. The U.S. landfill problems; the Environmental Protection Agency's definition of recycled paper; the de-inking process; the recycling of magazines; need for curbside collection programs; what readers can do to help. INSET: Congress wields the hammer (goals of the Resource Conservation and Recovery Act).

"The old woodpile lights up the town," *Canadian Geographic,* October/November 1991, p. 8.

Reports on a project in Kirkland Lake, Ontario, using waste wood, bark and branches from the local logging industry to generate power for the town. Clean-burning; reduces air pollution; reduces need for landfill sites; recommendation by Ontario's Department of Environment that the government give financial assistance to other such projects.

Austin, T., "Waste to energy? The burning question," *Civil Engineering,* October 1991, p. 35.

Looks at the challenges facing the waste-to-energy industry, particularly in the areas of recycling and legislation. Problems facing waste-to-energy development in California; efforts to coexist with recycling; waste-to-energy industry efforts to get some of the garbage sent to landfills; boost for industry from President George Bush; example of Lancaster County, Pa., recovery facility; community concerns about dioxin; strict emissions control. INSET: RDF redefined.

Berss, M., " 'No one wants to shoot Snow White,' " *Forbes,* Oct. 14, 1991, p. 40.

Examines the issue of recycling, which seems the aesthetically preferred method for dealing with the garbage crisis, although it can be pushed too far by oversupply. Half the states now have some kind of law mandating curbside recycling; questions whether recycling is the best way to deal with our landfill shortage; biggest oversupply is newsprint; Uncertainty of environmental improvement; landfill vs. recycling cost differentials; cites example of Gilliam County, Ore.

Hilts, P., "Green paper," *Publishers Weekly,* July 25, 1991, p. 26.

Reports that concern for the environment once fueled interest in recycled paper for publishing and now vanishing landfill sites are rekindling that flame. Shrinking landfills and growing waste; recycling goals for the paper industry; defining what is meant by the term recycled paper; different types of de-inked paper; answers for the future. INSET: The whiteness problem.

Back Issues

Great Research on Current Issues Starts Right Here... Recent topics covered by The CQ Researcher are listed below. Issues dated before May 10, 1991, were published under the name of Editorial Research Reports.

Back issues are available for $4.00 (subscribers) or $7.00 (non-subscribers). Quantity discounts apply to orders over ten. To order, call Congressional Quarterly 1-800-432-2250.

Future Topics

▶ *The Mafia*

▶ *Ozone Depletion*

▶ *Welfare Reform*

Mafia Crackdown

Has relentless prosecution fatally weakened the U.S. Mafia?

JOHN GOTTI

B ELONGING TO THE MAFIA, AMERICA'S MOST
powerful organized-crime group, seems to grow
riskier by the day. Thanks to aggressive prosecutors
and high-level turncoats, dozens of mob bigwigs in
cities across the country have been convicted and sentenced
to long prison terms in recent years. John Gotti of New York,
reputedly the top Mafia boss still in power, will face a similar
fate if the verdict is guilty in his current trial on murder and
racketeering charges. But while some law-enforcement
officials say the mob has been grievously weakened, others
point to its past resilience. If the mob does succumb, other
organized-crime groups like the Colombian drug cartels,
Chinese Triads and even outlaw biker gangs could move into
the Mafia's traditional turf.

CQ   **March 27, 1992 • Volume 2, No. 12 • 265-288**

Formerly Editorial Research Reports

COVER ART: BARBARA SASSA-DANIELS

THE CQ Researcher

March 27, 1992
Volume 2, No. 12

EDITOR
Sandra Stencel

MANAGING EDITOR
Thomas J. Colin

ASSOCIATE EDITOR
Richard L. Worsnop

STAFF WRITERS
Charles S. Clark
Mary H. Cooper
Rodman D. Griffin

PRODUCTION EDITOR
Laurie De Maris

EDITORIAL ASSISTANT
Thomas H. Moore

GRAPHICS
Jack Auldridge

PUBLISHED BY
Congressional Quarterly Inc.

CHAIRMAN
Andrew Barnes

VICE CHAIRMAN
Andrew P. Corty

EDITOR AND PUBLISHER
Neil Skene

EXECUTIVE EDITOR
Robert W. Merry

PUBLICATIONS MARKETING/SALES
Robert Smith

EDITOR, EBSCO PUBLISHING
Melissa Kummerer

The CQ Researcher (ISSN 1056-2036). Formerly Editorial Research Reports. Published weekly (48 times per year, not printed the first Friday of any month with five Fridays) by Congressional Quarterly Inc., 1414 22nd St., N.W., Washington, D.C. 20037. Rates are furnished upon request. Second-class postage paid at Washington, D.C. POSTMASTER: Send address changes to The CQ Researcher, 1414 22nd St., N.W., Washington, D.C. 20037.

Mafia Crackdown

BY RICHARD L. WORSNOP

THE ISSUES

Now York's current media idol isn't a sports hero or a rock star or even a Wall Street oracle. Far from it. The man of the moment is John Gotti, reputed head of the city's — and the nation's — most powerful Mafia family.* Currently on trial for murder and assorted racketeering charges, Gotti arrives at U.S. District Court in Brooklyn each day flashily dressed and radiating confidence. He's a crowd-pleaser, and he knows it.

Gotti's attire is obviously chosen for maximum visual impact. He favors custom-made, double-breasted suits (reportedly costing $2,000 each), set off by hand-painted silk ties and matching pocket squares ($500 per set). Hardly what you would expect from a guy who claims to make a living selling zippers and plumbing supplies. *New York Newsday* was so taken by Gotti's style that it began featuring " Today's Gotti Garb" during the trial.

Some experts on organized crime say the "Dapper Don," as the tabloids have dubbed the 51-year-old Gotti, is unworthy of the spotlight — either as a fashion plate or Mafia heavyweight. G. Robert Blakey, a law professor at the University of Notre Dame, says Gotti is "largely a creation of the media" and that "very little" would be accomplished by convicting him.

Blakey rates Paul Castellano, the Mafia chieftain whom Gotti is accused of murdering in 1985, as far more suc-

JOHN GOTTI

cessful than Gotti, by organized-crime standards. Castellano "was not in the public eye all the time, and therefore could be more effective," Blakey says. "Gotti is constantly in the public eye. He's a self-promoter." Also, Castellano "wasn't a thug, wasn't just mindlessly violent. Gotti is."

In Blakey's opinion, the recent plea-bargaining deal between New York City prosecutors and two sons of the legendary Mafia leader Carlo Gambino is "more significant" than the Gotti case. To avoid prison terms, Thomas and Joseph Gambino agreed on Feb. 26 to pay a $12 million fine and get out of the trucking business. (Prosecutors contended that virtually every garment manufacturer in New York City was forced to use one of the trucking companies controlled by the Gambino or Lucchese crime families.)

The Gambinos' deal, and others like it, have led many law-enforcement officials to regard the Mafia as a spent force. In city after city across the country, Mafia families have been splintered by prosecutors enforcing tough anti-racketeering laws. These

laws, enacted over the past two decades, enable prosecutors to attack criminal enterprises on a broad front, stripping them of their leadership and sources of illicit — and legitimate — revenue in one massive prosecution.

While the prosecutors battle on, ordinary citizens continue to find the exploits of old-time gangsters fascinating. For example, the critically acclaimed movie "Bugsy" is based on the underworld career of Benjamin "Bugsy" Siegel. *(See story, p. 276.)* Though he has been dead for 45 years, Siegel is still remembered as one of the founding fathers of Nevada's modern gambling industry. In 1946, he built the first of the elaborate postwar casinos, the Flamingo, on the outskirts of Las Vegas — the area known today as The Strip.

Sam Giancana, the Chicago mobster who was linked to President John F. Kennedy and actress Marilyn Monroe, also lives on in memory. On March 8, *Double Cross,* a book about him by his godson and brother, landed in sixth place in its first appearance on *The New York Times* best-seller list of hardcover non-fiction books.

Few of today's Mafiosi possess the aura of a Siegel or a Giancana. Indeed, organized-crime bosses prefer to keep their private and "business" lives hidden from outside scrutiny, insisting all the while that they are legitimate businessmen.

Because of this penchant for secrecy, most of what the typical American knows about organized crime comes from news accounts of high-profile court cases involving Mafia dons and underbosses, and from films and books. The resulting melange of fact, fiction and supposition leaves many people wondering where the fiction ends and fact begins. Here are some of the main questions that are asked about the nation's most notorious organized-crime group:

---

*Many law-enforcement officials refer to the Italian-dominated organized-crime "families" operating in the United States as the "Mafia," the name of the organized-crime group based on the Italian island of Sicily. *(See story, p. 274.)* Others prefer La Costra Nostra ("This thing of ours") or Cosa Nostra ("Our thing"), terms popularized by mob informer Joseph Valachi in 1963 congressional testimony.

New York's Mafia Families

In 1931, following a two-year Mafia war in the New York area, national mob leader Salvatore Maranzano divided the city's Mafia into five crime "families." At the time, the families were known by the names of the bosses who headed them — Bonnano, Gagliano, Luciano, Mangano and Profaci. The names changed as leaders died off or left the country, with the result that only one family still bears its original name. Maranzano himself was killed by rivals soon after creating the five families.

Today, according to law-enforcement officials, New York's Mafia is controlled by the following five families:

Bonnano Family: Estimated number of members: 75. The family is believed to be headed by Salvatore Vitale, the brother-in-law of the previous boss, Joseph Massina, who is serving a 10-year prison sentence for racketeering.

Colombo Family: Estimated members: 100. Victor Orena is acting boss in the absence of Carmine Persico, who is serving a long prison term for a racketeering conspiracy.

Gambino Family: Estimated members: 400-500. The Mafia group allegedly headed by John Gotti is the largest in New York and the country.

Genovese Family: Estimated members: 300-400. Vincent Gigante, the reputed leader, has been found mentally incompetent to stand trial on racketeering charges. Prosecutors suspect he is putting on an act.

Lucchese Family: Estimated members: 125. Defections and prosecutions have left this group's leadership in disarray. The boss, Vittorio Amuso, is awaiting trial on racketeering charges. Former boss Anthony Corallo, convicted in 1986 of similar charges, is in prison.

Is the American Mafia on its last legs?

For decades, the Mafia seemed almost invincible. Now some of its chroniclers say it is on the decline. They contend the Mafia is reeling from assaults by federal and state prosecutors, often working in tandem to enforce a new generation of anti-racketeering laws, principally the federal Racketeer Influenced and Corrupt Organizations Act (RICO) (see p. 277).

Government attorneys also are striving to sever longstanding links between the Mafia and labor unions that they say are mob-controlled. Other weapons in the prosecution arsenal include electronic surveillance to gather evidence and an improved witness-protection program to induce mobsters to testify against their associates.

This multifaceted attack has yielded dramatic results over the past decade, prosecutors say. They assert that Mafia gangs, or families, have been declawed in such mob strongholds as Cleveland, Denver, Milwaukee, New Orleans, Pittsburgh and Tampa. They cite the breakup of the Philadelphia mob as perhaps their crowning achievement. In November 1988, Mafia don Nicodemo "Nicky" Scarfo and 16 Philadelphia-Atlantic City associates were convicted on racketeering charges. Scarfo was sentenced to life in prison.

Putting a Mafia family's leaders behind bars can have a devastating ripple effect, prosecutors say, because unseasoned successors often are pressed into leadership roles before their time. Many of the replacements are "less disciplined and not interested in honor and respect but money and power," says Ronald Goldstock, director of the New York State Organized Crime Task Force. "They are untested and untrained."[1]

The Mafia also has been weakened by the migration of Italian Americans from inner-city neighborhoods to the suburbs, diminishing the mob's political clout near its base of operations. The process can be seen unfolding at a brisk pace in Lower Manhattan, where Chinatown is growing in area and population at the expense of neighboring Little Italy, traditional home of the Mafia in New York. In fact, Chinese expansion in many U.S. urban centers has been accompanied by the emergence of Chinese organized-crime groups that may become a significant problem in the future, some law-enforcement officials say. (See story, p. 270.)

The federal government's campaign to rid corrupt unions of mob influence represents a more serious threat to the Mafia's well-being. In June 1988 prosecutors launched their biggest anti-corruption initiative, filing racketeering charges against the International Brotherhood of Teamsters (IBT). "The IBT leadership has made a devil's pact with La Cosa Nostra," the Justice Department flatly asserted. Shortly before the case was to go to trial, in March 1989, union officials agreed that the union's top officers would henceforth be elected by secret ballots cast directly by rank-and-file members. Previously, those officers were chosen at a national convention whose delegates were local union leaders.

The new procedure received its first big test last December, when Teamsters members elected a president. Reform candidate Ronald Carey, head of a Teamsters local in Long Island City, N.Y., was considered the dark horse. But Carey confounded the handicappers and won by a decisive margin. He said his victory would mean "goodbye to the Mafia, goodbye to concessionary contracts, goodbye to those who have lined their pockets at their members' expense."

Carey has pledged to give rank-and-file members — ranging from truck drivers and brewery workers to warehousemen, food processors and police — more say in formulating Teamsters policy. Meanwhile, prosecutors and labor leaders are hoping that Carey's reforms will bring an end to Mafia infiltration and corruption of the Teamsters, as well as prompt changes in other infested unions.

Surveying the progress they have made against organized crime and union corruption over the past decade, many law-enforcement officials foresee more good news. Goldstock, for example, predicts the Mafia infrastructure "will fail and collapse of its own weight." He adds: "With instability at all levels and with continuing sociological change inevitable, if current law-enforcement efforts are maintained in the next five to 10 years, the mob is likely to be rendered totally unrecognizable from what it has been for the last 60 years."

Blakey makes essentially the same forecast, noting that the 30-year war on organized crime has passed through three distinct stages. "In the 1960s, we figured out who the mob leaders were," he says. "In the 1970s, we drafted the legislation to fight organized crime. And in the 1980s, we found out how to apply the legislation effectively."

Such optimism is not universally shared, however. Mafia expert James B. Jacobs, a professor at New York University Law School, says La Cosa Nostra is "a very entrenched feature of American society — extremely adaptable, extremely opportunistic and with a lot of money and resources. It's hard to believe they will just wither away and die out." [2]

Frederick Martens, director of the Pennsylvania Crime Commission, also says it is too early to start writing obituaries for the mob. "It reminds

me of the [predictions] that the Vietnam War was going to be won shortly," he says. He adds that the Mafia's imminent demise has been forecast before, only to prove false.

Indeed, celebrated Manhattan District Attorney Robert M. Morgenthau in 1970 compared the typical Mafia family to "a good football team." In flush times, it could afford to lose a few of its stars and fill the vacancies with reserve players. In New York, however, organized crime had reached the point "where there [were] no substitutes available," Morgenthau said. As a result, the mob had become "less attractive for people to be recruited into those spots." [3]

But 22 years after Morgenthau's optimistic assessment, the situation looks different. Martens believes today's Mafia is merely in a transitional phase in which "the weak are being culled out so that the organization can become stronger." As less dedicated members leave, "the old-timers are coming back into power — the old Sicilians.... In fact, all we're really witnessing, in many respects, is a changing of the guard."

How does the Mafia affect the daily lives of ordinary Americans?

The average American family can be excused for thinking it exists in a world completely apart from the Mafia. Law-abiding Americans don't seek out such traditional Mafia goods and services as pornography, prostitution, money-laundering and loansharking. Nevertheless, the Mafia impinges on the country's daily life in myriad ways.

Ronald Goldstock cites numerous examples, including "racketeering 'taxes' from the mob's involvement in various industries." In the indictment issued before New York's Gambino brothers struck a plea bargain with prosecutors, Manhattan District Attorney Morgenthau said payoffs to the Gambino family added from $3.50 to $7.50 to the cost of making every

$100 worth of clothing in New York. Since such costs are routinely passed along to consumers, people across the country unwittingly contributed to the mob when they bought apparel made in New York.

Mob activities also lower the quality of daily life in ways that are hard to measure, says Goldstock. Illicit drugs, a major source of income for the mob, not only blight the lives of those who become hooked but also hurt society as a whole "because of all the other kinds of crimes that flow from addicts needing money to support their habits."

Quality of life also suffers when mob pressure forces the use of substandard construction materials or tainted meat in food processing. Adulteration of food products typically entails bribing government inspectors, Goldstock says, or preventing inspectors from seeing the unhealthy products.

Above all, mob influence degrades the quality of life by undermining the integrity of democratic and social institutions. This happens when government officials and business leaders accept mob bribes, or when corrupt union leaders collaborate with the mob in labor-racketeering schemes, to cite two not-uncommon scenarios.

The New York City construction industry has long been under the mob's thumb, with secret pacts binding the Mafia and corrupt contractors and union officials in what amounts to a cartel, police officials say. "General contractors are told what suppliers to use and who [the] subcontractors will be," the President's Commission on Organized Crime noted in a 1986 report. "If a contractor does not comply, either he will never get the job (having been purposefully underbid by the cooperating companies) or he will get the job but will never be able to complete it." [4]

Such arrangements have flourished for years in part because of the exacting logistics of high-rise construction in New York. "Narrow city streets do

A Melting Pot of Organized Crime

Even if the Mafia loses its grip in the United States, other organized-crime groups — some tightly organized, others barely so — seem capable of filling the vacuum. FBI Director William S. Sessions referred to two of the groups in testimony before the Senate Permanent Subcommittee on Investigations on April 11, 1988: "There is evidence to suggest that in cities with large Asian populations, factions of the Japanese Yakuza, as well as the Chinese Triads, are attempting to establish footholds."†

Here are some of the main organized-crime organizations that law-enforcement officials say they are watching:

Chinese Triads: These secret criminal societies were formed in opposition to the Ching Dynasty, which ruled China from the 17th century until 1912. Many Triad members have moved from Hong Kong to the United States in recent years, partly in fear that the British protectorate's return to Chinese control in 1997 will jeopardize their wealth and freedom to operate. Triad activities include extortion, gambling, prostitution and the smuggling of narcotics and aliens.

Japanese Yakuza: The word literally means numbers that are worthless or losers, but Yakuza now refers to what police officials say may be the world's biggest organized-crime group. The Yakuza came into its own after World War II, when immense social and economic changes presented opportunities to expand racketeering and penetrate legitimate enterprises. Yakuza operations in the United States are concentrated in Hawaii, California and New York, states with large Asian-American populations.

Vietnamese Gangs: In some cases these groups are little more than packs of street thugs, preying almost exclusively upon members of their own ethnic community. Other Vietnamese crime groups are involved in sophisticated criminal schemes — extortion, gambling, drug trafficking and smuggling among them — that require organization and discipline.

Colombian Cocaine Cartels: Approximately 75 percent of the cocaine consumed annually in the United States comes from Colombia, where it is collected, processed and distributed by ruthless rings based mainly in Medellín and Cali. The rings' hired assassins kill not only informants but also their families and innocent bystanders. Their vicious modus operandi has been adopted by many American street gangs.

Jamaican Posses: Heavily armed Jamaican gangs known as posses suddenly emerged in the late 1980s as major distributors of crack, the crystalline form of cocaine that is relatively inexpensive and highly addictive. Many cities in the grip of the crack epidemic have experienced sharp increases in homicides, due in part to violent turf wars between rival drug gangs.

"Russian" Gangs: A significant number of criminals who emigrated from the former Soviet Union have continued their illegal activities in the United States. These "Russian" gangs, as they are known for the sake of convenience, deal in several organized-crime standbys — extortion, insurance fraud, counterfeiting, tax fraud, narcotics trafficking and the infiltration of legitimate businesses.

Biker Gangs: Hundreds of outlaw motorcycle gangs exist in this country, but four are particularly infamous: Hell's Angels, Outlaws, Bandidos and Pagans. Some people regard the gangs as a colorful if somewhat menacing feature of modern American life. Law-enforcement officials take a less romantic view, noting that outlaw bikers have done dirty work for the Mafia, including contract killings, drug trafficking and witness intimidation.

Prison Gangs: Over the past quarter-century, prison inmate groups have developed into self-perpetuating gangs that operate both behind bars and in society at large. Narcotics and weapons trafficking, extortion, robbery and murder are their chief activities.

---

†The subcommittee hearings, titled "Organized Crime: 25 Years After Valachi," were held April 11, 15, 21, 22 and 29, 1988.

not provide much storage space for building materials, so steel beams, concrete, brick and glass must be trucked to the job on a precise schedule geared to when they will be used," *Fortune* magazine reported.

"Construction sites in New York are enclosed by wooden fences, and Teamster foremen are posted at the gates to check the union membership of all drivers delivering materials," the article continued. "These foremen can withhold labor and disrupt deliveries. That power gives mob-run unions a lot of leverage."[5]

Ready-mix concrete is probably the mob's chief extortion tool in Manhattan. If the concrete fails to arrive on time, it not only will disrupt the construction schedule but also may hard-

en inside the drum. The Mafia also has infiltrated other key building trades in New York, among them painting, blasting, carpentry and drywalling, police say.

Bid-rigging and other abuses reportedly inflate New York building costs 20 to 35 percent above costs in big cities elsewhere, with more than half the excess reportedly flowing into Mafia coffers. But many contractors tolerate the system without complaint, knowing they can pass the mob tax along to consumers disguised as higher office or apartment rents. Indeed, the Mafia is often viewed within the New York building industry as a stabilizing force that enables construction schedules and profit targets to be met.

Other New York businesses dependent on timely delivery and pick-up of goods also have come under the mob's sway. As the recent plea-bargain deal with the Gambino brothers showed, the Mafia indirectly jacks up the retail price of clothes made in Manhattan's garment district by dictating which trucking companies the garment firms may patronize. "If you control the trucks, you control the industry," said prosecutor Eliot Spitzer in his opening statement at the Gambinos' trial.

The same observation applies to New York's Fulton Fish Market, a Mafia fiefdom for more than 60 years, police say. Crews of unloaders tell the drivers of refrigerated trucks delivering fish to the market where to park their vehicles; they then charge them a stiff fee for transferring the cargo to wholesalers' stalls. The unloaders charge about as much per pound to move fish from a truck to a stall as the freight bill for transporting the seafood hundreds of miles from the ocean to New York. Drivers who don't cooperate are often beaten, and their trucks vandalized.

The gouging resumes when retail merchants and restaurateurs show up shortly after midnight to place their orders. "Loaders" tell the purchasers where to park, what trucking company will deliver their fish and what the shipping and handling fee will be. The loading-unloading racket clearly inflates the retail price of fish in New York.

Waste removal is another truck-dependent New York enterprise with longstanding ties to the Mafia. Pickup and disposal of residential trash is handled by the city sanitation department. However, New York's 250,000 retail stores and businesses must use private haulers. The group consists of approximately 400 small carters, many of Italian extraction and controlled by the Mafia, who collect a share of the profits, according to police.

Awareness of the mob's role in disposing of New York's garbage is growing as the region's sanitary landfill edges closer to capacity.[6] Mafia-linked truckers, sometimes billing themselves as recyclers or experts on hazardous-waste disposal, have been accused of illegally dumping toxic materials — even in such tony suburbs as Tuxedo Park, N.Y.

Trucking isn't the only mode of transportation to feel the Mafia's crushing embrace. For generations, the mob has exacted tribute from New York's shippers and stevedores, according to law-enforcement officials. And for the past quarter-century, it has preyed upon John F. Kennedy International Airport, where dope smuggling and cargo theft are rampant.

The mob has "always prospered" on the New York waterfront, the President's Commission on Organized Crime declared in 1986. "The necessity for speed, plus the lack of rail connections to the piers, gave rise to the coveted 'loading' racket, which involved moving cargo from the pier floor to waiting trucks.... [L]oading generated extraordinary profits, and was a principal incentive for organized crime to infiltrate the ILA [International Longshoremen's Association]."[7]

Racketeers are interested in illicit cargo, too. Corruption of port employees gives the mob access to cargo shipment and storage areas, which in turn facilitates traffic in contraband (mainly narcotics) and stolen property (luxury vehicles and the like). All the while, incoming and outgoing legitimate cargo is stolen. "The magnitude of the problem at the ports and carriers most targeted for theft ... [is] simply not known," said the president's commission. "Cargo losses are often absorbed as part of the cost of doing business."[8] And those costs, as always, are passed on to consumers in the form of higher retail prices, freight rates, insurance premiums and so on.

Will reorganizing the federal government's organized-crime strike forces cripple the fight against the mob?

The strike-force concept originated with Henry E. Petersen, head of the Justice Department's organized-crime section in the mid-1960s. In 1967, Petersen put together a team of prosecutors and investigators from five federal agencies — including the FBI, the Internal Revenue Service, the Treasury Department and the Labor Department. The target: the Magaddino crime family of Buffalo, N.Y. The fledgling unit obtained 14 indictments against 31 individuals in its first year, proving the concept's effectiveness. By 1972, strike forces were operating in 18 cities, monitoring every significant organized-crime activity.

For nearly a quarter-century, the federal government's war against the Mafia and other organized-crime groups was spearheaded by these quasi-autonomous units — responsible to the Justice Department but not under the control of local U.S. attorneys. During that time, strike forces won convictions of dozens of Mafia leaders in cities across the country. But on Jan. 1, 1990, then-Attorney General Richard L. Thornburgh placed the strike forces under the control of local U.S. attorneys' offices.

In Thornburgh's view, the strike forces had outlived their usefulness. Merging them with U.S. attorneys' offices would lead to "substantial management benefits," he argued, by concentrating each jurisdiction's federal prosecution forces in a single unit. He also said the strike forces had been slow to respond to new organized-crime groups, such as the Colombian and Jamaican drug cartels and the increasingly powerful ethnic street gangs. *(See story, p. 278.)*

Thornburgh's decision has come under fire from several quarters. *(See "At Issue," p. 281.)* In an op-ed article in *The New York Times,* Sens. Sam Nunn, D-Ga., and Edward M. Kennedy, D-Mass., challenged the idea that U.S. attorneys are well-equipped to fight organized crime. "As political appointees, U.S. attorneys serve too briefly to develop the expertise and maintain the continuity required for organized-crime investigations," they wrote. "They give priority to investigations that can be resolved quickly and to high-profile local cases that often do not involve organized crime."

Nunn and Kennedy argued that strike forces, on the other hand, "concentrate on organized crime, coordinate the numerous federal, state and local agencies involved in particular investigations and develop the veteran investigators and prosecutors needed to build strong cases."[9]

Blakey feels it is too soon to judge Thornburgh's move. "The cases that are coming forward now have been in the pipeline for some time," he says. "To get an organized-crime prosecution, you've got to put something in the pipe and then wait two or three years for it to come out."

Blakey says, however, that the two prerequisites for an effective campaign against organized crime are "organization and will." The identity of the attacking force is of secondary importance. "If you can recruit enough competent people and organize and lead them properly through the strike forces, that's fine. If you can do it through the U.S. attorneys' offices, that's fine, too."

Goldstock also says the jury is still out on Thornburgh's decision. As originally conceived, he notes, the strike forces were to "take a regional approach" because "organized crime

is not confined to the federal district lines" that define the jurisdiction of U.S. attorneys' offices.

As things turned out, though, many strike forces had to operate within the confines of a single U.S. judicial district. Consequently, says Goldstock, "Instead of having one strike force for New York and New Jersey, there was one for the Southern District of New York, one for the Eastern District [of New York] and one for the District of New Jersey."

Goldstock also believes the strike forces failed to deliver on their mandate to "analyze organized-crime problems, in terms of both the [organized

crime] syndicates themselves and the activities the syndicates engaged in." Instead, the strike forces often were "following the dictates of the FBI rather than working with it as part of the Justice Department to develop strategies for [organized-crime] control."

In sum, Goldstock feels that, "While the strike forces did good things, they never did what they were capable of doing. If they had lived up to their potential, merging them into the U.S. attorneys' offices would be a great mistake. But if they were never going to do all that was expected of them, [Thornburgh's decision] would have a lesser impact." ∎

BACKGROUND

Uncertain Origins

Historians disagree about the origins of the Mafia. Some say the group dates from the ninth century, when it was a secret society opposed to Arab rule in Sicily. Another view holds that the Mafia originated in 1282 during a rebellion against French control of Sicily, and that the name is an acronym of the battle cry "Morte Alla Francia Italia Anela!" ("Death to the French Is Italy's Cry!"). According to a third theory, the Mafia was spawned by 19th-century Sicilian feudalism under the Bourbon kings.[10]

This much is certain: During the middle of the 19th century, wealthy Sicilian landowners hired Mafia members to keep the peasantry in line. Before long, the Mafiosi were extorting money and goods from the peasants. Mafia chieftains also acquired political clout after Italian unification in 1870, by which time they could deliver the Sicilian peasant vote to the highest bidder. A government crackdown on the Mafia in 1878 drove some Mafia leaders underground.

Others emigrated to America.

In the early years of this century, wrote reporter Ralph Blumenthal of *The New York Times,* "ties between the American Mafiosi and their more entrenched Sicilian brethren were strong and close. Sicilian Mafiosi could travel to the United States and start [crime] families of their own, provided they had the permission of their boss at home."[11]

Over time, the trans-Atlantic bonds frayed. Today, says Goldstock, the U.S. Cosa Nostra "is not a subsidiary or subdivision of the Sicilian Mafia. Instead, it is a distinctly American organization which, while drawing on … [Mafia] traditions, developed in response to the unique social forces and culture of the New World."

Probibition Provides a Mafia Bonanza

Organized crime entered an era of unprecedented prosperity and expansion during Prohibition (1920-33), when the federal government turned alcohol — a commodity that millions of Americans wanted — into an illicit product. Prohibition "brought the racketeer riches and respectability beyond his wildest dreams," Peter

Continued on p. 274

Chronology

Late 1800s *Mafia groups become politically influential after Italian unification in 1870.*

1878
A government crackdown on the Sicilian Mafia forces some members to go underground, others to emigrate to the United States.

1920s-1930s *Prohibition gives Italian-American hoodlums an opportunity to move from the fringes to the mainstream of organized crime in America.*

Jan. 17, 1920
The 18th Amendment to the Constitution, outlawing the manufacture and sale of alcoholic beverages, goes into effect.

1929-31
A Mafia civil war fought largely in the New York area ends with the division of New York City's Mafia into five crime families and the drafting of a standard organizational plan for Mafia families.

1931
Chicago mobster Al Capone is convicted on federal income-tax evasion charges.

1950s *Televised Senate hearings alert the public to the extent of organized crime in the United States.*

1950-51
A special Senate committee headed by Estes Kefauver, D-Tenn., holds hearings on organized crime in the United States. Many of the sessions are televised live, exposing a broad segment of the public to the problem.

Nov. 14, 1957
State police in Apalachin, N.Y., break up a conclave of more than 75 crime bosses from cities throughout the country.

1957
The Senate Select Committee on Improper Activities in the Labor or Management Field learns that many of the Apalachin participants were directly involved in labor-related businesses.

1960s-1970s *Concern about organized crime mounts, and tough federal laws are enacted to combat it.*

September-October 1963
Former Mafia member Joseph Valachi, a convicted murderer, describes the inner workings of organized-crime families at hearings held by a Senate subcommittee. Valachi says mob members call their organization La Cosa Nostra, or "This thing of ours."

January 1967
The federal government's first organized-crime strike force, including investigators from six agencies, is sent to Buffalo, N.Y., to attack the Magaddino Mafia family.

1970
President Richard M. Nixon signs the Organized Crime Control Act into law. Title IX of the measure is the Racketeer Influenced and Corrupt Organizations Act (RICO), which is to prove a potent weapon against the Mafia in later years.

1980s *Making full use of RICO as an anti-organized-crime weapon for the first time, prosecutors inflict heavy damage on the Mafia.*

Dec. 16, 1985
Paul Castellano, head of the Gambino Mafia family in New York City, is slain outside a Manhattan steakhouse. John Gotti emerges as his successor shortly afterward.

March 13, 1989
The Justice Department and Teamsters union reach an out-of-court settlement of a racketeering suit, altering the way national officers are elected and tightening efforts to curb corruption in the Teamsters.

1990s *The government's crackdown on the Mafia continues, though some observers detect a slackening of effort.*

Jan. 1, 1990
U.S. Attorney General Richard L. Thornburgh places the Justice Department's 14 organized-crime strike forces under the control of local U.S. attorneys' offices.

1992
John Gotti, the reputed head of New York's powerful Gambino Mafia family, goes on trial in U.S. District Court in Brooklyn on murder, racketeering and other criminal charges.

Italy's Mafia: Political Clout and More

The Italian Mafia has always been based on the island of Sicily and the southern mainland provinces of Calabria and Campania. Thus, it was possible for northern Italians to view organized crime as primarily a regional problem. Few people believe that today.

With the European Community (EC) scheduled to achieve full economic integration this year, law-enforcement officials on the continent worry that the Mafia will leap at the chance to extend its reach from one end of the EC to the other.

Traffic in drugs, chiefly heroin, provides the bulk of the Italian Mafia's revenue, according to law-enforcement officials. Cocaine is becoming more important, however, as drug lords from Colombia try to expand their market beyond the Americas. To gain a foothold in Europe, the Colombians have had to strike deals with the Mafia, which jealously guards its home turf.

As in the United States, Mafiosi in Italy have found it worthwhile to take over legitimate enterprises. In Sicily, for example, they have infiltrated the wine and citrus industries and assumed control of hospitals and soccer

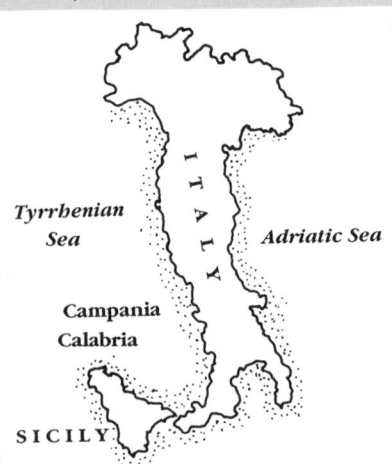

teams. Profitable in their own right, these acquisitions have helped augment the Mafia's already considerable political clout.

Subsidies provided by Italy's central government to raise living standards in the impoverished south give the Mafia another dependable income stream. Year after year, money flows out from Rome to finance development projects aimed at giving the backward region a modern infrastructure. Just as regularly, much of the money ends up in Mafia coffers — and the development projects often end up half-finished, if that.

A wave of revulsion against the Mafia erupted last August when Libero Grassi, a Sicilian industrialist, was gunned down in Palermo because he had refused to pay protection money to the mob. There was speculation that the public outrage would prod authorities into mounting a serious offensive against organized crime. Skeptics said that was unlikely to happen as long as the Mafia retained the ability — first acquired more than a century ago — to deliver blocs of voters to the political candidates of its choice.

Continued from p. 272
Maas wrote in *The Valachi Papers* (1968). "The entire underworld, then monopolized by the Irish, Jews, and, to a lesser extent, Poles, cashed in on the Prohibition bonanza.

"But for Italian racketeers, especially, it was a chance to at last move into the big time. Bootlegging was something they knew about. For years, Prohibition or not, thousands of home distillers had been operating in the ghettolike neighborhoods that Italian immigrants, like other ethnic groups before them, tended to crowd into after landing in this country. Thus, they had a running start on a huge market that had opened up, and from then on they bowed to no one."

In addition to making mobsters a lot of money, Prohibition helped or-

ganized crime in two other fundamental ways. Bootlegging, which had to overcome the same basic problems of production and distribution faced by legitimate businesses, taught gang bosses to run their organizations more efficiently. And widespread flouting of the liquor laws led to the systematic corruption of law-enforcement officials at all levels.

But the opportunities created by Prohibition also led to turmoil within the Italian-American underworld as rival groups maneuvered for market share. The jostling for advantage culminated in a Mafia civil war that broke out in 1929. Fought mainly in the New York area, the conflict ended in April 1931 with the assassination of Joe Masseria, head of the city's most powerful Mafia clan. Sal-

vatore Maranzano then emerged as the Mafia's national "boss of bosses" *(capo di tutti capi)*.

Moving swiftly, Maranzano divided the New York City Mafia into the five "families" that still operate there today. He also decreed that each family was to have a boss, underboss, counselor, lieutenants and soldiers. Moreover, all soldiers had to pledge absolute loyalty to the organization and work through a military-style chain of command. Attacking another family member in anger or violating a member's wife were strictly forbidden.*

The repeal of Prohibition in 1933 brought new opportunities for labor

---

*Maranzano did not live to see what came of his dictates. On Sept. 11, 1931, he was slain in his headquarters by five gunmen posing as law-enforcement officers.

racketeering and gambling. Capital amassed from bootlegging enabled the Mafia to finance new illicit enterprises and to penetrate legitimate business. During World War II, black-market sales of rationed consumer goods proved profitable, the narcotics trade boomed and mobsters moved to assert their control of gambling enterprises ranging from pinball and card games to race tracks and numbers. By war's end, mobsters were richer and more firmly entrenched than ever before.

Crackdown Begins

Increasing affluence, however, put the Mafia and other organized-crime groups under renewed scrutiny from law-enforcement officials. The conviction of Chicago crime kingpin Al Capone on tax-evasion charges in 1931 as well as the mob-busting activities of Thomas E. Dewey* in New York during the mid-1930s were early victories in the fight against organized crime.

But in the immediate postwar years, with federal officials seemingly more interested in communists than racketeers, the mob gained a valuable respite. Then, in 1950, U.S. Attorney General J. Howard McGrath launched a campaign against the "criminal conspiracy," bringing officials from across the country to Washington to consider the growing nationwide scope of organized crime.

Mayor De Lesseps S. Morrison of New Orleans, a city with a strong Mafia tradition, summed up the extent of the problem: "We do not have the whole picture, but each of us ... [has] seen

*Dewey was a U.S. attorney in 1935 when he was appointed a special prosecutor to investigate organized crime. In 1937 he was elected district attorney of New York County (Manhattan). He served as governor of New York from 1943 to 1955 and was the Republican nominee for president in 1944 and 1948.

small segments of ... organized crime. These pieces fit together in a pattern of mounting evidence concerning several highly organized syndicates whose wealth, power, scope of operations and influence have recently grown to alarming proportions." [12]

Meanwhile, Sen. Estes Kefauver, D-Tenn., alarmed by what he had learned from a 1948 study by a California crime commission, called in 1950 for a sweeping examination of organized crime in the United States. The Senate adopted his resolution by one vote. Hearings were held before a special committee from May 10, 1950, to May 1, 1951. Live telecasts of many "Kefauver committee" sessions were credited with increasing the public's awareness of organized crime and the breadth of its dealings.

Among the committee's major accomplishments was the first detailed study of criminal infiltration of legitimate businesses. Racketeers, it concluded, used unscrupulous business practices, violence, blackmail, extortion and fraud to touch virtually every aspect of business from advertising to transportation. The committee also discovered that professional gambling in the United States, especially illegal casinos, had become widespread.

In a book about his committee's work, Kefauver wrote: "A nationwide crime syndicate does exist in the United States ... despite the protestations of a strangely assorted company of criminals, self-serving politicians, plain blind fools and ... [the] honestly misguided." The Mafia is "no fairy tale," he continued, but a "shadowy international organization that lurks behind much of America's organized criminal activities." It is engaged in "almost every conceivable type of criminal violence, including murder ... smuggling ... kidnapping and labor racketeering." [13]

Dramatic confirmation of the Kefauver committee's conclusions came on Nov. 14, 1957, when state police broke up a conclave in Apalachin,

N.Y., of at least 75 crime bosses from all over the country, New York's Vito Genovese among them. Although 20 attendees were eventually found guilty of conspiracy to obstruct justice, the convictions were overturned. Even with grants of immunity, the government had been unable to break the conspiracy of silence surrounding the activities of the Mafia chieftains. Still, the meeting put organized crime back in the public eye.

Government Probes
Mob Ties to Labor

What little the government learned about the Apalachin powwow was revealed soon afterward by the Senate Select Committee on Improper Activities in the Labor or Management Field — the so-called McClellan committee. Chaired by Sen. John L. McClellan, D-Ark., the panel focused mainly on the underworld's links to labor unions. Meeting late in 1957, it learned, for example, that many of the Apalachin participants were directly involved in labor-related businesses: Nine owned construction companies; 16 were in garment manufacturing or trucking; and 11 were in the export-import business.

Committee investigators, led by Chief Counsel Robert F. Kennedy, learned that the crime syndicate not only had broadened its business activities but had infiltrated organized labor, including the Teamsters, one of the nation's largest unions. Investigators found that Teamster President Dave Beck of Seattle, suspected of having underworld ties, had illegally received more than $32,000 in union kickbacks and had stolen some $370,000 from the union's pension fund. Beck was convicted of tax evasion and sentenced to prison in 1959.

Beck's heir was Jimmy Hoffa, who had leaked information about his former boss to the committee. But following the Beck investigation, the committee in 1958 turned its attention to Hoffa and his rapid rise to

Hollywood and the Gangster

There is at least one offer a male film actor shouldn't refuse — a supporting role in a movie about organized crime. In the 65-year history of the Academy Awards, only three movies have won three nominations apiece for best supporting actor. All three pictures — "On the Waterfront," "The Godfather" and "The Godfather — Part II" — had mob-related plots.†

Another gangland epic leads the 1992 Oscar parade with 10 nominations. "Bugsy," based on the career of mobster Benjamin "Bugsy" Siegel, is a contender for best picture, best actor (Warren Beatty in the title role) — and, naturally, best supporting actor (Harvey Keitel and Ben Kingsley). (This year's Academy Awards winners will be announced March 30.)

Hollywood's fascination with the underworld goes back decades. In fact, a film called "Underworld" was a nominee for the "best-writing" Oscar at the very first (1927-28) Academy Awards ceremony. "Alibi," also about gangsters, was nominated the following year for both best picture and best actor (Chester Morris).

Nonetheless, some film historians say the dawn of the gangster-film era was in 1930, the year Darryl F. Zanuck assumed control of production at Warner Brothers. Zanuck decreed that the studio would plan its output with headline news in mind. The result was a torrent of violent organized-crime movies — from Warner Brothers and rival studios, too — that crested in 1931. Exhilarating to watch even today, the pictures created numerous stars, including James Cagney, Spencer Tracy, Edward G. Robinson, Clark Gable, Joan Blondell, Glenda Farrell and Jean Harlow.

Though Hollywood moguls insisted that gangster films moralized against crime, critics said they actually glamorized it. For instance, filmgoers instinctively identify with

Warren Beatty and Annette Bening in "Bugsy"
© 1991 TriStar Pictures, Inc.
Reprinted by permission

Edward G. Robinson as mobster Caesar Enrico (Rico) Bandello, who cries as he is gunned down at the end of "Little Caesar" (1930): "Mother of mercy, is this the end of Rico?"

Critics also objected to the philosophy of life espoused by the hero of "Quick Millions" (1931). Too nervous to steal and too lazy to work, the aspiring racketeer (played by Spencer Tracy) says a man is a fool to go into legitimate business when he can make a mint applying business methods to crime.

Screen artifice and gritty reality collided in 1934, when the infamous outlaw John Dillinger (the FBI's "Public Enemy No. 1") died in a hail of FBI gunfire on a Chicago street. Dillinger had just left a movie theater showing "Manhattan Melodrama," starring Clark Gable in one of the gangster roles that helped make him a screen idol.

Gangster flicks never again scaled the heights of popularity they attained in the early 1930s, but neither did they fall completely out of favor. Post-1930s films like "On the Waterfront," "The French Connection" (1971) and the first two "Godfather" movies testify to the genre's enduring hold on the public. All four pictures dominated the Academy Awards in their respective years.

On the other hand, "Prizzi's Honor" (1985), "The Godfather — Part III" (1990) and "Goodfellas" (1990) each won multiple Academy Award nominations but took home a grand total of only two Oscars, both for supporting roles.††

---

† Lee J. Cobb, Karl Malden and Rod Steiger were nominated for best supporting actor in "On the Waterfront" (1954); James Caan, Robert Duvall and Al Pacino for "The Godfather" (1972); and Robert De Niro, Michael V. Gazzo and Lee Strasberg for "The Godfather — Part II" (1974). De Niro was the only Oscar winner among the group.

†† Anjelica Huston for "Prizzi's Honor" and Joe Pesci for "Goodfellas."

---

leadership, his questionable business transactions with trucking companies and his association with members of organized-crime families. Hoffa testified at length before the committee under questioning from Kennedy and others. Hoffa's many appearances did not cost him his union presidency. However, they did fuel his reputedly intense hatred of Robert Kennedy.

When John F. Kennedy moved into the White House in 1961, he appointed Robert Kennedy, his brother, as attorney general. Citing organized crime and corrupt labor practices as his main concerns, Robert Kennedy fought for and obtained passage of various criminal statutes dealing with interstate racketeering. Underworld figures targeted for special attention included

mobsters Mickey Cohen and John Roselli on the West Coast, Sam Giancana in the Midwest and Carlos Marcello and Santo Trafficante in the South.

In the area of labor corruption, Kennedy's principal goal was putting Hoffa behind bars. After a series of federal indictments, the Teamster boss was finally convicted of jury tampering and fraud in 1964; he began serving a federal prison term in 1967. Granted executive clemency by President Richard M. Nixon in 1975, Hoffa disappeared later that year, apparently murdered.

In the fall of 1963, the McClellan committee held another round of hearings and listened to riveting testimony from ex-Mafia member Joe Valachi. His account of underworld doings provided, according to Justice Department officials, conclusive proof of the existence of a nationwide criminal network.

Valachi had agreed to testify after he was marked for execution by Vito Genovese when both were serving time in the Atlanta federal penitentiary. The Mafia's reaction to Valachi's testimony was said to be something approaching panic. FBI Director J. Edgar Hoover told McClellan that Valachi's oral history of gangland "shook [the mob] up." [14]

After the assassination of President Kennedy on Nov. 22, 1963, speculation arose that the Mafia may have been involved. *(See story, p. 280.)* Underworld figures, it was revealed in a later Senate probe,[15] had taken part in a Kennedy-era CIA plot to kill Cuban Premier Fidel Castro. But at the same time, Mafia leaders harbored a deep resentment over the Kennedy administration's unrelenting attack on organized crime.

Following its 1979 investigation of the Kennedy and Dr. Martin Luther King murders, the House Select Committee on Assassinations concluded that the late president was probably killed as a result of a conspiracy.* Blakey, the committee's chief counsel, suggested in a 1981 book, *The Plot to Kill the President,* that Kennedy was shot by a "rogue elephant" sub-group within the Mafia and that the accused assassin, Lee Harvey Os-

wald, Oswald's killer, Jack Ruby, and dozens of other individuals were all part of an elaborate underworld plot against the government in general and the Kennedy family in particular.

The murder of Oswald by Ruby, Blakey and his co-author, Richard N. Billings, argued, gave the entire episode the unmistakable imprint of the mob. If Ruby, a known underworld associate, was ordered to kill Oswald, they speculated, someone must have ordered Oswald to kill Kennedy.

New Laws Aid Crackdown

Lyndon B. Johnson, the slain president's successor, in 1965 opened a fresh offensive in the war against organized crime by creating the President's Commission on Law Enforcement and the Administration of Justice. Headed by Attorney General Nicholas deB. Katzenbach, the commission analyzed the federal failure to cope with organized crime and, in its 1967 final report, offered more than 200 suggestions for reducing crime.

These recommendations served as the basis for two major pieces of anti-crime legislation, both drafted principally by Blakey. The Crime Control and Safe Streets Act of 1968 made it easier to gather evidence about Mafia enterprises by authorizing court-ordered electronic surveillance at the federal and state levels. Two years later, President Nixon signed into law the Organized Crime Control Act, which expanded the investigative powers of grand juries, permitted the detention of recalcitrant witnesses and authorized the attorney general to protect cooperative federal and state witnesses and their families.

Title IX of the 1970 law was the potent Racketeer Influenced and Corrupt Organizations Act, known as RICO. RICO defined 32 "predicate

offenses" * as racketeering activities and made it a crime to use profits from those activities to establish, acquire, or operate a legitimate business involved in interstate or foreign commerce. Violations could be punished by up to $20,000 in fines and up to 20 years' imprisonment and could result in the forfeiture of any assets derived from the activity.

Borrowing from federal antitrust law, RICO included a civil section, too. It allowed anyone "injured in his business or property" by racketeering activity to sue the persons responsible and recover triple damages plus "a reasonable attorney's fee."

The White House hailed the 1970 statute that created RICO as a fulfillment of Nixon's 1968 campaign promise to restore the nation to law and order. But many critics saw it as a threat to the rights of individuals, warning that safeguards were needed to assure that the new legal weapons would be used only to fight organized crime.[16]

In any event, prosecutors were slow to appreciate RICO's potential as an anti-organized-crime tool. Then, in the mid-1970s, FBI agents began persuading assistant U.S. attorneys around the country to put this untried weapon into play. The Supreme Court made the agents' selling job easier by issuing decisions that endorsed prosecutions against strictly "illegitimate" enterprises, such as an organized-crime family,[17] and upheld broad application of RICO's forfeiture provisions.[18] Those two rulings, Blakey says, set the stage for RICO to become "the prosecutor's tool of choice in sophisticated crime."

There was much about RICO for prosecutors to cherish. For one thing, the 20-year prison term for a RICO vi-

---

*The seven-member Warren Commission, convened to investigate the assassination of President Kennedy, said in its Sept. 24, 1964, report that Lee Harvey Oswald had "acted alone" in killing Kennedy and Jack Ruby similarly had acted alone in slaying Oswald two days later.

---

*The offenses ranged from murder, gambling, arson and bribery to extortion, drug-dealing, embezzlement from pension or welfare funds and bankruptcy fraud. Offenses added since 1970 include trafficking in contraband cigarettes, state or federal obscenity violations, money-laundering and child pornography.

Attacking Organized Crime

When a Mafia bigwig like John Gotti goes on trial, everyone sits up and takes notice. But the names of most organized-crime figures don't ring a bell outside their home areas. And many are not affiliated with the Mafia. Here, drawn from a 1991 U.S. Justice Department report,† are some of the lesser-known individuals and organizations that ran afoul of the Racketeer Influenced and Corrupt Organizations Act (RICO) and other criminal laws in 1990:

Lonnie "Ted" Binion: A one-count indictment charged Binion and seven others with conspiracy to operate the Horseshoe Hotel and Casino in Las Vegas through a pattern of racketeering, including beatings, robberies and kidnappings of casino patrons. Binion is scheduled to go to trial in October.

Frank Cammarano: In a complex case, Cammarano was convicted of conspiracy to extort and of substantive extortion of two freight-forwarding companies operating out of New York's John F. Kennedy International Airport. He obtained $250,000 from the companies by promising to help end a three-year strike against them and head off further labor disputes with two Teamsters locals with ties to organized crime.

National On Leong Chinese Merchants Association: Four organizations and 29 individuals linked to the merchants group were charged with RICO and other offenses involving a multi-city gambling business dating from 1974. On Leong is the name of a Chinese tong (social group) long identified with organized crime.

Alberto Robinson: A reputed member of a Jamaican drug-dealing "posse," Robinson was indicted for the murder in Maryland of a posse member and for RICO violations. The posse to which Robinson belonged operated in New York, Philadelphia, Maryland, the District of Columbia and California, according to police.

Yakov Tilipman: Tilipman and three associates were indicted in Brooklyn in connection with alleged "C.O.D." frauds aimed at obtaining and fencing jewelry in cities across the country. Tilipman and two of the others named in the indictment were suspected of belonging to a major organized-crime group comprised of Russian immigrants. Theirs was the first case to be prosecuted as the result of a three-year probe of such groups. They pleaded guilty to conspiracy to commit wire fraud and to transport stolen property in interstate commerce. Tilipman, the ringleader, was sentenced to the jail time he had already served while awaiting trial. The others received probation.

Hieu Duc Tran: The leader of a Vietnamese armed-robbery gang, Tran was convicted of conspiracy and interstate transportation of stolen property relating to a violent home-invasion robbery. Such robberies, carried out by roving gangs, have become commonplace in Vietnamese-immigrant communities from Virginia to Texas to California.

Peter Vario: A member of New York's Lucchese organized-crime family, Vario was convicted of one RICO conspiracy charge and 13 counts stemming from his position as vice president of General Building Laborers Local 66, the largest construction union on Long Island. The charges involved extorting illegal payments from construction companies in the area.

Steven Wayne Yee: Yee and two other members of the Hell's Angels motorcycle gang were convicted of conspiracy and unlawful possession of firearms. The case centered on the murder of an innocent teenager whom the defendants mistakenly believed was a member of a rival biker gang. They received prison sentences ranging from 15 to 25 years and face state murder charges.

†U.S. Department of Justice, *Attacking Organized Crime*, 1991.

---

olation was longer than the sentence for most of the predicate offenses. RICO's forfeiture provision opened up a whole new area of punishment and, in combination with the longer prison term, gave prosecutors a strong hand in plea bargaining. At trial, the broad definition of "enterprise" allowed the government to present a more complete picture of a defendant's criminal activities and also helped persuade judges to allow ever-larger trials with multiple defendants.

In the early 1980s, the Justice Department began to turn RICO's full force against the mob. Testifying before the Senate Judiciary Committee in October 1987, Assistant Attorney General William F. Weld (now the Republican governor of Massachusetts) said the government had achieved "unprecedented successes" in obtaining RICO-based convictions of the heads and principal lieutenants of La Cosa Nostra families in Boston, Buffalo, Kansas City, Cleveland and Los Angeles, as well as four of the five principal families in New York City.

David C. Williams, director of the General Accounting Office's special investigations unit, told the Senate Permanent Subcommittee on Investigations in April 1988 that the RICO assaults on the mob would endure. Crime families were being forced to replace seasoned leaders, Williams said, with "inexperienced, violent wiseguys" lacking the skills to direct sophisticated financial enterprises. ∎

CURRENT SITUATION

Going After Gotti

For all their success in fighting organized crime over the past decade, prosecutors have yet to convict John Gotti, the reputed head of New York City's Gambino family, the largest Mafia group in the nation. Prosecutors say Gotti reigns over a criminal network that rakes in millions from construction and garment-industry extortion, loan-sharking, gambling and heroin. Gotti indignantly insists he is a legitimate businessman.

Gotti has walked away from serious criminal charges three times since 1986, the year prosecutors say he became a Mafia don. Assault and robbery charges against him were dismissed in 1986 after the victim, who had been beaten in a dispute over a double-parked car, first failed to appear in court and then said he could not identify Gotti and his co-defendant. In 1987, Gotti was acquitted in a federal racketeering case in which he was accused of participating for more than 18 years in a criminal enterprise involving loan-sharking, illegal gambling, armed hijackings and at least three murders.*

And in 1990, Gotti was found not guilty of assault and conspiracy in the 1986 shooting of John O'Connor, an official of a carpenters' union whose members had allegedly vandalized a restaurant owned by a

---

*George H. Pape, the foreman of the jury that acquitted Gotti in 1987, was indicted Feb. 24 on charges that he conspired with the mob to sell his vote and influence the jury in exchange for $60,000.

member of the Gambino family. With prosecutors unable to make a charge stick, New York's tabloids gleefully tagged Gotti with another moniker: "the Teflon Don."

Now Gotti is on trial again. He is charged with ordering the assassinations of five men, including former Gambino family chief Paul Castellano, who was gunned down in December 1985 as he stepped from his black Lincoln limousine outside a Manhattan steakhouse. The 13-count indictment also accuses Gotti of conspiracy to murder a sixth man, racketeering, obstruction of justice, illegal gambling and tax evasion. Gotti and his co-defendant, Frank "Frankie Locs" Locascio — the purported No. 2 man in the Gambino family at present — face life in prison if convicted. Both have been held without bail since their arrests 15 months ago.

Key Defection

The current Gotti trial, like the ones in 1987 and 1990, features taped conversations recorded through electronic surveillance of mob hangouts, mainly the Ravenite Social Club in Little Italy. But the tapes have taken second billing to the testimony provided by the chief prosecution witness, Salvatore "Sammy Bull" Gravano. Named in three murder counts in the Gotti indictment (he has admitted to those and 16 other murders), Gravano agreed last fall, after 10 months in jail, to break the Mafia vow of silence and testify against Gotti.

Gravano's defection raised eyebrows because he was not only Gotti's close friend but also served as his underboss. "I don't like Sammy, I love him," Gotti said in a Dec. 12, 1989, conversation recorded with an FBI bug. "I'm gonna go to jail and leave him in charge. So obviously, I gotta love the guy."

His opinion appears to have changed. "Mr. Gravano is a little man, full of evil, connivance, manipulation and vanity who has tried to clean his slate by admitting to 19 murders," Gotti's lawyer, Albert J. Krieger, told the jury when the trial began.

In his testimony about the murders of Castellano and his driver, Thomas Bilotti, Gravano said he and Gotti were waiting in a nearby car while several of their associates carried out the slayings. He and Gotti were there not as mere spectators, Gravano said, but as "backup shooters" if their services were needed.

After Castellano's murder, Gravano said, Gotti made him a captain in the Gambino family. Gravano was promoted in 1987 to *consigliere* (counselor), the third-highest position in the Mafia command structure, and in 1990 to underboss.

Having eluded conviction for so long, Gotti seems almost an obsession with some New York prosecutors. But other law-enforcement experts feel Gotti's media image greatly magnifies his true stature. A Gotti conviction, says Martens of the Pennsylvania

JFK Assassination and the Mafia: Is There a Link?

"Gangsters have always operated in a shifting, layered, shadowy world," Stephen Fox asserted in *Blood and Power*, his 1989 study of the Mafia. "They leave inscrutable histories replete with accident and misdirection, the imponderables of personality, appearances that correspond to no realities, and many surprises." † He could have been writing about the Mafia's interaction with the Kennedy family.

Several authors of books on the assassination of John F. Kennedy concluded that the president set the stage for his own murder by compromising himself with the mob. He had used the Mafia's services in a plot to kill Cuban Premier Fidel Castro, they reasoned, all the while backing the Justice Department's unrelenting assault on organized crime.

"It's understood by prosecutors and police," G. Robert Blakey and Richard N. Billings wrote in *The Plot to Kill the President* (1981), "that there is a line that must not be crossed. You are all right ... just as long as you do not 'sleep with them,' that is, you do not take [Mafia] favors, either money or sex. The prosecutor or cop or government official who does cross the line and takes action against them ... invites violent retribution." †† This, Blakey and Billings argued, is precisely what happened in Dallas.

John H. Davis took a similar tack in *Mafia Kingfish*, in which he advanced the theory that New Orleans Mafia chieftain Carlos Marcello played a pivotal role in John Kennedy's death. But Davis ended his book by acknowledging he had failed to prove his case: "Despite the overwhelming web of circumstantial evidence suggesting the complicity of the Marcello organization in the assassination ... and despite the fact that the president's murder did bear, in thinly disguised form, the fingerprints of a traditional Mafia execution, we are still uncertain about the precise details and extent of Carlos Marcello's suspected involvement in the crime." ‡

A new movie similarly portrays organized crime as the prime force behind the JFK assassination (with an assist from the CIA). In docudrama fashion, "Ruby" tells the story of Jack Ruby, the Dallas nightclub owner who gunned down accused Kennedy assassin Lee Harvey Oswald in the basement of Dallas' municipal building. The film argues that the Mafia, furious at Kennedy for not showing appreciation for its alleged help in swinging the 1960 election his way, killed the president out of revenge.

Director Oliver Stone, whose recent film "JFK" suggests the Kennedy assassination was the product of a broadly based conspiracy, dismisses the "Ruby" premise as wrongheaded. It is a myth concocted by "a bunch of New York tabloid writers who have always glamorized the mob and given them powers they do not possess," says Stone. "These people do not have one-tenth of the power ascribed to them by writers, and the people who've made 'Ruby.'"

The real danger, Stone adds, is that "if push comes to shove and the government is forced to accept a conspiracy theory, they're going to try and lay it off on the mob. I guarantee that's what they'll do." ‡‡

Be that as it may, the great majority of Americans believe the Kennedy assassination involved some kind of conspiracy. Only 11 percent of the respondents to a December 1991 *Time*-Cable News Network poll said they accepted the official Warren Commission explanation that Oswald, acting alone, killed the president. Asked to name one or more groups that might have been involved in an assassination conspiracy, 50 percent cited the CIA — and 48 percent cited the Mafia. ‡‡†

---

† Stephen Fox, *Blood and Power: Organized Crime in 20th Century America* (1989), p. 11.

†† G. Robert Blakey and Richard N. Billings, *The Plot to Kill the President* (1981), p. 339.

‡ John H. Davis, *Mafia Kingfish: Carlos Marcello and the Assassination of John F. Kennedy* (1989), p. 527.

‡‡ Quoted by Jeffrey Wells, "Riling Stone," *Entertainment Weekly*, Feb. 7, 1992, p. 12.

‡‡† The four other groups of possible conspirators listed in the *Time*-CNN poll were the Cuban government (picked by 34 percent of the respondents), anti-Castro Cuban exiles (19 percent), U.S. military leaders (18 percent) and the Dallas police (13 percent).

Crime Commission, would cause "not a ripple" in the war against crime.

"Why it is important to convict Gotti," he says, "is to prove to the public that Gotti is not bigger than government. But to argue that his incarceration will be the death knell of La Cosa Nostra is pure fantasy. After all, he's been in jail for more than a year now.

Did that end La Cosa Nostra?"

Ronald Goldstock also feels a Gotti conviction would be "largely symbolic." He doubts whether Gotti would have much of a future in the mob even after an acquittal. "He has not been a good leader for the Gambino family," he says. For one thing, Gotti "has been unable to avoid electronic surveillance. And while he has been acquitted [previously], largely because of jury tampering, those around him have been convicted on the basis of the same tapes that were directed at him. He has brought a great deal of attention to the mob, and he has created conflict within it

Continued on p. 282

At Issue:

Was it wise to put the Justice Department's organized-crime strike forces under the command of local U.S. attorneys' offices?

RICHARD L. THORNBURGH

Former U.S. Attorney General
FROM CONGRESSIONAL TESTIMONY, SEPT. 8, 1989

yes

*a*t the outset, let me point out that those who characterize this plan as one to abolish these offices, known popularly as strike forces, are mistaken. Our merger plan is, in fact, designed to strengthen the fight against organized crime through more efficient coordination and by making more resources available to the effort, by reducing confusion and overlapping jurisdiction, and providing overall management through a newly established Organized Crime Council in Washington.

What we are talking about to a large extent is a change that is more bureaucratic and managerial than substantive. To the public and to prospective targets of our organized-crime fight, the day following the consolidation will be very little different from the day preceding it. Over time, however, I believe this consolidation can lead to more prosecutions, more convictions and to a more effective enforcement program....

Today, however, we find ourselves in an era when the traditional elements of organized crime are changing their tactics and new criminal organizations and techniques are emerging. This, we feel, requires new approaches and a new configuration in our efforts....

Specifically, the consolidation will end prosecutor-shopping by investigative agencies and will eliminate the turf battles that have been noted in the present system. Further, the consolidation of the offices would centralize the accountability for prosecuting crime in a district and would encourage U.S. attorneys to dedicate their resources strategically to combat organized crime.

I would like to mention one other development which has occurred since the initiation of the strike force program in 1967. During this interval, the overall quality, quantity and independence of the U.S. attorneys and their assistants has measurably increased.

While I personally believe that the U.S. attorneys' offices in 1967 were up to the task of combating organized crime with appropriate support from Washington, what I believed then is now undeniably true. U.S. attorneys and their greatly enlarged staffs are now recognized as dedicated professionals widely respected within their districts....

Today's U.S. attorneys are the premier law-enforcement officials in this country. They have the capability, the determination, the commitment and, if this plan is implemented, will have the full authority to pursue major organized crime and other criminal enterprises on a comprehensive basis.

EDWARD A. MCDONALD

New York lawyer and former strike force member
FROM CONGRESSIONAL TESTIMONY, SEPT. 8, 1989

no

*m*y initial impulse is to rely on the old adage that has become a cliché in the current debate — "If it ain't broke, don't fix it." To be sure, the strike force program "ain't broke."... Indeed, during the past decade, the strike force program has flourished.

In city after city, the strike forces have successfully prosecuted the hierarchy of every significant organized-crime family. Countless labor racketeers, unscrupulous businessmen, corrupt public officials and large-scale narcotics traffickers, who had conducted their criminal activities for years with impunity and without detection, have been convicted. Forfeitures in the hundreds of millions have been obtained. And for the first time, industries that have been captured by organized crime face the prospect of being freed from that domination if the department's effort is not weakened.

Unquestionably, the achievements of the attorneys in the strike force program, never numbering more than 150, are unprecedented — not only in the history of the war against organized crime but in the annals of the entire Department of Justice as well.

In view of these successes and the cost-effective way in which they were achieved, any suggestion that the program be eliminated would appear to border on the inane. Nonetheless, the attorney general's public statements reveal a resolute commitment to abolish the strike force program, and in these circumstances, facile clichés and the cavalier reliance on an established record of accomplishment are not adequate in response....

"Merger" [will] have serious adverse consequences in the long run. The tenures of United States attorneys are measured by their accomplishments — while they are in office. They receive no credit for matters commenced and investigated during their terms that come to fruition after they leave office.

Consequently, many United States attorneys, who generally remain in office for only four or five years, are invariably motivated to produce short-term results. Thus, it is inevitable that United States attorneys, with more diversified agendas and shifting pressures and influences, will feel compelled to assign their best and most experienced attorneys to either what appear to be the more important matters of the day or to matters that can be quickly resolved. All this, of course, would be at the expense of the organized-crime program, which requires the long-term, intensive commitment of resources.

Continued from p. 280
between families. Most people in the mob recognize that he is a liability rather than an asset."

Mafia Defectors

Dramatic though they were, the Gotti trial's revelations about intrigue, treachery and violence in one Mafia family broke no fresh ground. Over the past several years, other organized-crime groups also have fallen prey to internal upheaval. Sometimes a single act of violence or betrayal triggers a chain reaction, virtually crippling a crime organization with minimal input from law-enforcement authorities.

Ripples from the botched assassination of Peter Chiodo, a *capo* (captain) in New York's Lucchese family, are still being felt. In May 1991, two men with pistols shot Chiodo 12 times as he was working on his car at a filling station on Staten Island. Chiodo survived. Believing that the shooting had been ordered by Lucchese family leaders, Chiodo decided to testify for the prosecution in a federal racketeering trial about alleged Mafia control of New York's lucrative window-installation industry.*

One of the most devastating Mafia turncoats is Philip Leonetti, former underboss of the Philadelphia-Atlan-

*The trial involved charges that Mafia leaders skimmed "tens of millions" of dollars through a conspiracy to control awarding of $142 million in window-replacement contracts at the New York City Housing Authority. Three men were convicted in October 1991, among them Venero "Benny Eggs" Mangano, reputed underboss of the Genovese family. Five men were acquitted, including John Gotti's older brother, Peter. On March 10, 1992, Peter Chiodo's 38-year-old sister, Patricia Capozzalo, was shot twice as she sat in her car in Brooklyn. Police surmised the attack may have been intended to discourage Chiodo from testifying in other trials of Mafia figures, including John Gotti.

tic City crime family and the nephew of that family's jailed leader, Nicodemo "Nicky" Scarfo. Although the two reportedly had a father-son relationship, Leonetti decided to testify for the government after he was convicted in 1988 along with Scarfo and 15 other mobsters. He has since built a reputation as an accomplished government witness, testifying in three

One of the most devastating Mafia turncoats is Philip Leonetti, former underboss of the Philadelphia-Atlantic City crime family and the nephew of that family's jailed leader, Nicodemo "Nicky" Scarfo.

1990 trials in Pennsylvania that resulted in convictions.

His New York courtroom debut is expected to take place at the Gotti trial, where prosecutors say they will ask him to establish that Gotti is indeed the head of the Gambino crime family. Leonetti is in the witness-protection program, along with his girlfriend and mother.

Why Key Mobsters Defect

Two factors are cited to explain the epidemic of defections. One is fear of incarceration, a concern that has intensified with the government's string of successful prosecutions of mob bigwigs. Authorities say, for example, that Gravano turned state's evidence because he dreaded the prospect of being separated for years from his wife and children.

The second factor centers on generational differences. Joe Pistone, a former FBI agent who infiltrated two Mafia families, recalled that older members

often complained about the younger members' lack of dedication. "'Our thing' was turning into 'my thing' within the Mafia," said Pistone, "just as the larger American society is facing the new realities of the 'me generation.'"[19]

A similar erosion of discipline has occurred in mob families based in Sicily. Tommaso Buscetta, a member of the Sicilian Mafia, defected in 1984 because he felt the organization he had known "no longer existed." Two years later, he provided key testimony in an unprecedented Palermo, Sicily, trial that resulted in the convictions of 435 Mafia members. In 1988, he told the U.S. Senate Permanent Investigations Subcommittee why he cooperated with Italian and U.S. authorities.

Buscetta argued, in effect, that the Mafia betrayed him, not the other way around. "Over the years, I have seen our organization change from within," he said. "I have seen money, drugs and greed corrupt and destroy the Cosa Nostra code of honor and loyalty to the families.... Today, the Mafia takes from everybody and gives nothing back. It exists only for the personal benefit of its members.... I no longer feel bound by the code of *omertá,* or silence."

Mafia defectors say that life under the government's witness-protection program will never rival the old days. Former hitman Nicholas "The Crow" Caramandi, who helped finger Nicky Scarfo in 1988, rhapsodized about his career as a mobster in a 1991 *Time* interview.

Belonging to the mob is "the greatest thing that a human could experience," he said. "At Christmas, people are bangin' on your door, dropping off gifts. If it rains, 25 umbrellas open up. If you walk into a restaurant, they'll chase the person out of the best table and put you there. There's just so much glamour and respect and money. The nightclubs, the broads. Broads just die over you. It's unbelievable."[20] ∎

OUTLOOK

Down But Not Out

As prosecutors go after more Mafia leaders, RICO doubtless will continue to figure in their game plans. In fact, says Ronald Goldstock, law-enforcement officials "ought to understand that RICO is a very flexible tool. Just because they have used RICO in one way, and succeeded, does not mean they ought to employ it only in that way in the future." A flexible approach is needed, Goldstock says, because "different groups and different criminal activities present different problems."

Goldstock sees no chance that the Mafia can change its operating methods enough to insulate itself from assault by RICO. He speculates that mobsters might try to manipulate the value of their assets in an effort to escape the full impact of RICO's forfeiture provisions. "But other than that, I don't think there's very much they can do."

Some observers give the Mafia the benefit of the doubt where long-term survival is concerned. "We're talking about an organization that has thrived in this country for 70 years," says Martens of the Pennsylvania Crime Commission. "Now, you might point to communism in the Soviet Union. That crumbled after 70 years, and I would agree everything runs its course. But I don't think [organized crime's] course is over by a long shot."

Jim Savage, associate editor in charge of investigations for *The Miami Herald* and a longtime Mafia-watcher, says the Mafia "is probably evolving and has been evolving since Prohibition. It is also becoming less visible. But to believe that the Mafia component of organized crime in this country is going to disappear is overly optimistic."

Meanwhile, increasingly powerful ethnic crime syndicates are claiming pieces of the faltering Mafia's underworld action. The lesson, said FBI Director William S. Sessions, is that "Crime is becoming more and more international in nature, and law-enforcement agencies from different countries must join together if we are to deter the international criminals." [21]

However, the mobility of today's organized criminals promises to make deterrence more difficult. Savage notes that the Colombian drug cartels based in Cali and Medellín seemed to have eclipsed the Mafia in South Florida some years ago. Now there is evidence, he says, that the Colombians have shifted much of their business to Southern California.

A recent Sunday talk show on Miami television underscored the economic impact of the move. It was almost "as if they were talking about the tourist industry or the citrus industry," says Savage. But the subject was drug money, and the program concluded that its disappearance from South Florida had deepened the area's recession.

With so much money at stake, it's no wonder that Robert Blakey, the father of RICO, hedges his bets about the mob's future. "That's why I say it's twilight [for the Mafia], not sunset." ∎

Notes

[1] Quoted in "The Great Mafia Roundup," *U.S. News & World Report*, April 16, 1990, p. 27.

[2] Quoted in the *Los Angeles Times*, Feb. 9, 1991, p. A23.

[3] Quoted by Victor S. Navasky, "A Famous Prosecutor Talks About Crime," *The New York Times Magazine*, Feb. 15, 1970, p. 96.

[4] The President's Commission on Organized Crime, *The Edge: Organized Crime, Business and Labor Unions*, March 1986, p. 21.

[5] Roy Rowan, "The Mafia's Bite of the Big Apple," *Fortune*, June 6, 1988, p. 131.

[6] For background, see "Garbage Crisis," *The CQ Researcher*, March 20, 1992, pp. 241-264.

[7] President's Commission on Organized Crime, *op. cit.*, p. 33.

[8] *Ibid.*, p. 36.

[9] Sens. Sam Nunn and Edward M. Kennedy, "A Move the Mob Would Like," *The New York Times*, June 19, 1989, p. A15. Nunn is chairman of the Permanent Investigations Subcommittee of the Senate Governmental Affairs Committee; Kennedy is a member of the Senate Judiciary Committee.

[10] August Bequai, *Organized Crime: The Fifth Estate* (1979), p. 14.

[11] Ralph Blumenthal, *Last Days of the Sicilians* (1988), p. 50.

[12] See Attorney General of the United States, Conference on Organized Crime, 1950.

[13] Estes Kefauver, *Crime in America* (1952), pp. 11-12.

[14] Quoted by G. Robert Blakey and Richard N. Billings in *The Plot to Kill the President* (1981), p. 221.

[15] U.S. Senate Select Committee to Study Government Operations with respect to Intelligence Activities, *Alleged Assassination Plots Involving Foreign Leaders*, 1975.

[16] For background, see "Racketeering Law Comes Under Attack," *Editorial Research Reports*, March 17, 1989, pp. 133-148.

[17] *United States v. Turkette*, 452 U.S. 576 (1981).

[18] *Russello v. United States*, 464 U.S. 16 (1983).

[19] Quoted in "Federal Government's Use of the RICO Statute and Other Efforts Against Organized Crime," report of the Permanent Investigations Subcommittee of the Senate Governmental Operations Committee, July 10, 1990. Pistone (with co-author Richard Woodley) wrote a book about his undercover work: *Donnie Brasco* [his undercover name]: *My Undercover Life in the Mafia* (1989).

[20] Richard Behar, "A Crow Turns Stool Pigeon," *Time*, June 17, 1991, p. 13.

[21] Address before the Commonwealth Club of California, San Francisco, Sept. 7, 1990.

Bibliography

Selected Sources Used

Books

Bequai, August, *Organized Crime: The Fifth Estate,* Lexington Books, 1979.

Bequai's study proceeds from a historic overview of organized crime to an examination of its main contemporary varieties and a critique of law-enforcement strategies aimed at combating them.

Blumenthal, Ralph, *Last Days of the Sicilians,* Timesbooks, 1988.

Blumenthal, a veteran reporter for *The New York Times,* describes how the FBI and other government agencies cracked the Pizza Connection case, which involved the funneling of tons of heroin and morphine base through U.S. pizza parlors, cafes and boutiques.

Cantalupo, Joseph and Thomas C. Renner, *Body Mike: An Unsparing Exposé by the Mafia Insider Who Turned on the Mob,* Villard Books, 1990.

This book tells how Cantalupo, a close associate of the late Mafia leader Joseph Colombo, became an undercover informer and state's witness against Mafia kingpins.

Cox, Donald W., *Mafia Wipeout: How the Feds Put Away an Entire Mob Family,* Shapolsky Publishers Inc., 1989.

Cox chronicles the rise and fall of Nicodemo "Nicky" Scarfo, the unusually vicious (even by Mafia standards) boss of the Philadelphia-Atlantic City crime family.

Davis, John H., *Kingfish: Carlos Marcello and the Assassination of John F. Kennedy,* McGraw-Hill Publishing Co., 1989.

Davis, whose previous books include *The Kennedys: Dynasty and Disaster,* explores the possibility — raised by some conspiracy theorists — that New Orleans Mafia boss Carlos Marcello played a pivotal role in the assassination of President Kennedy. In the end, though, Davis concludes that proof of Marcello's involvement in such a scheme (if one existed) is lacking.

Fox, Stephen, *Blood and Power: Organized Crime in 20th-Century America,* William Morrow and Co. Inc., 1989.

Fox traces the evolution of organized crime in the United States from the mid-19th century to the late 1980s. He devotes one chapter to the mob's alleged ties to the Kennedy family.

O'Brien, Joseph F. and Andris Kurins, *Boss of Bosses*

— *The Fall of the Godfather: The FBI and Paul Castellano,* Simon & Schuster, 1991.

O'Brien and Kurins, who are former FBI agents, present an in-depth profile of Paul Castellano, the New York Mafia boss whose murder John Gotti is accused of arranging.

Articles

Byron, Christopher, "There Goes the Neighborhood," *New York,* Jan. 15, 1990.

Byron attempts to unravel the mystery of how 22,000 tons of hazardous waste was dumped in the posh suburb of Harrison, N.Y., creating health problems and undermining local property values. Circumstantial evidence points to the involvement of Mafia-controlled waste-disposal firms.

Raab, Selwyn, "Running the Mob," *The New York Times Magazine,* April 2, 1989.

Raab, a *New York Times* reporter who has written extensively on the mob, examines the career of John Gotti and appraises the state of the Mafia in New York, long its national stronghold.

Reports and Studies

U.S. Senate Judiciary Committee and Permanent Investigations Subcommittee of the Senate Governmental Affairs Committee, *Status of the Department of Justice Organized Crime Strike Forces* (published proceedings of hearing held Sept. 8, 1989).

Former Attorney General Richard L. Thornburgh's proposal to merge the Justice Department's organized-crime strike forces with local U.S. attorneys' offices is hotly debated at a hearing.

Permanent Investigations Subcommittee of the U.S. Senate Governmental Affairs Committee, *Federal Government's Use of the RICO Statute and Other Efforts Against Organized Crime,* July 10, 1990.

This legislative report examines how prosecutors have used the Racketeer Influenced and Corrupt Organizations Act (RICO) to sow disarray among crime families.

Permanent Investigations Subcommittee of the U.S. Senate Governmental Affairs Committee, *Organized Crime: 25 Years After Valachi* (published proceedings of hearings held in April 1988), January 1991.

Various law-enforcement officials testify about the current strength of organized crime in the United States a quarter-century after Mafia turncoat Joseph Valachi testified before a Senate panel in 1963.

The Next Step

Additional Articles from Current Periodicals from EBSCO Publishing's Database

Actions & defenses

Magnuson, E. and C. Gorman, "Still the Teflon Don?" *Time*, Dec. 24, 1990, p. 19.

Reports that John Gotti, the alleged boss of the nation's largest and most vicious Mafia family, was charged last week with murder, racketeering and tax evasion. Having beaten federal and state prosecutors in three trials since 1986, he earned the tag "Teflon Don." How his arrogance has made him seemingly careless; acquittal in 1987 on similar charges; sensational rubout of Paul Castellano in 1985.

Raab, S., "FBI taped Gotti talks about fixing jury," *The New York Times*, Jan. 8, 1991, p. B1.

Tells about the secret tape recordings on which federal agents overheard the nation's most powerful Mafia boss, John Gotti, talk of trying to fix the jury in his state trial last January. The FBI withheld the information from state prosecutors who were trying to prove that he had engineered the shooting and wounding of a carpenters' union leader.

Asian crime

"Chinese criminals in America," *Futurist*, May/June 1991, p. 54.

Refutes claims that there is a "Chinese Mafia" in the U.S. Focus on the research and conclusions from the book "Chinese Subculture and Criminality: Nontraditional Crime Groups in America," by Ko-Lin Chin; overview of Chinese crime groups; role played in increased heroin trafficking in the U.S.

Kifner, J., "New immigrant wave from Asia gives the underworld new faces," *The New York Times*, Jan. 6, 1991, p. 1.

Presents a special report on Asian gangs in New York City. As waves of Chinese and Southeast Asian immigrants flood New York City in search of better lives, their expanding neighborhoods are being plagued by increasingly violent street gangs and new criminal enterprises that law-enforcement officials say may come to rival the Mafia in its heyday. Crimes concentrated in the hard-working Chinese community; types of crimes.

Books & reading

Fleischer, L., "Book review," *Publishers Weekly*, July 5, 1991, p. 34.

Discusses the book "Goombata," by Ernest Volkman and

John Cummings. The book is about the so-called "Teflon Don," a.k.a. Mafia crime lord John Gotti. How "Goombata" recently came to Gotti's attention and why he doesn't like the book; more about the Mafia and true-crime books.

O'Brien, J. F. and A. Kurins, "Conversations with the Godfather," *New York*, May 27, 1991, p. 30.

Discusses how in March 1983, the FBI bugged the fortress of "Big Paul" Castellano, then-head of the Gambino clan, and the godfather of New York's five mob families. The FBI eavesdropped on some 600 hours of conversation, hearing classic mobspeak — straight from the movies. Excerpts from the new book "Boss of Bosses — The Fall of the Godfather: The FBI and Paul Castellano," by Joseph O'Brien, Andris Kurins and Laurence Shames.

Patrick, V., "My son, the gangster," *The New York Times Book Review*, Aug. 25, 1991, p. 6.

Reviews the novel "Inherit the Mob," by Zev Chafets. The author maintains that the novel is in perfect keeping with Mr. Chafets' hilarious, warm look at one of organized crime's oft-neglected ethnic groups. INSET: "A movie in my head".

Stuttaford, G., "Forecasts: Nonfiction," *Publishers Weekly*, Nov. 29, 1991, p. 40.

Reviews the book "The Soviet Mafia: A Shocking Exposé of Organized Crime in the USSR," by Arkady Vaksberg, translated by John and Elizabeth Roberts.

Case studies

"Refuse you cannot offer," *Economist*, Feb. 23, 1991, p. 27.

Discusses the reasons why New York's garbage collection business is a stronghold of the regional organized-crime syndicates. Manhattan's Fulton Fish Market; Frank Wohl, a federal investigator; Mafia influence in the building trades; the Genovese crime family; details.

Behar, R., "A crow turns stool pigeon," *Time*, June 17, 1991, p. 11.

Presents an interview with Nicholas "The Crow" Caramandi, a Philadelphia hitman who fingered his Mafia boss to save his own skin. Killed one of his best friends; testified in 11 trials that have brought 52 convictions; right-hand man to Nicodemo "Nicky" Scarfo.

Behar, R., "Revving up for a cleanup?" *Time*, June 24,

1991, p. 36.

Discusses how the Teamsters union is at last cleaning up its act, thanks to the prodding of court-appointed officers who have forced dozens of mob-connected officials out of the union. Deal with the government in 1989 to settle massive racketeering suit; first free election of president and executive board; the candidates for president; about the union; lawyer James P. Hoffa, 50; current president, William McCarthy. INSET: "The Members Have Been Hurt So Badly."

Bernstein, A., "The teamsters and the mob: It may really be over," _Business Week_, June 17, 1991, p. 102.

Shows how the Teamsters, one of the most mob-connected unions in the nation, is on the verge of being cleaned up. The change will be dramatized on June 24 when the union holds a convention in Orlando to nominate candidates for president — and for the union's executive board. Top nominees for president, including R. V. Durham and Ron Carey; their backgrounds; cleaning up the union; changes to be made. INSET: Is Ryder in bad company? by A. N. Fins.

Black, A., "Joe Hill rides again," _New Statesman & Society_, May 24, 1991, p. 24.

Reveals that after many years of corruption and Mafia involvement, democracy is about to break out in America's biggest union — the Teamsters. Who the International Brotherhood of Teamsters (IBT) represents; the beginning of a Teamster civil war; fixing the union's leadership elections; U.S. government lawsuit; Teamsters for a Democratic Union (TDU); history of Mafia involvement; unions are big business; details.

Cook, J., "But where are the dons' yachts?" _Forbes_, Oct. 21, 1991, _1991 Forbes 400_, p. 121.

Questions why there are no Mafia chieftains among The _Forbes_ 400, and cites the case of mob boss John Gotti Jr. as an answer to that question. Background on John Joseph Gotti Jr.; estimated net worth; assets; the structure of a Mafia family; the hazards involved in doing business with the mob; a Mafia boss must adjust his lifestyle to the visible source of his income.

Manly, H. and C. Friday, "The banker vanishes," _Newsweek_, Jan. 7, 1991, p. 31.

Details the mystery behind the sudden disappearance of Rhode Island banker Joe Mollicone last November. Various theories on his disappearance; Mollicone's admitted association with Luigi Manocchio, a reputed leader of the Patriarca family, which allegedly controls organized crime in New England; Mollicone's failure to mention that the Heritage Loan and Investment Co. had been vandalized.

Raab, S., "Racketeering is still found at Fulton Fish

Market," _The New York Times_, Aug. 9, 1990, p. A1.

States that an "atmosphere of lawlessness" and brutality still prevail at the Fulton Fish Market in Manhattan (long investigated as a Mafia stronghold) two years after a federal administrator was appointed to help drive out the racketeers. Strong-arm tactics discourage suppliers from sending fish to New York, driving up retail prices for consumers.

Raab, S., "School bus pacts go to companies with ties to mob," _The New York Times_, Dec. 26, 1990, p. A1.

Presents a special report on school buses, unions and the mob. New York City, without competitive bidding, consistently awards the most expensive school bus contracts in the nation, and many have gone to companies linked to suspected organized-crime figures. Since the state pays almost 80 percent of the bus contracts, school officials have no incentive to cut costs.

Debates & issues

"The G-men and the million-dollar Mafia bug," _Newsweek_, June 24, 1991, p. 26.

Reports on the reaction of FBI brass to the newly released book "Boss of Bosses," written by FBI agents Andris Kurins and Joseph O'Brien regarding the pursuit of Mafia leaders. James Fox, chief of the FBI's New York office; FBI Director William S. Sessions; Kurins' and O'Brien's resignation from the bureau; trial of John Gotti; more.

Behar, R., "The underworld is their oyster," _Time_, Sept. 3, 1990, p. 54.

Presents a special report on organized crime which argues that while John Gotti may get the headlines, Vincent Gigante's mob family ranks as the real powerhouse in a $100 billion industry. Convictions and bloodletting; penchant for privacy; ridding the unions of mobsters. INSET: Is the Godfather insane, or crazy like a fox?

Bruning, F., "Taking money from gangsters," _Maclean's_, Oct. 7, 1991, p. 15.

Outlines the curious case of Thomas and Joseph Gambino, sons of deceased Mafia boss Carlo Gambino, who have for years raised funds for the Long Island Jewish Medical Centre, and recently laid out the better part of $2.3 million for a facility serving children with leukemia.

Raab, S., "2 FBI agents quit over royalties for Mafia book," _The New York Times_, June 14, 1991, p. A1.

Tells about the furor over whether two Federal Bureau of Investigation agents improperly published secret information on the sex life of a former New York Mafia boss and on FBI surveillance tactics. "Boss of Bosses" by Joseph F. O'Brien and Andris Kurins about the late Paul Castellano of the Gambino crime family; resignation of the two agents.

Raab, S., "A battered and ailing Mafia is losing its grip on America," *The New York Times,* **Oct. 22, 1990, p. A1.**

Presents a special report on the Mafia. Most of America's traditional Mafia families appear to be fading out of existence, except in the New York City area and in the suburbs of Chicago. The convictions of top Mafia leaders and their henchmen have dismantled thriving underworld organizations in Philadelphia, New Jersey, New England and elsewhere. How the public gains; other groups moving in take the Mafia's place.

Federal witnesses

Del Giudice, M., "The mobster who could bring down the mob," *The New York Times Magazine,* **June 2, 1991, p. 24.**

Profiles Phil Leonetti, a man who has gone from Mafia hit man to government witness. Decision to cooperate and enter the federal witness protection program; Leonetti's background; involvement with the Mafia; Leonetti's testimony and its possible implications for mobster boss John Gotti; more.

Raab, S., "How Gotti's No. 2 gangster turned his coat," *The New York Times,* **Nov. 15, 1991, p. B1.**

Discusses Salvatore Gravano's offer to testify against John Gotti, the nation's most powerful Mafia boss. Gravano, who as the No. 2 leader and underboss in the Gambino family is the highest-ranking Mafia defector to become a government witness, is providing information about the assassination of former Gambino boss Paul Castellano and others that Gotti is said to have ordered. He is also talking about the gang's illicit business deals, bribes and labor racketeering operations.

Sullivan, J.F., "41 charged in mob case based on informer," *The New York Times,* **Aug. 22, 1990, p. B1.**

Reports that 41 people, including members of six organized-crime families and two of their bosses, were charged with racketeering on the basis of almost 400 conversations secretly recorded by George Fresolone, an informer, who even recorded his own induction into the Bruno-Scarfo crime family in the Bronx on July 29.

Italy

"Italy's ever-growing monster," *Economist,* **July 27, 1991, p. 43.**

Discusses how Vincenzo Scotti, Italy's interior minister, promises victory in the fight against the Mafia and its cousins. Scotti claims that Italy now has the means and the right laws to crack organized crime. Why few Italians share his optimism; the various crimes committed by the Sicilian Mafia; the biggest-ever Mafia trial, which opened in Palermo in

1986; why the Italian government is struggling so badly against the Mafia.

Hinckle, P., "The war of the teens," *Newsweek,* **Dec. 24, 1990, p. 40.**

Reports that teenagers in Sicily have increasingly become the foot soldiers and casualties in the Mafia's struggles. The young *sicari* — hit-men — and the murder of Giuseppe Aredia in the Sicilian town of Gela; how the Mafia tactics have changed over the years; description of the city of Gela, whose alleyways are rich in cannon fodder.

Stille, A., "Where the bad fellows gather," *U.S. News & World Report,* **July 22, 1991, p. 39.**

Describes the Italian waterfront, Reggio Calabria, the murder capital of Italy, theater of war for Calabria's powerful Mafia gangs, and a monument to the futility of the government's 30-year effort to pull southern Italy up to the standards enjoyed by the more prosperous, law-abiding north. Putting the gangsters into office; losing control of the southern third of the country; price Calabria pays for lawlessness.

Japan

Miller, K.L., "Suddenly, the Japanese mob is out of the shadows," *Business Week,* **July 8, 1991, p. 29.**

Discusses the influence of Japan's underworld, which is home to some 3,300 yakuza — Japanese Mafia — gangs with nearly 90,000 members. What gangsters look like; what they do; now opening legitimate companies as fronts; wink-and-nod deals; why yakuza dealings strike a nerve; expanding overseas; unlikely to be subject in Japan to the same pressure the Mafia has faced in the U.S.; details.

New England

Raab, S., "U.S. says mob is drying up in New York," *The New York Times,* **Oct. 21, 1991, p. B1.**

States that New York's five Mafia families — Gambino, Genovese, Lucchese, Colombo and Bonanno — have deteriorated in recent months to the point that three are virtually out of business and two are crumbling. After 60 years of illicit expansion, they are succumbing to a decade of aggressive federal prosecution.

Segal, D., "Rogues island," *New Republic,* **Nov. 25, 1991, p. 9.**

Summarizes politics as usual in Rhode Island, were some 200,000 depositors were frozen out of their accounts after banker Joseph Mollicone Jr. vanished with $14 million and the mayor of Pawtucket was tape-recorded shaking down a contractor. Laying the blame on the General Assembly; Mafia presence; signs that Rhode Islanders have had enough.

Back Issues

Great Research on Current Issues Starts Right Here... Recent topics covered by The CQ Researcher are listed below. Issues dated before May 10, 1991, were published under the name of Editorial Research Reports.

SEPTEMBER 1990
Dangers of Alcohol
Western Alliance After the Cold War
Tobacco Industry
Right to Die

OCTOBER 1990
Organ Transplants
Energy Policy Options
Search for Arab Unity
Child Support

NOVEMBER 1990
Lotteries and Gambling
Post-Cold War Choices
Setting Limits on Medical Care
Multicultural Education

DECEMBER 1990
Cable TV Regulation
Americans' Search for Their Roots
Is Insurance System a Failure?
Why Schools Still Have Tracking

JANUARY 1991
Growing Influence of Boycotts
Should the U.S. Reinstate the Draft?
America's Archaeological Past
Peace Corps' Challenges in '90s

FEBRUARY 1991
Regional Impact of Recession
Puerto Rico's Status
Redistricting: Mapping Power
Nuclear Power

MARCH 1991
Acid Rain
Cost of the Gulf War
Reassessing Gun Laws
Future for Man in Space

APRIL 1991
Social Security
Canadian Crisis Over Quebec
California Drought
Electromagnetic Radiation

MAY 1991
School Choice
Racial Quotas
Animal Rights
U.S. and Japan

JUNE 1991
Children and Divorce
Teenage Suicide
Endangered Species
Europe 1992

JULY 1991
Teenagers and Abortion
Soviet Republics Rebel
Mexico's Emergence
Athletes and Drugs

AUGUST 1991
Sexual Harassment
Fetal Tissue Research
Oil Imports
The Palestinians

SEPTEMBER 1991
Police Brutality
Advertising Under Attack
Saving the Forests
Foster Care Crisis

OCTOBER 1991
Pay-Per-View TV
Youth Gangs
Gene Therapy
World Hunger

NOVEMBER 1991
Fast-Food Shake-Up
The Greening of Eastern Europe
Business' Role in Education
Cuba In Crisis

DECEMBER 1991
Retiree Health Benefits
Asian Americans
The Obscenity Debate
The Disabilities Act

JANUARY 1992
Term Limits
Oil Spills
Hunting Controversy
Alternative Medicine

FEBRUARY 1992
Threatened Coastlines
New Era in Asia
Assisted Suicide
Jobs in the '90s

MARCH 1992
Women and Sports
Underage Drinking
Garbage Crisis

Back issues are available for $4.00 (subscribers) or $7.00 (non-subscribers). Quantity discounts apply to orders over ten. To order, call Congressional Quarterly 1-800-432-2250.

Future Topics

▶ *Ozone Depletion*

▶ *Welfare Reform*

▶ *Politicians and Privacy*

PUBLISHED BY CONGRESSIONAL QUARTERLY INC., IN CONJUNCTION WITH EBSCO PUBLISHING

Ozone Depletion

Can global action rescue the deteriorating ozone layer?

U NTIL RECENTLY, SEVERE DEPLETION OF THE
Earth's protective ozone layer — which blocks
harmful solar radiation — was thought to be
confined to a "hole" over Antarctica. But in
February NASA scientists raised new concerns when they
reported that the 25-mile-wide layer apparently is thinning
over the Northern Hemisphere and other populated areas.
Findings to be released this month may even show that a
second hole has opened over northern New England, Canada,
northern Europe, Russia and China. Led by the United States,
once complacent governments are now scrambling to
accelerate the elimination of chlorofluorocarbons (CFCs) and
other chemicals that destroy ozone. Their response to this
global threat could provide a model for international
cooperation in combating similar environmental dangers.

THIS ISSUE

 April 3, 1992 • Volume 2, No. 13 • 289-312

Formerly Editorial Research Reports

April 3, 1992
Volume 2, No. 13

EDITOR
Sandra Stencel

MANAGING EDITOR
Thomas J. Colin

ASSOCIATE EDITOR
Richard L. Worsnop

STAFF WRITERS
Charles S. Clark
Mary H. Cooper
Rodman D. Griffin

PRODUCTION EDITOR
Laurie De Maris

EDITORIAL ASSISTANT
Thomas H. Moore

GRAPHICS
Jack Auldridge

PUBLISHED BY
Congressional Quarterly Inc.

CHAIRMAN
Andrew Barnes

VICE CHAIRMAN
Andrew P. Corty

EDITOR AND PUBLISHER
Neil Skene

EXECUTIVE EDITOR
Robert W. Merry

PUBLICATIONS MARKETING/SALES
Robert Smith

EDITOR, EBSCO PUBLISHING
Melissa Kummerer

The CQ Researcher (ISSN 1056-2036). Formerly Editorial Research Reports. Published weekly (48 times per year, not printed the first Friday of any month with five Fridays) by Congressional Quarterly Inc., 1414 22nd St., N.W., Washington, D.C. 20037. Rates are furnished upon request. Second-class postage paid at Washington, D.C. POSTMASTER: Send address changes to The CQ Researcher, 1414 22nd St., N.W., Washington, D.C. 20037.

Ozone Depletion

BY MARY H. COOPER

THE ISSUES

Scientists at the National Aeronautics and Space Administration (NASA) hadn't planned to hold a news conference on February 3. But, they decided at the last minute, their preliminary findings about Earth's upper atmosphere were too important to sit on. Earth's protective ozone layer,* they announced, was losing ozone much faster than anyone had predicted, exposing humans to higher amounts of harmful radiation.

Even more ominous, they said, it seemed likely that a highly depleted section of the ozone layer, known as a "hole," would develop over the Arctic, exposing populated areas of the Northern Hemisphere. A similar hole had first been observed over Antarctica in 1985.

The scientists based their startling announcement on new data collected over northern New England, eastern Canada and much of Europe and Asia. What their airborne instruments — carried aloft by a satellite and two high-flying planes — detected was the highest concentration of ozone-destroying chlorine monoxide ever measured in the atmosphere.

Chlorine monoxide is a derivative of an important family of synthetic chemicals that are known as chlorofluorocarbons (CFCs). They have enjoyed wide use for decades as coolants in refrigerators and air conditioners, propellants in aerosol spray cans, blowing agents in the manufacture of plastic and rubber foam products and as solvents in the production

---

*The ozone layer is a 25-mile-wide band above the Earth with a high but uneven concentration of ozone gas. Starting at an altitude of about 15 miles, it shields humans and other organisms from the most harmful effects of the sun's ultraviolet (UV) radiation.

of electronic equipment.

Once released into the atmosphere, CFCs drift upward until they reach the ozone layer, which begins in the stratosphere. As long as they remain in their original molecular form, CFCs are harmless. But intense ultraviolet radiation can break the CFC molecule apart, producing chlorine monoxide and setting off a series of reactions that destroy ozone. *(See diagram, p. 292.)*

High levels of chlorine monoxide are alarming enough by themselves. But NASA's scientists found evidence of even more worrisome atmospheric problems: high levels of bromine monoxide. A byproduct of halons, man-made chemicals used in fire extinguishers, bromine monoxide is even more destructive than chlorine monoxide.

Michael Kurylo, NASA's program manager for the study, estimated that the two chemicals could destroy 1 to 2 percent of the ozone layer daily during brief periods of late winter. At that rate, as much as 40 percent of the ozone over populous areas of the Northern Hemisphere could be de-

pleted by early spring, when ozone destruction ends each year. The resulting hole, scientists said, could be almost as serious as the one over Antarctica, where ozone depletion has been known to reach 50 percent.

In addition to high levels of ozone-destroying chlorine monoxide and bromine monoxide, the NASA team found reduced levels of nitrogen oxides, which protect ozone from the other two gases by converting them into harmless compounds before they have time to destroy ozone. The loss of nitrogen oxides, which scientists attribute to high levels of volcanic ash ejected into the stratosphere last summer during the eruption of Mount Pinatubo in the Philippines, diminishes the atmosphere's natural ability to recover from ozone depletion.

"The latest scientific findings indicate pretty clearly that the atmosphere all over the place, and not just in the polar regions, is nearly devoid of some of the constituents that protect ozone against depletion," says Michael Oppenheimer, senior scientist at the Environmental Defense Fund in New York City.

NASA was scheduled to complete its data-gathering flights in March and to announce its final observations by mid-April. At that time, says a NASA spokesman, scientists should know conclusively whether or not another ozone hole has actually opened over the Northern Hemisphere.

Meanwhile, recent findings are serious enough that several countries, including the United States, have taken new steps to slow ozone depletion. In 1987, for example, the main producers and consumers of CFCs and halons signed the Montreal Protocol, which mandated phasing out these destructive chemicals by the year 2000, or sooner. The phaseout was subsequently accelerated in

How Ozone-Depleting Agents Attack the Ozone Layer

Beginning in the stratosphere at an altitude of about 15 miles and extending up into the mesosphere, the 25-mile-wide ozone layer protects Earth by blocking out most of the sun's harmful ultraviolet light. Breakdown of ozone by chlorofluorocarbons and other chemicals allows harmful radiation to reach Earth.

1. Oxygen molecules in the stratosphere are transformed into ozone by solar ultraviolet (UV) radiation, which splits the oxygen molecule (top) and releases highly reactive oxygen atoms. The free oxygen atoms then bind to oxygen molecules to form ozone molecules, which also are broken up by UV radiation. This continuous creation and destruction of oxygen and ozone occurs normally in the stratosphere.

2. Once certain chemicals, chiefly chlorofluorocarbons (CFCs), reach the ozone layer, UV radiation bombards the CFC molecule, breaking off an atom of chlorine.

3. The free chlorine atom attacks an ozone molecule, breaking off one of ozone's three oxygen atoms to form one chlorine monoxide molecule and leaving one oxygen molecule.

4. When the chlorine monoxide molecule encounters a free oxygen atom, produced during the natural mixing of oxygen and ozone (step 1), the oxygen atom breaks up the chlorine monoxide molecule and binds to its oxygen atom, forming a new oxygen molecule and leaving behind a free chlorine atom.

5. The newly freed chlorine atom can continue to destroy ozone molecules for many years (steps 3 and 4). Oxygen molecules continue to break apart and form ozone (step 1), but this natural replenishing process is slowed in the presence of chlorine monoxide.

6. Because oxygen, unlike ozone, does not reflect UV radiation, the sun's potentially harmful UV rays penetrate the depleted areas of the ozone layer and reach Earth's surface.

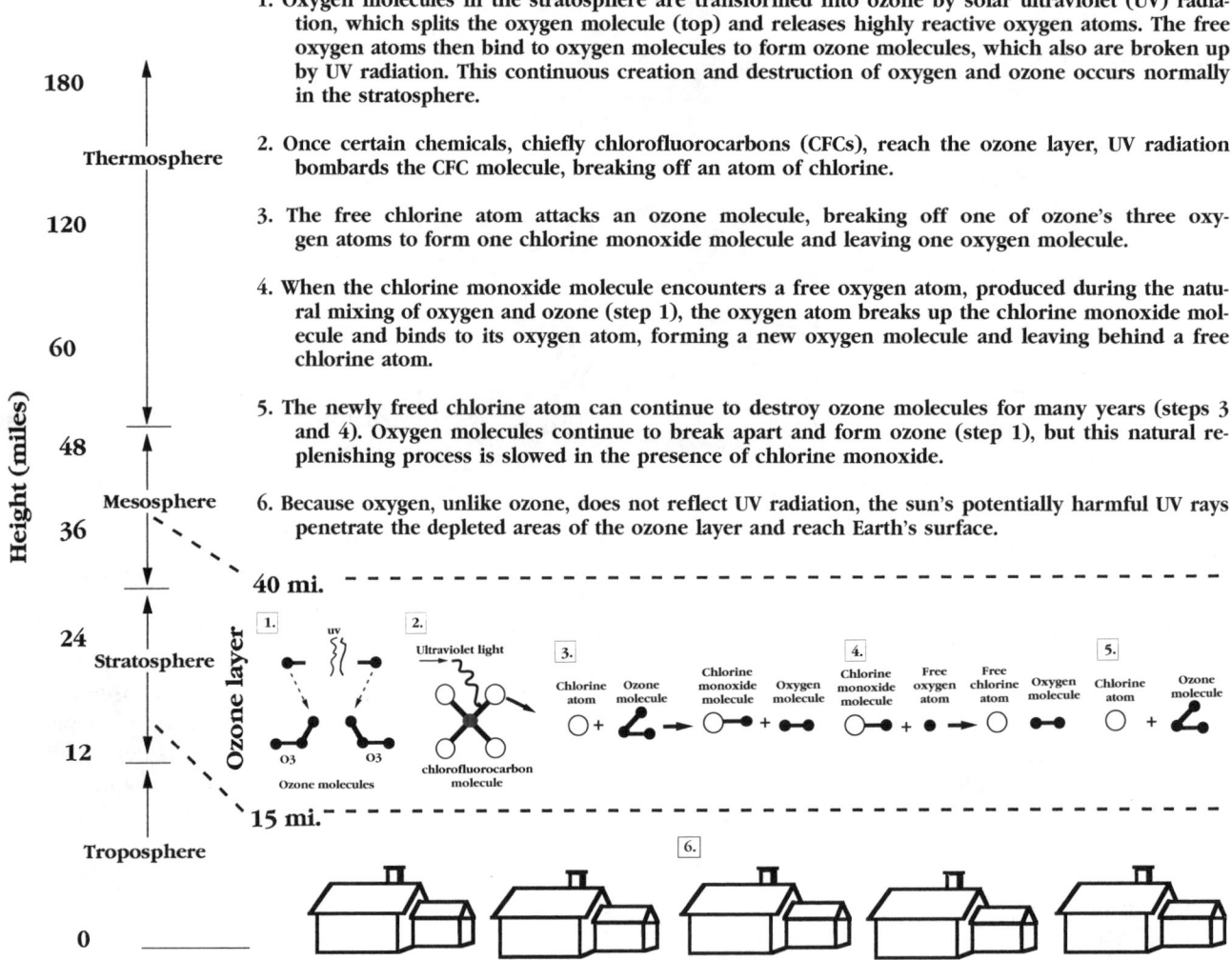

1990, and several signatories to the protocol have since committed themselves to beating the deadline.

As the United States and other nations work to slow ozone depletion, these are some of the questions being asked:

How dangerous is ozone depletion?

Ozone-destroying chemicals are extremely stable, so they last in the atmosphere for many decades. That means that even if production of all CFCs and halons stopped today, the chemicals already in the atmosphere would go on destroying ozone well into the 21st century. And because large quantities of these chemicals are contained in existing air conditioners and refrigerators, from which they continue to escape through mal-function or intentional venting, it may be a century before the ozone layer has built itself back up.

Just how devastating widespread ozone depletion would be is not known. But a 1975 government study on the environmental effects of an all-out nuclear war — which scientists say would destroy much of the ozone layer — provided a chilling glimpse of the aftermath. Ozone depletion of 50 percent, the study postulated, "would cause [skin] blistering after one hour of exposure. This leads to the conclusion that outside daytime work in the Northern Hemisphere would require complete covering by protective clothing.... It would be very difficult to grow many (if any) food crops, and livestock would have to graze at dusk if there were any grass to eat."

The study speculated that a 25 to 30 percent depletion of stratospheric ozone — which NASA's findings indicate already may have occurred over parts of the Northern Hemisphere — would make it "difficult to imagine" how survivors could carry out post-war recovery operations.[1]

Since the ozone hole opened over Antarctica in 1985, scientists have been assessing the impact of increased ultraviolet (UV) radiation on phytoplankton, the micro-organisms that make up the essential first link in the food chain that maintains all animal life in warm southern waters, including whales. Preliminary findings show that phytoplankton populations have dropped by up to 12 percent in areas where surface UV radiation has increased under the Antarctic ozone hole.

This is the first evidence outside the laboratory that links ozone depletion to damage of living organisms on Earth.[2]

Excessive UV radiation is also thought to disrupt photosynthesis, the process by which green plants use the sun's radiant energy to produce carbohydrates. Ozone depletion could thus cause reduced yields in crops such as soybeans and rice, crops that are essential to feeding large parts of the Third World.

Ultraviolet radiation has long been known to cause health problems in animals, including cataracts in humans — the leading cause of blindness. The United Nations Environment Programme (UNEP), which was set up in 1972 to foster international cooperation in protecting the environment, predicts that ozone depletion will cause an additional 1.6 million cases per year.

There are also preliminary reports of widespread blindness among rabbits, sheep, horses and cattle in southern Chile, where high UV radiation exposure resulted from the ozone hole over Antarctica.[3]

UNEP also foresees an annual increase of 300,000 cases of skin cancer, by the year 2000, particularly in Argentina and Australia, which have come under increased UV radiation. UNEP also estimates that a 10 percent depletion of the ozone layer would cause up to 26 percent more basal and squamous-cell skin cancers. The agency cites new evidence that UV radiation may also contribute to cancers of the lip and salivary glands. *(See box, page 300.)*

Other studies project that a 10 percent increase in UV penetration would cause up to a 9 percent increase in the incidence of the more deadly malignant melanoma among light-skinned people, the group that is most vulnerable to this virulent form of cancer.[4]

Ultraviolet radiation may also undermine the immune system's ability to ward off infectious diseases. This, says Margaret L. Kripke, an immunologist at the University of Texas' M.D. Anderson Cancer Center in Houston, is the biggest unknown health effect of UV radiation. Animal experiments have indicated that UV radiation may reduce lymphocytes' ability to destroy certain microorganisms that enter the body through the skin, such as Leishmania, malaria, schistosoma and the leprosy bacillus.

Although it is not known whether UV radiation actually reduces human resistance to these agents, Kripke testified last fall, "infectious diseases constitute an enormous public health problem worldwide, and any factor that reduces immune defenses ... is likely to have a devastating impact on human health."[5]

Kripke's research was particularly ominous for sun worshipers. She found that commercial sunscreen preparations, which protect against sunburn and other damage to the skin from UV radiation, don't block the immunosuppressive effects of UV radiation. Similarly, skin pigmentation, which protects darker-skinned people from skin cancers that are prevalent among Caucasians, doesn't seem to protect the immune system from UV damage.

Aside from not producing more ozone-depleting chemicals, is there a technological way to restore the ozone layer?

Scientists haven't hit pay dirt yet, but they are looking for so-called "technological fixes," or ways to eliminate ozone-destroying chemicals already in the atmosphere. Thomas Stix, a physicist at Princeton University, is investigating the use of lasers to blast CFCs in the lower atmosphere before they drift up into the stratosphere where they destroy ozone.

The trouble is, Stix acknowledges, there are already about 10 million tons of CFCs floating around today in the atmosphere. That's a lot of ozone-destroying potential, but the CFCs are mixed with other gases and account for only about one-billionth of the total atmosphere. "CFCs are very dilute," Stix says, "so in order to remove them from the atmosphere you need a process that is enormously selective." Stix, who calls his idea "flaky" given today's grasp of the problem, says the energy required to blast CFCs with existing technology would be prohibitive.

Still, if the process were improved by "a factor of 10 or 20," Stix says the cost of removing CFCs from the atmosphere by lasers could be brought down to about $1 a pound, "an amount of money that people would start to think could be worthwhile," especially if some of the more dire scenarios of ozone depletion were to take shape in coming years.

Another technological approach, put forward by three scientists from the University of California, calls for spraying such hydrocarbons as ethane or propane into the stratosphere over Antarctica.[6] The gases would, theoretically, stop the chlorine atoms from destroying the ozone.

The plan poses enormous technical problems, however, as its authors readily concede. For one thing, it would take hundreds of large aircraft several weeks to spray the hydrocarbons over Antarctica.

"Most responsible people feel that it is better to deal with the root cause of some of these environmental problems instead of assuming that there is a technological fix that's going to be a completely benign and beneficial solution," says Ralph Cicerone, a geoscience professor at the University of California at Irvine and lead scientist for hydrocarbon "injection," or spraying.

Cicerone agrees that many proposals to restore the ozone layer are unsound or dangerous. But he says it is wrong to dismiss them out of hand. "We think the only way to get to the bottom of these ideas is to go ahead and air them and expose them to the same level of criticism as a normal piece of science."

At present, however, scientists say that the only feasible solution to ozone destruction is the Montreal Protocol approach: stopping the production and emission of CFCs and other ozone-depleting chemicals. Even then, it would take decades before the ozone layer could be restored to its normal composition.

That's why Michael Oppenheimer calls for more drastic steps to eliminate CFCs than are currently called for under the treaty. Such steps, he says, could reduce the buildup of ozone depleters in the atmosphere projected for 2010 by almost half.

Is there a relationship between ozone depletion and global warming?

Ozone depletion and global warming are in some ways closely related.

A Multi-Talented Satellite

NASA's Upper Atmosphere Research Satellite (UARS) carries 10 scientific instruments to measure a wide range of atmospheric characteristics, including ozone levels (shown in maps at right). UARS instruments also measure chlorofluorocarbons and atmospheric temperature, pressure, wind velocity and solar ultraviolet radiation. Launched by the Space Shuttle, UARS flies at an altitude of 354 miles.

Source: NASA

CFCs have long been identified as "greenhouse gases," gases that trap solar heat inside Earth's atmosphere, much as the glass roof and walls of a greenhouse. Other greenhouse gases, such as carbon dioxide and methane, are far more plentiful than CFCs. Burning fossil fuels such as gasoline and heating oil produces most of the carbon dioxide emissions that constitute about half the greenhouse effect.

But CFCs are the most potent heat retainers of all the greenhouse gases: One CFC molecule has about 20,000 times more impact on global temperatures than one molecule of carbon dioxide. As a result, CFCs are thought to be currently responsible for as much as a fifth of the greenhouse effect that is now taking place.[7]

Since CFCs are such potent greenhouse gases, it would seem fair to deduce that curbing their production and release into the atmosphere should slow the process of global warming. Indeed, while the Bush administration has rejected proposals to set limits on carbon dioxide emissions, it contends that capping production of CFCs in the United States will reduce overall U.S. emissions of greenhouse gases.

"Elimination of these ozone-destroying chemicals ... is a double winner," wrote Sen. John H. Chafee, R-R.I. "First, it is absolutely essential if we are to stop destroying the ozone layer. Second, it is the most effective single step we can take to curb the ... greenhouse effect."[8]

But recent scientific findings suggest that the relationship between ozone depletion and the greenhouse effect is more complex than it first appeared. Because ozone absorbs as well as reflects ultraviolet and visible radiation, it retains heat from the sun. For that reason, when ozone is destroyed, that part of the atmosphere where the ozone loss occurs loses heat, as do areas immediately surrounding the depleted ozone layer. Scientists are now trying to determine if the cooling that occurs at the altitudes where ozone is lost spreads to lower altitudes and reduces temperatures on Earth.

"There is a lot of uncertainty about whether or not that cooling gets transmitted to the ground," says Sherwood Rowland, a chemist at the University of California at Irvine who, together with co-worker Mario Molina, first discovered the ozone-deplet-

Tracking Earth's Disappearing Ozone Layer

Low values of ozone (top) were mapped over a broad tropical band by NASA's Upper Atmosphere Research Satellite (UARS) on Jan. 11, 1992. The lowest values, shown in light gray, were measured at an altitude of about 13 miles. Depressed ozone levels are also shown north of Europe. On the same day, at the same altitude, the UARS also detected an abundance of the ozone-destroying chemical chlorine monoxide over northern Europe and Russia (bottom), shown in dark gray.

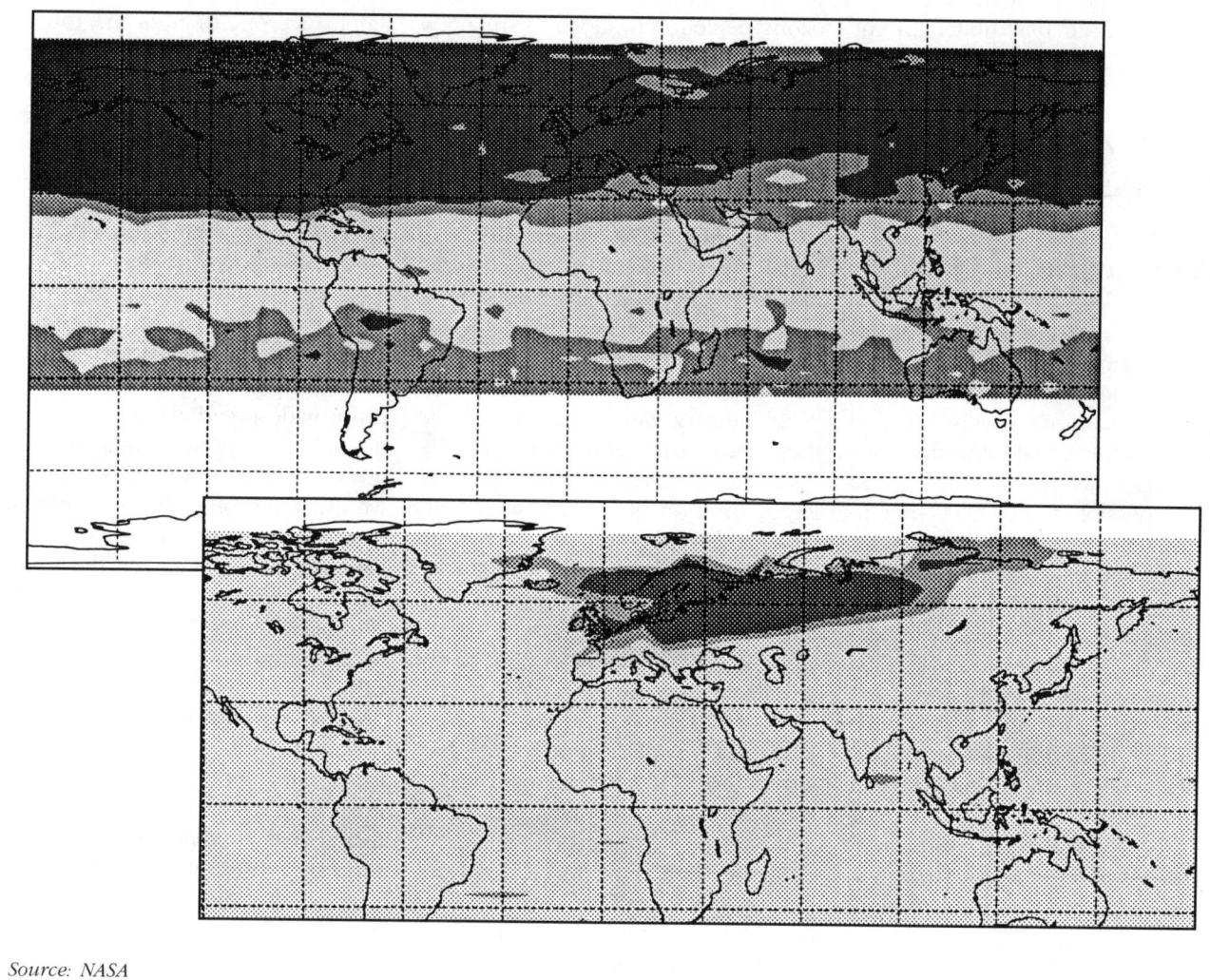

Source: NASA

ing effects of CFCs in 1974.[9] "That's the question that's being raised in the atmospheric science community."

The debate intensified last October, when a group of scientists postulated that the cooling effect caused by ozone loss in the lower stratosphere would cancel out the rise in temperature caused by CFCs' contribution to the greenhouse effect.

But Rowland calls this argument "greatly oversimplified." For one thing, he says, such a cancellation would occur only in latitudes where there is ozone depletion in the lower stratosphere. Because there has been no ozone depletion in the lower stratosphere over the tropics, he says, "that means they are saying the cancellation doesn't happen everywhere."

The debate became politicized after the Bush administration expressed support for the cancellation theory. Supporters of immediate action to curb greenhouse-gas emissions, such as UNEP, said that because the findings suggest that CFCs contribute much less to global warming than previously thought, the United States could no longer claim its efforts to curb CFC emissions were an adequate contribution to efforts to curb global warming.

For its part, the Bush administration claimed the findings meant that global warming is less of a threat than previously thought and held to its prediction that the United States' total emissions of greenhouse gases would be no higher by the year 2000 than they were in 1987 under current policy.

"Each of them put a political spin on what is still a very controversial and grossly oversimplified scientific conclusion," Rowland says. Meanwhile, the jury is still out on the overall contribution of CFCs and ozone depletion to global warming. ∎

BACKGROUND

Development of CFCs

The chemicals that have done so much damage to the ozone layer have only been around since 1930. Chlorofluorocarbons were hailed from the outset as safe and fire-resistant refrigerants. Extensively tested for their possible toxic effects on ambient air (the air we breathe), CFCs provided energy-efficient substitutes for ammonia — which was potentially explosive — in refrigerators. Inexpensive to produce, CFCs soon found many other uses as well.

Marketed under the trade name Freon by E. I. du Pont de Nemours & Co., the world's largest manufacturer of these chemicals, CFCs became the leading coolant for air conditioners as well as refrigerators. Their low cost enabled postwar generations of Americans to regard air conditioning as a standard item in their homes and cars.

Manufacturers eventually discovered a wide range of uses for CFCs. They served as propellants for spray cans, which were used in the 1960s and early '70s to apply everything from deodorant and hair spray to household cleaners and paint. Plastics manufacturers used CFCs to make foam products such as seat cushions, packing materials and insulation.

More recently, the electronics industry found that chlorofluorocarbons' chemical stability made them ideal cleaning solvents for removing dust and lint from components such as circuit boards and silicon chips.

In the early 1970s, when smog was becoming a major focus of environmental concern, manufacturers were seeking substitutes for the volatile organic compounds that constituted the bulk of cleaning solvents then in use. "Our industry went to CFCs because they were safer and more durable than other solvents," says Theresa Pugh, director of environmental affairs for the American Electronics Association. "CFCs were thought to be the miracle substances because they did not cause problems here on Earth, and we certainly had no reason to believe they caused problems elsewhere."

By 1974, CFC production had grown from 150,000 metric tons in 1960 to more than 800,000 metric tons.[10]

At the same time that CFCs were finding widespread industrial applications, other chemicals that were later found to deplete the ozone layer also were entering into use. Two other chlorinated compounds, methyl chloroform and carbon tetrachloride, found use as solvents for cleaning and degreasing metal parts in manufacturing industries and as ingredients in pesticides. Methyl chloroform also was used as a component of adhesives. Halons were developed for use in fire extinguishers. Like CFCs, halons are very stable chemicals, and they were adopted quickly for both industrial and home firefighting equipment.

First Signs of Trouble

Even as industry was finding new uses for CFCs in the early 1970s, scientists were beginning to link them to ozone destruction. In 1974, Ralph Cicerone, then at the University of Michigan, and his colleague, Richard S. Stolarski, investigated the possible effects on stratospheric ozone of chlorine released by NASA rockets. They concluded that a single atom of chlorine would destroy many thousands of ozone molecules.

However, because the number of rockets passing through the ozone layer was small, and no other sources of chlorine at that altitude had been identified, their findings did not cause widespread alarm.[11]

Findings reported later that year, however, showed that rocket engines were not the only source of chlorine in the stratosphere. Sherwood Rowland and Mario Molina at the University of California at Irvine decided to study CFCs after they are released into the atmosphere. They found that CFCs are so durable that they do not break down under the forces of solar radiation and precipitation in the lower atmosphere, but continue to float around in their original state for many years, eventually drifting upward into the stratosphere.

"What we did was to ask a question that hadn't been asked before: What is going to happen to the CFCs?" Rowland recalls. "The conclusion we came to was that nothing would happen quickly, but on the time scale of many decades CFCs would go away into the stratosphere and release chlorine atoms and then that the chlorine atoms would attack the ozone.... We concluded that there was danger to the ozone layer and ... that we should quit putting CFCs into the atmosphere."

Not surprisingly, Rowland and Molina faced hostile reactions from the

Continued on p. 298

Chronology

1970s *Scientists first recognize that chlorofluorocarbons (CFCs), used since the 1930s for refrigeration, air conditioning and other uses, may destroy the ozone layer.*

June 5, 1972
The United Nations Conference on the Human Environment opens in Stockholm. Participants proclaim the right of human beings to a healthy environment and their responsibility to protect and improve the environment for future generations. June 5 is celebrated each year thereafter as Earth Day. Later that year, the General Assembly establishes the United Nations Environment Programme (UNEP) to monitor the environment.

1974
Sherwood Rowland and Mario Molina, chemists at the University of California at Irvine, discover the ozone-depleting effects of CFCs.

1976
Congress directs the National Aeronautics and Space Administration (NASA) to expand its upper-atmosphere research program to study the ozone layer.

March 1978
The United States becomes the first country to impose limits on CFC use when the Environmental Protection Agency and the U.S. Food and Drug Administration ban the use of CFCs as propellants in aerosol spray cans.

1980s *Evidence of ozone loss due to CFCs and other chemicals continues to build, prompting many countries to phase them out of production.*

1985
A team of British scientists discovers the existence of an ozone "hole," a vast area of severe ozone depletion, in the stratosphere above Antarctica.

Sept. 16, 1987
The United States and 23 other countries sign the Montreal Protocol on Substances That Deplete the Ozone Layer, promising to halve their production and importation of CFCs and halons no later than 1999.

1989
Congress imposes an excise tax on the sale of CFCs and other chemicals that destroy ozone.

1990s *Pressure to accelerate the phaseout of ozone depleters builds as ozone loss is found to be more severe than previously thought.*

June 1990
Signatories to the Montreal Protocol revise the treaty to require the total elimination of CFC production and importation by the year 2000. They also agreed to establish a $240 million fund to help developing nations obtain technology that does not use ozone-depleting chemicals.

November 1990
With enactment of the Clean Air Amendments, the so-called London revisions become U.S. law. The measure requires the elimination of CFCs, halons and carbon tetrachloride by 2000; of methyl chloroform by 2002; and of hydrochlorofluorocarbons (HCFCs) by 2030. It also requires recycling and other measures to curb the release into the atmosphere of existing stores of ozone-depleting chemicals.

Sept. 12, 1991
NASA's Upper Atmosphere Research Satellite (UARS) is launched from the Space Shuttle *Discovery*. Its mission is to carry out the first systematic study of the stratosphere and to monitor the ozone layer.

Oct. 22, 1991
UNEP releases a report by 80 atmospheric scientists who conclude that ozone depletion has occurred over virtually the entire world, except perhaps a relatively narrow band around the tropics.

Feb. 3, 1992
Scientists announce preliminary findings from UARS measurements of alarmingly high levels of chlorine monoxide, a CFC byproduct that destroys ozone, above inhabited regions of northern New England, Canada, Europe and Russia.

Feb. 11, 1992
President Bush announces that the United States will voluntarily stop producing CFCs by Dec. 31, 1995, earlier than most other signatories to the Montreal Protocol.

June 1-12, 1992
Two decades after the first U.N. summit on the environment, 8,000 delegates from more than 160 nations are expected to meet at the U.N. Conference on Environment and Development in Rio de Janeiro, Brazil. The largest diplomatic conference ever held, the "Earth Summit" will focus on global environmental problems and sustainable development practices. A treaty to curb emissions of carbon dioxide and other heat-trapping greenhouse gases may also be signed.

U.S. Use of Ozone-Depleting Chemicals

Manufacturers in the United States currently use chlorofluorocarbons and halons in products ranging from foam packaging and insulation — the biggest category — to refrigeration, air conditioning and fire extinguishers. On Feb. 11, the White House committed the United States to unilaterally halting production of CFCs by Dec. 31, 1995.

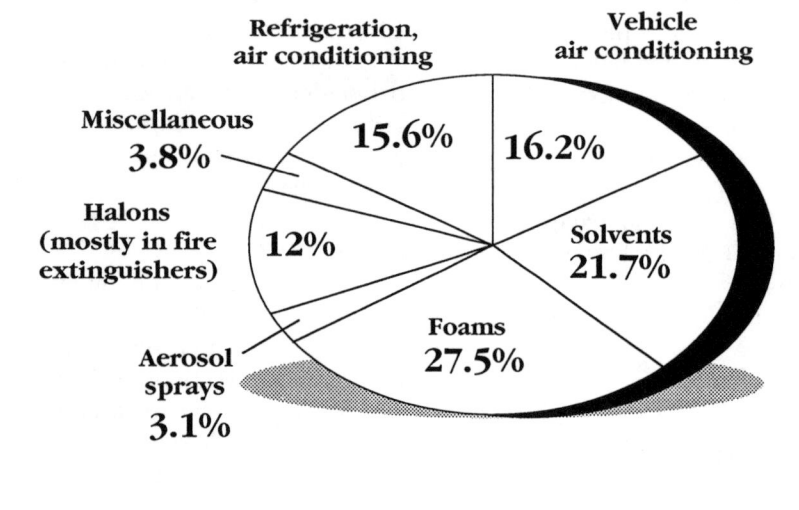

Refrigeration, air conditioning **15.6%**
Vehicle air conditioning **16.2%**
Miscellaneous **3.8%**
Halons (mostly in fire extinguishers) **12%**
Solvents **21.7%**
Aerosol sprays **3.1%**
Foams **27.5%**

Source: Environmental Protection Agency

Continued from p. 296

producers of CFCs when they published their results in 1974. "The public was probably more likely to believe it than the chemistry community," Rowland says. "Within the chemistry community then and still now there is a feeling that most environmental problems are really just public relations problems, that they are not real problems."

Rowland says the chemicals manufacturers set up the Committee on Atmospheric Science to discredit the two researchers' findings. Indeed, he adds that many critics dismissed their conclusions as "kooky. One of my favorites was an aerosol-propellant company that claimed [our results were] disinformation put out by the KGB."

But their data held up. In 1976, after a nationwide research effort involving NASA and the National Oceanic and Atmospheric Administration (NOAA), the National Academy of Sciences confirmed that CFC gases released into the atmosphere from spray cans were in fact damaging the ozone layer.

Two years later, after consumer boycotts had reduced the market for spray cans by almost two-thirds, the United States banned the use of CFCs as aerosol propellants in spray cans for most uses.[12]

Ozone Hole Discovered

Although other industrial nations continued to produce and use CFCs for aerosol sprays and other purposes, the international scientific community continued the search for data on ozone depletion launched by Rowland and Molina. During the early 1980s, most research was confined to computer models of the atmosphere. Then, in 1985, British scien-

tists discovered that ozone depletion had become so severe over a vast area of Antarctica that it amounted to a virtual "hole" in the ozone layer.

Still, resistance to the ozone-depletion theory remained so strong that the British team was refused additional government funding to continue their research. Ironically, they obtained backing instead from the U.S. Chemical Manufacturers Association, whose members had the most to lose from confirmation of Rowland and Molina's theory. Because of mounting pressure at home to find substitutes for CFCs, however, the American chemical industry wanted to resolve the issue once and for all before abandoning CFCs.[13]

Meanwhile, Rowland and other scientists were learning more about ozone depletion and why the phenomenon was so strong over the Antarctic.

They discovered that CFCs are concentrated over the South Pole because of strong circular winds known as the "polar vortex," which sweep unimpeded over the flat, barren continent of Antarctica. The vortex gathers the destructive gases from the surrounding atmosphere into a wide funnel over Antarctica, where they remain isolated during the dark, frigid winter months.

Equally important, they found that as CFCs break down, the resulting chlorine monoxide clings to the ice crystals that form clouds in the stratosphere. These ice crystals provide the surfaces needed for the catalytic reaction in which chlorine breaks down ozone.

With the return of sunlight to Antarctica during September and October, the beginning of spring in the Southern Hemisphere, solar radiation acts as a catalyst enabling the chlorine monoxide produced by CFCs to destroy the surrounding ozone layer.

As the days lengthen, the air over Antarctica warms up, breaking up both the stratospheric ice clouds and the polar vortex. The destruction of ozone slows as the chlorine atoms are once again bound into harmless chlorine nitrate and hydrogen chloride molecules, and the hole disappears as the vortex dissipates, allowing ozone from the surrounding regions to fill the void.

The final confirmation of Rowland and Molina's theory linking CFCs to ozone depletion came in 1987, when NASA undertook a series of aerial tests over Antarctica. From inside the ozone hole, the NASA instruments detected high concentrations of chlorine monoxide.

Montreal Protocol Signed

International reaction to the proof that CFCs were destroying the ozone layer was swift. On Sept. 16, 1987, just nine months after formal negotiations began, 24 nations signed the Montreal Protocol on Substances That Deplete the Ozone Layer. The agreement garnered an unprecedented degree of international support for such a sweeping program to protect the environment: The ratifying nations accounted for 99 percent of the world's production of CFCs and 90 percent of their consumption.[14]

The Montreal Protocol called for freezing halon emissions at 1986 levels by 1992; for halving CFC emissions by 1998; and halving CFC production and importation by 1999. To compensate for their low levels of production of ozone-depleting chemicals, developing nations were given an additional 10 years to meet these deadlines. By Jan. 1, 1989, the protocol had been ratified by enough countries to go into effect.

Richard Elliot Benedick, a Foreign Service officer who led the U.S. delegation in negotiating the Montreal Protocol, identifies several reasons for the treaty's overwhelming success. First, international cooperation among scientists allowed for the rapid discovery of CFCs' role in ozone depletion. Public opinion, which was then beginning to focus on environ-

mental issues throughout the industrial world, was also quick to press governments to act. Negotiations were supported by the UNEP.

Benedick also credits the United States for its leading role in gaining support for the treaty. The United States was the first producer of ozone-depleting chemicals to restrict their production, he points out in his account of the negotiations surrounding the protocol. In addition, Congress passed ozone-protection legislation as early as 1977, long before the governments of Western Europe responded at all.

The United States also was primarily responsible for the 1985 Vienna Convention for the Protection of the Ozone Layer, an agreement among the major CFC producers to collect additional data that led up to the Montreal Protocol.

"The U.S. government reflected its concerns over the fate of the ozone layer through stimulating and supporting both American and international scientific research," Benedick wrote. "Then, convinced of the dangers, it undertook extensive diplomatic and scientific initiatives to promote an ozone protection plan to other countries, many of which were initially hostile or indifferent to the idea."[15]

The drafters of the Montreal Protocol also assured its success by making the agreement flexible. As such, it could be rapidly amended to reflect subsequent changes in environmental conditions or new findings. And new findings were soon to test the agreement's flexibility.

The ozone hole over Antarctica continued to appear each September and October after its initial discovery in 1985. In 1988, scientists were en-

Leading CFC Polluters

The United States — the world's leading user of CFCs — and 23 other nations signed the Montreal Protocol Sept. 16, 1987, promising to halve their production and importation of CFCs and halons no later than 1999. However, not all of the world's polluters initially ratified the agreement. China and South Korea signed it after it was amended in 1990 to provide aid to developing countries seeking CFC substitutes. About 70 countries have now signed the agreement, but Pakistan and India, two of the CFC polluters on the list, remain holdouts.

	Chlorofluorocarbon emissions in 1989 (thousand metric tons)		Chlorofluorocarbon emissions in 1989 (thousand metric tons)
United States	130	Netherlands	6
Japan	95	Pakistan	6
Germany	34	Mexico	5
Italy	25	South Korea	5
United Kingdom	25	Poland	5
France	24	Belgium	4
Spain	17	Czechoslovakia	4
China	12	Greece	4
Canada	11	India	4
Australia	8	Portugal	4
South Africa	7	Yugoslavia	4
Brazil	6		

Sources: U.S. State Department; World Resources Institute

The Many Dangers of Ultraviolet Radiation

High in the stratosphere and mesosphere, the 25-mile-wide ozone layer provides vital health protection to humans down below by blocking the sun's damaging ultraviolet (UV) radiation. But when the concentration of ozone is depleted by chlorofluorocarbons and other agents that drift upward from Earth, harmful UV radiation hits Earth, causing serious health and environmental problems. Sun lovers should take note: Even the most powerful sunscreens don't block out UV radiation's damage to the immune system.

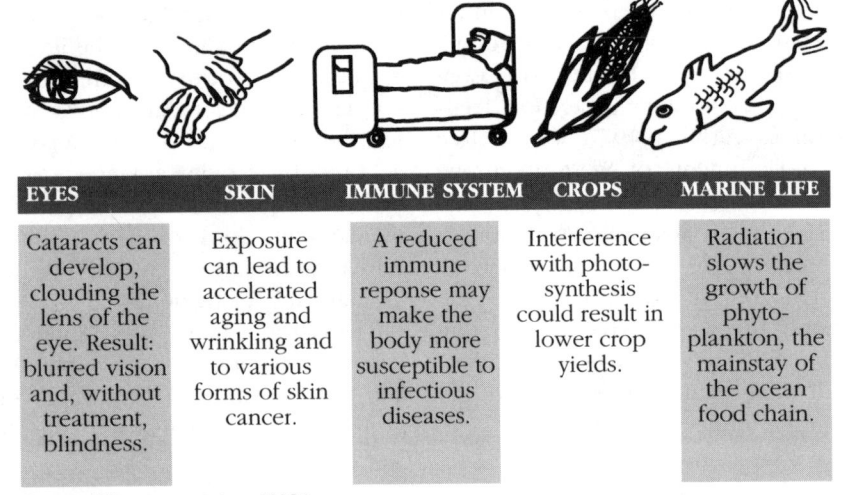

EYES	SKIN	IMMUNE SYSTEM	CROPS	MARINE LIFE
Cataracts can develop, clouding the lens of the eye. Result: blurred vision and, without treatment, blindness.	Exposure can lead to accelerated aging and wrinkling and to various forms of skin cancer.	A reduced immune reponse may make the body more susceptible to infectious diseases.	Interference with photosynthesis could result in lower crop yields.	Radiation slows the growth of phytoplankton, the mainstay of the ocean food chain.

Source: Time *magazine, NASA*

couraged to find that the hole was not as big as before. But the following year, the ozone hole reappeared, covering more than 15 million square miles.

Arctic Expedition Launched

The same year, NASA and NOAA launched an airborne expedition to the Arctic to investigate whether conditions were ripe near the North Pole for another ozone hole. Because the Arctic terrain is not as flat as that of Antarctica — and because temperatures at the North Pole do not fall as low as they do at the South Pole — the polar vortex was found to be weaker in the north. But the scientists did find higher than expected concentrations of chlorine compounds and concluded that an ozone hole could easily develop.

Because more people live at far northern latitudes than in southern Chile, Argentina, Australia and New Zealand, which border the area exposed to UV radiation in the Southern Hemisphere, an ozone hole over the Arctic would pose far greater risks to human health.

Other research revealed a new potential source of ozone depletion in areas far from the polar regions. American chemists Susan Solomon and Dave Hoffman found that sulfate particles spewed into the stratosphere by strong volcanic eruptions could act in much the same way as ice crystals in polar stratospheric clouds by providing surfaces on which chlorine and bromine compounds can destroy ozone more efficiently than when they are floating free.

Studying the impact of volcanic ash in the aftermath of the 1982 eruption of El Chichon in Mexico, Solomon and Hoffman found that ozone concentrations over the middle latitudes were significantly depleted. They concluded that ozone

depletion was likely following other major volcanic eruptions.

Although their research was limited to El Chichon, Solomon, a NOAA chemist in Boulder, Colo., says, "We found that similar processes could also take place on the liquid sulfuric acid and water particles that form following major volcanic eruptions."

The implications of Solomon and Hoffman's research are clear. While ice clouds form only over the polar regions, volcanic ash can travel anywhere. If volcanic ash does facilitate ozone depletion even in the absence of ice crystals, an ozone hole could open over any region on Earth.

In the summer of 1990, NASA reported that, globally, the ozone layer had been depleted by 2 to 3 percent over the previous two decades. It was also reported that the ozone layer had already begun to thin over the United States and other populated areas in the middle latitudes.

At the same time, the chemicals industry was quickly bringing into production substitutes for CFCs that are less damaging to the ozone layer. While not completely benign, these hydrochlorofluorocarbons, or HCFCs, were hailed as temporary substitutes for CFCs in many applications, particularly as coolants. Most important, the HCFCs and other substitute chemicals facilitated the rapid phaseout of CFCs.

Montreal Protocol nations were quick to respond to the news that ozone depletion was intensifying. In June 1990, in London, they amended the agreement to accelerate the phaseout of ozone-depleting chemicals. Under the new guidelines, all production and importation of CFCs and halons must stop by the year 2000. Other ozone-depleting agents, such as carbon tetrachloride and methyl chloroform, were added to the list of chemicals to be phased out of production. Developing countries still have an additional 10 years to meet the deadline. As a result of the new deadlines, chlorine pollution was expected by 2075 to fall below levels recorded prior to the first appearance of the ozone hole.

The amendments also addressed the special problems faced by developing nations. Although they produce few ozone-depleting chemicals, India, China and other countries have counted on introducing cheap refrigeration and air conditioning as part of their plans for modernization. They succeeded in convincing the industrial world to set up a fund to help them pay for the more expensive substitutes they will be forced to purchase, as well as information and equipment to help them produce environmentally sound refrigerators and air conditioners themselves.

Also in 1990, Congress passed the far-reaching Clean Air Act Amendments, which call for the complete phaseout of CFCs, halons and carbon tetrachloride by 2000, of methyl chloroform by 2002 and HCFCs by 2030. The law made the United States the first nation to legislate a ban on these chemicals. To reduce emissions of existing stores of ozone-depleting agents, the law called for regulations to require recycling of refrigerants and air-conditioning coolants. Finally, the new law mandated faster elimination of ozone-depleting substances if warranted by new scientific findings of damage to the ozone layer. ■

substances that destroy ozone. On Feb. 3, two months before the current study was scheduled for completion, NASA announced that the satellite had detected high levels of chlorine monoxide over Scandinavia and northern Eurasia, an area that includes London, Moscow and Amsterdam. The levels were comparable to concentrations found in the ozone hole over Antarctica.

NASA predicted that an ozone hole could open over the Northern Hemisphere this spring if chlorine monoxide levels remain high enough. Final results of the study are due in mid-April.

The bad news was not limited to the far north. NASA's satellite observations also showed ozone depletion over the tropics, which the agency suggested was due to plumes of ash from Mount Pinatubo. In addition, the satellite detected areas of low ozone across the western United States. These findings were confirmed by separate measurements taken in Boulder, Colo.

Confirming the satellite data were new findings from the NASA-led Airborne Arctic Stratospheric Expedition, which monitors ozone depletion from two specially equipped aircraft: the ER-2, a converted U-2 spy plane that gathers data at 70,000 feet, and the DC-8-72, a "flying lab" that operates at 41,000 feet. The expedition reported Feb. 3 that it had found even higher levels of chlorine monoxide than the satellite had over eastern Canada and northern New England. The readings — at 1.5 parts per billion by volume — surpass anything ever measured in either polar region.

"These findings have increased our concern that significant ozone loss will occur during any given winter over the Arctic in the next 10 years," scientists announced. "This is based on significant new data with improved instrumentation obtained with broader geographic and season-

CURRENT SITUATION

Vast Area at Risk

No sooner had the ink dried on the revisions to the Montreal Protocol than new information pointed to an even more dire situation. In October 1990, scientists found the lowest ozone levels ever recorded over Antarctica and discovered that the hole had stretched into southern Chile, including Punta Arenas, a city of 100,000. There was also further evidence that parts of Australia had been exposed to high levels of UV radiation when bits of the ozone hole broke away as the polar vortex weakened and drifted northward from Antarctica.

On Oct. 22, the UNEP and the World Meteorological Organization announced that ozone depletion had begun to occur at the middle and high latitudes of both the Northern and the Southern Hemispheres in spring, summer and winter.

"Ozone depletion in the middle and high latitudes means that it covers almost all of North America, Europe, the Soviet Union, Australia, New Zealand and a sizable part of Latin America," said UNEP Director Mostafa K. Tolba. "The only area with no indication of change, that is, no visible reduction of ozone, is the tropical belt around the Earth."

European researchers, building on Solomon and Hoffman's volcano-ash findings, are now predicting that last year's eruption of Mount Pinatubo threatens to erode the ozone layer to dangerous levels over much of Europe this spring. Researchers participating in the 17-nation European Arctic Stratospheric Ozone Experiment based in northern Sweden have yet to complete their experiments. But they issued a recommendation in early February that governments in Northern Europe should take more urgent steps to protect the ozone layer.

The most recent signs of severe ozone loss were detected by NASA's Upper Atmosphere Research Satellite (UARS), launched last September to monitor the ozone layer and measure

al coverage and the knowledge that past release of CFCs will increase chlorine substantially in the stratosphere in the decade to come."

U.S. Leadership on CFCs

For the most part, the United States has taken a leading role in protecting the ozone layer from manmade chemicals. Although it was the largest producer and consumer of CFCs, halons and other ozone-depleting substances, the United States was the first country to ban their use in spray cans and to translate into law the terms of international agreements to phase out their production and use altogether. The United States also provided the main impetus behind international negotiations leading up to the 1987 Montreal Protocol, which set deadlines for the elimination of ozone-depleting chemicals. It went beyond the terms of that agreement in 1989 when Congress passed a tax on the sale of CFCs in a further effort to speed their withdrawal from the market.

But the Bush administration's record on the issue of ozone depletion has been mixed. During the June 1990 meeting in London of signatories to the Montreal Protocol, other industrial nations proposed setting up a $240 million fund to help developing nations acquire the necessary technology to phase out CFC-based refrigerators and air-conditioning systems or to avoid purchasing such equipment at all. The Bush administration resisted such a step and only agreed at the last minute in order to prevent a breakdown in the negotiations.

On Feb. 6, in response to the warnings of severe ozone depletion over the Northern Hemisphere, the U.S. Senate voted 96-0 to direct the administration to accelerate the phaseout of ozone depleters. The White House quickly announced its support of the measure, and on Feb. 11 committed the United States to unilaterally halting production of CFCs by Dec. 31, 1995 — sooner than most of the other signatories.

But this did not placate some crit-

> **Although it was the largest producer and consumer of CFCs and other ozone-depleting substances, the United States was the first country to ban their use in spray cans and to translate into law the terms of international agreements to phase out their production and use.**

ics of the Bush administration's environmental policies, including the Senate resolution's author, Al Gore, D-Tenn. "The president has abdicated his responsibility," Gore told the Senate. "It is easy enough, after the ozone hole is pointed to and predicted above Kennebunkport, to say, 'OK, we will now think seriously about doing something.' Where was the president when the warnings came through so loudly and clearly for the last several years?"

Before the administration's stated support of the earlier deadline can take effect, the Environmental Protection Agency (EPA) must issue a regulation to that effect. Martha Dye, a spokeswoman for the agency's Global Change Division, said EPA would propose "in the beginning of April" a regulation moving up the deadline for phasing out CFC production to Dec. 31, 1995.

But the issuance of a regulation does not necessarily mean the terms of the regulation will immediately take effect, as other components of CFC phaseout demonstrate. One example is a recycling requirement for coolants from car air conditioners, which are the biggest single source of CFC emissions.

The 1990 Clean Air Act Amendments required that auto repair shops purchase equipment to recover and recycle CFCs from car air conditioners by Jan. 1, 1992. On Sept. 4, 1991, EPA issued a proposed regulation in compliance with the law.

Although the regulation took effect Jan. 1, Dye says, "We don't have the final regulations out yet, so it's a legal gray area." That is, auto repair shops "do have to comply, but there's nothing in place to stop them from not complying."

Industry Efforts Advance

Unlike many areas of environmental regulation, where industry resists making costly changes in its operations, the international effort to protect the ozone layer has been largely supported and even advanced by the makers of CFCs and other ozone depleters. Some industries are phasing out the use of CFCs faster than they are required under current guidelines.

The Society of the Plastics Industry, for example, has said its members will cease using CFCs in foam packaging by 1993 and in insulation material by 1995. Several makers of electronic equipment, including American Telephone & Telegraph Co., Motorola Inc. and Hughes Air-

Ozone: Pollutant or Protector?

Ozone's impact on human health and the environment varies dramatically depending on where it occurs in the atmosphere.

Heavy concentrations of ozone are not found naturally close to Earth but in the 25-mile-thick ozone layer high in the stratosphere. Here, ozone is a force for good. Because ozone reflects the sun's ultraviolet (UV) radiation, the layer serves as an essential shield, protecting life on Earth from the sun's harmful rays.

Ultraviolet radiation has been found to cause cataracts, the leading cause of blindness in humans, as well as certain forms of skin cancer. There is also evidence that it may undermine the body's immune system, making it more vulnerable to infectious disease. Because UV radiation also impedes the ability of plants to grow, heavy exposure could threaten food crops.

Close to Earth's surface, however, ozone is highly undesirable. Ozone is virtually absent on Earth under natural conditions. But when fossil fuels such as gasoline are burned during hot weather, tailpipe emissions from motor vehicles react in the presence of heat and sunlight to produce heavy concentrations of ozone, which is one of the main ingredients of urban smog.

At ground level, ozone does nothing to protect living organisms. Indeed, it is toxic to most. The gas causes respiratory problems and eye irritation in humans. Ozone can make an asthma sufferer twice as sensitive to the allergens that set off asthma attacks. When heavily polluted cities such as Los Angeles and New York issue smog alerts in the summer, advising elderly people and those with respiratory diseases to stay indoors, they do so because of high ozone readings. Plants also suffer in the presence of ozone, which is thought to reduce crop yields in the United States by up to 10 percent.†

The same steps being taken to protect ozone in the upper atmosphere can be used to reduce ground-level ozone: changing human activities that affect concentrations of the gas. On the ground, that means reducing tailpipe emissions. Indeed, cars coming on the market today are required to emit fewer pollutants. But because there are more cars on the road than ever before, ground-level ozone remains a problem.

---

†See World Resources Institute, *The 1992 Information Please Environmental Almanac,* 1992.

---

craft Co., have already begun using solvents that do not contain CFC-113 and other ozone-depleting chemicals.

"All the major electronics manufacturers have had very aggressive [conversion] programs," says Steve Seidel, deputy director of EPA's Global Change Division. "All plan to phase out use of CFC-113 well ahead of any schedule that has been recently announced."

Seidel also has praise for manufacturers of refrigerators, most of whom he says will have new products that do not contain CFCs ready by the end of 1994. "Everyone is doing a reasonably good job to a very good job," he says, in incorporating safe chemicals into their products.

In some cases, the move to non-CFC-based solvents has meant going back to cleaners that contain volatile organic compounds. "The sad thing is, they will contribute to ozone problems here on Earth where you and I live and breathe," says Theresa Pugh of the American Electronics Association. "One of the reasons our companies moved away from these solvents over the last 20 to 30 years was because they were considered to be pollutants."

But scientists also have come up with new, non-polluting solvents that can do the same job. One of these is a water-based compound made from oranges and other citrus fruits. "That has become a marvelous drop-in substitute for CFCs where the expense is relatively nominal by manufacturing standards," Pugh says.

Other substitutes are more controversial. HCFCs were introduced as a temporary substitute for CFCs used in refrigeration and air-conditioning systems for big buildings, known as "chillers." Although they are chemically similar to CFCs, these chemicals are less stable and break down more readily once they are released into the atmosphere. For that reason HCFCs are far less damaging to the ozone layer. According to Seidel, HCFC-123 is 98 percent less damaging to the ozone layer than CFC-11, the coolant it is replacing in many applications. "You could use an awful lot of that for a long time, and it will still be significantly better than continuing to use CFC-11," Seidel says.

The Clean Air Act Amendments require that HCFCs be phased out by 2030. Following the recent findings of severe ozone depletion in the Northern Hemisphere, the Bush administration announced that deadline would likely be moved up but stopped short of setting a new date for eliminating HCFCs. According to Martha Dye of EPA, the agency has received suggested phaseout dates ranging from 2000 to 2015 for the more destructive forms of HCFC.

But critics of current policy say HCFCs should be eliminated much faster. Scientists at the Institute for Energy and Environmental Research in Washington, for example, reported in February that some HCFCs are three to five times more damaging to the ozone layer than previously reported and called for their elimination sooner than the current deadline of 2030.[16]

While substitutes have been found for CFCs in most applications, there has been less progress in replacing halons, the main source of ozone-destroying bromine compounds.

"There is no good substitute for halons yet," says Michael Oppenheimer of the Environmental Defense Fund. Fortunately, the uses of halons are far more limited than those of CFCs, Oppenheimer says, and recycling efforts could eliminate the need to produce them. "There is ample time to develop a halon substitute because the existing bank of these chemicals is large enough that you don't need to produce any more." ■

OUTLOOK

Who Pays?

While the United States and other industrial nations are moving faster than anticipated to phase out ozone-depleting chemicals, progress has been much slower in finding an equitable division of the costs entailed in protecting the ozone layer.

Though the Montreal Protocol gave developing nations a 10-year grace period in which to adopt substitute chemicals for refrigeration and other applications, they asked for financial assistance in making the transition. Because such provisions were absent from the original 1987 agreement, India, China and many other developing nations refused to sign it.

Today, these countries account for only about 15 percent of world production of CFCs. But because they are eager to broaden popular access to refrigerators and air conditioners as part of an effort to rapidly modernize, the Third World could quickly become a major source of CFC emissions unless it accepts the CFC phaseout.

Although the Bush administration initially rejected the demand for financial assistance from the developing countries, it reversed course in July 1990, when the industrial nations agreed to set up a $240 million fund to help the Third World pay for refrigeration and other equipment that does not use ozone-depleting chemicals. The United States, by far the biggest producer and user of CFCs, agreed to provide 25 percent of the total.

Since the fund was set up, China and South Korea have signed the revised Montreal Protocol, bringing to about 70 the total number of countries committed to phasing out ozone-depleting chemicals. Other large developing countries, including India and Pakistan, however, have yet to do so.

As an added incentive for Third World nations to sign the protocol, the UNEP, together with the World Bank and the U.N. Development Programme, set up another fund to help poor countries pay for technologies that protect the environment. The Global Environment Facility, launched in November 1990, will provide grants and low-interest loans for ozone-related projects, but only to poor countries that signed the protocol.

"Earth Summit" Set for June

It will be harder to bridge the gap between the developed and the developing worlds that has been widening in the context of an upcoming meeting on the global environment. The U.N. Conference on Environment and Development, or "Earth Summit," scheduled to be held in Rio de Janeiro in June, will focus on global warming.

Most scientists concur that a build-up of carbon dioxide and other gases due to human activities is trapping solar heat inside the atmosphere. Whether this "greenhouse effect" has already begun to raise global temperatures is a matter of debate, as are various proposals for curbing global warming.

Like ozone depletion, this environmental threat involves the atmosphere and thus the entire world. For this reason, environmentalists and scientists say all nations must cooperate if efforts to stem global warming are to succeed.

As they did in the negotiations leading up to the Montreal Protocol, however, developing nations are arguing that because the industrial world is primarily responsible for the environmental problem, it must bear the primary responsibility for resolving it. They point out that the industrial world, with only a quarter of the world's population, consumes 80 percent of its fuel and mineral resources. They are especially critical of the United States, which consumes a third of these resources while accounting for only 5 percent of the world's population.[17]

Third World criticism of industrial nations' policies on global warming focuses on the Bush administration, which has long refused to help developing countries reduce their emissions of greenhouse gases. In contrast, the European Community already has committed $1.5 billion to such a fund.

When the Europeans promised in early March to set aside even more aid for developing nations, the Bush

Continued on p. 306

At Issue:

Has the National Aeronautics and Space Administration (NASA) exaggerated the threat of ozone depletion?

THE WALL STREET JOURNAL

Editorial entitled "Press-Release Ozone Hole"
FROM *THE WALL STREET JOURNAL,*
FEB. 28, 1992.

*i*f you're the average White House official, you will, of course, hit the panic button if you wake up one morning to read in the papers that NASA says an ozone "hole" may be opening up this winter. The frightening news story raises the possibility of "exposing people and plant life to higher levels of harmful ultraviolet radiation from the sun." Within 48 hours of widespread news reports on the NASA warning, the White House sent out EPA chief William Reilly to announce that "President Bush is very concerned" and that the administration would likely move up the date to phase out chlorofluorocarbons. This triggered a quick 96-0 Senate vote to ban the chemicals....

Does it make any difference if NASA was wrong? Or at the least, if the others jumped the gun on the agency's tentative conclusions?

In the course of doing reporting yesterday on the "Earth Summit" scheduled for June in Rio de Janeiro, we learned that NASA is expected to put out a second ozone report any day now.... Where the original NASA press release reported the "highest levels of chlorine monoxide — 1.5 parts per billion by volume — ever measured," more recent citings are down to 0.5 parts per billion....

To understand the degree to which these ozone Chicken Littles are panicking, it helps to review the scant evidence that set them in motion after the NASA press release appeared.

As NASA has been the first to acknowledge, the report is not finished. The famous 1.5-per-billion rating is based on the flight of one converted ER-2 airplane Jan. 20. But chlorine rates in the atmosphere are known to fluctuate wildly over the year. Arguing the destruction of the ozone layer on the basis of one day's, or a few weeks', data is a bit like announcing the comeback of retail on evidence that takes Neiman-Marcus' receipts from the day before Christmas and annualizes them....

We just can't buy this nobody-here-but-us-disinterested-scientists argument. Environmental science has become an arena fraught with political pressures. It is simply not clear to us that real science drives policy in this area. NASA's Mike Kurylo himself noted that a recent Time magazine cover story on the subject "played on sensationalism" and that "scientists have mixed feelings" about press releases.

Before agreeing that the sky is falling, we'd like to see more time spent on the data, starting with the likelihood that NASA now believes there won't be any ozone hole this year.

JAMES G. ANDERSON

Professor of chemistry, Harvard University.
FROM LETTERS TO THE EDITOR, *THE WALL STREET JOURNAL,* MARCH 23, 1992.

*a*s head scientist for the second Airborne Arctic Stratospheric Expedition (AASE II) in progress, I am responsible for the aircraft part of the scientific results in the Feb. 3 press briefing to which you refer. Prior to AASE II, results from six years of flights by this team into the Antarctic and Arctic stratosphere using a broad complement of instruments has (1) demonstrated that chlorofluorocarbons (CFCs) are responsible for the Antarctic ozone "hole," (2) isolated the specific reactions that control the rate of ozone destruction in the Antarctic stratosphere, and (3) revealed that the agent chlorine monoxide, proved to be directly responsible for ozone loss over the Antarctic, was present at equivalent levels within the Arctic stratosphere....

Even if your cited chlorine monoxide levels of 0.5 parts per billion correctly represent conditions in the lower stratosphere in mid-February (which they don't), that level still represents nearly 100 times the natural levels in the lower stratosphere. It is about an amount of chlorine monoxide sufficient to remove 20 percent of the ozone in the lower stratosphere by the end of February. The word "alarming" was not used in our briefing; what level of ozone thinning would elicit your concern?

You suggest the American people will be submitted to a crash project at great expense. Are you aware the principal U.S. producer of CFCs, Du Pont Co., is ahead of even the new White House schedule for phaseout? The intense scientific scrutiny examining the link between CFC release and ozone thinning engaged leading scientists in industry from around the world for nearly two decades. The case stands. Many of these scientists helped draft the international protocol cutting production of CFCs dramatically by 1996.

To equate the six-year, peer-reviewed research process exploring ozone in the polar stratosphere with the analysis of one day of receipts at Neiman-Marcus is your editorial prerogative....

Your final point strikes a powerful note of irony. Did the investigation behind your editorial comply with the standards you suggest? Thoughtful leadership in education, in science, in technology and public policy is crucial for this nation and is the responsibility of universities, industry, journalism and government. Perhaps it is time to review carefully evidence on matters that will affect generations to come.

Continued from p. 304

administration relented and offered $75 million. But it has yet to follow the Europeans' lead in promising to hold emissions of greenhouse gases to 1990 levels by the year 2000 or to set any such measurable limits on U.S. emissions.

Said President Bush in a March 24, 1992, message to Congress: "The United States will continue to restrain or reduce its net carbon dioxide emissions by improving energy efficiency, developing cleaner energy sources, and planting billions of trees in this decade. But an exclusive focus on targets and timetables for carbon dioxide emissions is inadequate to address the complex dynamics of climate change."

Many obstacles stand in the way of a broadly accepted international treaty to curb greenhouse gas emissions, and few experts predict that such an agreement will be ready for signature at the Earth Summit. "It was easy to get out of CFCs, but carbon dioxide is another story," says Steve Seidel of EPA.

That's because a curb on greenhouse gas emissions would require far more drastic economic disruption than the phaseout of ozone-depleting chemicals. To significantly slow the emissions of carbon dioxide, the most plentiful greenhouse gas, industrial nations would have to shift to non-fossil fuels, and developing countries would have to stop burning tropical forests. Both steps pose daunting economic and political challenges.

But the Montreal Protocol offers Earth Summit negotiators a reason for optimism and an important model on which to build a new treaty to protect the "global commons."

"As recently as 1986, people were saying, 'We can't do without CFCs for refrigerators, there's nothing else that works,'" Seidel recalls. "They were warning that cars wouldn't run, that computers wouldn't run without

CFCs, that there was nothing else out there — in short, that this would be the end of life as we know it. Clearly, those worst-case scenarios have not come true. In fact, the technological progress has really exceeded everyone's expectations." ∎

Notes

[1] National Research Council, *Long-term Worldwide Effects of Multiple Nuclear Weapons Detonations,* National Academy Press, October 1975, cited by Arjun Makhijani, Kevin Gurney and Anni Makhijani, *Saving Our Skins: The Causes and Consequences of Ozone Layer Depletion and Policies for Its Restoration and Protection,* Institute for Energy and Environmental Research, Feb. 19, 1992.

[2] See Marnie Stetson, "Saving Nature's Sunscreen," *Worldwatch,* March-April 1992, p. 35.

[3] See Julian Michaels, "S. American Research Focuses on Impacts of Ozone Depletion," *Christian Science Monitor,* Feb. 10, 1992.

[4] Findings from the scientific literature cited by Makhijani et al., *Ibid.*

[5] Kripke testified Nov. 15, 1991, at hearings on ozone depletion before the Senate Committee on Commerce, Science and Transportation.

[6] See R. J. Cicerone, Scott Elliott and R. P. Turco, "Reduced Antarctic Ozone Depletions in a Model with Hydrocarbon Injections," *Science,* Nov. 22, 1991.

[7] See, for example, Francesca Lyman, *The Greenhouse Trap,* World Resources Institute, 1990.

[8] Sen. John H. Chafee, "Stratospheric Ozone: The Problem," *EPA Journal,* January-February 1991.

[9] M. Molina and F. S. Rowland, "Stratospheric Sink for Chlorofluoromethanes: Chlorine At-

om-Catalysed Destruction of Ozone," *Nature,* Vol. 249, 1974.

[10] Chemical Manufacturers Association, *Production, Sales, and Calculated Release of CFC-11 and CFC-12 through 1987,* 1988.

[11] Richard S. Stolarski and Ralph J. Cicerone, "Stratospheric Chlorine: A Possible Sink for Ozone," *Canadian Journal of Chemistry,* Vol. 52, 1974. See Richard Elliot Benedick, *Ozone Diplomacy* (1991), p. 10.

[12] Benedick, *op. cit.,* pp. 27-28.

[13] *Ibid,* p. 30.

[14] See Daniel J. Kevles, "Some Like It Hot," *The New York Review of Books,* March 26, 1992. The original signatories to the Montreal Protocol were Belgium, Canada, Denmark, Egypt, Finland, France, West Germany, Ghana, Italy, Japan, Kenya, Mexico, the Netherlands, New Zealand, Norway, Panama, Portugal, Senegal, Sweden, Switzerland, Togo, the United Kingdom, the United States, Venezuela and the 12-nation European Economic Community (EEC). A total of 62 countries ratified the protocol.

[15] Benedick, *op. cit.,* pp. 205-206.

[16] Makhijani et al., *op. cit.*

[17] Kevles, *op. cit.,* p. 32.

Bibliography

Selected Sources Used

Books

Benedick, Richard Elliot, *Ozone Diplomacy: New Directions in Safeguarding the Planet,* Harvard University Press, 1991.

The author, a career Foreign Service officer, led the U.S. delegation in negotiations that in 1987 produced the Montreal Protocol on Substances That Deplete the Ozone Layer. That agreement established deadlines for the phaseout of chlorofluorocarbons (CFCs) and other chemicals that destroy the stratospheric ozone layer. Benedick describes the negotiating process and suggests ways the protocol may serve as a model for future environmental accords.

Gore, Sen. Al, *Earth In the Balance: Ecology and the Human Spirit,* Houghton Mifflin Co., 1992.

Sen. Gore, D-Tenn., has long pressed for stronger environmental policies in Congress. In this book he elaborates on the moral and philosophical precepts that lie behind his perception of environmental problems and policies aimed at correcting them. On the dilemma posed by continuing depletion of the ozone layer, he asks, "What does it mean to redefine one's relationship to the sky? What will it do to our children's outlook on life if we have to teach them to be afraid to look up?"

Articles

Kerr, Richard A., "New Assaults Seen on Earth's Ozone Shield," *Science,* Feb. 14, 1992.

This article reviews the data released by NASA scientists in February indicating that a vast area of the Northern Hemisphere may soon be exposed to heavy ultraviolet radiation due to severe depletion of the overlying ozone layer. While the unprecedented levels of chlorine monoxide detected earlier this year do not necessarily mean that an ozone hole has already opened over populated areas, they do indicate that one may well appear next winter or in coming years.

Kevles, Daniel J., "Some Like It Hot," *The New York Review of Books,* March 26, 1992.

This review of seven new books on environmental issues places ozone depletion in the context of other current problems, including the steady extinction of plant and animal species, global warming and the difficulties developing countries face in avoiding the pitfalls of traditional industrial development while providing better living conditions.

Renner, Michael G., "Forging Environmental Alliances," *Worldwatch,* November-December 1989.

Ozone depletion is just the first case of global environmental degradation to spur nations to negotiate an agreement to protect the atmosphere, also referred to as the "global commons." It will be far more difficult, but even more important, he writes, to draw up an international treaty to curb global warming. To achieve widespread agreement on global environmental issues, he concludes, nations must understand that their national security rests as surely on a sound environment as on military strength.

Reports and Studies

French, Hilary F., *After the Earth Summit: The Future of Environmental Governance,* Worldwatch Paper 107, Worldwatch Institute, March 1992.

Since the first United Nations global environmental summit was held in 1972, more than 100 international environmental treaties have been drawn up. But they are inadequate, the author contends, to effectively curb the growing destruction of Earth's habitat by human activities. Strengthening the United Nations and providing aid to developing nations are among the steps that need to be taken to improve international cooperation on environmental protection.

Makhijani, Arjun, Kevin Gurney and Annie Makhijani, *Saving Our Skins: The Causes and Consequences of Ozone Layer Depletion and Policies for Its Restoration and Protection,* Institute for Energy and Environmental Research, Feb. 19, 1992.

The authors report that some substitutes for CFCs, called hydrochlorofluorocarbons, or HCFCs, are far more damaging to the ozone layer than previously believed. They call on parties to the Montreal Protocol to speed up the elimination of these ozone depleters as well as CFCs.

Miller, Alan S., and Irving M. Mintzer, *The Sky Is the Limit: Strategies for Protecting the Ozone Layer,* World Resources Institute, November 1986.

Although later findings make part of this report somewhat dated, its description of atmospheric chemistry and its background information on CFC development, use and effects on stratospheric ozone are helpful in gaining an understanding of the dynamics of ozone destruction.

The Next Step

Additional Articles from Current Periodicals from EBSCO Publishing's Database

Case studies

Barry, J.B., "The main street solution," *Sierra,* **May/June 1991, p. 24.**

Considers local governments in North America and Europe who are addressing the issues of ozone depletion, global warming, and tropical deforestation. Irvine, California's chlorofluorocarbons (CFCs) law; Berkeley, California and Portland, Ore., banned polystyrene foam; Toronto, Ont., cuts carbon emissions; Germany and the Netherlands stop buying tropical timber; more.

Tharp, M. & M. Satchell, "California greening," *U.S. News & World Report,* **Nov. 5, 1990, p. 35.**

Describes California's Environmental Protection Act of 1990 ("Big Green") and argues that Tom Hayden's environmental initiative could radically change the face of the West Coast. Nine environmental initiatives nationwide; stringent new regulations on pesticide use, food safety, agricultural workers' health, oil-spill prevention, water pollution and cleanup, recycling, reforestation, and ozone depletion; major role in local politics.

Debates & issues

"Laughing stocking," *Discover,* **November 1991, p. 13.**

Reports on the worrisome increase in nitrous oxide (N2O), or laughing gas, in the upper atmosphere, where it destroys ozone, warms the planet more quickly than carbon dioxide and may be produced by the nylon manufacturing process. Other sources; no plans to regulate emissions.

Anderson, J.G., D.W. Toohey, et al., "Free radicals within the Antarctic vortex: The role of CFCs in Antarctic ozone loss," *Science,* **Jan. 4, 1991, p. 39.**

Describes observational data which attempt to link chlorofluorocarbons (CFCs) to the observed loss of ozone in the Antarctic stratosphere during the Southern Hemisphere's spring. Observed containment of chlorine concentrations much greater than normal; decrease in ozone concentrations; comparisons between observed ozone loss rate and predictions with rate-limiting radicals.

Fulmer, D., "Launching dirty?" *Ad Astra,* **September 1991, p. 6.**

Looks at how NASA faces growing concerns that its Solid Rocket Boosters (SRB) cause ozone depletion and acid rain. How the SRBs work; Pollution-causing solid fuels coming under increased criticism; damage to wildlife and flora; hybrid motor alternatives; NASA developing new solids; potential acid rain fallout.

Jenish, D., "The ozone holes," *Maclean's,* **Sept. 17, 1990, p. 70.**

Discusses chlorofluorocarbons (CFCs) and their effect on the Earth's ozone layer. How CFCs destroy ozone; society's dependence on CFCs; Montreal Protocol; how elimination of CFCs will affect industry.

Monastersky, R., "Summer ozone loss detected for first time," *Science News,* **Nov. 2, 1991, p. 278.**

Comments on an announcement from a United Nations scientific panel that reveals that over the last two decades the global ozone layer has thinned significantly during the spring and summer. Evidence of ozone thinning in the lower stratosphere; Montreal Protocol; chlorofluorocarbons (CFCs) and halons; comment of James Hansen, a climate modeler at NASA's Goddard Institute for Space Studies in New York City.

Monastersky, R., "The supersonic question," *Science News,* **Oct. 26, 1991, p. 270.**

Ponders whether fleets of high-speed jetliners will damage the ozone layer. Work of the National Aeronautics and Space Administration, which is exploring the possibility of developing a new breed of supersonic plane called high-speed civil transport (HSCT); computer studies that show that fleets of supersonic jets could weaken the ozone layer; new computer simulations that give different results; work of Debra K. Weisenstein and colleagues; more.

Stevens, W.K., "Summertime harm to shield of ozone detected over U.S," *The New York Times,* **Oct. 23, 1991, p. A1.**

States that for the first time, scientists have found the Earth's protective ozone shield to be weakened over the U.S. and other temperate-zone countries in summer, when the sun's harmful ultraviolet rays are the strongest and pose the greatest danger to people and crops. Ozone depletion has accelerated and will continue at that rate, requiring a faster phasing out of man-made chemicals that destroy ozone. Stricter controls to be sought.

Economic aspects

Carey, J., J. Weber, et al., "A red alert over the ozone," *Business Week,* **April 22, 1991, p. 88.**

Declares that despite thoughts a few months ago that the

Earth's protective ozone layer had been saved from a grim fate, a new study shows that the ozone layer actually shrank 50 percent more than previously estimated. International accords to eliminate ozone-destroying chemicals; 1990 Clean Air Act; push for brisker phaseout would find opposition; results of a thinning ozone; ending chlorofluorocarbons (CFC) use. INSET: More protection for the ozone layer?

Pollack, A., "Moving fast to protect ozone layer," *The New York Times*, May 15, 1991, p. D1.

States that the nation's leading electronics companies are moving more rapidly than they expected to phase out the use of industrial cleansers that damage the Earth's protective ozone layer. Alternatives to using chlorofluorocarbons.

Environmental aspects

"The price of ozone erosion," *Science News*, Dec. 7, 1991, p. 380.

Discusses the conclusions reached by a United Nations panel charged with assessing the environmental effects of ozone loss. Belief that thinning of the ozone layer can harm millions of people and the world's ecosystems; predictions regarding possible increases in the incidence of skin cancer and cataracts; testimony from Susan Weiler, head of the American Society of Limnology and Oceanography at a Senate hearing last month.

Carey, J., "Hot science in cold lands," *National Wildlife*, April/May 1991, p. 4.

Examines scientific research going on at both the Antarctic and the Arctic to determine man's effect on the Earth's environment and which of the regions' natural resources need the most protection. Similarities of two regions' resources; land and water life; focus of international political disputes; Antarctic Treaty pros and cons; examples of scientific studies being conducted; effect of Antarctic ozone hole on ecosystem. INSET: Wildlife Week focuses on polar regions.

Environmental aspects

Kadlecek, M. & D. Ritter, "Confusion in the air: Global warming and the ozone hole," *Conservationist*, November/December 1990, p. 54.

Discusses the confusion over global warming and the ozone hole, how they're related, and how humans can positively and negatively affect them.

Health aspects

Begley, S., "A bigger hole in the ozone," *Newsweek*, April 15, 1991, p. 64.

Reports that the Environmental Protection Agency pre-

dicts 200,000 more people will die of skin cancer due to the deteriorating condition of the ozone. What has been done about the production of chlorofluorocarbons (CFCs) since the discovery in 1987 of a hole in the ozone over Antarctica; how the problem if far graver than anyone thought; EPA's plans to intensify its efforts. INSET: Danger: Sunlight.

Bergofsky, E. H., "The lung mucosa: A critical environmental battleground," *American Journal of Medicine*, Oct. 21, 1991, p. 11s.

Comments on the effects of ozone on lung function, lung compliance and airway resistance and calls for efforts to control or limit damage by ozone or other environmental inhalants in individuals with lung disease or damage. Need for wider knowledge of the pharmacologic control of the mucous membrane; factors affecting lung mucosal function including tobacco smoke, environmental gases, allergens and more; federal standards for ozone levels; more.

Molfino, N. A., S. C. Wright, et al., "Effect of low concentrations of ozone on inhaled allergen responses in asthmatic subjects," *Lancet*, July 27, 1991, p. 199.

Investigates whether low ozone concentrations increase the airway response to allergens in atopic asthmatic patients. Studies seven asthmatic patients with seasonal symptoms of asthma and positive skin tests for ragweed or grass to determine whether exposure to low concentrations to ozone potentiates the airway allergic response.

Read, R. & C. Read, "Breathing can be hazardous to your health," *New Scientist*, Feb. 23, 1991, p. 34.

Reports on the health problems caused by air pollution and about clean air legislation in some countries. Vehicle exhaust emissions; photochemical pollution; World Health Organization estimates of premature deaths from air pollution; the London smog that killed 4,000 people; reactivity of sulfuric acid and acid aerosols; impact of ozone on the formation of acid from sulfur dioxide; culprits in car exhausts; more.

Skolnick, A. A., "Is ozone loss to blame for melanoma upsurge?" *Journal of the American Medical Association*, June 26, 1991, p. 3218.

Addresses the issue that the dramatic increase in malignant melanoma may result at least in part from increased radiation caused by the depletion of the Earth's ozone layer. Not much data is available to support this theory. Most believe the threat must be monitored.

Toon, O. B. & R. P. Turco, "Polar stratospheric clouds and ozone depletion," *Scientific American*, June 1991, p. 68.

Reports that although clouds rarely form in the dry Antarctic stratosphere, when they do they chemically conspire with chlorofluorocarbons to create the "ozone hole" that

OZONE DEPLETION

opens up every spring. Effect on food chain; implicated as cause of cancer, cataracts and immune deficiencies; destruction of ozone predicted to double over next few decades. INSET: Further reading.

International cooperation

"All together now," *Economist,* **Nov. 16, 1991, p. 109.**

Discusses how European countries are cooperating to research the ozone layer. 250 scientists from 17 countries involved; the five-month European Arctic Stratospheric Ozone Experiment; research tools and strategy; more.

Prevention

"Research notes: Hydrocarbons suggested as a means to counter ozone depletion," *The Chronicle of Higher Education,* **Nov. 27, 1991, p. A7.**

Considers an article in *Science* in which a team of atmospheric scientists proposed the use of squadrons of airplanes spraying hydrocarbon gases over the South Pole to arrest the increasingly alarming rate of ozone depletion. Research by Ralph J. Cicerone (University of California, Irvine) and colleagues; use of ethane and propane to scavenge the destructive chlorine atoms; complex air-circulation patterns.

Cicerone, R. J., S. Elliott, et al., "Reduced Antarctic ozone depletions in a model with hydrocarbon injections," *Science,* **Nov. 22, 1991, p. 1191.**

Suggests a concept for action to arrest Antarctic stratospheric ozone loss by injecting the alkanes ethane or propane into the Antarctic stratosphere. Numerical model of chemical processes; size of annual injections of ethane or propane needed to suppress ozone loss; hurdles concept must overcome.

Research

"Research notes: Antarctic ultraviolet radiation found to be twice normal level," *The Chronicle of Higher Education,* **Oct. 9, 1991, p. A14.**

Considers a report in *Geophysical Research Letters* which finds a persistent hole in the ozone layer above Antarctica last year resulted in that continent's receiving twice its normal dose of biologically damaging ultraviolet radiation. Research by John Frederick and Amy Alberts (University of Chicago); computer analysis of daily ultraviolet radiation measurements.

Appenzeller, T., "Ozone loss hits us where we live," *Science,* **Nov. 1, 1991, p. 645.**

Reports on recent findings that the ozone shield is eroding over temperate latitudes in summer. Previous prediction of ozone erosion by Atmospheric and Environmental Research (AER); reasons for AER's ozone model; possible

mechanisms driving mid-latitude losses; role of sulfate particles in mid-latitude ozone erosion; use of Total Ozone Mapping Spectrometer (TOMS) data.

Begley, S. & M. Hager, "Bring back the ozone layer!" *Newsweek,* **Nov. 4, 1991, p. 49.**

Reports that last week scientists convened by the United Nations Environment Programme unveiled satellite data showing summertime ozone loss of three percent in the 1980s, which was triple the loss in the 1970s. How to lessen the depletion; banning chlorofluorocarbons (CFCs); halons are also detrimental to the environment; possibility that greenhouse effect will become worse if ozone layer repairs itself.

Bowler, S., "Ozone hole hunters look north," *New Scientist,* **Oct. 19, 1991, p. 14.**

Describes the European Arctic Stratospheric Ozone Experiment that will scrutinize ozone in the stratosphere from November to March. EASOE is a response to growing concern over ozone levels in the Northern Hemisphere; amount of ozone depletion at middle northern latitudes; main difference between ozone loss between north and south.

Brune, W. H., J. G. Anderson, et al., "The potential for ozone depletion in the Arctic polar stratosphere," *Science,* **May 31, 1991, p. 1260.**

Examines the chemical state of the Arctic lower stratosphere in winter by analyzing data obtained in January and February 1989 during the Airborne Arctic Stratospheric Experiment and by comparing this data to data obtained in the Antarctic ozone hole in 1987. Mechanisms for ozone loss over Antarctica; assessment of ozone loss in the Arctic polar vortex for 1989; potential for large-scale ozone loss in the Arctic.

Flamstead, S., "The hole story," *Discover,* **January 1992, p. 40.**

Reports on research that shows that ozone depletion is occurring over the entire continental U.S. Description of ozone depletion process in the Antarctic; reliability of new evidence; impact of ozone depletion on crops and humans; ways to curb ozone depletion.

Pyle, J., "Closing in on Arctic ozone," *New Scientist,* **Nov. 9, 1991, p. 49.**

Reports on the European Arctic Stratospheric Ozone Experiment (EASOE), a European environmental science project that will study the stratospheric ozone and how it is destroyed around the Arctic. How ozone in Antarctic is being destroyed; what type of loss is expected to be found in the Arctic; recent measurements of ozone levels by satellite; how the study will be conducted. INSET: Tipping the ozone balance.

Schnell, R.C., S.C. Liu, et al., "Decrease of summer tropospheric ozone concentrations in Antarctica," *Nature*, June 27, 1991, p. 726.

Demonstrates that surface ozone concentrations at the South Pole in the austral summer decreased by 17 percent over the period 1976-90. Over the same period, solar irradiance at the South Pole in January and February decreased by 7 percent as a result of a 25 percent increase in cloudiness.

Schoeberl, M.R. & D.L. Hartmann, "The dynamics of the stratospheric polar vortex and its relation to springtime ozone depletions," *Science*, Jan. 4, 1991, p. 46.

Presents new information on structure of polar vortices during winter and their relation to polar ozone depletions. Large gradients of potential vorticity; concentration of conservative trace species; strong inhibition of inward mixing of heat and constituents; isolation of perturbed polar stratospheric chemistry associated with ozone hole; limited maximal areal coverage; implications for size of Antarctic hole; implications for Northern Hemisphere ozone hole.

Solomon, S., "Progress towards a quantitative understanding of Antarctic ozone depletion," *Nature*, Sept. 27, 1990, p. 347.

Reviews current information on the Antarctic ozone hole. Theories; toward a qualitative understanding; the quest to be more quantitative; interannual and interhemispheric differences; implications for other latitudes.

Stephenson, J.A.E. & M.W.J. Scourfield, "Importance of energetic solar protons in ozone depletion," *Nature*, July 11, 1991, p. 137.

Examines the depletion of stratospheric ozone caused by the reaction of ozone with nitric oxide generated by energetic solar protons, associated with solar flares. Methods; results; discussion.

Warr, K., "Ozone: The burden of proof," *New Scientist*, Oct. 27, 1990, p. 36.

Presents an overview of research and legislation surrounding the depletion of the ozone layer. The origins of concern; environmental cooperation and agreement on solutions. INSET: A quick look at ozone chemistry.

Restoration

McDonald, K.A., "Novel ideas to remedy global warming and ozone loss won't work, scientists say," *The Chronicle of Higher Education*, Jan. 8, 1992, p. A6.

Outlines the recent meeting of the American Geophysical Union in San Francisco, where many of the attending scientists warned that suggestions for counteracting the atmospheric problems caused by mankind could backfire,

triggering unexpected chemical reactions in the atmosphere that might exacerbate the very problems they sought to prevent. Tinkering with a system we don't understand; evidence of ozone depletion; Mount Pinatubo eruption; natural climate changes.

Volcanos

Berreby, D., "Acid-flecked candy colored sunscreen," *Discover*, January 1992, p. 44.

Examines the effects the Mount Pinatubo eruption in the Philippines is expected to have on the global climate and on ozone layer. Statistics on eruption; gassy concentrations in stratosphere; measurements of sunlight scattering by haze from Mount Pinatubo; temporary global cooling; impact on ozone layer.

Gribbin, J., "Volcanic dust threatens the ozone layer," *New Scientist*, Sept. 7, 1991, p. 27.

Focuses on the effect of volcanic eruptions on the ozone layer. New calculations on ozone depletion by the University of l'Aquila in Italy; amount of ozone layer that could be destroyed by Mount Pinatubo.

Monastersky, R., "Pinatubo's impact spreads around the globe," *Science News*, Aug. 31, 1991, p. 132.

Warns that the eruptions of Mount Pinatubo in June may increase the risk of skin cancer in North America next summer. Preliminary estimates of the volcano's effect on stratospheric ozone; sulfur dioxide gas in the stratosphere; possible thinning of the ozone layer; comment from Guy P. Brasseur of the National Center for Atmospheric Research (NCAR) in Boulder, Colo.; more.

Back Issues

Great Research on Current Issues Starts Right Here... Recent topics covered by The CQ Researcher are listed below. Issues dated before May 10, 1991, were published under the name of Editorial Research Reports.

SEPTEMBER 1990
Dangers of Alcohol
Western Alliance After the Cold War
Tobacco Industry
Right to Die

OCTOBER 1990
Organ Transplants
Energy Policy Options
Search for Arab Unity
Child Support

NOVEMBER 1990
Lotteries and Gambling
Post-Cold War Choices
Setting Limits on Medical Care
Multicultural Education

DECEMBER 1990
Cable TV Regulation
Americans' Search for Their Roots
Is Insurance System a Failure?
Why Schools Still Have Tracking

JANUARY 1991
Growing Influence of Boycotts
Should the U.S. Reinstate the Draft?
America's Archaeological Past
Peace Corps' Challenges in '90s

Back issues are available for $4.00 (subscribers) or $7.00 (non-subscribers). Quantity discounts apply to orders over ten. To order, call Congressional Quarterly 1-800-432-2250.

FEBRUARY 1991
Regional Impact of Recession
Puerto Rico's Status
Redistricting: Mapping Power
Nuclear Power

MARCH 1991
Acid Rain
Cost of the Gulf War
Reassessing Gun Laws
Future for Man in Space

APRIL 1991
Social Security
Canadian Crisis Over Quebec
California Drought
Electromagnetic Radiation

MAY 1991
School Choice
Racial Quotas
Animal Rights
U.S. and Japan

JUNE 1991
Children and Divorce
Teenage Suicide
Endangered Species
Europe 1992

JULY 1991
Teenagers and Abortion
Soviet Republics Rebel
Mexico's Emergence
Athletes and Drugs

AUGUST 1991
Sexual Harassment
Fetal Tissue Research
Oil Imports
The Palestinians

SEPTEMBER 1991
Police Brutality
Advertising Under Attack
Saving the Forests
Foster Care Crisis

OCTOBER 1991
Pay-Per-View TV
Youth Gangs
Gene Therapy
World Hunger

NOVEMBER 1991
Fast-Food Shake-Up
The Greening of Eastern Europe
Business' Role in Education
Cuba In Crisis

DECEMBER 1991
Retiree Health Benefits
Asian Americans
The Obscenity Debate
The Disabilities Act

JANUARY 1992
Term Limits
Oil Spills
Hunting Controversy
Alternative Medicine

FEBRUARY 1992
Threatened Coastlines
New Era in Asia
Assisted Suicide
Jobs in the '90s

MARCH 1992
Women and Sports
Underage Drinking
Garbage Crisis
Mafia Crackdown

Future Topics

▶ *Welfare Reform*

▶ *Politicians and Privacy*

▶ *Illegal Immigration*

THE
CQ Researcher

PUBLISHED BY CONGRESSIONAL QUARTERLY INC., IN CONJUNCTION WITH EBSCO PUBLISHING

Welfare Reform

Should welfare benefits be used to change recipients' behavior?

P OLITICIANS ACROSS THE COUNTRY ARE PUSHING proposals that use welfare benefits to try to change the behavior of families receiving government assistance. Wisconsin's "Learnfare" program, for example, cuts a family's welfare benefits if children skip school too often. A new law in New Jersey will deny additional benefits to single women if they have more children while on welfare. Welfare advocates call such proposals punitive and question their effectiveness, but the public appears to approve of the idea. The debate over what is often called "the new paternalism" comes as welfare rolls are reaching record levels. As the political season heats up, candidates in both parties are promising further reforms of the welfare system, but the exact shape of those changes — and their effects — remains to be seen.

 April 10, 1992 • Volume 2, No. 14 • 313-336

Formerly Editorial Research Reports

COVER ART: BARBARA SASSA-DANIELS

CQ Researcher

April 10, 1992
Volume 2, No. 14

EDITOR
Sandra Stencel

MANAGING EDITOR
Thomas J. Colin

ASSOCIATE EDITOR
Richard L. Worsnop

STAFF WRITERS
Charles S. Clark
Mary H. Cooper
Rodman D. Griffin

PRODUCTION EDITOR
Laurie De Maris

EDITORIAL ASSISTANT
Michael M. Taylor

GRAPHICS
Jack Auldridge

PUBLISHED BY
Congressional Quarterly Inc.

CHAIRMAN
Andrew Barnes

VICE CHAIRMAN
Andrew P. Corty

EDITOR AND PUBLISHER
Neil Skene

EXECUTIVE EDITOR
Robert W. Merry

PUBLICATIONS MARKETING/SALES
Robert Smith

EDITOR, EBSCO PUBLISHING
Melissa Kummerer

The CQ Researcher (ISSN 1056-2036). Formerly Editorial Research Reports. Published weekly (48 times per year, not printed the first Friday of any month with five Fridays) by Congressional Quarterly Inc., 1414 22nd St., N.W., Washington, D.C. 20037. Rates are furnished upon request. Second-class postage paid at Washington, D.C. POSTMASTER: Send address changes to The CQ Researcher, 1414 22nd St., N.W., Washington, D.C. 20037.

Welfare Reform

BY KENNETH JOST

THE ISSUES

Welfare has always been a sensitive subject in the United States, but this political season, hostility toward government assistance to the poor seems especially high. Financially strapped state governments are cutting or freezing welfare benefits, and politicians from President Bush on down are issuing calls for reform.

"We must work to reform our dismal welfare system," Bush declared Feb. 12 as he officially announced his campaign for re-election. Earlier, in his State of the Union address on Jan. 28, the president promised to speed up federal approval of state initiatives to reshape the most controversial welfare program — Aid to Families with Dependent Children (AFDC).

Bush's remarks signaled an intention to push the welfare issue in the fall campaign, but one of the leading Democratic presidential hopefuls — Arkansas Gov. Bill Clinton — was making welfare reform a theme of his campaign as well. Clinton has proposed setting a two-year limit on welfare benefits. "I want to erase the stigma of welfare for good by restoring a simple, dignified principle: No one who can work can stay on welfare forever," Clinton said in a speech last fall at Georgetown University in Washington.

At the state level, welfare reform is being pushed by leaders of both parties and all ideological persuasions. In Wisconsin, conservative Republican Gov. Tommy G. Thompson is optimistic about his new "Learnfare" policy of reducing benefits for welfare families whose children miss too many days of school. In New Jersey, liberal Democratic Gov. Jim Florio is taking credit for a new law that will

deny increased benefits to an unmarried mother who gives birth to another child while on welfare. And in California, moderate GOP Gov. Pete Wilson is pushing an initiative for the Nov. 3 ballot that would cut the state's relatively high welfare benefits by 25 percent and also deny increased benefits to women for children conceived after they went on welfare.

Clinton himself is claiming credit for implementing a successful welfare-to-work program in Arkansas and for helping shepherd a work-oriented welfare overhaul bill through Congress in 1988 (see p. 325). That law, the Family Support Act, required states to increase the number of welfare recipients participating in job training programs, increased federal funding for those programs and added other liberalizing benefit provisions. The main author of the bill, Sen. Daniel Patrick Moynihan, D-N.Y., said at the time it would "bring a generation of young American women back into the mainstream of American life."[1]

Those expansive hopes for moving welfare recipients into jobs would have been difficult to realize in the best of economic times. But the economic slump that began just as the law was being implemented left states with less money to start up or expand job-training and placement programs. The continuing recession also meant there were fewer jobs to move welfare recipients into. So, far from shrinking, the nation's welfare rolls have been climbing steadily in recent years. In July 1989, 3.75 million families, or nearly 11 million individuals, were collecting AFDC. By December 1991, the number of AFDC recipients had risen to a record 4.7 million families, or nearly 13.5 million people.

Confronted with growing welfare rolls and growing budget deficits, 39 states and the District of Columbia either froze or cut welfare benefits in 1991. (See table, p. 328.) With more cuts expected in 1992, welfare advocates were disheartened. "It's a bleak time that's getting bleaker," says Michael Katz, director of the urban studies program at the University of Pennsylvania in Philadelphia.

Trying to counter the anti-welfare mood, welfare advocacy groups and liberal academic experts such as Katz argue that much of the discontent with welfare stems from widely believed myths that have little or no basis in fact. Far from being generous, they argue, the value of AFDC benefits, measured in constant dollars, has declined by about 42 percent since 1970. (See table, p. 322.) Today, AFDC benefits average about $390 per month for a family of three — well below the federal poverty level of about $905 per month for a family that size.

Moreover, welfare advocates say, warnings about "welfare dependency" ignore findings that many families who receive AFDC benefits stay on welfare for a relatively short period.* Welfare advocates also maintain that statistical research has shown no positive link between welfare and illegitimacy. Despite a sharp rise in the illegitimacy rate in the United States in recent years, they point out, single-parent welfare families average

emphasizing personal responsibility. The bipartisan endorsement of the welfare-to-work principle in the 1988 reform act seemed to have ushered in a new philosophy — dubbed the "new paternalism" — of using financial incentives or penalties to change welfare recipients' behavior. And few politicians were willing to defend the un-

governor in 1967. "We are not going to perpetuate poverty by substituting a permanent dole for a paycheck," Reagan said in his first inaugural address as governor. As president in the 1980s, Reagan continued his attacks on the welfare system, presiding over an era of budget cuts for social services that saw sustained criticism of the effects of welfare on the poor.

The most influential — and most controversial — of those critiques came from sociologist Charles Murray, whose 1984 book *Losing Ground* assembled a mass of data to support the familiar arguments about welfare, work and personal responsibility. Changes in welfare policy during the 1960s and '70s, Murray argued, made it "profitable" for the poor "to behave in the short term in ways that were destructive in the long run." The result, he said, was an increase in poverty at the very time that anti-poverty programs were being created and expanded.[3]

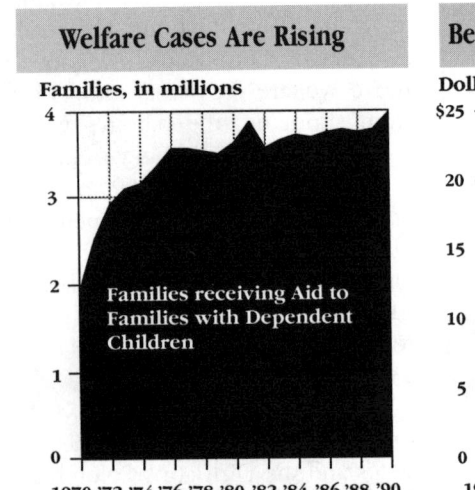

Welfare Cases Are Rising

Families, in millions

Families receiving Aid to Families with Dependent Children

1970 '72 '74 '76 '78 '80 '82 '84 '86 '88 '90

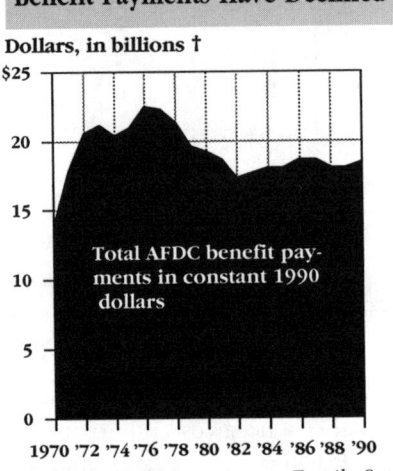

Benefit Payments Have Declined

Dollars, in billions †

Total AFDC benefit payments in constant 1990 dollars

1970 '72 '74 '76 '78 '80 '82 '84 '86 '88 '90

Sources: Office of Family Assistance and Office of Financial Management, Family Support Administration; 1991 Green Book; Statistical Abstract of the United States
† Figures do not include administrative costs

only 1.8 children — less than the national average.

These defenses of the welfare system seem to be having little impact, however, on an increasingly hostile public. Conservatives continue to press the argument fashioned during the 1980s that welfare actually aggravates poverty by reducing work incentives, encouraging family breakups and de-

popular system or resist what welfare advocates decried as punitive measures directed against the poor.

In this climate, more changes in state welfare systems are likely during the coming year. Here are some of the major issues that will affect the states' decisions:

Does the welfare system reduce recipients' work incentives?

Critics of public welfare long have argued that relief often backfires by allowing poor people to live on charity rather than encouraging them to better themselves through hard work. As one New York citizen remarked during a debate early in the 19th century: "The more paupers you support, the more you will have to support."[2]

Ronald Reagan voiced the same thought as California's newly elected

Murray's book — published under the auspices of a conservative think tank, the Manhattan Institute — touched off a vigorous debate that continues today. In one influential response, Robert Greenstein, director of the Center on Budget and Policy Priorities, accused Murray of misrepresenting data to make the point that welfare was more profitable than working at a minimum-wage job. As for the increase in the nation's poverty rate, Greenstein said the explanations were simple: a general economic slowdown, rising unemployment, stagnating real wages and a decline in the value of welfare benefits.[4]

Murray, now a fellow at the American Enterprise Institute in Washington, stands by his thesis, but in its broadest terms it has not won wide acceptance. "His interpretation of the evidence is a minority interpretation," says Brown University economist Robert Moffitt.[5] Even Murray's fellow conservatives stop short of complete agreement. Stuart Butler and Anna Kondratas of the conservative Heri-

---

*A 1983 study by Harvard Professors David Ellwood and Mary Jo Bane found that most families who received AFDC benefits stayed on welfare for less than two years. Other experts said the study understated the extent of long-term receipt of AFDC benefits by neglecting the fact that many people go on and off welfare several times. A follow-up study by Ellwood that counted such "multiple spells" over a 25-year period tended to confirm the other experts' contention. It showed that 30 percent of AFDC recipients had been receiving benefits for 1-2 years, 20 percent for 3-4 years, 19 percent for 5-7 years, and 30 percent for 8 or more years.

tage Foundation endorse Murray's main point — that welfare has increased rather than decreased poverty — but acknowledge that "there is plenty of room for uncertainty and disagreement over statistical details."[6]

Moffitt says, however, that on the specific issue of work incentives, the conservative critique appears to have some validity. "[T]he available research unequivocally indicates that the AFDC program generates nontrivial work disincentives," he wrote. The effect on income, though, is not substantial because people receiving AFDC payments tend to be employed, if at all, in low-wage, part-time jobs. Researchers estimate the work reduction prompted by AFDC payments ranges between 1 hour to 9.8 hours per week, compared with an average of 9 hours per week worked by AFDC recipients. Using the midpoint of that range, Moffitt calculates that a typical AFDC recipient's annual earnings are reduced only by $1,000 or so — not enough to "make a major dent in the poverty rate."[7]

One reason for the reduced labor effort among AFDC recipients, Moffitt points out, is time spent in child care by the mother. "Allowing the mother to take care of her children was the original purpose of the program," he writes. Public support for that policy diminished, however, as an increasing number of single women — especially single black women — with illegitimate children went on the welfare rolls. "What we're paying for is nonwork and single motherhood," says Robert Rector, the Heritage Foundation's current policy analyst for welfare issues.[8]

Does the welfare system contribute to the increasing rate of out-of-wedlock births and single-parent families?

To many observers, the welfare system would appear to encourage single-parent families and illegitimacy, since AFDC benefits are paid pri-

marily to women heading families with children and no spouse present.

As Charles Murray notes in *Losing Ground,* public concern about the link between welfare and illegitimacy dates to the 1950s, when the illegitimacy rate was low: just 4.5 percent of all live births in 1955. Today, the illegitimacy rate is 17 percent among whites and 63 percent among blacks. The number of families headed by single women also is increasing — rising from 6.2 million in 1980, or 12 percent of all families, to 8.4 million, or 24 percent of all families, in 1990.

Welfare advocates have tried to address concerns about the link between welfare and illegitimacy by offering AFDC benefits to some needy two-parent families under a program established as an option for the states in 1961 and made mandatory in 1988. Critics, on the other hand, have used the issue to argue for keeping benefits low and, more recently, to push proposals such as the one in New Jersey to deny additional benefits to unmarried women who have children while already on welfare.

As Moffitt points out, however, statistics do not confirm a clear, direct connection between welfare benefits and illegitimacy or families headed by females. Illegitimacy has risen steadily since 1960, among whites and non-whites, even though the value of AFDC benefits (measured in constant dollars) has been declining since the 1970s. The reduction in the value of welfare benefits also has not interrupted the increase in the percentage of households headed by single women.[9]

Others say non-economic factors — chiefly, changing social attitudes toward out-of-wedlock births and single parenting — have played a greater role in the trend than any economic incentives. This was the conclusion of Theodore Marmor, a political science professor at Yale University, Yale law Professor Jerry

Mashaw and New York lawyer-economist Philip Harvey in their 1989 book, *America's Misunderstood Welfare State.* Moffitt says the lack of economic opportunities for disadvantaged men may also be a factor. "Some people think it's the women who don't want the men around," he explains, "because the men don't have jobs, and they would have to support the men."

Despite these criticisms, Murray still argues that welfare is the key reason for increasing illegitimacy and single-parent families. "If you get rid of the welfare system, you would have a massive reduction in the number of children being born to single women," he says. "And you'd have many more children being given up by single women — not because the state says you have to but because the reality of the situation says to do it."

Will work-for-welfare programs help get people into jobs, off welfare and out of poverty?

The goal of getting welfare recipients into jobs and off public assistance, a recurrent theme throughout U.S. history, has been embraced in recent years by policy-makers across the political spectrum. But welfare advocates argue that the goal is harder to achieve than the public is led to believe — and all the more difficult in today's sluggish economy.

Ronald Reagan viewed California's 1971 work-oriented welfare reform act as one of his major accomplishments as governor. But analyzing the record after Reagan was in the White House, David L. Kirp, a professor of public policy at the University of California at Berkeley, found that the program managed only 1,000 placements at its peak — far from the stated goal of 30,000 jobs.[10]

At the outset, welfare critics confront the discomfiting fact that the job-training and placement programs welfare recipients need to find jobs are expensive. One Ohio program of-

Public Favors "Workfare"

Surveys show the public generally favors helping the poor, but the overwhelming majority believe able-bodied welfare recipients should work.

The government should help more needy people even if it means going deeper in debt

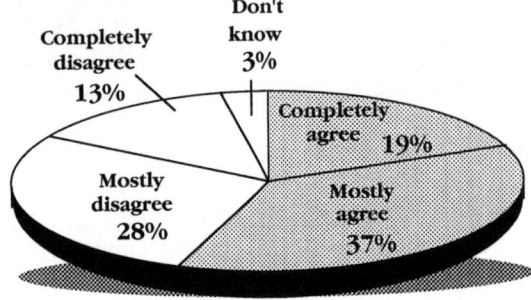

Poll conducted by *Princeton Survey Research Associates* for *Times Mirror,* **February, 1992**

Should all people on welfare who are capable of working, including women with children two years of age or older, be required to work or to seek job training?

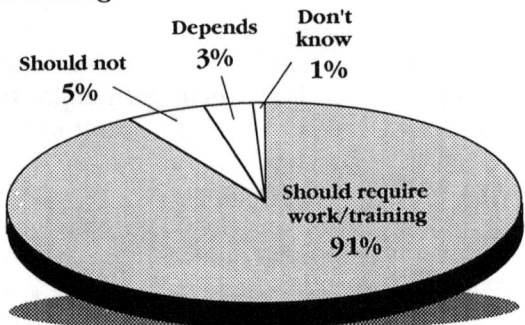

Poll conducted by *CBS News*/*New York Times, January 1992*

blunting the impact of the law even when it is fully put into effect.

Most broadly, though, liberal welfare advocates emphasize that work-for-welfare programs, or workfare, may increase welfare recipients' earnings without lifting them out of poverty. That was the central conclusion of an in-depth evaluation of 13 programs in 21 states completed in July 1991 by the Manpower Demonstration Research Corp. (MDRC), a New York-based think tank that evaluates government programs aimed at the disadvantaged.[13] Workfare fell short as an anti-poverty program, the report said, and needed to be supplemented by other policies — such as an expanded tax credit for the working poor.

But as Katz of the University of Pennsylvania argues, the consensus behind workfare may diminish support for other anti-poverty initiatives. "One danger is that it will lull legislators and public opinion into believing they have solved the problem of which the objects of new-style workfare are but one small part," he writes. In particular, Katz notes, workfare does not address the problem of unemployment and underemployment among men. In fact, jobless men may resent the special job-training and placement programs created for welfare mothers that are not available to them.[14]

Supporters of work-for-welfare programs acknowledge some of these difficulties, but respond by pointing to the importance of giving welfare recipients a sense of dignity and self-worth. More and more people across the political spectrum view welfare as a trap — a debilitating invitation to long-term dependency and poverty and a major cause of the creation of what some social scientists and politicians have labeled an "underclass" in America's inner cities.[15] From this perspective, workfare policies are not punitive, but supportive — and the short-term economic costs and benefits less important than the long-term social effects. ■

ten cited as a successful model estimates its cost at $6,000 per placement — the equivalent of about 18 months of AFDC benefits in the state.[11] As Butler and Kondratas write, "[C]onservatives are talking through their hats when they claim that workfare makes people independent and cuts costs immediately.... [T]here is no clear evidence that any savings in fact will be forthcoming in the short run."[12]

In addition, even though the proportion of women with children in the workplace has increased, requiring welfare mothers with young chil-

dren to work poses philosophical and practical problems. Conservatives may complain that welfare mothers should not be protected from the economic considerations that lead many other women to leave home and enter the workplace, but Congress still decided in the 1988 Family Support Act to exempt women with children under the age of 3 from mandatory job placement and training. The act also allows an exemption if child care is not available. Those two exemptions total about half of the AFDC caseload — thus

BACKGROUND

The Welfare 'System'

The U.S. welfare system is no system at all, but rather a conglomeration of assistance programs established at different times, funded and operated by different levels of government and built on differing — and sometimes conflicting — political philosophies.

Broadly defined, welfare includes any government assistance program where eligibility is determined on the basis of need — so-called means-tested programs. Spending on these programs totaled $210 billion in fiscal 1990 — $152 billion by the federal government and $58 billion by state and local governments.

Nearly three-fourths of that money was spent not on cash aid to the poor, but on "in-kind assistance" such as medical care (Medicaid), subsidies for food (food stamps, school lunch program), housing benefits or student aid. (See chart this page.)

The welfare debate tends to focus on cash-assistance programs, however, and most specifically on Aid to Families with Dependent Children. The federal government pays a little over half of the cost of the program, which totaled $21.2 billion (including administrative costs) in fiscal 1990. The states pay the rest, define standards for eligibility and set the level of benefits, which today range from $120 per month for a family of three in Mississippi to $924 per month in Alaska. (See table, p. 328.) The average monthly payment per case in 1990 was $377.

Poor families with children also receive direct cash assistance through a less visible program: the Earned Income Tax Credit (EITC), a form of negative income tax established during the Nixon administration and expanded in 1991 to cover families

with incomes up to $21,250. The credit, up to $2,000 for a family of four, is refundable — that is, the family gets a cash refund if the credit is greater than its tax bill. The cost in fiscal 1990: $5.9 billion.

Another federal program — Supplemental Security Income (SSI) — provides cash assistance to three categories of poor people: the elderly, blind and disabled. SSI, also established during the Nixon administration, essentially federalized what had been joint state-federal grant programs aimed at people who are generally considered unemployable.

Benefits are indexed to the cost of living; some states provide a supplement. Total state and federal cost in 1990: $17.2 billion.

Poor people who are not eligible for any of these programs may get help from so-called general assistance or general relief programs that are operated in all but six states. Some programs provide long-term help, while others are limited to emergency aid. Thirty of these programs are entirely state-funded; the rest use local funds or a state-local combination. The cost of general-assistance programs — $3.2 billion in

Programs for the Needy

Broadly defined, welfare includes any government-assistance program where eligibility is determined on the basis of need — so-called "means-tested" programs. Federal, state and local spending on these programs totaled $210 billion in fiscal 1990. Only about a quarter of that money was spent on cash aid to the poor, including Aid to Families with Dependent Children. Most of the money was spent on "in-kind assistance," such as medical care (Medicaid, etc.) or subsidies for food (food stamps, school lunch program).

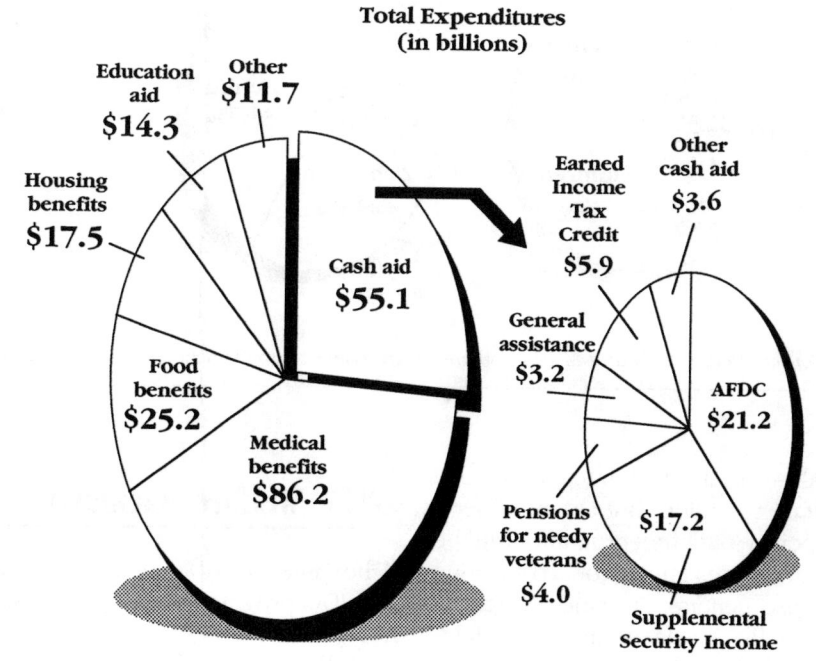

Total Expenditures (in billions)

Education aid $14.3
Other $11.7
Housing benefits $17.5
Food benefits $25.2
Medical benefits $86.2
Cash aid $55.1
Earned Income Tax Credit $5.9
Other cash aid $3.6
General assistance $3.2
AFDC $21.2
Pensions for needy veterans $4.0
$17.2
Supplemental Security Income

Source: Theodore R. Marmor, et al., *America's Misunderstood Welfare State* (1992 edition, forthcoming)

Facts About Welfare Families

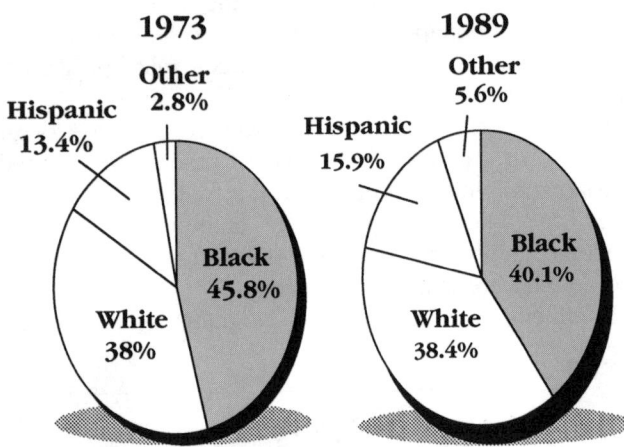

Less than half are black

Makeup of families receiving AFDC benefits

1973

Other 2.8%
Hispanic 13.4%
White 38%
Black 45.8%

1989

Other 5.6%
Hispanic 15.9%
White 38.4%
Black 40.1%

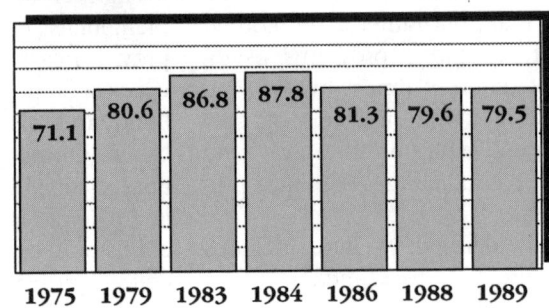

Most rely on AFDC as their only source of income

Percent of families with no reported income other than AFDC

1975	1979	1983	1984	1986	1988	1989
71.1	80.6	86.8	87.8	81.3	79.6	79.5

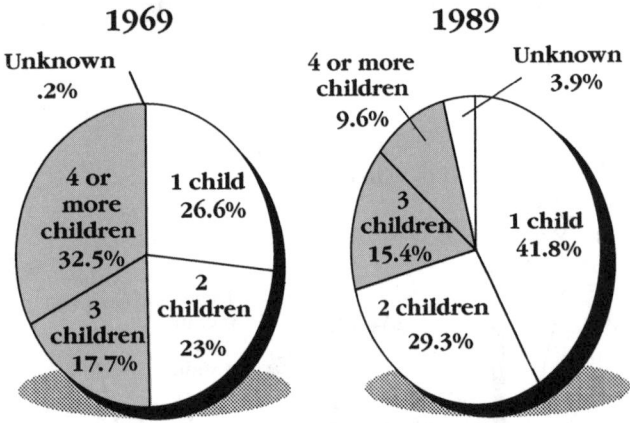

The percentage of AFDC families with three or more children is declining

1969

Unknown .2%
4 or more children 32.5%
3 children 17.7%
2 children 23%
1 child 26.6%

1989

4 or more children 9.6%
3 children 15.4%
Unknown 3.9%
1 child 41.8%
2 children 29.3%

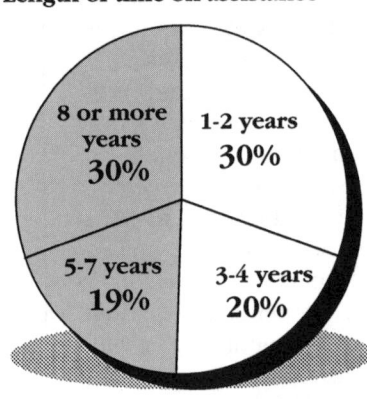

Almost half stay on welfare for 5 or more years

Length of time on assistance

8 or more years 30%
1-2 years 30%
5-7 years 19%
3-4 years 20%

Source: House Ways and Means Committee, Overview of Entitlement Programs: 1991 Green Book

1990 — is a small fraction of total welfare spending. But as one observer points out, the programs can be an attractive target for cost-cutting because general assistance recipients — chiefly, single people and childless couples who are not elderly or permanently disabled — are "perceived much less sympathetically" than other welfare recipients.[16]

The Welfare Backlash

The intensified debate over the AFDC program over the past several years has likewise been about more than money. As the authors of *America's Misunderstood Welfare State* point out, the $21 billion spent by state and federal governments on

AFDC in 1990 can be regarded as "a fiscal triviality."[17] Currently, federal spending on AFDC constitutes less than 1 percent of the total federal budget; state and local spending on the program amounts to about 1 percent of total state and local revenues.

The AFDC controversy stems largely from two recent social changes: the increasing proportion of out-of-wedlock children being supported by welfare payments and the increased acceptance of mothers working outside the home.

AFDC's origins lie in the turn-of-the-century child-welfare movement, which advocated so-called widows' pension laws to allow widows with dependent children to raise youngsters in the home rather than going to work or placing the children in a foster home or institution. Missouri passed the first such law in 1911. By 1919, 39 states had passed similar laws; by 1935, all but two states had them. By that time, most of the laws had been broadened to extend coverage to all needy mothers, including women with illegitimate children or women whose husbands for one reason or another were unable to support their families.[18]

Up until the New Deal in the 1930s, the federal government played virtually no role in social-welfare policy — reflecting the strength of states' rights and economic and religious philosophies that viewed direct aid to the poor as an invitation to idleness. The Great Depression, however, brought demands for the federal government to step in to get the economy moving again and to help the needy.

The centerpiece of the New Deal's social-welfare policy was the Social Security Act of 1935, most famous for establishing the federal program of old-age insurance and old-age assistance. The law also created a state-federal system of unemployment compensation. And Title IV of the act established what was then called Aid to Dependent Children (ADC), a program to give the states matching federal funds "to assist, broaden and supervise existing mothers' aid programs." *

Charles Murray says all three New Deal initiatives were aimed at help-

ing "upstanding citizens who had gotten a tough break or were too old to be expected to support themselves."[19] In fact, for the first 15 years or so, most of the people receiving ADC benefits were dependent white children with widowed mothers. But by the mid-1950s, an increasing number of welfare recipients were single black women with children. And, with the great postwar black migration to the North, welfare families were more visible in such major cities as Chicago and New York. The result was the welfare backlash.

As Murray writes, AFDC became the "bête noire of the social welfare system." Race played a major part in the change in public attitudes. Though the majority of welfare recipients were white, blacks were disproportionately represented on AFDC rolls and black AFDC families were larger than white ones.[20] In any event, the news media tended to focus on inner-city black women, depicting them — as Murray describes one magazine article — as "mindlessly accumulating children." The public came to view welfare as a system that bred immorality and irresponsibility.

Public officials responded with steps aimed at cutting off welfare payments to unwed mothers or stopping the in-migration of AFDC recipients. Some efforts failed. Louisiana tried to remove 23,000 illegitimate children from the welfare rolls, but was blocked by the federal government. New York legislators passed a bill requiring a year's residency before becoming eligible for AFDC, but Gov. Nelson A. Rockefeller vetoed it. Residency requirements were enacted or enforced in other states, however, as were so-called "man-in-the-house" rules that cut off AFDC benefits if a man was present in the household.

The most famous of the welfare restriction efforts came in the village of Newburgh, N.Y., where City Manager

Joseph Mitchell proposed a 13-point program that called for denying welfare to unmarried mothers if they had additional children, limiting AFDC to three months in any year and requiring able-bodied men to work or lose their benefits. New York's State Welfare Board blocked the proposals in 1962, but in the process Mitchell became a national figure.[21]

While race played a key role in the backlash against welfare, another important factor was the general lack of concern about poverty. The 1950s seemed at the time to be an era of peace and prosperity. As Trattner notes, liberal Harvard economist John Kenneth Galbraith could write confidently in his 1958 book *The Affluent Society* that poverty was "no longer a massive affliction [but] more nearly an afterthought."

The growing welfare rolls contradicted Galbraith's assumption, but most Americans viewed them as an isolated phenomenon whose causes lay with the failings of individuals rather than with society at large.

War on Poverty

Poverty was "rediscovered" in the 1960s, however, and the welfare backlash yielded to initiatives by Democratic Presidents John F. Kennedy and Lyndon B. Johnson that created federal programs aimed at helping the disadvantaged. But the moment was brief, and a new backlash began to set in during the second half of the decade.

The Kennedy administration's view of poverty was fixed on poor whites in Appalachia and inner-city black teenagers, and its most significant programs were aimed at regional development, job training and juvenile delinquency prevention. Two legislative initiatives, however, sought to deal with problems in the welfare system. Social Security amendments

---

*The program was renamed Aid to Families with Dependent Children in 1950.

Living on Welfare

Average monthly AFDC benefits were $377 in 1990, far below the federal poverty level of $868 per month for a family of three. The spending power of welfare benefits has declined by about 42 percent since 1970 because it has not kept pace with inflation.

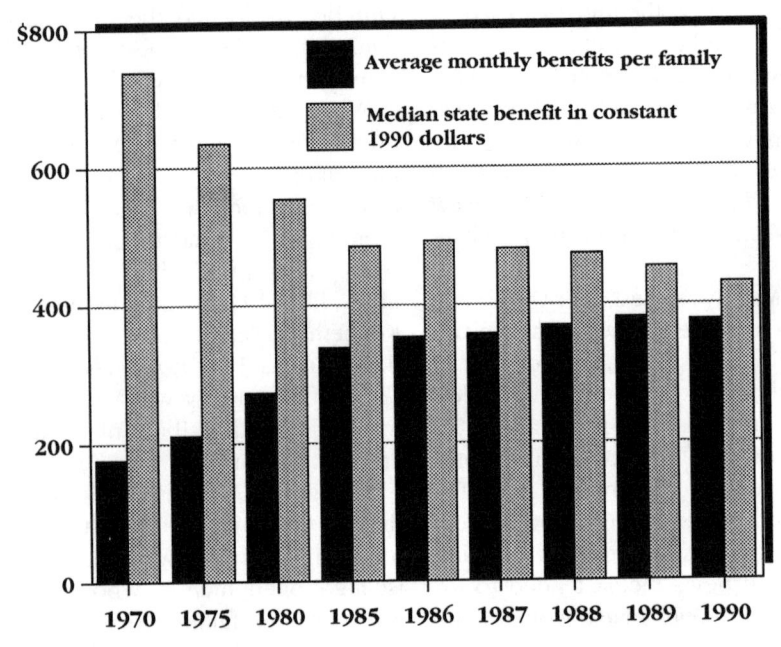

Legend:
- Average monthly benefits per family
- Median state benefit in constant 1990 dollars

Years: 1970, 1975, 1980, 1985, 1986, 1987, 1988, 1989, 1990

Sources: Family Support Administration; Congressional Research Service

passed in 1961 gave states the option to extend welfare benefits to needy families with an unemployed parent (AFDC-UP), a change aimed at reducing the incentive for desertion by jobless fathers. And the Social Service Amendments of 1962 provided federal matching funds for social services to welfare recipients, in the hope of helping them establish financial independence and get off welfare rolls.

Johnson, two months after succeeding the slain Kennedy, used his State of the Union message in January 1964 to declare "unconditional war on poverty." He followed with an omnibus Economic Opportunity Act that emphasized education (Head Start), manpower development (Job Corps) and community action rather than job creation or direct income support for the poor. But Johnson's

legacy also includes two programs that substantially expanded the number of poor people receiving direct assistance: Food Stamps, enacted in 1964, and Medicaid, created in 1965.

Murray argues that Johnson's Great Society programs represented a fundamental change in attitude — from "the dream of ending the dole to the institution of permanent income transfers." [22] The dream was, in any event, not being realized. Although the poverty rate was declining, more than 4 million people were added to the welfare rolls during the decade.

Much of that growth stemmed from an active welfare-rights movement that encouraged a greater proportion of eligible persons to apply for AFDC. [23] But whatever the reason, the increase in welfare spending, combined with the disarray of the

administration's anti-poverty programs and the urban riots of 1966-1968, disillusioned much of the American public and brought forth promises from politicians to clean up the "welfare mess."

Nixon, Carter and Reagan Advocate Reforms

Richard M. Nixon was one of those reform-minded politicians, but as president he surprised welfare advocates — and astonished his fellow Republicans — with a proposal that on its face appeared to expand assistance to the poor. Nixon's proposed Family Assistance Plan, announced in August 1969, called for needy families with children to be given $1,600 from the federal government. As a work incentive, families also would have been able to keep any earned pay until their income reached about $4,000.

The proposed plan was designed to appeal to conservatives by reducing the welfare bureaucracy and requiring anyone receiving assistance to work, with the exception of mothers with children under the age of 3. Those provisions did not win over conservatives, however. For their part, many liberals and most experts opposed the plan, calling the benefit levels too low and the work requirements punitive. The plan died when the Senate rejected it in 1972.

Nixon nonetheless presided over several major expansions of welfare programs that, as policy analyst Sar Levitan has written, exceeded Kennedy's and Johnson's initiatives in size and scope. [24] The food stamp program was made mandatory for the states in 1972, and eligibility was substantially eased. Aid for the elderly, blind and disabled was consolidated into the federalized Supplemental Security Income (SSI). The Earned Income Tax Credit was enacted to provide aid to the working poor. The welfare rolls continued to grow, while total spend-

Continued on p. 324

Chronology

1960s
Presidents John F. Kennedy and Lyndon B. Johnson push initiatives to help the poor. Conservative backlash helps Richard M. Nixon win 1968 election.

1962
Michael Harrington's book *The Other America*, dramatizing plight of the poor in urban ghettos and rural areas, influences Kennedy administration officials to begin developing anti-poverty policies.

1964
President Johnson declares "unconditional war on poverty" in his first State of the Union address. Later that year, Congress approves Economic Opportunity Act, containing job-training, community action and other anti-poverty programs, and the Food Stamps Act, providing food aid to the poor.

1966
Welfare-rights demonstrations in 16 cities culminate in August with the founding of National Welfare Rights Organization.

1967
Congress establishes Work Incentive Program (WIN) aimed at cutting off benefits to adults receiving Aid to Families with Dependent Children (AFDC) unless they accepted jobs or job-training. The program was generally viewed as a failure with few people placed in jobs and little savings in welfare costs.

1968
U.S. Supreme Court overturns "man-in-the-house" rules, which automatically cut off AFDC payments if a man was living the household.

Aug. 8, 1969
President Nixon proposes Family Assistance Plan to provide financial payments to poor families, including the working poor.

1970s
Broad income-support programs urged by Presidents Nixon and Carter both die in Congress, but less controversial federal welfare programs are expanded.

Oct. 4, 1972
Senate rejects Nixon's Family Assistance Plan.

1974
Aid programs for elderly, blind and disabled are consolidated into federal Supplemental Security Income (SSI) program. Earned Income Tax Credit is enacted to provide tax break for the working poor.

Aug. 6, 1977
President Carter announces "Program for Better Jobs and Income" to overhaul welfare system, but legislation fails to advance in Congress.

1980s
President Ronald Reagan presides over an era of cuts in programs to help the poor. Welfare-to-work programs are established in most states.

July 31, 1981
Congress approves the Omnibus Budget Reconciliation Act containing provisions Reagan requested to cut AFDC benefits for the working poor and allow states to require welfare recipients to participate in work programs.

1984
In his controversial book *Losing Ground*, Charles Murray argues that welfare has made poverty worse by rewarding dependency, joblessness and out-of-wedlock childbearing.

Oct. 13, 1988
President Reagan signs Family Support Act of 1988, requiring states to implement education, job training and placement programs for welfare recipients.

1990s
Budget woes lead many states to cut or freeze welfare benefits. Several states consider proposals to use incentives or penalties to try to modify welfare recipients' behavior.

Oct. 23, 1991
Democratic presidential candidate Bill Clinton proposes plan to provide health care and job training to welfare recipients but require those capable of work to take private or community jobs after two years.

Jan. 21, 1992
New Jersey Gov. Jim Florio signs bill that allows welfare mothers to earn more money without losing benefits but also bars increased benefits for women who have more children while on welfare.

Jan. 28, 1992
President Bush, in State of the Union address, says it's "time to . . . help reform the welfare system" and promises to ease federal review of welfare-reform initiatives by the states.

Continued from p. 322
ing on means-tested programs by all levels of government rose nearly 13 percent per year from 1968 to 1973.[25]

Like Nixon, Democrat Jimmy Carter entered the White House promising a complete overhaul of the welfare system. His "Better Jobs and Income" plan, unveiled in August 1977, was also a modified guaranteed annual income. But it differed from Nixon's proposal in that it provided universal coverage, higher benefits and public-service employment. Despite initial favorable reaction, though, Carter's plan also failed as conservatives balked at the cost and liberals faulted the benefit levels and job and work-training elements.

Ronald Reagan came to the White House in 1981 with a record of having strongly criticized the welfare system since his first campaign for governor of California in 1966. In his first budget as president, Reagan won congressional approval of sharp cuts in AFDC benefits estimated to save almost $4 billion over three years.

Ironically, in view of Reagan's "lift-oneself-by-the-bootstraps" philosophy, the most significant change reduced benefits for working AFDC recipients by limiting the "income disregard" — the amount subtracted from their earnings in calculating eligibility and benefits. The administration said welfare should be only a "safety net" for the extremely poor rather than an income supplement for the marginally needy. Critics countered that the change would discourage many welfare mothers from working.

Reagan and his supporters chose to place greater importance on a separate provision that permitted states to require most welfare recipients to participate in so-called workfare programs. Reagan had wanted to make workfare mandatory, but the Democratic-controlled Congress refused. Nonetheless, the optional provision paved the way for states to try to find ways of getting welfare recipi-

ents into jobs — the issue that dominated the welfare debate for the rest of the decade.

Welfare and Work

Congress had been trying to reorient the welfare system toward work since 1967, when it approved the Work Incentive Program — dubbed WIN. It called for cutting off AFDC benefits to adults or older out-of-school children unless they took jobs or participated in employment-training programs.

The program is generally regarded as a failure. States had discretion in administering the program: Many excluded women with young children, for example, thus reducing the number of participants. The program's major drawback, however, was lack of jobs and training slots. As the authors of *America's Misunderstood Welfare State* point out, most WIN participants "spen[t] most of their time in a category called 'holding'" — waiting for education, training or employment slots to open up.[26]

Despite this inauspicious beginning, a broad consensus emerged during the 1970s in favor of what came to be called workfare. Richard Nathan, one of the experts behind the movement and now provost of Rockefeller College at the State University of New York in Albany, says many commentators initially used the term to mean simply working off welfare grants, even in make-work jobs. By the early 1980s, however, the term reflected a broader concept of helping welfare recipients overcome dependency through employment training and education.[27]

By 1987, as many as 40 states were exercising their option under the 1981 Omnibus Budget Reconciliation Act to develop and operate welfare-to-work programs. The programs varied widely. Some were mandatory —

such as the one Bill Clinton developed in Arkansas. Others were voluntary — like the Massachusetts Employment Training program supported by Gov. Michael S. Dukakis, the Democratic Party's 1988 presidential candidate. Most were not well-funded, and only 10 programs operated statewide.

The programs produced mixed results. An initial assessment of five programs by the Manpower Development Research Corp. found positive responses among welfare clients enrolled in work programs, evidence of increased employment and increased earnings by participants and some cost savings for governments. But another study analyzing the same data said most program participants continued to rely on AFDC for most of their income, suggesting that they simply went on and off welfare rolls without achieving self-sufficiency. A broader study of 61 programs by the General Accounting Office (GAO) similarly concluded that the "modest" earnings increases were insufficient to move participants in the programs off welfare.[28]

In a more complete analysis published last summer, MDRC stuck to its conclusion that welfare-to-work programs had demonstrated the ability to produce "sustained increases in employment and earnings for single parents and a clear payoff on the public's investment." But at the same time, the study concluded that earnings increases had been "smaller and less consistent" among more disadvantaged welfare recipients, that caseload reductions "have not been dramatic" and that increases in people's standard of living "have been limited."[29]

These questions did not divert policy-makers from pushing work programs. But they did influence Congress in writing a work-oriented welfare overhaul in 1988. For conservatives, the lesson from the states was the programs could work and should be mandatory. To liberals, the states' experience showed the importance of strong

Learning From "Learnfare"

The idea sounds appealing: Get poor children to stay in school by cutting their families' welfare benefits if they skip school too often. Staying in school and developing a sense of personal responsibility, the theory goes, will help youngsters break out of the cycle of welfare dependency and make it on their own.

This is the notion behind Wisconsin's "Learnfare" program, which covers children ages 13 to 19 whose families are on welfare. Welfare reformers cheered Wisconsin's conservative Republican governor, Tommy G. Thompson, for pushing the program through a Democratic-controlled Legislature in 1987. They often cite Learnfare as an example of how states can use carrot-and-stick policies to encourage more responsible behavior by welfare recipients.

Under the program, which was put into effect in the fall of 1988, a family receiving Aid to Families with Dependent Children (AFDC) has its monthly benefits reduced by about $100 if a teenager misses two days of school in a month after previously accumulating at least 10 unexcused absences. "If your mother and father don't require you to go to school," Thompson says, "the state is going to be there to make sure you [do]." [†]

But the first detailed evaluation of Learnfare has questioned the program's effectiveness. A federally commissioned study — prepared by the Employment and Training Institute (ETI) of the University of Wisconsin at Milwaukee and released in February — found that the program had not improved overall school-attendance among high school students from welfare families.

According to the study, about a third of the students in the program had improved their attendance while over half had poorer attendance records. Graduation rates for the class of 1991 were the same for teenagers subject to Learnfare (18 percent) as for teens from families that had gone off AFDC and who therefore were no longer subject to the policy. In Milwaukee, the state's largest school district, truancy rates for students subject to Learnfare con-

**Wisconsin Gov.
Tommy G. Thompson**

tinued to increase during the three years covered by the study.

Gov. Thompson's welfare secretary disputed the report's findings. Secretary of Health and Social Services Gerald Whitburn issued a statement calling ETI "a liberal boutique," labeling the report "a faulted, biased product" and suggesting that stronger sanctions might be needed to reduce school truancy. In Washington, Jo Anne B. Barnhart, assistant secretary for children and families at the Department of Health and Human Services, also faulted the report's methodology. "I don't consider it to be an indication of whether Learnfare is working or not," she said. [††]

Wisconsin legislators divided along party lines. Democratic Assemblywoman Rebecca Young said the study confirmed the doubts voiced by lawmakers last July in rejecting Thompson's request to expand the program to younger students. "From all the evidence we have so far, it has not accomplished any of its goals, and it has created enormous hardships," she said.

But Republican Assemblyman John Gard said the study would not weaken support for the program. "I don't think anybody expected success overnight," Gard said. "But there are people it's going to help, and that's what we're after." [‡]

As for the public, Learnfare appeared to be popular — at least before the study came out. The state's GOP senator, Bob Kasten, told the Senate Finance Subcommittee on Social Security and Family Policy Feb. 3 that a poll by the Wisconsin Policy Research Institute measured 81 percent approval of the policy. And the *Milwaukee Journal* published a poll Feb. 18 indicating that 70 percent of Milwaukee residents favor reducing welfare benefits for families of children who skip school too often.

[†] Quoted in *Time*, Aug. 19, 1991, p. 19.

[††] Quoted in *The Washington Post*, Feb. 19, 1992, p. A17.

[‡] Young and Gard were quoted in *Education Week*, Feb. 19, 1992, p. 20

---

training and education programs and continued assistance to welfare recipients who did succeed in finding employment. With difficulty, both approaches were combined into the Family Support Act of 1988.

Family Support Act

Much of the credit for the 1988 welfare reform act went to Sen. Moynihan, a Democrat of sometimes unconventional views who had been a central figure in the national debate over welfare since the mid-1960s. As an assistant secretary of Labor in the Johnson administration, Moynihan wrote a controversial report blaming many problems of black Americans on the breakdown in family life and social structures. As a White House counselor to President Nixon, he had been the principal author of the unsuccessful Family Assistance Plan. And as a senator from New York, he had deepened his expertise and involvement in the issue as chairman of the Finance subcommittee with jurisdiction over welfare programs.

Political conditions were favorable for congressional action. President Reagan had called for welfare reform in his 1986 State of the Union address. The next year, the National Governors' Association made a bipartisan commitment to make welfare reform its top priority, with Democrat Clinton and Republican Gov. Michael N. Castle of Delaware designated to spearhead the issue on Capitol Hill. But the Reagan administration's initial proposal called for no new federal funds to support welfare-to-work programs, while the Democratic-controlled House passed a $7 billion bill emphasizing liberalized benefits rather than work programs.

Moynihan helped broker a compromise in the Senate and held it together in a House-Senate conference committee that concluded its work Sept. 27, 1988. The centerpiece of the bill, signed into law by Reagan on Oct. 13, was the Jobs Opportunities and Basic Skills Training Program — dubbed JOBS. Each state was required to implement a JOBS program for welfare recipients by Oct. 1, 1990, that would include education, job training and placement, plus support services such as child care and transportation. The federal government would pay 60 percent of the cost. States could set exemptions for a parent caring for children under the age of 3, but each state had to achieve participation by at least 7 percent of non-exempt AFDC recipients in 1990

and 20 percent by 1994.

Besides the JOBS program, the law also provided for strengthened child-support enforcement — reflecting the broadly shared view that the failure of non-custodial parents, typically fathers, to pay support was a principal factor in the poverty of families headed

The centerpiece of the 1988 Family Support Act was the Jobs Opportunities and Basic Skills Training Program — dubbed JOBS.

by females. It also required states to pay welfare benefits to needy two-parent families — the so-called AFDC-UP program, which only 28 states had enacted since it was made optional in 1961. And the act extended transitional child-care and Medicaid benefits to families in which the parent left the welfare rolls for a job.[30]

Implementing Reforms

Supporters of the 1988 welfare reform act hailed it as a sweeping overhaul. "I think the law has tremendous potential," says Nathan of Rockefeller College. He describes its key provisions — an emphasis on education, a balance between work requirements and service and transitional help for welfare recipients — as "something that both conservatives and liberals can see value in."

There were skeptics, however, from both ends of the ideological spectrum. Charles Murray predicted that the child-care benefits and extended Medicaid eligibility would

give low-income working women who had not been on welfare a financial incentive to quit their jobs and go onto welfare.[31] Murray claimed vindication for his prediction after the welfare rolls began climbing in July 1989, though most experts blamed the increase on the recession.[32]

Another conservative — Kate Welsh O'Beirne, vice president for government relations at the Heritage Foundation — predicted the law's costs would exceed any gains it made in dealing with welfare problems. "I think it provides expensive benefits to those best able to get off welfare on their own, and largely ignores the more hard-core population dependent on welfare," she said.[33]

For their part, some liberals minimized the importance of the law. Walter Trattner, in the 1989 edition of his history of social welfare in America, complained that the idea of forcing welfare mothers into work "was hardly novel, or very successful in the past."[34] The authors of America's Misunderstood Welfare State, published the same year, called the law's work-related provisions "a set of marginal adjustments to existing law" and warned against unrealistic expectations.[35] And, in fact, the nonpartisan Congressional Budget Office (CBO) issued a cautionary projection in January 1989 that the law would result in getting only 50,000 persons off welfare over five years — far from a major reduction.[36]

As the country drifted into recession in the summer of 1989, however, the welfare rolls across the country began to increase rather than decrease. By December 1991, after 29 consecutive monthly increases, AFDC cases had risen more than 20 percent, to nearly 4.7 million families. An analysis by the CBO showed that the caseload increase was steeper than during any of the three other recessions since 1970.[37] ∎

CURRENT SITUATION

Effects of Recession

The recession meant not only that the poor needed more help but that state governments had less money to provide assistance. With revenues hurt by the slowdown in the economy, states struggled to avoid budget deficits, and programs for the poor offered an inviting target for spending cuts. The result, according to a recent report, was the sharpest cuts in programs for the poor since the beginning of the Reagan years.

The report found that during 1991 AFDC benefits were cut across the board in five states and the District of Columbia, reduced for some families in three more states and frozen in 31 others.* General assistance — the relief programs run by state or local governments for people who do not qualify for unemployment compensation, AFDC or other welfare — was cut in 14 states and frozen in 13 others. Emergency cash assistance programs — programs aimed in part at avoiding homelessness — were cut in 12 states. And 10 of the 26 states that provide funds for low- or moderate-income housing cut those programs.[38]

Some cuts in general assistance were especially sharp. Michigan, for example, terminated cash aid and medical assistance for about 82,000 general relief recipients. Civil rights leader Jesse Jackson led a march to the state's Capitol to protest the cuts. In Massachusetts, about 10,000 general assistance recipients were to lose benefits. Ohio cut its general assis-

---

*California, Maryland, Michigan, Tennessee and Vermont cut benefits across the board. Georgia, Maine and New Mexico reduced benefits for some recipients. Texas increased benefits for a small number of families.

tance program in half, reducing benefits for most single individuals to $100 per month.

Michigan also reduced its AFDC benefits. The state initially proposed a 17 percent reduction. Though this was scaled back, Michigan eliminated a winter differential designed to help poor people with seasonally high heating bills. The result was the equivalent of a 6 percent cut on an annual basis. Other states cutting AFDC benefits included California (4.4 percent), with the second-highest benefits of any state; Tennessee (5 percent), with among the lowest benefits in the nation; and Maryland, where a 7 percent cut brought its level down to almost exactly the national average.

The states' budget woes also had a direct impact on participation in the JOBS program under the 1988 welfare reform law. More than 40 states had to limit their programs because of budget problems. "We are leaving money on the table this year, and we will do so for the next two years," said Claudia Langguth, deputy commissioner of the Texas Human Services Department.[39] According to the federal Department of Health and Human Services, the states will draw only about $565 million of the $1 billion the federal government has put up for the JOBS program in fiscal 1992.

For different reasons, states were having problems providing the transitional child-care and Medicaid benefits to cushion AFDC recipients' moves from welfare to work. The Center for Law and Social Policy, a liberal Washington advocacy group, estimated that just one out of 14 AFDC recipients eligible for subsidized child care were claiming the benefits. Lack of acceptable child care was one problem; some states insisted AFDC mothers send their children to licensed day-care centers rather than use informal arrangements with friends or relatives. As for Medicaid, the rules for extended cov-

erage were complicated, and states said they did not have enough staff to help guide AFDC recipients through the process.

Despite the problems, welfare administrators were claiming that they were implementing the JOBS program faster than the law required. A. Sidney Johnson, executive director of the American Public Welfare Association, told Moynihan's subcommittee Feb. 3 that about 500,000 individuals were participating in JOBS programs nationally — nearly one person in four among the nonexempt AFDC population. The biggest problem, Johnson said, was the lack of jobs to move welfare recipients into. "Job opportunities for those who graduate from our training programs simply do not exist today," he concluded.

Appearing before the same panel on March 30, however, researchers for the Rockefeller Institute of Government at the State University of New York in Albany questioned the support that state welfare bureaucracies were giving to the JOBS program. In a study of the implementation of the program in 10 states, researchers Irene Lurie and Jan Hagen said they found that state leaders had not "alter[ed] their public stance toward welfare or [made] a strong personal commitment to reform their welfare programs in light of the law."[40]

'The New Paternalism'

With the passage of the 1988 law, critics of the welfare system began shifting their attention away from getting welfare recipients into jobs and toward an array of initiatives to change welfare recipients' behavior in other ways through financial incentives and penalties. Critics said the policies — labeled "the new paternalism" — were punitive and would prove to be ineffectual, but the public seemed to approve of the idea.

State Budget Woes

Confronted with growing welfare rolls and growing budget deficits, 39 states and the District of Columbia froze or cut welfare benefits in 1991.

| State | AFDC Maximum Benefits for Family of Three | | | |
	January 1991 maximum benefit	January 1992 maximum benefit	% change	% change in purchasing power
Alabama	$124	$149	20.2%	16.5%
Alaska	891	924	3.7	0.6
Arizona	293	334	14.0	10.6
Arkansas	204	204	0	-3.0
California	694	663	-4.4	-7.3
Colorado	356	356	0	-3.0
Connecticut	680	680	0	-3.0
Delaware	338	338	0	-3.0
District of Columbia	428	409	-4.4	-7.3
Florida	294	303	3.0	0
Georgia†	280	280	0	-3.0
Hawaii	632	666	5.4	2.2
Idaho	317	317	0	-3.0
Illinois	367	367	0	-3.0
Indiana	288	288	0	-3.0
Iowa	426	426	0	-3.0
Kansas	409	422	3.2	0.1
Kentucky	228	228	0	-3.0
Louisiana	190	190	0	-3.0
Maine††	453	453	0	-3.0
Maryland	406	377	-7.1	-9.9
Massachusetts	539	539	0	-3.0
Michigan	525	459	-12.6	-15.2
Minnesota	532	532	0	-3.0
Mississippi	120	120	0	-3.0
Missouri	292	292	0	-3.0
Montana	370	390	5.4	2.2
Nebraska	364	364	0	-3.0
Nevada	330	372	12.7	9.3
New Hampshire	516	516	0	-3.0
New Jersey	424	424	0	-3.0
New Mexico†	310	324	4.5	1.4
New York	577	577	0	-3.0
North Carolina	272	272	0	-3.0
North Dakota	401	401	0	-3.0
Ohio	334	334	0	-3.0
Oklahoma	341	341	0	-3.0
Oregon	444	460	3.6	0.5
Pennsylvania	421	421	0	-3.0
Rhode Island	554	554	0	-3.0
South Carolina	210	210	0	-3.0
South Dakota	385	404	4.9	1.8
Tennessee	195	185	-5.1	-8.0
Texas‡	184	184	0	-3.0
Utah	402	402	0	-3.0
Vermont	679	673	-0.9	-3.9
Virginia	354	354	0	-3.0
Washington	531	531	0	-3.0
West Virginia	249	249	0	-3.0
Wisconsin	517	517	0	-3.0
Wyoming	360	360	0	-3.0

† Georgia and New Mexico delayed benefits for new recipients.
†† Maine cut benefits for some AFDC working families.
‡ Texas increased benefits for a small number of families.
Source: Center on Budget and Policy Priorities and Center for the Study of the States

"Ordinary Americans want to be generous toward the poor, but they also want to be demanding," Lawrence Mead, an associate professor of politics at New York University, said at the Feb. 3 hearing before the Senate Finance Subcommittee on Social Security and Family Policy. Mead, who had criticized the welfare system as overly permissive in his 1986 book *Beyond Entitlement,* said the new trend reflected a recognition that "direction is one thing that today's seriously poor clearly need."

The best known of the initiatives was in Wisconsin, where Gov. Thompson's "Learnfare" program provides for a 15 percent cut in an AFDC recipient's benefit if a teenage child misses school too often. Thompson claimed the program was a success, citing figures that the families of 6,600 teenagers had their benefits cut in its first full year, saving the state $3.3 million. But a study completed in February questioned the effects of the program on school truancy. *(See story, p. 325.)*

New Jersey enacted a more controversial provision in January, denying welfare mothers any increase in benefits if they had additional children while on AFDC. The provision was part of a package pushed by Assemblyman Wayne Bryant, a black representing the state's poorest city, Camden. Other parts of the bill allowed welfare mothers to marry without losing their benefits and to earn as much as 50 percent of their total welfare payment without having benefits cut. But the provision to deny the scheduled $64 per-child increase in benefits drew the most attention.

Bryant and others said the plan simply forced welfare mothers to confront the same economic factors that other families face in deciding whether to have children. "A middle-class wage earner does not go to his boss to say, 'I'm having another child, so I'm entitled to a raise,'" Bry-

Continued on p. 330

At Issue:

Should states attempt to limit the size of welfare families by denying welfare mothers additional benefits if they have more children?

Lawrence M. Mead

Associate Professor, Department of Politics, New York University
FROM TESTIMONY BEFORE SENATE FINANCE SUBCOMMITTEE ON SOCIAL SECURITY AND FAMILY POLICY, FEB. 3, 1992.

yes

*i*n recent months, governors and leading politicians in several states have proposed changes in local welfare policy that sound far reaching.... The California and New Jersey plans seek to limit the size of welfare families by denying welfare mothers additional benefits if they have further children while on the rolls. Economic incentives are proposed to encourage welfare mothers to marry.

The welfare proposals are only part of a new movement toward controlling the lives of the poor that has been called the "new paternalism." Not only in welfare, but in schools, clinics and homeless shelters, programs are asserting more authority over the way the chronic poor live than they used to....

[D]irection is one thing that today's seriously poor clearly need. Merely to dole out benefits is simply not enough to deal with their problems....

Advocates for the poor will claim that the benefit cuts are punitive, bound to cause suffering among the poor. I think it is premature to conclude that....

Whether the behavioral policies will have good effects, or any effects, is uncertain. Workfare is a well-supported policy because we have good evaluation studies and a long policy history to suggest what those programs can achieve.... We have no such studies of measures to promote marriage or limit childbearing. I doubt effects will be as large or as positive as for workfare. Family behavior probably is less subject to outside suasion of any kind than employment and education are....

There will probably be more resistance from the clients than in the case of workfare.... They will be less accepting of intervention in their family lives, which they, like other Americans, regard as a protected realm....

There is fear that the new policies may produce unintended consequences.... If welfare mothers get no more money if they have more children, the incidence of abortion may rise. One should bear in mind that the incidence is already high — a major reason why the size of welfare families has fallen sharply in the last 20 years.

On the other hand, it is hard to say that these policies should not be tried. If efforts to change lives through benefits alone have failed, then the more directive policies become unavoidable. The new paternalism is not a pleasant policy, but it is preferable to the alternative, which is continued destructiveness in poor communities.

Mimi Abramovitz and Martha Davis

Abramovitz is a professor of social welfare policy at Hunter College School of Social Work, City University of New York. Davis is a staff attorney at the NOW Legal Defense and Education Fund.
FROM *THE WASHINGTON POST*, FEB. 4, 1992.

no

a recent spate of legislative proposals in states across the country seeks to use welfare programs to control the behavior and family structure of poor women....

The dual purpose of these proposals is (1) to limit births by women on welfare and (2) encourage welfare mothers to marry as a way out of poverty. But both the assumptions underlying these proposals and the strategies they employ are misguided, falling heavily on women of color, and thus promising to fuel the politics of race.

First, the popular perception of a conniving female welfare recipient spurning marriage proposals in order to continue receiving benefits and surrounded by a half-dozen children is a myth, pure and simple. Although by restricting aid to all but a limited group of two-parent families AFDC forces many couples in need to live apart, solid empirical evidence has demonstrated again and again that the configuration of welfare benefits does not shape childbirth and marriage decisions.

Single-parent families on welfare average only 1.8 children — considerably less than the average national family size. The decisions of poor women to marry and have children are shaped by more potent and psychological forces than income, just as those of middle-class women are.

The "new paternalism" implicit in conditioning public assistance on conformity to traditional wife and mother roles is part of a predictable, if unsuccessful, cycle. As in the late 1940s and 1950s,... the government today resorts to making value-laden distinctions between "deserving" and "undeserving" women. These behavior-based distinctions were recognized as illegal during the 1960s, when states' attempts to deny welfare benefits to "illegitimate" children and to restrict unmarried women on welfare from having romantic attachments were squarely disallowed by the federal courts.

If the new welfare proposals will not affect family composition and have failed past legal tests, what will they do? They will deepen the already debilitating poverty of the average AFDC family....

The "new paternalism" in fact reflects a deep-seated societal distrust of the capacity of poor unmarried mothers to properly socialize their children.... [They] blame poverty on poor women rather than the adverse economic policies of business and the state.

Continued from p. 328

ant said at the Feb. 3 hearing. But Richard Nathan, who followed him to the stand, called the law "shooting at a popular and safe target" and predicted it would save the state little, if anything, in welfare costs.

Such criticisms have not stopped the idea from spreading. California Gov. Wilson included a provision to deny increased benefits to welfare mothers who have additional children in a broad welfare-cutting initiative being prepared for the November ballot; the plan also would require teenage mothers to live with a parent or guardian to continue receiving AFDC benefits.

In Wisconsin, Thompson developed a "Wedfare" proposal to allow married young couples to retain $200 of their independent income while on welfare, but the state Legislature rejected it. And in Maryland, Democratic Gov. William Donald Schaefer has proposed a plan to penalize AFDC recipients if their children do

not stay in school or if they do not get regular health care for their children. The plan is awaiting approval by the federal Department of Health and Human Services.

The politicians pushing these proposals often glossed over the practical difficulties in implementing them. Critics of the Wisconsin Learnfare program, for example, depicted it as an administrative nightmare with a high error rate in imposing penalties. Maryland legislators considering Schaefer's plan said that requiring the state to track compliance with the new requirements would add to the work of already burdened caseworkers. Those questions appeared to be doing little, however, to dampen interest in the ideas.

"Congress should not underestimate the anger that welfare causes today," Professor Mead told lawmakers Feb. 3. "[V]oters, very naturally, feel less generous toward the poor when they themselves are struggling. In 'hard times,' the 'abuses' in welfare become insupportable." ∎

issue by introducing a bill to raise spending for the JOBS program to $6 billion a year. "Let's find out how serious they are," Moynihan said. A spokesman for the Bush administration told Moynihan's Finance Subcommittee on Social Security and Family Policy on March 30 that the administration opposed the bill as too expensive.

The Democrats were walking a tightrope on the issue, though, hoping to please voters critical of the welfare system as well as welfare advocates. Presidential candidate Clinton epitomized the ambivalence. He touted his record of welfare reform as governor of Arkansas and offered a campaign proposal to limit AFDC recipients to two years of benefits.

But when Clinton was asked about New Jersey's plan to cut off additional benefits to women who had more children while on welfare, he took a more liberal-sounding stance. "I wouldn't sign that bill," he said in a Jan. 19 debate in New Hampshire. "What I would do is make welfare reform work. I would spend more money on health care, make sure they have child care, require them to go to work when they can and if, after the education program is complete and they haven't gone back to work, provide public-service employment."

Policy Proposals

The idea of setting time limits on AFDC benefits was not new: The conservative Heritage Foundation had included a four-year limit as part of an eight-part welfare reform agenda in 1987. But the new attention to the idea typified the yearning among experts, policy-makers and the public at large for some new approach — something more than tinkering — that would rescue the welfare system.

David Ellwood, a professor of public policy at Harvard University's John F. Kennedy School of Government, included time limits as part of one broad reform proposal. His plan

OUTLOOK

Political Moves

With the 1992 political season still in its early stages, welfare has already proved to be an appealing issue. It promises to become more volatile as the year continues.

President Bush's re-election campaign drew first blood when Vice President Dan Quayle traveled to New York City on Feb. 27 to decry what he called "the liberal vision of a happy, productive and content welfare state." At the same time, Bush's campaign began airing a commercial promising "to change welfare and make the able-bodied work."

Quayle's speech drew sharp reaction from New York Democrats, led

by Gov. Mario M. Cuomo, who had earlier predicted welfare would become "the Willie Horton issue" of 1992. "They've decided from their polls that a significant number of voters are susceptible to divisive and irrational arguments that welfare is largely to blame for the nation's economic ills," Cuomo said in a written statement following Quayle's speech.

Bush had raised welfare as an issue in his State of the Union address, and political advisers reported that the public gave the passage the second most favorable reaction of any issue in the address.[41] But Bush's only concrete "reform" was to promise to speed up federal approval of waiver requests from states wanting to change AFDC rules.

The day after Quayle's speech, Democrat Moynihan challenged the administration's commitment to the

also called for increased child-support enforcement and federal child-support insurance; health care, day care and tax credits for the working poor; and government jobs at minimum wage for welfare recipients who do not find jobs within the time limit. He estimated the cost of his plan at $30 billion a year.[42]

Public-service employment was also the focus of a plan announced in March by a group of Democratic senators led by Oklahoma's David L. Boren and Illinois' Paul Simon to create a new public jobs program reminiscent of the Works Progress Administration (WPA) set up by President Franklin D. Roosevelt. The plan — not yet formally introduced — would require welfare recipients other than women with young children to take public-service jobs unless they were already enrolled in education or training programs. As with Ellwood's plan, cost would be an obstacle. The senators conceded anything more than a pilot plan was unrealistic for the present.

Notes

[1] Quoted in *The New York Times,* Sept. 9, 1991, p. A12.

[2] Quoted in Walter I. Trattner, *From Poor Law to Welfare State: A History of Social Welfare in America* (1989), p. 53.

[3] For background on Murray's book, see "Working on Welfare," *Editorial Research Reports,* Oct. 10, 1986, pp. 729-752.

[4] Robert Greenstein, "Losing Faith in 'Losing Ground,'" *The New Republic,* March 25, 1985, p. 12. For a further exchange between Murray and Greenstein, see *The New Republic,* April 8, 1985, p. 21.

[5] See Robert Moffitt, *Incentive Effects of the U.S. Welfare System: A Review,* Institute for Research on Poverty, University of Wisconsin, March 1990.

[6] Stuart Butler and Anna Kondratas, *Out of the Poverty Trap: A Conservative Strategy for Welfare Reform* (1987), p. 4. Butler is the Heritage Foundation's director of domestic policy studies. Kondratas, a senior fellow at the foundation at the time, is now assistant secretary for community planning and development at the Department of Housing and Urban Development.

On the conservative side, ideas about changing welfare recipients' behavior through rewards or penalties continued to attract increasing interest. The proposed California welfare initiative promised to put the spotlight again on whether it is possible — and desirable — to try to affect childbearing decisions by denying welfare mothers additional benefits. *(See "At Issue," p. 329.)*

The debate over welfare reform reflects a wide agreement on general goals: getting welfare recipients into jobs and reducing long-term welfare dependency. But politically charged differences persist over benefit levels, funding for support programs and efforts to regulate welfare recipients' behavior. And overhanging the entire debate is the stark reality of economic hard times, which limit policymakers' options and strain public support for welfare policies while driving the welfare caseloads higher and higher.

Kenneth Jost is a free-lance writer in Washington.

[7] Moffitt, *op. cit.,* pp. 26-27.

[8] Quoted in *The Christian Science Monitor,* March 6, 1992, p. 4.

[9] Moffitt, *op. cit.,* p. 49.

[10] David L. Kirp, "The California Work/Welfare Scheme," *The Public Interest,* spring 1986.

[11] *The Wall Street Journal,* July 24, 1991, p. A1.

[12] Butler and Kondratas, *op. cit.,* p. 145.

[13] Judith M. Gueron and Edward Pauly, *From Welfare to Work* (1991).

[14] Katz, *op. cit.,* pp. 229-232.

[15] For background, see "Dealing With the Underclass," *Editorial Research Reports,* Nov. 10, 1989, pp. 633-648.

[16] Kathleen Sylvester, "The War Against the 'Able-Bodied' Poor," *Governing,* February 1992, p. 24.

[17] Marmor et al., *op. cit.,* p. 95.

[18] Trattner, *op. cit.,* pp. 201-203.

[19] Charles Murray, *Losing Ground* (1984), p. 17.

[20] Murray cites 1960 statistics that the mean number of children in female-headed AFDC families was 0.85 for whites and 1.57 for blacks; the percentage of such families with four or more children was 5.0 among whites, 16.5 among blacks.

[21] See Trattner, *op. cit.,* p. 282; and Joe R. Feagin, *Welfare and American Beliefs* (1975), pp. 74-75. For a current recollection of the Newburgh controversy, see *The New York Times,* March 9, 1992, p. B2.

[22] Murray, *op. cit.,* p. 25.

[23] Michael B. Katz, *The Undeserving Poor: From the War on Poverty to the War on Welfare* (1989), p. 106. Katz notes that the proportion of applicants accepted also increased, rising from 33 percent in 1960 to 90 percent in 1971.

[24] Quoted in Trattner, *op. cit.,* p. 316.

[25] Marmor et al., *op. cit.,* p. 94.

[26] *Ibid.,* p. 122.

[27] Richard Nathan, "Will the Underclass Always Be With Us?" *Society,* March-April 1987, summarized in Katz, *op. cit.,* pp. 225-226.

[28] Fred Block and John Noakes, *The Politics of New Style Workfare,* January 1988; General Accounting Office, *Work and Welfare: Current AFDC Programs and Implications for Federal Policy,* January 1987, cited in Katz, *op. cit.,* pp. 227-228.

[29] Gueron and Pauly, *op. cit.,* pp. 10-12.

[30] See *1988 Congressional Quarterly Almanac,* p. 349.

[31] Charles Murray, "New Welfare Bill, New Welfare Cheats," *The Wall Street Journal,* Oct. 13, 1988, p. A22.

[32] The most detailed analysis of the caseload increase, by the nonpartisan Congressional Budget Office, discounted Murray's theory. It said that the small number of children receiving child-care transition benefits — about 45,000 as of August 1991 — "seems to argue against this hypothesis." See Congressional Budget Office, *A Preliminary Analysis of Growing Caseloads in AFDC,* December 1991, p. 39.

[33] Quoted in *The Christian Science Monitor,* Dec. 28, 1990, p. 3.

[34] Trattner, *op. cit.,* p. 339.

[35] Marmor et al., *op. cit.,* p. 233-237.

[36] Congressional Budget Office, *Work and Welfare: The Family Support Act of 1988,* January 1989, p. 8.

[37] *A Preliminary Analysis of Growing Caseloads in AFDC, op. cit.,* pp. 25-27.

[38] Center on Budget and Policy Priorities/Center for the Study of States, *The States and the Poor: How Budget Decisions in 1991 Affected Low Income People,* December 1991. The Center on Budget and Policy Priorities is a liberal think tank in Washington. The Center for the Study of the States is a nonpartisan clearinghouse affiliated with the State University of New York in Albany.

[39] Kathleen Sylvester, "Welfare: The Hope and the Frustration," *Governing,* November 1991, p. 52.

[40] Jan L. Hagen and Irene Lurie, *Implementing JOBS: Initial State Choices,* Nelson A. Rockefeller Institute of Government, State University of New York, March 1992, p. 22.

[41] *The Washington Post,* Feb. 9, 1992, p. B1.

[42] See *The New York Times,* March 1, 1992, p. E3.

Bibliography

Selected Sources Used

Books

Butler, Stuart, and Anna Kondratas, *Out of the Welfare Trap: A Conservative Strategy for Welfare Reform,* **Free Press, 1987.**

Butler, director of domestic policy studies at the conservative Heritage Foundation, and Kondratas, a former Heritage Foundation fellow and Reagan administration official, set out a conservative plan for revising but not eliminating the welfare system.

Katz, Michael B., *The Undeserving Poor: From the War on Poverty to the War on Welfare,* **Pantheon Books, 1989.**

Katz, director of the urban studies program at the University of Pennsylvania, surveys political and intellectual attitudes toward poverty from the mid-1960s through the 1980s. He critiques the various conservative attacks on the welfare system written during the 1980s as well as media treatment of the so-called "underclass."

Marmor, Theodore R.; Jerry L. Mashaw and Philip L. Harvey, *America's Misunderstood Welfare State: Persistent Myths, Enduring Realities,* **Basic Books, 1990.**

The authors — two Yale professors and a New York lawyer-economist — argue that critics of the welfare system are fundamentally wrong in depicting the welfare system as "a failed enterprise." The welfare system, they argue, has lifted millions of people out of poverty, but many poor people remain in need of help because of structural economic problems. An updated paperback edition is due to be published this summer.

Murray, Charles, *Losing Ground: American Social Policy, 1950-1980,* **Basic Books, 1984.**

Sociologist Murray, now a fellow at the American Enterprise Institute in Washington, provoked a fierce national debate by arguing that federal welfare programs have made the poor less well off by acting as a disincentive to work and perpetuating single-parent families. On that basis, Murray recommends (and continues to favor) abolishing the federal welfare system in favor of limited assistance programs at the local level. The text is strongly written and argued, with supporting data published in notes and an appendix. The book also contains a 16-page bibliography.

Trattner, Walter, *From Poor Law to Welfare State: A History of Social Welfare in America (4th ed.),* **Free Press, 1989.**

Trattner, a professor at the University of Wisconsin in Milwaukee, updated this standard history of social welfare in America just as President Bush was succeeding Ronald Reagan in the White House. Written from an acknowledged liberal perspective, the book chronicles social-welfare policy from Colonial poor laws to the emergence of the welfare state, closing with a critical assessment of the Reagan-era "war on the welfare state." A bibliography appears at the end of each chapter.

Reports and Studies

Center on Budget and Policy Priorities/Center for the Study of States, *The States and the Poor: How Budget Decisions in 1991 Affected Low Income People,* **December 1991.**

This 85-page report was written by the Center on Budget and Policy Priorities, a liberal think tank in Washington, and the Center for the Study of States, a private research organization in Albany, N.Y., affiliated with the State University of New York. The report details actions in 40 states cutting or freezing aid to the poor during 1991 and calls the budget-driven moves the deepest welfare cuts in more than a decade.

Committee on Ways and Means, U.S. House of Representatives, *Overview of Entitlement Programs: 1991 Green Book,* **May 1991.**

This authoritative annual volume provides detailed, state-by-state statistics on benefit levels, eligibility standards, caseloads and expenditures for the Aid to Families with Dependent Children (AFDC) program.

Gueron, Judith M., and Edward Pauly, *From Welfare to Work,* **Russell Sage Foundation, 1991.**

The authors — president and senior research associate, respectively, of the Manpower Demonstration Research Corp. (MDRC) — report on the MDRC's evaluation of welfare-to-work programs in 21 states. Their central conclusion: well-run job-training and placement programs may help people get off welfare rolls, but may not raise their income enough to lift them out of poverty.

Moffitt, Robert, *Incentive Effects of the U.S. Welfare System: A Review,* **Institute for Research on Poverty, University of Wisconsin-Madison, March 1990.**

Moffitt, an economics professor at Brown University, describes the range of research findings on such issues as work incentives and the welfare system, long-term welfare "dependency," and the effects of the welfare system on family structure. The objectively written 120-page report, with detailed notes and a 12-page list of references, is an invaluable research tool.

The Next Step

Additional Articles from Current Periodicals from EBSCO Publishing's Database

Case studies

Allen, G., "The pain of poverty," *Maclean's,* **July 3, 1989, p. 38.**

Compares and contrasts the lives and financial problems of Canadian welfare mother Christine Roberts, 31, of Halifax, Nova Scotia, and American welfare mother, Kim Munson, 22, of Portland, Maine; Nova Scotia's Family Benefits and Family Allowances; U.S.' Aid to Families with Dependent Children (AFDC); finding work which provides both adequate money and benefits.

Barrett, T., "Getting tough on the poor," *Newsweek,* **Oct. 15, 1990, p. 33.**

Reports that over the past four years the Republican governor of Wisconsin, Tommy G. Thompson, has made the state a laboratory for welfare reform and set off a national debate in the process. Criticism of Thompson's actions; how he defends his programs.

Debates & issues

Bethell, T., "Keeping them on the plantation," *National Review,* **May 28, 1990, Special Supplement, p. 8-S.**

Criticizes Americans' current welfare-state philosophy that the government, rather than the individual citizen, is responsible for social change. Why legislation has been unable to solve the nation's worst problems; case study on public housing programs; importance of allowing the poor to make changes themselves, rather than remaining dependent on bureaucracy.

Dervarics, C., "Welfare reform/child support," *Single Parent,* **May/June 1989, p. 11.**

Discusses the problem of the working poor, often single parents who work full time but do not earn enough money to properly care for their families. Tax code; aid from Washington. INSET: Child support update.

Garland, S.B.; L. Therrien, et al., "Why the underclass can't get out from under," *Business Week,* **Sept. 19, 1988, p. 122.**

In an era of prosperity, legions of welfare mothers and inner-city youths face dead-end lives. Discusses the growth of the underclass unemployed and possible ways to reduce the problem.

Hinds, M., "Pulling families out of welfare is proving to be an elusive goal," *The New York Times,* **April 2,**

1990, p. A1.

Discusses the welfare system, which was overhauled by Congress in 1988 on the premise that people on public assistance did not need handouts so much as they needed a helping hand to find and keep a job. Subsidized child care and medical benefits; problems; effects on other services.

King, W., "Trenton panel supports bills on welfare," *The New York Times,* **Dec. 6, 1991, p. B1.**

States that the New Jersey Legislature moved to take up one of the most controversial proposals for improving the welfare system — deciding whether the state can discourage welfare mothers from bearing more children. Provisions of the six-bill package that would drastically revise the state's welfare system.

Purdum, T.S., "Spiraling welfare roll dominates Dinkins's report card," *The New York Times,* **Sept. 18, 1991, p. B1.**

Comments on the Mayor's Management Report, an annual survey on the state of New York City. Dark picture of the city's growing social problems and service burdens: climb in welfare roll; dirtier streets; more homeless families in temporary housing; more children in foster care.

Schram, S.F., "Welfare spending and poverty: Cutting back produces more poverty, not less," *American Journal of Economics & Sociology,* **April 1991, p. 129.**

Asserts that reducing welfare expenditures relative to need does not produce less poverty and dependency. Theories that welfare dependency is the major problem confronting public policy-makers; revision of Aid to Families with Dependent Children (AFDC); The Family Support Act of 1988; more.

Schwartz, J., "The moral environment of the poor," *Public Interest,* **spring 1991, p. 21.**

Discusses different approaches to dealing with the problem of poverty and comments on recent efforts that emphasize the restoration of the moral order as an essential component in the reduction of poverty. Work requirements for welfare recipients; quasi-military boot camps for young felons; moral vs. environmental approaches; "From the Depths: The Discovery of American Poverty," by Robert H. Bremmer; "How the Other Half Lives," by Jacob Riis; more.

Walsh, J., "Take this job or shove it," *Mother Jones,* **September 1988, p. 30.**

Analyzes new workfare programs to determine how well

they work for welfare recipients. Many states now operate programs to encourage welfare recipients to work; profiles of workfare participants.

Whitman, D., "A father's place in the welfare state," *U.S. News & World Report,* **Oct. 17, 1988, p. 41.**

Discusses the fathers of children on public assistance. Role in child rearing; eligibility for aid from welfare; reforms; child-support crackdown; example of Timothy McSeed, who was featured on 1986 television special on the black family.

Wilkerson, I., "Costly absences: Wisconsin ties welfare to attendance in school," *The New York Times,* **Dec. 11, 1989, p. A1.**

Examines the Wisconsin welfare program which ties family benefits to a child's school attendance, set up to hold welfare recipients accountable and to encourage children to stay in school to learn skills needed to get off welfare. Centerpiece of welfare reform; no more than two absences; program covers students ages 13 to 19; pros and cons of the system; new federal law in October 1990.

Wingert, P., "And what of deadbeat dads?" *Newsweek,* **Dec. 19, 1988, p. 66.**

Discusses the high number of fathers who give no emotional or financial support to their children, often despite court orders to do so. Talks about the welfare-reform bill that will allow automatic pay deductions and provide state support standards. New bill and effects; statistics.

Economic aspects

Connors, K.A., "The gathering storm: Welfare in a depressed economy," *Public Welfare,* **winter 1991, p. 4.**

Discusses the problems faced by state welfare agencies in the wake of the current economic crisis. Massive problems in the Northeast; reforming the welfare system; considering economic realities; magnitude of the federal debt.

Hammonds, K.H.; E.A. Benedek, et al., "The wolf comes knocking at nonprofit doors," *Business Week,* **Nov. 5, 1990, p. 95.**

Details how recession is wreaking havoc not only on welfare reform efforts but also on the nonprofit social service agencies that help poor people cope. How the new belt-tightening is forcing dramatic change in the way agencies operate; shrinking or eliminating programs; countering state cuts. INSETS: Where the pain is worst; even the United Way is struggling to make ends meet, by K.H. Hammonds & M.D. Sosland.

Employment training

"Against the odds," *Inc.,* **August 1991, p. 22.**

Examines the recent federal and state efforts to promote self-employment training as a way to get people off welfare. Looks at the pitfalls and problems of such programs.

"Research notes: Scholars assess job-training program in Massachusetts," *The Chronicle of Higher Education,* **Nov. 7, 1990, p. A5.**

Comments on a report issued by the Urban Institute which found that the widely publicized job-training program instituted for welfare mothers by the state of Massachusetts in 1983 has improved the recipients' chances of getting jobs and earning higher wages.

Dugger, C.W., "New York shifts on welfare: Education stressed over jobs," *The New York Times,* **Oct. 4, 1991, p. A1.**

States that the Dinkins administration has changed a strategy of quickly placing New York City's welfare mothers in mostly low-paying jobs in favor of a more expensive — and as yet unproven — investment in education and training. The aim is to eventually lead the women out of poverty into higher-paying jobs, improving their chances of staying off welfare and thus saving taxpayers money in the long run.

Mead, L.M., "The new welfare debate," *Commentary,* **March 1988, p. 44.**

Welfare reform, one of the hardy perennials of American politics, has been revived in Washington, D.C. But the politics of welfare has altered: where in the past controversy centered on the issue of expanded benefits, today debate has shifted mostly to "workfare" that is, proposals requiring that adult welfare recipients work or otherwise better themselves in return for support.

Sack, K., "Albany pact resolves fight over welfare," *The New York Times,* **June 21, 1990, p. B1.**

Reports that New York legislative negotiators reached a compromise on welfare reform, aimed at expanding educational opportunities and job training for mothers. The year-long delay in reaching the agreement cost the state millions of dollars in federal aid. Gains and losses.

Sherwood, K.E. and D.A. Long, "JOBS implementation in an uncertain environment," *Public Welfare,* **winter 1991, p. 16.**

Examines the Jobs Opportunities and Basic Skills Training (JOBS) Program and some of the mileposts it has passed since its inception in 1988. Passage of the Family Support Act (FSA) by Congress in 1988; welfare reform; Work Incentives Program (WIN); welfare-to-work programs in California and New Jersey before the implementation of the JOBS program; the Greater Avenues for Independence (GAIN) program and California Gov. George Deukmejian; more.

Family Support Act, 1988

Amidei, N., "What came in like a lion," *Commonweal,* **Oct. 21, 1988, p. 551.**

Opinion. Criticizes a new welfare reform bill which requires the unemployed to perform unpaid community service jobs, fails to help states with low benefits, and continues to provide incentives against part-time work.

Brockway, G. P., "Reality and welfare reform," *New Leader,* **Nov. 28, 1988, p. 14.**

Overview of Sen. Daniel Patrick Moynihan's, D-N.Y., new Family Support Act. Cost; "workfare" provision; its requirements.

Friedman, D., "Why the welfare mess gets messier," *U.S. News & World Report,* **Nov. 25, 1991, p. 30.**

Details the problems stemming from the reform of the welfare system in 1988, under a law authored by Sen. Daniel Patrick Moynihan, D-N.Y. Today, a record 13 million Americans — 2 million more than when the overhaul was enacted — are receiving checks from the Aid to Families with Dependent Children (AFDC) program. The core of the welfare plan, known as the Family Support Act (FSA); the missing jobs connection; loopholes; more. INSET: Where welfare woes mount.

Hylton, R. D., "The new welfare bill: When more isn't enough," *Black Enterprise,* **January 1989, p. 21.**

Discusses the new welfare bill, the government's latest attempt to overhaul the welfare system. Provisions of the bill. INSET: Significant changes in the welfare system.

Kaus, M., "Is it hype or true reform?" *Newsweek,* **Oct. 10, 1988, p. 45.**

Discusses the recently passed family welfare reform act, which is touted by many as a major reform, but actually provides compromise work requirements. It also allows states to make requirements for beefing up child-support collection and living arrangements. Bill; critics.

Lewis, A. C., "Getting on with it," *Phi Delta Kappan,* **February 1989, p. 428.**

Discusses how educators and states will be affected by the Family Support Act of 1988, known as welfare reform.

Udesky, L., "Welfare reform and its victims," *The Nation,* **Sept. 24, 1990, p. 302.**

Examines how the Family Support Act of 1988, which requires parents on Aid to Families with Dependent Children to work, is actually hurting the very people on welfare: children. How the reform programs put children in danger; what happens if a recipient refuses to work; how the workfare program is undermining its own goals.

Political aspects

Rainie, H., "State of the union," *U.S. News & World Report,* **Dec. 30, 1991 and Jan. 6, 1992, Outlook 1992, p. 36.**

Comments on how the 1992 presidential campaign will be dominated by debate over economic woes. No great prospect for relief in the coming election; Possibility that three great debates will take form; practical solutions to economic problems needed; the sense that the large-bureaucracy welfare state has failed to fix chronic social problems; an attempt to define America's role in a world devoid of military threats; more.

Roberts, S. V.; D. Gergen, et al., "Ready, set, propose," *U.S. News & World Report,* **Dec. 23, 1991, p. 24.**

Discusses how Democrats are in the middle of a full-blown debate about their sorry past and how to write a new post-liberal agenda. The conviction that the old liberal orthodoxies do not work anymore; the leading revisionist challenging party principles among the candidates; economic growth; welfare reform; health; more. INSETS: How the race is shaping up (lists the six candidates running and their aspirations); blueprint for a better government, by J. Buckley.

Research

Sonenstein, F. L. and D. A. Wolf, "Satisfaction with child care: Perspectives of welfare mothers," *Journal of Social Issues,* **spring 1991, p. 15.**

Examines Aid to Families with Dependent Children (AFDC) mothers' perspectives on their child care in 1983-1984, before welfare reform, to explore the characteristics of care that mothers are likely to seek. Data sources; AFDC mothers' use of child care; characteristics of care related to mothers' satisfaction; policy implications; discussion.

Teenage mothers

Wattenberg, E., "Minor mothers and welfare reform," *Public Welfare,* **fall 1991, p. 12.**

Tells how a Minnesota initiative provides lessons for implementing the 1988 Family Support Act's federal directives for minor mothers. Four mandates for adolescent parents; Aid to Families with Dependent Children (AFDC); eleven points of mandatory case plan for minor mothers; results of study of implementation phase of program by Center for Urban and Regional Affairs at the University of Minnesota; referrals of mothers to program; methods to reach mothers.

Back Issues

Great Research on Current Issues Starts Right Here... Recent topics covered by The CQ Researcher are listed below. Issues dated before May 10, 1991, were published under the name of Editorial Research Reports.

OCTOBER 1990
Organ Transplants
Energy Policy Options
Search for Arab Unity
Child Support

NOVEMBER 1990
Lotteries and Gambling
Post-Cold War Choices
Setting Limits on Medical Care
Multicultural Education

DECEMBER 1990
Cable TV Regulation
Americans' Search for Their Roots
Is Insurance System a Failure?
Why Schools Still Have Tracking

JANUARY 1991
Growing Influence of Boycotts
Should the U.S. Reinstate the Draft?
America's Archaeological Past
Peace Corps' Challenges in '90s

FEBRUARY 1991
Regional Impact of Recession
Puerto Rico's Status
Redistricting: Mapping Power
Nuclear Power

Back issues are available for $4.00 (subscribers) or $7.00 (non-subscribers). Quantity discounts apply to orders over ten. To order, call Congressional Quarterly 1-800-432-2250.

MARCH 1991
Acid Rain
Cost of the Gulf War
Reassessing Gun Laws
Future for Man in Space

APRIL 1991
Social Security
Canadian Crisis Over Quebec
California Drought
Electromagnetic Radiation

MAY 1991
School Choice
Racial Quotas
Animal Rights
U.S. and Japan

JUNE 1991
Children and Divorce
Teenage Suicide
Endangered Species
Europe 1992

JULY 1991
Teenagers and Abortion
Soviet Republics Rebel
Mexico's Emergence
Athletes and Drugs

AUGUST 1991
Sexual Harassment
Fetal Tissue Research
Oil Imports
The Palestinians

SEPTEMBER 1991
Police Brutality
Advertising Under Attack
Saving the Forests
Foster Care Crisis

OCTOBER 1991
Pay-Per-View TV
Youth Gangs
Gene Therapy
World Hunger

NOVEMBER 1991
Fast-Food Shake-Up
The Greening of Eastern Europe
Business' Role in Education
Cuba In Crisis

DECEMBER 1991
Retiree Health Benefits
Asian Americans
The Obscenity Debate
The Disabilities Act

JANUARY 1992
Term Limits
Oil Spills
Hunting Controversy
Alternative Medicine

FEBRUARY 1992
Threatened Coastlines
New Era in Asia
Assisted Suicide
Jobs in the '90s

MARCH 1992
Women and Sports
Underage Drinking
Garbage Crisis
Mafia Crackdown

APRIL 1992
Ozone Depletion

Future Topics

▶ *Politicians and Privacy*

▶ *Illegal Immigration*

▶ *Native Americans*

THE

CQ Researcher

PUBLISHED BY CONGRESSIONAL QUARTERLY INC., IN CONJUNCTION WITH EBSCO PUBLISHING

Politicians and Privacy

Should the news media probe politicians' private lives?

W HEN THE ALLEGED MARITAL INFIDELITY OF presidential candidate Bill Clinton was spotlighted by the media, the ensuing flap raised more than the immediate issues of adultery and the character of candidates. News professionals found themselves uneasy, divided and confused over the relentless pursuit of such a highly personal story. The fact that the initial source was a supermarket tabloid merely added to their discomfort. Since the late 1960s, in fact, the media have been regularly probing politicians' private lives (as well as their mental and physical health). Like the sex scandal that shattered the presidential candidacy of Gary Hart in 1987, the Clinton episode proves that journalists exercise tremendous power in American politics. But they are still struggling to write their ethical rule book.

 April 17, 1992 • Volume 2, No. 15 • 337-360

Formerly Editorial Research Reports

PHOTO CREDITS: WASHINGTON, P. 344, ARCHITECT OF THE CAPITOL COLLECTION; DUKAKIS, P. 346, RICHARD SOBOL; WILSON, P. 347, ROOSEVELT, P. 348, KENNEDY, P. 349 AND EISENHOWER, P. 350, LIBRARY OF CONGRESS.

COVER ART: BARBARA SASSA-DANIELS

THE CQ Researcher

April 17, 1992
Volume 2, No. 15

EDITOR
Sandra Stencel

MANAGING EDITOR
Thomas J. Colin

ASSOCIATE EDITOR
Richard L. Worsnop

STAFF WRITERS
Charles S. Clark
Mary H. Cooper
Rodman D. Griffin

PRODUCTION EDITOR
Laurie De Maris

EDITORIAL ASSISTANT
Michael M. Taylor

GRAPHICS
Jack Auldridge

PUBLISHED BY
Congressional Quarterly Inc.

CHAIRMAN
Andrew Barnes

VICE CHAIRMAN
Andrew P. Corty

EDITOR AND PUBLISHER
Neil Skene

EXECUTIVE EDITOR
Robert W. Merry

PUBLICATIONS MARKETING/SALES
Robert Smith

EDITOR, EBSCO PUBLISHING
Melissa Kummerer

The CQ Researcher (ISSN 1056-2036). Formerly Editorial Research Reports. Published weekly (48 times per year, not printed the first Friday of any month with five Fridays) by Congressional Quarterly Inc., 1414 22nd St., N.W., Washington, D.C. 20037. Rates are furnished upon request. Second-class postage paid at Washington, D.C. POSTMASTER: Send address changes to The CQ Researcher, 1414 22nd St., N.W., Washington, D.C. 20037.

Politicians and Privacy

By Charles S. Clark

The Issues

Hillary Clinton took shelter in what she called a "zone of privacy" during an extraordinary "60 Minutes" interview in January about the adultery allegations dogging the presidential campaign of her husband, Arkansas Gov. Bill Clinton. But judging from the flood of news coverage of the candidate and an ex-cabaret singer named Gennifer Flowers, privacy is a prerogative that politicians no longer enjoy.

Displayed that week in the *Star*, a supermarket tabloid, were partial transcripts of a telephone conversation Flowers said she had secretly taped between herself and the governor. The flirtatious dialogue, the partially deleted references to sex and the vague discussions of a strategy for fending off reporters were offered as proof of Flowers' claim that she had a 12-year love affair with Clinton.

"Sex, Lies and Audiotape" screamed front-page headlines in both the *New York Daily News* and *New York Newsday*. In marked contrast, *The New York Times, The Washington Post* and the *Los Angeles Times* relegated their stories to inside pages.

Appearing on CBS's "60 Minutes" with his wife, Clinton admitted to causing "pain" in his marriage but called Flowers' story untrue, acknowledging only a friendly but limited acquaintance with her. He also seemed to hint at something more, adding, "I think most Americans who are watching this tonight, they'll know what we're saying, they'll get it."

As the television networks and the newsweeklies jumped on the story, some troubling aspects of Flowers' account emerged. Critics pointed out that she had been paid in the six-figure range for her account. And the

Star refused to release the complete tapes or to have their authenticity independently verified.

Further doubts were raised when it was revealed that Flowers previously had denied rumors that she had been involved with Clinton. Finally, *Newsweek* uncovered inconsistencies in Flowers' account, among them mention of a hotel that had not yet opened at the time Flowers said she had been there with Clinton.[1]

The news media immediately showed signs of sharp disagreement over the coverage. Flowers' story is "a shabby accusation," said Al Hunt, Washington bureau chief for *The Wall Street Journal*. "I'm ashamed for my profession," said *New York Times* Executive Editor Max Frankel. "Newspapers are behaving like a bunch of dominoes," said *Miami Herald* Editor Doug Clifton, who years earlier had spied on presidential candidate Gary Hart *(see below)*. "Some low-rent publication publishes damning information with dubious sources and credibility, and then the 'higher' publications give up their independence."

But defenders of the coverage — and they were not confined to "rumormongers" in the tabloid press — saw the story as an indicator of Clinton's character. "If Anita Hill's stories about Clarence Thomas were judged relevant to his nomination for the U.S. Supreme Court, then why shouldn't Flowers' claims about Clinton be aired as well?" wrote *New York* magazine media critic Edwin Diamond.[2] "There's a woman standing there," said *Des Moines Register* Editor Geneva Overholser. "Is [the skepticism] because of her questionable morals, her peroxided hair? It's because we're uncomfortable with the subject."

The lack of consensus on the newsworthiness of the Clinton-Flowers story is the latest question mark in a conundrum the press has yet to resolve for itself: how to balance sound news practices and respect for privacy with the competitive demands that arise with a mesmerizing sex scandal.

The current preoccupation with the private lives of public figures — what perennial tabloid target Sen. Edward M. Kennedy, D-Mass., called political journalism "honed through the prism of *People* magazine"[3] — is a trend that dates from the late 1960s and early '70s. A generation of reporters egged on to aggressiveness by the Watergate scandal combined with new revelations about past presidents *(see p. 344)* to produce a cynical curiosity about the sex lives of politicians.

Suzanne Garment, author of the recent book *Scandal*, points out that the period also bred an alliance of old-fashioned morality with feminist disdain for men who womanize. "On the one hand we were seeing new habits of explicitness and a growing market for news about sex and public personalities," she writes. "On the other side we saw a growing hostility toward women who made a sexual display of themselves and an increasing disapproval of personal immorality in politicians."[4]

The media go through cycles of style and fashion, notes Dom Bonafede, a professor of communications at American University in Washington. In contrast with the 1960s, when film stars' visits to a president's hotel suite were winked at and ignored by reporters, there's more subjective analysis now. "In this day and age, if President Bush invited Madonna to go swimming with him, it would be reported," Bonafede says.

At the same time, the decline in the influence of political parties in the past two decades has magnified the importance of journalists in determining the fate of candidates. "No individuals are so entrusted with enormous yet nearly unchecked influence as are newspersons," University of Virginia government Professor Larry J. Sabato writes in *Feeding Frenzy*, his recent book on press excesses. "The abuses painfully visible during feeding frenzies damage the political fabric of America by cheapening public discourse, trivializing the campaign agenda, breeding cynicism and discouraging people from seeking public office."[5]

Newspaper editors struggling with declining readership are aware of the limits of the public's attention span for such topics as the federal budget deficit or affordable health care. The appetite for "inside dope" about sex among the rich and famous is obvious from the popularity of the tabloid press and its more recent cousin — tabloid TV. "The public goes for simplicity," says Duke University political scientist James David Barber. "They don't know what *deficit* means but they know what *adultery* means."

On a conscious level, however, the public seems to side with those who argue that a politician's private life should remain so. Only 25 percent of those responding to a recent poll agreed that voters should be informed about extramarital affairs and other private aspects of presidential candidates.[6]

When an intimate detail of a candidate's life suddenly barrels its way into publication, the public often takes its cue from the importance assigned the story by the media. Hence there is irony in the press' own confusion. *New York Times* Deputy Metropolitan Editor Michael Oreskes summed it up in a 1991 symposium on campaign coverage: "When you pick a president, the most important thing you are picking is ... someone whose judgment and strength and will are things that you respect and can count on.... But somehow, we twisted that idea, a good idea, and an idea that would be really helpful in understanding who we elect as president into a license to ask all sorts of questions about fundamentally unimportant things."[7]

As scandals and phony scandals play out on the campaign trail, here are some of the key questions being asked about politicians and privacy:

Are the news media too aggressive in probing the private lives of politicians?

Mainstream journalism reached the pinnacle of its pursuit of the adultery issue when it dug into the private life of Democratic presidential hopeful Gary Hart in May 1987. The coverage of Hart broke new ground in two important regards. A team of *Miami Herald* reporters spent hours furtively staking out Hart's Washington townhouse in order to verify the overnight presence of Donna Rice, a young woman who was not Hart's wife and whom the reporters had followed on a flight from Miami. Secondly, the evasive give-and-take that followed between Hart and the press gave *The Washington Post's* Paul Taylor his opening to ask Hart, after a series of questions on morality: "Have you ever committed adultery?"

Both Taylor and the *Herald* drew heavy criticism. "The notion was to put a citizen under surveillance," said Bill Kovach, then-editor of *The Atlanta Journal-Constitution*.[8] "That is a technique for police, not journalists." A poll showed that 63 percent of the *Herald's* own readers thought the coverage was excessive. Several *New York Times* columnists accused Taylor of deliberately trying for titillation, wondering whether reporters would soon be asking candidates about masturbation or impotence.

Defenders responded by noting that only weeks before the stakeout, Hart had vehemently denied rumors of womanizing and had actually dared reporters to follow him around. In the subsequent debate over "the character issue," many argued that Hart's deception showed poor judgment and a disturbing compulsiveness that voters should be informed of even if it made reporters feel sleazy. "Sometimes this job demands that we raise questions we'd rather not ask," Taylor said. "What I did was ask Gary Hart the question he asked for."[9]

The Hart affair also made editors and reporters wary of missing the next scoop. "This paper has tended to be very conservative about rumors," said *Rocky Mountain News* reporter Pam Maples. "After the Gary Hart story broke, there was guilt among some of the editors and reporters. You know, he was the hometown boy. Shouldn't we have been doing that story?"[10]

Politically, the legacy of the scandal was what syndicated columnist Charles Krauthammer called the "Hart Rule on Infidelity: For the offense to be fatal, it must be compulsive and current."[11]

As far as is known, that is not the situation with Bill Clinton. But that hasn't stopped assignment editors around the country from dispatching teams of reporters to sift through Clinton's past in search of women willing to kiss and

Public Supports Politicians' Right to Privacy

The overwhelming majority of those responding to a recent poll believe the press pays too much attention to candidates' private lives, at the expense of other issues. Charges related to a candidate's personal life should only be revealed, respondents said, if they are directly connected to the candidate's ability to perform public duties.

Should American voters be informed about the private lives of presidential candidates — including any extramarital affairs?

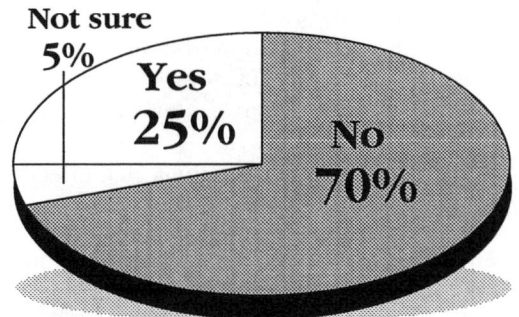

Not sure 5%
Yes 25%
No 70%

Does the press pay too much attention to a candidate's personal life?

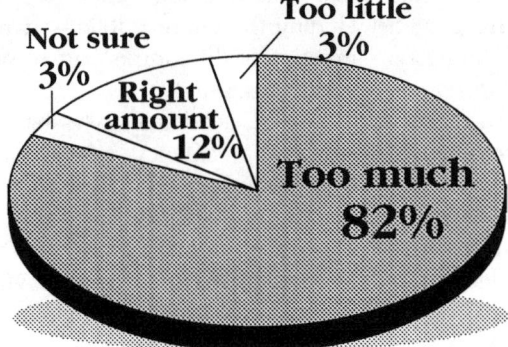

Too little 3%
Not sure 3%
Right amount 12%
Too much 82%

If a reporter learns something controversial about a candidate's life, should the reporter:

Make the information public and let voters decide how important it is................................25%

Or, should he or she respect the candidate's privacy unless the information has a direct connection to the candidate's public duties....69%

Not sure.. 6%

If a competing medium reveals charges about a candidate's personal life, should an editor:

Consider the charge to be news in itself and report it on that basis.........................4%

Check out the charges and do a story only if it can be independently verified...................42%

Ingore the charges unless they seem clearly connected to the candidate's public duties..... 50%

Not sure... 4%

Does media discussion of a candidate's personal life:

Crowd out discussion of the issues...................48%

Help reveal what candidates truly believe........16%

Not have much effect on the debate about the issues..28%

Not sure... 8%

Source: Poll conducted January 1992 by Yankelovich Clancy Shulman for Time

---

tell. It is a trend that many journalists frown upon. "When the press is confronted by such [sexual] behavior in a presidential candidate, it has no choice but to report it," wrote veteran *Washington Post* political reporter David S. Broder. "But the press has no such obligation to go rummaging in the closets of White House contenders for any past indiscretions that may fall out."[12]

But others argue that the press wasn't tough enough in ferreting out the extent of the scandal. The media are "letting Clinton lie," charged media watchdog Reed Irvine of the Washington-based Accuracy in Media. "If Gennifer Flowers had turned the tapes over to *The Washington Post* instead of the supermarket *Star*, Clinton would be finished as a presidential candidate."[13]

Author Garment confesses to some ambivalence on the coverage of Clinton, noting that if he indeed had affairs, they apparently happened a long time ago. But she also was startled that the press dropped the issue so quickly. "I don't think journalists have terrific self-confidence in this story," she says. "Clinton is the Democrat reporters think has the best chance to beat Bush, and they're hoping for a good race. Many can't be reporting it with enthusiasm, because they're of the same generation as Clinton and lived through the heyday of the sexual revolution."

The general public is as divided as the press over coverage of Clinton and the adultery issue. In a January poll by the Times Mirror Center for the People and the Press, 53 percent of the respondents said that if they headed a news organization they would report the Clinton-Flowers story, while 43 percent said they would not.

Nonetheless, the public does *not* appear to believe journalists who say

How Public Views Character Issues

Excessive drinking and tax evasion are considered more serious than infidelity or sexual orientation, according to a recent poll.

Should the following disqualify someone from becoming president of the United States?

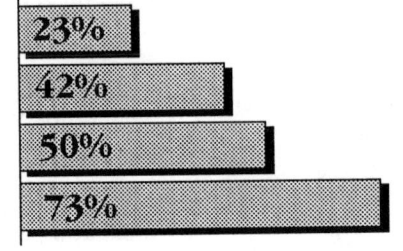

Having an extramarital affair	23%
Being gay or lesbian	42%
Having tax problems with the IRS	50%
Drinking too much	73%

Source: NBC/Wall Street Journal Poll, March 1992

they reported the story because it helped voters learn about Clinton's character. A full 73 percent of those responding to the Times Mirror poll said news organizations were driven more by the belief that the Clinton stories would draw large audiences.

Is an extramarital affair relevant to a politician's ability to handle public office?

"If he's going to cheat on his wife, he's going to cheat on America," a voter told NBC News soon after Clinton appeared on "60 Minutes." Contrast that with the New Hampshire secretary who told *Newsweek,* "We're voting for president, not pope."

Most Americans would not be uplifted by news that their political hero had engaged in an extramarital affair. But there are very different schools of thought on whether adulterers make bad political leaders.

"In the old days, a few good rumors about your sexual prowess would help you" as a candidate, comments Dean Keith Simonton, a psychology professor at the University of California at Davis who studies the personalities of presidents. "Nowadays, it's a sensitive issue."

The modern frankness on sexual matters has come hand in hand with a demand for emotional honesty. "Respect for the *public institution* of marriage is on the decline, while demand for the *private authenticity* of marriage is on the rise," noted the editors of *The New Republic.* "That is why we are now more willing to tolerate divorce than adultery in our presidents, a complete reversal of the attitudes of a generation ago."[14]

To many Americans with traditional and religious values, an extramarital affair by a candidate is disqualifying. "Adultery will always matter, just as all promise-breaking matters," wrote Gary Bauer, a Reagan administration adviser who now heads the Family Research Council in Washington.[15] The issue also appears to be more of a factor to Republicans than Democrats. In the January Times Mirror poll, 54 percent of Republicans said marital infidelity is something voters should consider in a presidential candidate, compared with only 33 percent of Democrats and 35 percent of independents.

But others cite a need for more-realistic expectations. "Politicians, like basketball players, have easy access

to women," says Debra Haffner, executive director of the New York City-based Sex Information and Education Council of the United States, referring to recent revelations about the sexual conquests of athletes Magic Johnson and Wilt Chamberlain. "In Washington, there's a general looking-the-other-way, and I'm always amazed when a politician's sex life becomes news because it's clearly an example of someone getting caught rather than a revelation of [rising] sexual activity."

Some even think that effective politicians and sexual conquests go together. As Gail Sheehy, author of *Character: America's Search for Leadership,* put it: "Wanting to charm women can easily go with a personality picture that includes charming and manipulating other people, including the entire public — which to my way of thinking is part of being a good president."[16]

Indeed, academics who have studied the presidency see an indirect correlation between having a mistress and being effective as a president. Professors Robert J. House of the University of Pennsylvania's Wharton School and William D. Spangler of the State University of New York at Binghamton, recently wrote: "Presidents who are tall and charismatic also tend to be better performers and to be rated as great or near great in surveys of political scientists.... Presidents who are tall and charismatic are more likely to have mistresses."[17]

David Winter, a University of Michigan professor who has studied the psychology of presidential behavior, says presidential adultery need not be a negative. "I'd rather have a president who's had an affair and caused pain, worked through to intimacy and handled a crisis and who sees himself as morally complex than a fundamentalist zealot who beats his wife or oppresses women," he says.

Simonton of the University of California notes that "charismatic leaders have a high need for the kind of power that can lead into war and to an autocratic style. And a need for power is often associated with sexual conquest," either in reality or by reputation.

To evaluate the effect of an active sexuality on presidential performance, Winter and many of his peers recommend consideration of other personality traits. As George Washington University historian Leo P. Ribuffo argues, President John F. Kennedy led a politically risky sex life, but his handling of the 1962 Cuban missile crisis was "prudent and thoughtful."

Duke University's Barber contrasts Kennedy with President Warren G. Harding (1921-23). "Harding was hungry for affection," Barber says. "So he had women and people in the White House playing poker and crooks causing scandals and was rated the worst president." With Kennedy, the sex was "much more trivial. It was hard to say if he knew the women's names. It tells you very little about Kennedy's presidency."

While the press is not the moral arbiter on adultery, journalists clearly play a role in how the issue affects politics.

"The moral and personal tone a president sets is as vital for the nation as his foreign policy," said Robert Caro, author of a best-selling biography of President Lyndon B. Johnson. "If we had known more about the character of some presidents, we might not have elected them. Nonetheless, there is an element of prurience — and not just with the press. What's wrong is that we give the sexual revelations such disproportionate weight."[18]

Is news coverage of sex scandals lowering standards of fairness and accuracy?

When tabloids report on Elvis sightings or the breakup of Prince Andrew's marriage to Sarah Ferguson, their "sources" can be as wispy as a rumor — an item printed in an obscure publication or a tip from a notorious liar. The mainstream press traditionally has required more rigorous verification.

In recent years, however, newspapers going for sassy "personality journalism" — as well as publications subject to manipulation by media-savvy political operatives — have unwittingly helped to spread "stories" later found to be false or unprovable. In *Feeding Frenzy,* Larry Sabato cites such examples as a 1988 story on vice presidential candidate Dan Quayle's purported drug use in the early 1970s (the source was a prisoner serving 50 years for drug smuggling and domestic terrorism) and a 1989 rumor that House Speaker Thomas S. Foley, D-Wash., was a homosexual (a story now known to have been generated by his political enemies).

"The new permissive approach," wrote *Time* magazine's Walter Shapiro, allows leading newspapers and the television networks "to write and broadcast artfully crafted stories about the rumors themselves, thereby spreading calumny while piously decrying it."[19]

According to Sabato, that's how the press went overboard in covering this year's claims against Clinton. Its first mistake, Sabato says, was printing references to unsubstantiated rumors about Clinton and marital infidelity even before Flowers came forward. The second was using the Flowers information simply because the *Star* had published it.

Clinton's hometown paper, the *Arkansas Democrat-Gazette,* took the restrained approach. "On the whole," said Editor John Starr, "I'd rather get beat on a story like this than scoop the world and be wrong."[20]

The potential harm from publicizing unverified charges was dramatized in a recent study by University of Virginia researcher Daniel Wegner. In an experiment demonstrating what is called the "innuendo effect," he showed that consumers of news, who in their haste often pay only partial attention to news reports failed to distinguish among three very different headlines: "Smith linked to mob; Is Smith linked to Mob? Smith Not linked to Mob."[21]

The use of rumors can also backfire and prevent a reporter from unearthing verifiable facts. Queries based on rumors are more easily dismissed by press spokesmen seeking to protect their candidates. "When people asked me a general, vague question like, 'Gee, we hear there are rumors,'" recalls Kathryn Bushkin, who was Gary Hart's press secretary in 1984, "I'd say 'Fine, if you can come back with something specific, then maybe there's something to talk about.'"[22]

The trend toward reporting rumors does not disturb all media-watchers. When it comes to sex, after all, there usually are only two witnesses. Editors nowadays may ease their requirements for multiple sources for every fact if they want to keep up with a breaking story that, for reasons beyond titillation, is becoming relevant to public discourse.

Press analyst Stephen Hess, a senior fellow at the Brookings Institution in Washington, says the current "short-term blip" toward reporting rumors is no worse than the situation in the 19th century, when newspapers were much more partisan. The Gary Hart stakeout, he says, shows "we have brought the standards of factual journalism to what used to be rumors."

Defending his paper's coverage of the Clinton-Flowers episode, *Washington Post* Managing Editor Robert G. Kaiser distinguished between investigative reporting and a need to report other breaking developments on campaigns. "If we didn't pay attention to the fact that Clinton's private life, subject of rumor or gossip for years, had become news," he said, "it would feed the anxiety among our readers that we know lots of things we don't share with them because of some conspiracy."[23] ∎

BACKGROUND

Sexual Politics

In the days of the Founding Fathers, the fledgling American press was considerably more partisan than it is today. Rumors were routinely planted and repeated in pamphlets and newspapers owned by fierce ideological activists. The following overview reveals a wide range of press responses to reporting on sexual matters involving American presidents and politicians:

Washington Whispers: One of the nation's earliest rumor victims was George Washington. Scholars today agree that Washington was the subject of four major public calumnies. Beginning in 1775, the commander of the Continental army was reported to have circulated a letter to other prominent figures offering sex with slave girls to visitors to his plantation, Mount Vernon. Washington also was said to have conducted an affair with a Tory woman named Mary Gibbons, and, separately, to have fathered an illegitimate son. After his death in 1799, Washington's enemies spread word that he had contracted his fatal illness in inclement weather during an assignation with the wife of a Mount Vernon overseer. Such reports usually appeared first in newspapers in London and then were reprinted by Loyalists in the Colonies.[24]

The best-known rumor about the first president didn't surface until 1877, when *The New York Herald* published the text of an intimate letter written by Washington in 1758 to Sally Cary Fairfax, the wife of his Loyalist friend and neighbor, George William Fairfax. It confessed coyly to a secret "object of my love," even though Washington at the time was preparing to marry Martha Dandridge Custis. This and a second sentimental letter Washington wrote decades later to Mrs. Fairfax in England led some historians to speculate that he had a lifelong infatuation with her.[25]

Hamilton's Secret: The adultery scandal of Alexander Hamilton, the nation's first Treasury secretary, was an early example of how the press can sometimes get a story wrong but eventually ferret out the truth. In July 1797, a sensationalistic journalist named James Callender published allegations that Federalist Party chief Hamilton had used Treasury monies for private financial speculations. Callender reproduced documents showing payments from Hamilton to a James Reynolds. To protect his reputation, the married Hamilton was left with the unenviable prospect of confessing the true purpose of the payments: blackmail paid from his own purse to cover up his long affair with Reynolds' wife.

George Washington

In a 1797 pamphlet, Hamilton explained how in 1791, Maria Reynolds had come to him pleading abandonment and asking for a loan. Hamilton was then lured into a sexual affair that continued even after her husband, by apparent prearrangement, caught them in the act. When Reynolds was imprisoned on an unrelated fraud charge, he tried fruitlessly to blackmail Hamilton into helping him. The Jeffersonians in Congress launched an investigation. Hamilton confessed all to the inquisitors, and his confession was leaked to Callender.[26]

Jefferson's Turn: In 1802, the same Callender got another "scoop." As a pro-Jefferson writer for the *Richmond Examiner*, Callender had been imprisoned for defaming President John Adams. When Jefferson became president in 1801, he pardoned Callender, who expressed gratitude by importuning Jefferson for a postmastership. Jefferson rejected him. So, from a new position on the *Richmond Recorder*, Callender began publishing articles accusing Jefferson of bribery and of having had an affair with Betsey Walker, the wife of his best friend when he was young. Jefferson was silent publicly, but he admitted to friends that the charge of seducing the married woman was the only truth in Callender's accusations.[27]

Then Callender published an article charging that Jefferson had fathered several mulatto children by a slave woman at Monticello, Sally Hemings. The charge inspired ribald poems in the anti-Jefferson press and mockery in the *New York Evening Post.*

The Sally Hemings story was repeated throughout the 19th century. English Professor Sidney P. Moss of Southern Illinois University more recently concluded that the story was motivated more by 19th-century politics than a search for truth. "The legendary nature of the story becomes plain enough," he wrote, "when we see it transmitted by the British, let alone the American press in all its grotesque accretions."[28] Less controversial was the affair that Jefferson, as a widower, carried on with a married woman named Maria Cosway while minister to France in the 1780s.

Jackson's Problem Marriage: When Andrew Jackson ran for president — unsuccessfully in 1824 and successfully in 1828 — his opponents, led by John Quincy Adams, attacked him with pointed rhetoric. "Ought a convicted adulterer and her paramour husband to be placed in the highest offices of this free and Christian land?" they asked.[29]

The charge stemmed from a complicated misunderstanding about Jackson's marriage in 1791 to a Nashville, Tenn., divorcee named Rachel

Continued on p. 347

Chronology

1960s
Extramarital affairs by Presidents John F. Kennedy and Lyndon B. Johnson go unreported by male-dominated press.

Oct. 2, 1964
News media report findings of controversial poll of psychiatrists concerning Barry Goldwater's fitness for the presidency. Goldwater later sues the person who commissioned the poll, becoming one of the few public figures to win a libel suit.

Oct. 14, 1964
Walter Jenkins, an aide to President Johnson, resigns after the press reveals that Jenkins had been arrested for homosexual activity in a YMCA.

1970s
Watergate-era investigative journalism spurs reporters to new aggressiveness. Loosening sexual mores make news coverage more explicit. Women's movement makes womanizing by candidates less acceptable among public and press.

July 31, 1972
Revelations about past electric-shock treatment force vice presidential candidate Thomas F. Eagleton of Missouri off the Democratic ticket.

Oct. 9, 1974
House Ways and Means Committee Chairman Wilbur D. Mills, D-Ark., is found drunk with stripper Fanne Foxe after she jumps into Washington's Tidal Basin.

Dec. 10, 1975
Special Senate committee headed by Frank Church, D-Idaho, reveals that Judith Campbell Exner was the mistress of President Kennedy and a top Mafia member.

May 23, 1976
The Washington Post reports that House Administration Committee Chairman Wayne L. Hays, D-Ohio, kept "typist" Elizabeth Ray on his payroll as his mistress.

1980s
Gay activists begin "outing" allegedly homosexual celebrities.

Oct. 3, 1980
Story breaks that Rep. Robert E. Bauman, D-Md., had been arrested for soliciting a male prostitute.

March 6, 1981
Wilmington (Del.) *News-Journal* breaks story that Rep. Thomas B. Evans, R-Del., had an affair with lobbyist Paula Parkinson.

May 3, 1987
After staking out the home of presidential candidate Gary Hart, *Miami Herald* publishes story alleging he had a sexual affair with Donna Rice. Hart later is forced out of the race.

June 3, 1987
Presidential prospects of Ohio Democratic Gov. Richard F. Celeste are undercut after Cleveland *Plain Dealer* reports allegations of three extramarital affairs.

Aug. 2, 1988
Several newspapers report Democratic presidential candidate Michael S. Dukakis' denials of unsubstantiated allegations that he sought psychiatric treatment.

Oct. 19, 1988
Stock market drops 43 points on rumor — later revealed as false — that *The Washington Post* was about to publish a story alleging that President Bush once had a mistress.

March 9, 1989
Defense secretary nominee John Tower is rejected by Senate after publication of allegations of drinking and womanizing.

Aug. 25, 1989
The Washington Times breaks story that a male prostitute operated a gay escort service from the apartment of Rep. Barney Frank, D-Mass.

1990s
Mainstream press covers rumors and follows lead of tabloids.

Oct. 28, 1990
Minnesota Republican gubernatorial candidate Jon Grunseth withdraws from race after *Minneapolis Star-Tribune* reports charges that nine years earlier he had invited four teenage girls to go swimming with him nude.

April 28, 1991
NBC's "Exposé" airs allegations from beauty queen Tai Collins that she had an affair with Sen. Charles S. Robb, D-Va.

Jan. 26, 1992
Democratic presidential candidate Bill Clinton appears with his wife on "60 Minutes" to respond to Gennifer Flowers' allegation that she and Clinton had an extramarital affair.

March 1, 1992
Sen. Brock Adams, D-Wash., drops re-election bid after *Seattle Times* publishes story on alleged past sexual abuse of female staffers.

Risks of Prying Into Mental-Health Problems

The privacy issue most often misconstrued by press and public alike involves the delicate area of mental health. It's not simply that rumors or evidence of current emotional troubles can tarnish a candidate's election prospects. Recent history has shown that the mere fact of having sought treatment for a mental problem in the past can be a political kiss of death.

The modern ground rules for handling this issue took shape in the fall of 1964, when Republican presidential candidate Barry Goldwater was subjected to an ethically questionable attack on his mental health. Pornographic magazine publisher Ralph Ginzberg, in a now-defunct magazine called *Fact,* published results of a poll he had commissioned in which he asked more than 2,400 psychiatrists to respond to the question, "Is Barry Goldwater psychologically fit to be president of the United States?"

A startling 1,189 of the psychiatrists responded "no," while only 657 said "yes." (A cautious 571 said they did not know enough to answer.) Medical authorities and many in the public were appalled at the survey.† Goldwater successfully sued Ginzberg, becoming one of the few public figures to win a libel suit. In response to the incident, the American Psychiatric Association adopted what it called "the Goldwater Rule." It forbids doctors from offering a psychiatric opinion on a public figure unless the psychiatrist has personally treated the official and has authorization to break patient-doctor confidentiality.

The damage that can be wrought by mental-health questions was made clear in July 1972. Democratic presidential candidate George McGovern had selected Missouri Sen. Thomas F. Eagleton as his running mate at the party convention in Miami. Several days later, *The Miami Herald* approached Eagleton with information that he had once undergone electric-shock treatment for depression. Before the story could be published, Eagleton disclosed that he had voluntarily hospitalized himself three times from 1960-66 for "nervous exhaustion and fatigue."

A distraught McGovern announced he was still behind Eagleton "1,000 percent." The intraparty and public uproar swelled, however, and columnist Jack Anderson reported unsubstantiated charges that Eagleton had been arrested several times for drunken driving. Under pressure, Eagleton withdrew from the race on July 31.

The mental-health controversy made another appearance in 1980, in a South Carolina congressional race. Democratic state Sen. Tom Turnipseed lost the election in the wake of repeated press coverage of the fact that he had once undergone electric-shock therapy. His opponent's campaign manager, Lee Atwater, the future chairman of the Republican National Committee, at one point in the campaign told reporters he wouldn't respond to charges by someone who had been "hooked up to jumper cables." A decade later, while dying from a brain tumor, Atwater wrote Turnipseed to apologize.††

In 1988, the rumor mill combined with the stigma about mental-health treatment to bedevil the presidential campaign of Democrat Michael S. Dukakis. At the July Democratic convention in Atlanta, supporters of extremist candidate Lyndon H. LaRouche Jr. had distributed fliers claiming, without any basis in fact, that Dukakis had been treated twice by a psychiatrist. Word shot round the political community, and some officials in George Bush's campaign encouraged reporters to investigate the story.

Michael S. Dukakis

With rumors flying that *The Detroit News* was about to break the story, some in the media succumbed to competitive pressures. After a *Boston Herald* reporter asked Dukakis about the rumors (the candidate shrugged them off), *The Boston Globe* described the exchange, though noting the lack of evidence. That was enough for *The Washington Times,* which ran a front-page story about Dukakis denying the rumors. Days later, the *Times* followed with a story headlined "Dukakis Kin Hints at Sessions," based on an interview with the candidate's sister-in-law. The story said merely that Dukakis may have spoken to a neighbor who is a psychiatrist.

Dukakis had to produce his doctor to confirm there had been no such treatment. Still, President Ronald Reagan was able to take a political jab at Dukakis when he was asked about the rumors. "I'm not going to pick on an invalid," Reagan quipped.‡ (Reagan later apologized for the remark.)

It seems unlikely that mental-health issues will soon lose their potential for singeing reputations of politicians. Dr. Jeremy Lazarus, chairman of the ethics committee of the American Psychiatric Association, says it is unfortunate that political candidates who've been treated for mental problems are stigmatized. Eagleton, he points out, is an example of someone who was successfully treated and went on to a distinguished political career. "If one has been treated for an emotional illness," he says, "it might make one a more sensitive, insightful person." A mental ailment "in and of itself is a problem only if it interferes with an official's duty to carry out his work."

† See *The New York Times,* Oct. 2, 1964.
†† See *The Wall Street Journal,* Aug. 11, 1988.
‡ See Jack Germond and Jules Witcover, *Whose Broad Stripes and Bright Stars?* (1989), p. 360, and Larry J. Sabato, *Feeding Frenzy* (1991), p. 153.

Continued from p. 344
Donelson Robards. Her estranged husband had been jealous when the young Jackson appeared smitten with his wife and eventually sought a divorce from the Virginia legislature. Jackson and Rachel then took off to Natchez, Miss., to get married, only to discover three years later that the Virginia legislature had simply given permission for divorce *proceedings.* They had a second wedding in 1794, but rumors of bigamy persisted throughout Jackson's career, causing him on more than one occasion to fight duels over his wife's honor.

Rachel died just before Jackson was inaugurated in 1829, shortly before the outbreak of another sex scandal, the Peggy Eaton affair. Peggy O'Neale, the divorced daughter of a saloon keeper and a woman with an unsavory reputation, had married Treasury Secretary John Eaton. The disapproving wives of Jackson's Cabinet members were inclined to believe stories that she had slept with 20 men, had had a miscarriage when her first husband had been at sea for a year and had traveled with Eaton before they were married.[30]

The women's snubs eventually divided the Cabinet along political lines. Jackson had to defend her as "chaste as a virgin" against attacks from Vice President John C. Calhoun. *The Washington Journal* accused officials who broke the Eaton boycott of trying to force "an unworthy person" on Washington society. The resulting fight resulted in the resignations of Eaton and Secretary of State Martin Van Buren and the firing of three Cabinet members loyal to Calhoun.

Garfield's Itch: President James A. Garfield, a schoolteacher and part-time Disciples of Christ minister, was torn between his aspirations as a rake and the "living grave of marriage." In 1858, he reluctantly married Lecretia "Crete" Rudolph, but continued to visit several women, among them his college friend Rebecca Selleck and Kate Chase, the daughter of Treasury Secretary Samuel P. Chase. In 1862, he also called on a woman in New York, Lucia Gilbert Calhoun, a widowed writer for *The New York Tribune*, to obtain all letters that might some day "cause trouble." *

When Garfield became a national political figure, rumors arose that he had visited a New Orleans brothel. On the eve of his election in 1880, a gossip column in the *New York Independent* asserted that Garfield's "moral purity" was not equal to "his intellectual acumen." He defended himself to his church, to Congress and the army, and no definitive proof of infidelity ever emerged.[31]

Cleveland's Child: The only presidential election that may have turned on a sex scandal was Grover Cleveland's. On July 21, 1884, just after the New York governor won the Democratic nomination, the *Buffalo Evening Telegram* ran a banner headline: "A *Terrible* Tale: A Dark Chapter in a Public Man's History. The Pitiful story of Maria Halpin and Gov. Cleveland's Son." Thus the story broke that when Cleveland had been mayor of Buffalo in 1881, he had a sexual relationship with a widow and may have been the father of her child. Cleveland's political allies, however, were startled at the unmarried candidate's advice: "Above all, tell the truth."[32]

So Cleveland acknowledged paternity, and the press and cartoonists went to town. "Ma! Ma! Where's my Pa?" Cleveland's opponents chanted. Came the Democratic rebuttal: "Gone to the White House Ha! Ha! Ha!" A winning strategy for Cleveland was said to have been hatched during a strategy

Woodrow Wilson

session with supporters from the reform group known as Mugwumps, who sensed vulnerability in the well-known corruption of Cleveland's Republican opponent, James G. Blaine.

"We are told that Mr. Blaine has been delinquent in office but blameless in private life, while Mr. Cleveland has been a model of official integrity but culpable in his personal relations," said a strategist. "We should therefore elect Mr. Cleveland to the public office which he is so well qualified to fill and remand Mr. Blaine to the private station which he is admirably fitted to adorn."[33]

Cleveland's success in overcoming the scandal allowed his supporters to chant, "Hurrah for Maria, hurrah for the kid. We voted for Grover and we're damned glad we did!" During his first term, the 49-year-old Cleveland caused more scandal when he married a 21-year-old. Reporters spied on the couple with telescopes during their honeymoon in Cumberland, Md. Cleveland accused the press of "doing their utmost to make American journalism contemptible."[34]

Wilson and the New Politeness: By the time Woodrow Wilson became president in 1912, much of the sensationalism of the partisan press and the late-19th-century "yellow journalism" had been superseded by fact-based publications. The rise of national wire services forced reporters to produce copy that would appeal to a variety of newspapers and their readers. Adolph Ochs bought *The New York Times* in 1896 and began the modern notion of publishing for a select readership of "thoughtful, pure-minded people."

The new politeness may be the reason the public never suspected a love affair between Wilson and a married New York socialite, Mary Al-

---

*In 1978, a Garfield biographer discovered references to an affair in Garfield's papers.

Checking Up on the President's Health ...

The most enduring cat-and-mouse game played by presidents and the press involves the commander-in-chief's health. More than one team of White House advisers has scurried to project an image of vibrant health for an ailing president. Even rumors about a chief executive's illness can spark a crisis over succession or an overnight shift in prospects for the opposition party.

One of the earliest instances of what today is called "spin control" was occasioned by a carbuncle (a painful inflammation beneath the skin) in George Washington's leg. The June 20, 1789, issue of a pro-Federalist newspaper, the *Gazette of the United States*, assured an anxious public that Washington was "much better" after only a "slight fever." In fact, the president was undergoing a risky incision.

President James Garfield is commonly thought to have died from an assassin's bullet in 1881. But modern readings of his autopsy link his death to the poor care he received from his attending physician, who encouraged the press to report that "a tide of hope is sweeping in."

In July 1893, President Grover Cleveland took a huge risk in undergoing major oral surgery in a makeshift medical facility aboard a yacht. To throw reporters and Congress off the scent, Cleveland announced he was taking a sailing vacation to Buzzards Bay, Mass. The next month, however, *The Philadelphia Press* ran the whole story, having been tipped off by the dentist who had anesthetized Cleveland.

Franklin D. Roosevelt

Woodrow Wilson's served his final 18 months in office suffering from arteriosclerotic brain disease. Wilson had been ill with various digestive and nerve ailments — reports of which were kept vague by his physician — until October 1919, when he suffered a massive stroke. From that point on, his wife, Edith, whose formal education had ended at age 12, received and sent all presidential messages and determined who would meet with the president.

Just before the Democratic National Convention in June 1920, party leaders were told by a White House doctor that Wilson was "permanently ill physically." Two days later, a *New York World* correspondent was summoned to meet with Wilson and reported that he was in tip-top shape, even though accompanying pictures showed him sitting with Mrs. Wilson as if dependent on her to hold papers for him to sign. Though they had originally pledged themselves to Wilson, Democrats at the convention nominated James M. Cox instead.

In 1944, President Franklin D. Roosevelt's health became a topic of speculation among reporters, who wondered if he was healthy enough to seek an unprecedented fourth term. Ross T. McIntyre, Roosevelt's physician, told reporters Roosevelt was only suffering from fatigue. McIntyre did call in a young Navy cardiologist named Howard Bruenn, who diagnosed arteriosclerosis, hypertension and imminent cardiac failure. McIntyre, however, kept Bruenn from talking to the press. Roosevelt won re-election. In February 1945, he traveled to Yalta in the Soviet

len Hulbert Peck. Beginning in 1907, the married Wilson had regularly visited the woman and eventually sent her more than 100 letters. When Mrs. Peck began divorce proceedings, there were rumors that Wilson would be named. Though the existence of the letters was known to journalists and Washington insiders, Theodore Roosevelt, one of Wilson's two opponents in 1912, declined to stoop to scandal-mongering. "You can't cast a man as a Romeo who looks and acts so much like an apothecary's clerk," Roosevelt said of Wilson.[35]

After Wilson's first wife died in 1915, Mrs. Peck visited the White House and Wilson agreed to help her financially. Months later, in the midst of his courtship of Edith Gault, Wilson was wrongly informed that Mrs. Peck was selling his love letters to potential blackmailers. He confessed his affair to Edith and pleaded forgiveness. They were married in December 1915.[36]

Harding's Secret: Some of the best-known philandering in the White House occurred under President Harding in the early 1920s. A decade before the election of the Ohio newspaper publisher, his wife almost sought a divorce over Harding's affair with a neighbor, Carrie

Phillips. (A cache of love letters from that affair was uncovered in 1963.[37])

Harding also had a long affair with a young woman from his hometown named Nan Britton. The public was unaware of this when Harding's administration, plagued by corruption and financial scandals, ended with his death from a stroke in 1923. But in 1927, Britton rocked the country with a book (privately published, as no major house would touch it) called *The President's Daughter*. It detailed Britton's hotel assignations with Harding and introduced the daughter she said the union produced. After an initial silence by re-

... The Ultimate Cat-and-Mouse Game

Union to confer with British Prime Minister Winston Churchill and Soviet Premier Josef Stalin. Photographs of the conference show the president looking ashen and ill. On April 12, 1945, at Warm Springs, Ga., he died of a cerebral hemorrhage.

In the 1950s, President Dwight D. Eisenhower set a White House precedent for candor about illnesses. His 1955 heart attack raised questions about his seeking a second term and about the succession of Vice President Richard M. Nixon. News of the president's illness caused the stock market to take its most dramatic plunge since 1929. Eager to avoid Wilson's mistakes, Eisenhower ordered his press secretary, James Hagerty, to tell all.

The same openness was evident during Eisenhower's intestinal inflammation in 1956. After Eisenhower's stroke in 1957, however, his aides panicked and covered up the extent of his disabilities. Eisenhower's chief legacy on the health issue was a letter of agreement he and Nixon signed stipulating that Nixon would decide whether the president could no longer perform his duties, and the president would decide when he was capable of resuming them. That principle was incorporated into the 25th Amendment on presidential succession, ratified in 1967.

Rumors about John F. Kennedy's health problems began to circulate shortly after the Kennedy forces had organized formally for the presidential contest. On June 14, 1959, the *Des Moines Register* reported that "whispers have been stating as a fact that Kennedy has Addison's

John F. Kennedy

disease," a condition caused by failure of the adrenal glands and characterized by weakness and low blood pressure. Kennedy and his spokesmen flatly denied it, and had his personal physician Dr. Janet Travell circulate a memo specifically denying that Kennedy had "classic Addison's." It was not until 1976, with publication of Joan and Clay Blair's *The Search for JFK*, that the public received confirmation that Kennedy had in fact battled Addison's since the late 1940s.

By the 1970s and '80s, the age of television had rendered it virtually impossible for the White House to disguise a president's poor health. In 1984, computer-made diagrams showing the location of President Ronald Reagan's cancerous colon polyps were broadcast around the world. Equally graphic coverage of Reagan's 1986 prostate surgery reportedly angered first lady Nancy Reagan.

But by then most people accepted the fact that the health of the president is too important to remain private — even, as President Bush discovered, if it's only a bout of stomach flu.

The following books were used as sources for this sidebar: Douglas Southall Freeman, *George Washington: A Biography, Vol. VI, Patriot and President* (1954); John Tebbel and Sarah Miles Watts, *The Press and the Presidency* (1985), p. 152; Edward B. MacMahon and Leonard Curry, *Medical Cover-Ups in the White House* (1987); Edwin A. Weinstein, *Woodrow Wilson: A Medical and Psychological Biography* (1981); Thomas C. Reeves, *A Question of Character: A Life of John F. Kennedy* (1991).

viewers (H. L. Mencken was the first to break it), the book became a bestseller.

Roosevelt's Charm: One of the great charmers of the American press was President Franklin D. Roosevelt (1933-45), who avoided scandal over two extramarital affairs. FDR had a decades-long relationship with Lucy Mercer, who had come to work as Eleanor Roosevelt's social secretary in 1913. Eleanor discovered the affair in 1918, when she found a letter from Mercer to FDR. At that moment, she wrote years later, "The bottom dropped out of my own particular world." [38]

Though the Roosevelts maintained a successful political union, their marriage was no longer a physical one. Reporters such as United Press International's Merriman Smith would later recall Roosevelt stopping his Hyde Park-bound train in New Jersey for a rendezvous with Lucy, whose married name was Rutherford. (She also was present when FDR died in Warm Springs, Ga., in 1945.)

During the White House years, FDR also had an affair with his own secretary, Missy Lehand. The executive mansion became divided between an Eleanor faction and a Missy faction, according to *Chicago Tri-*

bune White House correspondent Walter Trojan, a severe critic of Roosevelt's New Deal politics: "It was a frequent subject of conversation by various insiders, who wanted to show how much they knew." [39]

Trojan said he once found Eleanor crying and saying Franklin wanted to marry Lucy Rutherford. He offered the story to his editor, but it was rejected. So he passed it to controversial columnist Westbrook Pegler, who used the story but was reviled for doing so. The story was generally ignored. The public would learn of Roosevelt's affairs in 1968, with the publication of *Washington Quadrille,* a memoir by North Carolina editor and former Roosevelt aide Jonathan Daniels.

Laying Off Willkie: Despite his own situation, Roosevelt was not above using the adultery issue against his 1940 presidential opponent, Wendell L. Willkie. Though the Republican businessman was married to what he once called "a sane Indiana girl with a rare quality to bear with a restless and ... unsatisfactory husband," he openly continued a long affair with *New York Herald Tribune* Literary Editor Irita Van Doren.

Friends were puzzled that Willkie would show up at dinner parties sometimes with his wife, sometimes with Van Doren. When the candidate decided to hold a press conference in Van Doren's apartment, he assured aides, "Everybody knows about us — all the newspapermen in New York." [40] As the campaign heated up, he was pressured to assure journalists that he and Van Doren were just friends.

Years later, a White House tape recording surfaced showing that Roosevelt knew of Willkie's affair and had commented to his Interior secretary, Harold L. Ickes, that it showed poor political judgment. Roosevelt instructed Ickes to spread the word about Willkie through state legislators and members of Congress. FBI Director J. Edgar Hoover reportedly declined a request from Ickes to help. [41]

Eisenhower's Chauffeur: During World War II, the world grew accustomed to seeing photographs of Gen. Dwight D. Eisenhower with his attractive, young British chauffeur, Kay Summersby. There was ample speculation around Washington, but it wasn't until the early 1970s, after Ike died, that the public learned about the relationship. [42]

A 1974 biography of Harry S Truman by Merle Miller reported that Ike had written his superior, Gen. George C. Marshall, after the war asking for permission to divorce his wife and marry Summersby. Marshall supposedly threatened to bust him out of the Army. Summersby's memoir, *Past Forgetting: My Love Affair with Dwight D. Eisenhower*, was published in 1975. It reported that during one of the rare moments when she and the general were alone, Eisenhower had been impotent.

Kennedy's Appetite: President Kennedy, in historian Ribuffo's phrase, was a "world-class adulterer." A regular parade of sex partners was a pattern Kennedy established in his Navy days, and continued as a member of Congress beginning in the late 1940s and after his marriage in 1953. As intimates would later confirm, Kennedy's presidential campaign style included regular private sessions with movie stars and prostitutes. (Only 90 minutes before one of his 1960 debates with Richard M. Nixon, Kennedy reportedly had been in bed with a call girl. [43])

Kennedy's partners included stewardesses on his plane and several White House secretaries, two of whom were known by their Secret Service code names "Fiddle" and "Faddle." Kennedy's involvement with actress Marilyn Monroe and Judith Campbell Exner, the girlfriend of a top Mafia chieftain, left him a potential target for blackmailers.

The Kennedy escapades were known around Washington, and Kennedy even wondered whether Nixon would use the issue against him. Still, the largely all-male press corps had been instructed by editors that the topic was off-limits.

As veteran *Time* magazine correspondent Hugh Sidey recalls, the evidence of Kennedy's sex life was circumstantial, based on glimpses of him with women during off-hours. The only time Sidey broached the subject was as part of a regular weekly internal memo to his editors. He was angry because he had traveled to the family retreat at West Palm Beach, Fla., but couldn't interview any Kennedy spokesmen because the president and his aides were busy partying with young women. Sidey wrote "flippantly, intemperately" that there had not been such a sordid government "since the last days of Rome."

The memo was leaked to the Kennedy administration, and Sidey found himself in the office of Attorney General Robert F. Kennedy being threatened with a lawsuit. "I told Bobby that it may have been unwise for me to write like that because it leaked," Sidey recalls, "but I said, 'I won't take back the facts, because someday they may cause you problems.'"

The truth about Kennedy's sex life wasn't made public until 1975, when Exner's Mafia links were revealed in the course of a Senate committee investigation of abuses in the CIA.

Johnson After Hours: Since his Senate days in the 1950s, Lyndon Johnson had established a proud reputation for womanizing. He had what one journalist said amounted to a harem, "with Lady Bird as the head wife." [44] There was an oft-told tale about the young female White House aide who spent the night at the LBJ ranch in Texas and was awakened by a voice saying, "Move over honey, this is your president."

In 1982, biographer Robert Caro revealed Johnson's decades-long affair with Alice Glass, the wife of a newspaper publisher. As with Kennedy, reporters often spoke among themselves about Johnson's roving eye, but nothing was written publicly until after Johnson's death in 1973, when former aides began publishing their memoirs.

Continued on p. 352

Dwight D. Eisenhower

'Outing' of Gay Politicians Divides the Press

In June 1991, a member of Congress was standing in a gay bar in Northern Virginia when a man suddenly approached and splashed a drink in his face. The stunt, carried out by a member of the gay-activist group Queer Nation, was an effort to cause a scene and generate press coverage of the politician's reputed homosexuality. The incident was reported in *The Washington Post,* but without the politician's name. Accounts in *The Washington Times* and two papers in the House member's home state included the name.

The practice of "outing" is being used increasingly in the gay community to force prominent figures believed to be gay to "come out of the closet." Viewed by many as a loathsome invasion of privacy, the tactic is often intended to embarrass a gay public figure who has taken positions against the gay-rights movement. It has also been used to force into the open a gay person whom some feel is short-changing gays by declining to be a public role model.

Most of the news media decline to be manipulated into reporting on outings. Allegations of homosexuality are difficult to prove, and such information needs to be relevant, says Leonard Downie Jr., executive editor of *The Washington Post.* Even if other publications have used the politician's name, "there's no reason to follow the pack," Downie says.†

The question of when sexual orientation is relevant to a larger story has long ranked among the news executive's toughest calls. Informants often have their own motives for alleging someone is gay, and reputations — sometimes lives — are at stake. (Tom Pappas, the administrative assistant to a House member, committed suicide in 1988 the same day the *Post* implied he was gay in a long story on his unorthodox personnel practices.)

Long before the era of media-savvy gay activists, early versions of outings went on behind the scenes. During the administration of President Franklin D. Roosevelt, prominent foreign service officer William C. Bullitt repeatedly pressed for the firing of Sumner Welles, a rival of Bullitt at the State Department who in 1940 was said to have exposed himself and made sexual overtures to railroad porters aboard a train.

Welles was one of FDR's favorite aides, however, and the president declined to dismiss him, so Bullitt took his story to editors at *The Washington Times-Herald,* the *New York Daily News* and the *Chicago Tribune.* All three papers were anti-Roosevelt, but all considered the subject too hot to handle. Three years after the incident, on the eve of the 1944 election, Welles was quietly asked to resign after FBI Director J. Edgar Hoover persuaded the president that Welles was a political and security risk.††

A more partisan use of the tactic was recorded in 1964, during the final weeks of the campaign that would elect President Lyndon B. Johnson. One of LBJ's top aides, Walter Jenkins, was arrested in a Washington YMCA for "disorderly conduct" that involved sex with another male. When newsmen began investigating, Johnson aides Clark M. Clifford and Abe Fortas went to local editors and persuaded them not to run the story, assuring them that Jenkins was suffering from exhaustion and would soon resign.

But Johnson's rivals at the Republican National Committee warned the public that "the White House is desperately trying to suppress a major news story affecting the national security."‡ Jenkins resigned Oct. 14, after the story hit the papers. Johnson went on to win in a landslide over Barry Goldwater.

It was at the start of the 1990s, with AIDS on the policy agenda and a rising number of public officials now openly gay, that the media began confronting the practice of outing. One event came in the form of a Capitol Hill news conference at which the names of allegedly gay members of Congress were announced without evidence. No news outlets published the names. In another case, a U.S. senator's campaign billboards were defaced with charges that he is gay. The event was reported with the senator's name by several mainstream newspaper chains and by National Public Radio.‡‡

In August 1991, *The Advocate,* a Los-Angeles-based gay and lesbian biweekly, published a cover story about a top Defense Department official for the express purpose of outing him. The justification, the magazine said, was the fact that the Pentagon was actively enforcing its decades-old ban on homosexuals in the military, discharging up to 2,000 gays and lesbians who had recently seen action in the Persian Gulf War.

The impact was considerable. Though many major newspapers and television networks reported the story without using the official's name, he was fully identified in *The Detroit News,* the *New York Daily News* and *The Village Voice,* as well as in a Jack Anderson column on the outing that appeared in dozens of papers.

The phenomenon of outing may divide editors, but it is also hotly debated in the gay community. "It's a dirty business that hurts people," writes columnist and author Randy Shilts, who is openly gay. "It's bizarre ... for a minority fighting the moral judgments of fundamentalist preachers to set itself up in the business of compelling others to submit to their moral judgments."‡‡†

---

† Quoted in *The Washington Post,* July 10, 1991.
†† Gentry, Curt, *J. Edgar Hoover: The Man and the Secrets* (1991), p. 308.
‡ *Ibid.,* p. 579.
‡‡ Larry J. Sabato, *Feeding Frenzy* (1991), p. 208.
‡‡† *Los Angeles Times,* Aug. 7, 1991.

Continued from p. 350

The Scandal Era

By the late 1960s and early '70s, American culture was setting new standards for explicitness, and the press was no exception. The concept of "the public's right to know" had been gaining ground since the introduction of government "sunshine laws" in the 1950s. The definition of what was fair game for the press would expand over the next two decades.

During this era, reporters for the first time disclosed alcohol abuse among major political figures — among them, Sen. Thomas J. Dodd, D-Conn., Sen. Harrison A. Williams, D-N.J., and House Speaker Carl Albert, D-Okla. The first of what would become a stream of sex scandals unfolded. The press usually defended its disclosures by saying there was a rationale for violating a politician's privacy: A public official's behavior showed he was unfit for his job, for example, or there was a conflict of interest or a crime had been committed.

In 1974, Rep. Wilbur D. Mills, D-Ark., chairman of the House Ways and Means Committee, had his alcohol problem splashed onto the front pages when police found him in a wrecked car after his companion, a stripper named Fanne Fox, had jumped into Washington's Tidal Basin. In 1976, *The Washington Post* ended the career of powerful House Administration Committee Chairman Wayne L. Hays, D-Ohio, by revealing that he kept a young woman named Elizabeth Ray on his payroll as a typist when she actually served as Hays' mistress.

After Hart, All's Fair

The era's watershed sex scandal was the 1987 collapse of Gary Hart's presidential campaign. Ironically, the story came to light precisely because of agonizing by the press over its proper role in sex and privacy issues. *Miami Herald* Political Editor Tom Fiedler had touched off the scandal by scolding the tabloids and other publications for devoting space to Hart's denials of rumors that he was a womanizer.

Fiedler's column prompted an anonymous tip from a woman caller who said her friend was having an affair with Hart and that she was tired of lying by presidential candidates.[45]

The resulting stakeout in May, which revealed that Donna Rice had stayed overnight at Hart's Capitol Hill house, still produced denials from the candidate. "I am not stupid," Hart said. "If I had wanted to bring someone into a house, an apartment, meet with a woman in secret, I wouldn't have done it this way."

After *The Washington Post* informed Hart that it was preparing a story on another of his alleged affairs, he withdrew his candidacy. Since Hart was no longer running, the *Post* didn't run the story.

With the Hart example dominating the news, newspapers stepped up their explorations of state and local candidates. Within a month, *The* (Cleveland) *Plain Dealer* reported that Ohio Democratic Gov. Richard F. Celeste, who had been mentioned as a presidential possibility, had had extramarital affairs with three unidentified women. "Do you have a Gary Hart-type personal problem, sir?" a reporter asked Celeste.[46] The governor denied it, and the paper ran the story that undercut his presidential prospects.

The press' tendency to rummage through a candidate's past was taken to new levels during the 1990 Minnesota governor's race. Having been tipped off by a lawyer whose clients wanted Republican candidate John Grunseth to withdraw, the *Minneapolis Star-Tribune* quoted eyewitness accounts of a swimming party nine years earlier in which Grunseth had allegedly invited four girls under age 16 to swim with him naked. Grunseth denied the story and said it was a plant by Democratic rival Gov. Rudy Perpich. Grunseth hedged about whether he would withdraw from the race, but then the paper published a story about a woman who said she had a sexual relationship with Grunseth for nine years during his two marriages. He withdrew nine days before the election. ■

CURRENT SITUATION

Clinton's Denials

January's media focus on Bill Clinton's marital problems quickly blended into in a series of "character questions" raised by Clinton's escape from the draft during the Vietnam War and his wife's law firm's business dealings with his state government. Clinton has maintained a consistent, if somewhat hazy, story about Gennifer Flowers, though getting somewhat more specific in his denials.

He referred to her as "a woman I never slept with." He also confronted a TV reporter who felt compelled to ask if he'd ever committed adultery. "If I had," Clinton said, "I wouldn't tell you." His strategy for getting past the issue has been to portray each inquiry into his personal veracity as "an attack from the press," and to discourage voters from seeking perfection. "What you're doing is saying that if you want to be a politician, you have to be perfect, and if you're not, you need to be divorced," he told a TV reporter in Baton Rouge, La.

A poll conducted for *Newsweek* March 19-20 showed 76 percent of

Continued on p. 354

At Issue:

Was the adultery allegation against Bill Clinton worthy of the news coverage it received?

GENEVA OVERHOLSER

Editor, The Des Moines Register
**FROM SPEECH FROM PRESS-ENTERPRISE
LECTURE SERIES, UNIVERSITY OF CALIFORNIA
AT RIVERSIDE, FEB. 6, 1992**

yes

look at the Bill Clinton story. All that concentration on his sex life. As if that had anything to do with his fitness for leadership. Tut tut.

And indeed, all across America, editors are wringing their hands and regretting that they were forced to print this, er, uncomfortable news. We quake in our offices, waiting for the disapproving readers who will call and tell us that they are sorry that a once great newspaper has been turned into a scandal sheet. Can't tell the difference, they'll scold, between your rag and the *National Enquirer*. . . .

Do I embrace this? you ask, aghast? Do I approve of all this gossip? It's not up to me to embrace it, to approve it or to reject it. It's up to me to acknowledge it and, yes, to publish it. This, for heaven's sake, is human nature. . . . Have you ever listened to talk across a back fence? Heard its rhythms, how rich but irregular, listened to the subjects, some high-brow, some low? Well, we are the back fence. The little old country newspaper that told who was visiting whom? That was gossip. The people's curiosity about how the rich or famous — or the powerful — live? That is gossip.

Editors are the last people in the world who should decide that folks are just not up to making wise decisions if we give them some piece of information that we, personally, want to assure everyone we simply can't stand. I'm willing to bet that part of why [newspapers] have become less read is because we've become less gossipy, not more. . . .

Individual comfort cannot be the determinant of what we put in the newspaper. Nor, God forbid, can someone else's sense of what is proper. Cursed decorum! Take the Anita Hill-Clarence Thomas hearings. . . . The nation was riveted to the tube for days running, at least partly because — at last — Congress was dealing with something that really mattered in a lot of people's lives. . . .

Let us embrace openness, with all its rough edges, all its individual inconveniencing. . . . Yes, there are dangers. We may be sensational, lightweight, insensitive. But what of the dangers of our failing to call a crook a crook, a liar a liar. . .? There are legal constraints, commercial pressures, privacy interests. But we feed them all, with our timidity, our caution. Let our robustness ring out against them. Yes, it will be rough and untidy, raw and fractious. Why, it'll be a veritable cacophony — the sweet sound of democracy itself.

LANCE MORROW

Essayist, Time magazine
FROM *TIME*, FEB. 3, 1992

no

if America is only afternoon television, then people will care, in a slack-jawed way, whether Bill was unfaithful to Hillary with Gennifer. It is the kind of question asked on soap operas and on "Oprah" and "Geraldo" and "Donahue." When the program ends, the audience will mute a commercial and scratch itself, glance out of the window and see that reality still looks lousy. It will turn back to the television and click through the channels to find another hour of pointless junk. . . . But somehow the winter of 1992 feels a bit late for the prim old American Kabuki: the mayor caught in the whorehouse, the schoolmarm shaking her finger.

In the first place, the pseudo-moral attention lavished on this spectacle offends a sense of proportion and priorities. Did Bill Clinton have an affair with Gennifer Flowers? The question must get in line behind the real news: drugs and drug murders, AIDS deaths, illiteracy, a population getting dumber, 74,000 jobs lost at General Motors, Pan Am and Eastern folding, the highest homicide rate in the Western world. As for the sexual problems of America, they have less to do with consenting governors going to bed with other adults than with the abuse of children, with sexual violence and rape and incest. In any case, the nation cannot afford to waste good candidates. There are not many to spare. . . .

The Clinton mess . . . suggested something about a certain brainless overstimulation of American media life. . . . The rest of the world has been waiting for some time for America to mature on the subject of sex. Assume, however, that public interest in a candidate's sex life is not prurient, not a sort of freebasing of sleaze, but an honest curiosity about a politician's character. What does an extramarital affair reveal? On purely civic grounds, the public would be better off investigating the politician's other habits. Healthy diet? Does he drink too much? Does he drive a car recklessly? Does he read books?

Too much sexual buzz interferes with people's instruments and makes it harder to judge a candidate on important questions — his or her stability, judgment, decency, intelligence, ethics, strength of will, experience, truthfulness. . . .

Collective judgments based on gossip are always crude, often stupid, and sometimes stir up a lynch mob. Given the size of the job that needs to be done, it is time for America to get serious. At the very least, turn off the television set. And grow up about sex.

Continued from p. 352

respondents saying that marital infidelity would not keep them from voting for Clinton. Polls and most observers agreed, however, that his stature would be gravely damaged if it turned out he had been lying about the Flowers affair.

Brock Adams' Past

The press was put to another test on the privacy issue in March, this one involving charges of sexual harassment against Sen. Brock Adams, D-Wash. Adams dropped his 1992 reelection bid after the *Seattle Times* printed the results of its long investigation of allegations that Adams had fondled and, in some cases, drugged and raped women on his staff.

The story was based on claims by eight women who had previously worked for Adams, none of whom was willing to be named. The investigation had been prompted by calls to the paper from women reacting to the 1988 story of Kari Tupper, the daughter of

friends of the senator. She had told *Washingtonian* magazine that Adams had drugged her drink when she was at his house to discuss a job and that she had awakened in his bed to find him fondling her.

After its exposé appeared March 1, the Seattle paper was criticized for publishing, during an election year, unattributed allegations going back to the 1970s. The criticism was not unexpected. After agonizing for months, the editors had decided that the number of women making the claims made it a disservice not to print them. As a precaution, they obtained affidavits from seven of the eight women promising to testify in court if Adams sued for libel. Adams denied the charges but said he couldn't refute them because the sources were anonymous. Several women who had worked for him in recent years said they had never witnessed such behavior.

"What is a newspaper to do with such damaging information as that on Brock Adams?" asked a *New York Times* editorial. "Verify, verify, verify. Then publish what it believes to be the truth, however painful." [47] ■

United States show that in as many as 50 to 80 percent of marriages, at least one partner will have an affair at some point in the relationship. Combine that with the aphrodisiac effect of political power, and one can understand the estimate of the late political reporter Theodore H. White, who covered national campaigns from the late 1940s to the mid-1970s. In his memoirs, White wrote that he had met only three candidates who had not succumbed to casual sex on the campaign trail — Truman, George Romney and Jimmy Carter. [50]

Many observers have suggested the possibility that with the adultery issue on the table, President Bush may find himself confronting a reporter asking "the big A" question. An old, unsubstantiated rumor that Bush had a longtime relationship with an aide made the rounds during the 1988 presidential campaign, even causing the stock market to drop. Reporters investigating the rumor turned up nothing, though comedians such as Mark Russell and cartoonist Garry Trudeau continue to raise the allegation, as do political talk-show pundits. And Hillary Clinton, in an interview in the May issue of *Vanity Fair* magazine, is described by writer Gail Sheehy as being angry at the media's double standard in investigating her husband's personal life but not Bush's. Clinton later said she regretted making the remark.

To many political and journalistic observers, sex habits will continue to be seen as an indicator of character, and hence fair game for the press. "It's precisely when editors decide at Page 1 meetings," writes media critic Diamond, "that inquiries into the candidate's finances, for example, are important, while those about the candidate's sex life are not, that the short-circuiting of civic education begins. How can anyone argue that something is not relevant to the presidency until you know what that something is — compulsive sex,

OUTLOOK

A Call for Restraint

When politicians feature their families in brochures in order to get votes, "they are inviting the press into their private lives," said George Reedy, former press secretary to President Johnson. [48] The trouble is, the absence of clear boundaries between the private and public spheres often means that informed political debate gets overwhelmed by a carnival atmosphere in which all bedroom doors are flung open.

At a news conference in January, Gennifer Flowers was asked by a ra-

dio show prankster whether she and Gov. Clinton had used a condom. In 1987, Donna Rice endured an embarrassing fishing expedition from reporters at the Miami airport: "Have you slept with Gary Hart? *'No.'* Do you want to? *'No.'* Has he ever asked? *'No.'* " [49]

Time's Hugh Sidey says he is troubled by the trend toward asking about private matters and wonders whether it might not deter good candidates from running for political office. Sidey recalls the old saying: "The search for perfection is the enemy of what is just good." When it comes down to it, he adds, "Jefferson and Lincoln were very odd people."

Surveys cited by the Sex Information and Education Council of the

drug-taking, beating the draft?"

Others say interest in the issue may die off. "In a strange way, this election may be a turning point," says the Brookings Institution's Hess. "Clinton has had everything thrown at him. If he wins, he could do for adultery what JFK did for Catholicism and Nixon did for campaign losers, which is to provide a sort of journalistic inoculation."

What the press should strive to do, says Duke University's Barber, is present individual traits of candidates "not just as a blip" but in the larger context of their overall lives. In *The Wall Street Journal's* 1987 profile of presidential candidate Marion G. (Pat) Robertson, for example, the titillating fact that his first child was born less than nine months after he was married appeared not in the headline but well into the story. Such restraint requires confidence on the part of editors.

"If newspapers can say, 'I don't care what the competing publications are doing, this is what we do,' then it can be done on a higher plane," says *Miami Herald* Editor Clifton.

Larry Sabato offers a set of guidelines for minimizing press "feeding frenzies." He would have the press cover health questions that affect a politician's performance; incidents that reach police blotters or courts; sex with staff (coercion); sex that is compulsive; ongoing alcohol or drug abuse; and any illegal abuse or condoning of drug abuse, perhaps within the past decade. Sabato would have journalists avoid coverage of non-legal matters involving candidates' underage children; current extramarital activity as long as it is discreet, non-compulsive and not involving minors or staff; sexual orientation unless it is compulsive or with minors; and drug or alcohol abuse that is at least a decade old.[51]

But as Paul Taylor has written, journalism is "too unwieldy, untidy and plural a profession for rules." (The Code of Ethics of the Society of Professional Journalists pays heed to both a "right to privacy" and the "public's right to know.") News judgments are made case by case.

The recent concentration on reporting adultery is clearly the result of a trend that could taper off. Columnist Carl Rowan has called for editors who advocate questioning candidates about adultery to sign affidavits swearing that they themselves have never sinned.

"Was there really anything wrong 30 years ago — and is there anything wrong today — with respecting the privacy of politicians if personal conduct is not distorting public performance?" asks veteran TV journalist Bill Monroe. "The alternative is to get comfortable with the idea of sinful editors exposing sinful politicians, with the journalists emerging as the more dedicated hypocrites."[52] ∎

Notes

[1] "Substance vs. Sex," *Newsweek*, Feb. 3, 1992.

[2] "Crash Course: Campaign Journalism 101," *New York*, Feb. 17, 1992, p. 28.

[3] Quoted in *Washington Journalism Review*, May 1988, p. 38.

[4] Suzanne Garment, *Scandal* (1991), p. 175.

[5] Larry J. Sabato, *Feeding Frenzy* (1991), p. 23.

[6] The poll was conducted in January by Yankelovich Clancy Shulman for *Time* magazine.

[7] "Reporting the Presidential Campaign of 1992: Lessons from 1988," Marist Institute for Public Opinion, 1991, p. 18.

[8] Quoted in *Time*, May 18, 1987.

[9] Letter to the editors of *The New York Times*, quoted in Paul Taylor, *See How They Run* (1990), p. 70.

[10] Quoted in *Time*, July 10, 1989, p. 53.

[11] Column in *The Washington Post*, Jan. 31, 1992.

[12] Column in *The Washington Post*, Jan. 28, 1992.

[13] *AIM Report*, February-B 1992.

[14] Editorial in *The New Republic*, Nov. 13, 1989.

[15] *Family Research Council Washington Watch*, February 1992.

[16] Quoted in Burt Solomon, "White House Lore of Adultery Touches Good Leaders and Bad," *National Journal*, Feb. 1, 1992, p. 286.

[17] Letter to *The New York Times*, Feb. 10, 1992.

[18] Quoted in *Time*, May 18, 1987, p. 33.

[19] *Time*, July 10, 1989. p. 53.

[20] Quoted in *Editor & Publisher*, Feb. 8, 1992, p. 8.

[21] Reported in *The Washington Post*, March 16, 1992.

[22] Quoted in Sabato, *op. cit.*, p. 77.

[23] Quoted in *The Washington Post*, Jan. 28, 1992.

[24] John C. Fitzpatrick, *The George Washington Scandals*, Bulletin No. 1 of the Washington Society of Alexandria, 1929.

[25] James Thomas Flexner, *George Washington*, Vol. I (1965), p. 195.

[26] Steven O'Brien, *Alexander Hamilton* (1989), p. 93, and Shelley Ross, *Fall From Grace* (1988), p. 20.

[27] Virginius Dabney, *The Jefferson Scandals: A Rebuttal* (1981), p. 10.

[28] Quoted in *The New York Times*, Nov. 22, 1987.

[29] Stefen Lorant, *The Glorious Burden* (1976), p. 124.

[30] Paul Johnson, *The Birth of the Modern* (1991), p. 945.

[31] Margaret Leech and Harry J. Brown, *The Garfield Orbit* (1978), p. 194.

[32] Lorant, *op. cit.*, p. 384.

[33] Ross, *op. cit.*, p. 126.

[34] *Ibid.*

[35] *Ibid.*, p. 151.

[36] Edwin Weinstein, *Woodrow Wilson: A Medical and Psychological Biography* (1980), p. 290.

[37] Francis Russell, *The Shadow of Blooming Grove* (1988 edition).

[38] Cited in Joseph P. Lash, *Eleanor and Franklin* (1971), p. 220.

[39] Walter Trojan, *Political Animals* (1975), p. 134.

[40] Steve Neal, *Dark Horse: A Biography of Wendell Willkie* (1989), p. 43.

[41] Curt Gentry, *J. Edgar Hoover: The Man and the Secrets* (1991), p. 227.

[42] Stephen E. Ambrose, *Eisenhower: Soldier and President* (1990), p. 125.

[43] Joseph Reeves, *The Question of Character* (1991), pp. 95, 202.

[44] Robert Dallek, *Lone Star Rising: Lyndon Johnson and His Times* (1991), p. 189.

[45] Jack Germond and Jules Witcover, *Whose Broad Stripes and Bright Stars?* (1989), p. 182.

[46] Taylor, *op. cit.*, p. 72.

[47] *The New York Times*, March 6, 1991. For background, see "Sexual Harassment," *The CQ Researcher*, Aug. 9, 1991, pp. 537-560.

[48] Quoted in Dom Bonafede, "Scoop or Snoop?" *National Journal*, Nov. 5, 1988, p. 2791.

[49] Germond and Witcover, *op. cit.*, p. 198.

[50] Theodore H. White, *In Search of History* (1978), p. 529.

[51] Sabato, *op. cit.*, p. 218.

[52] Column in the *Washington Journalism Review*, June 1991, p. 6.

Bibliography

Selected Sources Used

Books

Barber, James David, *The Presidential Character: Predicting Performance in the White House*, Third Edition, Prentice-Hall, 1985.

A Duke University political scientist divides the presidents into categories based on their personality traits.

Garment, Suzanne, *Scandal: The Crisis of Mistrust in American Politics*, Times Books, 1991.

A former *Wall Street Journal* columnist now with the American Enterprise Institute for Public Policy Research surveys recent scandals involving sex and ethics. She argues that constant news coverage of scandals has distracted the public from the business of government.

Germond, Jack W., and Jules Witcover, *Whose Broad Stripes and Bright Stars? The Trivial Pursuit of the Presidency 1988*, Warner Books, 1989.

Two veteran political columnists weave a comprehensive narrative of the 1988 race rich in detail about press coverage. The book includes a chapter on the "self-destruction" of Gary Hart.

Lorant, Stefan, *The Glorious Burden: The American Presidency*, Author's Edition, 1976.

An overview of the presidency, told through more than 2,000 illustrations — including contemporary portraits, early daguerreotypes, photos and engravings — and 300,000 words of text, with special emphasis on electoral campaigns and losing candidates.

MacMahon, Edward B., and Leonard Curry, *Medical Cover-Ups in the White House*, Farragut Publishing Co., 1987.

A Georgetown University professor of orthopedic surgery and a Washington writer detail how the American public was deceived during the illnesses of numerous presidents. Includes many anecdotes about the press.

Ross, Shelley, *Fall From Grace: Sex, Scandal, and Corruption in American Politics from 1702 to the Present*, Ballantine Books, 1988.

A journalist weaves colorful anecdotes into a narrative of incidents that have embarrassed American politicians. She makes it clear that the behavior hasn't changed much, only the frankness of the coverage.

Reeves, Joseph, *A Question of Character: A Life of John F. Kennedy*, The Free Press, 1991.

A former admirer of President Kennedy surveys his life and arrives at negative conclusions about the man's behavior and values, noting Kennedy's sexual adventurism and drifting ethics as well as the political myth-making engineered by his family and advisers.

Sabato, Larry J., *Feeding Frenzy: How Attack Journalism Has Transformed American Politics*, The Free Press, 1991.

A University of Virginia government professor frequently quoted in the news media analyzes press coverage of recent scandals, near-scandals and unproven rumors. He argues for restraint and avoidance of the "pack mentality" that often blows stories out of proportion.

Taylor, Paul, *See How They Run: Electing the President in an Age of Mediacracy*, Alfred A. Knopf, 1990.

A *Washington Post* reporter who covered the 1988 presidential race offers eyewitness accounts and analysis of how modern political campaigns are covered. Taylor is the reporter who asked candidate Gary Hart the famous direct question about adultery.

Tebbel, John, and Sarah Miles Watts, *The Press and the Presidency: From George Washington to Ronald Reagan*, Oxford University Press, 1985.

Two journalism professors survey White House relations with the press throughout American history. Provides good detail on the rise and influence of various media empires.

Articles

Gup, Ted, "Identifying Homosexuals: What Are the Rules?," *Washington Journalism Review*, October 1988, p. 30.

A former *Washington Post* reporter now with *Time* magazine recounts from personal experience the discussions among editors regarding the sensitive issue of when a person's sexual orientation is newsworthy.

"Privates on Parade," *The New Republic*, Nov. 13, 1989.

A thoughtful essay endeavoring to provide some rules on when a public figure's private life should be reported on.

Hosenball, Mark, and Michael Isikoff, "Pssst. Inside Washington's Rumor Mill," *The New Republic*, Jan. 2, 1989.

Two Washington journalists reflect on press handling of recent privacy issues, noting several "stories" that were really false leads.

The Next Step

Additional Articles from Current Periodicals from EBSCO Publishing's Database

Addresses & essays

"Predators," *The New Republic*, Aug. 19, 1991, p. 9.

Editorial. Criticizes the press for its growing propensity to invade the private lives of public figures. Analysis of the unspoken claim that private acts, especially sexual ones, have a direct bearing on public acts; examples of recent press exposés of political figures; how the field of journalism should reform.

Greenfield, M., "The judges on the hill," *Newsweek*, Oct. 14, 1991, p. 80.

Opinion. States that Congress howls about the probing into their lives and asserts that when they break the rules, they ask for it. Politicians who have helped turn our national political discourse into what often seems an unending trial of various individuals' moral character; consequences of Washington's failure to discipline wrongdoers or act clearly and openly to repudiate misbehavior.

McLaughlin, J., "Political winter book," *National Review*, Feb. 5, 1988, p. 24.

Opinion. The return of Gary Hart to the presidential primaries brings the character issue to center stage. And other candidates have to be careful of making the character issue central, in an effort to discredit Hart, because front-runners of both parties are skating on thin ice.

O'Sullivan, J., "Race and sex again," *National Review*, Dec. 16, 1991, p. 6.

Editorial. Comments on how issues of race and sex are dealt with by politicians and the media. The Willie Horton issue; Sen. Bob Kerrey's, D-Neb., joke about ex-Gov. Jerry Brown and lesbians; Gov. Bill Clinton's reaction to the joke.

Books & reading

Lively, J., "A tragic pluralism," *TLS*, Sept. 6, 1991, p. 26.

Reviews Steven Lukes' book "Moral Conflict and Politics," a collection of a number of essays with a general unifying theme: a strong and urgent plea for the recognition of the reality and importance of the moral element in political decisions.

Case studies

Alter, J.; G. Carroll, et al., "Substance vs. sex," *Newsweek*, Feb. 3, 1992, p. 18.

Discusses whether tabloid charges about Gov. Bill Clinton's private life will hijack the political process. Hints of comparison between Clinton's situation and that of former President Franklin D. Roosevelt; the biggest difference; *Star* tabloid's sleazy tactics and reputation; the article is riddled with demonstrable inaccuracies; Clinton and his wife Hillary denounce the charges; classic media sex carnivals; inconsistencies.

Beachy, L., "Fatal attraction," *Newsweek*, Nov. 21, 1988, p. 45.

Summarizes the political suicide of former Sen. Gary Hart, at one time the Democratic front-runner, who was caught in a media web of marital infidelity from which he never could emerge. Hart's biggest problem was his appetite for action, which often got him into trouble, and raised troubling public questions about his judgment.

Handelman, D., "Campaignus interruptus: the fall and rise .. ," *Rolling Stone*, March 24, 1988, p. 72.

Chronicles the comeback campaign of former Sen. Gary Hart. Follows Hart's presidential campaign through the Iowa caucuses and the New Hampshire primary. Looks at Hart, his staff, and the sexual and financial scandals plaguing his campaign.

Leo, J., "Bob Kerrey's dirty little joke," *U.S. News & World Report*, Dec. 9, 1991, p. 26.

Comments on the "dirty joke" that Sen. Bob Kerrey, D-Neb., told Gov. Bill Clinton at a political roast in New Hampshire. A crew from C-SPAN recorded the joke, but the tape was shelved because the conversation was private and presumably out of bounds. Description of the joke, which involves Jerry Brown and two lesbians; analysis of the joke; gay organizations explode in rage; Kerrey apologizes; Clinton's campaign hung in the balance.

Shapiro, W., "The Teflon Twins of 1988," *Time*, Jan. 11, 1988, p. 30.

Notes that, in this political season of the character issue, nothing appears to stick to Pat Robertson and Jesse Jackson. They could be called The Teflon Twins of post-Reagan politics, unabashed and unapologetic about intemperate statements, personality flaws and boastful exaggerations on their resumes. Other candidates do not criticize them on their characters or their stands on the issues.

Conflicts of interest

"A dirty world," *Economist,* April 13, 1991, p. 25.

Reports on the revelations that Sen. Mark Hatfield, R-Ore., accepted gifts from James Holderman, a former president of the University of South Carolina. Details of the case; Hatfield's reputation; also covers the alleged sex scandal involving Sen. Brock Adams, D-Wash.; details.

Apple, R.W. Jr., "In Minnesota politics, a test of character," *The New York Times,* Oct. 30, 1990, p. A1.

Says that former Rep. Arlan Stangeland, R-Minn., is in trouble because he made several hundred calls to or from the phone of a Virginia woman who is a lobbyist. He says it was all business, but it has raised questions about his character.

Ethical aspects

Hook, J., "Votes slated before recess for Frank, Durenberger," *Congressional Quarterly Weekly Report,* July 21, 1990, p. 2273.

Elaborates on the likelihood of judgment being passed by the House and the Senate, before the August recess, on the ethics of two of their members, attempting to close two highly publicized cases that questioned the financial dealings of a senator and the sexual life of a House member. Details of Sen. Dave Durenberger's, R-Minn., case; Rep. Barney Frank's, D-Mass., case; outlook for Durenberger; neither sees himself in immediate political danger.

Meyerson, H., "Dilemmas for the Democrats," *Dissent,* winter 1987/88, p. 33.

Discusses problems facing the Democratic Party in 1988. The "character" issue; economic and social problems; fundraising and political action committees (PACs); high cost of campaigning; shrinkage of the Democratic Party base; future proposals.

Debates & issues

"Senate charade," *National Review,* Oct. 7, 1991, p. 10.

Speculates on how a future nominee to the U.S. Supreme Court may respond to questions from the Senate Judiciary Committee concerning that nominee's commitment to a constitutional right of privacy, and comments on how the current confirmation hearings for Judge Clarence Thomas serve as the latest evidence of a continued deterioration of the political process.

Clift, E., "Peccadillo politics and the new rules of conduct," *Newsweek,* April 9, 1990, p. 21.

Tells how, despite unrelenting media scrutiny into the private lives of politicians, the public seems to accept certain human foibles. Statements made by Clayton Williams, the GOP's gubernatorial candidate in Texas; Illinois Rep. Gus Savage; prejudice plays; media backlash; repentance.

Fineman, H., "Second thoughts on 'character cops,'" *Newsweek,* Aug. 12, 1991, p. 24.

Reports that journalistic "outing" is nothing new among heterosexuals, especially of Sen. Gary Hart, D-Colo., in 1987 when he was spotted frolicking on the boat "Monkey Business" with Donna Rice. How the media made "character-cop" reporting a standard feature in our politics; reviews the new book on character-cop craziness, "Feeding Frenzy," by Larry J. Sabato.

Henry, C., "Private sins, public office," *Christianity Today,* March 4, 1988, p. 28.

An analysis of the question of whether the public has "a right to snoop on its political leaders." Lists nine considerations to keep in mind when judging character and moral integrity in public life.

Henry, W.A. III and L. Williams, "To 'out' or not to 'out,'" *Time,* Aug. 19, 1991, p. 17.

Maintains that one of the hottest ethical issues for journalists these days is where to draw the line between two colliding rights: the individual's right to privacy and the public's right to know. Action of *The Washington Post* in not printing the name of a top Pentagon official who is allegedly gay; gay activists pursuing a political agenda using controversial tactics; when the media allows itself to be manipulated.

Lois, G. and B. Pitts, "Pre-emptive strike could have sunk Bush," *Advertising Age,* Oct. 14, 1991, p. 28.

Discusses how a pre-emptive strike in political advertising could have changed presidential politics. Political advertising that works will show the voters the essence of a candidate's character — or the character of his or her opponent. Ten secrets to political advertising; Dukakis vs. Bush; details.

Ornstein, N.J., "Sexpress," *The Atlantic,* October 1991, p. 24.

Focuses on the new standards concerning the American press' coverage of scandal. The competitive pressures related to sales and advertising; the placement of news; examples of stories involving John Towers, Nancy Reagan, Charles Robb and others; private behavior and public performance; public attitude toward the press.

Wilkins, R., "Dirty secrets," *Mother Jones,* July/August 1991, p. 14.

Faults the leadership of national politicians over the past four decades. Lack of responsibility to identify and solve national problems; television's effect; the way politics are conducted; need for leaders of moral courage.

Sexual behavior

"Coming out, or pushed?" *Economist,* **Aug. 4, 1990, p. 20.**

Reports that the scandal involving Rep. Barney Frank, D-Mass., and a male prostitute illustrates changing attitudes toward homosexuality in American politics. Disagreement between Republican and Democratic House members; question whether the mild reprimand Rep. Frank received would hurt Democrats at the polls.

"Limousine libertine?" *Time,* **July 31, 1989, p. 21.**

Outlines sexual harassment allegations against Rep. Gus Savage, D-Ill., who reportedly made advances toward a 28-year-old Peace Corps volunteer in Kinshasa, Zaire, Africa.

Berke, R.L., "Formal reprimand of Rep. Frank is urged by House's ethics panel," *The New York Times,* **July 20, 1990, p. A1.**

Reports that the House ethics committee voted to recommend that Rep. Barney Frank, D-Mass., receive a formal reprimand from the House for his relationship with a male prostitute. This is the latest development in what has been two years of turmoil over ethics on Capitol Hill.

Hook, J., "House reprimands Frank, refuses to censure him," *Congressional Quarterly Weekly Report,* **July 28, 1990, p. 2379.**

Addresses the formal reprimand of Rep. Barney Frank, D-Mass., for improperly using his office to help a male prostitute. House of Representatives has been struggling to end a grim string of ethics scandals that reached from its top leadership to the back benches. Debate about how harshly to punish Frank; Frank's crime; House's rejection of expulsion; the debate; Frank's public acknowledgement of his homosexuality; the year of politics and ethics; censure as a harsh reprimand.

McElwaine, S., "Washington, D.C. land of the sexually free?" *Cosmopolitan,* **April 1991, p. 174.**

Speculates on the sex lives of some famous politicians in Washington, D.C.: Sen. Edward M. Kennedy, D-Mass.; Sen. Christopher J. Dodd, D-Conn.; the new era of discretion.

Stanley, A., "Facing questions of private life, Kennedy apologizes to the voters," *The New York Times,* **Oct. 26, 1991, p. 1.**

Comments on Sen. Edward M. Kennedy's, D-Mass., speech at the John F. Kennedy School of Government at Harvard University to discuss his future in politics. His apology for his private life; his aim to mend his ways in the future.

Thomas, E.; M. Starr, et al., "Sobering times," *Newsweek,* **Dec. 9, 1991, p. 22.**

Relates how Sen. Edward M. Kennedy, D-Mass., the "cool" uncle, has talked to friends and family about moderating his lusty tastes and toning down his frat-brother behavior, while privately some friends question if the senator can truly change. Political necessity propelled the speech at Harvard's John F. Kennedy School of Government, citing "shortcomings" in his private life. Kennedy's unfavorable rating; Kennedy's public embarrassments; image of the Kennedy men.

Turque, B.; M. Miller, et al., "The age of 'outing,'" *Newsweek,* **Aug. 12, 1991, p. 22.**

Reports on the exposure of gays in the closet in the age of "outing," in which gay activists are pointing an unwanted spotlight on some of their community's most prominent members. How it has ignited a debate over privacy, political correctness and the road to equality and acceptance in an unaccommodating straight world. INSET: On the front lines: Where gay groups stand (list of gay groups).

Back Issues

Great Research on Current Issues Starts Right Here... Recent topics covered by The CQ Researcher are listed below. Issues dated before May 10, 1991, were published under the name of Editorial Research Reports.

OCTOBER 1990
Organ Transplants
Energy Policy Options
Search for Arab Unity
Child Support

NOVEMBER 1990
Lotteries and Gambling
Post-Cold War Choices
Setting Limits on Medical Care
Multicultural Education

DECEMBER 1990
Cable TV Regulation
Americans' Search for Their Roots
Is Insurance System a Failure?
Why Schools Still Have Tracking

JANUARY 1991
Growing Influence of Boycotts
Should the U.S. Reinstate the Draft?
America's Archaeological Past
Peace Corps' Challenges in '90s

FEBRUARY 1991
Regional Impact of Recession
Puerto Rico's Status
Redistricting: Mapping Power
Nuclear Power

Back issues are available for $4.00 (subscribers) or $7.00 (non-subscribers). Quantity discounts apply to orders over ten. To order, call Congressional Quarterly 1-800-432-2250.

MARCH 1991
Acid Rain
Cost of the Gulf War
Reassessing Gun Laws
Future for Man in Space

APRIL 1991
Social Security
Canadian Crisis Over Quebec
California Drought
Electromagnetic Radiation

MAY 1991
School Choice
Racial Quotas
Animal Rights
U.S. and Japan

JUNE 1991
Children and Divorce
Teenage Suicide
Endangered Species
Europe 1992

JULY 1991
Teenagers and Abortion
Soviet Republics Rebel
Mexico's Emergence
Athletes and Drugs

AUGUST 1991
Sexual Harassment
Fetal Tissue Research
Oil Imports
The Palestinians

SEPTEMBER 1991
Police Brutality
Advertising Under Attack
Saving the Forests
Foster Care Crisis

OCTOBER 1991
Pay-Per-View TV
Youth Gangs
Gene Therapy
World Hunger

NOVEMBER 1991
Fast-Food Shake-Up
The Greening of Eastern Europe
Business' Role in Education
Cuba In Crisis

DECEMBER 1991
Retiree Health Benefits
Asian Americans
The Obscenity Debate
The Disabilities Act

JANUARY 1992
Term Limits
Oil Spills
Hunting Controversy
Alternative Medicine

FEBRUARY 1992
Threatened Coastlines
New Era in Asia
Assisted Suicide
Jobs in the '90s

MARCH 1992
Women and Sports
Underage Drinking
Garbage Crisis
Mafia Crackdown

APRIL 1992
Ozone Depletion
Welfare Reform

Future Topics

▶ *Illegal Immigration*

▶ *Native Americans*

▶ *Jobs vs. the Environment*

Illegal Immigration

Does it damage the economy and strain social services?

A MERICA IS A LAND OF OPPORTUNITY, BUILT WITH the contributions of immigrants from all points on the globe. Yet according to public opinion polls, roughly two-thirds of Americans now believe the United States is being overrun and overburdened by the recent waves of newcomers. Most of the ire is reserved for those who enter the country illegally, the majority of whom are Mexicans. Recent efforts to staunch the flow — by passing tougher immigration laws and tightening enforcement along the U.S.-Mexican border — have proved futile. Illegal immigrants seem increasingly willing to take great risks and withstand terrible hardships to come to the United States — and to accept low wages once they're here. But contrary to popular perceptions, most experts say illegals probably are not a net drain on the economy.

CQ **April 24, 1992 • Volume 2, No. 16 • 361-384**

Formerly Editorial Research Reports

COVER ART: BARBARA SASSA-DANIELS

THE CQ Researcher

April 24, 1992
Volume 2, No. 16

EDITOR
Sandra Stencel

MANAGING EDITOR
Thomas J. Colin

ASSOCIATE EDITOR
Richard L. Worsnop

STAFF WRITERS
Charles S. Clark
Mary H. Cooper
Rodman D. Griffin

PRODUCTION EDITOR
Laurie De Maris

EDITORIAL ASSISTANT
Michael M. Taylor

GRAPHICS
Jack Auldridge

PUBLISHED BY
Congressional Quarterly Inc.

CHAIRMAN
Andrew Barnes

VICE CHAIRMAN
Andrew P. Corty

EDITOR AND PUBLISHER
Neil Skene

EXECUTIVE EDITOR
Robert W. Merry

PUBLICATIONS MARKETING/SALES
Robert Smith

EDITOR, EBSCO PUBLISHING
Melissa Kummerer

The CQ Researcher (ISSN 1056-2036). Formerly Editorial Research Reports. Published weekly (48 times per year, not printed the first Friday of any month with five Fridays) by Congressional Quarterly Inc., 1414 22nd St., N.W., Washington, D.C. 20037. Rates are furnished upon request. Second-class postage paid at Washington, D.C. POSTMASTER: Send address changes to The CQ Researcher, 1414 22nd St., N.W., Washington, D.C. 20037.

Illegal Immigration

BY RODMAN D. GRIFFIN

THE ISSUES

They slip into the San Diego rail yard furtively, preferably beneath the protective cover of darkness, jumping fences, eluding guards and dodging 200-ton locomotives in a perilous dash for the most elusive of prizes, a free ride to the north. "To be truthful, I have no idea of precisely where this train goes, other than it takes us to *el norte,*" says José Flores Osuna, an illegal Mexican migrant seeking work in the United States.[1]

Every day thousands of Mexicans and Central Americans surreptitiously cross the U.S.-Mexican border carrying little more than dreams of a better life. And they are not alone. Last year in the region around El Paso, Texas, the U.S. Border Patrol apprehended illegal entrants representing 75 nationalities.* Some are driven out of their homelands by war or political oppression, but most are bread-and-butter migrants hoping to trade poverty for prosperity.

Foreigners unauthorized to work in the United States can be found in restaurant kitchens, garment factories, tomato fields, parking garages and taxicabs, or pushing brooms and performing a host of other menial tasks whose common features are long hours and low pay. Despite passage of the long-fought-for 1986 Immigration Reform and Control Act (IRCA), which liberalized legal immigration in exchange for a promised crackdown on unlawful entry and employment, millions of illegals continue to flood into the United States, competing for scarce U.S. jobs, putting pressure on public services and arousing xenophobic fears.

---

*Ninety percent of those apprehended at the border are Mexicans.

The number of people caught at the U.S.-Mexican border dropped sharply from 1986 to 1989, after IRCA legalized more than 3 million aliens already living here. But apprehensions have increased dramatically in the past two years. More than 1 million people were intercepted last year, and apprehensions were up 15 percent in the first quarter of this year, leading many observers to claim, once again, that our borders are out of control.

"As Americans we must always remember that immigration helped make this country great," says U.S. Attorney General William P. Barr. "But as we welcome people in the front door . . . we see people crashing through the back door and the back window, violating our laws, flouting our sovereignty and ignoring our process."[2]

In a Sisyphean effort to staunch the flow along its southern border, the United States has recently added 300 Border Patrol agents, put up new stadium lights and constructed a 10-foot-high, solid-steel barricade along a 14-mile stretch of the frontier, just south of San Diego.

The fact that each night literally hundreds of men and women clamber over the barricade is testament to its ineffectiveness — and to the irresistible pull of U.S. jobs that on average pay eight times their equivalent in Mexico. "It doesn't matter how many people, horses, bicycles, helicopters or planes they use," says Javier Ortega, a 40-year-old auto body repairman from Guadalajara. "People will go. It doesn't matter if the fence is electric."[3]

Critics of the U.S. enforcement effort say it is a waste of time and resources and may even impede attempts to address the underlying problem — the huge economic disparity between the United States and Mexico. U.S. emphasis on police measures, such as the new wall, increases resentment and economic nationalism in Mexico, says Wayne A. Cornelius, director of the Center for U.S.-Mexican Studies at the University of California at San Diego. U.S. policies, he says, "make it more difficult for the Mexican government to adopt free-trade policies needed for a long-term solution."

But Americans are nearing the breaking point. The United States accepts 700,000 immigrants legally each year, more than the rest of the world put together. Many wonder how many more the country could absorb without causing a social breakdown. According to a poll conducted by the Gallup Organization last month, two-thirds of Americans want greater restrictions placed on immigration.

The brewing backlash against immigrants — even those here legally — is also evident in this year's election campaigning. Republican presidential aspirant Patrick J. Buchanan touched a nerve when he said: "I think God made all people good, but

Estimated Range of Illegal-Alien Population

Experts are hard-pressed to come up with solid figures on the number of undocumented aliens in the United States. According to The Urban Institute's "best estimate," the illegal population peaked in 1986, rising to between 3-5 million. The illegal population dropped following passage of the 1986 Immigration Reform and Control Act, which made it harder for illegal aliens to find work and allowed more than 3 million illegals already in the U.S. to obtain legal status. Since 1989, however, the number of illegal aliens has risen sharply, reaching 2.5 million to 4 million in 1992.

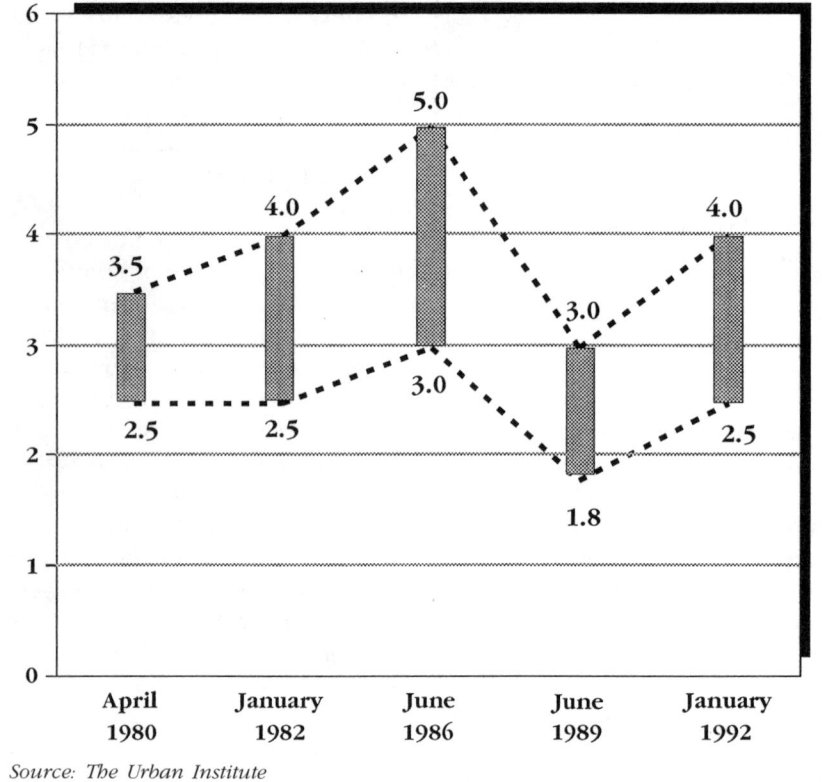

Millions of illegal immigrants

	April 1980	January 1982	June 1986	June 1989	January 1992

Source: The Urban Institute

if we had to take a million immigrants in, say Zulus, next year, or Englishmen, and put them in Virginia, what group would be easier to assimilate and would cause less problems for the people of Virginia?"[4]

In California, U.S. Senate candidate Rep. William F. Dannemeyer, R-Calif., has openly campaigned against illegal immigration, calling upon President Bush and California Gov. Pete Wilson, a Republican, to bring in the California National Guard and U.S. military to seal the border.[5]

Declaring war on illegal immigra-tion, adopting a Berlin Wall attitude, makes many experts and government officials uncomfortable. But what should the United States do? As policy-makers grapple with the issues of how to treat illegal immigrants once they're here — and how to prevent more from coming — these are some of the questions being asked:

Does illegal immigration damage or help the U.S. economy?

Obviously, legal immigration has profoundly influenced U.S. society. Numerous studies conclude that migrants enhance productivity in a number of ways. They accept temporary or marginal jobs, work hard, pay more in taxes than they take in services and establish vibrant small-business sectors. Bustling commercial areas from Koreatown in Los Angeles to Miami's Little Havana attest to the entrepreneurial verve of recent immigrants.

The equation, however, is more complex for illegal migrants. For one thing, they are a mysterious and — in a real, statistical sense — undocumented lot. *(See story, p. 366.)* There is little reliable data on their tax input and service use. Some pay taxes and function as active citizens in the community while others live quietly on society's fringes and are paid "off the books." Furthermore, most analyses still are based on 1980 census data and fail to reflect recent changes in immigration laws and the current economic downturn.

In the absence of hard data, discussion tends toward the polemical. Persistent perceptions that immigrants take jobs away from natives and are hard to assimilate into society have joined another growing viewpoint: that increasing numbers of newcomers strain public services. Suspicions of illegitimate use of welfare by undocumented migrants were so strong that Congress included provisions in the 1986 immigration law for a high-technology automated program — Systematic Alien Verification Entitlements (SAVE) — to weed unentitled aliens from the welfare rolls. So few were discovered that several states, including Texas, sacked SAVE because it cost more to operate than it saved.

Most experts say widely held assumptions that illegals are a net drain on the economy are probably erroneous. By law, illegal immigrants are barred from receiving federal welfare payments and a range of other benefits, including food stamps and unemployment compensation.[6] Fearing deportation, few file for the income-tax refunds owed them, and the vast majority are too young to apply for Social Security benefits — even if they dared. Illegals come to the United States to work, not to go on welfare.

At the same time, their children born in the United States can — and do — receive government assistance. Dependents of illegal residents tend to use education and neighborhood medical services, albeit sparingly, squeezing state and local revenues in areas where they are concentrated. "In a macro sense, any economist will say immigration — even illegal immigration — is always a gain to society," says Charles Keely, a migration expert at Georgetown University in Washington. "The problem is a distributional one. Taxes flow to the federal government, but services used are at the state and local levels."

Nowhere is the imbalance more acute than in Southern California, home to as many as 1 million undocumented migrants. In Los Angeles County, illegal immigrants — mostly from Mexico — generated almost $3 billion in assorted tax revenues during 1990-91, according to a recent study.[7] But the bulk of those funds — $1.7 billion — went to Washington in the form of income tax and Social Security levies. Related county costs — mostly in health and child care, jails and other justice-type expenses associated with the immigrant population — outpaced local tax inputs by nearly 3 to 1.

Los Angeles officials say that children born to illegal immigrants now account for more than 65 percent of all births at county-run hospitals, costing taxpayers $28 million a year. Federal welfare payments to U.S.-born children of illegal immigrants residing in Los Angeles County approach $250 million annually.[8] "The federal government is making out like a bandit," Keely says, "while Los Angeles is taking it in the neck."

Though few economists would deny that immigrant competition hurts low-skilled American workers, Law-rence Fuchs, former executive director of the U.S. Select Commission on Immigration and Refugee Policy and currently a professor at Brandeis University, says his research convinced him that illegal aliens "probably create more jobs than they take away." Douglas Massey, a sociologist at the University of Chicago, agrees. "Without illegal immigrants," he says, "many U.S. factories would go offshore. The garment industry in East Los Angeles ... would be in Taiwan or Mexico."

That's cold comfort to unemployed textile workers in Los Angeles, displaced by undocumented Mexicans working in sweatshops. Moreover, expanding the nation's gross domestic product on the backs of low-paid workers may not be morally just or economically sound. Billions of dollars' worth of wages are sent out of our economy. And hard-won benefits to American workers — the minimum wage, an eight-hour work day, pensions — are undermined by the enormous underground economy.

The larger issue concerns how undocumented workers affect the structure of the economy — making it more service-oriented and labor-intensive. Illegal immigration has almost certainly postponed greater mechanization, particularly in agriculture and manufacturing, which may be essential for U.S. industries if they are to compete in the global economy.

Would a national identification card diminish the flood of undocumented workers?

The novel idea behind IRCA was to hold businesses accountable for hiring improperly documented workers. But the employer-sanctions section of the 1986 law had to be watered down to win enactment because of opposition from employers, who resisted being deputized as border guards, and from civil rights groups that feared anyone with a Hispanic surname or Asian features might be subjected to the third degree. IRCA set fines and jail terms for employers who knowingly hire illegal aliens, but in practice the law is a sieve.

IRCA requires only that the employer examine any two of 17 proofs of citizenship, some of which, baptismal certificates for example, have thousands of acceptable variations. And the employer need only make a reasonable inspection of a worker's documents.

This lax standard has spawned a cottage industry in bogus documents. "The word is out that you can circumvent the law with fraudulent documents," says Duke Austin, spokesman for the U.S. Immigration and Naturalization Service (INS) in Washington. "You can pick up a Social Security card for $20 on just about any street corner in Los Angeles." Immigration experts estimate that at least 40 percent of undocumented workers carry fraudulent papers. Last September, the INS seized two printing presses and more than 250,000 phony ID cards in Los Angeles.[9]

The prevalence of counterfeit documents has prompted some experts to call for a national identification system. "If America were more adult about this issue, like some Western European nations," argues Robert Kuttner, the economics correspondent for *The New Republic* magazine, "we might save ourselves endless inconvenience by establishing a single official ID. Employers could ask to see it, and counterfeiting it would be a serious crime."[10]

Most advocates for reforming immigration documents don't go that far. But many agree with the University of Chicago's Massey, who says if the nation wants to control and deter undocumented migration, "there has to be some sort of employer-verification system." Massey contends that credit-card technology could easily be adapted to limit the hiring of undocumented workers. "VISA and American

Trying to Count the Nation's Shadow Population

When Americans complain about levels of illegal immigration, they invariably use the number of apprehensions at the U.S.-Mexican border as a gauge. And why not? That's what the press prints — and what public officials turn to when they discuss changing immigration policy. The problem is that these numbers are at best imperfect and, at worst, extremely misleading.

Last year, more than 1 million undocumented migrants were apprehended coming from Mexico. This was lower than the peak year of 1986 (see graph), but a significant increase for the second consecutive year. "The general rule of thumb is that for every one caught, three or four get across," says Ernesto Rodriguez, a migration expert at the University of Houston. "It's like going fishing and estimating the number of fish that got away. The fact is, no one really knows."

However, multiply even the most conservative estimates over the years and you've got quite a sum. It's that sort of simple arithmetic that led the U.S. Immigration and Naturalization Service (INS) to conclude back in the 1970s that there were between 8 million and 12 million illegal immigrants residing in the United States, with millions more en route.

"If you look at the data on apprehensions at the U.S.-Mexican border, there are some frightening numbers," says Jeffrey Passel, a senior research associate at The Urban Institute in Washington. But, he adds, they don't reflect the undocumented population in the United States. "Over 90 percent [of those apprehended] are Mexican, and 90 percent of those are adult males. If those numbers reflected the number of actual illegal immigrants, over the last 15 years there would be a big shortage of males in Mexico. That hasn't happened."

Several factors account for the discrepancy. First, much of the inflow consists of temporary migrants, generally seasonal laborers. These workers, known as sojourners, return to Mexico without fanfare. In fact, apprehension numbers along the Texas border go up substantially on Mondays when Mexican laborers have to report for work. Furthermore, apprehension statistics do not differentiate between arrests resulting from more aggressive law enforcement and those reflecting a real increase in illegal immigration; nor do they distinguish between the same individual arrested at different times and different individuals.

What all this means is that estimates of the undocumented population based on apprehension statistics are probably grossly exaggerated. Nowadays, with the benefit of more sophisticated census data, the estimates have been revised downward to between 2.5 and 4 million.† And contrary to what apprehension numbers may suggest, current research indicates that between 200,000 and 300,000 illegal aliens, fewer than 10 percent of those who are suspected of crossing the border, are being added annually to the population of the United States.††

These estimates are significant because they are constantly being used by policy-makers — and by immigration critics — to pursue their agendas. "You have to put this in context," cautions Frank Bean, a University of Texas demographer. "The numbers of the undocumenteds got exaggerated, and the drain on the welfare system that they were [thought to be creating] got exaggerated enormously."

At the same time, adds Passel, "To say the numbers aren't as great as some suggest doesn't mean that it's not a problem. Two-and-a-half to 4 million illegals in a country of 250 million is still quite a lot, especially when you consider that 1 million of them live in Southern California."

---

† These estimates don't include the 3.1 million undocumented migrants legalized under the 1986 Immigration Control and Reform Act.

†† Mexican border-crossers represent barely half that number. See Frank D. Bean, et al., eds., *Undocumented Migration to the United States: IRCA and the Experience of the 1980s* (1991).

Number of people caught entering the U.S. illegally each year

Express cards are used millions of times daily," he says. "Retailers simply call a number for verification."

"The technology is there," he adds. "What is lacking is the political will." Americans have a deep-rooted distrust of any form of government identification card. Until recently, Social Security cards included the disclaimer: "For Social Security and tax purposes — not for identification," even though Social Security numbers are now in standard use for driver's licenses, bank accounts, passport applications and so on.

Talk about an employment-verification system has met relentless opposition from a host of groups from the U.S. Chamber of Commerce to the American Civil Liberties Union, who liken identification cards to South African passbooks. Even the Social Security Administration opposes it.

"A national I.D. card may seem a logical solution," says Muzaffar Chishti, an immigration specialist with the International Ladies' Garment Workers' Union, "but for all sorts of social, political, civil libertarian reasons, it's not worth the price."

Nancy Cervantes, an attorney at the Coalition for Humane Immigration Laws in Los Angeles, agrees. "The prospect of a national I.D. card is a little scary. Already the practice of requiring Social Security numbers for driver's licenses encourages people to drive without a license. I don't think it's in the public interest to have more government intrusion than there already is."

Proponents of employment-verification cards say such Orwellian fears are misplaced. In fact, few people are seriously advocating a national I.D. card that must be carried around at all times. Rather, proponents insist, most proposals for reforming immigration documents are intended merely to enforce existing laws, and ultimately would lead to less discrimination. "America didn't need employment cards to intern the Japanese during World War II," says Fuchs. "Their absence is not what guarantees freedom and keeps fascism out of the U.S."

In any case, virtually everyone agrees that without a more consistent — and fraud-resistant — means of differentiating eligible workers from ineligible workers, employer sanctions won't work. "The whole document business has to be reformed," says Doris Meissner, a former acting commissioner of the INS and presently a senior associate at the Carnegie Endowment for International Peace. "We knew that when IRCA passed, but I don't know if we have the stomach for it."

Do illegal immigrants have any rights under U.S. law?

Whether Americans welcome them or not, once immigrants are here they have certain rights guaranteed by the Constitution. In earlier eras, however, some Americans assumed that undocumented aliens did not have any rights whatsoever — other than the right to humane treatment during deportation. Talk of a right to an American education, for example, would have been dismissed out of hand. Yet in 1982, the U.S. Supreme Court ruled that undocumented immigrant children had a right to go to school, invalidating a 1975 Texas law withholding educational funds for children not "legally admitted" into the country.

In an opinion written by Justice William J. Brennan Jr., the court held that the equal-protection clause of the 14th Amendment applied to all, regardless of citizenship status. Though public education is not a constitutional right, noted Brennan, "neither is it merely some governmental 'benefit' indistinguishable from other forms of social welfare legislation."

Education has "a fundamental role in maintaining the fabric of our society," Brennan said. To deny children the right of education, he concluded, would in the long run add to the problems and costs of unemployment, welfare and crime.[11]

Undocumented migrants have other rights, too. For example, all illegals have the right to apply for political asylum, a process that can take more than a year and effectively prolong their stay in the United States. Though relatively few illegals have any realistic hope of gaining asylum status, an increasing number are applying, knowing the system can't handle them (see p. 375). Those awaiting a ruling on asylum requests often take jobs and meld into the underground economy.

Since the 1970s, all workers, regardless of immigration status, have been entitled to the same labor protections and remedies. But despite these protections, illegal aliens are discriminated against in countless ways. "In theory," says attorney Nancy Cervantes, "undocumented workers are protected under labor laws. But in reality they have to put up with all kinds of discrimination. Without working papers, they are pushed out of the conventional work force."

Fears of workplace discrimination have intensified since IRCA was passed in 1986. Because the law makes it illegal to hire undocumented workers, some employers argue that federal labor legislation, including Title VII of the 1964 Civil Rights Act and the Fair Labor Standards Act, no longer covers illegal workers. Thus far, the courts have rejected this argument and held that undocumented workers can bring lawsuits against employers.[12]

For many illegals, however, that's a hollow victory. In order to exercise legal rights, an individual usually has to hire a lawyer. Although most illegal immigrant claims are paid on a contingency basis, problems arise when claims involve subtle discrimination or relatively minor physical injuries, such as broken limbs. "Who's going to take on a $1,000 claim?" asks Cervantes. "Not very many lawyers I know."

Most undocumented workers are not likely to persue their legal rights in any case. "If [illegals] make a claim against an employer, they fear they will be turned over to the INS," Cervantes says. "But even more important, they are afraid they'll lose their jobs."

Ultimately, most experts agree, the real danger for illegals is that they may become a permanent servant class — latter-day indentured servants needed for their labor but living as fearful, second-class citizens on the margins of society. This may not be bad for the economy, but many believe it corrodes the polity. As Lawrence Fuchs puts it: "We'd be a healthier society if the 14th Amendment covered everybody." ∎

BACKGROUND

Half-Open Door

Despite the generous words inscribed on the pedestal of the Statue of Liberty — "Give me your tired, your poor, your huddled masses yearning to breathe free...." — America has vacillated between welcoming immigrants and resenting them.

Thousands of Chinese laborers were brought to this country to build the railroads in the 19th century, and then excluded in a wave of anti-Chinese hysteria. The Chinese Exclusion Act of 1882 and its extensions effectively ended immigration of Chinese to the United States for over half a century. Other Asian groups were restricted through legislation passed in 1917 that created "barred zones" for Asian immigrants.[13]

Of course, the racist undertones of U.S. immigration policy were by no means reserved for Asians. Singling out Italians and the Irish as "wretched beings," *The New York Times* sounded the alarm in an editorial on May 15, 1880: "There is a limit to our powers of assimilation, and when it is exceeded the country suffers from something very like indigestion." A decade later, Francis Walker, who was then director of the Census Bureau, cited data in support of the argument that the United States was being overrun by "less desirable" immigrants, including newcomers from Southern and Eastern Europe who he described as "beaten men from beaten races."

In the 1920s, public concern about the nation's changing ethnic makeup prompted Congress to set up the national-origins quota system, limiting immigration. Measures passed in 1921, 1924 and 1929 were designed not only to restrict overall immigration but also to limit immigration from certain areas. Quotas were based on the share of the U.S. population having similar ancestry, effectively closing the door to Asians and Southern Europeans.

Quotas, of course, didn't stop the desperate. Legal barriers served to swell the ranks of those who came illegally — particularly Mexicans, whose only physical obstacle was to wade the Rio Grande River. The outbreak of the Mexican Revolution (1910-17) provided additional incentives to those considering a flight to the north. To help stem the flow, the United States in 1924 created the U.S. Border Patrol, the enforcement arm of the INS, which guards the 6,000 miles of U.S. land bordering Canada and Mexico.

Immigration and Nationality Act

Economic and political realities during the early 1940s forced the United States to relax its immigration policies. In 1941 China became a wartime ally against Japan, and two years later the Chinese exclusion laws were repealed. Moreover, partly to relieve U.S. wartime labor shortages and partly to legalize and control the flow of Mexican agricultural workers into the country, the United States in 1942 began the *Bracero* ("laborer") guest-worker program. Through a series of bilateral agreements primarily with Mexico but also including several Caribbean countries, Washington admitted temporary workers to pick crops in Western states.

Shortly thereafter, there was pressure to codify the scores of immigration laws that had evolved over the years. The result was the 1952 Immigration and Nationality Act, which despite numerous revisions still un-

Continued on p. 370

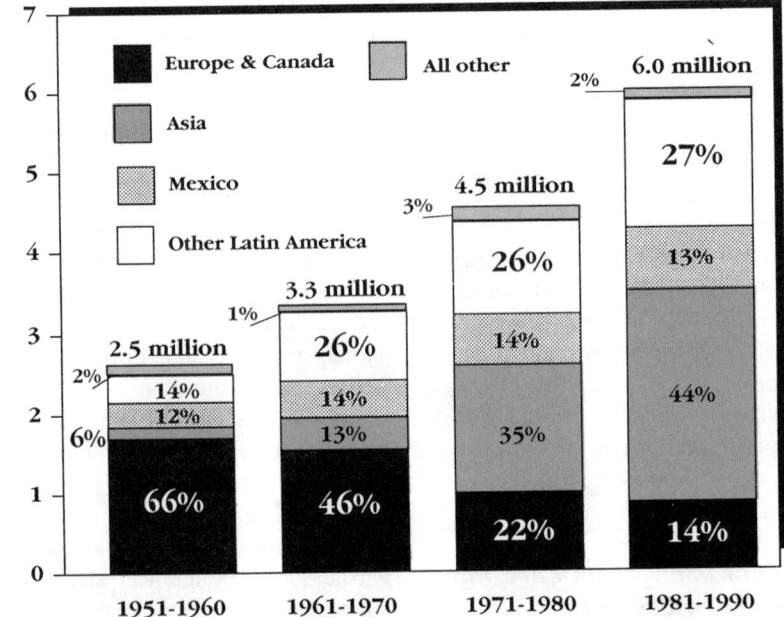

Where Immigrants Come From

As recently as the 1950s, two-thirds of the legal immigrants to the U.S. came from Europe and Canada. By the 1980s, that percentage had dropped to 14 percent. In the '80s, 44 percent of the nation's legal immigrants came from Asia and 40 percent came from Mexico and other Latin American countries.

Millions of immigrants

Legend:
- Europe & Canada
- Asia
- Mexico
- Other Latin America
- All other

1951-1960 — 2.5 million: 2%, 14%, 12%, 6%, 66%
1961-1970 — 3.3 million: 1%, 26%, 14%, 13%, 46%
1971-1980 — 4.5 million: 3%, 26%, 14%, 35%, 22%
1981-1990 — 6.0 million: 2%, 27%, 13%, 44%, 14%

Source: Immigration and Naturalization Service

Chronology

1800s
After successive waves of legal immigrants are admitted into the United States, resentment toward newcomers builds, and laws excluding certain nationalities are passed.

1845
The potato famine in Ireland propels hundreds of thousands to emigrate to the United States.

1875
Congress passes the country's first exclusion law, barring convicts and prostitutes from U.S. shores.

1882
The Chinese Exclusion Act prohibits the immigration of Chinese laborers to the United States.

1891
The Bureau of Immigration, the forerunner of today's Immigration and Naturalization Service (INS), is created by Congress.

1920s-1930s
Hard economic times prompt the nation to close the door to immigration, setting quotas intended to preserve the nation's ethnic makeup.

May 19, 1921
President Warren G. Harding signs legislation limiting annual immigration to no more than 3 percent of the tally of each nationality present in the United States at the time of the 1910 census.

May 28, 1924
U.S. Border Patrol is formed to police the Canadian and Mexican borders.

1940s-1950s
Labor shortages and expansion of the U.S. economy create magnet for Mexican laborers seeking work.

1942
U.S. initiates the *Bracero* guest-worker program, which allows Mexican agricultural workers to help ease labor shortages caused by World War II.

June 27, 1952
Immigration and Nationality Act codifies the hodgepodge of existing immigration laws and also permits law enforcement officers to search vehicles suspected of harboring aliens.

1954
U.S. Border Patrol launches "Operation Wetback," during which more than 1 million undocumented Mexican migrants, together with some U.S. citizens, are rounded up and deported to Mexico.

1960s-1970s
As the civil rights movement gathers momentum, the U.S. drops the biased quota system and admits more Asians and Latin Americans.

1965
Amendments to the Immigration and Nationality Act expand the preference system for allocating immigrant visas to relatives; the legislation also establishes a ceiling on immigration from the Western Hemisphere.

1980s
Tide of illegal immigration rises dramatically, prompting policy-makers to act.

March 17, 1980
Congress passes Refugee Act of 1980, with the goals of removing political standards from refugee policy and deciding refugee status on a case-by-case basis.

April 21, 1980
Fidel Castro opens the Cuban port of Mariel, leading to the exodus of some 129,000 Cubans to Florida, including criminals. Though most are accepted legally into the U.S., they strain U.S. society, focusing attention on immigration problems.

1986
The number of illegal aliens apprehended at the U.S.-Mexican border reaches a peak of 1.7 million.

Nov. 6, 1986
President Ronald Reagan signs the Immigration Reform and Control Act (IRCA), a landmark law that grants amnesty to illegal aliens who have resided in the U.S. since 1982 and for the first time introduces sanctions against employers who hire undocumented workers.

1990s
Immigration laws fail to deter illegals from coming to the U.S., creating public backlash against immigrants in general.

Nov. 29, 1990
President Bush signs the 1990 Immigration Act, which raises quotas of legal immigrants by 40 percent.

Feb. 10, 1992
Attorney General William P. Barr announces plan to improve policing of the U.S.-Mexican border by adding new lights and fencing and an additional 300 Border Patrol agents.

Legal Immigration to the U.S., 1820s-1980s

Large-scale immigration to the U.S. began in the late 1840s, spurred by revolutions and upheavals in Europe. The flow of immigrants was slowed by World War I, restrictive legislation and the Great Depression. The second great wave of immigration began to build after World War II. Over the next four decades, the composition of the immigrant population altered dramatically. (See graph, p. 368)

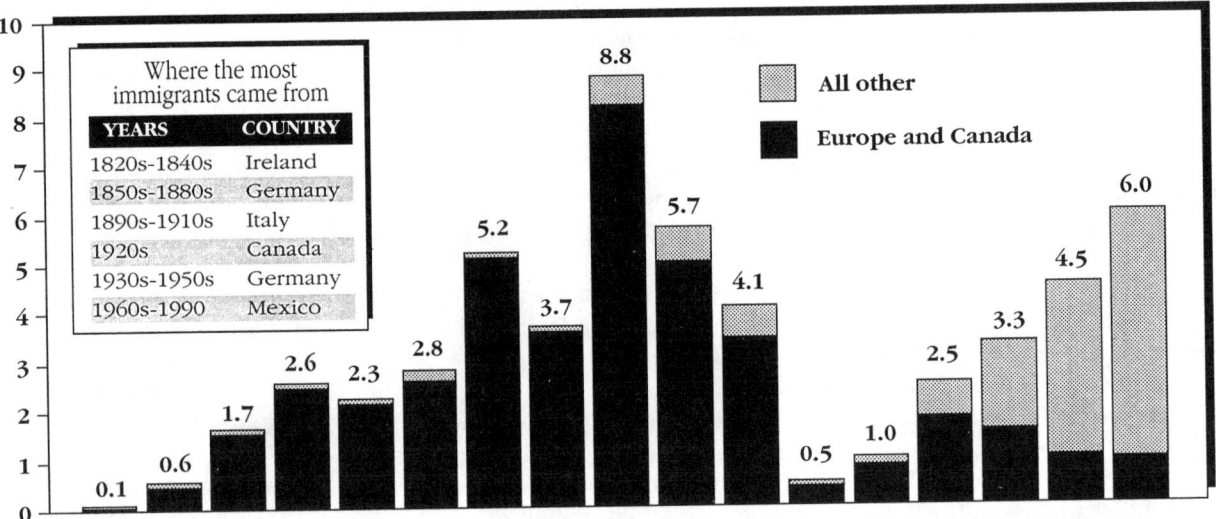

Millions of immigrants

Where the most immigrants came from	
YEARS	COUNTRY
1820s-1840s	Ireland
1850s-1880s	Germany
1890s-1910s	Italy
1920s	Canada
1930s-1950s	Germany
1960s-1990	Mexico

■ All other
■ Europe and Canada

Source: Immigration and Naturalization Service

Continued from p. 368
derpins much of U.S. immigration policy. That legislation, also known as the McCarren-Walter Act, retained the basic quota system favoring skilled workers and relatives of U.S. citizens, but also removed all racial prohibitions against naturalization and immigration.

'Operation Wetback'

Legal immigration, however, was no longer the principal issue for many government officials. Its cumulative impact had become overshadowed by the flood of illegals circumventing legal immigration channels. "Before 1944, the illegal traffic on the Mexican border ... was never overwhelming," the President's Commission on Migratory Labor noted in 1951, but in the past seven years, "the wetback traffic has reached entirely new levels.... In

its newly achieved proportions, it is virtually an invasion."[14]

In a desperate attempt to reverse the tide, the U.S. Border Patrol in 1954 launched "Operation Wetback." Nearly 500 INS officers were transferred from the Canadian perimeter and from large cities in the U.S. interior, joining some 250 patrol agents already along the U.S.-Mexican border. Agents swooped down on factories and farms, arresting any Hispanic-looking people who appeared not to belong. More than 1 million undocumented Mexican migrants, together with some U.S. citizens, were summarily deported.

Although Operation Wetback enjoyed popular support and served to bolster the prestige — and budget — of the INS, it exposed an inherent contradiction in U.S. immigration policy. The 1952 law contained a gaping

loophole, known as the Texas Proviso, an obvious concession to Texas agricultural interests who relied upon cheap labor.

"The Texas Proviso said companies or farms could knowingly hire illegal immigrants, but they couldn't harbor them," says Brandeis' Lawrence Fuchs. "It was a duplicitous policy. We never really intended to prevent illegals from coming."

Immigration Reform

U.S. immigration policy has undergone three important changes since the mid-1960s. The first involved increases in legal immigration brought about by the passage of the 1965 amendments to the Immigration and Nationality Act of 1952. By scrapping the by-then notorious system of national-origin quotas and by giving priority to family reunification as a basis for immigration admission, the amendments repaired "a deep and painful flaw in the fabric of American justice," President Lyndon B. Johnson declared at the time.

The second major change consisted of a shift in the national origin composition of immigrants. During the 1950s, nearly 70 percent of immigrants came from European countries or Canada. This figure dropped to about 20 percent during the 1970s and then to about 14 percent during the '80s. The percentage coming from Asian, Central American or Caribbean countries increased from about 30 percent during the 1950s to about 75 percent during the '70s. *(See graph, p. 368.)*

The third important shift was related to the resurgence in illegal immigration that began in 1964 when the *Bracero* program ended. The program was terminated largely because of public opposition to conditions under which migrant workers lived — and effective lobbying of labor, church and ethnic groups. But having opened the spigot, letting in millions of temporary Mexican laborers, officials found it impossible to stop the torrent. The number of illegal migrants coming from Mexico began to rise precipitously. At the same time, the number of persons who entered the country legally but stayed beyond their visa-expiration dates also began to escalate.

Partly in response to these trends, the Select Commission on Immigration and Refugee Policy was established in 1978 to study all aspects of U.S. immigration policy. The commission concluded in its final report that "one issue has emerged as most pressing — that of undocumented illegal immigration." [15] This perception came to be shared by the general public. Eighty-seven percent of respondents in an early 1980s survey in

Southern California thought that "the illegal immigration situation" was either "somewhat serious" or "very serious." The number of apprehensions on the border peaked in 1986 at 1.7 million, driven in part by the deepening economic crisis in Mexico.

"The simple truth is that we've lost control of our own borders," declared President Ronald Reagan, "and no na-

> ## The resurgence in illegal immigration began in 1964 when the *Bracero* program ended. Having opened the spigot, officials found it impossible to stop the torrent.

tion can do that and survive." [16] The president may have been overstating the case, but a compelling argument could be made that the decade-long increase in illegal immigration extracted a burdensome price on society — and on the public conscience. At a minimum, the illegal influx seemed unfair at a time when tens of thousands of legal petitioners were waiting to obtain entry visas. "What right do these people have to jump the queue?" many citizens asked.

Immigration Reform and Control Act

All of these factors contributed to a movement to do something about illegal immigration. On Capitol Hill, the debate was marked by cross-party alliances that Sen. Alan K. Simpson, R-Wyo., described as "the goofiest ideological-bedfellow activity I've ever seen." [17] Conservative anti-immigration think tanks teamed up with liberal labor unions and environmentalists favoring tighter immigration restrictions, while pro-growth groups and business interests joined

forces with their frequent adversaries in the Hispanic and civil rights communities in opposing such legislation.

After several false starts, Congress passed the Immigration Reform and Control Act (IRCA) in October 1986. The legislation was signed into law the following month. The new law was a compromise that contained something for everyone to hate. Its basic trade-off was a crackdown on the U.S. job market to make it much harder for illegal aliens to find work in exchange for a limited amnesty that would allow millions of illegals living in the country to become legal residents.

IRCA constituted the most sweeping revision of U.S. immigration policy in more than two decades. For the first time, the business community faced sanctions for hiring illegals. Employers found guilty of breaking the law can be assessed fines of up to $2,000 per worker and given jail terms for repeated offenses. The law also included a commitment to beef up enforcement along the 2,000-mile U.S.-Mexican border.

Since 1987, IRCA has allowed 3.1 million undocumented aliens to obtain legal status. Within two years, the number of aliens captured each year at the border fell by half, from a peak of more than 1.7 million in 1986 to fewer than 900,000 in 1989, leading some to proclaim the law a success. Said former INS Commissioner Alan Nelson in 1985: "Once word spreads along the border that there are no jobs for illegals in the U.S., the magnet no longer exists."

Politics vs. Economics

These days, illegal migrants come not only from neighboring countries but from far afield, some from halfway around the world. In February, U.S. officials seized a 150-foot

Taiwan-registered trawler off the coast of California, carrying 84 men from China who had survived 50 days in the vessel's fetid hold. Five ships carrying a total of about 600 people have been discovered since January, and as many as a dozen more are being monitored by the INS.

Experts say roughly 40 percent of the 200,000 to 300,000 people who become permanent illegal residents each year are actually people who overstay visas. The INS suspects that over the past two years, the number of visa overstayers from Ireland and Eastern Europe may have tripled. They get less attention because they are more difficult to track — and much harder politically to deal with. "To enforce immigration laws internally runs afoul of American citizens, they get all bent out of shape," says sociologist Douglas Massey. "Apprehending Mexicans at the border is easier. They'll voluntarily go home — and you generate apprehension numbers to justify the policy."

Even more important from a policy standpoint, the intellectual distinction between a political refugee, the unhappy victim escaping persecution, and an economic migrant, the enterprising fellow who sets off for greener pastures, is becoming more difficult to draw in practice. The distinction is more than academic. Historically, U.S. immigration law has been more receptive to political refugees, defined as anyone who is politically persecuted. In the past, this usually meant coming from communist countries. To open the door to economic migrants, officials reasoned, would be to invite a deluge.*

"It used to be clear," says the Car-

negie Endowment's Meissner. "Mexicans were economic, Cubans and Vietnamese were political. That changed when the Haitian boat people started coming in the 1970s. Their reasons for leaving were both political *and* economic. Are they any less endangered than Cubans? Possibly not."

Profile of Illegal Immigrants in the 1980s

- **About 55 percent came from Mexico and 22 percent from other Latin American countries.**
- **Nearly half were between the ages 15 and 27.**
- **About 53 percent were males.**
- **Nearly half lived in California; 32 percent lived in the greater Los Angeles-Long Beach area.**
- **Other states with large numbers of illegal aliens were New York (11.4 percent), Texas (9.1 percent) and Illinois (6.6 percent).**

Source: David E. Simcox, ed., U.S. Immigration in the 1980s *(1988)*

Treatment of Haitians and Central Americans

Yet in contrast to Cubans, who were granted immediate asylum once they reached U.S. shores, Haitians received — and continue to receive — a uniquely fierce rebuff. In the 1970s, they were routinely imprisoned while their applications were processed. In 1981, with the agreement of the Haitian government, the Reagan administration decided it would be simpler to intercept the Haitians' boats on the high seas and tow them back to Haiti.

The situation was further exacerbated during the 1980s by the increasing number of Central American refugees seeking political asylum in the United States. Since the vast majority were fleeing war-torn lands governed by non-communist regimes — notably El Salvador and Guatemala — their chances of obtaining political asylum were limited. So, like so many Mexicans, they came illegally.

For many human rights advocates, the plight of Central American refugees — like that of Haitian boat people — raised issues not only of

asylum rights but of possible discrimination. From 1981 through 1986, the federal government deported nearly 18,000 Salvadoran escapees while granting permanent-resident status to only 598.[18] Meanwhile, during the same time period, half of the Poles who applied were granted asylum.

"Whereas traditionally Cubans and Poles were accepted without significant questioning," says Ernesto Rodriguez, an immigration expert at the University of Houston, "Central Americans were grilled and usually not accepted despite the fact that lives were endangered. [Polish President] Lech Walesa would never have survived in Guatemala."

Concerned about the obvious inequities, churches and certain U.S. communities — Berkeley, Los Angeles, Chicago and others — began offering asylum to Central American refugees. By 1985, the sanctuary movement had spread to more than 200 parishes of virtually all denominations. Several leaders of that movement were put on trial in 1985 and accused of being part of an "alien smuggling conspiracy." Four years later, the sanctuary movement was vindicated when the U.S. government (in settling a lawsuit filed by a coalition of religious and refugee organizations) agreed to reconsider the cases of tens of thousands of Central Americans previously rejected for political asylum.

The much-lauded 1990 Immigration Act also contained a provision granting temporary amnesty for Salvadoran refugees.* But the act dealt primarily with legal immigration, raising quotas by 40 percent, and adding new emphasis on attracting skilled immigrants.[19] Experts say its impact on the growing masses coming by other means will be negligible. ∎

---

*Economic migrants can apply to emigrate, but their chances of acceptance are virtually nil, unless they have family in the United States or can offer special skills.

---

*A peace treaty ending El Salvador's civil war was signed on Jan. 16, 1992.

CURRENT SITUATION

Pressure From Mexico

They call it "El Calle de Muerte," the highway of death, a four-lane strip of concrete slicing through the center of the U.S. border town of San Ysidro, south of San Diego. In the last few years, some 97 Mexicans have been killed on Interstate 5, where thousands of cars and trucks speed daily to and from Tijuana, just across the border.[20] The trespassers, often in groups of up to 100, would run en masse through the border plaza and into ongoing traffic, knowing that Border Patrol agents were reluctant to make arrests for fear of causing accidents. The Mexican government began cracking down on their side of the border earlier this year.

Elsewhere along the porous, 2,000-mile border between the two countries, undocumented migrants play a cat-and-mouse game with border agents. The dangers are real. By the time they get into the United States, some 65 percent of the emigrants will have been robbed, beaten, extorted or raped by bandits or Mexican police. Even on the U.S. side of the border, there are reports of increasing brutality by the U.S. Border Patrol.[21]

The high-risk journey to *el norte* was exposed perhaps most dramatically in July 1987, when 18 Mexican men suffocated inside a sealed boxcar in the high desert of West Texas. They apparently were too fearful of being detected to call for help. "Yes, it's dangerous, but Mexico offers us nothing but misery," says Luis Lopez, a migrant headed for the cherry orchards of the Pacific Northwest. Back home, he says, a day's wages for repairing tires, his profession, does not even generate enough income to buy a pound of meat.[22]

Jorge Bustamante, president of Tijuana's College of the Northern Border, a leading center for immigration research, says despite IRCA's early success, the law has failed to deter illegal migrants. The situation "has returned to business as usual," Bustamante says. "Those who delayed migration in the past are now coming having observed that work is still available even for new arrivals lacking papers." Says the University of Chicago's Massey, "Everyone who tries to cross ultimately does."

IRCA's purported failure can be attributed to any number of factors, among them a big trade in counterfeit identity documents, an increase in labor contractors acting as middlemen for employers and weak INS enforcement of penalties against those who hire undocumented workers. Those employers who openly defy the INS often find that the law has no teeth. Since 1986, the INS has fined thousands of employers, but the average penalty in 1990 was a mere $850. No employers anywhere have gone to jail for breaking the law, and a 1991 study showed that roughly 50 percent of employers are not obeying the law.[23]

During the last six months, enforcement of employer sanctions jumped by more than half, but critics say given the law's lax standard, only the most blatant offenders are at risk.

Furthermore, the underlying economic reasons for the immigration flow have not changed on either side of the border. In Mexico, inflation has dropped sharply, and economic growth is up to 4 percent a year after nearly a decade of crisis. Yet 44 million Mexicans still qualify as impoverished, underemployment stands at 40 percent and real wages are at about what they were in 1980.[24] Each year more than a million new workers enter the Mexican work force, yet the economy is generating jobs for fewer than a quarter of that number.

To the north, anger in some states about the public burden of illegal immigrants has often obscured the easy availability of low-paying jobs in agricultural and service industries. In California, for example, lawn and gardening services have roughly doubled their work forces since the early 1980s. "Here we have the United States demanding cheap, exploitable labor," says Roberto Martinez of the American Friends Service Committee, a human rights group. "We need [illegal aliens]. We employ them."

In any case, most researchers believe that the law — whatever its toll on undocumented job seekers — won't slow migration. In fact, it could do the opposite. Researchers say the law's legalization of 3.1 million foreigners, 70 percent of whom were from Mexico, has had the unintended effect of attracting those immigrants' relatives and friends.

Underclass Status

Scholars and policy-makers disagree widely on the economic and social impacts of illegal immigration. But one thing they all can agree upon is that undocumented migrants form an underclass. "The detrimental impact of illegal immigration is by and large on illegals themselves," says Jeffrey Passel, a senior associate at the Washington-based Urban Institute, a think tank that conducts extensive immigration research. "It creates a class outside the mainstream that is exploitable in many ways: They are afraid to report crimes and are reluctant to go to hospitals or use public services. And unlike what we normally construe as the underclass, they have no means of improving their lot."

IRCA was supposed to correct this situation. By making jobs unavailable to illegals, it was thought the law

Common Myths About Illegal Immigration

The 1980s witnessed the largest wave of arrivals in the United States since the turn of the century. In recent years, some Americans have concluded that too many newcomers are being admitted, and too many of the "wrong kind" at that. Though it is difficult to separate the impact of illegal immigration from recent arrivals who are here legally, recent research† indicates several myths have arisen about both groups:

Myth 1: Mexicans make up nearly all illegal immigrants. Mexicans make up no more than 55 percent of the illegals in the United States. The balance come from all points on the globe, and most of them enter the country legally but overstay their visas.

Myth 2: People who cross the border illegally stay permanently. More than 3 million people illegally cross the U.S.-Mexican border each year. The common assumption is that they all stay but, in reality, more than nine out of 10 don't. Experts say only 200,000 to 300,000 become permanent inhabitants each year.

Myth 3: Illegal immigrants take jobs from native-born workers and legal immigrants. Illegal immigrants do take unskilled jobs from Americans, mostly minorities and legal immigrants in border states such as California and Texas. Illegals make up as much as 6 percent of the U.S. labor force and undoubtably push wages — and hence consumer prices — downward.

At the same time, immigrants, both legal and illegal, start businesses, consume goods and services and, in so doing, help the U.S. economy grow, benefiting all workers. According to the 1990 report of the President's Council of Economic Advisers, "numerous studies suggest that the long-run benefits of immigration greatly exceed any short-run costs. The unskilled jobs taken by immigrants in years past often complemented the skilled jobs typically filled by the native-born population, increasing employment and income for the population as a whole."

Myth 4: Most illegal immigrants work in agriculture, picking fruits and vegetables. In fact, researchers estimate only 9 percent of undocumented workers are pickers. Significantly larger numbers work in the service sector (hotels, restaurants, etc.), in industry and as domestic helpers. Some experts say the 1986 Immigration Reform

and Control Act (IRCA), which enabled 1.2 million temporary farm workers to become U.S. citizens, has encouraged more illegals to seek employment in urban areas.

Myth 5: Illegal immigrants depend heavily on welfare and other social services, placing a heavy burden on U.S. taxpayers. The legal status of immigrants — whether they are refugees, legal immigrants or undocumented — has a major effect on their use of welfare and all public services. Ironically, refugees, who garner the most public sympathy, tend to rely most heavily on welfare and Medicaid. Illegal immigrants are barred from most forms of government assistance and tend to avoid all contact with public officials.

Myth 6: Recent arrivals are being assimilated more slowly than previous waves of newcomers. Today's immigrants are often thought of as uneducated, unwilling to learn English and reluctant to become fully assimilated. Recent research findings, however, tell a different story. According to 1980 census data, of the immigrants who entered the United States from 1975 to 1980, almost 24 percent had completed four or more years of college. Only 16 percent of the U.S.-born population had an equivalent level of education. And contrary to popular beliefs, most second- and third-generation Hispanics are doing fine, about on a par with the record of Italian-Americans. Of the 40 finalists in the 1991 national high school science competition sponsored by Westinghouse Corp., 18 were foreign-born children of foreign-born parents. In Boston, 13 of the 17 public high school valedictorians in the class of 1989 were foreign-born.

Myth 7: U.S. immigration policy is becoming more restrictive. Anxiety about the economy and illegal immigration has created a false perception that the United States is closing the door on immigrants. In fact, the 1990 Immigration Act expanded immigration by 40 percent above previous levels, already the most generous in the world.

---

†Among the leading organizations conducting research on illegal immigration are the Washington-based Urban Institute, the Center for U.S.-Mexican Studies at the University of California at San Diego and the College of the Northern Border in Tijuana, Mexico.

would reduce the glitter of American society. To some degree, that has happened. But inadvertently, IRCA may have perpetuated a two-tiered labor market: one that is legal and one that is illegal. "Rather than curtailing the hiring of undocumented migrants,

employers seem to have adjusted to the increased risks IRCA posed by reducing the wages of undocumented workers," concludes a recent study assessing IRCA's labor impact.[25] In Los Angeles there are a hundred known day-labor corners, five times the num-

ber before IRCA, where workers congregate in the hope of gaining a day's work, pruning trees, hauling cement or mowing lawns.

Illegals without fake documents are also turning to newly proliferating sweatshops, underground manufacturing outfits that ignore state and federal laws. Experts estimate that as many as 7,000 sweatshops operate in New York City and Los Angeles alone. "Before IRCA, at least we had the semblance of competition in the workplace," says Chishti of the Ladies' Garment Workers' Union. "Now many illegal workers are segregated to sweatshops where employers hold them at their mercy."

Discrimination and Animosity

Critics say employer sanctions have adversely affected segments of the legal work force as well. Although supporters contend that job discrimination occurs independent of IRCA, a 1990 study by the General Accounting Office found "a serious pattern of discrimination" against legal immigrants, mostly Hispanics, as a result of the legislation.*

"The stunning thing is that it cuts across all geographical and occupational lines," says Chishti. "If this were happening to blacks or women, and not immigrants, people would be up in arms. But it's not getting attention." Chishti contends that reputable businesses have an incentive to hire "American-looking" applicants, while less reputable outfits "have gone from the back alley to the basement." The easiest way to avoid employer sanctions is to take workers off the payroll.

In the garment industry, where many illegals work, that practice is becoming more prevalent. The Labor Department's Apparel Industry Task Force suspects that more than a third of New York City's manufacturing contractors (sewing shops, textile factories, etc.) are not even registered.

"When we do head counts of employees and compare them to payroll,

nine out of 10 times they don't match up," says Joe Halik, a task force investigator. "Roughly half of the employees are not on the books. These outfits violate any number of laws — Social Security, child labor, workers' compensation, you name it."

Unfortunately, the loss in wages and working conditions of illicit workers isn't necessarily the gain of the legal work force. In fact, if the underground economy grows and prospers, it could usurp work from the legal sector. "Even if consumers and the economy in general benefit from lower product costs and lower fuel prices," says Charles Keely at Georgetown, "there's a social price. In certain parts of the country, public services will be strained and people may be pushed out of jobs."

Last year, such pressures led California's Gov. Pete Wilson to warn that the state's burgeoning number of immigrants and indigents will lead to a $20 billion deficit by the year 2000. He termed immigrants and the poor "tax receivers," as opposed to "taxpayers." After some Hispanics, Asians and congressional Democrats accused Wilson of race-baiting and scapegoating immigrants, he began to downplay the statements, focusing the blame on the federal government for cutting immigrant-assistance funds to the states.*

Nevertheless, Wilson's comments reflect growing anti-immigrant fervor sweeping the country. Some San Diegans took to expressing their concern with undocumented migration by staging "Light Up the Border" rallies. About once a month in 1989 and 1990, scores of San Diegans would line up their cars and shine their headlights at the border to register their opposition to illegal immigration. Rising incidents of violence

against immigrants suggest others have taken their animosity a step further. "Undocumented migrants are a very victimized and vulnerable group," says immigration-rights activist Cathi Tactaquin. "They are a much easier target than African Americans."

But like most other victims of poverty, the undocumented underclass is not composed solely of victims. According to the INS and other enforcement officials, crimes committed by illegal aliens are skyrocketing, fueled in part, critics say, by an unwieldy and impractical deportation process. Los Angeles and other cities say between 15 percent and 30 percent of the major crimes reported each year may be attributable to illegal aliens. At present, nearly 20 percent of the inmates in federal prisons are illegal aliens.[26]

"There's no doubt we have a major crisis, one that eventually could affect every city in the country," notes Rep. Lamar Smith, a Texas Republican whose congressional district in San Antonio is significantly affected by illegal immigration. "Yet the vast majority of the criminal aliens arrested each year never spend a day in jail." Law enforcement authorities say illegal aliens who commit crimes or those who have been released from jail after serving time are generally not held pending deportation hearings. This February, Attorney General Barr announced plans to hire 200 INS investigators to crack down on crimes by illegals.

INS Tries to Cope

By any objective standard, illegal immigration is an escalating problem. Put simply, the INS is overwhelmed. IRCA was supposed to increase the ranks of border patrol agents to as many as 6,000. Congress failed to provide the funding, however, and many of today's 3,800 agents are overworked and demoralized.

---

*Continuing employer discrimination, reaffirmed in subsequent studies, has inspired a movement to repeal employer sanctions, led by Sen. Edward M. Kennedy, D-Mass. Most experts say legislative action is extremely unlikely this year.

*California's predicament could worsen this year, when the 3.1 million immigrants made legal under IRCA, half of whom reside in California, become eligible for welfare.

Smuggling Humans: A Lucrative Trade

As the U.S. Immigration and Naturalization Service (INS) redoubles its efforts to seal U.S. borders, would-be trespassers are seeking professional help. Up to half the estimated 3 million illegals entering the United States successfully each year are now smuggler-assisted, according to immigration officials.

Borne into the U.S. on private jets, inside rusty trunks of old cars or aboard leaky fishing boats, the shipments of human cargo are surging. The Immigration Reform and Control Act of 1986 (IRCA) was supposed to curtail the flow, mostly by beefing up enforcement along the U.S.-Mexican border and by nabbing employers who hire illegal aliens. Instead, experts say, it has merely motivated undocumented aliens to plan their trips more carefully.

The sordid trade reaps as much as $1 billion in annual revenues and uses safe houses, bribes, fake documents and even involuntary servitude. "I don't think Congress intended to create a black market," says Douglas Massey, a sociologist at the University of Chicago, "but it seems that IRCA's only impact has been to increase the efficiency and cost of illegal entry."

From Guatemala to the Philippines to Mexico, smugglers brazenly promote their services in newspapers or on radio stations. At the top: Chinese citizens, from Taiwan, Hong Kong or the People's Republic, who generally pay $25,000 to $30,000 apiece. At the bottom: Mexicans and Central Americans, who are brought into the U.S. for $50 to $1,000 by professional smugglers known as "coyotes" because of their predatory habits.† "It's a sliding scale depending on how far you travel and how familiar you are with the system," says David Simcox, executive director of the Center for Immigration Studies.

Increasingly, shrewd smugglers are targeting the 1,800-mile U.S.-Canadian border. U.S. agents are so thinly spread along the northern frontier that most reports of illegal incursions come from patriotic farmers.

The Canadian route is the preferred one for would-be European and Asian immigrants who can't obtain U.S. visas (which they would overstay). Typically, the illegals fly to Montreal, then pay $1,500 to $5,000 to smugglers who take them by auto or truck to Winnipeg, central Canada's largest city. From there it's a short drive to a U.S. border so porous that at one point it's straddled by a golf course. A waiting car retrieves illegal entrants on a farm road and then takes them to Chicago or points east.

Not all illegal aliens can afford to travel in style — though the prices they pay suggest that they could. For $25,000 to $30,000, part of which goes to bribe Chinese officials, farmers and laborers from southern China are sailing to America crammed in the bellies of merchant vessels, often with little food or water. Since January, five ships carrying a total of 600 Chinese have been seized off the Pacific coast of the United States.

International Chinese crime syndicates, many with roots in ancient secret societies called triads or tongs, have begun to add their resources and muscle to the enterprise of human smuggling. "This is kind of 19th-century stuff now where the tongs are not just shipping illegals but trafficking in people as human slaves," says Peter Kwong, a professor of political science at the State University of New York at Old Westbury.††

"Most of them end up in pretty squalid conditions as indentured servants in restaurants and packinghouses and garment factories," adds Bruce Nicholl, an INS expert on Chinese smuggling. Others "can end up actually enslaved in triads as prostitutes or enforcers or drug runners or pickpockets." He says as many as 25,000 Chinese have entered the country illegally in the last three years, mostly brought in by air using forged papers; the ocean routes appeared to have been put into operation about a year ago.

Already faced with a difficult mission, the INS is now up against some of the world's most sophisticated smuggling operations. The INS has identified as many as 30 different smuggling routes into the United States, Nicholl says, but "every time we get a handle on what they are doing and how they are doing it, things change."

---

† "Coyotes" will sometimes lead a migrant across the border, store him in a safe house and then refuse to release him until his relatives in the U.S. pay a ransom. For more details, see Leo R. Chavez, *Shadowed Lives: Undocumented Immigrants in American Society* (1992).

†† Quoted in *The New York Times*, March 21, 1992.

The INS enforcement budget for 1992 comes to $946 million, twice what it was in 1985 but still about half that of the New York City Police Department. The lack of resources, acknowledges a senior INS official who asked not to be identified, reflects the longstanding "national ambivalence" toward illegal immigration.

"Every country has a right to control its borders," says college president Bustamante, "but the United States wants to have its cake and eat it, too. You want to stop illegal immigration, but you want and need cheap labor. It is a U.S. schizophrenia, wanting to open and close your borders at the same time."

Part of the blame for the morass, some experts say, belongs with the INS itself. Political pressures force the INS to jump back and forth between focusing on the border and the interi-

Continued on p. 378

At Issue:

Should the United States open its borders to more immigrants?

THE EDITORS OF THE WALL STREET JOURNAL

FROM AN EDITORIAL IN THE *WALL STREET JOURNAL*, JULY 3, 1990.

*t*he law of our land is now the 1986 Immigration Reform and Control Act (IRCA), which seeks to hound "illegal" immigrants and persists in sending anyone who hires them to jail or fining them. The U.S. Immigration and Naturalization Service has assessed millions of dollars in fines against employers under this law. In 1986, we offered an alternative. We wrote, "If Washington still wants to 'do something' about immigration, we propose a five-word constitutional amendment: 'There shall be open borders.'"

We added, "Perhaps this policy is overly ambitious in today's world, but the U.S. became the world's envy by trumpeting precisely this kind of heresy." A policy of liberal borders is no more or less radical than the notion that a democracy founded in a new, wild world could become the envy of all nations....

The price of freedom does not lie only in defending it through force of arms but also in proving its worth by extending it to the unfree. What is required now when many are tired of helping the huddled masses is leadership.

The consensus in Congress after the immigration law passed was that it would be modified if it proved discriminatory. Instead, there has been talk of creating an improved personal "document system," which sounds very much like a national identity card. Some elected official — Republican or Democrat — has to provide the leadership that will eliminate the abuse of immigrants.

We have no illusions that this will be easy.... Nativists cast their opposition to immigration in terms of protecting a cultural status quo.... Limits-to-growth types say we've run out of space.

Recall that when the Statue of Liberty was unveiled, an earlier generation of nativists had said that the Irish pouring into the U.S. would never assimilate. They did just fine. Recently, we've seen a number of works published allaying some of the most frequently heard criticisms and fears of the harm immigrants pose to U.S. society. The President's Economic Report [in 1990] advocated more liberal immigration restrictions, because of immigration's benefits.

Our support for more immigration isn't entirely for the benefit of the immigrants alone. This nation needs the rejuvenation that waves of new Americans bring. Latins, Vietnamese and West Indians are the new Irish, Italians and Poles....

The yearning masses offer us their talents, ambitions and obviously unbreakable spirit. In return, we acquire a renewed view of our own difficult past and, if we are true to that past, a reason for confidence in our future.

POPULATION-ENVIRONMENT BALANCE, A WASHINGTON-BASED ADVOCACY GROUP

FROM A POSITION PAPER, APRIL 1991.

*t*he United States cannot afford to continue to allow the rapid population growth we are experiencing, largely due to immigration. Approximately 2.7 million foreign-born job seekers will enter the U.S. labor market between 1991 and 1995, according to estimates by the Center for Immigration Studies.

Contributing to this total is the nearly 40 percent increase in legal immigration allowed by the Immigration Act of 1990. These figures do not include the effects on employment opportunities of net illegal immigration, which could total at least 1.25 million over this same period. How much more can we take? With the United States already suffering from serious unemployment and recessionary problems, the effect of increased immigration is to continue to import even more competition for our own citizens....

Emigration does not provide a net benefit for the country from which immigrants come, either. It is often the politically dissatisfied or economically unfulfilled who decide to leave.... These dissatisfied people ... are often the most motivated and best able to rectify the problems of their own societies. What, for example, would have happened to the Polish reform movement had Lech Walesa decided to emigrate to the United States?

Although most immigrants to the United States are relatively unskilled, a small number are skilled. Is it fair to other countries to allow the brain drain to the United States to continue? Their exodus is their country's loss.

Perhaps most important, many of the countries from which prospective immigrants come are countries with very high and entirely unsustainable population rates.... For example, if present trends continue, Central America will add 100 million people by the year 2020. As well, studies show that the perception of economic opportunity is an incentive to increase family size....

We simply must be realistic, for ourselves, for future generations, and for those who may want to come here. We must set limits on immigration at the "replacement" level of 200,000, which will help achieve population stabilization and thus safeguard our environment.

We are being unethical and unjust to our own people and to those from other countries by allowing excessive immigration and thus refusing to confront directly the carrying-capacity problem. Allowing high levels of immigration sends these countries the wrong signal, the signal that their high emigration and high birth rates can continue because the U.S. will provide a safety valve. This is neither good for other countries nor good for the United States.

Continued from p. 376

or. "When employer sanctions were passed in 1986," notes the Carnegie Endowment's Meissner, "they were implemented by de-emphasizing the border. It was a huge effort to get employer sanctions going, but it should not have been at the expense of the border. The agency tends to be highly reactive to pressures from the press and congressional hearings, and that is not the best way to go about its business."

Requests for Asylum Overwhelm System

The U.S.-Mexico border, of course, is only one facet of the illegal-immigration problem. The issue of illegals who request political asylum is a case in point. In December 1991, 1,250 foreigners — mostly from India, Bangladesh and Pakistan — requested political asylum upon arriving at New York airports. They had boarded U.S.-bound flights carrying bogus documents that they destroyed en route. Nevertheless, they are guaranteed a legal hearing under U.S. law.* The backlog of a quarter-million cases in immigration courts and the lack of space in detention centers means most will have an opportunity to meld into American society before their deportation hearings — often scheduled a year down the road.

The plight of the Haitian boat people evokes a more ticklish problem. Some 10,000 Haitians currently are being held in a detention center at Guantánamo Bay naval base in Cuba. In February, the Bush Administration's plan to repatriate them to Port-au-Prince was put on hold for six months, due to fierce criticism from human rights groups. While administration officials acknowledge that the political climate in Haiti has deteriorated since the September coup that deposed

*Following the Refugee Act of 1980, officials expected 2,000 claims a year. In 1989, 101,000 claims were filed.

democratically elected President Jean-Bertrand Aristide, they maintain that most of the boat people are economic migrants whose fears of persecution are not grounds for asylum.

"Under present laws, anyone can ask for asylum," says INS spokesman Duke Austin. "We can't hold them and we can't process them. It's absurd, the system is bankrupt." Austin says the only solution is to change the laws. "We should introduce summary exclusion, what other countries do, to sort out frivolous claims," he argues.

However, streamlining the asylum application process, like much of the legislative fine-tuning that was supposed to follow in IRCA's wake, may not be in the cards. "It took a lot of political maneuvering and political capital to get IRCA passed," says The Urban Institute's Passel. "I don't see anyone willing to invest more capital to change it. I fear we're left with a situation that will continue the status quo." ∎

OUTLOOK

Unstoppable Forces

"The U.S. has the most generous immigration policy in the world — and we should," says Lawrence Fuchs of Brandeis. "But you cannot have an immigration policy without enforcing it. There has to be a limit. We cannot sanction lawlessness." Indeed, few people argue that illegal immigration is a good thing. Even those who defend illegal immigrants say they would be better off being admitted legally.

As a practical matter, however, immigration control in democracies is highly imperfect. That's because of the range of legitimate reasons for entering the country, the obligations embedded in due-process-based legal systems, and economic interests and political values that are inimical to expulsion. People migrate across borders because of a combination of push and pull forces that are beyond any one country's control. And as the world shrinks, more and more of its poor will want to join the rich, without waiting for an invitation.

So long as the United States limits the number of newcomers, it is the explicit duty of the INS to enforce those limits. Despite the fact that apprehension numbers are creeping upwards, "the situation is better than it would have been in absence of IRCA," concludes David Simcox, executive director of the Center for Immigration Studies in Washington. "With each cost and risk factor — more Border Patrol agents, tighter enforcement of employer sanctions, greater use of sensors, additional fences — there is a fraction that won't take the risk. If we decrease the number by half, the impact over a decade would be tremendous."

That may be true. But if current trends are any indicator of what's to come, the United States would be lucky to stabilize the flow, much less reduce it. Moreover, an increasing number of experts believe that enforcement may not be the answer at all. "Washington and Mexico City cannot continue to look at immigration as a law enforcement problem, but must work to seek political solutions," says Primitivo Rodriguez, a spokesman for the Mexico-U.S. Border Program, a Washington-based, nonpartisan information clearinghouse on border issues. "If they don't, Mexico's chief export will continue to be capital, people and drugs." [27]

Since illegals are likely to remain in our midst, some argue that the only meaningful, and indeed compelling, question becomes a moral one: What can we do to rescue these individuals and their families from the afflictions they suffer because of their illegal status?

"Once illegals are in this country, we have to treat them fairly," says Muzaffar Chishti. "Factory raids in the middle of Brooklyn terrorize everyone. The problem is not that illegals are taking jobs. The problem is what they are getting paid and working conditions."

Many cities are tacitly accepting the reality of illegal immigrants. Throughout the country, communities are following Los Angeles' lead, setting up formal programs to help find jobs for day laborers, the majority of whom are undocumented.

North American Free Trade Agreement

Over the long term, many immigration experts — as well as the Bush administration — hope that the North American Free Trade Agreement, currently being negotiated among the United States, Mexico and Canada,[28] will bolster the Mexican economy and reduce the pressures south of the border to migrate. "The current levels of illegal migration are not inevitable," says Cornelius at the University of California at San Diego. "What happens on the Mexican side is what will determine the flow."

Economists, citing European experiences, suggest that migration will begin to ebb when Mexican pay rises from one-eighth the American equivalent to one-fourth. But some Mexican analysts have argued that such a shift would run counter to a basic equation of free trade: that new jobs will be created in Mexico precisely because of its low labor costs. And while most economists consider it inevitable that the wage gap will narrow, they say it could take up to two generations to occur.

"Free trade is not a quick fix," Cornelius acknowledges, "but it is not going to take decades. I think you could see some significant im-

provement in five to 10 years." That remains to be seen. Thus far, the issue of migration has been deliberately left off the table in free-trade discussions. By not dealing with the labor issue, it's impossible to predict the likely impacts. But some immigration experts are skeptical. "You can't set up a free-trade agreement without the movement of labor, the single-most important factor of production," says sociologist Massey.

Meanwhile, new laws allowing Mexican peasants to sell their community lands, along with an expected end to the huge subsidies that Mexico pays its corn farmers, could propel some new immigrants northward.

In the short term, notes Jeffrey Passel, the new laws, coupled with the proposed free-trade agreement, could spur more migration. "A little bit of prosperity enables people to leave," he says.

Whatever the time frame, as long as Mexico is poor and the United States has jobs, people will come, legally if they can and illegally if they must. The desperation was put most poignantly by Carlos Rivera, a 28-year-old restaurant worker, about to embark for *el norte:* "If the U.S. really wants to keep people out, they need to do it like East Germany did and put soldiers every 10 feet and shoot people — but even then we'll go." [29] ∎

Notes

[1] Quoted in the *Los Angeles Times,* Oct. 1, 1991.

[2] Quoted in *USA Today,* Feb. 11, 1992.

[3] Quoted in *The Washington Post,* Feb. 18, 1992.

[4] Remarks made on ABC-News' "This Week With David Brinkley," Dec. 8, 1991.

[5] See *The San Francisco Examiner,* Jan. 11, 1992.

[6] In 1984, Sidney Weintraub of the Lyndon B. Johnson School of Public Affairs at the University of Texas, in a widely respected eco-

nomic analysis of illegal immigrants, found that almost none of them used social services, and only one-fourth used public health services (particularly hospital emergency rooms).

[7] See the *Los Angeles Times,* Jan. 6, 1992.

[8] *Ibid.*

[9] See *The New York Times,* Feb. 19, 1992.

[10] Quoted in *Business Week,* Aug. 26, 1991, p. 14.

[11] Quoted in Ellis Cose, *A Nation of Strangers: Prejudice, Politics and the Populating of America* (1992), p. 191.

[12] For background, see Rachel Morello-Frosch, "Immigrant Women's Rights & Employer Sanctions Under the 1986 Immigration Reform and Control Act," *Equal Rights Advocates,* November 1991.

[13] For background, see "Asian Americans," *The CQ Researcher,* Dec. 13, 1991, pp. 945-968.

[14] Cose, *op. cit.,* p. 90.

[15] Cited in Michael Fix, ed., *The Paper Curtain: Employer Sanctions' Implementation, Impact, and Reform* (1991), p. 2.

[16] Quoted in *Newsweek,* June 25, 1984.

[17] Quoted in *National Journal,* May 19, 1990, p. 1206.

[18] Cose, *op. cit.,* p. 192.

[19] To avoid charges that whites again are being favored over Hispanics, blacks and Asians, the law increases the number of slots for family members of aliens, which will largely benefit non-Europeans. Under a separate provision of the law, Congress set aside 10,000 visas for foreigners who invest at least $1 million in a U.S. business that creates at least 10 new jobs.

[20] *USA Today,* Feb. 11, 1992.

[21] See Americans Friends Service Committee, *Sealing Our Borders: The Human Toll,* February 1992.

[22] Quoted in the *Los Angeles Times,* Oct. 1, 1991.

[23] Fix, *op. cit.,* p. 183.

[24] See "Mexico's Emergence," *The CQ Researcher,* July 19, 1991, p. 503.

[25] See Katharine M. Donato, et al., "Changing Conditions in the U.S. Labor Market: Effects of the Immigration Reform and Control Act of 1986," *Population Research and Policy Review,* scheduled for publication later this year.

[26] Daniel James, *Illegal Immigration: An Unfolding Crisis* (1991), p. 63.

[27] Quoted in *The Washington Times,* May 25, 1990.

[28] For background, see "North America Trade Pact: A Good Idea?" *Editorial Research Reports,* Dec. 8, 1989, pp. 681-696.

[29] Quoted in *The Washington Post,* Feb. 18, 1991.

Bibliography

Selected Sources Used

Books

Bean, Frank D., et al., eds., *Undocumented Migration to the United States: IRCA and the Experience of the 1980s,* The Urban Institute Press, 1991.

The Rand Corporation and The Urban Institute have collaborated to produce some of the most current and balanced research on the 1986 Immigration Reform and Control Act (IRCA) and the issue of illegal migration. This compilation of scholarly articles is no exception.

Chavez, Leo R., *Shadowed Lives: Undocumented Immigrants in American Society,* Harcourt Brace Jovanovich College Publishers, 1992.

Leo Chavez, an anthropologist at the University of California at Irvine, has put together an academic book that also manages to give a glimpse of what it is like to live as an undocumented immigrant in America. Extensive interviews with migrants provide valuable insights.

Cose, Ellis, *A Nation of Strangers: Prejudice, Politics and the Populating of America,* William Morrow and Co., Inc., 1992.

This book offers excellent background on the evolution of immigration law and policy in the United States, putting it in the context of the country's racial and cultural heritage. The author, a journalist, is a deft chronicler of America's schizophrenic attitude toward new immigrants.

Fix, Michael, ed., *The Paper Curtain: Employer Sanctions' Implementation, Impact, and Reform,* The Urban Institute Press, 1991.

The articles in this volume address the implementation, impact and reform of employer sanctions and selected programs authorized by the Immigration Reform and Control Act. The book is a useful guide to the complex legislation.

James, Daniel, *Illegal Immigration: An Unfolding Crisis,* University Press of America, Inc., 1991.

Daniel James first sets out to show how illegal immigration is a net drain on American society and then presents a concise argument for what the United States can do to limit the flow of illegals. The author attempts to give an unbiased view but draws primarily from literature generally opposed to immigration.

Articles

Barich, Bill, "La Frontera," *The New Yorker,* Dec. 17, 1990.

Barich offers a compelling and detailed journalistic account of what goes on along the U.S.-Mexican border. The article includes numerous quotes from illegals embarking on the journey to *el norte* but also discusses the main issues that constitute the "border problem."

Donato, Katharine M., et al., "Changing Conditions in the U.S. Labor Market: Effects of the Immigration Reform and Control Act of 1986," *Population Research and Policy Review,* scheduled for publication later this year.

The authors of this paper argue that the employer sanctions part of IRCA have not deterred illegal immigration but rather have contributed to the underground economy by causing a split in the labor market between documented immigrants and undocumented immigrants. Research suggests that undocumented workers are working less hours and making less money.

Meissner, Doris, "Managing Migrations," *Foreign Policy,* spring 1992.

The former acting commissioner of the U.S. Immigration and Naturalization Service discusses global migration issues, with a focus on the status of political refugees. She presents a balanced survey of the global migration problem.

Reports and Studies

American Friends Service Committee, *Sealing Our Borders: The Human Toll,* February 1992.

This controversial report by the AFSC's active Immigration Law Enforcement Monitoring Project includes extensive interviews with illegal immigrants suffering abuse on the border. The report contends that the U.S. Border Patrol is guilty of patterns of abuse against illegal aliens.

The Center for Immigration Studies, *Immigration Reform and Perishable Crop Agriculture: Compliance or Circumvention?* April 1991.

This report documents the impact of IRCA on the farming operations of four specific perishable commodities in various counties across the United States.

General Accounting Office, *Immigration Control: Deporting and Excluding Aliens From the United States,* October 1989.

Though a bit dated, this GAO report provides useful data and background on the Immigration and Naturalization Service, its mission, how it functions and some of the barriers it faces in enforcing U.S. immigration laws.

The Next Step

Additional Articles from Current Periodicals from EBSCO Publishing's Database

Addresses & essays

"Daybreak for some refugees," *America,* **Feb. 9, 1991, p. 115.**

Editorial. Applauds the United States government's agreement in a federal court in San Francisco to stop deporting illegal immigrants from El Salvador and Guatemala.

Becker, G. S., "Opening the golden door wider — to newcomers with knowhow," *Business Week,* **June 11, 1990, p. 12.**

Describes how the United States needs a new immigration policy that admits many more younger, skilled workers — and punishes illegal entrants. Why punishing illegal aliens would help; how admitting younger skilled workers can help alleviate shortages in engineering, nursing, computer programming and many other fields.

Sheehan, E. R. F., "The open border," *New York Review of Books,* **March 15, 1990, p. 34.**

Argues that the United States should focus its energies along the Rio Grande border on the drug trade rather than on illegal aliens. Difficulties faced by Central American refugees; torturous conditions of Mexican prisons; U.S. Immigration and Naturalization Service (INS).

Case studies

Glaberson, W., "6 are seized in smuggling illegal aliens," *The New York Times,* **May 5, 1989, p. A1.**

Reports on the arrest of six smugglers involved in bringing illegal Asian immigrants to Chinese sections of New York for work in low-paying jobs. Description of the practice of "arranging," which traps smuggled immigrants into working to pay back smugglers' fees; links to Hong Kong.

Kaihla, P. and K. Greer, "Toronto's firebrand," *Maclean's,* **Jan. 13, 1992, p. 16.**

Profiles Jamaican-born immigration counselor Dudley Laws, 57, sharp-tongued critic of the Toronto police. Two views of Laws: found guilty of assaulting his wife Monica, 34, (on appeal) and charged in October with seven counts of smuggling illegal aliens both ways across the U.S.-Canadian border. Supporters and detractors; Laws' background and comments on his radical message; abuse of blacks in Toronto; charges of institutionalized racism on the police force.

Maslen, G., "International notes: Australia deports a dozen Chinese students for visa violations," *The*
Chronicle of Higher Education, **Oct. 17, 1990, p. A48.**

Reports that Australia has deported about a dozen Chinese students for violating its visa regulations, the first to be sent back to China as part of a recent crackdown on illegal immigration. Poor attendance; no prosecution upon their return.

McGurl, M., "The quick, the dead," *The New York Times Magazine,* **Aug. 5, 1990, p. 20.**

Relates the author's experience as a teenager observing a dead man wash up on Florida's shore. Haitian illegal aliens drowned in a storm; rite of passage toward adulthood for the author.

Nelson, A. and N. Cousineau, "Rock-a-bye Nino," *Mother Jones,* **May/June 1991, p. 40.**

Relates the concerns of a white mother and her caregiver from El Salvador. The obstacle of economic reality; language problem; cultural problems; social relationship created by hiring an undocumented immigrant. INSET: Nanny confessions of an "illegal" caregiver, by B. Johnston-Hernandez.

Shaw, D., "Take a number and wait," *Washington Monthly,* **September 1989, p. 28.**

Account of an illegal immigrant's experience in obtaining U.S. citizenship under the amnesty program.

Debates & issues

Becker, G. S., "Barbarians at the gate — or an economic boon?" *Business Week,* **Oct. 7, 1991, p. 20.**

Presents the author's view's on the growing problem of immigration for the EC (European Community) as well as the U.S. Becker maintains that illegal aliens should be excluded from welfare and other subsidized social benefits and should not be allowed to gain legal status from periodic amnesty programs. Alternative approach; fallacious perceptions; the opening up of Eastern Europe and the Soviet Union can be a boon to the West.

Davidson, M., "The Mexican border war," *The Nation,* **Nov. 12, 1990, p. 557.**

Expresses concern over how illegal aliens entering through the U.S.-Mexican border near the San Diego area are being treated. "Light Up the Border" vigils; the Civilian Materiel Assistance group and its patrol of the border in Arizona; abuses by law enforcement officials; the Immigration Law Enforcement Monitoring Project and examples they describe in testimony before Congress.

Estrada, J. R., "**The journey to the Rio Grande,**" *World Press Review,* **April 1989, p. 30.**

Discusses the abuse suffered by illegal Central American immigrants to the United States when caught by Mexican officials. Accusations of extortion; human trafficking; rape; beating; deprivation; presented in "Uno Mas Uno."

Grant, L., "**Facing the consequences of illegal immigration,**" *USA Today,* **January 1991, p. 10.**

Contends that illegal immigration is swelling America's population beyond sustainability. Negative consequences of overpopulation; flaws in the arguments of those who oppose effective border patrols; recommendations for stemming the flow of illegal immigrants.

Magnuson, E., "**The re-greening of America,**" *Time,* **March 20, 1989, p. 30.**

Describes the surge of Irish immigrants to the U.S., many of whom are here illegally to escape debt-plagued Ireland, where unemployment has reached almost 19 percent nationally. Claims of U.S. discrimination against Irish immigrants; Irish immigration reform movement; fight for the right of illegal aliens to seek permanent residency.

McCormick, J., "**'We can't catch what's coming,'**" *Newsweek,* **Aug. 20, 1990, p. 45.**

Reports on Canada-based smugglers bringing illegal immigrants, drugs, and arms into the United States through the northern U.S. borders. Borders of the Plains states are guarded much less closely other borders; particular problems for North Dakota; drug and liquor trafficking.

Mydans, S., "**One last deadly crossing for illegal aliens,**" *The New York Times,* **Jan. 7, 1991, p. A1.**

Says that hundreds of illegal immigrants coming north from Mexico have been killed or injured in the past four years as they try to run across highways in an effort to avoid capture by immigration agents. Police officials say it is often impossible for drivers to avoid them. California highway authorities are trying to find ways to reduce the casualties.

Tasker, R., "**Asia's migrant laborers,**" *World Press Review,* **June 1990, p. 64.**

Discusses the current situation of Asian migrant workers; legal and illegal immigrants; boost to Asian economies; International Labor Organization (ILO); Association of Southeast Asian Nations (ASEAN); benefits for legal migrant workers.

Education

Stewart, D. W., "**Immigration and higher education: The crisis and the opportunities,**" *Educational Record,* **fall 1991, p. 20.**

Discusses American immigration and its effect in the nation's schools and adult education agencies. Rising immigrant population; 1990 Immigration Act; new kind of diversity; effect on higher education; curriculum change; language and access; admission of illegal immigrants; new realities.

Employment

Henderson, N., "**Singing the green card blues,**" *Changing Times,* **October 1989, p. 71.**

Discusses how many families are willing to risk breaking the law to hire an illegal immigrant to care for their children. How the risks are about to increase.

Kuttner, R., "**Illegal immigration: Would a national ID card help?**" *Business Week,* **Aug. 26, 1991, p. 14.**

Talks about how millions of illegal aliens or undocumented workers continue to flood the U.S. labor force, despite a long-fought 1986 immigration-reform law that liberalized legal immigration in exchange for what was supposed to be a crackdown on unlawful entry and employment. How this illegal system works; what the U.S. needs to do; the latest in a series of futile crackdowns; more.

Stevenson, R. W., "**U.S. work barrier to illegal aliens doesn't stop them,**" *The New York Times,* **Oct. 9, 1989, p. A1.**

Reports that though most companies are trying to comply with the 1986 immigration law, many illegal aliens still find jobs, either by using false identity papers or entering the underground economy where no records are kept and workers can be easily exploited. Fines or jail for employers; tough conditions in Mexico spur flight.

Europe

"**A programme, or a pogrom?**" *Economist,* **Nov. 23, 1991, p. 56.**

Discusses the new proposals by France's National Front, the political party headed by Jean-Marie Le Pen, which is anti-immigrant. Proposals have been drawn up by Bruno Megret, the reputed intellectual of the party; proposals include: Large deposit would be required to visit France; obligatory AIDS test to enter; illegal immigrants sought out and expelled; complete ban on Africans and Arabs from North Africa; details.

Phillips, A. and M. Kallenbach, "**The great escape,**" *Maclean's,* **Sept. 9, 1991, p. 23.**

Surveys the numbers of illegal Eastern European migrants who are joining the westward exodus from economic chaos and political instability and are being viewed with increasing alarm by governments from France to Austria. Italy's dramatic step: sending home most of the 45,000 Albanians; problems in Germany along the Oder and Neisse rivers;

pressure on the German government to amend the asylum law; pressure on other European governments.

Law & legislation

Pear, R., "Study finds bias, forcing a review of 1986 alien law," *The New York Times*, March 30, 1990, p. A1.

Says that a report by Congress' General Accounting Office found that the Immigration Reform and Control Act of 1986, which was intended to curtail illegal immigration, had produced a "widespread pattern of discrimination." Congress must thoroughly re-examine the law's merits.

Tobar, H., "No rights for migrant workers," *The Nation*, Sept. 19, 1988, p. 196.

Explains effects of the Immigration Reform and Control Act of 1986 on illegal immigrant workers and their employers. "Grandfather clause"; increased poverty; employer sanctions; resistance strategies.

Mexico

Borrell, J., "Journey along the border," *Time*, Oct. 24, 1988, p. 56.

Discusses a trip along the 2,076-mile boundary between the U.S. and Mexico, through Texas, New Mexico, Arizona, and California. Places where illegal immigrants enter the country by crossing the Rio Grande; prejudice and bad feelings between Mexicans and U.S. citizens; Border Patrol.

Golden, T., "Mexicans head north despite rules on jobs," *The New York Times*, Dec. 13, 1991, p. A1.

Discusses illegal immigration from Mexico into the U.S. Each night, hundreds of men and women clamber over the 10-foot-high barricade that separates the two countries, and experts say that the flow will almost certainly remain high for years. Free-trade agreement being negotiated with Canada by President Bush and Mexican President Salinas; feeling by many that free trade will take too long.

Shorris, E., "Borderline cases," *Harper's Magazine*, August 1990, p. 68.

Describes several shelters in the U.S. located on the border with Mexico that take in refugees. The terrible conditions of these shelters and the horrible stories of some of the refugees are recounted by the author, who once lived near the border.

Suro, R., "At a border crossing, a rarity: Illegal alien is caught," *The New York Times*, Oct. 15, 1989, p. A1.

Discusses the continuous flow of illegal aliens along the Tijuana border. Efforts of the Border Patrol to control, rather than stop, the flow; border crossing patterns; drug-related concerns.

Tharp, M., "Good neighbor policy," *U.S. News & World Report*, May 13, 1991, p. 23.

Describes recent protests — considered by some to be racially motivated — near the U.S. border with Mexico. Fear that growing vigilantism and intolerance spawned by mass rallies have contributed to a steep jump in hate crimes against Hispanics along the border; numbers of illegal immigrants crossing the border; immigration law.

Social conditions

Lorch, D., "Immigrants from China pay dearly to be slaves," *The New York Times*, Jan. 3, 1991, p. B1.

States that hundreds of illegal Chinese immigrants pay tens of thousands of dollars to become modern-day indentured servants in the New York City area in return for counterfeit identification papers and passage to the U.S. Smuggling network connected with Chinese organized crime.

Lyall, S., "Illegal Salvadorans fight poverty, winter and fear on L.I.," *The New York Times*, Dec. 25, 1989, p. 33.

Describes the poor and crowded conditions under which illegal Salvadorans are living on Long Island, where the estimated number of aliens ranges from 60,000 to more than 80,000, one of the largest Salvadoran populations in the country after California.

Taiwan

"Illegal, but wanted, in Taiwan," *The Economist*, March 2, 1991, p. 40.

Comments on the problem of illegal workers and other immigrants in Taiwan. February 28th deadline for illegals to surrender and be deported without punishment; numbers of illegal workers; economic pressures; concerns of the government; details.

Hoffman, J., "Mainland 'cousins' leave for Taiwan," *World Press Review*, March 1991, p. 29.

Discusses the growing number of mainland Chinese who have come to Taiwan, and the moral and political dilemma for Taiwan's Kuomintang (KMT) government of what to do with the illegal mainland immigrants. Popularity of Taiwan to the mainland Chinese; Taipei's "one country, one government" policy.

Back Issues

Great Research on Current Issues Starts Right Here… Recent topics covered by The CQ Researcher are listed below. Issues dated before May 10, 1991, were published under the name of Editorial Research Reports.

OCTOBER 1990
Organ Transplants
Energy Policy Options
Search for Arab Unity
Child Support

NOVEMBER 1990
Lotteries and Gambling
Post-Cold War Choices
Setting Limits on Medical Care
Multicultural Education

DECEMBER 1990
Cable TV Regulation
Americans' Search for Their Roots
Is Insurance System a Failure?
Why Schools Still Have Tracking

JANUARY 1991
Growing Influence of Boycotts
Should the U.S. Reinstate the Draft?
America's Archaeological Past
Peace Corps' Challenges in '90s

FEBRUARY 1991
Regional Impact of Recession
Puerto Rico's Status
Redistricting: Mapping Power
Nuclear Power

MARCH 1991
Acid Rain
Cost of the Gulf War
Reassessing Gun Laws
Future for Man in Space

APRIL 1991
Social Security
Canadian Crisis Over Quebec
California Drought
Electromagnetic Radiation

MAY 1991
School Choice
Racial Quotas
Animal Rights
U.S. and Japan

JUNE 1991
Children and Divorce
Teenage Suicide
Endangered Species
Europe 1992

JULY 1991
Teenagers and Abortion
Soviet Republics Rebel
Mexico's Emergence
Athletes and Drugs

AUGUST 1991
Sexual Harassment
Fetal Tissue Research
Oil Imports
The Palestinians

SEPTEMBER 1991
Police Brutality
Advertising Under Attack
Saving the Forests
Foster Care Crisis

OCTOBER 1991
Pay-Per-View TV
Youth Gangs
Gene Therapy
World Hunger

NOVEMBER 1991
Fast-Food Shake-Up
The Greening of Eastern Europe
Business' Role in Education
Cuba In Crisis

DECEMBER 1991
Retiree Health Benefits
Asian Americans
The Obscenity Debate
The Disabilities Act

JANUARY 1992
Term Limits
Oil Spills
Hunting Controversy
Alternative Medicine

FEBRUARY 1992
Threatened Coastlines
New Era in Asia
Assisted Suicide
Jobs in the '90s

MARCH 1992
Women and Sports
Underage Drinking
Garbage Crisis
Mafia Crackdown

APRIL 1992
Ozone Depletion
Welfare Reform
Politicians and Privacy

Back issues are available for $4.00 (subscribers) or $7.00 (non-subscribers). Quantity discounts apply to orders over ten. To order, call Congressional Quarterly 1-800-432-2250.

Future Topics

▶ *Native Americans*

▶ *Jobs vs. the Environment*

▶ *Litigation Reform*

Native Americans

Will the Columbus quincentenary highlight their problems?

D
ESPITE THEIR GREAT DIVERSITY, NATIVE
Americans share a fierce attachment to the land.
But of the 1.9 billion acres that Native Americans
roamed 500 years ago, only 46 million acres
remain in Indian hands today. The Indians' lost heritage helps
explain their outrage over this year's 500th anniversary
celebrations of Christopher Columbus' first voyage to the New
World. Columbus, to the Indians, was not a brave discoverer
but a savage despoiler who brought slavery, disease and
genocide. While Indians continue to battle oppressive social
and health problems, they also are fighting for new respect.
This includes denouncing the use of Indian names for
professional and school sports teams. Eliminating Indian team
names will help erase ethnic stereotypes, they say, making it
easier for Americans to see Indians as individuals.

C_Q   **May 8, 1992 • Volume 2, No. 17 • 385-408**

Formerly Editorial Research Reports

COVER ART: BARBARA SASSA-DANIELS

May 8, 1992
Volume 2, No. 17

EDITOR
Sandra Stencel

MANAGING EDITOR
Thomas J. Colin

ASSOCIATE EDITOR
Richard L. Worsnop

STAFF WRITERS
Charles S. Clark
Mary H. Cooper
Rodman D. Griffin

PRODUCTION EDITOR
Laurie De Maris

EDITORIAL ASSISTANT
Michael M. Taylor

GRAPHICS
Jack Auldridge

PUBLISHED BY
Congressional Quarterly Inc.

CHAIRMAN
Andrew Barnes

VICE CHAIRMAN
Andrew P. Corty

EDITOR AND PUBLISHER
Neil Skene

EXECUTIVE EDITOR
Robert W. Merry

PUBLICATIONS MARKETING/SALES
Robert Smith

EDITOR, EBSCO PUBLISHING
Melissa Kummerer

The CQ Researcher (ISSN 1056-2036). Formerly Editorial Research Reports. Published weekly (48 times per year, not printed the first Friday of any month with five Fridays) by Congressional Quarterly Inc., 1414 22nd St., N.W., Washington, D.C. 20037. Rates are furnished upon request. Second-class postage paid at Washington, D.C. POSTMASTER: Send address changes to The CQ Researcher, 1414 22nd St., N.W., Washington, D.C. 20037.

Native Americans

By Richard L. Worsnop

The Issues

This year's Tournament of Roses Parade in Pasadena, Calif., featured the usual New Year's Day extravaganza of marching bands and flower-bedecked floats. One member of the showy procession stood out, however. Riding his horse War Bonnet, Rep. Ben Nighthorse Campbell, D-Colo., cut a striking figure in his fringed buckskin suit, eagle-feather headdress and red-and-blue face paint. But Campbell, one of the parade's grand marshals and the only Native American in Congress,* was there to make a point, not a splash.

Campbell's point involved the parade's theme — "Voyages of Discovery" — marking the 500th anniversary of Christopher Columbus' first trip to the Americas. A direct descendent of the legendary explorer, Cristobal Colón, had been selected initially as the parade's grand marshal. But American Indian groups assailed Columbus as a racist exploiter and denounced Colón's selection as an insult to all native peoples of the Western Hemisphere.

Taken aback, parade officials quickly invited Campbell to share grand-marshal honors with Colón, a Spanish aristocrat. That only fanned the controversy's flames. Some Indians said Columbus should not be represented in the parade at all and urged Campbell not to appear. The congressman, an ardent supporter of Indian causes, "absolutely agonized" over his decision. He finally accepted

the invitation, he said, because it gave Native Americans a once-in-a-lifetime chance to lay their case before the non-Indian public.

"I saw 1992 as a time to reflect on and to mourn our tragic and unjust treatment for the past 500 years," Campbell said. "I saw it as a time for lawful and hopefully non-violent protests protected by a Constitution we did not write. And I saw it as a time ... to educate the non-Indian world about our lives." [1]

The discord in Pasadena reflected the kind of disagreement that often arises today when Indian and non-Indian sensibilities clash. Only a few decades earlier, Indians might not have protested, feeling that complaints of unjust treatment by whites went unheeded.

Now, for increasing numbers of American Indians, the self-imposed silence has ended. Over the past three decades, Indians have found a voice, and with it they are groping toward political and social unity. Indian activism began to emerge on a nationwide scale in the mid-1960s,

and it has continued to erupt intermittently since then. Along the way, white America began to respond to at least some Indian concerns, as the Rose Parade compromise showed.

The Columbus quincentenary has spawned acrimony elsewhere as well. Indian groups objected to the jubilee's primary theme — Europe's role in developing the Americas — and their protests forced white America to pay attention. Sponsors of several jubilee events reacted as Rose Parade officials did: by giving Native Americans equal billing with Europeans.

But some Indian activists reject such compromises. They argue that Columbus brought disease, slavery and other evils to the Western Hemisphere. Instead of honoring him as the "discoverer" of already-inhabited lands, they say Columbus should be vilified for despoiling what he found. *(See "At Issue," p. 401.)*

In a letter to the *Los Angeles Times,* Campbell added his voice: "At the time of Columbus' arrival in the New World, Native Americans had advanced cultures with strong family structures, devout religious beliefs, representative and elective governments, respect for elders, sophisticated medicine and an ecologically sound way of life." [2]

The controversy over the Columbus quincentenary reflects the growing influence of Native Americans on the nation's culture. Recent years have brought renewed interest in Indian art and spiritual values. Demands to stop using Indian names for athletic teams, dismissed at first, are winning converts among sportswriters, fans and players *(see below).* At the same time, the stereotypical, taciturn savages that once passed for Indians in vintage Hollywood westerns have been succeeded by the more complex Native Americans por-

---

*Campbell, whose father was Northern Cheyenne, is a great-grandson of Chief Black Horse, who fought in 1876 against Gen. George A. Custer at the Battle of Little Bighorn. The last previous Native American to serve in Congress was Rep. Clem R. McSpadden, D-Okla., a part-Cherokee who left office in 1975.

trayed (often by Indian actors) in movies like last year's top Oscar winner, "Dances With Wolves."

One reason why Indians are now getting more consideration may be that there are, suddenly, many more of them. Much of the increase, demographers suspect, has been caused by people identifying themselves for the first time as Indians on census forms. *(See story, p. 389.)*

At the same time, sympathy for Indians and their grievances — though slow to manifest itself — has been building for decades among non-Indians. Today, as a result, there's wide awareness of the Indians' crushing social, economic and health problems — rampant unemployment and underemployment, suicide and alcoholism. As far back as 1947, a surprising 38 percent of the respondents to a nationwide Gallup Poll said Indians had been treated unfairly by the federal government.

Nonetheless, certain Indian demands — including the return of millions of acres of their ancestral lands — inevitably provoke intense opposition when they clash with the interests of other population groups. With Native American activism on the increase, these are some of the key issues being raised:

Why have teams with Indian names stirred such anger among Native Americans?

Many sports fans profess bafflement over Native Americans' claims that Indian team names are demeaning and should be changed. If fans even think about team names, they

probably view them as no more than handy identification tags — and may even believe the names flatter Indians by linking them to skilled athletes.

Native Americans say this rationale completely misses the point. Appropriating Indian names and paraphernalia for sports use, they explain, is always offensive and sometimes blatantly racist. A particular sore point is the feathered headdress often worn by fans and team mascots. Andrea Nott, a community activist in Naperville, Ill., notes that Indians regard feathers as sacred symbols that must be earned before they can be worn. "It's analogous," she says, "to somebody dressing up as the pope, going out on the field, waving a cross and performing a mock communion." [3]

Suzan Shown Harjo, president of the nonprofit Morning Star Foundation, in Washington, D.C., which promotes traditional Native American culture, goes further. She feels "very strongly" that Indian names for

sports teams, such as Chippewas, Braves, Apaches and Chiefs, lower the self-esteem of Native American teenagers and thus contribute to their high suicide rate. Possibly as damaging, she says, is the stereotype of the drunken Indian passed out in the gutter, an image that may have especially dire consequences for young Indians. Realizing they have little chance of following in the footsteps of professional athletes, youths may emulate the other role model, she says.

Many high schools and colleges have bowed to the argument that portraying Indians as one-dimensional warrior figures robs them of their dignity. In the early 1970s, for example, Dartmouth College and Stanford University responded to protests by changing their nicknames.* More recently, St. John's University in New York City retired its ersatz Indian mascot, replacing him with a costumed student who looks "like a lion," says a school spokesman.

Five teams in major U.S. professional sports leagues have Indian names — baseball's Atlanta Braves and Cleveland Indians, football's Kansas City Chiefs and Washington Redskins and hockey's Chicago Blackhawks. None plans to change its name or logo, though some have quietly discarded Indian trappings of doubtful authenticity.

The Redskins marching band, for example, no longer struts to the beat of tom-toms; the cheerleading Redskinettes stopped wearing squaw wigs with feathered headbands years ago; and the team's fight song has been pared of its more offensive wording.

---

*Instead of the "Indians," teams are now named for colors at Dartmouth ("Big Green") and Stanford (Cardinal).

Did Newfound Pride Boost Indian Census?

In modern history, few racial groups have experienced a population bust-and-boom cycle matching that of American Indians. Some scholars estimate that as many as 12 million Indians inhabited what is now the United States at the time the first white man set foot on American shores. Others say the figure was probably below 1 million. There is general agreement, however, that whatever the original population might have been, war and disease caused it to plummet until perhaps the early 20th century. When the turning point came is also a matter of disagreement among the experts.

But no one doubts that Native America is now undergoing robust population growth. As recently as 1960, the U.S. census counted only 551,669 Indians, Eskimos and Aleuts. The total climbed to 827,268 in 1970, to 1.4 million in 1980 and to 1.9 million in 1990 — a virtual quadrupling in only 30 years.

Demographers say fertility alone cannot explain the new head count. According to Jeffrey S. Passel, of the Washington-based Urban Institute, the Indian population surge far exceeds projected growth from "natural increase" — births minus deaths. And since immigration and emigration are negligible factors in tracking Indian population, the explanation must lie elsewhere.

Passel and other experts suspect that people are more willing nowadays than they once were to identify themselves as American Indian on census forms. "We don't have studies to show whether the same people are labeling themselves as Indian, or what kinds of people are changing" their racial self-identification, says Passel. "But we've clearly seen an increasing tendency for people to answer that they're American Indian."

Newfound racial pride and cultural awareness may have been a factor. Passel also speculates that there "may be a certain romanticism on the part of the people answering the census — a tendency to romanticize their heritage."

He cautions, however, that simply listing oneself as Indian doesn't indicate the depth of an individual's sense of cultural belonging. Indeed, Passel says it may well be weak: "My impression is that most of these people [changing their racial identification to Indian] are not enrolled as tribal members." He hastens to add there is nothing improper about that. Each Indian tribe keeps its own rolls, he notes, and membership qualifications can vary widely.

Curiously, most of the unexpected population growth during the past decade occurred in Southern and Eastern states that historically have not had large Native American communities. Between 1980 and 1990, for example, the number of Alabama residents listing themselves as Indian on census forms rose from 7,583 to 16,506 — an increase of 118 percent. Over the same period, New Jersey's Indian population went from 8,394 to 14,970 — a 78 percent rise. Some demographers believe that urban Indians in these states opted for Native American identity for the first time in 1990, thus giving a misleading impression of actual population growth in the 1980s.

Many additional switches might have occurred if a hit movie sympathetic to Indians had been released earlier, Passel believes. "'Dances With Wolves' came out at the end of 1990," he says. "If it had come out before the census, [which was taken in April 1990], we'd have seen a lot more American Indians."

("Scalp 'em, swamp 'em ... we want heap more.") Similarly, the Chiefs bade farewell to the Indian-costumed mascot who patrolled Arrowhead Stadium's sidelines on horseback.

But that's as far as the five pro teams are now prepared to go, as millions of sports fans recently learned: The appearance of the Braves in the 1991 World Series and the Redskins in this year's Super Bowl gave angry Native Americans a double-barreled opportunity to beam their protest message to a nationwide audience.

At the Series, the Braves came under fire not only for their name but

also for their fans' behavior. Braves rooters bellowed an Indian "war chant" popularized at Florida State University (the "Seminoles") while brandishing foam-rubber tomahawks. The "tomahawk chop" quickly became a focal point of Indians' ire.

At the Super Bowl, the name Redskins was sufficient to fuel demonstrators' anger. "There is no more derogatory name" in professional sports, Harjo says. Two Redskins stalwarts, linebacker André Collins and defensive end Charles Mann, told a TV interviewer before the game that the team's name should be changed.

"It doesn't matter whether I personally find it derogatory or not," said Mann. "If they say it bothers them, then that's good enough for me."

However, team owner Jack Kent Cooke has said he won't budge. "The name was never intended to offend anyone," a Redskins policy statement declares. "Over the long history of the Washington Redskins, the name has reflected positive attributes of the American Indian such as dedication, courage and pride."

The four other pro teams with Indian names have taken similar positions. "Why would any team adopt a

The 10 Largest American Indian Tribes

Many of the nation's American Indians live on one of the 243 reservations in the contiguous 48 states. The Cherokee, based mainly on reservation lands in Oklahoma and North Carolina, are the nation's largest tribe. The Navajo, the second largest tribe, are based mainly in New Mexico, Arizona and Utah. New tribal census figures due to be released in 1993 may affect the rankings of some of the tribes.

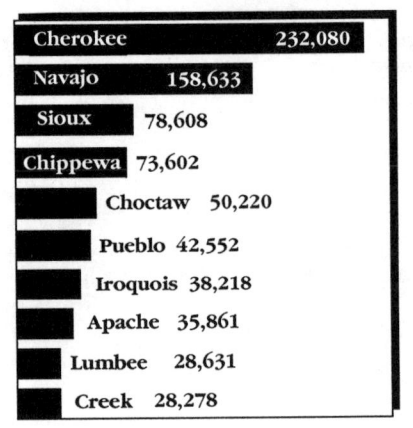

Cherokee	232,080
Navajo	158,633
Sioux	78,608
Chippewa	73,602
Choctaw	50,220
Pueblo	42,552
Iroquois	38,218
Apache	35,861
Lumbee	28,631
Creek	28,278

Source: 1980 Census

will help erase ethnic stereotypes, she says, making it easier for Americans to see Indians as individuals.

What accounts for the increasing militancy of American Indians on a broad range of issues?

To a great extent, the modern Indian-rights movement is rooted in reverence for land. Native Americans have never forgotten the vast territory they surrendered to the U.S. government more than a century ago. At the same time, they retain a deep attachment to the land they still hold. For tribal Indians, land is more than a source of food and work. It is an integral part of their religion and world view.

"We are not living in the past when we talk about our sacred treaties, sacred sites, or the visions handed down to us through the oral history of our ancestors," explained Tim Giago, editor and publisher of *The Lakota Times,* an Indian weekly (*see p. 402*). "We are talking about yesterday, today and tomorrow. To us they are all one and the same."[5]

Of the 1.9 billion acres roamed by Indian tribes 500 years ago, only about 140 million were left in Native American hands by the end of the 19th-century Indian wars. Today, 46.3 million acres remain — an area roughly the size of Nebraska. Tribes have been uprooted from their original grounds and transplanted into new preserves hundreds of miles away. The original treaty grants have been eaten away — by the government, corporations and private individuals. Indian groups say the process continues today. With a few notable exceptions, moreover, there is little chance that lands taken from the Indians can ever be fully restored to the tribes.

Despite the slim prospects for success, Indians continue to press their claims. One case in particular illustrates the high stakes involved — and the likelihood of disappointment for

name it didn't hold the highest respect for?" says Bob Moore, public relations director for the Kansas City Chiefs. He adds that "Sports teams are the last place to look for people who are mistreating minorities ... In some instances [they are] the highest-paid employees."

Bob DiBiasio, the Cleveland Indians' vice president for public relations, acknowledges that some people bristle at the team's logo, a cartoon of a grinning Indian. "But we haven't been under any pressure to change it," he says.

The Atlanta Braves, like the Redskins, obviously can make no such claim. Still, club President Stan Kasten says the team has no plans to change its name or logo, nor to issue any statements that might prolong the controversy. Does that mean the debate will just die down of its own accord? "Probably not," Kasten concedes.

The debate seems likely to drag on, if for no other reason than the news media and politicians have chimed in. In February, *The Oregonian,* in Portland, Ore., became the first major U.S. daily to banish team nicknames offensive to Native Americans.[4] WTOP-AM, an all-news radio station in Washington, D.C., followed suit with a similar policy. WTOP's proscribed list even includes the University of Notre Dame's Fighting Irish. And sportswriter Dave Kindred of *The Sporting News* has pledged not to mention Indian team names in his future columns for the weekly tabloid.

Possibly discerning a vote-getting issue, elected officials are also beginning to speak out. William P. Lightfoot Jr., a member of the Washington, D.C., City Council, introduced a Redskins name-change resolution on March 3. The proposal, which is still in committee, would not have the force of law if passed. In Missouri, meanwhile, state Rep. Vernon Thompson of Kansas City has introduced a bill that would prod the Chiefs to discourage fan behavior offensive to Native Americans. The bill was recently approved in committee and sent on to the General Assembly for possible action this year.

For those who find the Indian-name question overblown, Harjo offers a passionate argument. "It's not a peripheral issue at all," she insists. "It underlies many of our other concerns." Eliminating Indian team names

Indian claimants. In February 1972, Maine's Passamaquoddy and Penobscot tribes sued the state. They demanded the return of 12.5 million acres* — more than half the state's land area — and $25 billion in damages.

The two tribes acknowledged that the land had been relinquished more than 150 years earlier in treaties signed with local authorities. But the Indians claimed the pacts were invalid because they never were approved by the federal government, as required by a 1790 law *(see p. 393)*. A series of court rulings in the Indians' favor stirred alarm in Maine, where uncertainty over ownership of the disputed acreage led to the denial of bond issues, delays in construction projects and depressed real estate markets.

In the end, the Passamaquoddy and Penobscots settled for a good deal less than they originally sought. Under a 1980 agreement approved by Congress and the Maine Legislature, the tribes accepted a $27-million trust fund and 300,000 acres. In return, they surrendered all further land claims.

Indians' concern for land extends well beyond questions of ownership. Another longstanding grievance centers on desecration of natural sites regarded as sacred. At South Dakota's Mount Rushmore National Monument, for example, Indians say the four enormous busts of U.S. presidents carved into the Black Hills defile a spiritual landmark.

"We have fewer and fewer sacred sites that haven't been harmed, altered, encroached upon or destroyed," says Steven Moore, an attorney at the Native American Rights Fund, a Boulder, Colo., law firm. "There's a cumulative effect, too. The more sacred sites are destroyed, the

---

*The disputed land, in the northern part of Maine, embraced some 350,000 non-Indian residents and the city of Bangor.

weaker the community of Indians becomes, and the easier it is to destroy their sacred sites." [6]

For many years, Indians quietly endured such assaults on their culture. Their forbearance was based not on stoicism but on their impotence in the face of depredations by the dominant white society. When the Indian wars ended in the late 19th century, Native Americans found themselves broken as a people and without a voice in the management of their own affairs, their unity as tribes and nations lost, seemingly forever.

The Indians' few friends in the white world often shared the view that Indians were incapable of caring for themselves and meeting the challenges of daily life. In frontier society, the Indians' low economic, cultural and political state was taken as evidence of their inferiority.

Alcohol has been one of the Indians' constant problems. In the early 19th century, various federal, state and territorial laws banned the sale of liquor to Indians, but lax enforcement rendered them ineffective. The Indians of a century ago were weakened also by the tribal rivalries that whites exploited as they pursued a divide-and-conquer strategy.

But in recent years a cross-tribal cohesion, or "supertribalism," has emerged, giving Native Americans the confidence to press their demands as a distinct people. "For most, tribal identifications remain at least as strong and usually stronger," Harvard University sociologist Stephen Cornell wrote in *The Return of the Native*. "But increasingly for large numbers of Indians, Indian identity — as distinct from tribal identity — has become a conscious and important basis of action and thought in its own right." [7]

Ironically, an institution designed by whites to hasten the assimilation of Indians into mainstream America may have helped reinforce feelings of Indian solidarity. Off-reservation

boarding schools, introduced in the late 19th century and taught in English, provided young Indians from different tribes with a common language — often for the first time.

The multitribal experience yielded significant results in other ways, too. "It was at these schools," says Cornell, "that an Indian journalism — as opposed to tribal or community journalism — got its start. Lasting friendships and even marriages were made across distant tribal boundaries. Such relationships helped to break down traditional barriers to a common Indian consciousness." [8]

Should Indians rely on organized gambling as a prime source of income?

Like millions of their fellow Americans, many Indians dream of attaining financial security through gambling. But while others muse about winning a multimillion-dollar jackpot, Indians are gambling that their big payoff will come from running bingo halls, casinos and less familiar forms of legalized gaming. For many tribes, the dream already has become a reality.

In 1990, the most recent year for which complete statistics are available, revenue from gaming operations on Indian reservations accounted for slightly less than 0.5 percent of the $286.2 billion U.S. total from all legal gambling sources.[9] But that minuscule share still came to $1.3 billion — money that hard-pressed tribes say is crucial to their economic survival. Gambling is a key source of jobs on reservations, where unemployment rates above 40 percent are not uncommon.

Indian-sponsored bingo games began to proliferate after 1982, when the U.S. Supreme Court left standing a lower court's decision that Florida — and, by implication, other states — could not regulate bingo on Indian reservations if the game was legal elsewhere in the state. In 1987, the high court explicitly restated the prin-

Where Native Americans Live

The 1990 census showed a significant jump in the population of American Indians, Aleuts and Eskimos, from 1.4 million in 1980 to 1.9 million. Some of the increase, experts say, reflects non-demographic factors: People are more willing than they once were to identify themselves as American Indian on census forms. Indians live throughout the nation (bottom map) and comprise small but significant minorities in a number of states (map, top right). Indians also make up a sizable presence in several major metropolitan areas (table, top left).

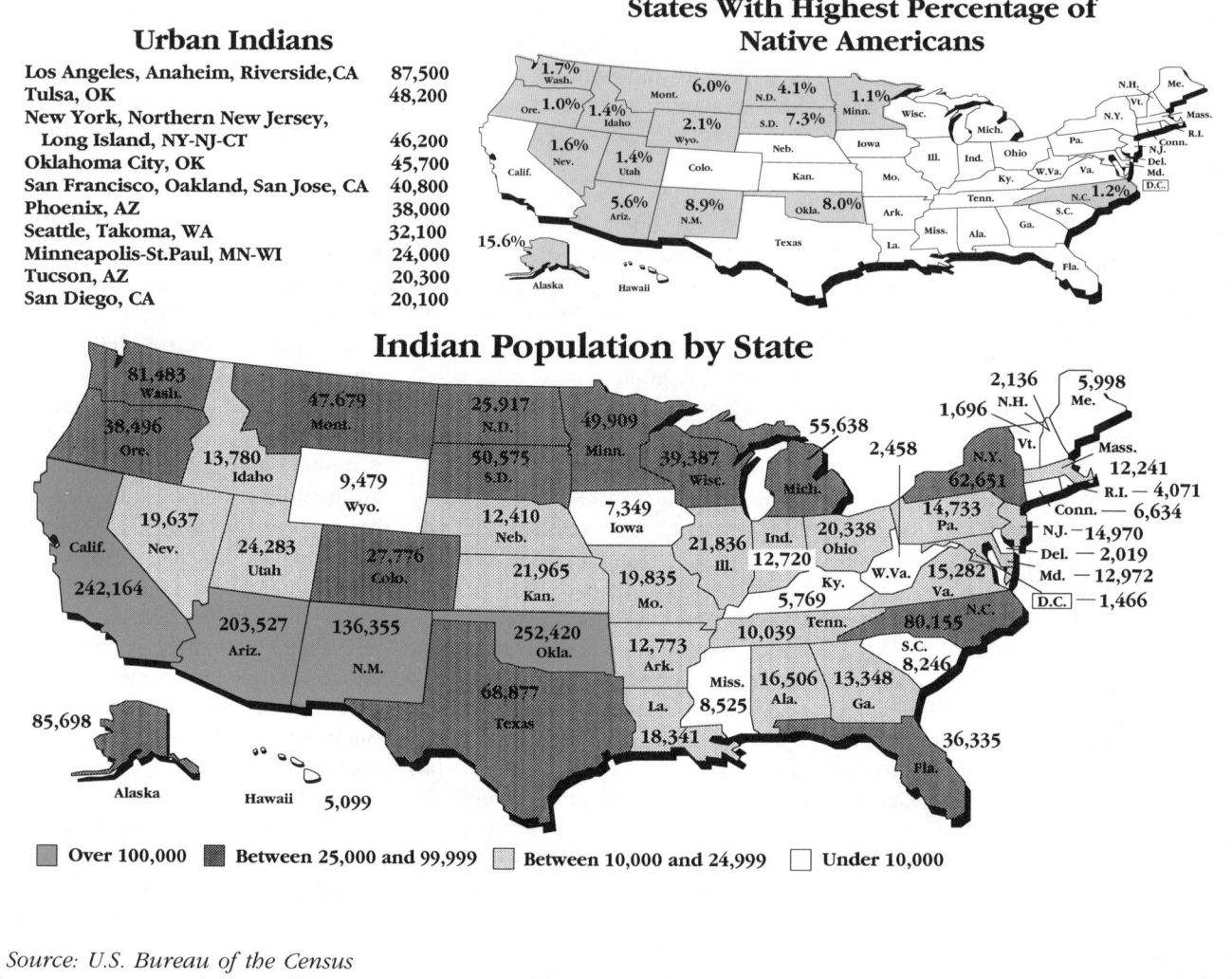

Urban Indians

Los Angeles, Anaheim, Riverside,CA	87,500
Tulsa, OK	48,200
New York, Northern New Jersey, Long Island, NY-NJ-CT	46,200
Oklahoma City, OK	45,700
San Francisco, Oakland, San Jose, CA	40,800
Phoenix, AZ	38,000
Seattle, Takoma, WA	32,100
Minneapolis-St.Paul, MN-WI	24,000
Tucson, AZ	20,300
San Diego, CA	20,100

States With Highest Percentage of Native Americans

Indian Population by State

Legend: Over 100,000 ■ Between 25,000 and 99,999 ■ Between 10,000 and 24,999 □ Under 10,000

Source: U.S. Bureau of the Census

ciple in *California v. Cabazon Band of Mission Indians.*

Nonetheless, the spread of gambling on tribal lands stirred anxiety among state and federal law enforcement authorities, who feared that organized crime would corrupt the games and defraud the tribes and their gambling patrons. Congress

sought to allay these concerns by passing the Indian Gaming Regulatory Act in 1988. The law defined three classes of gambling and applied differing regulatory standards to each:

Class I, consisting of traditional ceremonial gaming or social games for prizes of limited value, was placed under the tribes' exclusive

control. Class II, comprising bingo, lotto and certain card games, was made subject to oversight by a five-member National Indian Gaming Commission appointed by the president and confirmed by the Senate. Three commission seats were set aside for tribal members. Class III activities, including casino gambling, slot machines, horse and dog racing and jai alai, were prohibited unless they were legal in the state.

Many Native American leaders have denounced the 1988 law as an unwarranted intrusion on tribal sovereignty. Others oppose gambling on the grounds that it attracts unsavory elements to the reservations and fails to deliver the promised economic benefits.

Disagreement over gambling's merits can create serious tribal rifts. In 1989 the Mohawks of upstate New York split into pro- and anti-gambling factions and waged a brief civil war because all the profits from their six casinos were allegedly going to the casino operators and their non-Indian management team. Two tribe members died in the conflict.

Still, proponents of Indian gaming insist the industry is, on balance, a positive force. "If properly nurtured," says Leonard Prescott, chairman of the National Indian Gaming Association, "it will provide part of the solution to decades of reservation poverty and dependence on taxpayer-funded assistance." [10]

One venture being closely watched is the Foxwoods High Stakes Bingo and Gambling Casino, which opened Feb. 15 in Ledyard, Conn., near New London. Operated on reservation land by the Mashantucket Pequot nation, the huge facility — boasting 170 gaming tables and an atrium waterfall — is the first major casino on the East Coast outside Atlantic City, N.J. Tribal members are hoping for 4 million visitors and gross annual revenues of $100 million.

Connecticut officials opposed the casino but were overruled by Interior Secretary Manuel Lujan Jr., who noted that the Indian Gaming Regulation Act permits tribes to operate gambling facilities if such activity is legal in the state. Republican Gov. Lowell P. Weicker Jr., a staunch opponent of casinos, asked the Connecticut General Assembly to repeal the statute al-

lowing charities to raise money at so-called Las Vegas Nights, but the lawmakers refused.

Meanwhile, an Oklahoma tribe has launched the staid game of bingo into orbit by making innovative use of space technology. Telecast live each night from the Creek Nation Bingo Hall in Tulsa, MegaBingo is a 15-minute game beamed by satellite to 47 sites on 31 reservations in 10 states.[11] Each hall also is linked by a two-way audio network. The hookup not only facilitates instant identification of game winners but also enables the widely scattered MegaBingo tribes to communicate with each other throughout the day.   ■

BACKGROUND

Early Treaties

Native American tribes have always occupied a unique place in the United States. The U.S. government, like the European colonial governments before it, from the beginning treated tribes as sovereign nations.* Between 1778 and 1868, the U.S. Senate ratified no less than 370 treaties with Indian tribes, under which nearly 1 billion acres were ceded to the national government as white settlement spread into Indian country. The government in return pledged to protect the remaining Indian lands and resources. But throughout U.S. history, the federal government has vacillated between encouraging tribes to govern themselves on self-sufficient reservations and assimilating Indians into a predominantly white society.

The 1778 Fort Pitt Treaty with the Delaware Indians, the first between a tribe and the U.S. government, was a model of enlightenment. It invited friendly tribes, at a time of their own choosing, to send representatives to Congress and to join the union in a state of their own. Similarly, a treaty

with the Cherokees in 1785 provided: "The Indians may have full confidence in the justice of the United States respecting their interests; they shall have the right to send a deputy of their choice to Congress."

Two years later, in the Northwest Territory Ordinance of 1787, the government made its first major declaration of Indian policy: "The utmost good faith shall always be observed towards the Indians; their land and property shall never be taken from them without their consent; and in their property, rights and liberty, they shall never be invaded or disturbed.... Laws founded in justice and humanity shall from time to time be made, for preventing wrongs being done to them and for preserving peace and friendship with them."

One such law took effect July 22, 1790. Aimed at unscrupulous private land dealers, it declared that purchases of Indian territory were invalid unless made by a public treaty with the United States. The law also provided for the punishment of murder and other crimes committed by whites against Indians in Indian country.

Special Status Recognized by Supreme Court

Perhaps the two most important judicial decisions dealing with the special status of the Indian tribes were handed down by the Supreme Court in the early 1830s. In *Cherokee Nation v. Georgia* (1831), Chief Justice John Marshall asserted that Indi-

*Article I, Section 8 of the U.S. Constitution states that "the Congress shall have the power to regulate commerce with foreign nations and among the several states and with Indian tribes."

Seeking a Solution to Alcoholism

For the United States as a whole, alcoholism has long been a serious health problem. For Native Americans, it is nothing less than a calamity. Health officials estimate that alcohol abuse causes as many as one in every three Indian deaths. Indeed, the toll is so high that some believe Indians have a physiological inability to cope with alcohol that other races do not share. Research has uncovered no such trait, however.

Before the arrival of European settlers, Native Americans knew little about intoxicating beverages. An exception was pulque, a fermented drink made from the fleshy leaves of various desert plants. But white merchants soon established a flourishing alcohol trade with Indian tribes. Congress, alarmed by reports that alcohol made Indians violent, barred liquor sales to Native Americans in 1832.

The ban was lifted under legislation signed by President Dwight D. Eisenhower in 1953. Since then, tribes have had the option of permitting or banning alcohol sales on their lands. Today, such sales are allowed on only 93 of the 293 reservations in the 48 contiguous states.

Some Indian leaders and public health officials say that far from discouraging alcohol abuse, prohibition actually spurs the consumption of liquor and prevents young people from learning controlled patterns of drinking. A recent study† of New Mexico reservations that ban liquor found male residents often traveled miles to off-reservation bars for a night of heavy drinking. Some later died from exposure to cold or from being hit by cars while walking home.

Nonetheless, opinion surveys indicate that residents of reservations with prohibition strongly support the status quo. They fear that selling liquor on Indian land will lead to more interpersonal violence, cirrhosis of the liver, fetal alcohol syndrome and other chronic effects of alcohol abuse.

In a fresh approach to the drinking problem, some tribes are turning to ancient healing rituals. One therapy gaining wide acceptance is the "sweat lodge," a rigorous variant of the sauna bath. The lodge typically consists of a tent erected over a pit containing red-hot rocks. After the blanket-encased participants have gathered inside, a medicine man or spiritual adviser pours water over the rocks, instantly raising heat and humidity to the upper limits of tolerance. All the while, the adviser leads the chants and meditations of the purification process.

It is too soon to gauge the impact of sweat lodges on Native American alcoholism. At this point, certainly, no one touts them as a cure-all. But proponents say the lodges can help reacquaint alcoholic Indians with their spiritual roots, giving them the inner strength to overcome their addiction.

---

† Margaret M. Gallagher, et al., "Pedestrian and Hypothermia Deaths Among Native Americans in New Mexico," *Journal of the American Medical Association*, March 11, 1992, pp. 1345-1348.

---

ans "are in a state of pupilage. Their relation to the United States resembles that of a ward to his guardian." Indian tribes may thus "be denominated domestic dependent nations."

In the second case, *Worcester v. Georgia* (1832), the court held that a state, in this instance Georgia, could not enforce its laws on Indian lands. Indian tribes or nations, Marshall declared, "had always been considered as distinct, independent, political communities, retaining their original natural rights.... The Cherokee nation, then, is a distinct community occupying its own territory ... in which the laws of Georgia can have no force."

The two decisions collided, however, with harsh political reality, though they were based on standing treaties, not on some abstract idea of tribal sovereignty. President Andrew Jackson, Marshall's bitter foe, wanted Southern lands cleared of Indians and made available to whites. He responded to the rulings by ignoring them. "John Marshall has made his decision; let him enforce it," the president supposedly remarked after the *Worcester* ruling. Treaty rights were ignored, and the Cherokees were driven from their homelands.

The removal of the Cherokees, which took place during the winter of 1838-39, was one of the most infamous incidents in the history of U.S. Indian administration. More than 15,000 Indians embarked for the Oklahoma Territory on the "Trail of Tears," mostly on foot, since wagons were provided only for small chil-

dren and the old and infirm. One-fourth of the travelers died en route.

Vanishing Americans'

The forced immigration of the Cherokees set a pattern that was to recur as white America expanded westward throughout the 19th century. As events unfolded, most whites came to view Indians as "vanishing Americans" who were doomed to die off or be absorbed into the country's cultural mainstream. The U.S. cavalry confined defeated and demoralized tribes on large reservations carved from federally owned lands that at the time held little interest for set-

Continued on p. 396

Chronology

1700s *The U.S. government's early dealings with Indian tribes are conducted in a spirit of goodwill.*

1778
The government negotiates the nation's first treaty with an Indian tribe, the Fort Pitt Treaty with the Delaware Indians.

1787
The Northwest Territory Ordinance declares that "the utmost good faith shall always be observed towards the Indians" and that "their lands and property shall never be taken from them without their consent."

——— • ———

1800s *Relations between whites and Indians deteriorate as white settlers move westward, occupying traditional Indian lands.*

1824
The Bureau of Indian Affairs is created under the War Department. In 1849 it is transferred to the newly established Interior Department.

1830
Congress passes the Indian Removal Act, giving the president authority to resettle the Eastern tribes on unoccupied lands west of the Mississippi, to which they would be given perpetual title.

1876
Gen. George A. Custer and 264 members of his 7th Cavalry Regiment are killed by Sioux and Cheyenne warriors at Little Big Horn.

1890
For the first time, the U.S. census includes a full count of the country's Indian population (248,253).

Dec. 28, 1890
In the last great conflict of the Indian wars, at least 200 Sioux are massacred at Wounded Knee, S.D., by the 7th Cavalry under Col. James W. Forsyth.

——— • ———

1960s-1970s *U.S. Indians display new assertiveness in pressing their claims on state and local governments and proclaiming pride in their culture.*

1965
Indian groups band together to stage "fish-ins" in defense of Native American fishing rights in Washington state.

November 1969
Indian demonstrators gain national attention by seizing Alcatraz Island in San Francisco Bay. U.S. marshals evicted the last protesters in June 1971.

1969
N. Scott Momaday, a Kiowa, wins the Pulitzer Prize for his novel, *House Made of Dawn*. He is the first Indian so honored.

Nov. 2, 1972
Indians representing more than 200 tribes in the United States occupy the Bureau of Indian Affairs headquarters in Washington, renaming it "The Native American Embassy."

Feb. 27, 1973
Law-enforcement officers begin a two-month siege to end the American Indian Movement's occupation of the hamlet of Wounded Knee on the Pine Ridge Reservation in South Dakota.

1980s-1990s *The Reagan and Bush administrations stress the role of private enterprise in fostering Indian economic development.*

1989
After a two-year probe of fraud and mismanagement in agencies charged with overseeing Indian programs, a special Senate investigative committee recommends largely abandoning those agencies and funneling federal funds directly to tribal governments.

Nov. 28, 1989
President Bush signs into law legislation establishing a museum of American Indian history and culture as part of the Smithsonian Institution in Washington.

Nov. 28, 1990
President Bush signs into law legislation to prevent child abuse on reservations and to fund a variety of Indian health programs. The measure stemmed from hearings that revealed numerous cases of sexual abuse of Indian children by BIA employees.

Nov. 16, 1990
President Bush announces he will not sign a bill to establish preferences for Indian enterprises in the awarding of federal grants or contracts. Bush said the bill "would impose new, expensive and often duplicative program responsibilities on the secretary of the Interior that would be difficult to implement." The president also said he supported the goals of the legislation and was "committed to helping alleviate the widespread unemployment and underemployment on Indian reservations."

Canada's Indians Fight for Their Rights

Indians in Canada share many of the grievances and hopes voiced by Indians in the United States. This is hardly surprising, considering that many tribes have members in both countries. But the legal status of Canadian Indians differs in fundamental ways from that of U.S. Indians.

Unlike tribes in the United States, Canadian tribes are not treated as sovereign nations. The Indian Act of 1876 made Canada's Indians wards of the federal government. It also made their reservations, known in Canada as reserves, subject to both provincial and federal law.

While Indians in the United States can use their reservation land as collateral for loans, Canadian Indians cannot. The ban, Indian leaders say, acts as a daunting obstacle to economic advancement. "We are sitting on millions of dollars of real estate, and we can't use it to access financial institutions," says Darrell Boissoneau, chief of the Ojibwa tribe on Canada's Garden River First Nation Reserve, near northern Michigan.†

Still, Canadian Indians are making headway in their battle to win self-government — including the right to make their own laws and tax themselves. Their cause received an unexpected boost in June 1990 when the sole Indian member of the Manitoba legislature, Elijah Harper, a Cree, effectively killed a series of constitutional amendments known as the Meech Lake Accord, arguing that it failed to address the concerns of native peoples.††

A development of more tangible benefit to Canada's aboriginal peoples came May 4, when residents of the Northwest Territories approved the western boundary for the vast, new territory of Nunavut ("Our Land" in the Inukitut language). The vote followed a Dec. 16 announcement by the Ottawa government that it had reached agreement with leaders of the Inuits, or Eskimos, on a land-claim settlement

Newly designated Inuit territory of Nunavut

including the creation of the new territory in 1999. The accord calls for the existing Northwest Territories to be split into two sections — Nunavut, embracing 772,000 square miles in the north and east, and an unnamed western sector. Eskimo voters are expected to vote on ratification of the land claim agreement in November.

The Inuit are to come into outright ownership of 135,000 square miles within Nunavut — a subarctic territory slightly larger than New York, Pennsylvania and Ohio. They also will receive the equivalent of about $1 billion U.S. dollars over a 14-year period, as well as hunting and fishing rights in the rest of the sparsely populated Nunavut region. Parliament is expected to vote on legislation endorsing the new territory and land-claim settlement in early 1993.

However, things have not gone so smoothly for Canadian Indians when it comes to hunting and fishing rights on lands with majority non-Indian populations. In May 1991, for instance, Ontario Premier Bob Rae created an uproar when he announced that native Canadians would be allowed to hunt and fish for food, or for ceremonial purposes, in contravention of the province's wildlife laws. Many white Ontarians vehemently objected, claiming that Indians were depleting wildlife resources.

"It is not 1492," said Matthew Murphy, a spokesman for the Ontario Federation of Anglers and Hunters. "You cannot hunt and fish with abandon."‡

---

† Quoted in *Maclean's* magazine, March 16, 1992, p. 19.
†† For background information on the Meech Lake Accord, see "The Deepening Canadian Crisis Over Quebec," *Editorial Research Reports,* April 12, 1991, pp. 205-220; and "Will Canada Fall Apart?" *Editorial Research Reports,* May 11, 1990, pp. 269-284.
‡ *Ibid.,* p. 14.

Continued from p. 394

tlers. Eventually — when the lands were needed for homesteaders or when valuable resources were discovered on them — the government forced tribes to move once again.

In 1871, Congress ended the practice of making binding treaties with Indians. Instead, relations between the government and Indians would be governed by political "agree-

ments" requiring the approval of both houses of Congress instead of only the Senate.

Another milestone in U.S.-Indian relations came in 1887, when Congress passed the General Allotment Act to speed Indian assimilation. Sponsored by Sen. Henry L. Dawes, a Massachusetts Republican, the law gave the president authority to divvy up reservations into parcels and give

each Indian an allotment of land formerly owned in common by the tribe. Leftover tribal lands were to be opened to non-Indian homesteaders.

The Allotment Act signaled the ascendancy of the Bureau of Indian Affairs (BIA), which had been set up in the War Department in 1824 and transferred to the newly created Interior Department in 1849. After 1887, the bureau became the guardian of all Indians, assuming responsibility for the most picayune decisions — even about school attendance, feasts and dances. The bureau's philosophy, like the philosophy behind the Allotment Act, was to speed the Indians' melding into white society.

BIA officials made no secret of their intentions. "The Indians," Indian Commissioner Thomas Morgan said in 1889, "must conform to 'the white man's ways,' peaceably if they will, forcibly if they must." Morgan praised off-reservation boarding schools for their "liberalizing" influence, which "breaks the shackles of tribal provincialism." [12]

Between 1887 and 1934, tribal lands dwindled from 138 million acres to about 46 million acres. Most individual allotments were too dry for farming, and most Indians could make no productive use of their holdings. With BIA approval, many leased their lands to white ranchers.

New Century Brings New Policies

In the early decades of the 20th century, evidence mounted that assimilation policies were not improving Indian welfare. Through the Indian Reorganization Act of 1934, Congress prohibited future allotments of tribal lands, returned remaining surplus lands to the tribes and empowered them to adopt written constitutions and set up governments to manage their internal affairs.

But the gains achieved by the Reorganization Act were short-lived. Sentiment began to grow in Congress for the "termination" of all federal Indian programs, including economic assistance and social services. Termination became a reality under the Eisenhower administration. A resolution adopted by both the House and the Senate in 1953 declared it to be the "policy of Congress, as rapidly as possible, to make the Indians … subject to the same laws and entitled to the same privileges and responsibilities as are applicable to other citizens of the United States."

Under this policy, several tribes were removed from federal supervision, or "terminated," in the late 1950s and early '60s.[13] The policy eventually fell into disuse, but Indians continued to fear that the government someday would break up their reservations, consigning Native Americans to a permanent pauper class within white society.

Indian frustration gave rise in the late 1960s and early '70s to a militant Red Power movement that led to numerous demonstrations. In the fall of 1972, the so-called "Trail of Broken Treaties" caravan brought nearly 1,000 Indians to Washington, D. C., where they demanded the reaffirmation of treaties as the basis of Indian-federal relations.

Early in 1973, the American Indian Movement (AIM) occupied BIA offices at Wounded Knee, S.D., setting in motion a long siege by federal law enforcement officers. When it ended after more than two months, two Indians were dead, a U.S. marshal was paralyzed and dozens of other persons were wounded.*

Tribal Autonomy

The policy pendulum began to swing back toward tribal autonomy in the late 1960s, when Washington made tribal governments eligible for several federal social welfare and economic-development programs. In 1970, President Richard M. Nixon reorganized the BIA. Native Americans were given top-level bureau positions, and federal funding for Indian programs was expanded.

Congress endorsed Nixon's policy

---

*Wounded Knee held symbolic significance for the protesters: In 1890 at least 200 Sioux men, women and children had been massacred there by the U.S. cavalry. The slaughter marked the end of the Indian wars.

by passing the Indian Self-Determination and Education Assistance Act of 1974, which permitted tribes to assume control and operation of many federal programs on reservations. The law acknowledged the government's role as trustee but shifted much of the control of federal programs to the Indians. In the same year, Congress also passed the Indian Financing Act, which provided grants and loans to help Indians exploit and manage their own resources. Additionally, the government encouraged defense contractors to open electronics assembly plants on Indian lands.

Initiatives taken under these new laws met with mixed success. Many of the development projects were ill-conceived, plagued by inadequate financing and poor management. Several reservation motels and resorts ran consistent losses; tribally built industrial parks stood nearly empty. When the electronics market faltered, some firms closed their reservation plants. Indian militancy also hampered development on the reservations. Taken together, these failures made Indians wary of relying solely on federally financed development programs or plants managed by outsiders to bring economic growth.

Despite these setbacks, President Ronald Reagan issued a Jan. 24, 1983, policy statement calling for the creation of a "favorable environment" to make reservations more economically self-sufficient. To this end, he urged greater involvement by private industry. Both the tribes and the country as a whole, he declared, "stand to gain from the prudent development and management of the vast coal, oil, gas, uranium and other resources found on Indian lands."

Reagan Administration Cuts Aid

At the same time, however, the Reagan administration made significant cuts in federal assistance to Native Americans. In 1983 alone, aid was slashed by more than one-third, from $3.5 billion to $2 billion, affecting programs on every reservation. Few tribes were able to recoup their losses from other sources.

The Reagan approach came under heavy fire from some Indian-affairs experts. "The Reagan administration has emphasized elitism and uncontrolled exploitation under the aegis of private enterprise, thereby creating a new divisiveness within the Indian reservation community," charged Vine Deloria Jr. and Clifford M. Lytle in their book *The Nations Within*. "Further, Reagan's gospel of reliance on the private sector is absurd when applied to reservations, where the only private enterprise has been the non-Indian trader and the mixed-blood rancher or storekeeper."[14]

Reagan, however, was selective in his support of Indian business development. In 1988, he pocket-vetoed (refused to sign) a bill that would have provided $100 million for an Indian Development Finance Commission to make loans to Indian business. "The bill would have created an expensive and unnecessary new bureaucracy and duplicated currently existing programs," the president asserted.

Two weeks earlier Reagan had signed into law a bill to regulate high-stakes bingo games and other forms of gambling on reservations. The Indian Gaming Regulatory Act was inspired in part by the discovery that some tribes were seeking to purchase land far from their reservations for the purpose of creating new enclaves exempt from local gambling regulations. This could have led, some members of Congress feared, to Indian gaming operations in most of the 50 states.

When a similar measure was being debated by the House in 1986, Rep. Morris K. Udall, D-Ariz., said it was not surprising that Indians were seeking revenue from gambling. "Just as there are many states turning to lotteries and other gaming activity to fill the gap left by federal cutbacks, so, too, are the Indian tribes," he said.

Senate Review of BIA

Federal Indian policy has undergone little revision during the Bush administration, though an opportunity to change direction arose during the president's first year in office. After two years of investigating fraud and mismanagement in the BIA and other federal agencies responsible for overseeing Indian programs, a special Senate investigative committee recommended in late 1989 that the BIA be dismantled. Instead, the committee suggested funneling federal funds directly to tribal governments.[15]

Under the committee's proposal, tribes would have received their customary share of the federal Indian budget, but as unrestricted block grants. In addition, tribal governments would have had to follow a written constitution approved by tribal members. Tribes also would have been subject to federal laws prohibiting corruption and guaranteeing fair elections.

These requirements were aimed at preventing the types of graft and corruption by tribal leaders that were publicized during hearings held earlier in 1989. The most celebrated case involved Peter MacDonald Sr., the suspended chairman of the Navajo tribe. On Oct. 17, 1990, he was convicted in Navajo Tribal Court of accepting $400,000 in bribes and kickbacks from businesses and individuals seeking to do business with the tribe. He was sentenced to five years and 335 days in jail and fined $11,000.

The primary focus of the committee's investigation, however, was mismanagement at the BIA, which has responsibility for overseeing a myriad of federal programs affecting Indians. For instance, the committee found

Ben Nighthorse Campbell

that a $200-million-a-year minority-preference program set up to aid Indian-owned companies was instead funneling funds to front companies set up by non-Indian contractors. Although a BIA division chief was alerted to the problem, little was done.

The committee's report also cited examples of neglect and corruption in other federal agencies: The Interior Department's Bureau of Land Management failed to detect millions of dollars in theft of oil and gas on Indian lands; the Indian Health Service (IHS) diverted $70,000 in federal funds from a juvenile alcohol-abuse prevention program to finance a fitness retreat for IHS managers.

"American Indians, and the nation, are being badly served by federal programs that do not accomplish their goals and by individuals more interested in lining their pockets," declared Sen. Dennis DeConcini, D-Ariz., who chaired the Senate Indian Affairs Special Committee on Investigations.

Despite the seriousness of the committee's findings, no legislative action was taken. Most Indian leaders were not surprised. After all, Congress had cited federal agencies for mismanagement in their handling of Indian programs on 42 occasions in the previous 83 years. Each time, congressional investigators urged reforms that either were not adopted or proved ineffective.

"We have been the victims of so many changing federal policies," Cherokee Chief Wilma P. Mankiller told the panel. "The best solutions to our problems are within our own communities." Sounding a similar note, Colorado Rep. Ben Nighthorse Campbell complained that "Indians have never had any political clout and very little voice in congressional matters." ∎

CURRENT SITUATION

Legislative Victories

Though Indian policy has remained constant under President Bush, he has approved several measures of enduring significance. In November 1989, for example, he signed a bill establishing a national museum of American Indian history and culture as part of the Smithsonian Institution in Washington *(see p. 402)*.

In a related matter, Bush signed legislation in October 1990 to protect Indian grave sites and return human remains to the tribes. The bill sought to balance the emotional requests of Indian tribes for the return of ancestral remains with the scholarly interests of scientists and museum officials.* Under existing law, human remains unearthed on federal lands were considered government property, to be preserved in museums or educational institutions. The 1990 law exempted the Smithsonian from its provisions.

Actually, the Smithsonian had reached a separate accommodation with Indian leaders on the remains issue a year earlier. On Sept. 9, 1989, the museum agreed to examine its estimated 18,000 skeletal remains and burial objects to determine their origins. A five-member committee, including three Indians, would oversee the inventory. If a "preponderance of evidence" linked the objects to direct descendants of the deceased or to a specific tribe, the Smithsonian would — upon request — return the objects.[16]

---

*The Dickson Mounds Museum in Lewiston, Ill., believed to be the last institution in the country with Indian remains on display, closed April 3 in response to pressure from Native American activists. Indian remains had been removed from public display earlier in Alabama, Georgia, Kansas and Kentucky.

Native Americans scored another triumph — largely symbolic — last December when President Bush signed into law a bill changing the name of Montana's Custer Battlefield National Monument to Little Bighorn National Battlefield Park. The law also established a memorial to the Indians who fought in the 1876 battle of Little Bighorn, in which Gen. George A. Custer and all 264 men under his immediate command were killed by Chief Crazy Horse's band of Sioux and Cheyenne warriors.

During House debate on the bill, Rep. Campbell said naming the park after Custer had been a slap in the face to Indians. However, Rep. John D. Dingell, D-Mich., the only member to speak in opposition, said the name change "demeans the American soldiers who died at Little Bighorn."

Indians had lobbied for decades to rename the Montana battlefield. But affronts to Native American pride continue to occur. In the same month Bush signed the Little Bighorn legislation, the San Diego City Council voted to place a 23-foot bronze statue of the Spanish explorer Vasco Núñez de Balboa in the city's central park, which bears his name. The council accepted the statue as a gift despite strenuous opposition from Indians, who noted that Balboa had been beheaded in Panama after being tried on charges of treason and mistreatment of natives.

Health Problems

Indians suffer inordinately from a range of health problems. The Indian death rate from diabetes, tuberculosis and sudden infant death syndrome is substantially higher than it is for other Americans. Moreover, poverty and social isolation make many Indians vulnerable to chronic ailments like depression, as well as abuse of alcohol and drugs. Indeed, Indians are far more likely to die of alcoholism than other U.S. races, and fetal alcohol syndrome is a serious problem.[17]

Many of the Indians' health problems can be linked to their economic condition. According to the 1980 census, 28 percent of the nation's 1.4 million Indians lived in poverty. A quarter of all reservation houses lacked complete plumbing such as running hot and cold water, a flush toilet or an indoor bathtub or shower. About 16 percent lacked electric lighting.

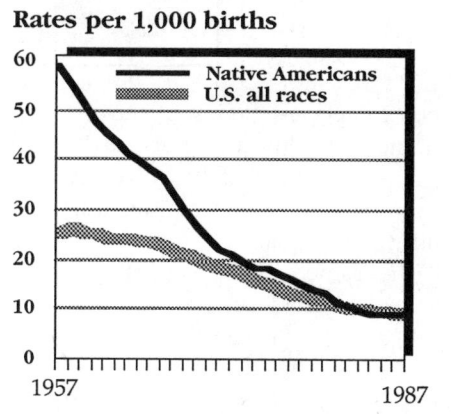

Infant Mortality Rates

Over the past three decades, the infant mortality rate for American Indian and Alaska Natives has been brought down to the U.S. average. However, the United States still has one of the highest infant mortality rates among industrialized countries.

Rates per 1,000 births

Native Americans
U.S. all races

1957   1987

Source: U.S. Public Health Service

Another part of the problem is Indians' isolation; many live in rugged areas where delivery of health care and retention of practitioners is iffy, at best. In some rural areas, for example, services must be rationed, with non-emergency cases sometimes waiting months for treatment.

Statistics underscore the problem with health-care delivery: On reservations, there are 96 doctors and 251 nurses per 100,000 people, compared with 208 doctors and 672 nurses for the general population. Indian health care "is abysmal," says Gerald Hill, head of the University of Minnesota Center for American Indian and Minority Health.[18]

All the same, some progress has been made. The Indian Health Service, created by Congress in 1921 to improve Indian health "to the highest level possible," has helped bring communicable diseases like tuberculosis, pneumonia and gastrointestinal ailments under control. The life expectancy of Indians has risen dramatically over the past few decades, infant mortality has been brought down to the U.S. average and more Indian preschoolers are regularly vaccinated than children in the general population. Today, most Indians die from the same killers that afflict the general public: heart disease, injuries, cancer, stroke and chronic liver disease, including cirrhosis.

Congress addressed Indian health and human-services issues in two laws enacted in 1990. One measure was inspired by findings of child molestation revealed in the 1989 report by the special Senate investigative panel *(see p. 398)*. According to the report, the BIA

Alcohol's Toll

More Native American men and women die from alcohol-related causes than any other racial group.

Native American deaths related to alcohol
Deaths per 100,000

■ Men
□ Women

34.7 — Native Americans (Men)
18.7 — Native Americans (Women)
19.1 — Blacks (Men)
7.1 — Blacks (Women)
9.8 — Whites (Men)
3.4 — Whites (Women)

Source: Alcoholism in Minority Populations

employed teachers who had admitted to sexual abuse of minors, including an individual who molested at least 25 Indian youngsters over 14 years. To guard against future offenses, Congress approved legislation seeking to ensure that workers dealing with Indian children didn't have criminal records. The law also prescribed fines and prison terms for anyone who did not report known instances of abuse.

A second law passed in 1990 mainly benefited urban Indians, who constitute about half the total Native American population. The law provided funds for immunization services, mental-health care, child-abuse treatment and a program of health awareness and disease prevention. Additional legislation of this kind may be proposed in response to new reports of serious health problems among Indians, especially youths.

According to a recent survey, a "sizable minority" of Native American students are particularly prone to suicidal tendencies, alcohol abuse and other unhealthful behaviors. "This is the most devastated group of adolescents in the United States," said Michael D. Resnick, an epidemiologist and one of the authors of the report.[19]

Youth Suicide Rate

Native American youths commit suicide at a far higher rate than youths of all other races.

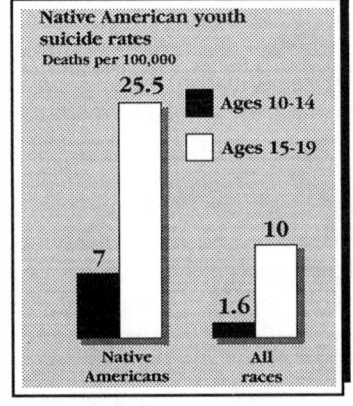

Native American youth suicide rates
Deaths per 100,000

■ Ages 10-14
□ Ages 15-19

25.5 — Native Americans (Ages 15-19)
7 — Native Americans (Ages 10-14)
10 — All races (Ages 15-19)
1.6 — All races (Ages 10-14)

Source: University of Minnesota

Business Prospects

Recent efforts by Native Americans to attain greater self-sufficiency through business development — a Reagan administration goal — are beginning to pay off. Though often lacking entrepreneurial experience, "Indians bring some real advantages to the business world," says Dan Fost, a contributing editor of *American Demographics* magazine. Their biggest edge, in his view, comes from the suspension of many local, state and federal taxes on Indian territory. "Reservations have no sales or property tax, so cigarettes, gasoline and other items can be sold for low prices."[20]

Steven L. A. Stallings, president of the National Center for American Indian Enterprise Development, in El Monte, Calif., feels value-added processes, such as finishing products made of metal or wood, form a business niche that Native Americans could profitably fill. He also sees a bright future in Indian-operated waste dumps. "We're not talking about nuclear waste or hazardous waste — just municipal waste," he says. "There's real opportunity and growing markets in refuse disposal."

Tourism also offers room for growth, in Stallings' opinion. He suggests Indians ought to experiment with on-reservation "boutique tourism," which he defines as "a bed-and-breakfast package giving people a Native American experience in a picturesque setting." He says marketing surveys indicate there is considerable

Continued on p. 402

At Issue:

Should Native Americans celebrate the 500th anniversary of Columbus' first voyage to the Americas?

MICHAEL S. BERLINER

Executive director, Ayn Rand Institute
FROM *LOS ANGELES TIMES*, DEC. 30, 1991

*t*he politically correct view is that Columbus did not discover America, because people had lived here for thousands of years. Worse yet is the assertion that Columbus' main legacy was death and destruction....

Did Columbus "discover" America? Yes, in every important respect. This does not mean that no human eye had been cast on America before 1492. It means that Columbus brought America to the attention of the civilized world — that is, to the civilizations of Western Europe, which were then emerging into an era of great creativity, scientific achievement and philosophical ferment. The result, ultimately, was the United States of America....

Before 1492, what is now the United States was sparsely inhabited, unused and undeveloped. The inhabitants were primarily wandering hunter/gatherers, living hand-to-mouth and day-to-day. There was virtually no change, no growth for thousands of years. There was no wheel, no written language, little agriculture and scant permanent settlement, but there were endless, bloody wars. With rare exception, life was nasty, brutish and short.

Whatever the problems it brought, the vilified Western culture also brought enormous, undreamed-of benefits, without which most of today's Indians would be infinitely poorer or not even alive.

Columbus should be honored, for in so doing, we honor Western civilization. But the critics do not want to bestow such honor, and this is the real reason for the opposition to celebrating Columbus as the discoverer of America. The critics' real goal is to denigrate the values of Western civilization and to glorify the primitivism, mysticism and collectivism embodied in the tribal cultures of American Indians. They decry the glorification of the West as "Eurocentrism." We should, they claim, replace our reverence for Western civilization with multiculturalism, which regards all cultures as morally equal. In fact, they aren't....

Underlying the political collectivism of the anti-Columbus crowd is a racist view of human nature. They claim that one's identity is primarily ethnic: If one thinks one's ancestors were good, one supposedly will feel good about oneself; if one thinks one's ancestors were bad, one will feel self-loathing. But it doesn't work; the achievements or failures of one's ancestors are monumentally irrelevant to one's worth as a person.

HANS KONING

Novelist and essayist
FROM *THE NEW YORK TIMES*, AUG. 14, 1990

*y*ou are spoiling the pleasure of our children," a woman said to an American Indian who was demonstrating outside a 1992 exhibition already circulating in the Southeast. That exhibition is called "First Encounters."

The miserable truth is that those first encounters on the Indian side quickly led to last encounters. The Indians of the Caribbean were destroyed within two generations by the Spanish discoverers. Not one of them was converted to the Catholic faith, which was supposedly a prime motive of those voyages. They died when they were hanged, in rows of 13, "in honor of the Redeemer and His 12 Apostles," according to the original Spanish documents.

They had their hands cut off when they did not bring in their quarterly quota of gold dust. Their chiefs were roasted on fires of green wood. When their cries kept the Spaniards awake, they were silenced with wooden slats put over their tongues. Ten years after the first landing, the miserable native survivors started killing themselves by eating poisoned roots.

Yes, Christopher Columbus was the first European to sail to America in recorded history. But Columbus set into motion a sequence of greed, cruelty, slavery and genocide that, even in the bloody history of mankind, has few parallels. He organized an extermination of Native Americans. He was also as mean, cruel and greedy in small matters as he was in vast ones.

I am not giving any radical opinions here. These aren't new facts. You can find them substantiated in the logs of Columbus' son, in the writing of Bartolomé de las Casas, a Spanish bishop and historian of the time, and in plenty of other period documents.

It may seem a pity to let go of dear national lore. But we can no longer in good faith celebrate this man and this occasion. We must look at our own past with open eyes.

We must end the phony baloney about the white man bringing Christianity, and about Columbus the noble son of the humble weaver. Our false heroes and a false sense of the meaning of courage and manliness have too long burdened our national spirit.

We must set out for a new harmony of races, for an atonement of past crimes. In that way, we have a truly New World to discover.

Continued from p. 400

interest in such tours among foreign visitors, particularly those from Germany, Japan and Scandinavia.

Stallings is less enthusiastic about the commercial possibilities offered by the revival of interest in Native American crops and foodstuffs. He cautions that food marketing is difficult to master. "We have some people who are in food products, mainly things like wild rice," he says. "But if you don't have the proper distribution channels to the retailer, it's a real tough business to be in."

The Navajos found a way around the problem. They grow a vegetable that is at once traditionally Indian and familiar to all — the potato. At their farm near Farmington, N.M., the Navajos last year harvested 112,000 tons of potatoes, which accounted for 40 percent, or $12.6 million, of the farm's gross revenues. About half the crop is marketed fresh; the rest goes into packaged chips. The Navajo tribe is now the biggest supplier of potatoes to Frito-Lay Inc., the country's largest snack-food company.[21]

Indian Newspaper Opens Washington Bureau

Another Indian enterprise, *The Lakota Times,* of Rapid City, S.D., is banking on increased Indian consciousness to expand its market. The weekly, which was founded in 1981 and now claims a 10,000 circulation, recently opened a Washington bureau because, says Publisher Tim Giago, "Almost all Indian tribes in the United States are impacted by the agencies in Washington."

Eventually, Giago plans to open several additional bureaus — "one in every area of the United States where there are large numbers of Indians." Each bureau "might serve 10 or 15 reservations, but it'll have its own section of the paper."

Because the paper supports sovereignty and tribal rights, its editorial policy on local matters relies heavily on feedback from readers. But on national issues, says Giago, tribal opinions tend to coalesce. "When there's a case that's going all the way to the Supreme Court or an issue involving sovereignty or signing compacts with states for gaming, the tribes take pretty much the same position. Tribes are really hanging together more strongly now." ∎

OUTLOOK

Plotting the Future

Christopher Columbus, though certainly no hero to Indians, has provided, ironically, a map of the future for Native Americans. As the Oct. 12 anniversary of the explorer's first landing in the Americas draws closer, Europeans and white Americans are looking back half a millennium and trying to put the famed mariner in historical perspective. Indians, on the other hand, are looking half a millennium ahead. "Enough with Columbus," says the Morning Star Foundation's Harjo. "Forget him. The important thing now is, what's next? Where do we see things going?"

To find out, the foundation two years ago took the lead in establishing the 1992 Alliance, a coalition of individual Indians and tribes. It called on "all people everywhere to join us on Oct. 12, 1992, in tribute to and thanksgiving for those indigenous people and nations who have survived the excesses of 'civilization,' especially those who remain as peoples with rich cultures and traditions." The alliance also challenged historians, teachers, scientists, journalists, clergy and others to re-examine their thinking about Native Americans.

Giago, for one, is cautiously optimistic: "For once, and the quincentennial of Columbus may be the year it could happen, white America can make an effort to see this nation through the eyes of the Indian people, and maybe then they will understand why Indians will never be assimilated into a melting pot that would destroy them as a people."[22]

New Indian Museum Hailed

Indian leaders see the National Museum of the American Indian, scheduled to open in the year 2000, as a workshop for crafting more positive perceptions of Native Americans. At the same time, the museum may help overcome Indians' longstanding suspicion of institutions that exhibit tribal paraphernalia and burial remains.

Harjo, a museum director, says it will be a "living" institution — not just a collection of art objects and implements but a forum for Indian intellectuals, artisans and performing artists. Moreover, tribal leaders are being consulted about artifacts under consideration for display. The inquiries are not to determine who "owns" a given item, or even who created it, but to identify the people whose cultural traditions it expresses.

Giago endorses the museum's collaborative approach, noting that "most Indians look at museums with jaundiced eyes, simply because that's where the remains of a lot of our ancestors were stored." Billing it as a living museum "shows we are a living, breathing, surviving culture."

Threats to Tribal Rights

Indeed, fighting perceived threats to the Indians' survival is an ongoing task, leaders say. One of their major worries is an apparent erosion of concern in both Congress and the courts for Native American rights.

Robert T. Coulter, executive director of the Indian Law Resource Center (ILRC) in Helena, Mont., notes that Indian tribes "have a lot of inherent rights that [in the past] have always been recognized by the courts," including aboriginal title to land, self-government, immunity from state taxation and freedom to hunt and fish. But in recent years, he says, "The courts have been limiting or doing away entirely with these rights, leaving Indian rights increasingly to Congress."

The trend has not gone unnoticed at the Native American Rights Fund, where attorneys feel that with the current conservative makeup of the Supreme Court, federal legislation offers Indians more hope for protection than the judicial system.

The trouble, says Coulter, is that Congress also has shown insensitivity to Indian rights. He says the Hoopa-Yurok Settlement Act of 1988 was especially galling to many Indians, not least the Yuroks. The law sought to conclude a 25-year-old dispute between the Hoopa and Yurok Indians over timber rights on the Hoopa Valley Reservation, California's largest. Court decisions handed down over that period had consistently upheld the Yuroks' claims to an equal share of timber profits.

But Congress, in effect, reversed the court rulings by awarding the reservation's timber rights to the Hoopas. The law also established membership standards for the Yurok tribe — a matter traditionally left for Native Americans to decide. Under the law, Indians of Yurok ancestry were given the choice of joining the Yurok tribe (and thus becoming eligible for government aid) and waiving all rights to sue the federal government in the future, or accepting a $15,000 lump-sum payment, in effect "terminating" their rights as Native Americans.

Coulter calls the settlement act "just an outrage, an absolute outrage." A suit filed by a group of Yurok Indians seeks to invalidate the 1988 act, alleging, among other things, that the provision on tribal membership violated their First Amendment rights of free association.

"If Congress can do this to the Yurok," says Curtis Berkey, director of the ILRC's Washington office, "it can do it to any tribe. Indians across the country will be watching this case to see what happens." [23] ∎

Notes

[1] Address before the National Congress of American Indians in San Francisco, Dec. 6, 1991.

[2] Letter in the *Los Angeles Times,* Jan. 9, 1992.

[3] Quoted in *The Chronicle of Higher Education,* Dec. 4, 1991.

[4] Letters and phone calls to *The Oregonian* have overwhelmingly opposed the paper's new policy, says Managing Editor Peter Thompson. Quoted in *Editor & Publisher* magazine, March 21, 1992.

[5] Tim Giago, "'Our Past Is a Part of Our Tomorrow,'" *The Christian Science Monitor,* March 27, 1992, p. 12.

[6] Quoted by Dan Baum in "Sacred Places," *Mother Jones* magazine, March/April 1992, p. 34.

[7] Stephen Cornell, *The Return of the Native: American Indian Political Resurgence* (1988), p. 107.

[8] *Ibid.,* p. 114.

[9] Eugene M. Christiansen, "U.S. Gaming Handle Up 14 percent in '90," *Gaming & Wagering Business* magazine, July 15-Aug. 14, 1991, p. 32.

[10] Leonard Prescott, "Gambling Offers Escape From Poverty," *USA Today,* Feb. 6, 1992. Prescott is a former chairman of Minnesota's Shakopee Sioux tribe.

[11] National Center for American Indian Enterprise Development, *Growing Market Opportunities for Indian Reservation Enterprises,* April 1991, pp. 71-72.

[12] Quoted in Cornell, *op. cit.,* pp. 56, 114.

[13] The terminated tribes included Wisconsin's Menominees, Oregon's Klamath and the Wyandotte, Peoria and Ottawa in Oklahoma. For background on the issue of termination, see *Congress and the Nation Vol. I, 1945-1964* (1965), published by Congressional Quarterly.

[14] Vine Deloria Jr. and Clifford M. Lytle, *The Nations Within: The Past and Future of American Indian Sovereignty* (1984), p. 259.

[15] See *Congressional Quarterly Almanac, Vol. XLV,* 1989, pp. 369-371.

[16] For background information on the controversy over Indian remains and artifacts, see "Is America Allowing Its Past to be Stolen?" *Editorial Research Reports,* Jan. 18, 1991, pp. 38-39.

[17] "The Indian Health Service: A Flawed Diamond," *Medicine & Health Perspectives,* March 2, 1992.

[18] Quoted in *USA Today,* Nov. 12, 1991.

[19] Quoted in *Education Week,* April 1, 1992.

[20] *American Demographics,* December 1991, p. 34.

[21] Guy Webster, "Digging Up Riches: Navajo Potato Fields Are Showing Big Profits," *Indian Business and Management,* December 1991, p. 9.

[22] Giago, *op. cit.,* p. 12

[23] Quoted by Susan E. Davis, "Tribal Rights, Tribal Wrongs," *The Nation,* March 23, 1992, p. 376.

Bibliography

Selected Sources Used

Books

Brown, Dee, *Bury My Heart at Wounded Knee: An Indian History of the American West,* **Holt, Rinehart & Winston, 1970.**

Brown's sobering account of the injustices experienced by American Indians, together with Vine Deloria's 1969 book, *Custer Died for Your Sins,* served as a rallying point for Indians during the militant 1960s and early '70s and also alerted white America to the depth of Native America's anger and sense of betrayal.

Cornell, Stephen, *The Return of the Native: American Indian Political Resurgence,* **Oxford University Press, 1988.**

Cornell, a Harvard University sociologist, traces the reawakening of Indian political consciousness and suggests that a new feeling of tribal solidarity helped the process unfold. He concludes that "The next stage of Indian-white relations remains unknown, but it seems certain that, in some substantial measure ... it will be Indian-made."

Deloria, Vine Jr., *Custer Died for Your Sins: An Indian Manifesto,* **The Macmillan Co., 1969.**

Deloria, a professor of Indian studies at the University of Arizona, writes that "The primary goal and need of Indians today is not for someone to feel sorry for us and claim descent from Pocahontas to make us feel better.... What we need is a cultural leave-us-alone agreement, in spirit and in fact."

Deloria, Vine Jr., ed., *American Indian Policy in the 20th Century,* **University of Oklahoma Press, 1985.**

Deloria and 10 other contributors cover a wide range of topics of concern to Indians, including tribal government, voting, cultural values, water rights and the evolution of federal policy toward Indian tribes.

Josephy, Alvin M. Jr., *Red Power: The American Indians' Fight for Freedom,* **American Heritage Press, 1971.**

This book largely consists of documents and speeches by or about Indians, dating from the pivotal 1960s and '70s. The concluding essay, by Vine Deloria Jr., is titled, "This Country Was a Lot Better Off When the Indians Were Running It."

Prucha, Francis Paul, *American Indian Policy in the Formative Years,* **University of Nebraska Press, 1962.**

Though much has changed since the period covered by Prucha (1790-1834), early developments in U.S. government policy toward Indian tribes provide valuable insights about current policy.

Thornton, Russell, *American Indian Holocaust and Survival: A Population History Since 1492,* **University of Oklahoma Press, 1987.**

Thornton explains why the population of American Indians declined for more than 400 years starting in about 1500, and then rebounded.

Articles

Durning, Alan Thein, "Native Americans Stand Their Ground," *World Watch,* **November-December 1991.**

Indians in the United States are not the only aboriginal peoples of the Western Hemisphere reasserting their rights. As Durning notes, similar native movements have arisen throughout the Americas, from the Arctic to Tierra del Fuego.

Kerr, Scott, "The New Indian Wars," *The Progressive,* **April 1990.**

Focusing mainly on Wisconsin, Kerr describes how Indians are becoming more assertive in claiming their rights under treaties negotiated more than a century ago with the federal government.

Reports and Studies

National Center for American Indian Enterprise Development, *Growing Market Opportunities for Indian Reservation Enterprises,* **April 1991.**

In this survey, the center assesses the profit potential of various business enterprises suitable for Indians living on reservations.

Subcommittee on National Parks and Public Lands, U.S. House Committee on Interior and Insular Affairs, *Custer Battlefield National Monument Indian Memorial,* **(published proceedings of hearing held Sept. 4, 1990).**

Witnesses debate a bill to establish a memorial at Montana's Custer Battlefield National Monument to honor the Indians who fought in the 1876 Battle of Little Bighorn.

Walke, Roger, *Federal Programs of Assistance to Native Americans,* **Congressional Research Service, (report prepared for the Senate Select Committee on Indian Affairs), December 1991.**

Proceeding alphabetically, Walke lists and briefly describes the numerous programs designed expressly to benefit American Indians.

The Next Step

Additional Articles from Current Periodicals from EBSCO Publishing's Database

Alcohol use

Hill, T.W., "Peyotism and the control of heavy drinking: The Nebraska Winnebago in the early 1900s," *Human Organization,* **fall 1990, p. 255.**

Describes the drinking practices of the Winnebago Indians from the early 1860s until the early 1920s and relates these drinking patterns to the changing sociocultural environment. Peyotism as a native therapeutic system; treatment of excessive drinking; relationship between Peyotism and abstinence; more.

Kolata, G., "A new toll of alcohol abuse: The Indians' next generation," *The New York Times,* **July 19, 1989, p. A1.**

Examines the devastating effects of alcohol abuse among Indians on the next generation. Negative influence of maternal drinking on infants' mental and physical health; efforts to control and punish maternal alcoholism; alcohol recovery program, Project Recovery, run by Jeaneen Grey Eagle at the Pine Ridge Reservation in South Dakota.

Books & reading

Kawashima, Y., "Book reviews," *Journal of American History,* **December 1991, p. 1047.**

Reviews the book "The Pequots in Southern New England: The Fall and Rise of an American Indian Nation," edited by Laurence M. Hauptman and James D. Wherry.

Robinson, W.S., "Book reviews," *Journal of American History,* **December 1991, p. 1046.**

Reviews the book "Pocahontas' People: The Powhatan Indians of Virginia Through Four Centuries," by Helen C. Roundtree.

Stuttaford, G., "Forecasts: Nonfiction," *Publishers Weekly,* **Jan. 6, 1992, p. 58.**

Reviews the book "Stolen Continents: The Americas Through Indian Eyes Since 1492," by Ronald Wright.

Case studies

Egan, T., "Back from oblivion, a tribe forges a future," *The New York Times,* **Nov. 25, 1991, p. A1.**

Describes how the Siletz American Indian tribe is struggling for the restoration of its land, its sovereign status and its tribal identity, which was taken from it in the 1950s as part of a government policy known as termination. The Indians have cleared a swath in the woods and constructed a new community of big homes and broad streets, where unemployment is well below the national average, drugs and alcohol are not allowed and the budget shows a healthy surplus.

Gruson, L., "Town learns the Indians are taking it all back," *The New York Times,* **Dec. 2, 1991, p. B1.**

Tells about Salamanca, N.Y., the only town in the country built almost entirely on an Indian reservation. Now the Seneca Indians are claiming ownership, the residents are up in arms, tensions are building and some families have obtained permits to dynamite their homes rather than turn them over to the Senecas.

List, S.K., "The great American Indian pencil," *American Demographics,* **January 1992, p. 34.**

Discusses The Blackfeet Indian Writing Co., Montana, its history, accomplishments and reputation. Founder Earl Old Person; Earth pencil; for more information; more.

Columbus, Christopher

Gregory, D., "A red light for Columbus," *History Today,* **December 1991, p. 5.**

Reports that Nelson Mandela, ANC leader, is the latest recruit to the movement opposing Columbus' Quincentennial celebrations. He has given personal assurance to the International Indian Treaty Council that he will join the protest planning to greet the replica ships of the *Nina, Pinta* and *Santa Maria* when they sail into San Francisco Bay on Oct. 12, 1992 — marking the day Columbus landed in the Americas. Further protest plans; the focus of the protests.

Harjo, S.S., "I won't be celebrating Columbus Day," *Newsweek,* **fall/winter91, Columbus issue, p. 32.**

Opinion. Asserts that for Native people, it is time for 500 years of suffering to come to an end. Obscene amount of money that will be lavished over the next year on parades, statues and festivals; pressure on Native people to be window dressing for Quincentennial events; need to enter a time of grace and healing; call to educate the colonizing nations of the bloodshed and destruction.

Helle, S. "Anthropologists examine commemorations of Columbus' fateful voyage," *The Chronicle of Higher Education,* **Dec. 18, 1991, p. A9.**

Focuses on how the commemoration of Christopher Columbus' 1492 voyage has degenerated into an argument over words such as encounter, invasion and conquest. Reaction at the American Anthropological Association's annual meeting to Indian scholars who have mobilized to challenge interpretations of the event; negotiations and compromises by the Library of Congress, the Newberry Library, the Smithsonian on displays for Columbus-related exhibits; marking, and marketing, the event.

Debates & issues

"What you don't know about Indians," Utne Reader, November/December 1991, p. 67.

Reprints an excerpt from the book "In the Absence of the Sacred: The Failure of Technology and the Rise of the Indian Nations," by Jerry Mander. The incorrect tendency of most Americans to think of Indian issues as tragedies of the distant past; avoidance of the current situation; "New Age" awareness of Indians' spiritual practices but lack of awareness of their political struggles.

Deloria, V. Jr., "Commentary: Research, redskins, and reality," American Indian Quarterly, fall 1991, p. 457.

Comments on observations and reflections of a personal nature on the present state of Indian-scholar/researcher relations. Author's complaints against researchers; shortcomings of the research done by writers Ruth Beebe Hill and Peter Matthiessen on the issue of Indian lifestyle; Indians at a great disadvantage due to misrepresentations written about their culture.

Hafford, W., "Along the way," Arizona Highways, October 1991, p. 2.

Opinion. Recounts how the traditionally peaceful Hopi Indians were pushed by American government interference to fight among themselves. Tells how the Hopis peacefully settled their problems, disregarding federal efforts.

Mathews, T., "The Custer syndrome," Newsweek, Sept. 30, 1991, p. 34.

Considers the Custer syndrome, known as the curse of the West. Questions about who owns the West. Native Americans who were in place long before white men came; the Sioux who took the Black Hills from the Crow before Custer; seductive power of the Western landscape; Big Horn Mountains in Wyoming; Washington's unfavorable role in the argument over the West; many myths of the West; comments by Paul Fees, senior curator of the Buffalo Bill Historical Center in Cody, Wyo.

Matthiessen, P. and B. Cronin, "The trials of Leonard Peltier," Esquire, January 1992, p. 55.

States that the American Indian leader Leonard Peltier has been serving two consecutive life sentences for the killing of two FBI agents in the June 26, 1975, shoot-out at Wounded Knee on the Pine Ridge Reservation in South Da-

kota. Demanded a federal review of the Treaty of 1868; the government's military response; 15 years served; "In the Spirit of Crazy Horse"; improper withholding of data and records; Mister X; details.

Drug use

Wallace, J. M. Jr., and J. G. Bachman, "Explaining racial/ethnic differences in adolescent drug use," Social Problems, August 1991, p. 333.

Studies whether the often large racial/ethnic differences in cigarette, alcohol, marijuana and cocaine use are attributable to racial/ethnic differences in background or important lifestyle factors. Results that indicate that controlling for background alone does not account for most racial/ethnic differences in drug use; drug use among Native American youth; more.

Economic conditions

"The landless landed," Economist, June 8, 1991, p. 31.

Presents the fifth in a series of articles examining ethnic groups in America, this one focusing on the American Indians. Standard of living; unemployment; poverty; diversity of the more than 300 tribes; economic outlook; example of the Navajos; tourism industry; alcohol; need for reform of land policies; Bureau of Indian Affairs; Peterson Zah, the elected leader of the Navajos; details.

Miller, A., "Indian Tribes, Incorporated," Newsweek, Dec. 5, 1988, p. 40.

Discusses the increasing number of Indian tribes turning entrepreneur, entering the business arena with force. Many tribes are trying to combat high unemployment, alcoholism and poor housing conditions with ingenuity, using large land-claim settlements to start businesses. Examples.

Smith, G. and K. Jarecke, "Shadow of a nation," Sports Illustrated, Feb. 18, 1991, p. 60.

Looks at the social conditions on the Crow Indian reservation in Montana. Importance of high school basketball to the community; poverty and alcoholism; profile of Jonathan Takes Enemy, a former basketball star at Lodge Grass High; problems most players have adjusting in college; more.

Education

Tice, T. N., "Indian children," Education Digest, October 1991, p. 33.

Discusses research by Danielle M. Hornett, which offers a perspective on why the achievement of Indian students declines the longer they stay in school after grade four. Social functioning and identity formation; need for longitudinal studies that trace individuals of diverse backgrounds through schools and identify obstacles to children's development within school systems; article in the Fall 1990 issue of *Action in Teacher Education*; more.

Gambling

Baker, J. N., D. Rosenberg, et al., "Gambling on the reservation," *Newsweek,* **Feb. 17, 1992, p. 29.**

Reports that Native Americans hope to make gambling casinos pay off. Tribes that face stricter regulation from the recently formed National Indian Gaming Commission; use of casinos to reduce welfare rolls; unemployment rates among Native Americans.

Johnson, K., "Betting, in harmony with nature," *The New York Times,* **Jan. 29, 1992, p. B1.**

Tells about the $58 million casino that is being built by the Mashantucket Pequot Indians in Connecticut and is scheduled to open Feb. 15. Conflicts between ancient tradition and hard-headed profit-making; hope that the casino will revive the tribe's economy.

Health aspects

Nakamura, R. M., R. King, et al., "Excess infant mortality in an American Indian population, 1940 to 1990," *Journal of the American Medical Association,* **Oct. 23, 1991, p. 2244.**

Describes the infant mortality experience of an American Indian community and demonstrates the utility of examining community-level mortality data. Describes a population-based historical review of infant death certificates at the Warm Springs Indian Reservation, in Oregon.

History

Bosveld, J., "Forgotten founders," *Omni,* **February 1992, p. 33.**

Considers the book "Forgotten Founders: How the American Indian Helped Shape Democracy," by Bruce E. Johansen, which describes how the Iroquois constitution, the Great Law of Peace, helped shape the basis for the U.S. Constitution. Meetings between Benjamin Franklin and Iroquois leaders; Franklin's view of the Iroquois system as a model on which to base the Union; congressional resolution acknowledging the contribution of the Iroquois; historical amnesia.

Law & legislation

Dumas, K., "Bill would permit crime prosecution," *Congressional Quarterly Weekly Report,* **Oct. 5, 1991, p. 2877.**

Considers the Senate Select Committee on Indian Affairs' approval of legislation (S 962) that would give tribes permanent authority over all Indians within the tribes' territory, allowing them to have authority to prosecute Indians who are not members of their tribes for misdemeanor crimes. Support from both the House and Senate; the Senate committee's approval of two other bills (S 1720 and S 1287).

Dumas, K., "Bills settle claim, offer tribes aid," *Congressional Quarterly Weekly Report*, **Nov. 16, 1991, p. 3389.**

Discusses how several bills aimed at benefiting Native American tribes were either passed by the House or approved for floor consideration the week of Nov. 11, 1991. The House's voice vote approval on legislation (HR 932) that would give the Aroostook Band of Micmac Indians federal recognition as an Indian tribe; veto threat; other legislation approved.

Research

Raymond, C., "Growth of scholarship on American Indians brings new insights about native cultures," *The Chronicle of Higher Education,* **Jan. 15, 1992, p. A8.**

Focuses on the insight recent research is providing into longstanding puzzles in the anthropology of tribes and into the remarkable resilience of Indian cultures in the face of enormous social, political and economic pressures over the 500 years since the arrival of Europeans. Explores the nature of resistance to colonialism, biases in traditional ethnographies, uses of oral histories, character of America's Colonial period; comments from scholars; uneasy relations.

Sports

"O-F-F-E-N-S-E," *U.S. News & World Report,* **Nov. 4, 1991, p. 22.**

Reports that fury over the Atlanta Braves' "tomahawk chop" cheer last week drew attention to team names that American Indians find offensive. Most Irish Americans have no problem with names like the Celtics and the Fighting Irish.

Giago, T., "I hope the Redskins lose," *Newsweek,* **Jan. 27, 1992, p. 8.**

Opinion. States that the national media have finally caught on to the complaints American Indians have been voicing for years. The media will gather in Minneapolis for Super Bowl Sunday on Jan. 26 to cover what will be the largest protest by American Indians against a professional football team in the history of the country. Complaint that Indians are people, not mascots; a new awareness of the Indian; efforts of Sen. Paul Simon, D-Ill.; a matter of dignity.

Reilly, R., "Let's bust those chops," *Sports Illustrated,* **Oct. 28, 1991, p. 110.**

Editorial. Denounces the way Native Americans have been caricatured by professional sports teams. Focus on the Atlanta Braves fans' "tomahawk chop" controversy and war cries during games; why such actions offend Native Americans.

Back Issues

Great Research on Current Issues Starts Right Here... Recent topics covered by The CQ Researcher are listed below. Issues dated before May 10, 1991, were published under the name of Editorial Research Reports.

OCTOBER 1990
Organ Transplants
Energy Policy Options
Search for Arab Unity
Child Support

NOVEMBER 1990
Lotteries and Gambling
Post-Cold War Choices
Setting Limits on Medical Care
Multicultural Education

DECEMBER 1990
Cable TV Regulation
Americans' Search for Their Roots
Is Insurance System a Failure?
Why Schools Still Have Tracking

JANUARY 1991
Growing Influence of Boycotts
Should the U.S. Reinstate the Draft?
America's Archaeological Past
Peace Corps' Challenges in '90s

FEBRUARY 1991
Regional Impact of Recession
Puerto Rico's Status
Redistricting: Mapping Power
Nuclear Power

MARCH 1991
Acid Rain
Cost of the Gulf War
Reassessing Gun Laws
Future for Man in Space

APRIL 1991
Social Security
Canadian Crisis Over Quebec
California Drought
Electromagnetic Radiation

MAY 1991
School Choice
Racial Quotas
Animal Rights
U.S. and Japan

JUNE 1991
Children and Divorce
Teenage Suicide
Endangered Species
Europe 1992

JULY 1991
Teenagers and Abortion
Soviet Republics Rebel
Mexico's Emergence
Athletes and Drugs

AUGUST 1991
Sexual Harassment
Fetal Tissue Research
Oil Imports
The Palestinians

SEPTEMBER 1991
Police Brutality
Advertising Under Attack
Saving the Forests
Foster Care Crisis

OCTOBER 1991
Pay-Per-View TV
Youth Gangs
Gene Therapy
World Hunger

NOVEMBER 1991
Fast-Food Shake-Up
The Greening of Eastern Europe
Business' Role in Education
Cuba In Crisis

DECEMBER 1991
Retiree Health Benefits
Asian Americans
The Obscenity Debate
The Disabilities Act

JANUARY 1992
Term Limits
Oil Spills
Hunting Controversy
Alternative Medicine

FEBRUARY 1992
Threatened Coastlines
New Era in Asia
Assisted Suicide
Jobs in the '90s

MARCH 1992
Women and Sports
Underage Drinking
Garbage Crisis
Mafia Crackdown

APRIL 1992
Ozone Depletion
Welfare Reform
Politicians and Privacy
Illegal Immigration

Back issues are available for $4.00 (sub-scribers) or $7.00 (non-subscribers). Quantity discounts apply to orders over ten. To order, call Congressional Quarterly 1-800-432-2250.

Future Topics

▶ *Jobs vs. the Environment*

▶ *Litigation Reform*

▶ *Salary Fairness*

PUBLISHED BY CONGRESSIONAL QUARTERLY INC., IN CONJUNCTION WITH EBSCO PUBLISHING

Jobs vs. Environment

Should jobs be sacrificed for the sake of environmental protection?

EFFORTS TO PROTECT THE NORTHERN SPOTTED owl have sparked an impassioned debate that echoes far beyond the endangered bird's habitat in the Pacific Northwest. Safeguarding the owl means setting limits on lumbering in the region's ancient forests. That means lost profits and lost jobs in one of the Northwest's leading traditional industries as well as in communities that support the logging industry. Hard-pressed residents of Washington, Oregon and northern California are unwilling to sacrifice "jobs for owls." Environmentalists counter that both will disappear within a few years if loggers continue to destroy what they say is a non-renewable resource. The Bush administration and others contend that the controversy is illusory, because economic growth and environmental protection are not incompatible.

INSIDE

THIS ISSUE

THE ISSUES...............................411
BACKGROUND..........................417
CHRONOLOGY..........................419
CURRENT SITUATION...............422
OUTLOOK................................426
BIBLIOGRAPHY.........................428
THE NEXT STEP.......................429

May 15, 1992 • Volume 2, No. 18 • 409-432

Formerly Editorial Research Reports

COVER ART: BARBARA SASSA-DANIELS

CQ Researcher

May 15, 1992
Volume 2, No. 18

EDITOR
Sandra Stencel

MANAGING EDITOR
Thomas J. Colin

ASSOCIATE EDITOR
Richard L. Worsnop

STAFF WRITERS
Charles S. Clark
Mary H. Cooper
Rodman D. Griffin

PRODUCTION EDITOR
Laurie De Maris

EDITORIAL ASSISTANT
Michael M. Taylor

GRAPHICS
Jack Auldridge

PUBLISHED BY
Congressional Quarterly Inc.

CHAIRMAN
Andrew Barnes

VICE CHAIRMAN
Andrew P. Corty

EDITOR AND PUBLISHER
Neil Skene

EXECUTIVE EDITOR
Robert W. Merry

PUBLICATIONS MARKETING/SALES
Robert Smith

EDITOR, EBSCO PUBLISHING
Melissa Kummerer

The CQ Researcher (ISSN 1056-2036). Formerly Editorial Research Reports. Published weekly (48 times per year, not printed the first Friday of any month with five Fridays) by Congressional Quarterly Inc., 1414 22nd St., N.W., Washington, D.C. 20037. Rates are furnished upon request. Second-class postage paid at Washington, D.C. POSTMASTER: Send address changes to The CQ Researcher, 1414 22nd St., N.W., Washington, D.C. 20037.

Jobs vs. Environment

BY MARY H. COOPER

THE ISSUES

In the Pacific Northwest, a popular bumper sticker reads, "Save a Logger. Kill an Owl." A few dead owls, indeed, have been found — nailed to fence posts near some of the region's more depressed communities. Such is the anger felt by residents of Washington, Oregon and California who depend on the timber industry for their livelihoods. They say that federal environmental policies have destroyed thousands of the industry's jobs and thousands more among the many businesses that support the timber industry.

The focus of this increasingly emotional debate is the northern spotted owl, a reclusive inhabitant of the Pacific Northwest's ancient forests. Two years ago, the rare bird was listed under the 1973 Endangered Species Act as threatened with extinction. The listing required that steps be taken to protect the owl's habitat — more than 6 million acres of old-growth forest. But the timber industry wants to harvest trees on the land. (See "At Issue," p. 425.)

The square-off between loggers and environmentalists reflects a fundamental problem for policy-makers that goes beyond the Pacific Northwest. As sensitivity to environmental degradation grows, such conflicts seem likely to intensify.

Although the signs of mounting public concern over the environment can be readily found in the demand for ecologically sensitive "green" products and the unexpected success of community recycling programs, such enthusiasm often dissipates when jobs are at stake. A recent poll found that only 4 percent of Oregon voters and 8 percent of Washington voters would be willing to protect

the owl at all if it cost 10,000 jobs or more. That is less than a third of the jobs that would be lost under the current protection plan (see p. 414).[1]

Despite the volatility of the issue, there is surprisingly little official government information about the impact of environmental regulations on employment. This year's annual report of the Council on Environmental Quality, an executive branch agency that advises the president on environmental issues, makes no mention of the matter.

"We have not studied this issue in the aggregate," concedes a senior environmental economist in the Bush administration, who spoke on condition he not be identified. "Part of the problem is the difficulty of getting those estimates. From a professional economist's viewpoint, it's difficult to separate out the effects of regulations or technological change from everything else that's going on in the economy."

Several non-governmental organizations, however, have studied the impact of environmental regulations

on employment. These studies mostly are limited to specific regions, ecosystems and industries, and their findings are in some cases controversial. But they provide a starting point in a widening debate.

For despite two decades of progress in cleaning up the nation's air and water and protecting fragile habitats, industrial and agricultural expansion is placing continued pressure on the environment. At the same time, popular concern for the environment continues to mount, resulting in increasingly stringent measures to prevent further damage. But in recessionary times such as these, the fear of unemployment can overwhelm the desire to protect the environment.

Here are some of the fundamental questions that arise when environmental protection conflicts with job security:

Do environmental regulations destroy jobs?

The spotted owl controversy is virtually the only instance where systematic studies have been conducted by the government to determine the impact of environmental regulation on employment. Over the next 25 years, the Interior Department predicts, 31,000 jobs will be lost in the Pacific Northwest as a result of current plans to protect the spotted owl. An alternative plan now being drawn up by Interior Secretary Manuel Lujan Jr. would reduce the job loss by about half.

The controversy involves more than 6 million acres of ancient forests that are slated to be set aside for the spotted owl under the terms of the Endangered Species Act. The law limits activities that place threatened species at additional risk. Much of the forested land is under the control of the Interior Department, which allows timber companies to harvest

How Voters Feel About the Northwest's Problems

According to surveys† of voters in the Pacific Northwest, 64 percent of Oregonians and 48 percent of Washingtonians are unwilling to risk job losses in order to protect the spotted owl and old-growth timber. Thirty-two percent of the Oregonians and 20 percent of the Washington state residents blamed environmentalists for the current situation in the region's forests.

To protect the spotted owl and old-growth timber, is the potential loss of jobs for people in the forest-products industry an acceptable risk?

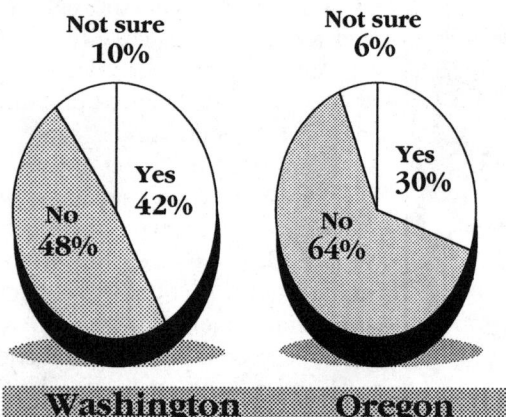

Who do you feel is most responsible for the current situation in the forests of the Pacific Northwest?

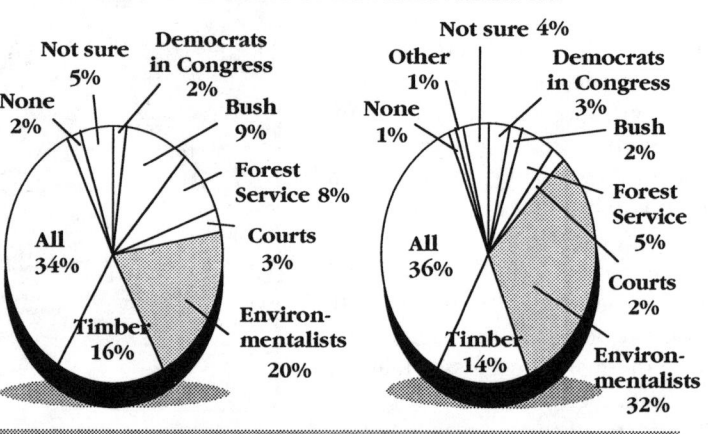

How many jobs for people in the forest products and related industries would you be willing to lose to protect the spotted owl and old-growth timbers?

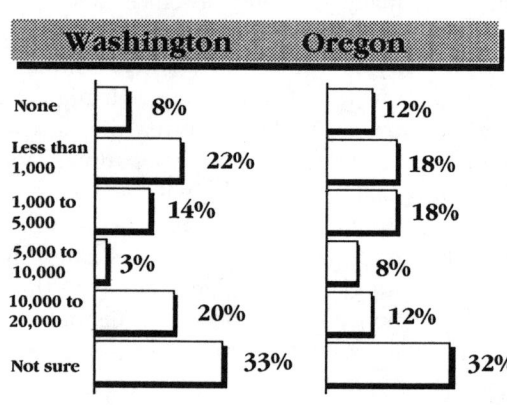

Who do you feel could best solve the current problems in the forests of the Pacific Northwest?

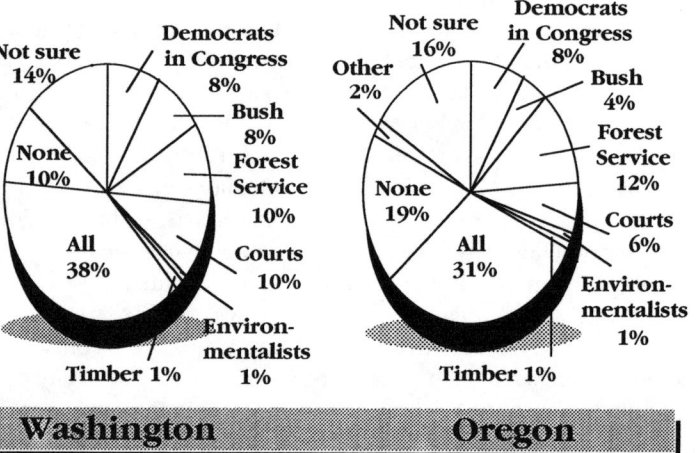

† *Washington voters were surveyed in February 1992, Oregon voters in March.*
Source: Political/Media Research, Inc., survey conducted for the Timber Industry Labor-Management Committee

trees on public land. Since the owl was listed as endangered in 1990, however, environmental groups have won court injunctions preventing further timber sales.

The timber industry and unions representing loggers and other workers say job losses will be much greater than the government estimates, and could reach 140,000.[2] Beginning

with a rally in Portland, Ore., in April 1990, before the logging ban even went into effect, protesting loggers and millworkers and their supporters took their cause to the streets of communities throughout the Northwest. Oregon's timber industry, probably the most potent political force in the nation's most timber-dependent state, recently helped finance an unsuccessful drive to recall first-term Democratic Gov. Barbara Roberts, who is seen as siding with environmentalists over the spotted owl.[3]

"In the last two years, that region out there lost 110 mills impacting about 11,000 workers," says economist Denny Scott of the United Brotherhood of Carpenters and Joiners of America. "Those are permanent shutdowns. The mills will never reopen, and those jobs are gone. While we had weak markets during that period, and we can't attribute every single job loss to the owl, certainly a large percentage of those jobs lost are the result of the listing of the owl and the subsequent injunction."

Under the Endangered Species Act, economic considerations may not be taken into account in decisions on whether to list a species as threatened or endangered. As a result, the law has long been targeted by industries whose activities it has restricted. In 1978, for example, the Tennessee Valley Authority was forced to postpone construction of the Tellico Dam on the Little Tennessee River until steps were taken to save the snail darter, an endangered fish whose habitat would be destroyed by the dam.*

Today, criticism of the act's indifference to economic repercussions centers around the spotted owl. But many other species currently are on the endangered species list or in the process of being listed, including the delta smelt, a fish native to the Sacramento-San Joaquin Delta in California, two kinds of salmon native to

*Construction on the Tellico Dam proceeded the following year, after Congress exempted the project from the Endangered Species Act. Although the snail darter subsequently disappeared from the waters around the dam, additional populations of the fish were later discovered elsewhere.

the Columbia River basin and as many as 60 species native to South Florida, including the Florida panther, the American crocodile and the Cape Sable seaside sparrow.

Only rarely, if ever, have government studies been undertaken to measure the impact these listings would have on local employment.

Loggers in Washington state's Olympic Peninsula and throughout the Pacific Northwest strongly opposed the 1990 listing of the northern spotted owl as endangered.

Photo: Mike Mills

The designation of salmon in the Columbia River and its tributaries, for example, would affect a vast part of the river system, which extends 900 miles into Idaho's Sawtooth Mountains. Eight large dams on the river would have to lower water levels to facilitate the annual migration of young salmon to the Pacific Ocean. That would raise electricity rates and reduce the amount of water available to local farmers and ranchers.

However, the National Marine Fisheries Service, which is responsible for drawing up a recovery plan for the salmon, has no mandate to assess the plan's economic impact on the affected area, much less to assess employment. Affected industry groups, however, often undertake studies to measure the impact of environmental regulation on jobs.

While the Endangered Species Act is currently the main focus of attention, industry critics say other environmental measures are also contributing to joblessness. The American Petroleum Institute (API), for example, estimates that environmental regulations have figured in the loss of more than 400,000 oil-industry jobs in the last decade. Just last month, Phillips Petroleum Co. announced 1,350 layoffs and cited environmental regulations as one of the reasons for the cutbacks.[4]

But just what portion of the industry's job losses can be traced to environmental protection is unknown. Bans on oil drilling off the coasts of North Carolina and Florida have contributed to the loss of jobs in this industry. But so too have general economic trends, such as falling oil prices and the subsequent reduction in oil drilling in the United States.

"We know from past experience that for every job created to operate an offshore rig there are almost four

Domain of the Northern Spotted Owl

Northern spotted owls can be found from southern British Columbia to northwestern California. Biologists say that about 6,000 of the shy creatures remain in the wild, and that they need 6 million acres of dense old-growth forest to survive. Logged forests offer less cover and protection from competing species, such as the barred owl and great horned owl.

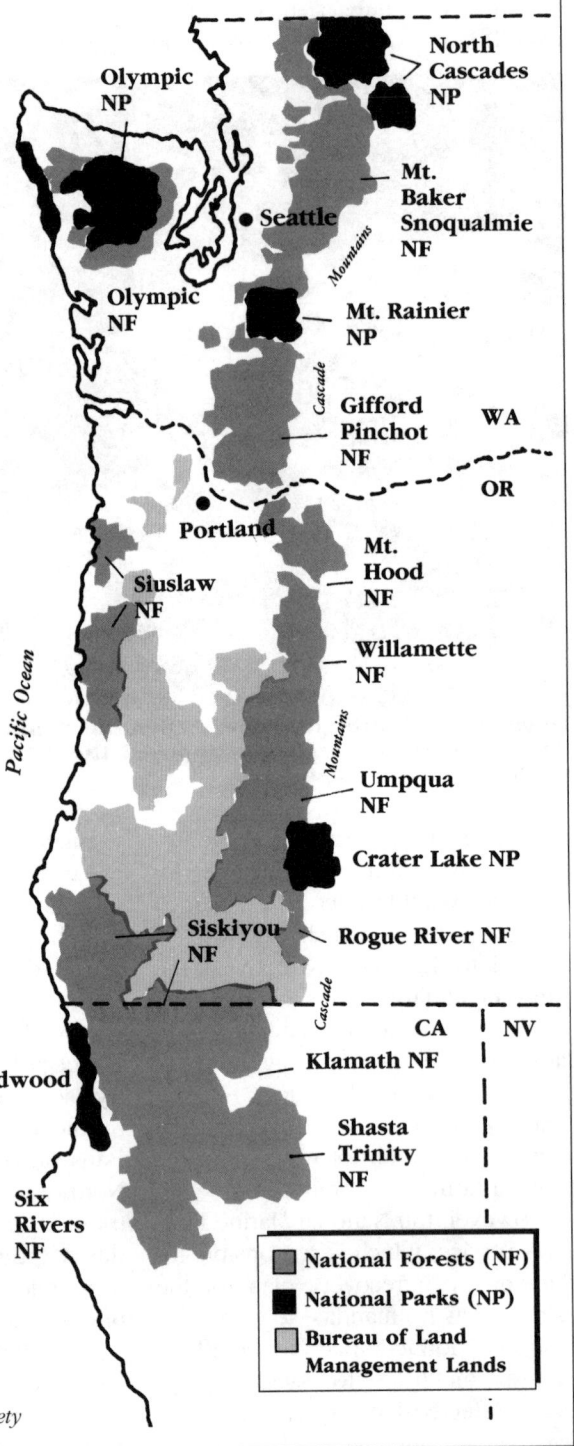

Olympic NP

North Cascades NP

Olympic NF

Seattle

Mountains

Mt. Baker Snoqualmie NF

Mt. Rainier NP

Cascade

Gifford Pinchot NF

WA

OR

Portland

Mt. Hood NF

Siuslaw NF

Pacific Ocean

Willamette NF

Mountains

Umpqua NF

Crater Lake NP

Siskiyou NF

Rogue River NF

Cascade

CA | **NV**

Redwood NP

Klamath NF

Shasta Trinity NF

Six Rivers NF

■ **National Forests (NF)**
■ **National Parks (NP)**
■ **Bureau of Land Management Lands**

Source: The Wilderness Society

onshore jobs," says William F. O'Keefe, chief operating officer of the API. "Since we weren't able to do that, the capital has flowed overseas," along with jobs for American workers.

Air-quality standards and numerous other environmental regulations introduced since the 1970s have also taken their toll on oil-industry employment. O'Keefe cites the case of a polluting oil refinery in Wyoming that Amoco was forced to shut down several months ago. "That put 200 people out of work because the cost of bringing that refinery into compliance couldn't be justified," he says.

Environmental-protection measures also prevent certain new jobs from becoming available. O'Keefe says the oil industry predicts that as many as 700,000 new jobs would be created throughout the nation's economy if Alaska's Arctic National Wildlife Refuge (ANWR) were opened to oil drilling, a proposal Congress rejected last fall.[5]

Measures to preserve water quality, a broad area of environmental concern, are the focus of a similar debate now raging in South Florida. Everglades National Park, a vast wetland that is home to numerous endangered species, has shrunk over the years as farmers have drained the marshes along its perimeter. Because much of the Florida peninsula drains into the Everglades, the park also is being damaged by industrial wastes and runoff from cities and agricultural land far to the north.

Of particular concern is runoff containing phosphorus, an ingredient of fertilizers that accelerates the growth of algae. The enhanced algal growth reduces oxygen in the water and thus threatens plants and animals in the Everglades. To curb the phosphorus pollution, the South Florida Water Management District Board has proposed flooding a 58-square-mile area north of the park to create a buffer area to filter out the phosphorus before it reaches the vast wetland. But this would destroy the sugar cane, vegetable and sod farms in the affected area. Further, the project's $400 million estimated cost would be raised through additional taxes on farmers.

According to local sugar growers, the effort to protect the Everglades would eliminate 15,000 jobs, including 7,000 in farming and 8,000 positions in the retail and other businesses that support farming. The casualties include farmers who would be forced out of business by the new tax.

"The authorities get very embarrassed and say they're doing plenty in terms of job-training assistance," says Robert Buker Jr., vice president of corporate affairs at giant U.S. Sugar Corp. "But what can you train a tractor driver to do who lives in the agricultural area [to be flooded]? These workers will have to relocate."

Aren't jobs also lost through environmental degradation?

For virtually every job lost to environmental regulation, environmentalists respond that even more jobs would be lost in an unregulated environment. This is particularly true, they say, for the so-called "extractive industries," such as logging, oil drilling and fishing, which use up finite resources.

In the Pacific Northwest, for example, no one disputes the fact that today's loggers and other workers will be affected by plans to save the spotted owl. But supporters of the conservation efforts say these same workers would find themselves without jobs in a decade or two anyway — if the industry continued cutting down the ancient trees.

"The issue has been billed as a conflict between jobs and the environment," writes Sen. Al Gore, D-Tenn. "But if the remaining 10 percent of old-growth forest is logged out, as the timber industry prefers, the jobs will be lost anyway. The only

question is whether the effort to create new jobs will begin now or later, after the forest is completely gone."[6]

Fishermen often protest limits placed on the number of fish they are allowed to catch. Recently, salmon fishermen have protested a sharp reduction in the Pacific salmon quota due to falling populations of several salmon species. "When people say environmental controls on catches are ruining these industries, that's not the problem," says Stephen M. Meyer, a professor of political science at Massachusetts Institute of Technology who is studying the impact of environmental controls on employment. "The problem is that short-term you can continue to do what you do and then completely eliminate the species — and then eliminate the industry entirely. Or you can cut the catch and let it reproduce. It's a tradeoff between extraction rates and profits, and it affects short-term jobs."

Environmentalists also point out that destruction caused by one industry often hurts the economic viability, and hence the employment rate, of other industries. Loggers in the Pacific Northwest typify the syndrome, says Lauren Mical, a spokeswoman for the Environmental Protection Agency (EPA). "Not only are they cutting down trees that are 300 years old and not replaceable," she says, "but they are also creating a major runoff problem." Logging promotes soil erosion, and the earth that washes into surrounding streams dirties spawning areas for salmon and other fish. This reduces the fish catch many miles downstream from the cut forests.

Industrial wastes, pollutants that enter the waterways from city storm drains and fertilizers used on farms and suburban lawns also find their way into the river systems and coastal waters of the industrial Northeast. "Because of the pollution, runoff and overfishing," Mical says, "fishermen in the Northeast have to go further and further out, and they just can't

make a living anymore."

In Massachusetts, Meyer says, a proposal by the New England Regional Fisheries Management Council to reduce fish catches by half over the next five years along much of the New England coast has sparked a sharp debate. "The program will literally shut down several major towns in southern Massachusetts and Rhode Island," he says. "The alternative is to let them keep going [at the current rate], and they will be out of business forever in three years. So from the point of view of the fisherman or the farmer or the forester, the choice is between losing the job now and losing it three years from now. He's not so worried about losing it three years from now."

Is economic growth compatible with environmental protection?

If measures to protect the environment result in immediate job losses in certain industries, there could be a point at which further regulation, affecting broad segments of American industry, would slow the rate of economic growth.

According to George Bush, who promised voters during the 1988 presidential campaign that he would be the "environmental president," the United States is in no danger of reaching that point under current policies. "As I often have stated, we can have both economic growth and a cleaner, safer environment," President Bush said in a March 24 statement to Congress. "Indeed, the two can be mutually supportive. Sound policies provide both."

Bush went on to identify technological change and international trade as two keys to economic growth that his administration has championed. (See story, p. 420.) Research into advanced materials, electric batteries and biotechnology, Bush said, is providing environmentally sound alternatives to some of the more damaging industries. Meanwhile, trade agree-

Owls and the Ancient Forests

Far from the heated debate over its future, the northern spotted owl carries on its reclusive, nocturnal existence in the ancient forests of the Pacific Northwest. The owls' range extends from southern British Columbia, southward through western Washington and Oregon into northwestern California. Typically, the owls take one mate for life, each pair claiming an average territory of 4,800 acres as its home range.

In addition to a lot of space, the owl requires old-growth forests for its survival. These woodlands contain large numbers of tall Douglas firs with thick canopies, as well as dead wood and fallen logs that are home to squirrels, wood rats and other small mammals that are staples of the owls' diet.

If their territory is left undisturbed, spotted owls are long-lived, often surviving a dozen years or more. But they are unable to adapt to radical changes in their environment. Unlike some birds, which raise more than one clutch of young in a summer, northern spotted owls usually have one clutch of one or two chicks a season. Only about 1 in 5 juveniles survives to adulthood after leaving the nest.

A special government group, the Interagency Scientific Committee, was set up in 1988 to study ways to save the bird from extinction. The group recommended that large tracts of forested land containing numerous owls offer a greater chance of long-term survival than the small, fragmented areas that increasingly characterize the owls' territory. Logging in the Pacific Northwest's ancient forests has destroyed vast tracts of the owl's habitat. Even if they do not clear-cut the land, loggers selectively remove the big, heavily leafed trees the owl requires for nesting and cover.

The owl population has shrunk with its habitat. The

Northern spotted owls

Photo: U.S. Fish and Wildlife Service

Environmental Protection Agency (EPA) estimates that there are only 6,000 spotted owls left in the world and that none have survived heavy logging in parts of Oregon, California and southwestern Washington.

The northern spotted owl is not the only species to face the risk of extinction as a result of deforestation in the Pacific Northwest. In fact, the owl is considered to be an "indicator species," whose declining population is symptomatic of broader environmental degradation within its habitat. The EPA has identified at least 200 rare and potentially threatened species of vertebrates in the old-growth forest, including the bald eagle, northern goshawk and marbled murrelet, which have suffered from habitat loss.

Because logging facilitates erosion, it also threatens fish in the streams that pass through the forests. Silt that washes into the streams adjoining logged forests destroys salmon and other fish that require clean water and gravel stream beds for spawning. As a result, EPA reports, 101 of 214 salmon stocks in the Pacific Northwest are at risk of extinction.

Extensive logging also threatens an important plant species — the Pacific yew. This small evergreen, which is native to old-growth forests of the Pacific Northwest, is the chief source of the chemical taxol, which has recently been found to be highly effective in the treatment of some forms of cancer. The heavy equipment that loggers use to harvest the large trees they seek for timber destroys small trees that are in their path, including the yews.†

---

†See "Saving the Forests," The CQ Researcher, Sept. 19, 1991.

---

ments promote growth that frees up resources to pay for environmental protection. He also cited the 1990 Clean Air Act amendments, which tightened emissions requirements for polluting industries and encouraged energy efficiency.

But the administration's stance on

environmental regulation appears ambivalent, as it has also recently acted to water down some of the same environmental regulations it touts as conducive to economic growth. In his Jan. 28 State of the Union message, Bush announced a 90-day moratorium on environmental and other regu-

lations as a temporary stimulus to the economy. The moratorium, which began in late January, is delaying the issuance of most new regulations that already have been mandated by Congress.

Further, the White House Council on Competitiveness, responding to industry pleas for relief, has cited the need for economic growth as its reason for trying to dismantle a broad array of environmental regulations. The council earlier this year proposed opening half of the country's remaining wetlands — vital breeding grounds for countless plant and fish species — to development.

"To overzealous regulators," said Vice President Dan Quayle, who heads the group, "you've met the enemy, and it's called the Competitiveness Council, and we are going to make sure the president's order is fully implemented."[7]

Many business executives agree with Quayle that environmental regulations are part of the economy's problem. In a recent poll of industry leaders, more than 73 percent of the respondents said that mandated investments in environmental programs had hampered their company's efforts to improve competitiveness, and more than 63 percent doubted that those investments to improve the environment would pay off in the long term.[8]

But environmentalists dispute the logic behind the council's anti-regulatory efforts. Michael Bean, an attorney for the Washington-based Environmental Defense Fund, points out that the three states with the most species protected under the Endangered Species Act — California, Florida and Hawaii — are also the fastest-growing states in the nation.

"If the listing of endangered species led to 'endangered species gridlock,' the term economists use, one would expect the most gridlock would be evident in these states," Bean says. "But the hypothesized conflict between jobs and the environment has been shown to be basically faulty."

Some environmentalists even assert that environmental-protection efforts eventually will promote more economic growth and more jobs than traditional industries — but only if

policy-makers and industrialists pursue environmentally sound goals. Known as "sustainable development," this path toward economic well-being hinges on avoiding activities that deplete natural resources and discarding traditional notions that link increases in productivity with progress.

"For years, industry has directed technological innovation toward reducing the need for human labor," writes Michael G. Renner of the

BACKGROUND

Belated Regulations

Environmental awareness is a relatively recent addition to the national consciousness. Indeed, it runs counter to the tradition of the American frontier, built over generations of experience. For most of the nation's history, as farmers and industrialists ran out of resources in one spot, they simply pulled up stakes and migrated further west.

It was not until the 1960s that the public at large began to comprehend the environmental damage caused by 200 years of uncontrolled industrial expansion. In *Silent Spring,* her inspiring 1962 best-seller, Rachel Carson linked the use of pesticides such as DDT to the abrupt decline of bald eagles and other birds and described serious water pollution in industrial centers.

Prompted by Carson's warnings, the first major environmental legislation emerged in the 1960s: the Clean Air Act of 1963, as well as laws protecting parklands, the water supply and endangered species. But it was not until 1970, following massive participation in the first Earth Day, that the environmental movement took off and set the stage for sweeping

Worldwatch Institute, an environmental research organization in Washington. "This strategy has worked well for managers interested in cost-cutting, but it has produced tremendous burdens for society at large. Now, the key to solving both the environmental and unemployment crises is to direct innovation toward improving the productivity of other inputs — that is, reducing the amount of capital, energy and materials needed to generate a dollar's worth of wealth."[9] ∎

laws curbing industrial pollution and protecting natural resources.*

Air pollution, which had blackened Pittsburgh and other Midwestern industrial cities since the turn of the century, was the first major focus of the decade's environmental legislation. The Clean Air Act amendments passed in 1970 set national air-quality standards that required industries to reduce smokestack emissions. The next two years saw a flurry of federal measures to curb water pollution, noise pollution, the production of harmful pesticides and ocean dumping of wastes.

Sen. Gore acknowledges the importance some of these earlier environmental laws had. "In the United States," Gore wrote, "... the Clean Water Act of 1972 has reduced pollution levels markedly. Twenty-five years ago, the Cuyahoga River in Cleveland became so polluted, it actually caught fire. Today, while it is still polluted, it is no longer flammable."[10]

From the beginning, affected industries have opposed environmental regulations as harmful to employment and profits. Their pleas were frequently ignored, however, until the OPEC oil embargo of 1973 began

---

*The first Earth Day celebration was held April 22, 1970, when some 20 million Americans participated in demonstrations and marches calling for action to protect the environment.

the nation's series of energy crises. As industries reeled from the sudden rise in energy prices, concern over the availability of affordable gasoline and heating oil began to erode the overwhelming support the environmental movement had enjoyed in the early years of the decade.

In 1975, President Gerald R. Ford declared: "I pursue the goal of clean air and pure water, but I must also pursue the objective of maximum jobs and continued economic progress. Unemployment is as real and sickening a blight as any pollutant that threatens the nation." [11]

Despite the continuing economic problems caused by rising energy prices, Jimmy Carter entered the White House in 1977 promising to strengthen environmental legislation. During his administration, air- and water-quality regulations were tightened as public pressure mounted in response to new disasters, including the discovery of toxic waste in New York's Love Canal as well as some of the nation's major rivers. But with the second oil crisis at the end of the decade, the struggle between jobs and the environment resurfaced.

Attitudes Change

The 1980s were marked by a reversal in the move toward environmental protection. Bolstered by widespread support among businessmen and landowners, President Ronald Reagan dismantled many existing environmental regulations as part of his campaign to deregulate the American economy during the first half of the decade. The new policy was moderated during Reagan's second term, when Congress passed several new measures, including new funding for cleaning up hazardous wastes and tighter controls over water purity, endangered species and pesticide production.

As Reagan's vice president, George Bush had supported deregulation and business development. But during the 1988 presidential campaign, he promised to usher in a new era of environmental concern. After his election, Bush signaled his commitment by appointing William K. Reilly, a respected environmentalist, to head the EPA. But the struggle between economic

Continued on p. 421

Executives' Views on Environmental Regulations

Complying with today's environmental regulations is more frustrating and time-consuming than it was in the past, industry executives report. According to 94.3 percent of the respondents to a recent survey, company managers now spend more time on environmental matters than they did three years ago. And 73.3 percent said that mandated investments in environmental programs hampered their company's efforts to improve competitiveness.

Are your company's operations managers now spending more time on environmental matters than they did three years ago?

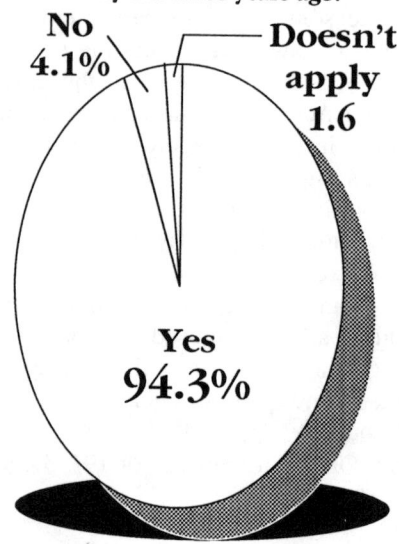

No 4.1%
Doesn't apply 1.6
Yes 94.3%

Have mandated investments in environmental programs hampered your company's efforts to improve competitiveness?

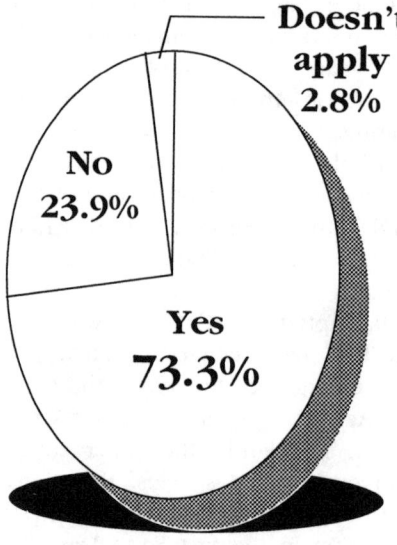

Doesn't apply 2.8%
No 23.9%
Yes 73.3%

In the long term, do you believe that environmental investments will enhance your company's competitiveness?

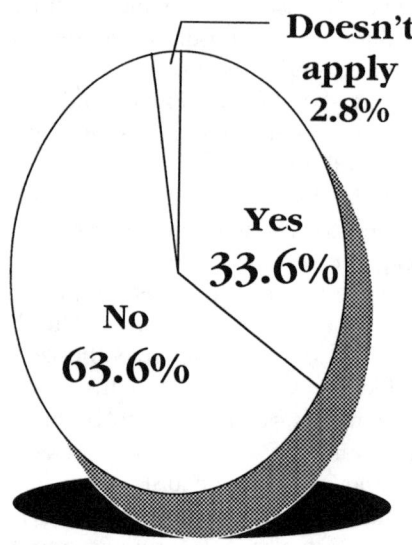

Doesn't apply 2.8%
Yes 33.6%
No 63.6%

Source: Industry Week *magazine, March 16, 1992*

Chronology

1960s *With the nation's polluted waterways and cities bearing testimony to decades of industrial contamination, public concern mounts over the high environmental cost of economic development.*

1962
In *Silent Spring,* author Rachel Carson documents the widespread harm to birds and other wildlife caused by pesticides as well as the damage to waterways from agricultural runoff. The book becomes a best-seller and a call to action.

1963
The first Clean Air Act authorizes state and local authorities to monitor and curb air pollution. The law initially focuses on reducing visible smoke and smog emitted from factories and other fixed industrial sites.

———— ● ————

1970s *As the environmental movement takes off, Congress enacts the world's strictest environmental protection laws.*

April 22, 1970
Twenty million Americans take part in the first Earth Day celebration. Later in the year, Congress passes amendments to the Clean Air Act. This landmark legislation replaces the existing regional environmental regulatory system with national standards on air pollution.

1972
The Clean Water Act becomes law, regulating the discharge of pollutants into waterways, storm sewers and reservoirs.

1973
Congress passes the Endangered Species Act. The law requires that decisions to list species as threatened or endangered be reached without considering the economic consequences, including unemployment, of those decisions.

1974
The first fuel-economy standards require automakers to produce energy-efficient cars to save fuel and reduce harmful emissions.

1976
Congress passes the Resource Conservation and Recovery Act (RCRA), regulating the disposal and treatment of solid and hazardous waste.

———— ● ————

1980s *Advocates of the Reagan administration's deregulation policy clash with environmentalists over the need for stricter environmental laws.*

December 1980
Congress sets up the "superfund" program to clean up hazardous chemical dumps.

1986
Congress puts additional money into the "superfund" program and reauthorizes the Safe Drinking Water Act.

January 1987
Fish and Wildlife Service receives the first petition requesting that the northern spotted owl be listed as endangered. In December the agency says the listing is not warranted.

1988
Several environmental organizations file suit challenging the government's finding that listing the northern spotted owl under the Endangered Species Act is not warranted. During his successful quest for the White House, George Bush promises voters he will be the "environmental president."

———— ● ————

1990s *As unemployment climbs, popular support for environmental protection is weakened by worries over job security.*

June 1990
The northern spotted owl is listed as threatened under the Endangered Species Act, activating measures to protect its habitat, the ancient forests of the Pacific Northwest. The timber industry protests that the move will cause widespread unemployment among loggers and other workers in the region who depend on the timber industry.

Nov. 15, 1990
President Bush signs amendments to the Clean Air Act whose goal is to cut emissions of 189 toxic air pollutants. The measure calls for a significant reduction in emissions that cause acid rain, smog, airborne toxic chemicals and substances that deplete stratospheric ozone. In an effort to protect industry and jobs, the law relies more heavily than before on market incentives such as voluntary compliance credits and performance standards.

January 1992
President Bush announces a 90-day moratorium on new regulations, including those affecting the environment, in an effort to save American businesses money and protect employment.

April 29, 1992
Still concerned about the nation's faltering economy, Bush extends the moratorium.

U.S. Lags in the 'Green' Marketplace

In the early 1970s, the United States took the global lead in promoting environmental action. While Europe's roadsides were littered with trash, and Japan's rapid industrial growth overwhelmed all environmental concerns, Congress was passing landmark measures to protect the nation's air and water. U.S. industry responded with technological brilliance — catalytic converters, smokestack scrubbers and water-filtration systems.

U.S. environmental leadership has eroded, however, in recent years. At the same time that nascent Green parties were winning seats in Europe's parliaments and introducing more stringent environmental standards, the Reagan administration was undermining environmental protection laws as part of its campaign to deregulate the economy. Japan quickly stepped in to satisfy American consumers' appetites for fuel-efficient, less-polluting cars while Detroit expended its energy on fighting fuel-economy standards.

Critics say that President Bush, the self-appointed "environmental president," has done little to enhance U.S. leadership in environmental affairs. Aside from the Clean Air Act amendments of 1990, which impose stricter standards on emissions of airborne pollutants, the past four years have seen relatively little progress in federal initiatives to protect the environment. Recently, the United States refused to adopt a timetable for reducing emissions of carbon dioxide as part of an international effort to curb global warming.†

The strictest measures to protect the environment are coming from state legislatures, led by California. Dealers there must begin selling pollution-free cars in 1998. By 2003, 10 percent of all new cars sold in the state must be free of harmful emissions. The only cars able to meet this standard run on batteries. Because California itself is one of the biggest auto markets in the world — and because other states are considering adopting its pollution standards — Detroit carmakers are rushing to meet the deadlines.

Electric cars are not entirely new, but Detroit has never put much effort into developing them. Older prototypes can only travel relatively short distances before the battery runs down. But with the huge California auto market at stake, Detroit is suddenly showing renewed interest in the electric car. General Motors took the lead, and already has developed a two-passenger model, the Impact, scheduled for production in the mid-1990s.

Ford, too, is gearing up. It has developed a conventional gasoline-powered car for the California market. The 1993 Escort, a subcompact, will meet the state's emissions standards for 1997 when it goes on sale in California later this month. Chrysler, meanwhile, has entered into a joint venture with Westinghouse Electric Corp. to develop a faster electric car with a longer travel range between rechargings.

But Detroit will face stiff competition in California from Japan and several European carmakers. Clean Air Transport Ltd., an Anglo-Swedish company, plans next year to introduce a car that runs on both gasoline and electricity. Italy's Fiat has already begun producing the tiny Panda Elettra, and BMW of Germany has also developed an electric prototype. Japan, Detroit's main competitor in the conventional car market, is weighing in with an electric car built by Nissan Motor Co. and another model under joint development by Mitsubishi Motors and Tokyo Electric Power Co.

Because of increasingly stringent pollution-control laws at home, these foreign companies were busy gearing up to develop low-emission vehicles at the same time Detroit was relaxing in the deregulatory climate of the past decade. Michael E. Porter, a professor of business administration at Harvard Business School, cites the example of fuel-efficiency standards, which the Reagan administration reduced. Today, he writes, "The strictest regulations in many of these areas are first introduced abroad. Foreign companies learn to deal with stricter standards before American firms, giving them an advantage when U.S. regulations catch up." ††

Both European and Japanese companies work much more closely with their governments in research efforts, a tradition that further enhances their ability to quickly develop new technologies. In 1990, for example, Japan's powerful Ministry of International Trade and Industry (MITI) presented a long-range plan for coordinating industry efforts to cope with environmental problems.

"The future holds great promise for technologies and products that are responsive to environmental concerns," says Michael Bean, an attorney for the Environmental Defense Fund. "The perception exists that Japan is way ahead of us on that. Just as they were way ahead of us in producing small, fuel-efficient cars, they are way ahead of us in producing new solar and other energy technologies. Our failure to capitalize on the future demand for that sort of technology will mean that the jobs to create those products will exist out of the country, not here."

---

† The U.N. Conference on Environment and Development, the so-called Earth Summit, begins June 6 in Rio de Janeiro, Brazil. One of its main aims is signing a treaty to limit emissions of carbon dioxide. As a result of U.S. opposition, negotiators in early May dropped language from the draft treaty requiring industrial nations to cut their emissions to 1990 levels by the year 2000.

†† Michael E. Porter, *The Competitive Advantage of Nations,* (1990), p. 525.

Continued from p. 418

and environmental concerns became apparent in the administration's policies. As the economy slid into recession — with unemployment surpassing 7 percent early this year — public support for strong environmental legislation characteristically weakened.

In the past, the struggle over regulations often pitted environmentalists against corporate interests in classic confrontation. For example, the fuel-economy standards set by Congress in 1974 were supported by environmentalists but loudly denounced by the auto industry as a threat to the survival of one of the country's key industries and the employer of hundreds of thousands of American workers.

More recently, however, the auto industry cited the same reasons for resisting a proposal to install pollution-control devices on new cars to trap the fumes that are released into the atmosphere when gasoline passes from the pump to the gas tank. But this time, the auto industry didn't fight the environmentalists. They wanted gas station operators to install more efficient vapor traps on their gas pump nozzles.

This choice pitted the auto industry against another corporate giant, the oil industry, which claimed it had already lost four times as many jobs as the carmakers.[12] At this point, the auto industry appears to have won the battle: President Bush, in a campaign stop in Michigan, told carmakers in March that they would not be required to install the devices, thus leaving the job of reducing gasoline fumes to the oil industry.[13]

Impact on Employment

Whether the clash over the burden of environmental protection is between environmentalists and corporate executives or between reluctant industries, the debate rarely includes the impact on employment. Although it is difficult to determine the precise toll environmental laws take on jobs in a given industry, extensive Labor Department studies suggest that economic and technological changes are causing an inexorable shift in certain industries and occupations over the long term.

For the most part, industries that cause the greatest environmental damage — mining, manufacturing and farming — are expected to lose jobs over the next 15 years. The service sector, with less of an impact on the environment, is expected to provide many more jobs, continuing a long-term trend. From 1987 to 1989, the Census Bureau reported in April, more than three-quarters of the people who entered the work force took jobs in the service sector. The largest number of new jobs was in retail stores and professional fields such as health care and education. Manufacturing industries accounted for only 13 percent of the new jobs.[14]

In fact, by the year 2005 the Labor Department expects job opportunities to decline in 30 occupations, and more than half are manufacturing jobs. The department projects that, even when jobs created by the so-called "peace dividend" are considered, almost 600,000 manufacturing jobs will be lost as a result of defense spending cuts, increased imports and technological advances and automation of assembly-line production. Almost 320,000 jobs for farmers and farm workers are expected to disappear by 2005 due to lower crop and livestock production. Job losses in mining, oil and gas drilling are expected to total 7,000; the 5,000 jobs lost in mining alone amount to a 20 percent drop in employment.[15]

Trend Favors 'Benign' Jobs

While the Labor Department does not attribute the occupational shifts to environmental regulations, the trend is clearly toward more environmentally benign jobs. Logging operations, for example, are expected to see a 2 percent fall in jobs over the next 15 years. During the same period, the number of forest and conservation positions will increase by 8 percent. Overall, 106,000 logging jobs will be lost and 43,000 conservation jobs gained.[16]

It is this long-term employment trend that some say has been ignored in the debate over jobs in the Pacific Northwest. "It's quite clear that timber employment in the Pacific Northwest is going down anyway," says Robert E. Jenkins Jr., vice president for science at the Nature Conservancy, a conservation organization based in Arlington, Va. "Even if the timber interests up there were allowed to cut every last tree that they would like to — which would probably be every last tree — it would still only stave off their day of reckoning for a few years."

A study of the Northwest's timber industry by the Wilderness Society, in Washington, D.C., found that almost 14,000 jobs already have been lost in the past decade due to automation and a shift in timber exports from milled products to raw logs.[17] In Jenkins' view, however, automation accounts for only part of the decline. "They are running out of timber," he says, "and it's just a question of whether you stop before you cut down the last tree or whether you stop some time before that."

The timber industry disputes some of the Wilderness Society's findings. Denny Scott of the carpenters union, for example, calls the study "basically flawed" because it downplays the role of regulations. "As long as the environmental community tries to make this false case that old-growth preservation does not impact negatively on unemployment, we're not going to get very far," he says.

Aid to Loggers Advocated

But Scott agrees with the environmentalists that not enough has been done to help workers make the transition to different employment. "Lives and industries and regional economies should have been planned for long before it was too late."

If the timber industry's long-term decline has been so obvious, why has the debate focused on the spotted owl and the Endangered Species Act? According to Bean of the Environmental Defense Fund, "People focus on the things they can understand and ignore what may be far more significant threats to employment."

Still, Bean cautions, "We cannot afford to be indifferent to the loss of even one job in the Northwest from this effort to preserve the forests."

Bean emphasizes the need for job training and other forms of government assistance for displaced workers in the region. "Without that," he says, "the perception is that there is a choice that must be made between protecting the environment and protecting jobs. This is a perception that is not beneficial to anyone's ultimate goals."

Despite evidence that employment shifts are occurring for other reasons, some representatives of industries that are losing jobs continue to blame environmental regulations. For years carmakers have faulted regulations mandating tighter emissions controls and better fuel economy for their lagging competitiveness.

"But foreign automakers [who compete in the United States] are required to meet the same pollution standards for their vehicles as American automakers are," says MIT's Meyer. "When you compare market shares over time, you see that American automakers are losing it. Since they are competing in markets where essentially environmental controls are equal, there must be another determinant." ∎

CURRENT SITUATION

Pollution Credits

American manufacturers, typically, have railed against the inflexibility of traditional environmental regulations. If a plant was unable to reduce its emissions of air pollutants, it was declared non-compliant. This meant shutting down, relocating to other areas, or even moving overseas, taking their jobs with them. In response to industry's complaints, lawmakers have introduced innovative ways to protect the environment while mitigating the impact on company profits and, indirectly, employment.

Rather than mandating changes for each plant through regulatory "command and control," as the traditional regulatory process is known, recent legislation takes a new tack. Free-market techniques such as tradable pollution credits give companies greater flexibility in meeting pollution limits.

Rules for using pollution credits were first spelled out in 1975, when the EPA allowed businesses to buy and sell credits, as authorized by the 1970 Clean Air Act. But the idea gained much broader application with the 1990 amendments to that law. They introduced a program, scheduled to begin in 1995, that will help utilities in the Midwest and along the East Coast cope with stricter standards governing emissions of sulfur dioxide, a pollutant produced by burning coal that causes acid rain. The program will allow utilities that emit less sulfur dioxide than the law allows to sell pollution credits to other utilities that are unable to meet the new standard.[18] The Tennessee Valley Authority, for example, plans to meet part of its clean air requirements by buying pollution credits from Wisconsin Power & Light Co., a relatively clean utility. The historic deal, announced May 12, is believed to be the first of its kind.

In regions where stringent local environmental regulations are forcing companies to take drastic steps to reduce emissions, such as New England and the industrial Midwest, pollution credits are already widely used. Southern California, a region that is plagued with some of the worst smog conditions in the country, has undertaken the nation's most ambitious free-market regulatory effort to date, affecting scores of industries. Regulators there have established pollution-credit programs for all three of the heaviest industrial pollutants — nitrogen oxide, sulfur oxide and reactive organic gas.

Although businesses are free to reduce their emissions however they can, by installing smokestack "scrubbers" or by reducing energy use, for example, the pollution-credit program is attracting a growing following among oil refineries and other plants with limited ability to meet pollution standards. Because demand for pollution credits is expected to increase as the 1995 deadline for stricter standards draws near, the Commodity Futures Trading Commission announced in late April that it would allow the Chicago Board of Trade to set up a market for buying and selling the credits.

The Bush administration has embraced pollution credits as a better way to clean up the environment than the traditional command-and-control system. The free-market approach is also more in line with the administration's commitment to deregulation, embodied by the Council on Competitiveness. Now, to broaden the appeal of these incentives, Bush recently extended pollution credits to the auto market. In a March 18 statement issued by the White House, he announced a new plan that would pay owners of old cars, which emit more pollutants than newer models, to get their clunkers off the road.

Under Bush's plan, utilities and other polluting industries would earn pollution credits by purchasing the cars. Auto companies and their employees, the administration says, would profit from the plan through enhanced auto sales, as consumers are expected to buy new cars to replace their old ones.

Farmers Eye Free-Market Techniques

Farmers in South Florida would like to see their regional regulatory agency take a similar approach toward pollution in the Everglades. The EPA has identified water pollution as one of the thorniest environmental problems, especially when it results from agricultural and urban runoff.[19] The South Florida Water Management District Board has proposed a plan to flood 58 square miles of farmland just outside the Everglades in an attempt to filter 150 tons of phosphorus out of the runoff.

But farmers and the local sugar industry say the flooding will drive 15,000 people out of work. They want a two-year reprieve to try to save those jobs through other techniques, such as lining drainage canals with phosphorus-absorbing limestone.

For farms that are unable to reduce phosphorus runoff, pollution credits could provide the answer, local growers say. "Just as the new Clean Air Act has acid-rain credits, we think they should have Everglades restoration credits so each farmer can have X amount of phosphorus come off his land," says Robert Buker of U.S. Sugar, which is based in Clewiston, near the area the government plans to flood. "Then, if he reduces more than that, he can sell the excess to someone else."

The farmers' plan, Buker says, would cost $30 million, much less than the estimated $400 million cost

A Flood Plan for the Everglades

A plan to flood 58 square miles of farmland (shaded area in large map) just north of the Everglades has upset local farmers and sugar growers. Regional water officials say the flooded area will help filter 150 tons of phosphorus out of the runoff that now pollutes the vast swamp, but farmers say the flooding will cost 15,000 local jobs. They want to try voluntary anti-pollution techniques, such as lining drainage canals with phosphorus-absorbing crushed limestone.

Source: Florida Sugar Cane League

of the government proposal. "If we can't meet their standards, then they can go ahead and flood the land," he says. "But give us a couple of years to reduce it on our own property and let the free market work first."

Voluntary Controls

Another market incentive to a cleaner environment was introduced last year by EPA Administrator

Reilly. He asked the country's 600 biggest industrial polluters to voluntarily reduce by a third emissions of the 17 most dangerous toxins by the end of 1992. By 1995, he asked that they cut these emissions by half of their 1988 levels. Reilly's appeal to the bottom line — that it is cheaper to prevent pollution than it is to clean it up once the toxins have left the plant — appears to have paid off: At least 200 companies have pledged to try to meet the voluntary standards.

Among the volunteers are 80 percent of the members of the American Petroleum Institute, which historically has resisted environmental regulation. But the voluntary approach struck a chord. "It's a question of the right balance in pursuing society's goals," says William O'Keefe of API. He cites cost estimates for complying with environmental regulations of between $100 billion and $200 billion in the 1990s and studies that indicate a third of that cost is related to waste. "That means companies aren't as efficient as they could be, they don't compete well and ultimately that hurts the consumer and the worker."

The realization that preventing pollution saves money in the long run is beginning to influence the way companies operate. Minnesota Mining & Manufacturing Co. (3M) set up a pollution prevention program in 1975, but it was not until the last few years that many other companies followed suit. Chevron Oil Co. set up a waste-reduction program in the late 1980s and has since reduced its toxic emissions by about 60 percent, O'Keefe said.

One of the better-known programs is Dow Chemical Co.'s WRAP ("waste reduction always pays") program. At its Pittsburg, Calif., plant, for example, Dow recycled a reactant used in the production of agricultural products, saving $8 million in raw materials and costs associated with environmental regulations governing the incineration of toxic wastes.

The effects of such waste-reduction schemes on employment are far from clear cut. "Our effort is to enhance what we're doing ... in waste- reduction efforts within our existing employment structure," says Joe Lindsly, who directs Dow's WRAP program. "So our efforts would have no impact whatsoever on employment."

But the Bush administration claims that voluntary waste-reduction efforts indirectly benefit employment. "These

are cases where the environment and jobs can be mutually supportive," says an administration environmental economist. "If there are cost savings, then those savings are freed up for expenditures elsewhere. Environmentally improving technologies make economic sense in their own right, and by making economic sense they tend to either increase the competitiveness of the company or expand jobs."

Stimulating Jobs

The EPA claims that environmental regulations provide a strong stimulus for new jobs throughout the U.S. economy. The Clean Air Act alone, the EPA estimates, will create as many as 25,000 new jobs over the next three years and an average of 20,000-40,000 full-time positions each year during the last half of the 1990s. Engineers, construction managers, field construction workers and supervisors and some equipment-manufacturing workers are expected to find new employment opportunities as a result of the new law.[20]

Critics of the EPA challenge the findings. "EPA says some of the regulations create jobs, but they are really just a reallocation of who bears the cost," says O'Keefe of the API, whose members have often found it less costly to close down polluting refineries and shift operations overseas rather than comply with environmental regulations. "They don't create jobs in a productive sense."

But there is ample evidence that environmental regulations do foster new technologies and industries that can provide new employment opportunities for more American workers, compensating for jobs lost when plants shrink their operations because of stricter standards. Stephen Meyer of MIT cites the heated debate now taking place in Massachusetts over a new statewide recycling bill,

which the plastics and glass bottling industries oppose, saying it will throw many people out of work.

"A crucial distinction needs to be brought out," Meyer says. "When the bottle and the plastics industries talk about lost jobs, they are talking about immediate, specific, individual jobs. They are not talking about real employment. From the microeconomic standpoint, it is true that Bill and Joe and Lucille and Wanda may in fact lose their jobs. But the net impact in every single case where recycling has been introduced has been a tremendous growth of jobs in the recycling industries."

Another argument often heard from industries facing environmental regulations is that any new jobs that may be created by replacement industries are menial and low-paying. Loggers in the Pacific Northwest, for example, are loath to give up their $14-an-hour wages if the only jobs they will find in the protected parklands are low-paying positions waiting tables or waxing skis. In the absence of adequate job training and incentives for alternative industries to relocate to the region, the loggers' concern is understandable.

The Promise of High Technology

The real promise for industry and employment from environmental protection measures lies in the high-technology field. For every $1 billion spent to control air pollution, the EPA estimates, up to 20,000 jobs are created in industries producing new technology.[21]

For example, the federal Clean Air Act and California's even stricter pollution standards created a ready market for the air-quality monitoring equipment made by Advanced Pollution Instrumentation, a San Diego firm. Edward Etess founded the company in 1988 in direct response to regulations requiring caps on carbon dioxide, sulfur dioxide, nitrogen ox-

Continued on p. 426

At Issue:

Can the northern spotted owl's ancient forest habitat be saved without causing widespread unemployment in the Pacific Northwest?

H. MICHAEL ANDERSON AND JEFFREY T. OLSON

The Wilderness Society
FROM *FEDERAL FORESTS AND THE ECONOMIC BASE OF THE PACIFIC NORTHWEST: A STUDY OF REGIONAL TRANSITIONS,* SEPTEMBER 1991

yes

ontroversy over the impact of logging on the northern spotted owl — considered an indicator of the ecological health of ancient forests — culminated in the listing of the owl as a threatened species in 1990. . . .

Adequate protection of ancient forests and biological diversity will necessarily entail substantial reductions in federal timber sales, compared to historic and planned levels. It is important to observe, however, that the Westside region has experienced a transition in the past 15 years that has significantly altered the economic base of the region. [The Westside region lies along the coastline of Washington, Oregon, and northern California, reaching inland to the west slope of the Cascade Mountains.]

The timber industry has become much less important to the region's overall economic health, employing just 4 percent of the total work force. At the same time, there has been tremendous growth and diversification in other sectors of the economy. Much of the transformation of the Westside's economic base is due to the influx of new residents and the increasingly urban character of the region's population. . . .

Timber-industry employment losses will occur throughout the region, mostly in response to productivity improvements — some 33,600 jobs by 2010. Reduced federal timber sale levels exacerbate the economic impact of the region's declining timber industry. . . .

As long as the Westside's rural, timber-dependent communities continue to rely on a shrinking timber industry, their future is clouded by the growing competitive disadvantage of the timber industry. Transition strategies are needed to facilitate economic growth in rural communities regardless of federal timber-sale levels. Reduction in future timber supplies, necessary to maintain biological diversity and healthy forest ecosystems, adds to the need for viable options. . . .

In the final analysis, the growth and vigor of the Pacific Northwest's economy, and the environmental concern of the region's residents, provide the key to achieving the dual goals of economic and economical well-being. The opportunity exists for the transition that is taking place in the Northwest economy, the timber industry and federal forest-management preferences to result in a reconciliation of environmental and economic values.

DENNY SCOTT

Economist, United Brotherhood of Carpenters and Joiners of America
FROM *ENVIRONMENTAL ACTION,* SPRING 1992

no

he Wilderness Society study . . . is a welcome addition to the literature concerning the transition taking place in the region's forest-products industry. The change — some call it crisis — has been rapid and disruptive.

Too little attention has been paid to the human, social and economic impacts of drastically reduced timber harvests, transition to second growth and other factors causing mind-numbing change in the Northwest forest industry. . . . Absent a coherent, well-crafted plan, the cost of old-growth preservation will fall disproportionately on forest workers and their timber-dependent communities.

This report's chief fault is that it buys into the frequently repeated — and misguided — thesis that job losses from old-growth preservation would be minimal when compared to the thousands of jobs that will be lost in any event to automation and technological change. This conclusion in based on a series of questionable assumptions.

To begin with, the report assumes that between 1990 and 2040 the job loss due to "productivity advances" in the timber industry will continue on the track it followed during the 1980s. Recent history, however, is not a reliable basis on which to estimate future worker displacement. The industry went through a surge of technological modernization in the 1980s that may not be sustained for the next 50 years. Assuming this high rate over such a long period, exaggerates job loss numbers and creates a misleading context for decision making. . . .

As a union representative, I see the faces behind the economic modeling that projects a "smooth transition." The model cannot begin to resemble what happens in the real world. The Pacific Northwest solid-wood industry lost 6,000 full-time direct jobs in 1990 and 5,000 jobs in 1991 due to permanent mill closures. While not all of these jobs were lost because of harvest reductions, it is certainly true that the majority were lost due to the federal court decision halting nearly all logging on Westside federal forests. How do these employment declines fit with the smooth sloping lines developed by the model? Will these jobs be restored before the long-term trend line in the model takes control? It is unlikely.

Continued from p. 424

ide and ozone. The firm produces and installs "sniffers," as the monitors are called, for all four of these gases.

"We felt that the market was going to really grow, which it has," says Etess. "The regulations are not only creating jobs in terms of building the analyzers, but also servicing, installing, calibrating and maintaining this equipment." He counts utilities, pulp and paper mills and refineries among the firm's main clients.

Etess says his firm employs 20 workers, ranging from highly skilled engineers to laborers. That's not a large number, especially compared with the hundreds of workers who can lose their jobs when a refinery closes. But Etess emphasizes the indirect job benefits that are resulting from the region's cleaner environment. "If you put money into pollution control, then California is getting cleaned up, and more people are going to come for tourism and other rea-

sons," he says. "That will create more jobs all around."

California's air-quality regulations — the strictest in the nation — have already stimulated new areas of research and production in the auto industry. State law will require that automakers begin selling cars with zero emissions in 1998 and that by 2003 non-polluting cars account for a tenth of all new autos sold in the state. The only cars that can meet that standard are fueled by electricity. But difficulties producing an electric battery capable of powering a car for long distances have kept such non-polluting vehicles off the road until now.

Because California is the biggest auto market in the country, its new standards have prompted Detroit to beef up research. As a result, all three domestic automakers have developed prototypes they hope to have ready for sale to California residents by the deadline. ■

now cut. The conservation group also calls for more generous government support for the region, including job training to help displaced loggers find new employment.

In an attempt at compromise, the Bureau of Land Management, which manages some of the federal forestlands in dispute, has asked the seven-member Endangered Species Committee, known as the "God Squad," to exempt timber sales from the timber-cutting restrictions imposed by the law on 4,426 acres of federal land in Oregon.* The committee has the authority to do so if it decides that the economic harm caused by the restrictions outweigh the benefits to the environment. A committee decision is expected this week.

Congress, meanwhile, is considering numerous proposals to defuse this and similar potential conflicts. At least a dozen bills focusing on the Pacific Northwest have already been introduced. One bill, drafted by Rep. George Miller, D-Calif., chairman of the House Interior and Insular Affairs Committee, would allow less logging in the Pacific Northwest than the timber industry is seeking, but would provide retraining assistance for forestry workers.[23]

A longer-term proposal to help preserve jobs and the environment was recently presented by Sen. Barbara A. Mikulski, D-Md., who is calling for a massive shift of research funding from the military to technology that can improve the environment. She has introduced legislation that would set up a "national environmental technologies agency," similar

OUTLOOK

New Approaches

Evidence that environmental regulations will enhance employment in the long run is of little consolation to the loggers of the Pacific Northwest who face unemployment today under current policy. Their dilemma was the focus of congressional hearings in March, where timber industry representatives and environmentalists clashed over saving jobs or the spotted owl's habitat.

The timber industry called for an amendment to the Endangered Species Act that would allow economic considerations to be taken into account during deliberations on whether or not to list a species as endangered. "Species values are the only

ones that count under the Endangered Species Act," said Sen. Slade Gorton, R-Wash., who testified in favor of such an amendment.[22]

Environmentalists resist changing the act, which they deem one of the most effective preservation measures on the books today. Instead, they are beginning to focus on ways to ease the transition from environmentally destructive industries such as logging to more sustainable economic activity.

The Wilderness Society, for example, has proposed several ways the timber industry could remain viable in the Pacific Northwest even after the spotted owl's habitat is protected. The industry could increase profits by producing more value-added products, such as lumber for furniture, instead of exporting raw logs. It could also retool mills to process second-growth timber rather than the irreplaceable old-growth stock they

---

*The Endangered Species Committee includes the Secretary of the Interior (Manuel Lujan Jr.), the Secretary of Agriculture (Edward Madigan), the Secretary of the Army (Michael P. W. Stone), the chairman of the Council of Economic Advisers (Michael J. Boskin), the administrator of the National Oceanic and Atmospheric Administration (John A. Knauss), the EPA administrator (William K. Reilly) and a citizen from the affected state (in this case, Oregon), appointed by the president. Five of the seven members must approve any exemption to the law.

to the Defense Advanced Research Projects Agency, which conducted research into military hardware throughout much of the Cold War.

"Environmental technology is a field America has an opportunity to take the lead on," Mikulski said at an April 13 press conference in Baltimore to announce her plan. "The National Environmental Technologies Agency will help the United States develop the technologies we need to find answers now to avoid cleanup later. And as new technologies emerge, jobs will be created through new environmental markets and industries."

A Campaign Non-Issue

During the 1988 presidential campaign, the environment was close to the top of the agenda. George Bush promised to be the "environmental president" if elected. Four years later, however, Bush is virtually silent on environmental protection, and so are the Democrats angling for the White House. "By and large, certainly none of the candidates is rushing forward to proclaim himself the environmental candidate as George Bush did in 1988," says Michael Bean of the Environmental Defense Fund. "I presume that part of the reason for that is the anxiety over jobs during a recession."

Bush, who has come under strong criticism for paying too little attention to domestic issues as the unemployment rate climbed to over 7 percent earlier this year, stands to lose the support of workers who side with the loggers in the spotted owl controversy if he broaches the subject.

According to Stephen Meyer of MIT, the Democratic front-runner, Gov. Bill Clinton, D-Ark., is just as eager to skirt the jobs-vs.-environment debate. "Clinton doesn't want to bring it up because he's catering to the unions," Meyer says, "and he's afraid that if he starts talking environment they're going to think lost jobs because they don't understand the is-

sue. So no one is bringing it up."

Clinton finally broke the silence in a speech he delivered in Philadelphia, appropriately enough on Earth Day, April 22. "Presidential leadership on the environment has become an endangered species," Clinton charged, as he called for tax penalties against "energy wasters," a national bottle bill to promote recycling and other environmental initiatives.[23] Vulnerable to criticism because of the severe water pollution in his state, Clinton admitted to having "made the choice from time to time for jobs" when forced to choose between stricter environmental standards and higher employment. He added that he was forced to make this choice "because my state was a poor one without either enough jobs or enough federal help to clean up the environment."[24]

President Bush ignored Clinton's challenge on the environment, repeating in a statement from the White House his prior claim that "we can have both economic growth and a cleaner, safer environment."[25] ∎

Notes

[1] The Timber Industry Labor-Management Committee released the results of the poll, conducted by Political/Media Research Inc. of Washington, D.C., on March 23.

[2] Union estimates were compiled by the United Brotherhood of Carpenters and Joiners of America and the American Federation of Labor and Congress of Industrial Organizations (AFL-CIO).

[3] See *The Washington Post*, May 10, 1992, p. A6.

[4] See *The New York Times*, April 4, 1992.

[5] See *Congressional Quarterly Weekly Report*, Nov. 9, 1991, p. 3274.

[6] Sen. Al Gore, *Earth in the Balance* (1992), p. 194.

[7] Address to the Republican National Committee winter meeting, Washington, D.C., Jan. 31, 1992.

[8] The survey was conducted earlier this year among 318 U.S. executives by *Industry Week* magazine and the Environmental Technology Exposition and Conference. See John H. Sheridan, "Environmental Issues Sap Executive Time," *Industry Week,* March 16, 1992.

[9] Michael G. Renner, "Saving the Earth, Creating Jobs," *Worldwatch,* January-February 1992, p. 11.

[10] Gore, *op. cit.,* p. 109.

[11] See Pamela Fessler, "A Quarter-Century of Activism Erected a Bulwark of Laws," in *Environment '90: The Legislative Agenda* (Congressional Quarterly Inc., 1990), p. 20.

[12] See William O'Keefe's letter to the editor, *The New York Times,* April 1, 1992.

[13] President Bush made the promise to automakers in a March 13, 1992, address to the Economic Club in Dearborn, Mich.

[14] Census Bureau, *Job Creation During the Late 1980s: Dynamic Aspects of Employment Growth,* April 15, 1992.

[15] See George Silvestri and John Lukasiewicz, "Occupational Employment Projections," *Monthly Labor Review,* November 1991.

[16] *Ibid.*

[17] The Wilderness Society, *Federal Forests and the Economic Base of the Pacific Northwest,* September 1991.

[18] See Jeffrey Taylor, "New Rules Harness Power of Free Markets to Curb Air Pollution," *The Wall Street Journal,* April 14, 1992.

[19] Environmental Protection Agency, *National Water Quality Inventory: 1990 Report to Congress,* 1992.

[20] ICF Resources, Inc. and Smith Barney, Harris Upham & Co., *Business Opportunities of the New Clean Air Act,* January 1992 (draft report commissioned by the EPA).

[21] See Keith Mason, "The Economic Impact," *EPA Journal,* January-February 1991.

[22] Sen. Gorton testified March 24 at joint oversight hearings on the Bush administration's response to the spotted owl crisis, held by the House Interior and Insular Affairs Subcommittee on National Parks and Public Lands; the House Agriculture Subcommittee on Forests, Family Farms and Energy; and the House Merchant Marine and Fisheries Subcommittee on Fisheries and Wildlife Conservation and the Environment.

[23] See Phillip A. Davis, "Miller Drafting Bill to End Northwest Forest Feud," *Congressional Quarterly Weekly Report,* April 4, 1992.

[24] Gov. Clinton spoke at Drexel University in Philadelphia, Pa., April 22, 1992.

[25] Statement issued by the White House April 22, 1992.

Bibliography

Selected Sources Used

Books

Borman, F. Herbert, and Stephen R. Kellert, *Ecology, Economics, Ethics: The Broken Circle*, Yale University Press, 1991.

In this collection of essays, several environmental experts bemoan the lack of long-term planning in current policy to protect the environment and suggest that the consequences of environmental degradation are far more threatening to the economy than is commonly recognized.

Gordon, Anita, and David Suzuki, *It's a Matter of Survival*, Harvard University Press, 1990.

Using traditional economic standards to assess environmental policy is flawed, the authors assert, because they fail to adequately measure the consequences of industrial development. According to these standards, they write, "Environmental degradation and activity to clean it up add equally to the economic health of society.... We have imposed an artificial intellectual construct, a human-created design, on the Earth at the expense of physical reality, and have then ravaged the globe for economic return."

Gore, Sen. Al, *Earth in the Balance: Ecology and the Human Spirit*, Houghton Mifflin Co., 1992.

When Gore, D-Tenn., ran for his party's presidential nomination in 1988, environmental issues were close to the top of his agenda. In this book, he resumes his criticism of Republican environmental policies. "The Bush administration and the entire U.S. government ought to understand the economic significance of a healthy environment as a kind of infrastructure supporting future productivity. If it is destroyed, many jobs now at risk will be lost."

Articles

Dowie, Mark, "American Environmentalism: A Movement Courting Irrelevance," *World Policy Journal*, winter 1991-92.

The dominant strategy of most environmentalists in the United States, support for laws to regulate pollution and other assaults on the environment, is doomed, Dowie writes. "No matter how big and clever environmental groups become, when it comes to lobbying Congress they will always be a mosquito on the hind quarters of the industrial elephant." To have any lasting impact, he says, U.S. environmentalism must grow into a broad-based movement.

Horton, Tom, "The Endangered Species Act: Too Tough, Too Weak, or Too Late?" *Audubon*, March/April 1992.

Of about 600 plants and animals that have won protection under the 1973 Endangered Species Act, only five — the American alligator, three birds and a plant — have recovered to the point where they have been taken off the list. For environmentalists, this fact illustrates the need for much greater funding to better implement the law, while detractors say it merely shows the law's ineffectiveness.

Renner, Michael G., "Saving the Earth, Creating Jobs," *WorldWatch*, January-February 1992.

The author suggests that a shift toward more sustainable development — economic activity that does not harm the environment or deplete natural resources — would create many more jobs than our current industrial economy.

Reports and Studies

Congressional Budget Office, *Environmental Regulation and Economic Efficiency*, March 1985.

This report, while somewhat dated, contains useful information on the economic costs of environmental regulation during a period of rapid increase in these regulations. While it does not directly address the issue of regulations' impact on jobs, the study concludes that "environmental regulation has not been a significant source of productivity loss in the private sector."

Hahn, Robert W., *U.S. Environmental Policy: Past, Present, and Future*, conference paper, American Enterprise Institute Annual Policy Conference, Nov. 27, 1991.

Hahn, a scholar at the American Enterprise Institute, a conservative think tank in Washington, contends that environmental regulations are becoming increasingly costly. "Future environmental regulations are much less likely to pass narrow benefit/cost tests that are based on the risks reduced. The reason is that we have already implemented most of the relatively easy fixes for cleaning up the environment."

Warren, Melinda, *Regulation on the Rise: Analysis of the Federal Budget for 1992*, Center for the Study of American Business, July 1991.

Federal spending on regulations of all types is at a record level and rising, the author writes. In 1992, it will cost $13 billion to fund the government's regulatory apparatus. "There is one area of the regulatory budget where President Bush has more than surpassed the spending pattern of any other president. Environmental regulation has grown at an astounding rate in the last few years, now comprising 38 percent of the entire regulatory budget."

The Next Step

Additional Articles from Current Periodicals from EBSCO Publishing's Database

Addresses & essays

Yandle, B., "Environmental feudalism," *Society,* November/December 1991, p. 45.

Argues that better solutions to the world's environmental problems will come from true environmentalists, not politicians, business, industry or new learning in economics. The effect on the environment of the market process; regional regulation and why it doesn't work; the need for national environmental regulation.

Canada

"A bird in the bush," *Maclean's,* June 24, 1991, p. 9.

Reports that the rare spotted owl may be moving into British Columbia. Under the Endangered Species Act, U.S. environmentalists have been using the owl to save West Coast old-growth forests. Now British Columbians are worried about logging jobs.

Allen, G., "A delicate balance," *Maclean's,* Dec. 16, 1991, p. 40.

Considers the balance between the harvesting of timber and the recreational, environmental and spiritual values inherent in Canada's forests, and notes a Decima poll found 6 in 10 Canadians believe more should be done to protect the environment even if it cost jobs. Criticisms of Canada's logging practices; international threat of a boycott of Canadian forest-products; changing Canadian forest management; effects of climactic changes on the forest; lessening impact.

Came, B., "Colliding cultures," *Maclean's,* Aug. 12, 1991, p. 10.

Examines the cultural clash between Quebec's Cree and Inuit peoples and the provincial government over Hydro Quebec's proposed Great Whale project on the Great Whale River. Hydroelectric generating station on the La Grande River; Quebec's need for jobs and electricity vs. the natives' traditional culture; social problems stemming from development; skepticism about environmental assessment; the Crees' efforts to preserve culture; Premier Robert Bourassa's support for development.

Pynn, L., "Logging with horse power," *Canadian Geographic,* August/September 1991, p. 30.

Applauds the resurgence of the use of horses in the logging industry in British Columbia. The call for more environmentally sensitive forestry practices; a small but growing fraternity; "Not hippies and not back-to-the-landers either";

even industry beginning to recognize the role for limited horse logging.

Case studies

"Wild and scenic river suffers from logging," *National Parks,* November/December 1991, p. 14.

Reports that the Skagit River, which runs through Mount Baker-Snoqualmie National Forest and North Cascades National Park in Washington, has been damaged by logging in spite of its designation as a wild and scenic river. The Forest Service's position; the National Parks and Conservation Association's position; the Wild and Scenic Rivers Act.

Davis, P.A., "'God Squad' called on to weigh timber interests, spotted owl," *Congressional Quarterly Weekly Report,* Oct. 5, 1991, p. 2854.

Examines Interior Secretary Manuel Lujan Jr.'s decision to convene the high-level Endangered Species Committee, known as the "God Squad," over a group of 44 timber sales on a small fraction of Oregon federal forestland that is also home to the threatened northern spotted owl. The committee's power to grant exemptions to the Endangered Species Act (PL 93-205) based on economics and jobs; the panel's makeup; comments from logging representatives and environmentalists; more.

McCarthy, S., "The last drive," *Canadian Geographic,* December 1991, p. 18.

Reports that environmental concerns have ended an era for the Gatineau River's log drivers. Recycling lowers amount of logs necessary; chipping the logs at the forest camp; trucking the chips to the paper mill; cost-effectiveness. INSET: Farewell to an era (pictorial history of river drives).

Pearce, F., "Rainforest rescue plan," *New Scientist,* Dec. 28, 1991, p. 7.

Reports on the launching last week of the first international project to help save a country's rain forest when several groups granted Brazil money for conservation in the Amazon basin. What the agreement stresses; who the members of the groups are; what the program will fund.

Proper, D.C., "A perfect stream," *Field & Stream,* January 1992, p. 30.

Describes the pristine condition of the Rock Creek watershed in Montana, and the conflicting concerns of sportsmen, environmentalists, and the logging industry, regarding the impact planned timber production will have on the area, beginning in 1992.

Corporations

"Goody two-shoes," *Economist,* **Nov. 2, 1991, p. 68.**

Describes how many companies are introducing aggressive environmental policies, partly to be good citizens, partly to beat the regulators. Profiles the work done by B & Q, Britain's largest do-it-yourself retailer, and Monsanto, an American chemical company. Styles; details.

Dwyer, P., "Clinton bashes business — but does he mean it?" *Business Week,* **Feb. 10, 1992, p. 97.**

Discusses how Arkansas Gov. Bill Clinton has passed out about $100 million in special tax breaks to entice companies to expand, and has been willing to hold off fixing environmental problems to keep plants open. In short, Gov. Clinton has been a lot friendlier to business than would-be President Clinton. Arkansas on cutting edge of economic development; mixed results; poor state; raising education standards.

Holusha, J., "Environmentalists assess corporate pollution records," *The New York Times,* **Dec. 9, 1991, p. D1.**

Comments on efforts made to appeal to socially conscious investors and to encourage companies to minimize pollution. The series of environmental profiles being published by the Council on Economic Priorities; statistical summaries of the environmental performance of all 500 companies in the Standard & Poor's Index, to be published early next year.

McMurdy, D., "Green is the color of money," *Maclean's,* **Dec. 16, 1991, p. 49.**

Scrutinizes the specter of expensive cleanup operations and protracted lawsuits that have elevated the environment from an abstract moral issue to one of fundamental business practice. Company officials have learned they must have a solid record of environmental performance to attract new investment from the public and retain their existing base of shareholders. Changing attitudes of the business community toward the environment; socially responsible investing; green quotient.

Debates & issues

"How conservation can hurt output," *Canadian Business,* **August 1991, p. 15.**

States that using less electricity may be good for the environment but there is a growing concern that it is having a negative effect on office productivity. Modified lighting and modern work situations; harms vision of computer users.

"Log on," *Economist,* **Nov. 9, 1991, p. 26.**

Discusses how environmentalists and bureaucrats, banded together to protect the ancient forests of the Pacific Coast, have followed the timber industry into the piney woods below the Mason-Dixon Line, where production is up 121 percent. The tactics of militant environmentalists; the South's attractiveness due to privately owned land and cheaper logging prices; environmental groups' lobbying to restrict timber harvest and clear-cutting in the South.

Coghlan, A., "Going green gives greater gains," *New Scientist,* **Aug. 31, 1990, p. 12.**

Argues that environmental policies within government can actually increase employment and income or at least make them no worse with regulation compared with the situation without it. The key error in traditional economic models; example; thought by economic guru David Pearce.

King, P. and J. Taliafer, "The war for the West," *Newsweek,* **Sept. 30, 1991, p. 18.**

Details how environmentalists, ranchers and loggers collide over the future of the frontier. Congress scheduled to debate the reauthorization of the Endangered Species Act; the Bureau of Land Management (BLM); cattleman John Falen's work; fights over timber; saving the salmon; Boston developer Mory Bergmeyer; rivers running dry. INSETS: Nature at risk: A reader's guide; firing lines (battlegrounds between environmentalists and businesses), by G. Gates and J. Schneidman.

Economic aspects

"Trees don't grow on money," *Economist,* **Aug. 10, 1991, p. 11.**

Reports on how difficult it is to combine preserved rain forests with economic development. Details on last year's Houston summit of the Group of Seven leading industrial nations conference on forest conservation; decision by governments in Geneva whether such agreement should be put to next year's environmental jamboree in Rio de Janeiro.

"Wealth of nature," *Economist,* **Jan. 18, 1992, p. 67.**

States that environmentalists who believe that economic growth leads to environmental damage argue that national-income accounts should reflect changes in a country's natural wealth. Uses Costa Rica as an example; spending on pollution prevention; Peter Bartelmus, the green guru of the United Nations statistics department.

Barber, L., "The 'ungreening' of America," *World Press Review,* **September 1991, p. 38.**

Reprints an article from the *Financial Times* of London that laments the downturn in fortunes for the green movement in America. Membership and revenues in organizations turn down; a "Chicken Little" backlash; the Persian

Gulf War; a weak economy; opposition from the White House. INSET: Back in the mother country (similar happenings in England) by J. Porritt from *New Statesman and Society*.

Sawhill, J. C., "We can have growth and still save endangered species," *USA Today,* **July 1991, p. 52.**

Rejects the current belief that conservation of rare species and economic growth are mutually exclusive. Case studies of how developers and ecologists have successfully worked together; dangers of losing species to extinction; economic advantages of protecting the world's "genetic warehouse."

Europe

"Greening of Europe benefits U.S. firms," *USA Today,* **December 1991, p. 6.**

Predicts that European companies will be looking to American consulting firms for help when new environmental regulations for the European Community (EC) go into effect over the next few years. Overview of common environmental regulations for the EC; types of United States firms that could benefit.

Lang, I., "Hungary: The pitfalls of growth," *Unesco Courier,* **November 1991, p. 25.**

Outlines Hungary's efforts to redress environmental damage caused by pollution-prone heavy industry. Limitations of the centrally planned economy; efforts to create a market-driven economy; the National Commission's preparations for the 1992 United Nations Conference on Environment and Development; energy policy; privatization of industry and agriculture; transportation as a source of pollution; national parks and conservation.

Law & legislation

Davis, P. A., "Economy, politics threaten species act renewal," *Congressional Quarterly Weekly Report,* **Jan. 4, 1992, p. 16.**

Notes that the Endangered Species Act, conceived in 1973, faces renewal in 1992, and considers how, fueled by the recession, an anti-environmental backlash has made the act a highly divisive issue in several states, most notably Oregon, California and Washington. The act's protection of the spotted owl, which has halted timber sales in timber dependent communities in Oregon; the Cabinet-level Endangered Species Committee, known as the "God Squad"; more. INSET: Endangered species.

Erickson, D., "Sustainable jobs," *Scientific American,* **November 1991, p. 92.**

Asserts that employment gains from environmental policies are likely to outweigh losses. Jobs which would be lost if the world moved away from fossil fuels; results of a study conducted by Michael G. Renner; dividends in international competitiveness stemming from environmental consciousness.

Lemonick, M. D., P. Dawson, et al., "Whose woods are these?" *Time,* **Dec. 9, 1991, p. 70.**

Discusses how conservationists calling for an overhaul of U.S. forest policy are being joined by employees of the Forest Service, many of them members of the Association of Forest Service Employees for Environmental Ethics. Managing lands for "multiple use"; consideration of the Forest Service as a federally subsidized logging agency; rising tide of anti-logging sentiment; Tongass Timber Reform Act; Ancient Forest Protection Act of 1991 proposal.

Wise-use movement

Alexander, C. P., A. Dorfman, et al., "Gunning for the greens," *Time,* **Feb. 3, 1992, p. 50.**

Suggests that economic anxieties and shifting political winds are threatening to produce a green-out effect that could make tree huggers feel as endangered as the California condor. Organization of ranchers, miners, loggers, developers and manufacturers in a "wise-use movement"; renewal of the Endangered Species Act and the clean water act; pressure to weaken the laws and spur economic growth; congressional division; anti-green and lawsuits; backlash.

Knox, M., "Meet the anti-greens," *Progressive,* **October 1991, p. 21.**

Reports that a determined band of organizations is working to defeat environmentalists who wish to restrict corporate encroachment and motorized recreation on public lands. The "wise-use" movement; help from the Unification Church, oil, mineral and timber companies, and political allies in the Senate; efforts of the arch-conservative American Freedom Coalition (AFC).

Satchell, M., "Any color but green," *U.S. News & World Report,* **Oct. 21, 1991, p. 74.**

Reports on the environmental issues — wilderness, logging, endangered species, wetlands, mining, grazing, recreation — that drew several hundred activists to Washington, D.C., in late September. The lobbyists were members of a burgeoning national coalition of grass-roots activists, and others, called the "wise-use" movement; definition of the wise-use movement; what they have accomplished so far; the roots of wise use; more. INSET: A wise-use sampler.

Back Issues

Great Research on Current Issues Starts Right Here... Recent topics covered by The CQ Researcher are listed below. Issues dated before May 10, 1991, were published under the name of Editorial Research Reports.

NOVEMBER 1990
Lotteries and Gambling
Post-Cold War Choices
Setting Limits on Medical Care
Multicultural Education

DECEMBER 1990
Cable TV Regulation
Americans' Search for Their Roots
Is Insurance System a Failure?
Why Schools Still Have Tracking

JANUARY 1991
Growing Influence of Boycotts
Should the U.S. Reinstate the Draft?
America's Archaeological Past
Peace Corps' Challenges in '90s

FEBRUARY 1991
Regional Impact of Recession
Puerto Rico's Status
Redistricting: Mapping Power
Nuclear Power

MARCH 1991
Acid Rain
Cost of the Gulf War
Reassessing Gun Laws
Future for Man in Space

APRIL 1991
Social Security
Canadian Crisis Over Quebec
California Drought
Electromagnetic Radiation

MAY 1991
School Choice
Racial Quotas
Animal Rights
U.S. and Japan

JUNE 1991
Children and Divorce
Teenage Suicide
Endangered Species
Europe 1992

JULY 1991
Teenagers and Abortion
Soviet Republics Rebel
Mexico's Emergence
Athletes and Drugs

AUGUST 1991
Sexual Harassment
Fetal Tissue Research
Oil Imports
The Palestinians

SEPTEMBER 1991
Police Brutality
Advertising Under Attack
Saving the Forests
Foster Care Crisis

OCTOBER 1991
Pay-Per-View TV
Youth Gangs
Gene Therapy
World Hunger

NOVEMBER 1991
Fast-Food Shake-Up
The Greening of Eastern Europe
Business' Role in Education
Cuba In Crisis

DECEMBER 1991
Retiree Health Benefits
Asian Americans
The Obscenity Debate
The Disabilities Act

JANUARY 1992
Term Limits
Oil Spills
Hunting Controversy
Alternative Medicine

FEBRUARY 1992
Threatened Coastlines
New Era in Asia
Assisted Suicide
Jobs in the '90s

MARCH 1992
Women and Sports
Underage Drinking
Garbage Crisis
Mafia Crackdown

APRIL 1992
Ozone Depletion
Welfare Reform
Politicians and Privacy
Illegal Immigration

MAY 1992
Native Americans

Back issues are available for $4.00 (subscribers) or $7.00 (non-subscribers). Quantity discounts apply to orders over ten. To order, call Congressional Quarterly 1-800-432-2250.

Future Topics

▶ *Too Many Lawsuits?*

▶ *Salary Fairness*

▶ *Nuclear Proliferation*

PUBLISHED BY CONGRESSIONAL QUARTERLY INC., IN CONJUNCTION WITH EBSCO PUBLISHING

Too Many Lawsuits?

Is a litigation explosion choking the nation's legal system?

ICE PRESIDENT DAN QUAYLE REVIVED THE simmering debate over the nation's legal system when he confronted lawyers last August with an administration-backed package of civil justice reform measures. Business groups and political conservatives agree with Quayle that legal rules have made it too easy — and too profitable — to go to court, resulting in costly strains on the judicial system, the economy and the nation's social fabric. Lawyers and other defenders of the system say the critics are exaggerating the costs and ignoring the benefits of permitting easy access to the courts. Congress is unlikely to act on the administration's proposals, but states also are being urged to adopt judicial reforms. Some states are considering proposals to make it more difficult for accident victims to recover compensation through the courts.

 May 22, 1992 • Volume 2, No. 19 • 433-456

Formerly Editorial Research Reports

Cover Art: Barbara Sassa-Daniels

The CQ Researcher

May 22, 1992
Volume 2, No. 19

EDITOR
Sandra Stencel

MANAGING EDITOR
Thomas J. Colin

ASSOCIATE EDITOR
Richard L. Worsnop

STAFF WRITERS
Charles S. Clark
Mary H. Cooper
Rodman D. Griffin

PRODUCTION EDITOR
Laurie De Maris

EDITORIAL ASSISTANT
Michael M. Taylor

GRAPHICS
Jack Auldridge

PUBLISHED BY
Congressional Quarterly Inc.

CHAIRMAN
Andrew Barnes

VICE CHAIRMAN
Andrew P. Corty

EDITOR AND PUBLISHER
Neil Skene

EXECUTIVE EDITOR
Robert W. Merry

PUBLICATIONS MARKETING/SALES
Robert Smith

EDITOR, EBSCO PUBLISHING
Melissa Kummerer

The CQ Researcher (ISSN 1056-2036). Formerly Editorial Research Reports. Published weekly (48 times per year, not printed the first Friday of any month with five Fridays) by Congressional Quarterly Inc., 1414 22nd St., N.W., Washington, D.C. 20037. Rates are furnished upon request. Second-class postage paid at Washington, D.C. POSTMASTER: Send address changes to The CQ Researcher, 1414 22nd St., N.W., Washington, D.C. 20037.

Too Many Lawsuits?

BY KENNETH JOST

THE ISSUES

The United States passed a milestone of sorts in 1990 when the number of new cases filed in state courts topped 100 million for the first time.

The caseload figures released by the National Center for State Courts[1] appeared to confirm the widely held image of lawsuit-happy Americans running to court to settle every conceivable dispute. This penchant for litigation, many people believe, clogs the judicial system and enriches lawyers while it strains social relations, undermines the political process and saps the nation's economic strength.

The release of the caseload figures came in April, while President Bush was promising to "end fraudulent lawsuits" in one of his early campaign commercials for the 1992 presidential race. Eight months earlier, Vice President Dan Quayle had renewed the debate over lawyers and lawsuits with a confrontational speech to the American Bar Association (ABA).

"Let's ask ourselves: Does America really need 70 percent of the world's lawyers?" Quayle said, expanding on the theme of a report on civil justice reform by the President's Council on Competitiveness, which he heads.* "Is it healthy for our economy to have 18 million new lawsuits coursing through the system annually? Is it right that people with disputes come up against staggering expense and delay?"

The ABA's outgoing president, Boston lawyer John J. Curtin Jr., followed Quayle to the lectern. "Anyone who believes a better day dawns

EQUAL JUSTICE UNDER LAW

TAKE A NUMBER

when lawyers are eliminated bears the burden of explaining who will take their place," he responded to Quayle, who stood at his side. Curtin challenged Quayle's suggestion that litigation hampers the nation's ability to compete with foreign countries and urged him to focus on "real problems" and "not be distracted by illusory ones."

The faceoff between Quayle and the lawyers last August gave the administration a week of favorable sound bites and commentary. Lawyer-bashing headlines adorned feature stories in *Time, Newsweek* and other publications.[2] Hardly anyone rallied to the lawyers' defense.

Since then, lawyers have tried to present their case in the court of public opinion. In one typical response, Bob Gibbons, president of the Association of Trial Lawyers of America, whose 60,000-plus members represent plaintiffs in personal-injury suits, called Quayle's critique "a distorted picture of litigation." Gibbons said Quayle and other critics grossly exaggerated the cost of litigation, wrongly

depicted personal-injury suits as the major component in rising civil caseloads and ignored findings that the vast majority of accident victims never seek compensation in court.[3]

But while the White House was winning the public relations battle, it made no headway in the legislative arena. An administration-backed bill to help businesses defend suits involving allegedly defective or dangerous products stalled after having been approved by a Senate committee in October.* Republican lawmakers introduced portions of the administration's package of civil justice reforms in the House and Senate in February, but those bills also appear to be going nowhere.

The administration faces an obstacle that has slowed all the efforts over the past three decades to make the legal system quicker, cheaper and fairer: Federal courts handle only a small portion of the nation's legal caseload — about 1.4 million cases in 1990. The state court systems have widely varying laws and rules for handling their 100 million cases. Federal legislation to change the rules for state courts has failed in part because of concerns about states' rights, forcing legal reformers to try to achieve their goals on a state-by-state basis.

Those efforts have borne some fruit. To try to contain the number of automobile accident suits, several states enacted no-fault insurance laws in the early 1970s. An increase in medical malpractice suits brought a

---

*President Bush established the interdepartmental council in March 1989 to review government regulations and policies for their effects on the country's competitiveness.

---

*Sen. Bob Kasten, R-Wis., the chief sponsor of the product liability bill, was unsuccessful in an effort to have the measure considered as an amendment to an unrelated voter-registration bill. On May 14 the Senate voted 53-45 to table Kasten's amendment after some supporters joined opponents in arguing against the maneuver on procedural grounds. A spokeswoman for Kasten said the senator will try again this year to force the bill onto the Senate calendar.

Number of Lawsuits Swells, But Most Are Minor

The number of new cases filed in state courts topped 100 million for the first time in 1990. This included about 13 million criminal cases and about 18 million civil cases.

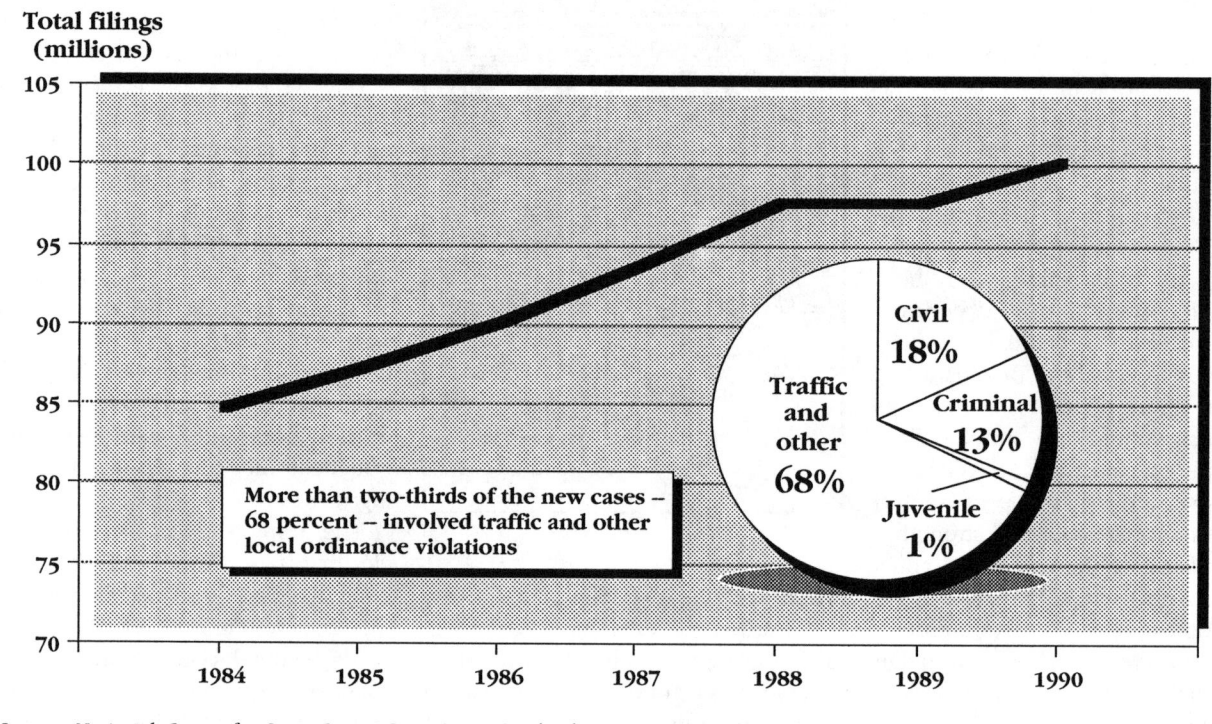

Total filings (millions)

More than two-thirds of the new cases – 68 percent – involved traffic and other local ordinance violations

Civil **18%**

Criminal **13%**

Traffic and other **68%**

Juvenile **1%**

Source: National Center for State Courts, State Court Caseload Statistics: Annual Report 1990, *April 1992*

wave of state reform laws beginning in the mid-1970s. And a broad increase in insurance premiums in the mid-1980s fueled another wave of reform measures aimed at controlling insurance costs and protecting businesses and local governments from expensive jury awards and settlements in personal-injury suits.

With the administration's prodding, those efforts are likely to be pressed anew in Washington and in many state capitals by influential lobbies representing businesses, doctors, local governments and others. Resisting their efforts will be the powerful trial lawyers' lobby and allied consumer groups, who defend existing legal rules as helping injured plaintiffs recover compensation and deterring unsafe practices.

As the debate over the legal system heats up, here are some of the key questions being asked:

Has there been a litigation explosion in the United States?

Americans are accustomed to momentous changes in the nation's social and economic affairs wrought not by legislative bodies or executive officials, but by the courts — often in lawsuits brought by private individuals or groups. Lawsuits have desegregated the nation's public schools, helped dismantle the monopoly telephone system, improved conditions in prisons and mental hospitals and funneled billions of dollars to victims of unsafe products, toxic chemicals, financial wrongdoing and medical injuries.

The public perception of a litigation explosion stems in part from these kinds of policy-laden cases and in part from the more novel — some say eccentric, some say frivolous — lawsuits that seem to have grown more common in recent years. A child sues his parents for "parental malpractice." A teenager sues a classmate for standing her up for a date to the prom.

Statistically, both kinds of cases represent a tiny fraction of the growing caseloads in state courts. Of the 100 million new cases filed in 1990, 68 million — more than two-thirds — involved traffic violations or other local ordinances. About 1.5 million cases involved juveniles. The cases that most concern the public — civil and criminal filings — totaled about

31.5 million. And most of those were, in a sense, minor cases. At least 60 percent of the 13.1 million criminal cases were for misdemeanors rather than more serious felonies. And domestic relations cases and small claims cases — many of which are collection matters — comprised the bulk of the 18.4 million civil cases. *(See chart, p. 438.)*

Most of the public debate has been focused on one particular kind of civil case: so-called tort suits, in which a person who has been injured tries to recover money for losses — medical expenses, lost wages and perhaps "pain and suffering" — from the person or organization he or she claims to have caused the injury. These are the cases that dominate the headlines: suits against doctors for malpractice, against airlines and aircraft manufacturers for airplane crashes, against pharmaceutical companies for faulty drugs or medical devices, against manufacturers for dangerous or defective products. The biggest cases involve claims for millions of dollars and result in jury verdicts or bargained settlements for big amounts — although rarely as much as sought in the original lawsuit.

Statistically, tort cases are on the rise in state courts. Deborah Hensler, a senior social scientist with the Rand Corporation's Institute for Civil Justice, estimates that about 955,000 tort suits were filed in state courts in 1989.[4] Tort suits have increased around 30 percent over the last seven years while the population grew about 5 percent. But the growth in tort cases has now leveled off — possibly because of the tort reform laws enacted in the late 1980s *(see p. 445)*. Meanwhile, other civil cases — suits over contracts or real estate — showed similar increases over the same time period and are now growing faster than personal-injury cases.

Critics of the legal system base their arguments less on statistics than on changes in the legal rules governing lawsuits and in legal and public attitudes toward lawsuits. In his influential book *The Litigation Explosion,*[5] Walter K. Olson, a senior fellow at the conservative Manhattan Institute, argues that a host of procedural changes have made it easier for plaintiffs to bring and win lawsuits. More broadly, he says, litigation has come to be viewed in markedly different terms: not as an unduly expensive and acrimonious process to be avoided if at all possible, but as a beneficial and productive way to compensate accident victims and deter unsafe or improper practices by individuals, businesses and government.

Supporters of the legal system say that lawsuits are not as easy for plaintiffs or as costly for defendants as the critics depict. "For plaintiffs as well as defendants, litigation is usually a miserable, disruptive, painful experience," writes University of Wisconsin law Professor Marc Galanter. Partly for that reason, he says, the vast majority of cases are either dismissed or settled before trial — and that rate has been increasing. One of the chief benefits of litigation, Galanter concludes, is that it supports "a vast system of bargaining in which almost all disputes are resolved by negotiation."[6]

Does the economic cost of litigation deter innovation and hurt U.S. competitiveness?

Critics of litigation claim that the costs of the civil justice system amount to what Vice President Quayle called "a self-inflicted competitive disadvantage." They argue that litigation hurts U.S. business not just by its direct costs — which they estimate at $80 billion to $100 billion — but also by the secondary effects of forcing manufacturers to pull some products from the market and to discontinue development of new ones.

The debate focuses on suits in which a plaintiff claims an injury resulted from a dangerous or defective product and seeks to collect damages from the manufacturer or seller. The rules governing product liability suits changed in favor of plaintiffs beginning in the 1950s and '60s. In the past several years, business leaders have used the innovation and competitiveness theme as their key argument in urging Congress to pass federal legislation to change the law in their favor.

The argument found an especially effective advocate in Peter W. Huber, an MIT-trained engineer turned lawyer. His 1988 book, *Liability,* catalogued a host of economic ills for U.S. manufacturers allegedly brought on by ill-founded suits invited by the liberalized rules for plaintiffs.[7] He argued that product liability suits had forced manufacturers to withdraw safe products from the market to cut or avoid legal costs and sapped the economic strength and innovativeness of such major industries as automobiles, chemicals, pharmaceuticals and small- aircraft manufacturing.

Statistics undercut Huber's arguments to some extent. The increase in product liability suits — a five- to eightfold increase in federal court cases from the mid-1970s to 1985 — was due in large part to what one researcher calls "epidemics" of suits about a single product.[8] In particular, suits for illnesses related to asbestos — the widely used insulating fiber now known to be a potent cancer-causing agent — have been a major component of the federal courts' product liability caseloads. As the General Accounting Office (GAO) and others have noted, with the exception of asbestos cases, product liability suits have actually been declining in federal courts over the past several years.

Studies by the GAO and The Conference Board, a business-oriented research group, also suggest that product liability costs are not major competitive factors for most industries. In a 1987 report, The Conference Board indicated that liability

Taking It to Court

More than 18 million civil cases were filed in state courts in 1990, split about evenly between trial-level courts and lower-level courts that mostly handle small claims. Statistical breakdowns available from 24 states indicate that domestic relations, small claims and other relatively minor cases comprise the bulk of the workload in trial-level courts, while tort suits constitute just 10 percent of the caseload.

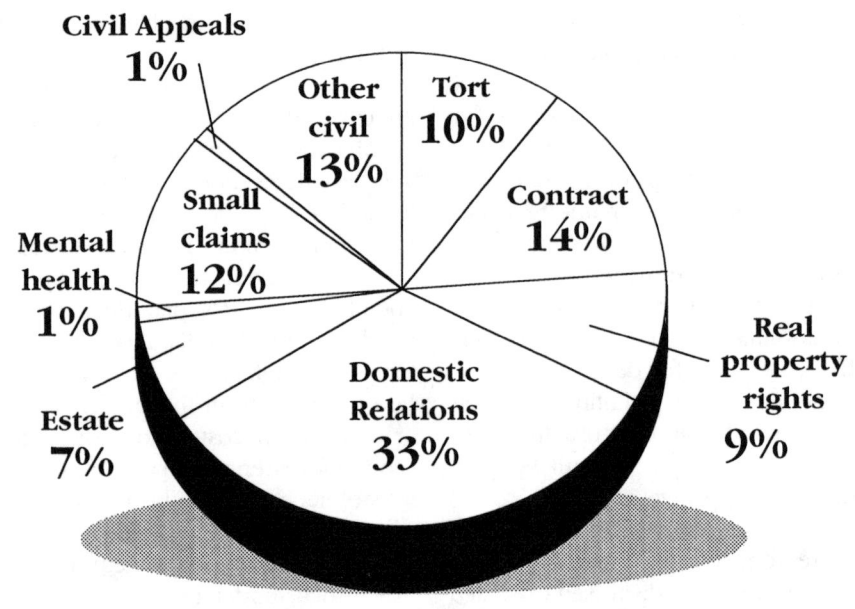

Civil Appeals
1%

Other civil 13%

Tort 10%

Small claims 12%

Contract 14%

Mental health 1%

Estate 7%

Domestic Relations 33%

Real property rights 9%

Source: National Center for State Courts, State Court Caseload Statistics: Annual Report 1990, *April 1992*

---

costs amounted to less than 1 percent of total costs for more than two-thirds of the companies surveyed. Several studies show the vast majority of product liability suits are either dropped or settled before trial for small amounts. And the Rand Institute for Civil Justice in 1985 produced a markedly lower estimate for the direct costs of the litigation system than the $80 billion figure claimed by critics of the system. The institute put the costs at between $29 billion and $36 billion.[9]

Huber contributed to a second influential book, *The Liability Maze,*[10] which he co-edited with Brookings Institution economist Robert E. Litan. The collection of papers written by a variety of experts sought to examine product liability's effects on safety

and innovation. The business coalition pushing federal product liability legislation touted the book as providing solid evidence that product suits had little effect on consumer safety but substantially reduced innovation in the industries studied. A closer reading, however, shows a more mixed message from the papers. Safety experts said litigation and the resultant publicity did contribute to product safety, while the three most critical papers about innovation were authored by experts with financial ties to the industries they were writing about.[11]

The Huber-Litan book nonetheless helped strengthen the critics' position as the Senate Commerce Committee moved toward a vote last fall on the product liability bill. Proponents of

the bill emphasized the innovation and competitiveness issue in winning 13-7 approval of the bill in October. Although two dissenting Democratic senators sharply challenged the thesis, the committee's bipartisan majority forcefully declared that the product liability system "has hurt our competitive position in world markets" because of excessive costs that result in higher prices for U.S. products.[12]

Should the losing party in a lawsuit be required to pay the winner's legal fees?

Critics of the legal system have a host of proposals aimed at making it more efficient and less expensive and correcting what they see as an imbalance in favor of plaintiffs and against business and other defendants.

For example, they want to: control the process called discovery, which allows both sides to gather evidence from the other before trial; limit the kinds of scientific evidence that can be offered to show, for example, links between chemical exposure and occupational illnesses; limit punitive damage awards — damages above the amount needed to compensate plaintiffs for their losses and designed to punish the defendant for unsafe or improper conduct; and encourage greater use of so-called alternative dispute-resolution techniques, such as mediation by non-judicial personnel. *(See story, p. 447.)*

The proposal at the top of the civil justice reform agenda, though, is simpler to understand than any of these. Currently, the typical rule in U.S. courts is that each side of a lawsuit is responsible for its own legal fees. Instead, critics want the losing party to pay the legal fees for the winning side. Adoption of this so-called "English rule" — followed in England and much of the rest of the world — would be, according to the Manhattan Institute's Walter Olson, "the single most important and constructive legal reform that ordinary citizens can fight for over the long term."[13]

While the idea has the strong backing of business groups and their supporters, proponents seek to depict the change as fairer to both sides. "The 'loser pays' rule ... is grounded in fairness — the equitable principle that a party who suffers should be made whole," the President's Council on Competitiveness stated in urging adoption of the idea for some federal court suits. "...[T]his approach will encourage litigants to evaluate carefully the merits of their cases before initiating a frivolous claim or adopting a spurious defense."

Plaintiffs' lawyers and consumer groups, however, fiercely oppose the idea. They insist that it would reduce access to the courts by making many plaintiffs wary of bringing lawsuits that could leave them stuck with their opponents' legal bills. In particular, they say litigants with ground-breaking lawsuits would be deterred. They note, for example, that many of the initial asbestos lawsuits were rejected before plaintiffs finally convinced courts that asbestos manufacturers should be held legally responsible for the serious diseases resulting from exposure to the substance.

Some critics also continue to press for limits on contingency-fee arrangements, which allow attorneys to take a specified percentage, usually one-third, of any settlement or jury award as their fee. The lawyer gets no fee if the plaintiff loses.

The practice has been controversial ever since its adoption in the late 19th century. Critics say it encourages litigation — and shady practices by a financially motivated lawyer once a lawsuit is filed. Supporters say contingent-fee arrangements are the only way that many ordinary citizens can bring a lawsuit. And some even suggest that the lawyer's financial stake in the outcome of the suit actually serves as a check on litigation — by making the lawyer reluctant to pursue a case that is likely to result in little or no fee.

The effects of changes in fee arrangements may be more complex, however, than partisans on either side of the debate suggest. Many legal observers, for example, believe jurors often award damages for "pain and suffering" in personal-injury cases in part to defray the plaintiff's cost in bringing the case. If attorney fees are added on top of those awards, some plaintiffs may collect a double recovery. At the same time, the prospect of collecting legal fees may lead some plaintiffs with legally strong but financially marginal claims to file lawsuits that they otherwise would not bring.

The Rand Institute's Deborah Hensler has suggested experimenting with fee-shifting in federal court contract cases between corporations. She argues that adoption of the practice in business cases could demonstrate its effects without creating new barriers to the legal system for individuals.[14]

The Bush administration also has called for limited experiments with fee-shifting. Its proposal would apply only to those cases filed in federal court because the opposing parties are from different states. And the fee-shifting would be limited to the amount the losing party incurred in its own case — thus preventing a successful party from running up the legal bills for the other side. ∎

BACKGROUND

Evolving Legal Doctrines

In 1842, Nicholas Farwell, a $2-a-day engineer for the Boston & Worcester Railroad, suffered a crushed hand when he was thrown from a derailed train in a switchyard. He sued the railroad, which blamed the accident on the switchman who allowed the train to be derailed.

In a famous opinion, *Farwell v. Boston & Worcester Railroad,* the Massachusetts Supreme Judicial Court sided with the railroad. Chief Justice Lemuel Shaw reasoned that Farwell had assumed the risk of a workplace accident when he took his job. The court said Farwell might recover from the switchman — his "fellow servant" — but the railroad itself had not been negligent and could not be held liable.

The so-called fellow-servant rule is the most notorious of several 19th-century legal doctrines that often protected railroads, mining companies and other business concerns from legal responsibility for the accidents and injuries that accompanied the industrial revolution in the United States. "The modern law of torts," legal historian Lawrence M. Friedman writes, "must be laid at the door of the industrial revolution, whose machines had a marvelous capacity for smashing the human body."[15]

Friedman and other legal scholars who have studied this period argue that courts in England and in the United States created these liability-limiting doctrines specifically to encourage industrial enterprise. Under these doctrines, compensation for accidents turned on who was at fault — in legal terms, negligence.

"Absolute liability" — what today is called "strict liability" — was "rejected ... or, more accurately, never even considered" because it "might have strangled the economy," Friedman writes. The doctrine of "contributory negligence" prevented accident victims from recovering damages if they had been partly at fault. The doctrine of "proximate cause" limited liability to damages closely connected to a defendant's actions — even if the defendant had been negligent. And — before the passage of so-called wrongful-death statutes — there was

Speaking of Lawyers…

"The first thing we do, let's kill all the lawyers."

— *Shakespeare,* Henry VI

"In all points out of their own trade they were the most ignorant and stupid generation among us, the most despicable in common conversation, avowed enemies to all knowledge and learning, and equally disposed to pervert the general reason of mankind in every other subject of discourse as in that of their own profession."

— *Jonathan Swift,* Gulliver's Travels

"The public regards lawyers with distrust. They think lawyers are smarter than the average guy, but use their intelligence deviously. Well, they're wrong. Usually, they're not smarter."

— *F. Lee Bailey, lawyer*

"Through the centuries, men of law have been persistently concerned with the resolution of disputes … in ways that enable society to achieve its goals with a minimum of force and maximum of reason."

— *Archibald Cox, Harvard law professor*

"There is far too much law for those who can afford it and far too little for those who cannot."

— *Derek Bok, former Harvard president*

"Doctors … still retain a high degree of public confidence because they are perceived as healers. Should lawyers not be healers? Healers, not warriors? Healers, not procurers? Healers, not hired guns?"

— *Warren E. Burger, former chief justice,*
U.S. Supreme Court

no recovery in fatal accidents since the only possible plaintiff was dead.

These doctrines spared railroads the cost of workplace injuries as well as damage to passengers, bystanders, livestock or property from crossing accidents, fires and so forth. In effect, Friedman argues, railroads and other emerging industries were given a subsidy at the expense of industrial-accident victims.[16]

Workers' Compensation

Legal doctrines pertaining to workplace accidents slowly evolved. Some courts created exceptions to the fellow-servant rule — for example, allowing recovery from an employer for accidents caused by a supervisor rather than a fellow employee. By 1910, the fellow-servant rule had been scrapped altogether in about half the states.

The broadest change, though, came from state legislatures rather than the courts. Workers' compensation laws created an administrative system requiring employers to pay workers for

workplace injuries without regard to who was at fault. Organized labor began lobbying for the change around the turn of the century and, between 1911 and 1948, succeeded in getting such laws enacted in all 48 states.

As Friedman describes the laws, both sides gave up something. Employers lost the court-made defenses to liability, including the fellow-servant rule, assumption of risk and contributory negligence. Employees lost the right to sue in court, and they were limited to recovering their medical expenses and a specified portion of their wages.

For much of the 20th century, the workers' compensation system was viewed largely as a success. In recent years, however, the costs have risen and the legal complexities have increased. Employer expenditures on workers' compensation rose from $1 billion in 1950 to $2 billion in 1960, $5 billion in 1970, $21 billion in 1980 and perhaps $50 billion today — almost equaling the rate of increase in tort litigation costs. Employers blame

this increase in part on new claims for compensation for job-related cancers and other occupational diseases, including such vaguely defined conditions as occupational stress.

But while employers complain about rising costs, employee groups and workers'-compensation attorneys view the system as stingy and increasingly difficult. They point out that benefit levels are not adjusted for inflation in most states, so that over time compensation becomes less and less adequate. Moreover, despite employers' complaints, most occupational-disease claimants do not receive compensation.[17]

No-Fault Insurance

If tort law was the child of the railroads, Lawrence Friedman writes, it was the adopted child of the automobile. Like the railroad, the automobile brought about efficient mass trans-

Continued on p. 443

Chronology

1800s *U.S. industrial revolution is accompanied by large number of workplace accidents, but legal doctrines prevent many workers from recovering compensation for their injuries.*

1842
Massachusetts Supreme Court adopts "fellow-servant rule" barring workers from suing employers for job-related injuries.

1870s
Lawyers begin to adopt "contingent fee" system — taking a fixed percentage of a client's recovery as their fee in personal injury cases. Many established lawyers criticize the practice, saying it encourages lawsuits.

—— • ——

1900-1950s *Tort law becomes more well-defined, with gradually liberalized rules helping accident victims to recover compensation for their injuries. Workers' compensation laws take job-related accidents out of the courts. Automobile accident cases become a major part of the workload of state courts.*

1911
Missouri becomes first state to adopt a law allowing workers to recover compensation for workplace injuries from employer-financed insurance system without regard to who was to blame for accident.

1916
New York Court of Appeals, in influential opinion written by Judge Benjamin Cardozo, allows car owner to sue manufacturer, not just dealer, for injury resulting from alleged defect.

1960s *Medical malpractice and product liability suits increase. Jury verdicts in personal injury cases also rise.*

1963
California Supreme Court establishes doctrine of strict liability for manufacturers for injuries resulting from defective or unreasonably dangerous products.

—— • ——

1970s *State legislatures pass no-fault auto insurance laws to try to keep accident cases out of courts and revise medical malpractice laws to try to limit costs for doctors and hospitals. Businesses begin to lobby for reform of product liability laws.*

1970
Massachusetts enacts nation's first no-fault automobile insurance law. About 24 states pass no-fault laws over next five years, but most leave room for court suits in many auto accident injuries.

1975
California enacts Medical Injury Compensation Reform Act, capping awards for pain and suffering in medical malpractice suits at $250,000 and limiting attorneys' fees. More than 20 other states enact medical malpractice reform laws over the next decade.

1978
Federal task force urges uniform national product liability law, but it is not adopted.

1980s *Insurance premiums rise and some insurers drop lines of coverage, leading to national debate over a perceived "insurance crisis." Tort reform measures are enacted in many states.*

May 30, 1986
President Ronald Reagan criticizes excessive jury awards in speech to American Tort Reform Association. But Reagan administration is viewed as giving only mild support to tort reform efforts in Congress.

—— • ——

1990s *Tort reform measures are viewed by some experts as having helped hold down insurance rates and slowed the increase in tort cases. Bush administration renews debate over "litigation explosion."*

March 4, 1991
Supreme Court says juries have wide latitude to impose punitive damages as long as they exercise discretion "within reasonable constraints."

Aug. 13, 1991
Vice President Dan Quayle, in speech to American Bar Association, calls U.S. liability system "a self-inflicted competitive disadvantage" and urges adoption of package of civil justice reform proposals.

Oct. 3, 1991
Senate Commerce Committee approves federal product liability bill in 13-7 vote. But supporters acknowledge it's unlikely to be enacted.

February 1992
American Bar Association "blueprint" for improving civil justice system calls for increased funding for courts and says tort reform should be left to the states.

Too Many Lawyers?

When Vice President Dan Quayle suggested last year that there were too many lawyers in the United States, his audience was understandably cool. After all, Quayle had been addressing the annual meeting of the American Bar Association (ABA).

But not all lawyers took umbrage at the question Quayle posed at the end of his speech: "Does America really need 70 percent of the world's lawyers?"

Some 650 California lawyers responding to a recent magazine poll agreed with the vice president. They represented about 76 percent of the lawyers who answered the unscientific mail-in poll in *California Lawyer* magazine, which is distributed to all of the state's 110,000 lawyers. Nearly half of the respondents — 47 percent — said they favored limiting the number of new lawyers admitted to the bar.

Poll results, published in the magazine's May issue, did not come from a statistically reliable, random sampling of the state's lawyers. But they do show that the anti-lawyer attitudes widespread among the public at large can be found even within the legal profession itself. And many of the respondents agreed with critics of the legal system that the rising tide of litigation stems directly from the growth of the U.S. lawyer population.

The number of lawyers in the United States has more than tripled in the past four decades — from 221,605 in 1951 to 777,119 as of December 1991, according to the ABA. The peak growth period was in the 1970s, when the lawyer population increased by more than 50 percent in 10 years, compared with a 40 percent increase during the 1980s.

Other professions also are increasing rapidly. The number of doctors, for example, increased 75 percent from 1971 to 1987, while the number of lawyers was increasing about 105 percent.

Barbara Curran, a researcher for the ABA-funded American Bar Foundation, attributes the legal profession's growth to a number of factors, including the post-World War II baby boom, the increased popularity of postgraduate degrees and, in particular, the increase in the number of women entering law schools since the 1970s. She declines to enter the debate over whether there are too many lawyers.

"The one thing that can be said is that [only] 5 percent of the lawyer population is not actively employed," Curran says. "So they are finding employment in the economy."

University of Wisconsin law Professor Marc Galanter describes the 70 percent figure cited by Quayle as vastly exaggerated. Galanter says critics of the legal system, including former Chief Justice Warren E. Burger, have been using the statistic since the early 1980s with no explanation of where it came from.

Compiling data from 49 countries, Galanter said he counted about 1.9 million lawyers as of the mid-1980s, with the U.S. number of 655,000 in 1985 amounting to about one-third of that total. He estimated a full count would show the U.S. lawyer population was between 25 percent and 35 percent of the worldwide total.[†]

Galanter's estimate for the number of lawyers in Japan has been challenged. The figure he used — 124,000 lawyers — is far higher than the approximately 14,000 members of the Japanese Federation of Bar Associations. But Galanter and many other experts say that a more meaningful tally for Japan should include the larger number of trained professionals who draft legal documents, serve as tax attorneys or work as government or in-house corporate advisers but are not members of the tightly controlled bar federation.

For its part, the ABA dismisses the critics' underlying premise: "There is no evidence that U.S. citizens bring more lawsuits because we have more lawyers," an ABA fact sheet declares.

Number of Lawyers Rising

The rate of increase in the number of lawyers has surpassed that of the general population, as reflected in the progressive decline of population/lawyer ratios from 1 lawyer per 695 people in 1951 to 1 lawyer per 340 people in 1988.

Year	Number	Ratio
1951	221,605	695:1
1960	285,933	627:1
1971	355,242	418:1
1980	655,191	360:1
1988	723,189	340:1
Dec. 1991	777,119	NA

Source: American Bar Foundation, American Bar Association, 1991

U.S. Leads the World

Lawyers per 100,000 population

U.S.	England & Wales	Germany
281	111	82

[†]Marc Galanter, "The Debased Debate on Civil Justice," *Institute of Legal Studies,* University of Wisconsin-Madison, February 1992. A version of the paper was published in *Legal Times,* Feb. 17, 1992, p. 26.

Continued from p. 440
portation at the cost of countless property-damaging, injury-inflicting and death-causing accidents. Those accidents landed in a 20th-century court system with a more developed set of rules for assigning responsibility and awarding compensation on the basis of who was at fault.

By the 1950s, auto accidents had become the bread-and-butter of the nation's civil courts — and the lawyers who practiced in them. The legal system for handling these cases was undergirded by private insurance. Most, but not all, drivers bought insurance to pay for injuries they caused to other drivers, passengers or pedestrians — so-called third-party coverage. Many drivers also had "first-party" coverage to pay their own expenses if they were hurt.

As auto insurance premiums rose in the 1950s and early '60s, many consumer-minded critics began arguing that using the court system to handle these cases was unnecessarily expensive and inefficient. Even worse, they argued, compensation often appeared to be arbitrary. Seriously injured accident victims might receive nothing if they were at fault or if the driver at fault was uninsured. On the other hand, some plaintiffs won seemingly excessive jury awards that covered not just their medical expenses but their "pain and suffering" as well.

Two legal scholars — Robert Keeton, then at Harvard Law School and now a federal judge in Boston, and Jeffrey O'Connell, then at the University of Illinois law school and now at the University of Virginia law school — crafted a solution: no-fault insurance. Based in part on the workers' compensation model, the plan called for mandatory auto insurance to pay accident victims predetermined amounts for their personal injuries without regard to who was at fault. In exchange for assured and speedy compensation, accident victims were to lose the right to sue in court.[18]

Some 24 states enacted some type of no-fault insurance law between 1970 and 1975, and supporters were pushing for federal legislation as well. But the drive stalled, largely because of the opposition of personal-injury lawyers and their national organization, the Association of Trial Lawyers of America.

These lawyers argued that no-fault deprived accident victims of the right to recover damages for injuries caused by someone else and instead limited them to inadequate compensation paid for from their own insurance. Proponents of no-fault charged that the lawyers simply wanted to keep auto cases in the courts to protect their own fees.

Today, no-fault supporters acknowledge that the laws have not brought insurance rates down, but they blame the disappointing results on a failure to stick to the original plan. While a few states enacted no-fault statutes that barred suits in all but the most serious accidents, most of the 24 no-fault states — 14, by O'Connell's count — enacted laws that provided only modest no-fault benefits and eliminated relatively few fault-finding claims. Eight states enacted what O'Connell called "add-on plans" that provided no-fault benefits in some cases without any restrictions on fault-based suits.[19]

No-fault gained some new momentum in the late 1980s, especially after California voters approved a 1988 ballot initiative requiring a 20 percent cutback in car insurance premiums.[20] But the interest faded. Today, the effort for a federal bill is moribund, while states grapple with the details of existing laws.

Medical Malpractice

The no-fault insurance debates of the early 1970s were followed by a second wave of tort reform proposals. These aimed at containing a sharp rise in lawsuits that blamed medical injuries on alleged negligence by doctors, other health-care providers and hospitals.

Medical malpractice suits had been rare in the 19th century and well into the 20th century. In the late 1960s and early '70s, however, the medical community was stung by what historian Friedman calls "a small but important group of cases that produced huge recoveries."[21] The number of claims against doctors rose from 1 per 100 physicians in 1960 to 2.5 per 100 physicians in the mid-1970s. And insurance costs soared. Premiums for hospitals rose 263 percent between 1960 and 1970, those for physicians other than surgeons increased 541 percent and those for surgeons rose 950 percent.[22]

Doctors spoke of a medical malpractice crisis and blamed it on "greedy, grasping, unethical shysters, stirred by their unconscionable contingent fees, who in turn stir up, or at least join with, ungrateful, unrealistic and ignorant patients."[23] Doctors believed that when lawyers presented these cases before juries with little understanding of medical procedures, the frequent result was an unjustified verdict in favor of a sympathetic plaintiff at the expense of a physician who had done nothing wrong.

Others said doctors were exaggerating the malpractice crisis and over-simplifying its causes.[24] The reasons for the surge in malpractice suits, they said, lay not just with lawyers and patients but with changes in the medical profession itself. Greater specialization had reduced the personal relationship between patient and doctor. Advances in medical knowledge had established links in some cases between medical injuries and improper medical procedures. And, as with other personal-injury lawsuits, rising health-care costs were a major reason for the increasing amounts paid out in settlements or jury awards.

Doctors succeeded in convincing

View From the Executive Suite

More than 80 percent of the executives responding to a recent survey say their decisions are increasingly affected by the fear of lawsuits, and 62 percent believe the legal system significantly hampers U.S. competitiveness.

Would you say that the fear of lawsuits has more or less impact on decision-making within your company today than it did 10 years ago?

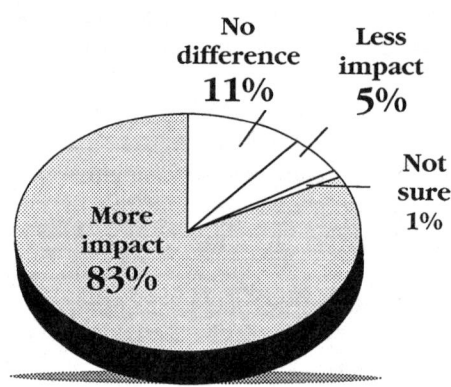

No difference **11%**

Less impact **5%**

Not sure **1%**

More impact **83%**

Do you feel that the U.S. civil justice system significantly hampers the ability of U.S. companies to compete with Japanese and European companies, or don't you feel that way?

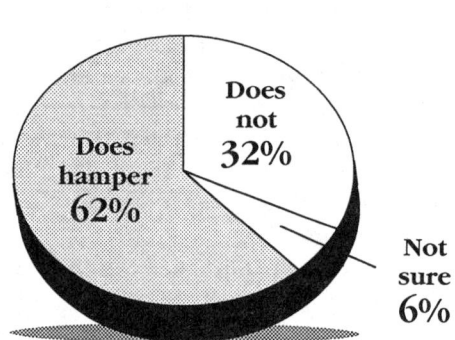

Does not **32%**

Does hamper **62%**

Not sure **6%**

In your company, would you say that the following have a major impact, a minor impact, or almost no impact on your business?

	Major impact	Minor impact	Almost no impact	Not sure
The high cost of defending and protecting the company from litigation	40%	49%	11%	0%
Fear of litigation that hampers the introduction of valuable new products or entry into new markets	10	47	42	1
Legal issues that divert valuable management time and energy from running the business	44	50	6	0

Source: Survey of 400 senior executives at corporations drawn from the Business Week *Top 1000. Interviews were conducted Jan. 27-Feb. 11, 1992, for* Business Week *by Louis Harris & Associates, Inc.*

much of the public, however, that the crisis required steps to make it harder for plaintiffs to win malpractice suits and to limit the amounts doctors had to pay in any successful suits. California led the way with a 1975 law that set a $250,000 cap on awards for pain and suffering in medical malpractice suits, limited lawyers' fees in such cases and added procedural burdens for plaintiffs. Over the next decade, 22 more states enacted similar reform laws.

While many of the reform statutes were relatively mild, they appeared to be having some effect in stabilizing malpractice insurance premiums and slowing the increase in claims filed. Premiums paid by doctors, which had increased from $1.9 billion in 1984 to $4 billion in 1987, dropped to $3.9 billion in 1988 and appeared to drop further in 1989 and 1990.[25] The rate of claims against doctors also appeared to stabilize, with such high-risk specialists as anesthesiologists, obstetricians and surgeons all reporting a drop in claims rates between 1985 and 1989.

A research team from Harvard University revived the debate over medical malpractice suits in March 1990, when it recommended a type of no-fault compensation system for medical injuries. The researchers said they found negligence in 1.3 percent of more than 30,000 records they studied from New York hospitals. Based on that rate, they estimated that the incidence of malpractice was 10 times greater than the number of claims filed in the state. To close that gap, the research team, led by Harvard law school Professor Paul Weiler, recommended a no-fault compensation system and argued it would be no more costly than the existing liability system.[26]

Looking to curb health-care costs, the Bush administration considered the no-fault plan as one possible way to reform the medical malpractice system. But after a year's study, the administration chose instead to propose more conventional reform proposals, including a financial incentive for states to adopt a $250,000 cap on pain-and-suffering awards. The administration's proposal failed to advance in Congress in 1991, but President Bush included a recycled version in a broad health-care reform plan he outlined in February.

Product Liability

A third wave of tort reform proposals began to emerge in the late 1970s to try to contain another surging category of litigation: product liability suits.

In less than a decade, the number of suits claiming injuries from dangerous or defective products increased by one count from 50,000 to 500,000 in the mid-1970s, while product liability insurance premiums increased an estimated 500 percent between 1950 and 1970.[27] Like doctors a few years earlier, manufacturers viewed the litigation explosion as a crisis and began searching for ways to make it harder for plaintiffs to win suits and to limit damage awards in any successful suits.

Unlike the doctors, manufacturers could point to a specific legal development as one cause of the rash of product-related suits: the development of the doctrine of "strict liability" for unreasonably dangerous or defective products.[28] In a key decision in 1963, the California Supreme Court ruled that plaintiffs did not have to prove a manufacturer had been negligent in order to recover damages.[29] Instead, manufacturers were held strictly liable for injuries resulting from a defect that made the product "unsafe for its intended use."

Within a decade, strict liability for suits based on manufacturing defects had been adopted in most states. Proponents argued the rule broke down artificial legal barriers to compensating accident victims and encouraged manufacturers to make safer products. Critics called it social engineering that penalized manufacturers solely because of their ability to pay. More recently, critics such as Peter Huber have charged that the rule discourages manufacturers from marketing some products or developing new ones, especially in such risk-laden fields as chemicals and pharmaceuticals.[30]

Strict liability is not as strict, though, as the critics depict. Manufacturers still have many lines of defense. They can show, for example, that the product was not "unreasonably" dangerous, that the product was not the cause of the injury, that they provided adequate warnings about the dangers of the product or that the consumer contributed to the accident. Moreover, in the most common types of product-related suits, courts have adopted balancing tests — for example, weighing the cost of designing a safer product against the benefit to the consumer — that resemble traditional negligence more than strict liability.

Product liability suits, nonetheless, were clearly exacting a toll on manufacturers, who turned to Congress and the state legislatures for relief. In the early 1980s, business groups were pushing for federal legislation to cap awards for pain and suffering at $250,000, bar repeated awards for punitive damages in separate cases and replace strict liability with negligence in product-related suits in state and federal courts. After those bills failed in Congress, they crafted less ambitious legislation in the late 1980s that would have provided manufacturers with some new defenses and raised the proof needed to win punitive damages. Despite a business-coalition lobbying drive with a $1.5 million budget in 1990, those bills also failed to pass.[31]

Business groups enjoyed greater success in the states. Between 1986 and 1989, 46 states enacted product liability legislation of some form. While some of the laws were relatively mild, and none provided the uniform national standards sought by business, they helped stem the rise in insurance premiums.

At the same time, two Cornell Law School professors — James Henderson and Theodore Eisenberg — detected a shift in judicial attitudes in favor of defendants in product suits. Based on an examination of court decisions between 1979 and 1988, they found the success rate for plaintiffs had declined markedly — from 55 percent to 37 percent in the appellate courts and from 40 percent to 32 percent at the trial level.[32]

The apparent change in the courts' handling of product liability suits and the slowed growth in the number of such suits did not stop the business groups' pressure for change. But with state reforms on the books and federal legislation acknowledged even by supporters to be most unlikely, the issue appears to be at a stalemate.

The Insurance 'Crisis'

In the early and mid-1980s, the debates over liability and litigation broadened as insurance costs soared, not just for doctors and manufacturers but for a broad range of businesses, local governments and nonprofit institutions. Insurers blamed the increases on an explosion of lawsuits, legal doctrines skewed in favor of plaintiffs and juries that awarded accident victims unjustified damage awards to be paid for by any available "deep-pocket" defendant with little regard for who was really at fault.

Premium increases of anywhere from 60 percent to as high as 1,500 percent were widely reported. Some insurance customers, such as day-care centers, nurse-midwives and some local governments, said they could not get insurance at any price. Figures from the Insurance Information Institute showed the industry's net profit dropped from 18.1 percent in 1978 to 1.8 percent in 1984. The sense of crisis was captured by a *Time* magazine cover story in 1986: "Sorry, America, Your Policy Has Been Canceled."[33]

Some industry critics, such as Robert Hunter of the National Insurance Consumer Organization, tried at the time to shift the blame for increased premiums away from the liability system. Hunter said insurers had underpriced coverage during the early 1980s in a competitive effort to attract dollars when high interest rates meant high returns for investments. When interest rates began to fall, Hunter said, insurance companies had to raise premiums sharply in order to try to make up for the lower rate of return on investments and for the previous underpricing.

But the public sense of a widespread insurance crisis caused by a liability system run amok led more than 40 states to enact general tort reform measures aimed at slowing the increase in insurance rates and costs.[34] Some bills capped damage awards for pain and suffering or limited punitive damages. Others provided for payment of damage awards over time rather than in a single lump sum. And some provided that damage awards be reduced by any amount a plaintiff received from another source, such as his or her own insurance.

The provisions most commonly included in the reform measures modified a legal doctrine called "joint and several liability" that was a special concern to municipal governments. The doctrine provides that if two defendants are found responsible for an injury, each one is "jointly liable" for damages and has to pay the entire award if the other fails to pay its share. Supporters of the doctrine say it protects an innocent plaintiff from a financial loss just because a judgment cannot be enforced against one

defendant. But local governments said that expansive liability rulings often meant they were stuck with an entire damage award when they were only minimally responsible.

In one prominently discussed case, for example, a driver high on drugs ran a stop sign and collided with another vehicle. A jury held the city of Los Angeles 22 percent responsible for the accident because of bushes obstructing the view of the stop sign. The jury awarded the brain-damaged plaintiff $2.16 million, and the city had to pay almost the entire amount because the driver was insolvent.

The reform measures took various approaches to limiting this form of extended liability. Some laws allowed joint and several liability only for di-

rect economic losses rather than the more amorphous pain and suffering awards. Some allowed joint liability only if the defendant was found at least 50 percent at fault. And a small number of statutes repealed joint liability altogether.

Today, the impact of the wave of tort reform legislation is subject to debate. Insurance premiums have continued to increase, though not sharply, while the industry's profits have improved. Two researcher have calculated that tort reform laws saved consumers $2.6 billion in insurance premiums.[35]

But critics say these trends prove the "crisis" was only a temporary industry cycle rather than a pervasive problem tied to legal trends. ∎

CURRENT SITUATION

Quayle's Reform Initiative

The Bush administration's interest in civil justice issues reportedly originated with Vice President Dan Quayle, a lawyer, who began looking into the area in December 1990 as a possible topic for the competitiveness council that he heads. The next month, Quayle named Solicitor General Kenneth W. Starr, the Justice Department's third-ranking official, to head an interdepartmental task force to draft a package of civil justice reform proposals.

Quayle's speech to the American Bar Association last August drew attention to 50 proposals that otherwise might have seemed too technical to merit public attention. Three sets of items contained in the 28-page report by the Council on Competitiveness were especially contro-

versial: requiring the losing party in a lawsuit to pay the other side's legal fees; making it harder for a plaintiff to win punitive damages; and revising the discovery process to mandate early disclosure of so-called "core information" but impose costs for additional document production on the party seeking the information.

The package sought to reduce the number of trials by encouraging use of mediation, arbitration or other "alternative dispute resolution" techniques; requiring a plaintiff to give formal notice to a defendant before filing suit; and requiring plaintiffs to pay trial costs if a jury award is less than the defendant's final settlement offer. Other items called for financial sanctions against unreasonable discovery requests and "unfounded assertions" in court filings. Several items were aimed at controlling the use of testimony from "expert" witnesses.

Only half of the items in the package envisioned federal legislation. The other items called for such steps as encouraging judicial action or drafting model legislative provisions

Continued on p. 448

Settling Out of Court: Alternative Dispute Resolution

When someone wishing to file a lawsuit enters the District of Columbia Superior Court Building in Washington, his final destination may not be a courtroom. Instead, the court may try to channel the problem into one of several alternate procedures for resolving legal disputes.

Small claims cases, for example, are referred to a judge who encourages the plaintiff and defendant to sit down with a mediator to try to work out a resolution acceptable to both sides. Civil suits for more than $2,000 may also be referred to mediation or to other techniques — called case evaluation and arbitration — that use local lawyers rather than judges to recommend or impose a settlement.

Proponents say alternative dispute resolution, or ADR, can help unclog the courts and can settle legal disputes more quickly and less expensively. The President's Council on Competitiveness puts "voluntary use of ADR techniques" at the top of its list of proposed civil justice reforms. Alternative dispute resolution has long had the backing of the American Bar Association (ABA), which says it has "the potential to become ... an effective and cost-expeditious settlement device for attorneys and litigants."

Praise for alternative dispute resolution is not universal, however. Austin Sarat, a professor in law and jurisprudence at Amherst College, calls ADR "a technocratic solution to a non-technocratic problem." Laura Nader, an anthropology professor at the University of California in Berkeley, says ADR "trades justice for harmony." †

Even some supporters of alternative dispute resolution concede that it has not achieved the benefits claimed by more enthusiastic proponents. Ohio Attorney General Lee Fisher says many of the mediation units established by state attorneys general in recent years — including the one in his own office — often amount to "nothing beyond a glorified intake procedure." Critics also have raised questions about private, for-profit mediation services that operate, as Sarat puts it, "under the shadow of the court."

Despite such concerns, the use of alternative dispute resolution has spread to more than 400 local court systems around the country. Washington's Superior Court — the local trial court for the nation's capital — established its ADR office in 1985. The division handles only a small fraction of the District court's annual flow of more than 141,000 civil cases. In 1991, judges referred about 2,300 small claims to mediation, along with 160 domestic relations matters. About 3,800 civil suits were referred to the division — 2,800 for mediation, 400 for case evaluation and just under 600 for arbitration.

These techniques resolve many, but not all, disputes. Mediation — in which the mediator takes a passive role, merely helping the parties fashion their own solution — has a settlement rate of about 50 percent. Case evaluation — in which lawyers recommend a settlement based on what they think the case would be worth if taken to trial — has a similar settlement rate. Arbitration — in which a lawyer hears evidence and issues a decision that may be binding or nonbinding depending on the parties' decision at the outset — has a higher disposition rate, about 70 percent.

District court officials say surveys show that about 80 percent of the people who have gone through the ADR process were satisfied with the service, whether or not they accepted the recommended settlement. As in most jurisdictions, Washington's ADR program is voluntary — at least in theory. But critics say an ADR program inevitably has an element of coercion. "There's an implicit threat that the situation will be worse if you come back to court," Sarat says.

In some place, alternative-dispute-resolution methods have been made mandatory. California requires couples to go to mediation before filing for divorce. Pennsylvania requires arbitration for disputes involving less than $10,000. "This adds another step to go through to get to court," Sarat says. "It hasn't simplified things; it's made them more complex."

Even the president of the American Arbitration Association, Robert Coulson, questions the wisdom of forcing arbitration or mediation on litigants. "Mandatory ADR verges on coercion," he says. "Even when a court-administered system is acceptable to most parties, there will be some who would rather obtain a trial in open court."

The critics' broadest fears, though, center on issues of public accountability. Laura Nader — sister of consumer activist Ralph Nader — complains that mediators and arbitrators do not keep public records of their cases. She also notes that some researchers have found that mediators "may adjudicate when they are supposed to be mediating."

Questions about public accountability have been heightened as ADR proponents have expanded their vision beyond resolving "minor disputes" to encompass more substantial legal disagreements. In fact, businesses have become the biggest ADR users — opting out of the public judicial system to get what they regard as quicker, less expensive and more private resolutions of their disputes. Despite the criticisms, alternative dispute resolution seems likely to grow as rising caseloads strain state court systems, and lawyers, litigants and the general public look for ways to cope.

---

† Sarat made the comment in an interview. For a written presentation of his views, see Austin Sarat, "Alternative Dispute Resolution: Wrong Solution, Wrong Problem," in Walter K. Olson, ed., *New Directions in Liability Law* (1988). Nader's remarks and following comments by Lee Fisher and Robert Coulson are from articles in the winter 1992 issue of *Forum,* a publication of the National Institute for Dispute Resolution in Washington.

Continued from p. 446

for states to consider. The administration had no legislation ready when the council's report was released in August 1991. When Republican lawmakers did introduce civil justice reform measures in early February, the bills included only a handful of the Quayle group's recommendations, steering clear of such controversial areas as discovery reform, financial sanctions and expert witnesses.

The Bar's Response

The ABA's decision to respond to Quayle in time for the same day's news coverage indicated the lawyers' sensitivity to renewed criticisms of the legal system. But with Quayle viewed by most observers as a decisive winner in the face-off, the ABA and other lawyer groups appeared to recognize the need for a more affirmative response.

In February, the ABA released its own, 150-page "blueprint" for improving the civil justice system. The reform package, released at the ABA's midyear meeting in Dallas, was highlighted by proposals to increase funding for state and federal courts and legal aid programs and to provide tax breaks for employer-provided prepaid legal service programs. But it urged that tort reform issues be left to the states, called for limiting discovery through better enforcement of existing rules and took no position on the "loser pays" rule for shifting attorney fees.

The ABA document responded item by item to the recommendations in the Council on Competitiveness report — by one rough count, agreeing with about 20, disagreeing with 12 and taking no position on the rest.[36] More generally, though, the ABA labeled the council's report "too narrow" because it failed to address the legal system's greatest problems: underfunding and inadequate access. The administration's agenda, the ABA concluded, "may please some busi-ness and industry groups, but will do little to bring justice to poor and middle-class Americans."

The ABA meeting also provided a forum for experts to challenge the statistical foundation of Quayle's August attack. At one session, University of Wisconsin Professor Galanter unveiled a paper disputing Quayle's assertion that the United States had 70 percent of the world's lawyers; Galanter said a better estimate was between 25 percent and 35 percent. And Rand researcher Hensler took issue with Quayle's description of the 18 million civil lawsuits filed in the United States in 1990 — "one for every 10 adult Americans" — as "making us the most litigious society in the world." Hensler said the bulk of the cases were routine filings for divorces, wills or small claims.

The better measure of litigiousness, Hensler suggested, was to look at what she called "discretionary" suits — contract and tort cases. She estimated they numbered about 2.5 mil-lion cases — 1.5 million contract suits and just under 1 million tort suits. "This amounts to one of these types of suits for every 75 adult Americans," Hensler said, "suggesting that we are a good deal less litigious than the vice president and the [competitiveness] council would have us believe."

The refutations and criticisms left administration officials unmoved. Speaking at one of the ABA sessions, Deputy Assistant Attorney General J. Mark Gridley brushed off the argument over counting lawyers. Whatever the number, he said, it "seems like a lot to legislators anyway."

Two weeks later, when a reporter for the *ABA Journal* asked Quayle's spokesman David Beckwith for reaction to the ABA's reform proposals, he was openly derisive: "Is this the one that calls for more money in the pockets of lawyers? More money for the Legal Services Corp.? More money for the Department of Justice to hire more lawyers to study laws? Have I missed anything?"[37]   ■

OUTLOOK

Drastic Changes Unlikely

The law's expense and delay have been the target of critics and legal reformers since Charles Dickens' 1853 novel *Bleak House* chronicled the wasting of a great estate through interminable court battles. For much of American history, such complaints came primarily from people of modest means. In the past 30 years or so, this popular dissatisfaction with the pace of justice has been augmented by growing complaints from business sectors about the cost of litigating and compensating personal injury suits.

The civil justice reform measures currently being debated by the Bush administration, the legal profession and others come out of this debate over tort suits. Some items, though, would have across-the-board effects on litigants and courts. The administration's decision to take on the issue has elevated the debate and encouraged the business groups clamoring most loudly for change.

The legal system has proved slow to change in the past, however. And many changes will have to overcome not just judicial inertia but also the entrenched opposition from those who benefit from existing legal doctrines, including consumer groups and substantial segments of the legal profession itself.

Action on these issues can come from any of 50 state legislatures and court systems, Congress or the federal judiciary itself. Here is what to look for on some of the major topics

Continued on p. 450

At Issue:

Has there been a litigation explosion in the United States?

WALTER K. OLSON

Senior Fellow at the Manhattan Institute
FROM *THE LITIGATION EXPLOSION*, 1991.

*a*merica's litigation explosion was not inevitable.... The trend proceeded gradually over decades and then quite suddenly moved into high gear in the late 1960s and 1970s, amid little real public debate. Taken together, the changes amount to a unique experiment in freeing the legal profession and the litigious impulse from age-old constraints....

The experiment has been a disaster, an unmitigated failure. The unleashing of litigation in its full fury has done grave harm and little lasting good....

America's common law tradition, like the legal tradition of every great nation, formerly viewed a lawsuit as an evil, at best a necessary evil....

These views shaped the most fundamental features of the old legal system. First and foremost were the ethical rules set up to control the legal profession itself. Yesterday's lawyers were specifically forbidden to "stir up litigation." ... The rules of legal procedure, until not long ago, provided a second line of defense. Their consistent theme was to narrow and focus a dispute within close limits....

The third line of defense against litigation was the most subtle yet vital of all.... Judges and lawmakers alike took care to spell out clear, definite lines of responsibility. Courts in particular tended to yield to the spirit of private contract — of letting people shape their own legal rights, responsibilities, and duties....

Squinted at from a distance, litigation would appear to have a brighter side. When successful, it brings some benefit ("relief") to the instigator: money, rights to visit a child, cessation of some local nuisance.... Maybe litigation is also a tough form of punishment and example-setting, which teaches those who misbehave an emphatic, not-soon-to-be-forgotten lesson.

The idea of treating lawsuits as vessels for "compensation" and "deterrence" is seductive. In no time at all you get to thinking of them less as a personal tragedy and more as a personal opportunity....

With each step along the way critics predicted and supporters seldom bothered to deny that more lawsuits would result. And that is exactly what happened. America did not begin litigating more and harder because its population suddenly took it into its head to become more contentious. We got more lawsuits because those who shaped our legal system wanted more lawsuits. The American litigation explosion was no enigmatic Big Bang out of a void. It had a long traceable fuse.

MARC GALANTER

Law Professor at the University of Wisconsin
FROM *NEW DIRECTIONS IN LIABILITY LAW*, 1988.

*c*urrent discussions of the litigation system display a sensitivity to the various kinds of costs, direct and indirect, that attend the system. One hears much of bizarre claims, immense jury verdicts, undeserved windfalls, the emergence of contingent-fee lawyers, the financial devastation of defendants and other horrors that befall the participants in specific cases. One also hears much about the deleterious effects of litigation in the large — that it dampens enterprise, distracts managers, makes doctors practice defensive medicine, increases the costs of products, keeps useful products off the market and so on.

One hears much less of the benefits of litigation — that in addition to its direct provision of compensation, it supports a vast system of bargaining in which almost all disputes are resolved by negotiation and that it stimulates a host of preventive activities by threatening and educating those engaged in the various activities that underlie injuries and disputes.

Respect for the available evidence suggests a more benign reading of the current situation.... The United States is not faced with an inexorable exponential explosion of cases but with a series of local changes, some sudden but most incremental, as particular kinds of troubles move in and out of the ambit of the courts....

Why is the bad face of law evident and its good face hidden to many? ... [T]wo points deserve mention. First, litigation implies accountability to public standards. This heightening of public accountability in the courts can be seen as a counter to deregulation in the executive branch of government, and as such is unwelcome in many quarters....

[L]itigation patterns have changed, too. The kind of litigation that once dominated the system — lawsuits to enforce market relations — has given way to tort, civil-rights and public-law cases that "correct" the market. It is litigation aimed "upwards" — by outsiders, clients, and dependents against authorities and managers of established institutions — that excites most of the reproach of the litigious society.

It is not claimed that the system is optimal, that its benefits outweigh all its costs, or that the current patterns of litigation represent the best way to achieve those benefits. But it should be recognized that the benefits are real and that any assessment of the social value of litigation must take them into account in comparing the net effects of present litigation patterns with those of proposed or likely alternatives.

Continued from p. 448

being debated:

Fee-shifting: The administration-backed bills in Congress would adopt the "loser pays" rule for cases brought in federal courts because they involve citizens from different states. Legal reformers want fee shifting to be widely adopted, but the change will face strong resistance in Congress or state legislatures from trial lawyers, consumer groups and others. Proposals to restrict or prohibit contingency fee arrangements would be even more strenuously opposed by trial lawyers and are unlikely to advance in the near future.

Punitive damages: Despite several studies questioning the frequency of punitive damage awards, more than 30 states have enacted restrictions of one form or another. And the U.S. Supreme Court, in a 1991 decision, *Pacific Mutual Life Insurance Co. v. Haslip,* provided a limited constitutional basis for challenging punitive damage awards if they are "unreasonable" or "extreme."

The administration is urging the states to require a higher level of proof — what is called "clear and convincing" evidence — for punitive damage awards and to prohibit any punitive damage award above the amount given for compensatory damages. Restrictive measures may continue to advance slowly in state legislatures. Meanwhile, three states — South Carolina, Virginia and West Virginia — have struck down their punitive damage laws because of the U.S. Supreme Court ruling, while some others have upheld their laws under the court's guidelines.

Discovery: Created to try to speed up and simplify the litigation process by requiring disclosure of information in advance of trial, discovery is today widely viewed as having turned into a nightmare. Lawyers on both sides swamp their adversaries with lengthy questionnaires called interrogatories or voluminous documents in response.

The administration's plan — not included in the bills introduced in Congress — combined early disclosure of "core information" about a case with numerical limits on additional discovery requests and cost-shifting provisions for the party seeking information to pay for the other side's cost of producing it.

Some corporate lawyers opposed mandatory disclosure. Plaintiffs' lawyers responded that without disclosure, the numerical limits would unduly hamper their ability to gather needed evidence. Despite the controversy, a federal judicial advisory group in April recommended a disclosure provision similar to the administration's proposal. The recommendation must be acted on by the U.S. Judicial Conference and the Supreme Court before adoption.[38]

Expert evidence: The administration has embraced the proposal of critics such as Peter Huber to change the broad interpretation of a provision in the Federal Rules of Evidence permitting use of expert testimony if it "may assist the trier of fact." They want to return to a standard adopted in a 1923 case, *Frye v. United States,* that allowed expert testimony only if it was generally accepted within the scientific community.[39]

The administration's plan was not included in the bills introduced in Congress. In addition, the Supreme Court in January declined to take a case raising the issue.

Alternatives to litigation: The apparent consensus in favor of alternative dispute-resolution techniques masks an important disagreement. The administration envisions out-of-court mediation or arbitration as a way of diverting cases from the legal system, while legal groups view these alternatives as low-cost forums for disputes that are not currently being brought into the courts. The programs are likely to continue to grow, but their impact on court caseloads remains to be seen.

Court funding: State courts, which handle 99 percent of the nation's litigation, are understaffed and underfunded in comparison with the federal judicial system. But state budgets are tight, many state court systems are experiencing cutbacks, and substantial budget increases are unlikely until the nation's economy gets out of its slump.

Product liability: The business coalition continues to push for federal legislation, but supporters acknowledge it is unlikely to be enacted. The movement for state legislation also appears to have crested.

Medical malpractice: President Bush's health-care reform plan announced in February included several provisions aimed at reducing medical malpractice litigation. He proposed financial incentives for the states to adopt tort reform measures and a number of steps, including fee-shifting, to encourage use of mediation or other alternatives to litigation.[40]

Some Democratic-written health plans also include provisions aimed at reducing medical malpractice litigation. But the whole issue is too complex and contentious for Congress to move on this election year. And as with product liability, the wave of reform laws at the state level appears to have crested.

No-fault auto insurance: Auto insurance rates continue to be a volatile issue — as shown by California voters' approval of a 1988 initiative requiring a 20 percent rollback in premiums. No-fault laws originally enacted in the 1970s, however, have been less successful than hoped in keeping cases out of the courts because they provided low benefits or continued to allow lawsuits in many types of cases. Today, the issue lacks momentum.

Overall, the most likely prognosis for the legal system appears to be for modest changes at most. Critics may view the slow pace of change as evidence of the need for more radical reforms, while the legal profession's defenders may lose interest in pushing for any change. Without some improvements, however, public disenchantment seems likely to grow.

The challenge for the opposing sides in this polarized debate is to avoid a stalemate and instead find common ground in moving toward the unrealized goal of speedy, affordable justice for all.

Kenneth Jost, a lawyer, is a freelance writer in Washington.

Notes

[1] National Center for State Courts, *State Court Caseload Statistics: Annual Report 1990,* April 1992. The caseload total includes civil, criminal, juvenile and traffic or other ordinance violation cases. The report covers all 50 states, Puerto Rico and the District of Columbia, whose local court system functions as a state court.

[2] "The Lawsuit Cha-Cha," *Time,* Aug. 26, 1991, p. 54; "Do We Have Too Many Lawyers?" *Newsweek,* Aug. 26, 1991, p. 58. Quayle addressed the ABA on Aug. 13, 1991.

[3] Bob Gibbons, "Propositions Built on Myth," *National Law Journal,* Oct. 7, 1991, p. 17.

[4] Deborah R. Hensler, "Taking Aim at the American Legal System: The Council on Competitiveness's Agenda for Legal Reform," *Judicature,* February-March 1992, p. 245.

[5] Walter K. Olson, *The Litigation Explosion: What Happened When America Unleashed the Lawsuit* (1991).

[6] Marc Galanter, "Beyond the Litigation Panic," in Walter Olson, ed., *New Directions in Liability Law* (1988), pp. 26, 29.

[7] Peter W. Huber, *Liability: The Legal Revolution and Its Consequences (1988).* Two law professors have sharply criticized Huber's legal analysis, calling it exaggerated, misleading and, in places, flatly wrong. See Mark M. Hager, "Civil Compensation and Its Critics: A Response to Huber," *Stanford Law Review,* Vol. 42, No. 2, January 1990, p. 539; and Joseph A. Page, "Deforming Tort Reform," *Georgetown Law Journal,* Vol. 78, No. 3, February 1990, p. 649.

[8] Terence Dungworth, *Product Liability and the Business Sector: Litigation Trends in the Federal Courts,* Rand Institute for Civil Justice, 1988, p. 49.

[9] Peter Huber calculates that the "indirect costs" of the liability system amount to $300 billion. For a critical analysis suggesting the figure is a "huge exaggeration," see Hager, *op. cit.,* pp. 547-551.

[10] Peter W. Huber and Robert E. Litan, eds., *The Liability Maze: The Impact of Liability Law on Safety and Innovation* (1991).

[11] See Kenneth Jost, "Tampering With Evidence," *ABA Journal,* April 1992, pp. 48-49.

[12] U.S. Senate Committee on Commerce, Science, and Transportation, *Product Liability Fairness Act,* 102nd Cong., 1st Sess., Report 102-215, Nov. 14, 1991, p. 2. See pp. 59-87 for the minority views of Sens. Ernest F. Hollings, D-S.C., and Al Gore, D-Tenn.

[13] Olson, *op. cit.,* pp. 337-338.

[14] Hensler, *op. cit.,* p. 250.

[15] Lawrence M. Friedman, *A History of American Law,* 2d. ed (1985), p. 467.

[16] Some tort-law experts have challenged this prevailing view of 19th-century developments. See Robert L. Rabin, "The Historical Development of the Fault Principle: A Reinterpretation," *Georgia Law Review,* Vol. 15, No. 4, summer 1981, pp. 925-961; and Gary M. Schwartz, "Tort Law and the Economy in Nineteenth-Century America: A Reinterpretation," *Yale Law Journal,* Vol. 90, No. 8, 1981, pp. 1717-1775.

[17] For background, see "Reforming Workers' Compensation," *Editorial Research Reports,* April 13, 1990, pp. 205-220.

[18] Robert Keeton and Jeffrey O'Connell, *Basic Protection for Traffic Accident Victims* (1965). See also Jeffrey O'Connell, *The Lawsuit Lottery: Only the Lawyers Win* (1979), pp. 157-175; and Jeffrey O'Connell and C. Brian Kelly, *The Blame Game: Injuries, Insurance, and Injustice* (1987), pp. 112-122.

[19] O'Connell, *The Lawsuit Lottery,* p. 161.

[20] For background, see "Curbing Auto-Insurance Premiums," *Editorial Research Reports,* April 27, 1990, pp. 237-252.

[21] Friedman, *op. cit.,* p. 685.

[22] Figures cited in Jeffrey O'Connell, *Ending Insult to Injury: No-Fault Insurance for Products and Services* (1975), p. 42.

[23] *Ibid.,* p. 39.

[24] A 1971 study by the Center for the Study of Democratic Institutions found that "most people who sustain medical injuries, whether through negligence or unavoidable accident, ... receive no compensation." A Harvard

University research team reached the same conclusion in a study completed in 1990. See Harvard Medical Practice Study, *Patients, Doctors, and Lawyers: Medical Injury, Malpractice Litigation, and Patient Compensation in New York,* 1990.

[25] *The New York Times,* June 11, 1989, p. A1; Sept. 23, 1990, p. A1.

[26] For background, see Paul Weiler, *Medical Malpractice on Trial* (1991).

[27] O'Connell, *Ending Insult to Injury,* p. 21.

[28] See Gary Schwartz, "Product Liability and Medical Malpractice in Comparative Context," in *The Liability Maze, op. cit.,* pp. 30-33.

[29] *Greenman v. Yuba Power Products, Inc.*

[30] See Huber, *op. cit.,* pp. 153-172.

[31] See Linda Lipsen, "The Evolution of Products Liability as a Federal Policy Issue," in Peter H. Schuck, ed., *Tort Law and the Public Interest: Competition, Innovation, and Consumer Welfare* (1991), pp. 247-261.

[32] James A. Henderson Jr. and Theodore Eisenberg, "The Quiet Revolution in Product Liability Law: An Empirical Study of Legal Change," *UCLA Law Review,* Vol. 37, 1990, pp. 479-553. For an opposing evaluation of the data, see Arthur Havenner, "Not Quite a Revolution in Product Liability," a "white paper" published by the Manhattan Institute in 1990. Havenner, an economist at the University of California-Davis, argues that the data show at best a stabilization in plaintiffs' claims, success rates and mean recoveries.

[33] *Time,* March 24, 1986, p. 26.

[34] The laws are compiled in *Tort Law and the Public Interest, op. cit.,* Appendix 1, pp. 262-265.

[35] See Glenn Blackmon and Richard Zeckhauser, "State Tort Reform Legislation: Assessing Our Control of Risks," in *Tort Law and the Public Interest, op. cit.,* pp. 272-300.

[36] *ABA Journal,* April 1992, p. 30.

[37] *Ibid.,* p. 31.

[38] See *Legal Times,* April 20, 1992, p. 6.

[39] See Peter W. Huber, *Galileo's Revenge: Junk Science in the Courtroom (1991).* For critical reviews, see *ABA Journal,* October 1991, p. 104; *Science,* Dec. 13, 1991, p. 1663.

[40] See *American Medical News,* Feb. 24, 1992, p. 35.

Bibliography

Selected Sources Used

Books

Enterprise Responsibility for Personal Injury, American Law Institute, 1991.

This two-volume study of liability issues by a group of 14 scholars was commissioned by the American Law Institute, a prestigious private legal study group. It provides a detailed, well-organized and thoroughly footnoted exposition of the issues, along with arguments for sweeping reforms in the legal system that stirred controversy among partisans on both sides of the debates.

Friedman, Lawrence M., *A History of American Law* (2d ed.), Simon & Schuster/Touchstone, 1985.

Friedman, a professor of law at Stanford University, completed this one-volume legal history of the United States in 1972 and revised it in 1985. His chapter on torts critically evaluates the development of tort law in the 19th century, while a final chapter quickly surveys 20th-century trends. Friedman comments on the debate over the "litigation explosion" in another book, *American Law* (W. W. Norton, 1984), a contemporary overview of the U.S. legal system.

Huber, Peter W., *Liability: The Legal Revolution and Its Consequences*, Basic Books, 1988.

Huber, formerly a senior fellow at the conservative Manhattan Institute, provided the intellectual underpinning for a renewed debate over tort law with this attack on expansive theories of legal liability. The book was widely praised by tort reform advocates but criticized as misleading and exaggerated by many defenders of existing legal doctrines.

Huber, Peter W. and Robert E. Litan (eds.), *The Liability Maze: The Impact of Liability Law on Safety and Innovation*, Brookings, 1991.

Huber and Litan, an economist at the Brookings Institution, commissioned papers by leading experts to examine the effects of product liability suits on safety and innovation. Business groups depict the book as proving that litigation has deterred product innovation with little enhancement of safety, although the individual papers actually give mixed answers to both questions.

O'Connell, Jeffrey and C. Brian Kelly, *The Blame Game: Injuries, Insurance and Injustice*, Lexington, 1987.

O'Connell, a professor at the University of Virginia Law School, has written prolifically about accident and insurance law since he co-authored the original no-fault auto insurance proposal in the 1960s. This book, cowritten with a former journalist, surveys the range of liability issues based largely on news accounts. Although dated, two of O'Connell's earlier books are also valuable: *The Lawsuit Lottery: Only the Lawyers Win* (Free Press, 1979) and *Ending Insult to Injury: No-Fault Insurance for Products and Services* (University of Illinois Press, 1975).

Olson, Walter K., *The Litigation Explosion: What Happened When America Unleashed the Lawsuit*, Dutton, 1991.

Olson, a senior fellow at the conservative Manhattan Institute, argues that the legal system has gone haywire by rewarding rather than discouraging people who resort to lawsuits. Olson also served as editor of a collection of papers representing various points of view in the liability debate. It was published by the Academy of Political Science in 1988 under the title *New Directions in Liability Law.*

Schuck, Peter H., *Tort Law and the Public Interest: Competition, Innovation, and Consumer Welfare*, Norton, 1991.

This collection of essays presented in 1990 by the American Assembly, a policy studies center at Columbia University, addresses the relationships between liability law, insurance, safety regulation, technological innovation, international trade and consumer interests.

Weiler, Paul C., *Medical Malpractice on Trial*, Harvard University Press, 1991.

Weiler, a Harvard Law School professor, says tort suits inflict "considerable harm" on doctors but medical injuries inflict "much greater harm" on patients. His thoroughly footnoted analysis concludes by urging a no-fault system to compensate victims of medical injuries.

Reports and Studies

Hensler, Deborah R., et al., *Compensation for Accidental Injuries in the United States,* Rand Corporation Institute for Civil Justice, 1991.

The Rand Corporation's Institute for Civil Justice has done extensive, highly regarded research on the actual workings of the civil justice system over the past decade. This report contradicts the popular notion of American litigiousness by showing that the vast majority of accident victims never seek compensation in the courts.

National Center for State Courts, *State Court Caseload Statistics: Annual Report 1990,* April 1992.

This annual report, prepared by the National Center for State Courts in Williamsburg, Va., since 1976, provides statistics on caseloads in the 50 state court systems.

The Next Step

Additional Articles from Current Periodicals from EBSCO Publishing's Database

Addresses & essays

Benson, S., "Why I quit practicing law," *Newsweek,* **Nov. 4, 1991, p. 10.**

Editorial. Discusses why the author decided to stop practicing law, and how he felt an overwhelming sense of relief after telling one of his firm's partners that he was leaving. Adversarial system of law; code of ethics; warlike atmosphere for attorneys; justice an insignificant concept; balancing inherent conflicts without sacrificing integrity; ethical behavior.

Coxe, D., "Tipping the scales," *Canadian Business,* **February 1990, p. 106.**

Opinion. Argues against "Americanizing" the Canadian legal system simply to take advantage of litigation profits. Canadian lawyers; maintenance and champerty.

Gergen, D., "America's legal mess," *U.S. News & World Report,* **Aug. 19, 1991, p. 72.**

Editorial. Suggests that help for America's legal system is on the way, courtesy of a study from the Council for Competitiveness, chaired by Vice President Dan Quayle. Sweeping overhaul of the nation's civil justice system; numbers of lawsuits and the enriching of the lawyers; medical bills and malpractice insurance; a closer look at the problem.

Gordon, J.S., "Reforming the law," *American Heritage,* **September 1991, p. 18.**

Argues that a thorough reform of the American legal system is needed. The problems involved in change; the benefit to lawyers of maintaining the status quo; evolution from English common law; several examples of historical necessity for change and the changes that took place.

Riga, P., "Capping a gusher," *Commonweal,* **Sept. 13, 1991, p. 502.**

Expresses outrage over the nation's present legal system. Causes for the vast amount of litigation and overcompensation of many victims; six proposals for reform, which includes changes in the concept of punitive damages, establishment of an arbitration board for automobile insurance claims and medical malpractice suits, setting an upper limit on awards, and more.

Sessions, W.S., "Fundamental changes in the legal system," *Vital Speeches,* **Jan. 15, 1992, p. 196.**

Presents a speech by the FBI Director William S. Sessions, "Fundamental Changes in the Legal System," delivered before the annual meeting of the North Carolina Bar Association in Raleigh, North Carolina in October 1991, concerning professional priorities in the legal system.

Weinberger, C.W., "Reforming our legal system," *Forbes,* **Sept. 30, 1991, p. 35.**

Opinion. Reflects publisher Casper W. Weinberger's impression that the President's Council on Competitiveness was correct in addressing to the American people the issue that the U.S. has too many lawyers chasing too many dollars through too many endless lawsuits.

Books & reading

Caldwell, G.G., "Law," *Journal of the American Medical Association,* **July 10, 1991, p. 281.**

Reviews the book "Demystifying the Law: An Introduction for Professionals," by Daniel A. Bronstein. Simplifies and summarizes the U.S. legal system for non-lawyer professionals.

Case studies

Huber, P., "Asbestos Jr.," *Forbes,* **Sept. 30, 1991, p. 170.**

Commentary. Presents the opinion of author Peter Huber concerning the issue of asbestos and its entanglement within our legal system. A staggering and increasing number of claimants; longevity of "pleural plaques" — freckles on the lungs lawsuits; poses various questions regarding the judicial system's stance on asbestos.

Debates & issues

"A plague of lawyers," *Economist,* **Aug. 10, 1991, p. 13.**

Reports on how America's litigiousness can be reduced without restricting access to the law. The reason there is an American hatred for lawyers; statistics on how America is over-lawyered and sue-happy; tortuous reforms; the link between lawyer and client; advice for juries.

"Are contingent fees unethical and illegal?" *USA Today,* **December 1991, p. 7.**

Questions the ethics and legality of contingent fees charged by plaintiffs' attorneys. How a contingent fee arrangement works; benefits for the attorney; disadvantages for the client; comments on the system by Lester Brickman, law professor at the Cardozo School of Law.

"Money clip," *U.S. News & World Report,* **Aug. 26, 1991 and Sept. 2, 1991, p. 18.**

Presents some proposed changes in the legal system from the President's Council on Competitiveness, led by Vice President Dan Quayle. Presents graphs comparing settlement of two actual cases, one by mediation and one by a jury.

"Uncommon law," *National Review,* **Sept. 9, 1991, p. 14.**

Evaluates the recent legal reforms proposed by Vice President Dan Quayle at the annual meeting of the American Bar Association (ABA). Overview of the vice president's package, which if enacted would curtail the continuing litigation explosion in the United States and help the ailing American economy; recommended additions; prospects for passage of the reforms.

Brimelow, P., "The plaintiff attorneys' great honey rush," *Forbes,* **Oct. 16, 1989, p. 197.**

Reports on the growth of the great American greed game perpetrated by plaintiff attorneys — lawyers who specialize in suing — who have created a $10-billion-per-year income. Explains how litigation has become so lucrative and gotten so out of hand. Liability crisis; contingent fee system; examples of large awards; judicial system; reform attempts; Ralph Nader. INSET: Brothers in bucks (discusses the group of lawyers in an exclusive club called the Inner Circle).

Cohn, B., "The lawsuit cha-cha," *Newsweek,* **Aug. 26, 1991, p. 58.**

Comments on how reformers and politicians are moving toward proposed changes in the nation's civil-liability system. Popularity of attacking lawyers; former President Jimmy Carter's criticism of the profession in 1978 for high costs, judicial delays and an emphasis on serving the privileged few; Vice President Dan Quayle's 50 recommendations to the American Bar Association to temper the nation's much-discussed litigation crisis; details.

Gergen, D. and T. Gest, "Ruling on Quayle v. lawyers," *U.S. News & World Report,* **Aug. 26, 1991 and Sept. 2, 1991, p. 44.**

Opinion. Suggests that the coming battle to overhaul the nation's legal system will be long, tedious, expensive, incomprehensible to outsiders, yet worthwhile. Speech by Vice President Dan Quayle, before the American Bar Association, proposing dozens of reforms, some already being explored by the 94 federal district courts. Formidable opposition from lawyers; key reforms under debate; possible outcome.

Hazard, G.C. Jr., "The role of the legal system in responses to public risk," *Daedalus,* **fall 1990, p. 229.**

Considers the importance of how the legal system shapes the responses to public risks as well as the social, political,

and economic environment in which public risks arise and are responded to. Part of solutions as well as problems; the legal system; command and control vs. markets; legal constraints on response mechanisms.

Holmes, S.A., "Workers find it tough going filing lawsuits over job bias," *The New York Times,* **July 24, 1991, p. A1.**

States that as the nation wrestles intellectually and politically with the issue of civil rights, the legal system appears to be growing increasingly inhospitable toward individual race and sex discrimination cases. Lawyers more and more are turning away such cases because they are time-consuming, difficult to win, and bring far less money than other civil litigation like personal-injury suits, which permit punitive damages.

Kasten, R.W. Jr., "Absurd product liability laws hurt business and consumers," *USA Today,* **July 1991, p. 49.**

Charges that impractical product liability laws are destroying American competitiveness and seriously decreasing the prospects of economic growth in America's future. High costs of frivolous product liability lawsuits; negative impact on businesses and consumers; recommended reforms for product liability laws.

Kritz, F.L., T. Gest, et al., "Lawyers on the lam," *U.S. News & World Report,* **March 25, 1991, p. 72.**

Comments on the increasing numbers of lawyers who are taking their clients' money and running for the hills. Checking malpractice insurance your lawyer carries, insisting on regular statements for escrowed monies; state protections and reimbursement panels; local bar associations.

Mahoney, R.J. and S.E. Littlejohn, "Innovation on trial: Punitive damages versus new products," *Science,* **Dec. 15, 1989, p. 1395.**

Discusses the effects strict liability, huge jury awards, and punitive damages are having on innovation, or scientific discovery transformed into valuable products, an asset for the United States in the global economy of today. The authors argue for legal reforms to control punitive damages, which they say are preventing new, safe products from reaching the market due to legal uncertainties.

Margolick, D., "A speech by Quayle on the legal system unsettles lawyers," *The New York Times,* **Aug. 14, 1991, p. A1.**

Discusses Vice President Dan Quayle's speech to the American Bar Association, in which he said that the US has too many lawyers, too many lawsuits, and too many excessive damage awards, with the result that the country is handicapped in world markets. Cool reception of his remarks; his return to the microphone to defend himself.

Olson, W., "The case against expert witnesses," *Fortune*, Sept. 25, 1989, p. 133.

Discusses the backlash that is beginning to develop among lawyers, and especially among judges, against expert witnesses that will testify to almost anything in a trial — for a fee.

Economic aspects

"CA newsnotes," *Consumer Alert*, September/October 1991, p. 7.

Comments on the "lawyers tax" added on to the price of consumer goods due to the out-of-control American tort system and the federal government's wetlands policy. Vice President Dan Quayle advocates reform of liability system; Dick Bryant's loss of value of North Carolina lot designated as wetlands by U.S. Army Corps of Engineers in 1988.

Law & legislation

Fenyvesi, C., "The high profits of failure," *U.S. News & World Report*, Sept. 30, 1991, p. 28.

Reports that in the wake of Vice President Dan Quayle's recent attack on the nation's expensive legal system, insiders predict that Congress will soon take the first step in capping runaway legal and accounting fees that drain the remaining assets of bankrupt corporations. Gives one example of Eastern Airlines' filing for bankruptcy; bankruptcies are expected to top 1 million this year.

Mass media coverage

Hans, V.P. and J.L. Dee, "Media coverage of law," *American Behavioral Scientist*, November/December 1991, p. 136.

Reviews and analyzes the impact of media coverage of law on the public's knowledge and views of law and the legal system by considering how the media presents law, crime and justice, and by discussing the impact of these media distortions on people's knowledge of and attitudes toward law and crime. An examination of the effect of media coverage of courtroom trials on juries; the impact of cameras in court on jurors; conclusion.

Waldman, A., "Hear ye! Hear ye! L.A. Law's in session," *TV Guide*, March 16, 1990, p. 7.

Summarizes some of the ways NBC's drama series "L.A. Law" has affected America's legal system, including an increase in law school applications and stereotyping specialized attorneys.

Medicine

Coyte, P.C., D.N. Dewees, et al., "Medical malpractice — the Canadian experience," *New England Journal of*

Medicine, Jan. 10, 1991, p. 89.

Describes the legal system for dealing with malpractice claims in Canada, contrasting it with that in the United States and suggesting reasons for the dramatically different liability costs imposed on physicians. Trends in malpractice liability; the Canadian system; effects of litigation; conclusions.

Ferrari, H.A., "Suing for restitution: The medical malpractice crisis," *USA Today*, January 1990, p. 49.

Explores the causes of today's medical malpractice crisis. Roles of the insurance industry and the legal profession; faults in the judicial system; possible solutions.

Jacobson, P.D., "Medical malpractice and the tort system," *Journal of the American Medical Association*, Dec. 15, 1989, p. 3320.

Examines medical malpractice and the tort system; review of medical professional liability data trends during the past 20 years; legal trends; suggested public policy measures possibly taken in response to these trends.

Joyce, C. "AIDS trial challenges U.S. legal system," *New Scientist*, Aug. 31, 1990, p. 11.

Reports on a controversial trial of an AIDS vaccine for pregnant women that is currently in limbo in the United States. The vaccine makers are afraid of being sued if any of the babies born to women in the trial suffer from birth defects.

Lemonick, M.D. and A. Purvis, "Lawyers to the rescue," *Time*, Feb. 10, 1992, p. 46.

Speculates on the effects of the more than 1,000 implant-related lawsuits already filed by women who claim they were disfigured or debilitated by silicone implants on trial lawyers and the American court system. Aggressive lawyers who advertise in newspaper, billboards and television; massive lawsuits and ambulance-chasing lawyers as a major part of the U.S. system for regulating medical products; fear of lawsuits pressures companies to be honest; lawyers' fees.

Personal injury

Kreindler, L.S., "Assuring compensation for wrongful death," *USA Today*, November 1991, p. 68.

Opposes artificial limits on money awards for victims who have suffered personal injury or death. How the nation's legal system developed the concept of compensating for pain with money; why money awards make accident victims or their families feel better; negative consequences of artificial limits or compensation.

Back Issues

Great Research on Current Issues Starts Right Here… Recent topics covered by The CQ Researcher are listed below. Issues dated before May 10, 1991, were published under the name of Editorial Research Reports.

NOVEMBER 1990
Lotteries and Gambling
Post-Cold War Choices
Setting Limits on Medical Care
Multicultural Education

DECEMBER 1990
Cable TV Regulation
Americans' Search for Their Roots
Is Insurance System a Failure?
Why Schools Still Have Tracking

JANUARY 1991
Growing Influence of Boycotts
Should the U.S. Reinstate the Draft?
America's Archaeological Past
Peace Corps' Challenges in '90s

FEBRUARY 1991
Regional Impact of Recession
Puerto Rico's Status
Redistricting: Mapping Power
Nuclear Power

MARCH 1991
Acid Rain
Cost of the Gulf War
Reassessing Gun Laws
Future for Man in Space

APRIL 1991
Social Security
Canadian Crisis Over Quebec
California Drought
Electromagnetic Radiation

MAY 1991
School Choice
Racial Quotas
Animal Rights
U.S. and Japan

JUNE 1991
Children and Divorce
Teenage Suicide
Endangered Species
Europe 1992

JULY 1991
Teenagers and Abortion
Soviet Republics Rebel
Mexico's Emergence
Athletes and Drugs

AUGUST 1991
Sexual Harassment
Fetal Tissue Research
Oil Imports
The Palestinians

SEPTEMBER 1991
Police Brutality
Advertising Under Attack
Saving the Forests
Foster Care Crisis

OCTOBER 1991
Pay-Per-View TV
Youth Gangs
Gene Therapy
World Hunger

NOVEMBER 1991
Fast-Food Shake-Up
The Greening of Eastern Europe
Business' Role in Education
Cuba In Crisis

DECEMBER 1991
Retiree Health Benefits
Asian Americans
The Obscenity Debate
The Disabilities Act

JANUARY 1992
Term Limits
Oil Spills
Hunting Controversy
Alternative Medicine

FEBRUARY 1992
Threatened Coastlines
New Era in Asia
Assisted Suicide
Jobs in the '90s

MARCH 1992
Women and Sports
Underage Drinking
Garbage Crisis
Mafia Crackdown

APRIL 1992
Ozone Depletion
Welfare Reform
Politicians and Privacy
Illegal Immigration

MAY 1992
Native Americans
Jobs vs. Environment

Back issues are available for $4.00 (subscribers) or $7.00 (non-subscribers). Quantity discounts apply to orders over ten. To order, call Congressional Quarterly 1-800-432-2250.

Future Topics

▶ *Salary Fairness*

▶ *Nuclear Proliferation*

▶ *Food Irradiation*

PUBLISHED BY CONGRESSIONAL QUARTERLY INC., IN CONJUNCTION WITH EBSCO PUBLISHING

Fairness in Salaries

Will outrage over soaring executive pay lead to reforms?

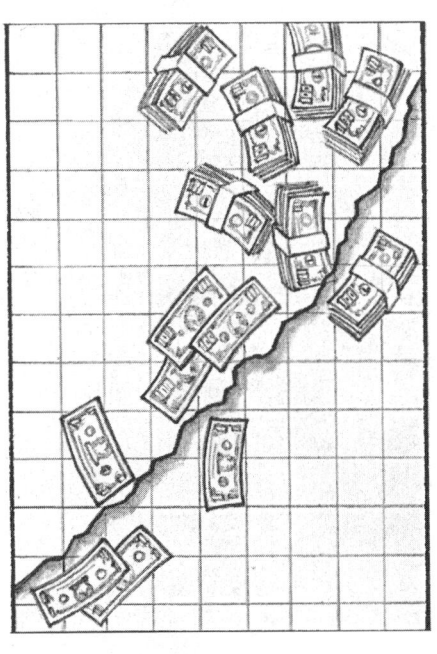

CORPORATE CHIEFS ARE ON THE HOT SEAT nowadays as the public reels with each report of a record-setting executive pay package. With salary and stock deals in the range of $80 million at companies such as Time Warner, H. J. Heinz and Coca-Cola, average wage earners beset by economic recession are reacting with anger and amazement. Disgruntled shareholders are descending on annual meetings to charge that officers are even being rewarded when company performance is poor. Defenders say high salaries are needed to attract top talent and to give executives an incentive to make tough decisions. But that hasn't stopped many boards of directors from rethinking methods of setting executive pay. Congress and federal regulators are also entering the fray.

 May 29, 1992 • Volume 2, No. 20 • 457-480

Formerly Editorial Research Reports

COVER ART: BARBARA SASSA-DANIELS

CQ Researcher

May 29, 1992
Volume 2, No. 20

EDITOR
Sandra Stencel

MANAGING EDITOR
Thomas J. Colin

ASSOCIATE EDITOR
Richard L. Worsnop

STAFF WRITERS
Charles S. Clark
Mary H. Cooper
Rodman D. Griffin

PRODUCTION EDITOR
Laurie De Maris

EDITORIAL ASSISTANT
Michael M. Taylor

GRAPHICS
Jack Auldridge

PUBLISHED BY
Congressional Quarterly Inc.

CHAIRMAN
Andrew Barnes

VICE CHAIRMAN
Andrew P. Corty

EDITOR AND PUBLISHER
Neil Skene

EXECUTIVE EDITOR
Robert W. Merry

PUBLICATIONS MARKETING/SALES
Robert Smith

EDITOR, EBSCO PUBLISHING
Melissa Kummerer

The CQ Researcher (ISSN 1056-2036). Formerly Editorial Research Reports. Published weekly (48 times per year, not printed the first Friday of any month with five Fridays) by Congressional Quarterly Inc., 1414 22nd St., N.W., Washington, D.C. 20037. Rates are furnished upon request. Second-class postage paid at Washington, D.C. POSTMASTER: Send address changes to The CQ Researcher, 1414 22nd St., N.W., Washington, D.C. 20037.

Fairness in Salaries

BY CHARLES S. CLARK

THE ISSUES

William A. Anders became a $9.35 million man in 1991. So it was no surprise when the chief executive officer (CEO) of General Dynamics Corp. was asked to defend his salary and stock bonus at a time when the giant defense contractor was planning 30,000 layoffs.

At the company's annual meeting in January, an employee who owns a modest 11 shares of stock stood up and told the former astronaut: "The confusion I have is why you need this extra incentive to do the job you were hired to do. For everyone else, if you do a good job, maybe you get a raise, but nothing like this."[1]

Anders' reply — that it is unreasonable to expect the head of a top defense contractor to work these days as "a hired hand" — embodied the clash of cultures that has become familiar in the corporate world of the 1990s. Business-page readers have been hit with a drumbeat of reports of eight-figure CEO paychecks — all of them combinations of base salary, bonuses and cashed-in stock — that are spiraling upward like an arms race: Time Warner Inc.'s Steven J. Ross took home $78.2 million in 1990; H. J. Heinz Co.'s Anthony J. F. O'Reilly garnered $74.8 million in 1991; and Coca-Cola Co.'s Roberto C. Goizueta bagged $86 million last year — $41,346 an hour. More than half of the 800 highest-paid executives surveyed by *Forbes* magazine for 1991 had earnings that topped $1 million. *(For this year's top 10, see p. 460.)*

The resulting uproar has led to a revival of the age-old debate over society's hierarchy of wealth and a fear of a "polarization of incomes," in the words of Rep. Martin Olav Sabo, D-Minn., a critic of rising CEO pay.

When President George Bush took

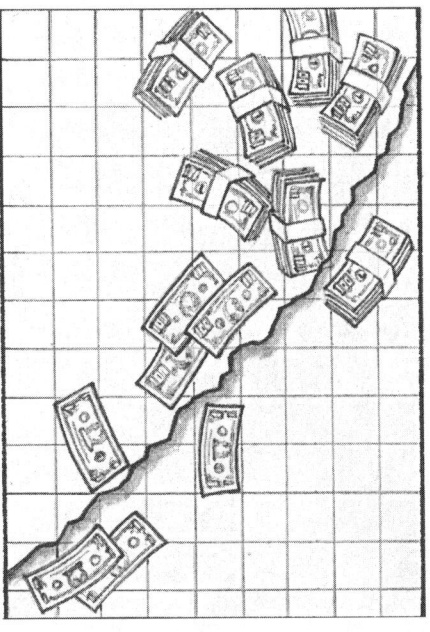

eight top U.S. executives to Japan in January, their pleas to Tokyo for trade concessions were all but overshadowed by reports of their average $2 million salaries — more than quintuple those of their Japanese counterparts.

The reports of CEO prosperity have also come amid a prolonged economic recession and nationwide disgust over some perks enjoyed by members of Congress, among them overdraft checking and subsidized health clubs. And such reports are appearing alongside a spate of studies asserting that the celebrated economic growth of the 1980s was of far greater benefit to the richest 1 percent of Americans than to the poor and middle classes.[2]

"There's a strong populist wind in America that's fed up with special deals for special people," says Ralph V. Whitworth, president of the Washington-based United Shareholders Association, which seeks to reform executive-pay practices. That furor spilled into the nonprofit sector this winter when controversy erupted over the "lavish lifestyle," manage-

ment irregularities and $473,000 salary of the head of the United Way of America, the nation's biggest charity.

The pay issue makes hay for both the political parties. Vice President Dan Quayle, citing the need to improve U.S. competitiveness overseas, has appealed to corporate boards to curtail "exorbitant salaries" paid to executives that are unrelated to productivity. Democratic presidential contender Bill Clinton has proposed changes in the tax code to thwart "self-serving CEOs" who "build an economy out of paper and perks instead of people and products." Among the public, as many as 72 percent feel that a CEO salary of $1 million is too much, a *USA Today* poll found in February. (And even 82 percent of business school deans, in another *USA Today* poll, agreed that the outrage over executive pay is justified.)

There is little doubt that CEO pay is rising at a record pace. In its recent annual survey, *Business Week* magazine calculated that average CEO pay for 1991 was 104 times that of an average factory employee; in 1980, the figure was only 42 times as much.[3] It's also clear that many executive pay hikes have been bestowed in spite of declining company profits and dividends. Towers Perrin, a New York City-based compensation consulting firm, has estimated that 1990 CEO pay rose 6.7 percent while shareholder value fell by 9 percent over the previous year.

The driving force behind the largess, according to shareholder activists and other critics, is a too-cozy relationship between CEOs and their boards of directors. "Only CEOs pick the people who set their salary," Nell Minor, president of Institutional Shareholder Services, a Washington consulting firm, told the Senate Governmental Affairs Oversight of Government Management Subcommittee, chaired by Sen. Carl Levin, D-Mich., last year. "If Bruce Springsteen, Jack Nicholson, Janet Jackson or Darryl Strawberry fail to perform, their salaries go down to zero. But when a CEO does badly, his pay almost never goes down." [4]

The emotional force of the issue has been dramatized by the threatened lawsuits and insults that have been hurled from corporate suites at Graef S. "Bud" Crystal, a top executive-compensation consultant who defected from the executive camp. Crystal gave up the $800,000 a year he commanded as a self-described "rubber stamp" for the desires of executives to become a $150,000 business professor at the University of California at Berkeley. Since 1988, he has authored an iconoclastic book on executive pay, *In Search of Excess,* launched a newsletter and testified unceasingly for reform of the pay practices of the CEOs he likens to "a cross between ancient pharaohs and Louis XIV."

The traditional secrecy surrounding aspects of executive pay has raised hackles at many levels of a society that itself has traditionally kept salary matters hush-hush. "People who make $20,000 have a hard time with others' high salaries, and they don't know what their doctors and dentists are making," observes Mark A. Abramson, president of the Council for Excellence in Government, a Washington business group that develops new ideas for public service and management.

When the sums are announced, the effect on morale can be devastating. "To succeed, a company requires a sense of shared commitment among its workers," writes *Newsweek* business columnist Robert J. Samuelson. "Instead, the CEO's mes-

sage is 'Hey, I got mine.' This spawns cynicism and indifference — even among would-be executives — that can hurt a company in dozens of ways from slipshod workmanship to unnecessary costs." [5]

As the ballooning executive sums

The Top CEO Breadwinners

Chief Executive	Company	1991 salary and bonus	Total pay with stock
		(in thousands of dollars)	
Anthony J. F. O'Reilly	*H.J. Heinz Co.*	$1,361	$75,085
Martin J. Wygod	*Medco Containment*	459	33,749
Leon C. Hirsch	*U.S. Surgical Corp.*	1,351	23,281
John C. Malone	*Tele-Communications Inc.*	454	18,934
Richard K. Eamer	*National Medical Enterprises Inc.*	1,538	17,497
Sanford I. Weill	*Primerica Corp.*	2,234	15,906
Hamish Maxwell	*Philip Morris Companies Inc.*	1,741	15,677
William P. Stiritz	*Ralston Purina Co.*	1,198	13,813
Richard L. Gelb	*Bristol-Myers Squibb Co.*	2,051	12,658
William A. Schreyer	*Merrill Lynch Co. Inc.*	4,500	11,530

Note: Coca-Cola's Roberto Goizueta doesn't appear on the list because his restricted stock can't be cashed in for several years.
Source: Business Week *magazine*

are paraded in public, the resulting outcry is prompting a re-examination of pay philosophies by corporations as well as government pay specialists, nonprofit groups and analysts of rank-and-file salaries. Here are some of the key issues being discussed:

Do top executives deserve their high salaries?

In the view from the executive suite, the tempest of headlines over executive pay is a distortion. "CEO pay levels are just now catching up to where they were 50 years ago," says the National Association of Manufacturers (NAM), citing a Harvard Business School study of 430 of the largest U.S. corporations. [6] A recent Towers Perrin survey found tremendous dissatisfaction among 270 corporate executives, with fewer than half believing that "pay is a good reflection of performance" at their workplace. Many gripe that pay largely reflects seniority and promotions rather than achievement, and that a

superstar often earns the same as a rank-and-file employee. [7]

Harvard Business School Professors Michael C. Jensen and Kevin J. Murphy write of the "damage" inflicted on U.S. corporations by executive-pay protesters at annual meetings, the business press, labor unions and political figures who become "uninvited guests" at the bargaining table. "As a result of public pressure," they write, "directors become reluctant to reward CEOs with substantial (and therefore highly visible) financial gains for superior performance," eroding the relationship between pay and performance and entrenching bureaucratic compensation systems. [8]

The most common defense of high corporate pay is a simple bow to supply and demand. Attracting — and retaining — top talent requires salaries that aren't easily trumped by a competitor, or more-lucrative offers from Wall Street, advocates say. A fact of life in today's corporate culture, Towers Perrin pay consultant Jim Moss explains, is its competitive nature, the need to "keep up with the Joneses." When CEOs see the new lists of who makes what, Moss says, "they want to know how they stack up."

Others note that the mammoth budgets of many large companies render the CEO's salary a drop in the bucket, given the thousands of employees he supervises. "A good manager can save an organization far more than his or her salary," says Thomas C. Dolan, president of the American College of Healthcare Executives in Chicago. [9]

Financial incentives are seen by many in business as the only fair way to reward top performers. "Put yourself in the executive's shoes," says Daniel C. Rowland, chairman of the American Compensation Association. "When you consider living expenses, $1 million may not go as far as some people think. And once you get there, you're looking for more."

Perhaps the principal justification for lofty executive pay, Murphy says, is the need to encourage the CEO to systematically make decisions that help shareholders. Often, these are tough decisions — getting out of the current business, closing plants and laying off employees. "They don't need high-powered incentives when all they're doing is growing the firm," Murphy says. "They love that anyway."

Pay critics point out, however, that CEO salaries are not just rising at entrepreneurial, rapidly changing companies such as those in California's Silicon Valley, but at stable, established firms where risks are relatively minimal. Would Coca-Cola's Goizueta have given less than his best if he had been paid a tenth as much? asks Graef Crystal. The head of one of the country's most venerable companies was paid $400 million over 11 years "for not messing up." [10]

"There's virtually no connection between pay and performance," says Whitworth of the shareholders' association, charging that pay-setting boards reward their CEOs merely on the size of a company. "I'm often asked, 'How much is enough? What else could one buy? Isn't there an amount of pay that is just obscene?'" Whitworth observes. But as long as an executive is performing for shareholders, he should be given as much as it takes to keep him working, Whitworth says. "I want to work him until he drops."

If executive pay were determined strictly on company profits or return to shareholders, the published rosters of top-paid executives would indeed be radically different. Calculations made regularly by the United Shareholders and *Business Week* and *Financial World* magazines show that hundreds of *Fortune* 500 executives would come out "overpaid" while many others would seem "underpaid" if pay were determined solely by the annual numbers.

In reality, personalities, negotiating tactics and a corporation's internal culture often affect pay. And of course, executives are happy to cite rising profits to justify an increase in their pay but will seldom mention a loss of revenues as a reason for taking a cut.

Salaries for Familiar Occupations

	1991 median annual salary†
Architects	$32,396
Automobile mechanics	20,020
Bank tellers	14,612
Bartenders	12,948
Brickmasons and stonemasons	25,480
Butchers and meat cutters	16,796
Bus drivers	19,656
Cashiers	11,336
Chemists (excluding biochemists)	35,724
Child-care workers	11,284
Clergy	23,868
College professors	39,312
Computer equipment operators	19,864
Computer systems analysts and scientists	41,184
Cooks (excluding short-order)	12,480
Electricians	27,976
Engineers	44,044
Farm operators and managers	18,928
Farm workers	12,428
File clerks	15,652
Garage and service station related occupations	11,648
Groundskeepers and gardeners (excluding farm)	13,988
Hairdressers and cosmetologists	13,676
Hotel clerks	12,896
Insurance sales people	26,676
Janitors and cleaners	15,184
Lathe and turning machine set-up operators	25,376
Librarians	27,092
Machine operators, assemblers and inspectors	17,472
Photographers	22,048
Police and detectives, public service	30,940
Real estate sales people	26,884
Registered nurses	32,968
Roofers	19,552
Sales workers, retail and personal services	13,676
Secretaries, stenographers and typists	18,564
Sheet metal workers	24,752
Street and door-to-door workers	14,456
Supervisors, guards	31,616
Taxicab drivers and chauffeurs	17,628
Teachers	28,080
Telephone line installers and repairers	32,708
Truck drivers, heavy	22,308
Waiters and waitresses	11,336
Welders and cutters	22,048

† *These annual salaries were derived by taking median weekly salaries and multiplying by 52. Economists caution that actual annual figures probably are slightly higher because weekly figures are weighted to account for weekly fluctuations.*
Source: *U.S. Department of Labor, Bureau of Labor Statistics*

The true reason executives command high pay in good times and bad, Crystal jests, is that "their greed glands are bigger." More seriously, he says, it's the values that are celebrated in business schools — minimize the risks and maximize the upside potential — that create expectations, which are then taken care of by the executive's peer group.

Each of us has our own internal yardstick, Crystal continues. "If you earn $50,000, you think someone who earns $5 million is a greedy pig; if you earn $20 million, you see $5 million as charity case." Hence a good way to predict CEO pay is to measure the pay of all the board members, he suggests. They're not setting the CEO's pay "in a vacuum."

Murphy, not surprisingly, rejects Crystal's critique of business school values. "We talk a lot about recognition for individual accomplishments other than money, and we talk about social issues," he says. But what stands out about the business school culture is that it produces individuals who "don't want to be missed in the noise," Murphy says. "It's not greed but a desire to make a difference that is noted. Few of our graduates want to be mid-level managers in a huge bureaucracy."

Are stock options good motivators for executives or sources of abuse?

Efforts to rein in executive pay are complicated by the fact that the bulk of the opulent pay packages consist of corporate stock, often in the form of stock options — the right to buy stock at a fixed price over what is usually a 10-year period. This financial perquisite has been dubbed "stealth compensation" by Sen. Levin because details of stock options are often buried in the dense legal prose of corporate financial statements. Because options are exercised only at some point in the future when the stock price has risen to a favorable level, accountants have trouble assigning a precise value when options are issued.

The technique of rewarding a top executive with company stock is used by about 90 percent of U.S. corporations as a way to "tie management's fortunes directly to those of the shareholder," The Business Roundtable noted in testimony prepared for Levin's Senate subcommittee last October. At fast-changing, high-tech firms, especially, stock options are viewed as effective attractions to executives as an incentive for making decisions that may pay off only in the long term. Indeed, a study by none other than maverick pay critic Crystal, using stock ownership data for executives over a 10-year period, found that the more stock the CEO owned, the more the shareholders earned.[11]

But as the executive pay debate has unfolded, many experts have emphasized the shortcomings of options. Shareholders and boards that approve salary packages often assume that options are not a debit on the account books. And in many companies, they

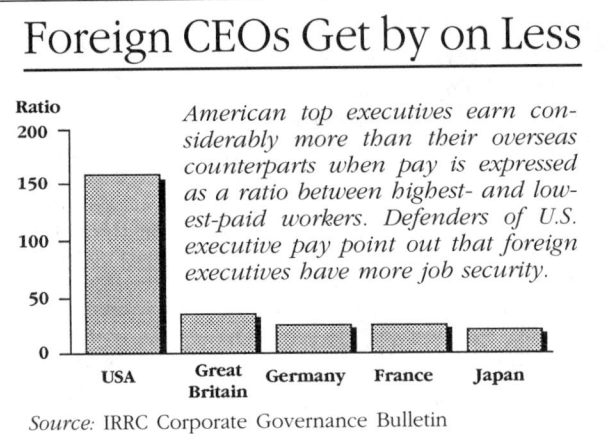

Foreign CEOs Get by on Less

American top executives earn considerably more than their overseas counterparts when pay is expressed as a ratio between highest- and lowest-paid workers. Defenders of U.S. executive pay point out that foreign executives have more job security.

Source: IRRC Corporate Governance Bulletin

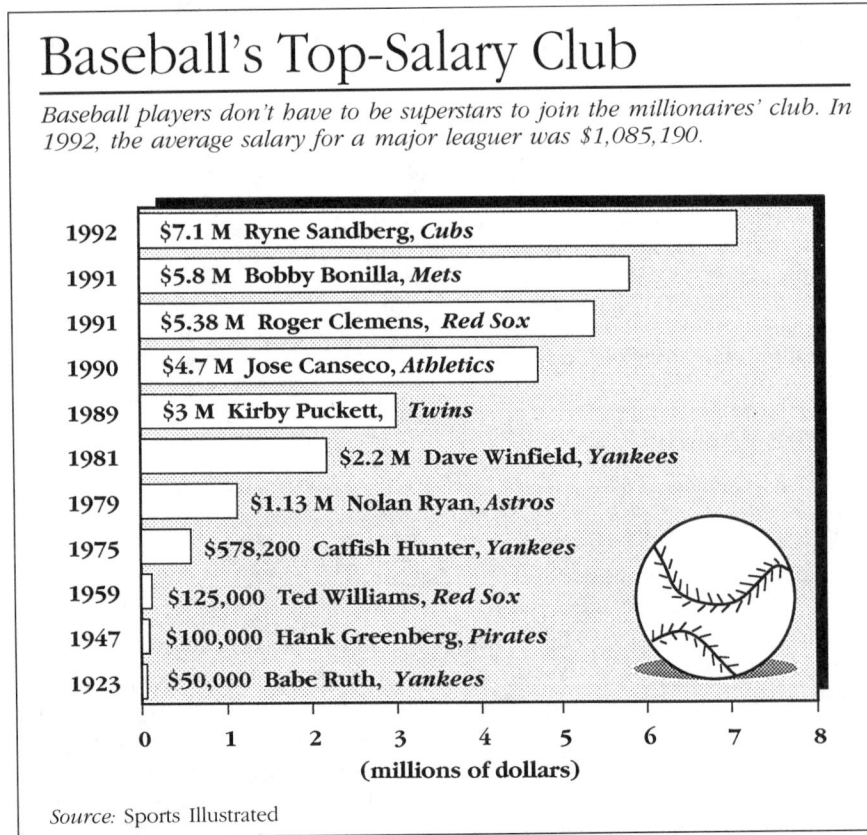

Baseball's Top-Salary Club

Baseball players don't have to be superstars to join the millionaires' club. In 1992, the average salary for a major leaguer was $1,085,190.

1992	$7.1 M Ryne Sandberg, *Cubs*
1991	$5.8 M Bobby Bonilla, *Mets*
1991	$5.38 M Roger Clemens, *Red Sox*
1990	$4.7 M Jose Canseco, *Athletics*
1989	$3 M Kirby Puckett, *Twins*
1981	$2.2 M Dave Winfield, *Yankees*
1979	$1.13 M Nolan Ryan, *Astros*
1975	$578,200 Catfish Hunter, *Yankees*
1959	$125,000 Ted Williams, *Red Sox*
1947	$100,000 Hank Greenberg, *Pirates*
1923	$50,000 Babe Ruth, *Yankees*

(millions of dollars)

Source: Sports Illustrated

are not recorded as such.

Fans of stock options often assume that the executive who owns the options is taking an investment risk similar to that of a stockholder. Critics point out, however, that an executive can control the timing of exercising his stock option, so there is little downside risk. They note that a company's stock can float up because of a general optimism that is unrelated to CEO performance, and that often a stock option transfers money to the CEO that some feel belongs to shareholders.

As New York City investment adviser David Norr told Levin's panel in January, "The failure to measure the cost of options, the failure to charge a cost to profits, even though the executive knows his wealth is increasing as the stock rises in price, the failure of management to hold on to the stock when it exercises options, the lack of risk involved with options … the lack of a need to put up cash to exercise options, all contribute to a failure to convert management to the viewpoint of owners."

Many CEOs have been eager to take more pay in the form of stock options, garnering what are called "megagrants" of as many as 4 million shares, as in the case of Heinz's O'Reilly. Such grants can be worth millions if the stock rises just a fraction of a point. And in mature or slow-growth companies, says Biomet Inc. chief executive Dane A. Miller, awarding more options doesn't really give an executive an additional performance incentive. "When you're already holding stock worth $100 million, what incremental value does an extra 100 shares have?" Miller asks. "At some point you're just satisfying an uncontrollable greed complex."[12]

Companies use loopholes to work stock options to the CEO's advantage, says Crystal. He cites four common techniques: CEOs are allowed to swap worthless options for those more likely to pay off; CEOs are giv-

Top-Earning Entertainers

Bruce Willis

Kevin Costner

		1991 earnings	1990 earnings
		(in millions)	
New Kids on the Block	*pop music group*	$54	$61
William H. Cosby Jr.	*actor, comedian, author*	58	55
Oprah Winfrey	*TV host, producer*	42	38
Madonna	*pop singer, actress*	24	39
Michael Jackson	*pop singer*	25	35
Kevin Costner	*movie actor, director*	50	9
Johnny Carson	*TV host, producer*	30	25
The Rolling Stones	*rock group*	11	44
Charles M. Schulz	*cartoonist*	25	26
Steven Spielberg	*movie director, producer*	27	23
Paul McCartney	*pop singer, composer*	15	34
Julio Iglesias	*pop singer*	23	22
Janet Jackson	*pop singer*	18	25
Bruce Willis	*movie actor*	15	28
Eddie Murphy	*movie actor, comedian*	16	26
Tom Cruise	*movie actor*	17	19
Arnold Schwarzenegger	*movie actor*	15	20
Aerosmith	*rock group*	12	22
Hammer	*rap singer*	22	11
The Grateful Dead	*rock group*	16	17
Sean Connery	*movie actor*	5	27
Billy Joel	*pop singer*	5	26
Jack Nicholson	*movie actor*	14	16
John Hughes	*movie producer, director*	20	8
Frank Sinatra	*singer*	14	13
Michael Douglas	*movie actor, producer*	12	15
Michael J. Fox	*movie actor*	3	23
Guns N' Roses	*rock group*	21	4
Stephen King	*novelist, screenwriter*	13	12
Siegfried & Roy	*illusionists*	15	10
Prince	*pop singer*	10	15
Andrew Lloyd Webber	*composer, producer*	12	12
Paula Abdul	*pop singer, dancer*	10	14
Sylvester Stallone	*movie actor*	10	13
Arsenio Hall	*TV host, comedian*	12	11
Tom Clancy	*novelist*	15	5
Xuxa	*pop singer, TV host*	10	9
Mel Gibson	*movie actor*	10	9
Matt Groening	*cartoonist*	8	10
Vanilla Ice	*rap singer*	13	5

Note: Rankings are based on combined 1990 and 1991 earnings.
Source: Forbes *magazine*

en options to buy at below-market prices from the start, guaranteeing a profit as long as the stock doesn't fall; companies cushion the blow of falling stock prices by piling on more shares (Apple Computer is well known for this); and companies replace stock options with "restricted stock," a designation that lowers the option price to a hypothetical "zero," thus assuring a profit (though the stock can't be converted to cash until the executive leaves the company).[13]

Defenders argue that stock options are worth nothing if the stock price sinks or freezes, so there is indeed a downside risk. The NAM says many option plans risk as much as half an executive's annual pay.

Even if options are in fact worth nothing, few executives seem willing to give them up. In a spring special section, The Wall Street Journal noted that corporate boards are not cutting executive pay packages as much as reshaping them to rely more on stock grants. Overall, cash compensation rose 3.9 percent in 1991, the lowest since 1982, the Journal said, but total compensation rose 4.2 percent.[14]

Should the government seek to curb excessive executive pay?

There are two principal ways in which the federal government could step into the executive pay dispute: by regulating the way corporate salaries are disclosed to shareholders, and by altering the tax code.

The regulatory approach is favored by Sen. Levin in his Corporate Pay Responsibility Act (S 1198). The bill would require the Securities and Exchange Commission (SEC) to force corporations to arrive at an absolute bottom line on an executive's total compensation, including long-range stock options, and to explicitly spell it out to shareholders. The bill would also require companies to accommodate activist shareholders who seek to reduce executive pay by forcing a shareholder vote on executive packages.

Levin's bill has met resistance (from the SEC itself, initially) and from business groups worried about government "micromanagement" of corporate governance. Permitting shareholder votes "will erode the independence of the board," the NAM said in March, and could cause pay matters to be "dictated by public relations concerns."[15] The Business Roundtable also objects, questioning whether votes on executive pay should be permitted to small shareholders, who can easily withdraw their investments if they don't like the way a company is being run.

Use of the tax code to rein in executive pay is the approach favored by Rep. Sabo. His Income

What Lawyers Earn

1991 salary

Top Corporate Counsels
Benjamin W. Heineman Jr.
General Electric Co. (Fairfield, Conn.) $1,051,628
James W. Walker Jr.
CIGNA Corp. (Philadelphia, Pa.) $644,000
Harold E. Kennedy
Foster Wheeler Corp. (Clinton, N.J.) $533,110

Partners at Top Firms†
Debevoise and Plimpton
(New York City) $637,000
O'Melveny & Myers (Los Angeles) $620,000
Winston & Strawn (Chicago) $500,000

Law Professors (median salary)
Dean $126,000
Full professor $ 81,463

First-year Associates
Cleary, Gottlieb, Steen & Hamilton
(New York City) $ 83,000
Jones, Walker, Waechter, Poitevent,
Carrere & Denegre (New Orleans) $ 50,000

Legal Services Lawyers (starting salary)
Alabama $ 25,631
Los Angeles $ 41,239

Public-interest Lawyers (starting salary)
Center for Constitutional Rights
(New York City) $ 29,000
Public Citizen Litigation Group
(Washington, D.C.) $ 22,300

† In the late 1980s, it was common for partners to earn well over $1 million.
Source: National Law Journal

Doctors' Rewards

The high earnings of specialists have produced a shortage of general and family practitioners.

Specialty	Mean income (in thousands)
General/family practice	$102.7
Internal medicine	152.5
General internal medicine	125.9
Cardiovascular diseases	262.2
Other internal medicine	174.6
Surgery	236.4
General surgery	196.1
Otolaryngology	219.8
Orthopedic surgery	283.3
Ophthalmology	213.0
Urological surgery	195.9
Other surgery	331.1
Pediatrics	106.5
Obstetrics/gynecology	207.5
Radiology	219.4
Psychiatry	116.5
Anesthesiology	207.4
Pathology	172.5
Emergency medicine	139.7

Source: American Medical Association

Disparities Act (HR 3056) would disallow business tax deductions for the salaries companies pay to executives in excess of 25 times the salary of their lowest-paid worker. (He chose 25 because that is approximately the ratio of the president's salary to the minimum wage.) It is intended, in Sabo's words, "to create some self-interest on the part of the people at the top in what happens to people at the bottom."

Such use of "pay caps," either mandated by the tax code or imposed voluntarily by a company's board of directors, reflects their backers' broad concerns about salary fairness in society. But opponents warn that caps would kill the goose that lays the golden eggs. "Incentives should be unlimited," says the compensation association's Rowland. "Exceptional results should bring exceptional compensation. Besides, it's difficult to come up with rational caps when you consider all that goes into determining a salary."

Caps are also opposed by many critics of rising executive pay. The

United Shareholders' Whitworth argues that ending tax deductibility would simply make shareholders pay twice. "It wouldn't be a deterrent to executives," he adds, "because it's not their money." Congress in 1984 limited tax deductibility on lavish executive severance packages known as "golden parachutes," he points out, but the multimillion-dollar packages are as golden as ever.

Crystal argues that salary caps wouldn't work because the "scoring system in the business world" is based on how much one earns. "It's a symbol," he says. "Executives care only about pre-tax income for comparison."

As for the public, 64 percent of those responding to a January NBC News-*Wall Street Journal* poll favored a law limiting tax deductibility of executive salaries that are more than 25 times that of the lowest-paid

worker. Of those opposed, 11 percent said it was because the limit was too high, 3 percent because it was too low, and 13 percent opposed it because they felt the government should not be involved in the issue. *(See "At Issue," p. 473.)* ■

Top-Paid Wall Street Investors

	1990 earnings
Bruce Kovner, *Caxton Corp.*	$95 million+
Henry Kravis, *Kohlberg Kravis Roberts*	$90 million+
George Roberts, *Kohlberg Kravis Roberts*	$90 million+
Irwin Jacobs, *Private investor*	$75 million+
Paul Tudor Jones II, *Tudor Investment*	$70 million+
Robert MacDonnell, *Kohlberg Kravis Roberts*	$70 million+
Donald Kelly and family, *D. P. Kelly*	$67.6 million
Jerome Kohlberg, *Kohlberg & Co.*	$60 million+
George Soros, *Soros Fund Management*	$60 million+
Michel David-Weill and family, *Lazard*	$55 million+
Michael Steinhardt, *Steinhardt Partners*	$50 million
John Weinberg, *Goldman, Sachs*	$35 million
Theodore Forstmann, *Forstmann Little*	$30 million+
Julian Robertson, *Tiger Management*	$25 million+
George Weiss, *George Weiss Associates*	$25 million+
Lawrence Hilibrand, *Salomon Brothers Inc.*	$23 million
James Chanos, *Kynikos Associates*	$20 million+
Martin Dubilier, *Clayton & Dubilier*	$20 million
Andrew Hall, *Salomon*	$20 million
Richard Rainwater, *Rainwater Inc.*	$20 million
Average retail broker	$79,169
Average institutional broker	$166,335

Sources: Financial World *magazine; Securities Industry Association*

BACKGROUND

History's 'Just Price'

"Money alone sets all the world in motion." A 1990s CEO defending a lavish pay package? No, it's a maxim of Publius, the first-century Roman governor of Malta. The issues raised by the executive pay fracas — fairness, hierarchy, the role of marketplace forces — have been framed and fought over for centuries.

The Greek philosopher Plato is known to have told his pupil Aristotle that no one in an organization should earn more than five times

what the lowliest worker earns. Plato also advanced the "just-price theory," that workers should be paid as much as it takes to retain the same social status as their parents. That notion was revisited during the Middle Ages, when the Catholic Church, under pressure from wealthy landowners to maintain social harmony, established wage schedules for skilled artisans, acknowledging their status over the unskilled.[16]

By the 14th century, salary levels were being determined by forces other than authorities' decrees. Artisans' wages were bid up by the newly formed craft guilds, and by 1562 urban workers in Britain who had come in from the farms benefited from the

first minimum wage act. By the 18th century, the industrial revolution in Europe and the United States had spawned the urban labor movements.

Scottish economist Adam Smith, in his 1776 capitalist classic *The Wealth of Nations,* popularized the notion of labor as a value to be exchanged and wages as something to be bargained for. In one of the earliest discussions of what became the modern corporation, Smith also warned of the dangers of not keeping corporate officers accountable for handling other people's money. He explained that they "wouldn't watch over it with the same anxious vigilance."

In 1817, British economist David Ricardo authored the influential Iron Law of Wages, which stated that "the natural price of labor is that price which is necessary to enable the laborers, one with another, to subsist and to perpetuate their race without increase or diminution." A few decades later, German social philosopher Karl Marx, the founder of modern communism, advanced the "surplus value theory," which held that one of the injustices of capitalism was that workers would receive only subsistence-level income even though it was their labor that produced profits.

By the end of the 19th century, German economist Johann Heinrich von Thuren had introduced the notion that differing contributions from individuals — different skills, knowledge and effort — should produce different levels of pay.

Modern Compensation

In the early 20th century, it was auto pioneer Henry Ford who, by paying his workers twice what competing companies were paying (and thus improving their consuming power), established the notion that different employers could pay different salaries. Banker J. P. Morgan asserted during this period that no executive should earn more than 20 times the salary of the least-paid worker. And the experience of World War I, which required that many government employees be ranked according to their skills, carried over into private industry's systems of performance appraisal and job evaluation.[17]

By 1923, the first federal job-classification system was established to prevent agencies from raiding one another's staffs. Also at this time, private-sector experts began designing evaluation systems that assumed motivators other than money — working conditions, job satisfaction, etc. By the 1930s, British economist John Maynard Keynes had formalized his "full-employment" theory, which assigned the government an active economic role and argued that high general wages would boost general economic health. Under President Franklin D. Roosevelt's New Deal, a series of labor laws was enacted that cemented the modern role of government as a force in arbitrating wage disputes.

The modern determinants of pay — supply and demand, collective-bargaining, legislation and corporate governance — were all in place by the period of economic expansion

following World War II. Corporations formed fully staffed personnel offices. Job-evaluation systems — which define and rank the worth of jobs on such factors as skill, effort, responsibility and working conditions — became widespread in the early 1950s.[18]

One of the best known is the Hay system, pioneered by Edward N. Hay and Dale Purves, which emphasizes

Top-Paid Washington Lobbyists

		1989 salaries
Jack Valenti	Motion Picture Association of America	$672,590
James H. Sammons	American Medical Association	623,167
Jason S. Berman	Recording Industry Association of America	551,731
Edward I. O'Brien	Securities Industry Association	511,159
Robert E. Vagley	American Insurance Association	474,122
Richard S. Schweiker	American Council of Life Insurance	473,937
Charles J. DiBona	American Petroleum Institute	468,408
Donald G. Ogilvie	American Bankers Association	450,932
John M. Damgard	Futures Industry Association	407,500
David Silver	Investment Company Institute	404,652

Source: National Journal

criteria of know-how, problem-solving and accountability. Another useful classification tool is the Labor Department's *Dictionary of Occupational Titles,* which describes and analyzes the complexity of each American job. In applying such systems, salary planners often choose key jobs as "benchmark jobs," assign them a salary and then use the benchmarks to assign salaries to the surrounding jobs in the hierarchy. In practice, such interdependence often means that top executive salaries are continually raised to keep them ahead of second- and third-level salaries that might go up on merit.

Job Evaluators' Formulas

In the 1950s, job evaluators developed what are called "maturity curves," mathematical formulas used to add pay for extra experience gained by technical and scientific workers. In government during the postwar period, certain agencies such as the Veterans Administration won special

augmented pay scales to attract medical and research talent. By the 1960s, it was common for corporate personnel managers to conduct intricate surveys of other employers to determine the market's "going rate" as an aid in determining in-house salaries. The practice continues today, motivated in part by awareness of potential lawsuits based on civil rights legislation and the doctrine of comparable worth (see p. 471).

Some job evaluators today rationalize differing salaries for different jobs with formal systems of salary classes. One approach sets up eight categories based on different lifestyles and the family budget required to maintain it. Planners then decide which employees belong in which class, ranging from $6 million and all the lavishness of such a lifestyle down to $10,500, which is below the poverty level.[19]

Whatever salary-evaluation method is used, the results have a tremendous impact on the attitudes of employees at all levels. "Compensation is one of the most critical communication tools available to an organization," writes Richard I. Henderson, a professor emeritus of management at Georgia State University. "It tells workers what management thinks of them.... Compensation becomes a very concrete, highly visible representation of the philosophy and values of the owners and leaders of the organization."[20]

Executive Pay

The modern system for determining executive pay began evolving after Congress first approved the use of stock options in 1950. By the 1960s, special packages for managers were

Continued on p. 468

Journalism Highs and Lows

TV anchors
Dan Rather, CBS	$3.6 million
Tom Brokaw, NBC	$2 million
Peter Jennings, ABC	$1.8 million
TV news directors (median)	$45,000
TV reporters (median)	$20,000
Average newspaper editor	$66,664
Average starting reporter	$20,722

Sources: USA Weekend; Forbes; American Newspaper Publishers Association; Radio-Television News Directors Association

Chronology

1930s *Strong wage laws are enacted under the Roosevelt administration's New Deal.*

1935
National Labor Relations (Wagner) Act assures employees the right to collective bargaining for wages, benefits and working conditions.

1938
Fair Labor Standards Act sets first minimum wage at 25 cents an hour.

1950s *Postwar expansion shapes modern U.S. corporation; corporations begin awarding stock to executives*

Sept. 23, 1950
President Harry S Truman signs Revenue Act of 1950, which permits corporations to offer stock options to executives.

1951
Advent of modern job-evaluation systems of Edward N. Hay and Dale Purves.

1960s *Executive-pay plans begin to emerge; new laws ban workplace discrimination.*

June 10, 1963
President John F. Kennedy signs Equal Pay Act requiring an employer to pay equal wages for men and women who work in the same establishment and whose jobs require the same skills and responsibility.

June 2, 1964
President Lyndon B. Johnson signs Civil Rights Act, which prohibits wage discrimination by sex and race under Title VII.

June 17, 1969
President Richard M. Nixon, using 1967 law, orders largest pay increase for federal workers in 44 years: Congressional salaries rise 40 percent, federal workers' salaries increase 15.6 percent.

1970s *The concept of comparable worth is developed. A decade-long stock market slump leads to new ways to measure executive pay.*

Aug. 15, 1971
Nixon imposes wage and price controls on executives and workers.

Aug. 15, 1972
Congress establishes blue-collar pay scales for government workers in line with local private-sector wages.

1973
Comparable worth originates in Washington state study by public-employees union.

Oct. 6, 1978
Civil Service Reform Act creates the Senior Executive Service and merit pay in government.

1980s *Leveraged buyouts lead to increased use of stock options. Earnings of athletes, entertainers and executives boom.*

June 8, 1981
The Supreme Court rules that wage discrimination under Title VII of the 1964 Civil Rights Act applies even when jobs are dissimilar.

June 27, 1984
Tax reform legislation limits the tax deductibility of corporate "golden parachute" pay packages.

Oct. 19, 1987
Stock market falls a record 508 points, eventually causing Wall Street salaries to drop.

Nov 18, 1989
Following yearlong controversy and defeat of a recommended 51 percent pay hike, Congress enacts a more-modest pay hike for senior federal executives, judges and lawmakers.

Nov. 17, 1989
President Bush ends a 10-year impasse and signs bill boosting minimum wage to $4.25 per hour.

1990s *Furor erupts over executive pay. Pay cuts begin.*

Oct. 24, 1990
Congress passes Federal Employees Pay Comparability Act to match government General Schedule salaries with private-sector pay.

July 17, 1991
Senate bans honoraria.

Feb. 13, 1992
Securities and Exchange Commission switches policy and forces companies to permit shareholders to initiate votes on executive pay.

April 1992
First votes on shareholder proposals to cut executive pay.

common, creating a hierarchy of executive levels whose slots become increasingly complex as one moved up the ladder. The higher the job, the tougher it became for job evaluators to describe jobs in clear terms that wouldn't vary with the personality of the incumbent.

By the 1970s, recalled pay expert Crystal, the start of a decade-long slump in the stock market made it clear that executive pay required more complicated calculations that didn't depend on a steadily rising market.[21] By then the field of compensation management was firmly established, and the foremost corporate executives were routinely employing "compensation consultants" to go to bat for them to win higher pay from boards of directors. Such consultants are themselves highly paid. "Smooth and sophisticated in their knowledge of the tax code and the market," in the words of Henderson, they are "a little bit of a technician but more of an ego-booster."

One of them was Graef Crystal. Shortly before quitting the field in disgust, the maverick consultant acknowledged the "fine line between a compensation consultant and a prostitute."[22] He recalled the reaction of a CEO when he had recommended, based on performance numbers, that his pay be cut. "Just who do you think is paying your bill, anyway?" the CEO demanded. Whitworth of the United Shareholders says such consultants are "like a good bird dog —

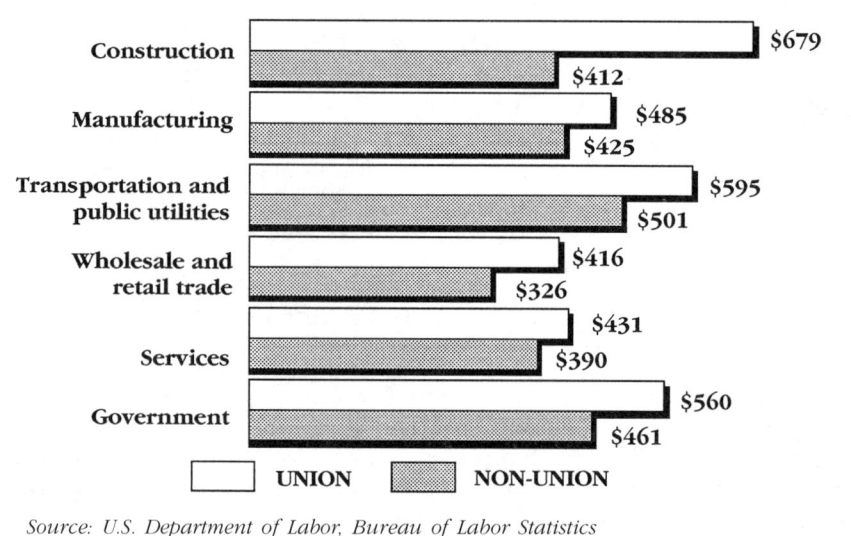

Union Paychecks Fatter

Weekly union pay continues to top pay in similar non-union jobs. In 1991, union members received on average a 4.8 percent increase, compared with a 4.3 percent increase for non-union workers.

Construction — $679 (UNION), $412 (NON-UNION)
Manufacturing — $485 (UNION), $425 (NON-UNION)
Transportation and public utilities — $595 (UNION), $501 (NON-UNION)
Wholesale and retail trade — $416 (UNION), $326 (NON-UNION)
Services — $431 (UNION), $390 (NON-UNION)
Government — $560 (UNION), $461 (NON-UNION)

□ UNION   ▨ NON-UNION

Source: U.S. Department of Labor, Bureau of Labor Statistics

they will hunt with anyone who's got a gun. They're paid to justify, not to rationalize."

Rowland of the American Compensation Association says that while some consultants will simply recommend what CEOs ask them to, "the majority I've worked with have high ethical standards and their own views as to what is fair. They're almost expected to go before the board with their own view."

Athletes and Entertainers

The startling CEO paychecks that began appearing in the 1980s have been viewed as the executive suite's answer to the sky-high pay of rock stars, movie stars and athletes. Celebrity salaries, of course, have been in the stratosphere for decades, at least since 1930, when it was pointed out to Yankee slugger Babe Ruth that he made $5,000 more than President Herbert Hoover. (The home-run king is said to have replied: "I had a better year than he did.") In the cur-

rent climate, however, athletes' and entertainers' salaries have come under industry fire.

In March, Chicago Cubs second baseman Ryne Sandberg became the first $7 million man in baseball, signing a four-year contract for $28.4 million. *(See table, p. 462.)* The Cubs said Sandberg, one of the club's most popular players, had been underpaid at $2.1 million the previous year. But other team owners warned that baseball could not survive such escalation, asserting that only those teams with lucrative television markets, such as the New York Yankees and the Boston Red Sox, would be able to bid for the best players.[23]

Gene Orza, general counsel of the Major League Players Association, replied that the owners have been saying the same thing for a century. "Players are paid based on revenues," he said. "Revenues go up, salaries go up."[24]

An April CBS News-*New York Times* poll asked the public whether baseball players are greedy when it comes to salaries: 39 percent re-

Wages: Men vs. Women

The "gender gap" in weekly earnings has narrowed in recent years, but female workers still earn less than males in many jobs.

Occupation	Women's wage	Men's wage	Wage gap
Mechanic/repairer	$392	$441	11%
Motor vehicle operator	289	383	25
Mail carrier	440	505	13
Construction worker	335	423	21

Source: Wider Opportunities for Women

Current Government Salaries

Public-sector pay continues to be generally less than salaries in the private sector, though legislation in 1989 and 1990 somewhat narrowed the gap. Most of the federal salaries listed reflect pay raises that took effect Jan. 1, 1992.

President of the United States
$200,000

House Speaker
$166,200

Vice President
$166,200

Chief Justice of
the United States
$166,200

Senate Majority
and Minority Leaders
$143,800

Cabinet Member
$143,800

Associate Justice
of the Supreme Court
$159,000

Joint Chiefs of Staff, chairman
$104,800

Senate and House Members
$129,500

Senior Executive Service,
top jobs
$112,100

Federal Appeals Judge
$137,300

Federal District Judge
$129,500

Governors

Arkansas	$ 35,000
Florida	$100,883
Michigan	$106,690
New Mexico	$ 90,000
New York	$130,000

Top General or Admiral
$104,800

Starting enlisted service member
$8,719

Federal Reserve

Chairman	$129,500
Governors	$119,300
Regional Presidents:	
New York	$245,000
Chicago	$209,000
Kansas City	$146,500

Foreign Service

Top	$83,502
Starting	$17,686

Surgeon General
$110,778

Director, National Institutes of Health
$143,800

Office of Thrift Supervision

Director	$119,300
Top regional director	$176,000

Government-sponsored enterprises
(quasi-governmental)

Federal Home Loan Mortgage
Corporation (Freddie Mac) Chairman
$1,049,837

Top NIH AIDS researcher
$110,000

Postmaster General
$138,900

Resolution Trust Corporation

President	$119,300
Senior vice president	$135,000

Federal National Mortgage Association
(Fannie Mae) Chairman
$1,120,352

Veterans Affairs physician
$93,558

Typical NASA engineer
$70,987

State Budget Officers

Student Loan Marketing Association
(Sallie Mae) President
$1,101,269

General Schedule

Arkansas		$ 49,199
Florida		$ 73,547
Michigan		$ 80,300
New Mexico		$ 53,123
New York		$ 96,662

GS-15 (top)	$83,502
GS-11 (mid-range)	$36,747
GS-1 (starting)	$11,478

Sources: Federal Register, *Council of State Governments, individual agencies*

---

sponded yes, and 50 percent agreed that the players were merely making what they can in the few years they have to play.

In Hollywood, studios have been worrying that company profits are being sliced by the high price of acting talent. A well-publicized example has been Jack Nicholson's reported $11 million for the 1989 movie "Batman," a deal that also included 10 percent of rentals and licensing fees. The studios blame the agents, saying the industry suffers because fewer movies are being made. "It's a freely negotiated market, and nobody forces any-

body to buy a talent if they don't think it's worth it," Nicholson's agent, Sandy Bresler, told *Daily Variety*. "If everybody says Actor A is overpriced, and after three pictures actor A doesn't deliver, that price will go down."[25] *(See list, p. 463.)*

This spring, several studio heads proposed that Hollywood rely more on good ideas than "overpriced talent" as a way to reverse declining profits. "Revenues would go up, the agents would have less leverage and lawyers would have less leverage if we made better movies," said Joe Roth, chairman of 20th Century Fox Film Corp.[26]

In the recording industry, the eye-popping multi-year contracts of Michael Jackson ($50 million) and Madonna ($60 million) are defended on the grounds that they are based purely on the stars' perceived ability to sell records. In that often cruel industry, most new albums fail, which is why unproven musical acts are usually signed for relatively little money. Recording company executives who can juggle the big sellers against the flops make out quite handsomely themselves. Charles Koppelman, chairman of SBK Records, for example, is reportedly worth $100 million.[27]

Union Reaction

Not surprisingly, the executive pay controversy has prompted some of the most vitriolic criticism from labor unions. "There's a sense of anger," says AFL-CIO spokeswoman Candice Johnson. "We're told we must keep wages low to be competitive with other countries when CEO salaries are off the charts compared with Japan and other industrialized nations."

During this spring's United Auto Workers strike against Caterpillar Inc., union members and commentators pointed out that the CEO of the Peoria, Ill., farm-equipment maker, Donald V. Fites, had received an 18.5 percent raise in 1991, bringing his salary to $503,486, while demanding wage freezes for workers making $16 an hour. Rowland of the compensation association agrees that a key problem with high executive pay that does not appear linked to performance is that it raises questions of equity that hamper management's ability to bargain with unions.

Union leaders themselves have been criticized for drawing salaries that dwarf those of average members. Ron Carey, newly elected president of the troubled International Brotherhood of Teamsters, this spring announced that one of his planned reforms was to sell the union's two corporate jets and take a pay cut from $225,000 to $175,000.

Government's Dilemma

The populist uproar over executive pay may fuel the vehemence of taxpayers who are upset with what they view as the high salaries in government. That's the view of Abramson of the Council for Excellence in Government, whose business-backed group works to ease the federal government's longstanding dilemma: the taxpayers' twin demands for good service and low-cost government.

Congress and the judicial and executive branches in recent years have weathered what many called a crisis caused by the inability of the government to recruit talented careerists and executives merely with "psychic rewards" and pay scales that are a fraction of private-sector salaries. "We firmly believe that people will cut their salaries in half to serve the nation, but asking them to cut their salaries significantly further may be asking too much," Abramson told a commission on federal salaries in 1988. As top-ranking government AIDS researcher Dr. Anthony Fauci told a similar panel that year, the National Institutes of Health (NIH) had "not been able to recruit a single senior research scientist from the private or academic sectors to engage in the independent conduct of a clinical or basic biomedical research program." [28]

The trouble is, in a country where the average annual salary is around $20,000, many citizens are outraged that their tax dollars should go to pay public employees salaries four or five times their own earnings. The issue is complicated by the traditional link between the pay levels of the three branches of government as well as the common reluctance of management to raise mid- and lower-level salaries without first raising salaries at the top.

As a way around the inevitable political firestorm, government salaries are raised only after a Rube Goldberg-like system in which a commission makes recommendations for approval first by the president and then Congress. The public, of course, directs its outrage at Congress, scoffing at the arguments of members who say they deserve higher pay because of the impact of their daily decisions and, more practically, because they have to maintain two homes.

"We think people should be paid

Top Salaries at Selected Nonprofits

Pressure on executives at nonprofits to raise money and operate like a business has boosted salaries at many nonprofits in the past decade.

American Cancer Society (Atlanta)	$ 208,231
American Heart Association (Dallas)	246,000
American Red Cross (Washington, D.C.)	200,000
Art Institute of Chicago	236,642
Boy Scouts of America (Irving, Texas)	223,375
Catholic Charities USA (Alexandria, Va.)	51,088
Columbia University (New York)	313,000
Ford Foundation (New York)	422,426
Friends of the Earth (Washington, D.C.)	50,400
Girl Scouts of the U.S.A. (New York)	133,845
Greenpeace USA (Washington, D.C.)	51,000
Harvard University (Cambridge, Mass.)	199,986
Heritage Foundation (Washington, D.C.)	319,367
Johns Hopkins University (Baltimore)	275,671
John D. & Catherine T. MacArthur Foundation (Chicago)	282,065
Andrew W. Mellon Foundation (New York)	375,560
National Black United Fund (Newark)	55,654
National Geographic Society (Washington, D.C.)	343,701
National Wildlife Federation (Washington, D.C.)	231,577
Nature Conservancy (Arlington, Va.)	185,000
New York City Opera	210,000
Salvation Army (Alexandria, Va.)	14,222
San Francisco Symphony	220,232
Save the Children Federation (Westport, Conn.)	204,593
U.S. Holocaust Memorial Council (Washington, D.C.)	200,000
University of California at Berkeley	175,000

Source: The Chronicle of Philanthropy

America's Economic Classes

No consensus has ever emerged on an official economic-class structure in the United States. Here is a proposed classification system based on earnings that was formulated by a Georgia State University management professor.

Class	Family of four annual income	% of U.S. population
Ultra rich	Over $1,000,000	less than .5
Wealthy	$225,000 to $1,000,000	less than 2
Upper middle	$85,000 to $225,000	6
Middle middle	$45,000 to $85,000	25
Lower middle	$22,500 to $45,000	37
Working poor	$12,500 to $22,500	17
Poverty	Up to $12,500	13

Source: Richard I. Henderson, Compensation Management: Rewarding Management Performance, *using figures from U.S. Census Bureau and Internal Revenue Service, 6th edition (publication forthcoming)*

for their education and skills," Abramson says, "but people don't think congressmen have skills. They want Jeffersonian citizens in Congress, like a hardware store owner, perhaps."

When the 1988 pay commission recommended a 51 percent pay raise, which would have boosted congressional pay from $89,500 to $135,000, the nation's talk show hosts had a field day. The National Taxpayers Union organized a mass mail-in of tea bags, recalling the Boston Tea Party tax revolt.

Consumer advocate Ralph Nader organized vocal opposition to the proposed congressional pay hike, arguing that money "does not buy integrity, dedication or commitment. At a time of deficits and program cuts, the commission's connection between money and quality is an insult to all qualified Americans — scientists, blue- and white-collar workers, civic leaders and state and local public officials — who would be delighted to fill a government position at $89,500 and significantly increase their salary while serving their country."

A January 1989 *Washington Post* poll showed that 85 percent opposed the pay raise for Congress, 82 percent opposed it for district court judges and 87 percent for the Cabinet.

Raises for Government Workers

After months of negotiating and quiet votes on the issue, Congress finally bit the bullet in late 1989 and approved a lesser pay raise for itself, judges and the topmost federal officials who make up the Senior Executive Service. That paved the way the following year for a raise for federal bureaucrats and blue-collar workers under the General Schedule to match those of the private sector. *(See chart of government salaries, p. 469.)*

Today, many agencies appear pleased with the new salaries, though some, such as the NIH, are still awaiting implementation of a special augmented-pay scale. A fear that future pay hikes won't keep up with living costs has caused many federal employees to plan early retirement at pension levels of their newly raised salaries.

U.S. government salaries are still low compared with those of other industrialized countries (which explains why the salaries of the mostly foreign employees at the World Bank and International Monetary Fund are high by Washington standards). And several U.S. agencies, financial regulators in particular, still have trouble recruiting experienced attorneys and accountants. Indeed, the director of the Office of Thrift Supervision,

which regulates the nation's savings and loans, earns less than some of his more-specialized underlings.

To Abramson, the pay dispute represents a fundamental issue of democracy. "Do we want upward mobility in government?" he asks "Should NIH be made up of first-class scientists or second-class ones who can't get university jobs?"

Gender Gap

The executive-pay flap is fought out over the earnings of only a few thousand people high up in *Fortune* 500 companies. In sheer numbers of people affected, however, the fairness issue with the widest implications is the salary gap between men and women. The 57 million women in the U.S. work force, according to the Institute for Women's Policy Re-

Most Americans Aren't CEOs...

The number of Americans who make it to the highest-paying jobs is dwarfed by the numbers in average-paying occupations.

	Number employed
CEOs of major companies	800
Actors and directors	47,000
Musicians and composers	28,000
Athletes	39,000
Authors	10,000
Managers	11,320,000
Engineers	1,739,000
Nurses	1,170,000
Teachers	3,246,000
Health technicians	1,027,000
Sales representatives	2,733,000
Secretaries	2,991,000
Food preparation and service occupations	2,477,000
Janitors	1,374,000
Mechanics	3,747,000
Homemakers	20,000,000
Unemployed	9,242,000

Sources: U.S. Department of Labor, Bureau of Labor Statistics; Census Bureau

search, earn only 71 cents for every dollar earned by men. (Though individual women executives earned as much as $23 million in 1991, they make up only 2.6 percent of *Fortune* 500 officers, according to the Washington-based Business and Professional Women's Foundation.)

One of the key proposals to remedy the so-called gender gap has been known since the early 1970s as "comparable worth," and more recently, "pay equity." It asserts that many of the traditional job-evaluation systems are biased in favor of men and that revised "gender-neutral" evaluations could be implemented that would better reward females working in "comparable" jobs.

According to Temple University sociologist Ronnie Steinberg, traditional job-evaluation methods such as the Hay system were built around 1940s-era stereotypes of "female jobs" and "black jobs," which were relatively low-paying.

Advocates of comparable-worth remedies argue that wage-setting is influenced by how society perceives elements of work and who does it. Firefighters, for example, don't spend every moment fighting fires, Steinberg says, but while waiting for emergencies do limited work around the station, maintaining equipment and cooking meals. "Yet we perceive their primary work to be that of firefighter," she writes. Contrast that with jail matrons, who, when not busy with prisoners, perform clerical duties that are weighted into the "value" of their work. That results in a lowering of their wages relative to jail guards, who have no assigned duties when not occupied by prisoners.[29]

About 20 state and local governments over the past two decades have implemented some sort of pay-equity program. At the request of Rep. Mary Rose Oakar, D-Ohio, Congress' General Accounting Office is at work on a pilot program to assess the possibilities for pay equity among federal employees. A poll for the National Committee on Pay Equity in December 1990 showed that 77 percent of registered voters would support a law requiring the same pay for men, women and minorities who work in jobs requiring similar skills and responsibilities, even if the jobs are different. Steinberg is designing what she intends to be a gender-neutral job-evaluation system based on skill, effort, responsibility and working conditions.

Pay equity is strongly opposed by many business groups as an infringement on management's rights to pay according to market forces. "The pay gap is closing the longer women remain in the work force," says Diane Generous, senior associate director for employee relations at the NAM. "But if you start artificially creating a pay scale, you will create a whole new set of problems." ∎

CURRENT SITUATION

Shareholder Activism

This spring brought unprecedented activism on executive pay among shareholders around the country. (One prominent attacker is a $7,200-a-year Indiana Catholic priest named Leo Conti.) Two of the country's largest institutional investors, the California Public Employees Retirement System and the California State Teachers Retirement System, have conducted negotiations on the issue with numerous companies. Following a go-ahead from the SEC, some 10 firms voted on shareholder-initiated executive pay questions.

Only one initiative passed, at Howard Savings Bank in Newark, N.J., according to Peg O'Hara, communications director of the Washington-based Investor Responsibility Research Center, which monitors corporate governance issues for institutional investors. O'Hara notes that even if they pass, shareholder initiatives to curb pay are advisory rather than binding. They have yet to be well-targeted at the truly non-performing companies, she adds, but "the movement is gathering steam."

In response to public pressure and face-to-face lobbying from the United Shareholders Association, many CEOs have been taking pay cuts. "I'm tired of being the poster boy for executive compensation," said Rand Araskog, CEO of International Telephone and Telegraph Corp., whose 1990 pay package of $11.4 million came down to $7.6 million for 1991.[30] The CEO's pay also fell at Xerox Corp. (7.3 percent), American Express Co. (39 percent) and International Business Machines Corp. (40 percent). The CEOs of all three major automakers took cuts, and United Airlines linked its CEO's future stock option gains to whether company stock rises by 15 percent a year.

SEC Chairman Richard C. Breeden recently reiterated a longstanding SEC view that market forces, not government, should set executive pay. "Boards that pay too little can expect to lose their best management talent," he said. "Boards that pay too much, by contrast, create unnecessary costs that must be absorbed by the shareholders that the boards represent."

Faced with pressure from Congress, however, Breeden in February announced new federal rules for clear disclosure of executive pay and agreed for the first time to require companies to permit shareholder-initiated votes on the issue. Also, at the SEC's urging, the Financial Account-
Continued on p. 474

At Issue:

Should the government step in to restrain rising executive salaries?

REP. MARTIN OLAV SABO, D-MINN.

Sponsor, Income Disparities Act
FROM *THE NEW YORK TIMES,* **MARCH 7, 1992**

President Ronald Reagan said a rising tide lifts all boats. But that is not the case when it comes to the salaries of American executives: Their salaries have skyrocketed in the last decade, while the pay of average workers has stagnated....

Recession-weary Americans find it hard to understand why, for example, Paul Fireman, Reebok's chief executive officer, earned $14.8 million a year, and Michael Eisner of Walt Disney pulls in $11.2 million. More unseemly is the $78.2 million that Steven Ross of Time Warner made in 1990 when stock options are included.... The Income Disparities Act ... would disallow business tax deductions for executive salaries in excess of 25 times the salary of the lowest-paid employee in the same organization....

This proposal doesn't cap executive pay. It would just mean that companies that want to compensate executives extravagantly wouldn't be subsidized through tax deductions for doing so. Most important, by linking the pay of those at the top with those at the bottom, we provide an incentive for executives to raise the salaries of their lowest-paid employees.

Why should government interfere with corporate pay? According to the 1990 census, 12 percent of adults living below the poverty line were full-time workers. Working people increasingly need government help to put food on their tables and roofs over their heads. So long as public resources are needed to support low-income workers, the government has a compelling interest in business pay scales.

The Income Disparities Act has a strong precedent. For decades, tax code provisions have been used to influence economic behavior: for example, the mortgage interest deduction and business tax credit for research and development. In the takeover boom of the 1980s, there was a furor over unnecessarily lucrative buyouts of top managers at companies being taken over. In 1984, Congress set a formula for determining if a golden parachute was excessive and took away business tax deductions for any settlement over the allowed amount....

Obviously, good management is critical to business, and executives should be paid in accordance with their responsibilities.... The Income Disparities Act acknowledges that businesses exist not only for shareholders and executives but also for their employees, clients and community.

PEARL MEYER

President, Pearl Meyer & Partners,
Executive compensation consultants
FROM *THE NEW YORK TIMES,* **APRIL 30, 1992**

There's something terribly wrong on the executive compensation scene these days, and it's not just the horde of overpaid chief executive officers portrayed in the news media. The problem is the effort by some legislators and consultants, wielding some slippery statistics, to micromanage a compensation system that has largely fulfilled its goal of spurring good performance and profits from American business.

Concentrating their fury on wide use of stock option plans, the new "pay police" have led the news media into a virtual pack attack on America's top executives, using catchy slogans such as "stealth compensation" and "reverse welfare." The few instances of real abuse — very highly compensated executives presiding over very poorly performing companies — are repeatedly trotted out, and their impact on each company's bottom line is exaggerated.

Certainly, the tempest has focused attention on genuine problems. There is a need to fine-tune stock and long-term thinking. Proxy statements should plainly set out how much top executives will earn that year — and explain why. And pay-for-performance bonus plans must make tough demands for results that warrant reward.

Those adjustments are being made — by companies themselves. In response to legitimate shareholder concerns, compensation committees are showing a healthy skepticism toward management proposals....

For the last four decades, stock options have instilled in executives a long-term shareholder view and have provided a vehicle for cash-strapped companies to compete for top talent in an open market.

Wealthy executives, even deserving ones, are an easy target. But it's fundamentally unfair to compare American executives with lower-paid peers in Japan — ignoring that in Japan, job security is absolute, insider trading and sizable perks are acceptable, and a chief executive officer is a first among equals....

Our struggling economy needs stimulation, not more bureaucratic restraint and regulation. Compensation simply cannot be made the scapegoat for every ill on the American economic scene. Government intervention will cripple the ability of American companies to retain and motivate their most effective leaders. To defuse this issue and keep government out of the boardroom, corporations must police themselves and convince stockholders, legislators and the news media that they can do it effectively.

Continued from p. 472

ing Standards Board, which sets bookkeeping rules for industry, this May announced plans to make it more costly for companies to reward their executives with stock options.

Sen. Levin has said that he is willing to drop his Corporate Pay Responsibility Act if the SEC accomplishes the same purpose administratively. Rep. Sabo, meanwhile, saw elements of his Income Disparities Act included in the House-passed tax bill in February, but it was vetoed by President Bush.

Nonprofits Re-evaluate

This spring's controversy at the United Way erupted with news reports of the "high salary," frequent first-class travel and mixing of business and personal relationships by president William Aramony. Though the 22-year veteran quickly resigned, many local United Way branches suffered a severe decline in donations, and nonprofit and charitable organizations around the country moved to re-evaluate their executive salaries.

Through most of their history, nonprofits were run by idealists who worked as much or more for their cause as for financial gain. In the past decade, however, as government support has shrunk, many charities and public-interest groups have been forced to adopt the methods of private business to bring in revenues. In the 1970s, explains Tom Gorski, vice president for public relations and marketing at the American Society of Association Executives in Washington, four-fifths of nonprofits' funds came from collecting dues. Nowadays half is from dues and the rest from revenue-enhancing activities, such as putting on conferences and selling publications.

Today, as Towers Perrin's Jim Moss points out, nonprofits have to decide

on the caliber of the top officer they wish to attract. "To the extent that you can find someone with a commitment to your cause, who also has the skills, you have a perfect match, but it is more difficult to find that match today," he says.

Charities must also deal with public scrutiny of how their budgets divide between administrative costs and direct aid to the needy. "There is a point where the salary becomes a burden, not because it causes a problem for the administration of the group but for the public perception," says Jennifer Anne Fisch, associate editor of *The Nonprofit Times*.[31]

Author Joseph Flinder, writing in the May 4 issue of *The New Republic*, defended the United Way's Aramony, noting that he had transformed a loose, $700,000-a-year alliance of community chests into a multimillion-dollar network that has raised $35 billion for the needy, tapped into a system of corporate payroll deductions and formed a successful fund-raising alliance with the National Football League. "No other country in the world relies on the nonprofit sector to provide human services to the extent we do," Flinder writes. "The time of the mendicant friars who took a vow of poverty is long past.... It's not just for amateurs anymore."

The United Way debacle has ex-

Salaries Vary Around the Country

State per-capita income figures provide a useful approximation of how salaries vary around the country. Per-capita income includes income from salaries, interest, dividends and government transfer payments, such as welfare.

State	1991 per-capita income	State	1991 per-capita income
Alabama	$15,567	Montana	$16,043
Alaska	21,932	Nebraska	17,852
Arizona	16,401	Nevada	19,175
Arkansas	14,753	New Hampshire	20,951
California	20,952	New Jersey	25,372
Colorado	19,440	New Mexico	14,844
Connecticut	25,881	New York	22,456
Delaware	20,349	North Carolina	16,642
District of Columbia	24,439	North Dakota	16,088
Florida	18,880	Ohio	17,916
Georgia	17,364	Oklahoma	15,827
Hawaii	21,306	Oregon	17,592
Idaho	15,401	Pennsylvania	19,128
Illinois	20,824	Rhode Island	18,840
Indiana	17,217	South Carolina	15,420
Iowa	17,505	South Dakota	16,392
Kansas	18,511	Tennessee	16,325
Kentucky	15,539	Texas	17,305
Louisiana	15,143	Utah	14,529
Maine	17,306	Vermont	17,747
Maryland	22,080	Virginia	19,976
Massachusetts	22,897	Washington	19,442
Michigan	18,679	West Virginia	14,174
Minnesota	19,107	Wisconsin	18,046
Mississippi	13,343	Wyoming	17,118
Missouri	17,842		

Source: U.S. Department of Commerce, Bureau of Economic Analysis

posed a nerve in the nonprofit community. "There's a contradiction," says Phil Dover, a marketing professor who has been a consultant to the United Way. "You want to run charity efficiently as a business. You want to run it with good management talent. At the same time, you want them almost to be the sackcloth and ashes type. Somehow, you've got to compromise."[32] ∎

OUTLOOK

A New Era?

While corporate boardrooms buzz with debate on the ups and ups of executive pay, society continues grappling with wider issues of salary fairness. What will happen to pay in the occupations for which there have been shortages of qualified applicants: teachers (median salary $28,080) and nurses (median salary $32,968)?[33] Will the market boost the classically low-paid occupations for which there is growing demand: social workers (median salary $24,232) and day-care workers (median salary $11,000)?

Answers will be considered at a time when most American workers are seeing only modest increases in pay. (White-collar raises are averaging 4.5 percent and blue-collar 4.4 percent, according to a recent Hewitt Associates survey of 2,000 companies.) And the economy as a whole, the Census Bureau reported this May, is seeing its most dramatic rise in lowest-paying jobs, from 12 percent of American jobs in 1979 to 18 percent in 1990.

The result may be an expanding revolt against executive grandeur. As Harvard business Professor Murphy says, "As long as there's a populist notion to go after the pay of the richest 1 percent, the general backlash to the excesses of the 1980s will continue."

Though Americans don't appear to begrudge the wealth of superstars in sports, entertainment or in the realms of inventors and entrepreneurs, they may have trouble grasping the "indispensability" of individual CEOs. As Biomet's Miller put it, "People buy Celtics tickets because they want to see Larry Bird, but no one buys a Coke because of its CEO."[34]

But neither average Americans nor their elected representatives sit on corporate boards. "I don't care what law they pass in Congress," says Gordon Wolf, a consultant with Towers Perrin. "Short of legislating a firing squad, the pay level of CEOs is not going to go down."[35]

Key Issue Is Non-Performance

To skeptics of the populist critique, the real issue is not high pay but the failure of many boards to fire a non-performing chief executive. "If the U.S. were beating the pants off its rivals, hardly anyone would care what its CEOs got paid," writes *Fortune* magazine reporter Geoffrey Colvin. "That's why just paying less isn't the answer, and paying for performance is."[36]

Paying for performance is a goal that is likely to be insisted upon by corporate shareholders. "The time is now waning when the CEO can say, 'It's my company, it's my board,' " says John Nash, president of the National Association of Corporate Directors. "It's going to be the shareholders' company."[37]

Noted management theorist Peter Drucker has called for a 20-to-1 ratio between top executive pay and that of the company's lowest-paid worker. It is seen as a way of improving teamwork and worker morale. (Half of all business school deans back the proposal, according to the *USA Today* poll.) Already, numerous companies have adopted their own ratios: At Ben and Jerry's Homemade ice cream in Waterbury, Vt., it's 7-to-1; at Independent Technologies in Freemont, Calif., no executive earns more than two-and-a-half times the average salary; and at Herman Miller Inc., a Zeeland, Mich., office furniture maker, the CEO gets no more than 20 times the average pay of $28,000.

There are many who feel that if some CEOs volunteer for cuts, others will follow and effect a change in corporate culture. "What big American companies need most is leadership," said John Kotter, a Harvard Business School professor. "I don't think you can encourage leadership with money. In fact, you can discourage it. The kind of people who make good leaders are not obsessed with money."[38]

Clearly looking over their shoulders, many boards of directors are re-evaluating procedures. They're entertaining proposals, for example, that pay-setting boards be composed of members with no links to the CEO. Others are pondering the recommendation of Crystal and other critics that they hire an independent compensation consultant to represent the board against the CEO's personal consultant.

Crystal recommends that companies abandon the practice of cushioning CEO stock losses with new stock grants, that they consider the "negative bonus," or pay cut, when corporate performance is poor and that the salaries of CEOs in foreign countries be used as benchmarks for setting U.S. pay.

"In the near-term, I'm encouraged," Crystal says. "I've shown that if we pick off some of the animals at the outer ends, we can start to turn the herd." He warns, however, that many companies will cut back only on the "flashy" parts of pay, such as cash, and that if the stock market continues its rise, another pay explosion could occur.

Rowland of the compensation association predicts that the gap between CEO and average pay will be based on the performance of each business. "If the company does well, the gap will widen; if the company does poorly, the gap will narrow and pay will drop," he says.

In many ways, high executive salaries are less a bottom-line issue than a symbolic one. "Executive pay generally is a minute fraction of total cost," said Michael D. Rose, chairman of Promus Companies, a casino and hotel operator. "But it's symptomatic. At companies where executive pay is out of line, you'll probably find other [areas] where they are not cost-conscious. It will be an indication of a not-very-demanding management and board."[39]

The recent burst of record-setting pay has led a few observers to speculate that a new era in the pay culture has dawned. "We're seeing the last vestiges of royalty," as management Professor Henderson puts it. "We're seeing the start of some kind of legitimate relationship between the CEO and rank-and-file, the start of a democratization of pay at work." ∎

Notes

[1] Quoted in *The Washington Post,* Jan. 16, 1992.

[2] Such studies have been released by the Congressional Budget Office, the House Ways and Means Committee, the Federal Reserve and the Center on Budget and Policy Priorities. Conservatives have challenged the methodology of the studies. (See *The Wall Street Journal,* editorial, May 11, 1992.)

[3] "What, Me Overpaid? CEOs Fight Back," *Business Week,* May 4, 1992, p. 142.

[4] Testimony before the Senate Governmental Affairs Oversight of Government Management Subcommittee, May 15, 1991.

[5] Column in *Newsweek,* Nov. 11, 1992, p. 55.

[6] Statement of the National Association of Manufacturers to the Subcommittee on Oversight of Government Management, Senate Governmental Affairs Committee, Jan. 31,
1992.

[7] "A Little Pain and a Lot to Gain," *The Wall Street Journal,* April 22, 1992.

[8] Michael C. Jensen and Kevin J. Murphy, "CEO Incentives: It's Not How Much You Pay, But How," *Harvard Business Review,* May-June 1990, p. 138.

[9] Quoted in *The Wall Street Journal,* April 14, 1992.

[10] Quoted in *The Washington Post,* March 20, 1992.

[11] "What Do You Know, Owning Shares Really Does Help Performance!" *The Crystal Report,* January-February, 1992, p. 1.

[12] Quoted in *Business Week,* May 4, 1992, p. 144.

[13] Graef Crystal, "Pay, Performance Have Vague Link," *USA Today,* April 27, 1992.

[14] "A Little Pain and a Lot to Gain," *The Wall Street Journal,* April 22, 1992.

[15] *Industry Week* magazine, March 2, 1992. p. 44.

[16] Richard I. Henderson, *Compensation Management: Rewarding Performance,* 4th edition (1985), p. 63.

[17] Thomas H. Patten Jr., *Fair Pay: The Managerial Challenge of Comparable Worth and Job Evaluation* (1988) p. 156.

[18] Henderson, *op. cit.,* p. 278.

[19] Robert E. Sibson, *Compensation* (1990), p. 102.

[20] Henderson, *op. cit.,* p. ix.

[21] Crystal, *op. cit.,* p. 216.

[22] Graef Crystal, *In Search of Excess* (1991), p. 12.

[23] For more on sports salaries, see "Free Agency: Pro Sports' Big Challenge," *Editorial Research Reports,* Feb. 9, 1990, p. 82.

[24] Quoted in *Sports Illustrated,* March 6, 1992, p. 16.

[25] Quoted in *Daily Variety,* Oct. 31, 1989.

[26] Quoted in *Daily Variety,* March 30, 1992.

[27] See *Forbes,* Sept. 30, 1991, p. 108.

[28] National Commission on the Public Service, *Leadership for America: Rebuilding the Public Service,* 1989, p. 34.

[29] Helen Remick and Ronnie Steinberg, "Comparable Worth and Wage Discrimination," *Center for Women in Government* (1984), p. 19.

[30] Quoted in *The Wall Street Journal,* April 27, 1992.

[31] Quoted in *The New York Times,* March 16, 1992.

[32] Quoted in *The New York Times,* March 16,
1992.

[33] Average salary figures for teachers ($34,413) and nurses ($34,462) provided by the National Education Association and the American Nurses Association differ slightly from the Bureau of Labor Statistics median weekly data used in the table on page 461.

[34] Quoted in *Business Week,* May 4, 1992, p. 142.

[35] Quoted in *The Wall Street Journal,* April 22, 1992.

[36] Geoffrey Colvin, "How to Pay the CEO Right," *Fortune,* April 6, 1992.

[37] Quoted in *The Wall Street Journal,* April 27, 1992.

[38] Quoted in *The Economist,* Feb. 1, 1992. p. 19.

[39] Quoted in *The New York Times,* Feb. 2, 1992.

Bibliography

Selected Sources Used

Books

Crystal, Graef S., *In Search of Excess: The Overcompensation of American Executives,* W. W. Norton & Co., 1991.

One of the country's foremost executive-pay experts, Crystal became disillusioned working as a mere "rubber stamp" for the pay desires of top executives and left his lucrative corporate consulting job to become a pay critic and business professor at the University of California at Berkeley. This story of his conversion describes how current executive pay is negotiated and proposes substantive reforms.

Henderson, Richard I., *Compensation Management: Rewarding Performance,* Reston Publishing Co. (Prentice-Hall), 4th edition, 1985.

A management professor emeritus at Georgia State University has assembled a comprehensive college textbook on the history, theory and practice of arriving at fair pay for all levels in the workplace. He surveys varying methods for evaluating jobs and applies a class analysis of American society.

Henrici, Stanley B., *Salary Management for the Nonspecialist,* AMACOM (American Management Association), 1980.

A retired manager of organization systems for Heinz USA reviews job-evaluation systems and such techniques as salary surveys used in arriving at pay rates. Includes a glossary of pay-related terms.

Thomas H. Patten, Jr., *Fair Pay: The Managerial Challenge of Comparable Job Worth and Job Evaluation,* Jossey-Bass Inc. Publishers, 1988.

A professor of management and human resources at California State Polytechnic University evaluates current and proposed systems for evaluating job worth to achieve workplace equity between men and women. He reviews management and legal issues.

Sibson, Robert E., *Compensation,* 5th edition, American Management Association, 1990.

The founder of a major human-resources consulting firm has updated this work several times since its first release in 1960. It is a how-to guide to corporate practices in compensation management, benefits design and work force recruitment.

Articles

Andrew Brownstein and Morris J. Panner, "Who Should Set CEO Pay? The Press? Congress? Shareholders?" *Harvard Business Review,* May-June 1992, p. 28.

Two New York lawyers criticize "populist" critics such as Graef Crystal for "zealousness" and "self-righteousness." They argue for a business solution to what has been turned into a political problem.

John A. Byrne, "What, Me Overpaid? CEOs Fight Back," *Business Week,* May 4, 1992, p. 142.

A prominent business magazine's annual list of top CEO salaries surveys the politics of the pay issue.

Carlson, Peter, "How the Rich Get Richer: Everything you wanted to know about executive compensation — but were too angry to ask," *The Washington Post Magazine,* April 5, 1992.

A Washington journalist describes his encounters with well-paid executives during his quest to understand the values of the corporate elite.

Colvin, Geoffrey, "How to Pay the CEO Right," *Fortune,* April 6, 1992, p. 61.

A Time Warner business journalist describes pay policies of several companies that have taken substantive measures to curb high CEO pay, among them, the replacement of stock options with grants awarded only if stock rises.

"Boss's Pay: Worthy of His Hire?" *The Economist,* Feb. 1, 1992.

The British newsweekly presents the current U.S. arguments for and against current executive pay levels.

Cordes, Helen, "How Much Dough for the Big Cheese?" *Utne Reader,* March/April 1992, p. 17.

An alternative journalist examines business and public reaction to skyrocketing executive salaries.

Jensen, Michael C. and Kevin J. Murphy, "CEO Incentives: It's Not How Much You Pay, But How," *Harvard Business Review,* May-June 1990, p. 138.

Two Harvard University business professors argue that newspaper headlines notwithstanding, executives are not receiving record salaries and bonuses. They favor big rewards for outstanding performance and meaningful penalties for poor performance.

The Next Step

Additional Articles from Current Periodicals from EBSCO Publishing's Database

Executives — Wages

Byron, C., "Strike it rich," *New York,* Feb. 17, 1992, p. 21.

Discusses controversy over the exorbitant salaries paid to some corporate heads. Specifics on two competing pieces of legislation introduced by Rep. Martin Olav Sabo, D-Minn., and Sen. Carl Levin, D-Mich.; the bills would set a ceiling on how much chief executives could be paid and give stock-holders more control over the process of setting chief-executive pay.

Colvin, G., "CEO pay: A hotter issue than ever," *Fortune,* Feb. 10, 1992, p. 10.

Looks at how the topic of chief executive salaries continues to be a hot issue, especially at annual shareholders meetings. Runaway CEO pay; cites examples of Chrysler's Lee Iacocca and Anthony J. F. O'Reilly of H.J. Heinz. Directors who set CEO pay know they're in trouble.

Colvin, G., "Stock options endangered," *Fortune,* Feb. 24, 1992, p. 11.

Comments upon the ever hotter issue of chief executive officer (CEO) pay. The current debate over what employee stock options are really worth; remarks from Securities and Exchange Commission (SEC) Chairman Richard Breeden; questions under investigation by the Financial Accounting Standards Board.

Cowan, A. L., "Magazine to drop column by expert on executive pay," *The New York Times,* Feb. 25, 1992, p. D1.

Says that *Financial World* magazine moved to sever its relationship with Graef S. Crystal, who writes on executive pay issues for the magazine, because of complaints about his column. Many companies whose executives have appeared overpaid, according to Crystal's calculations, object to his methodology in setting a value for stock options executives receive as part of their compensation.

Egan, J., "A shareholder's report card," *U.S. News & World Report,* March 2, 1991, p. 69.

Discusses the pertinence of a new tally by United Shareholders Association (USA) known as "Shareholder 1,000," which measures what investors care about: how a company's stock is doing and how its management creates value for investors rather than rewarding itself. The problems in executive compensation; the scores USA assigns to each of the 1,000 companies based on marks in four areas; Wal-Mart scored best in executive pay; Lawter International scored well; more.

"Getting the message," *Time,* March 23, 1992, p. 48

Offers a look at the companies currently reacting to stockholder gripes about executive greed by slashing the income of top management. Westinghouse Electric slashed the income of 14 top officials by as much as 62 percent, while IBM cut the top five by 40 percent and took smaller cuts from the next 60 executives. Action at Paramount's annual meeting.

"How sweet it was," *Time,* Feb. 24, 1992, p. 42.

Outlines a recent plan from the Securities and Exchange Commission that will allow anyone who owns $1,000 or 1 percent of a company's stock to insert a proposal in a firm's proxy statement that calls for a vote on an executive's compensation package. The agency has also zeroed in on stock-option grants. Reaction from corporate leaders, the Bush Administration and Sen. Carl Levin, D-Mich.

"Inside Interpublic labyrinth," *Advertising Age,* Nov. 18, 1991, p. S10 (special section).

Discusses how corporate compensation packages may be putting more executive-level pay at risk, but the degree of risk can be minimal. Interpublic compensation plan; long-term performance incentives; supplied personal financial planning and tax advice; retainer for director; serving on a committee; more.

Koretz, G., "CEO pay: Exorbitant, yes — illogical, no," *Business Week,* Aug. 19, 1991, p. 18.

Gives early results from the latest Hay Group Inc. executive compensation survey, which show a strong relationship between CEO annual cash compensation, particularly incentive payouts, and company profitability. Base salaries for CEOs in 40 large industrial companies; CEOs in companies whose profits were down; CEOs in companies with profit gains.

Labaton, S., "SEC proposal on executive pay expected," *The New York Times,* Feb. 13, 1992, p. D1.

States that the Securities and Exchange Commission, under pressure from lawmakers and shareholders to make companies more accountable for executive pay, will propose rules requiring publicly traded companies to disclose more fully how much their executives are paid and to give stockholders the right to vote on compensation. Details of the rules.

"Less perky, more practical," *Advertising Age,* Nov. 18, 1991, p. S10 (special section).

Comments that perquisites are taking a back seat as greater portions of executive compensation are being placed at risk in the form of incentive arrangements at leading U.S. corporations. Perks are less lavish and more practical; common perks; communications equipment; long-term incentive plans; more.

Levinson, M., "Lay off the pricey CEOs," *Newsweek,* Feb. 10, 1992, p. 44.

Describes the current witchhunt atmosphere concerning overpaid corporate officers. CEOs that treat the corporate treasury like a bank; suggestion that Congress has plenty of other serious economic issues it needs to address.

"Little companies, big rewards," *Forbes,* Nov. 11, 1991, p. 291.

Presents a listing of median compensation for chief executives of a *Forbes* 500 company. Compensation is for the company's most recent fiscal year.

Losee, S., "Posthumous paychecks for chief executives," *Fortune,* Oct. 7, 1991, p. 13.

Discusses how at least 15 percent of *Fortune* 500 CEOs have contracts that provide the oxymoronic "death benefit," a provision for their renumeration to continue for various periods should they die while in office. Occidental Petroleum's Armand Hammer was receiving a $2.3 million company salary nearly one year after his death, and he will continue to do so until 1998. Other executives with death benefits; why companies don't just increase life insurance; more.

McCarroll, K. Makihara et al., "Motown's fat cats," *Time,* Jan. 20, 1992, p. 34.

Compares the salaries and bonuses of the three U.S. auto-company chiefs (Chrysler's Lee Iacocca, Ford's Harold Poling and GM's Robert Stempel) with those of Japan's big three (Shoichiro Toyoda of Toyota, Honda's Nobuhiko Kawamoto and Nissan's Yutaka Kume). Japanese perks compared with American benefits: corporate jets, homes and home security services, stock options. Underwhelming financial performance of the companies represented; U.S. competitive position.

Neff, R. and J. Barnathan, "How much Japanese CEOs really make," *Business Week,* Jan. 27, 1992, p. 31.

Questions how much compensation Japanese executives actually receive compared with their American counterparts. Japanese compensation at $525,000 per year; U.S. at $3,200,000 per year; different business cultures; perks in U.S. and Japan.

"Next, the SEC should zero in on proxies," *Business Week,* March 2, 1992, p. 114.

Editorial. States that on Feb. 13 the Securities and Exchange Commission gave shareholders the right to question executive compensation through proxy resolutions, and proposed rules requiring that pay packages be disclosed in a more meaningful way. Suggests that the SEC should reform the proxy system to make managers more accountable to shareholders and shareholders more effective owners.

"Paying the boss," *The Economist,* Feb. 1, 1992, p. 13.

Discusses how America's corporate bosses have somehow managed to offend the public by paying themselves inordinate sums of money. As American companies report their financial results over the next few months, proxy statements sent to shareholders will reveal another batch of multimillion-dollar payments to chief executives last year, when the economy was in recession. Properly applied incentives; mulling reforms.

Samuelson, R.J., "The boss as welfare cheat," *Newsweek,* Nov. 11, 1991, p. 55.

Asserts that the way CEOs overpay themselves undermines U.S. business. Why we can't look to corporate America for moral leadership; comparison of CEOs to welfare cheats; the CEO pay boom between 1980 and 1990; CEO's salary as compared with the average worker's salary; stock options; poll of middle managers by *Industry Week* magazine; more.

"The golden coffin," *The Economist,* Sept. 21, 1991, p. 89.

Examines recent controversy over executive pay, which many people feel are far too exorbitant for a job not always well done. Shareholders beginning to challenge compensation schemes; the United Shareholders Association; example of Rand Araskog, who runs ITT; details.

"The prince of pay," *Forbes,* Sept. 30, 1991, p. 92.

Examines how Warner Communications' boss, Steve Ross, negotiated a compensation package for himself that allowed him to emerge as the country's best-paid chief executive of a major publicly traded company. Awarded for a job well done; Ross' cash compensation totaled $1.1 million; blueprint for Ross' earnings; Ross' 10-year bonus plan; details of contract with Time-Warner; various stock options.

Back Issues

Great Research on Current Issues Starts Right Here... Recent topics covered by The CQ Researcher are listed below. Issues dated before May 10, 1991, were published under the name of Editorial Research Reports.

NOVEMBER 1990
Lotteries and Gambling
Post-Cold War Choices
Setting Limits on Medical Care
Multicultural Education

DECEMBER 1990
Cable TV Regulation
Americans' Search for Their Roots
Is Insurance System a Failure?
Why Schools Still Have Tracking

JANUARY 1991
Growing Influence of Boycotts
Should the U.S. Reinstate the Draft?
America's Archaeological Past
Peace Corps' Challenges in '90s

FEBRUARY 1991
Regional Impact of Recession
Puerto Rico's Status
Redistricting: Mapping Power
Nuclear Power

MARCH 1991
Acid Rain
Cost of the Gulf War
Reassessing Gun Laws
Future for Man in Space

APRIL 1991
Social Security
Canadian Crisis Over Quebec
California Drought
Electromagnetic Radiation

MAY 1991
School Choice
Racial Quotas
Animal Rights
U.S. and Japan

JUNE 1991
Children and Divorce
Teenage Suicide
Endangered Species
Europe 1992

JULY 1991
Teenagers and Abortion
Soviet Republics Rebel
Mexico's Emergence
Athletes and Drugs

AUGUST 1991
Sexual Harassment
Fetal Tissue Research
Oil Imports
The Palestinians

SEPTEMBER 1991
Police Brutality
Advertising Under Attack
Saving the Forests
Foster Care Crisis

OCTOBER 1991
Pay-Per-View TV
Youth Gangs
Gene Therapy
World Hunger

NOVEMBER 1991
Fast-Food Shake-Up
The Greening of Eastern Europe
Business' Role in Education
Cuba In Crisis

DECEMBER 1991
Retiree Health Benefits
Asian Americans
The Obscenity Debate
The Disabilities Act

JANUARY 1992
Term Limits
Oil Spills
Hunting Controversy
Alternative Medicine

FEBRUARY 1992
Threatened Coastlines
New Era in Asia
Assisted Suicide
Jobs in the '90s

MARCH 1992
Women and Sports
Underage Drinking
Garbage Crisis
Mafia Crackdown

APRIL 1992
Ozone Depletion
Welfare Reform
Politicians and Privacy
Illegal Immigration

MAY 1992
Native Americans
Jobs vs. Environment
Too Many Lawsuits?

Back issues are available for $4.00 (subscribers) or $7.00 (non-subscribers). Quantity discounts apply to orders over ten. To order, call Congressional Quarterly 1-800-432-2250.

Future Topics

▶ *Nuclear Proliferation*

▶ *Food Irradiation*

▶ *Lead Poisoning*

THE CQ Researcher

PUBLISHED BY CONGRESSIONAL QUARTERLY INC., IN CONJUNCTION WITH EBSCO PUBLISHING

Nuclear Proliferation

Will the Soviet Union's collapse spawn a new arms race?

A LMOST 30 YEARS AGO, IN THE MIDST OF THE
U.S.-Soviet arms race, President John F. Kennedy
warned of the danger of nuclear proliferation.
Ironically, now that the Cold War is over, the
prospect has become a reality. The collapse of the Soviet
Union may have calmed fears of a nuclear Armageddon, but it
has aroused new concerns about the spread of nuclear
weapons. More than a dozen nations either have or are
feverishly trying to develop nuclear arsenals, including Third
World nations riven by religious and territorial disputes. If the
world fails to contain the spread of nuclear-weapons
technology, the balance of power that kept relative peace
during the four decades of the Cold War may be displaced by
a balance of terror.

C Q **June 5, 1992 • Volume 2, No. 21 • 481-504**

Formerly Editorial Research Reports

COVER ART: BARBARA SASSA-DANIELS

CQ Researcher

June 5, 1992
Volume 2, No. 21

EDITOR
Sandra Stencel

MANAGING EDITOR
Thomas J. Colin

ASSOCIATE EDITOR
Richard L. Worsnop

STAFF WRITERS
Charles S. Clark
Mary H. Cooper
Rodman D. Griffin

PRODUCTION EDITOR
Laurie De Maris

EDITORIAL ASSISTANT
Michael M. Taylor

GRAPHICS
Jack Auldridge

PUBLISHED BY
Congressional Quarterly Inc.

CHAIRMAN
Andrew Barnes

VICE CHAIRMAN
Andrew P. Corty

EDITOR AND PUBLISHER
Neil Skene

EXECUTIVE EDITOR
Robert W. Merry

PUBLICATIONS MARKETING/SALES
Robert Smith

EDITOR, EBSCO PUBLISHING
Melissa Kummerer

The CQ Researcher (ISSN 1056-2036). Formerly Editorial Research Reports. Published weekly (48 times per year, not printed the first Friday of any month with five Fridays) by Congressional Quarterly Inc., 1414 22nd St., N.W., Washington, D.C. 20037. Rates are furnished upon request. Second-class postage paid at Washington, D.C. POSTMASTER: Send address changes to The CQ Researcher, 1414 22nd St., N.W., Washington, D.C. 20037.

Nuclear Proliferation

By Rodman D. Griffin

The Issues

Last summer, Soviet soldiers looking for illegal drugs at a roadblock in Russia searched a truck and found, not drugs, but nuclear-weapons parts stolen from a Soviet bomb laboratory. In October, a Swiss businessman was caught in Zurich carrying samples of plutonium believed to be of Soviet origin. And in January, the Italian press reported that Soviet nuclear-tipped artillery shells had been offered for sale in Italy.[1]

Since the collapse of the Soviet Union last year, fear of the spread of nuclear weapons has mushroomed. The Soviet Union once controlled a stockpile of 27,000 nuclear warheads, including 15,000 portable and easily concealed tactical weapons.

Last month, three of the four newly independent republics with nuclear arms — Ukraine, Kazakhstan and Belarus — formally agreed to destroy all such weapons or turn them over to the fourth republic, Russia, by the end of the decade. But despite the landmark agreement, many potential hazards remain. The diversion of even a single nuclear weapon to terrorists or an unscrupulous state could have disastrous consequences.

Enriched uranium and plutonium, the key ingredients in nuclear weapons (see glossary, p. 493), are extremely valuable even in small quantities. Iraq alone has spent an estimated $15 billion trying to create plutonium. It only takes 15 pounds of it to make a bomb capable of leveling a city.

Thus far, there is no hard evidence that nuclear weapons or significant quantities of bomb-grade materials have been smuggled out of the former Soviet Union. But virtually all ex-

perts agree that conditions there are ripe for the emergence of a nuclear black market. "You can bet that right now arms merchants with big suitcases and big bank accounts are roaming around looking for [nuclear] merchandise," says Gary Milhollin, director of the University of Wisconsin's Project on Nuclear Arms Control, which tracks nuclear exports and the spread of nuclear weapons.

Just as the United States and the former Soviet Union are committing themselves to the biggest reduction of nuclear weapons in history, there is mounting concern that the world's most dangerous weapons could fall into the wrong hands. The breakup of the Soviet Union has provided both the greatest opportunity for disarmament and the greatest risk of proliferation since the dawning of the nuclear age.

On the one hand, the Cold War is over — and along with it the arms race that led to the accumulation of some 50,000 nuclear weapons by the two superpowers. As a result of the 1991 Strategic Arms Reduction Treaty

(START) and other recent arms control initiatives, the United States and the former republics of the old Soviet Union are drastically cutting their arsenals. If everything goes according to plan, all sides will reduce their stockpiles by 40 percent over the next five years.

On the other hand, the nuclear nightmare may be just beginning. "Beyond the borders of Russia and the newly sovereign republics lie other challenges to peace, to international order, and thus to us," CIA Director Robert M. Gates declared in December. "Foremost among these is the proliferation of weapons of mass destruction — nuclear, chemical and biological and related delivery systems — by nearly two dozen nations, forging arsenals of such destructive capacity as to defy all reason."[2]

In addition to the declared nuclear powers — the United States, Russia, China, Britain and France — and countries known to have nuclear weapons or the ability to assemble them quickly — Israel, South Africa, India and Pakistan — a number of countries also are thought to be on the brink of nuclear capacity. (See map, p. 488.)

North Korea began running a large research reactor in 1986 and now is reported to be building a reprocessing plant to turn the reactor's spent fuel (see glossary) into plutonium for weapons. Libya makes no secret of its nuclear envy and has purchased nuclear technology from several countries. Iran, spurred by Iraq's nuclear program, has begun to devote more research to its weapons goals and might be able to build a nuclear bomb within five to 10 years.

International safeguards set up to limit the spread of nuclear weapons have proved ineffective. The classic test case was Iraq, which despite being a signatory to the 1968 Nuclear

Strategic Nuclear Warheads in the Former Soviet Union

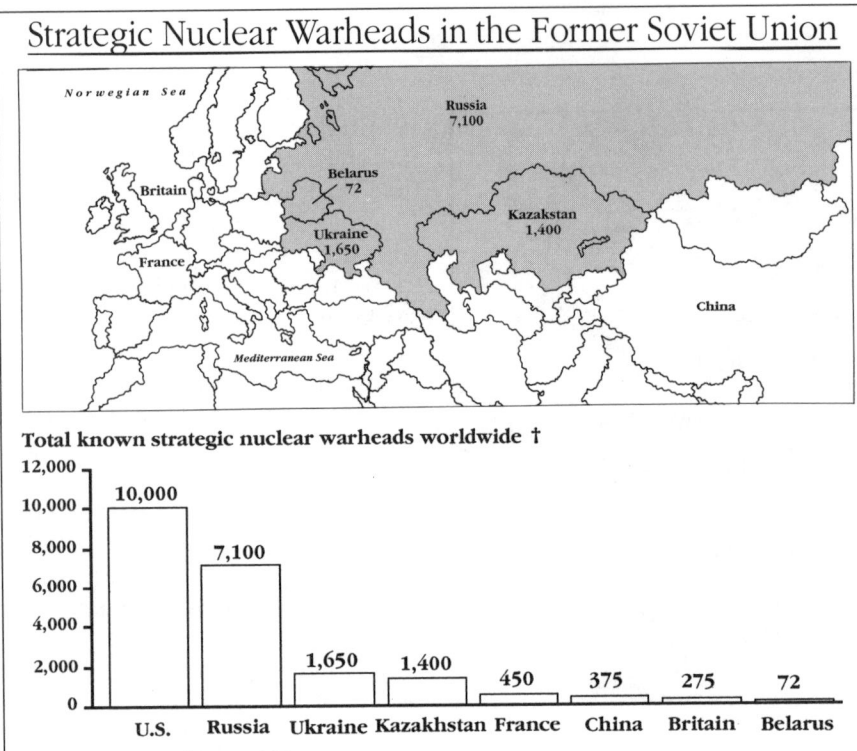

Total known strategic nuclear warheads worldwide †

10,000	7,100	1,650	1,400	450	375	275	72
U.S.	Russia	Ukraine	Kazakhstan	France	China	Britain	Belarus

† *Estimates as of May 1992*
Source: Arms Control Association

Non-Proliferation Treaty* (NPT), operated a clandestine program to develop nuclear weapons. Last year, following Iraq's defeat in the Persian Gulf War, Iraq's nuclear program was defused. But nuclear experts say Baghdad may have been just 18 months away from producing a bomb.

Like Iraq, many nuclear "wannabes" are inflamed by territorial and sectarian passions and are unfettered by the calculus of deterrence that prevented a nuclear confrontation between the superpowers over the four decades of the Cold War.

As the international community grapples with the seemingly unstoppable spread of nuclear technology, here are some of the pressing questions being asked:

*Under the treaty, "non-nuclear" signatories pledge not to develop nuclear weapons. In exchange, the "nuclear powers" agree to provide them with commercial nuclear technology, reduce their own arsenals, protect their non-nuclear allies from nuclear attack and prevent the exportation of nuclear technology to other countries.

What will happen to the former Soviet Union's nuclear arsenal?

When the 15 former Soviet republics became independent nations last December, there were suddenly four nuclear powers instead of one: Russia, Kazakhstan, Ukraine and Belarus. Power struggles raged within and between the new states, raising fears that a dispute could escalate into a nuclear conflict. Secretary of State James A. Baker III warned of a possible tragedy like Yugoslavia's bloody civil war, but played out with nuclear weapons.

In an effort to end economic and political chaos, 11 of the former republics agreed to form a loose confederation, the Commonwealth of Independent States. One of the commonwealth's first acts was to establish a new system for the control and use of nuclear weapons. After six months of difficult negotiations, it was agreed last month that only Russia, the largest state, would possess nuclear arms. The former Soviet re-

publics also agreed to adhere "in the shortest possible time" to the NPT as non-nuclear nations, and to abide by existing weapons treaties signed by the Soviet Union, including START.*

But even if the fragile commonwealth can control its arsenal, it will have a hard time living up to the disarmament commitments it has already made. One problem is that no one in the West really knows the exact number of nuclear weapons deployed in the commonwealth. Possibly even top Russian officials don't know, because competing military groups have custody of different types of weapons. Given this confusion, weapons or weapons materials could disappear and no one would know.

"There is a serious proliferation threat here," cautions Christopher Paine, a senior researcher at the Natural Resources Defense Council (NRDC), a private environmental group staffed by lawyers and scientists.[3] "The Soviet Union didn't maintain an elaborate system of nuclear material accountancy."

Equally frightening is the risk that some of Moscow's 15,000 small nuclear bombs and shells will leak into the Mideast arms bazaars from the 200-odd depots in which they are stored. "Traditionally, it has been thought that it takes a country about 10 years to develop nuclear weapons," says Leonard Spector, director of the Nuclear Non-Proliferation Project at the Carnegie Endowment for International Peace. "With the Soviet breakup, a country may be able to get a bomb in 10 months or 10 weeks."

Then there is the problem of what will happen to the former Soviet Union's sprawling nuclear establishment. *(See story, p. 486.)* Like the United States, the U.S.S.R. built a vast

*Upon ratifying the START treaty, the republics will begin to reduce strategic, long-range nuclear warheads on missiles and on bombers in three stages over a seven-year period. Military officials claim that tactical nuclear weapons have already been withdrawn from all former Soviet republics.

industry to support its nuclear arsenal, including stockpiles of nuclear material, laboratories, test sites, components factories, assembly plants and transport and storage facilities. The majority of Soviet uranium-processing plants are in the Asian republics of Kyrgyzstan and Tajikistan, now beyond the control of Moscow, creating the possibility of unregulated hard currency sales to Third World countries, especially nearby Pakistan, India and Iran.

"The only realistic thing to do," concedes Secretary of Defense Dick Cheney, "is to anticipate that one of the byproducts of the breakup of the Soviet Union will be a proliferation of nuclear capability."

Are current international safeguards adequate to deter countries such as Iraq and North Korea from obtaining nuclear weapons?

The principal bulwark against nuclear proliferation is the 1968 Nuclear Non-Proliferation Treaty (NPT). Under the treaty's safeguards agreement, signed by 143 countries, the International Atomic Energy Agency (IAEA), an independent arm of the United Nations based in Vienna, Austria, routinely inspects member countries with peaceful nuclear programs to make sure they are not secretly diverting the equipment and fuel to military use.

To accomplish that task, IAEA inspectors roam through "peaceful" nuclear power plants, sniff around munitions factories and pore over import/export records. If unsatisfied, the agency has the right to make a more detailed "special inspection." But, in practice, it has made only half a dozen over the last 20 years.

Moreover, because of an outdated network of rules that dictate when, where and how the IAEA can conduct inspections, critics say illicit bomb-builders can spruce things up before inspectors arrive. "The IAEA has limited oversight," argues Milhol-

lin of the Project on Nuclear Arms Control. "It can make inspections only in declared nuclear sites. The problem is everyone is making bombs in undeclared sites."

"The NPT regime was intended to be voluntary, not punitive," adds Janne Nolan, a senior fellow at the Brookings Institution, a Washington think tank. "Its success hinges on a degree of cooperation."

Those countries that choose not to cooperate encounter few obstacles. In fact, two of the world's five declared nuclear powers, France and China, refused to ratify the NPT until recently* and were busily trading nuclear secrets — as well as nuclear facilities — with little apparent concern about the consequences. *(See story, p. 494.)*

Many experts point to recent events in Iraq as demonstrating the total inadequacy of the IAEA safeguards. For more than a decade, the Iraqis were developing nuclear weapons right under the IAEA's nose. Before the Persian Gulf War, a single inspector from the IAEA would show up in Iraq twice a year. His visit announced long in advance, he would find an Iraqi official waiting for him at the airport. The Iraqis, in fact, could veto the selection of a particular inspector; they usually refused visas to any inspector without a Soviet or Eastern European passport.

IAEA officials say much of the criticism of the agency is unjustified. "I'm not ready to accept that [Iraq] was a failure of the system," says Hans Blix, the IAEA's director general. He insists that it is unfair to expect his inspectors to uncover an operation that even American intelligence had failed to detect before the gulf war. "Neither our inspectors nor any other inspectors can go like heroin dogs sniffing through every kilometer of a country," he says. "You

must, hence, have some information about where you should go — a building, a city — to search."[4]

In any case, the United Nations has been shocked into action. Under new guidelines approved by the IAEA Board of Governors in February, inspectors asserted the agency's right to conduct "challenge" inspections at "suspect sites" anywhere in a country, using intelligence information provided by member countries.* If the government balks, the IAEA can complain to the U.N. Security Council, setting up the kind of confrontation that most Third World countries prefer to avoid.

Even so, stopping the spread of nuclear weapons won't be easy. As more countries scramble to develop nuclear weapons — and as the IAEA's caseload and responsibilities mount — it becomes more apparent that the agency is both understaffed and underfunded. Indeed, the IAEA has just 212 inspectors and a $62 million budget — roughly the cost of a single fighter aircraft — to monitor more than 900 nuclear facilities worldwide.

Moreover, some experts, like Milhollin, believe the problems go beyond the IAEA to the very heart of the NPT. Many countries simply don't take the treaty seriously. Iraq isn't the only country to pursue nuclear weapons despite its signature. Iran, Libya and possibly North Korea are other examples. And the United States and the former Soviet Union have only recently begun to make good on their side of the NPT bargain: a pledge to reduce their own arsenals.

In addition, countless treaty signers have contributed to the spread of nuclear weapons by selling nuclear technology to non-nuclear states.

---

*China signed the treaty in March. France has pledged to sign it sometime this year.

---

*Technically, under the NPT, the IAEA always had the right to inspect suspect sites, even those the governments did not acknowledge. In practice, however, it has never exercised that right.

Nuclear Fallout: The Soviet Brain Drain

Imagine if IBM, Du Pont, Ford and General Dynamics all suddenly went bankrupt one day. From an employment standpoint, that is basically what has happened to the nuclear-weapons industry in the former Soviet Union. Only having the Soviet nuclear brain trust walking the streets looking for work is exponentially more dangerous than hordes of job-hunting engineers.

Robert M. Gates, director of the U.S. Central Intelligence Agency, told the Senate Governmental Affairs Committee in January that the Soviet "brain drain problem is the [proliferation issue] that causes us the greatest concern, more than a loss of materials or weapons."

Some 900,000 people work in the once-closed cities of the nuclear-weapons industry. Although only about 2,000 employees of the Soviet Ministry of Atomic Power and Industry have access to the most sensitive details of nuclear-bomb making, most of these scientists are paid less than Moscow bus drivers — about $6 or $7 a month.† The virtually worthless currency and shortages of most consumer goods increase the temptation for them to sell secrets or smuggle weapons parts or technology for foreign cash, much as German rocketeers sold their missile know-how abroad after the Nazis were defeated in World War II.

In December, there were reports that 60 or more Soviet nuclear-weapons scientists were already working in Brazil, India, Iran, Iraq and Pakistan, and earning $36,000 to $75,000 a year for their services.†† Another 19 top-level nuclear scientists have reportedly emigrated to Israel, and there are multiple accounts of Libya's unsuccessful attempt to lure weapons experts from Moscow's Kurchatov Institute of Atomic Energy.

"The grave danger is not scientists leaving for North Korea, Iraq or Libya," says William Potter, director of the Center for Russian and Eurasian Studies at the Monterey Institute of International Studies in California, "but rather that these countries might set up companies in Europe — similar to those set up by Iraq — that offer attractive employment opportunities. The only way to cope with this situation is to enhance intelligence cooperation and improve our monitoring capabilities. You can't block the movement of individuals, but you can monitor what skilled professionals are going where."

Western analysts say the fate of the Russian nuclear complex — as well as the brainpower that kept it running — partly depends on the U.S. government, which is still pondering its options and wary of aiding its former foes. Thus far, Washington has pledged $400 million to help dismantle Moscow's nuclear regime. Some of that money will go to help set up an International Science and Technology Center in Moscow designed to create research and development opportunities for displaced Russian weapons scientists. The European Community, Japan and Canada also have announced plans to support the center.

Even so, experts say some nuclear scientists will undoubtedly be left in the cold. "The United States should hire all of them and put them to work on some hard technical problem," says Thomas Neff, a physicist at the Massachusetts Institute of Technology. "It would be cheaper than buying a battleship." ‡

But Christopher Paine, a senior researcher at the Natural Resources Defense Council, a private environmental group with strong ties to Russian weapons scientists, urges caution. "It won't help our non-proliferation objectives if we suck the best and the brightest out of Russia," he says.

---

† After meeting with President Bush at Camp David on Feb. 1, Russian President Boris N. Yeltsin announced plans to increase scientists' salaries by as much as five times.

†† Cited in *Arms Control Today,* January/February 1992, p. 40.

‡ Quoted in *The New York Times,* Jan. 14, 1992.

German companies, for instance, provided Iraq with much of its nuclear technology.[5]

"What the IAEA does is vital," says Patrick Glynn, a research associate at the American Enterprise Institute, a Washington-based think tank. "But overall, it's a drop in the bucket. The IAEA's impact is similar to that of a safety belt in a car. It may encourage some to obey the law, but it's not going to stop nuclear proliferation."

Is nuclear deterrence still a valid concept?

For 42 years, the United States and the Soviet Union built as many nuclear weapons as they could on the theory that if the other country attacked first, each would want to have missiles to shoot back. Fears that any conflict could escalate to mutual destruction probably prevented direct confrontation between the two superpowers, and may have contributed to bringing them to the bargaining table.

From the U.S. vantage point, nuclear deterrence had another important component. During the Cold War, the U.S. policy of building large nuclear forces, tactical as well as strategic *(see glossary),* was also intended to offset Soviet superiority in conventional forces. Under the policy of "flexible response," tactical nuclear weapons were to be used if NATO's conventional defense forces were in danger of collapse. The missiles and bombers with nuclear warheads that made up the U.S. strategic forces were also to provide "extended" deterrence to protect America's European allies from conventional attack.

With the end of the Cold War, all that strategic thinking has been turned on its head. "The standard model of deterrence no longer applies," says Milhollin. "We are no longer dealing with a large country with strong conventional forces." Instead, he says, the new nuclear threat comes from regional conflicts in the Third World that may be even more dangerous. "The thought of North Korea with a couple of hidden nuclear bombs is more difficult to defend against than a Soviet ICBM [intercontinental ballistic missile]," he adds.

Rep. Les Aspin, D-Wis., chairman of the House Armed Services Committee, has warned against the danger of forces "undeterrable by the threat of retaliation, like Saddam Hussein." Spector at the Carnegie Endowment shares his concern. "If you're dealing with a dictator who has a distorted view of the world and who controls information to his citizens, you can't count on him to behave rationally," he notes. "As it is, Saddam Hussein took risks and exposed his country to enormous losses [during the gulf war] that could have been avoided. It is quite plausible he would use nuclear weapons."

The threat of retaliation — including a nuclear one — may, in fact, have kept the Iraqi dictator from using the chemical and biological weapons he is known to possess. Nevertheless, the mere prospect of "undeterrable" dictators possessing weapons of mass destruction poses a serious dilemma for policy-makers. Spector argues that even with small nuclear arsenals, Third World dictators could drastically alter the geo-political equation. "Would the Democrats in Congress have voted for the war if the nuclear danger was there?" he asks, recalling that the Sen-

ate vote authorizing force was a close 52-47. Possibly not.

More frightening, if a terrorist organization claimed to have smuggled a "suitcase" bomb into New York and delivered an ultimatum, what would the president do? Patriot missiles would be no consolation.

Some Defense Department officials argue that the prospect of nuclear "undeterrables" is itself sufficient reason for pursuing more sophisticated

nuclear-weapons systems, including the Strategic Defense Initiative (SDI), the multibillion-dollar program to develop nuclear defense in outer space. But the NRDC's Paine warns: "Reserving the nuclear option to deter all forms of conflict could be destabilizing and lead to greater proliferation. If we argue that we must develop a new range of nuclear devices for use against non-nuclear states, what will that tell every country in the world?" ■

BACKGROUND

Nuclear Dominoes

The capability of the atomic bomb awed even its architects. J. Robert Oppenheimer, director of the Manhattan Project, the top-secret U.S. initiative that developed the first A-bomb, said after the first successful atomic test in the New Mexico desert in the summer of 1945: "A few people laughed, a few people cried.... We knew the world would never be the same."

Oppenheimer couldn't have known just how right he was. On Aug. 6, 1945, the United States ushered in the nuclear age by dropping an atomic bomb on the Japanese city of Hiroshima. In an instant, thousands of people were killed as Hiroshima was engulfed by a raging firestorm.* Two weeks later, the Japanese surrendered, ending World War II and fulfilling claims by some scientists and policy-makers that atomic weapons might indeed be instruments of peace.

The first nuclear weapons were so successful, in fact, that national security seemed to demand that they con-

tinue to exist. The production plants and laboratories were kept operating and expanding, not only in the United States and the Soviet Union but in other countries as well. The implications of nuclear weapons seemed enormous. No nation possessing the technical and financial means to do so seemed to feel that it could afford to be without an atomic arsenal. The nuclear arms race was on.

Shortly after the end of World War II, the United States offered to share its nuclear knowledge with the world, provided an adequate system of policing could be established to ensure that no nation used this knowledge for anything but peaceful purposes. The Soviet Union flatly rejected this proposal — and detonated its own nuclear bomb in 1949. The other world powers soon followed — Britain in 1952, France in 1960 and China in 1964.

Non-Proliferation Regime

Since the 1960s, the world has relied on the 1963 Limited Test Ban Treaty, the 1968 Nuclear Non-Proliferation Treaty (the NPT went into effect in 1970) and an agreement among major nuclear supplier states, known as the London Suppliers Agreement of 1976, to control the spread of nuclear weapons.

---

*The A-bomb dropped at Hiroshima killed 142,000 people, and the one dropped at Nagasaki three days later killed 79,000.

The Nuclear Family

There are five declared nuclear powers (the United States, Russia, Great Britain, France and China), four undeclared ones (Israel, India, Pakistan and South Africa) and at least eight developing nations with nuclear potential (North Korea, Iraq, Iran, Libya, Algeria, Taiwan, Argentina and Brazil).

Declared nuclear powers:

1. United States

- Developed atomic bomb in 1945; only country to use nuclear weapons in war.
- Nuclear arsenal consists of some 22,000 strategic and tactical nuclear warheads.
- Under arms control treaties, has agreed to dismantle several thousand nuclear warheads, but hopes to leave nuclear options open.
- Signed Non-Proliferation Treaty (NPT) in 1970.

2. Russia

- Soviet Union developed A-bomb in 1949.
- During 1980s built up the largest nuclear arsenal in the world, consisting of 27,000 strategic and tactical nuclear warheads.
- Following collapse of the Soviet Union, Russia — as well as Ukraine, Kazakhstan and Belarus — agreed to nuclear arms reductions called for under 1991 Strategic Arms Reduction Treaty (START). Russia emerges as sole nuclear power. Republics have all agreed to sign NPT.

3. Great Britain

- Became a nuclear power in 1952.
- Nuclear arsenal consists of 275 strategic weapons and some 100 tactical warheads.
- Plans to continue developing next generation of nuclear submarines.
- Signed NPT in 1968.

4. France

- Joined "nuclear club" in 1960.
- Nuclear arsenal consists of 450 strategic nuclear weapons and some 125 tactical warheads.
- Has no plans to reduce nuclear arsenal.
- Has pledged to sign NPT in 1992.

5. China

- Exploded first A-bomb in 1964.
- Has estimated 500 strategic and tactical nuclear warheads.
- Signed NPT in March 1992.

Countries that have undeclared nuclear weapons or could produce small numbers quickly:

6. Israel

- Thought to have obtained first nuclear weapons in late 1960s.

This regime has put the brakes on many countries' nuclear weapons programs, and persuaded other nations — Taiwan, Egypt and South Korea, for example — not to start, or to abandon efforts early on. The prediction often heard in the 1960s that some 30 nations would have the bomb within 30 years has mercifully fallen short. There are now five known nuclear powers and four undeclared ones.

But with two or three new nations going nuclear each decade, the international safeguards regime can hardly be called a success. Controls have been least effective where they are most needed — with aggressive na-

- Probably has 100-200 undeclared A-bombs.
- Thought to have deployed short-range nuclear-capable missiles.
- Has not signed NPT.

7. India
- Tested nuclear device in 1974.
- Has essentials for 40-60 A-bombs and may be building undeclared nuclear arsenal.
- Has greatly expanded nuclear weapons production capability in recent years; reportedly designing hydrogen bomb.
- Not party to NPT.

8. Pakistan
- Apparently obtained material for first nuclear weapon in 1986.
- Probably has essentials for 5-10 A-bombs.
- Tested nuclear-capable short-range missile in 1989; U.S. canceled military aid in 1990 due to suspicions about nuclear-weapons program.
- Not party to NPT.

9. South Africa
- Able to build nuclear weapons since 1980-81.
- Possible undeclared arsenal of 15-25 nuclear weapons.
- Signed NPT in 1991.

States having technical infrastructure and apparent interest in acquiring nuclear weapons:

10. North Korea
- Has built large research reactor and may be building plutonium plant that could soon allow production of nuclear weapons.
- Under heavy pressure from U.S., Japan and China to abandon nuclear-weapons program.
- Signed NPT in 1985, but until this month had not permitted inspections by International Atomic Energy Agency (IAEA).

11. Iraq
- Believed to have been 12-18 months from developing a nuclear device prior to Persian Gulf War. Program has been set back perhaps a decade or more by subsequent United Nations actions.
- Experts say Iraqi dictator Saddam Hussein is still attempting to produce weapons-grade material.
- Signed NPT in 1969.

12. Iran
- Probably 5-10 years away from building nuclear weapons.
- Some nuclear installations and weapons research inherited from Shah; reactivating nuclear-research program.
- Signed NPT in 1970.

13. Libya
- Many years away from actually building nuclear weapons.
- Reportedly has attempted to purchase nuclear-weapons materials several times since the 1970s, including in the aftermath of the Soviet break-up.
- Signed NPT in 1975.

14. Algeria
- Building a heavily guarded nuclear reactor that many experts believe is intended to produce plutonium.
- Not party to NPT.

15. Taiwan
- Has sizable nuclear-power program, but lacks facilities to produce material for weapons.
- Built secret lab to extract plutonium in 1987, but dismantled unit under U.S. pressure before plutonium was obtained.
- Signed NPT in 1970.

16. Argentina
- Has had nuclear-weapons program for several decades, not under international inspection.
- Civilian government has pledged not to develop nuclear weapons.
- Signed nuclear non-proliferation pact with Brazil in 1991, calling for joint monitoring of nuclear facilities. Also signed safeguards agreement, permitting inspections under IAEA supervision.
- Not party to NPT.

17. Brazil
- Has pursued nuclear-weapons capability since the mid-1970s.
- Ruling civilian government opposed to nuclear arming, but military would keep option.
- Signed non-proliferation pact with Argentina in 1991, and is submitting to inspections of nuclear facilities similar to those called for under NPT.
- Not party to NPT.

Sources: Carnegie Endowment for International Peace; Arms Control Association

tions like Iraq.

Critics say the regulatory mechanisms embodied in the NPT are deeply flawed. The NPT divided the world into nuclear haves and have-nots, using the arbitrary criterion of each country's nuclear capacity in 1967. The have-nots promised not to acquire nuclear weapons, while the haves promised, in Article 6 of the treaty, "to pursue negotiations in good faith on effective measures relating to the cessation of the nuclear arms race at an early date." The preamble also committed nuclear states to "the discontinuance of all test explosions of nuclear weapons."

The idea of forswearing the bomb in exchange for a vague future promise of arms control seemed a bad bargain to many have-nots. India, Pakistan, Israel, South Africa, Argentina and Brazil, among others, refused to sign the treaty, citing discrimination.

From the have-nots' point of view, the treaty continues to be a dud. Although none of the have-nots that signed the treaty has acquired the bomb — Iraq was close — the superpowers went from 3,000 strategic nuclear weapons at the time of the NPT's signing to some 23,000 at the time of the Soviet Union's fall. Bitterness about this failure to disarm has been the principal point of contention at each of the NPT review conferences, held every five years. (The next one is scheduled to be held in 1995.)

The second leg of the non-proliferation regime is the 1963 Limited Test Ban Treaty, which prohibits atmospheric nuclear tests but allows underground tests — which at the time were unverifiable — to continue. Because it treats all parties equally, even the NPT critics have signed it. Its main success has been environmental, cutting nuclear fallout. But underground nuclear tests continue. The United States has scheduled six for this year.

Export Controls
Nuclear export guidelines constitute the other main protection against nuclear proliferation. In 1976, seven industrial countries — Canada, West Germany, France, Japan, the Soviet Union, Britain and the United States — collectively referred to as the Nuclear Suppliers Group,* endorsed a uniform code for conducting interna-

---

*The Nuclear Suppliers Group now has 27 members.

The Iraqi Bomb — And Where It Came From

This is the actual Iraqi bomb design described in secret documents seized by the International Atomic Energy Agency last year in Baghdad. Experts say that before the Persian Gulf War, Iraq was within 18 to 24 months of producing this bomb, which is roughly the size of a beach ball. Iraq is believed to have had all the necessary components except enough highly enriched uranium.

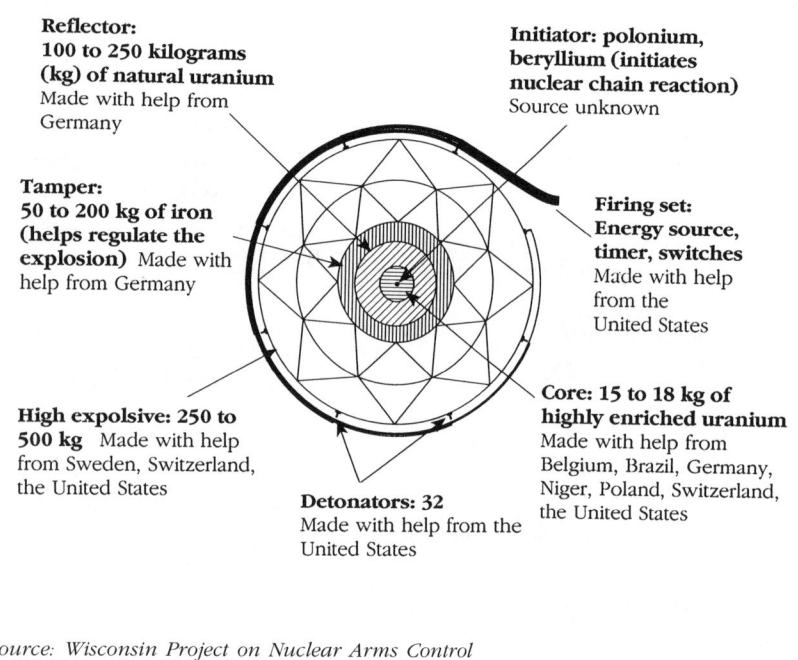

Reflector: 100 to 250 kilograms (kg) of natural uranium Made with help from Germany

Initiator: polonium, beryllium (initiates nuclear chain reaction) Source unknown

Tamper: 50 to 200 kg of iron (helps regulate the explosion) Made with help from Germany

Firing set: Energy source, timer, switches Made with help from the United States

High explosive: 250 to 500 kg Made with help from Sweden, Switzerland, the United States

Core: 15 to 18 kg of highly enriched uranium Made with help from Belgium, Brazil, Germany, Niger, Poland, Switzerland, the United States

Detonators: 32 Made with help from the United States

Source: Wisconsin Project on Nuclear Arms Control

tional nuclear sales. The voluntary guidelines were intended to eclipse the trade in so-called "trigger items" that are critical to nuclear weapons production. The fact that many members of the suppliers group are themselves leading proliferators says something about its effectiveness.

The truth is that the West has tolerated proliferation within the family. "Not all 'proliferation' is bad from our perspective," Jim Hinds, a deputy assistant secretary of Defense for negotiations policy, told a Senate committee in 1989. "It may be very much in our interest to assist our friends and allies in developing the same kinds of [nuclear] technology for the purposes of stability."[6]

Pakistan's weapons program, for example, was widely known and widely ignored, because Washington needed Pakistan to help the Afghan rebels, or *mujahedeen,* in their war against the Soviet-backed Afghan government. In 1985 Congress passed a requirement that for Pakistan to qualify for U.S. aid, the president had to certify each year that Pakistan does not possess a nuclear device and that renewal aid will "reduce significantly" the risk of its getting the bomb. Only in 1990 did a president refuse to certify. And the same day aid to Pakistan stopped, the Bush administration went to Congress to ask for its reinstatement.[7]

Similarly, U.S. concern that India might be driven further toward the Soviet Union led President Jimmy Carter to continue to supply that country, Pakistan's bitter adversary, with nuclear fuel. This was contrary to the sense of the Nuclear Non-Proliferation Act of 1978, which requires that such services be discontinued if non-weapons states do not accept international safeguards on all their nuclear facilities.

"In the United States, non-proliferation has ranked at the bottom of the food chain, somewhere near human rights," says Brookings' Janne Nolan. "And except for the rhetoric, that hasn't changed."

The Iraq Debacle

Last March, when the Pentagon ordered the destruction of Iraq's nuclear infrastructure after the gulf war, President Bush exulted, "Our pinpoint attacks have put Saddam Hussein out of the nuclear bomb-building business for a long time to come."[8] As it turns out, his exuberance was premature.

Since the war's end, it has become clear that much of Iraq's top-secret nuclear-weapons program survived the relentless U.N.-backed air assault intact. It has also become evident that the program was more advanced than anyone had previously thought.

During the 1980s, no one doubted that Iraq had nuclear ambitions.* The question was how long it would take them to succeed. Before the war, the U.S. intelligence community set the estimate at a reassuring five to 10 years. Now experts conclude that Iraq was 12 to 18 months from having a nuclear device.

As part of the treaty that ended the war, the United Nations has been sending international teams of in-

Continued on p. 492

*In 1981, suspicions about Iraq's nuclear intentions led the Israelis to bomb its Osirak reactor, which was under construction.

Chronology

1930s-1940s Cold War following World War II ignites a nuclear arms race.

1938
German scientists Otto Hahn and Fritz Strassman split the nucleus of an atom, setting the stage for the development of nuclear weapons.

August 1945
The United States drops nuclear bombs on Hiroshima and Nagasaki, Japan, ending World War II.

September 1949
The Soviet Union conducts its first atomic explosion.

—— • ——

1950s As the Cold War swings into high gear, the United States and the Soviet Union emerge as superpowers. Other nations seek to join the "nuclear club."

1957
The International Atomic Energy Agency (IAEA) is established with a dual mission: to prevent the misuse of nuclear technology for armaments and to promote the peaceful use of nuclear power. Also in 1957, the launch of Sputnik shows that the Soviets have the capability to launch nuclear missiles.

—— • ——

1960s Superpower tensions inspire international efforts to develop a non-proliferation regime.

October 1962
President John F. Kennedy confronts the Soviets over nuclear missiles in Cuba. The missiles are withdrawn.

1963
The United States and the Soviet Union sign the Limited Test Ban Treaty, prohibiting atmospheric nuclear tests.

July 1, 1968
Sixty-two nations, including the United States and the Soviet Union, sign the Nuclear Non-Proliferation Treaty (NPT), under which non-nuclear states pledge not to develop nuclear weapons in exchange for security guarantees.

—— • ——

1970s Nations continue to trade nuclear technologies and to put other foreign-policy objectives ahead of non-proliferation.

1974
India tests a "peaceful nuclear device."

1978
Congress passes Nuclear Non-Proliferation Act of 1978, requiring that the practice of sending nuclear fuel to non-nuclear states be discontinued if the states do not accept safeguards on all their nuclear facilities.

—— • ——

1980s Superpowers pump billions of dollars into their nuclear stockpiles. Several Third World countries undertake nuclear-weapons programs of their own.

1981
Israel bombs Iraq's Osirak nuclear reactor, setting back Saddam Hussein's nuclear-weapons program.

1990s Danger of nuclear proliferation in the Third World emerges as the world's greatest security risk.

April 1991
U.N. Security Council passes Resolution 687, authorizing the destruction of Iraq's non-conventional weapons, ballistic missiles and related production capabilities.

July 31, 1991
The U.S. and the U.S.S.R. sign the Strategic Arms Reduction Treaty, pledging to cut their nuclear arsenals.

Aug. 11, 1991
China indicates it plans to join the NPT, thereby following the lead of two other longtime holdouts, South Africa and France.

Sept. 27, 1991
President Bush announces unilateral elimination of U.S. tactical nuclear weapons in Europe and Asia. Soviet President Mikhail S. Gorbachev responds with a proposal for deeper cuts in nuclear arsenals.

December 1991
Soviet Union dissolves. Congress passes the Soviet Nuclear Threat Reduction Act of 1991, authorizing $400 million to help dismantle nuclear weapons in the new Commonwealth of Independent States.

Dec. 13, 1991
Brazil and Argentina pledge not to build nuclear arms.

Jan. 30, 1992
North Korea agrees to open its nuclear installations to scrutiny.

Feb. 26, 1992
Board of Governors of the IAEA agrees to measures designed to improve the agency's ability to detect secret nuclear-weapons programs.

Continued from p. 490

spectors into Iraq to search for, and destroy, any remaining Iraqi nuclear weapons or research facilities. Armed with CIA information culled from an Iraqi defector, IAEA inspectors knew where to go and what to look for. What they found was startling.

In a series of unannounced raids, the nuclear inspectors discovered secret rooms filled with documents and other evidence outlining an elaborate bomb-building program of the magnitude of the Manhattan Project during World War II.[9] Saddam Hussein, inspectors discovered, allowed his

scientists to pursue several methods of building a bomb simultaneously, including the use of calutrons, a technology discarded by the United States for weapons purposes in 1945.

The remarkable discoveries about the scope, equipment and innovation in Iraq's nuclear program "was proof that there has been a steady transferal of weapons technology around the world," says Nolan, including missiles and high-performance conventional weaponry. "Iraq was a wake-up call for us," she adds, "telling us there are highly motivated countries out there that still seek these weapons." ■

their longstanding hostility.

France and China, both notorious exporters of nuclear-weapons technology, last year finally agreed to sign the NPT so that all of the declared nuclear powers today are committed, at least theoretically, to the cause of non-proliferation.

CURRENT SITUATION

Hopeful Signs

Compared with the destructive fury contained within today's advanced nuclear weapons, the Hiroshima bomb was a mere stick of dynamite. The science of destruction has advanced so far that within the 20,000-plus nuclear arsenal of the United States, a single bomb now contains the explosive power of 1,500 Hiroshima bombs.

Fortunately, the powers of diplomacy have progressed along with the powers of science. Foreign policy has come a long way since the 1950s, when Secretary of State John Foster Dulles enunciated the doctrine of "massive retaliation," and President Dwight D. Eisenhower could assert, with some aura of believability, "I see no reason that [nuclear weapons] shouldn't be used just exactly as you'd use a bullet or anything else."[10]

Even when their bilateral relations were far from amicable, Washington and Moscow often cooperated to lim-

it nuclear proliferation. In the aftermath of the gulf war, the non-proliferation regime may be the strongest it's ever been. The political and financial leverage of the world's industrial giants has persuaded several nuclear-capable states to forgo weapons development in the expectation of greater benefits to their broader national interests.

Russia has emerged from the rubble of the old Soviet Union anxious to do its bit to keep the vast Soviet nuclear arsenal under control. The end of the Cold War has all but eliminated the specter of a U.S.-Soviet nuclear Armageddon.

South Africa, much as it did with racial apartheid, has decided to scrap nuclear weapons. The country, which is believed to have had parts for a dozen or so weapons for about 10 years, signed the NPT last July and now is opening up all its facilities to international inspection.

Brazil and Argentina, the two giants of South America, last fall announced plans to forgo nuclear weapons and to undertake a program of confidence-building measures, including inspecting each other's nuclear facilities and exchanging military experts to watch troop maneuvers in an effort to defuse

Nuclear Hot Spots

But while these developments are encouraging and even cast doubt on the military usefulness of nuclear weapons, the urgency in preventing their spread to other states is "as great as ever," according to Ronald F. Lehman, director of the U.S. Arms Control and Disarmament Agency. "In a few trouble spots, like the Korean peninsula, the Mideast and South Asia, time is running out," he adds.

Korean Peninsula

In testimony before the House Foreign Affairs Committee in February, CIA Director Gates predicted that North Korea could possess a nuclear weapon from "within a few months to a few years."[11] Few developments would be more destabilizing for the region — and the world. South Korea would immediately seek its own nuclear weapons, experts say, and Japan — bound to the United States by a defense treaty — might do the same. More than likely, China and Russia, too, would feel compelled to react to such a nuclear time bomb on their borders.

Citing satellite photographs, the United States has alleged that a 100-building complex near Yongbyon, 60 miles north of the North Korean capital of Pyongyang, includes a nearly completed plutonium reprocessing center capable of producing large volumes of weapons-grade plutonium that could be fabricated into crude nuclear weapons.

North Korea has denied the accu-

Nuclear Physics 101: A Glossary of Terms

Atomic bomb: A bomb whose energy comes from the fission *(see below)* of uranium or plutonium.

Heavy water: A manufactured form of water in which the hydrogen atoms are replaced by the heavier isotope of the element, deuterium. The higher density of heavy water allows it to perform a number of exotic functions, including the cooling and controlling of nuclear reactors that create plutonium, the explosive metal at the core of nuclear weapons. Also used in medical research and in cooling some nuclear-power reactors.

Highly enriched uranium: Uranium in which the percentage of uranium-235 nuclei has been increased from the natural level of 0.7 percent to some level greater than 20 percent, usually around 90 percent. One of the two possible fuels essential for making nuclear weapons.

Hydrogen bomb: A weapon that derives its energy largely from nuclear fusion *(see below)*. Also known as a thermonuclear bomb.

Kiloton: The explosive force of 1,000 tons of TNT.

Megaton: The explosive force of a million tons of TNT.

Nuclear fission: The splitting of the nuclei of atoms into fragments, a process that releases energy.

Nuclear fusion: The fusion of lightweight atomic nuclei into a nucleus of heavier mass, with a resultant loss in the combined mass, which is converted into energy.

Nuclear reprocessing: Chemical treatment of spent reactor fuel to separate the plutonium and uranium from the unwanted radioactive-waste byproducts and from each other.

Plutonium: An isotope occurring naturally in minute quantities, which is manufactured artificially when uranium-238, through irradiation, captures an extra neutron. It is one of the two materials that have been used for the core of nuclear weapons, the other being highly enriched uranium.

Spent fuel: Fuel elements that have been removed from the reactor after use because they contain too little explosive material and too high a concentration of unwanted radioactive byproducts to sustain reactor operation. Spent fuel is highly radioactive.

Strategic nuclear weapons: Using delivery systems such as aircraft and rockets, the nuclear powers are capable of launching warheads with nuclear yields of many megatons. Their deployment is intended to deter others from attacking.

Tactical nuclear weapons: Nuclear weapons of comparatively small yield, usually less than 10 kilotons, designed for battlefield use.

---

sations and says all of its nuclear sites are for civilian purposes. Instead of fingering the North, the country's leaders say, the world should focus its attention on South Korea, where U.S. forces have hundreds of nuclear weapons.* Nonetheless, until this month, President Kim Il Sung never permitted full-scope inspections by the IAEA, despite the fact that North Korea signed the NPT in 1985.**

The Carnegie Endowment's Leonard Spector believes the fundamental reason why North Korea is relenting is that the Kim Il Sung regime is tot-

---

*In November, South Korean President Roh Tae Woo unilaterally announced that "the Republic of Korea ... will not manufacture, possess, store, deploy, or use nuclear weapons." His pledge not to "store" nuclear weapons was widely seen as official confirmation of reports that all U.S. nuclear weapons deployed in South Korea were slated for removal.
**IAEA inspectors were still in North Korea as this report went to press.

tering, and in desperate need of international recognition as well as economic assistance. Japan has refused to assist North Korea until the nuclear issue is resolved. North Korea has also become isolated politically as its allies — notably China and the former Soviet Union — have improved their relations with South Korea.

But Spector — and others — say it is too soon to render a verdict on North Korea's nuclear program. Like Iraq, it is conceivable that Kim Il Sung is concealing his nuclear-weapons ambitions. "North Korea will be the litmus test for the IAEA," Spector says. "If we can pull them back convincingly from their weapons program, we will have begun to contain the proliferation problem."

The Middle East

The situation is even more complex in the volatile Middle East. Since the end of the Persian Gulf War, President Bush has stressed the need to curb the spread of nuclear, chemical and biological weapons in the region. Last May, he formally announced a new Middle East Arms Control Initiative, calling for an end to destabilizing arms flows in the region. The initiative also called upon Middle Eastern states to implement a verifiable ban on the production and acquisition of weapons-usable nuclear material and to sign the NPT.

So far, there has been little progress. Although Iraq's nuclear capability has been set back, there is no assurance that Saddam Hussein isn't already back in the bomb-building business. As Iraq's leading nuclear physicist Jaffar Dhia Jaffar told IAEA inspectors last November: "You can bomb our buildings. You can destroy our technology. But you cannot take it out of our heads. We now have the capability." [12]

Dr. Strangelove's Global Bazaar

Using various stratagems, a number of nations, including some of the leading boosters of non-proliferation, have abetted the spread of nuclear weapons. Some countries have been blatant nuclear proliferators, trading weapons technology wholesale. Others have been more subtle — technically obeying export laws that restrict sales of nuclear technology, but nonetheless full participants in the export game. Here are some of the key players:

France: The French bear a special responsibility for nuclear proliferation, refusing to sign the 1968 Nuclear Non-Proliferation Treaty (NPT) until this year, and egregiously flouting the treaty's safeguards regime.

France has a long list of dubious export credits: sending a nuclear reactor and reprocessing plant to Israel; offering to build uranium-reprocessing plants in Pakistan and South Korea; sending power reactors and fuel to South Africa; providing fuel for India's U.S.-built power reactors after the United States cut off nuclear fuel to India; and sending a nuclear reactor and bomb-grade fuel to Iraq.†

Germany: Although Germany itself does not have nuclear weapons, German companies have provided much of the technology that has enabled others to acquire them. In the case of Iraq, Germany supplied more of that country's mass-destruction machinery than all other countries combined, according to Gary Milhollin, director of the University of Wisconsin's Project on Nuclear Arms Control.

Germany not only sold Iraq most of its centrifuge equipment but also furnished an entire chemical-weapons industry. Germany also was Iraq's greatest supplier of missile technology, including the parts that enabled Iraq to extend the range of its Scud missiles, used during the Persian Gulf War.

But Germany's ominous trade practices extend beyond Baghdad. German corporations and middlemen transferred critical components, whole plants and heavy water (see glossary, p. 493) to India and Pakistan. The sales were made despite repeated protests from the United States and Great Britain to the German government.

Soviet Union: While trumpeting their supposed opposition to the spread of the bomb, the Soviets also have contributed to the spread of nuclear-weapons technology. They secretly helped India make plutonium in the mid-1980s; they sprinkled nuclear-capable missiles across the Middle East; and they offered long-range rocket technology to Brazil and India.

During the mid-1980s, using German middlemen as a conduit, the Soviet Union sold India at least 80 tons of Ukrainian-produced heavy water in violation of the Nuclear Non-Proliferation Treaty (NPT). Eight tons are enough to produce plutonium for about six bombs per year.

United States: The United States has contributed to the development of nuclear weapons programs in several countries, notably India, Pakistan, Iran and Iraq. Between 1984 and 1990, at least 29 licenses to U.S. companies were for exports to facilities that U.N. teams have since found were directly involved in Saddam Hussein's nuclear-weapons program.††

According to experts, Washington's greater sin has been its willingness to give other foreign-policy concerns priority over non-proliferation. The United States sold heavy water to India, in violation of its NPT commitment, and for years overlooked Pakistan's nuclear program, out of fear that those countries would be driven into the Soviet camp. Similarly, the United States has consciously ignored Israel's nuclear arsenal, while harshly criticizing nuclear programs in other Middle East countries.

China: The Chinese have been accused of running a veritable supermarket specializing in nuclear, chemical and missile technologies. According to Milhollin, China gave Pakistan full design details of a 25-kiloton atomic bomb — twice as powerful as the Hiroshima weapon — as well as enough weapons-grade enriched uranium to fuel two nuclear weapons.

Milhollin calls the transfer "one of the two greatest acts of proliferation in history," the other being Israel's joint testing of a nuclear bomb with South Africa in 1979.

Of all nuclear proliferators, China is believed to be the most active, currently helping Algeria build a nuclear reactor and having provided Pakistan with missiles capable of carrying nuclear warheads in 1991. The Chinese government has the least to lose by proliferating — the country is already politically isolated — and the most to gain. Despite recently joining the NPT, Beijing desperately needs foreign currency and desires clout in the Third World.

---

† That reactor was destroyed by Israeli fighters in 1981, before it was completed. See Paul Leventhal, "Why Bother Plugging Export Leaks?" Orbis, spring 1992, p. 167.

†† Gary Milhollin, "Building Saddam Hussein's Bomb," The New York Times Magazine, March 8, 1992, p. 33. Also see U.S. News & World Report, Nov. 25, 1991, p. 34.

There are increasing concerns that the lack of sufficient export controls in the Commonwealth of Independent States might permit Middle Eastern countries with nuclear ambitions to gain access to Soviet nuclear-weapons scientists, weapons-grade nuclear materials and even nuclear weapons themselves.

After having been stymied for the past decade, there are reports that Libya is aggressively seeking nuclear capability. U.S. officials say Libyan leader

Muammar el-Qaddafi has offered Pakistan billions of dollars for nuclear technology and is in the market for Soviet specialists willing to barter their knowledge. In December, Libya tried to lure several Russian atomic scientists to work there at $2,000 a month.

Iranian militants have proclaimed that they want to pick up the torch from Iraq for a Muslim atomic bomb, ostensibly to counter Israel's nuclear arsenal. Tehran is also believed to be concerned about obtaining nuclear weapons to balance a resurrected Iraq somewhere down the road.

Algeria, with extensive Chinese help, is building a reactor at a remote and heavily guarded site south of Algiers that Western experts believe is intended to produce plutonium for nuclear arms.

The catalyst for nuclear war in the Middle East would most likely involve Israel. Though absolute proof is lacking, it is widely believed that Israel possesses the largest nuclear arsenal outside of the five declared nuclear powers. Based on U.S. intelligence reports, leaks from within Israel's nuclear establishment and other sources, Spector estimates that Israel may have as many as 100 nuclear weapons.[13] Seymour M. Hersh, a Pulitzer Prize-winning investigative reporter, puts the number at several hundred.[14]

From the Israeli perspective, nuclear weapons are the deterrent of last resort. The Israeli government has pledged it will "not be the first nation to introduce nuclear weapons into the Middle East," but it has declined to sign the NPT and professes a need to keep its options open. Israel has been invaded by its Arab neighbors three times in its 44-year history, and a majority of Israelis regard nuclear weapons as a justifiable part of their small nation's defense. A poll conducted last year revealed that 91 percent of the Israelis supported the development of nuclear weapons as a means to deter Arab aggression, and 88 percent support using the bombs in certain circumstances.[15]

Of course, there is also the risk that building nuclear weapons may make Israel less safe in the long run. Israel "has started an arms race in the Middle East for weapons of mass destruction," says Michael Klare, professor of peace and world security studies at Hampshire College in Amherst, Mass. "The danger is that Arab nations such as Iraq will not rest until they have weapons to counter them."

India and Pakistan

Of all the regions where countries are suspected of having nuclear weapons, experts fret most over the situation in India and Pakistan. Both nations now have nuclear arms — or the material and ability to put them together quickly. And both have sophisticated aircraft capable of delivering nuclear bombs to their targets, and are at work trying to improve the range and accuracy of their ballistic missiles.

"South Asia seems to be the highest-temperature nuclear flash point in the world at this time," notes Gary Milhollin. "You have all the ingredients — a border dispute, historic rivalry, mutual suspicion and no nuclear doctrine in either country."

The catalyst for Pakistan's weapons program was India's 1974 test of a "peaceful" nuclear device. Pakistan publicly vowed that it would match India's nuclear status and privately began an elaborate secret effort to acquire the means to do so.[16] Its success provides a vivid case study of how an ambitious nation can overcome technical problems and international opposition to join the nuclear club.

The potential for disaster is hardly abstract. In May 1990 a dispute over Kashmir brought the two countries careening to the brink of nuclear war. U.S. officials who intervened to halt the conflict were dismayed to learn that neither India nor Pakistan had seriously considered the effects of nuclear weapons and had no conception of how to stop a war that had gone nuclear.

"India and Pakistan are playing a very dangerous game," says Milhollin. "The potential [to deploy nuclear weapons] creates fear in the other side, but in this instance the other side has the means to put fear into operation. They've wandered into a morass."

Tensions between the two countries remain high. Today Pakistan is believed to have acquired all the necessary material for two nuclear bombs and enough uranium for 10. After officially denying having a nuclear program for years, Shahryar Khan, the country's foreign minister, admitted in Washington in February that "the capability is there: elements which, if put together, would become a [nuclear] device."[17]

Experts believe India's nuclear arsenal is even larger. Although the New Delhi government insists it has never actually constructed nuclear bombs, most experts believe that the country has enough components to build between 40 and 60 nuclear weapons.

Recently, the United States has stepped up pressure on both countries to negotiate an arms agreement. In response, Pakistan has volunteered to sign the NPT if India does. Pakistani Prime Minister Nawaz Sharif says he is also ready to discuss a nuclear-free zone in South Asia. However, given that both nations have had weapons capability for so long, the prospects for ridding the region of the nuclear threat are dim.

"In South Asia we're dealing with an after-the-fact situation," says Spector. "Nuclear weapons have been there for 18 years. It's much harder to roll back nuclear capability than it is to stop it before it is achieved."

Export Challenges

Until recently, the West has either winked at other countries' nuclear-weapons programs or actively aided them. The Nuclear Suppliers Group (see p. 489) met in March 1991 for

Plutonium: Arms Race Legacy

During the Cold War, the United States and the Soviet Union spent trillions of dollars building weapons of awesome destructive force. But now that the arms race is over, experts are finding that disabling these nuclear warheads is uncharted territory.

Recent arms treaties have spelled out how delivery systems, such as rockets and cruise missiles, should be crushed, burned, cut up or otherwise reduced to rubble. But none has addressed the most basic challenge of all: destroying the nuclear warheads that have kept the world on edge for so long.

The crux of the problem is what to do with the 100 tons of weapons-grade plutonium, and the 500-700 tons of highly enriched uranium (some of it now in weapons), thought to have been produced by the Soviet nuclear-weapons industry over the past 40 years. Both are valuable — and extremely dangerous — commodities.†

The United States has offered $400 million in emergency funds to help the Commonwealth of Independent States dismantle and store its nuclear weapons. But with estimates that it will cost $100 billion to $300 billion for the United States to clean up its own nuclear-weapons waste,†† that contribution seems a mere pittance.

"If you look at the problem on the U.S. side, and then think of the Russian case, it's a disaster waiting to hap-

pen," says William Potter, director of the Center for Russian and Eurasian Studies at the Monterey Institute of International Studies in California. "The economic situations in the former republics are so desperate that there are not funds for routine maintenance and repairs at nuclear sites."

The accident at the Chernobyl nuclear-power plant in Ukraine alerted the world to the poor standards of Soviet civilian reactors. The Soviets' safety record in the weapons industry has been even worse, and some analysts wonder whether the Russian weapons industry can be trusted with the complex task of nuclear disarmament.

The United States, which has experience taking weapons apart, can only dismantle two or three a day, meaning it will take up to three years to eliminate the agreed-on weapons. The commonwealth, which has little experience, would need at least 10 years to destroy its weapons.

---

†Japan is the only country investing heavily in so-called "breeder" nuclear reactors that use plutonium as fuel. Tokyo plans to begin importing large quantities of plutonium from Europe in the fall. The prospect that the fuel could be hijacked on the high seas has aroused fears around the globe. For details, see *The New York Times*, Nov. 25, 1991, and the *Los Angeles Times*, Feb. 23, 1992.

††See "Nuclear Weapons Complex Braces for Overhaul," *Congressional Quarterly Weekly Report*, April 25, 1992, p. 1066.

---

the first time in 13 years. Meanwhile, the number of suppliers of nuclear-weapons technology is growing rapidly. Several nations that are not parties to the major agreements limiting exports of critical technologies — notably China, India, Israel, Brazil and Argentina — have begun to increase their nuclear exports.[18]

Furthermore, since the breakup of the Soviet Union, the strict export laws that controlled trade in that country have been eased, raising concerns about "loose nukes" — the proliferation of Soviet nuclear technology throughout the world. Already, private companies have sprouted up in Russia peddling nuclear technology. One such company, the CHETEK Corp., has advertised the sale of "peaceful nuclear explosives."[19]

Non-proliferation experts acknowledge that preventing dangerous ex-

ports won't be easy. A major obstacle to stopping the spread of nuclear-weapon technology is that the peaceful atom is hard to isolate from the military atom. For instance, centrifuges that enrich uranium for commercial power plants can also enrich it for bombs.

Even the most stringent laws and the most efficient enforcement authorities can be evaded by a sophisticated clandestine acquisition network that uses front companies and intermediaries to act as unsuspicious clients. Iraq, for instance, acquired most of its nuclear-weapons technology legally.

In the five years before the Persian Gulf War, the U.S. Commerce Department licensed more than $1.5 billion worth of strategically sensitive American exports to Baghdad. Many were for direct delivery to nuclear weapon sites, chemical weapon sites and missile sites. Major U.S. companies like Hewlett-

Packard, Honeywell, International Computer Systems and Rockwell, among others, sold high-performance electronics to Iraq's missile research center, called Saad 16, and to the Iraqi Atomic Energy Commission.[20].

Since then, the export-control regime has been strengthened. Embarrassed by the Iraq debacle, most countries are keeping a closer eye on what they export. In the United States, the Senate on April 9 passed a non-proliferation bill aimed at imposing new sanctions against companies and countries that promote nuclear arms. The Omnibus Nuclear Proliferation Control Act of 1992, sponsored by Sen. John Glenn, D-Ohio, would prevent U.S. firms found to be promoting nuclear proliferation, and foreign firms engaged in illicit nuclear deals, from applying for U.S. government

Continued on p. 498

At Issue:

Should the United States sign a comprehensive test ban on nuclear weapons?

REP. MARTIN OLAV SABO, D-MINN.

Member of the House Appropriations, Budget and Select Intelligence Committees
FROM *THE CHRISTIAN SCIENCE MONITOR,* **MARCH 24, 1992.**

yes

in next year's budget, President Bush calls for the Department of Energy to spend $474 million on the testing of nuclear weapons. The Defense Nuclear Agency will allocate at least another $100 million. This is not only wasteful but counter to U.S. security interests.

It is wasteful because it is unnecessary. Since we are not producing any new nuclear weapons, we obviously won't be testing any. The Pentagon claims that repeated testing is needed to ensure the reliability and safety of weapons already in the arsenal. Reputable scientists and several government agencies have concluded, however, that those few warhead systems that need to be tested — the electronic and other non-nuclear components — can be examined separately from the actual explosive warhead. The Defense Nuclear Agency already does substantial testing of this kind. . . .

More than being a waste of money, however, nuclear testing can threaten U.S. national security by undermining efforts to control the spread of nuclear weapons. The proliferation of nuclear weapons may be the chief threat America faces in the new, post-Cold War era. . . .

There are two ways to deal with nuclear proliferation. One is to continue and strengthen the steps we have already taken. This strategy would tighten controls on the export of sensitive nuclear technology, encourage more states to adhere to the Non-Proliferation Treaty [NPT], strengthen the International Atomic Energy Agency and improve intelligence-gathering capabilities in the area of nuclear weapons development. All of these efforts would require the active cooperation of Russia, Japan, the European powers and developing countries with nuclear potential. Continued U.S. nuclear testing undermines this international effort to reduce the nuclear threat. . . .

The other way — the administration's choice — is to continue going it alone: continue nuclear testing, devote minimal attention to technology controls, allow the NPT to fail and spend $100 billion deploying an unproven system to intercept nuclear missiles.

In my view, the administration's approach is . . . a reactive policy that assumes we can do little to stop nuclear proliferation. It is not enough. We must play an active role in a coordinated, international effort to halt the spread of nuclear weapons. An essential part of this strategy is to stop U.S. nuclear weapons testing — now.

HARRY REID, D- NEV.

Member of the Appropriations and Environment & Public Works Committees
FROM STATEMENT IN *THE CONGRESSIONAL RECORD,* **FEB. 27, 1992.**

no

the problem in the world today is not nuclear testing. It is nuclear weapons. To eliminate testing before we eliminate nuclear arms would not only undermine our country's military security but also endanger our public safety. As long as arms exist, testing is necessary to ensure that those weapons may be safely stored.

In May 1990, for example, Defense Secretary Dick Cheney acknowledged a safety problem with U.S. nuclear artillery shells in Europe. . . . The safety problems were confirmed through testing at the Nevada test site in 1988 and 1989. Because the problems were identified through testing, they were fixed, and accidents were prevented.

The use of nuclear weapons is a horrible thought, but it is that horror which has maintained the peace; it may be that horror which in the end causes the abandonment of war as an instrument of national policy. . . .

However, as long as we rely upon those weapons to keep the peace, we must test them to maintain an effective and credible deterrence posture. We need to know that the weapons in our arsenal are safe and reliable. We need to know that they will survive an attack. We need to know their effect on our equipment and that of our enemy. It has been the testing program, which, by teaching us to create smaller, more accurate and more efficient weapons, has enabled us already to [cut] our nuclear arsenal.

Perhaps as importantly, we also need to test to know the future. We test nuclear weapons to verify computer modeling, maintain scientific vitality and to avoid technological surprises. . . .

We must remember that the Nevada nuclear test site is a highly complex scientific operation, which involves literally hundreds of scientists and engineers and thousands of highly skilled technicians. You neither create nor deactivate such a facility with the wave of some magic wand. If we were to stop testing and then decide a year or two from now to begin again, where would we be?

We do not know what would have happened if Saddam Hussein had exploded a nuclear weapon in the atmosphere over the battlefield. We do not know what would have happened to our equipment. We think we know, but we are not sure. We need to test. It would be unsafe, impractical and unwise not to, and it would send a signal of complacency to Third World countries currently developing these weapons of mass destruction.

Continued from p. 496

contracts. The legislation also would impose penalties against banks and other financial institutions that knowingly assist nations to acquire the bomb. The bill, which has strong bipartisan support, has been referred to the House Foreign Affairs Committee.

But the problem of dual-use items, those that can be used for both peaceful and military purposes, will likely remain. The Bush administration opposes a measure, sponsored by Rep. Edward J. Markey, D-Mass., that would impose strict new unilateral controls on dual-use items, such as supercomputers and special steel alloys, and on nuclear technology and highly enriched uranium. The administration says the bill would undermine commerce.[21]

In fact, in April the administration changed U.S. export laws to make it easier to export highly advanced computers, which critics say could be used in making bombs. For example, regulations were eased on supercomputers, which critics note were invented for the purpose of making weapons.[22]

"The profit motive invariably dictates non-proliferation policy," says Paul Leventhal, director of the Washington-based Nuclear Control Institute. "Basically, it's greed. There is always an excuse of commerce or foreign policy grounds to ratchet down export controls in favor of unrestricted trade." ■

bomb is worthless unless the IAEA's bomb-busters — or other regional inspectors — are given real clout. At a minimum, experts say, that means the right to carry out challenge inspections on short notice. It means more random inspections of nuclear facilities, including undeclared sites. And most important, it means violators should be hit with U.N. sanctions — including the use of force, if necessary.

Whether or not the rejuvenated IAEA has the will to move beyond its traditional reporting role, and take on more of a police function, is unclear. "It's premature to make a judgment," says Leonard Spector. "We'll have to see what happens in North Korea and Iran." Some groups, like the Union of Concerned Scientists, argue in favor of a more direct role by the U.N. Security Council. Indeed, some analysts say a new international institution with its own means for space surveillance may be needed for monitoring the spread of nuclear weapons.

OUTLOOK

Balance of Terror

Almost 30 years ago, President John F. Kennedy warned of the danger of nuclear proliferation. Ironically, it is now that the Cold War is over that the prospect has become a reality. "Nuclear proliferation is the most salient security threat we face today," says Patrick Glynn at the American Enterprise Institute. If the world fails to contain the spread of nuclear weapons, the balance of power that kept relative peace for four decades of the Cold War may be displaced by a balance of terror.

But despite a plethora of new proliferation risks, most experts are cautiously optimistic about the future. "The overall picture is positive," says former Ambassador Jonathan Dean, an arms control adviser to the Union of Concerned Scientists and a former NATO-Warsaw Pact negotiator.

As the industrialized nations tighten up on critical exports and the rivalry among the superpowers gives way to

cooperation, analysts say there is as good an opportunity now as there ever will be to stop the bomb-builders. After all, today's nuclear delinquents got their start in the days when rival big powers egged them on, or at least turned a blind eye.

Two recent developments, in particular, show future promise in the non-proliferation field: the establishment of nuclear-free zones, where the production of plutonium and highly enriched uranium is banned, and the emergence of a framework for bilateral inspections by potentially hostile neighbors, such as that instituted in Brazil and Argentina.

For some nations, there is a new awareness that the nuclear arms race isn't worth the price. In the long run, says the Wisconsin Project's Gary Milhollin, the Argentina-Brazil example will be followed by antagonists such as Pakistan and India. "Sooner or later, you have to choose between bombs and breakfast cereal," he says.

But clearly, for regional agreements to work, it will take more than good will, especially where there is a history of mutual suspicion. As Iraq has shown, the promise not to build the

Ban Nuclear Tests?

Since the NPT's inception, the nonnuclear states have repeatedly castigated the nuclear states for not expanding the 1963 Limited Test Ban into a Comprehensive Test Ban, to cover underground tests. At a U.N. conference in January 1991, the United States and Britain were the only countries to oppose negotiating a ban on all nuclear tests. U.S. officials claim testing is still necessary to ensure safety. (The Soviet Union suspended nuclear testing in October 1991, and France announced a moratorium in April.)

"By not agreeing to a test ban," says Brookings' Janne Nolan, "the United States gives other countries a pretext to say the industrialized countries haven't lived up to the NPT commitment in good faith." The NPT comes up for renewal in 1995.

Disagreement over a comprehensive test ban underscores a more fundamental problem: the NPT's inherent double standard. While the treaty attempts to prevent non-weapons states from acquiring nuclear weapons, it permits the weapons states to retain them, further develop them and acquire more. Thus, as much of the world is disarming, Britain plans to go ahead with building four Trident submarines with multiple-warhead ballistic missiles, and U.S. strategists are contemplating new, more technologically sophisticated, nuclear weapons.

Having won the Cold War, the United States and some of its allies are loathe to close the nuclear door. "The world is safer if the United States has a substantial nuclear capability," says Patrick Glynn. "You don't get international gangsters like Saddam Hussein or Kim Il Sung to disarm by moral example."

The problem, of course, is that developing new weapons systems may act as a disincentive for other nations to abstain. The nuclear genie may never be put back in the bottle, and the discrimination inherent in the NPT may not be avoidable. But some analysts say there are ways nuclear tensions could be reduced.

"The kinds of conflicts we can anticipate are not ones in which nuclear weapons can play a constructive role," writes Paul C. Warnke, who was director of the Arms Control and Disarmament Agency during the Carter administration. "Only by devaluing them — stripping them of their special-status symbolism — can we avoid increasing the risk that regional conflicts and civil wars will be rendered exponentially more dreadful by the spread of nuclear weapons."[23]

In the final analysis, the success of the non-proliferation regime will depend on the United States — and its willingness to rethink its role in the new world order. In order to de-legitimize nuclear weapons, many experts are calling upon the Bush administration to support the test ban, sign a moratorium on the production of weapons-grade nuclear materials* and open U.S. facilities to the international inspection it demands of others.

Attempts to prevent nuclear proliferation by denying nations access to nuclear technology or by destroying a nascent nuclear infrastructure might delay the attainment of such capabilities. But most observers agree that military actions are unlikely to eliminate motivations, and may even reinforce them.

---

*The United States hasn't made highly enriched uranium since 1964 and in 1988 shut down the last of its plutonium factories. Despite having stockpiles of these materials to last for decades, the U.S. opposes a moratorium.

"We have to answer the fundamental question, 'What will be the protection for countries that forswear nuclear weapons?'" says the NRDC's Christopher Paine. "The Pentagon says put them under the nuclear umbrella, but that's not realistic. We're not going to be able to protect everyone. The superpower-first approach won't work in today's world."

But until the United Nations — or some other international body — proves itself capable of dealing with nuclear transgressors, the world will be on edge. The bottom line is that so long as nuclear weapons are considered vaunted instruments of policy, countries will demand to have them — and the world will be a less safe place to live. ∎

Notes

[1] See *Arms Control Today,* January/February 1992, p. 40.

[2] Quoted in the *Los Angeles Times,* Jan. 19, 1992.

[3] The NRDC, headquartered in New York, has worked closely with Soviet scientists on disarmament issues and is acknowledged even by Washington officials to have the best contacts within the Russian nuclear-weapons establishment.

[4] Quoted in the *Los Angeles Times,* Jan. 20, 1992.

[5] For a detailed account, see Gary Milhollin, "'Building Saddam Hussein's Bomb," *The New York Times Magazine,* March 8, 1992, p. 30.

[6] Quoted in *The New Republic,* Jan. 28, 1991, p. 22.

[7] Thus far, aid to Pakistan has not been reinstated, though there is pressure in Congress to do so. For background, see Gerrard C. Smith and Helena Cobban, "A Blind Eye to Nuclear Proliferation," *Foreign Affairs,* summer 1989, p. 53.

[8] Quoted in *The Bulletin of the Atomic Scientists,* September 1991, p. 14.

[9] For a more detailed account, see *U.S. News & World Report,* Nov. 25, 1991, p. 24.

[10] Cited in *Technology Review,* August/September 1991, p. 27.

[11] Quoted in *The New York Times,* May 7, 1992.

[12] Quoted in *U.S. News & World Report,* Nov. 25, 1991, p. 42.

[13] Leonard Spector, *Nuclear Ambitions* (1990), p. 149.

[14] Seymour M. Hersh, *The Samson Option* (1991), p. 318. Hersh also alleges that shortly after Iraqi Scud missiles began falling on Tel Aviv during the Persian Gulf War in January 1991, Israel rolled nuclear missiles out of silos and placed them on launch pads aimed at Iraq. Israeli Prime Minister Yitzhak Shamir refuses to confirm or deny that story.

[15] Cited in *Scholastic Update,* Feb. 21, 1992, p. 8.

[16] In a stormy season between U.S. Secretary of State Henry A. Kissinger and Pakistani Prime Minister Zulfikar Ali Bhutto in 1976, Bhutto promised that the Pakistanis would "eat grass if we have to" in pursuit of the bomb.

[17] Quoted in *The Economist,* March 14, 1992, p. 47.

[18] See William C. Potter, "The New Nuclear Suppliers," *Orbis,* spring 1992, p. 199.

[19] For a more detailed account of the former Soviet Union's new nuclear entrepreneurs, see *Arms Control Today,* January/February 1992, p. 33.

[20] See Milhollin, *op cit,* p. 30.

[21] The Markey bill was incorporated into the Export Administration Reauthorization Act, which passed the House Oct. 30, 1991. The Senate version of the reauthorization measure passed Jan. 22, 1992. Bush has said he will veto the bill, which is now in conference.

[22] See *The New York Times,* April 24, 1992.

[23] Writing in *The Bulletin of the Atomic Scientists,* May 1992, p. 37.

Bibliography

Selected Sources Used

Books

Hersh, Seymour M., *The Samson Option*, Random House, 1991.

Hersh, a Pulitzer Prize-winning investigative reporter, has put together an informative, somewhat controversial and highly readable book on how Israel developed nuclear weapons. Hersh also offers fascinating insight into how U.S. administrations have dealt with Israel's nuclear capability.

Potter, William C., *International Nuclear Trade and Nonproliferation*, Lexington Books, 1990.

This collection of country-by-country essays on the nuclear-weapons trade is somewhat dry, but it provides useful background on how several Third World countries are emerging as suppliers of nuclear-weapons technology.

Spector, Leonard S., *Nuclear Ambitions: The Spread of Nuclear Weapons 1989-90*, Westview Press, 1990.

Considered by many experts to be the seminal work on nuclear non-proliferation, this comprehensive study examines the nuclear-weapons programs of all the countries seeking to join the "nuclear club." In each case, the programs are put into their regional and political context.

Articles

Bethe, Hans A., Kurt Gottfried and Robert McNamara, "The Nuclear Threat: A Proposal," *The New York Review of Books*, June 27, 1991, p. 48.

The authors offer a detailed proposal of how to reduce nuclear tensions. They conclude that the United States must take bold disarmament steps if there is to be any hope for stopping the spread of nuclear weapons.

Leventhal, Paul L., "Why Bother Plugging Export Leaks?" *Orbis*, spring 1992, p. 167.

This article focuses on how countries have contributed to nuclear proliferation by exporting so-called "dual-use" nuclear technology to states bent on developing nuclear armaments. Leventhal also makes suggestions for how the non-proliferation regime could be strengthened.

Milhollin, Gary, "Building Saddam Hussein's Bomb," *The New York Times Magazine*, March 8, 1992, p. 30.

Milhollin provides an illuminating look at how Iraq managed to come so close to developing a nuclear bomb, despite international efforts to derail his nuclear program. The article documents how U.S. firms — as well as the Commerce Department — indirectly contributed to Saddam Hussien's arsenal.

Potter, William C., "Exports and Experts: Proliferation Risks From the New Commonwealth," *Arms Control Today*, January/February 1992, p. 32.

The author, director of the Center for Russian and Eurasian Studies at the Monterey Institute for International Affairs, examines the proliferation risks in the former Soviet Union, including the flight of Soviet nuclear scientists and the uncontrolled spread of weapons-grade materials.

Rathjens, George W., and Marvin M. Miller, "Nuclear Proliferation after the Cold War," *Technology Review*, August/September 1991, p. 25.

The article discusses how the end of the Cold War has diminished risks of a nuclear Armageddon but triggered new dangers in the Third World. It also discusses the issue of whether the United States should sign the Comprehensive Test Ban Treaty.

Smith, Gerard C., and Helena Cobban, "A Blind Eye to Nuclear Proliferation," *Foreign Affairs*, summer 1989, p. 53.

Though a bit dated, this article contains useful background on U.S. proliferation policy over the past few decades. The authors are critical, but generally balanced.

Warnke, Paul C., "Missionless Missiles," *The Bulletin of the Atomic Scientists*, May 1992, p. 36.

The former head of the U.S. Arms Control and Disarmament Agency critiques U.S. arms control policy and makes suggestions for the future.

Reports and Studies

Davis, Zachary S., and Warren H. Donnelly, *Non-Proliferation: A Compilation of Basic Documents on the International, U.S. Statutory, and U.S. Executive Branch Components of Non-Proliferation Policy*, Congressional Research Service Report for Congress, Dec. 18, 1990.

This compilation of the most critical non-proliferation legislation and treaties is very useful as reference material.

Union of Concerned Scientists, *A Program for World Nuclear Security*, February 1992.

The Union of Concerned Scientists is a nonprofit organization of scientists and other citizens concerned about science issues, including nuclear arms control. This 30-page study closely examines the current situation in the former Soviet Union and makes proposals for the future, based on strategic arms reductions.

The Next Step

Additional Articles from Current Periodicals from EBSCO Publishing's Database

Commonwealth of Independent States

"Resetting the nuclear clock," *Time,* **Feb. 17, 1992, p. 53.**

Reveals that Washington has been given assurances that all strategic missiles in Ukraine, Kazakhstan and Belarus would be eliminated within seven years, while all tactical nuclear weapons concentrated in Russia, Ukraine and Belarus will be either decommissioned or withdrawn to Russia by July. Lingering fear of Russian dominance.

Fessler, P., "More U.S. involvement sought in post-Soviet affairs," *Congressional Quarterly Weekly Report,* **Jan. 4, 1992, p. 27.**

Discusses how leading congressional Democrats and Republicans have continued to push the Bush administration for a more aggressive response to potential nuclear, economic and political threats in the former Soviet Union. The fate of thousands of unemployed nuclear experts and the 27,000 nuclear weapons spread throughout the former nation; implications of the strategic arms treaties signed with former Soviet President Mikhail S. Gorbachev; exchange programs; more.

Friedman, T. L., "U.S. says 4 Soviet republics vow to carry out nuclear-arms cuts," *The New York Times,* **Dec. 19, 1991, p. A1.**

Says that the leaders of all four of the crumbling Soviet Union's republics that have long-range nuclear missiles have promised to carry out all cuts in nuclear weapons required of them under agreements made between President Mikhail S. Gorbachev and President George Bush. The republics will also accept American advisers to help them dismantle the warheads.

Friedman, T. L., "Yeltsin rebuffed by Asian republic on nuclear arms," *The New York Times,* **Dec. 18, 1991, p. A1.**

Says that President Nursultan A. Nazarbayev of Kazakhstan took issue with the comments made by President Boris N. Yeltsin of Russia that eventually all Soviet republics would eliminate nuclear weapons except Russia. Nazarbayev declared that his republic would retain its nuclear missiles as long as Russia does.

Gilmartin, P. A., "Bush faulted for foot-dragging on weapon disposal initiative," *Aviation Week,* **Feb. 10, 1992, p. 22.**

Elaborates on the reaction of Senate Armed Services Committee Chairman Sam Nunn, D-Ga., and others to the Bush administration's failure to provide concrete proposals to spur the dismantlement of former Soviet nuclear weapons. Congressional authorization of $400 million for the Soviet Union; ensuring "sensible expenditures"; providing alternative employment for former Soviet weapons scientists; recent negotiations on dismantling nuclear and chemical weapons; storage capacity.

Nelan, B. W., J. Carney, et al., "Scrambling for the pieces of an empire," *Time,* **Jan. 13, 1992, p. 25.**

Outlines progress made by the Commonwealth of Independent States toward sharing the inheritance of the former union. The states agreed that intercontinental ballistic missiles be centrally controlled and that Ukraine, Belarus and Kazakhstan will destroy their nuclear weapons or give them to Russia. Reasonable confidence the nuclear weapons are under firm control; eight states will operate under a single military command; Yeltsin's power grab.

Watson, R., J. Barry, et al., "Nukes on the loose," *Newsweek,* **Dec. 16, 1991, p. 32.**

Raises the questions of who will get control of the 27,000 nuclear warheads housed in the Soviet Union's far-flung arsenal as the empire breaks up. Warning from Soviet President Mikhail S. Gorbachev; the nuclear problem is at the top of Secretary of State James A. Baker III's visit to Russia; conditions provided by the new Strategic Arms Reduction Treaty (START); provides a listing of how many fingers may be on the nuclear button; quick fix.

Debates & issues

"Nuclear halt," *Nation,* **Dec. 30, 1991, p. 835.**

Editorial. Argues that the time is now for major unilateral nuclear arms cuts, as the threat of instant proliferation of nuclear powers is represented in the breakaway Soviet republics. Secretary of State James A. Baker III's warning that the U.S. may now face a "Yugoslavia with nukes" — the former Soviet Union; President George Bush's Sept. 27 announcement on arms reduction; the elimination of a whole class of nuclear weapons; risks of nuclear accidents; details.

"Power to the bomb-busters," *The Economist,* **Nov. 23, 1991, p. 16.**

Discusses the different countries now trying to build nuclear weapons. Proposes that it can be stopped, but it will take courage, money and a lot of cooperation among world powers. Nuclear Non-Proliferation Treaty (NPT); export controls; international Atomic Energy Agency (IEAA); pressure on cheaters; details.

"Semipalatinsk, west," *The Economist,* Jan. 18, 1992, p. 25.

Examines the factories, reactors and stores for making nuclear weapons that are scattered across America, and how demand for their products is low. Waste problems; overcapacity of nuclear fuel reported by Department of Energy (DOE); tritium leak in South Carolina; pressure to close other nuclear weapons plants.

"The ash heap of history," *National Review,* Jan. 20, 1992, p. 14.

Questions the Bush administration's nostalgia for the efficient system of command and control over nuclear weapons. Why the administration is so eager to reconstitute the entire Soviet nuclear arsenal; advocates of Gorbachev; distrust of Gorbachev by both the reformers and the hardliners; the commonwealth is torn by disagreements about economic and military policy; more.

"When nukes spread," *The Economist,* Jan. 18, 1992, p. 18.

Discusses how the breakup of the Soviet Union has only complicated the world nuclear arms question. Problem of new nuclear powers; Nuclear Non-Proliferation Treaty (NPT); unemployed weapons scientists; emergency measures; no system foolproof.

Budiansky, S. and B. B. Auster, "Tackling the new nuclear arithmetic," *U.S. News & World Report,* Jan. 20, 1992, p. 38.

Reports how the Soviet Union's demise has left the U.S. pondering how many nuclear weapons it needs. Arms controllers who have been calling for substantial cuts in America's nuclear arsenal have found a surprising ally with Gen. Lee Butler, the new commander of the Strategic Air Command. Details the review of U.S. nuclear-weapons policy ordered by General Butler; the Strategic Arms Reduction Treaty; the uncertainties facing America's nuclear planners.

Gilmartin, P. A., "U.S. officials assess status of former Soviet weapon programs," *Aviation Week,* Jan. 20, 1992, p. 27.

Considers recent testimony before Congress that indicates the reform military leadership of the former Soviet Union is continuing to develop and test strategic weapons, but U.S. officials are heartened by the consolidation of Soviet tactical nuclear weapons. Soviets currently capable of activating Soviet nuclear weapons; effects of further deterioration in the Commonwealth of Independent States; comments from Central Intelligence Agency Director Robert M. Gates.

Milhollin, G. and G. White, "Too many fingers on the nuclear button?" *New Scientist,* Dec. 14, 1991, p. 6.

Opinion. Questions what the West should do about Soviet nuclear weapons. Ukraine's nuclear weapons; options available; what the West should do.

Morrocco, J. D., "Soviet military breakdown worries U.S. as control over nuclear arms splinters," *Aviation Week,* Dec. 16, 1991 and Dec. 23, 1991, p. 20.

Highlights U.S. officials' concerns about the effects of the unstable situation in the Soviet Union on the control and security of the Soviet arsenal of some 30,000 nuclear weapons, some of which continue to be aimed at the U.S. Control of the weapons in the hands of the Ministry of Defense and the General Staff; uncertainty as Russia and the other republics sort out weapons ownership and establish new control procedures; distribution of Soviet weapons; Robert Gates' testimony.

Post, T. and P. Hinckle, "Selling nuclear missiles — and minds," *Newsweek,* Jan. 13, 1992, p. 29.

Comments that the scariest fallout from a collapsed Soviet Union could be an international black market for nuclear fuel and weapons scientists. Cites example of last year's Italian undercover operation; details; questions concerning Soviet involvement in the Italian case; KGB investigation; potential brain drain of former Soviet nuclear scientists; questions who will pay for the destruction of Soviet strategic missiles. INSET: How great a (nuclear) threat?

Sanders, J. and R. Caplan, "Nuclear security and the Soviet collapse," *World Policy Journal,* winter 1991, p. 135.

Presents an interview with Daniel Ellsberg, a former State and Defense Department official, and a senior research associate of the center for Psychological Studies in the Nuclear Age at Harvard Medical School. Questions about command and control of the former Soviet Union's nuclear arsenal. Dangers posed by the breakdown of Soviet central control over nuclear weapons; consolidation of central control over nuclear weapons; individuals acting on their own; more.

Defense allocations

Norris, R. S. "U.S. strategic nuclear forces, end of 1991," *Bulletin of the Atomic Scientists,* January/February 1992, p. 49.

Outlines the major changes made in all three legs of the U.S. strategic triad last year and notes continuing fiscal constraints, changing operational requirements, implementation of START and a possible START II treaty would cause the strategic arsenal to decrease further by the late 1990s. Presents, in chart form, the type of weapon (ICBMs, bomber/weapons), name, launchers, year deployed, yield (megatons), total warheads and total megatons.

Schneider, K., "U.S. plans big cuts in its production of nuclear arms," *The New York Times,* **Dec. 17, 1991, p. A1.**

States that, nearly half a century after a secret atomic experiment led to the development of a mammoth government nuclear weapons industry, the Bush administration announced plans to slash the complex to four production plants in the South and Midwest and a test site in Nevada. Diminished need for a far-flung nuclear weapons industry; closings outlined.

Towell, P. "Bush expected to cut back on warheads, new weapons," *Congressional Quarterly Weekly Report,* **Jan. 25, 1992, p. 180.**

Notes that President George Bush will present his fiscal 1993 defense budget against a backdrop of expectations that it will embody revolutionary changes in longstanding U.S. defense policy. Possible proposals in Bush's State of the Union address; reductions in nuclear warheads and sophisticated new weapons; cutbacks in production of the B-2 stealth bomber and *Seawolf*-class submarine; effects of the Soviet Union's collapse; more.

Developing countries

Church, G.J., R. Ben-Yishai, et al., "Who else will have the bomb?" *Time,* **Dec. 16, 1991, p. 42.**

Focuses on the issue of uncontrolled atomic proliferation in the Third World, North Korea and Iraq, compliments of China and other suppliers. Estimates are that North Korea will have deliverable nuclear weapons in 1993, Iran and Algeria in six or seven years, while Brazil, Argentina and South Africa appear to be abandoning their programs. Rundown on what U.S. and allied intelligence sources already know or suspect; efforts to contain proliferation; China.

Lagarde, D., "The highest bidder gets the weapons," *World Press Review,* **December 1991, p. 11.**

Reprints an article from *La Truffe* of Paris that discusses the search by Third World countries for "technology mercenaries" from developed countries to assist them in making nuclear weapons. German engineers helping Libya's Qaddafi; Brazilians helping Iraq; Algeria turns to China.

Rizvi, G., "Has China sold out the Third World?" *World Press Review,* **December 1991, p. 12.**

Reprints an article from *Dialogue* of Bangladesh which discusses China's signing last summer of the Nuclear Non-Proliferation Treaty (NPT) after 20 years of holding out.

European Community

"La force d'Euro-frappe?" *The Economist,* **Jan. 18, 1992, p. 48.**

Reports that President François Mitterrand of France not-

ed at a conference in Paris that only two of the 12 European Community (EC) states — France and Britain — possessed nuclear forces. For the first time, a French president has put a question mark over the continuation of the policy of strict national independence.

Iraq

Albright, D. and M. Hibb, "Iraq's bomb: Blueprints and artifacts," *Bulletin of the Atomic Scientists,* **January/February 1992, p. 30.**

Focuses on U.N. and International Atomic Energy Agency inspectors working in Iraq, and their discovery of the nuclear weapons program archives in Baghdad outlining Iraq's investment in facilities to develop and make nuclear weapons. Showdown in the parking lot; work on an implosion device; the January-May 1990 progress report on Iraq's work; the calutron program; centrifuges. INSETS: Hostages, headlines, and hype; procurers and panderers.

Hedges, S.J., P. Cary, et al., "Saddam's secret bomb," *U.S. News & World Report,* **Nov. 25, 1991, p. 34.**

Details how money and an obsession with weapons of mass destruction very nearly made Iraq a nuclear power. The process through which John Googin, a veteran of the Manhattan Project, America's crash program to build an atomic bomb during World War II, discovered a calutron plant in Iraq. Saddam Hussein's secret nuclear weapons program; Iraq's American suppliers. INSETS: Iraq's doomsday weapon; the growing nuclear fold.

Korea

Sanger, D.E., "Bush warns Seoul on pace of pacts with North Korea," *The New York Times,* **Jan. 6, 1992, p. A1.**

States that President George Bush, on his arrival in Seoul, South Korea, warned the leadership against moving too fast in dealings with the Communist North before hard evidence emerged that it is ending reported efforts to produce nuclear weapons.

Nuclear Non-Proliferation Treaty

Arkin, W.M., D. Durrant, et al., "Nuclear weapons headed for the trash," *Bulletin of the Atomic Scientists,* **December 1991, p. 14.**

Suggests President George Bush's Sept. 27 disarmament initiatives, and Soviet President Mikhail S. Gorbachev's Oct. 5 response, signaled the beginning of the end for nuclear weapons. Criticism of Bush's initiative on three grounds; promotion of the B-2 stealth bomber for conventionally armed power projection; "star wars" recast as ground-based interceptor for rogue missile attack; change in attitude of U.S. military to nuclear power; contradictions, paradoxes.

Back Issues

Great Research on Current Issues Starts Right Here... Recent topics covered by The CQ Researcher are listed below. Issues dated before May 10, 1991, were published under the name of Editorial Research Reports.

NOVEMBER 1990
Lotteries and Gambling
Post-Cold War Choices
Setting Limits on Medical Care
Multicultural Education

DECEMBER 1990
Cable TV Regulation
Americans' Search for Their Roots
Is Insurance System a Failure?
Why Schools Still Have Tracking

JANUARY 1991
Growing Influence of Boycotts
Should the U.S. Reinstate the Draft?
America's Archaeological Past
Peace Corps' Challenges in '90s

FEBRUARY 1991
Regional Impact of Recession
Puerto Rico's Status
Redistricting: Mapping Power
Nuclear Power

MARCH 1991
Acid Rain
Cost of the Gulf War
Reassessing Gun Laws
Future for Man in Space

APRIL 1991
Social Security
Canadian Crisis Over Quebec
California Drought
Electromagnetic Radiation

MAY 1991
School Choice
Racial Quotas
Animal Rights
U.S. and Japan

JUNE 1991
Children and Divorce
Teenage Suicide
Endangered Species
Europe 1992

JULY 1991
Teenagers and Abortion
Soviet Republics Rebel
Mexico's Emergence
Athletes and Drugs

AUGUST 1991
Sexual Harassment
Fetal Tissue Research
Oil Imports
The Palestinians

SEPTEMBER 1991
Police Brutality
Advertising Under Attack
Saving the Forests
Foster Care Crisis

OCTOBER 1991
Pay-Per-View TV
Youth Gangs
Gene Therapy
World Hunger

NOVEMBER 1991
Fast-Food Shake-Up
The Greening of Eastern Europe
Business' Role in Education
Cuba In Crisis

DECEMBER 1991
Retiree Health Benefits
Asian Americans
The Obscenity Debate
The Disabilities Act

JANUARY 1992
Term Limits
Oil Spills
Hunting Controversy
Alternative Medicine

FEBRUARY 1992
Threatened Coastlines
New Era in Asia
Assisted Suicide
Jobs in the '90s

MARCH 1992
Women and Sports
Underage Drinking
Garbage Crisis
Mafia Crackdown

APRIL 1992
Ozone Depletion
Welfare Reform
Politicians and Privacy
Illegal Immigration

MAY 1992
Native Americans
Jobs vs. Environment
Too Many Lawsuits?
Fairness in Salaries

Back issues are available for $4.00 (subscribers) or $7.00 (non-subscribers). Quantity discounts apply to orders over ten. To order, call Congressional Quarterly 1-800-432-2250.

Future Topics

▶ *Food Irradiation*

▶ *Lead Poisoning*

▶ *Hard Times for Libraries*

Food Irradiation

Does using radiation to sterilize food pose a health hazard?

A
MERICAN CONSUMERS DEMAND SAFE FOOD. BUT
opponents of radiation say they should avoid food
treated with radiation. Proponents of food irradiation say the process kills disease-causing organisms
and retards spoilage without significantly impairing taste,
texture or nutritional content. Opponents passionately
disagree, noting that radiation forms new chemicals inside
food that may be harmful — especially if ingested over a
lifetime. Although the U.S. Food and Drug Administration has
approved irradiation for several different foods, consumers
and food producers seem wary. Groups opposed to
irradiation have dominated the debate by exploiting one of
the enduring legacies of the Atomic Age — the public's
deep-seated fear of radioactivity — though opponents and
supporters agree that irradiation can't make food radioactive.

  June 12, 1992 • Volume 2, No. 22 • 505-524

Formerly Editorial Research Reports

CQ Researcher

June 12, 1992
Volume 2, No. 22

EDITOR
Sandra Stencel

MANAGING EDITOR
Thomas J. Colin

ASSOCIATE EDITOR
Richard L. Worsnop

STAFF WRITERS
Charles S. Clark
Mary H. Cooper
Rodman D. Griffin

PRODUCTION EDITOR
Laurie De Maris

EDITORIAL ASSISTANT
Michael M. Taylor

GRAPHICS
Jack Auldridge

PUBLISHED BY
Congressional Quarterly Inc.

CHAIRMAN
Andrew Barnes

VICE CHAIRMAN
Andrew P. Corty

EDITOR AND PUBLISHER
Neil Skene

EXECUTIVE EDITOR
Robert W. Merry

PUBLICATIONS MARKETING/SALES
Robert Smith

EDITOR, EBSCO PUBLISHING
Melissa Kummerer

The CQ Researcher (ISSN 1056-2036). Formerly Editorial Research Reports. Published weekly (48 times per year, not printed the first Friday of any month with five Fridays) by Congressional Quarterly Inc., 1414 22nd St., N.W., Washington, D.C. 20037. Rates are furnished upon request. Second-class postage paid at Washington, D.C. POSTMASTER: Send address changes to The CQ Researcher, 1414 22nd St., N.W., Washington, D.C. 20037.

COVER: The flowerlike emblem called a "radura" is the international symbol of irradiation. Under FDA regulations, it must be displayed on all irradiated foods sold in the United States.

Food Irradiation

BY RICHARD L. WORSNOP

THE ISSUES

The strawberries that went on sale Jan. 25 at Laurenzo's Italian Market in North Miami Beach, Fla., looked luscious: deep red, plump and glistening. No wonder customers that day bought 400 pints off the back of a truck in the store's parking lot.

This was no routine merchandising coup, however, for these were no ordinary strawberries. As Laurenzo's customers knew, the fruit had been exposed to carefully controlled doses of gamma rays in a new plant not far from Tampa, Fla. — the first in the nation devoted exclusively to food irradiation. Radiation treatment, supporters say, extends the shelf life of strawberries and other foods without significantly impairing taste, texture or nutritional content.

Opponents of the process challenge these claims, asserting that nutrient loss from irradiation is often unacceptably high. Moreover, they say irradiation results in the formation of new chemicals, known as radiolytic products, that may prove harmful. At the very least, opponents argue, more studies are needed to identify and evaluate these substances. Finally, opponents contend that if food-irradiation facilities like the one in Mulberry, Fla., were built across the country, the chances of a serious nuclear accident would be greatly increased.

As the combatants trade barbs, consumers find it difficult to discern where the truth lies. The debate "is often reduced to ad hominem attacks and selective use of facts," notes the Center for Science in the Public Interest, a research group based in Washington, D.C. "Opponents fail to acknowledge benefits; proponents fail to recognize

safety and other concerns."

To complicate matters, actions by public officials send mixed signals to consumers. For instance, the U.S. Food and Drug Administration (FDA) has declared irradiation safe for preserving certain foods, and the Agriculture Department recently proposed rules governing the irradiation of fresh poultry. The World Health Organization issued a statement May 27 describing food irradiation as a "perfectly sound" way to preserve world food supplies. On the other hand, Maine, New Jersey and New York have enacted laws barring the sale of irradiated food. Similar legislation is being considered in a number of other states (see p. 516).

In some respects, irradiated food holds considerable appeal for health-conscious shoppers. Tests show that low to moderate levels of irradiation can retard ripening and spoilage, kill insects and microorganisms and inhibit sprouting. Moreover, opponents and advocates agree that irradiation does not make food radioactive.

All the same, many people instinctively recoil from the idea of radiation-treated food. The reason is "not difficult to fathom," the World Health Organization noted in a report. "Negative public attitudes toward virtually everything associated with radiation

are found all over the world. In millions of people's minds radiation is associated with war on a scale the Earth has never seen, with accidents that pose health threats lasting for generations and with nuclear wastes that will still be dangerous 10,000 years from now." [1]

Because such feelings are so widespread and firmly held, irradiation advocates bear a heavy burden of proof as they try to persuade people that irradiated food entails few risks.

Here are some of the key questions experts and laymen have discussed since food-irradiation technology emerged some 30 years ago:

Is irradiated food safe and nutritious?

Though no one claims irradiated food is radioactive, many people feel it is somehow tainted. Opinion on this point tends to be highly polarized, with irradiation proponents insisting that numerous tests have shown the process to be safe and opponents citing other tests that support their position. It is unclear whether any further testing could yield results acceptable to both sides.

To a great extent, food-irradiation enthusiasts say, resistance to the technology reflects fear of the new. "We must not forget that there were many who vigorously opposed, on safety grounds, the introduction of electricity, the use of the automobile and even the pasteurization of milk," says Scott Pattison, executive director of Consumer Alert Inc., a pro-irradiation group based in Modesto, Calif. "Today, it may sound strange that anyone would oppose the pasteurization of milk — but several decades ago many did." [2]

Irradiation supporters acknowledge, however, that it may be harder to persuade people to accept irradiated food than it was to persuade

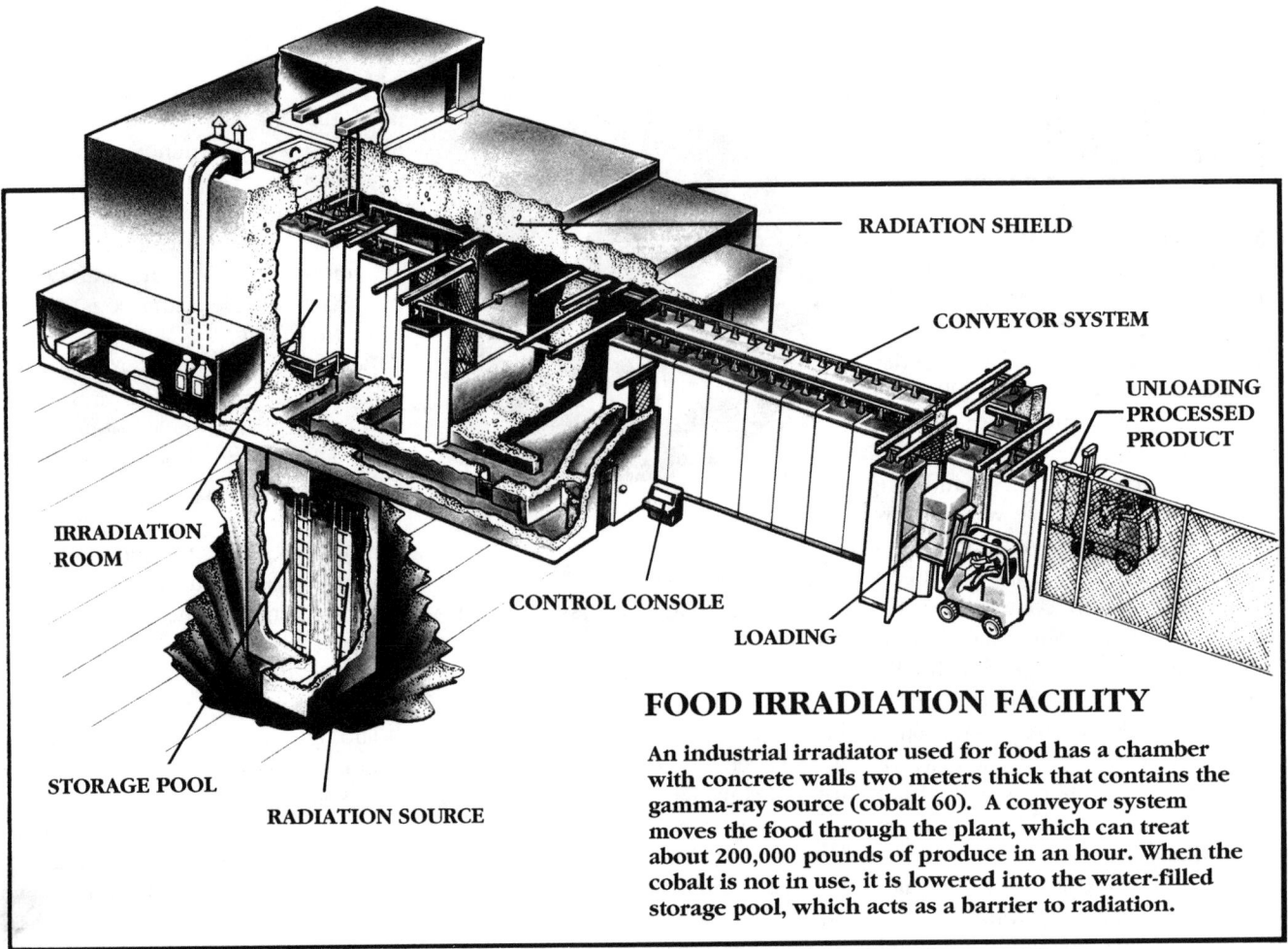

RADIATION SHIELD

CONVEYOR SYSTEM

UNLOADING
PROCESSED
PRODUCT

IRRADIATION
ROOM

CONTROL CONSOLE

LOADING

STORAGE POOL

RADIATION SOURCE

FOOD IRRADIATION FACILITY

An industrial irradiator used for food has a chamber
with concrete walls two meters thick that contains the
gamma-ray source (cobalt 60). A conveyor system
moves the food through the plant, which can treat
about 200,000 pounds of produce in an hour. When the
cobalt is not in use, it is lowered into the water-filled
storage pool, which acts as a barrier to radiation.

Source: Nordion International Inc.

them to drink pasteurized milk. According to columnist John McClung of *Produce Business* magazine, the monthly journal of the Alexandria, Va.-based United Fresh Fruit and Vegetable Association, the main sticking point is that food irradiation involves the use of radioactive materials.

Since "the term 'radioactive' carries a strong negative image," McClung wrote, "it is difficult for most of us to do a 180-degree turn and accept the positive side of the technology, especially for something as intimate as our food supply."[3]

That "positive side" is irradiation's versatility as a food preservative. Radiation inactivates the bacteria, molds and yeasts that cause most food spoil-

age, and it lengthens the shelf life of fresh produce by retarding the biological changes that make fruits and vegetables age. For instance, radiation delays the ripening of green bananas, inhibits the sprouting of potatoes, onions and garlic and prevents the greening of endive. Radiation also destroys disease-causing pests, including insects and parasitic worms, that damage food in storage.

As is true of many other methods of preservation, irradiation alters the chemical and physical properties of food. Some of the changes are clearly beneficial: Beans, for example, acquire a softer texture, making them easier to cook. In addition, irradiation increases the yield of juice from

grapes and speeds the rate at which plums dry.

However, some of the chemical changes that food undergoes during irradiation are difficult to identify, let alone characterize as helpful or harmful. At issue are the compounds called radiolytic products (RPs), which are formed during cooking because of the interaction of heat energy with fat, protein, carbohydrates and other food components.

In the irradiation process, food is exposed to a form of ionizing radiation — gamma rays strong enough to knock electrons out of the atoms of food, thus changing its chemical structure. The process also creates charged particles called ions, which can combine with other ions to form new chemicals.

The difficulty scientists have is that roasting, broiling, frying or any other method of cooking also changes the chemical composition of food. Indeed, the Coalition for Food Irradiation contends that "irradiation develops fewer radiolytic products than can be found in a barbecued steak."[4]

The key question is whether irradiation results in the formation of unique radiolytic products (URPs) — substances that no other preservation method yields. Available evidence seems inconclusive.

In the late 1970s, the FDA set up an internal task force to look into the matter. The committee estimated that up to 10 percent of all RPs may be unique to irradiated food. It also concluded there was little chance that an unusually toxic URP would be formed in significant amounts at the low radiation dosage — 1 kiloGray — normally used on most food.

Edward S. Josephson, a nutrition expert who has studied food irradiation for more than 30 years,* went further than the FDA committee. Testifying before the House Subcommittee on Health and the Environment in 1987, he asserted that "no compounds that are unique to foods processed with ionizing energy have … ever been found." He challenged "anyone voicing a contrary opinion" to come forward with documentation.

Skeptics retort that irradiation advocates have yet to prove conclusively that irradiated food does not contain minute amounts of chemicals that can cause cancer or genetic side effects. According to the authors of a book questioning the need for food irradiation, "it is safest to assume that there is no safe level of exposure to such chemicals; any dose can cause the initial damage that develops into

---

*Josephson currently is an adjunct professor of food science and nutrition at the University of Rhode Island.

Measuring Irradiation

Absorbed radiation is measured in units called "Grays." The amount of Grays refers to the level of energy absorbed by a food from ionizing radiation that passes through the food during the irradiation process.

In the past, the term "rad" was commonly used. It is an acronym for "radiation absorbed dose."

In a typical diagnostic X-ray or nuclear-medicine procedure, the patient receives a radiation dose of 10 rads or less; 10 rads are equivalent to 1/10,000 of the radiation of 1 kiloGray, the normal dosage for most irradiated foods.

100 rads = 1 Gray (1 Gy).

1,000 Grays = 1 kiloGray (1 kGy).

---

a cancer. Damage to the genetic blueprint may cause miscarriage or defects in future generations. The fact that a chemical change is small does not eliminate the risk."[5]

Dr. George L. Tritsch, a scientist at Roswell Park Memorial Institute Cancer Research Center in Buffalo, N.Y., takes a similar position. "Until one knows what compounds are produced [in irradiated food], one cannot be assured that no carcinogens are being formed," he wrote. "The amounts are irrelevant, since food is consumed during the entire lifetime, and only a single carcinogenic insult is needed to produce a malignant tumor that becomes evident decades later."[6]

Irradiation's effect on the nutritional content of food is another point of contention. That there is some nutrient loss is not in dispute — only how much. The FDA maintains that nutrient losses from low radiation doses "appear to be of no dietary significance." Others offer more guarded assessments. Charles Galina, a nuclear consultant in Springfield, Ill., says nutrient losses from irradiation "have never been significant but are usually higher in [heat-treated] food."[7] And Kathleen Tucker, co-author of *Food Irradiation: Who Wants It?* (1987), questions irradiation promoters' claims that vitamin losses are roughly comparable to those that occur in cooking. She notes that "many

foods will be cooked after irradiation, so total losses will increase."[8]

Tucker also says it would be deceptive to sell irradiated fruits and vegetables with artificially lengthened shelf lives as "fresh" produce. The reason is that fruits and vegetables steadily lose nutrients after picking, whether they are irradiated or not. In other words, a fresh-looking irradiated tomato will be less nutritious than an equally fresh-looking but unirradiated one that left the vine more recently.

Irradiation foes frequently point out that the bacterium responsible for botulism, a form of acute food poisoning, is resistant to the low radiation dosages commonly used on food. This means a perilous situation could develop if irradiation destroys the organisms that produce spoilage symptoms, such as an "off" odor or flavor, but fails to kill the botulism pathogens. In that case, an unwitting consumer might purchase and eat contaminated food and fall seriously ill.

Some opponents of food irradiation charge that the process could create mutant strains of bacteria and viruses that might pose a greater public-health hazard than any known pathogens. But others say the possibility is far-fetched. According to Dr. Donald B. Louria, chairman of the department of preventive medicine and community health at Rutgers Univer-

Radiation Phobia Arouses Fears

As advocates of irradiated food are keenly aware, many people regard "radiation" as a scary concept that evokes unimaginable horrors. "It is associated with atomic bomb explosions and nuclear-reactor accidents such as those at Chernobyl and Three Mile Island," observed Dale Blumenthal, a staff writer for *FDA Consumer*.†

The fear extends well beyond the still limited realm of food irradiation. According to Dr. Robert Henkin, director of nuclear medicine at Loyola University Medical Center in Maywood, Ill., "Radiation hysteria is a major issue facing medical imaging. There are more inappropriate articles on radiation effects and scientifically unfounded data being presented now than ever before."††

Radiation phobia frustrates physicians because some patients resolutely refuse to undergo radiation treatment even if advised that it is the most effective way of treating a serious disease like cancer or hyperthyroidism. Some people even balk at the idea of reporting to a hospital's nuclear medicine unit for diagnostic tests.

George H. Pauli and Clyde A. Takeguchi, food irradiation researchers at the U.S. Food and Drug Administration (FDA), concede that some consumers "may react so negatively to the mere thought of food irradiation that they will never find the process acceptable." Nonetheless, they believe most consumers "will accept irradiated products if they are convinced that their fears are being addressed appropriately by responsible authorities. This requires that information be conveyed accurately to avoid the confusion and mistrust that result from contradictory messages."‡

Unfortunately, discussion of food irradiation mostly takes place in professional journals that consumers are not likely to know about, let alone read. Thus, they can fall prey to the "intentional and unintentional dissemination of misinformation which preys on the fears of those not scientifically versed in this field," says Edward S. Josephson, a nutrition expert at the University of Rhode Island with more than 30 years of experience in food irradiation.

According to Josephson, many consumers tend to confuse the effects of irradiation with those of fallout from nuclear weapons tests or reactor accidents. Actually, there is no correlation between the two. When food is exposed to ionizing radiation, the energy that the food absorbs is converted to heat, causing the temperature of the food to rise slightly. Once the exposure ends, so does the process of heat-creation. Both proponents and opponents of irradiation agree that the food does not become radioactive.

Nuclear fallout, on the other hand, is inherently radioactive and thus continues to irradiate everything it comes into contact with — people, animals, plants, air, water and soil — until the radioactivity drops to a safe level through decay. This can take decades, or longer.

For instance, many sites used for atmospheric nuclear weapons tests from the late 1940s to the early 1960s still are uninhabitable because of contamination from fallout. Areas in the former Soviet Union that experienced heavy fallout from the 1986 nuclear-power plant explosion at Chernobyl also are likely to be off-limits to humans for years to come.

---

† Dale Blumenthal, "Food Irradiation: Toxic to Bacteria, Safe to Humans," *FDA Consumer*, November 1990, p. 12.

†† Quoted by Anita Warren, "Radiation Phobia: It Could Be Hazardous to Your Health," *Nuclear Industry*, third quarter 1991, p. 20.

‡ George H. Pauli and Clyde A. Takeguchi, "Irradiation of Foods — An FDA Perspective," *Food Reviews International*, 1986, p. 80.

---

sity's School of Medicine and Dentistry in Newark, N.J., irradiation-caused mutation is "a theoretical concern. But I don't think there are enough data to support it. Microorganisms are mutating all the time."

Both sides in the food-irradiation debate complain of a shortage of studies designed to answer key questions about the safety and nutritional content of irradiated food. One difficulty is that the FDA is required by law to treat irradiation as a food additive rather than a food-preservation process *(see p. 512)*.

When testing a chemical food additive, FDA researchers feed massive amounts of the substance to laboratory animals. The aim is to find the highest level of consumption that produces no ill effects. Once this is done, the agency applies the "rule of 100" in setting the maximum allowable consumption of the additive for humans. That is, the human consumption level is set at no more than 1 percent of the largest amount deemed safe for animals.

However, this approach is impractical for testing irradiated food products since the food itself — not just a minuscule part of it — is the substance being tested. And laboratory animals, being small, cannot be fed irradiated poultry or vegetables or fruit in massive enough amounts to permit meaningful scientific conclusions to be drawn.

Hoping to close the knowledge gap, the FDA in 1981 established an Irradiated Foods Task Group to review all existing toxicity studies relating to irradiated food. The panelists examined more than 400 such studies but concluded that only five had been properly conducted. According to the task group's interpretation of the data, all five studies found no adverse effects from the irradiated foods fed to test animals.

Instead of cooling off the controversy, this finding brought it to a fresh boil. Michael Colby, the director of Food & Water Inc., a New York City-based anti-irradiation group, says it is "outrageous" that the FDA can cite only five outside studies that support the safety of eating irradiated food. "Something's drastically wrong," says Colby, noting that Food & Water has called for "long-term toxicological studies" that will "definitely prove or disprove the safety question" once and for all. In his view, food irradiation is a "frivolous" and "easily replaceable" technology.

Louria says researchers in his department concluded that two of the five studies cited by the FDA were "methodologically flawed, either by poor statistical analyses or because negative data were disregarded." In a third study, the researchers found that animals fed irradiated food experienced weight loss and miscarriage — "almost certainly due to irradiation-induced vitamin E dietary deficiency."[9]

One study in particular — not one of the five named by the FDA task group — often figures in discussions of food-irradiation safety. Carried out in the mid-1970s by the National Institute of Nutrition in Hyderabad, India, it looked at the effects of feeding irradiated and unirradiated wheat to 15 severely undernourished children. Five children were given unirradiated wheat, five got freshly irradiated wheat and five ate irradiated wheat that had been stored for at least three months.

Subsequent tests showed that the children who ate freshly irradiated wheat developed unusually high levels of chromosomal abnormalities in their blood. No such changes were observed in the two other groups.

Several months after the freshly irradiated wheat diet was withdrawn, the chromosomal abnormalities disappeared.

Irradiation opponents cite the Indian study as lending substance to their fears. But some experts, including a number of irradiation foes, say the Indian study is unreliable because the sample was too small, the participants were not randomly selected and the statistical methodology was murky. A somewhat similar Chinese study conducted in the mid-1980s seemed to contradict the Indian findings but it, too, has been faulted as inconclusive.

In Louria's opinion, the studies should not be dismissed out of hand. Rather, they should serve as a point of departure for "a study in the United States in which you would feed irradiated food to people of different ages and income groups. We would try and settle this issue."

He says the study would be "perfectly ethical," since "no one would be hurt." That is because any chromosomal abnormalities that occurred "would go away as soon as the irradiated diet ceased." Louria surmises that "If such a study is done with a large enough population and is methodologically correct, we're not going to see anything." Still, he says, "That doesn't obviate the fact that it has to be done."

Do food-irradiation facilities pose a safety hazard?

To most opponents of food irradiation, food safety is just one of a set of interrelated concerns. High on the list of other worries is nuclear safety — the potential hazard that radioactive isotopes used to irradiate food pose to workers in the processing plant and residents of the surrounding community.

As a result, food irradiation has attracted the interest of anti-nuclear activists who do not ordinarily become involved in nutrition issues. One of

them is Diane D'Arrigo, radioactive waste project director of the Nuclear Information and Resource Service (NIRS), a Washington-based group that promotes alternatives to nuclear power. NIRS is only "peripherally involved" in food irradiation, says D'Arrigo, but is "absolutely opposed" to it. The group feels food irradiation will add to the nation's mounting nuclear waste disposal problems.[10]

Since the new Florida plant has been open for only five months, its operator, Vindicator of Florida Inc., has yet to establish a track record for safety. The records of the approximately 40 other irradiation plants in the United States, most of which sterilize medical equipment and cosmetics, have been less than spotless.

For instance, the Nuclear Regulatory Commission shut down an irradiation plant in Rockaway, N.J., in June 1986 for "very serious" and "willful" violations of safety procedures. In a similar incident at the same plant nine years earlier, the dismantling of a safety device had led to the near-lethal exposure of workers to radiation.

The most serious U.S. irradiation accident occurred in 1988 at a plant in Decatur, Ga., near Atlanta. Leakage from one or more of the facility's 252 capsules of radioactive cesium 137 contaminated more than 25,000 gallons of water in a tank used to insulate the cesium when it's not in use, prompting state officials to order a shutdown. A truckload of some 10,000 contaminated milk cartons was intercepted after the leak was discovered. But other contaminated products, already shipped from the plant, reportedly were not tracked down and retrieved.

Four years later, cleanup work is still under way at the facility, which remains idle. The final cleanup bill is projected at $35 million. In view of strict new environmental regulations and community opposition, officials of the Georgia Department of Natural

Resources say it is doubtful the plant will ever reopen, even if the company that owns it applies for a new operating permit.

While acknowledging that accidents have happened and may happen again, irradiation backers insist the technology is fundamentally safe. According to a report prepared by the American Council on Science and Health, a consumer-education group, "It is impossible for a 'meltdown' to occur in a food-irradiation plant. An irradiator is not a nuclear reactor. It is simply a processing plant containing a shielded area where foods are exposed to a source of ionizing radiation. The radiation sources used in food irradiation cannot explode."[11]

Thomas G. Martin III, director of safety and radiation protection at the U.S. Army Natick Research and Development Laboratories in Natick, Mass., wrote more than a decade ago that, "The safety history of facilities using large radiation sources has been one which justifies some pride. The number of serious accidents reported is very small, and with the right program and facilities even these could have been avoided." To that end, he recommended a "continuing program of education and training of personnel."[12]

Irradiation proponents further contend that shipping radioisotopes presents minimal risk. Nordion International Inc., a Canadian company, says it has made more than 2,000 shipments of cobalt 60 in lead-shielded containers over the past 20 years "without a transportation mishap." Nordion, which built the Vindicator plant's irradiator and supplies it with cobalt 60, takes back spent cobalt for disposal after it has exceeded its economically useful life of about 15 years.

At the Center for Science in the Public Interest, Michael Jacobson concedes that one food irradiation plant, or even several, would not pose significant environmental or public health hazards. "But if irradia-

tion is widely adopted as the way to promote food safety, there will be thousands of plants," he says. "And there you're multiplying the risks tremendously. There will inevitably be some safety glitches and some poorly trained workers who don't under-

stand the power of radioactive chemicals and allow accidents to happen."

In Jacobson's opinion, "It's not worth the price of having all of these facilities scattered around the country when we could be investing in safer alternatives" to food irradiation. ■

BACKGROUND

Early Discoveries

The two discoveries that made food irradiation possible both occurred a little less than 100 years ago. In 1895, German physicist Wilhelm von Roentgen discovered X-rays.* The next year, French physicist Antoine Henri Becquerel discovered radioactivity and its associated ionizing radiations — alpha, beta and gamma rays. The rays cause whatever material they strike to produce electrically charged particles called ions.

Scientists were quick to discern potential applications of Roentgen's and Becquerel's work. For instance, studies published at the Massachusetts Institute of Technology in 1904 reported on ionizing radiation's ability to kill microorganisms. U.S. and British patents for using ionizing radiation to rid food of bacteria were issued in 1905.

However, several decades passed before further progress took place. During World War II, a group of MIT scientists, working under contract to the Army, demonstrated the feasibility of preserving ground beef by exposing it to X-rays. This breakthrough was followed in the late 1940s by a spurt of food-irradiation research involving the federal government (chiefly the Atomic Energy Commission), private industry

and universities, working singly or in combination.

The "atoms for peace" plan proposed by President Dwight D. Eisenhower in an address to the U.N. General Assembly in December 1953 gave further impetus to food irradiation. Eisenhower urged that experts "be mobilized to apply atomic energy to the needs of agriculture, medicine and other peaceful activities." Irradiating food to rid it of contamination and extend its shelf life seemed to be just the sort of activity the president had in mind.

At that time, the FDA did not have the regulatory authority over food irradiation that it possesses today. Nonetheless, the agency became involved by recommending that wholesomeness* testing be conducted before any irradiated food was marketed.

Irradiation Ruled a Food Additive

Congress heeded the FDA's advice when it appended the Food Additives Amendment of 1958 to the Food, Drug and Cosmetic Act of 1938. The amendment defined sources of radiation (including radioactive isotopes, particle accelerators and X-ray machines) intended for use in food processing as "food additives." It also required a pre-market safety review prior to the issuance of an FDA regulation permitting the radia-

Continued on p. 514

---

*X-rays are highly penetrating electromagnetic radiation of much shorter wavelength than visible light.

*FDA wholesomeness tests seek to determine that a food product is microbiologically, nutritionally and toxicologically safe.

Chronology

1890s Two discoveries by European physicists lay the groundwork for today's food-irradiation technology.

1895
Wilhelm von Roentgen of Germany discovers X-rays, highly penetrating electromagnetic radiation of much shorter wavelength than visible light.

1896
Antoine Henri Becquerel of France discovers radioactivity and its associated ionizing radiations — alpha, beta and gamma rays.

— • —

1950s Tentative steps toward food irradiation are taken in the United States and Europe.

1953
Food irradiation becomes one of the technologies earmarked for development under President Dwight D. Eisenhower's "atoms for peace" proposal. The U. S. Army begins research.

1957
West Germany approves the irradiation of spices, but outlaws irradiation of all foods the following year.

1958
The Soviet Union approves irradiation of potatoes.

1958
In amending the Food, Drug and Cosmetic Act of 1938, Congress defines sources of radiation intended for use in food processing as "food additives."

1960s The U.S. Food and Drug Administration (FDA) gives food irradiation a major boost, then has second thoughts.

Feb. 15, 1963
The FDA approves the use of gamma radiation to preserve canned bacon. It is the first rule issued by the agency regarding gamma radiation in food processing.

Aug. 21, 1963
The FDA approves gamma irradiation to control insect infestation of wheat and wheat products.

October 1964
The FDA approves irradiation of potatoes to inhibit sprouting.

July 1966
The FDA issues labeling requirements for food treated by radiation.

October 1968
The FDA rescinds its approval of irradiated bacon. The action dampens interest in food irradiation.

— • —

1980s The FDA shows new enthusiasm for food irradiation during the administration of President Ronald Reagan.

July 1983
The FDA approves radiation of spices and vegetable seasonings.

July 1985
The FDA approves gamma radiation of pork to control *trichinella spiralis,* the parasite that causes trichinosis.

1985
The Environmental Protection Agency (EPA) gives irradiation a boost by banning the use of ethylene dicromide (EDB) as a fumigant to disinfest crops after harvest.

April 1986
The FDA issues a set of rules on irradiation of fruits and vegetables, pork and spices and herbs. Also, the agency requires irradiated whole foods to be labeled with the words "treated with radiation" or "treated by irradiation" as well as a flowerlike symbol called a "radura."

— • —

1990s Food irradiation moves closer to commercial reality, though controversy over the practice remains intense.

May 1990
The FDA approves irradiation of poultry.

January 1992
Vindicator of Florida Inc. opens the nation's first plant designed expressly for food irradiation in Mulberry, Fla. Strawberries are the first food product irradiated at the plant.

May 1992
The U.S. Agriculture Department endorses irradiation as a method for killing salmonella and other harmful bacteria in raw poultry.

May 1992
Senate Agriculture Committee Chairman Patrick J. Leahy, D-Vt., asks Agriculture Secretary Edward Madigan to commission a study by the National Research Council's board of agriculture "to determine if irradiation is an appropriate means of food preservation."

May 27, 1992
The World Health Organization describes irradiation as a "perfectly sound" way to preserve food.

Continued from p. 512

tion of specific food products.

As FDA researchers George H. Pauli and Clyde A. Takeguchi noted in a survey of food-irradiation regulations, treating irradiation as an additive rather than a process strikes many people as odd. But they argued that it is consistent with the agency's treatment of other "indirect food additives" used in food processing.

"For example," they wrote, "a filter membrane is considered a food additive because its components might migrate to food under conditions of use. Yet there is no confusion in recognizing that filtering is a process and that the filter is an additive (albeit not an intentional additive or ingredient). In the same way, irradiation is considered a process, and a source of radiation is an additive because its use affects the characteristics of a food." [13]

Regulatory Environment

The FDA's first regulation approving the use of gamma radiation in food processing was published Feb. 15, 1963. It provided for the use of sealed sources of cobalt 60 for preserving canned bacon. (Two subsequent rules permitted the processing of canned bacon with electron-beam radiation and X-rays.) On Aug. 21, 1963, the agency issued a rule permitting the irradiation of wheat and wheat flour to combat infestation by insects. And on July 8, 1964, it approved the irradiation of white potatoes to inhibit sprout development. All this rulemaking seemed to portend a new era in food preservation.

But it was not to be. The Army, which had initiated the campaign for irradiated canned bacon, asked the FDA in 1968 to approve preserving canned smoked ham with gamma rays from cobalt 60 or cesium 137. It said the method would significantly reduce canned-ham spoilage in tropi-

cal areas like Vietnam and improve the product's flavor.

However, the commissioner of the FDA, James L. Goddard, said in an April 1968 letter to the commander of the Army Quartermaster Research and Engineering Center in Natick, Mass., that he did not believe Army tests on animals had shown that the irradiated ham would be safe for human consumption. The smoked-ham review, Goddard added, also had "raised questions about previously approved regulations for irradiated food, such as canned bacon."

In a separate letter to Atomic Energy Commission Chairman Glenn T. Seaborg, Goddard warned: "Future studies to support the safety of irradiated food will require a more rigid adherence to established protocol and a more careful analysis of all available data than have been evident thus far."

On July 30, 1968, FDA officials told members of the congressional Joint Committee on Atomic Energy that some laboratory animals fed irradiated meat had developed cancer and cataracts, and that the reproduction rate of others had dropped. Nearly a month later, on Aug. 24, the agency proposed to revoke its three regulations governing the irradiation of canned bacon. The revocation was issued as a final rule on Oct. 17, 1968.

The FDA action sent shock waves through the food industry and discouraged interest in food irradition as a commercial venture for years to come. It also wrecked the Army's timetable for petitioning the FDA to approve plans for irradiating other foods, including pork sausage, chicken, beef, hamburger, shrimp, codfish cakes, tuna — even oranges and fruit compote.

Research Continues

Nonetheless, research into the radiation chemistry of food products continued. In 1979, for example, the FDA established the Bureau of Foods' Irradiated Food Committee (BFIFC) to re-

view existing policy and make recommendations about toxicological testing standards for irradiated food. The committee's report, published in 1980, sparked a controversy that still colors the food-irradiation debate. [14]

The only relevant safety issue, BFIFC decided, would be the production of harmful radiolytic products in food during irradiation. Thus, the panel examined all available data on such substances obtained by the Army's high-protein food-sterilization program. Only six of the 65 substances identified by Army researchers could not be identified as being present also in non-irradiated foods. The six substances were found in beef irradiated at 50 kiloGrays, a very high dosage.

The BFIFC concluded that as many as 40 percent of the foods eaten by humans could withstand irradiation, but it estimated that only 10 percent of a typical person's food intake would be irradiated. Even a diet consisting mainly of food irradiated at the low 1 kiloGray level, the committee determined, would not be likely to contain a significant amount of harmful radiolytic products.

The committee therefore declared in its report that food irradiated at dosages not exceeding 1 kiloGray is safe for human consumption and that animal tests are called for only when food is irradiated above 1 kiloGray. However, the committee also concluded that a food constituting only a tiny fraction of the human diet (for instance, a spice like cinnamon) could be irradiated at doses of up to 50 kiloGrays without need for toxicological testing.

The rationale for waiving the requirement for animal-feeding tests at low radiation dosages was that the test substance (irradiated food) consisted of a minute quantity of target material (radiolytic products) diluted in a large amount of non-hazardous matter. Thus, the committee saw no point in conducting tests on hundreds or thousands of laboratory animals if

Preserving Food Throughout the Ages

Irradiation is a relatively recent addition to the long list of food-preservation techniques. Thousands of years ago, humans learned to make many foods last longer by drying them in the sun. Drying, salting, smoking and various fermenting processes were the sole ways of preserving food other than cooking.

Sugar and spices helped make the results more palatable. Only later did research show that smoking and fermentation added potentially harmful chemicals to food. Indeed, some of the earliest food-preservation methods, if introduced in the United States today, would surely be challenged, if not prohibited, by the Food and Drug Administration.

Early in the 19th century, Napoleon was the catalyst for a major food-preservation advance. At the time, food for soldiers and seamen consisted of salt-preserved meat, bread and a few dried items such as beans. The monotonous, vitamin-poor diet led to frequent outbreaks of scurvy. Napoleon, determined to find a reliable way to feed his troops, offered a 12,000-franc prize in 1809 to the person who devised a safe and dependable food-preservation process.

The winner was Nicolas Appert, a French chemist and confectioner, who had observed that food heated in sealed containers was preserved if the container was not reopened or the seal did not leak. Appert and others first used glass bottles, which were replaced by tinned-iron canisters. But since canners of the early 19th century had no knowledge of how food spoiled, their canned goods frequently went bad. It remained for another Frenchman, Louis Pasteur, some 50 years later, to note the relationships between microorganisms and food spoilage — a discovery that largely removed the risk from canning.

The next major advance in food preservation came with Clarence Birdseye's development of freezing techniques in the early 1920s. Birdseye, who worked for the U.S. Fisheries Association, began work on the process in 1917; by 1925 his General Seafoods Co. was producing and selling frozen fish. In 1930 the General Foods Corp., which had bought Birdseye's patent and trademarks, introduced a full line of frozen food products. But canned goods accounted for the bulk of the preserved food market until World War II, when canned-goods shortages helped build a mass market for frozen foods.

Today, fresh fruits and vegetables are preserved for much longer periods by shipping them in trailer trucks that have controlled atmospheres. Air, which contains decay-causing oxygen, is pumped out of the interiors of refrigerated trucks and replaced with inert nitrogen. A head of lettuce will emerge fresh from this atmosphere after up to a three-week storage period.

Freeze-drying is one of the key developments in food preservation since World War II. Water is removed from freeze-dried foods by changing it from a solid (ice) to a gas (water vapor) without letting it pass through the intermediate liquid phase — a process known as sublimation. Freeze-drying takes place in a vacuum at very low temperatures, conditions that help explain its high cost. There is little loss of texture, flavor or nutritional value.

Because freeze-drying is expensive, the World Health Organization concluded that, "Its use seems justified only when the food being processed is very heat-sensitive, and the resulting product must meet the highest possible standards of quality."†

By the 1970s, freeze-drying was widely used for coffee, soup mixes and other dehydrated convenience foods. Some meat is freeze-dried, and other processes keep meats edible for extended periods. Antibiotics added to water-filled chilling tanks, for example, prolong the freshness of poultry.

† World Health Organization, *Food Irradiation: A Technique for Preserving and Improving the Safety of Food* (1988), p. 14.

---

the tests were incapable of providing scientifically useful information.

FDA officials agreed with this analysis. The Bureau of Foods' Irradiated Foods Task Group,* formed later that year, also concluded that toxicology tests on food products irradiated at 1 kiloGray or below are not needed to support a conclusion that such foods are safe to eat.

---

*The Bureau of Foods is now the Center for Food Safety and Applied Nutrition.

The findings of the BFIFC and the task group formed the basis of FDA regulations issued April 18, 1986. These rules (1) allow manufacturers to irradiate fruits and vegetables at doses not exceeding 1 kiloGray to inhibit growth and ripening and destroy insect pests; (2) permit processors to irradiate dry or dehydrated spices and herbs at doses of up to 30 kiloGrays to kill microorganisms; (3) require that irradiated foods be labeled as such at both the

wholesale and retail levels; (4) require that manufacturers maintain records of irradiation and make them available to FDA inspectors; and (5) require that irradiated whole foods be labeled with the words "treated with radiation" or "treated by irradiation" as well as a flowerlike symbol called a "radura." Also incorporated into the April 1986 regulations was a rule issued the previous July approving the irradiation of pork at doses of up to 1 kiloGray to control the trichinosis microorganism.

Two other federal regulations bear on the irradiated food debate. In 1985, the Environmental Protection Agency (EPA) prohibited the use of ethylene dibromide (EDB) as a post-harvest crop fumigant. And in May 1990, the FDA approved the irradiation of poultry at doses of up to 3 kiloGrays. The two actions were seen as a potential bonanza for commercial irradiators. No satisfactory chemical substitute for EDB was at hand when the EPA banned its use, and the poultry industry was reeling from media reports of salmonella contamination. Irradiation, its supporters felt, could easily solve both problems. ■

CURRENT SITUATION

Business Plays It Safe

The hoped-for business opportunities have failed to materialize, however. Instead, major food companies have publicly renounced irradiation, often at the behest of consumer groups like Food & Water and the New York-based Interfaith Center on Corporate Responsibility (ICCR).

The list of corporations that have said no to irradiation includes food manufacturers like Beechnut, Kellogg's, Kraft and Ralston Purina; poultry producers like ConAgra, Foster Farms, Perdue and Pilgrim's Pride; fast-food restaurant empires like Arby's, Kentucky Fried Chicken, McDonald's and Pizza Hut; and supermarket chains like A & P, Kroger, Pathmark and Publix.

A company joining the non-irradiation faction typically does so with a terse statement. For instance, Publix Super Markets Inc. says only that it "will not sell any irradiated produce, meat, seafood. We listen to our customers, and our customers are telling us they do not want these irradiated products." The McDonald's Corp.'s policy, first enunciated in its 1989 annual report, simply says the company "does not use irradiated food products in the preparation of food sold at McDonald's restaurants."

Corporate policy on irradiation, as on any other business practice, is not necessarily engraved in stone. Public relations Director Ron Bottrell of the Quaker Oats Co. says his company won't use irradiated foods "until consumer confidence in the process reaches a level where we feel more comfortable with it."

Quaker Oats adopted its policy, Bottrell says, after telling a consumer group about five years ago that one of its varieties of Rice-a-Roni contained irradiated mushroom bits. The disclosure triggered a consumer boycott, which in turn prodded Quaker Oats executives into action. Zapped mushroom bits were "not something we wanted to stake our consumer loyalty and company reputation on," says Bottrell.

In some parts of the country, selling irradiated food is against the law. New Jersey and New York enacted two-year bans in 1989, and Maine approved a permanent ban.* At the local level, Cleveland, Ohio, and its suburb of Lakewood have prohibited the distribution of irradiated food products. Michael Colby of Food & Water says similar legislation is under study in Maryland, North Carolina, Vermont and Philadelphia.

---

*New York has extended its ban for another two years. The New Jersey ban, which expired Jan. 1, has not been renewed. However, Michael Colby of Food & Water says he expects an extension bill to be approved during the current session of the Legislature.

Florida's New Plant

Despite the many obstacles in their path, food irradiation proponents can point to some successes. The most noteworthy of these was the opening this January of the nation's first food-irradiation plant in Mulberry, Fla.

Cobalt 60, the plant's radiation source, is embedded in thin rods called "pencils." When not in use, the rods are submerged in water that shields workers from radiation. To protect outsiders, the room housing the radiation apparatus is encased in concrete walls six to eight feet thick.

Products to be irradiated move on conveyor belts to the source, which is hoisted out of the water by remote control when needed. The radiation dose depends not only on time of exposure but also distance from the source. Food items needing only a small dose can move through the irradiator continuously. Items like poultry, which needs a larger dose, might pause briefly at the source to get the required exposure.

Delivering the correct radiation dosage is crucial, since different foods require different amounts of radiation to produce the desired result. If less than the intended dosage is applied, the intended effect — destruction of microorganisms, say — may not be achieved. Conversely, an excessive dose may spoil the food product's taste and texture, making it unmarketable.

Vindicator opened the Mulberry plant in the wake of a hostile media campaign by Food & Water. One of the group's radio spots, which were broadcast on more than 50 Florida radio stations, attracted particular attention. "What if you found out those fresh fruits and vegetables everyone keeps telling you to eat more of might kill you?" a male voice asked. "No joke. Because supermarkets have started selling radiation-exposed foods."

The campaign seems to have had

Limited Global Acceptance of Irradiated Foods

Food irradiation inspires at least as much debate overseas as it does in the United States. Though the process has been endorsed by three specialized agencies of the United Nations — the Food and Agriculture Organization, the International Atomic Energy Agency and the World Health Organization — the official policies of individual U.N. member countries vary considerably.

Some 35 nations permit food irradiation, with South Africa and Thailand the most tolerant users. Each has authorized the irradiation of 18 different food items, more than any other country. Indeed, only South Africa sanctions the irradiation of bananas, avocados, litchi nuts, almonds, cheese powder and ginger. (Worldwide, the three foods most commonly irradiated are spices, onions and potatoes.)

At the opposite end of the scale is Japan, which only permits irradiating potatoes, a fringe component of the rice-based Japanese diet. Japan prohibits the importation of all irradiated foods.

Four Eastern European countries — Bulgaria, Czechoslovakia, Hungary and Poland — have approved food irradiation only on an experimental, provisional or test-marketing basis. A second cluster of nations has effectively banned the practice, including Australia, Denmark, Germany, Luxembourg, New Zealand and Sweden.

In the United States, the campaign against food irradiation has been led by organizations such as Food & Water, the Interfaith Center on Corporate Responsibility and antinuclear groups. Similar groups abroad also have adopted the cause. The International Organization of Consumers' Unions, representing consumer groups in 70 countries, including the United States, is seeking a global moratorium on food irradiation until a reliable testing method is devised to tell whether food has been irradiated.

---

little impact at Laurenzo's Italian Market in North Miami Beach. Owner David Laurenzo says that customers shopping for strawberries seemed more concerned about price than about radiation. When the irradiated berries went on sale Jan. 25, he says, they were priced at $2 a pint to reflect the Vindicator processing fee; non-irradiated berries were $1.89. On the first day of the sale, Laurenzo's sold 400 pints of irradiated berries and 600 pints of untreated berries.

After Laurenzo's lowered the price of irradiated berries to $1.89, they sold at roughly the same volume as non-irradiated ones. And when the store re-ordered non-irradiated berries and priced them at $2.19 a pint, the remaining irradiated berries — still priced at $1.89 — outsold them. Through all the price fluctuations, the cartons containing the irradiated berries were labeled in accordance with FDA rules, and literature summarizing the pros and cons of irradiation was posted nearby.

According to Laurenzo, no buyers of the irradiated strawberries complained afterward about their taste or texture: "The widest response was, 'What's the big deal? If you want to buy them, buy them. If you don't, don't.'"

Meanwhile, the Vindicator irradiation plant is keeping busy, according to Executive Vice President Harley Everett. He says that the plant has run tests on "probably two dozen different kinds of foods" and has done commercial processing of citrus fruit, tomatoes, dry ingredients, spices and packaging.

Food & Water representatives, who have monitored the plant since January from a nearby rented apartment, report seeing only sporadic evidence of irradiation orders being filled. From mid-January to March 1, they say they observed only five trucks, believed to be carrying irradiated produce, leaving the premises. Concluded Michael Upledger, managing editor of the Food & Water newsletter: "The food industry and consumers appear to be giving Vindicator and the irradiation technology a resounding 'no thank you.'" [15] ■

OUTLOOK

Poultry Irradiation

To become a significant force in food processing, irradiators will first have to overcome the deep-seated resistance of many consumers. They also will need to move beyond their precarious beachhead in seasonal produce and begin handling year-round foods like meat, poultry and seafood. Industry executives recognize this, but the required government approval for some irradiation uses still is lacking. In addition, meat, poultry and seafood producers are wary of irradiation because of the consumer backlash it might unleash.

All the same, food-irradiation advocates discern a few hopeful signs. On May 6, for example, the Agriculture Department issued proposed regulations permitting the irradiation of raw poultry products to kill disease-causing bacteria. The rules implement the FDA

In Search of Alternatives

Food irradiation, opponents say, is essentially a matter of choice. Michael Jacobson, executive director of the Center for Science in the Public Interest, puts it this way: "Is there, for any proposed use of irradiation, another approach that is about as effective, about as economical, about as safe?"

Sweden, for example, has "pretty much eliminated dangerous bacteria from poultry by taking a systems approach," Jacobson says, "making sure that chicken feed and breeder stocks are free of salmonella, cleaning chicken coops to protect them from bird droppings and rat pellets that can spread bacterial diseases."

The Swedish method might not yield such satisfying results in the United States, Jacobson acknowledges. "Sweden lies in a very northern latitude. Conditions there are different from, say, summertime Arkansas, where the heat makes it easier for bacteria to spread." Also, he notes, many more chickens are raised and slaughtered in the United States than in Sweden. Still, Jacobson thinks that added attention to cleanliness "can go a considerable way toward reducing salmonella" in the U.S. poultry industry.

Michael Colby, executive director of the anti-irradiation group Food & Water, recommends that the seafood industry follow a similar course. Instead of relying on irradiation, he says, "Cook seafood correctly. Inspect seafood. Get the federal government inspecting seafood, and let's not allow seafood to be caught or trapped in filthy waters."

Chemical alternatives to irradiation also are available to combat food contamination, opponents say. At the International Poultry Exposition in Atlanta, Ga., in January, Rhône-Poulenc Inc., an agricultural-chemical maker, described a dipping treatment that may offer a simple, effective and inexpensive answer to the salmonella problem.

The treatment calls for immersing poultry carcasses for 15 seconds in a solution of trisodium phosphate (TSP).

"At this stage, we do not claim that this treatment eliminates salmonella," said Bill Swartz, the firm's director of technology. "But we have consistently demonstrated [significant] reductions in salmonella counts in inoculated chickens."† Moreover, the company claims that tests at Pennsylvania State University's Sensory Laboratory showed TSP had no discernible effect on poultry taste, texture or color.

Before the TSP process can be used commercially in the United States, Rhône-Poulenc will have to obtain clearance from the FDA and the Agriculture Department. Confident that approval will be forthcoming, the company says it expects the process to be in widespread use in about 18 months.

Meanwhile, Dr. Donald B. Louria, chairman of the department of preventive medicine and community health at Rutgers University's School of Medicine and Dentistry in Newark, N.J., feels genetic engineering will produce many of the purported benefits of food irradiation. The technology recently received a boost from the FDA, which announced on May 25 that foods developed through genetic modification are not inherently hazardous and, with rare exceptions, should not require extraordinary testing and regulation before going on the market.

"Some people think it will be a long time before genetically altered food is available," says Louria. "I don't. I think we'll start having it two or three years from now."

---

† Quoted in "Poultry Treatment Puts Big Chill on Salmonella," *Prepared Foods*, March 1992, p. 88.

regulation of May 1990 permitting the irradiation of raw poultry at doses of up to 3 kiloGrays. The deadline for public comment on the Agriculture Department proposal is July 6.

Vindicator's Everett welcomed the department's move, saying: "That's the main reason we built the plant. We expect poultry to become our largest-volume product. 'Pasteurizing' poultry is something that's been necessary forever."

According to Pattison of the pro-irradiation group Consumer Alert, irradiated poultry could become a popular product among the elderly. "I can't tell you how many elderly people have contacted us out of concern over salmonella in poultry," he says. "I have the feeling that some older people are not eating chicken or turkey right now because of that fear."[16]

Calls for More Research

The poultry question is not the only food-irradiation issue currently under consideration at the Agriculture Department. Sen. Patrick J. Leahy, D-Vt., chairman of the Senate Agriculture Committee, on May 4 asked Agriculture Secretary Edward Madigan to commission a study by the National Research Council's board of agriculture "to determine if irradiation is an appropriate means of food preservation."

This is the sort of study that food-irradiation foes have been demanding for years. As the operating arm of the National Academy of Sciences and the National Academy of Engineering, the research council commands great respect in both governmental and scholarly circles.

Continued on p. 520

At Issue:

Is irradiated food safe to eat?

SCOTT PATTISON

Executive director, Consumer Alert, Inc.
FROM *CONSUMER ALERT STATEMENT,* NOV. 4, 1991

*t*hroughout history, advances in technology have served to improve the quality of life for all people. New technologies lead to improved products, a cleaner environment, increased efficiency and lower prices. We must avoid emotional responses to new technology and calmly and rationally look at the scientific research involving the new technology.

We must not forget that there were those who vigorously opposed, on safety grounds, the introduction of electricity, the use of the automobile and even the pasteurization of milk. Today it may sound strange that anyone would oppose the pasteurization of milk — but several decades ago many did. Now we demand that our milk be pasteurized and we recognize that pasteurization prevents us from ingesting life-threatening food-borne diseases....

Food irradiation merely involves the purifying of food by ionizing energy.... The process has been found to be completely safe and is endorsed by the American Medical Association, the World Health Organization and the United Nations Food and Agriculture Organization. The technology is in widespread use in over 30 developed countries around the world. Millions of people throughout the world safely consume irradiated food each and every day for protection from contaminated food.

The U.S. Department of Agriculture has approved this process (which does not make food radioactive, by the way) for treatment of spices, grains, fruits, vegetables, pork and poultry. The full weight of creditable scientific authority stands behind the safety of irradiation....

Food irradiation was first used during World War II, and later for patients with low resistance to infection and, more recently, for astronauts in the space program. The food industry has taken its time to get around to irradiation because there are a variety of other, equally safe, ways to protect foodstuffs today. Nevertheless, irradiation technology shows such particular promise, that its time has come.

Nutritional values of foods are always affected to some degree during any kind of processing. Irradiation is no exception. But repeated tests have shown that the nutritional value of irradiated foods is *not* significantly impaired. Irradiated food is as good as any foods processed by any other commercial method used today.

RICHARD PICCIONI

Senior staff scientist, Accord Research and Educational Associates
FROM CONGRESSIONAL TESTIMONY, JUNE 19, 1987

*w*e feel that there is no assurance in the scientific literature or the arguments of the FDA [Food and Drug Administration] that the widespread irradiation of food will not be a significant, if silent, threat to the public health. In summary, we feel the FDA has adopted scientifically indefensible criteria for assessing, and in their view, demonstrating, the safety of irradiated foods.

Treatment of food with ionizing radiation presents issues of food safety qualitatively unlike those posed by any other food-processing method or food additive. The large amount of energy contained in ionizing radiation provides the potential for exceedingly complex chemical transformation of food components, including the production of mutagenic or carcinogenic substances which were not present, or were present in far smaller amounts, before irradiation.

This potential far exceeds that of ordinary heat processing, microwave radiation, etc., because the energy contained in each "quantum" of gamma radiation is so great. At the same time, because the production of these "radiolytic products" takes place within the food itself, it is impossible to design a toxicological test in which animals are exposed to exaggerated doses of these products, the chemical identity of which remains largely unknown. Thus toxicologists are limited to biological testing which is thousands of times less sensitive than the testing typically required of other chemical additives or pesticide residues.

It should be clearly understood that without toxicological testing at exaggerated doses, the carcinogenic risk to large human populations ingesting any additive or residue is impossible to assess. Exposure of test animals to exaggerated doses is the most basic tool in use in estimating carcinogenic risk. In the case of food irradiation, this tool is simply not available.

At the same time, evidence from other types of experiments provides a strong indication that mutagens and/or carcinogens are indeed present in irradiated foods. What such experiments are unable to provide, however, is a quantitative estimate of the risk. In the absence of such an estimate, it is completely irresponsible to proceed with the sale and distribution of irradiated foods. Consequently ... approvals by the FDA for food-irradiation processing should be immediately rescinded.

Continued from p. 518

Leahy suggested that the proposed study should cover such issues as (1) the dangers, if any, to consumers from changes in food caused by irradiation; (2) the potential health impact of irradiation-caused nutritional losses; (3) the relative costs and benefits of alternative food-preservation methods; and (4) the dangers to workers and community residents from the transport, use and disposal of radioactive materials. Whether the study will in fact take place depends largely on the availability of financing.

The main value of a National Research Council study, says Michael Jacobson, is that it "can address, to some extent, social values that the FDA really doesn't take into account. It can look at alternatives. It's not the FDA's job to look at alternatives. All it does is determine whether a particular substance is safe or not."

The broader scope of a research council study, in Jacobson's view, "certainly would give Congress a foundation on which to build a policy. If the council said food irradiation is safe — no nutritional concerns, no toxicological concerns — that certainly would pull the rug out from under the critics." Jacobson thinks the council might also decide to call attention to the various trade-offs involved. For instance, it could stress that the bacteria-killing power of irradiation comes at the cost of accepting some risk to workers.

Looking further ahead, expert opinion on food irradiation spans the spectrum of possibility. Pattison, who is optimistic, feels the process will become "accepted and common" within the next 10 years. At the same time, though, he believes irradiation "will never be a huge, major industry."

Whatever the outcome, Pattison says it should be shaped by free-market forces. "If irradiation is deemed safe, and I believe it has been, then we should allow it to be used. But if the market determines there are oth-

er, more effective ways to preserve food and prevent contamination, then we should allow that to happen."

Jacobson is more skeptical, saying he doesn't see "anything more than very limited use of irradiation" over the next few years. Some unforeseen public-health catastrophe could alter public opinion, he says, citing a hypothetical mass outbreak of salmonella from contaminated chicken. Barring that, Jacobson says he hopes popular pressure for safer food "stimulates the kind of research that's needed to come up with alternatives" to irradiation.

Some irradiation critics say that cost considerations will inevitably limit the industry's prospects. According to Professors Noel F. Sommer and F. Gordon Mitchell of the University of California-Davis department of pomology,* a food-irradiation plant must operate around the clock, every day of the year, to take full advantage of its capital investment. That is because the radioactive isotopes used cannot be switched on and off; they decay whether they are in use or not.

"The peak period of harvesting and handling most fruits and vegetables seldom exceeds five months at any location," Sommer and Mitchell noted. "It is not certain to what use irradiation facilities could be placed during the off-season. At present, there are few commercial uses for irradiation other than sterilizing surgical and medical equipment, spices and a limited amount of packaging."[17]

The fact that some foods do not respond well to irradiation also crimps the industry's potential. For instance, the taste and odor of irradiated milk and dairy products have been described as "chalky" or "scorched." Fatty and oily foods also suffer, ending up as "musty" or "nutty."

The bleakest prediction about food irradiation comes from Michael Colby

of Food & Water. What the nuclear establishment and the irradiation industry "want more than anything," he says, "is for Food & Water and the millions of consumers who actively oppose this technology to go away." That is not going to happen, he vows: "We will always be around to monitor the situation and educate consumers and the food industry about irradiation's dangers."

The irradiation industry "is not dead right now," Colby concedes. "But," he insists, "it's dying." ∎

Notes

[1] World Health Organization, *Food Irradiation: A Technique for Preserving and Improving the Safety of Food* (1988), p. 48.

[2] Consumer Alert statement concerning the food-irradiation plant in Mulberry, Fla., Nov. 4, 1991. Pattison's office is in Arlington, Va.

[3] John McClung, "Irradiation and 20/20," *Produce Business*, January 1992, p. 6.

[4] From *The Facts of Food Irradiation*, an undated white paper prepared by the Coalition for Food Irradiation.

[5] Tony Webb, Tim Lang and Kathleen Tucker, *Food Irradiation: Who Wants It?* (1987), p. 30.

[6] Letter to the editor in *Chemical and Engineering News*, Jan. 2, 1986.

[7] Quoted in *USA Today*, Feb. 24, 1992.

[8] Testimony before House Subcommittee on Health and the Environment, June 19, 1987.

[9] Donald B. Louria, "Zapping the Food Supply," *The Bulletin of the Atomic Scientists*, September 1990, pp. 34-35.

[10] For background on the nuclear waste issue, see "Will Nuclear Power Get Another Chance?" *Editorial Research Reports*, Feb. 22, 1991, pp. 123-124.

[11] American Council on Science and Health, *Irradiated Foods*, December 1988, p. 18.

[12] Thomas G. Martin III, "Radiation Protection and Health Physics in Food Irradiation Facilities," in Edward S. Josephson and Martin S. Peterson, eds., *Preservation of Food by Ionizing Radiation*, (1981), vol. I, p. 249.

[13] George H. Pauli and Clyde A. Takeguchi, "Irradiation of Foods — An FDA Perspective," *Food Reviews International*, 1986, p. 81.

[14] A. P. Brunetti, et al., *Recommendations for Evaluating the Safety of Irradiated Foods*, U.S. Food and Drug Administration, 1980.

[15] Michael Upledger, "Vindicator Opens," *Safe Food News*, spring 1992, p. 11.

[16] For background, see "How Safe Is Your Food?" *Editorial Research Reports*, Nov. 18, 1988, pp. 581-596.

[17] Noel F. Sommer and F. Gordon Mitchell, "Gamma Irradiation — a Quarantine Treatment for Fresh Fruits and Vegetables?" *HortScience*, June 1986, p. 359.

*Pomology is the science and practice of fruit growing.

Bibliography

Selected Sources Used

Books

Derosier, Norman W., *The Technology of Food Preservation*, The Avi Publishing Company Inc., 1970.

Derosier treats irradiation as just one of several food-preservation techniques developed over the centuries. His tone throughout is dispassionate, making it easier for readers to evaluate irradiation as an alternative to the preservation methods that preceded it.

Josephson, Edward S. and Martin S. Peterson, *Preservation of Food by Ionizing Radiation*, CRC Press Inc., 1982.

This three-volume work is mainly for specialists. However, it also contains a valuable historical survey of food irradiation and an examination of radiation-protection issues.

Murray, David R., *Biology of Food Irradiation*, Research Studies Press Inc., 1990.

Murray, who wrote this after serving as the Australian Conservation Foundation's representative on the Consumers' Health Forum, often is vitriolic in his criticism of food irradiation, which tends to undermine his arguments.

Webb, Tony; Tim Lang; and Kathleen Tucker, *Food Irradiation: Who Wants It?* Thorsons Publishers Inc., 1987.

As the title of the book makes clear, the co-authors are no fans of food irradiation. They conclude: "Only coordinated local and national campaigns involving a broad coalition of interests ... can bring about the moratorium on further developments and the public review of all the risks and benefits that is now urgently needed."

Articles

Begley, Sharon (with Elizabeth Roberts), "Dishing Up Gamma Rays: Are the Benefits of Irradiated Food Worth the Risks?" *Newsweek*, Jan. 27, 1992.

In effect, Begley answers the question posed in the title of her article with a slightly qualified "no."

Blumenthal, Dale, "Food Irradiation: Toxic to Bacteria, Safe for Humans," *FDA Consumer*, November 1990.

With an even hand, Blumenthal reviews the arguments for and against irradiated food. There are useful quotes from professional publications not available in most public or school libraries.

Hecht, Marjorie Mazel, "First U.S. Food Irradiation Plant Opens in Florida," *21st Century*, fall 1991.

Hecht, who writes frequently on food irradiation, provides an upbeat account of the January opening of the Vindicator irradiation plant at Mulberry, Fla.

Leslie, Jacques, "Food Irradiation: Emotional Opposition Persists in the Face of Scientific Evidence that the Process Is Harmless," *The Atlantic*, September 1990.

Scientific opinion is nowhere near as heavily in favor of food irradiation as Leslie appears to think. But he sets forth the chief arguments of both sides with clarity and fairness.

Sommer, Noel F., and Gordon F. Mitchell, "Gamma Radiation — A Quarantine Treatment for Fresh Fruits and Vegetables?" *HortScience* (monthly journal of the American Society for Horticultural Science), June 1986.

Sommer and Mitchell, professors of pomology (the science of raising fruit) at the University of California at Davis, contend that the effects of irradiation on fruits and vegetables are more damaging than irradiation proponents say.

Warren, Anita, "Radiation Phobia: It Could Be Hazardous to Your Health," *Nuclear Industry*, third quarter 1991.

The main focus of the article is people's fears about the medical applications of radioactive substances. But similar fears underlie the widespread popular resistance to irradiated food.

Reports and Studies

American Council on Science and Health, *Irradiated Foods* (third edition, December 1988).

The council lays out the case for irradiated food in a brisk, easy-to-read manner. Critics' complaints about the technology are noted but not dealt with in detail.

Subcommittee on Health and Environment, U.S. House Committee on Energy and Commerce, *Food Irradiation* (published proceedings of hearing held June 19, 1987).

Various witnesses offer sharply opposed views on food irradiation, including several experts whose views are most often cited in professional journals and the media.

World Health Organization, *Food Irradiation*, 1988.

This is a relatively straightforward presentation of the pros and cons of food irradiation. The reader should bear in mind, however, that WHO has long been a strong supporter of the technology.

The Next Step

Additional Articles from Current Periodicals from EBSCO Publishing's Database

Books & reading

Unklesbay, N., "Books," *Journal of the American Dietetic Association,* **May 1991, p. 626.**

Reviews the book "Biology of Food Irradiation," by David R. Murray.

Debates & issues

"Divine intervention," *Consumer Alert,* **November 1990, p. 3.**

Discusses Mulberry, Fla.'s, decision to allow the installation of a food irradiation plant to preserve citrus for export. Town council initially turned down request after the town was visited by New Jersey-based anti-nuclear organization Food & Water.

Abramov, V., "Food irradiation — scientists' toy or everyman's joy?" *World Health,* **April 1989, p. 28.**

Discusses the health benefits of new food irradiation technology. Public fear of irradiation due to lack of education about the process; importance of the procedure for world food supplies.

Begley, S. and E. Roberts, "Dishing up gamma rays," *Newsweek,* **Jan. 27, 1992, p. 52.**

Questions whether the benefits of irradiated food are worth the risk. Cites example of Vindicator of Florida Inc.; the appeal of irradiated food; opposition; estimates from the U.S. Food and Drug Administration; threat to workers and the public; how an irradiation facility works; additional details.

Evans, S. J., "Processed progress?" *History Today,* **July 1990, p. 4.**

Looks at possible food catastrophes of the present. Overprocessed foods; irradiation; London Science Museum's "Food for Thought" exhibition.

Godfrey, E. H., "Zapping chickens," *American Health,* **September 1990, p. 90.**

Examines the use of irradiation to kill salmonella in poultry and questions irradiation safety. Details.

Hirshorn, S., "Food irradiation," *Canadian Consumer,* **1990 No. 3, p. 39.**

Studies the controversy over the risks and advantages of food irradiation. Why certain foods are irradiated; critics' charges that the process is unnecessary and unsafe; policy statement on food irradiation issued by the Consumers' Association of Canada (CAC); consumer reaction to the process. INSETS: Irradiation: How safe for workers and the environment?; approvals and controversies.

Kretchmar, L. and A. E. Serwer, "Did Sam Whitley zap shareholders?" *Fortune,* **March 23, 1992, p. 121.**

Reports that Sam Whitley, the folksy chief executive officer (CEO) of tiny Vindicator of Florida Inc., is betting he will hit paydirt with a food preservation process called irradiation. However, Whitley may be guilty of misleading shareholders in his company.

Lamb, L., "Food irradiation meets the opposition," *Utne Reader,* **July/August 1990, p. 20.**

Discusses developments around food irradiation, including states which have banned irradiated food; FDA approval of irradiating poultry; a 1988 radiation leak at the Decatur, Ga., plant of Radiation Sterilizers Inc.

Leslie, J. and A. E. Cober, "Food irradiation," *The Atlantic,* **September 1990, p. 26.**

Discusses the emotional opposition to food irradiation that persists in spite of scientific evidence that the process is harmless. Kills salmonella and other harmful bacteria; extended shelf life; radiolytic products (RPs) in low concentrations; opponents' arguments and tactics.

Rohter, L., "Era of irradiated foods nears as qualms persist," *The New York Times,* **Jan. 21, 1992, p. A1.**

Reports that the first food irradiation plant in the U.S. now stands ready for service. Many scientists regard irradiation of food as a safe and efficient way to retard spoilage and kill organisms that cause illness, and they think it will help both growers and consumers. But opponents argue that "zapping the food supply" robs food of some of its nutritional value and requires the use of dangerous nuclear material — perhaps increasing the risk of cancer and birth defects.

Weiss, R. "The gamma-ray gourmet," *Science News,* **Dec. 19, 1987 and Dec. 26, 1987, p. 398.**

The technology of irradiation of fresh foods with gamma rays as a means of extending shelf life is stimulating a nationwide debate over its safety and usefulness. Discusses the advantages and disadvantages of food irradiation.

International aspects

Dickman, S., "Compromise eludes EC," *Nature,* Jan. 24, 1991, p. 273.

States that the European Community (EC) has once again failed to gain community-wide approval for food irradiation. General application of the technique remains controversial; negotiations broken down over the labelling of products containing irradiated food.

Rao, R., "Limited use approved in India," *Nature,* Nov. 23, 1989, p. 334.

Reports that India's National Monitoring Agency has approved limited irradiation tests to kill bacteria that cause food deterioration. Past controversy; plans.

Law & legislation

"Comment on proposed FDA regulations in the 1980s," *FDA Consumer,* September 1990, p. 6.

Reports on consumer reactions to four proposed Food and Drug Administration regulations on: irradiated foods, biological products, food labeling, and sulfites in food.

"Update on federal regulations," *Journal of the American Dietetic Association,* July 1990, p. 931.

Provides an update on federal regulations for a variety of dietetics-related concerns. Food labeling; minor ingredients need not be listed in quantitative order; irradiation labeling; irradiation of poultry; "spices" defined; GRAS ("generally regarded as safe") binding and flavoring agents in meat and poultry; sulfites on fresh potatoes loses GRAS status; FD&C Red No. 3 ruling; low-fat dairy formulations.

Blumenthal, D., "Food irradiation," *FDA Consumer,* November 1990, p. 11.

Reports that the Food and Drug Administration recently issued a rule defining the use of irradiation as a safe and effective means of controlling salmonella and other food-borne bacteria in raw poultry. Poultry and illness; explanation of the irradiation process; consumer concern. INSETS: Poultry producers respond; measuring irradiation.

Research

Zeman, N. and L. Howard, "Beagle rays," *Newsweek,* Nov. 12, 1990, p. 5.

Notes that for 27 years, the Department of Energy conducted experiments in which 3,700 beagles were exposed to radiation in order to study its effects. Dogs fed radiation-laden food for a year and a half and left to live out their lives; conclusion that exposure to low-level radiation isn't so dangerous.

Signs & symbols

Brown, P. L., "In a world of symbols, one brings confusion," *The New York Times,* Jan. 30, 1992, p. C1.

Discusses the government-approved symbol for fool irradiation, a process in which food is treated with gamma rays produced by radioactive cobalt. The symbol, known as the radura, depicts a leafy flower enclosed in a half-broken circle, and will be required on all packages of meat and produce that have been irradiated. But some consumer advocates think the design is too friendly.

Back Issues

Great Research on Current Issues Starts Right Here... Recent topics covered by The CQ Researcher are listed below. Issues dated before May 10, 1991, were published under the name of Editorial Research Reports.

DECEMBER 1990
Cable TV Regulation
Americans' Search for Their Roots
Is Insurance System a Failure?
Why Schools Still Have Tracking

JANUARY 1991
Growing Influence of Boycotts
Should the U.S. Reinstate the Draft?
America's Archaeological Past
Peace Corps' Challenges in '90s

FEBRUARY 1991
Regional Impact of Recession
Puerto Rico's Status
Redistricting: Mapping Power
Nuclear Power

MARCH 1991
Acid Rain
Cost of the Gulf War
Reassessing Gun Laws
Future for Man in Space

APRIL 1991
Social Security
Canadian Crisis Over Quebec
California Drought
Electromagnetic Radiation

MAY 1991
School Choice
Racial Quotas
Animal Rights
U.S. and Japan

JUNE 1991
Children and Divorce
Teenage Suicide
Endangered Species
Europe 1992

JULY 1991
Teenagers and Abortion
Soviet Republics Rebel
Mexico's Emergence
Athletes and Drugs

AUGUST 1991
Sexual Harassment
Fetal Tissue Research
Oil Imports
The Palestinians

SEPTEMBER 1991
Police Brutality
Advertising Under Attack
Saving the Forests
Foster Care Crisis

OCTOBER 1991
Pay-Per-View TV
Youth Gangs
Gene Therapy
World Hunger

NOVEMBER 1991
Fast-Food Shake-Up
The Greening of Eastern Europe
Business' Role in Education
Cuba In Crisis

DECEMBER 1991
Retiree Health Benefits
Asian Americans
The Obscenity Debate
The Disabilities Act

JANUARY 1992
Term Limits
Oil Spills
Hunting Controversy
Alternative Medicine

FEBRUARY 1992
Threatened Coastlines
New Era in Asia
Assisted Suicide
Jobs in the '90s

MARCH 1992
Women and Sports
Underage Drinking
Garbage Crisis
Mafia Crackdown

APRIL 1992
Ozone Depletion
Welfare Reform
Politicians and Privacy
Illegal Immigration

MAY 1992
Native Americans
Jobs vs. Environment
Too Many Lawsuits?
Fairness in Salaries

JUNE 1992
Nuclear Proliferation

Back issues are available for $4.00 (subscribers) or $7.00 (non-subscribers). Quantity discounts apply to orders over ten. To order, call Congressional Quarterly 1-800-432-2250.

Future Topics

▶ *Lead Poisoning*

▶ *Hard Times for Libraries*

▶ *Prescription Drug Prices*

PUBLISHED BY CONGRESSIONAL QUARTERLY INC., IN CONJUNCTION WITH EBSCO PUBLISHING

Lead Poisoning

Are children suffering because of weak prevention efforts?

W ELL OVER A DECADE AFTER THE FEDERAL government banned most leaded paint and ordered leaded gasoline phased out, the number of children defined as victims of lead poisoning is actually growing. That's because health officials now know that even low levels of lead can cause serious permanent neurological problems. They also know that particles of lead — one of the most toxic substances in the environment — can be found almost anywhere, often spread by tailpipe emissions from cars that used leaded gasoline. Critics of efforts to control lead poisoning say not enough is being done and that children — particularly minority children living in run-down inner-city housing — are needlessly suffering from what health officials call the most preventable of all childhood diseases.

 June 19, 1992 • Volume 2, No. 23 • 525-548

Formerly Editorial Research Reports

COVER ART: BARBARA SASSA-DANIELS

June 19, 1992
Volume 2, No. 23

EDITOR
Sandra Stencel

MANAGING EDITOR
Thomas J. Colin

ASSOCIATE EDITOR
Richard L. Worsnop

STAFF WRITERS
Charles S. Clark
Mary H. Cooper
Rodman D. Griffin

PRODUCTION EDITOR
Laurie De Maris

EDITORIAL ASSISTANT
Michael M. Taylor

GRAPHICS
Jack Auldridge

PUBLISHED BY
Congressional Quarterly Inc.

CHAIRMAN
Andrew Barnes

VICE CHAIRMAN
Andrew P. Corty

EDITOR AND PUBLISHER
Neil Skene

EXECUTIVE EDITOR
Robert W. Merry

PUBLICATIONS MARKETING/SALES
Robert Smith

EDITOR, EBSCO PUBLISHING
Melissa Kummerer

The CQ Researcher (ISSN 1056-2036). Formerly Editorial Research Reports. Published weekly (48 times per year, not printed the first Friday of any month with five Fridays) by Congressional Quarterly Inc., 1414 22nd St., N.W., Washington, D.C. 20037. Rates are furnished upon request. Second-class postage paid at Washington, D.C. POSTMASTER: Send address changes to The CQ Researcher, 1414 22nd St., N.W., Washington, D.C. 20037.

Lead Poisoning

BY MARY H. COOPER

THE ISSUES

Three-year-old Beverly Mielke was not the stereotypical victim of lead poisoning. She wasn't Hispanic or African American. She didn't live in a run-down, inner-city housing project. And she hadn't ingested flaking paint by putting her dirty fingers in her mouth. In fact, she came from a middle-class family in St. Paul, Minn., and probably had never even come in contact with the peeling paint so often associated with lead poisoning. Beverly was poisoned in the sandbox at her neighborhood day-care center.

Beverly was lucky. The source of her poisoning in 1984 was discovered early, and she didn't suffer permanent injury. But her father, Howard Mielke, a toxicologist, was so appalled by the ease with which his daughter had been exposed to harmful levels of lead that he launched a statewide investigation of lead in the environment.[1]

He discovered that dangerous amounts of this highly toxic metal can be found almost anywhere.* One of the main sources, Mielke found, was lead particles that had been spewed from the tailpipes of cars and trucks that used leaded gasoline. As a result, areas near busy roadways — including playgrounds, sidewalks and back yards — are often so tainted that they far exceed federal lead-pollution standards for hazardous-waste dumps. Yet federal laws do not require such places to be monitored or cleaned up.

Like Howard Mielke, other middle-class parents are finding to their sur-

prise and horror that lead is poisoning their children, often leading to permanent neurological damage — and in rare cases death. The exposure often comes not from paint chips, once considered the main source of lead poisoning, nor tailpipes, but from the lead-laden paint dust produced during old-house renovations. Young children — who are more susceptible to lead poisoning than adults because their nervous systems are still developing — inhale the dust or ingest it with contaminated food after layers of old lead-based paint are sanded and scraped.

"In general, these cases are increasing somewhat," says Dr. John F. Rosen, a pediatrician at Montefiore Medical Center's lead-poisoning center in New York City. "Most frequently, they involve old, stately homes outside the city, usually in rather affluent suburbs such as Westchester County, homes that the parents have purchased without any knowledge of the real possibility of leaded paint being present."

Such cases illustrate one of the

most heartbreaking ironies in the field of public health. Well over a decade after the federal government took steps to eliminate lead from paint and gasoline — two of the leading sources of lead in the environment — lead poisoning in children appears to be far more serious than previously thought.[2]

The federal actions, to be sure, dramatically lowered the average blood-lead levels in children after 1980, from 12.8 micrograms per deciliter to about 4 to 6 micrograms, according to the Environmental Protection Agency (EPA). But meanwhile, researchers discovered that even small amounts of lead can cause irreversible damage in children.

Based on these findings, the federal Centers for Disease Control (CDC) last October lowered the threshold blood-lead levels at which children are considered to be poisoned from 25 micrograms to 10 micrograms. Now, the CDC estimates, about 3 million children under age 6 — between 10 and 15 percent of the nation's preschoolers — are victims of lead poisoning. Using the new threshold, that's at least 10 times more children than in 1980.[3]

The newly discovered risks of lead poisoning have attracted widespread media coverage. *Newsweek* magazine, for example, ran a cover story on the situation last July 15. But as these articles point out, there's still scant public awareness of what Dr. Louis W. Sullivan, the secretary of Health and Human Services (HHS), calls "the No. 1 environmental threat to the health of children in the United States."

In its natural state, embedded in ore deposits below the Earth's surface, lead poses no health risks. It is only after lead is mined and applied to products ranging from curtain weights to batteries that it becomes a problem. That makes lead poisoning,

---

*Mielke, now a professor of toxicology at Xavier University of Louisiana, in New Orleans, conducted similar investigations of environmental lead in Louisiana and found comparable pollution levels.

in theory, entirely preventable. "Lead poisoning is the most common preventable disease in the pediatric age group," Rosen says. "I consider it to be a national disgrace that such a widely pervasive condition continues to threaten this country's most important resource for the future, its children."

But because lead is so pervasive, the cost of removing it is enormous. Deciding how best to use limited resources to remove the most dangerous sources of lead is the subject of an ongoing debate among health professionals, policy-makers and manufacturers who produce or use lead. Here are some of the key questions they are wrestling with:

How serious is lead poisoning?

Lead poisoning has been recognized as a potentially fatal condition for centuries — and for decades as a widespread affliction among children of the poor. A potent neurotoxin, lead can disrupt the functioning of many organs, even causing convulsions, coma and death. Among adults, exposure to lead at high enough levels to cause symptoms of poisoning usually occurs at industrial sites where lead is being processed or used in manufacturing. Symptoms of the disease in adults include a loss of hand strength and coordination known as "wrist drop," kidney malfunction, high blood pressure, shortened attention spans and lowered fertility.

Young children, however, are most vulnerable to lead. The metal impedes the development of the central nervous system, causing mental retardation, learning disabilities and behavioral disorders, as well as kidney disease, hearing loss and impaired growth. Poisoning can occur even be-

fore birth if the mother is exposed to lead, because lead in the mother's blood passes through the placenta to the developing fetus.

The lead industry stands virtually alone in disputing lead's effects on human development and health.[4] But the level at which lead becomes toxic has been hotly debated for more than a decade.

Sources of Lead Poisoning

Children in the U.S. are exposed to lead from a variety of sources. However, an estimated 12 million children under 7 were exposed to lead paint, the main source of lead poisoning in children.

Source	Millions of children †
Leaded paint	12.0
Leaded gasoline	5.6
Stationary sources *(lead smelters, factories and buildings that burn recycled oil)*	0.233
Dust/soil *(from all sources)*	5.9-11.0
Water/plumbing	10.4
Food *(contaminated by airborne particles, cooking water and containers)*	1.0

† Children are usually exposed to multiple sources of lead in the environment.
Source: Centers for Disease Control

The controversy erupted in 1979, when Dr. Herbert L. Needleman, a professor of psychiatry and pediatrics at the University of Pittsburgh, found that lead at very low doses causes reduced mental capacity among young children.[5] Other researchers, at least one of whom has received funding from the lead industry, challenged Needleman's findings because of his alleged mishandling of the data. The scientific dispute has raged on ever since, with Needleman's challengers demanding a peer review of the case and Needleman charging them with conflict of interest. *(See story, p. 529.)*

Even as the debate over Needleman's research dragged on through the 1980s, other studies confirmed his

findings. Several federal agencies have acted on these findings in the past two years, issuing a series of strategic plans to reduce children's exposure to lead. This action culminated in the CDC's lowering of the blood-lead level at which a child is defined as poisoned, from 25 micrograms per deciliter to 10 micrograms. At the same time, HHS Secretary Sullivan called for the universal screening of all preschool children, preferably before their first birthday.

Screening for the presence of lead in the blood is usually the only way to detect lead poisoning because the symptoms of the disease are not readily discernible at the lower threshold blood levels that now indicate poisoning. Although the full extent of lead poisoning among the nation's young will be unknown until many more children are screened, the government estimates that 10-15 percent of American children under age 6 have toxic levels of lead. But today, only 10 percent of the children in this age group are screened by doctors and other health-care providers, as the CDC recommends. That means the vast majority of lead-poisoning cases go undetected.

The pace of lead screening may soon pick up. "We recommend that pediatricians pay attention to the CDC statement on lead poisoning, which defines high-risk and low-risk children," says Dr. J. Routt Reigart, chairman of the American Academy of Pediatrics' environmental health committee and director of general pediatrics at the Medical University of South Carolina in Charleston. "If the parents provide positive answers to questions on the quality of housing and other indicators of lead in the environment, the committee feels

A Rare Peek at a Scientific Feud

Charges of scientific misconduct rarely are heard beyond the halls of academia, but a recent case involving research into lead poisoning broke that tradition. Dr. Herbert L. Needleman faced his accusers in an unusual public showdown in April over his groundbreaking research more than a decade ago.

Needleman, a professor of psychiatry and pediatrics at the University of Pittsburgh, reported in the March 1979 issue of *The New England Journal of Medicine* that lead caused serious neurological damage at concentrations far lower than scientists had previously thought. His findings spurred policy-makers to radically reduce threshold blood-lead levels — the concentration of lead in blood considered to constitute poisoning. The findings also spurred the expansion of programs to treat poisoned children and prevent exposure to the highly toxic metal.

Numerous subsequent studies confirmed Needleman's findings of lower IQ scores among Boston schoolchildren exposed to only small amounts of lead. But Claire B. Ernhart, a professor of psychiatry and reproductive biology at Case Western Reserve University in Cleveland, Ohio, and Sandra W. Scarr, a psychologist at the University of Virginia, in Charlottesville, charged that Needleman's methods had been flawed, casting doubt on his conclusions.

Needleman responded to the accusations by pointing out that Ernhart had received funding from the lead industry for her own research and thus had a financial interest in playing down the metal's toxicity. The charges and countercharges escalated into increasingly acerbic exchanges of articles and letters in scientific journals.

The dispute intensified after Ernhart and Scarr gained access to some of Needleman's original data as they prepared to testify as expert witnesses on behalf of the owners of a lead smelter, which the federal government charged with pollution. In a May 1991 appeal to the National Institutes of Health's Office of Scientific Integrity, Ernhart and Scarr claimed the data demonstrated that Needleman had skewed his findings to show a definite link between low-level lead exposure and impaired intellectual development. NIH then presented the case to the University of Pittsburgh, where a panel of scientists recommended a formal investigation.

Normally an inquiry into scientific misconduct would proceed in secret. At Needleman's request, however, the university held a public hearing. The two-day forum left both parties disappointed. Needleman claimed he had been denied a fair trial because he was not allowed to subpoena certain witnesses. Ernhart said she was "appalled" by Needleman's accusation that her objections to his research stemmed from a financial interest in the lead industry.[†]

Many scientists familiar with the dispute side with Needleman. "Recently, [the lead] industry has attempted a revival of its tactics ... to single out one scientist and then to challenge the veracity and integrity of his or her research," testified Dr. Ellen Silbergeld, a toxicologist at the University of Maryland Medical School, at recent congressional hearings on lead toxicity. "The focus of their attack on Herbert Needleman is unsubstantiated, and the tactic of using the NIH process of investigating scientific fraud is deplorable. Dr. Needleman's work was critically reviewed by an EPA expert panel nearly 10 years ago and found to be reliable in design, analysis and interpretation.... Even if industry succeeds in confusing public opinion, its campaign is insufficient."[††]

[†] Quoted by Joseph Palca, "Lead Researcher Confronts Accusers in Public Hearing," *Science*, April 24, 1992.

[††] Silbergeld testified March 27, 1992, before the Senate Governmental Affairs Subcommittee on Consumer and Environmental Affairs.

---

those children need to be tested twice, once at one year of age and again at 18 to 20 months."

Even among children who are diagnosed with lead poisoning, medical treatment of the disease is of limited value, and then only in severe cases. Children with blood-lead levels of more than 35 micrograms per deciliter undergo chelation therapy, which involves the intravenous administration of a chemical that binds with lead in the bloodstream and then is excreted in the urine. But chelation cannot remove all the lead in a child's body; traces end up in the teeth and bones. More important, by the time doctors intervene, the lead usually has caused irreversible neurological damage.

Improvements in chelation therapy may come with a new drug, DMSA, which recently won approval from the Food and Drug Administration (FDA). DMSA can be taken orally and is more effective in binding with lead. Up to now, the drug has been successfully administered in China, mainly in adults.

"For ease of treatment, DMSA potentially offers a major advantage," says Rosen, whose clinic at Montefiore Hospital serves the largest number of lead-poisoned children in the country. "Our concern is that it has been used with a very limited number of kids in the United States, and that oral administration of the drug may actually enhance the absorption of lead into the bloodstream."

Even if the new drug is adopted, Rosen says, all children in his clinic would continue to be hospitalized for

Levels of Childhood Lead Poisoning

Health officials recommend intervention when children have blood-lead levels as low as 10 micrograms per deciliter, the level at which the Centers for Disease Control now says children are considered to be poisoned. The CDC lowered the level last October from 25 micrograms per deciliter.

CDC class	Blood-lead concentration (micrograms per deciliter)	Comment
I	9 or less	A child in class I is not considered to be lead-poisoned.
IIA	10-14	Many children with blood-lead levels in this range should trigger communitywide prevention activities. Children in this range may need to be rescreened more frequently.
IIB	15-19	Children should receive nutritional and educational interventions and more frequent screening. If the blood-lead level persists in this range, environmental investigation and intervention should be done.
III	20-44	Children should receive environmental evaluation and remediation and a medical evaluation. Such children may need pharmacologic treatment of lead poisoning.
IV	45-69	Children will need both medical and environmental intervention, including chelation therapy.
V	70 or higher	A child with Class V lead poisoning is a medical emergency. Medical and environmental management must begin immediately.

Source: Centers for Disease Control

five days — as they are for intravenous chelation therapy — to make sure the new drug is taken correctly. "After that, the children are discharged to a 'safe' house near the hospital, where they live with their families until their apartments or houses are de-leaded."

Even with improvements in treatment, chelation therapy can't reverse neurological damage — learning disabilities, lowered IQs and behavioral problems. According to the Alliance to End Childhood Lead Poisoning, an advocacy group in Washington, an 11-year study showed that lead-poisoned children failed grades in school at seven times the average rate and were six times as likely as non-poisoned children to have reading disabilities.

Are current efforts to combat lead poisoning adequate to the task?

Industries that use lead in their products point to the dramatic fall in average blood-lead levels in recent years. "We have to put the problem into perspective," says Steven Sides, director of health, safety and environmental affairs for the National Paint and Coatings Association (NPCA) in Washington.

"Today we are seeking to protect kids with lead levels below what we of an earlier generation were exposed to," Sides explains, citing the lower federal blood-lead levels. "That's no excuse for inaction, but it does show the tremendous strides that have been made. Most people know we're winning the fight against childhood lead poisoning."

Housing industry spokesmen agree with this optimistic assessment. "Lead poisoning has gone down very rapidly over the past 15 years," says Dick Morris, senior technical adviser for the National Association of Home Builders (NAHB) in Washington. Morris cites EPA findings that the percentage of children with blood-lead levels of more than 25 micrograms per deciliter — the old threshold level — fell from 10.7 percent during the 1976-80 period to just 1 percent in 1990.

Even considering the new lead-poisoning threshold of 10 micrograms per deciliter, Morris views the trend as very encouraging. More than 90 percent of children exceeded that level in the 1976-80 period, while only 15 percent did in 1990. "That's still a lot," he says, "especially considering CDC studies that show adverse health effects at over 10 [micrograms per deciliter], but even CDC doesn't call for environmental remediation until you get to blood levels of 20 [micrograms] or more."

Like paint manufacturers, the housing industry has a big stake in the way health officials approach lead poisoning. That's because paint chips and dust from lead-based paint in homes are still identified as the major causes of childhood lead poisoning. Both industry groups support the CDC's calls for universal screening to find young victims of lead poisoning and treat them quickly. But they oppose calls for preventive measures such as banning lead in all types of paints and coatings (including primer for cars) and removing old paint from housing.

Requiring the removal of old lead paint "would reduce homeowner equity, increase the price of all housing and result in an increase in abandonments [by landlords] and homelessness," says the NAHB.[6] And paint companies say it would be costly to find alternatives to products that contain lead.

But many health professionals are adamant in their calls for widespread lead abatement, or removal, in existing housing. "About 75 percent of all housing in the United States built before 1980 contains lead," says Rosen. "There are an estimated 1.3 million tons of lead paint in this country's housing. It's a national disgrace."

The Alliance to End Childhood Lead Poisoning estimates that almost 4 million houses and apartments have chipping and peeling lead paint or hazardous levels of lead dust. Children ingest paint dust and chips when they put their fingers in their mouths after touching contaminated surfaces. Because hand-to-mouth activity is high in small children, they can ingest a substantial amount of lead.

In addition to paint dust, soil often contains high levels of lead that was emitted from the tailpipes of vehicles once fueled with leaded gasoline. Lead particles are present in the air in regions where leaded gasoline is still used, mainly agricultural areas; where catalytic converters are not heavily used; where recycled motor oil, which often contains high concentrations of lead, is burned for fuel; and near lead smelters and plants that use lead.

Drinking water in many parts of the country still contains excessive levels of lead, usually because of lead pipes and lead solder used in residential plumbing systems. Some ceramic dishes leach lead contained in the glaze into food and beverages. All these sources are now the focus

of a wide range of efforts to reduce contact with lead.

Is lead poisoning mainly a disease of the poor?

Cases of lead poisoning among middle-class children have been the focus of numerous magazine stories and television news features over the past year. Often, the young victims' parents unwittingly exposed them to lead dust while renovating older homes. These examples are startling because they underscore the lack of general awareness of the risks of lead exposure even among well-educated, affluent parents who wouldn't dream of skimping on their children's health care.

But these children of affluence are not the main victims of lead poisoning. While the disease affects children of all races and economic status, the highest rates of poisoning occur in poor, inner-city neighborhoods,

where minority children are likely to live. Rosen, whose lead-poisoning clinic treats 250 children a year, says that "about 45 percent of the children the clinic admits are African American, more than half are Hispanic and a very small portion are Caucasian."

Confirming this anecdotal evidence, the CDC concluded in a landmark 1988 study that 68 percent of all poor, inner-city black children were lead-poisoned — a percentage that is surely higher now that the blood-lead threshold has been reduced.

By comparison, the CDC found that 36 percent of poor, inner-city white children suffered lead poisoning. Indeed, the agency found that African American children were between 10 and 30 percent more likely to get lead poisoning than white children at all income levels, both inside and away from cities.[7] Subsequent studies have found a similarly disproportionate occurrence of lead poison-

---

Damaging Effects of Lead

Children suffer increasingly serious health problems as their exposure to lead increases. Health officials recently discovered that even low levels of exposure can cause irreversible damage, including deficits in neurological and behavioral development.

Lowest blood-lead level at which effect is seen (micrograms/deciliter)	Neurologic effects	Other effects
10-15 (prenatal and postnatal)	Deficits in neurological and behavioral development; electrophysiological changes	Reduced gestational age and weight at birth; reduced size up to age 7-8 years
15-20		Impaired vitamin D metabolism
less than 25	Lower IQ, slower reaction time	
30	Slowed nerve-conduction velocity	
40		Reduced hemoglobin
70	Damage to peripheral nerves	Anemia
80-100	Brain damage	Colic, other gastrointestinal and kidney effects

Source: Centers for Disease Control

The Nation's Old Houses Pose Health Hazards

Older homes, which contain substantial levels of lead paint, tend to be concentrated in certain areas of the country. Urban areas in the Northeast and upper Midwest have the highest percentages of dwellings built before 1940. The Department of Housing and Urban Development estimates that 57 million dwelling units contain lead paint.

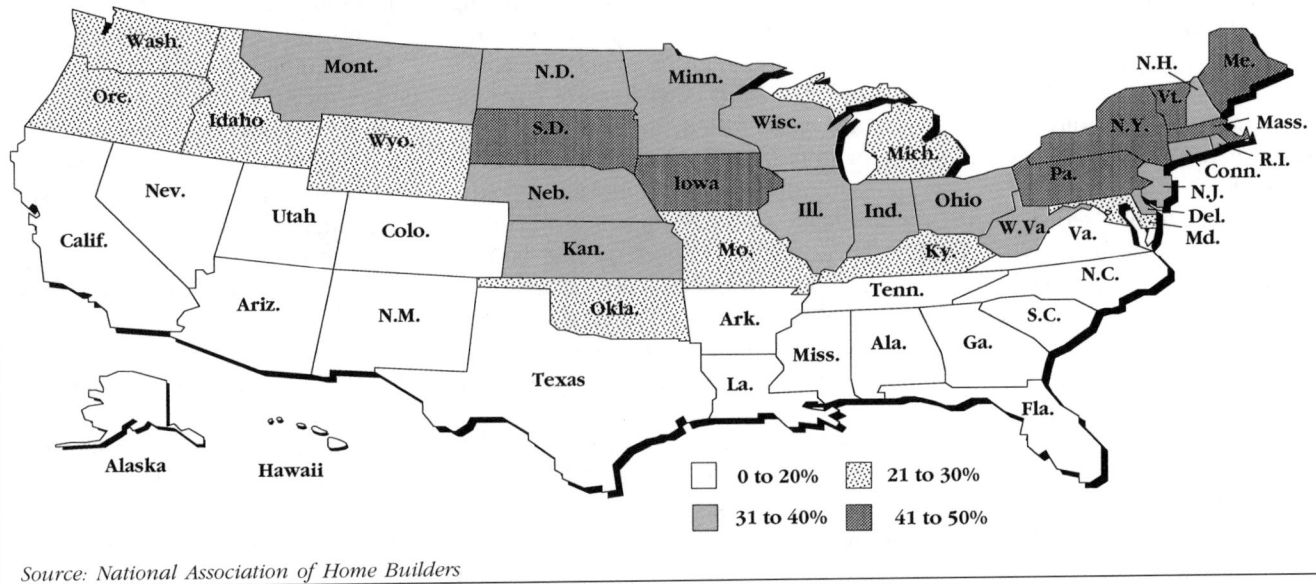

☐ 0 to 20%	▨ 21 to 30%
▦ 31 to 40%	▩ 41 to 50%

Source: National Association of Home Builders

ing among Hispanic children as compared with white children.[8]

Dr. Ellen K. Silbergeld, a professor of toxicology at the University of Maryland Medical School in Baltimore, says a similar racial and social breakdown among lead-poisoned children occurs in her city as well. "There is no evidence suggesting genetic anomalies that would make children of one race more vulnerable to lead poisoning than any other," she says. "It needs to be stressed that the incidence

of lead poisoning comes down to who's living where." Black, inner-city families are more likely to live in deteriorating housing near factories, dumps and highways — sources of high lead contamination.

Some public health experts suggest that lead poisoning may go far in explaining the high rate of learning disabilities, behavioral problems and school dropouts among minority children. "It is bound to be a contributor," says Rosen. ∎

BACKGROUND

Lethal Legacy

In its natural state, lead lies below the Earth's surface and presents no danger to humans or other living organisms. It was not until lead deposits were mined that lead poisoning

began to take its toll.

According to Dr. Clair Patterson, a geochemist at the California Institute of Technology, the ancient Greeks first mined the soft, dense metal in their search for silver deposits, which often are present in lead ore. The Greeks' invention of silver coins for currency came as they were running out of arable land in their homeland on the Attica peninsula — which was

rich in lead and silver — and were forced to obtain grain from abroad. "At the same time that the Greeks were becoming very rich and powerful with their newfound coins," Patterson explains, "contamination from lead began to be seen in that region."

But it was another important commodity in ancient Greek culture — wine — that spread lead contamination far beyond the mines and refineries and into the general population. Early vintners had a problem storing wine, Patterson says. The yeast used to turn the sugar in grapes into alcohol in time turned the brew into an unpalatable acid. Efforts to completely remove the yeast after fermentation proved ineffective. When they tried to kill the yeast by heating the wine, the yeast residue, known as sapa, continued to make it sour-tasting. "But when they boiled the sapa in pots made of pure lead," Patterson says, "the Greeks found a way to turn green wine into wine that would

Continued on p. 534

Chronology

1950s *Leaded house paint applied over the past half century begins to deteriorate, causing a noticeable increase in the incidence of childhood lead poisoning.*

1953

The paint industry issues voluntary standards limiting lead to 1 percent of the ingredients of house paints. The industry cuts the limit by half in 1962.

1970s *As the dangers of lead poisoning become more apparent, governments assume a more activist role in limiting exposure to lead.*

1971

Congress passes the Lead Based Paint Poisoning Prevention Act, which prohibits the use of leaded paint on surfaces that are accessible to children and sets up grants for lead-poisoning screening and treatment. Massachusetts adopts the most sweeping state law in the country to prevent lead poisoning. The statute requires the removal of peeling paint from windowsills and other surfaces that are accessible to small children in all dwellings where a child under 6 years of age resides.

1973

Congress amends the Lead-Based Paint Poisoning Prevention Act to prohibit the use of paint containing more than 0.5 percent lead in federally funded housing as well as toys and other products with which young children might come into contact.

1977

Gradual phaseout of leaded gasoline — in use since the 1920s — begins after the Ethyl Corp., the leading U.S. producer of lead additives for gasoline, loses its court challenge to the phaseout. The Consumer Product Safety Commission issues regulations banning the use of leaded paint for residential and most other uses.

1979

Dr. Herbert Needleman reports that exposure to low levels of lead can lower IQ scores in children and cause other serious neurological effects. His findings lead to a gradual tightening of various regulations aimed at limiting exposure to the metal. Although subsequent studies confirm his findings, Needleman's work comes under vehement criticism from two researchers, one of whom receives funds from the lead industry.

1980s *Childhood lead poisoning becomes a back-burner issue during this decade of deregulation.*

1980

The Food and Drug Administration reaches an agreement with the food-processing industry to phase out the use of lead-soldered cans, a leading source of lead contamination of food. Massachusetts expands its lead statute by requiring doctors and other health-care providers to screen all preschool children for lead poisoning. The law also requires day-care providers to ensure that all children in their care undergo screening by age 2.

1986

Amendments to the 1973 Safe Drinking Water Act tighten regulations on lead in drinking water and ban the installation of lead pipes in water systems and the use of lead solder to connect plumbing joints and fittings. California passes a childhood lead-poisoning prevention program expanding screening efforts in the state.

1988

The federal Lead Contamination Control Act prohibits the use of lead-lined tanks in water coolers — widely used in schools across the country.

1990s *Federal agencies turn their attention once again to the issue of lead poisoning as evidence mounts that very low levels of exposure can seriously harm young children.*

1990

The Environmental Protection Agency finds that 10-15 percent of children have blood-lead levels of more than 10 micrograms per deciliter, down from more than 90 percent during the period 1976-80. The improvement is a result of the phaseout of leaded gasoline and leaded paint.

Oct. 7, 1991

Despite the reduction in blood-lead levels, Secretary of Health and Human Services Louis W. Sullivan calls lead poisoning "the No. 1 environmental threat to the health of children in the United States" and lowers the blood-lead threshold from 25 to 10 micrograms of lead per deciliter. He also calls for universal screening of all children by their first birthday. Under the new standard, about 4 million children under age 6 are considered to be lead poisoned, about 10 times as many as under the old standard.

A Flawed Fetal-Protection Policy

The danger of lead poisoning does not just begin at birth. Developing fetuses also are at risk if pregnant women are exposed to lead and it enters their bloodstream. Fetal exposure to lead can cause premature birth, low birthweight and impaired neurological development. Because lead is present in many manufacturing processes, an estimated 7.75 million workers are exposed to lead each year and about 400,000 babies are born with toxic blood-lead levels.

To reduce the risk of prenatal lead poisoning, some companies have introduced so-called fetal-protection policies barring women of child-bearing age from work involving exposure to lead. One such company was Johnson Controls Inc., the nation's leading producer of lead-acid car batteries. In 1982 the Milwaukee firm declared it would no longer allow women of child-bearing age to work at these jobs unless they proved they were sterile.†

At the time Johnson Controls imposed its policy, Gloyce Qualls was 32 years old and was making about $350 a week as a burner, using a torch to melt the lead that went into the batteries. She was forced to take a job that paid only $200 a week. To get her old job back, she underwent sterilization.

Women's advocates denounced the policy. "If a toxin primarily affects men, the toxin is banned," said Dr. Maureen Paul of the Reproductive Hazards Center at the University of Massachusetts in Worcester. "If it affects women, the women are banned." ††

Several of Qualls' co-workers subsequently challenged the controversial policy, which the company claimed was a necessary defense against lawsuits brought by employees on behalf of their children born with defects. The case made its way to the U.S. Supreme Court, which in March 1991 ruled against the company. Excluding fertile women from hazardous jobs, the court found, amounts to illegal sexual discrimination in the workplace.

"Decisions about the welfare of future children must be left to the parents who conceive, bear, support and raise them rather than to the employers who hire those parents," wrote Justice Harry A. Blackmun. "Women as capable of doing their jobs as their male counterparts may not be forced to choose between having a child and having a job."

The ruling means that manufacturers must warn workers of potential workplace hazards instead of transferring them out of harm's way and, where possible, reduce their exposure. In the case of Johnson Controls, the firm had to reduce the workers' exposure to lead by installing powerful ventilation systems or, where possible, finding alternatives to lead.

---

† See "Equal Rights, Equal Risks," *Newsweek,* April 1, 1991.

†† Quoted by Rebecca Norris in "Double Jeopardy," *American Health,* March 1991, p. 32.

Continued from p. 532

stay sweet for years." But their discovery also greatly increased human exposure to lead.

The Greeks eventually ran out of silver deposits. As their civilization waned, they passed on their skills in lead and silver mining to the up-and-coming Romans. They increased lead production tenfold, Patterson says, by mining vast deposits in Spain.

Patterson and his colleagues followed recipes for sapa and wine production that had been discovered among Roman ruins and found extremely high lead levels in the batch they brewed. "It was enough to produce drastic lead poisoning, and in fact many people in Southern Europe were poisoned with lead during the Roman era."

In addition to wine production and storage vessels, the Romans used lead for pipes for aqueducts, sophisticated plumbing systems, tableware and copper cookware, which they lined with lead to block the taste of copper. The widespread lead poisoning they apparently suffered has been cited as a major cause of the fall of the Roman Empire.[9]

Lead Use Spreads in Europe and the New World

Lead production dropped in the Middle Ages but resumed with a vengeance after the Spanish discovered vast silver and lead deposits in the New World. Over a period of two centuries, Patterson says, Spanish galleons carried more than 40,000 tons of silver to Europe, where it was used for coinage, as in ancient Greece. Europeans continued to use lead in plumbing systems and to make pots and pans for cooking and storing food and wine. They also found new uses for lead, such as roofing material and solder for stained-glass windows.

"Spanish silver broke Europe out of the doldrums of the Middle Ages and spurred business enterprise all over the world," Patterson says. "Lead production also went up gigantically, and then lead poisoning was no longer a regional disease confined to Southern Europe."

In North America, lead was one of the first metals to be mined and was valued by early European settlers for making shot. But lead's toxicity was also well-known at the time. In a letter to a friend dated July 31, 1786, Benjamin Franklin described examples of lead poisoning from the use of lead in stills used to ferment rum. He also described the symptoms of lead poisoning he had experienced while working in a print shop in London some years earlier.

Franklin had been warming lead type before a fire to make it easier to handle in cold weather. "But an old Workman observing it, advis'd me not to do so, telling me I might lose the Use of my Hands by it, as two of our Companions had nearly done .... This, with a kind of obscure Pain that I had sometimes felt as it were in the Bones of my Hand when working over the Types made very hot, induc'd me to omit the Practice." [10]

Franklin's discovery was nothing new. Fumes from melting lead type had been recognized as a hazard to print-shop workers for several centuries. During the Industrial Revolution, children living near lead smelters were found to suffer from severe lead poisoning. It was during this period that paint manufacturers began to use white lead in residential paint. Lead makes paint spread more evenly and resist wear. Indeed, the best-quality paint at the time was 70 percent lead by weight. [11]

20th-Century Reaction

Although alternatives to lead additives for paint were introduced in Europe and the United States in the 1920s and '30s, leaded paint continued to be the covering of choice for homes, apartments, schools and hospitals in the United States until the early 1940s. Then, paint companies began replacing white lead, or lead carbonate, with less expensive pigments for most of their interior residential paint.

By the 1950s, however, the older, lead-based paint that had been ap-plied over several decades had become so deteriorated that lead poisoning was common among children who ingested paint flakes and dust. For many years, lead poisoning was diagnosed only in children with enough lead exposure to produce severe symptoms, such as paralysis, convulsions and death. The introduction of blood tests for lead in the 1940s and '50s showed that many more children were affected than had previously been recognized. [12]

In 1953, the paint industry issued voluntary standards limiting lead to 1 percent of the ingredients of house paints. The industry tightened the standard in 1962 to 0.5 percent. On the evidence of widespread lead poisoning among children, state and local public-health agencies started educational programs to inform apartment dwellers and homeowners of the dangers they faced if deteriorating leaded paint wasn't removed or covered with non-lead paint.

These programs were most active in large cities with vast tracts of older, dilapidated housing. It was not until 1972, however, that Congress passed the Lead-Based Paint Poisoning Prevention Act limiting the lead content in consumer paints to no more than 0.5 percent. In 1978, Congress lowered the lead limit to 0.06 percent, thus instituting a virtual ban on leaded paint for consumer uses.

Contamination Continues Despite Paint Ban

The ban on leaded paint blocked the main source of lead poisoning in children. But lead contamination from other sources remained a problem. Leaded gasoline, first introduced in the 1920s to improve engine performance, had become the fuel of choice by the 1940s. When research indicated that airborne lead particles were greatly increasing human exposure to the metal, the Ethyl Corp., the leading U.S. manufacturer of tetraethyl lead — the lead compound used in gasoline — argued that leaded fuel was not to blame.

Leaded gasoline continued to be sold without restrictions until 1973. But even after 1977, when the federal government mandated its phaseout, leaded gasoline was widely used, in part because leaded regular gas generally was priced lower than any other grade available at the pump.

In recent years, as older cars gradually have been replaced with newer models that run only on unleaded gasoline, the phaseout of leaded fuel has accelerated. In some communities, local air-quality standards have also forced gas stations to stop selling leaded fuel. But even today leaded gasoline is still available in many parts of the country.

The impact of such measures as the phaseout of leaded gasoline can be seen in Patterson's studies of lead levels in polar ice. "The ice records we examined showed an increase of atmospheric lead by a factor of 300 during the Industrial Revolution, and a decrease by a factor of five after 1970," he says, an improvement he attributes to the phaseout of leaded gasoline.

But the improvements are slight when compared with the virtual absence of lead exposure in pre-industrial times. According to another study conducted by Patterson and his colleagues, skeletons of modern humans contain about 1,000 times more lead than those of ancient American Indians who did not mine the metal.

Until the late 1970s, lead was commonly used as soldering material for metal food cans. Patterson and his co-workers found that the level of lead in tuna was 10,000 times higher after it was packed in lead-soldered cans than it was before packing. The FDA, however, found a much lower addition of lead to the food in soldered cans and merely recommended that alternative canning materials be used rather than banning lead solder outright. Because alternatives were readily available, lead soldering for food

The Rise and Fall of Leaded Gas

Manufacturers began adding lead to gas in the early 1940s. Use of leaded gas peaked between 1965 and 1975 and then plummeted after the federal government began phasing out lead additives in 1977.

Amount of lead used (1,000 tons)

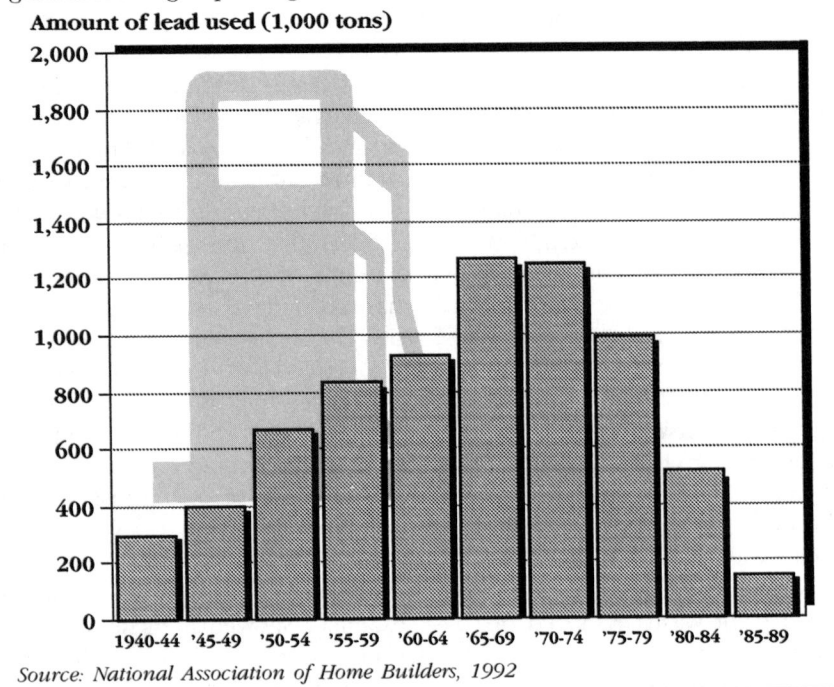

Source: National Association of Home Builders, 1992

cans has been virtually eliminated. This step alone, the FDA reports, accounts for much of the 90 percent decrease in the lead found in food purchased in U.S. grocery stores since 1982.[13]

Major Lead Sources

Despite the growing list of banned uses of lead, the world continues to mine more than 6 million tons of lead annually. More than 400,000 tons are mined in the United States, which ranks second in world production after Australia. (Before it broke up, the Soviet Union was the world's leading source of lead.) Most American lead comes from Missouri, the rest from several Western states. Once it is excavated, lead ore is smelted in a blast furnace to produce lead bullion. It then goes to a refin-

ery, where the lead is separated from other accompanying minerals, including silver, zinc and copper.

Not all the lead that ends up in manufactured products comes from newly mined ore, however. According to the New York-based Lead Industries Association, some 90 percent of lead in American products is recycled. In 1988, the association reports, some 800,000 tons of the metal were reclaimed in secondary lead smelters, mostly from scrapped automobile batteries.

Today, about 80 percent of all lead consumed in the United States is used to make large storage batteries, mostly for automobiles, trucks and boats. Lead-acid batteries are the sole source of power for electric vehicles such as forklifts, wheelchairs and golf carts, and they are the only batteries that are now commercially available to power electric cars. These non-polluting vehicles are expected to replace gasoline-

powered cars over the next few decades in California and other parts of the country affected by heavy air pollution. Lead storage batteries also provide backup power for hospitals, airports and other essential facilities.

The remaining 20 percent of lead used in the United States goes into manufacturing a variety of products, including medical X-ray shielding, soldering material for electronic circuit boards, industrial coatings, such as the primer coat for automobiles, ammunition and weights. Lead-chromate pigments, valued for their bright, durable colors, are used in paints for road markings, bridges and other industrial uses where there is relatively little danger of human exposure. Here are the major sources of industrial lead found in the United States:

Lead-Based Paint: The main source of lead poisoning in children continues to be lead-based paint. According to Rosen of the Montefiore Medical Center, "99.9 percent of the kids we see were poisoned by leaded paint, which they ingested either as chips or as dust" from deteriorating walls and other surfaces. It was once believed that children had to swallow whole chips of leaded paint to become poisoned. It was also thought that many children who ate paint chips suffered from pica, a behavioral disorder characterized by compulsive ingestion of dirt and other non-edible material.

Pica is no longer considered an explanation for most cases of lead poisoning. "Pica is a very rare pathological behavioral disturbance in children," Rosen says. "We see it only very, very rarely." Rather, health professionals now agree, lead poisoning most often stems from everyday activity. "It's the normal hand-to-mouth activity that is typical of young children and toddlers that is the root or conduit of lead ingestion in about all of the cases," Rosen says.

In addition to chipping and peeling, painted surfaces also deteriorate by gradually shedding minute particles of paint. This gradual wearing away is most pronounced on moving surfaces such as window sashes and door frames. The leaded-paint dust then settles on floors near doorways and on windowsills, places where small children often crawl or place their hands.

The CDC estimates that 3 million tons of lead from paint still remain in about 40 million dwellings across the country. Almost 2 million of these are believed to be in poor condition and pose serious risks of lead exposure.[14] That fact, together with the realization that normal children — not those with behavioral disorders — are the main victims of lead poisoning, makes it clear that many more children are vulnerable to the disease than was once believed.

Representatives of the paint and housing industries say that not all the remaining leaded paint poses a threat. "We don't believe that intact leaded paint is a significant hazard to the general population," says Dick Morris of the NAHB. Morris says that health officials became concerned that children might be contaminated by chewing on building surfaces following several cases of lead poisoning during the 1960s and early '70s among children who had chewed on cribs that were covered with leaded paint. "We have asked CDC for statistics indicating that children chew on building surfaces and become poisoned from doing that, but they say they don't know of any such studies," Morris says.

Leaded Gasoline: Dust may be the leading pathway of lead into children's bodies, but leaded paint is not always its source, paint-industry representatives are quick to make clear. "There may be leaded paint in an older home, but there is also soil contamination from leaded gasoline," says Steve Sides of the NPCA. "You can clean up the contaminated dust,

but if you open a window or the kids track it in, you will recontaminate the home. When the paint is intact, however, the source of the lead-dust exposure is going to be something else."

Indeed, a study of the soil around Interstate 880 in Oakland, Calif., showed lead levels that exceeded federal guidelines for hazardous waste sites. Had the area been an industrial site, it would have qualified for federal "superfund" support to clean it up. Two-thirds of the children living near the freeway had high blood-lead levels. As a result of the study, Oakland closed its contaminated playgrounds — one of the few local governments to do so.[15] The EPA has found that lead levels in the soil near other heavily traveled roadways can exceed 10,000 parts per million, about eight times higher than the lead contamination found along I-880.[16]

After the phaseout of leaded gasoline began in 1977, health officials noted a significant drop in blood-lead levels. One national survey showed a drop of 5.8 micrograms per deciliter from 1976 to 1980, which was attributed primarily to the reduction in airborne lead particles that accompanied the gradual switch to unleaded gasoline.[17] Of course, the phaseout only affects exposure to airborne lead. Most of the lead particles emitted from vehicle tailpipes are still present in the soil. And leaded gasoline is still sold in many areas of the country because the phaseout law exempted cars made before 1975 and all farm equipment. As of 1990, leaded gasoline still accounted for 9 percent of U.S. gasoline sales in the United States.[18]

Many experts agree that leaded gasoline is an important source of lead poisoning but stress that the main culprit remains leaded paint. "A larger number of children have lead-contaminated dust from gasoline as the principal source of exposure, but those kids tend to be the ones with low blood-lead levels of 15 micrograms and under," says Karen Florini,

an attorney at the New York-based Environmental Defense Fund, which has been campaigning to stop lead poisoning since the 1970s. "But it is also true that the children with higher blood-lead levels are getting poisoned from paint."

Recycled Oil: A major source of lead exposure — and one that is often overlooked — is recycled engine oil. Consumers who drop their used crankcase oil off at a recycling center in the belief that it will be re-refined or disposed of in an environmentally safe manner are sorely mistaken, says Erik Olson, a senior attorney for the Natural Resources Defense Council (NRDC), a New York-based environmental group. "Recyclers do not generally re-refine used motor oil, but rather sell it as is to be burned as fuel," Olson says.

After it is blended with other grades of oil, the contaminated used motor oil is burned in industrial boilers and in furnaces to heat office buildings and apartment houses. Except in California, which has banned the practice, Olson says, "burning used oil is now the leading cause of airborne lead emissions."

Smelters: High concentrations of airborne lead particles are present inside and around "primary" lead smelters, which process lead ore, and "secondary" smelters, which recover the metal from recycled batteries and other used products. The Lead Industries Association reports that there are 20 primary and secondary lead smelters in the United States. Smelters are the main source of lead poisoning among plant workers and neighbors. The children of employees of smelters and other lead-using industries are also exposed to lead when their parents bring lead dust home on their clothing or shoes.

In addition to smelters, small recycling operations throughout the country ship lead from used batteries and other products to secondary smelters. According to James Foster, a spokes-

Urban Areas Where a Majority of Preschoolers Have Lead Poisoning

Lead poisoning is a serious problem in many urban areas (known as standard metropolitan statistical areas, or SMSAs). In the cities shown on the map below, at least 50 percent of the children ages 6 months to 5 years were estimated to have blood-lead levels above 10 micrograms per deciliter, the new threshold level for lead poisoning.†

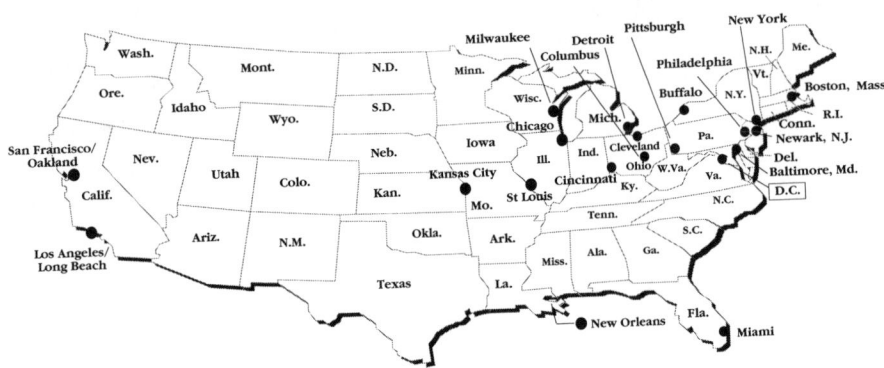

Areas With Populations of 1 Million or Less

At least 50 percent of the young children in these urban areas exceed minimum lead-poisoning levels.

Anderson, Ind.	51.8%
Battle Creek, Mich.	50.6
Bridgeport, Conn.	52.6
Columbus, Ga.	50.6
Cumberland, Md.-W.Va.	53.4
Decatur, Ill.	50.0
El Paso, Tx., and Las Cruces, N.M.	50.4
Fall River, Mass.-R.I.	51.6
Glen Falls, N.Y.	52.0
Harrisburg, Pa.	53.8
Jackson, Miss.	50.2
Jersey City, N.J.	71.1
Johnstown, Pa.	53.4
Joplin, Mo.	52.3
Lancaster, Pa.	52.7
Memphis, Tenn.-Ark.-Miss.	50.9
Montgomery, Ala.	51.8
New Haven-West Haven, Conn.	50.3
Paterson-Clifton-Passaic, N.J.	59.7
Providence-Warwick-Pawtucket, R.I.-Mass.	50.2
Reading, Pa.	51.0
Savannah, Ga.	51.8
Shreveport, La.	51.2
South Bend, Ind.	50.0
Springfield, Ohio	51.4
Trenton, N.J.	59.2
Vineland-Millville-Bridgeton, N.J.	52.8
Williamsport, Pa.	50.2
York, Pa.	50.0

Areas With Populations Over 1 Million

At least 50 percent of the young children in these areas exceed minimum lead-poisoning levels. In the New York-New Jersey area, 490,977 children — an amazing 74.7 percent of the area's total number of young children — are afflicted.

SMSA	Est. no. of children	% of children	SMSA	Est. no. of children	% of children
Baltimore, Md.	98,857	58.5	Miami, Fla.	64,150	51.2
Boston, Mass.	122,862	69.4	Milwaukee, Wisc.	66,110	56.7
Buffalo, N.Y.	54,012	61.8	New Orleans, La.	64,845	57.7
Chicago, Ill.	371,952	61.5	New York, N.Y.-N.J.	490,977	74.7
Cincinnati, Ohio-Ky.-Ind.	65,746	54.6	Newark, N.J.	95,230	70.7
Cleveland, Ohio	95,304	64.7	Philadelphia, Pa.-N.J.	221,654	62.0
Columbus, Ohio	48,738	50.6	Pittsburgh, Pa.	86,921	58.9
Detroit, Mich.	186,768	56.5	St. Louis, Mo.-Ill.	99,705	55.7
Kansas City, Mo.-Kan.	58,019	50.5	San Francisco-Oakland, Calif.	114,921	55.5
Los Angeles-Long Beach, Calif.	380,905	58.2	Washington, D.C.-Md.-Va.	122,406	51.7

† These estimates are based on data analyzed for the Public Health Service's Agency for Toxic Substances and Disease Registry. Due to sampling limitations, the agency dealt only with white and black children ages 6 months to 5 years.
Source: Environmental Defense Fund, 1990

man for the Occupational Safety and Health Administration (OSHA), these "battery-breaking" operations are sources of heavy lead contamination among workers.

At one such operation, conditions were particularly appalling. "The workers took batteries off trucks and then broke them into their component parts, which included large amounts of toxic acid as well as lead," Foster recalls. "Some had to stand along a moving belt above a large vat of acid.

These workers suffered acute lead poisoning, including headaches and palsied limbs."

Water: The EPA estimates that drinking water causes 10-20 percent of the lead exposure in children. About 20 percent of the population, EPA suggests, is exposed to levels of lead in water of at least 20 parts per billion, a concentration that increases blood-lead levels in children by as much as 3.5 micrograms per deciliter. Infants who drink formula mixed

with contaminated tap water are most vulnerable to poisoning from water.

Lead can leach into the water supply from waste dumps containing batteries and other lead products or as airborne particles emitted when leaded fuel is burned. But the main sources of lead contamination of water are the individual plumbing systems that carry municipal water from the underground main to the household faucet.

Because of lead's malleability, municipal water authorities used it for the lines serving neighborhoods built in the early 1900s. These lead pipes are still present in many older systems. For the same reason, lead pipes were widely used for household plumbing before 1930. Even when lead plumbing was replaced by pipes made of copper and other metals, plumbers until recently joined them with lead solder.

Amendments enacted in 1986 to the Safe Drinking Water Act banned the use of both lead pipes and lead solder in plumbing. Congress also passed the Lead Contamination Control Act in 1988 to ban water coolers with lead-lined tanks, which were used in schools across the country. Critics charge, however, that most states have failed to comply with the 1988 law.[19]

Local water conditions also affect lead contamination. Acidic and soft water, for example, are corrosive and make lead in the pipes or solder leach more easily into the water supply, while hard water coats the pipe surfaces with a layer of minerals. But any type of hot water, or even cold water that sits for several hours in the pipes, can be contaminated with lead.

Food: While paint chips and dust explain most cases of childhood lead poisoning, the main source of exposure to lead in adults is food. Food is contaminated in the fields by farm machinery exhaust, in processing if it is packed in lead-soldered cans and in preparation if it is washed or cooked in lead-tainted water.

Until 1980, more than 90 percent of metal food cans had lead-soldered seams. The FDA reached an agreement that year with food processors and can producers on the voluntary phaseout of lead solder. Because the phaseout was voluntary and did not apply to imported food, statistics on the presence of lead solder in food cans are inconsistent: food processors and can makers reported in 1988 that only 5.8 percent of U.S. food cans contained lead solder. But *Con-*

sumer Reports the following year estimated that a quarter of the cans were lead-soldered.[20]

Another source of lead in food is the glaze that coats most ceramicware. "We believe that the largest single source of lead in the diet is lead that migrates into food from lead-glazed ceramicware — the plates, cups, coffee mugs, bowls, pitchers and other articles we use in our homes," said FDA Deputy Com-

CURRENT SITUATION

▌Government's Response

Despite the growing evidence of lead's toxic effects at lower and lower doses and the fact that lead poisoning is preventable, the federal government has only recently begun to coordinate efforts to combat it.

During most of the 1980s, childhood lead poisoning became what the Alliance to End Childhood Lead Poisoning calls an "orphan" issue that received too little attention from any of several federal agencies with responsibility in the area. "For the past 20 years, [the Department of Housing and Urban Development's] general approach to the hazards of lead-based paint has been denial — and its unstated but steadfast policy goal to do as little as possible," the group said.[22]

In July 1988, the CDC's Agency for Toxic Substances and Disease Registry issued a landmark report describing childhood lead poisoning as an epidemic. Other agencies quickly followed suit with several "strategic plans" aimed at coordinating the federal effort to eliminate the disease.[23] These efforts culminated Oct. 7, 1991, in CDC's adoption of a stricter thresh-

missioner Michael R. Taylor at recent hearings on this issue.[21]

The FDA, which tightened its ceramicware standards last September, estimates that about 300 million pieces of china sold in the United States each year contain levels of lead that would be deemed toxic even under the old, less strict standard. Only California requires ceramicware makers to test for lead content and label all products they sell in the state.   ■

old for lead poisoning and its call for universal screening in children.

Critics Call for More Action
But despite the initial flurry of reports, critics charge that the federal government is not doing enough to rid housing of dangerous leaded paint, a process called lead abatement. "The federal government has allocated money for lead abatement, but it is now bogged down in the HUD bureaucracy," says Lillian Wilmore, director of the National Toxics Campaign Fund's lead-pollution prevention project in Boston. "They are still trying to figure out a process for getting the funds out there, while we want them to treat lead abatement as an emergency. They don't need to study this problem a lot longer. It's just outrageous."

EPA also is accused of foot-dragging in efforts to purify drinking water. The agency was required by the 1986 amendments to the Safe Drinking Water Act to adopt tougher lead levels for drinking water. "EPA fought that requirement for many years, and only issued them last year as a result of a lawsuit," says Erik Olson of the NRDC.

The new regulations require water authorities to reduce water acidity where necessary and, if that fails, to replace lead service lines. "The problem is, they have eight years to try corrosion control and another 15 to replace the lines," Olson says. "So it will be another 23 years in many com-

How to Avoid Exposure to Lead

Lead can enter the body in a variety of ways, and from many sources. Although adults are vulnerable to higher levels of exposure, children under age 7 are most susceptible to injury. For this reason, the following tips are especially important for households with pregnant women, infants and young children. But even if families observe all these precautions, they cannot assume their children are safe. The soil and dust in playgrounds, back yards, day-care centers and even at home may contain lead.

Paint: This is still the most common source of childhood lead poisoning. The first step is finding out if lead paint was used in your apartment or house. About half the houses built before 1978 contain some lead paint. Older houses, built before 1950, are much more likely to have lead paint. Any chipping or peeling lead paint poses an immediate threat to children. If the paint is in good condition or has been painted over, leave it alone or have it removed only by contractors who are trained and certified in lead abatement. Abatement is expensive, and many local governments provide subsidies to low-income families for deleading their homes. If you are renovating an older home, have your children live elsewhere while surfaces are being sanded or scraped and then rent a special vacuum cleaner to remove fine paint dust.

Water: Utilities have more than two decades to comply with the EPA's strict new standards for lead levels in drinking water. Meanwhile, ask your local utility for the names of EPA-certified laboratories to test your drinking water; the cost should be under $50. Soft water is more likely to be lead-contaminated than hard water, and acidic water also poses a threat. Both cause lead pipes or solder in the home plumbing system to leach lead into the water. Homes built before 1930 may contain lead pipes. Homes built between 1978 and 1988 also pose special risks because it takes time for mineral deposits to cover any lead in the plumbing system. (Lead solder was banned in 1988.) To reduce lead in the water, let the tap flow for a minute or two before drinking or cooking with water that has stood in the pipes overnight or for several hours. Use only cold water for cooking. Be especially careful if you feed a baby formula mixed with tap water.

Food: Most U.S. canners no longer use lead solder, once a major source of lead contamination of food. Imported food cans, however, may still be soldered with lead. The other major source of lead in food is the clear glaze that covers most ceramicware. In California, ceramic dishes, pitchers and mugs must now bear a warning label if lead levels in the glaze exceed the state standard. The state attorney general and the Environmental Defense Fund have compiled an extensive list identifying which popular brands and patterns of china meet California's lead standards.

Some types of china are more likely than others to pose a lead hazard — old or damaged pieces, hand-crafted pieces that may have been improperly fired, dishes with painted or raised decal-type decorations that are not covered by a glaze. Do not use these for serving food or beverages. Do not routinely serve hot or acidic foods, such as tomato-based foods, on heirloom china or any dishes that have damaged glaze because these foods can leach lead out of the glaze. Ceramic pitchers should not be used to store acidic juices. Coffee mugs with leaded glazes pose a potential threat because coffee and tea are both hot and acidic.

Glass dishes and stoneware dishes (heavy pieces with a dull surface) do not contain lead. Some manufacturers now used unleaded glaze on their conventional china. To determine the lead content of dishes you use frequently, contact the manufacturer or test them yourself using special kits that cost less than $30. Two kits are mentioned in the June 1990 issue of *Consumer Reports*. Do not use leaded-crystal decanters to store anything you plan to drink.

---

munities before everyone gets water that EPA considers safe." Moreover, utilities in small communities are exempted from the regulations, no matter how much lead is in the water.

The CDC's call for universal screening seems likely to face similar delays in implementation. The current federal blood-lead screening program can test only a few tens of thousands of children a year. Under the new guidelines, children expected to test positive for lead poisoning number in the millions. That leaves much of the burden of screening on financially strapped state and local governments.

State Initiatives

Efforts to combat lead poisoning at the state and local levels vary enormously. Fewer than half the states have active lead-screening programs. About 20 states and many cities and counties, however, regulate the amount of lead paint in public housing and in some cases require abatement.[24]

Two states — Massachusetts and California — stand out for their programs to screen children and remove leaded paint from housing. Since 1971, Massachusetts has required owners and landlords to remove

Continued on p. 542

At Issue:

Should the federal government launch a nationwide lead-abatement program?

ENVIRONMENTAL DEFENSE FUND

FROM *LEGACY OF LEAD: AMERICA'S CONTINUING EPIDEMIC OF CHILDHOOD LEAD POISONING,* MARCH1990.

*t*he massive amounts of information on lead's toxicity — bolstered by recent findings on low-exposure-level effects — as well as indications of children's current exposure levels, reveal an urgent need for an aggressive federal program to control America's continuing epidemic of lead poisoning.

To be effective, such a program must provide a mechanism not only to stop adding lead to children's environments but also to remove it from the areas where they are most heavily exposed: their homes. And, to be politically feasible, it must respond to current budgetary realities the nation now faces.

The Environmental Defense Fund proposes creation of a National Lead Paint Abatement Trust Fund, to be financed by placement of a substantial excise fee on the production and importation of lead. Proceeds from the fund initially would be devoted to the removal of deteriorating lead-based paint from the group of highest-risk homes.....

The program would be implemented jointly by the Environmental Protection Agency and the Department of Health and Human Services. It would contain provisions to enable it to reflect market conditions and, where possible, accomplish secondary goals of improving housing and creating employment opportunities by hiring and training workers for abatement programs.

In addition, by avoiding the slow and resource-intensive process of developing a regulatory approach to control continuing uses of lead in products, it would yield results far more quickly than would more traditional approaches.

While the proposed program would not alleviate every aspect of the nation's current lead-poisoning epidemic, it would constitute a pragmatic and timely next step.

Lead poisoning already burdens America with millions of dollars of costs each year — both the direct costs of medical treatments and the indirect social costs of special education, lost income and a less productive citizenry. Lead poisoning also imposes grave handicaps on individual children, their families, and their communities. For them and for the nation as a whole, these handicaps will only intensify as the transition to the 21st century's "information age" continues....

NATIONAL ASSOCIATION OF HOME BUILDERS

FROM *LEAD EXPOSURE PREVENTION MANUAL,* 1992

*t*he problem of lead exposure in children is declining rapidly, although about 3 million children under the age of 6 may still suffer adverse health effects from lead exposure.

Most lead exposure in children is caused by lead in house dust. The primary source of lead in soil is emissions from leaded gasoline. A secondary source is deteriorated exterior lead paint. Lead from both sources has accumulated in the soil over the years. The lead is brought into houses on shoes and pets. In addition, a small percentage of children are exposed by eating contaminated soil and lead paint chips.

The most cost-effective solution to the problem is cleaning lead dust and chips from housing, covering bare urban soil in high-traffic areas and repairing peeling paint. This can be accomplished by educating the public, physicians, remodelers, owners of rental property and government employees on the need for in-place management of dust, soil and paint. Homeowners and renters should be urged to thoroughly clean their homes. Owners should promptly repair defective paint.

Since lead in drinking water causes some exposure, parents should be taught to not allow children to drink "first flush" tapwater. A standard of care for owners of rental property should be defined and protection from liability provided to them if they follow it. Remodelers should be urged to use methods that create less dust, and to clean more thoroughly upon completion. Blood screening should be greatly expanded.

Abatement of intact lead paint is not a cost-effective solution to the problem. Requiring abatement of intact paint is likely to increase children's blood-lead levels, the cost of all housing, bankruptcies, abandonments and homelessness. For these reasons, legislation and regulations should not require abatement of intact lead paint. Voluntary abatement using encapsulation, enclosure and replacement — already done unintentionally on a large scale — can be increased through education.

We believe that the above strategy will reduce childhood lead poisoning more quickly and more effectively than strategies aimed at elimination of intact lead paint, and will do so at a fraction of the cost.

Continued from p. 540

peeling paint from easily reached surfaces, such as windowsills, in all dwellings where there is a child under age 6.

In 1988 Massachusetts adopted the most extensive lead-poisoning prevention measure in the country, requiring sellers of homes to provide information about lead paint and give buyers 10 days to have the house inspected for potential lead hazards. The law also requires training and licensing of contractors and workers involved in lead-paint inspection and abatement and prohibits occupants from staying in the dwelling during cleanup operations. Finally, the law requires doctors to screen children and day-care providers to ensure that all children have been screened by age 2.

California also has an extensive screening program. And it is the only state that requires makers of ceramicware to test their products for lead leaching from the glaze and to attach warning labels to all pieces that exceed the state's stringent lead standards for tableware.

Among local governments, the city of Baltimore has an extensive screening program, testing about 26,000 children each year. When a child tests positive for lead poisoning, health officials order an inspection of the child's home. The city also inspects day-care centers for lead paint. Tenants can request inspections of their apartments, and if a lead-paint hazard is present, the landlord is required to remove the deteriorating paint. [25]

But even these far-reaching state and local programs are not without problems. In Massachusetts, for example, the law prohibits landlords from renting to families with children under 7 if there is lead paint in the dwelling. "People in Boston are extremely disturbed about the cost of lead abatement, which is out of reach not only for homeowners but also for many small landlords," Wilmore says. "This problem is aggravating the housing crisis here because many are simply refusing to rent to families with small children." ∎

Lead abatement can cost up to $10,000 for a medium-size home. To help lower-income families and child-care centers pay for abatement, Rep. Benjamin L. Cardin, D-Md., has introduced a measure (HR 2922) that would set up a trust fund from an excise fee on lead sales and imports. This "polluter pays" approach to funding would yield an estimated $1 billion a year, which would be paid out in grants to local governments that set up effective lead-removal programs. The excise fee would be higher for newly mined lead than for recycled lead, as an incentive for industry to find alternatives to lead and to use only recycled lead for most other applications.

Debate Continues

Critics of lead-paint abatement programs say that the costs of such ambitious programs exceed their benefits. "It's just not prudent for people to spend a lot of money on paint, which is only one source of the lead problem," says the NPCA's Steve Sides.

Dick Morris of the NAHB agrees, predicting that abatement requirements would place an unfair burden on homeowners. "We think it would be extremely damaging to homeowners if they were required to abate before they sold their homes," Morris says. "The money they thought they had in equity to use to move up to a better house would be greatly reduced. So it would really slow down home sales."

But health professionals reject this reasoning. Reigart of the American Academy of Pediatrics, while endorsing the CDC's goal of universal screening, also points out the need for more primary prevention of lead poisoning. "This includes abatement and more action from the federal government. In general, we have supported the various lead bills in Congress, including Waxman's proposal."

To break the deadlock, participants in the lead-abatement debate

OUTLOOK

Legislative Proposals

To lend greater uniformity to local efforts to combat childhood lead poisoning, several legislators have introduced measures at the federal level. In addition to calling for a major increase in funding for these programs, some proposals go beyond the CDC guideline calling for universal screening and emphasize prevention. Because leaded paint is still the leading cause of lead poisoning among children, these proposals focus on ways to prevent exposure from this source.

The Lead Contamination Control Act (HR 2840), introduced July 10, 1991, by Rep. Henry A. Waxman, D-Calif., would require landlords to inspect apartments or houses built before 1980 for the presence of lead-based paint before renting them. It also would require sellers of houses built before 1980 to give purchasers a 10-day opportunity to have the dwelling inspected for lead. That information would allow buyers to proceed with abatement or to take special precautions during renovation and thus avoid exposing their children to lead in the first place. Because improperly handled abatement can aggravate an existing lead problem by stirring up lead-tainted dust, Waxman's bill would also require contractors to be trained in abatement techniques.

are seeking a legislative compromise that focuses on identifying and removing the most serious lead paint hazards from all federally assisted housing. This approach, first included in a bill introduced in March by Sen. Alan Cranston, D-Calif., was subsequently redrafted as Title X of the Senate's National Affordable Housing Act, which is up for reauthorization this year.

However lawmakers act on the issue this year, the prevalence of lead poisoning among inner-city, minority children is becoming a key issue among civil rights advocates. "A lot of communities are getting more and more upset, as people of color conclude that if it were a different kind of neighborhood something would be done about lead poisoning," says Wilmore of the National Toxics Campaign Fund. And she says their frustration is often justified. "I believe there is a factual basis in saying those communities have suffered the most. Where water is contaminated, theirs is the most contaminated, and the same holds true for lead-contaminated air and soil."

Wilmore acknowledges the importance of identifying victims of lead poisoning no matter what their social, economic and racial circumstances. But she says distinctions must be made between poisoned children whose families have the resources to delead their homes and those who do not. Indeed, she says, poor communities should be the focus of any new initiatives to prevent lead poisoning. "We have to be very careful to focus on the worst injury and the highest-risk children and take some action there. We all know who those children are and where they live." ■

Notes

[1] Dr. Mielke's story was featured on an ABC News "Primetime" segment entitled "Hidden Poison," on July 25, 1991.

[2] In 1977 federal regulations took effect requiring the phaseout of leaded gasoline. The phaseout was an indirect response to the 1970 Clean Air Act, which set auto emission standards. To meet those standards, automakers developed catalytic converters, which only operate in cars using unleaded gas. As a result, the Environmental Protection Agency phased out leaded gasoline for most vehicles. By 1986, lead additives in gasoline had declined by 90 percent. Also in 1977, the Consumer Product Safety Commission banned lead in residential and most other paints. Paints used in road markings and certain industrial coatings were exempted from the ban.

[3] Secretary of Health and Human Services Louis W. Sullivan announced the changes in blood-lead standards Oct. 7, 1991. The CDC is an HHS division.

[4] See *A Review of Blood Lead Trends and Health Effects,* a study prepared by the Center for Information on Toxicology & Environment for the Lead Industries Association, April 1992.

[5] H. L. Needleman et al., "Deficits in Psychologic and Classroom Performance of Children with Elevated Dentine Lead Levels," *The New England Journal of Medicine,* March 29, 1979.

[6] National Association of Home Builders, *Lead Exposure Prevention Manual,* 1992, p. 1.

[7] Centers for Disease Control, Agency for Toxic Substances and Disease Registry, *The Nature and Extent of Lead Poisoning in Children in the United States: A Report to Congress,* July 1988.

[8] O. Carter-Pokras, J. Pirkle, G. Chavez and E. Gunter, "Blood Lead Levels of 4-11 Year-Old Mexican American, Puerto Rican and Cuban Children," *Public Health Reports,* July-August 1990.

[9] For a detailed historical account of this theory, see S. C. Gilfillan, "Lead Poisoning and the Fall of Rome," *Journal of Occupational Medicine,* February 1965.

[10] From Franklin's letter to Benjamin Vaughan, reproduced and distributed by the Philadelphia Department of Public Health.

[11] See National Association of Home Builders, *op. cit.,* p. 3.

[12] See Karen L. Florini, George D. Krumbhaar, Jr., and Ellen K. Silbergeld, *Legacy of Lead: America's Continuing Epidemic of Childhood Lead Poisoning,* Environmental Defense Fund, March 1990.

[13] From March 27, 1992, testimony by Michael R. Taylor, FDA's deputy commissioner for policy, before the Senate Governmental Affairs Ad Hoc Subcommittee on Consumer and Environmental Affairs.

[14] Centers for Disease Control, *op. cit.*

[15] From "Hidden Poison," ABC News "Primetime," July 25, 1991.

[16] Environmental Protection Agency, *Air Quality Criteria for Lead,* Vol. IV, 1986.

[17] *Ibid.*

[18] Florini et al., *op. cit.,* p. 19.

[19] See National Resources Defense Council, *The Lead Contamination Control Act: A Study in Non-Compliance,* June 1991.

[20] *Ibid.,* p. 20.

[21] Taylor testified March 27, 1992, before the Senate Governmental Affairs Subcommittee on Consumer and Environmental Affairs.

[22] Alliance to End Childhood Lead Poisoning, "Federal Update and Policy Analysis," January 1991.

[23] Department of Health and Human Services, "Strategic Plan to Eliminate Childhood Lead Poisoning," February 1991; Environmental Protection Agency, "Integrated Lead Strategy," 1990; Department of Housing and Urban Development, "Comprehensive and Workable Plan for the Abatement of Lead-Based Paint in Privately Owned Housing," December 1990.

[24] Florini et al., *op. cit.,* p. 30.

[25] *Ibid.,* p. 32.

Bibliography

Selected Sources Used

Books

World Resources Institute, *World Resources 1992-93*, Oxford University Press, 1992.

While airborne lead pollution from industrial emissions and vehicle exhaust is falling in the United States and other industrial nations, it is increasing in many developing countries, this book notes. In Mexico City, for example, seven out of 10 newborns had higher blood-lead levels than the World Health Organization's threshold for poisoning.

Articles

Blakeslee, Sandra, "The Lead-Calcium Time Bomb," *American Health*, November 1990.

Lead poisoning may pose threats to adults as well as children, the author reports, citing new scientific evidence. When lead enters the human body, it tends to travel in tandem with calcium, which is why the metal settles in bones and teeth. Under certain conditions, such as pregnancy, lactation and old age, when the body needs more calcium than is provided in the diet, bones release calcium — and with it, lead — into the bloodstream. Episodes of lead poisoning can thus recur throughout a person's lifetime.

Brough, Holly, "Minorities Redefine 'Environmentalism,'" *World Watch*, September-October 1990.

Mainstream environmental organizations, says Brough, "sometimes accused of valuing pandas or parks above people," may not adequately represent the interests of minorities. Poor blacks, especially, are more likely than better-off white Americans to live in a polluted environment, near landfills, toxic-waste dumps and factories that emit toxic fumes and particulate matter. Their homes are more likely to contain deteriorating lead paint, resulting in a higher incidence of childhood lead poisoning. The author calls on mainstream environmental groups to become advocates for environmental improvements that will affect minorities as well as the general public.

Suplee, Curt, "Water Works," *The Washington Post Magazine*, April 26, 1992.

The author follows the Washington area's water supply from its three main river sources to the tap. His description of the myriad contaminants that enter raw river water and the chemicals the utilities dump into it to kill them is enough to quench the strongest thirst. Like many older cities, lead pipes still carry some of the city's water to the tap. Still, Washington residents can take heart from the knowledge that the city's water supply is among the less lead-contaminated city water systems in the country.

Waldman, Steven, "Lead and Your Kids," *Newsweek*, July 15, 1991.

This cover story recounts the experiences of several families in which young children suffered from lead poisoning. In some cases, parents inadvertently exposed their children to danger by scraping or sanding leaded paint during renovations, releasing clouds of small lead particles that the children breathed or ingested. Parents of small children need to be better informed about the dangers of lead and ways to minimize exposure, the article concludes.

Reports and Studies

Agency for Toxic Substances and Disease Registry, U.S. Department of Health and Human Services, *The Nature and Extent of Lead Poisoning in Children in the United States: A Report to Congress*, 1988.

Although convulsions and other extreme symptoms of lead poisoning that were common in the 1960s and '70s are far less widespread today, millions of children are suffering less visible but long-term effects of exposure to lead at low levels. This report found that black children were between 10 and 30 percent more likely to be victims of lead poisoning than white children at all income levels.

Karen L. Florini, George D. Krumbhaar, Jr., and Ellen K. Silbergeld, *Legacy of Lead: America's Continuing Epidemic of Childhood Lead Poisoning*, Environmental Defense Fund, March 1990.

Perhaps the most widely read report on lead's toxicity and steps the federal and state governments have taken to limit exposure to the metal, the report offers a comprehensive review of the sources and pathways of lead exposure. It also presents a proposal for reducing lead poisoning, based on an excise fee on the production and importation of lead. The fee's proceeds would pay for a federal program to remove leaded paint from dwellings.

National Association of Home Builders, *Lead Exposure Prevention Manual*, 1992.

This membership association opposes government mandates for removing leaded paint from homes, saying lead abatement often increases the risk of exposure by releasing large amounts of lead dust into the air. More useful, the group says, would be a widespread education program instructing parents to thoroughly clean their dwellings to reduce their children's exposure to lead. In addition to its legislative agenda, the association provides a detailed rundown on each state's laws dealing with lead and provides addresses where consumers can obtain more information on their states' provisions to reduce lead poisoning.

The Next Step

Additional Articles from Current Periodicals from EBSCO Publishing's Database

Case studies

Foley, D., "Case of the 'anemic' diagnosis," *Prevention,* September 1991, p. 106.

Details the story of Fran Wallace, who was diagnosed with a rare, genetic blood disease called porphyria due to lead poisoning from ceramicware dishes. How Wallace's husband and son were also affected; the symptoms of lead poisoning; getting the lead out. INSETS: Heavy-metal supersleuths (information on lead poison control); the lead in your life.

Schirmer, J., H.A. Anderson, et al., "Fatal pediatric poisoning from leaded paint — Wisconsin, 1990," *Journal of the American Medical Association,* April 24, 1991, p. 2050.

Summarizes the investigation of a child who died from poisoning associated with ingestion of lead-based paint in Wisconsin. Includes an editorial note from the Centers for Disease Control, Atlanta, Ga.

Debates & issues

Berney, B., "Lead and racism," *Environmental Action,* September/October 1991, p. 21.

Focuses on the link between lead-paint poisoning and racism. The fact that deteriorated lead paint is most often found in slum housing in minority communities; results of a study by Dr. Herbert L. Needleman during 1979 and the early 1980s in Boston, Mass.; lead as a case that demonstrates the effectiveness of toxic-use reduction as a strategy; estimates; the estimated cost to eliminate lead paint from the nation's housing stock over the next 10 years.

Greeley, A. "Getting the lead out ... of just about everything," *FDA Consumer,* July/August 1991, p. 26.

Reports that consumption of products that contain lead continues to be a health concern despite steps taken by several government agencies to cut down on exposure to this metabolic poison. Facts on lead; why children are so vulnerable; drugs; safe blood levels; government standards; future; what specific agencies are doing. INSET: How to avoid lead exposure.

Needleman, H.L., "Childhood lead poisoning: A disease for the history texts," *American Journal of Public Health,* June 1991, p. 685.

Editorial. Discusses the numerous sources of lead and how these sources cause childhood lead poisoning. Why

federal policy has undergone a historic change; how lead adversely affects children; the abundant experimental literature on low-level lead intoxication; Assistant Secretary for Health James O. Mason's four-step plan to eradicate childhood lead poisoning; reasons for lack of action on lead.

Palca, J., "Get-the-lead-out guru challenged," *Science,* Aug. 23, 1991, p. 842.

Explores the 10-year-old dispute over the credibility of data on the effects of low-level lead exposure on intelligence, which was published by Dr. Herbert L. Needleman of the University of Pittsburgh. Claims by critics of Needleman's scientific misconduct; history of Needleman's claims about lead poisoning; first claims of serious methodological flaws in Needleman's paper; involvement of Environmental Protection Agency (EPA) special panel.

Shenon, P., "Despite laws, water in schools may contain lead, study finds," *The New York Times,* Nov. 1, 1990, p. A1.

States that four years after the government imposed tough rules to limit the amount of lead in drinking water, federal auditors warn that hundreds of thousands of American children may still be drinking lead-contaminated water at school. Gives results of the auditors' study.

Yulsman, T., "Lead hazards at home," *The New York Times Magazine,* April 28, 1991 (supplement), p. 28.

Emphasizes that the risk of lead hazards at home is more widespread than once thought, but there are ways to minimize your family's exposure. Federal government estimates of the lead content of houses built before 1980; studies of lead poisoning levels in children; one example of lead poisoning; need for lead-level testing in homes built prior to 1980; more. INSETS: Hidden sources of lead; how to avoid the hazards of lead.

Food storage

"Lead crystal," *Harvard Health Letter,* February 1992, p. 8.

Presents some follow-up and feedback on the possible dangers of eating or drinking food stored in lead-crystal decanters. Possibility of the lead leaching out in an acidic environment; more.

"Plumb brandy," *Harvard Health Letter,* April 1991, p. 7.

Considers the little serious consideration that has been

given to possible dangers of alcoholic beverages stored in decanters and drinking glasses made with lead crystal. How the Roman Empire may well have hastened its own undoing by ingesting enormous quantities of lead; work of Conrad Blum, a physician, and Joseph H. Graziano, a researcher in pharmacology, at Columbia University College of Physicians and Surgeons.

"Tainted wrappers for the staff of life," *Consumer Reports,* **March 1991, p. 141.**

Warns consumers about potential lead exposure from plastic bread bags. The lead may rub off or flake off onto food when people turn the bag inside out and use it to store other food. Levels of lead found in samples; how the lead from labels contaminates the environment.

"Two agencies look at lead in wine," *FDA Consumer,* **November 1991, p. 2.**

Reports that a program to reduce consumers' exposure to lead from table wines was announced in September by the Food and Drug Administration (FDA) and the Bureau of Alcohol, Tobacco and Firearms. Long-term plans that include eliminating the use of lead foil capsules to cover the outside rim and cork of some wine bottles; how wine consumers can reduce their lead exposure.

Law & legislation

"Committee moves to restrict some uses of lead," *Congressional Quarterly Weekly Report,* **Aug. 3, 1991, p. 2163.**

Declares that legislation (S 391) designed to improve the environment and protect children from lead poisoning won the approval of the Senate Environment and Public Works Committee on Aug. 1. Approved by voice vote; Environmental Protection Agency; action came after the filing of several federal suits; recycling mandates; landlord disclosures of the use of lead paint.

"Lead exposure bill stalls in markup," *Congressional Quarterly Weekly Report,* **Nov. 2, 1991, p. 3206.**

Considers a House Energy and Commerce subcommittee's failure to complete the markup of popular legislation (HR 2840) aimed at lowering the alarming statistics of lead exposure, especially in young children. Voice-voted amendment of the section of the bill dealing with water; the authorization of five fiscal years, before beginning in fiscal 1992, to help state and local water systems implement the bill's requirements; more.

"Senate panel approves low-lead bill," *Congressional Quarterly Weekly Report,* **April 20, 1991, p. 982.**

Highlights a Senate Environment subcommittee's first push to sweeping legislation to prohibit the use of lead in many products and to ban sales of leaded gasoline in urban

areas. Designed to limit children's exposure to lead; lead poisoning prevalence among children in U.S.; bill (S 391); approved by Toxic Substances Subcommittee; restrictions and banning.

Blum, A. and S. Harowitz, "New lead-paint rules ahead," *Kiplinger's Personal Finance Magazine,* **January 1992, p. 76.**

Reports that bills now before Congress may help get rid of lead-paint poisoning by mandating standards for laboratory analysis of lead in paint, soil and blood. Also pending are standards for certification and training programs for lead inspectors and removers. Outlook of the bill; why none of these proposals would help middle-income homeowners financially; cost of removing lead-based paint.

Dumas, K., "Lead weights: Congress wary of costs and mandates," *Congressional Quarterly Weekly Report,* **Nov. 9, 1991, p. 3286.**

Cites conflicts surrounding legislation (HR 2840) voice-vote approved by the House Energy and Commerce Subcommittee on Health and the Environment on Nov. 4, 1991 that would tighten federal regulations on lead in water, homes, schools, soil and food. The Bush administration's opposition to the bill; the bill's key provisions; details. INSET: The lead threat.

Zylke, J.W., "Preventive medicine's latest goal: Getting lead out to protect children," *Journal of the American Medical Association,* **July 17, 1991, p. 315.**

Reports on the government's initiative to prevent childhood lead poisoning, now in its third year. Reports from government agencies; reports from the Centers for Disease Control; call for lowering of definition of lead poisoning; "multi-tiered approach" to intervention; impact of report recommendations.

Prevention

"Who will get the lead out?" *U.S. News & World Report,* **Oct. 21, 1991, p. 18.**

Discusses how the message declared by the Department of Health and Human Services (HHS) that lead poisoning is one of the most common pediatric health problems in the U.S., is undisputed. The question of who would provide the prevention; HHS Secretary Louis W. Sullivan's announcement of the new guidelines; symptoms of lead poisoning; the approximate number of children with lead poisoning in the U.S.; suggestions by Rep. Henry A. Waxman, D-Calif.

Hilts, P.J., "U.S. opens a drive to wipe out lead poisoning among children," *The New York Times,* **Dec. 20, 1990, p. A1.**

Discusses the federal government's plans to eliminate lead poisoning in children over the next decade. Nearly

900,000 units of public housing and about 57 million homes still have lead paint. Hazards; details of the government's plan.

Jaroff, L., A. Blackman, et al., "Controlling a childhood menace," *Time*, Feb. 25, 1991, p. 68.

Considers the 3 to 4 million American children (one out of every six) under 6 years of age that have lead poisoning. "Strategic plan" developed by the Department of Health and Human Services; elusive goal of total prevention; lead-based paints and leaded gasoline; effects of lead on the bloodstream, oxygen, and enzymes in the brain and nervous system; symptoms; effective treatment; four-point HHS plan. INSET: Some unexpected sources of trouble.

Mason, J.O., "U.S. Public Health Service's strategic plan to eliminate childhood lead poisoning," *Journal of the American Medical Association*, April 24, 1991, p. 2049.

Presents a commentary on childhood lead poisoning from the chief of the U.S. Public Health Service. Lead poisoning is the No. 1 environmental disease that faces children; lead-based paint is the major source; strategic plans to eliminate the problem outlined.

Sherrid, P., "A nontoxic childhood," *U.S. News & World Report*, March 4, 1991, p. 56.

Reports that safeguarding children from lead, radon and other pollutants may be easier than parents think. Presents a guide for first tackling those problems that are easiest to solve. Lead paint, drinking water; electromagnetic fields and childhood cancer; radon testing; pesticides; passive smoking. INSET: Who you gonna call? (free pamphlets on several subjects).

Research

"Deadly lead dust," *Home Mechanix*, October 1991, p. 25.

Discusses new evidence that airborne lead dust is the primary cause of lead poisoning. The U.S. Department of Housing and Urban Development's new testing and abatement procedures; the Lead Exposure Task Force formed by the Remodelers Council of the National Association of Home Builders; health professionals' new concern; where to get more information.

"Lead: New levels of concern," *Science News*, Oct. 19, 1991, p. 252.

Informs that the Centers for Disease Control (CDC) has lowered its "threshold for concern" for blood-lead levels in the wake of mounting evidence that levels previously thought to be safe can cause developmental disorders in children. Announcement by the CDC of several "levels of concern" and recommendations for thresholds at each level;

lead levels and low-birthweight babies; more.

"Lead's reduced stature," *Science News*, Sept. 21, 1991, p. 189.

Comments on a study of 1,454 Mexican American children indicating that too much lead in the bloodstream can hinder growth. Analysis of data from the Hispanic Health and Nutrition Examination Survey; average height reductions; comment of A. Roberto Frisancho, a biological anthropologist at the University of Michigan's Center for Human Growth and Development in Ann Arbor.

Testing

Burgower, B., "Lead alert: Is your child at risk?" *Ladies' Home Journal*, February 1991, p. 62.

Discusses the problems of dangerously high levels of lead being found in schools' drinking water. Environmental Protection Agency investigation; problems with law enforcing tests of schools' water supplies; what parents can do.

Henderson, N., J. Goldwasser, et al., "Testing your child for lead," *Kiplinger's Personal Finance Magazine*, December 1991, p. 98.

Gives advice on testing your child for lead poisoning. The recent Centers for Disease Control guidelines indicate that there are dangers at lead levels as low as 10 micrograms per deciliter. Previous guidelines; details of the test; cost.

Henderson, N. and S. Buri, "How to test your water for lead," *Kiplinger's Personal Finance Magazine*, October 1991, p. 105.

Includes some advice for those consumers who should have their water tested for lead. Who's at risk; health concerns; getting your water tested; what to do if you find lead in your water.

Therapy

"New drug to treat lead poisoning," *FDA Consumer*, June 1991, p. 2.

Reports that the first oral medication approved for the treatment of severe lead poisoning in children was approved by the Food and Drug Administration on Jan. 30. Details on the drug; recommended course of treatment.

Nightingale, S.L., "Succimer (DMSA) approved for severe lead poisoning," *Journal of the American Medical Association*, April 10, 1991, p. 1802.

Announces that the U.S. Food and Drug Administration has approved Succimer for the treatment of lead poisoning in children with blood-lead levels above 45 micrograms per deciliter. This is the first oral medication approved to treat severe lead poisoning in children.

Back Issues

Great Research on Current Issues Starts Right Here... Recent topics covered by The CQ Researcher are listed below. Issues dated before May 10, 1991, were published under the name of Editorial Research Reports.

DECEMBER 1990
Cable TV Regulation
Americans' Search for Their Roots
Is Insurance System a Failure?
Why Schools Still Have Tracking

JANUARY 1991
Growing Influence of Boycotts
Should the U.S. Reinstate the Draft?
America's Archaeological Past
Peace Corps' Challenges in '90s

FEBRUARY 1991
Regional Impact of Recession
Puerto Rico's Status
Redistricting: Mapping Power
Nuclear Power

MARCH 1991
Acid Rain
Cost of the Gulf War
Reassessing Gun Laws
Future for Man in Space

APRIL 1991
Social Security
Canadian Crisis Over Quebec
California Drought
Electromagnetic Radiation

MAY 1991
School Choice
Racial Quotas
Animal Rights
U.S. and Japan

JUNE 1991
Children and Divorce
Teenage Suicide
Endangered Species
Europe 1992

JULY 1991
Teenagers and Abortion
Soviet Republics Rebel
Mexico's Emergence
Athletes and Drugs

AUGUST 1991
Sexual Harassment
Fetal Tissue Research
Oil Imports
The Palestinians

SEPTEMBER 1991
Police Brutality
Advertising Under Attack
Saving the Forests
Foster Care Crisis

OCTOBER 1991
Pay-Per-View TV
Youth Gangs
Gene Therapy
World Hunger

NOVEMBER 1991
Fast-Food Shake-Up
The Greening of Eastern Europe
Business' Role in Education
Cuba In Crisis

DECEMBER 1991
Retiree Health Benefits
Asian Americans
The Obscenity Debate
The Disabilities Act

JANUARY 1992
Term Limits
Oil Spills
Hunting Controversy
Alternative Medicine

FEBRUARY 1992
Threatened Coastlines
New Era in Asia
Assisted Suicide
Jobs in the '90s

MARCH 1992
Women and Sports
Underage Drinking
Garbage Crisis
Mafia Crackdown

APRIL 1992
Ozone Depletion
Welfare Reform
Politicians and Privacy
Illegal Immigration

MAY 1992
Native Americans
Jobs vs. Environment
Too Many Lawsuits?
Fairness in Salaries

JUNE 1992
Nuclear Proliferation
Food Irradiation

Back issues are available for $4.00 (subscribers) or $7.00 (non-subscribers). Quantity discounts apply to orders over ten. To order, call Congressional Quarterly 1-800-432-2250.

Future Topics

▶ *Hard Times for Libraries*

▶ *Prescription Drug Prices*

▶ *Alternative Energy*

PUBLISHED BY CONGRESSIONAL QUARTERLY INC., IN CONJUNCTION WITH EBSCO PUBLISHING

Hard Times for Libraries

Will budget cuts diminish their community role?

FREE ACCESS TO INFORMATION IS OFTEN SAID TO be a cornerstone of democracy. That principal is embodied in the nation's system of public libraries. But in many cash-strapped communities, access to at least some library services is no longer free. Budget cuts have forced some librarians to start charging daily fees to those who borrow best-selling books or current videos. Many are charging library patrons for online computer searches. User fees are just one way libraries are coping with budget cuts. Orders for books and periodicals are being slashed, operating hours curtailed, staff furloughed or laid-off and branches closed. The American Library Association and local "Friends of the Library" groups are trying to mobilize public opinion and convince government officials that libraries are vital parts of their communities and deserve adequate funding.

 June 26, 1992 • Volume 2, No. 24 • 549-572

Formerly Editorial Research Reports

COVER ART: BARBARA SASSA-DANIELS

THE CQ Researcher

June 26, 1992
Volume 2, No. 24

EDITOR
Sandra Stencel

MANAGING EDITOR
Thomas J. Colin

ASSOCIATE EDITOR
Richard L. Worsnop

STAFF WRITERS
Charles S. Clark
Mary H. Cooper
Rodman D. Griffin

PRODUCTION EDITOR
Laurie De Maris

EDITORIAL ASSISTANT
Michael M. Taylor

GRAPHICS
Jack Auldridge

PUBLISHED BY
Congressional Quarterly Inc.

CHAIRMAN
Andrew Barnes

VICE CHAIRMAN
Andrew P. Corty

EDITOR AND PUBLISHER
Neil Skene

EXECUTIVE EDITOR
Robert W. Merry

PUBLICATIONS MARKETING/SALES
Robert Smith

EDITOR, EBSCO PUBLISHING
Melissa Kummerer

The CQ Researcher (ISSN 1056-2036). Formerly Editorial Research Reports. Published weekly (48 times per year, not printed the first Friday of any month with five Fridays) by Congressional Quarterly Inc., 1414 22nd St., N.W., Washington, D.C. 20037. Rates are furnished upon request. Second-class postage paid at Washington, D.C. POSTMASTER: Send address changes to The CQ Researcher, 1414 22nd St., N.W., Washington, D.C. 20037.

Hard Times for Libraries

By Charles S. Clark

The Issues

It's been a sobering spring for residents of Fairfax County, Va., an affluent Washington suburb. Local officials confronting a $200 million revenue shortfall have been threatening unprecedented cuts in social programs and services, including the possible closing of 15 of the county's 22 public libraries (see p. 566).

The impact of the crunch is already visible: Information desks often have signs that say "temporarily closed." Answering machines defer telephone reference questions, and the fine charged adults for overdue books has doubled to 20 cents a day. A new $10 surcharge is being levied for on-line computer searches, and there is a new $24 fee for using the public meeting room.

Services have been seriously affected by a 30 percent cut in the materials budget: All spending on non-print items (compact discs, videocassettes and Books on Tape) has been eliminated; dozens of newspaper and periodical subscriptions have been canceled; Bookmobile service has been discontinued; and the county has ended cable television broadcasts of programming tied to library collections. The final insult comes at 6 p.m.; the library staff, which used to work until 9 p.m., is locking up for the night.

The Fairfax County Public Library system is the nation's third busiest — behind those in New York City and Los Angeles. But while its budget problems are serious, Fairfax has not had to cut its library services as drastically as many other communities.

In Worcester, Mass., six of the seven library branches have closed. In Detroit, six branches have cut the number of hours they're open each week from 40 to 20. In Atlanta, the library

system was forced to close its highly praised day-care centers for "at-risk" children. More than 40 percent of the libraries responding to an American Library Association survey last year said they have had to postpone hiring and terminate, furlough or reduce the hours of some employees.[1]

"At a time when the problems of cities have become acute," says historian and former Librarian of Congress Daniel J. Boorstin, "it is ironic and tragic that city libraries are reducing their hours of service."

Many in the library field say the current cutbacks are worse than those of the Great Depression. "In 1937, for example, all branches of the Queens Borough Public Library [in New York City] were open six days a week as long as 12 hours a day," recalls the borough's library director, Constance B. Cooke. "Compare that to the scenario of early this year, [when] 30 percent of them were open only two or three days a week, six to seven hours a day."[2]

Public libraries aren't the only ones affected; academic libraries also are feeling the pinch. "Librarians worry that years from now researchers will be frustrated by 'holes in the early 1990s' in research collections because certain scholarly works weren't purchased," *The Chronicle of Higher Education* noted recently. Students complain that librarians refuse to check out books when the libraries are shortstaffed, and at least one library requires students to supply their own paper for photocopying.[3]

"It's a silent crisis," says Patricia Glass Schuman, president of the 55,000-member American Library Association (ALA). "And no one realizes it's a problem because libraries have very few enemies." In most cases, libraries fall victim to budget cuts by default. "People say libraries are wonderful, but they are a lower priority than police or firefighters," says June Garcia, president of the Public Library Association.

"With the tax base dwindling, the crime rate going up and the infrastructure deteriorating ... potholes become more important than books," adds Patrick O'Brien, director of public libraries in Dallas, Texas.[4]

Even in affluent Montgomery County, Md., libraries are competing for increasingly scarce resources with various social service agencies. "If there are only two programs [in the county] for child abuse, would you want to cut one of them?" asks the county's library director, Agnes Griffin. "Libraries are a harder case to make," she says, partly because they are sometimes seen as a "frill" that mainly benefits middle- and upper-income citizens.

Library advocates are trying to mobilize public opinion. The ALA has launched a wide-ranging public relations campaign to convince "the policy-makers who spend our tax dollars that Americans value library services and want to see them fully supported." The group points out that libraries receive only about 1 percent of all tax dollars but are used by 66 percent of Americans.

"In cities, a public library is essential to making a neighborhood a community," says Carol Henderson, an official in the ALA's Washington office. She notes that *Money* magazine uses the quality of libraries as one of the factors in its annual ranking of the nation's most livable cities.

Librarians also make the case that they are on the front lines in tackling various social problems — disseminating information on the AIDS crisis, for example, and providing services to the homeless and unemployed. "Libraries have traditionally tried to provide a welcome environment for anyone and a non-judgmental attitude toward anyone who tries to use us," says Public Library Association President Garcia. "It's one reason we encounter the social concerns and challenges of our society."[5] (See story on the homeless, p. 562.)

"[Now] is a perfect moment for a new assault on the consciousness of both the politicians and the electorate," *Library Journal* Editor in Chief John N. Berry III wrote recently. "It is time to work for a new wave of citizen outrage, time for us and our friends to tell them that libraries are not just another budget target."[6]

As the budget battles proceed, here are some of the issues on which libraries' prospects will turn:

Should the federal government play a stronger role in easing the library budget crunch?

"Because an educated and informed public is the lifeblood of democracy, librarians also help to preserve our nation's great experiment in liberty and self-government," President Bush proclaimed during National Library Week in April.

As the president's remark indicates, there is no shortage of enthusiasm in Washington for the country's

15,481 public library branches.* But any notion of a federal rescue effort is tempered by the fact that more than 80 percent of public library funding comes from local governments; only 1.4 percent comes from the federal government. *(See chart, p. 553.)*

The tradition of local control, which dates from the public library's origins in the 19th century, is regarded as a plus by most in the library profession. "There are two basic views of libraries," says the ALA's Schuman. "One is that they're good for recreational reading and the other is that they're a social agency. The beauty of local control is that each community gets the mix it wants."

Though federal funding in the 1950s and '60s did much to encourage local support for libraries *(see p. 561)*, the clear trend over the past 12 years has been to cut the federal share. The Reagan administration consistently proposed zero funding for the Education Department's library appropriation, only to have Congress restore the money annually at basically a flat rate.

The Bush administration has generally proposed cuts less severe than those supported by President Ronald Reagan. The fiscal 1993 budget Bush proposed in January called for a 76 percent cut from the previous year's library funding level. The president asked for a total of $35 million for libraries, all of it to be used to support adult literacy programs — a cause supported by first lady Barbara Bush.

The library community was less than pleased. "It forces us to run just to stay in place," says the ALA's Schuman, whose organization recommended a $207 million appropriation for fiscal 1993. "Bush calls himself the education president, but he

---

*According to the American Library Association, there are 8,968 public library systems in the country, 3,438 academic libraries, 1,735 government libraries, 9,051 special libraries and 92,538 school libraries.

hasn't delivered on his promises."

Rep. Major R. Owens, D-N.Y., the only professional librarian in Congress, had a similar reaction. "Bush talks more than he is willing to pay," he says, adding that he is confident Congress will restore the money Bush is seeking to cut. Owens would like to see a dramatic increase in federal spending on libraries. "Just as we do with education spending," he says, "the federal government should fund libraries at about 25 percent, but we would still give them lots of local control."

The Bush plan, offered as part of a larger "America 2000" education reform strategy, reflects the administration's interest "in how the public library functions in the 21st century, not the 1930s," says William D. Hansen, assistant Education secretary for management and budget.

Hansen mentions the Library Services Act of 1956, which gave grants to states to expand library services in rural areas, and the 1964 Library Services and Construction Act, which provided funds for new library buildings, services for the handicapped and interlibrary loan programs.

These programs were "very successful," he says. "Now it's time to look at new ways that libraries can be leveraged with government assistance." As an example, he cites the Education Department's planned "Smartline" computer network, which will transmit instructional materials to public libraries and schools.

Hansen says Bush's fiscal 1993 education budget — a proposed increase of $1.6 billion plus $600 million more for the Head Start program for disadvantaged preschoolers — "came out of the hide of other domestic programs." "He's put his money where his mouth is," Hansen adds.

But Henderson of the ALA says it is misleading to say that the decades-old federal library programs have completed their mission. It assumes that today's rationale is the same as the

1950s goal of getting libraries to rural areas, she says. "It says nothing about whether funds are adequate for today's libraries."

Henderson says the ALA would like to see a modest expansion of federal library funds to help pay for such high-cost items as library services for the blind and other disabled individuals and for non-English-speakers. "Since the 1960s, the federal government has also helped share resources across political boundaries, which redounds to the benefit of a whole area," she adds.

ALA President Schuman believes "the federal government could also make library funding more equitable," easing some of the regional disparities caused by libraries' reliance on revenues from property taxes. Garcia of the Public Library Association says Washington could be more active in helping to standardize computer software used by libraries and in sharing technology and catalogs that often are too expensive for individual libraries to purchase.

Many librarians emphasize the need for federal grants to preserve the crumbling, aging volumes that sit on many library shelves. The Association of Research Libraries estimates that there are 80 million such volumes around the country. "It's a national cultural heritage at risk," says Duane Webster, executive director of the association's Washington office. "The enormity of the problem requires a national response." *

Are user fees and privatization good solutions to the budget crunch?

Libraries facing financial drought are turning increasingly to various types of user fees. Many are charging daily fees, for example, to those who

---

*The National Endowment for the Humanities has a multimillion-dollar program to copy brittle books onto microfilm. It is projected to cover about 3 million books in the next 20 years.

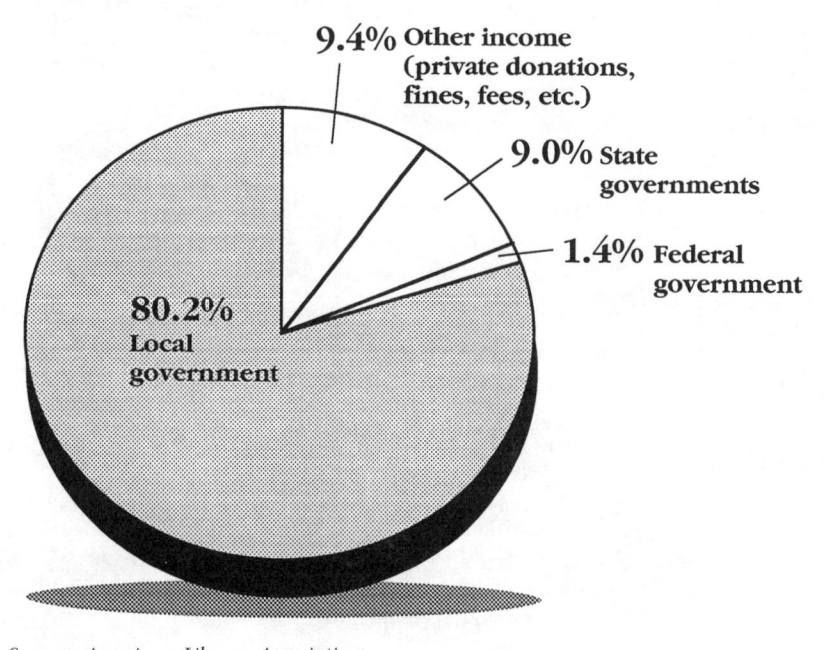

How Libraries Are Funded

Public libraries receive the bulk of their funds from local governments.

- 9.4% Other income (private donations, fines, fees, etc.)
- 9.0% State governments
- 1.4% Federal government
- 80.2% Local government

Source: American Library Association

---

borrow best-selling books or current videos, or charging out-of-town users for borrowing privileges.

The advent of computerization in libraries has sometimes made user fees seem the wave of the future. An estimated 200 to 300 libraries have fee-based information services, according to For Your Information, a fee-based research and document delivery service that works out of the Los Angeles County Public Library.[7] About a hundred college and university libraries now rely on revenues from fee-based research services offered to local businesses, *The Chronicle of Higher Education* reports.[8]

Advocates defend user fees as being financially necessary, but they also argue that the fees encourage a better understanding of the financial limitations of local government. They say fees limit waste and overconsumption while encouraging management improvements to control growth and reduce demand for expensive library services.[9]

But many librarians still oppose the fee concept. As far back as 1977, the ALA approved a resolution stating that charging user fees for information services "is discriminatory in publicly supported institutions." Current ALA President Schuman even questions the trend toward charging for online computer searches. "Just because the information is in a different format doesn't mean ipso facto that you should charge money," she says. "Some people won't be able to afford it."

A similar view was expressed by technology analyst Barbara Smith in *Library Journal.* "Would a town want or wish to support a police station that charged victims for criminal databank searches performed in conjunction with an investigation?" she asked. "Unless a public library is willing to modify its mission, the charging of user fees is inconsistent and unsupportable."[10]

An Entrepreneur at the Library of Congress

In his five years as Librarian of Congress, James H. Billington has stirred up plenty of shelf dust in his effort to bring the nation's foremost public library into the Information Age.

Billington helped persuade Congress to increase the library's budget, enabling the institution to begin processing a massive backlog of uncataloged acquisitions, install an elaborate computer center and launch a pioneering sound, text and visual archive known as "American Memory."† But there is one Billington project that is drawing decidedly mixed reviews: his proposal to begin charging user fees for specially tailored services.

Billington described the rationale behind the plan in a speech to a business group in May: "A lawyer in San Francisco wants our law library to find and send him copies of all the relevant court decisions on divorce law in Chile. Or an author ... wants us to find and provide copies of all our hundreds of pictures of Mark Twain. Or a research scientist in Houston wants us to translate, and mail all our recent Japanese journal articles on satellite technology.... We believe that such highly specialized requests should be met ... but that the costs of the extra effort required ... should be paid by the person requesting the extra service, not by the taxpayer."

Following a year of negotiations with librarians and business representatives, the fee proposal has now taken the form of a bill (S 2747) introduced this May by Sen. Claiborne Pell, D-R.I. It would update the Library of Congress' 90-year-old authorization to charge local libraries small fees for preparing card catalog cards; help disseminate the library's information products and services; and create a revolving fund to allow the library to recover costs for providing specially tailored products. Basic services — such as cataloguing, inter-library loan and book preservation — would continue to be supported by taxpayers.

The plan has garnered little enthusiasm from the Amer-

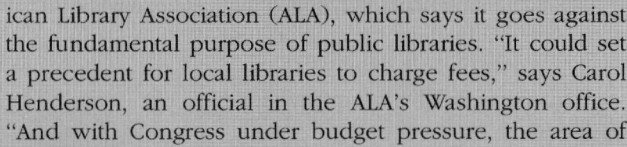

James H. Billington

ican Library Association (ALA), which says it goes against the fundamental purpose of public libraries. "It could set a precedent for local libraries to charge fees," says Carol Henderson, an official in the ALA's Washington office. "And with Congress under budget pressure, the area of charging fees may be where all the library's innovative expertise goes in the future." The ALA has been working with the library to more clearly specify which services would require which fees.

Another group that has expressed concerns about the plan is the Information Industry Association (IIA), the Washington trade group for companies whose work includes compiling government information and marketing it in electronic and print formats. IIA members warn that the bill could endanger public and entrepreneurial access to government information, increase the risk of copyright infringement†† and allow the taxpayer-supported Library of Congress to unfairly compete with private-sector information marketers.

"The library wants a blank check," says IAA Vice President and General Counsel Steven J. Metalitz. "It wants in on any information service for a fee with minimal oversight and accountability."

Billington is hoping to win the skeptics over. "We're not trying to make money or have flashy new services," he told *National Journal*. "There is no more noble mission than just keeping this [institution] going. But what people don't realize is that it's an endangered species. The whole library profession is an endangered species. And therefore, it has to be dynamic to survive."‡

---

† The new program will enable the Library of Congress to send schools and libraries electronic copies of photos, manuscripts, music, films and sound recordings.
†† For more on copyright issues, see "Artists' Rights and Copyrights," *Editorial Research Reports,* May 13, 1988, pp. 246-256.
‡ Quoted in *National Journal,* March 21, 1992, p. 698.

The key, says Garcia of the Public Library Association, is whether "the fee becomes a barrier to anyone because of their economic level." It's one thing, she says, if a library merely wants to encourage rapid turnover by charging a fee for borrowing current best-sellers, such as the latest Danielle Steele novel. "If you *have to pay,* however, it's a different kind

of values statement."

Some librarians note that user fees don't actually cover costs and can discourage library use. In the 1970s, recalls Dallas Public Library Director O'Brien, a decision to charge non-city residents $10 to borrow 5 items and $25 for 15 items reduced library use by 15 percent and prompted suburban libraries to consider retaliating with

their own fees. A similar plan in Kansas City, Mo., produced similar results. "It was projected that user fees would raise a half-million dollars in revenue," says Kansas City's public library director, Daniel J. Bradbury. "But it was a dismal failure and probably purchased instead about $500,000 of bad will in the community." [11]

Another frequently mentioned alternative in library-financing debates is privatization. But the notion that a for-profit company could come in and run a public library has not progressed much beyond buzzword status. In Fairfax County, for example, a blue ribbon panel convened last year to explore ways out of the county's budget crunch recommended privatization for libraries, but the panel offered not a single model or case study where such methods had been tried.

Privatization might work in certain areas, says Garcia, such as custodial work, purchasing and cataloging, but not in librarianship itself. "Where the public good becomes subverted by profit mechanism, public service would suffer," she says, particularly service for children. "Library service is extraordinarily labor-intensive," notes O'Brien. "We're not at the point where people can sit by a library computer and do it all alone."

The only area where privatization has made headway in libraries is in the federal government, a trend actively opposed by the ALA. The operations of more than a hundred federal libraries have been contracted out to commercial firms over the past decade, with libraries at the Department of Labor, the Department of Housing and Urban Development and the National Oceanic and Atmospheric Administration going to foreign firms.[12] Most recently, the library at the Department of Health and Human Services was replaced by a self-service online information service and fax machine.

Since 1987, the White House Office of Management and Budget, which monitors costs incurred by federal agencies, has circulated a policy document that suggests which services agencies could cost-effectively contract out. Libraries were included along with cafeterias and cleaning services. After lobbying from the ALA, officials at OMB recently agreed to remove libraries from the list, but

OMB says it will leave it up to individual agencies whether to contract out their libraries.

Has computerization aggravated library budget problems?

The onslaught of computerization in American libraries over the past decade has prompted some taxpayers to question whether libraries that are having trouble keeping their doors open should continue investing in high-tech gadgetry.

In Grosse Point, Mich., for example, senior citizens organized groups called Citizens Against Unnecessary School Extravagance and Citizens for Accountable Government to oppose a 1991 referendum that called for spending $7.8 million on public library improvements, including a new building, media center and computer systems. The measure was defeated.

Computers unquestionably have given librarians and library users powerful new research capabilities, but they often carry a high price tag. The online article research database called InfoTrac, for example, has been judged by users to be faster and more up-to-date than the long-venerated *Reader's Guide to Periodical Literature*. But InfoTrac's magazine index costs about $3,600 a year, compared with $160 a year for the green-bound *Reader's Guide*.

But most librarians believe computer-based information services are well worth the initial expense. "Take the *Encyclopaedia Britannica*," says Gloria Konsler, vice president for libraries at the Board of Education in Grosse Pointe. "It costs $1,149" and takes up a lot of space. By contrast, the same or a comparable encyclopedia available on CD-ROM* stores much more information in much less space. And, says Konsler, the soft-

---

*CD-ROM stands for Compact Disc-Read Only Memory, a format in which information is provided on discs that are playable on a compact disc player and personal computer.

ware can be updated every year for about $900.

"Computers provide a payback in less than five years," says Vera Fessler, associate library director for technical operations in Fairfax County. "We can deliver the same service in fewer hours." Fessler, who teaches computer librarianship at Catholic University in Washington, says computers also have allowed librarians to offer new services. About 150 public libraries currently offer remote access by home computer, she says, allowing users to reserve books online even when the building is closed.

Other librarians point to savings in acquisition budgets from current and planned international data base services. The Online Computer Library Center (OCLC), launched in the 1970s by a consortium of universities in Ohio, now links networks in 46 countries and provides access to more than 22 million text items. It has saved local libraries hours of backroom cataloging work, enabling staff to attend to the public.

In the next few years, the federal government will oversee installation of a cross-country fiber-optic cable "information superhighway" known as the National Research and Education Network (NREN), which will link public libraries, government and industry to countless databases.

"We have more information in computers than has ever been printed," marvels O'Brien. "And we can harness the economies of scale afforded by computers to keep libraries open."

The growing number of electronic data bases has prompted a debate over whether libraries should acquire new materials or simply arrange to gain access to them. Last year, the library at Virginia Polytechnic Institute and State University, in Blacksburg, Va., reported that it had canceled $300,000 in academic journal subscriptions because library users were more interested in journal articles available from electronic data bases around the world.

"The bottom line is that we will be spending more of our budget for access to information and less on ownership of information," VPI librarian Paul M. Gherman wrote. "This change strikes at the basic economic model of libraries, which traditionally have bought information once and shared it many times with their users."[13]

Some question this change in the way libraries spend their money. "The reasoning goes, 'Harvard will buy it, so I won't,'" O'Brien says. "Does that mean everyone bombards Harvard to access [the material]? What's the payback for Harvard? What will we do when no one's acquiring?" ∎

BACKGROUND

Intellectual Democracy

The public library is a characteristically American institution, its history a tale of private and government heroics to create benefits for the public at large.

The first library in North America appeared in 1638, when the Rev. John Harvard bequeathed 300 volumes from his private collection to an exclusive college in Cambridge, Mass., that would bear his name. Other private and church libraries were established in the late 17th century, including a number of "revolving libraries," small private collections that were transported from town to town.

In 1731 Benjamin Franklin made history by launching the Library Company of Philadelphia, a unique subscription library that would be copied around the country and in Europe. Because books were expensive, members banded together to share their copies. "Franklin's very simple but hitherto unthought-of device was a new and radical departure," wrote one historian. "Its effect was toward a more even distribution of intellectual wealth, the establishment of an intellectual democracy."[14]

Franklin saw the library as a way to "improve the general conversation" of common men and later as an inspiration to rally colonists to de-fend their political rights. It succeeded. As one Philadelphian wrote in a letter to a friend on the eve of the American Revolution: "You would be astonished at the general taste for books which prevailed among all orders in this city. The librarian assured me that for one person of distinction and fortune there were 20 tradesmen that frequented this library."[15]

Several towns in New England stake a claim to having the oldest tax-supported library in the United States, but most historians give the honor to Peterborough, N.H. In 1833, a Rev. Abiel Abbott persuaded citizens of that town to use state money to start the Peterborough Town Library. At the same time he launched a fee-based "social" library, the Peterborough Library Company.

"Obviously, Abott did not see the new public library as a competitor of the social library, but such competition began almost immediately," historian Jesse H. Sherea wrote in *Foundations of the Public Library* (1949). "As early as 1834, dues in the social library began to lapse, and in 1853 the minutes of that institution record: 'Since the establishment of the town library, very few books have been taken from the [private] library.'" The fee-based library soon closed.

The concept of public libraries would steadily spread. In the 1850s, Massachusetts and New Hampshire became the first states to permit localities to collect taxes for libraries.

The city of Boston opened its public library in 1853.

The Library Profession

That same year, Charles C. Jewett, an official at the Smithsonian Institution in Washington, called a convention of prominent librarians in the hope of launching a national library and a uniform catalog of holdings in all American libraries. His plans were thwarted by a general financial panic in 1857 and then by the Civil War.

Still, librarians pressed on, demonstrating a commitment to creating non-elitist collections of books. Justin Winsor, who became superintendent of the Boston Public Library in 1868, was among those to plead for more public libraries: "It is a very easy matter to form a library to suit the wants of specific conditions of people; but it is not so easy to gather such books as will afford the greatest and most varied interest to all sorts of readers."[16]

By 1875, all states of the union had created state libraries for use by government officials, the judiciary and nearby public. Public libraries had also proliferated, ballooning from 779 in 1850 to 3,682 in 1876, when the nation celebrated its centennial.

It was during the centennial year that a 25-year-old Amherst College librarian named Melvil Dewey helped found the American Library Association in Philadelphia. (It's now based in Chicago.) Though best known for inventing the Dewey decimal book-classification system, Dewey furthered a library philosophy that emphasized mass education. The library should reach out and be "less a reservoir than a fountain," he said.[17] Dewey also wrote what would become the ALA's slogan: "the best reading for the greatest number at the least cost."

One of the concrete steps taken to further library democracy in this period was to permit patrons to person-

Continued on p. 558

Chronology

1700s-1800s *Birth of public libraries in the U.S.*

1731
Benjamin Franklin creates a subscription library in Philadelphia.

1800
President John Adams creates the Library of Congress.

1833
Petersborough, N.H., establishes first tax-supported public library.

1876
American Library Association (ALA) is founded in Philadelphia. It later moves to Chicago.

1890
Massachusetts approves funding for the Boston Public Library.

1930s *Depression forces libraries to slash budgets in spite of rising use. New Deal allots federal money to rebuild and replenish libraries.*

1936
U.S. Office of Education creates Library Services Division.

1950s-1960s *Congress expands federal support for libraries.*

June 19, 1956
Congress passes Library Services Act, which gives grants to states to expand library services in rural areas.

Feb. 11, 1964
President Lyndon B. Johnson signs Library Services and Construction Act, which expands federal aid for public library construction and school library improvements.

1970s *General revenue-sharing in early '70s boosts federal aid to local libraries, but cuts in federal funds later in decade prompt protests.*

July 20, 1970
President Richard M. Nixon signs law creating National Commission on Libraries and Information Science to advise the executive and legislative branches on national library and information policies and plans.

May 8, 1973
Public libraries across the country dim lights to protest cuts in federal library spending.

May 29, 1974
New York City Mayor Abraham D. Beame announces plans for library cuts in response to city's fiscal crisis.

June 6, 1978
California voters approve Proposition 13 cap on property taxes, which leads to cuts in library budgets.

Nov. 15-19, 1979
First White House Conference on Library and Information Services.

1980s *Cutbacks in federal support force libraries to turn to private fundraising. Computer data bases revolutionize information industry.*

Oct. 1, 1985
Revenue-sharing program expires.

Dec. 12, 1985
President Ronald Reagan signs Balanced Budget Act, which later forces staff cuts and reduced hours at the Library of Congress.

1990s *ALA launches protest rallies and media campaign to staunch budget cuts.*

March 15, 1990
President Bush signs amendments to 1964 Library Services and Construction Act.

July 25, 1991
President Bush signs National Literacy Act.

Dec. 9, 1991
President Bush signs High-Performance Computing Act, creating an information "superhighway" known as the National Research and Education Network.

July 9-13, 1991
Second White House Conference on Library and Information Services.

Aug. 14, 1991
President Bush signs National Commission on Libraries and Information Sciences Act to improve operations of the commission.

March 11, 1992
ALA launches "Call for America's Libraries," to encourage public to register support for libraries.

April 5-11, 1992
During National Library Week, newspaper, radio and television features focus attention on budget cuts.

Continued from p. 556

ally browse in the stacks. "This obviously democratic move was made tentatively," one library historian wrote, "against the severest opposition by many conservative librarians and library boards, who were concerned about theft, mutilation and increased wear and tear."[18]

In other innovations, librarians in Cleveland, Ohio, and Worcester, Mass., pioneered the practice of lending book collections to classrooms in public schools. And thanks to the example set by Minerva Sanders, a public librarian in Pawtucket, R.I., public libraries began opening to children. Sanders "was something of a 'radical' who believed in a people's library," one historian wrote. "She had introduced open shelves, had encouraged workingmen to come to her institution and was most interested in children at a time when they were considered noisy nuisances. In 1887, Sanders welcomed youngsters to a corner of the reading room where she had provided four tables and chairs, lowered because she had ordered a large segment of the legs cut off."[19]

Leveraged Philanthropy

The late 19th century became known as the age of robber barons, but it also was a time of celebrated philanthropy. The names of such tycoons as John Jacob Astor, James Lennox, Samuel J. Tilden and Enoch Pratt became associated with generous bequests to public libraries. But none was more celebrated than Andrew Carnegie, the multimillionaire steel magnate from Scotland.

As a working-class youth in Allegheny, Pa., in the 1850s, Carnegie had been profoundly affected by his experience using a library for working boys that had been made possible by a bequest from a Col. James Anderson. For the rest of his life, Carnegie would view libraries as "the People's University." After he made his fortune, Carnegie embarked on a

philanthropic mission on behalf of libraries, eventually donating more than $56 million to finance construction of 1,679 libraries in 1,412 communities, and 830 more overseas.[20]

Carnegie's generosity was magnified because he conditioned his bequests on a promise of future support from local governments. He felt voters would support government spending for libraries "because no class in the community is to be benefited so clearly and so fully as the great mass of the people, the wage-earners, the laborers, the manual toilers."[21] After his death in 1919, Carnegie's grants to libraries continued through the Carnegie Corp.

Government officials began getting the idea. By end of the 19th century, all states had given localities authority to raise taxes for libraries. At this time, New York, Maine and Rhode Island became the first states to appropriate annual sums (averaging $100-$500) to libraries that met state standards. In 1890, Massachusetts became the first state to establish a state library commission. By 1900, there were 1,700 public libraries in the nation that owned at least 5,000 books.

Reaching the Public

Public libraries entered the 20th century with a new eagerness to reach out in the manner of Melvil Dewey's "fountain." In Washington County, Md., horse-drawn wagons began carting portable libraries into rural areas. In Dayton, Ohio, library carts were brought onto factory floors. In Minneapolis, the public library in 1910 set up a special reading room for unemployed men. The New York Public Library, founded in 1895 with money from the Astor, Lenox and Tilden family fortunes, moved to a huge new building on Fifth Avenue in 1911. In that first year it lent 8 million books, a third of them to children.[22]

Urbanization created a rising social consciousness that furthered the mission of libraries. "Earnest young people sought work in the slum areas as nurses, teachers, pastors and social workers," wrote library historian Ernestine Rose. "Some of them drifted to libraries, feeling that in these also lay an opportunity to reach the submerged masses."[23] With the Library of Congress leading the way, public libraries began serving the blind with special reading rooms and books printed in Braille.

The group that may have benefited most from free access to libraries were the recent immigrants, who poured into the country in record numbers early in the century. Libraries boosted their collections of holdings in Russian, Yiddish, Italian, Hungarian and other languages, and hired staffers who spoke foreign languages. English-language instruction became common at libraries, along with courses on "Americanization," or how to negotiate the naturalization process.[24]

One of the immigrants' great success stories also became a library success story. John Defarrari, the son of an Italian immigrant fruit vendor, become a multimillionaire investor and in 1947 donated $1.5 million to the Boston Public Library. He said he made his fortune by studying corporate reports in the library's statistical room.

The exceptions to this open access, of course, were the racially segregated libraries primarily in the South. In his famous memoir *Black Boy*, author Richard Wright described how he posed as an errand boy for a white library card-holder in order to borrow a book by H. L. Mencken. It was a situation that would endure until the civil rights sit-ins in the late 1950s and early '60s.

National Mobilizations

During World War I, libraries were at the forefront of wartime civic-mindedness. "You can't beat a read-

Celebrating Libraries

Among the most enthusiastic users of the nation's libraries have been its writers. An anthology of writers' tributes to public libraries was published last year. Here are excerpts from *Reading Rooms: America's Foremost Writers Celebrate Our Public Libraries with Stories, Memoirs, Essays and Poems,* edited by Susan Allen Toth and John Coughlan (Doubleday, 1991).

"Libraries — those temples of learning, those granite-and-marble monuments — do not appear to most people as places of passion or even vital activity. Local newspapers don't cover the library beat as ardently as they do city hall; protests don't usually erupt for television cameras on the library steps; the mayor doesn't invite visiting celebrities to be feted and photographed in the Main Reading Room. For most Americans, the library is a reassuring and stable presence, there when they need it, and until then, to be comfortably taken for granted."
— *Susan Allen Toth, editor of* Reading Rooms

"The library was a place where most of the things I came to value as an adult had their beginnings. Art was there, poetry, history and words. Millions of words. Trillions. Politicians have come and gone since many of them were written, empires have risen to temporal glory and collapsed into decay. But those words remain as powerful as they were when I was a boy and will be there long after I'm gone."
— *Pete Hamill, reporter and novelist*

"For many, the public library is the only quiet place in an unquiet world; a refuge from the violence and ugliness outside; the only space available for privacy or work or thought. For many it is the only exposure to books waiting on open shelves to be taken home, free of charge. As a former student put it: 'In a library, it's hard to avoid reading.'"
— *Bel Kaufman, teacher and novelist*

"You would not want to say that [the New York Public Library] has the smell of the tomb of its steady, underpaid clerks; but it does have the smell of a tomb and that is not unpleasant for a day of study. Damp winter shrouds on the backs of chairs. Bright, determined scholars, using the minutes, the hours, and the bibliographies, the footnotes falling into line obediently, like little soldiers in the ranks of documentation."
— *Elizabeth Hardwick, essayist, novelist and a founder of* The New York Review of Books

"There it was, as soon as you walked up the great marble steps [of the New York Public Library] off Fifth Avenue. "On the Diffusion of Education Among the People Rest the Preservation and Perpetuation of Our Free Institutions." It said that to you as you entered the great hall, in gold letters on the pylons facing the Fifth Avenue entrance. The entrance also read: "The library is open every day of the year 9 a.m.-10 p.m., Monday-Saturday, 1-10 Sunday."
— *Alfred Kazin, literary critic*

"Often, while waiting for the books to come up from the mysterious depths of the library, I would stroll along the outer aisles glancing at the titles of the amazing reference books which lined the walls. Thumbing those books was enough to set my mind racing for days. Sometimes I sat and meditated, wondering what question I could put to the genius which presided over the spirit of this vast institution that it could not answer."
— *Henry Miller, novelist*

"Here is where people,
One frequently finds,
Lower their voices
And raise their minds."
— *Richard Armour, English professor and author of light verse and humorous prose*

ing army," one prominent librarian said. The ALA's Library War Service responded by shipping 7 million donated books to the 4.5 million U.S. troops overseas.[25]

Community support for public libraries continued during the Depression, when libraries were nicknamed "breadlines of the spirit." As in economic hard times today, libraries became vital centers for the unemployed, even as their operating funds were cut back. From 1929-33, one report said, the circulation at public libraries in 77 cities of more than 100,000 people went up by 33 percent, while expenditures fell by the same amount.[26] To raise funds, libraries in Cleveland began sponsoring "overdue weeks," in which more affluent citizens were asked to intentionally keep books out so that their fines could aid the library.

By 1935, about 63 percent of the country was served by libraries. As part of President Franklin D. Roosevelt's New Deal, the Works Progress Administration spent more than $18 million to put more than 27,000 Americans to work in libraries, build-

Making Do With Less . . .

Most state library agencies and public library budgets have been affected by the recession. The following roundup is based on responses to a survey conducted by The Council of State Governments. Five states did not respond to the survey.

Alabama: Three years of budget cuts have forced the public library service to cut 27 jobs, or 36 percent of the staff, to reduce or eliminate services, to cut average annual acquisition spending from $400,000 to $200,000, and to recruit volunteers to maintain minimal services.

Alaska: Fiscal 1992 budget cuts eliminated five full-time positions, resulting in termination of Statewide Media Service, which provided curriculum-support videotapes to school districts.

Arizona: Fiscal problems delayed authorization of state funds to match federal construction grants. Libraries have imposed a hiring freeze and across-the-board budget cuts.

Arkansas: General hiring freeze. No state funds allocated for acquisition of circulating books or reference materials. Seventy percent of periodical subscriptions were canceled.

California: Shortage of state funds delayed receipt of federal library construction funds and forced a hiring freeze.

Colorado: Materials budget cut by 7.5 percent; library newsletter to be published less frequently. Three prison libraries opened with aid from the state Corrections Department. Library for the Blind and Physically Handicapped moved to expanded and renovated facility.

Connecticut: Hiring and salary freeze. State library lays off 15 workers and eliminates Saturday hours.

Delaware: Reduced service for patrons of the Library for the Blind and Physically Handicapped.

Florida: State library agency has experienced intermittent hiring freezes over past two years.

Georgia: State library aid cut by 5 percent; state library agency staff cut by 36 percent. End of direct library ser-

vice for state government. New emphasis on data base searching for reference services. Addition of two state-funded library positions.

Idaho: State library agency print shop closed and service contracted out. Four new library clerical positions authorized by Legislature.

Illinois: Hiring freeze in all but critical positions.

Indiana: Hiring freeze initiated after budget is cut by 3 percent. Out-of-state travel cut by 50 percent. Two positions eliminated to free up funds for computer upgrade.

Iowa: Six positions eliminated.

Kansas: State operating budget for libraries cut by $69,110, with reductions in communications, travel and acquisitions. Aid to local libraries cut by $30,309.

Kentucky: State library budget cut by 5 percent; four positions eliminated. Planned expansion of state interlibrary loan program in question.

Lousiana: Serious budget cuts made in fiscal years 1988-89. State library funded on "standstill" reduced level since then.

Maine: State library budget cut by 15 percent; nine positions eliminated.

Maryland: Four positions eliminated and two vacancies frozen because of "economic crisis." State Library Network cut budget by 25 percent. State aid to counties cut by $65 million, producing cuts in aid to local libraries.

Massachusetts: Revenue shortfall forces state agency furloughs of two to eight days.

Michigan: State aid to public libraries cut by 9.2 percent in fiscal 1990-91, but boosted to record level for fiscal 1991-92. Some staff reductions through attrition. Evening hours eliminated at state libraries on Mondays and Wednesdays.

Minnesota: Film and video collection terminated; several state library agency publications discontinued. Staff cuts in reference service.

Mississippi: Half-million-dollar budget cut eliminates some positions; $59,000 cut from book budget; audio-

ing, cataloging, indexing and driving bookmobiles to rural areas.

Not everyone was pleased with the role of libraries as spiritual breadlines, however. In a letter to *The Saturday Evening Post*, a New York City resident complained: "Now the public libraries ... are simply loathsome. All the chairs in the Magazine Room and Newspaper Room are filled with down-and-outers, the overflow from

Bryant Park and Central. All the marble seats on the stairs are filled with more down-and-outers, their feet swathed in newspapers. . . . I think it is the smell I resent the most rather than the actual presence of these people." [27]

When prosperity returned, it was wartime again. The ALA book drives for World War II netted 17 million books for the troops overseas. The

Army alone would hire 1,000 librarians during the war years. [28]

Postwar Boom

The postwar economic expansion accelerated the growth of America's suburbs, where a functional library became part of every leafy-green landscape. Describing the new facilities, historian Rose wrote: they are designed "to meet your needs, and

... Recession's Impact on State Library Budgets

visual services terminated. Hiring freeze with some exceptions. State stopped printing letterhead and routine forms for local libraries.

Missouri: Hiring freeze forces staff to assume extra duties.

Montana: Operations budget cut by 8 percent, changing some full-time positions to part-time.

Nebraska: University of Nebraska film service discontinued.

Nevada: Job vacancies frozen; 12 percent cut in operating budget forces reductions in state aid to local libraries; loss of six full-time and six part-time positions; cuts in operations and materials acquisition.

New Hampshire: "Library Comes to You" book-delivery service to isolated areas terminated. State film collection disbanded. Law library closed two days a week. Hiring freeze, some layoffs and furloughs.

New Jersey: Eighteen state library positions eliminated. Hiring freeze, except for two vacancies in manager positions.

New Mexico: Self-imposed reductions in collections and services following re-examination of library agency mission.

New York: Despite some budget cuts and staff reductions, the state agency has enhanced several programs related to information resources and foreign trade. Small-business federal contract information service continued fully funded. Library support program for developmentally disabled wins a competitive grant.

North Dakota: State agency considering establishing the state's first regional library systems.

Ohio: Budget cuts forced elimination of seven state library positions.

Oklahoma: Full funding for production of CD-ROM bibliographic data base to be available to 300 libraries.

Oregon: State aid to public libraries cut by 4.8 percent. Three state positions abolished. Materials budget cut by a third.

Rhode Island: Four state library employees laid off; hiring freeze imposed; cuts in state aid to local libraries and in services for disadvantaged and minority populations. Grant from National Endowment for the Humanities permits hiring of one full-time librarian and one part-time clerk.

South Carolina: Hiring and salary freeze imposed. Budget for services is in a "holding pattern."

South Dakota: Reorganization of public services workload in reference, interlibrary loan and circulation. State library is unable to fill key network coordinator positions because of low salaries.

Tennessee: Budget cut of 14 percent forces elimination of 17 positions in state library and archives and 12 in regional system. Salaries frozen. Weekend hours at state library and archives discontinued. Additional staff reductions expected.

Utah: State Legislature funded a new paraprofessional program for Library for the Blind and Physically Handicapped and $106,000 in state aid to public libraries.

Virginia: Only impact of state budget restrictions has been delays in hiring.

Washington: Across-the-board library budget reduction of 2.5 percent.

West Virginia: Began installation of satellite dishes at every public library; fax machine network extended to more than 100 libraries; program launched to provide all libraries with print and video resources for literacy instruction.

Wisconsin: Spending on library materials cut by 10 percent. Interstate travel curbed, hiring slowed. Some staff cuts through attrition.

Wyoming: Hiring freeze, staff travel curbs, plans under way for future 12 percent budget cut. Legislature authorized some expansion of services in collection on natural resources and state planning materials.

Source: The Council of State Governments, *1991 State Library Agencies Financial Survey*

---

to avoid giving you an inferiority complex. No high steps — you go right in. No turnstiles or crowded counters with lynx-eyed attendants — you walk through a wide door, and after you enter you find the return desk at one side, and books around the walls. Nearby is an information desk. Is the librarian in attendance busy at something? Never mind. Go right up and interrupt her.

Her chief business is to attend to your wishes." [29]

In 1956, decades of lobbying by the ALA bore fruit when Congress passed the Library Services Act, which provided funds to encourage states to extend library services to rural areas. In 1964, President Lyndon B. Johnson's Great Society spawned the Library Services and Construction Act, which gave state agencies au-

thority to distribute federal money to local libraries for new buildings, services for the handicapped and interlibrary loan programs. Urban libraries saw their funds increase sevenfold the following year; the act was extended in 1966. College libraries would benefit from the 1963 Higher Education Facilities Act and the 1965 Higher Education Act.

Continued on p. 563

Libraries Struggle Over Rules on the Homeless

The Library of Congress calls them "special patrons." They are not scholars or researchers, but the increasing number of homeless people who use the nation's most prestigious book repository as a daytime shelter. They sleep in its reading rooms, wash in its lavatories and, according to some officials, hamper the library's ability to serve its regular users.

The homeless problem is not confined to America's big-city libraries, however. In the affluent community of Morristown, N.J., hostility toward the homeless who frequent the town's library led to a highly publicized legal battle over whose rights prevail in a public library.

The situation began in the summer of 1989, when Richard Kriemer, a 40-year-old homeless man who had grown up in Morristown, incurred the wrath of other library users because of his body odor and his habit of staring at women and following them around the reading room. The library responded by issuing new rules permitting the eviction of patrons who annoy other users with their staring or their offensive body odor.

Kriemer immediately challenged the rules and retained a lawyer from the American Civil Liberties Union. "The haves don't want to look at the have-nots," he told *The New York Times*.†

In May 1991, a district judge ruled that the library had violated Kriemer's "First Amendment rights to receive ideas." Those who want to avoid the sight and smell of the homeless "should revoke their condition, not their library cards," wrote Judge H. Lee Sarokin of the federal district court in Newark.

The controversial opinion made international news and divided the nation's librarians, who were sent scurrying to come up with acceptable patron guidelines. An editorial in *The Wall Street Journal* criticized the judge for making Kriemer a hero and for ruling that "a homeless person's right to offend and disturb takes precedence over the rights of society at large."††

Kreimer, who already had been awarded $150,000 in damages after he sued the Morristown Police Department for harassment, in early March settled with the library for an undisclosed amount. But a few weeks later, on March 23, an appeals court overturned the lower court's ruling, backing the library's right to set patron-exclusion rules.

Many librarians describe the appeals court ruling as a "win-win" decision for libraries and patrons. The judge affirmed a library's status as a "limited public forum," notes Patricia Glass Schuman, president of the American Library Association. "That means libraries can set regulations — you can't come in and make a speech — but it also means people have 'a right to know'" — regardless of whether they have a home or not.

"The body odor question is a behavior issue, not a homelessness issue," Schuman adds. "We wouldn't want to see library regulations that eliminate a whole class of people."

The publicity surrounding the Morristown case prompted similar actions elsewhere. In Las Vegas, Nev., a group called the Homeless Rights Coalition filed a suit that prompted a change in local library policies in January.

Previously, Las Vegas-Clark County libraries would eject patrons who had body odor that could be detected from six feet away. Following months of negotiations with the Homeless Rights Coalition, library officials agreed to a consent decree that requires them to call one of three local representatives of the homeless before evicting anyone because of offensive body odor. Failure to comply results in a $250 fine for the library.

The agreement also affirms that patrons need not carry personal identification in order to read newspapers and magazines in the library, and that they may bring personal belongings as long as they fit in the library's 24-by-18-by-20-inch storage boxes.

Since the decree, Las Vegas library officials have complained that homeless advocates are taking longer than the stipulated 30 minutes to arrive at the scene. They plan to return to court to refine the agreement. "We're trying to make the library free and equal to everyone," said library Director Charles Hunsberger. "But some people want to use the library as a shelter for the homeless."‡

Some communities have gone out of their way to make the homeless feel welcome. In Portland, Ore., a librarian created a special storefront library especially for the homeless. In Tulsa, Okla., the public library set up showers and a telephone service. In San Francisco, the public library began issuing library cards to the homeless even though they have no fixed address.

Such moves are welcomed by homeless activists. "Concerns such as body odor and disheveled appearance are part of the reality of being homeless," says Maria Foscarinis, director of the Washington-based National Law Center on Homelessness and Poverty. "It's not fair to prevent access to exactly the kinds of places that might help the homeless escape."

"It's a very hard problem," admits Morristown librarian Barbara Rice. "We want to serve everyone in the community. But we're not social workers."‡‡

---

† Quoted in *The New York Times*, Sept. 15, 1989.

†† *The Wall Street Journal*, June 12, 1991.

‡ Quoted in *American Libraries*, February 1992, p. 127.

‡‡ Quoted in *The New York Times*, op cit.

Continued from p. 561

Budget Cuts Begin

In 1970, the need for a national body to coordinate library policy at the local, state and federal levels prompted creation of the National Commission on Libraries and Information Science. It set up shop just in time to witness the first rounds of library budget cuts that are still being felt today.

The tone was set when President Richard M. Nixon proposed a fiscal 1974 budget calling for a cut in federal library spending from $140 million to zero. In May 1973, public libraries across the country dimmed their lights or went by candlelight to protest. Congress restored much of the money, but as the oil crisis, a recession and inflation set in, many local libraries began shutting their doors.

During New York City's fiscal crisis in 1974, Mayor Abraham Beame announced a "crisis budget" that would involve mass closings of libraries. Construction of new branches was temporarily halted and dozens of employees were laid off, but in the end, no libraries were closed. Efforts to close branches of the Queens Borough Public Library were headed off by community protests and a lawsuit filed by the National Association of Colored People (NAACP) charging racial discrimination.

Beginning in these troubled times, the District of Columbia Public Library began cutbacks that would drop 30 percent of its staff over the next decade. The Chicago Public Library began reductions that would shrink its staff from 2,400 employees to 1,400 employees today.

In several reports in the mid and late 1970s, the National Commission on Libraries and Information Science warned that the nation's libraries were "grossly underfunded." "Public library needs and problems are similar to those of schools," one report said. "It is a responsibility of each state to provide for both an adequate and financially equitable distribution of services. It is logical therefore that public libraries and public schools have comparable forms of financial support."

In 1979, during the Carter administration, 2,000 library professionals gathered at the first White House Conference on Library and Information Services. Of 3,000 resolutions passed at the state and territorial meetings that preceded the conference, more than 60 percent dealt with the need for new funding. (Many others dealt with the impending wave of computerization.)

"Over history's time, the destruction of libraries, whether by war or dictatorship, has been viewed as a serious blow to freedom and democracy," consumer advocate Ralph Nader told the gathering. "In New York, it's seen merely as a way to save some money."

Although Congress declined to follow up on the conference's recommendation for a large increase in federal aid, many participants said the meeting helped galvanize grassroots support for local libraries around the country.

Cuts Under Reagan

The Reagan administration inaugurated an era of diminished federal funding for libraries. Federal funds represented 3.7 percent of public library moneys in 1982, but are down to 1.4 percent today.

In 1986, the Library of Congress got caught in the federal budget wars, and had its budget cut for the first time. The library terminated 300 temporary employees and shortened reading hours by a third. Following a protest vigil on the sidewalks outside the library, the hours of service were restored several weeks later.

Also in 1986, during the time when President Reagan was encouraging a "New Federalism," the general revenue-sharing program expired, leaving states and localities even more on their own to maintain libraries. In many regions, library cuts were deep. Shasta County, Calif, for example, which is home to 143,000 people, had no library service for seven months in 1988. San Francisco began a budget crunch in 1984 that would cut library services by 24 percent over the next eight years, despite a 27 percent boost in demand.

The budget cuts came at a time of steady inflation. According to the ALA, the average price of hardcover books doubled from $19 to $40 from 1977-90, while the costs of periodical subscriptions went up 400 percent.

There was some good news for libraries during this period. From 1988-89, 111 new library buildings went up in the United States, the greatest number since 1979.[30]

Militant Librarians

By the 1990s, the years of budget battles had produced a new militant attitude among librarians. "We have not spoken out before," Richard M. Dougherty, then president of the ALA, told a 1991 rally in Atlanta. "In a way, people take libraries for granted until the doors close."[31]

In the summer of 1991, the ALA organized a five-day whistle-stop tour called "Rally on Wheels." Protesters carrying placards saying "Libraries are Worth It" stopped at cites between Atlanta, where the ALA had just met, and Washington, where the Second White House Conference on Libraries and Information Services was set to begin. They presented the White House with 500,000 signatures from library supporters. The rallies prompted such ideological opposites as the Rev. Jesse Jackson and Rep. Newt Gingrich, R-Ga., to make common cause. As Gingrich told one rally, "Cutting library budgets is the technique most likely to return us to barbarism."[32]

At the conference in Washington, 2,000 delegates gathered to hear speeches from President Bush, first lady Barbara Bush and Marilyn Quayle, wife of the vice president. Education Secretary Lamar Alexander spoke of the important role for libraries in the administration's America 2000 education reform plan, though critics pointed out that the plan mentions libraries only once. In the end, the conference endorsed 95 recommendations, among them initiatives in literacy programs for children and the disadvantaged, multilingual programs, rural library aid, the fiber-optic "information superhighway" and finally, a vow to "fund libraries sufficiently to aid U.S. productivity."

These recommendations will be the "core agenda for many groups for the 1990s," said J. Michael Farrell, chairman of the National Commission on Libraries and Information Science. *Library Journal* called the conference a success because it "has given new birth to the citizen movement for libraries that began in 1979, and it has added some key Republicans to the roster of library supporters."[33] ∎

"at risk" youth the use of homework centers and computers. "The rationale is that if we put more money into libraries now and keep our youth off the street, we'll be putting less money into jails and police protection later on," says Carol Young, the library's administrative analyst.[35]

Since 1989, the Seattle Public Library has run an after-school program for "latchkey" children. Known as SPLASH, for Seattle Public Library's After-School Happenings, it uses its $250,000 budget to provide reading programs, homework help and entertainment for "at risk" 4 to 14 year olds whose parents are not at home in the afternoons.

CURRENT SITUATION

Local Politics

Library advocates say the surest way to maintain funding for public libraries is to build community political support. And the best way to accomplish that, they say, is to have tax revenues and local bond issues that are specifically tied to libraries.

"If you have dedicated taxes on the local level, support for libraries is way at the top with police and fire departments," says Rep. Owens. In Kansas, for example, state law earmarks a certain percentage of every dollar of property taxes (it varies by locality) for libraries. In Las Vegas, libraries get a percentage of the sales and motor vehicle taxes.

Experts have found that bond issues are most likely to be approved by voters when they deal with libraries separately from other public services. In 1990, *Library Journal* reports, 80 percent of the library ballot referendums passed, a figure similar to other years. The bond issues seem to pass more often during special

elections than during general elections, when many other issues are on the ballot.[34]

Political support for libraries appears closely related to the state of an area's economy. One of the most robust library systems in the country right now is in Salt Lake City. "Utah is one of the lighthouse economies of the nation, with a No. 1 financial-effectiveness rating," explains Dennis Day, director of the Salt Lake City Public Library. The Legislature tries to attract new businesses to the state, he says, by highlighting the area's low crime rate and generous support for the symphony orchestra and the library. That generosity is preserved, Day adds, "through meaningful communication" with city and state officials. "We try not to be greedy in order to maintain credibility. We present a library budget and they know it's real."

In communities with severe social problems, libraries can dramatize their worth to budget-makers by intertwining themselves in social programs. For example, the San Diego, Calif., public library has seen its budget increased by 16 percent since it joined the police and parks departments in a "Neighborhood Pride" program aimed at reducing crimes by youth gangs. Among other things, the library offers

Fundraising Activities

For the past decade or so, the plight of public libraries has been confronted most determinedly by local "Friends of the Library" volunteer groups. There now are more than 2,300 tax-exempt "friends" groups around the country, according to the Philadelphia-based Friends of Libraries USA. (Ten years ago, there were virtually none.) They organize book sales, celebrity auctions and letter-writing campaigns on behalf of libraries, and quite often retain the services of professional fundraisers.

Professionals can make the difference when libraries are competing for funds with many other worthy causes. "The library doesn't have the same prestige that the symphony and the ballet have," says Sandy Dolnick, executive director of Friends of Libraries USA. "We have a hard time appealing to people who want to give to prestigious causes."[36]

Librarians and "friends" groups are careful to emphasize that the work of fundraisers is intended "to make a good library great," not to substitute for basic services. "More parsley on

Continued on p. 566

At Issue:

Will computers render traditional libraries obsolete?

S. Michael Malinconico

Professor, School of Library and Information Studies, University of Alabama, Tuscaloosa
FROM *LIBRARY JOURNAL*, MAY 1, 1992

yes

Unrelenting, accelerating change has brought libraries and librarians to the threshold of a new era, radically different from even the recent past....

Electronic information technologies are diminishing the central role of traditional libraries. Online catalogs and their associated communication networks allow ready access to the collective holdings of numerous libraries....

Access to other library collections is no mere convenience — it is a matter of urgent necessity. Because of the amount of information produced each year and the costs to acquire and organize it, individual institutions are able to satisfy with their own resources an ever diminishing fraction of their users' needs....

The increasing availability of information in machine-readable form permits many information needs to be satisfied with decreased involvement of libraries and librarians.... For example, CD-ROMs allow individuals to own specialized collections of information sources and to carry them with them, instead of traveling to conventional libraries to consult them.... Electronic journals ... are more timely and less costly to produce, distribute, index and maintain than are conventional journals....

When connected to ... networks, the [personal computers] that many people own can function as workstations, bringing an unprecedented richness of information resources to their desktops.... It is ironic that the new information services simultaneously increase user need for the assistance of information specialists and reduce the contact they have with them.... Many users who need assistance may not seek it because they are reluctant to appear unable to deal with high-technology systems. For many of them ... the connection between information services and library services will grow weaker. Users will be more likely to seek advice from colleagues or technical specialists than from librarians or information specialists....

With the reduced importance of physical libraries, librarians and information specialists will need to be pro-active and promote their special services to their user communities. They will need to function more like consulting information engineers than traditional, passive information resource custodians and dispensers of documents.

Those who are successful in this endeavor will enjoy satisfying careers and earn the status and respect long due, but not achieved by, the library profession. Librarians who cling to the old paradigms of librarianship may find themselves curators of infrequently used, increasingly irrelevant information museums.

Patricia Glass Schuman

President, American Library Association
FROM *WHOLE EARTH REVIEW*, WINTER 1991

no

Predictions ... about electronic technology too often cause us to assume that the future will just happen, not that we can play a key role in inventing it.... Two major assumptions are at work here. The first is that we are moving toward a paperless society. Books will soon be historic artifacts, and full-text electronic publishing will hold sway. The second assumption is that hardware and software will be readily available, usable, affordable, desirable and satisfying to everyone....

An individual must be literate in order to negotiate our complex social, political, economic and work environment. But ... 23 million adult Americans cannot read above a fifth-grade level.... An educated user also needs an awareness of the value of information and the financial wherewithal to use it.

What does our fantasy about direct home delivery of information services really mean in a society where 25 percent of households below the poverty line have no telephone? Only 13 percent of U.S. households own a personal computer. Only 10 percent have modems. Seventeen percent of all white children use a computer at home, while only 6 percent of black and Hispanic children do. Rather than providing universal delivery, there is a very real possibility that technology could widen the gap between the information-rich and the information-poor....

Which brings us to perhaps the most dangerous of our fantasies ... that libraries must decide whether they are in the book-delivery business or the information-delivery business.... Adopting the vocabulary ... of a business can be dangerous for the library profession.... The production, management and sale of information is something quite different from the provision of access. It implies efficiency, not equity. Just look at what the concept of managing information has done to public access to government information: cutbacks, privatization, increased user fees....

No machine can compete with a creative, knowledgeable, flexible, professional librarian, one who provides interpersonal interaction, information evaluation, communication, synthesis and judgment.... The role of the librarian is to distinguish between data and information, between facts and knowledge. Libraries must be concerned not only with the what and the how but with the why. Access means more than mere physical location. It means the connection of ideas to people. Our challenge is not just to provide more information, or even the right answers. Our challenge is to help people formulate the right questions.

Continued from p. 564

the potatoes, never the potatoes themselves," as one librarian put it.[37] "Although the funds are useful to the library," another said, "the primary benefit is public support and public relations."[38]

Libraries must also be careful to keep donated money in a separate account, notes O'Brien of the Dallas library. "If it shows up as a credit on the budget, politicians will be tempted to reduce tax-dollar support," he says.

Because "friends" groups and librarians themselves are restricted in their freedom to lobby political officials, local citizens' groups can make a huge difference. In Dallas, budget cuts throughout the 1980s prompted a public relations professional named Freda Gale Stern to conclude that the City Council needed to hear the voices of library users. She founded the Citizens for Library Excellence to encourage letters and phone calls to the council and eventually won restoration of evening hours at branch libraries and a $75,000 appropriation for book restoration. "We were a catalyst for support that was already there," Stern recalls. "It was just a matter of asking."

Signs of Hope

This year, the ALA has been engaged in its most active library boosterism ever. Its "Call for America's Libraries" campaign offered an 800 telephone number to citizens wishing to express their concerns over library budget cuts. With help from several corporations and a $3,200 donation from the Association of American Publishers, the campaign drew 75,000 calls in four weeks, with such comments as, "I'd rather give up my food stamps than the library." This month the ALA presented Congress with a pro-library petition containing some 300,000 signatures.

The organization also has conducted more than 200 "radio rallies," in which Patricia Schuman and other ALA officials participate in local talk shows to discuss the ramifications of the budget cuts. Schuman reminds listeners, for example, that the average book is in print for only nine months; if a financially strapped library postpones the purchase, it may never be able to acquire the book.

There is plenty of evidence that such cries of outrage are having an effect. A survey just released by the Public Library Association shows that 65 percent of the responding libraries had received a budget increase this year; 16 percent had been hit with a decrease and 18 percent reported no change.

In Fairfax County this June, the Board of Supervisors turned around and voted to come up with $400,000 to prevent closing any libraries, having received more phone calls and letters on the issue than on any other in memory.

This spring, the city of Chicago opened the nation's largest municipal library. After months of budget squabbles and threats to lay off city workers and cut hours at the 80 branch libraries, Mayor Richard M. Daley reversed himself and the city aldermen allocated new library money.

In New York City in June, Mayor David N. Dinkins reversed an earlier position and persuaded the City Council to restore $13.3 million that had been slated for cuts at the city's 205 library branches. "Like schools and churches, libraries are part of the heart and soul of a neighborhood and a city," Dinkins said.

New York's move comes with strings attached, however. The funds are to be used only to keep branches open for more hours, according to Mimi Koren, director of public affairs at the Queens Borough Public Library. "There is nothing for books, and we lost two-thirds of our book budget last year," she says. "We're still unhappy that we can't keep the level of library services." ∎

OUTLOOK

Will Libraries Survive?

A common view of the future of public libraries was set out recently by a private citizen. "Construction will soon begin on the 'new' main branch of our public library system," a reader wrote in a letter to the *San Francisco Chronicle*. "It will be obsolete before most of us ever see it. Shortly after the 1995 scheduled completion date, technology will have advanced to the point where companies currently in existence will be providing complete 'library' services to the comfort of our living rooms. All at a cost incidental even to our poorest citizens. Our 'new library' will continue to serve a function for which anyone who uses the main branch is all too painfully aware. At over $100 million, the most expensive homeless shelter in the world!"[39]

This notion of a computerized "library without walls" may have a place in libraries' future, says O'Brien of the Dallas Public Library, but it won't replace the neighborhood library. "There's a need to interact, with people serving people," he says. "Libraries are one of the only face-to-face services left where kids can come with no appointment and get professional service from someone with a master's degree, who assigns no grades, makes no judgments. We don't care what you look like or smell like. It's the greatest democratic institution ever created."

That institution also shows remarkable capacity to change with the times, adapting the notion of free public access to an ever broadening array of media and services. In Pikes Peak, Colo., 14,000 commuters a year find carpools through the library's computerized matching system. In Salem, Ore., the library lends audiovisual equipment and computers. In Pittsburgh, Pa., the Carnegie library shares work space and a computer network with local community and housing activists.

"The value of libraries is such a common-sense observation," says Rep. Owens. "It has the least bureaucracy, the buildings are already there and it's open to everyone." Owens is optimistic that the upsurge of interest in education will help libraries regardless of which administration is in power.

The argument for library funding invites a long-term perspective. "It costs about $2,000 to teach an adult illiterate to read and write," notes Richard C. Wade, the New York University professor who headed the New York Governor's Commission on Libraries. "It costs $8,000 [a year] to put someone on welfare; and it costs $50,000 to put someone in prison" — the same $50,000 that a philanthropic fund recently gave to keep the Crown Heights library in Brooklyn open one more day a week.[40]

On the central but politically volatile question of how to fund libraries, the public appears evenly divided. Forty-four percent of those responding to a poll conducted by the Library Research Center at the University of Illinois said they favored increasing taxes to help pay for libraries, while 41 percent said they favored library user fees. Only 8 percent of the respondents favored reducing library services. (By contrast, 73 percent of librarians responding to a separate survey said they favored tax hikes, and only 9 favored user fees.[41])

History has demonstrated that the library profession attracts highly committed individuals, and that shows no signs of changing. At the Pasadena,

Calif., Public Library this spring, staff members agreed to forgo pay raises to keep library services going. Mayor Jess Hughston said he was "flabbergasted" by their sacrifice, adding, "I think it's setting an example for the rest of the city."[42]

Such a commitment comes from viewing public libraries as "part of what made this nation," says Salt Lake City librarian Dennis Day. He became committed in 1964 when he was doing research at a library in Dayton, Ohio. He had checked out a book on the aerodynamics of birds in flight, and there on the endpaper was the signature of a previous borrower, aviation pioneer Orville Wright.

"The great thing about library service in the United States is that, like so many other things, it's a hybrid," says Daniel Boorstin. "There's no national system, so it's a movement, and it's important that it continue as a movement. We have the greatest national library in the world because of the support of Congress and the American taxpayer."

"Public libraries," Boorstin concludes, "can develop and catalyze and keep alive a love for books." ∎

Notes

1 "Library Budgets Survey '91: Hard Times Continue," *Library Journal*, January 1991, p. 14.

2 Constance B. Cooke, "Save our Libraries," *Penthouse*, July 1992, p. 84.

3 Julie L. Nicklin, "Rising Costs and Dwindling Budgets Force Libraries to Make Damaging Cuts in Collections and Services," *The Chronicle of Higher Education*, Feb. 19, 1992, p. 1.

4 Quoted in *The* (Baltimore) *Sun*, Jan. 5, 1992.

5 Quoted in Rob Gurwitt, "Shelving Tradition in the Library," *Governing*, March 1992, p. 24.

6 Editorial in *Library Journal*, March 15, 1992.

7 Cited in *National Journal*, March 21, 1992, p. 695.

8 *The Chronicle of Higher Education, op. cit.*

9 See "About Fees: A Sampling of Recent Commentary," *American Libraries*, October

1986, p. 676.

10 Barbara Smith, "A Strategic Approach to Online User Fees in Public Libraries," *Library Journal*, Feb. 1, 1989, p. 33.

11 Quoted in Judy Quinn, "Daniel J. Bradbury: Librarian of the Year," *Library Journal*, January 1992, p. 47.

12 Patricia Glass Schuman, "Making the Case for Access: ALA Needs You," *RQ*, winter 1989, Vol. 29, No. 2., p. 166.

13 Paul M. Gherman, "Setting Budgets for Libraries in the Electronic Era," *The Chronicle of Higher Education*, Aug. 14, 1991.

14 Joseph Leroy Harrison, *The Public Library in the United States* (1894), quoted in Paul Dickson, *The Library in America* (1986), p. 2.

15 Ernestine Rose, *The Public Library in American Life* (1954), p. 15.

16 *Ibid.*, p. 19.

17 *Ibid.*, p. 203.

18 *Ibid.*, p. 28.

19 C. H. Cramer, *Open Shelves, Open Minds* (1972), quoted in Dickson, *op. cit.*, p. 36.

20 Dickson, *op cit.*, p. 46.

21 Quoted in Sidney Ditzion, *Arsenals of a Democratic Culture* (1947), cited in Dickson, *op cit.*, p. 48.

22 *Ibid.*, p. 66.

23 Rose, *op cit.*, p. 38.

24 U.S. Education Department, "Partners for Lifelong Learning: Public Libraries and Adult Education," November 1991, p. 9.

25 Dickson, *op cit.*, p. 74.

26 *Ibid.*, p. 119.

27 Quoted in Susan Allen Toth and John Coughlan, *Reading Rooms* (1991), p. 110.

28 Dickson, *op. cit.*, p. 127.

29 Rose, *op cit.*, p. 199.

30 *Time*, Jan. 15, 1990, p. 72.

31 Quoted in *The New York Times*, July 8, 1991.

32 Quoted in John Berry and Judy Quinn, "Consensus Out of Chaos," *Library Journal*, August 1991, p. 42.

33 *Ibid.*

34 *Library Journal*, June 15, 1991, p. 48.

35 Quoted in Patricia Glass Schuman "The Silent Crisis:—The Erosion of America's Libraries," forthcoming *USA Weekend*.

36 Quoted in Holly Hall, "Financially Strapped Libraries Try Fund Raising," *The Chronicle of Philanthropy*, June 18, 1991, p. 24.

37 Jeffrey R. Krull, "Private Dollars for Public Libraries," *Library Journal*, January 1991, p. 65.

38 Dwight F. Burlinggame, "Public Libraries and Fundraising: Not So Strange Bedfellows," *Library Journal*, July 1990, p. 52.

39 *San Francisco Chronicle*, May 16, 1992.

40 Quoted in *New York Times*, Feb. 10, 1992.

41 *Library Journal*, April 1, 1992. p. 54.

42 Quoted in the *Los Angeles Times*, March 18, 1992.

Bibliography

Selected Sources Used

Books

Dickson, Paul, *The Library in America: A Celebration in Words and Pictures,* Facts on File Publications, 1986.

A Washington-based author and lover of libraries has assembled a rich anthology of photographs and text reprints that dramatize the story of the library movement and the role libraries have played in U.S. history and culture.

Rose, Ernestine, *The Public Library in American Life,* Columbia University Press, 1954.

A librarian offers a discussion of the genesis of the American public library with emphasis on the nature of the services it has offered library users.

Toth, Susan Allen and John Coughlan, eds., *Reading Rooms: America's Foremost Writers Celebrate Our Public Libraries with Stories, Memoirs, Essays and Poems,* Doubleday, 1991.

This anthology offers warm recollections and tributes to libraries in the words of prominent American writers, both highbrow and popular. The forward by Librarian of Congress Emeritus Daniel J. Boorstin provides a capsule history of the American public library.

Articles

Hall, R.B., "Still a Boom for Bonds?" *Library Journal,* June 15, 1991, p. 48.

Reports that while operating budgets are tightening, libraries are still making gains on capital improvement issues.

Kurzweil, R., "The Future of Libraries Part 1: The Technology of the Book," *Library Journal,* January 1992, p. 80.

Discusses the technology of books, which constitute such an integral element of our society — both reflecting and shaping its culture — that it is hard to imagine life without them. The life cycle of technology; precursor stage; invention; development; maturity; obsolescence; from goat skins to CD-ROM; more.

Nicklin, J.L., "Rising Costs and Dwindling Budgets Force Libraries to Make Damaging Cuts in Collections," *The Chronicle of Higher Education,* Feb. 19, 1992, p. A1.

Discusses the waning buying power of academic libraries, noting that in an era of rising costs and dwindling resources, college libraries are making cuts that could ultimately damage the nation's collections of scholarly works. Forcing a fundamental reshaping of the mission of research libraries; individual problems at some universities; statistics from the Association of Research Libraries; cutting staffs and consolidating operations; integrating groups of libraries.

Quinn, J. and M. Rogers, "Library budgets Survey '91: Hard Times Continue," *Library Journal,* January 1992, p. 14.

Reports that as state and local budget cuts get deeper, so too does the crisis for librarians and library service across the country. Library staff layoffs and freezes; rising service demands; local victories; comments from librarians across the country by state; Arizona, cuts of 1-5 percent in FY91, 1992; Maine, 15 percent reduction in FY91 and so far 13 percent for FY92; Brooklyn Public Library budget impact; details.

Quinn, J. and M. Rogers, "National Poll Reveals Tensions Between Librarians and the Public," *Library Journal,* Feb. 15, 1992, p. 108.

Presents the results of a National Opinion Poll on Library Issues. Suggests the public favors some censorship, and wants adult literacy and latchkey programs, but aren't sure how to fund them. Librarians do not want censorship.

"Setting Budgets for Libraries in Electronic Era," *The Chronicle of Higher Education,* Aug. 14, 1991, p. A36.

Contends that the way in which research libraries spend their budgets for books and other printed materials in an age of electronic communication poses broad implications for libraries, journal publishers and university presses. Paul M. Gherman details how Virginia Polytechnic Institute's libraries are handling the budget crunch.

Reports and Studies

1991 State Library Agencies Financial Survey, *The Council of State Government,* 1992.

Annual report summarizing data on libraries collected by the chief officers of state library agencies. The latest report looks at the impact the recession is having upon state library agencies.

The Next Step

Additional Articles from Current Periodicals from EBSCO Publishing's Database

Acquisitions

Dick, J. T., "Secondhand videos," *Library Journal,* **Nov. 15, 1991, p. 49.**

Recommends considering buying secondhand movie tapes, saying they can stretch your library budget dollar. Cost of new wholesale videos; how libraries, unless they charge a fee, are stuck subsidizing a pricing system designed to reap profits for movie studios unable to share directly in video rental receipts; large catalog to choose from; whom to call about buying videos; how the industry views pre-viewed.

McMillen, L., "Recession pushes libraries to cut back on acquisitions of literary archives," *The Chronicle of Higher Education,* **Feb. 19, 1992, p. A29.**

Considers the state of the market for literary archives and manuscripts: in a word — depressed. Time and patience to place an archive; comments from Bart Auerbach, consultant to Christie's; endowments that generate funds to buy materials; changing shape of literary studies; university libraries with major archives of 20th century writers; University of Texas, Austin; donations; disadvantageous tax laws.

Addresses & essays

Dougherty, R. M., "ALA faces hard times; how will we react?" *American Libraries,* **May 1991, p. 460.**

Addresses the effect the recession has had on libraries. Plight of the New York City public libraries, one of the most visible examples; American Library Association's agenda; focusing energy on personnel-related issues; progress being made.

MacLeish, A., "Libraries in the contemporary crisis," *Library Journal,* **June 15, 1991, p. S10.**

Presents an article originally published in the November 1939 issue of "Library Journal" by author and poet Archibald MacLeish concerning his own ignorance of American libraries. He states that is is upon American libraries that the burden of his education must fall; claim that education is not an altogether adequate answer to those who ask for a chance to work usefully and creatively; educating the people of this country to the value of the democratic tradition the have inherited; more.

Books

"Reading between the videos," *The Economist,* **Feb.**

29, 1992, p. 29.

Discusses how the American book industry recently released a study showing that 60 percent of American households bought no books over the course of an entire year, prompting the media to declare books "a dying form of communication." Less talked about is the 40 percent rate of "aliteracy," which is the number of Americans who can read but choose not to. Cut in federal funding of libraries.

Hoffert, B., "The paperback bind," *Library Journal,* **July 1991, p. 51.**

Considers the rising use of paperbacks in the nation's libraries, not only because the price is right, but because so many patrons want paperbacks. Fully 95 percent of "Library Journal's" respondents carry paperbacks, and on average spend 17 percent of their budgets on them, allocating 8 percent to mass market and 9 percent to trade titles. Readers before budgets; choosing a format; pitching paperbacks to libraries. INSET: The reverse deal: From paperback to hardcover.

Budget allocations

Anderson, A. J., S. Pridham, et al., "Why isn't the public library an essential service?" *Library Journal,* **March 1, 1992, p. 62.**

Presents a case study, in which the library's budget was to be cut by 40 percent over the next year, bringing the director of the library to the conclusion that the library was not an essential service. Analysis I: Suggests changing the director's inability to act in a crisis; questions what to do about the proposed cut; analysis II: Suggests that the major issue is whether a public library ever constitutes an essential service; possible solutions.

Burgin, R. and P. Hansel, "Library management: A dialogue," *Wilson Library Bulletin,* **January 1992, p. 73.**

Opinion. Presents rules for budget requests. Be honest; don't whine; do your homework; be brief; more.

Gerhardt, L. N., N. Rawlinson, et al., "Emergency library action," *School Library Journal,* **May 1991, p. 4.**

Editorial. Presents a proposal for an Emergency Library Action Committee to deal with the effects of budget cuts on libraries. Lack of action by the American Library Association; assertion that local budget cuts are a national crisis; proposal to plan and execute actions to convince voters that libraries are a basic responsibility of government; plans for advertisements on local radio and TV.

Case studies

"Enoch Pratt plans to give five branches to local groups," *American Libraries,* **January 1992, p. 7.**

Reports that due to budget cuts in early December, Enoch Pratt Free Library in Baltimore, Md., plans to shut down as many as five of its 28 branches by March 15, unless community groups take over their operation. Origin of the plan to relinquish control to local organizations; partial reprieve; narrowed mission; Program Director Anna Curry's mixed feelings; fears about the long-term effects.

"New Jersey libraries fight funding blues," *American Libraries,* **February 1992, p. 131.**

Offers a look at the fiscal problems plaguing several New Jersey libraries. In Jersey City, six libraries and all library programming is threatened by an 8 percent budget cut; Newark Public Library is implementing severe reductions in staff, hours, and services; Montclair Public Library is curtailing hours in an effort to hold its budget down for 1992, despite a 15 percent increase in borrowing in 1991; more.

Gill, J.F., "Bookshelves of the vanities," *Washington Monthly,* **June 1991, p. 42.**

Reports that although celebrities like Tom Wolfe, Jackie Onassis and Oscar de la Renta are raising millions to save the main New York Public Library, the neighborhood branches are dying. The myopia of tax deductible New York charity; current crisis considered worse than that which existed during the Great Depression; government's responsibilities.

Jaschik, S., "Frustration at U. of Tennessee: Proposed 10 percent budget increase becomes a 10 percent cut," *The Chronicle of Higher Education,* **Sept. 4, 1991, p. A35.**

Details current frustrations among administration and faculty members of the University of Tennessee (Knoxville) over a review of campus operations that resulted in cuts in virtually every program. Effects of increases in class size; fewer faculty members; library hours; separation of athletic and academic budgets.

Lee, F.R., "New Yorkers fear for literacy as libraries cut back," *The New York Times,* **March 6, 1991, p. B1.**

Discusses the plight of New York City's public libraries. To help close a budget gap that exceeds $2 billion over the next 16 months, the city has slashed $14.7 million from its budget of about $133 million for library operations, and state financing is expected to be cut about 10 percent.

Mestrovic, M., G. Feldman, et al., "Publishing at NYPL: Alive and well," *Publishers Weekly,* **May 31, 1991, p. 46.**

Reports that at a time of grave budgetary crisis in the public sector, the New York Public Library's innovative trade and scholarly book publishing program is drawing international interest from would-be emulators. Richard Newman, manager of publications for the library; origins of the commercial publishing program; other publishing projects in development; more.

Quinn, J. and M. Rogers, "Brooklyn PL begins 'adopt-a-branch'," *Library Journal,* **December 1991, p. 33.**

Reports that the Brooklyn Public Library (BPL) has begun an 'Adopt-a-Branch' program, in which civic or business organizations donate money to supplement library services that have been cut by New York City's budget. BPL's program does not restrict money to capital improvements; the Kaplan fund, the only donor so far; the latest cut, the Homework Hotline; more.

Quinn, J. and M. Rogers, "Despite some beneficence, NYPL management still draws fire," *Library Journal,* **Oct. 1, 1991, p. 14.**

Reports on an update to the news that the New York Public Library (NYPL) has made the historic move to transferring $1.23 million of private monies from its research libraries to fund branch libraries. States that the financial arrangement is that nearly half the money $500,000 is actually a loan, and a little more than a quarter of it is coming from a 'quasi-endowment.'

Quinn, J. and M. Rogers, "New Yorkers rally for libraries — but is anyone listening?" *Library Journal,* **July 1991, p. 15.**

Discusses the plans by New York City Mayor David Dinkins to cut the city's library budgets by one-third, or $42 million, and details the protests scheduled in the city against that action. City Hall rally.

College & research libraries

Nicklin, J.L., "Libraries drop thousands of journals as budgets shrink and prices rise," *The Chronicle of Higher Education,* **Dec. 11, 1991, p. A29.**

Considers a survey from the Association of Research Libraries which found at least 50 of its 119 member institutions this year plans to cancel an average of $140,000 worth of subscriptions. Duane E. Webster, executive director of the association, comments on the vicious circle of cancellations leading to price increases forcing more cancellations. Increases at Oxford, England's Pergamon Press PLC; actions taken at Princeton, Harvard; cancellations, budget cuts.

Quinn, J. and M. Rogers, "ARL libraries fight for their 'place' on campus," *Library Journal,* **June 15, 1991, p. 16.**

Considers how Association of Research Libraries (ARL) members are reshaping their services as budget crises and threats to higher education loom. ARL/OMS (Office of Management Services) Financial Strategies Quick-Spec Survey Tabulation; work of Pru Adler, ARL's lobbyist; restrictions; more.

Debates & issues

DeBruyne, B., "Latchkey solutions," *School Library Journal,* **February 1992, p. 42.**

Reviews the book "Latchkey Children in the Library & Community: Issues, Strategies, and Programs," by Frances Smardo Dowd.

Flagg, G., "The recession and public libraries," *American Libraries,* **May 1991, p. 381.**

Reveals the results of an American Library Association's survey concerning the economic climate of libraries throughout the United States. Budget cut at the New York Public Library that forced layoffs and service cutbacks; outlook in the Northeast including Massachusetts, Pennsylvania, New Jersey, New York and New Hampshire; economic difficulties in Texas; problems in Wyoming, New Mexico, and other mountain states; the midwest and south.

Schuman, P. G. and J. Berry, "Tough times bring tough questions," *Library Journal,* **Nov. 1, 1991, p. 52.**

Suggests responses to questions concerning library finances. How money can be demanded for libraries when there isn't enough to cover such urgent needs as health, police, education and drug problems; how to answer if there is a lot of fat in the library budget; questions concerning new material; intellectual freedom questions; more.

Homeless

"Homeless men set up house in Maine State Library crawl space," *American Libraries,* **January 1992, p. 7.**

Recounts the story of two homeless men who made a home in a five-foot-high crawl space above a third floor ceiling in the Main State Library in Augusta for almost three months. How they gained access to what security officials call "a heavily secured building"; objects that they stole; how they were caught.

Brennan, M., "All I really need to know I learned in the library," *American Libraries,* **January 1992, p. 38.**

Presents a formerly homeless man's first-person account of his not-so-distant "schooling" in the Boston Public Library. His transformation from a homeless ex-con and day laborer into a full-time free-lance writer in less than a year; his life before the library; a dilemma with no easy answers; the route to first magazine sale; the episode of the lady in the ragged pea coat.

Landgraf, M. N., "Library cards for the homeless,"

American Libraries, **November 1991, p. 946.**

Highlights "Camp Agnos," a collection of 6,000 homeless people in San Francisco's Civic Center Plaza, and how San Francisco found a solution to the problem of homeless people borrowing library books. The problem of "permanently homeless" residents; responsible management of the library's resources; attorney Lisa Parsons, director of the San Francisco Bar Association's Homeless Advocacy Project; San Francisco Public Library's (SFPL) "open-door" policy; more.

International aspects

"A bad fairy in the library," *The Economist,* **June 29, 1991, p. 52.**

Examines why the British public-library system is fast falling into decay. Problems being caused by local government; cuts in spending; lawsuit threatened by the Library Association; British Arts Minister Tim Renton; details; outlook.

Sankowski, A., "Requiem for Polish libraries," *Wilson Library Bulletin,* **January 1992, p. 15.**

Relates the financial difficulties of Poland's libraries since the transition from socialism to democracy. Polish libraries under socialism; needs of Polish libraries; who uses Polish libraries; consequences of financial difficulties; details of the problem.

Technological aspects

Berry, J., "CD-ROM: The medium of the moment," *Library Journal,* **Feb. 1, 1992, p. 45.**

Presents the results of the CD-ROM Market Study, which states that public librarians expect to spend much more this fiscal year on CD-ROM services than their academic and special library colleagues. CD-ROM outsells online databases; special libraries are the online market; CD-ROM library collections; budgets, vendors and services; selecting CD-ROM; outline outlook; Cahners Research.

Rogers, M., "Online/CD-ROM '91 draws librarians," *Library Journal,* **December 1991, p. 46.**

As prices for online searching rise and budgets fall, many stalwart onliners say they are switching to CD-ROM as a thrifty means of providing information. Online/CD-ROM '91 Conference and Exposition held in San Francisco, November 11-14; computer guru Ted Nelson; 'Computer literacy'; Project Xanadu; cutting-edge CDs; CD-ROM standard in libraries; comments from Barbara Quint; more.

Back Issues

Great Research on Current Issues Starts Right Here... Recent topics covered by The CQ Researcher are listed below. Issues dated before May 10, 1991, were published under the name of Editorial Research Reports.

DECEMBER 1990
Cable TV Regulation
Americans' Search for Their Roots
Is Insurance System a Failure?
Why Schools Still Have Tracking

JANUARY 1991
Growing Influence of Boycotts
Should the U.S. Reinstate the Draft?
America's Archaeological Past
Peace Corps' Challenges in '90s

FEBRUARY 1991
Regional Impact of Recession
Puerto Rico's Status
Redistricting: Mapping Power
Nuclear Power

MARCH 1991
Acid Rain
Cost of the Gulf War
Reassessing Gun Laws
Future for Man in Space

APRIL 1991
Social Security
Canadian Crisis Over Quebec
California Drought
Electromagnetic Radiation

MAY 1991
School Choice
Racial Quotas
Animal Rights
U.S. and Japan

JUNE 1991
Children and Divorce
Teenage Suicide
Endangered Species
Europe 1992

JULY 1991
Teenagers and Abortion
Soviet Republics Rebel
Mexico's Emergence
Athletes and Drugs

AUGUST 1991
Sexual Harassment
Fetal Tissue Research
Oil Imports
The Palestinians

SEPTEMBER 1991
Police Brutality
Advertising Under Attack
Saving the Forests
Foster Care Crisis

OCTOBER 1991
Pay-Per-View TV
Youth Gangs
Gene Therapy
World Hunger

NOVEMBER 1991
Fast-Food Shake-Up
The Greening of Eastern Europe
Business' Role in Education
Cuba In Crisis

DECEMBER 1991
Retiree Health Benefits
Asian Americans
The Obscenity Debate
The Disabilities Act

JANUARY 1992
Term Limits
Oil Spills
Hunting Controversy
Alternative Medicine

FEBRUARY 1992
Threatened Coastlines
New Era in Asia
Assisted Suicide
Jobs in the '90s

MARCH 1992
Women and Sports
Underage Drinking
Garbage Crisis
Mafia Crackdown

APRIL 1992
Ozone Depletion
Welfare Reform
Politicians and Privacy
Illegal Immigration

MAY 1992
Native Americans
Jobs vs. Environment
Too Many Lawsuits?
Fairness in Salaries

JUNE 1992
Nuclear Proliferation
Food Irradiation
Lead Poisoning

Back issues are available for $4.00 (subscribers) or $7.00 (non-subscribers). Quantity discounts apply to orders over ten. To order, call Congressional Quarterly 1-800-432-2250.

Future Topics

▶ *Alternative Energy*

▶ *Prescription Drug Prices*

▶ *Alzheimer's Disease*

Alternative Energy

Can renewable energy sources replace fossil fuels?

F
OSSIL FUELS HAVE BEEN THE PRIME MOVER OF
industrial life for some 200 years. The burning of
coal and oil have saved inestimable amounts of time
and labor while substantially raising living standards
around the world. But many scientists now say the use of
fossil fuels, which account for 85 percent of U.S. energy use,
contributes to global warming and could ultimately threaten
the planet's future. That concern, coupled with America's
growing dependence on insecure fuel sources, has sparked
new interest in alternatives. Unlike in the 1970s, however, this
time renewable energy may be more than just a fad. Technological advancements have made the economics of wind and
solar power much more competitive. Moreover, public utilities
are beginning to consider the environmental costs of cheap
fossil fuels.

C_Q   July 10, 1992 • Volume 2, No. 25 • 573-596

Formerly Editorial Research Reports

THE ISSUES

BACKGROUND

CURRENT SITUATION

OUTLOOK

SIDEBARS

FOR FURTHER INFORMATION

COVER ART: BARBARA SASSA-DANIELS

THE CQ Researcher

July 10, 1992
Volume 2, No. 25

EDITOR
Sandra Stencel

MANAGING EDITOR
Thomas J. Colin

ASSOCIATE EDITOR
Richard L. Worsnop

STAFF WRITERS
Charles S. Clark
Mary H. Cooper
Rodman D. Griffin

PRODUCTION EDITOR
Laurie De Maris

EDITORIAL ASSISTANT
Michael M. Taylor

GRAPHICS
Jack Auldridge

PUBLISHED BY
Congressional Quarterly Inc.

CHAIRMAN
Andrew Barnes

VICE CHAIRMAN
Andrew P. Corty

EDITOR AND PUBLISHER
Neil Skene

EXECUTIVE EDITOR
Robert W. Merry

PUBLICATIONS MARKETING/SALES
Robert Smith

EDITOR, EBSCO PUBLISHING
Melissa Kummerer

The CQ Researcher (ISSN 1056-2036). Formerly Editorial Research Reports. Published weekly (48 times per year, not printed the first Friday of any month with five Fridays) by Congressional Quarterly Inc., 1414 22nd St., N.W., Washington, D.C. 20037. Rates are furnished upon request. Second-class postage paid at Washington, D.C. POSTMASTER: Send address changes to The CQ Researcher, 1414 22nd St., N.W., Washington, D.C. 20037.

Alternative Energy

By Rodman D. Griffin

THE ISSUES

In the 1980s, the future course of U.S. energy policy seemed as straight as a smokestack. Conventional fossil fuels — oil, coal and natural gas — were slated to propel the United States well into the 21st century. The Reagan administration demonstrated its commitment to fossil fuels by opening up federal lands for oil exploration and sending U.S. warships to protect oil-shipping lanes in the Persian Gulf in 1987.[1]

These were not happy times for advocates of the "soft energy path." With oil plentiful and cheap, interest in alternative-energy sources — hydropower, solar energy, wind turbines, geothermal energy, among others — rapidly waned. Government subsidies, which had kept the renewable energy industry thriving during the early 1980s, expired in 1985. Federally funded research, the industry's springboard to the future, also dried up — withering from $1 billion in fiscal 1981 to less than $116 million in 1989.

But today there is new energy in renewables. Technologies have greatly improved. Declining costs are making many alternative energy sources economically competitive with conventional power plants. Utilities, prodded by new state regulations, are realizing they can make a profit not only by producing electricity but also by designing and marketing conservation measures for homes and businesses. And the Persian Gulf War has made it clear that fossil fuels are not only finite but dangerous to rely on.

Fossil fuels now account for 85 percent of U.S. energy use. Domestic oil demand climbed from 15.7 million barrels a day in 1985 to 17 mil-

lion barrels in 1990.* Meanwhile, domestic oil production has been declining. As a result, the United States — the world's largest energy consumer — now imports roughly 50 percent of its crude-oil and petroleum products. A fourth of those imports comes from the politically volatile Middle East. If nothing is done, experts warn, the United States will need to import two-thirds of its oil by the year 2000.[2]

Concern about U.S. dependence on oil imports is not the only factor behind the renewal of interest in energy alternatives. Even before the Earth Summit in Rio de Janeiro last month, policy-makers and politicians from around the globe were responding to public concerns about the buildup of harmful greenhouse gases, due primarily to the burning of fossil fuels (see p. 579).

President Bush's National Energy Strategy, submitted to Congress in 1991, relied heavily on fossil fuels

*Demand fell slightly in 1991, to 16.6 million barrels a day.

and nuclear power. (For details on Bush's plan, see p. 580.) But even environmentalists concede that the Bush administration has shown more interest in renewable energy than its predecessor.

"Renewable energy has enormous promise for clean and abundant supplies," says J. Michael Davis, assistant Energy secretary for conservation and renewable energy. Collectively, alternative energy sources "can contribute significantly to our economic and energy security," he adds.

At present, renewables supply just 8 percent of total U.S. energy demand — 13 percent of the nation's electrical consumption. Most of that energy (86 percent) comes from hydropower and the burning of biomass (wood, wood wastes, agricultural wastes and municipal wastes).

Even if the government does nothing to encourage greater reliance on renewables, a study published by the Department of Energy concludes, their share of the U.S. energy equation will double over the next 40 years because of likely technological and economic developments.[3]

Duane Sunderman, director of the National Renewable Energy Laboratory in Golden, Colo., is even more upbeat about the potential for renewables. By increasing research and development (R&D) and overcoming constraints such as storage capacity during those times when the sun doesn't shine or the wind doesn't blow, the contribution of alternative energy sources could increase tenfold, he says. "The resources are unlimited and wait only upon technological progress for harvesting."

But moving toward an alternative energy future will not be easy. Unlike a decade ago, when the world believed oil should be conserved because the supply was running out, any action today to limit fuel use or

U.S. Energy Sources

Fossil fuels — oil, coal and gas — provide 85 percent of all energy used in the United States. Renewable energy sources supply just 8 percent, and most of that comes from hydropower and the burning of biomass (wood, wood wastes, agricultural wastes and municipal wastes).

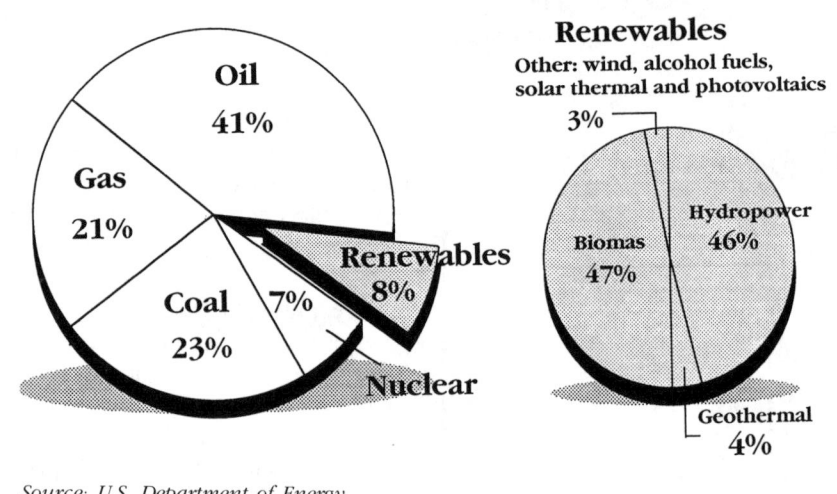

Oil 41%

Gas 21%

Coal 23%

Renewables 8% 7%

Nuclear

Renewables
Other: wind, alcohol fuels, solar thermal and photovoltaics
3%

Hydropower 46%

Biomas 47%

Geothermal 4%

Source: U.S. Department of Energy

develop alternatives runs against the economics of cheap oil. The price of oil — now around $20 a barrel — has proved in the last 20 months to be more stable than almost anyone had expected; even a war in the Persian Gulf did not move it higher for long. In addition, the price of coal is low and has remained stable, and the price of natural gas is declining in the United States.

Nevertheless, there is an emerging consensus that alternative energy sources should not be sold short. "Ironically, cheap oil may be too expensive for the economy," says Jeff Alson, an alternative fuels expert at the federal Environmental Protection Agency. With a mounting trade deficit and sputtering economy, the United States can no longer afford its $55 billion oil-import bill, Alson says. "Those dollars are no longer coming back in the form of export revenue."

As policy-makers grapple with the complex — and at times conflicting — information on the energy front, here are some of the questions being asked:

Has the potential for alternative fuels been oversold?

In 1979, the authors of *Energy Future,* a highly touted report by the Harvard Business School, projected that oil prices would rise to at least $35 a barrel and possibly even $85 a barrel by the late 1980s. At those prices, a host of new alternative energy technologies would come online, they said. Extrapolating on the data, they predicted that solar energy could provide 20 percent of U.S. energy output by the year 2000.[4] It presently accounts for less than 1 percent.

Obviously, ascertaining the future impact of alternative fuels is a complicated — and risky — endeavor. "Let's face it, many of these projections are built on quicksand," says Joel Darmstadter, senior researcher at Resources for the Future, a Washington-based environmental group. "We've all been playing the projections game for a long time. And we've usually been proven wrong."

For critics, the lackluster perfor-

mance of alternative energy sources to date is proof that they will never live up to their expectations. "The idea that we'll be able to light the city of Los Angeles on the basis of solar panels is nonsense," says Jerry Taylor, director of natural resources at the CATO Institute, a conservative think tank in Washington. "Solar power may be a smart energy choice for certain industries, but its role is on the margins."

Stan Field, an energy analyst at SRI International, a nonprofit consulting firm based in Palo Alto, Calif., expresses similar views. "Wind, geothermal and solar power can produce minute quantities of energy that can't possibly be powerful enough to subdue OPEC [the Organization of Petroleum Exporting Countries]," he says. "Research on these alternatives has generated press, but not results."

Such sentiments are not uncommon, especially among proponents of conventional energy sources. Other experts, however, say the problem is not that alternative energy sources are being oversold, but that they are being underdeveloped. "Federal and state agencies and regulators have not generally endorsed renewables as a significant part of their energy policy objectives," says Gregory M. Rueger, senior vice president of Pacific Gas & Electric Co. (PG&E), the nation's largest investor-owned utility. "This has created a self-fulfilling prophecy in terms of the role of renewables. Because they are unrecognized, they are underused. And because they are underused, they remain unrecognized."[5]

Rueger maintains that alternative energy sources will be an essential part of the future energy picture. By the year 2000, he says, hundreds of conventional power plants built in the 1940s, '50s and '60s will be wearing out. Their replacements may well come from the diverse spectrum of alternative fuels.

Obviously, the contribution of renewables could be significantly higher than it is presently. But how much higher? Predictions vary tremendously. Public Citizen, a Ralph Nader organization, proclaims "it is technically feasible to double the contribution of renewable energy technologies in the next five years and to at least triple it by the year 2000."

But Davis at the Department of Energy says attempts to estimate the overall potential of renewable technologies — or to set specific goals — can be misleading. "To say that we want to achieve 'X' percentage of our energy from renewables by a certain year is interesting, but almost meaningless," he cautions. "How would we get there? With which specific technologies? In which sectors? In what time frames? At what levels of investment? These are the meat of the issue. Goals we put on ourselves just wash over all that."

Should the government subsidize alternative energy technologies?

Supporters argue that renewables need a "technology push" and a "market pull" during the next 10 years to reach widespread use. The technology push would come from research — both private and government-funded. Already, research projects have dramatically lowered the costs of renewable energy. But proponents say that effort needs to be followed up with demonstration projects that prove the technologies are cost-effective and dependable.

The pull would come from a growing market for alternative energy sources, perhaps with federal subsidies or government mandates that require use of renewables. "We've made major investments before, with the national highway system and rural electrification development," says Michael Brower, a physicist and director of research at the Union of Concerned Scientists (UCS). "But now we're in a period where that sort of policy is widely opposed. The

thing is, it wouldn't take much to give renewables a nudge."

A coalition of more than a dozen energy and environmental groups, including the Union of Concerned Scientists, requested a reintroduction of tax incentives for renewables, plus $1 billion in direct R&D assistance for this year — four times the amount requested by the Bush administration.

Any mention of government encouragement rankles free marketeers. They argue that force-feeding technologies can result in wrong choices and would impose unacceptable economic costs. "Every time the government steps in, it slows things up," observes Carleton Jones, Houston-based director of the energy division of the Arthur D. Little consulting firm.[6]

Even some in the alternative energy industry oppose government hand-outs. "We shouldn't subsidize any energy sector, whether oil or solar," says Steve Baer, president of Zomeworks, an Albuquerque-based solar manufacturing company. "Any time you do that, directly or indirectly, you end up distorting markets and harming industry. We should have learned from the experiences of the early 1980s."

A lot of the tax incentives put in place during the Carter administration "turned out to be tax shelters instead of energy producers," admits Nicholas Lenssen, an energy researcher at the Worldwatch Institute, an environmental group in Washington. "In the future, we don't want to give incentives for increasing energy-producing facilities, but to provide energy services."

According to the UCS's Brower, "there is no such thing as free enterprise in the energy business. There has always been a big network of subsidies, incentives and penalties." For example, in nuclear power, there is a cap on liability for accidents; fuel reprocessing is heavily subsidized,

and the cost of plant decommissioning is virtually ignored.[7] For coal, there is low-cost leasing for mining on federal lands. And for oil, there are limits on company liability for oil spills,[8] as well as tax breaks for oil exploration.

All told, federal subsidies to conventional energy technologies amounted to $41 billion in 1984. Four years later, conventional energy technologies received 92 percent of all federal energy subsidies, while renewable energy technologies received roughly 3 percent and conservation programs 5 percent.[9]

"Federal incentives for the oil industry aren't that great anymore," argues Gus Ensz, a spokesman for the American Petroleum Institute, the oil industry's Washington-based trade group.

Environmentalists disagree. According to the Alliance to Save Energy, which is presently analyzing data on energy subsidies, fossil fuels still receive the lion's share of federal R&D moneys as well as tax breaks. (See graph, p. 578.)

Federal tax legislation in 1986 diluted the value of the oil depletion allowance, which reduces the taxes paid on oil production. But the oil industry still benefits. In 1990, for instance, independent oil and gas companies received some $650 million from the oil depletion allowances; this was more than four times the entire federal R&D budget for renewables.

"As long as there are subsidies for other fuels, we'll have an unequal situation," says Eric Heitz, a program officer at the San Francisco-based Energy Foundation, a nonprofit organization that provides private research grants to energy companies.

If the government fails to pitch in more money now, proponents say America will lose its competitive edge in the alternative energy field. "Currently, Japan and many of our other international competitors are using tax and other market incentives

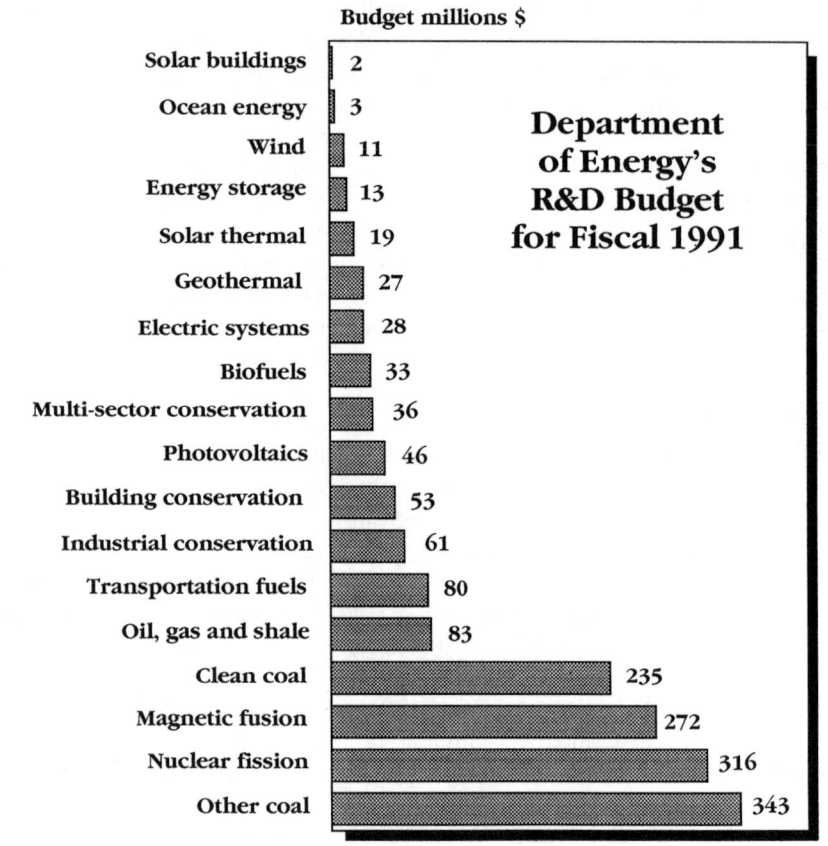

Where the Money Goes

Nuclear power and fossil fuels — oil, coal and gas — receive the lion's share of federal funds for energy research and development.

Budget millions $

Department of Energy's R&D Budget for Fiscal 1991

Category	Budget
Solar buildings	2
Ocean energy	3
Wind	11
Energy storage	13
Solar thermal	19
Geothermal	27
Electric systems	28
Biofuels	33
Multi-sector conservation	36
Photovoltaics	46
Building conservation	53
Industrial conservation	61
Transportation fuels	80
Oil, gas and shale	83
Clean coal	235
Magnetic fusion	272
Nuclear fission	316
Other coal	343

Sources: Budget of the United States, Fiscal Year 1992; Clinton J. Andrews, Princeton University

to build their domestic renewable energy industries," says Scott Sklar, executive director of the Solar Energy Industries Association in Washington. "We're almost at the point of no return. If we relinquish our technology lead, we will face a repeat of the VCR syndrome — by default letting international companies usurp our role in the industry."

Not all alternative energy advocates agree that subsidies are the answer, however. "Gasoline or carbon taxes may be a more realistic approach than turning to subsidies," says Pietro Nivola, an energy expert

and visiting fellow at the Brookings Institution, a Washington think tank. "When you enter the subsidies game, everyone stakes a claim. How do you determine who gets what? You set up a situation ripe for boondoggles."

Do the environmental benefits of alternative energy sources outweigh the higher costs?

One of the principal barriers to the commercialization of alternative energy technologies is that current energy markets ignore, for the most part, what economists call "market externalities" — the social and environ-

mental costs and risks associated with fossil-fuel use. As Joel Darmstadter at Resources for the Future puts it: "We've done inexcusably too little to factor the environment into our energy transactions. Compelling evidence exists, locally and globally, that energy does a lot to hurt the environment. That's not been reflected in energy prices."

Social and environmental costs take many forms. Coal-fired power plants and automobiles, for example, damage human health and reduce agricultural production by contributing to acid rain and air pollution. Overreliance on imported oil makes the United States vulnerable to supply disruptions and price increases and requires large naval fleets to defend Persian Gulf shipping. Nuclear power creates a public-safety hazard as well as a radioactive-waste disposal problem.

"In addition to developing technology and building markets, utilities have to find a way to explicitly take into account environmental and social values," says Brian Thomas, R&D administrator of Puget Sound Power & Light in Bellevue, Wash. "During the planning stage of adding new capacity, the external costs associated with each type of generating system need to be considered."[10]

To some degree, of course, that's already happening. Regulations governing the energy industry, such as requirements for double-hulls on oil tankers, strict environmental standards for oil-drilling rigs and emission controls on power plants and automobiles, are factored into the prices consumers pay for energy. But critics say environmental regulations don't begin to cover the damage caused by fossil fuels and nuclear power. If externalities were taken into account, says Nicholas Lenssen of Worldwatch, "the price of imported oil per barrel would increase anywhere from $50 to $100."

Clearly, the game of externalities is

no trivial pursuit. It is a serious political tug of war over federal subsidies, market share, cleanup costs and economic development worth hundreds of billions of dollars. "The bottom line is that it takes fewer resources to deliver the same amount of energy through fossil fuels," says CATO's Jerry Taylor. "Prices are a reflection of relative scarcity." Taylor argues that environmental disputes should be left to the courts to address on a case-by-case basis.

Many environmentalists concede that there is no reliable mechanism for measuring environmental damage, or for that matter, placing a value on clean air. Often externalities are hard to value, such as the loss of a scenic valley to a hydroelectric dam. The people who bear external costs may be nowhere in sight, like a fisherman halfway around the world whose waters are fouled by a spill from a U.S.-bound tanker. Future generations will be the ones to cope with radioactive waste produced by today's nuclear-powered generating plants.

Nevertheless, as a practical matter, most environmental advocates say the cost of dirty fuels — notably coal, but also oil — could be nudged upward. "We don't even have to go the whole way, but we should start moving in that direction," says Sklar. "As it is, the cost of energy is not market-oriented in the true sense. We are not taking into account the risks."

To be fair, no alternative energy source is environmentally cost-free. To the unsympathetic eye, sprawling wind farms on mountain ridges are eyesores — and the turbines themselves kill large numbers of birds. Geothermal energy, produced by converting subterranean hot water and steam into electricity, can adversely affect the water table. And the electric transmission lines necessary to bring many renewables online cause electromagnetic fields with unknown health effects.[11]

Partly in response to increased public concern about the impacts of acid rain and global climate change, regulatory commissions in many states are now grappling with difficult questions of how to include environmental externalities in utility resource planning. So far, at least 15 states have developed procedures for including environmental costs in resource planning.[12]

In Wisconsin, for example, utilities that are considering building new power plants are required to favor non-fossil fuels even if they cost up to 15 percent more than fossil fuels.

And in New York, regulators assign an environmental penalty of 1.4 cents per kilowatt-hour to new coal-fired power plants. Other options — including putting a carbon-based tax on all fossil fuels — also are being discussed. (*See At Issue, p. 589.*)

"Even if you believe global warming is hogwash, it makes business sense for utility managers to take the possibility of it occurring seriously," says Brower of the Union of Concerned Scientists. "In the future it is likely that there will be controls that will impose costs." ∎

BACKGROUND

The Reign of Oil

For some 200 years, fossil fuels have been the prime mover of industrial life. They have saved inestimable amounts of time and labor while substantially raising living standards around the world. But scientists say the use of fossil fuels ultimately could change the planet's climate and threaten its future.

Atmospheric concentrations of carbon dioxide, the principal cause of global warming, have grown by more than 25 percent since the Industrial Revolution. Fossil-fuel burning and forestry and agricultural practices are responsible for most of the man-made contributions to the gases in the atmosphere that act like a greenhouse to raise the Earth's temperature.

Climatologists widely disagree over the exact impact of fossil fuels on the environment, but most agree that heavy dependence on them will not be sustainable over the long term. In addition to the environmental concerns, current patterns of oil production and consumption, and the political alignments that accompany them, are leading the United States

— and the world — into a future laden with uncertainty.

It has only been in the past 20 years that U.S. policy-makers have given serious thought to switching to cleaner, more abundant energy alternatives — or to saving energy. The reason is not just a lack of interest in so-called "green" issues. Until the 1970s, the cost of oil and other fossil fuels was relatively low and stable.

Through most of the century, increases in supplies of fossil fuels kept pace with demand. The fears of the early 1970s that the world was about to run out of fuel have proved groundless. In 1950, the world's proven reserves of oil — the amounts recoverable under then-current economic and operating conditions — stood at 100 billion barrels; by 1970 they had risen to 550 billion barrels, and by 1990 to over 1 trillion. Proven reserves of coal and natural gas also have increased strikingly.[13]

The existence of substantial oil reserves does not imply that the price of energy will remain low indefinitely, however. Indeed, the oil-price shocks of 1973-74 and 1979 served notice of the volatility of oil prices.

In 1979, the inflation-adjusted price of crude oil was six times higher than its 1973 level. It has since fallen precipitously, but guessing even the medium-term trend is a crapshoot. The one certainty, says Vahan Zanoyan, an analyst with the Washington-based Petroleum Finance Co., is that the price of oil is cyclical. Periods of low prices, such as the past decade, inevitably lead to large cuts in exploration and development by the oil industry, and a loss of interest in conservation and alternatives among consumers. As capacity limits are reached and demand increases, the stage is set for a new rise in prices.

Energy Strategies

George Bush is not the first president to offer a plan for America's energy future. The oil embargo of 1973 prompted President Richard M. Nixon to launch Project Independence, an ambitious campaign to "set as our national goal, in the spirit of Apollo, with the determination of the Manhattan Project, that by the end of this decade we will have developed the potential to meet our own energy needs without depending upon any foreign energy sources."

Congress responded to Nixon's plan by approving several energy conservation measures and reorganizing the federal energy bureaucracy. Among other things, Congress created the Energy Research and Development Administration to direct federal research into the better use of existing fuels and the development of new sources of energy. During the Ford administration, Congress established mandatory fuel efficiency standards for new automobiles and set up a program to apply energy-efficiency ratings to appliances.

Jimmy Carter unveiled his National Energy Plan in April 1977, shortly after taking office. Carter called his energy policy "the moral equivalent of war," and his battle plan included some 200 proposals to promote energy efficiency and reduce the nation's

dependence on oil imports — among them the creation of the Department of Energy to centralize energy planning. He also called for a tax on gas-guzzling autos, tax incentives to improve residential energy efficiency and substantial increases in federal funding for research into synthetic fuels, solar energy and other alternative energy sources. Alternative energy was so "in" that the president even had solar panels installed on the White House roof.

Reagan's Policy Switch

Carter's efforts eventually succumbed to the Reagan push in the other direction, a game plan which, according to then-budget director David A. Stockman, required "only two policies — strategic [oil] reserves and strategic [military] forces." As oil gushed into the world market in the early 1980s — partly the result of oil and gas deregulation, which led to massive exploration efforts — interest in renewables rapidly waned. Subsidies that had kept the industry thriving expired in 1985. Symbolic of the times, Reagan removed the solar panels from the White House.

"Our industry was decimated," declares solar expert Scott Sklar. The number of solar-equipment manufacturers in the water- and space-heating end of the business fell from 185 to 20 following the removal of the subsidies. And the survivors were none too healthy. For example, Florida-based American Energy Technologies Inc., a manufacturer of solar collectors, saw its employment shrink from 75 people to a mere eight. (Now it's back to 20.)

"The effect of the policies of the Reagan administration on the solar industry was almost unbelievable," says Sklar. "Today, solar water-heating units are installed in only 1.2 million buildings in the United States,*

---

*The city of Tokyo has as many buildings with solar water-heating units as the entire United States.

and solar accounts for less than 1 percent of electricity production. If the government would have just maintained its level of incentives of the 1970s — even with no increase — today we'd have 5 million buildings with solar. And solar would account for 5 percent of all electricity."

The impact of Reagan's policies on other renewable technologies was equally heavy. Consider wind power. "Back in the subsidy era," reflects Michael Bergey, president of Bergey Windpower Co. in Norman, Okla., "I had 40 competitors. Now I have only one. And my company is only one-third the size it once was."

Amid this dire news, the bright spot has been in the area of conservation, also commonly referred to as energy efficiency. "It is much cheaper to save energy than to produce new sources," says Michael Shepard, director of energy policy at the Rocky Mountain Institute (RMI), a nonprofit research group in Snowmass, Colo.

From the initial "oil shock" in 1973 through the 1980s, more "new" energy was obtained through efficiency than all other sources of supply — seven times as much, according to RMI's research director, Amory Lovins. While the U.S. gross national product (GNP) grew by nearly half over that period (including 20 million new homes and 50 million more vehicles), energy use rose just 7 percent. The amount of energy needed to produce a dollar of GNP actually declined 20 percent — from 25,000 to 20,000 British thermal units (Btus).[14]

Bush's Energy Strategy

By the time George Bush was elected, the nation faced a web of energy crises, highlighted by Iraq's invasion of Kuwait in August 1990, which caused oil prices to more than
Continued on p. 582

Chronology

1950s-1960s
While America expands oil exploration efforts and increases its dependence on fossil fuels, some scientists and energy planners begin to consider alternatives.

1953
The United States becomes a net energy importer.

1954
Bell Laboratories develops the first photovoltaic cell. The Supreme Court rules in favor of government control of the wellhead price of natural gas.

1957
The government-owned Shippingport nuclear power plant begins supplying steam to an electric utility near Pittsburgh.

———— • ————

1970s
Oil prices shoot upward, prompting first serious efforts to reduce oil dependency and develop a more balanced energy policy.

1973-74
Arab countries embargo sales to the U.S. for five months, leading to rationing and lines of motorists waiting to buy gas; the price of Saudi Arabian light crude oil increases 450 percent, to $11.65 per barrel.

1975
Congress creates the Strategic Petroleum Reserve; automobile fuel efficiency standards are established; cars average 15.8 miles per gallon.

April 1977
President Jimmy Carter unveils his National Energy Plan, declaring it the "moral equivalent of war." Carter's plan includes incentives for the development of renewable energy and conservation.

1978-79
Revolution in Iran cuts off its oil exports, causing panic stockpiling in consuming countries, commonly referred to as the "second oil shock."

1979
A partial core meltdown occurs at Pennsylvania's Three Mile Island nuclear power plant, near Harrisburg.

———— • ————

1980s
As an international oil glut develops, oil prices plummet, and President Ronald Reagan scales back alternative energy efforts except for nuclear power.

1985
Tax subsidies for most renewable energy industries expire.

1986
Members of the Organization of Petroleum Exporting Countries (OPEC) boost production in an internal struggle for market share, causing oil prices to collapse; Chernobyl nuclear accident in the Soviet Union hinders prospects for nuclear power.

1989
Alaskan oil production begins to decline; largest U.S. oil spill occurs in Alaska's Prince William Sound.

1990s
Increasing public concern about global warming and U.S. oil dependence sparks new interest in alternative energy.

1991
New cars average 28.1 miles per gallon.

March 1991
President Bush sends his National Energy Strategy to Congress, retaining the country's focus on fossil fuels and nuclear power, but also requesting more money for renewable energy research.

April 1991
Texas Instruments Inc. announces breakthrough in photovoltaic (PV) technology that it says could cut costs in half, from 30 cents to 15 cents per kilowatt-hour.

November 1991
Iowa-Illinois Gas & Electric Co., a Midwest utility, tentatively agrees to enter into a joint venture with U.S. Windpower Inc. to develop the first major wind-energy project outside California.

May 27, 1992
Following an earlier Senate vote, the House passes sweeping legislation aimed at stemming the nation's oil dependence.

June 1992
Leaders from more than 100 countries sign a treaty at the Earth Summit in Rio de Janeiro, in principle, committing their countries to lessening the impacts of fossil-fuel use.

Rethinking the Nuclear Option

The 110 atomic power plants operating in the United States provided one of every five watts of electricity consumed here last year. Uranium, the fuel used to generate nuclear power, is "so plentiful that it's hard to conceive of it ever running out," says Carl Goldstein, a spokesman for the U.S. Council for Energy Awareness (USCEA), the trade association for manufacturers, utilities and other companies in the nuclear power business. "And ... you're not dependent on any one part of the world for uranium the way you are for oil."

Yet the political reality is that nuclear power has lost its economic, technological and popular charm. Since 1973, the year of the Arab oil embargo, every order placed in the United States for a nuclear plant has been canceled — more than 100 in all. There have been no U.S. orders at all since 1978, when the Iranian Revolution came to a boil. That's the legacy of the industry's environmental record, poor construction-management, cost overruns, regulatory instability and the 1979 partial core meltdown at the Three Mile Island nuclear power plant near Harrisburg, Pa.

Symbolic of the industry's demise is the case of the Shoreham nuclear power plant on Long Island, N.Y. Last month, demolition crews began tearing down the facility, which cost $5.5 billion to build and generated electricity for only 30 hours. There was nothing technically wrong with the plant, which was licensed by the Nuclear Regulatory Commission in 1985. Its problems were political. The plant was located close to New York City on the heavily populated north shore of Long Island. Local governments and New York state rejected the company's emergency evacuation plans and blocked its operation.†

Whether nuclear power is a dinosaur heading for oblivion or a promising technology heading for a new era of growth depends on who is doing the analyzing. "We either stop now or start the next generation of orders," says Goldstein.

Faced with aging plants and growing demand, utilities must start building some new power plants. Electricity demand, the fastest-growing energy sector, is projected to grow 40 percent in the next decade. Proponents, including the Bush administration, say nuclear power could meet much of that demand.

The administration's National Energy Strategy (NES) recommends doubling production of nuclear-generated electricity by the year 2030. "Nuclear power is a proven electricity-generating technology that emits no sulfur dioxide, nitrogen oxides or greenhouse gases," the NES proposal states.

That's the good news. The downside of nuclear power — the safety of reactors and the disposal of radioactive waste — continues to challenge researchers. To date, there is no long-term dump site for the 22,000 tons of radioactive waste that already exist. Nuclear's "second coming" will require solutions to these problems.

In hope of revitalizing nuclear power's prospects, the president's strategy recommends halving the number of steps in nuclear-plant licensing, doubling the license period to 40 years, standardizing reactor design and accelerating the selection of a site to store the nation's commercial and military nuclear wastes. General Electric and Westinghouse are already working on designs for smaller, simpler and less expensive plants that they hope can be pre-certified by the Nuclear Regulatory Commission and then sold "off the shelf" to utilities.

But even if the industry can surmount its technical problems, it faces another big obstacle — the public's widespread fear of nuclear power. In two recent polls, more than 75 percent of Americans reported that they believed nuclear power to be important. The same percentage of respondents, however, rejected or reserved judgment on putting a nuclear plant in their own neighborhoods.††

---

† See *The Washington Post*, June 18, 1992.

†† Cited in *Omni*, May 1991, p. 85. For background, see "Will Nuclear Power Get Another Chance," *Editorial Research Reports*, Feb. 22, 1991, pp. 113-128.

Continued from p. 580
double in a matter of weeks.* Meanwhile, concerns about global warming, air pollution and acid rain — all linked to the burning of fossil fuels — were escalating. To top it off, America's wanton use of imported energy was beginning to take its toll on the trade deficit.[15]

In response to the new pressures, Bush set his secretary of Energy, James D. Watkins, to work. For nearly two years, department officials scoured the country for ideas, visiting 48 states, holding 18 public hearings, reviewing some 200,000 pages of material. The result was Bush's National Energy Strategy, submitted to Congress in March 1991. The administration hailed it as a "comprehensive foundation for a cleaner, more efficient and more secure energy future."

Among other things, the plan offered to enhance domestic oil production, simplify gas pipeline regulations and streamline the process for obtain-

---

*Prices quickly dropped to the pre-invasion level when the Bush administration announced it would use the Strategic Petroleum Reserve to buffer the shock. The resolve of the United Nations to oust Iraq from Kuwait also served to calm the international oil market.

ing permits for nuclear power plants. Many energy analysts, however, have expressed fear that Bush's strategy would not avert a future energy crisis because it tilts too heavily toward promoting existing energy sources and technologies.

"The National Energy Strategy is almost silent on renewables — solar and wind get particularly short shrift," says George Preston, a vice president at the Electric Power Research Institute (EPRI), the research arm of the utility industry. "We may have made a lot of progress in advancing these technologies, but we still have a long way to go in getting decision-makers in the utilities and the government to fully appreciate their potential."

Bush did ask for $521 million in conservation R&D and state grants (vs. a request of $325 million for fiscal 1992) and $250 million for renewable energy (vs. $143 million for fiscal '92).

Legislators critical of Bush's strategy responded by introducing some 80 energy bills, most offering a different vision of the nation's energy future. The House and the Senate each have passed versions of the energy plan and it is currently in conference.[16] From the standpoint of alternative energy, the House version is substantially stronger, since it includes a package of tax incentives for renewable energy, cars that run on alternative fuels and energy efficiency.

But both bills would encourage independent, non-utility companies to get into the electric-generating business by exempting them from regulation by the Securities and Exchange Commission. If this provision becomes law, energy companies could sell their output to any utility that would buy it, even across state lines.

Though largely unheralded, experts say this change to the 1935 Public Utility Holding Company Act could alter the utility business as radically as the breakup of AT&T

changed the telephone industry. Equally important, experts say it would open the door to renewable energy, which is conducive to small operators. Although dozens of differences between the two bills have yet to be resolved, analysts are confident new energy legislation will emerge sometime this year.

Looking for Alternatives

Ultimately, the hope for tackling the greenhouse effect — as well as gaining energy independence — lies in the development of non-fossil energy sources to a point where they are cheaper and easier to use than their fossil rivals. That won't be easy. As technical improvements in alternative energies occur, they may well be matched by improvements in conventional energy sources. Moreover, as Brookings' Pietro Nivola points out, "You have a product concentrated in the Middle East, where governments can undercut the price at which other technologies would come on stream."

That, coupled with America's failure to plan its energy policy beyond the next few years, makes it difficult for the country to get on a sustainable energy path. Nuclear power, once thought of as too cheap to meter, has become financially — and politically — untenable. (*See story, p. 582.*) No new nuclear power plants have been ordered since 1978.

That leaves renewable energy sources as the principal alternatives to fossil fuels. Today, hydropower* and the burning of biomass (wood and wood wastes, agricultural crops and municipal wastes) are the most entrenched of the renewable technologies, accounting for 46 percent and 47 percent, respectively, of renewables' total energy output. Geothermal contributes 4 percent; other technologies — wind, alcohol fuels, solar thermal and photovoltaics — produce 3 percent.

---

*Despite hydropower's important role in America's energy picture, its future is limited. Despite the country's 49,000 dams, most suitable sites for hydroelectric power already have been developed, and environmentalists oppose development of many of the others. ∎

CURRENT SITUATION

▌Tilting at Windmills

Wind farms got off to a turbulent start in the early 1980s. In order to harvest time-limited tax credits, thousands of faulty machines were rushed into production, and some $2.5 billion were sunk into wind projects, many of them ill-conceived. As a result, rotor blades broke off some poorly designed turbines, rotors lost efficiency after getting encrusted with dead insects and some were put at the wrong height to get

the most out of local winds. By 1985 the federal government had withdrawn the tax incentives and cut research grants by 90 percent.

"Wind developed a reputation for not working, and it had the stigma of a tax scam," says Robert Thresher, the wind-program manager at the National Renewable Energy Laboratory in Golden, Colo.[17] Eventually the problems caused power companies to back away.

Today, wind power, among the cleanest and most competitive of renewable energy sources, is making a brisk comeback. Unlike traditional power sources, wind energy involves relatively simple, cheap equipment that is amenable to cost-cutting through mass production. Engineers

Continued on p. 586

Driving Out Oil Dependency ...

Any serious discussion of breaking America's petroleum addiction has to focus on transportation. Vehicles guzzle more than 11 million of the 17 million barrels of oil Americans consume daily, and most of that goes into cars, trucks and buses. Transportation is 97 percent oil-dependent; electricity generation is only 5 percent oil-dependent.

Moreover, automobile fumes contribute more than half of the carbon monoxide in the air, a third of the nitrous oxides, a quarter of the hydrocarbons and nearly a third of the carbon dioxide.† "Motor vehicles generate more air pollution than any other single human activity," says Deborah Bleviss of the Washington-based International Institute for Energy Conservation.

Conventional wisdom holds that the clean cars of tomorrow exist only in blueprints. In fact, they already exist, and range from General Motors Corp.'s high-performance electric sportscar, the "Impact," to hundreds of United Parcel Service vans running on compressed natural gas. So why do these marvels of efficiency seldom make it to the showroom?

General Motors Corp.'s electric sportscar, the "Impact"

The reason, some say, has nothing to do with technology — and everything to do with the marketplace. Take the example of the Volvo LCP 2000. This prototype sedan is more crashworthy than required by law, accelerates from 0 to 60 in 11 seconds and could be priced competitively. It gets 81 miles per gallon (mpg) on the highway and 63 mpg in the city. "It feels like a Honda Civic," says Lee Schipper of the Lawrence Berkeley Laboratory in California. "But it was allowed to die because fuel prices fell and Volvo felt that it wouldn't pay off. Most of the world today wants to buy cars that are bigger and more powerful."

That ambition is a strong indication of how far away this country is from the ultimate solution — breaking the public's love affair with the private car. Even with tougher fuel-efficiency standards down the road, a long-term solution may lie in vehicles that dispense with refined crude altogether. Here is a look at some of the most likely alternatives to gasoline:

Methanol: In the United States, methanol, an alcohol that can be made from coal, wood, natural gas or other materials, is emerging as the main rival to gasoline for private cars.†† Since it is liquid, today's cars could adapt to it with only minor technical changes.

The clear favorite of automakers, methanol is a cleaner and cheaper fuel than oil and yields more horsepower and acceleration (it's a popular fuel for race cars). It produces no particulate emissions, and carbon-dioxide emissions are projected to be from 5 to 10 percent lower than gasoline's. "It's the alternative technology that's the furthest along and the most feasible," says Chrysler engineer D. C. Van Raaphorst.

Methanol has many drawbacks, though. Cars powered by it are sometimes hard to start when the temperature falls below 50 degrees Fahrenheit. Mechanics are leery of its toxicity; it can burn the skin and peels paint. Moreover, methanol is environmentally suspect. It doesn't lower nitrogen-oxide emissions much, and compared with gasoline, it releases much more formaldehyde, a potent carcinogen and contributor to smog.

Natural gas: Natural gas vehicles (NGVs) not only contribute a lot less to local smog than do gasoline vehicles, they also emit 25 percent less carbon dioxide, which means less risk of global warming. Because the fuel is so much cleaner than gasoline, vehicles running on it require less maintenance and fewer oil changes.

Proponents contend natural gas is no fantasy fuel — some 500,000 NGVs are already on the road. But only 30,000 of them are in the United States — about one car in 6,000. Canada, with one-tenth of the U.S. population, has an NGV fleet two-thirds as large. The fuel itself is 30-50 percent cheaper than gasoline, and likely to stay that way, given that the United States has substantial reserves of untapped natural gas.

However, converting to natural gas vehicles poses a chicken-and-egg dilemma. Detroit might be more willing to devote more resources to developing NGVs if there were a solid market for them, and mass production would eliminate the high cost of retrofits. Buyers would be attracted to NGVs low operating costs — if they could readily refuel them. And gas station owners would install natural gas compressors if there were enough demand to make that investment profitable. But no one seems willing to make the first move.

Experts say the likely transportation niche for NGVs is for vehicles that travel local routes and can be centrally fueled, such as buses, delivery vans, garbage trucks and taxicabs — in all, about 10 percent of American vehicles. These so-called fleet vehicles make up some 20 percent of road transportation, presently consuming about as much oil as the U.S. imports from the Persian Gulf.

... The Push to Develop Clean Cars

Electric: Driven by tougher emission standards, especially those being imposed in California — which wants "zero emission" vehicles to account for 10 percent of new car sales by 2003 — every major car company has an electric-car project under way.

Environmentally, electric cars have always made sense. They do produce a few pollutants indirectly because power plants must generate the electricity needed to charge the batteries. But even after taking these into account, electric cars release 98 percent less carbon monoxide and nitrous oxides, and 25 percent less carbon dioxide than conventional cars, according to Steve McCrea at the Electric Auto Association in Belmont, Calif. Says McCrea: "It's easier to clean one smokestack than a million tailpipes."

One drawback is that electric cars can be lackluster performers, often because of awkward trade-offs between acceleration and range. The prototype of GM's Impact has a top speed of 110 mph and a range of 120 miles, but that's largely a result of the car's aerodynamic shape and high-tech components.

Electric cars also are expensive: According to some estimates, the price of an electric car is likely to be 20-40 percent higher than an equivalent gas-powered car, depending on the type of batteries. And the batteries will need replacing, perhaps every two or three years (charge: roughly $1,500).

Last October, Detroit's Big Three automakers formed the U.S. Advanced Battery Consortium, a four-year collaborative R&D effort with the U.S. government to pour $260 million into new battery technology that will give electric cars longer range. The sodium-sulfur battery, a promising new technology, can store two to three times as much energy as the lead-acid battery and may be ready for the marketplace by the mid-1990s. Last autumn, Japan's Ministry of International Trade & Industry announced a similar program. Already, Nissan contends it has a battery that can be recharged in only 15 minutes, compared with two to eight hours for most others.

Even when electric cars hit the road commercially — GM expects to have the Impact in showrooms by 1995 — experts say they are likely to function primarily as second cars for commuters.

Looking ahead: While clean-air laws could aid a switch to other fuels, legislators aren't sure which alternatives to promote, since even experts disagree about the trade-offs involved. Each possibility reduces some pollutants, but sometimes at the price of more serious ones. All the available choices require technical retooling and time for consumer acceptance.

Last October, alternative vehicles got a big boost when nine Eastern states and the District of Columbia promised to adopt tough new smog-reduction rules first imposed by California in 1990.‡ With other states mulling similar moves, it seems almost certain that large numbers of new U.S. cars and trucks will have to run on natural gas or methanol starting in 1997. On top of that, the new rules mandate that by 1998, 2 percent of all new vehicles will have to run on electricity. That will hit 10 percent by 2003, or nearly 500,000 vehicles annually in states that have agreed to the rules so far.

Nevertheless, most experts believe it's far too early to write the obituary for Henry Ford's internal-combustion engine. The move to supplant gas-guzzlers has inspired the auto industry to tinker more seriously with advanced two-stroke engines and new gas turbines that promise to give cars more oomph and less exhaust. They are also experimenting with lighter materials, such as ceramic engines and plastic side panels, to improve mileage efficiency.

"Oil has been fueling the transportation sector for 70 years," notes Jeff Alson, assistant director of the Environmental Protection Agency's auto emissions lab in Ann Arbor, Mich. "It is *the* fuel. Everything is designed around it." Changing that will take a revolution in thinking.

Moreover, motorists may be wary of shifting fuels, especially if they can't find anywhere convenient to fill up. In the meantime, so-called flexible-fuel vehicles (FFVs) and hybrid cars, which can run on electricity or gasoline, could break the gridlock.

An FFV will be able to detect which type of fuel its tank has been filled with — even if it is a mixture — and will automatically adjust the engine. FFVs use specially modified engines with sensors that measure the quality of the fuel flowing to the engine. Volkswagen has developed an FFV capable of running on any carbon-based liquid fuel, from diesel to alcohol.

The drawback is that these "transition" vehicles will never perform as optimally as one designed specifically for one fuel. But most experts agree it is unrealistic to rely on any of the current alternatives beyond the near term. The wild card is how fast companies can improve alternative-vehicle technology. "The alternative-fuel lobbies are fighting each other as much as they are fighting the gasoline industry," says Alson. "But none of the alternative fuels will make an impact until any of them does."

---

† Technology Review, May/June 1990, p. 22.

†† An alternative fuel with similar qualities is ethanol. For more details, see *Replacing Gasoline: Alternative Fuels for Light-Duty Vehicles*, Congressional Office of Technology Assessment, 1990.

‡ The states are New York, New Jersey, Pennsylvania, Massachusetts, Maryland, Delaware, New Hampshire and Maine.

Continued from p. 583

have used advanced technology to make wind turbines that are far more efficient and cost effective than their predecessors. Since 1980, costs have dropped from nearly 40 cents per kilowatt-hour to 7-9 cents. The next generation of wind turbines could bring costs down to 5 cents by 1995, according to industry specialists.

In a sense, wind power has come full circle. In the early 1900s, most of the electricity on U.S. farms was provided by windmills. Those were replaced during the 1930s when the Rural Electrification Administration wired the countryside.

"Wind is the renewable electric source that will move fastest into the marketplace," predicts Worldwatch's Lenssen. Technological breakthroughs in wind power have re-energized the manufacturers of wind-power equipment and attracted the interest of foreign competitors.* Utilities are conducting wind surveys and starting pilot projects. And a new breed of wildcatter is scurrying to buy up wind rights — licenses to erect what may be the oil wells of tomorrow.

"From the bids we've made in 1991, it's clear we're approaching the point where wind will be the energy resource that others have to beat" to get utility contracts for new generating facilities, says Alexander Ellis, vice president of U.S. Windpower Inc. in Livermore, Calif., the world's leading manufacturer of wind turbines.[18]

The total wind power generating capacity in the United States already

Cost of Electricity From Wind

Federal R&D Investment FY 1981-1990 $243 million

Source: U.S. Department of Energy

exceeds 1,600 megawatts (MW),* with most of the 18,000 turbines located along a few mountain passes in California. Sixteen states have wind-energy potential equal to or greater than California's, according to the Department of Energy.[19]

Last November, a Midwest utility, Iowa-Illinois Gas & Electric Co., tentatively agreed to enter a joint venture with U.S. Windpower to develop a 250 MW wind farm in Iowa, the first major U.S. wind-energy project outside California.

Experts say today's models of wind generators are capable of meeting 10 percent of America's energy demand, and within 30 years, newer versions could provide for a quarter of the nation's power needs. But because energy is unavailable when the wind isn't blowing, critics say wind power will never be more than a supplemental source of electric power, even in high-wind areas such as the Great Plains.[20]

To be sure, wind energy isn't expected to become a significant power source nationally for at least a decade. Most utilities regard it skeptically, because they "are used to generating plants that you can turn on and off" when desired, says Carl Weinberg, manager of research and development at PG&E, which has helped pioneer wind power in California.

Despite America's early lead in wind technology, the major markets for wind technology are now in Europe, according to the Washington-based American Wind Energy Association. Today there is only one major American manufacturer in a position to compete against European or Japanese companies, the association says, and the European wind development effort is five to 10 times larger than the U.S. Department of Energy's. The countries with the largest wind development programs are Germany, the Netherlands and Denmark.

Solar Eclipsed?

Solar energy is the dream technology of environmentalists. During the 1970s, even politicians and businessmen hailed it as the answer to the energy crisis. The idea of harnessing an abundant energy supply generated enough megawatts of excitement to light up a billion-dollar industry. Yet, like wind power, solar failed to produce much actual electricity. Big companies that flirted with solar energy, including Arco, Exxon, Shell and Motorola, have since left the field.

Cost of Electricity From Photovoltaics

Federal R&D Investment FY 1981-1990 $596 million

Source: U.S. Department of Energy

Nevertheless, most experts still believe solar power probably will be the foundation of a sustainable energy economy.

The solar industry has three segments: photovoltaics, solar thermal and solar buildings. The "hot" sector of the industry, even during the downturn of the last decade, has been photovoltaics (PV). Photovoltaic cells are semiconductor devices —

---

*New technologies include variable speed rotors, light and more durable blades and refinements in site placements.

*One megawatt equals 1,000 kilowatts. The 1,600 megawatts generated by windpower is enough electricity to meet the residential needs of a city the size of San Francisco. A conventional coal-fired plant delivers about 600 megawatts.

the material is typically silicon — that generate an electrical current when they absorb photons (discrete particles of light).

In addition to being classically simple, PV cells make no noise and emit no pollutants. They require little maintenance, and can be fabricated in virtually any size, so they are especially useful in remote areas with no access to the utility electric grid. In the United States, it costs on average $10,000 a mile to put in an electrical line.

During the past two decades, the cost of photovoltaic power has fallen from $30 a kilowatt-hour to just 30 cents. (This figure is composed almost entirely of manufacturing costs, since solar power requires no fuel.) That's still four to six times the cost of power generated from fossil fuels. Nevertheless, photovoltaics have carved out impressive niche markets. Sales of PV systems topped $300 million in 1991, with two-thirds of U.S.-manufactured equipment being exported to the developing world. Applications include everything from powering wristwatches to lighting walkways and navigation beacons.

Some experts say the key to the future of photovoltaics, however, lies in whether the technology can successfully enter the electric-power grid, which would require costs to drop to the 10-15 cent per kilowatt-hour range. While demand for photovoltaics is not yet large enough to warrant mass production, the situation could change within five years. Many utility companies — even in New England, with its substantial cloud cover — are examining whether adding photovoltaic systems to

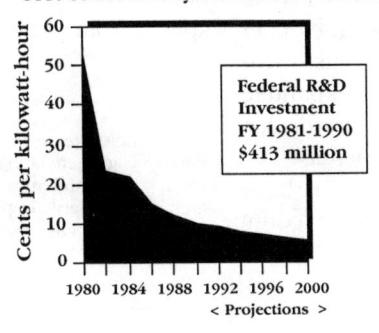

Cost of Electricity From Solar Thermal

Cents per kilowatt-hour

Federal R&D Investment FY 1981-1990 $413 million

60 50 40 30 20 10 0

1980 1984 1988 1992 1996 2000
< Projections >

Source: U.S. Department of Energy

homes and businesses could help meet customers' demands during peak daytime hours.

Also holding promise in the future is solar-thermal, a technology that converts solar energy into heat by focusing the sun's rays with a mirror onto a fluid. The heated fluid then boils water to create steam, which in turn drives a turbine to generate electricity. In essence, the sun plays the role of coal, gas or oil in a conventional steam-turbine plant.

At present, the only commercial-scale operation is a nine-plant system built and run by Luz International Inc. in California's Mojave Desert. It generates 150 megawatts of electricity, at a cost of 8 cents per kilowatt-hour.* That's competitive with Southern California's "peak power" rates. Current research could lead to solar-thermal costs dropping to 5 cents per kilowatt-hour by the end of the decade.[21]

But solar thermal has major drawbacks: It requires intense sunshine, available only in the Southwest in this country, and takes up large amounts of space. Luz International's solar collectors occupy three square miles. "For solar-thermal power to be commercial, you'd have to pave over the Mojave Desert," quips CATO's Jerry Taylor. "If that were to actually happen, environmentalists would go ballistic."

The solar building technology, which uses the sun to provide electric-

ity for water heaters, space heating and lighting in buildings, has been the most depressed sector of the solar industry. Still, the 1.2 million buildings in the United States with "active" solar systems (which use pumps, fans and other mechanical components) displace some 1,400 megawatts of electricity, an amount of power equal to two nuclear power plants. Many more have "passive" systems that rely on the building design itself.

Energy specialists say advances in solar-building technologies could have a profound impact. Some 37 percent of the nation's energy is consumed in residential and commercial buildings. Some experts say solar installations could provide up to 80 percent of a building's energy requirements.[22]

Not-So-Hot Prospects

Natural heat trapped in rocks and fluids beneath the Earth's surface has become a key energy resource in the United States. More than 2,800 megawatts of installed geothermal capacity now exists — practically all of it in California, where it generates enough electricity for 3 million households at costs of between 4 cents and 8 cents per kilowatt-hour. Conventional geothermal energy is extracted by drilling wells in places where hot rock and ground water have come together naturally, providing a ready supply of superheated water or steam.

Geothermal technology would seem to have an almost limitless potential. The Interior Department estimates that a staggering 1.2 million quads (quadrillion Btus) of geothermal energy underlie 3.4 million acres of U.S. land. Yet, like hydropower, surging growth in geothermal's share of the nation's energy mix is doubtful. That's because many of the geysers and hot springs that could provide geothermal power are not accessible.

*This figure is slightly lower than the DOE's estimated average cost because the facility also uses natural gas, which has lower generation costs. California also offers a small subsidy for using renewable technologies. Luz International declared bankruptcy earlier this year, but industry specialists say that was largely because of planning problems, rather than technology.

Trapping the remainder of the geothermal resource — hot dry rock, pressurized brines and magma located 30 miles below the Earth's crust — would require great leaps in technology. Another problem is that it is a regional resource. Historically, all of U.S. land with geothermal development potential is in the West, most of it away from major electricity markets.

Cost of Electricity From Geothermal

Federal R&D Investment FY 1981-1990 $434 million

Source: U.S. Department of Energy

Even where geothermal energy has been a proven success, technical problems abound. Consider The Geysers, a massive geothermal field north of San Francisco. It has a generating capacity of 1,500 megawatts of electricity, less than the 2,000 megawatts it was expected to produce. Worse yet, steam pressure in the wells is plummeting, raising the specter that the $3.5 billion investment will run dry.

But the underlying problem at The Geysers — and the danger for geothermal development everywhere — is overdevelopment of a poorly understood resource. Since 1989, more than five separate utilities have tapped into The Geysers' geothermal field. "Put simply, there are too many straws in the teapot," says Thomas Box of Calpine Corp., one of the firms operating in The Geysers.[23]

Energy From Biomass

It may surprise some, but the leading renewable energy source in the United States is biomass. Currently, wood accounts for some 84 percent of biomass' energy production. This is mostly in the paper and forest-products industries, which use the technology to meet more than half of their own energy needs.

Experts say biomass' share of the renewables' overall market is likely to shrink as other new technologies climb higher on their growth curves. But that doesn't mean that biomass energy won't continue to grow.

Although some 170 billion tons of biomass resources are grown annually, "less than 1 percent is currently consumed for fuel," explains Christopher Flavin, vice president and senior researcher at Worldwatch Institute. "Thus, there is a potential for greatly expanded biomass energy use." In particular, there is a projected increase in waste-to-energy plants, or garbage incinerators, which already account for 14 percent of the electricity gen-

erated by biomass.[24]

Moreover, biomass energy is relatively inexpensive. Production of electricity from biomass costs between 6 and 8 cents per kilowatt hour — competitive with a conventional coal-fired generating plants.*

Biomass-burning generates carbon dioxide and is perhaps the most polluting form of renewable energy. But new technologies are being developed to reduce harmful emissions. The negative effects of biomass on global warming can be further reduced through sustainable forestry practices, in effect matching the amount of carbon dioxide removed from the atmosphere from photosynthesis.

---

*Since there are so many different technologies involved in generating energy from biomass, each with a different cost structure, no cost-comparison graph is presented here. Generally speaking, though, experts say costs have remained stable for the past decade. ∎

OUTLOOK

Barriers Remain

The Electric Power Research Institute believes that, even if the annual growth rate in electric demand is as low as 1.4 percent, the nation will need as much as 250,000 megawatts of new energy capacity by the year 2010. That is the equivalent of building some 400 large coal or nuclear plants in the next 18 years. Many other organizations, including the American Gas Association, have come up with similar forecasts of future power needs.[25]

Meanwhile, the world is still experiencing a glut of low-cost fossil fuels, especially oil. And lower fuel costs have meant lower prices for

electricity. That's bad news for renewable energy. In the current economic climate, analysts say, there is little incentive for the private sector to seek or develop alternative fuels. Although in the long run this will probably change, it may take several years for excess supplies to be absorbed by rising demand, and thus prices are likely to remain relatively low for some time.[26]

Though willing to assist, the Bush administration is unwilling to give renewables the nudge proponents say they need. "We've seen a fundamental institutional change for the nuclear and coal industries," notes Scott Sklar, "but the administration is not willing to undertake fundamental change to transition to renewables."

Sklar singles out the admini-

Continued on p. 590

At Issue:

Should the U.S. impose a carbon tax to encourage the development of alternative energy sources?

CHARLES KOMANOFF

Director of a New York-based consulting firm
FROM *THE WASHINGTON POST,* MARCH 6, 1989.

by taxing all fossil fuels — coal, petroleum and natural gas — we can, in one simple measure, trim $50 billion from the federal deficit, encourage alternative energy and help the environment as well.... Such a tax would help balance the budget while providing incentives to make America more fuel-efficient, but without the regional or sectoral conflicts that a new gasoline tax might provoke.

One variant of a fuels tax could be pegged to each fuel's contribution to the greenhouse effect — the buildup of carbon dioxide that is gradually heating the Earth's atmosphere....

Fifty billion dollars per year could be derived from a carbon-based tax on all fossil fuels in the following manner: $10 billion would come from a 10-cent-a-gallon levy on gasoline; $17 billion from surcharges on one-half to one cent per kilowatt-hour on power generation, primarily coal-fired; $8 billion from taxing natural gas used by industry, offices and homes; and $15 billion from truck and jet fuel, petrochemicals, home-heating oil, coal used in steel-making and other sources....

Unlike with a gas tax, there is little chance of crippling sensitive sectors such as the auto industry or farm states, undermining the economy at large and reducing taxable income. No one group would bear more than a fraction of the total burden. Indeed, since the wealthy consume a greater share of electricity from manufactured goods than gasoline, a carbon tax would be less regressive than a gas tax.

Without the punitive taint of a gasoline-only tax, positive features such as energy efficiency can be emphasized. Opportunities for conservation would abound, particularly in the price-sensitive industrial sector....

The strongest objections to the carbon tax may be expected from customers of all-coal utilities, who would face 10 to 15 percent increases in electricity rates. Yet the real price of coal-fired power has fallen 8 percent in the 1980s, providing a cushion for a fuels tax that begins to redress atmospheric damage from burning coal. And utilities could soften the blow by offering rebates and other incentives for energy-saving lights and appliances, and by pursuing investments in efficient power generation.

No tax is a panacea, and no one wants to curb disposable income and slow the economy. But a carbon-based fossil fuels tax that fights pollution without discriminating against any one region, class or economic sector may be the least stressful option for cutting the deficit.

ROGER W. GALE

President, Washington International Energy Group, a consulting company
FROM *THE WALL STREET JOURNAL,* JULY 6, 1990.

recent converts to free-market principles ... support a carbon tax as a fix to the global warming problem that would work far more smoothly than complex command-and-control regulations on carbon dioxide and other greenhouse gases. That may sound practical, but it would entail a number of drawbacks.... First, it would fall more heavily on some parts of the country than others. Western coal- and oil-producing regions and Midwestern coal-burning regions would both be hit hard.

Second, domestic coal, which supplies 60 percent of America's electricity and will be even more crucial in the future unless nuclear power is revived, would be hit disproportionately hard if a tax is levied that does not consider environmental-control technologies that alter actual emissions. Coal exports could be mortally wounded.

Third, a carbon tax could reduce American competitiveness and inadvertently encourage more imports of oil. Swapping part of the budget deficit for a larger trade deficit may not be prudent policy.

Fourth, many utilities are scampering to finance billions of dollars in upgrades to meet the acid-rain provisions of the Clean Air Act legislation.... These same utilities would be the most likely candidates to pay a hefty carbon tax.

Fifth, a carbon tax ... might not lead to significant carbon dioxide cuts if industry decided it was cheaper to pay a tax than to clean up older plants. Instead of encouraging energy efficiency, it could bias the energy industry against new capital investments.

Sixth, carbon dioxide is not the only greenhouse gas. A meaningful first response to global climate change is to develop a greenhouse-gas index that compares the impacts of various gases on the environment and allows countries to establish their own priorities among the various greenhouse gases.... Finally, before Congress and the administration move any farther down the carbon-tax path, they must earmark the revenue for environmental and energy projects. More likely, the revenue would go for increased government spending in other areas.

A carefully constructed strategy makes sense once we know more about global warming and the pacing of necessary actions. And a carefully constructed increase in taxes also makes sense. It could be devastating to the United States, however, to get carried away by a naive belief that fixing the deficit and the environment is only a matter of working out a few mechanical details, such as applying a carbon tax.

Continued from p. 588

stration's refusal to extend tax credits for solar power beyond one year, which industry says is essential to plan effectively.

The growth of renewable energy is further slowed by other, more subtle market barriers. Experts say society's emphasis on short-term profits works to the disadvantage of alternative technologies, many of which cost more up front than fossil fuel technologies but save money in the long run because of lower fuel costs. Private consumers often demand a payback period of just two to three years for their investments. In addition, the poor economic performance of some early projects has also given them a bad name in financial circles.

Perhaps most important, however, utilities have been reluctant to experiment with new technologies. "Utilities don't have incentives to use alternatives and are not innovative," says Michael Brower of the Union of Concerned Scientists. Rather than choosing the least-cost alternative, he says, they generally take the path of least resistance: building conventional power plants.

"It's as if utility managers say, 'We've never used them before, why switch now?'" Brower says. "They are not dedicated to renewable energy."

Historically, utility commissions allowed electric companies to incorporate the cost of pollution control into their rate base, thereby shifting costs to customers. That may seem reasonable at first glance, but it removes any incentive to build anything but coal-fired plants, which are reliable and cheap to operate.

The 1990 amendments to the Clean Air Act may help change that. The act offers a cash incentive to utilities that invest in conservation and renewable energy, as long as their regulators ensure that efficiency investment is at least as profitable as buying new plants.

Utility Reform

While President Bush and the Department of Energy may continue America's reliance on the development of fossil fuels, states are thinking differently. And, increasingly, they have the power to carry through on their decisions.

"We are at the frontier of a utility regulation revolution," says Worldwatch's Lenssen. Leading the way is the state of California, the acknowledged capital of alternative energy. In that state, utilities are finding it makes sense to link energy efficiency to profits, something utilities call demand-side-management.[27]

Starting in 1989, state regulators and environmentalists devised a variety of incentives for utilities to invest in energy efficiency, resulting in "ne-gawatts" — actual reductions in the amount of electricity generated.

Over the next 10 years, PG&E projects it can save 37 billion kilowatt-hours of electricity — and save customers $3.5 billion in the process. Two other California utilities — Southern California Edison Co. and the Los Angeles Department of Water and Power — have taken the initiative a step further, voluntarily setting targets to reduce carbon dioxide by 20 percent by the year 2000.

During that timespan, California, one of the fastest growing states in the country, plans to build no new coal or oil-fired electric plants, instead relying on a combination of energy efficiency (75 percent), renewable energy (12.5 percent) and natural gas (12.5 percent) to meet energy demand.

"When you compare the U.S. energy plan and the California energy

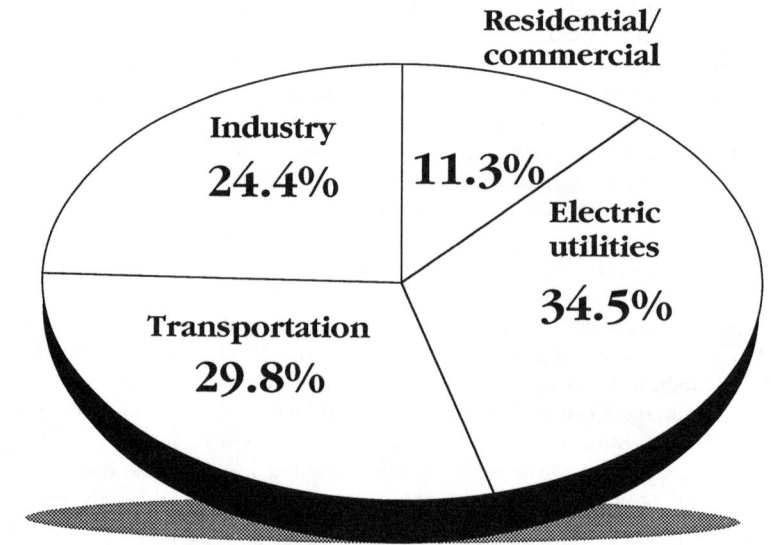

Sources of Carbon Dioxide Emissions

Electric utilities are the biggest source of carbon dioxide emissions in the United States. California and other states are trying to curb carbon dioxide emissions by encouraging conservation and incorporating environmental costs into utility rates.

Residential/commercial

Industry 24.4%

11.3%

Electric utilities 34.5%

Transportation 29.8%

Note: Figures are for 1988.
Source: Energy Information Administration

plan, both set up roughly 20 years ago, the difference is striking," says David Goldstein, co-director of the energy program at the Natural Resources Defense Council. According to Bush's National Energy Strategy, the United States would meet its future needs primarily with new sources of fossil fuels: coal (37 percent), natural gas (29 percent) and oil (3 percent).

California's plan is not pie in the sky. In 1980, nearly half of the state's power came from burning oil; today only 1 percent does — roughly the same as it gets from burning waste. Unlike in much of the rest of the country, electric and gas rates in California are calculated to reflect the avoided cost of building new generating capacity — including environmental costs.

"The results have been dramatic," says Goldstein. "When each category of renewable energy is considered, more capacity has been added in California than in the rest of the world combined."

Energy experts say other states are beginning to follow California's example.* More and more, utilities are hesitant to invest in long-term, conventional power plants. Instead they're looking to smaller, modular projects, buying from independent power producers, and thinking about natural gas and renewables.

None of this means the end of the fossil-fuel era is near. On the contrary, fossil fuels are likely to dominate the energy scene for decades to come. According to PG&E's Weinberg, the nation's energy strategy should be considered an investment portfolio. Within that portfolio, fossil fuels will play a lead role, but they should be considered like high-risk stocks, cheap to buy but with the

payoff risky, depending on fuel prices and environmental concerns. Renewables cost more to buy but have steady yields, with low risks and environmental impacts. "Each option uses different technologies, has different risks and different impacts on the environment," says Weinberg. "Just as we need to balance our investment portfolio, we need to balance our energy portfolio."

Solar expert Scott Sklar agrees. "Utilities have to enter into a whole new social contract," he says. "It used to be the more kilowatts delivered, the more money you made. Now it's what is the best service for customers. That may mean 'negawatts,' it may mean renewable energy, or it may mean enhancing the performance of conventional fuels. It is only through a diverse resource base that we can stave off oil price shocks and environmental catastrophes." ∎

Notes

[1] For background, see "Persian Gulf Oil," *Editorial Research Reports*, Oct. 30, 1987, pp. 565-576.

[2] For background, see "Oil Imports," *The CQ Researcher*, Aug. 23, 1991, pp. 585-608.

[3] Department of Energy, *The Potential of Renewable Energy: An Interlaboratory White Paper*, March 1990.

[4] Robert Stobaugh and Daniel Yergin, eds., *Energy Future: Report of the Energy Project at the Harvard Business School* (1979), p. 213.

[5] Quoted in *The Christian Science Monitor*, March 14, 1991.

[6] Quoted in *Industry Week*, April 1991, p. 67.

[7] For background, see "Will Nuclear Power Get Another Chance?" *Editorial Research Reports*, Feb. 22, 1991, pp. 113-128.

[8] See "Oil Spills," *The CQ Researcher*, Jan. 17, 1992, pp. 25-48.

[9] U.S. Export Council for Renewable Energy, *Renewable Energy for the World*, 1990, p. 8.

[10] Quoted in *EPRI Journal*, June 1991, p. 21. The journal is published by the Electric Power Research Institute.

[11] See "Electromagnetic Fields: Are They Dangerous?" *Editorial Research Reports*, April 26, 1991, pp. 237-252.

[12] Eight of the 15 states have formulas for assessing environmental costs in energy planning. They are California, Colorado, Massachusetts, New York, New Jersey, Oregon, Vermont and Wisconsin. See I. C. Bupp and Gary Simon, *Quiet Revolution: Integrated Resource Planning and the Future of U.S. Electric Power*, Cambridge Energy Research Associates, April 1992, p. 9.

[13] "Energy and the Environment Survey," *The Economist*, Aug. 31, 1991.

[14] A British thermal unit is the quantity of heat required to raise the temperature of a pound of water one degree Fahrenheit.

[15] In 1991, imported oil accounted for 66 percent of the U.S. trade deficit.

[16] The Senate bill passed on Feb. 19 by a vote of 94-4; the House version passed on May 27 by a 381-37 margin. Two of the more controversial issues — raising the Corporate Average Fuel Economy (CAFE) standards for cars and opening the Arctic National Wildlife Refuge to oil exploration — were dropped. For background, see "House Gives Energy Bill Big Win; Lengthy Conference Expected," *Congressional Quarterly Weekly Report*, May 30, 1992, p. 1530.

[17] Quoted in *Time*, Jan. 13, 1992, p. 48.

[18] Quoted in *The Wall Street Journal*, Sept. 6, 1991.

[19] Department of Energy, *Conservation and Renewable Energy Technologies for Utilities*, 1991, p. 20.

[20] In parts of California where wind farms are located, high winds tend to coincide with periods of high-peak electricity needs, in the late afternoon.

[21] Department of Energy, *op. cit.*, p. E-2.

[22] See *Industry Week*, Feb. 4, 1991, p. 57.

[23] For details, see "Geothermal Tragedy of the Commons," *Science*, July 12, 1991, p. 134.

[24] For a more detailed description of the pros and cons of this technology, see "Garbage Crisis," *The CQ Researcher*, March 20, 1992, pp. 241-264.

[25] See Philip C. Cruver, "Lighting up the 21st Century," *The Futurist*, January/February 1989, p. 30.

[26] The DOE forecasts that the real price of crude oil will not go up appreciably until after the turn of the century. See Michael Brower, *Cool Energy: The Renewable Solution to Global Warming* (1990), p. 74.

[27] David Moskovitz, "Renewable Energy: Regulatory Barriers and Opportunities," draft paper for the World Resources Institute, December 1991.

---

*Other states committed to utility reform include Washington, Oregon, Wisconsin, New York, Massachusetts, Minnesota, Rhode Island and Connecticut.

Bibliography

Selected Sources Used

Books

Brower, Michael, *Cool Energy: The Renewable Solution to Global Warming,* Union of Concerned Scientists, 1990.

This survey of renewable energy technologies, currently being updated, contains useful data and is generally a good primer on alternative energy.

Stobaugh, Robert, and Daniel Yergin, eds., *Energy Future: Report of the Energy Project at the Harvard Business School,* Random House, 1979.

When it first came out, this book was widely cited as the most authoritative source on alternative energy. Sections on the history of resource development are insightful.

Articles

Idelson, Holly, "House Gives Energy Bill Big Win; Lengthy Conference Expected," *Congressional Quarterly Weekly Report,* May 30, 1992, p. 1530.

This is a good summary of the main differences between the House and Senate energy bills, which are now in conference.

Fischetti, Mark, "Here Comes the Electric Car — It's Sporty, Aggressive and Clean," *Smithsonian,* April 1992, p. 34.

The author discusses the technology triumphs and setbacks in developing electric cars. The article also provides background on the politics of bringing electric cars into the marketplace.

Voight, Keith, "Electric Vehicles: Fast Lane to Practicality," *Electric Perspectives,* May/June 1992, p. 13.

The article discusses the leading electric-vehicle prototypes and has a separate section on the development of batteries for electric cars.

White, David C., et al., "The New Team: Electricity Sources Without Carbon Dioxide," *Technology Review,* January 1992, p. 43.

Three academics — David White, Clinton Andrews and Nancy Stauffer — take the view that the world must reduce its dependence on carbon-based fuels. They provide a survey of the leading alternatives — notably solar, wind and geothermal power. The article also contains an interesting section on how fossil fuels can be used more efficiently.

Reports and Studies

Alliance to Save Energy, et al., *An Alternative Energy Future,* April 1992.

This joint industry study by the Alliance to Save Energy, the American Gas Association and the Solar Energy Industries Association provides a detailed look at energy use in the United States. The study contains extensive data on renewable energy, including projections for the future.

Congressional Office of Technology Assessment, *Replacing Gasoline: Alternative Fuels for Light-Duty Vehicles,* 1990.

This report covers all the main substitutes for gasoline, including natural gas, methanol, ethanol and electric. It is an unbiased and thorough examination of each technology, with data on costs, emissions, etc.

Department of Energy, *The Potential of Renewable Energy: An Interlaboratory White Paper,* March 1990.

Widely cited by energy experts as well as in the media, this report examines the role of alternatives based on several scenarios, roughly broken down as "business-as-usual," "R&D incentives" and "market incentives." The data compiled for this study serve as the foundation for many other non-governmental studies.

Flavin, Christopher, and Nicholas Lenssen, *Beyond the Petroleum Age: Designing a Solar Economy,* Worldwatch Paper 100, December 1990.

The authors, both at the Worldwatch Institute, argue that the end of the fossil fuel age is in sight, and that countries must start planning for the transition. Some of the projections for the role of renewable are optimistic, but overall the report contains useful information.

U.S. Energy Information Administration, *1992 Annual Energy Outlook,* January 1992.

Although this study has text describing the energy market and prospects for future energy sources, it is primarily a source for up-to-date energy data.

Union of Concerned Scientists, et al., *America's Energy Choices: Investing in a Strong Economy and a Clean Environment,* 1991.

Four nonprofit environmental organizations co-authored this study documenting the need for a national energy policy. The report concludes that reducing fossil-fuel use is essential to America's long-term economic well-being. The project includes proposals for how the nation can get on a "sustainable energy path."

The Next Step

Additional Articles from Current Periodicals from EBSCO Publishing's Database

Addresses & essays

"Energy security: Alternatives to oil," *Society,* **May/June 1991, p. 2.**

Asserts that the United States must drastically reduce its dependence on outside energy sources. Search for ways to cut oil imports; super-efficient appliances; development of methanol (wood alcohol), ethanol (grain alcohol), natural gas, electricity and hydrogen.

"Renewable energy — key to the future," *USA Today,* **December 1991, p. 12.**

Contends that the technologies are at hand to begin the transition away from oil and coal toward renewable energy. Importance of developing energy from sunlight, wind, water, plant and subsurface heat; problems with the nuclear alternative to fossil fuels.

Fischer, M. L., "Kick the oil habit," *Sierra,* **July/August 1991, p. 6.**

Presents the Sierra Club's proposal for a comprehensive alternative energy strategy that relies on energy efficiency and reducing the need for petroleum.

Lovins, A., "Oil-free energy," *Good Housekeeping,* **April 1991, p. 92.**

Looks at alternative energy sources. Benefits; passive solar; wind; garbage; how much energy and money can be saved.

Morris, D., "Making fossils of fossil fuels," *Utne Reader,* **May/June 1991, p. 42.**

Proposes plant-based products as environment-friendly alternatives to fossil fuels. The uses of hydrocarbons that were made from a carbohydrate; politics as obstacle to use of fuel alcohol and hemp; plant-matter-based plastics being produced by companies on the rise.

Automobile design & construction

"The car that drinks cocktails," *The Economist,* **Sept. 28, 1991, p. 95.**

Looks at the effects that the combination of technology and environmental worries are having on the design of new types of car engines. The internal-combustion engine; advanced two-stroke engines; the gas turbine; work by General Motors, Ford, and others; alternative fuels, such as ethanol and methanol; flexible-fuel vehicles (FFVs); electric cars; details; outlook.

McCarroll, T., J. Szczesny, et al., "No fuel like a new fuel," *Time,* **March 18, 1991, p. 66.**

Describes the new Impulse, General Motors' experimental electric car that runs on 10-volt batteries and gets 120 miles with each fill-up. Uncertain oil supplies have sparked interest in alternative fuels and the race for a clean, dependable substitute for gasoline is in full gear. Methanol, compressed natural gas and hydrogen; winning over the driving public. INSET: Easing gas pains.

Woodruff, D., T. Peterson, et al., "The greening of Detroit," *Business Week,* **April 8, 1991, p. 54.**

Looks at several alternative-fuel cars now making their way into the spotlight. The U.S. government and the European Commission have demanded that automakers drastically reduce harmful exhaust emissions, and shows their attempts to do so. New models; three ways to go. INSETS: Is America finally ready for the gasless carriage? by D.Woodruff; clean cars in 13 years?; big oil sees the future — and it's clean gasoline, by M. Ivey, R. Buderi, et al.

Zygmont, J., "Alternative engines: Sputtering to life after years of experimentation," *Omni,* **March 1992, p. 16.**

Considers today's development of alternative engines. Focuses on alternatives that promise to improve both the quality of car motors and the prospects for energy use and the environment. Effects of the latest California clean air laws; research at Ford, Chrysler and General Motors; electric, jetlike turbine engines; hybrid vehicles combining electric drive with small internal-combustion engines; technical hurdles; cost.

Books & reading

Davis, J. D., "Book reviews: Economics, development, energy and environment," *International Affairs,* **April 1991, p. 345.**

Reviews the book "The economics of natural gas: pricing, planning and policy," by DeAnne Julius and Afsaneh Mashayekhi.

Plotkin, S. E., "Books of note," *Environment,* **March 1992, p. 28.**

Reviews the book "Review of Alternative Transportation Fuels: An Environmental and Energy Solution," edited by Daniel Sperling.

Case studies

"A watt saved is a watt gained," *The Economist,* March 16, 1991, p. 24.

Looks at the state of alternative energy in California. Claims of having the cleanest energy in the world; solar energy; windmills; geothermal power; Luz International; natural gas; details.

Uda, J. R., "Prophets of an energy revolution," *National Wildlife,* December/January 1992, p. 10.

Discusses the work of Amory and Hunter Lovins of the Rocky Mountain Institute (RMI) who are giving energy advice to utilities and businesses. Education of Amory Lovins; commitment to alternative energy sources; criticisms from energy sources; criticisms from energy establishment; formation of RMI; advisory work; statistics on energy wasted in United States (US); companies and utilities interested inenergy efficiency. INSET: Throwing away $300 billion (energy-saving tips).

Debates & issues

Begley, S., "The road not taken," *National Wildlife,* August/September 1991, p. 10.

Examines the pros and cons of several kinds of alternative fuels for U.S. cars, as well as the reasons cars using these fuels aren't yet available in showrooms. Opposition from Big Three automakers; buying factors in cars; gas-saving tips; why the fuel-efficient Volvo LCP2000 prototype died; compressed natural gas (CNG); methanol; electric cars; hydrogen. INSETS: Whatever happened to a balanced energy policy? by M. Hager; untitled (Bryan-Gorton Motor Vehicle Fuel Efficiency Act).

Elmer-DeWitt, P. and D. Carres, "Gee, your car smells terrific!" *Time,* July 22, 1991, p. 48.

Reviews recent developments in the field of cleaner-burning gasolines, and notes that Atlantic Richfield, eighth-largest U.S. oil company, has developed a gasoline that will cut toxic emissions nearly 50 percent. Producing designer-gasolines; cleaner fuels are more expensive; California's new fuel standards; possible death knell to alternative fuels.

Grable, R., "Alternative fuels," *Motor Trend,* December 1991, p. 108.

Examines the pros and cons of the most popular alternative fuels including propane, the alcohol family and natural gas. Reasons for interest in alternative fuels; description of propane fuel and how a propane engine works; savings of natural gas systems; details of different alcohol fuels; performance comparison of alternative fuels and gasoline.

Kleiner, A., "Oily wastes and wants," *Discover,* May 1991, p. 30.

Examines the feasibility of distilling oil from wood as an alternative fuel source. Benefits; origin of idea; development of pyrolysis method; "entrained flow" pyrolysis reactor; how the system works; prototype reactor; possible applications.

Smith, E. T., "Conservation Power," *Business Week,* Sept. 16, 1991, p. 86.

Asserts that conservation power is an idea that is igniting an energy revolution. Trendsetters; simple technology; energy statistics for American industry; the search for ideas about alternative sources of energy; prospects for changes in energy policy this year; architects and buildings gearing toward energy efficient buildings; "feebate" program in California; programs for highways; need for a comprehensive energy policy from Washington.

Templeman, J. and K. L. Miller, "Fill 'er up — with hydrogen, please," *Business Week,* March 4, 1991, p. 59.

Discusses how the Persian Gulf War piqued interest in alternative fuels, and new clean air laws make hydrogen a more realistic fuel choice than it was before. Benefits of using hydrogen-powered cars; wasting energy; problems with hydrogen; how the process works; how the fuel should be stored. INSET: The pluses and minuses of hydrogen cars.

Ethanol

Ainsworth, E., "Ethanol's billion-bushel potential," *Farm Journal,* May 1991, p. 13.

Considers several predictions for corn demand by 1995 for use in the alternative fuel ethanol. Use of the fuel is supported by members of the American Petroleum Institute, National Corn Growers Association and the American Soybean Association; other organizations affected; projecting price increases; impact on soybean markets.

Hoke, F. and C. Renaud, "Grow your own fuel," *Environment,* November 1991, p. 22.

Reports that in an effort to reduce air pollution, Gado NV, a buscompany in the Netherlands, is planning to run its fleet of buses on ethanol, an alternative to conventional fuels. Ethanol produces a cleaner emission than diesel fuel and is renewable; why products such as grass, wood, and even municipal solid wastes might be a more efficient source of ethanol; reducing the amount of government subsidies for untilled land.

Lynd, L.R., J.H. Cushman, et al., "Fuel ethanol from cellulosic biomass," *Science,* March 15, 1991, p. 1318.

Examines ethanol produced from cellulosis biomass as a large-scale transportation fuel. Production and utilization; air-quality impact; biomass feedstocks; processing options; global climate change implications; environmental impacts.

Government policy

Heede, R. and R. Bishop, "Corporate wealth through waste," *Sierra,* **July/August 1991, p. 16.**

Presents information from Richard Heede and Robert Bishop, two analysts with the Rocky Mountain Institute, the nation's premier energy-efficiency think tank. Together they examined the controversial oil provision section of President Bush's National Energy Strategy. Compares Bush's plan with an alternative energy policy based on efficiency to find effects on cost, consumption, and import of oil over next 20 years; Bush's plan boosts imports; geologically and economically improbable.

Watkins, J. D., "Administration energy proposal," *Congressional Digest,* **May 1991, p. 136.**

Summarizes the Bush administration's National Energy Strategy, proposed energy policy legislation. Looks at energy efficiency, renewable energy, alternative fuel use and more.

Natural gas

Tanzer, A., "Preferred fuel," *Forbes,* **Dec. 23, 1991, p. 40.**

Discusses how natural gas is in huge oversupply in the U.S., yet Asia is extremely greedy for every bit it can get. Gas-rich countries; the expense of producing natural gas; the Green movement; the deliveries of natural gas by pipeline across borders will commence in Asia within the decade; focus; analysts' predictions.

Wald, M. L., "Natural gas as auto fuel gets a push in New York," *The New York Times,* **Sept. 14, 1991, p. 21.**

Tells of a garage that was opened in Staten Island by Metropane Inc. that can convert hundreds of vehicles a month from gasoline to natural gas. In the next few months, nearly 20 filling stations offering natural gas will open in New York City. Advantages of natural gas.

Nuclear energy

Collingwood, H., "Alternative power down East," *Business Week,* **May 13, 1991, p. 52.**

Announces how Maine utilities have switched to hydropower and activated an oil-fired electric generating plant in the wake of a crippling hydrogen fire at Maine Yankee Atomic Power Co.'s Wiscasset nuclear plant on April 29. A quarter of Maine's electricity is supplied by the nuclear plant; outlook.

Szoke, A. and R. W. Moir, "A practical route to fusion power," *Technology Review,* **July 1991, p. 20.**

Explains how small underground nuclear explosions could supply the world's electricity for centuries to come. Proposed peaceful nuclear explosions system (PNE); building a PNE power plant; planning development and costs; obstacles still to be resolved; advantages over other energy alternatives.

Winner, L. "Fear and loathing on the nuclear bandwagon," *Technology Review,* **August/September 1991, p. 74.**

Reflects on a steady decline in public approval of nuclear power since the mid-1970s. Efforts of the industry to sway popular sentiment toward nuclear power as the only alternative to dependence on foreign oil; emphasis on nuclear power in President Bush's energy plan; why the public's fear of nuclear power should be taken seriously.

Propane

Oldham, J. and J. Dunne, "The alternate fuel report: Propane-powered Buick," *Popular Mechanics,* **August 1991, p. 91.**

Reports on a Buick LeSabre that uses propane as an alternative fuel.

Quayle, C., "Propane for cars? It's a gas!" *Environment,* **March 1992, p. 23.**

States that the National Propane Gas Association is extolling the virtues of propane as the most viable alternate fuel. Number of motor vehicles worldwide that are running on propane; driving range of a car running on propane; more.

Renewable energy

Bauerlein, M., "Renewable energy: The little engine that does," *Utne Reader,* **May/June 1991, p. 17.**

Discusses the research of new renewable energy technologies. California wind and solar energy plants; some renewable energy used unwisely; developing countries dependence on imported oil; need for commitment from President Bush's administration and corporations for alternative energy exploration.

Menzel, P., S. Nadis, et al., "Alternative sources: A status report," *Omni,* **May 1991, p. 50.**

Examines the current status of research and development into renewable energy sources. Solar energy; biomass energy; nuclear energy; solar-based hydrogen system; geothermal energy; wind power.

Wald, M. L., "Putting Windmills Where It's Windy," *The New York Times,* **Nov. 14, 1991, p. D1.**

Discusses the wind energy farm that the Iowa-Illinois Gas and Electric Co. of Davenport, Iowa, and U.S. Windpower of Livermore, Calif., want to build in the Upper Midwest. At full production, the plant would be able to meet the electricity needs of 100,000 households and would be cost-competitive with new electric plants fired by coal or natural gas.

Back Issues

Great Research on Current Issues Starts Right Here... Recent topics covered by The CQ Researcher are listed below. Issues dated before May 10, 1991, were published under the name of Editorial Research Reports.

DECEMBER 1990
Cable TV Regulation
Americans' Search for Their Roots
Is Insurance System a Failure?
Why Schools Still Have Tracking

JANUARY 1991
Growing Influence of Boycotts
Should the U.S. Reinstate the Draft?
America's Archaeological Past
Peace Corps' Challenges in '90s

FEBRUARY 1991
Regional Impact of Recession
Puerto Rico's Status
Redistricting: Mapping Power
Nuclear Power

MARCH 1991
Acid Rain
Cost of the Gulf War
Reassessing Gun Laws
Future for Man in Space

APRIL 1991
Social Security
Canadian Crisis Over Quebec
California Drought
Electromagnetic Radiation

MAY 1991
School Choice
Racial Quotas
Animal Rights
U.S. and Japan

JUNE 1991
Children and Divorce
Teenage Suicide
Endangered Species
Europe 1992

JULY 1991
Teenagers and Abortion
Soviet Republics Rebel
Mexico's Emergence
Athletes and Drugs

AUGUST 1991
Sexual Harassment
Fetal Tissue Research
Oil Imports
The Palestinians

SEPTEMBER 1991
Police Brutality
Advertising Under Attack
Saving the Forests
Foster Care Crisis

OCTOBER 1991
Pay-Per-View TV
Youth Gangs
Gene Therapy
World Hunger

NOVEMBER 1991
Fast-Food Shake-Up
The Greening of Eastern Europe
Business' Role in Education
Cuba In Crisis

DECEMBER 1991
Retiree Health Benefits
Asian Americans
The Obscenity Debate
The Disabilities Act

JANUARY 1992
Term Limits
Oil Spills
Hunting Controversy
Alternative Medicine

FEBRUARY 1992
Threatened Coastlines
New Era in Asia
Assisted Suicide
Jobs in the '90s

MARCH 1992
Women and Sports
Underage Drinking
Garbage Crisis
Mafia Crackdown

APRIL 1992
Ozone Depletion
Welfare Reform
Politicians and Privacy
Illegal Immigration

MAY 1992
Native Americans
Jobs vs. Environment
Too Many Lawsuits?
Fairness in Salaries

JUNE 1992
Nuclear Proliferation
Food Irradiation
Lead Poisoning
Hard Times for Libraries

Back issues are available for $4.00 (subscribers) or $7.00 (non-subscribers). Quantity discounts apply to orders over ten. To order, call Congressional Quarterly 1-800-432-2250.

Future Topics

▶ *Prescription Drug Prices*

▶ *Alzheimer's Disease*

▶ *Infant Mortality*

PUBLISHED BY CONGRESSIONAL QUARTERLY INC., IN CONJUNCTION WITH EBSCO PUBLISHING

Prescription Drug Prices

Should the government regulate prescription drug prices?

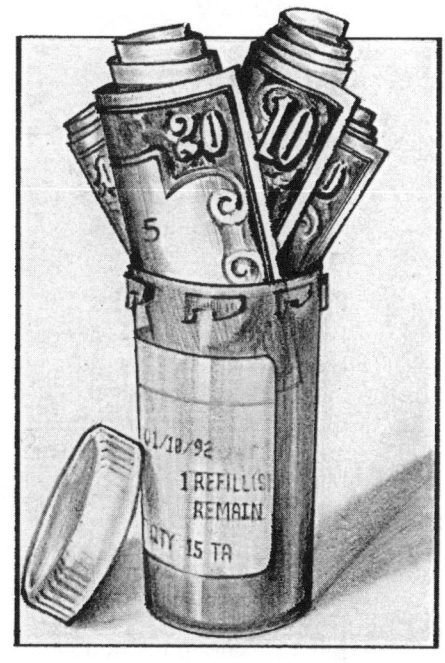

THE U.S. PHARMACEUTICAL INDUSTRY IS AMONG the most profitable sectors of the nation's otherwise lagging economy. It's also one of the few bright spots on the international trade scene. But an increasing number of consumer advocates, as well as some lawmakers, say that many prescription drugs are becoming so costly they are beyond the reach of those they could help. Condemning pharmaceutical companies for spending as much marketing their products as they do inventing new ones, the critics say it is time for the federal government to step in and regulate drug prices. Drug manufacturers contend that their products not only help lower medical costs by preventing costly hospitalization and surgery but also reduce the toll in human suffering.

CQ | **July 17, 1992 • Volume 2, No. 26 • 597-616**

Formerly Editorial Research Reports

COVER ART: BARBARA SASSA-DANIELS

CQ Researcher

July 17, 1992
Volume 2, No. 26

EDITOR
Sandra Stencel

MANAGING EDITOR
Thomas J. Colin

ASSOCIATE EDITOR
Richard L. Worsnop

STAFF WRITERS
Charles S. Clark
Mary H. Cooper
Rodman D. Griffin

PRODUCTION EDITOR
Laurie De Maris

EDITORIAL ASSISTANT
Michael M. Taylor

GRAPHICS
Jack Auldridge

PUBLISHED BY
Congressional Quarterly Inc.

CHAIRMAN
Andrew Barnes

VICE CHAIRMAN
Andrew P. Corty

EDITOR AND PUBLISHER
Neil Skene

EXECUTIVE EDITOR
Robert W. Merry

PUBLICATIONS MARKETING/SALES
Robert Smith

EDITOR, EBSCO PUBLISHING
Melissa Kummerer

The CQ Researcher (ISSN 1056-2036). Formerly Editorial Research Reports. Published weekly (48 times per year, not printed the first Friday of any month with five Fridays) by Congressional Quarterly Inc., 1414 22nd St., N.W., Washington, D.C. 20037. Rates are furnished upon request. Second-class postage paid at Washington, D.C. POSTMASTER: Send address changes to The CQ Researcher, 1414 22nd St., N.W., Washington, D.C. 20037.

Prescription Drug Prices

BY JULIE ROVNER

THE ISSUES

Two-year-old Justin Smith was born eight weeks premature and with a long list of medical problems. Among other things, the Salt Lake City, Utah, child wasn't growing. Then Justin began receiving a drug known as human growth hormone. "He's gained nearly five pounds since last August, when he had his first hormone shot," Justin's mother, Cindy, told a Senate subcommittee in January. "Before the hormone treatments, it took him 10 months to gain one pound."

As the world's leader in developing new drugs, America's pharmaceutical industry can point to many such stories with happy endings. But, increasingly, the last chapter comes at a steep price.

In Justin's case, the hormone that will help him to live a normal life costs a whopping $36,000 per year. Luckily for the Smiths, medical insurance helps pay the bills. But the family's monthly premiums skyrocketed because of the new expenses. So did the fees paid by the company Justin's father works for — and in August they likely will rise an additional 60 percent. "My biggest fear is that [the company's high premiums] could cost my husband, Brad, his job," Cindy Smith told the Senate Judiciary Subcommittee on Antitrust, Monopolies and Business Rights.

She has good reason to worry, and so do millions of other Americans. Over the past decade, prices for prescription drugs have risen nearly three times faster than prices for other products. And drug prices rose even faster than other health-care services. The increases have forced millions of Americans of limited means to stop taking the medicines they need, or to

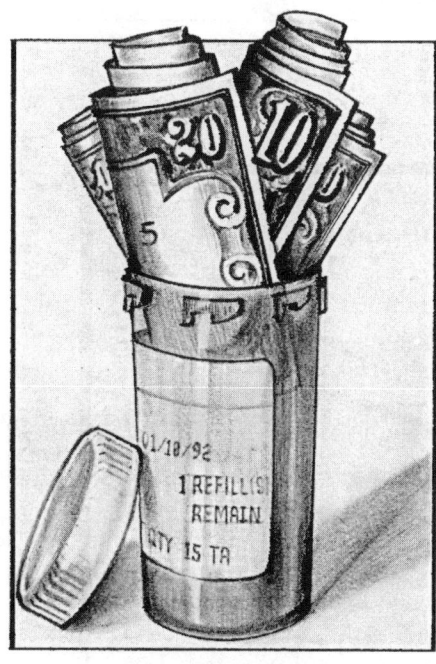

cut back their prescribed doses.

To Sen. David Pryor, D-Ark., the most outspoken congressional critic of the drug industry, these "shameful and unrelenting price increases" have reached "crisis" proportions. "For the 12th year in a row," Pryor said in February, "prescription drug price inflation has been the leader of the pack in pushing up the cost of medical care in our country.... Over 5 million people over 55 now say they are having to make choices between food and their prescription drugs — between fuel for their home for heat or paying for prescription drugs. If that is the case, what kind of a country have we become?" [1]

These higher prices, moreover, have produced "excessive and unconscionable profits" for pharmaceutical companies, according to a scathing staff report issued last September by the Senate Special Committee on Aging, chaired by Pryor. "At a time when Americans are scrimping and saving to afford their medications, the drug industry's annual average 15.5 percent profit margin more

than triples the 4.6 percent profit margin of the average *Fortune* 500 company," Pryor wrote in the report's introduction. [2]

Recently developed drugs like Justin Smith's are often particularly expensive. Consider Clozaril, which was approved by the Food and Drug Administration (FDA) in 1989 to treat schizophrenia. Since the much-vaunted drug can cause a potentially fatal blood disorder in a small number of patients, its maker, Sandoz Pharmaceuticals Corp., took the unusual step of requiring users to take weekly blood tests. Included in the cost of prescriptions, the tests helped push the drug's yearly cost to $10,000 per patient. [3]

Similarly, the cost of combating AIDS, at least initially, was frightfully expensive. AZT, the first drug approved to treat HIV, the human immunodeficiency virus that causes AIDS, cost nearly $10,000 per year when it went on the market in 1987. But AIDS activists protested, pointing out that the drug actually had been developed by government researchers at the National Institutes of Health. Ultimately, the outcry prompted the manufacturer, Burroughs Wellcome Co., to reduce the price. A subsequent discovery that the drug works at half its original dose brought the cost down to its current level of about $3,000 annually. [4]

Because most Americans' health insurance doesn't cover prescription drugs, even inexpensive medications can cause hardship. According to the Washington-based Employee Benefit Research Institute (EBRI), nearly three-quarters of all prescriptions are paid for directly by the patient. While a two-week supply of antibiotics for a strep infection might not throw most middle-class families into a financial tailspin, the modest cost of daily "maintenance" doses for such conditions as diabetes, high blood pressure

The High Cost of Drugs

Over the past decade, prices for prescription drugs have risen nearly three times faster than prices for other products. And drug prices rose even faster than other health-care services.

Inflation index

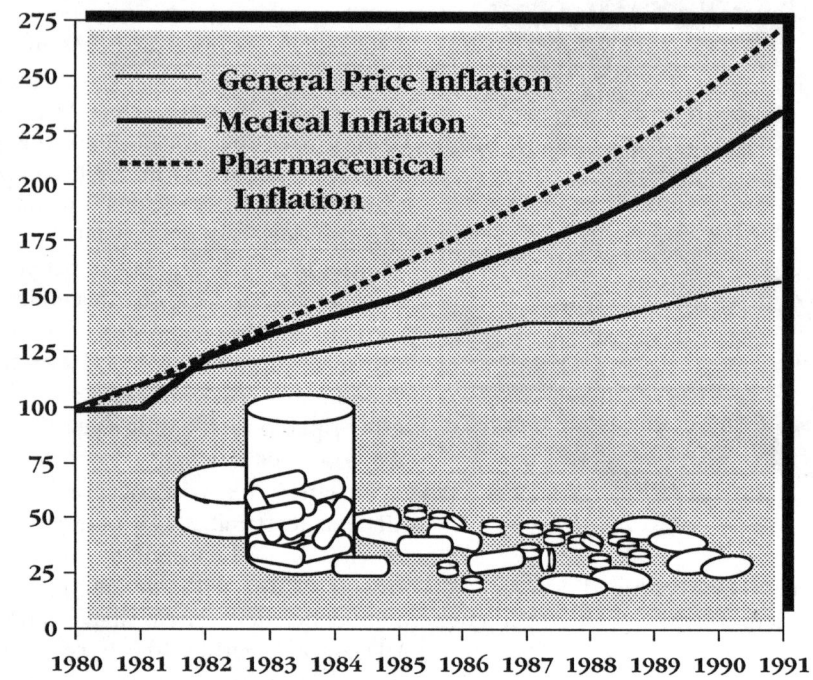

General Price Inflation

Medical Inflation

Pharmaceutical Inflation

1980 1981 1982 1983 1984 1985 1986 1987 1988 1989 1990 1991

Sources: Bureau of Labor Statistics; Congressional Research Service

and arthritis can add up quickly.

For elderly Americans especially, prescription drugs are a bitter pill. Seniors use the most prescription drugs of any age group — consuming roughly 30 percent of all drugs sold in the United States annually — and they are also the least likely group to have insurance coverage for prescriptions. That's because Medicare, the federal health-care program for the elderly and the disabled, does not cover most outpatient prescription medications.* Compounding the problem, many senior citizens live on fixed incomes.

The situation has drawn the ire of the influential American Association of Retired Persons. According to the

---

*Medicaid, the joint federal-state health program for the poor, does pay for some prescriptions.

33-million-member group, "Prescription drug consumers, who are more often elderly, are held hostage by whatever pricing structure a pharmaceutical company wishes to adopt."[5]

Drugmakers, of course, do offer an explanation. In essence, says the Pharmaceutical Manufacturers Association (PMA), it's the drugmakers themselves who have been taken hostage, by skyrocketing research and development (R&D) costs. According to the PMA, drugmakers spend an average of $231 million to bring each new drug to market.[6] That covers testing the drug for safety and effectiveness and then satisfying the FDA, which must approve all drugs sold in the United States.

Research and development is so costly, says a PMA spokesman, that 12 of the top 30 U.S. pharmaceutical firms last year actually lost money or

earned less than shareholders might have received from a savings account.

Furthermore, said Richard J. Kogan, president and chief operating officer of Schering-Plough Corp. and a past president of the PMA, "The pharmaceutical industry has proven that its products save lives, avoid premature deaths and save billions of dollars in costs resulting from disease. The industry is not part of the health-care cost problem in America, but instead is a vital part of the solution."

One thing is certain: Despite continuing debate on Capitol Hill over health costs, drug prices haven't been lowered. Not that Congress hasn't tried. As early as 1984, it sought to spur competition by making it easier for generic copies of brand-name drugs to be brought to market after expiration of the original patent.

In 1988, the Medicare Catastrophic Coverage Act provided outpatient prescription drug coverage for the first time. But after Medicare recipients balked at being asked to help pay for the new benefits through higher premiums, Congress repealed the law in 1989.[7]

Congress stepped back into the drug-pricing issue in a small way in 1990. It required drug companies to give the same discounts to state Medicaid programs that they provide to other bulk-drug purchasers, such as hospitals and health maintenance organizations. In many cases, however, the drugmakers didn't lower prices for Medicaid but raised them for everyone else. That simply fueled the fire for further legislative action on pricing. As Congress continues to grapple with the drug-price issue, here are some of the key questions being asked:

Are prescription drug prices too high?

When Sen. Pryor's Special Committee on Aging released its sharply critical staff report on pharmaceutical industry profits last September, it issued a dire warning: If prices continued rising at the current pace, a prescription that cost $20 in 1980 would be nearly $121 by the year 2000 — an increase of more than 500 percent. Alternatively, if drug manufacturers limited price hikes to current projected increases in the general rate of inflation, that same $20 prescription would cost only $49.72 by the turn of the century.[8]

According to the report, pharmaceutical prices rose at almost three times the general rate of inflation from 1980 to 1990. While the general inflation rate was 58 percent during the 10-year period, prescription drug prices rose 152 percent.

Drug-price increases even outpaced increases in overall health-care spending. On average, the Aging committee noted, pharmaceutical prices rose 18.5 percent more each year during the 1980s than total health-care costs. At the same time, health-care costs were escalating twice as fast as the general rate of inflation.

Industry critics say drug-price inflation is continuing in the 1990s. In 1991, for example, the Consumer Price Index increased just 3.1 percent, while prescription drug prices increased 9.4 percent.

Expensive new drugs like AZT and Clozaril have helped shove the drug-inflation rate sky-high. But critics say pharmaceutical manufacturers also have been raising prices for drugs that have been on the market for decades. For example, the price of Dilantin, a drug widely used since the early 1950s to prevent epileptic seizures, has risen 69 percent since 1985, an average annual increase of more than 11 percent.[9]

As proof that drug companies are charging too much for their products, industry critics point to the manufacturers' high profit margins. In 1991, the average profitability (as a percent of sales) of drug companies was 12.8 percent — four times the *Fortune* 500 average of 3.2 percent. (*See graph, p. 600.*)

According to the Aging committee, pharmaceuticals led all U.S. industries in 1990 in three commonly used profitability measures: percentage of return on sales, percentage of return on assets and percentage of return on stockholders' equity. The report cited an analyst's prediction that pharmaceutical profits will climb 18 percent each year over the next few years because of the expected introduction of several "extremely high-priced" new drug products.

Even drug manufacturers say the outlook is healthy. According to the PMA, worldwide U.S. drug sales are expected to reach a record of $75.2 billion in 1992, up 11.7 percent from $67.3 billion in 1991.[10]

But while they boast that their industry is thriving, drug manufacturers say critics — particularly Sen. Pryor and his committee staff — have distorted their profit picture.

PMA Executive Vice President Robert F. Allnutt told reporters in May that drug costs have remained a relatively constant share of total U.S. medical expenses. In 1960, he said, outpatient prescription drugs accounted for 0.53 percent of the gross national product (GNP), while total health-care costs represented 5.3 percent of GNP. By 1990, total health costs had risen to 12.2 percent of GNP, but spending on prescription drugs had risen to only 0.58 percent.

Spending on prescription drugs is also only a small part of total health-care costs, drug manufacturers point out. Such spending has actually dropped, from 8.9 percent of the total spent on health needs in 1965 to 4.8 percent in 1990.[11]

And, despite what Pryor's committee claims, says the PMA, drug-price inflation is actually slowing. The association notes that the drug portion of the Producer Price Index, which measures manufacturers' prices (not the prices consumers pay), rose by only 7.8 percent in 1991, compared with 8.1 percent in 1990.

"By no stretch of the imagination can one say that increases in prices of pharmaceuticals are somehow driving up health-care expenditures," Allnutt said.

Drugmakers defend their profits, too, noting that the industry is a risky one whose investors expect high returns for the risks they take. According to the PMA, only one of every 4,000 compounds tested will result in a drug that is approved by the FDA. "Those who invest in the pharmaceutical industry would not support this high-risk R&D enterprise if they did not expect to get a better rate of return than they could with safer investments, such as Treasury bonds," says the PMA.

Pryor derided that argument. "Other *Fortune* 500 companies, whose profit margins are one-third that of the drug industry, do not appear to have trouble attracting sufficient capital," he said.

Do high research and development costs justify higher drug prices?

One reason drug prices have steadily risen, manufacturers say, is because the costs of discovering and developing new drugs have increased even more. In 1976, according to the PMA, bringing a new drug to market cost approximately $54 million. That swelled to $125 million in 1987 and $231 million in 1990.[12]

In fact, say drug producers, companies plow most of their profits right back into the search for new drugs. The PMA reported in January that its member companies will spend an estimated $10.9 billion in 1992 on research and development, an increase of 13.5 percent over the $9.6 billion they spent in 1991. It's also more than the total spent by the federal government for R&D in the health field, and roughly three times the average for all U.S. industries that conduct research. This year's projected spending, PMA adds, continues a

Drug Company Profits

In 1991, the average profitability of the 10 top U.S. drug companies was 15.5 percent. For all U.S. drug companies, it was 12.8 percent — four times the Fortune *500 average of 3.2 percent.*

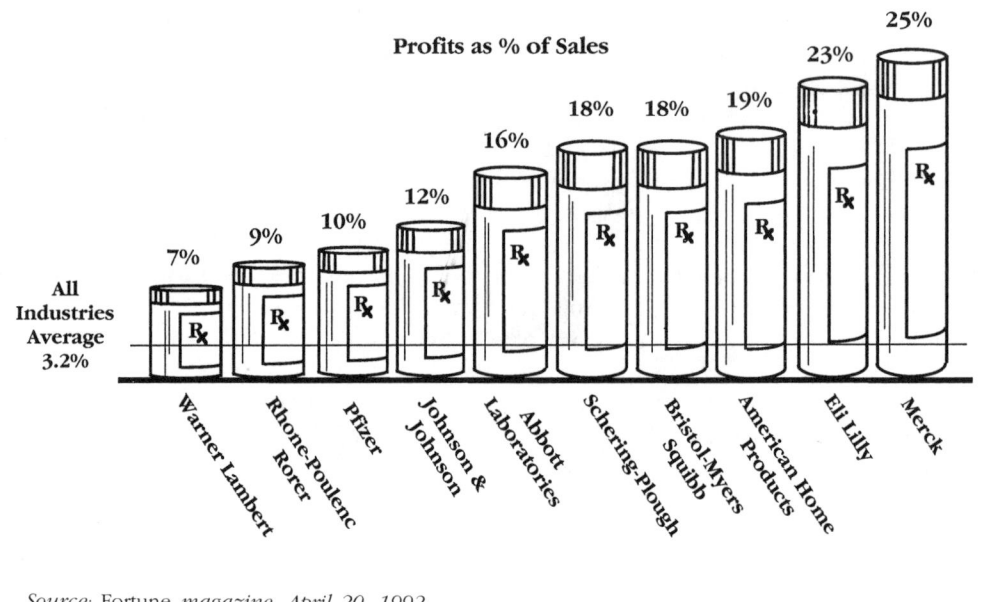

Profits as % of Sales

All Industries Average 3.2%

7% — Warner Lambert
9% — Rhone-Poulenc Rorer
10% — Pfizer
12% — Johnson & Johnson
16% — Abbott Laboratories
18% — Schering-Plough
18% — Bristol-Myers Squibb
19% — American Home Products
23% — Eli Lilly
25% — Merck

Source: Fortune *magazine, April 20, 1992*

trend for industry spending on R&D to double roughly every five years.

In short, the drugmakers maintain that the combined costs of bringing new drugs to market and the returns expected by investors justify the industry's price increases.

The risks are so great, says the PMA, that only 30 percent of all drugs approved in the 1970s earned back their investment — but consumers and lawmakers only focus on superstar drugs like Tagamet and Zantac, two anti-ulcer drugs that literally earn billions every year. "Obviously, the ones that pay off, pay off big," PMA's Allnutt said in May.

Critics, however, say they would take industry arguments about research costs more seriously if not for the fact that drugmakers spend more on marketing and promotion than they do on R&D. In 1991, according to the Aging committee staff report, projected advertising and marketing

expenditures for the average drug company were 25 percent of sales, compared with only 22.5 percent of sales for research and development.

In fact, said the report, some expenditures that companies count under R&D are actually promotion efforts. "These so-called research activities help the companies collect the data they need to design their lavish marketing and promotional campaigns," the report said. "Such marketing research expenditures are lumped into claimed research and development expenditures, and manufacturers are then able to write them off at a significant cost to the American taxpayer."

Industry officials counter that they spend a smaller proportion of their incomes on marketing than many other industries. In addition, because of the unique nature of the pharmaceutical business, the PMA says that such spending is "necessitated by more than ordinarily rapid innovations that

require extensive and detailed explanation."

Finally, the drug industry doesn't market its products directly to consumers, but primarily to the doctors who make the prescribing decisions. And that is a very expensive proposition involving legions of "detail" men and women who make individual office visits to practitioners.

Industry foes say drug companies spend too much of their R&D budgets developing so-called "me-too" drugs, which simply offer another way to treat an already treatable ailment or illness. According to a 1989 report by the Senate Aging committee staff, 84 percent of all new drugs introduced by the 25 largest prescription drug manufacturers were rated by the FDA as having "little or no potential for therapeutic gain" when compared with already available medications.

But the drugmakers say that is not their goal, merely an unfortunate side-effect of the industry's hit-or-miss nature. "No company sets out to develop a 'me-too' drug," says the PMA. "The hope is always for a breakthrough. But drug development is a long, serendipitous process full of surprises. Sometimes it results in a breakthrough, often it results in only a small therapeutic advance."

Do prescription drugs save the medical system money?

Drugmakers' chief defense against accusations of overcharging is that their products actually lower the nation's total health bill by reducing or eliminating hospital stays and averting costly surgery.

Vaccines to prevent childhood diseases are cited as a prime example. "In 1983, the nation's health bill for measles, mumps and rubella vaccination programs came to $100 million," Merck President P. Roy Vagelos noted in 1991. "According to the U.S. Public Health Service, the cost of these diseases, in contrast to the cost of preventing them, would have been $1.4 billion."[13]

In an effort to bolster those claims, Schering-Plough commissioned a study, released in March 1991, showing that over the next 25 years drugs will prevent 9 million cases of heart disease and save 5 million lives. During that same time, drug intervention will reduce deaths from lung cancer by 662,000 and lower new arthritis cases by 2.1 million.[14]

During that quarter-century, according to the study, pharmaceuticals would reduce projected spending for cardiovascular disease by $211 billion, spending for lung and colon-rectal cancer and leukemia (a form of cancer) by $14 billion and spending for arthritis by $170 billion. Over the next 10 years, it projected, spending for AIDS would decline by an estimated $11 billion.

Direct medical costs will also decline thanks to new pharmaceutical products, the study found, including $1.7 billion in savings for the three cancers, $10 billion for arthritis and $68 billion for Alzheimer's disease (primarily due to a decreased need for expensive nursing home care).

Other analysts say that advances in medications provide benefits that cannot be readily quantified. "It is impossible to account for improvements in quality," wrote Alan Reynolds, director of economic research for the conservative Hudson Institute in Indianapolis, Ind. "A 1991 drug that saves your life may cost a bit more than the 1980 equivalent that left you dead, but that is qualitative progress that cost money to achieve;

Top 10 U.S. Drug Companies

	1991 SALES	1991 PROFITS
	(in millions)	
Johnson & Johnson *New Brunswick, N.J.*	$12,447	$1,461
Bristol-Myers Squibb *Princeton, N.J.*	11,298	2,506
Merck *Rahway, N.J.*	8,603	2,122
Pfizer *New York, N.Y.*	7,144	722
American Home Products *New York, N.Y.*	7,103	1,375
Abbott Laboratories *Abbott Park, Ill.*	6,922	1,089
Eli Lilly *Indianapolis, Ind.*	5,726	1,315
Warner-Lambert *Morris Plains, N.J.*	5,167	35
Rhône-Poulenc Rorer *Collegeville, Pa.*	3,824	327
Schering-Plough *Madison, N.J.*	3,688	646

Source: Fortune *magazine, April 20, 1992*

it is not inflation."[15]

But the fact that prescription drugs may be less expensive than other forms of medical technology is beside the point, says Sen. Pryor. "While drugs are sometimes less expensive than other medical interventions, they are not cost-effective if they are unaffordable," he declared.

Would government regulation help reduce prices?

The United States is the only Western nation that doesn't control the costs of prescription drugs.[16] Pryor and other critics of the drug industry say government regulation of prices is needed because prescription drugs, like health care in general, is an unusual market because intermediaries (usually doctors) determine the demand.

"The drug is prescribed by a physician who is often unaware or little concerned with drug costs," says H. C. Eastman, a professor of economics at the University of Toronto.

"The consumer, for his part ... considers the drug essential to his health and lacks the knowledge to find a cheaper product with similar therapeutic effect when that is possible."

Supporters of price regulation also ask why prescription drugs should not be regulated like other "utilities" that are deemed necessary for survival, such as water and electricity. "Drugs are important to our health," said Rep. Henry A. Waxman, D-Calif, chairman of the House Energy and Commerce Subcommittee on Health and the Environment, which oversees drug prices. "We must guarantee that they are denied to no one simply because they cost too much."[17]

Pryor says federal action on prices is justified by the tremendous profits drug companies make. "Now, how do they make these enormous profits?" he asked on the Senate floor in March. "One, by outright price gouging of our American citizens who can least afford the medications — the elderly, the poor and the other vulnerable parts of the American population."[18]

But drugmakers counter that price controls would do little more than guarantee that drugs are available to no one — in effect hurting just those people Pryor says he wants to help. "Innovative pharmaceutical companies are in business to make money, as well as to market new medicines," wrote Merck President Vagelos, "and, unless they do both, they would be out of business, and the flow of new medicines would be reduced."[19]

Adds Reynolds of the Hudson Institute: "What is unconscionable is not high profit, but a demagogic political attack that aims to convert one of this country's most competitive industries into a regulated utility, on a par with the Postal Service."[20]

Finally, says PMA President Gerald J. Mossinghoff, price controls simply do not work. "Naked price controls are an absolute failure, and I think the history of the world has shown that," he told reporters in May. "Price controls are so foreign to the free-market system and so damaging to the free-market system that I think Congress will be wise enough not to do it."

Which side is right? The nonpartisan Employee Benefit Research Institute had this to say in a January 1992 report on drug prices: "Other things being equal, it is likely that policies that restrict prescription drug prices will reduce drug industry profitability. Whether such policies would lead to reduced investment in future products is an unanswered question." [21] ■

BACKGROUND

Government Regulation

The federal government's formal involvement with the drug industry began in 1906 with the passage of the Pure Food and Drug Act. Among other things, the new law called for government analysis of the ingredients in so-called "patent medicines," which promised "to end cancer and the tobacco and morphine habits, to enlarge female 'busts,' and to bring on abortion." [22]

At the time, makers of patent medicines were in direct competition with physicians. Ads in newspapers and magazines frequently sought to deter the public from seeing doctors, recommending their products instead. "The doctor did no good," announced the headline on one ad from the Lydia Pinkham Co., which invited women to write for confidential advice about their health problems.

But while the increasingly powerful American Medical Association was beginning to agitate against drugmakers who were advertising their nostrums directly to the public, it took journalistic muckrakers to make the law a reality. It was ultimately pushed through Congress over manufacturers' objections after turn-of-the-century revelations in *Colliers* and other popular magazines about patent medicines that contained opium and even poisons.

One *Colliers* article revealed, among other things, how a fast-selling concoction called "Liquozone" was actually 99 percent water. Another report revealed that in the late 1890s the Pinkham Co. was still encouraging women to write to Mrs. Pinkham for advice ("Do you want a strange man to hear all about your particular diseases?" asked one ad) even though she had been dead since 1883. [23]

The coup de grâce for patent medicines came, somewhat ironically, with publication of Upton Sinclair's *The Jungle,* which so graphically depicted the unsafe and unsanitary conditions in Chicago's slaughterhouses that Congress was prompted to pass a law encompassing drugs as well as food.

What is today's Food and Drug Administration in fact began in 1901 as the Agriculture Department's Bureau of Chemistry, headed by the legendary Dr. Harvey W. Wiley, whose agitation for increased federal oversight of food and drugs earned him the nickname "father of the pure food law."

But the 1906 act was hardly the cure-all the drug industry needed. As health policy expert Paul Starr wrote: "The law affected only the most arrant fakes. It did not require the disclosure of all contents, except in the case of narcotics; it only banned statements on the label of a drug about its composition that were 'false and fraudulent.' This rule did not initially apply to claims about the effectiveness of drugs, nor to statements made in newspaper advertisements."

After some initial caution, drugmakers discovered they could resume making bold claims, even intimating that their drugs now met a federal standard of purity and effectiveness." [24]

Tougher Law Heralds Modern Era

By 1938, it was clear that a firmer federal hand was required, and Congress passed the Food, Drug and Cosmetic Act (FDCA), which remains the basis of modern drug regulation. Like the 1906 law, the FDCA grew out of a public health emergency. This time, the law was prompted by an incident in which more than 100 people died after taking sulfanilamide, a new "miracle" drug whose ingredients included a substance used to make anti-freeze. [25]

In addition to bringing cosmetics and medical devices under the purview of the federal government, the 1938 law required pre-market government approval of drugs for safety. Proof of effectiveness was not added to the law until 1962.

Pricing Controversies

The modern pharmaceutical industry is in many ways a creature of the federal government. It was born of necessity during World War II, when the government helped coordinate research into developing antibiotics like penicillin and treatments for malaria, which plagued troops in the Pacific.

Today, pharmaceutical companies conduct more than half of all U.S. biomedical research and development. According to the PMA, the prescription drug industry is the largest single spender on health-care R&D in the country. The projected $10.9 billion that private companies will put into research and development in 1992 is larger than the $9.7 billion

Continued on p. 606

Chronology

1900s-1930s
Outrageous claims of patent medicines are exposed by muckrakers, prompting congressional action to regulate drugs.

1906
Congress passes the Pure Food and Drug Act, which provides for government analysis of patent medicines and prohibits false and misleading claims.

1938
Congress passes the landmark Food, Drug and Cosmetic Act (FDCA), which dramatically increases federal oversight of prescription drugs by requiring, among other things, that drugs be proven safe before they can be offered for sale.

———— • ————

1950s-1960s
Congress begins trying to regulate drug prices.

1959
In lawmakers' first major attempt at regulating prescription drug prices, Sen. Estes Kefauver, D-Tenn., chairman of the Senate Judiciary Subcommittee on Antitrust and Monopoly, begins hearings on the drug industry's pricing, patent and business policies.

1961
Sen. Kefauver's committee concludes that drug prices are "unreasonable" and that some companies have unfair competitive advantages because of the 17-year period of patent exclusivity. Kefauver introduces legislation to, among other things, shorten the period of patent exclusivity to three years.

1962
The discovery that the drug Thalidomide causes severe birth defects helps prompt passage of amendments to the FDCA, including a requirement that drug companies give the Food and Drug Administration (FDA) information on adverse drug reactions and documentation of effectiveness.

———— • ————

1980s
Drug-price increases outpace the rise in overall health spending, and expensive new drugs push the drug-inflation rate higher.

1983
Congress passes the Orphan Drug Act, which provides tax and other incentives to encourage the development of drugs to treat rare diseases.

1984
Congress passes the Drug Price Competition and Patent Term Restoration Act, which makes it easier to market generic copies of drugs whose patents had expired and also gives drugmakers patent extensions to make up for time lost due to the FDA's slow review process.

1986
Sales of Tagamet, a revolutionary anti-ulcer medication introduced by SmithKline in 1977, hit the $1 billion-a-year mark — the first drug to break that barrier.

1988
Congress passes the Medicare Catastrophic Coverage Act, which provides outpatient prescription drug coverage for the first time.

1989
Congress repeals the Catastrophic Coverage Act after recipients balk at being asked to help pay for the new benefits.

1990s
Several members of Congress introduce legislation to cope with high drug prices; some drugmakers pledge to limit price hikes, and the pharmaceutical industry mounts a public relations offensive.

1990
Sales of Glaxo's Zantac, a drug similar to Tagamet but with fewer risks of adverse reactions, reach $2.4 billion, a new record for a single drug in a single year. Congress passes the Medicaid drug price law, which requires drugmakers to give the same discounts to the joint federal-state Medicaid program they offer to other bulk-drug purchases.

November 1991
Sen. David Pryor, D-Ark., introduces the Prescription Drug Cost Containment Act, which ties special tax breaks to drugmakers' willingness to link price hikes to the inflation rate. Sen. Pete Stark, D-Calif., proposes Medication Price Control Act, which denies research and development tax credits to drug companies if their new products increase in price more than 2 percent above the Consumer Price Index.

January 1992
Pharmaceutical makers hire a public relations firm to publicize the industry's positive contributions to health care.

February 1992
At least five drugmakers pledge to limit price increases to the inflation rate.

June 1992
Sens. Nancy Landon Kassebaum, R-Kan., and Howard M. Metzenbaum, D-Ohio, introduce a bill to eliminate provisions of the Orphan Drug Act giving companies a monopoly on marketing rights for drugs whose sales top $200 million.

The Drug Approval Process

Drugs are more expensive and more time-consuming to develop than nearly any other consumer product. According to the Pharmaceutical Manufacturers Association, it takes an average of 12 years and $231 million to bring a new drug to market.

At the heart of the complex process is the Food and Drug Administration (FDA), which is required under the federal Food, Drug and Cosmetic Act to approve all prescription drugs for safety and effectiveness before they can be sold.

Here are the key steps in the FDA's review process:

Discovery: Once a new drug (known as a "chemical entity") is developed, it undergoes pre-clinical testing in animals to determine its safety and effect on specific ailments. This phase usually takes 3.5 years.

Investigational New Drug Application: If a drugmaker believes a chemical entity shows promise, it files an application with the FDA for designation as an Investigational New Drug. If the FDA doesn't reject the application within 30 days, the company may begin the following three-phase human-testing process:

Phase One Clinical Trials take approximately one year and test a drug's safety in healthy volunteers (those without the ailment the drug is meant to treat).

Phase Two Clinical Trials take about two years and reveal how the drug works on 100 to 300 volunteer patients who suffer from the target ailment.

Phase Three Clinical Trials are the most elaborate, requiring up to three years and 1,000 to 3,000 patients to verify the drug's effectiveness and monitor potential adverse reactions.

In response to the urgent need for drugs to treat AIDS, an "expedited process" was authorized in 1989 that combines phases two and three of the clinical trials for drugs that show early promise in treating life-threatening illnesses.†

New Drug Application: If a drug "passes" all three clinical trials, the company may file a New Drug Application seeking FDA approval. Only about one of every five drugs that begin human testing make it this far. These voluminous submissions — sometimes running to 100,000 pages — must include all the scientific information gathered during testing. By law, the FDA is required to review the applications within six months, but in practice the agency almost never meets the deadline. For example, it took the FDA an average of two and a half years to rule on drugs approved in 1991.

Approval: Even after a drug is approved by the FDA — and only one of every 4,000 or so drugs that undergo preclinical testing makes it to market — studies continue. Drug manufacturers must continue to provide the FDA with data on adverse reactions, quality control and, in some cases, a drug's long-term effects.

---

†The anti-AIDS drug DDC, approved by the FDA June 22, was the first medication approved under the new fast-track process.

Continued form p. 604
the federal government will spend on the research institutes and components of the National Institutes of Health, which research a vast array of health problems, including heart disease, cancer and AIDS.

In addition to the vast sums it spends on R&D, the drug industry can also brag about its healthy overseas sales — one of the few bright spots for U.S. industry — a fact drug companies never fail to remind those who would tamper with their operations. "The industry is one of very few American businesses which currently enjoy a positive balance of trade, estimated to be nearly $1 billion in 1992," the PMA trumpeted in a February fact sheet. Indeed, of 97 new drugs introduced to world markets between 1975 and 1989, U.S. companies were responsible for 47, according to the association,

But while drug companies like to tout their strong international position, industry critics say U.S. consumers are getting a raw deal compared with buyers overseas. Americans on average pay 62 percent more for prescription drugs than Canadians and 54 percent more than the average European, according to the Senate Aging committee.

And often, the committee found, those higher prices are for the exact same drugs. Premarin, for instance, an estrogen-replacement for women, cost 233 percent more in the United States than in Canada in 1989. Likewise, Synthroid, used to treat thyroid ailments, cost U.S. consumers 277 percent more than Canadians.

The PMA disputes the claims of the committee's report, pointing out, among other things, that Canada is more reliant on generic drugs than the United States. But the industry group does acknowledge that a study comparing the purchasing power of consumers in 24 developed nations puts the United States about in the middle, with Americans paying more than consumers in the United Kingdom, Canada and Japan, but less than buyers in Italy, France and Germany.

Among all health costs, drug prices are of special concern to consumers because in most cases it is the consumers themselves, rather than insurance companies, who pay the bills.

In 1989, nearly three-fourths of all spending on prescription drugs in the United States (72.4 percent) was paid out-of-pocket, according to the January 1992 study by the EBRI. By contrast, consumers themselves paid only 5 percent of hospital bills and 19 percent of doctors' charges.[26]

The elderly are particularly hard-hit by rising drug prices. Many live on fixed incomes that increase, if at all, only as much as general inflation. In addition, Medicare does not cover most outpatient prescription drugs. And senior citizens are by far the largest users of prescription drugs.

Not surprisingly, the combination of lower-than-average insurance coverage and higher-than-average use leaves many senior citizens in a difficult position. According to the Aging committee, 15 percent of the elderly say they can't pay for their medications. And an August 1991 report by the Congressional Budget Office found that 60 percent of elderly citizens are at risk for catastrophic out-of-pocket prescription drug costs.

Price-Regulation Efforts

Over the years, Congress has made frequent — although seldom successful — attempts to regulate prescription drug prices.

The first dates back to 1959, when Sen. Estes Kefauver, D-Tenn., chairman of the Senate Judiciary Subcommittee on Antitrust and Monopoly, began a series of hearings on the drug industry's pricing, patent and business practices. The resulting report, issued in 1961, concluded that drug prices were "unreasonable," with companies enjoying unfair advantages, including patents that allowed a single company exclusive rights to market a drug for 17 years.[27]

Kefauver introduced legislation based on the information uncovered in the hearings that would, among other things, have shortened the period of patent exclusivity to three years.

But it was less Kefauver's hearings than the thalidomide scare in the summer of 1962* that helped prompt passage of that year's amendments to the Food, Drug and Cosmetic Act. Many of the Kefauver bill's safety provisions were included in the law, including requiring drug firms to provide the FDA with more information about adverse drug reactions and requiring pre-market documentation of effectiveness. But the controversial pricing provisions were dropped.

It was not until 1984 that Congress squarely addressed the drug-price question with passage of the Drug Price Competition and Patent Term Restoration Act. The law embodied a compromise that gave drugmakers something they had been seeking for years — patent extensions to make up for time lost due to the FDA's slow review process. At the same time, the law made it easier to bring to market "generic" copies of drugs whose patents had expired. Sponsors hoped that helping to foster the development and quick approval of generic drugs — which generally retail for 50 to 80 percent less than their brand-name counterparts — would spur competition and bring overall prices down.[28]

Under the new law, makers of generics wouldn't have to demonstrate safety and efficacy, but only that their copies were "bioequivalent" to the original drug, or acted in the same way. In exchange for simplifying the approval process, brand-name makers were allowed to recoup up to five years of exclusive marketing rights under patent law — often the amount of sales-time lost waiting for the FDA to finish its review.

However, Congress did not anticipate the tremendous economic advantage that the first generic to be approved would have. Because that first copy often ended up with as much as half the generic market, some drugmakers illegally tried to get an advantage. FDA officials were bribed to slow down competitors' applications. And some makers cheated on testing, actually submitting the brand-name drug for testing instead of their copy, thus ensuring that the generic would be deemed equivalent to the brand-name product.*

Controversy Over Medicare Coverage

The next major battle between Congress and the drug industry was over the 1988 Medicare Catastrophic Coverage Act. The law was originally intended merely to close coverage gaps that left the elderly and disabled beneficiaries of the program subject to unlimited hospital and doctor costs. But senior citizen groups successfully lobbied for provisions to provide the first-ever large-scale Medicare coverage of outpatient prescription drugs.

The ink on the new law was barely dry, however, before Congress was flooded with complaints from elderly citizens outraged about having to help foot the bill for the new benefits. There was an added problem: With drug prices rising rapidly, so were estimates of how much the new drug benefit would cost.

In late 1988, Sen. Pryor, who was just taking over as chairman of the Senate Special Committee on Aging, said he thought some of the complaints were being prompted by the drug industry. The drugmakers, he speculated, feared that broad inclusion in the Medicare program would lead to price controls. "I frankly think there's a lot of [drug company] greed out there," Pryor told reporters. "Those medicines that old people have to have are the ones that are

---

*Thalidomide, a sedative then on the market in Europe, was found to cause severe birth defects if taken by pregnant women.

*Eight drug companies and 29 individuals have been convicted of abusing the fast-track process for approving generic drugs.

the most expensive. They say they need to spend all this money on research, and I just don't buy that."[29]

The complaints ultimately forced Congress to repeal the Catastrophic Coverage Act in 1989, but the ill will toward the drug companies persisted among Pryor and other backers of the act.

The next year, however, gave Pryor another chance to discipline the drugmakers. In 1990, Congress passed legislation he co-authored that required drug companies to provide the same discounts to the joint federal-state Medicaid program they routinely granted to other bulk purchasers, such as hospitals and the Department of Veterans Affairs.

But it turned out to be in many ways a hollow victory. By mid-1991,

it was apparent that many drug companies were circumventing the intent of the law by raising prices for other customers rather than lowering them for Medicaid programs. A Sept. 25 study by the inspector general for the Department of Health and Human Services found that of 101 drugs checked, prices had been raised for 90, and 28 percent of the boosts were of 20 percent or more.[30]

The PMA argued that its members had no choice on the price hikes. Drugmakers could not, the organization said, afford to give to Medicaid, which represents roughly 15 percent of the drug market, the same discounts given to the Department of Veterans Affairs, which represents just 1 percent.   ■

tax-incentive approach." But to the PMA, "The carrot is non-existent; the stick a veritable two-by-four."

The controversial bill ties the drug industry's eligibility for a special tax break designed to spur investment in Puerto Rico to its willingness to hold price increases to the general inflation rate. *(See story, p. 610.)* In effect, drug companies could have their tax credits reduced by up to 20 percent for each percentage point drug prices increase above the inflation rate.

The measure would also establish a Prescription Drug Policy Review Commission for "analyzing trends in national and international prescription drug prices and making recommendations on providing or improving coverage, reimbursement and financing for prescription drug coverage under federal health-care programs."

The drug industry vehemently opposes S 2000. According to the PMA, the bill "would undermine longstanding and highly successful U.S. policy, is unwise and discriminatory and would violate the three main tenets of U.S. tax policy — fairness, simplicity and economic growth."

Thus far, sentiment in Congress seems to be on the side of the drug industry. When Pryor offered a slightly amended version of S 2000 as a floor amendment to another bill in March, it was defeated by a 61-36 vote.[33] "This measure, far from controlling prices, will dramatically increase those prices and ultimately be a great drag upon the American people and the economy," said Sen. Hank Brown, R-Colo.

In the House, Rep. Stark is taking a slightly different approach. A bill he introduced last November would deny R&D tax credits to drug companies if their new products increased in price more than 2 percent above the Consumer Price Index. The bill would also deny R&D tax credits for the expenses associated with developing "me-too" or copycat drugs that do not add new medicines to the

CURRENT SITUATION

Price War Escalates

Judging from the rhetoric that has been flying between congressional critics and the drug industry, the feud over prices has reached critical mass.

By far the most outspoken critic has been Aging committee Chairman Pryor, whose tirades against the drug industry seem to come almost weekly. "It seems like nothing that we in Congress do or say will get the drug manufacturers to understand that we have had enough of their reckless pricing behavior," he said last September. "They obviously have no shame."[31]

Another critic has been Sen. Edward M. Kennedy, D-Mass., chairman of the Labor and Human Resources Committee, which oversees the FDA. "[T]here is a line between profits and profiteering," he said last October. "No industry should have carte blanche to raise

prices without regard to the consequences for the public."[32]

And Rep. Pete Stark, D-Calif., chairman of the House Ways and Means Subcommittee on Health, took the drug industry to task on the House floor last Nov. 19. "Never have so few made such gross amounts of money from so many sick people," he said.

In response, the drugmakers tend to zero in on Pryor. "It must be clear to everyone by now that Sen. Pryor has a vendetta against the pharmaceutical industry," said the PMA's Allnutt. "In one area after another, he uses selective facts to paint a distorted picture in order to make his point."

Several Bills Address Issue

But this is a war of action as well as words. In Congress, Pryor, Stark and others have introduced several bills to limit prescription drug prices. With his penchant for fiery rhetoric, the media-conscious Pryor has won high visibility for his Prescription Drug Cost Containment Act, known on Capitol Hill as S 2000. Introduced last November, it uses what Pryor calls "a businesslike, carrot and stick

Does the Orphan Drug Act Need Fixing?

Congress sought to help a unique group of disease sufferers when it passed the 1983 Orphan Drug Act. These were people who, because of their rare disorders, had fallen through the cracks of the profit-motivated U.S. pharmaceutical business. The law was designed to stimulate the development of medications to treat uncommon disorders — generally defined as those afflicting fewer than 200,000 people — by providing incentives for the drugmakers.

Since the law's passage nine years ago, 60 new drugs to treat rare disorders have been approved, compared with only 10 in the decade before. The bad news is that some of those drugs are prohibitively expensive. Ceredase, for instance, the Genzyme Corp.'s breakthrough treatment for Gaucher's disease approved in 1991, costs an average of $350,000 per year, making it the most expensive drug in medical history.† And EPO, an anti-anemia treatment for patients undergoing kidney dialysis, costs about $8,000 annually and earns more than $350 million a year for its manufacturer, Amgen Inc.

Needless to say, creating unaffordable drugs — and windfall profits — hadn't been lawmakers' intent. The idea was simply to stimulate the development of drugs for a patient base so small that sales would almost certainly never recoup the costs of development. The law's incentives included tax credits and, crucially, seven years of "market exclusivity" for drugs that were otherwise not patentable.††

One reason for the high profits and prices has been the Food and Drug Administration (FDA) policy of granting "orphan" status to drugs long before the drugs themselves are approved. As a result, by the time approval is granted the patient base may exceed 200,000. Thus, several important drugs for AIDS — whose patient base has grown exponentially — are still considered orphan drugs. This includes aerosol pentamidine, used to treat AIDS-related pneumonia, which earned $131 million in 1991 for Fujisawa USA.

The flexibility of the Orphan Drug Act compounds the situation. While orphan drugs are usually developed for a specific disease, once approval has been granted they can be used to treat other ailments, broadening the sales potential. Human growth hormone (HGH), for example, was approved to treat a rare form of dwarfism. Now, however, doctors prescribe HGH for a variety of conditions, including obesity, aging and even to encourage the growth of children with dysfunctional pituitary glands.

Some observers think the law needs to be changed. "Billion-dollar drugs neither need nor deserve the special monopoly protections of the Orphan Drug Act," said Abbey Meyers, executive director of the National Organization for Rare Disorders, in New Fairfield, Conn..

She gets no argument from Rep. Henry A. Waxman, D-Calif., chairman of the House Energy and Commerce Subcommittee on Health and the Environment and one of the law's authors: "Drugs that are profitable are not orphans. Sponsors are very interested in claiming heritage."

But Robert K. Dresing, president and chief executive officer of the Cystic Fibrosis Foundation, is among those who want the law untouched. "Orphan drug development has worked beautifully since 1984," he said. "Drug companies finally are willing to take a risk on people with orphan diseases. Tinkering with [the law] now will destroy the integrity of the program, and promising research efforts to save lives will be abandoned."

And, adds Gerald J. Mossinghoff, president of the Pharmaceutical Manufacturers Association (PMA), a proposal to eliminate the problem by capping sales "in fact could become a cap on research."

Congress has already tried to address the matter. In 1990, it passed a bill that would have paved the way for price competition by allowing two or more companies to share the exclusive marketing rights if they were developing the same orphan drug at approximately the same time. The law also would have terminated market exclusivity if a drug affected more than 200,000 people.

President Bush, however, vetoed the measure, echoing the PMA's concern that it would "certainly discourage development of desperately needed new orphan drugs."‡

---

† National Organization for Rare Disorders, New Fairfield, Conn.

†† See *1982 CQ Almanac*, Congressional Quarterly, p. 490.

‡ See *1990 CQ Almanac*, Congressional Quarterly, p. 577.

---

market. "We should not reward inflators with tax breaks," Stark said.

Stark also wants to take the industry to task for alleged abuses of the 1983 Orphan Drug Act, which provides tax breaks and other incentives to encourage the development of drugs for diseases that afflict so few people that companies would otherwise not be able to recoup their investments through sales. *(See story above.)*

Stark's Orphan Drug Windfall Profits Tax Act would limit, but not eliminate, the profits drug companies may reap from orphan drugs. "The only way to correct these abuses without discouraging the development of orphan drugs is to create a windfall profits tax that will recapture excessive benefits of market monopoly," Stark said. His bill, he added, "will still allow for a huge profit to be made by companies producing true orphan drugs."

The Puerto Rico Tax Break

One of the major debates between the drug industry and price-conscious lawmakers centers around a special tax break that encourages employment in Puerto Rico and other U.S. territories.

Officially known as Section 936 of the Internal Revenue Code, the tax break has been around in various forms since 1921. It was last revised in 1976 to help Puerto Rico and other U.S. territories attract manufacturing jobs. In essence, it allows firms to deduct a portion of income earned in the territory from any taxes owed.

In a May 1992 report, the General Accounting Office (GAO) estimated that from 1993 through 1997, the credit will allow U.S. companies to deduct $15 billion in taxes they would otherwise owe the federal government.†

According to the GAO, the pharmaceutical industry has claimed about half the tax benefits provided under Section 936. Other industries that use the tax break include electronics companies, food producers, apparel manufacturers and makers of medical devices.

Backers of the credit say it has been a boon to Puerto Rico's economy. The Puerto Rico USA Foundation, a pro-business group that includes U.S.-based companies that use the credit, estimates that corporations claiming Section 936 tax credits account for more than one-third of the island's total employment, directly providing more than 115,000 jobs and another 200,000 indirect jobs.

Critics, however, led by Sen. David Pryor, D-Ark., point out that drug companies who operate in Puerto Rico save in taxes considerably more than they pay in wages. According to the GAO report, drug firms reaped an average of $70,788 in Section 936 credits per employee in 1987 while paying average wages of only $26,512. Those credits were three to four times greater than the average credit received by the next-largest industry, electrical and electronic equipment manufacturers, the GAO found.

Pharmaceutical companies also employ fewer people in Puerto Rico than other types of firms. In 1987 — the same year drug companies claimed more than half of all the Section 936 credits — they employed only 18,000 of more then 100,000 workers for U.S. companies. By contrast, electrical and electronic equipment makers employed 23 percent of the workers but claimed only 16 percent of the tax credits.

"We are handing over American tax money to the pharmaceutical industry, which is not resulting in additional jobs in Puerto Rico, but inflated bottom lines for drug company reports," Pryor said at a May 14 press conference. "To ask the American taxpayer to ... continue to subsidize the most profitable industry in the country through the Section 936 tax credit is not only unfair, it is a disgrace."

Legislation introduced by Pryor last November *(see p. 608)* would link the amount of the Section 936 credit that drug companies could claim to the wages paid employees in Puerto Rico and to whether or not they keep drug price increases in line with the general inflation rate.

Puerto Ricans in Civic Action, a pro-statehood group, agrees with Pryor that the credit should be restricted. "Corporations are more interested in transferring income to reduce their tax liability than in making fixed investments and creating jobs," the group says.

But the U.S. Senate apparently has other ideas about Section 936. In March, Pryor tried to append an amended version of his plan to the tax bill President Bush ultimately vetoed. The veto didn't matter — Pryor's plan was soundly rejected on the Senate floor by a 61-36 vote.

Senators, it seemed, were convinced by the Pharmaceutical Manufacturers Association (PMA), which argued that Pryor's plan "is unwise and discriminatory and would violate the three main tenets of U.S. tax policy — fairness, simplicity and economic growth." ††

The PMA also blasted the accuracy of the GAO's May report. If the agency had taken into account independent contractors and temporary workers employed by drug companies in Puerto Rico, the group said, the average tax break per job would be $14,800 rather than $71,000. The PMA also cited a 1990 GAO study showing that pharmaceutical companies actually pay higher than average taxes — 28 percent in 1987 compared with 27.8 percent for all industries.

---

† Pharmaceutical Industry: Tax Benefits of Operating in Puerto Rico, General Accounting Office, May 1992.

†† "Fact Sheet," Pharmaceutical Manufacturers Association, Nov. 20, 1991.

Meanwhile, a Senate coalition led by Nancy Landon Kassebaum, R-Kan., and Howard M. Metzenbaum, D-Ohio, is taking a different approach to orphan drugs. A bill they have introduced would eliminate the provision granting companies a monopoly on marketing rights for drugs whose sales top the $200 million mark. A companion bill was introduced in the House in April by Reps. Gerry E. Studds, D-Mass., and Henry A. Waxman, one of the Orphan Drug Act's original authors.

Members of Congress are also still dealing with the angry fallout from a 1990 law that required drugmakers to provide the same discounts to Medicaid that they were routinely granting to other bulk prescription-drug buy-

Continued on p. 612

At Issue:

Are drug companies charging too much?

RON POLLACK

Executive Director, Families USA Foundation
FROM *SENIOR WATCH,* **JULY 1992.**

yes

Americans like to think of themselves as wise consumers. We shop and compare, clip and save and buy on sale. Yet we're paying a whole lot more for the same old medications.

We're getting a raw deal when you compare what we're charged with what Europeans and Canadians pay for the same drugs.

The U.S. Special Committee on Aging found that, between 1980 and 1990, the price of prescription drugs shot up almost three times as fast as prices in general. The committee, chaired by a real consumer advocate — Sen. David Pryor, D-Ark. — found that while general inflation drove other prices up 58 percent, drugs skyrocketed 152 percent!

Your local pharmacist isn't getting rich on these price increases. The drug manufacturers are. The big drug companies reap profits three times as high as other big corporations.

Drug companies say they need the money for research and development. But the shocking fact is that the drug companies spend a billion dollars more on lobbying and advertising every year than on research!

To really get a perspective on how badly inflated American prescription drug prices are, just compare them with drug prices in other countries. The Italian Pharmaceutical Manufacturers Association found that Americans pay more than three times as much as the average European pays for prescription drugs.

One example is Ativan. This prescription drug is made in the United States, but Sen. Pryor's investigation found the average U.S. price for 100 one mg. tablets was $48.96. In Canada, the average price was $7.18.

Tylenol with codeine was also vastly more expensive in the United States than in Canada.

The fact is, the drug companies are simply overcharging the American consumer, and senior citizens are getting the worst of it. Prescription medication for senior citizens is often a matter of life and death. But many seniors can't just afford to fill prescriptions on a regular basis. Some older Americans wind up skipping pills, endangering their health by taking their medicine less often than they're supposed to. Others cut down on food or turn the heat way down to pay for their medicine.

It is wrong that our parents should have to face these hard choices. The big drug companies are making higher and higher profits, while the elderly cannot afford to buy the prescription drugs they need. For older Americans — for all of us — this is a bitter pill to swallow.

PHARMACEUTICAL MANUFACTURERS ASSOCIATION

FROM *GOOD MEDICINE: A REPORT ON THE STATUS OF PHARMACEUTICAL RESEARCH,* **MARCH 1992.**

no

In recent years, the rising cost of health care has become a national issue. The price of prescription drugs is also being questioned. While we now have more medicines to treat more diseases, they cost more than in the past. It is important to understand, however, the underlying factors that affect the price of drugs.

The unique characteristic of the pharmaceutical industry is its large investment in the discovery and development of new medicines — and R&D is expensive. Modern research has become much more complex as we have learned more about the human body and about diseases that have been previously untreatable.

Adding to the expense of the research and development effort is the fact that it now takes an average of 12 years to bring a new drug to market. . . .

Moreover, for every drug compound that makes it to patients, up to 5,000 do not. And those that fail exhaustive safety and effectiveness testing must be abandoned at considerable expense. Economists at Tufts University calculated that the average cost of a new drug exceeds $230 million.

To meet the demands of this costly process, the industry has doubled its investment in R&D every five years since 1970 — to nearly $11 billion in 1992. This exceeds the total biomedical research expenditure of the U.S. government.

Despite the high R&D costs, prescription drug expenditures have fallen as a percentage of the nation's total health bill, representing just five cents of each health-care dollar.

Drug products not only improve health, they hold down the total cost of health care. Drugs shorten hospital stays by speeding up recovery and by eliminating the need for surgery in many instances. They also reduce the number of days lost from work or other productive activities.

Despite the undeniably important role they play in America's free market system, "advertising" and "promotion" have somehow earned a bad name in our society. In the case of pharmaceutical marketing, these activities are sometimes called "needless" expenditures that increase the cost of prescription medicines without offsetting benefits.

The opposite is true. Pharmaceutical advertising and promotion inform physicians of the value of new and existing products and of their effectiveness and side effects. Availability of sound prescribing information is indispensable to the proper use of a new and powerful drug. Without it, prescription drugs cannot fulfill their therapeutic potential — and may even cause harm.

Continued from p. 610

ers, such as hospitals and health maintenance organizations. In many cases, drug companies have responded not by providing lower prices for Medicaid but by raising prices for everyone else.

In February, Kennedy's Labor and Human Resources Committee unanimously approved a bill that would enable U.S. Public Health Service agencies, such as family planning clinics and community health centers, to purchase drugs at the lower of a set discount rate or the price negotiated by the Department of Veterans Affairs. The drug industry did not oppose the measure, which was negotiated by Chairman Kennedy and Orrin G. Hatch of Utah, the panel's ranking Republican. A House companion bill, introduced by Reps. Jim Cooper, D-Tenn., and Ron Wyden, D-Ore., is awaiting action by Waxman's subcommittee.[34]

And prescription drug prices are also not escaping inclusion in proposals to overhaul the entire national health system. A proposal drafted by Stark would have created a "national formulary," a list of drugs that the government would pay for after comparing similar medications and choosing those with the best cost-benefits ratio. It also would have set maximum prices for prescription drugs. Stark withdrew the formulary proposal under pressure from fellow Democrats, but provisions to set maximum prices are part of the House Democrats' health bill.

Drug Firms React

None of this activity is being lost on drug companies, which are taking concrete action as well as stepping up public relations efforts.

So far, according to the PMA, at least five major companies — Merck, Bristol-Myers Squibb, Pfizer, Glaxo and ICI — have pledged to limit price increases to no more than the general inflation rate. Together, the PMA notes, the companies sell one-third of all U.S. pharmaceuticals.

The PMA is also increasing its efforts to reach the general public. In January, the organization hired a public relations firm to conduct a $7 million campaign to "emphasize the value of the industry's contributions to health and health-care cost containment through research."[35]

"While we may be able to convince half a million doctors to use a particular medicine, we appear to be unable to convince the public at large of our virtues and the absolute need for our very being," said PMA Chairman Paul E. Freiman at the organization's annual meeting in May.

Individual companies are also helping the public relations drive, led by Merck, one of the largest U.S. drugmakers. *(See table, p. 602.)* Not only was Merck one of the first companies to link price hikes to the inflation rate, it also has begun a major program to provide drugs at reduced prices, and in some cases free, to the needy. One of its biggest giveaways involved a program begun in 1987 to distribute its anti-worm medication to villagers in Africa and South America at risk for river blindness. As of 1991, more than a million people had received the drug.

"The special nature of its products demands that the pharmaceutical industry, more than perhaps any other, be responsible to social needs," wrote Merck President Vagelos. "If a pharmaceutical company can meet these demands of the market — innovation and reasonable pricing — profits will follow."[36] ∎

OUTLOOK

Impact of Competition

For American consumers, the key questions are whether normal market forces will moderate rising drug prices, whether drug companies will keep prices from escalating faster than inflation or whether the government will step in.

There is some evidence that market forces alone will help bring prices down. One factor is the growing presence of generic copies of brand-name drugs. The credibility of the generics industry was badly marred by a series of scandals in the past five years involving company officials bribing FDA workers to approve their drug applications first or submitting fraudulent applications. But many industry observers predict that the copycat industry will overcome its bad press and continue to provide increasing price competition for brand-name drugs, as Congress sought with the 1984 generic-drug law.

Indeed, generics do have a major impact on drug prices, studies have found. "Once a product goes off-patent, and a generic copy is available, the pioneer drug commands only 51 percent of the marketplace within two years," said Sen. Hatch, a co-author of the 1984 law. "This allows competitive forces to begin to reduce the cost of the drug."

And more and more drugs will be eligible for competition in the coming years. This year, patents will end for drugs with annual sales of $1.9 billion, and in 1993, competition can begin for drugs with $2.6 billion in sales. That compares to drugs with sales of only $363 million that went off-patent in 1991.[37]

Insurers Scrutinize Prices

Rising drug prices also will be slowed by the increase of third-party payments for drugs by private insurers and company insurance plans. As more and more consumers obtain drug coverage, those who pay the bills will be looking more closely at drug prices, just as they now scrutinize what doctors and hospitals charge. On the increase are "utilization review" programs for drugs, in which companies or insurers study doctors' prescription patterns as well as patient-use patterns and often question the appropriateness of drug therapies.

Such programs can encourage doctors to prescribe less expensive medications that are shown to work equally well. But utilization review is not just about price. "Properly implemented, utilization review can identify cases in which drugs are prescribed inappropriately, in insufficient amounts, or excessively," noted the Employee Benefit Research Institute.[38]

Utilization review may have yet another effect on drug prices — forcing companies to revamp sales and marketing efforts they aim at doctors. "With gimlet-eyed review boards at corporations and insurance companies exerting more control over which medicines get prescribed, drugmakers must learn to pitch drugs on the basis of economy as well as therapy," reporter Brian O'Reilly wrote in *Fortune* magazine.[39]

For the moment, those in Congress who want the government to control drug prices remain a distinct minority. For every David Pryor, the industry's arch foe, there is also an Orrin Hatch, one of the drugmakers' leading defenders.

"Competitive forces must work to bring down the prices of drugs," said Hatch. "Let's not talk about developing new regulatory systems, taking away patent protections, removing market forces or treating the pharmaceutical industry differently than any other industry in America. These kinds of solutions will only lead to the drying up of the development of new, important therapies for Americans."[40] Instead, said Hatch, Congress needs to improve FDA's speed

in reviewing new drugs and revise patent laws so biotechnology products can be better protected.

But with heightened public concern about rising health prices in general, even the drug industry's friends suggest caution. "I urge the representatives of the medico-pharmaco industry in this country to engage in good-faith efforts to make the market work for the benefit of the American people," said Sen. Dave Durenberger, R-Minn., "If they do not, their behavior will be the evidence used to sentence them to a verdict they will regret."

Given the intense emotions the drug-price dilemma has spawned, friends and foes agree, however, that the situation requires action. As Rep. Waxman said five years ago, speaking for many critics of the drugmakers: "Unless the industry can provide an adequate explanation for these price hikes, one can only conclude that what is going on is greed on a massive scale."[41] ∎

Notes

[1] Statement on the Senate floor, Feb. 5, 1992.

[2] The figures cited by Pryor are for 1990. See "The Drug Manufacturing Industry: A Prescription for Profits," a staff report of the Senate Special Committee on Aging, September 1991, p. 7.

[3] See *The Washington Post,* May 26, 1992.

[4] See the *Los Angeles Times,* April 11, 1991.

[5] Statement submitted to the House Ways and Means Subcommittee on Health, June 11, 1991.

[6] Pharmaceutical Manufacturers Association press briefing, May 19, 1992.

[7] *1989 CQ Almanac,* Congressional Quarterly, p. 184.

[8] "The Drug Manufacturing Industry: A Prescription for Profits," *op. cit.,* pp. 7, 30.

[9] "Facts Countering Drug Industry Fiction Regarding Research and Development," Senate Special Committee on Aging, October 1991.

[10] Pharmaceutical Manufacturers Association, press release, Jan. 15, 1991.

[11] Pharmaceutical Manufacturers Association,

press briefing paper, May 1992, p. 8.

[12] Pharmaceutical Manufacturers Association press briefing paper, May 19, 1992, p. 2.

[13] P. Roy Vagelos, "Are Prescription Drug Prices High?" *Science,* May 24, 1991, p. 1083.

[14] The study was conducted by the Battelle Medical Technology Assessment and Policy Research Center in Washington, D.C.

[15] Alan Reynolds, "An Unproductive War Against Drugs," *Forbes,* Nov. 11, 1991.

[16] Senate Special Committee on Aging.

[17] Opening statement at hearing of the Subcommittee on Health and the Environment, April 21, 1987.

[18] *Congressional Record,* March 11, 1992, p. S 3183.

[19] Vagelos, *op. cit.*

[20] Reynolds, *op. cit.*

[21] "Issue Brief," Employee Benefit Research Institute, January 1992, p. 18.

[22] See Louis Filler, *The Muckrakers* (1976), pp. 148-156.

[23] Paul Starr, *The Social Transformation of American Medicine* (1982), p. 128.

[24] *Ibid.,* p. 131.

[25] *Congress and the Nation, Vol. I,* Congressional Quarterly, p. 1160.

[26] Employee Benefit Research Institute, *op. cit.,* p. 10.

[27] *Congress and the Nation, Vol. I, op. cit.,* p. 1181.

[28] *1984 CQ Almanac,* Congressional Quarterly, p. 451.

[29] Quoted in the *1989 CQ Almanac,* Congressional Quarterly, p. 154.

[30] See *Congressional Quarterly Weekly Report,* Oct. 5, 1991, p. 2875.

[31] Press conference, Sept. 24, 1991.

[32] Opening statement at Senate Labor and Human Resources Committee hearing on drug prices, Oct. 16, 1991.

[33] See *Congressional Quarterly Weekly Report,* March 14, 1992, p. 662.

[34] *Congressional Quarterly Weekly Report,* Feb. 8, 1992, p. 311.

[35] "Medicine and Health" newsletter, Jan. 24, 1992.

[36] Vagelos, *op. cit.,* p. 1084.

[37] *Fortune,* July 29, 1991, p. 60.

[38] Employee Benefit Research Institute, *op. cit.,* p. 13.

[39] *Fortune, op. cit.,* p. 63.

[40] Statement at hearing of the Labor and Human Resource Committee, Oct. 16, 1991.

[41] Opening statement before the Subcommittee on Health and the Environment, April 21, 1987.

Bibliography

Selected Sources Used

Books

Filler, Louis, *The Muckrakers*, Penn State University Press, 1976.

Filler's meticulously detailed account of the rise and fall of the muckraking journalists of the turn of the century includes an account of the exposés that led to passage of the 1906 Pure Food and Drug Act.

Starr, Paul, *The Social Transformation of American Medicine*, Basic Books, 1982.

Starr also looks at the events leading to the 1906 law. But his study of the U.S. medical profession approaches the subject from the vantage point of doctors who found themselves in direct competition with makers of patent potions.

Welch, Henry and Felix Marti-Ibanez, eds., *The Impact of the Food and Drug Administration on our Society*, MD Publications Inc., 1956.

Published on the occasion of the Food and Drug Administration's 50th anniversary, this collection of essays provides a fascinating, if somewhat outdated, look at the FDA's workings, from the perspective of agency officials, physicians and representatives of the food and drug industries themselves.

Articles

O'Reilly, Brian, "Drugmakers Under Attack," *Fortune*, July 29, 1991.

Reporter O'Reilly presents an exhaustive and thoroughly readable examination of how the drug industry got to be so profitable — and why those profits may not last.

Reynolds, Alan, "An Unproductive War Against Drugs," *Forbes*, Nov. 11, 1991.

Reynolds, director of economic research for the Hudson Institute, a conservative think tank in Indianapolis, Ind., defends the drug industry's prices. He says controlling drug prices would lead to the downfall of a highly successful industry.

Vagelos, P. Roy, "Are Prescription Drug Prices High?" *Science*, May 24, 1991.

This article by the president of Merck & Co., Inc., one of the nation's largest drugmakers, provides a fact-filled, comprehensive and remarkably objective look at the drug-pricing issue from the drug industry's perspective.

Reports and Studies

Employee Benefit Research Institute, *Prescription Drugs: Coverage, Costs and Quality*, January 1992.

A fact-filled, objective discussion of who pays for prescription drugs, drug-price inflation and some of the major policy issues under discussion.

Pharmaceutical Manufacturers Association, *Good Medicine: A Report on the Status of Pharmaceutical Research*, March 1992.

This report by the drug industry's Washington-based trade association challenges many of the arguments made by the congressional committee reports. The association contends that prescription drugs improve health while containing health-care costs.

Staff of the House Energy and Commerce Subcommittee on Health and the Environment, *Second Staff Report on Price Increases for Prescription Drug and Related Information*, April 21, 1987.

The second of two studies looking at drug-price increases during the 1980s (the first was completed in 1985), this study focuses on comparisons between the amount of money drugmakers spend on research and development and the sum they devote to marketing and promotion.

Staff of the Senate Special Committee on Aging, *Prescription Drug Prices: Are We Getting Our Money's Worth?* July 18, 1989.

This introduction to a variety of prescription drug-price issues looks at who uses prescription drugs, who pays for them and the relative values of new drugs.

Staff of the Senate Special Committee on Aging, *The Drug Manufacturing Industry: Prescription for Profits*, Sept. 21, 1991

This far more critical study details drug-price inflation throughout the 1980s and examines the industry's record on profits as well as spending on marketing and promotion. It also includes international price comparisons and a discussion of the Section 936 tax credit for corporations operating in Puerto Rico, which is used by many drug manufacturers.

U.S. General Accounting Office, *Tax Benefits of Operating in Puerto Rico*, May 1992.

According to this GAO study, the pharmaceutical industry has claimed about half the tax benefits provided under Section 936.

The Next Step

Additional Articles from Current Periodicals from EBSCO Publishing's Database

Consumer information

Henderson, N. and J. Goldwasser, "Cut the cost of prescription drugs," *Changing Times,* June 1991, p. 83.

Suggests that consumers use discount mail-order services for prescription drugs they use routinely in order to keep costs down. Eligibility; cost comparisons.

Podolsky, D., "How to swallow prescription prices," *U.S. News & World Report,* Oct. 7, 1991, p. 96.

Reports that prescription prices have been going up fast, and suggests a few steps that can bring costs down more than consumers might expect. Pharmaceutical manufacturers contend the higher prices support costly research into new drugs; check to see if there is a cheaper alternative drug; mail-order pharmacies; Medicare assistance.

Debates & issues

"Priceless medicines," *The Economist,* Oct. 26, 1991, p. 14.

Considers the pace of innovation in the pharmaceutical industry and the rocketing prices companies are charging for their treatments. The government as the biggest customer in the pharmaceutical industry; why U.S. drug prices are the highest in the world; the charge of profiteering; four ways the government can keep the cost of drugs down; Britain's Pharmaceutical Price Regulations Scheme (PPRS); approaches in European countries.

Merline, J.W., "Drug prices," *Consumers' Research Magazine,* November 1991, p. 38.

Reports on the 152 percent increase in prescription drug prices between 1980 and 1990 and shows what might be contributing to these increases. Excessive sales, marketing, and advertising expenditures; drug prices higher in the U.S. than in other countries; the surge in generic drugs; more.

Pollack, A., "Both heart drugs are effective; Doctors prescribe the costly one," *The New York Times,* June 30, 1991, p. 1.

Declares that two drugs for treating people with heart attacks are equally effective in saving lives, according to two important studies, but one drug, TPA, costs $2,200 a dose while the other, streptokinase, costs only $76 to $300. American doctors tend to prescribe more expensive drug; considering costs in medical decisions; marketing; battle between the drugs; details.

International aspects

Kolata, G., "Why drugs cost more in U.S.," *The New York Times,* May 24, 1991, p. D1.

According to one study, Americans paid an average of 54 percent more than Europeans for 25 commonly prescribed drugs. Comparison with other countries; debate over how the U.S. can control its drug costs; reasons why drug costs are so high in the U.S.; the elderly and chronically ill affected the most.

Law & legislation

Freudenheim, M., "Drug makers face pressure to restrain price increases," *The New York Times,* May 11, 1991, p. 1.

Tells of the efforts being made to keep drugmakers from raising prices far more rapidly than the general rate of inflation. New federal law that requires them to cut prices to Medicaid programs; patients told about lower-priced, alternative drugs; price controls suggested.

Orphan drugs

Gershon, D., "Orphan drug windfalls?" *Nature,* Jan. 30, 1992, p. 381.

Highlights Congress' concern that a handful of companies are exploiting the exclusive marketing provisions provided by the Orphan Drug Act and charging patients exorbitant prices for orphan drugs. Bills in the House and Senate that would open up the market to competition.

Pharmaceutical industry

"Pills sans frontiers," *The Economist,* Nov. 9, 1991, p. 89.

Highlights the gathering of more than 1,000 drug-industry representatives and regulators from America, Europe and Japan on Nov. 5-7 in Brussels to put the final touches on a draft of international standards on the data that drug firms must produce to get their new pharmaceuticals approved. The needless repetition of testing for approval; a cut in R&D costs that should drop drug prices; the need for governments to accept foreign data; three aspects of drug testing.

Back Issues

Great Research on Current Issues Starts Right Here... Recent topics covered by The CQ Researcher are listed below. Issues dated before May 10, 1991, were published under the name of Editorial Research Reports.

JANUARY 1991
Growing Influence of Boycotts
Should the U.S. Reinstate the Draft?
America's Archaeological Past
Peace Corps' Challenges in '90s

FEBRUARY 1991
Regional Impact of Recession
Puerto Rico's Status
Redistricting: Mapping Power
Nuclear Power

MARCH 1991
Acid Rain
Cost of the Gulf War
Reassessing Gun Laws
Future for Man in Space

APRIL 1991
Social Security
Canadian Crisis Over Quebec
California Drought
Electromagnetic Radiation

MAY 1991
School Choice
Racial Quotas
Animal Rights
U.S. and Japan

Back issues are available for $4.00 (subscribers) or $7.00 (non-subscribers). Quantity discounts apply to orders over ten. To order, call Congressional Quarterly 1-800-432-2250.

JUNE 1991
Children and Divorce
Teenage Suicide
Endangered Species
Europe 1992

JULY 1991
Teenagers and Abortion
Soviet Republics Rebel
Mexico's Emergence
Athletes and Drugs

AUGUST 1991
Sexual Harassment
Fetal Tissue Research
Oil Imports
The Palestinians

SEPTEMBER 1991
Police Brutality
Advertising Under Attack
Saving the Forests
Foster Care Crisis

OCTOBER 1991
Pay-Per-View TV
Youth Gangs
Gene Therapy
World Hunger

NOVEMBER 1991
Fast-Food Shake-Up
The Greening of Eastern Europe
Business' Role in Education
Cuba In Crisis

DECEMBER 1991
Retiree Health Benefits
Asian Americans
The Obscenity Debate
The Disabilities Act

JANUARY 1992
Term Limits
Oil Spills
Hunting Controversy
Alternative Medicine

FEBRUARY 1992
Threatened Coastlines
New Era in Asia
Assisted Suicide
Jobs in the '90s

MARCH 1992
Women and Sports
Underage Drinking
Garbage Crisis
Mafia Crackdown

APRIL 1992
Ozone Depletion
Welfare Reform
Politicians and Privacy
Illegal Immigration

MAY 1992
Native Americans
Jobs vs. Environment
Too Many Lawsuits?
Fairness in Salaries

JUNE 1992
Nuclear Proliferation
Food Irradiation
Lead Poisoning
Hard Times for Libraries

JULY 1992
Alternative Energy

Future Topics

▶ *Alzheimer's Disease*

▶ *Infant Mortality*

▶ *The Homeless*

Alzheimer's Disease

Are researchers close to finding an effective treatment?

A
LZHEIMER'S DISEASE RANKS HIGH ON THE LIST OF
elderly people's deepest fears. Unpreventable and
untreatable, the disorder gradually destroys the
brain's ability to remember, reason or even
recognize familiar places and faces. Family members,
meanwhile, can only look on helplessly as they grapple with
the grueling, round-the-clock job of caring for an Alzheimer's
victim. To make matters worse, very little public assistance is
now available for Alzheimer's patients or caregivers.
Researchers nonetheless are confident that an effective
treatment for Alzheimer's will be found before the end of the
decade. Some even predict a cure. Government health
officials hope they are right, because people over 65 — the
individuals most vulnerable to Alzheimer's — constitute the
nation's fastest-growing age group.

CQ **July 24, 1992 • Volume 2, No. 27 • 617-640**

Formerly Editorial Research Reports

COVER ART: BARBARA SASSA-DANIELS

CQ Researcher

July 24, 1992
Volume 2, No. 27

EDITOR
Sandra Stencel

MANAGING EDITOR
Thomas J. Colin

ASSOCIATE EDITOR
Richard L. Worsnop

STAFF WRITERS
Charles S. Clark
Mary H. Cooper
Rodman D. Griffin

PRODUCTION EDITOR
Laurie De Maris

EDITORIAL ASSISTANT
Michael M. Taylor

GRAPHICS
Jack Auldridge

PUBLISHED BY
Congressional Quarterly Inc.

CHAIRMAN
Andrew Barnes

VICE CHAIRMAN
Andrew P. Corty

EDITOR AND PUBLISHER
Neil Skene

EXECUTIVE EDITOR
Robert W. Merry

PUBLICATIONS MARKETING/SALES
Robert Smith

EDITOR, EBSCO PUBLISHING
Melissa Kummerer

The CQ Researcher (ISSN 1056-2036). Formerly Editorial Research Reports. Published weekly (48 times per year, not printed the first Friday of any month with five Fridays) by Congressional Quarterly Inc., 1414 22nd St., N.W., Washington, D.C. 20037. Rates are furnished upon request. Second-class postage paid at Washington, D.C. POSTMASTER: Send address changes to The CQ Researcher, 1414 22nd St., N.W., Washington, D.C. 20037.

Alzheimer's Disease

By Richard L. Worsnop

The Issues

Alzheimer's disease, the scourge of the elderly, is as terrifying in its way as AIDS. Once stricken, Alzheimer's victims gradually lose the ability to remember, to reason, even to recognize familiar places and faces — including their own image in a mirror. They lose, in short, the very mental attributes that define a human being. The ability to perform routine physical functions goes next. And all these losses are irreversible.

Eventually, Alzheimer's sufferers become unable to feed themselves or to chew and swallow. As the body and its immune system weaken still further, patients fall prey to opportunistic infections, much as AIDS patients do. Death often follows the onset of a disease like pneumonia.

The duration of Alzheimer's, from inception to death, varies with the individual's age, overall health and quality of treatment. The typical victim lives for seven to nine years after diagnosis. In some cases, however, the disease can take 20 years to run its course.

An estimated 4 million Americans have Alzheimer's disease (also known as Alzheimer's or AD), and the number is expected to rise sharply as the population ages. Alzheimer's is the nation's fourth leading cause of death, accounting for some 100,000 deaths annually.[1] Only heart disease, cancer and stroke claim more lives. Yet federal funding for Alzheimer's research, due to reach $280 million by the end of the current fiscal year, lags well behind funding for heart disease, cancer and AIDS.

One reason for the spending gap is that Alzheimer's is not a glamour disease like polio or muscular dystrophy. The vast majority of AD victims

develop the disease late in life, often past the age of 80. Consequently, there is no Alzheimer's "poster child" to elicit sympathy and donations.

Alzheimer's also suffers from spotty name recognition. The disorder received its name less than 100 years ago (see p. 624), and not much was known about its possible causes as recently as 20 years ago.

The situation is rapidly changing, though. As the number of AD patients increases, family members are clamoring more insistently for relief from the burdens the disease imposes on them. Though relatively little assistance is available now, some health officials foresee a substantial increase in public and private support as awareness of Alzheimer's and its related problems spreads.

Chief among these problems is the devastating impact of Alzheimer's on caregivers. (See story, p. 630.) Those who tend to a parent, spouse, sibling or friend with Alzheimer's undergo severe strain, for it is quite literally a round-the-clock job. To cite just one example, since many Alzheimer's patients have difficulty sleeping, they are liable to awaken in the middle of the night and start shrieking. In an effort to convey the nature of AD caregiving, the authors of a manual on the subject titled it *The 36-Hour Day*.

Caring for a stranger with Alzheimer's is stressful enough. When the patient is a close relative, however, the emotional burden can become all but overwhelming. Numerous caregivers have spoken eloquently of their despair and helplessness as they watched Alzheimer's crush the essence of a beloved family member.

"One of the worst memories for my sister and me is of my mother opening her mouth, screaming at the top of her lungs, hitting her cheeks and then pointing desperately at her tongue, and then breaking into tears," television actress Shelley Fabares told a congressional subcommittee two years ago. "She could no longer speak. She knew in stages what was happening to her, but she was absolutely trapped inside her own body."[2]

Testifying before the same panel, actress Angie Dickinson described her sister's struggle with Alzheimer's. "People kind of laugh at us old folks who forget what we had for dinner last night or where we ate," she said, referring to herself. "But we need to let the public know that Alzheimer's victims forget how to eat, not where they ate."

In the same vein, the two psychiatrists who wrote *The 36-Hour Day* noted that "People with dementing illnesses forget things quickly. For the person with a memory impairment, life may be like constantly coming into the middle of a movie: One has no idea what happened just before or what is happening now."[3]

The lack of an effective treatment for Alzheimer's, to say nothing of a cure for it, compounds the anguish of family

Death Rate Increases

The age-adjusted annual death rate† for Alzheimer's disease increased from 0.4 deaths per 100,000 persons in 1979 to 4.2 deaths per 100,000 persons in 1987. Two factors may be responsible for the increase, according to the federal Centers for Disease Control. First, the incidence of Alzheimer's may have increased. Second, heightened awareness of Alzheimer's may have caused physicians to diagnose the disease more frequently.

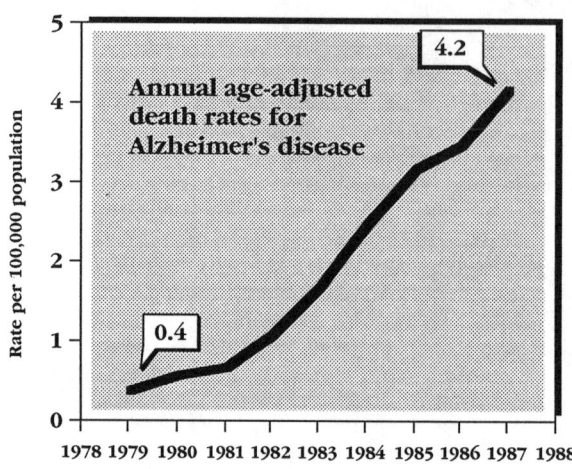

Annual age-adjusted death rates for Alzheimer's disease

Death Rates for Alzheimer's by Age and Race (per 100,000 persons)

Age	White		Black	
	1979	1987	1979	1987
50-59	0.3	0.6	0.2	0.4
60-69	1.7	4.8	0.8	3.2
70-79	2.7	28.4	1.0	16.4
80 and over	3.8	108.8	1.4	45.3

† Age adjustment eliminates the differences in observed rates that result from age differences in population composition.
Source: "Mortality From Alzheimer's Disease — United States, 1979-1987," Journal of the American Medical Association, Jan. 16, 1991.

caregivers. "Unlike patients who suffer from heart disease, Alzheimer's patients can't assert any control over the course or severity of their illness," the National Institute on Aging has noted. "Unlike people at risk of AIDS, we can't prevent ourselves from getting Alzheimer's disease."[4]

Amid all this frustration, researchers nonetheless express confidence that ways will be found to arrest or reverse the brain damage caused by Alzheimer's. They even hold out hope of reaching medical science's ultimate goal with respect to any disease — developing a drug or procedure that will prevent it.

First, though, researchers must identify the cause or causes of AD. The list of suspects includes genes, toxins, infectious agents, blows to the head and disruption of the body's immune system, acting singly or in combination. The roster may grow longer as laboratory studies probe unexplored areas.

While heartened by the buoyant forecasts of AD specialists, people who fear they may be at risk for developing Alzheimer's remain dissatisfied. They want action and expert counsel now. Here is the question that people worried about Alzheimer's ask most often:

What causes Alzheimer's disease?

Although Alzheimer's disease was identified shortly after the turn of the 20th century, it was not until the 1970s that scientists began to gain important insights into its etiology. At that time, recalls Dr. Leonard L. Heston, a professor of psychiatry at the University of Washington, "no one knew of any causes of Alzheimer's, let alone any good bets for a cause." Research has come "an awfully long way" since then, he says, "and it's accelerating."

AD has two telltale physical features, always found together — abnormalities in the brain known as neuritic plaques (clumps of beta-amyloid protein outside brain cells, or neurons) and neurofibrillary tangles (twisted, spaghetti-like fibers inside damaged neurons). First identified in tandem in 1906 by Alois Alzheimer, a German neuropathologist (see p. 624), these plaques and tangles are found only in humans.

Alzheimer made his discovery while conducting an autopsy of a deceased patient. Even today, autopsy remains the only reliable way of confirming a diagnosis of AD. Theoretically, the presence of tangles and plaques could be established through a biopsy. This entails drilling a hole in the patient's skull, inserting a thin tube and removing a sample of brain tissue. But since the procedure is considered extremely hazardous, especially for people of advanced age, it is not used in Alzheimer's cases. Also, a positive result would be of no benefit to the patient.

In any case, the plaques and tangles constitute a nagging mystery that has impeded the search for what triggers AD. The reason is that medical science still does not know whether the plaques and tangles cause the disease or are merely its byproducts.

Over the past decade, much Alzheimer's research has focused on the beta-amyloid protein that is the building block of the plaques. Many scientists suspect that these abnormal structures are indeed a cause of the disease, though probably not the only one.

In 1990, a research team headed by Dr. Bruce Yankner of Children's Hospital in Boston found that beta-amyloid caused nerve cells growing in culture to degenerate. Alzheimer's specialists were intrigued by the Yankner team's report because the nerve cells were from the hippocampus, a part of the brain where memories of the recent past are stored. Inability to recall recent events is one of the earliest symptoms of Alzheimer's.

The following year, Yankner and his colleagues reported on a similar experiment involving live rats. Synthetic beta-amyloid was injected directly into the animals' hippocampus and cerebral cortex, another brain area that is severely affected in human Alzheimer's. "We tried to create an experimental plaque," Yankner said, adding: "The animals showed profound neuronal degeneration around the plaques." [5]

The Boston researchers went on to demonstrate that another common brain protein can neutralize the harmful effects of beta-amyloid. They injected the rats used in the beta-amyloid experiment with substance P, a brain chemical that assists in the perception of pain. In a way not yet understood, substance P protected the rats from beta-amyloid damage. The earlier substance P was administered, the greater the degree of protection it provided.

These results pointed to another area of research that may prove fruitful. If science could develop a simple test for detecting elevated levels of beta-amyloid — by analyzing a blood or tissue sample, say — doctors could prescribe substance P to arrest the disease's progress.

However, many researchers doubt that AD will be conquered that easily. Their skepticism stems from awareness that several other potential causes of Alzheimer's are under investigation. Moreover, none of the suspects has been ruled out as a contributing factor.

Links to Aluminum

In recent years, aluminum has emerged as a major focus of attention. The most common metal found in the Earth's crust, aluminum serves no biological function and is routinely expelled from the body. But researchers discovered in 1989 that Alzheimer's patients often live where the water supply contains unusually high levels of the metal. When these victims' brains were dissected, the diseased parts were found to be rich in aluminum.

This finding raised the possibility that aluminum plays a part in triggering Alzheimer's. To test the hypothesis, a group of New York and Toronto researchers gave 25 AD patients desferrioxamine, a drug that flushes aluminum from the body, over a two-year period. During that time, the 25 patients suffered only half the mental deterioration experienced by 23 untreated Alzheimer's patients in a control group.

No firm conclusion can be drawn from this one study, however, because other research indicates that aluminum deposits form in brains that have already been impaired by Alzheimer's. One small-scale study suggested that aluminum may accumulate in AD patients' brains because they have defective transferrin, a blood protein to which aluminum normally binds in the blood stream. According to another theory, Alzheimer's somehow perforates the blood-brain barrier, allowing aluminum to migrate from the blood stream into brain tissue.

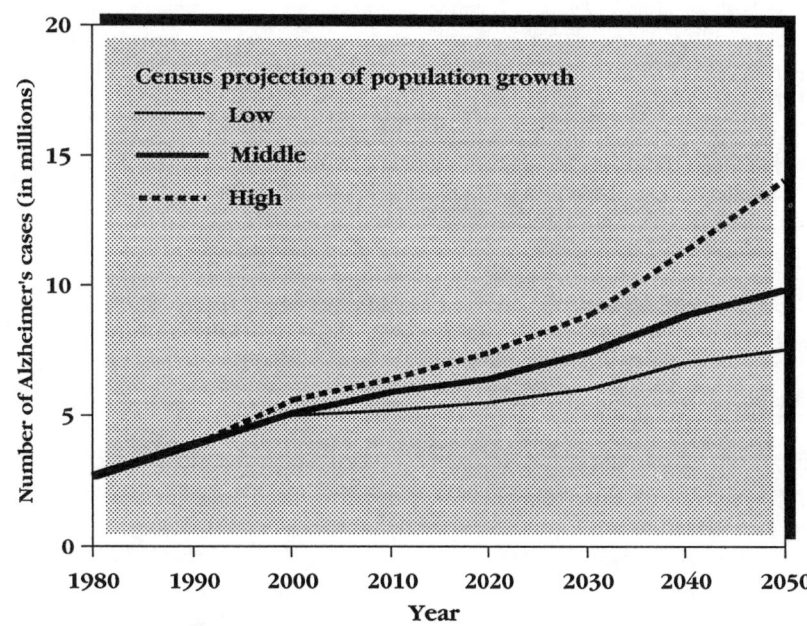

Incidence Expected to Increase

The estimated number of persons 65 and older in the United States with Alzheimer's disease (AD) was 2.88 million in 1980. The number had risen to about 4 million by 1990. By the year 2050, the number of older Americans with AD is expected to be between 7.5 million and 14.3 million, depending on the rate of population growth.

Number of Alzheimer's cases (in millions)

Census projection of population growth
— Low
— Middle
••••• High

Year

Source: Denis A. Evans et al., "Estimated Prevalence of Alzheimer's Disease in the United States," The Milbank Quarterly, Vol. 68, No. 2, 1990.

Reaction to Invalidation of Mice Experiments

Many Alzheimer's specialists feel handicapped by the lack of a laboratory animal "model" for studying the disease. Their prayers seemed answered last year, when three teams of researchers announced the development of genetically engineered strains of mice that presumably would allow scientists to test highly experimental therapies not appropriate for human subjects. In all three cases, the researchers transferred into their mice human genes for making beta-amyloid, a protein that forms the abnormal plaques found in the brains of AD victims.

Assuming they proved reliable, mouse models would enable medical investigators to examine the pathological lesions at an early or intermediate stage of brain deterioration. Most previous studies of beta-amyloid deposits in AD victims' brains were based on tissue obtained through autopsy.

Researchers were still relishing the prospect of working with transgenic mice when two of the three mouse studies were abruptly retracted earlier this year. One study was withdrawn because the scientists who had conducted it were unable to reproduce their results. The other was retracted because its authors had misidentified abnormal brain deposits as beta-amyloid.

The surviving model is viewed as too incomplete as a disease model to use in realistic tests of potential treatments. "It's a real disappointment that no one has yet been able to produce a mouse with Alzheimer's-like pathology," said Dr. Dennis J. Selkoe, a neurologist at Harvard Medical School.†

However, some Alzheimer's experts feel the withdrawal of the two mice studies was no great setback. Dr. Leonard L. Heston, a professor of psychiatry at the University of Washington, says an animal model for Alzheimer's will eventually be found. At the same time, he questions whether one is really needed.

"It's awfully hard to tell when an animal is demented, as in Alzheimer's disease, and whether it is depressed or has schizophrenia," Heston says. "On the biological level, human and animal brain mechanisms are quite different in many important respects. We produce the same proteins, by and large, as animals do, but the regulation is different."

Dr. Fred Gage, a professor of neuroscience at the University of California-San Diego, takes a similar view. "The two studies were retracted so quickly that no damage was done," he says. "It was just science cleaning up its own act."

Although Gage feels "it would be great" to have an animal model for Alzheimer's, he says "it's a very complicated issue to say you're modeling something. Because what is it that you're really modeling? Are you modeling the visual pathology of the brain? Or are you modeling the disease? If you define the disease as these plaques and tangles [the telltale signs of Alzheimer's in human victims' brains] then you'd be satisfied if you got a mouse with plaques and tangles. But the disease is a lot more complicated than that."

Gage believes that researchers eventually will "come up with three or four models that have good features about them. We'll learn something from all of them. They'll interface at a certain point that gives us information that will be useful toward understanding the human clinical disease."

† Quoted by John Rennie, "The Mice That Missed," *Scientific American,* June 1992, p. 20.

Head Injuries

In separate studies published in 1989 and 1991, British researchers speculated that head injury may be a cause of Alzheimer's. In the earlier study, G. W. Roberts of the Clinical Research Center in Harrow, England, noted that the brains of boxers who had developed the punch-drunk syndrome* contained tangled nerve fibers similar to those in the brains of AD victims. Roberts deduced that blows to the head "may be a predisposing factor or environmental trigger for Alzheimer's disease."

The second British study, by Dr. Gareth Roberts of St. Mary's Hospital Medical School in London, found beta-amyloid plaques in the brains of head-injury victims that were identical to the deposits in AD sufferers. According to Roberts, the plaques begin to form within hours or days of a serious blow to the head. "Our next stage," Roberts wrote last December in the British medical journal *The Lancet,* "is to work out how much of a head trauma will trigger amyloid production and to see if we can manipulate the response by using different drugs."

Genetic Puzzle

Even if it turns out to be a cause of AD, head trauma would account for only a small percentage of Al-

*The medical term for punch-drunk syndrome is *dementia pugilistica.*

zheimer's cases. Establishing a genetic cause, which many scientists are currently trying to do, could have much broader import. Research has shown that about half of each generation in certain families acquires early-onset Alzheimer's from a genetic defect. Early-onset AD strikes victims in their 40s and 50s. The triggering mechanism is a mutation on chromosome 21* in the gene encoding the amyloid precursor protein (APP), parent molecule of the beta-amyloid protein that forms neuritic plaques.

This is not the only link between chromosome 21 and Alzheimer's. As has long been known, people with Down's syndrome are born with three copies of chromosome 21 instead of the normal two. Moreover, Down's syndrome sufferers almost always develop the brain lesions characteristic of AD prematurely, by their 40s or 50s. The mental capabilities and behavior of Down's syndrome patients deteriorate markedly at about the same time.

Early-onset Alzheimer's accounts for only a tiny percentage of AD cases. The more common form of the disease typically manifests itself after age 65. Dr. Allen D. Roses, a professor of neurology at Duke University, believes that late-onset Alzheimer's also is of genetic origin. However, his research indicates that the responsible gene is on chromosome 19, not chromosome 21. He surmises that it is some sort of "housekeeping gene that is supposed to keep cells tidy and operational but burns out with age." [6]

In Roses' opinion, "We could all potentially, with some escapees, develop the disease by 120 years of age." However, "Since none of us live that long, what we see is the beginning of the curve" — that is, patients who begin to display AD symptoms in their 60s, 70s and 80s. [7]

A third researcher, Dr. Timothy Bird of the University of Washington, also has studied large families in which Alzheimer's seems to be genetically transmitted. But he concluded that none of the persons he examined appeared to have an AD gene on either chromosome 19 or 21. If he is correct, a gene on still another chromosome could be the causative agent.

Chemical Imbalance Theory

As efforts to solve the genetic puzzle go forward, some researchers are revisiting an early theory — that Alzheimer's begins with a chemical imbalance in the brain. Since the mid-1970s, it has been known that AD is somehow related to a deficiency of acetylcholine, a substance that transmits signals between brain cells. An adequate supply of acetylcholine is especially important in brain areas where memories are stored.

Current brain-chemistry research centers on choline, the substance from which acetylcholine is derived. Because it is the material from which brain cells form their outer membranes, choline is important in its own right. And according to a team of researchers from the Boston area, choline also plays some sort of role in Alzheimer's disease. In a report published earlier this year, Dr. Richard J. Wurtman of the Massachusetts Institute of Technology (MIT) and his colleagues said that brain samples taken from persons who had died from Alzheimer's contained 40 percent to 50 percent less choline than is present in normal brain tissue. They also found abnormally high levels of a substance formed by the breakdown of choline and molecules chemically related to it. [8]

Taken together, the Boston team's findings indicated that defects in the processing of choline and related molecules cause the brain-cell membranes of Alzheimer's victims to decay. The researchers found no such

damage in the brains of persons who had died from other forms of dementia, such as Parkinson's disease.

Other Possibilities

At least three other potential causes of Alzheimer's are being studied at present. One possibility is a slow-acting virus that could be present in a person's body at birth but does not become active until decades later. The only way to prove that a virus causes AD is to implant brain tissue from an infected animal into a healthy one and then wait — possibly for years — for the disease to appear. In the meantime, notes Leonard Heston of the University of Washington, "because the virus itself cannot be shown to be present unless transmission occurs, the possibility is virtually impossible to *disprove*." [9]

Some researchers believe Alzheimer's results from malfunctioning of the body's immune system. They base their belief on the neuritic plaques made of beta-amyloid that are one of the disease's distinctive signatures. Amyloid is present in the tissues of persons suffering from numerous immune-system breakdowns. The fact that it is found at the very site of injured tissue in AD patients strongly suggests, these researchers feel, that Alzheimer's also is an immune disorder.

Because menopause and aging are accompanied by changes in the body's hormonal makeup, some researchers are looking into the possibility that the key to the Alzheimer's mystery will be found in the endocrine system. A hormone called nerve growth factor (NGF), needed to maintain nerve cells in developing nervous tissue, has attracted particular interest.

Dr. Fred Gage, a professor of neuroscience at the University of California in San Diego, has successfully transplanted tissue genetically engineered to produce NGF into the damaged brains of rats, resulting in nerve

---

*Each human cell contains 23 pairs of chromosomes, which consist of coiled DNA (deoxyribonucleic acid) that carries genetic material.

cell survival and improvement of function. The experiments may lead eventually to clinical trials involving Alzheimer's patients and persons suffering from other degenerative diseases of the brain. *(See story, p. 632.)*

With so many possible causes under investigation, there is a growing conviction in the medical community that Alzheimer's will turn out to be not a single disorder but a set of closely related ones, each requiring a different treatment or treatments. Heston of the University of Washington likens the situation to cancer: "There are a lot of different ways to get different cancers — even different ways to get colon cancer, for example." He believes researchers will identify numerous causes of Alzheimer's, each accounting for perhaps 2 to 10 percent of the total caseload.

Gage also thinks AD will turn out

to be "a little bit like cancer" in that "it's not going to be a single disease with a single trigger that, when fired, elicits Alzheimer's disease." This means, in turn, that it may be difficult to devise a single diagnostic test to tell a physician "before a patient starts exhibiting behavioral symptoms that there's a 100 percent chance he's going to get the disease."

Dr. Barry Reisberg, a professor of psychiatry at the New York University School of Medicine, points to another eventuality. It is "definitely" possible, he says, that the main cause of Alzheimer's is something no one suspects as yet. "In the absence of any convincing evidence as to what the cause is," Reisberg says, "it may be one of the causes we're currently speculating on, or it may turn out to be a surprising cause." ∎

ly. It commences with enfeeblement of memory, particularly the memory of recent impressions. The sensations are feeble; the attention, at first fatiguing, at length becomes impossible; the will is uncertain and without impulsion; the movements are slow and impractical."[11]

Another key development came in 1898, when the German neurologist Otto Ludwig Binswanger introduced the term "presenile dementia" to describe the progressive impairment of mental function in young or middle-aged persons. Binswanger's finding was to have a fateful influence on the next major advance in scientific knowledge about dementing disorders.

Work of Alois Alzheimer

The advance occurred in November 1906, when neuropathologist Alois Alzheimer described a recent case of his to the South West German Society of Neurologists. The case involved a 51-year-old woman who suffered from depression, loss of memory, diminished ability to reason and "progressive jealousy" — a highly unusual set of symptoms for a person of her age.[12]

When the woman died four years after her initial consultation with Alzheimer, the doctor decided to apply a newly available tissue stain to a slice of her brain taken at autopsy. On examining the tissue sample through a microscope, he noticed the two abnormal structures — neuritic plaques and neurofibrillary tangles — that are the hallmarks of the disease that now bears his name.

Important as Alzheimer's discovery was, its significance was not adequately understood at the time. Because the patient was relatively young when her disorder first became apparent, scientists concluded that her dementia was of the presenile type. Her condition was so classified in a standard psychiatry text published in 1910. Only presenile dementia was

BACKGROUND

Early Research

Alzheimer's disease undoubtedly existed long before it acquired its name. The literature of ancient civilizations contains occasional references to senile dementia, as in this observation by the Greek playwright Sophocles in the fifth century B.C.: "All evils are engrained in long old age, with vanished, useless actions, empty thoughts."

Many centuries later, Shakespeare came closer to the mark in *King Lear*. Toward the end of the play, after noting that his age is "fourscore and upward," the distraught monarch tells his daughter Cordelia: "I fear I am not in my perfect mind./ Methinks I should know you, and know this man;/ Yet I am doubtful; for I am mainly ignorant/ What place this is; and all the skill I have/ Remembers not these garments; nor I know not/

Where I did lodge last night."[10]

Though the outward signs of senile dementia were unmistakable, almost nothing was known about its underlying causes. It was widely assumed that loss of mental capacity was an inevitable consequence of old age's "hardening of the arteries." But the disorder was of scant concern to society at large, because few people reached the age level at which dementia of the Alzheimer's type most often strikes.

The first important scientific work on dementia dates from the 19th century. James Prichard, an English psychiatrist, established a rough framework for subsequent research in 1837. He did so by describing four stages in the progression of dementia: (1) impairment of recent memory, (2) loss of reason, (3) incomprehension and (4) loss of instinctive action.

Jean Etienne Dominique Esquirol, a French psychiatrist, was the first scientist to employ the term "senile dementia." In 1838, he wrote that "Senile dementia is established slow-

Continued on p. 626

Chronology

1900s
The telltale signs of Alzheimer's disease in human brain tissue are described for the first time.

November 1906
At a meeting of the South German Society of Neurologists, neuropathologist Alois Alzheimer presents his findings about the disease that now carries his name.

1970s
As research intensifies, the American public becomes aware for the first time that Alzheimer's is a disorder, not a natural part of the aging process.

1977
At a joint meeting, members of three federal agencies with interest in various aspects of the aging brain stress the importance of distinguishing between Alzheimer's-type dementia, other irreversible forms of dementia and the reversible dementias.

1980s
As government funding of Alzheimer's research increases, various studies report progress in establishing the cause or causes of the disease.

1980
Families, physicians and health-care professionals from seven cities across the country meet at the National Institutes of Health and form the Alzheimer's Disease and Related Disorders Association. Now based in the Chicago, the group has been renamed the Alzheimer's Association.

October 1984
The National Institute on Aging (NIA), one of the National Institutes of Health, announces the establishment of five Alzheimer's disease (AD) research centers.

October 1985
NIA announces the establishment of five additional AD research centers.

1986
President Reagan signs into law the Alzheimer's Disease and Related Dementias Services Research Act, which establishes the Council on Alzheimer's Disease in the Department of Health and Human Services.

February 1987
A scientific research team in Boston reports finding a genetic link to early-onset AD on chromosome 21, one of the 23 pairs of coiled DNA (deoxyribonucleic acid) that carry genetic material in human cells.

January 1989
A British researcher suggests that head injuries such as those experienced by most boxers may be a contributing factor to AD.

January 1989
A British government study concludes that adults who drink water with high concentrations of aluminum run a 50 percent greater risk of developing AD than people whose water contains virtually no aluminum.

November 1989
On the basis of a study of elderly people living in East Boston, Mass., the National Institute on Aging estimates that 4 million Americans over age 65 may have Alzheimer's disease — nearly twice the previous estimate.

1990s
New studies spur speculation that Alzheimer's, like cancer, may be not just one disease but a cluster of diseases with multiple causes.

April 1990
A British study suggests aluminum may accumulate in the brains of AD victims because they have defective transferrin, a protein to which aluminum normally binds in the blood stream.

May 1990
Researchers at Duke Medical Center in Durham, N.C., report finding evidence that a gene on chromosome 19 is associated with late-onset (after age 65) AD, the most common form of the disease.

April 1991
Sen. Bill Bradley, D-N.J., introduces legislation to provide "functionally disabled" individuals with up to $2,400 a year in temporary caregiver services of various kinds. The "respite care" bill was drafted with the help of the Alzheimer's Association.

March 1992
John Kingery, 82, an Alzheimer's victim, is found abandoned at a dog-racing track in Coeur d'Alene, Idaho.

March 1992
Researchers in Boston report finding chemical deficiencies in the brains of people who died of AD, suggesting new treatments for the disorder. The researchers say levels of choline and ethanolamine, which brain cells use to build their surrounding membranes, were 40 to 50 percent lower than in normal brain tissues.

Celebrity Victims

Celebrity affords no protection against Alzheimer's disease. The disorder has claimed the lives of film actors Rita Hayworth, Edmund O'Brien and Arthur O'Connell; essayist and humorist E. B. White; magazine illustrator Norman Rockwell; mystery writer Ross McDonald; jazz saxophonist Charlie Barnet; and former middleweight and welterweight boxing champion Sugar Ray Robinson. Sir Rudolf Bing, 90, former general manager of New York's Metropolitan Opera, is a current sufferer.

For various reasons, the cases of Hayworth, Robinson and Sir Rudolf attracted especially wide interest. Admirers of Hayworth, one of the most glamorous film stars of the 1940s, were shocked to learn she had fallen victim to AD after her Hollywood career faded. Before her illness was properly diagnosed, rumors had circulated that she was suffering from acute alcoholism.

For the last six years of her illness, which ended with her death in 1987 at age 68, Hayworth was cared for by her daughter, Yasmin Aga Khan Jeffries. Testifying in 1983 before a congressional subcommittee concerned with appropriating money for Alzheimer's research, Princess Yasmin said the disease had reduced her mother to "a state of utter helplessness." The princess has played a major role in the growth of the Alzheimer's Association, and she is a national vice chairman of the group.

The revelation that Robinson was an Alzheimer's victim was no less shocking than the news about Hayworth. Robinson was admired in his prime not only for his ring prowess but also, like Hayworth, for uncommon physical grace. AD took that away, too. By coincidence, a study that sought to determine whether boxers are predisposed to Alzheimer's was presented at the annual meeting of the American Academy of Neurology just three days after Robinson's death in 1989.

The study's author, Professor Patricio Reyes of Thomas Jefferson University in Philadelphia, had tracked eight elderly former boxers over a five-year period. All eight, Reyes concluded, probably had Alzheimer's. He acknowledged, however, that head trauma may have been only part of the picture. "I'm not saying that boxing causes Alzheimer's," he said. "I think it should be viewed as a possible predisposing factor for susceptible individuals."†

Sir Rudolf first began to exhibit Alzheimer's-like symptoms around the time his first wife died in 1983. Friends noticed sporadic memory lapses that became more frequent as time passed. However, his apparent illness did not attract popular attention until his marriage in January 1987 to Carroll Douglass, a woman 38 years his junior with a history of mental illness. Longtime associates of Sir Rudolf charged that Douglass had married him for his money.

The newlywed Bings received intense media coverage as they journeyed to Florida, the Caribbean and Britain during most of 1987. Reporters noted that Sir Rudolf, famed for his imperious manner while in charge of the Met, now seemed meek and uncommunicative.

After the Bings returned to New York that November, Sir Rudolf's legal guardian initiated a series of actions that culminated in annulment of the marriage in September 1989. Sir Rudolf was then placed in the Hebrew Home for the Aged in the Bronx. Visitors give differing accounts of his condition, with some describing him as alert and others expressing shock at the deterioration of his memory.

Such contrasting impressions are not uncommon. Though brain damage from Alzheimer's is progressive and irreversible, patients in the early and middle stages of the disease can have "good days" when their condition seems improved.

---

† Quoted by Beverly Merz, "Is Boxing a Risk Factor for Alzheimer's?" *The Journal of the American Medical Association*, May 12, 1989, p. 2598.

Rita Hayworth

Classico San Francisco, Inc. photo

Continued from p. 624

then regarded as a disease. Senile dementia was still assumed to be an inescapable byproduct of aging.

Labeling the newly named Alzheimer's disease as a form of presenile dementia effectively put it on a scientific back-burner for decades to come, for presenile dementia is quite rare. Interest in Alzheimer's revived only in the 1960s, when British researchers examined tissue from the brains of relatively young, deceased dementia sufferers and compared it to tissue from the brains of deceased elderly patients.

Both sets of samples exhibited the telltale plaques and tangles noted by Alzheimer. The finding clearly suggested that Alzheimer's disease was much more prevalent than previously believed. Before long, AD was on the way to becoming the major field of scientific inquiry that it is today.

Advances Since the 1970s

A key breakthrough came in 1976, when British researchers found lower than normal levels of acetylcholine in the brains of AD victims. Acetylcholine is one of several brain chemicals crucial to memory and learning. The finding inspired pharmaceutical companies to develop drugs that increased acetylcholine levels in the brain. One approach was to provide the body with the raw material to produce more of the chemical. But the effort failed. Researchers surmised that Alzheimer's rendered the body incapable of making aceylcholine from its component molecules.

Two other developments spurred Alzheimer's research, especially in North America and Western Europe. The life expectancy of persons in developed countries was increasing, which meant that the pool of potential AD victims was expanding as well. In addition, research suggested Alzheimer's was at least a contributing factor in about 70 percent of all cases of dementia in persons age 65 or older.

As the long-range implications of these trends became clearer, public-health officials realized that finding an effective treatment or cure for AD should be made a top priority. Failure to bring the disease under control, they reasoned, could doom the health-care systems of advanced countries to eventual collapse from the ever-rising costs of treating Alzheimer's patients.

Concerns About Federal Funding Spur Private Initiatives

However, the mounting sense of urgency was not matched by a corresponding surge in federal funding for Alzheimer's research in the United States. Government spending for that purpose has increased over the years, but it still lags well behind the sums earmarked for cancer, heart disease and AIDS. One reason why Alzheimer's has failed to attract more public financing is that most of its victims are perceived as being near the end of their life cycle whether a cure is found or not.

Seizing the initiative from Washington, seven private caregiver groups banded together in 1980 to form the Alzheimer's Disease and Related Disorders Association* to help families of AD sufferers. Starting with a first-year budget of $85,000, the association has grown to be the nation's largest nonprofit health organization, with annual spending of $30 million.

The Alzheimer's Association promotes research into AD and other types of dementia as well as support for the afflicted and their family members. To this end, it sponsors 1,600 support groups around the country and presses for federal legislation to provide long-term health care, respite care for family members of AD victims and nursing-home reform. It also supports similar efforts at the state level.

Growing Federal Involvement

Since the mid-1980s, the federal government has become more active in combating Alzheimer's. Under omnibus health legislation enacted in 1986, the Council on Alzheimer's Disease was established in the Department of Health and Human Services (HHS) and directed to coordinate research, establish a mechanism for sharing information and identify the most promising research areas.

The law also established within HHS the Advisory Panel on Alzheimer's Disease, composed of researchers, service providers, experts in the financing of long-term care and representatives of groups concerned with the problems of AD victims and their families. The panel's mandate was to assist in identifying priorities and emerging issues.

Furthermore, the omnibus health bill directed the National Institute on Aging (NIA) to set up a clearinghouse on Alzheimer's to compile, archive and distribute information about research, programs and projects dealing with AD and related dementias. The clearinghouse, called the Alzheimer's Disease Education and Referral Center (ADEAR), was established in 1989. Among other services, it translates the latest scientific and technical information about Alzheimer's into language ordinary people can understand, identifies gaps in the current literature and develops new publications to fill those gaps. The center also operates a national toll-free hot line (1-800-438-4380) for persons seeking information on AD.

Prevalence of Alzheimer's

Interest in Alzheimer's, already building steadily, shifted into overdrive in November 1989. Nine researchers from the Boston area that month published the results of a study suggesting the number of Alzheimer's cases in the United States was much greater than previously thought.[13]

Until then, the researchers noted, most studies designed to ascertain the nationwide incidence of AD had "been conducted among outpatients referred for evaluation or among persons admitted to tertiary-care medical centers,* chronic-care institutions or psychiatric hospitals." These studies concluded that from 2 million to 2.5 million Americans suffered from Alzheimer's.

The Boston researchers took a different approach. Confining their

---

*The group shortened its name to the Alzheimer's Association Inc. in 1988. Its headquarters are in Chicago.

*Tertiary care is the aspect of inpatient care dealing with illnesses or conditions requiring specialized techniques, such as coronary artery bypass surgery, renal dialysis or treatment of severe burns.

study to East Boston, a working-class community of 32,000 people, they strove to interview as many of the over-65 residents as possible. Community response was positive, as 3,811 age-eligible residents (80.5 percent of the total) took part in a population survey that included a simple memory test. In stage two, 467 individuals underwent more elaborate clinical evaluation, in part to rule out other causes of mental impairment.

After tabulating their data, the researchers found that 10.3 percent of elderly East Boston residents had probable Alzheimer's disease. For those 65 to 74 years old, the rate was 3.0 percent; for those age 75 to 84, it was 18.7 percent; and for those over 85, it was 47.2 percent.

The researchers cautioned that their study was possibly flawed. For one thing, they noted, their population survey covered only non-institutionalized persons. "If institutionalized individuals had been in-cluded," they said, "it is likely that our prevalence estimates … would have been higher."[14]

Brushing aside these caveats, leading Alzheimer's specialists across the country hailed the East Boston study as a significant addition to the growing body of knowledge about the disease. The National Institute on Aging paid the study the ultimate compliment of extrapolating its prevalence results to the American population as a whole. Thus, the official estimate of U.S. Alzheimer's cases virtually doubled from 2 million-plus to 4 million-plus.

Commenting on the East Boston study in an editorial, *The Journal of the American Medical Association* said it was "likely to be disturbing to the general public, given the widespread fear of Alzheimer's disease, and should receive the careful attention of health planners and physicians: the fastest growing segment of our population is this same group of persons more than 85 years old."[15] ■

such basic functions as the ability to (14) sit up, (15) smile and (16) hold up one's head.

The 16 steps may seem insignificant in themselves. But each denotes a specific stage in the progressive loss of mental competence experienced by Alzheimer's sufferers. To establish the link between functional and mental capacity, researchers gave AD patients tests adapted from those devised for infants and small children by the Swiss psychologist Jean Piaget.

According to Piaget, children's intellectual development proceeds in genetically determined stages that always follow the same sequential order. A similar sequence, operating in reverse, occurs in Alzheimer's patients. The 16 steps cited by Reisberg act as signposts of cognitive decay.

Paying for Care

Though the families of AD sufferers welcome any news of progress toward an effective treatment or cure, their most immediate concern is paying for the cost of caring for a stricken loved one. As these families soon learn, home care and institutional care are both expensive, and the availability of public or private financial support is extremely limited.

According to the Alzheimer's Association, AD costs the nation about $90 billion a year — including the costs of diagnosis, treatment, nursing-home care, informal care and lost wages.

A recent study using 1981-82 data found that home care for dementia patients averaged $11,700 a year. Updating that figure by applying the average annual inflation rate for medical care of 8 percent, Stephen McConnell, the Alzheimer's Association's senior vice president for public policy, estimated the 1992 cost at $25,259.

Institutional care, as might be expected, costs a great deal more. The

CURRENT SITUATION

Research Continues

Research conducted since the East Boston study has yielded new insights into the mystery of Alzheimer's. For instance, Dr. Barry Reisberg of the New York University School of Medicine notes that "We're just beginning to truly track the course of the disease." Earlier studies were able to track only about a third of its course, he says. By utilizing the more complete knowledge now available, says Reisberg, "We might be able to determine what factors are involved not only in the course but perhaps also in the cause of the disease."

Studies published between 1990 and 1992 determined that an Alzheimer's patient passes through what Reisberg calls "16 functional stages and substages from normality to the most severe dementia." In descending order, the patient goes from (1) decreased ability to handle a complex job to (2) decreased ability to handle such complex activities of daily life as (3) managing finances, (4) complex meal preparation and (5) complex marketing skills. Next comes (6) loss of ability to pick out clothing properly, (7) or to put on clothing properly, followed by (8) loss of ability to handle the mechanics of bathing properly. Then (9) progressive difficulties with continence and (10) toileting occur, followed by (11) very limited speech ability and (12) inability to speak more than a single word. Next comes (13) loss of ambulatory capacity. Last to go are

study that used 1981-82 data found that nursing-home care for dementia patients averaged $22,300 a year. Updating this figure with the 8 percent inflation factor, McConnell arrived at an average bill of $48,144 for 1992.

Support for Long-Term Care

The main problem facing most families of Alzheimer's patients is the lack of a national program of long-term health care. As recently as 1988, Congress seemed poised to adopt some such program. Rep. Claude Pepper, D-Fla., introduced a bill that year to provide home health-care benefits to disabled persons of all ages, and Congress passed the much-touted Catastrophic Health Care Act of 1988. But Pepper's bill went down to defeat, and the Catastrophic Health Care Act was largely repealed in 1989. Advocates of repeal objected to the law's funding mechanism, which placed the burden for increased costs entirely on the better-off elderly. They also pointed to the legislation's failure to offer what older voters wanted most, insurance coverage for long-term care.

Today, reform of the entire health-care system has replaced long-term health care as the leading health-related issue before Congress. But long-term care has by no means been forgotten. On April 9, House and Senate Democrats announced a plan to help underwrite both home-based and institutional care for all Americans who need it.[16] The program's first-year cost was estimated at $45 billion. To pay for benefits, the House sponsors would impose a 1 percent payroll tax on workers and employers and a 2.5 percent tax on unearned income, as well lower the amount of property not subject to federal inheritance taxes from $600,000 to $200,000. Senate sponsors left open the question of financing.

Gaps in Insurance Coverage

In the absence of a federally funded program of long-term care, fam-

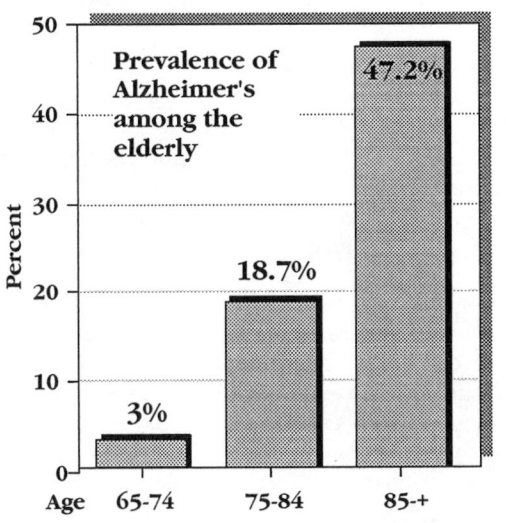

Scourge of the Elderly

The prevalence of Alzheimer's among older Americans may be much higher than previously thought. A study published in November 1989 indicated that among those 64 to 74 years old the prevalence rate for Alzheimer's was 3 percent; for those age 75 to 84, it was 18.7 percent; and among those over 85, it was 47.2 percent.

Prevalence of Alzheimer's among the elderly

Age	Percent
65-74	3%
75-84	18.7%
85-+	47.2%

Source: Denis A. Evans et al., "Prevalence of Alzheimer's Disease in a Community Population of Older Persons," Journal of the American Medical Association, *Nov. 10, 1989.*

ilies of Alzheimer's victims can turn to a number of generally unsatisfactory options. Many private insurers offer long-term care policies, and elected officials have been promoting them as a way of holding down government spending on health care. The trouble is that private insurance for long-term care often provides unrealistically low benefits, rules out payments to family members who perform home-care services, excludes coverage for pre-existing conditions and/or charges very high premiums.

In a generally negative survey of long-term care insurance published last summer, *Consumer Reports* stated: "Even though state regulators require all policies to cover Alzheimer's disease, policyholders with the disease may be denied benefits if they are physically able to perform the activities of daily living. If a company uses an activities standard to judge whether the policyholder is entitled to benefits, and if it doesn't specifically allow people whose only problem is severe memory loss to qualify, patients with Alzheimer's disease

may be uncovered."[17]

For workers who are diagnosed with Alzheimer's prior to retirement age, Social Security disability insurance can provide a measure of financial relief. The program is designed to aid disabled wage earners below age 65. Under Social Security guidelines, a person is considered disabled when a physical or mental condition prevents him or her from working and when the condition is expected to last — or has lasted — for at least 12 months or is likely to result in death. Applicants must supply medical evidence of their condition and prove that it keeps them from working. Benefits are pegged to the person's past earnings.

Supplemental Security Income (SSI) is another federal program that helps individuals who are disabled or have little or no income or assets. SSI provides benefits even when money is available from other sources, including Social Security. To qualify as a disabled person, an AD patient must prove that he is essentially unemployable. If the patient also is

Caring for Alzheimer's Victims

For every victim of Alzheimer's disease (AD), there is at least one additional sufferer: the person or persons in charge of the victim's care. The caregiver's job is physically and emotionally exhausting, and it may last for years.

"In many ways, dementia is like death," the late Dr. Monica Blumenthal of the University of Pittsburgh School of Medicine once said. "It is the death of the mind. Most family members who are close to the patient will go through some phase of mourning which is often more grievous than that produced by death itself." †

There are no shortcuts to ease the strain of Alzheimer's caregiving. But knowledge of what lies in store can help family members approach the task in an orderly way. Personal finance is one example. If Alzheimer's is diagnosed early, the patient may still be alert enough to participate in planning his or her financial future. "Legal advice should be sought as soon as possible," the Alzheimer's Association advises, "not only for the protection of the patient but for the economic survival of the caregiving family."

Alzheimer's caregivers soon learn that patients respond well to familiar surroundings and set routines. "In daily life, try to maintain a routine that features well established landmarks such as regular meals," counsels Dr. Leonard L. Heston of the University of Washington. "Make life predictable. Avoid breaks in routine whenever possible, and be especially mindful of the total dose of disruption over time. If some disturbance of routine is necessary, minimize its intensity." ††

Understanding the reason for an AD victim's baffling or infuriating behavior can lessen the psychic toll on caregivers. For instance, a patient may give every indication of comprehending a simple spoken instruction, yet fail to follow it. The explanation is simple, if heartbreaking. "When a person with a dementing illness does not understand what you told him," wrote the authors of a caregiving manual, "the problem is not inattentiveness or willfulness, but an inability of the malfunctioning brain to make sense out of the words it hears." ‡

Whether knowledgeable about the disease or not, many family caregivers eventually reach the breaking point. Among the patient behaviors most often cited as a cause of burnout are persistent wandering outside the home, falls and other household accidents, disturbed sleep, hostile outbursts, inability to bathe and to dress and, above all, incontinence. Toileting a parent or sibling is the chore that family caregivers usually are the most reluctant to perform.

It is at this point, in fact, that many families of Alzheimer's patients decide the time has come to consider a nursing home. According to Heston, such facilities "are almost certain to be needed during a dementing illness." Thus, they "should be investigated *before* the caregiver's burden becomes intolerable, and the caregiver should not decide on an alternative alone; the family should participate." ‡‡ Doing this groundwork well in advance helps relieve the guilt that family members feel when consigning a stricken loved one to institutional care.

---

†Quoted in American Association of Retired Persons, *Coping & Caring: Living With Alzheimer's Disease*, 1986, p. 4.

††Leonard L. Heston and June A. White, *The Vanishing Mind: A Practical Guide to Alzheimer's Disease and Other Dementias* (1991), pp. 109-110.

‡Nancy L. Mace and Peter V. Rabins, *The 36-Hour Day* (1981), p. 31.

‡‡Heston and White, *op. cit.*, p. 119.

over 65, he may get a higher payment by qualifying as an "aged" rather than a disabled person. In any event, SSI beneficiaries must apply for any other payments they may be entitled to under Social Security. If those payments are in fact forthcoming, SSI benefits can be reduced correspondingly.

Medicare and Medicaid, the two main entitlement programs that underwrite medical expenses, are of only partial help to Alzheimer's sufferers. When an eligible AD patient requires skilled nursing care, Medicare will pick up the entire bill for the first 20 days. It also will pay a part of the cost of 80 additional days of skilled care. Support then ceases, since persons suffering from dementia are assumed under Medicare guidelines to need only custodial care. Some exceptions are granted, but eligibility rules are strict and the level of assistance modest.

Medicaid, a federal-state program intended to provide medical coverage for the very poor, has emerged as one of the main sources of support for Alzheimer's patients needing institutional care. At present, Medicaid helps pay for about half of all nursing-home stays. But there is a catch: An AD patient in long-term care can qualify for Medicaid only if he has minimal income and cash assets.

Some individuals qualify for Medicaid upon admission to a nursing home. Others qualify only after months or years of paying for institutional care have consigned them to the ranks of the very poor — a demeaning process known as a "spend-down." Once eligible for Medicaid, a nursing home patient with no spouse or dependents must turn over to the institution all income, including that from Social Security. However, the patient is allowed to keep $30 to $50 a month for personal needs.

For one small group of persons needing long-term care, even Medicaid is not a viable option. These individuals have the misfortune of being in the "Medicaid gap." That is, their income is too low to allow them to pay the costs of nursing-home care from their own pockets, but too high to permit them to qualify for Medicaid.

Relatives of Alzheimer's patients caught in the Medicaid gap sometimes try to achieve eligibility by giving up a pension or some other steady source of funds. The tactic seldom succeeds. A report published last year found that the Florida Department of Health and Rehabilitative Services, which administers the state's Medicaid program, approved only 8.7 percent of attempts to reduce the income of nursing-home patients during the spring of 1990.

The report's authors concluded: "Although studies of spend-down deplore the possibility of becoming impoverished in old age, ironically, not being able to become impoverished poses an even greater dilemma. In comparison to receiving no government support, spending down one's income to obtain Medicaid eligibility appears to be a preferable option." [18]

Many male Alzheimer's patients served in the armed forces during World War II or the Korean War. As a result, it may be worthwhile for their families to see if treatment is available at one of the hundreds of health-care facilities operated throughout the country by the Department of Veterans Affairs (VA). VA medical facilities offer a wide range of services, but budgetary constraints have obliged the department to give first priority to veterans with service-related disabilities and to low-income veterans who cannot finance their own care.

Toll on Caregivers

The vast majority of Alzheimer's victims are cared for at home by family members, at least in the early and middle stages of the disease. *(See story, p. 630.)* Family members feel a sense of obligation to the patient, and they may also lack the money to pay for institutional care over an indefinite period.

But the physical and psychic toll on Alzheimer's caregivers mounts swiftly, leaving many of them exhausted and depressed. A partial solution to the problem is "respite care" provided on a regular basis by a trained professional. Family caregivers can use the time off to run errands, meet with friends and catch up on lost sleep. Thus refreshed, they are better able to cope with the relentless grind of caregiving.

Little respite care is now available. But under legislation introduced last year by Sen. Bill Bradley, D-N.J., it would become generally available throughout the country. Bradley's bill (S 972), which the Alzheimer's Association helped draft, would provide "functionally disabled" individuals with up to $2,400 a year in temporary caregiver services of various kinds.

Bradley claims the measure would save more than its estimated price tag of $2 billion a year. "For as little as $7 a day, which this bill provides, we could save over $70 a day in institutional costs," he said. "To allow caregivers to continue to provide the quality of life, dignity and love that they want to provide to their family members who have functional limitations, is more than a good investment; it's common sense." [19]

Both the Bradley bill and a companion House measure (HR 2106) have been stranded in committee since April 1991. Nevertheless, the Alzheimer's Association remains hopeful that the legislation, or something very much like it, eventually will be enacted. According to the group's senior vice president, Stephen McConnell, the association advocates a national program of caregiver support "both in its own right and as a steppingstone" to a more comprehensive program of long-term health care.

Incidents of 'Granny Dumping'

Making respite care more widely available could help combat an emerging problem called "granny dumping." According to the monthly newsletter of the American Association of Retired Persons (AARP), "Elderly and often confused Americans are being shockingly abandoned in small but growing numbers on hospital emergency room doorsteps across the country. Sometimes they are abandoned by children who have come to regard aging parents as a nuisance. And sometimes they are dropped off by family or friends who are simply exhausted by the pressures of caregiving." [20]

A granny-dumping incident this spring made headlines across the country. John Kingery, 82, was found abandoned March 21 at a dog-racing track in Coeur d'Alene, Idaho. Labels had been cut from his clothing and notes misidentifying him as "John King" — but correctly noting that he was an Alzheimer's victim — had been attached to his wheelchair. Kingery was unable to say who he was or where he lived.

It transpired that he was a retired autoworker who had been placed early in March in a Portland, Ore., nursing home by Sue Gifford, a daughter by his second marriage. Gifford reportedly checked him out of the nursing home the morning of March 21. She has been charged in Portland with kidnapping and perjury and could get up to 15 years in prison if convicted. Gifford also has been charged with stealing nearly $10,000 that was supposed to pay for Kingery's nursing home care. She is accused of cashing

Other Causes of Dementia

Though Alzheimer's disease is the most common form of dementia, it is far from the only one. Before a diagnosis of probable Alzheimer's can be made, a physician must rule out other potential origins of the patient's mental deterioration. Here are some of the leading possibilities:

Parkinson's disease: A progressive disorder of the central nervous system, Parkinson's disease (PD) affects an estimated 1 million Americans. Victims lack sufficient dopamine, a substance crucial to the central nervous system's control of muscle movement. Consequently, PD sufferers experience tremors and stiffness in limbs, impaired speech and difficulty in walking and getting in and out of chairs. Some eventually develop dementia and Alzheimer's. Conversely, some Alzheimer's patients develop Parkinson's.

Huntington's disease: Only about 25,000 Americans suffer from Huntington's disease, an inherited disorder that weakens both mind and body. Symptoms include intellectual decline, irregular and involuntary movement of limbs and facial muscles, personality change and loss of memory. A genetic marker linked to Huntington's disease has been located on chromosome 4, but the precise gene has yet to be identified.

Pick's disease: Pick's disease is a rare brain disorder that, like Alzheimer's, resists early diagnosis. But there is a key distinction between the two disorders: The average age at onset of Pick's disease is 52.8 years, and death follows after a period averaging 6.5 years. After people reach the mid-50s, new cases of Pick's are rare. With Pick's, moreover, changes in personality and behavior may precede and be more severe than memory loss.

Creutzfeldt-Jakob disease: A transmissible infectious agent, probably a virus, causes the rare, fatal brain disorder known as Creutzfeldt-Jakob disease (CJD). Early symptoms include failing memory, behavioral changes, and loss of coordination. The course of the disease is usually rapid, rarely lasting more than two years.

Multi-infarct dementia: This form of mental deterioration results from multiple small strokes (infarcts) in the brain. Often the strokes are so tiny that the first few produce no noticeable symptoms. But the cumulative damage may eventually manifest itself as full-blown dementia. Persons who undergo several large strokes also can become demented.

This by no means exhausts the list of potential causes of dementia. Other conditions that can cause or mimic dementia include depression, brain tumors, nutritional deficiencies, head injuries, hydrocephalus, infections like AIDS, meningitis and syphilis, drug reactions and thyroid disorders.

Source: Alzheimer's Association Inc.

---

his pension checks while Medicaid paid his nursing home bills. Kingery, meanwhile, now lives in a Kentucky nursing home, near children from his first marriage.

Family members are not the only parties to granny dumping. Some short-staffed nursing homes have been known to transfer difficult patients to hospitals rather than attempt to provide treatment themselves. Moreover, elderly people living alone can become so desperate that they go to hospital emergency rooms and, in effect, abandon themselves. Such cases create a dilemma for hospitals, because Medicare will not reimburse them for custodial care. ∎

OUTLOOK

Scientists Are Optimistic

From one perspective, the future of Alzheimer's disease in the United States looks unrelievedly bleak. Applying the East Boston formula to current population projections, the nation will have between 7.5 million and 14.3 AD cases by the year 2050. *(See graph, p. 621.)* Even if the cost of medical services remains steady between now and then, the total bill for Alzheimer's care in 2050 will be about $315 billion annually. With inflation factored in, the sum would be vastly greater.

These dire projections assume no significant progress in treating Alzheimer's over the next half-century or so. And that is not a likely scenario, leading researchers say. Though no cure or effective treatment has yet been found, scientists express confidence that a major breakthrough will come within a few years, perhaps by the end of this decade.

Gene D. Cohen, acting director of the National Institute on Aging (NIA) in Bethesda, Md., says his agency's goal is "to fundamentally alter the course of Alzheimer's disease by the end of the decade." He likens the current state of research to "a television game show where we're getting more pieces of the puzzle. They just haven't all connected yet." Each identification of an abnormal occurrence in the Alzheimer's process "increases the chance that a new intervention can be developed to al-

Continued on p. 634

At Issue:

Is a federally funded program the best way to provide long-term care for the elderly?

SEN. JOHN D. ROCKEFELLER IV, D-W.Va.

Chairman, Senate Medicare and Long-Term Care Subcommittee
FROM *THE NEW ENGLAND JOURNAL OF MEDICINE,* OCT. 4, 1990

Some may greet the report [of the Bipartisan Commission on Comprehensive Health Care, also known as the Pepper Commission] as a non-event — just another set of recommendations to sit on the shelf, as the problems of Americans in getting and paying for health care continue to grow. For some, it has become far easier to bemoan our inability to act than to tackle the problems we all face.

But I see the commission's work in a different light and intend to use it accordingly. I believe the commission's efforts provide an opportunity at long last to come to grips with a rapidly growing health-care crisis. The president and the Congress have a choice. We can continue to duck our heads and hope this issue will not bring the nation to its knees, or we can use the commission's recommendations as the rallying point for building the political consensus that can make universal coverage for health and long-term care a reality....

A look at the outcome of the commission's deliberations gives a good indication of what, in fact, it takes to build political consensus. The commission basically faced two separate tasks — reform of the nation's existing system for insuring medical or health care, and creation of a system for insuring assistance in the tasks of daily living that we call long-term care. The commission voted overwhelmingly (11 to 4) in favor of a major government initiative in long-term care.

First, this initiative would establish government or social insurance to keep resources intact for severely disabled people at home or with the potential to return home after a short nursing home stay, and second, it would establish a floor of protection against impoverishment for all nursing home users, no matter how long they stay....

On long-term care, the political gains in taking a stand are substantial and the costs are relatively small. Most Americans — rich and poor, old and young — see themselves at risk of impoverishment if they or their family members need long-term care. They support government action to ensure their protection. At the same time, no entrenched system of private insurance is threatened by government expansion, and providers stand to gain considerably from broader public support. Finally, the elderly and their families are politically organized and active in demanding government help.

STUART M. BUTLER

Domestic policy studies director, the Heritage Foundation
FROM *THE NEW YORK TIMES,* AUG. 21, 1989

rep. Claude Pepper had a dream. He wanted to steer a new program through Congress to provide government help for the nursing home costs of elderly Americans that would be financed by a payroll tax on workers.... But this type of social insurance is not the answer. In fact, the Medicare experience shows that it would be a recipe for financial disaster.

Politicians are quick to hike benefits but slow to raise taxes to keep the system financially sound. And when the government picks up the tab, neither the seniors nor those providing the services are very interested in controlling costs. That's why Medicare's inflation-adjusted costs have far outstripped the projections made at its inception in 1965.

America spends nearly $50 billion annually on nursing home care, with government at some level picking up about half the cost. A new program simply would substitute federal dollars for private dollars. Further, it would encourage more Americans to dump their elderly parents into nursing homes rather than caring for them themselves. And, with the government paying the bills, costs would escalate. Great for the nursing home industry; bad for taxpayers.

Thus, within a few years, government could be spending $100 billion annually — four times the amount it now spends on nursing home costs.

A better answer is private long-term insurance. Protecting family assets from potential loss is what private insurance is all about. We protect our investment in a car or home through insurance. And middle-class breadwinners protect their dependents by insuring the family's most productive asset — their own lives.

Safeguarding family resources from heavy, unexpected nursing home costs is no different. In each case, the risk can be assessed and an appropriate premium calculated....

Working Americans must start thinking of long-term care insurance as a normal family purchase — so that policies are bought early in life when rates are low. The federal government should act as a catalyst by stressing the need for such insurance. Even more important, it should change the tax code to encourage potential buyers — just as it did many years ago to foster the growth of life insurance....

Heavy nursing home costs can be a crippling blow for a family. But that potential blow is insurable. Government needs only to stimulate the demand for such coverage.

Continued from p. 632
ter that step." Alzheimer's "is a cascade of things that are going wrong," says Cohen, adding: "If you could interrupt that cascade at any point, you could have a profound effect" in combating the disorder.

Even limited progress would have far-reaching significance. "For example, if you could delay the onset of Alzheimer's disease by five years, you could cut the incidence of it in half," Cohen says. "That would have a truly profound effect from a public-health standpoint, because more people would die of other causes before they developed Alzheimer's."

In pursuing its campaign against Alzheimer's, the NIA observes what Cohen calls "a hierarchy of approaches." The main concern at present is relieving the disease's symptoms. The next goals, in ascending order of importance, are slowing the disease's course, arresting it, reversing it to some extent, curing it and, finally, preventing it.

Reversing the damage inflicted by Alzheimer's will entail finding "more effective ways to bring about regeneration in brain cells like the regeneration in other tissues, such as skin," Cohen says. "We have found that cells which are still alive can regenerate following damage to those cells. It's a different situation if a cell has been totally destroyed. There, the goal is to see to what extent the brain can generate new cells even in the face of destruction."

Help for Caregivers

Just as researchers are confident AD will be vanquished, McConnell of the Alzheimer's Association feels sure there will be a "significant increase" in government aid to Alzheimer's victims and their family caregivers. "The reason is that there are just too many people involved," he says. "It's going to be too big a political problem to avoid. Also, the nation's demographics are changing dramatically." He

notes that family caregivers "are not young, for the most part. They're in their 60s and 70s. So they have their own health-related issues."

In the future, much of the pressure for a publicly funded program of long-term health care will come from the baby-boom generation. "Baby boomers are going to be entering their 50s when their elderly parents will need assistance," McConnell says. "And that huge part of the population is going to be saying, 'Wait a minute. We can't do this by ourselves. We need help.' "

Bill Keane, vice chairman of the Alzheimer's Association's public policy committee, told a congressional subcommittee in May that a comprehensive long-term care program would cost about $5 a week per taxpayer. "That is $260 a year — a number taxpayers understand and, according to public opinion polls, are willing to pay, if it buys real protection against the massive long-term care costs they fear." [21]

In the meantime, Alzheimer's researchers also are pressing for financial aid. Cohen of the NIA observes, for example, that a congressional advisory panel has recommended that government spending on AD research be virtually doubled, to $550 million.

In Heston's view, money spent on Alzheimer's research is likely to yield ample dividends. "Biomedical research does cost a lot," he concedes. "But those who pay taxes to support research … might find it comforting to reflect that the amounts spent on research are a minute proportion of the amounts now being spent on treatments (which are largely ineffective) and on custodial care. Money spent on research is a wise investment in the best humanistic sense. For millions of us, it is our best single hope." [22]

Notes

[1] Estimate of the Chicago-based Alzheimer's Association Inc. In many cases, death is officially attributed to a secondary illness such as pneumonia.

[2] Testimony at a joint hearing of the House Select Committee on Aging and the Senate Labor and Human Resources Committee's Subcommittee on Aging, April 3, 1990.

[3] Nancy L. Mace and Peter V. Rabins, *The 36-hour Day* (1981), p. 24.

[4] National Institute on Aging, "Alzheimer's Disease: New Research Frontiers," statement submitted to House Select Committee on Aging and the Senate Labor and Human Resources Committee's Subcommittee on Aging in connection with their joint hearing on April 3, 1990.

[5] Quoted by Jean Marx, "New Clue Found to Alzheimer's," *Science*, Aug. 23, 1991, p. 857.

[6] Quoted in *Business Week*, Aug. 13, 1990, p. 119.

[7] Quoted in *The Journal of the American Medical Association*, Jan. 16, 1991, p. 310.

[8] Richard J. Wurtman, et al., "Evidence for a Membrane Defect in Alzheimer's Disease Brain," *Proceedings of the National Academy of Sciences of the United States of America*, Vol. 88, issue No. 5 (March 1992), pp. 1671-1675.

[9] Leonard L. Heston and June A. White, *The Vanishing Mind: A Practical Guide to Alzheimer's Disease and Other Dementias* (1991), p. 85.

[10] *King Lear*, Act IV, Scene 7.

[11] Jean Etienne Dominique Esquirol, *Des Maladies Mentales* (1838).

[12] In his written account of the case, published in 1907, Alzheimer said the woman's "entire behavior bore the stamp of utter perplexity."

[13] Denis A. Evans, et al., "Prevalence of Alzheimer's Disease in a Community Population of Older Persons," *Journal of the American Medical Association*, Nov. 10, 1989, p. 2551. A somewhat different version of the study was published in *The Milbank Quarterly*, Vol. 68, No. 2 (1990).

[14] *Ibid.*, p. 2555.

[15] "Alzheimer's Disease in the Community," *The Journal of the American Medical Association*, Nov. 10, 1989, p. 2591.

[16] See Julie Rovner, "Long-Term Care Plan Unveiled," *Congressional Quarterly Weekly Report*, April 11, 1992, p. 957.

[17] "An Empty Promise to the Elderly?" *Consumer Reports*, June 1991, p. 429.

[18] Jill Quadagno, et al., "Falling Into the Medicaid Gap: The Hidden Long-Term Care Dilemma," *The Gerontologist*, August 1991, p. 526.

[19] Remarks on the Senate floor, April 25, 1991.

[20] Robert P. Hey and Elliot Carlson, " 'Granny Dumping': New Pain for U.S. Elders," *AARP Bulletin*, September 1991.

[21] Testimony before Subcommittee on Medicare and Long-Term Care of the Senate Finance Committee, May 13, 1992.

[22] Heston and White, *op. cit.*, p. 156.

Bibliography

Selected Sources Used

Books

Aronson, Miriam K., ed., *Understanding Alzheimer's Disease,* Charles Scribner's Sons, 1988.

The chapters in this collection of articles by various contributors are grouped under four headings: (1) definitions, diagnosis and treatment; (2) how to cope; (3) legal and financial aspects; and (4) [future] directions.

Heston, Leonard L., and June A. White, *The Vanishing Mind: A Practical Guide to Alzheimer's Disease and Other Dementias,* W.H. Freeman and Co., 1991.

In language that lay readers can easily grasp, the authors set forth the basic information about Alzheimer's disease: its signs, symptoms and associated disorders; what can and cannot be done to treat it; suspected causes; availability of professional care and financial assistance; and how to care for an Alzheimer's patient at home.

Light, Enid, and Barry D. Lebowitz, *Alzheimer's Disease Treatment and Family Stress: Directions for Research,* Hemisphere Publishing Corp., 1990.

The book devotes nearly equal attention to the problems faced by Alzheimer's victims and those faced by the family members who carry the main burden of caregiving.

Mace, Nancy L., and Peter V. Rabins, *The 36-Hour Day,* The Johns Hopkins University Press, 1981.

In exhaustive detail, psychiatrists Mace and Rabins explain what it is like to live with an Alzheimer's victim and what steps prospective caregivers should be prepared to take when the disease strikes a loved one.

Reisberg, Barry, ed., *Alzheimer's Disease,* The Free Press, 1983.

This 58-item anthology will be of interest mainly to health professionals who already are well acquainted with the pathology of Alzheimer's. In his preface, Reisberg expresses hope that "presenting the enormous recent advances in the field will stimulate other medical investigators to further discoveries in this important but still largely unexplored illness. The real hope is that this volume will immediately enable clinicians to better serve Alzheimer's patients and their families."

Articles

Evans, Denis A., et al., "Prevalence of Alzheimer's Disease in a Community Population of Older Persons," *The Journal of the American Medical Association,* Nov. 10, 1989; and Evans, Denis A., et al., "Estimated Prevalence of Alzheimer's Disease in the United States," *The Milbank Quarterly,* Vol. 68, No. 2, 1990.

These somewhat different accounts are both based on the study in East Boston, Mass., that prompted the National Institute on Aging to revise its estimate of the number of Alzheimer's cases in the United States sharply upward.

Quadagno, Jill, et al., "Falling Into the Medicaid Gap: The Hidden Long-Term Care Dilemma," *The Gerontologist,* August 1991.

The authors explore the plight of persons who have too little income to pay for nursing-home care out of their own pockets yet too much income from regular sources to qualify for Medicaid.

Reports and Studies

American Association of Retired Persons, *Coping & Caring: Living With Alzheimer's Disease,* 1986.

Liberally sprinkled with anecdotes, this brief overview of Alzheimer's explains what the disease as well as what it is not and provides numerous tips to caregivers.

Alzheimer's Association, *Time Out! The Case for a National Family Caregiver Support Policy,* 1991.

The association stresses the urgency of helping those who now bear the primary burden of caring for Alzheimer's patients. "This informal caregiving system is the very embodiment of family values in our society," it says. "But it is at great risk — from the pressures of caregiving itself, from demographics, and from changing family structures. It would cost at least $54 billion to replace this system with full-time paid care."

U.S. Congress, Office of Technology Assessment, *Confused Minds, Burdened Families: Finding Help for People With Alzheimer's and Other Dementias,* July 1990.

A highlight of this report is a chronological review of growing federal involvement in Alzheimer's research.

U.S. House Select Committee on Aging and Subcommittee on Aging of the Senate Labor and Human Resources Committee, *Alzheimer's — The Unmet Challenge for Research and Care* (published proceedings of joint hearing held April 3, 1990).

Expert and celebrity witnesses testify about their own firsthand experiences with Alzheimer's disease and discuss various treatment strategies.

The Next Step

Additional Articles from Current Periodicals from EBSCO Publishing's Database

Case studies

Corbett, J., "A father's death," *Commonweal,* **Nov. 9, 1990, p. 633.**

Describes the death of the author's father, James A. Corbett, a university professor, from Alzheimer's disease.

Firlik, A. D., "Margo's logo," *Journal of the American Medical Association,* **Jan. 9, 1991, p. 201.**

Provides a look at the relationship between a medical student and a 55-year-old woman with Alzheimer's disease. The patient's cheerful and peaceful disposition inspires the student.

Webb, A., "An exhausting responsibility," *Maclean's,* **Aug. 19, 1991, p. 33.**

Describes Victoria, British Columbia, resident Jacqueline James' struggle to care for her family and her 77-year-old mother Ethel Reynolds, who suffers from Alzheimer's disease. Adult day care and other arrangements; decision to put her mother in a nursing home.

Debates & issues

"Alzheimer's disease: What to expect?" *Harvard Health Letter,* **April 1991, p. 8.**

Reports that two recently published investigations have sought to answer questions concerning what will happen to an individual ill with Alzheimer's disease after being diagnosed. The investigations appeared in the Sept. 19, 1990 issue of *Annals of Internal Medicine* and in the August 1990 issue of *Archives of Neurology.*

"Alzheimer's patients: A growing burden," *Futurist,* **January/February 1991, p. 42.**

Presents highlights of the study "Confused Minds, Burdened Families," prepared by the U.S. Office of Technology Assessment (OTA). Focus on the growing national burden of Alzheimer's disease; proposed plan to coordinate a national effort to deal with the disease and the problems it causes.

Brownlee, S., "Alzheimer's: Is there hope?" *U.S. News & Report,* **Aug. 12, 1991, p. 40.**

Describes the debilitating mental disorder now afflicting almost four million Americans known as Alzheimer's disease. Research into the two proteins involved in the death of nerve cells in brain regions essential to memory, emotions and thought. No cure or effective treatment; types of brain abnormalities: tangles and plaques; environment and genes; desperate need for ways for families to cope. INSETS: Alice's story; nursing the mind.

Fackelmann, K. A., "Probe turns up flaws in Alzheimer's study," *Science News,* **Feb. 2, 1991, p. 70.**

Investigates the Food and Drug Administration findings of a study that reveals serious flaws in a 1986 research report claiming dramatic improvements in Alzheimer's patients on the experimental drug tetrahydroaminoacridine (THA). How THA reportedly works; reasons for criticisms; differences between research report and lab records; denial of 1986 report's authors.

Weiler, P. G., J. E. Lubben, et al., "Cognitive impairment and hospital use," *American Journal of Public Health,* **September 1991, p. 1153.**

Reports that an increasing number of older people are at higher risk for developing Alzheimer's disease or another dementia. The resultant cognitive impairment has been well identified as one of the risk factors for nursing home placement. Presents results of a study of the association between cognitive impairment and hospital use.

Diagnosis

Newbern, V. B., "Is it really Alzheimer's?" *American Journal of Nursing,* **February 1991, p. 50.**

Shows how careful assessment can reduce the risk of a misdiagnosis of Alzheimer's disease. Effects of drugs on elderly people; delirium and pseudodelirium. INSETS: Common drug interactions that can produce confusion, by I.M. Burnside; the mini-mental status examination, by M. Folstein; causes of acute confusion in the hospitalized elderly, by M.D. Foreman; continuing education test.

Thomas, P., "Is there a test?" *Harvard Health Letter,* **January 1991, p. 1.**

Details current information on Alzheimer's disease. The diagnosis cannot be made without microscopic examination of brain tissue and the fundamental cause of the disease is not known. Alzheimer's disease-associated protein (ADAP); radiologist seeking to expand their role in diagnosis; symptoms; work of Harvard neurologist Dennis Selkoe and associate professor of neurology at the Boston University School of Medicine, Dr. Richard Myers. INSET: In the doctor's office.

Moral & religious aspects

Brack, B. "**Rational suicide: My mother's story,**" *Christian Century,* **Nov. 13, 1991, p. 1054.**

Editorial. Relates the story of the author's mother's battle with Alzheimer's disease, and how they decided on a plan of euthanasia that would finally liberate her mother from the humiliating disease. The slow painful deterioration of her mind; why suicide should not be spoken of as a selfish act; the lack of a treatment for Alzheimer's disease; Christian objections to rational suicide in cases of terminal illness.

Goodwin, J.S., "**Mercy killing: Mercy for whom?**" *Journal of the American Medical Association,* **Jan. 16, 1991, p. 326.**

Argues against the mercy killing of Alzheimer's patients. Comments that mercy killing is the ultimate selfish act.

Physiological effect

Cowley, G., "**Brain killer or bystander?**" *Newsweek,* **March 4, 1991, p. 54.**

Reveals new clues about the causes of Alzheimer's disease. Describes how beta amyloid, a protein fragment, has aroused great interest. The aberrant molecule, a small piece of a normal protein called APP, invariably shows up in victims' brains, surrounded by masses of dead neurons. Why the role of the disease remains unclear; writing in the British journal, *Nature.*

Ezzell, C., "**Alzheimer's alchemy,**" *Science News,* **March 7, 1992, p. 152.**

Discusses a new theory, proposed by Dennis J. Selkoe and some of his colleagues in Alzheimer's research, that Alzheimer's disease is a quantitative exaggeration of something that happens normally in all human beings. Exploration of all phases of beta amyloid production for clues as to why some people make more of the destructive protein than others; estimates from the National Institute on Aging on how many Americans are now afflicted with Alzheimer's; more.

Selkoe, D.J., "**Amyloid protein and Alzheimer's disease,**" *Scientific American,* **November 1991, p. 40.**

Contends that when amyloid protein fragments accumulate excessively in the brain, Alzheimer's disease may be the result. Asserts that understanding how these fragments form could provide a key to successfully treating this affliction. The role of neuropathologists; investigations of underlying genetic causes; the greatest challenge to students of Alzheimer's disease.

Reference materials

Forsythe, E., "**Book reviews,**" *Age & Ageing,* **September 1991, p. 386.**

Reviews the book "Living with Alzheimer's Disease and Similar Conditions," by G. Wilcock.

Jarvik, L., "**Book reviews,**" *Age & Ageing,* **January 1991, p. 74.**

Reviews the book "Alzheimer's Disease — The Long Bereavement," by Elizabeth Forsyth.

Kelechi, T. and A. Nevins, "**Audiovisual reviews,**" *The Gerontologist,* **October 1991, p. 715.**

Reviews the audiovisual "Alzheimer's Disease: Pieces of the Puzzle," produced by the Arizona Long-Term Care Gerontology Center and Biomedical Communications.

Martyn, C., "**Bookshelf,**" *The Lancet,* **Nov. 24, 1990, p. 1285.**

Reviews the book "The Epidemiology of Alzheimer's Disease and Related Disorders," by Anthony F. Jorm.

O'Malley, P.E. and A. Nevins, "**Audiovisual reviews,**" *The Gerontologist,* **October 1991, p. 716.**

Reviews the audiovisual "Dealing with Alzheimer's: A Common Sense Approach to Communication," produced by Karen Feldt.

Research

"**Panning aluminum,**" *The Economist,* **June 8, 1991, p. 84.**

Looks at how the discovery of a possible link between aluminum and Alzheimer's disease may soon lead to a treatment for the victims of Alzheimer's. Work by Donald McLachlan, Theo Kruck, and colleagues at the University of Toronto and the New York Institute for Basic Research in Developmental Disabilities; use of the drug desferrioxamine; details.

Bayles, K. A. and C. K. Tomoeda, "Caregiver report of prevalence and appearance order of linguistic symptoms in Alzheimer's patients," *The Gerontologist,* **April 1991, p. 210.**

Presents results of a longitudinal study of disease effects on communication of Alzheimer's patients. Interviews of primary caregivers regarding the existence and appearance order of linguistic symptoms; most and least prevalent symptoms; methods; results; more.

Burns, A., R. Jacoby, et al., "Neurological signs in Alzheimer's disease," *Age & Ageing,* **January 1991, p. 45.**

Examines the frequency of neurological phenomena in a representative population of patients with Alzheimer's disease (AD) to relate these phenomena to cognitive impairment and cerebral appearance as assessed by computer tomography (CT) scan. Catchment area of the study; satisfaction for criteria clinical diagnosis of AD suggested by two groups; use of the CAMCOG to determine cognitive function; more.

Erickson, D., "Love and terror," *Scientific American,* **April 1991, p. 148.**

Considers whether a chemical messenger holds the key to treating Alzheimer's disease. Cholinergic hypothesis; controversial Alzheimer's drug called Cognex; other acetylcholinesterase inhibitors; Hoechst-Roussel's inhibitor HP-029; software therapeutics; more. INSET: A plague of plaques, by J. Rennie.

Kolata, G., "Alzheimer's researchers close in on causes," *The New York Times,* **Feb. 26, 1991, p. C1.**

Discusses researchers' new findings that many, if not most, cases of Alzheimer's disease have a genetic basis — a dramatic switch in the understanding of the disease from just a few years ago, when many scientists estimated that no more than 10 percent of the cases were inherited. New tools of neurochemistry and molecular biology are being used to investigate what happens in Alzheimer's patients' brains as wave after wave of nerve cells inexorably die. Role of chromosomes 21 and 19.

Marx, J., "Boring in on beta-amyloid's role in Alzheimer's," *Science,* **Feb. 7, 1992, p. 688.**

Discusses recent research in which the role of the beta-amyloid protein has been linked to Alzheimer's disease. Presence of beta-amyloid in healthy cells; research into factors that cause more beta-amyloid deposits to form in brains of Alzheimer's patients; impact beta-amyloid modulation might have on Alzheimer's treatment or prevention; history of research into beta-amyloid as cause of Alzheimer's; research into how beta-amyloid is made in cells; role of amyloid precursor proteins.

Wheeler, D. L., "Limited supplies of brain tissue hamper research," *Chronicle of Higher Education,* **Nov. 13, 1991, p. A8.**

Outlines the effects a shortage of brain tissue is having on research into schizophrenia, Alzheimer's and Parkinson's disease and Tourette's syndrome. Difficulties of getting brain tissue; need for brain tissue from the severely mentally ill; "control brains" to compare with abnormal ones; requests for brain donations.

Wright, L. K., "The impact of Alzheimer's disease on the marital relationship," *The Gerontologist,* **April 1991, p. 224.**

Compares caregiver-Alzheimer's afflicted spouse dyads with healthy married couples. Differences on levels of companionship and total marital quality; differences in levels of sexual activity; review of the literature; method; results; more.

Yanker, B. A. and M. M. Mesulam, "Beta-amyloid and the pathogenesis of Alzheimer's disease," *New England Journal of Medicine,* **Dec. 26, 1991, p. 1849.**

Focuses on the recent developments in the study of the molecular pathogenesis of Alzheimer's disease and tries to bring them together into what is becoming a coherent framework. Typical clinical presentation of Alzheimer's disease; histopathological changes of Alzheimer's; statistics on the percentage of cases of dementia in persons over age 65 caused by Alzheimer's; molecular origin of the amyloid plaques in Alzheimer's disease; neurofibrillary tangles.

Social aspects

Conrad, E., "When grandma has Alzheimer's," *Working Mother,* **January 1992, p. 60.**

Presents tips for helping one's child deal with a grandparent's Alzheimer's disease. Book entitled "Grandpa Doesn't Know It's Me"; create ways for your child and your ailing parent to share activities; focus on emotional bonds; more.

Teri, L. and R. G. Logsdon, "Identifying pleasant activities for Alzheimer's disease patients: The Pleasant Effects Schedule-AD," *The Gerontologist,* **February 1991, p. 124.**

Discusses the benefits and problems involved in identifying pleasant activities for the Alzheimer's patient. Presents the Pleasant Events Schedule, a tool which can help professional and family care providers identify and monitor activities that are enjoyable to individual patients. Gradual loss of ability to perform rewarding and enjoyable activities in people with Alzheimer's disease; alleviating depression;

providing a sense of accomplishment.

Therapy

"A drug for Alzheimer's?" *Harvard Health Letter,* **July 1991, p. 8.**

Covers controversy of the drug now known as tacrine that in 1986 showed promising results in 14 patients with Alzheimer's disease. Tacrine's potential to cause liver damage; benefits of the drug; articles in various medical magazines concerning the drug.

"A thorny question for Alzheimer's drug," *The New York Times,* **April 4, 1991, p. A1.**

Discusses tacrine, a drug proposed for the treatment of Alzheimer's disease. It has helped some patients' ability to remember things but did not dramatically improve their condition, and it carries risks of liver damage. Debate over how effective a drug must be to enter the marketplace.

Eagger, S. A., R. Levy, et al., "Tacrine in Alzheimer's disease," *The Lancet,* **April 27, 1991, p. 989.**

Studies the efficacy and safety of tacrine (tetrahydroaminoacridine) plus lecithin in a randomized, double-blind, placebo-controlled, crossover study in patients with probable Alzheimer's disease. Tacrine produced an improvement in key outcome measures roughly equivalent to the deterioration which might have occurred over six to 12 months.

"This hospital patient has Alzheimer's," *American Journal of Nursing,* **October 1991, p. 44.**

Presents an American Nursing Association continuing education article with multiple-choice examination on helping a hospitalized Alzheimer's patient recover from serious illness without exacerbating the Alzheimer's dementia. Creating a supportive environment; consistency; anti-fatigue strategies; communication clues; assessment tips; meeting everyday needs; stages of Alzheimer's; catastrophic behavior; beyond discharge. INSET: "Incidentally, this patient has memory problems...."

Levine, D., "Attacking Alzheimer's," *American Health,* **December 1991, p. 9.**

Details the existing treatments used to alleviate some of the more disturbing symptoms of Alzheimer's disease. Includes psychotherapy, anti-depressant drugs and reminiscence therapy. Research; benefits of treatments.

O'Brien, J. T., S. Eagger, et al., "Effects of tetrahydroaminoacridine on liver function in patients with Alzheimer's disease," *Age & Ageing,* **March 1991, p. 129.**

Reports on detailed liver function analysis tests for 30 patients with Alzheimer's disease who were treated with tetrahydroaminoacridine. Percentage of cases that experienced a benign elevation of aspartate transaminase; clinical hepatitis; gender differences in hepatotoxicity; Benzodiazepine as a hypnotic; more.

Teri, L. and D. Gallagher-Thompson, "Cognitive-behavioral interventions for treatment of depression in Alzheimer's patients," *The Gerontologist,* **June 1991, p. 413.**

Presents two strategies for treating depression in Alzheimer's patients. Cognitive therapy; behavioral intervention; cognitive distortions; negative events.

Toufexis, A., G. Bellafante, et al., "Still no relief from Alzheimer's," *Time,* **July 29, 1991, p. 52.**

Summarizes recent requests by Warner-Lambert of the Food and Drug Administration for permission to market the drug tacrine as the first drug treatment for Alzheimer's, and the rejection of the agency's advisory panel of the request. Danger of significant liver damage; lowering scientific standards by using limited marketing, a strategy used for release of AIDS drugs.

Back Issues

Great Research on Current Issues Starts Right Here... Recent topics covered by The CQ Researcher are listed below. Issues dated before May 10, 1991, were published under the name of Editorial Research Reports.

JANUARY 1991
Growing Influence of Boycotts
Should the U.S. Reinstate the Draft?
America's Archaeological Past
Peace Corps' Challenges in '90s

FEBRUARY 1991
Regional Impact of Recession
Puerto Rico's Status
Redistricting: Mapping Power
Nuclear Power

MARCH 1991
Acid Rain
Cost of the Gulf War
Reassessing Gun Laws
Future for Man in Space

APRIL 1991
Social Security
Canadian Crisis Over Quebec
California Drought
Electromagnetic Radiation

MAY 1991
School Choice
Racial Quotas
Animal Rights
U.S. and Japan

JUNE 1991
Children and Divorce
Teenage Suicide
Endangered Species
Europe 1992

JULY 1991
Teenagers and Abortion
Soviet Republics Rebel
Mexico's Emergence
Athletes and Drugs

AUGUST 1991
Sexual Harassment
Fetal Tissue Research
Oil Imports
The Palestinians

SEPTEMBER 1991
Police Brutality
Advertising Under Attack
Saving the Forests
Foster Care Crisis

OCTOBER 1991
Pay-Per-View TV
Youth Gangs
Gene Therapy
World Hunger

NOVEMBER 1991
Fast-Food Shake-Up
The Greening of Eastern Europe
Business' Role in Education
Cuba In Crisis

DECEMBER 1991
Retiree Health Benefits
Asian Americans
The Obscenity Debate
The Disabilities Act

JANUARY 1992
Term Limits
Oil Spills
Hunting Controversy
Alternative Medicine

FEBRUARY 1992
Threatened Coastlines
New Era in Asia
Assisted Suicide
Jobs in the '90s

MARCH 1992
Women and Sports
Underage Drinking
Garbage Crisis
Mafia Crackdown

APRIL 1992
Ozone Depletion
Welfare Reform
Politicians and Privacy
Illegal Immigration

MAY 1992
Native Americans
Jobs vs. Environment
Too Many Lawsuits?
Fairness in Salaries

JUNE 1992
Nuclear Proliferation
Food Irradiation
Lead Poisoning
Hard Times for Libraries

JULY 1992
Alternative Energy
Prescription Drug Prices

Back issues are available for $4.00 (subscribers) or $7.00 (non-subscribers). Quantity discounts apply to orders over ten. To order, call Congressional Quarterly 1-800-432-2250.

Binders are available for $15.00. To order call 1-800-638-1710.

Future Topics

▶ *Infant Mortality*

▶ *The Homeless*

▶ *The Overworked American*

PUBLISHED BY CONGRESSIONAL QUARTERLY INC., IN CONJUNCTION WITH EBSCO PUBLISHING

Infant Mortality

Why is the U.S. death rate high compared with other nations?

THE UNITED STATES SPENDS MORE MONEY ON health care per person than any other country. Yet an American baby is less likely to reach its first birthday than a baby born in 21 other nations. Experts trace the problem to the inability of pregnant women from poor families to get early and continuous prenatal care. Without it, doctors can't screen for potentially serious medical problems. If untreated, these conditions can cause birth defects, the leading cause of infant death in the United States. Early prenatal intervention also can help pregnant women improve their diets and stop abusing alcohol, tobacco and other drugs that greatly increase the chance that they will give birth to low-birthweight infants, which are far more likely to succumb than other babies.

 July 31, 1992 • Volume 2, No. 28 • 641-664

Formerly Editorial Research Reports

COVER ART: BARBARA SASSA-DANIELS

THE CQ Researcher

July 31, 1992
Volume 2, No. 28

EDITOR
Sandra Stencel

MANAGING EDITOR
Thomas J. Colin

ASSOCIATE EDITOR
Richard L. Worsnop

STAFF WRITERS
Charles S. Clark
Mary H. Cooper
Rodman D. Griffin

PRODUCTION EDITOR
Laurie De Maris

EDITORIAL ASSISTANT
Michael M. Taylor

GRAPHICS
Jack Auldridge

PUBLISHED BY
Congressional Quarterly Inc.

CHAIRMAN
Andrew Barnes

VICE CHAIRMAN
Andrew P. Corty

EDITOR AND PUBLISHER
Neil Skene

EXECUTIVE EDITOR
Robert W. Merry

PUBLICATIONS MARKETING/SALES
Robert Smith

EDITOR, EBSCO PUBLISHING
Melissa Kummerer

The CQ Researcher (ISSN 1056-2036). Formerly Editorial Research Reports. Published weekly (48 times per year, not printed the first Friday of any month with five Fridays) by Congressional Quarterly Inc., 1414 22nd St., N.W., Washington, D.C. 20037. Rates are furnished upon request. Second-class postage paid at Washington, D.C. POSTMASTER: Send address changes to The CQ Researcher, 1414 22nd St., N.W., Washington, D.C. 20037.

Infant Mortality

By Mary H. Cooper

The Issues

More than 4 million babies were born in the United States last year. An appalling number of them — 36,500 — never survived infancy, defined as the first year of life. With an infant mortality rate of 9.8 deaths per 1,000 infants in 1989, the latest year for which final data are available, the United States ranked 22nd in protecting its most vulnerable citizens. (*See table, p. 644.*)

Japan's infant mortality rate — the lowest in the world — was less than half that of the United States. Even Singapore and Hong Kong, developing nations whose standards of living few Americans would envy, fared better than the U.S.

To be sure, the United States appears to be improving. In 1990, the infant mortality rate was 9.1 deaths per 1,000 births, according to provisional data issued by the National Center for Health Statistics. In 1991, the agency estimates, the mortality rate was down to 8.9. But experts attribute the improvement in infant survival mainly to advances in technology to save sick babies, not to improved health among newborns.

Indeed, the progress masks a disturbing trend that provides the key to understanding why so many infants die in the United States. Last year, for the first time since 1978, the number of low-birthweight babies increased. Babies who weigh less than 5.5 pounds at birth are 40 times more likely to die in their first month than babies of normal weight. And the main reason why babies are born underweight is lack of prenatal care by mothers who cannot afford to go to the doctor or who don't know how to nurture the developing fetus.

Early medical care is essential to a

healthy pregnancy and a healthy baby. In the view of many physicians, including Dr. Richard H. Aubry, director of obstetrics at Crouse Irving Memorial Hospital and the State University Health Science Center in Syracuse, N.Y., all women of child-bearing age should be treated with the possibility of pregnancy in mind. "Before pregnancy occurs," Aubry says, "we can help correct nutritional problems, improve lifestyle problems such as abuse of alcohol, cigarettes and drugs, as well as uncover and treat medical problems."

Equally important, Aubry says, is prenatal care commencing during the first trimester of pregnancy. This allows doctors to screen for a variety of potentially serious health problems, including anemia, urinary tract infections and diabetes. These conditions can cause birth defects — the leading cause of infant deaths — if they are not corrected early in pregnancy.

One of the most important functions of prenatal care is dating the pregnancy, and this can only be done accurately if the woman is ex-

amined during the first trimester. "If the woman comes in at five months or later, you don't know if her baby is small because it is early in the pregnancy or because she is growing a small baby," Aubry says. "And the two situations require entirely different treatments."

Because infant mortality is largely preventable, health professionals, social workers and child advocates express frustration at its persistence, especially in light of the impassioned controversies surrounding related issues, such as abortion and teen sexuality. The deeply divisive national debate over abortion rights, for example, often stops at the moment of birth. "Whatever you think about the fetus, we as a society have to recognize that if you're born alive you're a person," says Dr. Michael Durfee, a child psychiatrist and coordinator of Los Angeles County's child abuse prevention program. "Babies are dying."

Likewise, Durfee says, the controversy over distributing condoms at high school clinics ignores the fact that condoms can help reduce the incidence of infant death from AIDS. "The main cause of AIDS in infancy is fetal contamination from an infected mother," he notes.

Even in the cold light of economic analysis, infant mortality exacts a heavy toll on American society. It costs hospitals nearly eight times as much to care for a low-birthweight baby (about $21,000 in 1990) as it does to handle a normal delivery ($2,842 on average). In 1990, the hospital costs of caring for low-birthweight infants exceeded $2 billion. These excess costs further strain the U.S. health-care system, which is already more expensive than those in other industrial nations.

As experts grapple with high infant mortality, here are some of the questions they are asking:

What are other countries doing to protect infants?

The 21 countries with lower infant mortality rates than the United States generally provide a wider range of publicly financed health and social services than the U.S. "What it all boils down to is a focus on prevention," says Rae K. Grad, executive director of the National Commission to Prevent Infant Mortality, which Congress established in 1987 to develop solutions to the problem. "Of course, one of the ways they invest in prevention is to grant universal access to health care, so that the lack of insurance is not a barrier to preventive care."

In Japan, for example, government health insurance covers nearly three-quarters of all health expenditures. In many other industrial nations, public health insurance accounts for an even higher percentage of total outlays for health care. In the United States, by contrast, the government covers just over 40 percent of health-care costs. In fact, the United States is the only Western democracy except South Africa that does not provide basic universal access to health care.

As many as 40 million Americans have no health insurance, including 10 million women of childbearing age. Because most health insurance in the United States is provided as a benefit of employment, a worker who is laid off or fired typically loses health insurance along with the job. But employment does not assure access to health care. While almost all large firms offer some health coverage, over the past decade the percentage of medium-size and large firms that cover the full cost of health insurance for their employees and their dependents has plummeted from 51 percent to 23 percent.[1]

The smaller the company the less likely workers and their families are to receive health benefits: The Health Insurance Association of America reports that only a third of the firms employing fewer than 10 workers offer any kind of health coverage at all. The Labor Department estimates that 1 million Americans lose their health insurance each year due to unemployment or reduced coverage for employed workers and their families.[2]

Without health insurance, many pregnant women can't receive early and regular medical attention throughout pregnancy, which is vital to a healthy birth outcome. Babies born to women who didn't receive care before delivery are three times more likely to be born at low birthweight and four times more likely to die than those whose mothers began to receive care during the first trimester of pregnancy.[3]

Without health insurance, many pregnant women cannot afford the seven or eight doctors' appointments that are needed to provide adequate prenatal care. Although affordable health care is not the only key to infant health, a 1989 study found that infants born to parents with no insurance were 30 percent more likely to fall ill or die than those born to insured parents.[4]

There are sound financial, as well as social and moral, reasons why other countries invest in preventive care for pregnant women. For every $1 spent on a pregnancy, an estimated $3 is saved in after-delivery hospital costs. "If you have a baby born tiny, [the United States] can do a better job of saving it," says Grad. "But with limited dollars, other countries put their money at the front end, not at the back end as we do."

Other Western democracies do not stop at public health insurance. "The key to their success is a whole range of social supports," says Joseph Liu, a health analyst for the Children's Defense Fund (CDF), a Washington-based advocacy group. "This includes income supports as well as access to health care."

The United States, however, is one of the few Western democracies that does not have a national maternity-leave policy allowing employed mothers to stay home for several months after giving birth with com-

U.S. Ranks 22nd In Protecting Infants

Twenty-one countries had lower infant mortality rates than the United States in 1989, the latest year for which final data are available.

Rank	Country	Infant Mortality Rate †
1	Japan	4.6
2	Sweden	5.8
3	Finland	6.0
4	Singapore	6.6
5	Netherlands	6.8
6	Canada	7.2 ††
7	Switzerland	7.3
8	France	7.4
9	Hong Kong	7.4
10	Federal Republic of Germany	7.4
11	Ireland	7.6
12	German Democratic Republic	7.6
13	Norway	7.7
14	Australia	8.0
15	Spain	8.1 ††
16	Austria	8.3
17	United Kingdom	8.4
18	Denmark	8.5
19	Belgium	8.6
20	Italy	8.8
21	Greece	9.8
22	United States	9.8
23	Israel	9.9
24	New Zealand	10.2

† Number of infant deaths per 1,000 live births.
†† Rate for 1988.
Source: Office of International Statistics, National Center for Health Statistics

pensation and without fear of losing their jobs. And less than one-fifth of the U.S. gross domestic product (the nation's domestic output of goods and services), is devoted to government social spending in general, which benefits pregnant women and infants along with the general population. Most other Western democracies spend more on their citizenry's basic needs.[5]

Why are infant mortality rates higher among minorities?

One of the most disturbing aspects of infant mortality in the United States is its overwhelming incidence among minority populations. The situation is especially dismal for black Americans. The infant mortality rate among black babies (17.7 deaths per 1,000 births) is about twice that of whites (8.2 deaths per 1,000 births). Similarly, the percentage of black babies born at low birthweight, 13.2 percent, is double the percentage for white babies. (*See graph, p. 646.*) Black American babies are as likely to be born underweight as babies in the Third World nations of Cameroon, Guinea-Bissau and Zaire.[6]

A clue to understanding why so many more black babies die in infancy is found in other statistics on prenatal care. A quarter of all American women — but 40 percent of black women — don't receive prenatal care in the crucial first trimester of pregnancy.

Infant mortality rates among other minority groups are more uncertain because of imprecise classifications on infant death certificates. One recent study suggests that American Indians fared almost as poorly as blacks, while infants born to Asian-Americans did better than whites.[7] Hispanic infants have a higher mortality rate than whites, but figures for this group vary widely because there is no consensus about who should be defined as Hispanic.[8]

The most obvious explanations for the high infant mortality rate among minorities are unemployment, poverty and the consequent lack of access to health care. Blacks and Hispanics are more likely to lack health insurance than whites, and they constitute a disproportionately large and growing segment of the uninsured population, according to government statistics. Members of both groups are more likely than whites to belong to poor families without a working adult. Because most health insurance coverage is provided by employers and is expensive to buy out-of-pocket, both these conditions make it difficult to obtain commercial health-care coverage.[9]

Still, other factors may be at work. Kenneth C. Schoendorf and his colleagues at the federal Centers for Disease Control (CDC) in Atlanta studied the effects education and social conditions have on infant mortality among black and white Americans. They found that even in families where both parents graduated from college, and presumably have higher incomes and better access to health care than the population at large, infant mortality still was twice as high among blacks as whites.[10] The discrepancy was due entirely to the higher incidence of low birthweight among black infants, even those of college-educated parents.

Schoendorf says more research is needed to explain why black college-educated parents are more likely to have low-birthweight babies than white college-educated parents. One possible explanation: Education and the resulting rise in living standards are not sufficient to erase the physical effects of poverty that may have oc-

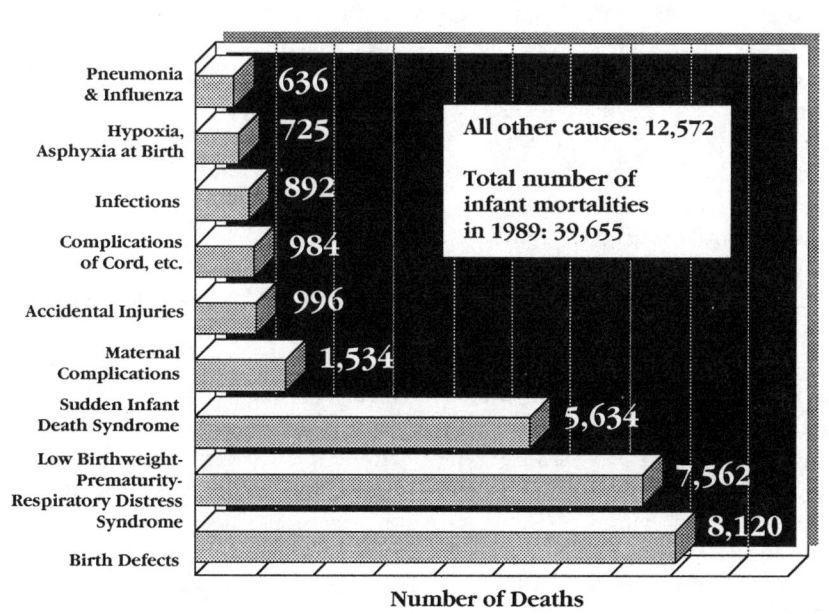

Leading Causes of Infant Mortality

Birth defects, low birthweight and Sudden Infant Death Syndrome were the leading causes of infant deaths in 1989.

Cause	Number of Deaths
Pneumonia & Influenza	636
Hypoxia, Asphyxia at Birth	725
Infections	892
Complications of Cord, etc.	984
Accidental Injuries	996
Maternal Complications	1,534
Sudden Infant Death Syndrome	5,634
Low Birthweight-Prematurity-Respiratory Distress Syndrome	7,562
Birth Defects	8,120

All other causes: 12,572

Total number of infant mortalities in 1989: 39,655

Number of Deaths

Source: March of Dimes Birth Defects Foundation

Low Birthweight Linked to Infant Mortality

The infant mortality rate among black infants is about twice that of white infants. The primary reason is that black women are much more likely to have low-birthweight babies.

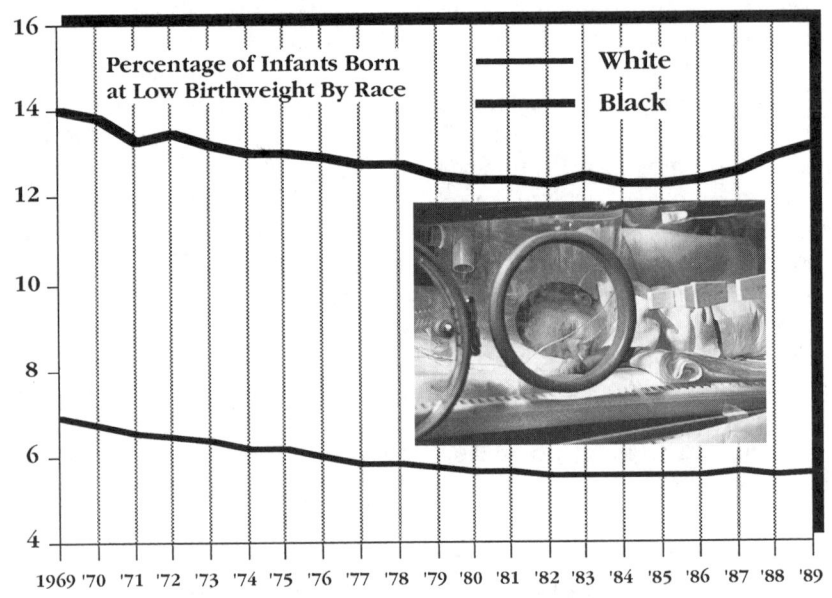

Percentage of Infants Born at Low Birthweight By Race

— White
— Black

16
14
12
10
8
6
4

1969 '70 '71 '72 '73 '74 '75 '76 '77 '78 '79 '80 '81 '82 '83 '84 '85 '86 '87 '88 '89

Source: National Center for Health Statistics
Photo: National Commission to Prevent Infant Mortality

curred during the mother's early development. But, says Schoendorf, "more information has to come out before we can definitely associate those conditions with prematurity or really bad birth outcomes, and not just a few ounces off birthweight."

Other health professionals find little ambiguity in the CDC findings. "It would be a mistake to deduce that women of similar educational levels are similar socially," says Paul H. Wise, director of Harvard University's Institute of Reproductive and Child Health. "The general social conditions among similarly educated black and white women are vastly different. Black college-educated women have lower incomes and more fragile family lives."

Wise says that the negative influence of stress caused by discrimination on black women's reproductive

health is still a matter of speculation. But he says the disparity in infant mortality rates between black and white Americans sends a clear message to policy-makers that programs providing prenatal and infant care need more funding.

Is infant mortality more a social and economic problem than a medical problem?

High infant mortality among the nation's poor suggests that it is not strictly a medical problem or even as simple a problem as coverage by health insurance. "Just because people have insurance doesn't mean they will get the care they need," says Martha King, manager of the Maternal and Child Health Project for the National Conference of State Legislatures in Denver.

Indeed, for many women, a range of social and economic barriers block the way to a healthy pregnancy. The main obstacle is poverty, which is spreading. Today, more American children than ever — 12 million under the age of 18, or one in five — are living in poverty.*

Two years ago, Congress tried to improve access to prenatal care for poor women and infants by expanding eligibility for Medicaid to pregnant women whose incomes were 133 percent of the official poverty level (*see p. 654*). But this measure has been of limited help. "We still provide no help for these women before they get pregnant," says Liu of the Children's Defense Fund.

Once a woman learns she is pregnant, she often does not have immediate access to prenatal care under Medicaid. Although some states have simplified the application form, many have not, and the complexity of applying for Medicaid deters many women.

In one typical case described by the National Commission to Prevent Infant Mortality, a woman made nine trips to various offices and clinics over a six-week period just to begin prenatal care and receive Medicaid eligibility. "All too often," the commission concluded, "a positive pregnancy test turns out to be the end — rather than the beginning — of a woman's contact with perinatal and pediatric services."[11]

Even if she manages to make all the required trips and fill out the application forms, says Liu, "it can take four to six weeks after the woman applies for Medicaid at the welfare office before she receives her Medicaid card. Depending on how long the state takes to complete the application process, the delays can easily deprive her of care during the first three months of pregnancy."

*Poverty is currently defined by the Labor Department as an annual income of $13,950 or less for a family of four.

Infant Mortality in the Nation's Capital

Washington, D.C., consistently ranks among the cities with the highest infant death rates in the nation. In 1989, when the U.S. infant mortality rate was 9.8 deaths per 1,000 births, the nation's capital suffered the highest infant mortality rate in the nation: 26 deaths per 1,000 births.

As in other parts of the country, the main culprits are low birthweight, poverty, poor nutrition and lack of prenatal care. "Although we saw some improvement in 1990, low birthweight is the key to infant mortality here," says Patricia Tompkins, director of the city's Office of Maternal and Child Health.

Tompkins says the city government offers many services to low-income pregnant women and infants, and that her office is waging a campaign to improve their access to those services. To help the working poor, for example, four of the city's 11 public health clinics that serve pregnant women and children now have evening hours.

One of the biggest problems Tompkins faces is the per-

How Other Cities Fare

1988 infant mortality rate per 1,000 births for cities with populations above 500,000

City	All	White	Black
San Jose	7.8	7.8	†
San Diego	8.1	7.6	13.9
San Francisco	8.4	9.6	†
Dallas	9.3	8.2	12.3
San Antonio	9.5	8.9	†
Los Angeles	10.1	8.3	20.2
Phoenix	10.9	10.1	23.5
Jacksonville	11.3	9.6	14.7
Houston	11.3	10.4	17.0
Milwaukee	12.1	7.8	17.5
Indianapolis	12.6	9.7	20.1
New Orleans	12.7	†	15.5
New York	13.2	11.0	18.3
Boston	13.9	8.4	22.1
Columbus	14.2	12.5	18.0
Chicago	15.2	9.9	21.0
Cleveland	17.0	12.2	20.9
Philadelphia	17.5	12.0	22.5
Memphis	17.6	9.0	21.6
Baltimore	18.0	12.9	20.4
Detroit	21.0	13.6	23.1
Washington, D.C.	23.2	19.9	26.0

† *Too few infant deaths in these populations to calculate infant mortality rate.*
Source: National Center for Health Statistics

vasive sense of isolation that often separates poor women from the services that are available to them. Tompkins tells of one young mother who was found feeding her baby nothing but water because she couldn't afford to buy infant formula. "What she didn't know," Tompkins says, "was that there was a public health clinic two blocks away from where she lived and that even the neighborhood pharmacy would have given her the formula at no cost if she had only asked."

In an attempt to bridge the information gap, Tompkins' office has issued the "Moms' Resource Book," listing the locations where pregnant women and mothers can obtain the services they need.

Tompkins is also counting on the Bush administration's Healthy Start demonstration project (*see p. 656*) to help cut infant mortality in the District. Due to begin later this year, Healthy Start will concentrate new initiatives and funding in the District and 14 other communities with high infant mortality rates. "Healthy Start will take down some of the barriers of isolation," Tompkins says.

But a pregnant woman who receives her Medicaid card still cannot count on prompt medical attention. Many doctors will not accept Medicaid patients who come to them when they find out they are pregnant — and they aren't obligated to do so.

"In most major cities, if you go through the Yellow Pages, maybe a quarter of the obstetricians and gynecologists will see [Medicaid patients]," Liu says. The problem is even more severe in many rural areas. Nearly 1,500 non-metropolitan counties had no practicing obstetrician in 1988, and the number of physicians providing obstetric care continues to decline nationwide.[12]

In addition to the financial and provider barriers to prenatal care, there are what Liu calls personal barriers that must be addressed if prenatal care is to succeed. An essential component of prenatal care is information on such matters as special nutritional requirements during pregnancy and the need to avoid tobacco, alcohol and drugs. Immigrants who don't speak English may not understand their health-care providers, or they may not be familiar with the foods doctors and nurses suggest for a healthy diet.

Lack of transportation to prenatal care clinics is another significant obstacle to obtaining care, especially in rural areas, where the infant mortality

rate is often as high as it is in large cities. Getting prenatal care may require women to travel great distances several times during pregnancy in areas that often are not served by public transportation.

Prenatal health care is essential for more than medical reasons. "There is nothing magical about seven or eight visits to the doctor's office," says Liu. "What that prenatal care does is provide opportunities for the pregnant woman to hook up to other services she needs to help her infant survive."

Ideally, Liu says, providers of prenatal care should make sure the woman has adequate housing and enough money to give herself and

Infant Mortality Rates

The states shaded gray on the map below had infant mortality rates above the national average for 1989, the latest year for which final data are available.†

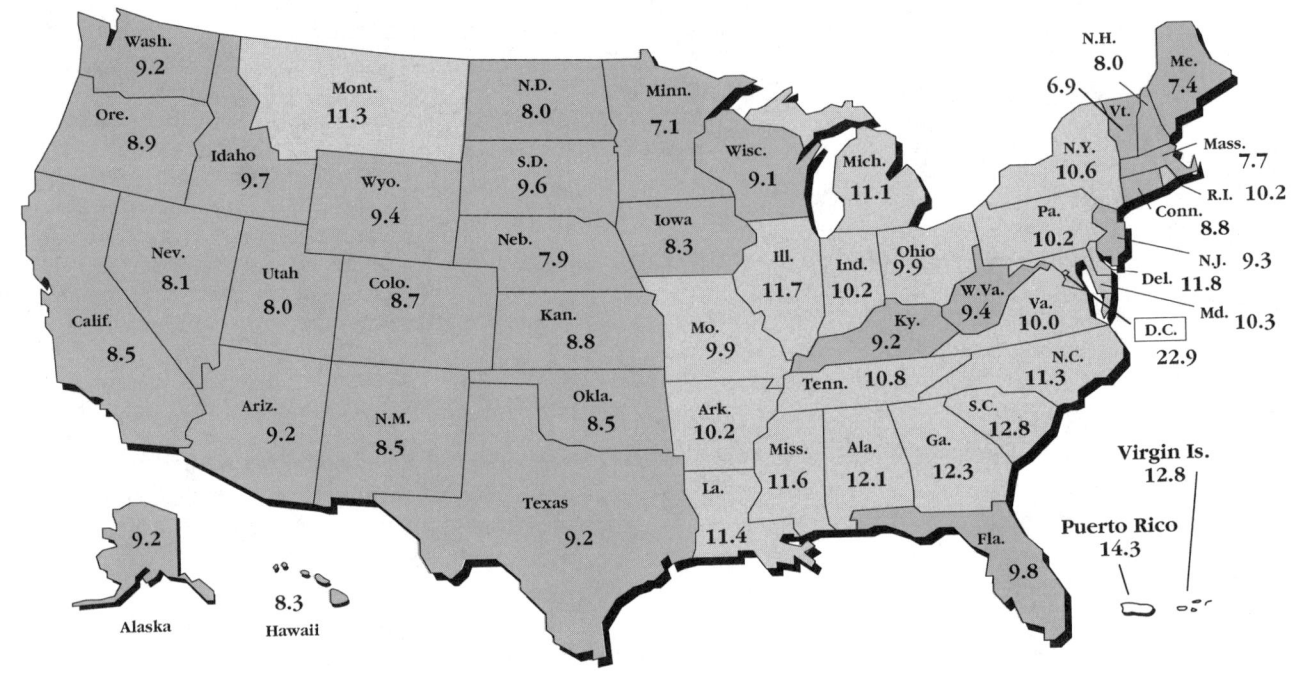

Wash. 9.2
Ore. 8.9
Mont. 11.3
N.D. 8.0
Minn. 7.1
N.H. 8.0
6.9
Vt.
Me. 7.4
Idaho 9.7
Wyo. 9.4
S.D. 9.6
Wisc. 9.1
Mich. 11.1
N.Y. 10.6
Mass. 7.7
R.I. 10.2
Nev. 8.1
Utah 8.0
Colo. 8.7
Neb. 7.9
Iowa 8.3
Ill. 11.7
Ind. 10.2
Ohio 9.9
Pa. 10.2
Conn. 8.8
N.J. 9.3
Del. 11.8
Calif. 8.5
Kan. 8.8
Mo. 9.9
W.Va. 9.4
Va. 10.0
Ky. 9.2
D.C. 22.9
Md. 10.3
Ariz. 9.2
N.M. 8.5
Okla. 8.5
Ark. 10.2
Tenn. 10.8
N.C. 11.3
S.C. 12.8
Virgin Is. 12.8
Texas 9.2
La. 11.4
Miss. 11.6
Ala. 12.1
Ga. 12.3
Fla. 9.8
Puerto Rico 14.3
Alaska 9.2
Hawaii 8.3

† Note: The nation's infant mortality rate in 1989 was 9.8 deaths per 1,000 infants.
Source: National Center for Health Statistics

her child a healthy diet. If these conditions are lacking, he says, health-care providers should help her contact housing authorities and obtain income support, such as the Special Supplemental Food Program for Women, Infants and Children — better known as WIC (*see p. 650*). "Without prenatal care, we have no ability to provide these other services," Liu says.

Many states and localities are trying to overcome the myriad social and economic barriers that deter poor women from obtaining prenatal care. But even where these services exist, poverty itself adds a final, psychological barrier to care.

In the District of Columbia, where infants' chances of survival are no better than they are in Jamaica, health-care providers say many women are so isolated by poverty that they don't

believe the community will help them. (*See story, p. 647.*) Patricia Tompkins, who heads the District's maternal and child-care program, says part of her agency's job is to build trust among the city's poor women and to "get the word out" about the city's services. "Citizens who are isolated from the mainstream tend to distrust government," she says. "The distrust comes from a sense that government doesn't care." ∎

BACKGROUND

Early Progress

The U.S. infant mortality rate is high only by contemporary standards. At the turn of the century, one American child in 10 did not survive the first year of life. The nation's infant mortality then was no better than today's rate in less developed countries

in Sub-Saharan Africa and Asia.

The leading causes of infant death in 19th-century American cities were the same as those that still plague many Third World nations: infectious diseases and diarrhea resulting from contaminated water and poor sanitary conditions. Well into the 1900s, city-dwelling infants were more likely to succumb than babies born in rural areas. Even among black Americans living in abject poverty in the rural

Continued on p. 650

Chronology

1900-1930s The federal government begins to assume a role in protecting infants.

1908
New York City creates the country's first agency for child hygiene, aimed at improving health conditions for infants and children.

1912
Julia C. Lathrop, a health and education reformer, becomes the first chief of the Federal Children's Bureau, the first federal agency charged with child welfare.

1921
Congress passes the Maternity and Infancy Act, creating the first federal program to promote maternal and child health.

1935
The Social Security Act goes into effect. Title V of the act, which was modeled after the earlier Maternity and Infancy Act, provides grants to the states to improve maternal and child health and welfare.

1940s-1950s Medical advances, such as the introduction of antibiotics, and improved living standards for most Americans help cut the nation's infant mortality rate.

1953
The Department of Health, Education and Welfare — later renamed the Department of Health and Human Services — is created out of the old Federal Security Agency and elevated to Cabinet status.

1960s Programs set up as part of President Lyndon Johnson's Great Society address the problems of maternal and infant health.

1962
Economic assistance to needy children receives separate funding with the creation of Aid to Families with Dependent Children (AFDC), one of the cornerstones of the federal welfare system.

1965
Congress establishes Medicaid, a joint federal-state program providing public health insurance for the poor, as well as Medicare for the elderly.

1970s The U.S. infant mortality rate continues to decline, thanks to federal programs to help pregnant women and infants and to continuing medical advances, including neonatal intensive care units for low-birthweight babies.

1970
Congress establishes the National Health Service Corps, which helps medical students to pay for their training in exchange for their pledge to work in areas of the country that lack adequate health-care services.

1972
The Special Supplemental Food Program for Women, Infants and Children — better known as WIC — is set up to combat malnutrition, a major cause of low birthweight and death among infants. The program provides food and vouchers to buy food to eligible pregnant women, nursing mothers and children under age 5.

1980s The Reagan administration's campaign to reduce federal spending for domestic programs results in cutbacks for many maternal and child health initiatives.

1981
The Omnibus Budget Reconciliation Act causes most working poor to lose eligibility for welfare and, with it, coverage by Medicaid. Title V programs are consolidated into the Maternal and Child Health Services block grant, leaving the states to administer programs and assume greater responsibility for their funding.

1987
Congress sets up the National Commission to Prevent Infant Mortality.

1989
Congress passes legislation authorizing about $100 million to pay for home visits to pregnant women, create a maternal and infant health handbook and help place medical care and other maternal and infant services under one roof. Under the '89 budget act, the states are required to extend Medicaid coverage to pregnant women and young children with family incomes that are 133 percent of the poverty level.

1990s Black infants continue to die at twice the rate of white babies.

1991
The Bush administration unveils Healthy Start, a demonstration project aimed at halving infant mortality in 15 communities over the next five years.

Continued from p. 648

South, infant mortality was lower than it was among blacks who migrated to the cities in search of better living conditions.

In essence, the rapid influx of rural blacks and European immigrants into the manufacturing centers of the Northeast and Midwest led to overcrowded tenements and overwhelmed water and sewer systems, fostering the spread of disease and contamination of food and water.[13]

Sanitary reforms, including the construction of modern water and sewer systems, helped bring about a rapid fall in infant mortality during the first half of the century. Additional improvements came with the spread of pasteurization, which curtailed diseases caused by contaminated milk, and educational programs that taught mothers how to care for their babies. On the medical front, the advent of antibiotics greatly reduced infant deaths from to pneumonia and other bacterial infections, while vaccines vanquished such killers as measles, whooping cough and polio.

New Deal Launches Federal Aid

Federal welfare policies, meanwhile, were also helping to combat high infant mortality. Beginning in the 1930s with President Franklin D. Roosevelt's New Deal, needy families with children first became eligible to receive federal income support under the Social Security Act of 1935. Initially designed to deter child starvation during the Great Depression, a program jointly administered by the federal and state governments allocated cash benefits to single-parent families and families with unemployed or disabled parents.

The economic stimulus provided by World War II diverted public attention from poverty programs until the 1960s. In 1962, during the administration of President John F. Kennedy, Aid to Families with Dependent Children (AFDC) became a separately

funded program. Kennedy's successor, Lyndon B. Johnson, introduced other measures to help poor families with children as part of his War on Poverty.

A key program was Medicaid, the federal health insurance plan for the poor. Since it was launched in 1965, Medicaid has been a crucial source of aid to pregnant women and infants, providing free prenatal and hospital care and, when needed, postnatal care for both mothers and infants. The federal-state matching program now serves about 26 million low-income people.

Community and Migrant Health Centers were also established during the Johnson administration. Today numbering more than 550, they provide preventive and primary health care to uninsured people in areas poorly served by hospitals and doctors.

Another welfare program is specifically aimed at reducing malnutrition — one of the leading causes of low birthweight and death among infants. The Special Supplemental Food Program for Women, Infants and Children (WIC) was introduced in 1972 during the Nixon administration as a $20 million amendment to the 1966 Child Nutrition Act. WIC enables state health departments to distribute food and food vouchers each month to eligible pregnant women, nursing mothers and their infants and children under age 5.[14]

Why Babies Die

As medical advances and improved living standards have greatly reduced the risk of infant death from infectious diseases over the past several decades, the causes of death during the first year of life have changed. Today, low birthweight, resulting from premature delivery or other problems arising during fetal development, is one of the biggest

risk factors in infant mortality. It also is occurring more frequently, accounting for 7 percent of all births in 1989, up from 6.9 percent in 1978.

Infants born under 5.5 pounds at birth are 40 times more likely to die in the first month of life, and 20 percent more likely to succumb within their first year, than other babies. Among all infants who die at any time during the first year of life, 60 percent had low birthweight.

There are many reasons why babies are born under normal weight. Many of them have to do with the mother's social and economic conditions — poverty, poor nutrition and lack of access to medical care — and are therefore preventable if she receives early prenatal care.

Some health-care analysts blame pregnant women for the persistence of low-birthweight infants and high infant mortality, saying they bear the responsibility for failing to protect the developing fetus by abusing alcohol and other substances and by making other foolish lifestyle choices. (*See "At Issue," p. 657.*)

Substance Abuse During Pregnancy

Because they may withhold such information, no one knows exactly how many women smoke cigarettes, drink alcohol or use such illegal drugs as cocaine or heroin during pregnancy. "We have very serious problems determining how many women abuse substances," says Liu of the Children's Defense Fund. "Also, the science is not very clear at this point on what the toxic effects of the various substances are."

It is clear, however, that fetal development can be impaired in many ways by maternal substance abuse throughout pregnancy and even during the months before conception. Taken alone, few of the conditions that result from substance abuse appear to cause infant death. But when combined with the other problems

The Mystery of Sudden Infant Death Syndrome

Sudden Infant Death Syndrome, also known as SIDS or crib death, has long ranked among the leading — and most mysterious — causes of death among infants in the United States.†

Suggested causes run the gamut from obscure genetic abnormalities to child abuse. Known risk factors include low birthweight, lack of prenatal care and a mother who is poor or who smokes. As is true for infant mortality from all causes, SIDS is more likely to strike black infants than white infants. The death rate from SIDS is 226 deaths per 100,000 black infants and 124 deaths per 100,000 white infants.††

Most of the major risk factors for SIDS are more prevalent among black women than among white women. Yet no single cause or set of causes has yet emerged to explain why an estimated 5,600 babies die each year in the United States from this perplexing malady.‡

One of the more popular theories — first advanced in 1985 by a doctor in Hong Kong to explain the British colony's low incidence of SIDS — attributes SIDS to the face-down sleeping position. In many countries, including the United States, parents traditionally place infants face down to prevent them from choking. In countries where the new findings have prompted parents to put babies on their backs, however, SIDS rates have fallen. In Australia alone, crib death declined by 30 percent after a nationwide publicity campaign advised parents to do so.‡‡

It is not known how many infant deaths that are attributed to SIDS are really due to other causes. "There is a very serious question about how to define SIDS," says Joseph Liu, senior health associate at the Children's Defense Fund in Washington, D.C. "In some states, when the mortician fills out the death certificate, if he doesn't know the cause of death, he writes down SIDS. We don't know how many cases may be from suffocation on poorly designed mattresses, medical factors or even abuse."

Many deaths that are attributed to SIDS actually may be the result of child abuse. The National Committee for Prevention of Child Abuse estimates that 1,106 children under age 5 died of abuse in 1991, including 597 infants.

"Almost all the deaths from child abuse occur at the hands of caretakers — parents, other relatives or babysitters," says psychiatrist Michael Durfee, coordinator of Los Angeles County's child abuse prevention program. "SIDS cases have been mismanaged in some states because no autopsy was performed." To better differentiate between SIDS and homicide, Durfee says, 25 states have set up multiagency teams to examine the cause of death in children.

---

† SIDS is officially defined as the sudden death of an infant under one year of age that remains unexplained after a post-mortem investigation, an examination of the scene of death and a review of the case history.

†† Figures from the SIDS Clearinghouse in McLean, Va.

‡ Figure from the National Center for Health Statistics. The SIDS Clearinghouse says there are 7,000 SIDS deaths each year.

‡‡ See "Cot Deaths: Looking Up?" *The Economist*, May 9, 1992.

---

that often occur among substance abusers — such as poor nutrition, physical abuse from partners and neglect of adequate care — substance abuse contributes to infant mortality.

Smoking has long been associated with low birthweight among infants, even when the pregnancy is carried to term. Babies born to the 20 percent of all pregnant women who are known to smoke are twice as likely to be underweight at birth than nonsmokers' babies.[15] Alcohol is also harmful to fetal development. If a pregnant woman drinks heavily, her baby may suffer from fetal alcohol syndrome, whose symptoms include facial deformities and mental retardation.

A recent survey estimated that almost 20 percent of all pregnant women — 739,200 each year — use at least one illegal drug during their pregnancies.[16] Illegal drug use can result in the birth of an addicted baby who suffers the same withdrawal symptoms as adult addicts.

During the 1980s, the rising number of cocaine users included many pregnant women. There are indications that cocaine use is declining in some major cities and with it the rate of infant deaths.

Still, babies born in New York City to women who used cocaine during pregnancy died at three times the average rate in 1989, though it is unclear to what extent death was due to the drug.[17]

AIDS and Other Sexually Transmitted Diseases

Closely associated with increased drug use during the 1980s has been the rise of AIDS and other sexually transmitted diseases among pregnant women and their newborns. The decade-long AIDS epidemic, fueled by sexual contact and contaminated needles, is increasingly affecting women and their babies. Recent data suggest that three women out of every 2,000 who give birth in the United States are infected with HIV, the virus that causes AIDS.[18]

Because the virus can be passed on to the developing fetus, many babies of HIV-positive women are already infected at birth. While AIDS can take many years to develop in infected adults, the disease progresses much faster in infants. About a third of the babies who are exposed to HIV before birth will develop AIDS within 18 months of birth. Many others die before their first birthday.

Other sexually transmitted diseases are also on the upswing among pregnant women. The most common conditions — syphilis, gonorrhea, chlamydia and genital herpes — can cause low birthweight and other physical problems. Syphilis kills 40 percent of the babies who contract the disease from their mothers.

Risks of Teen Pregnancies

The 1980s also saw a rise in the number of babies born to adolescents. After declining from the mid-1950s through the mid-1970s, adolescent pregnancy rose during the last decade. By 1989, more than a half-million babies, or about 13 percent of all babies born in the United States, had teenage mothers.[19]

For a variety of reasons, teenagers are more likely than older women to give birth to underweight babies. Many teens have not reached the physical maturity needed to carry a pregnancy to term. In some cases, young adolescents don't realize they are pregnant during the first trimester.

Even when unmarried teens — who account for two-thirds of teen mothers — realize they are pregnant, many try to hide their condition from family and friends and are reluctant to seek prenatal care. Without such care, many teens know little of how to eat properly and care for themselves to foster a successful birth outcome. As a result, teens are especially at risk for anemia, toxemia and premature delivery — as well as inadequate weight gain during pregnancy, which contributes to low birthweight.

Birth Defects

Birth defects are the main cause of infant death in the United States,

contributing to the deaths of about 8,000 American infants each year, according to the March of Dimes Birth Defects Foundation in White Plains, N.Y. "Birth defects are very democratic," says the organization's president, Dr. Jennifer L. Howse. "They hit everybody."

Heart defects are the most common fatal abnormality, followed by respiratory defects and malformations of the central nervous system, such as spina bifida and anencephaly.

The rate of infant mortality from birth defects remains high despite recent advances in diagnostic techniques and preventive medicine. Amniocentesis, for example, can detect major congenital birth defects. Preventive weapons include the development of a vaccine against rubella, or German measles, and the discovery that folic acid, a vitamin supplement, may prevent spina bifida and other fatal defects of the central nervous system.

The incidence of birth defects is not known with precision because there is no nationwide requirement to report them on birth certificates. According to Howse, the causes of many birth defects are unclear, though maternal exposure to toxic materials at the workplace and elsewhere are thought to contribute significantly to some congenital anomalies.

Sudden Infant Death Syndrome and Child Abuse

Sudden Infant Death Syndrome, also known as SIDS or crib death, claims nearly 6,000 infants each year in the United States. The average age at death from SIDS is 8 months.

SIDS has been recognized as a leading killer of infants for centuries. But its causes remain unknown. Explanations range from suffocation to defects in the cardiorespiratory system. Some researchers say a large but unknown portion of infant deaths attributed to SIDS are, in fact, the result of homicide or neglect. (See story, p. 651.)

The occasional newspaper accounts

of newborn babies miraculously saved from a dumpster before the garbage truck arrives hint at the role child abuse may play in infant mortality. For every newborn who is saved from death by neglect, abuse or homicide, an unknown number succumb without a trace.

Based on death-certificate information, the National Committee for the Prevention of Child Abuse in Chicago calculates that 1,106 children under age 5 died from abuse in 1991. More than half of those, almost 600 babies, were infants. But even among infants whose bodies are discovered and a cause of death is registered on the death certificate, the incidence of death by abuse probably is grossly underestimated.

"You don't need a weapon to kill a child that age," says Dr. Michael Durfee of Los Angeles County's Child Abuse Prevention program. "If you drown or suffocate an infant there need be no lesions, and the death may be classified as SIDS. There is no way of telling for sure, even if bruises are present."

Substance abuse by parents is often associated with infant death from neglect and homicide. Children of alcoholics, for example, suffer injuries as much as three times the rate of other children.[20] "If someone is intoxicated and leads a chaotic life, they often can't get a child to age 2," Durfee says. "They may shake, drown or throw them to death."

Funding Cuts in the '80s

Most of the leading causes of infant mortality are closely associated with poverty. Low birthweight occurs most frequently in babies whose mothers received little or no prenatal care in the early stages of pregnancy. Other causes — substance abuse, teen births, SIDS, sexually transmitted diseases and even child abuse — are more often encountered in poor families.

Federal programs to help poor pregnant women and new mothers care for themselves and their infants contributed to the rapid decline in infant mortality from 1965 until the early 1980s. Since that time, however, funding for many of the programs for this segment of the population has been cut, leading the United States to slip from 15th to 22nd place in world rankings for infant survival.

Upon taking office in 1981, President Ronald Reagan set about fulfilling his campaign pledge to "get the government off our backs" by reducing federal spending for domestic programs, including those benefiting pregnant women and infants. "The biggest improvement in infant survival came after the implementation of the Medicaid program, which enabled women to get timely prenatal care," says Liu of the Children's Defense Fund. "In the 1980s, the improvement in the infant mortality rate slowed."

One reason for the slowdown was the fall in Medicaid eligibility during the 1980s. Many Medicaid recipients, for example, lost coverage in 1981, when the Omnibus Budget Reconciliation Act removed most working poor from the welfare roles.[21]

The 1981 budget act also amended Title V of the Social Security Act to provide for a Maternal and Child Health Block Grant for the states to provide health-care services to needy women and children. States are required to provide matching funds equal to 75 percent of the federal grant. But during the 1980s federal funding of the grant fell by almost 40 percent, after adjusting for inflation. Because of this cut and deteriorating economic conditions that required state and local governments to reduce services, public health clinics in most communities suffered overall cuts in funding.

Federally funded Community and Migrant Health Centers, which are lo-

Medicaid Eligibility Levels

States are required to offer Medicaid coverage to pregnant women and young children with family incomes that are 133 percent of the official poverty level.† They are allowed to offer coverage to individuals with family incomes that are 185 percent of the poverty level. Twenty-four states now offer the highest benefit.

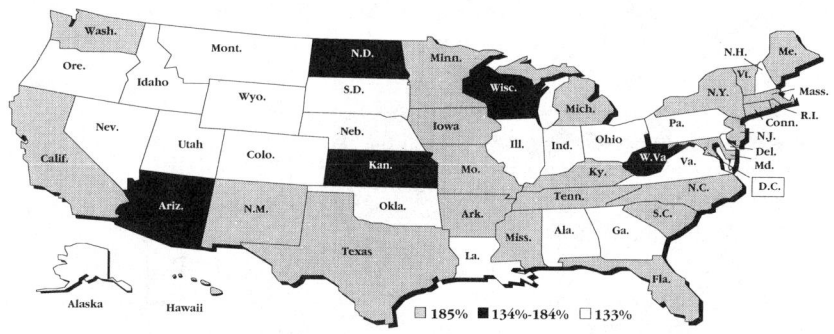

†*Note: Poverty currently is defined by the Labor Department as an annual income of $13,950 or less for a family of four.*
Sources: National Governors' Association; March of Dimes Birth Defects Foundation

cated in poor areas with few doctors and high infant mortality, have for more than 25 years served mostly the uninsured as well as those who are eligible for Medicaid. Funding for these centers fell by a third during the 1980s. "The Medicaid card does not have a lot of meaning at a time like this, when there is a shortage of health-care providers in many areas," says Laura Summer, a health policy analyst at the Center on Budget & Policy Priorities in Washington.

Part of the problem, Summer says, stems from cuts in funding for the National Health Service Corps. This federal program covers the cost of medical training for medical students, who then repay the government by serving in community facilities in underserved areas. Because of a 64 percent cut in the corps' budget from 1981 to 1991, Summer says, "the program is really only a shadow of its former self," producing far fewer doctors than it did in the past.

WIC, which distributes food to low-income pregnant women and in-

fants, is widely recognized as one of the most effective federal programs in reducing infant mortality. According to the Agriculture Department, which administers the program, every federal dollar spent on WIC saves as much as $3 in medical care by helping prevent low birthweight and other problems that require infants to be hospitalized. Although funding for WIC increased steadily during the 1980s, it never was enough to meet the need and by the end of the decade served only about half of the eligible population.[22]

Increasing Need for Services

At the same time that federal and state funding of health and welfare programs fell, poverty spread, increasing the demand for these services. The recession of 1981-82 and severe cutbacks in many sectors of the economy during the 1980s left many workers jobless and prompted employers to cut back on health benefits for those workers who remained employed. According to the

Children's Defense Fund, 18 percent of all U.S. children, or 1.2 million children, lived in poverty in 1989, up from 16 percent a decade earlier.

Alarmed by the persistent infant mortality rate, Congress began in the mid-1980s to require the states to provide Medicaid coverage for those who were then ineligible for AFDC, regardless of whether the family breadwinner was employed.

Under the Omnibus Budget Reconciliation Act of 1989, states were required to offer coverage to pregnant women whose family income fell below 133 percent of the poverty line, or $18,500 for a family of four. In 1991, Medicaid coverage was extended further to include the first 60 days after delivery for eligible mothers and the first year of life for their infants.

Technology's Role

Although funding for health services for low-income pregnant women and infants is declining at a time when demand for these services is growing, the infant mortality rate is holding steady. The reason, analysts say, is the improvement in caring for low-birthweight babies, who now make up 7 percent of all newborns. Even very-low-birthweight babies, those under 3.5 pounds, often can be saved in hospitals equipped with the latest technology.

One such facility is Long Beach Memorial Medical Center in California. Its neonatal intensive-care unit treats more than 5,000 babies each year. Most of them are underweight and 10 percent of them are born drug-addicted. Babies who survive the first two weeks are likely to be released from the hospital. Although most survive that long, many have lingering respiratory, cardiac and other problems and don't reach their first birthday.

The costs of saving such children are immense. Nationwide, some $2.5 bil-

lion — more than half of the total cost associated with newborns — is spent each year to save premature babies. That's more than $21,000 for each low-birthweight infant, compared with an average $2,842 in hospital costs for a normal delivery and about $500 to give prenatal care to a pregnant woman.[23]

"It makes much more sense to save 300 babies for the same cost of

CURRENT SITUATION

State Initiatives

The drop in federal funding for preventive programs benefiting pregnant women and infants has led many states to offer additional services on their own. In 1991 alone, says Martha King of the National Conference of State Legislatures' Maternal and Health Project, 350 new initiatives were introduced. "There are a variety of ways the states are approaching the problem," she says. "The most common way, which is the path of least resistance, is to expand Medicaid eligibility."

The 1989 budget reconciliation act required states to offer Medicaid coverage to pregnant women and young children with family incomes that are 133 percent of the poverty level. The law also allowed states to cover individuals with incomes 185 percent of the poverty level. Twenty-four states now offer the higher benefits. (See map, p. 653.) "Mississippi — one of the poorest states in the country — was among the first to provide the maximum coverage for pregnant women and should be commended," King says.

Other states offer a wide variety of services:

what it takes to put very fancy technology in use for one child," says Rae Grad of the National Commission to Prevent Infant Mortality. "It's not that the child isn't valuable — it certainly is, and if it were my baby I'd want that life-saving equipment. But we have limited resources, and prevention is a much more effective way to prevent infants from dying." ■

• In California, the Healthy Black Babies program serves more than 3,000 pregnant women in black communities. The program is aimed at communities like Los Angeles, where the black infant mortality rate is 20.2 deaths per 1,000 births, more than twice the national average.

• South Carolina offers its large population of low-income pregnant women an economic incentive to seek care by giving them discount coupons for goods and services every time they go to the doctor for prenatal care. This and other incentives for prenatal care helped reduce South Carolina's infant mortality rate by 18 percent during the 1980s.

• Washington state has a comprehensive program to aid low-income women and their infants. Known as "First Steps," the program was providing services to one in three babies born in the state in 1990, its first year.

To avoid delays in qualifying, the program streamlined the application process. The program also offers prenatal services for illegal aliens who are not eligible for Medicaid. To encourage doctors to accept new Medicaid patients, the program increased Medicaid reimbursements for services rendered to First Step clients. To remove other obstacles to timely prenatal care, the program provides child care and transportation to and from the doctor's office. Finally, First Step offers treatment for alcohol and other substance abuse for pregnant women who are chemically dependent.

A Little "Baby Love" Goes a Long Way in North Carolina

Southern states have long had some of the highest infant mortality rates in the nation. Poverty, especially among the region's large black population, is a major factor, along with the lack of health-care providers in many rural counties.

In 1984, the Southern Governors' Association and the Southern Legislative Conference launched a campaign to change things by improving prenatal care for low-income women. By 1989, the resulting Southern Regional Project on Infant Mortality had helped reduce infant mortality from 12.8 deaths per 1,000 births to 11.5 deaths per 1,000 over the five-year period, a 10 percent improvement.

One of the most successful state initiatives prompted by the effort is North Carolina's Baby Love program. Launched in 1987, it was the first program in the region to utilize coordination of care, or case management. Every participant is assigned to a nurse or social worker who helps her gain access to a variety of prenatal and postnatal services, including health screening, child care, family counseling, Medicaid, the Special Supplemental Food Program for Women, Infants and Children (WIC) and instruction in nutrition and parenting. After a client gives birth, the case manager helps her obtain family-planning services and pediatric care.

Baby Love caught on quickly and is now operating in all 100 of North Carolina's counties, which are free to tailor local programs to meet their residents' needs.

One of the program's greatest benefits, says Marcia Roth, special assistant for planning and program development at North Carolina's Division of Maternal and Child Health, is making it easier for pregnant women to gain access to services offered by many different health and welfare agencies. "Maternity care coordination looks at a broad range of needs of pregnant women, not just WIC but also housing, transportation, child care, even help in getting the electricity turned on," she says.

Part of Baby Love's success can be attributed to North Carolina's efforts to enable more women in the state to qualify for health-care coverage under Medicaid. Essentially, the state dropped the assets test for Medicaid eligibility, which often excluded poor women whose families owned land, and discounted parental income in determining eligibility for pregnant teens.

By 1991, half the women in the state who were enrolled in Medicaid also participated in Baby Love, a total of almost 19,000 women. Even more women are expected to benefit from a recent expansion of the program to include women who do not qualify for Medicaid, including illegal aliens, prison inmates and some women whose income exceeds the current cap of 185 percent of the official poverty level.

In recent months, Baby Love has hired 50 outreach workers to seek out pregnant women who may not know of the prenatal services to which they are entitled. "We recruit these women from the lay community to offer more intensive services to women who need home-visiting and extra support," Roth says. The outreach workers function in "much the same way as resource mothers in South Carolina and some other states."

Baby Love has proved cost-effective, an important factor given state and local funding problems. In its first two years, the program saved Medicaid more than $2 million, or $2.10 for every dollar spent to run the program in North Carolina.

Above all, the program is meeting its goal of reducing infant mortality. "In 1988, North Carolina had the highest infant mortality in the country — 12.6 deaths per thousand," Roth says. "At that point, some legislators were saying Baby Love, which was only in its second year, was a failure. But in 1989 the rate went down to 11.5 and in 1990, the most recent year for which we have data, it was down to 10.6 per 1,000."

Among North Carolina women covered by Medicaid, those who did not receive Baby Love's services had a 21 percent higher rate of low-birthweight babies, a 62 percent higher rate of very-low-birthweight babies and a 23 percent higher infant mortality rate than women who participated in Baby Love.†

"We've cited Baby Love often as a good example of how states can overcome some of the problems associated with infant mortality," says Madalene Milano, communications director of the National Commission to Prevent Infant Mortality. "They have made a wholehearted effort to fix these problems, including fragmented health and social services."

---

† Low-birthweight babies are those who weigh less than 5.5 pounds at birth. Very-low-birthweight babies weigh less than 3.5 pounds at birth. Statistics from Southern Regional Project on Infant Mortality, *Building Blocks: Infant Mortality Prevention Strategies*, April 1992.

Many other states have begun offering similar services, though few programs are as comprehensive as Washington's. Southern states, with some of the highest infant mortality rates in the nation, are adopting home-visiting services to help their low-income and largely rural populations. (*See story about North Carolina's program, above.*)

Virginia's Resource Mothers program, started in 1985, recruits and trains women to seek out pregnant women in their communities who may have difficulty obtaining prena-

Prenatal Care Services Offered by States

A drop in federal funding for programs benefiting pregnant women and infants in the 1980s led many states to offer enhanced services on their own. Services include nutritional and psychological counseling and home visits.

	Care coordination/case management	Risk assessment	Nutritional counseling	Health education	Psychosocial counseling	Home visiting	Transport
Alabama	X	X				X	
Alaska	X	X	X			X	
Arizona							
Arkansas	X	X	X	X	X	X	
California	X	X	X	X	X	X†	
Colorado							
Connecticut		X		X		X	
Delaware	X	X	X	X	X	X	
District of Columbia							
Florida							
Georgia	X	X		X†		X†	
Hawaii	X	X	X	X			
Idaho	X	X	X		X	X	
Illinois	X	X					
Indiana							
Iowa	X	X	X	X	X		
Kansas		X	X	X		X	
Kentucky							
Louisiana	X	X					
Maine							
Maryland	X	X	X	X	X	X	
Massachusetts	X	X	X	X	X		
Michigan	X	X	X	X	X	X	X
Minnesota	X	X	X	X	X	X	
Mississippi	X	X	X	X	X	X	X
Missouri	X	X					
Montana							
Nebraska							
Nevada	X	X	X	X	X	X	
New Hampshire	X	X	X	X	X	X	
New Jersey	X	X	X	X	X	X	
New Mexico	X						
New York	X	X	X	X	X	X	
North Carolina	X	X		X		X	
North Dakota							
Ohio	X	X	X	X	X	X	
Oklahoma							
Oregon	X	X	X	X		X	
Pennsylvania	X	X	X	X	X	X	
Rhode Island							
South Carolina	X	X	X	X	X	X	
South Dakota							
Tennessee	X	X				X	
Texas							
Utah	X	X	X	X	X	X	
Vermont	X					X	X
Virginia	X	X	X	X		X	
Washington	X	X	X	X	X	X	X
West Virginia	X	X	X	X			
Wisconsin							
Wyoming							

† *Future implementation date.*
Source: Joshua M. Wiener and Jeannie Engel, Improving Access to Health Services for Children and Pregnant Women, *The Brookings Institution, 1991*

tal care. Margaret Konefal, director of the Norfolk-based program, is pleased with the results. "We see pregnant women gaining weight appropriately, healthy babies being born, teenagers staying in school, their babies getting well-child checkups, subsequent pregnancies being delayed and more confidence developing among the new parents and grandparents," she said.[24] Since the program began, the low-birthweight rate for teens who were home-visited has dropped to 6 percent — lower than the national rate of 9.4 percent for teens and even below Virginia's 9.6 percent rate.

Healthy Start Project

The Bush administration has set a goal of reducing infant mortality by 31 percent, to no more than 7 deaths per 1,000 births, by the year 2000.[25] Since President Bush took office in 1989, federal spending for primary-care services, including the National Health Service Corps, Community and Migrant Health Centers and the Maternal and Child Health Block Grant, has increased by 51 percent, totaling $6.3 billion in fiscal 1992. Bush's budget request for fiscal 1992 would raise spending for primary care services to $7.6 billion.

Bush also appointed a task force to study the causes of the country's high infant mortality rate and recommend solutions to the problem. In the fall of 1990, the task force presented a list of 18 recommendations costing a total of $500 million each year, including broader eligibility for Medicaid.

Reluctant to support such a big increase in federal spending, however, the White House shelved the report.[26] "The Bush administration never liked the task force recommendations for Medicaid expansion,"

Continued on p. 658

At Issue:

Is parents' behavior to blame for the nation's high rate of infant mortality?

NICHOLAS EBERSTADT

Researcher, Harvard University's Center for Population and Development Studies, and Visiting Scholar; the American Enterprise Institute.
FROM *THE WALL STREET JOURNAL*, JAN. 20, 1992.

Why does America produce so many low-birth-weight babies? The answer may have much to do with the behavior of parents-to-be. Evidence suggests that the attitudes, practices and life styles of many American parents — including many who are neither poor nor poorly educated — are exposing U.S. babies to unfamiliar and unnecessary hazards....

CDC [Centers for Disease Control] data show that one of the maternal characteristics most strongly associated with low birthweight is out-of-wedlock childbearing. And regardless of a mother's race or age, infant mortality is higher for out-of-wedlock births. (CDC data tend to ignore the important role fathers play in infants' well-being.)...

Unwed mothers, of course, are not the only parents to engage in practices prejudicial to infant health, nor are nicotine and "tar" the only hazardous substances to which a fetus can be exposed. Illegal drug use during pregnancy can hurt a fetus, although data on the prevalence of such practices are hard to come by....

Such behavior by mothers-to-be is all too characteristic of the infant mortality problem in modern America. And unfortunately, the traditional tools of social policy are not easily applied against dangerous parental behavior. Despite ever-greater schooling for the population at large, the proportion of babies receiving no prenatal care, or care delayed until the last trimester of pregnancy, is slightly higher today than it was in the mid-1970s. Education can be highly effective when lack of knowledge is a constraint; it fares less well when the problem is a lack of motivation.

Key elements in the social policy and public health communities appear determined not to confront the problem — or even to acknowledge its existence....

Medical advances and increased health expenditures promise the continuation of progress against U.S. infant mortality. Unless the problem of hazardous parental behavior is controlled, however, the infant mortality rate is likely to remain needlessly high. It may well be that our government and legal systems, which prize liberty, are not particularly suited to enforce model behavior upon negligent parents-to-be. But it is not too much to ask our leaders and health specialists to speak plainly about what it is that really ails our nation's babies.

JENNIFER L. HOWSE

President, March of Dimes Birth Defects Foundation
FROM *THE WALL STREET JOURNAL*, FEB. 27, 1992.

No one would deny parents play a significant role in the health and well-being of their child, both before and after birth. But Mr. Eberstadt's accusation that our country's high rate of infant death is due to the misbehavior of parents is as far-fetched an answer as any ancient superstition. It is also misleading and unfair.

Mr. Eberstadt is perhaps unaware that every day in America women who did everything "right" during pregnancy — that is, they got good prenatal care, they were married to the father of the child, they neither smoked nor drank nor abused drugs — nevertheless give birth to babies with birth defects or low birthweight....

Mr. Eberstadt is correct that perinatal survival rates in the U.S. appear to be the best in the world. But his conclusion about the meaning of this statistic is wrong: It provides a measure of access to high-tech care for the sickest infants, not an accurate picture of access to preventive prenatal services.

Adequate prenatal care is not available, affordable or accessible to every pregnant woman who needs it. Eight million women of childbearing age have no health insurance; most live in low-income working families who cannot afford a physician's fee. Pregnant women covered by Medicaid do not fare much better; in many areas of the U.S., private physicians do not accept Medicaid patients. At some clinics, pregnant women wait months for an appointment. Mr. Eberstadt also ignores the fact that drug-treatment programs and drinking- and smoking-cessation programs are not generally available to pregnant women who need them.

Mr. Eberstadt gives the false impression that research, education and prenatal care cannot help reduce the incidence of infant mortality in America. The March of Dimes, on the other hand, has great hopes for the success of these approaches. It is our experience that most parents want their babies to be born healthy....

We urge Mr. Eberstadt to stop blaming victims of infant mortality and spend more time looking for workable solutions to the problem. Across the nation, communities are working to reduce infant mortality, whether through President Bush's "Healthy Start" initiative, community health centers or infant-mortality study committees. More federal funding, combined with local initiatives, may turn the tide. Nothing less than our country's economic future and moral conscience are at stake.

July 31, 1992   657

Continued from p. 656
says the CDF's Liu. "Its stance is a strong portrayal of how poorly the United States compares with other industrial nations in preventing infant mortality and providing basic care for pregnant women and infants."

One of the task force's recommendations, however, was singled out by the White House as the centerpiece of the administration's efforts to reduce infant mortality. Unveiled in 1991, the "Healthy Start" project will provide funding to 15 communities to help them cut their infant mortality rate by half over five years.* Although the targeted communities are still completing plans to implement Healthy Start later this year, most of the initiatives the administration proposes for the program mirror efforts that many states are already undertaking on their own.

Criticism of the Program

Healthy Start came under fire last year because the administration initially sought to pay for the program with funds from the Title V Maternity and Child Health Block Grants and the Migrant Health Center program. Rejecting that funding plan, Congress appropriated less than half of Bush's request for Healthy Start in fiscal 1991 and 1992. The president has requested $143 million for fiscal 1993, which begins Oct. 1, but few observers expect Congress to appropriate the full amount.

The main criticism of Bush's initiative is that, by targeting only a few communities, it provides too little assistance to make a dent in infant mortality. "It is a very reasonable approach to have community-based initiatives to foster cooperation among

all the health and social service agencies that pregnant women need," says Laura Summer of the Center on Budget & Policy Priorities. "It would be a terrific approach for all communities, yet many will see their health and social services deteriorate over the next few years.... What is needed is not so much new strategies as new funding for the programs we know work." Those, most health experts agree, include WIC, Medicaid, the Community and Migrant Health Centers and the National Health Service Corps.

Even those who welcome Healthy Start say more is needed. Like many experts in the field of infant health, March of Dimes President Howse says universal access to quality prenatal care should be the first priority of government action. "That means all pregnant women should receive core services, including prenatal visits, coverage of labor and delivery costs and pediatric care for infants through the first year of life," she says.

Congress Tackles the Issue

Several proposals to improve access to prenatal care are now before

Congress. They include a "one-stop-shopping" bill recently introduced by Sen. Bill Bradley, D-N.J., which would eliminate some of the barriers to prenatal care. Under this approach, already offered in many states, low-income women would gain access to a panoply of welfare and health services from a single source, instead of having to apply at numerous different agencies offering prenatal care.

Another proposal, the Healthy Beginnings Act, introduced last year by Rep. Joseph P. Kennedy II, D-Mass., embraces home visiting, which has helped reduce infant mortality in several states, as well as in Japan and other countries with low infant mortality rates.

Several other pending measures would expand required Medicaid coverage of pregnant women and children to include families with family incomes of up to 185 percent of the federal poverty level. Current law sets the required cutoff at 133 percent of poverty. Other measures would expand the services offered under Medicaid. A bill introduced by Rep. Charles B. Rangel, D-N.Y., for example, would permit states to cover substance-abuse treatment. ■

---

*The 15 communities are: Northern Plains Reservations (S.D., N.D., Iowa, Neb.); Baltimore; Birmingham, Ala.; Boston; Chicago; Cleveland; Detroit; Lake County (Gary), Ind.; New Orleans; New York; Oakland, Calif.; Philadelphia; Pittsburgh; Pee Dee Region, S.C. and Washington, D.C.

OUTLOOK

Universal Access

The broader goal of universal access to health care for the entire population, including pregnant women and infants, is the main focus of several major health reform measures now before Congress. Lawmakers of both parties remain divided over the best way to achieve that goal.

President Bush's "Comprehensive Health Reform Program," issued Feb. 6, would retain the present system of private health insurers, expanding

coverage by offering tax credits and deductions to uninsured Americans to help them purchase coverage. Other Republican-backed measures differ from the administration proposal. A House bill introduced June 4 by Minority Leader Robert H. Michel, R-Ill., would make insurance more affordable to employees of small businesses but lacks the tax-based provisions contained in the administration's bill.

Democratic lawmakers also are divided on health-care reform. Some, such as Reps. Marty Russo, D-Ill., and Jim Moody, D-Wis., would replace the current system with a national health insurance plan similar to those of other industrialized nations. Other Democrats support a more gradual reform, such as a "play-or-pay" approach embodied in last year's proposal (S 1227) by Senate Majority Leader George J. Mitchell, D-Maine. This approach would require businesses to either offer health insurance benefits to their workers or contribute to a public fund that would provide benefits.

The Democratic Party's platform commits to neither approach, insisting only that major health-care reform be among the top priorities of Gov. Bill Clinton of Arkansas if the newly chosen Democratic candidate emerges victorious from the November presidential election.

No one is predicting that Congress will pass major legislation affecting maternal and infant health in this election year. Even after the election, a major push to improve the country's infant mortality rate will require a fundamental shift in health-care priorities. After all, says Rae Grad of the National Commission to Prevent Infant Mortality, Medicare already provides universal access to health care for the elderly. But unlike elderly Americans, who have considerable political clout, she says, children have no political voice.

"It really boils down to what people care about," Grad says. "Everyone gives you the right line by expressing concern about infant mortality, so we are fighting a battle without an enemy." For there to be a significant fall in infant mortality in the United States, she says, "People have to understand in their heart of hearts that children, honest to God, are important to the future of this country." ■

Notes

[1] The Hay Group, *Benefits Report,* 1991.

[2] See "Blueprints for National Health Insurance," *The Washington Post,* Dec. 4, 1990.

[3] Health Resources and Services Administration, Department of Health and Human Services, *Healthy Start,* May 1992.

[4] Paula Braverman *et al.,* "Average Outcomes of Lack of Health Insurance Among Newborns in an Eight County Area of California, 1982-1986," *The New England Journal of Medicine,* Aug. 24, 1989.

[5] See "Why We Should Invest in Human Capital," *Business Week,* Dec. 17, 1990.

[6] Data from UNICEF, *State of the World's Children 1992,* and National Center for Health Statistics, cited by Children's Defense Fund, *Analysis of Final 1989 U.S. Birth Statistics,* Dec. 18, 1991.

[7] See Robert A. Hahn, Joseph Mulinare and Steven M. Teutsch, "Inconsistencies in Coding of Race and Ethnicity Between Birth and Death in U.S. Infants: A New Look at Infant Mortality, 1983 through 1985," *The Journal of the American Medical Association,* Jan. 8, 1992.

[8] See José E. Becerra *et al.,* "Infant Mortality among Hispanics: A Portrait of Heterogeneity," *The Journal of the American Medical Association,* Jan. 9, 1991.

[9] See Agency for Health Care Policy and Research, Department of Health and Human Services, "Minorities: Health Insurance Coverage," *National Medical Expenditure Survey,* April 1992.

[10] Kenneth C. Schoendorf *et al.,* "Mortality Among Infants of Black as Compared with White College-Educated Parents," *The New England Journal of Medicine,* June 4, 1992.

[11] National Commission to Prevent Infant Mortality, *One-Stop Shopping: The Road to Healthy Mothers and Children,* April 1991, p. 8.

[12] March of Dimes Birth Defects Foundation, *Infant Survival in Rural America,* August 1991.

[13] See Samuel H. Preston and Michael R. Haines, *Fatal Years: Child Mortality in Late Nineteenth-Century America* (1991).

[14] See "Praise Is High, Funds Are Low for Welfare that Works," *Congressional Quarterly Weekly Report,* June 27, 1992.

[15] Health Resources and Services Administration, *op. cit.*

[16] National Commission to Prevent Infant Mortality, *Troubling Trends Persist: Shortchanging America's Next Generation,* March 1992.

[17] See Celia W. Dugger, "Cocaine Use and Infant Mortality Decline Together in New York City," *The New York Times,* April 20, 1991.

[18] National Commission to Prevent Infant Mortality, *Troubling Trends Persist, op. cit.*

[19] *Ibid.*

[20] See Polly E. Bijur *et al.,* "Parental Alcohol Use, Problem Drinking and Children's Injuries," *The Journal of the American Medical Association,* June 17, 1992.

[21] See Joshua M. Wiener and Jeannie Engel, *Improving Access to Health Services for Children and Pregnant Women* (1991).

[22] See Democratic Policy Committee, *From Cradle to Grave: Too Often a Short Distance for American Children,* Nov. 15, 1990.

[23] National Commission to Prevent Infant Mortality, *Troubling Trends Persist, op. cit.*

[24] Quoted in National Commission to Prevent Infant Mortality, *Home Visiting: Opening Doors for America's Pregnant Women and Children,* July 1989.

[25] Department of Health and Human Services, *Healthy People,* National Health Promotion and Disease Prevention Objectives, September 1990.

[26] See Robert Pear, "Study Says U.S. Needs to Battle Infant Mortality," *The New York Times,* Aug. 6, 1990.

Bibliography

Selected Sources Used

Books

Wiener, Joshua M. and Jeannie Engel, *Improving Access to Health Services for Children and Pregnant Women*, The Brookings Institution, 1991.

Improving health-care insurance in the United States is essential to reducing the country's high infant mortality rate, the authors write. Wiener and Engel also call for improvements in the health-care delivery system.

Articles

Guntheroth, Warren G., and Philip S. Spiers, "Sleeping Prone and the Risk of Sudden Infant Death Syndrome," *Journal of the American Medical Association*, May 6, 1992, pp. 2359-2362.

All studies in this review of the literature showed an increased risk of SIDS when infants are placed face down in their cribs. The authors advise physicians to recommend that parents avoid the prone position for infants during the first six months.

Schoendorf, Kenneth C., Carol J.R. Hogue, Joel C. Kleinman and Diane Rowley, "Mortality among Infants of Black as Compared with White College-Educated Parents," *The New England Journal of Medicine*, June 4, 1992, pp. 1522-1526.

Even in families where both parents graduated from college, and presumably have higher incomes and better access to health care than the population at large, infant mortality is twice as high among blacks as whites. The discrepancy is traced to the higher incidence of low birthweight among black infants, even those of college-educated parents.

Reports and Studies

Children's Defense Fund, *The Health of America's Children*, 1991.

Extensive tables illustrate the lack of appreciable improvement in maternal and infant health in the United States over the past decade. Little progress can be expected, the report concludes, until all Americans obtain health insurance and access to basic health services, including prenatal and pediatric care.

CIGNA Corp., *Infant Health in America: Everybody's Business*, 1992.

Although infant mortality is most prevalent among the poor, this study shows that infants of working mothers who are covered by health insurance plans are not immune. It also found that the nation's employers and workers spent about $5.6 billion in health care for treating babies who were born with defects or low birthweight, conditions that cause infant mortality.

General Accounting Office, *Early Intervention: Federal Investments Like WIC Can Produce Savings*, April 1992.

Since its creation in 1972, the Special Supplemental Food Program for Women, Infants and Children — better known as WIC — has helped pregnant women and mothers feed themselves and their infants healthy foods. Funding for this federal program is currently $2.6 billion. The General Accounting Office found that prenatal WIC benefits reduced the rate of low-birthweight births by 25 percent and very-low-birthweight births by 44 percent. It also concluded that every federal dollar invested in WIC benefits saves nearly $3 in health-care expenses in the infant's first year of life.

March of Dimes Birth Defects Foundation, *Birth Defects and Infant Mortality*, December 1991.

As advances in medical technology have helped save premature infants and others born with low birthweight, infections and other causes, birth defects have emerged as the leading cause of death among infants.

National Commission to Prevent Infant Mortality, *Troubling Trends Persist: Shortchanging America's Next Generation*, March 1992.

Since Congress established the commission in 1987, it has published several reports calling attention to infant mortality. In this report, the commission, chaired by Gov. Lawton Chiles, D-Fla., points out that many other countries do a better job of protecting their infants than the United States while spending far less money on health care. Preventive care, the commission concludes, would go far in improving the U.S. infant mortality rate.

White House Task Force on Infant Mortality in the United States, *Infant Mortality in the United States*, Nov. 30, 1989.

This official report of a task force created by the Bush administration to recommend steps to reduce the infant death rate lists 18 measures, costing about $500 million a year. The administration has instead launched a less costly demonstration project called Healthy Start, which will provide enhanced services to pregnant women and infants in 15 communities where the infant mortality rate is exceptionally high.

The Next Step

Additional Articles from Current Periodicals from EBSCO Publishing's Database

Addresses & essays

Hein, H.A., "Do we have the infant mortality rate we desire?" *Journal of the American Medical Association,* **July 3, 1991, p. 114.**

Presents a commentary decrying the high infant mortality rate in the United States. Offers suggestions to remedy the problem by a nationwide educational approach coupled with programs to meet human needs.

Novello, A.C., C. Degraw, et al., "Healthy children ready to learn: An essential collaboration between health and education," *Public Health Reports,* **January/February 1992, p. 3.**

Details the "Healthy Children Ready to Learn" initiative. Attention to the availability of prenatal care, infant mortality, inadequate nutrition during pregnancy and childhood; first steps toward successful achievement of the readiness goal; critical role of parents in shaping a healthy environment conducive to school readiness; Healthy People 2000; racial differences in infant mortality rates; more.

Case studies

"Physician program cut infant death rate by 45 percent," *American Journal of Public Health,* **November 1991, p. 1428.**

Details how physicians serving poor Miami neighborhoods under a controversial national program, the National Health Service Corps, cut the infant death rate by 45 percent, according to a study in the September issue of "Obstetrics and Gynecology."

Klitsch, M., "Postponing infant mortality," *Family Planning Perspectives,* **September/October 1991, p. 197.**

Reports that rates of infant mortality declined by 18 percent in Tennessee during the 1980s, with the most impressive improvements among very low-birthweight infants during the neonatal period. Research in Tennessee; details of the study; conclusions.

Monmaney, T., "Saving babies," *American Health,* **July/August 1991, p. 23.**

Profiles Rae K. Grad, executive director of the National Commission to Prevent Infant Mortality. Grad's efforts to make prenatal care more available to the poor; frustration with Congress and the Bush administration.

Piper, J.M., "Preventing and postponing death: Trends in Tennessee infant mortality," *American Journal of Public Health,* **August 1991, p. 1046.**

Determines whether reductions in Tennessee infant mortality have been achieved during the 1980s and quantifies any evidence of a postponement effect by reviewing vital records data for 1979 through 1988. Methods; results; discussion.

Debates & issues

Cowley, G., L. Wilson, et al., "Children in peril," *Newsweek,* **summer 1991, p. 18.**

Reports that American children remain the most neglected in the developed world, revealing that despite medical advances, astonishing numbers die or suffer needlessly. Statistics on infant mortality; substance abuse; contagion; lead poisoning; injuries; poverty.

Eberstadt, N., "America's infant-mortality puzzle," *Public Interest,* **fall 1991, p. 30.**

Discusses how during the 1980s, America's infant mortality rate became a focus of increased attention, commentary, and public concern, and how America still has an unusually high rate in comparison with other countries. Historical perspectives; reliability of data; poverty and medical care; biological and behavioral factors; illegitimacy; parental practices and infant health; local-level data; the limits of policy intervention.

Korte, D., "Infant mortality: Lessons from Japan," *Mothering,* **winter 1992, p. 82.**

Reports that Japan has the lowest infant mortality rate in the world and that per capita, Japan spends half as much money on health care as does the United States. The picture behind the numbers; access to prenatal care; infant mortality rates; prematurity and low birthweight; social support; breastfeeding; maternal health records; medical intervention; Cesarean rates; midwifery; marital and age factors; what can be learned from the Japanese picture.

Mason, J.O., "Reducing infant mortality in the United States through 'Healthy Start,'" *Public Health Reports,* **September/October 1991, p. 479.**

Asserts that the United States comes off poorly when compared with international standards of annual reductions in infant mortality. Goals set forth in "Healthy People 2000"; infant mortality, 1983-85; the Mexican-American difference; early prenatal care; health insurance coverage; need to improve access to and quality of prenatal care; reducing prenatal substance abuse; narrowing minority health disparities; more.

Mosley, W. H. and P. Cowley, "The challenge of world health," *Population Bulletin,* **December 1991, p. 2.**

Discusses the gross discrepancies in life expectancy that exist worldwide, and states that reducing these discrepancies is the challenge of the 1990s. Indicators of health status; more. INSETS: Sources and limitations of mortality data; low-birthweight babies; combating malaria; tobacco: a global health problem; sexually transmitted diseases, HIV infection and AIDS; "diseases of affluence" and the poor.

Skolnick, A. A., "North Carolina's maternal health campaign ignores smoking, maternal health advocates fume," *Journal of the American Medical Association,* **Dec. 25, 1991, p. 3399.**

Highlights the outrage expressed by many maternal and child health advocates over educational materials put out by North Carolina's campaign to reduce infant mortality. The brochures and posters neglect to warn against the hazards of smoking, even though they mention alcohol, illicit drugs, and other dangers to a healthy pregnancy.

Stehlin, D., "Infant apnea monitors help parents breathe easy," *FDA Consumer,* **June 1991, p. 16.**

Discusses how home monitors are helping parents detect if their infants are not breathing properly. Apparent life-threatening events; apnea monitors; government standards; false alarms; memory monitors; life with a monitor. INSET: Does apnea cause Sudden Infant Death Syndrome?

Government programs

"For women and infants in 15 U.S. communities — a 'Healthy Start,'" *Public Health Reports,* **November/December 1991, p. 737.**

Focuses on a new effort by the federal government to reduce infant mortality in the U.S. by 50 percent in five years. The government has selected 15 communities to receive special funds for prenatal and postnatal care for impoverished women and children. "Healthy Start"; focus of the activities of the successful applicants.

"Neighborhood women serve as maternal-child health advocates in Chicago," *Public Health Reports,* **September/October 1991, p. 595.**

Details the Resources, Education and Care in the Home (REACH)-Futures, a program designed to reduce infant mortality by promoting primary health care of mothers and infants, parenting skills, and knowledgeable use of resources. Why REACH-Futures is unique; coordination of the program by the University of Illinois Hospital and Clinics in collabo-

ration with the Chicago Department of Health and West Side Future; more.

Health aspects

Kleiner, E. "Midwifery: A resource for low-income communities," *Mothering,* **winter 1992, p. 24.**

Reports that midwifery is emerging as a practical and effective solution to the soaring infant mortality rate reported in depressed neighborhoods. Midwife-staffed birthing centers for low-income women; the needs for these birthing centers; midwife as a companion and guide.

Minorities

"Minority infant mortality much higher than reported," *Jet,* **Jan. 27, 1992, p. 28.**

Reports that infant mortality among blacks and some other minorities is much higher than records indicate, according to the Centers of Disease Control. Results of study; role of racial classifications.

Hahn, R. A., J. Mulinare, et al., "Inconsistencies in coding of race and ethnicity between birth and death in U.S. infants," *Journal of the American Medical Association,* **Jan. 8, 1992, p. 259.**

Examines the consistency of the racial and ethnic classification of U.S. infants between birth and death and its impact on infant mortality rates. "Healthy People 2000," and the goal of reducing disparities in health among different segments of the population including racial and ethnic groups; remarkable inconsistencies in the coding of race and ethnicity of infants at birth and death; more.

Nakamura, R. M., R. King, et al., "Excess infant mortality in an American Indian population, 1940 to 1990," *Journal of the American Medical Association,* **Oct. 23, 1991, p. 2244.**

Describes the infant mortality experience of an American Indian community and demonstrates the utility of examining community-level mortality data. Describes a population-based historical review of infant death certificates at the Warm Springs Indian Reservation, Ore.

Polednak, A. P., "Black-white differences in infant mortality in 38 standard metropolitan statistical areas," *American Journal of Public Health,* **November 1991, p. 1480.**

Considers how the United States black-white difference in the infant mortality rate continues to persist. Presents results of a study that examines the black-white difference in infant mortality rate in 38 large standard metropolitan statistical areas in relation to socioeconomic status indicators and an index of residential segregation.

Prevention

Cohen, D.L., "Home visits help combat a host of childhood problems," *Education Digest,* **January 1992, p. 57.**

Reveals in a condensed reprint from *Education Week* that policy analysts from varied sectors are convinced that the lack of basic child-rearing knowledge is leading to increased infant mortality, child abuse, and school dropout rates. Their advancing of a strategy that rests on neighbor helping neighbor; home visits; the value of a skilled home visitor; breaking the cycle; individual concern.

Kleiner, E., "Businesses offer prenatal education," *Mothering,* **winter 1992, p. 26.**

Reports that each year the 40,000 infant deaths and 11,000 low-birthweight babies are costing businesses millions of dollars in health insurance. In order to help this, several businesses have begun providing prenatal care programs for their employees. Hope for healthier mothers and babies; examples of participating businesses; for more information.

Research

"Infant mortality — United States, 1988," *Journal of the American Medical Association,* **Oct. 9, 1991, p. 1912.**

Summarizes final 1988 infant mortality data in the United States, based on information from death certificates compiled by the Centers for Disease Control's (CDC) National Center for Health Statistics' Vital Statistics System. Compares findings with those for 1987; editorial note from the CDC.

"Infant mortality — United States, 1989," *Journal of the American Medical Association,* **March 4, 1992, p. 1182.**

Summarizes 1989 infant mortality data based on information from death certificates compiled through the Vital Statistics System of the Centers for Disease Control's (CDC) National Center for Health Statistics and compares findings with those for 1988. Overall postneonatal mortality rate for 1989; impact of short gestation and low birthweight; differences in infant mortality between black and white infants; editorial note from the CDC; current efforts to reduce infant mortality.

Dusitsin, N., S. Chompootaweep, et al., "Development and validation of a simple device to estimate birthweight," *American Journal of Public Health,* **September 1991, p. 1201.**

Reports that low birthweight is the major factor associated with the death of infants within the first four weeks of life. Details how a circular nomographic chart which was developed so that birthweight could be computed from a

newborn baby's chest and mid-arm circumferences is being used in Thailand's rural areas.

Ezzell, C., "Routine screen hints at fetal death risk," *Science News,* **July 6, 1991, p. 5.**

Discusses the results of a retrospective study comparing second-trimester alpha-fetoprotein levels of pregnant women whose babies died late in the pregnancy with those who successfully carried their babies to term. Test for babies with neural-tube defects; statistics on alpha-fetoprotein levels and fetal deaths.

Small, M. F. and M. Hellweg, "A reasonable sleep," *Discover,* **April 1992, p. 82.**

Examines the research of anthropologist James McKenna, who claims that co-sleeping, or having babies sleep in a bed with their parents, is developmentally beneficial and could also have an influence on the rate of sudden infant death syndrome (SIDS). How idea of independent sleep for babies developed in Western culture; how McKenna became interested in subject; details of sleep experiments. INSET: Medical research on SIDS, by L. Oliwenstein.

Sudden Infant Death Syndrome

"SIDS and seals," *Discover,* **February 1992, p. 7.**

Looks at the possible connection between Sudden Infant Death Syndrome (SIDS) and northern elephant seals, according to marine biologist Michael Castellini of the University of Alaska. How seals hold their breath during sleep; irregular heartbeats of young sleeping seal pups; possible problems of human infants in controlling heartbeat and respiration.

McKenna, J.J., "SIDS research," *Mothering,* **winter 1992, p. 44.**

Discusses Sudden Infant Death Syndrome (SIDS) and urges scientists to consider whether the cultural pattern of solitary infant sleep has had harmful psychological or emotional effects on infants. Impact on parents; epidemiology of SIDS; definition of SIDS; statistics; possible causes of SIDS; cross-cultural epidemiology of SIDS; co-family sleeping research and its preliminary findings; for more information.

Weintraub, B. "Can seal pup biology help save infant lives?" *National Geographic,* **April 1992, preceding p. 1.**

Reports on a study by researchers at the University of Alaska who are examining elephant seal pups who may give clues to identifying infants at risk for Sudden Infant Death Syndrome (SIDS). The pups normally experience periods of apnea; no documented cases of seal pups falling victim to SIDS; also it has been found that seal pups have erratic heartbeats during this time.

Back Issues

Great Research on Current Issues Starts Right Here... Recent topics covered by The CQ Researcher are listed below. Issues dated before May 10, 1991, were published under the name of Editorial Research Reports.

JANUARY 1991
Growing Influence of Boycotts
Should the U.S. Reinstate the Draft?
America's Archaeological Past
Peace Corps' Challenges in '90s

FEBRUARY 1991
Regional Impact of Recession
Puerto Rico's Status
Redistricting: Mapping Power
Nuclear Power

MARCH 1991
Acid Rain
Cost of the Gulf War
Reassessing Gun Laws
Future for Man in Space

APRIL 1991
Social Security
Canadian Crisis Over Quebec
California Drought
Electromagnetic Radiation

MAY 1991
School Choice
Racial Quotas
Animal Rights
U.S. and Japan

JUNE 1991
Children and Divorce
Teenage Suicide
Endangered Species
Europe 1992

JULY 1991
Teenagers and Abortion
Soviet Republics Rebel
Mexico's Emergence
Athletes and Drugs

AUGUST 1991
Sexual Harassment
Fetal Tissue Research
Oil Imports
The Palestinians

SEPTEMBER 1991
Police Brutality
Advertising Under Attack
Saving the Forests
Foster Care Crisis

OCTOBER 1991
Pay-Per-View TV
Youth Gangs
Gene Therapy
World Hunger

NOVEMBER 1991
Fast-Food Shake-Up
The Greening of Eastern Europe
Business' Role in Education
Cuba In Crisis

DECEMBER 1991
Retiree Health Benefits
Asian Americans
The Obscenity Debate
The Disabilities Act

JANUARY 1992
Term Limits
Oil Spills
Hunting Controversy
Alternative Medicine

FEBRUARY 1992
Threatened Coastlines
New Era in Asia
Assisted Suicide
Jobs in the '90s

MARCH 1992
Women and Sports
Underage Drinking
Garbage Crisis
Mafia Crackdown

APRIL 1992
Ozone Depletion
Welfare Reform
Politicians and Privacy
Illegal Immigration

MAY 1992
Native Americans
Jobs vs. Environment
Too Many Lawsuits?
Fairness in Salaries

JUNE 1992
Nuclear Proliferation
Food Irradiation
Lead Poisoning
Hard Times for Libraries

JULY 1992
Alternative Energy
Prescription Drug Prices
Alzheimer's Disease

Back issues are available for $4.00 (subscribers) or $7.00 (non-subscribers). Quantity discounts apply to orders over ten. To order, call Congressional Quarterly 1-800-432-2250.

Binders are available for $15.00. To order call 1-800-638-1710.

Future Topics

▶ *The Homeless*

▶ *The Overworked American*

▶ *NATO's Evolving Role*

The Homeless

How can the complex problems of the homeless be overcome?

WHEN HOMELESSNESS BEGAN ATTRACTING national attention in the early 1980s, U.S. cities initially responded by providing the barest of accommodations — a roof and one meal. That response was borrowed from the past, when the typical homeless person was a white, middle-aged alcoholic. But today's new generation of homeless is young, poorly educated and increasingly composed of families, often from minority groups. Many also suffer from severe mental illness or substance abuse. To help such people, providers are building small, resource-centered facilities designed to change peoples' lives, even if it means singling out those individuals with the motivation to improve. Critics say this approach discriminates against the hard-luck cases. Others say the emphasis should be on preventing homelessness in the first place.

C
Q
August 7, 1992 • Volume 2, No. 29 • 665-688

Formerly Editorial Research Reports

FOR REFERENCE

Do Not Take From This Room

COVER ART: BARBARA SASSA-DANIELS

CQ Researcher

August 7, 1992
Volume 2, No. 29

EDITOR
Sandra Stencel

MANAGING EDITOR
Thomas J. Colin

ASSOCIATE EDITOR
Richard L. Worsnop

STAFF WRITERS
Charles S. Clark
Mary H. Cooper
Rodman D. Griffin

PRODUCTION EDITOR
Laurie De Maris

EDITORIAL ASSISTANT
Michael M. Taylor

GRAPHICS
Jack Auldridge

PUBLISHED BY
Congressional Quarterly Inc.

CHAIRMAN
Andrew Barnes

VICE CHAIRMAN
Andrew P. Corty

EDITOR AND PUBLISHER
Neil Skene

EXECUTIVE EDITOR
Robert W. Merry

PUBLICATIONS MARKETING/SALES
Robert Smith

EDITOR, EBSCO PUBLISHING
Melissa Kummerer

The CQ Researcher (ISSN 1056-2036). Formerly Editorial Research Reports. Published weekly (48 times per year, not printed the first Friday of any month with five Fridays) by Congressional Quarterly Inc., 1414 22nd St., N.W., Washington, D.C. 20037. Rates are furnished upon request. Second-class postage paid at Washington, D.C. POSTMASTER: Send address changes to The CQ Researcher, 1414 22nd St., N.W., Washington, D.C. 20037.

The Homeless

BY EILEEN QUIGLEY

THE ISSUES

Gregory Parmenter had been the assistant manager of a drugstore chain in Washington, D.C., but constant marijuana use gradually devastated his life and he drifted into the uncertainty of construction work. Three and a half years later, he ended up in a rat-infested city shelter where he saw "one man stabbed to death and another man beaten to death."[1]

In time, Parmenter managed to stop his pot smoking, and he found his way to McKenna House. Founded by Franciscan monks, the private, nonprofit residential facility in the District of Columbia guides homeless men back into society by helping with résumés, job searches, apartment hunting and, importantly, giving them a telephone number prospective employers can call. Participants can stay up to three months if they remain drug- and alcohol-free. Of the 550 men who have made it through McKenna House since its start in the mid-1980s, 70 percent have obtained jobs and affordable housing.

Facilities like McKenna House — offering homeless people a wide range of survival skills and services — have been starting up all across the United States in recent years. The new programs reflect the awareness that homeless people need more than just a roof over their heads. But there is a catch: Some of the new full-service resource centers are selective, working only with the homeless clients they deem most likely to respond to treatment and assistance.

Such programs have come a long way from the days of the Great Depression, when down-on-their-luck Americans were given shelter — and not much more — in spartan, make-

shift spaces in synagogue and church basements, or in cavernous halls, such as New York City's armories. That policy prevailed into the early 1980s, when the ranks of the homeless swelled once again and an outpouring of compassion led public and private organizations to provide the homeless with the customary hot meal and a cot.

By the end of the decade, however, it was generally recognized that the "eats and sheets" approach did not begin to address the serious problems that afflict many of the homeless. Experts now say roughly one-third of the homeless struggle with economic problems often associated with limited job skills and poor education; one-third are severely mentally ill; and one-third are addicted to drugs or alcohol. In addition, increasing numbers of women and children, many from minority groups, have joined the stereotypical homeless person: a middle-aged, alcoholic, white male.

Armed with their new perceptions of the homeless, experts realized that

the shelter approach "often made matters worse because [it] perpetuated the notion that the homeless simply needed a bit more money, food and a place to stay for the night." The end result, one expert concluded, "has been that the expensive transitional and rehabilitative services, that the homeless most need are shortchanged, and the focus becomes warehousing the homeless in barebones shelters."[2]

But just as the complex needs of the homeless were being understood, compassion for the homeless appeared to wane. America's patience seemed to be wearing thin with a problem that didn't respond to a quick-fix.

Policy analysts and homeless-care providers went back to the drawing boards. The housing solutions they devised hinged on homeless people finding the motivation to change. There was child care for single mothers who had job skills but could not get to work, as well as those who needed to develop skills; life-management skills, such as balancing a checkbook, paying the rent on time or interviewing for jobs; general equivalency diplomas (GEDs) for high school dropouts; and drug and alcohol recovery programs.

"In the mid to late 1980s, we all woke up and realized that we had to do something more than provide a temporary fix," says Charles Ridings, executive director for Catholic Charities on the Hawaiian island of Maui, which is constructing a $5.5 million, five-acre campus for the homeless. "We saw that there were deeper social problems nationwide and that there had to be an evolution from the Band-Aid approach to one that will break the chain of homelessness."

Today, homeless providers across the country are working with programs that can make a real change in

The Census Bureau Counts the Homeless

As part of the 1990 census, the Census Bureau surveyed more than 39,000 sites where homeless people are found. The bureau cautions that the tally of 459,209 people does not represent the total U.S. homeless population but a numerical snapshot on the March night the count was taken.

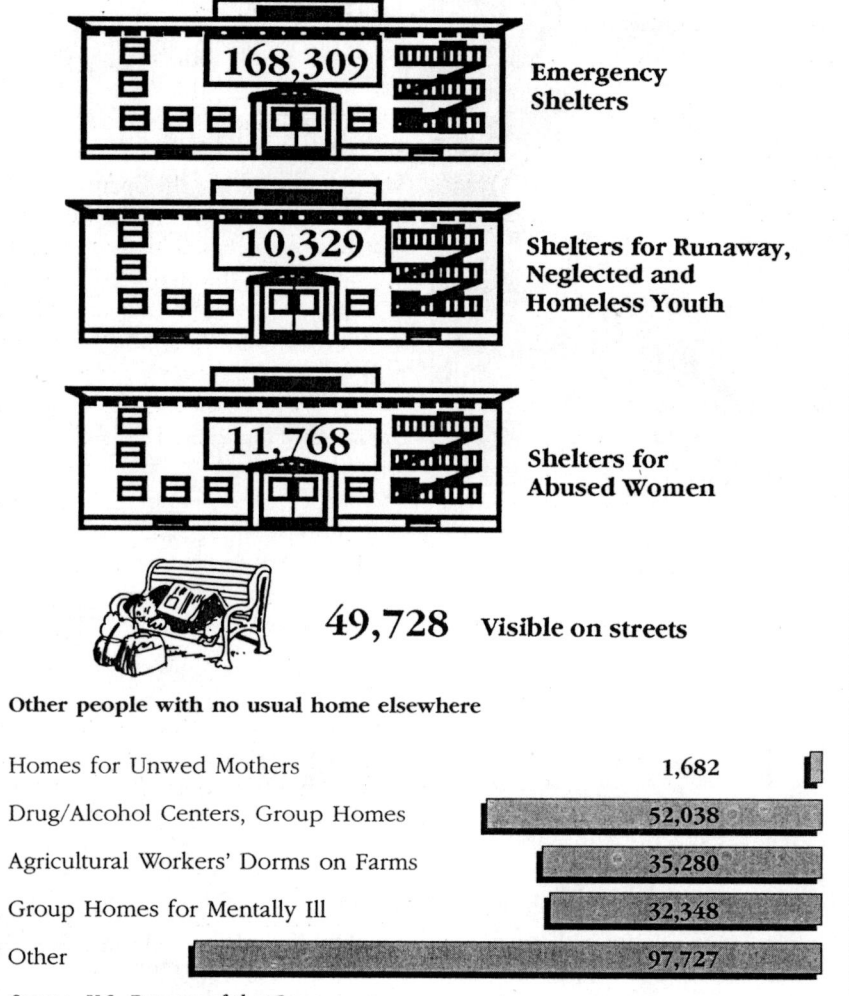

168,309 — **Emergency Shelters**

10,329 — **Shelters for Runaway, Neglected and Homeless Youth**

11,768 — **Shelters for Abused Women**

49,728 — **Visible on streets**

Other people with no usual home elsewhere

Homes for Unwed Mothers	1,682
Drug/Alcohol Centers, Group Homes	52,038
Agricultural Workers' Dorms on Farms	35,280
Group Homes for Mentally Ill	32,348
Other	97,727

Source: U.S. Bureau of the Census

olescent Alcohol and Drug Endeavor (BLAADE) discovered recently in Seattle. The group wants to house recovering teens in an old inn in a traditionally liberal neighborhood of single-family dwellings near the University of Washington. But residents' vocal NIMBY ("not in my back yard") response has complicated the approval process.[3]

While many homeless programs today embrace the new transitional approaches, others are looking at ways to prevent homelessness in the first place. Programs in several states provide landlord-tenant mediation, backrent assistance and lessons in budgeting that teach families to manage their households. The National Housing Institute, a public-policy organization in Orange, N.J., and the American Affordable Housing Institute, a policy research center at New Jersey's Rutgers University, studied seven such prevention programs throughout the country and found thousands of families had escaped homelessness through mediation — and at a fraction of the cost of shelters or welfare hotels. *(See story, p. 677.)*

While there is general agreement that policies that deal with the fundamental causes of homelessness are most effective, soaring budget deficits and decreasing tolerance for the homeless make these expensive programs difficult to implement. Here are some of the questions that experts are asking as they seek solutions to the homelessness problem:

Is the number of homeless people growing?

The answer to this most fundamental question about homelessness is endlessly debated. Experts' estimates of the number of homeless range from 200,000 to 3 million. Advocates for the homeless call estimates by the federal government far too low, while government officials consider the advocates' numbers grossly overblown.

peoples' lives, even if it means picking individuals who seem more receptive to change. Critics call this selection process "creaming." Others maintain that focusing aid on the "cream of the crop" is better than letting everybody drown together.

"We don't think of our process as creaming," says Mary Case, executive director of St. Vincent de Paul Village, a Catholic diocese facility for homeless individuals, children and

families that occupies an entire city block in San Diego. "We serve those who are motivated to change. We are not designed for people who want to sit around."

Such residential programs do best, studies show, when they are placed in well-established communities that aren't plagued by urban blight. All too often, however, targeted communities want nothing to do with these facilities, as the Black and Latino Ad-

The most recent attempt to count the nation's homeless took place the evening of March 20, 1990, and early the next morning. Surveyors from the U.S. Bureau of the Census fanned out across the land, visiting more than 39,000 specific sites frequented by the homeless, ranging from emergency shelters and homes for abused women to farm dormitories and refuges for runaways. The count was 459,209 people, but Census officials emphasize that it is only a numerical snapshot of the homeless on that particular night, not an estimate of the total number of homeless.[4] (*See table, p. 668.*)

Counting the homeless is understandably difficult, given their mobility. According to the National Resource Center on Homelessness and Mental Illness, "most individuals who live on the streets do so episodically, moving between shelters, single-room-occupancy (SRO) hotels, the homes of friends and relatives and the streets."[5]

In addition, many shelters don't have the staff to keep accurate data. As Ellen Baxter and Kim Hopper observed in their landmark 1981 study, *Private Lives/Public Spaces,* "The estimates [of the number of homeless] that do surface from time to time are notoriously unreliable, subject to wild discrepancies depending upon the methods of estimation used, the source of the figures, the time of the year, and we strongly suspect, the purpose from which the numbers are put forth."[6]

Although the exact number of homeless Americans remains elusive, some studies seem to indicate the number is rising. A 1988 study by the U.S. Conference of Mayors found increased requests for emergency shelter in all but three of the 27 cities it surveyed. The number of emergency shelter beds in the 27 cities had increased by an average of 13 percent over the previous year, and transitional housing units increased an average of 25 percent. The survey estimated that 22 percent of the requests for

emergency shelter went unmet, and that shelter was particularly lacking for homeless families, the severely mentally ill and substance abusers.[7]

Some analysts caution that requests for shelter don't necessarily prove that the number of homeless is increasing. Randall K. Filer, who studied homelessness for the Manhattan Institute, a New York-based policy research group, has noted that the growing number of shelters could mean that the total homeless population is increasing or that "a constant population may be more likely to sleep in shelters."[8]

Filer also argues that "the more generous the programs for the homeless are, the greater the number will be as people respond to the incentives created." If shelters were not available, he speculates, poor people would not end up on the streets but might find sanctuary with families or friends.

Would more affordable housing eradicate homelessness?

Some experts believe that if more affordable housing were available, homelessness would be significantly curtailed. "In the first line of analysis,

homelessness is a housing problem," assert James D. Wright and Julia A. Lam. "Between the late 1970s and the early 1980s, the poverty population increased sharply, while the supply of low-income housing dwindled just as sharply."[9]

Others, such as University of Massachusetts sociologist Peter H. Rossi, author of a major study of homelessness, *Down and Out in America,* argue that a "large proportion of the homeless could be housed in existing housing, if they had the income to pay for it."[10] Still other studies seem to indicate that the problem may be a combination of decreasing housing supply *and* declining wages, compounded by increasing numbers of people seeking affordable housing.

One thing is certain: During the 1980s, the Reagan administration's shift from building new affordable housing to more reliance on the private market translated into a decline of about 1 million rental units during the decade. At the same time, according to a General Accounting Office (GAO) study, the demand for affordable rental units increased by about 2 million households. "With

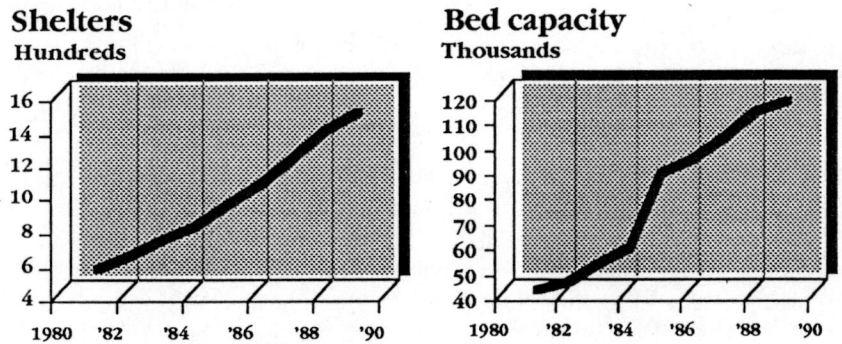

Number of Shelters on the Rise

Since the early 1980s, the number of shelters and shelter beds has steadily risen in U.S. cities with populations of 100,000 or more.†

Shelters
Hundreds

Bed capacity
Thousands

† *Note: The tally includes welfare hotels and private and public voucher programs but excludes domestic violence shelters. New York City is included in the figures for bed capacity but not the number of shelters.*
Source: Martha L. Burt, Over the Edge: The Growth of Homelessness in the 1980s

too few affordable units to house a growing number of lower income households, there is a greater likelihood that more people are at risk of becoming homeless," the GAO concluded.[11]

Conservatives point out that President Ronald Reagan's cuts could not have been felt during the 1980s because it can take five to 10 years to complete public housing units after Congress authorizes them. According to a paper published by the Heritage Foundation, a conservative Washington think tank: "The 1980s have been boom years for public housing. Yet this upswing coincides with the emergence of large homeless populations."[12] In short, says author William Tucker, blame for the shortage should be tied to local factors, such as rent control and strict zoning regulations, not federal policy.

One of those local factors was the precipitous loss of single-room occupancy (SROs) hotels. For decades, SROs harbored people hovering at or below the poverty line, as well as many of the approximately 430,000 patients released from state mental hospitals over the past 30 years (see p. 672). In the 1970s, many SROs were "gentrified" — converted into condominiums — or replaced by luxury apartment buildings.[13]

While housing costs rose and supplies fell, the 1980s also saw an increase in the number of poverty-level, or near-poverty households. According to William C. Apgar Jr, associate director of the Joint Center for Housing Studies at Harvard University, "some 7.7 million renters have incomes at or below the poverty level, an increase of 56 percent from the 1974 level."[14]

To make matters worse, writes Ellen L. Bassuk, an associate professor of psychiatry at Harvard and president of the Better Homes Foundation, the "median rents of unsubsidized, low-income apartments climbed from $255 to $360, [while]

the maximum amount of AFDC [Aid to Families with Dependent Children] available to a family of three — even when taken together with food stamp benefits — bought 26 percent less in 1990 than it did in the early 1970s."[15]

Should caregivers be selective in helping the homeless?

Almshouses of the early 1800s used a two-tiered classification system in which the "worthy" poor received relief while "undeserving" vagrants were disciplined in the workhouse. This distinction remained until the Progressive-era reforms of the early 1900s.[16] To some extent, a similar weeding out is occurring today.

St. Vincent de Paul Village in San Diego, for example, reserves its plusher accommodations for people who are recently homeless or who demonstrate the motivation to pull their lives together. St. Vincent's, which has been featured on CBS' "60 Minutes," ABC's "Nightline" and the front-page of *The Wall Street Journal*, cost $15 million to build and has an annual budget of $6 million.

Across the courtyard from the facility's airy, semi-private rooms with telephones is a dormitory for the harder cases, mainly alcoholics, drug addicts and the mentally ill. "We are dealing with the higher-functioning individual who can handle care coordination," says Executive Director Mary Case. "We can't deal with everybody."

Critics of the policy say leaving addicts and the mentally ill out of the equation excludes most of the homeless. Ridings of Catholic Charities in Maui responds that programs like his and St. Vincent's don't "cream" as much as they invite self-selection among the homeless themselves. "We're not lining up 12 people and saying, 'OK, this six goes and this six stays,'" he explains. "What we're doing is attracting motivated people who want to be helped with their transition back to the community." Ridings also says his program can assist what he calls the "manageably mentally ill," whose symptoms can be curbed by regular medication.

Critics also contend that transitional programs that are too cushy only serve to institutionalize homelessness. But both Case and Ridings note that the strict rules at well-run shelters discourage clients from feeling too comfortable. "The men and women in the long-term program tend to want to move on after experiencing such a highly structured environment," says Case.

Still another concern is that the transitional facilities will drain what little funding there is from long-term solutions, such as constructing permanent housing. While that may be true to some extent, Ridings concedes, he says that in Maui the state and local governments decided that the private sector would be more effective at providing housing. Besides, he adds, disadvantaged people still need to learn skills to function.

"If you eliminate money for the homeless programs," Ridings says, "you would still find a population that lacked the skills to get their bills paid, to deal with everyday living. There would still be the need for case management."

Are Americans becoming less compassionate toward the homeless?

When the media spotlighted homelessness in the 1980s, the public was sympathetic. An October 1989 Gallup Poll found that 60 percent of the people surveyed wanted to increase government spending on programs for the homeless, even if it meant higher taxes. However, public opinion began to shift in the early 1990s, as the homeless became increasingly visible to the public and people felt overwhelmed by the problem.

A *Washington Post*-ABC News Poll of 1,003 adults in 1990 found that only 58 percent would be willing to pay higher taxes to help the homeless, compared with 71 percent in September 1989. Young people, especially, seem discouraged by the problem's stubbornness. A *New York Times*/CBS News Poll in January found that 55 percent of 1,376 respondents between 18 and 29 thought that people had become so accustomed to seeing the homeless that they were no longer upset by them.

There are other indications that the public is less tolerant of the homeless. In Washington, D.C., a City Council subcommittee voted in May 1990 to weaken a 1984 ordinance that guaranteed shelter to anyone requesting it. District officials had said the measure was too costly, prompting the subcommittee to cap spending for the homeless.[17]

During the same period, Atlanta began making arrests for loitering, public drunkenness and blocking traffic near the city's convention hotels. More than 100 people were arrested in March 1990, when the International Olympic Committee visited the city to appraise its bid to host the 1996 Summer Games.

In New York City, transit officials banned panhandling in the subways, and a U.S. Court of Appeals upheld the ban in May 1990, ruling that panhandling is not a form of constitutionally protected free speech and in some instances "is nothing less than assault."

A recent letter in *The New York Times* reflected the "compassion fatigue" many Americans have over the hordes of homeless people they see on a typical day: "You walk with your eyes either downcast or looking straight ahead. You ignore. Years ago, when you'd see one or two beggars in as many days, you gave. Now there are just too many."[18]

Six years earlier, even as polls were still showing strong support for homeless programs, one Stuart D. Bykofsky vented similar frustrations in *Newsweek*: "There are people living

How the Public Views the Homeless

There are some indications that the public is becoming less compassionate toward the homeless. But most people feel the homeless are not responsible for their plight, and the vast majority thinks the government can do a lot about the problem.

Do you personally see homeless people around your community or on the way to work, or is the problem only something you have seen on television, or have read about?

	Personally see	Only see on television or read about
January 1992	58%	39%
December 1990	54	45
January 1989	51	48
January 1986	36	59

Do you think that when most people see the homeless they feel upset, or do you think that most people have gotten so used to seeing the homeless that they don't feel upset by them?

	Feel upset	Do not feel upset
Total adults	42%	44%
18-29 year olds	35	55
30-44 year olds	44	45
45-64 year olds	45	41
65 and older	45	30
Men	37	50
Women	47	39

Do you think that most homeless people are homeless mainly because of their own fault, or are most homeless people homeless mainly because of circumstances beyond their control?

Own fault	22%
Circumstances beyond their control	55
Both	20
Don't know/No answer	3

Is homelessness something the government can do a lot about, or is homelessness a problem that is beyond the government's control?

Can do a lot about	70%
Beyond control	22
Don't know/No answer	8

*Source: CBS News/*New York Times *Poll, based on telephone interviews with 1,376 adults nationwide conducted Jan. 6-8, 1992*

on the streets of most American cities, turning sidewalks into dormitories.... They have got to go. I don't know, exactly, when they got the *right* to live on the street. I don't know, exactly, when I lost the right to walk through town without being pestered by panhandlers. I do know I want them off my sidewalk. If you think I am heartless for saying that, can I send them to live on *your* sidewalk?" [19]

Church groups report that donations for homeless programs are down and complaints about shelter programs are up. Some people feel that giving money to the homeless, whether by tossing a coin into an outstretched cup or by funding an organized program, only hurts the homeless person because the money may be used to purchase drugs or alcohol. Most of all, Americans question the allocation of resources because they don't see the situation improving.

Campaigns to discourage panhandling have begun in many cities, often revealing the deep anger on both sides of the homeless issue. In Seattle, merchants in historic Pioneer Square pass out cards asking tourists and residents not to reward begging with money. To discourage the homeless from congregating in the area, the beleaguered merchants also removed the slats on six benches and removed a seventh bench altogether.

The merchants said they were protesting the vandalism of the park benches and the nearby park itself, where as many as 50 homeless people often gathered. The homeless picketed the merchants, and Ken Cole, director of the Pike Market Senior Center and the Downtown Food Bank, called the removal of the benches "a highly organized hate crime ... by people who have a vested financial interest in the area." ■

or foster care, built shelters for the mentally ill and retarded and provided stipends for widows and injured workers.

New Deal reforms passed in the wake of the Great Depression included several new programs to prevent large-scale poverty and homelessness, including Social Security. World War II provided work for millions of Americans, and the ranks of the homeless dipped considerably during the prosperous 1950s. By the early 1960s, the homeless were mostly represented by the older, white male tipplers of skid row.

Deinstitutionalization

In February 1963, President John F. Kennedy called on Congress to take a "bold new approach" toward the seriously mentally ill, a challenge that would have profound implications for the homeless problem. Kennedy urged the creation of Community Mental Health Centers (CMHCs) to replace existing mental institutions.

Encouraged by the salutary effects that new psychotropic drugs had on psychotic mental patients, the nation embarked on a plan to release them to their communities and the new CMHCs.

From the outset, however, there was evidence that many recently released patients were not receiving the aftercare they needed to remain functional. Provisions often hadn't been made to forge a working relationship between the mental institutions and the CMHCs, and many of the mentally ill fell through the cracks.

The population of the country's mental institutions was 505,000 in 1963; today it is roughly a quarter of that, and many deinstitutionalized people are living on the street. As Dr.

BACKGROUND

Living on Skid Row

"Except for a vague knowledge of the 1930s," writes Temple University historian Kenneth L. Kusmer, "people are generally unaware that vagrancy and street begging have a long history in America." [20]

Prior to the widespread homelessness caused by the Depression, many poor Americans had a taste of life without shelter. Some were veterans of the Civil War in the 1860s, and others helped to build the railroads or picked crops. When their work was done, they moved on in search of other jobs.

The depression of the 1870s had seen a dramatic rise in indigence and the emergence of the hobo. Kusmer notes that the "increasing number of homeless men during the very period

when the United States was emerging as an industrial nation was no coincidence. The new vagrancy was an indigenous aspect of a country in rapid transition from an agricultural and small-town society to one centered in great cities." [21]

As more people moved off the land and commerce gathered around urban centers, the homeless gravitated to "skid rows" in cities across the country. The name came from Seattle's Yesler Way, the road used to skid logs from the forest to the mill. Many loggers frequented the saloons and brothels that grew up along the road, and the term skid row became synonymous with degradation.

Beyond the skid rows, other members of the population were homeless, too, including widows and children, the mentally ill and the retarded. They lived in almshouses until the early 1900s, when the Progressive era ushered in reforms that placed children up for adoption

Continued on p. 674

Chronology

1930s *The federal government begins to provide a wide range of programs for transients and the homeless.*

1933
A Depression-era census conducted by the National Committee on Care of Transient and Homeless finds some 1.2 million persons (or 1 percent of the nation's population) homeless in mid-January.

1933-1935
Programs financed by the Federal Emergency Relief Administration (FERA) provide shelter, food, medical care, clothing, cash and jobs for transients and the homeless. The two-year program assists 375,000 people.

1935
FERA is replaced with specialized programs that meet individual needs, including the Works Progress Administration, which creates jobs on public works projects, and the Social Security Act. They establish — for the first time — an ongoing relief role for the federal government.

1960s *Pensions, unemployment insurance, Medicaid and Medicare help decrease the number of people on the streets. But deinstitutionalization of the mentally ill sets the stage for increasing numbers of homeless people.*

1963-1965
A major analysis of homelessness in New York is completed by the Bureau of Applied Social Research at Columbia University. The study finds 35 lodging houses and missions caring for 5,773 destitute men.

1963
Congress passes the Community Health Centers Act, which deinstitutionalizes an estimated 430,000 mentally ill people.

1970s *The courts become involved in homelessness for the first time in the country's history.*

1972
The Supreme Court decriminalizes vagrancy and also rules that laws requiring residency as a condition for assistance are unconstitutional.

Oct. 2, 1979
The first right-to-shelter lawsuit, *Callahan v. Carey*, is filed in New York State Supreme Court by homeless advocate Robert M. Hayes. Judge Andrew R. Tyler rules Dec. 5, 1979, that the state and city must provide "clean bedding, wholesome food and adequate supervision and security." Within 10 days, New York City opens its first public shelter in 50 years on Ward's Island.

1980s *The nation awakens to the problems of the homeless.*

1981
A study by Ellen Baxter and Kim Hopper garners considerable attention with its detailed portrayal of New York City's homeless problem.

September 1982
A controversial survey by the Community for Creative Non-Violence, a homeless advocacy organization in Washington, D.C., contends that 1 percent of the population, or 2.2 million people, lack shelter.

October 1982
A 55-city survey by the U.S. Conference of Mayors shows that only 43 percent of the demand for emergency services for the homeless is met.

May 1984
The Department of Housing and Urban Development finds the number of homeless ranges from 192,000 to 586,000, with the "most reliable estimate" being 250,000 to 350,000. Homeless advocates protest that the estimates are too low.

July 1987
Congress passes the Stewart B. McKinney Homeless Assistance Act, which provides emergency shelters, health care, job training and other programs.

November 1988
Congress reauthorizes the McKinney Act for two years.

1990s *The shift continues from an emergency response to the homeless to long-term solutions.*

1990
Congress again reauthorizes the McKinney Act.

May 1992
The U.S. Census Bureau releases the results of a nationwide survey of homeless people taken on one night in March 1990. Census officials caution that the tally — 459,000 people found in a variety of shelters and on the street — only represents a numerical snapshot of the homeless situation on the night of the survey, not the total of U.S. homeless.

Affordable Housing: Out of Reach for Many

During the 1970s, federally funded new construction and rehabilitation projects added an average of 197,000 rental units a year. That number fell 53 percent, to 93,000 units a year, in the 1980s, according to Martha L. Burt, director of social services research programs at The Urban Institute in Washington. In a recent study of the growth of homelessness in the 1980s, Burt concludes that "there is an absolute shortage of appropriate rental units to accompany poorly housed families.... [T]he problem is not simply an inability to afford what exists." †

The overall housing picture was just as bleak, according to William C. Apgar Jr., associate director of the Joint Center for Housing Studies at Harvard University. "Measured in 1988 dollars," he wrote, "the number of privately owned, unsubsidized units renting for less than $300 fell by nearly 2.9 million units from 1974 to 1985. During the 1980-85 period alone, the number of units renting for less than $300 dropped by slightly more than 1.6 million." ††

Apgar notes that from "1974-1985, the loss of low-cost, privately owned unsubsidized stock was tempered by a considerable increase in the number of low-cost subsidized units." But he emphasizes that "increases in the number of households receiving subsidies have not been sufficient to offset the decline" in low-cost housing.

Studies examining the percentage of income that renters put toward rent suggest how rising housing costs have increasingly strapped low-income people. A joint study by the Center on Budget and Policy Priorities and the Low-Income Housing Information Service found that in 1985 nearly 6 million renters nationwide with incomes below the poverty line‡ spent at least 30 percent of their incomes on housing costs (which included rent and utili-

ties). More than 3 million poor renters spent at least 70 percent of their income on housing. Homeowners were also strapped by house payments: Nearly 2 million low-income homeowners spent at least half their income on housing costs in 1985, and more than 1 million spent 70 percent.#

With low-income housing supplies falling and costs rising, the demand shows no sign of abating. In a 1989 survey of 27 cities in the United States, the U.S. Conference of Mayors found a 72 percent increase in demand for assisted housing by low-income families and individuals during the previous year. "With the decline in federally assisted housing programs, none of the survey cities expect to be able to meet the housing needs of low-income households in the foreseeable future," the report said.###

---

† Martha L. Burt, *Over the Edge: The Growth of Homelessness in the 1980s* (1992), pp. 32-33.

†† William C. Apgar Jr., "Which Housing Policy is Best?" *Housing Debate Policy*, Vol. 1, Issue 1, Fannie Mae, 1990.

‡ Poverty currently is defined by the Labor Department as an annual income of $13,950 or less for a family of four.

Paul A. Leonard, Cushing N. Dolbeare, and Edward B. Lazarre, *A Place to Call Home: The Crisis in Housing for the Poor*, Center on Budget and Policy Priorities and Low Income Housing Information, 1989. Also see *The State of the Nation's Housing*, published by The Joint Center for Housing Studies at Harvard University in 1989. It reported that some renters were paying 75 percent of their income in rent, and 6.6 million poverty-level households were paying more than 50 percent.

Lilia M. Reyes and Laura DeKoven Waxman, *A Status Report on Hunger and Homelessness*, The U.S. Conference of Mayors, December 1989.

Continued from p. 672

E. Fuller Torrey noted, "[r]ather than deinstitutionalization, which implied that alternative community facilities would be provided, what took place was simply depopulation of the state hospitals. It was as if a policy of resettlement had been agreed upon but only eviction took place." [22]

The 1970s found the courts involved in the homeless issue for the first time in the country's history. In 1972, the Supreme Court decriminalized vagrancy and decided that it was unconstitutional to require residency when determining whether

someone was eligible for public assistance. New York City homeless advocate Robert M. Hayes filed the first right-to-shelter suit in 1979. His victory in *Callahan v. Carey* meant the city had to provide beds, food and security for homeless men.

In the next few years homeless advocates were in and out of the courts, filing suits to require humane conditions for the homeless. Indeed, though New York agreed in a 1981 consent decree to improve conditions in its shelters, homeless advocates had to obtain an additional 19 court orders to force full compliance.

Crisis in the 1980s

The marked increase in the number of street people in the 1980s was initially attributed to the 1981-82 recession and federal budget cuts made by the Reagan administration. While the latter part of the 1980s witnessed falling unemployment and new jobs in certain sectors, the number of homeless people didn't drop. Several factors explain why. Reductions in resources available for the seriously mentally ill and chemically dependent meant that some people could not get Social Security Disability Insurance, and those who were still eligible often received less assistance.

In addition, state mental hospitals toughened their admission requirements and lowered their lengths of stay, sometimes releasing patients into the community without aftercare — or even a place to live. When The Urban Institute, a public policy research organization in Washington, D.C., undertook a study of homeless people in 1987, it found that slightly more than half the adults had been institutionalized for mental problems, drug dependency or criminal actions.[23]

State court decisions in the 1970s decriminalizing public drunkenness also increased the number of homeless. "In 1968, about 40 percent of all arrests in the United States were for vagrancy, public drunkenness and disorderly conduct," Associate Editor David Whitman of *U.S. News & World Report* told a conference sponsored by the Heritage Foundation. "Today, fewer than 15 percent of the arrests are for such offenses. That means that there are hundreds of thousands of drunks who were once locked up overnight but are now left on the streets."[24]

The situation has been further complicated by changes in the labor market and in housing availability. Unskilled day-labor jobs that transients depended on have largely disappeared. And much of the nation's stock of low-income housing is gone as well. During the 1950s, '60s and even the '70s, Americans suffering from mental illness or drug dependency were often able to find decent shelter in lodging houses and single-room-occupancy (SROs) hotels. But aggressive urban development in the 1960s and '70s dramatically upgraded or demolished them by the thousands.

In her study of homelessness, Martha L. Burt, director of the social services research program at The Urban Institute, notes that even the poorest Americans historically paid for housing when they could afford to, "including alcoholics whom one might expect to spend all their money on drink." Burt reasons that since little evidence suggests these people now prefer to live on the streets, then "changes in resources and in housing options are the proximal causes of their increasing homelessness in the 1980s."[25]

Debate Over Numbers

The long-running debate over the extent of the nation's homelessness began in 1980, when Mitch Snyder, a homeless activist with the Community for Creative Non-Violence (CCNV) in Washington, D.C., entered the fray.* Snyder asserted that official data on the homeless were insufficient. His organization then undertook a 14-city phone survey of agencies that aided the homeless. From this rather unscientific sampling, CCNV "concluded that approximately 1 percent of the population, or 2.2 million people, lacked shelter" and that the number would reach 3 million or more in 1983.[26]

Although CCNV's alarming statistics were challenged, the ensuing media coverage prompted the Department of Housing and Urban Development (HUD) the following year to gather official data on the homeless. The agency spent six months reviewing 100 local and national studies and conducting more than 500 interviews with homeless providers in 60 cities. HUD's report, released in May 1984, determined that on an average night from December 1983 to January 1984, there were between 192,000 and 586,000 homeless, with a "most reliable range" of

---

*A genius at generating publicity, the colorful Snyder attracted the support of film star Martin Sheen and other celebrities, who often slept with Snyder on downtown heating grates. He once went on a hunger strike to force President Ronald Reagan to release funds for a shelter in the District. Snyder committed suicide in 1990.

Counting Homeless Children

Every night between 61,500 and 100,000 American children sleep in emergency shelters, abandoned buildings, cars or on the streets. Estimates of the annual number of homeless children range from 273,000 to 500,000.

Estimates of the Number of Homeless Children

Annually:

U.S. Department of Education (1989)	273,000
General Accounting Office (1989)	310,000
National Coalition for the Homeless (1990)	500,000

Nightly:

Urban Institute (1988)	61,500
General Accounting Office (1989)	68,000
National Academy of Sciences (1988)	100,000

Source: Children's Defense Fund

250,000 to 350,000.[27]

Predictably, HUD's report was greeted by a chorus of complaints from homeless advocates, who charged the agency with minimizing the homelessness problem. But in 1986, Harvard researchers Richard Freeman and Brian Hall, in a report for the National Bureau of Economic Research, concluded that the much maligned HUD numbers had been "roughly correct."[28]

Counting the homeless is important, of course, for without accurate data it is difficult to gauge how big, and how costly, aid programs must be. In the view of S. Anna Kondratas, a former assistant secretary at HUD, "the numbers are of critical political significance at the federal level. If the U.S. is swamped with millions of homeless Americans, then a better case can be made for treating the matter as a federal problem." If they are closer to the HUD figures, then the "main burden of responsibility for the homeless ... is with state and local governments and private organizations."[29]

Who Are the Homeless?

In recent years, the politically charged debates about the actual number of homeless people have given way to in-depth studies of the reasons why people are homeless. The sobering truth is that the homeless are a heterogeneous lot requiring a diverse array of assistance.

The typical homeless person of today is no longer a transient, often alcoholic, older white man but rather a younger man or woman, increasingly with children and, disproportionately, a minority.

According to a Conference of Mayors study, 46 percent of the homeless are single men; 36 percent are families with children; 14 percent are single women; and 4 percent are unaccompanied youth. The racial breakdown is 51 percent black, 35 percent white and 14 percent "other." And 24 percent are employed in full- or part-time jobs, and 26 percent are veterans.[30]

A 1987 Urban Institute study found that almost half the homeless have not finished high school; one out of five single homeless persons reported prior hospitalization for mental problem; 35 percent had had inpatient treatment for chemical dependency; 56 percent had been in jail five or more days; one out of four had served time in state or federal prisons; and three-quarters of the adults with children were non-white and predominantly female.[31]

Finally, most studies have found that between 30 and 40 percent of all homeless people suffer from serious mental illness, such as schizophrenia, manic-depression or clinical depression. ∎

CURRENT SITUATION

The McKinney Act

Today, instead of merely supplying emergency shelter, providers are advancing programs for the homeless that address their myriad physical, financial, emotional and educational problems. Some clients just need help with budgeting or with landlord-tenant mediation. Others, such as drug addicts or sufferers from severe mental illness, may need a wide range of services. Then there is the increasing number of homeless women and children who need day care, education and jobs.

Many assistance providers consider case management the most effective way to deliver help to the homeless. Case workers assigned to specific clients provide individual attention and help them extract assistance from a fragmented and complicated delivery system.

Experts also say that programs have the best chances of success when they keep their size smaller; select clients motivated to change; and use highly structured programs, since clients, particularly in drug rehabilitation, respond to strict rules.

Congress Responds

On Capitol Hill, the debate over how to deal with the homeless problem culminated in the Stewart B. McKinney Homeless Assistance Act, which became law in July 1987. The act, initially authorized at $490.2 million, included nearly 20 programs to address homelessness. In addition to emergency shelter and food, the act provided medical care, mental-health care, permanent housing, educational programs and job training. Congress reauthorized the act for $1.2 billion for the 1988-91 period.

The Senate Subcommittee on Housing and Urban Affairs, in its report on the reauthorized McKinney Act, concluded that the most cost-effective way to assist people was with preventive programs aimed at helping them *before* they become homeless, rather than to pay later for expensive emergency solutions such as shelters, welfare hotels and transitional housing. Subsequent amendments to the act have emphasized prevention programs that offer short-term financial aid or counseling to people in danger of eviction or mortgage foreclosure.

The McKinney Act encouraged the federal government to stop "viewing the homeless problem as some kind of episodic emergency that happened when the weather got cold or the economy went sour," said *U.S. News*

Continued on p. 678

An Ounce of Prevention

One of the best ways to deal with homelessness, experts agree, is to keep people from losing their homes in the first place. The National Housing Institute and the American Affordable Housing Institute at Rutgers University recently issued a report on seven programs designed to keep struggling families in their homes. The two groups found that "prevention is cheaper, as well as more compassionate, than waiting until people become homeless and then paying for shelter."[†]

The prevention programs studied encourage families to take responsibility for their homes, requiring them to budget properly to ensure stability after they receive assistance. All but one of the programs have been operating for five years or more. Here are highlights of some of the programs:

The Eviction Prevention/Rent Bank Program in Connecticut has provided free landlord-tenant mediation and money to help pay back rent since 1989. Mediators can draw up to two months rent or $1,200, whichever is less, from a "rent bank" to cover the gap between what the tenant can pay and what is sought by the landlord.

About half the cases referred to mediation do not result in agreements. In those cases that are successful, the mediator must monitor the agreement after 14, 30, 90 days and six months to see that it is followed. Funding for fiscal 1990 was $1.2 million for mediation and $2 million for the rent bank.

The program is proving cost-effective: For example, in New Haven, where it costs $7,000 to shelter a family in a motel room for 100 days, the average rent bank payment was $960. In 50 percent of the successfully mediated cases, no rent bank money was paid out at all. In Hartford, 46 evictions were prevented and of these, 33 percent of back rent was paid by the tenants. The bank covered the $21,933 balance.

The Rental Assistance Program (RAP) in Maryland provides small monthly rent supplements for up to a year to stabilize low-income families who are either homeless or facing critical housing needs. The program, which aims to create long-term housing self-sufficiency, began in 1986 and is run by the state Department of Housing and Community Development. Grants are based on geographic location and size of the family. The average grant is $175, or $2,100 per year. The maximum grant is $250.

After a local housing agency approves the housing selected by the family, it draws up a contract between the agency, the landlord and the tenant. The state pays the landlord directly. Funding for the program was $2 million in fiscal 1991. As of April 1990, more than 3,100 households had been successfully housed with the help of RAP payments. The majority (70 percent) were helped before becoming homeless; the rest were already homeless families who were able to move into permanent housing through the program.[††]

Based on figures from fiscal 1987 and 1988, 34 percent of the households had become self-sufficient and no longer needed assistance of any kind. At least 80 percent had found housing and were able to make housing payments on their own.

The Pennsylvania Homeowner Emergency Mortgage Money Assistance Program was one of the nation's first homeless prevention initiatives and has provided loans to avoid foreclosure since 1983. The loans help homeowners with delinquent mortgages and offer monthly mortgage assistance for up to three years. State laws require lenders to tell homeowners in danger of foreclosure about the programs, and homeowners then have 30 days to contact one of 31 credit-counseling agencies. Lenders must delay foreclosure for roughly 90 days while the emergency loan is being processed.

The assistance program sends checks for mortgage arrears directly to the lender. All money must be repaid, but no payment is due until homeowners are paying no more than 35 percent of their income for housing. The program received $7.5 million in the 1989-90 funding year from the state's general fund. By mid-1990, more than $12 million had been repaid, or 17 percent of the funds used.

The Home Ownership Protective Effort (HOPE) is a nonprofit program begun in 1983 that offers counseling and support for low- and moderate-income households in danger of losing their homes. The program helps with budgeting and may negotiate with creditors on the client's behalf, as well as assist with emergency cash for food needs. In 1991, HOPE was operating in 19 locations in five states — Pennsylvania, Ohio, Kentucky, Texas and Colorado.

Only households referred by a participating lender are accepted. In addition to financial and mediation services, HOPE may also help enroll people in job training or educational courses. HOPE is paid a monthly per-client fee by a participating lender and a flat rate per client by utility companies. More than 2,300 households have been helped since 1983. A little less than one-third of them brought all mortgage payments current, and less than 5 percent of them ended up in foreclosure.

"The intensive, case management approach of HOPE provides just the right balance between no-nonsense practicality and concerned, knowledgeable support that many families need to get their lives back on track," notes *Shelterforce*, a magazine on affordable housing published by the National Housing Institute in Orange, N.J.

[†] See "Preventing Homelessness," *Shelterforce*, November/December 1991, pp. 12-16.
[††] *Ibid.*, p. 14.

Continued from p. 676

& *World Report's* David Whitman. But he found the act's requirements "far too complicated" for providers to comprehend: "The fact is that it takes an expert in federal grantsmanship to understand what the McKinney Act is about."[32]

Similarly, people who work on the frontlines with the homeless appreciate the bill's intent but doubt its ultimate impact. "Although the McKinney Act was a promising first step, the funds were spread too thin and were not directed to supplying permanent housing or long-term services," Ellen Bassuk of Harvard Medical School wrote in an article on homeless families.[33]

New York's Quandary

At the outset of his first term, New York City Mayor David N. Dinkins stated that he was deeply committed to homeless families and single adults. In conjunction with several other efforts to improve the city's shelter system, Dinkins appointed a Commission on the Homeless in September 1991 chaired by Andrew M. Cuomo, who is the head of HELP, a nonprofit program that houses 500 homeless people, and New York Gov. Mario Cuomo's son.

In February, the commission released a 118-page analysis of the city's homeless problem, *The Way Home: A New Direction in Social Policy.* In a cover letter to Dinkins, the commission described the city's system as a "creature of cumulative improvisation, having evolved by fits and starts over decades ... [and] characterized by makeshift arrangements, Byzantine procedures and entrenched bureaucracies." It called for a "wholesale restructuring with new, radically different policies, priorities and programs."

The commission concluded that:

• No single group defines the homeless, and no class distinctions can be drawn about the population. Rather, there are distinctive overlapping subgroups within the homeless population.

• The approach to the problem must be tailored to the individual.

• Reform is less a matter of additional resources than it is better use of existing resources.

• The shelter system is not designed to help a family escape poverty or dependence on government assistance.

The report also documented heavy drug and alcohol addiction and mental health problems among shelter residents. The highest level of drug abuse — 80 percent — occurred in the armories, huge facilities where the annual $18,000 cost of a bed equals, ironically, the annual cost of drug treatment. Fully 85 percent of the homeless people surveyed for the study said they would enter a treatment program if one were available.

While the commission report spelled out several specific recommendations, it ultimately recommended that care for the homeless should be administered not by the city but through private, community-based nonprofit organizations, which possess the expertise to provide effective and efficient services, including the siting and construction of new facilities.

The Cuomo report was generally praised for its thoroughness and straightforward recommendations. In a Feb. 20, 1992, editorial, *The New York Times* called it "an intelligent opportunity." The fact that a reallocation of existing funds was recommended rather than an increase in costs made the plan particularly appealing.

Still, some observers found several of the proposals problematic because they depended on the approval of state officials — including Gov. Cuomo — and the federal government.

Others doubted there was enough money available for drug treatment. Manhattan Borough President Ruth W. Messinger questioned whether private agencies with their own political constituencies would do a better job of providing services or save more money than the city.[34]

Overall, however, city officials and others concerned with homelessness seemed to have reached a consensus — to the surprise of many — that treatment and training are essential to helping the homeless to get back on their feet and that large shelters must be replaced with smaller programs tailored to meet the needs of different groups. "While the call for 'housing, housing, housing' is misguided, so are the calls for 'services, services, services,'" the report asserts. "The truth is that both are necessary."[35]

Mayor Dinkins' office took no action on the report for three months and then authorized six "work groups" to further study different aspects of homelessness. The mayor deferred until 1995 the main step of developing small programs to replace the armories. Commented a *New York Times* editorial: "The report invites speculation that the Mayor prepares to put off opening the new sites in order to avoid offending neighborhoods before his re-election campaign. Mayor Dinkins' dilatory pace threatens to squander the best opportunity yet to give help to the homeless."[36]

Beyond Shelter

While changes in New York's homeless policies may be long in coming, other cities already have had success with transitional or permanent facilities in so-called "scattered sites" away from the drugs and crime of public housing developments. The Seattle Housing Authority, for example, has placed hundreds of individuals and families in such facilities in safe, quiet neighborhoods.

Funded with a $50 million tax levy in 1986, Seattle's program focuses on tenants in public housing projects who pay their rent on time, maintain their apartments in good condition and don't disturb their neighbors.

"I am an advocate of using scattered-site housing to reward people who are successful in the projects," said Maryanne Russ, executive director of the Council on Large Public Housing Authorities in Washington, D.C. "Among the consequences are that you have people who will take better care of the place, cause fewer management problems and reduce maintenance costs."[37]

Another successful approach is the "supported SRO," a rooming house typically run by a private, nonprofit organization and staffed with caseworkers. There are some 1,700 such facilities in New York City, 750 in Chicago and 500 in San Francisco. The caseworkers visit residents every day, seeing that they take their medication and helping them find job training or treatment.

The newly created Corporation for Supportive Housing, a nonprofit group based in New York, plans to offer seed money, technical assistance, training and financial counseling to supported SROs throughout the country. In addition, the Pew Charitable Trusts, the Ford Foundation and the Robert Woods Johnson Foundation have contributed $10 million to help the corporation tap local matching funds for the construction of new supported-housing facilities.

Making Clients Toe the Line

When homeless advocates talk about giving the homeless more than just a roof over their heads, they are talking about places like The Neighborhood Center of St. Benedict the Moor. It was founded seven years ago in a drug-infested section of the

---

Getting Tough on the Homeless

Some local governments have tried to sweep the homeless from streets, airports and other public places by enacting new ordinances, by singling out homeless people for arrest under anti-loitering and public-nuisance statutes and by unequal enforcement of public-intoxication codes.

City	Anti-homeless action
Atlanta	Aggressive begging ordinance Habitual panhandling statute Prohibition on loitering in vacant buildings Periodic sweeps of downtown area Permit fee required for street vendors Unequal enforcement of other laws
Chicago	Anti-begging ordinance (2,400 arrests in 1990) Sweeps of O'Hare Airport and Grant Park Unequal enforcement of other laws
Dallas	Aggressive panhandling ordinance Unequal enforcement of public intoxication code Recent zoning changes barring new shelters downtown
Las Vegas	Loitering ordinance Public-nuisance statute Trespassing statute Anti-begging ordinance (not currently enforced) Homeless people barred from public library
Miami	Loitering ordinance Prohibition on sleeping in public Park curfews and codes against storing possessions Sweeps prior to the Orange Bowl Parade Unequal enforcement of other laws
New York City	Prohibition on begging, sleeping and loitering in subways Park codes against sleeping in park, leaving possessions unattended, and building unlicensed structures Destruction of shantytowns
San Francisco	Prohibition of "intent to lodge" in public (50 arrests from July to October 1990) Prohibition on sleeping in public Park curfews and prohibition on unlicensed structures Anti-begging ordinance (Invalidated in *Blair v. City of San Francisco*, Sept. 24, 1991)
Seattle	Aggressive panhandling ordinance Park curfews
Washington, D.C.	Prohibition against begging in the "Metro" system Anti-begging ordinance (currently not enforced) Aggressive panhandling ordinance currently before City Council Prohibition of "disorderly conduct" and public drunkenness Park curfews and sweeps

Source: National Law Center on Homelessness & Poverty

South Bronx to give housing and counseling to recovering drug addicts. In order to qualify for an apartment, residents must first enroll in a 90-day treatment program. Once at the center, they are required to attend five weekly self-help meetings, enroll in outpatient therapy, work or go to school and pay their share of the rent.

Despite the constant temptation of drugs sold just outside the center's entrance, drug abuse is not the center's biggest problem. According to Dr. Herbert Kelber, executive vice president of the Center on Addiction and Substance Abuse at Columbia University and a former deputy director of the Office of National Drug Control Policy, drugs are less of a problem for the homeless than the lack of counseling and opportunities to develop job skills.[38]

McKenna House in Washington, D.C., where former marijuana abuser Gregory Parmenter received job training, boasts an amazing success rate. Director Hagos Weldegiorgis credits the residents' high motivation and the 24-hour attention they receive. "Our clients come to us when they are really ready to turn their lives around, and we work with them every day, step-by-step," he says. "When you're dealing with people in recovery, if you're not working with them every day, the recovery is always in question."

McKenna residents stay for three months, during which time they must attend at least one meeting per day of Narcotics or Alcoholics Anonymous.

Comprehensive Programs for Homeless Families

In San Diego, Project Genesis offers a similarly intensive program — but for homeless families. Funded by a $434,000 state emergency shelter grant and $1.78 million from HUD, the project's parent, the Interfaith Council, bought four apartment buildings and a child-care center. Lo-

cal businesses and volunteers renovated and furnished the apartments before the first families arrived in December 1991.

"We wanted to make sure that we were providing a long-term solution to those problems people face," said the council's Ed Paradis. "People have to be willing to work very hard."[39]

Every family receives individual and group counseling. A tenants' cooperative provides after-school care, and the center also has its own day-care and preschool center.

Homeless families can also find comprehensive care in Salt Lake City, Utah, where a $4 million, 23-unit transitional housing facility built by the Travelers Aid Society offers private rooms for families as well as a school, a medical clinic and a wide range of counseling and educational services.

"Case management works with families and with individuals to help them become self-sufficient," says Assistant Director Leslie R. Russell, who notes that each of the organization's four caseworkers specializes in an area of major client need: mental health, alcohol and drug recovery, vocational rehabilitation and medical problems.

Travelers Aid has been serving Utah's homeless since 1923. In 1985, the Society took over the city's emergency shelter system, and in 1988 the organization was chosen to operate the Salt Lake Community Shelter and Resource Center. Open 24 hours a day, the center operates an on-site medical clinic and educational programs for youngsters and adults. In fiscal year 1990-91, the center served an average of 310 men, 30 women, and 27 families every 24 hours — more than 8,700 different homeless people over the year.

A Boon for Job-Seekers

The Seattle Worker Center has pioneered an innovative way to apply today's technology to the problems of the homeless. One of the major

difficulties homeless people face when they are trying to find work is how to be contacted by prospective employers. With the Worker Center's voice mail service, homeless job-seekers can get around the problem. Individual voice mailboxes allow homeless men and women to call in from a pay phone and pick up messages from employers as well as from their caseworkers or doctors.

Since the voice mail program began in May, nearly 100 people have obtained boxes and 20 have already left the program, which serves 13 agencies. The center was formed to assist area shipyard workers who were displaced by mechanization in local ports and has been serving the economically disadvantaged in Seattle since 1986.

Miami's Crackdown

Not all cities always handle their homeless with creative aid programs, let alone sympathy and forbearance. Ever since the mid-1980s, when the homeless problem became highly visible, some local governments have been literally trying to sweep the problem away.

Chicago has initiated a "homeless relocation program" under which it periodically expels all homeless people from airport terminals. In Las Vegas, Nev., the homeless are singled out for arrest under the city's anti-loitering and public-nuisance ordinances during sweeps of the downtown area. And in Miami, Fla., the city's penchant for homeless-free streets, especially during the Orange Bowl parade, led to court action.[40]

In December 1988, the American Civil Liberties Union (ACLU) sued Miami on behalf of 6,000 homeless people. This past June, in closing arguments before Federal District Judge C. Clyde Atkins, the ACLU asserted

Continued on p. 682

Should the homeless mentally ill be reinstitutionalized?

CHARLES KRAUTHAMMER

Syndicated columnist
FROM *THE NEW REPUBLIC*, FEB. 8, 1988.

Why should a civilized society have to prove that a person's mental incapacity will lead to death before it is permitted to save that person? Should not degradation be reason enough?

The standard for involuntary commitment of the homeless mentally ill is wrong. It should not be dangerousness but helplessness. We have a whole array of laws (e.g., on drug abuse and prostitution) that prohibit certain actions not primarily because they threaten life but because they degrade the person. In order to override the liberty of the severely mentally ill, one should not be forced to claim ... that life is at stake, but that a minimal human dignity is at stake....

For the homeless who are clearly mentally ill, why should it be necessary to convince a judge that, left alone, they will die? The vast majority won't. It should be enough to convince a judge that, left alone, they will suffer....

Moreover, the suffering is needless. It can be mitigated by a society that summons the courage to give the homeless mentally ill adequate care, over their objections if need be. In a hospital they will at the very least get adequate clothing and shelter....

A sensible approach to the problem begins with the conviction that those helpless, homeless and sick are the responsibility of the state. Society must be willing to assert control even if protection and treatment have to be given involuntarily. These people are owed asylum. Whether the asylums should be large or small, rural or urban is a matter of debate.... What should by now be beyond debate is that the state must take responsibility for the homeless mentally ill....

Rebuilding an asylum system is one problem we can and should throw money at. It will take a lot. The way to do it is to say to Americans: You are pained and offended by homelessness. We propose to get the most wretched, confused and disruptive of the homeless off the street and into clean and humane asylums. We need to pay for them. We propose capping the mortgage interest deduction: less of a tax break on your house so that others can be housed....

Society must not leave the ordinary citizen with no alternatives between ignoring the homeless and playing Mother Teresa. A civilized society ought to offer its people some communal act that lies somewhere in between, such as contributing to the public treasury to build an asylum system to care for these people.

MICHAEL J. DEAR AND JENNIFER R. WOLCHMAN

FROM THEIR BOOK *LANDSCAPES OF DESPAIR: FROM DEINSTITUTIONALIZATION TO HOMELESSNESS*, 1988.

The many unanticipated and sometimes undesirable side effects of deinstitutionalization could not have been foreseen without knowledge of later transformations in the social, political and economic climates. Moreover, despite the dilemmas that faced community-based services, they took the first step in delivering what many had called for but which institution-based services has historically failed to provide: humane, caring support for the dependent. Thus deinstitutionalization was — and is — a necessary stage in the evolution of modern human services.

On the other hand, reinstitutionalization is a step backward in our commitment to progressive service-support systems. We do not doubt that a small number of the service-dependent will always require a secluded, protected living situation; but there is no need, either economic or therapeutic, for such quarters to be provided in large-scale institutions. The onus should be on the advocates of reinstitutionalization to demonstrate the requirement for "new asylums"....

We believe that the earlier arguments in favor of deinstitutionalization retain their validity.

The future archaeologist of human services is likely to discover one of two landscapes at the end of the 20th century. The first is a landscape of despair. The perfect metaphor for this terrain is provided by the homeless who nightly populate the California beaches of Santa Monica and Venice.... This portrait of the landscape of despair presages the collapse of the human-service system and an abandonment of those in need.

An alternative archaeology is invoked by the many engravings of 19th-century asylums. These massive, isolated structures epitomized their creators' search for order, control and "cure".... The trend toward reinstitutionalization will again take the service-dependent out of sight and out of mind. Only the ghosts of the incarcerated will be left to haunt the community....

Instead of these alternative archaeologies, we call for a landscape of caring ... in which the potential and promise of deinstitutionalization will be realized. In it, community-based care is the norm....

The general long-term objective must be to realize the community-based alternative promised by deinstitutionalization. This includes a full range of transitional living arrangements for the diverse service-dependent populations, as well as specific programs of care, social integration and employment.

Continued from p. 680

that the city's arbitrary arrests of homeless people, at the request of merchants and tourists, had been discriminatory and unconstitutional.

The city said it made arrests only in response to complaints by residents or to uphold the law and claimed it had no express policy directed at the homeless. "We can't allow them to rule the community because of their plight," Assistant City Attorney Leon Firtel told the judge. "We're losing sight of the neighborhoods and business community. This is wrong."[41]

If the judge rules for the ACLU, it may seek damages of up to $50 million, which is based on ACLU estimates of $10,000 to $15,000 for each homeless person involved. Any damages won will be donated to a social service institution, the ACLU says. As of Aug. 4, the judge had not ruled. ∎

OUTLOOK

Uncertain Future

Two years ago, police in riot gear tore down a shantytown built by homeless people in a park on New York City's Lower East Side. When the squatters moved to a vacant lot, the police returned and again evicted them. But the homeless were soon back.

In cities throughout the country, and in rural areas as well, the homeless seem to have become fixtures on the local scene. And many studies indicate the homeless likely are increasing in numbers. The problem is so complex it has not responded to the quick-fix. What's needed, experts say, is a multifaceted response, only one piece of which is affordable housing. The emerging consensus is that a wide range of services — from health care to job training — must be provided, but on a small scale and with adequate supervision.

In addition, prevention programs have shown that homelessness can be avoided in many cases, and with relatively modest price tags. But prevention programs and integrated case management approaches often face resistance. As New York Mayor David Dinkins discovered, the public doesn't want to house the homeless in its back yard.

Funding continues to be a major stumbling block. According to the National Housing Institute, "Federal [funding] of the McKinney Act continues to fall short of the mark, pitting the already homeless against the near homeless in a battle for scarce federal resources."[42]

Where drug treatment is concerned, funding for these prevention programs is particularly troublesome. Current drug and alcohol recovery programs are not capable of meeting the demands of those who have decided to quit drinking or taking drugs, to say nothing of those who might be convinced to quit if programs were available. As Martha Burt of The Urban Institute notes, "[a] war on drugs cannot succeed if it concentrates on punishment without providing adequate treatment, and without affecting the social conditions that make drug-taking and drug-dealing attractive."[43]

Homeless people who are fortunate enough to get into short-term recovery programs have considerable difficulty staying clean and sober due to the lack of long-term, follow-up programs. According to David Whitman of U.S. News & World Report, "roughly 75 percent of all public inebriates who come in for detoxification [are] ... back on the streets in a few days without any referral for aftercare."[44]

Data have only recently been compiled on the incidence of AIDS among the homeless, and the statistics are disturbing. On July 15, 1992, the National Commission on AIDS released a study that indicated almost 15 percent of homeless people in the United States are infected with HIV and that about half of all AIDS patients are, or are about to become, homeless.

Beyond just a place to sleep, the homeless need jobs, health care, education, and a sense of community. As Ellen Bassuk observes, unless "a multidimensional understanding of the origins of homelessness is reached along with acknowledgment of the heterogeneity of homeless family needs, we will continue to formulate ineffective policies."[45]

The growing number of young, unskilled, minorities who are homeless may reflect a larger structural problem in the country's economy and educational system. It may well be that until more fundamental changes take place to alter the way that poor and disenfranchised people enter the nation's economy, the homeless will remain a haunting national specter. ∎

Eileen Quigley is a fellow at the Discovery Institute in Seattle, Wash.

Notes

[1] Quoted in Gina Kolata, "Drugs and Homeless: Case Studies of Lost Dreams," *The New York Times*, May 30, 1989.

[2] "Rethinking Policy on Homelessness," *The Heritage Lectures*, December 1988, No. 194.

[3] For background on the NIMBY phenomenon, see "Not In My Back Yard!" *Editorial Research Reports*, June 9, 1989, pp. 305-320.

[4] U.S. Census Bureau, "Fact Sheet for 1990 Decennial Census Counts of Persons in Selected Locations Where Homeless Persons Are Found," May 7, 1992.

[5] National Resource Center on Homelessness and Mental Illness for The Interagency Council on the Homeless, *Reaching Out: A Guide for Service Providers*, December 1991, p. 7.

[6] Ellen Baxter and Kim Hopper, *Private Lives/Public Spaces: Homeless Adults on the Streets of New York City*, Institute for Social Welfare Research, 1981, p. 8.

[7] Lilia M. Reyes and Laura DeKoven Waxman, *A Status Report on Hunger and Homelessness*, The U.S. Conference of Mayors, December 1989, pp. 2-3.

[8] See "What We Really Know About the Homeless," *The Wall Street Journal*, April 10, 1990.

[9] James D. Wright and Julia A. Lam, "Homelessness and the Low-Income Housing Supply," *Social Policy*, spring 1987.

[10] Quoted in Robert K. Landers, "Why Homeless Need More Than Shelter," *Editorial Research Reports*, March 30, 1990, p. 175.

[11] General Accounting Office, *Homelessness: Too Early To Tell What Kinds of Prevention Assistance Works Best*, April 1990, pp. 8-9.

[12] William Tucker, "America's Homeless: Victims of Rent Control," *The Heritage Foundation Backgrounder*, No. 685, Jan. 12, 1989, p. 2.

[13] See E. Fuller Torrey, M.D., *Nowhere To Go: The Tragic Odyssey of the Homeless Mentally Ill* (1988), p. 22.

[14] William C. Apgar Jr., "Which Housing Policy is Best?" *Housing Debate Policy*, Vol. 1, No. 1, Fannie Mae, 1990, p. 12.

[15] See Ellen L. Bassuk, "Homeless Families," *Scientific American*, December 1991, p. 68. The Better Homes Foundation, based in Newton, Mass., was founded in 1988 by the editor-in-chief of *Better Homes and Gardens* magazine to assist homeless families. It is largely supported by donations from subscribers.

[16] See Rick Beard, *On Being Homeless: Historical Perspectives*, Museum of the City of New York, 1987, p. 92.

[17] See Gwen Ifill, "Sympathy Wanes for the Homeless," *The Washington Post*, May 21, 1990, p. A1.

[18] See David Feldstein, "Legions of Homeless Make People Indifferent," *The New York Times*, Feb. 20, 1992.

[19] See Stuart D. Bykofsky, *Newsweek*, Dec. 1, 1986.

[20] Quoted in Beard, *op. cit.*, p. 21.

[21] *Ibid.*, p. 23.

[22] Torrey, *op. cit.*, p. 4. Also see Rael Jean Isaac and Virginia C. Armat, *Madness in the Streets: How Psychiatry and the Law Abandoned the Mentally Ill* (1990).

[23] See Martha L. Burt, *Over the Edge: The Growth of Homelessness in the 1980s* (1992).

[24] Quoted in *The Heritage Lectures*, *op. cit.*, p. 44. Whitman wrote the cover story on homelessness for the Feb. 29, 1988, issue of *U.S. News & World Report*. He is now a senior writer for the magazine.

[25] Burt, *op. cit.*, p. 213.

[26] Mary Ellen Hombs and Mitch Snyder, *Homelessness in America, A Forced March to Nowhere*, Community for Creative Non-Violence (1982), p. xvi.

[27] HUD Office for Policy Development and Research, *A Report to the Secretary on the Homeless and Emergency Shelters*, May 1, 1984.

[28] Quoted in Isaac and Armat, *op. cit.*, p. 3.

[29] S. Anna Kondratas, "A Strategy for Helping the Homeless," *The Heritage Foundation Backgrounder*, No. 431, 1985, p. 6.

[30] Reyes and Waxman, *op. cit.*, p. 2.

[31] Cited in *The Heritage Lectures*, *op. cit.*, pp. 20-21.

[32] *The Heritage Lectures*, *op. cit.*, p. 49.

[33] Bassuk, *op. cit.*, p. 72.

[34] See Sam Roberts, "Another Panel to Look at Proposals on Homeless," *The New York Times*, Feb. 22, 1992.

[35] The New York City Commission on the Homeless, *The Way Home: A New Direction in Social Policy*, February 1992, p. 13.

[36] *The New York Times*, May 23, 1992.

[37] Quoted in Paul Shukovsky, "More than a House: Shelter from Fear," *Seattle Post-Intelligencer*, Feb. 26, 1992, p. A1.

[38] See David Gonzalez, "Bronx Apartments Provide a Shelter From Addiction's Storm," *The New York Times*, June 30, 1992, p. A17.

[39] Quoted in Mary Curran-Downey, "Project Genesis Means More Than a Shelter for Homeless Families," *San Diego Union-Tribune*, May 18, 1992.

[40] See "Go Directly to Jail," National Law Center on Homelessness & Poverty, December 1991.

[41] Quoted in *The New York Times*, June 20, 1992.

[42] David C. Schwartz et al., *Preventing Homelessness*, National Housing Institute, October 1991, p. 8.

[43] Burt, *op. cit.*, p. 225.

[44] *The Heritage Lectures*, *op. cit.*, p. 47.

[45] Bassuk, *op. cit.*, p. 74.

Bibliography

Selected Sources Used

Books

Baxter, Ellen and Kim Hopper, *Private Lives/Public Spaces: Homeless Adults on the Streets of New York City***, Institute for Social Welfare Research, 1981.**

In their landmark study of New York's homeless, the authors followed people on the streets and in shelters, conducting numerous interviews with the same individuals over the course of their investigation. The study describes the lives of different types of homeless people and offers policy recommendations.

Burt, Martha L., *Over the Edge: The Growth of Homelessness in the 1980s***, The Urban Institute Press, 1992.**

One of the nation's leading experts on homelessness, Burt became scholar in residence at the Russell Sage Foundation in 1991 to study homelessness in depth. That work led to *Over the Edge*, a data-filled examination of the factors underlying the surge in homelessness in the 1980s. Based on information from 147 cities, it is considered by many experts as the definitive study of the subject.

Isaac, Rael Jean and Virginia C. Armat, *Madness in the Streets: How Psychiatry and the Law Abandoned the Mentally Ill***, The Free Press, 1990.**

Isaac and Armat examine deinstitutionalization of the mentally ill and the anti-psychiatry backlash that arose in the 1960s. They discuss the failure of community mental health centers to adequately care for those who were released from institutions.

Rossi, Peter H., *Down and Out in America***, The University of Chicago Press, 1989.**

Rossi, acting director of the Social and Demographic Research Institute at the University of Massachusetts, explains why poverty and homelessness trouble the United States and proposes remedies.

Torrey, E. Fuller, M.D., *Nowhere To Go: The Tragic Odyssey of the Homeless Mentally Ill***, Harper & Row, Publishers Inc., 1988.**

Torrey, a clinical and research psychiatrist specializing in schizophrenia, ran a clinic for mentally ill homeless women and has written extensively about mental illness. His book is a blistering indictment of deinstitutionalization.

Reports and Studies

Federal Task Force on Homelessness and Severe Mental Illness, *Outcasts on Main Street***, February 1992.**

This study, 18 months in the making, offers a strategy to end homelessness among the severely mentally ill.

The Heritage Lectures, *Rethinking Policy on Homelessness***, December 1988.**

The essays in this collection grew out of a 1988 conference on homelessness sponsored by The Heritage Foundation and *The American Spectator* magazine.

General Accounting Office, *Homelessness: Too Early to Tell What Kinds of Prevention Assistance Work Best***, April 1990.**

Provisions of the McKinney Act directed the General Accounting Office (GAO) to study and report on various homeless prevention programs implemented by recipients of McKinney Act grants. The GAO determined that few providers have the resources to collect follow-up data on clients that would help determine the success of homeless prevention programs.

Kondratas, S. Anna, *A Strategy for Helping America's Homeless***, The Heritage Foundation Backgrounder, No. 431, May 6, 1985.**

Kondratas, a former assistant secretary for community planning and development at HUD, calls for less federal involvement in homelessness and more state aid.

New York City Commission on the Homeless, *The Way Home: A New Direction in Social Policy***, February 1992.**

In this extensive report on homelessness, the commission calls for "radically different policies" in managing the city's homeless, including major private-sector involvement.

Reyes, Lilia M. and Laura DeKoven Waxman, *A Status Report on Hunger and Homelessness***, The U.S. Conference of Mayors, December 1989.**

This report contains the fruits of the conference's 1989 survey of 27 cities to assess the status of hunger and homelessness in urban America.

Schwartz, David C., Donita Devance-Manzini and Tricia Fagan, *Preventing Homelessness***, National Housing Institute and the American Affordable Housing Institute, October 1991.**

Researchers looked at state and local homelessness prevention programs around the country and found that they aided thousands of families on the edge of eviction and were, on average, more cost-effective than shelters.

The Next Step

Additional Articles from Current Periodicals from EBSCO Publishing's Database

Addresses & essays

Bassuk, E. L., "Homeless families," *Scientific American,* **December 1991, p. 66.**

Examines the plight of homeless mothers and children and the far-reaching societal impact of their situation and suggests long-term policy decisions to address the diverse needs of these families. Rates of family homelessness; single-parent families lead homeless population; rupture in community, family ties; plummeting financial assistance programs; today's housing market; reasons for isolation; employment problems; substance abuse and mental illness; homeless children.

Books & reading

"Book reviews," *Journal of Community Health,* **December 1991, p. 333.**

Reviews the book "Under the Safety Net: The Health and Social Welfare of the Homeless in the United States," edited by Philip W. Brickner, M.D., Linda Keen Scharer, MUP, Barbara A. Conanan, RN, MS, et al. An authoritative volume on the social and health problems of the homeless.

"Booklist," *Horn Book Magazine,* **March/April 1992, p. 216.**

Reviews the book "No Place to Be: Voices of Homeless Children," by Judith Berck.

Mohan, B., "Book reviews," *Social Work,* **January 1992, p. 94.**

Reviews the book, "Inventing a Non-Homeless Future: A Public Policy Agenda for Preventing Homelessness," by Madeline R. Stoner.

Torkelsen, S. E., "Book reviews," *Child Welfare,* **January 1992, p. 93.**

Reviews the book "Homeless Children and Youth: A New American Dilemma," edited by Julee H. Kryder-Coe, Lester M. Salamon, and Janice M. Molnar.

Case studies

"A moment of joy," *Newsweek,* **Dec. 30, 1991, p. 52.**

Presents a photo essay of Rosalie Johnson, who lives at Jamaica Armory, a homeless shelter operated by New York City. She collected cans to buy shoes for the St. Mary's Church Christmas dance, hosted by the homeless men at the Borden Avenue Veterans Residence, Queens.

"My daily dives in the dumpster," *Harper's Magazine,* **December 1991, p. 19.**

Recounts how the author has been forced into urban scavenging since becoming homeless after working 10 years as an attendant at the state hospital in Austin, Texas. What he collects from dumpsters; the stages of scavenging; types of foods he eats from dumpsters; how he began; lessons he has learned.

Brennan, M., "All I really need to know I learned in the library," *American Libraries,* **January 1992, p. 38.**

Presents a formerly homeless man's first-person account of his not-so-distant "schooling" in the Boston Public Library. His transformation from a homeless ex-con and day laborer into a full-time freelance writer in less than a year; his life before the library; a dilemma with no easy answers; the route to first magazine sale; the episode of the lady in the raggedy peacoat.

Brown, C., "A last good place to live," *Harper's Magazine,* **February 1992, p. 48.**

Describes life at Bailey House, the nation's first residence for the homeless with AIDS in New York, N.Y. Tensions that exist; how Bailey House was started; what it is like when someone dies at Bailey House; some of the residents; the people who work there.

Ellis, D., "Star of his own sad comedy," *Time,* **March 9, 1992, p. 62.**

Profiles Richard Kreimer, 42, who filed a civil rights suit against Morristown, N.J., alleging a pattern of police harassment — and won a $150,000 out-of-court settlement. His lawyer is negotiating another cash settlement stemming from a First Amendment suit now under appeal. Kreimer's background in Morristown; his years there living on the street; his rejection of the middle class ethic and the local shelter; his plan to be the homeless Ralph Nader.

Morgan, T., "Fear and dependency jostle in shelters," *The New York Times,* **Nov. 4, 1991, p. A1.**

Describes the homeless shelter in the Atlantic Avenue Armory in Brooklyn. It is dimly lighted and unheated — the kind of city shelter that has frightened many homeless people into staying on the streets. Yet many of the 900 men who sleep there have grown increasingly comfortable with the facility.

Tierney, J., "Mole returns to hole," *The New York Times,* **Nov. 30, 1991, p. 21.**

Tells about John Joseph Kovacs, 49, who lived alone in a tunnel under Riverside Park in New York City for 17 years. Last March he headed upstate to become the first student in a program training the homeless to become organic farmers. A film company offered to buy rights to his story, and things looked good for him. But now he is back in the tunnel.

Vargas, B., "A test of faith," *Essence*, January 1992, p. 33.

Recounts the experience of the author and her four children during their first time in a New York City shelter. How they became homeless; failure of the system to help the so-called middle-class person who is having a hard time financially; difficulties faced living in the shelter; lessons learned; how they survived until she found an apartment and job.

Debates & issues

"Deaths among homeless persons — San Francisco," *Journal of the American Medical Association*, Jan. 22, 1992, p. 484.

Summarizes the results from a review of records of homeless decedents from the San Francisco Medical Examiner's (ME) Office, which was conducted in order to characterize causes of death among homeless persons in San Francisco during 1985-1990. The study was conducted by the Health Care for the Homeless Program. Location of death; presence of alcohol or drugs; editorial note from the Centers for Disease Control.

Doblin, B.H., L. Gelberg, et al. "Patient care and professional staffing patterns at McKinney Act clinics providing primary care," *Journal of the American Medical Association*, Feb. 5, 1992, p. 698.

Describes the patient care and staffing patterns of the 157 clinics that receive federal funding to provide care for the homeless. Concludes that current financial constraints may be impeding the ability of clinics serving the homeless to ensure adequate access to high-quality care. Methods; results; conclusion; obstacles to physician recruitment in 82 clinics providing health care to the homeless; more.

Dugger, C.W., "Dinkins panel urges rent subsidy in overhaul of care for homeless," *The New York Times*, Jan. 31, 1992, p. A1.

States that a mayoral commission is recommending a sweeping overhaul of New York City's troubled shelter system, including introducing rent subsidies to help the homeless pay for housing. The commission would offer the homeless a richer array of services, including drug treatment, psychotherapy and job training, in smaller settings. But it would also require the homeless to take steps like enrolling in a drug-treatment program to qualify for subsidized permanent housing.

Lorch, D., "Despite pledge, New York uses welfare hotels," *The New York Times*, Feb. 7, 1992, p. A1.

Tells about the Kennedy Inn near Kennedy International Airport in New York City. Sometime in the coming weeks, with the arrival of 150 homeless families, the inn will become the largest for-profit welfare hotel in a city that not long ago had pledged it would stop using welfare hotels. Uproar among advocates for the homeless, officials and residents of neighborhoods near the airport.

Mathews, J., "Rethinking homeless myths," *Newsweek*, April 6, 1992, p. 29.

States that new questions have arisen about the best way to provide housing and help for America's homeless. Ways that officials are dealing with the problem; turning shelters into transitional housing; importance of education and creating jobs.

Morganthau, T., S.D. Lewis, et al. "A tough winter," *Newsweek*, Dec. 2, 1991, p. 26.

Reports that nationwide, the combination of recession and middle-class taxpayer revolts has created a multistate fiscal crisis that may well mean new cutbacks in government spending for the poor and the homeless. Epidemic of homelessness and unemployment in Detroit; percent of Americans in poverty; Medicaid costs soaring; the Family Support Act of 1988, which requires the states to provide education and job training for adult recipients of AFDC; more details.

Whitman, D., "Exodus of the 'couch people,'" *U.S. News & World Report*, Dec. 23, 1991, p. 30.

Details how some cities may be encouraging homelessness, and highlights what can be done to overcome the problem. The exodus of the "couch people" stems from a shortage of affordable housing; description of the "couch people"; reassessing the problem; those liberals who now oppose open-ended benefits, including Philadelphia's Mayor W. Wilson Goode; more.

Drug use

Dugger, C.W., "Drug abuse mars shelters, panel in New York says," *The New York Times*, Feb. 16, 1992, Section 1, p. 1.

Discusses how a New York City mayoral commission found in a recent survey that 80 percent of the homeless men housed in vast armory shelters and 30 percent of adults in shelters for families abuse drugs or alcohol. System's overhaul urged; city's program found unable to help the homeless fight crippling disabilities; first-time urine testing added to the survey; extreme poverty, mental illness, AIDS, domestic violence, lack of education or job skills; more.

Dugger, C.W., "Gambling on honesty on the homeless," *The New York Times,* Feb. 17, 1992, p. B1.

Analyzes the results of a survey documenting that crack use is widespread among the homeless in New York City, and deals with the question of whether releasing those results will set off a backlash against the homeless or prove that society must do more to help them.

Education

James, W.H., A.J. Smith et al., "Educating homeless children," *Childhood Education,* Annual Theme Issue 1991, p. 305.

Describes a school-based transition initiative for homeless children designed for the Seattle School District in Washington, which began in 1989 at B.F. Day Elementary. Kids Organized on Learning in School (KOOL-IS) program addresses the need for coordination of health, social and educational services for homeless children; adapts interprofessional case management model of Center for the Study and Teaching of At-Risk Students (C-STARS), University of Washington.

Richardson, L., "New York schools falling behind homeless," *The New York Times,* Jan. 2, 1992, p. A1.

Discusses the problem of truancy among homeless students in the New York City public schools. The obstacles that confront the thousands of homeless children living in the city's temporary shelters; the stigma attached to homelessness.

Exhibitions

Adams, R., "Smithsonian horizons," *Smithsonian,* May 1992, p. 12.

Describes how museums can put things the way they really are. The Smithsonian's exhibit on the homeless, "Etiquette of the Undercaste"; details of a just-published study by Martha L. Burt; why one cannot readily characterize a "typical" homeless person.

Health aspects

Navarro, M., "Recalcitrant patients a threat as TB returns," *The New York Times,* April 14, 1992, p. A1.

Discusses the comeback that tuberculosis has made, especially among homeless people and those infected with the HIV virus that causes AIDS. The problem of people who do not complete treatment and can develop drug-resistant strains of the disease and infect others with it.

Schlosstein, E., P. St. Clair, et al., "Referral keeping in homeless women," *Journal of Community Health,* December 1991, p. 279.

Examines factors associated with referral keeping among 118 homeless women screened for health-care needs in Seattle. Homeless women at high risk for acute and chronic physical disorders; model programs, such as Health Care for the Homeless; methods; results; discussion.

International aspects

Cole, J., "Housing hits where it hurts," *New Statesman & Society,* Dec. 20, 1991, p. 9.

Investigates the housing and homelessness crisis in England. Brief overview of various housing policies since the postwar period to the present; major problems with the Conservative Party's "right to buy" program; failure to acknowledge the need for government intervention to help those on the fringes of the free market.

Mollins, C., J. DeMont, et al., "No fixed address," *Maclean's,* Jan. 20, 1992, p. 20.

Portrays some of the Canadians who, by misfortune or choice, mismanagement or fate, are homeless, and those who help them. *Maclean's* staff members spend 24 hours on Jan. 3 logging the lives of dozens of these homeless people; reasons for their homelessness; estimated numbers of homeless in Canada.

Research

"Research notes: New data on homeless families result from Stanford U. research," *The Chronicle of Higher Education,* Nov. 27, 1991, p. A7.

Considers research conducted by Sanford Dornbusch and colleagues that found parents of homeless families tend to be younger, less educated and less likely to have histories of substance abuse or mental illness than do other homeless adults. Nine interrelated studies; other key findings.

Bohanon, C., "The economic correlates of homelessness in sixty cities," *Social Science Quarterly,* December 1991, p. 817.

Examines variations in the rate of homelessness across 60 metropolitan areas in the United States. The statistical analysis confirms the notion that homelessness is an economic problem. Empirical analysis; implications; concluding remarks.

Franklin, D. and P. Long, "Homelessness is a housing problem," *Health,* February/March 1992, p. 15.

Comments on a recent survey that studied nearly 700 homeless women and shows how most of these women tended to have more social ties to relatives and friends than did a comparison group of their housed peers. Only 4 percent had ever been hospitalized for mental problems; differences between homeless women and women in subsidized housing; no single "homeless type."

Back Issues

Great Research on Current Issues Starts Right Here... Recent topics covered by The CQ Researcher are listed below. Issues dated before May 10, 1991, were published under the name of Editorial Research Reports.

JANUARY 1991
Growing Influence of Boycotts
Should the U.S. Reinstate the Draft?
America's Archaeological Past
Peace Corps' Challenges in '90s

FEBRUARY 1991
Regional Impact of Recession
Puerto Rico's Status
Redistricting: Mapping Power
Nuclear Power

MARCH 1991
Acid Rain
Cost of the Gulf War
Reassessing Gun Laws
Future for Man in Space

APRIL 1991
Social Security
Canadian Crisis Over Quebec
California Drought
Electromagnetic Radiation

MAY 1991
School Choice
Racial Quotas
Animal Rights
U.S. and Japan

JUNE 1991
Children and Divorce
Teenage Suicide
Endangered Species
Europe 1992

JULY 1991
Teenagers and Abortion
Soviet Republics Rebel
Mexico's Emergence
Athletes and Drugs

AUGUST 1991
Sexual Harassment
Fetal Tissue Research
Oil Imports
The Palestinians

SEPTEMBER 1991
Police Brutality
Advertising Under Attack
Saving the Forests
Foster Care Crisis

OCTOBER 1991
Pay-Per-View TV
Youth Gangs
Gene Therapy
World Hunger

NOVEMBER 1991
Fast-Food Shake-Up
The Greening of Eastern Europe
Business' Role in Education
Cuba In Crisis

DECEMBER 1991
Retiree Health Benefits
Asian Americans
The Obscenity Debate
The Disabilities Act

JANUARY 1992
Term Limits
Oil Spills
Hunting Controversy
Alternative Medicine

FEBRUARY 1992
Threatened Coastlines
New Era in Asia
Assisted Suicide
Jobs in the '90s

MARCH 1992
Women and Sports
Underage Drinking
Garbage Crisis
Mafia Crackdown

APRIL 1992
Ozone Depletion
Welfare Reform
Politicians and Privacy
Illegal Immigration

MAY 1992
Native Americans
Jobs vs. Environment
Too Many Lawsuits?
Fairness in Salaries

JUNE 1992
Nuclear Proliferation
Food Irradiation
Lead Poisoning
Hard Times for Libraries

JULY 1992
Alternative Energy
Prescription Drug Prices
Alzheimer's Disease
Infant Mortality

Back issues are available for $4.00 (subscribers) or $7.00 (non-subscribers). Quantity discounts apply to orders over ten. To order, call Congressional Quarterly 1-800-432-2250.

Binders are available for $15.00. To order call 1-800-638-1710.

Future Topics

▶ *The Overworked American*

▶ *NATO's Evolving Role*

▶ *Marine Mammals*

THE CQ Researcher

PUBLISHED BY CONGRESSIONAL QUARTERLY INC., IN CONJUNCTION WITH EBSCO PUBLISHING

Work, Family and Stress

Can overworked Americans cope with today's time crunch?

MORE AND MORE AMERICANS ARE SHOUTING, "Stop the world, I want to get off!" Opinion polls reveal rising numbers who feel stressed, while some studies suggest a decline in leisure time and an increase in how much people work. Two-career families are especially buffeted by this trend. As the baby-boom generation negotiates parenthood and middle age, concerned groups are pushing workaholics to shift out of overdrive and spend more time with their families. The business world is trying to become more "family friendly," but managers are under pressure to remain economically competitive. Conflicts between work and family continue to raise questions about the roles of men and women, questions that society has been struggling with since women first entered the work force in large numbers three decades ago.

 August 14, 1992 • Volume 2, No. 30 • 689-712

Formerly Editorial Research Reports

COVER ART: BARBARA SASSA-DANIELS

CQ Researcher

August 14, 1992
Volume 2, No. 30

EDITOR
Sandra Stencel

MANAGING EDITOR
Thomas J. Colin

ASSOCIATE EDITOR
Richard L. Worsnop

STAFF WRITERS
Charles S. Clark
Mary H. Cooper
Rodman D. Griffin

PRODUCTION EDITORS
Laurie De Maris
Sarah E. Merritt

EDITORIAL ASSISTANT
Michael M. Taylor

GRAPHICS
Jack Auldridge

PUBLISHED BY
Congressional Quarterly Inc.

CHAIRMAN
Andrew Barnes

VICE CHAIRMAN
Andrew P. Corty

EDITOR AND PUBLISHER
Neil Skene

EXECUTIVE EDITOR
Robert W. Merry

PUBLICATIONS MARKETING/SALES
Robert Smith

EDITOR, EBSCO PUBLISHING
Melissa Kummerer

The CQ Researcher (ISSN 1056-2036). Formerly Editorial Research Reports. Published weekly (48 times per year, not printed the first Friday of any month with five Fridays) by Congressional Quarterly Inc., 1414 22nd St., N.W., Washington, D.C. 20037. Rates are furnished upon request. Second-class postage paid at Washington, D.C. POSTMASTER: Send address changes to The CQ Researcher, 1414 22nd St., N.W., Washington, D.C. 20037.

Work, Family and Stress

By Charles S. Clark

The Issues

In the go-go years of the 1980s, more than a few American households awoke to find that life had dealt them a rude surprise. "Our careers are important to us," a 37-year-old female lawyer told an inquiring sociologist. "Before we had children, we would work hard and play some, too. We used to go out a lot together, sometimes to a different movie every night. We bicycled weekends.

"But when our [law] practices got up to 55 hours a week and Kevin was born, we went into a state of siege. No one tells you how a child turns your life around. For a while, there we were, just surviving, very little sleep, no sex, little talk, delight in Kevin and adrenaline. We just say hello in bed before dropping off."[1]

What the victims of such chaos began calling the "family time famine" would only worsen as an economic recession ushered in the 1990s. "Workers are weary, parents are frantic and even children haven't a moment to spare," a *Time* magazine cover story proclaimed.[2]

The frustration was evident in a 1990 Roper Organization poll, which found that for the first time in 15 years, more respondents (41 percent) said the most important thing in their lives was leisure rather than work (36 percent). A CNN-*Time* poll in 1991 showed 61 percent agreeing that "earning a living today requires so much effort that it's difficult to enjoy life." And in a 1991 survey for the Hilton Hotels Corp., more than half of the 1,010 Americans questioned said they would gladly sacrifice a day's pay for an extra day off.[3]

The craving for more time was shown to be exacting a toll on people's health. Scientists expressed amaze-

ment at the number of Americans who were sacrificing sleep to get more done and showing up at work visibly drowsy.[4] "Stress is running like fire through the American workplace," said an official of Northwestern National Life Insurance Co., which surveyed its employees this year and found that 65 percent suffered from exhaustion and insomnia.[5]

In 1991, Harvard University economist Juliet B. Schor analyzed the time crunch in her provocative best-seller, *The Overworked American: The Unexpected Decline of Leisure*. Schor argued that Americans in the past two decades, in sharp contrast with their trade competitors in Europe, have increased their work hours by the equivalent of a full month per year. (*See chart, p. 698.*) Using statistics that some dispute (*see story, p. 693*), Schor blamed the trend on a decline in real wages, a rise in consumer materialism and the tendency of companies to avoid the expense of hiring new employees and paying them fringe benefits by having current employees work overtime.

The reasons for the time shortage are manifold. The galloping pace of new technology is a clear factor. Americans now command each other to "fax it!" rather than wait for the mail, and they grow impatient with their preprogrammed telephones when they are forced to dial a number manually.

The information explosion is also adding pressure. The dazzling array of specialized publications, the thousands of advertisements glimpsed per day, the scores of channels on cable TV, the 24-hour news broadcasts all combine to overwhelm today's hurried consumer with an overload of choices.

"Too much information violates our senses and even becomes harmful," notes business writer Jeff Davidson in his recent book, *Breathing Space: Living and Working at a Comfortable Pace in a Sped-Up Society*. "As you receive more information, you experience stress, anxiety, even helplessness. Your perception of breathing space is adversely and directly influenced by the more news, information and details that you ingest, or believe you have to ingest."[6]

Another source of stress is the recession itself, which has been prompting struggling companies to "smartsize," notes Barbara Otto, a spokeswoman for 9to5, a Cleveland-based workplace-rights organization. By trimming their payrolls of middle managers to reduce costs, firms are forcing lower-ranking employees — particularly women — to do overtime to absorb the work without increasing their pay and without looking at the impact on their child-care arrangements, she says.

Finally, time has become a precious commodity to the once self-indulgent members of the baby-boom generation — 60 percent of whom are now parents — who want to slow down and hang out with their children.

The big shift — which some have dubbed "the new familism" — was documented in "family values" surveys commissioned by Massachusetts Mutual Life Insurance Co. in 1989 and again in 1991. Over the two-year period, the polls showed a 20-point rise in the number of people who felt they were not spending enough time with their children. And the trend has been building.

Studies by the University of Maryland based on detailed "time diaries" kept by American families showed that parents spent 40 percent less time with their children in the 1980s than they did in the 1960s, a drop from 30 hours a week to 17 hours.[7] The effects of the "parenting deficit" — the rise of latchkey children, increased drug abuse and sexual promiscuity — have been noted, particularly now that the first children who were raised in the dual-career families of the 1970s are old enough to articulate resentment. (A CNN-*Time* poll of 18-to-29-year-olds in 1990 showed that 64 percent planned to spend more time with their children than their parents did.)

With families of the 1980s exhausted from a lifestyle built on shortcuts — "quality time" appointments with children, "grazing" for food instead of sitting down to family meals — it's small wonder that a new array of activist groups has emerged to try and shift society out of overdrive. Some are organizing interested parents, some are campaigning for a shorter workweek, some are negotiating for more flexible workplace rules and some are seeking help from government, among them liberals concerned about children in poverty and conservatives promoting "family values."

"Something has changed about the ability of a family to take care of its members," says Fran Sussner Rodgers, founder of Work/Family Directions, a Boston consulting firm that counsels corporations on work-family issues. "The question is, 'What is the solution?'" As experts search for the answer, here are the key issues being discussed:

Is the dual-career family to blame for the modern-day time crunch?

In the collective memory of modern Americans squeezed for time are vivid black-and-white images from the television world of the 1950s: genial fathers strolling home to be greeted by neatly dressed children and serene, well-coiffed housewives named June Cleaver or Harriet Nelson. Such images stand in stark contrast to the reality of life in today's two-career families.

"Increasingly, family schedules are intricate applications of time-motion principles, with everything engineered to the minute and with every piece designed to fall in the right place in the right time," writes Barbara Dafoe Whitehead, a social historian at the New York City-based Institute for American Values, a research organization concentrating on family issues. "When a shoe is lost, or a cold car engine fails to turn over, or the baby fills his diaper just after he's been zipped into his snowsuit, or the staff meeting runs late, the whole intricate schedule can unravel and fall apart."[8]

It should come as no surprise that some blame the intensified pace on the movement of mothers into the work force. The notion that career women neglect their families has been articulated in recent years by University of Chicago classicist Allan Bloom in his mid-1980s best-seller, *The Closing of the American Mind*, and by author Michael Levin in his 1988 critique, *Feminism and Freedom*.

Among policy experts, there is new concern that a mother's "unbridled careerism" is psychologically harmful to her children. As Karl Zinsmeister of the Washington-based American Enterprise Institute for Public Policy Research recently wrote: "For years, one of the most cogent criticisms of American sex roles has been the argument that many fathers get so wrapped up in earning and doing at the workplace that they become dehumanized, losing interest in the intimate joys of family life and failing to participate fairly in domestic responsibilities. Now it appears workaholism and family dereliction have become equal-opportunity diseases, striking mothers as well as fathers."[9]

Women themselves in recent years have shown signs that the "superwoman" desire to "have it all" may be more trouble than it's worth. In the 1980s, many observers became alarmed by news reports of the rising number of heart attacks among women and of safety problems at daycare centers. Yankelovich Clancy Shulman's annual Monitor survey[10] found that the number of American women who say that enough money would get them to stop work jumped from 35 percent in 1987 to 56 percent in 1990. In 1990, the Bureau of Labor Statistics for the first time in decades noted a 200,000 drop in the number of women in the work force. But economists attribute the slight decline at least in part to the recession and the difficulties would-be working mothers have in finding child care.

To most women and men, however, returning to the idyllic days of June Cleaver is hardly an option. "It's a crazy argument — unless society first makes major changes," says Ellen Galinsky, co-president of the Families and Work Institute in New York City, which researches workplace family policies. "It might not be crazy for some families because it's a personal decision, but to do it en masse would require a lot more family support."

Currently, about 58 percent of U.S. households with children have two

Continued on p. 694

Is the Time Crunch Real or Imagined?

Notwithstanding the many "trend" stories in the news, the notion that Americans are overworked and overscheduled may in fact be an overstatement. Popular writings in recent years suggesting that "Americans have run out of time," in *Time* magazine's phrase, have relied on anecdotes from stressed-out individuals and on opinion polls, such as a famous Louis Harris poll showing that Americans in 1989 were working 20 percent more than they did in 1973 and were enjoying 32 percent less free time.

Only last year, the time-crunch theory was bolstered with some economic data that many experts promptly called into question.

In her 1991 best-seller, *The Overworked American*, Harvard University economist Juliet B. Schor argued that a century-old trend toward increased leisure time was reversed during the past two decades, and that a month of extra work had been added to the average American's burden. Annual work time rose by 158 hours from 1969-89, Schor asserted in an updated study she co-authored for the Economic Policy Institute, while paid time off for vacations, holidays, sick leave and personal days shrank by 15 percent.†

Schor's numbers, as she acknowledges, conflict with others in the field. The federal Bureau of Labor Statistics (BLS) reports that the average workweek actually shrank slightly, from 39.9 hours in 1969 to 39.6 hours in 1989 and to 39.3 hours in 1991. (BLS economists note that the arrival of women in the work force spread the work among more people and hence kept workweek numbers stable.)

A well-known study by University of Michigan economists F. Thomas Juster and Frank P. Stafford found that average weekly leisure time grew by six hours from 1965-1981. And a rise in leisure hours also was reported by the Americans Use of Time Project, a series of studies headed by University of Maryland sociologist John B. Robinson. It found that from 1965-1985, men's free time stabilized at about 40 hours a week while women's leisure time grew from 34 to 39 hours.†† The reasons for the increase include the fact that women are doing less housework and that people are marrying later and having fewer children.

Schor explains in her book that she found flaws in the Michigan and Maryland figures, calling their samples "unrepresentative" because, she says, they fail to correct for differences in age groups, the size of the respondents' cities, dips in the economy and a shortage of female respondents. She produced her adjusted numbers by combining some of the Michigan figures with data from the federal government's Current Population Survey, which the Census Bureau performs for the Bureau of Labor Statistics (BLS).

To Robinson, Schor's figures are problematic because "she doesn't look at leisure hours, she only infers them from the Bureau of Labor Statistics data." His methods rely on detailed "time diaries," or logs, kept by respondents. "They are much more accurate in measuring work and household chores than people's estimates given in a 3-10 second interview with the BLS," he says. He says Schor misrepresents the Michigan and Maryland data and "adds on the time-diary data only when it fits what she wants."

Robinson cautions that he is "not unsympathetic" to Schor's thesis that Americans work harder and are under more stress than people in other countries. The argument just can't be made using time studies, he says.

The "central paradox," as his own studies show, is that the supposed rise in leisure time has still left Americans feeling that their leisure is declining: 32 percent of his time-diary respondents in 1985 said they feel more rushed, as opposed to 28 percent in 1975.‡ Robinson suggests that it may be a result of the baby boomers having entered the 36-50 age bracket, a time when parenting and home-owning obligations cut into free time. Baby boomers, he and others have noted, get lots of media coverage.

How Much Free Time?

More than half the people responding to a recent poll said that compared to five years ago, they felt they had less free time.

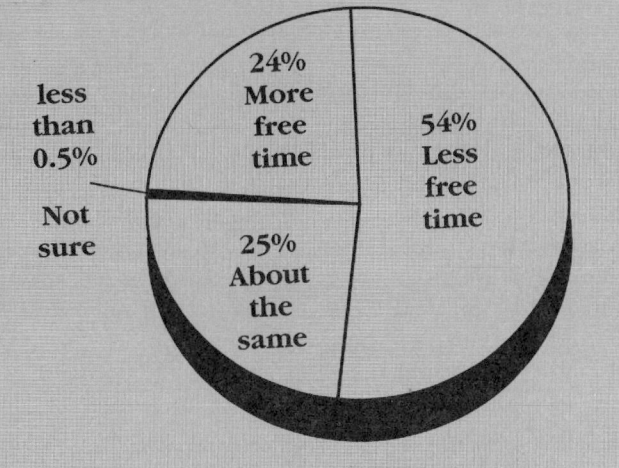

24% More free time

less than 0.5% Not sure

54% Less free time

25% About the same

†Juliet B. Schor and Laura Leete-Guy, *The Great American Time Squeeze: Trends in Work and Leisure 1969-1989*, Economic Policy Institute, February 1992.

††John P. Robinson, "Time's Up," *American Demographics*, July 1989, p. 33.

‡John P. Robinson, "Time's Squeeze," *American Demographics*, February 1990, p. 30.

A Glossary of New Work Options

Efforts to juggle work and family over the past two decades have produced a multitude of alternatives to the classic 9-to-5 routine. The most common options include:

Regular part-time work: Voluntarily reduced work hours, with prorated employee benefits.

Flexitime: Employees choose their starting and quitting times as long as they put in the required minimum. (Attendance may be mandatory during prescribed "core hours.")

Flexiplace: Employees work at home all or part of the week, usually with electronic communication to the office. (Also called telecommuting.)

Job sharing: Two similarly qualified individuals each work part-time to share the tasks and responsibilities of a single job. Benefits are pro-rated.

Compressed work week: Normal five-day 40-hour week is condensed to four 10-hour days or some variation, allowing employees a three-day weekend.

Phased retirement: Gradual reduction of work hours for employees nearing retirement age.

Split-shift parenting: Work hours for couples arranged so that hours never overlap (usually involving a night shift) so that one parent is always available for the children.

Sequencing: Women halt their careers when they become mothers and then resume them when their children are older (see p. 702).

Sources: Association of Part-Time Professionals; New Ways to Work

---

Continued from p. 692
breadwinners, compared with only 18.6 percent in 1960, according to the Bureau of Labor Statistics. Women's participation in the work force is expected to grow in coming decades as the economy experiences a shortage of skilled labor. As for the traditional nuclear family — an employed husband, homemaker wife and children — it's now found in only 15 percent of U.S. households, according to the Census Bureau.[11]

Clearly, many women work because they're ambitious or seek personal satisfaction. ("My brain would turn to mush if I stayed home" is a common refrain.) "Studies show that working mothers have higher self-esteem and get less depressed than housewives," writes Arlie Hochschild, a sociologist at the University of California at Berkeley.[12]

But polls and other data show that the majority of mothers work out of economic necessity (see p. 700). "The middle-class package of a home, car, health care and college have increased beyond the cost of living in the 1980s," notes Rep. Patricia Schroeder, D-Colo., whose Select Committee on Children, Youth and Families has held a series of hearings on the theme of "briefcases and babies."

University of Maryland economist Frank Levy has calculated that payments on a typical house in the 1950s cost 14 percent of an average 30-year-old American's gross income; by the mid-1980s, the figure had risen to 44 percent. What's more, Hochschild notes, in about a fifth of American households today, the woman's contribution to the family budget is higher than the man's.

For both economic and personal career reasons, many women see the stay-at-home option as a luxury they can't afford, even temporarily. "Many women say they want to quit because the degree of stress has become unmanageable," observes Barbara Geiger-Green, administrator of the Association of Part-Time Professionals in Falls Church, Va. "But they want to remain viable in the work force. Most want a little piece of both actions."

Notwithstanding the recent shift in attitudes away from work and toward the family, the decades-old influx of women into the work world shows few signs of abating in the long run. In 1991, the American Council of Education's survey of 211,000 college freshmen at 410 campuses showed the number of females who were planning to become full-time homemakers at only half of 1 percent.

Are workplace managers doing enough to accommodate work and family conflicts?

For decades, one of the most vocal critics of women who leave their children for work has been conservative activist Phyllis Schlafly. "I believe babies need moms," she now says. "But I urge young women to choose a career for part-time work, and I support flexible [workplace] options."

The solution to the time famine that attracts support across the political spectrum is the movement to make the workplace "family friendly." The smorgasbord of benefits that many companies have begun to offer includes varying combinations of on-site child care, financial aid or referral services for child care, job sharing, voluntary part-time work with benefits, maternity leave, leave for adoptive parents or employees with elderly relatives who are sick, flexitime, telecommuting (see story, p. 704) and flexible combinations of benefits, known as "cafeteria" plans.

In the past five years, several hundred American companies have created "work-family manager" positions. The Communications Workers of America and the International Brotherhood of Electrical Workers have negotiated work and family benefits language in separate sections of their contracts. Major corporations are also pooling resources to stretch dollars that are spent, for example, on child-care benefits. International Business Machines (IBM) has formed a team with American Express, Sears and Allstate, while Kodak has joined with Xerox and Bausch & Lomb.[13]

A recent survey of 1,000 major firms by Hewitt Associates found that 66 percent are providing some form of help with child care, 36 percent help with elder care, 53 percent offer flexible scheduling and 51 percent offer parental leave. According to the *Corporate Reference Guide to Work-Family Programs*, published in 1991 by the Families and Work Institute and the Ford Foundation, the most family-friendly companies are Aetna Life and Casualty, Corning, IBM and Johnson & Johnson.

The main reason companies are pitching in, notes the institute's Galinsky, is to stay competitive with rival companies in recruitment and retention of quality employees. She also notes that in the long run, family benefits will sweeten a company's bottom line by keeping employees loyal.

The Child Care Action Campaign, a New York City advocacy group, says breakdowns in efficiency because of employee turnover cost U.S. businesses $3 billion a year. Others note that the costs of replacing employees who leave when they have children is higher than offering the experienced employees reduced or flexible schedules. The Alexandria, Va.-based Society for Human Resource Management has calculated the cost of replacing a $12,000 employee at $4,000 for recruiting, $1,200 for training and $6,000 for the lost

productivity — a total of $11,200 in just the first year.

But another key reason companies are becoming family-friendly, according to Lynn O. Hayes, co-author of *The Best Jobs in America for Parents Who Want Careers and Time for Children Too*, is new sympathy from top management. More and more "gatekeepers in the business world are themselves part of the two-career chaos or are seeing their own sons and daughters struggle with it," she says.

Despite a number of well-publicized changes, however, corporate resistance to family-friendly flexibility remains pervasive, specialists agree. The demand for a shorter work week, as Juliet Schor observed, goes against many executives' views of how to keep their companies profitable. Three-fourths of the CEOs in a *Fortune* magazine poll said "competing with [the] Japanese will require us to push managers harder," she noted.[14] In fact, shorter work hours are classified by the Commerce Department as a negative "leading economic indicator," points out University of Iowa Professor Benjamin K. Hunnicutt, author of *Work Without End.*[15]

"Employers see a slippery slope," says Maria Lacquer, executive director of the Association of Part-Time Professionals. "They say, 'If I let one employee do it, I'd have to let everyone, and no work will get done.' There's also a perception that managers and supervisors resent it because they can't schedule meetings or take time off themselves."

"For the most part," says Diane Generous, senior associate director of employee relations of the National Association of Manufacturers in Washington, "the manager's attitude remains, 'I came up the hard way, I sacrificed, took time from my kids, and everyone should do it if he expects to move up.'"

"It's hard to change corporate culture," says consultant Fran Sussner Rodgers. "Companies think of re-

sponding to family issues as doing someone a favor. They think of whether Chuck's needs are greater than Sally's, but they should be thinking of how to take care of each employee's contribution. Creative managers should know how to use [family benefits] to make the most of people."

Many companies adopt the goal of implementing work-family policies but then leave those policies unimplemented. By Galinsky's survey, 68 percent of companies in 1990 said they were planning to launch programs, but only 21 percent actually did. She divides companies into three phases of progress: those that are cautiously supportive, those that have announced commitments from their executives and those that have actually integrated work-family policies into the corporate culture, which so far includes only 2 percent of companies. By 2 to 1, Galinsky's surveys show, supervisors thought they would be more flexible than employees thought they would. And most employees were worried that if they took advantage of family-friendly policies, their careers would be jeopardized.

Finally, Galinksy notes, there is a gap between the haves and have-nots in the distribution of family-friendly benefits, one that favors large companies that employ many professionals. A study by the Washington-based Urban Institute surveyed companies to determine how family-friendly benefits broke down among income classes. Flexitime was offered to 26 percent of employees from high-income families but to only 13 percent of those from low-income families; the work-at-home option was available to 16 percent of upper-income families but to only 4 percent of low-income families; and "cafeteria" benefits packages were available to 9 percent of employees from high-income households but to only 5 percent of the poor.[16]

Top Causes of Stress Among Men and Women

Only two areas were found to be more stressful for men than women, according to recent polls. Half of the working men surveyed (compared with 44 percent of the women) considered their co-workers a source of stress, and 40 percent (compared with 36 percent of the women) cited their bosses.

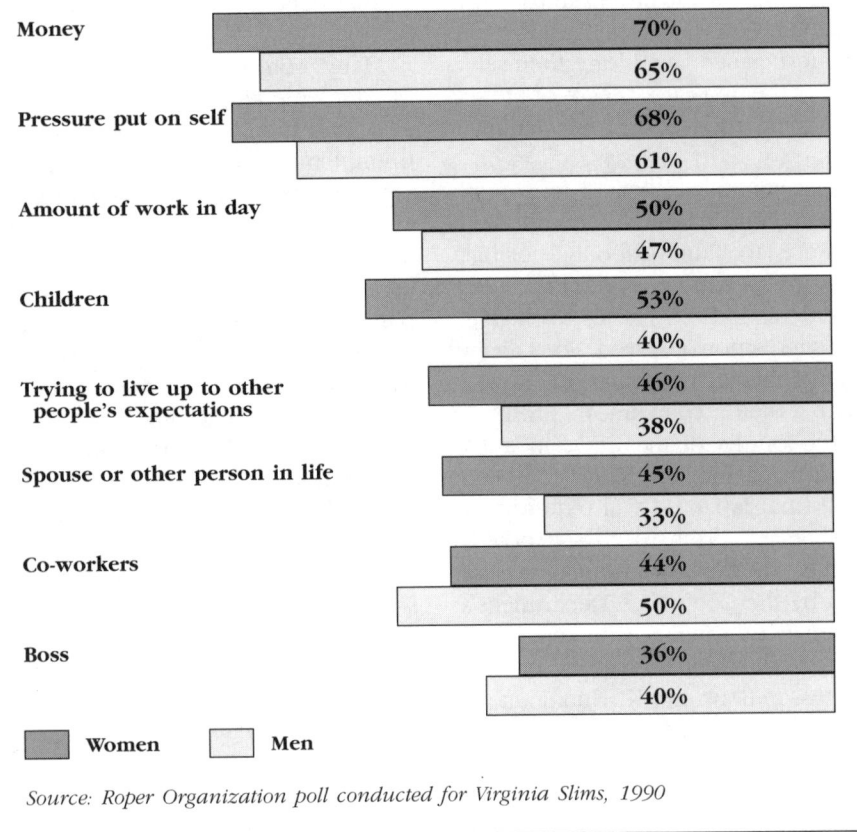

	Women	Men
Money	70%	65%
Pressure put on self	68%	61%
Amount of work in day	50%	47%
Children	53%	40%
Trying to live up to other people's expectations	46%	38%
Spouse or other person in life	45%	33%
Co-workers	44%	50%
Boss	36%	40%

Source: Roper Organization poll conducted for Virginia Slims, 1990

Is there a role for government in relieving work-family stress?

If there is consensus on the need for a family-friendly workplace, the unanimity breaks down on the issue of what the government should do to make it happen. To Schor and other liberals concerned about overwork, the United States should emulate such countries as Germany, Canada and Sweden by requiring businesses to limit the workweek, lengthen vacations and provide time off to new parents. "Germans are noting that the United States does not have a safety net," observes Galinsky. They can see "we're leading such stressed-out lives that we're losing our edge" in productivity.

The current vehicle for such an approach is the Family and Medical Leave Act. The version of the bill agreed to by House-Senate conferees Aug. 5 would require businesses with more than 50 employees to give workers up to 12 weeks of unpaid leave after the birth or adoption of a child or for the serious illness of the worker or an immediate family member. The bill enjoys broad bipartisan support, but it seems unlikely that sponsors can muster the two-thirds majority needed to override President Bush's promised veto (see p. 703).

To conservatives, the best way government can restore family life is not by issuing edicts to business but through income tax relief. The Washington-based Heritage Foundation, in a recent paper discussing the "family time famine" attributes the entry of mothers into the work force to rising taxes. Census data indicate that the average working mother earns about 32 percent of total family income, the foundation notes, but two-thirds of her earnings go to federal taxes that have been raised steadily since World War II. "In fact, if federal tax rates as a percentage of family income were restored to 1948 levels, and if the average employed mother in a two-parent family were to leave the labor force entirely, the family would see only a moderate dip in real post-tax income." [17]

The Washington-based Family Research Council, which promotes a "family values" agenda, has called for the government to make it easier for parents to stay home through a new young-child tax credit. Over the long term, it recommends removal of various disincentives for old-age employment, such as the Social Security earnings test, on the idea that parents with young children would be more willing to stay home and forgo income if they could count on working longer into their retirement years.

The gap between liberal and conservative philosophies is wide not only because of differing views on whether government should place burdens on business but also because of differing visions of the ideal structure of society. "The Left envisions the workplace as the center of life for adults, and day care and school as the center for children," says William R. Mattox Jr., director of policy analysis at the Family Research Council. "We want the home as the center for mother, father and children."

To Rep. Schroeder, the conservatives' talk of family values is a "great speech with no action." "The Right still holds onto the mindset that you shouldn't have a family unless you can afford it," she says. "It says, 'Don't take your caregiver problems into the workplace, and the government has no role.'" In a reference to first lady Barbara Bush, she adds, "Conservatives are simply telling American families to get a Barbara. We say these children are this nation's future. That's why so many corporate CEOs are now concerned." ■

BACKGROUND

The Industrial Pace

Americans who are bowled over by the hectic pace of modern life can take comfort in the fact that the tendency toward busyness stretches far back in human history. In ancient Greece, Plato warned "how foolish it was to run from leisure by working too much," covering up a fear of freedom and getting caught in the "webs of luxuries, power, politics and excessive amusements."[18]

Though leisure in ancient times was enjoyed primarily by the affluent, modern critics of overwork frequently point to the large number of holidays that were enjoyed by the common people. The ancient Romans celebrated some 200 public festivals a year and spent less than a third of their waking hours at work, notes McGill University architecture Professor Witold Rybczynski in his recent study of leisure, *Waiting for the Weekend*. In the Middle Ages, the Christian world celebrated 115 holidays, and the workday, though stretching as long as 16 hours in summer, is thought to have equaled just eight hours when afternoon naps and refreshment breaks were factored in.

It was the 18th-century Industrial Revolution, led by England and the United States, that urbanized what previously had been farm economies and introduced the worker to increasingly long work days. "Before capitalism, most people did not work very long hours at all, and the tempo of life was slow," writes Juliet Schor. "When capitalism raised their incomes, it also took away their time."[19]

Long workdays prompted one of the earliest strikes in American history, launched in 1791 by Philadelphia carpenters. Their demand for a 10-hour day was opposed by many employers who, mirroring today's managers, worried about falling behind foreign competition. "Shorter hours represented a workingclass brand of Jeffersonian liberalism, in which leisure was liberation from bosses, capitalism and toil," writes the University of Iowa's Hunnicutt.

A 70-hour, six-day workweek was standard practice in the 19th century, but following demands by social reformers and labor unions it dropped to 60 hours by the turn of the century. It wasn't until 1908 that a New England spinning mill became the first American factory to adopt the five-day week, partly as a concession to Jewish employees who couldn't work on the Saturday Sabbath and who didn't want to offend Christians by working on Sunday. The mill's 50-hour schedule was adopted by enlightened auto magnate Henry Ford in 1914 and soon emulated widely, though it drew heavy criticism from business groups.

During the Great Depression, the scarcity of jobs prompted employers to shorten hours to spread work around, and the workweek fell from 50 hours to 35 hours. When the Kellogg Co. switched to six-hour days in 1930, workers' productivity rose by some 4 percent.[20]

The 40-hour week was mandated by the 1938 Fair Labor Standards Act, hard-won by labor unions as part of President Franklin D. Roosevelt's New Deal. World War II would postpone its implementation, but by the late 1940s, 40 hours had become standard, and remains largely so today.

After a two-century march toward a shortened workweek, the labor movement, as Schor says, simply gave up the fight. "Once the Second World War began, the pressure for longer hours was unstoppable," she writes. "The immediate postwar years witnessed a surge of pent-up consumer demand. The baby boom and the spread of home ownership encouraged the acquisition of consumer goods. . . . The nation was locked into a pattern of work and spend. Leisure was left out of the loop."[21]

Indeed, postwar America's rising enchantment with work is told in figures from the Bureau of Labor Statistics: In 1948, 13 percent of Americans with full-time jobs worked more than 49 hours a week; by 1979 the total had risen to 18 percent; and by 1989, it was up to 24 percent.

The Culture of Work

The lack of leisure time that Americans complain of today is a product not just of economic pressures but of cultural values as well. For much of recent American history, leisure was viewed with Calvinist suspicion. In the 1920s, when the automobile had begun making vacations affordable and advertising was creating a mass-consumer culture, popular books warned that leisure would lead to laziness and drunkenness. Political pundit Walter Lippmann wrote of the "problem of leisure" in *Woman's Home Companion* magazine, warning that leisure offered difficult choices and that people would squander it on mass entertainments.

By the 1950s, amid the postwar

How Hard Do Americans Work?

Americans work harder than their European trade competitors, but not as hard as the Japanese. Japan tallies more hours per worker, and shorter vacations, than any other industrialized nation.

Country	Annual hours worked, per employee	Annual paid vacation, by law or by agreement
Belgium	1,572	5 weeks
Canada	1,887	3 weeks
Denmark	1,595	5 weeks
France	1,610	5 to 6 weeks
Germany	1,603	5-1/2 to 6 weeks
Italy	1,858	4 to 6 weeks
Japan	2,155	15-1/2 days
Netherlands	1,592	4 to 5 weeks
Norway	1,614	4 weeks, 1 day
Sweden	1,539	5 to 8 weeks
United Kingdom	1,856	4 to 6 weeks
United States	1,951	2-1/2 weeks

Sources: Laura Leete-Guy and Juliet B. Schor, The Great American Time Squeeze, *briefing paper published by the Economic Policy Institute; Canadian Manufacturers' Association; Embassy of Japan*

prosperity, church groups were meeting to debate the pitfalls of leisure, academics had formed departments of leisure studies and historian Arthur M. Schlesinger Jr. warned that increased leisure "was the most dangerous threat hanging over American society."

The prevailing cultural ethos in the decades that followed would do much to trounce leisure under the boot of the work ethic. The turning point in this process was captured in William H. Whyte Jr.'s 1956 classic, *The Organization Man*, which described the suburbanizing society of the 1950s as dominated by men who drew their identities from their role in their corporations, blurring the traditional line between work and personal life.

The "organization man," wrote Whyte, "is [as] sensitive to the bogy of overwork and ulcers as his forebears were to the bogy of slothfulness. He believes in leisure, but so does he believe in the Puritan insistence on hard, self-denying work.... That up-ward path toward the rainbow of achievement leads smack through the [corporate] conference room."[22]

The Cost of High-Pressure Living

Such attitudes, which in the 1960s would help provoke the hippie counterculture, were lamented by author Walter Kerr in 1965 in his popular book *The Decline of Pleasure*. Kerr wrote, "We are all of us compelled to read for profit, party for contacts, lunch for contracts, bowl for unity, drive for mileage, gamble for charity, go out for the evening for the greater glory of the municipality and stay home for the weekend to rebuild the house."[23]

By the 1970s, the terms "workaholic" and "hurry sickness" had been coined to describe that increasingly common personality who is driven by time pressure to perform several tasks at once, who has difficulty standing in line or doing nothing and who impatiently interrupts and completes other people's sentences. Corporate executives were warned that such be-havior can presage a heart attack.

In their 1974 book, *Type A Behavior and Your Heart*, two cardiologists said that the Type A personality "has staked his innermost security upon the pace of his status enhancement. This pace in turn depends on a *maximal* number of achievements accomplished in *minimal* amount of time, achievements recognized as significant by constantly changing groups of his peers and superiors."[24]

By the 1980s, the fast-forward style had swept millions of average Americans into a disturbing "cult of busyness," in the phrase of business journalist Amy Saltzman. In her 1991 book, *Downshifting: Reinventing Success on a Slower Track*, Saltzman fashioned a metaphor for the era from an encounter with a friend who "from a distance had the look of the '80s: hurried, determined, I've-got-somewhere-to-go-and-I'm-going-to-get-there-quickly self-confidence.

"As we moved closer, however ... the image seemed to lose its neat, glossy edges. In her haste to get wherever she was going, she had buttoned her black wool coat so that one side hung lower than the other; her mustard-colored cashmere scarf was ... in danger of slipping off her shoulder, small pastel slips of paper overflowed from her Filofax notebook. The uniform was right ... but the overall picture was slightly off-center."[25]

Motherhood vs. Career

Having spent the 1960s and '70s blazing their way into the work force, American women in the '80s found themselves emotionally tugged between the workplace and the home fires. A barrage of headlines stoked the self-doubt: "You can't do everything," *USA Today* warned. "Pressed for success, women career-

Continued on p. 700

Chronology

1960s Birth of the modern women's movement.

1963
Betty Friedan publishes her groundbreaking book, *The Feminine Mystique*, urging women to work outside the home.

1967
A congressional panel hears testimony predicting that by 1985, Americans would be working just 22 hours a week and would be able to retire at age 38.

———— • ————

1970s Women pour into the work force, fomenting public debate over the merits of raising children in day-care centers. Americans become aware of the dangers of "workaholism."

1970
Swedish economist Staffan Linder publishes his seminal book, *The Harried Leisure Class*, arguing that economic growth in the United States caused an increasing scarcity of leisure time.

1971
The first major corporate day-care center is opened in Cambridge, Mass., by the Stride-Rite shoe company. Rhona and Robert Rapoport publish *The Dual Career Families*, one of the earliest studies of modern-family life.

Dec. 9, 1971
President Richard M. Nixon vetoes a $2 billion child-care bill, saying it would weaken the family.

1974
Publication of *Type A Behavior and Your Heart*, by Meyer Friedman and Ray H. Rosenman, sounds the alarm about growing "workaholism."

Oct. 15, 1989
In a boost to working women, Congress passes the Pregnancy Disability Act banning discrimination on the basis of pregnancy and requiring health plans to cover pregnancy.

———— • ————

1980s Women continue moving into the work force, but news reports of stress and unsafe child care give many second thoughts; expanding economy accelerates the pace of life; work-family issues emerge as a corporate benefits issue.

1984
Marjorie Hansen Shaevitz publishes her book, *The Superwoman Syndrome*.

1985
Pediatrician T. Berry Brazelton publishes *Working and Caring*.

April 11, 1988
President Ronald Reagan proclaims National Child Care Awareness Week.

January-February 1989
An article by Felice N. Schwartz in the *Harvard Business Review* creates a furor over what comes to be called "the Mommy track" for women in the work force.

1990s Americans complain of feeling burnout and time-crunch pressure; work-family issues rise to the top of corporate agendas.

June 29, 1990
President Bush vetoes a bill to require businesses to offer parental leave.

Nov. 5, 1990
President Bush signs the Child Care Act to spend $22.5 billion over five years to aid with child care.

1991
Juliet B. Schor publishes *The Overworked American: The Unexpected Decline of Leisure*.

November 1991
House and Senate pass separate versions of the Family and Medical Leave Act, a measure similar to the one President Bush vetoed in 1990.

January 1992
The Joint Economic Committee releases "Families on a Treadmill," a report showing that two-earner couples with children by 1989 were working more but earning less than in 1979.

Aug. 5, 1992
House and Senate conferees approve a compromise version of the Family and Medical Act. President Bush has said that he will veto the measure, which is awaiting final congressional action.

Good Parent vs. Good Professional

Many of the hard-edged qualities cultivated by successful professionals are directly at odds with the patient, selfless elements of good nurturing, says author Sylvia Ann Hewlett.

Qualities needed to succeed in chosen career	Qualities needed to meet needs of child
Long hours and one's best energy.	Time to be together as a family and energy for the hard tasks of parenting.
Mobility.	Stability.
A prime commitment to oneself.	Selflessness and a commitment to others.
Efficiency.	A tolerance for chaos.
A controlling attitude.	An ability to let go.
A drive for high performance.	An acceptance of difference and failure.
Orientation toward the future.	Appreciation of the moment.
A goal-oriented, time-pressured approach to the task at hand.	An ability to tie the same pair of shoelaces twenty-nine times with patience and humor.

Source: Sylvia Ann Hewlett, When the Bough Breaks, *1991*

ists are cheating themselves," reported *The Washington Post.*

News magazines and talk shows were filled with accounts of feuds between career mothers and homemakers as well as horror stories about unsafe day-care centers and studies purporting to show the psychological harm of child care outside the family. Working mothers confronted with a sick child or a no-show baby sitter found themselves afraid to explain the situation to demanding supervisors and resorting to alibis about "car trouble."

The emerging pull of family duties was clearly stronger on career women than on men. "I believe most women choose to conserve their time and energy in ways that men do

not," says Halcyone H. Bohen, a Washington D.C., clinical psychologist, "mainly by not seeking leadership in the same ways men do.... They do so in part because they want to, in part because men do not participate equally in parenting."

Topping off the media blitz was a controversial article in the *Harvard Business Review* in 1989 by corporate consultant Felice N. Schwartz, which gave rise to the term "mommy track." Though Schwartz did not use the term (it was coined by *The New York Times* in describing her concept), she shook up current feminist thinking by arguing that corporations should recognize two types of female employees: "career primary" and "career-and-family" women.

Schwartz's opening sentence contained the politically incorrect admission that "the cost of employing women in management is greater than the cost of employing men." Angry feminists accused her of setting the revolution back by giving ammunition to the prejudices of male executives. (In her new book, *Breaking with Tradition: Women and Work, the New Facts of Life*, Schwartz refines her thesis, asserting that the shortage of skilled labor makes women invaluable to the future of corporate management. She also says that corporations should consider a "parent track" for women and men and that managers should "learn how to measure productivity instead of counting hours spent in the office."[26])

To feminists such as Susan Faludi, author of the much-heralded 1991 book *Backlash: The Undeclared War on American Women*, all the guilt-inducing stories were part of an effort by anti-feminists and a trend-hungry press to pressure working women to go back to the kitchen. "Journalism replaced the 'pro-family' diatribes of fundamentalist preachers with sympathetic and even progressive-sounding rhetoric," she wrote. "It cosmeticized the scowling face of anti-feminism while blackening the feminist eye. In the process, it popularized the backlash beyond the New Right's wildest dreams."[27]

Trying to "Have It All"

To others, however, the change in women during the 1980s was a personal realization, a change from within that is experienced only when one becomes a mother. "Susan Faludi and [*Ms.* magazine founder] Gloria Steinem don't have children," notes *Washington Times* syndicated columnist Suzanne Fields.

The feeling of frustration brought on by straining to "have it all" was also noted by prominent pediatrician T. Berry Brazelton, who recorded the

Continued on p. 702

Who's Doing the Housework (Or Should Be)

What is the single easiest solution to the time crunch in today's two-income families? The clear answer for many is for men to share more of the cooking, cleaning and child care. In a 1990 poll conducted by the Roper Organization for Virginia Slims cigarettes, 69 percent of women and 64 percent of men cited increased housework by men as the solution — nearly twice the number of respondents who chose flexible work hours or more day-care centers.

"The second shift," as housework is called by Arlie Hochschild, a sociologist at the University of California at Berkeley, burdens women with as much as an extra month's worth of labor every year, she estimates, creating a wide "leisure gap" between the sexes.

Feminists and other observers see this as a sign of a "stalled revolution" in gender relations. "It was unrealistic 20 years ago" to assume that men would take up the housework abandoned by women who entered the work force, says Edward Zigler, a Yale University psychology professor. "Fathers today are more helpful and nourishing, but the fact of the matter is we're far away from a 50 percent split."

The most reputable systematic data, derived from "time diaries" kept by households being polled, show that men perform about one-third of household chores and have been increasing their share, according to University of Maryland researchers.† "While married men's 34 percent of housework in 1985 is still far from the 50 percent that would denote equality," says Joseph Pleck, a scholar of work-family issues at Wellesley College's Center for Research on Women, "the increase from men's 20 percent share of housework and child care in 1965 is substantial."

Marital feuds over housework are complicated by long-standing cultural and psychological differences between the sexes. "Most women cook dinner and most men change the oil in the family car," Hochschild writes in her book, *The Second Shift: Working Parents and the Revolution at Home*. "But dinner needs to be prepared every evening about six o'clock, whereas the car oil needs to be changed every six months, any day around that time, any time that day." ††

Women suffer more stress from housework, Hochschild says, because their tasks involve more rigid deadlines. Moreover, men often make a "fetish" out of a single household task, she adds, making pies, grilling fish or baking bread, and then converting "a single act into a substitute for a multitude of chores for the second shift." ‡

Many men, of course, see it differently. "There's some legitimacy to those arguments, and I don't believe men should come home, prop their feet up on a recliner and order the wife around," says William R. Mattox Jr., director of policy analysis at the Family Research Council. "But I've never heard women complain that men are doing the bulk of carpentry and yard work. I've heard women say they'd rather do two hours of dusting inside in the air conditioning than do an hour of yard work in the hot sun."

Hostility over chore-sharing can threaten a marriage. The arguments are often a "stand-in for 'Does what I want matter, does what's important to me make a difference to you?'" says Halcyone H. Bohen, a Washington, D.C., clinical psychologist who has studied work and family conflict. She counsels men and women to pay more attention to their feelings and to "slow down enough to realize what's behind all the pressure and irritation with each other."

Male resistance to increased housework is frustrating to many in the women's movement. "It's easier to pass legislation than to make more equitable personal relationships," laments Patricia Ireland, president of the National Organization for Women (NOW).

But critics of feminism caution women not to push men into becoming so-called "house-husbands." "Men are throwing up their hands and going into the woods to beat tom-toms," says *Washington Times* syndicated columnist Suzanne Fields, referring to the new men's movement led by Robert Bly. "The notion that women can re-create men in their own image is a foolish idea. And women wouldn't like the new men, anyway."

Wealthier families, of course, have long finessed the housework problem by hiring a housekeeper, a solution that dismays Hochschild and other feminists because it allows men to avoid taking on the consciousness of "the second shift."

For the time being, observers agree, average two-earner families appear to be coping with the housework problem by simply tolerating dirtier homes. Rep. Patricia Schroeder, D-Colo., who in the 1960s and early '70s was in the vanguard of the movement of women into the work force, dedicated her 1989 autobiography, *Champion of the Great American Family*, to her husband, Jim, "for giving up home-cooked meals, darned socks and a dust-free home."

---

† See John P. Robinson, "Who's Doing the Housework?" *American Demographics*, December 1988, p. 24.

†† Arlie Hochschild, *The Second Shift: Working Parents and the Revolution at Home* (1989), p. 8.

‡ *Ibid.*, p. 47.

Continued from p. 700

following confession in his 1985 book, *Working and Caring:* "I'm a lawyer in town," said a tearful women who had brought her young son to Brazelton as a patient. "Suddenly, I don't want to go back to work at all. I was counsel for a woman's rights organization and had bought completely into their beliefs. I waited as long as I dared to have this baby, though we both wanted him. I love my work and resented the idea of having to leave it even for a month. After he was born, I suddenly fell completely in love. I couldn't eat or sleep or think of anything but my baby. I don't care about work any longer.

"I realize I'm a woman without a culture. I can't believe in the woman's movement in the same way I did in the past. And I have no good models to follow as a mother who must go back to work." [28]

"What has happened," says consultant Fran Rodgers, "is that a generation of women got out of college believing we could do it all. We worked our tails off. But it is obvious that after 20 years, we're not succeeding, with or without children. A whole generation of women paid a tremendous price, and now we get to that middle-age sigh: Was it worth it? Where was the support? For years the burden of change was on women. Now there is an understanding that men and workplaces have to change."

The Daddy Track

"Men need more and more support and preparation to become successful nurturers," writes Brazelton. "A father who allows himself to be excluded with no chance to feel competent and important to his baby will be angry and will often undermine his wife's role."

The notion that men should assume a larger share of the work-family burden gained ground steadily in the past two decades. In a Roper poll conducted for Virginia Slims cigarettes, the number of respondents who said that a husband who stays home loses respect shrank from 68 percent of women and 58 percent of men in 1970 to only 19 percent and 21 percent, respectively, in 1990.

There are now nine states (plus the District of Columbia) that require employers to offer some sort of paternity leave. "We had one of the biggest, toughest guys in the company ask for parental leave," the chief executive of a major bank told *Fortune* magazine, "[and] then nobody thought it so odd anymore." [29]

"The attitude is actually out there — yes, fathers should get involved," said Joseph H. Pleck, a researcher at Wellesley College's Center for Research on Women. "But there is also the attitude that fathers should not reduce their commitment to the job, never forget that their primary responsibility is to earn an income." [30]

In a 1990 survey of 1,000 companies by the accounting firm of Robert Half International, 31 percent offered paternity leave, but only 1 percent of male employees had taken advantage of it. "Men get conflicting, if subtle, pressure from their women in these matters," notes psychologist Bohen. "*She* may talk a lot about wanting *him* to share 50-50. But she also wants him to succeed in his career — which often means working the longest hours right in the years when the pressures on families are the greatest."

Rodgers notes that "the workplace is more unforgiving for men, and the family types are thought of as the odd ducks. That's part of it, but the big issue is how men and women think about life at home. Generally, the man trades off family time and women trade careers. It's deeper than we understand."

A Third Option for Women?

"We're in a period of transition," says Patricia Ireland, president of the National Organization for Women (NOW). Feminists "are accused of trying to live politically correct personal lives, but what we really want is more choices. I despair when young women ask me which choice they should make. I say, 'Pick a good one.'"

One approach to finessing the work-family dilemma that emerged during the 1980s is the option called "sequencing." Numerous successful American career women — among them Supreme Court Justice Sandra Day O'Connor, former United Nations Representative Jeane J. Kirkpatrick and Labor Secretary Lynn Martin — are cited by backers of sequencing for having spent years at home during their early career years raising children.

"Let me assure you that many other women with perhaps lesser talent have also reached their goals through sequencing," says Edith U. Fierst, a Washington, D.C., attorney. "Studies I have made of successful sequencers include nearly 100 women. Almost without exception, these women are well-satisfied with the way they dealt with the family/career dilemma and with their careers." [31]

The drawbacks to sequencing lie mostly in the image it creates in the eyes of workplace managers. "Employers don't like to see a gap in an employee's history," notes Barbara Geiger-Green of the Association of Part-Time Professionals. "If they don't see a significant achievement other than raising children, if they see you're not involved with the community or making money, they assume you are not motivated, or lazy."

Sequencing also imposes "opportunity costs," Galinsky points out. "There's a feeling that you can never regain the income lost from sequencing. Our focus groups show that women are worried about divorce and the family's need for a second earner." Women feel a strong need to keep their hand in, she adds, because there are others ready to take over their jobs.

∎

Workplace Stress: Is the Computer a Friend or Foe?

The computer revolution has given the modern workplace an array of new options and improved efficiency. But far from having a calming effect on overworked employees, computerization has itself become a source of increasing psychological stress.

This paradox was examined as early as 1984 by Craig Brod, a Berkeley, Calif., psychotherapist, in a book called *Technostress: The Human Cost of the Computer Revolution*. Brod described strange new complaints he was hearing from his patients: "Those who worked with computers — from clerical workers to CEOs to computer programmers — consistently revealed to me the striking effects that computers were having on their personal and professional lives. Not only were they contending with easily recognizable stress reactions such as headaches and fatigue, they were beginning to internalize the standards by which the computer works: accelerated time, a desire for perfection, yes-no patterns of thinking."

Brod wrote of "techno-centered experts' annoyance with human inefficiency" and noted their difficulties in making the break between life at work and home. "Being a good mother is about interruptions," one computer user told him during a discussion of her relationships with her children. "Right now, I just can't tolerate interruptions."

By offering so much power, Brod observes, computers broaden our view of what we *can* and *should* do. "The person is immersed in processing information, which overshadows normal sensory awareness.... Meals are skipped and meetings missed as a problem is pursued.... But symptoms of an overtaxed mind are not as easily recognized as those of an overtaxed body, so hardworking computer users bend their minds to questionable limits."

The most potent stress-inducing aspect of computers is the ability they give supervisors to tally operators' keystrokes, and thus "measure" their productivity. Monitoring keystrokes has been cause for concern among labor unions, including the Communications Workers of America (CWA). In a CWA-commissioned study released in 1990, engineering professors at the University of Wisconsin compared workers whose keystrokes were being monitored against a control group. Consistently, they found, the monitored workers suffered 12-16 percent more depression, tension, fatigue and back pain.

A study released in July by the National Institute of Occupational Safety and Health had similar results, noting that users of visual display terminals were more prone to stress-related injuries even when they followed recommended procedures for proper posture. "The study points to the need to address psychological factors, especially work pressure and job insecurity," the institute said.†

Congress is now considering legislation (HR 1218) introduced by Rep. Pat Williams, D-Mont., that would discourage clandestine workplace monitoring of keystrokes by requiring employers to tell workers when the monitoring might take place.

---

† Quoted in *The Washington Post*, July 21, 1992.

CURRENT SITUATION

Support for Family Leave

Sen. Albert Gore, D-Tenn., on the day this July when he was selected as running mate for Democratic presidential candidate Bill Clinton, made a highly partisan comment on the central policy issue in the current debate over work and family stress. The Republicans "claim to be pro-family," Gore said, "but when we pass legislation for the people of this country which gives mothers and fathers a chance to have a little time off from work when a child is seriously injured, or when a child is first born, the Bush-Quayle administration vetoes it because they're afraid that it's going to cost money to the wealthy and powerful of this country."

The Family and Medical Leave Act, which would expand to businesses across the country the mandatory unpaid-leave requirement that is currently the law in 23 states, has passed both the House and Senate and is awaiting final approval. President Bush, who vetoed an earlier version of the bill in November 1990, has vowed to veto this one as well.

The act is a top priority of several organizations that exist to shift the country's direction on work and family issues. The Shorter Work-Time Group of Boston, a coalition of labor- and women's-rights activists, healthcare specialists, economists and work-family consultants, has folded the bill into its national campaign for a six-hour day and 30-hour week. The bill is "a minuscule and pathetic attempt to deal with the problem because the leave is unpaid and lasts only nine months," says spokeswoman Barbara Brandt. "But it's better than nothing, and it's representative of the issue."

Also solidly behind the act is Parent Action, a Baltimore-based group co-founded by T. Berry Brazelton. It has set up a state-by-state network of parents who want to create more time and money for families, lobby for affordable health care, expand community services and "promote respect for the role of parenting."

Finally, the act is favored by several work-family consulting groups, among them San Francisco-based New Ways to Work. It has been working with corporate executives to promote flexible work options and is doing research and advocacy work for "economic justice," according to co-founder Barney Olmsted. Her group hopes to demonstrate, for example, that the recent trend among companies toward involuntary part-time work with meager benefits is not cost-effective. "We want to make sure people don't have to trade their safety net in order to reduce their stress in coping with full-time work," she says.

Business Opposition

Mandated family leave is opposed by the Concerned Alliance of Responsible Employers (CARE), a coalition of the National Association of Wholesalers, the National Association of Manufacturers (NAM), the Society for Human Resource Managers and the U.S. Chamber of Commerce. "Uncle Sam doesn't have any more money," says Mary Tevenner, senior director of government relations for the wholesalers' association, "so he's going to the next deep pocket — private enterprise."[32]

The NAM's Diane Generous, who herself recently negotiated a permanent part-time arrangement with her employer following the birth of her second child, says that "companies should be as accommodating as they can be, but we can't lose sight of the fact that the reason for their existence is profit — we're not talking charity here. Passing legislation won't

change attitudes. What if a company has a parental-leave policy but treats its employees like dirt?"

Opposition to family leave is particularly strong among small businesses, which often "tailor special needs to special employees in order to keep them," notes Terry Hill, spokeswoman for the Washington-based National Federation of Independent Business. In 1991, the federation polled 950 owners of small and medium-size companies on existing family-leave policies and found that 90 percent routinely grant requests for leave. But 55 percent said they would be more likely to reduce other employees' benefits if family leave was mandated by the government.

The Family Research Council opposes the Family and Medical Leave Act because its nine-month leave provision is too short for the bonding process between mother and child, according to spokesman Mattox. As an alternative, his group supports the Family Protection Act introduced in the House by Rep. Charles W. Stenholm, D-Texas, and in the Senate by Sen. Orrin G. Hatch, R-Utah. It would not guarantee a job slot to parents who leave work to stay home with children but would encourage companies to give special consideration to such former employees who want to return.[33]

OUTLOOK

Slowing Down

"Living in the moment means being aware of your power in the present," counsels business writer Jeff Davidson in his prescription for relief from rapid living. "It is not a recipe for accomplishment. It is observing the finely woven canvas of your life while you are also living it. It is giving yourself permission to be who you are. It is resting when you are tired. It is not having to strive."[34]

Such an overhaul of one's lifestyle is easier said than done. In a parody of Americans' penchant for over-scheduling, *USA Today* once calculated the typical day of a well-rounded someone who is determined to accomplish everything in the amount of time experts recommend: 30 minutes of exercise, 45 minutes for personal grooming, 2-4 hours with children and spouse, 45 minutes for reading the newspaper, 1.5 hours for commuting, 7-10 hours for working, 1-2 hours for housekeeping and chores, 50 minutes for sex and intimacy, plus

another 15 minutes for such activities as cooking and eating dinner, taking care of plants, reading a book, listening to music and sleeping. It's all doable — in a 42-hour day.[35]

It is also not clear that all Americans truly wish to slow down. Hunnicutt argues that cutting back on work would "force an increasingly secular people to confront traditional religious questions, such as, 'What is worth doing for its own sake?'" "Americans," he concludes, "thus run headlong from free time back to the relative security of finding new problems to solve, new and 'serious' tasks to perform, new frontiers to open and more work to do."[36]

But for the rising numbers of American families feeling trapped like "a squirrel in a cage," change will be sought through shifts in attitudes and policies at the societal level. "It is important not to have the family adopt to needs of the workplace but to have the workplace do the giving," says Juliet Schor.

"There is still a gender gap in understanding what others are going through," observes Fran Rodgers. "If a man's wife dies of breast cancer,

Continued on p. 707

At Issue:

Should the government act to alleviate the work-family time crunch?

ARLIE HOCHSCHILD

Professor of sociology, University of California at Berkeley
FROM HER BOOK, *THE SECOND SHIFT: WORKING PARENTS
AND THE REVOLUTION AT HOME,* 1989

yes

We really need a Marshall Plan for the family. It would look to other progressive industrial nations for a model of what could be done. In Sweden, for example, upon the birth of a child, every working couple is entitled to 12 months of paid parental leave, nine months at 90 percent of the person's salary plus an additional three months at about $300 a month. The mother and father are free to divide this year off between them as they wish. Any working parent of a child under eight has the opportunity to work no more than six hours a day, at six hours' pay. Parental insurance offers parents money for work time lost to visit a child's school or care for a sick child. That's "pro-family" policy.

An honestly pro-family policy in the United States would give tax breaks to companies that encourage "family leave" for new fathers, job sharing, part-time work and flextime. Through comparable worth, it would pull up wages in "women's" jobs. It would go beyond half-time work (which makes it sound like a person is only doing "half" of something else that is "whole") by instituting lower-hour, more flexible "family phases" for all regular jobs filled by parents of young children.

The government would give tax credits to developers who build affordable housing near places of work and shopping centers, with nearby meal-preparation facilities. It would create warm and creative day-care centers. If the best day-care comes from elderly neighbors, students, grandparents, they could be paid to care for children. Traveling vans for day-care enrichment could roam the neighborhoods as the ice-cream man did in my childhood.

In these ways, the American government could create a "safer environment" for the two-job family. It could draw men into children's lives, reduce the number of children in "self-care," and make marriages happier. These reforms could even improve the lives of children whose parents divorce, because research has shown that the more involved fathers are with their children before the divorce, the more involved they are with them afterwards. If the government encouraged corporations to consider the long-range interests of workers and their families, they would save on long-range costs due to higher incidence of absenteeism, turnover, juvenile delinquency, mental illness and welfare support for single mothers.

WILLIAM R. MATTOX JR.

Director of policy analysis at the Family Research Council
FROM *A WORKING PAPER PREPARED FOR THE INSTITUTE
FOR FAMILY VALUES,* 1992

no

Parents in the United States today devote roughly 40 percent less time to child-rearing activities than did parents a generation ago.... From a patriarchal perspective, the shift stems from a significant increase in the number of employed married mothers. From an egalitarian perspective, the shift stems from the fact that the increase in labor force activity by married mothers has not been offset by a corresponding decrease in hours of paid employment by married fathers. In either case, there is a growing consensus that the increase in time devoted to wage-earning activities has been driven by both economic and cultural forces.

Growing economic pressures, however, are not the only reason families spend less time together....A recent Pennsylvania State University study found that the rise in two-earner white families since 1960 has been driven more by a preference for a higher standard of living than by economic necessity....

Some experts believe our nation's government and business policy-makers should respond to America's growing parenting deficit with a massive effort to socialize child-rearing — day care for infants and toddlers, mandatory preschool for young children, after-school programs for latchkey kids, longer school days.... Indeed, some steps toward such a brave new world have already been taken.

Thankfully, there is a growing recognition that easing work-family tensions in these ways places a much higher premium on enabling parents to work than on encouraging them to parent. In addition, there is a growing recognition among people across the political spectrum that government programs, however well-designed, are inferior to strong families.

Rather than expanding the scope of government to replace families, policy-makers should seek to help parents fulfill their child-rearing responsibilities by giving special attention to promoting pro-child tax relief; home-based employment and other family-friendly work policies....

While there is clearly a need for governments and business policies that give parents greater economic autonomy, it would be a mistake to suggest that policy changes are the sole key, or even the primary key, to greater parent-child interaction. Indeed, no dramatic change in parent-child interaction is apt to take place so long as the predominant cultural message of our time is one that says family time should take a back seat to career aspirations and material gain.

Telecommuting: Beating the Stress of the Daily Drive

Flip on any morning radio traffic report and you can tell why the most stressful of the workaday tasks is simply driving to work. Drivers who get out of their cars "exhausted, irritable and unable to unwind" suffer both at work and at home, reporting adverse effects on "blood pressure, mood, frustration tolerance, [frequency of] illness, work absences, job stability and overall life satisfaction," according to a recent study of commuters.†

Women commuters often suffer more than men because their jobs are often further away (the husband's workplace is likely to have been the stronger factor in the couple's choice of where to live), and mom is more likely to be saddled with extra driving to drop the children off at day care.

In the booming 1980s, the number of Americans hooked on commuting shot up from 81 million in 1980 to 100 million in 1990, according to the Census Bureau. Simultaneously, over the past decade, a growing number of people have sought relief from the rat race through "telecommuting."

The term, coined in 1973 by Los Angeles management consultant Jack Nilles, refers to the growing practice of allowing employees — usually equipped with personal computers, modems and fax machines — to perform their jobs at home. The savings in commuting stress is paralleled by an easing of highway gridlock and reduced air pollution, which is why telecommuting has been encouraged by local governments in heavily polluted areas such as Southern California.

An estimated 6.6 million Americans are telecommuters for at least part of the workweek, according to the New York City consulting firm Link Resources. The number has recently been growing at 20 percent a year.

About half of telecommuting households have children under 18, which is one reason why activists concerned about work-family conflicts have begun promoting telecommuting as a way to foster more family togetherness. William R. Mattox Jr., director of policy analysis at the Family Research Council, says that technologies such as computers and fiber optics could create a "neo-agrarian technical revolution" that would put workers back in their homes, as they were before the 19th-century Industrial Revolution lured them away from their farms.

With telecommuting and other home businesses, parents who've been starved for time with their children could continue lucrative and creative careers, even if they advanced at a slower pace. Mattox foresees work arrangements similar to those on college campuses, in which work could be done without "eyeball supervision."

"Flexibility is the key," says Chuck Hanson, a Seattle market planner who telecommutes to his job at GTE Northwest. "If things aren't going well, I take a break and make it up in the evening, or sometimes I go for a jog. It's a lot less stressful, and I'm more productive. I can get done at home in a few hours what it takes a whole day to do in the office." ††

Already, companies that have experimented with telecommuting have reported positive results for workers and management. In 1991, Bell Atlantic arranged for volunteer telecommuters to keep journals and participate in focus groups. Nearly all reported an increase in morale, job satisfaction and quality of family life. Each saved a monthly average of $55 in gas, parking and car depreciation, and productivity improvements ranged from 5 percent to 40 percent. Most recently, the federal government completed a successful pilot program that is expected to make it common for federal employees to telecommute.

Telecommuting does have its drawbacks. Labor unions have resisted for fear of worker exploitation, though successful pilot programs have recently won approval from union locals for clerical workers at the University of Washington and among service representatives at Illinois Bell in Chicago.‡ Some communities have worker-safety ordinances and restrictions against business activity in residential areas that discourage the practice. Such restrictions might be overridden under telecommuting legislation being prepared by Sen. Conrad Burns, R-Mont.

Other disadvantages are interruptions from one's children, isolation from colleagues, resentment from co-workers whose jobs don't lend themselves to telecommuting and complications in the scheduling of staff meetings. Many managers still don't trust employees to apply self-discipline and stay busy, observers report.

Telecommuting also raises the possibility of increasing a worker's stress level. Experts say that the main problem with any home-based business is the psychic risk that one can never can mentally "punch out."

"The home has been defined as a place of nurturance, refuge and recuperation," writes business journalist Roxane Farmanfarmaian. "The essence of the workplace is performance, productivity; the aggressive, even warlike, projection of one's own products into the world. When the two zones overlap, steps must be taken to see that each is preserved or enhanced." ‡‡

---

† Raymond W. Novaco, Wendy Kliewer and Alexander Brouquet, "Home Environmental Consequences of Commute Travel Impedance," *American Journal of Community Psychology*, Vol., 19, No. 6., p. 881. The Federal Highway Administration this August came to similar conclusions.

†† Quoted in *The Washington Post*, May 10, 1992.

‡ *The Wall Street Journal,* May 6, 1992.

‡‡ Roxane Farmanfarmaian, "Worksteading: The New Lifestyle Frontier," *Psychology Today*, November 1989, p. 37.

Continued from p. 704
leaving two kids, a company will go to the nth degree to help the man, but a single mother dealing with child care every day is virtually ignored."

Society's lack of respect for the full-time homemaker, notes Ellen Galinsky, is a sign that nurturing in general — of children, of the elderly — is not respected in the work world. "That has to change," she says. "We have to get to the point where we respect differences."

Impact of Demographic Change

The argument for reshaping society to accommodate the dual-career family may well be borne out demographically. The Census Bureau projects that the share of women who work will grow to 75 percent by the year 2000, as a predicted shortage of skilled labor has its effect. That could mean that the shorter workweeks and generous parental-leave policies common in Europe will continue to be touted as a model.

"These demographic changes are happening all over the world," observes Yale University psychologist Edward Zigler, "but other countries have the infrastructure that allows someone to be both a worker and a mother." American "families can function either way, but they're going to be more or less hassled depending on the infrastructure."

Even the notoriously hard-driving Japanese, who are America's biggest trade competitors, have set up a government commission to promote shorter work hours and boost leisure time "to make our working lives less stressful," as Prime Minister Kiichi Miyazawa put it.[37]

Americans, however, given their tradition of high-energy ambition, are not likely to solve the modern-day time crunch very quickly. "Most of us would probably choose to enjoy more leisure if extra leisure had no cost," writes Brookings Institution economist Gary Burtless. "But additional leisure does have a cost. Those who work for a living would have to give up some time on our jobs and forfeit some wages. Those who cook or work around the house might have to tolerate less palatable meals, less attractive lawns and less sanitary kitchens. Given these trade-offs, most of us strike the best bargain we can."[38] ∎

Notes

[1] Quoted in Arlie Hochschild, *The Second Shift: Working Parents and the Revolution at Home* (1989), p. 209.

[2] Quoted in "How America Has Run Out of Time," *Time*, April 24, 1989, p. 58.

[3] See *The Wall Street Journal*, Aug. 5, 1991.

[4] Natalie Angier, "Cheating on Sleep: Modern Life Turns America into the Land of the Drowsy," *The New York Times*, May 15, 1990.

[5] Quoted in *The Wall Street Journal*, May 5, 1992.

[6] Jeff Davidson, *Breathing Space: Living and Working at a Comfortable Pace in a Sped-Up Society* (1991), p. 26.

[7] William R. Mattox Jr., "The Parent Trap: So Many Bills, So Little Time," *Policy Review*, winter 1991, p. 6.

[8] Quoted in Mattox, *op. cit.*, p. 7.

[9] *Ibid.*, p. 6.

[10] An annual tracking survey of consumer values that Yankelovich has conducted since 1970. About 90 percent of the questions remain the same every year.

[11] *Work and Family Today: 100 Key Statistics,* Bureau of National Affairs, May 1991.

[12] Hochschild, *op. cit.*, p. 4.

[13] See *The Wall Street Journal*, Oct. 17, 1991.

[14] Juliet B. Schor, *The Overworked American: The Unexpected Decline of Leisure* (1991), p. 152.

[15] Benjamin K. Hunnicutt, "No Time for God or Family," *The Wall Street Journal*, Jan. 4, 1990.

[16] The Urban Institute, *National Child Care Survey,* 1990.

[17] Robert Rector, "How to Strengthen America's Crumbling Families," *Heritage Foundation Backgrounder*, April 28, 1992.

[18] Quoted in Amy Saltzman, *Downshifting: Reinventing Success on a Slower Track* (1991), p. 201.

[19] Schor, *op cit.*, p. 44.

[20] *Ibid.*, p. 154.

[21] *Ibid.*, p. 78.

[22] William H. Whyte Jr., *The Organization Man* (1956) p. 18.

[23] Walter Kerr, *The Decline of Pleasure* (1965), p. 39.

[24] Meyer Friedman and Ray H. Rosenbaum, *Type A Behavior and Your Heart* (1974), p. 93.

[25] Saltzman, *op. cit.*, p. 20.

[26] See Felice N. Schwartz, "Women as a Business Imperative," *Harvard Business Review,* March-April, 1992, p. 105.

[27] Susan Faludi, *Backlash: The Undeclared War on American Women* (1991), p. 77.

[28] T. Berry Brazelton, *Working and Caring,* (1985) p. xv.

[29] Alan Deutschman, "Pioneers of the New Balance," *Fortune*, May 20, 1991, p. 60.

[30] Quoted in *The Washington Post*, July 7, 1992.

[31] Edith U. Fierst, speech to the Family Research Council in Washington, May 8, 1992.

[32] Quoted in Richard Louv, "Bringing Up Baby," *Best of Business Quarterly*, fall 1991, p. 34.

[33] See "The Family Leave Bill Returns In Time for GOP Convention," *Congressional Quarterly Weekly Report, Aug. 8, 1992, p. 2364.* Numerous other family-oriented bills are pending in Congress. For background, see Robert Pear, "Family Values: Hard to Define, Harder to Afford," *The New York Times,* June 7, 1992, p. E4.

[34] Davidson, *op. cit.*, p. 169.

[35] *USA Today*, April 13, 1989.

[36] Quoted in *The Wall Street Journal*, Jan. 4, 1990.

[37] Quoted in *The New York Times*, March 3, 1992.

[38] Quoted in *The Wall Street Journal*, Jan 4, 1990.

Bibliography

Selected Sources Used

Books

Brazelton, M.D., T. Berry, *Working and Caring*, Addison-Wesley Publishing Co., 1985.

One of the country's foremost pediatricians uses case studies from his practice to offer advice to parents on coping with the pressures of balancing work with the raising of children.

Davidson, Jeff, *Breathing Space: Living & Working at a Comfortable Pace in a Sped-Up Society*, MasterMedia Limited, 1991.

A business writer surveys the factors in modern life that contribute to hurry and stress. He offers ways to reorganize to "help you handle the deluge of information, have greater control over your life and feel better about each day."

Faludi, Susan, *Backlash: The Undeclared War Against American Women*, Crown Publishers, 1991.

A *Wall Street Journal* reporter and feminist surveys the current state of gender relations. She maintains that "the last decade has seen a powerful counter-assault on women's rights, a backlash, an attempt to retract the handful of small and hard-won victories that the feminist movement did manage to win for women.... This counter-assault is largely insidious: In a kind of pop-culture version of the Big Lie, it stands the truth boldly on its head and proclaims that the very steps that have elevated women's position have actually led to their downfall."

Goldscheider, Frances K. and Linda J. Waite, *New Families, No Families?: The Transformation of the American Home*, University of California Press, 1991.

In this study for the Rand Corp., two sociologists analyze time-diary and demographic data to discuss changes in recent decades in who performs housework and child care.

Hewlett, Sylvia Ann, *When the Bough Breaks: The Cost of Neglecting Our Children*, Basic Books, 1991.

An economist and consultant to corporations analyzes the state of families in modern America, arguing for major changes by government and business to ease the "parenting deficit."

Hochschild, Arlie, *The Second Shift: Working Parents and the Revolution at Home*, Viking, 1989.

A University of California at Berkeley sociologist reports on years of in-depth interviews with couples on how they divide household chores and child care. She analyzes the impact on marriages and society.

Kabat-Zinn, Jon, *Full Catastrophe Living: Using the Wisdom of Your Body and Mind to Face Stress, Pain and Illness*, Delacorte Press, 1990.

A professor of medicine who founded the Stress Reduction Clinic at the University of Massachusetts describes health effects of stress caused by work, other people, roles in society, accelerated time and world events. He offers a program of "mindfulness meditation" for relief.

Saltzman, Amy, *Downshifting: Reinventing Success on a Slower Track*, Harper Collins, 1991.

An editor at *U.S. News & World Report* examines the hectic pace of American life in the 1980s and offers alternatives to the emphasis on careers.

Schor, Juliet B., *The Overworked American: The Unexpected Decline of Leisure*, Basic Books, 1991.

A Harvard University economist interprets recent economic data to argue that Americans are working more than they did in previous decades. She proposes European-style shorter workweeks, longer vacations, and more equitable sharing of housework and child care between men and women.

Schroeder, Pat, *Champion of the Great American Family: A Personal and Political Book*, Random House, 1989.

This autobiography by a Democratic House member who chairs the Select Committee on Children, Youth and Families includes the author's views on how the political and business worlds are handling the issues of women, careers and child-rearing.

Reports and Studies

Free to Be Family: Helping Mothers and Fathers Meet the Needs of the Next Generation of American Children, Family Research Council, Washington, D.C., 1992.

A policy group led by a former Reagan administration domestic policy adviser prepared this analysis and blueprint for change to arrest the decline of the family caused by the rising incidence of divorce, premarital sex and crime.

Work and Family Today: 100 Key Statistics, Bureau of National Affairs, May 1991.

A Washington, D.C., publisher of legal and economic information has assembled a grab-bag of up-to-date facts relating to work and family, including sources.

The Next Step

Additional Articles from Current Periodicals from EBSCO Publishing's Database

Addresses & essays

O'Mara, P., "Consideration for the child," *Mothering,* **spring 1992, p. 6.**

Offers some considerations — for both parents and policy-makers — concerning the nature of the child and the needs of the family. Considerations that a comprehensive family policy would reflect; assumptions of the past no longer work; in addressing the needs of families; the nature of the child; more.

Schor, J.B. and B. Maddocks, "Workers of the world, unwind," *Technology Review,* **November/December 1991, p. 24.**

Calls for changes in the traditional workplace system of working long hours with little leisure time. Rising level of time spent at work; decline of leisure time; growth of productivity has been matched with a growth in spending; many businesses call for longer hours; Americans work more than most other countries; solutions offered; problems that may be encountered; more.

Books & reading

"Annotated listing of new books," *Journal of Economic Literature,* **March 1991, p. 215.**

Reviews the book "The protestant work ethic: The psychology of work-related beliefs and behaviors," by Adrian Furnham.

Gloyer, J., T.E. Jones, et al., "Book reviews," *School Library Journal,* **February 1992, p. 78.**

Reviews the book "Busy! Busy! Busy!," by Jonathan Shipton, illustrated by Michael Foreman.

Kuttner, R., "No time to smell the roses anymore," *The New York Times Book Review,* **Feb. 2, 1992, p. 1.**

Reviews the book "The Overworked American: The Unexpected Decline of Leisure," by Juliet B. Schor, which examines how working time has steadily increased to the point where the average worker now puts in the equivalent of an additional month of work, resulting in the "shrinkage of leisure ... has created a profound structural crisis of time" for Americans of nearly all social groups. INSET: Used and trapped by time (Juliet B. Schor), by S. Strom.

Mergen, B., "Book reviews," *Journal of American History,* **September 1991, p. 705.**

Reviews the book "For Fun and Profit: The Transformation of Leisure into Consumption," edited by Richard Butsch.

Raymond, C., "Studies of housework," *The Chronicle of Higher Education,* **March 4, 1992, p. A13.**

Reviews the book "Feeding the Family: The Social Organization of Caring as Gendered Work," by Marjorie L. DeVault, which argues that social organizations, rather than women's inherent character, shape the idea that women should do "caring work."

Vigilante, R., "Workingman's blues?" *National Review,* **April 27, 1992, p. 47.**

Reviews the book "The Overworked American: The Unexpected Decline of Leisure," by Juliet B. Schor.

Debates & issues

"Americans' leisure time on the rise," *USA Today,* **December 1991, p. 10.**

Suggests that the amount of spare time that Americans have has increased, not decreased, over the past 25 years. Research conducted by John P. Robinson, director of the Americans' Use of Time Project; causes of the added leisure hours; how they are used.

"Lagging family benefits," *Consumers Digest,* **March/April 1992, p. 16.**

Reveals that a National Research Council report entitled "Work and Family: Policies for a Changing Work Force" has found employee benefits no longer match their needs. Many employers have not responded with family-targeted benefits; a third of employees have no paid sick leave; most women have no paid leave for pregnancy.

Castro, J., "Work ethic — in spades," *Time,* **Feb. 17, 1992, p. 57.**

Presents some statistics from Juliet Schor's new book, "The Overworked American," which found Americans are working 163 more hours a year than in 1970 and more than 7 million Americans hold two or three jobs to make ends meet. Reaction to Japanese Prime Minister Kiichi Miyazawa's remarks that Americans are lazy, greedy and lack a work ethic.

Collins, G., "Why no one wants to work anymore," *Working Woman,* **November 1991, p. 160.**

Looks at the amount of free time most people have and contemplates what they do with it. Trading success for quality leisure time; calling in sick to avoid the stress of work; why some would rather get by on less money and have more time to themselves.

Corcoran, E. and P. Wallich, "Trading leisure time for more goods?" *Scientific American*, September 1991, p. 176.

Opinion. Looks at conflicting reports by economists that Americans are working more hours than they did just 20 years ago. Hazy data on work hours; reasons for interest on work and leisure injuries; differences in data and interpretations; statistics on American productivity and leisure time.

Haggard, L. M. and D. R. Williams, "Identity affirmation through leisure activities: Leisure symbols of the self," *Journal of Leisure Research*, January 1992, p. 1.

Presents a paper that focuses on the process of identity definition and expression, termed self-affirmation, and the potential role of leisure activity participation in the self-affirmation process. Studies; methods; results; details.

Hall, T., "Time on your hands? It may be increasing," *The New York Times*, July 3, 1991, p. C1.

Debunks the notion that people are busier today than formerly. According to a study by a University of Maryland professor of psychology, the opposite is true. He says that since 1965, men have gained seven hours of free time in a week, and women, six.

Hamilton, R. F., "Work and leisure," *Public Opinion Quarterly*, fall 1991, p. 347.

Discusses Louis Harris' recent book "Inside America," which has reported that there has been a substantial increase in work between 1973 and 1985 and a corresponding decrease in the availability of free time. What data from the Current Employment Statistics of the Department of Labor and the National Opinion Research Center's General Social Surveys show; Current Population Survey results; the increased participation of leisure-time activities; Harris's results.

Kleiner, E. "A shift in maternal values," *Mothering*, spring 1992, p. 33.

Reports that a nationwide survey of mothers with children 18 or younger reveals that moms today believe they communicate better and spend more time with the family than their mothers did. Houses aren't as clean as their mothers' as housekeeping is no longer a top priority; healthy shift in values; survey depicts a generation of mothers who realize the importance of sharing feelings and thoughts with their children; overall top priorities.

Lieberman, A., "Using our leisure time," *Futurist*, September 1991, p. 60.

Opinion. Ponders how leisure-time choices will be made as Americans head into the 21st century. Increasing impor-

tance of leisure time; prediction that home-based activities will likely characterize, to an increasing extent, Americans' entertainment preferences in the future.

Mattox, W.R. Jr., "America's family time famine," *Children Today*, November/December 1990, p. 9.

Examines the effect of a lack of parental time, attention and affection on children of today's overextended parents. Parents spend 40 percent less time with their children than in 1965, according to sociologist John P. Robinson; time pressures of two-income households and single-parent families; decline in family size causing children to miss out on interaction with siblings; effects of growing economic pressures; role of cultural factors.

Rademaekers, W., "The oh so good life," *Time*, July 9, 1990, p. 80.

Examines a society that has long been praised for an overgrown work ethic and is now turning its restless energies to the cultivation of leisure. "Never in our history have we lived so well"; inheriting all the fruits of an economic miracle.

Economic aspects

"Not for the money," *Psychology Today*, May/June 1992, p. 22.

States that when mothers join the work force, up to 68 percent of their income goes for work-related expenses such as child care, transportation, taxes and lunch money. Those who benefit most; statistics and findings; elements that policy strategies aimed at increasing the standard of living of low-income families need to focus on; more.

Meade, J. and A. Christ, "Take control," *Men's Health*, January/February 1992, p. 38.

Discusses how our earnings are in a race with our expenses and our expenses are winning. We have to work more just to break even, and free time is scarce. American life is experiencing loss of control; having purpose will pull you through; know what your goals are; set priorities; get rest; more.

Strassels, P. N., "A spouse's income costs as well as pays," *Nation's Business*, March 1989, p. 66.

Advises two-income couples to calculate precisely what their "second" income is really worth after taxes and extra expenses are taken into account.

Health aspects

Nyborg-Andersen, I., "How to get a good night's sleep," *Ladies' Home Journal*, October 1991, p. 54.

Discusses the effects of sleep deprivation from which many people with busy schedules are suffering. Enhancing sleep quality; tips for ways to get the best rest possible.

Research

"Working mothers found 'not guilty,'" *Tufts University Diet & Nutrition Letter,* **April 1992, p. 1.**

Reports on a study that found that children of working mothers eat just as well as children of non-working mothers. Details of the study; shortcomings of the study.

Chavira-Prado, A., "Work, health, and the family," *Human Organization,* **spring 1992, p. 53.**

Discusses how material conditions surrounding the family can affect its gender structure by influencing men's and women's status. Work and health conditions of an undocumented Mexican migrant population in southern Illinois influence women's status within the family; conditions that threaten the physical and economic survival of the entire family; differences between men's and women's interpretations of ideology; more.

Cimmarusti, R.A., "Family preservation practice based upon a multisystems approach," *Child Welfare,* **May/June 1992, p. 241.**

Describes an approach to family preservation work that is based upon a multisystems model. Public Law 96-272 and demand for home-based, time-limited family preservation programs; framework for family preservation work in Illinois; Federal Adoption Assistance and Child Welfare Act of 1980; managing the goals of child protection and family empowerment; areas of assessment in the multisystems model; more.

Cornish, E., T. Willard, et al., "How Americans use time," *Futurist,* **September 1991, p. 23.**

Interviews John P. Robinson, a sociology professor at the University of Maryland, College Park, and director of the Americans' Use of Time Project. How the project was conceived and developed; how much time people spend on diverse daily activities; leisure time vs. work time; changing trends in the use of time.

Kilborn, P.T., "Tales from the digital treadmill," *The New York Times,* **June 3, 1990, Section 4, p. 1.**

Describes how, among 88 million people with full-time jobs last year, nearly 24 percent spent over 49 hours on the job, according to the Bureau of Labor Statistics. How the work ethic has changed; problems; why the change came about.

Samdahl, D.M., "Leisure in our lives: Exploring the common leisure occasion," *Journal of Leisure Research,* **January 1992, p. 19.**

Presents a study which explores the common leisure occasion — those informal, unstructured leisure situations

which emerge throughout the day — in attempt to understand the situational factors conducive to its appearance.

Work ethics

"Changing attitudes toward work," *USA Today,* **August 1991, p. 16.**

Contends that America's work ethic is fading fast. Recent surveys on how Americans feel about work; impact on the nation's competitiveness in the global market; analysis of the decline of the work ethic; arguments by some that refute the decline.

"Why has hard work fallen on hard times?" *Christianity Today,* **Feb. 10, 1992, p. 34.**

Excerpts the book "Why America Doesn't Work," by Charles Colson and Jack Eckerd. Traces the decline of the work ethic in America, with proposals for change.

Lipset, S.M., "The work ethic, then and now," *Journal of Labor Research,* **winter 1992, p. 45.**

Discusses how, despite many beliefs to the contrary, the work ethic is alive and well worldwide because people inherently like to work for various reasons in many diverse cultures. Ancient history of the human race speaks eloquently to the inherent disdain for work; Protestantism brought a major shift in traditional attitudes; attitudes toward work; management; more.

Posner, M., "Whatever happened to spare time?" *World Press Review,* **September 1991, p. 26.**

Reprints an article from the *Globe and Mail* of Toronto that examines the work ethic and how we spend our leisure time. The Industrial Revolution; the progress myth; consumerism; corporate pressures; working as hard at leisure as at the job.

Sheehy, J., "The work force of tomorrow?" *Harvard Business Review,* **September/October 1990, p. 234.**

Observes the work ethic of the future work force. Aversion to hard work; lack of respect for managers, customers and often co-workers; focus on a human resource professional's experiences working in a fast-food business to study the psyche and behavior of tomorrow's corporate recruits.

Working mothers

Crosby, F.J. and B. Plotkin, "I'm OK, they're OK," *Working Mother,* **March 1992, p. 43.**

Explores the ways working women and their children are surviving and thriving. How working mothers benefit from a sense of accomplishment and fulfillment; research conducted by Faye J. Crosby, Ph.D. and detailed in her book "Juggling"; benefits of combining the roles of worker and mother; positive impact on children.

Back Issues

Great Research on Current Issues Starts Right Here... Recent topics covered by The CQ Researcher are listed below. Issues dated before May 10, 1991, were published under the name of Editorial Research Reports.

Back issues are available for $4.00 (subscribers) or $7.00 (non-subscribers). Quantity discounts apply to orders over ten. To order, call Congressional Quarterly 1-800-432-2250.

Binders are available for $15.00. To order call 1-800-638-1710.

Future Topics

▶ *NATO's Evolving Role*

▶ *Marine Mammals*

▶ *Domestic Partners*

THE CQ *Researcher*

PUBLISHED BY CONGRESSIONAL QUARTERLY INC., IN CONJUNCTION WITH EBSCO PUBLISHING

NATO's Changing Role

Does the old Atlantic alliance have a post-Cold War role?

I N 1949, THE UNITED STATES, CANADA AND 10 European nations established the North Atlantic Treaty Organization to defend North America and Europe from Soviet aggression. For more than 40 years, the U.S.-dominated alliance helped keep the Cold War cold. With the demise of the Soviet Union and the disbanding of its Eastern European alliance, the Warsaw Pact, the old military threats virtually disappeared. But even as other threats to European security are arising, such as the savage fighting in the former Yugoslavia, alliance members on both sides of the Atlantic are expressing uncertainty about NATO's relevance in the new Europe. Moreover, some European members are seeking greater autonomy from the United States and a greater defense role for distinctly European organizations.

C_Q **August 21, 1992 • Volume 2, No. 31 • 713-736**

Formerly Editorial Research Reports

COVER ART: BARBARA SASSA-DANIELS

CQ Researcher

August 21, 1992
Volume 2, No. 31

EDITOR
Sandra Stencel

MANAGING EDITOR
Thomas J. Colin

ASSOCIATE EDITOR
Richard L. Worsnop

STAFF WRITERS
Charles S. Clark
Mary H. Cooper
Rodman D. Griffin

PRODUCTION EDITORS
Laurie De Maris
Sarah E. Merritt

EDITORIAL ASSISTANT
Michael M. Taylor

GRAPHICS
Jack Auldridge

PUBLISHED BY
Congressional Quarterly Inc.

CHAIRMAN
Andrew Barnes

VICE CHAIRMAN
Andrew P. Corty

EDITOR AND PUBLISHER
Neil Skene

EXECUTIVE EDITOR
Robert W. Merry

PUBLICATIONS MARKETING/SALES
Robert Smith

EDITOR, EBSCO PUBLISHING
Melissa Kummerer

The CQ Researcher (ISSN 1056-2036). Formerly Editorial Research Reports. Published weekly (48 times per year, not printed the first Friday of any month with five Fridays) by Congressional Quarterly Inc., 1414 22nd St., N.W., Washington, D.C. 20037. Rates are furnished upon request. Second-class postage paid at Washington, D.C. POSTMASTER: Send address changes to The CQ Researcher, 1414 22nd St., N.W., Washington, D.C. 20037.

NATO's Changing Role

BY MARY H. COOPER

THE ISSUES

On Christmas Day 1991, the giant red Soviet flag atop the Kremlin was lowered for the last time. In its place rose the white, red and blue flag of czarist Russia. That symbolic act marked not only the demise of the Soviet Union but also the end of the nuclear standoff between the United States and the Soviets.

"We live in a new world," declared Soviet President Mikhail S. Gorbachev as he announced his resignation that day. "The Cold War has ended, the arms race has stopped, as has the insane militarization that mutilated our economy, public psyche and morals. The threat of world war has been removed."

Not only had the Soviet Union broken up, but its former member republics and allies were embracing the democratic and capitalistic models of the West and the empire's military alliance, the seven-nation Warsaw Pact, had disbanded.*

"By the grace of God, America won the Cold War," exulted President Bush in his State of the Union address Jan. 28. "There are still threats. But the long, drawn-out dread is over."

One of the greatest changes brought about by the historic upheavals in the Soviet Union involved the United States and its 15 allies in the U.S.-dominated North Atlantic Treaty Organization (NATO).** For more than 40 years, NATO's sole pur-

---

*In 1955 the Soviet Union signed the Warsaw Pact with Albania, Bulgaria, Czechoslovakia, East Germany, Hungary, Poland and Romania. Albania withdrew in 1968.

**U.S. allies in NATO are Belgium, Canada, Denmark, France, Germany, Greece, Iceland, Italy, Luxembourg, the Netherlands, Norway, Portugal, Spain, Turkey and the United Kingdom.

pose had been to defend Western Europe and North America from Soviet aggression. Now, thanks to Gorbachev and Russian President Boris N. Yeltsin, the West's traditional nemesis to the East was gone.

Indeed, Yeltsin, pressed by the urgent need for economic aid from his country's former enemies, hurried to Washington early this year with proposals to slash the nuclear and conventional arsenals he had inherited.

For the European members of NATO, Yeltsin's proposal made it likely that they could undertake a long-awaited demilitarization of their territory. For the United States, there was hope of a "peace dividend" — defense savings that could be used to combat growing domestic problems. "[W]e can stop making the sacrifices we had to make when we had an avowed enemy that was a superpower," Bush declared. "Now we can look homeward even more and move to set right what needs to be set right." [1]

But the euphoria accompanying the Cold War's demise soon gave way to anxiety. Without the Soviet Union's iron grip, old ethnic, religious and national rivalries resurfaced. Fighting broke out between Christian Armenians and Muslims over the disputed Nagorno-Karabakh region of the former Soviet republic of Azerbaijan, while ethnic rivalries also threatened the stability of the newly independent governments of Moldova and Georgia. Among the old Warsaw Pact allies, ancient frictions between Czechs and Slovaks have scuttled the democratic government of Czechoslovakia, which now seems likely to split in two along ethnic lines.

The most devastating breakdown of the old European order, of course, has occurred in Yugoslavia. [2] In 1991, after a decade of growing unrest, all of the Balkan nation's republics broke away except Serbia and Montenegro. But Serbian forces have tried to retain control over parts of Croatia and Bosnia-Herzegovina. The hostilities that began in Croatia last year ended in a cease-fire this January. But since March, Serbian insurgents armed by Yugoslav President Slobodan Milosevic have been fighting in Bosnia-Herzegovina to expel the country's Croats and Slavic Muslims.

Western Europeans fear that the regional hostilities could escalate, perhaps saddling them with thousands of unwanted refugees. In fact, the region's economic recession already has produced domestic pressure to curtail immigration and a rise in nationalism that threatens the move toward greater political unity of the 12-nation European Community *(see p. 718)*.

The rapidly changing situation throughout Europe poses a particular dilemma for NATO. The 43-year-old alliance was based on a commitment among all 16 members to consider an attack against any one of them as an attack against them all. "The NATO

How NATO Works

Shortly after it was established in 1949, the North Atlantic Treaty Organization (NATO) set up headquarters in Paris. In 1967, after France withdrew from the alliance's military command, NATO moved to Brussels, Belgium, where today its vast bureaucracy helps to coordinate the alliance's defense of Europe and North America.

NATO's political leadership is provided by the organization's North Atlantic Council, comprised of representatives of all 16 members; each has an equal voice in decision-making. Guided by a secretary general, the council meets weekly to set policy and oversee all NATO activities.

NATO's integrated military structure, also based in Brussels, is divided into the Europe, Atlantic and Channel commands. Thirteen of the allies contribute national military forces to the three commands. The exceptions are France, Spain and Iceland, which has no armed forces.

Under normal circumstances, the forces that are allocated to NATO remain under their national commands. Control passes to NATO only during a crisis and upon the assent of the individual alliance members, who also decide together how to equip and train these forces and where to deploy them.

The Supreme Allied Commander Europe (SACEUR) oversees the defense of the European area of NATO and commands land and air forces from his headquarters 30 miles outside Brussels. This most critical of NATO's three commands covers 3 million square miles from northern Norway to Southern Europe, including the entire Mediterranean Sea, and from the Atlantic Coast to the eastern border of Turkey. Gen. Dwight D. Eisenhower was NATO's first SACEUR. Today that command is held by U.S. Gen. John M. Shalikashvili.

The Supreme Allied Commander Atlantic (SACLANT) oversees the Atlantic Ocean from the North Pole to the Tropic of Cancer, and from the Atlantic Coast to the coasts of Europe and Africa, excluding the British Isles and the English Channel. Headquartered in Norfolk, Va., SACLANT controls naval and air units that defend vital sea lanes and support SACEUR's land operations.

The Commander-in-Chief Channel (CINCHAN) commands naval and air forces covering the area from the southern part of the North Sea through the English Channel. Based in Northwood, United Kingdom, CINCHAN defends merchant shipping and strategic approaches to Western Europe.

allies no longer have a common adversary in the old sense," says David P. Calleo, director of European studies at the Johns Hopkins University School of Advanced International Studies in Washington. "It was a great incentive to alliance unity, having the Russian army in the middle of Germany."

Today, however, allies on both sides of the Atlantic are expressing uncertainty about NATO's relevance for the defense of the new Europe. Moreover, some European members of the alliance are seeking greater autonomy from the United States and a greater defense role for distinctly European organizations, such as the Western European Union *(see p. 726)*. At the same time, they are loath to cut themselves off altogether from the expansive American military umbrella.

For its part, the United States may

also be turning inward. Although Americans supported U.S. military intervention last year to drive Iraqi forces out of Kuwait, they seem to be more concerned about solving domestic problems, even at the expense of foreign involvement.

With the military and political climate in Europe constantly changing and Western Europeans expressing increasing desire for more autonomy, here are some of the crucial questions being asked:

Now that the Cold War is over, has NATO outlived its usefulness?

As cynics viewed NATO, its original purpose was "to keep the Russians out, the Germans down and the Americans in." Indeed, when NATO was founded in 1949, its main goals were blocking the westward advance of Soviet power and preventing the

buildup of hostile forces in Germany. Success, the European allies agreed, would require a strong American presence in Europe.

Today, however, the equation has changed. "The Russians couldn't be further out, since the Soviet Union has disappeared," says Eugene J. Carroll Jr., a retired rear admiral who is now deputy director of the Center for Defense Information in Washington. "The Germans are not going to be inhibited in any way, shape or form by the presence of Americans troops — any time that we are in the way of their internal policies, we're going to be asked to leave forthwith. And to keep the Americans in doesn't serve any purpose. There's nobody to defend Europe against."

Apart from changes that have affected the original members of NATO and the Warsaw Pact, Carroll says, the very terms of the alliance treaty are outdated. "The North Atlantic Treaty was a defensive agreement," he says. "Today, there is simply no threat of attack by an external power, absolutely none — not now and probably not in the foreseeable future."

Other observers are more cautious. "I think that all kinds of new, fundamental instabilities threaten Europe's security," says Simon Serfaty, a professor at the Foreign Policy Institute at the School of Advanced International Studies, "and for that reason the alliance deserves to remain in effect."

But the altered state of global security, Serfaty adds, requires a change in NATO. When the alliance's main adversary was the Soviet Union, U.S. dominance of NATO could be justified because the United States alone possessed the nuclear capability to deter the Soviet nuclear threat. With the dramatic reductions of nuclear weaponry envisioned in recent arms control agreements, however, U.S. dominance may no longer be justified. "Some reforms are necessary," Serfaty says, "and there needs to be a better sharing of leadership among the allies."

There are also calls for NATO to end its traditional stricture against taking military action outside the territory of its member states. According to this view, some of the most serious threats to alliance members lie beyond Europe and North America. The Middle East, for example, is the main energy source for most NATO allies. But when Iraq invaded Kuwait in August 1990 and threatened the West's oil supplies, it was not NATO but rather a coalition of countries pieced together by the United States that intervened militarily to expel Iraq.

"The first thing I think we need to do with NATO," says Rep. Patricia Schroeder, D-Colo., who has long called on the European allies to shoulder more of NATO's expenses, "is to get a commitment that they can act out of region for regional interests."

Will U.S. interests be served by proposed changes in NATO's role?

Over the past two years, NATO members have agreed to several changes in the alliance to reflect the changing security situation in Europe. The NATO force structure, or deployment of troops and armaments, is to become less reliant on the large concentrations of troops and tanks that traditionally were deployed along the border that once divided East and West Germany. Because the threat of a sudden invasion of NATO territory has dissipated, fewer troops will be deployed in Europe by the mid-1990s. Many NATO forces will be based in their home countries and will be trained for varied new combat conditions. Some will belong to rapid-reaction forces, which can be quickly transported to crisis areas, perhaps even outside NATO territory.

Like most other NATO members, the United States will reduce its forces now deployed in other allied countries. Under plans drawn up by the Bush administration, the number of U.S. troops in Europe will drop to 150,000 by 1995, less than half the 307,000 contingent in 1989.

Some defense experts agree with the administration that it is in the interests of the United States to maintain a substantial military presence on the continent. "I think we can do it at lower troop levels than we now have, perhaps at even slightly lower troop levels than the administration has suggested with NATO's reorganization," says R. James Woolsey, a Washington attorney who served as the U.S. ambassador and negotiator for the 1990 Conventional Forces in Europe (CFE) treaty, which calls for cuts in non-nuclear forces throughout Europe. "But I think you have to have something over there that you could with a straight face call several brigades' worth of troops, plus a few air wings, in order to be a serious and major component in the security arrangements of Europe."

Even though World War II ended more than 40 years ago, Woolsey says that a U.S. military presence in Europe is necessary "to keep the European continent from going haywire again. The history of the continent is such that someone has tried to dominate it six times over the last four centuries. Europe is sufficiently important and sufficiently closely tied to American security that we have three times in the 20th century had to intervene massively in order to keep that from happening."

The Cold War cost the United States billions of dollars, but the cost in human life was negligible compared with U.S. participation in the two world wars. And that, Woolsey says, is thanks largely to American leadership in NATO.

Other experts agree that NATO continues to serve American interests in Europe but criticize the administration's plan to maintain 150,000 troops there. The huge deployment, they say, is a not-so-subtle way to influence the politics of America's European allies rather than a means of defending them.

"What I hear the administration saying is that NATO is how we gain respect in Europe," says Rep. Schroeder. "They don't want to bring the [number of] troops down because they see the European Community becoming stronger and more viable and more of a trading competitor. They seem to be saying, 'By golly, the only way we have some leverage in Europe is with NATO.'"

In Schroeder's view, it is the European allies who will ultimately profit if the U.S. government tries to use NATO as a tool of political manipulation against them. With most of the threats to alliance security coming today from outside NATO territory, such as Bosnia and the Persian Gulf, she says, American forces would likely bear the burden of intervention. "NATO will just say, 'Well, gee, if you're here, great. Thanks for sending all the money over and thanks for spending it all on our economy. And, oh, by the way, if anything rises up, you guys will have to go take care of it because it's out of area.' I just don't buy that argument at all, and I don't think Americans are going to buy it."

If the government's reason for having a U.S. presence in Europe is to maintain a strong U.S. voice in European affairs, says Carroll, there are better ways to go about it than deploying large numbers of U.S. troops. "I think we ought to be trying to play a very strong economic role in Europe and thinking about our strategy with respect to trade and European Community unification," he says. "I don't believe any longer that [dominating] NATO gives us any leverage on those problems. In fact, I think it's a negative influence, inhibiting progress on the trade, commercial and financial relationships with Europe, elements where we need progress." ∎

ern and Western Europe.

Both the nuclear threat and geography shaped NATO's strategy. The Soviet Union and its Warsaw Pact allies deployed ground troops all along the border in East Germany. Based close to their home territories, these forces could have mounted a full-scale invasion of Western Europe with little or no warning. To counter this threat, NATO also deployed the bulk of its forces in Germany, along the western side of the same border. The largest contingent of these forces was American.

BACKGROUND

Anti-Soviet Mission

When NATO was created out of the rubble of World War II, there was no question about its mission, or the pre-eminent role of the United States in the alliance. The Soviet Union was consolidating its grip over the Eastern European countries it occupied — Poland, eastern Germany, Czechoslovakia, Hungary, Bulgaria and Romania. Fearing that Joseph Stalin would continue his push westward, the United States, Canada and 10 Western European countries on April 4, 1949, signed the North Atlantic Treaty to stop the Soviet advance along a line that ran through Germany.

The treaty made no distinction among its members, eventually numbering 16 nations. (Greece and Turkey joined NATO in 1952, West Germany in 1955 and Spain in 1982.) Rather, it emphasized the collective nature of the alliance as a joint endeavor among equals. Article V of the treaty also made clear NATO's purely defensive purpose: "The parties agree that an armed attack against one or more of them in Europe or North America shall be considered an attack against them all."

NATO also was intended to be a temporary arrangement, at least in the mind of Gen. Dwight D. Eisenhower, the first Supreme Allied Commander in Europe. "Eisenhower said that if we Americans were still in Europe 10 years later, the whole venture would have been a failure," recalls Eugene Carroll of the Center for Defense Information. "He had a clear view of NATO as an organization that was created for a particular purpose, which was to provide a shield for Western Europe and the democratic nations to rebuild their social, political and economic structures free of fear from foreign aggression, but only until such a time that they could take over the responsibility themselves."

The temporary arrangement that Eisenhower had envisioned for NATO became steadily more permanent after September 1949, when the Soviet Union exploded its first nuclear bomb. As the only other nation that possessed a nuclear capability, the United States inherited the role of counterweight to the Soviets. The Cold War had started.

Over time, the two superpowers stockpiled growing quantities of nuclear weapons, their home-based strategic nuclear missiles bolstered by intermediate- and short-range nuclear weapons deployed throughout East-

European Community

Stoked by Marshall Plan aid, the economies of Western Europe boomed during the 1950s and '60s. With their security protected as well by the American nuclear umbrella that constituted NATO's ultimate deterrent, several Western European countries undertook a drive toward unity, hoping to break the region's cycle of warfare.

The European Community (EC) was created in 1957 with the aim of eventually creating a United States of Europe. The original six members — Belgium, France, Italy, Luxembourg, the Netherlands and West Germany — were later joined by Denmark, Ireland and the United Kingdom in 1973; by Greece in 1981; and by Portugal and Spain in 1986.

But real progress toward European unity proved sporadic. For many years the EC was little more than a customs union, known as the Common Market, that regulated trade among the members and with the rest of the world.

All the members of the European Community except Ireland were also members of NATO. But there were early attempts to set up autonomous European defense structures as well.

Continued on p. 720

Chronology

1940s-1960s
NATO and the Warsaw Pact build up their forces in Europe amid tense U.S.-Soviet relations.

April 4, 1949
The United States, Canada and 10 Western European countries establish the North Atlantic Treaty Organization (NATO) to provide collective self-defense under U.S. leadership against possible attack by the Soviet Union and its Eastern European allies. Four more European nations later join NATO, bringing its membership to 16.

September 1949
The Soviet Union explodes its first nuclear device, igniting the nuclear arms race.

1954
The Western European Union (WEU), eventually to number nine members, is established to serve as a forum to discuss European security.

1955
The Soviet Union sets up the Warsaw Pact with seven countries of Eastern Europe — Albania, Bulgaria, Czechoslovakia, East Germany, Hungary, Poland and Rumania. Albania later leaves the alliance.

1957
NATO adopts a new "massive retaliation" strategy calling for the use of nuclear weapons in response to a major Soviet attack. Six European countries — Belgium, France, Italy, Luxembourg, the Netherlands and West Germany — set up the European Community (EC). They are later joined by Denmark, Ireland, the United Kingdom, Greece, Portugal and Spain.

1967
NATO adopts a new strategy, later dubbed "flexible response," which calls for maintaining military forces capable of deterring attack by their sheer strength and countering an attack if it should occur. Resentful of U.S. influence in European security matters, France pulls out of NATO's integrated military structure.

———— • ————

1970s-1980s
East-West tensions abate as détente flowers between the United States and Soviet Union and, after 1985, political and economic reforms sweep the Soviet Union.

1972
The members of NATO and the Warsaw Pact as well as the neutral and non-aligned countries of Europe set up the Conference on Security and Cooperation in Europe (CSCE) to reduce the risk of war. Three years later, it produces the Helsinki Accords requiring advance notification of troop maneuvers in Europe.

1989
East Germans tear down the Berlin Wall and oust their Communist government. Communist regimes in Czechoslovakia, Hungary, Poland, Bulgaria and Romania also fall.

———— • ————

1990s
The collapse of the Soviet bloc leaves a power vacuum that gives rise to regional conflicts in Eastern and Central Europe and forces NATO to change its strategy.

Oct. 3, 1990
German unification is completed with the merger of East Germany into the Federal Republic.

November 1990
The Conventional Forces in Europe (CFE) treaty, signed by members of NATO and the Warsaw Pact, calls for significant cuts in non-nuclear forces from the Atlantic to the Urals.

March 1991
The Warsaw Pact disbands.

November 1991
Meeting in Rome, NATO members approve the alliance's new Strategic Concept, emphasizing crisis management as a central NATO mission. They also set up the North Atlantic Cooperation Council to broaden cooperation with all the CSCE countries of Central and Eastern Europe.

Dec. 25, 1991
The 74-year-old Soviet Union is disbanded. Several of its 15 constituent republics proclaimed their independence earlier in the year. The 12 members of the European Community sign a treaty in Maastricht, the Netherlands, that would make the WEU the community's defense organization.

1992
Serbian forces wage a campaign of "ethnic cleansing" to drive Croats and Slavic Muslims from the newly independent republic of Bosnia-Herzegovina, killing nearly 9,000 people and leaving a million more homeless by early August. France and Germany agree to set up a "Eurocorps" of 35,000 troops — possibly the foundation of a new EC army.

1994
All remaining forces from the former Soviet Union are scheduled to withdraw from Poland and Germany.

1995
Under plans drawn up by the Bush administration, the number of U.S. troops in Europe will drop to 150,000.

In a Changing World, Where Does NATO Fit In?

Many NATO members (shaded areas) also belong to distinctly European groups, underscoring uncertainty about the alliance's future role in the defense of Europe.

North Atlantic Treaty Organizatio (NATO)
Belgium
Canada
Denmark
France
Germany
Greece
Iceland
Italy
Luxembourg
Netherlands
Norway
Portugal
Spain
Turkey
United Kingdom
United States

Warsaw Pact (disbanded March 1991)
Bulgaria
Czechoslovakia
East Germany
Hungary
Poland
Romania
Soviet Union

European Community (EC)
Belgium
Denmark
France
Germany
Greece
Ireland
Italy
Luxembourg
Netherlands
Portugal
Spain
United Kingdom

Western European Union (WEU)
Belgium
France
Germany
Italy
Luxembourg
Netherlands
Portugal
Spain
United Kingdom

Continued from p. 718

A 1952 treaty setting up the European Defense Community was prepared but never ratified. Another defense organization, the Western European Union (WEU), was set up outside the community in 1954 to further European integration and security through increased cooperation among the seven member nations: Belgium, France, West Germany, Italy, Luxembourg, the Netherlands and the United Kingdom; Spain and Portugal joined later.

Today, the WEU functions as a consultative body on security matters. But efforts to give the WEU a clear military role were actively opposed by the United States. "A lot of the groundwork for building a coherent and meaningful European security organization needed to be done 10 or 20 years ago, and it wasn't done," says Ted Galen Carpenter, director of foreign policy studies at the Cato Institute in Washington. "It wasn't done to a large extent because Washington didn't want it done. It felt that any competing organization would automatically undermine U.S. control of NATO."

U.S. Dominance Resented

As the European allies gained in economic strength, however, tensions mounted over U.S. dominance of the alliance. France in particular resented the overwhelming American role in Europe's security arrangements, and in 1967 President Charles de Gaulle withdrew his country from NATO's integrated military command. (France remains outside NATO's military structure but retains political membership.)

As more and more nuclear weapons were deployed in Europe in the early 1980s, West German opposition to the American presence also grew. Because their country was the likely field of battle for any military action against NATO, many Germans opposed the nuclear deployments as well as the large American bases in their country. An active peace movement, calling for the withdrawal of American nuclear and conventional forces from Europe, gained popular support and spread to other NATO countries, including the United Kingdom, the Netherlands, Belgium and Italy.

Tensions also built among the European allies over America's hostile relations with the Soviet Union. Led by West Germany, the European allies tended to support closer political relations with the Soviet Union and Eastern Europe throughout the 1970s and '80s. For their part, successive American presidents feared that détente would reduce the Germans' commitment to NATO.

End of the Cold War

The end of the 1980s found the Soviet bloc in crisis. Decades of heavy defense spending and the inability of centrally planned economies to provide an acceptable standard of living forced the communist leadership to embark on a series of reforms. Mikhail Gorbachev, who took over the Kremlin in 1985, gradually introduced market forces into the Soviet economy while relaxing state controls over political expression.

Even before the Soviet Union's official demise last Christmas, its former allies in Eastern Europe took advantage of the weakened empire to break free of Soviet political domination. Communist regimes in Poland, Bulgaria, Czechoslovakia, Hungary and Romania were voted or thrown out of office in 1989 and replaced with democratically elected governments by the end of the year.

In the first step toward German unification, East Germans in 1989 tore down the Berlin Wall, the Cold War's most poignant symbol. On Oct. 3, 1990, East Germany ceased to exist after its merger with the Federal Republic, and a unified Germany appeared on the map of Europe for the first time since the fall of the Third Reich. Meanwhile, the "Evil Empire," in President Ronald Reagan's phrase, slowly disintegrated as Georgia, Moldova and the Baltic republics of Estonia, Latvia and Lithuania declared their independence. Eight other Soviet republics joined the exodus.

Concessions by Gorbachev and Yeltsin

In an effort to gain Western economic support for his massive reforms, Gorbachev made unprecedented concessions in arms control negotiations with the United States. The 1987 treaty between the United States and Soviet Union banning intermediate-range nuclear forces (INF) in Europe was followed in 1988 by Gorbachev's unilateral cut in the Warsaw Pact's nuclear forces.

Following in Gorbachev's footsteps, Russian President Yeltsin, under similar pressure to resuscitate his country's ailing economy, has continued to offer to reduce the nuclear arsenal his nation inherited from the Soviet Union. During a June visit to Washington, Yeltsin proposed even more drastic cuts in strategic weapons than were envisioned in the Strategic Arms Reduction Treaty (START) that Bush and Gorbachev signed barely a year ago.

While the nuclear threat has been progressively reduced by continuing negotiations between the United States and the Soviet Union, and now Russia, even greater progress has been made in reducing the non-nuclear military threat to Europe's security. In 1989, NATO and the Warsaw Pact opened a new set of talks to cut conventional armed forces on both sides. The Conventional Forces in Europe (CFE) treaty, which was signed in November 1990 and went into effect this June, requires both NATO and the former members of the Warsaw Pact to reduce their troops, tanks and other non-nuclear forces throughout Europe, from the Atlantic to the Urals.

In many respects, the CFE treaty favored NATO. "The numerical limitations worked in such a way that the NATO countries had to come down in about all categories to levels very slightly below what they had had before," says R. James Woolsey, who negotiated the treaty's terms on behalf of the United States. For example, the Warsaw Pact had deployed more than 60,000 main battle tanks, compared with NATO's 23,000. Thus, Woolsey says, the treaty required NATO to make much less drastic force reductions to meet the target level of 20,000 tanks.

"Whatever happens, the Conventional Forces Agreement of 1990 makes impossible the sort of massive surprise attack that NATO's defenses were designed to counter," wrote David Calleo of Johns Hopkins University. "Any thrust into Western territory would require a long and rather transparent redeployment of conventional forces."[3]

Since the 1991 demise of the Warsaw Pact, many of the Soviet Union's former military allies have sought security ties with their former Cold War adversaries. In response to the appeals of their newly elected governments, NATO organized the North Atlantic Cooperation Council to provide a forum in which NATO members can meet with their former Warsaw Pact counterparts to share information and concerns about security issues throughout Europe. The new council has already met several times since its first official convocation last December.

NATO Reforms

As the old East-West order was crumbling, NATO began to reassess its forward-defense, flexible-response strategy and the force structure that strategy required. *(See story, p. 724)*. Most of the allies, including the United States, agreed that the reduced threat of immediate attack enabled them to cut their defense budgets and reduce their deployments of troops and equipment in Europe. In July 1990, NATO announced that it would make significant changes in both strategy and force structure. These changes were formally adopted at a NATO summit meeting in Rome in December 1991.

Because most of the Soviet forces had been withdrawn from eastern Germany, Poland and other major deployment sites, NATO decided to reduce the number of its divisions by 22 percent and the brigades by 13 percent by 1996. There would be cuts in almost all allied forces, including offensive and reconnaissance aircraft, heavy bombers, mine sweepers, aircraft carriers and ballistic-missile submarines.

Much of the equipment that is being pulled back from the old North European front is being redeployed to the southern region of NATO, including Spain, Italy, Greece and Turkey, which is now considered to be more vulnerable to attack. Sources of potential trouble in the Mediterra-

nean include the spread of ethnic conflict now raging in the Balkans, the rise of Islamic fundamentalism in northern Africa, the continuing Arab-Israeli crisis and threats to the West's supply of oil from the Persian Gulf.

While the changes have not altered NATO's defensive posture, the eruption of regional conflicts after

> **In a significant departure from precedent, the allies declared in December 1991 in Rome that their forces may in the future be sent outside NATO territory to defend their vital interests.**

the Soviet bloc's collapse suddenly dispersed the security threats to NATO from a concentrated zone along the East-West divide to the far more vast area of Eastern and Central Europe. In a significant departure from precedent, the allies declared in December 1991 in Rome that their forces may in the future be sent outside NATO territory to defend their vital interests. Among these interests, NATO declared, might be a "disruption to the flow of vital resources," a clear reference to oil from the Middle East.

NATO Forces Redeployed

In light of its new policy, NATO decided to replace many of its permanently deployed, heavily armed forces with smaller, more mobile forces capable of responding to varied situations. More of the forces would be stationed in their home countries and kept at lower readiness levels, but trained to respond quickly

to crises that may arise. And in addition to the main defense forces that made up the bulk of forward-deployed troops during the Cold War, there would be immediate-reaction forces kept at peak readiness, rapid-reaction forces able to back them up, as well as augmentation forces that could be brought into action if the initial conflict spread.

Information on what contribution each allied country, including the United States, will make to the new NATO military force is still largely classified. But NATO has disclosed plans to put 5,000 troops into the immediate-reaction force, which could be sent on short notice to any threatened area to demonstrate solidarity within the alliance. Command of this force would rotate among NATO members. The rapid-reaction corps would come under British command and consist of several divisions deployed in different NATO regions. Its air component is expected to be led by a German officer.

The main defense force will consist of each ally's forces as they are now committed to NATO. In addition, there will be six multinational corps made up of forces from Belgium, Denmark, Germany, the Netherlands and the United States. Some will be based in Germany. The United States plans to station two divisions in Germany beyond its contribution to the multinational corps in Germany. One U.S. NATO brigade will be stationed in the United States.[4]

Post-Cold War Crises

No sooner had the old order maintained by the Cold War started to crumble than new crises began to erupt in the power vacuum left by the collapse of the Soviet Union and its alliance. While the democratic revolution in Eastern Europe proceeded with almost no violence, regional conflicts that had been kept under control by Moscow broke out in several of the former Soviet republics as soon as they gained their independence.

But the first serious international crisis of the post-Cold War era erupted in the Middle East. On Aug. 2, 1990, Iraqi President Saddam Hussein, who had long received Soviet support, sent troops into Kuwait, threatening to cut off its oil exports. The U.N. Security Council responded to the attack by imposing economic sanctions against Iraq. When these didn't force Iraq to withdraw, President Bush called for joint international action. On Aug. 6 he deployed a U.N.-authorized American military force called Operation Desert Shield to Saudi Arabia. When Saddam still refused to withdraw his troops, the mission was upgraded to Operation Desert Storm. The U.S.-led coalition of 28 countries, including 10 European Community members, attacked Jan. 16, 1991, and forced the Iraqis out of Kuwait by the end of February.

"Even though some of the NATO countries provided troops and equipment for Desert Shield and Desert Storm, it is, I think, very revealing that they did so as individual powers," says the Cato Institute's Carpenter. "NATO as an organization did not get involved in this."

Indeed, only two NATO members — Britain and France — contributed both ground and air forces to the coalition facing Iraq. Italy and Canada sent air forces only. Europe's most powerful nation, Germany, refused to send forces. Arguing that their postwar constitution forbids the deployment of troops outside NATO territory, the German government limited its participation to an $11 billion contribution to the $80 billion effort.

Although the interruption of oil supplies from the region constituted a threat to NATO security, the alliance did not act because the conflict was out of NATO's territory. "There was no way NATO was going to respond to the invasion of Kuwait," says Eugene Carroll of the Center for Defense Information. "We gradually got grudging support from several of the NATO allies plus relatively active support from France and the United Kingdom, but it was not in the name of NATO and, honestly, not even in the name of the United Nations. This was all arranged by U.S. diplomacy and military coordination."

Trouble in Yugoslavia

The post-Cold War era also saw major conflict in Yugoslavia. The fighting began in 1991 in newly independent Croatia and spread early this year to Bosnia-Herzegovina, which also split off from Yugoslavia. This new development poses a far more immediate threat to NATO security than the Persian Gulf War because the hostilities are much closer to home. But in this case as well, NATO allies were divided over how to respond and failed to adopt a common strategy for dealing with a potential threat to their own security.

As in the Persian Gulf crisis, the principal multinational response to the Balkan conflicts came from the U.N. Security Council, which imposed economic sanctions against Yugoslavia. "NATO was ineffective and unresponsive when the situation blew up in Yugoslavia," says Carroll. "The Balkans are regarded as out of area. Nobody had attacked a member of NATO, so the NATO organization couldn't agree to respond."*

In contrast to its leading role in the Persian Gulf, the Bush administration has been reluctant to intervene in Bosnia. It wasn't until mid-June that it agreed to take part in the U.N.-sponsored airlift of food and humanitarian supplies to the Bosnian capital of Sarajevo, which had been under siege by Serbian forces fighting against Bosnian independence.

Additional conflicts undoubtedly will arise in the former Soviet bloc as ethnic and religious conflicts that were repressed under communist regimes erupt. "The key factor is that the new threats are much smaller in nature," says Carpenter. "They are simply not the same kinds of problems as the threat of Soviet-led aggression was during the Cold War. NATO was at least a reasonably effective vehicle for dealing with that kind of problem. It is not in any way an effective arrangement for dealing with these sorts of difficulties." ∎

---

*According to NATO Secretary General Manfred Woerner, NATO members have given themselves until Aug. 24 to decide whether to send troops to ensure delivery of humanitarian aid to Sarajevo, the besieged Bosnian capital. Meanwhile, the U.N. Security Council voted on Aug. 13 to allow military force, if necessary, to support relief operations, and on Aug. 14 France offered to send 1,100 troops.

CURRENT SITUATION

Europe's Ambivalence

At the same time that Eastern Europe was shedding its Soviet-dominated political and economic structure, the European Community was gathering new momentum toward unification. In 1985, the community launched a program to remove all remaining barriers to commerce within the EC by the end of 1992. As the initiative, known as EC-92, got under way, support grew for further unification in foreign and defense policy as well.[5]

The push for a common European

Continued on p. 726

Responding to the Changing World Order ...

In July 1990, NATO announced that it would make significant changes in both its strategy and force structure. Members of the 16-nation alliance agreed that the crumbling of the eastern bloc had reduced the threat of immediate attack. In response to the new NATO policies, which were formally adopted at a NATO summit in Rome in December 1991, most alliance members decided to cut their defense budgets and reduce their troop deployments in Europe. Iceland, which has no military forces, is not included in the major changes listed below.

UNITED STATES

Defense Budget: Plans to cut defense spending from $314 billion to $292 billion (in constant 1990 dollars) from 1989 to 1992, a 7 percent drop. Proposed budget for 1993 is $266 billion (in 1990 dollars).

Armed Forces: 2,029,600 active, 1,926,400 reserves. Plans 30 percent cut in the number of divisions and 42 percent cut in the number of brigades contributed to NATO by 1995. U.S. troops in Europe will fall from 307,000 to 150,000 (117,000 in Germany) by 1995.

Weapons Programs: More than 100 new and existing weapons programs to be terminated from 1991 through 1993. Ground-launched tactical nuclear weapons have been eliminated; tactical nuclear weapons are being removed from surface ships; and submarines, strategic bombers and Minuteman III intercontinental ballistic missiles are now off alert.

CANADA

Defense Budget: $11.4 billion in 1991. Plans to reduce defense expenditures by 5 percent over the next five years.

Armed Forces: 86,600 active, 64,500 reserves. All 6,600 troops are being withdrawn from Germany. The all-volunteer armed forces will be cut to 76,000 active troops, while reserves will be increased.

Weapons Programs: Uncertain.

UNITED KINGDOM

Defense Budget: $43.6 billion in 1991. Plans to cut defense spending by 7 percent between 1989 and 1992.

Armed Forces: 300,100 active, 347,200 reserves. Plans 21 percent cut in total forces by 1995. Also plans to bring home troops from Germany, leaving 29,000 there, down from 67,000. U.K. will lead NATO's new rapid-reaction corps.

Weapons Programs: Some procurement programs have been cut or delayed, but few have been canceled.

Plans to continue modernizing strategic nuclear weapons while eliminating ground-launched tactical nuclear weapons.

FRANCE

Defense Budget: $37.3 billion in 1991. Spending cuts of less than 1 percent from 1989 to 1992.

Armed Forces: about 453,100 active, 1,314,500 reserves. Reorganizing military into smaller, more flexible forces. Conscription term cut from 12 months to 10 months. Army reduced by 60,000. About 10,000 troops will stay in Germany as part of new Franco-German "Eurocorps."

Weapons Programs: No plans to reduce strategic nuclear arsenal until the U.S. and former Soviet arsenals are comparable in size to France's. A few major procurement programs have been canceled, others cut back.

GERMANY

Defense Budget: $34.4 billion in 1991. Spending cut 5 percent from 1989 to 1992.

Armed Forces: 476,300 active, 1,009,400 reserves. Germany added 61,000 East German troops upon unification. Plans to pare active force to 370,000 by 1995. Will participate in all six NATO multinational corps and contribute to immediate- and rapid-reaction forces. Debate continues in Germany over whether or not the nation's constitution allows German forces to be deployed outside the NATO area. Conscription term has been reduced from 15 to 12 months.

Weapons Programs: Canceling and delaying some procurement plans but continuing those that will help create more mobile and flexible forces.

BELGIUM

Defense Budget: $3.3 billion in 1991. Cutting spending by 21 percent.

Armed Forces: 85,450 active, 234,000 reserves. Will lead a NATO multinational corps, reduce overall force levels and withdraw all but 3,500 troops from Germany. Cutting troop levels by 18 percent by 1995. Conscription term being cut from 12 to 8 months.

Weapons Programs: No major procurement programs changed.

THE NETHERLANDS

Defense Budget: $8.3 billion in 1991. Plans 5 percent spending cut.

... Most NATO Allies Reduce Budgets and Troop Levels

Armed Forces: 101,400 active, 152,400 reserves. Plans smaller and more mobile forces. Cutting troop levels by 17 percent, moving toward all volunteer army with conscription term cut from 14 to 12 months in 1990; will reduce tanks, artillery and aircraft allocated to NATO.

Weapons Programs: Canceled a few programs.

LUXEMBOURG

Defense Budget: $100.2 million in 1990. Plans spending increases.

Armed Forces: 800 active. No changes planned in its sole battalion of military forces.

DENMARK

Defense Budget: $2.9 billion in 1991; 1 percent spending cut from 1989 to 1992.

Armed Forces: 29,400 active, 72,700 reserves. No immediate plans for major change in defense policy; continues to rely on reserves for the bulk of troops. Conscription term of 9 to 12 months, depending on service.

Weapons Programs: No cancellations of major weapons programs are planned.

NORWAY

Defense Budget: $3.8 billion in 1991; 1 percent spending cut from 1989 to 1992.

Armed Forces: about 32,700 active, 345,000 reserves. Still debating whether to downsize or expand military forces.

Weapons Programs: Some weapons programs have been delayed, but there have been no major cancellations.

TURKEY

Defense Budget: $4.4 billion in 1991; 3 percent spending increases annually from 1991 through 1995. Relies heavily on military assistance from NATO allies.

Armed Forces: 579,200 active, 1,107,000 reserves. Conscription term of 18 months. Plans substantial cuts in personnel and restructuring of forces to improve mobility and flexibility to better respond to regional crises, such as the Persian Gulf War.

Weapons Programs: Modernization of equipment emphasized. Will receive transfers of tanks, armored personnel carriers and artillery from NATO forces leaving Germany.

GREECE

Defense Budget: $4.5 billion in 1991. Plans 3 percent spending cut from 1989 to 1992. Receives military assistance from U.S. and other allies.

Armed Forces: 158,500 active, 406,000 reserves. Conscription term of 19 to 23 months, depending on service. Plans to increase sea and air forces for NATO.

Weapons Programs: Like Turkey, will receive transfers of equipment from NATO forces leaving Germany.

ITALY

Defense Budget: $21.3 billion in 1991. Spending cut 8 percent from 1989 to 1992.

Armed Forces: 361,400 active, 584,000 reserves. Conscription term of 12 months. Plans 25 percent cut in total personnel, 40 percent cut in conscripts, as support grows for all-volunteer service.

Weapons Programs: Still procuring major weapons but spending cuts may force cancellations.

PORTUGAL

Defense Budget: $1.5 billion in 1990. Slight spending increases planned for 1989 to 1992.

Armed Forces: 61,800 active, 190,000 reserves. Dismantling garrison army, adding more mobile brigades. Plans to cut conscription from 15 months to 8 months. May go to all-volunteer force.

Weapons Programs: Plans to improve capabilities with NATO transfers, new naval equipment and aircraft. No major procurement programs canceled.

SPAIN

Defense Budget: $9 billion in 1991. Plans 15 percent spending cut.

Armed Forces: 257,400 active, 2,400,000 reserves. Developing a rapid-reaction force. Decreasing conscription term from 12 to 9 months in move to 50 percent volunteer army. Plans to reduce total personnel from current level.

Weapons Programs: Some army procurement programs have been canceled and some navy and air force programs have been postponed.

Sources: General Accounting Office; International Institute for Strategic Studies

Continued from p. 723

defense had been brewing for many years, especially in France, which pulled out of NATO's military command in 1967. France sought greater autonomy to develop its own defense structure, including a nuclear arsenal, and it wanted to be free of American interference.

As the push toward unification among the European Community developed, France became the leading proponent of a communitywide defense organization able to act independently of NATO on European security issues. In December 1990, with momentum building for military action against Iraq, the European Community adopted amendments to its charter to allow for participation in collective security organizations in Europe.

The Western European Union

The means for developing a common defense arrangement was already at the EC's disposal. The Western European Union had been set up in 1954 as a forum for discussing cooperative defense policy. After members rejected the creation of a European Defense Community as an integral part of the emerging European Community the same year, the WEU evolved into a nine-member consultative body of countries that belong to both the EC and NATO.

Today, the WEU is Western Europe's only forum coordinating matters of defense. Although it is not officially part of the European Community, the WEU is made up of all the EC nations except Denmark, Greece and Ireland. But in nearly four decades, the WEU, overshadowed by U.S.-dominated NATO, has never played a major role in Europe's defense.

Stung by criticism of their failure to take unified action in the Persian Gulf War, EC members have tried to strengthen the Western European Union. Supporters of a stronger WEU — led by German Chancellor Helmut Kohl and French President François

Mitterrand — want it to become a link between the European Community and NATO by merging it into the EC. A stronger WEU, they say, would become a true "European pillar" of NATO.

The question of which organization would control the WEU — the European Council or NATO — is still in dispute. France and Germany want the organization to answer to the EC. "That could mean, of course, the European contingent would be virtually independent of NATO and the United States and, thus, unacceptable to Washington," writes Axel Krause, an editor of *The International Herald Tribune*, in his book about European integration. "Britain, not surprisingly, remained the United States' staunchest ally in the simmering debate."[6]

The European Community reached a compromise over its internal dispute about the WEU's role in a treaty the 12 members signed in Maastricht, Netherlands, in December 1991. The new treaty, which must be ratified by all member governments, is best known for proposing a single European currency by 1999. But the treaty also identifies the WEU as the European Community's defense body. It gained the support of the British and other strong supporters of the Atlantic alliance by requiring the WEU to cooperate with NATO.

Rise of the "Eurocorps"

Both the French and German governments insist that they continue to support NATO as well as the presence of U.S. troops in Europe, and only want to strengthen the alliance's European pillar. To that end, they announced in May the expansion of a Franco-German brigade, created only last October, into a new "Eurocorps." Expected to number 35,000 troops by 1995, the new force could provide the beginnings of a new EC army.

While the French have always clearly stated their desire to reduce America's say in Europe's defense,

German reasons for participating in the corps are more complex. On the one hand, Chancellor Kohl has repeatedly expressed his strong support for NATO as well as a strong U.S. role in the alliance. On the other hand, his country boasts the strongest economy in Europe and is a leader in the drive toward European unification.

Further complicating the German position are fears, especially among Europe's smaller countries, that the Eurocorps may be the first sign that a reunited Germany will try once again to dominate Europe, this time in league with France. "The Germans are in a little bit of a bind now," says Simon Serfaty of the Johns Hopkins Foreign Policy Institute. "They have to reassure the Europeans. But at the same time, to play the card of European unity is to get in bed with the French."

The United Kingdom, which maintains the closest ties with the United States of any EC member, is resisting any steps that could undermine the U.S. presence in Europe. David Owen, a former British foreign secretary, concedes that the "European countries will have to take a larger share of the burden from the United States within NATO than hitherto, and to do so there is merit in a coherent European view sometimes being coordinated by the WEU in advance of NATO meetings." But, he goes on to say, "it is in Europe's interests for the United States to keep some forces assigned to NATO based in Europe.... If U.S. forces are totally withdrawn ... it will not be long before America sees its own security starting only at its shoreline."[7]

What Role for the CSCE?

Another multinational organization that has assumed broader functions since the end of the Cold War is the Conference on Security and Cooperation in Europe (CSCE). Created in 1972, the CSCE includes the members of both NATO and the Warsaw Pact as well as the neutral and nonaligned countries of Europe. It produced the 1975 Helsinki Accords requiring advance notification of troop maneuvers and permitting the freer movement of people and information across national boundaries. Today, the organization has 52 members and is the only truly pan-European organization that deals with security issues.

Still, the CSCE has remained at the fringe of the defense community. With no armed forces at its disposal, it is even less prepared than the WEU to assume an immediate role in the continent's defense. The political will to strengthen the CSCE also is lacking because the biggest powers in Western Europe favor the WEU.

CSCE members, who include the United States, decided in July to give some additional clout to the organization by setting up a commission on national minorities to mediate ethnic and religious disputes in the former East bloc. They also agreed to give the organization the power to send peacekeeping forces, which would be provided by NATO, into disputed areas if all parties involved in the dispute want the forces. The conference stopped short, however, of sending observers to existing conflicts in Moldova and Nagorno-Karabakh.

For their part, many former Warsaw Pact nations are seeking closer security ties with NATO. "What the Poles, Czechs, Hungarians and a number of other Eastern Europeans really want is the chance over time to be associated with a security arrangement that the United States is part of," says James Woolsey, U.S. negotiator for the conventional forces treaty. "That's what gives the whole system some glue, from their point of view."

Slow Response to Balkan Unrest

For all the apparent support of a bigger role for Europeans in the continent's defense, none of the European defense organizations have been able to stop a war from breaking out in their midst. The ongoing conflict in Yugoslavia found the European Community initially unable to formulate a common stance. Germany tried to break the logjam in December 1991 by recognizing the independence of Croatia and Slovenia. Other community members followed suit,

> "What the Poles, Czechs, Hungarians and a number of other Eastern Europeans really want is the chance over time to be associated with ... the United States."

but little agreement on further action has materialized beyond diplomatic efforts. Even the repeated efforts by the EC foreign ministers to mediate cease-fires between Croats and Serbs have failed.

On July 10, more than three months after Serbs began their campaign to annex much of Bosnia, the WEU and NATO agreed to send naval and air task forces to the Adriatic Sea. Their mission: help enforce U.N. sanctions against Yugoslavia by intercepting ships delivering arms and other banned equipment to Serbian forces in Bosnia.

But proposals to use WEU ground forces to open land corridors for relief efforts in Bosnia were vetoed by the United Kingdom, which announced it would not supply ground troops for such an effort, even if the U.N. Security Council issued a new resolution approving it. President Bush also decided against sending troops into Bosnia, effectively ruling out NATO involvement.

According to the Cato Institute's Carpenter, the Europeans are not the only ones to blame for the failure to create an effective regional defense apparatus. "We in the United States may be paying a price for Washington's insistence throughout the Cold War on having a U.S.-dominated NATO be the sole security vehicle for dealing with European security affairs," he says. "Now the Europeans are having to try to come up with a substitute, unfortunately in the midst of several regional crises. It's a little like forming a fire department when the house is on fire."

U.S. Ambivalence

The reluctance of the United States to surrender its dominant role in European security has hardly diminished in the wake of the Cold War. An internal planning guide for the U.S. Department of Defense that was leaked to the press in February advocated that the United States build a "new world order" based on "convincing potential competitors that they need not aspire to a greater role or pursue a more aggressive posture to protect their legitimate interests."[8] In essence, the United States was to remain the world's sole superpower, and would oppose efforts by its allies to assume greater autonomy in the field of defense.

Although it was never officially endorsed, the Pentagon document prompted a flurry of protests both in the United States and among NATO allies trying to carve out an enhanced role for the Western European Union. A later version of the same document, also leaked to the press, struck a much more conciliatory tone. The document, known as the Defense Planning Guidance for fiscal 1994-99, endorsed the concept of a "base force" of 1.6 million U.S. troops, which the Bush administration has proposed as an adequate U.S. military force for the post-Cold War era. While the document emphasized the administration's commitment to cooperate with allies and the United Nations, it also stressed its determination "to act independently, as necessary, to protect our critical interests."[9]

The Bush administration proposes reducing U.S. forces in Europe from 210,000 currently deployed there to about 150,000 by 1995 to comply with NATO's new force-structure goals. At the same time, however, President Bush has publicly stated his intention to maintain a strong U.S. leadership role in NATO and expressed misgivings about European attempts to strengthen the WEU.

"If, my dear friends, your ultimate aim is to provide independently for your own defense, the time to tell us is today," Bush told the allies at the November 1991 NATO summit in Rome. "If you want to go your own way, say so. If you don't need us any longer, say so."

Supporters of continued strong U.S. leadership of NATO say Bush is right to discourage the development of a European defense organization outside the existing alliance. "All the European countries, even at their level of sophistication and worldliness and prosperity," says James Woolsey, "have a very hard time getting together and adopting a cohesive position on security issues without our being the catalyst. It doesn't mean the United States needs to be heavy-handed; it can be behind the scenes. But it just seems not to work without us."

Woolsey says the European deadlock over policy toward the Balkan conflict underscores his point. "The Europeans showed how cohesive they can be without the United States being involved during their backing and forthing about Yugoslavia," he scoffs. "Certainly it hasn't been any

model of effectiveness since we got involved, but even the U.N. sanctions couldn't have been done without the United States taking the lead."

The Europeans were not the only voices of indecision surrounding the Balkan crisis, however. No sooner had the Bush administration declared that a strong NATO under American leadership was necessary to prevent instability than war broke out in the Balkans. "Yet when the chaos and violence in Yugoslavia provided a first, rather dramatic example of such instability, Americans quickly declared that coping with the Yugoslav situation was up to the Europeans," writes former Defense Secretary James R. Schlesinger. "The fact that I personally think that it was the correct policy does not vitiate the more impressive fact that this political decision undermined our own more general argument for the continued role of our forces in Europe."[10]

Other critics say the administration errs in emphasizing NATO as the main vehicle for protecting American interests in Europe. "Our concern in Europe," says Carpenter, "is preventing a large-scale expansionist power from controlling the population, the technology and the resources of Central and Western Europe, because that by its very nature would pose a threat to our security. It's not to try to solve every low- or medium-level case of disorder that might erupt

somewhere in Europe. That is something that can and should be managed by the powers in that region to the extent that they deem those threats relevant to their own security." An autonomous European military force would be appropriate to handle such local threats, he adds.

In the long run, U.S. efforts to retain American primacy, or dominance, in NATO may work against American interests. "Primacy is an example of trying to micromanage European affairs," Carpenter says. "That wasn't even particularly healthy during the latter stages of the Cold War because it fostered an unhealthy European dependence upon the U.S. security guarantee. In a post-Cold War period, I think that insisting on U.S. primacy is more likely to create friction with the European nations than anything else."

Congressional advocates of lower defense spending agree with this assessment. Rep. Schroeder, who has long called for the European allies to shoulder a greater burden of NATO's costs, says they should also have greater autonomy in their own defense arrangements. "I think it must be very frustrating to be a European because they hear Congress yelling at them about burden-sharing," she says, "but every time they try to do something about it, here comes the administration and slaps them across the face. So they're caught between these two very different messages." ∎

OUTLOOK

European Unity

In addition to the mixed U.S. signals coming from across the Atlantic, events in Europe are raising obstacles to the development of a European defense structure. The main impediment has been the outbreak of

hostilities in the Balkans, which presented the EC with a crisis it was not yet prepared to take on. Months of bickering over whether and how to intervene in that conflict have stalled the process of building the very institutions required to do so.

Then, on June 2, Danish voters rejected the Maastricht treaty, which the European Community's leaders had signed just six months before.

Continued on p. 730

At Issue:

Is France trying to torpedo NATO?

JEANE J. KIRKPATRICK

Senior fellow, American Enterprise Institute
FROM THE *LOS ANGELES TIMES*, JUNE 21, 1992

yes

*i*n the name of a "European Europe," France does not merely oppose U.S. policy proposals regarding Europe's markets and security, it opposes significant American participation in these areas.

In General Agreement on Tariffs and Trade (GATT) negotiations, France is the chief opponent of freer trade. It has opposed with determination North and South American and British moves to eliminate barriers and subsidies to trade, especially in agriculture. In theory as well as practice, France is advocating free trade — but only within the European Community.

In the security domain, France has advocated a Franco-German "Eurocorps" with only the most ambiguous links to the North Atlantic Treaty Organization (NATO). The French withdrew from NATO's integrated command in 1967, shut NATO bases on French soil and expelled U.S. troops from France. They adopted an ill-defined, consultative relationship with the alliance.

Now, although they do not say so outright, they would like the whole of Europe to have the same relationship with NATO that France has had since 1967. They believe that NATO and the United States should have no significant role in Europe's future unless Europe becomes the object of a major, and unexpected, attack from some unsuspected source.

To this end, they have dragged their feet on authorizing NATO troops to perform peacekeeping functions in Europe at the request of the United Nations and the Conference on Security and Cooperation in Europe.... Similarly, they dragged their feet on the establishment of the North Atlantic Cooperation Council (NACC), a forum in which members of NATO meet with former members of the Warsaw Pact....

Is it a hostile act when the French seek a reduced U.S. role in Europe? Without a doubt, "Europe for the Europeans" carries an American-exclusion clause.... The notion that Americans and Canadians have enough in common with democratic Europe to spend lives and capital, but not enough to be appropriate security and trading partners, is curious and unpersuasive. It is also unfriendly.

Neither the United States nor Canada is part of Europe. But they and Europe are part of the same Western civilization. American participation in World Wars I and II and in the long Cold War was based on the conviction that civilization unites what geography separates. It was based on the view that democratic institutions, individual rights and rule of law are more compelling measures of proximity than miles or kilometers.

MICHEL ROCARD

Former prime minister of France
FROM *IN SEARCH OF A NEW WORLD ORDER: THE FUTURE OF U.S.-EUROPEAN RELATIONS*, 1992

no

*i*n the field of security, fear is particularly acute that the very symbol of transatlantic relations, NATO itself, might be in jeopardy. For a long time, it is true, misunderstanding marred relations between France, anxious to preserve its policy of independence, and the United States, whose main concern was to maintain the . . . alliance.

I am one of those people who consider that this opposition was often very damaging: In those days cooperation on security matters could take place only in the context of NATO, and I have always been firmly convinced that security is an area for international cooperation, and regretted that Europe was not yet able to take charge of this grand project.

Today, however, that is no longer true. NATO is undeniably a solid reference point in a world in complete turmoil. Its know-how, its experience must be preserved, and I for one would be in favor of France intensifying its cooperation with NATO. But there is more to it than that. Who can fail to see that under the combined pressure of the disintegration of the communist bloc and the new international stakes that are emerging, transatlantic relations lose their world-embracing dimension to become one piece among others in the machinery of planetary stability? . . .

The Euro-Atlantic debate certainly seems at times to take on a surrealistic tone. And yet the question is simple enough; can Europeans be confronted on their own territory with crises that do not concern the United States? . . . Rightly or wrongly, the United States decided that its interests and its idea of international stability were not at stake in [Yugoslavia], and it let the European Community act. This is the type of crisis Europeans may have to suffer on their own soil in the years to come, and it is for this reason that Europe must have the military means to support its policy, so that it is ready to act as and when required. Diplomatic mediation alone is clearly not enough....

Only the manifest determination and ability of Europeans to defend themselves can permit new transatlantic relations to take shape. Nobody can be defended against his will. I have long been in favor of a European defense system. Today I rejoice that this idea has met with a broad consensus among my fellow Europeans, who decided in Maastricht to make the Western European Union the instrument of this policy.... One should not fall into the trap, therefore, of criticizing Europeans because they are not yet able to achieve their goal, as if in so doing one hoped to prevent them from achieving it.

Continued from p. 728

This treaty would take the EC further along the path to unity by calling for a common currency as well as bringing the Western European Union into the community as the official coordinating body of its common defense.

The Danish vote caused an uproar among supporters of European unity, who fear it may be a harbinger of growing uncertainty in Europe about the process itself. That uncertainty has been fueled recently by the insistence of the German central bank to raise interest rates to combat inflation there. Because other EC currencies are linked to the German mark, other member countries had to raise their interest rates as well, worsening the recessionary conditions that plague much of Europe.

"Both anti-Brussels and anti-German, the [Danish] vote was a nationalist rejection of large new transfers of sovereignty," writes George Ross, a professor of labor and social thought at Brandeis University. "Worse still, the vote reflected the broader distrust of establishment politics and parties that has recently been spreading across Europe and North America."[11]

The Danish vote may be a fluke, however. The real test of the Maastricht treaty will come in September, when voters in France, European unity's strongest supporter, decide in a referendum whether to accept its terms. Simon Serfaty of the Johns Hopkins Foreign Policy Institute sees little chance that the treaty, and the process it represents, will be reversed. "What matters is the process of European unification, which keeps moving on," he says. "Every new achievement creates the need for more achievements, unless the member states are willing to pull out, which can no longer be done."

In fact, Britain, the traditional holdout against European unity, is committed to it by now, Serfaty says. "Even Margaret Thatcher, the strongest prime minister of Britain since Winston Chur-

chill, could not pull her country out of the European Community," he says. "The community is now past the single market and is moving in the direction of the United States of Europe." And that, Serfaty adds, means in the end a European defense organization that can act independently of NATO and the United States.

America's New Role

NATO ministers took a further step along the path toward out-of-area intervention in June, when they agreed to make alliance forces available for peacekeeping missions. Although the terms of this new function for NATO forces were not spelled out, the continuing conflict in the Balkans could be a candidate for NATO's first foray outside its territory.

At the same time, reports of atrocities committed against inmates of Serbian detention camps in Bosnia have increased the pressure for American intervention in the conflict. On Aug. 4, Arkansas Gov. Bill Clinton, the Democratic presidential candidate, called on the United States to ask the U.N. Security Council to demand the detention camps be closed. He also said the United States "should be prepared to lend appropriate support, including military, to such an operation."

Clinton's call for a more aggressive U.S. stance in the Yugoslav crisis was echoed by members of Congress and outside organizations. President Bush subsequently called for a U.N. resolution authorizing the use of force, if necessary, to facilitate delivery of humanitarian assistance to Bosnia. But he repeated his reluctance to send U.S. troops to the Balkans.

Beyond the immediate crisis, however, whoever wins the election this fall will have to come to grips over the next four years with the changing security situation in Europe as well as changing priorities at home. America's role in NATO will depend to a great extent on how far the European allies

proceed toward unity on defense matters. Beyond that, however, American voters seem increasingly eager for the long-awaited peace dividend.

"People just aren't real interested in foreign policy issues these days," says Rep. Schroeder. "If you get up and say you're going to give a speech on foreign policy, they all say, 'Gee, I remember I left the beans on the stove.' It's just not where people's heads are right now. Like it or not, the administration is going to find itself constantly being pushed to downsize over there." ∎

Notes

[1] From President Bush's State of the Union address, Jan. 28, 1992.

[2] For background, see "Balkanization of Eastern Europe (Again)," *Editorial Research Reports*, Nov. 3, 1989, pp. 617-632.

[3] David P. Calleo, *NATO: Reconstruction or Dissolution?* Johns Hopkins Foreign Policy Institute, 1992, p. 2.

[4] See U.S. General Accounting Office, *NATO: A Changing Alliance Faces New Challenges*, July 1992, pp. 12-14.

[5] For background, see "Europe 1992," *The CQ Researcher*, June 28, 1991, pp. 417-440.

[6] Axel Krause, *Inside the New Europe* (1991), p. 278.

[7] David Owen, "Atlantic Partnership or Rivalry?" in Henry Brandon, ed., *In Search of a New World Order: The Future of U.S.-European Relations* (1992), p. 29.

[8] Quoted in *The New York Times*, March 8, 1992, p. A1.

[9] Quoted in *The New York Times*, May 24, 1992, p. A1.

[10] James R. Schlesinger, "An American Assessment: 'Hands Across the Sea' Less Firmly Clasped," in Brandon, *op. cit.*, p. 146.

[11] George Ross, "After Maastricht: Hard Choice for Europe," *World Policy Journal*, summer 1992, p. 502.

Bibliography

Selected Sources Used

Books

Brandon, Henry, ed., *In Search of a New World Order: The Future of U.S.-European Relations*, Brookings Institution, 1992.

Eight current and former high-ranking officials and analysts from the United States, the United Kingdom, France, Germany and Italy explain how their countries are changing their defense policies in the post-Cold War era. A clear difference of opinion over NATO's role in Europe is seen between those in Britain and the United States who want to retain a strong U.S. presence in Europe and others who want the European allies to assume a stronger role.

Calleo, David P., *Beyond American Hegemony: The Future of the Western Alliance*, Basic Books, 1987.

According to Calleo, U.S. dominance of NATO may be counterproductive if it continues into the 1990s at a time when the European allies are demanding greater autonomy and the United States needs to direct greater attention to domestic problems. Calleo's position today (the book was written before the end of the Cold War) enjoys considerable support among analysts who see fewer threats to Europe.

Carpenter, Ted Galen, ed., *NATO at 40: Confronting a Changing World*, Lexington Books, 1990.

The contributors to this volume agree that the alliance must adjust to the new security situation in Europe, but they differ widely over the degree of change that needs to be made. The editor, director of foreign policy studies at the conservative Cato Institute, is an outspoken critic of NATO who calls for a reduction in U.S. forces in Europe.

Krause, Axel, *Inside the New Europe*, HarperCollins, 1991.

An editor of *The International Herald Tribune* looks at the economic and political forces that are driving the 12-member European Community to unify and to assume a greater role in Europe's security arrangements. He shows how business leaders and politicians worked together to launch the unification process.

Sbragia, Alberta M., ed., *Euro-Politics: Institutions and Policymaking in the "New" European Community*, Brookings Institution, 1992.

The European Community's evolving social and monetary policies are examined to assess the organization's ability to unify as planned under the 1990 Maastricht treaty. The volume also presents an update on the community's initiative to remove all remaining barriers to internal trade by the end of this year, known as EC-92.

Sloan, Stanley R., ed., *NATO in the 1990s*, Pergamon-Brassey's, 1989.

Fourteen defense experts from both sides of the Atlantic address issues facing NATO in the 1990s, including political pressure for change in Europe, the alliance's role in out-of-area crises, burden-sharing among the allies and the shift in force structure away from nuclear weapons to flexible conventional forces.

Articles

Livingston, Robert Gerald, "United Germany: Bigger and Better," *Foreign Policy*, summer 1992, pp. 157-174.

American and European squeamishness over Germany's unification are unfounded, the author writes, as the republic that has emerged in the postwar period identifies closely with European unity, not German nationalism. Germany's historical ties to Eastern and Central Europe and its fears of instability in those regions are evident in the country's early recognition of Croatia and leadership role in funneling Western aid to Russia.

Ross, George, "After Maastricht: Hard Choices for Europe," *World Policy Journal*, summer 1992, pp. 487-513.

The latest push toward political union among the European Community's 12 members faces obstacles after Danish voters rejected a treaty calling for a common defense organization and a single currency. The community's longstanding goal of expanding its membership while pressing on with unification faces new obstacles in the continent's rapidly changing security environment.

Tiersky, Ronald, "France in the New Europe," *Foreign Affairs*, spring 1992, pp. 131-146.

European unity has long been a central aim of French leaders, including President François Mitterrand. The emerging Franco-German partnership as the locomotive for European political union is likely to endure, though the roles each country will play in a unified Europe remain uncertain.

Reports and Studies

U.S. General Accounting Office, *NATO: A Changing Alliance Faces New Challenges*, July 1992.

The collapse of NATO's traditional nemesis, the Soviet Union, has prompted the alliance to change its strategic concept to face a variety of threats to European security.

The Next Step

Additional Articles from Current Periodicals from EBSCO Publishing's Database

Books & reading

Eberle, J., "Book reviews: Security and arms control," *International Affairs,* **October 1991, p. 779.**

Reviews the book "The Origins of NATO," edited by Joseph Smith.

Howard, M., "Shooting at a moving target," *TLS,* **March 13, 1992, p. 7.**

Reviews six new books dealing with European security and the future of NATO. Includes Alpo M. Rusi's "After the Cold War: Europe's new political architecture"; "European Security Towards 2000," edited by Michael C. Pugh; "Securing Peace in Europe, 1945-62: Thoughts for the post-Cold War era," edited by Beatrice Heuser and Robert O'Neill; Richard H. Ullman's "Securing Europe"; John Leech's "Halt! Who Goes Where? The future of NATO in the new Europe."

Hyde-Price, A., "Book reviews: Security and arms control," *International Affairs,* **October 1991, p. 777**

Reviews the book "European Defence Cooperation: America, Britain and NATO," edited by Michael Clarke and Rod Hague.

Wells, S. F., "Reviews of books: United States," *The American Historical Review,* **April 1992, p. 643.**

Reviews the book "NATO and the United States: The Enduring Alliance," by Lawrence S. Kaplan.

Europe, defenses

"Europe's security clubs," *The Economist,* **Feb. 15, 1992, p. 60.**

Gives a list of several security organizations in Europe. Conference on Security and Cooperation in Europe (CSCE); Council of Europe; North Atlantic Treaty Organization (NATO); more; details.

"The European Community's new army," *Forbes,* **Nov. 25, 1991, p. 33.**

Expresses the view of Publisher Casper W. Weinberger, which states that the French and German proposal to form a joint army unit of at least 50,000 troops as a nucleus of an independent European defense force rightly caused consternation to the United Kingdom, Americans and other strong supporters of NATO. The French-German plan confirms the worst suspicions; reasoning behind proposal; unclear details; the basic absurdity of the proposal; an attempt to undermine NATO.

"Esprit de korps," *National Review,* **Nov. 18, 1991, p. 18.**

Questions the wisdom behind a recent joint initiative by French President François Mitterrand and German Chancellor Helmut Kohl to promote a common European security policy. Such a policy would call upon the European Community to develop a common foreign policy toward Washington and Moscow and also a Franco-German military brigade. Anti-Americanism in Europe is suicidal; the importance of maintaining the North Atlantic Treaty Organization (NATO).

"Esprit de korps," *National Review,* **June 22, 1992, p. 18.**

Contends that any military moves that would weaken the NATO alliance are dangerous for the nations of the West, and more dangerous for France. Emergence of Franco-German army corps; why the French are under a delusion if they think they can be a counterweight to German power by themselves.

"The German delusion," *The New Republic,* **Nov. 11, 1991, p. 8.**

Argues there is no need to become alarmed over the possible obsolescence of NATO, because the European Community countries, particularly Germany, are ready to bear more military and diplomatic responsibility in Europe and beyond. Suggests that while in the long term the German economy will prosper, in the short term NATO is unlikely to be replaced by the Western European Union anytime soon.

Owen, K., "Europe seeks news defense identity," *Aerospace America,* **January 1992, p. 12.**

Discusses options for the pattern of defense cooperation which should accompany the continuing advance toward European political union. The response of the European Community (EC) and the North Atlantic Treaty Organization (NATO) to the aspirations of the newly democratic East European nations; NATO's historic concern with European defense integration.

Riding, A., "French and Germans plan an army corps despite NATO fears," *The New York Times,* **May 23, 1992, p. 1.**

States that the leaders of France and Germany approved formation of a 35,000-member joint army corps with the aim of turning it into the nucleus of a future European army. Concern in Washington and London that they may be undermining NATO; corp's missions; other members of the Western European Union invited to join.

North Atlantic Treaty Organization

"A time of decision for the NATO alliance," *Department of State Dispatch,* **Nov. 11, 1991, p. 823.**

Presents remarks by President Bush at the NATO summit, Rome, Italy, November 1991, concerning military strategy and approval of a fundamentally new strategic doctrine for Europe. Four defining questions; revolutionary forces at work in the Soviet Union; the American perspective. INSET: Post-Cold War opportunities for security and partnership.

"Enough reserves?" *The Economist,* **Aug. 17, 1991, p. 45.**

Reviews NATO's new plans for its main defense forces, outlined in May, and discusses why these plans depend on large numbers of reserves. 'Reserve' means different things in different countries; NATO armies will also need reserve units; the problem of equipment; how attitudes should change toward reserves if NATO's new strategy will have to be believed.

"Fact sheet: North Atlantic Treaty Organization," *Department of State Dispatch,* **Dec. 16, 1991, p. 898.**

Presents a rundown on NATO today, following the Rome Declaration on Peace and Cooperation issued after the November 1991 meeting, signaling the vitality of the alliance in adapting to security needs in a post-Cold War world. The new NATO security policy; the trans-Atlantic partnership; history of U.S.-NATO relations; Soviet arms. INSETS: NATO background; NATO structure; Rome NATO summit: Reaching out to the East.

"Is America a part of Europe?" *National Review,* **March 2, 1992, p. 26.**

Presents former President Richard M. Nixon's views on the position of the United States in newly unified Europe. U.S. role in the North Atlantic Treaty Organization (NATO); how U.S. should maintain its presence in Europe; relationship of Eastern Europe with U.S. and NATO; curbing arms sales; restructuring NATO for new missions; framework for common transatlantic home; more.

"NAC meeting overview," *Department of State Dispatch,* **Dec. 23, 1991, p. 904.**

Presents excerpts from a press conference by Secretary of State James A. Baker III, NATO Headquarters, Brussels, Belgium, December 1991, concerning the meeting of the North Atlantic Council and the major role the alliance should play in the transformation of the Soviet Union. Need for a coordinated Western effort; problems faced in the Soviet Union; NATO's role in collective engagement; joint efforts in accelerated destruction of nuclear weapons. INSET: Trip to former Soviet republics.

"NATO seeks closer ties to former Soviet states," *Aviation Week & Space Technology,* **Jan. 13, 1992, p. 28.**

Discusses NATO's intent to establish formal ties with Russia, Ukraine, Belarus and other newly independent states of the former Soviet Union as it already has with former Warsaw Pact members. The first meeting will likely take place in Prague Jan. 31 with the intent of helping the new governments transfer military industrial capacity to civilian purposes. Other possible meetings of the NATO foreign ministers.

Fenyvesi, C., "NATO moves east," *U.S. News & World Report,* **Nov. 4, 1991, p. 31.**

Reports that although President Bush last week discouraged Czechoslovakia's desire to join the North Atlantic Treaty Organization, the alliance will soon establish formal ties with former parts of the Soviet empire. What senior NATO officials say about next week's summit in Rome; reaction of the Baltic States; NATO will not currently offer the East European nations security guarantees.

Javetski, B., P. Oster, et al., "NATO: A new mission for an old cold warrior," *Business Week,* **May 25, 1992, p. 49.**

Discusses how when Western foreign ministers gather in Oslo on June 4, they are likely to create a bold new mission for the North Atlantic Treaty Organization (NATO). In a break with the tradition confining NATO military operations to Western Europe, sources say the ministers will approve plans to use NATO troops as peacekeepers in eastern Europe and points beyond. Tampering with NATO's identity; plan fraught with obstacles.

Knight, R., R.Z. Chesnoff, et al., "Compromise in Rome," *U.S. News & World Report,* **Nov. 18, 1991, p. 68.**

Reports on Eastern Europe's security problems that are compounded by the woeful state of the region's armed forces. By agreeing to formalize links with its former Warsaw Pact foes, the North Atlantic Treaty Organization (NATO) is shifting its boundaries eastward and going some way toward meeting Czechoslovak, Hungarian and Polish demands for 'security guarantees.' Risks stirring up new pressures for change; the compromise reached at NATO's Rome summit.

Knight, R. and B.B. Auster, "Alliance without an enemy," *U.S. News & World Report,* **Nov. 11, 1991, p. 50.**

Reports on how the North Atlantic Treaty Organization (NATO) is becoming a vehicle for keeping the U.S. in Europe. Its latest attempt to adapt to changing times; NATO's political leadership is groping for a new role and a new rationale; details of the old NATO; what keeps NATO from adapting new realities; why the centerpiece of the Rome summit — a decision to widen NATO contacts with Poland, Czechoslovakia, Hungary and the Baltic States — is risky.

Mecham, M., "Signing NATO's new strategy may be the easy part for summit," *Aviation Week & Space Technology,* Nov. 4, 1991, p. 27.

States NATO will approve at the Rome summit this week the most sweeping revision of its basic military doctrine since its formation 42 years ago. Emergence of a NATO that will emphasize its political role in crisis management; NATO force cuts and drawdown of both the East and West's conventional forces; the United States as observer only; factors driving the alliance between France and Germany; desire to direct national resources away from military spending' NATO's charter.

Mecham, M., "NATO stresses politics, not military to assure security in unstable '90s," *Aviation Week & Space Technology,* March 16, 1992, p. 31.

States members of the Commonwealth of Independent States, the former Warsaw Pact and the Baltics see NATO as a security umbrella to protect them against potential regional conflicts, and have joined the organization's newest group, the North Atlantic Cooperative Council, which now has 35 members. NACC meeting set for April is concerned with organizing militaries; NATO's political agenda; comments from U.S. Army Gen. John Galvin, NATO's supreme allied commander.

Mecham, M., "NATO strategy review moves faster on political rather than military front," *Aviation Week & Space Technology,* Nov. 11, 1991, p. 83.

Studies the 16-page strategy document from the North Atlantic Treaty Organization that formally integrates its political and military roles. Estimates that it will be the mid-1990s before the new military doctrine is filled out in detail. Little debate about the military component of the strategy, which relies heavily on air power; awaiting a resolution of how the continent's leaders will define their own security identity; formal declarations.

Nelan, B.W., D. Benjamin, et al., "Au revoir, U.S.?" *Time,* Nov. 11, 1991, p. 64.

Summarizes the policy statement from this week's NATO summit in Rome, where the 16 member heads of state and government are expected to wrangle over how to produce a separate 'European defense identity' and how they should be linked to the U.S. and the alliance as a whole, and what happens to U.S. units on the continent. A military discussion and a highly political substance; a Euroarmy feasible in the very long term; aid to the Warsaw Pact; isolationism.

Nelson, D.N., "NATO — means, but no ends," *Bulletin of the Atomic Scientists,* January/February 1992, p. 10.

Recounts the NATO November summit in Rome, and argues it highlighted NATO's failure to address the most basic questions it faces in a post-Cold War world: the "Western question," the "Eastern question," and the "American question." Failure to reveal how the West's security forces would work together; ponderous indecision on handling the ethnic rivalries and territorial disputes in Eastern Europe; provide genuine collective security throughout Europe or retrench.

Steel, R., "NATO's afterlife," *The New Republic,* Dec. 2, 1991, p. 18.

Suggests that now that NATO, formed to provide war-shocked Europeans with a security blanket until they could take care of themselves, is no longer necessary, the United States is unwilling to let it die. American ability to exert pressure on Europe is sharply reduced; European certainty that the U.S. will pull most of its forces out of Europe.

Sullivan, S., A. McDaniel, et al., "The birth of a new NATO," *Newsweek,* Nov. 18, 1991, p. 32.

Reports that the declaration signed in Rome last Friday recognizes that, despite the end of the threat that brought American troops to European soil in the first place, Europe still sees value in political-military concord with the United States. NATO no longer designed to repel a Warsaw Pact invasion; envisions rapid-deployment forces to deal with a multitude of new and unpredictable risks; NATO arsenals; deal last week will keep NATO going; details.

Whitney, C.R., "NATO, victim of success, searches for new strategy," *The New York Times,* Oct. 26, 1991, p. 1.

Discusses the question: How much longer will the U.S. continue to be the key to European security? This question is on practically everybody's lips in private conversation at NATO headquarters in Brussels, where 4,000 military officers and diplomats are trying to put the finishing touches on a sweeping new strategy in time for a meeting of the alliance's 16 leaders in Rome on Nov. 7 and 8.

Nuclear weapons

Heuser, B., "What nuclear strategy for post cold-war Europe?" *ORBIS,* spring 1992, p. 211.

Addresses two broad questions that have emerged from the confusion of NATO and the European Community: are nuclear weapons still needed to secure peace in Europe; and are alliances still needed to provide the framework for nuclear guarantees. The changed variables; new threats and threat perceptions; the impact of technological change; future for tactical nuclear forces; nuclear weapons in different contingencies; nuclear weapons and alliance options; conclusion.

Young, T., "The need for NATO-Europe's substrategic

nuclear weapons," *ORBIS,* spring 1992, p. 227.

Discusses the twofold problem associated with the future role of nuclear weapons in NATO strategy, as the author sees it. The absolute number of nuclear forces available to NATO will diminish as short-range nuclear forces are withdrawn from service; this change in NATO is taking place just as the breakup of the Soviet Union increases the likelihood of nuclear proliferation in the Middle East; the Bush initiative; considerations for forces and strategy; obstacles; more.

World politics

"CIS outlines security concerns," *Aviation Week & Space Technology,* **April 13, 1992, p. 15**

Recounts the meeting between military chiefs of the Commonwealth of Independent States and the 16 members of NATO's military committee that was the initial effort to develop a "workplan" for increased contact with the ex-Soviet empire and a request for joint training exercises with NATO forces. Refining strategy elements; consensus on headquarters, functions and staffing; ratification.

"Fact sheet: Who belongs to what," *Department of State Dispatch,* **Feb. 10, 1992, p. 98.**

Presents a listing of membership by country in selected international organizations. Includes, among others, APEC (Asia-Pacific Economic Cooperation), Arab League, ASEAN (Association of South East Asian Nations), CIS (Commonwealth of Independent States), COCOM (Coordinating Committee for Multilateral Export Controls), Council of Europe, CSCE (Conference on Security and Cooperation in Europe), Group of Seven, NATO, OPEC (Organization of Petroleum Exporting Countries), WEU (Western European Union).

"Opening the skies," *The Economist,* **March 28, 1992, p. 38.**

Describes how an "open skies" treaty was signed on March 25 by 25 countries, including all 16 members of NATO (North Atlantic Treaty Organization), plus the five Eastern European ex-members of the Warsaw Pact and Russia, Ukraine, Belarus and Georgia. For the first time it legalizes aerial snooping at short notice over somebody else's territory. Plugging the intelligence gap; attempts to avoid regional conflicts.

"The road to Maastricht," *The Economist,* **Nov. 23, 1991, p. 15.**

Discusses the details to be discussed at the Maastricht summit, and how Britain and Prime Minister John Major should respond to the agenda. Monetary union; political union; European Community (EC) solidarity; Britain's lack of vision; action Major should take.

Cowell, A., "Bush challenges partners in NATO over

role of U.S." *The New York Times,* **Nov. 8, 1991, p. A1.**

Says that President Bush challenged his European allies to state clearly whether they wanted America to withdraw from Europe's defense. As leaders of the Western alliance unveiled their first major strategic shift in 24 years, he was rapidly assured that they did not. The exchange was made as NATO leaders offered their former adversaries in Eastern Europe a formal link to the Western military alliance, but withheld any commitment to safeguard their security.

Lepgold, J., "The United States and Europe: Redefining the relationship," *Current History,* **November 1991, p. 353.**

States that as Europe begins to reassess its security and economic needs, the United States increasingly finds that it is no longer the central actor in determining how best to meet those needs. Cites issues of concern to both the United States and Europe, the results of which will help redefine the nature of U.S.-European relations. The changing role of NATO; the European Community's Common Agricultural Policy (CAP); more.

Treverton, G. F., "The new Europe," *Foreign Affairs,* **1991/1992 Special issue, p. 94.**

States that no one on either side of the Atlantic has much idea how to reshape the American connection to Europe after the disappearance of the Soviet threat — or whether a reshaping is really necessary. German reunification's effect on European Community (EC); how open warfare in Yugoslavia has dashed pan-European dreams and strained Europe's center; future of NATO.

Back Issues

Great Research on Current Issues Starts Right Here... Recent topics covered by The CQ Researcher are listed below. Issues dated before May 10, 1991, were published under the name of Editorial Research Reports.

FEBRUARY 1991
Regional Impact of Recession
Puerto Rico's Status
Redistricting: Mapping Power
Nuclear Power

MARCH 1991
Acid Rain
Cost of the Gulf War
Reassessing Gun Laws
Future for Man in Space

APRIL 1991
Social Security
Canadian Crisis Over Quebec
California Drought
Electromagnetic Radiation

MAY 1991
School Choice
Racial Quotas
Animal Rights
U.S. and Japan

JUNE 1991
Children and Divorce
Teenage Suicide
Endangered Species
Europe 1992

JULY 1991
Teenagers and Abortion
Soviet Republics Rebel
Mexico's Emergence
Athletes and Drugs

AUGUST 1991
Sexual Harassment
Fetal Tissue Research
Oil Imports
The Palestinians

SEPTEMBER 1991
Police Brutality
Advertising Under Attack
Saving the Forests
Foster Care Crisis

OCTOBER 1991
Pay-Per-View TV
Youth Gangs
Gene Therapy
World Hunger

NOVEMBER 1991
Fast-Food Shake-Up
The Greening of Eastern Europe
Business' Role in Education
Cuba In Crisis

DECEMBER 1991
Retiree Health Benefits
Asian Americans
The Obscenity Debate
The Disabilities Act

JANUARY 1992
Term Limits
Oil Spills
Hunting Controversy
Alternative Medicine

FEBRUARY 1992
Threatened Coastlines
New Era in Asia
Assisted Suicide
Jobs in the '90s

MARCH 1992
Women and Sports
Underage Drinking
Garbage Crisis
Mafia Crackdown

APRIL 1992
Ozone Depletion
Welfare Reform
Politicians and Privacy
Illegal Immigration

MAY 1992
Native Americans
Jobs vs. Environment
Too Many Lawsuits?
Fairness in Salaries

JUNE 1992
Nuclear Proliferation
Food Irradiation
Lead Poisoning
Hard Times for Libraries

JULY 1992
Alternative Energy
Prescription Drug Prices
Alzheimer's Disease
Infant Mortality

AUGUST 1992
The Homeless
Work, Family and Stress

Back issues are available for $4.00 (subscribers) or $7.00 (non-subscribers). Quantity discounts apply to orders over ten. To order, call Congressional Quarterly 1-800-432-2250.

Binders are available for $15.00. To order call 1-800-638-1710.

Future Topics

▶ *Marine Mammals*

▶ *Domestic Partners*

▶ *Violence in Schools*

THE CQ Researcher

PUBLISHED BY CONGRESSIONAL QUARTERLY INC., IN CONJUNCTION WITH EBSCO PUBLISHING

Marine Mammals vs. Fish

Will overexploited oceans become the next global ecology concern?

EFFORTS TO PROTECT MARINE MAMMALS HAVE been extremely successful. Certain species of whales, dolphins and sea lions are rebounding hearteningly. But now scientists say there are new concerns — about fish stocks. As commercial fishing by the overbuilt and poorly regulated U.S. fishing fleet intensifies, marine mammals increasingly come into conflict with fishermen, becoming entangled in their nets or competing for the same fish. As a result, virtually all of the nation's fish are under stress or in serious decline. Without action, experts say, there won't be enough fish for marine mammals — or for fishermen. And the problem isn't limited to the United States. Environmentalists fear that overexploited oceans will replace tropical rain forests as the next global ecology concern.

CQ | **August 28, 1992 • Volume 2, No. 32 • 737-760**

Formerly Editorial Research Reports

CQ Researcher

August 28, 1992
Volume 2, No. 32

EDITOR
Sandra Stencel

MANAGING EDITOR
Thomas J. Colin

ASSOCIATE EDITOR
Richard L. Worsnop

STAFF WRITERS
Charles S. Clark
Mary H. Cooper
Rodman D. Griffin

PRODUCTION EDITORS
Laurie De Maris
Sarah E. Merritt

EDITORIAL ASSISTANT
Michael M. Taylor

GRAPHICS
Jack Auldridge

PUBLISHED BY
Congressional Quarterly Inc.

CHAIRMAN
Andrew Barnes

VICE CHAIRMAN
Andrew P. Corty

EDITOR AND PUBLISHER
Neil Skene

EXECUTIVE EDITOR
Robert W. Merry

PUBLICATIONS MARKETING/SALES
Robert Smith

EDITOR, EBSCO PUBLISHING
Melissa Kummerer

The CQ Researcher (ISSN 1056-2036). Formerly Editorial Research Reports. Published weekly (48 times per year, not printed the first Friday of any month with five Fridays) by Congressional Quarterly Inc., 1414 22nd St., N.W., Washington, D.C. 20037. Rates are furnished upon request. Second-class postage paid at Washington, D.C. POSTMASTER: Send address changes to The CQ Researcher, 1414 22nd St., N.W., Washington, D.C. 20037.

COVER: A white-sided dolphin and a squid being hauled aboard a Japanese drift-net ship in the North Pacific. (© Greenpeace/Dorreboom — Used with permission)

Marine Mammals vs. Fish

BY RODMAN D. GRIFFIN

THE ISSUES

New England fishermen have mined the fertile waters of the Gulf of Maine for centuries, hoping to find a mother lode of cod, flounder and haddock. Each year, their nets inadvertently ensnare dozens of whales and dolphins, and untold numbers of sea birds and untargeted fish species that end up being wasted.

For decades, it seems, few people noticed or cared. The so-called "by-catch" was part of the price of having a commercial fishing fleet. Recent scientific data, however, have conservationists and marine biologists alarmed. Among the yearly casualties off New England's coast are some 2,000 harbor porpoises, a species that is becoming increasingly rare. "The by-catch of harbor porpoises is twice the level at which their population can be sustained," notes Michael Payne, a marine biologist at the National Marine Fisheries Service (NMFS), the government body charged with regulating the nation's fisheries.

The porpoises' dwindling numbers have led a group of environmental organizations — including the International Wildlife Coalition, the Sierra Club and the Center for Marine Conservation — to petition that the species, whose total estimated population is 45,000, be listed as "threatened" under the 1973 Endangered Species Act.[1] Theoretically, that would ensure the porpoise better protection from fishermen.

"We understand that fishermen don't want to kill harbor porpoises. It's like running over a dog with a car," says Dave Wiley, senior scientist at the International Wildlife Coalition in Falmouth, Mass. "But so far we haven't saved even one harbor por-

poise. We need to see some action — soon."

Under federal law, the NMFS is obliged to respond to the environmentalists' petition by sometime next month. Even if the harbor porpoise isn't listed as threatened, most experts, including fishermen, agree that something will be done to limit the use of gill nets in certain areas off the New England coast.*

But while the public rallies behind the lovable harbor porpoise, scientists say the real tragedy is the depletion of fish stocks. "If haddock and yellowtail flounder were mammals, they would be listed as endangered," says Ed Lima, a third-generation fisherman and executive director of the Cape Anne Vessel Association in Gloucester, Mass.

These days, fishermen return to port telling tales not of bountiful catches, but of working twice as hard to catch half the number of fish they

*A fish swimming head first into a gill net becomes ensnared once the head and gills pass through the netting.

caught just a few years ago. And what they do catch is mostly "trash fish," species like skate and dogfish that Americans don't eat and fishermen would prefer to avoid catching.

The decline of the New England fishery has attracted the most attention, but fish stocks are under pressure everywhere in the world. In the Gulf of Mexico, the once-abundant red snapper have been overfished. Swordfish, prized for their high price, have been decimated in the Atlantic. In the Pacific, some Asian boats fish illegally with vast drift nets, dubbed "walls of death." Up to 40 miles long, they entrap tens of thousands of marine mammals and millions of young migrating salmon each year. (See story, p. 746.)

"There has been flagrant mismanagement of fisheries," says Michael Sutton, senior program officer at the World Wildlife Fund. "But the environmental community is partly to blame. We've been out to lunch on this issue. Fish are in much worse shape than most marine mammals ever were."

Fifteen years ago, the United States declared a 200-mile boundary around its shores, banning most foreign trawlers that had plundered America's waters. It was, proponents said, the only way to save beleaguered New England fishermen — and to salvage U.S. fisheries. It worked, until Americans themselves began overfishing.

Of America's important fish stocks, 42 percent are overfished, according to a report published earlier this year by the National Oceanic and Atmospheric Administration.[2] Scientists say 14 of the most valuable species — haddock, striped bass and Atlantic bluefin tuna among them — are threatened with commercial extinction, meaning that too few would remain to justify the cost of catching them.

Only drastic conservation will re-

Depletion of Fish Stocks

The following table includes a sampling of fish and shellfish species that are overexploited. Those marked with a bullet are being fished to the maximum level, but without damaging spawning stocks.

Northeast
Atlantic cod
Pollock
Yellowtail flounder
Haddock
Atlantic halibut
Redfish
Atlantic salmon
American lobster
Sea scallop
Surf clam•

Atlantic Migratory Fish
Swordfish
Bluefin tuna
King mackeral (Gulf of Mexico)
Spanish mackeral

Atlantic/Gulf of Mexico
Grouper
Red porgy
Red snapper
Shrimp
Spiny lobster

Pacific Coast
Pacific herring•
Pacific ocean perch

Pacific whiting•
Salmon

Pacific Migratory Fish
Albacore tuna
Blue marlin
Yellowfin tuna•

Alaska/Bering Sea
Greeland turbot•
King crab•
Mackeral•
Pacific cod•
Pollock•
Rockfish•
Sablefish•
Salmon•
Tanner crab•
Yellowfin sole•

Nearshore Fish
Abalone
Atlantic hard clam
Bay scallop
Oyster (Atlantic)
Pacific razor clam
Striped bass (Pacific)

Source: National Marine Fisheries Service, 1992

store these threatened stocks. However, a five-to-10-year fishing ban to allow rebuilding could spell economic disaster for segments of the fishing industry. "What are we preserving the stocks for, if you're going to put the fishermen out of business?" asks Tony Verga, executive director of the Gloucester Fisheries Commission, which oversees one of the nation's oldest — and largest — fishing fleets.

Virtually all the remaining commercial fish stocks — including many of those in Alaskan waters — are now being harvested to their limits. Further fishing pressure could put more species in jeopardy. Between 1986 and 1991, the finfish and shell-fish catch off the lower 48 states declined by 500 million pounds, from 4.8 billion pounds to 4.3 billion. Even more serious, spawning stocks have been decimated.

"We have two choices — conserve and develop a sustainable resource, or squander and destroy it," says Roger E. McManus, head of the Center for Marine Conservation, in Washington, D.C. "Our record so far is abysmal." [3]

There is a growing belief among environmentalists that the world's overexploited and ailing oceans will replace tropical rain forests as the next global ecology concern. The stakes are high. More than half of the human populace depends on fish for most of the animal protein it consumes; in some developing nations, fish is often the only source of animal protein for many people. [4]

In the United States, both the fiercely independent fishing industry and the NMFS, which tries hard to regulate it, are struggling over ways to control overfishing, reduce the number of boats, curb the waste of by-catch fish and find more efficient ways to manage and harvest the stocks. At present, fisheries are the least regulated of public resources. Unlike oil leases or grazing permits or timber sales on public lands, America's fish resources can be used free of charge. Enforcement of even the lax regulations is spotty, compliance is weak and there is simply no real incentive for individual fishermen to conserve fish stocks.

As the debate over how to manage the complex marine ecosystem heats up, here are some of the questions being asked:

Can marine mammals be protected without undermining the fishing industry?

At the risk of oversimplification, there are basically two ways in which marine mammals and fishermen come into conflict. First, marine mammals become entangled in fishing gear, as in the case of the harbor porpoise*. And second, marine mammals and humans compete for some of the same fish resources.

Perhaps the most notorious conflict between marine mammals and fisheries involves the incidental killing of some 6 million dolphins over the past two decades in purse-seine nets** used by tuna fishermen in the Eastern Tropical Pacific. Under in-

---

*Federal regulations that require shrimp trawlers to use turtle excluder devices (TEDs) have successfully reduced the number of endangered sea turtles that are trapped in nets in the Gulf of Mexico.
**These very large nets can be closed like a drawstring purse once they are set.

tense public pressure, the tuna industry has modified its fishing techniques and equipment. As a result, dolphin mortality rates have been cut to one-fifth of what they were five years ago. (*See story, p. 748.*)

Since passage of the Marine Mammal Protection Act (MMPA) in 1972, it has been illegal to hunt marine mammals commercially in the United States. But fishermen have been allowed to kill a certain number incidentally as part of normal fishing practices. Management has become a game of numbers: How many marine mammals can be killed incidentally without endangering the population?

Attempting to balance the needs of the fishing industry with its mission to protect marine mammals, the NMFS is currently developing new guidelines for maximum acceptable mortality rates for each species of marine mammals. The new regulations are bound to be controversial, with critics already saying the numerical approach diverts attention from more important issues, such as developing new fishing technologies that will limit the number of marine mammals killed, and ultimately drive the number down to zero.

Even more problematic is the issue of competition for food sources.* "One responsibility of the NMFS is to determine whether fisheries are limiting the recovery of endangered whale populations," says Peter Tyack, a marine biologist at the Woods Hole Oceanographic Institute in Woods Hole, Mass. "The entire question of multispecies, or ecosystem, management and the effects of competition between human fisheries and marine mammals on prey populations has been overlooked."

Competition may already be a seri-

ous problem in the Arctic, where 95 percent of marine mammals in the United States dwell. During the past 30 years, populations of the huge Stellar sea lions have declined by as much as 90 percent in some areas.[5] No one knows exactly why the population has plummeted. In the Bering Sea, populations of fur seals and sea birds have also dropped significantly. These declines coincide with the rise of commercial fishing for Alaskan pollock, a common groundfish, leading scientists to suggest that fishermen and marine mammals are competing for the same prey — and that the fishermen are winning. The commercial value of the pollock fishery has grown 25 times in the last five years.

"There are complaints that it's either sea lions or fishermen — that you can't have both," says the NMFS' Michael Payne. "That's just not true. The cause for the decline of the Stellar sea lion is more complex than simple cause-and-effect." Moreover, he says, creating buffer zones around significant breeding places for Stellar sea lions in the Bering Sea will ultimately help alleviate the problem.

Others say more drastic action is necessary. "As we overharvest the oceans, it often puts commercial fisheries in direct conflict with marine mammals that are using the same fish as prey sources," says Nina Young, a marine mammalogist at the Center for Marine Conservation. "We need to carve out a piece of the pie and allocate it to marine mammals." There is a move afoot to include a provision in next year's reauthorization of the Marine Mammal Protection Act requiring that a certain amount of fish be preserved for marine mammals.

Fishing interests — and the representatives they elect to Congress — strongly oppose such measures. "Environmental groups think that we must protect the fish for the marine mammals — and for the natural eco-

system," says Rep. Don Young, R-Alaska. "I can't figure out what people are going to eat. You're not supposed to eat meat anymore. You can't eat fish. Just how far do these extremists want to go?"[6]

The Stellar sea lion, which was declared a "threatened" species in 1990, may, in fact, be a special case since its population is known to be steadily declining. For many other marine mammals, protection under the MMPA has enabled their populations to flourish. That raises a separate set of issues — and problems. For example, California sea lions were once nearly hunted out of existence. In the past 20 years, they have increased their numbers more than sixfold. Fishermen say this once "threatened" species is now preying on endangered fish stocks.

One highly publicized battleground is in Seattle, where a group of some 150 sea lions have been congregating at Ballard Locks along the Lake Washington Ship Canal, feasting on steelhead trout worth millions of dollars a year to Puget Sound fishermen. Since the sea lions discovered the locks seven years ago, the number of steelhead successfully navigating the fish ladder over the locks on their way to spawn each year has dropped to below 1,000 from about 7,000.* Fishermen blame the sea lions, and some have taken the matter into their own hands and started shooting their competitors. Environmentalists counter that sea lions are a convenient scapegoat, and that the real problem is loss of habitat.[7]

In any case, incidents of violence against marine mammals are becoming increasingly common. At least 51 baby seals and sea lions have been shot in the Pacific off Northern California this year, either by people shooting for fun or by fishermen up-

---

*Scientists say rough calculations of fish consumption by cetaceans — whales, dolphins and porpoises — indicate that in many areas they consume about the same amount of fish as humans.

*Fish ladders are elaborate man-made structures that allow fish to pass upstream with no more effort than they would use to swim against natural river rapids.

Status of Marine Mammals Under Protection

Twenty-one species of marine mammals are listed as endangered or threatened under the 1973 U.S. Endangered Species Act. Scientists say that after two decades of protection under that statute and the Marine Mammal Protection Act (1972), some species have begun increasing in number while others still face serious survival problems.

COMMON NAME	STATUS	RANGE	TREND
Manatees and Dugongs			
West Indian manatee	E	Southeastern U.S.; Central and South America	Unknown (but officials are concerned about its high mortality rate in Florida and Georgia)
Amazonian manatee	E	South America	Unknown
West African manatee	T	West Africa	Unknown
Dugong	E	Indian Ocean; Southeast Asia	Unknown
Otters			
Marine otter	E	Western South America	Unknown
Southern sea otter	T	Central California coast	Increasing
Seals and Sea Lions			
Hawaiian monk seal	E	Hawaiian Archipelago	Unknown (but pup counts declining)
Caribbean monk seal	E	Caribbean Sea and Bahamas	Believed extinct (last sighting in 1957)
Guadalupe fur seal	T	West coast of Baja California	Unknown (possibly increasing)
Mediterranean monk seal	E	Mediterranean Sea, northwestern Africa	Declining
Steller sea lion	T	North Pacific Rim	Declining
Whales and Porpoises			
Gulf of California harbor porpoise	E	Gulf of California, Mexico	Uncertain (probably declining)
Northern right whale	E	Northeast Atlantic Ocean	Stable (but only 350 probably left in north Atlantic; nearly extinct in Pacific)
Southern right whale	E	Southern oceans	Uncertain
Bowhead whale	E	Arctic Ocean and adjacent seas	Increasing
Humpback whale	E	All oceans	Unknown in eastern Pacific; possibly increasing in northwest Atlantic
Gray whale	E	Eastern and western North Pacific; Bering Sea	Unknown (possibly increasing in certain areas)
Blue whale	E	All oceans	Stable in U.S. waters (possibly increasing); decreasing in Antarctic
Finback or fin whale	E	All oceans	Unknown
Sei whale	E	All oceans	Unknown
Sperm whale	E	All oceans	Unknown

Source: Marine Mammal Commission, Jan. 31, 1992

set that the creatures sometimes steal fish from their nets.* While adult seals are adept at avoiding hunters, the pups make easier targets.

Most experts say it is doubtful that the expanding population of California sea lions poses any serious threat to the fishing industry. But down the road, that could change, especially for those marine mammals that thrive under federal protection. "We may reach a point where marine mam-

---

*Under the Marine Mammal Protection Act, fishermen can shoot marine mammals if they jeopardize fishing gear or the safety of fishermen.

mals are in conflict with another species, and we'll have to choose between and among species," says Nancy Foster, director of the NMFS' Office of Marine Mammal Protection. "It's a difficult question. And unfortunately, there are no easy answers."

Should the United States condone commercial whaling for species that are no longer endangered?

As recently as 25 years ago, whales were hunted mercilessly, their flesh turned to food, their oil to industrial lubricants and their ambergris to perfume. It is estimated that there

are now just 700 giant blue whales left on Earth; in the 1920s there were 250,000. Nine species of whales are still listed as endangered under the Endangered Species Act.

For centuries, whales symbolized the mystery and immense power of nature, inspiring, like Herman Melville's Moby Dick, a mix of awe and fear. During the past 20 years, the image of the fearsome behemoth was replaced with a gentler vision: the whale as an intelligent, friendly giant, a kindly singer of ethereal ballads. The public embraced the gentle-giant image, and it was that perception that fueled the "Save the Whales" campaign of the 1970s. The effort culminated in 1985 with the International Whaling Commission (IWC) banning commercial whaling.[8]

The seven-year-old ban effectively collapsed this June when Norway said it would begin hunting minke whales again and Iceland quit the whaling commission. Japan, which now takes 330 whales a year for "research" purposes but sells the meat to expensive restaurants, also wants minke hunting reopened.

At issue is whether the species has recovered enough to hunt without danger of extinction. Technically, the IWC moratorium was imposed because of insufficient scientific evidence to continue whaling. Now, with more data in hand, most scientists conclude the minke population may be large enough to permit controlled hunting. The IWC's best estimates are that there are 86,000 minkes in the Northern Hemisphere and 600,000 in the Southern Hemisphere (whales do not cross the equator to migrate or mate).

Nevertheless, most anti-whaling nations are still fervently opposed to the killing of whales. "Even if whales could be harvested in a sustainable manner, we believe the moratorium should remain in force," says the World Wildlife Fund's Michael Sutton. "There is no humane way to kill a 10-ton mammal, there is no conservation benefit from commercial whaling and there is no human need to continue." Indeed, not counting subsistence hunting by aboriginal groups, which most environmental organizations don't oppose, the countries that continue whaling — Japan, Norway and Iceland — are all relatively prosperous.

Moreover, many scientists say there is continuing uncertainty regarding the role of whales in oceanic ecosystems. No one knows, for instance, where minke whales mate or calve. In addition, the estimates of whale populations aren't precise. As one researcher put it, counting whales is

like walking through New York's Central Park with blinders on, counting dogs and then estimating the number of dogs in New York state.

Even whale proponents concede that these days most arguments against limited whale hunting are based primarily on emotion rather than science. "Personally, I'm opposed to the killing of whales," says Woods Hole whale expert Peter Tyack, "but as a policy issue, it is cultural imperialism to say it's immoral to kill a whale." That's especially true, he says, for a meat-dependent society such as the United States, which annually slaughters millions of cows. "The human killing of whales is a non-issue biologically," he adds. "I am much more concerned about high toxicity levels in whales and the depletion of their feeding stocks."

Over time the whaling holdouts will probably be forced to relent. The pressure of the anti-whaling nations on the IWC is just too strong. Technically, it would take a three-quarter majority of the 37-member body to overturn the moratorium, and that's highly unlikely.

Of course, that hasn't stopped Norway from mobilizing its fleet. But the pressure is mounting. There is already a bill pending in the U.S. Congress to embargo Norwegian fisheries' products. More important, Iceland and Norway both want to become full members of the European Community, which would ultimately prevent them from whaling. And in the case of Japan, there's concern about trade sanctions and the country's environmental image. "Japan is trying to look greener every day," explains Sutton. ∎

BACKGROUND

The Last Frontier

Efforts to exploit marine resources go back as far as recorded history. The first maritime people, believed to be Baltic fishermen of the Mesolithic era — around 10,000 years ago — did not regulate their fisheries. They did not have to. Their populations were so small and their corresponding impact on marine resources so minuscule that there was no need to constrain their fishing effort.

One of the earliest documented instances of severe overfishing occurred nearly 3,000 years ago along the Peruvian coast, where the depletion of marine resources, possibly accentuated by a climatological catastrophe similar to the El Niño phenomenon, forced the coastal ancestors of the Incas to develop more diversified food sources.[9]

In more recent history, itinerant whalers had wiped out North Atlantic

gray whales by the early 18th century and reduced those in the western Pacific to perhaps a few dozen. The latter remain listed as an endangered species, but some experts say they may already be extinct.

Industrialization of Fishing

The systematic raping of global fisheries is even more startling. The industrialization of the fishing industry was epitomized by the great fleets of factory ships that roamed the North Atlantic from the 1950s through the 1970s. The ships were huge, some exceeding 300 feet in length, and capable of bringing in as much as 500 tons of fish in a single haul and of processing over 250 tons a day.

These fleets specialized in fishing in cold waters, where the largest aggregations of single species in the sea are found, catching mainly herring and perch that were in high demand in European and North American markets. Because of their processing capacity, the ships could stay at sea longer than any fishing vessels ever before — sometimes for a year or more. Each was a floating factory, and the fleet itself a kind of roving industrial complex, where even the by-catches of untargeted species and the scrap from the on-board processing operations were reduced to fish meal.

In the 1970s, the Soviet fishing fleet alone — then the largest in the world — contained more than 700 big trawlers, 100 factory ships, 2,800 smaller side trawlers and more than 500 support vessels, including refrigerated fish carriers, supply ships and fuel tankers. Prior to the imposition of the 200-mile territorial limits, the Soviet fleet mined the rich Georges Bank fishery off the New England coast. First concentrating on cod and herring, and then, as those stocks declined, turning their attention to haddock, the Soviet ships "paced out in long diagonal lines, plowing the best fishing grounds like disk harrows in a field," writes fisheries expert William W. Warner.[10]

For many of the small-scale fishermen who lived along the coastlines that were being exploited by these roving fleets, the result was economic disaster. Not only did the offshore fleets deplete the stocks they had traditionally depended on, but the floating factories could usually out-compete them because of the economies of scale they enjoyed.

Marine Mammals

The public became concerned about marine mammals well before there was any talk about the long-term impacts of overfishing. "As a society we've decided marine mammals deserve special status and should be treated differently from fish," says the NMFS' Foster. "They are perceived as man's special friends."

Marine mammal preservation has become a key environmental issue

— as evidenced by the ubiquitous "Save the Whale" T-shirts that surface each summer. Last year hundreds of thousands of Americans went on whale-watching cruises and some 40 million visited marine mammal exhibits.

Part of their appeal owes to their presumed intelligence. During the 1970s, scientists began analyzing whale songs and social behavior, and many people held out the hope that marine mammals might turn out to be so intelligent that they could offer troubled humans philosophical guidance. At a minimum, they might provide navigational insights and assist the Navy.

There also are biological reasons for concern about marine mammals. Once a species is depleted to certain levels, recovery may be impossible. "Dolphins and whales are slow to reproduce," explains Ken Norris, a professor emeritus of natural history at the Long Marine Laboratory at the University of California-Santa Cruz. "They may have only 12 young in 30 years, compared with skipjack tuna that have a million eggs a year. You can take a lot of fish without destroying their reproductive potential. That's just not the case for marine mammals."

Before the passage of the Marine Mammal Protection Act (MMPA) in 1972, conservation and protection of marine mammals in areas under U.S. jurisdiction were the responsibility of coastal states or international authorities such as the International Whaling Commission, the North Pacific Fur Seal Commission and the International Commission on North Atlantic Fisheries. But the conservation efforts of some of these bodies were not very effective.

Of particular concern were the IWC's weak regulation of commercial whaling, the large "incidental" take of dolphins by the U.S. tuna fleet in the Eastern Tropical Pacific and the clubbing of "baby" harp seals in the

North Atlantic. By the late 1960s, many people feared that certain marine mammal species and stocks were in danger of extinction because of human activities.

The Marine Mammal Protection Act established a moratorium on taking marine mammals in U.S. waters and importing marine mammals and marine mammal products into the United States. However, there were some exemptions. The moratorium did not apply to Indians, Aleuts or Eskimos in coastal Alaska who hunted marine mammals for subsistence. Under a permit system, the act also allowed killing and importing marine mammals for scientific research; for education and public display; and, incidentally, in the course of commercial fishing operations.

In 1973, the Endangered Species Act was enacted, joining the MMPA as the principal means employed by the United States to protect endangered marine mammals. The act's defined purpose was "to provide a means whereby the ecosystems upon which endangered species and threatened species depend may be conserved." It mandated that federal agencies formulate recovery plans for endangered species and establish management priorities for their protection, especially those threatened by the long-term effects of economic development.

Despite the new laws, some marine mammal populations, such as the northern right whale, have failed to recover, and others like the West Indian manatee are in rapid decline, under pressure from rampant coastal development. But overall, Foster says, the laws have removed the sense of crisis. "They allow us to focus on other aspects of conservation," she says, "such as marine mammal-fisheries interactions and habitat."

When the MMPA is up for reauthorization next year, the likely areas of focus will be the impact of the NMFS' new guidelines governing interac-

Continued on p. 746

Chronology

1940s-1960s

Despite some efforts to regulate fisheries, both marine mammals and fish are generally thought of as commodities that are inexhaustible in supply.

1946

The International Whaling Commission is set up to regulate the whaling industry, which by then had driven numerous whale species to the brink of extinction.

1952

The United States, Japan and Canada reach an agreement — the International Convention for the High Seas Fisheries of the North Pacific Ocean — to regulate Japanese high-seas drift-net salmon fisheries to minimize their harvest in areas where they may encounter salmon originating from North American rivers.

1970s

Fueled by the "Save the Whales" campaign, the American public assumes an emotional stake in saving marine mammals from extinction, prompting passage of a network of laws to protect them.

1972

Congress passes the Marine Mammal Protection Act, establishing a moratorium on taking marine mammals in U.S. waters and importing marine mammals into the United States.

1973

Congress enacts the Endangered Species Act, strengthening marine mammal protection by mandating that federal agencies formulate recovery plans for endangered species and establish management priorities for their protection.

1976

Congress passes the Magnuson Fishery Management and Conservation Act. The law extends the exclusive economic zone (EEZ) in waters off U.S. coasts from 12 to 200 miles, restricts fishing in U.S. waters by foreign fleets and creates eight regional management councils to oversee the fishery.

1980s

Subsidized by federal loan guarantees, the U.S. fishing industry rebuilds its fleet and begins overfishing territorial waters.

Nov. 23, 1988

Congress reauthorizes the Marine Mammal Protection Act, exempting fishermen from punishment for incidental kills of marine mammals for five years, so long as they participate in a program to provide scientific data on where they fish and the amount of "by-catch."

April 20, 1989

The National Marine Fisheries Service (NMFS) publishes initial guidelines for marine mammals-fisheries interaction, placing each fishery in one of three categories. Those fisheries that cause higher rates of marine mammal kills are subjected to closer government monitoring.

June 1989

Two hundred scientists sign letter decrying the lack of management of the nation's fisheries and calling for a moratorium on new entries into the nation's fisheries.

Dec. 22, 1989

The U.N. General Assembly agrees to a non-binding resolution banning high-seas drift-netting.

1990s

Policy-makers and fishermen acknowledge fisheries crisis and begin to take steps to deal with complex issues of managing marine resources.

March 30, 1990

The U.S. Department of Commerce publishes final rules concerning the standards foreign nations must meet for dolphin protection in order to export tuna to the United States.

April 12, 1990

In a surprise development, three major U.S. tuna canners — Starkist, Bumble Bee and Van Camp (Chicken of the Sea) — announce that they will terminate buying and selling tuna captured with dolphins.

October 1990

The U.S. imposes an embargo on Mexican tuna due to unacceptably high dolphin-mortality rates.

Nov. 26, 1990

NMFS lists the Stellar sea lion as a "threatened" species under the Endangered Species Act.

Oct. 4, 1991

The Antarctic Treaty Protocol on Environmental Protection is signed by 24 nations to conserve whales and seals, and their habitats in Antarctica.

Nov. 25, 1991

Under strong U.S. pressure, the Japanese government formally agrees to ban drift-net fishing.

June 1992

The North Pacific Fishery Management Council institutes a moratorium against new boats entering the offshore fisheries for the next three years.

Drift Nets: Stripmining the Sea

It began as a small, experimental fishery in 1978. Within a decade, the squid drift-net fleet in the North Pacific would become the largest — and most destructive — fishery on earth. By 1990, a combined fleet of about 800 Japanese, Taiwanese and South Korean vessels were deploying between 10,000 and 20,000 miles of net per night, so-called "walls of death" that kill nearly every animal that swims into them.†

The annual catch of squid by the drift-net fleet was estimated to be between 200,000 and 300,000 metric tons in 1990, worth more than $600 million. But squid wasn't all the drift-netters caught. Experts say up to 70 percent of the harvest is "by-catch" — unwanted species that are dumped over the side, almost always dead or dying.††

In 1990, Japanese drift nets alone unintentionally entrapped some 41 million non-targeted fish and marine mammals — including an estimated 450,000 sea birds, 35,000 whales and dolphins and literally millions of sharks. There are reports that the drift-net fleets, which have not limited their quarry to squid, have nearly exhausted the South Pacific of albacore tuna and are beginning to put a dent in salmon stocks in the North Pacific.‡

Ironically, much of the impetus for the creation of the high-seas squid drift-net fishery came, indirectly, from U.S. actions. In the late 1970s, when the United States established an exclusive economic zone extending 200 miles from its shores, hundreds of Japanese vessels were displaced from salmon fishing. Seeking new resources, Japanese companies converted many of their salmon drift-net boats and middle-distance trawlers into squid drift-net vessels.

For both the U.S. government and environmental groups, one of the biggest obstacles to banning high-seas drift-net fishing has been the fact that the resources of the open ocean are owned by no one, and are governed by no one. "This has encouraged an attitude of greed and exploitation, and discourages sound management practices," says Mark Tennant, president of the SouthEast Alaska Coalition Opposed to Pirated Salmon.

For more than a decade, Japan, Taiwan and South Korea sought to defend the wholesale slaughter on the ground that evidence about the environmental damage it causes is incomplete. Yet they showed little interest in monitoring the impact of their drift-net fisheries, and for a long time resisted efforts by the United States to initiate observer programs.

Under heavy international pressure, the three Asian nations finally agreed to a non-binding 1989 United Nations resolution requiring all countries involved in drift-net fishing to dismantle their fleets by the end of this year.‡‡ They were supposed to be cut in half by the end of June, but few experts believe that has yet happened.

"Even if the ban is enforced, it amounts to little more than squeezing a balloon," says Ben Deeble, a Seattle-based fisheries expert at the environmental group Greenpeace. "They will simply move off the high seas into their own coastal zones — or they'll continue to do it illicitly."

William Perrin, a marine biologist for the National Marine Fisheries Service in La Jolla, Calif., shares his concern. "The U.N. resolution doesn't affect small-scale drift-netting, or that which takes place within a country's 200-mile national waters," he says.

Earlier this year a South Korean drift-netter was reported in El Salvador's territorial waters, and three Taiwanese drift-netters were nabbed just off the coast of Somalia, in East Africa. More distressing, there are reports that China and Panama are right now equipping their fleets to fish with drift nets.

Meanwhile, Sen. Bob Packwood, R-Ore., and Sen. Ted Stevens, R-Alaska, have introduced legislation that would impose sanctions against countries that continue drift-netting. If the bill passes, it would limit the use of U.S. port facilities by drift-netting nations, strengthen the role of the Coast Guard and employ military satellites to track foreign fishing fleets. Even so, it will be hard to control offenders. As the NMFS' Perrin puts it, "It's a big ocean — and the financial incentives are great."

---

† A typical drift net deployed by one vessel might be 40 miles long and dangle 30 to 100 feet under water.

†† See Todd Campbell, "Net Losses," *Sierra*, April 1991, p. 48.

‡ See Eugene H. Buck, *Driftnets: A Controversial Fishing Method*, Congressional Research Service Report for Congress, Sept. 20, 1990.

‡‡ In the fall of 1990, the U.S. Congress and the International Commission for the Conservation of Atlantic Tunas banned the use of fishing nets longer than 1.5 miles. On Nov. 25, 1991, Japan signed an additional agreement with the U.S. to end drift-netting.

Continued from p. 744
tions between marine mammals and commercial fishing operations, the fishing rights of Alaskan natives and the brewing conflict between animal rights groups and those wishing to display marine mammals.

Fisheries Mismanagement

Public concern for the marine environment also inspired changes in laws governing U.S. fisheries. However, the outcome was markedly different. In 1976, Congress passed the Magnuson Fishery Management and Conservation Act. The law extended the exclusive economic zone (EEZ) in waters off U.S. coasts from 12 to 200 miles, restricted fishing in U.S. waters by foreign fleets and created eight regional management councils to oversee the fishery. Under its umbrella the domestic fishing fleet revived and prospered — at least for a while.

Designed to preserve the U.S. domestic fishing fleet and rebuild fish stocks, the Magnuson act was a victim of its own success. Ironically, the nation managed to gain control of its coastal oceans, but in so doing simply traded overfishing by foreigners for unrestrained fishing by domestic fishermen.

"We saw huge Soviet and Polish factory ships, all lit up like cities, banging away at the fishing stock," says Jeff Pike, a former fisherman and now legislative assistant to Rep. Gerry E. Studds, D-Mass. "Then we'd look at the small wooden boats out of New Bedford and Gloucester. It seemed inconceivable you could overfish the stock."

The government soon discovered it was much easier to say "no" to the Soviet fleet than to say "no" to its own. In the debate over how to manage the fisheries, fishermen had made it clear that they were not interested in having bureaucrats in Washington tell them how to fish. Neither was Congress interested in constructing a new federal fishery bureaucracy. Instead, the council system was created.

But some experts believe the councils, made up largely of fishing industry representatives appointed by the secretary of Commerce, bumbled their mission by failing to balance the biological realities of fish management with the economic demand of fishermen to sell more fish. By their own admission, the councils tilted toward the latter. In 1981, for example, the New England council caved in to pressure from fishermen to remove all catch quotas on cod, haddock and flounder. That led to the disastrous depletion of the most valuable commercial species.

"We missed a tremendous oppor-

tunity to wisely and sustainably manage our marine resources," says Carl Safina, senior scientist at the Audubon Society's Scully Marine Center on Long Island, N.Y. "The councils have been in place 16 years, and they still haven't come up with a definition of overfishing. If you haven't defined it, how can you possibly prevent it from happening?" Reporting on the amount and location of catches by fishermen is generally not mandated under the law.

Meanwhile, the rust-bucket American fleet was gradually replaced — thanks to more than $500 million in federal loan guarantees — with efficient, high-tech boats. A $1.3 billion fleet of some 70 factory vessels, American registered but mostly owned by Japanese, Scandinavian and South Korean interests, now plies the Gulf of Alaska and the Bering Sea. In New England, the fleet of otter trawlers — boats that fish for

species that live on the ocean floor — grew from 590 in 1976 to more than 1,000 in the early 1980s.

The fishing capacity of the new boats is staggering and, more than anything else, has exacerbated the destructive pressure on the fish stocks. "Overcapitalized" is the term the U.S. fishing industry uses to describe its unhappy condition. Just a decade ago, many fishermen still used binoculars and oil-can buoys to mark and relocate productive areas. Today, even the smallest vessels employ depth finders and sophisticated electronics that can pinpoint a single fish at depths of up to 600 feet. Radio signals can guide a captain to within 50 feet of a favorite hot spot, and enable him to fish near rocky bottoms or wrecks that he had to avoid in the past for fear of tearing up expensive nets. Fishermen can even get ocean temperatures faxed to their boats via satellite. ∎

CURRENT SITUATION

New England's Crisis

To many marine biologists, the tattered state of America's fisheries can be attributed to weak leadership by the National Marine Fisheries Service. "Until recently, the NMFS failed to vigorously push for scientifically sound fishing practices," notes John Twiss, executive director of the Marine Mammal Commission in Washington.

Nowhere is the nation's fisheries crisis more apparent than in New England, where fishermen find themselves in dire straits, victims of a get-it-while-you-can mentality that could exhaust stocks beyond recovery. Last year the region's fishermen

caught 95,000 metric tons of groundfish, less than half what they caught a decade earlier. The reduction in landings of groundfish costs the region at least $350 million and 14,000 jobs per year, according to a 1990 report from the Massachusetts Offshore Groundfish Task Force.[11]

There have been booms and busts before, as ports such as New Bedford and Gloucester, Mass., grew over the centuries from colonial towns into bustling commercial centers. But scientists say this time is different, because the fleets are so big and the technology so good that fish literally have nowhere to hide.

"You don't need very good statistics to know what's going on," says Vaughn Anthony, a researcher at the Woods Hole Oceanographic Institute. "If you want to harvest large amounts of fish, you need to keep certain spawning stock in place." An-

Continued on p. 750

Can Society Save Dolphins ...

There was a time when a person could grab a tuna salad sandwich at lunch without worrying about killing dolphins. Tuna were caught by rod, line and hook. When a boat found a school, powerful men lined the rail, yanking the fish out of the water and back over their heads onto the deck. That practice went on for centuries.

As in every other industry, however, the technology of tuna fishing suddenly changed. In the 1960s, tuna fishermen began switching to purse seines, mile-long nets that are wrapped around a school of fish and then closed at the bottom. The whole net is then winched on board the boat. Almost overnight, the tuna industry was revolutionized.

But there was a catch. For reasons scientists don't fully understand, several species of dolphins habitually swim with schools of yellowfin tuna. (This heavily fished species runs larger, is easier to process and thus brings a premium price from canners.)

Until the 1960s, the presence of the leaping dolphins simply flagged the location of schools of tuna. But with the advent of purse seine nets, dolphins often were ensnared along with the tuna, and the dolphins frequently drowned in the nets.

By the early 1970s, nearly half a million dolphins were dying each year as a direct result of tuna fishing. The problem was particularly acute in the warm waters of the Eastern Tropical Pacific (ETP), which stretches from California to northern Chile and out to the Hawaiian islands, where much of the tuna for the U.S. market is caught.

Setting on dolphins, as the fishing method is called,

didn't set well with a generation raised on the television series *"Flipper."* Congress responded by passing the Marine Mammal Protection Act in 1972, requiring U.S. fishermen to use techniques that would reduce — although not eliminate — the number of dolphin deaths. Even with new nets and new maneuvers, however, up to 20,000 dolphins were dying each year in nets thrown from U.S. tuna boats and perhaps 80,000 more in the nets of foreign vessels.

Though environmental groups called for tuna boycotts in the late 1970s, the turning point came in 1988 when Sam LaBudde, a biologist at the Earth Island Institute in San Francisco, shipped out as a cook on a Panamanian tuna boat and filmed 200 dolphins drowning in nets.[1] The gruesome spectacle, which was viewed on prime-time TV by millions of Americans, turned the stomachs of tuna fish lovers and dolphin lovers alike. Before that, there was no hard evidence to confirm what environmentalists had long maintained.

The most crucial tuna-dolphin battle may actually have been won in school lunchrooms all across America. When students went to their school boards in the 1980s demanding that tuna be taken off the menus, companies finally noticed. In April 1990, the StarKist, Bumble Bee and Van Camp (Chicken of the Sea) seafood companies — suppliers of nearly 75 percent of all canned tuna consumed in the United States — pledged to quit buying tuna caught in association with dolphins.[2]

The U.S. government went a step further, banning tuna imports from Mexico, Venezuela and the island of

How Many Dolphins Die?

The estimated number of dolphins killed by U.S. and foreign tuna purse-seine fleets in the Eastern Tropical Pacific Ocean has steadily dropped since passage of the Marine Mammal Protection Act in 1972.

Year	U.S. Vessels	Non-U.S. Vessels
1972	368,600	55,078
1973	206,697	58,276
1974	147,437	27,245
1975	166,645	27,812
1976	108,740	19,482
1977	25,452	25,901
1978	19,366	11,147
1979	17,938	3,488
1980	15,305	16,665
1981	18,780	17,199
1982	23,267	5,837
1983	8,513	4,980
1984	17,732	22,980
1985	19,205	39,642
1986	20,692	112,482
1987	13,992	85,185
1988	19,712	59,215
1989	12,643	84,336
1990	5,083	47,448
1991	891	25,000 †

† *Preliminary estimate*
Source: Marine Mammal Commission

… And Still Savor Tuna Fish?

Vanuatu (formerly New Hebrides), which had unacceptably high dolphin-kill rates. Furious over the embargo, Mexico filed a protest with the General Agreement on Tariffs and Trade (GATT), a pact that binds 109 nations to a set of international trade rules. A GATT dispute panel ruled in Mexico's favor, concluding that one country may not foist environmental laws upon another.

State and federal lawmakers — including the Bush administration — continue responding to unabated demand for a dolphin-safe world. Rep. Barbara Boxer, D-Calif., for example, has introduced a bill in Congress that would force U.S. tuna boats to stop setting on dolphins by the end of 1992 and require the same of any country exporting tuna to America.

Overall, the dolphin-protection movement has been extremely successful. Dolphin mortality worldwide has been cut dramatically in recent years through net modifications, legislation, captain training and observer monitoring programs. While 130,000 dolphins were killed in tuna fishing expeditions across the globe in 1986, the number dropped to an estimated 25,000 in 1991, according to a detailed report by the National Research Council (NRC).[3] Even Mexico has cut dolphin mortality in half in the past two years.

However, it is still not clear whether the "dolphin-safe" label on tuna fish cans really means dolphin-safe tuna. "Enforcement of the ban may not be practical or possible," concluded the NRC report. Tuna fishermen can easily ship tuna caught with dolphins to foreign ports where it may be canned and sold in U.S. markets as dolphin-safe. "The ban may even increase dolphin mortality if it drives boats out of the more closely regulated nations' fisheries," the report added. Nearly 60 percent of the tuna fleet in the ETP now sails under the flags of Latin American nations, which have notoriously lax environmental standards.

Experts say the tuna industry has become so decentralized over the past decade that it would be extremely difficult to track down the contents of a can of tuna. Most of the tuna fleet and two of the three major companies (Bumble Bee and Van Camp) are now foreign owned — and thus subject to less U.S. regulation.[4] The United States, which consumes nearly a third of the world's tuna, imports much of the product. The U.S. fleet last year brought in only 11 percent of the world's catch and was responsible for fewer than 5 percent of dolphin mortalities.

Furthermore, most of the U.S. fleet that hasn't been mothballed or reflagged now fishes for tuna in the calmer political waters of the western Pacific. "There is no question that some fishermen have moved to other areas to avoid scrutiny," says Nancy Foster, director of the Office of Marine Mammal Protection at the National Marine Fisheries Service. "You can never know for certain if tuna is 'dolphin-safe.' Data is only as good as the honesty of those involved. It's 50 percent faith."

Others are even more skeptical. "Dolphin-safe standards deal only with the [Eastern Tropical Pacific]. That's a very shortsighted point of view," says Tracy Romine, coordinator of the tuna-dolphin project at Greenpeace. "Other fisheries operate out-of-sight and out-of-mind.... Clearly a lot more has to be done."

Greenpeace and other environmental groups advocate multilateral regulations that would require observers on all tuna boats,[5] training for ship captains and mandates for implementing dolphin-friendly fishing technologies, including modifications in netting material and design.

As long as America maintains its voracious appetite for tuna, experts say some dolphins will likely be killed — but a lot less than before. "Despite what environmental extremists say, fishing in association with dolphin, when done correctly, is ecologically sound," says Teresa Platt, manager of a tuna fleet still working in the eastern Pacific. "It targets large, old yellowfin — which helps avoid overfishing the resource — while releasing 99.8 percent of all dolphin unharmed. Canners who support an international tuna-dolphin management regime are correct: We can protect the mammals while allowing fishermen to continue their unique way of life."[6]

---

[1] See Kenneth Brower, "The Destruction of Dolphins," *The Atlantic*, July 1989, p. 35.

[2] For background, see "The Growing Influence of Boycotts," *Editorial Research Reports*, Jan. 4, 1991, pp. 1-16.

[3] National Research Council, *Reducing Dolphin Mortality from Tuna Fishing*, 1992.

[4] Bumble Bee was sold to a Thai company in 1989. Van Camp Seafood, producers of Chicken of the Sea, was sold to an Indonesian company in 1988.

[5] At present, observer presence is as low as 5 percent in some parts of the world.

[6] Quoted in *National Fisherman*, May 1992.

Continued from p. 747
thony notes that the spawning stock for certain species of fishes is one-twentieth what it was when the Magnuson act passed in 1976.

Most experts agree that resolving the crisis will require major changes in the management of the New England fishery. "Unless the depleted stocks of groundfish are allowed to rebuild, no one will earn a living in the ground fishery," cautions Eleanor Dorsey, staff scientist at the Conservation Law Foundation, a Boston-based environmental organization that filed a lawsuit in June 1991 against the U.S. secretary of Commerce over the diminished fish stocks.

In response to the lawsuit, the New England Fisheries Management Council has agreed to draft a plan to rebuild the fish stocks. The current proposal under consideration would limit fishermen's days at sea by 10 percent every year for five years, increase the net-mesh size to reduce the catch of small, juvenile fish and ban newcomers to the industry. Similar measures are being debated on Capitol Hill, where fisheries committees in both the House and the Senate have approved legislation intended to reduce fishing in New England by 50 percent over the next seven to 10 years.[12]

Hard Choices for Fishermen

Either way, a storm lies on the horizon for fisherman. Straining to pay off mortgages on expensive boats, many fishermen say they don't have the luxury of not catching as much as they can as fast as they can. "How are you supposed to pay your bills when your ability to make a living is cut in half?" asks Tony Verga. Fellow Gloucester fisherman Joseph Testaverde expresses similar sentiments. "When the 200-mile line came in, the government said, 'Invest, capitalize, get bigger, get better.' Now we're too big, and they say go the other way," he laments.

Rooted in the Colonial era and steeped in tradition, New England fisheries have long resisted regulation. In general, fishermen argue that the situation would improve if loopholes in existing laws were closed, such as those allowing the devastating practice of pair trawling, where a vast net is stretched between two boats working together, effectively sweeping the ocean clean.

But even some fishermen concede it may be too late for that. "I used to be strongly opposed to any kind of limited entry in fisheries," says Dick Allen, vice president of the Atlantic Offshore Fish Association in Newport, R.I. "But I've come to feel we have to have some way of rationally allocating fishery resources just as we do other resources." At this point, Allen adds, fishermen should be willing to make short-term sacrifices to reap the long-term benefits of rebuilding the stocks.

Canadian fishermen who fish the Atlantic waters off Newfoundland face similarly bleak prospects. This July, the Canadian government announced a two-year moratorium on all fishing for cod. But unlike in the United States, which has no tradition of bailing out fishermen, the Canadian government has set up an extensive relief program for the province's 19,000 fishermen.

"If the sort of disaster that has besieged the New England fishery had hit the American Farm Belt, the government would have pulled out the stops," complains Zeke Grader, executive director of the Pacific Coast Federation of Fishermen's Associations, an umbrella group that represents 24 fishing organizations. "But for fish, a high protein source, it's 'Sorry, Charlie.' I'm not advocating subsidies. But we have to do something."

Exactly what is a hotly contested topic. Besides attempting to rein in the fleet, efforts are being made to develop an industry for underutilized fish, such as skate and dogfish. This

spring, Sen. Edward M. Kennedy, D-Mass., proposed legislation that would allocate more than $7 million in research-and-development monies to help fund that effort.

Northwest's Response

In contrast to New England, fisheries in the Northwest, developed in recent decades, more readily accept tight controls. There are not only limits on the number of fishing permits issued but also on the number of fish that can be caught and on the number of days that can be fished. Nonetheless, problems abound.

"The NMFS views Alaska as their showcase," says Ben Deeble, a Seattle-based fisheries expert at the environmental group Greenpeace. "But we have a different view. The fisheries look better, but that's because Alaska had more fish to start with." In the view of Deeble and others, Alaska's high-tech, industrial-strength fleet has too many boats, and there is enormous waste.

Consider the case of Alaska's pollock fishery. In the cold, greenish waters of the Gulf of Alaska and north in the vast, stormy Bering Sea is America's greatest seafood larder — an estimated 36 billion pounds of bottom-dwelling cod, sole, flounder, perch, mackerel, and, most of all, walleye pollock. During the last decade, this has been America's fastest-growing fishery. And with the development have come many of today's most alarming concerns about environmental depletion, waste, excessive fishing competition and government management at cross-purposes.

In 1980, fishermen harvested about 100,000 metric tons of pollock and other common groundfish off Alaska. The dockside value of these fish at 5 cents a pound was about $1 million. Ten years later the catch approached

Continued on p. 752

Fishing Atlantic Bluefin to the Brink of Extinction

What weighs 1,500 pounds, can go from 0 to 55 miles per hour in less than 10 seconds and costs about $65,000? Answer: a Porsche — or a tuna. Not an ordinary tuna, but a fully mature Atlantic bluefin tuna, one of the most majestic of all creatures in the wild. Last winter a single fish was auctioned off in Tokyo for $68,503 — $95.65 a pound.

The similarities between Porsches and bluefins don't end with the hefty price tag. Like Porsches, bluefin are designed for speed. When they hit top speed, their pelvic, pectoral and front dorsal fins all retract into slots.

They swim with mouths agape, supercharging their blood-rich muscles with oxygen, in a process similar to that of a jet engine. To maintain balance at high speeds, they have horizontal stabilizers protruding from the base of their hard, sickle tails. Restrained from swimming, they suffocate and drown.[†]

Among the most advanced of fishes, the sleek bluefin are biological marvels. In contrast to most fish, they are warm-blooded, at times maintaining body temperatures 38 degrees above that of surrounding seawater.

Until recently, the majesty of these pelagic Olympians was lost on virtually everyone, even environmentalists. People thought of them not as wildlife but as a commodity — just another kind of fish, albeit bigger and more capable of putting up a good fight. (Novelist Ernest Hemingway was known to get drunk and use bluefin carcasses for punching bags.)

Two decades ago, giant bluefins (defined in the trade as those over 310 pounds) sold for just a few pennies a pound and were used primarily for pet food. While the Japanese had long relished giant bluefin, eaten raw as sushi (with rice) and sashimi (without rice), the Atlantic stock had been largely unavailable for that market because no one had figured out how to get it there, fast, fresh and cost-efficiently.

Two events in the 1980s changed that. First, an enterprising Boston fishmonger discovered that for the Japanese no price is too high to pay for something as beautiful and delicious as bluefin. And second, sushi bars proliferated in the United States. By 1986, bluefin was selling wholesale for $12 a pound. Even a moderately sized giant can fetch $10,000 at dockside, enough for a down payment on a Porsche.

Such demand has rendered sportfishing for giants more than sport — it's a serious business. Since 1970, fishing for bluefin has increased more than twentyfold, driving the population down from 319,000 to 30,000 in 1990, according to a study conducted by the International Commission for the Conservation of Atlantic Tunas (ICCAT). "The last buffalo hunt is taking place in the oceans," warns Carl Safina, senior scientist at the Audubon Society's Scully Marine Center on Long Island, N.Y.

As far as is known, humankind has failed to wipe out any of the pelagic, or migratory, fishes. They are mightily prolific, producing millions of eggs each. Biological extinction would take an awful lot of doing. But bluefin could be the first to go. In the 19th century, the last few buffalo were spared because tracking them down didn't make economic sense; one animal wasn't worth a house or even a horse. But given Japanese sushimania, it just might pay to track down the last bluefin. As it is, boats are willing to stay out two weeks to kill one fish. Few can resist joining the hunt.

Scientists say there's a population threshold, below which bluefin tuna may not be able to function, migrate or mate. "Maybe we're already below it," suggests Michael Sutton, senior program officer at the World Wildlife Fund. "Bluefin lay millions of eggs because they are subject to predation. They don't lay that many eggs to make up for overfishing."

Why hasn't there been greater effort to protect these majestic fish? When Congress passed the Magnuson Act in 1976 to manage marine resources within the 200-mile zone offshore, all tuna were exempted from regulations because of active lobbying by commercial tuna fishermen on the West Coast. Prior to 1991, quotas for bluefin hadn't changed for 10 years, despite scientific evidence of their decline.[††]

Commercial fishermen point the finger at sport fishermen, who they say are taking all the small fish before they have a chance to reproduce. Sport anglers say the blame lies with the commercial boats, which net the lion's share of the catch. "They may both be right," laments Sutton. "But it's like rearranging deck chairs on the *Titanic*. It won't matter. There won't be any tuna for anyone."

[†] See Ted Williams, "The Last Bluefin Hunt," *Audubon,* July-August 1992, p. 14.

[††] The United States and Japan initially proposed that ICCAT members accept a 50 percent cut in bluefin quotas, but under pressure from Canada they eventually agreed to a 10 percent cut. Photo: Harry Upton, Center for Marine Conservation

Continued from p. 750
2 million metric tons with a value of $2 billion. By 1990, one out of every three pounds of fish landed in all of the United States was Alaskan pollock.

Anxious to exploit the resource and reap big profits, some 70 factory ships are locked in fierce competition with thousands of small vessels in the Bering Sea and the Gulf of Alaska. The North Pacific Fishery Management Council has responded to the pressure by shortening the season, not by limiting how many boats can fish. The year-round pollock season now lasts only five and a half months, and is getting shorter all the time.

Alaska's solution to the problem of overfishing may be preferable to New England's neglect, but it is less than perfect. With hindsight, experts say it's easy to see the effects of a shrinking fishing season and growing fishing fleet. The amount of waste is mindboggling.

The processing machines on factory trawlers cannot handle pollock that are too small. If each boat was assigned a quota of pollock, a boat that ran into schools dense with undersized fish might sail away without worrying about wasting time and move elsewhere rather than net and kill millions of pounds of unusable pollock. But when the quota is assigned to the fleet, individual boats are competing against each other and they scramble as fast and as hard as they can, no matter what gets wasted.

"The way it is, a captain says, 'I don't care if I can only keep half of the [catch], at least I can keep half.' So he keeps on fishing," explains Bruce Buls, spokesman for the American Factory Trawlers Association.[13]

The result: In 1990, Alaskan trawlers fishing for pollock and cod jettisoned some 20 million pounds of halibut — worth about $24 million —

because they were an unwanted by-catch.* That compares with just 70 million pounds actually brought to market. They also reported throwing away 550 million pounds of groundfish because they were the wrong size or to save space for more valuable species. Larry Cotter, a Juneau, Alaska, fisheries consultant and former by-catch chairman for the

Among other problems, observers say the high pressure placed on fishermen to work in dramatically shortened seasons sacrifices safety.

NMFS regional management council, calls the waste "a national scandal and an unconscionable disgrace."[14]

The 20-Minute Fishing Season

In a similar vein, so many fishermen compete for the valuable Pacific halibut that the entire year's quota — once harvested over a leisurely six-month season — is now taken in two frantic 24-hour periods. With some 6,000 boats vying to get maximum fish aboard in minimum time, the carcasses are poorly handled, many are not cleaned quickly enough and shore-side processors are overwhelmed with huge volumes all at once. Virtually all of the domestic catch has to be frozen or it will go bad. Because frozen halibut is less prized than fresh, fishermen are paid only one-third to one-half the price.

---

*Fishing everywhere produces by-catch. For example, for every pound of shrimp hauled from the Gulf of Mexico, nine pounds of unwanted fish are brought up in the nets and tossed overboard, usually dead or dying.

And, amazingly, the 24-hour halibut free-for-all is not even the shortest of Alaskan fishing seasons. There are so many herring boats that the "season" in some places lasts just 20 minutes, with fishermen deploying airplanes to help them find the schools of spawning herring. The black cod season used to run 200 days. Now it is down to 15 to 18 days. Yellowfin sole was a year-round fishery. Now it lasts two and a half to four months.

Among other problems, observers say the high pressure placed on fishermen to work in dramatically shortened seasons sacrifices safety. The one-day halibut "openers," for example, are conducted regardless of weather. Last year, in storm-torn seas, one Coast Guard officer recalled logging 13 Mayday calls from sinking vessels in a single hour, many of them ignored by fellow fishermen who did not dare put a year's wages on the line to help a stranger.[15]

"The way things have evolved, we're forced to use slash and burn techniques on the fisheries. That's the way they are set up," says Dean Adams, a third-generation fisherman in Kodiak, Alaska. In the past, Adams notes, a fishermen could grow old, if not necessarily wealthy, on the sea. Today, he says, the demands to work 16 hours or more — and often around the clock — to get the most out of the foreshortened season, has driven out all but the reckless.

This June, after two years of anguished deliberation, the North Pacific Management Council took a first step to try to contain the mess. It voted to institute a temporary moratorium against new boats entering the offshore fisheries for the next three years. Presumably, this will prevent things from becoming worse in the short run, although many believe it will do little to make them better. ∎

Continued on p. 754

At Issue:

Should fishermen be allocated individual quotas to help control overfishing?

THE EDITORS OF NATIONAL FISHERMAN

National Fisherman is a monthly publication that serves the fishing industry
FROM *THE NATIONAL FISHERMAN,* MAY 1991.

yes

for all practical purposes, commercial fishermen have been playing by rules that were written when fisheries still had plenty of room to grow. In recent years, the playing field and the players have changed a lot, while the rules have changed only a little.

There are now more boats and fewer fish, and estuaries are less productive due to water pollution and habitat loss. Competition and concern for the resource is keener than ever before. Management regulations often serve only to penalize the law-abiding captain, as others choose to disregard the rules. These conditions have reached the critical stage in some fisheries, forcing boat owners out of business or into marginal profitability.

It is long past time for the industry to take a stand and do its part to turn this situation around. Commercial fishermen must act now if they want viable fisheries in 10 or 20 years.

Our best hope is a system in which fishermen own a share of the resource — in both a real and a moral sense. Ownership clearly provides the motivation to conserve and manage the fishery for the long haul.

Along with this commitment comes certain side benefits, including better financial stability for one's business, the ability to plan for the future, an opportunity to collect better scientific data for the fishery's benefit and, ultimately, improved profitability.

Only a handful of resource ownership programs are in operation around the world, and none of them is perfect. Among many areas of concern are warnings that such systems could destroy fishing communities as local owners sell their ownership rights to large companies. There are also arguments that owned-quota programs do little to reduce the incidental take of non-target and juvenile fish.

Under a typical ownership scheme, the fishermen who choose to remain can buy shares [individual transferable quotas] from those who decide to leave the industry, thereby increasing the former group's investment and commitment to the fishery. An effective ownership program would encourage and then directly reward responsible management and fishing activities.

We urge industry leaders in every port to investigate the various approaches to resource ownership. Each area could develop a version that suits the conditions of the fishery. Over the long run, it may be the most important thing that could be done to ensure the future of the fishing industry.

ERIC A. JOHNSON

A commercial fisherman in Portland, Maine.
FROM *COMMERCIAL FISHERIES NEWS,* MARCH 1989.

no

privatization of the fishing industry by any name is by its very nature exclusionary. If it weren't, it would be unable to reduce fishing pressure. Regardless of the "size of the pie," a prudent businessman is not going to give up part of his portion to a potential competitor. Given a small biomass and subsequently small number of ITQs (individual transferable quotas), entry into the industry becomes virtually impossible.

Quota systems, whether individual or industrial or industrywide, require either enforcement or voluntary compliance. The principal failing of every management plan of the past 10 years has been due in part to an inability to enforce regulations. . . .

Privatization of the resource will result in a radical change in the nature of the industry, leading ultimately to the ownership of the resource by a few large companies. If I hold a number of shares of a resource and decide to sell out, I will look for the best price I can get. That best price will invariably come from those whose holdings are large enough to permit the capital expense of such a purchase, not from someone trying to buy a boat and get in. . . .

Quotas have already proven unworkable. While the concept looks sound, it fails to permit the effort necessary for the financial well being of a boat. While touted as a working system, closer examination reveals that quotas penalize the successful and the efficient while artificially keeping the marginal operation afloat.

Quota schemes either distribute the catch based on history, allowing no room for growth; or, if set for the industry at large, result in periods of furious activity followed by mandated inactivity. In an attempt to catch their share of such a quota, fishermen are forced to fish whether conditions are favorable or not. Moreover, if a man owns a boat and has all the attendant expenses he will find a way to fish, quotas or no. . . .

What then is the solution to our management woes? I believe that the best way to attempt to manage is by regulating gear. . . . Next, the consequences of gear violations must be such that they truly provide a deterrent. A fine . . . that is easily recouped in a trip is not adequate. Perhaps the loss of the right to fish the boat for an extended period would be more effective. . . .

The important decisions aren't often popular and rarely easy to make. But if our goals are the protection of the freedoms we value and the stocks we depend on, ITQs aren't the answer — better enforcement is.

Continued from p. 752

OUTLOOK

Individual Quotas

With virtually all of the nation's fisheries under stress or in decline, many experts say U.S. fisheries policy is in need of radical overhaul. "At this point we can't assume equilibrium conditions in our fisheries," says Saul Saila, professor emeritus of oceanography at the University of Rhode Island. "They are completely out of whack. The concept of open access to fisheries is no longer viable." If fish stocks are allowed to rebuild over the next decade, Saila says, the long-term yields of many valuable fish species would be two to five times what they are today.

For its part, the National Marine Fisheries Service favors the introduction of individual transferable quotas, called ITQs. Under such a system, boat owners would be given a permit, based on their previous fishing history, allowing them to harvest a fixed amount of finfish or shellfish each year. The permits could be leased, sold or passed on in a family. (See "At Issue," p. 753.)

"We need to get fishermen to act more like farmers — give them an ownership privilege and a vested interest in the stocks," argues the NMFS' conservation chief, Richard Schaefer. "Fishermen don't own a fish until it's flopping around on the deck. If they own it before it is caught, they will manage it rationally." [16]

The ITQ system is already being utilized with some success in New Zealand, Australia and parts of Canada. But critics are skeptical. "People point to the privatization of New Zealand's fisheries as a success," says legislative expert Jeff Pike. "But my understanding is that as many people are managing the fishery as there are fishermen. It's a tremen-

dous waste of resources."

It is also worth noting that enforcement of ITQs in New Zealand is made easier by the fact that the country's fishing fleet is comprised mostly of large trawlers owned by a few companies. They process their catch at only a few designated places, and their product goes almost entirely into export. In contrast, the much larger U.S. fleet contains a hodgepodge of independent-minded, part-time operators, middle-sized trawlers and huge factory vessels. [17]

As one might expect, most U.S. fishermen vehemently oppose ITQs, which they contend will inevitably put independent operators out of business. "ITQs will destroy us," says Gloucester fisherman Ed Lima. "Corporations will buy up permits and swallow us like corporate farms gobbling up family farmers." Lima points to the New England surf clam industry as evidence. Before the ITQs were introduced in 1990, there were 175 to 180 clamming boats. Now there are only 65, and most of those are Canadian- and Japanese-owned, according to Lima.

Pollution's Toll

The battle for control over the nation's fisheries is far from over. Managing the resource in a sustainable way will require some hard choices for policy-makers — and a substantial amount of pain for fishermen. Ironically, experts say overfishing may be one of the more manageable problems concerning the nation's fisheries. The more daunting challenge may involve other man-made factors affecting fish production — pollution, water diversion, dam building and the destruction of coastal wetlands.

The bays and estuaries that are the breeding grounds and nurseries for fully 75 percent of commercial-seafood species are being increasingly

befouled by sewage, industrial waste water and runoff from cities and farms. At any given time, fully one-third of the nation's oyster, clam and other shellfish beds are closed because of contamination. Some 27 species of marine mammals and birds in American coastal waters are now listed as threatened or endangered, and the rising phenomenon of mass die-offs of dolphins and seals is blamed on toxins like PCB (polychlorinated biphenyl) that are rapidly accumulating in the marine environment. [18]

This year hundreds of dead and dying dolphins have washed up on the shores of the eastern Mediterranean in what has become an almost yearly occurrence. "With the die-offs of dolphins and humpback whales off the Atlantic coast in the late 1980s and more recently in the Mediterranean, it's hard not to conclude that pollution is playing a role," says the Marine Mammal Commission's John Twiss. "The dolphins have high levels of PCBs, which are known to reduce ability to resist disease." *

Whales and dolphins may have sounded the alarm, but fish are being affected, too. In a recently completed six-month study, the Consumers Union found detectable levels of PCBs, which have been linked to cancer and developmental disorders, in 43 percent of salmon samples and 25 percent of examined swordfish. [19]

"Fish are like sponges," explains Ellen Haas of Public Voice for Food and Health Policy, a consumer advocacy group in Washington, D.C. "They are highly susceptible to absorbing contaminants in water."

The report by Consumers Union has the seafood industry and the

---

*Most scientists, however, are reluctant to pin the blame solely on pollution. While analyses show high levels of toxic man-made chemicals, the widespread die-offs don't fit known patterns of disease or chemical dumping. In 1988, the NMFS set up the Marine Mammal Tissue Bank to help establish a data base on marine mammal die-offs.

Food and Drug Administration on the defensive. "The perception that seafood is unsafe is untrue," FDA Commissioner David Kessler declared in May in an effort to dispel public fears. "The vast preponderance of seafood that reaches the consumer is safe, clean and free of contaminants and chemicals."[20]

Nevertheless, the presence of high levels of toxins in some fish is a concern to health-conscious Americans, who over the last few decades have been eating less porterhouse and more tuna, which is high in protein but low in calories, fat and cholesterol. Overall U.S. fish consumption is up 50 percent since 1960 and nearly 25 percent in the past 10 years alone.

Aquaculture

With most of the ocean's fisheries in trouble, a new industry has been spawned. Initially thought of as a supplement to commercial fishing, fish farms are increasingly being thought of as an alternative source of fish. "At a time when there are rising health concerns on the part of consumers about the effects of pollution on seafood, fish farming gives you the power to control both the purity of the aquatic environment and what the fish are fed," argues Peter Shea, senior vice president of Chiquita Brands, the diversified food company known for its bananas. Chiquita Brands purchased a large aquaculture operation based in Southern California in 1990.

Moreover, a recent government report concludes that fish farming "could alleviate the conflicts between the need for fish as food and the view of fish as a recreational or aesthetic resource."[21] A trend toward domesticated fish would also reduce conflicts between fisheries and marine mammals.

In the past decade, rapid advances in aquaculture technology and the introduction of new species have changed the business from a low-in-

tensity speculative project to a high-powered, billion-dollar enterprise. The industry has been growing at a rate of 20 percent a year for each of the last 10 years. "In a decade or two, aquaculture will account for 30 to 40 percent of the fish population of the world," says oceanographer Saul Saila. Presently, fish farms account for roughly 13 percent.

The United States ranks far behind other countries in fish farming, with most of the U.S. effort concentrated in oysters, freshwater trout and catfish. But the potential is tremendous. Farm-bred salmon in Norway, for example, already account for 250 million pounds of production, more than all the world's natural stocks. And three-fourths of the shrimp the American public eats today is cultured.

In the future, fish farms will no doubt help satisfy consumers' growing appetite for fish, and in the process maybe even help natural fish stocks replenish. But even with the inevitable rise in aquaculture, it is hard to conceive of a world without fishermen. As Audubon's Carl Safina puts it: "You can't raise swordfish or bluefin tuna or codfish in ponds." ∎

Notes

[1] For background on the law, see "Endangered Species," *The CQ Researcher*, June 21, 1991, pp. 393-416.

[2] National Oceanic and Atmospheric Administration, *Our Living Oceans*, U.S. Department of Commerce, 1992, p. 16.

[3] Quoted in *U.S. News & World Report*, June 22, 1992, p. 65.

[4] See James R. McGoodwin, *Crisis in the World's Fisheries* (1990), p. 3.

[5] For details, see *Marine Mammal Commission: 1991 Annual Report to Congress*, Jan. 31 1992, p. 24.

[6] Quoted in *National Fisherman*, January 1991.

[7] See J.R. Sullivan, "The Battle of Ballard Locks," *Sea Frontiers*, August 1991, p. 42, and *The Wall Street Journal*, April 3, 1992.

[8] See "Whaling: End of an Era," *Editorial Research Reports*, Sept. 27, 1985, pp. 717-736.

[9] See James R. McGoodwin, *op. cit.*, p. 52. El Niño is a warm ocean current that develops after late December along the coast of Ecuador and Peru that sometimes causes catastrophic weather conditions.

[10] William W. Warner, *Distant Water: The Fate of the North Atlantic Fisherman* (1983), p. 6.

[11] Massachusetts Offshore Groundfish Task Force, *New England Groundfish in Crisis — Again*, December 1990.

[12] The New England Groundfish Restoration Act was sponsored in the House by Gerry E. Studds, D-Mass., and in the Senate by John Kerry, D-Mass. If resulting legislation passes the full Congress and is signed into law, it will supersede the plan now being drafted by the management council.

[13] Quoted in the *Los Angeles Times*, June 29, 1992.

[14] Quoted in *U.S. News & World Report, op. cit.*, p. 75.

[15] See the *Los Angeles Times*, June 28, 1992.

[16] Quoted in *U.S. News & World Report, op. cit.*, p. 75.

[17] For a detailed discussion of ITQs, see James Wilson, "Question: How to Reduce Fishing Effort?" *Commercial Fisheries News*, March 1989.

[18] For background, see "Threatened Coastlines," *The CQ Researcher*, Feb. 7, 1992, pp. 97-120.

[19] See "Is Our Fish Fit to Eat," *Consumer Reports*, February 1992, p. 112.

[20] Quoted in *Time*, June 29, 1992, p. 71.

[21] See *Marine Aquaculture: Opportunities for Growth*, Committee on Assessment of Technology and Opportunities for Marine Aquaculture in the United States, 1992.

Bibliography

Selected Sources Used

Books

McGoodwin, James R., *Crisis in the World's Fisheries,* Stanford University Press, 1990.

This book is a useful overview of the global fishing crisis. Much of the space is devoted to the history of fishing cultures — and to the dilemmas faced by Third World fishing communities.

Sherman, Kenneth, *et al,* eds., *Food Chains, Yields, Models, and Management of Large Marine Ecosystems,* Westview Press, 1991.

This collection of academic essays represents the collective efforts of oceanographers, fishery biologists and ecologists to assess the state of marine ecosystems.

Warner, William W., *Distant Water: The Fate of the North Atlantic Fisherman,* Little Brown, 1983.

The author provides an intimate description of how the Atlantic Coast fisheries off New England were plundered by foreign factory fleets. The book contains extensive interviews with fisherman.

Articles

Brower, Kenneth, "The Destruction of Dolphins," *The Atlantic,* July 1989, p. 35.

This article focuses on the tuna-dolphin controversy, and includes significant background on how the public became aware that dolphins were dying in large numbers.

Campbell, Todd, "Net Losses," *Sierra,* March-April 1991, p. 48.

A griping first-hand account of the environmental costs of drift-netting.

"Fishing in the Global Pond," *National Fisherman Yearbook,* December 1991.

This special issue of the monthly publication *National Fisherman* focuses on the status of America's fisheries.

Satchel, Michael, "The Rape of the Oceans," *U.S. News & World Report,* June 22, 1992, p. 64.

This cover story on overfishing takes a critical look at the fishing industry and the exploitative fishing techniques that have been employed for the past two decades.

Stirrup, Marion, "A Sea Lion Mystery," *Sea Frontiers,* March-April 1990, p. 46.

Stirrup examines the probable causes for the precipitous decline in the Stellar sea lion population in the Bering Sea.

This is a good case study of the clash between marine mammals and a valuable commercial fishery (for Alaskan pollock).

Reports and Studies

Marine Mammal Commission, *1991 Annual Report to Congress,* Jan. 31, 1992.

A thorough, comprehensive status report on marine mammal populations. The report is unbiased and contains detailed descriptions of each specific case where a marine mammal population is in jeopardy, and what the likely or suspected causes are.

National Research Council, *Reducing Dolphin Mortality from Tuna Fishing,* National Academy Press, 1992.

The most definitive work on the tuna-dolphin controversy to date, this balanced study analyzes the mortality rates of dolphins caught in purse-seine nets. The report concludes that one of the most dramatic ways to reduce dolphin mortality is to train ship captains.

National Oceanic and Atmospheric Administration, *Our Living Oceans,* Department of Commerce, 1992.

This extensive report discusses the status of U.S. fisheries, broken down by region and fish species. The report concludes that 42 percent of the nation's fisheries are overfished and that an even larger percentage is currently being fished to full capacity.

National Marine Fisheries Service, *Revised Proposal to Govern Interactions between Marine Mammals and Commercial Fishing Operations,* National Oceanic and Atmospheric Administration, Nov. 20, 1991.

The NMFS's proposal to manage interactions between marine mammals and fisheries has gone through several review stages. Formal guidelines are expected to be released soon. It's likely that fisheries where a high number of marine mammals are killed will be subjected to closer government monitoring.

Subcommittee on Fisheries and Wildlife Conservation and the Environment, Committee on Merchant Marine and Fisheries, *Hearing Proceedings: New England Groundfish Restoration Act of 1991 (HR 2919),* U.S. House of Representatives, 102nd Congress, Sept. 23, 1991 and Oct. 2, 1991.

The testimony presented on the crisis in the New England fishery provides useful insight into how both marine biology experts and fishermen perceive the problem.

The Next Step

Additional Articles from Current Periodicals from EBSCO Publishing's Database

Books & reading

Barnett, J.B., "Book reviews: Science & technology," *Library Journal*, February 15, 1991, p. 218.

Reviews the book "The Living Ocean: Understanding and Protecting Marine Biodiversity," by Boyce Thorne-Miller and John Catena.

Fishing industry

"Ghost nets reap a harvest of death," *National Geographic*, August 1990, p. 142.

Reports that the grim toll taken in marine life on the high seas by huge, nearly invisible drift nets continues, despite attempts at international regulation; various species caught; resolutions for tougher restrictions on drift-net fishing.

"Swim with the dolphins," *Newsweek*, April 23, 1990, p. 76.

Reports that StarKist tuna, Bumble Bee Seafoods Inc. and Chicken of the Sea announced last week that they would no longer accept fish caught in nets that also kill dolphins.

Campbell, T., "Net losses," *Sierra*, March/April 1991, p. 48.

Presents an eyewitness report of the Greenpeace schooner *Rainbow Warrior's* two-month voyage through North Pacific drift net fishing grounds to gather data and document the destruction. Drift nets used by Japan, South Korea and Taiwan drown seabirds and mammals; South Pacific Forum banned drift nets in the Tasman Sea; the United Nations' 1989 anti-drift-net resolution; problems with enforcement; effects on North American salmon fishing.

Dugger, A., "Gillnet fisheries: A worldwide concern," *Sea Frontiers*, January/February 1990, p. 20.

Summarizes the worldwide concerns about gill-net fisheries, including accidental killings, incidental catches and hazards to seagoing traffic.

Hoke, F. and R. Lyhus, "Farther and deeper," *Environment*, November 1990, p. 24.

Examines how fishing techniques — from destructive dynamiting of reefs to dense fleets of boats working offshore areas — have significantly altered shallow coastal systems and are affecting progressively deeper habitats farther from shore.

Just, H., & B. Stearns, "Drift nets," *Field & Stream*,

March 1990, p. 152.

Examines the destructive impact of drift-net fishing on sport fishing, sea mammals and "incidental by-catch" (nontarget fish species). Destruction of future generations of fish; Japan's drift-net fleet; reasons why drift nets are so deadly; United Nations' moratorium; U.S. Rep. Gerry E. Studds' amendment. INSET: How you can help.

MacKenzie, D., "Whaling nations threaten unilateral action," *New Scientist*, July 14, 1990, p. 22.

Reports that whaling nations Japan, Norway and Iceland threaten to form a rival body to the International Whaling Commission (IWC). The IWC's continued rejection of proposals; accusations that the IWC is unscientific.

McCredie, S., "Controversy travels with driftnet fleets," *Sea Frontiers*, January/February 1990, p. 13.

Discusses the controversy over squid drift-netting, which involves 30,000 miles of net each night and kills nearly every animal that swims into it, and the enormous damage the practice could be causing to the ocean's ecology and resources. Drift net operations; recent ecological victories; incidental fish caught; trade concerns; international controls.

Shabecoff, P., "3 companies to stop selling tuna caught with dolphins," *The New York Times*, April 13, 1990, p. 1.

Reports that the nation's three top sellers of canned tuna announced today that they would stop buying tuna that is caught in nets that also trap and kill dolphins. Together the three companies — the H.J. Heinz Company, owner of StarKist brand, the Van Camp Seafood Company, which markets Chicken of the Sea, and Bumble Bee Inc. — account for nearly 70 percent of the canned tuna sold in the U.S. Reason for the decision; other methods for finding tuna.

Skorupa, J., "Stripmining the sea," *Popular Mechanics*, November 1990, p. 106.

Describes various incidents in which Taiwanese vessels have been caught fishing in prohibited waters. Explains how Pacific Rim nations are using drift-netting — the most destructive technology ever invented to catch fish — threatening the vitality of the world's oceans.

Stevens, W.K., "Large drift nets move to Atlantic," *The New York Times*, August 14, 1990, p. A1.

Says that huge, super-efficient drift nets, of the kind that ignited a storm of international protest in the Pacific Ocean, have been spotted for the first time in the Atlantic near the

Caribbean, raising fears that Atlantic marine life could be threatened and that commercial and sport fisheries important to the eastern U.S. could be devastated.

Williamson, L., "Fish un-limited," *Outdoor Life,* June 1992, p. 53.

Reports that overfishing, habitat loss and pollution have pushed fisheries to their limit — and the results could be devastating. Specifics on National Marine Fisheries Service (NMFS) report; problems at Columbia River Basin, Chesapeake Bay and other waters; plans to restore marine fishery.

Government policy

"Cleared bill would ensure 'dolphin safe' tuna." *Congressional Quarterly Weekly Report,* November 3, 1990, p. 3750.

Announces that the Senate on Oct. 27 cleared legislation calling on the administration to pursue an international agreement to end use of large-scale drift nets on the high seas. Magnuson Fishery Conservation and Management Act; increase of maximum penalty for violating United States fishing laws.

"Drift net sanctions OK'd by House," *Congressional Quarterly Weekly Report,* February 29, 1992, p. 465.

Discusses the House's unanimous approval of a bill (HR 2152) on Feb. 25, 1992, which would strengthen a United Nations policy against large-scale drift-net fishing by imposing U.S. sanctions on countries that continue the practice.

"Fishing nations agree to stop 'strip mining' the world's seas," *International Wildlife,* March/April 1992, p. 29.

Announces that Japan and Taiwan have agreed to stop their fishing fleets' use of huge drift nets by the end of 1992. South Korea is expected to do the same. United Nations resolution; U.S. Congress' pressure; dangers of drift nets.

"Marine sanctuaries bill strengthens local input," *Congressional Quarterly Weekly Report,* May 16, 1992, p. 1340.

Details the House Merchant Marine and Fisheries Committee's voice-vote approval of a bill (HR 4310) on May 14, 1992, which would streamline the creation of new underwater marine sanctuaries and allow greater local input into those sanctuaries. Reauthorization of the national marine sanctuaries program through fiscal 1996; establishment of a new Coastal Sanctuary Foundation; funding for the program; sponsor Dennis M. Hertel (D-Mich.).

"Norway sharpens harpoon for minke whale," *New Scientist,* July 7, 1990, p. 20.

Summarizes the main purpose of this week's meeting of the International Whaling Commission in Noordwijk, in the Netherlands. Some of the die-hard whaling nations are pressing for the moratorium on commercial whaling to be lifted for the minke whale. Opposition by scientists to lifting the moratorium; controversy.

"Stronger drift net ban OK'd by Merchant Marine," *Congressional Quarterly Weekly Report,* October 5, 1991, p. 2862.

Reports that the House Merchant Marine and Fisheries Committee approved legislation (HR 2152) that aims to strengthen enforcement of international agreements barring drift-net fishing. Allows the president to ban imports from nations that allow drift-net fishing and impose sanctions on countries that do not abide by the United Nations resolution on net fishing.

Eliot, J.L., "Walls of death, drift nets will kill no more," *National Geographic,* April 1992, p. 142.

Reports that Japan and Taiwan have agreed to cease fishing with drift nets by the end of the year. South Korea may soon follow suit bowing to a United Nations resolution; size of the nets; they had been used for squid and tuna.

Ewing, T., "Japan and Taiwan refuse international ban," *Nature,* December 14, 1989, p. 726.

Reports that several South Pacific nations have agreed on a ban on drift-net fishing in their territorial seas and exclusive economic and fishing zones. Criticism from Japan and Taiwan; details.

Marine animals

"Britain signs deal to protect dolphins," *New Scientist,* May 16, 1992, p. 8.

Reports on the Agreement on Small Cetaceans that was recently drawn up under the Bonn Convention. Why this agreement is needed; its aim; who has signed it so far.

"Buying sanctuary," *The Economist,* June 1, 1991, p. 12.

Discusses a potentially permanent way to save the whale. Possible threat of Japan, Norway and Iceland leaving the International Whaling Commission (IWC); difficulty of monitoring whaling; arguments for banning whale hunting; use of money to end whaling; details.

"End of the line for sharks?" *USA Today,* June 1990, p. 10.

Warns that many of the world's sharks are heading toward extinction. Impact of sharks' bad public image and overfishing; why sharks are important.

"Good hunting?" *New Scientist,* July 14, 1990, p. 19.

Argues against Japan and Norway's excessive killing of whales. Asserts the global value of not rendering a species extinct; need for whalers to learn from scientists how to best pursue whaling.

"Sharks. Predators that need our protection," *National Geographic,* **December 1990, p. 146.**

Explains how East Coast commercial and sport fishermen, who kill sharks to the tune of more than 22,000 metric tons a year, are threatening the viability of the mako, sandbar and blacktip.

"Sharks find a friend in Washington," *U.S. News & World Report,* **November 20, 1989, p. 16.**

Highlights the National Marine Fisheries Service's 100-page protection plan to save sharks. Annual shark take along the East Coast is expected to be 11,000 tons; new regulations to put limits on number taken.

"The struggle for dolphin safety," *Mother Earth News,* **February/March 1992, p. 16.**

Reports that tens of thousands of dolphins continue to die at the hands of tuna fishermen each year, despite the fact that all tuna sold in the United States is now deemed "dolphin safe." Purse-seine nets kill 100,000 dolphins a year; incidental-take permits; North American Free Trade Agreement (NAFTA); General Agreement on Tariff and Trade (GATT).

"U.S. extends use of turtle protectors," *International Wildlife,* **January/February 1992, p. 26.**

Announces that the Department of Commerce has ordered Atlantic shrimpers to use turtle excluder devices (TED) year-round through 1992. Previously the agency required TED use from May 1 to September 1. The TEDs prevent sea turtles from becoming caught in shrimp nets.

Graham, F., "Feeding frenzy," *Audubon,* **March 1990, p. 10.**

Presents University of Miami shark specialist Samuel "Sonny" Gruber's recommendations for shark conservation. Increase in commercial shark fishing; demand for shark fins; need to change people's thinking about sharks.

Leaf, M., "Turtle rescue," *Omni,* **April 1989, p. 35.**

Discusses turtle excluder device (TED) nets, expected to give sea turtles a chance to escape nets. A new law, which goes into effect May 1, requires the use of TED nets by shrimp fishermen.

Morowitz, H.J., "Balancing species preservation and economic considerations," *Science,* **August 16, 1991, p. 752.**

Discusses the economics and ethics questions involved in the measurement of how much a species is worth. Questions about benefits to individuals or society; impact of growth of human population on biodiversity; impact of hu-man pollution; arguments for the importance of species preservation; examples of difficulties in assigning value to species.

Ross, P.E., "Man bites shark," *Scientific American,* **June 1990, p. 31.**

Reports that shark populations are plunging due to a growing taste for the meat and the fins. Sharks check populations by feeding on the weak; plans for the shark to go on the list of managed species; shark fins prized by chefs, but plans are ahead for limited harvesting.

Rudloe, A. and J. Rudloe, "Shrimpers and lawmakers collide over a move to save the sea turtles," *Smithsonian,* **December 1989, p. 44.**

Account of the bitter fight between fishermen and the United States government over the requirement that fishermen use turtle excluder devices, (TEDs), to keep sea turtles from drowning in their nets. Endangered sea turtles are symbols of environmental conflict; economics of shrimping; legislation and enforcement.

Williams, T., "The exclusion of sea turtles," *Audubon,* **January 1990, p. 24.**

Examines the opposition of shrimpers in the Gulf of Mexico to the use of turtle excluder devices (TEDs), which modify their nets to prevent the catching of sea turtles. Comments by shrimpers in Aransas Pass, Texas; Kemp's ridley turtles; policies of the National Marine Fisheries Service (NMFS) and Secretary of Commerce Robert Mosbacher; violence and threats of violence.

Oceans

"Closing the open oceans," *Environment,* **January/February 1992, p. 21.**

Reports how marine scientists are considering an idea to establish reserves in the open oceans, due to concern that the high seas will lose their relatively pristine nature because of pollution and overfishing.

Satchell, M., "The rape of the oceans," *U.S. News & World Report,* **June 22, 1992, p. 64.**

Examines the plight of America's oceans as overfishing, pollution and poor management threaten their future survival. The precipitous decline of New England's groundfish; where disaster is striking; close to half of United States coastal finfish stocks are now overexploited; how pollution is taking its toll on sealife; 90 million metric tons of seafood eaten in the world annually; the national scandal in Alaska; more. INSET: Can sharks survive?

Back Issues

Great Research on Current Issues Starts Right Here... Recent topics covered by The CQ Researcher are listed below. Issues dated before May 10, 1991, were published under the name of Editorial Research Reports.

FEBRUARY 1991
Regional Impact of Recession
Puerto Rico's Status
Redistricting: Mapping Power
Nuclear Power

MARCH 1991
Acid Rain
Cost of the Gulf War
Reassessing Gun Laws
Future for Man in Space

APRIL 1991
Social Security
Canadian Crisis Over Quebec
California Drought
Electromagnetic Radiation

MAY 1991
School Choice
Racial Quotas
Animal Rights
U.S. and Japan

JUNE 1991
Children and Divorce
Teenage Suicide
Endangered Species
Europe 1992

JULY 1991
Teenagers and Abortion
Soviet Republics Rebel
Mexico's Emergence
Athletes and Drugs

AUGUST 1991
Sexual Harassment
Fetal Tissue Research
Oil Imports
The Palestinians

SEPTEMBER 1991
Police Brutality
Advertising Under Attack
Saving the Forests
Foster Care Crisis

OCTOBER 1991
Pay-Per-View TV
Youth Gangs
Gene Therapy
World Hunger

NOVEMBER 1991
Fast-Food Shake-Up
The Greening of Eastern Europe
Business' Role in Education
Cuba In Crisis

DECEMBER 1991
Retiree Health Benefits
Asian Americans
The Obscenity Debate
The Disabilities Act

JANUARY 1992
Term Limits
Oil Spills
Hunting Controversy
Alternative Medicine

FEBRUARY 1992
Threatened Coastlines
New Era in Asia
Assisted Suicide
Jobs in the '90s

MARCH 1992
Women and Sports
Underage Drinking
Garbage Crisis
Mafia Crackdown

APRIL 1992
Ozone Depletion
Welfare Reform
Politicians and Privacy
Illegal Immigration

MAY 1992
Native Americans
Jobs vs. Environment
Too Many Lawsuits?
Fairness in Salaries

JUNE 1992
Nuclear Proliferation
Food Irradiation
Lead Poisoning
Hard Times for Libraries

JULY 1992
Alternative Energy
Prescription Drug Prices
Alzheimer's Disease
Infant Mortality

AUGUST 1992
The Homeless
Work, Family and Stress
NATO's Changing Role

Back issues are available for $4.00 (subscribers) or $7.00 (non-subscribers). Quantity discounts apply to orders over ten. To order, call Congressional Quarterly 1-800-432-2250.

Binders are available for $15.00. To order call 1-800-638-1710.

Future Topics

▶ *Domestic Partners*

▶ *Violence in Schools*

▶ *Public Television*

THE

CQ Researcher

PUBLISHED BY CONGRESSIONAL QUARTERLY INC., IN CONJUNCTION WITH EBSCO PUBLISHING

Domestic Partners

Should unmarried partners get a wider range of benefits?

F
amily values has become a hot issue in this
presidential election year. But does the term refer
only to traditional families — married couples with
children? A growing number of American
households now consist of two unmarried adults, often of the
same sex. These domestic partners are clamoring for job,
housing and health benefits comparable to those routinely
extended to married couples. Many cities, colleges and
businesses have initiated benefit programs that recognize
domestic partners, and more could follow suit. Conservatives
are alarmed by the trend, fearing that domestic partnerships
will undermine the institution of marriage and perhaps even
lead to the legalization of same-sex marriage. Others worry
that domestic-partnership benefits will drastically increase
health-care costs.

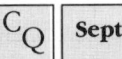 **September 4, 1992 • Volume 2, No. 33 • 761-784**

Formerly Editorial Research Reports

COVER ART: BARBARA SASSA-DANIELS

The CQ Researcher

September 4, 1992
Volume 2, No. 33

EDITOR
Sandra Stencel

MANAGING EDITOR
Thomas J. Colin

ASSOCIATE EDITOR
Richard L. Worsnop

STAFF WRITERS
Charles S. Clark
Mary H. Cooper
Rodman D. Griffin

PRODUCTION EDITOR
Sarah E. Merritt

EDITORIAL ASSISTANT
Michael M. Taylor

GRAPHICS
Jack Auldridge

PUBLISHED BY
Congressional Quarterly Inc.

CHAIRMAN
Andrew Barnes

VICE CHAIRMAN
Andrew P. Corty

EDITOR AND PUBLISHER
Neil Skene

EXECUTIVE EDITOR
Robert W. Merry

PUBLICATIONS MARKETING/SALES
Robert Smith

EDITOR, EBSCO PUBLISHING
Melissa Kummerer

© 1992 Congressional Quarterly Inc.

The right to make direct use of material contained in The CQ Researcher is strictly reserved to newspaper, magazine, radio and television clients of the service. Others wishing to quote from the reports for other than academic purposes must first obtain written permission.

The CQ Researcher (ISSN 1056-2036). Formerly Editorial Research Reports. Published weekly (48 times per year, not printed the first Friday of any month with five Fridays) by Congressional Quarterly Inc., 1414 22nd St., N.W., Washington, D.C. 20037. Rates are furnished upon request. Second-class postage paid at Washington, D.C. POSTMASTER: Send address changes to The CQ Researcher, 1414 22nd St., N.W., Washington, D.C. 20037.

Domestic Partners

By Richard L. Worsnop

The Issues

Family values, a deceptively simple term, has emerged as one of the themes of the 1992 presidential campaign. Leaders of both parties hail families as the nation's primary source of social and economic stability. But Republicans and Democrats seem to have two quite different notions of what constitutes a family in today's America.

Vice President Dan Quayle, speaking in San Francisco May 19, soon after the riots in Los Angeles, said, "Children need love and discipline. They need mothers and fathers. A welfare check is not a husband. The state is not a father. It is from parents that children learn how to behave in society."

Carrying his argument further, Quayle attacked the television show "Murphy Brown," spawning heated comment. "It doesn't help matters when prime-time TV has Murphy Brown — a character who supposedly epitomizes today's intelligent, highly paid, professional woman — mocking the importance of fathers by bearing a child alone and calling it just another lifestyle choice," the vice president said. "I know it is not fashionable to talk about moral values, but we need to do it."

Three months later, on Aug. 20, Quayle hoisted the family values banner at the Republican National Convention in Houston: "Americans try to raise their children to understand right and wrong — only to be told that every so-called 'lifestyle alternative' is morally equivalent. That is wrong." For the vice president, the traditional household unit of a husband, wife and children is clearly paramount.

Democratic presidential nominee Bill Clinton has fashioned a broader concept of family. In his July 16 ac-

ceptance speech at the Democratic National Convention in New York City, the Arkansas governor proclaimed his faith in "an America that includes every family: every traditional family and every extended family, every two-parent family, every single-parent family and every foster family. Every family."

But whether one agrees with Quayle or Clinton, population studies show that living arrangements in the United States are becoming increasingly diverse. For instance, a 1990 Census Bureau survey of 57,000 homes found that only 26 percent of American families consisted of a married couple with one or more children under age 18. In 1970, by contrast, 40 percent of American families fit that traditional mold. The remaining 74 percent of families in the 1990 survey were non-traditional, a category including single and divorced parents, unmarried heterosexual and homosexual couples, extended and intergenerational families, as well as married couples without children under age 18.

Next year, the Census Bureau is due to publish data providing an even closer look at non-traditional U.S. families. The study will focus on people who consider themselves "unmarried partners" — a category added to census forms for the first time in 1990, joining "single," "married," "roommate" and "boarder." The term unmarried partners, or domestic partners, usually refers to heterosexual or homosexual couples. However, some experts extend the definition to handicapped, elderly and other single people living together in group homes.

Both supporters and opponents of domestic partnerships are eagerly awaiting the Census Bureau study. Supporters hope it will put added pressure on local governments and private businesses to provide spousal benefits to the live-in partners of employees. Over the past decade, several dozen municipalities and companies across the country have begun offering benefits like bereavement leave, hospital visitation rights and health insurance coverage to unmarried partners. Public and private policy-makers "are adopting a concept of family more in line with the way people actually live," says Professor Arthur Leonard of New York Law School, an authority on domestic-partnership law.[1]

Sociologist Jessie Bernard predicted many current trends in family formation in a book published 20 years ago. "Not only does marriage have a future," she wrote, "it has many futures. There will be, for example, options that permit different kinds of relationships over time for different stages in life, and options that permit different lifestyles or living arrangements according to the nature of the relationships." Traditional marriage will still be available, she said, "But it will not have a monopoly; it will not be the only choice open."[2]

One of those choices, Bernard said, would be cohabitation out of wedlock. Many young couples decide to live together without exchanging marriage vows, often for financial reasons. Elderly couples may elect to do so because Social Security benefits based on a former spouse's earnings are cut in half upon remarriage. Similarly, a divorced woman may be reluctant to remarry for fear of losing alimony payments.

But these examples account for only a small fraction of the nation's non-traditional relationships, critics of domestic partnerships insist. They say the movement is being driven by homosexual-rights activists intent on securing legal recognition of same-sex marriage. *(See story, p. 768.)*

Both sides in the debate recognize that the key finding in next year's Census Bureau study will focus on same-sex couples. If a person lists himself or herself as an "unmarried partner" of a person of the same sex sharing the same home, the natural inference will be that both partners are homosexual. Consequently, the bureau's total count of "unmarried partners" of the same gender could spark a fierce policy dispute.

Opponents of gay and lesbian rights challenge the commonly cited estimate, dating from the first Kinsey Report in 1948, that about 10 percent of the American population is homosexual. Actually, says Robert Knight, director of the Family Research Council's Cultural Studies Project, "the incidence of homosexual behavior in the general population is less than 3 percent and may be as little as 1 percent."[3] If the Census Bureau study supports that lower estimate, the campaign for domestic-partnership rights could suffer a crippling setback.

The American public seems receptive to the concept of domestic partnership, even though the issue is still evolving. In a survey of 1,220 people

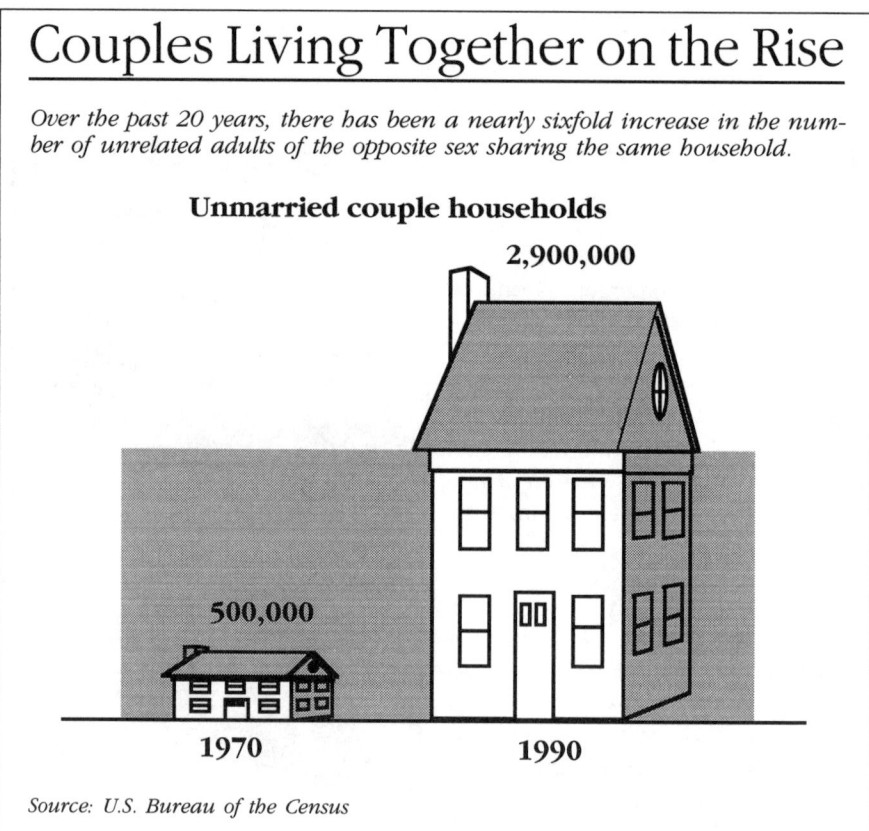

Couples Living Together on the Rise

Over the past 20 years, there has been a nearly sixfold increase in the number of unrelated adults of the opposite sex sharing the same household.

Unmarried couple households

2,900,000

500,000

1970   1990

Source: *U.S. Bureau of the Census*

conducted in 1989, the Massachusetts Mutual Life Insurance Co. found that 74 percent of the respondents defined family as "a group who love and care for each other." Only 22 percent chose the more legalistic description of "a group of people related by blood, marriage or adoption."[4]

As might be expected, feelings about homosexual couples appear far more ambivalent. A *Time*/CNN poll taken in November 1989 found that 54 percent of the respondents thought same-sex couples should be permitted to receive medical and life-insurance benefits from a partner's policy; 37 percent opposed the idea. However, legalization of homosexual marriage was resoundingly rejected, 69 percent to 23 percent.

Since the movement for domestic-partnership rights is barely a decade old, many Americans have only a vague notion of the issues involved. Experience suggests, however, that

discussion will continue to center on two fundamental questions:

Should unmarried couples be given the many legal rights enjoyed by married couples?

Supporters and opponents of domestic partnership approach the issue from sharply different angles. For proponents, domestic-partnership benefits can be justified on grounds of fairness alone. "In most workplace situations, employee benefits packages, or fringe benefits, comprise as much as 40 percent of a worker's total compensation," asserts the National Gay & Lesbian Task Force. "Marital status most often determines an employee's eligibility for entitlements such as sick, bereavement or parenting leave, health and dental insurance, disability and retirement benefits, family assistance and discount buying privileges."[5] From this perspective, extending spousal benefits to domestic partners is simply a matter of providing equal compensation for equal work.

Ivy Young, director of the task force's Families Project, says the campaign for domestic-partnership rights is a natural response to social changes in the United States since World War II. "Society always outpaces the law it creates," she says. "So the law is constantly catching up with the reality."

For example, notes Young, most current family law was written with the traditional family in mind. Today, though, "only one-fourth of American families are nuclear families. And an even smaller percentage consists of traditional families, with mother in the home, father in the workplace and two kids. Barely 10 percent of the population fits that description." The main reason is that wives and mothers have entered the work force in large numbers over the past 30 years or so.

It goes without saying that family policy conceived decades ago ignores non-traditional living arrangements, especially those involving homosexual couples. But non-traditional households "are families nonetheless," says Young, "whether they consist of a single parent, two adult working parents or intergenerational or extended families with grandparents or an aunt and uncle or somebody else living in the home. It's another instance of policy needing updating to keep pace with the reality of American family life."

Those who oppose spousal benefits for domestic partners argue that such a policy will eventually undermine the institution of traditional marriage and, by extension, society itself. Domestic partnership, says the Family Research Council's Knight, represents "an attempt to take the moral capital from marriage and the family and apply it elsewhere. In effect, it says society has no stake in upholding and promoting two-parent families. And it reduces marriage to the level of roommates."

Domestic-partnership ordinances now in force usually allow a person to register a new partnership six months or more after the breakup of an earlier one. "When you can kick somebody out and reapply in six months," says Knight, "it undercuts the whole notion of commitment and fidelity." He adds that, "At a time when so many social ills have been traced to loose sexual standards, the answer always seems to be, let's loosen them a little more and see if that helps. It never does. It always makes things worse."

Young vigorously disputes the charge that domestic partnership poses a threat to marriage. "People who put that argument forward are absolutely ignorant of what a marriage license provides," she says. "The difference between domestic partnership and marriage is the difference between the Wright brothers' plane and an SST. There are an incredible number of privileges, protections and benefits that come with the civil recognition of a couple's union — that is to say, a marriage license and the civil recognition of that. A domestic-partnership ordinance doesn't even begin to *touch* the vast array of entitlements that come with a marriage license."

A domestic-partnership ordinance, Young adds, "is not the same as a gay-marriage bill. They're completely separate items." She notes that "In many cities where domestic-partnership ordinances are in place — Berkeley [Calif.], for instance — 85 percent of the people who register as domestic partners are heterosexual couples."

According to Thomas F. Coleman, a Los Angeles attorney who is an authority on family diversity issues, the domestic-partnership movement has made only sporadic gains thus far because many individuals who stand to benefit from it are unaware of their latent political clout. "People are fighting individually, they're not organizing politically," says Coleman, who is executive director of the

Spectrum Institute's Family Diversity Project. "But some traditional civil rights organizations like the ACLU [American Civil Liberties Union] are beginning to take up the cause."

Since domestic partners have such diverse backgrounds, Coleman says they "are not a natural constituency that views itself as a group of people with common interests and goals, as members of the gay community do, or the women's movement, or blacks or Hispanics. But the potential is there for quite a backlash by unmarried people against being continually battered by laws and policies and practices and negative words by politicians."

Will domestic-partnership rights impose an unacceptable financial burden on society?

Some opponents of spousal benefits for domestic partners say the nation simply cannot afford to adopt such a program on a broad scale. But no one really knows whether that is true. Elected officials are understandably wary, for domestic partnership is a concept with a very short track record. Insurers and employers, with little secondhand experience to guide them, are unsure how many additional people will apply for benefits.

The uncertainty does not end there. Many city officials and business executives worry that the partners of some homosexual employees will seek costly treatment for AIDS, possibly jeopardizing the coverage of others enrolled in group insurance plans. However, some precautions are available to insurers. Liberty Mutual Insurance Co., which provides domestic-partner coverage, insists on a one-year wait before providing benefits to a partner, to guard against both pre-existing conditions and the possibility that a casual friend will be misrepresented as a domestic partner.

In a 1991 survey of 50 San Francisco Bay area employers, the benefits consulting firm A. Foster Higgins & Co. Inc. found that 90 percent rated

What Constitutes a Family?

According to a recent opinion poll, a bare majority of Americans feel that a man and a woman who have lived together a long time make up a family, but only about half that number recognize gay couples, with or without children, as family units.

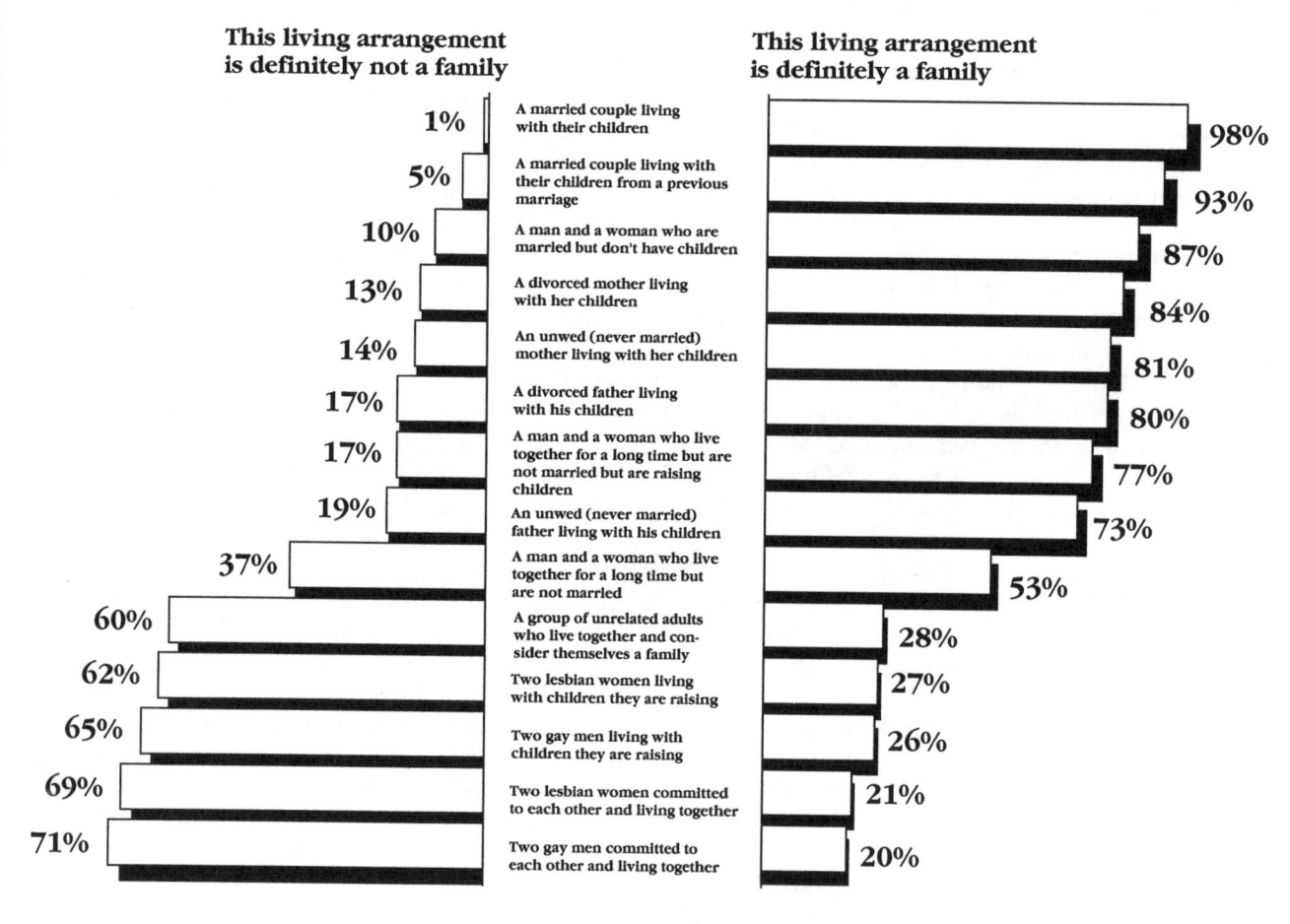

This living arrangement is definitely not a family

1%	A married couple living with their children
5%	A married couple living with their children from a previous marriage
10%	A man and a woman who are married but don't have children
13%	A divorced mother living with her children
14%	An unwed (never married) mother living with her children
17%	A divorced father living with his children
17%	A man and a woman who live together for a long time but are not married but are raising children
19%	An unwed (never married) father living with his children
37%	A man and a woman who live together for a long time but are not married
60%	A group of unrelated adults who live together and consider themselves a family
62%	Two lesbian women living with children they are raising
65%	Two gay men living with children they are raising
69%	Two lesbian women committed to each other and living together
71%	Two gay men committed to each other and living together

This living arrangement is definitely a family

A married couple living with their children	98%
A married couple living with their children from a previous marriage	93%
A man and a woman who are married but don't have children	87%
A divorced mother living with her children	84%
An unwed (never married) mother living with her children	81%
A divorced father living with his children	80%
A man and a woman who live together for a long time but are not married but are raising children	77%
An unwed (never married) father living with his children	73%
A man and a woman who live together for a long time but are not married	53%
A group of unrelated adults who live together and consider themselves a family	28%
Two lesbian women living with children they are raising	27%
Two gay men living with children they are raising	26%
Two lesbian women committed to each other and living together	21%
Two gay men committed to each other and living together	20%

Source: Survey by the Roper Organization, February 1992, as published in The American Enterprise, *July/August 1992.*

"cost of additional coverage" as their chief concern in deciding whether to offer fringe benefits to their workers' domestic partners. Similarly, Foster Higgins reported that "benefit professionals, insurance carriers and HMOs [health maintenance organizations] alike are most concerned about the financial implications and administrative burdens of adding domestic-partner coverage."[6]

Insurers cite similar concerns in defending their reluctance to add domestic partners to existing coverage plans. Some say they would consider covering domestic partners if they had a longstanding relationship with the client company and the size of the group to be covered was large enough to present an acceptable underwriting risk.

But few insurance vendors have actually taken the plunge. The city of West Hollywood, Calif., which has a sizable homosexual population, was turned down by 16 insurers before

deciding to self-insure the health-care coverage of its roughly 150 municipal employees and their spouses and dependents, including domestic partners. Since the self-insurance program took effect in 1989, only about six domestic partners have been enrolled in the city's plan at any given time.

Kevin Fridlington, the city's benefits manager, says no AIDS-related claims have been filed by domestic partners of municipal employees. On the other hand, he reports that the benefits program has taken some "dramatic hits" from AIDS-related claims filed by employees.

The experience of Berkeley, Calif., which instituted the nation's first domestic-partnership benefit plan in December 1984, parallels that of West Hollywood in many respects. The city, with about 1,625 municipal employees, pays the entire cost of insuring its workers' partners, 116 of whom are covered at present. No participating partner has ever filed an AIDS claim.

Nancy Adler, Berkeley's benefits representative, estimates that domestic-partner coverage accounts for about $125,000, or 2.8 percent, of the city's overall health insurance costs of $4.5 million. "Our experience with domestic partners has been very good," she says.

When Berkeley's two health maintenance organizations originally agreed to the city's domestic-partnership plan, they raised premiums by 2 percent in anticipation of increased costs. One of the HMOs, Kaiser Permanente, later said that the city's risk is no greater with domestic partners than it was when coverage was limited to spouses and children.[7]

Other health-care experts have reached similar conclusions. According to Lyn S. Thompson, vice president of Consumers United Insurance Co. of Washington, D.C., "Smoking and exercise are better predictors of who will file claims than are sexual orientation or marital status." Consumers United routinely includes domestic partners in its health-care coverage.

In Thompson's opinion, "approximately 80 percent of all disease and illness starts with poor coping skills. Things like anxiety, stress and repressed anger have far more to do with who gets sick and who does not than does one's sexual preference — or one's gender, for that matter."

Several reasons are cited to explain why participation in domestic-partner benefit plans is less than many observers had expected. For one thing, many partners already have coverage under their own work-related group health insurance plans. In addition, some partners not covered under other insurance forgo the benefits because they do not want to publicly acknowledge their homosexuality.

But the main reason why participation is low may be that employer-provided health benefits for domestic partners are considered taxable by the Internal Revenue Service (IRS). The agency announced its policy in May 1990 in response to a query from the city of Seattle, which includes domestic partners in its benefit program for municipal employees. Unless the domestic partner is a legal spouse or qualifies as a dependent under Section 152 of the Internal Revenue Code, the IRS declared, the fair-market value of the employer-provided benefits will be taxed as ordinary income. In general, Section 152 defines dependents as relatives by blood or marriage.

Summing up the current situation, the Foster Higgins study concluded: "It's too early to determine the direction most employers will go. Domestic-partner health coverage is a complex issue that many are uncomfortable with. Clearly, those employers adding coverage are pioneers. But the question remains whether others will follow in large numbers."[8] ∎

BACKGROUND

Church's Early Role

The traditional family, bound together by marriage, has long been the Western world's basic household unit, ensuring the cohesion and continuity of society as a whole. Until the 16th century, however, marriage could be effected by the man and the woman themselves, acting alone and without formal ceremony. Words of commitment were spoken by them, though almost always in private. Moreover, the sacramental act was not the exchange of vows but physical consummation of the union.

The Council of Trent, in 1563, gave the church a prominent role in solemnizing marriages. A valid wedding ceremony, the council decreed, must be performed before a priest and in the presence of at least two witnesses. This new pronouncement of canon law applied only in countries that had remained faithful to the Roman Catholic Church after the Reformation.

England, which broke with Rome during the reign of King Henry VIII, was not one of those countries. However, Lord Hardwicke's reform of the marriage laws in 1753 made it necessary, for a marriage to be held legally valid, to go through a ceremony in accordance with Church of England rites. Informal or "common law" marriages thereafter became virtually impossible in England. *(See story, p. 771.)*

Nonetheless, such marriages remained acceptable in newly settled overseas territories of the European powers, including what is now the United States. During the early days on the Western frontier, a minister or a justice of the peace — to say nothing of a church — often was not readily available. Even today, common-law marriage is recognized in 13 states and the District of Columbia.*

---

*The 13 states that recognize common-law marriages are Alabama, Colorado, Georgia, Idaho, Iowa, Kansas, Montana, Ohio, Oklahoma, Pennsylvania, Rhode Island, South Carolina and Texas. In addition, 16 states (Arizona, Arkansas, California, Delaware, Hawaii, Maryland, Minnesota, Missouri, Nebraska, New York, North Carolina, Oregon, Tennessee, Virginia, Washington and West Virginia) recognize common-law marriages that are valid in the states where contracted, even though they do not recognize such marriages contracted in their own states.

Controversy Over Same-Sex Marriages

Of the many controversies associated with domestic partnership, same-sex marriage strikes the most sparks. All 50 states and the District of Columbia prohibit such unions. Moreover, the notion violates fundamental precepts of organized religion, and polls show that Americans oppose it by overwhelming margins. Even so, same-sex marriage is now being openly discussed — sometimes approvingly. *(See "At Issue," p. 777.)*

"Gay marriage would simply recognize a consistent cross-cultural, trans-historical minority and allow that significant minority to also participate in an important social institution," a contributor to *Commonweal* magazine wrote last fall.†

He went on to cite two other prospective benefits: "In the wake of AIDS, encouraging gay monogamy is simply rational public health policy. Just as important, gay marriage would reduce the number of closeted gays who marry heterosexual partners, as an estimated 20 percent of all gays do, in an effort to conform to social pressure — but at enormous cost to themselves, their children and their opposite-sex spouses."

But Robert Knight, director of the Family Research Council's Cultural Studies Project, says that sanctioning same-sex marriage would "destroy the idea of [traditional] marriage as the symbol of legitimacy and the foundation of social relations and society itself. It would open the door to a more relativistic view of sexual relations. Once you say, in effect, that traditional marriage is no better or worse than any other arrangement, and you adjust your legal system to reflect that belief, you are advancing the gay-rights agenda."

In a case that was closely followed by homosexual-rights groups and their opponents, two Washington, D.C., men in 1990 sued the District of Columbia government for $1 million for denying them a marriage license and violating the city's human rights laws, which outlaw discrimination on the basis of sexual orientation. The city's marriage laws expressly prohibit polygamous and incestuous marriages, but not same-sex ones. The plaintiffs, Craig Dean and Patrick Gill, said they sought not only the respect and recognition that marriage bestows but also its attendant legal advantages, including automatic inheritance and the right to decide on medical care for each other.

In a decision handed down Dec. 31, 1991, Judge Shellie F. Bowers of D.C. Superior Court ruled against Dean and Gill. Citing their argument that the early Christian church was "ambivalent but tolerant" about same-sex marriage, Bowers declared: "[O]ne of the most important characteristics of fundamental moral principles is that they are immutable — not simply malleable reflections of the mores of the moment. The Ten Commandments are as relevant today as they were at Mount Sinai, and their observance or non-observance no less consequential. Thus, if homosexual marriage were anathema to Christian religious dogma and morally repugnant, it would still be so, regardless of the number of clergy willing to participate in such a ceremony or the number of centuries over which they did so." ††

---

† Brent Hartinger, "A Case for Gay Marriage," *Commonweal*, Nov. 22, 1991, p. 681. Hartinger is a Seattle-based freelance writer.

†† *Craig Dean and Patrick Gill v. District of Columbia*, Dec. 31, 1991 (civil case no. 13892-90).

As informal marriages became less common in the United States, social disapproval of non-traditional households grew. Unmarried opposite-sex couples occupying the same residence were often said to be "living in sin." At the same time, adult same-sex couples portrayed themselves as "roommates" to cloud the nature of their relationship.

The 'Palimony' Lawsuit

The social upheaval of the 1960s brought a loosening of sexual mores and seemingly increased acceptance of unconventional living arrangements. These trends, in turn, eventually gave rise to the notion that unmarried domestic partners might have legally enforceable property rights similar to those enjoyed by married couples. This novel premise was put to the test in *Marvin v. Marvin*, a decade-long court action that received extensive media coverage in the United States and overseas and is still discussed in American law journals.

The plaintiff in the case was Michelle Triola Marvin, a singer who lived with Academy Award-winning film actor Lee Marvin for seven years beginning in 1964. The couple separated in 1970, shortly after Triola had legally changed her name to Marvin. According to testimony, Lee Marvin provided monthly support payments for 14 months, then abruptly terminated them.

In February 1972, Michelle Marvin filed suit against him, claiming she was entitled to half the $3.8 million he had earned while they lived together as well as $100,000 to compensate her for the loss of her career. She based her claim on a remark she said Lee had once made to her: "What I have is yours, and what you have is mine."

Continued on p. 770

Chronology

1970s *The influential Marvin v. Marvin "palimony" case begins wending its way through the courts.*

February 1972
Michelle Triola Marvin, a former live-in companion of film actor Lee Marvin, files suit seeking one-half of the $3.8 million he had earned during their seven-year relationship. A trial court's dismissal of the suit is later affirmed by the California Court of Appeal.

December 1976
Ruling in Michelle Marvin's favor, the California Supreme Court reverses earlier judicial decisions in the case and remands her suit to a lower court for trial.

April 1979
Judge Arthur K. Marshall of California Superior Court in Los Angeles orders Lee Marvin to pay $104,000 to Michelle Marvin "so that she may have the economic means to re-educate herself and to learn new employable skills."

1980s *Numerous municipalities, nonprofits, unions and private companies enact ordinances or adopt policies offering certain spousal benefits to the unmarried domestic partners of their employees.*

August 1981
Reversing Judge Marshall, the California Court of Appeal rules that Lee Marvin does not have to pay $104,000 to Michelle Marvin.

October 1981
The California Supreme Court affirms the appellate court ruling in *Marvin v. Marvin* — the case's last chapter.

December 1984
Berkeley, Calif., becomes the first U.S. municipality to offer benefits to the domestic partners of municipal workers.

July 1989
The New York Court of Appeals rules in the case of *Brashchi v. Stahl Associates* that the term family "should not be rigidly restricted to those people who have formalized their relationship by obtaining . . . a marriage certificate or an adoption order."

1990s *As the domestic-partnership movement gathers momentum, conservative opposition to it becomes more vocal.*

December 1990
At the urging of Los Angeles attorney Thomas F. Coleman, an expert on domestic-partnership law, non-traditional families begin registering with the California secretary of state's office to gain legal status as unincorporated nonprofit groups under the state's Corporation Code.

April 1991
Montefiore Medical Center in New York City becomes the largest private employer in the country to provide health benefits for homosexual employees and their partners. Lotus Development Corp. of Cambridge, Mass., adopts a similar policy in September 1991.

November 1991
The Minnesota Court of Appeals grants guardianship of Karen Kowalski, a 35-year-old woman left brain-damaged and quadriplegic by a 1983 auto accident, to Karen Thompson, her lesbian lover. According to the court, Kowalski and Thompson "are a family of affinity, which ought to be accorded respect."

April 1992
Despite strong opposition by local religious leaders, the District of Columbia approves legislation granting benefits to the domestic partners of city employees.

May 1992
Vice President Dan Quayle, speaking about "family values" in San Francisco, attacks a TV sitcom. "It doesn't help matters when prime-time TV has Murphy Brown — a character who supposedly epitomizes today's intelligent, highly paid, professional woman — mocking the importance of fathers by bearing a child alone and calling it just another lifestyle choice," Quayle says.

June 1992
In a statement sent to U.S. Catholic bishops, the Vatican endorses discrimination against homosexuals in such areas as housing, employment, health benefits and military service. Such a policy, the statement says, will help promote the traditional family and protect society.

July 1992
In his acceptance speech at the Democratic convention, presidential nominee Bill Clinton envisions an America that includes "every traditional family and every extended family, every two-parent family, every single-parent family and every foster family. Every family."

July 1992
In approving the District of Columbia appropriations bill for fiscal 1993, the Senate approves language barring implementation of the city's recently enacted domestic-partnership law.

Continued from p. 768

At first, the case went badly for Michelle Marvin, whose attorney, Marvin Mitchelson, built a national reputation in the 1970s for representing clients in such "palimony" cases. A trial court's dismissal of her charges was subsequently affirmed by the California Court of Appeal. In December 1976, however, the California Supreme Court struck down the earlier decisions and remanded the case to lower court for reconsideration. In doing so, the high court endorsed the proposition that unmarried couples had certain rights and obligations.

"In summary," said the court, "we base our opinion on the principle that adults who voluntarily live together and engage in sexual relations are nonetheless as competent as any other persons to contract respecting their earnings and property rights.... So long as the agreement does not rest upon illicit meretricious consideration [that is, payment for sexual services], the parties may order their economic affairs as they choose, and no policy precludes the courts from enforcing such agreements."

The court went on to observe that "The mores of society have ... changed so radically in regard to cohabitation that we cannot impose a standard based on alleged moral considerations that have apparently been so widely abandoned by so many."

In an opinion issued April 17, 1979, Judge Arthur K. Marshall of the California Superior Court in Los Angeles concluded that no express or implied contract existed between Michelle and Lee Marvin. Without a contract, the judge said, there was no legal basis for approving a property settlement comparable to that between a husband and wife. To sanction a settlement under such conditions, he said, would be tantamount to recognizing the concept of common-law marriage, which California abolished in 1895.

Nonetheless, Marshall awarded Mi-

chelle $104,000 as an "equitable remedy." * The money, he said, could be used "for rehabilitation purposes so that she may have the economic means to re-educate herself and to learn new, employable skills or to refurbish those utilized, for example, during her most recent employment and so that she may return from her status as companion of a motion picture star to a separate, independent but perhaps more prosaic existence."

Michelle Marvin's triumph was to be short-lived. In August 1981, the state Court of Appeal overturned the $104,000 award, declaring that it was "without merit in either equity or law." Two months later, the state Supreme Court declined to reinstate the award, bringing the Marvin case to an end.

Fallout from the Marvin Case

In the meantime, the Marvin case had inspired a spate of multimillion-dollar lawsuits featuring other celebrities and their spurned housemates. Among those sued for support by former lovers were actors James Daly and Nick Nolte and popular music stars Alice Cooper, Rod Stewart, Ringo Starr and Peter Frampton.

But a 1979 Illinois case involving two non-celebrities drew the most attention from legal scholars. In *Hewitt v. Hewitt,* Victoria Hewitt said she was entitled to a half share of the profits and properties acquired by her and Robert Hewitt during the 15 years they lived together in an unmarried "family relationship."

The court rejected her claim, declaring in effect that the interests of society must take precedence over those of individuals. "[H]ave the increasing number of unmarried cohabitants and changing mores of our society reached the point at which

---

*The sum is approximately equal to a weekly salary of $1,000 — the highest scale Michelle Marvin ever earned as a singer — over two years.

the general welfare of the citizens of this state is best served by a return to something resembling the judicially created common-law marriage our legislature outlawed in 1905?" the court asked. Answering that rhetorical question in the negative, the Illinois court said issues of public policy in the domestic relations field were best left to the legislature.

Judicial recognition of mutual property rights between unmarried cohabitants, the court added, would violate the state's recently enacted Marriage and Dissolution of Marriage Act, whose stated objective was to "strengthen and preserve the integrity of marriage and safeguard family relationships."

Impact on Domestic Partnerships

Opinion is split on whether *Marvin v. Marvin* and the cases that followed in its wake helped energize the domestic-partnership movement. Robert Knight of the Family Research Council thinks there is a connection. The Marvin case, in his view, "was definitely a steppingstone toward delegitimizing marriage. It was an attempt to do an end run around marriage."

Ivy Young of the National Gay & Lesbian Task Force disagrees. "Domestic-partnership issues are more about protecting families than about fretting over who gets what if you split up," she says. "It's about obtaining rights that everyone else is entitled to, ranging from something as simple as discount membership at the local Y all the way up to and including health benefits in the workplace. It wouldn't be fair to say *Marvin* was the genesis of the movement. It really arose from the changing nature of the family, particularly since World War II."

Attorney Thomas Coleman takes a middle position. He believes *Marvin* "gave unmarried people some hope that they weren't going to be treated as outcasts by the courts." That hope, in turn, encouraged them to perse-

The Evolution of Common-Law Marriage

Domestic partnership is often confused with the centuries-old custom of common-law marriage, and no wonder. Common-law marriages are recognized in more than a dozen states and the District of Columbia *(see p. 767)*, enabling a man and a woman to live together as husband and wife without going through either a civil or a religious ceremony. After they have cohabited for a specified length of time, typically seven years, their union acquires the status of marriage.

Common-law marriage was widespread in the United States during the pre-independence period and through much of the 19th century. Michael Grossberg, the author of *Governing the Hearth: Law and the Family in 19th Century America* (1985), attributes its popularity to the American ethic of individualism and esteem for personal privacy. By the end of the 19th century, however, social reformers had succeeded in replacing common-law marriage with mandatory formalities meant to strengthen the marital bond.

Around the same time, the U.S. Supreme Court affirmed the continuing validity of common-law marriage in some circumstances. In the 1877 case of *Meister v. Moore,* the court held that a statute mandating wedding formalities should not be regarded as the only legal route to marriage, provided the legislature had refrained from declaring that it was. Common-law marriage must remain available unless specifically forbidden, the court ruled, "because marriage is a thing of common right, because it is the policy of the State to encourage it, and because ... any other construction would compel holding illegitimate the offspring of many parents conscious of no violation of the law."

One of the chief objections to common-law marriage is that it promotes loose sexual behavior by allowing couples to cohabit without taking on the responsibilities that a civil or religious ceremony imposes. Domestic relations expert Homer H. Clark Jr. disagreed. "The assertion that common-law marriage encourages vice is ... fallacious, since common-law marriage has precisely the opposite effect," Clark wrote in *The Law of Domestic Relations in the United States* (1968). "Recognizing nonceremonial unions gives them status and to that extent reduces vice."

But Clark took a less indulgent view in a 1976 *Willamette Law Journal* article on "The New Marriage." Persons who "wish to undertake [property] rights and duties ... have a clearly defined method for doing so [that is, by marrying]," he wrote. "Those who do not wish to undertake them have an equally clearly defined method for avoiding them, that is, by not marrying. Those who advocate the freedom that accompanies the refusal to marry but who at the same time wish the law to impose property rights and duties upon cohabiting but unmarried people are indulging in the great American dream of wishing to have their cake and eat it too."

When Clark wrote that article, the influential case of *Marvin v. Marvin* was winding its way through the California courts *(see p. 768)*. The case centered on a claim by Michelle Triola Marvin, who had lived with film actor Lee Marvin for seven years, that she was entitled to half of the $3.8 million he had earned during their time together.

According to some experts, *Marvin v. Marvin* gave impetus to the domestic-partnership movement by establishing that unmarried couples, at least in California, could make legally enforceable contracts governing the disposition of property. Los Angeles attorney Thomas F. Coleman, an authority on domestic-partnership law, believes that *Marvin* may have done more than that. "The more rights that are built for unmarried couples," he says, "the more we're returning to common-law marriage through the back door."

vere in their quest. To that extent, Coleman thinks, *Marvin* did "lend some steam" to the domestic-partnership movement.

Recent Rulings

State and federal laws prohibiting discrimination based on marital status have both helped and retarded the spread of domestic partnership. Safeguards against such discrimination vary widely in scope. For instance, states have outlawed marital-status bias in housing, employment, public accommodations and the granting of credit. In 1974, moreover, Congress enacted the Federal Equal Credit Opportunity Act, which bars discrimination on the basis of marital status in all credit transactions.

The trouble is that most of these laws fail to say precisely what is meant by "marital status" or what constitutes discrimination based upon it. As a result, courts have been left to supply their own definitions and remedies. In general, they have tended to adopt one of two contrasting approaches: a narrow, all-or-none construction of the law, or a broad, more inclusive interpretation.

Under the narrow view, courts find marital-status discrimination unlawful only when a person is treated differently solely because he or she is single, married, divorced, separated or

Recognizing Domestic Partners

More than two dozen cities, counties and other local jurisdictions across the country have adopted laws or policies that extend benefits to the domestic partners of government employees. The range of benefits varies widely. Some communities offer extensive health and dental benefits to employees' domestic partners; others extend sick and bereavement leave to employees in domestic partnerships, but offer no other benefits.

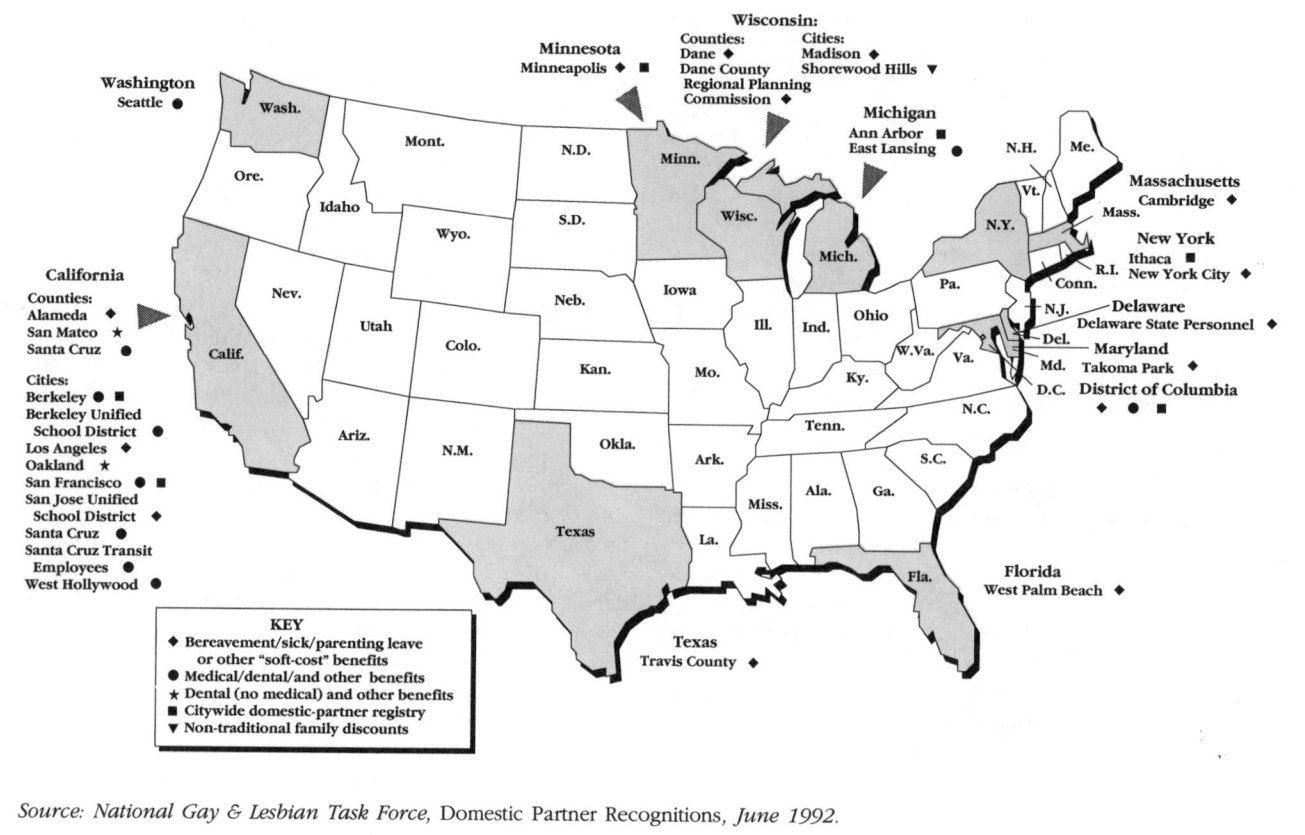

Washington
Seattle ●

Minnesota
Minneapolis ◆ ■

Wisconsin:
Counties: Cities:
Dane ◆   Madison ◆
Dane County   Shorewood Hills ▼
Regional Planning
Commission ◆

Michigan
Ann Arbor ■
East Lansing ●

Massachusetts
Cambridge ◆

New York
Ithaca ■
New York City ◆

Delaware
Delaware State Personnel ◆

Maryland
Takoma Park ◆

District of Columbia
◆ ● ■

California
Counties:
Alameda ◆
San Mateo ★
Santa Cruz ●

Cities:
Berkeley ● ■
Berkeley Unified
 School District ●
Los Angeles ◆
Oakland ★
San Francisco ● ■
San Jose Unified
 School District ●
Santa Cruz ●
Santa Cruz Transit
 Employees ●
West Hollywood ●

Florida
West Palm Beach ◆

Texas
Travis County ◆

KEY
◆ Bereavement/sick/parenting leave
   or other "soft-cost" benefits
● Medical/dental/and other benefits
★ Dental (no medical) and other benefits
■ Citywide domestic-partner registry
▼ Non-traditional family discounts

Source: National Gay & Lesbian Task Force, Domestic Partner Recognitions, *June 1992.*

widowed, as the case may be. Courts adopting this approach thus will strike down a policy based on marital status only if the policy affects every individual within a given marital category.

The narrow view of marital-status discrimination often comes into play in cases challenging local housing policies, as when an unmarried couple is refused accommodations available to married couples. For example, the 1981 case of *Prince George's County v. Greenbelt Homes Inc.* involved a couple who had been barred from a cooperative housing development because they were not husband and wife.

The plaintiffs in *Prince George's* argued that since their application would have been accepted had they been married, the cooperative's policy discriminated against them because each was single. The Maryland Court of Appeals disagreed. It held that "neither complainant ... was denied membership [in the cooperative] *individually* because of his or her *individual* status. While each separately had a marital status, collectively they did not. Only marriage as prescribed by law can change the marital status of an individual to a new legal entity of husband and wife."

In sum, courts adopting the narrow view of marital-status discrimination say that unmarried plaintiffs have no protection because the chal- lenged policies do not affect all unmarried applicants, only those who choose to live with an intimate partner outside the bounds of wedlock. Challenges fail, that is, when the disputed policy considers a person's marital status in conjunction with some other factor.

The narrow view of marital-status bias obviously works to the disadvantage of domestic partners, especially those of the same sex. Opposite-sex domestic partners can overcome the narrow view's strictures by marrying, should they choose do so, but same-sex partners do not enjoy that option.

Unlike courts adhering to the narrow view, courts adopting a broader interpretation of marital-status bias hold that the identity or position of one's partner may be taken into account in deciding whether a policy is unlawfully discriminatory. The broad view protects plaintiffs from policies based on marital-status classifications even when those policies affect only a portion of the protected group.

California Court's Broad View of Discrimination

The California Court of Appeal's decision in the 1976 case of *Atkisson v. Kern Housing Authority* showed how the broad view of marital-status discrimination is applied in practice. In *Atkisson,* a divorced mother of six children challenged a local public-housing policy prohibiting her boyfriend from living with her. The court held that the policy, which barred low-income housing tenants from living with anyone of the opposite sex not related to the tenant by blood, marriage or adoption, illegally discriminated on the basis of marital status. The court declared that the policy "automatically exclude[d] all unmarried cohabiting adults; a class of persons defined by their marital status."

Some legal scholars are troubled by the fact that laws barring marital-status discrimination have created a protected class quite different from the other groups usually covered by civil rights statutes. Persons defined by race, sex, national origin or physical disability usually cannot alter those conditions. In contrast, some individuals have several spouses over the course of a lifetime, meaning that they alternate between being single and being married.

The state's traditional interest in promoting marriage as a source of social stability also gives some experts pause. Government, in their view, is trying to have it both ways. On the one hand, it encourages marriage by granting husbands and wives certain legal rights not available to single persons. On the other hand, it enacts laws penalizing discriminatory policies and practices that favor persons of a particular marital status — usually married couples.

Some legal scholars are troubled by the fact that laws barring marital-status discrimination have created a protected class quite different from other groups usually covered by civil rights statutes.

Key Issues in New York Case

The case of *Braschi v. Stahl Associates Co.*, decided by the New York Court of Appeals in 1989, seemed to crystallize some key domestic-partnership issues.

It began with an action initiated by a tenant, Miguel Braschi, for a preliminary injunction against an evicting landlord. Braschi and Leslie Blanchard had lived together as a couple for more than 10 years in Blanchard's rent-controlled New York City apartment, until Blanchard's death in September 1986. The two men considered themselves spouses, as did their friends and families. Their social, familial and financial lives were fully intertwined.

In his effort to forestall eviction, Braschi cited a New York City regulation stating that a landlord may not dispossess "either the surviving spouse of the deceased tenant or some other member of the deceased tenant's family who has been living with the ten-

ant." But the term "family" is not defined in the city's rent-control ordinance, and the measure's legislative history does not specifically refer to the non-eviction provision.

In finding for Braschi, the court said the intended safeguard against sudden eviction "should not rest on fictitious legal distinctions or genetic history, but instead should find its foundation in the reality of family life." Factors to weigh in evaluating a family relationship, the court held, are "its exclusivity and longevity, the level of emotional and financial commitment, the manner in which the parties ... conducted their everyday lives and held themselves out to society, and the reliance placed upon one another for daily family services." Blanchard and Braschi's relationship, the court ruled, met this test.

Domestic-partnership activists hailed the *Braschi* decision, while conservatives expressed dismay. The thrust of the court's opinion, *The Wall Street Journal* declared in an editorial, "is to diminish incentives for marriage by anyone, meaning that on this most important and private relationship the law of contracts increasingly will be superseded by ad hoc decisions by judges. Given the view of the world held by some judges, that doesn't sound like progress to us."

But the legal reasoning in *Braschi* apparently failed to impress some jurists, as indicated by a case decided two years ago by the Surrogate's Court for New York County (Manhattan).* When Thomas Cooper died in February 1988, his longtime companion, Ernest Chin, entered a claim against the will on the ground that he was a "surviving spouse." He said

---

*The Surrogate's Court for New York County has jurisdiction over probate, adoption, guardianship and about 60 miscellaneous matters.

the only reason he and Cooper had never wed was that state law barred same-sex marriages. Chin complained that this distinction denied him equal protection of the law.

The court rejected Chin's claim, asserting that the state had "a compelling interest in fostering the traditional institution of marriage ... whether based on self-preservation, procreation, or in nurturing and keeping alive the concept of marriage and family as a basic fabric of our society." It also declared that *Braschi* was inapplicable because "There is a great distinction between being part of a family entitled to the protection of rent control laws because of public policy and legislative intent, and in being the surviving spouse of a decedent." [9]

CURRENT SITUATION

New Partner Laws

In its present form, the domestic-partnership movement is barely a decade old. The San Francisco Board of Supervisors approved an ordinance in 1982 extending health benefits to the partners of city employees, but the measure was vetoed by then-Mayor Dianne Feinstein, who called the legislation "vague and unclear."

Seven years later, the supervisors unanimously passed a somewhat weaker law recognizing gay, lesbian and unmarried heterosexual couples by offering them certificates similar to marriage licenses. Eligible couples could obtain a certificate by publicly filing a declaration of domestic partnership with the city clerk and paying a $35 fee. However, the measure was defeated in a referendum held in November 1989.

In 1990, a watered-down version of the defeated certificate ordinance was placed on the San Francisco ballot and was approved by 54 percent of the voters.* This law, still on the books, defines domestic partners as "two people who have chosen to share one another's lives in an intimate and committed personal relationship of mutual caring, who live together and have signed a declaration of domestic partnership in which they have agreed to be jointly responsible for basic living expenses."

To obtain a certificate, partners must verify that they are not married to other mates and are at least 18 years old; are not related in a way that would legally bar marriage; share living expenses; and have been free of previous domestic partnerships for at least six months. Dissolving a domestic partnership in San Francisco requires the filing of a separate petition with the city clerk.

Under city law, domestic partners in San Francisco are accorded family hospital-visitation rights — an important benefit for many partners of AIDS victims. However, the city certificate does not give partners the full array of entitlements available to married couples. In other words, domestic partners have no automatic rights to inherit or jointly accumulate property, to seek spousal support after divorce or to obtain power of attorney.

Pioneers Include Cities, Colleges, Companies and Nonprofits

More than two dozen cities, counties and other local jurisdictions across the country have adopted laws or policies benefiting domestic partners, mostly during the past three years. *(See map, p. 772.)* California has been the most active state in this respect. Many of the municipalities with domestic-partnership laws or policies are large cities like Los Angeles, Minneapolis and New York, or college communities like Cambridge, Mass., Ithaca, N.Y., and Ann Arbor, Mich.

Moreover, some colleges and universities have adopted domestic-partnership policies of their own. A 1990 study by the National Gay & Lesbian Task Force found that 23 colleges and universities offered same-sex partners of their employees one or more of eight specified family-type benefits, such as parental leave and medical insurance.[10] Several additional colleges have adopted similar policies since then, including Oberlin, Ohio State, Pitzer College (Claremont, Calif.) and the State University of New York-Purchase.

About three dozen private organizations, including companies, advocacy groups and labor unions, have adopted some sort of domestic partnership or alternative family benefits program. The list includes Ben & Jerry's Homemade Inc., Levi Strauss Co., *The Village Voice*, Greenpeace International, the Human Rights Campaign Fund, the National Organization for Women, the National Treasury Employees Union, Local 476 of the American Federation of Government Employees and the Oil, Chemical and Atomic Workers International Union.

The range of benefits available to domestic partners varies considerably. Some organizations offer extensive health and life insurance coverage while others provide only "soft-cost" benefits like bereavement, sick and paternity leave.

In April 1991, mammoth Montefiore Medical Center in New York City began providing health benefits to the partners of its homosexual employees. The change in Montefiore's benefits policy applied only to persons who were unable to marry because of the legal prohibition against same-sex marriage. The center has about 10,000 employees.

---

*The effective date of the law was Feb. 14, 1991 — Valentine's Day.

Five months later, in September 1991, Lotus Development Corp., with 3,100 workers, announced it would offer the partners of its homosexual employees the same benefits enjoyed by the spouses of married employees. The computer firm said it was not offering the same benefits to the domestic partners of unmarried heterosexual employees because those couples had the option of marrying, while homosexual couples did not.

Legal Support

Meanwhile, other developments affecting the domestic-partnership movement were occurring on the legal front. In May 1989, for example, the Denver City Council repealed a 36-year-old zoning ordinance that prohibited unmarried couples from living in some of the city's more affluent neighborhoods. An estimated 6 to 8 percent of the city's single-family houses were covered by the rule. The old law was replaced by a measure allowing two adults not related by blood, marriage or adoption to live in the same house with their children.

In December 1990, Thomas Coleman came up with the idea of harnessing a section of the California Corporation Code to the cause of domestic partnership. The loosely written section had been used mainly to register unincorporated nonprofit groups such as fraternities, garden clubs and homeowners' associations. Coleman encouraged non-traditional families to register with the secretary of state's office to gain similar legal status.[11]

Coleman acknowledges that a registration certificate is, at present, mainly an ego-booster to the family that receives it. However, he hopes the official recognition that the document confers may eventually help non-traditional families obtain tangible benefits now denied them. Coleman says at least six other states —

Private Sector Recognition

The companies and organizations listed below are among the growing number of private sector concerns that recognize domestic partners in employee or member health-benefit plans.

American Civil Liberties Union, San Francisco, Calif.
American Friends Service Committee, Philadelphia, Pa.
American Psychological Association, Washington, D.C.
Ben & Jerry's Homemade, Inc., Waterbury, Vt.
Beth Israel Medical Center, New York, N.Y.
Committee of Interns and Residents Staff Union, New York, N.Y.
Crum & Forster Insurance Corp. (health benefits for unmarried
     heterosexual couples in common-law marriages), Basking Ridge, N.J.
Gardener's Supply Co., Burlington, Vt.
Greenpeace International, Washington, D.C.
Human Rights Campaign Fund, Washington, D.C.
Lambda Legal Defense & Education Fund, New York, N.Y.
Levi Strauss Company, San Francisco, Calif.
Lotus Development Corp., Cambridge, Mass.
MCA/Universal, Hollywood, Calif.
Minnesota Communications Group/Minnesota Public Radio, St. Paul, Minn.
Montefiore Medical Center, New York, N.Y.
National Gay & Lesbian Task Force Policy Institute, Washington, D.C.
National Organization for Women, Washington, D.C.
Para Transit, Inc. Sacramento, Calif.
***The Village Voice*, New York, N.Y.**

Source: National Gay & Lesbian Task Force, Domestic Partner Recognitions, *June 1992.*

Michigan, New Jersey, Oregon, Virginia, West Virginia and Wisconsin — have similar registration laws on their statute books.

In a court ruling of special interest to homosexual domestic partners, the Minnesota Court of Appeals last Nov. 17 overturned a lower court decision and awarded guardianship of a brain-damaged, quadriplegic lesbian to her longtime lover. The appeals court held that the lower court had abused its discretion in awarding guardianship of Sharon Kowalski, 35, to a family friend of her parents instead of to Karen Thompson, her lover. Thompson had been battling Kowalski's parents for guardianship ever since Kowalski was disabled in a 1983 auto accident.

"All the medical testimony established that Sharon has the capacity reliably to express a preference in this case, and she has clearly chosen to return home with Thompson if possible," the court said. "This choice is further supported by the fact that Thompson and Sharon are a family of affinity, which ought to be accorded respect." Thompson's lawyer, M. Sue Wilson, commented: "This seems to be the first guardianship case in the nation in which an appeals court recognized a homosexual partner's rights as tantamount to those of a spouse."

Legal Setbacks

Notwithstanding such victories, the domestic-partnership movement has suffered its share of legal setbacks in recent years. For one thing, various courts have held that landlords may refuse to rent residential property to unmarried couples on religious grounds. A case decided last November by the California Court of

Appeal in Los Angeles laid out the issue with almost textbook clarity. The plaintiffs were an elderly Roman Catholic couple who had refused to rent an apartment to a young woman and her boyfriend because they considered sex out of wedlock to be "a mortal sin."

The California Employment and Fair Housing Commission had awarded the young couple $7,480 in damages, ruling that the landlords violated state housing laws barring "marital-status" discrimination as well as the Unruh Civil Rights Law, which prohibits arbitrary discrimination.[12] It was the landlords' challenge of the commission's action that was heard by the Court of Appeal.

In finding for the elderly couple, the court held that, "Although the law has ... acknowledged a societal trend toward cohabitation without marriage, it has not affirmatively promoted it as a matter of government policy." Noting that the "sincerity and depth" of the landlords' religious convictions "are unquestioned," the court went on to rule that, "No paramount and compelling state interest overbalances the landlords' legitimate claim of the free exercise of religion, and the landlords are entitled to an exemption" from state anti-discrimination laws.

Much of the backlash against non-traditional living arrangements is directed at homosexuals. For instance, a law that took effect June 15 in Springfield, Ore., prohibits the city from "promoting, encouraging or facilitating homosexuality." It also blocks protection of homosexuals from discrimination in employment and housing. The Springfield ordinance was enacted in response to a campaign by homosexuals last spring for an anti-discrimination law.

A domestic-partnership law enacted in April in Washington, D.C., also has come under heavy fire because of the numerous benefits it offers to the partners of homosexual city employees. The law allows partners to register with the city as couples and gives those who work for the District government new medical leave. It also gives tax incentives to private employers who agree to insure domestic partners, and it requires local hospitals to accord partners the same visiting rights as spouses. The D.C. City Council approved the law despite strenuous opposition from area church leaders, including Cardinal James A. Hickey, the Roman Catholic archbishop of Washington.

Congress may yet have the last word on the matter. In approving the fiscal 1993 appropriations bill for the District on July 30, the Senate agreed to language barring the city from implementing its domestic-partnership law. Sen. Trent Lott, R-Miss., who led the Senate campaign against the law, told his colleagues: "We must begin to take a stand for the family. We must make the difficult moral decisions of right and wrong, and we must reach the conclusion, based on evidence and moral precepts, that all lifestyles are not equal. We must decide that the institution of traditional marriage is preferable and superior, and our policies should reflect that conclusion and its moral imperative." The D.C. law's fate now rests with the House-Senate conference committee that will iron out differences between the two chambers' versions of the appropriations bill this fall.

Vatican Assails Gay Rights

By coincidence, the battle over Washington's domestic-partnership law came at a time when gay and lesbian rights groups were assailing a Vatican document that suggested some forms of discrimination against homosexuals are justified. The document, issued in mid-June by the Congregation of the Doctrine of the Faith, restated longstanding Catholic doctrine on homosexuality.

Archbishop Daniel E. Pilarczyk of Cincinnati, president of the National Conference of Catholic Bishops, issued a statement June 22 explaining the document's intent. "The congregation's concern," he said, "is that proposals to safeguard the legitimate rights of homosexual persons not have the effect of creating a new class of legally protected *behavior,* that is, homosexual behavior, which, in time, could occupy the same position as non-discrimination against *people* because of their race, religion, gender, or ethnic background.

"The document rightly warns against legislation designed more to legitimate homosexual behavior than to secure basic civil rights and against proposals which tend to promote an equivalence between legal marriage and homosexual lifestyles."

Spokesmen for the Archdiocese of Washington and the National Council of Catholic Bishops would not say whether the Vatican document was meant to apply to domestic-partnership laws like the District of Columbia's. But many individuals caught up in the issue, pro or con, agreed that it probably did. ■

OUTLOOK

Uncertain Future

According to Robert Knight of the Family Research Council, the domestic-partnership movement's recent setbacks show that "a backlash is developing." Up till now, he says, there has been "a feeling of inevitability about these kinds of laws, because the media has pushed them full-throttle. There wasn't much resistance, because people didn't know what the laws would involve and didn't know how to resist them."

Now, Knight says, the tide of opin-

Continued on p. 778

At Issue:

Should homosexual marriages be recognized legally?

ANDREW SULLIVAN

*Editor, The New Republic**
FROM *THE NEW REPUBLIC,* AUG. 28, 1989

yes

gay marriage squares several circles at the heart of the domestic-partnership debate. Unlike domestic partnership, it allows for recognition of gay relationships, while casting no aspersions on traditional marriage. It merely asks that gays be allowed to join in.

Unlike domestic partnership, it doesn't open up avenues for heterosexuals to get benefits without the responsibilities of marriage, or a nightmare of definitional litigation. And unlike domestic partnership, it harnesses to an already established social convention the yearnings for stability and acceptance among a fast-maturing gay community.

Gay marriage also places more responsibilities upon gays: It says for the first time that gay relationships are not better or worse than straight relationships, and that the same is expected of them. And it's clear and dignified. There's a legal benefit to a clear, common symbol of commitment. There's also a personal benefit.

One of the ironies of domestic partnership is that it's not only more complicated than marriage, it's more demanding, requiring an elaborate statement of intent to qualify. It amounts to a substantial invasion of privacy. Why, after all, should gays be required to prove commitment before they get married in a way we would never dream of asking of straights?

Legalizing gay marriage would offer homosexuals the same deal society now offers heterosexuals: general social approval and specific legal advantages in exchange for a deeper and harder-to-extract-yourself-from commitment to another human being. Like straight marriage, it would foster social cohesion, emotional security and economic prudence. Since there's no reason gays should not be allowed to adopt or be foster parents, it could also help nurture children. And its introduction would not be some sort of radical break with social custom.

As it has become more acceptable for gay people to acknowledge their loves publicly, more and more have committed themselves to one another for life in full view of their families and their friends. A law institutionalizing gay marriage would merely reinforce a healthy social trend. It would also, in the wake of AIDS, qualify as a genuine public health measure. Those conservatives who deplore promiscuity among some homosexuals should be among the first to support it.

*This article was written by Sullivan before he became editor of the magazine.

BRUCE FEIN

Former U.S. Associate Deputy Attorney General
FROM *ABA JOURNAL,* JANUARY 1990

no

authorizing the marriage of homosexuals, like sanctioning polygamy, would be unenlightened social policy. The law should reserve the celebration of marriage vows for monogamous male-female attachments to further the goal of psychologically, emotionally and educationally balanced offspring.

As Justice Oliver Wendell Holmes noted, the life of the law has not been logic; it has been experience. Experience confirms that child development is skewed, scarred or retarded when either a father or mother is absent in the household.

In the area of adoption, married couples are favored over singles. The recent preferences for joint child-custody decrees in divorce proceedings tacitly acknowledge the desirability of child intimacies with both a mother and a father....

A child receives incalculable benefits in the maturing process by the joint instruction, consolation, oversight and love of a father and mother — benefits that are unavailable in homosexual households. The child enjoys the opportunity to understand and respect both sexes in a uniquely intimate climate. The likelihood of gender prejudice is thus reduced, an exceptionally worthy social objective....

To deny the right of homosexual marriage is not an argument for limiting other rights to gays, because of community animosity or vengeance. These are unacceptable policy motivations if law is to be civilized. Several states and localities protect homosexuals against discrimination in employment or housing. In New York, a state law confers on a homosexual the rent-control benefits of a deceased partner. Other jurisdictions have eschewed special legal rights for homosexuals, and the military excludes them. Experience will adjudge which of the varied legal approaches to homosexual rights has been the most enlightened.

Sober debate over homosexual rights is in short supply. The subject challenges deep-rooted and passionately held images of manhood, womanhood and parenthood, and evokes sublimated fears of ... ostracism or degradation.

Each legal issue regarding homosexuality should be examined discretely with the recognition that time has upset many fighting faiths and with the goal of balancing individual liberty against community interests. With regard to homosexual marriage, that balance is negative.

Continued from p. 776

ion has decisively turned. "People are saying, maybe we ought to re-examine these laws and see if they would be a social good or a social detriment. I think we'll see more and more efforts to overturn existing gay-rights laws and to oppose new ones. Not out of hatred of homosexuals, but because of fear of the consequences these laws bring."

In contrast, Ivy Young of the National Gay & Lesbian Task Force feels current trends favor the spread of domestic-partnership laws. She predicts the 1993 Census Bureau report on unmarried partners will prove to be "another indication that families are what people create, not what a few individuals fantasize about. We can't turn back the clock. This is not pre-World War II. And families, for any number of reasons, are structuring themselves in different ways."

Instead of talking about diversity, Young thinks more cities should set up family diversity task forces, as Los Angeles, Minneapolis and San Francisco have done. "First, the task forces looked at what constituted families in those cities. Then they looked at existing laws and policies affecting families. Finally, they discussed what needed to be done to update the laws and policies to fit current conditions."

The Los Angeles Task Force on Family Diversity, which issued its final report in May 1988, conducted the most comprehensive study of family structure ever undertaken by an American city. Among other things, the task force recommended that Los Angeles grant sick and bereavement leave to municipal employees with domestic partners. Although the City Council was willing to do so, municipal unions balked, fearing that it might jeopardize benefits to the dependents of married city workers.

However, Thomas Coleman's Family Diversity Project, which opened talks with the recalcitrant unions after the task force disbanded, eventually persuaded two major unions to in-

corporate the leave proposal into their contracts, Local 18 of the International Brotherhood of Electrical Workers, with 8,172 members, and the American Federation of State, County and Municipal Employees, with 5,197 members in Los Angeles.

Two other smaller unions later followed suit. As a result, more than 15,000 employees — a majority of the city's unionized work force — now have the domestic partner leave benefit. City Councilman Michael K. Woo, who is expected to run for mayor in 1993, has proposed amending the Los Angeles Administrative Code to extend the benefit to non-unionized municipal employees.

Coleman, principal author of the Los Angeles task force's final report, believes the domestic-partnership movement will continue to spread, though on a "spotty" basis. "It's going to be grass roots, from the bottom up," he says. However, he cautions that "There still are 12 states that make it illegal for a man and a woman to cohabit out of wedlock, and 25 states that outlaw private sex between consenting adults, especially same-sex couples."

In Coleman's view, the nation's changing demographics will eventually produce changes in the law. He notes that 1990 census data show a majority of the adults in San Diego, as well as in Alameda, Los Angeles and Sacramento counties, are not married. In fact, 43 percent of the adults in California are single.

"Of course, not every unmarried adult is living with somebody out of wedlock," says Coleman. "Some are living with siblings, or adult parents, or by themselves. Some have never wed, some are divorced, some are widowed. But one thing they all have in common is they're not currently married, and a lot of them face discrimination — in obtaining automobile insurance, for example. So there is a growing political awareness among this constituency."

Lyn Thompson of Consumers United Insurance Co. foresees no "cataclysmic breakthrough" that will put domestic-partner benefits within reach of all who qualify for them. The pervasiveness of homophobia, she feels, will act as a brake on domestic partnership for some time to come. "Here we're brushing against the issue of what the Bible says and what the preachers say. But society is changing, and the people in it are changing also. Institutions historically take much longer to respond to change than people do."

Notes

[1] Quoted in *U.S. News & World Report,* Aug. 21, 1989.

[2] Jessie Bernard, *The Future of Marriage* (1972), p. 302.

[3] The Family Research Council is a conservative think tank in Washington, D.C., that aims to preserve the "traditional" family.

[4] Massachusetts Mutual Life Insurance Co., *American Family Values Study,* 1989.

[5] National Gay & Lesbian Task Force, *Domestic Partner Recognitions,* June 1992.

[6] A. Foster Higgins & Co. Inc., *Domestic Partner Health Care Coverage — 1991 Employer Survey Results,* 1991, p. 1.

[7] Hewitt Associates, *Domestic Partners and Employee Benefits 1991,* 1991, p. 15.

[8] Foster Higgins, *op. cit.,* p. 7.

[9] See *Estate of Cooper,* Dec. 28, 1990.

[10] The 23 institutions offering benefits to same-sex partners were Bowdoin, Brown, Columbia, Florida International, Georgia State, Grinnell, Harvard Law School, Hiram, Mission, Moorehead State, New York University Law School, North Dakota, Occidental, Princeton, Stanford, State University of New York-Stony Brook, Teachers College (Columbia), Union Theological Seminary and the universities of Colorado, Michigan, Oregon, Tampa and Wisconsin.

[11] According to the California secretary of state's office, 500 to 600 families have registered as associations under the California Corporation Code.

[12] The law is named for Jesse M. Unruh, a former Speaker of the California Assembly.

Bibliography

Selected Sources Used

Books

Bernard, Jessie, *The Future of Marriage*, Bantam Books, 1972.
Bernard, a sociologist, foresaw many current developments in American family life in this book written well before the domestic-partnership movement was born.

Curry, Hayden, and Denis Clifford, *A Legal Guide for Lesbian and Gay Couples*, Nolo Press, November 1991.
Essentially a how-to manual, this book examines the laws affecting homosexual couples and offers advice on such matters as drafting a "living together" contract, home ownership and medical emergencies.

Sloan, Irving J., *Living Together: Unmarrieds and the Law*, Oceana Publications Inc., 1980.
Sloan reviews the evolution of case law regarding domestic partnership in the 1970s, paying particular attention to the court decisions in *Marvin v. Marvin*, *Hewitt v. Hewitt* and *McCall v. Frampton*.

Articles

Riche, Martha Farnsworth, "The Future of the Family," *American Demographics*, March 1991.
The seemingly traditional households of baby-boomers mask fundamental changes in family lifestyles affecting all age groups, says Farnsworth. She concludes that companies looking beyond the traditional concept of family "will attract and keep more customers" than their competitors.

Turner, Scott, "In Praise of Family," *New England Law Review*, summer 1991.
Turner looks at the legal ramifications of the *Braschi v. Stahl Associates Inc.* decision.

Reports and Studies

A. Foster Higgins & Co. Inc., *Domestic Partner Health Care Coverage 1991 Employer Survey Results*, 1991.
Fifty public and private employers in the San Francisco Bay area are interviewed about their views on domestic partnership. Most express wariness about the idea of providing benefits to the unmarried partners of their workers.

Family Diversity Project, *Official Registration of Families With the Secretary of State*, May 1991.
Attorney Thomas F. Coleman, who originated the idea, describes how non-traditional families can gain official recognition as nonprofit associations by registering with the California secretary of state. He also enumerates possible future benefits of registration.

Family Research Council, *Sexual Disorientation: Faulty Research in the Homosexual Debate*, June 1992.
The council challenges assertions by gay- and lesbian-rights groups that about 10 percent of the American population is homosexual and that homosexuality is "an immutable, genetically based sexual orientation."

Hewitt Associates, *Domestic Partners and Employee Benefits, 1991.*
Case studies of selected public and private domestic partnership benefit plans are augmented by discussions of their tax implications, the attitudes of insurance companies and proof-of-partnership issues.

Lambda Legal Defense & Education Fund, *Domestic Partnership: Issues and Legislation*, 1992.
This packet of materials is divided into two parts: an overview and summary of domestic partnership legal issues and facsimiles of domestic partnership ordinances and registration forms from cities around the country. Also included is the full text of the New York Court of Appeals' ruling in *Braschi v. Stahl Associates Inc.*, a landmark in domestic partnership case law.

National Gay & Lesbian Task Force Policy Institute, *Domestic Partner Recognitions*, June 1992.
Domestic partnership laws and policies in force in various communities, companies and organizations are summarized. Excerpts from court decisions and policy resolutions provide additional perspective.

National Gay & Lesbian Task Force Policy Institute, *Domestic Partners/ Non-Traditional Family Recognition in Campus Benefit Policies 1990 Survey*, 1991.
In both summary and tabular form, this booklet sets forth the results of a nationwide survey of colleges and universities. A list of campus contacts for domestic partnership queries is included.

Task Force on Family Diversity, City of Los Angeles, *Strengthening Families: A Model for Community Action*, 1988.
Domestic partners constitute just one of the non-traditional family structures covered in this exhaustive study of living arrangements in the nation's second-largest city.

The Next Step

Additional Articles from Current Periodicals from EBSCO Publishing's Database

Books & reading

"Daddy is out of the closet," *Newsweek,* Jan. 7, 1991, p. 60.

Reports that the Boston-based Alyson Publications Inc. is publishing the first two books featuring gay and lesbian parents in a new line of books for and about children of gays.

Stier, H., "Book reviews," *American Journal of Sociology,* May 1991, p. 1587.

Reviews the book "Informal Marriage, Cohabitation and the Law, 1750-1989," by Stephen Parker.

Throop, J.R., "Out of the closet, into the chancel," *Christianity Today,* Nov. 4, 1988, p. 49.

Book review of "Living in Sin? A Bishop Rethinks Human Sexuality," by Episcopal Bishop John S. Spong. Spong proposes changes in the church's historic position on sexual morality. He supports the cohabitation of couples without marriage, the blessing of homosexual unions, and the blessing of divorce.

Employee benefits

"A new kind of spouse in the house," *U.S. News & World Report,* Aug. 21, 1989, p. 13.

Trend giving homosexual and unmarried couples benefits once reserved for married couples; examples of laws redefining the term family.

Halcrow, A., "A numbers game," *Personnel Journal,* March 1992, p. 4.

Opinion. Comments on a letter from a reader who was displeased with an article about extending health benefits to unmarried domestic partners of employees. Explains why it is important to keep things in perspective when dealing with numbers in this case, numbers of homosexuals in the population and work force.

Hammond, K.H., "Lotus opens a door for gay partners," *BusinessWeek,* Nov. 4, 1991, p. 80

Examines Lotus Development Corp.'s decision to grant benefits to gay workers' "spouses." Gay and lesbian leaders hail Lotus' actions as a milestone; Lotus' new policy has touched a nerve; fears of various companies in violating laws prohibiting homosexuality; details behind Lotus' decision; cost; private issues; details of the terms of coverage; employers granting benefits to gay workers' companions

find the costs lower than expected; redefining the "family"; minimum backlash.

Laabs, J.J., "Living arrangements," *Personnel Journal,* December 1991, p. 25.

Gives a variety of numbers and percentages on living arrangements in American households. Number of households consisting of unmarried heterosexual and gay couples; shared income; employers who provide benefits for unmarried partners; more.

Laabs, J.J., "Unmarried ... with benefits," *Personnel Journal,* December 1991, p. 62.

Reports that covering employees' non-marital domestic partners by providing health insurance and other benefits is a reality for a growing number of employers and a hotly debated question for many others. Details on programs under way at Ben & Jerry's Homemade Inc. and Lotus Development Corp.; variations on the benefits theme. INSET: Organizations that offer domestic-partner benefits.

Wiatrowski, W.J., "Family-related benefits in the workplace," *Monthly Labor Review,* March 19, 1990, p. 28.

Studies the emergence and subsequent expansion of employer-provided benefits since 1915, fueled in part by the changing needs of employees and their families. War years and boom years from 1915-1929; Great Depression and World War II from 1930-1944; return to prosperity in the period 1945-1959; changes from 1960-1974; plans for the 'new' family from 1975-1989.

Government policy

"'Family' redefined," *Christianity Today,* April 21, 1989, p. 44.

A landmark San Francisco ordinance known as the domestic-partnership proposal would, if passed, give legally married status to homosexual couples and unmarried couples living together. Most benefits to these couples would be in real estate and rental contracts.

"Will you join me in civil unionlock?" *The Economist,* May 2, 1992, p. 59.

Discusses how three French Socialist deputies have put forward proposals for a new contract of civil union, which will give some legal protection to the new array of unmarried couples in France. Illegitimacy rate in France; husbands admitting to adultery; details of the proposals.

Digitale, R., "San Francisco set to define 'family,' " *Christianity Today,* **Oct. 20, 1989, p. 44.**

Reports that San Francisco voters will soon vote on a proposal that would allow homosexual couples and unmarried heterosexual couples who live together to register their relationships. Once registered, such couples would be eligible for benefits now given only to married couples. Opposition from church groups; forecasting the outcome; economic aspects.

Jenish, D., "A couple's revolt," *Maclean's,* **Sep. 16, 1991, p. 55.**

Reports that Walter and Elaine Schachtschneider have appeared in court to challenge, under the Charter of Rights and Freedoms, the legality of Revenue Canada's discriminatory treatment of married couples. The couple claims the federal Income Tax Act treats married and unmarried couples differently, contrary to the charter's provision of equal treatment under the law. Details of the suit; decision expected in several weeks from Judge Robert King.

Heterosexuals

"Fornication dealt a blow," *Christianity Today,* **Oct. 22, 19, 1990, p. 56.**

Comments on a recent lawsuit faced by Layle French, a Christian man who chose not to rent a house to a woman who planned to live in it with an unmarried man. Charges of discrimination; ruling in favor of French.

"Marriage: practice makes imperfect?" *Psychology Today,* **July/August 1988, p. 15.**

Reports that a Yale University study has concluded that women who cohabitate with their partners before marriage are 80 percent more likely to separate or divorce than women who do not live with their spouses before marriage.

"Tea for you and your POSSLQ," *U.S. News & World Report,* **May 15, 1989, p. 17.**

Discusses POSSLQs (partners of opposite sex sharing living quarters). Rise in unmarried couples living together; Denver, Colo., City Council zoning ordinance changed.

"Union begun in legal marriage is more stable than any other," *Family Planning Perspectives,* **January/February 1992, p. 2.**

Asserts that co-residential relationships that begin with marriage appear inherently more stable than either nonmarital unions or marriages that begin as non-marital unions. The ongoing study The National Longitudinal Study of the High School Class of 1972; study results; conclusions.

"Victory for unwed couple," *Christianity Today,* **Sept. 22, 1989, p. 44.**

Reports on a ruling by the California Fair Employment and Housing Commission that required a landlord to rent a one-bedroom apartment to an unmarried couple. The landlord had refused the rental for religious reasons.

"Young adults choose alternative to marriage, remain single longer," *Family Planning Perspectives,* **January/February 1991, p. 45.**

Examines the continuing trend that began in the late 1950s and intensified in the mid-70s, where an increasing number of young adults in the United States are postponing or forgoing marriage, and many are remaining with their parents or are setting up households as unmarried couples. Statistics published by the U.S. Bureau of the Census; median age at first marriage; marriage; living arrangements; more.

Balakrishnan, T.R. & Z. Wu, "Attitudes towards cohabitation and marriage in Canada," *Journal of Comparative Family Studies,* **spring 1992, p. 1.**

Investigates the attitudes toward cohabitation and marriage in Canada with a focus on the structural variables that mold such attitudes. Changes in the nuptiality patterns in Canada in the past two decades; average age of brides at first marriage; the uniqueness of Quebec Society as a distinct ethno-cultural and linguistic group and how these differences were handled in the study; more.

Blum, A. & R.R. Roha, "Legal side of living together," *Changing Times,* **Oct. 19, 1990, p. 73.**

Observes that people who live together have fewer legal rights than married couples. Importance of written living-together agreements; what to include; estate planning. INSET: Legal tangles of living together.

Brower, M. & D. Waggoner, "Living in sin? Not in her apartments, vows Christian landlady Evelyn Smith," *People,* **Dec. 11, 1989, p. 113.**

Discusses the legal battle going on between Chico, Ca., landlady Evelyn Smith, 57, and a cohabitating couple she refused to rent an apartment to, Ken Phillips, 30, and Gail Randall, 26. The couple claims discrimination on the basis of marital status, while Smith says their being unmarried violates her religious beliefs, and forcing her to rent to them is unconstitutional.

Brown, R., "New dilemma for black professionals: 'Living together' or marriage?" *Ebony,* **December 1989, p. 96.**

Several black professional couples discuss their reasons for choosing cohabitation over marriage. Some couples have married after living together for several years. Examines such issues as financial security, commitment, and social approval (or disapproval).

Bumpass, L.L., J.A. Sweet, et al., "The role of cohabita-

tion in declining rates of marriage," *Journal of Marriage & the Family,* **November 1991, p. 913.**

Examines the role cohabitation plays in declining rates of marriage. The national survey of families and households; marital and non-marital union formation; characteristics of cohabitors; marriage expectations; summary and conclusions.

Bushnell, C., "Tales of almost living together," *Mademoiselle,* **May 19, 1990, p. 200.**

Presents a scenario of a woman's dilemma over cohabitating with her boyfriend. INSET: Living together: the truth and the consequences.

Carroll, G., "Marriage by another name," *Newsweek,* **July 24, 1989, p. 46.**

Talks about the effect of celebrities' common-law marriage lawsuits, like those of actor William Hurt and baseball star Dave Winfield, on the number of disputes among the public. Past legality of such marriages; current status.

Cherlin, A., "Recent changes in American fertility, marriage, and divorce," *Annals of the American Academy of Political & Social Science,* **July 19, 1990, p. 145.**

Discusses recent trends in fertility, marriage, and divorce in the period since 1965 in the United States. Cohabitation; continuing postponement of marriage; rise in birth rates to women in their 30s; fertility focus for the future on upbringing and education of children.

Clarke, C.V., "Financial strategies for unmarrieds," *Black Enterprise,* **October 1989, p. 94.**

Offers advice to unmarried couples that live together on how to arrange finances to avoid financial and legal pitfalls. Setting up a partnership agreement; establishing joint credit and joint savings accounts; joint tenancy agreements.

Colella, U. & E. Thomson, "Cohabitation and marital stability: Quality or commitment?" *Journal of Marriage & the Family,* **May 1992, p. 259.**

Uses data from the 1987-88 National Survey of Families and Households to examine whether couples who cohabited before marriage reported lower-quality marriages, lower commitment to the institution of marriage, more individualistic views of marriage, and greater likelihood of divorce than couples who did not cohabit. Data; analyses and results; conclusions.

DeMaris, A. & K.V. Rao, "Premarital cohabitation and subsequent marital stability in the United States: A reassessment," *Journal of Marriage & the Family,* **February 1992, p. 178.**

Presents a study assessing whether cohabitors would show higher odds of marital dissolution, compared with non-cohabitors, whether this difference would vary by differences in the nature of the cohabiting relationship, and whether any differences found in the risk of divorce between cohabitors and noncohabitors could be accounted for by a greater length of time at risk. Data and methods; results; discussion.

Engeler, A., "Living together," *Glamour,* **January 1991, p. 150.**

Summarizes research into cohabitation that shows it often creates candidates for later divorce, not stronger marriages. Risks of cohabiting; how marriage changes attitudes; communication gap; how fighting can help; examples. INSET: Living together: Who's doing it?

Fennelly, K. & N.S. Landale, "Informal unions among mainland Puerto Ricans: Cohabitation or an alternative to legal marriage?" *Journal of Marriage & the Family,* **May 1992, p. 269.**

Examines the meaning of informal unions among mainland Puerto Rican women with data from a survey of Puerto Rican women residing in New York City and its surrounding counties in 1985. Comparison of the characteristics of women in informal unions to those of women who are single and women who legally married; whether Puerto Rican women define their informal unions as non-marital cohabitation or a form of marriage; the predictors of informal unions.

Harmon, T., "The juicy truth about living together," *Glamour,* **December 1989, p. 122.**

Account of the author's feelings about moving in with his girlfriend. Presents a list of new things live-ins don't know they have to deal with including personal idiosyncrasies, and mementos from the past.

Jacoby, S., "Can you cheat and still be faithful?" *Glamour,* **June 19, 1990, p. 224.**

Discusses the new morality of unmarried lovers and who decides if certain behavior is "cheating" or faithful. Gives example situations and how different people interpreted them in a relationship.

Malveaux, J., "Premarital insurance," *Essence,* **Feb. 19, 1990, p. 32.**

Gives advice on prenuptial or cohabitation agreements, including raising the subject and what should be included in the agreement.

Mare, R.D., "Five decades of educational assortative mating," *American Sociological Review,* **February 1991, p. 15.**

Discusses changes in patterns of assortative mating and educational attainment over the past 50 years. Women's participation in the labor force and cohabitation between unmarried persons; changes in timing of schooling and marriage; changes in the expectation of both sexes regarding marriage; data and methods; more.

Mehren, E., "I was an unwed stepmother," *Newsweek,* **Oct. 23, 1989, p. 12.**

Talks about social parenting, describing households where there is a residential adult of the opposite sex who is not married to the parent of the children, and how the author lived in such a situation as an unmarried stepmother.

Polonko, K.A. & J.D. Teachmand, "Cohabitation and marital stability in the United States," *Social Forces,* **Sept. 19, 1990, p. 207.**

Tests the hypothesis that cohabitation increases the results of marital disruption in the United States. More time in union of cohabitants; data; descriptive results; multivariate results; discussion.

Schoen, R., "First unions and the stability of first marriages," *Journal of Marriage & the Family,* **May 1992, p. 281.**

Uses the National Survey of Families and Households to examine the relationship between premarital cohabitation and marital instability among U.S. women born between 1928 and 1957. Definition of cohabitation; data and methods; results; summary and conclusions.

Stets, J.E., "Cohabiting and marital aggression: The role of social isolation," *Journal of Marriage & the Family,* **August 1991, p. 669.**

Examines the difference between physical aggression among cohabiting couples and that among married couples by using data from the National Survey of Families and Households. Tests the speculation that cohabitors are more likely to be socially isolated than married persons. Background; social support; social control; method; results; discussion.

Valvur, A., "Moving into her place," *Cosmopolitan,* **Oct. 19, 1990, p. 128.**

Recounts a man's experiences when he moves into his girlfriend's apartment. Possessions; compromises; other adjustments.

Homosexuals

"Homosexual families and the law," *Newsweek,* **July 17, 1989, p. 48.**

Talks about the recent focus on the legal rights of homosexual couples as families. The New York State Court of Appeals ruled gay couples who live together for 10 or more years are a family. In San Francisco a referendum will be held on giving city benefits to unmarried couples.

"Surge of lesbian moms to present legal problems,"

Jet, **March 20, 1989, p. 37.**

Discusses reproductive law and how it relates to lesbian mothers, according to Sandra Garcia, a University of South Florida professor.

Brownworth, V.A., "Stonewall +20," *The Nation,* **July 3, 1989, p. 5.**

Editorial. Describes how civil rights for gay men and lesbians have not changed during the 20 years after the Stonewall riot. Justice Byron R. White's majority opinion that sexual acts are not protected by the Constitution; examples of discrimination.

Chideya, F., J. Seligmann, et al., "Variations on a theme," *Newsweek,* **winter/spring, 1990, p. 38.**

Discusses new types of family units, including gay and lesbian couples and unmarried heterosexual couples, and how the public is more willing recently to accept and recognize them as families. Legal developments defining families; statistics on new types of families; examples of successful units; desire to be parents; options.

Leonard, A.S., "Report from the legal front," *The Nation,* **July 2, 1990, p. 12.**

Reviews major developments in laws that are on the cutting edge of gay and lesbian rights. Sodomy laws; anti-gay discrimination by the military; family rights for homosexual partners.

Margolick, D., "Lesbian child-custody cases test frontiers of family law," *The New York Times,* **July 4, 1990, p. 1.**

Comments on the case of a lesbian couple, with a child, who decided to split up, and how, in cases like this, the children's interests do not even arise in court. The judges' task of handling what amounts to divorces involving people who cannot legally marry.

Rebeck, G., "Gay families begin to win recognition," *Utne Reader,* **September/October 1990, p. 34.**

Details the legislative battles being fought over issues concerning such non-traditional family groups as gays and lesbians, and the resulting reforms that are gradually being implemented.

Stoddard, T.B., "Gay marriages: Make them legal," *The New York Times,* **March 4, 1989, p. 27.**

States the opinion that gay marriages should be made legal, as marriage is a basic civil right and is not merely for procreation.

Back Issues

Great Research on Current Issues Starts Right Here... Recent topics covered by The CQ Researcher are listed below. Issues dated before May 10, 1991, were published under the name of Editorial Research Reports.

FEBRUARY 1991
Regional Impact of Recession
Puerto Rico's Status
Redistricting: Mapping Power
Nuclear Power

MARCH 1991
Acid Rain
Cost of the Gulf War
Reassessing Gun Laws
Future for Man in Space

APRIL 1991
Social Security
Canadian Crisis Over Quebec
California Drought
Electromagnetic Radiation

MAY 1991
School Choice
Racial Quotas
Animal Rights
U.S. and Japan

JUNE 1991
Children and Divorce
Teenage Suicide
Endangered Species
Europe 1992

Back issues are available for $4.00 (subscribers) or $7.00 (non-subscribers). Quantity discounts apply to orders over ten. To order, call Congressional Quarterly 1-800-432-2250.

Binders are available for $15.00. To order call 1-800-638-1710.

JULY 1991
Teenagers and Abortion
Soviet Republics Rebel
Mexico's Emergence
Athletes and Drugs

AUGUST 1991
Sexual Harassment
Fetal Tissue Research
Oil Imports
The Palestinians

SEPTEMBER 1991
Police Brutality
Advertising Under Attack
Saving the Forests
Foster Care Crisis

OCTOBER 1991
Pay-Per-View TV
Youth Gangs
Gene Therapy
World Hunger

NOVEMBER 1991
Fast-Food Shake-Up
The Greening of Eastern Europe
Business' Role in Education
Cuba In Crisis

DECEMBER 1991
Retiree Health Benefits
Asian Americans
The Obscenity Debate
The Disabilities Act

JANUARY 1992
Term Limits
Oil Spills
Hunting Controversy
Alternative Medicine

FEBRUARY 1992
Threatened Coastlines
New Era in Asia
Assisted Suicide
Jobs in the '90s

MARCH 1992
Women and Sports
Underage Drinking
Garbage Crisis
Mafia Crackdown

APRIL 1992
Ozone Depletion
Welfare Reform
Politicians and Privacy
Illegal Immigration

MAY 1992
Native Americans
Jobs vs. Environment
Too Many Lawsuits?
Fairness in Salaries

JUNE 1992
Nuclear Proliferation
Food Irradiation
Lead Poisoning
Hard Times for Libraries

JULY 1992
Alternative Energy
Prescription Drug Prices
Alzheimer's Disease
Infant Mortality

AUGUST 1992
The Homeless
Work, Family and Stress
NATO's Changing Role
Marine Mammals vs. Fish

Future Topics

▶ *Violence in Schools*

▶ *Public Television*

▶ *Women in the Military*

THE

CQ Researcher

PUBLISHED BY CONGRESSIONAL QUARTERLY INC., IN CONJUNCTION WITH EBSCO PUBLISHING

Violence in Schools

Can anything be done to curb the growing violence?

A GROWING NUMBER OF SHOOTINGS INVOLVING students in small-town and suburban schools has experts convinced that school violence is no longer just a big-city phenomenon. While some experts blame a breakdown in school discipline, others point to drugs and gangs. And some say schools merely reflect an increasingly violent society, whose attitudes are passed on through television and movies to children who lack the traditional counterweights of parental guidance, community kinship or religion. As violence mounts, many teachers and criminologists argue for a crackdown on hard-core troublemakers through toughened expulsion policies. But other educators believe that schools must take on the basic task of teaching students to resolve conflicts peacefully — a lesson that many children no longer seem to receive at home.

 September 11, 1992 • Volume 2, No. 34 • 785-808

Formerly Editorial Research Reports

COVER ART: BARBARA SASSA-DANIELS

THE CQ Researcher

September 11, 1992
Volume 2, No. 34

EDITOR
Sandra Stencel

MANAGING EDITOR
Thomas J. Colin

ASSOCIATE EDITOR
Richard L. Worsnop

STAFF WRITERS
Charles S. Clark
Mary H. Cooper
Rodman D. Griffin

PRODUCTION EDITOR
Sarah E. Merritt

EDITORIAL ASSISTANT
Michael M. Taylor

GRAPHICS
Jack Auldridge

PUBLISHED BY
Congressional Quarterly Inc.

CHAIRMAN
Andrew Barnes

VICE CHAIRMAN
Andrew P. Corty

EDITOR AND PUBLISHER
Neil Skene

EXECUTIVE EDITOR
Robert W. Merry

PUBLICATIONS MARKETING/SALES
Robert Smith

EDITOR, EBSCO PUBLISHING
Melissa Kummerer

© 1992 Congressional Quarterly Inc.

The CQ Researcher (ISSN 1056-2036). Formerly Editorial Research Reports. Published weekly (48 times per year, not printed the first Friday of any month with five Fridays) by Congressional Quarterly Inc., 1414 22nd St., N.W., Washington, D.C. 20037. Rates are furnished upon request. Second-class postage paid at Washington, D.C. POSTMASTER: Send address changes to The CQ Researcher, 1414 22nd St., N.W., Washington, D.C. 20037.

Violence in Schools

BY SARAH GLAZER

THE ISSUES

In what city is school violence such a concern that a vice principal and security guards have been issued bulletproof vests? Detroit, New York, Los Angeles? Guess again. The answer is Parkland, a middle-class suburb of Tacoma, Wash.

Unlike the big-city schools that have made headlines recently with shootings and stabbings on school grounds, Parkland's Washington High School has been relatively peaceful. There have been no shootings, and only two guns have been confiscated — an air-gun one student wanted to show a schoolmate and a .38-caliber revolver a student from another school brought to a concert.

But when teenagers were involved in three shootings, one fatal, only blocks away from the campus earlier this year, the union representing school security guards demanded the bulletproof vests. In one incident, a rival gang member died when he was shot in the chest at point-blank range by a Washington High dropout. In another incident, a student from the school fired at a group of youths in front of a bowling alley, wounding one youngster. In the third shooting, the same teenager returned to a recreation center with a gun after an argument and wounded a student from another school.

To make matters worse, says Peter McIntyre, who recently left the school after 11 years as principal, several of the youths were members of Tacoma gangs that are starting to make their presence felt on campus. "Sometimes kids get in a fight, and they'll say, 'My [gang] brother is going to be here.' "

Across the nation, in suburbs like Parkland and in rural towns once considered safe havens from big-city

shootings, schools are encountering gun violence for the first time. Consider a sampling of incidents from the 1991-92 school year:

- In Obetz, Ohio, a 12-year-old student fired five shots from a .22-caliber pistol in a middle school cafeteria during lunch period, hitting a student in the head; miraculously, he recovered.

- In Baldwin Park, Calif., two boys, about 8 and 10, robbed a teacher at gunpoint, leading officials to bar teachers from working in school after hours.

- In Greenwood, S.C., a high school student was shot in a school hallway following a fight.[1]

"It's still accurate that most youth homicide is occurring in urban areas, but more and more weapons activity and gang activity is getting out of urban areas," says George E. Butterfield, deputy director of the National School Safety Center (NSSC) in Westlake Village, Calif., which advises school districts on safety measures.

Most startling to experts are the high numbers of students in high school and junior high who say they

regularly carry weapons — and increasingly handguns. "I'm surprised there aren't more homicides in schools, considering the data about how many kids carry guns," says Charles Patrick Ewing, a professor of law and psychology at the State University of New York-Buffalo and an expert on juvenile homicide.

Ewing has found that juvenile homicides tend to be spur-of-the-moment efforts to even a score, aided by the impersonal nature of guns. "I've had kids say, 'All I did was pull the trigger,' " he says. "What at one time might have been a bloody nose becomes a gun slaying."

But guns are not the only problem. According to a 1990 survey by the national Centers for Disease Control (CDC), one in five high school students carries a weapon at least once a month for self-protection or use in a fight. Knives or razors were the most popular weapons, followed by clubs and then guns. Approximately one out of 20 students said they carry a firearm.[2]

Experts say the frequency of youthful weapons-carrying helps to explain the high rate of youth-related homicide. More than 11,000 persons died between 1980 and 1989 as a result of homicides committed by high school-age youths using firearms, cutting instruments or blunt objects, according to FBI statistics.[3]

Young black males have a higher probability of dying in a gunfight than any other segment of the population. The homicide rate for black males 15-19 nearly doubled between 1984 and 1988. According to the CDC's Youth Risk Behavior Survey, 39 percent of black male students said they carried a weapon, and of those more than half carried a firearm.*

---

*The 1990 Youth Risk Behavior Survey is the first of several periodic surveys that will track young people's behavior over time.

Gun Violence in the Nation's Schools

The Center to Prevent Handgun Violence examined gun violence in both public and private schools from September 1986 to September 1990. Here is a sampling of what they found based on a review of more than 2,500 newspaper articles on shooting incidents in schools:

 At least 71 people — 65 students and 6 school employees — had been killed with guns at schools; another 201 were severely wounded; and 242 individuals were held hostage at gunpoint.

 Shootings or hostage situations in schools had occurred in at least 35 states and the District of Columbia.

 Males are most frequently the offenders (93%) as well as the victims (76%).

 Schoolchildren ages 14-17 are most at risk of gun violence at school.

 Gun violence in schools occurs most often in hallways (25%) and in classrooms (19%).

 Gang or drug disputes were the leading cause of school gun violence (18%). Longstanding arguments (15%), romantic disagreements (12%), fights over material possessions (10%) and accidents (13%) are also common causes of gun violence.

 Handguns were the overwhelming choice of firearm (75%) for those who committed gun violence in schools.

Source: Center to Prevent Handgun Violence

There are no national statistics indicating whether violence in schools nationwide is on the rise. *(See story, p. 789.)* But individually, school districts report disturbing increases in weapons-related incidents. In March, Prince George's County, Md., a Washington suburb, experienced its first shooting since 1985. A 16-year-old sophomore fired a handgun into a chemistry class, narrowly missing another student, the apparent target.

In Detroit, student assaults on teachers rose 900 percent from 1985 to 1990, according to the NSSC. In Cleveland, the number of serious incidents rose from 5,953 in 1990 to 7,022 last year. Fifty-two guns were seized in Cleveland schools, more than double the previous year's total.

In two highly publicized incidents, New York City recently experienced the first student killings in more than a decade. One student was killed and a teacher seriously wounded by wild gunfire in November 1991 at Thomas Jefferson High School in Brooklyn. Both were bystanders in a hallway when a 14-year-old drew a gun to even the score following a fight between his older brother and another student. Then on Feb. 26, less than an hour before Mayor David N. Dinkins was scheduled to address the school, a student pulled out a .38-caliber pistol and killed two classmates, one of them his partner in an earlier robbery.

Violence in schools — counting robberies, vandalism, arson and assaults — reached a national peak in the mid-1970s, according to available data. While it is not clear whether violence

has increased since then because no one has done a comparative study, experts have no doubts that the extent of the shootings and the deadliness of the weapons are unprecedented.

In some school districts, the increase in violence can be traced to the arrival of gangs.[4] Kenneth S. Trump, a nationally recognized authority on school gangs and coordinator of a special youth gang unit in the Cleveland Public Schools, says he now gets inquiries from principals with gang problems in such unlikely places as Oberlin, Ohio, and affluent Kansas suburbs. "Kids in the suburbs look to the cities and say, 'That's cool' and copy the big-city gangs," he says.

Experts also blame the violent behavior on a growing tolerance for violence in a generation raised on gory TV programs and movies and a surprising inability among adolescents to find non-violent ways of dealing with one another. *(See stories, pp. 792, 802.)*

Many experts say that's because children now spend much of their free time without adult guidance, either because they come from stressed one-parent homes or a family where both parents work full time. At Harvard University's School of Public Health, Assistant Dean Deborah Prothrow-Stith, author of *Deadly Consequences*, a study of teenage violence, blames adult attitudes toward violence. She cites the phrase "Make my day," from the violence-packed Clint Eastwood movie "Dirty Harry," as symptomatic of the lack of thought about consequences that has "cut across class." The macho slogan, she says, was embraced by everybody from poor blacks and middle-class whites to former President Ronald Reagan.

But others blame the violence on the small number of adolescents who commit most of the nation's youth crime[5] and school officials who balk at taking strong disciplinary action. According to sociologist Jackson Toby, director of the Institute for

Has the Level of School Violence Increased?

Are America's schools more violent than they used to be? It's hard to say. No recent study has tried to compare today's level of school violence with earlier levels, largely because national statistics have not been compiled in a consistent manner from year to year.

The last major national study, commissioned by Congress and produced by the National Institute of Education, was issued in 1978. By then, an upward trend in school violence since the early 1970s had peaked and was even showing modest signs of decline.

A striking indication of changed student behavior by the time of the study was the statistic from annual teacher surveys showing that the risk of a teacher being attacked by a student had doubled since 1956. However, the risk had not changed much from 1974 to 1978.†

The 1978 report, which was based on surveys and interviews with principals, teachers and students, contains no tables totaling gun fatalities — a rare event for the 1970s but a growing public preoccupation in the '90s. School vandalism and personal theft were the most common offenses reported.

By today's standards, the levels of violence in the 1978 report seem pretty mild. For example, only 1.3 percent of secondary students reported being attacked at school in a typical one-month period, and only 4 percent of those attacks required medical attention.

While there is no precise comparison with those statistics, some recent surveys suggest today's students are more likely to be seriously injured at school. For example, in a survey of 31 public high schools in Illinois during the 1989-90 school year, 8 percent of students reported being attacked in school or on the way to school. Of those, 8 percent reported being cut and 4 percent said they had been shot.††

Nationwide statistics on school violence may be available in the years ahead. The Centers for Disease Control (CDC) in Atlanta has initiated a series of school-based surveys to help determine whether school violence is going up or down. The surveys will ask questions about the fighting and weapon-carrying habits of a representative sample of students in grades 9-12 in all 50 states and the District of Columbia. Known as the Youth Risk Behavior Survey, it was first undertaken in 1990. The second survey will take place this school year.

Results of the 1990 CDC survey were widely reported earlier this year. One of the most startling findings was that 20 percent of high school students carried a weapon at least once in the month preceding the survey. (The study did not ask whether the weapons were carried onto school grounds, although it has been reported that way in a number of journal and newspaper articles.)

In another series of questions about school fighting, the CDC survey found that nearly 8 percent of all high school students had been in at least one fight that resulted in an injury requiring treatment by a doctor or nurse.‡

Efforts to assess trends in school violence may run into resistance from school officials. "There's gross underreporting of violence in schools ... because principals want parents to feel schools are safe and that they are good administrators," says Paul M. Kingery, director of the health promotion program at Texas A&M University.

The 1978 report to Congress, for example, found that interviews with students yielded 22 times the number of attacks, shakedowns and robberies reported by principals. The authors of the study speculated that in addition to wanting to protect a school's reputation, principals were often unaware of attacks on students.

Only two states, California and South Carolina, collect and publicize statistics on school violence annually, according to the National School Safety Center in Westlake Village, Calif. When the Center to Prevent Handgun Violence in Washington, D.C., decided to tally recent school shootings, it was forced to turn to newspaper accounts because so few states would release data, spokeswoman Vanessa Scherzer says. The center counted 227 shootings or hostage incidents on school property between September 1986 and September 1990. At least 71 people were killed on school grounds and 201 severely wounded during the four years.

---

† National Institute of Education, *Violent Schools — Safe Schools*, 1978, p. 33. The institute is now the Department of Education's Office of Educational Research and Improvement.

†† Illinois Criminal Justice Information Authority, *Trends and Issues '91*, 1991.

‡ "Physical Fighting Among High School Students — United States 1990," *Morbidity and Mortality Weekly Report*, Feb. 14, 1992, pp. 91-94.

Criminological Research at Rutgers University, the civil rights granted to juveniles in the 1960s and '70s by the Supreme Court *(see "Chronology," p. 795)* and the national preoccupation with the dropout rate has made schools increasingly reluctant to expel badly behaved students. "Most schools in most big cities have given up and keep kids in school who are sufficiently troublesome that it's very difficult to maintain an educational program," Toby says.

As educators and security experts try to cope with the problem of school violence, here are some of the questions they are asking:

How much can or should schools do to protect students and teachers?

Growing numbers of schools are installing security devices once reserved for nabbing airport terrorists and department store shoplifters. One-quarter of the nation's large urban school systems now use hand-held or walk-through metal detectors, according to the National School Safety Center. And some 245 of the nation's 15,000 school districts have police or security departments, according to the National Association for School Safety and Law Enforcement Officers; 156 school districts have uniformed officers, often with arrest powers, and in 102 districts they are armed. New York City's school security force, slated to reach 2,600 officers this fall, is the sixth-largest police force — of any kind — in the nation.

But is this the kind of atmosphere the nation wants in its schools? At Thomas Jefferson High School in Brooklyn, it takes from 7:30 a.m. to 10 a.m. to funnel all 3,000 students into the gym, where they are frisked with hand-held metal detectors and their book bags are probed. Some students have to miss a first-period class as a result.

"It doesn't resemble what I knew as school," says the NSSC's George Butterfield, who visited Jefferson as a safety consultant. "We [adults] would be incensed."

Indeed, parents, administrators and school boards tend to resist such security measures until a violent incident shocks the community into action, says Karen W. Powe, director of the National Education Policy Network at the National School Boards Association (NSBA) in Alexandria, Va.

Parents and staff at Thomas Jefferson High initially prevented the use of metal detectors after the school was cited as the most violent in the city in 1988. Principal Carol A. Beck explained at the time that she didn't want to create a prisonlike atmosphere.[6] The school began using the detectors last December.

A similar debate surfaced in Prince George's County this spring after the first school shooting in seven years. Suzanne M. Plogman, chairman of the county's Board of Education, says a majority of the panel opposed metal detectors. "When you put metal detectors in buildings, that's a statement that schools are violence-ridden, out of control and unsafe," she says, "and that's not a fair statement about the schools in our system."

But Board Vice Chairman Marcy C. Canavan, reversing her previous opposition, plans to push for detectors. "I understand the reasons for the opposition," she said. "I just don't want to wait for someone to be killed."

At Jefferson High, students told the NSSC that they liked the metal detectors, both for protection from classmates' weapons and, in a sad commentary on their huge school, for the extra personal attention they received during security checks. After the school started using metal detectors on a roughly once-a-week basis, 32 weapons were confiscated from individuals, and 89 were found on school premises. Detectors weren't used on the day of the fatal February shootings.

The New York City public schools report that since the introduction of metal detectors in 1988, serious incidents have declined by 58 percent in schools with scanners and by 43 percent in schools without them. "The number of firearms we're seizing is decreasing because kids are stashing them [outside school]," says James S. Vlasto, spokesman for New York school Chancellor Joseph A. Fernandez. Vlasto says security guards often find guns hidden behind bushes and garbage cans on days when detectors are used. Students want to have a weapon handy, he says, because "they fear going to and from school."

Security experts say there is no evidence that a metal detector will solve the problem of violence, even though it offers a highly visible symbol to the community. "It's very labor-intensive, very expensive and the net results don't show a difference one way or another," says Peter D. Blauvelt, chairman of the board of the National Association for School Safety and Law Enforcement. "New York City is the classic example: They can't say whether it's successful or not, but they don't know what else to do."

Walk-through metal detectors can cost up to $10,000 each, and X-ray units designed to detect weapons in book-bags can run $17,000. Because of the expense, school systems can't afford to place them at every school. Instead, like New York, they move the metal detectors around on a random basis.

Some school districts that experimented with metal detectors found them an exercise in frustration. Students can sneak weapons through bathroom windows or unguarded entrances at recess, and it is hard to guard multiple entrances on a spread-out suburban campus.

"We tried [detectors], but they proved worthless," says Rochester, N.Y., teachers' union President Adam Urbanski. "They couldn't afford to have them everywhere — only in two or three places and only on certain days. Eventually, the pattern became clear. On Tuesdays and Thursdays, kids became more creative about weapons."

In addition, some school districts are reluctant to enter into new security measures that could open them to lawsuits or constitutional challenges. The threat of litigation from parents and students is a particular problem with metal detectors, says Gwendolyn H. Gregory, deputy general counsel of the NSBA.

In 1985 the Supreme Court established current constitutional standards for lawful searches of students in *New Jersey v. T.L.O.* The court ruled that, unlike police officers, who must show "probable cause" to conduct a search, school officials need only have a "reasonable suspicion" that the search will uncover illegal activity. It's not clear, however, whether such blanket security checks as metal detector stations would come under the Supreme Court's definition of a "search."

If so, the searches could be severely restricted. "The question is: Do you have reasonable suspicion to search that person?" says Gregory. In the absence of specific guidance from the Supreme Court, the NSBA points school districts to guidelines worked out under a consent decree between the American Civil Liberties Union and Detroit schools. The school system agreed to notify students in advance when it was planning to use metal detectors, and to use them only if there was a problem with guns.

Anti-gang dress codes have also raised constitutional questions in the past. In 1987, a high school student in Midlothian, Ill., challenged a rule forbidding boys to wear earrings. Darryl Olesen Jr. argued that the policy violated his First Amendment right of free expression. However, a U.S. District Court judge dismissed the suit, calling the policy "rational."[7]

Should teachers be given more information about potentially violent students?

In response to the growing climate of violence, teachers are demanding to be informed about students with records of juvenile delinquency or misbehavior in school. In many states, however, schools are barred from seeing juvenile court records under state confidentiality laws. In 1989, in response to teachers' concerns, the California Legislature required school districts to tell teachers about students who had injured another person or attempted to do so.[8]

The NSSC has urged that juvenile records be shared with schools. "Our juvenile justice system protects the privacy of the serious youthful offender to such an extent that the rest of society often is left at risk," says the organization's executive director, Ronald D. Stephens.[9]

The American Federation of Teachers (AFT), the nation's second largest teachers' union, is pushing for more information-sharing on the grounds that serious incidents could be prevented if students with violent backgrounds could be identified and sent to special alternative programs.

Alternative schools for students with behavior problems, while highly praised in some localities, have been resisted in others as discriminatory "dumping grounds" for minorities and undesirables. And many school districts simply have no alternative school to turn to.

Nowhere has the conflict between the rights of the individual student and the school community as a

Guns in American Schools

Intentional shootings (graph at left) were much more common than other types of school incidents involving guns. Five causes sparked most of the shootings (graph at right); incidents involving drugs and gangs topped the list.

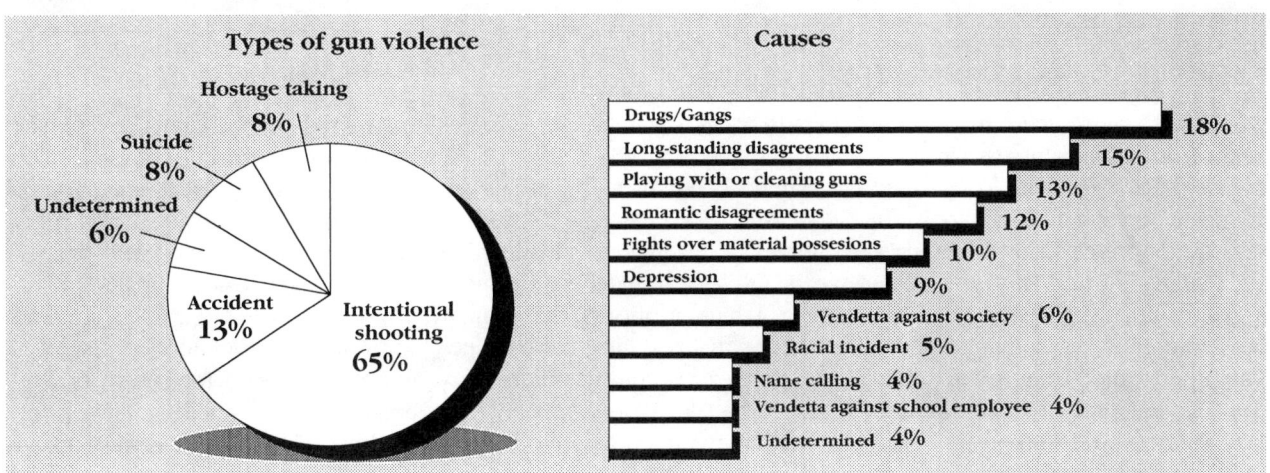

Types of gun violence

Hostage taking 8%
Suicide 8%
Undetermined 6%
Accident 13%
Intentional shooting 65%

Causes

Drugs/Gangs 18%
Long-standing disagreements 15%
Playing with or cleaning guns 13%
Romantic disagreements 12%
Fights over material possesions 10%
Depression 9%
Vendetta against society 6%
Racial incident 5%
Name calling 4%
Vendetta against school employee 4%
Undetermined 4%

Source: Center to Prevent Handgun Violence

The Cycle of Violence

"If gangs and drugs disappeared tomorrow from our poorest neighborhoods, our young black men would continue killing each other at grossly unacceptable rates, as they have done throughout this century," Deborah Prothrow-Stith, assistant dean of Harvard University's School of Public Health, wrote in *Deadly Consequences*, her 1991 book on teenage violence.

Today, the chance that a black male born in the United States will be murdered is 1 in 27. By contrast, the chances for a white male are 1 in 205, for a white female 1 in 496, and for a black female 1 in 117.[†]

Prothrow-Stith, who teaches violence-prevention classes to inner-city 10th graders in Boston, says the students are interested in learning tactics for avoiding fights. However, they "had no faith that fighting could be prevented, and they were fearful of looking cowardly in the eyes of their peers."[††]

Prothrow-Stith still believes fighting and even homicide can be prevented because they result from how individuals relate to one another. As proof, she points out that most murders occur not between strangers but between people who know one another, often intimately.

For young black males living in crime-ridden urban neighborhoods, the mental and emotional equipment that is needed to alter those intimate relationships has often been crippled, Prothrow-Stith suggests. A bleak sense of the future, seething anger at society because of racial discrimination and a lack of reasoning skills have produced a deadly recipe for violence, she says. As a group, black males have the lowest school performance of any segment of the population. And some never gain the language and analytical skills that help children use words instead of weapons in moments of stress or anger.

Experts say that most violent conflicts among school-age children can be traced back to long-simmering disputes. While gang or drug disputes account for many school shootings, a variety of personal conflicts — long-standing arguments, romantic disagreements and fights over possessions — account for a larger share of the shootings, according to the Center to Prevent Handgun Violence, in Washington, D.C.[‡] *(See graph, p. 791)*

But what makes young people decide that guns are the only way to solve a dispute? Kenneth S. Trump, a nationally recognized authority on school gangs and coordinator of a special youth gang unit in the Cleveland Public Schools, says students are reacting as much to the perception of violence as to its reality: "A kid turns on the 6 o'clock news, hears the number of weapons confiscated in school and what clicks in the kid's mind is, 'My school's not safe, I've got to bring a gun to my school.'"

George E. Butterfield, deputy director of the National School Safety Center (NSSC) in Westlake Village, Calif., says he finds such reactions understandable in crime-ridden neighborhoods. Students in New York have responded to the daily onslaught of neighborhood shootings much like adults in California who rushed to gun stores after the Los Angeles riots, he says.

"There's a perception that law enforcement is understaffed," he adds. "In a strange way, it's a healthy person who says, 'I have to take my life into my hands.' You have young people saying, 'This is the world I live in.' It's not a lack of self-esteem."

[†] Deborah Prothrow-Stith, *Deadly Consequences* (1991), p. 17.

[††] *Ibid.*, p. 24.

[‡] Center to Prevent Handgun Violence, *Caught in the Crossfire*, September 1990, p. 2.

whole been more acute than in the area of discipline. Rutgers University sociologist Jackson Toby, who advocates greater use of expulsion, says the Supreme Court's landmark 1975 ruling in *Goss v. Lopez* made it "very difficult" for schools to expel violent or disruptive students. The court ruled that every child has an "entitlement" to education that cannot be taken away, even for a few days' suspension, without due process of law. "As a result," Toby writes, "many central-city schools have tended to abandon

expulsion as the ultimate enforcer of discipline."[10]

Safety is such a big issue in Rochester — where a student stabbed a teacher to death nine years ago — that teachers are making it a higher priority than salary increases in upcoming contract negotiations, according to union President Urbanski. Approximately 100 teachers have been assaulted annually by students in the past four school years, the union says.

The union's main demand is that teachers, parents and principals be

permitted to write the disciplinary code for their own schools. This would permit a local school team to overrule board suspension rules, which the union considers dangerously weak. Under board policy, according to Urbanski, students cannot be recommended for long-term suspension for "mere possession" of dangerous weapons. Rather, school officials must prove that the student "brandished the weapon with intent to use."

The policy practically invites students to bring weapons to school,

Urbanksi says. He contends that concern about safety and discipline underlies middle-class flight from Rochester's public schools, where about 70 percent of the majority black and Hispanic student population now comes from families living below the poverty level.

While Urbanski blames school board members for a weak discipline code, other teachers blame principals. "One of the major complaints of teachers is they send kids to the [principal's] office and the kids come back" thumbing their noses at teachers, says AFT spokesman Bruce Goldberg. "Politically, administrators are sometimes reluctant to back up teachers because they fear reprisals in the local community."

Public schools have come under increasing fire in recent years for using expulsion and suspension policies in a way that falls most heavily on the shoulders of minority children. Eventually, some child advocates argue, such children become "push-outs" from the school system.

In a highly publicized 1988 case, Joe Clark, principal of Eastside High School in Paterson, N.J., was threatened with dismissal by his school board after expelling 66 students without due process or board approval. He insisted the students were "hoodlums, thugs and pathological deviants." Clark, who won national attention for wielding a baseball bat to keep drug pushers away, had already ejected more than 300 students at the time for absenteeism, tardiness and disruption in school.[11]

Not everybody applauded Clark's tough-guy approach. Prominent in the debate was the fact that Eastside's student body was largely black and Hispanic, and about a third were from families on welfare. "If the students were not poor black children, Joe Clark would not be tolerated," commented Los Angeles Principal George McKenna, whose Washington Preparatory High School has been plagued with neighborhood shootings. "Our role is to rescue and be responsible."[12]

When it comes to curbing school violence, many teachers support the creation of alternative schools, especially for those who have been suspended or expelled for carrying weapons, says the AFT's Goldberg. "We can't just send them home for three weeks and expect them to come back all reformed," he says. But alternative schools are expensive, Goldberg concedes. The solution, he says, is federal assistance to school districts: "This is not just a local problem, anymore. It's a national problem."

Can schools change youngsters' behavior?

Many educators are coming to believe that more than strict discipline is needed to counter youthful violence. Traditional discipline may even be counterproductive, engendering hostility without teaching children alternatives, the authors of some of the newest curricular approaches argue. They believe that educational programs that show children how to resolve disputes peacefully — even at the preschool level — offer the best long-term solution.

One reason for an early start is that elementary schools are already seeing the kind of inability to get along that erupts into violence at older ages. Lillian M. Brinkley, immediate past president of the National Association of Elementary School Principals in Alexandria, Va., reports that principals across the country are "more concerned than they were eight to 10 years ago about whether young children can handle problems in the correct manner, rather than handling them in the same way as their big brothers or sisters. More children are not following the rules and regulations of schools, more children are showing disrespect for authority and teachers, more children are getting involved in fighting, more children are trying to solve their own problems with guns or knives."

Part of what is causing teenagers to react violently, says Marilyn Watson, program director of the Child Development Project in San Ramon, Calif., is that they have not "bought into the social system, and that buying-in takes place in elementary school." Watson's project is in its 11th year of an ambitious educational experiment aimed at teaching children to build cooperative, caring relationships with one another starting in kindergarten.

In one of the few long-term comparative studies of such an effort, children in the program were better at resolving conflicts, such as arguments over toys, than those without the training.[13]

It sounds simple, but these are the sorts of skills that young killers, muggers and rapists lack, says Ronald G. Slaby, a developmental psychologist at Harvard University. In a study comparing adolescents incarcerated for violent offenses with high school students from similar demographic backgrounds, Slaby and co-author Nancy G. Guerra found big differences in how young people solved social problems. Highly aggressive youths tended to attribute hostility to other people, to search for few facts in trying to understand a situation and to have difficulty envisioning alternative solutions.[14]

Using a curriculum that has now been expanded for testing in three Boston middle schools in neighborhoods with high murder rates, Slaby said he succeeded in changing habits of thinking among incarcerated youths and found a marginal improvement in recidivism. The juveniles showed improved problem-solving skills in tests that asked what they would do in hypothetical conflict situations. Example: If a new kid has the last ball on the ballfield and you want to play, what do you do: Bash the kid or ask if he'd like to play catch?[15]

"Habits of thinking can be changed," Slaby says. "To the extent we're successful in changing those, the behaviors will also change."

Some are skeptical. "If a kid has wasted five to six years of his life hating school, acting out and being a troublemaker, it may be too late to do anything about it," says sociologist Toby. "It's a tragic thing to say about someone who's 16, but sometimes it's irreversible."

Is it too much to expect schools to teach something once taught at the mother's knee? Former teacher Urbanski thinks it may be, though he supports the violence-prevention curricula gaining increasing currency in public schools. "Even if all of us [teachers] became a cross between Albert Einstein and Mother Teresa," he says, "it wouldn't solve the problem, because children exist in families more than schools."

Harvard's Deborah Prothrow-Stith authored a violence-prevention curriculum program now used in thousands of schools. "Yes, it works," she says. "No, it's not enough to prevent the problem because children have been raised by us, and this society has a problem glorifying and endorsing violence." She advocates nothing less than a full-scale public health campaign against violence, just like the national efforts to curb smoking and highway deaths.

Should gun owners be held criminally responsible if children injure themselves or others with the adult's weapon?

On New Year's Day 1992, 4-year-old Jesus Valencia picked up his grandfather's .22-caliber pistol and shot himself in the heart, dying almost instantly. The mixture of horror over the tragedy and sympathy for the grandfather that many observers felt reflects the controversy over the California law under which Jesus' grandfather, C. Nicholas Conchas, was subsequently charged.

The Children's Firearm Accident Protection Act of 1991 makes adults who negligently store loaded weapons within reach of children criminally liable if a child is injured or killed. Conchas faces a possible sentence of three years in jail and a $10,000 fine if convicted. Nine other states now have similar laws.*

Handgun Control Inc., the national citizens lobby against handguns, has made such laws its highest legislative priority for combating violence in schools. The organization points to a Florida School Boards Association study, which found that 88 percent of weapons confiscated from Florida students over a two-year period came from the students' own homes.[16]

"A lot of legislation trying to deal with possession of guns by children penalizes the child and leaves the adult owner completely untouched, without any responsibility," says Davis S. Weaver, assistant director for state legislation at Handgun Control. "That is bad public policy because there's no deterrent for adults."

A case in point, says Weaver, is the first arrest made under Florida's 1989 parental responsibility law, the first in the nation. Willie W. Green was charged with violating the new law in October 1989 when his visiting 8-year-old granddaughter shot herself

---

*The 10 states with child-accident prevention laws are Florida, Iowa, Connecticut, Maine, Virginia, California, New Jersey, Wisconsin, Maryland and Hawaii.

in the thumb with a gun she found in his room. "The arrest and trial of this grandfather did more to save lives than any law is going to do," Weaver says. "Every gun owner in the state of Florida had to say, 'You mean I could be arrested for leaving my gun in the night table? Whoa.'"

But not everyone sees it that way. "The individual [who was charged] has lost or suffered already, and then to file criminal charges I don't think is good legislation," says E. O. "Red" McAllister, executive director of the Dade County (Fla.) Public Schools special investigative unit. "If it was, it would be prosecuted more vigorously — and it's not."

Although the National Rifle Association (NRA) supported passage of the law in Florida, it opposes similar statutes under consideration in Ohio, New York and Illinois. *(See At Issue, p. 801)* Handgun Control says the NRA's position is determined solely by the strength of its lobby in each state. But spokesman Paul Blackman says the NRA supported the Florida law because it gives prosecutors discretion to charge someone with a misdemeanor instead of a felony.

Blackman argues that such laws may prevent childhood accidents with guns, but not school shootings. "Since most of the violence with guns in schools involves violent children," he says, "what you have to do is punish them. The problem of schools is violence, not guns." ■

BACKGROUND

Breakdown in Discipline

By the standards of 50 years ago, today's violent schools are literally unbelievable. "When I went to school, it was unthinkable to hit a teacher or even say something [rude] to a teacher," says sociologist Jackson

Toby, 66. "If you have teachers in control and students afraid of teachers, they behave themselves. Now teachers are afraid of students."

Disciplinary standards in American schools have changed radically over the past century, although some would argue the changes were, on balance, for the better. Historically, the strongest influence may have been the rise of the progressive edu-

Continued on p. 796

Chronology

1800s *Concept of juvenile delinquency emerges, enabling young offenders to be treated as delinquents, not adult criminals.*

1824
Establishment of the House of Refuge in New York City, the first training school aimed at keeping minors out of jail.

1830s
Renowned educator Horace Mann crusades against excessive corporal punishment in schools.

1847
The nation's first publicly funded school for delinquents is founded in Massachusetts.

1899
Illinois establishes the first statewide court especially for children.

—— • ——

1910s *Study of child psychology advances; progressive education movement challenges emphasis on strict discipline in U.S. public schools.*

1918
National Education Association issues report repudiating mastery of academic subject matter as a goal for secondary education. The report, promoting instead such progressive education goals as command of fundamental processes and worthwhile use of leisure, had a pervasive influence on American public schools until the 1950s.

1919
Progressive Education Association is established.

1940s-1950s *A rise in juvenile delinquency following World War II revives public support for a return to school discipline even as educators embrace progressive education.*

1955
Progressive Education Association disbands.

1955-56
The National Education Association polls teachers in response to newspaper accounts portraying juvenile gangs and crime as growing problems. Ninety-five percent of teachers describe students as well-behaved.

1957
Launching of the satellite *Sputnik I* by the Soviet Union catalyzes criticism of progressive education as overly sentimental and permissive. In response, schools revise curricula and disciplinary approaches.

—— • ——

1960s *Urban high schools hire large numbers of young, idealistic teachers in the face of student population increases; Vietnam war protests and college demonstrations trickle down to high schools; statistics on school crime are published for the first time.*

1967
In *Gault v. Arizona* the Supreme Court holds that children brought before a juvenile court are entitled under the Bill of Rights to the same procedural protections accorded to adults on trial. The decision fosters a growing reluctance to send youngsters away to training schools, especially for offenses such as truancy or misbehavior, which would not be crimes if committed by an adult.

1970s *School administrators reduce use of suspensions in response to court cases requiring due process for students who misbehave; schools establish security forces as reports of vandalism, burglary, assault and arson reach a peak in the mid-1970s.*

1975
In *Goss v. Lopez*, the Supreme Court rules that children cannot be suspended from school without due process.

1978
National Institute of Education publishes a report to Congress, "Violent Schools — Safe Schools," showing that school violence is national in scope.

—— • ——

1980s-1990s
Homicides increase among young people, propelled by the sharp upturn in gunshot deaths of young black males.

1989
Florida becomes the first state to make it a felony for a gun owner if children injure themselves or others with the adult's gun.

June 10, 1992
Surgeon General Antonia C. Novello declares deaths and injuries from gunshots a public health crisis. The *Journal of the American Medical Association* reveals that gunshot wounds are the second leading cause of death among all high school-age children.

Gun Wounds Killing More Teenagers

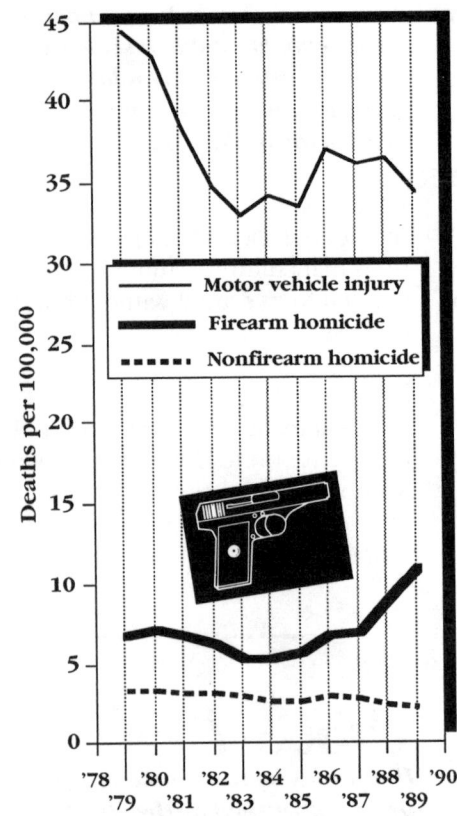

Deaths per 100,000

- — Motor vehicle injury
- ▬ Firearm homicide
- - - Nonfirearm homicide

Motor vehicles were the leading cause of death by far among teenagers 15 to 19 years of age from 1979-1989. But while teen deaths from car accidents decreased in the late 1980s, firearm homicides rose sharply. Non-firearm homicides declined or remained stable.

Source: Centers for Disease Control

'78 '79 '80 '81 '82 '83 '84 '85 '86 '87 '88 '89 '90

Continued from p. 794
cation movement, which opposed authoritarian methods and encouraged teachers to recognize the individual in students.

Beginning with experimental private schools in the teens and 1920s, progressive principles gradually gained wide acceptance during the first half of this century. Critics, however, blamed the movement's permissiveness for encouraging a breakdown of educational standards and behavior.

In the 1960s, the anti-establishment views of college students trickled down to the high schools, further contributing to disorder in the classroom. Many of those same young, idealistic college graduates were hired as teachers in the midst of a student population explosion in urban schools. According to Robert J. Rubel, author of *The Unruly School*, a history of school misbehavior, student baiting of teachers became the prevalent form of school disorder in the 1960s.[17]

Teachers in suburban and rural schools still demand more of their students in terms of attendance and homework than those in inner-city schools, Toby says, but it is their ability to back up their demands with suspensions that controls the violence.

Some critics of today's lax discipline point to the recent success Roman Catholic schools have had with minority students. Parochial schools are much more likely to improve the educational achievements of poor and minority students, and have lower dropout rates than public schools, concluded a 1987 study.[18]

Parochial school students, unlike public school students, "realize if they don't live up to the standard of the school, they will have to leave," Toby says.

Rising Use of Guns

Although surveys of school violence have been conducted from time to time, there are no national figures to indicate whether the overall level has increased in recent years. *(See story, p. 789.)* Yet Surgeon General Antonia C. Novello and other public health experts recently declared gun violence a public health crisis, particularly among young black males.[19]

In 1986, gun homicides became the second leading cause of death among teenagers 15-19, and gunshot fatalities have been increasing more rapidly than any other cause of death in that age group. Statistician Lois A. Fingerhut of the National Center for Health Statistics in Hyattsville, Md., attributes the increase in the teen homicide rate from 1979 to 1989 solely to "murder by guns." The rate for homicides by other methods actually decreased over the decade, she says.[20] *(See graph, above.)*

Some experts believe the skyrocketing toll can be explained at least in part by high rates of weapon-carrying and fighting among high school students. And students' perceptions that their schools are violent places also appear to be common. More than three-quarters of American teenagers believe that threats of violence against students are a problem in their schools, and more than 53 percent believe their schools have problems with students carrying weapons, according to a recent survey.[21]

Rural Areas at Risk

In the 1970s, surveys found that students and teachers in rural schools were less likely to be robbed or assaulted than those in big-city schools. In 1978, for example, the National Institute of Education reported that assaults on teachers were nine times as common in inner-city as in rural schools.[22] But more recent studies suggest that the most violent of crimes, homicide, is spreading beyond big cities. While the firearm homicide rate for teenagers remains highest in the inner cities, large increases in teenage gun deaths occurred for the first time in suburban areas and small towns; in suburbs, the rate increased an average of 23 percent annually from 1987 to 1989.[23]

In rural America, several surveys show the widespread extent of weapons-carrying. In Iowa, 23 percent of high school students carry a weapon to school, according to a survey of 1,773 students conducted by the Iowa Department of Education. By contrast, only 20 percent of high school students said they carried a weapon at least once in the month preceding a nationwide survey released last year by the CDC. (Students were not asked if they carried the weapon to school in the nationwide survey.)

Boys in small-town Texas carry handguns to school at twice national rates, according to a 1988 survey of 1,004 eighth- and 10th-graders from 23 central Texas communities. Paul M. Kingery, author of the study and director of the health promotion program at Texas A&M University, repeated the survey in 1990 and found that the rate of handgun-carrying to school had almost doubled among boys and girls.[24] Texas youths have also become inventive about carrying items that might not be recognized by adults as weapons, such as metal hair combs with teeth sharpened for stabbing, Kingery said.[25]

In surveys, teachers say that violence has gotten worse in schools. The extent of the change is revealed by a survey taken in 1940 and 1980, in which teachers were asked to list the top seven public school problems.[26] In 1940, talking out of turn, chewing gum, cutting in line, dress code infractions and littering were top problems. By 1980, three new entries had made the list: rape, robbery and assault. *(For complete list, see below.)*

Behind the Violence

With gunshot deaths among teens increasing, the cause can be found at least partly in the easy availability of guns. "There are just a tremendous number of firearms available on the streets and in homes," says Blauvelt of the National Association for School Safety and Law Enforcement. "I think carrying weapons has become a glamorous thing — just like dressing like a gang-banger," says the NSSC's Butterfield.

Nearly half of all male students and one-third of all students said they could easily obtain a handgun in a recent survey of Seattle public high schools. As gun sources, most students cited friends, buying a gun on the street or from a gun shop or getting one from home.[27]

The spread of gangs and drug traffic has also been implicated in the increasing violence among high school youths. While surveys show that kids are starting to say no to using drugs, "they're saying 'yes' to drug sales," reports Cleveland gang expert Kenneth Trump. He candidly admits to young audiences that they can make money as a drug-dealing gang member — for one or two years. But when he asks them to think of someone they know who has been in a gang at least four years, he finds, "Most kids, if they're honest, know of situations where a kid has been shot."

Yet gangs only explain part of what is happening in schools. In Cleveland, Trump estimates only 7-10 percent of violent incidents are gang-related. And outside of major cities, gangs and drugs are not major causes of homicide among young males, crime statistics indicate. Even in inner-city slums, they are probably more of a symptom than a cause.

Child Abuse a Factor

For teenagers who kill, there is more than emptiness at home. There

---

Public Schools Problems: 1940 vs. 1980

The top in-school problems identified by U.S. teachers in 1940 seem insignificant when compared with more serious concerns identified in a similar survey in 1980.

1940	1980
Talking Out of Turn	Drug Abuse
Chewing Gum	Alcohol Abuse
Making Noise	Pregnancy
Running in Halls	Suicide
Cutting in Line	Rape
Dress Code Infraction	Robbery
Littering	Assault

Source: CBS News broadcast cited by Sen. John Glenn, D-Ohio, in a statement before the Senate Committee on Governmental Affairs, March 31, 1992.

Leading the Nation in School Violence

In the 10 states listed bleow, at least 48 people died from gun-shot wounds and 156 were wounded in public and private schools from September 1986 to September 1990. The estimates are based on a review of newspaper articles on shooting incidents in schools by the Center to Prevent Handgun Violence.

States	Number of Incidents	Deaths	Woundings
California	29	16	45
Florida	25	10	10
New York	23	3	21
Texas	17	4	10
Georgia	14	1	15
Maryland	10	1	9
Michigan	9	3	6
Missouri	8	3	6
North Carolina	7	0	12
Illinois	7	7	12

Source: Center to Prevent Handgun Violence

CURRENT SITUATION

Gun-Free Zones

In response to shootings involving school-age children, federal, state and local lawmakers have passed legislation to bar guns at the school door. In 1990, Congress made it a felony to bring guns within 1,000 feet of any school under the "gun-free school zones" provision of the 1990 crime prevention package.

Modeled after drug-free school zones, which were aimed at adult drug dealers, the gun-free zones may be irrelevant when it comes to guns brought by schoolchildren. "How do you prosecute a sixth grader?" asks Vanessa K. Scherzer, a spokeswoman for the Center to Prevent Handgun Violence, an educational group in Washington, D.C.

Handgun Control Inc., the center's lobbying counterpart, supports gun-free zones but focuses on the passage of state laws penalizing adults who leave guns where children can get them. Ten states have passed such laws since 1989 *(see p. 794)*, and similar legislation was defeated in Georgia, Colorado and Missouri, where the National Rifle Association lobbied against it. The NRA says it opposes the law in those states where the statute would limit a prosecutor's flexibility to reduce the charge from a felony to a misdemeanor.

Whether such laws will deter adult gun owners remains to be seen. In California, C. Nicholas Conchas, the first person charged under the state's parental-responsibility law, plans to challenge the statute as unconstitutional. Conchas was charged in January in connection with the accidental gunshot death of his 4-year-old grandson. Conchas' attorney argued

is usually a history of abuse, often brutal, starting when a child is too young to understand what is happening.

In *Kids Who Kill*, psychologist Charles Patrick Ewing predicts that the annual number of juvenile homicides will continue to skyrocket, rising from 2,555 in 1990 to 8,000 by the year 2000. What seems to be driving this increase, he says, is an increase in child abuse, a characteristic he invariably finds in the backgrounds of young killers.

Adolescent homicides are often characterized by gratuitous "overkill": stabbing someone 46 times instead of once; emptying a gun into a victim's head. "To dehumanize a person to that extent — to treat them like a

piece of meat — I believe you yourself have to have been dehumanized," Ewing says.

As a consultant in legal cases involving juvenile killers, Ewing is now hearing about cases "in all walks of life," not just the inner city. He theorizes that the phenomenon, though still minor, is spreading in part because economic pressures, changes in family structures and drug use have pervaded the suburbs.

"We're much more one society now because of television and other media," Ewing adds. "Things that might never have occurred to some of these kids are now part of their consciousness." ■

that the statute was written too broadly and did not allow for due process.[28]

One difficulty in enforcing such laws may be the reluctance of prosecutors to charge an already grieving parent or grandparent. In Florida, staff analyst Brent Taylor of the House Criminal Justice Committee reports that since passage of the law, "The issue has died. There didn't seem to be a lot of prosecutions under it."

Focus on Relationships

Bowing to what some educators have dubbed the "fourth R" — for relationships — well over half the nation's school districts now employ educational approaches aimed at preventing violence. These efforts at "conflict resolution" vary widely. While some schools spend weeks training teachers to rethink their basic assumptions about conflict, others only ask teachers to spend a few minutes of health class discussing the dangers of guns.

Many schools train selected students to act as "peer mediation" teams. At DuVal High School in Prince George's County, Md., students involved in a dispute may be referred by a teacher to mediation before a full-fledged fight erupts. A team of two students who have received two days of training hears both sides and comes up with an agreement for both parties to sign. According to Peter Blauvelt, the system has reduced suspensions and fights at DuVal by half since the program was started three years ago.

Other community- and school-based violence-prevention programs for young adolescents utilize a variety of other methods — education, counseling, therapy, parent education, trips and well-baby care — according to the Carnegie Council on Adolescent Development in Washington, D.C. Many programs are offered in cooperation

with local businesses, churches and community centers. In Milwaukee, Wis., the Centro de la Comunidad Unida (United Community Center), which tries to discourage young Latinos from joining gangs, sponsors basketball games on Friday nights from 8 p.m. until midnight, when young people are most likely to be drinking or otherwise getting into trouble.[29]

Ensley High School in Birmingham, Ala., provides comprehensive health and social services for youngsters considered at risk for becoming violent. Ensley's Extra Help Services Clinic asks students on a confidential health form for information about drug and alcohol use, their ability to talk with their parents and their use of violence as a way to handle problems. The clinic provides counseling and classes that help students avoid violence by teaching them techniques for defusing anger and managing stress.[30]

The Violence Prevention Curriculum for Adolescents differs from traditional conflict-resolution training by confronting students' assumptions about the inevitability of violence "up front," says its creator, Deborah Prothrow-Stith. At the start of the 10-session program, students compile a class list of what makes them angry. Before students learn to resolve conflicts non-violently, they first complete an exercise in which they weigh the costs and benefits of fighting. "The aim is to create a desire to prevent fighting and a belief that it can be done," says Prothrow-Stith.

While some schools have seized on such programs, others still shy away from them. "Until the first shooting, they're still in the denial phase," says Karen Powe of the NSBA. "The tendency is to do nothing until they're scared by incidents." ∎

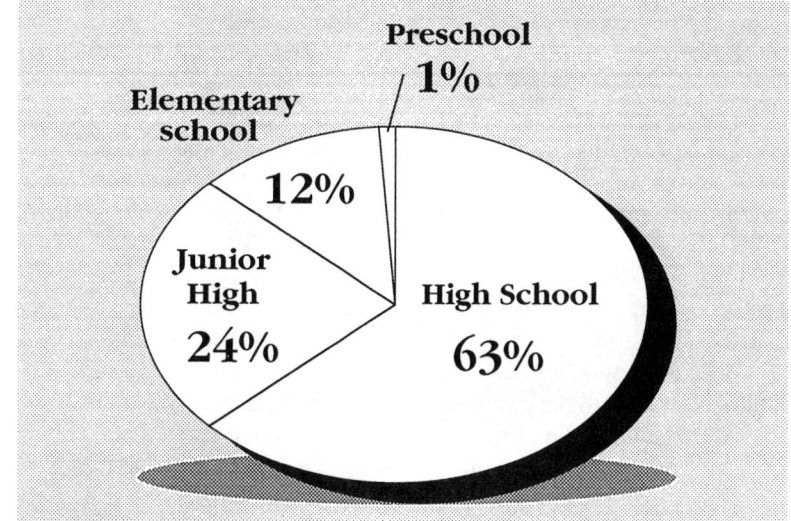

Schools Affected by Gun Violence

Incidents involving guns in schools occurred in high schools more than twice as frequently as at any other grade level.

Preschool 1%

Elementary school 12%

Junior High 24%

High School 63%

Source: Center to Prevent Handgun Violence

OUTLOOK

Early Intervention

School officials and authorities on children have a growing interest in schools taking over functions previously taught in the home: building self-esteem, learning to share and learning to cool down and think before fighting. That's because most violent youths share a common history of abuse at the hands of their parents. In a recent report to Congress, the General Accounting Office (GAO) reported that preschool programs combined with home visits early in a child's life could "reduce later delinquency and violent behavior."[31]

The GAO pointed to a widely cited 1984 study of black children from poor families who attended the Perry Preschool in Ypsilanti, Mich. The study followed the lives of 123 children, starting in 1962. The children were randomly assigned either to a group that attended preschool or a group that did not. By age 19, the preschool graduates were less likely to have been arrested, had lower numbers of arrests for serious crime and reported fewer violent behaviors than the control group. They were also more likely to be employed.[32]

However, even advocates of the latest violence-prevention curricula are rarely able to gauge their impact. "Often ... programs have been disseminated widely without any proof of their effectiveness," says Renee Wilson-Brewer of the Education Development Center, in Newton, Mass., which markets Prothrow-Stith's curriculum.[33] Wilson-Brewer authored the Carnegie Council study last year surveying 51 violence-prevention programs, the majority of them in schools. The study concluded it was "impossible to state with conviction which types of violence-prevention programs ... reviewed are most effec-

tive." According to Wilson-Brewer, almost none of the programs followed up on participants after the program had ended to see how their lives were affected, usually because they lacked the funds.[34]

Aside from insufficient funding, the biggest problem cited by violence-prevention experts is "overworked ... burned-out" teachers.[35] Some teachers are resentful when a new curriculum is introduced because they don't believe in it, others because it increases their workload, the Carnegie survey reported. And it's disheartening when one small program is expected to solve a school's violence problems, some trainers commented, without the aid of counseling, parent involvement or efforts to change the overall school environment.

Turning Schools into "Homes"

Indeed, some inner-city school administrators are becoming convinced that they must turn their schools into comprehensive, round-the-clock social service centers. They say that many of their students spend hours at home alone without adult guidance and that parents often seem to lack the time and the knowledge it takes to instill the basic values of a civilized society.

"We've got to find the money to make schools focal centers for the community — not just for children, but for parents, too," says principal Lillian Brinkley of Willard Model Elementary School in Norfolk, Va. Her ideal vision of the school would encompass parenting and adult education classes as well as branches of social service agencies. "When I have the students here for five hours, I have to be mother, father, social worker to get my work done," she says. "We've become more than teachers and dispensers of knowledge."

At Brooklyn's Thomas Jefferson High, where more than half the male students suffer a puncture wound as a result of violence, principal Carol

Beck has set up a "grieving room" staffed with guidance counselors to help students deal with the shootings of their classmates. Following the February incident, she dispatched psychologists into nearby housing projects to defuse tensions before they escalated into more violence.

Beck says she would like to build a dormitory for her students who don't have stable homes. And, she told a congressional committee this spring, if she had the money she would keep the school building open on nights and weekends to provide academic and athletic activities for students and their families.[36]

Even this may not be enough. Because violent children so often come from families where parents abuse them, programs that visit a child's home starting at infancy have the most impressive track records, according to the GAO. The Prenatal/Early Infancy Project in Elmira, N.Y., which worked with mothers most at risk for abusing their children, found fewer cases of abuse among mothers who had received regular home visits from nurses compared with those who had not. An evaluation of similar services offered by the Parent-Child Development Center in Houston, Texas, showed that five to eight years after families received the services, their children were rated by teachers as significantly less disruptive and hostile in school than similar children whose mothers did not receive services.[37]

It sounds expensive, but so is juvenile delinquency. Holding juvenile delinquents in custody cost taxpayers $1.7 billion in 1988, or an average annual per-resident expense of $29,600, according to the Justice Department. By contrast, evaluators estimate the Perry Preschool program returned $3-$6 for every dollar invested in it because of the savings from reduced crime and welfare payments and increased income from employment.

Continued on p. 802

At Issue:

Should gun owners be prosecuted if children injure themselves or others with the adult's gun?

SARAH BRADY

Chair, Handgun Control Inc.
SEPT. 11, 1992*

yes

Many Americans believe that my involvement in the campaign for sensible gun laws began immediately after the 1981 shooting of my husband, former White House Press Secretary James Brady. In fact, the incident that really spurred me into joining the movement against handgun violence was a near-tragic gun incident involving my son, Scott.

While visiting relatives one summer, my then 5-year-old son and I hopped in the pick-up truck of a relative, when Scott picked up and started playing with a toy he found sitting on the seat. As I took the gun from my son, I realized to my horror that what he was waving around was a real, loaded Saturday night special. I couldn't believe that the Brady family had nearly suffered another handgun tragedy.

Every day in this country, a child is accidentally killed with a gun, and countless more are seriously injured. In almost every case, these weapons were stored carelessly within easy reach of the child, loaded and unsecured. According to the Centers for Disease Control, over 1 million elementary-age, latch-key children have access to guns. Loaded, easily accessible guns in the home also contribute to hundreds of teenage suicides and a growing number of gun-related incidents in our nations's schools.

In 1989, Florida became the first state in the nation to enact a law which recognized that adult gun owners have a responsibility to keep their weapons locked away from children. Leaving a loaded firearm where one knows or reasonably should know that a child may gain access to it, can result in criminal charges. Organizations on both sides of the gun debate, Handgun Control, Inc., and the National Rifle Association, endorsed Florida's child safety law. Nine other states have adopted similar statutes aimed at preventing gun tragedies, and Congress will be looking at related gun safety legislation next year.

The point of these laws is not to confiscate guns, and it is not to punish grieving parents. Rather it is to promote the safe and responsible storage of firearms — before a tragedy happens. We use seat belts to prevent serious injury in car accidents. We put up fences around swimming pools to prevent child drowning. We must store guns safely away from children to prevent gun injury and death. However, should a child be killed or injured as a result of negligence, criminal charges must apply.

The accidental shooting death of a child is one of the most tragic aspects of America's gun violence epidemic. It is also one of the most preventable.

MARION P. HAMMER

2nd Vice President, National Rifle Association
SEPT. 11, 1992*

no

Pesticides and cleaning solutions under the sink. Plastic bags lying in a closet. Matches on the table. These common household items are just some of the potential hazards that could lead to the tragic injury or even death of a child. Parents know of these dangers. So they teach their children not to play with matches and not to touch the pesticides. Parents teach safety.

With a firearm now in an estimated one out of every two households in America, responsible parents are also teaching their children to be safe around firearms. The NRA's "Eddie Eagle" program has spread a simple but important message: "If you find a gun: Stop! Don't Touch. Leave the area. Tell an adult."

But rather than help teach children to be safe, there are those who argue that the way to prevent accidents is to punish parents after the accident occurs. These people contend that passing laws to send parents to jail if their firearm is misused by a child will cause such accidents to decrease.

Actually, there are currently laws on the books in every state dealing with accidents caused by negligence. Yet groups like Handgun Control Inc. continue to single out firearm accidents, even though such accidents are already decreasing.

From 1967 to 1990, the number of accidental firearm deaths in the United States dropped from 2,986 to 1,400. During the same period, the population, the number of gun owners and the number of firearms owned increased substantially. This is also the same time period during which the NRA intensified its safety-training effort. Today, the 30,000 NRA certified instructors teach nearly 1 million firearm owners a year. The more that people, including children, know about firearms and their potential dangers, the less an accident is likely to occur.

In spite of the decreasing number of firearm accidents, some people continue to sensationalize the pain and trauma suffered by families involved in an accident to push their own agenda of removing firearms from families. Putting parents in jail would not reduce accidents. It would only further injure a family that is already hurting.

Parents are responsible for the conduct and safety of their children. But, just like the police, parents cannot always be there. Teaching children safety is the only way to prevent an accident from occurring. Education and responsible parenting are the keys to preventing tragic accidents — not emotional rhetoric designed to drive a hidden agenda.

*Both articles were written for *The CQ Researcher.*

TV and the Breakdown of Values

"Our children are subjected to some of the most insidious forms of brain-washing developed by mankind," Carol A. Beck, principal of Brooklyn's violence-wracked Thomas Jefferson High School, told a congressional panel in March. Specifically, she pointed to "the constant ... violence portrayed in the media [and] the constant message that easy money can provide them with all the benefits our society has to offer, and that hard work, honesty and moral character are not always attributes of successful Americans." †

Beck is not alone. Increasingly, school officials and others are taking seriously the impact of violent television programs on young people's behavior. In fact, child-development experts say infants as young as 14 months imitate behavior they see on TV, and children up to age 4 are often unable to distinguish fact from fantasy. In moments of stress, says psychiatrist Brandon S. Centerwall of Seattle, Wash., adolescents are likely to revert to their earliest, most visceral memories of TV violence.††

For children who are already aggressive, TV violence may simply confirm their worst instincts. The more frequently children watched television at age 8, the more serious the crimes for which they were convicted by age 30, University of Illinois psychologist Leonard D. Eron found in a long-term study of 875 boys and girls. One explanation, says Eron, is that children who are more aggressive to start with tend to be less popular with their peers and are likely to spend more time alone watching television. The violence they see on TV may reassure them that their own behavior is appropriate.‡

Of course, TV is often a reflection of messages that the larger society is giving children. Deborah Prothrow-Stith, assistant dean of Harvard University's School of Public Health, starts her presentations to inner-city high school students by apologizing. "From your very first cartoon through 'Lethal Weapon 3,'" she tells them, "we have told you violence is the hero's way to solve the problem: Hit back, be the Rambo. That's just not the way it is. You've been to enough funerals to know it's painful, tragic and rarely solves the problem and often leads to revenge and more violence."

High school students appreciate the entertainment value in a good fight, Prothrow-Stith learned. She also found that fights usually develop in stages, as schoolmates carry stories from one side to the other, ratcheting up the drama. "They say, 'Man, what you going to do about it?' Someone says 3 o'clock at the corner, and you go and there's a large crowd there. We encourage fighting. We're there at 3 o'clock on the corner."

But television and movies probably wouldn't have the same impact if it weren't for the void that many students now feel at home, experts say. "Parents are not staying together, and kids are not living with their first parents anymore," says Paul M. Kingery, director of the health promotion program at Texas A&M University. "People are working more hours outside of home. TV is much more exciting than reality."

---

† Testimony of Carol A. Beck before the Senate Committee on Governmental Affairs, March 31, 1992.

†† Brandon S. Centerwall, "Television and Violence," *Journal of the American Medical Association*, June 10, 1992, pp. 3059-3063.

‡ Testimony of Leonard D. Eron before the Senate Committee on Governmental Affairs, March 31, 1992.

Similarly, a Syracuse University research program that provided day care and home visiting to very poor, predominantly black families found the average juvenile justice cost per child was $186 for the home-visiting group and $1,985 for a control group. Only 6 percent of children who received the services underwent probation as teenagers, compared with 22 percent of the control group.[38]

How much schools can do by themselves to shape character is still unclear. But experts inside and outside the education system agree that since schools reflect the larger society, Americans will have to alter their own attitudes toward violence before they can expect their children to change. Schools may be the earliest opportunity society has to do that.

Sarah Glazer is a free-lance writer in Washington, D.C.

Notes

[1] Incidents reported in Donna Harrington-Lueker, "Blown Away," *American School Board Journal*, May 1992, pp. 21-27.

[2] "Weapon-Carrying Among High School Students, 1990," *Morbidity and Mortality Weekly Report*, Oct. 11, 1991, pp. 681-684. Note: The CDC survey did not ask students whether they had carried a weapon to school but only if they had carried one at least once in the month before the survey.

[3] See National School Safety Center, *Weapons Statistics*, October 1991, p. 1.

[4] For background, see "Youth Gangs," *The CQ Researcher*, Oct. 11, 1991, pp. 753-776.

[5] According to the General Accounting Of-

fice, an estimated 79 percent of all serious, violent juvenile crime is committed by 7 percent of the youths. See testimony of Gregory J. McDonald, GAO director of human services, before the Senate Committee on Governmental Affairs, March 31, 1992, p. 3.

[6] See "Protection Racket," *The Economist*, Nov. 30, 1991, p. 29, and testimony of Carol A. Beck before the Senate Committee on Governmental Affairs, March 31, 1992.

[7] Harlan Draeger, "Judge backs school ban on male earrings as 'anti-gang,'" *Chicago Sun-Times*, Dec. 2, 1987, p. 23.

[8] For a review of state confidentiality laws, see James A. Rapp et al., *The Need to Know: Juvenile Record Sharing*, National School Safety Center, 1989.

[9] *Ibid.*, p. 4.

[10] Jackson Toby, "Crime in the Schools," in James Q. Wilson, ed., *Crime and Public Policy* (1983), p. 79.

[11] See Ezra Bowen, "Getting Tough," *Time*, Feb. 1, 1988, pp. 52-58.

[12] *Ibid.*

[13] "The Killing Grounds: Can Schools Help Stem the Violence?" *The Harvard Education Letter*, July/August 1991, p. 5.

[14] Ronald G. Slaby and Nancy G. Guerra, "Cognitive Mediators of Aggression in Adolescent Offenders: 1. Assessment," *Developmental Psychology*, 1988, pp. 580-588.

[15] Nancy G. Guerra and Ronald G. Slaby, "Cognitive Mediators of Aggression in Adolescent Offenders: 2. Intervention," *Developmental Psychology*, 1990, pp. 269-277.

[16] National School Safety Center, *School Crime and Violence Statistical Review*, August 1992, p. 18. For background see "Reassessing the Nation's Gun Laws," *Editorial Research Reports*, March 22, 1991, pp. 158-171.

[17] Robert J. Rubel, *The Unruly School* (1977), pp. 70-71, 150.

[18] James S. Coleman and Thomas Hoffer, *Public and Private High Schools: The Impact of Communities* (1987).

[19] See Philip Hilts, "Gunshots Killing More Teen-Agers, *The New York Times*, June 10, 1992, p. A19.

[20] Lois A. Fingerhut et al., "Firearm and Nonfirearm Homicide Among Persons 15 through 19 Years of Age," *Journal of the American Medical Association*, June 10, 1992, p. 3048.

[21] "Survey Suggests Most U.S. Teens Find Violence, Weapons in Schools," *Education Week*, June 3, 1992, p. 2.

[22] National Institute of Education, *Violent Schools-Safe Schools* (1978).

[23] Fingerhut, *op. cit.*, p. 3050.

[24] In 1988, 6 percent of the boys in the Texas survey said they carried a handgun at least once in the past year compared with 3 percent of the youths in the 1989 *National Adolescent Student Health Survey: A Report on the Health of America's Youth*, conducted by the Association for the Advancement of Health Education in Reston, Va. Forty percent of boys in the Texas sample carried a knife to school, compared with 23 percent in the national sample.

[25] Paul M. Kingery et al., "Rural Communities near Large Metropolitan Areas: Safe Havens from Adolescent Violence and Drug Use?," *Health Values*, July/August 1991, p. 47.

[26] The two surveys, broadcast by CBS News in 1987, were cited by Sen. John Glenn, D-Ohio, chairman of the Senate Committee on Governmental Affairs, in his opening statement for hearings on youth violence prevention, March 31, 1992.

[27] Charles M. Callahan et al., "Urban High School Youth and Handguns," *Journal of the American Medical Association*, June 10, 1992, pp. 3038-3042.

[28] The Associated Press, "Grandfather Will Challenge Gun Law," *San Jose Mercury News*, March 25, 1992, p. 1B.

[29] "Public Health Attacks Violence," *Medicine and Health Perspectives*, June 22, 1992.

[30] Gregory J. McDonald, General Accounting Office, Testimony before the Senate Governmental Affairs Committee, March 31, 1992, p. 12.

[31] General Accounting Office, *Reducing Youth Violence*, March 31, 1992, p. 9.

[32] John R. Berrueta-Clement et al., *Changed Lives: The Effects of the Perry Preschool Program on Youths Though Age 19*, High/Scope Educational Research Foundation, 1984.

[33] Testimony of Renee Wilson-Brewer before the Senate Governmental Affairs Committee, March 31, 1992.

[34] Renee Wilson-Brewer et al., *Violence Prevention for Young Adolescents: A Survey of the State of the Art*, September 1991, p. 56.

[35] *Ibid.*, pp. 17-18.

[36] Testimony of Carol A. Beck before the Senate Committee on Governmental Affairs, March 31, 1992.

[37] General Accounting Office, *op. cit.*, pp. 11-12.

[38] *Ibid.*, p. 10.

Bibliography

Selected Sources Used

Books

Ewing, Charles Patrick, *Kids Who Kill*, Avon Books, 1990.

A collection of readable case histories and some statistics about youngsters who have committed homicide.

Prothrow-Stith, Deborah, *Deadly Consequences*, HarperCollins Publishers, 1991.

This well-written book discusses the causes of violence among today's teenagers and proposes a public health approach to fighting it. The author, an assistant dean at the Harvard School of Public Health, presents an excellent mix of research, statistics and anecdotes about her own experience teaching adolescents at inner-city Boston schools.

Rubel, Robert J., *The Unruly School: Disorders, Disruptions and Crimes*, Lexington Books, 1977.

Though dated, this book provides a useful historical perspective on school misbehavior and violence from the 1950s through the 1970s and social changes that spurred growing unruliness among students.

Articles

Callahan, C.M., et al., "Urban High School Youth and Handguns: A School-based Survey," *Journal of the American Medical Association*, June 10, 1992, p. 3038.

One of the most recent surveys of students' gun-carrying habits, this one in Seattle public schools, reports that many students believe guns are easy to obtain. Published in a special issue devoted to violence.

Fingerhut, Lois A., et al., "Firearm and Nonfirearm Homicide Among Persons 15 through 19 Years of Age," *Journal of the American Medical Association*, June 10, 1992, pp. 3048-3053.

This widely cited article reports that gun homicides are now the second leading cause of death among high school-age youth. It finds that young black males in the inner cities have the highest rates of death from gun homicides, but rates are also increasing among young people in the suburbs.

Hickey, Neil, "How Much Violence?" and "The Experts Speak Out," *TV Guide*, Aug. 22-28, 1992, pp. 10-23.

This special issue of *TV Guide* is devoted to the question "Is TV Violence Battering our Kids?" The answer is yes, say the magazine's editors. In a survey of an 18-hour day of television programs in Washington, D.C., the magazine found that cartoons are the most violent form of television program. The issue reports research findings that TV violence can lead children to real-life violence and presents a panel discussion between experts on violence and network representatives.

Toby, Jackson, "Crime in the Schools," *Crime and Public Policy*, ICS Press, 1983, p. 69.

The Rutgers University sociologist says that one of the main contributors to school violence has been declining use of suspensions and expulsions.

"Weapons in Schools," *Juvenile Justice Bulletin*, Office of Juvenile Justice and Delinquency Prevention, U.S. Department of Justice, October 1989.

A good overview of problems that schools are experiencing with weapons, measures they are taking and controversies surrounding those measures.

Reports and Studies

Caught in the Crossfire: A Report on Gun Violence In Our Nation's Schools, Center to Prevent Handgun Violence, 1990.

This report, based solely on newspaper accounts, provides statistics on school shootings that occurred from September 1986 to September 1990. It looks at causes, locations and types of schools affected.

Violence Prevention for Young Adolescents: A Survey of the State of the Art, Carnegie Council on Adolescent Development, September 1991.

A survey of school and community programs aimed at preventing teen violence.

Violent Schools — Safe Schools: The Safe School Study Report to the Congress, National Institute of Education, 1978.

The last major national study of violence in schools, this report contains interesting contrasts as well as parallels to today's concerns.

Weapons Statistics, National School Safety Center, October 1991.

Rates of weapon-carrying among students, as reported in the most well-known current studies, are summarized in this report.

Youth Violence Prevention, Hearings before the Senate Committee on Governmental Affairs, March 31, 1992.

Soon to be available from the committee, these hearings should provide one of the best sources of information on the topic of youth violence. The hearings featured testimony from numerous prominent experts.

The Next Step

Additional Articles from Current Periodicals from EBSCO Publishing's Database

Books & reading

Huffman, C.A., "Book review: Junior high up," *School Library Journal*, November 1991, p. 140.

Reviews the book "Teen Violence," by Susan S. Lang.

White, L.K., "Book review: Junior high up," *School Library Journal*, September 1990, p. 264.

Reviews the book "Teenage Violence," by Elaine Landau.

Clothing

"Robberies push Detroit's school board to propose district-wide dress code," *Jet*, Jan. 1, 1990, p. 28.

Reports on a proposed dress code by the Detroit Board of Education, due to violent incidents in the public schools over designer clothing items.

Darnton, N., "Street crimes of fashion," *Newsweek*, March 5, 1990, p. 58.

Reports on the two-year-old trend in the poor sections of American cities (New York, Detroit, Newark, N.J., Los Angeles) where more and more kids are resorting to violence, including killing, for cool clothes. Athletic and leather jackets; sneakers; down parkas. Totemlike power; revival of mandatory dress codes in schools.

Galloway, J.L., J. Trimble, et al., "Your jacket or your life," *U.S. News & World Report*, Feb. 26, 1990, p. 14.

Reports that school dress codes are becoming more common in the face of violent crime triggered by the theft of "starter jackets" in Chicago, Air Jordan sneakers, and Nike shoes in Detroit. Banning various adornments.

Murder

"Violence in American schools," *Pediatrics for Parents*, January 1992, p. 5.

Reports that in the past five years, 65 students and six school workers were killed at school by guns. Statistics from the Centers for Disease Control (CDC); children carrying weapons; examples.

Gregory, S.S., L. Morrow, et al., "Childhood's end," *Time*, March 9, 1992, p. 22.

Recounts the double murder in Brooklyn's Thomas Jefferson High School, where Khalil Sumpter, 15, allegedly shot Tyrone Sinkler, 16 and Ian Moore, 17, at point-blank range with a .38-caliber revolver. Both students died. Gun violence in New York City, Los Angeles, Houston and Boston; guns as a fetish of manhood; accessibility; children kill children for earrings, jackets and tennis shoes.

Nordland, R., "Deadly lessons," *Newsweek*, March 9, 1992, p. 22.

Reports that kids with guns are setting off an arms race of their own across the country — as a double murder in New York City showed. Considers whether American schools are doomed to become free-fire zones. Details of the recent outbreak of violence at New York City's Jefferson high school that left two teenagers dead.

Prevention

"Preventing school violence," *The Futurist*, July/August 1990, p. 52.

Describes preventive measures against school violence. Controversial metal detectors; alarm systems; two-way intercoms; effect on students; more.

Bjorklund, B., & D. Bjorklund, "Battling the schoolyard bully," *Parents*, April 1989, p. 195.

Discusses schoolyard bullies and their violence, also research that shows it's a more serious problem than previously thought. Advice to parents for dealing with bullies; research findings.

Eddowes, E.A. & J.R. Hranitz, "Violence: A crisis in homes and schools," *Childhood Education*, fall 1990, p. 4.

Examines the increasing violence in American schools and homes and discusses the role of educators, legislators, parents and psychologists in reducing the incidence of violence. Statistics on violence in schools; battered women and domestic violence; changes in the family unit; children as the victims of violence; need for teaching conflict resolution skills and responsible citizenship; suggestions.

Gest, T., "These perilous halls of learning," *U.S. News & World Report*, March 13, 1989, p. 68.

Report that recent tragedies in schools have resulted in preventive action. Crimes; murders; positive approach; drills; security measures. INSET: A tragic report card (school crimes).

Harrington-Lueker, D., "Protecting schools from outside violence," *Education Digest*, December 1989, p. 46.

Reports on what schools in Greenwood, S.C., and Winnetka, Ill. are doing to develop a total security plan in the wake of major violent incidents in elementary schools there. Important components of any school security plan.

Hayes, L., "Reducing school violence," *Phi Delta Kappan*, December 1991, p. 334.

Discusses how the U.S. Justice Department should release statistics on schools that have reduced violence, such as a middle school in Albuquerque, N.M., that reduced violence by teaching gang members techniques of conflict resolution.

Kantrowitz, B., E. Salholz, et al., "How to keep kids safe," *Newsweek*, March 9, 1992, p. 30.

Reports that school violence has become a dismal fact of life, yet many educators continue to respond with not-in-my-schoolyard denial. Describes the Schools Are For Education (SAFE) program that is being used in Chicago's public schools; strategies schools are adopting to help kids avoid being victims of crimes involving firearms.

McFadden, R.D., "Security and schools," *The New York Times*, March 2, 1992, p. A1.

States that parents, educators and elected leaders are haunted by violence at New York City schools. Visits to four high schools provide a look at security, the culture of weapons, the proud academic atmosphere in some schools and tensions in others.

Monaghan, P., "Summer programs at Portland campus aims to help poor teen-agers steer clear of gangs' violence," *The Chronicle of Higher Education*, Aug. 15, 1990, p. A23.

Describes a summer program at the Cascade campus of Portland Community College which pays students to attend, and has 16 students identified by school counselors, police gang units or other agencies as at risk of becoming involved with gangs. Improving writing and math skills; facing the hazards of growing up poor; keeping track of the students through high school.

Ostling, R.N., "Shootouts in the schools," *Time*, Nov. 20, 1989, p. 116.

Reports on ways educators are trying to cope with classroom violence. Security measures and the cost; training of staff.

Steinberg, A., "How schools can help stem violence in today's youth," *Education Digest*, November 1991, p. 40.

Informs that school people concerned about violence can choose from a growing number of prevention curricula. New curriculum for middle schools that is due to be published by the Educational Development Center (EDC) in

Newton, Mass.; the EDC's Health Promotion Program for high schools, developed by Deborah Prothrow-Stith of Harvard University's School of Public Health.

Steinberg, J., "Dinkins promises money for safety in worst schools," *The New York Times*, March 2, 1992, p. A1.

Tells of New York City Mayor David N. Dinkins' program to identify the 40 most dangerous public high schools and middle schools in the city and to bolster security at them. He was responding to a plea from school Chancellor Joseph A. Fernandez, following the shooting deaths of two students by a third one at Thomas Jefferson High School on Feb. 26. Cost of the program; skepticism that the program would halt the violence.

Stephens, R.D., "Bullies and victims: Protecting our schoolchildren," *USA Today*, September 1991, p. 72.

Probes the increased bullying and intimidation that has invaded many of America's schools and communities. Examples of schoolyard bullying; common characteristics of bullies; impact on victims and society; proposals for combating this pervasive problem; focus on a four-step program of prevention.

Teachers

Garza-Lubeck, M., "A student pulled a knife: The contributing circumstances and aftermath," *Equity & Excellence*, summer 1990, p. 41.

Presents a case study of a threatened knifing involving a student and his teacher. Provides an in-depth examination of in-school violence from a variety of perspectives — perpetrators, victims, and others indirectly involved. Examines the factors that contributed to both the attempted knifing and the school administration's response.

Martin, D., "Teachers strive to rise above the grip of despair," *The New York Times*, Feb. 29, 1992, p. 25.

Tells how the escalating violence in Thomas Jefferson High School in New York City (two students were shot to death by a third on Feb. 26) has brought profound disillusionment for the teachers. Their locked classroom doors no longer bring a feeling of security. Their reasons for teaching in a such a school.

Violence

"A blackboard jungle," *Maclean's*, March 16, 1992, p. 30.

Presents a report from Washington correspondent Hilary Mackenzie regarding crime in U.S. schools that is reaching epidemic proportions. Nowhere is the situation more bleak than in the poorest parts of Washington, where the District of Columbia Public School Security Service has logged 52 weapons incidents already in this school year. Culture of drugs and gang violence turning schools into armed camps; comments from students on owning guns; violence on school property.

"Physical fighting among high school students — United States, 1990," *Journal of the American Medical Association*, June 10, 1992, p. 3009.

Presents self-reported data about the prevalence and incidence of physical fighting among high school students in the United States during 1990. The Youth Risk Behavior Survey; percentage listings by race/ethnicity and sex; editorial note from the Centers for Disease Control; more.

Bell, A., "Campus showdown," *Teen Magazine*, November 1988, p. 54.

Discusses violence in the nation's high schools. Cliques; turf fights; "peer terrorism"; use of weapons and bombs; role of drugs and alcohol; how teenagers deal with society's hostility; materialism; violence among girls; how school systems are trying to prevent campus violence.

Burke, D., "A study in fear," *Maclean's*, May 22, 1989, p. 42.

Examines gang violence in the Montreal, Quebec school system. Racial and ethnic hatred; struggle to cope with students from a wide variety of ethnic backgrounds; comments by police; incidents at Metro (subway) stations.

Hardy, J.E., S. Manning, et al., "Violent youth," *Scholastic Update*, April 5, 1991, p. 5.

Explores some of the most disturbing examples of violence by and against teens. Gang warfare; killing for status clothes; hate crimes; violence in schools; battered and sexually abused girlfriends.

Lee, F.R., "Violence is scarce in schools, police find," *The New York Times*, Feb. 13, 1990, p. B1.

Says that five New York City police officers, all of whom were men age 20 or 21 years old, who spent seven months undercover as high school students, found little evidence of drug use, weapons, or gang activity in the schools. They reported that virtually all of the violence and drug use attributed to students goes on outside schools.

Lee, F.R., "When violence and terror strike outside the schools," *The New York Times*, Nov. 14, 1989, p. B1.

Reports that though violence in schools is still a major problem, it's violence outside of schools that frightens most students in New York City. Gang and posse violence; antiviolence measures inside schools.

Menacker, J., W. Weldon, et al., "School order and safety as community issues," *Phi Delta Kappan*, September 1989, p. 39.

Reports on research into the lawlessness, danger, and lack of discipline perceived to be found in inner-city schools. Results show, however, that schools are islands of safety in dangerous communities. Policy decisions and recommendations for communitywide solutions are discussed.

Zinsmeister, K., "Growing up scared," *The Atlantic*, June 1990, p. 49.

Reports on the increasing problem of violent crime involving children in the United States. Family breakdown; bolstering healthy families; housing vouchers; holding parents responsible; violence in the schools; problems with the correction system; RID ("regimented inmate discipline") program for juvenile offenders.

Weapons

"Protection racket," *The Economist*, Nov. 30, 1991, p. 29.

Discusses the problems of guns in New York City's schools. In-school shooting of a 16-year-old student by a 14-year-old; nearly 500 under-16-year-olds shot in New York this year; weapons possession up 14 percent from last year; views of the teachers' union; details.

"Students and weapons: A deadly combination," *NEA Today*, March 1992, p. 32.

Reports that one in five high school students sometimes carries a gun, knife, or other weapon with the intention of using it if necessary. Findings by researchers with the Centers for Disease Control; recent incidents of violent crime in public schools across the United States; examples.

"Weapon-carrying among high school students," *Journal of the American Medical Association*, Nov. 6, 1991, p. 2342.

Presents prevalence and incidence of self-reported weapon-carrying among U.S. 9-12 graders during 1990. Statistics on homicides committed by high school-age youths using firearms, cutting instruments, or blunt objects; the 1990 national school-based Youth Risk Behavior Survey; strategies employed by school systems to confiscate weapons and deter students from bringing weapons onto school grounds; editorial note from the Centers for Disease Control (CDC); more.

Hedges, S.J., G. Witkin, et al., "Kids who kill," *U.S. News & World Report*, April 8, 1991, p. 26.

Discusses the prevalence of youths killing with and being killed by guns. States that every 100 hours, more youths die on the streets than were killed in the Persian Gulf. Focuses on several youths who have been killed within the last year by youths with guns; the reasons why youths feel the need to carry a gun; the gang connection; easy access to the purchase of guns; the schools crack down; violence prevention; more.

Back Issues

Great Research on Current Issues Starts Right Here... Recent topics covered by The CQ Researcher are listed below. Issues dated before May 10, 1991, were published under the name of Editorial Research Reports.

MARCH 1991
Acid Rain
Cost of the Gulf War
Reassessing Gun Laws
Future for Man in Space

APRIL 1991
Social Security
Canadian Crisis Over Quebec
California Drought
Electromagnetic Radiation

MAY 1991
School Choice
Racial Quotas
Animal Rights
U.S. and Japan

JUNE 1991
Children and Divorce
Teenage Suicide
Endangered Species
Europe 1992

JULY 1991
Teenagers and Abortion
Soviet Republics Rebel
Mexico's Emergence
Athletes and Drugs

AUGUST 1991
Sexual Harassment
Fetal Tissue Research
Oil Imports
The Palestinians

SEPTEMBER 1991
Police Brutality
Advertising Under Attack
Saving the Forests
Foster Care Crisis

OCTOBER 1991
Pay-Per-View TV
Youth Gangs
Gene Therapy
World Hunger

NOVEMBER 1991
Fast-Food Shake-Up
The Greening of Eastern Europe
Business' Role in Education
Cuba In Crisis

DECEMBER 1991
Retiree Health Benefits
Asian Americans
The Obscenity Debate
The Disabilities Act

JANUARY 1992
Term Limits
Oil Spills
Hunting Controversy
Alternative Medicine

FEBRUARY 1992
Threatened Coastlines
New Era in Asia
Assisted Suicide
Jobs in the '90s

MARCH 1992
Women and Sports
Underage Drinking
Garbage Crisis
Mafia Crackdown

APRIL 1992
Ozone Depletion
Welfare Reform
Politicians and Privacy
Illegal Immigration

MAY 1992
Native Americans
Jobs vs. Environment
Too Many Lawsuits?
Fairness in Salaries

JUNE 1992
Nuclear Proliferation
Food Irradiation
Lead Poisoning
Hard Times for Libraries

JULY 1992
Alternative Energy
Prescription Drug Prices
Alzheimer's Disease
Infant Mortality

AUGUST 1992
The Homeless
Work, Family and Stress
NATO's Changing Role
Marine Mammals vs. Fish

SEPTEMBER 1992
Domestic Partners

Back issues are available for $4.00 (subscribers) or $7.00 (non-subscribers). Quantity discounts apply to orders over ten. To order, call Congressional Quarterly 1-800-432-2250.

Binders are available for $15.00. To order call 1-800-638-1710.

Future Topics

▶ *Public Television*

▶ *Women in the Military*

▶ *Depression*

Public Broadcasting

Will political attacks and new technologies force big changes?

THE NATION'S PUBLIC BROADCASTING SYSTEM is at a crossroads. Conservatives have stepped up attacks on its alleged liberal bias, politicians wary about budget deficits have been eying its federal funding and advocates of privatization say that it has been rendered obsolete by cable television. Public TV officials are re-evaluating the complex community of stations and bureaucracies that was spawned by President Lyndon B. Johnson's Great Society of the 1960s. As they brush up against private competition in a technologically evolving marketplace, many of these officials are reorganizing and making a case that public broadcasting is more needed than ever before. They contend that amid increasing commercialization, only public broadcasting offers quality educational programming and broad community access to the public airways.

C_Q **September 18, 1992 • Volume 2, No. 35 • 809-832**

Formerly Editorial Research Reports

THE CQ Researcher

September 18, 1992
Volume 2, No. 35

EDITOR
Sandra Stencel

MANAGING EDITOR
Thomas J. Colin

ASSOCIATE EDITOR
Richard L. Worsnop

STAFF WRITERS
Charles S. Clark
Mary H. Cooper
Rodman D. Griffin

PRODUCTION EDITOR
Sarah E. Merritt

EDITORIAL ASSISTANT
Michael M. Taylor

GRAPHICS
Jack Auldridge

PUBLISHED BY
Congressional Quarterly Inc.

CHAIRMAN
Andrew Barnes

VICE CHAIRMAN
Andrew P. Corty

EDITOR AND PUBLISHER
Neil Skene

EXECUTIVE EDITOR
Robert W. Merry

PUBLICATIONS MARKETING/SALES
Robert Smith

EDITOR, EBSCO PUBLISHING
Melissa Kummerer

The CQ Researcher (ISSN 1056-2036). Formerly Editorial Research Reports. Published weekly (48 times per year, not printed the first Friday of any month with five Fridays) by Congressional Quarterly Inc., 1414 22nd St., N.W., Washington, D.C. 20037. Rates are furnished upon request. Second-class postage paid at Washington, D.C. POSTMASTER: Send address changes to The CQ Researcher, 1414 22nd St., N.W., Washington, D.C. 20037.

Public Broadcasting

BY CHARLES S. CLARK

THE ISSUES

Public broadcasting celebrated its 25th birthday this year immersed in what seems to have become one of its regularly scheduled programs: fending off attacks from conservatives.

In a symphony of criticism that trailed its recent reauthorization bill through Congress, public broadcasting was variously labeled "an upper-middle-class entitlement program," "a government frill we can no longer afford" and a liberal mouthpiece for promoters of homosexuality.

On the floor of the Senate in June, Sen. Bob Dole, R-Kan., led a charge to freeze public broadcasting funds, complaining of "big private profits from a so-called nonprofit network; big bureaucracies and big salaries . . . and the steady stream of documentary cheerleading for left-wing interests."

"The liberals love it," Dole said. "They have their own network. We are talking about political documentaries which come as close to being an editorial page as an institution such as broadcasting has."

Singled out for fire among recent Public Broadcasting Service (PBS) documentaries were reports by two veteran journalists: Bill Moyers' "America: What Went Wrong?" which examined economic decline during the 1980s, and William Greider's "The Betrayal of Democracy," which looked at the role of lobbyists and political action committees in alienating voters from government. Critics also blasted a PBS decision in 1990 not to broadcast a British environmental documentary, "The Greenhouse Conspiracy," which downplayed concerns about global warming.

The most vehement anger was directed at "Tongues Untied," a 1991 National Endowment for the Arts-supported documentary on gay black

men. The program was rejected by more than 200 of the nation's 340 public television stations when PBS sent it out on its national feed. "We're noticing that [PBS stations] are showing an inordinately high number of programs dealing with homosexuality," said the Rev. Donald Wildmon, who heads the American Family Association in Tupelo, Miss. "We do not think the government should be endorsing the homosexual lifestyle."[1]

Weighing in on the issue were an array of conservative media-watchdog groups and some vocal individuals who began devoting almost full time to attacking public broadcasting. Author David Horowitz, a leftist activist during the 1960s who became a neoconservative and Dole speechwriter in the 1980s, began publishing stinging critiques of the "leftist slant" of PBS foreign policy documentaries from his Studio City, Calif.-based organization, the Committee on Media Integrity (COMINT). And Laurence Jarvik, a communications scholar at the conservative Heritage Foundation in Washington, D.C., began flooding public

broadcasting officials with requests for proprietary financial information and making speeches calling for the sale of PBS' funding agency, the private, government-created Corporation for Public Broadcasting (CPB), to the private sector. *(See "At Issue," p. 825.)*

Public broadcasting officials and liberal groups point out that the current assault is not occurring in a vacuum. "The Corporation for Public Broadcasting is the right wing's latest target in their ongoing culture war," said Melanne Verveer, vice president of the Washington-based First Amendment advocacy group People for the American Way. "This vital public entity has become the victim of a campaign of distortion and smears."

"These are contentious times," says PBS Executive Vice President Bob Ottenhoff. "People's positions about issues are hardening and narrowing, and they're less willing to accept the views of others. Public broadcasting plays a role as reflector of what goes on in the nation in politics and in lifestyle."

The controversy goes "deeper than just PBS," agrees David J. Brugger, executive director of the Association of America's Public Television Stations. "It has to do with changes in our culture that the right wing doesn't agree with. Public broadcasting is visible — we get into people's living rooms — so we're being used to help them raise the issue."

While public broadcasting has been a political hot potato since its founding as an educational tool *(see p. 818)*, liberals and conservatives now agree that vast changes in technology — the rise of cable television, in particular — have blown today's public broadcasters into uncharted waters.[2] The array of stations, boards and foundations that make up the public broadcasting community have assembled multiple task forces in the past two years to map the future (*see p. 826*).

"The core function of public television is threatened because the economics of television have fundamentally changed," concluded a 1991 consultant's study. It noted that the long-established format of terrestrial broadcasting was now a more expensive way of distributing programs than cable TV, videocassettes and laser discs. Pointing to new competition from educational cable distributors and textbook publishers, it recommended that public TV concentrate on revenue-enhancing activities and strengthen its national programming to compete on the basis of quality.[3]

To some, the new landscape means that public broadcasting must emulate and compete with private broadcasters — should it continue to exist at all. The current debate over public broadcasting is occurring "at a time of tremendous change in the communications industry and show business," noted the Heritage Foundation's Jarvik. Specifically, he points to what he sees as models in "an explosion of private media outlets" in Europe with the collapse of communism, privatization moves in French public television and the recent move by Britain's BBC to offer an advertising-supported satellite channel.[4]

To others, however, the current crossroads is seen as a chance not to privatize or convert public broadcasting into a profit center but to reassert a vision of public broadcasting as an educational island in a sea of commercial interests, assuring that community, consumer, labor and environmental groups have access to the nation's airwaves.

"There's a connection between the [current effort by] the commercial-oriented right wing and the big changes in technology," says Jeffrey A. Chester, co-director of the Center for Media Education in Washington, a new research and advocacy group specializing in public media. "This could be precisely the moment to restructure the system and reinvigorate public telecommunications."

As critics and supporters of public broadcasting continue the debate, here are the main questions on which the outcome will turn:

Is there a liberal bias in public broadcasting?

In 1990, PBS aired "The Race to Save the Planet," a documentary series inspired by environmental alarms sounded by the Worldwatch Institute in Washington. It was promptly blasted as one-sided, anti-business and anti-technology by the Media Research Center, a conservative group based in Alexandria, Va.

Linda Harrar, the series' producer, responded: "We made no efforts to avoid particular points of view. There are ways of confusing the public in putting Ping-Pong matches onto television. . . . You come up with a program that's virtually impossible for the audience to sort out."[5]

Complaints of a liberal bent at PBS are not confined to conservative activists. *New York Times* TV critic Walter Goodman has written that "like news professionals everywhere, the producers of PBS documentaries tend to be politically on the left, and unlike more restrained journalists, they have shown little compunction about pushing their own opinions."[6] A long list of *New York Times* critiques of "one-sided" PBS programs over the past decade was inserted into the *Congressional Record* this spring by Sen. Dole.[7]

The Washington-based Center for Media and Public Affairs, a research organization that analyzes how news and entertainment media treat social and political issues, also has concluded that public television's programming is biased in liberals' favor. After viewing 225 documentaries that aired on Washington-area public television station WETA, the center's analysts issued a report stating that the programs were "far more consonant with the beliefs and preferences of contemporary American liberals than those of conservatives."[8] *(See story, p. 813.)*

Few critics have cataloged PBS' alleged biases as extensively as David Horowitz, who launched his Committee on Media Integrity with an essay called "Missing Balance in PBS History." Citing language in the 1967 Public Broadcasting Act requiring "strict adherence to objectivity and balance" in programs of a controversial nature, Horowitz slammed public TV for consistently portraying American foreign policy as that of an "expansionist, militaristic predator" and for failing to highlight the "epic of human perseverance in the defense of liberty" that marked the end of the Cold War. He was particularly critical of programs by Bill Moyers dealing with alleged legal and constitutional violations by the CIA over the years and by the Reagan administration during the Iran-contra scandal.

"There is no serious effort at finding a balance" at PBS, Horowitz says today. "They make no difference between prime-time shows and non-prime-time shows, and no difference between talking heads, where opinions are clearly those of the speakers, and documentaries, which are reconstructed realities."

Moyers fired back with an ad hominem attack on Horowitz, accusing the former leftist of having his own "shrill bias" and wanting a media that is subservient to his own "self-righteous authoritarian" agenda. "What constructive purpose could it serve to celebrate America's leadership, as Horowitz would have us do," Moyers wrote, "when America's leaders are doing such a good job themselves from a bully pulpit that commands millions more viewers than PBS could ever hope for?"[9]

PBS officials respond to the bias charge by stating that it is Congress that has the authority to decide whether public broadcasters are maintaining proper balance in their shows, which

In Search of Liberal Bias

This March saw publication of the only study that has attempted to systematically determine whether public television's programming is imbalanced in liberals' favor. The Washington-based Center for Media and Public Affairs, under the sponsorship of several foundations, analyzed 225 documentaries that aired on Washington-area public station WETA from April 1987 to March 1988. Trained coders examined 35,094 segments of the programs to determine their politically relevant topics and themes, sources of information and opinions. The major topics were war and national defense, environment, the status of women and minorities, constitutional interpretation, health care, religion and South Africa's apartheid system.

Analysts S. Robert Lichter, Daniel Amundson and Linda S. Lichter concluded that the programs were "far more consonant with the beliefs and preferences of contemporary American liberals than those of conservatives.... The preponderance of opinion questioned justifications for armed conflict and nuclear development, supported the primacy of environmental concerns over human needs, asserted that American society discriminates against women and minorities, upheld liberal interpretations of constitutional rights ranging from gay rights to search-and-seizure provisions and condemned the failings of America's allies far more frequently than its Marxist opponents." †

The study was attacked in public forums by officials from the Public Broadcasting Service (PBS), who pointed out that it examined only 1 percent of the 6,100 annual hours of PBS programming. And media critics faulted the study for not factoring in the array of conservative talk shows that are regulars on PBS.

Others derided the methodology, particularly the way it broke programs down into "units" that could be characterized as liberal positions. In the study's discussion of the documentary on the early civil rights movement, "Eyes on the Prize," for example, "racial discrimination is described as a condition of American society 50 times without a single dissenting opinion," noted Josh Daniel, an independent producer writing in the film journal *The Independent*. "These 50 speakers do not necessarily oppose segregation; they merely cite instances of discrimination in our society ... a dubious liberal stance."

Michael Tracey, director of the Center for Mass Media Research at the University of Colorado, called the study a "weapon in the jihad against public broadcasting" that "doesn't begin to examine the real philosophical problems that cling to any debate about balance, diversity, objectivity and impartiality.... Nowhere do the authors examine what liberalism and conservatism mean." ††

---

† S. Robert Lichter, Daniel Amundson, Linda S. Lichter, "Balance and Diversity of PBS Documentaries," Center for Media and Public Affairs, March 1992.

†† Josh Daniel, "Uncivil Wars: The Conservative Assault on Public Broadcasting," *The Independent*, August-September 1992, p. 20.

---

reach 87 million viewers weekly. "Congress has made it clear that CPB is to emphasize maximum protection from interference in program content to allow the greatest freedom for the expression of ideas from diverse sources," says a CPB statement.

PBS officials also point to a 1975 District of Columbia Circuit Court ruling saying that political views have to be balanced not within the same program or series but across the PBS schedule. A national poll done for PBS in 1990 by Statistical Research Inc. found that 79 percent of public TV viewers did not consider the viewpoint of PBS news and public affairs programs to be either conservative or liberal.

A detailed statement of PBS policy in selecting programs appeared in a 1990 letter to critic Horowitz from PBS programming chief Jennifer Lawson. "PBS seeks to be ideologically diverse as one would expect from a system that has no central news division, more than 300 independent stations, a wide range of funding sources and one which showcases the work of more than 200 producers a year," the letter read. "PBS may reject a program because it does not meet PBS journalistic standards or simply because another program does a better job of telling the same story. But there is no PBS political agenda, and no program is rejected because it favors one viewpoint over another." [10]

David Fanning, executive producer of "Frontline," the PBS documentary series that is a favorite target of conservatives, emphasizes that his show is planned around a rigorous editing process based on investigative journalism, not political labeling. "Our role is asking questions of people in power," he says. "By definition, for the last 12 years, we've had conservative administrations, so it's inevitable that we will have questions directed at those agencies and policies."

Many public broadcasters acknowledge, however, that the nature of their mission lends itself to a perception of liberalism. "If you're questioning the status quo, if you're looking at things that are going wrong in society, if you're

Who Pays for Public Broadcasting?

In 1990 individual subscribers provided more money for public radio and television than any other funding source. Income from the federal government (for the Corporation for Public Broadcasting and federal grants and contracts) amounted to about one-sixth of public broadcasting's total income.

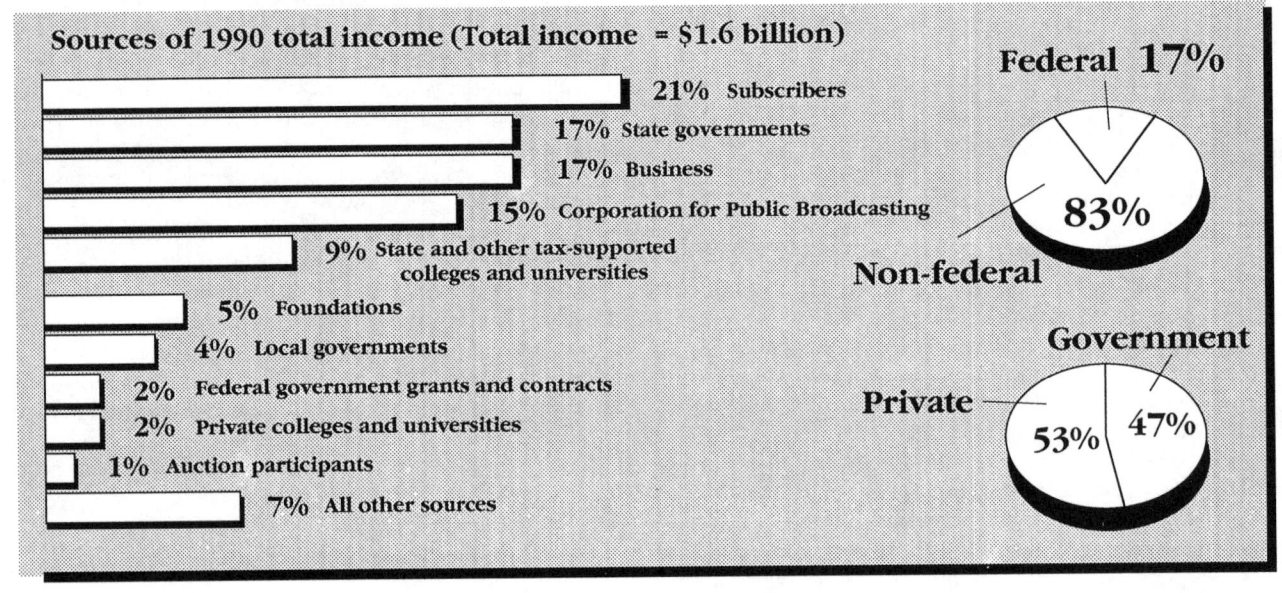

Sources of 1990 total income (Total income = $1.6 billion)

- 21% Subscribers
- 17% State governments
- 17% Business
- 15% Corporation for Public Broadcasting
- 9% State and other tax-supported colleges and universities
- 5% Foundations
- 4% Local governments
- 2% Federal government grants and contracts
- 2% Private colleges and universities
- 1% Auction participants
- 7% All other sources

Federal 17%
83% Non-federal

Government 47%
Private 53%

Source: Corporation for Public Broadcasting

looking at what the problems are, the warts and the difficulties are, you could say that has some kind of political bias," PBS President Bruce Christiansen said on ABC's "Nightline" in May.

As PBS officials are well aware, they must also deal with attacks from the left. The New York City-based media-watchdog group Fairness and Accuracy in Reporting (FAIR) has long argued that the PBS schedule is lopsided with conservative talk shows such as those hosted by William F. Buckley and John McLaughlin as well as "pro-corporate" business shows, including Louis Rukeyser's "Wall $treet Week" and Adam Smith's "Money World."

"I would agree that's there's lots of liberals on the documentaries," says FAIR Research Director Steve Rendall, "but there are far fewer of them than there are McLaughlin-type shows, which are weekly and topical and so

have more impact."

In 1990, FAIR published a study of the guests appearing on PBS' "MacNeil/Lehrer NewsHour" and found a preponderance of white males. (During a 40-month period surveyed, 92 percent of the guests were white, and 89 percent were male.) In addition, the group argues that PBS should provide a "counterweight" to conservative shows with more programs from the point of view of labor and consumers.[11]

Has cable TV eliminated the need for public television?

"The original argument for public television was that over-the-air broadcasting allows only a few competitors who are driven to seek a broad — and low — common denominator," syndicated columnist George F. Will wrote this spring. "That argument has been obviated by technology — by cable and the onset of 'narrowcasting'

to many small segments of the American audience."[12]

Cable TV's audience share in recent years has ballooned — from 14 percent for basic cable in 1983-84 to 24 percent in 1990 — while PBS's has remained stable at about 3 percent.[13] The Federal Communications Commission (FCC) released a study in June 1991 noting that "with the advent of commercial viewer-supported programming on cable, many of the needs public television was intended to fill have begun to be met by cable. In the future, government funding of public television may have to be justified on different grounds."

Cable enthusiasts report that the Disney Channel outspends public TV on children's programming $120 million to $56 million. And conservative media critic Reed Irvine, chairman of Washington-based Accuracy in Media, says that PBS has been outdone in public affairs programming by the cable-transmitted C-SPAN, which covers congressional debate and other government proceedings "at a fraction of the cost without all the filter of commentary." "This is what Congress had in mind in setting up PBS," Irvine asserts.

In defending against the cable onslaught, public TV advocates note that only 61 percent of U.S. households are wired for cable, according to the National Cable Television Association, whereas public TV is available in 98 percent of households — and without the monthly subscription fee that is beyond the means of poorer households.

Public TV advocates also raise questions about quality. "You click through the 54 channels of cable, and half the time there's nothing on but old movies," says Beth Courtney, executive director of Louisiana Public Broadcasting. "We are original programming producers, and we don't have to make a profit like commercial TV." *

Public broadcasters cite surveys in which two-thirds of cable subscribers say one of the reasons they pay for cable is to get better reception for public stations. And in a recent Roper Organization survey, public television outranked cable for being interesting, stimulating, imaginative, educational, informative and important, though cable beat out public TV for variety.

Above all, critics laud the educational value of PBS' children's programming. "It's easy to put junk on cable and say it's good enough for children," puppeteer and longtime TV star Shari Lewis said on a Washington news show this spring. "The goal of public television's programming is education not entertainment," Sen. Daniel K. Inouye, D-Hawaii, told the Senate during this June's debate. "Put simply, 'The New Mickey Mouse Club' and 'Masters of the Universe' cannot be compared with 'Sesame Street' and 'Mister Rogers.' "

"Frontline" producer Fanning says that while he admires much of what CNN and C-SPAN have added to cable, they have a "short-term interest and a fraction of public TV's audience." And, he adds, they lack the resources to delve into the past with the "consideration of an author who has carefully picked his way through a subject."

Jeffrey Chester of the Center for Media Education expresses alarm at the FCC's recent approval of a plan that will allow telephone companies to enter the cable TV business through a new service called "Video Dialtone," which allows callers to order TV shows over phone lines. He predicts that more American consumers will begin supporting public TV if they're confronted with prospects of a "vaster wasteland" dominated by hundreds of pay-per-view cable channels, monthly charges of $50 and pro-

hibitive access charges that make it difficult for independent producers to get on television.

Is government funding for public broadcasting still merited?

The contentiousness of public broadcasting, its reputation for liberalism and its role in providing programming that the networks might reject as indecent, could all be avoided, say conservative critics, if no taxpayer dollars were involved.

Robert Knight, director of cultural studies at the Family Research Council in Washington, D.C., recently excoriated PBS for broadcasting "Portrait of a Marriage," a drama that portrayed nude lesbian sex. "Taxpayers shouldn't be forced to support shows that undermine traditional values," he says. If PBS programs were subjected to the free market, "then the good stuff would make it, and all the pro-Sandinista, pro-Palestine Liberation Organization, pro-

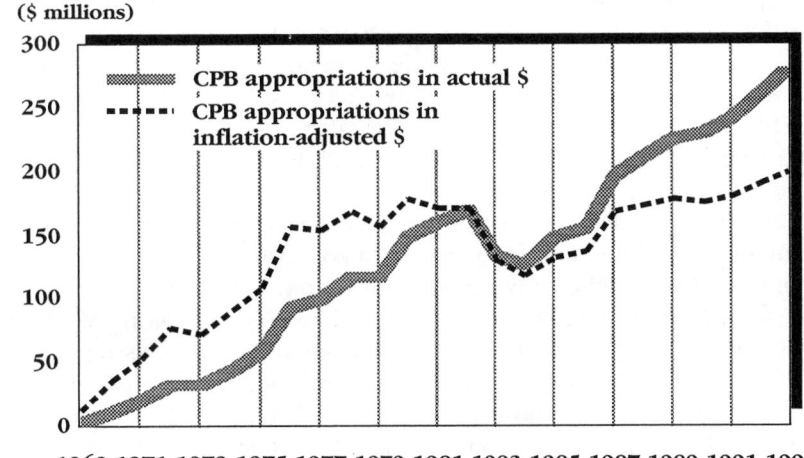

Federal Funding for the CPB

Congressional funding for the Corporation for Public Broadcasting dropped sharply in the early years of the Reagan administration. Funding has risen steadily since the mid-1980s to nearly $300 million. However, when the figures are adjusted for inflation relative to 1982-84 dollars, the increases tend to level off.

($ millions)

CPB appropriations in actual $
CPB appropriations in inflation-adjusted $

1969 1971 1973 1975 1977 1979 1981 1983 1985 1987 1989 1991 1993

Source: Corporation for Public Broadcasting

*Public TV produces some 1,600 hours of television annually.

homosexuality stuff would die."

Advocates of privatization also see ammunition in the six-figure salaries of some public broadcasting officials. And they note the $58 million endowment of the Children's Television Workshop, creators of "Sesame Street," and the $641,244 salary of the president of its product division. Also questioned are the profitable spinoff operations — the licensing of "Sesame Street" toothbrushes and lunchboxes, as well as the seven-figure production deals enjoyed by Bill Moyers and other producers whose private companies benefit from exposure on public TV.

"Despite perpetual pleas of poverty, public broadcasting is already a lucrative venture on both a local and national level," Jarvik writes. As evidence of the potential for self-sufficiency, he points to videotapes, recordings and books spun off the highly successful PBS series "The Civil War"; the new chain of stores in the Boston area devoted to selling WGBH tote bags and coffee mugs, among other merchandise; and the *Wireless* catalog of recordings and products that has earned millions for Minnesota Public Radio through the popularity of Garrison Keillor's "A Prairie Home Companion."

Finally, say those who would defund public broadcasting, the most successful PBS programs —"Sesame Street," "The Civil War" and "Cosmos," for example — would have little trouble finding a home in the private market. "With our country's debt over $4 trillion," says Rep. Philip M. Crane, R-Ill., "it is foolish to continue funding costly and non-essential programs ... that are inherently better suited for the private sector.... Already the vast majority of public radio and television stations are operated by private sources such as universities and nonprofit community organizations.... Eliminating federal funding ... would do little to threaten public broadcasting's future as private sup-

How U.S. Compares With Other Nations

The federal government spends far less per person on public broadcasting than some other nations.

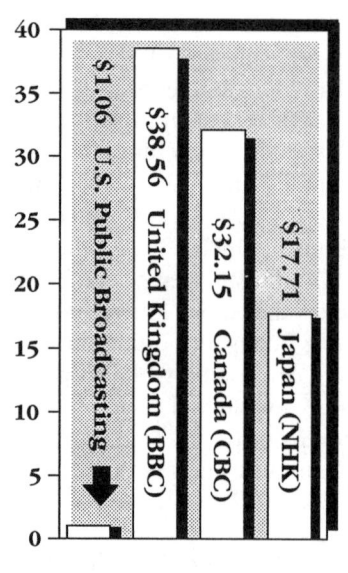

(U.S. dollars)

$1.06 U.S. Public Broadcasting

$38.56 United Kingdom (BBC)

$32.15 Canada (CBC)

$17.71 Japan (NHK)

Source: Corporation for Public Broadcasting

port is robust and growing." [14]

Rebuttals to all these arguments were laid out during this year's congressional debate as public broadcasters found themselves rearticulating the reasons for their existence. On the salary question, Bill Baker, president of New York City's WNET-TV, says that public television salaries are "generally in the basement compared with commercial TV"— he took an 80 percent pay cut when he switched.

Children's Television Workshop spokesmen note that its highest salaries go for recruiting the most talented sales people, who are paid based on their sales of the licensed products. The licensing revenues, in turn, are precisely what has enabled the workshop to survive without di-

rect federal aid since 1982. *(See story, p. 817.)*

Ken Burns, producer of "The Civil War," says he is mystified by the suggestion that his public TV success has made him rich. He's still repaying the government grants he received for the five-year project, he says, and plowing money back into his next project, a documentary about baseball. "You can't punish the 1 percent of public television films that are successful," he says. "The U.S. government may order a bomber plane and buy some copies, but then that manufacturer is free to sell others at full profit. In rare instances of success [at public broadcasting], we ought to be overjoyed that we're getting the message out to people."

The undeniable appeal of "The Civil War" has made Burns one of public broadcasting's key advocates. He has made it clear that he would never have made the series without CPB seed money because he wasn't yet famous as a producer and because he was proposing a decidedly non-commercial 11-hour documentary made from still pictures and talking heads.

The value of public broadcasting "has nothing to do with the defense of our country, but it makes our country worth defending," he says. "We ought to be able to allocate a minuscule fraction of our budget for rich intellectual history rather than allow a marketplace to dominate an illiterate country where people know every cast member of 'Gilligan's Island' but can't name six presidents."

Other prominent spokesmen, such as Moyers, argue that society still needs alternative broadcasting that allows for long, uninterrupted narratives, talk, art and culture that aren't motivated solely by market forces. "There ought to be a place where the bottom line is not making a buck," adds Louisiana's Courtney. "Just because you have bookstores doesn't mean you don't need public libraries."

Continued on p. 818

Even Big Bird Has His Critics

When Sen. Bob Dole, R-Kan., led the attack on public television this spring, he bemoaned the way his opponents were accusing him of wanting to "kill Big Bird." Indeed, the pure-hearted characters of "Sesame Street" have long been deputized by public TV supporters as effective allies in lobbying. But not everyone considers the cuddly creatures beyond reproach.

"'Sesame Street' is just another kids' show," said Laurence Jarvik of the conservative Heritage Foundation. "No better than 'Underdog' or 'The Flintstones.' What did the taxpayers get for their investment in 'Sesame Street?' A generation of kids who spray graffiti on the walls of New York City. If 'Sesame Street' was so effective, why do we have such a literacy problem?" †

Though embraced by educators since its creation in 1968, "Sesame Street" has dismayed intellectuals who believe that its catchy tunes and rapid-paced parodies of advertising cause children to grow up with short attention spans.

"'Sesame Street' encourages children to love school only if school is like 'Sesame Street,'" writes New York University communications Professor Neil Postman in his book *Amusing Ourselves to Death*. He complains that the show relieves parents of their responsibility to teach children, oversimplifies ideas by forcing them into visual forms and misleads children into assuming that learning must be fun.

Psychologists Jerome and Dorothy Singer, who direct Yale University's Family Television Research and Consultation Center, have chided "Sesame Street" for the subtle aggressiveness of some of its characters, in contrast to the non-violent "Mr. Rogers' Neighborhood." To others, the show is too wholesome and unrepresentative of the bleak environments many children grow up in. "'Sesame Street' for all its good intentions," writes child psychologist Robert Coles, "fails to inspire the very ones for whom it was primarily created — the ghetto children of our big cities, or those isolated in our rural slums: migrant children; Appalachia's hollow children; boys and girls who live on our Indian reservations or in the barrios along the Rio Grande." ††

Among educators and media analysts, however, the clear consensus on "Sesame Street" is thumbs-up. "It teaches good values and an appreciation for learning," observes Kathryn C. Montgomery, a communications scholar who heads the Campaign for Kids' TV in Washington. She says Postman and other critics are too categorical in dismissing television as a learning tool. "It's too powerful a medium to write off," she says. "If we can harness its power and help children, then we should."

The Children's Television Workshop, the New York City-based nonprofit group that created "Sesame Street,"

CTW/Richard Termine

has been hearing the criticisms for two decades and is well armed with studies to rebut them. "Sesame Street" is watched in 63.3 percent of TV households with children under 6, or more than 10 million households, it reports. The shows have been translated for broadcast in more than 80 countries. A 1989 survey of 1,000 mothers of preschool children nationwide showed that 75 percent named "Sesame Street" as their child's favorite show.

The planners of "Sesame Street" work to fulfill some 600 specific educational goals, all aimed at teaching cognitive skills and presenting the diversity of the world. "The dialogue on 'Sesame Street' closely resembles that of a mother talking to her child, with simple sentences, much talk about the here and now, repeated emphasis on key terms and an avoidance of abstract terminology," observed one team of psychologists.‡ Also, the show's teaching of vocabulary and counting takes place free from commercial interruption.

How effective is the program? Studies giving high grades to "Sesame Street" go back to 1970. A group of 943 children, mostly from disadvantaged families, was tested by the Educational Testing Service (ETS) of Princeton, N.J., after a portion of them had watched 26 weeks of "Sesame Street" during its debut season. The watchers outscored the non-watchers by an average of 40 points, displaying better knowledge of the alphabet, numbers, body parts and shapes.

The majority of studies in the 1970s and '80s showed that "Sesame Street" improves children's vocabularies, according to Aletha Huston, author of *Big World, Small Screen: The Role of Television in America,* published this year in cooperation with the American Psychological Association. The studies would also suggest that "Sesame Street" improves social skills, such as cooperating with peers.

Currently under way is one of the largest longitudinal studies of how preschool children use and are affected by mass media. It is being conducted by Huston and John Wright, both professors of human development at the University of Kansas. Preliminary findings, Wright says, make "Sesame Street" look good in comparison with the more violent shows of commercial TV. Ironically, the study is being performed at a facility named for a prominent U.S. senator: the Robert S. Dole Center for Human Development.

---

† Quoted in *The New York Times*, April 30, 1992.

†† Writing in *The New York Times*, Nov. 13, 1988.

‡ M.L. Rice, A.C. Huston, R.T. Truglio and J.C. Wright, "Words from Sesame Street: Learning Vocabulary While Viewing," *Developmental Psychology*, Vol. 26, No. 3 (1990), pp. 421-428.

Continued from p. 816

The suggestion that an old standby like "Sesame Street" could simply walk over to a commercial station is rebutted by Children's Television Workshop spokesmen, who point out that few commercial stations would devote three and four hours a day to showing it uninterrupted by commercials.

As Sen. Tim Wirth, D-Colo., noted during the debate, taxpayers shell out only 17 percent of public broadcasting's revenues, about $1 per person, compared with $40 per citizen for broadcasting in the United Kingdom, $32 in Canada and $18 in Japan. (*See graphs, pp. 814, 816.*)

One of the hardest-hitting defenses of government support for public broadcasting came from San Francisco broadcast engineer Marshall Turner, until recently CPB's chairman. The purpose of public broadcasting, he said, relates to the difference between a country and a market: "A country is a body politic and a culture that, if successful, enables a people to make good collective decisions, express their purposes, share some common values, protect themselves, develop to their full potential, and enhance their lives. Markets are vigorous, challenging, flexible and ultimately truthful. Their ability to learn, react and satisfy inspires admiration. But markets have no thoughts, values or higher purposes beyond their reflexive response to needs. Few people have knowingly fought or died for a market." [15] ∎

BACKGROUND

Early History

Public broadcasting has been a political football since its first stirrings in the 1920s and '30s. It began with a movement among educational, labor and religious groups to set aside some channels on the nation's radio dial for instructional programming. "The goal was to make radio more democratic," says Erik Barnouw, author of *Tube of Plenty: The Evolution of American Television,* "because of a feeling that social needs couldn't be met by advertising-supported radio."

Communications writer James Rorty lambasted what he called the "jabberwocky" noise of commercial radio in the 1930s, asking, "Is it any wonder ... that the stimuli of art, science, religion are progressively expelled to the periphery of American life to become marginal values, cultivated by marginal people in marginal time?" [16]

Under the sponsorship of Sen. Robert F. Wagner, D-N.Y., an amendment to create educational radio channels was nearly included in the landmark 1934 legislation that created the Federal Communications Commission. It was defeated after lobbying from the national radio networks, whose spokesmen promised that they could donate adequate radio time to educational programming because advertising sales during the Great Depression were not steady enough to fill all broadcast hours.

In the mid-1930s, the FCC created the Federal Radio Education Committee, and the Rockefeller Foundation commissioned a study on the influence of radio on children and adults. [17]. The non-commercial radio time given over to nonprofits and educational broadcasters gave vent to often-experimental work by young talents, including director Orson Welles and conductor Leonard Bernstein, who would become more famous after they switched to commercial broadcasting.

In the 1940s, the FCC had become sympathetic to educational broadcasters, giving them a portion of the FM radio band. And with the TV industry mushrooming, President Harry S Truman appointed an FCC commissioner named Frieda B. Hennock, who launched a crusade to allocate a group of channels for educational use. Initial resistance to the educational channels from commercial networks was eventually overcome, and in 1952 the FCC announced that the addition of the new Ultra-High Frequency (UHF) band would allow it to reserve channels for 242 educational television stations nationwide.

Educators expressed hope that this would relieve teacher shortages and other problems in disadvantaged school districts. Throughout the Eisenhower administration, however, the government provided no finances to the fledgling stations, which relied on foundations and local fundraising.

"A Vast Wasteland"

In 1961, the Kennedy administration's FCC chairman, Newton N. Minow, made history with a tough speech to the National Association of Broadcasters. He excoriated commercial television as "a vast wasteland ... a procession of game shows, violence, audience participation shows, formula comedies about totally unbelievable families, blood and thunder, mayhem, violence, sadism, murder, western badmen, western goodmen, private eyes, gangsters, more violence, and cartoons. And endlessly, commercials — many screaming, cajoling and offending." [18]

Minow's comments did not please network and TV station executives, particularly when he hinted that in the future, broadcast licenses might become more difficult to renew.

Under Minow, the FCC awarded the first federal grants for construction of educational television stations, and in 1962, it won passage of the All-Channel Receivers Act, which required manufacturers of televisions to outfit all sets with UHF receiving equipment. President John F. Kennedy hailed it as a boost to the consumer movement.

Continued on p. 820

Chronology

1950s Fledgling educational radio and TV stations struggle for funds from foundations.

April 13, 1952
Federal Communications Commission reserves 242 TV channels for educational purposes.

1960s Kennedy and Johnson administrations inaugurate era of federally funded public broadcasting.

July 10, 1962
President John F. Kennedy boosts educational television by signing the All-Channel Receiver Act requiring all TV sets to carry UHF channels.

Jan. 24, 1967
Carnegie Commission issues report "Public Television: A Program for Action."

Nov. 7, 1967
President Lyndon B. Johnson signs Public Broadcasting Act, creating Corporation for Public Broadcasting.

Dec. 3, 1968
CPB offers first grant, to "Black Journal" television program.

1969
Public Broadcasting Service created by CPB and local stations. "Sesame Street" launched.

1970s Nixon administration's attack on public television results in major changes in federal funding policy.

Feb. 6, 1970
National Public Radio (NPR) founded by CPB and local stations.

1971
NPR launches its first live nationwide broadcast with coverage of Senate hearings on Vietnam. "Masterpiece Theater" debuts on PBS. "All Things Considered" debuts on NPR.

June 1972
President Richard M. Nixon vetoes CPB appropriation.

1973
PBS and CPB sign partnership agreement on programming relationship and long-range funding goals. PBS provides gavel-to-gavel coverage of Senate Watergate hearings.

Dec. 31, 1975
President Gerald R. Ford signs Public Broadcasting Financing Act establishing long-range, advanced funding for public broadcasting.

1976
"MacNeil/Lehrer Report" debuts.

March 1, 1978
Public TV satellite service begins.

1978
NPR transmits Panama Canal Treaty debates in the first live radio broadcast of Senate floor proceedings.

1979
Carnegie Commission issues second report on public TV.

1980s Reagan budget cuts force public broadcasters to seek new funding. Conservatives attack PBS' alleged liberal bias.

1981
TV Guide magnate Walter Annenberg gives $150 million to CPB.

1982
"American Playhouse" debuts as the first public television series produced by a consortium of stations.

1983
MacNeil/Lehrer expands to become first one-hour news show. CPB bails out NPR's $9.1 million deficit.

1984
FCC permits "enhanced underwriting," lowering the barrier against outright sponsorship.

1988
Congress authorizes $200 million to replace public radio and TV satellites.

1989
Satellite Educational Resources Consortium links rural and disadvantaged high schools to specialized teachers.

September 1989
Independent Television Service formed.

1990s Conservatives gear up for multi-pronged attack on public television.

1990
CPB releases report "Meeting the Mission in a Changing Environment." "The Civil War" series attracts record audience.

June 3, 1992
Key Senate debate on bill calling for a 50 percent CPB funding hike and requiring improved monitoring of objectivity and balance. The bill is approved by Congress and signed by President Bush Aug. 27.

Continued from p. 818

Financial Support

By the mid-1960s, several philanthropic organizations had embraced educational television. The Ford Foundation, headed by former Kennedy National Security Adviser McGeorge Bundy, had given $100 million to 100 educational stations and to planners of an envisioned national network. The foundation had been particularly active in building what would become one of public TV's flagship stations, WNET in New York.

A sign of the foundation's interest in educational broadcasting was its hiring of Fred W. Friendly, a former CBS news official who had quit in protest over the network's refusal to broadcast one of the first congressional hearings that questioned the Vietnam War.[19] Friendly set to work conceptualizing a national educational network and satellite system to broadcast programs that would ask "viewers to face ethical, political and moral dilemmas of such profound complexity that the only way to escape is by thinking."

At the same time, President Lyndon B. Johnson and officials at the Department of Health, Education and Welfare asked the Carnegie Corporation to convene a commission of prominent educators and broadcasters to study educational TV. After Johnson spoke of the need for educational TV in his January 1967 State of the Union address, the Carnegie Commission released *Public Television: A Program for Action*. It called for a "new and fundamental institution in American culture" that would better serve the public's need for regional and local diversity in ways beyond mere education.

Bestowing the more broadly symbolic name of "public television," it called for a decentralized system of local stations nourished by grants from a federally chartered non-governmental agency that would pro-

duce no national programming but would be a "heat shield" to protect stations from government interference. The agency would be financed through a federal appropriation as well as a tax on television receivers.

Public television, author E. B. White wrote in a famous letter to the commission, "should be the visual counterpart of the literary essay, should arouse our dreams, satisfy our hunger for beauty, take us on journeys, enable us to participate in events, present great drama and music, explore the sea and the sky and the woods and the hills. It should be our Lyceum, our Chautauqua, our Minsky's and our Camelot."[20]

Creation of the Public Broadcasting System

Hearings and debate on a legislative proposal went on through much of 1967. The proposed tax on television sets was opposed by the Electronic Industries Association, which succeeded in getting it dropped, while conservatives in Congress (among them then-Rep. Robert Dole) expressed wariness. The proposal would create a "Frankenstein monster" that could turn into a propaganda machine, warned Rep. Albert W. Watson, R-S.C.[21] Republicans insisted on safeguards such as local control and a provision requiring fairness, objectivity and balance.

On Nov. 7, 1967, President Johnson signed the Public Broadcasting Act creating the Corporation for Public Broadcasting. He proclaimed that it would "make our nation a replica of the old Greek marketplace, where public affairs took place in the view of all citizens." But Johnson, beset by domestic political unrest over the Vietnam War, also warned that "in weak or even in irresponsible hands, it could generate controversy without understanding; it could mislead as well as teach; it could appeal to passions rather than reason."[22]

By 1969, the loose confederation of public TV and radio stations was at-

tracting both government and foundation funding. But it had a problem. There was no quick way for local stations to share programming around the country.

"All we had were 'the bicycled tapes,'" recalled veteran Washington public radio broadcaster Susan Stamberg, "meaning I'd do something and mail a tape of it off to Boston. Boston would mail the same tape to Philadelphia. Philadelphia would mail it to someone else. We could never do anything national and live with one another; we could never do anything topical."[23]

The solution to the lack of interconnection was the founding of the Public Broadcasting Service in 1969, and National Public Radio (NPR), in 1970, both as station-owned cooperative organizations that distribute programming, though only NPR could produce original shows. *(See story, p. 821.)*

Nixon Targets PBS

With the Vietnam War raging and the American counterculture visible throughout news and entertainment programming, the new PBS would soon begin mixing its broadcasts of "Sesame Street" and "The Forsyte Saga" with politically sensitive satires such as "That Was the Week That Was" and "The Great American Dream Machine." Other PBS shows produced by former NBC newsman Sander Vanocur and Canadian broadcaster Robert MacNeil raised questions about the Vietnam War and exposed alleged inequities in the American banking system. The Nixon administration was not pleased.

Clay Whitehead, director of the White House Office of Telecommunications Policy, reprimanded PBS officials, saying that news commentary, particularly from the Eastern intellectual establishment, was bound to invite a lot of political attention. In

Continued on p. 822

National Public Radio Comes of Age

National Public Radio (NPR) has logged a lot of sign-ons since its fledgling days as the "hippie radio" of the 1970s. Back then, the modest string of campus and small public stations filled countless hours of airtime with part-time reporters' extended dispatches on Third World revolutionary summits and the like.

Today, NPR occupies a central niche in American journalism. Its lengthy news reports and cultural backgrounders attract 9.8 million listeners a week. It draws steady support from foundations, corporations and member stations. (Only 2 percent of its funding comes from the federal government.) And, like its competitors in the mainstream media, it provokes critics of all political stripes.

The new status of NPR can be seen in its expanded roster of 12 foreign correspondents — in 1985 there were only two — plus numerous stringers. "Our main news and analysis is, to millions [of listeners], not a supplement but full comprehensive coverage," says John Dinges, managing editor of NPR news. "We're using fewer BBC reports, and we can choose our own targets and go after them." Dinges regards NPR as the "journalistic lifeline" in small towns, rural areas and suburbs where "there is dissatisfaction with local media."

To old-timers who valued NPR for its alternative, social-activist reportage, the latest incarnation contains hints of a sell-out. "NPR is picking up the slack and becoming CBS," a disgruntled NPR reporter told *The Washington Post Magazine*. "The staff walks into their morning meeting with their *New York Times* and *Washington Post*, and it's real easy for that to become their world." †

The clash over the mimicking of commercial media was dramatized in a 1988 episode in which NPR Foreign Editor John McChesney was fired after he had decided to send only two reporters and an editor to cover a Moscow summit between President Ronald Reagan and Soviet leader Mikhail S. Gorbachev. Vice President for News Adam Clayton Powell III overruled McChesney and sent 10 reporters at a cost of $70,000. "Given our budget, spending that amount on something that was little more than a big photo opportunity was so far out of line with what NPR had been doing as to be ludicrous," McChesney told *Columbia Journalism Review*.

"There is always tension between covering breaking news and the features we're famous for," says NPR spokeswoman Mary Morgan. "We sound less alternative to people because our reporters are no longer independent."

The content of the in-depth reports on NPR's "All Things Considered" and "Morning Edition" for years has irked conservatives. In the early 1980s, *The Washington Times* routinely called for defunding of National Public Radio for its allegedly leftward coverage of Nicaragua and Grenada. More recently, the National Rifle Association leveled a major attack on its coverage of gun control.

In an effort to systematically search for a liberal bias at NPR, the Washington-based Center for Media and Public Affairs surveyed coverage of the 1988 presidential campaign. While it found that NPR focused on policy issues more than the television networks, which concentrated more on candidate tactics, the center deduced the existence of a gender gap that it said produced a "liberal slant." Female reporters, the center said, tend toward liberalism, and the heavily female on-air staff at NPR gave Democratic candidate Michael S. Dukakis roughly equal amounts of praise and criticism but gave negative reports on Republican George Bush by a factor of 3 to 1.††

The most recent attack on NPR has come from conservative lawmakers and critics bothered by the role NPR reporter Nina Totenberg played in the explosive confirmation hearings of Supreme Court Justice Clarence Thomas in September 1991. Totenberg and another reporter received a leak from a still-unnamed source on the Senate Judiciary Committee that enabled them to break the story of sexual harassment charges against Thomas by Anita F. Hill. To David Horowitz of the Committee on Media Integrity, the leak was evidence of liberal "collusion" at NPR.

"It was not an accident that the torpedo-Thomas forces contacted Totenberg," says Horowitz. By his own "impressionistic" measures, Horowitz says, NPR's top political reporters — Totenberg, Cokie Roberts, Linda Wertheimer and Daniel Schorr — are all liberals. "The problems with Totenberg wouldn't have occurred if there had been a conservative in their stable," he says.

NPR's Dinges calls the criticism an "ill-founded attempt to personalize the attacks" around Totenberg, "as if she had a stake in the story and was not telling it appropriately. It's like attacking Bob Woodward because of Watergate. Her reporting was pristine."

NPR staff emphasize that their coverage should be judged not on whether an individual report is balanced, but whether over the course of time a variety of viewpoints are represented. "We have become more rigorous on questions of fairness and balance," Dinges says. "We discuss it. We ask whether our treatment of one side is emotional, while the other is just the facts. But radio is a unique medium, and its very personal dialogue doesn't always lend itself to cookie-cutter, 50-percent-X and 50-percent-Y journalism."

---

† Marc Fisher, "The Soul of a News Machine," *The Washington Post Magazine*, Oct. 22, 1989, p. 40.

†† S. Robert Lichter and Richard E. Noyes, "Choice or Echo? 1988 Election Coverage on National Public Radio," *Center for Media and Public Affairs*, November 1990.

Public TV's Total Income

In the decade from 1980 to 1990, public television's total income more than doubled, reflecting growing support from private and public funding sources.

($ in millions)

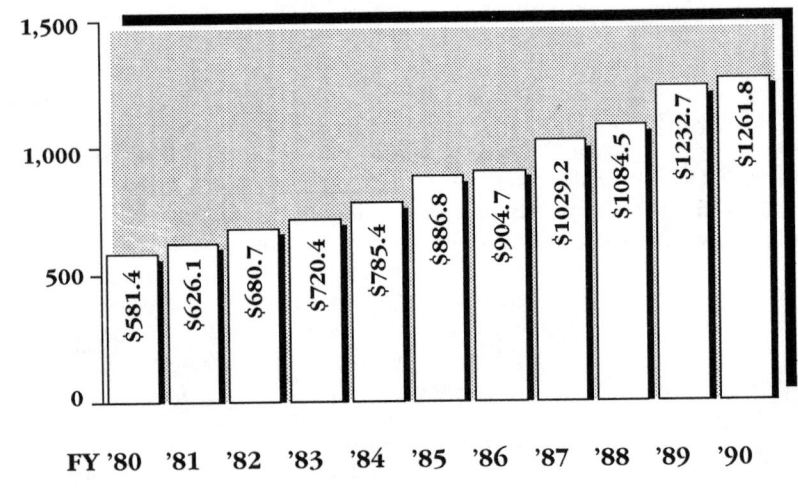

FY '80	'81	'82	'83	'84	'85	'86	'87	'88	'89	'90
$581.4	$626.1	$680.7	$720.4	$785.4	$886.8	$904.7	$1029.2	$1084.5	$1232.7	$1261.8

Source: Corporation for Public Broadcasting

cal appointees on the CPB board and pressuring the CPB to study its relations with PBS and its potential for taking a stronger role in programming. He also won restrictions on the CPB's ability to accept and accumulate foundation money and greater diffusion of CPB money directly to local stations.

But in the long run, as then-Nixon aide Antonin Scalia (now on the U.S. Supreme Court) wrote in a memo, any "attempt to cut back on public broadcasting as a whole would be doomed to failure because of strong support from education interests, minority groups and liberals, but also from Congressmen whose districts contain stations which contribute to local education." [27]

Nixon's crackdown would taper off after the pressures of the Watergate scandal overwhelmed his agenda. Ironically, in the summer of 1973, PBS provided the only gavel-to-gavel coverage of the Senate committee hearings on Watergate.

Advanced Funding

In reaction to Nixon's pressure, public broadcasting began what would be an ongoing effort to secure steady corporate underwriting. Major changes in federal funding procedures were enacted in 1975, during the Ford administration, among them a three-year advanced-funding schedule — designed to insulate public broadcasting from momentary political passions. "It was one of the real victories that public television ever achieved," said then-CPB Vice President Cortland Anderson. "It's clear to me that the advanced-funding mechanism is the only way to keep politics out of public broadcasting."

In 1979, the Carnegie Corporation empaneled its second commission, which issued a report on the future of public broadcasting that reiterated the ideal. "Intelligently organized and adequately funded public broadcasting can help the creative spirit to flourish," it read. "It can reveal how

Continued from p. 820
February 1972, Republican National Committee Deputy Chairman Lyn Nofziger circulated copies of the annual public broadcasting bill drafted by House Democrats with a note reading, "The Corporation for Public Broadcasting is a victim of fiscal irresponsibility and partisan non-objectivity in its hiring practices and programming." [24] The administration began criticizing PBS for wanting to become "a fourth network."

The situation came to a head in June 1972, when President Richard M. Nixon vetoed the public broadcasting authorization bill. As Nixon aide Patrick J. Buchanan would later explain, the White House would not tolerate an increase in funding when it could look at the PBS schedule and see that Sander Vanocur was "a notorious Kennedy sycophant," MacNeil was a person who is "definitely anti-administration," Elizabeth Drew was "definitely not pro-administration,"

"Washington Week in Review," "Black Journal" and "Bill Moyers' Journal" were "unbalanced against us" and the one conservative offering, William F. Buckley's "Firing Line," was "a fig leaf." [25]

Subsequent proposals to cancel those shows drew thousands of letters and opposition from the American Civil Liberties Union, the National Association of Educational Broadcasters, Congress, the public and the press. Nixon's position was clear, recalled former Texas Instruments Chairman Ralph Rogers, who was active in public TV at the time. "Public TV could sing anything from 'Sesame Street' to 'Aida' and it could dance all it wanted," he said, "but there was to be no federal money in support of public affairs news or analysis that might be critical of the Nixon administration." [26]

Congress passed a compromise bill that Nixon would sign, and Nixon succeeded in getting his own politi-

we are different and what we share in common. It can illuminate the dark corners of the world and the dark corners of the mind. It can offer forums to a multitude of voices. It can reveal wisdom and understanding — and foolishness too. It can entertain us. Above all, it can add to our understanding of our own inner workings and of one another."

But the report also warned that public television was now "fatally flawed." Minorities were not represented enough in PBS programming, it said, and with the impending blossoming of cable TV, public TV should consider a "grand alliance," a joint venture with cable for a money-making cultural TV system.

The Reagan Cuts

The Reagan administration came to Washington in 1981 recommending that the CPB be abolished. Public broadcasting officials scrambled to save their funding, and federal funds were eventually cut by about 25 percent. When NPR suffered a gaping $9.1 million budget deficit in 1983, however, it required a bailout from the CPB.

At the same time, CPB began relying on one of the biggest philanthropic gifts in history, a 1981 gift of $150 million over 15 years from *TV Guide* Publisher Walter Annenberg, for use in programming and college-level courses. Meanwhile, PBS stations stepped up their on-air pledge drives, annoying many viewers, critics noted, by interrupting programming with "begathons" that use "snob appeal" to extract donations in exchange for totebags and other premiums.

Also at this time, new FCC regulations permitted PBS to experiment with forms of on-air acknowledgments of corporate aid, though resulting revenues were deemed inadequate to replace federal funding. By this time, PBS's long association with corporate sponsors — the familiar presence of Mobil, Exxon and

Gulf led wags to dub it the Petroleum Broadcasting Service — earned it some derision from commentators.

"The spectacle of this old hooker [public broadcasting] announcing that she had discovered a method of going all the way without losing her virginity is pretty comical, because there's nothing especially non-commercial about public television," wrote then *Harper's* magazine Editor Michael Kinsley in 1983. The reliance on business backing now meant that business dictated the agenda of PBS programs, in the view of Patricia Aufderheide, a professor of communications at American University who writes regularly about PBS.

The mid-1980s saw publication of the memoirs of Herb Schmertz, the Mobil public relations whiz who had been instrumental in creating "Masterpiece Theater" in the 1970s. He criticized PBS fundraisers for claiming the popular show had been threatened by budget cuts when in fact it came free from corporate underwriters. He was also candid in admitting that Mobil's sponsorship was part of a strategy of "ambush marketing" to reach upscale consumers who were suspicious of advertising.

"When we give certain publics a reason to identify with the projects and causes that we have chosen to support," Schmertz wrote, "they will translate that identification into a preference for doing business with us." Viewers are left feeling "enriched and ennobled," and surveys showed that Mobil was now "the thinking man's gasoline." [28]

Political Tensions

Later in the 1980s, political tensions arose at the CPB partly because of a perception among PBS officials that the White House was applying pressure on the CPB. "They were turbulent times, with a lot of backbiting," recalls former CPB Chairman Howard Gutin, now a documentary producer in San Antonio, Texas.

In 1985, CPB President Ed Pfister resigned after the CPB board voted to

withdraw support for sending a delegation of public broadcasting officials to Moscow at a time when U.S.-Soviet relations were tense. In June 1985, some in public TV blamed White House pressure for the decision by other PBS officials to broadcast a documentary prepared by Accuracy in Media as a rebuttal to PBS' 13-part series "Vietnam: A Television History," which AIM had found too favorable to the North Vietnamese. It sets a precedent, one TV critic warned. What if a fundamentalist group wanted to rebut a documentary on how the universe was created? he asked. [29]

PBS, in turn, was attacked by Reagan officials for its 1986 broadcast of the nine-part series "The Africans," which National Endowment for the Humanities Chairwoman Lynne V. Cheney, in rejecting a Washington public station's application for grant money, had called "worse than unbalanced, this film frequently degenerates into an anti-Western diatribe. I fail to understand how a public television station of WETA's stature and reputation could be involved with a series that extols the virtues of [Libyan leader Muammar el-] Qaddafi." [30]

A turning point came in 1986, when at a CPB board meeting in Boston, CPB board member and *National Review* Editor Richard Brookhiser proposed that the CPB commission a scientific study to determine whether PBS programming had a leftward bias. "It is inappropriate for a presidentially appointed group to be conducting a content analysis of programming," said PBS Vice President Barry Chase after the board had unanimously rejected the plan. "It indicates that some people on the CPB board don't fully understand the appropriate constraints on them." [31]

Structural Changes

As the decade neared its end, public TV received steady federal

Viewer Support for Public TV

Viewer support for public television rose steadily from 1980-1990. The amount of money collected more than tripled, reaching $272.5 million; the number of members doubled, and the average contribution nearly doubled.

	Dollars in Millions	Members in Millions	Average Contribution
FY80	$77.9	2.6	$29.96
FY81	102.4	2.9	35.31
FY82	111.8	3.3	33.88
FY83	147.0	3.5	42.00
FY84	160.0	3.8	42.11
FY85	180.0	3.9	46.15
FY86	200.2	4.2	47.67
FY87	230.2	4.7	48.98
FY88	240.5	4.7	51.17
FY89	262.0	5.2	50.40
FY90	272.5	5.2	52.40

Source: Corporation for Public Broadcasting

those programs that have valuable ancillary markets, says Chester, they've opened a "Pandora's box. Becoming a vertically integrated monopoly might make PBS more viable, but it distorts its original mission. And it makes PBS more politically vulnerable." ∎

CURRENT SITUATION

Legislative Funding Battle

The flap over public broadcasting that came to a head in Congress this summer took shape in the fall of 1991. Conservative lawmakers such as Reps. Dick Armey, R-Texas, and Philip Crane had introduced legislation to abolish the CBP, and in November a group of conservative senators led by Dole delayed floor consideration of the CPB's three-year reauthorization legislation by applying a "hold," a routine stalling procedure.

The hold caused an uproar in the public broadcasting community. Public TV stations around the country stepped up an active lobbying campaign in anticipation of a conservative attack. They used local donor lists to encourage their viewers to write to their members of Congress on behalf of public broadcasting.[33] In March, public radio station KCRW of Santa Monica, Calif., took the unusual step of encouraging donors to send money by broadcasting round-the-clock bulletins about "a cabal" of Republican senators who were holding up federal funding.

Dole and conservative critics such as Horowitz and Jarvik were appalled at what they saw as a one-sided propaganda stance being taken by the public station. (Public radio and television officials

funding but underwent important structural changes. In 1988, Congress appropriated $24 million to create the Independent Television Service (ITVS) "to expand the diversity and innovativeness of programming available to public broadcasting."

It was a response to years of complaints by independent producers about the unresponsive PBS bureaucracy. "The whole point of ITVS is to do programming so risky the stations wouldn't attempt it on their own," said Lawrence Daressa, a member of the National Coalition of Independent Public Broadcasting Producers, which had lobbied for the money. "We shouldn't even try to be inclusive.... It should be a laboratory for broadcast innovation."[32]

Conservative critics, alarmed at such independent productions as the controversial "Tongues Untied," have blasted the ITVS as a boondoggle, noting that in more than three years it has yet to produce a single program.

In 1990, in response to task force reports on the financial prospects of public broadcasting, the CPB autho-

rized PBS to create a new position, known informally as "programming czar." Contrary to PBS' tradition of decentralization, the new czar — currently PBS Executive Vice President Jennifer Lawson — presides over a $100 million fund to encourage production of nationally visible programming. The rationale, says Courtney of Louisiana, is to give someone more authority over the "fractious lot" of public station officials who often vote for each other's tried-and-true programming and take few chances that might produce popular new national programming at a reduced cost.

To some independent producers and critics of PBS, however, a program czar risks furthering PBS' reputation as a centralized bureaucracy that is feathering its own nest and that of its stations. Such fears intensified this summer when PBS said it would seek to maximize revenues by retaining many of the ancillary rights to programs (videocassette versions for schools, for example) that formerly were left to independent producers and distributors. If this means that PBS now supports only

Continued on p. 826

At Issue:

Should the Corporation for Public Broadcasting be privatized?

LAURENCE JARVIK

Former Bradley resident scholar, The Heritage Foundation
FROM "MAKING PUBLIC TELEVISION PUBLIC," HERITAGE BACKGROUNDER, JAN. 18, 1992

yes

for two decades, reformers have tried to change the public broadcasting system, calling for more fairness, honesty and integrity. They have all failed.

The basic reason is structural. The present public broadcasting system is a private corporation that depends on public tax revenues. Such a contradiction leads to endless confusion and disputes between broadcasters concerned primarily with independence and free speech and lawmakers who must assure that the taxpayers' dollars are spent according to law.

Designed during the Great Society of the 1960s, public broadcasting is a bureaucratically complex subculture that remains impervious to reform.... Despite being on the receiving end of federal tax dollars, the CPB staff are hostile to objectivity and balance, and guard their secrets carefully....

The logical and practical solution to the public television mess is to make public television private. Given the increasingly commercial nature of the giant enterprise known as public television, and the cultural offerings of many cable stations, the American public probably would not even notice the difference. Once privatized, however, Public Broadcasting Service (PBS) programmers no longer would be able to indulge themselves with the taxpayer's money, and the federal deficit could be reduced.....

Privatization could be achieved by selling the CPB to the public as a publicly held corporation with stockholders. In such a structure, PBS and National Public Radio would be partially owned subsidiaries of CPB. These subsidiaries also could be sold, if required. The community service grants, currently payable to local stations, would be the equivalent to the network compensation received by commercial affiliates.

A fully private CPB would have a target audience extremely attractive to advertisers — upscale, affluent and educated viewers and listeners. It also would be subject to the same market pressures and regulatory restrictions as any commercial network. And a free market in "public" television has other advantages. The private sector can deliver far more efficiently and economically than the public sector....

The current public broadcasting system is obsolete, overly expensive and doomed to be the center of continuous political controversy. So long as taxpayer dollars go to a system without taxpayer accountability, conflicts are inevitable, and decisions will be made with an eye to political expediency rather than to efficient operations or quality of service.

JEFFREY A. CHESTER

Co-director, Center for Media Education
FROM THE MONOGRAPH "A HERITAGE BETRAYED: FIVE CONFUSIONS," SPRING 1991.

no

the Heritage Foundation's desire to hold a sheriff's auction of CPB has only one problem: There is nothing to sell. CPB's only "asset" is its appropriation; its only function is to funnel federal funds to public television. The federal appropriation Heritage wants to eliminate is CPB's only asset....

CPB is in essence an endowment, a foundation, not a business — an endowment to subsidize and prod public television to do precisely the kind of public service programming commercial television wouldn't.... In reality a privately held "CPB" would be no different from any other start-up film production company free to invest in any production that could make money.... A privately owned CPB would be accountable to the short-term, financial interests of its shareholders but unaccountable to the rest of the American public and our long-term interests as a democratic society. Heritage's unwillingness to make this elementary distinction reveals its habitual confusion of plutocracy with democracy....

Commentators as radical as the *Harvard Business Review* have made the distinction between a corporation's shareholders and its stakeholders. A corporation's stakeholders include its employees, the communities where they work, customers and the environment. A corporation's accountability to its shareholders is restricted to maximizing quarterly dividends and stock appreciation. Congress created the CPB to supplement the programming that would be produced by network television in response to shareholders' interests with programming responding to the long-term interests of a democratic society....

Heritage forgets that in a democracy (in contrast to a market), citizens are called upon not simply to consume products but to participate in producing and developing society, its culture, politics and values. Therefore what should distinguish public from commercial television is that public TV is made for citizens not consumers....

Public TV cannot be judged by the quantity of its viewers but the quality of their experience. Public TV's ultimate constituency is not tonight's Nielsen families nor the satisfaction of immediate consumer demand. Its commitment is to the audience not as they are but as they might become. Public TV's real constituency is the future — and the future, almost definitionally, is not ready for commercial exploitation.

Continued from p. 824

say there are no regulations against on-the-air advocacy of legislation.)

In early June, the Senate finally took up the 1991 Public Telecommunications Act, which sought $1.1 billion for the CPB over three years, a 50 percent increase. Opponents argued not for abolishment of CPB but for a funding freeze. "For the most part, I would acknowledge PBS provides valuable service," said Sen. Jesse Helms, R-N.C. But "we need more disclosure and accountability. The public has a right to know how the taxpayers' money is being spent.... There are millions of Americans out there who share the view that the programming on public television is not balanced."

Defenders of the funding hike emphasized the educational efforts of PBS. "This is one thing that works in this country," said Sen. Al Gore, D-Tenn., the Democratic vice presidential candidate.

The proposed freeze was defeated, and the reauthorization was approved in the Senate June 3, 84-11, with federal money authorized at $310 million in 1994, $375 million in 1995 and $425 million in 1996. But critics succeeded in winning passage of two important amendments — extension to midnight of the current 6 a.m.-to-8 p.m. ban on public TV broadcasts of programming considered indecent and a requirement that

CPB examine public programming on a regular basis for "quality, diversity, creativity, excellence, innovation, objectivity and balance."[34]*

"If there is a lesson to be learned," said CPB Chairwoman Sheila Tate, "it is that a perceived imbalance is as important to address as a real imbalance."

The House approved the bill on Aug. 4, and lobbying resumed as it wended its way to President Bush's desk. KCRW of Santa Monica warned its listeners of a possible veto during its summer pledge drive. *The National Review* called on the president to veto the bill to "remind voters that it's Congress that authorizes and appropriates the tax dollars." The American Family Association took out a full-page ad in *The Washington Times* asking, "Do you want 1.1 billion of your tax dollars supporting nude lesbian sex and a push for homosexuality on PBS?"

At the Republican convention in Houston in August, delegates approved a platform with language deploring "the blatant political bias of the government-sponsored radio and television networks," and looking "forward to the day when public broadcasting is self-sufficient." Despite conservatives' concerns, President Bush signed the funding bill on Aug. 26.   ∎

---

* CPB's first report on program content is due in January 1993.

ually re-examine their role.

Several blue-ribbon panels are at work doing that. The Twentieth Century Fund of New York City will report early next year. The Carnegie Corporation has commissioned a book by Kennedy FCC Chairman Newton Minow and Northwestern University Professor Craig LeMay on public service TV programming. The John D. and Catherine T. MacArthur Foundation and the Benton Foundation have been convening roundtables of scholars to discuss future research in the field.

Fundraising will continue to be a challenge. In New Jersey, the Republican-controlled Legislature is considering abolishing the state Public Broadcasting Commission and selling off cash-strapped WNEJ to New York's WNET.[35] And Democratic presidential candidate Bill Clinton recently commented in a C-SPAN interview that while he supports public television, he considers it a lower priority for federal spending than income- and job-creating programs.

Finally, PBS' airing of corporate messages that more and more resemble advertising are drawing attention from the Internal Revenue Service, which asks why such corporate grants should be considered tax-deductible charitable contributions and why public TV stations pay no taxes on them.[36]

Public TV lobbyists, meanwhile, have requested that Congress accelerate consideration of future CPB bills so that authorizations are delayed less frequently. The recent debate and new provisions requiring CPB to monitor program content left the public broadcasting community with "a better understanding and a better ability to demonstrate that it can be accountable to taxpayers," says Gerald Hogan, CPB's vice president for federal relations.

The long-term strategy, notes lobbyist Brugger, is to emphasize public broadcasting's potential roles in pub-

OUTLOOK

Self-Examination

"We are a self-righteous crowd who believe that what we are doing is essential to democracy itself," PBS President Bruce Christiansen said in a speech in July.

Indeed, futurists Alvin Toffler and John Naisbitt have written in a CPB publication that public broadcasting "will become increasingly important to be able to put events in broader and deeper context."

But with the country divided by a political and culture "war," with a federal budget deficit looming and technological change still galloping ahead, public broadcasters seem destined to contin-

Continued on p. 828

In the Current Climate, PBS Highlights Education

At pledge-drive time, public television spotlights its highbrow "Masterpiece Theater" and the gentle "Mr. Rogers." But when legislators brandish a budget knife, public TV zooms in on the serious lectures, homework and exams.

"The nation's largest classroom," as the Public Broadcasting Service (PBS) dubs itself, reaches 29.5 million students at 70,000 schools with such PBS standbys as National Geographic Society nature programs, which teachers praise for their high production values.

Two-thirds of the nation's 3,000 colleges offer PBS-prepared courses, and more than 2 million adult Americans have earned college credit through PBS since 1981. A survey commissioned by cable television's Arts and Entertainment Network in 1991 found that PBS classroom programming was used by 55 percent of educators, compared with only 12 percent who used "CNN Newsroom" and 11 percent who used "A&E Classroom."

"Sesame Street" has become such a staple at day-care centers around the country that there is now a PBS program to train day-care providers in techniques for enhancing children's viewing, reinforcing the lessons with reading, art, music and drama.

In the information age, of course, instructional programming has come a long way from the days of single-angle cameras trained on a drab science teacher and his clay volcano. PBS is a leader in the growing field of "long-distance learning," in which adult night-school students receive lectures on their home computers or via cable television. PBS has also acquired six transponders on a new satellite, *Telstar 401*, to be launched in 1993 by American Telephone & Telegraph Co., which will greatly augment the amount of transmission time PBS can devote to academic programming.

Just as education has traditionally been handled by states and localities, the bulk of public TV education comes from state and municipal public stations. Some 23 states are members of public TV's Satellite Education Resource Consortium. Stations in Kentucky, Nebraska, South Carolina and Wisconsin have led a trend toward active partnerships — a form of "team teaching" — between public television professionals and full-time educators to take advantage of communications technologies.

Nowhere has the development been more dramatic than at Kentucky Educational Television (KET) in Lexington. For much of the 1980s, the impoverishment of Kentucky's public schools caused concern among education reformers. College deans complained that Kentucky high school graduates were spending their freshman years finishing up high school-level courses. An alarming 78 high schools in the state offered no courses in physics, and 40 percent of the state's foreign-language teachers held only a minor degree in their specialty language.

Spurred by legislation and a 1989 Kentucky Supreme Court ruling that mandated funding equity among schools, KET joined with education officials to outfit each public school with the latest equipment for long-distance learning. At a cost of $3,000 per school, each received a television, videocassette recorder, computer, modem, printer, portable telephone and 12 specially designed key pads. Now, via a linkup with a commercial satellite, students in the most remote or rural areas take KET-transmitted courses electronically from the best teachers in the state. They study physics, German, Japanese and Latin — the "high-need, low-numbers" subjects, in the words of Virginia G. Fox, executive director of KET.

Students reach teachers by telephone with the key pads, which allow their responses to be recorded in individual files and tabulated to give the teacher an instant measure of how lessons are being absorbed. More than 5,000 adult Kentuckians have now received general equivalency diplomas via TV. Kentucky public broadcasters are working with teachers to better integrate educational programming into lesson plans. "We spend money on the last mile, the last foot and the last inch," Fox says. "The program is only half of it. If the audience is not ready to receive the program, then teachers can't use it."

Public television's presence in the debate over education reform has provoked some discontent among private-sector providers of instructional programming. Businesses that produce programming for Oklahoma State University, the Black Colleges Satellite Network and others are represented in Washington by Shelly Weinstein, president of the National Education Telecommunications Organization. In seeking federal loan guarantees for the purchase of another satellite, to be shared by private educational programming providers, she recently accused PBS of treating private providers as competitors. "PBS's goal to create a critical mass of satellite capacity with public monies is not to build an infrastructure to transport more and more ... [but] to add revenue sources and outlets for PBS's programs," she told the Senate Commerce Committee's Communications Subcommittee.

Bob Ottenhoff, senior vice president at PBS in Alexandria, Va., says that some program providers have misunderstood PBS's policy because current transmission technology has limited capacity and forces private program providers to wait in line to use it. Public TV's coming new satellite will be available to all private providers, he says. "We've thrown out the net as wide as we can. We will be known as the most important neighborhood for educational telecommunications."

Continued from p. 826

lic-private partnerships, helping to harness new technologies, and in education, one of the few areas of the federal budget where new spending is likely. As Virginia G. Fox, executive director of Kentucky public television, puts it, "When Bob Dole can prove that they've solved the problem of undereducated people, when they have provided total access, when cable is free and available to 99 percent of American households, then I'll let go of public TV."

Politics of the Tube

"At a time when America is fragmenting as a community — both in the culture war and in the sense that the networks are no longer dominant," notes conservative critic David Horowitz, "there is an important slot for public broadcasting. It wouldn't take that much to reform the system to give conservative Republicans confidence that it has diversity, and it would be healthy for the media and country."

To Laurence Jarvik, who recently left the Heritage Foundation to work with Horowitz's Center for the Study of Popular Culture, there is a role for public broadcasting only if the enterprise is a market failure. "But just to assume market failures" is dangerous, he says. "With that, you could rationalize a national journalism, and you'd be on a slippery slope to government propaganda."

"There is too much contentment inside American public television," says Michael Tracey, a public TV sympathizer who directs the Center for Mass Media Research at the University of Colorado. "One of the more obvious reasons why the right has had so much success is that it nurtured think tanks like the Heritage Foundation, adopted a public role and captured the intellectual high ground of the 1980s. Whether there is real stuff in their intellect, whether it is the self-serving ideology of a wealthy elite, whether their utterances are those of the new barbarians

are all significant questions. The fact remains, however, that they won."[37]

Whether the recent victors really were the conservative critics or the public broadcasters who will be receiving new monies, it is clear that public broadcasters are likely to continue operating in a climate of easily incited controversy. "The biggest problem with the idea of public broadcasting," observed John Wicklein, a former CPB public affairs director, "is that there are 250 million views of what it should be."[38] ∎

Notes

[1] Quoted in *The Washington Times*, June 28, 1991.

[2] For background, see "Does Cable TV Need More Regulation?" *Editorial Research Reports*, Dec. 7, 1990, pp. 698-711.

[3] Quoted in Corporation for Public Broadcasting, "Strategies for Public Television in a Multi-channel Environment," March 1991.

[4] Laurence Jarvik, "After Privatization: Public Television in the Cultural Marketplace," Heritage Foundation lecture, May 21, 1992.

[5] Quoted in Media Research Center, *Media Watch*, December 1990.

[6] The New York Times, March 22, 1992.

[7] See *Congressional Record*, June 3, 1992, p. S 7432.

[8] S. Robert Lichter, Daniel Amundson and Linda S. Lichter, "Balance and Diversity of PBS Documentaries," Center for Media and Public Affairs, March 1992.

[9] Writing in *Current*, May 27, 1991.

[10] Reprinted in the newsletter *COMINT*, spring 1991.

[11] Jeff Cohen, "PBS Tilts Toward Conservatives, Not the Left," *Extra*, June 1992.

[12] Column appearing in *The Washington Post*, April 23, 1992.

[13] Cited in Jarvik, *op. cit.*

[14] *Congressional Record*, July 28, 1992, p. H 6744.

[15] Quoted in *Current*, March 2, 1992.

[16] Quoted in Erik Barnouw, *Tube of Plenty:*

The Evolution of American Television (1990), p. 74.

[17] George H. Gibson, *Public Broadcasting: The Role of the Federal Government* (1977), p. 39.

[18] Quoted in Barnouw, *op. cit.*, p. 300.

[19] David Horowitz, *The Problem with Public TV*, Center for the Study of Popular Culture, 1991, p. 6.

[20] Quoted in Patricia Aufderheide, "Public Television and the Public Sphere," *Critical Studies in Mass Communication*, June 1991, p. 168.

[21] Quoted in Gibson, *op. cit.*, p. 143.

[22] Quoted in Aufderheide, *op. cit.*, p. 168.

[23] Corporation for Public Broadcasting, "From Wasteland to Oasis," *1991 Annual Report*, p. 6.

[24] Quoted in Gibson, *op. cit.*, p. 177.

[25] *Ibid.*, p. 191.

[26] Quoted in Patricia Aufderheide, "Public TV Tunes Out the Big Picture," *In These Times*, July 4-17, 1990.

[27] Aufderheide, *Critical Studies in Mass Communication, op. cit.*, p. 168.

[28] *Ibid.*

[29] Howard Rosenberg, writing in the *Los Angeles Times*, June 4, 1985.

[30] Horowitz, *op. cit.*, p. 21.

[31] *Ibid.*

[32] Quoted in Patricia Aufderheide, "Toward Anti-Television: The Independent Production Service and the Future of Public Broadcasting," *After Image*, March 1989, pp. 4-5.

[33] See Carol Matlack, "Public Broadcasters' New Lobby Tool," *National Journal*, Jan. 18, 1992, p. 163.

[34] Public stations that go off the air at or before midnight could begin airing such programs at 10 p.m.

[35] See *The New York Times*, July 24, 1992.

[36] See Laura Bird, "Public TV Plugs Getting Closer to Network Ads," *The Wall Street Journal*, Aug. 10, 1992.

[37] Quoted in *Current*, June 22, 1992.

[38] Quoted in Keith Dunnavant, "PBS: Dynamo or Dinosaur?" *Media Week*, Feb. 24, 1992. p. 19.

Bibliography

Selected Sources Used

Books

Barnouw, Erik, *Tube of Plenty: The Evolution of American Television,* Second Revised Edition, Oxford University Press, 1990.

This condensed version of a three-volume work by a Vermont-based historian describes the economics, technologies, politics and cultural changes that came with the development of television, beginning with the early days of radio at the turn of the century.

Gibson, George H., *Public Broadcasting: The Role of the Federal Government, 1912-76,* Praeger Publishers, 1977.

A St. Lawrence University history professor gives a blow-by-blow account of the political, policy, legal, technological and bureaucratic forces that created today's public broadcasting establishment.

Lashley, Marilyn, *Public Television: Panacea, Pork Barrel or Public Trust?,* Greenwood Press, 1992.

A University of Maryland professor of Afro-American studies worked in cooperation with the Brookings Institution in Washington, D.C., to produce this analysis of the weaknesses and strengths of public television, concentrating on the role minorities play in the public TV field and in its programming. The author laments the fact that "public TV's mandate to provide programming, employment and audience diversity is subordinate to securing increased appropriations from one year to the next."

Postman, Neil, *Amusing Ourselves to Death: Public Discourse in the Age of Show Business*, Viking, 1985.

A New York University communications professor takes a dim view of the effects of television on the quality of debate, thinking and reading in current American life.

Articles

Behrens, Steve, "Foundations Renew Interest in PTV," *Current,* Aug. 3, 1992, p. 1.

The author, who is editor of the biweekly newspaper devoted to public telecommunications, reports on the numerous private foundations showing renewed support for public television.

Daniel, Josh, "Uncivil Wars: The Conservative Assault on Public Broadcasting," *The Independent,* August-September 1992, p. 20.

An independent filmmaker provides a history of the current controversy and analysis of the conservative organiza-

tions and individuals who are attacking public broadcasting.

Jarvik, Laurence, "Monopoly, Corruption, and Greed: The Problem of Public Television," *The Heritage Lectures,* Feb. 25, 1992.

The author, until recently a scholar at the conservative Heritage Foundation in Washington, D.C., argues that federal funding of public television contributes to the system's weakness and should be eliminated.

Jarvik, Laurence, "After Privatization: Public Television in the Cultural Marketplace," *The Heritage Lectures,* May 21, 1992.

Continuing his attack on public television, the author contends that public television, as a "truly private entity," would thrive in competition with new commercial communications services.

Reports and Studies

Corporation for Public Broadcasting, *From Wasteland to Oasis: Retrospective 1967-92,* 1991 annual report.

The private, nonprofit corporation authorized by Congress to distribute funds to public television and radio stations celebrated its first quarter-century with an illustrated history of its accomplishments.

Horowitz, David, *The Problem with Public TV: A Monograph from the Committee on Media Integrity,* Center for the Study of Popular Culture, December 1991.

Horowitz, who with Peter Collier is author of best-selling biographies of the Kennedy and Rockefeller families, is a former editor of the defunct leftist magazine *Ramparts.* This history of public television is told along the theme of its creation during the Vietnam War in the 1960s.

The Next Step

Additional Articles from Current Periodicals from EBSCO Publishing's Database

Debates & issues

"PBS's enemies list," *National Review*, April 13, 1992, p. 19.

Comments on a memo from the president of the Association of America's Public Television Stations to all station managers, congressional liaisons, public information directors and development directors, concerning a "battle" against conservatives. Organizations, publications and people listed in the memo; more.

"The taxpayer's Wagner," *The Economist*, May 30, 1992, p. 31

Considers whether American taxpayers should finance the Corporation for Public Broadcasting (CPB). Details of an argument against the practice as articulated by columnist George F. Will; opposing statements made by Sharon Percy Rockefeller; why public television is under attack for its alleged left-wing bias.

Geier, T., M. Horn, et al., "Let them eat cable," *U.S. News & World Report*, May 25, 1992, p. 25.

Discusses the fierce battle Congress faces over the future of public television. The Senate is expected to vote soon on a funding bill; Robert Dole, R-Kan., denies conservatives are targeting public broadcasting; public TV considered too liberal; why the elitism claims are among the most hotly debated; public TV's advocates; more.

Horowitz, D., "The politics of public television," *Commentary*, December 1991, p. 25.

Discusses public television, which was created by the Public Broadcasting Act of 1967. One of the last vestiges of the "Great Society"; its private benefactors; its organizational complexities; some of its broadcasting luminaries; its alleged left-wing bias; attempts to put it out of business.

Lewyn, M., "Is PBS really worth it?" *Newsweek*, Dec. 24, 1990, p. 10.

Argues that it's time to start thinking about ending government support for public TV. Questions why a bankrupt government should continue subsidizing public TV at the cost of $200 million a year. Other channels providing programming that only PBS once did; cable television's competition.

Morse, M., "Where's the public in public broadcasting?" *Utne Reader*, January/February 1990, p. 33.

Analyzes the ways in which public television and radio raise funds. Questions whether the public's interest is being served by public broadcasting. Relationship between corporate funding and skewed programming decisions; politics of program funding; threat of cable television.

Ouellette, L., "The right wing targets public TV," *Utne Reader*, May/June 1992, p. 45.

Cites the claims made by the right wing that public television has a "leftist bias" and is a "misuse of public funds." An all-out war against "subsidized cultural dissidence"; quotes articles in "Alternet," "Columbia Journalism Review," "Current" and two others.

Rosen, J., "Chatter from the right," *Progressive*, March 1988, p. 26.

Reports that the conservative biweekly "National Review" supplies the hosts for three political talk shows on public television, all of them backed by corporate money. Discusses the oversupply of entertaining, glib, right-wing commentators.

Shannon, E., and R. Zoglin, "Public TV under assault," *Time*, March 30, 1992, p. 58.

Focuses on recent attacks by conservatives and a growing number of election-year critics on Capitol Hill against public television; delay in funding for the Corporation for Public Broadcasting; candidate's attacks on "Tongues Untied," and "Maria's Story"; Heritage Foundation report concerning privatizing PBS.

Economic aspects

"Dark days loom for some public stations," *Broadcasting*, May 6, 1991, p. 24.

Reports that state funding shortfalls may jeopardize the continued competitiveness, and in some cases the continued existence, of some non-commercial television and radio stations in Tennessee and North Carolina. Two, and perhaps three, of seven public TV stations in Tennessee could go off the air next year.

"March: Like lion for PBS," *Broadcasting*, March 25, 1991, p. 24.

Discusses the success of public TV stations earlier this month with improving viewer response to on-air fundraising efforts over last year. States that public TV stations during the important March 2-17 fundraising drive received $36.7 million in pledges, according to figures supplied by the Public Broadcasting Service.

"PBS faces possible rough road for pledge drives," *Broadcasting*, Feb. 25, 1991, p. 33.

Reports that public television could be facing some difficulties next month as it enters its most important on-air fundraising period of the year. Stations are hopeful that viewers will respond favorably to public TV's coverage of the Persian Gulf and of PBS' popular "The Civil War" series. Estimated 45,000 volunteers nationally would be helping raise money; PBS has funded a weekend edition and prime-time updates of "MacNeil/Lehrer NewsHour."

De Llosa, P., and D. Seligman, "Quacking on public tv," *Fortune*, April 20, 1992, p. 189.

Presents an argument in favor of privatizing the Corporation for Public Broadcasting (CPB). Resistance of public broadcasting to balancing its public-affairs coverage; denial that quality broadcasting is uneconomical.

Education

Harrell, L., "Distance learning," *Childhood Education*, winter 1991, p. 96-M.

Reports that despite the many benefits of distance learning, some controversy still exists. Threats to new teachers who are looking for work but are being replaced by public television classrooms; concerns about students' ability to learn in this kind of classroom.

Shelton, H.H., "Math/science teacher training program expanded," *Childhood Education*, fall 1991, p. 32G.

Discusses how Thirteen/WNET and Texaco announced at an Aug. 1 press conference that the success of their 1990 jointly sponsored pilot program to train math and science teachers in the skillful use of public television resources warranted its continuation and expansion. How the original program was developed; comments from contributors.

Government policy

"Congress feathers Big Bird's nest,' *Newsweek*, June 15, 1992, p. 59.

Reports that last week the Senate authorized $1.1 billion in federal funds for public broadcasting through 1996. How this amount reflects a 50 percent boost over current levels; why conservatives rail against taxpayer underwriting of public television.

"Public broadcasting can be dealt with by reforming it, not killing it," *Broadcasting*, June 8, 1992, p. 55.

Presents a commentary on public broadcasting reform by Federal Communications Commission (FCC) Commissioner Ervin S. Duggan. Critics of the Senate's decision to reauthorize the Corporation for Public Broadcasting; public television's roots in the robust tradition of populism; problems with restructuring public broadcasting for the 21st Century; more.

Mills, M., "Senate tunes out critics, boosts public TV, radio," *Congressional Quarterly Weekly Report*, June 6, 1992, p. 1598.

Details the Senate's approval of bill (S 1504) that would authorize a 50 per cent increase in funding for public broadcasting. Complaints that public radio and television programming is rife with "elitism, sweetheart deals and one-sided partisanship"; the Senate's rejection of Trent Lott's (R-Miss.) amendment to keep authorized levels for the Corporation for Public Broadcasting (CPB) at $275 million a year; other amendments; more. INSET: An unlikely champion.

Television programs

Beschloss, S., "Local vs. central: Civil War at PBS," *Channels*, Dec. 3, 1990, p. 52.

Looks at the success of the PBS series "The Civil War" and the pros and cons of a more centralized plan for PBS. Jennifer Lawson, PBS executive vice president of national programming and promotion services, is a key figure in the new system, which is intended to improve the ability to compete with cable.

Gallagher, J., "Balance is watchword at CPB meeting," *Broadcasting*, June 29, 1992, p. 35.

Covers the Corporation for Public Broadcasting awards banquet at the PBS annual meeting in San Francisco. CPB Chairwoman Sheila Tate's remarks that "a pereceived imbalance [in public television programming] is as important to address as a real imbalance"; the Senate's approval of the CPB authorization bill on June 3, 1992; the increased promotion of children's programs; new fall programs.

Goodman, W., "Public TV juggles a hot potato," *The New York Times*, Sept. 3, 1989, Section 2, p. 1.

Discusses the controversial documentary film "Days of Rage," a public television offering about the Palestinian uprising in Israel. Charges that its pro-Palestinian focus is discriminatory; impact on public television and its goals.

Hedegaard, E., "Beyond Masterpiece Theater," *Mother Jones*, October 1989, p. 49.

Comments on a new law that will expand the creative boundaries of PBS' programming. Possible programs that may follow; funding and individual station's rights.

Lowe, V., "PBS show tries race relations," *Black Enterprise*, February 1992, p. 32.

Announces that the public television series "Sesame Street" is airing a "race relations curriculum" aimed at introducing viewers to various cultural backgrounds. Public Broadcasting Service (PBS); helping children to celebrate differences; focus on the contributions of African-Americans, Native Americans, Latinos and Asian Americans; more.

Back Issues

Great Research on Current Issues Starts Right Here... Recent topics covered by The CQ Researcher are listed below. Issues dated before May 10, 1991, were published under the name of Editorial Research Reports.

MARCH 1991
Acid Rain
Cost of the Gulf War
Reassessing Gun Laws
Future for Man in Space

APRIL 1991
Social Security
Canadian Crisis Over Quebec
California Drought
Electromagnetic Radiation

MAY 1991
School Choice
Racial Quotas
Animal Rights
U.S. and Japan

JUNE 1991
Children and Divorce
Teenage Suicide
Endangered Species
Europe 1992

JULY 1991
Teenagers and Abortion
Soviet Republics Rebel
Mexico's Emergence
Athletes and Drugs

AUGUST 1991
Sexual Harassment
Fetal Tissue Research
Oil Imports
The Palestinians

SEPTEMBER 1991
Police Brutality
Advertising Under Attack
Saving the Forests
Foster Care Crisis

OCTOBER 1991
Pay-Per-View TV
Youth Gangs
Gene Therapy
World Hunger

NOVEMBER 1991
Fast-Food Shake-Up
The Greening of Eastern Europe
Business' Role in Education
Cuba In Crisis

DECEMBER 1991
Retiree Health Benefits
Asian Americans
The Obscenity Debate
The Disabilities Act

JANUARY 1992
Term Limits
Oil Spills
Hunting Controversy
Alternative Medicine

FEBRUARY 1992
Threatened Coastlines
New Era in Asia
Assisted Suicide
Jobs in the '90s

MARCH 1992
Women and Sports
Underage Drinking
Garbage Crisis
Mafia Crackdown

APRIL 1992
Ozone Depletion
Welfare Reform
Politicians and Privacy
Illegal Immigration

MAY 1992
Native Americans
Jobs vs. Environment
Too Many Lawsuits?
Fairness in Salaries

JUNE 1992
Nuclear Proliferation
Food Irradiation
Lead Poisoning
Hard Times for Libraries

JULY 1992
Alternative Energy
Prescription Drug Prices
Alzheimer's Disease
Infant Mortality

AUGUST 1992
The Homeless
Work, Family and Stress
NATO's Changing Role
Marine Mammals vs. Fish

SEPTEMBER 1992
Domestic Partners
Violence in Schools

Back issues are available for $4.00 (subscribers) or $7.00 (non-subscribers). Quantity discounts apply to orders over ten. To order, call Congressional Quarterly 1-800-432-2250.

Future Topics

▶ *Women in the Military*

▶ *Depression*

▶ *U.S. Auto Industry*

Women in the Military

What role should women play in the shrinking military?

T HE PERSIAN GULF WAR WAS A WATERSHED
event for women in the military. For the first time,
American women were stationed alongside men in
a prolonged conflict. The stellar performance of
more than 40,000 female troops during the war has mobilized
many in Congress — and some in the military — to push for a
broader role for women in the armed forces, including
combat. But many observers contend that the male-dominated
military culture is not prepared to accept women as equals. As
evidence they point to recent disclosures about pervasive
sexual harassment, including the widely publicized Tailhook
incident. The controversy comes at a difficult time for the
armed forces, which are under federal mandate to reduce
their ranks by 25 percent by 1995.

C
Q **September 25, 1992 • Volume 2, No. 36 • 833-856**

Formerly Editorial Research Reports

COVER ART: BARBARA SASSA-DANIELS

THE CQ Researcher

September 25, 1992
Volume 2, No. 36

EDITOR
Sandra Stencel

MANAGING EDITOR
Thomas J. Colin

ASSOCIATE EDITOR
Richard L. Worsnop

STAFF WRITERS
Charles S. Clark
Mary H. Cooper
Rodman D. Griffin

PRODUCTION EDITOR
Sarah E. Merritt

EDITORIAL ASSISTANT
Michael M. Taylor

GRAPHICS
Jack Auldridge

PUBLISHED BY
Congressional Quarterly Inc.

CHAIRMAN
Andrew Barnes

VICE CHAIRMAN
Andrew P. Corty

EDITOR AND PUBLISHER
Neil Skene

EXECUTIVE EDITOR
Robert W. Merry

ASSOCIATE PUBLISHER
John J. Coyle

EDITOR, EBSCO PUBLISHING
Melissa Kummerer

The CQ Researcher (ISSN 1056-2036). Formerly Editorial Research Reports. Published weekly (48 times per year, not printed the first Friday of any month with five Fridays) by Congressional Quarterly Inc., 1414 22nd St., N.W., Washington, D.C. 20037. Rates are furnished upon request. Second-class postage paid at Washington, D.C. POSTMASTER: Send address changes to The CQ Researcher, 1414 22nd St., N.W., Washington, D.C. 20037.

Women in the Military

BY RODMAN D. GRIFFIN

THE ISSUES

Bill Baxter is not the sort of man to speak ill of the military. A pilot in the Naval Reserve and a proud member of the National Rifle Association, he believes fervently in a strong defense. He attends Plymouth Haven Baptist Church, talks about "family values" and considers himself a dyed-in-the-wool Republican. An American flag flaps in the breeze outside his Alexandria, Va., home. The last thing he ever imagined he would do was write to Rep. Patricia Schroeder, D-Colo., a longtime critic of military policies, pleading with her to hold the U.S. armed forces accountable for the sexual harassment of women.

But that was before last year's convention of the Tailhook Association,* when his wife, Lt. Cmdr. Roxanne Baxter, was one of 14 officers, and at least 36 women in all, who said they were mauled by a "gantlet" of Marine Corps and Navy aviators. It was before the Navy sought to whitewash the unseemly events in the Las Vegas hotel corridor, before one of the women, Lt. Paula Coughlin, a helicopter pilot and admiral's aide, decided to step forward and tell her story publicly, and before the subsequent public and political furor that has sent the Navy scurrying to buff up its image. *(See story, p. 844.)*

"I've watched Roxanne's hassles throughout her career, one straw after another, and I've finally gotten sick of it," Bill Baxter says, explaining his decision to speak out. "Her career progression has been halted solely because she is a woman." Several times over the years, Roxanne Baxter, a transport pilot whose assignments have included ferrying mail and supplies to aircraft carriers, was left behind during lengthy tours at sea that would have furthered her career.

On her one extended sea tour, in which she was the only woman among 500 men, she was the brunt of smutty skits, her husband says. And once, Baxter was forcibly removed from an office by a man who did not want to take orders from a woman, then told that if she pressed charges she would lose her job as a department head. Last spring, she was passed over for promotion to full commander, despite glowing assessments from many colleagues.[1]

Roxanne Baxter's experience is all too common. In September 1990, in the first major study of sexual harassment in the military, the Pentagon concluded that nearly two-thirds of the 20,000 women surveyed experienced some form of harassment, including touching, pressure for sexual favors and rape. *(See list, p. 838.)* The Pentagon report, which took two years to complete, described pervasive deni-

gration of women in an atmosphere where policies aimed at preventing abuse are frequently not enforced.

The Tailhook publicity has emboldened other women to come forward. The Army is investigating reports that dozens of female soldiers were assaulted in Saudi Arabia by Army men during the Persian Gulf War. The head of an Air Force fighter wing in South Korea recently was relieved of his command for making a derogatory remark to a female officer.

As disclosures about sexual misconduct in the armed forces continue to emerge, officials find themselves struggling not only with the practical problems of how to integrate women into their ranks but also with the deeper military-culture dilemma. After years of indoctrination about how to be aggressive under extraordinary combat conditions, these men are under new pressure to check their behavior around women and keep sexually offensive comments to themselves.

"Until Tailhook, we dealt too often with sexual harassment at the local level, one case at a time, rather than understanding it as a cultural issue," Adm. Frank B. Kelso II, the chief of naval operations, told the House Armed Services Committee in July.

Seen in that light, the Tailhook debacle, which has already cost H. Lawrence Garrett III his job as secretary of the Navy, may be a blessing in disguise. Much as shipboard race riots in 1972 led to racial reforms within the Navy, the embarrassing incident is prompting serious efforts to stamp out sexual harassment.

Last summer then-Acting Navy Secretary J. Daniel Howard announced a policy of "zero tolerance" toward sexual harassment and ordered all personnel to devote a full day to sensitivity training. And just last week, Sean O'Keefe, appointed in July by President Bush as the new acting Navy sec-

---

*The Tailhook Association, a private organization for Navy and Marine Corps pilots, takes its name from the hook on planes that snags an arresting cable when they are landing on aircraft carriers.

retary, upped the ante. He asked his standing committee on women in the Navy for recommendations by Sept. 30 on new proposals to end sexual harassment, including participation by more women in fleet training exercises.

Women, like blacks, had long served in their own units, and integration did not begin on a grand scale until the all-volunteer military was launched in 1973. It took women nearly two decades to make a significant impact, but now they represent about 11 percent of all American armed forces personnel and are considered vital to military readiness. More than 40,000 women were deployed in the Persian Gulf War — the first major test of the integration of women into the military. By virtually all accounts, they performed admirably — even in the heat of battle.

Tradition and military culture, the realities of women's performance in the gulf and constrained opportunities for military women are converging to create tension in the armed services. Women's advocates are pushing for an expanded role for women, including combat. "Our policies on utilization of women are dictated by laws passed in 1948," says Carolyn Becraft, a military analyst in Washington and former Army officer. "The premise of these laws is no longer valid. We're looking at this from a World War II mind-set."

Last year, Congress repealed the final laws that barred women from combat aircraft. But the Pentagon has delayed changing its policy, pending the report of a special presidential panel, the Commission on the Assignment of Women in the Armed Forces, expected in mid-November. The pervasive accounts of sexual misconduct that have emerged in recent months have stoked the fires for change.

The controversy comes at a difficult time for the military. Under a 1990 federal mandate, the armed forces must reduce their ranks by 25

percent by 1995. As policy-makers, military personnel and the public debate what role women will play in the shrinking military, here are some of the questions being asked:

Do rules excluding women from combat deny them equal opportunities for advancement?

Some 1.5 million American women are veterans today. Another 211,000 serve on active duty. But while many of these women are willing to risk their lives for their country, their country is reluctant to let them.

Despite repeal of the combat-exclusion laws for pilots, military policy does not permit women to serve in positions that bring them into direct combat. As a result, roughly half of the nation's 1.9 million military jobs are off-limits to women.[2] Culturally, Americans have, until recently, rejected the notion of women going into direct combat where they could lose their lives or be captured. Many still feel deep ambivalence. (*See poll results, p. 837.*)

Yet many military women complain that combat is the missing step on their career ladders. Officially, they have an equal shot at all non-combat jobs. But because combat is the surest ticket to promotion, women's chances for moving into the top spots are slim. (Although the proceedings of military promotion boards are secret, it is common knowledge that the system favors officers with combat service.) Today, just 11 women hold the rank of general or admiral, out of a total 1,021 slots.* Although a 1989 General Accounting Office (GAO) study showed that women are generally promoted at a rate similar to that for men, the study also concluded that combat-exclusion blocks most women

---

*It takes on average 23 years to reach the rank of general, and back in 1971 women made up fewer than 2 percent of the armed forces. Nevertheless, women are still underrepresented in the higher echelons, holding only 1.1 percent of the top jobs.

from the higher echelons.[3]

"Instead of a glass ceiling, they have a lead ceiling," says Becraft. As long as combat-exclusion persists, she says, opportunities for women will remain limited.

Yet even among military women, there is not unanimity on the subject. While female officers see their career opportunities diminishing as they become more senior, enlisted women are less subject to career disappointment, partly because their expectations are lower to begin with. "It's absolutely true that officers are more supportive of ending combat exclusions than enlisted personnel," says Becraft. "Enlisted women are like blue-collar workers in their career progression. I don't think they want to be in the infantry."

In any case, many military men believe equal opportunity for women in the military will undermine national security. "The military is not a jobs program, nor is it an equal-opportunity program," contends John Luddy, a Marine Corps Reserve infantry officer and defense analyst at the Heritage Foundation. "Putting women in combat will weaken the fighting ability that is the key to winning battles and wars. It is not worth a single life to provide equal opportunity."

That argument, however, has lost some of its validity in the aftermath of the Persian Gulf War (*see p. 842*). Moreover, the lines distinguishing combat and combat support are blurred. For instance, women are allowed to fly Air Force refueling planes, officially a "combat-support" job, yet some observers say this is more dangerous than flying a bomber, a "combat" job.

"To a certain extent women have the worst of both worlds," says Lawrence J. Korb, former assistant secretary for Defense under Ronald Reagan and now a senior fellow at the Brookings Institution. "They can't go into those jobs with the highest probability of promotion to the top of the organization. But they are still in danger."

Even the Joint Chiefs of Staff concede there is a double standard at work. "I believe the combat-exclusion law is discrimination against women [and] that it works to their disadvantage in a career context," Gen. Merrill McPeak, the Air Force chief of staff, told the Armed Services Committee in July. "[But] I still think it is not a good idea for me to have to order women into combat. Combat is about killing people. I'm afraid that even though logic tells us that women can do that as well as men, I have a very traditional attitude about wives and mothers and daughters being ordered to kill people." The other Joint Chiefs expressed similar reservations.

The problem with this attitude, retired Army Gen. Evelyn "Pat" Foote argues, is that it "develops a whole male cadre and officer corps that doesn't know how to work with women." So long as officers in the combat branches are practicing "a different sheet of music," she says, they will not know how to use women to their full capabilities. The end result, she says, is that trained and qualified women are prevented from performing where they are needed.

Is the military culture prepared to accept women as equals to men?

"By and large, compared to civilian society, the military offers a better opportunity for women to be all that they can be," says Anne Stone, a research associate at the Women's Research and Education Institute in Washington. "Flawed though it may be, the military has given women, and minority women in particular, an opportunity to get training and education."

Operation Desert Storm accustomed the public to seeing women as full-fledged soldiers. But the war did little to remove the most stubborn barrier to female acceptance in the military: the traditional views of military men — and women. As Gen. Carl E. Mundy, Jr.,

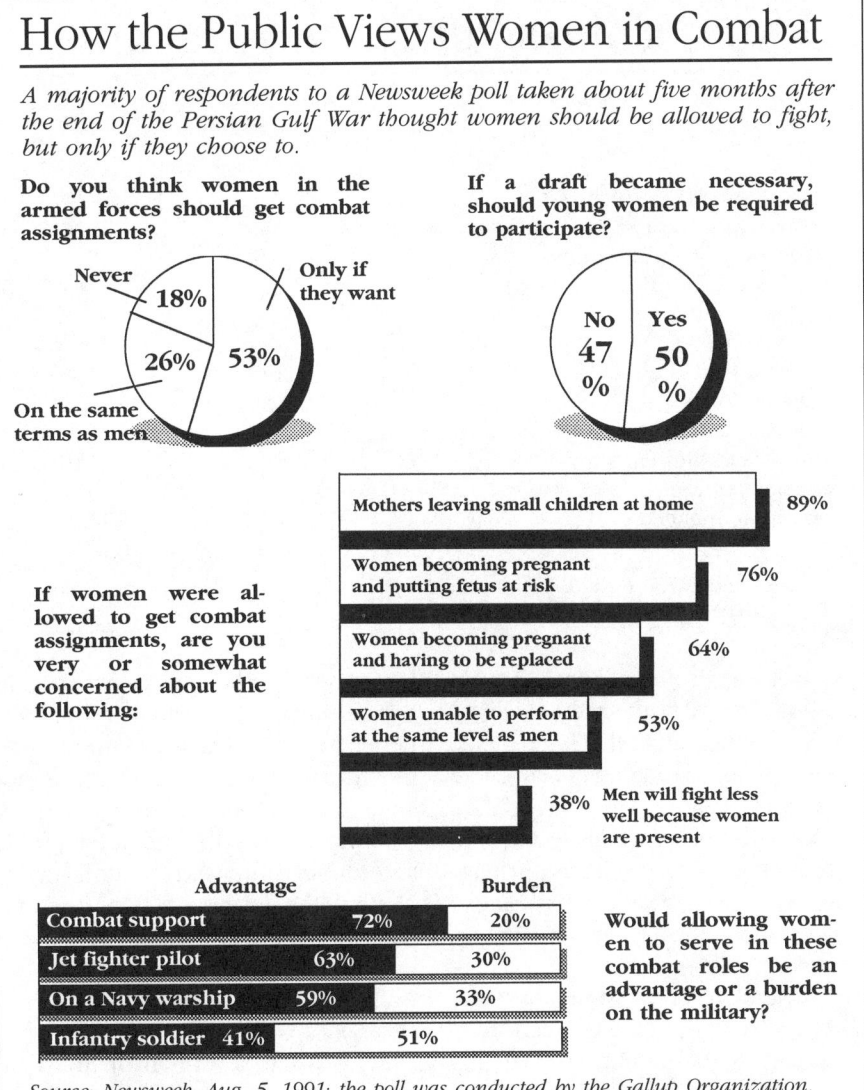

How the Public Views Women in Combat

A majority of respondents to a Newsweek poll taken about five months after the end of the Persian Gulf War thought women should be allowed to fight, but only if they choose to.

Do you think women in the armed forces should get combat assignments?

Never 18%
Only if they want 53%
On the same terms as men 26%

If a draft became necessary, should young women be required to participate?

No 47%
Yes 50%

If women were allowed to get combat assignments, are you very or somewhat concerned about the following:

Mothers leaving small children at home 89%
Women becoming pregnant and putting fetus at risk 76%
Women becoming pregnant and having to be replaced 64%
Women unable to perform at the same level as men 53%
Men will fight less well because women are present 38%

Would allowing women to serve in these combat roles be an advantage or a burden on the military?

	Advantage	Burden
Combat support	72%	20%
Jet fighter pilot	63%	30%
On a Navy warship	59%	33%
Infantry soldier	41%	51%

Source: Newsweek, Aug. 5, 1991; the poll was conducted by the Gallup Organization.

commandant of the Marine Corps, told the Armed Services Committee: "In the elite organizations of all the armed forces, there is that spirit of 'We're a band of brothers.'"[4] In other words, if you're a female, don't apply.

But most experts say accepting women as equals within the military brotherhood will require more than just giving them jobs and benefits. "There are guys who seem to be saying, 'I want to keep you in your place and remind you that you are not one of the boys. You're not my drinking partner or my fishing partner, and you never will be,'" says

Capt. Jamie Conway, an Army intelligence officer.[5]

In recent years, nonetheless, the climate for women in the military has steadily improved. "When I began basic training 11 years ago, it was: 'Female do this. Female, do that,'" says Sgt. 1st Class Terese Blount, a re-enlistment administrator at Fort Bragg, N.C. "They don't do *that* anymore." Yet, both officers and enlisted personnel say many barriers and biases must still be overcome.

The armed forces have their roots in time-honored masculine traditions. The uniforms, rituals and authoritarian struc-

Sexual Harassment in the Military

A majority of women in the military (and a small percentage of men) reported experiencing some type of sexual harassment while on the job.

Type of Sexual Harassment	Female	Male
Actual or Attempted Rape or Sexual Assault	5%	1%
Pressure for Sexual Favors	15%	2%
Touching, Cornering	38%	9%
Looks, Gestures	44%	10%
Letters, Calls	14%	3%
Pressure for Dates	26%	3%
Teasing, Jokes	52%	13%
Whistles, Calls	38%	5%
Attempts to Get Participation	7%	2%
Other Attention	5%	1%
None Experienced	36%	83%

Percentages do not add up to 100 percent because respondents could select more than one answer. Data in the table are weighted to represent the active military population.
Source: Defense Manpower Data Center

ture that permeate military life help transform boys into effective soldiers — into men. Taken as a whole, the armed forces have resisted attempts at gender integration. During World War II, a spontaneous campaign arose to sabotage the new women's military organizations, with GIs engaging in widespread slander of their female counterparts, targeting morals and character. Hence, initial integration was resisted by men, even when women were assigned to traditional tasks, such as nursing and filing.

Now the age-old, male-dominated military culture is colliding with a new reality that includes women in cockpits and more than likely in combat. But it remains an open question how quickly attitudes can be changed. Scholars speculate that men resist initial integration because they find it threatening — particularly in the more elite factions, such as fighter pilots. The very fact of a woman succeeding in the military dilutes the macho mystique and reflects poorly upon the concept of the dominant male. "Essentially, they have invaded an elite male testing ground," notes political scientist Patricia Shields.[6]

Among the most debilitating obstacles military women face is sexual harassment. "All of my 20 years ... in this business tell me that if you cannot share the equal risks and hazards in arduous duty, then you are not equal," says Cmdr. Rosemary Mariner, a senior analyst for the Joint Chiefs and former jet squadron commander. "And if the institution can discriminate against you, then it's not a big leap for ... bigots to decide that, 'Well, I can harass you and I can get away with it.'"

Retired Marine Col. Paul Roush, a leadership professor at the U.S. Naval Academy, agrees. "Women as professionals will not be fully legitimized until the combat exclusion is eliminated," he says. "Its continuation perpetuates second-class status and expectations of substandard performance for women." Until servicewomen stand on equal ground with their male counterparts, Roush believes, reducing sexual misconduct will be difficult.

Luddy of the Heritage Foundation takes a different position. "The logic that leads one to conclude that women are second-class citizens in the military is ridiculous," he says. "The data-processing man in the Marine Corps isn't a second-class citizen. He's a Marine, no

different from the infantryman. The same goes for women. I have no problem with women in senior roles."

But many career servicewomen believe they are being denied such roles. "We're not getting the jobs with meat," says an Army major at the Pentagon who asked not to be identified. "Generally, the females are on another career track."

Experts say the younger generation of military men, with greater experience working with women as peers, are more apt to treat female colleagues as equals. But full acceptance within such a male-dominated institution will take time. "Women will continue to have problems in the military so long as they are a distinct minority," says Martin Binkin, a senior fellow at the Brookings Institution. "Research indicates that groups behave a certain way until a threshold is reached. Integration problems existed at universities such as Yale and Princeton when they first went coeducational."

Should the military have a separate career track for mothers?

Women soldiers shipping off to war became a familiar media theme of Desert Storm. Many women volunteered to go, even if it meant leaving young children behind. A new image, the military mom, was suddenly thrust into the public consciousness. With it came another kind of storm, this one over whether mothers should be sent into war zones where they risked capture or death.

The intense media attention greatly increased public awareness and sympathy for families separated by war, particularly when children were left with no parent at home. Child-advocacy groups argued that, during the war, many children from military families feared they would lose their only parent or both parents. In a *Newsweek* poll conducted in July 1991, five months after the war ended, 89 percent of those surveyed felt uneasy about the prospect of mothers with young children going to war.

Rep. Barbara Boxer, D-Calif., tried to address this situation when she introduced legislation in January 1991 to prevent both of a child's parents from being sent to a war zone.[7] Many of her feminist colleagues, however, opposed this legislation because they saw it as a setback for women's rights.

"If women seek equality in the military, there should come with it equal responsibility and equal liability," says Anne Stone. Jean Jackson, chairwoman of the Defense Advisory Committee on Women in the Services (DACOWITS), a 40-member civilian panel that advises the secretary of Defense, agrees. "The vast majority of women we've interviewed haven't expressed any desire for a 'mommy track,'" she says. "Everyone has child-care problems; they're not unique to the military."

As with the rest of society, the professional costs of establishing a "mommy track" for the military would be quite high. Such a policy could limit the advancement of parents, because, as Shirley Sagawa and Nancy Duff Campbell of the National Women's Law Center note, "decisions regarding enlistment, training and promotions rest on the individual's ability to perform during wartime."[8]

Ironically, experts say women have become so entrenched in the military, in so many important roles, that it would be hard for the Pentagon to hand out many exemptions for mothering while maintaining an effective military. "It's more likely the Pentagon will start trying to screen out mothers," predicts Charles Moskos, a Northwestern University sociologist who specializes in military matters.

That is precisely what concerns women's-rights advocates and lawmakers like Rep. Schroeder. With the military facing personnel reductions of 25 percent by 1995, Schroeder fears the public outcry about military mothers is simply playing into the Defense Department's hands. "You can imagine who they'd love to throw out first," she says. "It

doesn't make any difference how well they perform. Having people on the outside raising all these questions is really helpful to them because it gives them license to say, 'Well, gee, it's been really nice having you here. Now go home.'"

The furor about mothers in the Persian Gulf conflict has raged out of proportion to the numbers involved. According to the Pentagon, the war left 17,500 families without the custodial parent. Of these, about 1,200 were families with both parents in the gulf. Of the rest, the great majority were families headed by single men.

Carolyn Becraft says women in the military are held under different scrutiny than men. "With single mothers, they're subject to criticism for being 'a bad mother,' while with single fathers, the attitude is, 'Oh, the poor guy.' Why isn't anyone asking if we need a 'daddy track?'"

Ultimately, the central issue has to do with military readiness. Service members' availability to deploy in the event of war becomes the paramount imperative. The Pentagon asserts that 9 percent of military women were unable to ship out during the gulf war, compared with 2 percent of the men. The difference is attributed largely to pregnancy.

Indeed, pregnancy poses special problems for the military, disrupting unit cohesion in a unique way: Pentagon officials say that during Desert Storm more than 1,200 pregnant women were evacuated from the gulf region — the equivalent of two infantry battalions.[9] However, focusing on time lost due to pregnancy can be misleading. Studies indicate that men have lost more time for abusing drugs and alcohol than women have for drug and alcohol abuse and pregnancy combined.[10] Similarly, a recent GAO study of the effect of single parents on readiness reported that if anything they had a better record than those who were unmarried without children.[11] ∎

How Many Women Serve?

Women made up 11 percent of total military personnel in fiscal 1991, up from 8.9 percent a decade earlier.

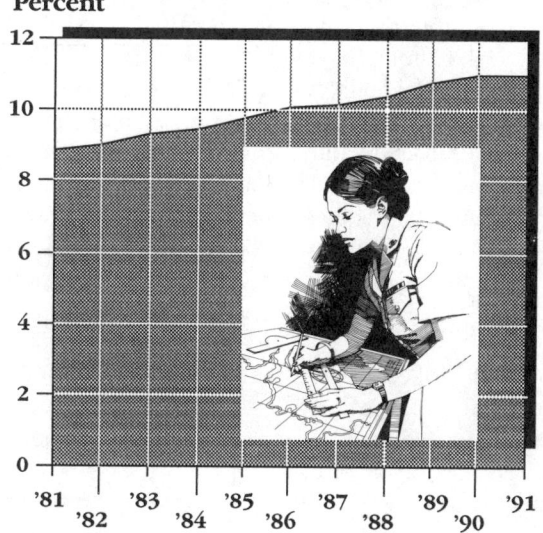

Percent

Source: Defense Manpower Data Center

BACKGROUND

Man's Domain

Traditionally, service in the military of the United States, as in most other industrialized nations, has been a male calling. Except as nurses, the formal association of women in the military is a relatively recent phenomenon. "Serious interest in defining the role of women in the armed forces did not awaken until the beginning of World War II," write Martin Binkin and Shirley J. Bach, "and it was not until 1948 that women achieved permanent military status."[12]

Formal barriers, of course, didn't stop some women from taking up arms. During the Revolutionary War, Molly Pitcher achieved legendary acclaim after assuming the duties of her wounded husband as a cannoneer. Disguised as men, small numbers of women served in combat roles in every war before the 20th century in which the United States became involved. Officially, however, women's participation in the military had been narrowly limited to nursing, clerical and logistical-support jobs, such as doing laundry and sorting mail.

In other countries, differing circumstances and social customs have led women into mainstream military roles. For example, women have participated actively in China's revolutionary movements for the past 150 years. During World War II, about 1 million Russian women reportedly served with combat units as machine gunners, snipers and tank and artillery crew members.

When World War II broke out, the only women permitted in the U.S. armed services were nurses. But manpower needs caused the precursor to the Women's Army Corps (WAC) to be established in May 1942, followed shortly thereafter by the Navy's WAVES (Women Accepted for Voluntary Emergency Service) and the Coast Guard's SPARs (from the Guard's motto, "Semper Paratus: Always Ready"). Women were allowed into the Marine Corps in 1943. The Army Air Corps used women as transport pilots, radio operators and airplane mechanics, as well as stenographers and telephone operators.* For the most part, however, women were cordoned off in separate auxiliaries.

The Women's Armed Services Integration Act of 1948 gave permanent status to military women, but with the proviso that there would be a 2 percent ceiling on the proportion of women in the services (excluding nurses). No female generals or admirals were to be permitted. For the next two decades, women averaged only a little over 1 percent of the armed forces, and nearly all of them did "traditional" women's work, in health care and clerical jobs.

In addition to the 2 percent quota, American women after World War II were indirectly excluded from service through policies that mandated their discharge upon marriage or pregnancy. These policies resulted in first-term attrition rates sometimes as high as 80 percent during the 1950s.

Women's New Status

With the emergence of the Cold War, the assumptions surrounding national security changed. The highly technical nuclear era led to new national security goals such as containment and deterrence, which required a large standing force. During the 1950s and '60s, the armed forces relied upon the male draft to meet its manpower needs.

Under pressure from the expanding role of women in the labor force and

---

*Women in the Air Force (WAF) was created in 1948, after the Air Force had become a separate service.

from the heavy manpower demands of the Vietnam War, the Department of Defense established a task force in 1966 to reassess the role of women in the armed forces. The study group established directions in which women's programs should evolve and laid the groundwork for the expansion that was to occur several years later.

Partly as a result of the study, several significant changes were made in 1967 in the status of military women. Provisions of the law that limited the career opportunities available to women officers were altered, first to allow them to hold permanent grades up through colonel (captain in the Navy) and later general, and, second, to remove existing differences between men and women with respect to retirement provisions. The 1967 law also struck down the 2 percent cap on female enlistees.[13]

By no means was the American public sold on the idea of women in the military. The lukewarm attitude of young civilian women in the early 1970s is reflected by a survey commissioned by the Army in 1972. Asked to rate their degree of favorability toward women's military service, 65 percent reported unfavorably.

Starting in the 1970s, a series of barriers fell in relatively rapid succession. While numerous factors precipitated the military's inclusion of women, several clearly were critical: congressional passage of the Equal Rights Amendment in 1971, the abolition of the draft and the subsequent creation of the all-volunteer force in 1973. These milestones marked the beginning of the era when the military was forced to compete with institutions of higher learning and civilian employers for the nation's young adults. With the women's movement gaining momentum, it became increasingly difficult to deny women the educational and career opportunities that the military offered.

Several judicial decisions were also significant. In 1973, the Supreme Court

Continued on p. 842

Chronology

1900s-1950s *Like most other industrialized nations, the United States relies on young males to staff its military, keeping women in separate auxiliaries and limiting their roles to "traditional" female jobs, such as nursing.*

1901
The U.S. Army establishes an auxiliary for nurses.

May 14, 1942
The Women's Army Auxiliary Corps (WAAC) is created, paving the way for women's corps in each branch of the armed forces.

1948
Congress passes the Women's Armed Services Integration Act establishing a permanent place for women in the armed forces but limiting them to 2 percent of the active-duty force.

———— ● ————

1960s-1970s *The military begins to turn to women to help bolster its ranks in response to stress from the Vietnam War, pressure from the feminist movement and problems in recruiting high-quality males.*

1967
The government lifts the 2 percent ceiling on female enlisted strength in the U.S. military and opens all but the top officer ranks to women.

1970
The draft ends in the United States.

June 11, 1970
Anna Mae Hayes, of the Army Nurse Corps, and Elizabeth P. Hoisington, the director of the WACs, become the first female U.S. generals.

May 14, 1973
The Supreme Court rules that dependents of military women can receive the same entitlements as those offered for the dependents of military men.

Oct. 7, 1975
President Gerald Ford signs law permitting women to attend service academies.

———— ● ————

1980s *Women fill high-tech slots in the military and play an increasingly important role in providing military readiness, but still suffer from discrimination.*

July 20, 1988
The Department of Defense issues a memorandum defining sexual harassment and stating that it "will not be condoned or tolerated in any way."

December 1989
Army Capt. Linda Bray leads a military police unit in Panama that comes under enemy fire, becoming the first U.S. woman to command troops in combat.

———— ● ————

1990s *Combat-exclusion policies get heavy pressure as women survive their first real test in battle and revelations of widespread sexual harassment plague the armed forces.*

June 8, 1990
Navy Cmdr. Rosemary Mariner becomes the first woman to command a fleet jet aircraft squadron.

January 1991
Some 40,000 female soldiers are deployed in the Persian Gulf and play integral combat-support roles during the conflict, the first large-scale U.S. military operation since the establishment of the all-volunteer force.

July 31, 1991
Following an earlier House vote, the Senate eliminates regulations that prohibit women in the Air Force and Navy from flying combat missions.

Sept. 7, 1991
Some 36 women, including 14 military officers, are allegedly sexually harassed by Navy and Marine Corps aviators at the Tailhook Association convention in Las Vegas.

Dec. 5, 1991
President Bush signs the National Defense Authorization Act for FY 1992, which includes a provision repealing the 43-year-old restriction on women flying combat missions in the Air Force, Navy and Marines.

April 3, 1992
Thirty-nine women become the first female cadets at Japan's National Defense Academy.

May 28, 1992
The Senate Armed Services Committee notifies Defense Secretary Dick Cheney that the promotions of more than 4,500 Navy and Marine officers will be held up pending investigation of whether any on the list were involved in the Tailhook incident.

June 2, 1992
Lt. Col. Anne E. Dunwoody becomes the first female battalion commander in the 82nd Airborne Division.

June 26, 1992
Secretary of the Navy H. Lawrence Garrett III resigns over the Tailhook incident.

Continued from p. 840

ruled that dependents of military women could receive the same entitlements as those offered for the dependents of military men. That decision, coupled with a separate federal court ruling that a woman could not be involuntarily discharged if she became pregnant or if she had dependents less than 18 years old, removed significant impediments to the retention of military women. Another federal court decision forced the Navy to open certain categories of ships to women.[14]

In the ensuing years, the proportion of women in the military soared, rising from less than 2 percent of the force in 1972 to more than 8 percent in 1980. Under pressure for equality, even the military's most sacrosanct institutions were obliged to give way: In 1975, Congress ordered West Point and the other military academies to admit women.[15] The Women's Army Corps was abolished in 1978, leading to the direct assignment of women soldiers to non-combat branches of the Army.

The military's growing reliance on women owed partly to factors beyond its control. Facing a sharp drop-off in the pool of eligible males as the baby boomers passed out of recruitment age in the mid-1970s, the Carter administration had to embark on a huge personnel buildup — or risk abandoning the new all-volunteer army.

Women were also needed to boost the quality of personnel. In 1980, more than a quarter of all new male recruits — and almost half the male recruits in the Army — had abilities ranked "below average." Moreover, the armed forces were losing their top male technicians to high-paying jobs in the private sector, ceding many of the high-tech communications, electronics and scientific specialties to women.

The Reagan administration confronted those realities when it tried to limit the female buildup — and toyed with the idea of reinstituting the draft. After a formal study, the

Army closed 23 military occupational specialties (MOSs) to women based on their "combat probability." But when Army teams toured units worldwide, they found there were few men trained to take the women's places — particularly in biological, chemical and nuclear specialties. As a result, 12 of the MOSs were re-opened, and Defense Secretary Caspar W. Weinberger advised top brass in 1983 that "the combat-exclusion rule should be interpreted to allow as many as possible career opportunities for women to be kept open."[16]

Women have been "the margin of success" for the all-volunteer force, says military sociologist Charles Moskos. Were it not for the women recruits, with their superior formal education and test scores, their places would have had to be filled by "lower-quality" male volunteers.

But within the ranks of the military at all levels there persisted just below the surface a deep well of resistance, and even resentment, to the growing incursion of women into previously all-male preserves. Critics perceived the expanded use of women as part of a social action program rather than as the product of sound military policy planning.[17]

Even today, although the Defense Department recognizes that women "contribute significantly to the high degree of readiness which we currently enjoy" and says they "will be provided full and equal opportunity with men,"[18] it seems evident that the services would really prefer to have "high-quality" males than females. During the 1980s, when recruitment of such men became easier, the services relaxed their efforts to recruit more women. As a result, the proportion of females in the military has stabilized over the past few years.

"Women are the spigot," says Carolyn Becraft. "When [the services] need them, they open it up and they bring them in. When recruiting of

males is good, they close it up."

Persian Gulf War

Women played important combat-support roles in the invasion of Grenada in 1984, the U.S. raid on Libya in 1986 and the Panama invasion in 1989. But for the most part, their lives were never in serious jeopardy. The Persian Gulf War provided the first real test for American women in prolonged combat.

More than 40,000 women were sent to the Persian Gulf to fill a wide variety of non-traditional jobs, many under austere and hazardous conditions. Army women were an integral part of the invading force, piloting aircraft with troops and supplies, setting up complex traffic routes for the invading forces and following directly behind with logistical support. Air Force women flew and were crew members of AWACS transports, tankers and reconnaissance aircraft. Navy women piloted helicopters and reconnaissance aircraft and served on supply, repair and hospital ships. Marine Corps women served support functions with ground units.

By virtually all accounts, women in the gulf proved their mettle. Thirteen women died, including five who were considered combat fatalities, and two more were taken prisoner.

While the conflict was too limited and the casualties too few to provide confident assessments, several general observations seem warranted, according to Binkin of the Brookings Institution. First, against many predictions that Americans were not prepared to accept female casualties — and especially women POWs — the public did not appear to react any differently than it did to male casualties and POWs.[19] Second, the participation by women in military operations so near to the front lines, especially the parts played by a

Continued on p. 844

What Jobs in the Military Are Open to Women?

Women have become an integral part of the U.S. armed forces. Their numbers in the military have steadily increased from less than 2 percent in 1972 to more than 11 percent (209,494) in March 1992. The exact policy on military jobs open to women varies from service to service. What follows is a rough breakdown of combat-related assignments women are eligible for, and the roles women played in the Persian Gulf War. The Army, Navy and Marines all set separate recruiting goals for men and women based on program needs; the Air Force does not.

Army: There is no statute that explicitly restricts the assignment of women in the Army, but it is Army policy to exclude women from positions it determines would have routine engagement in direct combat. Direct combat has been defined as "engaging an enemy with individual or crew-served weapons while being exposed to direct enemy fire, a high probability of direct physical contact with the enemy, and a substantial risk of capture."

> **Number of jobs open to women:** 52 percent
> **Women on active duty:** 75,633 (11.8 percent)
> **Women deployed in the Persian Gulf War:** 30,855

At the end of 1991, 286 of 331 of all career fields, or Military Occupational Specialties (MOSs) were open to enlisted women, and 205 of 214 of officer specialties were open to women. Examples of closed career fields include the infantry, armor (tanks) and field artillery.

During the Persian Gulf War, women were assigned to forward support units, flying helicopters to transport personnel, air defense artillery, military police and medical search and rescue in the battle area, among other things. About 270 women served with U.S. Patriot missile battalions. Eleven Army women lost their lives during the conflict, five in combat situations. Two women, a truck driver and a flight surgeon, were among the 25 U.S. POWs.

Air Force: The Air Force has, for several years, had a higher percentage of women than the other services primarily because a very small percentage of Air Force personnel serve in direct combat positions. Air Force women have been trained as pilots and air crew and assigned to Minuteman missile crews and Airborne Warning and Control System (AWACS) aircraft, among other posts. No women have been assigned to fighters, bombers, gunships and most helicopters, despite the removal of the legal ban against women in combat aircraft in December 1991.

> **Number of jobs open to women:** 97 percent
> **Women on active duty:** 70,346 (14.5 percent)
> **Women deployed in the Persian Gulf War:** 4,246

During the gulf war, women served in military airlift, aerial refueling, communications, intelligence and a wide variety of support activities. Female pilots also flew AWACS reconnaissance aircraft, tactical transport and aeromedical airlift aircraft.

Navy: Job assignments for Navy women are restricted by statute and Navy policy: Women cannot serve on ships, or fly aircraft, that are expected to be engaged in a combat mission. However, women are allowed to serve temporary duty on combat ships as well as to train men to fly combat planes. The Navy fielded the first female military pilot and astronaut. Some 8,500 Navy women currently serve on more than 70 ships.

> **Number of jobs open to women:** 59 percent
> **Women on active duty:** 54,912 (10.2 percent)
> **Women deployed in the Persian Gulf War:** 4,246

Of 98 enlisted career fields in the Navy, 81 are open to women; of 27 officer career fields, 25 are open to women. Examples of closed jobs include those specifically associated with submarines, such as submarine sonar technician and gun or missile crew members.

During the gulf war, women served on hospital, supply and repair ships, and served in Navy construction battalions and as public affairs officers. Women Navy pilots flew helicopters and reconnaissance aircraft.

Marine Corps: The Marine Corps has the smallest percentage of women, largely because a higher proportion of Marines than members of the other services serve in combat roles. Sixty-three of 102 officer and 299 of 357 enlisted career paths are open to women. Many

> **Number of jobs open to women:** 20 percent
> **Women on active duty:** 8,603 (4.6 percent)
> **Women deployed in the Persian Gulf War:** 1,232

new career paths have been opened, and women serve as Marine security guards for U.S. embassies overseas, for example. Examples of jobs closed to women are combat engineers, infantry and tanks. In addition, all pilot positions remained closed to women at the end of 1991.

The women Marines who served in Saudi Arabia during the gulf war were the first female Marines deployed to any conflict since the Vietnam era. They were assigned to logistics, intelligence, transportation, aviation support and public affairs duties.

Sources: Women's Research and Educational Institute; Congressional Research Service; Department of Defense

The Tailhook Convention ...

When drunken Navy and Marine Corps fliers fondled, slapped and even stripped women guests at an aviators' convention in Las Vegas last September, they dropped a bomb that may do what no other episode of sexual harassment by American sailors has done: force a revolution in the U.S. Navy's treatment of women in its ranks.

At last year's annual convention of the Tailhook Association, a private organization for Navy and Marine Corps pilots, as many as 100 junior officers allegedly assaulted and harassed at least 36 civilian women and fellow officers, including an admiral's aide, Lt. Paula Coughlin, who publicly described the attack on her. The scandal, which escalated when the Naval Investigative Service failed to get to the bottom of the incident during a months-long inquiry, has toppled the secretary of the Navy, H. Lawrence Garrett III, tarnished the brass and badly sapped morale.

Until this summer, few Navy officers took the unseemly incident seriously. "There is a sense in the tactical air community that what happened was acceptable social conduct and that allegations concerning conduct had been blown out of proportion," the Navy inspector·general said in an April report on its Tailhook investigation, which failed to identify any suspects.

That was the view of the commanding officer of the first Tailhook victim to come forward publicly. "That's what you get when you go to a hotel party with a bunch of drunken aviators," Rear Adm. John W. Snyder Jr. is said to have told Coughlin, after she told him of being assaulted.†

Some outside commentators share that view. "The people who should be booted out of the service are the female officers who complained," columnist Charley Reese of the *Orlando Sentinel* wrote of the Tailhook episode in early July. "If a grown woman can't handle some friendly drunks in a public place, then she's hardly qualified to command men in the much more serious and stressful environment of war." ††

By most accounts, the atmosphere was hardly friendly. Beyond the offensive porno films, strippers and prostitutes hired by squadrons to "entertain" aviators in hospitality suites, there also was a "gantlet" of airmen in a third-floor corridor. Depending on who was manning the gantlet, pats on the bottom became gropes and grabs. Women who came off the elevator and didn't want to go down the gantlet were shoved against their will. At least three women were bitten, one severely. Snapshots turned over to investigators reportedly reveal a 17-year-old girl stripped of her jeans and panties being passed down the gantlet.

That the scandal occurred *after* the Persian Gulf War, in which women achieved new military equality by sharing hazardous desert duty with men, speaks volumes about sexism in the Navy, critics say. After months of stonewalling by officers, Congress is focusing the Navy's attention. For much of the summer, some 4,500 Navy and Marine Corps promotions were held up for fear of approving the advancement of a Tailhook offender. While other factors are also at play, Rep. John P. Murtha, D-Pa., chairman of the House Appropriations Defense Subcommittee, pegged his decision to cut 10,000 Navy headquarters jobs to that service's "obstruction and arrogance" in the Tailhook affair. Sexual harassment is also being cited as a reason for why women should be allowed in combat roles.

Many fliers believe they are the victims of a Washington witch hunt that will sweep up the innocent along with the guilty. Indeed, to indict the entire military — or even the entire Navy — on the basis of the lewd behavior at Tailhook

Continued from p. 842
female helicopter pilot in an air assault operation deep into Iraq and by a female doctor captured during a behind-the-lines search and rescue mission, blurred further the distinctions between combat and support duties. In fact, during the war the majority of the 122 Americans killed died in combat-support roles, not in actual combat.

On balance, the conflict did much to earn women the respect of their male peers that had proven so elusive under peacetime conditions and is likely to buttress the case for removing all remaining occupational barriers for women in the military. Defense Secretary Dick Cheney said on March 2, 1991: "Women have made a major contribution to this [war] effort. We could not have won without them."

Commanders in the field echoed similar sentiments. "Desert Storm was a bit of a watershed for me in terms of my own thinking as it pertains to women in the Marine Corps," said Lt. Gen. Walter E. Boomer, commanding general of the Marine Corps Combat Development Command in Quantico, Va. "I looked around, and I had women in the middle of combat." [20] ■

CURRENT SITUATION

The Combat Question

Only a few years ago, the likelihood of seeing American women in combat seemed virtually nil. "There are some things that are difficult politically, and some things that are impossible politically," Rep. Les Aspin, D-Wisc., chairman of the House

… More Than Just 'Boys Being Boys'

would be unfair. No more than 10 percent of the Navy's 16,000 active-duty aviators even attended the convention.

If Tailhook '91 were a completely isolated event, it might have been easier to stomach. But the gantlet dates back at least to 1986, and senior brass have always eagerly flocked to the rowdy convention. In many ways, experts say, the Tailhook scandal was predictable in a culture that prizes edge-of-the-envelope performance and has a long tradition of port-of-call hedonism.

Tailhook, at bottom, was seen not just as a failure of culture but of leadership. "You have to question the wisdom of the Navy's top leadership in going there; your mere appearance legitimizes that kind of behavior," says military analyst Lawrence J. Korb, a Navy flight officer in the early 1960s and assistant Defense secretary for manpower under Ronald Reagan. After all, the government paid $190,000 to fly aviators to Las Vegas and is somewhat responsible for their behavior.

During one question-and-answer session at the convention, a number of aviators in the audience who opposed allowing women to fly in combat wore buttons that read "Not in my Squadron." The Navy's assistant chief of naval operations for air warfare, Vice Adm. Richard M. Dunleavy, was a member of the panel and was assigned to field questions from the floor. When a woman asked Dunleavy when women would be allowed to fly in combat, a legitimate question given that both the Senate and House had voted in favor of it, the admiral ducked under a table. The audience hooted and hollered.

"There were nine admirals on the panel, and all nine sat there silently," comments Paul Roush, a leadership professor at the U.S. Naval Academy. "That indicates a gross failure in leadership. By tolerating that, they sig-

naled it was open season on women."

Moreover, the military top brass initially dismissed the gantlet as "boys being boys" and blamed it on heavy drinking. Some Pentagon officials still fret (privately, of course) that curbing Navy pilots' sexual feistiness will remove the edge they need for combat. Experts, however, reject those claims as ridiculous. "Sexism is not a prerequisite for bravery," says Korb. "Many of this country's greatest war heroes were respectable family men."

Even more galling — and damaging — was the subsequent cover-up. Investigators from two separate Navy agencies had been stymied by a wall of silence put up by pilots and their commanders, but the agencies had each made their own fumbles. The Naval Investigative Service omitted important documents from its report; the Naval Inspector General's office failed to put its chief investigator on the case. The public uproar prompted the Navy to call in the Defense Department's Office of the Inspector General, a larger agency with subpoena powers.

Once the investigation is completed, more heads may roll. But if the Navy is to right itself after Tailhook, it will take a sustained commitment to change. Last summer, then-Acting Navy Secretary J. Daniel Howard declared a policy of "zero tolerance" of sexual harassment, adding: "There's a subculture here, the macho-man idea, the hard drinking, skirt chasing that goes with the image of the Navy and Marines. That crap's got to go." ‡

---

†Adm. Snyder has since lost his command for not taking "timely" action on Coughlin's complaint.

†† Quoted in *The Washington Post*, July 14, 1992.

‡Quoted in *U.S. News & World Report*, July 13, 1992, p. 26.

Armed Services Committee, said in 1985. "Changing the combat-exclusion laws is one of the impossibles." [21]

Since then, a lot has changed. The experience of women in the Persian Gulf War has energized the debate and altered America's thinking. For a long time, justification for excluding women from combat was based on public opposition. But now the public favors at least an option for those who make the grade. The 1991 *Newsweek* poll taken after Desert Storm found that nearly eight of 10 Americans thought women should be allowed to fill combat jobs.

On Dec. 5, 1991, President Bush signed into law the Defense Authorization Act for fiscal year 1992, which included an amendment repealing the laws excluding women from flying combat aircraft in the Navy and Air Force. The only remaining law that precludes women from combat is a vintage 1948 statute excluding women from combat duty aboard ships.

But many in Congress and the military establishment still feel ambivalent. In what observers say was an attempt to thwart the momentum of Congress to repeal all the

combat-exclusion laws, a group of powerful senators, led by Sam Nunn, D-Ga., John Glenn, D-Ohio, and John McCain, R-Ariz., lobbied for setting up a presidential commission to study the future role of women in the military. The 15-member commission, appointed by the president in March, is scheduled to make its recommendations by Nov. 15.

"Dick Cheney and the Defense Department have hid behind the commission," says Brookings' Lawrence Korb. "For years, the Pentagon used to say, 'It's not us, it's

Congress that won't let you in planes and on ships.' From what has been leaked so far, it appears they want to roll the whole thing back. The commission is stacked with people opposed to women in combat."

Fine Line Between Combat and Combat Support

In the interim, a bulwark of policies still keeps women out of the trenches and off combat aircraft. These restrictions have produced a military rife with anomalies. In the Navy, for example, women can't serve on destroyers, but they serve on supply ships that sail as part of the same carrier battle group. In the Army, women are barred from infantry and artillery specialties, but can serve in some missile and signal units that operate close to combat.

Individual paradoxes aside, the distinction between combat and noncombat jobs is broadly eroding. In the era of cruise missiles and other "smart weapons," front lines are not necessarily more vulnerable than rear supply lines. "The harm's-way myth has been exploded," says Binkin. "The distinction between combat and combat support is razor-thin."

Much of the opposition to women in combat has come from senior male brass, who raise a battery of objections — everything from unit cohesion to the pregnancy rate (about 10 percent of enlisted women are pregnant at any time). Military commanders argue that logistical problems such as fraternization and the need for separate bathrooms and sleeping facilities would interfere with the operation of combat divisions. They also contend that the protectiveness men feel toward women would hamper performance in battle. Others feel women don't have the right physical stuff for combat: Pentagon studies have shown that women have only 55 percent the muscle strength and 67 percent the endurance of their male counterparts.*

---

*An infantry soldier's pack, weapon and ammunition weigh about 70 pounds.

But many military experts dismiss the size and strength objections as irrelevant in today's high-tech Army, where fewer than 10 percent of jobs require actual infantry duty. Warfare has become a lot more technological, demanding more brains than brawn, they say. "It takes the same strength to pull a lanyard on a howitzer as it does to start up a washing machine," quips the Naval Academy's Roush, a retired Marine Corps artillery officer. Fewer and fewer soldiers in uniform ever come face-to-face with their enemies.

Proposals to allow some women into combat on a trial basis have been rejected outright by the military — and by Congress. In 1990, Rep. Schroeder introduced legislation to establish a four-year test for women to be deployed in combat units. She couldn't get enough support for the proposal, even from her Democratic colleagues.

Other countries have experimented with different roles for women in the military. Israel allowed them to fight alongside men in its war of independence in 1948 but has since sharply restricted them to support roles.[22] Since Canada opened all combat positions, except submarines, to women in 1989, the results have been mixed. Few women choose to join infantry or armor units, and only a handful have passed a grueling 10-week basic training course.

In the United States, the issue of women in combat may end up being much ado about very little. Surveys suggest that few enlisted women in the military are yearning for combat duty. Some argue that there is no need to exclude the exceptional women from the infantry: Just set rigorous standards for admission and apply them equally to men and women. One problem that many see with this solution is that it would eliminate any logical justification for excluding women from a draft.

Since women themselves are divided on this issue, one proposed option is to permit women who meet the criteria to be assigned to combat positions, but not unless they volunteer. Some women believe this would provide equal opportunity for those who want it while respecting the views of those who see a different role for women. Others say it would be unfair to permit women a choice that is not available to men, and that to make the choice available to both men and women would make it difficult for the services to function.

Sexual Harassment

Much of the debate over the future role of women in the military has focused on sexual harassment. The Tailhook scandal is the Navy's — and the military's — most serious incident of sexual misconduct to date. But it was hardly out of the blue.

Some experts believe the Navy's shipboard culture breeds sexism. "On average, Navy men spend 10 to 14 years on sea duty. The guys live in a male world entirely," explains Brookings' Binkin. "When I heard about Tailhook, I wasn't surprised. The elite fliers have always been part of a very macho culture."

Navy machismo has gotten the service into trouble before. Some of its officers have been anything but gentlemen. In 1987, Pentagon investigators uncovered "morally repugnant behavior" on a Navy salvage ship cruising the western Pacific, which included the captain's performing oral sex on a prostitute in front of his crew. In 1990, a female midshipman at the U.S. Naval Academy resigned after she was handcuffed to a urinal by male midshipmen. Rapes reported on Navy bases and ships around the world have nearly tripled over the past five years despite cuts in the number of sailors.[23]

As bad as the Navy's record is, a 1990 Pentagon study concluded that a higher percentage of women in the Army and Marine Corps suffer sexual

Women on Active Duty in the Armed Forces

The Air Force boasts the highest percentage of women in any branch of the armed forces, while the Marine Corps has the lowest percentage.

	Women officers	Women as percentage of total officers	Women enlisted personnel	Women as percentage of total enlisted personnel	Total women officers and enlisted personnel	Women as percentage of total officers and enlisted personnel
Army	12,162	12.1%	63,471	11.7%	75,633	11.8%
Navy	8,255	11.8%	46,657	10.0%	54,912	10.2%
Air Force	13,069	13.8%	57,277	14.6%	70,346	14.5%
Marine Corps	651	3.3%	7,952	4.7%	8,603	4.6%
Total	34,137	12.0%	175,357	11.2%	209,494	11.3%

Source: Defense Manpower Data Center. Figures are as of June 30, 1992.

harassment, ranging from demeaning jokes to violent sexual attacks.[24] The Army is investigating reports that dozens of female soldiers were sexually assaulted in Saudi Arabia by their Army comrades. A 1992 government report on sexual harassment at the military academies found that roughly two-thirds of the female cadets at West Point experienced some form of sexual harassment.[25]

"The military's best-kept secret — rampant sexual violence — is now out in the open," comments Rep. Schroeder. Independent estimates based on surveys of U.S. military personnel indicate that over the last 20 years, 5 percent of all females in the armed forces — as many as 60,000 women — have suffered some form of sexual violence, she says.[26]

System Deemed Insensitive to Harassment Problem

Once charges are brought, experts say military justice is swift and sure. The problem is, charges aren't often brought. "Military women are more hesitant to come forward," says Kathy Gilberd, co-chair of San Diego's Military Law Task Force. "They're afraid they won't be taken seriously." Too often, they have reason. This summer,

Jacqueline Ortiz, an Army reservist, told the Senate Veterans' Affairs Committee of being "forcibly sodomized" while serving in Saudi Arabia. When she reported the attack, she was called a liar. Only after the adverse publicity did the Army charge a sergeant in her unit with sexual assault.

Those who deflect sexual advances risk being labeled by some men as lesbians, a threat that can cost a woman her military career. *(See story, p. 850.)* Those who dare to complain are often branded as "too soft." Such is the backdrop against which women in the armed forces must determine whether it is worth registering a complaint against a male colleague.

Three lawmakers are drafting legislation that would urge the services to adopt policies aimed at rooting out abuse of women.[27] These include keeping better records on allegations of harassment, weighing a service member's sensitivity to women's concerns as a factor in promotion, creating better education programs on proper behavior between service members of opposite sexes and instituting procedures to protect women from reprisals for filing complaints of harassment or abuse.

The prevalence of sexual harassment in the military may have some-

thing to do with the way soldiers are trained. One way the military motivates young men to train and fight and kill is by manipulating their insecurities. At its most elementary levels, the mastery of military skills often is equated with sexual conquest. "The military teaches men to kill and challenges their sexuality if they fail," says Gilberd. "That may be a good way to motivate young men, but it is dangerous to society. Training that equates sex and violence encourages men to act violently toward women."

But according to sociologist Charles Moskos, a member of the presidential commission studying the role of women in the services, military training equates masculinity and violence, not sex and violence. "We are asking men in combat to do an essentially irrational thing — put themselves in a position where they are likely to get killed," he argues. "One of the only ways to convince men to do that is to appeal to their masculinity. You cannot have an androgynous military. All soldiers are not Phil Donahue or Alan Alda, but they are not all brutes in uniform either."[28]

Moskos says it would be naive to expect sex-related problems to disappear from the military. Rather, he predicts as more women enter the military and work more closely with men in a wider variety of jobs, sex-related problems and sexual relationships may increase. Others think harassment will decrease as women become more integrated — and accepted — in the armed forces. Military statistics indicate that where men and women are members of the same unit, harassment is less common.

In a step that many believe will lead to a better working relationship between military men and women, the Marine Corps announced in August that it plans for the first time to integrate basic training at its Quantico, Va., facility. The Navy, Army and Air Force already have integrated training programs. ■

OUTLOOK

The New Military

In a sense, the military is in a better position to deal with sexual harassment than the rest of society. "The military has the hammer to mandate changes," explains Jennifer Eaves, a former Navy chief petty officer and research analyst at the Center for Strategic and International Studies. "It may not be able to regulate attitudes, but it sure can regulate behavior."

Some senior officials are comparing the now-notorious Tailhook episode — and the cover-up afterwards — to the race riots aboard the aircraft carriers *Kitty Hawk* and *Constellation* in 1972. Those led to major changes in the way the service deals with race issues. Today, though far from perfect, the Navy — and the military, generally — may be one of the most colorblind institutions in America.

Similarly, a decade later, when the issue was prevalent drug use in its ranks, the military came down hard. The triggering event took place in May 1981, when an airplane crashed during a night landing on the carrier *Nimitz,* killing 14 and injuring 48. Six of the dead had been smoking marijuana, it turned out, leading the Navy to implement a rigid "zero-tolerance" drug policy.

It may take time, but most military

personnel believe the armed forces will become more hospitable to women — and emerge from the current crisis better for it. Among other things, changing times are forcing the military and Congress to re-examine the roles of females and military couples. The days when commanding officers told enlisted men, "If the military wanted you to have a wife, you'd have been issued one," are long gone. The proportion of married troops of both sexes among the lower enlisted grades has doubled since the draft ended. A third of the enlisted ranks and 90 percent of the career force are now married. And since two-thirds of the women who marry while in uniform pick a spouse who is also in the military, there are many more all-service families.

"Family and child-care problems will not be resolved as long as the military promises more than it can possibly deliver," warns Elaine Donnelly, a member of the president's commission and a bitter opponent of women in combat. "Before the next war begins, a balance must be found in the three-way conflict of interest among children, their parents and the requirements of national defense."[29]

Experts say family and child-care issues will indeed pose some of the most difficult — and controversial — dilemmas for military leaders as well as soldiers. But most of those challenges mirror those faced by society at large. "If it were up to the military,

they would like single people," says Lawrence Korb. "In fact, they'd prefer the same race, gender and sexual orientation. It makes it all much easier. But this is 1992; we have a voluntary military" that competes with jobs in the private sector.

Moreover, in a volunteer environment the services constantly have to balance military needs with the normal, legitimate needs of families. "When you have a career force that is 90 percent married, you can't tell people they can't have children," says Korb.

Expanding Horizons

For the most part, the younger generation of military men who went to college with women and have played on teams with them is more prepared to accept them as professional equals. "It is clear from testimony before the president's commission that both enlisted men and officers who have worked with women favor an expanded role for women in the military," says DACOWITS' Jean Jackson.

While the actual number of women in the military will decrease as the military down-sizes, observers say the proportion of women is apt to remain roughly the same, at 11 percent. "What's important now — and presently lacking for women — is the political commitment of our political leaders and senior military officials," says Carolyn Becraft. "I'm talking about Dick Cheney. If their agenda is to utilize the best talent available, we should give women opportunities for combat."

The first chinks in the armor of this male-dominated institution have already appeared. The combat-exclusion policies will most likely be eased beginning next year, first in the Navy and Air Force, but in the Army and Marine Corps, too. Most experts agree there is little objective reason to prevent women from flying combat aircraft and sailing aboard combat vessels. In fact, most scientific evidence suggests that female pilots generally can withstand wrenching G-

Continued on p. 851

At Issue:

Should women be allowed in combat?

BECKY CONSTANTINO

Former chairwoman, Defense Advisory Committee on Women in the Services
FROM *TESTIMONY BEFORE THE SENATE ARMED SERVICES COMMITTEE, SUBCOMMITTEE ON MANPOWER AND PERSONNEL,* JUNE 18, 1991.

yes

t he performance of American servicewomen in the Persian Gulf War calls into question existing combat restrictions for women — and highlights the benefits of fully using the capabilities of all personnel to further enhance combat readiness and to optimize the quality of the military. The time has come to give the chain of command the flexibility to use their best people to accomplish the tasks which our country asks of them....

Physical gender differences which could negatively impact combat readiness would be valid reasons for closing positions for women. But limitations based on substantiated rationales would be more acceptable than the current limitations, which are strictly gender-related with an assumed intent of protecting the military women's exposure to hostile fire.

Servicewomen go through the same training, make the same sacrifices and sign the same contract as servicemen. They want an opportunity to fulfill their commitments and serve their country to the best of their abilities. They do not expect special treatment or want standards to be reduced to assure their success.... They know that equal opportunity means equal responsibility, and they are willing to accept the responsibility and corresponding risks.

Sometimes those who fight in opposition to women being in the military and in combat roles forget the reason these women join. They join for the same reasons the men join — to be full-fledged defenders of our country and our military.

The spirit of the U.S. servicewoman was captured when Maj. Marie Rossi said: "I think if you talk to the women who are professionals in the military, we see ourselves as soldiers. We do not really see it as man versus woman."

As a nation, we now know what we will do if women become prisoners of war. We will wear yellow ribbons for them and pray for their early return. We now know what we will do if women die for their country. We will grieve for them and bury them beside their brothers in Arlington Cemetery.

The lesson of the gulf war is that those who support a strong defense and those who want to expand opportunities for women in the military are on the same team. In spite of the inequities servicewomen face, they set aside personal frustrations and become part of a team whose objective is to protect and defend the United States.

GEN. ROBERT H. BARROW

Former commandant, U.S. Marine Corps
FROM *TESTIMONY BEFORE THE SENATE ARMED SERVICES COMMITTEE, SUBCOMMITTEE ON MANPOWER AND PERSONNEL,* JUNE 18, 1991.

no

t he issue of women in combat is not about women's rights, equal opportunity or career assignments for enhancement purposes for selection to higher rank. It is most assuredly about combat effectiveness, combat readiness, winning the next conflict, and so we are talking about national security.

Those who advocate change have some strange arguments, one of which is that there is a de facto women-in-combat situation already, that women have been shot at, that they have heard gunfire, that they have been in areas where they could have been hit with missiles. But exposure to danger is not combat; combat is a lot more than that. It is a lot more than getting shot at or even getting killed by being shot at. Combat is finding and closing with and killing or capturing the enemy. It is killing, that is what it is.

And it is done in an environment that is often as difficult as you can possibly imagine — extremes of climate, brutality, deaths, dying. It is uncivilized, and women cannot do it. Nor should they be even thought of as doing it. The requirements for strength and endurance renders them unable to do it. And I may be old-fashioned, but I think the very nature of women disqualifies them for doing it. Women give life, sustain life, nurture life, they do not take it.

I just cannot imagine why we are engaged in this debate about even the possibility of pushing women into the combat part of our profession. The most harm that could come would probably come to what it would do to the men in that kind of situation. I know in some circles it is very popular to ridicule something called male bonding, but it is real, and one has to have experienced it to understand it.... It is cohesiveness. It is mutual respect and admiration. It is one for all and all for one....

The other attendant problems to being in a combat situation — sexual harassment, fraternization, favoritism, resentment, male backlash — would be insurmountable for anyone to deal with. Who would deal with it? Not some faceless political appointee over there in the Pentagon, but the corporals and the sergeants and the lieutenants and the captains would have to maintain good order and discipline and also fight the war....

If you want to make a combat unit ineffective, assign some women to it. It is a destructive proposition, and the thing that puzzles me about this, there is no military requirement for it.... We have all the men we need for those requirements....

Gays in the Military

It took nearly a year for the military to formally acknowledge the Tailhook scandal — and to do something about it. In contrast, when Navy Lt. Tracy Thorne, a 25-year-old navigator/bombardier, announced on ABC's "Nightline" last May that he is gay, the Navy quickly moved to discharge him.

When it comes to homosexuals, the armed forces' enforcement of its "zero-tolerance" policy is swift and sure. The Pentagon — which officially bans gays from uniformed service — expels about 1,000 men and women every year on account of their sexual preference. In some cities near military bases, vice squad detectives routinely help military police hunt down soldiers at gay and lesbian bars.

According to the Department of Defense (DOD), "homosexuality is incompatible with military service." † The prohibition applies not only to those who admit to homosexual activity but also to those who merely profess homosexual inclinations. Their presence, officials argue, would risk security and weaken discipline.

Despite the ban, however, between 100,000 to 200,000 of the roughly 2 million members of the U.S. armed forces are gay, lesbian or bisexual, according to Allan Berube, author of *Coming Out Under Fire*. Most elude detection by being discreet. "The question is not, 'What happens if we let gays in the military?'" says Berube. "At least 99 percent stay and serve."

Gay advocates say it's time to bring policy in line with that reality. Last May, several members of Congress — led by Patricia Schroeder, D-Colo., Gerry E. Studds, D-Mass., and Barney Frank, D-Mass. — introduced a bill aimed at dismantling what Schroeder calls the "last bastion of discrimination in the military."

Last year, Defense Secretary Dick Cheney was forced to concede that the security argument was "a bit of an old chestnut" after *The Advocate*, a gay magazine, "outed" a senior civilian DOD official who had access to classified materials during the gulf war.†† But while gay civilians are welcome in the Pentagon, Cheney insists that barring gays from the armed forces is necessary to preserve discipline and morale in close quarters.

To others, however, the Pentagon's justifications for keeping gays out of the military reflect deep-seated prejudice. "It's based on the assumption that all homosexuals are sex maniacs and somehow incapable of acting maturely," says Joe Steffan, a star student who resigned from the Naval Academy in 1987, two weeks before final exams, after his superiors learned that he was gay.

The plight of gays in the military is even worse for women than for men. Like the combat-exclusion ban for women, critics say the military's ban on gay and lesbian service members encourages sex discrimination, including lesbian-baiting. Women are much more likely to come under fire than men, gay-rights advocates charge, in part because the presence of women in the services has never been fully accepted. DOD statistics indicate that women are three times more likely than men to be investigated and discharged for homosexuality, and in the Marine Corps the rate of discharge is eight times higher for women than men.

Though any hint of homosexual activity means close scrutiny, gay military personnel say a good deal of wayward heterosexual activity is tolerated, even tacitly approved, by the military hierarchy. At the end of the gulf war, for example, a Nevada brothel called the Mustang Ranch offered free passes to returning soldiers. "For some reason," says Bridget Wilson, of the Military Law Task Force in San Diego, "going to a whorehouse in their dress blues is not a problem."

By and large, the presence of gay soldiers is not a major issue for the American public. A March 1991 Gallup survey showed that 69 percent of those interviewed felt that homosexuals should be allowed to serve in the armed forces, up from 51 percent in 1977. The policy can be overturned only by an act of Congress, a decision by the secretary of Defense or a Supreme Court ruling. So far, the court has upheld the ban in all the cases it has agreed to hear, but this year a California state court ruled that the military cannot merely state its policy on gays; it must defend it.

Critics of the Pentagon's policy believe it's only a matter of time before the ban against gays, like earlier ones against blacks and women, becomes a thing of the past. Arkansas Gov. Bill Clinton has vowed that if elected president he will overturn the ban. If nothing else, it is expensive keeping gays out: Government reports show it costs tens of millions of dollars every year to recruit, investigate, dismiss and replace gay personnel ($28,000 for each enlisted member and $121,000 for each officer).‡

Meanwhile, many gay soldiers continue to play it safe, lying about their sexual preference, fabricating heterosexual relationships, laughing at gay slurs, even entering into camouflage marriages. "It was frightening and horrible having to watch yourself all the time," recalls Capt. Dusty Pruitt, a 13-year veteran who was discharged in 1986. "The closet is a horrible place to be, and the military is in a deep closet."‡‡

---

† Department of Defense Directive 1332.14, Jan. 28, 1982.

†† Two DOD-commissioned studies have concluded that homosexuals in the military do not pose a national security risk. See *Defense Force Management: DOD's Policy on Homosexuality*, General Accounting Office, June 1992, p. 3.

‡ *Ibid.*, p. 4.

‡‡ Quoted in *Time*, Aug. 19, 1991, p. 16.

Continued from p. 848

forces better than their male counterparts, largely because women are smaller and have more body fat. Women are already flying some of the nation's most sophisticated aircraft, including the F-14 Tomcat fighter.

If Arkansas Gov. Bill Clinton wins the presidential election in November, many more barriers to women in combat could fall. Since combat exclusion is largely a matter of policy, not law, it would only take a presidential order to open up most combat slots. On the campaign trail, Clinton has said that he favors greater opportunities for military women.

The issue of women in the infantry is clearly the most problematic. "The key issue is not whether women can do the job individually," says Martin Binkin. "Some obviously can. The issue is what effect women in combat roles will have on the effectiveness of the organization — and ultimately on national security. Over time, we might change the culture, but whether we want to is another question."

Whatever conclusions emerge from the deliberations of the presidential commission, women have passed another milestone. The next step will be to begin devising policies reflecting the new political environment and the realities of the modern military. It boils down to tapping the best talents from a shrinking pool of young potential recruits to do the jobs required by a military that grows smaller but more technologically demanding each day.

"That goal," says retired Maj. Gen. Jeanne Holm, "can best be served by a gender-neutral, best-qualified personnel system that matches individual talents and aptitudes with the legitimate, validated requirements of the jobs that have to be done, without artificial, unrelated constraints."[30]

Indeed, some have questioned whether it is right to expect military men to face the risks inherent in the military profession while protecting women who take the same oath, draw the same pay, get the same training and wear the same uniform.

Today, an increasing number of military women are saying no, among them Capt. Debra Dubbe, an Air Force Academy graduate who served as a navigator on a refueling tanker during the Grenada invasion. "There is no difference in women or men taking risks — or dying," she says. "I signed up to be an officer, and if it means having to die, that's what I agreed to do." A female enlisted paratrooper who landed in Panama with the 82nd Airborne Division is even more blunt: "If they are going to let us wear the uniform, then they ought to let us defend it. Otherwise, don't let us wear it."[31] ■

Notes

[1] See *The New York Times,* July 24, 1992.

[2] For background, see "Should Women Be Allowed Into Combat?" *Editorial Research Reports,* Oct. 13, 1989, pp. 570-583.

[3] See *Women in the Military: Career Progression Not a Current Problem but Concerns Remain,* U.S. General Accounting Office, September 1989.

[4] Quoted in the *Los Angeles Times,* July 31, 1992.

[5] Quoted in *Army Times,* July 27, 1992.

[6] Writing in Charles C. Moskos and Frank R. Wood, eds., *The Military: More Than Just a Job?* (1988), p. 107.

[7] Boxer's bill, the Military Orphans Prevention Act, never got out of committee.

[8] Quoted in *Ms.,* May/June 1991, p. 90.

[9] See Col. David H. Hackworth, "War and the Second Sex," *Newsweek,* Aug. 5, 1991, p. 28.

[10] Maj. Gen. Jeanne Holm, *Women in the Military* (1992; revised edition), p. 387. See also, *Navy Times,* Jan. 6, 1992, for details of a three-year study on pregnancy and its effect on the Navy by the Naval Personnel Research and Development Command.

[11] General Accounting Office, "Reserves and Readiness: Appraising the Total Force Policy," 1991.

[12] Martin Binkin and Shirley J. Bach, *Women and the Military* (1977), p. 4. Unless otherwise noted, information in the Background Section on the history of women in the military is based on chapter 2 of Binkin and Bach's book.

[13] *Ibid.,* p. 14.

[14] The court cases are *Frontiero v. Richardson, Crawford v. Cushman* and *Owens v. Brown,* respectively. See Carolyn H. Becraft, "Military Women: Policies and Politics," *The Bureaucrat,* fall 1991, p. 9.

[15] For an interesting account of one of the first women cadets at West Point, see Carol Barkalow, *In the Men's House* (1990).

[16] Quoted in *Newsweek,* Nov. 11, 1985, p. 37.

[17] See Holm, *op. cit.,* p. 382.

[18] Quoted in a Defense Department fact sheet, "Women in the Military."

[19] The fact that one of the female POWs, Maj. Rhonda Cornum, a flight surgeon, was sexually abused by her captors has not become a major issue, largely because she has dismissed its significance as simply one of the risks of war. See "The Matter-of-Fact Major's War Story," *The Washington Post,* Aug. 8, 1992.

[20] Quoted in an interview in *Armed Forces Journal International,* August 1992, p. 41.

[21] Quoted in *Newsweek,* Nov. 11, 1985, p. 38.

[22] See *Editorial Research Reports, op. cit.,* p. 579.

[23] See *The Orange County Register,* May 18, 1992.

[24] Melanie Martindale, *Sexual Harassment in the Military: 1988,* Defense Manpower Data Center, 1990.

[25] See *DOD Service Academies: Status Report on Reviews of Student Treatment,* U.S. General Accounting Office, June 2, 1992.

[26] Quoted in the *Los Angeles Times,* Aug. 13, 1992.

[27] The legislation is being drafted by Reps. Patricia Schroeder, D-Colo., Marilyn Lloyd, D-Tenn., and Beverly B. Byron, D-Md. See *Congressional Quarterly Weekly Report,* Aug. 1, 1992, p. 2293.

[28] Quoted in *Army Times,* July 27, 1992.

[29] Quoted in *National Review,* Nov. 18, 1991, p. 41.

[30] Quoted in Holm, *op. cit.,* p. 506.

[31] *Ibid.,* p. 507.

Bibliography

Selected Sources Used

Books

Barkalow, Capt. Carol, *In the Men's House,* Poseidon Press, 1990.

Barkalow, a member of the first female graduating class at West Point, has written a readable and insightful account of the trials and rewards of life as a woman in the U.S. Army.

Binkin, Martin, and Shirley J. Bach, *Women and the Military,* The Brookings Institution, 1977.

This book is dated but useful as background on how the role of women in the military has evolved over the century.

Holm, Maj. Gen. Jeanne, *Women in the Military: An Unfinished Revolution,* Presidio Press, 1982 (1992 revised edition).

This book, first published in 1982, is perhaps the most authoritative source on the subject. It includes good history as well as numerous current interviews and discussion of the political process as it affects women's roles in the armed forces. The revised edition covers the role of American military women in all post-Vietnam military operations, including the Persian Gulf War.

Mitchell, Brian, *Weak Link: The Feminization of the American Military,* Regnery Gateway, 1989.

Mitchell, a former Army officer, has written a polemic against extensive use of women in the military. His views are radical and worth reading for perspective, but he backs up few of his suppositions with objective data.

Moskos, Charles C. and Frank R. Wood, eds., *The Military: More Than Just a Job?,* Pergamon-Brassey's, 1988.

This book contains chapters by various scholars on the broad issue of women in the military. The editors note "the number of military women will almost surely increase in the near and middle future. The core issue for military women is not the combat-exclusion rule but the development of a modus vivendi among military life, marriage and especially parenthood."

Articles

Becraft, Carolyn H., "Military Women: Policies and Politics," *The Bureaucrat,* fall 1991, p. 9.

Becraft is one of the leading proponents of women in the military. This article covers the major events since the all-volunteer force was instituted in 1973, and explains how the various administrations have approached the broader issue of women in the military.

Binkin, Martin, "The New Face of the American Military: The Volunteer Force and the Persian Gulf War," *Brookings Review,* summer 1991, p. 7.

Binkin looks at the broader picture of how the all-volunteer force has fared in recent years. He supports women in combat aircraft and aboard combat ships but feels less certain of women in infantry roles. He also concludes that more study is necessary on the impact of women in combat and on the question of the draft.

Salholz, Eloise, "Deepening Shame," *Newsweek,* Aug. 10, 1991, p. 30

This journalistic investigation into what happened at the 1991 Tailhook convention in Las Vegas provides detail of the scandal and puts it into the context of how the military has dealt with revelations of sexual misconduct in the past.

Seigle, Greg, "Boys Will Be Boys," *Army Times,* July 27, 1992.

The author has conducted extensive interviews with military personnel on the subject of sexual harassment and discrimination in the military. What results is an interesting patchwork of views and experiences of women in the military.

Reports and Studies

Collier, Ellen C., *Women in the Armed Forces,* Congressional Research Service Issue Brief, July 21, 1992.

This CRS issue brief provides a sketch of the major issues relating to women in the military. Although it contains little detail, it poses the critical questions and frames the debate: Should the armed forces expand recruitment of women? Should women be barred from combat positions? What provisions are there for motherhood?

***Defense Force Management: DOD's Policy on Homosexuality,* U.S. General Accounting Office, June 1992.**

On the basis of its policy of excluding homosexuals from the military, the Department of Defense annually expelled an average of about 1,500 men and women between 1980 and 1990. One interesting finding of the report: Lesbians are eight times as likely to be expelled as gay men.

***Women in the Military: Career Progression Not a Current Problem but Concerns Remain,* U.S. General Accounting Office, September 1989.**

Although policy and other factors such as combat exclusion can impede women's career progression, promotion data from 1986 through 1988 show that women are being promoted at rates similar to men. They are, however, still being excluded from the top echelons.

The Next Step

Additional Articles from Current Periodicals from EBSCO Publishing's Database

Books & reading

"Editors' bookshelf," *American Heritage*, December 1990, p. 110.

Reviews the book "For God, Country, and the Thrill of It: Women Airforce Service Pilots in World War II," by Anne Noggle. A tribute to fellow members of the World War II civilian unit that was the first group of women ever to fly U.S. military aircraft.

"History bookshelf," *American History Illustrated*, July/August 1991, p. 25.

Reviews the book "For God, Country, and the Thrill of It: Women Airforce Service Pilots in World War II," by Anne Noggle.

"Mulishness," *The Economist*, April 13, 1991, p. 84.

Reviews the book "Those Bloody Women: Three Heroines of the Boer War," by Brian Roberts. Discusses the involvement of Lady Sarah Wilson, Hansie van Warmelo, and Emily Hobhouse in the Boer War.

Hartmann, S.M., "Book reviews," *Journal of American History*, March 1991, p. 1409.

Reviews the book "One Woman's War: Letters Home from the Women's Army Corps, 1944-1946," by Anne Bosanko Green.

Itkin, S., "Book reviews: Social sciences," *Library Journal*, August 1991, p. 117.

Reviews the book "On Final Approach: The Women Airforce Service Pilots of World War II," by Byrd Howell Granger.

Itkin, S., "Book reviews: Social sciences," *Library Journal*, Feb. 1, 1992, p. 108.

Reviews the book "Women Pilots of World War II," by Jean Hascall Cole.

Mellett, E., "Book reviews," *School Library Journal*, March 1992, p. 265.

Reviews the book "Women in the Military," edited by Carol Wekesser and Matthew Polesetsky.

Showalter, D.E., "Book reviews: Social sciences," *Library Journal*, June 15, 1992, p. 88.

Reviews the book "Women Marines: The World War II Era," by Peter A. Soderbergh.

Stuttaford, G., "Forecasts: Nonfiction," *Publishers Weekly*, Jan. 1, 1992, p. 44.

Reviews the book "Women Pilots of World War II," by Jean Hascall Cole.

Debates & issues

"GI Jane," *National Review*, Aug. 26, 1991, p. 15.

Comments on the recent U.S. Senate vote to lift combat restrictions on women fighter pilots. Flaws in its decision-making process that included neither debate nor an actual study of the performance of women soldiers during Desert Storm; why the proposal should not have been approved.

"Let women vie for combat roles," *Aviation Week & Space Technology*, Aug. 5, 1991, p. 7.

Editorial. Argues that women should be evaluated for combat roles based on their capabilities and willingness to serve, just as in the civilian sector. Bill currently in Congress; Persian Gulf War.

"Lost cause," *The Economist*, April 27, 1991, p. 26.

Comments on the fight being put up by the last two state-supported military schools that refuse to admit women cadets. The Virginia Military Institute; The Citadel, in Charleston, S.C.; women troops who served in the gulf war; details; outlook.

"Women in combat — the 1 percent change," *U.S. News & World Report*, Aug. 12, 1991, p. 8.

Reports that the Senate has called for a study to determine whether women who aren't pilots should also be given combat roles. Those women make up 99 percent of the military's female force.

Bagnall, N., "A contrary view," *World Press Review*, December 1990, p. 72.

Editorial. Discusses why women should not be allowed in combat. Moral reasons; physical; their detrimental effect in the combat area.

Barkalow, C. & G. Carroll "Women have what it takes," *Newsweek*, Aug. 5, 1991, p. 30.

Opinion. Presents argument of Army Capt. Carol Barkalow, 32, of Clifton Park, N.Y., as to why females should have the right to fight in wars. Issue of how qualified a female should be; how pregnancy in the military should be treated; why women would be good fighters in war.

Clift, E., B. Kantrowitz, et al., "The right to fight," *Newsweek,* **Aug. 5, 1991, p. 22.**

Discusses the measure that the U.S. Senate this week will take up to let women be combat pilots. The issue has ignited sharp debate on the potential disruption of U.S. military readiness, but it pivots on one key question: Are women really ready to be professional killers? Feelings of the nation's women in uniform regarding equality in military service.

Donnelly, E., "What did you do in the Gulf, mommy?" *National Review,* **Nov. 18, 1991, p. 41.**

Argues against allowing women into combat. Because all soldiers in close combat are interdependent and rely on the strength, stamina and speed of all unit members, gender-norming practices that fudge the truth about most women's physical ability are counterproductive and detract from the military's responsibility to deter aggression or win a war with as few casualties as possible.

Elshtain, J. B., "Feminism and war," *Progressive,* **September 1991, p. 14.**

Proposes that, while a few military men may balk, sending women into combat seems to be an idea whose time has come. The issue of female advancement to high-ranking positions in the military; legislative sponsorship by liberal women politicians; ethical considerations of effects on the children.

Ferrato, D., J. Ralston, et al., "Women's work," *Life,* **May 1991, p. 52.**

Explores the role played by women in the Persian Gulf by refuting several common myths about women in combat. Myths include the following: women can't perform under pressure; sexual tensions and primitive living conditions make the combat zone no place for a woman; mothers shouldn't and don't want to go to war; the public isn't ready for female POWs or women in body bags. INSET: The way they war (photo history of women in the military).

Fuentes, A., "Equality, yes — militarism, no," *The Nation,* **Oct. 28, 1991, p. 13.**

Describes the ongoing debate about whether or not women should be allowed in military combat missions. Conservative types think the inclusion of women will sabotage male bonding on the front lines, and the equal rights advocates argue that dropping all barriers to women in the military is not only fair, it contributes to military preparedness. The number of women fighting in Desert Storm; the Pentagon's perspective; combat restrictions and rank; more.

Gilmartin, P.A., "Proposed policy shift on women in combat meets resistance," *Aviation Week & Space Technology,* **June 24, 1991, p. 81.**

Covers the opposition of senior U.S. military officials to a congressional effort to repeal a law banning women from flying combat missions. A repeal would not require the Air Force, Navy and Marine Corps to place women in combat roles but would allow it. The Army is not covered by the law but bans women from such roles as a matter of policy.

Johnson, J. & E. Mitchell, "The thin gray gender line," *Time,* **July 1, 1991, p. 66.**

Reports that federal Judge Jackson L. Kiser has ruled that all-male Virginia Military Institute, which has maintained a single-sex admissions policy since its founding in 1839, may continue to discriminate. The decision goes against a 1982 Supreme Court ruling that forbids gender discrimination in schools receiving federal or state funds; barring women from the school effectively curtails their access to the Old Dominion's old-boy network; jarring decision.

Johnson, J., "The new top guns," *Time,* **Aug. 12, 1991, p. 31.**

Recounts the recent Senate vote to overturn a law barring women from flying combat missions, which has won little support from military brass. Opponents of the measure; supporters of the policy; push by female officers and civilian feminists.

Moskos, C., "Army women," *The Atlantic,* **August 1990, p. 70.**

Examines the life, the sentiments and the aspirations of women in the U.S. Army. Women in combat and changes in the role of women in the military; background; daily life; sexual harassment; proposal for a trial program of women in combat.

Norden, E., "Right behind you, Scarlett!" *American Spectator,* **August 1991, p. 14.**

Argues against post-gulf war moves to allow American women in front-line combat roles in the next war. Comparison with Israel Defense Forces (IDF); there women can hold all military offices but must be evacuated in the event of hostilities; claims that women should only be in combat if the situation is desperate.

Nordheimer, J., "Women's role in combat: The war resumes," *The New York Times,* **May 26, 1991, p. 1.**

Considers women's role in combat. Confusion in the Persian Gulf War about how close women were supposed to get to the front lines; comment by Sgt. Sheri L. Barbato, a Persian Gulf War veteran; House's approval of a military budget bill that included a provision repealing restrictions on women flying combat aircraft.

Palmer, E.A., "Senate debates rights, role of women warriors," *Congressional Quarterly Weekly Report,* **June 22, 1991, p. 1687.**

Examines the expanding role of women in the armed

forces and the question of whether or not women should serve in combat capacity. Fiscal 1992 defense authorization measure (HR 2100 — H Rept 102-60); provision permitting Air Force, Navy and Marine Corps to use women as combat pilots; question of using women in front-line ground combat; women in the Persian Gulf War; current law bars women from combat roles; women and the draft; details.

Rothstein, L., "War of words over women warriors," *Bulletin of the Atomic Scientists,* **December 1991, p. 6.**

Outlines the current inconsistencies among feminist groups concerning the issue of excluding women from combat roles in the armed forces. Statement from retired Marine Gen. Robert H. Barrow; Senate overturning of a law banning women from flying planes in combat; no consensus among women in the military.

Schmitt, E., "Senate votes to remove ban on women as combat pilots," *The New York Times,* **Aug. 1, 1991, p. A1.**

Reports that the Senate voted overwhelmingly to overturn a 43-year-old law that bars women from flying warplanes in combat. Strong reservations of chiefs of the four uniformed services; strong support in Congress because of women's performance in the Persian Gulf War.

Wright, C., "G.I. Jill," *The New Republic,* **Oct. 21, 1991, p. 16.**

Describes the double standard of behavior that is policy in the Air Force and the emphasis on sexuality that persists in the "real" military world. Sexual harassment inside and outside the military academies; how women perpetuate sexism; comments from a 1989 readers' poll in "Military Lifestyle."

History

Erickson, J., "Night witches, snipers and laundresses," *History Today,* **July 1990, p. 29.**

Describes the contributions of Soviet women in the Great Patriotic War. Soviet women in World War II; Soviet women as nurses, combat pilots, navigators, snipers, gunners, paratroops, tank crews, as front-line "laundresses" in field bath/laundry units and mine clearers; women of the home front in the labor force.

Evans, K., "Memories of war-time victories," *American Visions,* **December 1991, p. 26.**

Follows the actions of the 6888th Central Postal Battalion, 800 black women who made up the only battalion of African American women, as they served in the European Theater of Operations in World War II. The Advisory Committee on Negro Troop Policy; HR 4906, which created the Women's Auxiliary Army Corps.; details. INSET: "One Woman's Army" (a book by Charity Adams Earley).

Kageleiry, J. & R. Tobey, "War and reunion," *Yankee,* **December 1991, p. 82.**

Presents the World War II recollections of former servicemen and servicewomen attending recent reunions of the Women's Air Force Service Pilots (WASPS), the sailors of the USS *Massachusetts,* the 168th Engineer Battalion, and the Iwo Jima survivors of Connecticut.

Persian Gulf War, 1991

"First U.S. female fatalities," *The New York Times,* **Feb. 28, 1991, p. A1.**

Refers to an article on page A13 ("Scud's lethal hit takes first 2 female soldiers," by D. Terry) telling of at least two women who were reported to be among the 28 American soldiers who were killed in an Iraqi missile attack on this week.

"Women in the military: The first POW?" *Newsweek,* **Feb. 11, 1991, p. 20.**

Reports on the disappearance last week of Melissa A. Rathbun-Nealy, 20, of Newaygo, Mich., and a colleague, David Lockett, and the belief that they were captured by Iraqi soldiers after the pair's vehicle got stuck in the sand during a supply mission. The possibility of a female POW raises new questions about the role of women in the military.

Beck, M., R. Wilkinson, et al., "Our women in the desert," *Newsweek,* **Sept. 10, 1990, p. 22.**

Discusses the role of women in the military and how they are not allowed in combat but can support the combat units. Number of women in Operation Desert Shield is classified; hypocrisy of Pentagon policies toward women; objections to women on the front lines; employment opportunities for women in the military.

Myers, W. S., "Women of the war," *Women in Business,* **January/February 1992, p. 15.**

Profiles several American Business Women's Association (ABWA) members who hung up their business suits for camouflage fatigues during the Persian Gulf War.

Schmitt, E., "War puts U.S. servicewomen closer than ever to combat," *The New York Times,* **Jan. 22, 1991, p. A1.**

Comments on the fact that the Persian Gulf War has drawn servicewomen closer to the front lines than any other war in America's history.

Sciolino, E., "Women in war: Ex-captive tells of ordeal," *The New York Times,* **June 29, 1992, p. A1.**

Describes the ordeal of Maj. Rhonda Cornum, a 37-year-old flight surgeon from upstate New York, who was captured in Iraq in the Persian Gulf War. Her treatment has since become an issue in the debate over whether women in the military should be allowed into combat.

Back Issues

Great Research on Current Issues Starts Right Here... Recent topics covered by The CQ Researcher are listed below. Issues dated before May 10, 1991, were published under the name of Editorial Research Reports.

MARCH 1991
Acid Rain
Cost of the Gulf War
Reassessing Gun Laws
Future for Man in Space

APRIL 1991
Social Security
Canadian Crisis Over Quebec
California Drought
Electromagnetic Radiation

MAY 1991
School Choice
Racial Quotas
Animal Rights
U.S. and Japan

JUNE 1991
Children and Divorce
Teenage Suicide
Endangered Species
Europe 1992

JULY 1991
Teenagers and Abortion
Soviet Republics Rebel
Mexico's Emergence
Athletes and Drugs

AUGUST 1991
Sexual Harassment
Fetal Tissue Research
Oil Imports
The Palestinians

SEPTEMBER 1991
Police Brutality
Advertising Under Attack
Saving the Forests
Foster Care Crisis

OCTOBER 1991
Pay-Per-View TV
Youth Gangs
Gene Therapy
World Hunger

NOVEMBER 1991
Fast-Food Shake-Up
The Greening of Eastern Europe
Business' Role in Education
Cuba In Crisis

DECEMBER 1991
Retiree Health Benefits
Asian Americans
The Obscenity Debate
The Disabilities Act

JANUARY 1992
Term Limits
Oil Spills
Hunting Controversy
Alternative Medicine

FEBRUARY 1992
Threatened Coastlines
New Era in Asia
Assisted Suicide
Jobs in the '90s

MARCH 1992
Women and Sports
Underage Drinking
Garbage Crisis
Mafia Crackdown

APRIL 1992
Ozone Depletion
Welfare Reform
Politicians and Privacy
Illegal Immigration

MAY 1992
Native Americans
Jobs vs. Environment
Too Many Lawsuits?
Fairness in Salaries

JUNE 1992
Nuclear Proliferation
Food Irradiation
Lead Poisoning
Hard Times for Libraries

JULY 1992
Alternative Energy
Prescription Drug Prices
Alzheimer's Disease
Infant Mortality

AUGUST 1992
The Homeless
Work, Family and Stress
NATO's Changing Role
Marine Mammals vs. Fish

SEPTEMBER 1992
Domestic Partners
Violence in Schools
Public Broadcasting

Back issues are available for $4.00 (subscribers) or $7.00 (non-subscribers). Quantity discounts apply to orders over ten. To order, call Congressional Quarterly 1-800-432-2250.

Future Topics

▶ *Depression*

▶ *U.S. Auto Industry*

▶ *Apprenticeships*

THE CQ Researcher

PUBLISHED BY CONGRESSIONAL QUARTERLY INC., IN CONJUNCTION WITH EBSCO PUBLISHING

Depression

Why does the disorder afflict so many people?

I N THE UNITED STATES ALONE, IT IS ESTIMATED that severe depression affects more than 15 million people. Depression is so widespread that it is sometimes called "the common cold of mental illness." It is also the most treatable of mental disorders, with up to 80 percent of patients showing marked improvement after therapy. Nonetheless, only about 30 percent of depression sufferers seek professional help. Those who don't often feel the condition carries a stigma. The pain endured by untreated or misdiagnosed depression sufferers is also felt by society at large. According to the government, depression costs the nation some $27 billion a year, chiefly in reduced productivity and lost work time. Despite the problems, researchers remain cautiously confident of further progress in understanding and treating the debilitating affliction.

C_Q   October 9, 1992 • Volume 2, No. 37 • 857-880

Formerly Editorial Research Reports

COVER ART: BARBARA SASSA-DANIELS

THE CQ Researcher

October 9, 1992
Volume 2, No. 37

EDITOR
Sandra Stencel

MANAGING EDITOR
Thomas J. Colin

ASSOCIATE EDITOR
Richard L. Worsnop

STAFF WRITERS
Charles S. Clark
Mary H. Cooper
Rodman D. Griffin

PRODUCTION EDITOR
Sarah E. Merritt

EDITORIAL ASSISTANT
Michael M. Taylor

GRAPHICS
Jack Auldridge

PUBLISHED BY
Congressional Quarterly Inc.

CHAIRMAN
Andrew Barnes

VICE CHAIRMAN
Andrew P. Corty

EDITOR AND PUBLISHER
Neil Skene

EXECUTIVE EDITOR
Robert W. Merry

ASSOCIATE PUBLISHER
John J. Coyle

EDITOR, EBSCO PUBLISHING
Melissa Kummerer

The CQ Researcher (ISSN 1056-2036). Formerly Editorial Research Reports. Published weekly (48 times per year, not printed the first Friday of any month with five Fridays) by Congressional Quarterly Inc., 1414 22nd St., N.W., Washington, D.C. 20037. Rates are furnished upon request. Second-class postage paid at Washington, D.C. POSTMASTER: Send address changes to The CQ Researcher, 1414 22nd St., N.W., Washington, D.C. 20037.

Depression

BY RICHARD L. WORSNOP

THE ISSUES

"If there is a hell upon Earth, it is to be found in a melancholy man's heart." So wrote the British scholar Robert Burton more than 350 years ago in his classic treatise, *The Anatomy of Melancholy.* Millions who suffer from depression, the modern term for the condition Burton described, would readily agree with him.

More disabling than the blues or the blahs that everyone goes through now and then, depression clouds concentration, retards work performance and dims interest in life itself. Dr. Frederick Goodwin, director of the National Institute of Mental Health (NIMH), likens depression to a "spectrum" ranging from minor to severe, with numerous gradations in between.

The most serious form of the disorder is called clinical depression, episodes of which typically last nine to 12 months. Clinical depression is accompanied by "a heavily achy feeling, very vague and difficult to localize," Goodwin says, and by "a sense that thinking is so difficult it's like slogging through molasses to get from one thought to another."

Indeed, in its extreme form depression is among the most excruciating mental disorders known and is often linked to suicide. In the United States alone, it is estimated that severe depression affects more than 15 million people and that 15 percent of them may eventually attempt suicide.[1] Moreover, a person hospitalized for depression is about 30 times more likely to commit suicide than a non-depressed person. A family history of suicide also indicates a predisposition to depression.[2]

Besides torturing individuals, depression wreaks havoc on society as

a whole. According to the Alcohol, Drug Abuse and Mental Health Administration, a branch of the U.S. Department of Health and Human Services (HHS), depression costs the nation about $27 billion a year, mainly in reduced productivity and lost work time.

Losses that are inexpressible in dollars may be the hardest of all to bear. A recent HHS publication on depressive disorders noted that "research may never be able to capture the complexities in an individual's life as the result of one or more episodes of clinical depression or a series of them: potentials never developed, roads not taken, love lost, jobs lost, relationships ended. Multiplied by millions, the cumulative result of the disruptions caused by depression is indeed beyond measurement."[3]

Similarly, experts say they can't be sure just how widespread depression is because many sufferers don't seek treatment or have mild cases, and personal physicians often misdiagnose actual depression as a physical ailment. And in some cases, a depressive reac-

tion to stress has become part of an individual's personality and is thus unrecognizable as an abnormal mental state. The vagueness of the borderline between a passing phase of dejection within the normal range of mood shifts and a pathological depression adds to the difficulty of making an exact count.

However, some generalizations can be made. According to HHS, 10 percent of all Americans (6.6 percent of the females and 3.5 percent of the males) will experience at least one depressive disorder during any six-month period. No wonder, then, that depression has been called "the common cold of mental illness." *(See story, p. 863.)*

The disorder can victimize any family — even the nation's first family. In a 1990 magazine interview, Barbara Bush disclosed that she had found herself seriously depressed in 1976, shortly after she and George Bush returned from China, where he served as chief of the U.S. Liaison Office. Mrs. Bush called her experience "one of the best things that ever happened to me. First of all, I didn't do anything about it except to sweat it out.... It makes you much more sympathetic for people who have depression."[4]

Perhaps the most vivid account in recent years of depression's impact came from novelist William Styron, whose works include *Lie Down in Darkness* and *Sophie's Choice.* In *Darkness Visible,* a "Memoir of Madness" published in 1990, Styron described a bout of severe depression that began shortly after he had renounced alcohol. Depression, he asserted, is "a wimp of a word" for an affliction that amounts to nothing less than a "howling tempest in the brain."[5]

"Afternoons were ... the worst," Styron explained, "beginning at about 3 o'clock, when I'd feel the horror, like some poisonous fogbank, roll in upon my mind, forcing me into bed. There I would lie for as long as six hours, stuporous and virtually paralyzed, gazing at the ceiling and waiting for that moment of evening when, mysteriously, the crucifixion would ease up."[6]

Though depression has received widespread coverage in newspapers and general interest magazines over the past decade or so, many people remain ignorant or fearful of it. A nationwide survey conducted last year for the National Mental Health Association found that 43 percent of those interviewed believed that depression resulted from personal or emotional weakness. If a spouse or child were getting treatment or counseling for depression, the survey found that 53 percent of those polled would tell their friends, while 30 percent would not want them to know.[7] *(See poll, p. 861.)*

Such attitudes may account for the reluctance of many depression sufferers to seek treatment. The NIMH estimates that only 30 percent of depression victims seek professional help. Some sufferers remain untreated because they and their family members fail to recognize that something is amiss; others are so disabled that they lack the strength or will to summon professional help. And some depression victims, especially the very young or the very old, are misdiagnosed and incorrectly treated.

The situation leaves health-care professionals frustrated, for they call depression the most treatable of all mental disorders. Studies consistently show that at least 80 percent of depression sufferers enjoy marked improvement after drug treatment, psychotherapy, electroconvulsive (electroshock) therapy, or a combination of treatment modes. Most sufferers, moreover, can be helped on an outpatient basis. Relief is often felt within weeks.

The stigma still attached to depression suggests that, at the very least, the mental-health community needs to mount a vigorous public-education campaign to combat misconceptions

about the disorder. As experts struggle to improve the treatment — and understanding — of depression, here are some of the most frequently asked questions they encounter about the disorder:

Is depression caused by chemical imbalance or psychological problems?

Depression has no single cause. Pressing societal problems may foster depression, as can major personal setbacks like a divorce or business failure. But experts say the mainsprings of the disorder often lie within an individual sufferer's psyche.

Freud and his followers theorized that depression has its roots in early childhood, when the most significant experience often is the loss of a parent's love. The loss can reflect physical separation, the parent's conscious or unconscious rejection of the child or the child's mistaken belief that he is being rejected.

It follows, then, that experts find in depression a strong component of anger against a loved one with whom the sufferer identifies. "Depression is rage against someone else turned inside against yourself," said Theodore Reik, a friend and colleague of Freud.[8] The "someone else" is often the parent who failed to supply the needed emotional security in infancy or early childhood — or the parent who failed the child by dying. This anger may be repressed until it boils up in the form of a self-despising depression at a critical time later in life.

The incidence of depression is highest among people between the ages of 25 and 44. In this group, and generally among working-age adults, the struggle against depression may lead to alcoholism, marital infidelity, gambling or compulsive overwork. It has even been theorized that the manic phase of a manic-depressive illness — characterized by hyperactivity, boastfulness and euphoria — represents a desperate effort to forestall the feared misery of the "down"

phase of the illness.*

Adolescents are also highly susceptible to periods of depression. Much of the behavior of today's alienated youth — dropping out of school, rejecting middle-class lifestyles, resorting to drugs — is seen by many experts as an effort to forestall an impending depression. Furthermore, mental-health experts have identified depression as one of the leading causes of suicide among adolescents. Since the 1950s, the teenage suicide rate in the United States has tripled.[9]

Depression in old age is all too familiar. Social neglect intensifies a tendency that accompanies a decline of energy, a loss of status due to retirement, the death of contemporaries or worsening of physical ailments. Much of the older person's psychological distress is related to his physical condition. Nutritional neglect, common among elderly persons living alone, aggravates the psychic problem.

Dr. Nathan Billig, director of the geriatric psychiatry program at Georgetown University Medical Center in Washington, notes that depression in the elderly "is compounded by the fact that it is one of the great masqueraders of medicine. Depression in older adults, unlike in younger people, frequently first shows itself as a physical problem — headaches, low back pain, chest symptoms, bowel disturbances — and may not be thought of as a primary problem to be treated."[10]

A depressed older person sometimes is misdiagnosed as having Alzheimer's disease or some other dementia-causing disorder, for the symptoms are strikingly similar to depression.[11] Both are marked by confusion, disorientation and memory failure. If depression is the cause but isn't identified, the patient may be consigned to custodial care instead of

---

*In manic-depressive illness, the mood of the sufferer usually swings from overly "high" and irritable to sad and hopeless and then back again, with periods of normalcy in between, according to the National Institute of Mental Health.

receiving treatment.

When a loss triggers depression in an old person, it need not have occurred recently. According to Billig, the condition can arise from "the reliving of losses sustained earlier in life that were not satisfactorily worked through, mourned, or otherwise dealt with. They may resurface because of some current reminder and then complicate our present mental state, making us more vulnerable to depression in the here and now." [12]

Over the past decade, researchers have gathered evidence indicating that depressive illnesses run in families. For instance, studies show that rates of depression consistently are higher among children of depressed parents than among the general population.

In fact, research involving twins has strengthened suspicions that vulnerability to depression can be inherited. Scientists have demonstrated that if one identical twin suffers from depression or manic-depressive illness, there is a 70 percent likelihood that the other twin also will be afflicted. Among fraternal twins, however, as with siblings, parents or children of the sufferer, the risk drops to about 25 percent.[13] Since identical twins have identical genes, while siblings and other blood relatives have only half as many genes in common, the differing incidence rates for depression strongly suggest genetic involvement (see p. 872).

The quest for knowledge about the causes of depression often centers on psychobiology. Basic research in neurochemistry, neuroendocrinology and neurophysiology presents tantalizing clues to the links between complex processes in the human nervous system and an individual's mood states.[14]

The role of neurotransmitters — chemical "messengers" that transmit electrical signals from one nerve cell (neuron) to another — figures prominently in most hypotheses about the biochemical origins of depression. In carrying out this func-

What People Think About Depression

A sizable number of the respondents to an October 1991 poll for the National Mental Health Association indicated they felt there was a stigma attached to depression and that they would not seek treatment.

Which of the following do you think of as health problems, and which do you think of as signs of personal or emotional weakness?

	Health Problems	Personal/ Emotional Problems	Not Sure
Alcoholism	34%	58%	8%
Depression	46%	43%	11%
Obesity, or being overweight	48%	38%	14%

If your spouse or child were getting treatment or counseling for depression, would this be something you would tell friends or something you would not want friends to know?

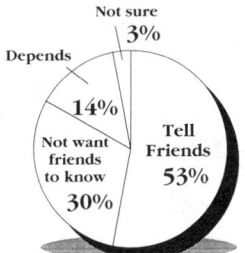

Not sure 3%
Depends 14%
Tell Friends 53%
Not want friends to know 30%

Have you, or has someone in your family, ever sought the help of a psychiatrist, psychologist, or counselor?

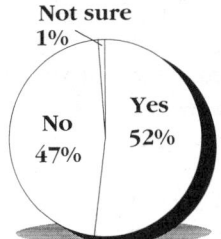

Not sure 1%
No 47%
Yes 52%

How did you/your family member deal with depression?

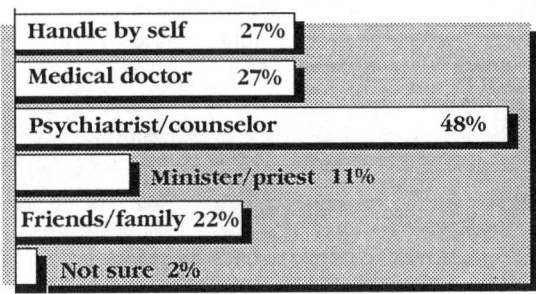

Handle by self	27%
Medical doctor	27%
Psychiatrist/counselor	48%
Minister/priest	11%
Friends/family	22%
Not sure	2%

If a doctor prescribed a pill because you were suffering from ...

	Yes	No	Not Sure
An infection, would you take an antibiotic pill?	94%	4%	2%
A sleeping problem, would you take a sleeping pill?	59%	34%	7%
Depression, would you take an antidepressant pill?	63%	27%	10%
Being overweight, would you take a weight loss pill?	43%	50%	7%

Note: Percentages do not always add up to 100 percent.

Source: Peter D. Hart Research Associates, Inc.

tion, neurotransmitters regulate the complex processes that shape thought, feeling and behavior.

At one time, it was thought that depression was caused by a deficit of two neurotransmitters — either serotonin or norepinephrine (pronounced no-ruh-puh-NEFF-rin) — at critical locations in the central nervous system. By implication, the manic phase of manic-depressive illness was attributed to excess norepinephrine or serotonin. More recent research suggests that a third neurotransmitter, dopamine, may also be involved in mood disorders.[15]

Some conditions once considered precursors of depression are no longer under suspicion. For years, mental-health experts believed that women often experienced a special form of depression during menopause. Research has since established that change-of-life depression does not differ from depressive illness at other ages and that women most susceptible to menopausal depression usually have a prior history of the disorder.

Similarly, the "empty-nest" syndrome has been discredited as a trigger of depression in older women. Women without children to care for, the theory held, were prone to feel useless and then despondent. However, studies have uncovered no significant increase in the rate of depression among female empty-nesters. (Depression among men in the empty-nester age bracket is usually viewed as a response to retirement.)

Is there too much emphasis on drug therapy in treating depression?

For many years, psychotherapy, also called "talk" therapy, was the primary tool for treating mental illness. *(See story, p. 871.)* In recent decades, however, drug therapy has come into widespread use, especially for treating depression. Psychiatrists generally hail drugs for making mental-health care more convenient and affordable. But some voice misgiv-

ings, arguing that talk therapy — or a combination of talk therapy and drugs — often produces more lasting results than medication alone.

"There is certainly a group of physicians — not just psychiatrists but also internists — who are too fast to throw medication into patients [for mental disorders]," says Dr. Lawrence Hartmann, a Boston psychiatrist and past president of the American Psychiatric Association. "I think some clinicians think that is clearly unwise. Many patients think it's unwise. Some patients who are themselves physicians think it's unwise."

According to Hartmann, "medication should be thought of as a very interesting adjunct to treatment of depression, but not the only thing we've got."

However, psychiatrists J. Raymond DePaulo Jr. and Keith Russell Ablow, authors of *How to Cope With Depression*, caution that psychotherapy isn't a cure-all for depression. "The techniques are clearly inappropriate for patients who are so depressed that they find it difficult to communicate; these therapies are equally ill-advised for those who are suffering with psychotic symptoms or are suicidal. Psychotherapy in which the therapist is passive, rather than supportive and actively interacting with the patient, may be misinterpreted by the patient and may worsen the sense of hopelessness and guilt."[16]

DePaulo, director of the Johns Hopkins University Hospital Center for Affective Disorders, rejects the idea that too much emphasis is placed on drugs. "If we're overselling biological treatments, we're not doing a very good job of it," he says. "Epidemiological data suggest most people who would benefit from antidepressant medicines aren't getting them. Medications are clearly helpful for moderately severe to severe clinical depressions, but only about 20 to 30 percent of people with those disorders are receiving drug therapy."

However, according to Dr. Brian Doyle, a Washington, D.C., psychiatrist and former Georgetown University professor, there is too much emphasis on "drugs alone as a treatment for mental disorders." He says, "Clinical research studies indicate that a combination of medication and psychotherapy is the most effective treatment for clinical depression. Medication alone is often helpful, but medication and psychotherapy together give better results."

Ablow, associate medical director at Tri-City Community Mental Health Centers in Lynn, Mass., agrees that a combination of drug and talk therapy generally works best. "We really need to marry [antidepressant] medications to an understanding of patients' lives," Ablow says. "The next frontier in treating depression may be a re-realization that while these disorders could have roots in biochemistry and anatomy and genetics, some of the roots are in peoples' life stories. We need to pay attention to both."

Eventually, he says, "we will find it's not sufficient to use the medical model of diagnosing syndromes and then matching those syndromes to appropriate medications in the mental health field. We'll realize that the kind of suffering that we're dealing with is much more complex than any list of symptoms can capture."

But health insurers' reimbursement practices make it difficult to pursue such a holistic approach, Ablow says. These practices make it more lucrative for mental-health-care services to prescribe an antidepressant than to provide psychotherapy. As a result, patients are deprived of "the synergy that can occur from having one person who is both their confessor and an investigator of the themes in their lives — and the person who's very closely tracking their improvement so their medications can be tailored."

Goodwin of the NIMH agrees that drugs and psychotherapy are both crucial in treating depression. Drugs

The Wide World of Depression

According to the National Institute of Mental Health, the incidence of depression is highest among persons between the ages of 25 and 44. But the condition afflicts people in all age brackets, and care givers are now focusing more sharply on small subgroups within them.

For instance, while depression has long been recognized as a common affliction of the elderly, it is now viewed as especially acute among elderly hospital patients. According to Dr. Jonathan T. Stewart of the Department of Veterans Affairs Medical Center in Gainesville, Fla., at least 35 percent of the nation's hospitalized elderly suffer from depression. He says their disorder is rarely diagnosed. "Left untreated, [depression] can increase length of hospital stay, impair compliance with treatment and rehabilitation of the physical illness, and, in many cases, slow recovery," says Stewart.†

Adolescent depression also has come under increasing scrutiny, largely because of the sharp rise in teenage suicide. Now the spotlight may be shifting toward depression among pre-teenagers. Surprising as it may seem, children as young as 5 are currently taking antidepressants.

Most children with depression go undiagnosed because they fail to exhibit symptoms characteristic of depressed adults — fatigue, low self-esteem, social withdrawal and suicidal fantasies. A depressed child, by contrast, is more likely to be restless, aggressive, hyperactive and moody. Parents tend to dismiss such behavior as "a phase" of growing up, and often they are right. But sometimes the child's behavior points to a more serious form of inner turmoil.

Researchers have found that certain habits may be indicative of depression. For instance, two studies published in September 1990 in *The Journal of the American Medical Association* reported that smokers are more likely than non-smokers to have suffered from depression. Both studies also concluded that severe depression seems to make it extremely difficult for smokers to kick the habit. The findings lent support to the theory that smokers unconsciously "medicate" themselves with nicotine, which is believed to have mood-altering properties.

In a more startling development, Robert J.W.M. Howard and Roland M. Valori of Maudsley Hospital in London reported two years ago in the *Journal of the Royal Society of Medicine* that wearers of tinted eyeglasses are more likely than others to suffer from depression and hypochondria. After testing 20 patients who wore tinted shades and 20 others who did not, Howard and Valori concluded that the first group displayed not only higher levels of depression and psychosomatic illness but also more obsessive-compulsiveness, phobic anxiety and psychosis.

The researchers said their findings supported a theory set forth in 1984 by Dr. Patrick D. Trevor-Roper in his book *The Eye and Its Disorders*, that neurotics favor tinted lenses in the belief they will protect the wearers' "frail sensibilities . . . from the light of day."

---

†Jonathan T. Stewart, "Diagnosing and Treating Depression in the Hospitalized Elderly," *Geriatrics*, January 1991, p. 64.

---

usually are the treatment of choice at the severe end of the depression spectrum, he says, while psychotherapies are most effective at the milder end. "The middle of the spectrum is where it's most appropriate to have combinations of drugs and psychotherapy," he says.

Goodwin notes that research involving combinations of drugs and psychotherapy shows "different responses to each treatment." In this connection, he cites a study involving a group of depressed women who displayed physiological symptoms such as sleep and appetite disorders as well as low self-esteem and chronic interpersonal difficulties. When some of the women underwent psychotherapy alone, their self-esteem and interpersonal skills improved, but their other symptoms did not.

A second subgroup only received antidepressant drugs. The sleeping and eating patterns of these patients returned to normal, but their self-esteem and interpersonal relationships remained impaired. The third subgroup got both drugs and psychotherapy and "did better in both spheres," reports Goodwin.

Such findings help explain why NIMH research activities are almost evenly divided between drug therapy and psychotherapy. Psychotherapy accounts for 52 percent of the agency's current research budget, Goodwin says, and drug therapy for 48 percent. "But a number of studies combine the two," he adds.

Are some drugs better than others in treating depression?

As with psychotherapy, psychiatrists have several options when choosing a drug for a depressed patient. John Cade, an Australian psychiatrist, discovered in 1949 that lithium, a naturally occurring chemical element, relieves the symptoms of mania. Lithium compounds have been found effective in relieving depressive episodes, too. As a result, lithium is now the medication of choice for manic-depressive illness, also known as bipolar disorder.

Two other classes of chemical antidepressants were discovered

Recognizing Symptoms of Depression

Depression can be revealed by the presence of any of several physical, mental and psychological symptoms. According to experts, professional treatment, including a medical evaluation, should be sought when four or more of the following symptoms persist for more than two weeks or are causing impairment of ordinary functioning:

- Persistent sad, anxious or "empty" mood;
- Loss of interest or pleasure in ordinary activities, including sex;
- Decreased energy, fatigue, being "slowed-down";
- Sleep disturbances (insomnia, early-morning waking, or oversleeping);
- Eating disturbances (loss of appetite and weight, or weight gain)
- Difficulty concentrating, remembering, making decisions;
- Feelings of hopelessness, pessimism;
- Thoughts of death or suicide; suicide attempts;
- Irritability;
- Excessive crying;
- Chronic aches and pains that don't respond to treatment.

Source: National Institute of Mental Health

soon after lithium. In 1956, American psychiatrist Nathan S. Kline found that the tuberculosis drug iproniazid elevates the mood of depressed patients. Iproniazid was the first of the antidepressants known as monoamine oxidase inhibitors (MAOIs). Such drugs are useful in combating all forms of depression. However, MAOIs are thought to be especially effective in treating persons suffering from extreme anxiety and social phobias, which often cause increased sleep and appetite.

MAOIs impede the functioning of monoamine oxidase, an enzyme that helps deactivate chemical messengers, including norepinephrine and serotonin, emitted by neurons. This allows more neurotransmitters to travel from cell to cell. In ways not fully understood, the increased neurotransmitter volume eventually relieves the sufferer's symptoms.

MAOIs, however, can have a number of serious side effects, including high blood pressure. Patients taking the drugs are warned to avoid a long list of foods and medications, including yogurt, figs, cheese, beer, wine, sour cream, avocados, pills for the common cold, decongestants and certain pain relievers.

In 1957, Swiss psychiatrist Roland Kuhn found that a third class of antidepressant drugs, called tricyclics,* is remarkably effective against depression. Tricyclics also increase the volume of norepinephrine and serotonin, but in a somewhat different way than MAOIs do. Once a neurotransmitter goes from one nerve cell to another, it is reabsorbed by the originating cell, which then deactivates it. But tricyclic drugs block the return of norepinephrine and serotonin, allowing the level of those two key substances to increase in the space between neurons.

Tricyclics also have undesirable side effects, though not so serious as those that accompany MAOIs. Patients on tricyclics may experience drowsiness,

---

*Tricyclics are named for the three-ring chain in their chemical structure. Newer drugs called heterocyclics have four or more rings.

lightheadedness, blurred vision or constipation. However, these and other side effects often subside or disappear over time.

In recent years, Prozac has emerged as perhaps the best-known antidepressant of all. The trade name for fluoxetine, Prozac differs from other antidepressants in that it acts only on serotonin. Prozac was hailed as a wonder drug soon after it came on the market in 1988. But a number of former users have sued the manufacturer, Eli Lilly and Co., claiming that Prozac made them suicidal (see p. 871).

Some patients suffering from major depression can obtain temporary relief simply through sleep deprivation. On the other hand, the same individuals usually relapse when they return to sleep, even if only for an hour or so.

"With some notable exceptions, sleep deprivation by itself is probably not a very useful treatment for depressed patients because after they have responded to the procedure, they tend to relapse when they resume normal sleep," writes Dr. Thomas A. Wehr of the National Institute of Mental Health. "Deprivation appears to be more useful when it is combined with antidepressant drugs, which seem to sustain the effect of the procedures." [17]

Is electroconvulsive therapy a safe and reliable approach to treating depression?

Electroconvulsive therapy (ECT) is once again gaining favor as a depression treatment. Also known as electroshock therapy, ECT first came into use for severe depression in the late 1930s, then fell out of favor as the perception grew that it was too extreme an approach. Now, however, improved techniques have made ECT the treatment of choice in some situations, especially when fast results are sought. It is not clear, however, whether the technique is being used more often than in the past or is just getting more positive media attention.

The treatment consists of applying

As the Days Dwindle Down ... Depression Flourishes

As days grow shorter and grayer with the approach of winter, some people become irritable and lethargic and find it increasingly hard to concentrate. They may suffer from seasonal affective disorder (SAD), a form of depression that afflicts an estimated 10 million persons in the United States.†

Frederick A. Cook, the Arctic explorer, provided a vivid description of the effects of prolonged darkness on the human psyche. "The curtain of blackness which has fallen over the outer world has also descended upon the inner world of our souls," Cook wrote in his journal on May 16, 1898. "Around the tables ... men are sitting about sad and dejected, lost in dreams of melancholy ... For brief moments some try to break the spell by jokes, told perhaps for the 50th time. Others grind out a cheerful philosophy; but all efforts to infuse bright hopes fail."

The fact that SAD peaks in the Northern Hemisphere around Christmas and New Year's Day led many people to assume the disorder was merely a form of holiday blues. But that theory collapsed with the discovery that SAD strikes most of its victims below the Equator in June and July — the Southern Hemisphere's midwinter.

Light therapy is the most commonly recommended treatment for SAD. It entails several hours a day of exposure to artificial illumination 10 to 15 times brighter than the light in a typical room at night. Researchers have found that extra light in the morning does more to enhance mood than light administered later in the day.††

Nonetheless, researchers still don't know why or how light therapy combats SAD. Some believe it does so by altering the levels of certain neurotransmitters in the brain — chemicals that act as messengers between nerve cells. In this connection, there is evidence that light affects the body's ability to produce or make use of serotonin, a neurotransmitter that helps induce feelings of calm and well-being.

At one time, it was thought that artificial light, like sunlight, inhibited the production of melatonin, a hormone manufactured by the brain's pineal body that induces sleepiness and impedes reaction time. But the hypothesis became suspect when it turned out that SAD patients who improve with light therapy lose melatonin at the same rate as patients who show no improvement after treatment.

Individuals who suffer from SAD or two other behavioral disorders — carbohydrate-craving obesity (CCO) and premenstrual syndrome (PMS) — tend to engage in bouts of overeating and excessive weight gain. The binges usually occur at predictable times: late afternoon or evening in the case of CCO; just prior to menstruation in PMS; and in the fall and winter for SAD.

Some researchers believe the craving for carbohydrates that is characteristic of all three disorders stems from cyclical disruptions of a feedback mechanism in the central nervous system. At such times, the theory goes, the brain fails to respond when carbohydrates are eaten. Consequently, the craving for them persists longer than it ordinarily would.

The only sure cure for SAD is said to be the arrival of spring. But some people even dread the prospect of warmer weather, knowing that it will trigger a bout of summer seasonal affective disorder (SSAD). Though much less prevalent than SAD, SSAD shares many of the same symptoms. To obtain relief, SSAD sufferers are advised to avoid high temperatures and spend their summer vacations in cool northern latitudes.

---

† Susan Gilbert, "Harnessing the Power of Light," *The New York Times Magazine,* April 26, 1992, p. 17.

†† Richard J. Wurtman and Judith J. Wurtman, "Carbohydrates and Depression," *Scientific American,* January 1989, p. 72.

---

electrodes to the patient's head at precise locations and delivering a low-voltage electric shock for less than a second. The treatments are typically repeated every few days until a course of six to 12 treatments have been given.

The purported drawbacks have been temporary loss of memory and uncertainty over the effect of repeated doses on brain function. Recent improvements in ECT seek to minimize possible hazards by lowering the number of treatments

required or by applying an electrode to only one side of the head.

According to Dr. Max Fink, a professor of psychiatry at the State University of New York-Stony Brook and editor of the journal *Convulsive Therapy*, much of the criticism leveled against ECT is unfounded — particularly memory loss. "Yes," he says, "there *is* a period of confusion after each [treatment]. And, yes, some things are forgotten that seem striking at the time. However, you will find that, on average, patients

do better on neuropsychological tests three to six weeks after a course of ECT than they did at the beginning. If anything, memory function and recollection improve with ECT."

The reason, he says, is that the memory loss attributed to ECT actually is a product of the depression itself. Depressed persons "are withdrawn, apathetic, they do not record the events around them. So when they recover, they look back on that period and say it's all a blank. Depressive illness interferes with memory rather markedly."

Fink also challenges the notion that ECT is unsafe. When the technique was first developed, he notes, patients were treated without anesthesia and often developed anoxia — the medical term for absence of oxygen in blood or tissue. As a consequence, says Fink, many patients experienced severe memory loss that sometimes persisted for months. The early treatments, administered without general anesthesia, also caused pronounced convulsions that sometimes resulted in broken bones. All that changed with the introduction of the muscle relaxant succinylcholine chloride in 1953 and, in 1963, the use of oxygenation.

Today, says Fink, ECT is "no different than giving a person a pill." Patients have undergone hundreds of ECT sessions with no ill effects, he says. "Again, it's no different than saying, 'How often can you take a pill? How often do you give a person with diabetes insulin?' There's no limit. If they're alive, they take insulin. It works."

The NIMH's Goodwin reports that "the main utilizers of ECT are successful doctors, lawyers and businessmen who become depressed and want to get over it as soon as possible. They don't want to wait out the time it takes for a drug to work. So they get ECT in an outpatient setting and are essentially recovered in a week to 10 days." ∎

BACKGROUND

An Ancient Malady

Depressive disorders were as familiar to ancient societies as they are to the modern world. Disciples of Hippocrates, the fifth-century B.C. Greek physician regarded as the father of medicine, wrote that melancholia was associated with "aversion to food, despondency, sleeplessness, irritability, restlessness." Any 20th-century psychiatrist would instantly recognize the symptoms. There is a world of difference, however, between ancient and contemporary theories on the origins and treatment of depression.

For some 2,000 years, from Hippocratic times to the late 17th century, the diagnosis and treatment of disease was based on the humoral theory. It held that physical and mental disorders stemmed from an oversupply of one of four bodily fluids — blood, phlegm, yellow bile and black bile. By the same token, good health indicated that the four "humors"

were in balance. Depression was attributed to an excess of black bile, the "cold and dry" humor.

Galen, a Greek physician who lived about 600 years after Hippocrates, elaborated on the humoral theory. He contributed the idea of four basic temperaments, each linked to one of the humors: the sanguine, buoyant type; the phlegmatic, sluggish type; the choleric, quick-tempered type; and the melancholic, dejected type.

As late as the 17th century, bloodletting and purgatives were recommended for combating melancholia. Medical practitioners believed these treatments would rid the body of black bile and restore the patient to health. In addition, the patient was to be given warm and moist foods to counteract the cold and dry influence of the offending humor.

Burton's *The Anatomy of Melancholy*, first published in 1621, included practically everything then known about the subject. "This humor of melancholy," he wrote, "is a disease so grievous, so common, I know not wherein to do a more general service

and spend my time better than to describe means how to prevent and cure so universal a malady, an epidemical disease, that so often, so much, crucifies the body and mind."

The instant and enduring popularity of *Anatomy* justified Burton's dedication; the author himself oversaw the publication of six editions during the 19 years between 1621 and his death. Burton, who said melancholy was "something I can speak [about] out of ... painful experience," thought a sickness in society was partly responsible. His vast miscellany of fact and fancy included a discourse on reforms needed for a less depression-prone society.

Dr. Johnson's 'Vile Melancholy'

Samuel Johnson, the English lexicographer and critic, was among the 18th century's most notable depression sufferers. He complained of his "vile melancholy" and said he "felt himself overwhelmed ... with perpetual irritation, fretfulness, and impatience; and with a dejection, gloom, and despair, which made existence misery."

It was Dr. Johnson, in fact, who made "depression" a synonym for "melancholy." In 1761 he wrote in his diary of being "under great depression." Two years later, referring to the deceased British poet William Collins, Johnson observed that he had "languished some years under that depression of mind which enchains the faculties without destroying them, and leaves reason the knowledge of right without the power of pursuing it." [18]

While Johnson hardly found depression attractive, the condition had acquired an almost fashionable aura in some literary circles by the 18th century. The publication in 1774 of Goethe's *The Sorrows of Young Werther* set off waves of imitative *Weltschmertz*, or world-weariness, all over Europe. Many young people

Continued on p. 868

Chronology

17th Century
As the Renaissance recedes into history, a major work is published on the mental disorder now known as depression.

1621
The Anatomy of Melancholy, by the English scholar Robert Burton, meets with great popular acclaim and soon is published in several editions. The work, regarded as both an artistic achievement and a scientific treatise, sums up medical-psychological thought on melancholia from the time of Hippocrates to Burton's day.

1940s-1950s
Most of the first drugs found to be useful in treating depression are discovered by accident and without knowledge of how they work.

1945
British Prime Minister Winston Churchill's defeat at the polls triggers another of his recurrent spells of depression, deeper than a normal reaction to disappointment in politics.

1949
Australian psychiatrist John Cade discovers that lithium, a naturally occurring chemical element, relieves the symptoms of mania. Lithium compounds prove to be an effective treatment for depression as well.

1953
The introduction of succinylcholine chloride, a muscle relaxant, greatly eliminates violent convulsions during electroconvulsive therapy (ECT) for severe depression and other mental disorders. The convulsions sometimes caused broken bones.

1956
American psychiatrist Nathan Kline discovers that the tuberculosis drug iproniazid elevates the mood of depressed patients. Iproniazid is the first of the antidepressant drugs classified as monoamine oxidase inhibitors (MAOIs).

1957
Swiss psychiatrist Roland Kuhn discovers that imipramine, the first member of the drug family called tricyclics, is remarkably effective in treating depressive disorders.

1970s
Despite widespread press coverage noting that depression is both ubiquitous and readily treatable, the disorder still carries a stigma.

1972
Fluoxetine, the generic name for the antidepressant Prozac, is discovered by scientists at Eli Lilly and Co.

1972
Democratic vice presidential nominee Thomas F. Eagleton resigns from the ticket after confirming media reports that he was treated for depression during the 1960s. During two of his hospitalizations, Eagleton received electroconvulsive therapy.

1980s-1990s
Prozac, initially hailed as an antidepressant wonder drug, becomes the target of multimillion-dollar lawsuits alleging that it triggers violent or suicidal behavior in some users.

January 1988
Eli Lilly introduces Prozac, billing it as not only a highly effective antidepressant but also one of the safest and easiest to tolerate.

May 1990
Barbara Bush discloses in an interview in *U.S. News & World Report* that she found herself seriously depressed in 1976, shortly after she and George Bush returned from China, where George Bush served as chief U.S. liaison officer.

July 1990
Rhonda Hala, a secretary in upstate New York, sues Eli Lilly for $150 million, charging that Prozac had made her slash herself more than 150 times and try repeatedly to commit suicide.

1990
Former Sen. Lawton Chiles, D-Fla., comes out of political retirement to seek his party's nomination for Florida governor. At the same time, he acknowledges that rumors about his mental condition are true. "I've had depression and sought treatment," Chiles says. He goes on to win the general election by a margin of 57 percent to 43 percent.

September 1991
The U.S. Food and Drug Administration's Psychopharmacological Drug Products Advisory Committee unanimously agrees that available scientific data do not prove a causal link between antidepressants — including Prozac — and suicidal or other violent behavior.

September 1992
Eli Lilly reports that 27 civil suits seeking damages for alleged side effects of Prozac have been dismissed and that no such suit against the company has been successful. In addition, the company says there have been no acquittals in the estimated three dozen criminal cases in which defendants cited their Prozac use as a mitigating factor.

Continued from p. 866

adopted the manner and attire of Goethe's young hero, some even emulating Werther's suicide.

Melancholy also was a characteristic feature of the Romantic Era, which spanned the last decade of the 18th century and the early 19th century. The premature deaths of three major English poets of that period — Keats, Shelley and Byron — contributed to the mournful temper.*

But social upheaval, in part caused by the disruption of family stability by rapid industrialization, fostered a more hopeless outlook on life than a mere fad for melancholy could achieve. In *The Tower and the Abyss: An Inquiry Into the Transformation of the Individual*, Princeton University historian Eric Kahler in 1957 traced the development of "a deep uneasiness ... which, from the 18th century onward, kept stirring in minds of people unceasingly and increasingly up to our present time." At the same time he noted "a steady growth of man's self-reflection and psychological introspection" that began in the Renaissance and culminated with modern psychoanalysis. These two forces, together with the proliferation of new modes of literary and artistic expression, interacted to create a "new sensibility" and a growth of the malaise.

This sense of inner discontent, of being engulfed in nothingness, was known in the 19th century as *mal du siecle* (sickness of the century). "The *mal du siecle* passed over without interruption into the condition of the *fin de siecle* [end of the century] which was identified with decadence and morbid gloom," wrote Kahler. The influential writers of the period

---

*Keats died of tuberculosis in Rome in 1821 at 26. Shelley drowned in 1822 in the Gulf of Spezia a month before his 30th birthday. Byron died in 1824 at 36 of fever contracted while helping Greek rebels in their struggle for independence from the Turks.

— Nietzsche, Ibsen, Strindberg, Dostoevsky, Tolstoy — were hardly purveyors of merriment.

"What else did these great authors express ... but the deep unrest, uneasiness and alarm at the effects of our modern middle-class civilization: the increasing hollowness and precariousness of conventional values, the derangement of human relations."

20th-Century Anxiety

The uneasiness continued into the next century, gaining momentum in the period of disillusionment following World War I. The malaise originated in Europe but spread to the United States. Among the conditioning factors, according to Kahler, were "loss of religion and, with it, the firm personal foundation of values ... and ... finally, loss of orientation in the maze of the modern world, the loss of meaning, of inner security, the feeling of forsakenness, anxiety and alienation."

Modern industrial civilization has been indicted countless times as a leading cause of psychic distress among vulnerable individuals. Henry David Thoreau's comment in *Walden* that "The mass of men lead lives of quiet desperation" has often been applied to 20th-century man. In 1950, sociologist David Riesman's *The Lonely Crowd: A Study of the Changing American Character* described the anxiety and psychic isolation of many Americans — maladies that have become more pronounced in the intervening 42 years.

In 1970, Alvin Toffler ascribed the psychic disarray characteristic of the depressed state to "future shock," that is, the inability to adjust to the swift pace of change. As a result, he said, the individual becomes "tense, anxious ... irascible ... [reaching a] final stage of emotional exhaustion" like the weary soldier in battle who loses the will to live.[19]

Sounding a similar note, U.S. diplomat George F. Kennan decried the disorienting effect of modern life in his memoirs, published in 1989. "A man's life ... is too long a span today for the pace of change," he wrote. "If he lives more than half a century, his familiar world, the world of his youth, fails him like a horse dying under its rider, and he finds himself dealing with a new one which is not really his."[20]

New Insights

The 20th century, meanwhile, brought new understanding of depression as a distinct mental disorder. In 1899, the German psychiatrist Emil Kraepelin proposed a category of mental disorders called manic-depressive psychosis, comprising manic, depressed and mixed states. Kraepelin, however, was concerned mainly with diagnostic classification and did not accept the theory of unconscious mental activity championed by psychoanalysts.

At the same time, however, Kraepelin helped make the treatment of depressive illness more humane. His "rest-cure" program included bed rest, constant care, nutritious food in small portions at frequent intervals, warm baths instead of sedatives for insomnia and safeguards against suicide attempts. Caregivers were encouraged to be "gentle, friendly and assuring."

It remained for Freud to supply the dimension that was missing from Kraepelin's work. In "Mourning and Melancholia," an influential paper published in 1917, the Viennese psychiatrist drew a sharp distinction between the two mental states. Although mourning "involves grave departures from the normal attitude to life," he wrote, "it never occurs to us to regard it as a pathological condition and to refer it to mental treatment. We rely on its being overcome after a certain lapse of time, and we look upon any interference with it as useless or even harmful."

But melancholia, Freud noted, is

Continued on p. 870

Talking About Depression — a Glossary

Affective: Refers to mental experiences that include moods, emotions and motivations. Affective experiences are often distinguished from cognitive abilities such as intelligence, memory and reasoning.

Affective disorders: Narrowly, the syndromes of depression, mania or mixed states; more broadly, also includes anxiety states, such as panic disorder.

Anxiety disorders: Disorders in which debilitating anxiety is a central feature. The anxiety comes on as sudden panic attacks or is the result of a phobia, an obsession or a compulsion. Anxiety symptoms are frequently associated with depression.

Atypical depression: A moderately severe form of affective illness that combines long periods of depression with short intervals of relief. Sleep and appetite are often increased. The onset of atypical depression may seem closely tied to distressing life events. Its victims frequently come to suffer from prominent anxiety symptoms and abnormal behaviors (e.g., eating disorders)

Bipolar disorder: Affective illness in which episodes of depression keep company with episodes of mania. Persons who have experienced only manic episodes are also referred to as bipolar.

Bright-light therapy: Also called phototherapy, a treatment for depression in which the patient is exposed to bright lights for several hours each day. The therapy was inspired by seasonally depressed individuals, some of whom experience depression during winter months when sunlight is less plentiful.

Bulimia: An excessive appetite for food accompanied by an insistence on remaining thin. The conflicting goals lead to abnormal behaviors, such as binge eating and then purging (making oneself vomit). Eating disorders are frequently associated with atypical depression.

Dysphoric mania: A mixed affective disorder combining the high energy levels, racing thoughts and pressured speech of mania with fearful or sad, rather than elated, mood.

Imipramine: A tricyclic antidepressant. Trade names include Tofranil, SK-Pramine and Presamine.

Iproniazid: The first monoamine oxidase inhibitor used to treat depression (1956). Iproniazid was originally used in the treatment of tuberculosis.

Learned helplessness: The passive acceptance of painful stimuli after a period during which escape from pain has been blocked. Learned helplessness has been proposed as an explanation for depression.

L-tryptophan: The major building block of the neurotransmitter serotonin. L-tryptophan may prove helpful in treating depression.

Major depression: The affective illness marked by decreased self-esteem, inability to concentrate and lack of energy. When major depression occurs in the setting of past manic episodes, the patient is said to have bipolar disorder.

Mania: The "high" phase of affective illness marked by elation, increased energy, increased activity, and, often, decreased judgement.

Manic-depressive illness: Affective illness in which episodes of both mania and depression have occurred; bipolar disorder.

Mixed affective disorder: An affective disorder in which symptoms of depression and mania exist simultaneously.

Neurotransmitter: A chemical messenger released by neurons. The neurotransmitters noreponephrine and serotonin have been most closely linked to affective illness.

Obsessive-compulsive: Refers to being troubled by significant obsessions or compulsions. Obsessions and compulsions are common in depression, but each may appear independently.

Panic attack: A sudden period of intense fear or discomfort, usually lasting minutes, during which the victims may be short of breath, dizzy, or nauseated. They may also experience chest pain, heart palpitations, hot or cold flashes or muscle cramps. Often there is a sense of impending doom, as if death is imminent. Panic attacks are common in depression, but they may appear independently.

Phobia: An unreasonable fear that is closely related to a particular situation. Fear of crowds is one example. Phobias are frequent companions of atypical depression.

Premenstrual syndrome: Irritability, bloating, abdominal pain and occasional depressive symptoms that occur during the days prior to menstruation. Premenstrual syndrome sometimes becomes "wedded" to full-blown major depressive episodes, particularly atypical depressions.

Psychotherapy: A treatment for psychiatric disorders in which support, reassurance and reeducation of the patient, rather than medication, form the basis of treatment. Many different techniques are used, including psychoanalysis and cognitive therapy.

Sleep therapy: A treatment for depression in which the sleep-wake cycle is altered. A patient might, for example, be kept awake during one full night or during specific hours of several nights.

Source: "How to Cope with Depression: A Complete Guide for You and Your Family," by J. Raymond DePaulo, Jr., M.D. and Keith Russell Ablow, M.D.

Continued from p. 868
"a profoundly painful dejection, abrogation of interest in the outside world, loss of the capacity to love, inhibition of all activity, and a lowering of the self-regarding feelings to a degree that finds utterance in self-reproaches and self-revilings, and culminates in a delusional expectation of punishment." He concluded that the melancholic's self-reproaches "are reproaches against a loved object which have been shifted away from it to the patient's own ego."

Political Leaders' Woes

Growing awareness of the prevalence of depression has sparked interest in the emotional problems of political leaders past and present. Abraham Lincoln was one of the great figures of history plagued by melancholy. "This brooding and often sombre [sic] man ... so sad and so haunted-looking," as Carl Sandburg described him, showed at times certain classic symptoms of depression: hypochondria, despair, withdrawal and mood shifts from one extreme to another.[21]

During his law-studying days in New Salem, Ill., in the 1830s, Lincoln was "a homely joker who could go gloomy and show it," wrote Sandburg. "It was noticed he had two shifting moods, one of the rollicking, droll story, one when he lapsed silent and solemn beyond any bystander to penetrate."[22]

In 1841, the year of his broken engagement to Mary Todd, Lincoln suffered so severe a period of depression his friends feared he would commit suicide. "I am the most miserable man living," Lincoln wrote his law partner John T. Stuart. "If what I feel were equally distributed to the whole human family, there would not be one cheerful face on Earth."[23]

Winston Churchill was another great leader who knew spells of deep depression from early life onward. Churchill called these episodes his "black dog." In the diary of his physician, Lord Moran, Churchill is quoted as saying in 1944: "When I was young, for two or three years the light faded out of the picture. I did my work. I sat in the House of Commons, but black depression settled on me."[24]

Churchill's defeat at the polls in 1945 triggered another spell of depression, deeper than a normal reaction to disappointment in politics. "He brooded over his repudiation by his countrymen until it began to prey on his mind," Moran wrote. "I was troubled ... because he seemed to be sinking into a state of melancholy that I could not fully explain."[25]

Recalling that several of Churchill's ancestors had similar tendencies, the doctor asked: "Was there not something more behind this despair? Could it be that the shock of his defeat had stirred up the inborn melancholia of the Churchill blood?"[26]

Anthony Storr, a noted British psychiatrist, speculated that Churchill's bouts with depression actually helped him rally England at a time when, by all rational calculations, the country must either surrender or be destroyed. "Only a man who had known and faced despair within himself could carry conviction at such a moment," wrote Storr. "Winston Churchill was such a man, and it was because, all his life, he had conducted a battle with his own despair that he could convey to others that despair can be overcome."[27]

Eagleton Controversy

Depression emerged unexpectedly as an issue in the 1972 U.S. presidential election campaign. Democratic vice presidential nominee Thomas F. Eagleton, responding to reports that had been leaked to the news media, disclosed that he had been hospitalized three times in years past for depression. The Missouri senator explained that he had suffered the breakdowns as a result of exhaustion from driving himself too hard while campaigning. During two of the hospitalizations, in 1960 and 1966, he had received electroconvulsive therapy. There had been no recurrences of the trouble since 1966, Eagleton said, and he considered himself fully cured.

Eagleton's disclosures ignited a furious debate over his fitness for high office. But even those who felt Eagleton should be disqualified empathized with someone who had suffered so familiar an affliction. Others thought Eagleton presented no unusual risk but rather showed commendable judgment and character in having sought medical help when he needed it for a temporary condition.

Eagleton claimed his mail was heavily in favor of his staying on the ticket. A Gallup Poll showed 59 percent of Americans thought the experience did not render him unfit for the presidency, while 28 percent thought it did; 13 percent were undecided. At the same time, there was concern that people in public life, many of them hard-driving and subject to uncommon depression-provoking stress, would become more reluctant to seek medical help if they ever faced similar breakdowns.

In the end, Eagleton withdrew as a candidate. The Democratic presidential nominee, Sen. George S. McGovern of South Dakota, said at a news conference with Eagleton on July 31, 1972, that Eagleton's health was "not a factor" in his withdrawal but that debate on the question was diverting attention from the "great national issues that need to be discussed" in the campaign.

Florida's Lawton Chiles

Depression reappeared in American politics in 1990, when former Sen. Lawton Chiles, D-Fla., came out of political retirement to seek his party's nomination for Florida governor.

---

*Eagleton's place on the Democratic ticket was taken by former Peace Corps Director R. Sargent Shriver.

Four Approaches to 'Talk' Therapy

Partly because there is no miracle drug for depression, psychotherapists (such as psychiatrists and psychologists) often treat depressed patients with a combination of drug therapy and one of four basic types of "talk" therapy:

Psychoanalytic therapy, which originated with Freud and others, seeks to uncover the unconscious childhood conflicts believed to underlie the patient's symptoms. According to Freud, the mental struggle to keep conflicts repressed eventually surfaces as telltale signs of psychiatric disorder. Freud's followers often see depression as anger against someone else that has been turned against oneself following a loss. Exposing the true source of the anger, the theory goes, enables the patient to cope with the experience more effectively, and find relief.

Cognitive therapy is typically used on moderately depressed patients whose illness is thought to flow from chronic feelings of low self-esteem and a pessimistic outlook on life. Consequently, the goal of cognitive therapy is to alter the patient's negative mental habits. "The therapist confronts the patient with the distortions in his or her self-image and view of the world," according to psychiatrists J. Raymond DePaulo and Keith Russell Ablow. "Role playing, the daily recording of negative thoughts, and the demonstration of success in assigned simple tasks at home might be used to augment discussions."

Interpersonal therapy can relieve depressive symptoms by re-establishing ties between the patient and persons close to him when broken relationships are the cause — or the result — of the depression. To this end, friends and family members also may take part in the counseling sessions. *Behavioral therapy,* as the name suggests, focuses on leading the patient away from abnormal or destructive behavior and toward more positive conduct.

On the day he announced his candidacy, Chiles told reporters that rumors about his mental condition were true. "I've had depression and sought treatment," Chiles said. "I think I was depressed about what was going on in the state. Now I'm going to do something about it." [28]

Chiles said he had been taking Prozac since retiring from the Senate in January 1989 because he felt "burned out." Acknowledging that his depression could become an issue in the primary and general election campaigns, he said he was just then completing his treatment with the drug.

Rep. Bill Nelson, who had been the early front-runner in the Democratic gubernatorial primary, served notice that he regarded Chiles' depression as a political issue. "I can assure you that I'm not burned out," he said. "I'm ready to govern this state. We Democrats lost an important U.S. Senate seat two years ago when Lawton Chiles decided he was suddenly burned out with public service. Which job is the more mentally and physically and emotionally demanding, governor or U.S. senator?" [29]

In the end, Florida voters seemed not to care very much about Chiles' depression. The former senator flattened Nelson in the primary, 69 percent to 31 percent, and went on to beat incumbent Gov. Bob Martinez in the general election, 57 percent to 43 percent. ∎

CURRENT SITUATION

Prozac: Wonder Drug?

At the time Chiles was campaigning for the Florida governorship, his depression medication was coming under intense scrutiny. Prozac, put on the market in 1988 by Dista Products Co., a division of Eli Lilly and Co., initially was hailed as a wonder drug — not only a highly effective antidepressant but also one of the safest and easiest to tolerate.

Early experience indicated Lilly's claims were justified. Prozac was easier to prescribe — it had fewer side effects than other antidepressants — and also seemed to relieve a broader range of ailments, from depression and anxiety to bulimia and obsessive-compulsive disorder. In addition, Prozac did not cause the weight gain and low blood pressure associated with some other antidepressants.

Nonetheless, clinical tests showed Prozac can cause some unpleasant side effects. For instance, it provokes feelings of anxiety and agitation in as many as 15 percent of users, and some patients complained of headaches, nausea and insomnia.

Despite these drawbacks, physicians and patients quickly made Prozac the nation's best-selling antidepressant. Patients not suffering from depression reportedly pleaded with their doctors to prescribe Prozac as an all-purpose mood enhancer.

Then, on July 17, 1990, the Prozac story took an unexpected turn. A secretary and mother of two children in upstate New York, Rhonda Hala, sued Lilly for $150 million, charging that Prozac had made her slash herself more than 150 times and try repeatedly to commit suicide. Within weeks, several other multimillion-dollar damage suits making suicide allegations were filed by former Prozac users. Meanwhile, the Citizens Coalition for Human Rights, a group affiliated with the Church of Scientology, mounted a massive advertising campaign asserting that the drug causes violent behavior.

Lilly says that the "Prozac defense" has been raised by defendants in 37 criminal cases. The company says it has been named in about 100 civil suits seeking damages because of Prozac use; 27 of the cases have been dismissed, and none has succeeded, Lilly says.

The campaign to discredit Prozac suffered a serious setback a little more than a year ago. The U.S. Food and Drug Administration's Psychopharmacological Drug Products Advisory Committee, a group of non-governmental medical experts from around the country, unanimously agreed on Sept. 20, 1991, that available scientific data did not prove a causal link between Prozac or other antidepressants and suicidal or other violent behavior. Consequently, the panel voted 6 to 3 against recommending label changes, sought by the Public Citizen Health Research Group, warning that suicidal thinking has been linked to Prozac use. (*See "At Issue," p. 873.*)

Through all the furor, psychiatrists have continued to hold Prozac in generally high regard. "It's an excellent drug whose key constituency is persons who are treatment-resistant to tricyclic antidepressants," says Dr. Alan Romanoski, an assistant professor of psychiatry at Johns Hopkins University in Baltimore.

Because Prozac is "aggressively marketed," says Romanoski, it "might be overused" and probably should not be the drug of first choice for most patients. "Some people think it's a magic bullet for all depressive disorders," he says. "But there is no magic bullet. However, there is a population of patients for whom it *should* be the first-line drug."

Dr. Elliott Gershon, chief of the neurogenetics branch of the NIMH intramural research program, describes Prozac as a "very efficacious" drug that is "safer than most." The reason, he says, is that "the risk of suicidal impulse — a very real hazard in depression — is very much less likely to appear than to disappear" among patients taking Prozac.

The key point, says psychiatrist DePaulo, is that "it's very important we continue to have multiple treatment choices, especially since we don't have one drug that will get everyone well. The advantage Prozac has over other antidepressants is simply that, for most patients, it has fewer side effects. The advantage for the doctor is that it's yet another different kind of drug."

At the same time, says DePaulo, "we've got to keep in mind that all these drugs are limited. If any one of them was perfect, all the others would vanish in a flash. Our research ultimately will lead us to a singularly effective treatment, but we haven't reached that point yet." ∎

irregular heartbeat. Similarly, says NIMH Director Goodwin, ECT may play a role, "at least sometimes, in interrupting cyclic recurrences of depression."

NIMH also is interested in gauging whether regularly spaced ECT treatments — perhaps every four weeks — can prevent the disorder from returning to persons with highly recurrent forms of depression or manic-depressive illness.

A longer-range goal at the NIMH and other research centers is locating genetic markers for some forms of depression. The quest is important, says Goodwin, because "whenever you have a treatable disorder, you want to find a way to identify the individual child as early as possible."

"If you allow a person to go through several episodes of depression in adolescence or early adulthood before they're identified [as being depression-prone]," Goodwin notes, "they may have failed in school and developed a lot of bad relationships and deflated self-esteem. By the time you finally treat them, you can wipe out the illness, but in the meantime they've accumulated all these problems from having spent years essentially derailed from life."

NIMH's intramural research program is currently conducting a study with several other institutions to find a genetic cause of manic-depressive illness. NIMH psychiatrist Gershon, a participant in the study, predicts that in five to 10 years, "we'll either have found a genetic cause or determined that the methods we are using will not succeed in finding one. That would raise questions as to whether such a cause exists."

Some psychiatrists are investigating the possibility that all types of depression will turn out to have a common chemical pathway in the brain. A conference on neuroscience research held at the Yale University Medical School in late 1991 seemed to suggest that evidence supporting that hypothesis might soon be forth-

OUTLOOK

Future Research

Future advances in combating depression could come in a number of areas. For instance, although the NIMH concentrates mainly on drug therapy and psychotherapy, it has received half a dozen grants totaling about $2 million for research on electroconvulsive therapy.

One theory NIMH researchers will investigate holds that ECT works in somewhat the same way a defibrillator delivers an electric shock to interrupt an

At Issue:

Should the Food and Drug Administration require the antidepressant drug Prozac to warn users about possible suicidal impulses?

PUBLIC CITIZEN

A consumer advocacy organization founded by Ralph Nader
PETITION TO THE FOOD AND DRUG ADMINISTRATION,
MAY 23, 1991

yes

*f*luoxetine [Prozac] is an effective medication in many patients with clinical depression (the only indication it is approved for by the Food and Drug Administration), including patients whose depression has been resistant to other drug therapy. Evidence of its usefulness in the treatment of other psychiatric disorders, including obsessive-compulsive and eating disorders, is still emerging, but the drug appears promising in clinical trials under carefully controlled conditions. Because of the benefits that may be attributed to [Prozac], and the lower risk of injury and death associated with overdoses of [Prozac] than tricyclic antidepressants, we do not propose the drug be banned. However, the evidence linking [Prozac] to suicidal [thinking] is alarming and strongly indicates the need for caution in the use of this medication.

In response to reports of suicidal [thinking] among [Prozac] users, Eli Lilly and Company now mentions "suicidal ideation" in Prozac's label, but only in a long list of other adverse effects toward the end of the label, under the heading "Postintroduction Reports." There is no mention that suicidal [thinking] may be related to [Prozac] use in the "Precautions" section of the label that deals with suicide.

Given the seriousness of suicidal [thinking] as an adverse effect, and the widespread distribution of the drug by non-psychiatrists to patients with diverse symptoms who are unlikely to be closely monitored for the emergence of suicidal thoughts, this is not an adequate response. A box warning ... is necessary to inform physicians and patients of the unexpected possibility that Prozac may induce suicidal [thinking].

ELI LILLY AND COMPANY

Pharmaceutical company that manufactures Prozac
COMPANY STATEMENT, ISSUED MAY 23, 1991

no

*t*he position advocated by the Public Citizen Health Research Group is unfounded and unnecessary.

The approved labeling for Prozac is consistent with current medical and scientific information. No additional warnings are needed. There is no credible evidence in the medical literature that Prozac causes increased suicidal thinking or suicidal actions. This medical literature encompasses more than 2,000 published articles and more than 20 years of medical and scientific research.

Suicidal thinking and acts are tragic symptoms of depression. They are caused by the disease, not by the therapy — including Prozac — that is used to treat the disease. In 1991, the U.S. Food and Drug Administration and an independent scientific advisory committee both concluded that current research data show "no credible evidence" of a causal link between antidepressant medications, including Prozac, and suicidal or violent behavior. The scientific evidence shows that Prozac and other antidepressant medicines have been effective in lowering suicidal thinking and also appear to protect against aggressive behaviors.

Thirty-two thousand patients have participated in Prozac clinical trials. It is widely accepted by regulatory agencies and physicians in more than 50 countries and has been used by more than 3.5 million people worldwide. In an evaluation of more than 3,000 clinical trial patients with depression, serious suicidal thoughts occurred less often in people receiving Prozac than in people using other treatments. The weight of medical opinion worldwide clearly supports the safety and effectiveness of Prozac for the treatment of depression.

---

coming, spurring the development of more effective and faster-acting antidepressants.

Now, almost a year later, a common chemical pathway for depression seems a more distant prospect. Dr. Ronald Duman, a professor of molecular neuropharmacology at Yale and a conference participant, re-

ports some "slow but steady progress." His current feeling is that depression and other psychiatric illnesses will turn out to be "something like blood disorders, where there are many causes, not just one. But once you find a cause, you can start to direct specific types of treatment toward it."

Another possibility is that researchers will isolate a genetic cause of certain depressive disorders. "It's really a very long-term type of research," says Duman, involving molecular biology techniques. He foresees no significant developments for 10 to 20 years.

Psychiatrist Pedro Delgado of the
Continued on p. 875

Where to Get Help

Several private organizations, as well as the National Institute of Mental Health, have programs to educate the public and encourage further research into affective disorders, including:

The Depression/Awareness, Recognition and Treatment (D/ART) Program is a national public education campaign on depressive illnesses that was launched in 1988 by the National Institute of Mental Health (NIMH), a component of the Alcohol, Drug Abuse and Mental Health Administration. The D/ART program disseminates information about the symptoms and treatment of depressive illnesses. For more information, contact D/ART, NIMH, Room 10-85, 5600 Fishers Lane, Rockville, MD 20857; (301) 443-4140.

The Depression and Releated Affective Disorders Association (DRADA) is a nonprofit organization that focuses on manic-depressive illness and depression. DRADA distributes informational materials, conducts educational meetings and runs Young People's Outreach programs for high school counselors and nurses. The association helps support groups and provides leadership training programs and consultation for those groups. DRADA helps support research on the causes and treatment of depressive and manic-depressive disorders; it co-sponsors, with The Johns Hopkins School of Medicine Department of Psychiatry, an annual research-education symposium for both professionals and interested laypersons. The association serves members in many states. For more information, contact DRADA, The Johns Hopkins University School of Medicine, 600 N. Wolfe St., Baltimore, MD 21205; (301) 955-4647.

The National Alliance for the Mentally Ill (NAMI), the nation's largest self-help support and advocacy organization for people with serious mental illnesses and for their families. The alliance includes nearly 1,100 affiliated support groups and 140,000 families. For more information, contact NAMI, 2101 Wilson Blvd., Suite 302, Arlington, VA 22201; (703) 524-7600.

The National Alliance for Research on Schizophrenia and Depression (NARSAD) is committed to ending mental illness through research. Consisting of private citizens, psychiatrists and scientists, NARSAD raises funds to find the causes, treatments, cures and preventions of severe mental illnesses, primarily schizophrenia and depression. Areas of research to be funded are determined by a scientific council, and grants are allocated to scientists throughout North America. For more information, contact NARSAD, 60 Cutter Mill Road, Suite 200, Great Neck, NY 11021; (516) 829-0091.

The National Depressive and Manic-Depressive Association (NDMDA) is a patient- and family-based organization of more than 250 groups throughout the United States, Canada and overseas. NDMDA, representing more than 35,000 patient and family members, views affective disorders as biochemical in nature and often treatable with a program of psychotherapy and medication. For more information, contact NDMDA, 730 N. Franklin, Suite 501, Chicago, IL 60610; (312) 642-0049.

The National Foundation for Depressive Illnesses (NAFDI), established in 1983 by a group of prominent psychopharmacologists and laypeople, provides information about affective disorders as well as a state-by-state doctor referral list. For more information, contact NAFDI, P.O. Box 2257, New York, NY 10016; (800) 248-4344.

The National Mental Health Association (NMHA), founded in 1909, promotes mental health and the improved care and treatment of people with mental illnesses. A volunteer group concerned with all aspects of mental health and mental illnesses, NMHA has chartered organizations in most states. This citizens network supports and participates in nationwide programs of advocacy, education, information and volunteer services. The association also serves the public interest as the public-policy voice for mental health issues in Congress and in state legislatures. The NMHA information center is a major source of mental health information for the general public. For more information, contact NMHA, 1021 Prince St., Alexandria, VA 22314; (703) 684-7722 or (800) 969-6642.

Source: How to Cope with Depression: A Complete Guide for You and Your Family, *by J. Raymond DePaulo, Jr., M.D., and Keith Russell Ablow, M.D.*

Continued from p. 873

University of Arizona College of Medicine, another Yale conference attendee, reports that "We really haven't gone any further toward identifying a common mechanism" for depression since then. He now thinks the question of whether depression has one cause or multiple causes is "up in the air." Delgado is confident that research with laboratory animals bred to exhibit behavior consistent with clinical depression in humans will provide "a lot of very, very important information" about "whether there can be multiple pathways through which a drug can alleviate depressive disorders."

Delgado believes animal studies "may very well lead to novel drugs." He notes that almost all antidepressants now in use "were either discovered by accident or are relatives of drugs that were discovered by accident," before much was known about the brain. "We would find a drug that worked," Delgado says, "but we wouldn't know anything about what it did. And all the drugs that followed were based on the ones discovered earlier."

Now, in contrast, animal studies are helping scientists to understand "how the brain is dysfunctional in depression," Delgado says. That knowledge "might prove to be the impetus for developing new kinds of medications" for depression sufferers.

But, cautions Ablow, it is "possible that life experiences create the chemical imbalances" in the brain that antidepressants are taken to counteract. It follows that "preventive psychiatry" could help nip depression in the bud. "People really need to be reached early on and counseled to avoid drawing the kinds of conclusions about their lives — sometimes formed when they are children or adolescents — that set the stage for these disorders." ∎

Notes

[1] See Constance Holden, "Depression: The News Isn't Depressing," *Science*, December 1991, p. 1450.

[2] Marilyn Sargent, *Depressive Illnesses: Treatments Bring New Hope*, National Institute of Mental Health booklet, 1989, p. 9.

[3] U.S. Department of Health and Human Services, *Information About D/ART and Depression*, 1991.

[4] "The Hidden Life of Barbara Bush," *U.S. News & World Report*, May 28, 1990, p. 27.

[5] William Styron, *Darkness Visible* (1990), p. 26. The title alludes to the poet Milton's description of hell in *Paradise Lost* as a place where there is "no light, but rather darkness visible."

[6] *Ibid.*, p. 58.

[7] The poll was conducted by Peter D. Hart Research Associates Inc. in October 1991.

[8] Erika Padan Freeman, "Theodore Reik: A Conversation," *Psychology Today*, April 1972.

[9] For background, see "Teenage Suicide," *The CQ Researcher*, June 14, 1991, pp. 369-394.

[10] Nathan Billig, *To Be Old and Sad: Understanding Depression in the Elderly* (1987), p. 4.

[11] For background, see "Alzheimer's Disease," *The CQ Researcher*, July 24, 1992, pp. 617-640.

[12] Billig, *op. cit.*, p. 9.

[13] Sargent, *op. cit.*, p. 10.

[14] For background, see "Biology Invades Psychology," *Editorial Research Reports*, July 8, 1988, pp. 341-352.

[15] Sargent, *op. cit.*, p. 11.

[16] J. Raymond DePaulo Jr. and Keith Russell Ablow, *How to Cope With Depression* (1989), p. 139.

[17] Thomas A. Wehr, "Improvement of Depression and Triggering of Mania by Sleep Deprivation," *The Journal of the American Medical Association*, Jan. 22-29, 1992, pp. 550, 549.

[18] Samuel Johnson, *Lives of the English Poets* (1905), p. 338.

[19] Alvin Toffler, *Future Shock* (1970), p. 306.

[20] George F. Kennan, *Sketches From a Life* (1989), p. 183.

[21] »Carl Sandburg, *Abraham Lincoln* (one-volume edition, 1954), p. 37.

[22] *Ibid.*, p. 70.

[23] *Ibid.*, p. 146.

[24] Lord Moran, *Churchill* (1966), pp. 179-180, 331-332.

[25] *Ibid.*, p. 331.

[26] *Ibid.*, p. 332.

[27] Anthony Storr, "Winston Churchill's Black Dog," *Esquire*, January 1969, p. 95. Storr's views on Churchill's mental state also appear in his book *Churchill's Black Dog, Kafka's Mice: And Other Phenomena of the Human Mind* (1989).

[28] Chiles made his remarks April 12, 1990, in a meeting with reporters from *The Palm Beach Post*, *The St. Petersburg Times* and the *Tampa Tribune*.

[29] Nelson is quoted in an Associated Press dispatch of April 13, 1990, datelined Tallahassee, Fla.

Bibliography

Selected Sources Used

Books

Beck, Aaron T., et al., *Cognitive Therapy of Depression*, The Guilford Press, 1979.

In a lengthy work geared to clinicians and researchers, the authors examine how cognitive therapy is used to treat moderately depressed patients whose illness is thought to arise from chronic feelings of low self-esteem and an exaggeratedly pessimistic outlook on life. Psychotherapists' interviews with depressed and suicidal patients are included.

Billig, Nathan, *To Be Old and Sad: Understanding Depression in the Elderly*, Lexington Books, 1987.

The author, director of the geriatric psychiatry program at Georgetown University Medical Center in Washington, provides information on recognizing depression in the elderly and helping sufferers to find relief. Written for the lay reader, especially concerned family members, the slim volume includes case studies and information about drug therapy.

DePaulo, J. Raymond Jr., and Keith Russell Ablow, *How to Cope With Depression*, McGraw-Hill Publishing Co., 1989.

In this overview, DePaulo and Ablow examine the symptoms, causes and treatment of depression in its various guises. They also include a list of organizations that provide information on and encourage research into the disorder.

Hirschfeld, Robert, *When the Blues Won't Go Away*, Macmillan, 1991.

Hirschfeld, chairman of the Department of Psychiatry and Behavioral Sciences at the University of Texas Medical Branch at Galveston, focuses on forms of chronic, low-grade depression that often are dismissed by those who suffer from them as simply "the blues."

Jackson, Stanley W., *Melancholia and Depression: From Hippocratic Times to Modern Times*, Yale University Press, 1986.

This historical survey traces prevailing notions about depression, including extensive excerpts from noted works on the subject by Galen, Robert Burton and Sigmund Freud.

Styron, William, *Darkness Visible: A Memoir of Madness*, Random House, 1990.

An expanded version of an article that originally appeared in *Vanity Fair,* this short book describes the novelist's harrowing encounter with depression.

Articles

Dowling, Colette, "Rescuing Your Child From Depression," *New York*, Jan. 20, 1992.

Writing from personal experience with a manic-depressive husband and a deeply depressed daughter, the author contends that most parents fail to recognize children's depression symptoms, which can differ markedly from symptoms in adults. She offers tips to concerned parents on symptoms to look for in their children.

Grady, Denise, "Wonder Drug — Killer Drug," *American Health*, October 1990.

Grady reviews Prozac's roller-coaster ride during 1990, when the widely used antidepressant suddenly became a target of multimillion-dollar damage claims. What happened to Prozac "could have happened to nearly any new drug that so quickly became popular and widely regarded as extraordinarily safe," Grady observes.

Potter, William Z., et al., "The Pharmacological Treatment of Depression," *The New England Journal of Medicine*, Aug. 29, 1991.

This authoritative article offers guidelines for deciding which medications are most effective in treating various types of depressive disorders.

Stewart, Jonathan T., "Diagnosing and Treating Depression in the Hospitalized Elderly," *Geriatrics*, January 1991.

Stewart, assistant chief of the psychiatry service at the Department of Veterans Affairs Medical Center in Gainesville, Fla., examines the links between medical illness and depression in the hospitalized elderly, some 35 percent of whom are believed to suffer from depressive disorders.

Wartik, Nancy, "Jerry's Choice: Why Are Our Children Killing Themselves?" *American Health*, October 1991.

Depression, a disorder usually associated with the middle-aged and elderly, has emerged as a serious problem among adolescents as well. Wartik offers reasons for the disturbing trend.

Reports and Studies

Alcohol, Drug Abuse, and Mental Health Administration, U.S. Department of Health and Human Services, *Information About D/ART and Depression*, 1991.

Written in question-and-answer format, this booklet from the Public Health Service's Depression/Awareness, Recognition, and Treatment Program (D/ART) summarizes what is known about depression's symptoms and treatment.

The Next Step

Additional Articles from Current Periodicals from EBSCO Publishing's Database

Books & reading

Adams, J., "Book reviews: Social sciences," *Library Journal,* **June 1, 1992, p. 154.**

Reviews the book "Beyond Depression: A Practical Guide for Healing Despair," by Andrew Canale.

Andreasen, N. & D. L. Dunner, "Book forum," *American Journal of Psychiatry,* **April 1992, p. 564.**

Reviews the book "Depressive Disorders: Facts, Theories, and Treatment Methods," edited by Benjamin B. Wolman and George Stricker.

Brown, L. S., "Reviews," *Psychology of Women Quarterly,* **March 1992, p. 133.**

Reviews the book "Sex Differences in Depression," by Susan Nolen-Hoeksma.

Hudson, L., "Intimate dangers," *TLS,* **June 19, 1992, p. 10.**

Reviews the book "Silencing the Self: Women and Depression," by Dana Crowley Jack, which argues that men see the danger of intimacy as "entrapment," whereas women sense a danger in isolation.

Huffman, C. A., "Book reviews," *School Library Journal,* **March 1992, p. 263.**

Reviews the book "Straight Talk about Anxiety and Depression," by Michael Maloney and Rachel Kranz.

Markowitz, J. C., "Book forum," *American Journal of Psychiatry,* **April 1992, p. 563.**

Reviews the book "Psychotherapy for Depression," by T. Byram Karasu.

Ross, H. M., "Is your diet making you depressed?" *Health News & Review,* **Summer 1992, p. 4.**

Reports that according to the author's book "Fighting Depression," no one has to stay depressed if they use vitamins and nutrients to lift the debilitating cloud from themselves. Low blood sugar could be the cause of depression or even the total cause; the amount of food you should eat; frequent high-protein snacks; more.

Causes

"10 physical reasons you may be depressed," *Prevention,* **June 1992, p. 69.**

Presents ways to treat depression that really isn't "all in your mind." Case study of how a sunlight deficiency led to one man's depression; physical illness masquerading as an emotional problem; as many as 75 hidden physical causes of chronic depression; listing of 10 of the most commonly identified physical reasons behind mental consequences; prescription drugs; thyroid problems; premenstrual syndrome; hormonal disturbances; more.

"Blues of the birth," *Psychology Today,* **March/April 1992, p. 18.**

Offers a look at several reasons for postpartum depression. Americans are unrealistic; fantasy version of events; disappointment inevitable; urge for mothers to be gentle on themselves.

"Powerless chemistry of depression," *Science News,* **June 13, 1992, p. 396.**

Looks at the belief of some psychologists that "learned helplessness" is at the root of some cases of human depression. Report in the June 1991 issue of *American Journal of Psychiatry,* which suggests that people who show evidence of elated activity by a particular chemical messenger in the brain are most likely to feel powerless and at the mercy of others; view of psychologist Jacqueline A. Samson and her colleagues; norepinephrine; more.

Bower, B., "Here comes the sun," *Science News,* **July 25, 1992, p. 62.**

Focuses on research involving seasonally recurring depression which is also known as seasonal affective disorder or SAD. Preliminary support for the "sleeper effect" of simulated dawn; symptoms of SAD that are not usually seen in cases of non-seasonal depression; use of bright lights to treat SAD; how simulated dawns may affect circadian processes; The Society for Light Treatment and Biological Rhythms in Bethesda, Md.; details of several studies.

Fackelmann, K. A., "Beta blockers, depression: Breaking the link," *Science News,* **April 4, 1992, p. 213.**

Reports on a new study that may force doctors to re-examine the evidence linking beta blockers with depression. Work of Roselie A. Bright of the Food and Drug Administration (FDA) in Rockville, Md., and Daniel Everitt of the Presbyterian Medical Center in Philadelphia; possible impact of confounding factors including use of benzodiazepines; report in the April 1, 1992 issue of the *Journal of the American Medical Association;* more.

Diagnosis

Donohue, T., R. Sliman, et al, "Recognition of depression by internal medicine residents," *Journal of Community Health,* June 1992, p. 143.

Studies the ability of internal medicine residents to recognize depressive symptoms in a population of lower socio-economic primary-care patients. Introduction; methods; results; patient characteristics; multiple-regression analysis; discussion; emerging consensus that depression is an illness that can be effectively treated.

Physiological effect

Bower, B., "Depression, early death noted in HIV cases," *Science News,* July 25, 1992, p. 53.

Comments on a report presented at the VIII International Conference on AIDS in Amsterdam, which stated that depressed men in the early stages of infection with the AIDS virus (HIV) suffer a more rapid decline than their non-depressed counterparts. Comment of physician Jeffrey H. Burack of San Francisco General Hospital, who directed the investigation; study details; more.

Bower, B., "Depression boosts blood-vessel disease," *Science News,* March 28, 1992, p. 196.

Looks at a study by George A. Kaplan and his co-workers which found that mild to moderate depression may substantially increase the impact of several known contributors to a blood-vessel disease that can lead to heart attack or stroke. Study of 1,225 Finnish men; findings about depression, smoking and fibrinogen; comment of Robert Anda, a physician and epidemiologist at the Centers for Disease Control in Atlanta; more.

Research

"Depression gets anxious," *Science News,* Nov. 9, 1991, p. 295.

Reveals that anxiety symptoms often coexist with severe depression even though the two are treated separately in the current manual of psychiatric diagnoses. Report from psychiatrist Paula J. Clayton in the November issue of *American Journal of Psychiatry,* which warns that "anxious depression" is extremely resistant to standard therapies and drugs for depression; details of a study headed by Clayton; funding from the National Institute of Mental Health; more.

"Iceberg of depression," *Lancet,* April 18, 1992, p. 985.

Comments on a new report suggesting that clinical depression is under-recognized and undertreated. Estimates on the percentage of people in North America and Western Europe who will experience depression at some time in their lives; why people do not seek help; causes of child-hood depression, including bereavement and sexual abuse; tricyclic antidepressants; other treatments; more.

"Mental disorders more likely in jail," *Science News,* Oct. 26, 1991, p. 268.

Discusses a study of Chicago inmates that indicated that schizophrenia, severe depression and mania occur up to three times as often among men in urban jails as among men in the population at large. Statistics on those suffering from mental disorders and those who also abuse alcohol or illicit drugs; lack of mental health treatment alternatives; suggestions from Karen M. Abram and Linda A. Teplin of Northwestern University Medical School in Chicago for improving the situation.

Bower, B., "Marked questions on elderly depression," *Science News,* Nov. 16, 1991, p. 310.

Details a consensus statement from a 14-member panel of mental health clinicians and researchers that warns that the majority of people aged 65 or older who are struggling to cope with depression go undiagnosed and untreated. Concern that many primary-care physicians regard depression as a normal part of aging; problems caused by the definition of severe or "major" depression; tricyclic antidepressant drugs; the depressed elderly and electro-shock therapy; more.

Holden, C., "Depression: The news isn't depressing," *Science,* Dec. 6, 1991, p. 1450.

Summarizes research described at a recent Yale Medical School conference on the neurobiology of affective disorders at which it was reported that progress is being made in decoding the biological factors underlying depression. Depression's various and numerous triggers; how antidepressant drugs work; actions of two classes of antidepressants on neurotransmitter systems; serotonin's possible role in depression; stress. INSET: Imprinting depression on the brain.

Jessee, P. O., B. H. Ladewig, et al., "Children held hostage," *Journal of Family Issues,* March 1992, p. 65.

Examines how strain, family coping and family hardiness were related to depressive affect among mothers of children who were held hostage by two gunmen in a private church-sponsored elementary school. Details of the hostage-taking; study methods and results; perceived control as a dimension of hardiness; impact of the use of social and spiritual support; more.

Keitner, G. I., C. E. Ryan, et al., "Recovery and major depression: Factors associated with twelve-month outcome," *American Journal of Psychiatry,* January 1992, p. 93.

Discusses how the authors examined the probability of recovery from a major depressive episode 12 months after hospital discharge, the factors most closely associated with recovery, and the patterns of improvement between patients who recovered and those who did not. Method; results; conclusions; details.

Nolen-Hoeksema, S., "Responses to depression and their effects on the duration of depressive episodes," *Journal of Abnormal Psychology*, November 1991, p. 569.

Presents a study that proposes that the ways people respond to their own symptoms of depression influence the duration of these symptoms. Responses to depressed mood; mechanisms by which response styles influence depression duration; conclusion.

Smith, J. M., "Contrasts between symptoms of summer depression and winter depression," *Journal of the American Medical Association*, March 4, 1992, p. 1192.

Highlights a study by T. A. Wehr, et al., that compared the symptoms of depression in 30 patients with recurrent summer depression and 30 sex-matched patients with recurrent winter depression. Symptoms of winter depressives, including carbohydrate cravings and hypersomnia; symptoms of summer depressives, including decreased appetite and insomnia; more.

Smith, J. M., "Prospective study of postpartum blues: Biologic and psychosocial factors," *Journal of the American Medical Association*, Nov. 27, 1991, p. 2817.

Presents an abstract from the *Archives of General Psychiatry* of an article by Michael W. O'Hara et al. concerning the potential biologic and psychosocial causative factors for the postpartum blues. Summarizes a prospective study and its results.

Ziporyn, T., "True blue?" *Harvard Health Letter*, February 1992, p. 1.

Looks at three distinctive, though possibly related patterns to postpartum depression. Maternity "baby" blues; postpartum neurotic depression (postnatal depression); postpartum psychosis; why doctors do not readily accept postpartum depression as being a real concern; biologically plausible explanations for postpartum psychiatric illness; inconsistent criteria. INSETS: What's in a name? (postpartum depression); support groups.

Therapy

"Red, white, and blue, blue, blue," *Psychology Today*, March/April 1992, p. 8.

Looks at the latest update on clinical depression and shows how the numbers are still increasing — particularly among the young. According to the National Institute of Mental Health, a culture of pessimism is manifest in the decreasing age at which depression sets in, an increasing rate

of teen suicide, and a two to three times higher rate for women. Existence of temporal trends; more.

Bower, B., "Depression therapy gets interpersonal," *Science News*, Dec. 21, 1991, p. 404.

Presents intriguing findings resulting from a study of depression. Half of the patients whose depression cleared with a drug-therapy approach, who then received one hour of psychotherapy per month remained depression-free for three years. Consistent focus of therapy on improving social skills and relations with others; possible cost-effective treatment of depression; study by Ellen Frank and her colleagues at the University of Pittsburgh School of Medicine.

Eisenberg, L., "Treating depression and anxiety in primary care," *The New England Journal of Medicine*, April 16, 1992, p. 1080.

Looks at some studies of depression and the implications of findings for primary-care physicians. Study by Kenneth Wells and his colleagues; findings about the relation between depression and disability; the tendency of some primary-care patients to somatize their emotional distress; physicians who unwittingly collude with patients in ignoring psychiatric problems; why patients with psychiatric disorders should be treated by mental health specialists; more.

Holden, C., "Open season on depression," *Science*, May 22, 1992, p. 1137.

Announces the launching of a new project on depression. Nationwide screening program; started by Douglas Jacobs, a Harvard psychiatrist; pilot program; plans and hopes for the future.

Perry, P. & M. J. Scholz, "Helping a patient cope with pain-related depression," *RN*, April 1992, p. 111.

Gives advice to health-care professionals on helping a patient cope with pain-related depression. Encourage patient to seek further evaluation; tests that might be considered, including the Beck Depression Inventory; Hamilton Rating Scale for Depression; scores.

Wehr, T. A., "Improvement of depression and triggering of mania by sleep deprivation," *Journal of the American Medical Association*, Jan. 22, 1992, p. 548.

Discusses cases in which sleep depresses mood and sleep deprivation elevates it in certain individuals with mood disorders. Questions about whether sleep manipulations or other biologic mechanisms can be harnessed as routine treatments for depression and mania; case of author William Styron; the paradox of sleep deprivation and depression; case of a 34-year-old man with bipolar (manic-depressive) illness; more.

Back Issues

Great Research on Current Issues Starts Right Here... Recent topics covered by The CQ Researcher are listed below. Issues dated before May 10, 1991, were published under the name of Editorial Research Reports.

MARCH 1991
Acid Rain
Cost of the Gulf War
Reassessing Gun Laws
Future for Man in Space

APRIL 1991
Social Security
Canadian Crisis Over Quebec
California Drought
Electromagnetic Radiation

MAY 1991
School Choice
Racial Quotas
Animal Rights
U.S. and Japan

JUNE 1991
Children and Divorce
Teenage Suicide
Endangered Species
Europe 1992

JULY 1991
Teenagers and Abortion
Soviet Republics Rebel
Mexico's Emergence
Athletes and Drugs

AUGUST 1991
Sexual Harassment
Fetal Tissue Research
Oil Imports
The Palestinians

SEPTEMBER 1991
Police Brutality
Advertising Under Attack
Saving the Forests
Foster Care Crisis

OCTOBER 1991
Pay-Per-View TV
Youth Gangs
Gene Therapy
World Hunger

NOVEMBER 1991
Fast-Food Shake-Up
The Greening of Eastern Europe
Business' Role in Education
Cuba In Crisis

DECEMBER 1991
Retiree Health Benefits
Asian Americans
The Obscenity Debate
The Disabilities Act

JANUARY 1992
Term Limits
Oil Spills
Hunting Controversy
Alternative Medicine

FEBRUARY 1992
Threatened Coastlines
New Era in Asia
Assisted Suicide
Jobs in the '90s

MARCH 1992
Women and Sports
Underage Drinking
Garbage Crisis
Mafia Crackdown

APRIL 1992
Ozone Depletion
Welfare Reform
Politicians and Privacy
Illegal Immigration

MAY 1992
Native Americans
Jobs vs. Environment
Too Many Lawsuits?
Fairness in Salaries

JUNE 1992
Nuclear Proliferation
Food Irradiation
Lead Poisoning
Hard Times for Libraries

JULY 1992
Alternative Energy
Prescription Drug Prices
Alzheimer's Disease
Infant Mortality

AUGUST 1992
The Homeless
Work, Family and Stress
NATO's Changing Role
Marine Mammals vs. Fish

SEPTEMBER 1992
Domestic Partners
Violence in Schools
Public Broadcasting
Women in the Military

Back issues are available for $4.00 (subscribers) or $7.00 (non-subscribers). Quantity discounts apply to orders over ten. To order, call Congressional Quarterly 1-800-432-2250.

Future Topics

▶ *U.S. Auto Industry*

▶ *Apprenticeships*

▶ *Hispanics*

U.S. Auto Industry

Have U.S. automakers turned the corner on quality?

T HE GLOBAL ECONOMIC SLUMP HAS HIT U.S. automakers hard. Fearful about their jobs, many American consumers are in no mood to buy even a utilitarian family car, much less a luxury model that can run $40,000. Consumers in Europe and Japan are also steering clear of auto dealerships. But there are a few bright spots in this otherwise dismal picture. The Big Three U.S. automakers have made big improvements, and buyers have noticed, after more than a decade of shunning Detroit in favor of Japanese products. American consumers who are in a car-buying mood increasingly are buying American. They seem to be coming back to U.S. products to get what they abandoned them for in the 1980s: reliability, selection and price.

C_Q **October 16, 1992 • Volume 2, No. 38 • 881-904**

Formerly Editorial Research Reports

Cover Art: Barbara Sassa-Daniels

CQ Researcher

October 16, 1992
Volume 2, No. 38

Editor
Sandra Stencel

Managing Editor
Thomas J. Colin

Associate Editor
Richard L. Worsnop

Staff Writers
Charles S. Clark
Mary H. Cooper
Rodman D. Griffin

Production Editor
Sarah E. Merritt

Editorial Assistant
Michael M. Taylor

Graphics
Jack Auldridge

Published By
Congressional Quarterly Inc.

Chairman
Andrew Barnes

Vice Chairman
Andrew P. Corty

Editor and Publisher
Neil Skene

Executive Editor
Robert W. Merry

Associate Publisher
John J. Coyle

Editor, EBSCO Publishing
Melissa Kummerer

© 1992 Congressional Quarterly Inc.

The CQ Researcher (ISSN 1056-2036). Formerly Editorial Research Reports. Published weekly (48 times per year, not printed the first Friday of any month with five Fridays) by Congressional Quarterly Inc., 1414 22nd St., N.W., Washington, D.C. 20037. Rates are furnished upon request. Second-class postage paid at Washington, D.C. POSTMASTER: Send address changes to The CQ Researcher, 1414 22nd St., N.W., Washington, D.C. 20037.

U.S. Auto Industry

By Mary H. Cooper

The Issues

Car dealerships across the country are in the doldrums. After a dismal showing in 1991, when they had hoped to benefit from an economic recovery that never materialized, dealers have seen little improvement in 1992.

The cars certainly look good. Sleek, aerodynamic sedans with sculpted headlights and sport-utility vehicles rugged enough to conquer the roughest off-road trail, this year's offerings from Detroit's Big Three seem likely to gain ground in the hot contest with Japanese automakers. Inside, too, the new cars offer many improvements, including simplified instrument panels, anti-lock brakes and driver's-side air bags. And consumers have noticed: Surveys indicate that domestic cars are steadily becoming more reliable.

So why aren't Americans buying? The answer may lie more with the economy than with Detroit. Anxious about job security, consumers aren't making major purchases. This is especially true for pricey new cars, which cost an average of $16,666 for domestic models and $19,000 for imports.

The United States is not alone in suffering from the effects of economic stagnation. Automakers in Europe are facing similar problems. Even the Japanese, who for decades seemed immune to serious economic setbacks, are feeling the pinch. Problems at home, highlighted by the falling Tokyo stock market, pose the most severe challenge in 20 years to Japan's powerful auto industry.

But there are bright spots on this otherwise gloomy horizon. The Big Three U.S. automakers — General Motors, Ford and Chrysler — seem to have learned the lessons the Japanese taught

them in the 1970s and '80s. All three have incorporated major elements of the design, management and production techniques that have helped endear Japanese automotive products to U.S. consumers.

Ford has made the biggest strides in regaining market share from the Japanese, who accounted for 30 percent of all cars sold in the United States through August, unchanged from the same period last year. If current sales trends continue, the Taurus sedan could dethrone the Honda Accord as the best-selling car in America this year, a title it's held for three years.

For now, however, the stylish Taurus is still Detroit's sole contender for the honor. In short, the domestic auto industry — especially General Motors — faces daunting challenges. Whether the Big Three can recapture their position as the world's leading producers of quality vehicles will depend on several factors.

Here are two key questions being asked about the future of the U.S. auto industry:

Have American cars finally caught up with the competition?

Detroit has indeed come a long way in bridging the quality gap that separated U.S. products and imports from Europe and Japan. In the 1970s and early '80s, years of successive energy crises, Japanese automakers won over American consumers by producing economical, fuel-efficient cars while Detroit was slow to shift away from its traditional gas-guzzlers.

In the 1980s, when U.S. demand shifted back toward more luxurious cars — a segment the Big Three had long dominated — Japanese and European carmakers again gained ground by coupling comfort with better reliability. [1] U.S. carmakers suffered the ultimate humiliation in 1989, when Japan's Accord became the best-selling car in America. It was the first time an import had occupied that coveted position, and Detroit has been trying ever since to win it back.

Today, competition in the U.S. auto market is, if anything, even tougher. "Customers are much more demanding and much more knowledgeable than ever before," says Maryann N. Keller, a leading auto industry analyst and managing director of Furman Selz Mager Dietz & Birney, a New York consulting firm. "Cars are so expensive that people do a lot more shopping before they buy."

Nonetheless, Detroit automakers are staging something of a comeback in the U.S. as design changes and years of restructuring begin to pay off. Although the Taurus sedan has undergone only superficial redesign since its introduction in 1986, it and the similar Mercury Sable have drawn kudos for their reliability and easy handling as well as their design.

Ford is not alone in recapturing American customers. Chrysler Corp., the smallest U.S. automaker, has carved out segments in the domestic

Economic Stagnation Slows Car Sales

Lingering economic stagnation has put a damper on U.S. auto sales of foreign and domestic cars. Among U.S. carmakers, Ford has made the strongest gains in closing the gap with Japanese producers.

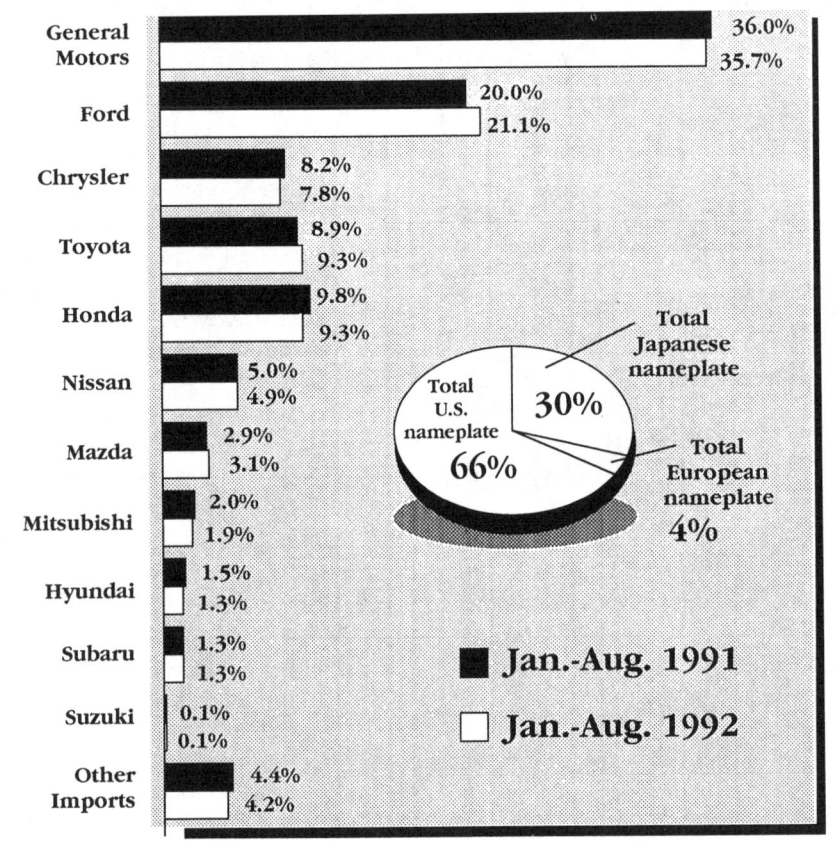

	Jan.-Aug. 1991	Jan.-Aug. 1992
General Motors	36.0%	35.7%
Ford	20.0%	21.1%
Chrysler	8.2%	7.8%
Toyota	8.9%	9.3%
Honda	9.8%	9.3%
Nissan	5.0%	4.9%
Mazda	2.9%	3.1%
Mitsubishi	2.0%	1.9%
Hyundai	1.5%	1.3%
Subaru	1.3%	1.3%
Suzuki	0.1%	0.1%
Other Imports	4.4%	4.2%

Total U.S. nameplate 66%

Total Japanese nameplate 30%

Total European nameplate 4%

Source: The Wall Street Journal, *Sept. 4, 1992.*

auto market beyond the traditional sedan. In 1983, Chrysler combined the commercial van and the family sedan to create the immensely successful minivan.

Considering that some 900,000 minivans were sold last year, Chrysler's leadership in this segment of the market is a significant asset to the company. Ford also has recently made strong inroads into the sport-utility market with its Explorer.

Chrysler is counting on expanding its share of the basic family-sedan market with its new LH series. Early reports from auto analysts have been positive about the series, whose "cab-forward" design expands interior room. "It's priced quite high, and I'm not sure that it's significantly better than the Taurus and Sable," Keller says. "But it is a significantly better car than the General Motors offerings in the midsize segment."

Some analysts expect the LH series to challenge both Taurus and Honda for the top spot. "They are very impressive," says Harley Shaiken, an auto industry expert and professor of work and technology at the Universi-

ty of California at San Diego. "They are not the kind of break that the first Taurus represented, with its very distinctly different style, but in a way the LH cars may be the next generation Taurus."

General Motors, the only one of the Big Three still losing money, continues to suffer from management errors of the past decade — principally failing to restructure its operations to become more efficient. But GM still dominates the U.S. market, accounting for almost 36 percent of car sales in the first eight months of the year. The company's Saturn, introduced in 1990, is also a recognized challenger to foreign compacts. Produced using Japanese quality-control techniques, the Saturn enjoys high ratings for reliability and customer satisfaction. *(See chart, p. 894.)*

Have American cars in general caught up with the Japanese offerings in terms of quality? "Not quite," Keller says. "But they are getting better."

Is the Japanese auto industry as much of a threat to the U.S. industry as before?

In the 1970s and '80s, Japanese automakers seemed impervious to setbacks. While repeated energy crises devastated Detroit, they were a godsend to Japanese producers, who already were making the energy-efficient, inexpensive cars U.S. consumers suddenly wanted.

But Japan's success was hardly a matter of luck. For decades, the country's automakers sought to incorporate the best features of American mass production in making hassle-free cars. Now, however, Japanese automakers finally are showing signs of vulnerability. After wrenching reorganization efforts, Detroit is re-emerging as a contender. Some of its new cars are already challenging the Japanese, and even better products can be expected in the future.

A second strike against the Japanese is the worldwide economic slump. Indeed, Japanese automakers are not only having trouble selling cars in Europe and the United States; consumers at home haven't been able to take up the slack. Compounding their problems, the recent slide in the Tokyo stock market has raised the cost of capital at a time when most Japanese automakers are paying for ambitious investments in new plants and equipment.

Finally, Detroit's improving reliability is creating a new breed of American consumer: the "crossover," someone who trades in an import for an American model. "By the end of the 1980s and early '90s," Shaiken says, "people still bought American cars in large numbers, but there was a lingering, generalized feeling that the Japanese were simply the standard. Now, I think that's been a little tarnished, and the increases in quality of U.S.-built cars and a host of new models have given the industry a major opening."

Japanese carmakers also slipped in the U.S. market by failing to respond quickly to changing consumer demands. The booming minivan and sport-utility market is thin on Japanese offerings. And while the luxury field is dominated by the Japanese nameplates — Acura, Lexus and Infiniti — especially in terms of customer satisfaction, there are few new Japanese models closer to the middle of the passenger car market. And Nissan's brand-new Altima sedan has not received the acclaim of Chrysler's LH series, with which it will compete.

Despite such problems, Japanese automakers are hardly standing still. The leading producers are undergoing a restructuring process of their own in an attempt to improve profitability and compensate for labor shortages caused by a rapidly aging population. Although little is yet known about the precise steps they will take, several carmakers have revealed that they will reduce the number of models offered each year, stretch out the period between model changeovers and rely more heavily on automation.

"The Japanese industry is going through a period of important and rather far-reaching changes," says Shaiken, who spent the summer in Japan studying its auto industry. "A new generation of plants that have come on line in the last year or so in many of the major companies are extremely impressive. They are very flexible, highly automated and productive. But they have labor-force problems they are going to have to deal with in the 1990s."

The Japanese industry's restructuring may cause a shakeout that could leave some of the smaller automakers out of the passenger-car business. "I think it's a fair guess as to whether they are facing severe difficulties that they're having trouble working their way out of or if they're on their way to some next stage or level of competitiveness," says Michael S. Flynn, associate director of the University of Michigan's Office for the Study of Automotive Transportation. "I don't think anyone will know that for a few more years." ■

BACKGROUND

Japan Speeds Ahead

Until the late 1970s, Detroit had little competition in the global auto market. The Big Three dominated the U.S. market and also were a major force in Western Europe, both through exports and sales of U.S. cars assembled in Europe. Even as late as 1978, in the midst of an energy crisis, the Big Three held more than 82 percent of the U.S. market.

That year, however, Japanese automakers claimed 12 percent of the U.S. market — about twice the share of the European producers, who for many years had provided virtually the only competition to Detroit in the United States. By 1982, the Japanese were selling nearly 2 million cars in the United States and had strengthened their market share to 23 percent, more than four times that of the European automakers; the U.S. share, meanwhile, had dropped below 75 percent.

Initially, better fuel economy led American consumers to abandon their gas-guzzling American behemoths for the no-frills, energy-efficient "econoboxes" made by Toyota, Datsun, Honda and other Japanese companies. They soon discovered a hidden benefit: Japanese cars were generally more reliable and held their value longer than domestic cars.

Such superior products catapulted Japanese automakers' share of world motor-vehicle production from less than 1 percent in 1955 to more than 25 percent by 1980.

Japanese automakers produced superior automobiles through a revolutionary way of designing, manufacturing and assembling cars. Known today as "lean production," the Japanese system was based on the mass-production techniques developed by Henry Ford and GM's legendary Alfred Sloan. But the Japanese — led by Toyota production guru Taiichi Ohno — improved on that system to produce cars with far fewer defects.

Essentially, the Japanese deeply involved their workers in the manufacturing process, organizing them into teams responsible for stopping the assembly line whenever a defect was discovered and finding — and eliminating — its cause. With fewer defects, Japanese cars needed fewer costly fixes at the end of the assembly line and, most importantly, after they were sold. "The whole foundation of lean production is no defects — otherwise it doesn't work," says Maryann Keller. "But lean production is far more than that. You have to design a car so that it can be produced with a minimum number of people."

The Japanese also developed the space-saving "just-in-time" inventory system, in which only the parts needed for a given production run are stored in the factory. "Lean production ... is 'lean' because it uses less of everything compared with mass production — half the human effort in the factory, half the manufacturing space, half the investment in tools, half the engineering hours to develop a new product in half the time," wrote James P. Womack and his coworkers at the Massachusetts Institute of Technology's International Motor Vehicle Program.[2]

Detroit Finally Reacts

With its near monopoly of the booming domestic car market, Detroit was slow to react to the Japanese onslaught. As sales of Japanese cars mounted, Chrysler, the smallest of the Big Three automakers, was pulled back from the brink of bankruptcy by a federally guaranteed bailout in 1980 (see page 889). Although Chrysler suffered periodic financial crises throughout the 1980s, it managed to improve its product lines and market share.

Ford also suffered an early setback but moved quickly to learn the secrets of Japanese production. In 1979, Ford purchased 24 percent of Mazda, gaining a firsthand look at lean production. After 1982, when Ford's very survival was in question, the company spent the rest of the decade steadily incorporating new manufacturing elements into its domestic and overseas plants. One result of Ford's efforts was the extremely popular Taurus, introduced in 1986.

General Motors, the biggest of the Big Three, was the slowest to change.

In 1984, GM and Toyota entered into a joint venture to produce Toyota-designed cars for sale in the United States at a Toyota-managed GM factory in Fremont, Calif. Once the New United Motor Manufacturing Inc. (NUMMI) plant reached peak operations in 1987, it turned out cars one-and-a-half-times faster than a traditional GM plant in Massachusetts — with a third of the defects.[3]

But the NUMMI plant was the exception, as GM failed to incorporate the principles of lean production throughout the rest of its vast operations (see page 890). GM's widely publicized effort to reorganize its five divisions — Buick, Cadillac, Chevrolet, Oldsmobile and Pontiac — in the 1980s failed to make the company more efficient. Despite its status as the world's largest corporation, GM by the end of the 1980s was finally faced with the need to radically over-

---

Flexible production systems, which permit different models to be produced on the same assembly line, enabled Japanese automakers to offer an unprecedented array of models and options. The Big Three, and to a lesser extent European carmakers, have tried to follow suit. The result is a plethora of choices within a given model type affecting everything from engine size to safety features.

---

haul its operations.

Meanwhile, the 1980s posed new challenges to Japanese automakers. In response to a 1981 voluntary restraint agreement with the United States — capping at 2 million the number of cars, vans and station wagons they could export to this country — Japanese producers began setting up "transplant" facilities in the United States. In addition to its venture with GM in California, Toyota opened a wholly owned facility in Kentucky, Honda opened a plant in Ohio and Nissan set up operations in Tennessee. Assembling cars in these plants with American workers — most of them non-union — helped the Japanese skirt the import restrictions.

Global Market of the 1990s

Today's auto market is much changed from the days before Japanese automakers came on the scene. For one thing, there are far more choices. Flexible production systems, which permit different models to be produced on the same assembly line, enabled Japanese automakers to offer an unprecedented array of models and options. The Big Three, and to a lesser extent European carmakers, have tried to follow suit. The result is a plethora of choices within a given model type affecting everything from engine size to safety features. (See story, p. 896.)

Another change is higher prices. Once the first choice of bargain-hunters, Japanese imports rapidly increased in price after the voluntary restraints went into effect in 1981. Permitted to sell only a limited num-

Continued on p. 888

Chronology

1960s
Domestic automakers continue to dominate the U.S. market despite early signs of interest in Japanese imports.

1966
Toyota introduces the Corolla, which becomes a best-seller in the U.S.

1969
Nissan, known as Datsun in the United States, introduces the 240Z, the first popular Japanese sports car.

— • —

1970s
Successive oil shocks drive U.S. consumers to fuel-efficient Japanese cars.

1971
Honda develops the CVCC engine, the first in the world to comply with the 1970 Clean Air Act.

1973
After the first oil crisis, Honda's Civic CVCC gains in U.S. popularity.

1975
Nissan replaces Germany's Volkswagen as the leading exporter of cars to the United States.

1979
Ford buys a quarter-interest in Japan's Mazda, which serves as a model for the No. 2 U.S. automaker in its quest to improve product quality.

— • —

1980s
Japan continues to build market share in the United States by meeting consumer demand for quality and luxury.

1980
Pushed toward bankruptcy by its failure to keep up with Japanese competition at the low end of the market, Chrysler is bailed out with a federally guaranteed $1.2 billion loan. Lee A. Iacocca, Chrysler's new chairman, begins a long campaign to redesign the company's products.

1981
Under pressure from the U.S. government, Japan agrees to voluntarily limit car exports to the United States.

1982
Honda begins assembling the popular Accord at its motorcycle plant in Marysville, Ohio. It is the first of several Japanese "transplant" facilities set up to get around auto-export restrictions to the U.S. market.

1983
Chrysler introduces the minivan and continues to dominate this growing segment of the U.S. market. General Motors, the world's biggest corporation, belatedly starts to overhaul its five divisions — Buick, Cadillac, Chevrolet, Oldsmobile and Pontiac.

1984
GM enters into a joint venture with Toyota to build Japanese-designed cars at GM's Toyota-managed plant in Fremont, Calif.

1985
GM launches its Saturn project. The company builds a state-of-the-art plant in Spring Hill, Tenn., and hires United Auto Workers members under an innovative contract that, following the Japanese model, grants more worker participation on the shop floor.

1986
Ford introduces the Taurus, incorporating design changes that help make it the best-selling domestic model. Honda introduces the Acura, cater-ing to growing demand for luxury. Nissan opens a plant in England, the first major Japanese transplant in Europe.

1989
New luxury lines from Japan come on the market with Toyota's Lexus and Nissan's Infiniti. The Honda Accord becomes the best-selling car in the United States. Mazda introduces the popular Miata sports car.

— • —

1990s
Auto sales drop as the decade opens with a worldwide economic slump that hurts even the Japanese automakers.

1990
Struggling General Motors hits a home run with the Saturn compact. Ford enters the sport-utility segment, long dominated by Chrysler's Jeep, with its instantly popular, upscale Explorer.

1991
A lingering recession causes the worst year for the auto industry since 1983. GM announces plans to close 21 plants by 1995, with an expected loss of 74,000 North American jobs.

1992
Detroit gains market share for the first time since 1989, as Ford's Taurus threatens to bump the Honda Accord from the No. 1 spot in U.S. sales.

1993
Contracts between the UAW and the Big Three are up for renewal. Negotiations are expected to focus on GM, whose restructuring will likely eliminate tens of thousands of jobs by the mid-1990s.

Detroit vs. the Imports: U.S. Car Sales

American automakers still far outsell European and Japanese producers, but the gap has narrowed in recent years. During Detroit's 1978 - 1982 sales plunge, Japanese manufacturers made great strides, approaching the two-million mark in sales.

Millions of cars

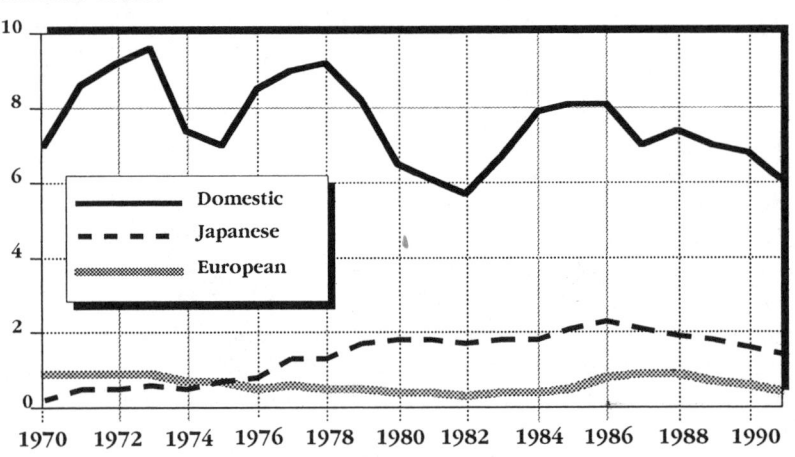

Source: Motor Vehicle Manufacturers Association of the U.S. Inc. (domestic sales); Ward's Automotive Yearbook (import sales).

Continued from p. 886

ber of cars in the United States, Japanese automakers began producing more luxurious models — with higher profit margins — for export. Soon Toyota was offering Camrys along with Corollas, and Honda was exporting pricey Accords and Preludes as well as Civics. With the arrival of Lexus, Acura and Infiniti, "Japanese" by 1990 no longer was synonymous with economical.

Though restrictions to the U.S. market didn't cover European producers, some followed the Japanese strategy. Saab and Volvo, which once made small cars for the economy-minded, began targeting upper-middle-class buyers. Among foreign producers, only the Japanese continue to sell a wide range of cars and small trucks to maintain demand for their products among all U.S. consumers.

As the range of choices — and prices — has grown, so too has consumer savvy. "What makes this mar-

ketplace of the 1990s different is the fact that most people who are buying cars today are repeat customers," says Maryann Keller. In the 1970s, she explains, the baby-boom generation was just coming of age, and many inexperienced buyers were walking into showrooms. "People who buy the first of anything might be dazzled by advertising," Keller says.

"But once you've owned a car for four or five years and you've had to take it back for service, you learn quickly what you want, what's relevant and what isn't. You don't make the same mistakes when you go back to buy a second time. So right now, the auto industry has to deal with a knowledgeable customer base."

Adding to automakers' woes is the current sales slump. Sales of light trucks, including minivans and sport-utility vehicles, have been strong this year, but not strong enough to offset the sag in passenger-car demand. Accounting for two-thirds of all vehicle

sales, cars are the automakers' mainstay. With consumer confidence low, even the hefty rebates many automakers are offering to clear out the 1992 models haven't stemmed the decline in sales. As a result, the companies most able to thrive in today's changed marketplace are not necessarily the ones that looked most promising a decade ago. ∎

CURRENT SITUATION

Detroit Enters the Race

Nearly a century ago, Henry Ford made mass production possible through his invention of the moving assembly line, launching the Model T and the global auto industry in 1913. Today, the company he founded has gone further than the other American automakers to integrate lean-production techniques into the manufacturing process. Ford was also the first American automaker to react to the new competitive challenge from Japan. In 1980, the year Ford posted its first losses in a quarter-century, the company launched its Taurus program, aimed at improving quality using the teamwork principles company executives had observed in Japan.

Ford put together planners, designers, engineers and assembly workers to come up with a completely redesigned vehicle based on the best features of 50 midsize cars from around the world. The company won United Auto Workers (UAW) support by providing special training for the 900 workers on the project in return for flexible job classifications and other union concessions. The company also involved 400 parts suppliers in the project to better assure component quality. Introduced in 1986, the Taurus was an immediate success. The entire model year run sold out within months.[4]

The Taurus owes its success to improved product quality and design — and persuasive marketing spearheaded by the familiar slogan, "At Ford, Quality Is Job 1." "With its six-cylinder, conventional engine, the Taurus wasn't much engineering-wise, especially compared with the multivalve engines of the Japanese," says Harley Shaiken. "Nonetheless, Ford was able to redefine a market through a very effective product."

In addition to its success in the midsize family-sedan market, Ford has scored a huge success with the Explorer, an upscale sport-utility vehicle. Ford also makes the most popular vehicle in the United States — the F-Series full-size pickup truck.

Despite an aggressive marketing program — attractive leasing terms and lucrative dealer incentives to sell the model — analysts predict Ford won't unseat the Honda Accord as America's best-selling car this year. Still, the continued popularity of the Taurus and the look-alike Mercury Sable has helped buoy Ford in today's stagnant auto market. Ford's share of the U.S. car market was 21 percent in the first six months of 1992, up almost a percentage point from all of 1991, thanks mostly to record sales for the Taurus and Sable.

A similar increase in the company's share of the domestic truck market, at 30 percent in the first half of the year, is traced to strong demand for the Explorer as well as for the new full-size Econoline van and Club Wagon. Ford is banking on several new products to further expand sales across the market, including the sporty Ford Probe, the Lincoln Mark VII luxury coupe, the Mercury Villager, a new front-wheel-drive minivan and the redesigned Ford Ranger pickup.

Ford also owes its ability to weather the 1980s to its size and global presence. The fourth-largest industrial corporation in the world and second-largest maker of cars and trucks,

Ford employed 157,000 workers at plants in most of the 50 states, part of a total of 332,700 people in 26 countries at the end of 1991. Ford vehicles, led by the subcompact Ford Fiesta, account for 12 percent of the European auto market. In Britain, where Ford has been the leading auto seller for 15 years, the company controls 24 percent of the market. Even in the Japanese-dominated Far

Harold A. Poling
Chairman of the Board and
Chief Executive Officer
Ford Motor Co.

East, Ford ranked first in total vehicle sales in Taiwan and in car sales in Australia last year.[5]

Ford will not emerge unscathed from the current downturn in auto sales, however. Slow sales have idled company plants in Dearborn, Mich., and Ontario, Canada. And the company is holding average price increases to below 1 percent for the 1993 models to boost sales. But auto analysts say that Ford's quality-improvement campaign and its global presence position it well for the 1990s. "It happens to be in its North American market probably the best marketer, the best developer of trucks and the cleverest company with respect to automobiles in terms

of being able to get good use out of very old products," Keller says. "Overall, Ford is certainly one of the strongest, if not the strongest, auto company in the world," she adds. "And it's not because Ford has beaten up on the Japanese. It's because Ford got better by itself."

Chrysler: Back From the Brink

Led by its flamboyant chairman, Lee A. Iacocca, Chrysler also regained the ground it lost in the late 1970s to Japanese competition. By 1984, the company had repaid the $1.2 billion in loans used to bail it out three years earlier and had raised more than $1 billion more on its own to redesign its entire product line.

Like its counterparts in Detroit, Chrysler forged a strategic alliance with a Japanese firm, in this case Mitsubishi, which it used as a model for incorporating lean-production techniques and expanding its product offerings. But Chrysler is much smaller than Ford or GM, accounting for just 12 percent of the U.S. auto market in 1991, and lacks a global presence. It has only one small overseas plant, a joint venture in Austria that assembles vans for the European market.

The slump in sales in 1991 — the worst year for the industry since 1983 — hit Chrysler hard. In an effort to staunch the red ink, the company sold its 50 percent interest in the joint venture with Mitsubishi, Diamond-Star Motors Corp. Even so, its net loss totaled $795 million for the year. Chrysler's financial troubles peaked again this summer, when several banks in an international consortium initially refused to renew their loans to the automaker, threatening a new $6.8 billion package Chrysler needs to continue its three-year-old restructuring program. The crisis passed in August when the lenders agreed to renew the deal. "Chrysler has been very strapped for cash," says Michael Flynn. "But the company has a new line of very attractive vehicles, and it looks like it has survived its latest financial brush with death."

Lee A. Iacocca
Chairman
Chrysler Corp.

Chrysler's ability to survive at all over the past decade is due largely to its success in producing innovative vehicles to meet changing consumer demand. In 1983, Chrysler produced the first minivan, carving out a new market segment that it has dominated ever since, largely with the popular Plymouth Voyager and Dodge Caravan. Chrysler Jeeps, which pioneered the sport-utility segment, remain leaders in that category. Chrysler has quickly answered new challenges to Jeep's leadership, such as the Ford Explorer, with a new upscale model, the Jeep Grand Cherokee.

Chrysler's performance in the passenger-car market has been less successful, and the company has been hounded by persistent quality problems. Its ability to make headway in this key segment is riding heavily on the new LH series, the company's first new passenger car in a decade. All four models — the Dodge Intrepid, Eagle Vision, Chrysler Concorde and Chrysler New Yorker, due out early next year — have innovative cab-forward design, which expands interior space and improves aerodynamics. Although the cars were recalled shortly after they were introduced to fix a faulty steering

component, they have received glowing reviews from the automotive press. *AutoWeek* magazine, for example, awarded the LH series its "best in show" title at the 1992 North American International Auto Show in Detroit.

But the LH cars are an exception to Chrysler's tactics under Iacocca. "One of Chrysler's strategies has been to avoid the Japanese, so that its products are essentially not in competition anywhere with them," Keller says. "The Japanese don't have minivans to speak of, they're not really in the sport-utility vehicle market and, while they are in the midsize car market with the Honda Accord and the Toyota Camry, it's a market that had opportunities for Chrysler."

Chrysler faces an important transition at the end of this year, when Iacocca is due to retire. He is to be succeeded by Robert J. Eaton, whose promotion Iacocca supports. But at the same time, the outspoken Iacocca reportedly is displeased with the board of directors' decision to limit his own post-retirement role in the company. Unless it is resolved, the succession issue could further complicate Eaton's already tough job steering Chrysler through its financial problems.

General Motors' Growing Pains

General Motors, the biggest of the Big Three, has been the slowest to adapt to the competitive challenges of the past decade. Unlike Ford and Chrysler, GM didn't respond quickly to the loss of market share to Japanese imports. As a result, says Michael Flynn, "Today, GM is more like Ford and Chrysler were in 1982 in terms of competitive realities." It is the only one of the Big Three that has not returned to profitability in North America, and its share of the passenger-car market in August sank to 30.9 percent, down from 32 percent the year before — GM's poorest showing since the 1930s. Indeed, GM lost $7 billion last year in its North American operations.

One reason for the delayed re-

sponse lies with GM's domestic dominance. Because it was the leading carmaker, controlling almost half the market in the early 1980s, GM had a big cushion against falling sales and could remain profitable longer than its two domestic rivals. Even though the company lost $1 billion in 1982, it remained the world's largest company and had little debt to weaken its financial position. "Ford and Chrysler were hit by Japanese imports in the 1970s and lost serious market share," says Flynn. "General Motors didn't really lose that much until the early 1980s."

But management's misreading of market trends also slowed GM's ability to change. When Japanese imports cut into the American market, the company's response was to stop making cars in market segments with Japanese competition, not to become a lean producer like its domestic rivals. Even its successful joint venture with Toyota in California seemed to be lost on GM's management as a viable model for change. "Since GM didn't face a crisis in the 1980s and failed to find any opportunities for growth, it was simply not able to face up to the challenge," noted MIT's Womack and his colleagues.[6]

Robert C. Stempel
Chairman
General Motors

Another major obstacle to GM's ability to change was its organizational structure. Each of the company's five automotive divisions was vertically organized, with separate operations from design through assembly. Until the mid-1970s, this structure had worked well. By the 1980s, however, GM had become a top-heavy, management-laden company insensitive to changing customer demands. "GM was making decisions like it made autos, with even the smallest queries having to travel from office to office, through layers of bureaucracy, before a decision was made," wrote Mark Potts and Peter Behr. "It was a system that buried innovation and penalized those who bucked the status quo." [7]

In 1983, two years after becoming GM chairman, Roger B. Smith launched the first major company reorganization in more than half a century. The plan was to consolidate GM into two groups, one combining Buick, Oldsmobile and Cadillac, the other joining Chevrolet, Pontiac and GM of Canada. But the vast reorganization failed to eliminate the company's vertical integration or to produce the quality and design innovations of its domestic competitors. By the mid-1980s, the company had lost 13 points of market share. "That was a period when GM was accused of having look-alike cars and pricing their cars too high," says Michael Flynn.

Stempel Tries to Cut Costs

With its market share still dwindling, GM has embarked on a new reorganization plan. Last December, Robert C. Stempel, who succeeded Smith in 1990, announced plans to close 21 plants by 1995, with an expected loss of 74,000 North American jobs. A key objective of the restructuring is cutting the high cost of components made by company-owned suppliers. GM recently decided to put all components out to bid, or "outsource" them, whenever outside suppliers would charge less.

To GM's dismay, Stempel's cost-cutting effort backfired. When the giant automaker announced it would eliminate 240 union jobs at a tool and die shop in Lordstown, Ohio, members of the union at the neighboring metal-stamping plant went on strike. Because GM's Saturn plant in Tennessee depended on shipments from the Lordstown stamping plant, production of the company's best-seller abruptly stopped. Before a compromise was reached nine days later, nine more plants were idled; the delay cost GM some $70 million. [8]

"Once the strike began, the leverage of the Lordstown plant was considerable," says Harley Shaiken. "Then the regional and national leaders of the UAW sought to use that to essentially send a very clear message to GM that certain kinds of downsizing were going to cause trouble with the union."

GM's outside directors reportedly have warned Stempel to stand up to the UAW and hasten the downsizing or risk losing his job. [9]

The only really bright spot on GM's horizon today is the Saturn. In 1985, GM launched its Saturn project, aimed at producing a new small car from the ground up, outside GM's existing organization. The company built a new plant, in Spring Hill, Tenn., equipped it with state-of-the-art equipment and hired UAW workers under an innovative contract that gave workers more voice in production decisions. Seven years later, the Saturn plant is widely

The Best-Selling Cars in America for 1991

For the third year in a row, Honda's Accord won the title, but industry experts say Taurus is a contender this year. Several cars made the list despite less-than-glowing reliability ratings.

Model	Type	Where Made	*Consumer Reports'* Reliability Rating
1. Honda Accord	Compact	U.S. and Japan	Much better than average
2. Ford Taurus	Mid-size	U.S.	Average
3. Toyota Camry	Mid-size	U.S. and Japan	Much better than average
4. Chevrolet Cavalier	Compact	U.S.	Worse than average
5. Ford Escort	Small	U.S.	Worse than average
6. Chevrolet Corsica/ Beretta	Compact	U.S.	Worse than average
7. Chevrolet Lumina	Mid-size	U.S.	Worse than average
8. Honda Civic	Small	U.S. and Japan	Much better than average
9. Toyota Corolla	Small	U.S. and Japan	Much better than average
10. Ford Tempo	Compact	U.S.	Much worse than average

Sales are for calendar year 1991, including models from both the 1991 and 1992 model years. U.S. includes cars produced in the United States, Canada and Mexico.

Sources: Motor Vehicle Manufacturers Association of the United States Inc.; Consumer Reports, April 1992.

Honda Accord
Best-selling car in America for the last three years, it faces a strong challenge from Ford's Taurus.

Plymouth Voyager LX AWD
Chrysler produced the first minivan in 1983 and has dominated the field with the Voyager and Dodge Caravan.

Ford Taurus LX
Introduced in 1986, the hugely popular mid-range car earned its success with improved quality and design.

admired as the one place where GM, the industry laggard, competes with the best of them. "It works extremely well," says Shaiken. "Saturn does what the popular perception of the Japanese approach is, but which does not really exist even in Japan. Our perception of Japan exists in reality at Saturn, not in Japan."

Today, the Saturn has placed GM squarely back into the running in the small-car market, which it had abandoned in the mid-1980s. After only two years, Saturn ranks high in customer-satisfaction ratings and this year may even outsell both the Toyota Corolla and Honda Civic, perennial low-end favorites.

GM broke precedent among domestic automakers in setting a non-negotiable sticker price for the Saturn. This haggle-free approach has been so well-received by customers that other producers are trying it.

GM is taking several steps to improve its sales in North America. Other models are now receiving praise, including Cadillac and the Buick Electra. The company also reduced prices on several 1993 models to boost sales. In September, GM issued a new credit card that enables users to get rebates toward the purchase of most GM cars and trucks equal to 5 percent of purchases. A consumer using the card to buy $1,000 worth of clothes, for example, gets a $50 credit on a new GM vehicle.

Despite its varied attempts to regain market share, comments Shaiken, "there is a general sense of floundering in the company." Maryann Keller blames the automotive giant's managers. "General Motors' management for the last 10 years allowed a steady deterioration in every aspect of competitiveness," she says. "It is the high-cost producer, and it's making cars that the public doesn't want to buy." Today, Keller adds, "General Motors cannot be deemed to be competitive against either Ford or Chrysler — you don't even have to consider the Japanese because that just complicates the issue."

Japan Feels the Pinch

After revolutionizing the U.S. auto market during the 1980s and forcing its Detroit competitors to restructure, Japanese automakers are finally showing signs of vulnerability. All but one of the five major Japanese companies that sell cars and trucks in this country are losing money here — as much as $4 billion last year alone. The losses seem likely to mount, as Japanese companies have lost 1.4 percent of market share so far this year. [10]

One reason for the Japanese carmakers' setback in the U.S. market has been their failure to keep up with consumers' fickle tastes. For more than a decade, Japanese producers kept one step ahead of demand, offering small economical cars when Americans faced energy shortages and later a wider range of cars, including luxury models, as the energy crises passed. Honda, for example, made its debut in the American market in the early 1970s with its tiny N600, followed by the subcompact Civic. By 1980, it had also introduced the larger Accord and the sporty Prelude. In

1986, Honda created a new division, Acura, to produce luxury cars.

A similar pattern has been followed by other Japanese producers. Like Honda, all debuted in this country with small sedans such as the Toyota Corolla and the Datsun 510 (as Nissan marketed its vehicles before the early 1980s). And like Honda, two of them later established new divisions — Toyota's Lexus and Nissan's Infiniti — to meet the growing U.S. demand for luxury cars. Smaller Japanese companies, Mazda and Mitsubishi, also introduced luxury models in the late 1980s.

But in the last few years the Japanese automakers seem to have lost their edge. "Not all Japanese cars launched in the last few years have been successful," Keller says. It's not that the upscale imports have failed to catch on. Acura, Lexus and Infiniti are among the highest-ranking cars on the market among consumers who can afford their $20,000-plus prices. And the Accord appears likely to chalk up its fourth straight year as America's best-selling car.

Where the Japanese producers are slipping is in the emerging-market segments. It is mainly Chrysler and Ford that have taken the initiative in the booming minivan and sport-utility segments. Japanese models of both types are available, notably the Toyota Previa minivan and Nissan Pathfinder utility vehicle, but they are far behind Detroit's offerings in sales.

One reason for the Japanese slowdown is the rise in value of the yen, which reached a record high in September. As Japan's currency appreciates, so too does the price of Japanese automobiles and other products. As a result, American consumers are finding Japanese imports less of a good buy than they have in the past, especially since Detroit has steadily improved the quality of its own products.

The Japanese carmakers are also hurting at home, where an economic downturn has dampened demand for vehicles. The downturn has made Japanese banks more skittish in their lending policies at a time when most Japanese automakers are seeking financing for major restructurings, necessitated by the shortage of labor. Says Keller, "The Japanese right now are being forced to put in automation where they'd rather have a human being, but they don't have the human being or the human being is now 55 years old and therefore is much less capable of carrying out strenuous work than he could have done 25 years ago. So in many cases the automation does not enhance productivity."

The crunch has come at an especially bad time for Japan's automakers, who for several years have been building new transplant facilities in the United States and Europe in an effort to bypass current or anticipated restrictions on Japanese imports. "My own belief is that they're exhausted, that their capital resources and human resources have been really stretched the last few years by the significant expansion in North America," says Michael Flynn.

Japanese producers also are grappling with the breakdown of their legendary supply networks, or *keiretsu*. Each keiretsu consists of several companies that supply components and services to others in the group and also have part ownership in them. For years, Japan's critics

Chrysler Concorde
One of four models in the well-received
LH series, it features innovative,
space-saving cab-forward design.

Ford Explorer
Success with this upscale sport-utility
vehicle helped earn Ford a big presence
in the domestic truck market.

General Motors Saturn SL 2
Non-negotiable sticker price and high
customer satisfaction put GM back in
the small-car race.

Top Models in Customer Satisfaction — 1991

Money talks when it comes to auto reliability, according to a poll of 34,000 car owners. Only three of the 11 models on the list — the Saturn sedan and coupe and the Honda Civic — cost less than $25,000. Respondents based their assessments mainly on their cars' repair and reliability records. Led by luxury nameplates Lexus and Infiniti, Japan leads the pack in customer satisfaction. But a hopeful sign for Detroit is the high ranking of GM's Saturn, which claimed the only two places for domestic models. Mercedes Benz is the sole European carmaker on the list.

Model Ranking		Base Prices
1.	Lexus LS 400	$46,000
2.	Lexus ES 300 (formerly the ES 250)	$27,500 - $28,400
3.	Infiniti Q45	$45,400
4.	Infiniti G20	$19,500
5.	Saturn Sedan	$9,195 - $11,495
6.	Infiniti J30 (formerly the M30)	$34,000
7.	Acura NSX	$63,000 - $67,000
8.	Mercedes Benz 190 (tie)	$28,950 - $34,900
	Saturn Coupe	$10,995 - $12,795
10.	Honda Civic (tie)	$8,400 - $15,850
	Toyota Cressida	$24,428

Base prices given are for the 1993 models, except for the Acura and Cressida, which are 1992 prices.

Source: J. D. Power and Associates (rankings).

have pointed to these tightly knit relationships between automakers and suppliers as a key to their strength, and a barrier to U.S. parts companies seeking access to the lucrative Japanese market. But today, Keller says, "keiretsu is a penalty, an enormous cost burden, especially for the smaller Japanese auto companies."

Isuzu, for example, is bogged down by inefficient, undercapitalized suppliers that are "dependent on Isuzu for just about everything." Except for Toyota, which encouraged its suppliers to seek business outside Toyota, Keller says Japanese automakers "can no longer afford to support their parts suppliers. The Japanese right now want to break down this system."

Japanese Forced to Change

The combination of all these problems is forcing the Japanese to change the way they produce cars.

"The Japanese are in a period of transition, not a crisis, but a far-reaching transition," says Harley Shaiken. Signs of change include the lack of automotive breakthroughs that U.S. consumers have come to expect from Japan, as well as a gradual decrease in the number of different models offered by each nameplate and a slowing down of the model cycle. Over the longer term, Shaiken predicts, the Japanese industry will undergo a shakeout. Suzuki, he says, is already feeling the pinch, while Isuzu may leave the passenger car business and make only trucks. "The smaller producers are getting hammered," Shaiken says.

A shakeout is likely to leave Japan's leading exporters — Toyota, Nissan and Honda — with a stronger grip on the global market than before. But here, too, much depends on how each company weathers the

current setback. Nissan, which expects to lose money for the first time since 1951, is banking on a strong U.S. showing of its new Altima sedan, built in Nissan's Smyrna, Tenn., assembly plant.

The luxury divisions of the three big Japanese carmakers also may face rough times in the U.S. market. Although Acura, Lexus and Infiniti all receive among the highest customer-satisfaction ratings, their high prices limit sales in this depressed market. Acura, for example, just raised prices for its 1993 models by between 2.5 and 4.2 percent, pushing the base price of its Legend sedan from $28,000 to $29,200. Lexus has raised its prices by as much as 6.1 percent. The base price of the 1993 Lexus SC300 sports coupe is $34,700, up $2,000 from last year's model.[11]

The high value of the yen is also forcing the Japanese producers to hike prices on more basic models at a time when domestic automakers are holding the line on many models. The base price of the redesigned 1993 Toyota Corolla stands at $11,198, up 19 percent from last year and more than its U.S. competitors, such as the Saturn sedan and Ford Escort (The base price for the cheapest Saturn model, the manual transmission SL, is $9,190, up from $8,395 in 1992; most of the increase is attributed to the addition of a driver's-side air bag. The base price for the cheapest Escort is $8,355, virtually unchanged from 1992.)[12]

European Shakeout

Like their counterparts in North America and Japan, European consumers are avoiding auto showrooms. Car sales in Europe fell 15 percent in July from the same period in 1991. The plunge was especially steep in Britain, whose auto industry has been declining for years. Sales are even flat in Germany, the continent's biggest car market. In addition to persistent economic stagnation throughout the continent, Europe faces an uncertain political future. French voters last month narrowly approved the Maastricht Treaty, which calls for greater monetary and political cooperation among the 12 members of the European Community. But support for European unification has waned in recent months, and ambivalence over the issue has dampened economic activity.

Even before the most recent turn in Europe's road to unification, far-reaching changes were jeopardizing many famous European automobile nameplates. Long subsidized and protected by import restrictions, several large automakers, including Fiat of Italy, Renault of France and Britain's Rover, face mounting competition. The European Community's program to eliminate trade barriers among its members means that such "national champions" will no longer enjoy protection from foreign imports.

Some European carmakers are better prepared to weather the changing market conditions. Germany's Volkswagen enjoys considerable market share throughout the United States and much of Europe. Makers of luxury cars, such as BMW, Volvo and Daimler-Benz — producer of the Mercedes Benz — also have weathered Europe's rapidly changing economic conditions by concentrating their efforts on luxury cars, largely for export.

All the European producers, however, face a formidable challenge from Japanese automakers, which for years were virtually closed out of the European market by strict import limits. In the late 1980s, Japanese companies began to overcome the barriers in much the same way they did in the more penetrable U.S. market. Led by Nissan, which set up a transplant operation in England, Japanese carmakers have begun to establish production facilities on the continent to meet the local-content rules that limit the number of finished cars they are allowed to export to Europe. ■

OUTLOOK

Political Realities

The rapidly changing global market for automobiles holds news both good and bad for U.S. automakers. Stagnant economic conditions are making it hard for Detroit to sell its products at home and abroad. At the same time, the Big Three in general have the strongest lineup in years and face somewhat weaker competition from their foreign rivals than at any time in the past decade.

But political developments in the United States may pose daunting challenges to the domestic automakers. The proposed North American Free Trade Agreement (NAFTA) has raised fears that U.S. automakers will relocate many of their operations to Mexico, where wages are much lower. (*See "At Issue," p. 897.*) The agreement, which would create a free-trade area embracing the United States, Canada and Mexico, would immediately eliminate tariffs on cars assembled in Mexico and remove tariffs on light trucks and auto parts within five years of ratification.*

Although Bush administration officials insist that the trade agreement

---

*Under rules for free-trade agreements, the president, in consultation with Congress, drafts legislation that puts the agreement in force. Once the legislation is submitted to Congress, both houses will vote whether to accept or reject it as it is written; they cannot amend the legislation. Each house has 90 congressional working days to act on the measure.

will help U.S. industry and workers by boosting overall trade among the three countries of North America, critics say it will further erode the industry. Arkansas Gov. Bill Clinton, the Democratic presidential candidate, has endorsed NAFTA but calls for greater protection for U.S. workers. Meanwhile, House Majority Leader Richard A. Gephardt, D-Mo., led an offensive by congressional Democrats who called on President Bush to either renegotiate the treaty or leave it to "the next administration" to do so. [13]

If NAFTA survives the ratification process, auto analysts agree that the agreement's impact on industry jobs will depend to a large degree on how the Big Three use it. "If they simply go to Mexico to chase cheap labor, we're going to lose a lot of jobs," says Michael Flynn. "If they try to integrate Mexico into a three-country strategy, then there's hope."

In Keller's view, however, conditions in Mexico limit Detroit's ability to shift parts production and car assembly south of the border. "I don't think that Mexico is going to be able to handle a flood of investment very quickly," she says. "The roads are horrific, the electricity is not always assured, and there is very high employee turnover in most of the parts plants that are already there."

The U.S. auto industry and related businesses employ some 13 million people, accounting for about 1 in 10 jobs in the country. With the presidential election only weeks away, both President Bush and Gov. Clinton have campaigned heavily in Detroit and other parts of the Midwest that rely heavily on the auto industry. Both Bush and Vice President Dan Quayle charged that Clinton's support for higher fuel-economy standards would result in a massive loss of jobs in the region. Clinton and his running mate, Sen. Al Gore, D-Tenn., have called for raising Corporate Average Fuel Economy, or CAFE, standards to 40 miles per gallon by 2000

How Automakers Are Building Safer Cars

It's safer than ever to sit behind the wheel of a new car. The number of motor vehicle traffic deaths in the United States fell from 54,633 in 1970 to 46,800 in 1990, even as the number of vehicles on the road multiplied. By 1990, the death rate per 100 million vehicle miles — a more exact measurement of vehicle safety — was 2.3, down from 3.5 a decade earlier.†

While stiffer penalties for drunken drivers have contributed to the falling death rate, it's clear that many lives have also been saved by safety features that help drivers avoid accidents and survive crashes.

The federal government began regulating auto safety in 1966, when Congress passed the National Traffic and Motor Vehicle Safety Act. The law required that beginning in the 1968 model year, cars had to be equipped with seat belts, padded instrument panels and shatter-resistant windshields. The law also set up the National Highway and Traffic Safety Administration, which has steadily expanded required safety features.

The latest additions are anti-lock brakes and air bags. Anti-lock brakes rely on special sensors in each wheel to detect road-surface conditions and transfer this information to the car's computer. When the driver slams on the brakes, the computer tells the brake on each individual wheel how to respond, thereby reducing or eliminating skidding.

Installed in the steering column and the passenger-side dashboard, air bags inflate upon impact, preventing contact with the windshield. Although air bags were tested in the early 1950s and ready for use by the 1970s, automakers resisted government regulations requiring air bags for two decades. It was not until the 1990 model year that all new cars had to be equipped with either automatic seat belts or driver's-side air bags.

Just over half the 1992 model cars that were sold in the first half of this year had air bags, according to the Highway Loss Data Institute, up from only a third of last year's models. "This is the first time in the more than 20 years that the air bag's efficacy has been known that a majority of new cars had them installed, at least on the driver's side," says Chuck Hurley, a senior vice president at the institute, a research organization supported by the insurance industry. The group predicts that two-thirds of the 1993 models will be equipped with air bags on the driver's side.

Despite the proven efficacy of air bags, they cannot be found everywhere. General Motors, which pledged to install air bags in all of its cars by 1975, today has them in only 38.3 percent of its lineup and is the only domestic automaker that falls below the industry average for air bag installation, the institute reports. Minivans and sport-utility vehicles, among the most popular sellers today, are classified as light trucks, which do not yet fall under the stringent regulations that apply to passenger cars. The rationale for allowing looser standards for light trucks, Hurley explains, was that "they are most often used to carry cargo, not people — though you have to wonder what the regulators think the drivers are." Indeed, most minivans and sport-utility vehicles are used as passenger cars and are popular among families with small children.

Safety standards are finally catching up with this reality. Congress last year passed a law requiring driver and passenger air bags in all cars by the 1998 model year and in lights trucks and vans by 1999. Due to growing consumer demand for safety features, however, Hurley predicts that the industry will beat those deadlines. "Companies are having a very hard time selling cars without air bags," he says.

Even among passenger cars, however, passenger-side air bags have been slow to arrive. Auto-industry analyst Maryann Keller attributes the delay to technical problems. "The passenger-side bag is much larger, and installing an air bag in the [dashboard] does require quite a bit of reworking."

Like most new safety features, anti-lock brakes and air bags are adding to price inflation, a phenomenon Keller says goes hand in hand with federal safety regulations. She recalls the regulation requiring automakers to install bumpers that could sustain an impact of 5 mph. "Then, courtesy of Ronald Reagan, bumper standards came down to 2.5 mph. The bumper at 5 mph was significantly heavier and stronger and much more expensive. But the auto industry did not give me a rebate when they put weaker bumpers on cars."

Similarly, Keller predicts, "Air bags in due course will come down substantially in cost because after any new technology is learned the cost will come down. But as it does, the initial price will remain unchanged. That's the way all regulation works."

---

† Motor Vehicle Manufacturers Association of the United States Inc., *MVMA Motor Vehicle Facts & Figures '92* (1992), p. 91.

to reduce pollution of the environment by auto emissions. "Clinton hasn't seen the estimates showing that increasing fuel economy standards by 13 miles per gallon would cost as many as 300,000 jobs nationwide," Quayle told a Michigan audience. "The advocates of higher CAFE standards call that 'progressive.' I call it irresponsible." [14]

Gore countered Quayle's criticism by pointing out the loss of auto industry jobs during the administrations of Ronald Reagan and Bush. "They are trying to talk about every-

Continued on p. 898

At Issue:

Will the North American Free Trade Agreement lead to job losses in the U.S. auto industry?

ALAN REUTHER

Legislative director, International Union, United Automobile, Aerospace and Agricultural Implement Workers of America
FROM *SUMMARY OF TESTIMONY BEFORE THE HOUSE WAYS AND MEANS SUBCOMMITTEE ON TRADE,* SEPT. 22, 1992

yes

*t*he North American Free Trade Agreement (NAFTA) is an issue of great importance to our union and to all American workers. Unless NAFTA is renegotiated, we are concerned that it will result in the loss of many thousands of U.S. auto jobs, as well as the jobs of workers in affected communities. We have experienced the type of North American economic integration that is supported by the Bush administration first hand, and we believe that it has contributed to lower living standards and pressure to lower workplace standards throughout the continent. The terms of the NAFTA auto provisions will set the future course for the continuation of this process....

U.S. negotiators accepted NAFTA auto provisions that protect Mexican and Canadian production, but refused to adopt equivalent protections for American workers. Thus, a serious imbalance among the three countries has been endorsed by the Bush administration....

The UAW also strongly opposed the inclusion of Mexican vehicles as "domestic" under the U.S. Corporate Average Fuel Economy (CAFE) standards because this would facilitate the transfer of small-car production to Mexico. But the Bush administration accepted the inclusion of Mexican values as "domestic." For the U.S.-based companies, this provision gives a green light to the concentration of small-car production in Mexico.

The UAW also strongly opposed reduction or elimination of the 25 percent tariff on imports of light trucks, since this would encourage the shift of light truck production to Mexico. The administration agreed to reduce this tariff by 60 percent upon implementation of the agreement and to phase it out over the next five years. The most common practice for import-sensitive products is to phase them out over the longest possible time. The administration failed to do even that....

The UAW urges Congress to reject the agreement as negotiated, and to expand the terms of the debate to make it clear that increased trade does not, by itself, make Americans better off. The United States needs to adopt a strategy that improves the lives of auto workers in each of the three countries negotiating the NAFTA. But it can do so only if we focus on the total trade picture, not just exports to Mexico.

CARLA A. HILLS

United States Trade Representative
FROM *TESTIMONY BEFORE THE SENATE FINANCE COMMITTEE,* SEPT. 8, 1992.

no

*w*hen the president launched these negotiations 14 months ago, he promised an agreement that was in the best interests of the American worker and farmer, consumer and exporter. And he has delivered on that promise and more. U.S. autos and light trucks will enjoy a greater access to Mexico, the fastest-growing major auto market in the world. With this agreement Mexican tariffs will be cut in half on light trucks and passenger cars immediately. Within five years, duties on three-quarters of U.S. auto parts to Mexico will be eliminated.

Mexican trade balancing and local content requirements, which have effectively kept out U.S. exports of U.S. vehicles and parts will entirely be eliminated in 10 years. Strict rules of origin will restrict benefits of the auto provisions to North American products. To obtain the preferential treatment, autos must contain 62.5 percent North American content, considerably more than the 50 percent required under the U.S.-Canada agreement....

These extensive market-opening provisions, and the rules designed to support them, will generate new export opportunities for our entrepreneurs, and new jobs for our workers. As a result, we believe that adjustment pressures on the U.S. economy will be minimal.

Some have raised fears that U.S. firms will relocate en masse in Mexico because of lower-wage labor. But the fact is that labor rates are only one determinant of plant location. If wages were the only factor, many less-developed countries would be economic superpowers.

Businesses base their investment decisions on a range of factors that determine productivity, such as the quality of infrastructure, availability of capital, interest rates, access to technology and education of the work force; and based on all the factors, on average, U.S. workers remain at least five times more productive than their Mexican counterparts.

To those who ask, how can we compete against lower-wage Mexican labor, the answer is, we are already competing, and successfully so. Our trade balance has swung from almost $6 billion deficit in 1987 to a projected $7 billion surplus this year....

By tearing down Mexico's tariffs, which are 2.5 times as high as our own, this agreement will level the playing field, not flood it.

Continued from p. 896

thing except jobs, when under their leadership, 1 in 10 autoworkers are losing their jobs," Gore said. "That's not a prediction. That's a cold, hard fact." [15]

Lessons From Japan

Regardless of who wins in November, U.S. automakers will continue to face an uphill climb in their quest to recover the share of the North American market they lost in the 1980s. In all probability, trade policy and industry regulations will have less impact on Detroit's competitiveness than will the industry's ability to continue improving the way it manufacturers automobiles. In their ongoing restructuring efforts, the Big Three are likely to continue following the lean-production model offered by Japan.

But auto analysts advise U.S. automakers against emulating the Japanese indiscriminately. "There's an enormous amount that has been learned and can be learned from the Japanese," says Harley Shaiken. "But, and I say this in direct violation of the conventional wisdom, in many ways the Japanese model has been too influential in Detroit."

The recent strike against GM's Lordstown stamping plant illustrates Shaiken's point. The strike was effective in part because General Motors had adopted the Japanese inventory system of just-in-time delivery at its highly efficient Saturn plant. Within hours of the strike at Lordstown, Saturn had to shut down because it depended on regular delivery of parts from the idled plant. The nine-day strike cost GM sales of one of its few popular models.

It is in labor relations that Detroit may have the most to learn from Japan. The three-year contracts between the UAW and the Big Three are up for renewal next fall. Because GM is undergoing the most sweeping restructuring of U.S. automakers, it probably faces the toughest negotiations. "For the UAW," says Shaiken, " clearly job security is going to be central."

Another key bargaining point will be health care. Health coverage adds about $800 a vehicle at GM, and the company has already forced salaried (non-union, white-collar) workers to begin making copayments on their health insurance premiums. It is expected to ask its union production workers to do the same. "The UAW is going to fight that one very hard," Shaiken predicts. "This is one of a whole range of issues that the Japanese don't have to deal with because they have a national health system."

U.S. automakers would also do well to study the social and demographic differences between the United States and Japan as they contemplate further automation, advises Maryann Keller. The Japanese auto companies are now investing heavily in new automation to compensate for a serious labor shortage. "We have this knee-jerk reaction that more automation is good," she says. "If anything, we have a surplus of labor, so it may not be to our benefit to automate the way they do."

Instead of copying the Japanese, Keller says, Detroit should find its own solutions to the unique problems posed by the U.S. market. "I'm not suggesting for a second that we shouldn't learn from the Japanese. But the Japanese don't look to us for the solutions to their [specific] problems; they find them within themselves, because all solutions are going to eventually be culturally based." ∎

Notes

[1] For background, see "Automakers Face Trouble Down the Road," *Editorial Research Reports*, July 14, 1989, pp. 381-396.

[2] James P. Womack, Daniel T. Jones and Daniel Roos, *The Machine That Changed the World* (1990), p. 13.

[3] *Ibid.*, pp. 82-83.

[4] See Davis Dyer, Malcolm S. Salter and Alan M. Webber, *Changing Alliances* (1987), pp. 236-237.

[5] Ford Motor Co., *Annual Report 1991*, p. 4.

[6] Womack et al., *op. cit.*, pp. 238-239.

[7] Mark Potts and Peter Behr, *The Leading Edge* (1987), p. 175.

[8] See Joseph B. White and Neal Templin, "A Swollen GM Finds How Hard It Is to Stick with Its Crash Diet," *The Wall Street Journal*, Sept. 9, 1992.

[9] Warren Brown and Frank Swoboda, "GM Directors Warn Chairman About UAW," *The Washington Post*, Oct. 13, 1992.

[10] See Jerry Flint, "Detroit Takes the Offensive," *Forbes*, Sept. 28, 1992, pp. 108-112.

[11] See "Honda's Acura Luxury Car Division, Porsche's U.S. Unit Raise 1993 Prices," *The Wall Street Journal*, Sept. 9, 1992.

[12] See Bradley A. Stertz, "Toyota Unveils Longer, Wider, Costlier Corolla," *The Wall Street Journal*, Sept. 3, 1992.

[13] Gephardt criticized the agreement in a statement Sept. 10.

[14] Quayle addressed the Economic Club of Grand Rapids on Aug. 28.

[15] Gore spoke at an outdoor rally in Detroit on Aug. 29.

Bibliography

Selected Sources Used

Books

Shook, Robert L., *Honda: An American Success Story*, Prentice Hall, 1988.

This history of Honda's progress from a small manufacturer of motorcycles to producer of the best-selling car in the United States illustrates the development of innovative manufacturing techniques by all Japan's automakers.

Womack, James P., Daniel T. Jones and Daniel Roos, *The Machine That Changed the World*, HarperCollins, 1990.

The result of a five-year study by the Massachusetts Institute of Technology's International Motor Vehicle Program, this book chronicles the passage from craft production during the early years of auto manufacturing, through Henry Ford's revolutionary mass production, to the so-called lean production in practice today. Introduced by Toyota and other Japanese carmakers, lean production entails the efficient use of resources and teamwork to greatly reduce waste and defects in auto production.

Articles

Consumer Reports, Annual Auto Issue, April 1992.

Every April, the monthly magazine of the Consumers Union publishes an entire issue on the current year's auto lineup. It includes new-car ratings and reliability records of older models, as well as articles on new safety features and tips on how to buy both new and used cars.

Fenster, J. M., "How General Motors Beat Ford," *Audacity: The Magazine of Business Experience*, fall 1992, p. 50.

The author tells the story of how General Motors took advantage of changing consumer preferences to best Ford in the U.S. auto market of the 1920s as a way of illustrating Japan's success in penetrating the same market 50 years later. (This is the first issue of *Audacity*, published by *Forbes* and *American Heritage*.)

Flint, Jerry, "Detroit Takes the Offensive," *Forbes*, Sept. 28, 1992, p. 108.

Japanese automakers, distracted by growing economic problems at home, have failed to keep up the initiative they have shown over the past two decades in predicting shifts in U.S. consumer demands. As a result, Detroit has set the pace in the popular minivan and sport-utility segments of the market.

"Lexus Leads, Saturn Flies High with Luxury Makes in

CSI Top Tier," *The Power Report*, July 1992, p. 1.

This year's Customer Satisfaction Index, compiled yearly by J. D. Power and Associates, an international marketing information firm, is dominated by such luxury nameplates as Lexus, Infiniti, Acura and Mercedes-Benz. But fourth-ranked Saturn "set a new level of excellence in the lower-priced segments that competitors may be forced to equal."

Morici, Peter, "Free Trade with Mexico," *Foreign Policy*, summer 1992, p. 88.

The North American Free Trade Agreement, which the Bush administration presented for Senate ratification in September, is opposed by representatives of U.S. workers who fear it will encourage employers to move to Mexico for cheap labor. Morici argues that the broader market the treaty would bring will help the U.S. compete with Japan.

Rowley, Anthony, "Ease Up, Japan," *Far Eastern Economic Review*, Aug. 6, 1992, p. 52.

Cars account for almost a quarter of Japan's exports. But as economic troubles at home pose new challenges to Japanese automakers, business leaders disagree over whether they should continue to emphasize export markets or focus instead on profit-making.

Stewart, Thomas A., "Brace for Japan's Hot New Strategy," *Fortune*, Sept. 21, 1992, p. 62.

Flexible manufacturing methods allowing the assembly of many different models on a single assembly line have enabled Japanese carmakers to offer a seemingly endless array of models and options to consumers.

Reports and Studies

Congressional Budget Office, "How the Economic Transformations in Europe Will Affect the United States", December 1990.

The European Community's program to eliminate barriers to internal trade, due to take effect Dec. 31, 1992, will have little impact on U.S. auto exports, according to the CBO, because most of the cars that domestic automakers sell in Europe are produced in European facilities. U.S. carmakers may, in fact, be helped by plans to phase out the government subsidies some European carmakers enjoy.

Motor Vehicle Manufacturers Association of the United States Inc., *MVMA Motor Vehicle Facts & Figures '92*, 1992.

The domestic auto industry's yearbook includes a wealth of data on production, sales, regulations, imports and other elements of the U.S. market in cars, trucks and buses.

The Next Step

Additional Articles from Current Periodicals from EBSCO Publishing's Database

Books & reading

Zetka, J. R., "Reviews," *Contemporary Sociology,* January 1991, p. 51.

Reviews the book "Restructuring the Automobile Industry: A Study of Firms and States in Modern Capitalism," by Dennis Patrick Quinn.

Corporations

"Cars: Another big name to be junked?" *Fortune,* June 15, 1992, p. 14.

Reports that Chrysler may soon discontinue either the Eagle or Plymouth. Why this move might be adopted in an effort to cut costs; how the Eagle name became a part of Chrysler; how there is often life after discontinuation for many cars; Studebakers; Edsels; De Sotos; more.

"Make Saturn the standard-bearer," *BusinessWeek,* Aug. 17, 1992, p. 118.

Editorial. States that General Motors Corp. and the United Auto Workers (UAW) should move more quickly toward the kind of partnership that has produced such stunning quality at Saturn Corp. Should whip dealers into shape; working closely with suppliers; other recommendations.

"Success at a price," *The Economist,* June 27, 1992, p. 80.

Discusses how General Motors Corp.'s Saturn is winning top marks for quality and selling faster than it can be built, but the only trouble is that Saturn is still losing money. Entirely new car company; putting its faith in people; car specifics; boosting production to stem losses.

Flint, J., "The LH factor," *Forbes,* June 8, 1992, p. 50.

States that by itself, Chrysler Corp.'s new LH model line isn't going to save the company, but it sends a proud signal both to Wall Street and to car buyers that there's lots of life in old Chrysler. Comparison to K cars that saved the company a decade ago; favorable reviews in the media; importance of image.

Horton, C. & R. Serafin, "GM stalls spending," *Advertising Age,* Feb. 24, 1992, p. 2.

Reports that General Motors Corp. is holding the line on 1992 ad budgets, with total spending expected to be flat or slightly down compared with the estimated $1.2 billion spent in 1991. Insiders' expectations; no massive cuts in spending; premium on new-product launches; Ford Motor Co. and Chrysler Corp.; more.

Kerwin, K., "Meanwhile, Chevy is sulking in the garage," *BusinessWeek,* Aug. 17, 1992, p. 90.

Discusses how while wunderkind Saturn Corp. basks in the limelight with its hot-selling new cars, Chevrolet has been shunted aside by General Motors Corp. Holding onto the truck market; all the money going to Saturn; leaving Chevrolet naked.

Levin, D. P., "Ford plans $3 billion outlay to raise production levels," *The New York Times,* April 14, 1992, p. D1.

Discusses Ford Motor Co.'s announcement of a $3 billion investment in new machinery and plant space, some of which will be used to build a new minivan in late 1993. This will affect a number of plants in the U.S. and Canada and should result in 1,300 new jobs at Ford's truck plant in Louisville, Ky. Rebound in vehicle sales expected.

Moreau, D. & K. Young, "Chrysler tries to make a comeback — again," *Kiplinger's Personal Finance Magazine,* June 1992, p. 34.

Describes the possible profit-making impact of Chrysler's new generation of cars. The new mid-size LH models as styling and engineering successes; recession-year revenues for 1991; efforts to slash production costs; thoughts about the future of the company.

Schiller, Z., D. Woodruff, et al., "GM tightens the screws," *BusinessWeek,* June 22, 1992, p. 30.

Discusses how on June 2, General Motors Corp. told its 5,700 suppliers that they've got lots more to do. GM's plans to winnow its suppliers down to those who can offer highest quality at cheapest price; shifting strategy; sharing the pain of cutting back; how vendors see GM's new rules.

Treece, J. B, "The board revolt," *BusinessWeek,* April 20, 1992, p. 30.

States that after years of humiliating erosion in market share, rivers of red ink and mind-boggling management miasma, General Motors Corp. has entered a period of seismic upheaval rarely seen in American business history. What's happening at GM is far more than a simple acceleration of a business plan to close down plants and shed tens of thousands of workers. INSET: "It's now become a we-they situation" (profiles GM Chairman Robert C. Stempel).

Government policy

Cloud, D. S., "Japan, Bush are targets of new Democratic bill," *Congressional Quarterly Weekly Report,* **May 9, 1992, p. 1240.**

Unveils House Democrats' new trade legislation (HR 5100) on May 7, 1992, that seeks to cap U.S. sales of Japanese cars at current levels and force the Bush administration to negotiate an agreement with Japan to buy more U.S. automobiles before the cap could be raised.

Flint, J., "The case for protection," *Forbes,* **Feb. 17, 1992, p. 44.**

Questions whether General Motors, Ford and Chrysler are expendable. Comments from Robert C. Stempel, chairman of General Motors; Chrysler Chairman Lee Iacocca; 33 percent loss of business to foreigners; arguments for protection of United States auto industry; recommendations.

International aspects

"Ford and Chrysler outpace Japanese in reducing costs," *The New York Times,* **June 18, 1992, p. D1.**

States that Ford Motor Co. and Chrysler Corp. have increased the efficiency of their factories and workers so much in recent years that their basic cost of producing a car is now less than that of their Japanese rivals. Comparison of cost of producing cars.

"The all-American car — not," *World Monitor,* **June 1992, p. 7.**

Discusses how the Wisconsin management consulting firm of Runzheimer International released a report that said no American car produced by any U.S. automaker is wholly American made.

Baker, S., D. Woodruff, et al., "Detroit south," *BusinessWeek,* **March 16, 1992, p. 98.**

Discusses how Mexican workers are emerging as a low-cost, high-quality work force that will help reshape the North American auto industry. In February, General Motors Corp. stunned Americans with factory closings across the United States and Canada that would shift some jobs to Mexico. Amount of cars made in Mexico; setting company quality records; ravenous home market in Mexico; labor-intensive manufacturing; predictions for the industry.

Levin, D. P., "U.S.-Japan auto chiefs hold talks," *The New York Times,* **May 19, 1992, p. D1.**

States that the chief executives of American and Japanese automakers agreed to establish working groups to stimulate Japanese purchases of American auto parts and distribution of American vehicles in Japan — a small but telling step toward soothing strained trade relations caused by automotive competition. But there are still vast differences over the pace and methods for easing tensions.

Rauch, J., "Drive shaft," *The New Republic,* **April 13, 1992, p. 15.**

Discusses the reasons why the Big Three automotive manufacturers cannot compete in the Japanese market. Redesigning the dashboard; moving the floor pedals and gearshift; rearranging the connecting assemblies; major adjustment costs; Japanese market expensive to enter and virtually closed; Japanese companies in the U.S.; more.

Ross, D. C., "Chrysler, Ford, and Saturn ready right-hand drivers," *Motor Trend,* **April 1992, p. 30.**

Announces plans of Chrysler, Ford and Saturn to make right-hand-drive vehicles for overseas markets.

Sanger, D. E., "A defiant Detroit still depends on Japan," *The New York Times,* **Feb. 27, 1992, p. A1.**

Comments on the continuing confusion about what constitutes an American car. Is it a Honda made in Ohio, or a Ford minivan also produced in Ohio in a joint venture with Nissan? There were 164,352 thoroughly Japanese vehicles produced in Japan last year that were sold as Chryslers, Dodges and Chevrolets. The Big Three's continuing dependence on Japanese manufacturing.

Marketing

"Are automobile dealers editing your local newspaper?" *Consumer Reports,* **April 1992, p. 208.**

Discusses the amount of control auto dealers have over the local press. *Consumer Reports'* telephone survey of 50 randomly chosen daily newspapers last December and January; Friction, real and anticipated, from car dealers; every inch of advertising is important to the papers today; a city editor in Oklahoma makes a comment; Warren Brown, auto writer for *The Washington Post*; Allan Wilbur, spokesman for the 19,000-member National Automobile Dealers Association.

Horton, C. & R. Serafin, "Automakers focus on service," *Advertising Age,* **July 6, 1992, p. 3.**

Reports that consumer service is emerging as a key marketing battleground in the automobile industry. Building a good product and strong image are no longer enough; new industry benchmarks for coddling luxury car buyers; Lexus placed first on the 1992 Customer Satisfaction Index; comments and examples; chart depicting the results of the 1992 J. D. Power & Associates Consumer Satisfaction Index.

Horton, C. & R. Serafin, "Recovery is good news for U.S. auto marketers," *Advertising Age,* **June 22, 1992, p. 3.**

Reports that U.S. auto marketers are winning share of an improving market, while imports face rougher times. John Hammond, a senior partner at J. D. Power & Associates;

prediction of a continued but modest economy for the overall auto industry; three elements that will combine to give the domestics the edge in the business; how market share is changing.

Serafin, R., "Pontiac ads bring excitement to sales," *Advertising Age,* July 20, 1992, p. 12.

Reports that excitement is back in Pontiac's sales performance with a new comparative ad campaign getting a lot of credit for a strong rebound by the General Motors Corp. division. Pontiac sales are up to 10.9 percent; description of the commercial; spot from D'Arcy Masius Benton & Bowles; advertising pits the full-size Bonneville against luxury imports; Pontiac's background.

Serafin, R., "Regional assault," *Advertising Age,* April 27, 1992, p. 4.

Reports that Ford Motor Co. and General Motors are stepping up regional ads and promotions aimed to win back import buyers. Both are trying to capitalize on recent "Buy American" sentiment; key to converting import buyers; what the campaigns include; different efforts and promotions.

Serafin, R., "The graying of the minivan," *Advertising Age,* June 15, 1992, p. 4.

Reports that Lincoln-Mercury is mapping out its biggest launch ever, an estimated $40 million advertising campaign starting in September 1992 for the Mercury Villager minivan. Target audience; significant revamp of its advertising.

Performance

"A blunt warning," *Maclean's,* Jan. 27, 1992, p. 27.

Outlines the warning from the Big Three North American automakers to Ontario's government that enacting labor law reforms that enhance union rights could trigger a new round of plant closings. General Motors of Canada Ltd. maintains the new laws will put it at a disadvantage compared with GM plants in the United States.

"American car sales speed past imports," *U.S. News & World Report,* June 15, 1992, p. 14.

Reports that sales of American-made cars are bouncing back, while foreign-auto makers are struggling to lure buyers in the United States. Increase in sales of American-made autos in May; the proportion of imports from Japan; percentage of American-made cars with Japanese nameplates; number of American nameplates among top 10 in quality; foreign-car makers that left the U.S. market in the past year.

"Propping up Detroit," *The Economist,* Feb. 15, 1992, p. 75.

States that the case for helping General Motors, Ford and Chrysler is a protectionist classic: full of talk about dumping, subsidies and unfairness. In its Feb. 17 issue, *Forbes* maga-

zine decided that Detroit's capitalists need more tools than others, in an article entitled "The Case for Protection." Advantages; disadvantages; "excess capacity costs"; health and labor costs; analysis of the protectionist argument.

Flint, J., "Detroit's crisis: too many competitors, too much capacity, too few buyers," *Forbes,* Jan. 6, 1992, p. 120.

Explains that in the past 12 months General Motors, Ford and Chrysler had $7 billion in net losses and even greater auto operating losses in North America. Too much competition; questions whether foreign manufacturers suffer equally; consumer durables groups are hurting; exception; projected recovery. INSET: Honda: the most efficient "American" carmaker.

Henry, J., "No waking up from nightmare," *Advertising Age,* March 30, 1992, p. S-50.

Focuses on automobile dealers in the Northeast, where many dealers last year were getting hammered for the third or fourth year. Comments from individual dealers; selling used cars, promoting service and parts and cutting advertising; Rhode Island froze the bank accounts of about a third of the state's residents, some of whom still don't have their money; falling numbers of dealerships in the region; tailoring operations to shore up the Northeast.

Horton, C., J. M. Winski, et al., "Calif. dream turns urgent," *Advertising Age,* March 30, 1992, p. S-26.

Considers evidence of a new commitment by the domestic automakers to the California market, which traditionally accounts for 11 percent of all U.S. sales of cars and light trucks. California as a problem and an opportunity for the domestic auto market; traditional Camaro market; General Motors' $3 billion experiment; Saturn; Chrysler's research.

Levin, D. P., "Car sales fell in mid-March; Trucks rose," *The New York Times,* March 25, 1992, p. D1.

Reports that sales of North American built vehicles fell 2.7 percent in mid-March, as automakers continued to feel the decline in fleet sales of cars to rental companies. Light-truck sales were higher. Details and statistics.

Levin, D. P., "February's vehicle sales rolled down," *The New York Times,* March 5, 1992. p. D1.

Reports that sales of North American-made cars and light trucks dipped 13.6 percent in late February, as most analysts concluded that evidence of a recovering automotive market remained slim. Other recent economic signposts have pointed to a slowly emerging recovery, with the latest report showing the third increase in four months in orders to the nation's factories.

Levin, D. P., "For Detroit, time to buckle down," *The New York Times,* Jan. 13, 1992, p. D1.

Analyzes the U.S. auto industry's entrance into a new and critical phase in which it must seek its own strategies to keep from being overwhelmed by competitors and a floundering economy. President Bush's mission to Japan; slumping car sales; erosion of market share.

Levin, D. P., "U.S. sales of vehicles jump 23.9 percent," *The New York Times*, July 7, 1992, p. D1.

Says that the nation's auto industry reported strong sales for late June, propelled by what executives said was rising consumer confidence and a stronger economy. "Buy America" preference among consumers; statistics.

Levin, D. P., "Vehicle sales jumped to 18.3 percent in late April," *The New York Times*, May 6, 1992. p. D1.

Reports that sales of North America-built cars and light trucks rose 18.3 percent in late April. While automotive analysts said the gain fell short of a full-fledged recovery, it provided a lift to beleaguered automakers and retail dealers. The total sales of domestic vehicles, 399,253, compared to 300,075 in the comparable period of 1991.

Pomice, E., "A balky balance sheet," *U.S. News & World Report*, April 20, 1992, p. 54.

Reports that the Big Three American automakers lost nearly $10 billion on North American car operations last year. The problem for Detroit; total North American auto overcapacity could fall this year; Ford is in the best financial shape of the Big Three; why General Motors' recovery could be more painful; why the history of the American auto industry is gloomy.

Reibstein, L., F. Washington, et al., "The hardest sell," *Newsweek*, March 30, 1992, p. 50.

Reports that American automakers have made great strides in improving their cars, now they must convince consumers that there's no more quality gap. U.S. auto executives who insist that they are suffering from a perception problem; renewed efforts by the Japanese to raise the quality standard; liabilities of brand-loyalty disadvantages.

Roberts, S. V., "Tears and fears in America's new civil war," *U.S. News & World Report*, March 9, 1992, p. 8.

Announces that after reporting an annual loss of $4.5 billion last week, General Motors said it would close 12 plants, representing 16,000 jobs, a down payment on a previously announced plan to fire 74,000 workers by 1995. The job scarcity has sparked a new civil war; how the auto industry is trying to make up for lost time; the other sectors of the United States economy that seem to be doing better.

Singleton, C. J., "Auto industry jobs in the 1980s: A decade of transition," *Monthly Labor Review*, February 1992, p. 18.

Provides a historical overview of the United States auto-

mobile market, with an emphasis on factors that affected output and employment trends during the 1980s. How the auto market remained fairly consistent throughout most of the 20th century; impact of growth during the 1980s of foreign competition in the domestic market; employment analysis through the 1980s; basic factors that determine the employment level data on related industries.

Taylor, A., "Auto showdown gridlock," *Fortune*, Dec. 30, 1991, p. 8.

Outlines the bleak future of the automobile industry, despite lower interest rates and rampant price cutting, Americans refuse to buy new cars. U.S. automakers predict slight uptick in 1992; possibly break even as costs are held in check; profit margins; rebates; Detroit's Big Three; rental car companies; more.

Statement of Ownership, Management, Circulation

Act of Aug. 12, 1970: Section 3685, Title 39, United States Code

Title of publication: The CQ Researcher. Date of filing: October 8, 1992. Frequency of issue: Weekly (Except for 1/3, 5/1, 7/3, 10/2/92). No. of issues published annually: 48. Annual subscription price: $296.00. Location of known office of publication: 1414 22nd Street, N.W., Washington, D.C. 20037-1097. Names and addresses of publisher, editor and managing editor: Publisher, Neil Skene, 1414 22nd Street, N.W., Washington, D.C. 20037-1097; Editor, Sandra Stencel, 1414 22nd Street, N.W., Washington, D.C. 20037-1097; Managing Editor, Thomas J. Colin, 1414 22nd Street, N.W., Washington, D.C. 20037-1097. Owner: Congressional Quarterly, 1414 22nd Street, N.W., Washington, D.C. 20037. Known bondholders, mortgagees, and other security holders owning or holding 1 percent or more of total amount of bonds, mortgages or other securities: none.

Extent and Nature of Circulation	Average Number of Copies Each Issue During Preceding 12 Months	Actual Number of Copies of Single Issue Published Nearest to Filing Date
A. Total number of copies printed (Net Press Run)	6,476	6,370
B. Paid Circulation		
1. Sales through dealers and carriers, street vendors and counter sales	—	—
2. Mail subscriptions	4,797	4,774
C. Total paid and/or requested circulation	4,797	4,774
D. Free distribution by mail carrier or other means. Samples, complimentary, and other free copies	473	416
E. Total distribution (Sum of C and D)	5,270	5,190
F. Copies not distributed		
1. Office use, left over, unaccounted, spoiled after printing	1,206	1,180
2. Returns from news agents	—	—
G. TOTAL (sum of E and F — should equal net press run shown in A)	6,476	6,370

Back Issues

Great Research on Current Issues Starts Right Here... Recent topics covered by The CQ Researcher are listed below. Issues dated before May 10, 1991, were published under the name of Editorial Research Reports.

APRIL 1991
Social Security
Canadian Crisis Over Quebec
California Drought
Electromagnetic Radiation

MAY 1991
School Choice
Racial Quotas
Animal Rights
U.S. and Japan

JUNE 1991
Children and Divorce
Teenage Suicide
Endangered Species
Europe 1992

JULY 1991
Teenagers and Abortion
Soviet Republics Rebel
Mexico's Emergence
Athletes and Drugs

AUGUST 1991
Sexual Harassment
Fetal Tissue Research
Oil Imports
The Palestinians

SEPTEMBER 1991
Police Brutality
Advertising Under Attack
Saving the Forests
Foster Care Crisis

OCTOBER 1991
Pay-Per-View TV
Youth Gangs
Gene Therapy
World Hunger

NOVEMBER 1991
Fast-Food Shake-Up
The Greening of Eastern Europe
Business' Role in Education
Cuba In Crisis

DECEMBER 1991
Retiree Health Benefits
Asian Americans
The Obscenity Debate
The Disabilities Act

JANUARY 1992
Term Limits
Oil Spills
Hunting Controversy
Alternative Medicine

FEBRUARY 1992
Threatened Coastlines
New Era in Asia
Assisted Suicide
Jobs in the '90s

MARCH 1992
Women and Sports
Underage Drinking
Garbage Crisis
Mafia Crackdown

APRIL 1992
Ozone Depletion
Welfare Reform
Politicians and Privacy
Illegal Immigration

MAY 1992
Native Americans
Jobs vs. Environment
Too Many Lawsuits?
Fairness in Salaries

JUNE 1992
Nuclear Proliferation
Food Irradiation
Lead Poisoning
Hard Times for Libraries

JULY 1992
Alternative Energy
Prescription Drug Prices
Alzheimer's Disease
Infant Mortality

AUGUST 1992
The Homeless
Work, Family and Stress
NATO's Changing Role
Marine Mammals vs. Fish

SEPTEMBER 1992
Domestic Partners
Violence in Schools
Public Broadcasting
Women in the Military

OCTOBER 1992
Depression

Back issues are available for $4.00 (subscribers) or $7.00 (non-subscribers). Quantity discounts apply to orders over ten. To order, call Congressional Quarterly 1-800-432-2250.

Future Topics

▶ *Apprenticeships*

▶ *Hispanics*

▶ *Physical Fitness*

PUBLISHED BY CONGRESSIONAL QUARTERLY INC., IN CONJUNCTION WITH EBSCO PUBLISHING

Youth Apprenticeships

Can they improve the school-to-work transition?

D
ESPITE THE PREMIUM SOCIETY PUTS ON A
college education, four out of five high school
graduates do not get a college degree. For
millions of young Americans, this can mean a
future of dead-end jobs. A movement is growing to create a
school-to-work transition system centered around the
centuries-old concept of apprenticeship. As early as the 10th
grade, students would combine academics with on-the-job
training as a way to meet today's growing demand for a
literate, "high-performance" work force. The idea is so new
a consensus has yet to emerge on how to go about it. But
business executives and government officials agree that
the future of the U.S. work force may depend on some
such action.

 October 23, 1992 • Volume 2, No. 39 • 905-928

Formerly Editorial Research Reports

COVER ART: BARBARA SASSA-DANIELS

CQ *Researcher*

October 23, 1992
Volume 2, No. 39

EDITOR
Sandra Stencel

MANAGING EDITOR
Thomas J. Colin

ASSOCIATE EDITOR
Richard L. Worsnop

STAFF WRITERS
Charles S. Clark
Mary H. Cooper
Rodman D. Griffin

PRODUCTION EDITOR
Sarah E. Merritt

EDITORIAL ASSISTANT
Michael M. Taylor

GRAPHICS
Jack Auldridge

PUBLISHED BY
Congressional Quarterly Inc.

CHAIRMAN
Andrew Barnes

VICE CHAIRMAN
Andrew P. Corty

EDITOR AND PUBLISHER
Neil Skene

EXECUTIVE EDITOR
Robert W. Merry

ASSOCIATE PUBLISHER
John J. Coyle

EDITOR, EBSCO PUBLISHING
Melissa Kummerer

The CQ Researcher (ISSN 1056-2036). Formerly Editorial Research Reports. Published weekly (48 times per year, not printed the first Friday of any month with five Fridays) by Congressional Quarterly Inc., 1414 22nd St., N.W., Washington, D.C. 20037. Rates are furnished upon request. Second-class postage paid at Washington, D.C. POSTMASTER: Send address changes to The CQ Researcher, 1414 22nd St., N.W., Washington, D.C. 20037.

Youth Apprenticeships

BY CHARLES S. CLARK

THE ISSUES

Paul Nurkala entered his junior year of high school with one foot in the present and the other planted squarely in the future. The 17-year-old begins his day in West Bend, Wis., at 7:30 a.m. with the usual classes in American literature, government and math. By mid-morning, however, Nurkala joins 11 other selected students in the school's graphics lab, where he learns the fundamentals of offset printing and photographic-plate making.

At noon, Nurkala reports for work at Serigraph Inc., a local printing firm, where, unlike most employees, he is guaranteed a broad exposure to all aspects of company operations. By 3 p.m. he's free for the day.

"I'm not one who looks forward to going to school," says the former B and C student, who says he's now making A's and B's. "But I like this because I don't have to spend four hours a night on homework."

Nurkala's schedule still leaves time to be with friends, go to football games and participate on the swim team. In two years, he will receive a certificate from the state attesting to his high school graduation and his job training. He will then be a likely candidate for a full-time job at the printing firm, and he will have a range of other educational options from technical school to a four-year college.

"The on-the-job training is the main advantage, and I get paid," Nurkala says. "And it leaves me a step ahead of the guys coming out of high school because I can run a one-color press."

Paul Nurkala is one of 23 students in Wisconsin's new youth apprenticeship program, a modern adaptation of a centuries-old concept that has

been sparking interest around the country. Led by efforts in Wisconsin, Oregon, Pennsylvania and Arkansas, youth apprenticeship projects have sprung up in some 20 states since 1990. And more than 50 pilot projects have been sponsored by the Labor Department and such private groups as the Washington-based National Alliance of Business.

Both President Bush and Arkansas Gov. Bill Clinton, the Democratic presidential nominee, have actively pushed for a national youth apprenticeship effort. Eight youth apprenticeship bills were introduced in the last session of Congress, and the subject is likely to gain more attention when the 103rd Congress convenes in January 1993.

"People are coming to see it's a very attractive training scheme — to learn by doing," said Robert W. Glover, an authority on apprenticeships at the Lyndon B. Johnson School of Public Affairs at the University of Texas in Austin. "It combines earning and learning — and both of these features are attractive to school-weary youth." [1]

Building better futures also cultivates maturity in young people, apprenticeship advocates say. "Apprenticeship has always done more than teach a specific trade," writes Cornell University human development Professor Stephen Hamilton. "Learning to work means learning to be an adult." [2]

The ascent of youth apprenticeship up the policy agenda stems from a confluence of trends in income growth, global economic competition and educational theory. It also reflects concern in business, government and academia about the perilous and growing mismatch between the future demands of the workplace and the quality of the nation's up-and-coming workers.

"Most of the kids coming out of high school have relatively low problem-solving skills," said Paul Whitley, vice president of Tyson Foods Inc. in Russellville, Ark., which has just launched an apprentice program. "They have poor math skills, poor reading skills and poor communication skills. We're on a collision course as the labor market shrinks and the need for more and better skills increases." [3]

"In our country, for the 80 percent who do not attend or may not complete college, there is no defined path to a job or career," observed Rep. Carl C. Perkins, D-Ky., during July hearings on his School to Work Transition and Skill Standards Development Act *(see p. 916)*. There is "only a hodgepodge of want ads, dead-end jobs and career counseling with no link to the job market or needs of employers." [4]

The lack of preparedness among non-college-bound youth has been forcefully documented. Over the past 15 years, economists say, the earnings gap between professionals and skilled workers widened from 2 percent to 37 percent, and the gap between professionals and clerical workers increased from 47 to 86 percent.[5] The General Accounting Office estimates that about 9 million of the nation's 33 million 16-to-24-year-olds lack the skills needed for entry-level jobs.[6]

During this period of blue-collar economic decline, the skills in demand have also become highly technical. "It hasn't been all that long since a kid could drop out of school and find a job as a mechanic," said a Rockbridge County, Va., math teacher involved with new programs to link school with work. "But now you can't even balance a tire without knowing how to work a computer."[7]

What's more, the changing workplace does not bode well even for college-educated job seekers of the future unless they have technical training. By the year 2000, the federal Bureau of Labor Statistics predicts, only 30 percent of jobs in America will require a college education.

"Our front-line workers ... may be the least skilled among those of all the major industrial countries," assert labor specialists Ray Marshall and Marc Tucker in a new book, *Thinking for a Living: Work, Skills and the Future of the American Economy.* In advocating apprenticeships and other education and training reforms, they argue that trade competitors such as Germany and Japan will force U.S. industry to invest more in "human-resource capital," tapping the skills of the rank and file.[8]

Similar thinking was apparent in an influential 1990 study, *America's Choice: High Skills or Low Wages!,* in which a commission of executives, labor leaders and former Labor secretaries laid out a plan to create a "high-performance work force." To restore economic growth, they proposed "mobilizing our most vital asset, the skills of our people — not just the 30 percent who will graduate from college — but the front-line workers, the people who serve as bank tellers, farm workers ... data-entry operators, laborers and factory workers."[9]

The push for apprenticeships comes at a time when educators are emphasizing "contextual learning," which stresses the practical and concrete over the theoretical (*see p. 918*). "The trend now in pedagogy is to push applied education, which reaches more people and in which people learn better," says Dale Hudeleson, information director of the American Vocational Association in Alexandria, Va.

The modern vision of youth apprenticeship is broader than the traditional apprenticeships associated mainly with construction and metalworking crafts. Drawing inspiration from successful apprentice programs in Germany (*see story, p. 917*) and other European countries, the concept includes apprenticeships in health care, financial services, culinary arts and child care as well as in government and nonprofit organizations.

At its heart, Sen. Sam Nunn, D-Ga., said last November when introducing a youth apprenticeship bill, the program should require "certifiable skills, involve employers as direct participants with a stake in the individual students' academic and skills training achievement and be an integral part of the school curriculum, available to all students, not an add-on or adjunct program, and [should carry] prestige in school and community."

"Apprenticeships can't be like college or vocational school," says M. Blouke Carus, a Peru, Ill., businessman. "They must be outcome-based like a chef's school. When you finish you must be able to bake a muffin, not just say that you completed 1,000 hours of muffin training."[10]

Though noble intentions permeate the apprenticeship movement, it meets skepticism from unions, who worry about undercutting their decades-old apprentice program for older workers. (*See story, p. 909.*) Another question mark is the commitment of employers, who profess an interest in education but spend far less on long-term training than their overseas rivals. (*See chart, p. 911.*)

But to its boosters, youth apprenticeship seems the ideal way to motivate aimless young people while offering businesses an invaluable resource: a long-term supply of employees with more up-to-date skills than those taught in traditional vocational education.

"The Germans have a saying that if you're trained in something, it makes you easier to retrain," notes the University of Texas' Glover. "Right now, our kids in high school don't see a connection between what they're doing in school and what happens afterward. We have to make that connection."

Whether the effort can succeed is likely to hinge on the following issues:

Is it fair to ask a 10th grader to commit to an apprenticelike career path?

"This friend of mine ... had a friend who made $50,000 her first year [working] in physical therapy," an Arkansas mother told an interviewer discussing apprenticeships. "Well, that's what my daughter wants to do now. Three weeks ago, it was a graphic artist. And before that she's marrying a millionaire and moving to Beverly Hills."[11]

Adolescents are known for indecision about their goals in life. And what sticks in the craw of many students and parents pondering apprenticeship is the fear that committing oneself at age 16 to a "vocational track" means giving up a chance for economic and social mobility.

"I'm not asking [my daughter] to be an honors graduate," said another Arkansas parent. "I just say, 'Pass so you don't have to go to summer school. So you can graduate with your class. And then you can make these commitments later on. Just learn a little self-discipline.' But in no way would I ever not want her to be in the mainstream. If you lose track

Who Owns Rights to the Word 'Apprenticeship'?

The most vocal resistance to the youth apprenticeship movement centers not on the goals or methods of the program but on the use of the name. Many union and state government officials argue that the word "apprentice" should be reserved for the decades-old "registered apprentice" program, which is strictly defined by federal and state regulations to refer to the 43,000 highly structured, multi-year training programs that have been negotiated around the country in collective-bargaining agreements.

"The rush to embrace apprenticeship ... is leading to efforts that could undermine the very pillars of its value," warns Barbara Green, chairwoman of the Federal Committee on Apprenticeship and senior vice president of the Greater New York Hospital Association. "No one questions the motives or intentions of the youth apprenticeship advocates, but loose application of the term could undermine confidence in one of the few effective training strategies we have in this country."†

Registered apprentices can apply to 800 apprenticeable occupations — primarily in construction and metalworking trades. There are currently about 300,000 apprentices nationwide, with an average age of 29. Their program requires 2,000 hours of on-the-job training supervised by a journey-level worker as well as 240 hours of related classroom time, under rules last updated in 1977. A registered apprenticeship typically lasts three to five years.

The Federal Committee on Apprenticeship, a labor, employer and educator group that advises the Labor Department, emphasizes the distinction between registered and youth apprenticeships. In a January statement, the committee said that a registered apprenticeship "(a) combines supervised, structured, on-the-job training with related theoretical instruction and (b) is sponsored by employers or labor/management groups that have the ability to hire and train in a work environment."

Union spokesmen add that in a registered apprenticeship, state and federal regulations determine the type and amount of related instruction, the manner of supervision, the appropriate ratios of apprentices to journey persons, the selection process for apprentices, recruitment procedures, wage progression and safety procedures.

In a youth apprenticeship, by contrast, students begin at age 16 rather than in their 20s; there are a variety of possible outcomes; academic and work-related competencies are integrated into the regular high school program; and youth apprenticeship would not, in itself, lead to a "journeyworker" certification.

"Every high school youngster with a part-time job is not a youth apprentice," observes Donald Grabowski, president of the National Association of State and Territorial Apprenticeship Directors in Albany, N.Y. "There is concern among state officials that if youngsters get involved with programs labeled apprentice and then realize that there is a state and federal program, they will ask for [the same] credential certificate. No one to our knowledge is opposed to youth apprenticeships, but people must realize what's involved. It must be a meaningful experience that leads somewhere, not just to a warm feeling all over."

Youth apprenticeship boosters originally began by using the phrase "school-to-work programs" and avoided using "the Big-A apprenticeship," according to James Van Erden, administrator of the Labor Department's Office of Work-Based Learning. "But then a lot of people, including President Bush, began using 'youth apprenticeship,' which caused some heartburn. I tell my friends in labor that they will never see us use the term apprentice without the word 'youth' in front of it."

Garrison J. Moore, director of research and development at the National Alliance of Business in Washington, says "it is unfortunate that the term 'youth apprenticeship' was adopted because it sounds blue-collar," when in reality there is more potential for apprenticeships in the service industries.

Laurence Steinberg, a psychologist at Philadelphia's Temple University who has written widely on teenagers' employment issues, is wary of using the label youth apprenticeship for a smorgasbord of programs without differentiating between good ones and bad ones that exploit kids. "If you began giving a work-study credit for wrapping hamburgers," he says, "it would only be a short cry from having McDonald's call it a 'restaurant apprenticeship.'"

---

† Letter to Robert W. Glover of the Center for the Study of Human Resources, University of Texas, Austin, Aug. 12, 1992.

---

socially, then you've lost."[12]

Hostility toward "tracking" became a major issue in Oregon in 1991 during the legislature's debate on a major education-reform bill. In addition to spawning a youth apprentice program, the act that was

eventually approved required all 10th graders in Oregon to pass a skills-assessment test and then to choose between academic and vocational pathways.

This "outmoded system of tracking would isolate and stigmatize

those students most in need of help ... and would be the end of schooling for many students," an irate reader wrote *The* (Portland) *Oregonian*. "Those with the most difficulty in school, the least family support and the greatest need for more schooling [would not be] employable beyond dead-end, minimum-wage jobs."[13]

A professor at Portland State University wrote in to speculate that employers liked the vocational plan and were using "the language of democracy to cover a real agenda: lowering the expectations of working class children ... thus creating workers who accept their 'places' and who will be less disruptive."

In addition, Oregon parents, particularly minorities, worried that 10th graders' choices are determined by factors beyond their control. "If you were told all your life you're not college material, then when you are given a choice, what choice will you make?" asked a Portland attorney.

Youth apprenticeship backers acknowledge the risks of tracking but emphasize that a properly designed program would expand rather than narrow a student's options. "It's hard to find a high school sophomore or parent of a sophomore who says college should not remain an option," says Cornell's Hamilton. "Such a program would never attract any kids."

Glover agrees with critics of tracking that if "we take the existing system and force young kids to make a decision, it would be a disaster." But he envisions apprenticeship as part of a whole new system of "educational infrastructure" that would make the high school curriculum more pragmatic and provide guidance counselors with more current information on the job market.

"We already permit them to make life choices in the 10th grade — and our young people are making the wrong choices," says a report from Jobs for the Future, a Cambridge, Mass., consulting firm. "An educational system more closely tied to the world of work will provide 10th graders better information upon which to make the choices they are already making."[14]

Robert J. Massey, an Arlington, Va., management consultant, points out that encouraging an early apprenticeship is better than loading up students with loans to put them through trade schools to learn skills they can't use for anything. "It's like offering a drink to an alcoholic," he says, referring to proprietary schools that concentrate more on profits from loans than on applicable technical instruction.

Others see benefits in the additional academic pressure that public school students would feel if forced to choose an early career path. "If failure to gain admittance to a particular set of high schools definitively eliminates a whole set of future opportunities," writes Professor Thomas Bailey of Columbia University Teachers College, "then students may be motivated to apply themselves more consistently in elementary school."[15]

Many who've wrestled with the tracking issue say that middle- and upper-class communities should simply tone down their snobbery about having everyone strive for college. "Where are they going to get the tradespeople who make their lives work?" asks Ellen Carlos, coordinator of apprentices at Fairfax County, Va., Public Schools. Carlos also pooh-poohs the fear that apprentices lose out on mainstream social life. "Apprentices go to parties on top of working for spending money 10-15 hours a week," she says. "It's just that they're working as electricians or machinists instead of slinging hash. Is that less fun?"

Most observers of high school career planning at least agree that the present system fails to launch many students on productive working lives. As one Wisconsin parent put it, "We've got two very clear tracks right now — college prep and nowhere prep."[16]

Will employers embrace youth apprenticeship?

"The primary concern of more than 80 percent of employers is finding workers with a good work ethic and appropriate social behavior — reliable, a good attitude, a pleasant appearance, a good personality," noted the *America's Choice* report.

The problem presented by youth apprenticeship, notes youth-employment specialist Samuel Halperin, study director of the W. T. Grant Foundation in Washington, D.C., is that many U.S. firms resist a three-or-four-year hiring commitment and prefer college graduates because they don't believe high school graduates are mature.

What's more, the well-publicized training programs at such firms as Xerox Corp., General Electric Co., Motorola Inc. and American Express Co., are not emulated at most companies. Few firms are actively upgrading their work forces, preferring to "dumb down" tasks and hire less costly part-timers, analysts note. A 1990 survey of 250 mid-size companies by the Grant Thorton accounting firm found that even though two-thirds of the respondents agreed they had a productivity problem, more than half considered it minor, and most would solve it by replacing people with machines. *(See "At Issue," p. 921.)*

Many employers don't want to pay more for training. The bulk of the $30 billion per year currently spent on training involves less than 1 percent of U.S. firms and is less than half what is spent by most of our European trade competitors, according to the Alexandria, Va.,-based American Society for Training and Development. *(See table, p. 911.)* As consultant Massey points out, investment in plant and equipment shows up on the account books as a positive asset, but training expenses are merely a debit. (The Labor Department is exploring ways to change this.)

From a manager's point of view, youth apprentices might add to training costs because participants are guaranteed a rotation through different parts of the company and would hence be relieved of certain demands for productivity. "There is a conflict between the worker role and the learner role," says Hamilton. "There's no formula for working it out."

A further complication, notes Quint Rahberger, Oregon's apprenticeship and training administrator, is that "employers in this litigious society are wary of violating child labor laws, hazardous-work orders" and insurance regulations, issues that designers of a national apprenticeship initiative would have to tackle.

Despite such obstacles, youth apprenticeship advocates are busy promoting their concept in the business community. "Companies shouldn't be passive advisers and think that now that they've sent computers into the schools they've done their job," says James D. Van Erden, administrator of the Labor Department's Office of Work-Based Learning.

"Employer endorsement is the key to the whole thing," says Glover. A national initiative would require "industrywide structural supports," he says, perhaps something akin to Germany's private craft and trade "chambers," business groups that administer apprentice programs and socialize training costs by collecting dues from all companies whether or not they participate in training.

"Currently, there aren't many jobs set up for apprenticeable skills," observes Anthony P. Carnevale, chief economist for the American Society for Training and Development. "We have to build up the demand side because it's the job that creates the need for training, not the apprenticeship that creates the job."

Because many youth apprenticeships are envisioned in service industries such as health care and insurance, notes Garrison J. Moore, director of research and development at the National Alliance of Business, "there is a cultural barrier. The companies say, 'We're white-collar, [apprenticeship is] blue collar.'" Companies also have the attitude that their managers are so special that they have to customize them, Moore says. His group seeks to change

that culture and create industry apprenticeship standards that would encourage "portability and transferability" among companies.

Many companies are having success at tapping into the skills of young students, Moore adds, even though they might not call it appren-

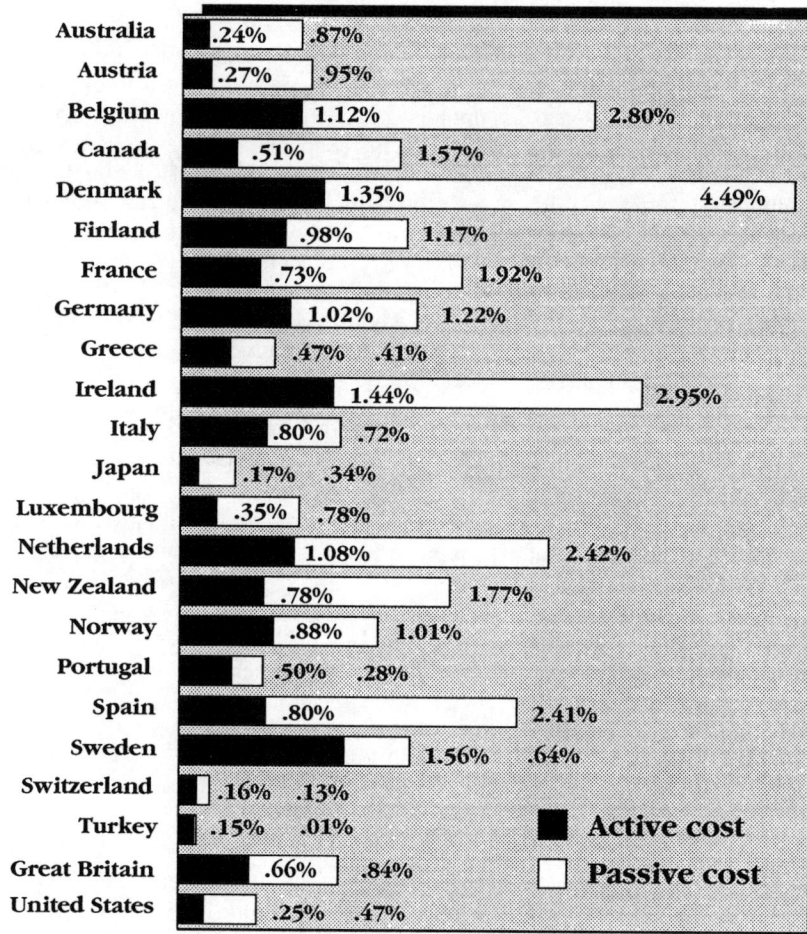

How Nations Compare in Spending on Training

Other nations invest far more than the United States on training and job counseling as well as unemployment insurance needed to support the unemployed while they are being retrained. Sweden's unusually high rate of "active" costs reflects education reforms in the 1960s that drastically raised education requirements.*

Percentage of 1989 gross domestic product

Nation	Active cost	Passive cost
Australia	.24%	.87%
Austria	.27%	.95%
Belgium	1.12%	2.80%
Canada	.51%	1.57%
Denmark	1.35%	4.49%
Finland	.98%	1.17%
France	.73%	1.92%
Germany	1.02%	1.22%
Greece		.47% .41%
Ireland	1.44%	2.95%
Italy	.80%	.72%
Japan		.17% .34%
Luxembourg	.35%	.78%
Netherlands	1.08%	2.42%
New Zealand	.78%	1.77%
Norway	.88%	1.01%
Portugal		.50% .28%
Spain	.80%	2.41%
Sweden	1.56%	.64%
Switzerland		.16% .13%
Turkey	.15%	.01%
Great Britain	.66%	.84%
United States		.25% .47%

■ **Active cost** □ **Passive cost**

*Passive costs mainly include unemployment insurance; active costs are mainly for training and job counseling.

Source: U.S. Dept. of Labor; Organization for Economic Cooperation and Development

An Array of Options Linking School With Work

Youth apprenticeships are among an array of programs designed to help high school students make the transition from school to work. What characterizes apprenticeship is on-the-job training administered by a professional, the awarding of a standardized certificate and the hope that it would be an option for all students, not just special cases. Other alternatives for those who don't attend a four-year college include the following:

Vocational Education: Created in the 19th century, high school voc. ed. programs have traditionally offered all students such practical courses as typing, home economics and shop. For a select group of students, they offer hands-on training in technical skills such as auto repair and mechanical drawing.

Tech Prep: Short for technical preparation (also called "2+2"), this program links two years of high school with two years of community college or technical-school study focusing on math, science, computers and technologies. Tech prep offers an associate degree and prepares students for specific occupations in such broad areas as computers or engineering. A tech prep grant program was formalized under the 1990 Carl D. Perkins Vocational and Applied Technology Education Act Amendments.

Cooperative Education: A longstanding approach that alternates study with work. High school students receive credit for their work hours and often receive only the minimum academic instruction needed for a high school diploma.

Community Colleges: Primarily open-enrollment local colleges that offer adult and vocational education and two-year degrees.

Trade Schools: For-profit schools that offer practical instruction in such fields as hair styling, computers, dental technology and trucking.

Career Academies: Over the past two decades, corporations in Philadelphia, New York and Los Angeles and elsewhere have sponsored simulated work environments, a "school within a school," in such fields as health, insurance and finance. Employers help design the curriculum and often provide students with summer jobs.

Focused Schools: Schools identified by the National Center for Research in Vocational Education for their success in integrating academic and vocational studies to create a special identity. Examples are Aviation High School, the High School of Fashion Industries and the Chicago High School for Agricultural Sciences.

School-Based Enterprise: Students provide services or produce goods in such enterprises as school restaurants, construction projects, farms, child-care centers, auto repair shops or production of school yearbooks or campus newspapers.

Mentoring: Corporation-sponsored one-to-one relationships between an older employee and a part-time worker still in high school. Mentors are often volunteer employees or retirees. Mentoring takes place at school or at the workplace.

Alternative Schools: Known for their individualized instruction and flexible scheduling, these experimental schools integrate remedial reading, writing and math instruction into all subjects, providing work/study options at the students' own pace. They also offer personal and career counseling, day care, family education and referrals to other agency services.

Youth Community Service: Led by Minnesota in 1987, several states are appropriating money to allow recent high school graduates or dropouts to work full time in such areas as conservation, recreation and historic preservation. There is increasing interest in federal renewal of the 1930s Civilian Conservation Corps.

Job Corps: Dropouts or poorly prepared students in limited numbers are eligible for a residential training, counseling and remedial education program under the Jobs Corps, funded under the federal Job Training Partnership Act.

Sources: *Real Jobs for Real People: An Employer's Guide to Youth Apprentice*, National Alliance of Business, September 1987; *State Initiatives for School and the Workplace*, Council of State School Officers, 1991.

ticeship. At the Kroger grocery chain, for example, high school students who were recruited as baggers have gone on to management slots, and at Ross clothing stores, even the lowest-level employees are "cross-trained" so that a backroom clerk can fill in helping customers.

Not all employers are temperamentally suited to supervise apprentices. As Fairfax County's Ellen Carlos points out, "youth apprentices need supportive parents and employer sponsors who will give them that time off for beach week, who know that junior proms are important enough to allow that af-

ternoon off to get fit for a tux."

Should the federal government play a role in promoting youth apprenticeship?

The fact that the Bush administration and Gov. Clinton both are pushing youth apprenticeship initiatives suggests that a successful program will require federal leadership (see p. 920).

In one of the most influential proposals on apprenticeships, prepared for the Progressive Policy Institute in Washington, scholars Robert I. Lerman of American University and Hillard Pouncy of Swarthmore College wrote: "Washington's role is chiefly to act as a catalyst for efforts by local school systems and business to harmonize their curricula, job training and hiring practices. Ultimately, the purpose of these efforts is to gain national credibility for apprentices as highly trained workers whose skills are occupationally specific, portable enough to be valuable for a variety of employers and critical for taking effective advantage of additional training." [17]

In an era of reluctance to create new federal bureaucracies, Lerman and Pouncy, along with Sen. Nunn, have proposed creating a National Youth Apprenticeship Institute. The public-private partnership would be directed by representatives of business, labor and education and clearly differentiated from federal jobs programs targeted at the disadvantaged. The institute would specify skills required to enter and succeed in an occupation, develop a system for certifying trainers and apprentices and monitor the quality of work-site training.

"If youth apprenticeship is to be a national program, available to all, there has to be a federal role," says Hilary Pennington, president of Jobs for the Future. "The goal would be to ensure maximum mobility and opportunity and regulate standards of quality."

Pennington would strengthen the Bush administration's current approach, which favors using the existing federal-state framework to funnel seed money to apprenticeship demonstration projects. "What is not thought through is the federal role as a catalyst for creating private-sector structures like Europe's trade and craft chambers," she says. Pennington also would step up the federal role in promoting nationally recognized standards to as-sess the skills represented by a completed apprenticeship. "But each industry would have to set its own standards," she adds.

Youth apprenticeship "won't happen by itself," asserts Carnevale. "Some Republican circles assume that market pressures will drive us toward those jobs. Either that won't happen at all or it will take too long. Government can step in to make the match. If the jobs were out there, we wouldn't have to push educators too much — they'd step up and meet it."

Glover agrees that government is needed to create an "infrastructure" for apprenticeship, but he emphasizes that industry would have to be the main player, creating an ongoing "feedback system" that would synchronize schools and work sites. The degree of federal involvement "is a sticky issue," he says. "The more we try to structure and regulate the program, the less attractive it is to employers. The more we try to attract employers, the less leverage we have in its structure."

"Any federal apprenticeship effort should spell out rules and set up the system and help develop standards so that [an apprenticeship] can travel, like a college degree," says William H. Kolberg, president of the National Alliance of Business. "But the real work will be done school by school, company by company, community by community. The government establishes a general pattern, but each state goes its own way."

Oregon's Rahberger agrees that "states are the laboratories" for the youth apprenticeship movement. "Unfortunately, federal resources come with strings attached," he says, strings that "will impede unless there's a clearer federal policy on education." Oregon's philosophy, he says, differs from federal policy in that it seeks "education for all youth, regardless of their living arrangements and family ties — there's no disposable youth, no throwaways."   ■

BACKGROUND

Time-Honored Practice

Young people seeking a trade have been signing on with master craftsmen since the days of ancient Babylon, Egypt and Greece. It was during the Middle Ages in Europe that apprenticeships became institutionalized under craft guilds. A master blacksmith or mason, for example, gave an apprentice food, shelter and care during illnesses in exchange for work and a commitment of time. When the training was complete, the "graduate" would agree to move to another town (hence the term "journeyman") so as not to compete with his master.

Centuries later, the guilds would lose their influence during the industrial revolutions of the 18th and 19th centuries. The tradition of apprenticeship, however, continued ad hoc. Benjamin Franklin, for example, was a printer's apprentice in New England in the 1720s.

In the early 19th century, apprentice programs gave America's fledgling unions early momentum in recruiting. By the 20th century, however, the assembly-line system had put apprenticeships in disfavor. "The factory system made a long period of apprenticeship unattractive to boys who could get immediate employment in the factory," write labor experts Marshall and Tucker. "More important, under the factory system the old, independent masters were no longer independent and it no longer paid them to teach aspirants the trade. As workers themselves became interchangeable parts, it no longer paid an employer to invest heavily in the skills of the worker, who could get up and take his skills with him whenever he wished." [18]

In the early 20th century, apprenticeships became the province of labor unions, which began working with

Union Apprentices in the United States

Not to be confused with youth apprenticeship programs, registered apprenticeships are operated by traditional construction craft unions. The average age of registered apprentices is 29. In the past few years, the number of apprentices has been rising steadily, while female and minority participation has risen slightly.

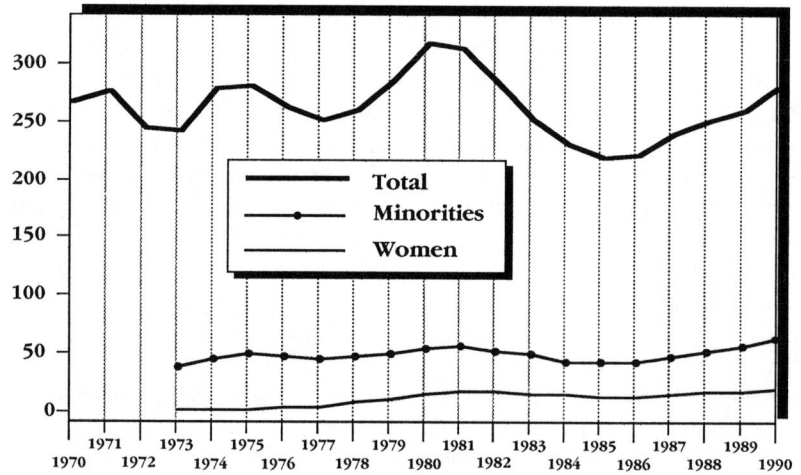

Note: No data on women or minorities were collected before 1973.

Source: U.S. Bureau of Apprenticeship and Training

state governments to erect a system of regulation. In 1911, Wisconsin became the first state to enact a law governing "registered" apprenticeships. Employers were not uninterested — as early as 1912, a Chicago business group sent an emissary to study the successful apprentice program already in wide use in Germany.

This period also saw the rise of systematic vocational education, advanced by educators who were worried that high schools were not meeting the needs of students who, in the words of educator James Russell, would "do the rougher work of life." Beginning with the 1917 Smith-Hughes Act,* vocational education was characteristically a federally oriented endeav-

*The Smith-Hughes Act authorized grants to the states for vocational education in public schools and other institutions below college level.

or, in contrast with mainstream public schooling, which was controlled by states and localities.

Federal Involvement

President Franklin D. Roosevelt's New Deal saw creation in 1933 of the U.S. Employment Service, an agency that sends representatives into schools to administer tests, counsel students and offer job placement. In 1934, union stewardship of apprenticeships was recognized with the chartering of the Federal Committee on Apprenticeship, made up of business and labor representatives who advise the Labor Department.

Most important, in 1937 Congress passed the National Apprenticeship Act. Using the Wisconsin law as a

model, it set up a joint federal-state framework of apprenticeship programs in numerous occupations. Because unions were worried that the law might be used to train future strikebreakers, they successfully lobbied to place responsibility for the law's enforcement in the Labor Department instead of leaving it to one of the federal government's education agencies.

Since 1937, some 5 million Americans have been trained as registered apprentices. "Union apprenticeship programs in the building trades and electrical-mechanical trades are arguably the best job-training programs in history," Andrea Dobson, a union official who is vice chair of the Oregon Workforce Quality Council, testified before the House Employment Opportunities Subcommittee on June 17.

A major initiative of the administration of President John F. Kennedy was passage of the 1962 Manpower Development and Training Act (MDTA), which represented the first peacetime effort by the federal government to assess the country's labor needs and retrain workers with obsolete skills. Expanded in 1963, the act also provided federal funding for union apprenticeships, though today's union officials recall that training under MDTA was "limited and fragmented."

The year 1963 also saw passage of a federal vocational education bill that shifted the emphasis from instruction in specific occupations to targeting hard-to-employ youth. In an era of dramatic hikes in federal spending as part of President Lyndon B. Johnson's Great Society, federal training efforts were boosted further by Johnson's 1964 Economic Opportunity Act and the creation that year of the Job Corps program to provide employment programs for disadvantaged youth. In 1965, Johnson also backed amendments to the MDTA that expanded federal job-training efforts.

In the early 1970s, President Richard

Continued on p. 916

Chronology

1930s New Deal launches federal registered-apprenticeship program.

1937
Congress enacts National Apprenticeship Act (Fitzgerald Act) providing federal and state regulation of registered-apprenticeship programs.

1960s Expansion of federal spending on training and youth job programs.

March 5, 1962
President John F. Kennedy signs Manpower Development and Training Act (MDTA) providing federal money to retrain workers, including registered apprentices and youth.

1963
Congress enacts Vocational Education Act and amends MDTA to better target youths from age 16.

Aug. 11, 1964
Congress passes President Lyndon B. Johnson's Economic Opportunity Act creating Job Corps to train youth.

Oct. 16, 1968
Johnson signs Vocational Education Act Amendments.

1970s Nixon administration disperses federal jobs programs to states. Carter-era attempts at apprenticelike youth programs.

July 12, 1971
President Richard M. Nixon signs Emergency Employment Act providing 150,000 public-service jobs.

Dec. 12, 1973
Nixon signs Comprehensive Employment and Training Act (CETA) decentralizing manpower programs and sharing revenues with states.

Sept. 29, 1976
Congress passes Education Act Amendments.

Aug. 5, 1977
President Jimmy Carter signs Youth Employment and Demonstration Projects Act.

Oct. 15, 1978
Congress amends CETA act to focus on the disadvantaged.

1980s President Ronald Reagan cuts federal Bureau of Apprenticeship and Training in half. CETA replaced by Job Training Partnership Act. Education reform gets underway.

December 1980
Congress rejects lame-duck President Jimmy Carter's $3 billion-a-year job and education aid for unemployed youth.

Oct. 13, 1982
President Ronald Reagan signs bill replacing CETA with Job Training Partnership Act, eliminating public-sector jobs.

Aug. 8, 1984
Congress passes Carl D. Perkins vocational-education act with 15 references to apprenticeship.

1987
Hudson Institute's *Workforce 2000* report warns of mismatch between workers and skills demanded and rise of services over manufacturing; Labor Department launches "Apprenticeship 2000" program.

1988
Publication of W. T. Grant Foundation's *The Forgotten Half*, making a case for education and training initiatives for non-college-bound youth. Congress passes Omnibus Trade and Competitiveness Act.

Sept 1989
Governors led by Bill Clinton of Arkansas meet with President Bush at education summit in Charlottesville, Va., stating new goals for human-resource-based education.

1990s Interest in youth apprenticeship mounts.

1990
Publication of *America's Choice: High Skills or Low Wages!* calling for drastic changes in training and education to compete in high-performance work organization. Congress amends Carl Perkins vocational act.

1991
Wisconsin and Oregon pass legislation and become first states to convert the *America's Choice* report into action on apprenticeship.

January 1992
President Bush releases Job Training 2000 program to steamline federal job training.

April 1992
Bush proposes National Youth Apprenticeship Plan.

July 1992
Clinton proposes youth apprentice program as part of his "Putting People First" economic plan.

Continued from p. 914

M. Nixon, after a long fight with Congress, succeeded in dispersing many of the 1960s federal jobs programs by turning the funds over to the states. As part of a compromise, Congress passed the 1973 Comprehensive Employment and Training Act (CETA), which created public-sector jobs in areas of high unemployment.

Experiments Under Carter

CETA would be expanded in 1978 during the administration of President Jimmy Carter and combined with the federal government's first efforts at something resembling the current proposals for youth apprenticeships. Under the 1977 Youth Employment Demonstration Project Act, the Labor Department funded city-based youth apprenticeship projects in Cleveland, Houston, Nashville, New Orleans, Des Moines and Rockford, Ill., plus statewide projects in New Jersey and Rhode Island.[19]

Some 3,000 apprentices received training, of whom 60 percent were eventually placed in jobs, at an average cost of $1,384 in federal wage subsidies. The programs were largely successful, according to a 1981 evaluation: 95 percent of the youths expressed satisfaction, and 63 percent of the employers recommended that other employers join.[20]

Less successful were several other initiatives under Carter, including an apprentice program within the federal government and the National Industry Promotion Plan, designed to extend apprenticeship beyond construction and manufacturing, and another effort that sought to create apprenticeships through a consortium of small businesses. Analysts said the lack of national standards or models forced their cancellation when federal funding ran out.

The Carter programs contained "lots of enthusiasm and received lots of money but did not result in much learning," says Cornell's Hamilton.

"There was too much too soon, and the stress on getting kids in jobs overwhelmed any efforts at research" on what makes apprenticeships work.

Cuts Under Reagan

Under President Ronald Reagan, CETA was replaced by the 1982 Job Training Partnership Act, which eliminated CETA's public-sector jobs and emphasized structured partnerships with businesses to create employment in depressed areas. Also under Reagan, the U.S. Employment Service was severely curtailed (at its peak in 1963, it had served 600,000 students in half the nation's high schools). Finally, staff size at the federal Bureau of Apprenticeship and Training was sliced in half. (Robert Glover, who was then chairman of the Federal Committee on Apprenticeship, says he quit his post to protest the "disinterest, inactivity and neglect on the part of [the Reagan] administration" in maintaining the apprenticeship program.)

Reagan budget-cutters were less successful in the 1984 debate over reauthorization of the federal vocational education law. The Carl D. Perkins Vocational Education Act boosted federal spending on vocational programs, particularly for the handicapped and disadvantaged at 28 percent more than Reagan had requested. The bill also encouraged the concept of apprenticeship.

Education Reform

The current momentum of the youth apprenticeship movement is attributable in great part to the general push for educational reform during the 1980s. The 1983 Education Department report *A Nation at Risk* spurred a nationwide re-examination of a failing public school system, but with an emphasis not on applied learning but on returning to traditional academic standards. Indeed, not

long after the report's release, then-Education Secretary William J. Bennett outlined his ideal high school curriculum at mythical James Madison High School and mentioned vocational courses only as electives.[21]

Later in the decade, however, as America's declining fortunes in international trade became apparent, businesses grew concerned about work-force quality and began what today has become active involvement in education.[22]

In 1988, the lack of jobs skills and poor literacy rates among the 50 percent of the country's youth who do not attend college was alarmingly documented in *The Forgotten Half*, a report by a commission of educators, social scientists, union leaders and business executives sponsored by the W. T. Grant Foundation. "A century ago, a high school education was thought to be superfluous for factory workers, and a college degree was the mark of an academic or a lawyer," the report noted. "Between now and the year 2000, for the first time in history, a majority of all new jobs will require some postsecondary education."[23]

The bleak prognosis echoed what had been asserted the previous year in *Workforce 2000*, a Labor Department report prepared by the Indianapolis-based Hudson Institute, which warned of a mismatch in skills and jobs of the future and predicted the further demise of manufacturing and the rise of service jobs.

The advantages to the country — and American business in particular — of a new effort to equip undereducated youth with marketable job skills was driven home to many in the 1990 report *America's Choice*. It called for raising educational standards for non-college-bound students by requiring all 10th-graders to pass a general knowledge test before earning a nationally recognized "Certificate of Initial Mastery." And, more broadly, the report linked such educational reform

Continued on p. 918

Lessons From the German Model of Apprenticeship

Boosters of youth apprenticeships look with envy at the well-oiled vocational-education systems in Denmark and Sweden. They draw lessons from Japan, where employers work hand-in-glove with high schools to keep educational achievement high and to recruit promising young job candidates.

But the most frequently cited model for a successful apprenticeship system is in Germany. The product of centuries-old traditions and an economic miracle that built Germany up from the ruins of World War II, the apprenticeship system is credited by German business leaders with being a major component in the engine that has made their country Europe's No. 1 economic power.

For 20 years, U.S. legislators, executives and education officials have been touring the academic and work sites that comprise Germany's "dual" system of education, so-called because it combines classroom and workplace instruction and because it represents a public-private partnership.

Two-thirds of Germany's young people participate in some aspect of the vocational system, and a whopping 1.8 million of them currently bear the title of apprentice. "German apprentices are far less likely than U.S. vocational high school students to regard themselves as losers, relegated to a lower track compared to college-bound youth," notes Cornell University human development Professor Stephen Hamilton in his book on apprenticeship.[†] Indeed, some 15 percent of Germany's college graduates have also earned apprenticeship certificates.

Though a few large German companies such as Daimler Benz and Siemens have notable apprentice programs, nine out of 10 apprentices are employed by the 500,000 German companies with fewer than 500 employees — the firms that create two-thirds of Germany's gross national product.[††] The two-to-four-year programs cost an average of $18,000, close to the tab for one year at an American Ivy League university.

Company participation in apprenticeships is voluntary, but since nearly all German firms belong to regional or industry-based craft or commerce chambers, they are all required to help finance the training of workers. (Indeed, many train more than they can employ.) It is the chambers that set apprenticeship standards and supervise training and examinations.

German students begin exploring occupations in the 7th grade, when many are already tracked either toward *gymnasia* (schools for the university-bound) or toward a combination academic-technical program. By age 16, the latter group begins spending as many as four days a week on a work site learning such concrete skills as bookkeeping, electrical engineering or auto mechanics.

In exchange for on-the-job training, students receive stipends averaging $400 a month and take interim and final exams supervised by their employers. More than half the apprentices remain with the firm where they trained (though companies are not obligated to hire them), and a larger share spend their careers in the same occupation, according to a study by the Progressive Policy Institute.[‡]

"The result," write labor specialists Ray Marshall and Marc Tucker in their new book, *Thinking for a Living: Education and the Wealth of Nations*, "is a work force among the most highly skilled on the face of the earth, a youth unemployment rate that is among the lowest of all the advanced industrial nations and a sense of self-worth and competence among those starting out at work that would be the envy of all Americans who care about their kids."

"Germany says that an 18-year-old, with training, can be a valuable citizen," says Samuel Halperin, study director in the Washington, D.C., office of the W. T. Grant Foundation. "Plus, even if apprentices leave a job, employers feel they have made an investment, that taxing themselves is part of building long-range prosperity."

Whether such cooperation between employers and youth could be transplanted to American soil is the $64,000 question among advocates of youth apprenticeships. They point to stark cultural, governmental and economic differences between Germany and the United States. "They have stronger unions [representing 46 percent of the work force]," Hamilton notes, "and their executives have a sense of civic responsibility that goes beyond maximizing profits." Finally, he says, more German business are financed by German banks rather than the stock market, which affords them a long-term view on such issues as investing in training.

Some observers of the German method also express concern about rigid entry requirements as well as the dependence on personal connections and style to win coveted jobs. They say these aspects of the program perpetuate inequality between the genders and discriminate against foreign workers.

"We don't want the German system per se," says Anthony P. Carnevale, chief economist at the Alexandria, Va.-based American Society for Training and Development. "It's bureaucratic and regulated, and it tracks by social class. We can't buy the German system and install it here. We want something evolutionary."

[†] Stephen Hamilton, *Apprenticeship for Adulthood* (1990), p. 144.

[††] "Think Small: The Export Lessons to be Learned From Germany's Mid-sized Companies," *Business Week*, Nov. 4, 1991, p. 58.

[‡] Robert I. Lerman and Hillard Pouncy, "Why America Should Develop a Youth Apprenticeship Program," Progressive Policy Institute Policy Report, March 1990.

How Education Affects Young Families

Lack of education had a dramatic impact on the income of young families with children during the 1973-90 period.† Income fell in all categories where the family head didn't have a college degree. In 1990, college graduates earned $11,700 more than college students without degrees, and high school grads had twice the income of dropouts. During the period studied, poverty rates increased at all educational levels.

| | Median Income | | Poverty Rate | |
	1973	1990	1973	1990
High School Dropout	$18,842	$10,213	32.2%	56.6%
High School Graduate	$28,410	$20,000	11.1%	28.0%
1 - 3 Years of College	$31,710	$27,000	8.1%	18.2%
College Graduate	$37,757	$38,700	2.1%	5.8%

† *Figures are adjusted for inflation. Young families are defined as those headed by persons under 25 years old.*

Source: Figures compiled by Professor Andrew Sum of Northeastern University, cited in testimony by Dr. Samuel Halperin before the House Subcommittee on Census and Population, July 28, 1992.

Continued from p. 916

to proposals for revolutionary changes in the way businesses are managed.

To catch up with their overseas competitors, the report said, U.S. firms should tap the strengths and skills of the average front-line worker to create a "high-performance work force." This meant abandoning the century-old, top-heavy, hierarchical mass-production systems associated with early-20th century management theorist Frederick Winslow Taylor. "Under the Taylor system, more planners are needed to develop procedures, more schedulers, more set-up and maintenance people, more checkers," the report noted. In the new "high-performance" work organization, "the guiding principle . . . is to reduce bureaucracy by giving authority to direct workers for a wide variety of tasks." [24]

The fundamental changes proposed in the *America's Choice* report had a wide impact on leaders in government, business, labor and academia but were particularly inspirational to advocates

of youth apprenticeship. The report was lauded as forward-looking by Marshall and Tucker, who wrote that the 1983 *Nation at Risk* "report said the problem was decline and it could be solved by restoring lost standards; the 1990 [*America's Choice*] report said the problem was a failure to reach targets to which the country had never before aspired." [25]

'Contextual' Learning

Interest in youth apprenticeship has coincided with a re-examination of the benefits of vocational education. Historically, writes Paul E. Barton, director of the Policy Information Center of the Educational Testing Service (ETS), there was a "wall between academic/general and vocational education." There was a tendency among vocational advocates not to see value in academics that do not have obvious application and a belief that their stu-

dents would not sit still for academic course work. "On the academic side," Barton writes, "there has been a tendency to belittle vocational education as being second-class, or to believe this was not the best way to prepare for employment." [26]

But nowadays, education specialists increasingly emphasize the value of practical — as opposed to theoretical — instruction that is applied in a concrete situation. "Contextual education," explains Columbia University Teachers College Professor Sue E. Berryman, is effective because it replicates the learning process of the young child, "who is the most spectacular learner."

In the early years of a human life, she writes, "(1) learning takes place in context. Children learn during their first five years in the midst of meaningful, ongoing activities and receive immediate feedback on the success of their actions; (2) Parents and friends serve as models for imitative learning and provide structure to and connections between their experiences; (3) Learning is functional. Concepts and tools are acquired as tools to solve problems; (4) The need for and purpose of the learning are explicitly stated for the child." [27]

In an apprenticeship or any school environment more oriented toward the work world, such theory would have English students writing practice business letters instead of book reports on *The Rhyme of the Ancient Mariner*, and students of auto mechanics would stay literate in the increasingly technical language of manufacturers' parts manuals.

Apprentice programs that were well integrated into school curriculums, advocates argue, would turn out students far better prepared for the ever-changing job market than students in traditional vocational education, where 60 percent of the participants "end up in jobs that have nothing to do with the training they receive in high schools," assert

Lerman and Pouncy.

New emphasis on contextual learning might also motivate students to take their studies more seriously. "Most kids think [academic] educational methods are torture devices invented by teachers," says Cornell's Hamilton. "And they get that idea because they can see that no one in the workplace is doing these things." Concrete student accomplishments in high school might, in turn, prompt employers to take high school job applicants more seriously, asking to see transcripts, for example, which currently they seldom do.

"Most employers look at the high school diploma as evidence of staying power, not of academic achievement," says the *America's Choice* report. "They realized long ago that it is possible to graduate from high school in this country and still be functionally illiterate. As a result, the non-college-bound know that their performance in high school is likely to have little or no bear-

ing on the type of employment they manage to find." [28]

Such a change in school curricula would have to be accompanied by new efforts by school guidance counselors to understand and inform students of the realities of the current job market. A 1980 ETS survey showed that only 4 percent of counselors spent more than a third of their time on job placement, while fully 34 percent spent that much time on students' choice of high school courses, 30 percent spent that much time on college admissions, 27 percent on attendance and discipline problems and 25 percent on long-term career planning.

"Higher education is doing a great job of selling college," says Oregon's Rahberger. "And in college prep, there are catalogs, and everyone understands the criteria." But if guidance counselors could be asked to compare college prep and practical, job-related counseling, "the question would be, which gives you more bang for your buck?" ∎

ginning this fall, 100 paid slots at six schools will be offered to high school juniors for a two-year period and matched with registered training agents at companies around the state. The Wisconsin program, established after state officials looked at Germany's vocational education program, is part of a larger "School-to-Work Initiative" passed by the Legislature that provided funds for 10th grade "gateway assessment," tech prep (*see glossary, p. 920*) and postsecondary enrollment options.*

Business groups have several pilot apprentice programs up and running. Since 1990, the National Alliance of Business has presided over the Quality Connection Consortium, a collaboration with BankAmerica, San Francisco's Mission High School, Sears, Roebuck & Co., and the DuPage County (Illinois) Area Occupational Education System. It is one of six of demonstration projects to receive grants from the Labor Department.

Also since 1990, Jobs for the Future has been operating a foundation-supported National Youth Apprenticeship Initiative at 10 sites, giving high school students apprenticeships in manufacturing, office technology and health care. Similar foundation grants have been awarded under the umbrella of the Council of Chief State School Officers in Washington, as part of its general efforts to promote career-oriented education over past programs that seemed merely to explore a student's lifestyle, talents and interests.

Finally, in Minneapolis, Minn., a nonprofit organization called Next Innovations has launched a pilot apprentice program that enables 18-to-24-year-olds to work in nonprofit community development.

Faced with a shortage of funds for

CURRENT SITUATION

Demonstration Projects

Youth apprenticeship has clearly moved from the talk to the action stage. Today there are more demonstration projects under way than at any time in U.S. history. In Maine, apprenticeship pilot projects began this fall in three schools under the supervision of Maine Technical College and state agencies. Maine's Republican governor, John R. McKernan Jr., got the inspiration for the program after watching apprentices at work in Germany and Denmark.

This fall in Arkansas, one of the

first state-funded apprentice programs placed 246 apprentices at 70 companies. One component of the program is a five-year apprenticeship for high school juniors offered by the Metalworking Connection, a consortium of 67 small fabricating companies organized at Henderson State University. It took shape after Gov. Clinton witnessed something similar in Italy. The program draws on money from the state's Educational Excellence Trust Fund, which is supported through sales taxes and a 1991 one-half of 1 percent hike in the Arkansas corporate income tax.

Oregon and Wisconsin were the first states to model a youth apprentice program on the recommendations of the *America's Choice* report. Oregon's program is part of a comprehensive education-reform law. Be-

*The German Marshall Fund of the United States, which seeks to strengthen U.S.-European relations, sponsored the trip by Wisconsin officials.

registered-apprentice programs, many labor officials worry that youth apprenticeships might exploit cheap labor and aid non-union firms in recruiting. But some of their anxiety is dissipating. Last April, the Federal Committee on Apprenticeship released a statement saying "the nation should develop a comprehensive, seamless youth training program and education system that responds to needs of all industries and all young people." And in July, the National Association of Governmental Labor Officials recommended tying youth apprentice programs to existing apprenticeship programs.

Clinton vs. Bush

For the first time in U.S. history, youth training has become a major issue in a presidential campaign, notes the National Alliance of Business' Kolberg. Both President Bush and Gov. Clinton have offered worker-training proposals that include youth apprenticeships. Their main difference on the general topic of training has been over funding. Clinton favors a 1.5 percent payroll tax, a proposal that Bush attacked vehemently as a burden on small business. Bush favors a voluntary approach with government encouragement.

Youth apprenticeship has been a Clinton pet project for years. His wife, Hillary, served on the commissions that produced *The Forgotten Half* report in 1988 and the *America's Choice* report in 1990. The latter report was prepared under the chairmanship of a key Clinton adviser, Ira C. Magaziner, an economic consultant based in Providence, R.I. Clinton has told his state's current apprentices, "You are real important to the state of Arkansas. We don't have a person to waste." [29]

The Clinton-Gore economic plan calls for creation of "a national apprenticeship program by bringing business,

labor and education leaders together to offer non-college-bound students skills training, with the promise of good jobs when they graduate." Clinton has proposed spending some $10 billion over four years on the program. On the campaign trail, he often says, "The only way America can compete and win in the 21st century is to have the best-educated, best-trained work force in the world."

Clinton's proposal was dismissed as "a costly mandate, a tax on every worker and his wages," by the Bush-Quayle campaign's assistant press secretary, Darcey Campbell. "For every problem facing the nation, Bill Clinton seems to have a new tax in mind," she says.

Though Bush's Labor Department first announced grants for youth apprenticeship demonstration projects as early as 1990, it was during this election year that administration activity was stepped up under Labor Secretary Lynn Martin.

In January 1992, Bush announced a "Job Training 2000" initiative that was expanded and submitted as legislation in April. It would create a federal-state-local framework to develop partnerships among businesses, schools and labor organizations.

"Far too many of our young people leave school poorly equipped for a rapidly changing and increasingly sophisticated workplace," Martin said in May. "Voluntary apprenticeship programs can enable them to enter the work force with real work experience, a skills certificate and a meaningful high school diploma."

President Bush's original proposal, introduced by Rep. Bill Goodling, R-Pa., and Sen. Bob Dole, R-Kan., would have provided $55 million to set up partnerships with labor, business and schools. Following the Republican National Convention in August, Bush doubled the proposed spending on apprenticeship to $100 million annually for five years, coupled with a $2 billion adult training

proposal and $1 billion for a nationwide Youth Training Corps to work in parks, recreation areas and low-income housing.

Van Erden of the Labor Department's Office of Work-Based Learning says the increased funding was not an election-year ploy but rather a reaction to the fact that states such as Wisconsin and Maine had proceeded faster in launching apprenticeship demonstration projects than expected. This meant there was a need to speed up implementation of the national plan, he says.

Markley Roberts, assistant director of economic research and development at the AFL-CIO, attacked Bush's training initiatives as "long on rhetoric and short on substance." "We support efforts to facilitate the transition from school to work," Roberts says. "However, we oppose efforts to undercut child labor laws and the Fair Labor Standards Act under the guise of promoting youth apprentice programs."

John R. Kroger, deputy policy director of the Clinton campaign, called Bush's proposal "a very cynical attempt to use the language of apprenticeships without actually doing anything. It would make only a marginal difference and, frankly, provide a tax break to corporations that are already establishing apprenticeship programs." [30]

Carnevale of the American Society for Training and Development says the Clinton and Bush approaches actually are very similar. But, he adds, Clinton's willingness to spend more money on apprenticeship and training makes it appear that he has the more substantive commitment.

Pennington of Jobs for the Future agrees that apprenticeships "are more central to Clinton's agenda," but gives Bush's Labor Department credit for advancing the issue, even if belatedly. Regardless of who wins in November, she says, apprenticeship will remain a hot topic. ∎

Continued on p. 922

At Issue:

Are U.S. businesses likely to embrace youth apprenticeship?

ROBERT I. LERMAN AND HILLARD POUNCY

Lerman is a professor at American University and Pouncy is a professor at Swarthmore College
FROM *PROGRESSIVE POLICY INSTITUTE REPORT*, MARCH 1990.

yes

We believe youth apprenticeship can help us fulfill four urgent national goals: First, offering serious training and entry-level jobs to large numbers of non-college youth will increase the supply of skilled workers. The opportunity to acquire marketable skills will be particularly important to minorities and women, who will make up a disproportionately large part of new entrants to the work force.

Since employers will be providing and paying for most of the training, the skills will be in fields they expect to need. In fact, quality and relevant training will do more to raise productivity than increased physical capital....

Second, as the productivity of non-college youth increases, a rise in their wages will follow. Their increased earning power will reduce the income gap between them and college-educated workers. We can expect employers to build on the capacities of apprentices by developing new job ladders and providing additional career training....

Third, word of promising new career options and the chance to begin job training by 11th grade will filter down to high school and junior high students. This could well achieve more improvement in academic skills than most school reforms currently under discussion....

Fourth, the enhanced education, training and careers of non-college youth will revive hope among youth who today are harming themselves through drugs and early parenthood.... It is conceivable that a large, effective youth apprenticeship program will help bring today's urban underclass into the mainstream of economic and social life....

Unlike other initiatives, this job-based education strategy is inclusive, not exclusive; it is productivity-enhancing, not simply redistributive; and it promotes the incentives to learn and earn instead of discouraging work. The program can perhaps do the most for young minority workers, yet in a way that neither stigmatizes them nor gives them advantages over white workers.

Now is the time to bring the apprenticeship idea to the center stage for the public, business and labor leaders and government policy-makers. Once people understand the program and its potential future benefit, large-scale implementation can proceed. It might take years before youth apprenticeships are sufficiently widespread to begin to generate major effects. But we believe the public will support the program and, most important, will recognize that long-term problems require long-term solutions.

THOMAS BAILEY

Bailey is a professor at Columbia University Teachers College
FROM *EDUCATIONAL RESEARCHER*, forthcoming issue.

no

According to all apprenticeship models, some formal, structured education will take place on the job. Why would employers participate? Certainly some will be willing to take on apprentices out of a sense of collective responsibility. This is probably the primary motivation for corporate participation in "adopt-a-school" programs, but it is not likely to sustain a mass effort.

Employers can also have a direct interest in participating. If they see individual apprentices as their future employees, training costs can be considered investments in the future of their own operation....

High turnover among young workers in particular lowers the probability that apprentices will be the future employees. Moreover, a mass youth apprenticeship program would have to involve many employers who may not have the job openings that would allow them to hire all of their graduating apprentices. And to the extent that youth apprenticeship also opens up future educational opportunities for the graduates, a successful youth apprenticeship program will lead to many separations as students go on to higher education, thus further weakening the incentives that employers have to invest in the training of young apprentices.

Reducing the cost of apprentices, whether through lower "training" wages or direct subsidies, is another alternative. [But] legislated training wages ... run the risk of antagonizing older workers.... Furthermore, lower apprenticeship wages work best as an incentive for employers when they are otherwise required to pay higher wages....

Current employer-training practices for production workers do not suggest a strong interest in training. As many people have emphasized, employers rarely hire teenagers for so-called career-ladder jobs that require some training. Moreover, even older production workers receive little training. Most firm-based training in this country still goes to managerial, sales and professional workers....

There needs to be some overarching institution that employers and workers (and unions, where they exist) trust that can coordinate individual employers' participation and that can help the schools work with business. At least in early stages, if employer participation is dependent on cajoling by individual schools, then the approach is doomed to remain marginal and at the mercy of the energy and commitment of individual enthusiasts.

Do Counselors Help Everyone?

Students who plan to work after high school get relatively little help from guidance counselors. Helping students choose their high school courses gets the most attention, followed by help with college selection and admission. Only 4 percent of the counselors spent at least a third of their time helping non-college-bound students with job placement.

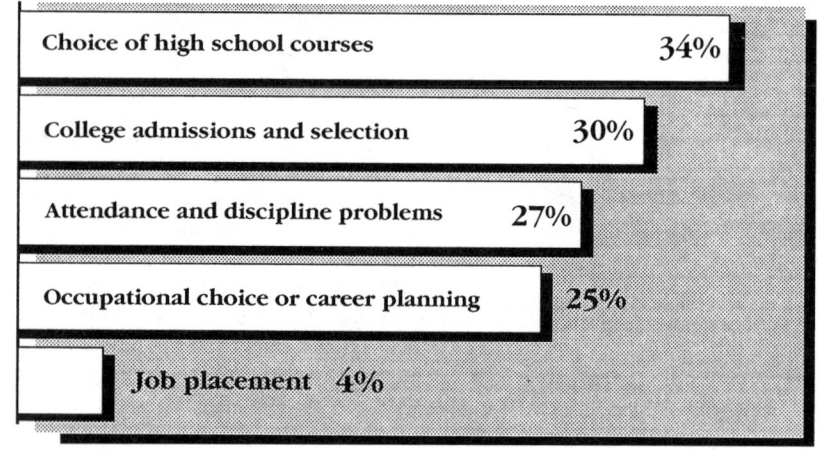

Choice of high school courses   **34%**

College admissions and selection   **30%**

Attendance and discipline problems   **27%**

Occupational choice or career planning   **25%**

Job placement   **4%**

Activities are listed at which counselors spent more than 30 percent of their time.

Source: Educational Testing Service, 1990.

Continued from p. 920

OUTLOOK

A Limited Option?

"I am willing to pay for, indeed insist upon, the education of my neighbors' children," says economist Lester C. Thurow of the Massachusetts Institute of Technology, "not because I am generous but because I cannot afford to live with them uneducated."[31]

If the idealism behind youth apprenticeship is to be converted to reality, major obstacles must be overcome. By the strictest definition, there are currently fewer than 2,000 youth apprentices nationwide, according to Jobs for the Future, and a realistic effort would still envision only about 100,000, according to the University of Texas' Glover.

"It's an option only for a certain few types who are motivated and mature," says Carlos of Fairfax County. "It was never proposed as a cure-all — there aren't enough employers who can give the individual attention."

An Education Department report on combining school and work called apprenticeship "a limited option" so long as the United States "lacks labor-market institutions that can articulate and enforce a social contract" — such as those in Germany. "Historically, it was worker mobility that caused apprenticeship agreements to unravel in the U.S. But worker mobility is a cherished right in a free society," the report observed.[32]

Others point out that apprenticeship may have trouble catching fire with the public as long as it is associated with unions, and unions are out of favor. Union officials themselves remain skeptical. "We in labor try to do what's best for our community," says Charles Bradford, the apprenticeship director for the International Association of Machinists and Aerospace Workers. "It's not union members who need the minimum wage, civil rights and health care — we have those in our contracts. But look at what I'm dealing with now. In 1980, I had 29,000 registered apprentices; now I only have 9,000. Given [the job losses in] the Rust Belt, how can you tell me government and management are serious" about apprenticeships?

An Evolutionary Process

Still, apprenticeship backers such as Robert Glover expect to see real movement on this front. "We will see it blossom under whatever name we call it because of the need to improve competitiveness," he says. Glover is concerned, however, about whether it will succeed on a large enough scale to be significant. "It will not work on moral suasion and community goodwill alone," he adds. "It has to be presented in terms of industry self-interest."

The movement toward youth apprenticeship will be evolutionary, observes Carnevale. "We clearly haven't pushed it far enough since we're not really disagreeing on how to do it. We're still in the talking stage." Pennington of Jobs for the Future says real progress will take 11 or 12 years, but she is "bullish — as long as we can help companies understand what it is intended to be." Kolberg of the National Alliance of Business is optimistic about a national system of "employer on-the-job training in which the non-college-bound young person can aspire to make $50,000 a year."

As long as poverty and unemployment remain high among youth, proposals for youth apprenticeships will seem relevant. (After the Los Angeles riots in May, Rep. Maxine Waters, D-Calif., was heard telling President Bush, "You've got to talk about real job training, apprentice training, especially in construction industries; you've got to teach life-management skills — how to negotiate, don't punch out your supervisor, teach people how to go.")[33]

Yet some apprenticeship advocates are leery of targeting poor and minority youth. "Such a strategy can easily backfire," warn Lerman and Pouncy. "When programs deal only with the most disadvantaged and least educated, the participants easily become stigmatized."[34]

Halperin of the W. T. Grant Foundation stresses the importance of making youth apprenticeship part of a whole *system* of options that help people go "from being an adolescent to being a good citizen and worker." It should not be a separate entity with multiple "funding streams that work against one another," he says. "It will take a feat of political engineering and a battle royal in Congress because the devil is in the details."

"I'm amazed and delighted at all the attention given to youth apprenticeships," says Cornell's Hamilton. "But I'm worried that it might lead to a few efforts that won't work, and then people will give up." Given the array of other vocational options — high school academies, occupation-oriented high schools and tech-prep programs, observes Columbia's Bailey, the country "may be able to incorporate many of the benefits of youth apprenticeship without having to wait until employers are ready to play a central role."[35]

Whether or not a new system develops under the label of youth apprenticeship, the American way of training is primed for some major changes. "Companies can't just buy employees, now they have to make them," says Curtis Plott, executive vice president of the American Society of Training and Development.[36]

"Some company or industry has a chance here of making a real breakthrough for the country," says consultant Massey. "We've got to do a better job of growing people. The current education system is like the metaphor of the lathe. We round off the core and then throw away all the chips." ∎

Notes

[1] Quoted in Charles Dervarics, "Apprenticeships: Tradition in Today's Economy," *Technical Skills & Training*, August/September 1990, p. 19.

[2] Stephen Hamilton, *Apprenticeship for Adulthood* (1990), p. 2.

[3] Quoted in Lonnie Harp, "Demands of Information Age Revive Old Idea of Apprenticeship," *Education Week*, June 5, 1991.

[4] Hearings on the School to Work Transition and Skill Standards Development Act were held May 6, 1992, before the Education and Labor Subcommittee on Employment Opportunities.

[5] *America's Choice: High Skills or Low Wages!*, National Center for Education and the Economy, 1990, p. 20.

[6] GAO estimate cited by Sen. Sam Nunn, D-Ga., in a statement introducing his Youth Apprenticeship Act on Nov. 26, 1991.

[7] Neal Thompson, "Rockbridge County, Va.: Weaving Together Academics and Work," *Hands and Minds: Redefining Success in Vocational Technical Education*, Education Writers Association, 1991, p. 19.

[8] Ray Marshall and Marc Tucker, *Thinking for a Living: Work, Skills and the Future of the American Economy* (1992), p. 58.

[9] *America's Choice, op. cit.*, p. 15.

[10] Quoted in Brian S. Moskal, "Apprenticeships: Old Cure for New Labor Shortage?" *Industry Week*, May 6, 1991, p. 30.

[11] Quoted in *Voices from School and Home: Arkansas Parents and Students Talk About Preparing for the World of Work and the Potential for Youth Apprenticeship*, Jobs for the Future, April 1991, p. 16.

[12] *Ibid.*, p. 24.

[13] *The Oregonian*, June 27, 1991. For background, see "Why Schools Still Have Tracking," *Editorial Research Reports*, Dec. 28, 1990, pp. 745-760.

[14] William E. Nothdurft and Jobs for the Future, "Youth Apprenticeship, American Style: Report of a Conference," December 1990.

[15] Thomas Bailey, "Can Youth Apprenticeship Thrive in the United States?" forthcoming paper, *Educational Researcher*.

[16] Quoted in *Real Jobs for Real People: An Employer's Guide to Youth Apprenticeship*, National Alliance of Business, June 1992, p. 27.

[17] Robert I. Lerman and Hillard Pouncy, "Why America Should Develop a Youth Apprenticeship System," Progressive Policy Institute, March 1990, p. 3.

[18] Marshall and Tucker, *op. cit.*, p. 21.

[19] General Accounting Office, *Transition from School to Work: Linking Education and Worksite Training*, August 1991, p. 36.

[20] Lerman and Pouncy, *op. cit.*, p. 9.

[21] See Hamilton, *op. cit.*, p. 12.

[22] For background, see "Business's Role in Education," *The CQ Researcher*, Nov. 22, 1991, pp. 873-896.

[23] W. T. Grant Foundation, *The Forgotten Half* (1988), p. 8.

[24] *America's Choice, op. cit.*, p. 39.

[25] Marshall and Tucker, *op. cit.*, p. 86.

[26] Educational Testing Service, *From School to Work: A Policy Information Report*, 1990, p. 19.

[27] Sue E. Berryman, "Designing Effective Learning Environments: Cognitive Apprenticeship Models," Institute on Education and the Economy Brief, September 1991.

[28] *America's Choice, op. cit.*, p. 45.

[29] Cited in David S. Broder column, "What Clinton's All About," *The Washington Post*, July 5, 1992.

[30] Quoted in Rochelle Stanfield, "The Forgotten Half," *National Journal*, May 2, 1992, p. 1049.

[31] Quoted in *The Forgotten Half, op. cit.*, p. 92.

[32] Education Department, *Combining School and Work: Options in High Schools and Two-Year Colleges*, March 1991, p. 9.

[33] Quoted in *The Washington Post*, May 19, 1992.

[34] Lerman and Pouncy, *op. cit.*, p. 3.

[35] *Educational Researcher, op. cit.*

[36] Quoted in *The Wall Street Journal*, March 18, 1991.

Bibliography

Selected Sources Used

Books

Hamilton, Stephen F., *Apprenticeship for Adulthood: Preparing Youth for the Future,* The Free Press, 1990.

A Cornell University professor of human development gives an account of his year in Germany spent examining the German system of youth apprenticeship. He offers thoughts on how such a system might be adapted in the United States.

Marshall, Ray and Marc Tucker, *Thinking for a Living: Work, Skills, and the Future of the American Economy,* Basic Books, 1992.

A former Carter administration Labor secretary and the president of the National Center on Education and the Economy outline their plan for an educational and industrial system that links social and economic needs.

Articles

Harp, Lonnie, "Demands of Information Age Revive Old Idea of Apprenticeship," *Education Week,* June 5, 1991.

The history and current status of youth apprenticeship are outlined by an education reporter.

McKenna, Joseph F., "Apprenticeships: Something Old, Something New, Something Needed," *Industry Week,* Jan. 20, 1992.

A business writer quotes top authorities on youth apprenticeship as they examine the German system and discuss how it might be adopted in the United States.

Reports

Council of Chief State School Officers, *State Initiatives for School and the Workplace,* 1991.

A Washington-based national group of school officials outlines nationwide activities surrounding school and work issues, among them youth apprenticeship.

Education Writers Association, *Hands and Minds: Redefining Success in Vocational Technical Education,* W. T. Grant Foundation, 1992.

A team of journalists conducted on-site interviews with high school students and teachers who are involved with new experiments linking school with work in Virginia, California, Delaware and Massachusetts.

Educational Testing Service, *From School to Work: A Policy Information Report,* 1990.

The organization that administers and evaluates the nation's standardized high school tests offers data and discussion of the complex issues surrounding adolescents' transition from school to work.

Lerman, Robert I. and Hillard Pouncy, *Why America Should Develop a Youth Apprenticeship System,* Progressive Policy Institute, March 1990.

Professors at American University and Swarthmore College offer a detailed argument for apprenticeship, calling it the answer to "a fundamental domestic challenge in the 1990s."

National Alliance of Business, *Real Jobs for Real People: An Employer's Guide to Youth Apprenticeship,* 1992.

A Washington business group concerned with training prepared this comprehensive history and explanation of how youth apprentice programs might work.

National Center on Education and the Economy, *America's Choice: High Skills or Low Wages: The Report of the Commission on the Skills of the American Workforce,* June 1990.

A bipartisan commission headed by former Reagan administration Labor Secretary Bill Brock offers a plan for revolutionizing American schools and work sites by linking school with work.

Nothdurft, William E. and Jobs for the Future, *Youth Apprenticeship, American Style: A Strategy for Expanding School and Career Opportunities,* December 1990.

This summary of a conference of government officials, educators, labor leaders and business executives outlines issues raised in establishing a national youth apprenticeship effort.

Shenon, Carol, *Union Perspectives on New Work-Based Youth Apprenticeship Initiatives,* Jobs for the Future, January 1992.

A writer with the AFL-CIO's Human Resources Development Institute reports on interviews with labor leaders about their concerns about youth apprenticeships and their effect on registered-apprentice programs.

W. T Grant Foundation, *The Forgotten Half: Pathways to Success for America's Youth and Young Families,* November 1988.

A commission of educators, government officials, labor leaders and business executives assembled data and reported on what they view as the country's disturbing neglect of its non-college-bound youth.

The Next Step

Additional Articles from Current Periodicals from EBSCO Publishing's Database

Books & reading

Rorabaugh, W.J., "Book reviews," *Technology & Culture,* **April 1991, p. 427.**

Reviews the book "Apprenticeship: From Theory to Method and Back Again," edited by Michael W. Coy.

Education

"Job training by apprenticeship," *Fortune,* **June 29, 1992, p. 16.**

Reports that starting this fall, high school students in Maine will have the option of being apprenticed in various pilot programs. Details of on-the-job training; support for the project by Gov. John R. McKernan, Jr. hopes to develop a skilled labor pool.

"Missing bridge," *The Economist,* **Feb. 9, 1991, p. 30.**

Examines the growing call for vocational training as an alternative bridge between school and career. Concern about competitiveness and the widening gap between rich and poor; lack of trained workers; the Job Training Partnership Act; apprenticeship programs; steps taken by the Labor Department; details.

Celis, W., "Oregon to stress job training in restructuring high school," *The New York Times,* **July 24, 1991, p. A1.**

Discusses Oregon's education plan, the first in the nation to establish a statewide apprenticeship program and make students choose between job training or a college-preparatory curriculum after 10th grade. The plan grew out of increasing concern that public schools have done a poor job of serving students who do not go to college. Other provisions of the plan.

Darch, G., R. Gersten, et al., "Apprenticeship and intensive training of consulting teachers: A naturalistic study," *Exceptional Children,* **December 1990/January 1991, p. 226.**

Assesses the impact of a model for intensive training of consulting teachers. Impact of intensive training on performance compared with teachers receiving standard training; significant differences in those areas of the job related to instructional improvement; low-income schools in a large metropolitan area; method; results; discussion.

Deutschman, A., M.D. Fefer, et al., "Why kids should learn about work," *Fortune,* **Aug. 10, 1992, p. 86.**

States that to achieve a better work force — with a better work ethic — companies should help forge links between academic subjects and business needs. States that are creating apprenticeship programs for high school students who are not bound for college; assertion that work does build character; why children seem to be absorbing less and less about their parents' working lives.

Hamilton, M.A. & S.F. Hamilton, "A progress report on apprenticeships," *Educational Leadership,* **March 1992, p. 44.**

Discusses apprenticeship, an ancient practice that has recently re-emerged as a promising strategy for improving education, especially for those who enter the work force immediately after high school. Basic principles of German apprenticeship; apprenticeship projects in America.

Harbrecht, D. & S.H. Wildstrom, "A fleeting victory for conservative democrats?" *Business Week,* **May 11, 1992, p. 49.**

Describes how some conservative Democrats fear that if their prescriptions go anywhere in the next four years, it will be because President Bush has shown a sudden fondness for such Democratic notions as a national youth apprenticeship program and a new college-loan program for middle-class parents. Republicans in disguise; education and health plans.

Hilton, M., "Shared training: learning from Germany," *Monthly Labor Review,* **March 1991, p. 33.**

Urges U.S. employers to look to Germany to learn how to make systematic, long-term investments in worker training. Overview of the German two-tiered system of training: apprenticeship, and further training; major role played by industry associations; how U.S. investments in training compare; recommended changes. Appendix: A note on the validity of the investment estimates.

Hoerr, J., "Making high school diplomas tickets to the workplace," *Business Week,* **July 9, 1990, p. 76.**

Opinion. Argues the need in the United States for a link between high school and the workplace to help non-college youths acquire skills and get channeled into stable, well-paying jobs. The "forgotten half"; teachers are career-illiterate; broad outlines for an apprenticeship program.

Linden, E., "An old idea makes a comeback," *Time,* **June 12, 1989, p. 71.**

Examines apprenticeship and how a number of educators and researchers would like to see more of it in the classrooms. Why the need for apprenticeships; results of current programs.

Novack, J., "Earning and learning," _Forbes,_ May 11, 1992, p. 150.

States that labor unions and educators don't think much of the idea, but apprenticeships are finally getting a bit of the attention they deserve. Examples of apprenticeships; spurring interest at schools; common in Europe; floundering of youth who don't go to college or drop out; advantages of apprenticeships.

Roditi, H. F., "High schools for docile workers," _Nation,_ March 16, 1992, p. 340.

Offers a look at the innovations in education that will give business a pivotal role in determining what young people should know and be able to do upon graduation. "Youth apprenticeship" programs; High Skills, Competitive Workforce Act of 1991; "Education for work" idea; details of the work and commitment; problems with these innovations; what they must do in order to succeed; programs with balance.

Schroeder, K., "Oregon makes tracks," _Education Digest,_ September 1991, p. 74.

Reveals that the Oregon state legislature has made its educational system the first in the country with a statewide apprenticeship program. Requirement that after grade 10 students must choose either a job-training or college-preparatory curriculum; support from Oregon Gov. Barbara Roberts; opponents of tracking; more.

Simms, M.C., "Are apprenticeships the answer?" _Black Enterprise,_ February 1992, p. 57.

Examines whether the European apprenticeship system may be a good model for American students. Improving the school-to-work transition; stay-in-school programs; belief that the U.S. needs a new system for producing good workers; Germany's "dual system"; possible problems if America adopts this system; more.

Szabo, J.C., "Learning and working — together," _Nation's Business,_ June 1992, p. 34.

Studies the ways apprenticeship programs benefit participating high school students and the firms that train them. How such programs work; support from the U.S. Department of Labor; why school-to-work transition programs are important for American business success; case studies of several successful apprenticeship programs. INSET: For more information on training programs.

Toch, T., "Crafting the work force," _U.S. News & World Report,_ Aug. 19, 1991, p. 63.

Describes recent changes in employment that are causing

policy-makers to rethink the school-to-work transition for the nation's workbound students and considers recent support for a national system of youth apprenticeships. Labor Department Secretary Lynn Martin's support of an apprenticeship system; nine pilot programs; establishing an Institute of Youth Apprenticeship to conduct pilot programs nationwide; Legislation in Wisconsin and Arkansas; the European experience.

Waldrop, T., "They are engineered like no other students in the world," _Newsweek,_ Dec. 2, 1991, p. 61.

Reports that the German reverence for trade crafts is at the heart of a high school system considered the best in the world. Gymnasium students train for the university entrance exams, known as the Abitur; apprentice system; 8 percent of all pupils drop out of Germany's multitrack high-school programs; more details.

History

Jacoby, D., "Legal foundations of human capital markets," _Industrial Relations,_ spring 1991, p. 229.

Examines the decline of traditional craft apprenticeships in the U.S. that has been widely attributed to legal impediments that prevented employers from holding apprentices long enough to recapture investment costs. Analysis of early 20th-century law; law that enforce indentures; more.

Jacoby, D., "The transformation of industrial apprenticeship in the United States," _Journal of Economic History,_ December 1991, p. 887.

Discusses how a nearly century-long decline in the use of apprenticeship was halted in the early 20th century as numerous attempts, particularly by corporate employers, were made to revitalize this institution. Human capital and agency theory; bonded apprenticeship and schooling; the minimum wage and apprenticeship; extension classes; conclusions.

Industries

"Ameco builds new training center to meet growing need for aircraft technicians," _Aviation Week & Space Technology,_ July 6, 1992, p. 50.

Highlights the $2.6 million apprentice training center now under construction by Beijing's Aircraft Maintenance and Engineering Corp. The center is expected to help satisfy China's growing need for qualified aircraft, avionics and aeroengine technicians. The school's first 48 students will graduate this year from an accelerated two-year course. Funding was provided by Ameco, Air China and the German government.

"Lowering turnover by using apprentices," _Inc.,_ May 1992, p. 145.

Outlines how Jim Fuchs, and his company, Fuchs Copy Systems, West Allis, Wis., developed an apprentice system for area high school and college students that not only gives the apprentice a feel for the copier business but also cuts servicing time and gives Fuchs a pool of technical people he needs. Comments from Fuchs on his relationship with his technicians.

"Slow train," *The Economist,* Mar. 2, 1991, p. 30.

Examines the initiative, involving the retraining of workers to make them more competent and competitive, being supported in North Carolina by Gov. James G. Martin. Prospect of shortages of skilled labor; expectations of low-skilled jobs to be lost during this decade; search for models of apprenticeships and regional economic development; the "tech prep" program of Joseph Grimsley; details.

Fleischer, L., "Less than peanuts," *Publishers Weekly,* June 14, 1991, p. 40.

Reports that the Gallopade Publishing Group has developed an apprenticeship program to help solve its personnel problems. Success of the program; more.

Goethals, H., "Mexico polishes its silversmiths," *Americas,* November/December 1990, p. 13.

Reports that the Mexican school, Centro Platero de Zacatecas, located in Mexico's historic mining region, is offering a one-year program to train apprentices in the production of high-grade silver jewelry. How the school drills its students in the principles of design, silver fabrication and other aspects of silver; criteria for admission.

Goldberger, P., "Beyond the master's voice," *The New York Times Magazine,* Oct. 13, 1991, p. 32.

Considers how most architects start as apprentices, reinterpreting the style of a mentor, then moving out on their own. Robert Venturi's work influenced by Frederic Schwartz; Frank Lloyd Wright's mentor, Louis Sullivan; Rick Mohler and Paul Muller, both who have taken Venturi's design stance and remade it on their own terms.

Wentz, L., "Ex-Soviet trainees wanted," *Advertising Age,* April 27, 1992, p. I-39.

Reports that Saatchi & Saatchi Advertising is trying to find trainee positions for young former Soviets by sending a mailing late this month or early next month to the top 100 multinational companies in Europe. Details of the project; once the apprenticeships are completed; what the task aims to do; cost.

Back Issues

Great Research on Current Issues Starts Right Here... Recent topics covered by The CQ Researcher are listed below. Issues dated before May 10, 1991, were published under the name of Editorial Research Reports.

APRIL 1991
Social Security
Canadian Crisis Over Quebec
California Drought
Electromagnetic Radiation

MAY 1991
School Choice
Racial Quotas
Animal Rights
U.S. and Japan

JUNE 1991
Children and Divorce
Teenage Suicide
Endangered Species
Europe 1992

JULY 1991
Teenagers and Abortion
Soviet Republics Rebel
Mexico's Emergence
Athletes and Drugs

AUGUST 1991
Sexual Harassment
Fetal Tissue Research
Oil Imports
The Palestinians

Back issues are available for $4.00 (subscribers) or $7.00 (non-subscribers). Quantity discounts apply to orders over ten. To order, call Congressional Quarterly 1-800-432-2250.

SEPTEMBER 1991
Police Brutality
Advertising Under Attack
Saving the Forests
Foster Care Crisis

OCTOBER 1991
Pay-Per-View TV
Youth Gangs
Gene Therapy
World Hunger

NOVEMBER 1991
Fast-Food Shake-Up
The Greening of Eastern Europe
Business' Role in Education
Cuba In Crisis

DECEMBER 1991
Retiree Health Benefits
Asian Americans
The Obscenity Debate
The Disabilities Act

JANUARY 1992
Term Limits
Oil Spills
Hunting Controversy
Alternative Medicine

FEBRUARY 1992
Threatened Coastlines
New Era in Asia
Assisted Suicide
Jobs in the '90s

MARCH 1992
Women and Sports
Underage Drinking
Garbage Crisis
Mafia Crackdown

APRIL 1992
Ozone Depletion
Welfare Reform
Politicians and Privacy
Illegal Immigration

MAY 1992
Native Americans
Jobs vs. Environment
Too Many Lawsuits?
Fairness in Salaries

JUNE 1992
Nuclear Proliferation
Food Irradiation
Lead Poisoning
Hard Times for Libraries

JULY 1992
Alternative Energy
Prescription Drug Prices
Alzheimer's Disease
Infant Mortality

AUGUST 1992
The Homeless
Work, Family and Stress
NATO's Changing Role
Marine Mammals vs. Fish

SEPTEMBER 1992
Domestic Partners
Violence in Schools
Public Broadcasting
Women in the Military

OCTOBER 1992
Depression
U.S. Auto Industry

Future Topics

▶ *Hispanics*

▶ *Physical Fitness*

▶ *Privitizing Government Services*

THE CQ *Researcher*

PUBLISHED BY CONGRESSIONAL QUARTERLY INC., IN CONJUNCTION WITH EBSCO PUBLISHING

Hispanic Americans

Can they find economic prosperity and political power?

W ITH SALSA NOW OUTSELLING KETCHUP, IT'S
clear that Hispanics have established a vivid
presence in American life far beyond ethnic
enclaves like Miami's Little Havana and the
barrios of East Los Angeles. Although Latinos comprise 9
percent of the U.S. population, they are still groping for a
collective identity — and a stronger political voice. This year's
election could sweep more Hispanics into office than ever
before. Meanwhile, many Latinos are finding the social
equality and economic prosperity enjoyed by earlier
immigrants to be illusive, with Hispanic children especially
hard hit. Adding to the problems, growing numbers of illegal
immigrants are putting inner cities under tremendous stress,
pitting Latinos against blacks and other minorities in the
competition for scarce jobs and limited social services.

 October 30, 1992 • Volume 2, No. 40 • 929-952

Formerly Editorial Research Reports

COVER ART: BARBARA SASSA-DANIELS

CQ Researcher

October 30, 1992
Volume 2, No. 40

EDITOR
Sandra Stencel

MANAGING EDITOR
Thomas J. Colin

ASSOCIATE EDITOR
Richard L. Worsnop

STAFF WRITERS
Charles S. Clark
Mary H. Cooper
Rodman D. Griffin

PRODUCTION EDITOR
Sarah E. Merritt

EDITORIAL ASSISTANT
Michael M. Taylor

GRAPHICS
Jack Auldridge

PUBLISHED BY
Congressional Quarterly Inc.

CHAIRMAN
Andrew Barnes

VICE CHAIRMAN
Andrew P. Corty

EDITOR AND PUBLISHER
Neil Skene

EXECUTIVE EDITOR
Robert W. Merry

ASSOCIATE PUBLISHER
John J. Coyle

EDITOR, EBSCO PUBLISHING
Melissa Kummerer

The CQ Researcher (ISSN 1056-2036). Formerly Editorial Research Reports. Published weekly (48 times per year, not printed the first Friday of any month with five Fridays) by Congressional Quarterly Inc., 1414 22nd St., N.W., Washington, D.C. 20037. Rates are furnished upon request. Second-class postage paid at Washington, D.C. POSTMASTER: Send address changes to The CQ Researcher, 1414 22nd St., N.W., Washington, D.C. 20037.

Hispanic Americans

BY RODMAN D. GRIFFIN

THE ISSUES

Next week, Democratic candidate Nydia M. Velázquez will almost certainly become the first Puerto Rican woman to be elected to the U.S. House of Representatives. She is running in New York's heavily Democratic 12th District, created under the Voting Rights Act to grant a "safe seat" in Congress to Latinos in the predominantly Hispanic area.

Destiny was clearly on Velázquez's mind back in September when she declared: "Carpetbaggers, move over! Our time has come." The former New York City Council member embodies the hopes and dreams of many Hispanic Americans, who are grossly underrepresented in Congress. They account for 9 percent of the U.S. population but fewer than 1 percent of the nation's elected officials.

Getting to this point wasn't easy. First, Velázquez had to defeat Stephen J. Solarz, D-N.Y., a popular nine-term congressman and senior member of the Foreign Affairs Committee. With four Latinos in the race, Solarz had gambled that he could tally enough votes to win in the new district, which contains a slice of his old territory, carved up by redistricting *(see p. 941)*. He lost, and now Hispanics hope Velázquez's stunning upset will be a harbinger of what's to come.

Across the country, this election could galvanize Hispanics — long viewed by pundits as "the sleeping giant" — into a political force. Observers say congressional reapportionment could give Hispanics as many as nine new representatives in Congress. (There are presently 11 Hispanics among 535 members.) The National Association of Latino Elected and Appointed Officials (NALEO) expects that 4.5 million Latinos will

vote in this presidential election, an increase of more than 20 percent over 1988.

Latinos' impact in the Electoral College could be even greater: Hispanics make up 18 percent of the total population of nine states — California, New York, Texas, Illinois, Florida, New Jersey, Colorado, Arizona and New Mexico — that together contribute 202 of the 270 electoral votes needed to get to the White House. "Hispanics could hold the swing vote in several key states, notably California and Texas," says NALEO Director Harry Pachon.

The growth of the U.S. Hispanic population is one of the most startling phenomena in American social history. As recently as 1950, the U.S. census counted fewer than 4 million residents on the U.S. mainland who would today fall under the category Hispanic, broadly defined as those who share a Spanish-language heritage and trace their roots to Spanish-speaking countries. By 1990, the Hispanic population had ballooned to 22.4 million. This growth (eight

times as fast as the non-Hispanic population during the past decade) has been accompanied by geographic dispersion and broader representation of national origins in the group.*

Historically, the great majority of this population was of Mexican origin and concentrated in the Southwest and California. Today, Hispanics are visible in virtually every major city and include large concentrations of Cubans and Puerto Ricans as well as identifiable clusters of groups from the Caribbean (Dominicans), from Central America (Salvadorans, Guatemalans and Nicaraguans) and growing concentrations of South American nationalities. *(See chart, p. 938.)* Analysts project that there will be 30-35 million Hispanic Americans by the year 2000, or 11 to 12 percent of all U.S. residents. If so, they would constitute the largest American minority, outnumbering blacks.

The notion that Hispanics represent a unified block, however, is misleading. The word Hispanic, to begin with, is a catchall term embracing new penniless illegal immigrants from Guatemala, wealthy political exiles from Cuba and Mexican-American families that have been living in what is now the Southwestern U.S. for 300 years or more. Aside from speaking Spanish, these groups often have little in common. *(See story, p. 933.)*

Nevertheless, as a group, Hispanics have left an indelible imprint on U.S. culture. You can't walk down a street in urban America without encountering the flavors and inflections of Latino culture. *(See story, p. 942.)* From singer Gloria Estefan to actor Edward James Olmos to ballplayer José Canseco, Hispanics have become marquee figures in American

---

*Roughly half the growth in the Hispanic population results from natural increase, and the other half from immigration.

society. Salsa has displaced ketchup as the nation's leading condiment, and some McDonald's now sell *fajitas*. Even Madonna, America's pop icon, has recorded songs in Spanish. At times, it's hard to tell if Latinos are being Americanized or if America is being Latinoized.

The rising Hispanic influence on American society is confounded by deeply disturbing news on how individual Hispanics are faring in this land of opportunity. They are less likely than other major racial or ethnic groups to complete high school, less likely to have health insurance and more likely than blacks to be segregated in inner-city schools, according to a 1991 report by the National Council of La Raza (NCLR).[1]

Indeed, Hispanics are disadvantaged on virtually every measure. The median income for Hispanic men, for example, is less than two-thirds the figure for non-Hispanic men — $14,141 compared with $22,207 — even though Hispanic men are more likely to be working or looking for work than any other group, including white males. Meanwhile, according to the Children's Defense Fund, Hispanic children in recent years accounted for more than half the children who entered into poverty. "Regrettably, there are not that many positive things that we can crow about," says Raúl Yzaguirre, president of NCLR.[2]

Latino leaders assert that Hispanics are underrepresented in government jobs and job-training programs and that many social programs tend not to reach Hispanics. Federal enforcement of civil rights in education, for example, relies on victims of discrimination to file complaints. But many Hispanics are reluctant to complain or are unaware of the grievance process. In other cases, they aren't eligible because they aren't citizens or legal residents.

One measure of Hispanic frustration with their worsening plight is the largely overlooked role they

played in the violence — and suffering — during the Los Angeles riots last spring.* According to the Los Angeles Police Department, Hispanics accounted for more than half of those arrested citywide during the riots. Nineteen Hispanics died in the violence, just three short of the number of black fatalities. And while newscasts featured standoffs between embittered blacks and Korean shop owners, the L.A. mobs ravaged about as many Hispanic businesses as Korean-owned ones.

During the next decade, increased competition for low-skilled jobs could cause cleavages between blacks and Hispanics as well as between Latino subgroups. Already there has been a public backlash against immigrants — and Hispanics in particular. According to opinion surveys, Hispanics are perceived as "lazy" and "unpatriotic," despite having the highest labor force participation rate of any ethnic group and the highest proportion of Medal of Honor winners. A poll conducted by the Gallup Organization in March found that 64 percent of those surveyed favored tighter immigration restrictions; 69 percent felt there are too many Hispanics.

As social scientists and policy-makers try to dispel myths about Latinos and grapple with how to keep the most impoverished among them from sinking into a permanent underclass, here are some of the questions being asked:

Why hasn't the Latino population explosion translated into political power?

"The 1980s will be the decade of the Hispanics," declared NCLR's Raúl Yzaguirre in 1978. Pollsters predicted that Hispanics would soon become a "voting time bomb."[3] But 14 years later, Latinos have largely failed at translating their numeric strength into political and

*The riots were triggered by the acquittal of four white police officers in the beating of Rodney King, a black motorist.

economic clout. "If anything, we retrogressed in the '80s," Yzaguirre says.

A 1989 study by the Southwest Voter Registration Education Project (SVREP) found that Latinos vote less, attend fewer political rallies and make fewer campaign contributions than other Americans.[4] Out of 13.8 million Hispanics of voting age, just 4.4 million registered in 1990. And out of that group, just 2.9 million reported that they actually voted. That made up just 3.5 percent of the total electorate.

One reason for the low turnout, says NALEO's Pachon, is that the Hispanic population is younger than the population at large, and young people generally are less likely to vote. Another reason is that 38 percent of voting-age Hispanics are not citizens, according to the U.S. Census Bureau. To some extent, that's a natural result of the immigration process. It takes five years of permanent residency before one can apply for citizenship. Several million Hispanics simply have not been in the country long enough to be citizens.[5]

"Beyond these obvious explanations, the political system itself has changed enormously," says Peter Skerry, director of Washington programs at UCLA's Center for American Politics and Public Policy. "We don't have strong local political organizations to draw the poor and unskilled into the political process. People don't come here because they want to vote, they come here because they want to make a living, to better themselves socially and culturally." Unlike blacks, whose churches and organizations provided an institutional base for the fight against segregation, Hispanics have lacked a political superstructure. Moreover, many Hispanics come from countries where elections, if held at all, are rigged and meaningless.

Involving Latinos in the political process takes time and organization. Disappointed by their lack of progress in the last decade, Hispanics are determined to turn the tide. Activists have

The Trouble With Being "Hispanic"

Though Latinos have had a continuous presence in this country for centuries, they have been slow to gain recognition. One problem is identity. The word "Hispanic" appeared as a census term only in 1980 — and it remains more convenient than precise: It applies to people of white, black, Indian and, frequently, thoroughly mixed ancestry who hail from countries that sometimes seem to have little in common except language and historical traditions. And the black-white dichotomy that characterizes American thinking on minorities leaves little room for Latino concerns.

For most Hispanics, the Spanish language is the most visible and charged symbol of their common cultural heritage. This is true even though about one-fourth of all Hispanics do not speak the language of their forebears.†

Many use the word Hispanic only when distinguishing themselves from Anglos (another catchall term meaning all non-Hispanic whites). Even less than Asians, Hispanics are hardly a race. If anything, Latin America has been the world's leading melting pot, yielding every possible mixture of European, African and indigenous strains.

When they meet in the U.S., Hispanics feel as much rivalry as camaraderie. Many of the first Cubans who fled from Castro were middle class or even wealthy. Other Hispanics call them "the hads" (los tenía) because so many of their sentences supposedly begin, "In Cuba, I had ...." These Cubans, in turn, contrast themselves with others who fled in the 1980 boatlift from the port of Mariel, a minority of whom had been inmates of prisons or mental hospitals. The word Marielito, flung by one Cuban American at another, can be a fighting insult.

Likewise, a Mexican American is extremely unlikely to look to a Cuban American for political leadership. Their values and experiences are often diametrically opposed.

But for all their diversity, Hispanics do share some common characteristics. Though many immigrate from rural areas, in the U.S. they have overwhelmingly become an urban population. As many as 90 percent live in cities or suburban towns. Hispanics also frequently display what U.S. Anglos have come to regard as old-fashioned

virtues: devotion to God, to family and, despite Anglo misconceptions about siestas and the "do it mañana" attitude, to work. Even the concept of machismo has a different ring in Hispanic than in Anglo ears. Asked to define the essence of masculinity, 54 percent of Hispanics responding to a 1984 Yankelovich survey answered that the ideal man above all else "is a good provider to his wife and family," vs. 34 percent of all Americans.

Even so, misperceptions about Hispanics tend to overshadow the reality. Perhaps unduly influenced by the 1950s Broadway play (and later film) "West Side Story," many Anglos feel Hispanics are prone to violence and gang warfare. Youth gangs are a problem in some areas, but police generally report that barrio crime rates at worst are no higher than in poor black and white areas. Illegal immigrants in particular seem to be less the perpetrators than the victims of crimes, which they often are reluctant to report.

In order to enhance their individual rights and collective identity, people of Latin decent are more and more accepting the term Hispanic. "The system creates incentives for Hispanics to lump themselves together, so they do it. It makes good sense," says Rodolfo O. de la Garza, a government professor at the University of Texas at Austin. In the political arena, it has obviously helped Latinos gain "safe seats" in Congress, through aggressive redistricting in recent years. It also pressures society to dole out more jobs and entitlements.

But there is a downside, too. "It generalizes a problem rather than acknowledging a particular phenomenon," adds de la Garza. "For example, this country has had an impact on perpetuating Puerto Rican poverty. You can't fix it if you treat it as a generic 'Hispanic' issue."

Some observers say there are other drawbacks as well. "In emulating the political example of blacks and claiming status as a racial minority group, Hispanics run the risk of being stigmatized as a group beyond help or hope," says UCLA political scientist Peter Skerry.

---

† Peter Skerry, "E Pluribus Hispanic?" *Wilson Quarterly*, summer 1992, p. 64.

adopted a grass-roots strategy that has led to successes in getting Hispanics on local school boards and in political redistricting. In 1974, there were 800 elected and appointed Latino officials; today there are 4,200. This year's election will undoubtedly bump up those numbers further. "The point is that we are emerging politically at a time when people are

turning off to politics, when civic participation is dropping," says SVREP President Andrew Hernández.

Indeed, the voting Hispanic electorate has grown 50 percent in the last decade. Increasingly, that has made a difference at the polls. For example, Hispanic voters played a pivotal role in Gov. Ann W. Richards' victory in Texas in 1990, giv-

ing her 80 percent of their vote. "If Dianne Feinstein had the same support, she would be governor of California," says Hernández. (Feinstein received 66 percent of Hispanic votes.) Hispanics were also critical to the victory of Harold Washington in his 1983 race for mayor of Chicago and in David Dinkins' 1989 victory in New York.

In the coming decade, some 5 million Hispanics will become eligible for citizenship, thanks in part to the amnesty program that granted legal residency to undocumented immigrants who had lived in the United States for five years.* Even so, experts say larger numbers are still unlikely to translate into a unified political voice. Contrary to popular belief, Latinos don't represent a voting block. "There is no Hispanic community politically," explains Rodolfo O. de la Garza, a professor of government at the University of Texas. "You can't talk about the 'Hispanic' vote. Cubans vote overwhelmingly Republican while Mexicans and Puerto Ricans are strongly Democratic."

Are Latinos having more difficulty assimilating into American society than other immigrant groups?

When you look at places like East Los Angeles or Miami — and even neighborhoods in South Chicago — it's easy to get the impression that Hispanics aren't melding into the American mainstream. Immigrants to the U.S. and their children have always tended to live together, of course. But the trend seems stronger, or at least more visible, among Hispanics. For one thing, their sheer numbers enable Hispanics to colonize bigger chunks of bigger cities than previous waves of immigrants could.

Perhaps more important, many Hispanics have kept close ties to their home country and continue to practice its traditions because, in many cases, they expect to go back one day after building a nest egg here. Ultimately, sociologists say, this can make assimilation more difficult. "To be Mexican in Texas isn't the

---

* Some 3.1 million illegal immigrants became eligible for citizenship under the Immigration Reform and Control Act (IRCA), landmark immigration legislation passed in 1986. See "Illegal Immigration," *The CQ Researcher*, April 24, 1992.

same as being a Pole in Chicago. They have a sense that this is home turf," notes UCLA's Skerry.

While most European and Asian immigration has occurred in clearly defined waves, the movement of people across the Rio Grande has been an almost continual stream, especially in this century. The steady flow has meant that no matter how quickly young people learn English and American ways, their community retains the status of an immigrant, Spanish-speaking minority group. To many Anglos, Hispanic insularity seems, to put it bluntly, un-American.

Cultural assimilation is a complex phenomenon. In many minds, the term itself, and underlying concept of absorption into a dominant culture, is both overly simplistic and offensive. A better term, advocacy groups argue, is acculturation, which implies the mutual influence of various cultural groups on each other.

Academic researchers tend not to define assimilation as abandoning one's heritage, or becoming indistinguishable from the dominant culture. Rather, they look at whether the grandchildren and great-grandchildren of immigrants approach national averages on several yardsticks, including how long they stay in school, their proficiency in English and their earnings.

For the families of European immigrants who flooded American shores early this century, each successive generation climbed higher on the socioeconomic ladder. By the third generation, most experts say ethnic background ceased to be an important factor in social or economic standing. Some sociologists fear the same may not be true for many Hispanics. To be sure, much of the Cuban-American population, enriched by thousands of well-educated and wealthy refugees who left the island in the early 1960s, is secure in the middle and upper economic classes. But Puerto Ricans have lagged significantly behind. *(See story, p. 944.)*

And Mexican-Americans — by far the largest group of Hispanics (63 percent) — are twice as likely as non-Hispanics to be poor, and their parents are three times less likely to have completed college.

Experts disagree over why Mexican Americans have stalled in their journey to the mainstream. Some argue that because Mexican Americans have been in this country so long their problems have little to do with the standard difficulties of immigration or assimilation, and more to do with discrimination against minorities.

"It's not an assimilation issue, it's the way in which this particular society treats these people," says Cecilia Muñoz, a senior policy analyst at NCLR. "It's classic discrimination," in education, access to social services, employment and housing, she says. "People haven't assumed it applies to Hispanics the way it has to African Americans, but in fact it does." A 1990 Urban Institute study concluded that Anglos are 52 percent more likely to receive job offers than Hispanics with the same job qualifications.[6]

Others contend that statistics on low earnings and high dropout rates among Mexican Americans are skewed by the high numbers of recent, Mexican-born immigrants, many with low educational and skill levels. Linda Chavez, staff director of the U.S. Commission on Civil Rights during the Reagan administration and author of *Out of the Barrio*, a book on Hispanic assimilation, says that while Mexican Americans may be behind today, they parallel the many European groups that eventually joined the mainstream. "It will take time," says Chavez. "It took 50 years for Italian immigrants as a group to catch up in education with other Americans." Italian Americans achieved parity in education in 1972.

"People on the left say Hispanics aren't assimilating because they're different from other ethnic groups and need to preserve their culture," says de la Garza, "and people on the

---

right say they can't do it because they don't love this country enough. But neither group has any evidence to back up their views." A recent national survey of Hispanics, conducted by de la Garza and three colleagues, found that 90 percent of native-born Mexican Americans speak English all or most of the time at home.[7] Less than 1 percent of native-born Mexican Americans speak only Spanish. "With very few exceptions, Hispanics are assimilating in American culture as much or more than other immigrant groups," he adds. Studies show that one-third of Hispanics marry non-Hispanics, and by the third generation half of all Mexican Americans speak only English and no Spanish.

The critical distinction that most research on Hispanics fails to take into account is whether those surveyed are native born or foreign born. Says de la Garza: "It would be virtually impossible for any society to absorb millions of people with low education characteristics and move them into the middle class. You can't judge success at incorporation into American society by that standard."

Are Hispanics on a collision course with African Americans?

After the L.A. riots, the media portrayed the Rodney King verdict and the carnage that followed as a classic case of cause and effect: white injustice and black rage. At the very least, it is now clear that the riot was a class rebellion as well as a race revolt. "It was the failure of the justice system to serve minorities, which is something Latinos can identify with," says Sergio Muñoz, news director of KMEX television, Los Angeles' largest Spanish-language television station. "The trigger was black. But the underlying reality was the interracial, inter-ethnic tensions of life in the inner city."[8]

Once solidly united in the drive for equality, blacks and Hispanics are now often at odds over such issues

as jobs, immigration and political empowerment. At the root of the quarrels is a seismic demographic change: Early in the next century, Hispanics will outnumber African Americans for the first time.

Though the differences were long submerged, they have recently burst into the open. As their numbers have grown, Hispanics have demanded a larger slice of the economic and political pie. Blacks, long accustomed to being the senior partner in the minority coalition, fear that those gains will come at their expense. In Houston, for example, blacks and browns have clashed over school board realignments and a proposed City Council expansion. "The big question is, Where do you draw the lines?" says Franklin Jones, a political scientist at Texas Southern University. "As Hispanics strengthen their push toward inclusion, we'll see more conflicts."

Increasingly, these long-simmering tensions are flaring into violence, es-

pecially in cities where one of the groups has a monopoly on political power. The feud over who will rebuild Los Angeles after the riots is only the most recent sign of discord. In May 1991, Hispanics in black-controlled Washington went on a two-day rampage after a Latino man was wounded by a black police officer. In Cuban-dominated Miami the following month, blacks briefly rioted following the overturn of the conviction of a Hispanic police officer for killing two black motorcyclists.

Underlying the disputes is the growing divergence between the two groups, reinforced by mutual suspicion. Black and Hispanic leaders, says Alejandro Portes, a sociologist at Johns Hopkins University, "see everything as a zero-sum game. If blacks get something, Latinos lose something, and vice versa." Many African Americans believe that Latinos are benefiting from civil rights victories won by blacks with little help

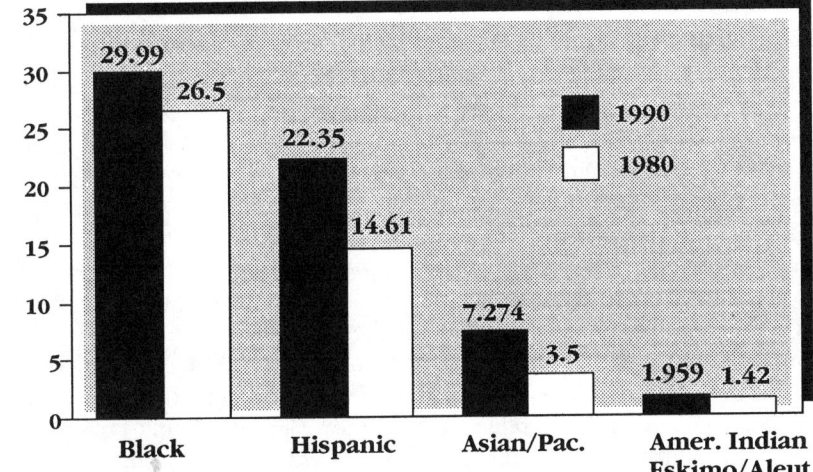

U.S. Minority Population Growth 1980-1990

The Hispanic population grew 53 percent between 1980 and 1990 — five times as fast as the total population growth and eight times as fast as non-Hispanics. At their current growth rate, Hispanics will become the largest ethnic minority in the United States by the turn of the century.

Population (millions)

	1990	1980
Black	29.99	26.5
Hispanic	22.35	14.61
Asian/Pac.	7.274	3.5
Amer. Indian Eskimo/Aleut	1.959	1.42

Source: U.S. Census Bureau

How Hispanics Compare

Hispanics lagged behind non-Hispanics in various economic and social indicators in 1991, including education levels. But Hispanics as a group had higher household incomes, lower unemployment and fewer female-headed households than blacks did that year.

	Non-Hispanics	Blacks	Hispanics	Mexicans	Puerto Ricans	Cubans	Cent. and S. Americans
Population (in millions)	227.4	30.9	21.4[†]	13.4	2.4	1.1	3.0
Median household income	$30,513	$18,676	$22,330	$22,439	$16,169	$25,900	$23,568
Percent households with income of $50,000 or more	25.4	11.9	13.4	11.6	11.9	19.8	15.7
Percent female-headed households	11.4	47.8	19.1	15.6	33.7	15.3	21.5
Percent urban households	72.8	N/A	91.8	90.5	95.2	95.7	97.0
Percent households owning or buying home	65.8	42.4	39.0	43.5	23.4	47.3	22.2
Percent completed high school	80.5	66.7	51.3	43.6	58.0	61.0	60.4
Percent with four or more years of college	22.3	11.5	9.7	6.2	10.1	18.5	15.1
Percent unemployed	6.9	12.4	10.0	10.7	10.3	6.4	10.3
Percent of individuals below poverty level	12.1	31.9	28.1	28.1	40.6	16.9	25.4

† *Note: This figure does not include the 1.6 million people in the category "other Hispanic."*
Source: U.S. Census Bureau; Wilson Quarterly, summer 1992.

from Hispanics. For example, Martin Luther King Jr. Hospital in South-Central Los Angeles was built to serve poor blacks following the Watts riots in 1965. Today, more than half the babies born there are Hispanic.

"During the height of the civil rights movement, Hispanics were conspicuous by their absence," says Arthur Fletcher, chairman of the U.S. Commission on Civil Rights. "They kept asking, 'What about us?' But rather than joining us in fighting the system, Hispanics were fighting us for the crumbs. And that in large part is still what's going on." [9]

For their part, some Latinos complain that blacks are unwilling to treat them as equals in the civil rights struggle. In Los Angeles County, for example, blacks, who make up 10 percent of the population, hold 30 percent of the county jobs. Hispanics, who constitute 33 percent of the population, hold only 18 percent of the jobs. "Blacks think we want to take jobs away from them, so they're fighting us tooth and nail," says Raúl Nuñez, president of the Los Angeles County Chicano Employees Association. "They are doing the same thing to us that whites did to them."

Many advocacy groups and civil rights leaders play down the con-

flicts, contending that they are largely a product of media hype. "We need to put to rest the black-brown myth," says Margarita Roque, executive director of the Congressional Hispanic Caucus. "After the Mount Pleasant [Washington] episode, everyone tried to put a black-brown face on it. It didn't matter that leaders in both camps said that's not the issue. It is about not having access or a voice in our community." Frank Morris, dean of graduate studies at Morgan State University in Baltimore, agrees. "Overall, it is wrong to say there is great tension between blacks and browns," he says. "Even in East Los

Angeles, attention is focused on drugs and gangs. The evidence overwhelmingly points to poverty as the determining factor for inner-city conflict."

Nevertheless, with immigration at record levels and the economy in recession, there is increased competition for jobs, housing and entitlements. The collision of cultures is most striking in places like South Los Angeles, which within the last decade has been transformed from a segregated black community to a Latino barrio. "The Spanish people are out there, and they're willing to [work] for less and less money," a black laborer told the *Los Angeles Times*. "There's two totally different cultures. That's where the problems start." [10] ■

BACKGROUND

Mexican Migrants

The habitual treatment of Mexican Americans as new immigrants irks those of Mexican decent, whose ancestors in the United States predate Colonial settlements at Plymouth and Jamestown. The frustration was poignantly put by an elderly Mexican American in Texas earlier this century when he said, "I didn't cross the border, the border crossed me — several times."

Indeed, the Spanish names of many Western cities — Los Angeles, San Francisco, Santa Fe — bear witness to the settlements of the early Franciscan friars. After the United States waged war with Mexico and acquired California and the Southwestern states in 1848 under the Treaty of Guadalupe Hidalgo, the Mexican people living there were expected to adopt the Anglo culture.

The first real Mexican migration, which began with the building of the railroads across the American Southwest, resulted in half a million Mexicans living in the United States by 1900. Though they weren't the preferred Northern European stock, Mexicans didn't experience the same exclusion as Asians. All Mexicans living in the territories acquired from Mexico were granted citizenship. In 1897, a U.S. district court ruled that the skin color of Mexicans was irrelevant to the issue of naturalization. [11] The vast majority, however, had no interest in citizenship. Why bother to become an American citizen when the land one loved, the land of family, language, and *la raza* (the people or race) was so close by?

Eligibility for citizenship, of course, didn't stop discrimination. "The Mexican American has been the black man of the Southwest," notes Ronnie Lopez, executive assistant to former Arizona Gov. Bruce Babbitt. "There have been rapings and lynchings.... People's land was taken from them." [12]

Immigration Trends

The immigrant waves of the first quarter of the century brought another three-quarters of a million legal immigrants from Mexico.* The immigrant flow ebbed during the Great Depression, when many recent Mexican arrivals voluntarily returned to their homeland. At that time, the U.S. also tightened its immigration policy and deported some 400,000 Mexicans (including many born in the United States).

Mexican immigration to the United States picked up again slightly in the 1940s, spurred by wartime labor shortages. In 1942, the nation initiated the "Bracero" guestworker program, under which large numbers of temporary

_____

*During the same period, some 15 million legal immigrants came from Europe.

workers were transported north. The program was supposed to end with the war but lasted until Congress refused to renew it in 1964. The Mexican guestworkers — 4.8 million over the life of the program — worked in at least 38 states, mostly picking fruit and vegetables in the Southwest. [13]

Throughout the next three decades, a large number of Mexican immigrants crossed the Rio Grande, giving the border cities, towns, and barrios that grew up around them a distinctive border culture. It was in such places that the noted Mexican-American labor leader César Chávez grew up, attending more than 30 schools before the seventh grade.

It was also from such barrios that more than 1 million Mexicans were deported in 1953 and '54, as part of "Operation Wetback" to deter illegal immigration. In a synchronized series of raids, some 750 U.S. Border Patrol agents swooped down on factories and farms, arresting any Hispanic-looking people who appeared not to belong.

At the time, Operation Wetback enjoyed popular support, but it is now considered one of the more embarrassing episodes of U.S. immigration history. More important, because the demand for cheap labaor was voracious, it failed to slow the tide of illegal Mexican immigration.

The fast urbanization of the Southwest in recent decades absorbed Mexican-American barrios that had begun as agricultural labor communities. The barrios remained, but the population was no longer concentrated in agricultural work. Other barrios grew out of former labor camps that brought together railroad workers and miners.

Simultaneously, as migrants gravitated toward cities, central-city barrios developed with large populations, such as the South Bronx and East Los Angeles, where by 1960 approximately 135,000 people of Mexican origin made up more than three-quarters of the total population.

Who Are America's Hispanics

The nation's population of 22.4 million mainland Hispanics includes many different nationalities, but the majority — 63 percent — are Mexican Americans.

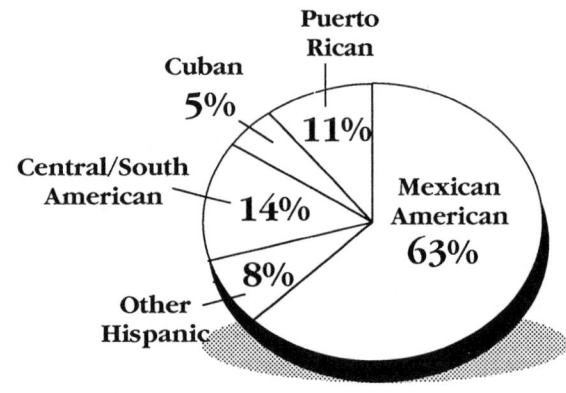

Source: *U.S. Census Bureau, The Hispanic Population in the United States, March 1991.*

Many Cultures

Although the Mexican-American population continued to grow as well as spread over time, its share of the total Hispanic population was reduced from 70 percent in 1950 to 63 percent in 1990. The change is attributed to the influx and spread of Puerto Ricans, Cubans and immigrants from Central and South America.

In the 1950s, Puerto Ricans launched America's first large-scale airborne migration as job opportunities and affordable plane travel attracted some 45,000 island residents annually to the mainland. Puerto Rico was a territory of the United States from the time of the Spanish-American War in 1898 to 1952, when it achieved status as a commonwealth, a unique relationship in which Puerto Rico remains part of the United States but governs itself. While the 1950 census had counted only 70,000 persons of Puerto Rican background on the mainland, by 1980 there were 2 million.[14]

Although many Cuban Americans arrived during the same time frame, their experience was markedly different. The vast majority came in the wake of the Cuban Revolution in 1959, driven out by the communist rule of Fidel Castro. And even though many arrived with financial and educational resources, they have, as political refugees, received substantial financial assistance from the federal government.

Following separate paths to the United States, these groups settled in different regions. More than two-thirds of Puerto Ricans live in the Northeast; about three-fifths of Mexican Americans live in the West; almost two-thirds of all Cuban Americans live in Florida. In South Florida, more than a million Cuban Americans have spread so rapidly beyond Miami that they sometimes refer to the entire 25-mile stretch from Miami to the Everglades as Calle Ocho (Eighth Street), after the main drag of Miami's Little Havana.

Even in cities with several Hispanic groups, each tends to live in distinct neighborhoods. In Chicago, for example, Mexican Americans are concentrated in the Little Village and Pilsen districts, while Puerto Ricans cluster in Logan Square and Humboldt Park. Intermarriage among Hispanic groups similarly appears infrequent, except perhaps among Puerto Ricans, Dominicans and other Central or South Americans in New York City.[15] "Hispanics don't live among themselves, they don't interact with each other and they don't necessarily have positive images of each other," says Rodolfo de la Garza.

Mixed Welcome

The 1960s brought fundamental change to U.S. immigration policy. The transformation was embodied in the Immigration and Nationality Act of 1965, which opened the doors to ethnic diversity and abolished the quota system that had given preference to certain European nationalities for the previous 40 years. In effect, the policy shift rolled out the welcome mat for Latin Americans — as well as Asians — who had historically been excluded from legal immigration channels.

In place of the old system, the 1965 legislation substituted an overall annual ceiling of 170,000 immigrants for the Eastern Hemisphere plus a 20,000 annual per-country limit based on a complicated visa-preference system that stressed employment skills and close family ties with persons already in the United States. Countries in the Western Hemisphere became subject to a 120,000 overall annual ceiling.

As a result of the legislation, Hispanics' presence in the United States surged. By the late 1970s, Latin Americans made up 42 percent of total immigrants, and Europeans were down to 13 percent (from 68 percent in the 1950s).[16]

Meanwhile, during the 1960s many Latinos remained outside the U.S. mainstream. In general, they had little economic clout, lacked political

Continued on p. 940

Chronology

1800s *Prior to the U.S.-Mexican War, the border between the two countries is loosely defined.*

Feb. 2, 1848
Treaty of Guadalupe Hidalgo ends the U.S.-Mexican War, awarding the United States the northern half of Mexico.

1898
Following the Spanish-American War, Puerto Rico obtains unique status as a U.S. territory.

•

1900-1930s *Hard economic times prompt the U.S. to tighten its immigration laws and force Mexicans who enter the U.S. illegally to return to Mexico.*

May 28, 1924
U.S. Border Patrol is formed to police the Mexican border.

•

1940s-1950s *Labor shortages and expansion of the U.S. economy create magnet for Mexican laborers seeking work.*

1942
U.S. initiates the *Bracero* guest-worker program, which allows Mexican agricultural workers to help ease labor shortages.

1952
Puerto Rico becomes a U.S. commonwealth.

1954
U.S. Border Patrol launches "Operation Wetback," which rounds up and deports more than 1 million undocu-mented Mexican migrants, together with some U.S. citizens.

•

1960s *The U.S. drops its biased quota system for immigrants, permitting more Latinos to enter the country legally.*

Oct. 3, 1965
President Lyndon B. Johnson signs the Immigration and Nationality Act, opening the door to more legal immigrants from Latin America.

Jan. 2, 1968
The Bilingual Education Act is enacted by Congress, providing funds for teacher training and a variety of experimental programs.

•

1970s *Feeling job discrimination and exclusion from the political process, Latinos begin to organize grass-roots efforts to increase political access.*

1975
The Voting Rights Act is extended to include Latinos. The act requires bilingual ballots in certain areas and puts redistricting under U.S. scrutiny.

1976
The Congressional Hispanic Caucus is formed to help Latino leaders formulate a common political agenda.

•

1980s *Latinos struggle economically and for the most part fail to achieve political power.*

April 21, 1980
Fidel Castro opens the Cuban port of Mariel, leading to the exodus of some 129,000 Cubans to Florida, including criminals. Though most are accepted legally into the U.S., they strain U.S. society, focusing attention on immigration problems.

1982
Amendments to the Voting Rights Act oblige certain local jurisdictions to redraw electoral district lines to elect more Hispanic and black candidates.

1986
Illegal aliens apprehended at the U.S.-Mexican border reach a peak of 1.7 million; the Immigration Control and Reform Act is passed to slow illegal immigration.

1987
Hispanics are elected mayor in 68 cities across the United States.

•

1990s *Immigration laws fail to deter illegals from coming to the U.S., creating public backlash against immigrants in general, and Hispanics in particular.*

Nov. 29, 1990
President Bush signs into law a bill allowing immigration to climb from about 500,000 persons annually to about 700,000 for the first three years of the act.

April 29, 1992
The verdict in the Rodney King trial ignites riots in Los Angeles; more than half of those arrested are Hispanic.

Where Hispanics Live

Hispanics are heavily concentrated in a few states, especially New Mexico (38 percent), California (26 percent) and Texas (26 percent). Regionally, 45 percent of the nation's Hispanics live in the West, compared with 21 percent of the total U.S. population. Just 8 percent live in the Midwest, compared with 24 percent of the total population.

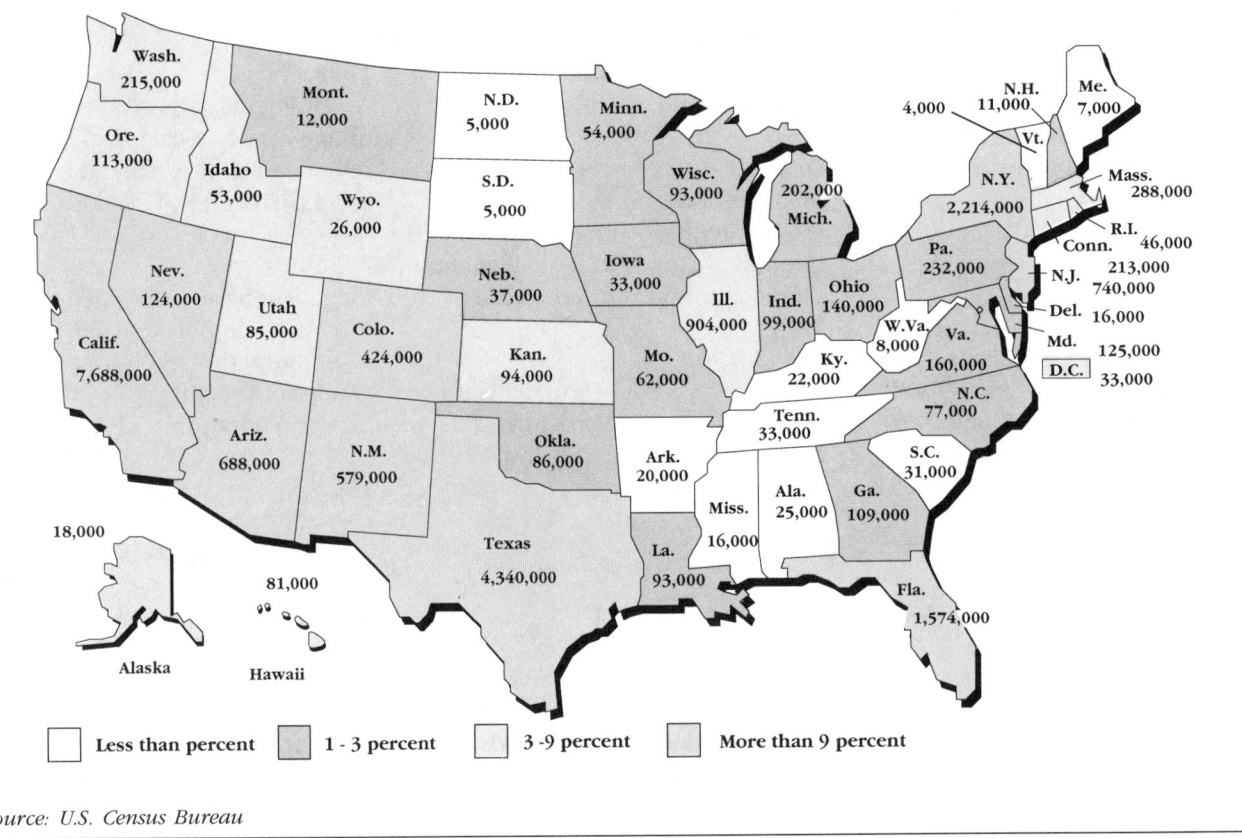

Wash. 215,000
Ore. 113,000
Idaho 53,000
Mont. 12,000
N.D. 5,000
Minn. 54,000
Wisc. 93,000
N.H. 11,000
Me. 7,000
4,000
Vt.
Wyo. 26,000
S.D. 5,000
N.Y. 2,214,000
Mass. 288,000
Nev. 124,000
Utah 85,000
Neb. 37,000
Iowa 33,000
202,000
Mich.
Pa. 232,000
R.I. 46,000
Conn. 213,000
N.J. 740,000
Calif. 7,688,000
Colo. 424,000
Kan. 94,000
Mo. 62,000
Ill. 904,000
Ind. 99,000
Ohio 140,000
W.Va. 8,000
Va. 160,000
Ky. 22,000
Del. 16,000
Md. 125,000
D.C. 33,000
Ariz. 688,000
N.M. 579,000
Okla. 86,000
Ark. 20,000
Tenn. 33,000
N.C. 77,000
S.C. 31,000
Miss. 16,000
Ala. 25,000
Ga. 109,000
18,000
Texas 4,340,000
La. 93,000
Fla. 1,574,000
81,000
Alaska
Hawaii

☐ Less than percent   ▨ 1 - 3 percent   ☐ 3 - 9 percent   ☐ More than 9 percent

Source: U.S. Census Bureau

Continued from p. 938
power and failed to catch the civil rights wave. Unlike blacks, who had been a part of the national consciousness for well over a century, Hispanics were virtually unknown to most Americans and ignored by policymakers. While most experts believe Hispanics didn't experience quite the same racial prejudice, they were nonetheless discriminated against.

In many Southwestern states, poll taxes and literacy tests kept Mexican Americans out of voting booths. In addition, local ordinances often required segregated housing, schools and public accommodations. Until the mid-1970s, the overwhelming majority of

Latinos in the Southwest attended segregated schools, not because state law required it (as with blacks), but as a matter of local practice and policy. The impact on education, self-esteem and professional opportunity was no less devastating. As recently as the 1960s, signs saying "No dogs or Mexicans allowed" were commonly posted outside restaurants, restrooms and bus stations throughout Texas and parts of the Southwest.

Rising Latino Militancy

Discontent among Latinos at the time spawned the so-called Chicano movement. Many of the political groups associated with the movement, such as the

Alianza Federal de Pueblos Libres (National Alliance of Free Peoples) and the Brown Berets,[17] promoted radical alternatives to the status quo, preferring socialism, for example, to capitalism. The Chicano movement's emphasis on the distinctiveness of Mexican culture, and its general resistance to cultural assimilation, aroused fears of biculturalism in the American mainstream.

By the mid-1970s, Latino militancy gave way to efforts to work within the system. Addressing the issue of political empowerment for Hispanics, Congress in 1975 extended the Voting Rights Act of 1965 to apply to Latinos. The law mandated the use of bilingual ballots in jurisdictions where more than 5 percent of the citizens of voting age were Spanish speakers.* The measure also required that any proposed changes in electoral jurisdictions be put under federal scrutiny to prevent discrimination against minorities.

Hispanic advocates say discrimination generally took two forms. The first involved the drawing of district lines to reduce the effectiveness of the Latino vote in a given jurisdiction. This was accomplished either by "cracking," dividing potential Latino voters among many districts, or by "stacking," packing all the potential Latino voters into a single district where they could have elected multiple officials if divided into two or more districts. The second type of discrimination involves at-large electoral systems, which Latino leaders say are inherently biased against minority groups.**

The Power of Redistricting

Even more important — and controversial — were the 1982 amendments to the Voting Rights Act, obliging local jurisdictions to jiggle their electoral district lines with the aim of electing more Hispanic and black candidates. The amendments made it legal for any Hispanic to charge discrimination if election results showed that the number of Latinos elected was not proportionate to the group's population in a particular district.

Over the past decade, Hispanic legal groups, such as the Mexican-American Legal Defense and Educational Fund, have relied on the federal courts to reverse discriminatory electoral boundaries. There are many examples of reapportionment to help minority candidates, but two of the

*The law also applied to Alaskan natives, American Indians and Asian Americans.

**Under an at-large electoral system, voters choose more than one candidate in a broad area. Since Hispanics represent a small percentage of the general population in most cities — and people tend to vote along racial and ethnic lines — Hispanic candidates don't fare well.

most notable are the judicially mandated redistrictings that occurred in Chicago and Los Angeles.

In Chicago, the newly drawn electoral map in the mid-1980s created districts that facilitated the election of Latinos to the state Senate, the state House of Representatives and the Chicago Board of Aldermen. In Los Angeles, under prodding from the federal courts, the county Board of Supervisors also altered traditional boundaries to create a Latino-majority district. Today, Latinos still hold only two of 15 City Council seats, despite making up 33 percent of the city's population. "Power is supposed to be in the numbers," says civil rights activist Frank Villalobos. "We have the numbers, but we don't have the power." [18]

Some experts say redistricting to help Latinos will ultimately prove counterproductive. "Affirmative action in the electoral arena makes respectable the notion that we should vote for candidates on the basis of skin color," argues Linda Chavez. "Under that scenario, so long as 70 percent of the population is white, there will be a ceiling on black and Hispanic candidates. I'd like to see a Hispanic or black president. Affirmative action will assure they'll never get that opportunity."

"What destroys the fabric of communities is not emerging political groups — but efforts to keep people out," counters SVREP's Hernández. "Historically, Anglos vote against Mexican Americans, period, regardless of qualifications. This happened before redistricting — and it still happens today. That's the reason we've prevailed in court."

"This year we are celebrating the 500th anniversary of Hispanics in the hemisphere," adds Roque. "To say the system will eventually bring us in isn't enough. At the rate we're going, we would need another 500 years. The system has been used against us for hundreds of years." ∎

CURRENT SITUATION

Downward Mobility

Today, some 22.4 million Hispanics live in the U.S., about 9 percent of the population, up from less than 3 percent in 1950. An estimated 6.5 million of the 13.5 million legal immigrants in the last three decades have been Hispanics. On top of that, 2.5 million to 4 million illegal immigrants from Mexico and other Spanish-speaking countries have settled in the U.S.* And the proposed North American Free Trade Agreement, by strengthening economic ties between Mexico and the U.S., might very well increase illegal immigration in the short run rather than diminish it.

The media often portray the nation's diverse Hispanic population as a group of impoverished, newly arrived immigrants from Mexico or Central America. Experts say the truth is more complex. A significant share of the Hispanic community has moved into affluence since 1970, and upscale Hispanic households are one of the nation's fastest-growing market segments. For instance, the number of Hispanic households with an income above $50,000 grew from 191,000 in 1972 to 638,000 in 1988, a 234 percent increase (in 1988 dollars). [19] Moreover, according to University of Chicago sociologist Douglas Massey, as incomes have increased, Hispanic families have tended to move up and out of ethnic enclaves and into more affluent, racially mixed suburbs, contrary to popular perceptions. [20]

At the same time, however, numerous studies conclude that Hispanics as a group are failing to make the same progress as other minorities, including

*These estimates don't include the 3.1 million undocumented migrants legalized under the IRCA amnesty program.

The Latinoization of American Culture

A decade ago, who would have thought that salsa would displace ketchup as America's leading condiment — or that tortillas would outsell bagels, not to mention English muffins and pita bread? Well, they have. Even fast-food burger joints now dish out nachos — *con salsa*. Mexican-American food is now the leading ethnic food among non-Hispanics, according to the National Restaurant Association.

Things that once seemed foreign now seem as American as ... a burrito. With Anglo teenagers dancing the *lambada*, speaking "Spanglish" among themselves ("Hey dude, catch ya' mañana") and eating *fajitas*, American culture seems positively Latinized. The Broadway show "Tango Argentino" inspired a tango craze in 1985. David Byrne and Paul Simon released albums heavily influenced by Latin music. And Linda Ronstadt recorded Mexican songs.

On street corners and in retail stores and offices, English has increasingly collided with Spanish. Anglos whose ancestors picked up such Spanish words as *bronco, tornado* and *incommunicado*, for instance, now freely use such Spanish words as *gracias, bueno, amigo* and *por favor*. Actors Raúl Julia and Rita Moreno are household names, and novels by Carlos Fuentes and Isabel Allende are instant best-sellers.

Yes, but is this really new? Was there ever a time without a Mexican spitfire in the movies, a hacienda-style suburb down the road, a Latino crooner singing "*Cuando Cuando*" to the stars? And in the past, hasn't the U.S. joined the conga line, bought the Trini Lopez album, then moved on heedlessly to something else? It has, and it did. But this time the prospects are different. Latin influences that were once just a pinch of spice for most Americans are becoming a vital part of the wider culture.

Demographics are the main reason. Hispanics are by far the fastest-growing ethnic group in the country. More American high school and university students sign up for Spanish than for any other foreign language.

Another reason is more subtle. The creative work being done by Hispanics today is more recognizable to Americans than ever before. Paintings and music that spring from Latin sources are being filtered through a north-of-the-border sensibility. Popular films like "La Bamba," a 1987 biography of teenage singer Richie Valens, convey the story of Chicano life, as told through myths of immigrant struggle and showbiz martyrdom that are distinctly American.

Increasingly, too, Hispanic artists and entertainers are courting the mass "crossover" audience in English. Thus, the popular rock group "Los Lobos" sings lyrics in both English and Spanish, and many of the nation's Latino theaters, such as the Hispanic American Arts Center in Manhattan, perform primarily in English.

Equally important, undiluted Spanish influences seem less threatening than in the past. Latino markets are among the fastest-growing in the nation, and three Spanish-language national television networks — Univision, Galavision and Telemundo — have emerged to serve them, recently joined by a Spanish-language version of CNN. There are some 350 Spanish-language newspapers in the U.S. and 331 Spanish-language radio stations, compared with 67 in 1976.

Major U.S. advertisers, eager to tap the estimated $185 billion in spending power wielded by Spanish-speaking Americans, have ventured into Spanglish to promote their products.† In some cases, attempts to sprinkle Spanish through commercials have produced embarrassing gaffes. A Braniff airlines ad in the mid-1980s that sought to tell Spanish-speaking audiences they could settle back *en* (in) luxuriant *cuero* (leather) seats, for example, inadvertently said they could fly *encuero* — without clothes. A fractured translation of the Miller Lite slogan told readers the beer was "Filling, and less delicious."

Whatever the cultural medium, the Latino influence is here to stay. In a sense, it is a reminder that the roots of Spanish culture go deep into American life. Though stereotyping is still prevalent in the arts, as in life, cultural osmosis is slowly changing the American psyche. "In the process of incorporating Hispanics into American culture, we're building something bigger and better," says Charles Kamasaki, vice president of the National Council of La Raza. "It's a two-way street. The norms of the dominant culture are changing as well."

---

†For details, see *Fortune*, Nov. 21, 1988, p. 186.

---

blacks. Median income of Mexican Americans in the Southwest, for example, was 57 percent of non-Hispanic median income in 1959, and exactly the same percentage in 1989. Education, earnings, poverty rates and other indicators are also static.[21]

Educational Woes

The faces behind these statistics are not just those of newly arrived immigrants. A study published this year by the University of Texas at Austin found that a long trend of educational advancement from one Mexican-American generation to the next has stopped.[22] Members of the second generation, for example, were more likely to have attended college than those of the third generation today. "It seems that as they faced economic hardship in the 1980s, second-generation parents were less willing or less able to emphasize education for their children than immigrant parents," says Frank D. Bean, a co-author of the study. "It is discouraging news for the future, because the educational gap is growing between Mexican Americans and Anglos."

The implications become very real in San Antonio, Texas, where 56 percent of the population is Hispanic, the vast majority U.S.-born. Nearly half of the Hispanic students in the San Antonio area do not graduate from high school,* and Hispanic teenage girls there are four times more likely to give birth than white girls. Fully 40 percent of Latino households are in substandard housing, many in projects spilling over with young Mexican Americans who seem to have lost their youthful dreams and see no clear path of escape. Many teenagers say they have little incentive to stay in school when they see few good jobs even for high school graduates. [23]

As a result, many Hispanics in San Antonio and elsewhere are finding their role models on the streets rather than in the classrooms, where few of their teachers are Hispanic. Even for those teenagers who stay in school, the odds against success can be formidable. Schools in Mexican immigrant neighborhoods are often inferior, and the language barrier limits parental involvement. "When a 17-year-old makes it to 10th grade," says Rogelio H. Torres, principal at Austin High School in Houston, "that's more education than anyone their parents know ever had, and so they think it is okay for them to drop out and take a minimum-wage job. They just don't seem to see that their children are ending on the losing end of a society divided between the haves and the have-nothings." [24]

Richard Farias, executive director of

---

*According to the 1990 census, nationwide 45 percent of Hispanics dropped out of high school, compared with 23 percent of blacks and 17 percent of whites.

the Houston-based Association for the Advancement of Mexican-Americans, says that too often teachers and counselors encourage Hispanics and other minority kids to find jobs or go to vocational school when they fall behind. Says Farias: "I've had more than one kid say that they've been told by teachers, 'You're not going to make it. You might as well drop out.'" [25] The credential that would do them the most good — a college degree — seems hopelessly out of reach.

Economic Problems

Part of the problem, of course, is the anemic economy. In the past, generations of Mexican immigrants found their way into the economic mainstream by working in factories and warehouses, on docks and at construction sites. Across the country, many of these steppingstone jobs disappeared in the 1980s, even as low-paying, insecure jobs in the service sector multiplied.

The ready availability of menial work has proved a magnet for large numbers of immigrants from Mexico and Central America, who find that life on the minimum wage here is an improvement. Many teenagers are also drawn to these jobs, often leaving school to help support their families. In these jobs, experts say, today's Hispanic children see little prospect for the upward mobility so vital to the immigrant experience of the past, and many of them end up learning the youth culture of inner-city poverty with its welfare dependency, drug use and teenage sex.

"There is a growing schism between poor Latinos, on the one hand, and middle-class Latinos on the other," says Hernández. "The middle class evolved out of 1960s; they had secure jobs and sent their kids to college. For the poorer class, the ladder isn't there." This schism was evident in this year's L.A. riots, when middle-class, mostly Mexican-American, neighborhoods in East Los Angeles remained relatively quiet and unscathed while areas dominated

by poorer, newly arrived Mexicans and Central Americans became caught up in the violence and looting. [26]

Most experts agree that the greatest obstacle that Hispanics face is poverty. "In the Hispanic community, it's not that people aren't working. Often the father works two jobs and the mother one, and they still can't make ends meet," says Roque.

To combat the discouraging trends, the Congressional Hispanic Caucus last year introduced legislation that would, among other things, establish early-intervention programs for elementary-school students and grant scholarships to college students who would teach in disadvantaged areas. In addition, a number of alternative high schools have been established for students in predominantly Hispanic communities. In San Antonio, for example, a business-education partnership set up in 1988 now embraces eight local high schools. Hispanics who maintain B averages and a 95 percent attendance rate are guaranteed four years of college or preference for career-track jobs for those not college bound.

Similarly, in Houston, the private George I. Sanchez High School boasts a graduation rate of 95 percent of the senior class. The key to that school's success, says principal Mark Gilbert-Cougar, is that in addition to a standard curriculum, the school provides social services that deal with unstable homes, drug and alcohol abuse and teen parenthood.

Such innovative programs are the exception, not the rule. They require substantial commitment and investment on the part of taxpayers and private businesses as well as policy-makers. Analysts say these parties seldom agree on strategy and are up against an entrenched education bureaucracy.

Bilingual Battleground

The real education battle involving Hispanics is being fought over bi-

Why Are Puerto Ricans in Such Dire Straits?

In the United States, illegal Mexican immigrants, like Salvadorans, Dominicans and others who are undocumented, are likely to be part of an underclass. Confined by their legal status to temporary or unstable jobs, often exploited by employers and usually unable to avail themselves of the protection or benefits of the civic culture, they find themselves struggling on the margins of society.

In contrast, Puerto Ricans have had U.S. citizenship since 1917 and full access to welfare benefits, health care and government-funded job-training programs. And yet census data reveal that Puerto Ricans are the worst-off ethnic group in the United States. For a period in the mid-1980s, nearly half of all Puerto Rican families were living in poverty.

Mexican Americans, who are no more proficient in English than Puerto Ricans, less likely to have finished high school and more likely to have arrived here very recently, have a much lower poverty rate. The *Journal of the American Medical Association* reported last year that Puerto Rican infant mortality was 50 percent higher than among Mexican Americans, and nearly three times as high as among Cubans.†

The statistics also show Puerto Ricans to be much more severely afflicted by what might be called the secondary effects of poverty, such as family breakups and not trying to find employment — which work to ensure that poverty will continue beyond one generation. In 1991, females headed 34 percent of Puerto Rican families, compared with 16 percent of Mexican-American families. Puerto Rican families are more than twice as likely as black families to be on welfare, and 50 percent more likely to be poor.

Why are Puerto Ricans in such dire straits? One paradoxical reason is the very fact that Puerto Ricans are free to come and go as they please; many indeed do travel back and forth between the mainland and Puerto Rico. As a sales executive who was born in Brooklyn but now lives on the island put it: "Puerto Ricans always dream of coming back [to Puerto Rico], and that dream has prevented them from settling down and their offspring from progressing." ††

When middle-class blacks move out of black ghettos, they tend to relocate to more prosperous black neighborhoods, but still serve as examples to the community. Middle-class Puerto Ricans who move back to Puerto Rico can hardly function as economic role models and political leaders for those who remain on the mainland. "There is no distinctive middle-class Puerto Rican neighborhood in the United States," laments Ramón Daubón of the National Puerto Rican Coalition.

Conservatives who criticize the role of the welfare system in creating the Puerto Rican underclass say that since other Hispanic groups have labor-force participation rates and family structures markedly different from those of Puerto Ricans, the real issue is availability of government checks, not jobs. Other than Cubans, Puerto Ricans are the only Spanish-speaking ethnic group for whom full U.S. citizenship (and thus welfare benefits) is guaranteed. "What should be an advantage for Puerto Ricans — namely citizenship — has turned into a liability in the welfare state,," says Linda Chavez, staff director of the U.S. Commission on Civil Rights under Ronald Reagan. "They have been smothered by entitlements."

Still others say the plight of Puerto Ricans has been made worse by circumstances beyond their control. During the past few decades, the contraction of the unskilled-labor market in New York and other Northeastern cities, where the majority of Puerto Ricans live, hit the community disproportionately hard. "What I see is a community that came here and put all its eggs in one basket, namely the garment industry and manufacturing," says Angelo Falcón, president of the Institute for Puerto Rican Policy.‡ When the unskilled jobs began to disappear, Puerto Ricans, who had little education and so were not well prepared to find other kinds of work, began to fall into drugs, street crime and family dissolution.

More than likely, it is a combination of these factors that has crippled Puerto Rican progress. Perhaps more important, the question of whether Puerto Ricans as a group have sunk into an underclass has been overshadowed by the debate over the island's political status. There are 3.5 million Puerto Ricans on the island and 2.75 million on the mainland. Part of the population would like the island of Puerto Rico to become independent, another part wants statehood and a third group favors continued status as a commonwealth. ‡‡ This national schizophrenia has given Puerto Ricans a perpetual identity crisis.

---

† *Journal of the American Medical Association,* Jan. 9, 1991, p. 217.

†† *Time,* July 8, 1985, p. 37.

‡ Quoted in Nicholas Lemann, "The Other Underclass," *The Atlantic,* December 1991, p. 102.

‡‡ For background, see "Puerto Rico: The Struggle Over Status," *Editorial Research Reports,* Feb. 8, 1991, pp. 81-96.

lingual language programs, one policy area where Mexican Americans, Puerto Ricans and Cuban Americans do speak with one voice. Since the mid-1960s, advocacy groups — and many educators — have felt that promoting native language skills would ultimately help Latinos and other recent immigrants learn English. When the Bilingual Education Act was introduced in 1967, its sponsor, Sen. Ralph Yarborough, D-Texas, said as much. "My purpose in doing this," he declared in the Senate, "is not to keep any specific language alive ... but just to try to make those children fully literate in English."[27] Recent surveys indicate that the vast majority of Latinos value bilingual education for the same reason.

Critics, however, contend that bilingual education will impede Hispanic assimilation in American life and result in a separate Spanish-language "track" for Hispanic children. "It is important to stress that the purpose of 'language-rights' proponents is not to protect the right of individuals to speak whatever language they choose in private — a right no one is disputing — but to promote the use of a language other than English in public activities," argues Linda Chavez.[28]

Although Hispanic leaders dispute that that is their intention, the Reagan administration, which strongly opposed bilingual education, shared those fears. Such concerns combined to produce the U.S. English movement, a lobbying group organized in the early 1980s to press for a constitutional amendment to declare English the official American language. Since then, some 19 states have passed so-called "English Only" laws primarily aimed at Spanish speakers. So far, they have not been tested in the courts and have had little impact on bilingual-education programs.

In the interim, many of the earlier studies denouncing bilingual education, promoted by former Secretary of Education William J. Bennett, have come under closer scrutiny. A widely touted — and often criticized — Department of Education study concluded in 1991 that students with limited

English proficiency participating in bilingual programs improved their skills in mathematics, English language and reading as fast or faster than students in the general population.[29]

Meanwhile, the debate over bilingual education still rages. (See "At Issue," p. 946.) "We no longer have the luxury of ideology," says Michael Fix, an immigration expert at the Urban Institute. Whether the solution is complete English immersion or bilingual programs, he says, "special compensatory training [and a plan for action] is critical." In many cities, the task of educating immigrant students has become an enormous burden. In Los Angeles, 39 percent of the city's students don't speak English well, and in Seattle, 21 percent come from homes where English is not the family's first language.

At present, the only federal funds available to help limited English proficiency (LEP) students, the majority of whom are Hispanic, are those provided under the Bilingual Education Act. That amounts to $170 million this year, half the amount allocated a decade ago. Many educators and advocacy groups now contend that since the problem of language proficiency is so great, money allocated under the Elementary and Secondary Education Act, so-called Chapter 1 funds, should be made available to help students learn English.[30]

"Language is the most salient issue of the future for Hispanics," says Fix. "There is a definite correlation between poverty and poor educational performance. New Hispanics have the additional disadvantage of lacking fluency in English." ∎

same urban and family stress brought about by high levels of immigration with an economy in recession.[31]

At the eye of the storm is the burgeoning population of Latinos. Hispanic Americans are a predominantly young population (median age: 26 — compared to 34 for non-Hispanics) with a relatively high birth rate. Even if all illegal immigration could be stopped, the Hispanic population would still grow. Some 40 percent of legal immigrants are from Mexico and Central America, and they follow the classic pattern of sending for spouses, children and parents once the first family member has established a home in the U.S.

There are signs that Latinos, like Asians, are beginning to add political muscle to their already considerable economic and demographic clout. However, the weight of this population has also put pressure on social services and on relations with other racial and ethnic groups vying for the same scarce resources. This is particularly true in the nation's cities, where 90 percent of Hispanics live. "Blacks are losing the struggle in labor markets," says Vernon Briggs, a labor economist at Cornell University. "They are being pushed out by new immigrants, mostly Hispanic, who compete directly with them for jobs." Newcomers take one of every three new jobs created in the labor force (40 percent in Los Angeles), according to Briggs.

Others say that pointing the finger at Hispanic immigrants is unfair. "A lot of economic dislocation has nothing to do with immigration. It has to do with the globalization of the economy," comments the Urban Institute's Fix. "The problem of structural unemployment for young American blacks began during the mid-1980s under Reagan at a time when the economy was thriving. Now that we're in a recession, black unemployment is blamed on Mexican immigration. It's more complex than that."

Fix argues that immigration policy cannot be disconnected from immi-

OUTLOOK

Mounting Tension

"No nation in history has proven as successful as the United States in managing ethnic diversity," writes Lawrence Fuchs, former executive director of the Select Commission on Refugee and Immigration Policy. "No nation before had ever made diversity itself a source of national identity and unity." Yet at the same time, Fuchs adds, no nation has faced the

At Issue:

Do bilingual education programs help Hispanic children learn English and assimilate into American culture?

KENJI HAKUTA, JENNIFER O'DAY AND MARSHALL SMITH

Hakuta is a professor of education, O'Day is a research associate and Smith is the dean of the School of Education at Stanford University
WRITTEN FOR *THE CQ RESEARCHER*, OCTOBER 1992.

YES

*S*ince 1968, the government has offered limited financial support for local and state districts to start bilingual education programs for students who speak Spanish or other non-English languages. The primary program model is that of transitional bilingual education which does not attempt to produce bilingual students, but rather to ease the "transition" to English-only classrooms.

These programs have overall been effective, when implemented by well-trained and fully bilingual teachers, in allowing students time to continue to keep up with the curriculum while learning English. But the unfortunate fact is that the programs make limited instructional use of the native language while the student is learning English, and try to move the students into "mainstream" monolingual English classrooms as quickly as possible. Speed, not quality, is the primary yardstick used by policy-makers to measure the effectiveness of transitional bilingual education programs.

Ironically, while educators and the public support foreign language programs to develop bilingualism among native English speakers, they discourage the development of native language skills on the part of the non-native English speakers, insisting that the native language be replaced by English. This subtractive form of bilingualism is wasteful.

First, we know how difficult it is for monolingual English students to achieve even marginal levels of bilingualism through foreign language study. Bilingualism is a resource in great demand these days of global competition; imagine have a free-trade agreement with Mexico without a bilingually competent labor force.

Second, considerable research evidence shows that there are both cognitive and social benefits to be reaped from bilingualism, including greater mental flexibility.

Moreover, the development of bilingualism among non-native English-speaking students can be accomplished efficiently and at no cost to English by upgrading the model of transitional bilingual education to an enrichment model of two-way or developmental bilingual education. Research indeed suggests that strongly developed skills in the native language leads to more rapid development of English.

Finally, the developmental programs provide supportive environments for *all* children to become bilingual. Properly implemented, developmental bilingual education programs can be the silver bullet that removes the country from the grips of monolingualism and produces the highly desirable goal of multilingually competent nation.

U.S. ENGLISH

A non-profit organization that advocates English as the official language of the United States
WRITTEN FOR *THE CQ RESEARCHER*, OCTOBER 1992.

NO

*b*ilingual education as an educational technique can have a variety of definitions. It can mean the teaching of some subject matter in the student's native language while introducing students to English slowly (transitional bilingual education). It can mean a program designed to maintain the student's home language and culture (native language-based instruction), with little instruction in English. It can refer to teaching subject matter in two languages, one of them English (two-way bilingual education). Or it can represent, as it does to most non-professionals, a way to help students feel comfortable and present subject matter in a language the student understands.

Because of the many different ways bilingual education is interpreted and implemented, research as to its effectiveness in teaching English becomes entangled in the non-standardization of definitions and the debate over student outcomes. The research conducted on bilingual education programs have many methodological flaws and limitations and, consequently, findings are many times unclear.

Two recent studies, frequently cited by bilingual advocates, known as the Longitudinal Study and the Immersion Study, are no exception. A recent National Academy of Sciences panel found an absence of clear findings in these studies and concluded that the findings are very difficult to generalize to a wider population.

The most controversial methodology involves the use of native language-based instruction. From California to New Jersey, evidence exists which demonstrates the ineffectiveness of this method of bilingual education in teaching English and in assisting students to integrate fully into the school community and society at large. Limited English proficient (LEP) students, especially Latino students, continue to drop out of school at an alarming rate. Parents are distressed that transitional bilingual education has not equipped their children with the necessary English skills to be successful in school.

Native language-based bilingual education programs segregate, involuntarily, LEP students into "separate-but-equal" classes, inhibiting the development of their English language skills, thereby reducing their opportunities for mobility. Without English language skills, they are unable to move into higher education or better jobs.

We believe that learning English quickly (in three years) along with their English-speaking peers is the best way for LEP students to get ahead academically and socially.

grant policy. "We can't bring in increasing number of people without thinking of how institutions will adapt, how we'll serve that population and how accessible services are," he notes. "To believe that immigrants will make their way — as they always have — is no longer tenable. The soup is getting watered down." In order to help inner-city Hispanics get on track, without undermining programs to serve struggling African Americans, Fix says urban programs will have to be redesigned.

The Next Generation

Looking over the horizon, it is the fate of Hispanic teenagers that most concerns urban sociologists and other experts. In the United States, nearly a third of all Mexican Americans, about 14 million people, are younger than 16, compared with less than a fifth of the non-Hispanic population. These young people will soon make up the fastest-growing segment of the labor force. Hispanics are projected to make up 17 percent of the labor force in 2005, compared with just under 10 percent in 1990.

And yet, as a group they are perhaps the least prepared of all minorities to compete in the global economy. Latinos are overrepresented in occupations expected to decline, such as farming, machine operators and household workers, and underrepresented in growth-sector jobs, such as those in science, computers and health care.[32]

Experts differ widely over remedies, but they essentially agree that the cause of the problem is poverty — and that the key to change is education. "If Hispanics don't graduate from college, they won't break into professional fields," says Linda Chavez. "They may not become an underclass, but nor will they rise from the lower middle class."

Some say that it is America, and not Hispanic immigrants and their descendants, that is in trouble, and that young Latinos simply are becoming more like the young people they see around them. Their problems are not unlike those that plague many young Americans in the nation's inner cities: drugs, early pregnancy and high dropout rates.

"When you're downtrodden and you can't get into the mainstream, it's not necessarily because you don't want to assimilate," adds Beverly Ellerman, executive director of the National Hispanic Leadership and Policy Development Institute. "To move up the economic ladder, you need educational opportunity. The Latino community is trying to mobilize itself. The whole society is worrying about the next generation — whether black, brown, Asian or Indian." ■

Notes

[1]National Council of La Raza, *State of Hispanic America 1991: An Overview*, February 1992. The National Council of La Raza, the nation's largest Hispanic organization, works to improve opportunities for Hispanics.

[2]Quoted in *The Washington Post*, Feb. 7, 1992.

[3]*Newsweek*, April 9, 1990, p. 18.

[4]Maria Antonia Calvo and Steven J. Rosenstone, *Hispanic Political Participation*, Southwest Voter Research Institute Inc., 1989, p. 2.

[5]Some communities, like Takoma Park, Md., have passed measures to permit residents who haven't yet gained citizenship to vote in local elections. Generally, however, state legislatures — which the U.S. Constitution charges with defining the electorate — oppose such election-law changes.

[6]See Harry Cross, et al., *Employer Hiring Practices: Differential Treatment of Hispanic and Anglo Job Seekers*, 1990.

[7]Rodolfo O. de la Garza, et al., *The Latino National Political Survey* (forthcoming).

[8]Quoted in *The New York Times*, May 24, 1992.

[9]*Time*, July 29, 1991, p. 15.

[10]*Los Angeles Times*, March 30, 1990. For a more detailed discussion of black-Hispanic relations, see Jack Miles, "Blacks vs. Browns," *The Atlantic*, October 1992, pp. 41-68.

[11]Lawrence H. Fuchs, *The American Kaleidoscope: Race, Ethnicity, and the Civic Culture* (1990), p. 134.

[12]Neal R. Pierce and Jerry Hagstrom, "The Hispanic Community — A Growing Force to be Reckoned With," in F. Chris Garcia, ed., *Latinos and the Political System* 1988, p. 12. The Reclamation Act of 1902 dispossessed many Mexican Americans of property rights thought to have been guaranteed by the Treaty of Guadalupe Hidalgo.

[13]For background, see Congressional Quarterly, *Congress and the Nation Vol. I* (1965), pp.762-767.

[14]Fuchs, *op. cit.*, p. 293.

[15]Peter Skerry, "E Pluribus Hispanic?" *Wilson Quarterly*, summer 1992, p. 66.

[16]See Leon F. Bouvier, *Immigration and Its Impact on U.S. Society*, Population Reference Bureau Inc., September 1981.

[17]See Leobardo F. Estrada, F. Chris Garcia, et al., "Chicanos in the United States: A History of Exploitation and Resistance," in Garcia, *op. cit.*, p. 28.

[18]Quoted in the *Los Angeles Times*, Sept. 2, 1992.

[19]*American Demographics*, August 1990, p. 40.

[20]In contrast, blacks tend to experience greater residential segregation. See Douglas S. Massey and Nancy A. Denton, "Trends in the Residential Segregation of Blacks, Hispanics, and Asians: 1970-1980," *American Sociological Review*, December 1987, p. 802.

[21]*Forbes*, March 20, 1992, p. 77.

[22]Frank Bean, Jorge Chapa, et al., *Educational and Socio-Demographic Incorporation Among Hispanic Immigrants to the United States*, University of Texas at Austin, fall 1991.

[23]See *The Washington Post*, June 21, 1992.

[24]Quoted in *The New York Times*, Jan. 20, 1992.

[25]Quoted in *Newsweek*, Aug. 19, 1991, p. 60.

[26]For background, see "Hispanics' Tale of Two Cities," *U.S. News & World Report*, May 25, 1992, p. 40, and *The New York Times*, May 11, 1992.

[27]*Congressional Record*, Dec. 1, 1967, p. 34703. For background, see also, "Bilingual Education: Does it Work?" *Editorial Research Reports*, March 11, 1988, pp. 126-139..

[28]Linda Chavez, *Out of the Barrio* (1991), p. 40.

[29]U.S. Department of Education, *The Longitudinal Study of Immersion Strategy, Early-exit and Late-exit Transitional Bilingual Education Programs for Language-Minority Children*, (1991). The four-year study tracked the academic progress of Spanish-speaking students in California, Texas, Florida, New York and New Jersey in several types of programs.

[30]In 1991, Chapter I provided $6 billion. The Elementary and Secondary Education Act is up for reauthorization next year.

[31]Fuchs, *op. cit.*, p. 492.

[32]*Occupational Outlook Quarterly*, winter 1991/92, p. 44.

Bibliography

Selected Sources Used

Books

Chavez, Linda, *Out of the Barrio: Toward a New Politics of Hispanic Assimilation*, Basic Books, 1991.

Chavez argues that for the most part Hispanics are doing a good job at assimilating into American society. The author, staff director of the U.S. Commission on Civil Rights in the Reagan administration, also makes a bold case against bilingual education programs.

Fuchs, Lawrence H., *The American Kaleidoscope: Race, Ethnicity, and the Civic Culture*, Wesleyan University Press, 1990.

This large book on immigration and American pluralism covers a lot of territory, including the role of Mexican Americans, Puerto Ricans and Cuban Americans in American society. One of the nation's leading experts on immigration, Fuchs is an excellent source on the evolution of U.S. immigration policy.

Garcia, F. Chris, ed., *Latinos and the Political System*, University of Notre Dame Press, 1988.

The 28 essays in this anthology explore the significance of the Latino constituency in the U.S. in both local and national politics. The authors, mostly academics, also assess the degree to which political power is being achieved by Latino political organizations.

de la Garza, Rodolfo O., and Louis DeSipio, eds., *From Rhetoric to Reality: Latino Politics in the 1988 Elections*, Westview Press, 1992.

This book presents a comparative analysis of Latino political participation in the 1988 U.S. election. The authors focus on case studies of states with the largest Latino populations and examine media strategies and polling methods as well as actual participation.

de la Garza, Rudolpho O., et al., *The Latino National Political Survey*, Westview Press, forthcoming.

This collection of surveys by four leading Hispanic scholars — Rodolfo O. de la Garza, Angelo Falcon, F. Chris Garcia and John Garcia — presents some of the most up-to-date data on opinions of native-born and foreign-born Mexican Americans, Cuban Americans and Puerto Ricans.

Portes, Alejandro, and Robert L. Bach, *Latin Journey: Cuban and Mexican Immigrants in the United States*, University of California Press, 1985.

Portes and Bach profile Cuban and Mexican immigrants as they arrived, then traces them over time as they settled in U.S. communities. The text also provides substantial background on Hispanic history in the U.S.

Shorris, Earl, *Latinos: A Biography of the People*, W.W. Norton & Company, 1992.

Shorris, a contributing editor at *Harper's* magazine, presents an anecdotal history of Latinos, told mostly through biographical sketches of individual immigrants who have come to the U.S. in search of a better life.

Articles

Miles, Jack, "Browns vs. Blacks," *The Atlantic*, October 1992, pp. 41-68.

Miles argues that behind the Los Angeles riot lay a grim economic competition between Latinos and African Americans, which poses a challenge to U.S. domestic and foreign policy, as well as to sentimental attitudes about immigration.

Lemann, Nicholas, "The Other Underclass," *The Atlantic*, December 1991, pp. 96-110.

Most people think of inner-city poverty as a black phenomenon. Lemann notes that Puerto Ricans are the worst-off ethnic group in the country, even though Puerto Rico itself has made great progress against poverty and there is a growing Puerto Rican middle class on the mainland.

Reports and Studies

Bureau of the Census, U.S. Department of Commerce, *1990 Census Profile: Race and Hispanic Origin*, June 1991.

This is a good source for raw census numbers on the Hispanic population.

National Association of Latino Elected and Appointed Officials, *The Latino Vote in 1992*, 1992.

This study offers an in-depth look at voting patterns of Hispanics with an eye toward the upcoming election.

National Council of La Raza, *State of Hispanic America 1991: An Overview*, February 1992.

This overview is a useful primer on how Hispanics are faring in terms demography, education, poverty, health and civil rights. The data cited is thoroughly documented.

Southwest Voter Registration Education Project, *The Southwest Voter Registration Education Project Legacy: 1974-1990*, 1990.

This is an excellent recap of what SVREP has accomplished in terms of increasing Hispanic voter participation over the past two decades.

The Next Step

Additional Articles from Current Periodicals from EBSCO Publishing's Database

Books & reading

Fuchs, L. H., "The secrets of citizenship," *The New Republic,* March 23, 1992, p. 37.

Reviews the book "Out of the Barrio: Toward a New Politics of Hispanic Assimilation," by Linda Chavez, which is so preoccupied with an attack on ethnic-conscious policies and the power brokers who advocate them that it tells virtually nothing about the history of Hispanic population in the United States.

Marquez, B., "Book reviews: American politics," *American Political Science Review,* June 1992, p. 542.

Reviews the book "The Politics of Hispanic Education," by Kenneth J. Meier and Joseph Stewart Jr.

Perez-Lopez, R., "Book reviews: Reference," *Library Journal,* May 15, 1992, p. 88.

Reviews the book "Hispanic Resource Directory, 1992-1994," by Alan Edward Schorr.

Education

Kantrowitz, B. & L. Rosado, "Falling further behind," *Newsweek,* Aug. 19, 1991, p. 60.

Reports that two recent studies conducted at the University of Texas at Austin found that the longer Mexican-American families are in the United States, the lower their children's educational level sinks. Differences among various Hispanic ethnic groups; why so many Hispanic youngsters leave school; poverty, the single greatest obstacle to schoolwork; what the Congressional Hispanic Caucus is doing to combat the trend; statistics on failure.

Lieb, K., "Technology update: 11 colleges with Hispanic enrollments form satellite network," *The Chronicle of Higher Education,* July 15, 1992, p. A19.

Describes the consortium established by 11 colleges and universities with substantial Hispanic enrollments that is based on an educational satellite network linking the campuses. The nationwide network will use existing satellite channels. Sharing both credit and non-credit courses and teleconferences; institutions included in the consortium; contact point for more information.

Suro, R., "Hispanics in despair," *The New York Times,* Nov. 4, 1990, p. 25.

Addresses the problem of Hispanic students succumbing to urban poverty, English illiteracy and the American system of education. Problems magnified by the fact that school-age Hispanics are the fastest-growing segment of the American population; President George Bush's Executive Order on "Education Excellence for Hispanic Americans"; Education Secretary, Lauro F. Cavazos' call for reassessment.

Wolford, T. E., "Elusive excellence," *Hispanic,* March 1992, p. 52.

Discusses the Bush administration's most recent offering to the Hispanic community, that being the implementation of an Executive Order on Educational Excellence for Hispanic Americans. The goals for the commission focus heavily on devising ways to improve federal efforts regarding Hispanic education; in September 1991, the commission was finally named and the office, headed by John Florez, became operational; Raúl Yzaguirre, commission member; more.

Employment

"Top 25 places for Hispanics to work in the federal government," *Hispanic,* April 1992, p. 28.

Presents *Hispanic* magazine's 1992 Federal recruitment survey in the federal work force. Lists 25 places in federal government for Hispanics to work. Hispanic recruitment survey (survey form).

Armstrong, M.J., "Florida gains diversity," *Soil & Water Conservation News,* July/August 1992, p. 12.

Reports that the Hispanic American Cultural Effort (HACE) has recognized the Soil Conservation Service Florida state office for its support of the Hispanic program and its success in recruiting Hispanic employees. Less than four years ago, the Florida office had three Hispanic employees; it now has eight; the office hired several soil scientists from Puerto Rico; more.

Heller, M., "People power," *Hispanic,* June 1992, p. 17.

Looks at how Hispanic employee associations are helping employees and companies achieve cultural diversity in the workplace. SOMOS, the association at U.S. West Market Research Group; formation of SOMOS; HISPA, the Hispanic Association of AT&T employees; the importance of providing networking opportunities; the Hispanic Leadership Council at Levi Strauss & Co.; more.

Murguia, E. & E.E. Telles, "Phenotypic discrimination and income differences among Mexican Americans,"

Social Science Quarterly, **December 1990, p. 682.**

Examines the earnings of Mexican American males and demonstrates that Chicanos with a dark and native American phenotype receive significantly lower earnings than those of a lighter and more European phenotype.

Puente, T., "Opportunity knocks," *Hispanic,* **April 1992, p. 40.**

Explores an educational program, Project 1000, striving to increase the number of Hispanics seeking graduate degrees. Started by Professor Gary Keller, Arizona State University; financial assistance; Graduate Record Examination (GRE) assistance; fields of education where shortages exist; information available.

Reyes, D., "From the minors to the big leagues," *Hispanic,* **April 1992, p. 72.**

Explores the involvement and growth of Hispanic businesses throughout the country. Involvement in legislation; Actions necessary to reach the big leagues of the business world.

Politics & government

Bullock, C.S. & S.A. MacManus, "Structural features of municipalities and the incidence of Hispanic council members," *Social Science Quarterly,* **December 1990, p. 665.**

Examines the impact of various structural arrangements on Hispanic city council representation in U.S. cities with 1980 populations over 25,000. The research demonstrates that use of different Hispanic population size thresholds to select units for analysis and differences in the methodological treatment of outliers produce different results.

Chavez, L., "Hispanics vs. their leaders," *Commentary,* **October 1991, p. 47.**

Expresses the opinion that Hispanic leaders who insist that Hispanics remain separate with their culture and language intact are doing their constituents a grave disservice. The necessity of assimilation; suggested remedies to correct low Hispanic voter turnout; description of the outrages of entitlement politics.

Coughlin, E.K., "Political survey notes differences among Latinos," *Chronicle of Higher Education,* **Sept. 11, 1991, p. A12.**

Surveys the findings of a report from the Latino National Political Survey, begun in 1988 with support from the Ford Foundation and other organizations, which is the first comprehensive study of the political values and behavior of the Latino population in the U.S. Initial results; "economic individualism"; comments on the survey at the meeting of the American Political Science Association.

Reinhold, R., "Mexican politicians look north of border," *The New York Times,* **Dec. 8, 1989, p. A1.**

Reports that the migration of millions of Mexican workers into the United States in search of jobs has brought a new influx: Mexican politicians and leaders in search of their influence, money and votes. The attention is focused mainly on the greater Los Angeles area, which now has the largest concentration of people of Mexican origin, about 3 million, anywhere outside Mexico City.

Religion

"The new evangelization and Hispanics in the United States," *America,* **Oct. 19, 1991, p. 268.**

Discusses why it is important to have programs of evangelization and catechesis that are specially directed to Hispanic Catholics in the United States. Sects; their evangelical foundation; why they are successful; who can learn from sects; Catholic Church called to be more welcoming, communal; need to emphasize centrality of Christ Jesus.

Deck, A.F., "The crisis of Hispanic ministry: Multiculturalism as an ideology," *America,* **July 14 & July 21, 1990, p. 33.**

Discusses some of the basic issues of the Catholic Hispanic ministry movement in the United States. Argues that the ideology of multiculturalism plays into certain dysfunctional tendencies found in religious institutions such as fear of conflict.

Matovina, T.M., "Hispanic Catholics in the United States: No melting pot in sight," *America,* **Mar. 16, 1991, p. 289.**

Lists seven differences between today's Hispanics and European Catholic immigrants who arrived from 1820-1920 which present a defense against assimilationist pressures. Hispanic ministry would be enhanced by seeing America as a stew pot rather than a melting pot.

Tapia, A., "Viva los evangelicos!" *Christianity Today,* **Oct. 28, 1991, p. 16.**

Explores the ways that America's growing Hispanic population is affecting the North American church. Statistics on the dramatic rise of Hispanic immigrants; impact on United States culture in general; why many are turning to the Protestant denominations; cultural differences in the way they worship; challenges faced as the two cultures merge; how they can grow together. INSET: Generation gap.

Social conditions

"Hispanics — the new underclass," *USA Today,* **September 1991, p. 6.**

Contends that during the past two decades, Hispanics have replaced blacks as the American underclass. Includes highlights of "The Emerging Hispanic Underclass," a report conducted for the Rand Corporation.

"Simmering suburbs," *Hispanic,* January/February 1992, p. 42.

Announces that suburbia is becoming the new melting pot of Hispanic culture. In 1990 census, Hispanic population had often doubled or tripled; booming areas; the Hispanic contribution; more.

Hartman, M. & P. Skerry, "Latin mass," *New Republic,* June 10, 1991, p. 18.

Considers the plight of Hispanic immigrants living in Washington, D.C. Common characteristics of Hispanics in the nation's capital; critical differences between Washington Hispanics and those in other American cities; why the recent Mount Pleasant area riots should not be considered as an indicator of future riots elsewhere; how politicians of both parties have failed to address the real needs of America's Hispanic population.

Heller, M., "Know your rights," *Hispanic,* May 1992, p. 46.

Discusses the Know Your Rights Project, developed by the National Council of La Raza (NCLR), which seeks to educate the Hispanic community on their legal rights. Cases of discrimination; statistics on complaints filed with the U.S. Equal Employment Opportunity Commission; reports of civil rights violations; more.

Jaen, V., "Chicano discrimination," *Equity & Excellence,* Summer 1990, p. 21.

Refers to one group of Spanish-speakers in the U.S. — the Mexican-Americans or Chicanos. Discusses the rapid growth of the Spanish language, due to two factors: immigration and high birth rates. States that both material and social conditions determine the fate of a language; the affect of bilingual education on the Spanish language; more.

Klitsch, M., "Hispanic ethnic groups face variety of serious health, social problems," *Family Planning Perspectives,* July/August 1991, p. 186.

Draws some observations primarily from a group of articles published in a special issue of the *Journal of the American Medical Association* that highlighted the health problems and needs of Hispanic Americans. U.S. Hispanic population; reproductive characteristics; birthweight; infant mortality; health insurance coverage; improving Hispanic health.

Krajewski-Jaime, E.R., "Folk healing among Mexican-American families as a consideration in the delivery of child welfare," *Child Welfare,* March/April 1991, p. 157.

Describes traditional health beliefs and practices among Mexican-American families and comments on the need to find ways to incorporate these practices in cross-cultural service provision. Possibility of inappropriate assessment based on the differences between the health beliefs of the predominant care provider and the minority client; "curanderismo"; definition of folk healing; natural and supernatural forces; imbalances of heat and cold; more.

Lemann, N., "The other underclass," *The Atlantic,* December 1991, p. 96.

Discusses inner-city poverty among Puerto Rican-Americans. The growing Puerto Rican middle class in the United States; history of America's relationship with Puerto Rico; studies about poverty and its relationship to waves of Puerto Rican immigration; comparisons between Puerto Ricans and black Americans.

Machado, M., "Hot cities," *Hispanic,* January/February 1992, p. 36.

Discusses how and why Hispanics flock to the five biggest cities in America. Mix of family and opportunity; worries; statistics in Los Angeles, New York, Miami, Chicago, and Houston; reasons for coming and staying; benefits; more.

Padgett, T., E. Salholz, et al., "The push for power," *Newsweek,* April 9, 1990, p. 18.

Describes how the number of Hispanics — the nation's fastest-growing group — could be approaching 25 million, or 10 percent of the total U.S. population, following results from the 1990 census. Hispanics see this as their ticket to fuller participation in American life. Lack of progress in the last decade; Latino talent. INSET: Looking ahead: Hispanics on the move.

Schwartz, J., "One-quarter of Hispanics move every year," *American Demographics,* April 1992, p. 12.

Reports that Hispanic households have the highest mobility rate among racial and ethnic groups. Twenty-six percent of Hispanic households move every year; minority householders move more because they rent; age affects mobility; source for more information.

Waldrop, J., "The Mexican May," *American Demographics,* May 1992, p. 4.

Discusses advertising to Hispanic Americans. Cinco de Mayo (fifth of May) festivals good place to reach Mexican Americans; over 22 million Hispanic Americans counted in 1990 census; choosing between English and Spanish; serving Hispanic consumers more complex than adding new products and hiring a translator; more.

Back Issues

Great Research on Current Issues Starts Right Here... Recent topics covered by The CQ Researcher are listed below. Issues dated before May 10, 1991, were published under the name of Editorial Research Reports.

APRIL 1991
Social Security
Canadian Crisis Over Quebec
California Drought
Electromagnetic Radiation

MAY 1991
School Choice
Racial Quotas
Animal Rights
U.S. and Japan

JUNE 1991
Children and Divorce
Teenage Suicide
Endangered Species
Europe 1992

JULY 1991
Teenagers and Abortion
Soviet Republics Rebel
Mexico's Emergence
Athletes and Drugs

AUGUST 1991
Sexual Harassment
Fetal Tissue Research
Oil Imports
The Palestinians

SEPTEMBER 1991
Police Brutality
Advertising Under Attack
Saving the Forests
Foster Care Crisis

OCTOBER 1991
Pay-Per-View TV
Youth Gangs
Gene Therapy
World Hunger

NOVEMBER 1991
Fast-Food Shake-Up
The Greening of Eastern Europe
Business' Role in Education
Cuba In Crisis

DECEMBER 1991
Retiree Health Benefits
Asian Americans
The Obscenity Debate
The Disabilities Act

JANUARY 1992
Term Limits
Oil Spills
Hunting Controversy
Alternative Medicine

FEBRUARY 1992
Threatened Coastlines
New Era in Asia
Assisted Suicide
Jobs in the '90s

MARCH 1992
Women and Sports
Underage Drinking
Garbage Crisis
Mafia Crackdown

APRIL 1992
Ozone Depletion
Welfare Reform
Politicians and Privacy
Illegal Immigration

MAY 1992
Native Americans
Jobs vs. Environment
Too Many Lawsuits?
Fairness in Salaries

JUNE 1992
Nuclear Proliferation
Food Irradiation
Lead Poisoning
Hard Times for Libraries

JULY 1992
Alternative Energy
Prescription Drug Prices
Alzheimer's Disease
Infant Mortality

AUGUST 1992
The Homeless
Work, Family and Stress
NATO's Changing Role
Marine Mammals vs. Fish

SEPTEMBER 1992
Domestic Partners
Violence in Schools
Public Broadcasting
Women in the Military

OCTOBER 1992
Depression
U.S. Auto Industry
Youth Apprenticeships

Back issues are available for $4.00 (subscribers) or $7.00 (non-subscribers). Quantity discounts apply to orders over ten. To order, call Congressional Quarterly 1-800-432-2250.

Future Topics

▶ *Physical Fitness*

▶ *Privitizing Government Services*

▶ *Paying for College*

THE CQ Researcher

PUBLISHED BY CONGRESSIONAL QUARTERLY INC., IN CONJUNCTION WITH EBSCO PUBLISHING

Physical Fitness

Has the fitness boom of the 1970s and '80s run out of steam?

TODAY, IF NATIONAL POLLS ARE TO BE BELIEVED, millions of Americans exercise at least three times a week, doing everything from jogging and cycling to aerobic dancing and weight training. But the image of a nation of exercise fanatics may be an illusion. Public health experts say that only about 10 percent of adult Americans exercise regularly. In essence, say the experts, the fitness boom that began 20 years ago has run out of steam. While the debate continues over how many adult Americans actually exercise, there is more universal concern about the nation's children. Numerous studies indicate U.S. youngsters are in generally poor shape, though one influential researcher believes that while some children are quite unfit, youth fitness isn't a public health problem.

C_Q **November 6, 1992 • Volume 2, No. 41 • 953-976**

Formerly Editorial Research Reports

CQ Researcher

November 6, 1992
Volume 2, No. 41

EDITOR
Sandra Stencel

MANAGING EDITOR
Thomas J. Colin

ASSOCIATE EDITOR
Richard L. Worsnop

STAFF WRITERS
Charles S. Clark
Mary H. Cooper
Rodman D. Griffin

PRODUCTION EDITOR
Sarah E. Merritt

EDITORIAL ASSISTANT
Michael M. Taylor

GRAPHICS
Jack Auldridge

PUBLISHED BY
Congressional Quarterly Inc.

CHAIRMAN
Andrew Barnes

VICE CHAIRMAN
Andrew P. Corty

EDITOR AND PUBLISHER
Neil Skene

EXECUTIVE EDITOR
Robert W. Merry

ASSOCIATE PUBLISHER
John J. Coyle

EDITOR, EBSCO PUBLISHING
Melissa Kummerer

The CQ Researcher (ISSN 1056-2036). Formerly Editorial Research Reports. Published weekly (48 times per year, not printed the first Friday of any month with five Fridays) by Congressional Quarterly Inc., 1414 22nd St., N.W., Washington, D.C. 20037. Rates are furnished upon request. Second-class postage paid at Washington, D.C. POSTMASTER: Send address changes to The CQ Researcher, 1414 22nd St., N.W., Washington, D.C. 20037.

COVER ART: BARBARA SASSA-DANIELS; LINE DRAWINGS: *HANDBOOK OF CALISTHENICS AND GYMNASTICS,* 1882

Physical Fitness

BY MARC LEEPSON

THE ISSUES

Consider the ubiquitous urban jogger. There he is, out on the pavement, determinedly getting in his daily run. There she is, stalled at a red light, grimly running in place. Why do people do these little sidewalk dances in public? Why, in fact, do hordes of American adults continue to jog and slog through rain, sleet, snow and gloom of night?

The one-word answer, as any dedicated jogger will tell you, is aerobics. But the benefits of aerobic exercise, especially warding off heart disease and shedding excess pounds, are only derived by keeping the heart working — continuously — at 60-80 percent of its capacity during a 20-30 minute workout.

Now, let's move indoors, into your neighborhood health club. In the mirrored aerobics room, women in sleek Lycra tights (and a few panting men) are jumping around to the driving beat of pop singer Paula Abdul. Upstairs, equally resolute men and women are rowing, skiing, stair-stepping and cycling on rows of gleaming, high-tech, computerized contraptions.

The joggers, aerobicizers and exercise-machine users are the very visible embodiment of a physical fitness boom that began in this country about 20 years ago. These days, if the polls are to be believed, tens of millions of Americans work out at least three times a week, not only jogging and rowing and cycling but also doing dance aerobics, weight training, lap swimming and working out on rowing machines.

But the image of a nation of exercise fanatics may be an illusion. While polls do indicate that up to 50 percent of adults get regular exercise, more exacting investigations by public health experts reveal that the true figure is

probably much lower — perhaps only 10 percent of the adult population.

In essence, say the experts, the exercise boom that began 20 years ago never fulfilled its promise.

"My guess is that nothing really changed," says Carl Caspersen, an authority on physical activity at the Atlanta-based federal Centers for Disease Control (CDC). "Certainly less than 10 or 15 percent of American adults follow the prescribed aerobic exercise program of [exercising] at least three times a week for 20-30 minutes per session at a steady rate." And that low percentage, adds Caspersen, an exercise physiologist/epidemiologist, "has been the same since the early 1970s."

In short, Americans may be in worse shape than they think they are. As experts examine physical fitness in the United States, here are the questions they are asking:

How many Americans really exercise regularly?

To read the sports-participation polls and exercise-equipment market-

ing surveys, it would seem that the fitness boom that began in the early 1970s continues unabated. Annual Gallup polls invariably indicate that between 40 and 51 percent of adults exercise daily.[1] The annual Prevention Index survey conducted by the Harris Poll for *Prevention* magazine put the figure at 34 percent in 1991.[2] And a survey conducted by American Sports Data Inc. reported that some 43.4 million American adults exercised regularly last year.[3]

The Sports Data survey also found that 16.7 million Americans belonged to health clubs in 1991. There were more than 12,000 commercial health and athletic clubs in 1991, according to IRSA: The Association of Quality Clubs, a Boston-based trade group. That figure does not include thousands of fitness facilities run by hospitals, hotels, corporations, schools, universities and municipalities. "Throughout the 1980s, the number of [commercial] clubs basically doubled," says Steve Goodfriend, the trade group's research manager.

Sales figures for equipment were just as impressive. Manufacturers last year racked up some $1.55 billion in wholesale sales of exercise equipment, not to mention a tidy $6.4 billion in wholesale sales of adult athletic shoes, about a 2 percent annual increase.[4] Basketball and running/jogging shoes accounted for nearly half the total.

Notwithstanding such sales figures, many experts question the results of surveys attempting to show how much regular exercise people actually get. The high sales do not necessarily mean that the exercise machines or shoes are regularly used. "We believe [the polls] are really quite inflated," says Christine Brooks, an associate professor at the University of Michigan's Sports and Fitness Market Research Lab.

"The general belief is that about

Americans' Exercise Habits

Although national polls in recent years have indicated that up to 50 percent of adult Americans exercise regularly, a more exacting poll used by epidemiologists came up with far different results: Only 8.1 percent of male adults and 7 percent of females engage in regular and appropriate physical activity, defined as aerobic exercises done at least three times a week for 20-30 minutes per session at a steady rate.

	Sedentary	Irregularly Active	Regularly Active but Not Appropriate Physical Activity	Regularly Active and Appropriate Physical Activity
Gender				
Male	24.8%	30.9%	36.2%	8.1%
Female	30.2%	31.3%	31.5%	7.0%
Age				
18-29	18.3%	30.1%	41.5%	10.1%
30-44	24.2%	34.5%	33.7%	7.7%
45-64	32.7%	31.9%	30.8%	4.7%
65 and older	42.6%	25.0%	24.9%	7.5%
Education				
Less than 9 years	49.2%	25.9%	20.2%	4.7%
9-11 years	35.5%	31.4%	28.3%	4.9%
12 years	26.9%	32.7%	34.4%	6.0%
13 years or more	18.5%	31.1%	39.3%	11.1%
Race				
White	27.1%	31.1%	34.1%	7.7%
Black	31.9%	31.2%	30.0%	6.9%
Other	30.4%	28.8%	33.8%	7.1%
Occupational Activity				
Light	28.2%	30.1%	33.5%	8.2%
Moderate	25.1%	33.9%	34.9%	6.1%
Heavy	27.8%	33.3%	33.4%	5.5%
Income				
Less than $7,000	35.1%	26.0%	30.5%	8.5%
$7,000 to $14,999	32.1%	30.0%	31.6%	6.3%
$15,000 to $24,999	28.1%	32.0%	33.4%	6.5%
$25,000 to $39,999	22.9%	33.3%	36.4%	7.5%
$40,000 or more	19.0%	32.6%	37.9%	10.5%

Source: U.S. Public Health Service, Centers for Disease Control, 1985 National Health Interview Survey, Health Promotion and Disease Prevention Questionnaire.

The nation's fitness profile, Brooks adds, "doesn't seem to have changed since 1980, based on comparisons that we have of data available to us."

The CDC's Caspersen not only has analyzed the national polls but also has designed and conducted his own surveys since 1983. He contends that about 50-60 percent of the adult population is either sedentary or "irregularly active," 31-36 percent are moderately active and that the rest of the population — only about 15 percent — follow the "appropriate" three-to-five-times-a-week aerobic exercise formula. *(See table at left.)*

What accounts for the significant differences between Caspersen's results and the national polls? In large part the answer has to do with the way the surveys are structured. The national polls tend to use "open-ended" questions, Caspersen explains. "They say, 'At any time in a typical week in the past year, about how often do you do high-intensity exercise vigorous enough to cause increased breathing and shortness of breath?'" That type of question, he says, encourages people to overestimate.

"What happens," Caspersen says, "is if anybody throughout the entire course of a year was running, cycling, swimming or jogging or doing something vigorously even for some short little burst of time, they're not so much going to lie or embellish their report, but take credit for something that they really didn't do every week."

As an epidemiologist, Caspersen seeks quantifiable, reliable data. He asks people specific questions about recent activities, such as during the previous two weeks. "We said, 'If you were exercising, what exactly were you doing? How many minutes was it? How many times per week?' We're asking for finite information. They're not just going to start averaging." Such surveys, he says, "get much more conservative estimates because we're talking about something that's very finite in time and not subject to a lot of guessing games or

20 percent of the adult population 18 and older are what we call regularly active," Brooks explains. "That's exercising at least three times a week on a regular basis. About 30 percent are in and out of the fitness market as the whim strikes them and about 50 percent are still fairly sedentary."

allowing for much embellishment."

Caspersen, Brooks and other analysts also question the statistics gathered by the equipment manufacturers. "It's hard to tell how good their data are," Brooks says. Sporting-goods surveys "tend to be a little bit inflated." Industry statistics, Caspersen adds, are little more than "slick marketing.... They're really only interested in selling a product, and they'll sell that in any way they can."

Then there's the question of the actual use of the products. "Certainly people seem to be buying equipment, if you believe what they say," Brooks notes. "But, then again, the use of it is an erratic type thing." Caspersen says: "There is a propensity for Americans ... to be quite interested in high-tech gadgetry and the latest fad.... The bottom line is, are they really sitting on this thing and using it every day?"

A survey conducted for *The Wall Street Journal* in 1989 tried to answer that question. It found that about 75 percent of the buyers of rowing machines, treadmills and other home equipment do not use them as much as they had planned to. "The first excuse is they don't have enough time," says Thomas Doyle, who directed the survey. "The second is that they don't have enough discipline." Of the more than 15 million exercise bicycles sold from 1984-89, Doyle says, "a lot of garages, basements and attics must be populated with them."[5]

Are American children out of shape?

While the debate continues over how many adult Americans exercise regularly, there is more universal concern about the condition of the nation's children. The federal government has been involved in encouraging children to exercise and take part

in sports ever since a 1954 survey found extremely poor fitness levels among schoolchildren.

The President's Council on Physical Fitness and Sports, founded in 1956 *(see p. 963)*, has been one of the leading advocates of youth fitness. "Forty percent of children 5 through 8 show at least one heart disease risk factor, whether it's physi-

---

The 1990 California Physical and Health-Related Fitness Test reported that 83 percent of fifth-graders, 79 percent of seventh-graders and 74 percent of ninth-graders in the nation's most populous state didn't meet minimum standards on four out of five tests.

---

cal inactivity, obesity, elevated cholesterol or high blood pressure," says Christine Spain, director of research, planning and special projects at the council. "A study done by the [Health and Human Services] Department ... showed that only 36 percent of American schoolchildren, grades 1-12, are enrolled in daily physical education, and that could have a lot to do with it — that P.E. is on the decrease." *(See table, p. 958.)*

The council has funded a national survey of schoolchildren's physical fitness every 10 years since 1965. The latest survey, in 1985, found that "youth fitness in the U.S. did not improve in the 10 years from 1975 to 1985, and in some cases there was a decline," Spain says.

The survey measured the perfor-

mance of boys and girls 6-17 in nine tests, including bent-knee sit-ups, pull-ups, 50-yard dash, standing long jump and the one-mile run/walk. The 1985 results found "significant improvements" compared with a survey published in 1958, but "no general gains" over the 1965 and 1975 test data. The survey concluded: "There is still a lower level of performance in important components of physical fitness by millions of our youth."[6]

More recent surveys, including a 1989 youth fitness test sponsored by the Amateur Athletic Union (AAU), have reported similar results. The AAU measured 10 million children and adolescents in tests similar to the council's. The percentage of children who scored "satisfactory" in the AAU survey dropped from 43 percent in 1980 to 32 percent in 1989. The survey revealed "a creeping problem that in 30 years can be a very serious one for the overall health of our society," said Wynn Updyke, dean of Indiana University's School of Health, Physical Education and Recreation, who directed the study.[7]

The 1990 California Physical and Health-Related Fitness Test reported that 83 percent of fifth-graders, 79 percent of seventh-graders and 74 percent of ninth-graders in the nation's most populous state didn't meet minimum standards on four out of five tests (pull-ups, sit-ups, one-mile run/walk, sitting stretch and an optional body-fat composition test). "It's pretty clear the kids just aren't fit," said Bill Honig, California's superintendent of public instruction.[8]

State education officials in Virginia obtained similarly dismal results after administering a basic fitness test in 1991. The findings — dubbed the "couch potato index" — revealed that fewer than one in four Virginia

Physical Education in High School

The percentage of high school students enrolled in physical education classes ranged from a high of 96 percent in New York State to a low of 24 percent in South Dakota. The percentage of students attending daily P.E. classes ranged from 4 percent in New York to 46 percent in Alabama.

	Percentage of Students Enrolled in Physical Education	Percentage of Students Attending Daily Physical Education Classes
Nationally	49%	42%
Selected States		
Alabama	52%	46%
Georgia	40%	35%
Idaho	46%	40%
Nebraska	47%	34%
New Mexico	48%	43%
New York*	96%	4%
Puerto Rico	27%	20%
South Carolina	38%	34%
South Dakota	24%	15%
Utah	61%	37%
Selected Cities		
Chicago	88%	74%
Dallas	39%	33%
Ft. Lauderdale	40%	32%
Jersey City	78%	62%
Miami	51%	45%
Philadelphia	72%	41%
San Diego	67%	55%

Does not include New York City
Source: Centers for Disease Control, Morbidity and Mortality Weekly Report, Aug. 21, 1992.

state high school students could pass minimum requirements for sit-ups, stretching, pull-ups and the mile run. *(See p. 963.)*

What's behind the disheartening condition of the nation's youth? The experts cite everything from the prevalence of video games and VCRs to the declining number of physical education classes. The U.S. Department of Health and Human Services (HHS) found in 1986 that only 36 percent of American schoolchildren had daily physical education classes.[9]

In response, the agency recommended last year that by the year 2000 the nation increase to at least 50 percent the percentage of children who participate in daily P.E.

The main reason for the comparatively low number of physical education classes has been a scarcity of local funds. "Increasing physical education is a fairly significant financial undertaking," says Judith Young, executive director of the National Association for Sport and Physical Education, which represents physical education teach-

ers. "If a school system has [P.E. classes] one day a week in elementary [schools], and they want to have three days a week for every child, then that would have a great impact on the teaching force required."

But despite the nation's weak economy, says Young, parents, teachers and school boards seem to support P.E. classes. "We have not seen great, extensive cuts, ultimately, although there have been many, many proposals to cut back on physical education," she points out. "In the end, through various means, some kind of program is maintained typically. But we certainly haven't seen expansion in any significant ways."

While public health analysts widely agree on the poor state of children's fitness, some observers question the seriousness of the situation. One of the most outspoken is Steven Blair, director of epidemiology at the Dallas-based Cooper Institute for Aerobics Research, who has written widely on the subject. "Clearly, there are some children who are quite unfit, and certainly there's a segment that is overweight," Blair says. "But I think it's relatively small."

Blair maintains that the alarming reports by the President's Council and other surveys tend not to address the issue of what desired fitness levels should be. "In order to understand the magnitude of the problem," he says, "we have to set standards, and then we can apply the standards to appropriately selected samples. So if you don't know what an acceptable level is, how can you possibly classify someone as being unfit?"

Blair also suggests that fitness levels among children are no worse than they have been in previous decades. "I hold out the possibility that maybe they are. We don't have as much data as we would like on this and many other issues. But there are absolutely no credible data that any reputable epidemiologist or public health statistician would accept that indicate we're on the downward path."

Blair believes that only about 20 percent of American children are "at risk because of low fitness." But he does warn about other fitness-related problems among children, including "the great rise ... in video games and [other] sedentary pursuits." On the other hand, he says, "in the last decade that we had a big increase, presumably, in the number of video games out there, I suspect there's also been quite an increase in the number of children playing soccer." ■

BACKGROUND

Early Fitness Booms

The current American "fitness boom," one commentator wrote in 1986, "is a cyclical phenomenon, predominantly middle class, layered by money, sex, religion, charismatic entrepreneurs and fear of an early death. What else is new?" [10]

Indeed, American proponents of exercise date back to the Colonial era. Benjamin Franklin, for example, in addition to advocating early to bed and early to rise, urged his countrymen to engage in swimming and running as early as 1743. Benjamin Rush (1746-1813), a prominent Philadelphia physician, prescribed exercise for an array of health problems.

The first widespread American fitness movement started in the 1830s, a period of "profound change in the way many Americans were living and working," says historian Stephen Nissenbaum. The most pronounced societal changes involved the young nation's first steps toward industrialization. More Americans began to work outside their homes, and fewer people produced their own food. That meant that more people than ever began to rely on others for the necessities of life — and found free time for recreation.[11]

Other important social factors of the 1830s were shifting national attitudes about religion and widespread concerns about the fate of the nation following the deaths of such revered leaders as Thomas Jefferson and John Adams (both died on July 4, 1826). While historians have noted a general feeling of optimism during the period, especially regarding the strength of the individual and the entrepreneur, many Americans nonetheless were losing faith in the second, less charismatic, generation of American leaders.

"Fearing the social fabric might disintegrate, some individuals turned for reassurance to mending their own bodies," wrote William Bennett, a former editor of *The Harvard Medical School Health Letter*.[12] This, in turn, led to the emergence of what historian Harvey Green characterized as a "coterie of health reformers — dietary faddists, water-cure specialists, animal magnetizers and electromagnetizers and physical educators." [13]

One notable member of the coterie certainly fit in the "charismatic entrepreneur" category. Sylvester Graham was a Presbyterian minister who lectured widely in the 1830s on the efficacy of vegetarianism and temperance. Graham — whom Ralph Waldo Emerson called "the prophet of bran bread and pumpkins"— decried the use of processed flour and chemical additives in bread. Graham also advocated what he called "active exercise" for adults and children. He called on Americans to visit gymnasiums to "swing upon and climb the poles, and ropes and ladders and vault upon the wooden horse," or, better yet, to "walk and run, and jump, or labor on the farm." Above all, Graham urged Americans to "avoid sedentary habits." [14]

Graham was hardly alone. Other influential fitness advocates of the 1830-50 period included Edward Hitchcock of Amherst College, the nation's first physical education professor; William Alcott, the popular author of nearly 100 self-help books, who espoused regular exercise and proper hygiene and diet; James C. Jackson, a physician who touted the all-purpose "water cure," as well as the benefits of calisthenics and gymnastics; Catharine Beecher, an early exponent of stress-reduction and the healing powers of fresh air; and H. H. Sherwood, a physician who viewed the body as a magnet and most physical problems as resulting from the body's magnetic forces being out of equilibrium.

The 1860s Athletic Revival

A second fitness movement began in the 1860s, largely influenced by the recent wave of German immigrants. The newcomers, many of them physicians, brought to this country a strong interest in sports, calisthenics and gymnastics. Calisthenics, popular fitness author J. Madison Watson wrote in 1863, are designed "to further the proportionate development of the body; render the joints more flexible in all directions; give the pleasing and graceful

appearance of firmness, steadiness and dexterity in the positions and in the use of the limbs; and secure physical beauty, muscular strength and robust health." [15]

During this era, physical education in schools and organized exercises among adults, which had begun in a few American colleges in the 1830s, became common, especially in urban areas. This second fitness wave, lasting roughly from 1860-90, featured "a more secular approach" among health reformers, Green wrote, based on widespread dissemination of new scientific and technological discoveries.

The second half of the 19th century also saw the growth of the sanitation movement, which focused on improving ventilation and household toilet practices. Also popular was the wilderness cure, in which city dwellers with health problems lived simply in tents or rudimentary cabins for extended periods.

Many health sanitariums prospered in this era. Sanitariums helped the health conscious give up tobacco, tea, coffee, meat, fried foods and drugs. Many offered low-calorie diets and exercise programs. The Battle Creek Sanitarium in Michigan, started by Ellen White (known as the

"prophetess of health" because of her religious visions), had become one of the most popular in the nation by 1890. John Harvey Kellogg, a physician who directed the sanitarium, advocated vegetarianism and abstaining from both alcohol and "sexual misconduct."

In the late 1870s, Kellogg began serving a healthy breakfast food he devised called Granula. The wheat flour, cornmeal and oatmeal concoction, which he later renamed Granola, is considered the nation's first breakfast cereal. Kellogg's brother, William, went on to found the giant company bearing the family name, igniting a breakfast cereal "boom" in the early 1890s.[16]

Among the new healthy cereal products were several others that are still served today — including Henry D. Perky's Shredded Wheat (developed in 1892), C. W. Post's Grape-Nuts (1898) and Kellogg's Corn Flakes (1906) — as well as many short-lived cereals such as Force Flakes, Mapl-Flakes, Ceru-Fruto, Norka Malted Oats, Golden Manna, Vim Wheat Flakes and Kellogg's Granose Wheat Flakes.

19th-Century Workout

The athletic revival after the Civil War also saw a renewed interest in "physical culture," especially gymnastics and calisthenics and sports. Physical culture was especially popular in the rapidly industrializing Northeast, where by 1860 more than half the population lived in cities and towns. Entrepreneurs and local governments built gymnasiums by the thousands beginning in the 1860s. "The idea of encouraging physical development dovetailed with increasingly cultural worries about emotionally overtaxing both the young and the mature in an increasingly urban, bureaucratic and sedentary society,"

Green noted.[17]

Women, for the first time, were encouraged to participate. Foremost among those who pushed for women to exercise was Dioclesian Lewis, a physical education instructor who had studied gymnastics in Europe and condemned the use of corsets and other restrictive female garments. Lewis was an innovator in the gym, introducing the exercise rings and a series of popular exercises using lightweight, wooden dumbbells.

Also popular in 19th-century gyms were parallel bars, vaulting bars, dumbbells, horizontal ladders, weights and pulleys, suspended rings, wooden horses, springboards and wands. Wooden clubs shaped like bowling pins and known as "Indian clubs," or "scepters," became widely popular in this era. "Nothing can be better calculated to invigorate the respiratory system, expand the chest, call into action the muscles of locomotion and the principle structures around the joints, and enlarge and strengthen the mus-

Continued on p. 962

Chronology

1820s-1830s
The first organized fitness programs begin in the United States, mainly in the Northeast.

1821
Exercise and calisthenics for women become part of the educational program at Emma Willard's school in Troy, N.Y.

1823
Round Hill School is established in Boston by Harvard University Professors George Bancroft and J.G. Cogswell with the specific purpose of integrating regular physical education into the curriculum.

1826
The nation's first college gymnasium opens at Harvard.

1830
Edward Hitchcock establishes a physical fitness program at Amherst College in Massachusetts.

1850
The American Vegetarian Society is founded.

1855
Charles Ottingnon and George Weyprecht open the first two public gymnasiums in New York City.

1860s-1890s
During the period that becomes known as the "Athletic Revival," Americans develop renewed interest in health and physical fitness, largely influenced by German immigrants who bring a strong interest in sports, calisthenics and gymnastics.

1866
The first "parlor gymnasiums," rudimentary weight-training devices for home use, and the first rowing machines are developed.

Late 1880s
Bicycles become widely popular in the United States.

1950s
Concern about the nation's low level of physical fitness leads to federal government support of fitness standards.

1954
Nearly 58 percent of American schoolchildren fail six simple fitness tests in a study by two New York University researchers, compared with a 9 percent failure rate among Italian, Swiss and Austrian children.

July 16, 1956
President Dwight D. Eisenhower creates the President's Council on Youth Fitness to help design and implement physical fitness programs in the nation's schools. It becomes the President's Council on Physical Fitness and Sports in 1968.

1960s
Interest in physical fitness increases.

1966
Runner's World magazine begins publication.

April 1968
Dr. Kenneth A. Cooper publishes *Aerobics*. The best-selling book is credited with launching the fitness boom of the 1970s and '80s.

1970s-1990s
The age of the exercise video.

1977
James Fixx's *The Complete Book of Running*, a paen to the physical and spiritual benefits of jogging, becomes a No. 1 best-seller.

March 1982
Actress Jane Fonda's first exercise video, "Jane Fonda's Workout," is released. It goes on to spend more than three years atop the national video sales charts.

1985
The President's Council on Physical Fitness and Sports releases a report on youth physical fitness that finds "no general gains" compared with tests taken in 1965 and 1975. The survey concludes "there is still a lower level of performance in important components of physical fitness by millions of our youth."

1987
A Gallup Poll reports that 51 percent of American adults say they participate in a daily fitness program, compared with 24 percent in 1961. The figure drops to 49 percent in 1987, the year that Gallup discontinues the annual poll.

November 1989
Dr. Dean Ornish of the Preventive Medicine Research Institute in California presents evidence that a low-fat diet combined with exercise and relaxation programs can reverse coronary artery disease without the use of cholesterol-lowering drugs.

1991
The state of Oregon sets a goal calling for 90 percent of the state's adults to be doing some type of aerobic exercise for 20 minutes at least three times a week by the year 2010.

From Jogging to Boxing: Aerobics Grows Up

What some have called the "aerobics revolution" began nearly a quarter-century ago, following the publication of an article on fitness in the March 1968 issue of *Reader's Digest* by an Air Force surgeon named Kenneth H. Cooper. Cooper's article and best-selling book, *Aerobics*, published the following month, set out the exercise theory that soon induced millions of Americans to undertake a regular exercise program that included aerobic exercises like jogging, walking and swimming.

Cooper's theory — now slightly modified — has been universally accepted by the medical community. It holds that regular aerobic exercises significantly increase the strength and efficiency of the heart, lungs and blood vessels — the all-important cardiovascular system. The key to physical fitness is activity that induces the heart to work harder, thereby improving the body's ability to use oxygen.

Cooper, who now heads the Aerobics Center, a nationally known exercise clinic in Dallas, says exercises that get the heart beating at 60-80 percent of its capacity should be performed nonstop for 20-30 minutes, three-to-five times per week. This has become known as the "traditional" exercise prescription.

"If you follow that prescription, we can be pretty confi-dent that you will achieve and maintain an adequate level of fitness, and that amount of exercise and fitness will be associated with health benefits," says Steven Blair, director of epidemiology at the Cooper Institute for Aerobics Research, which is affiliated with the Aerobics Center.

In the beginning, running, jogging and rapid walking were the aerobics exercises of choice. But in the last two decades, aerobicizers have branched into everything from lap swimming and low-impact dancing to machines for rowing, cycling, stair-climbing and cross-country skiing and circuit training, a form of continuous weight lifting using light weights.

"The latest rage on the fitness frontier," according to *The New York Times*, is aerobic boxing — especially among young, professional women. Workouts typically include boxing drills, work on the heavy punching bag, plus sit-ups, rope skipping and 3 minutes of fast-paced shadow boxing. But after a while, boxing fever hits.

"Male or female, it doesn't matter," said Ira Becker, who owns Gleason's Gym in Brooklyn. "They learn the craft, and eventually they're going to say, 'Let's box.' It's inevitable."†

---

† Quoted in Molly O'Neill, "The Lace is in the Gloves," *The New York Times*, Aug. 30, 1992.

Continued from p. 960

cles of the forearm, the upper arm, and the shoulder, as well as the abdominal and spinal muscles," fitness author Watson said of the Indian club.[18]

Exercise equipment designed to be used at home first appeared in the 1860s. By the end of the century, exercise-conscious Americans could choose from an assortment of home-gym equipment, including rowing machines and a variety of strength-building apparatuses predating today's gleaming Nautilus and Universal gym systems, including those using wires and pulleys, rubber bands, ropes, rings and dumbbells.

Era of "Regeneration"

The next wave of fitness mania began in the years preceding the turn of the century and lasted until just before World War II. During this era of "regeneration," as Green called it, there were crime waves in many large cities as well as racial and ethnic tensions, periodic labor unrest and other social upheavals, including the devastating Great Depression.[19]

Bicycling became a national craze in the 1880s at the start of the regeneration era. The period's leading fitness entrepreneur was author and publisher Bernarr Macfadden, a bodybuilder who branched out into the "healthatorium" business. Macfadden pushed many cures, preaching the benefits of regular exercise, fresh air, avoidance of spicy foods and medicines and frequent sexual intercourse. Macfadden, who reached his height of popularity in the early 1920s, also was known for his white-supremacist views and his infatuation with Benito Mussolini, the Italian dictator.

Another popular health guru, Horace Fletcher (the "Moses of mastication"), gained notoriety for his advice on how to eat properly. Fletcher held that each morsel should be chewed slowly and thoroughly in order to — among other things — cure obesity, indigestion and skin problems. "Fletcherizing" was wildly popular in the early 20th century and counted novelist Henry James, industrialist John D. Rockefeller and Sir Arthur Conan Doyle, the creator of Sherlock Holmes, among its enthusiastic adherents.*

---

*One of today's most popular health entrepreneurs, Jay Kordich, the self-proclaimed "Juiceman," advocates a form of Fletcherizing. Kordich, in his best-selling book, *The Juiceman's Power of Juicing* (1992), urges his followers to "chew" vegetable juice, swirling it "around in your mouth for 30 to 60 seconds before swallowing." Doing that, he says, makes the juice warmer and sweeter before swallowing it, and "more important, the warm juice stimulates and mixes with a digestive enzyme in the saliva called ptyalin. This process accelerates digestion and ultimate absorption."

'60s Fitness Boom

In the boom years after World War II, studies began to show prosperity's negative impact on the American people. After a 1954 study reported extremely poor fitness levels among schoolchildren, President Dwight D. Eisenhower — whose personal physician, Dr. Paul Dudley White, was an outspoken exercise advocate — created the President's Council on Youth Fitness in 1956 to help design and implement physical fitness programs for U.S. schools.

President John F. Kennedy broadened the program in 1961, putting more emphasis on helping schools design fitness programs rather than concentrating on team sports. The new emphasis seemed to pay off with marked improvements in physical testing results in 1965.[20] The council, which changed its name to the President's Council on Physical Fitness and Sports in 1968, began promoting fitness for adults in 1962.

The nation's fourth, and latest, physical fitness wave began in the late 1960s. One event that sparked new interest, especially in running and jogging, was the 1968 publication of *Aerobics* by Air Force surgeon Kenneth H. Cooper. Cooper, who now heads his own fitness institute in Dallas, set out the exercise theory that soon prompted millions of Americans to undertake regular aerobic exercise programs. (*See story, p. 962.*)

Another influential jogging proponent of the 1970s was James Fixx, a former magazine editor who in early middle age turned to running, lost an enormous amount of weight and overcame a two-pack-a-day cigarette smoking habit. Fixx's *The Complete Book of Running* became a best-seller in 1977.

Then there was George Sheehan, an iconoclastic New Jersey cardiologist turned magazine columnist, author, lecturer and running proselytizer.

"Sheehan is not just running's doctor but its reigning philosopher," Fixx wrote. "To read Sheehan rejuvenates one's faith that running really is as important as it seems."[21]

Spurred on by Sheehan and the other fitness gurus, America underwent "a physical fitness renaissance" in the 1970s, according to Richard Keelor, a former director of program development for the President's Council. Nearly half of all Americans in a 1977 Gallup Poll, for example, reported that they exercised daily — twice the percentage recorded in 1961. And for the next decade, opinion polls and sales of running shoes continued to indicate that almost half of all adult Americans exercised regularly.

The New Moderation

In recent years, at the same time that public health experts started reassessing Americans' exercise habits, many fitness experts began moderating their guidelines. The prescription changed from the three-to-five-day-a-week aerobics routine to a less intense regimen. As Kenneth Cooper said in a 1987 interview: "I used to think that it didn't make any difference how far you ran if you had a good, strong musculoskeletal system and no underlying cardiovascular problems.... Now I say that if you run more than 15 miles a week, it's for something other than aerobic fitness."[22]

Cooper went on to praise other, less strenuous types of aerobic exercise, such as walking, swimming and low-impact aerobic dancing. The latter, which became very popular in the late 1980s, is a gentler, less-demanding form of aerobic dancing.

In low-impact aerobics, instructors never urge their classes to "go for the burn," a phrase made famous by actress Jane Fonda in her phenomenally popular first exercise video in 1982. Fonda joined the new moderation exponents in the late 1980s. In her continuing series of exercise tapes, Fonda no longer exhorts her followers to push themselves until they feel pain. Fonda and most of the other popular home video exercise personalities (including Kathy Smith, Judi Sheppard Missett and Jacki Sorensen) offer routines that feature sensible, cautious workouts, many of the low-impact type.*

The new emphasis on moderation followed widespread reports of injuries caused by too much aerobic exercise. Called "overuse" injuries by sports-medicine specialists, they include stress fractures, pulled muscles, ruptured tendons, tennis elbow, tendinitis, bursitis, sore back and shin splints. There also seemed to be far

Model Cindy Crawford's exercise video was the nation's most popular in early October.

---

* "Jane Fonda's Workout" has sold more than a million tapes worldwide. Sales of exercise videos reached their peak in the late 1980s and have steadily declined since then. For the week ending Oct. 11, 1992, only one exercise video — model Cindy Crawford's "Shape Your Body Workout" — made *Billboard* magazine's top 20 listing of best-selling videos. Other currently popular exercise tapes include Kathy Smith's "Instant Workout" and Fonda's "Low-Impact Aerobics."

Aerobic Exercise and Weight Control

It is universally accepted that obesity is a threat to health. But agreeing on the best way to lose weight — and keep it off — is another matter. Researchers know that popular diets are often ineffective and that the common practice of continually gaining and losing weight (known as "yo-yo dieting") is harmful.

Recent research has given new credence to the genetic "set-point" theory advanced by the 1983 book, *The Dieter's Dilemma: Eating Less and Weighing More*. According to authors William Bennett and Joel Gurin, weight control is genetically predetermined — which tends to explain why some people can eat a lot and not gain weight and others can consume relatively few calories and balloon out.

Other recent studies, on the other hand, suggest that weight loss is a simple matter of mathematics: If you consume more calories than you burn, you gain weight, and vice versa. These studies have provided strong evidence that virtually anyone can lose weight by maintaining a diet low in fat and high in whole grains and fruits and vegetables (complex carbohydrates).

The one certainty in the weight-loss debate is exercise.

Virtually all health professionals say a program of aerobic exercise and/or weight training should be an integral part of any diet. "The best way to lose weight," said exercise physiologist Bryant Stamford, who directs the University of Louisville School of Medicine's Health Promotion and Wellness Center, "is through a combination of a good, prudent diet and exercise." †

Exercise helps in weight control in several ways. Aside from burning calories, it helps regulate the appetite, increases the metabolic rate and reinforces the discipline needed to make positive dietary and lifestyle changes, such as quitting smoking and eating less fat. Plus, a regular exercise program can bring about less quantifiable results.

"In a successful diet, the satisfaction and elevated self-esteem derived from [exercising] may be more important than the actual calories burned," said Mary-Giselle Rathgeber of the Preventive and Sports Medicine Center in New York City.††

† Quoted in *The Washington Post*, Jan. 10, 1989.
†† Quoted in *The New York Times*, June 18, 1990.

---

more serious problems. "Too many widows wrote and told me about so-and-so who followed my guidelines and had a heart attack," Cooper said in 1987.

Another moderating factor was a short-lived but nonetheless effective mid-1980s "backlash" against excessive exercise. In a controversial 1984 book, *The Exercise Myth*, Henry A. Solomon, a New York cardiologist, argued against a steady diet of strenuous aerobics, calling it useless at best and dangerous — "a public health hazard" — at worst. No scientific evidence surfaced linking aerobic exercise and health problems. But Solomon's book and other medical warnings influenced many exercisers to scale back.

Ultimately, common sense played a major role in moderating behavior. "The biggest reason why people quit [exercising] is because it hurts," says Christine Brooks of the University of Michigan. The traditional aerobic prescription is "very strict," and some who try to run, say, five days a week can be discouraged by the inevitable aching muscles that follow.   ■

CURRENT SITUATION

The Benefits of Fitness

Those who continue to exercise do so for many reasons. Many people equate exercise with good looks, popularity and sex appeal. But the experts say that the main motivation is for better health. Numerous clinical studies in recent years have provided strong evidence that regular exercise helps prevent heart disease — the nation's No. 1 cause of death

— as well as several other serious health problems, including obesity and diabetes.

For example, a review of recent fitness and health clinical studies in 1989 done by the U.S. Preventive Services Task Force, a government-appointed panel of experts, found "a strong association between physical activity and decreased risk of several medical conditions, as well as overall mortality." The report found strong "evidence" that exercise can cut the risk of developing coronary heart disease among men, and hypertension, obesity and osteoporosis among post-menopausal women. The group's conclusion: Physicians should counsel all healthy adults "to engage in a program of regular physical activity tailored to their health status and personal life-style." [23]

In 1989, an eight-year study of more than 13,000 adults found a "strong" relationship between physical fitness and longevity. "Moderate levels of physical fitness that are attainable by most adults appear to be protective against early mortality," researchers at the Institute for Aerobics Research concluded. The study has been described as "the most extensive analysis yet of the effects of fitness on longevity." [24] It found that exercise seemed to be a factor in warding off cardiovascular diseases and cancer deaths in "the more fit men and women," and that the millions of adults who get little or no exercise constitute "an important public health problem." [25]

A clinical study of 41 randomly selected heart disease patients at the Preventive Medicine Research Institute in Sausalito, Calif., found for the first time in 1989 that a low-fat diet, combined with exercise and relaxation programs, can reverse coronary artery disease without the use of cholesterol-lowering drugs. The study, the Lifestyle Heart Trial, put heart patients on an extremely low-fat vegetarian diet, a regime of daily relaxation exercises and a minimum of 30 minutes of exercising (usually walking) three times a week.

The study, which was announced at the annual meeting of the American Heart Association in 1989, "offers strong scientific evidence that life-style changes alone can actually reverse the progression of atherosclerotic plaques in coronary arteries," said Dr. Claude Lenfant, director of the federal National Heart, Lung and Blood Institute.[26]

Exercise got another boost in a 1991 research study, which strongly indicated for the first time that exercise can prevent the onset of adult diabetes, which affects nearly 12 million Americans. The study, conducted by researchers at the University of California's School of Public Health and the Stanford University School of Medicine's Department of Health Research and Policy, examined nearly 6,000 men who graduated from college in the 1930s and '40s. The results showed that those who took part in vigorous or moderate exercise programs had far

fewer cases of diabetes than those who did little or no exercise. " These findings strongly support the position that persons who are at substantial risk for [non-insulin-dependent diabetes mellitus] should . . . maintain a high level of physical activity in their daily lives," wrote Dr. Edward Horton of the University of Vermont College of Medicine.[27]

Doctors today are even recommending that many arthritis patients can gain relief from their pain through aerobic exercise. In the past, they either discouraged exercise or recommended only light stretching. But studies have discovered that arthritis patients derive physical as well as psychological benefits from swimming, walking and other less-demanding aerobic activities.

"In recent years, there's been a dramatic turnaround in our exercise recommendations," said Teresa J. Brady, the Arthritis Foundation's medical adviser. "New evidence is showing that more intense, aerobic activity is safe and beneficial as long as the exercise is carefully selected to fit the person's body conditioning and the state of their arthritis." [28]

The American Heart Association (AHA) now equates the lack of exercise with smoking and high blood pressure and high cholesterol levels as significant risk factors for developing heart disease. Exercise, the AHA said, can help cut the risk of developing coronary heart disease, as well as "help control blood lipid abnormalities, diabetes, and obesity." Persons "of all ages," the AHA recommended, "should include physical activity in a comprehensive program of health promotion and disease prevention, and should increase their habitual physical activity to a level appropriate to their capacities, needs and interest." [29]

The AHA reported that activities such as walking, hiking, stair-climbing, calisthenics, jogging, running, bicycling, rowing and swimming, as well as sports such as tennis, basketball and touch football, are "especially beneficial when per-

formed regularly." The AHA singled out "brisk walking" as "an excellent choice."

The national rate of death from heart disease, which rose steady from the 1920s through the '50s, has fallen more than 55 percent since it reached a peak of 220 per 100,000 population in 1963. (See graph, p. 966.) The decline began to accelerate rapidly in the early 1970s and continues to do so. But health researchers do not attribute this significant change solely to exercise. They point also to a national decrease in cigarette smoking and recent advances in cardiac-care technology.

Helping Couch Potatoes

Despite virtual scientific assurances that regular exercise provides positive health benefits, about half the adult population does very little or no exercising. That fact has led public health analysts to rethink their emphasis on the importance of the 20-30-minute aerobics session three times a week — what is widely called the "traditional" exercise prescription.

The consensus of opinion today is that the old prescription is still valid, but that it may not be appropriate for most Americans. Public health analysts now say that sedentary Americans can benefit even from a moderate aerobic program or simply by doing a few minutes of other physical activity on a daily basis.

"The traditional recommendations weren't wrong, and they aren't wrong today," says Russell Pate, chairman of the University of South Carolina's Department of Exercise Science. "However, there are very important health benefits associated with regular activity at a lower level than described in those guidelines. There is still great benefit to be associated with more modest levels of activity."

The best way to "enhance the health of the population overall," Pate says, would be to "get a sizable fraction of the essentially inactive people doing something. The health gains would be

Meeting the President's Challenge

Schoolchildren who score at or above the scores listed below for their age and sex qualify for the Presidential Physical Fitness Award from the President's Council on Physical Fitness and Sports, chaired by actor Arnold Schwarzenegger.

	Age	Curl-ups (Timed one minute)	Shuttle run (seconds)	V-Sit-reach (inches)	or Sit and reach (centimeters)	One-mile run (minutes/seconds)	Pull-ups
Boys	6	33	12.1	+3.5	31	10:15	2
	7	36	11.5	+3.5	30	9:22	4
	8	40	11.1	+3.0	31	8:48	5
	9	41	10.9	+3.0	31	8:31	5
	10	45	10.3	+4.0	30	7:57	6
	11	47	10.0	+4.0	31	7:32	6
	12	50	9.8	+4.0	31	7:11	7
	13	53	9.5	+3.5	33	6:50	7
	14	56	9.1	+4.5	36	6:26	10
	15	57	9.0	+5.0	37	6:20	11
	16	56	8.7	+6.0	38	6:08	11
	17	55	8.7	+7.0	41	6:06	13
Girls	6	32	12.4	+5.5	32	11:20	2
	7	34	12.1	+5.0	32	10:36	2
	8	38	11.8	+4.5	33	10:02	2
	9	39	11.1	+5.5	33	9:30	2
	10	40	10.8	+6.0	33	9:19	3
	11	42	10.5	+6.5	34	9:02	3
	12	45	10.4	+7.0	36	8:23	2
	13	46	10.2	+7.0	38	8:13	2
	14	47	10.1	+8.0	40	7:59	2
	15	48	10.0	+8.0	43	8:08	2
	16	45	10.1	+9.0	42	8:23	1
	17	44	10.0	+8.0	42	8:15	1

Arnold Schwarzenegger

Source: President's Council on Physical Fitness and Sports, which also supplied the photograph

far greater than if we focused our attention on the people who are already pretty active, and tried to get them into the very high active category."

"That fact," he says, "was not accepted during the early part of the most recent fitness boom. I'm certainly not all negative about what happened in the late 1960s and '70s because I think it changed some things about our society that really needed to change."

One of the most important societal changes, Pate says, was the acceptance of the image of "exercise as a part of one's life." Before the aerobics boom, Pate says, many people viewed runners and joggers as "kooks." By the mid-1970s, though, aerobic exercising had become "socially desirable behavior." During the 1970s, however, exercise proponents "may have inadvertently communicated that if you're not doing a rather high level of activity, you might as well forget it — if you're not running road races, you're not really an exerciser."

Another leading exponent of the modified exercise prescription, Steven Blair, says that "doing something is better than doing nothing. It is clear to me that if you're really a couch potato, and very unfit, just getting up and moving around is probably better for you than continuing to sit in your recliner 15 hours a day."

Integrating Exercise Into the Daily Routine

Blair's thinking has changed primarily in response to data showing that only about 10 percent of adults are exercising at higher levels. "We've been promoting that approach for 20-25 years," he says, "and if we have less than 10 percent of the adult American population signed on, that's evidence to me that we need to be thinking about some alternative approaches." Most of those who do not exercise, he says, have proven that they're not going to undertake a rigorous aerobics routine.

Blair encourages inactive types to integrate more physical activity into their daily lives. He advocates "taking the stairs instead of elevators and escalators; not driving around the mall for 10 minutes looking for a parking spot close to the door, just simply parking and getting out and walking; and interspersing short walks — two, three, four or five minutes over the course of the day."

Instead of doing some activity non-stop for 20-30 minutes, Blair says, those who are "very sedentary and unfit" should try to accumulate 30 to 40 minutes of walking during the week. "I'm always careful to say that I don't know that the benefits are exactly the same as taking one 30-minute walk," Blair says, "but I think the evidence suggests they're comparable."

The latest recommendations on exercise and health promotion by the American Heart Association conform to what Blair, Pate and the overwhelming majority of exercise experts now counsel. The new AHA recommendations call for "persons of all ages" to engage in regular aerobic exercise. But the AHA alternatively recommends daily "low-intensity" activities such as "walking for pleasure, gardening, yard work, housework, dancing and prescribed home exercise."[30]

The most popular low-intensity exercise, walking, is also the world's oldest exercise. Walking — and its cousin, slow jogging — also is among the easiest, safest and least expensive fitness activities. Walking's main low-intensity advantage is that

Heart Disease on the Decline

The national rate of death from heart disease — the nation's No. 1 cause of death — began to decline rapidly beginning in the 1970s, a time when diets improved, smoking dropped, cardiac-care improved and more Americans began exercising regularly.

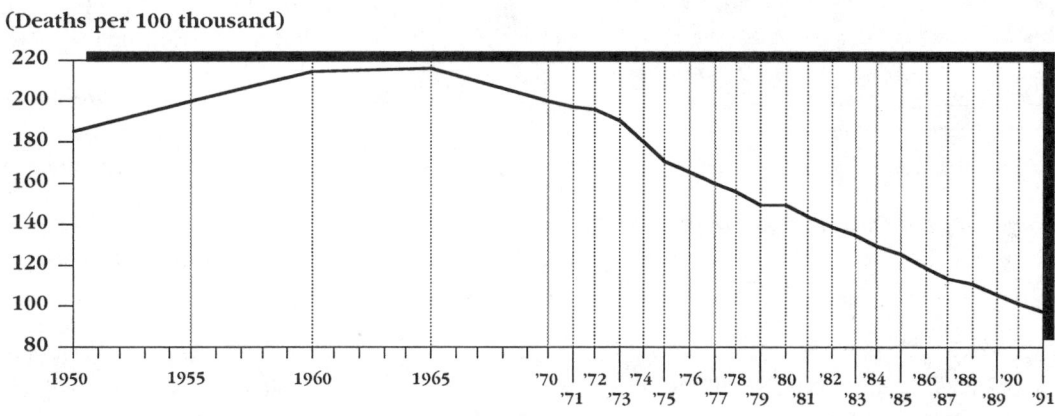

(Deaths per 100 thousand)

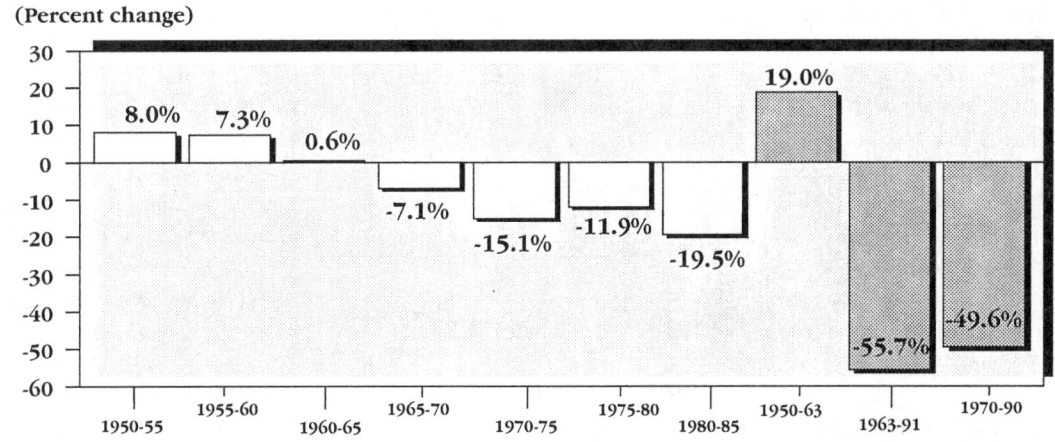

(Percent change)

Source: National Center for Health Statistics, Vital Statistics of the U.S.

The Fastest-Growing Exercises

More Americans jog and lift weights for their exercise than other activities. But stair-climbing machines, mountain bikes and treadmills have registered phenomenal growth in recent years, while running and weight lifting, by comparison, almost stood still.

Exercise	Participants, 1991 (in thousands)	Percent Change (1987-1991)
Cross-country ski machine	7,477	+119
Roller blading	6,212	+103**
Stair-climbing machine	17,140	+790
Mountain biking	5,047	+234
Treadmill	13,580	+209
Resistance machines	17,610	+15
Free weights	30,448	+24
Running/jogging	32,875	0

Source: American Sports Data Inc. "Fifth Annual Study of U.S. Sports Participation," 1992

it puts much less stress on the body than running or jogging. Research has shown that with each step, the legs of a runner or high-impact aerobicizer absorb the impact of more than four times the body's weight. That compares with just two and half times body weight for walking.

Walking and other low-impact exercises have other important, if less measurable, benefits. "There's no question that those who take it slow and easy enjoy it more and stay in much longer than those who push it and hurt themselves," notes Michigan's Brooks.

Jane Brody, the longtime *New York Times* health columnist, testified personally to the "compensations" of walking after a series of skiing injuries forced her to stop jogging. "Walking is turning out to be more enjoyable, adaptable and accessible for me," Brody said. "It is also an activity I should be able to pursue the rest of my life."[31] ∎

OUTLOOK

End of a Boom Cycle?

If history is a guide, interest in exercise is cyclical, and the nation may be nearing the end of the latest fitness boom. Indeed, since the begin-

ning of the 1970s, skeptics have viewed the interest in exercise as a passing fad popularized by affluent young adults.

In fact, each of the nation's four distinct fitness booms has been spurred largely by affluent American adults with leisure time on their hands and worries about health problems and longevity. While the current cycle may be ending, barring total economic collapse there likely will always be affluent, health-conscious Americans ready to launch a new cycle.

Christine Brooks believes that the driving force behind the current interest in fitness is not so much affluence itself but the "future orientation" of people in the upper-income brackets. Such Americans, Brooks says, are generally "better able to see into the future and prepare for the future." They see the prospect of heart disease, and they see that exercise can help prevent it. The less affluent, she says, "tend to live for now, from day to day, week to week."

Another clue to what may happen in the near future is the fact that since the 1830s all of the nation's fitness booms have been fed by entrepreneurs selling new products that capture the fancy of the consuming public. And there is no reason to think that situation will change in the immediate future.

"The latest fad is stair climbing," says Carl Caspersen of the Centers for Disease Control. "And who knows what the next new machine will be." One survey estimated that some 17 million Americans worked out regularly on stair-climbers in 1991, an almost eightfold increase compared to four years earlier.[32]

That is not an inconsiderable number. But as Caspersen also notes, expensive machines like stair-climbers "don't capture 90 percent of the population. You really just get the well-to-do who can afford these things and put them in their houses."

Continued on p. 971

At Issue:

Are the majority of America's children and youth physically unfit?

THE NATIONAL ASSOCIATION FOR SPORT & PHYSICAL EDUCATION

FROM *FIT TO ACHIEVE THROUGH QUALITY, DAILY PHYSICAL EXERCISE,* **1992**

yes

*a*merica's schoolchildren are being shortchanged. Physical education in our nation's schools is often forgotten or overlooked. It lacks adequate funding to support quality programs. As a result, studies show that the vast majority of America's children and youth are both inactive and unfit....

Most children are not getting enough quality physical education to understand how and why they should keep themselves healthy and fit throughout their lifetime. Recess and after school playtime do not meet the need. Consider these facts:

Among 5-8 year olds, 40 percent have significant cardiac risk factors like obesity, high blood pressure, high cholesterol and inactive lifestyles.

Most 6-17 year olds cannot run a quarter of a mile.

Seventy percent of girls and 40 percent of boys 6-12 years old can do no more than one pull-up.

The United States Department of Health and Human Services announced *Healthy People 2000: National Health Promotion and Disease Prevention Objectives* in September 1990. One of the 21 priority areas is called "Physical Activity and Fitness."

Here are two of the objectives: Increase to at least 50 percent the proportion of children and adolescents in first through 12th grade who participate in daily school physical education; 36 percent now participate. Increase to at least 50 percent the proportion of school physical education class time that students spend being physically active, preferably engaged in lifetime physical activities; students now spend 27 percent of their class time being physically active....

Congress, whose members are deeply concerned about children receiving inadequate time for physical education, passed the National Physical Education Resolution in 1987. In this landmark document, Congress urged state and local education officials to require every student from kindergarten to 12th grade to have a daily, high-quality physical education.

Joining NAPSE in supporting the Physical Education Resolution were the American Academy of Pediatrics, American Heart Association, American Medical Association, National Association of Elementary School Principals and National Education Association. But there is still much work to be done.

STEVEN N. BLAIR

Director, Division of Epidemiology, Cooper Institute for Aerobics Research
FROM *RESEARCH QUARTERLY FOR EXERCISE AND SPORT,* **JUNE 1992**

no

*i*t has long been surprising to me that the physical education profession and public health authorities so uncritically accepted the blanket conclusion that our children and youth were not physically fit. How could teachers (especially elementary teachers), who observe children several hours a day, believe that most children are inactive? How could parents accept this conclusion? Anyone who has taught or raised children should know that they are physically active.

Nonetheless, we have been bombarded by propaganda over the past 35 years in both the professional and lay literature that deplores the status of youth fitness in the United States. Perhaps the most egregious example of overstatement was attributed to then-Secretary of Health, Education and Welfare Joseph Califano: "Some 29 million adolescents are in poor condition." The truth is that in the mid-1980s there were no more than 25 million Americans between the ages of 11 to 17. I do not recall that anyone questioned the accuracy of Califano's statement; most seemed to be willing to believe anything bad that was said about the fitness of American children and youth....

Are American children and youth physically fit? It is astonishing to me that many professionals have answered this question, in virtually all cases, negatively, without defining physical fitness and setting an acceptable standard for it. A fundamental principle of measurement is that if one wants to categorize individuals on any variable, cut-points or criteria must be developed to define the categories....

The physical education profession resisted establishing, and some within it continue to resist, criteria for determining fitness. Many were willing to label generations of American children and youth as unfit but would not define what determines an acceptable level of physical fitness. Thankfully, this situation has been changing, and criterion-referenced standards are now available....

Although I suggest in this commentary that children and youth in the United States are not as unfit as the doom sayers indicate, I do think that some children and youth are unfit, and this group needs to be identified and programs to help them improve should be implemented. If, as I suspect, approximately 20 percent of our children are at risk because of low fitness, the national total equals between 8 and 9 million school-age individuals. These are the persons who should receive our major attention and efforts.

The Importance of Stretching and Strength

The centerpiece for any exercise regimen, experts say, should be a regular program of aerobic exercise such as walking, running, jogging, swimming, dancing, cycling or rowing. But a complete exercise program should include two other components: stretching and strength training. Stretching eases muscular tension and promotes overall flexibility. Strength training — either simple calisthenics or weight training with free weights or machines — helps build the muscles needed for everyday activities, for aerobic exercises and for sports.

Exercise physiologists say that nearly every adult can benefit from doing as little as 5-10 minutes of stretching and strength training two or three times a week. "I continue to feel as though [aerobics] should be the centerpiece" of all exercise programs, said Russell Pate, chairman of the Department of Exercise Science at the University of South Carolina. "But some attention to maintenance of strength and flexibility is important as well."

Stretching: Many exercisers begin and end their aerobics routines with a few minutes spent stretching the major muscle groups: the legs, back, stomach, chest and arms. The most important things to remember during stretching, the experts say, are to stretch out slowly and steadily and not to bounce or overstrain. Many people use the system of exercises involved in yoga, an ancient Hindu discipline.

Stretching, notes Bob Anderson, who coaches professional and Olympic teams on how to loosen up properly, "is the important link between the sedentary life and the active life. It keeps the muscles supple, prepares you for movement and helps you make the daily transition from inactivity to vigorous activity without undue strain.... Stretching before and after you work out will keep you flexible and help prevent common injuries such as shin splints or Achilles' tendinitis from running, and sore shoulders and elbows from tennis."†

Strength Training: Calisthenics — such as push-ups and sit-ups — will build strength. But weight training, with either barbells and dumbbells or weight machines, such as Nautilus (below) and Universal, is more efficient. Weight training, when done regularly and properly, helps exercisers gain muscle mass and strength. Weight training also can help in losing or gaining weight, shaping and toning muscles and improving posture.

The basic theory behind strength training is the overload principle: To gain strength a muscle must be worked more intensely than it usually is used. Muscle growth comes from progressive resistance: Muscles grow and gain strength when they are forced to perform proportionally heavier work. A good way to begin a weight-training program is to take a beginner's course at a health club or gym, or simply to begin doing sit-ups (for the abdominal muscles) and push-ups (for the chest, shoulder and upper arm muscles) at home. All fitness experts advise all beginners to start slowly and increase gradually.

---

†Bob Anderson, *Stretching* (1982), p. 9.

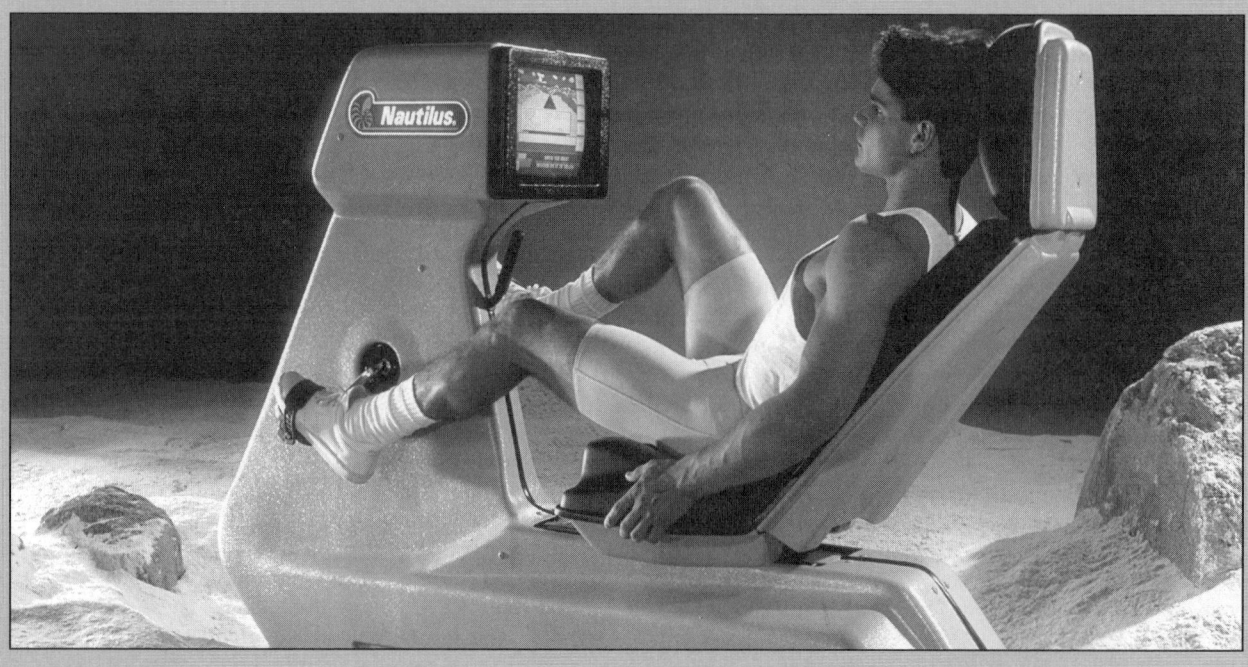

Nautilus

Continued from p. 968

Stair-climbing is among the more rigorous aerobic exercises — and just the type of activity that public health specialists are not recommending for inactive adults. But support for a traditional program of aerobic exercises, including stair-climbing — is not dead. In fact, the official policy of the state of Oregon is to encourage the state's adults to do some type of aerobic exercise for 20 minutes at least three times a week by the year 2010.

That policy became state law last year when the Oregon legislature enacted "Oregon Benchmarks," a package of 160 goals for the state. One of the goals was the aerobics recommendation. If the policy survives, the fitness boom will have a long life — at least in Oregon. ∎

Marc Leepson is a free-lance writer who lives near Washington, D.C.

Notes

[1] The Gallup Organization discontinued its daily exercise poll in 1987, when 49 percent of those questioned said they did some form of daily exercise.

[2] See *American Demographics*, October 1991, pp. 10-11.

[3] "Fitness Boom Reaches Plateau," American Sports Data Inc., April 1, 1992. The survey was based on interviews with 15,000 adults and defined regular exercise as participating in a fitness activity 100 times or more in the previous year.

[4] Sporting Goods Manufacturers Association, "SGMA 1991 Industry Financial Study, Top-Line Report," March 1992. The industry sold nearly 284 million pairs of adult athletic shoes in 1991.

[5] Quoted in *The Wall Street Journal*, Oct. 31, 1989.

[6] President's Council on Physical Fitness and Sports, "Youth Physical Fitness in 1985," March 20, 1986, pp. 5, 6 and 9.

[7] Quoted in *Sports Illustrated*, Oct. 2, 1989, p. 28.

[8] Quoted in the *Los Angeles Times*, Oct. 15, 1990.

[9] Office of Disease Prevention and Health Promotion, *Healthy People 2000: National Health Promotion and Disease Prevention Objectives*, 1991, p. 101. A federal survey released this summer reported that 49 percent of high school students nationwide were enrolled in physical education classes, 42 percent attended daily PE classes and 81 percent of those who went to class exercised 20 or more minutes per class. See Centers for Disease Control, "Participation in School Physical Education and Selected Dietary Patterns Among High School Students United States, 1991," *Morbidity and Mortality Weekly Report*, Aug. 21, 1992, p. 600.

[10] Robert Lipsyte, "What Price Fitness?" *The New York Times Magazine*, Feb. 16, 1986, p. 32.

[11] Stephen Nissenbaum, *Sex, Diet and Debility in Jacksonian America: Sylvester Graham and Health Reform* (1980), p. 4.

[12] Writing in *The New York Times Book Review*, March 23, 1986.

[13] Harvey Green, *Fit For America: Health, Fitness and Sport in American Society* (1986), p. 12.

[14] Quoted in Nissenbaum, *op. cit.*, p. 120.

[15] J. Madison Watson, *Hand-Book of Calisthenics and Gymnastics: A Complete Drill-Book for Schools, Families and Gymnasiums* (1882), 11th edition, pp. 119, 251.

[16] See Gerald Carson, *Cornflake Crusade* (1957) and Green *op. cit.*, pp. 308-309.

[17] Green, *op.cit.*, p. 182.

[18] Watson, *op. cit.*, p. 257. Several sports became popular during this period — including baseball, football, track and field, rowing, boxing, tennis and golf — as did bodybuilding and weight lifting. Among the nation's most famous musclemen was George Windship, a Harvard Medical School graduate known as the "Roxbury Hercules." Another was Eugene Sandow, a Prussian-born self-promoter who, Green noted, "not only performed feats of strength but also preached the gospel of health, in his books if not in his prodigious eating and drinking behavior."

[19] Green, *op. cit.*, p. 213.

[20] For background, see "Physical Fitness Boom," *Editorial Research Reports*, April 14, 1978, pp. 270-271.

[21] James F. Fixx, *The Complete Book of Running* (1977), pp. 248-249. Ironically, Fixx died of a heart attack in 1984 at 52 while jogging. Sheehan, now in his early '70s, continues to run and write about it.

[22] Quoted by Robert Reinhold in an interview in *The New York Times Magazine*, March 29, 1987, p. 16.

[23] Writing in *The Journal of the American Medical Association*, June 23, 1989, pp. 3597, 3588.

[24] By the editors of *University of California, Berkeley Wellness Letter*, "One Small Step...," January 1990, p. 1.

[25] Steven N. Blair, *et al.*, "Physical Fitness and All-Cause Mortality," *The Journal of the American Medical Association*, Nov. 3, 1989, p. 2401.

[26] Quoted in *The New York Times*, July 21, 1990.

[27] *The New England Journal of Medicine*, July 18, 1991, p. 197.

[28] Quoted in *The Washington Post*, Sept. 22, 1992.

[29] Gerald F. Fletcher, *et al.*, "Statement of Exercise," *Circulation*, July 1992, pp. 340, 341.

[30] *Ibid.*, p. 341.

[31] Writing in *The New York Times*, March 9, 1989.

[32] American Sports Data Inc., "Fifth Annual Study of U.S. Sports Participation," April 1, 1992.

Bibliography

Selected Sources Used

Books

Cooper, Kenneth, *Aerobics*, M. Evans, 1968.

In this best-selling book, then-U.S. Air Force surgeon Kenneth H. Cooper lays out the exercise program widely credited with beginning the age of aerobics. Cooper also is the author of *The New Aerobics* (1970), *Aerobics for Women* (1972) and *The Aerobics Way* (1977).

Fixx, James F., *The Complete Book of Running*, Random House, 1977.

Fixx, a former magazine editor, began running to lose weight. After loosing 60 pounds and giving up smoking and a sedentary lifestyle, Fixx wrote this popular, self-help book that called running "an antidote to what ails us." Fixx died of a heart attack while jogging in 1984 at age 52. His death was attributed to advanced atherosclerosis, which probably stemmed from decades of inactivity and heavy cigarette smoking before he began running.

Green, Harvey, *Fit for America: Health, Fitness, Sport and American Society*, Pantheon, 1986.

Green, a social historian at the Strong Museum in Rochester, N.Y., presents a serious study of the varied health, fitness and sports movements in America from 1830 to 1940. Green examines the serious as well as the pseudo-scientific side of fitness movements, tracing the origins of, among many other things, aerobic exercise, home exercise equipment, bodybuilding and health foods.

Articles

Blair, Steven N., "Are American Children and Youth Fit? The Need for Better Data," *Research Quarterly for Exercise and Sport*, June 1992.

Blair, director of Epidemiology at the Cooper Institute for Aerobics Research, argues that current standards for measuring children's physical fitness are inadequate, and that teachers, parents and public health authorities have uncritically accepted poor fitness assessments of schoolchildren. Blair calls for better fitness guidelines for youths and concludes that "approximately 20 percent of our children are at risk because of low fitness." That compares with other estimates of 40-50 percent.

Fletcher, Gerald F., *et al.*, "Statement on Exercise: Benefits and Recommendations for Physical Activity Programs for All Americans," *Circulation*, July 1992.

This article reports on the official findings of the American Heart Association's Committee on Exercise and Cardiac Rehabilitation, which were issued early in 1992. The com-

mittee recognizes lack of exercise as a "significant risk factor for heart disease." The article explains why and how "persons of all ages should include physical activity in a comprehensive program of health promotion and disease prevention."

Harris, Sally S., *et al.*, "Physical Activity Counseling for Healthy Adults as a Primary Preventive Intervention in the Clinical Setting," *Journal of the American Medical Association*, June 23, 1989.

The authors estimate that 40 percent of the adult population is "predominantly sedentary" and suggest that moderate activities such as brisk walking can help Americans cut their risk of heart disease, diabetes, obesity and other problems.

Roberts, Scott O., and Pam Staver, "Fit Kids," *American Health*, September 1992.

Specialists in youth fitness, the authors cite studies showing that many children and teenagers are not physically fit and recommend ways young people can shape up through exercise programs and organized sports.

Reports and Studies

Caspersen, Carl J., "Physical Activity Epidemiology: Concepts, Methods, and Applications to Exercise Science," *Exercise and Sport Science Reviews*, American College of Sports Medicine, Vol. 17, 1989.

Caspersen, a leading expert on exercise epidemiology at the federal Centers for Disease Control, provides a brief overview of the science of epidemiology as applied to physical activity. His research strongly indicates that fewer than 10 percent of adult Americans exercise regularly. Caspersen's estimate, which is widely accepted, compares to national polls indicating that 45-50 percent of adults exercise regularly.

President's Council on Physical Fitness and Sports, *Youth Physical Fitness in 1985*, March 20, 1986.

This latest in a series of reports produced every 10 years by the council is widely cited as evidence that, as the report states, "there is still a low level of performance in important components of physical fitness by millions of our youth." The study measured 19,200 boys and girls ages 6-17 in a series of fitness tests.

The Next Step

Additional Articles from Current Periodicals from EBSCO Publishing's Database

Children

"Vigorous physical activity among high school students — United States, 1990," *Journal of the American Medical Association,* Feb. 26, 1992, p. 1052.

Examines the prevalence of vigorous physical activity among U.S. students in grades 9-12. The national school-based Youth Risk Behavior Survey (YRBS); physical activity and reduced risk of chronic diseases in adults; percentage of students who reported being vigorously active three or more times per week; editorial note from the Centers for Disease Control (CDC); more.

"Young and unfit?" *Lancet,* July 4, 1992, p. 19.

Editorial. Comments on the popularity among children of passive pursuits such as television and computer games; determining whether these pursuits will lead to a generation of unfit people; assessing fitness; need to increase everyone's opportunities for everyday exercise; more.

Hales, D., "Are girls and boys equally fit?" *Working Mother,* May 1992, p. 78.

Observes that grade-school girls tend to be less physically fit than boys of the same age. Research conducted on the issue at the Johns Hopkins School of Medicine in Baltimore; importance of teaching good health to children; what parents can do.

Legwold, G., "Student fitness," *Better Homes & Gardens,* April 1992, p. 70.

Discusses the small amount of physical education children have in schools and suggests steps to take if you're worried about your child's level of exercise at school. Most kids spend more time watching television on Saturday mornings than they do in physical education each week; Ask your school how physical education could be expanded to 30 minutes a day; volunteer to help classes.

Marwick, C., "Pondering how to squeeze fitness programs into schools' budgetary, time constraints," *Journal of the American Medical Association,* Feb. 5, 1992, p. 616.

Discusses the status of physical education programs in the wake of ever tighter budgets and pressures to include more academic subjects. View of Judith C. Young, Ph.D., executive director of the National Association for Sport and Physical Education (Reston, Va.); concerns raised by the National Children and Youth Fitness Study II which took place more than four years ago; more.

Rosen, M.D., "A family affair," *Ladies' Home Journal,* June 1992, p. 90.

Discusses the benefits of fitting fitness into family life. Examples; statistics on adults' and kids' fitness levels; how to find an enjoyable family exercise; benefits of family exercise; family exercise goals. INSETS: Sticking with it; A little homework... (fitness program booklet).

Schlosberg, S., "Exercise and your child," *Shape,* June 1992, p. 54.

Examines the importance of exercise to children's lives. Discusses increase in childhood obesity and the best types of exercise for children. Emphasis during exercise; controversial opinions about exercise; how parents can help; benefits.

Physiological effect

"Babies fuss over post-exercise milk," *Science News,* July 18, 1992, p. 47.

Reports that babies don't like to nurse after their mothers have exercised heavily. New study that shows that babies may fuss throughout or even refuse post-exercise feedings. Work of Janet P. Wallace and her co-workers from the Adult Fitness Program at Indiana University in Bloomington; lactic acid; article in the June 1992 issue of *Pediatrics*; more.

"Diabetes at bay," *Health & Fitness Magazine,* March 1992, p. 22.

Discusses the benefits that exercise has on reducing your chances of suffering diabetes and if you are diabetic, exercise can reduce your need for insulin. Study; results; exercise keeps your bones strong.

"Does exercise boost immunity?" *University of California Berkeley Wellness Letter,* March 1992, p. 6.

Discusses how some physical fitness experts hypothesize that the effect of exercise on immunity may be a double-edged sword. If one works out moderately, they may indeed boost their body's ability to fight off colds and other illnesses. But exercise long and intensely and they may unwittingly depress their immune system and leave themselves more prone to such infections. Marathoners and colds; the upshot.

Andrews, J., "A case of endurance," *Health & Fitness Magazine,* March 1992, p. 18.

Presents a report on stamina and endurance as it is an important part of a total fitness program. The importance of oxygen; endurance sports; circuit training; the 40-minute circuit workout; Fartlek training; nutrition; a natural asset.

Gutfeld, G., L. Rao, et al., "Fit to work," _Prevention,_ March 1992, p. 15.

Reports that being in tip-top shape may reduce absenteeism on the job. Suggests that if companies help their current employees get into shape, they may reduce absenteeism even more. Cardiovascular fitness; study; results; comments.

Howard, B., "Brighten your sex life," _Reader's Digest,_ June 1992, p. 33.

Gives advice on how a couple can improve its sex life, using regular exercise as a catalyst. Discusses recent research supporting exercise's role in increasing libido. Fitness benefits; self-image; endorphin release. Beginning an exercise program.

LaForge, R., "Exercise and the immune system," _Executive Health's Good Health Report,_ April 1992, p. 6.

Discusses the controversy in the medical community about whether or not physical fitness from an exercise program will enhance a person's natural resistance to disease. How the immune system functions; components of the immune system, including macrophages and lymphocytes; mixed research results on the effects of exercise; how to become fit and minimize the risk of infection; more.

Mueller, T., "Run for your life," _Women's Sports & Fitness,_ August 1992, p. 12.

Gives the results of a study by Harvard epidemiologist Rose Frisch, which concluded that long-term exercise lowers the risk of breast cancer in women. How study was conducted; differences in rates of breast cancer.

Sheehan, G., "Exercise should be comfortable," _Hope Health Letter,_ April 1992, p. 3.

Reports that the gospel of fitness, exercise does not have to be painful to be effective, in fact, the more comfortable it is, the better it is for you. People believe the opposite; shortness of breath and aching muscles; different message; pace determined by listening to what your body tells you; comfort zone as a guide to determine exercise pace; more.

Psychological effect

"Power exercises," _Ebony,_ July 1992, p. 52.

Presents comments by black executives in various fields who discuss the importance of a regular fitness routine as a way of reducing job-induced stress. John E. Jacob, National Urban League president and chief executive officer; Jennifer Lawson, Public Broadcasting Service executive vice president; Dr. Joseph E. Lowery, president of the Southern Christian Leadership Conference; others; part of a special fitness section.

"Sweat and serenity," _Health & Fitness Magazine,_ February 1992, p. 12.

Discusses the new burgeoning selection of exercise class

styles with more and more emphasis on the mind. Activities to offset the tensions in peoples lives; focus on relaxation; different programs; comments from different health clubs; for more information; information on winning a year's membership to St. Alban's Health & Racquet Club (England).

Anderson, O., "Mind over matter," _Runner's World,_ May 1992, p. 26.

Suggests that a sharpened physical performance can be achieved by developing stronger psychological skills. Elements of Jeffery Simons' psychological skills training (PST); body checking; relaxing; objectifying fatigue; eliminating distractions; conjuring positive self-images; more.

Canter, M, D. Garr, et al., "The overly anxious need not apply," _Men's Health,_ July/August 1992, p. 14.

Quotes _Fit for Success_ author James Rippe, M.D. In rising to the top, the ability to handle stress is more important than a born talent for management; exercise to cope with stress; conditioned bodies pump out less adrenaline and more endorphins; these brain chemicals promote feelings of well-being.

Cohn, L.D. & N.E. Adler, "Female and male perceptions of ideal body shapes," _Psychology of Women Quarterly,_ March 1992, p. 69.

Examines whether women overestimate the desirability of thin figures among female peers as well as male preferences for thin female figures, as recent studies have demonstrated. Method; results; discussion.

Custer, S.J. & C.R. Doty, "Assessment of self-motivation and selected physiological characteristics as predictors," _Journal of Health Education,_ May/June 1992, p. 232.

Presents an investigation that was conducted to determine if self-motivation and selected physiological characteristics could be used to predict whether persons would complete a structured exercise/fitness program in a corporate setting. Method; results; discussion; more.

Gaudoin, T., "Level best," _Harper's Bazaar,_ July 1992, p. 82.

Examines the anxieties and frustrations caused by a weight loss/exercise plateau. Defining fitness plateauing; why it happens; distinguishing between plateauing and burnout; causes of fitness plateaus; differences between male and female attitudes toward working out; tips from experts on countering the psychological and physical problems associated with exercise.

Wilson, J., "Make peace with your body," _Woman's Day,_ June 23, 1992, p. 32.

Presents the author's reflections on how she changed from a former workout fanatic to someone who is comfortable with her body and exercises enough to stay healthy. Comment of Michael O'Shea, Ph.D., director of the Sports Training Institute in New York City; research that shows that women tend to overestimate body size.

Research

Downing, S., "The hour of power," *Women's Sports & Fitness*, March 1992, p. 13.

Considers whether morning or afternoon workouts are more beneficial. When aerobic and anaerobic capacity is highest; when strength peaks; Competition training suggestions; body's circadian rhythm.

Gutfeld, G., L. Rao, et al., "Stroll to a healthier heart," *Prevention*, June 1992, p. 16.

Reports that new research suggests that a regular stroll can powerfully reduce women's heart-disease risk — without necessarily having to improve actual cardiovascular fitness. Data and results of the study.

King, S., "Passing the test," *Shape*, July 1992, p. 40.

Examines fitness assessments and their accuracy. Tells how to get the most out of a fitness test. Health screening; cardiovascular endurance; body composition; flexibility; strength. INSET: What's your PAR-Q? (Physical Activity Readiness Questionnaire).

Kuzdek, C., "Small work-outs, big benefits," *Women's Sports & Fitness*, April 1992, p. 12.

Reports that a Stanford University study shows that short bouts of exercise throughout the day have similar weight-loss and health benefits to one long workout. How the study was conducted; examples of short-bout exercises.

Sheehan, G., "Too legit to quit," *Runner's World*, March 1992, p. 16.

Asks the question of why some people habitually exercise and others do not, and looks at a recent study by Lise Gauvin at the Concordia University in Montreal that may help answer the question. Significant differences in motivation among four groups of individuals: autonomous exercisers, fitness program enrollees, fitness program dropouts and sedentary individuals.

Trends

"Inside-out workout," *American Health*, March 1992, p. 122.

Discusses tai chi, a form of exercise that millions of people in China practice. One tenet is that fitness of body's internal organs important as external muscles; 'stomach moving'; describes abdominal exercise.

"Knock 'em out boxing workout," *Shape*, June 1992, p. 58.

Examines the growing interest in non-fight boxing-based fitness programs, such as Executive Boxing, held at Bodies in Motion in Los Angeles. Discusses the mental and physical benefits of boxing. Sample workout schedules; equipment needed; wrapping wrists; stance; training tips; moves.

Brody, L., B. Gordon, et al., Buri, S. & J. Clark, "Cash for clean living: How wellness pays," *Kiplinger's Personal Finance Magazine*, June 1992, p. 104.

States that if your are physically fit, you can benefit when buying insurance. Description of some medical or fitness tests; rewards for non-smokers; discounts for those who have good exercise habits; disability insurance; car insurance; other considerations.

LaForge, R., "Splish, splash ... the joys of aquatic fitness," *Executive Health's Good Health Report*, May 1992, p. 6.

Discusses the advantages of aquatic fitness. The five big benefits — safer for joints, water's soothing and therapeutic nature, enhancement of blood flow, fulfillment of cardiorespiratory fitness, and its uniqueness; getting started by working on skill then endurance; walking in water; tethered swimming; water aerobics; important reminders. INSET: Aquatics: Points to consider.

LaForge, R., "Stepping out: A look at the newest fad," *Executive Health's Good Health Report*, July 1992, p. 6.

Discusses the benefits of step exercise, the most popular among all aerobic group exercises offered at fitness centers. Similarities to aerobic dance, with its rhythmic stepping to the cadence of music; benefits such as cardiorespiratory endurance, agility and balance and coordination; movement patterns; calories burned per minute; more. INSET: Getting started? Consider these points (tips).

Thomas, J.B., "In-line skating," *Better Homes & Gardens*, June 1992, p. 42.

Reports on in-line skating or "blading" which is the hottest fitness craze to hit the streets. Closer to ice skating than roller skating; the fitness advantages; safety advice.

Wadyka, S., "No mean feet," *Health & Fitness Magazine*, March 1992, p. 72.

Offers a look at the safe and challenging form of exercise known as power walking. Low impact alternative; the walking craze in America; scientific proof of walking's advantages; frequency, intensity, and time; adding handweights; how fast you should be walking; stretches that should be done; power walking classes available in England.

Back Issues

Great Research on Current Issues Starts Right Here... Recent topics covered by The CQ Researcher are listed below. Issues dated before May 10, 1991, were published under the name of Editorial Research Reports.

APRIL 1991
Social Security
Canadian Crisis Over Quebec
California Drought
Electromagnetic Radiation

MAY 1991
School Choice
Racial Quotas
Animal Rights
U.S. and Japan

JUNE 1991
Children and Divorce
Teenage Suicide
Endangered Species
Europe 1992

JULY 1991
Teenagers and Abortion
Soviet Republics Rebel
Mexico's Emergence
Athletes and Drugs

AUGUST 1991
Sexual Harassment
Fetal Tissue Research
Oil Imports
The Palestinians

Back issues are available for $4.00 (subscribers) or $7.00 (non-subscribers). Quantity discounts apply to orders over ten. To order, call Congressional Quarterly 1-800-432-2250.

Binders are available for $15.00. To order call 1-800-638-1710.

SEPTEMBER 1991
Police Brutality
Advertising Under Attack
Saving the Forests
Foster Care Crisis

OCTOBER 1991
Pay-Per-View TV
Youth Gangs
Gene Therapy
World Hunger

NOVEMBER 1991
Fast-Food Shake-Up
The Greening of Eastern Europe
Business' Role in Education
Cuba In Crisis

DECEMBER 1991
Retiree Health Benefits
Asian Americans
The Obscenity Debate
The Disabilities Act

JANUARY 1992
Term Limits
Oil Spills
Hunting Controversy
Alternative Medicine

FEBRUARY 1992
Threatened Coastlines
New Era in Asia
Assisted Suicide
Jobs in the '90s

MARCH 1992
Women and Sports
Underage Drinking
Garbage Crisis
Mafia Crackdown

APRIL 1992
Ozone Depletion
Welfare Reform
Politicians and Privacy
Illegal Immigration

MAY 1992
Native Americans
Jobs vs. Environment
Too Many Lawsuits?
Fairness in Salaries

JUNE 1992
Nuclear Proliferation
Food Irradiation
Lead Poisoning
Hard Times for Libraries

JULY 1992
Alternative Energy
Prescription Drug Prices
Alzheimer's Disease
Infant Mortality

AUGUST 1992
The Homeless
Work, Family and Stress
NATO's Changing Role
Marine Mammals vs. Fish

SEPTEMBER 1992
Domestic Partners
Violence in Schools
Public Broadcasting
Women in the Military

OCTOBER 1992
Depression
U.S. Auto Industry
Youth Apprenticeships
Hispanic Americans

Future Topics

▶ *Privitizing Government Services*

▶ *Paying for College*

▶ *U.S. Policy in the Pacific*

THE CQ Researcher

PUBLISHED BY CONGRESSIONAL QUARTERLY INC., IN CONJUNCTION WITH EBSCO PUBLISHING

Privatization

Should the private sector provide more public services?

A LL ACROSS THE COUNTRY, REVENUE-PINCHED governments are turning to private firms as a way of saving money without impairing the delivery of services like trash collection and street paving. Indeed, it is an article of faith among conservatives — and a growing number of liberals — that nearly all government programs operate more efficiently under private management. Some critics caution, however, that privatization is no panacea. They contend that contracting out public services to private interests often ends up costing taxpayers more, not less. In addition, labor leaders say any cost savings from privatization come from reduced wages and benefits for workers. Still, privatization is likely to remain a popular option for government officials as long as resistance to tax increases stays high.

C Q **November 13, 1992 • Volume 2, No. 42 • 977-1000**

Formerly Editorial Research Reports

THE ISSUES

BACKGROUND

CURRENT SITUATION

OUTLOOK

SIDEBARS AND GRAPHICS

FOR FURTHER INFORMATION

COVER ART: BARBARA SASSA-DANIELS

November 13, 1992
Volume 2, No. 42

EDITOR
Sandra Stencel

MANAGING EDITOR
Thomas J. Colin

ASSOCIATE EDITOR
Richard L. Worsnop

STAFF WRITERS
Charles S. Clark
Mary H. Cooper
Rodman D. Griffin

PRODUCTION EDITOR
Sarah E. Merritt

EDITORIAL ASSISTANT
Michael M. Taylor

GRAPHICS
Jack Auldridge

PUBLISHED BY
Congressional Quarterly Inc.

CHAIRMAN
Andrew Barnes

VICE CHAIRMAN
Andrew P. Corty

EDITOR AND PUBLISHER
Neil Skene

EXECUTIVE EDITOR
Robert W. Merry

ASSOCIATE PUBLISHER
John J. Coyle

The CQ Researcher (ISSN 1056-2036). Formerly Editorial Research Reports. Published weekly (48 times per year, not printed the first Friday of any month with five Fridays) by Congressional Quarterly Inc., 1414 22nd St., N.W., Washington, D.C. 20037. Rates are furnished upon request. Second-class postage paid at Washington, D.C. POSTMASTER: Send address changes to The CQ Researcher, 1414 22nd St., N.W., Washington, D.C. 20037.

Privatization

By Richard L. Worsnop

The Issues

In 1989 autos were being abandoned on Chicago streets faster than municipal towing crews could haul them away. Instead of exhorting the city crews to do better, newly elected Mayor Richard M. Daley turned the job over to private, neighborhood-based companies. The independent towers paid the city $25 per vehicle, which they then sold for scrap. Before long, the abandoned-auto problem was under control.

All parties benefited from Daley's decision. The city saved an estimated $2.5 million a year, the private operators made money and Chicagoans were spared the sight of thousands of curbside eyesores. As an added bonus, the city workers formerly in charge of abandoned-car towing were reassigned to patrols monitoring illegal parking in the downtown area.

Junked autos tell only part of the still-unfolding Chicago privatization story. Under Daley, custodial companies have replaced city janitors, saving the city some $900,000 a year. Private firms have won street-paving contracts in certain wards, spurring municipal paving crews in adjacent wards to perform more efficiently. In addition, the mayor has contracted out the management of city-owned parking lots and is moving to privatize some municipal health clinics and the maintenance of street and traffic lights.

Last April's flood, which sent millions of gallons of water coursing through the basements and sub-basements of buildings in the "Loop," Chicago's central business district, may help speed the pace of local privatization. When it came out that city officials had been told, before the flood, about a leak in an underground tunnel but

did nothing, Daley fired the acting head of the transportation department and two of his aides. He also said he was looking "very closely" at the job performance of all municipal employees. "You contract more of the work out," he said. "You have to do it. It works better." [1]

But Daley's interest in promoting more private sector involvement in what traditionally have been government services stems from more than just a desire for improved job performance. He and other government executives see privatization as a convenient way of curbing costs at a time when local tax revenues are stagnant and federal aid is less generous and less reliable than in the past. Indeed, a committee of independent business analysts warned in 1990 that Chicago would face a budget shortfall of up to 24 percent by 1995 if new sources of revenue were not found. Rather than raise city taxes and possibly trigger a middle-class exodus to the suburbs, Daley turned to the private sector for help.

Many other government leaders

have done the same thing. All across the country, state and local officials — liberals and conservatives alike — are jumping aboard the privatization bandwagon. "It is not government's obligation to provide services, but to see that they're provided," says New York's Democratic Gov. Mario M. Cuomo. [2] In the same vein, Massachusetts Gov. William F. Weld, a Republican, declared in his 1991 inaugural address that he hoped to lead a government that will "steer rather than row."

Privatization advocates say nearly every government service can be contracted out or sold, at least in part. For instance, more than a dozen states now use privately built and operated correctional facilities, and other states are expected to adopt similar policies. *(See story, p. 985.)* Conversion of state-owned highways to privately owned toll roads is considered another likely growth area.

At the local level, the array of choices may be wider. Communities have struck deals with private concerns to run their vehicle fleets, zoos and homeless shelters, manage sports and recreational facilities, administer public-school lunch programs and operate mass transit systems. *(See graphs, p. 983.)*

The cost-cutting potential of privatization is what most appeals to fiscally strapped state and local governments. According to the National Association of Counties, some 40 percent of counties with populations of more than 100,000 face revenue shortfalls averaging $8.3 million this year. Moreover, the National League of Cities reports that more than 25 percent of cities face budget deficits of at least 5 percent in 1992.

Privatization, as practiced in the United States, follows no single pattern. The most common form is contracting out, where the government contracts with a private sector organi-

Leading Candidates for Privatization

The Reason Foundation, a leading advocate of privatization, has identified thousands of state and local enterprises that it says would be good candidates for sale or lease to the private sector. These enterprises generate sufficient revenue to at least cover their costs, the foundation says, and therefore they can be profitable under private ownership.

Enterprise Type	Estimated Number	Estimated Market Value (in $ billions)
Airports (Commercial)	87	29.0
Electric Utilities	2,010	16.7
Gas Utilities	800	2.0
Highways and Bridges	n/a	95.0
Parking Structures	37,500	6.6
Ports	45	11.4
Turnpikes	8	7.4
Water Systems	34,461	23.9
Wastewater Facilities	15,300	30.8
Waste-to-Energy Plants	77	4.0
Total Estimated Value		**$226.8**

Source: Robert W. Poole Jr., David Haarmeyer and Lynn Scarlett, "Mining the Government Balance Sheet: What Cities and States Have to Sell," The Reason Foundation, 1992

zation to provide a specific service, such as processing Medicaid claims or janitorial services, instead of providing the service itself.[3] Other forms include (1) the sale of public assets to private purchasers; (2) lease-back arrangements, under which private parties buy or build public facilities that are then leased to government agencies; and (3) vouchers, which consumers may use like cash toward a government-approved purchase such as food, housing or education.

Sales of public assets to private interests have been relatively infrequent in this country, at least at the federal level. The reason is not hard to find. In contrast to many other nations, the United States has no tradition of government ownership of "the commanding heights" of the economy — railroads, airlines, telecommunications, mining, the steel industry and so on. (*See story, p. 991.*)

And despite success stories like Chicago's, U.S. critics of privatization caution that it is no panacea. "The private sector has no magic wand," insists Al Bilik, president of the AFL-CIO's public employee department in Washington. "Their 'savings' are achieved through paying substandard wages, inadequate benefits, creative accounting methods and a host of other questionable business practices that earn profits simply by cutting corners on quality and placing a large burden on their employees."[4]

Paul Starr, a Princeton University sociology professor who has often written and testified on the subject, feels privatization advocates are "heroically selective" in their preference. "Given the American experience with defense production, construction projects and health care — all mostly produced privately with public dollars — it is remarkable that anyone could see a path toward budgetary salvation simply by shifting the locus of service production from the public sector to the private sector," he says.[5]

According to John D. Donahue, an assistant professor of government at Harvard University, privatization should be evaluated on a case-by-case basis. "To ask whether bureaucrats or private contractors perform better *in general* is as meaningless as asking whether, *in general,* an ax or a shovel is the better tool," he wrote in a book-length critique of privatization. "It depends on the job." [6]

Nonetheless, Donahue has concluded that governments often choose an ax when a shovel is clearly called for. "Sadly," he wrote, "there is no reason to expect the political process to lead to the right pattern of privatization. Unless we are luckier or more careful than we are likely to be, political pressures will tend to retain for the public sector functions where privatization would make sense, and to privatize tasks that would be better left to government." [7]

To complicate matters further, privatization has become an ideological flashpoint. Conservatives, Donahue says, "typically welcome private delivery of public goods and services as the next best thing to cutting them out of the government budget altogether," whereas most liberals "lament private delivery as a retreat from the principle of collective action." [8]

Bombarded with conflicting advice by privatizers and their opponents, taxpayers often have trouble discerning where the truth lies. Here are some of the questions about privatization that most concern them:

Does privatization improve service and lower costs?

For privatization supporters, it is an article of faith that virtually any government program or agency will operate more efficiently and at lower cost under private management. "Proponents view government as an unnecessary and costly drag on an otherwise efficient system," wrote John B. Goodman and Gary W. Loveman, assistant professors at Harvard Business School. [9]

A 1987 nationwide survey of city and county officials conducted by the accounting firm Touche Ross & Co. (now Deloitte & Touche) lends support to Goodman and Loveman's statement. Asked to list the advantages of contracting out government services, 74 percent of the respondents cited "cost savings" while 33 percent picked "higher-quality service." [10]

Ernest J. Berger, a Republican member of the Fairfax County (Va.) Board of Supervisors, says the savings attributable to privatization come about for many reasons. As he sees it, a private company tries to deliver first-rate service because it wants its contract renewed. "The private sector, because of free-market competition, always has incentive to perform," says Berger. "Government just doesn't have that incentive and drive." [11]

According to Stuart M. Butler, director of domestic policy studies at the Heritage Foundation, a conservative think tank in Washington, improved efficiency from contracting out has "far more to do with the impact of private sector management techniques and incentives than [with] the innate quality of the workers themselves." Consequently, he says, an employee who performed poorly for government managers "often turns out to be very efficient under the private sector." This means, says Butler, that governments can make programs work better by privatizing only their management, not their entire work force. [12]

Donahue says privatization can provide better community services because private companies often have more incentive to innovate than local governments. Whereas a local government's payoff from innovation usually does not extend beyond city limits, a private contractor "can claim proprietary rights to innovations, diffuse new methods throughout its operations and use technological advances as a competitive edge to expand its market." [13]

Sale of public assets to private purchasers opens up additional opportunities for government economies, privatizers say. By selling off assets like airports or utilities, governments realize a one-time windfall. The benefits do not end there, however. Once in private hands, the formerly tax-exempt properties become a steady source of revenue from real estate and corporate income taxes.

Critics of privatization argue that its supposed benefits often are short-lived or non-existent. Far from producing dramatic savings, they say, contracting out may shove costs above their previous levels. The reason, says Linda Lampkin, director of research for the American Federation of State, County and Municipal Employees (AFSCME), is that "The government must develop the bids ... prepare the contracts ... [and] monitor those contracts. It may even have to hire some people to do that job, actually increasing employment." [14] Moreover, she says, government supervisors often end up training the contractor's employees and sometimes have to complete their work for them.

According to Lampkin, difficulties typically begin at the start of the contracting-out process. They arise not from what is in the contract, but from what has been left out. That is because "anything that is not in that contract, the contractor can ask for more money to perform," Lampkin says.

Another source of trouble is "low-balling," or submitting an artificially low bid. The objective is to win the job and then extract higher rates from the government once the opportunity to switch contractors has passed. The cost overruns accompanying many Pentagon deals with defense contractors are the best-known examples of low-balling at the federal level.

At the local level, low-balling can occur in contracting for such services as trash collection, which require expensive equipment. "After contracting out such a service," AFSCME asserted in a booklet highly critical of privatization, "a municipality often sells its equipment, leaving it no realistic alternative but to use a contractor. The contractor who gets a contract with a 'low-ball' bid can thus obtain substantial price increases on subsequent contracts because the government is left with no options."[15]

One of the strongest arguments of privatization advocates is that introducing competition into the supply of basic services benefits all parties — government, the private sector and taxpayers. In this connection, Donahue observed: "Organizations (including public ones) that must match the pace set by ambitious rivals are virtually always more efficient than organizations (including private ones) that are secure against challenge."[16]

Phoenix is often cited as a successful example of public-private rivalry in delivering a basic service — in this case, garbage and trash collection. In the late 1970s, the Arizona metropolis allowed private companies to bid against its Public Service Department in three of the five local refuse-collection districts.

The department lost the right to serve two of the districts in that first round of competitive bidding. Stung by the experience, it hired managers from the private sector and took other steps to cut costs and improve productivity. As a result, the Public Service Department has regained service rights in all five Phoenix districts.

The discipline imposed by competitive bidding has left a lasting imprint on the way the department operates, says Sherwood Rogers, a public works administrative assistant. "We had to change our whole way of thinking," he says. "For instance, we're now used to looking at a profit and loss sheet." The department, which is audited once a month, also closely monitors its operating expenses on an ongoing basis. That's because, says Rogers, "Any time our costs exceed those of the next-lowest bidder, they get to serve the district."

Notwithstanding the results achieved

in Phoenix, privatization critics say competition for the delivery of basic services often yields only fleeting benefits. "Once a company has the contract and has acquired all the expertise, training and equipment required to do the job, it is very costly for the jurisdiction to switch to another contractor and begin again," says the AFL-CIO's Al Bilik. "The company knows that it has a lock on the contract, so it can increase its rates or perform sloppy work."[17]

Does privatization threaten the well-being of public workers?

Public employees overwhelmingly look upon privatization with suspicion or hostility. Their attitude flows from the belief that the contracting out of services or sale of government assets brings lower wages and fringe benefits and fewer opportunities for advancement.

Experience with privatization has done little to soften public workers' feelings. Forty-six percent of the respondents to a 1989 Touche Ross survey of state government officials said employee groups in their states had taken a position on privatization, "and in all cases that position was negative toward the concept." Touche Ross commented that the finding "represents a sad commentary on our ability to communicate with the employee groups and labor unions in our state governments."[18]

A survey of state comptrollers taken this year by Apogee Research Inc., a consulting firm based in Bethesda, Md., came up with similar results. Of the respondents, 46 percent claimed not to know how organized labor in their states felt about privatization. Among those who did have such knowledge, 90 percent said unions were strongly negative or somewhat negative toward the concept; the remaining 10 percent said unions were mildly or strongly in favor of it.[19]

The survey findings did not surprise Al Bilik. Public employees dislike privatization, he says, because

they understand that "unless the privatizers can reduce the cost of labor, they can't compete." He adds that "Public sector contracting, with its emphasis on temporary and part-time employment, is nothing more than a corollary to the move in the private sector toward a contingent (part-time, temporary, leased) work force."[20]

Labor spokesmen also contend that the negative effects of contracting out fall with particular force on women and minorities, who are employed in great numbers by public agencies and often earn better pay than they could in the private sector. Also, government service offers job security and employee rights that private employers are increasingly reluctant to grant.

To some privatization experts, such arguments are quite beside the point. Donahue, for instance, notes that "it is hard to discern any democratic mandate for [income] redistribution through the municipal payroll." He also says there is a "certain arbitrariness" to making worker self-interest a central issue in the privatization controversy. "If street-sweeping should be public so that street-sweepers will be well-paid," he says, "why not barbering or flower arranging? Equally troubling is the fact that city workers are frequently better off than many of the taxpayers who pay their salaries."[21]

Donahue also suggests that public employees may not be as powerless as they sometimes portray themselves. "The relative infrequency of private sector street-cleaning, turf maintenance and janitorial services may be because janitors, street-sweepers and lawn workers are much better off in the public sector, know it, and are able to defend their interests," he writes.[22]

According to the California-based Reason Foundation, a leading advocate of privatization, most states and cities that contract out services require that affected public employees either be hired by the private contrac-

Continued on p. 984

Privatization Trends in the Nation's Cities

A 1992 Reason Foundation survey of the nation's 24 largest cities found that a high percentage had hired private companies to provide one or more services, including street towing, garbage collection and operation of homeless shelters, homeless food programs and drug and alcohol treatment centers.

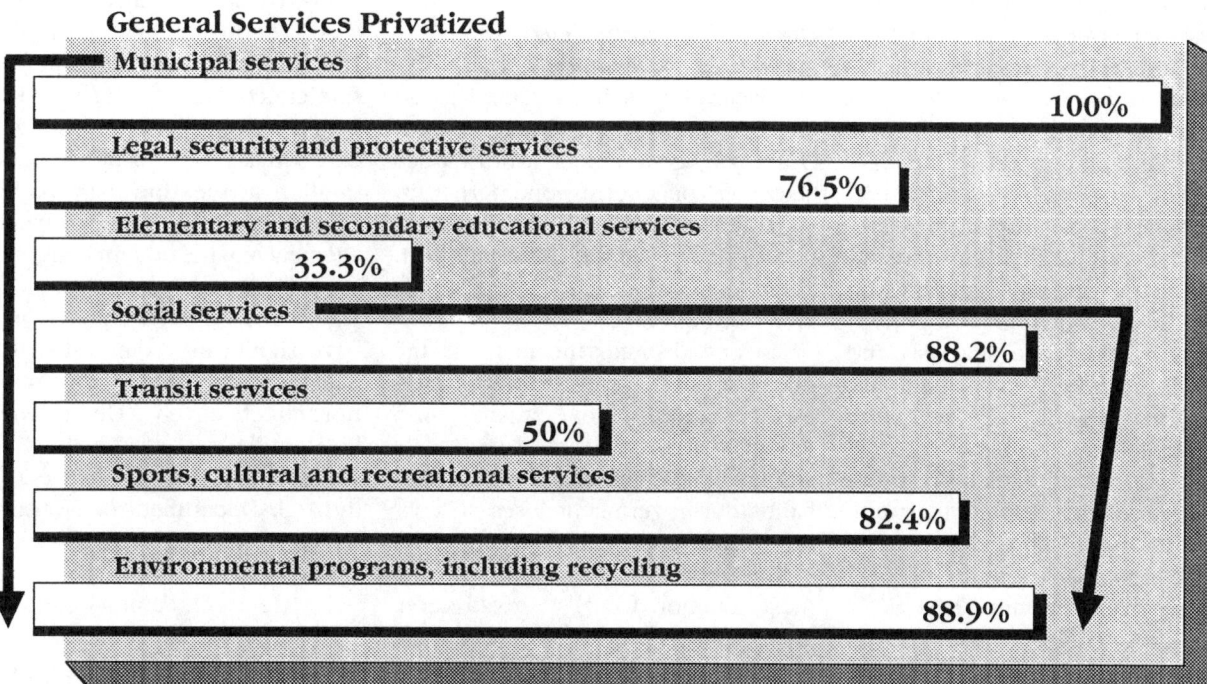

General Services Privatized

- Municipal services — **100%**
- Legal, security and protective services — **76.5%**
- Elementary and secondary educational services — **33.3%**
- Social services — **88.2%**
- Transit services — **50%**
- Sports, cultural and recreational services — **82.4%**
- Environmental programs, including recycling — **88.9%**

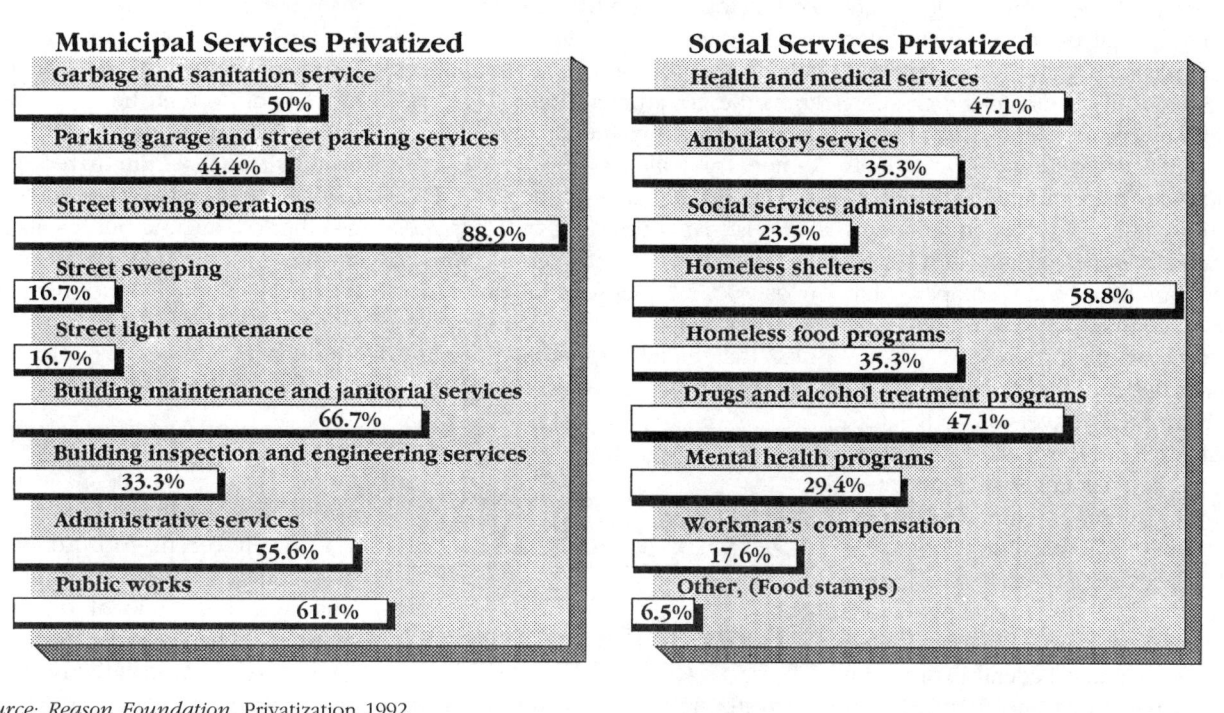

Municipal Services Privatized

- Garbage and sanitation service — **50%**
- Parking garage and street parking services — **44.4%**
- Street towing operations — **88.9%**
- Street sweeping — **16.7%**
- Street light maintenance — **16.7%**
- Building maintenance and janitorial services — **66.7%**
- Building inspection and engineering services — **33.3%**
- Administrative services — **55.6%**
- Public works — **61.1%**

Social Services Privatized

- Health and medical services — **47.1%**
- Ambulatory services — **35.3%**
- Social services administration — **23.5%**
- Homeless shelters — **58.8%**
- Homeless food programs — **35.3%**
- Drugs and alcohol treatment programs — **47.1%**
- Mental health programs — **29.4%**
- Workman's compensation — **17.6%**
- Other, (Food stamps) — **6.5%**

Source: Reason Foundation, Privatization 1992

Continued from p. 982

tor or be reassigned to a job in another government department. Moreover, governments often stipulate that the salaries of such workers not be reduced below their former level. "Thus, layoffs of public employees come slowly, occur over an extended period of time and typically result from natural attrition in the work force."[23]

A report issued in June by the World Bank lent support to the view that public workers have little to fear from privatization.[24] The study examined 12 divestitures of government-owned assets in four countries at various levels of economic development — Britain, Chile, Malaysia and Mexico. "In no case in the sample," the report stated, "did divestiture make workers as a whole worse off." To make the divestitures more palatable, governments offered their employees the right to buy shares in the privatized companies and, in some cases, generous severance pay.

The President's Commission on Privatization, a blue-ribbon panel created during the Reagan administration (see p. 989), recommended in its final report that the government offer similar incentives to federal employees. Specifically, it urged the creation of an employee stock ownership plan (ESOP) that would give federal workers an opportunity "to join corporations that bid for government-operated commercial activities, or to become owners of any company that won a contract."[25] So far, nothing has come of that proposal.

Stuart Butler of the Heritage Foundation has urged conversion of the U.S. Postal Service and Amtrak — the federally operated passenger rail network — from government to employee ownership. Employee-owned firms operating within the existing Postal Service framework would be able to compete more effectively with private firms like United Parcel Service and Federal Express, he told a congressional subcommittee. "In this way, the overall framework of the

Postal Service could be maintained, with uniform pricing and assurance of service, but the spur of private ownership and competition would be introduced to invigorate the service and to reward postal workers."[26]

Does privatization curb the growth of government?

Privatization is often touted as an effective way to "downsize" or "rightsize" government, and reduce taxpayers' bills correspondingly. Critics contend, however, that privatization can have just the opposite effect. There is evidence to support the views of both sides.

No one disputes the fact that the sale of a public asset to private interests shrinks the government's size, though perhaps only by a minuscule amount. Once the property changes hands the government loses all control over it, presumably forever.

The effects of contracting out, the most common form of privatization, are less clear-cut. In such cases the government retains managerial authority, including the right to make sure the contractor lives up to the terms of the service agreement. Although shifting jobs from public to private employees trims the government payroll, privatization critics say the savings may be temporary or illusory.

The reason, says Princeton's Paul Starr, is that contracting out "expands the set of claimants on the public treasury."[27] Defense companies and their workers, he notes, soon recognize that military-spending increases are in their best interest. By the same

token, the private companies that build federally funded highways acquire a stake in bigger construction expenditures while private suppliers of health services under Medicare clamor for higher fees.

Even when privatization does succeed in reducing the size or power of government, there may be unforeseen side effects that offset the anticipated benefits. According to H. George Frederickson, a professor of public administration at the University of Kansas, "downsizing, rightsizing, cutback management and the other means of reducing the size and costs of government, when combined with deregulation, have significantly diminished the capacities of some units of government to function effectively." He says the combination helped spawn the financial scandals that surfaced in the 1980s at the U.S. Department of Housing and Urban Development (HUD) and in the savings and loan industry.[28]

Dr. Henry M. Raimondo, an economist and associate professor of urban planning and policy at Rutgers University's Eagleton Institute of Politics, feels that voter pressure on governments to pare public payrolls is one of the main forces propelling the contracting-out movement. Voters, he says, view reduced public-sector employment as firm evidence of improved governmental efficiency, "regardless of whether contracting out results in cost savings or not." Meanwhile, though, the private workers performing the former public services constitute "almost a hidden government work force." ∎

BACKGROUND

Roots of the Controversy

Privatization is a relatively recent concept because direct govern-

mental involvement in the economy is relatively recent, too. Adam Smith, the Scottish economist, summed up what was conventional thinking for centuries when he declared in The Wealth of Nations (1776) that "no two characters seem more inconsis-

Continued on p. 986

Containing Prison Costs Through Privatization

Professor Charles W. Thomas, director of the University of Florida's Private Corrections Project, says states can save millions of dollars by letting private firms build and operate correctional facilities. By privatizing prisons, Thomas says, governments can save "15 to 25 percent of capital outlay" for construction of new facilities. Savings in operating costs generally run between 10 and 15 percent, he says, "closer to 15 percent if it's privately designed and constructed, and closer to 10 percent if it's a pre-existing facility."

Fourteen states already have privately operated prisons: Alabama, California, Colorado, Florida, Kansas, Kentucky, Louisiana, Nevada, New Mexico, Oklahoma, Rhode Island, Tennessee, Texas and Washington.

According to the most recent survey conducted by the Private Corrections Project, the combined capacity of the nation's 60 privately operated prisons was 19,513 on June 30, 1992. The actual number of prisoners housed in private facilities was 17,317.† (See table below.)

Another way of gauging the growth of private prison management is to chart the fortunes of the industry leader, Corrections Corp. of America (CCA). This year CCA is expected to become the first private corrections firm to post revenues of more than $100 million.

Though ample growth opportunities remain, private prison managers are not welcome everywhere. "Many jurisdictions still lack the enabling legislation required for contracting out" prisons to private management firms, says Professor Thomas. "Particularly in jurisdictions where the power of organized labor is strong, political opposition to privatization initiatives remains formidable." ††

The privatization of prisons disturbs some students of government. Since private operators of prisons are intent on making a profit, critics say, they may cut corners by neglecting the legal rights and physical well-being of inmates.

John D. Donahue, an assistant professor of government at Harvard University, framed the issue this way: "Are the people now bidding to run prisons entering the industry in order to make money by brutalizing inmates? Almost certainly they are not. Are there within our society people who would be willing to make money by brutalizing inmates? Almost certainly there are. And without robust measures to guarantee the conditions of confinement, the business people least constrained by scruples are likely to enjoy a competitive advantage in the imprisonment industry." ‡

In Thomas' view, worries that prisoners will be mistreated in privately managed correctional facilities are greatly overblown. He notes, for example, that Texas has four such facilities. The management contracts required that all four facilities be accredited by the American Correctional Association (ACA) within a specified period, as indeed they were.

"On the other hand," says Thomas, "no correctional facility operated by the Texas Department of Criminal Justice has ever obtained ACA accreditation. That's one of the paradoxes of the business. You'll see a state agency impose a higher performance standard on private managers than it does on itself — even though Texas law requires private vendors to operate at least 10 percent below state cost levels."

---

† Charles W. Thomas and Suzanna L. Foard, "Private Adult Correctional Facility Census," Private Corrections Project, Center for Studies in Criminology and Law, University of Florida, June 30, 1992.

†† Charles W. Thomas, "Growth in Corrections Accelerates," *PWFinancing*, July-August 1992, p. 12.

‡ John D. Donahue, *The Privatization Decision* (1989), p. 170.

Private Correctional Facilities Census

Management firm	Total facilities under contract	Rated capacity of facilities in operation	6/30/92 facility population totals	New facilities to open within 12 months	Capacity expansion within 12 months
Concepts, Inc.	5	2,544	1,528	1	200
Cornell/Cox Associates	1			1	300
Correctional Management Affiliates, Inc.	4	584	535	2	646
Corrections Corporation of America	17	6,616	5,970	1	832
Detention Services, Inc.	1	500	491	0	0
Dismas House Charities	1	100	95	0	0
Eclectic Communications	3	590	554	0	0
Eden Detention Center	1	565	565	0	0
Esmor, Inc.	2	423	369	0	0
Group 4 - ICS	1	300	125	0	0
Gary White & Associates	1	240	260	0	0
Management Training Corp.	1	400	400	0	0
Mid-Tex Detention	2	736	740	0	0
PPATHI	1	0	0	1	1,248
Pricor, Inc.	2	644	614	0	0
U.S. Corrections Corp.	3	1,350	1,350	0	0
Volunteers of America	2	117	104	0	0
Wackenhut Corrections Corp.	12	3,804	3,617	2	1,976
TOTALS	60	19,513	17,317	8	5,202

Source: Private Corrections Project, Center for Studies in Criminology and Law, University of Florida, June 30, 1992

Continued from p. 984

tent than those of trader and sovereign." By that he meant people tend to spend the money of others more freely than they do their own.

To illustrate his point, Smith cited Britain's East India Company, which began purely as a trading organization that was able to pay a "moderate dividend" to its shareholders. In time, though, the company took on what amounted to governmental responsibilities as well. Mixing private and public functions was a mistake, Smith wrote, because the company eventually was "obliged to beg extraordinary assistance of [the British] government in order to avoid immediate bankruptcy."

In the United States, Smith's views on the proper role of government vis-á-vis private enterprise colored economic policy for nearly 150 years after *The Wealth of Nations* was published. Until World War I, the federal government engaged in only a narrow range of activities and (except during the Civil War) imposed essentially no taxes other than the tariff. Moreover, wrote economist Steve H. Hanke, "Most states assumed only a few responsibilities. Local governments had a wider range of activities, but not many by present standards." [29]

The Progressive Movement

Conditions began to change with the rise of the progressive movement around the turn of the 20th century. The movement gave voice to discontent with the vast social changes caused by industrialization after the Civil War. During the 1890s, for example, reform mayors such as Hazen Pingree in Detroit, James Phelan in San Francisco and Samuel Jones in Toledo, Ohio, were elected on platforms promising municipal ownership of public utilities.

Urban reformers often were frustrated, however, because state legislatures, controlled by railroads and large corporations, blocked munici-

pal agitation for greater home rule. As a result, progressives turned their attention to gubernatorial politics. Their most noteworthy success was the election of Robert M. La Follette, who served as governor of Wisconsin from 1901 to 1906.

Among other achievements, La Follette won from the Legislature a state banking-control measure and an anti-lobbying law aimed at big corporations. Furthermore, corporate taxes were raised, a railroad commission was formed to set rates and a conservation commission was established. Similar laws and policies came into force in other states where progressives attained positions of power.

As progressives gained strength at the state level, they began to seek comparable influence in national politics. Some headway was made against the great corporate trusts during Theodore Roosevelt's presidency, when Congress approved two important laws regulating the railroads.* Meanwhile, a series of exposés by muckraking journalists led to the passage of federal laws such as the Pure Food and Drug Act and the Meat Inspection Act (both 1906), which sought to combat abuses in the food industry.

Roosevelt's successor as president, William Howard Taft, was a staunch opponent of progressivism. But Woodrow Wilson, who followed Taft, endorsed many progressive measures. For instance, the Federal Reserve Act (1913) reformed the currency system, the Clayton [Antitrust] Act and the Federal Trade Commission Act (both 1914) extended government regulation of big business, and the Keating-Owen Act (1916) restricted the use of child labor.

American entry into World War I effectively brought an end to the short but intense period of progressive reform in the United States. Although La Follette ran for president

---

*The two railroad-regulation laws were the Elkins Act (1903) and the Hepburn Act (1906).

as the Progressive Party nominee in 1924, the 1920s were a period of resurgence for both conservative Republicanism and big business. In the heady postwar economic climate, government regulation of private enterprise no longer commanded popular support.

The pendulum swung back again after the Great Depression took hold in the early 1930s. Hoping to jumpstart the enfeebled economy, President Franklin D. Roosevelt revived the old progressive agenda under the banner of the New Deal. Once again, the federal government asserted a leading role in shaping national economic policy. Congress and the Supreme Court generally went along, though often with great reluctance. The chief criticism of the New Deal was that it greatly centralized authority in the federal government and, through congressional delegations of power, vastly extended the power of the president and executive agencies.

Republican Support

World War II sent progressivism into hibernation once again. And with the 1952 election of Dwight D. Eisenhower, the first Republican to occupy the White House in 20 years, reaction against government interference in the economy began to swell. In 1955, the old Bureau of the Budget issued a policy directive discouraging federal agencies from producing for themselves any "product or service [that] can be procured from private enterprise through ordinary business channels."

That policy has remained in force ever since, under both Democratic and Republican administrations. However, conservatives complain that it is honored more in the breach than the observance. Joseph R. Wright Jr., deputy director of the Office of Management and Budget (successor to the Bureau of

Continued on p. 989

Chronology

1950s
Private enterprise finds a more congenial atmosphere in Washington as the Republican Eisenhower administration takes control of the White House, ending 20 straight years of Democratic rule.

1955
The Bureau of the Budget (forerunner of the Office of Management and Budget) issues a policy directive stating that "the federal government will not start or carry on any commercial activity to provide a service or product for its own use if such product or service can be procured from private enterprise through ordinary business channels."

1960s
The Tennessee Valley Authority, one of the chief monuments of the New Deal, becomes an early candidate for privatization.

Oct. 28, 1963
Sen. Barry Goldwater of Arizona, destined to be the 1964 Republican presidential nominee, proposes that the federally owned TVA be sold to private power interests. The authority, argues Goldwater, "would be better operated and would be of more benefit for more people if it were part of private industry."

1980s
Conservative administrations in the United States and Britain promote privatization and deregulation to break what they see as bureaucratic strangleholds on the economy.

1981
Congress privatizes the National Consumer Cooperative Bank by passing legislation (signed by President Reagan) directing the Treasury to dispose of its bank stock by Dec. 31, 1981.

Nov. 21-28, 1984
The British government sells its 50.2 percent stake in British Telecommunications PLC (British Telecom) for $4.8 billion — the largest single public stock offering in history. By encouraging purchases of small blocks of stock by numerous individual investors, the government makes it unlikely that a future Labor government could succeed in renationalizing the company.

1986
By barring the use of tax-exempt financing, accelerated depreciation and investment tax credits for environmental infrastructure projects, the Tax Reform Act makes water and wastewater-treatment facilities less attractive as candidates for full private ownership.

March 26, 1987
More than 18 million shares of Consolidated Rail Corp. (Conrail), the federally owned freight carrier, are sold to the public for $1.65 billion in what Transportation Secretary Elizabeth Hanford Dole calls "the largest privatization in U.S. history."

1987
The British government sells the former British Airports Authority (BAA) for $2.5 billion. BAA's properties included the three main London airports (Heathrow, Gatwick and Stansted) and four airports in Scotland.

1990s
Under recession-induced pressure to trim costs, state and local governments turn increasingly to privatization of public services.

1990
South Pointe Elementary School in Dade County, Fla., becomes the nation's first public school to be operated by a private, for-profit company (Education Alternatives Inc.).

Dec. 18, 1991
President Bush signs into law the Intermodal Surface Transportation Efficiency Act, which provides that a state may impose tolls on non-Interstate highways, bridges and tunnels, or even sell them to private enterprise, as long as the state transportation agency retains proper oversight.

December 1991
The British government sells about 26 percent of British Telecom for nearly $10 billion.

1991
Massachusetts Gov. William F. Weld expresses interest in selling the Massachusetts Turnpike, a state-owned toll road. In response, the American Trucking Associations and two other private parties submit unsolicited purchase offers.

February 1992
New York Gov. Mario M. Cuomo announces he will entertain serious proposals from private interests wishing to buy the 512-mile New York State Thruway, the nation's longest toll road.

April 30, 1992
President Bush signs an executive order aimed at helping state and local governments sell or lease to private interests such publicly owned "infrastructure assets" as roads, bridges and airports.

The School Choice Debate

One of the most hotly debated privatization proposals of recent years is school choice, designed to give families a much broader range of options in deciding where to educate their children.† Many students of school choice trace the movement's origins to a 1962 book by economist Milton Friedman, *Capitalism and Freedom*. In this work, Friedman expounded his idea for government-funded vouchers that would permit parents to send their children to any school — public or private — of their choice.

Privatization critics say the voucher idea is deeply flawed. In any general school choice program, Professor Paul Starr of Princeton University told a congressional panel in 1987, students attending private schools "would have to receive public funds that they are not now getting, and taxes would have to be raised accordingly."† Moreover, private schools might decide to raise their tuition fees, reasoning that families of students already enrolled would be able to afford them.

"And precisely because many schools would want to retain their exclusive images," Starr added, "they would very likely set their tuition high enough above the voucher to keep out students whom they perceive as unattractive." Should all this happen, Starr said, a public school student from a family of modest means would have no more "choice" of schools than he or she did before the voucher program began.

Starr went on to dispute the claim that vouchers and other forms of privatization would curb interest-group agitation for higher government spending. To the contrary, he said, "Private landlords, private schools and private health plans would all agitate for vouchers to be worth as much money as possible. The higher the monetary value, the greater their income."

In Starr's view, one of the chief drawbacks of education vouchers cannot be measured in dollars. A general voucher plan, he said, "could well drain much of the energy and life from local government." That is because many people initially become involved in their communities out of concern for their children's education. "Remove education to the marketplace," he said, "and the tendencies toward political uninvolvement, evident from declining voter participation, are only likely to be intensified."

Policy-makers should keep in mind, he added, that "all markets are not the same, and where public institutions have assumed important democratic functions, as in the case of the schools, the shift toward market alternatives may jeopardize core values of our society."

Despite such objections, President Bush gave school choice a prominent place on his administration's domestic agenda. At a White House Workshop on Choice in Educa-

tion held shortly before his inauguration, Bush said choice programs would "give parents back their voices and their proper determining roles in the makeup of children's education, and they give schools a chance to distinguish themselves from one another."

"America 2000," the education reform program Bush unveiled at a White House ceremony in April 1991, did not propose financing school choice programs directly. Instead, the federal government would have provided financial incentives to state and local governments to develop school choice policies. The Bush program also called for changes in the Chapter 1 program of federal aid to schools with disadvantaged students†† to allow federal dollars to follow a low-income student if he or she transferred to another school, even if the new school was a private or parochial one.

Attempts to enact key elements of America 2000 went nowhere. In the waning days of the 102nd Congress, Education Secretary Lamar Alexander recommended that Bush veto the Neighborhood Schools Improvement Act, an $800 million block grant to states and schools. The legislation contained hardly any of the president's education reform proposals, including those pertaining to school choice. But Senate Republicans succeeded in killing the bill before it even reached Bush's desk.‡

The incoming Clinton administration is likely to take a different approach to school reform. For instance, the 1992 Democratic Party platform assailed Bush's "efforts to bankrupt the public school system — the bedrock of democracy — through private school vouchers." At the same time, the platform expressed support for reforms like "site-based decision-making and public school choice, with strong protection against discrimination."

---

† For background, see "School Choice," *The CQ Researcher*, May 10, 1991, pp. 253-276.

‡ Testimony at hearing of the Subcommittee on Antitrust, Impact of Deregulation and Privatization of the House Committee on Small Business, June 11, 1987.

†† Under the Chapter 1 program, a school receives money if a large proportion of its students qualify as needy under either the federal school-lunch program or the Aid to Families With Dependent Children program. The money must be spent on remedial classes and services for those children, unless a school's poverty rate exceeds 75 percent, in which case Chapter 1 funds can be spent on schoolwide programs.

‡ See Jill Zuckman, "Dead Again: School Reform Done In by Both Sides," *CQ Weekly Report*, Oct. 3, 1992, p. 3052.

Continued from p. 986
the Budget) noted that a revised version issued in 1960 allowed for exceptions in cases where "procurement from commercial sources involved higher costs."[30]

As conservatives began to displace moderates and liberals as the dominant force in the Republican Party after World War II, calls for privatization of government enterprises became more insistent. Sen. Barry Goldwater of Arizona, who was to be the 1964 Republican presidential nominee, created a stir when he suggested in an Oct. 28, 1963, letter to Rep. Richard Fulton, D-Tenn., that the Tennessee Valley Authority (TVA) be sold to private interests. Goldwater argued that the massive public power network "would be better operated and would be of more benefit for more people if it were part of private industry." He added that "it would be a benefit and a great boon to Tennessee to have TVA placed on the tax rolls."

The suggestion was widely denounced, even by Southern Republicans, because TVA (one of the New Deal's proudest achievements) was highly esteemed in the region it supplied with electric power. But Goldwater stood his ground. In a February 1964 press release, he said he meant only to turn "a federal white elephant into a more productive and useful part of our economy — without in any way penalizing the people of the Tennessee Valley or taking anything away from them."

Because he lost the 1964 election to incumbent President Lyndon B. Johnson, Goldwater never got the chance to put his ideas about TVA into practice. Indeed, the concept of privatization had not yet acquired its present name. Business writer and consultant Peter F. Drucker is credited with originating the term in his 1969 book *The Age of Discontinuity.* And Anthony H. Pascal, a Rand Corp. analyst, examined the private delivery of public services in a study published three years later.[31]

Reagan's Commitment

By the time Ronald Reagan was inaugurated as president in 1981, privatization had become a prime domestic goal of the Republican Party. One of the administration's first efforts to privatize government assets involved the sale of millions of acres of federally owned land, mostly in Western states. "I want to open as much land as I can," said Reagan's Interior secretary, James G. Watt. "The basic difference between this administration and the liberals is that we are market-oriented. We are trying to bring our abundant acres into the market so that the market will decide the value."[32]

The land-sale proposal was hailed by private industries that stood to benefit from it and by economic analysts who shared the administration's view that private enterprise is more competent than government to manage a large-scale land program. However, the plan ran into strong opposition from ranchers, who voiced alarm at losing access to land they had long used as for grazing livestock, and from private real estate speculators and state land managers, who feared massive sales of public land could depress property prices throughout the region for years to come.

When the dust settled, it was clear the opponents had carried the day. In July 1983, Watt withdrew lands controlled by the Interior Department from the sale program. Department officials said he had come to regard the plan as a political liability to Reagan, especially in the West. After Watt resigned as Interior secretary on Oct. 9, 1983, little more was heard of the land-sale program.[33]

The Reagan administration still was committed to privatization, however. The issue returned to the spotlight in January 1984 with the publication of the final report of the President's Private Sector Survey, popularly known as the Grace commission.* The blue-ribbon panel cited numerous "random examples of bureaucratic absurdity" and predicted the federal government would post annual deficits of $1 trillion or more by the end of the century unless spending were brought under control. To do this, the commission called for adoption of private sector management practices.

The Grace commission's chief privatization proposal concerned the sale of federally subsidized power to customers in the Northwest at one-third the private-market rate. If the federal power were sold at market prices, the panel stated, there would be a three-year increase in revenues of $4.5 billion. This amount, it said, equaled the combined three-year federal income taxes of 675,000 American families with median incomes.

The administration, meanwhile, was pursuing privatization elsewhere. In 1981, President Reagan signed legislation directing the Treasury to dispose of its stock in the National Consumer Cooperative Bank by the end of the year. The bank was left to function as a private entity without further outside assistance.

Five years later, in March 1987, the administration sold the government's 85 percent stake in Conrail,[34] the federally owned freight carrier, for $1.65 billion — a deal that Transportation Secretary Elizabeth Hanford Dole hailed as "the largest privatization in U.S. history." She predicted it would "break ground for more privatizations to come."

Later that year, Reagan appointed the President's Commission on Privatization and directed it to study and evaluate past and current privatization ventures by U.S. and foreign governments and develop a framework for future privatization efforts. The commission's report, submitted

---

*The commission got its name from its chairman, J. Peter Grace, chairman and chief executive officer of W. R. Grace & Co.

to the White House on March 18, 1988, went well beyond previous proposals by the president to trim the size of the federal government and sell off many of its assets.

In presenting the report, commission Chairman David F. Linowes* described federal agencies as "muscle-bound to the point of paralysis when it comes to considering more effective alternatives." Government, he added, "should not be in the business of business."

Among the panel's 78 recommendations were (1) repeal of the statutes that give the U.S. Postal Service a monopoly on delivering letter mail; (2) sale of Amtrak, the government-owned passenger rail network; (3) sale of the federal government's $250 billion loan portfolio of housing, business, agricultural and education loans; (4) private operation of airport traffic-control towers, with the federal government continuing "to regulate the national airspace" and remaining responsible for air safety; (5) converting U.S. military commissaries and federal, state and local correctional facilities to private management; and (6) issuing vouchers for public-school education to give parents a greater choice of elementary and secondary schools for their children and to create competition among local school systems.

"Our report," Linowes said, "is not about money, budgets, or political ideologies. It is about programs and services and restoring to the American people their basic rights and obligations upon which our nation has been built."[35]

Because the report of the President's Commission on Privatization was issued at the start of the 1988 presidential campaign season, nothing was done to implement it before Reagan left office the following January. ∎

---

*Linowes, a Democrat, is a professor of political economy and public policy at the University of Illinois.

CURRENT SITUATION

State and Local Initiatives

The chief impetus for privatization today is coming not from Washington but from state and local governments. States and localities find themselves in a double bind as the recession causes revenues to stagnate or shrink and popular resistance to higher taxes to stiffen. In these straitened circumstances, contracting out public services and selling public assets seem increasingly attractive options.

To the surprise of some observers, Massachusetts is the state that has embraced privatization most wholeheartedly. Under former Gov. Michael S. Dukakis, the 1988 Democratic presidential nominee, the Bay State had acquired the derisive nickname "Taxachusetts" — a reference to its purportedly bloated public payroll and free-spending ways. But under Republican Gov. William Weld, Massachusetts sails by a different fiscal compass.

Weld characterizes his administration's approach as "entrepreneurial government," which he defines as formulating policy "with an eye more toward the results than the process."[36] Privatization, deregulation and tax-cutting are his principal tools.

Since Weld took office, Massachusetts has saved an estimated $8 million by having the private sector provide health care for its prison inmates. Moreover, it has privatized the state lottery's courier service* (which estimates say will save taxpayers more than $2.75 million), and moved mentally retarded residents of mental hospitals to private

---

*The Massachusetts Lottery Commission's courier service performed such chores as delivering instant-winner tickets and supplies to lottery outlets. The commission now uses United Parcel Service to do the job.

facilities (which will save an estimated $140 million over three years). Weld also is weighing privatization of rental-car inspections and collection of child-support payments.

Last winter, the American Trucking Associations (ATA) submitted an unsolicited offer to buy the Massachusetts Turnpike after press reports indicated Weld was interested in selling it. The Reason Foundation estimates the value of the 135-mile toll road at $500 million. The ATA also has expressed interest in purchasing the New York State Thruway. Although initial reaction from Albany was negative, Gov. Cuomo announced in February 1992 that he would entertain serious offers. The 512-mile thruway is worth $1.9 billion, according to the foundation.

Progress in Indianapolis

At the local level, one of the leading proponents of privatization is Mayor Stephen Goldsmith of Indianapolis, elected to his first term in 1991. A lawyer and former prosecutor, Goldsmith teaches a management course at Indiana University's School of Public and Environmental Affairs from January through April of each year. Among the topics covered in the course are "comparing public and private management" and "privatization."

Soon after Goldsmith took office in January, he ordered sizable layoffs of municipal employees. He insisted, however, that reducing the city payroll was not his overriding aim. "My goal, quite frankly, isn't even to privatize city government," he told local businessmen. "My goal is to produce the most efficient service at the lowest cost, maybe by government, maybe by some of you in the room."[37] Elaborating on that thought in a March interview, the mayor said: "For many services, the obligation should be on government to explain why it needs to do them instead of the private sector, rather than the other way around."[38]

To help him formulate and imple-

Continued on p. 992

Privatization: A Global Trend

The U.S. government lags well behind many foreign governments in privatizing public services, and for good reason: There is much less to privatize in the United States than there is overseas. In the late 1970s, when privatization efforts began, nearly 7 percent of employees in "other developed market economies" worked in state-owned businesses, compared with just 2 percent in the United States.†

Britain has been the global pace-setter in privatization since the Conservative Party came to power in 1979 and began dismantling much of the welfare state built by the Labor Party. By 1987 the government of Prime Minister Margaret Thatcher had sold off more than $20 billion in state assets, including British Airways, British Gas and a large chunk of British Telecom.

Under Prime Minister John Major, Britain is still pursuing privatization. The country's total public-asset sales of more than $19 billion in 1991 led the world for the third year in a row. Most of that amount came from the government's sale of 22 percent of British Telecom for almost $10 billion — the largest single privatization deal on record.

Other member countries of the European Community (EC) have adopted different approaches to privatization. The subject has always been especially touchy in France, whose state-owned firms account for about one-third of gross domestic product. During France's 1988 presidential campaign, President François Mitterrand sought to defuse the issue by proclaiming his so-called *ni-ni* (neither-nor) doctrine. He pledged that, if re-elected, he would put a halt to both nationalizations and privatizations.

Mitterrand won a second term, but the *ni-ni* policy soon developed leaks. In what amounted to a partial privatization, the state-owned car manufacturer Renault in 1989 agreed to a stock swap and limited merger with Volvo, the Swedish automaker. And the 1990 takeover of Union de Transport Airiens (UTA), a private French airline, by government-owned Air France was widely viewed as a nationalization in all but name.

By necessity, the most ambitious privatization program in the EC is Germany's. There the task is selling off or closing down thousands of businesses formerly owned by the defunct communist state of East Germany. Treuhandstalt (literally, Trusteeship Institute), a holding company set up in June 1990 to handle the job, began operating with more than 10,000 companies for sale. By the end of 1991, it had disposed of all or part of 5,000 enterprises and raised more than $10 billion. (The Treuhandanstalt portfolio also includes 28 percent of eastern Germany's farmland and two-thirds of its forest acreage.)

The second 5,000 companies controlled by Treuhandanstalt undoubtedly will be harder to unload than the first 5,000. Before reunification with West Germany, East German industry was reputed to be the most efficient and technologically advanced in the Soviet bloc. "In reality," *The Economist* noted, "many of the 'people's companies' were pollution-ridden, industrial museums, with well-trained but unmotivated labor and enormous debts." ††

Daunting as privatization of eastern Germany may be, converting Russia's state-owned enterprises to private ownership promises to be far more difficult and time-consuming. To speed the process, the government on Oct. 1 began distributing vouchers that will enable every citizen to buy shares in newly privatized factories, shops and businesses. The vouchers, which have a face value of 10,000 rubles, may also be traded or sold. Some key industrial sectors, including gold mining, arms manufacturing and oil production, are to remain under government control.

In Latin America, meanwhile, privatization is credited with sparking a regional economic revival, notably in Argentina and Mexico. Argentina has privatized the state-owned airlines, telephone company, TV stations, oil fields and water company and hopes to net $3.5 billion.

Privatization is further advanced in Mexico. Between 1982, when the Mexican program began, and 1990 the number of companies owned by the public sector declined from 1,155 to 280. The proceeds have been used largely to reduce the country's domestic debt. As a result, Mexico's budget deficit declined from 17 percent of gross domestic product in 1982 to 1.9 percent of GDP in 1991.‡

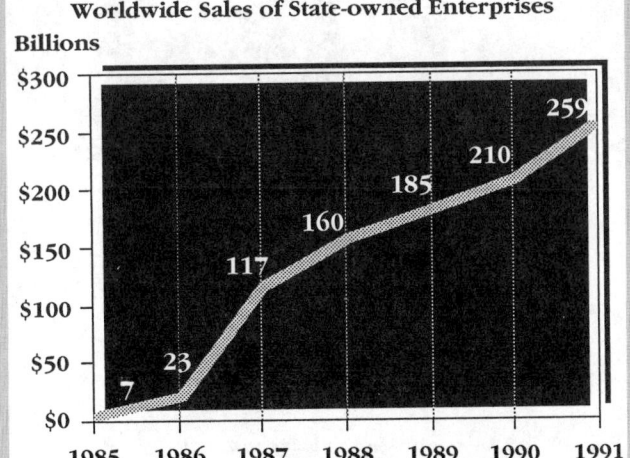

Worldwide Sales of State-owned Enterprises

Billions

Source: Reason Foundation, Privatization 1992

---

† John B. Goodman and Gary W. Loveman, "Does Privatization Serve the Public Interest?" *Harvard Business Review,* November-December 1991, p. 32.

†† "Privatising East Germany," *The Economist,* Sept. 14, 1991, p. 22.

‡ For background on privatization in Mexico, see "Mexico's Emergence," *The CQ Researcher,* July 19, 1992, pp. 489-512.

Continued from p. 992

ment his privatization plans, Goldsmith appointed a panel of volunteers called the Service, Efficiency and Lower Taxes for Indianapolis Commission (SELTIC). Headed by Mitch Daniels, vice president of corporate affairs at Indianapolis-based Eli Lilly and Co., the panel was directed to review all government services to determine if they should even continue to exist. One of SELTIC's first tasks was to study the feasibility of selling the sewer-billing service oper- ated by the Indianapolis Department of Public Works as well as the city's sewage-treatment plants.

Matt Ridenour, director of management services in the mayor's office, reports progress on both fronts. The city has agreed to let the Indianapolis Water Co., a private utility, take over the sewer-billing, starting in January. Indianapolis officials expect the deal to save the city $1.8 million a year.

In addition, the city has held talks with British, French and U.S. firms about taking over Indianapolis wastewater treatment plants through either purchase or some sort of contractual deal. Ridenour says sale of the plants could raise about $100 million, most of which would be earmarked for urgently needed capital improvements. "At a time when city and state governments are strapped and even the federal government is strapped," he says, "there's really no other way for us to take on the kinds of major improvements to keep our infrastructure up and running."

Numerous other city services in Indianapolis have been privatized or are potential candidates for privatization. Proposals currently under study include turning city golf courses and parks over to private management firms. "Virtually everything's a [privatization] target," says Ridenour, "from the way we fill potholes to the way we treat sewage to the way we issue permits."

M. Jenkins

All across the country, revenue-pinched cities are turning to private firms to provide services like trash collection.

Infrastructure Assets

Congress gave certain kinds of state-level privatization a boost when it passed the Intermodal Surface Transportation Efficiency Act of 1991 (ISTEA), signed into law by President Bush last Dec. 18. Reversing 70 years of federal opposition to toll roads, the law permits federal highway funds to be funneled into four kinds of user-fee projects: (1) construction of new toll highways, bridges and tunnels, except on the Interstate system; (2) rebuilding of

existing toll facilities, including those already part of the Interstate system; (3) rebuilding as toll roads any existing highway not in the Interstate system; and (4) rebuilding as toll facilities any bridge or tunnel, including those in the Interstate system.

Such projects may be privately owned, ISTEA says, provided the state transportation agency has a contractual relationship with the private operator. The law also provides that the federal matching share can run as high as 50 percent for toll highways and up to 80 percent for bridges and tunnels. In addition, states are free to use the federal money as grants or as loans, as they see fit. The option enables them to establish state revolving loan funds to make the dollars from Washington stretch.

Supporters of ISTEA say it will help states deal more effectively with the mounting problem of "crumbling infrastructure." Instead of scrambling for more tax revenue to finance bridge and road repairs, state governments can now turn the job over to private enterprise and realize a one-time windfall besides.

The law may also facilitate the construction of new, special-purpose intercity tollways. Indeed, notes the Reason Foundation, the American Trucking Associations has "begun talking about the creation of a 'second Interstate highway system' for trucks, outside the reach of federal highway taxes. This might be possible via the purchase of a set of existing turnpikes in the Eastern United

Continued on p. 994

At Issue:

Does privatization improve service and lower costs?

STUART B. BUTLER

Director of Domestic Policy at the Heritage Foundation
FROM TESTIMONY BEFORE THE SUBCOMMITTEE ON ANTI-
TRUST, IMPACT OF DEREGULATION AND PRIVATIZATION OF
THE HOUSE COMMITTEE ON SMALL BUSINESS, JUNE 11, 1987.

Privatization is a worldwide phenomenon. It has been estimated that more than 50 countries are actively engaged in large-scale privatization activities....

Why is this move to privatization so pervasive? There are several reasons. One is that countries outside the U.S. have for many years attempted to deliver basic services and stimulate economic growth through centralized government ownership and control. But experience has proven that this approach is not successful. Indeed, countries such as Britain have experienced slow growth and poor services precisely because of extensive central ownership. Even the socialist countries now recognize there must be reduced government control in the economy and in the delivery of basic services.

Second, there is a growing appreciation of the value of competition and entrepreneurship in the delivery of services. It is becoming widely understood that encouraging private firms to bid for government services spurs innovation and efficiency, leading to better services at lower cost. Moreover, scholars and politicians are having second thoughts about activities that once were considered to be natural monopolies and core government functions, such as basic utilities. Experience shows that these often can be made to be highly competitive without increasing the unit cost of production. This has led to the growing interest in privatizing telecommunications, electricity production, and other services previously assumed to need government ownership to obtain economies of scale.

Third, budget pressures have induced foreign governments — and governments lower down the U.S. federal system — to explore privatization simply as a means of reducing budget costs. These governments have found that outlays can be reduced without reductions in quality through sensible and cautious use of the private sector. As the experience of public sector managers improves in the use of private contractors, we are seeing steady improvements in the quality and efficiency of such privatization.

As Congress explores ways of reducing the heavy federal deficit and examines ways of improving America's competitive position, it should look carefully at privatization. Of course, it would be naive of proponents of privatization to contend that simply transferring a function to the private sector of itself guarantees cost savings and an improvement in the quality of services. While the potential benefits of privatization are very clear ... it has to be recognized that privatization raises many issues that need to be addressed.

PAUL STARR

Professor of Sociology at Princeton University
FROM *PROSPECTS FOR PRIVATIZATION,* 1987.

Conservatives who favor privatization read the record as proving the superiority of private providers, but this is an act of heroically selective attention. Given the American experience with defense production, construction projects, and health care — all mostly produced privately with public dollars — it is remarkable that anyone could see a path toward budgetary salvation simply by shifting the locus of service production from the public sector to the private sector.

Advocates of privatization show an undue tenderness toward private contractors and an undue hostility toward public employees. They indulge private contractors for their history of cost overruns; they rebuke public employees for their history of wage increases. But their preference for private provision actually reflects a deep underestimate of the skills that private firms can deploy. They underestimate the capacity of the contractors to manipulate to their own advantage the incentives that are held out to them for better performance. And they underestimate the contractors' capacity to influence political decisions, either illegitimately through bribery or legally through campaign contributions and lobbying. Missing from the case for privatization is any clear sense of feedback effects — the reaction back upon the government of the enlarged class of private contractors and other providers dependent on public money.

So, if partial privatization is to reduce public spending, it cannot be expected to achieve its effect by reducing spending pressure. Private firms have to be far more efficient. Some evidence does not suggest the private producers have lower costs, but the picture is complicated by the following: First, contrary evidence from other studies shows no difference in costs or even higher costs among commercial providers. Second, there are pervasive differences in the services performed by public and private organizations, particularly because of differences in their clientele, such as exist between public and private schools, hospitals and social services as the result of the 'creaming' of client populations by private institutions. Third, studies usually lack any evidence about the quality of services, thereby making it difficult to judge whether lower costs result from greater efficiency or deteriorating quality. And, fourth, some private firms' lower costs stem from lower wage levels and greater use of part-time workers with fewer fringe benefits.

Continued from p. 992

States, as their bonds are retired over the next few years." [39]

President Bush gave further encouragement to the privatization movement in an executive order issued this spring. [40] The directive's aim was to help cities and states privatize "infrastructure assets" like roads, tunnels, bridges, power plants, mass transit, rail systems, airports, waterways, housing, schools, prisons and hospitals.

To this end, the order greatly eased an existing regulation that had undermined numerous state and local privatization proposals. The regulation stated that when a state or city sold a facility built with federal aid, the seller must repay a percentage of the proceeds corresponding to the share originally contributed by Washington.

Bush eased the rule by declaring that state and local governments selling an infrastructure asset may first recoup in full the unadjusted dollar portion of their total project costs, including any incidental fix-up outlays. If any money remains, the federal government may recoup its share, minus accumulated depreciation. All funds left after that stay with the seller.

"Taxpayers will still come out ahead" under the Bush executive order, according to Reason Foundation President Robert W. Poole Jr. "The facilities will remain in use by the public, so the [federal] grants will have accomplished their intended purpose. And the privatized facilities will begin paying federal corporate income taxes." [41]   ∎

my. What then?

Irwin David of Apogee Research feels "there is a risk of privatization losing momentum if the economy picks up steam." At the same time, he thinks the move to privatize should endure because "there will never be enough money for state or local governments or the federal government to do what we're asking them to do."

David also believes President-elect Bill Clinton will be a supporter of privatization. "I haven't seen anything specifically that he's mentioned, but people I've talked to who were active in his campaign say he thinks private sector involvement continues to be valid. So I don't see a major change [in privatization policy] at the federal level during the Clinton administration."

Henry Raimondo of Rutgers feels "privatization will always be bouncing around somewhere. We're going to be hearing about it for at least the rest of this decade." In his opinion, "any public manager or any politician will talk about privatization. They'd be foolish not to."

As for Clinton, Raimondo feels the president-elect "has blurred the line so much about positions we would think of as traditionally Republican that he's promising, it seems to me, a more aggressive federal government." The Bush administration "may talk privatization," says Raimondo, "but we might actually see more of it under Clinton." ∎

OUTLOOK

Clinton's Position

Although privatization has made great strides in the United States, experts say its potential has only been scratched — partly because of the barriers that existed before Bush's April 30 executive order. To gauge the impact of that order, three members of the Reason Foundation surveyed the country's "total salable state and municipal enterprises" and estimated their market value. Their conclusion: The combined value of all such assets is $226.8 billion. [42] *(See table, p. 980.)*

The "principal candidates for sale to private investors," the study concluded, are the nation's 87 largest airports, which handle 90 percent of the country's scheduled air passenger traffic. If all those airports were sold, the study estimated they would fetch a combined $28.95 billion. [43]

Still, airports account for slightly

less than 13 percent of the value of the state and city assets covered in the study. The others included electric and gas utilities, highways and bridges, parking structures, ports, turnpikes, water system, wastewater facilities and waste-to-energy plants.

Whether government assets are sold is obviously up to state and local officials to decide, depending upon circumstances that cannot be foreseen. The 1992 Apogee Research survey of state comptrollers suggested that contracting out will continue to be more popular than asset sales as a privatization option. Ninety-four percent of the responding comptrollers said they thought contracting out of state services would increase in their states in the next decade, while only 28 percent said sales of state assets to private interests would grow over that period. [44]

Above all, the future of privatization in the United States may hinge on political and economic developments not always easy to foresee. Suppose, for example, there is a marked improvement in the econo-

Notes

[1] Quoted in *The Wall Street Journal,* May 28, 1992.

[2] Quoted in *The New York Times,* May 28, 1985.

[3] Apogee Research Inc., *State Government Privatization 1992,* 1992, p. 1.

[4] Al Bilik, "Privatization: Defacing the Community," *Labor Law Journal,* June 1992, p. 340.

5 Paul Starr, "The Limits of Privatization," in *Prospects for Privatization* (1987), Steve H. Hanke, ed., p. 128.

6 John D. Donahue, *The Privatization Decision* (1989), p. 84.

7 *Ibid.,* p. 13.

8 *Ibid.,* p. 221.

9 John B. Goodman and Gary W. Loveman, "Does Privatization Serve the Public Interest?" *Harvard Business Review,* November-December 1991, p. 28.

10 Touche Ross & Co., *Privatization in America,* 1987, p. 5.

11 Op-ed page column in *The Alexandria (Va.) Journal,* Aug. 15, 1992.

12 Testimony at a hearing of the Subcommittee on Antitrust, Impact of Deregulation and Privatization of U.S. House Committee on Small Business, June 11, 1987.

13 Donahue, *op. cit.,* p. 142.

14 Testimony at a hearing of the Subcommittee on Antitrust, Impact of Deregulation and Privatization of the U.S. House Committee on Small Business, June 11, 1987.

15 American Federation of State, County and Municipal Employees, *Passing the Bucks,* May 1984, p. 15.

16 Donahue, *op. cit.,* p. 218.

17 Bilik, *op. cit.,* p. 340.

18 Touche Ross & Co., *State Government Privatization in America,* 1989, p. 2.

19 Apogee Research Inc., *op. cit.,* p. 11.

20 Bilik, *op. cit.,* p. 339. For background on the growing use of contingent workers, see "Jobs in the '90s," *The CQ Researcher,* Feb. 28, 1992, pp. 169-192.

21 Donahue, *op. cit.,* pp. 146-146.

22 *Ibid.,* p. 149.

23 Reason Foundation, *Privatization 1992,* 1992, p. 11.

24 World Bank, *The Welfare Consequences of Selling Public Enterprises: Case Studies From Chile, Malaysia, Mexico and the U.K.,* June 1992.

25 President's Commission on Privatization, *Privatization: Toward More Effective Government,* March 1988, p. 141. For more information on employee stock ownership plans, see "New Styles in Work-Place Management," *Editorial Research Reports,* Feb. 26, 1988, pp. 104-105.

26 Testimony at hearing of the Subcommittee on Antitrust, Impact of Deregulation and Privatization of the U.S. House Committee on Small Business, June 11, 1987.

27 Starr, *op. cit.,* p. 128.

28 H. George Frederickson, "Painting Bull's-Eyes Around Bullet Holes," *Governing,* October 1992, p. 13.

29 Steve H. Hanke, "Privatization Versus Nationalization," in Hanke, *op. cit.,* p. 1.

30 Joseph R. Wright Jr., "Let's Get the Feds to Use the Private Sector," *The Privatization Review,* winter 1987, p. 28.

31 Anthony H. Pascal, "Clients, Consumers and Citizens: Market Mechanisms for the Delivery of Public Services" (paper presented at the Conference on Centrally Planned Social Change, Quail's Roost, N.C., April 1972).

32 Quoted in *The New York Times,* July 3, 1982.

33 The immediate cause of Watt's resignation had nothing to do with federal land sales. He was forced to quit because of adverse public reaction to his remarks about a special commission studying Interior Department coal-leasing policies. At a Sept. 21 breakfast meeting with lobbyists at the U.S. Chamber of Commerce in Washington, Watt said the commission had "three Democrats, two Republicans, every kind of mix you can have. I have a black, a woman, two Jews and a cripple. And we have talent."

34 The remaining 15 percent of Conrail stock was owned by the carrier's current and former employees. The line was formed in the mid-1970s from the Penn Central and six other smaller railroads.

35 Press release accompanying final report of the President's Commission on Privatization, March 18, 1988.

36 Quoted by Jacob Weisberg, "The Boston Slasher," *The New Republic,* Dec. 9, 1991, p. 19.

37 Remarks before members of the Indianapolis Chamber of Commerce, Indiana Convention Center, Jan. 30, 1992.

38 Quoted by columnist John Krull in *The Indianapolis News,* March 27, 1992.

39 Reason Foundation, *op. cit.,* p. 22.

40 Executive Order 12803, "Infrastructure Privatization," April 30, 1992.

41 Robert W. Poole Jr., "Invest in Infrastructure — Privatize," *The Wall Street Journal,* May 5, 1992.

42 Robert W. Poole Jr., David Haarmeyer and Lynn Scarlett, "Mining the Government Balance Sheet: What Cities and States Have to Sell," Reason Foundation, April 1992. Poole is president of the foundation, Haarmeyer is a policy analyst and Scarlett is vice president of research.

43 The study assumed a price of $61 per air passenger at each airport. *Ibid.,* p. 4.

44 Apogee Research Inc., *op. cit.,* p. 5.

Bibliography

Selected Sources Used

Books

Donahue, John D., *The Privatization Decision,* **Basic Books, 1989.**

Donahue, an assistant professor of government at Harvard University, weighs the arguments for and against privatization and suggests a few guidelines.

Finley, Lawrence K., ed., *Public Sector Privatization: Alternative Approaches to Service Delivery,* **Quorum Books, 1989.**

Finley, an associate professor of management at Western Kentucky University in Bowling Green, contributes an introductory chapter setting forth some of the key issues in alternative delivery of government services.

Hanke, Steve H., ed., *Prospects for Privatization,* **The Academy of Political Science, 1987.**

The 21 contributors to this collection analyze the economics of privatization as well as its potential as a tool for controlling the growth of government.

Hudgins, Edward L., and Ronald D. Utt, eds., *How Privatization Can Solve America's Infrastructure Crisis,* **The Heritage Foundation, 1992.**

The seven essays in this collection assess how the private sector can build and operate infrastructure facilities, including roads and bridges, transit systems, airports and prisons.

Articles

Goodman, John B., and Loveman, Gary W., "Does Privatization Serve the Public Interest?" *Harvard Business Review,* **November-December 1991.**

Goodman and Loveman, assistant professors at the Harvard Business School, examine the pros and cons of privatization and conclude that the real issue is managerial accountability, not the form of ownership.

Thomas, Charles W., "Correctional Facility Privatization — How It Redefines Legal Rights of Prisoners," *The Privatization Review,* **winter 1991.**

Thomas, director of the Private Corrections Project at the University of Florida's Center for Studies in Criminology and Law, analyzes the impact of privatization on the constitutional and legal rights of inmates of privately operated correctional institutions.

Reports and Studies

American Federation of State, County and Municipal

Employees, *Passing the Bucks: The Contracting Out of Public Services,* **May 1984.**

AFSCME, a labor union representing workers directly affected by privatization, argues that contracting out of public services often ends up costing taxpayers more money, not less.

Apogee Research Inc., *State Government Privatization 1992,* **1992.**

This study presents the findings of a survey answered by officials (including 19 comptrollers) representing 158 agencies in 29 states. Among other things, the respondents give their views on the future of privatization.

President's Commission on Privatization, *Privatization: Toward More Effective Government,* **March 1988.**

With a few minor qualifications, the commission strongly endorses privatization and makes numerous recommendations for contracting out or sale of federal services or assets. According to the panel, the "impact of privatization ... is only beginning to be felt."

Reason Foundation, *Mining the Government Balance Sheet: What Cities and States Have to Sell,* **April 1992.**

The authors identify government-owned assets in the United States that could be sold or leased to private interests. These properties, they estimate, have a combined market value of $226.8 billion.

Reason Foundation, *Privatization 1992,* **1992.**

This report summarizes 1991 privatization developments in the United States and foreign countries. It is divided into three main sections: contracting out, infrastructure and sale of state assets and enterprises.

Subcommittee on Antitrust, Impact of Deregulation and Privatization, U.S. House Committee on Small Business, *Impact of Deregulation and Privatization* **(published proceedings of hearings held June 3 and 11, 1987).**

Various experts testify on the advantages and disadvantages of privatizing government services, particularly at the federal level.

Subcommittee on Antitrust, Impact of Deregulation and Privatization, U.S. House Committee on Small Business, *Report of the President's Commission on Privatization* **(published proceedings of hearing held March 28, 1988).**

Supporters and skeptics offer critiques of a report on privatization issued earlier the same month.

The Next Step

Additional Articles from Current Periodicals from EBSCO Publishing's Database

Books & reading

"Annotated listing of new books," *Journal of Economic Literature,* **March 1992, p. 295.**

Reviews the book "Privatization and Deregulation in Global Perspective," edited by Dennis J. Gayle and Johnathan N. Goodrich (Greenwood, 1990).

Herrmann, K.J., "Book reviews," *Social Work,* **September 1991, p. 463.**

Reviews the books "Privatization: An Economic Analysis," by John Vickers and George Yarrow (M.I.T. Press, 1988) and "Privatization: The Key to Better Government" by E.S. Savas (Chatham House, 1987).

Levin, H.M., "Book reviews," *Teachers College Record,* **Summer 1991, p. 640.**

Reviews the book "Privatization and Educational Choice," by Myron Lieberman (St. Martin, 1989).

Shearing, C.D., "Book reviews," *Canadian Journal of Criminology,* **January 1992, p. 107.**

Reviews the book "Privatizing Criminal Justice," edited by Roger Matthews (Sage, 1989).

Teske, P., "Book reviews: Comparative politics," *American Political Science Review,* **December 1991, p. 1490.**

Reviews the book "The Political Economy of Public Sector Reform and Privatization," edited by Ezra N. Suleiman and John Waterbury (Westview, 1990).

Economic aspects

"Infrastructure privatization accelerates," *Civil Engineering,* **March 1992, p. 18.**

Looks at the acceleration of privatization of infrastructure projects such as the $8 billion English Channel Tunnel. The trend was discussed at a recent conference on project financing and construction in the 1990s. Global needs for infrastructure rebuilding; probable conservative investing in infrastructure projects by banks; design/build contracts expected; privatization risks; needed revenue stream for private-sector investors.

"It's time for the cities to restructure," *Business Week,* **June 1, 1992, p. 122.**

Editorial. States that in order to maintain political support for help to the cities, municipal governments are going to have to face the fact that they are perceived as unwieldy and inefficient. Need to restructure; privatizing as many government services as possible; other recommendations.

Deitch, J., "A rush to privatize government services," *The New York Times,* **May 31, 1992, p. 1.**

Reports that from one end of New Jersey to the other, hundreds of municipalities and in dozens of county and state agencies, officials are experimenting with a concept that stands the traditional notion of government on its head: privatization. The contracting out of government services to private companies; what private companies have been hired to do; public employee unions' concern over job losses; advantages and disadvantages of the idea; more.

Friday, C., J. McCormick, et al., "Taking the town private," *Newsweek,* **March 4, 1991, p. 52.**

Considers how hard-pressed governors and mayors try again to farm out public services. Privatization has been growing since the 1970s. Under pressure to shed costs, state and local governments have been quietly contracting with private concerns to handle all manner of mundane tasks. Problems in Massachusetts; belief that only well-defined, repetitive tasks should be privatized; how prisons have highlighted the limits of privatization.

Norman, J.R., "Unforeseen consequences," *Forbes,* **Sept. 16, 1991, p. 150.**

Questions the decision to privatize the operation of noncombat Navy ships to private firms through competitive bids. Suspicions concerning Raymond T. McKay, president of the Marine Engineers Beneficial Association; continuing contractor probe; dubious connections with reputed crime family; more expansion; winning friends in influential places.

Pattison, S., "Privatizing public works," *Consumers' Research Magazine,* **July 1991, p. 40.**

Considers how local and state governments saddled with huge deficits are increasingly looking to privatize some public services. Details on a survey by the Mercer Group reported in *The Wall Street Journal* which found that localities that privatize were extremely pleased with the results.

Weinberger, C.W., "Privatization and item vetoes — good for states and Washington," *Forbes,* **Aug. 19, 1991, p. 33.**

Editorial. Comments on the virtues of privatizing some government-managed institutions and item vetoes. Distressed state governments; prospects for privatizing the whole U.S. Postal Service; sale of Amtrak; more.

Wildstrom, S.H., "Privatization," *Business Week,* May 18, 1992, p. 61.

Reports how since the Landsat satellite imaging program was taken over by a General Electric/Hughes Aircraft venture in 1984, some prices have gone up by as much as 4,500 percent. Complaints to Congress.

Education

"Next — McSchool," *Nation,* June 15, 1992, p. 807.

.Editorial. Discusses how Benno C. Schmidt Jr. is leaving Yale to plan the privatization of secondary and primary education on a scale never before imagined in a democratic society. Leader of Whittle Communications' "core design team"; creating a national chain of a thousand or more private schools; purpose is to improve public education; comment against this idea by Jonathan Kozol; details.

Blumenstyk, G., "College officials and policy experts ponder implications of 'privatizing' state colleges," *Chronicle of Higher Education,* May 13, 1992, p. A25.

Points out a number of signs of privatization of public higher education and considers the reasons behind this movement. Drops in state funding leaving public institutions with greater responsibility for meeting their budgets; moves by college officials in Florida, Illinois, Maryland and North Carolina to obtain more autonomy from their state governments; use of private colleges to meet educational needs of certain students; growing dependence on tuition; comments.

Honig, B., "Why privatizing public education is a bad idea," *Brookings Review,* winter 1990, p. 15.

Presents a rebuttal to a proposal by John E. Chubb and Terry M. Moe to transform our public schools from democratically regulated to market-driven institutions. Honig says that Chubb and Moe's basic charge that current reform efforts have not succeeded is dead wrong. He says California's comprehensive approach has made real progress. Other objections to the proposal: cult schools will result; plan violates the Constitution; lack of accountability; more.

Lewis, A.C., "Public education and privatization," *Phi Delta Kappan,* April 1992, p. 580.

Discusses the issue of public funding for private schools. "Politics, Markets, and American Schools," by John Chubb and Terry Moe; proposal of Sen. Orrin G. Hatch, R-Utah to fund experimental voucher proposals for low-income parents failed by vote of 57-36; issue of public aid to private schools will someday reach the U.S. Supreme Court; more.

Wilson, D.L., "U. of Minn. drops plan to privatize its computer services," *Chronicle of Higher Education,* Nov. 6, 1991, p. A26.

Outlines the new computer consolidation plan the University of Minnesota has developed that will include layoffs of some university computer specialists (who have civil service status), but with number and timing uncertain. Previous plan that involved privatization and extensive layoffs; possible conflicts of interest between the Minnesota Supercomputing Center and vice president for academic affairs Ettore F. Infante; employee concerns.

Yudof, M.G., "The burgeoning privatization of state universities," *Chronicle of Higher Education,* May 13, 1992, p. A48.

Opinion. Argues that just as involvement with government may distort the mission of private universities, decreasing state support and increased reliance on external financing may distort the mission of public institutions. Informal study of funding for leading state universities from legislative funds and other-than-state sources; obvious and deeper causes of a reduction in state support; growth of massive subsidies; market influence on educational priorities; restoring trust.

Research

"Escaping the heavy hand of the state," *Economist,* June 13, 1992, p. 73.

Cites a new study conducted by the World Bank that states that the privatization of state-owned firms, all the rage with economic reformers, really does create wealth. Discussion of the study at a recent conference in Washington, D.C.; analysis of the data compiled in the study.

"Hot, at last," *Economist,* June 13, 1992, p. 76.

States that although privatization can encourage economic success, it can hardly guarantee it. The case of Amersham International; how Amersham began as an offshoot of Britain's Atomic Energy Authority; details of entrepreneurial benefits this firm has enjoyed.

Bruggink, T.H., "Privatization versus groundwater central management: Public policy choices," *American Journal of Economics & Sociology,* April 1992, p. 205.

Comments on a group of free-market natural resource economists who argue that the current system of limited property rights for groundwater users should be replaced by a new system of freely transferable property rights. Critical appraisal of their case for privatization; examines groundwater hydrology, common property, contamination and other third-party effects to determine the set of circumstances under which privatization would work best; more.

Goodman, J.B. & G.W. Loveman, "Does privatization serve the public interest?" *Harvard Business Review,* November/December 1991, p. 26.

Questions whether or not the current privatization trend

in governments around the world will serve the public interest. Supporters' claims that privatization brings improved efficiency and better quality; critics' warnings that profit will replace public interest in decision-making processes. Why privatization has gained popularity. List and summaries of several major publications on the concept.

Transportation

"Bob, you joker you," *Aviation Week,* June 1, 1992, p. 19.

Presents quotes from Robert J. Aaronson, president of the Air Transport Association, at a meeting in Houston over privatization of Los Angeles International Airport. Aaronson, frustrated by the fees, taxes and regulatory costs burdening the industry, suggested "privatizing the White House, and maybe Dan Quayle's vice presidential mansion next."

"Privatization could leave major airports in debt, port authority chairman warns," *Aviation Week,* May 25, 1992, p. 34.

Presents comments by Richard Leone, chairman of the 12-member board of the Port Authority of New York and New Jersey, which oversees the agency operating John F. Kennedy International, Newark International and LaGuardia airports, along with several other transportation facilities. Privatization in communities where you can't build anymore; several reasons airports should remain public; managing legal, community and intra-government problems.

"Right move on airport privatization," *Aviation Week,* May 11, 1992, p. 7.

Editorial. Asserts that President Bush's Executive Order on Infrastructure Privatization issued on April 30, promises improved airport capacity and is timely and important. City councils in communities large and small should review the order to determine whether to sell such public assets as airports, sewage treatment plants and transit systems to the private sector. Financial attractiveness; opposition from U.S. airlines; benefits for local and state governments.

Bancroft, T., "Privatization?" *Forbes,* June 24, 1991, p. 44.

Reports that even though the number of flights by major carriers under air-traffic control has grown a total of 15 percent since 1985, the system seems to be getting weaker. Tells how the controllers' equipment has not kept pace with new technologies. Why the federal bureaucracy is to blame; the $12 billion modernization plan for the industry. Problems getting the plan started; why the money isn't going toward the system.

Ott, J., "Bush order opens door for airport privatization," *Aviation Week,* May 11, 1992, p. 24.

Considers reaction to President Bush's recent executive order allowing privatization of airports that offers a full range of options for partnerships, removes a layer of politics and provides for entrepreneurial development of airports and adjacent sites. Evolution of airports into a mixture of quasi-public, municipal or state entities; Transportation Department analysis; comments concerning the Metropolitan Washington Airports Authority; airline reaction.

Pattison, S., "Privatizing airports," *Consumers' Research Magazine,* September 1991, p. 40.

Examines how privatization of public services continues to be a way in which financially strapped state and local governments can save taxpayer funds, while improving services to consumer. How selling LaGuardia and Kennedy airports could save New York money; other countries that have begun the privatization process.

Pattison, S., "Privatizing bus routes," *Consumers' Research Magazine,* June 1992, p. 40.

Reports that a proposal to privatize many of New Jersey's bus routes is getting serious attention in the state. The chairman of the state Assembly Transportation Committee, Alex DeCroce, has sponsored a bill to begin turning New Jersey Transit's bus routes over to private companies in the next two years. Plan could save New Jersey millions of dollars; opponents of the plan; more.

Seligman, D., "Infrastructure for sale," *Fortune,* Dec. 30, 1991, p. 139.

Suggests that the Massachusetts Turnpike may be privatized. Privatizing turnpikes is not something done every day in the U.S., but there is a devastatingly logical case for privatizing infrastructure nowadays. Familiar proposition that private managers manage better; Massachusetts Gov. William F. Weld's comments; more.

Back Issues

Great Research on Current Issues Starts Right Here... Recent topics covered by The CQ Researcher are listed below. Issues dated before May 10, 1991, were published under the name of Editorial Research Reports.

MAY 1991
School Choice
Racial Quotas
Animal Rights
U.S. and Japan

JUNE 1991
Children and Divorce
Teenage Suicide
Endangered Species
Europe 1992

JULY 1991
Teenagers and Abortion
Soviet Republics Rebel
Mexico's Emergence
Athletes and Drugs

AUGUST 1991
Sexual Harassment
Fetal Tissue Research
Oil Imports
The Palestinians

SEPTEMBER 1991
Police Brutality
Advertising Under Attack
Saving the Forests
Foster Care Crisis

Back issues are available for $4.00 (subscribers) or $7.00 (non-subscribers). Quantity discounts apply to orders over ten. To order, call Congressional Quarterly 1-800-432-2250.

Binders are available for $15.00. To order call 1-800-638-1710.

OCTOBER 1991
Pay-Per-View TV
Youth Gangs
Gene Therapy
World Hunger

NOVEMBER 1991
Fast-Food Shake-Up
The Greening of Eastern Europe
Business' Role in Education
Cuba In Crisis

DECEMBER 1991
Retiree Health Benefits
Asian Americans
The Obscenity Debate
The Disabilities Act

JANUARY 1992
Term Limits
Oil Spills
Hunting Controversy
Alternative Medicine

FEBRUARY 1992
Threatened Coastlines
New Era in Asia
Assisted Suicide
Jobs in the '90s

MARCH 1992
Women and Sports
Underage Drinking
Garbage Crisis
Mafia Crackdown

APRIL 1992
Ozone Depletion
Welfare Reform
Politicians and Privacy
Illegal Immigration

MAY 1992
Native Americans
Jobs vs. Environment
Too Many Lawsuits?
Fairness in Salaries

JUNE 1992
Nuclear Proliferation
Food Irradiation
Lead Poisoning
Hard Times for Libraries

JULY 1992
Alternative Energy
Prescription Drug Prices
Alzheimer's Disease
Infant Mortality

AUGUST 1992
The Homeless
Work, Family and Stress
NATO's Changing Role
Marine Mammals vs. Fish

SEPTEMBER 1992
Domestic Partners
Violence in Schools
Public Broadcasting
Women in the Military

OCTOBER 1992
Depression
U.S. Auto Industry
Youth Apprenticeships
Hispanic Americans

NOVEMBER 1992
Physical Fitness

Future Topics

▶ *Paying for College*

▶ *U.S. Policy in the Pacific*

▶ *Smoking in Public*

Paying for College

Is the price of a college education too high?

I N THESE LEAN TIMES, A COLLEGE DEGREE IS
considered especially vital to success. But for more
than a decade, the cost of higher education has been
growing at almost twice the rate of inflation. With
sluggish economic conditions threatening job security across
the country, parents and prospective students alike are
increasingly questioning whether they can afford the high cost
of a bachelor's degree — and if it's worth the expense. They
frequently complain that schools are charging more and
giving less. Indeed, colleges and universities have been
struggling to survive serious funding cutbacks by raising
tuition, increasing class size, cutting faculty and dropping
academic programs. Meanwhile, concern over the U.S. budget
deficit is eroding support for federal student-aid programs.

C_Q   **November 20, 1992 • Volume 2, No. 43 • 1001-1024**

Formerly Editorial Research Reports

COVER PHOTO: KEVIN SCHUMACHER

CQ Researcher

November 20, 1992
Volume 2, No. 43

EDITOR
Sandra Stencel

MANAGING EDITOR
Thomas J. Colin

ASSOCIATE EDITOR
Richard L. Worsnop

STAFF WRITERS
Charles S. Clark
Mary H. Cooper
Rodman D. Griffin

PRODUCTION EDITOR
Sarah E. Merritt

EDITORIAL ASSISTANT
Michael M. Taylor

GRAPHICS
Jack Auldridge

PUBLISHED BY
Congressional Quarterly Inc.

CHAIRMAN
Andrew Barnes

VICE CHAIRMAN
Andrew P. Corty

EDITOR AND PUBLISHER
Neil Skene

EXECUTIVE EDITOR
Robert W. Merry

ASSOCIATE PUBLISHER
John J. Coyle

© 1993 Congressional Quarterly Inc.

The CQ Researcher (ISSN 1056-2036). Formerly Editorial Research Reports. Published weekly (48 times per year, not printed the first Friday of any month with five Fridays) by Congressional Quarterly Inc., 1414 22nd St., N.W., Washington, D.C. 20037. Rates are furnished upon request. Second-class postage paid at Washington, D.C. POSTMASTER: Send address changes to The CQ Researcher, 1414 22nd St., N.W., Washington, D.C. 20037.

Paying for College

By Mary H. Cooper

THE ISSUES

Gerard is a 19-year-old sophomore at the University of Wisconsin-Madison, the flagship of the state's well-regarded public university system. A native of suburban Chicago, some 200 miles away, he chose Wisconsin because of its program in journalism and communications. But Gerard may transfer to the University of Illinois. It's not that Wisconsin has disappointed him: He's still enthusiastic about the course offerings, and the social life in "Madtown" is hard to beat. The problem is money.

In the year since Gerard enrolled, tuition for out-of-state students has risen more than 9 percent. Like other public colleges and universities, Wisconsin charges more for out-of-state students than state residents. The increase pushed Gerard's tuition from $6,927 to $7,571. And that doesn't include room and board, books and other expenses, which bring his annual bill to more than $12,000.

Wisconsin's tuition increase is not unusual. Hit by falling tax revenues in recent years, states around the country have for the first time reduced funding for higher education. *(See map, p. 1012.)* As a result, public institutions have had to raise fees.

According to a recent survey by the College Board, a nonprofit organization committed to raising academic standards and broadening access to higher education, tuition at public colleges and universities is up 10 percent over last year. That's the second-straight year of double-digit increases — and three times the inflation rate. Private institutions raised tuition by 6 to 7 percent. And these increases are less steep than in recent years. *(See graph, p. 1005.)*

Students were protesting tuition increases at San Diego State University.

Kevin Schumacher

As tuition has risen faster than personal income, students and their families have been scrambling to find additional funding. Gerard, for example, stayed in Madison last summer and got a job. He also applied to a variety of programs offering grants and loans, but ran into a brick wall. "All I got was a Stafford loan *(see glossary, p. 1014)* for $1,600, which covered about half the tuition for one semester," he says. "I searched everywhere, we tried everything, but that's all I could get." Gerard's father, a magazine-publishing executive, earns more than $50,000 a year, which made the family ineligible for most financial aid, even though Gerard is one of five children, two currently in college.

"My parents put a second mortgage on the house," Gerard says, "and my mother just got a job as an accountant for a record company, even though she didn't really want to."

For his part, Gerard is trying to find more part-time work, but the competition is stiff: Half of the university's students hold jobs. He's at an additional disadvantage because he doesn't qualify for the federally supported "work-study" program.

"We originally had an arrangement that my parents would help me pay for college, and then when I got out of school, I would start paying them back," Gerard says. But the recent tuition increases — and the prospect of more to come — have disrupted their plans. "It hasn't come down to where I have to drop out of school," he says. "But if I can get accepted, I'm probably going to transfer to Illinois, just because I would be paying in-state tuition."

Gerard's financial problems are hardly unique. As students across the country try to balance the desire for a college degree with the search for funding, these are some of the questions they and their parents are asking:

Are students from middle-income families being squeezed out of higher education?

Family income largely determines how the rapid rise in college costs affects students. Affluent families often include the cost of their children's higher education in their investment strategies years before the bill actually comes due. For low-income families, there are scholarships and federally supported financial-aid packages. *(See story, p. 1010.)*

But middle-income families must often struggle for years to set aside college funds. Over the past decade, however, the cost of higher education has risen much faster than the value of most investments. Few middle-income investors will have accumulated the sums needed to put one or more children through four years of private college, where tuitions and fees alone now average $10,498 a year. If room and board, books and supplies, transportation and other costs are thrown in, the average yearly cost of private college is $17,027. *(See table, p. 1004.)*

How Much College Costs

Tuition and fees at four-year public colleges and universities averaged $2,315 in 1991-92, compared with $10,498 at private schools. Overall, the cost of a year at a public school averaged $8,071, compared with $17,027 at private schools. Tuition and fees at two-year schools averaged $1,292 at public schools and $5,621 at private institutions.

Average College Costs 1991-92

4-Year Colleges	Public Colleges		Private Colleges	
	Resident	Commuter	Resident	Commuter
Tuition and fees	$2,315	$2,315	$10,498	$10,498
Books and supplies	528	528	531	531
Room and board*	3,526	1,549	4,575	1,762
Transportation	497	843	487	794
Other	1,205	1,238	936	1,036
Total	$8,071	$6,473	$17,027	$14,621
2-Year Colleges				
Tuition and fees	$1,292	$1,292	$5,621	$5,621
Books and supplies	502	502	512	512
Room and board	-	1,592	3,750	1,558
Transportation	-	926	517	812
Other	-	970	866	941
Total	-	$5,282	$11,266	$9,444

* Room not included for commuter students
- Insufficient data

Note: The figures are weighted by enrollment to reflect the charges incurred by the average undergraduate enrolled at each type of institution.

Sources: The College Board, as published in The Chronicle of Higher Education *(Oct. 21, 1992)*

Although tuitions and fees at public institutions are rising faster today than at private institutions, public schools are still a bargain, averaging $2,315 in tuition and fees ($8,071 if other costs are included). For a traditional, four-year undergraduate program away from home, that comes out to $32,284, compared with $68,108 for a private college degree.

As a result, many bright middle-income students are shifting their sights away from prestigious private institutions to the flagship institutions of statewide systems, such as the University of Michigan, the University of California-Berkeley and the University of North Carolina-Chapel Hill. According to one survey, 28 percent of college freshmen now say low tuition was an important reason for choosing their school, up from 21 percent the year before.[1]

"What we're now seeing is a gentrification of the public flagship universities because students with family incomes of $60,000 to $100,000 don't qualify for much in the way of aid at private colleges," says Arthur M. Hauptman, an authority on college financing and consultant to the American Council on Education. "They see that the public flagship theoretically offers a pretty good education at one-fifth the price."

While this shift may help some middle-income families, Hauptman says it undermines the mission of public schools: to broaden access to higher education by subsidizing colleges with taxpayers' money. "Since there are only a limited number of slots at the flagships," he says, "the wealthier kids from suburban schools with better grades and better test scores squeeze out poorer kids, who then go to a state college or a community college or the regional, private liberal arts college that will offer them $5,000 in aid. Or they don't go to college at all."

Representatives of private institutions say these concerns may be exaggerated. Richard F. Rosser, president of the National Association of Independent Colleges and Universities, points out that the average family income of students at private and public colleges and universities is actually about the same: $36,000. While that confirms the movement of middle-income students toward public schools, Rosser says, it also shows that "private colleges are not just the reserve of the elite or the upper class. It's not true and, frankly, it has never been true."

While concerns over college affordability focus on the middle class, there is evidence that the poor are also suffering, despite the widespread availability of financial aid to low-income students. In a recent study, Charles F. Manski, a professor of economics at the University of Wisconsin-Madison, found that four-year college attendance among high-income high school graduates has risen from 54 to 60 percent since the 1970s. But the percentage of lower-income youth going on to four-year institutions is essentially unchanged at 27 percent.[2]

Meanwhile, the cost of graduate school poses an even higher barrier. Spending additional time to obtain a master's degree, Ph.D. or professional degree in medicine or law simply means that much more time spending rather than earning money. "We've loaded our students with so much debt by the time they get out," says James B. Appleberry, president of the American Association of State Colleges and Universities, "that many are unwilling to go on to graduate study and go back in debt again, forgoing yet again their ability to buy consumer products. That's a very sad scenario for the future of this country."

Is the quality of higher education going down at the same time tuition is going up?

As college costs continue to rise, students and their families are looking more carefully at what they are getting for their money. Increasingly, they are finding that the college experience falls short of their expectations.

" The cost of education has been going up while the quality has been going down," says Stacey Leyton, president of the United States Student Association. In the public sector, especially, "classes are being cut out, library hours are being shortened and lectures are being canceled.

"It's very difficult for students now to get into the classes they need," Leyton says. "In the California community colleges, they joke that getting into a community college is like getting a hunting license: Admission is the signal to hunt for classes."

In the past, the problem was acute for first- or second-year students, she says, but now it is affecting everyone. In many cases, public colleges are even cutting out classes that seniors need to graduate. "Some are only being offered once every two years," Leyton says, "so people will have to wait for another year because they can't fulfill their require-

ments on time."

Apart from cuts in course offerings and student services, some schools are coming under closer scrutiny over the ways they allocate increasingly precious operating funds. Stanford University came under fire last year for using $500,000 in federal research grant money for non-academic purposes, including the renovation of President Donald Kennedy's official residence.

Salary inequities are also raising eyebrows — and hackles. According to an editorial in the student daily at the University of Colorado-Boulder, the school pays its football coach $360,000 a year, seven times the average professor's salary. "So when you run across that rare professor who exudes a love of learning, and of life, let him or her know," advises the editorial. "It might be the only re-

ward for a job well done."[3]

Prestigious research universities like Stanford, Harvard and Princeton, which are private, and Colorado, North Carolina and Virginia, which are public schools, are coming under fire for more than the way they spend funds. These much-vaunted institutions offer broad fields of study at both the undergraduate and graduate levels. Their emphasis on research draws prominent scientists and other experts, who are encouraged not only to continue researching and publishing but also to teach.

But as more and more students flock to research universities, pressure is building, especially on the public schools, to improve the quality of undergraduate instruction. "For the past several decades, there has been an expanding and concerted effort from within the public higher

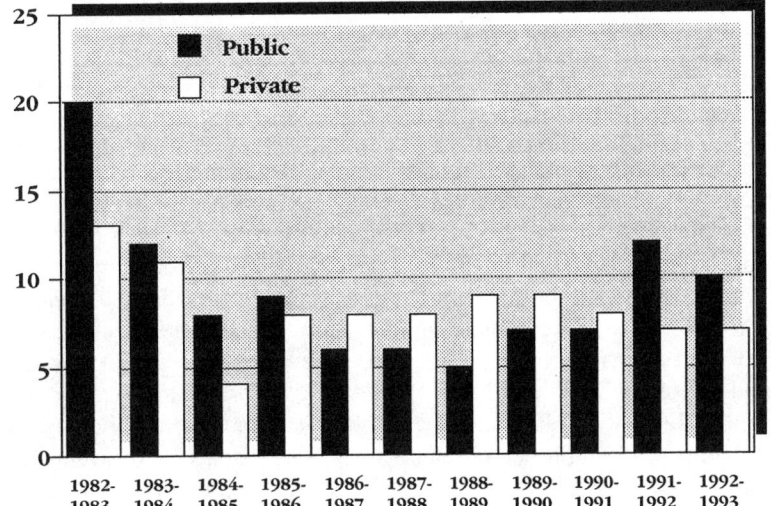

Tuition on the Rise

Tuition at public colleges and universities climbed by 10 percent this year, the second year in a row of double-digit increases. Increases in tuition at private colleges held at 7 percent, the same as in 1991-92.

Percent increase

Sources: *The College Board, as published in* The Chronicle of Higher Education *(Oct. 21, 1992)*

Some Fields Pay Better Than Others

Earnings among college graduates are significantly affected by their major field of study. Bachelor's degrees in economics, engineering, mathematics and business brought the highest earnings; home economics, education, English/journalism and liberal arts had the lowest. For holders of advanced degrees, those with professional degrees (medicine and law) and those in physical science, engineering and business had the highest earnings.

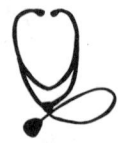

Field of study	Average monthly earnings	
	Bachelor's degrees	Advanced degrees
Agriculture/forestry	$2,154	------
Biology	$1,640	------
Business/management	$2,330	$3,210
Economics	$2,756	------
Education	$1,181	$1,962
Engineering	$2,670	$3,369
English/journalism	$1,431	$1,749
Home economics	$1,079	------
Law	------	$3,808
Liberal arts/humanities	$1,346	$1,587
Mathematics/statistics	$2,548	------
Medicine/dentistry	------	$5,607
Nursing/pharmacy/technical health	$1,367	$2,116
Physical/earth sciences	$1,467	$4,050
Psychology	$2,067	$2,482
Religion/theology	------	$1,975
Social sciences	$1,674	$2,377

Sources: U.S. Department of Commerce, What It's Worth? Educational Background and Economic Status: Spring 1987, *as published in* Occupational Outlook Quarterly, *summer 1992*

education system to emulate the research-dominated model of higher education," concludes a recent congressional report. "Along the way, the higher education system began to equate this search for prestige with quality. Therefore, by this reasoning, the higher the university's prestige, the better the quality of education provided.

"Unfortunately, not only is there a lack of support for this view, but there is convincing evidence that its pursuit has had a detrimental effect on the education provided to our nation's students, especially those at the undergraduate level."[4]

As professors dedicate more time to research, they spend less time with undergraduate students, employing graduate students to teach many of their courses. "In other words, parents are paying ever-increasing tuition to have students teach students," the report states. Because universities reward research more than teaching, according to the report, professors spend a maximum of eight hours a week in the classroom, on average.

Further, because professors are abdicating their responsibility for advising students, universities are forced to hire additional support staff, producing "administrative bloat" that

pushes up costs and thus tuition. And, due to budgetary constraints, universities are disproportionately cutting back undergraduate courses and consolidating sections, creating huge classes. The report cites a marketing class at Colorado that had 618 students and an introductory political science class at the University of Illinois-Urbana with 1,156 students.

The victim of the quest for prestige through research, the report concludes, is the "exasperated and poorly treated undergraduate. *They* are the ones who are taking the cutbacks on the chin in the form of [teaching assistants] posing as professors, fewer class selections, over-enrolled required courses, shorter library hours and eliminated departments."[5]

While they agree that their institutions need to improve undergraduate education, spokesmen for both public and private research institutions criticize the congressional report. "That study was a gross distortion and a terrible oversimplification," says Rosser of the National Association of Independent Colleges and Universities. "It assumes that all colleges and universities apparently are research universities or, if they are not, they are trying to be like that. The great bulk of the institutions in my organization are four-year undergraduate colleges where teaching has always been primary."

If anything, Rosser says, undergraduates are getting even more for their money. "If you go back 20 or 30 years, there was no such thing as career counseling, and financial aid was just in its infancy. Today, all you have to do is cut out the career-planning and placement office and you're going to have parents and students all over the place demanding an audience with the president."

Spokesmen for schools where research clearly is emphasized defend that practice. "The mission of the large public research universities is to do research in the public interest," says C. Peter Magrath, president of the National Association of State Universities and Land-Grant Colleges, whose members include the big flagship universities. "I think it's one of the things that works well for the United States, and they are funded for this by both state and federal support." At the same time, Magrath also recognizes that "more attention must be given to undergraduate education."

Finally, experts point out that the mission of most postsecondary schools is confined to teaching at the undergraduate level. These include virtually all four-year liberal arts colleges, both public and private, and community colleges, which usually grant a two-year associate degree that can be applied toward a four-year degree at most colleges and universities. *(See story, p. 1018.)*

Is the investment of tens of thousands of dollars in an undergraduate degree likely to pay off in today's job market?

That's a very real question to a recent college graduate who now works at the U.S. Student Association in Washington. When her tuition unexpectedly doubled, she had to take a full-time job to supplement her student loans. But she still graduated owing $20,000. "She says now if she had known she would graduate with that much debt, she probably wouldn't have started college in the first place," says association President Leyton.

But Leyton would hardly support that choice. "Studies show that a college degree will increase your earning power," she says. "Also, a lot of people say that a college degree now is worth what a high school diploma was worth about 20 years ago. So to compete in the job market, a degree is almost a necessity."

Indeed, Labor Department studies show that college graduates are facing a more competitive job market than in the 1980s. Only about seven out of 10 graduates who enter the labor market between 1990 and 2005 can expect to find jobs requiring a college degree, compared with about

eight out of 10 from 1984 to 1990, according to one study.[6]

The major field of study a student chooses has a significant impact on the degree's value. According to Daniel Hecker, an economist at the Bureau of Labor Statistics, graduates with bachelor's degrees in business, economics, engineering and mathematics had the highest earnings, while majors in education, English/journalism, home economics and liberal arts had the lowest. *(See table, p. 1006.)* The graduate degrees that produced the highest career earnings were in business, engineering, law, medicine and science.[7]

The economic benefits of a bachelor's degree are less obvious when students accumulate huge debts they have to pay off after graduation. In 1986, the latest year for which the Department of Education has data, half of all four-year-college graduates had some debt, up from a third in 1977. And the median debt had more

than doubled, from $2,000 to $4,800, over the same period.

Those figures tell only part of the story, however. "I don't get so tense about middle-income or upper-income students [borrowing money], and I certainly don't get so upset about stories of people who wind up as lawyers who have a lot of debt, because the fact is they tend to get a lot of economic return from their education," says Michael S. McPherson, a professor of economics at Williams College in Massachusetts. "But if you look at where lower-income people go to college, if you look at their probabilities of completion, at the kinds of jobs they get after college, it's not as gold-plated an investment for them as it typically is for more affluent students."

In general, McPherson says, college is an economically sound investment if you complete a bachelor's degree. But about half of all youth who enroll in college never obtain a degree, according to one study.[8] "If

How Education Affects Earnings

Average monthly earnings rise sharply for workers with higher degrees, primarily because of higher pay scales but also because workers with higher educational levels have lower unemployment rates.

Educational level	Average monthly earnings	Percent premium over high school graduates
Professional	$4,003	335%
Doctorate	$3,637	295%
Master's degree	$2,378	158%
Bachelor's degree	$1,829	99%
Associate degree	$1,458	58%
Postsecondary vocational school	$1,088	18%
Some college but no degree	$1,088	18%
High school graduate	$921	0%

Sources: U.S. Department of Commerce, What It's Worth? Educational Background and Economic Status: Spring 1987, *as published in* Occupational Outlook Quarterly, *summer 1992*

those people are borrowing a lot," McPherson says, "then it's much less obvious that there's a real payoff to going to college."

As long as the student makes it through graduation, then, investing in a college education appears to pay off in time. But when it comes to choosing between a private and a public institution, the evidence is more subjective. "It is probably the case that a Harvard, Yale or Princeton is worth the difference in price, in terms of your economic prospects, the job market and graduate school," says Arthur Hauptman. "But in terms of the also-ran private colleges, I don't think you can make that case credibly. People will pay more for those private colleges because they want small classes, an intimate campus and real professors teaching, not because the job market values those schools more than public institutions." ■

1970s, undergraduate students numbered more than 11.5 million in 1979.[11] During the 1980s, when funding problems began to emerge, the increases in enrollment slowed somewhat. Even so, there were 14.3 million students in the nation's 3,535 institutions of higher education at the beginning of the 1992 academic year — nearly 10 times the number of college students in 1939.

BACKGROUND

Postwar College Boom

The end of World War II unleashed three decades of unprecedented economic expansion in the United States. With their growing prosperity, American workers began sending their children to college. Many college students of the 1950s, '60s and '70s were the first members of their families to go beyond high school. The ranks of college students grew from 1.5 million in 1939 to 2.7 million by 1949 and 3.6 million in 1959.[9]

Until the mid-1960s, however, access to higher education was often limited by a family's ability to pay for it, or by the availability of the G.I. Bill. "Up to that point, either the states appropriated money for public colleges and tuition was kept so low that you could get in, or, where tuition was high, low-income people simply couldn't go," says James Appleberry of the American Association of State Colleges and Universities.

In the 1960s and '70s, both the federal and state governments took far-reaching steps to improve access to higher education. To help high school graduates without the money or time to spend in traditional, four-year programs, states across the country set up networks of community colleges offering two-year associate degrees. Designed to have broad appeal, community colleges offered low tuition, convenient locations for commuter students, night courses for working students and open enrollments for anyone with a high-school diploma or its equivalent.

The federal government's efforts to improve access to higher education centered around financial-aid programs aimed at lower-income students. The biggest step in that direction was the Higher Education Act, which President Lyndon B. Johnson signed in 1965. The law created a set of programs offering grants and loans to students in varying amounts according to their families' ability to pay for college. As a result of the law and later amendments, federal funds awarded to students skyrocketed from $782 million before the law went into effect to $19.7 billion a decade later.[10]

The combination of state and federal initiatives led to a boom in college attendance. During the 1960s, total enrollment at public and private institutions more than doubled, exceeding 8 million students by the end of the decade. Thanks largely to the new community colleges, the public sector's share of enrollment increased during the 1960s, accounting for almost 80 percent of all enrollment.

After further increases during the

Rising College Costs

With so many more students attending college than ever before, why haven't tuitions gone down? After all, any businessman can tell you that the more you make of a product the less it will cost to produce each item. Likewise, as college enrollments have expanded, it would seem logical that the costs of educating each student in a given institution would go down. But instead, tuitions have skyrocketed, increasing at about twice the rate of inflation during the last decade alone. The reasons for the rising cost of higher education can be found in the way colleges are funded. And those reasons differ between public and private institutions.

Because public colleges and universities depend overwhelmingly on tax revenues, their financial health mirrors their states' economies. When the economy is booming, high tax revenues from businesses and individuals as well as from taxes on sales and other transactions raise the pool of funds available for higher education. In recessionary times, tax revenues fall, shrinking the pool of funds for higher education. "At public colleges, tuitions are going up quite rapidly right now because they are so dependent on state funding," says college financing consultant Arthur Hauptman. "When state funds dry up, tuition is one of the things they

Continued on p. 1010

Chronology

1960s *Following two decades of rising college enrollments, a federal financial-aid program is introduced to expand access to higher education among lower-income youth.*

1965

The Higher Education Act creates a set of programs offering grants and loans to college students on the basis of family income. These include Pell grants, which recipients do not have to repay; Guaranteed Student Loans, later known as Stafford loans, which students must repay after graduation; and Work-Study programs, which enable students to pay for part of their education by working during the school year at on-campus or public-sector jobs. The law also authorizes a number of programs offering loans to families of students to help pay for college.

— • —

1970s *Boosted by federal student-aid programs, college enrollments continue to rise.*

1970-71

Federal student aid exceeds $10.5 billion for the academic year, up from $782 million in 1963-64. Student aid provided by the states also rises dramatically over the same period, from $230 million to $755 million. At the same time, colleges and universities give out more than $3 billion, more than double the amount of aid awarded by institutions in 1970-71.

1974

As appropriations for federal student-aid programs fail to keep pace with the annual rise in college tuitions, loans begin to outweigh

grants in the mix of federal student-aid packages. As the trend continues over the next decade, the amount of federal student loans is three times the amount awarded as grants by 1984.

1975

The number of students enrolled at American public and private institutions in the fall of this year tops 11 million. That's up from just under 6 million in 1965, when the Higher Education Act went into effect, and almost 10 times the number of college students who were enrolled in 1939.

October 1979

Congress creates the Department of Education. Among its responsibilities is the administration of federal student-aid programs.

— • —

1980s *College tuition and fees rise at almost twice the rate of inflation.*

1989

President Bush convenes an "education summit" with the nation's governors. Among its goals is a substantial increase in the proportion of qualified high-school students who go on to college by the turn of the century.

— • —

1990s *With a rise in the population of college-age Americans, the number of college graduates is expected to increase. But the number of jobs requiring a bachelor's degree is expected to fall dramatically during the decade.*

July 23, 1992

President Bush signs the Higher Education Act Amendments of 1992. The measure, reauthorizing the 1965 Higher Education Act, makes federal aid more widely available to middle-income students and increases the maximum amount that needy students can get through the Pell grant and Stafford loan programs. A separate loan program would be available to students regardless of family income.

Sept. 2, 1992

A federal district court rules that the Massachusetts Institute of Technology (MIT) and eight other private Northeastern institutions — the so-called Ivy League schools — violated antitrust law by sharing information on financial-aid applications and agreeing to a common aid offer to applicants to one or more members of the group. Although the association, known as the Overlap Group, disbanded and all the other schools agreed to discontinue the practice before the ruling, MIT argued that the collaboration did not violate antitrust law and that it broadened access to education to needy students. MIT announces it will appeal the decision.

Nov. 3, 1992

Gov. Bill Clinton, D-Ark., wins the presidential election. During the campaign, he presented a plan to replace most of the federal student-loan programs with a National Service Trust Fund. Students could borrow up to $10,000 annually from this fund regardless of family income, on condition that they pay off their debt through payroll deductions from subsequent job earnings or by giving two years of public or military service.

Paying for College: How to Get Help

If there's one piece of advice that advisers give financially strapped high school students, it's never to rule out a college or university because they can't afford the tuition. "For heaven's sake, if you want to go to a particular school, go see if you might be accepted and then go and talk with the financial-aid officer to see what's available," says Richard F. Rosser, president of the National Association of Independent Colleges and Universities. "Over 65 percent of the students in our colleges are getting financial aid of some kind."

Students should think twice, however, before applying for aid from a "reach" school — a school where their odds of being admitted are slim. "Although most admissions offices will select the majority of each class on the basis of merit alone, in borderline cases preference may be given to those with the ability to pay," says *The Insider's Guide to the Colleges*, a leading college directory.†

Prospective college students should make the search for financial aid an integral part of the application process. Even those who do not expect to qualify because their family income is too high should take the time to apply to several aid sources, experts say.

And time is what it will take. Students should contact each school's financial-aid office to learn how to apply for federal, state and institutional, or campus-based, assistance. In most cases, they can submit a single standardized form — usually The College Board's College Scholarship Service's Financial Aid Form (FAF) or the American College Testing Program's Family Financial Statement (FFS) — for both federal and institutional aid. These forms, several pages long, ask for even more details about a family's financial situation than the federal income tax return

On the basis of this information, the agencies assess the family's ability to pay for college and pass that information on to the schools where the student has applied for aid. They, in turn, will decide how much assistance to offer, based on the calculated "expected family contribution" and the funds at their disposal. Because much aid is granted on a first-come, first-served basis, students should submit all required forms as soon as possible after Jan. 1.

Federal aid consists primarily of Pell grants, three loan programs — Stafford, PLUS and SLS loans — and work-study, a program that allows students to earn money to help pay for school. Some students, mostly those from lower-income families, receive help from more than one federal program, though federal-aid packages have included more loans than grants in recent years.

Students who don't qualify for federal aid may get help from the schools themselves. Most private schools offer need-based grants and loans, as well as merit and athletic scholarships, in order to draw students who otherwise would be forced to attend less expensive public institutions. Public colleges and universities also offer aid to students who do not qualify for federal grants and loans.

Experts generally advise students whose aid applications are rejected to plead their case directly by calling or writing the school's financial-aid administrator. Explaining financial obstacles that are not adequately reflected on the standardized forms may change the school's assessment of need. Decisions are final, however, on applications for federal or state aid.

High-school seniors are often bombarded with mailings from private tuition-assistance services offering to find sources of financial aid. Although some of these firms may indeed uncover valuable sources of money from private companies, veterans' groups and foundations, aid experts warn that many fail to hold to their promise. In any case, students can turn up most of these less-known sources of aid at any public library.

The Nov. 3 presidential victory of Gov. Bill Clinton, D-Ark., may mean new financial-aid possibilities as early as next year. During the campaign, Clinton promised that, if elected, he would introduce a new National Service Trust Fund, which would essentially dismantle the current federal aid system. Under the proposal, all students, regardless of family income, could receive $10,000 a year to pay for college. Upon graduation, they would repay the government doing two years of public service work or through payroll deductions from another job.

---

† Staff of *The Yale Daily News*, ed., *The Insider's Guide to the Colleges, 1992*, (1991), p. 23.

Continued from p. 1008
use to make ends meet."

During the eight-year U.S. economic expansion that began in 1982, state funding of public higher education increased. This occurred in spite of the growing share of state budgets that went to pay for Medicaid and other federal programs that states are required to fund. "Higher education's share of the state tax dollar went down slightly during the 1980s, but the growth in state revenues was large enough from the economic growth of the period to balance that out," Hauptman says. As a result, he says, state funding for higher education doubled over the decade, from $20 billion in 1980 to $40 billion in 1990. Even when adjusted for inflation, the increase amounted to 25 percent.

But if public school tuitions so closely track the states' economic health, why do they only go up in bad times and fail to come back down when state coffers fill with tax revenues during recoveries? One reason is the tendency of colleges to offer new services in flush times and resist cutting back when the economy turns sour. "Once you build up a budget, it's not easy to crunch it down," Hauptman says. "There tends to be a roller-coaster effect, which is, I think, one of the unhealthy things about how states fund education."

Sure of better times to come, public institutions are loath to cut services and tend to raise tuitions to tide themselves over until public funding rises again. "Because of this relationship between tuition and state funding," says Hauptman, "public-sector tuitions tend to grow faster during a recession, which I think is a basic fault of the underlying system."

The Squeeze on Private Colleges

Private colleges and universities also respond to overall economic conditions, but in a different way from their counterparts in the public sector. Private schools receive the bulk of their funds directly from the consumers of their services — students and their families. As a result, Hauptman explains, "private college tuitions tend to moderate somewhat during recessions because they are higher to begin with, and people are more likely to feel squeezed during recessions to pay their tuitions." Private school tuitions, up 7 percent this year, are in fact rising less quickly today than public school tuitions, which rose 10 percent.

But private sector tuitions have failed to decrease as much as one would expect during the current economic slowdown. Hauptman attributes this trend to a change in tuition policy among private schools over the past decade. Until the 1980s, private institutions tended to hold tuition increases below the rate of inflation in an effort

to compete with each other for highly qualified students.

"During the 1980s, private colleges chose to compete for a dwindling number of traditional college-age students not by lowering the price, which would be what you would normally expect, but by competing in the quality of what they provided," Hauptman says. They began charging higher tuitions and using part of the surplus funds for financial aid to draw more needy and minority students and thus improve diversity among their students, for higher faculty salaries to draw more prestigious professors and for investing in new services and facilities.

"If you go to nice private colleges today," Hauptman says, "typically there are a couple of new buildings on campus that were built in the last 10 years." More often than not, he says, these are not academic facilities but recreational buildings or dormitories. "If you go to a small liberal arts college in the middle of nowhere, you will find a new performing arts center or a new indoor track or swimming pool." Thus, although tuitions at private colleges and universities increased dramatically during the 1980s, the increase did not necessarily reflect an improvement in the quality of education.

Spokesmen for private institutions defend their record, blaming much of the rise in tuitions on new administrative expenses over which the colleges have little control. Administrative costs are the fastest-growing component of college expenditures, according to a recent congressional report, increasing more than 60 percent from 1975 to 1985, when administrative staffs at colleges and universities grew three times as fast as faculty.[12]

Richard Rosser, who was president of De Pauw University in Indiana before he became president of the National Association of Independent Colleges and Universities, points to the increase in crime and other societal changes as a major reason for the higher administrative costs. "I saw our security force increase eightfold in the 10 years I was a college president," he says. "We had to add administrative staff for financial-aid administration, career counseling and psychological counseling, as well as do our level best to keep our campuses drug-free and do whatever we could to keep down the use of alcohol. All this demands an increase in staff." ∎

CURRENT SITUATION

Improving Quality

Although there is little sign of moderation in the pace of tuition hikes, public and private colleges and universities are making new efforts to provide students with more for their money. In large part, they are responding to students and their families, who feel they receive a poor return on their investment in higher

education. In a recent poll of registered voters, high college costs and declining education standards ranked second and fifth, respectively, among voters' chief concerns, ahead of concern over the nation's economy.[13]

For starters, many educators say, the balance between teaching and research should be restored at institutions where students complain that professors ignore undergraduate teaching. That can be done by adjusting salaries to make teaching more attractive, says James S. Fairweather, an associate professor of higher education at Pennsylvania State University. In a study of faculty pay scales, Fairweather found that schools

Waning State Support for Higher Education

Public colleges and universities in 17 states — including such populous ones as California, Florida, Illinois, New York and Ohio — are receiving lower state appropriations this year than two years ago. The East was particularly hard hit; only four of the states were located west of the Mississippi. Overall, state appropriations for higher education are about 1 percent less than they were two years ago — probably the first two-year drop in the country's history, according to a study by the Center for Higher Education at Illinois State University.

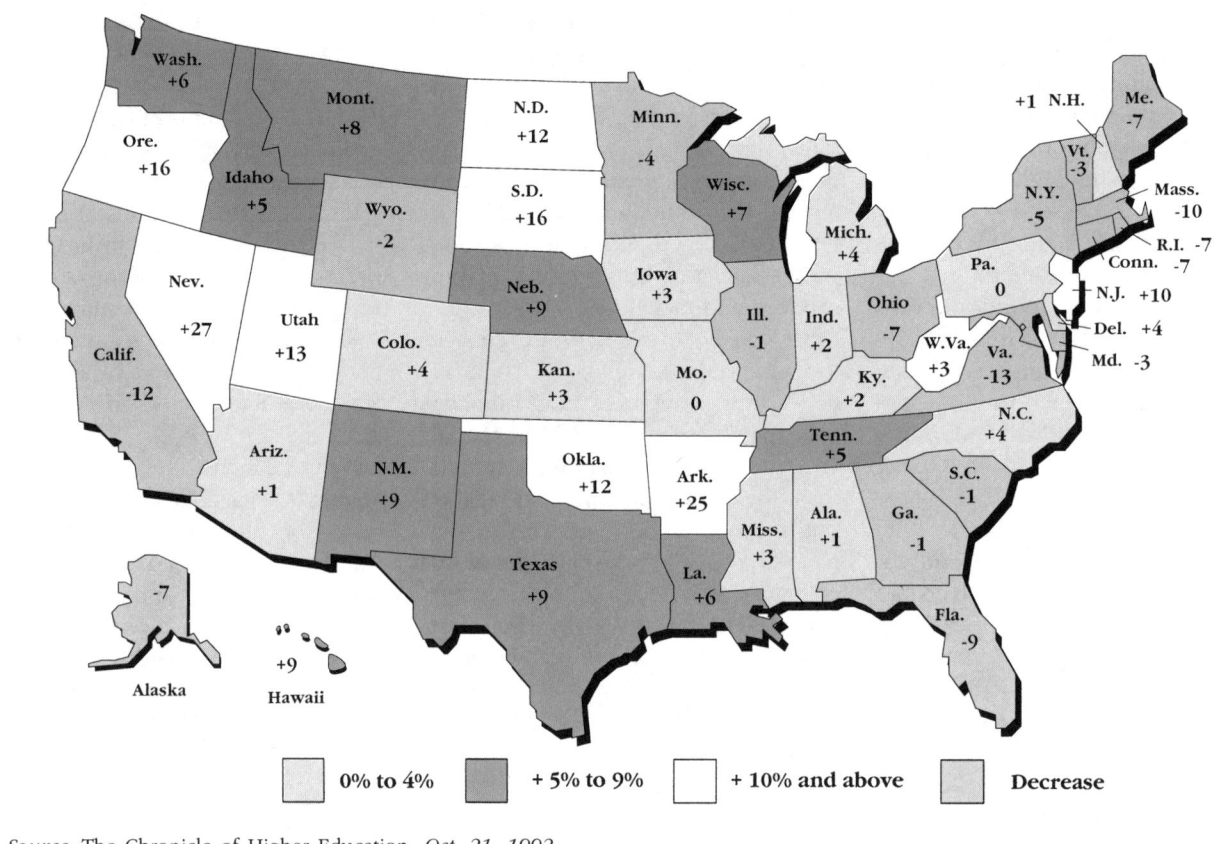

0% to 4%	+ 5% to 9%	+ 10% and above	Decrease

Source: The Chronicle of Higher Education, *Oct. 21, 1992*

reward professors more for doing research than teaching.[14] "We're actually still following the postwar agenda set in the wake of the Soviet launch of Sputnik, which really pushed everybody to do research," Fairweather says.

"I'm not interested in bashing higher education," Fairweather adds, "because we are doing things that pretty much people asked us to do, and we're doing a lot of things well." But the fact remains, he says, that "the people who are doing research and publishing are getting paid the most because we really haven't had a

new national agenda to replace that reward system."

Some states and private research institutions have taken steps on their own to restore the balance between research and undergraduate teaching. The California State University system, for example, mandates a minimum number of courses professors are required to teach each semester. The public universities in Ohio, including Ohio State, are also examining ways to place greater emphasis on undergraduate education.

Other big institutions have set up

"living-learning" facilities that combine dormitory and classroom areas to give undergraduate students a more tangible link to the school's academic resources. The University of Maryland, for example, introduced such a center for 100 honors students this fall in the hope of attracting talented and motivated students to its flagship campus at College Park.

"The public universities are working like heck to maintain and in some cases to improve the quality of undergraduate education," says Magrath of the National Association of State Universities and Land-Grant Colleges. "They are really addressing the issue of the appropriate emphasis on undergraduate teaching and balance, and they're doing that in the face of very difficult fiscal challenges."

The University of Oregon, for example, has undertaken a new program to increase teaching by full professors for first- and second-year undergraduates. The fact that Oregon is making this change is especially telling, Magrath says, because higher education in the state has suffered severe funding cutbacks due to a new law that funnels a quarter of all education revenues to elementary and secondary schools.

To pay for the new undergraduate program, the university will increase tuition for out-of-state students. "These new initiatives emphasizing undergraduate teaching aren't always headline news," Magrath says. "But they have been going on in many cases for quite a while and certainly with considerable intensity in the last couple of years, despite fiscal stress on the states."

But some experts fear that in the push to re-emphasize undergraduate teaching, schools may fail to address the underlying causes of its decline in recent years: salary inequities that give greater rewards to researchers. "I'm concerned with some of the states demanding that their public universities improve teaching just by forcing professors to spend more hours in the classroom," says Fairweather. "That's got nothing to do with reward structure, and it may even make things a little worse."

Funding Woes

Revenue shortfalls caused by the ailing economy have left most states with inadequate funds to operate all their higher-education programs. Magrath estimates that about 40 state systems have had to make more than one midyear cut in expenditures to meet their budgets during the past two

years. "State support for higher education is deteriorating," he says. "In a lot of states, where 10 years ago 18 percent of the state budget was going to higher education, now it's down to 14 percent." According to the Illinois State University's Center for Higher Education, state appropriations for higher education this year are about 1 percent less than they were two years ago, the first actual drop in funding in the nation's history.[15]

The crunch in funding varies widely, mirroring the economic fortunes of the states themselves. Nowhere has higher education been harder hit than in California, home of the country's biggest higher-education system, including the

Range of Tuition at Four-Year Colleges

One hundred schools accounting for 15.6 percent of private-school enrollments are charging tuition and fees of $15,000 or more in 1992-93. Among public colleges, 96 are in the highest category, charging $3,000 or more for tuition and fees.

	Number of colleges	Average tuition and fees	Proportion of total enrollment
Private Institutions			
$15,000 or more	100	$16,661	15.6%
$14,000 - $14,999	29	$14,533	3.1%
$13,000 - $13,999	34	$13,444	3.3%
$12,000 - $12,999	61	$12,447	6.0%
$11,000 - $11,999	82	$11,492	8.0%
$10,000 - $10,999	104	$10,442	10.6%
$9,000 - $9,999	110	$9,529	10.5%
$8,000 - $8,999	138	$8,483	10.0%
$7,000 - $7,999	118	$7,466	7.7%
$6,000 - $6,999	97	$6,480	6.7%
$5,000 - $5,999	84	$5,498	4.7%
$4,000 - $4,999	84	$4,477	5.2%
$3,000 - $3,999	66	$3,576	2.0%
$2,000 - $2,999	45	$2,556	5.5%
$1,000 - $1,999	7	$1,621	0.1%
Less than $1,000	10	$457	1.0%
Total	**1,169**	——	**100%**
Public Institutions			
$3,000 or more	96	$3,689	17.8%
$2,500 - $2,999	107	$2,745	20.9%
$2,000 - $2,499	84	$2,236	15.6%
$1,500 - $1,999	150	$1,718	25.5%
$1,000 - $1,499	100	$1,344	18.8%
Less than $1,000	17	$873	1.4%
Total	**554**	——	**100%**

Note: Includes only those institutions that provided final or estimated 1992-93 tuition and fees by Sept. 10, 1992

Sources: The College Board, as published in The Chronicle of Higher Education *(Oct. 21, 1992)*

A Glossary of Financial Aid

Campus-based Aid: Three federally supported student-aid programs are available at both public and private colleges and universities: Perkins Loans (*see below*), Supplemental Educational Opportunity Grants and Work-Study Aid.

Cost of Attendance: Includes tuition and fees, room and board and miscellaneous expenses (transportation, books, supplies, etc.).

Expected Family Contribution: The amount that a family is expected to pay for all its dependents to attend college in a given year. Factors that go into determining the amount are parents' income and assets, medical and unusual expenses, family size and the number of family members attending postsecondary schools.

Independent Student: One who is considered to be financially independent of his or her parents. Students over age 24 and veterans usually fall into this category.

Merit Scholarship: A grant from a college, private corporation or foundation usually awarded solely for academic achievement or special skill in music or athletics, not on the basis of need.

Need-based Aid: Schools offer this kind of aid through grants, loans and work-study jobs, solely on the basis of need. Sources are the federal and state governments as well as college funds. Most aid packages cover only a portion of the student's "unmet need," the difference between the expected family contribution and the cost of attendance.

Need-Blind Admissions: Used at a small number of institutions, this policy guarantees that an applicant's ability to pay for college will not be considered in the admissions process. Some institutions will cover all admitted students' unmet need, while others pay only a portion of those costs.

Pell Grant: A federally funded grant, or gift, that does not have to be repaid — available to eligible undergraduates with demonstrated financial need.

Perkins Loans: Federally funded, low-interest loans that are offered directly by the postsecondary institution to needy students.

Stafford Loans: Formerly called Guaranteed Student Loans, these low-interest loans are available from commercial banks and other lenders. The federal government pays the interest while the student is in school and guarantees the lenders a minimum rate of return in case of default.

Supplementary Educational Opportunity Grants: Federally funded grants for needy students that are offered directly by the schools.

Title IV Programs: The main source of financial aid for students at both public and private institutions, they include all student-aid programs administered by the Department of Education and authorized under the 1965 Higher Education Act, as amended, which receives annual appropriations from Congress. Programs include Pell grants, Perkins loans, Work-study, Supplemental Educational Opportunity Grants, Stafford Loans, Supplemental Loans for Students, and Parent Loans for Undergraduates.

Work-study Programs: Often federally supported, these programs offer part-time employment to pay for postsecondary education. Students typically work 10 to 20 hours a week.

---

prestigious nine-campus University of California, California State University's 20 campuses and a vast network of community colleges. Allocations to these schools have been reduced largely because tax revenues generated by the state's big defense industry have been eroded by federal cutbacks in military spending.

But California is not alone. "Massachusetts is another basket case, and Connecticut has had a lot of problems, as have Maryland and Virginia — problems are basically all over," says Magrath. "There are only a handful that have not had severe or at least moderate problems," including Utah, Arizona and New Mexico.

"State schools are looking for revenue any way that they can," says education-funding expert Michael McPherson. Most colleges and universities are trying to avoid drastic cutbacks in course offerings and support services by raising tuitions and fees. Average tuitions for state residents went up by 10 percent this year, three times the rate of inflation.

Most state schools charge from two to three times as much for out-of-state students, and some of the universities that receive many out-of-state applications are capitalizing on their popularity. The University of Colorado at Boulder, near some of the country's best skiing, charges out-of-staters five times the tuition paid by Colorado residents. State systems, including Colorado's, generally cap out-of-state enrollment at around a third of the student body. But this year 55 percent of Boulder's first-year students are from out of state, a shift that will help balance the school's budget because out-of-state students pay more than the actual cost of their education.

Tuition hikes alone cannot compensate for the funding shortfall in most public schools, however. Colleges and universities all over the country are cutting faculty positions, freezing salaries and increasing teaching loads. Many schools are hiring part-time professors because they can pay them much less than tenured faculty and don't have to provide pension or health benefits.[17]

Most public schools are coping with fiscal problems by cutting courses and services to students, increasing class size and making it harder for students to complete their required coursework in the traditional four-year period. "In addition to reducing the number of classes, a lot of schools are keeping libraries open fewer hours, and they're reducing academic-support services," Leyton says.

Although it is in less dire financial straits than many public institutions, the University of Arizona, for example, is canceling its remedial language and math classes for the 40 percent of incoming students, largely Hispanic, who need them. "They're going to have those students take the classes off campus," she says. "Financial aid will no longer cover the remedial courses, and they will not count for credit." The cuts, Leyton adds, "will disproportionately affect students of color and non-traditional students, those who are returning to school, who have been in the work force and because of the recession have lost their jobs and are going back to school."

Many of those students, like those at other public schools facing cutbacks, will be forced to drop out. A large number of these dropouts will already owe student loans and will thus be returning to a depressed job market with a burden of debt and no degree to show for their effort.

As state schools assess their funding dilemmas, some are looking for ways to gain greater independence from the state governments whose fiscal conditions can vary dramatically from year to year. "Traditionally, the [arrangement] has been that the states provide the bulk of the money and then they provide fairly close control over what the institutions do," McPherson says. "A lot of public school presidents now are at least

quietly thinking that maybe it would be a better deal to follow the lead of Penn State or Temple University." They and some other so-called publicly supported schools in Pennsylvania receive a smaller amount of money from the state than do most state institutions, but they enjoy greater freedom to set tuition levels and design course programs.

Strain on Private Colleges

Although they do not depend heavily on state funding, private colleges and universities are also facing fiscal strains. Many are coping with funding shortages by making the same kinds of changes taking place at public schools — cutting course offerings, merging class sections and cutting student services. But private institutions can only go so far in cutting back programs without hurting enrollment. Students who do not qualify for financial aid but cannot afford private school tuitions are flocking to public institutions in search of an affordable education. As a result, private institutions are having to hold down tuition increases while maintaining quality instruction to woo applicants.

As a whole, tuitions at private four-year colleges and universities stood at an average $10,498 this academic year, according to the College Board. While that is much higher than tuitions at most public institutions, the increase in private tuitions — 7 percent over last year — is now less than the increase in the public sector (10 percent last year).

A few private schools are actually freezing tuitions for a year or more to attract new students. Wells College, a women's liberal arts school in Aurora, N.Y., for example, is freezing tuition for the next five years beginning next fall. But the tactic is risky. "For that to work, the additional income has to offset what the school might have lost in students if their tuition had gone up," says Richard Rosser of

the National Association of Independent Colleges and Universities. "In other words, at some point they've got to cover their costs."

Fiscal difficulties are leading some schools with need-blind admissions policies to re-examine their commitment to this important tool for recruiting high-achieving, low-income students. Need-blind policies guarantee that qualified students will not be denied admission because of their inability to pay and that the school will cover any costs the student can't afford. "There are a number of private schools that have moved away from need-blind admissions because they are reducing the overall amount of financial aid that they are giving out to students," says the U.S. Student Association's Leyton.

Need-blind admissions policies faced another challenge this year when the Massachusetts Institute of Technology's use of the policy led to charges it was violating the 1890 Sherman Antitrust Act. For more than 30 years, officials of MIT and all eight Ivy League schools — Harvard, Princeton, Yale, Brown, Columbia, Dartmouth, Cornell and the University of Pennsylvania — had met annually to share information about financial-aid applicants who had been accepted at more than one of the schools. To avoid a bidding war over the most highly qualified students, the Overlap Group, as the officials were called, would agree to a uniform financial-aid offer for these top applicants.

After the Justice Department brought antitrust charges against the schools in 1991, all but MIT agreed in an out-of-court settlement to stop sharing financial-aid information. MIT, however, defended the practice, arguing that the schools are non-commercial organizations and thus lie outside the realm of antitrust laws. The Cambridge, Mass., institution also claimed that the practice helped needy students by enabling the schools to allocate financial aid more efficiently than they could working independently. On Sept. 2, 1992, U.S. District Judge Louis C. Bechtle of the

Federal District Court in Philadelphia ruled against MIT, which says it will appeal the decision. (See "At Issue," p. 1017.)

Aid From Congress

Amid protests from middle-income families that they could no longer send their children to college without help, Congress last summer offered some relief. The measure, which reauthorizes the Higher Education Act of 1965, makes federal aid available to more middle-income students by allowing students to deduct the value of the equity in their families' home or farm from calculations to determine the students' eligibility for aid.

Congress also increased the amount of money that lower-income, full-time students can obtain through guaranteed student loans, or Stafford loans. The hike was from $2,625 to $3,500 for second-year students; from $4,000 to $5,500 for third- and fourth-year students; and from $7,500 to $8,500 for graduate students. The limit for first-year students remains at $2,625. Congress also authorized a new loan program, now awaiting congressional funding, for all students regardless of family income.

The reauthorization measure included a controversial new program designed to save money by issuing federal loans to students directly through their schools, eliminating commercial banks as the middlemen for these transactions. The banks opposed the program, as did President Bush. Bowing to Republican lawmakers' fears of alienating middle-class voters during an election year, however, Bush withdrew his threat to veto the bill. He signed it into law July 23.[18]

While the new law was welcomed as improving federal student-aid programs, many experts say it doesn't go nearly far enough. Most of the criticism falls on the low priority given to grants, or outright gifts, for low-income students. In the past, grants comprised the bulk of federal aid, but today more money is available as loans, which must be repaid.

"We're happy that the law opens up access to loan programs for more middle-income students, who have been complaining that they couldn't get any help getting through school at all," says Stacey Leyton. "But we're pushing for more grants because students are graduating with unreasonable debts. Low-income students are supposed to be mainly receiving grants, and they're barely getting any grants right now."

Although the reauthorization measure raised the annual funding limit from $2,400 to $3,700 for Pell grants, the main federal student-grant program, actual grant awards have not reached authorized levels since the 1979-80 academic year, according to the College Board.[19] "That's happening while tuition is going up and while state and institutional aid is often decreasing because of financial problems," Leyton says. "So the trends are pretty negative right now for federal financial aid."

Some critics even say that low-income students, the main beneficiaries of federal aid, may be pushed out of higher education unless Pell grants are greatly increased. "I'm not a fan of low-income students having to borrow much to go to college," says Michael McPherson. "As states realign their priorities, public tuitions are going up so fast that unless Pell grants are beefed up there are going to be some states where there is really no institution where poor kids can afford to go to school." ∎

OUTLOOK

More Tuition Increases?

Prospective college students should not pin their hopes for an affordable education on the possibility of lower tuitions in the future. As long as the economy continues to falter, states likely will keep a lid on funding for higher education, and public institutions can be expected to raise tuitions and fees to make up for the loss. "None of us is naive enough to think that the states are going to be throwing buckets of dollars at universities," says Magrath of the Association of State Universities and Land-Grant Colleges. "Everyone assumes that fiscally it's going to be very, very tight."

Recent developments on campuses across the country this fall support that prediction. After eliminating seven academic departments and one of its colleges earlier this year, the University of Maryland announced in October that students at most campuses will face tuition increases in spring 1993 and again next fall. These will be the fourth and fifth semesters in a row that students at Maryland's public colleges and universities will face tuition increases.[20]

In neighboring Virginia, where tuition increases at public institutions rose 13 percent in the current academic year — the highest such increase in the nation — voters approved a $472.4 million bond issue to pay for new buildings to accommodate an expected rise in enrollment of 65,000 students during the 1990s. This expected increase will be repeated across the nation as the children of the "baby boomlet" that began in the late 1970s reach college age.

Magrath says that current funding trends threaten the public schools' mission of offering a college degree to all who desire it. "I do worry that if reasonable public support for higher education continues to erode, tuitions are

Continued on p. 1018

At Issue:

Is the practice of sharing financial-aid information unfair to students?

On Sept. 2, 1992, a federal judge ruled that MIT violated antitrust laws by sharing information about financial-aid applicants with the eight Ivy League schools — Brown, Columbia, Cornell, Dartmouth, Harvard, Princeton, the University of Pennsylvania and Yale. To avoid bidding wars over the best students, the schools, known as the "Overlap Group," met each year to agree on uniform aid offers to students who had been accepted at more than one institution. Although the group has disbanded, MIT is appealing the decision.

U.S. DISTRICT JUDGE LOUIS BECHTLE

U.S. District Judge for the Eastern District of Pennsylvania
FROM *U.S. VS. BROWN UNIVERSITY*, SEPT. 2, 1992.

yes

the ways in which our nation profits when our many great institutions of higher education open their doors to those who for too long were denied the privilege of attending college are immeasurable. These policies send an important signal to a large segment of our society that persons need not presume they are unable to attend college for fear of not being able to afford what has become the extraordinary cost of higher education. Nor can it be denied ... that cultural and economic diversity contributes to the quality of education and enhances the vitality of campus life. What can be questioned, however, is whether the scheme whereby the Ivy Overlap Schools conspire to remove price as a facet of competition for students is a necessary ingredient to achieve these ends.

The court is unconvinced because there is no evidence supporting MIT's fatalistic prediction that the end of the Ivy Overlap Group necessarily would sound the death knell of need-blind admissions or need-based aid....

The message to be gleaned from MIT's defense is that the moment the Ivy Overlap Group schools are no longer able to jointly eliminate price competition, they will immediately bow to faculty pressure to enroll the very highest caliber student at high cost and at the expense of needy students, leaving behind hollowed principles of equality of educational access and opportunity and the resultant societal benefits which they have so ardently underscored....

Can the Ivy Overlap Group members' purposes be so fragile that their primary goals of having the most desirable students outweighs their ability, without Overlap, to pursue diligently even an imperfect policy of promoting the virtue of student diversity and the advantages of making available to needy students the benefits of these elite educational institutions? Will there also be lost the value to be gained by signaling to all prospective students that they can in fact aspire to attend an Ivy Overlap Group institution even though their families may be of limited means? The court thinks not. If MIT and the other Ivy League schools were to so easily abandon these objectives merely because Overlap was not in play, then the court could only conclude that their professed dedication to these ends was less than sincere.

CHARLES M. VEST

President of the Massachusetts Institute of Technology
FROM *MIT NEWS RELEASE*, SEPT. 2, 1992.

no

the Massachusetts Institute of Technology intends to appeal the decision and fight very hard to win it. We believe we have not violated the Sherman Antitrust Act and the principles for which we are standing up are the correct ones. We are quite confident that the appellate court will understand that.

From MIT's perspective [the case is] very simple. [It's] about the ability of educational institutions to distribute charitable funds in the form of financial aid in a manner that they believe does the most social and educational good. In our case that is the desire to distribute undergraduate financial aid solely on the basis of the need of the individual students and their families with the understanding that merit has been established through the admissions process....

When I go around this country to raise money for MIT, a typical donor will say, "I was able to go to MIT because of financial aid. Otherwise that education would not have been possible. I want to make it possible for the next generation of young men and women." I do not believe donors give money in the expectation that it will be given to people who don't need it. That's a very important principle and one of the basic reasons MIT chose to fight this. Second, we have believed all along that the Sherman Antitrust Act didn't apply to us and we were not in violation of the law....

Merit aid has its place. I want to be extremely clear that MIT does not believe that its philosophy on financial aid should be imposed on other colleges and universities which operate in different contexts. For example, most large public institutions do not have the level of endowment and private support that allows them to provide need-based aid for all their students, particularly their out-of-state students. In their own context they may decide they need to distribute some portion of their aid on the basis of merit in order to maintain a high quality student body. Their needs may be quite different from those of MIT and the Ivy League schools. But at MIT all of the students admitted are highly meritorious and have met very high academic standards. We believe our limited resources should go to helping those who need it most.

Community Colleges Feel the Crunch

The same financial pressures that are forcing four-year colleges and universities to tighten their belts are also squeezing the nation's 1,150 community colleges, junior colleges and technical schools. Reduced course offerings, overcrowded classrooms, more part-time professors and cuts in budgets for libraries and other students services are fast becoming the norm in two-year institutions.

Now public community colleges are facing a particularly alarming prospect: the need to put limits on enrollment. Since their inception and rapid expansion in the 1960s and '70s, community colleges have opened their doors for most programs to virtually all who completed high school, in the process offering many low-income and minority youths a unique educational opportunity. About a quarter of the students who get two-year associate's degrees go on to earn a bachelor's degree from a four-year school. Enrollment caps threaten to close that door to many disadvantaged high-school graduates.

"We believe very strongly in the open-door philosophy," says David Pierce, president of the American Association of Community and Junior Colleges. "The thought of enrollment management has given us great trouble and distress, and we expect it to be only a temporary emergency response to an extraordinary financial situation."

But with economic stagnation thrusting a double-edged sword at community colleges, many schools see little choice but to limit the number of students they admit. While falling tax revenues mean skimpier state and local funding, the main source of community college support,

laid-off workers are turning to community colleges in droves to learn new skills. As a result, the average age of students enrolled at two-year schools is 30.†

The return to school of older people seeking new skills is nothing new for community colleges, which have always enrolled more workers and job seekers during economic downturns. But this time they are returning to school at the same time that many college-age youths are choosing community colleges over four-year institutions, either because they can't afford the higher tuitions or because they fail to gain admittance. Moreover, with highly qualified middle-income students increasingly choosing public colleges and universities over private schools for financial reasons, fewer spaces are available to marginally qualified students, who in turn are shifting their focus to community colleges. This year, for the first time, more than half the freshmen at all postsecondary schools were enrolled at community colleges.

Pierce predicts that the overcrowding at community colleges that has caused some schools to curtail enrollment "will be resolved within another couple of years." But his prediction may be overly optimistic. Unless competition for admission to public four-year colleges eases, there is little indication that demand for space at two-year colleges will let up anytime soon.

---

†See Anthony DePalma, "Community Colleges Forced to Restrict Access, and Goals," *The New York Times*, Nov. 11, 1992, p. A1.

Continued from p. 1016
going to get so high that a lot of individuals who really want to go to a public college are going to be shut out, particularly minorities," he says. "Or, we're going to have a kind of shell game where you all can come but you're going to have to hang around a long time because you can't get into the courses that you need to graduate. At some point, if you keep slashing and burning, there's going to be an erosion of quality."

Although they do not depend directly on state funding, private colleges and universities are also expected to face continuing fiscal pressures in the foreseeable future. To keep financially pressed students

from shifting to less expensive public schools, private institutions have to demonstrate they provide superior education. That means small classes, a variety of course offerings and professors who teach — all costly goals.

Clinton to the Rescue?

Although there is no sign that college costs will stop rising anytime soon, Arkansas Gov. Bill Clinton's Nov. 3 presidential victory offers new hope for improvements in financial aid to students. During the campaign, Clinton presented a sweeping proposal that would insulate students and

their families from tuition increases.

Clinton's plan is to largely dismantle the current 30-year-old federal financial-aid system (which dispenses grants, loans and work-study opportunities), leaving intact only the Pell grant program. The other aid programs would be replaced by a National Service Trust Fund, which would "give" all students, regardless of income, $10,000 a year to attend the college of their choice. Upon graduation, instead of having to pay off a bank loan, the students would work off the loan by spending two years as teachers, police officers or other public service workers. Those who eschewed public service could repay the government through deductions from their paychecks once they were employed.

Critics of Clinton's proposal say it is too expensive. With concern growing over the federal budget deficit, lawmakers may be reluctant to approve a program that its supporters estimate will cost as much as $13 billion. But Clinton has contended his program will save taxpayers money by eliminating the $2.5 billion that the government currently absorbs in defaults on student loans and another $1.5 billion in service charges that commercial banks charge each year to issue student loans under the current $10.4 billion program.

On Nov. 12, at his first news conference since the election, the president-elect said that the amount students could borrow had yet to be determined, voicing concern that the program not prompt private schools to raise tuitions.

Indeed, college funding experts, including supporters of the Clinton proposal, worry that the new program might, in Magrath's words, "provide a backdoor subsidy to private colleges."

But above all, Magrath says, experts want any new federal student-aid program to support the states' basic commitment to higher education by "really enabling students to go to public colleges without being priced out of the market." ∎

Notes

[1] "Colleges — Best Buys," *Money*, Sept. 2, 1992.

[2] Charles F. Manski, *Parental Income and College Opportunity*, Democratic Study Center, Aug. 26, 1992.

[3] Clint Talbot, "Welcome to the Fun, Crazy World of CU," *Colorado Daily*, Welcome Back Fall 1992, p. 18.

[4] "College Education: Paying More and Getting Less," staff report to the Select Committee on Children, Youth, and Families, presented at hearings Sept. 14, 1992, pp. 2-3.

[5] *Ibid.*, p. 5.

[6] Kristina J. Shelley, "The Future of Jobs for College Graduates," *Monthly Labor Review*, July 1992. For background, see "Youth Apprenticeships," *The CQ Researcher*, Oct. 23, 1992, pp. 905-928.

[7] Daniel E. Hecker, "College Earnings and Why They Vary," *Occupational Outlook Quarterly*, summer 1992.

[8] Manski, *op. cit.*, p. 5.

[9] See Michael S. McPherson and Morton Owen Schapiro, *Keeping College Affordable* (1991).

[10] *Ibid.*, p. 26. Amounts are in constant 1989-90 dollars.

[11] *Ibid.*, p. 22.

[12] Select Committee on Children, Youth, and Families, *op. cit.*, p. 3.

[13] *Washington Post*-ABC News poll reported in *The Washington Post*, Nov. 3, 1992, p. A9.

[14] James S. Fairweather, "Teaching and the Faculty Reward Structure: Relationships between Faculty Activities and Compensation," National Center for Postsecondary Teaching, Learning and Assessment, June 1992.

[15] See Scott Jaschik, "1 Percent Decline in State Support for Colleges Thought to Be First 2-Year Drop Ever," *The Chronicle of Higher Education*, Oct. 21, 1992, p. A21.

[16] See Ian Olgeirson, "Gates Opened to Non-Residents," *Campus Press*, Aug. 24, 1992, p. 1. *Campus Press* is a student newspaper at the University of Colorado-Boulder.

[17] See Brooke A. Masters, "Part-Time Profs: New Campus Class," *The Washington Post*, Oct. 21, 1992, p. A1.

[18] For background, see Jill Zuckman, "Student Loan Agreement Opens Door to All," *Congressional Quarterly Weekly Report*, June 20, 1992, pp. 1799-1801.

[19] The College Board, *Trends in Student Aid: 1982 to 1992*, September 1992.

[20] See Lisa Leff, "Tuitions at U-Md. Are Going Up Again To Offset State Cuts," *The Washington Post*, Oct. 31, 1992.

Bibliography

Selected Sources Used

Books

Anderson, Martin, *Impostors in the Temple: American Intellectuals Are Destroying Our Universities and Cheating Our Students of Their Future*, Simon & Schuster, 1992.

The author, a domestic-policy adviser to Presidents Richard M. Nixon and Ronald Reagan, decries the emphasis many universities give to academic research over teaching undergraduates. Because of corrupt practices, mismanagement and poor assessment of faculty performance, he writes, universities are shunning their commitment to teaching, even as they charge higher tuitions.

Boyer, Ernest L., *Scholarship Reconsidered: Priorities of the Professoriate*, Carnegie Foundation for the Advancement of Teaching, 1990.

Boyer offers a solution to the tug-of-war over research and teaching commitments by university faculty. Universities that are the focus of complaints over undergraduate education can improve their record by rewarding quality teaching as highly as they do scholarly research.

The College Board, *The College Cost Book 1993*, College Entrance Examination Board, 1992.

The College Board, which administers the Scholastic Aptitude Test (SAT), provides a step-by-step guide to the process of paying for college, including applications for student aid. It also includes the costs and aid policies of 2,800 colleges.

Huber, Richard M., *How Professors Play the Cat Guarding the Cream: Why We're Paying More and Getting Less in Higher Education*, George Mason University Press, 1992.

The author, a former dean at Hunter College in New York City, paints a dismal picture of academic life at research and doctoral-granting universities in which students are unable to complete their graduate requirements in four years because courses are over-enrolled and faculty teaching loads have fallen to half the level of 50 years ago.

McPherson, Michael S., and Morton Owen Schapiro, *Keeping College Affordable: Government and Educational Opportunity*, The Brookings Institution, 1991.

States can no longer afford to subsidize public higher education to the extent they have in the past. A fairer way to finance colleges and universities, the authors suggest, would be for public institutions to raise tuitions closer to the cost of providing education and for the federal government to offer more student aid for needy students.

Articles

"Campus of the Future," *Time*, April 13, 1992, pp. 54-60.

This cover story examines recent changes on college campuses. Funding problems are likely to cause further changes, including the disappearance of many small liberal arts colleges with meager endowments and greater emphasis on science and technology as well as on undergraduate teaching.

Shelley, Kristina J., "The Future of Jobs for College Graduates," *Monthly Labor Review*, July 1992, pp. 13-21.

Openings for jobs requiring a college degree are likely to fall over the next decade, a period when the number of degrees awarded is projected to rise. As a result, college graduates are expected to encounter a more competitive job market than graduates of the 1980s.

Sowell, Thomas, "The Scandal of College Tuition," *Commentary*, August 1992, pp. 23-26.

Sowell decries the rise in college costs, which he traces to higher faculty salaries, more administrative staff and wasteful spending for non-academic purposes. The price spiral could be halted, he writes, if colleges were forced to respond more directly to the competitive marketplace.

Reports and Studies

Robert M. Sweeney, *Report of the States*, American Association of State Colleges and Universities, February 1992.

The study traces the impact of economic stagnation on state funding of higher education and looks at steps states have taken to compensate for the loss.

Congressional Budget Office, *Student Aid and the Cost of Postsecondary Education*, January 1991.

Although the federal student-aid programs in place for more than 25 years have succeeded in expanding access to higher education, the system contains flaws. Subsidizing tuition for everyone, as the public schools do, unnecessarily benefits higher-income families, the report concludes.

El-Khawas, Elaine, *Campus Trends, 1992*, American Council on Education, July 1992.

Funding problems are raising new concerns about the affordability of higher education, especially in light of an expected growth in enrollment over the next decade. The report traces these developments and reviews efforts many institutions are undertaking to improve education quality.

The Next Step

Additional Articles from Current Periodicals from EBSCO Publishing's Database

Books & reading

"College dollars," *Black Enterprise*, August 1992, p. 40.

Discusses the book "Scholarship Directory: 1992 Minority Guide To Scholarships and Financial Aid," from Tinsley Communications Inc. Price and ordering information.

Caine, S.P., "Book reviews," *Journal of American History*, June 1992, p. 278.

Reviews the book "The Origins of Federal Support for Higher Education: George W. Atherton and the Land Grant College Movement," by Roger L. Williams.

Grun, L., "College guides that make the grade," *Library Journal*, June 1, 1992, p. 83.

Looks at a number of national guides for college education to regionally accredited undergraduate institutions. Yearly number of Americans that attend college for the first time; types of assistance offered for students, their families and counselors; questions concerning cost, scholarships, special services and social activities; catalogs and videocassettes that can be obtained from individual institutions; contact points; more. INSET: The developing schedule (upcoming subjects).

Corrupt practices

"University on trial for rigging prices," *New Scientist*, July 4, 1992, p. 9.

Reports that the U.S. Justice Department is accusing some of America's most prestigious universities of operating a cartel and conspiring to raise the price of a college education. Some of the universities included; The Massachusetts Institute of Technology has contested the charges; cost to attend one of these schools per year.

Mead, W.R. & E. Peck, "The great tuition scam," *Rolling Stone*, Oct. 3, 1991, p. 109.

States that professors and administrators are stealing college from students, explaining that administrators and senior faculty are doing their best to live like princes on the tribute of their undergraduate serfs. Donald Kennedy, the president of Stanford University who will enjoy the use of a $1,200 antique fruitwood commode in his house, which he fraudulently charged as "overhead" on federal research grants; Charles Sykes' book "ProfScam."

Sowell, T., "Price gouging," *Forbes*, June 24 1991, p.

109.

Discusses the wave of academic fraud and misconduct currently washing across America's educational institutions. Questions why the people responsible for this fraud, including the exchange of tuition and financial information, are not punished, as would be a businessman committing the same type of crime.

Wilson, R., "Consortium of 32 colleges issues guidelines on limits to discussion of student aid," *The Chronicle of Higher Education*, Oct. 30, 1991, p. A35.

Enumerates the guidelines issued by the Consortium on Financing Higher Education (comprised of 32 colleges and universities) aimed at helping higher-education officials decide what they can safely talk about in discussions of financial aid, admissions, tuition and budget setting. The Justice Department's investigation of the Overlap Group; Ivy League universities sign a consent decree.

Economic aspects

"Saving for college," *Consumer Reports*, October 1991, p. 661.

Gives advice on saving money for your child's college tuition. Put college funds in child's name for tax advantages; United States Savings Bonds Series EE; CollegeSure CDs; college savings bonds; stock mutual funds; when to start and how much.

"The nation: Resources," *The Chronicle of Higher Education*, Aug. 28, 1991, p. 35.

Presents, in chart form, a number of statistics on costs, revenues and expenditures affecting higher education. Includes, among others, average costs at public and private institutions, sources of voluntary support, revenues and expenditures of colleges and universities, range of tuition at four-year institutions, Defense Department contracts to nonprofit organizations, total return on college endowments, holdings of university research libraries.

"Tuition rising, despite recession," *USA Today*, May 1992, p. 4.

Notes that college tuition fees are continuing to increase despite the current recession. Statistics on costs and related expenses from the College Board's annual survey of United States colleges; negative implications for future students.

Bergsman, S., "In search of money for college," *Black Enterprise*, August 1992, p. 39.

Deals with the expense of sending a child to college and discusses the available scholarship money that goes unclaimed every year; comment from Saryl Zegerson Schwartz of Pathfinders, a company that helps people find scholarship money; why applications for funding are often rejected; books on scholarships; more.

Blumenstyk, G. & J. Mercer, "CUNY's unusual new tuition package draws questions and criticism," *The Chronicle of Higher Education*, April 22, 1992, p. A30.

Describes the tuition plan introduced by the City University of New York last week, which some members of the state legislature claim violates a state education law requiring all students enrolled in programs "leading to degrees" pay the same tuition, unless they are from out of state.

Blumenstyk, G., "Florida's prepaid-tuition program stirs skepticism amid success," *The Chronicle of Higher Education*, July 1, 1992, p. A24.

Focuses on the Florida Prepaid College Program, now in its fifth year, which has enrolled more than 123,000 participants, has a $26 million surplus and generates about $3 million in annual revenues for the businesses that help sell and manage it.

Collison, M., "Private colleges unveil tuition discounts and loans to woo middle-income students," *The Chronicle of Higher Education*, June 24, 1992, p. A27.

Lists a number of private colleges that have recently instituted tuition discounts and loan programs to lure middle-income students, the latest salvo in the admissions battle.

Dumaine, B. & S.L. Kirsch, "Married with a couple of teens," *Fortune*, Fall 1991, p. 133.

Presents some simple but overlooked principles of investing that will help people pay for their children's college tuition as well as save for their own retirements. Make sure you've got at least six months of after-tax salary in liquid investments; how to protect a college nest egg; borrowing money.

Evangelauf, J., "At public colleges, more double-digit tuition growth," *The Chronicle of Higher Education*, March 11, 1992, p. A29.

Focuses on a survey by the College Board that found in academic 1991-92 the average tuition went up 12 percent at public four-year colleges, 13 percent at public community colleges and 7 percent at private four-year colleges. Politically and economically nervous private institutions; states not willing or able to put money into preserving quality and maintaining low tuition; tuition increases in select states; more.

Jelks, F.N., "How to save money for college," *Consumers' Research Magazine*, May 1992, p. 10.

Discusses the major vehicles for college savings frequently offered to parents; stocks, mutual funds, life insurance and zero-coupon bonds; more.

Kantrowitz, B., "Ask your boss about this idea," *Newsweek*, March 16, 1992, p. 65.

States that college-tuition assistance could become this decade's most sought-after perk. Discusses other dramatic examples of the increasing corporate involvement in education. Asserts that these family-friendly benefits add up to greater worker loyalty and productivity.

Kosnett, J., "Financial woes plague college budget offices," *Kiplinger's Personal Finance Magazine*, May 1992, p. 16.

Asserts that a growing number of four-year colleges are headed for serious financial straits. Threats to departments with few majors or high operating costs; increases in tuition costs to nearly untenable levels; problems for private or religious colleges.

Wallace, T.P., "The inequities of low tuition," *The Chronicle of Higher Education*, April 1, 1992, p. A48.

Opinion. Argues that the expansion of the scope and missions of state colleges and universities has not been accompanied by a comparable evolution in fiscal policies and practices. Public higher education must overhaul its policies and financial strategies and acknowledge that states no longer can or will provide the bulk of public college and university budgets.

Weiss, S., "CUNY tuition plan: Biggest increase yet but a free semester," *New York Times*, April 15, 1992, p. A1.

Discusses the tuition increase plan of the City University of New York, believed to be the first of its kind in the nation. The increase will be coupled with a promise that if freshmen make it up to their senior year, they may attend their last semester before graduation free.

Government policy

"Legislation could provide college aid, teachers," *Congressional Quarterly Weekly Report*, July 20, 1991, p. 1992.

Discusses briefly Sen. Edward M. Kennedy's urging of more grant money to help college students pay their tuition and to provide financial aid for minority doctoral students in exchange for a promise to teach in college. Legislation S 1499, S 1500; reauthorization of the Higher Education Act; likely to spark administration opposition; Pell grant award system.

"State notes: Briefly noted," *The Chronicle of Higher Education*, June 3, 1992, p. A25.

Says the State of Michigan has begun selling tax-free bonds, to be sold for as little as $300, that are being promoted as an alternative to the state's prepaid-tuition program, which has been tentatively suspended. Also notes voters in Campbell County, Wyo., have rejected a proposal that would create a new community college district with authority to levy property taxes.

"Who deserves college tuition help?" *U.S. News & World Report,* **June 10, 1991, p. 12.**

Details the differences in the Bush administration plan for financial aid to college students as opposed to the congressional plan. Increasing aid to the poorest students and making Pell grants available to children of families making as much as $50,000.

Blumenstyk, G., "State notes: Pennsylvania enacts programs to help families save for college," *The Chronicle of Higher Education,* **April 15, 1992, p. A28.**

Outlines Pennsylvania's college credit and savings-bond programs enacted recently to help families save for college. The Tuition Account Program will allow families to buy credits equivalent to the cost of tuition at a state college or community college. The state would then pay the institution when the students redeem the credits and enroll.

Blumenstyk, G., "States plan to spend $1.2-billion on student aid, up 3.9 percent overall," *The Chronicle of Higher Education,* **March 25, 1992, p. A1.**

Considers figures from a new National Association of State Scholarship and Grant Programs report, which found that while the 1990-91 increase on student aid was 7.7 percent, the 1991-92 figures are 3.9 percent, and 11 states expect to make cuts in student aid funding. Additional assistance through tuition waivers and special grants; spending in individual states; state fiscal problems affecting appropriations for financial aid; contact point for copies of the report.

DeLoughry, T.J., "College officials urge Congress to adopt new Pell grant formula," *The Chronicle of Higher Education,* **May 13, 1992, p. A25.**

Investigates the compromise formula worked out by officials representing public and private colleges that would provide enough money to pay living expenses for students at the lowest-cost institutions and additional money to students at higher-priced institutions. Proposed changes to the "needs analysis" system; unclear if lawyers would adopt the proposed Pell grant changes; adding "tuition sensitivity"; comments on the proposed policy.

DeLoughry, T.J., "Alexander would deny Pell Grants to students to pay off program's deficit," *The Chronicle of Higher Education,* **June 17, 1992, p. A22.**

Considers the request of Education Secretary Lamar Alexander for Congress to pay for a Pell grant program shortage of $1.4 billion by tightening the eligibility rules and eliminating grants for at least 374,000 students. Background of the Pell grant shortage; other cost cutting measures announced by President Bush; review by House and Senate appropriations subcommittees; reaction of student leaders; comments from David Mertes, California Community Colleges.

DeLoughry, T.J., "Recession takes toll on U.S. student aid," *The Chronicle of Higher Education,* **June 10, 1992, p. A1.**

Highlights the effects of the recession, the rising tide of bad loans and high default rates on federal student aid programs. Greater demand for aid has coincided with increases in tuition; probably deficit of about $1.4 billion in the Pell grant programs; allocating work-study funds; problems at individual institutions; comments on the rising default rate.

DeWitt, K., "Battle is looming on U.S. college aid to poor students," *The New York Times,* **May 27, 1991, p. 1.**

Discusses the Bush administration's plan to increase federal college tuition grants for the poor and eliminate them for about 400,000 students whose families earn more than $10,000 a year. The plan is part of an overhaul of the Federal Higher Education Act and has already met heavy criticism in Congress.

Mercer, J., "State notes: Maine free-tuition for the unemployed faces November vote," *The Chronicle of Higher Education,* **April 15, 1992, p. A28.**

Outlines the $9.9 million bond issue approved by the Maine Legislature to pay the tuition of 3,000 unemployed people at any of the state's six technical colleges. The plan is subject to the approval of voters in November.

School selection

Collison, M., "More freshmen say they are choosing colleges based on costs," *The Chronicle of Higher Education,* **Jan. 22, 1992, p. A33.**

Presents statistics from the survey, "The American Freshman: National Norms for Fall 1991," based on responses from 210,000 students enrolled at 421 colleges and universities, and which found 27 percent of the students had selected their colleges because of low tuition. Students choosing a college based on offers of financial aid; working students; personal and academic issues; contact point for copies of the report.

Back Issues

Great Research on Current Issues Starts Right Here... Recent topics covered by The CQ Researcher are listed below. Issues dated before May 10, 1991, were published under the name of Editorial Research Reports.

MAY 1991
School Choice
Racial Quotas
Animal Rights
U.S. and Japan

JUNE 1991
Children and Divorce
Teenage Suicide
Endangered Species
Europe 1992

JULY 1991
Teenagers and Abortion
Soviet Republics Rebel
Mexico's Emergence
Athletes and Drugs

AUGUST 1991
Sexual Harassment
Fetal Tissue Research
Oil Imports
The Palestinians

SEPTEMBER 1991
Police Brutality
Advertising Under Attack
Saving the Forests
Foster Care Crisis

OCTOBER 1991
Pay-Per-View TV
Youth Gangs
Gene Therapy
World Hunger

NOVEMBER 1991
Fast-Food Shake-Up
The Greening of Eastern Europe
Business' Role in Education
Cuba In Crisis

DECEMBER 1991
Retiree Health Benefits
Asian Americans
The Obscenity Debate
The Disabilities Act

JANUARY 1992
Term Limits
Oil Spills
Hunting Controversy
Alternative Medicine

FEBRUARY 1992
Threatened Coastlines
New Era in Asia
Assisted Suicide
Jobs in the '90s

MARCH 1992
Women and Sports
Underage Drinking
Garbage Crisis
Mafia Crackdown

APRIL 1992
Ozone Depletion
Welfare Reform
Politicians and Privacy
Illegal Immigration

MAY 1992
Native Americans
Jobs vs. Environment
Too Many Lawsuits?
Fairness in Salaries

JUNE 1992
Nuclear Proliferation
Food Irradiation
Lead Poisoning
Hard Times for Libraries

JULY 1992
Alternative Energy
Prescription Drug Prices
Alzheimer's Disease
Infant Mortality

AUGUST 1992
The Homeless
Work, Family and Stress
NATO's Changing Role
Marine Mammals vs. Fish

SEPTEMBER 1992
Domestic Partners
Violence in Schools
Public Broadcasting
Women in the Military

OCTOBER 1992
Depression
U.S. Auto Industry
Youth Apprenticeships
Hispanic Americans

NOVEMBER 1992
Physical Fitness
Privatization

Back issues are available for $4.00 (subscribers) or $7.00 (non-subscribers). Quantity discounts apply to orders over ten. To order, call Congressional Quarterly 1-800-432-2250.

Binders are available for $15.00. To order call 1-800-638-1710.

Future Topics

▶ *U.S. Policy in the Pacific*

▶ *Smoking in Public*

▶ *The CIA*

THE CQ Researcher

PUBLISHED BY CONGRESSIONAL QUARTERLY INC., IN CONJUNCTION WITH EBSCO PUBLISHING

U.S. Policy in Asia

What role should America play in the post-Cold War era?

AMERICAN RELATIONS WITH ASIA ARE AT A historic turning point. For more than 40 years after World War II, the naval might of the United States protected its allies in the Far East from the threat of Soviet aggression. The presence of American forces also served as a stabilizing influence in the entire region. Now, with the Soviet threat virtually gone, regional tensions that had been suppressed by Cold War considerations have resurfaced. Arms sales throughout the Far East are on the rise, and there are signs that China is preparing to play a more aggressive role in the region. As the Clinton administration prepares to take over the White House, Asian leaders are seeking reassurances that the United States will maintain its diplomatic and military presence in Asia.

 November 27, 1992 • Volume 2, No. 44 • 1025-1048

Formerly Editorial Research Reports

CQ Researcher

November 27, 1992
Volume 2, No. 44

EDITOR
Sandra Stencel

MANAGING EDITOR
Thomas J. Colin

ASSOCIATE EDITOR
Richard L. Worsnop

STAFF WRITERS
Charles S. Clark
Mary H. Cooper
Rodman D. Griffin

PRODUCTION EDITOR
Sarah E. Merritt

EDITORIAL ASSISTANT
Michael M. Taylor

GRAPHICS
Jack Auldridge

PUBLISHED BY
Congressional Quarterly Inc.

CHAIRMAN
Andrew Barnes

VICE CHAIRMAN
Andrew P. Corty

EDITOR AND PUBLISHER
Neil Skene

EXECUTIVE EDITOR
Robert W. Merry

ASSOCIATE PUBLISHER
John J. Coyle

EDITOR, EBSCO PUBLISHING
Melissa Kummerer

The CQ Researcher (ISSN 1056-2036). Formerly Editorial Research Reports. Published weekly (48 times per year, not printed the first Friday of any month with five Fridays) by Congressional Quarterly Inc., 1414 22nd St., N.W., Washington, D.C. 20037. Rates are furnished upon request. Second-class postage paid at Washington, D.C. POSTMASTER: Send address changes to The CQ Researcher, 1414 22nd St., N.W., Washington, D.C. 20037.

U.S. Policy in Asia

BY

THE ISSUES

Nowhere has the end of the Cold War left political relations more unsettled than in Asia. For more than 40 years, the global competition between the United States and the Soviet Union defined relations between the superpowers and the nations of the Far East and, to a large extent, among the Asian countries themselves. Now, with the Soviet threat virtually gone, regional tensions that had been suppressed by Cold War considerations have resurfaced.

As President Bush observed last January during a visit to Australia: "The Cold War is over, but the threat of communism, which for so many decades occupied our energies, is now replaced by the instabilities of ethnic rivalries and regional conflicts." [1]

In fact, many analysts believe the threat of military conflict in the Far East is greater now than it was before the end of the Cold War. Territorial disputes have broken out from the Kurile Islands north of Japan to the Spratly Islands in the South China Sea.* In addition, arms purchases in the region have risen sharply. The countries of Asia and the Pacific purchased 35 percent of the military equipment (excluding small arms) sold internationally in 1991 — a higher total than any other region, including the Middle East. [2]

Total military spending also is on the

---

*The Kurile Islands, a chain of some 56 islands and islets stretching roughly 750 miles from northern Japan to Russia's Kamchatka Peninsula, were Japanese territory from 1875 to 1945, when they were ceded to the Soviet Union at the Yalta Conference. Japan itself has never conceded the loss of the islands, however, and has made the return of at least the four large islands closest to Japan a precondition for major aid programs to Russia. For information on the Spratly islands, see pp. 1028, 1039.

rise. The $6.8 billion defense budget unveiled by Chinese leaders last March was 50 percent higher than the one announced in 1989. Japan's military budget, which first surpassed China's in 1985, climbed to $35 billion in 1992, making the small but wealthy country the world's third-largest defense spender, according to one estimate. [3] But the most dramatic increases in defense spending have been in Southeast Asia. Singapore, Malaysia and Thailand have all projected 5 to 6 percent annual increases in military spending over the next several years. [4]

The increase in regional tensions and the rise in defense spending and arms purchases can be traced in part to uncertainty about America's commitment to the region. "The threat is, to some extent, what would happen if the United States were to withdraw" its forces, Defense Secretary Dick Cheney observed late last year. "Our presence ... in the Western Pacific is reassuring to an awful lot of people in that part of the world. If we were to withdraw, there would be pressures on other governments

to try to fill that vacuum." [5]

Despite repeated assurances by President Bush that the United States intends to maintain its commitment to the Far East, many in the region doubt that America will keep its current force levels. "There's great uncertainty about the U.S. presence," says Thomas McNaugher, a foreign policy analyst at the Brookings Institution in Washington. "Most people who go to Southeast Asia come back talking about how Asians don't expect the United States to stick around."

The election of Arkansas Gov. Bill Clinton as the next American president has heightened those concerns. "There's an impression [in Asia] that Clinton wants to focus almost exclusively on domestic policy," observes Bruce Porter, assistant director of the Olin Institute for Strategic Studies at Harvard University.

That concern was reflected in a recent statement from two of Asia's most powerful leaders — Japanese Prime Minister Kiichi Miyazawa and South Korean President Roh Tae Woo. Meeting in Tokyo on Nov. 8, five days after Clinton's election, Miyazawa and Roh urged the president-elect to maintain America's diplomatic and military presence in Asia, saying the U.S. role was essential to stability in the region. [6]

Clinton tried to reassure the Asian leaders during his first post-election news conference, held Nov. 12 in Little Rock. Clinton said he hoped Washington "can continue to be a force for the security of South Korea" and that "some day Korean people will be reunited in a democratic and free society."

As the new administration prepares to assume office, here are some of the issues in Asia that it will face:

Can the United States contain an increasingly strident China?

Over the past two years, as Cold War tensions faded, China has demonstrated a determination to assume a more

China	
Military personnel	3,030,000
Navy:	
Surface combatants	54
Submarines	46
Patrol and coastal	860
Combat aircraft	5,850

dominant regional role. That determination has been expressed most obviously by its arms purchases, which not only have risen dramatically, but also have been weighted toward the types of equipment and technology that will give China new capabilities to influence events beyond its borders.

The desire to increase its military profile was among the reasons for China's purchase earlier this year of 24 Russian-made Su-27 fighter planes. The Su-27s, unlike China's F-7 fighters, can take advantage of in-flight refueling technology, which the Chinese recently purchased, possibly from Pakistan or Iran.[7] Midair refueling would allow Chinese pilots to fly greater distances.

Experts say it will probably be several years before the Chinese air force can use the refueling technology effectively. But eventually, it could make a big difference. "The long-term implication is that China may be more effective in using its military power in a regional capacity," G. Keith Jacobs, an analyst of the Chinese military, told *The New York Times.* "This is a development that will have only a slight impact in the middle of the decade but could become far more serious late in the 1990s."[8]

Western diplomats also have expressed concern about Chinese inquiries last summer about buying an aircraft carrier from the cash-starved, former Soviet republic of Ukraine. And China has for the past several years been pouring funds into the development of a new generation of destroyers and frigates.

"There is no doubt that the Chinese navy is going to sea at a much higher rate ... in much greater numbers and exercising at higher levels of sophistication," Vice Adm. Stanley Arthur, vice chief of U.S. naval operations, said recently. "My feeling is they are prepared to move throughout the region very comfortably, confident in their ability to logistically support their ships much farther away from home ports."[9]

Western analysts are alarmed not only by recent trends in China's arms purchases, but also by China's diplomatic behavior. The most dramatic move came last February, when China claimed sovereignty over the entire chain of the Spratly Islands in the South China Sea. In June, China announced that it had signed a contract with an American oil company — Crestone Energy Corp. of Denver, Colo. — to explore for oil on the islands, which also are claimed by Vietnam, Taiwan, Malaysia, the Philippines and Brunei (*see p. 1039*).

China's new assertiveness has made other countries in the region nervous. China's territorial claims on the Spratlys were the main topic of conversation at a meeting of the Association of Southeast Asian Nations (ASEAN)* in Manila in July. The foreign ministers of the member countries urged the United States to maintain a counterbalancing military presence in the area. A failure to do so, warned Philippine President Fidel V. Ramos, could lead to "perilous developments."

The U.S. response was less than reassuring to many in the region. While President Bush promised that the United States would maintain an Asian presence, the administration specifically declined to give assur-

---

*ASEAN is an organization — comprised of Thailand, Singapore, Indonesia, Malaysia, the Philippines and Brunei — whose main purpose is to coordinate regional economic policy.

ances regarding the Spratlys. According to some Asian officials, the United States has wrongly assumed that the ASEAN countries are capable of taking care of themselves. "Our MiGs won't deter the [Chinese] if they decide to do something," a Malaysian defense official said in July.[10]

Are the Koreas headed for unification, or conflagration?

In the near term, most analysts agree that the most likely place where warfare could erupt in Asia is Korea. With the world's fifth-largest military force (North Korea) faced off against the ninth-largest (South Korea) across 150 miles of common border, the potential for conflict is great.

On the surface at least, the confrontation — which has lasted since the end of the Korean War in 1953 — seems to be edging toward resolution. The leaders of North and South Korea have publicly committed themselves to working toward the peaceful unification of the country. Over the past year the pace of negotiations has been stepped up; the eighth round of unification talks took place in September in Pyongyang, the capital of North Korea.

One reason for the renewed interest in unification is North Korea's increasing sense of isolation. Its old ally, the Soviet Union — pressed by its growing economic crisis, and no longer interested in Korea as the site of Cold War confrontation — had cut aid to North

South Korea	
Military personnel	633,000
Navy:	
Surface combatants	38
Submarines	4
Patrol and coastal	81
Combat aircraft	418

Defense Spending in Asia Is Increasing

An upsurge in regional tensions following the end of the Cold War has prompted an increase in arms purchases and total defense spending in most Asian countries.

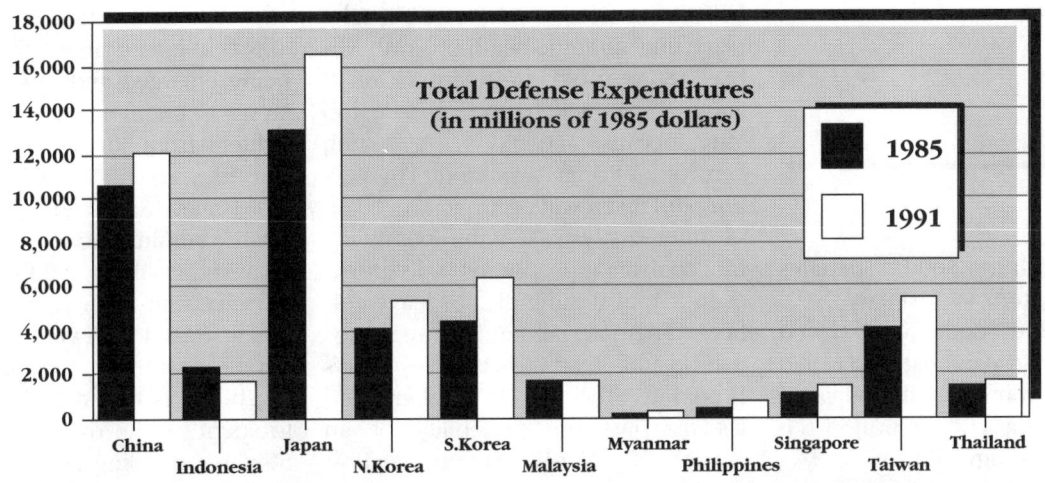

Total Defense Expenditures (in millions of 1985 dollars)

Legend: 1985, 1991

China, Indonesia, Japan, N.Korea, S.Korea, Malaysia, Myanmar, Philippines, Singapore, Taiwan, Thailand

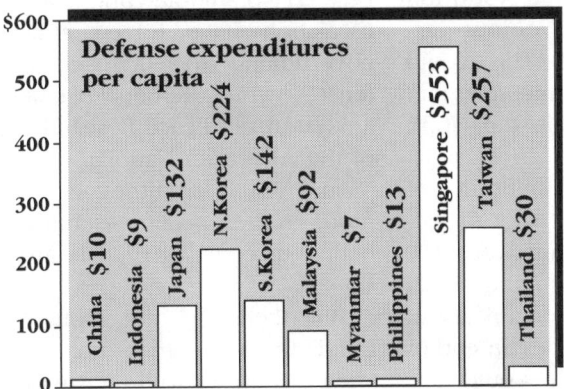

Defense expenditures per capita

China $10, Indonesia $9, Japan $132, N.Korea $224, S.Korea $142, Malaysia $92, Myanmar $7, Philippines $13, Singapore $553, Taiwan $257, Thailand $30

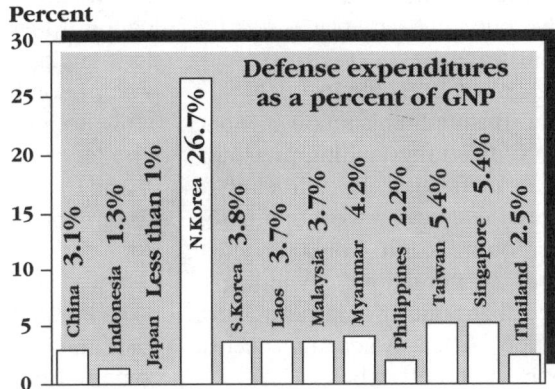

Defense expenditures as a percent of GNP

China 3.1%, Indonesia 1.3%, Japan Less than 1%, N.Korea 26.7%, S.Korea 3.8%, Laos 3.7%, Malaysia 3.7%, Myanmar 4.2%, Philippines 2.2%, Taiwan 5.4%, Singapore 5.4%, Thailand 2.5%

Note: Information was not available for Cambodia and Vietnam. Complete figures for Laos were not available for the graphs on total defense expenditures and defense expenditures per capita.

Source: International Institute for Strategic Studies, The Military Balance: 1992-1993, *1992*

Korea even before its own disintegration. Even worse, from the North Koreans' perspective, the Soviets established diplomatic relations with South Korea in September 1990.

China also has improved relations with South Korea in recent years. Indirect trade between China and South Korea, which had been a paltry $500 million in 1987, suddenly jumped to between $3 billion and $4 billion in 1988. According to some estimates, trade between the two countries will reach $10 billion this year. In October 1990, the two countries acknowledged the growing importance of their trade relationship by opening semi-diplomatic "trade bureaus" in each other's capital. In August 1992, China and South Korea formally established diplomatic relations.

These events did not go unnoticed by the North Koreans, who suddenly seemed more interested in the unifi-

North Korea	
Military personnel	1,132,000
Navy:	
Surface combatants	3
Submarines	26
Patrol and coastal	379
Combat aircraft	732

cation talks with the South. The talks gained momentum in February 1992, when North and South Korea signed a non-aggression pact that also called for joint development of the peninsula's resources and cooperation in science and technology.

But every time the unification talks appear to be on the verge of a major breakthrough, they hit a snag — usually one put in place by the North Koreans.

In October 1991, for example, just after the Bush administration met one of the North's longstanding preconditions to unification by agreeing to withdraw all nuclear weapons based in the South, North Korea issued a new set of conditions, including a demand that South Korea not receive protection from American nuclear weapons based elsewhere.

Similarly, though North Korea has several times announced that it would submit to international inspection of its nuclear installations — one of the conditions the United States and South Korea have insisted upon — it has consistently backed away from allowing such inspections at the last moment.[11]

Distrust of North Korea's intentions led the United States and South Korea to announce on Oct. 9 that a planned withdrawal of a portion of the approximately 35,000 U.S. troops stationed in South Korea would not take place until questions about North Korea's nuclear program were resolved.[12]

Despite all the problems, many analysts believe that citizen demands will force both the North and South to proceed toward unification. "There's going to be increasing sentiment for unification," says Bruce Porter. But he believes unification won't actually take place until after the death of North Korea's 80-year-old president, Kim Il Sung. "That will happen before too long, because the old man's getting very old," Porter says, "but I'm very doubtful that it will occur before."

Other analysts say the possibility of confrontation won't disappear even if Kim Il Sung dies or leaves office. "There are all kinds of scenarios that could lead to trouble," says Brookings' Thomas McNaugher, "and it's not just the possibility of an adventurist North moving against the South."

He envisions a scenario in which civil war breaks out in the North following Kim's death as various factions fight for power. This could prompt South Korea to intervene militarily to protect those in the North who favor unification.

And even the peaceful unification of Korea could increase regional tensions. "I think a lot of Japanese are very nervous about Korean unification," notes Porter, "even if it's on a peaceful basis and even if it involves an end of communism. [Unification] would turn Korea into a very large power, both economically and militarily."

Should the United States do more to limit the arms race in Asia?

Defense spending rose in nearly all Asian countries in 1990 and 1991. (See graph, p. 1029.) Although official figures for 1992 have not yet been released, analysts report a sharp increase in weapons buying in the past year, especially in the ASEAN countries of Southeast Asia.

Of all the countries of the region, "only Vietnam appears not to be engaged in any significant upgrading of its naval capabilities," notes the Far

Eastern Economic Review — an exception the Hong Kong-based magazine attributes to Vietnam's "acute economic problems, the almost complete suspension of military ties with Moscow and the absence of other foreign sources of military assistance."[13]

Naval forces aren't the only ones being enlarged and modernized. Malaysia is planning to buy 30 MiG-29 fighters from Russia. Singapore purchased a squadron of F-16 jets from the United States in 1990. And the Bush administration recently approved the sale of 150 F-16s, the most advanced air-to-air fighters in America's arsenal, to Taiwan (see below).

One reason for the weapons-buying binge is that the money is there to spend. "The rising trend of Asian military spending contrasts with other regions, such as the Middle East, Latin America and Africa, where depressed commodity prices and debt escalation have forced almost all governments to cut back on defense," writes Robin Luckham, an analyst at the Peace Research Centre of the Australian National University. "Some Asian countries have spent more on their military establishments mainly because they can afford to do so."[14]

But there's clearly more to the trend than countries not knowing what else to do with their money. In Southeast Asia in particular, the driving force behind the arms race is distrust among the nations, fueled by uncertainties about the continuing presence of U.S. forces.

"There's a lot of local competitiveness," observes James Clad, an Asia specialist at the Carnegie Endowment for International Peace in Washington. "And on top of that there's the idea that, whatever happens, the world is not going to be as safe and secure as it was during the long period of unrivaled U.S. 7th Fleet supremacy."

The looming presence of China is adding to the uncertainty. "We have been getting all kinds of reports about the Chinese going into the former Soviet Union and picking the shelves clean [of arms] at fire-sale prices," an unnamed U.S. official told *The New York Times*. "They are buying not only weapons, but advanced technologies so that they can upgrade their own weapons and make them more exportable. They are the ones who have started the arms race in the region."[15]

China's new assertiveness is of particular concern to Taiwan. Traditionally one of Asia's biggest defense spenders, Taiwan has recently gone on a buying spree. The Taiwanese navy recently finalized an agreement to build 12 frigates in cooperation with the United States, and Taiwan is purchasing another 16 frigates from France. The island has also purchased four minesweepers from Germany and two submarines from the Netherlands.

Taiwan's most controversial arms deal is the recently announced purchase of 150 F-16 fighters from the United States. China has objected to the sale, arguing that it violates U.S.-China agreements on Taiwan. Indeed, according to a State Department spokesman, under a 1982 Chinese-American communiqué, the United States pledged that its arms sales to Taiwan "will not exceed either in qualitative or quantitative terms the level of those supplied in recent years since the establishment of diplomatic relations between the United States and China, and that it intends to gradually reduce its sale of arms to Taiwan."[16]

The Bush administration justified the F-16 sale on China's recent purchase of Su-27 fighters from Russia, a deal the administration said would upset the military balance between China and Taiwan. Others, including President-elect Clinton, said the administration was motivated more by election-year concerns — since the deal would save thousands of jobs at General Dynamics Corp.'s aircraft plant in Fort Worth, Texas.

Some analysts, in fact, have pointed to the F-16 deal as evidence that the United States is trying to capitalize on Asia's arms-buying spree. "In

Views From the U.S. and Japan

Japanese opinion is divided over whether the United States should maintain its current level of military influence in the Asia-Pacific region. Most Americans, however, believe it is necessary in order to keep the region stable.

Détente in the Far East

Sweeping changes have taken place in the world since the Cold War between the United States and the Soviet Union ended. Do you think a détente, or easing of political and military tension, is also in progress in the Asia-Pacific region or not?

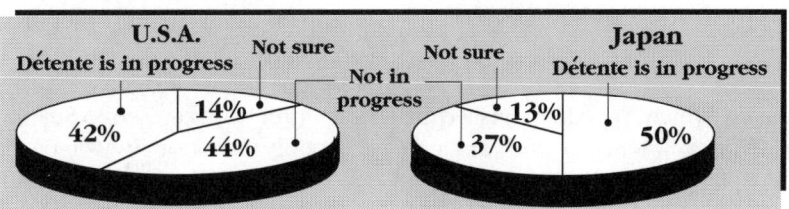

Japan — A Militarist Threat?

Do you feel there is a danger of Japan again emerging as a threatening militaristic nation as it was before World War II, or not?

	United States		Japan	
	1992	1991	1992	1991
Danger	36%	30%	18%	15%
No danger	62%	68%	76%	78%
Not sure	2%	2%	6%	7%

The Long Arm of Uncle Sam

In order to keep the Asia-Pacific region stable, do you think that it is necessary for the United States to maintain the same military influence over this area as it has now, or not?

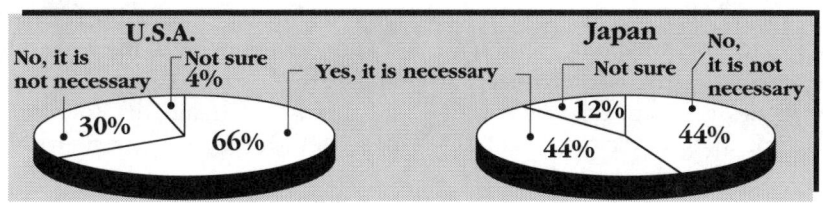

Who Benefits From the Security Treaty

Do you think the U.S./Japan benefits from the Security Treaty between the United States and Japan, or not?

	United States		Japan	
	1992	1991	1992	1991
Yes, U.S./Japan benefits	44%	52%	42%	50%
No, U.S./Japan does not benefit	43%	38%	21%	23%
Not sure	13%	10%	18%	17%
Other/no answer	—	—	9%	10%

Source: Polls conducted in April 1992 by Louis Harris and Associates Inc. and Asahi Shimbun, a Tokyo newspaper.

Taiwan

Military personnel	360,000
Navy:	
Surface combatants	33
Submarines	4
Patrol and coastal	93
Combat aircraft	518

a year in which President Bush is in Fort Worth waving F-16s around, we're not helping political trouble in the region at all," says a U.S. foreign policy analyst who asked not to be identified because of her relationship with the Bush administration. The analyst argues that the United States should use its aid and trade leverage to discourage the current level of weapons buying. "We could, for example, be doing much more through our security relationship with Thailand to control its military, and we're not doing it," she says.

To be effective, the analyst adds, such an effort "would have to be a multilateral effort that we organized or pushed," otherwise countries intent on arming could simply turn elsewhere for weapons. She notes that Japan already has taken steps to link its development aid to lower defense spending in recipient nations.

But other analysts argue that it is through selective arms sales that the United States can convince its allies of its commitment to the region. "I guarantee you that our allies in Asia were very relieved after they heard about [the sale of F-16s to Taiwan]," a Bush administration official told *The New York Times*. "It restores a little bit of geopolitical balance at a time when the Chinese have really been throwing their weight around."[17]

President-elect Clinton has not indicated whether he will support the sale of F-16s to Taiwan. But Clinton on sev-

eral occasions has taken a position significantly more critical of China than that adopted by the Bush administration, which may indicate that he would not cancel the F-16 agreement merely to keep China happy.

Should the United States encourage Japan to remilitarize?

For more than a decade, many U.S. government officials have called for greater "burden sharing" by our allies, particularly Japan. As early as 1981, President Ronald Reagan coaxed Japanese Prime Minister Zenko Suzuki into accepting responsibility for patrolling sea lanes up to 1,000 miles from Japanese shores, a responsibility formerly held by the U.S. 7th Fleet. And the United States has continually pressed Japan to assume a greater share of the cost of maintaining U.S. forces in Japan.

The Persian Gulf War increased tensions between the United States and Japan. U.S. officials were unhappy with Japan's slow response to U.S. entreaties for financial support for Operation Desert Storm and its decision not to send any troops to the region.

In June 1992, Japan finally bent to pressure from the United States and passed a bill modifying its Constitution to allow Japanese soldiers to be deployed abroad as long as the operation was under the aegis of the United Nations. In September, Japan began sending troops to Cambodia to monitor peacekeeping operations there. (*See story, p. 1038.*)

But some American analysts believe that urging Japan to assume a larger military role may be a serious mistake. "The problem is that what makes sense in a bilateral relationship [between the United States and Japan] doesn't always work for other parties' perceptions," says James Clad.

Indeed, many of the countries that experienced Japanese military aggression before and during World War II — including Korea, China, Russia and Singapore — get understandably nervous at any sign of a resurgent Japanese mili-

tarism. "The suspicions and the tensions that have existed since World War II are continuing," says Bruce Porter. "There's profound distrust about Japanese intentions. And unlike in Europe, where there's been a process of integration occurring, and you've had NATO for all these years, in Asia there's nothing similar to pull these states together."

Such concerns were evident after Japan passed the bill allowing for the limited foreign deployment of its forces. Singapore's senior minister, Lee Kuan Yew, spoke for many in the region when he warned: "Allowing Japan to once again send its forces abroad is like giving a chocolate liqueur to an alcoholic. Once the Japanese get off the wagon, it will be hard to stop them."[18]

Not all the countries in Asia fear a greater military role for Japan. Thailand — which was not occupied by Japan during World War II — proposed in 1990 that the two countries conduct joint military-training operations. "We don't feel threatened by the Japanese military, and we know that Japan is not interested in the military at all," a spokesman for Thai Prime Minister Chatichai Choonhavan said at the time. "In fact, what we're trying to do is get Japan more involved."[19]

But many, if not most, of those in the region — including a majority of the Japanese themselves — don't want the Japanese government to take on a greater military role. "The trouble with America is that you are

Japan

Military personnel	246,000
Navy:	
Surface combatants	64
Submarines	17
Patrol and coastal	11
Combat aircraft	539

always trying to encourage us to increase our military capability," Masao Kunihiro, one of the leading opponents of the bill allowing Japanese troops to participate in peacekeeping operations, said recently. "I know that the day will come when you will regret it."[20] ∎

BACKGROUND

Superpower Battleground

The beginnings of the Cold War between the Soviet Union and the United States had immediate and violent implications for the countries of Asia. Nowhere was the disruption greater than in Korea. Occupied by Japan before and during World War II, Korea at war's end was occupied by the Soviet Union in the North and U.S. forces in the South. The Soviets blocked Korean efforts at reunifying the country, and in 1948 the Democratic People's Republic of Korea, or North Korea, was officially formed under Kim Il Sung, who still holds power. The South responded by forming the Republic of Korea, with Syngman Rhee as president.

On June 25, 1950, North Korea, armed primarily by the Soviet Union, invaded the South. With the backing of the U.N. Security Council, U.S. troops counterattacked and by the end of October had driven North Korean troops back almost to the Chinese border. At that point, China sent its troops across the Yalu River to support the North Koreans, eventually forcing a stalemate in the war with the country divided along its present border.

The conflict did have one beneficial side effect, particularly for South Korea: The dollars spent by the large U.S. military contingent that stayed behind helped to energize South Korea's economy — as did generous aid from America and preferential access to U.S. markets.

In the 40 years since the Korean War, South Korea has become one of the world's leading industrialized nations. North Korea, on the other hand, is one of the world's poorest countries, despite having a generous assortment of natural resources.

Both countries have devoted an inordinately large portion of their resources to defense. South Korea regularly spends 4-6 percent of its gross national product (GNP) on its military. North Korea spends at least 10 percent of its meager resources on defense.* Some experts believe North Korea spends as much as 15-20 percent of its GNP on the military.[21]

Disagreements Over Taiwan

Korea was not the only site of superpower tensions in Northeast Asia in the years following World War II. The island of Taiwan, off the Chinese mainland, was one of the main sources of friction between the United States and China.

Ruled by Japan from 1895 until 1945, Taiwan was taken over by Chinese Nationalists in 1949. Led by Chiang Kai Shek, the Nationalists fled to the island after losing control of mainland China to the Communists. Both the Nationalist government on Taiwan and the Communist government on the mainland claimed to be the legitimate rulers of all of China. The United States backed the claim of the Nationalists.

When Chinese troops entered the Korean War in October 1950, the United States immediately sent the U.S. 7th Fleet to the Formosa Strait to protect Taiwan from an expected Chinese invasion. As it turned out, China did not press the Taiwan issue until after the Korean War ended.

---

*By comparison, the United States spends 6-7 percent of its GNP on the military.

In September 1954, the government in Beijing announced it was going to reclaim its territory from the Nationalists. In early 1955, the Communists pushed Nationalist forces — evacuated by the U.S. Navy — from two small island groups just off the coast of China. Over the next three years, the Communists repeatedly attacked the U.S.-armed Nationalists on two of the islands — Quemoy and Matsu.

While the Soviet Union did not get directly involved in this conflict, it did promise to use Soviet nuclear weapons against the United States if U.S. nuclear weapons were used against China, a move that was under active consideration by the Eisenhower administration. As a result of a firm U.S. statement in support of the Nationalists — backed up by a large buildup of U.S. naval forces — this U.S.-Soviet missile crisis ended in a standoff.

How Japan Benefited

The country of Northeast Asia that was least affected by the Cold War was, ironically, Japan. Following World War II, the former colonizer of Korea and Manchuria was occupied by a more benevolent power — the United States. Instead of punishing Japan, the Truman and Eisenhower administrations saw Japan as a potential bulwark against Soviet and Chinese encroachment and, as a result, the Americans sought to rebuild the Japanese economy.

The strategic importance of Japan became clearer with the outbreak of the Korean War. Japan — only 80 miles across the water from the southern coast of Korea — served as an excellent staging area for U.S. forces during the war.

Japan benefited from the conflict in two important ways: First, American spending on the war helped boost Japan's economy. Secondly, and more important over the long run, the United States relieved Japan of the need to provide for its own defense.

For the next several decades, Japan was able to focus on economic development and trade, aided both by concessionary access to U.S. markets and by American protection allowing Japan to divert only a fraction of its resources to defense. Indeed, under the new constitution written for Japan by the United States, Japan was forbidden to undertake military expeditions and was limited to spending no more than 1 percent of its gross national product on defense.

China's Role

China is the giant that ties Northern and Southern Asia together. And for most U.S. policy-makers of the Cold War era, China was the political as well as the geographical center of the Far East.

"After the Korean War, the United States began to construct its overall strategy in the Western Pacific around the containment of China," notes Harry Harding, a China specialist at the Brookings Institution. "Policy planners in Washington regarded China's invasion of Tibet in 1950, its support for the Communist revolution in Vietnam, its involvement in the Korean conflict and its ties with revolutionary Communist parties in Southeast Asia as evidence enough that Peking's ultimate goal was the Communist seizure of power across Asia."[22]

The initial U.S. response to this perceived threat was a series of mutual defense treaties. "Although some of these alliances were formally justified as efforts to deter the re-emergence of a military threat from Japan," Harding writes, "their real objective was to contain the expansion of Chinese influence in Asia."[23]

Besides committing itself to protecting Taiwan, the United States signed defense agreements with Ja-

pan, South Korea, the Philippines and Thailand. The United States also tried in 1954 to create a Southeast Asian version of NATO — the Southeast Asian Treaty Organization (SEATO). But despite its name, the organization included only two countries in Southeast Asia — Thailand and the Philippines. SEATO never achieved the coherence of NATO, and the alliance was essentially abandoned in 1974.

During the Cold War period, rela-

During the Cold War period, relations between the United States and China often were determined by the wider conflict between the U.S. and the Soviet Union.

---

tions between the United States and China often were determined by the wider conflict between the U.S. and the Soviet Union. In fact, for most of the 40 years following World War II, the United States continually sought to play the Chinese off against the Soviets.

Fears of Soviet expansionism and concerns about the continuing war in Vietnam — where U.S. troops were battling Soviet- and Chinese-supplied North Vietnamese — led President Richard M. Nixon to recognize China's Communist government in 1972, a move the United States had resisted since 1949. Nixon hoped Chinese pressure would force the North Vietnamese to the bargaining table, where some accommodation could

be reached. The Nixon administration also felt closer U.S.-China ties would force the Soviet Union to pay more attention to its own borders and less attention to such places as Cuba, Angola and Vietnam.

China had its own reasons for responding to Nixon's overtures. With Soviet forces arrayed across the Sino-Soviet border, the Chinese were at least as interested as the Americans in containing Soviet power. And just as the United States sought Chinese cooperation on the issue of Vietnam, the Chinese sought U.S. cooperation on the issue of Taiwan. China's leaders also wanted access to U.S. markets and technology.

At first, it looked like both the United States and China might get what they wanted. By 1975, the United States was able to end its involvement in the Vietnam War — though it is not clear how much the Chinese helped with the disengagement. For its part, China received a rather vague commitment from the United States on Taiwan. In a communiqué released in Shanghai at the end of President Nixon's 1972 visit to China, the United States indicated that it would "not challenge" the idea that Taiwan was part of China — a proposition even the Nationalist government on Taiwan accepted. The United States also indicated its intention to withdraw all American forces from Taiwan at some point in the future.

In late 1978, the United States finally broke off diplomatic relations with Taiwan and agreed to pull out its remaining military forces. The following year, Washington and the Communist government in Beijing exchanged ambassadors for the first time.

Hopes for the U.S.-China alliance remained high in the early 1980s. According to Harry Harding, the two countries "agreed on the desirability of

Continued on p. 1036

Chronology

1940s-1950s
Asia undergoes major changes as a world war finally ends and the United States becomes involved in two regional conflicts.

Sept. 2, 1945
On the battleship *U.S.S. Missouri*, Japan signs treaty ending World War II.

1948
With Soviet backing, North Korea declares its status as a separate country.

1949
Chinese Nationalists, defeated by the Communists, flee the mainland for Taiwan.

June 25, 1950
The Korean War begins as North Korean troops invade South Korea. U.S. troops, already stationed in South Korea, counterattack with United Nations approval.

October 1950
Chinese troops enter the Korean War in support of North Korea. The U.S. 7th Fleet is sent to block the Formosa Strait to protect Taiwan from China. Also in 1950, President Harry S Truman sends a 35-man contingent to Vietnam to help the French maintain colonial control.

July 27, 1953
An armistice is declared in Korea.

1955
U.S. military advisers arrive in South Vietnam, marking the beginning of the U.S. role in South Vietnam.

1960s-1970s
The Vietnam War dominates U.S. policy in Asia.

1968
During the Tet offensive in January and February, Viet Cong guerrillas attack Saigon, Hué and some provincial South Vietnamese capitals. On Oct. 31, President Lyndon B. Johnson orders a halt to bombing of North Vietnam. Peace talks begin in Paris.

Summer 1970
President Nixon initiates bombing and ground invasion of Cambodia.

1972
Nixon recognizes the Communist government of China.

April 1975
President Gerald R. Ford pulls the last U.S. forces out of Vietnam. That same month, Communist Khmer Rouge guerrillas seize power in Cambodia.

1979
The United States agrees to withdraw its recognition of Taiwan and to pull out both military and diplomatic personnel.

December 1979
Vietnamese forces invade Cambodia and quickly set up a puppet government in Phnom Penh.

* * *

1980s-1990s
Relative calm settles over Asia, with Vietnam pulling out of Cambodia and North and South Korea signing a non-aggression pact.

1981
At America's urging, Japan agrees to patrol sea lanes up to 1,000 miles from Japan.

1988
China sinks two Vietnamese gunboats in waters around the contested Spratly Islands, killing more than 70 Vietnamese sailors.

1989
After a costly occupation, Vietnam pulls its last troops out of Cambodia.

June 1989
Chinese troops crack down on political demonstrations in Tiananmen Square in Beijing.

1990
Japanese reluctance to aid in the allied fight against Iraq in Operation Desert Storm sours U.S.-Japanese relations.

September 1990
Soviet Union establishes diplomatic relations with South Korea.

October 1991
Cambodian rebels sign peace agreement with Cambodian government.

February 1992
U.N. Security Council votes to send a peacekeeping force to Cambodia. In an unrelated development, North Korea and South Korea sign a non-aggression pact. China passes a new territories law, claiming the Spratly Islands in the South China Sea as a Chinese territory.

June 1992
Japanese Diet allows Japanese troops to be deployed abroad for the first time since World War II.

August 1992
China and South Korea open formal diplomatic relations.

October 1992
The United States drops plans to withdraw troops from South Korea, at least until North Korea permits inspection of its nuclear facilities.

New Era in Asia

As the Clinton administration prepares to take over the White House, Asian leaders are seeking reassurances that the United States will maintain its diplomatic and military presence in Asia.

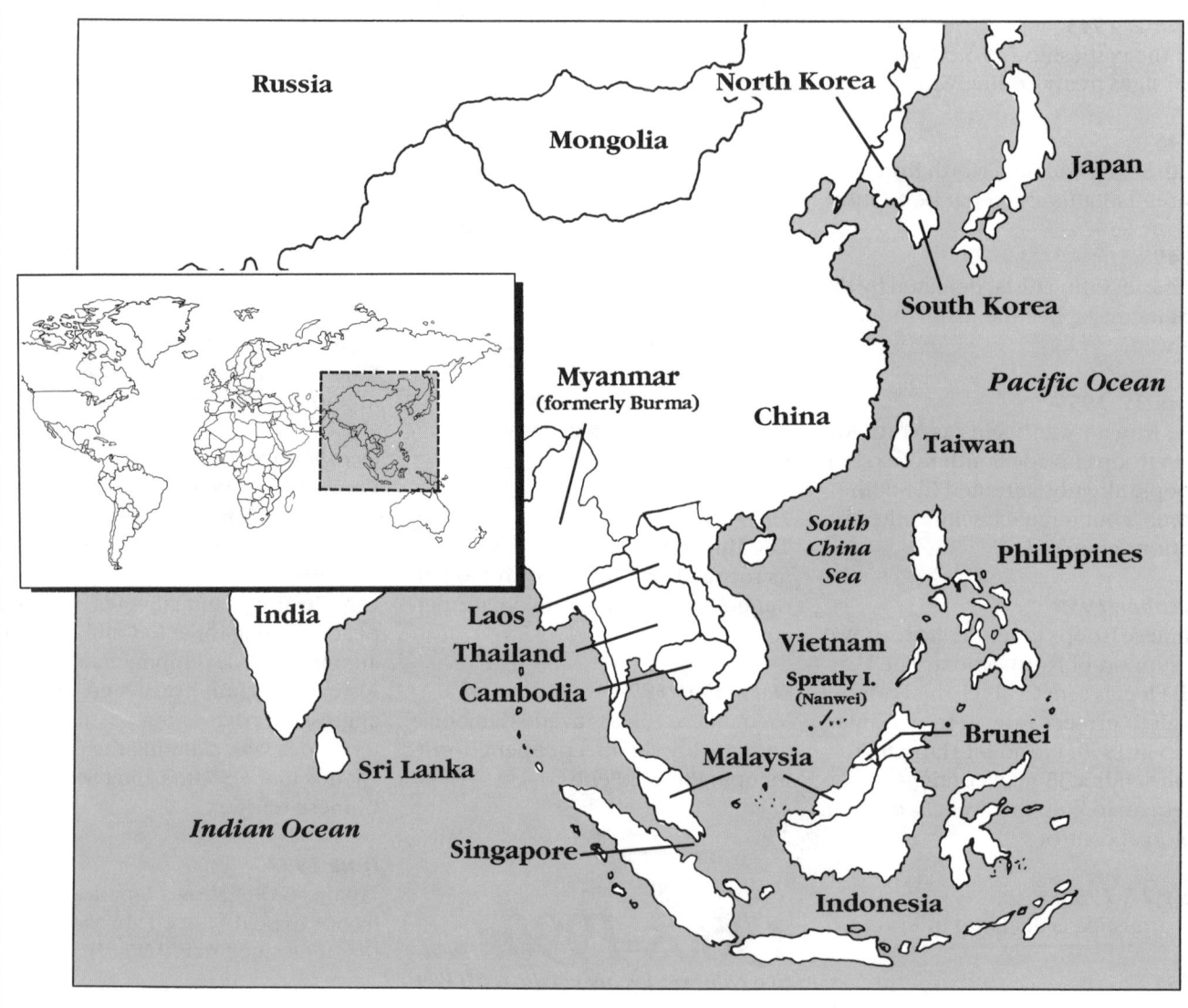

Continued from p. 1034
undertaking parallel or complementary actions on key regional disputes. The two worked together to deny the new pro-Vietnamese government in Phnom Penh [Cambodia] a seat in the United Nations and discussed ways of supporting the Cambodian resistance to the Vietnamese intervention. They also agreed on the need to oppose the Soviet invasion of Afghanistan, with the United States reimbursing Peking for some of the costs of transporting Chinese arms and equipment to the Afghan rebels."[24]

But despite the positive signs, relations between China and the United States never improved as much as either side had hoped. China was upset over continuing U.S. arms sales to Taiwan — which increased from

$208 million in 1978 to $267 million in 1980 — and over the refusal of the United States to sell advanced military equipment to China. The United States, in turn, was agitated over Chinese arms sales to Third World countries, especially in the Middle East, and over Chinese support for the Khmer Rouge guerrillas who took power in Cambodia in 1975. (*See story, p. 1038.*)

There also were important changes in the underlying interests that held the Sino-American relationship together. "As the threat of a consolidation of Vietnamese control over Cambodia seemed to wane," Harding writes, "the commonalties between Peking and Washington ... became less significant, and the divergences over the Khmer Rouge assumed greater salience. Just as the decline of the Soviet threat reduced the global rationale for Sino-American strategic cooperation, so did the ebbing of Vietnamese power in Indochina remove some of the regional foundation for a geopolitical alignment between Peking and Washington."[25]

The waning of Cold War frictions between the United States and the Soviet Union and China's brutal crackdown on demonstrators in Tiananmen Square in June 1989 put additional strains on the U.S.-Sino relationship. In response to the Tiananmen incident, the United States — along with most of the international community — imposed a series of diplomatic and trade sanctions against China.

But the Bush administration rescinded most of the sanctions within six months. The administration also blocked congressional challenges to China's "most-favored-nation" trading status — a trade classification that ensures that China receives the same trade access to U.S. markets as most other U.S. trade partners. (*See "At Issue," p. 1041.*) ■

their neighbors, particularly China.

Dispute Over U.S. Bases in the Philippines

Fears that the U.S. presence in the Far East might diminish increased last year when the United States and the Philippines failed to reach an agreement on keeping the two huge U.S. bases in the Philippines — Subic Bay Naval Station and Clark Air Base.

The presence of the American bases had been a source of friction in U.S.-Filipino relations, particularly since the overthrow of President Ferdinand E. Marcos in 1986. In September 1991, the Philippine Senate rejected an extension of the agreement that had allowed the United States to maintain its bases.

The Navy is scheduled to finish pulling out of Subic Bay by the end of November 1992. The Air Force already has abandoned Clark Air Base, which was virtually buried in ash from the eruption of Mount Pinatubo last year. The Subic Bay facilities — which were large enough to handle the maintenance of several carrier battle groups at one time — were considered a greater strategic loss to the United States.

Despite the problems with the Philippines, President Bush has repeatedly stated, as he did last January during a speech to the Australian Parliament, that America's role and purpose as a Pacific power "will remain constant.... We intend to re-
Continued on p. 1039

CURRENT SITUATION

Post-Cold War Problems

In the Far East, as in Europe, the Cold War forced nationalistic and ethnic rivalries into suspension, but it did nothing to cure them. Now that the Cold War is over, those rivalries are once again creating problems in both parts of the world.

But Asia specialists warn that comparisons between Europe and Asia must be made very cautiously, for the historical differences between the two regions are as important as the similarities. One important difference is that in Europe the Cold War was largely a two-party affair, while in Asia there was always a third major player — China. And because of the region's long history of colonial occupation, all three superpowers tended to look on their Asian allies as clients rather than true partners. For these reasons, Asia never developed a regional security organization along the lines of NATO.

"The post-Cold War arms race in Southeast Asia is a follow-up consequence of the fact that you never had a neat lineup in Cold War terms in Asia," explains James Clad. "You never had the equivalent of the Warsaw Pact on the one side and NATO on the other. It was always a question of alignments, jockeying for position and advantage."

The absence of a regional security alliance is partly responsible for the post-Cold War power vacuum in Asia. As the Soviet threat recedes, and the raison d'être for the U.S. presence becomes less self-evident, many countries in the region are turning their eyes nervously toward

Philippines	
Military personnel	106,500
Navy:	
Surface combatants	1
Patrol and coastal	42
Combat aircraft	54

Cambodia: The War Drags On

While 1975 marked the end of the Vietnam War, it was far from the end of conflict in the region. Cambodia, weakened by U.S. and Vietnamese incursions during the war and by a collapsing regional economy, was easy prey to Cambodian Communist guerrillas known as the Khmer Rouge, who took power in April 1975.

Over the next four years, the Khmer Rouge carried out a brutal social transformation, sealing off the country from outside contact, virtually clearing the cities of people, establishing strictly regulated communes in the countryside and killing any Cambodians who objected or who did not "fit in," mainly educated Cambodians, merchants and students. While the world silently watched the genocide, as many as 2 million people may have been executed.

But Pol Pot and his Khmer Rouge miscalculated: They attacked ethnic Vietnamese during their domestic purges and, eager to acquire land they considered historically Cambodian, they conducted border raids into Vietnam. In response, the Vietnamese invaded Cambodia in December 1979, quickly routed the Khmer Rouge forces and set up a puppet government in the capital, Phnom Penh.

The Vietnamese victory forced the Khmer Rouge forces into northwest Cambodia, where they immediately began fighting the Vietnamese-backed troops of the new Cambodian government. Ironically, the Khmer Rouge often found itself allied with two other smaller, non-communist armies that had previously fought the Khmer Rouge regime — the National Army of Prince Norodom Sihanouk, whose government was overthrown during the Vietnam War, and the Khmer People's National Liberation Front, led by Son Sann, a former prime minister under Sihanouk.

During the following decade of war, the United States funneled aid to the non-communist groups, primarily through Thailand and Malaysia. The Khmer Rouge received the bulk of their aid from China and from selling access to timber and gem fields in northeast Cambodia to Thai entrepreneurs.

Vietnam, strained by the costs of occupying Cambodia and under international pressure to leave, finally withdrew in 1989, leaving behind a much strengthened Cambodian regime in Phnom Penh led by Hun Sen, a former Khmer leader. The warfare inside Cambodia continued, but with Vietnam largely out of the picture the backers of each Cambodian faction pressed for a peaceful resolution. On Feb. 29, 1992, the United Nations Security Council voted to send a 22,000-man peacekeeping force to Cambodia at a cost of almost $2 billion.

But there has been little other progress since then. In fact, some analysts worry that the situation may be deteriorating, largely as a result of the Khmer Rouge's refusal to disarm according to the plan.

"The Khmer Rouge are in a situation where they may head into a Sendero Luminoso [Peru's violent revolutionary guerrillas, the Shining Path] type status," says Michael Vlahos, a project director at the Center for Naval Analysis. But in the end, Vlahos argues, "the Khmer Rouge don't have a lot of options. If they stay truculent, they'll get squeezed. They have Thailand on the one side and Vietnam on the other, and it's not like they have the sort of fortresslike situation of Cuba. And China can't effectively provide the kind of support that they once did."

The United Nations had, in fact, hoped that when China agreed to stop supplying the Khmer Rouge, after the signing of the peace accord, the Khmer Rouge would be forced into continuing to comply with the terms of the agreement. That hope has not been met, largely for two reasons: Khmer Rouge forces reportedly buried large caches of weapons and supplies before the United Nations arrived; and the Khmer Rouge appear to be receiving aid from Thailand.

In fact, Thai companies with close ties to the military are doing a lot of business in northwestern Cambodia, particularly in timber and gems. The Khmer Rouge are reportedly allowing tens of thousands of miners and loggers to cross the Thai-Cambodian border to work, while U.N. observers are kept away.† There is little question that the Khmer Rouge are receiving healthy profits from the operations.

Thailand has long claimed parts of northwestern Cambodia, and some analysts have speculated that the Thais and the Khmer Rouge might conceivably make a deal giving Thailand land in return for helping the Khmer Rouge regain control of Cambodia.

"The Thais never succeeded in occupying Cambodia in a military way, but now they can colonize the country with money," says a Western diplomat.††

Cambodia's Military	
Military personnel	135,000
Navy:	
Patrol and coastal	12
Combat aircraft	17

---

† See *The Washington Post*, Aug. 12, 1992.

†† Quoted in the *Far Eastern Economic Review*, June 25, 1992.

Continued from p. 1037

main engaged no matter what the changing security arrangements of our time."

During Bush's trip to Asia, U.S. officials announced that the United States and Singapore had agreed to move the logistical command center for the U.S. 7th Fleet, which had been based at Subic Bay, to Singapore. The United States also let it be known that it was seeking similar base-access agreements with Malaysia and Thailand.

The U.S. Pacific Command includes 383,000 personnel, 237 ships and about 300 fighter aircraft. Force levels are somewhat lower than they were in the 1980s. Most of the personnel and equipment are based on the U.S. mainland and in Hawaii and Guam, with most of the remainder

---

U.S. Forces:

Pacific fleet:
Surface combatants (including 5 aircraft carriers)	116
Submarines	61

South Korea:
Military personnel	35,500
Combat aircraft	84

Japan:
Military personnel	39,300
Combat aircraft	78

Russian Forces:

Pacific Fleet:
Surface combatants	54
Submarines	86
Navy combat aircraft	319

Russian Far East:
Combat aircraft	460

---

stationed in Japan and Korea.

As far as Western analysts can tell, the Russian Pacific Command also is somewhat smaller. There are 63 surface warships and 98 submarines in the Russian Pacific Fleet; 47 divisions of ground troops and more than 500 fighter planes are assigned to the Far East.

"The Soviet naval forces in the Pacific haven't actually been reduced much, though good figures are hard to find," says Brookings' Thomas McNaugher. "But they aren't being perceived as much of a threat. The fleet has held maneuvers, but that's mostly to keep the ships from getting rusty. According to the commander of the fleet, some of the ships are actually being leased for commercial purposes."

During a recent visit to South Korea, Russian President Boris Yeltsin indicated that his country was eager to slash its armed forces in the Far East and improve relations with its Asian neighbors. "We intend to noticeably cut our military potential, including its Far Eastern component," Yeltsin told the South Korean National Assembly Nov. 19. Departing from his prepared text, Yeltsin said that within the next two or three years Russia might stop building submarines for military purposes.

China's Intentions

As the Cold War ended, a new threat began to emerge in the Far East: China increased its purchases of sophisticated military equipment and technology and demonstrated a new territorial aggressiveness.

China's military could never be ignored. The country possesses an estimated 250-350 nuclear warheads, deployed on missiles, bombers and submarines. But while its nuclear forces alone qualify China as a member of the geopolitical big leagues, it is the country's increased spending on conventional weaponry that

makes many in the region nervous.

In March 1992 the Chinese government announced it was increasing its military budget by 13.8 percent — an increase of about 50 percent over 1989 levels — at a time when external threats to China were lower than they had been in many years. Even more troubling to other countries in the region was that China was buying equipment — such as midair refueling technology, aircraft carriers and submarines — that would allow it to extend its power far beyond its own borders.

This indicates, some analysts argue, that China is clearly preparing to assume a more decisive role in regional affairs. "What we are now witnessing is a Pax Sinica in the making, in place of a reluctant Pax Americana and an impotent Russia," writes B. A. Hamzah, assistant director-general of Malaysia's Institute of Strategic and International Studies.[26]

The place where China is most obviously flexing its muscles is in Southeast Asia. In February 1992, China passed a territories law that, in essence, puts all of the South China Sea, including the Spratly Islands, under Chinese jurisdiction. China has long claimed the Spratlys, as have Vietnam, Malaysia, Brunei, the Philippines and Taiwan. China even backed up its claim with an attack on two Vietnamese gunboats in 1988, an attack that killed scores of Vietnamese sailors. But passage of the new territories law, and the announcement a few months later that China had contracted with an American oil company to explore for oil in the area (*see p. 1028),* was perceived as an indication that China was raising the stakes in the Spratlys.

The belief that there may be large oil and gas reserves on and near the islands clearly has made the Spratlys a hot property. But so far, there is no hard proof that drilling efforts will pay off, certainly not in the immediate future. For this reason, some analysts see more than economic motives behind China's interest in the Spratlys. "The situation offers China a chance to 'teach lessons' that aren't lessons that necessarily involve a protracted encounter, like Korea would," says James Clad of the Carnegie Endowment.

Arthur Waldron, a professor at the Naval War College in Providence, R.I., offers a similar explanation for China's behavior. "What we've got is a China that doesn't really have a superpower role," he explains. "There is no great defining conflict anymore, so they're simply a regional power. They don't have to worry so much about the Soviet border, they've got a fair amount of money in the bank, they've observed the technological level of warfare — the gulf war had a very sobering effect on them — and they decided that they had better increase their military capacity."

Some analysts believe China's increased defense spending and its more strident diplomatic posturing may be more for domestic than foreign consumption. The government in Beijing was shaken by the level of popular outrage over its crackdown on demonstrators in Tiananmen Square in 1989, and China's leaders may be looking for ways to keep the military happy, and to give it something to do.

"There was almost civil war over Tiananmen," notes Michael Vlahos, a project director at the Center for Naval Analysis in Washington. "There's an attempt perhaps to make the army a symbol of the continuing vitality and motivation of the central state to survive." Vlahos also conjectures that China's increasing stridency over the Spratly Islands "may be an attempt to use external issues as lightning rods to keep the army as coherent as possible, and to keep in people's minds the loyalty of the military."

The military appears to be gaining increasing power at the highest levels of Chinese politics. In October, Chi-

na's leaders met to hammer out the shape of government policies for the next five years and to decide who would staff critical positions. For the first time, a career general was chosen to sit on the Politburo Standing Committee, the highest political body in China.

What makes these changes all the more critical is that China is on the verge of major political transition. Deng Xiaoping, China's 88-year-old leader, is understood to be in fading health, and most analysts expect a scramble for power when he dies or is incapacitated.

"We've had stability more or less since 1949," Waldron observes, "and that's largely been the product of a cohesive leadership group that might squabble among themselves, but nevertheless held the country together. Of course, those people are almost all gone, and they will be gone soon. Communism, is largely discredited, and China is facing political challenges equivalent to what we've seen in the Soviet Union."

The critical question as far as regional security is concerned, Waldron adds, "is whether this transformation is going to be successful, whether it will lead to a stable successor regime, or whether it will lead to a protracted struggle for succession. That has to be in the background of any security discussion." ∎

OUTLOOK

China's Political Future

Some Western analysts fear that the passing of power to a new generation of Chinese leaders could have unpredictable results, particularly in foreign affairs. "The instinctive feeling of Chinese politicians who don't have a lot of foreign policy experience is that China is the world's leading country and that China is the center of everything," says Waldron. "This is a very powerful cultural inheritance, and I don't think that they particularly welcome the United States. I think a more seasoned Chinese politician would understand that Japan is a tremendous threat to China potentially, and that China is not capable of coping with Japan alone. Therefore an alliance with the United States that leashes Japan is very much in China's interest."

But Waldron is not convinced that seasoned politicians will win out in China's power struggle. "Who's going to come into power now is a very big question, and it's tied up with the whole issue of democratization in China," he says. "Once you start having popular participation, then nationalistic policies can become appealing. So I think there's some danger that a highly contested democratic political structure would lead to a more irresponsible foreign policy."

Harvard's Bruce Porter says "there are a lot of people [in the United States] who think China is going to emerge as an expansionist power in the next decade or so." Waldron agrees. "I'm not worried because I'm afraid China is going to lay waste to Asia," he says. "I'm worried that this is going to start an arms race, and particularly if there's no longer a power out there in a position to arbitrate and help keep order."

Other analysts fear China might go in another direction equally fraught with risks: internal fragmentation. There already are signs that Beijing's control over the provinces is weakening, particularly in the economically booming region on the southern coast. "The south is showing that it has the economic power and eventually the political coherence to stand up to the north," says

Continued on p. 1042

At Issue:

Should the United States continue to grant China "most-favored-nation" trade status?

PRESIDENT GEORGE BUSH

FROM A MESSAGE TO CONGRESS VETOING LEGISLATION THAT WOULD HAVE LIMITED CHINA'S MOST-FAVORED-NATION TRADE STATUS IN 1993 UNLESS BEIJING MADE PROGRESS IN HUMAN RIGHTS, TRADE AND WEAPONS NON-PROLIFERATION, SEPT. 28, 1992.

i share completely the goals of this legislation: to see greater Chinese adherence to international standards of human rights, free and fair trade practices and international non-proliferation norms. However, adding broad conditions to China's MFN [most-favored-nation] renewal would not lead to faster progress in advancing our goals....

Our policy of comprehensive engagement lets the Chinese know in no uncertain terms that "business as usual" is not possible until they take steps to resolve our differences. Through multiple, focused measures, we are eliciting the results we seek.

This year China joined global efforts to control the spread of nuclear weapons and ballistic missiles by declaring adherence to the Missile Technology Control Regime's (MTCR) guidelines and parameters and signing the Nuclear Proliferation Treaty (NPT). Chinese behavior remains MTCR-consistent, and we have begun a dialogue with the Chinese on their responsibilities under the NPT. We continue to monitor vigilantly China's weapons export practices. We have used the sanction authorities available successfully and remain prepared to do so again if necessary.

We have made progress on the resolution of outstanding trade issues with our agreements to protect Intellectual Property Rights and to ban prison labor exports. I will not allow, however, market access to remain a one-sided benefit in China's favor while our bilateral trade deficit grows....

The limited steps China has taken on human rights are inadequate. But our human rights dialogue gives us an avenue to express our views directly to China's leaders. Significant improvement in China's human rights situation, including freedom for all those imprisoned solely for the peaceful expression of their beliefs, remains our objective. It is easy to be discouraged by the pace of progress in this area. But it would be a serious mistake to let our frustration lead us to gamble with policies that would undermine our goals....

MFN is a means to bring our influence to bear on China. Comprehensive engagement is the process we use to transform this influence into positive change. The relationship between these two key elements of our China policy is a powerful one, and the absence of one element diminishes the potency of the other.... Engagement through our democratic, economic and educational institutions instead of confrontation offers the best hope for reform in China. MFN is the foundation we need to engage the Chinese.

SEN. GEORGE MITCHELL, D-MAINE

Senate Majority Leader
FROM A RESPONSE TO PRESIDENT BUSH'S VETO, OCT. 1, 1992. THE SENTATE FAILED TO OVERRIDE THE PRESIDENT'S VETO.

p resident Bush's veto of this legislation continues his failed China policy.... The failures of the administration's China policy are clear and conclusive; they are indisputable. Instead of creating a new world order, where nations honor their obligations to respect international standards of behavior, the administration's policy continues the practice of the old order, an old order which should have fallen away with the collapse of Soviet Communism.

Instead of encouraging China to recognize and respect the rights of its own citizens as human beings, the administration's policy — and its supporters in the Senate — has reconfirmed the Chinese Communist leaders, reassured the Chinese Communist leaders in their arrogant disregard for human decency. Instead of earning respect for American trade laws, and encouraging other countries to observe those laws, the administration's policy ... lets the Chinese government profit by unfair trade at the expense of American workers and American businesses.

Instead of giving life to the honorable American ideal of national self-determination, the administration's policy ... contributes to the continued enslavement of Tibet, the continued exploitation of Tibetan lands, the eradication of Tibetan culture, the suppression of Tibetan religion....

It ought to be a source of shame that instead of standing for change and working for democracy, self-determination and human rights, this administration has paid lip service to American ideals ... making excuse after excuse for the conduct of the Chinese Communist dictators.

The administration's policy has not moved China toward democracy. It is still run by Communist tyrants. It is not making China respect international trade law. It is not turning China into a reliable member of the international community. It is a failure on all counts....

The administration's policy has rested on a hope, a hope that the Chinese regime would improve its behavior. That hope has not been realized. It is time to replace personal hope with national incentives for change. The vetoed bill is a real incentive for change. It is narrowly targeted to the real source of the problem, the Chinese Communist leaders, not the Chinese people. It asks only that China live up to international commitments already freely accepted by China, the same thing the world community expects of every other nation. Nothing more. It does not place our policy in a straitjacket.

Armed Forces in the Asia-Pacific Region

Among the countries of the Far East, China, North Korea and Vietnam have the largest militaries.

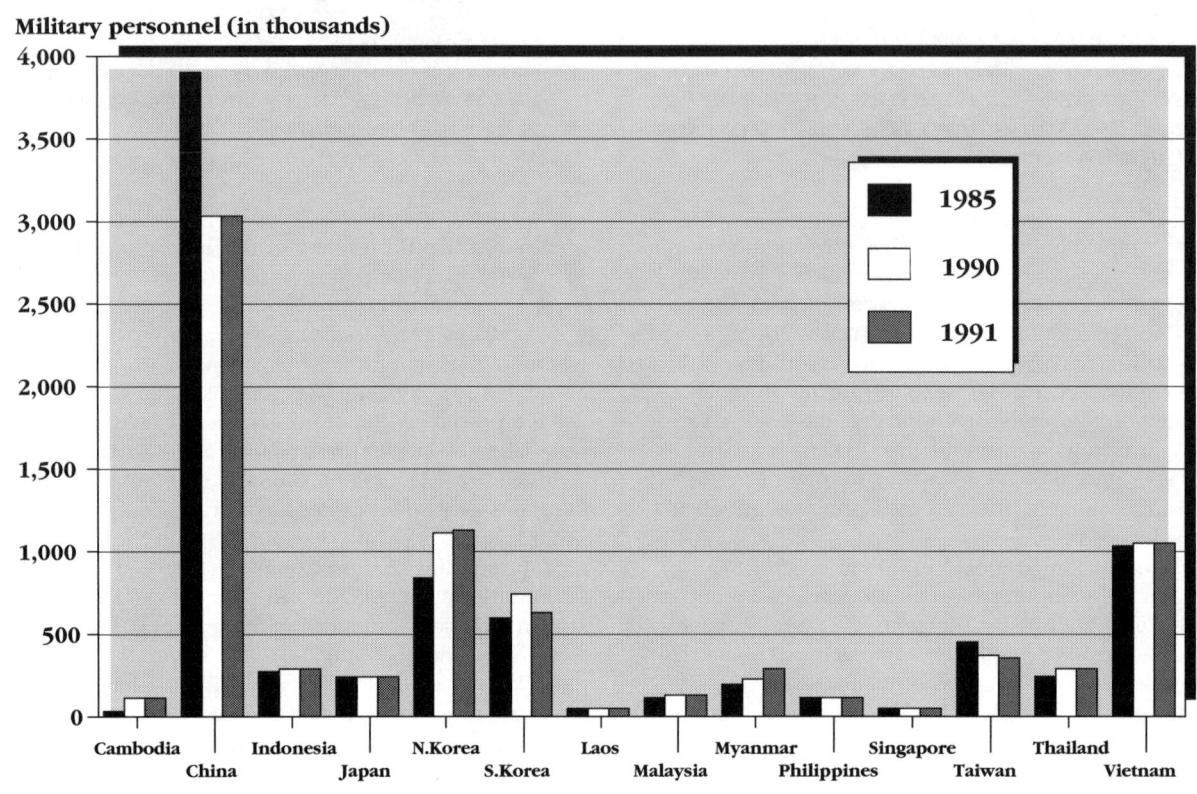

Military personnel (in thousands)

Legend: 1985, 1990, 1991

Countries (x-axis): Cambodia, China, Indonesia, Japan, N.Korea, S.Korea, Laos, Malaysia, Myanmar, Philippines, Singapore, Taiwan, Thailand, Vietnam

Source: International Institute for Strategic Studies, The Military Balance: 1992-1993, *1992*

Continued from p. 1040
Vlahos of the Center for Naval Analysis. "A watershed moment may soon come in which Beijing will have to demonstrate its control over southern China. If they can't do that, it would be an indication that China is breaking up. Their attempt to assert authority itself might lead to such a crisis."

U.S.-Japan Relations

For the past several decades, the United States has served as something of a referee in the Far East, buffering potential enemies and in many cases serving as an arbitrator of disputes. Its most important function has been to serve as a deterrent to Chinese encroachment and Japanese remilitarization.

Sohei Miyashita, head of Japan's Defense Agency, observed recently that if the United States does not maintain its forces in Asia, Japan would have to spend more on defense — a move that would make Japan's neighbors nervous. "A U.S. presence in Asia will also prevent Japan from re-emerging as a major militarist state," Miyashita said.[27]

For that reason, some experts think the United States should stop encouraging Japan to assume greater military responsibilities. A remilitarized Japan "would certainly trigger a counter buildup in China," says Bruce Porter. "There's a lot of concern that in the next decade we could see a Sino-Japanese arms race. The way to prevent that is to maintain the U.S. presence."

President-elect Clinton has indicated that he intends to do just that, but he also has called for greater cuts in defense spending than the Bush administration supported. And Clinton has expressed support for trade policies that could further irritate relations between the United States and

Japan. Some analysts have speculated that souring trade relations could ultimately lead to a break between Japan and the United States.

If that happened, former Sen. Howard H. Baker, R.-Tenn., and former Deputy Assistant Secretary of Defense Ellen L. Frost hypothesized, "one could see a resurgence of that element of the Japanese political psyche that identifies itself as Asian rather than Western in the modern industrial sense. Perceiving — and subconsciously exaggerating — a common heritage of race, geography, culture and history, Japan's leaders would shun the West, downgrade their global goals, halt or reverse their commitments to open their markets and pursue an agenda in Asia that could run counter to Western ideals."

"Criticism of the United States would become sharper and more vocal," Baker and Frost continued. "Japan's economic power in the region would solidify into a de facto trade and investment grouping, while the General Agreement on Tariffs and Trade (GATT) rules were ignored. Rather than relying on quiet diplomacy Tokyo would publicly criticize Washington for failing to understand Japanese goals in Asia. Meanwhile, in Japan, advocates of military autarky [independence] would accelerate autonomous programs and retreat from cooperative defense arrangements with the United States." [28]

Does Clinton's election make such a scenario more likely? "What you say in a campaign and what you do in reality may not be exactly the same thing," notes Porter. "I think the general consensus in both parties is that we don't want trade wars. We may see a Clinton administration take a tougher negotiating position, but I think they'll do everything they can to avoid things getting out of hand." ∎

Patrick G. Marshall is a free-lance writer in Seattle and a specialist on Asia.

Notes

[1] Address to a special session of the Australian Parliament, Jan. 2, 1992, reprinted in the *Congressional Quarterly Weekly Report*, Jan. 4, 1992, p. 36.

[2] See *The Economist*, June 20, 1992.

[3] *The Military Balance, 1992-1993*, The International Institute for Strategic Studies, 1992.

[4] James Clad and Patrick Marshall, "Southeast Asia's Hidden Arms Race," *Chicago Tribune*, May 23, 1992.

[5] Quoted in *The Washington Post*, Nov. 11, 1991.

[6] See *The Washington Post*, Nov. 9, 1992.

[7] China has not acknowledged obtaining the refueling technology. See *The New York Times*, Aug. 23, 1992.

[8] *Ibid.*

[9] Quoted in the *Far Eastern Economic Review*, Aug. 13, 1992.

[10] Quoted in the *Far Eastern Economic Review*, July 23, 1992.

[11] For background, see "Nuclear Proliferation," *The CQ Researcher*, June 5, 1992, pp. 481-504.

[12] See *The New York Times*, Oct. 10, 1992.

[13] *Far Eastern Economic Review*, Aug. 13, 1992.

[14] Luckham, Robin, "The Military, the Developmental State and Social Forces in Asia and the Pacific: Issues for Comparative Analysis," in *The Military, the State and Development in Asia and the Pacific* (1991), edited by Viberto Selochan, p. 26.

[15] Quoted in *The New York Times*, Sept. 3, 1992.

[16] Cited in *The New York Times*, Sept. 4, 1992.

[17] Quoted in *The New York Times*, Sept. 3, 1992.

[18] Quoted in the *Far Eastern Economic Review*, June 25, 1992.

[19] Quoted in *The Washington Post*, May 9, 1990.

[20] Quoted in *The New York Times*, June 1, 1992.

[21] See Lawrence E. Grinter, "Policy of the United States Toward East Asia: Tough Adjustments," in *Security, Strategy and Policy Responses in the Pacific Rim* (1989), edited by Young Whan Kihl and Lawrence E. Grinter, p. 38.

[22] Harry Harding, *A Fragile Relationship: The United States and China Since 1972* (1992), p. 28.

[23] *Ibid.*

[24] *Ibid.*, p. 93.

[25] *Ibid.*, p. 183.

[26] Writing in the *Far Eastern Economic Review*, Aug. 13, 1992.

[27] Quoted in *Japan Times*, Aug. 17, 1992.

[28] Howard H. Baker and Ellen L. Frost, "Rescuing the U.S.-Japan Alliance," *Foreign Affairs*, spring 1992, p. 106.

Bibliography

Selected Sources Used

Books

Becker, Elizabeth, *When the War Was Over: Cambodia's Revolution and the Voice of its People*, Simon & Schuster, 1986.

Becker's book covers events only up to 1985, but it helps readers understand how the Khmer Rouge came to power in 1975, why Vietnam invaded Cambodia in 1979 and how the non-communist rebels fit into the equation.

Clad, James, *Behind the Myth: Business, Money and Power in Southeast Asia*, Grafton, 1989.

Clad, a longtime correspondent in Southeast Asia for the *Far Eastern Economic Review,* draws a detailed picture of the freewheeling economies and politics of the countries of the region. Clad's book goes a long way toward explaining the vitality of the area as well as the mutual suspicions — and resulting arms purchases — that plague the region.

Harding, Harry, *A Fragile Relationship: The United States and China Since 1972*, Brookings Institution, 1992.

This book provides an excellent history of relations between the United States and China from just before President Richard M. Nixon's 1972 trip to China, which led to the reopening of relations between the two countries, through 1989, when Chinese troops cracked down on political demonstrations in Tiananmen Square in Beijing.

International Institute for Strategic Studies, *The Military Balance: 1992-1993*, Brassey's, 1992.

This annual report from the London-based International Institute for Strategic Studies is an invaluable resource for finding military force levels and equipment worldwide. The book also provides summaries of defense spending broken down by country and by region.

Karnow, Stanley, *Vietnam: A History*, Viking, 1983.

Karnow has produced what is arguably the best, and certainly the most readable, history of the U.S. involvement in Vietnam.

Kihl, Young Whan, and Lawrence E. Grinter, *Security, Strategy and Policy Responses in the Pacific Rim*, Lynne Reinner Publishers, 1989.

This collection of essays by security analysts examines the major strategic issues of both the North Pacific and South Pacific. The essays discuss not only general political and historical developments but also tactical considerations facing military planners.

Palmer, Norman D., *The New Regionalism in Asia and the Pacific*, Lexington Books, 1991.

This book tends to be academic and theoretical, but it has valuable background information on the development, and lack of development, of regional organizations in Asia.

Selochan, Viberto, ed., *The Military, the State and Development in Asia and the Pacific*, Westview, 1991.

Written just before arms sales in Southeast Asia really took off, this book shows surprising prescience about military trends in the region. It also explores the relationship between the military establishments and the governments in the region, and how that relationship may have affected the countries' development patterns.

Sheldon, Simon, *The Future of Asian-Pacific Security Collaboration*, Lexington Books, 1988.

This book was written before the end of the Cold War, but it provides a wealth of historical detail, as well as insight on the tactical concerns of military planners in Asia.

Articles

Baker, Howard H., and Ellen L. Frost, "Rescuing the U.S.-Japan Alliance," *Foreign Affairs*, spring 1992.

Howard Baker, a former U.S. senator from Tennessee, and former Deputy Assistant Secretary of Defense Ellen Frost examine the tensions in U.S.-Japanese relations. They believe the alliance must be maintained in order to preserve stability in Asia and U.S. interests in the region.

Crowe, William J. and Alan D. Romberg, "Rethinking Pacific Security," *Foreign Affairs*, spring 1991.

Crowe, a former chairman of the Joint Chiefs, and Romberg examine the changed situation for U.S. forces in the Pacific following the Cold War. They argue that while changes in force structure are indicated, an overall reduction in the military commitment to the region is not.

Oksenberg, Michael, "The China Problem," *Foreign Affairs*, summer 1991.

Oksenberg, a noted China watcher, surveys the tensions that have afflicted the U.S.-China relationship since the violence at Tiananmen Square in 1989. Oksenberg argues for a U.S. policy of maintaining "constructive engagement" with China on the grounds that the Chinese government is already in a period of fundamental change.

The Next Step

Additional Articles from Current Periodicals from EBSCO Publishing's Database

China

"China: Bush vs. the democrats — again," *U.S. News & World Report,* **June 15, 1992, p. 12.**

Reports that President Bush has again endorsed renewal of China's most-favored-nation (MFN) trading status even as complaints continue over Beijing's human rights abuses, weapons sales to Mideast countries and nuclear testing. Democrats' vow to overturn MFN; introduction of new bills to keep the low tariffs of MFN status for private businesses and joint ventures.

Cloud, D., "House tries again to restrict MFN status for China," *Congressional Quarterly Weekly Report,* **July 25, 1992, p. 2160.**

Reports on the House's overwhelming approval of legislation (HR 5318) on July 21, 1992, which would place stiff conditions on the continuation of normal trade relations between the United States and China. The House's vote on a resolution (H J Res 502) that would withdraw China's MFN status immediately; President Bush's veto threat; conditions that would be placed on China; Bush's decision to renew MFN treatment for China through July 1993; more.

Cranford, John, "House committee tries anew to press China for reforms," *Congressional Quarterly Weekly Report,* **July 4, 1992, p. 1933.**

Covers the House Ways and Means Committee's continued attempt to put stiff conditions on the continuation of normalized trade between the U.S. and China, as they gave their voice-vote approval of a bill (HR 5318) on July 2, 1992, which puts restrictions on trade with China. The subjection of U.S. imports of goods from China to high tariffs; China's progress in addressing human rights, trade and weapons proliferation concerns; the Jackson-Vanik waiver; other action; more.

Kristof, N.D., "As China looks at world order, it detects new struggles emerging," *The New York Times,* **April 21, 1992, p. A1.**

Presents the third article of a series on "After the Cold War," focusing on China. China, with its nuclear warheads, 3 million troops and significant territorial disputes with its neighbors, could present challenges to any Western-oriented plan or a new international order. China's struggle between capitalism and the remaining Communist countries; its growing friction within the Western alliance.

Schmitt, E. & E. Sciolino, "China said to sell parts for

missiles," *The New York Times,* **Jan. 31, 1992, p. A1.**

Says that American intelligence reports indicate that China is continuing to sell missile technology to Syria and Pakistan despite statements by Chinese leades that they are willing to curb missile exports. Importance of the issue.

Talbott, S., "How not to break China," *Time,* **Aug. 3, 1992, p. 53.**

Argues that while the leaders of the People's Republic of China richly deserve trade sanctions on the part of the U.S., the people don't. Congressional efforts to find ways to beat up on Deng Xiaopingand his hard-line protégé, Premier Li Peng; George Bush's contribution to the problem by coddling the Deng-Li gerontocracy; efforts of the Senate to restrict trade with China; examples of how trade sanctions can backfire; elements in bill from Rep. Don J. Pease (D-Ohio).

Economic policy

"Go east, America," *National Review,* **Aug. 17, 1992, p. 17.**

Asserts that America is the only nation that doesn't seem to realize that the U.S. has critical interests in the Pacific Rim region. Popular sentiment throughout Asia for a more prominent American role as a regional power; the need for an American commitment to supporting the GATT aim of a free-trading order.

"The booming Orient," *The Economist,* **June 27, 1992, p. 12.**

States that the long-term economic threat to Japan could come not from its market meltdown, but from China. Reaction from the United States to the rise of East Asia as a financial center; Tokyo the leading center for international banking; newly competitive world of international finance.

Hong Kong

"Bill seeks guidelines for Hong Kong policy," *Congressional Quarterly Weekly Report,* **May 9, 1992, p. 1261.**

Reports on the Senate Foreign Relations Committee's unanimous approval of a bill (S 1731) to establish new guidelines for U.S. policy toward Hong Kong after China takes control of the British colony in 1997. Sponsor Mitch McConnell (R-Ky.); the committee's resolution criticizing Myanmar's, formerly Burma, involvement in drug trafficking (S Con Res 107); details.

"Hong Kong bill passes Senate," *Congressional Quarterly Weekly Report,* **May 23, 1992, p. 1463.**

Discusses the Senate's voice-vote approval of a bill (S 1731) on May 21, 1992, to ensure that the U.S. maintains separate economic and trade relations with Hong Kong even after the British colony comes under the control of China in 1997. Sponsor Mitch McConnell (R-Ky.); more.

Japan

"Beefing up yen diplomacy," *Time,* **June 22, 1992, p. 27.**

Says Japan's parliament last week cast crucial votes to authorize sending troops overseas for the first time since World War II to participate in carefully circumscribed U.N. peacekeeping operations. The move is a victory for the government which was stung by Western criticism of Tokyo's painless pay-your-way yen diplomacy.

"Giant step for Japan," *Newsweek,* **June 22, 1992, p. 49.**

Reports that the Japanese Diet's lower house voted to give final approval to a compromise bill allowing Japanese troops to join United Nations (U.N.) peacekeepers. Ban from frontline duties; protests by left-wing legislators; conditions for military deployment.

"Meeting the Japanese challenge," *USA Today,* **May 1992, p. 16.**

Presents the views of House Majority Leader Richard A. Gephardt, D.-Mo., urging the United States government to use foreign policy on behalf of America's economic interests, particularly in its relationship with Japan. Overview of the persistent trade deficit with Japan; importance of dismantling Japan's trade barriers; proposed legislation that would give President Bush the power to do so, known as the Trade Enhancement Act.

Ritch, D., "American topics: Third world welcome," *World Press Review,* **June 1992, p. 39.**

Argues that President Bush should not have discussed exports in a recent visit to Japan, but rather the more far-reaching problem of Japanese disinvestment in the United States. Current American nationalist sentiment; why ardent nationalism should be relegated to museums.

Korea

"The real goal of Korean reunification should be democracy," *Forbes,* **Aug. 17, 1992, p. 35.**

Offers commentary by Caspar W. Weinberger, who states that beyond the proposals of South Korea-North Korea citizen exchanges and the reuniting of dispersed families, the North has resisted any specific measures that would move the countries closer to reunification. Estimates of costs of

reunification; President Roh Tae Woo of South Korea; recommendations.

Buchsbaum, H., "In the thick of it," *Scholastic Update,* **March 20, 1992, p. 13.**

Studies American policy toward the Koreas, nearly 40 years after the end of the Korean War. How the region has changed since the 1950s; continuing United States military presence in South Korea; why this is now being challenged; current status.

Il, H.S., "New hope on the road to reunification," *World Press Review,* **July 1992, p. 18.**

Cites a report in the *Statesman,* an independent periodical published in New Delhi, India. Consideration of North and South Korea's attempts to achieve reunification by 1995; why the prospects for reunion are better than ever; how the successive fall of communist states has isolated North Korea.

MacFarquhar, E., "Driving to a reunion?" *U.S. News & World Report,* **April 20, 1992, p. 44.**

Discusses the outcome of the opening-day ritual of a few thousand students gathered at Seoul National University shouting anti-American slogans and exchanging messages of solidarity with Kim Il Sung University, 121 miles away in Communist Pyongyang. Reason why South Korea's autocracy is evolving in democratic ways; why South Koreans are in no hurry to unite with their northern cousins; the affect the Germanys has had on Seoul and Pyongyang; more.

Military policy

"America and Asian security in an era of geoeconomics," *Dispatch,* **May 25, 1992, p. 410.**

Presents an address by Richard H. Solomon, assistant secretary for East Asian and Pacific affairs, before the Pacific Rim Forum, San Diego, Ca., May 1992, concerning the structure of economic, political and security institutions in a post-Cold War world. Replaying old political and ethnic rivalries with high-tech weaponry; how flows of trade, finance and technology shape the power realities and politics of today; the Asia-Pacific region as a pacesetter; conclusions.

"Pursuing U.S. objectives in Asia and the Pacific," *Dispatch,* **April 6, 1992, p. 272.**

Presents a statement by Richard H. Solomon, assistant Secretary for East Asian and Pacific Affairs, before the Senate Foreign Relations Committee, Washington, D.C., March 1992, concerning a range of issues pertaining to Thailand, Vietnam, Cambodia, Laos, South Korea, Japan and Hong Kong. Normalization plan presented to the Vietnamese; prisoners of war/missing in action accounting; POW/MIA investigations in Laos; economic and trade-related issues.

Acharya, A., "The association of Southeast Asian nations: 'Security community' or 'defense community'?" *Pacific Affairs,* summer 1991, p. 159.

Looks at the proposal for an ASEAN defense community which would represent a major shift from the hitherto preference for bilateral security ties among members. Argues that the idea of an ASEAN defense community not only faces serious barriers, but if implemented, would undermine ASEAN's role as a "security community." Background; evolving bilateral military ties among ASEAN states; problems and prospects of an ASEAN "defense community."

Giarelli, A., & M. Ram, "Cooperative vigilance," *World Press Review,* April 1992, p. 30.

Covers the speech by President Bush during a visit to Singapore, in which he stated America's intentions to remain in the Asia-Pacific region. The relocation of U.S. presence to Singapore, after abandoning two bases in the Philippines; the key elements of U.S. strategy for Asia; the promotion of economic integration of the Asia-Pacific countries; more.

Philippines

"Uncle Sam keeps his hands off," *New Statesman & Society,* May 22, 1992, p. 6.

Editorial. Studies the recent presidential elections in the Philippines. How the United States chose not to participate in the process; consequent freedom and openness of the elections; future forecast for the nation under probable winner Fidel Ramos.

Vietnam

"Vietnam: Humanitarian exceptions to the embargo," *Dispatch,* May 4, 1992, p. 360.

Presents a statement by State Department Spokeswoman Margaret Tutwiler, Washington, D.C., April 1992, concerning the U.S. granting of an exception to the economic embargo with Vietnam to permit commercial sales to meet basic human needs. Also restrictions have been lifted on projects by non-governmental and nonprofit organizations in Vietnam. Decision for the two steps; need for Vietnam to sustain its support for the Cambodian peace process.

Borrus, A., P. Engardio, et al., "Good morning, Vietnam!" *Business Week,* June 22, 1992, p. 48.

Discusses how after 17 years of forced separation, corporate America's courtship of Vietnam is suddenly gaining intensity, and the United States' economic embargo against Vietnam is crumbling. Relaxing sanctions step by step; cooperation in accounting for missing American GIs; what is egging the United States companies on; list of companies dealing in Vietnam.

Collingwood, H., "Is another cold war ending?" *Business Week,* March 9, 1992, p. 44.

States that businesses lobbying to end the trade embargo with Vietnam could get their wish by early summer. One stumbling block is the dispute over accounting for United States servicemen still missing in action.

Depke, D.A., "Going back: More trade with Vietnam," *Business Week,* May 11, 1992, p. 46.

Reports how just 10 days after lifting a ban on direct communication links with Vietnam, the State Department took two more big steps on April 29 toward easing the 17-year United States embargo on trade with Hanoi. Permitting sales of medical supplies and other goods; increasing cooperation by Hanoi in accounting for missing U.S. soldiers.

Back Issues

Great Research on Current Issues Starts Right Here... Recent topics covered by The CQ Researcher are listed below. Before May 1991, reports were published under the name of Editorial Research Reports.

MAY 1991
School Choice
Racial Quotas
Animal Rights
U.S. and Japan

JUNE 1991
Children and Divorce
Teenage Suicide
Endangered Species
Europe 1992

JULY 1991
Teenagers and Abortion
Soviet Republics Rebel
Mexico's Emergence
Athletes and Drugs

AUGUST 1991
Sexual Harassment
Fetal Tissue Research
Oil Imports
The Palestinians

SEPTEMBER 1991
Police Brutality
Advertising Under Attack
Saving the Forests
Foster Care Crisis

OCTOBER 1991
Pay-Per-View TV
Youth Gangs
Gene Therapy
World Hunger

NOVEMBER 1991
Fast-Food Shake-Up
The Greening of Eastern Europe
Business' Role in Education
Cuba In Crisis

DECEMBER 1991
Retiree Health Benefits
Asian Americans
The Obscenity Debate
The Disabilities Act

JANUARY 1992
Term Limits
Oil Spills
Hunting Controversy
Alternative Medicine

FEBRUARY 1992
Threatened Coastlines
New Era in Asia
Assisted Suicide
Jobs in the '90s

MARCH 1992
Women and Sports
Underage Drinking
Garbage Crisis
Mafia Crackdown

APRIL 1992
Ozone Depletion
Welfare Reform
Politicians and Privacy
Illegal Immigration

MAY 1992
Native Americans
Jobs vs. Environment
Too Many Lawsuits?
Fairness in Salaries

JUNE 1992
Nuclear Proliferation
Food Irradiation
Lead Poisoning
Hard Times for Libraries

JULY 1992
Alternative Energy
Prescription Drug Prices
Alzheimer's Disease
Infant Mortality

AUGUST 1992
The Homeless
Work, Family and Stress
NATO's Changing Role
Marine Mammals vs. Fish

SEPTEMBER 1992
Domestic Partners
Violence in Schools
Public Broadcasting
Women in the Military

OCTOBER 1992
Depression
U.S. Auto Industry
Youth Apprenticeships
Hispanic Americans

NOVEMBER 1992
Physical Fitness
Privatization
Paying for College

Back issues are available for $4.00 (subscribers) or $7.00 (non-subscribers). Quantity discounts apply to orders over ten. To order, call Congressional Quarterly 1-800-432-2250.

Binders are available for $15.00. To order call 1-800-638-1710.

Future Topics

▶ *Smoking in Public*

▶ *The CIA*

▶ *Eating Disorders*

THE CQ Researcher

PUBLISHED BY CONGRESSIONAL QUARTERLY INC., IN CONJUNCTION WITH EBSCO PUBLISHING

Crackdown on Smoking

Are bans on tobacco use unfair to smokers?

S MOKERS LIGHT UP AT THEIR PERIL NOWADAYS. An aggressive anti-smoking movement of health experts, public-interest groups and individuals offended by smoking has led to a wave of bans on smoking in the workplace, in restaurants and in public places. Some firms even limit hiring to employees who don't smoke — on or off the job. Fueling the crackdown is an array of studies warning that exposure to passive, or secondhand, smoke from active smokers can be fatal to nonsmokers — particularly children. Politicians, administrators and worksite supervisors face a delicate policy dilemma as cries of unfair treatment are heard from smokers'-rights groups, civil libertarians and a familiar veteran of struggles over smoking: the powerful U.S. tobacco industry.

C Q **December 4, 1992 • Volume 2, No. 45 • 1049-1072**

Formerly Editorial Research Reports

COVER: SIGN OF THE TIMES OUTSIDE A BANK IN WASHINGTON, D.C. (PHOTOGRAPH BY R. MICHAEL JENKINS)

December 4, 1992
Volume 2, No. 45

EDITOR
Sandra Stencel

MANAGING EDITOR
Thomas J. Colin

ASSOCIATE EDITOR
Richard L. Worsnop

STAFF WRITERS
Charles S. Clark
Mary H. Cooper
Rodman D. Griffin

PRODUCTION EDITOR
Sarah E. Merritt

EDITORIAL ASSISTANT
Michael M. Taylor

GRAPHICS
Jack Auldridge

PUBLISHED BY
Congressional Quarterly Inc.

CHAIRMAN
Andrew Barnes

VICE CHAIRMAN
Andrew P. Corty

EDITOR AND PUBLISHER
Neil Skene

EXECUTIVE EDITOR
Robert W. Merry

ASSOCIATE PUBLISHER
John J. Coyle

EDITOR, EBSCO PUBLISHING
Melissa Kummerer

The CQ Researcher (ISSN 1056-2036). Formerly Editorial Research Reports. Published weekly (48 times per year, not printed the first Friday of any month with five Fridays) by Congressional Quarterly Inc., 1414 22nd St., N.W., Washington, D.C. 20037. Rates are furnished upon request. Second-class postage paid at Washington, D.C. POSTMASTER: Send address changes to The CQ Researcher, 1414 22nd St., N.W., Washington, D.C. 20037.

Crackdown on Smoking

BY CHARLES S. CLARK

THE ISSUES

In rain, in snow, in freezing wind, smokers huddling outside buildings from which they've been banished are familiar sights in the 1990s. The habit that for decades symbolized glamour and suave sexuality is today a divisive stirrer of passions that is forcing a new segregation of society.

Among the 46 million Americans who flout the health warnings against smoking are desperate souls who've been caught blowing smoke in airplane lavatory bowls and disconnecting smoke alarms in smoke-free hotels.

"For smokers, their latest trip to the bottom of the social heap has been a long and painful one," writes Foster Gunnison Jr., a veteran of what he calls the smokers'-liberation movement. "It all adds up to a full-scale pogrom. Once-high-flying smokers have been publicly vilified, humiliated and ridiculed. They have been systematically lied to and lied about. They have been assaulted, spat upon, and in at least one case murdered. . . . In the classic mold of social scapegoating, smokers have been stigmatized, ghetto-ized and threatened with cultural annihilation."[1]

"Smokers *are* being made to feel like social pariahs," declares John F. Banzhaf III, a George Washington University law professor who founded the anti-smoking group Action on Smoking and Health (ASH). "The nonsmokers' movement is more successful than any other tobacco-control method. The social pressures are more important than even the health information."

A whopping 88 percent of Americans now say they find cigarette smoke annoying, according to a recent survey by the National Center for Health Statistics, including a third of all smokers. The number of adults who support total bans

on smoking (rather than milder restrictions such as no-smoking sections) rose from 19 percent in 1983 to 33 percent in 1992, according to a poll released in June by the American Lung Association. Of 10 features offered in restaurants, separate smoking sections ranked No. 1 in importance in a 1990 poll for the National Restaurant Association.

In the past two decades, 541 local laws have been passed to require nonsmoking areas in workplaces, schools, government buildings, public facilities and restaurants. Forty-six state legislatures have taken action against smoking. *(See map, p. 1060.)* And as many as 34 percent of all U.S. companies have totally banned smoking, compared with only 2 percent in 1986, according to a 1991 survey by the Bureau of National Affairs.

The impetus for the anti-smoking movement goes beyond the familiar science that links smoking to 434,000 annual deaths from heart disease, cancer, stroke and other maladies. The broader issue is passive smoke — also called secondhand smoke, sidestream smoke, involuntary smoking and environmental

tobacco smoke (ETS). It contains 4,000 chemicals, including benzene, ammonia and hydrogen cyanide, many of which are poisonous or cancer-causing to otherwise healthy nonsmokers.

The Environmental Protection Agency (EPA) this year released a draft report (still subject to final approval) that reviewed the major published studies and classified secondhand smoke as a Class A carcinogen, meaning it is a cancer-causing agent for which there is no safe level of exposure. The EPA linked passive smoke to thousands of deaths from lung cancer and heart disease as well as new cases of respiratory infection and asthma. Children of smokers, medical authorities have reported, are more vulnerable to wheezing, coughing and sputum production than children of nonsmokers, and nonsmoking women who are married to smokers are more likely to give birth to smaller babies.

Most dramatically, the Coalition on Smoking OR Health — an alliance of the American Heart Association, the American Lung Association and the American Cancer Society — announced this summer that people exposed to passive smoke have a 30 percent increased risk of death from heart disease. By one estimate, passive smoking kills 53,000 Americans every year.[2]

Adding heart disease to the known risks from smoking, such as lung cancer, is "the final nail in the tobacco coffin," said Fran Du Melle, deputy managing director of the Lung Association. Such findings, as Assistant Surgeon General John Duffy has put it, mean "there is no such thing as a nonsmoker in America today. As long as we all have to live and work around smokers, we must accept some of the risks of smoking."[3]

Authoritative medical evidence, however, has not produced a national consensus on the banning of smoking. Far from it. Increasingly vocal "smokers'-rights" groups, allied with some civil libertarians, have decried the work of governmental "nannies" who "refuse to treat smokers as adults."

Small businesses, particularly restaurants, hotels and transit providers, have warned that smoking bans will cost them the clientele that sustains their livelihoods. And finally, the powerful U.S. tobacco industry, a $45-billion-a-year giant with vast resources in advertising, lobbying and political-campaign contributions, has taken on the anti-smoking crusaders with an elaborate strategy that includes attacks on the medical evidence attesting to the dangers of secondhand smoke.[4]

"What's losing in this whole debate is science, which has become political," says Walker Merryman, a vice president of The Tobacco Institute. "What's also losing are the business people who have to try to operate when their economic life is threatened."

Some 200 anti-smoking groups nationwide have been trying to make an end run around the formidable tobacco lobby. Loosely affiliated with such organizations as the Berkeley, Calif.-based Americans for Nonsmokers' Rights and the Group Against Smokers' Pollution (GASP) in College Park, Md., these grass-roots groups have been pushing for restrictions on public smoking from local town and city councils. (See poll results, p. 1062.)

The tobacco industry has counterattacked. In September 1991, a confidential industry memo was leaked confirming what anti-smoking activists had observed: Tobacco strategists were concentrating lobbying efforts not on flatly opposing all anti-smoking laws but on encouraging states — among them Virginia and Wyoming — to adopt loosely written laws that pre-empt localities from approving tougher crackdowns on smoking.

While both sides have claimed victories, the issue of secondhand smoke clearly has emerged as a linchpin of the tobacco-policy debate. "It scares the hell out of the tobacco industry," says

Scott Ballin, vice president of the American Heart Association. "Nonsmokers are most vocal about the need for a clean indoor-air law. The industry will lose if we take away the opportunity to smoke in 90 percent of public places."

Beyond dispute is the fact that secondhand smoke has radically altered the battlefield of the tobacco wars. "When I used to talk to smokers in bingo halls and restaurants," says Robert A. Rosner, executive director of the Smoking Policy Institute, a Seattle-based consulting firm, "I'd get a lot of lip, a lot of fist-pounding on the table. Now the smokers are running up the white flag. They say, 'My kids smoke, and I hate it.' Ten years ago they would say, 'You owe me, I have a right to a place to smoke.' Now they say, 'Give me a place, even if it's outside. But you just can't legislate it out of my life.' "

How the smoking-policy issue is ultimately resolved is likely to hinge on the following questions:

Is medical research conclusive on the dangers of passive smoking?

The risks of secondhand smoke were discussed in medical literature as early as 1950.[5] But the first important evidence linking it to cancer comes from morbidity studies conducted in the early 1980s in Greece and Japan. In the most famous one, Japanese epidemiologist Takeshi Hirayama compared the death rates from lung cancer among nonsmoking women who were married to smokers with death rates of nonsmoking women who were married to nonsmokers.[6]

Because Japanese housewives spend a lot of time in the home and rarely smoke, they were regarded as an ideal group for a study of secondhand smoke. Hirayama found that women married to smokers had a 40 percent greater lung cancer rate. The study also showed that the cancers were worse in the homes of heavy smokers. The study made front-page news around the

world, and the tobacco industry took out full-page newspaper ads alleging a statistical error in the study.

As other medical studies weighed in with similar results, evaluations of the scientific literature were undertaken by the National Research Council and the U.S. surgeon general. In 1986, both released reports concluding that secondhand smoke is harmful and sometimes fatal. In 1991, the National Institute for Occupational Safety and Health (NIOSH) released a review of 12 major studies of environmental tobacco smoke and concluded that it is a potential carcinogen, recommending that all preventive measures be used to minimize occupational exposure.

More studies honed in on specific risks. Also in 1991, Pap smears of 145 healthy nonsmoking women in Washington, D.C.-area hospitals showed nicotine levels were higher among those who had been exposed to secondhand smoke, raising the risk of cervical cancer by at least 50 percent.[7] In August of this year, University of North Carolina researchers reported that children of smokers showed a 38 percent higher chance of ear infections.[8] And in October, a study of 283 people who died in Greece from 1986-90 — the first time autopsy lung tissue was used to check a link between cancer and secondhand smoke — showed lung lesions were "significantly higher among deceased nonsmoking women married to smokers rather than to nonsmokers."[9]

Of particular interest to specialists has been the EPA draft report, *Respiratory Health Effects of Passive Smoking.* Its alarm against secondhand smoke was endorsed by the EPA's own scientific advisory board as well as the American Medical Association. It has been attacked, however, by other scientists, smokers'-rights activists, and, not surprisingly, the tobacco industry.

"It is unfortunate for everyone that EPA is apparently serving up the same kind of science that gave us the Alar and Dioxin scares, where the result was lost jobs for apple growers

Why Some Employers Don't Restrict Smoking

Employers without workplace smoking policies say they haven't acted mainly because of lack of employee demand, not cost, according to a survey of 833 human-resource executives. While a small minority of U.S. employers don't have such policies, most say they plan to implement them in the next two years.

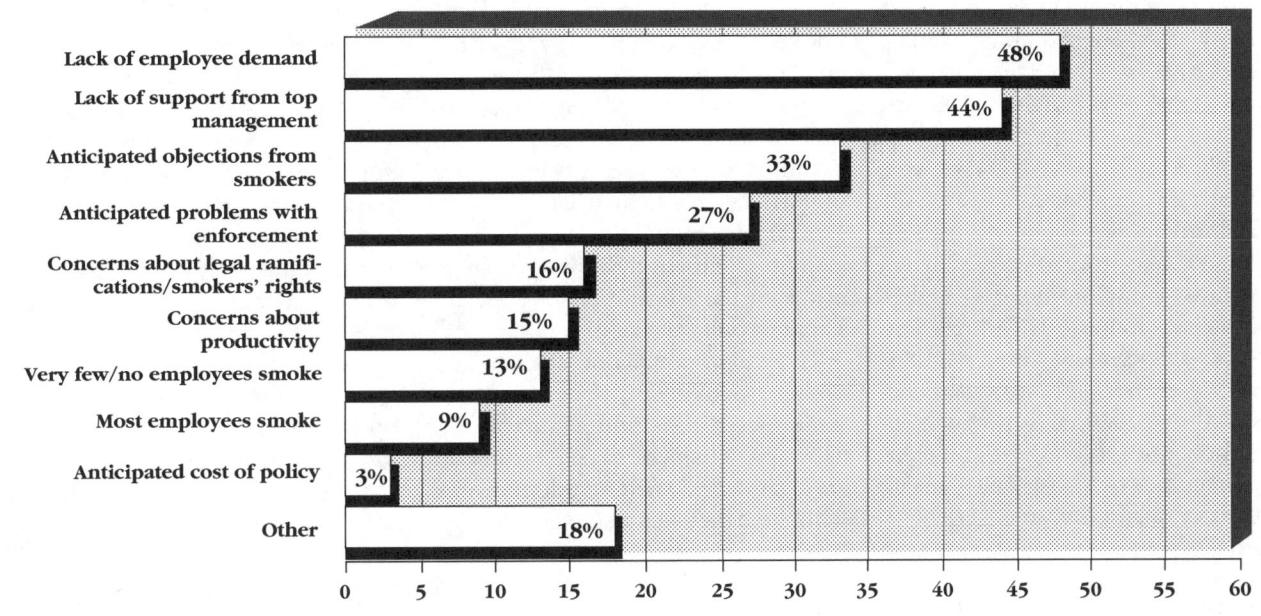

Source: *"Smoking in the Workplace," Bureau of National Affairs, August 29, 1991*

and lost homes and dollars for the residents of Times Beach [Missouri]," said Tobacco Institute spokeswoman Brennan Dawson.

The institute publicized contrary testimony from scientists. The EPA seems to have ignored its expert panel's counsel that "science should never be adjusted to fit policy," testified Gary Flamm, a biochemist at the American College of Toxicology and a former Food and Drug Administration consultant on carcinogens. Less than a third of the 30 published studies used by the EPA showed a "statistically significant association"between marriage to a smoker and increased risk of lung cancer in nonsmoking spouses, Flamm said.

As the EPA draft was circulated for public comment, insiders in the tobacco debate became familiar with a professional artist and smokers'-rights sympathizer from Connecticut named Martha Perske. She began bombarding EPA officials and members of Congress with detailed objections to the EPA's methodology, saying scientific data are being misused by government agencies to further the political agenda of those advocating a smoke-free America. She complained that the EPA had changed criteria for measuring statistical significance from its first draft of the report to its second. And she said the agency failed to consider factors known as "confounders" — such as diet, socioeconomic background, alcohol, drugs and other air pollution — that may explain the higher cancer rates.

For its general campaign against crackdowns on smoking, The Tobacco Institute has assembled a roster of scientists whose work in some way challenges the establishment's view of secondhand smoke, many of whom it hires as consultants. In 1989, the institute helped sponsor an international symposium on environmental tobacco smoke at McGill University in Montreal attended by 80 scientists from 20 countries. *(See story, p. 1059.)* Out of the symposium, the institute said, a conclusion emerged that "the claim that exposure to ETS increases the risk of nonsmoker cancer cannot be supported with the weak and inconsistent data available."

To argue that the effects of secondhand smoke are being exaggerated, the institute cites a 1990 Transportation Department study of tobacco smoke aboard airliners to make this contention: Passengers in the seats immediately adjacent to the smoking section "would have to fly 266 trips from New

York to Tokyo — about 7,500 hours in flight — to be exposed to the nicotine equivalent of one cigarette."

To Banzhaf of Action on Smoking and Health (ASH), the flaw in the institute's approach is that it takes each study in isolation and tries to poke a hole in it. "Although a study standing by itself may not be statistically significant," he says, "when you get dozens of them pointing in the same direction, it is."

To Stanton A. Glantz, a University of California at San Francisco medical researcher and former president of Americans for Nonsmokers' Rights, the "tobacco industry is hiring scientific consultants to say the world is flat." This gives politicians "a fig leaf to say the evidence is not conclusive," he argues. "But the only scientists or experts who don't believe [that secondhand smoke is dangerous] have some financial connection to the tobacco industry."

Glantz says he has offered to go on the radio to debate another scientist who will present the view that passive smoke is not dangerous, but the only people the industry has offered are "shills who are being paid."

Tobacco Institute spokesman Merryman replies that scientists who question the evidence on passive smoke do not speak out for fear "they will be drawn and quartered by Glantz and labeled as dupes of the tobacco cartel."

Are anti-smokers too militant?

John Banzhaf crossed the smoking controversy's Rubicon in 1985 when, during a televised debate, he poured a glass of water on a cigar being smoked by his opponent, who had lit up to make a point about freedom.

"Allergies to smoking have increased amazingly in recent years," his victim, Fordham University law Professor Ernest van den Haag, later wrote, "a sudden increase that suggests that many of them are hysterical, or faked, to justify the imposition of the nonsmokers' preference on smokers." [10]

The chief complaint against anti-smoking activists has been that they are self-righteous and fanatical. "It's nobody's business what we're doing," griped a Fort Lauderdale-area school teacher this fall as a statewide smoking ban took effect in Florida schools. "It's like the nonsmokers are purposefully going out of their way to make our lives miserable." [11]

Anti-smokers "reek of self-righteousness, insufferably so," says Merryman. "They speak with a moralistic fervor that parallels Prohibition and accuse us of enticing kids and women, of ruining families. Like Gladstone said of Disraeli, they are inebriated by the exuberance of their own verbosity."

Other critics attack donor-funded health groups such as the heart, lung and cancer associations for being "elitist." James T. Bennett, an economist at George Mason University in Fairfax, Va., says the principal goal of such groups is the "alteration of the lifestyles of American citizens in ways pleasing to the upper classes."

"Today's educated elite favors exercise, frowns on obesity and disdains smoking as hopelessly déclassé," he writes. "Smoking cigarettes and chewing tobacco are the vices of the lower-middle class, that pool of the tasteless and icky masses who are too stupid to make their own decisions." [12]

Anti-smoking health groups are also accused of feathering their own nests, spending more on salaries and fund-raising than research. It's an industry that provides "employment for an army of smoker-bashers and, for many, the opportunity to amass personal fortunes," writes Fred Phillis, a Trumbull, Conn., public relations consultant and smokers'-rights activist. [13]

If some anti-smokers are indeed too militant, they are a minority. The recent poll by the National Center for Health Statistics shows that only 4 percent of adults will ask a smoker to put out his cigarette. Fully 52 percent simply move elsewhere, and 40 percent do nothing. The image of self-righteous anti-smokers is "some-

(c) 1992, Washington Post Writers Group. Reprinted with permission.

thing the tobacco industry has done a great deal to promote," says GASP spokesman Willard K. Morris. "But what we ask is reasonable and right, and our position is more and more understood and sympathized with."

"The biggest misconception is that we're out to deprive someone of their rights," adds Ahron Leichtman, executive director of the Cincinnati-based Citizens for a Tobacco-Free Society. "We're out to protect ourselves from health hazards." *(See "At Issue," p. 1065.)*

"Are firemen self-righteous for getting people out of burning buildings?" asks medical researcher Glantz. "I'm a scientist, and if I see someone putting poison in the water supply, it's only prudent that I act."

"We're here to reduce the No. 1 killer in America," says Ballin of the Heart Association. "Here's one product that probably shouldn't have been legal in the first place, that is virtually unregulated and takes 400,000 lives a year. We have an obligation to our donors and the American public to be active."

When individual anti-smoking activists do display impatience, experts remind them that smokers — particularly the estimated 90 percent who would like to quit — need sympathy rather than scolding. They are enduring a withdrawal process that requires changing some of their most ingrained behaviors. "I'm telling you, I wanted a cigarette so bad I cried," recalled one would-be quitter. "I was so nervous I could hardly carry on at work, and I couldn't hide it. After awhile, I would just shake."[14]

The smug nonsmoker's "'Kiss-me-I'm-a-nonsmoker' button just doesn't cut it," says Rosner of the Smoking Policy Institute. "If the addiction were heroin, you wouldn't simply approach them and say, 'Come on, a

little will power will kick that smack habit.' I favor education for nonsmokers to get them out of the faces of smokers."

"While we're quick to turn the argument toward rights, as a smoker I can't help but feel picked on," writes Paul O'Brien, president of New England Telephone Co., who created a smoke-free workplace for his 27,000 employees. "For a smoke-free policy to succeed, it's important for nonsmokers to be supportive of smokers."[15]

R. Michael Jenkins

Is there an authentic smokers'-rights movement, or was it created by the tobacco industry?

"The strength of the tobacco-control movement has always been the depth and breadth of grass-roots commitment," asserts the newsletter of Americans for Nonsmokers' Rights. "The tobacco industry envies this, and also knows their own presence is unwelcome. That's why they fund numerous 'smokers'-rights' groups to create the illusion of a grass-roots movement of smokers."

The very notion of a smokers'-rights movement draws skepticism from many because, as Rosner notes, smokers often welcome restrictions as an incentive to quit. "Smokers' rights is a

legitimate position, but the groups suffer from a lack of members," he says. In a typical city where 100,000 people smoke, for example, proposed restrictions on smoking might generate only 100-200 letters of protest.

"I've never run into a genuine grass-roots group of smokers'-rights advocates," says anti-smoking activist Glantz. What he does encounter, he says, are average-seeming citizens in audiences at TV shows and public forums who raise technical questions about tobacco and health research that sound suspiciously like they've been planted.

Glantz has written extensively on the tobacco industry's behind-the-scenes funding of local political organizers and business groups with such names as Taxpayers United for Fairness and the Beverly Hills Restaurant Association, which seem to spring up whenever a locality is considering anti-smoking ordinances. The groups use computer data bases, glossy mailouts and public relations professionals, but "the tobacco industry never acknowledges that it is a highly integrated campaign that is run centrally," Glantz says.

The creation of smokers'-rights groups to thwart local restrictions on smoking was lauded by R.J. Reynolds Tobacco Co. Chairman James W. Johnston, who, according to Glantz, declared in 1990, "This is something I wish we had done a decade ago."[16]

The Tobacco Institute's Merryman acknowledges the industry's involvement with local political groups. "Obviously, we're going to make people aware of what's going on in Congress and at their city council and encourage individual customers to write letters," he says. "They need us to gather materials on the technical issues. Besides, the anti-smokers do a good job of telling their adherents what to say."

R.J. Reynolds spokeswoman Maura Payne says her company receives thousands of inquiries on its toll-free telephone line from smokers complaining that they're not being treated fairly, or griping about taxes. "They look to the industry as a natural ally," she says, "and many are daunted because they have never written to their congressmen or testified before a city council."

Reynolds also encourages smokers'-rights activity through its five-year-old customer magazine, *Choice*, which reports on local lobbying techniques. The number of smokers'-rights groups fluctuates with pending legislation, Payne says, but many of the groups have ongoing activities such as running booths at state fairs and adopting a highway. The groups ally themselves with local retailers when economic issues arise, such as ordinances to ban single-pack sales of cigarettes. Finally, Payne says, many of the groups now include nonsmokers concerned about civil liberties and governmental abuse of the power to tax.

Independent of the tobacco industry, according to its literature, is the new United Smokers of America Association. Based in Frankfurt, Ky., it says it represents nearly 1,000 smokers'-rights groups around the country that are often funded by bake sales and collecting aluminum cans. "For years, anti-tobacco fanatics have worked hard and spent millions (much of it our own tax dollars) to make us feel isolated, guilty and undesirable in an intolerant world," writes Dave Brenton, editor of the association's *American Smoker's Journal*. "We are committed to the belief that smokers are good, hard-working, decent, fun-loving people, who have been subjected to very unfriendly treatment of late and deserve much better."

The colorful, glossy magazine, which was co-founded by a printer who believes in the cause, operates on a shoestring budget funded by about 1,000 subscribers, says spokesman Fred Phillis. Its articles bemoan the fate of business owners who feel they were ruined by local smoking bans, ridicule the Environmental Protection Agency and hold up the Prohibition period as a "parallel" to the anti-smoking movement. Advertisements feature books such as British statistician Peter H. Lee's *Environmental Tobacco Smoke and Mortality*, a challenge to prevailing medical views. For the $18.95 subscription fee, readers also receive discount coupons and opportunities to use special travel, life insurance and financial-planning services.

The smokers'-rights constituency has also stimulated the creation of *Smoking Singles*, a bimonthly magazine/matchmaking service based in New York City, and a collection of snappy comebacks to complaints by anti-smokers published by Smokers Club International of San Diego. (Sample: "Do you know I hate it when you smoke?" Smoker's reply: "Do you know I hate it when you breathe?")

Individual members of smokers'-rights groups firmly deny that they are creations of the tobacco industry, saying they merely rely on the industry's magazines for information and strategy for opposing the anti-smokers movement. "I really enjoy smoking," says Gloria Kelber, who heads a group near Chicago. "I don't have many vices, and a person's got a right to use a legal product." ■

BACKGROUND

Early Crackdowns

The modern movement against smoking has antecedents dating back to the 15th century. One of Columbus' crewmen, Rodrigo de Jerez, returned from the New World smoking a strange leafy substance that fellow Spaniards took as a sign of possession by the devil. He was imprisoned by the Spanish Inquisition.

In 1603, a ban on tobacco was handed down in England by King James I, who called smoking "a custom loathsome to the eye, hateful to the nose, harmful to the brain and dangerous to the lungs." In Rome, several popes made it a policy to excommunicate smokers, while in China, Turkey, Persia and Russia smokers were executed, flogged or had their nostrils slit. And in the early 19th century, the city of Berlin implemented a smoking ban "because nonsmokers have a clear right not to be annoyed." [17]

In the early 19th century, U.S. temperance advocates opposed smoking because they thought the habit encouraged a thirst for alcohol. Health reformers also linked smoking to cancer, tooth decay, baldness and licentiousness, though others championed tobacco for its healing powers and as a superior alternative to drinking.

In the latter part of the 19th century, the anti-smoking movement picked up steam after mass production made tobacco products available to the common man. Middle-class reformers began warning that cigarettes were laced with opium. They linked smoking with the decadent wealthy, with foreign immigrants and with the corruption of youth. An anti-cigarette league, headed by Chicagoan Lucy Page Gaston, claimed a membership of 300,000 in the United States and Canada. Though its lobbying was countered by the American Tobacco Co., 14 states, beginning with Washington in 1893, outlawed the manufacture, sale, possession, advertising and use of cigarettes, and another 21 states considered such legislation. In 1901, the Supreme Court ruled that ciga-

Continued on p. 1058

Chronology

1960s
Decades-old image of smoking as glamorous is challenged by health authorities. Beginning of government crackdown.

Jan. 11, 1964
U.S. Surgeon General Luther L. Terry releases landmark report endorsing medical studies' findings that smoking causes cancer.

1965
Congress passes law requiring health warning labels on tobacco products.

1967
In response to a complaint by New York attorney John F. Banzhaf III, Federal Communications Commission rules that Fairness Doctrine requires radio and television stations to devote substantial airtime to anti-smoking messages. First World Conference on Smoking and Health convenes in New York City.

1970s
Environmental movement and energy-conservation measures prompt concern over indoor air quality. Grass-roots anti-smoking groups formed. Tobacco industry perceives a threat.

1971
Following a request from Action on Smoking and Health (ASH), United Airlines becomes first carrier to have separate smoking and nonsmoking sections. Groups Against Smoking Pollution (GASP) branches form around the country.

1972
A report including a chapter on hazards of secondhand smoke is published by the U.S. surgeon general.

1973
Civil Aeronautics Board requires all airlines to create nonsmoking sections. Arizona becomes first state to pass a comprehensive law protecting nonsmokers.

1975
Third World Conference on Smoking and Health pressures major health organizations to restrict smoking in their offices.

1976
In landmark legal case, office worker Donna Shimp of New Jersey wins an injunction prohibiting smoking in her office. American Cancer Society launches first Great American Smokeout campaign to encourage smokers to quit.

1977
California anti-smoking activists launch ballot-initiative campaign for statewide clean indoor air law, defeated after tobacco industry lobbying.

1979
Civil Aeronautics Board requires airlines to segregate pipe and cigar smokers on flights; soon pipes and cigars are banned. Tobacco Institute launches ad campaign against nonsmokers'-rights movement.

1980s
Government and medical authorities warn of dangers of secondhand smoke. Efforts at banning smoking shift to local level, drawing opposition from industry.

1981
GASP groups in California unite as Californians for Nonsmokers' Rights and shift strategy to seek local ordinances. Insurance companies begin offering nonsmokers discounts on life insurance premiums.

1983
San Francisco passes country's first strong workplace anti-smoking ordinance.

1986
Californians for Nonsmokers' Rights becomes Americans for Nonsmokers' Rights. U.S. Surgeon General C. Everett Koop and National Research Council issue reports warning that secondhand smoke can cause lung cancer and other ailments.

December 1987
Congress passes experimental smoking ban on airline flights of two hours or less. General Services Administration bans smoking in its 6,900 federal buildings. New York City passes comprehensive smoking ordinance.

1988
California adopts Proposition 99, the most far-reaching anti-smoking education program in the country, funded by raising the cigarette tax.

Nov. 14, 1989
Congress extends smoking ban to all airline flights in the lower 48 states.

1990s
Anti-smoking activists and tobacco industry continue locking horns over local anti-smoking ordinances.

1990
Interstate Commerce Commission bans smoking on interstate buses.

May 1992
Environmental Protection Agency releases draft report, subject to final approval by EPA chief, calling second-hand smoke a carcinogen.

Continued from p. 1056

rettes were a legitimate article of commerce but that states had the right to prohibit their sale.[18]

During this period, alarms were also sounded about secondhand smoke. Employers refused to hire smokers, and bills went before Congress to require cigarette packages to be labeled as poison or stamped with a skull and crossbones. Celebrities spoke out against smoking, among them Henry Ford, Thomas A. Edison and baseball player Honus Wagner, who demanded that the tobacco companies' new baseball cards bearing his likeness be destroyed (the main reason a Wagner is today the rarest card).

In 1910, when the Nonsmokers' Protective League was founded in New York, *The New York Times* editorialized that "anything that may be done to restrict the general and indiscriminate use of tobacco in public places, hotels, restaurants, railroad cars will receive the approval of everybody whose approval is worth having." The movement weakened, however, with the onset of World War I and the cigarette ration, and lost further ground in the 1920s, when the suffragette movement prompted many women to take up smoking.

The Spitting Precedent

A colorful chapter from turn-of-the-century U.S. history — the nationwide crackdown on tobacco chewing — still inspires anti-smoking activists. Many chewers were in the habit of spitting tobacco juice on public sidewalks, which risked the spread of diseases such as tuberculosis. In 1897, three Philadelphia women organized the Women's Health Protective Association, posting signs reading, "Don't Expectorate on the Sidewalk." In 1905, after cities had begun passing anti-spitting ordinances, Pennsylvania Gov. Samuel W. Pennypacker argued that "spitting is a gentleman's constitutional right."

Four years later, reform-minded attorney Sam Scovile of the Pennsylvania Tuberculosis Society argued back: "The object of law is the protection of the public. The great majority of our public have not yet learned to use their own rights so as not to injure the rights of their neighbors. Every man has, for example, the inalienable right to spit on his own domain. In fact, the right of expectoration seems to be as constitutional in America, judging from appearances, as the right to life, liberty, and the pursuit of happiness. If, however, by exercising this right a citizen spreads disease and death, or encourages others to do so, he should be impelled to forgo this American birthright."[19] The demise of the spittoon in the 1920s is regarded by modern anti-smoking groups as auguring the fate of the ashtray.

Activism on the Rise

Today's anti-smoking activists got their start in the 1960s, alarmed, as was much of the country, by the 1964 report of Surgeon General Luther L. Terry endorsing the view of many medical authorities that smoking causes cancer.

The tobacco industry, which since the early 1950s had been challenging such findings, was a powerful force in Washington. But the anti-smokers had little political clout, recalls ASH founder Banzhaf, who as a young lawyer in 1967 won a landmark Federal Communications Commission ruling stating that the Fairness Doctrine required broadcasters to balance tobacco advertisements with ads about smoking risks. "Where could we go for money? The nonsmokers, who mostly didn't care? The Seventh-day Adventists? The small number of [smoking] victims? Liberal do-gooders?"

For Banzhaf's small organization, the answer was to pressure government agencies. In 1969, ASH examined available medical literature on the effects of secondhand smoke and filed a petition with the Civil Aeronautics Board demanding nonsmoking sections on airplanes.

The movement toward smoke-free transportation was catching on elsewhere. The Penn Central Railroad released two surveys in 1969 showing overwhelming preference among commuters for nonsmoking cars. "A continuing problem concerns a minority of daily riders who gain gratification from smoking in nonsmoking cars, much to the annoyance of their nonsmoking brethren," read a Penn Central brochure. "Gentle prods by railroad employees and officials, even by fellow commuters, seem not to help alleviate the situation. In these instances, may we urge consideration as the noble cause to be pursued."[20]

At the same time, the American environmental movement was making advances that would culminate in the 1970 Clean Air Act, which helped galvanize the movement to improve indoor air. It was then that ASH helped prompt what Banzhaf called "the opening gun in the war for nonsmokers' rights." He telephoned the head of United Airlines on behalf of an air traveler who was recuperating from a respiratory ailment. Could the airline create a nonsmoking section to protect the passenger during a flight to Florida? United complied, and other airlines soon followed suit. Separate nonsmoking sections were required beginning in 1973.

"The impact of the ban in the air reflected itself on the ground," Banzhaf says. "It became clear that even though at no time did a majority of Americans smoke, most people thought the majority smoked. This began to change when people began to see the smoking section much less crowded. And they began to like the nonsmoking section."

Citizens' Groups in the 1970s

By the early 1970s, citizens who were offended by smoking were organizing local groups. GASP was found-

The Worldwide Crackdown on Smoking

I n France, few sights have been more familiar than the beret-sporting café habitué puffing a filterless Gauloise. But he may now be a vanishing species. On Nov. 1, an anti-smoking law went into effect throughout France that imposes fines of $120-$260 for individuals who light up in restricted areas and $600-$1,200 for businesses that don't provide separate smoking and non-smoking sections. On French trains, posters observe that "from now on, the only thing smoking in the bar will be the cup of coffee."

Though about 40 percent of the French smoke, 84 percent say they favor the new law.† But restaurants have complained about the expense of new ventilating equipment and griped that the no-smoking sections will spoil their decorating schemes and cost them their regular clientele. Others say that the government has not done enough to prepare the population. "You cannot change habits overnight," said a spokesman for France's major labor union. "We think the only way to [implement] this law in workplaces is for there to be harmonious talks and agreements among workers."

France has joined some 63 countries in enacting anti-smoking legislation, according to the World Health Organization (WHO), up from 47 in 1986. The bans focus on hospitals, government buildings, nurseries, schools, trains, buses, aircraft, theaters, sports arenas and elevators. Each May, WHO's World No-Tobacco Day encourages governments, communities and individuals to press for tobacco-free public places and, ultimately, a tobacco-free society.

The smoking bans already in effect vary widely. Finland prohibits smoking in all public places, except where smoking is specifically allowed; in Malta, Papua-New Guinea and Senegal local administrators designate sites where smoking is permitted; South Korea and Sweden want to ban or reduce public smoking while relying on voluntary cooperation; and New Zealand requires all employers to prepare a written smoking policy in consultation with employees.

Of particular note to Americans was the landmark Canadian legislation enacted in 1988. For years, a complex lobbying war had been waged by grass-roots anti-smoking activists and health groups in Canada. They roped national politicians into taking stands on smoking and challenged the more-cautious members of Canada's med-ical establishment to speak out.

The package that eventually passed took far-reaching steps that had long been fought over. It banned tobacco advertising (though this was later overturned by courts as a violation of free speech), slapped cigarettes with the largest sales-tax hike in Canadian history (from 40 cents to $1.10 per pack — seven times the U.S. rate) and implemented a Nonsmokers'-Rights Act that prohibits smoking in all federal offices and on all domestic airline flights and restricts it in most public transportation.

American anti-smoking activists predicted that Canada's move would trigger similar U.S. legislation. Even Canada's top tobacco-industry lobbyist agreed. "There is no question that the health lobby is international, well-coordinated and networked," said William H. Neville, president of the Canadian Tobacco Manufacturers' Council, "and therefore [the legislation] is going to be encouragement for similar forces in other jurisdictions." ††

But others maintain that Canada's action won't affect the United States. "They've got a very different legal system," says Scott Ballin, vice president of the American Heart Association. "Their constitution is totally different. They don't grow that much tobacco. They had an uphill [political] battle, but in this country we have things to overcome that they don't."

Since passage of Canada's law, says Tobacco Institute spokesman Walker Merryman, not only has the country's advertising ban been struck down but Canadian smokers annoyed at the tax have been creating a "nightmare" for government officials by driving across the U.S. border to buy cigarettes. Merryman acknowledged, however, that the ban on public smoking has not fomented an observable backlash among smokers.

The U.S. tobacco industry has good reason to keep tabs on the worldwide smoking crackdown, given its overseas marketing strategy: The share of American cigarette manufacturing that is slated for export rose, according to the Agriculture Department, from 10 percent in 1986 to 26 percent in 1991.

---

† *The Washington Post*, Nov. 2, 1992.

†† Morton Mintz, "No Ifs, Ands, or Butts," *Washington Monthly*, July-Aug. 1990, p. 30.

---

ed by Marylander Clara L. Gouin in 1971 to help local groups across the country circulate anti-smoking literature and sell posters, buttons and such novelty items as nonsmokers' ties.

GASP also produced a "Bill of Rights" declaring that: "Nonsmokers have the right to breathe clean air, free from harmful and irritating tobacco smoke. This right supersedes the right to smoke when the two conflict. Nonsmokers have the right to express — firmly but politely — their discomfort and adverse reactions to tobacco smoke.... Nonsmokers have the right to take action through legislative channels, social pressures or any other legitimate means — as individuals or in

State Laws Restricting Smoking in Public

A majority of state legislatures have passed laws restricting or banning smoking in public places; most of the states with weak or non-existent anti-smoking laws are in the South.

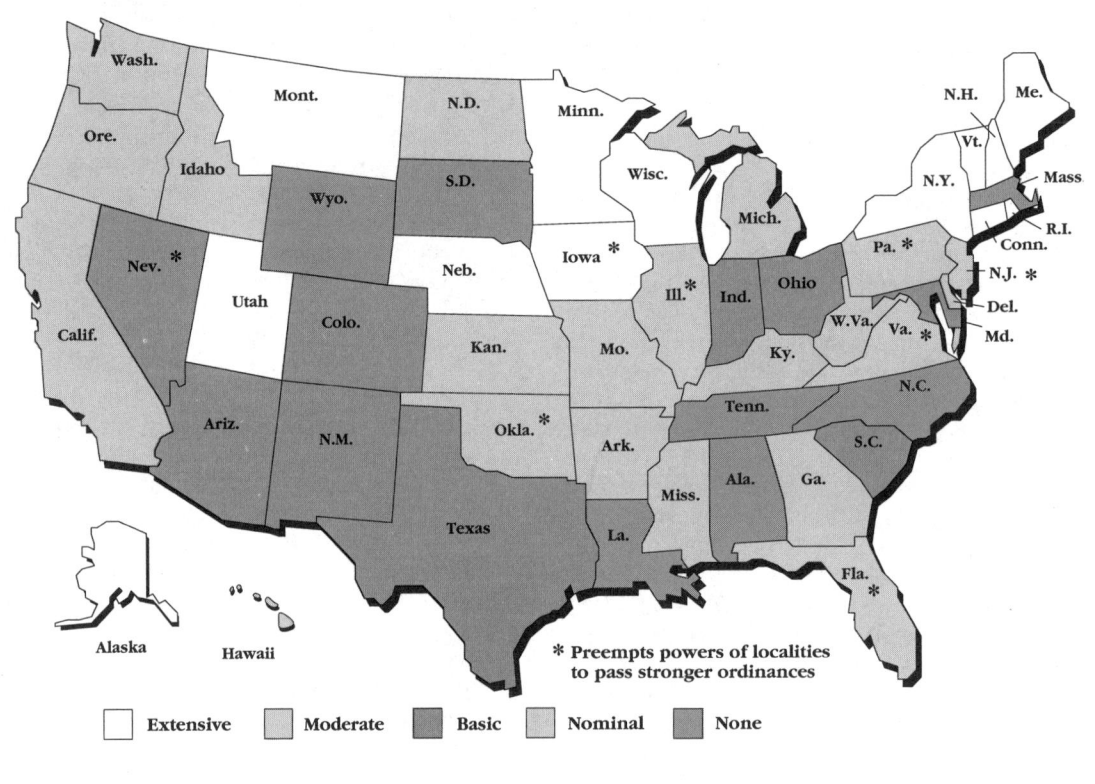

* Preempts powers of localities to pass stronger ordinances

Extensive   Moderate   Basic   Nominal   None

Source: Coalition on Smoking OR Health, October 1992

groups — to prevent or discourage smokers from polluting the atmosphere and to seek the restriction of smoking in public places."

With scant funds and little medical expertise, activists in Arizona and Minnesota lobbied successfully for passage of the first state indoor clean air laws. GASP groups were joined in the mid-1970s by Californians for Nonsmokers' Rights, which would later become Americans for Nonsmokers' Rights. Efforts were made to pass statewide restrictions on public smoking in California and Florida, but were defeated.

The tobacco industry, meanwhile, continued focusing on medical re-search that linked serious illnesses to smoking. In 1972, a Tobacco Institute official, in a memo that would emerge years later, advised the industry to stick with its "brilliantly conceived" strategy of "creating doubt about the health charge without actually denying it, advocating the public's right to smoke without actually urging them to take up the practice and encouraging objective scientific research as the only way to resolve the question of health hazard." [21]

But the rise of grass-roots anti-smoking groups could no longer be ignored. The Roper Organization, in a confidential study for the tobacco industry that would emerge in 1980, presented tobacco executives with disturbing results from its sixth biennial national opinion survey. The poll found that the number of Americans who believed that smoking is harmful to nonsmokers' health had risen from 46 percent in 1974 to 58 percent in 1978. The nonsmokers'-rights issue is "the most dangerous development to the viability of the tobacco industry that has yet occurred," Roper said. "The pressure for segregated facilities will change from a ripple to a tide."

Office Worker's Landmark Suit

The anti-smoking movement was aided in 1976 by a landmark court case that upheld an employee's right to a smoke-free work environment. In *Shimp v. New Jersey Bell Telephone*, office worker Donna Shimp complained of severe nose, throat and eye irritation, headaches, nausea and vomiting. Her physicians declared that she was allergic to cigarette smoke. At first the company installed an exhaust fan near her work space. When the situation did not improve, management asked her to work at a different location, a move that amounted to a demotion and pay cut. After fruitlessly complaining to government agencies, she finally sued for injunctive relief, asking the court to require management to remove the smoke from her work area.

"The evidence is clear and overwhelming," the judge wrote. "Cigarette smoke contaminates and pollutes the air, creating a health hazard not merely to the smoker but to all those around her who must rely upon the same air supply. The right of an individual to risk his or her own health does not include the right to jeopardize the health of those who must remain around him or her in order to properly perform the duties of their jobs. The portion of the population which is especially sensitive to cigarette smoke is so significant that it is reasonable to expect an employer to foresee health consequences, and to impose upon him the duty to abate the hazard which causes the discomfort." [22]

Victories in the 1980s

In 1980, the EPA conducted a national study of environmental smoke at bars, bowling alleys, workplaces and restaurants. It found that where smoking was permitted, the level of air pollution exceeded the standards of the Clean Air Act.

Momentum was building for the nonsmokers'-rights movement. In 1983, nonsmokers handed the tobacco lobby its first major defeat, winning passage of comparatively mild workplace smoking restrictions in San Francisco. The nonsmokers spent only $130,000 on lobbying, compared with the $1.3 million spent by their opponents in the industry, and the new policy drew worldwide attention.

Also galvanizing was the 1986 release of governmental studies warning about environmental tobacco smoke. The most important was by the surgeon general. *The Health Effects of Involuntary Smoking* said that ETS causes lung cancer and other disease in nonsmokers and noted that children of smokers have increased frequency of respiratory symptoms. Most significant, the report said, "The simple separation of smokers and nonsmokers within the same airspace may reduce but does not eliminate the exposure of the nonsmoker to environmental tobacco smoke."

The 1986 studies, recalls Banshaf, were a turning point. "Lots of people who were willing to tolerate sore eyes and a drippy nose were not willing to tolerate the risk of lung cancer," he said.

The war against public smoking intensified. At the First World Conference on Nonsmokers' Rights, held in Washington in 1986, the owner of the new Nonsmokers Inn in Dallas reported saving thousands of dollars a year by having nonsmoking employees and guests. Continental Airlines began cutting fares by 10 percent for nonsmoking passengers. U.S. hospitals began banning smoking at work by employees, physicians, patients and visitors. The General Services Administration imposed smoking bans in government buildings, affecting more than 1 million federal employees.

Congress Tests Ban on Planes

But the greatest victory for the anti-smokers came in December 1987, when Congress passed an experimental smoking ban on domestic airline flights of two hours or less. Vigorously opposed by the tobacco industry, the ban won the day largely because of dramatic testimony from flight attendants. For the first time in history, they noted, high numbers of flight attendants had been flying for 20 years or more, and that disproportionate numbers of them were experiencing chronic inflammation of the lungs as well as throat polyps.

R. Michael Jenkins

Public Attitudes About Smoking

An increasing proportion of Americans prefer a total ban on smoking in restaurants and in the workplace rather than restrictions. A large majority of both smokers and nonsmokers consider smoke inhaled by nonsmokers as harmful to children.

Smoking in Restaurants

	No Restrictions	Smoking Areas Set Aside	No Smoking At All	Don't Know	**Total**
1992	4%	62%	33%	1%	100%
1989	8%	66%	23%	3%	100%
1987	8%	74%	17%	1%	100%
1983	10%	69%	19%	2%	100%

Smoking in the Workplace

	No Restrictions	Smoking Areas Set Aside	No Smoking At All	Don't Know	**Total**
1992	5%	64%	30%	1%	100%
1989	10%	65%	21%	4%	100%
1987	11%	70%	17%	2%	100%
1983	15%	64%	17%	4%	100%

Indicate the extent to which you agree with the following statement: Passive smoking or secondhand smoke is harmful to infants and young children.

	Male	Female	Current Smoker	Former Smoker	Non-Smoker	**Total**
Strongly agree	58%	68%	42%	69%	75%	64%
Agree	35%	28%	47%	26%	23%	31%
Disagree	3%	3%	6%	1%	1%	3%
Strongly disagree	1%	–	1%	1%	0%	–
Don't know	3%	1%	4%	3%	1%	2%

Source: The Gallup Organization Inc., June 1992

"Years ago, a doctor asked me, after I had had a chest X-ray, how many cigarettes I smoked," one said at a 1989 hearing on the issue. "I told him I had never smoked, and he said I had the lungs of a two-pack-a-day smoker. He blamed my spots on the secondary smoke on the airplane. Help. I dread working a smoking section."[23]

In 1989, after the American Associ-ation for Respiratory Care released a survey showing that 84 percent of airline travelers supported the smoking ban, Congress made it permanent and extended it to almost all domestic flights.

But the tobacco industry fought back. In 1987, tobacco giant Philip Morris embarked on an unusual new lobbying effort to water down an an-ti-smoking ordinance in Pittsburgh.[24] Having unsuccessfully opposed the draft ordinance on economic and smokers'-rights grounds, Philip Morris began marketing what it called "an accommodation program." As an alternative to the international symbol for no smoking — a lit cigarette with a red slash through it — the tobacco maker created a new symbol with an accompanying text that said, "Smokers and Nonsmokers welcome." It displayed the symbol on billboards and on stickers given to restaurant owners throughout Pittsburgh, sparking protests from health groups and anti-smoking activists.

In November 1989, then-Surgeon General C. Everett Koop criticized the program as "a ploy to convince the public that smoking restrictions were an attack on civil rights rather than a health matter." Philip Morris eventually dropped the Pittsburgh campaign, but not its general efforts to thwart restrictions on smoking.[25] ■

CURRENT SITUATION

California Leads the Way

The primary battleground in the smoking-policy war has long been California, where dozens of localities have passed smoking bans and where the tobacco lobby, according to one study, has given double the amount of campaign contributions per state legislator that it has to lawmakers in Washington.[26]

Ordinances banning all smoking in workplaces or restaurants passed this year in Clayton, Laguna Beach, Larkspur, Novato, Oakland and Solana Beach. While San Francisco rejected a smoking ban this year, bans have been passed in the city's surrounding juris-

Continued on p. 1064

Hiring and Firing Smokers

It is one thing for employers to prohibit smoking at the workplace. It is another to prohibit employees from smoking when they're *off* the job. The issue of whether people should be hired and fired over smoking has suffused the smoking debate with broader questions of discrimination and civil liberties.

In 1987, Oklahoma City firefighter Greg Grusendorf lost his job for taking three puffs of a cigarette during his lunch break. Smoking on or off the job violated department policy. Grusendorf challenged his dismissal but lost. The judge found that smoking was not comparable to the fundamental and intimate privacy rights protected by the Constitution and that the fire department's policy had the legitimate goal of protecting the health of employees who perform dangerous physical work.

Legal precedent also exists, however, favoring smokers' rights. In Minnesota in 1988, a job applicant alleged discrimination when an employer refused to hire him, claiming he was an increased disability risk because he smoked. The applicant appealed to the state Human Rights Commission, which ruled that the employer's rejection amounted to discrimination if it was based solely on concern about the disability risk. In other words, the employer would have to prove that smoking would impair the man's job performance or injure other employees. That not being the case, the commission ordered him hired.

Concern over rising health insurance costs has prompted many companies to openly favor employees who don't smoke. An estimated 6,000 firms have such policies, according to the Administrative Management Society in Washington. Turner Broadcasting in Atlanta has declined to hire smokers since 1988. Phoenix-based U-Haul International gives nonsmoking employees a $130-per-year discount for health insurance. A 1991 survey by the Bureau of National Affairs in Washington found that 2 percent of the nation's companies hire nonsmokers exclusively, 8 percent have a stated preference for nonsmokers and 7 percent allow individual supervisors to decide against hiring smokers.

Smokers'-rights activists, with backing from the tobacco industry and the American Civil Liberties Union (ACLU), have been crying foul. *Choice*, the smokers'-rights magazine published by R.J. Reynolds Tobacco Co., asks its readers to watch out for newspaper classified ads that specify nonsmoking applicants and send them to Reynolds. The magazine reports on alleged discrimination against smokers and other individuals, such as the airline ticket agent who was fired for not wearing makeup or the police officer who was removed from patrol duty because a tatoo on his forearm made a bad impression.†

The magazine also exhorts smokers to write their state legislators demanding new or broadened laws to combat workplace discrimination against private behavior. Some 25 states and the District of Columbia have enacted laws within the past several years protecting persons who smoke outside the workplace. Some laws specifically cite smoking as a protected right off-premises, others have broader protection for any lawful activity. Some offer plaintiffs a right to bring suit for lost wages or injunctive relief and attorneys' fees. And some exempt religious organizations, schools, or employers — such as health organizations — for which a smoking restriction may be a bona fide occupational qualification.

In vetoing one such bill in March 1991, Utah's Republican Gov. Norman H. Bangerter warned that such a law would create an "unwarranted intrusion into the relationship between employers and employees." And he expressed "displeasure and resentment at the misinformation campaign waged by the tobacco industry to convince Utahans that this bill is somehow necessary to protect their 'fundamental right of privacy.'" President-elect Bill Clinton, as Arkansas' Democratic governor, vetoed a smokers'-rights bill last year.

John F. Banzhaf III, a George Washington University law professor who heads Action on Smoking and Health (ASH), has been battling efforts by the smokers'-rights movement to pass anti-discrimination laws. He sees the potential for abuse of laws intended to protect the rights of minorities.

"There is no rational basis for refusing to hire a black or a woman, because race and sex are immutable characteristics," he says. "Smoking is not. On the face of it, the laws sound good in that a boss has no business in what happens off the premises. But the ACLU is taking money from the tobacco industry. The ACLU used to take unpopular, underfunded cases, but that's not the situation here. The tobacco industry is equipped to fund its own defense openly and directly, without the need for a front."

Denying that it is fronting for tobacco interests, the ACLU says there is sizable public support for its positions on general privacy. A 1992 nationwide poll by the National Consumers League, for example, showed majorities of up to 96 percent agreeing that employers had no right to regulate private activities such as smoking, diet, dating, moonlighting or the expression of political views. The ACLU does not oppose workplace smoking bans, says Lewis Maltby, director of the group's task force on civil liberties in the workplace. It only opposes bans on legal products — such as tobacco, alcohol and junk food — consumed in the privacy of a person's home.

---

† "Is Your Employer Watching You?" *Choice*, September, 1991, p. 2.

Continued from p. 1062
dictions. A smokers'-rights bill to bar discrimination in hiring passed the state Assembly this fall but was vetoed by Republican Gov. Pete Wilson.

What would have been one of the nation's toughest smoking bans went before the San Diego City Council Oct. 26. The council voted it down 6 to 2 but promised to revisit the issue. The city's hospitality industry warned against economic losses and layoffs, citing a familiar but undocumented estimate that restaurant business declined by 30 percent after Beverly Hills implemented a restaurant smoking ban. "In San Diego, 20 percent of tourists are from the countries with a much higher percentage of smokers than San Diego's population," argued Anne Evans, owner of two San Diego hotels.[27]

Such arguments were countered by Americans for Nonsmokers' Rights, which cited studies showing that after smoke-free restaurant ordinances passed in Bellflower, Calif., and Aspen, Colo., business actually improved because of new visits from nonsmokers.

Stanley R. Kiker, executive vice president of the California Restaurant Association, notes that a study from the California State Board of Equalization (the agency that collects sales taxes) showed that smoking bans have not hurt restaurants. But the strong impression from individual owners is that bans do hurt, he says. "The concept of nonsmoking restaurants has grown in the past several years, but there's not as rapid a demand as some of the proponents indicate," he says. "There are still lots of nonsmokers who live with or have friends who go out to eat with smokers and concede the evening to the smoker."

Though for years Kiker's group opposed smoking bans, for the past two years it has pressed for a statewide ban which, instead of "chopping up" the market from locality to locality, would at least put all restaurants on the same competitive footing. "You can't be just a little bit pregnant," Kiker says. "If smoke is a health hazard, it's a hazard wherever."

Federal Action

In Washington, the science advisory board to the EPA on Oct. 27 approved the draft report classifying secondhand smoke as cancer-causing, leaving it to departing EPA Administrator William K. Reilly to give an expected approval to the finding. EPA has also prepared a draft "Guide to Workplace Smoking Policies," also not yet released.

The 102nd Congress, during its final weeks, acceded to lobbying by veterans' groups and overturned a ban on smoking in all veterans hospitals that had been ordered by recently dismissed Veterans Affairs Secretary Edward J. Derwinski. On the children's front, Sen. Frank R. Lautenberg, D-N.J., and Rep. Richard J. Durbin, D-Ill., who authored the airline smoking ban in the late 1980s, introduced the Smoke-Free Children's Programs Act in August 1992. It would require federally funded programs such as Head Start, health and day-care programs to establish a nonsmoking policy if they provide services to children under age 5. No action was taken on the bill, and it is expected to be reintroduced in 1993.

The anti-smoking movement is setting its sights on passage of a nationwide workplace smoking ban from the Occupational Safety and Health Administration (OSHA). Unlike EPA, OSHA has regulatory authority over environmental tobacco smoke. As far back as 1987, groups such as ASH, the American Public Health Association and the Public Citizen Health Research Group have lobbied OSHA for a workplace ban. In May 1991, a U.S. appeals court upheld a decision made by OSHA in September 1990 not to proceed on the issue because workplace tobacco smoke did not pose "grave danger." In September 1991, however, OSHA requested public commentary on the issue in the *Federal Register*.

ASH, meanwhile, has asked OSHA to ban workplace smoking or restrict it to well-ventilated areas. The idea of going through OSHA, an ASH newsletter explains, is to provide a national minimum standard, but one that would not preclude enforcement of stricter state and local laws. A uniform OSHA standard would make enforcement easier, ASH says, because everyone would know that smoking is restricted. Finally, the tobacco industry's political clout would have little effect because the final word would be left with federal courts.[28] A nationwide workplace ban would cost the tobacco industry $4 billion a year, according to a study released by Glantz in November.

By November 1992, OSHA had received 1,200 comments on workplace smoking, and though there is hope for a ruling on a national smoking ban by the end of the year, action may have to wait for the incoming Clinton administration. ∎

OUTLOOK

Getting Smokers to Quit

"I'm 57 years old, I've never broken a law in my life and all of a sudden I'm a criminal," a New York City smoker recently told *New York* magazine. "I'm getting punished for a dirty habit I picked up when it was a great thing to do."[29]

Though complaints are inevitable, rules governing smoking have been implemented largely with success in workplace environments, where the same people gather from day to day. "Smoking policies resolve conflicts, keep people focused on their jobs and are a positive influence," says

Continued on p. 1066

At Issue:

Are smoking bans justified?

AHRON LEICHTMAN

Executive Director, Citizens for a Tobacco-Free Society

yes

*i*f someone came up to you with an aerosol can and sprayed a mist about you containing more than 4,000 chemical compounds, many of which are pharmacologically active, toxic, mutagenic and carcinogenic — what would your reaction be?

Or suppose you were dining in a restaurant and the person at the next table spat upon you, or the waiter slapped you or pinched you? Would you sit idly by while the manager spoke to you about spitters' rights, slappers' rights or pinchers' rights? Would you calmly suggest that these folks be placed in a separate section in the restaurant where they couldn't harm you? No, you'd probably want them arrested and put in jail. That's where people who commit assault and battery are sent.

We haven't done that to smokers. For decades, we've permitted them to smoke virtually anywhere and any time. But tobacco smoke is now widely recognized as the most serious indoor air pollutant — a leading source of toxic chemicals.

The Environmental Protection Agency is expected to declare tobacco smoke a class A carcinogen (the classification reserved for the most lethal environmental hazards, such as asbestos, benzene and radon). The next and most logical step is to protect the public health by banning smoking in all enclosed public places. Smoking should be prohibited from workplaces where most people spend eight hours a day and where it may be impossible to restrict smoking to separate ventilated areas.

Secondhand smoke is a first-class disaster for more than 200 million Americans who have made the decision not to smoke. Despite recent public opinion polls that show overwhelming support for public smoking bans, a rich and powerful tobacco industry has thus far blocked federal bans in places other than the airliner cabin....

The Tobacco Institute — a nonscientific lobby similar to the Flat Earth Society — continues to deny that tobacco smoke is harmful. Only in the bizarre world of the tobacco industry can lobbyists justify the misrepresentation of factual information to make it appear that the controversy over smoking and health remains an open one.

The problem of nonsmokers being forced to breathe secondhand smoke should not be treated as a mere nuisance to be resolved by good manners, but as a severe threat to life and health requiring government action.

People who are addicted to tobacco should be shown compassion and helped to overcome their addiction if they want help, but they should not be permitted to inflict harmful chemicals — the waste products of their addiction — on others who have no choice in the matter.

WALKER MERRYMAN

Vice President, The Tobacco Institute

no

*g*enerally speaking, the American public is a pretty accommodating bunch. They tend to dislike unfair treatment of selected groups in our society. So, it should not be surprising that two public opinion polls in the last year show overwhelming support for treating smokers and nonsmokers fairly.

In December 1991, Gallup Organization researchers indicated, "About two-thirds [of Americans] prefer separate smoking areas ... rather than a total ban" on smoking. In an interesting twist, the report noted that "support even for these limits has fallen slightly, while backing for no restrictions has grown."

Similarly, when the American Lung Association released another Gallup Poll in June of this year, public preference for no restrictions or separate sections outpaced support for total smoking bans by margins of more than 2 to 1.

Anti-smoking groups will find little support in an article published in the October 1992 issue of the *Journal of the American Medical Association*. The AMA claims that this study is significant because it is the first to use autopsy samples in environmental-tobacco-smoke research.

However, the study's authors state that none of the subjects in the study died of diseases related to cancer. The researchers say they looked at lung tissue samples and observed cell changes they believe "may be lung cancer risk indicators" or were "possibly precancerous lesions." However, the significance of the observed cell changes is unknown. Furthermore, none of the individuals were interviewed for this study before they died to determine if they ever had been exposed to smoking or what other environmental influences they may have encountered in their lives.

This study, like much of the environmental-tobacco-smoke literature, raises many more questions than it aswers and adds little to the debate.

In the end, most Americans will continue to reject extreme appeals to banish smokers from society and will instead favor sensibly accommodating smokers and nonsmokers.

Tobacco Smoke and Sick-Building Syndrome

The battle over workplace smoking bans inevitably drifts into debates over building ventilation. "Cigarette smoke is often mistaken as the primary cause of indoor air pollution," says The Tobacco Institute. "Tobacco smoke is visible; allergenic fungus, bacteria and invisible gases and fumes that cause symptoms such as coughing, sneezing and watery eyes are not."† Hence, the industry argues, banning smoking is not the most important step toward purifying a building's air — especially if the root of the problem is a phenomenon called sick-building syndrome.

First defined by the World Health Organization (WHO) in 1982, sick-building syndrome refers to the nausea and dizziness experienced by workers in buildings that, while often poorly ventilated, contain inordinate amounts of tobacco smoke, organic chemicals, radon gas and fibers such as asbestos and fiberglass insulation.

WHO has estimated that up to 30 percent of the world's modern buildings have such indoor air problems. An American ventilation-consulting firm in the 1980s found that nearly 40 percent of the buildings it studied contained dirty ductwork, some afflicted with "a pet cemetery of dead rodents, pigeons, snakes and cockroaches."††

Healthy Buildings International (HBI), in Fairfax, Va., specializes in eradicating sick-building syndrome. "Activities such as copying, duplicating, smoking, cooking etc. all add to the indoor burden," reads HBI's literature, but the "real culprit often lies in the improper operation and maintenance, and faulty design and construction, of buildings, causing the structure to trap polluted air." HBI says that from 1980-1991 it found that the top cause of discomfort in buildings was allergenic fungi (33.4 percent of cases), followed by dust (26.6 percent). Tobacco smoke was the ninth-most-significant cause at only 2.8 percent of cases.

On June 10, 1992, the "NBC Nightly News" reported that HBI had received financial support from the tobacco industry for several years and that one of its primary functions is to divert public attention from considering bans on smoking. A former HBI employee who had been fired said HBI President Gray Robertson had boasted of the wealth he'd made from the tobacco industry. The ex-staffer also described being coached by HBI on how to appear convincing to clients while declining to recommend workplace smoking bans.

Anti-smoking activists seized on the report, calling HBI a "front group" for the tobacco industry that offers expert testimony and releases surveys to the public but never recommends that clients restrict smoking. "This public relations tactic is part of HBI's broader strategy of fighting for the tobacco industry's interests at the community, state and national levels," charges the Advocacy Institute, a grass-roots lobbying group in Washington. "Their efforts range from trying to convince businesses not to adopt no-smoking policies to influencing governments to not pass clean indoor air laws, and they seem to be willing and able to travel to any community, regardless of size or location, to accomplish their goals."

HBI's Robertson acknowledged to NBC that tobacco accounts for 20 percent of his firm's consulting fees. But in a later interview he said tobacco interests were represented by only three clients on a list of 250 that includes banks, hospitals, universities and government agencies. And he says that his firm has acknowledged it publicly when they have testified at the behest of the The Tobacco Institute, "but we never change our story." The reason HBI doesn't recommend smoking bans is that "our clients are usually landlords who have some tenants who want to accommodate smokers. We offer them options — designated areas or smoking lounges — and we don't recommend that they permit smoking, either. A smoking ban is a quick fix that addresses the cause not the symptom. We do a better job than a quick fix."

Walker Merryman, a spokesman for The Tobacco Institute, also denies that HBI is a tobacco industry front. He says the institute only learned of HBI by accident several years ago, when HBI did some work in the institute's building.

---

† *Smokers' Rights in the Workplace: An Employee Guide,* The Tobacco Institute, p. 7.
†† *Ibid.*

Continued from p. 1064

Rosner of the Smoking Policy Institute.

Their influence in encouraging smokers to cut down or quit is demonstrable. When the Johns Hopkins University Medical Center in Baltimore went smoke-free in the late 1980s, 30 percent of its smokers stopped within a year, and those who continued smoked 19 percent fewer cigarettes, reports Glantz.

By some reckonings, a total workplace ban is best for easing the way for smokers to quit. A partial ban that leaves some smoke in the air "is like forcing people who're on a diet to be with people who are constantly eating strawberry shortcake and chocolate sundaes," says Banzhaf. On the other hand, Rosner emphasizes that it is unfair to make smokers second-class citizens by designating a poorly ventilated smoking area that "smells like something crawled in there and died." He and other consultants stress the importance of soliciting employees' views and providing educational materials and plenty of advance warning before cracking down against smoking. Unions, in particular, have often resisted smoking bans if they're imposed by management rather than negotiated in collective bargaining.

The cost of smoking policies — consultants, employee-education campaigns, smoking-cessation programs and new ventilation equipment for designated areas — can be a factor in an organization's decision. But cost is probably only a short-term factor. Comparing smoking and nonsmoking employees, one study estimated that a smoker is absent 50 percent more often, uses the employer's health insurance 1.5 times more, has an accident rate twice as high and takes more time per day in breaks.[30]

"A lot of companies will drop $5,000 on helping an employee who's addicted to illegal drugs but won't shell out $150 on tobacco," complains Rosner. He calls for more insurers to emulate King County Medical/Blue Shield of Seattle, which in 1990 became the first major insurer to cover smoking cessation as a standard benefit and award group discounts on premiums to organizations that ban smoking.

Anti-Smokers' Split

The momentum achieved by the anti-smoking movement shows few signs of abating. This fall, Kentucky, one of the biggest tobacco-producing states, announced plans to limit smoking in state offices by 1993. In Montreal, the International Civil Aviation Organization at its annual meeting passed a resolution to intensify its studies into the safety aspects of banning smoking on all international flights. And building managers belonging to the International Facility Management Association predicted in a survey that companies with smoke-free offices would grow from 56 percent today to 96 percent by the year 2020.

Anti-smokers risk becoming divided, however, between their grassroots, militant faction and their professional, "establishment" wing. Several activists — Banzhaf of ASH, Morris of GASP, Leichtman of Citizens for a Tobacco-Free Society and Glantz of the University of California — have criticized the heart, lung and cancer associations saying they are allocating too few funds for anti-smoking efforts and being too cautious in taking on the powerful tobacco lobby. "They're afraid of lawsuits and losing donor funds" if they get involved in controversies, says Morris.

Ballin of the Heart Association responds that each type of group has its own role in the battle. "We bring a scientific credibility that no one else has," he says. "We have petitions pending and have beaten up on many members of Congress and the administration. This charge comes out of frustration among people outside of Washington [who are vexed by] the power of the tobacco industry." He adds that the donor-funded groups were founded with the mission of conducting biomedical research, and that in addition to anti-smoking work, they must tend to

---

Reasons for Smoking — or Quitting

Among the 2,500 employees of Blue Cross/Blue Shield of Maryland, most of those who quit smoking after the company implemented a workplace smoking ban say they stopped for health reasons. Eighty percent of the smokers, however, didn't quit after the policy was implemented, saying they smoked for enjoyment or because they were under stress.

Reasons For or Against Smoking

	Yes	No
Why quit smoking?		
Fear of losing job	24%	76%
Peer pressure	15%	85%
Information provided in a smoking-cessation program, pressure from family members	39%	61%
Personal concern for health	87%	13%
Increased restriction on smoking in public	20%	80%
Pressure from clients	0%	100%
Increased social view of smoking as a "dirty habit"	42%	58%
Why not quit smoking?		
I enjoy smoking	95%	5%
Unable to quit, even through a smoking-cessation program	29%	71%
I do not want my employer to tell me to quit smoking	75%	25%
Many of the clients I deal with smoke	68%	32%
One or more of the people in my household smoke	53%	47%
Most of my friends smoke	51%	49%
I am under too much stress	77%	23%

Source: Indiana School of Business, 1992

education and advocacy efforts in such areas as nutrition, exercise and high blood pressure.

Smoke-Free by 2000?

As smoking policy is fought out in legislatures, town councils and executive suites, action is also moving to the courts. The Supreme Court in January will hear the case of a Nevada prisoner who objected to sharing a cell with a five-pack-a-day smoker. His case was brought by the Washington-based consumer group Public Citizen.

Smoking by adults is increasingly an issue in child-custody fights, with nonsmoking parents more successful at winning custody. A group called Parents Against Secondhand Smoke (PASS) was founded in Watertown, Mass., this year after a custody fight.

Banzhaf says ASH may sue restaurants that lure children in with advertising and then place them at tables where smoking is permitted, inasmuch as some of them may suffer serious asthma attacks. In August, Leichtman went to court to charge a radio talk-show host with assault and battery and violating his right to privacy for blowing smoke in his face. Finally, smoking activists, says Phillis of the United Smokers' Association, are threatening legal action against "corrupt government officials" if EPA approves its pending report on the dangers of environmental tobacco smoke.

In the long term, says The Tobacco Institute's Merryman, it will be very difficult for the anti-smoking movement to push the portion of the American population that smokes below 25 percent. "In going to local legislative hearings," he says, "I've seen some smokers'-rights groups emboldened by the excesses and zealotry of their adversaries. In a perverse way, we ought to be grateful to anti-smoking groups for pushing us and starting a backfire."

Glantz acknowledges that the tobacco industry has been "somewhat successful in slowing things down." But 10 years ago, he adds, his non-smokers' movement was "all hypothetical, less well-dressed and had fewer glossy reports" than it does today. The irony of the situation, he says, is that it's like finding a cure for AIDS but not using it. "We know how to stamp out tobacco," he says. "The real cure for cancer is politics."

The surgeon general's office wants a smoke-free America by the year 2000. That doesn't mean there won't be smokers, Banzaf explains, only that there won't be public smoking places — just as there isn't "a spitting section of a company cafeteria." In the future, he says, "smoking will be an act confined to consenting adults, in private." ∎

Notes

[1] Foster Gunnison Jr. "The Smoker's Manifesto," *American Smoker's Journal*, Premier Issue, summer 1992, p. 5.

[2] Stanton A. Glantz and William W. Parmley, "Passive Smoking and Heart Disease: Epidemiology, Physiology, and Biochemistry, *Circulation*, January 1991, p. 1.

[3] Quoted in Jennifer Stock, "The Need for a Safe, Healthy, and Smoke-Free Workplace," *World Smoking & Health*, American Cancer Society, summer 1990, p. 3.

[4] For background, see "Tobacco Industry on the Defensive, But Still Strong," *Editorial Research Reports*, Sept. 21, 1990, pp. 537-552.

[5] The case involved a child whose symptoms of severe asthma were found to come and go as the mother smoked, quit and then resumed smoking. See Stanton A. Glantz, *Tobacco Biology & Politics* (1992), p. 23.

[6] *Ibid.*, p. 24.

[7] Reported in *The Washington Post*, March 12, 1991.

[8] Reported in *USA Today*, Aug. 5, 1992.

[9] Reported in *The New York Times*, Oct. 7, 1992.

[10] Ernest van den Haag, "Smokers Have Rights, Too," *The New York Times*, April 9, 1985.

[11] Quoted in *The Miami Herald*, Oct. 1, 1992.

[12] James T. Bennett and Thomas J. DiLorenzo, *Official Lies: How Washington Misleads Us* (1992), p. 222.

[13] Fred Phillis, "How the Anti-Smokers Have Gotten Rich and Powerful on Public Funds," *The Connecticut Smoker*, Vol. 1., No. 1.

[14] Quoted in David Krogh, *Smoking: The Artificial Passion,* (1991), p. 71.

[15] Stock, *op. cit.*, p. 5.

[16] Bruce Samuels and Stanton A. Glantz, "The Politics of Local Tobacco Control," *Journal of the American Medical Association*, Oct. 15, 1991, p. 2110.

[17] Jack E. Henningfield, *Nicotine: An Old-Fashioned Addiction* (1985), p. 95.

[18] Cassandra Tate, "In the 1800s, Antismoking Was a Burning Issue," *Smithsonian*, July 1989, p. 107.

[19] Clara L. Gouin and Willard K. Morris, "The Spitting Image of Smoking," *American Lung Association Bulletin*, March 1976.

[20] Quoted in *American Lung Association Bulletin*, December 1975.

[21] Glantz, *op. cit.*, p. 34.

[22] Quoted in Steve Allen and Bill Adler Jr., *The Passionate Nonsmoker's Bill of Rights: The First Guide to Enacting Nonsmoking Legislation* (1989), p. 161.

[23] Testimony of Susan Bianchi-Sand, president, Association of Flight Attendants, House Public Works and Transportation Subcommittee on Aviation, June 22, 1989. By 1989, smoking restrictions in public places or workplaces had been adopted by 513 U.S. cities with populations over 25,000. Comprehensive laws (affecting workplaces, restaurants and public places) were in effect in 165 cities, according to a study in the *Journal of the American Medical Association*.

[24] Nancy A. Rigotti, Chris L. Pashos, "No-Smoking Laws in the United States: An Analysis of State and City Actions to Limit Smoking in Public Places, *Journal of the American Medical Association*, Dec. 11, 1991, p. 3162.

[25] Bruce E. Samuels, Michael Evans Begay, Anna Russo Hazan and Stanton A. Glantz, *Philip Morris's Failed Experiment in Pittsburgh*, University of California, San Francisco, 1992.

[26] *Extinguishing Proposition 99: Political Expenditures by the Tobacco Industry in California Politics in 1991-1992*, Institute for Health Policy Studies, University of California, San Francisco, September, 1992.

[27] Writing in the *San Diego Union-Tribune*, Oct. 18, 1992.

[28] ASH, *Smoking and Health Review*, March-April, 1992.

[29] "Butt Heads," *New York*, March 23, 1992, p. 26.

[30] Elaine H. Fry, "Not Smoking in the Workplace: The Real Issue," *Business Horizons*, November-December 1990.

Bibliography

Selected Sources Used

Books

Allen, Steve and Adler, Bill Jr., *The Passionate Non-smoker's Bill of Rights: The First Guide to Enacting Nonsmoking Legislation*, William Morrow & Co., 1989.

The famed entertainer/talk-show host teamed up with a Washington journalist to produce this history, analysis and how-to guide for the anti-smoking activist.

Galloway, Arlene, *The Smoke-Free Guide: How to Eliminate Tobacco Smoke From Your Environment*, Qualy Publishing, 1988.

A Canadian registered nurse offers detailed pointers on how to implement smoking bans in homes and offices.

Glantz, Stanton A., *Tobacco Biology and Politics: An Expose´ of the Fraud and Deception the Tobacco Companies Have Used to Hoodwink Consumers for 85 Years*, 1992.

A University of California at San Francisco medical researcher who founded Americans for Nonsmokers' Rights surveys the health and policy issues surrounding smoking and criticizes the conduct of the tobacco industry.

Henningfield, Jack E., *Nicotine: An Old-Fashioned Addiction*, Chelsea House Publishers, 1985.

In this volume from an encyclopedia of psychoactive drugs, experts discuss the medical, psychological, historical, cultural and political aspects of tobacco use.

Krogh, David, *Smoking: The Artificial Passion*, W.H. Freeman and Co., 1991.

A University of California science editor examines motivations for smoking, the personalities of smokers and methods for kicking the habit.

***Smokers' Rights in the Workplace: An Employee Guide*, The Tobacco Institute.**

A 12-page compendium of questions and answers dealing with smokers' rights and how they can deal with complaints and policies about smoking in the workplace.

Articles

Samuels, Bruce and Stanton A. Glantz,, "The Politics of Local Tobacco Control," *Journal of the American Medical Association*, Oct. 16, 1991, p. 2110.

Researchers at the University of California at San Francisco detail systematic efforts of the tobacco industry to oppose anti-smoking ordinances at the state and local levels.

Sullum, Jacob, "Smoke and Mirrors," *Reason*, February 1991, p. 28.

An editor at a libertarian magazine argues that anti-smoking activists impose their personal preferences on those who are less health-obsessed.

Sylvester, Kathleen, "The Tobacco Industry Will Walk a Mile to Stop an Anti-Smoking Law," *Governing*, May 1989, p. 34.

A journalist analyzes the tobacco lobby's strategy for heading off anti-smoking ordinances and laws through intense campaigns at the state level.

"All Fired Up Over Smoking: New Laws and Attitudes Spark a War," *Time*, April 18, 1988, p. 64.

The nationwide battle over smoking in restaurants and workplaces is surveyed by a team of *Time* correspondents.

Reports and Studies

Americans For Nonsmokers' Rights, *Major Local Smoking Ordinances in the United States*, U.S. Health and Human Services Department, September 1989 (updated edition forthcoming).

This compilation by a major anti-smoking group is a city-by-city listing of the content and timing of smoking laws around the country.

Coalition on Smoking OR Health, *State Legislated Actions on Tobacco Issues*, 1991.

An advocacy alliance of the American Heart Association, the American Lung Association and the American Cancer Society compiled this state-by-state breakdown of smoking-related laws around the country.

Hanauer, Peter, Glenn Barr and Stanton A. Glantz, *Legislative Approaches to a Smoke-Free Society*, American Nonsmokers' Rights Foundation, 1986.

Activists with the nation's largest anti-smoking group compiled a handbook for lobbyists seeking new laws against smoking.

The Next Step

Additional Articles from Current Periodicals from EBSCO Publishing's Database

Activists

"Anti-smoker groups rally on world no-tobacco day," *Consumer Affairs Letter,* **May 1992, p. 3.**

Observes the World Health Organization's World No-Tobacco Day on May 31, 1992. This year's theme, "Tobacco-Free Workplace"; the 40 countries that have enacted national legislation to control workplace smoking; the Environmental Protection Agency's draft of its risk assessment on environmental tobacco smoke.

"Progressives plug in," *Progressive,* **July 1992, p. 12.**

Discusses how the Advocacy Institute's Smoking Control Access Research Center (SCARC) has developed a computer network to solve the problems associated with the balancing act of national advocacy of causes. SCARCNet links 200 anti-smoking activists around the country; forum for strategic brainstorming provided.

Corporations

"Sick buildings get a breath of fresh air," *Science News,* **Feb. 15, 1992, p. 109.**

Reports on a study by Charlene W. Bayer and Christopher C. Downing of the Georgia Institute of Technology in Atlanta, which examined whether pumping air into a building could reduce the level of indoor pollutants. Office workers who become ill from exposure to copy machines, furniture and cigarette smoke in poorly ventilated buildings.

"The employer pays for employee behavior," *Executive Health's Good Health Report,* **April 1992, p. 8.**

States that a four-year study of 45,976 employees showed that their lifestyle had a direct effect on their absenteeism, their health-care costs and their expense to the employer. Risks included current smoking, excessive alcohol intake and obesity.

Lesmes, G.R., "Corporate healthcare costs and smoke-free environments," *American Journal of Medicine,* **July 15, 1992, p. 48S.**

Presents results from two studies that were combined to assess potential market impact for programs to reduce health risks, as well as to define how small businesses can better control their operating expenses. Significant increase in recognition of impact of employee smoking on healthcare costs; what cessation programs are most successful; details.

Miller, R., "Health communication through workplace
smoking discouragement posters," *Journal of Health Education,* **May/June 1992, p. 250.**

Describes how one corporation produced posters designed to discourage tobacco smoking in the employee population by using data from an employee-union survey.

Moll, L., "Tangible benefits for better health," *Vegetarian Times,* **April 1992, p. 22.**

Discusses the efforts of U.S. companies to control health-care costs by offering financial rewards to employees who strive to stay healthy. Majority of companies either penalize tobacco users or reward non-users; some reward employees on positive results from wellness checkups.

Wernick, S., "Office smoke," *Working Mother,* **June 1992, p. 20.**

Contends that nonsmokers suffer when their office-mates smoke. Health problems associated with smoky offices; costs of the problem for the employer; highlights of research conducted on the issue.

Government policy

"Joint commission KOs smoking in hospitals," *American Journal of Nursing,* **March 1992, p. 108.**

Announces new conditions laid down by the Joint Commission on Accreditation of Healthcare Organizations. All accredited hospitals will have to be completely smoke-free within the next two years.

Cowley, G., "A quit-now drive that worked," *Newsweek,* **April 6, 1992, p. 54.**

Reports that California's anti-smoking initiative, Proposition 99, is facing budget cuts as a result of state fiscal pressure. Rationale for proposed cuts in the program; details of criticism from anti-smoking activists; other state and national proposals for similar anti-smoking campaigns.

Hamilton, D.P., "EPA defines hazards of tobacco smoke," *Science,* **July 24, 1992, p. 471.**

Focuses on the Environmental Protection Agency's draft review of the health effects of passive smoking. Expected action by the Occupational Safety and Health Administration.

Levine, D., "Smoking: Risks — and benefits?" *American Health,* **March 1992, p. 22.**

Discusses the effects of the movement to ban smoking for all hospital patients, staff and visitors in facilities for the addicted and mentally ill. Michael Greeman of the Veterans

Administration Medical Center in Minneapolis said smoking is the sole source of pleasure for some psychiatric patients; Dr. Phillip Sinaikin at Fair Oaks Hospital in Summit, N.J. comments; prescription tobacco.

Physiological effect

"Death by association?" *Harvard Health Letter,* **March 1992, p. 8.**

Announces that the largest investigation to date has strengthened the linkage of passive smoking to lung cancer, particularly with respect to pulmonary adenocarcinoma, the most common type of lung cancer among women in the U.S. Study; findings; results; conclusion; details.

"Do long noses save dogs from passive smoking?" *New Scientist,* **March 28, 1992, p. 16.**

Reports on a study that reveals long noses may protect dogs who live with heavy smokers from lung cancer. Possible reason why; study that found short-nosed dogs were more likely to develop lung cancer; drawback of long noses.

"Indoor air pollution and acute respiratory infections in children," *Lancet,* **Feb. 15, 1992, p. 396.**

Editorial. Comments on how the need to reduce the exposure of young children to tobacco smoke in all countries is self-evident, but it is even greater in less developed countries that need better methods of heating and cooking to control indoor pollution.

"Pardon my carcinogen," *Time,* **Aug. 3, 1992, p. 28.**

Gives figures from an Environmental Protection Agency review board that found "environmental tobacco smoke" (secondhand smoke) leads to about 3,000 cases of lung cancer a year in the U.S. and 300,000 cases of respiratory disease. The tobacco industry has attacked the report.

"Passive smoke and pregnancy," *Reader's Digest,* **March 1992, p. 31.**

Discusses a study reported in the journal *Neurotoxicology and Teratology* on the effects of active and passive smoke on children in the womb. The study finds that children of mothers who smoked suffered long-term problems in intelligence, visual/spatial abilities, behavior and other areas.

"Passive smoking and your heart," *Consumers' Research Magazine,* **April 1992, p. 13.**

Discusses the effects of environmental tobacco smoke (ETS) and the risk of nonsmokers developing lung cancer. Only seven of 32 published studies report statistically significant increased risk; relationship to cardiovascular disease; risk factors for cardiovascular disease; active tobacco smoking questioned as risk factor; more. INSETS: What is ETS?; the ETS social movement.

"Poison at home and at work," *Newsweek,* **June 29, 1992, p. 55.**

Covers a new report alleging that secondhand smoke or environmental tobacco smoke (ETS) poses a fatal health risk. Studies conducted by the U.S. Environmental Protection Agency (EPA).

"Smoked out of school," *Health & Fitness Magazine,* **March 1992, p. 58.**

States that the schoolwork of smokers' children could suffer because they sleep badly, according to the magazine *GP.* Children of smoking mothers are five times more likely to suffer impaired sleep from snoring; study; details.

"Smoking husbands pose risk," *Executive Health's Good Health Report,* **April 1992, p. 1.**

Present results from the first three years of a five-year study at Louisiana State University in New Orleans, which conclude that nonsmoking women have an increased risk of lung cancer if their husbands smoke.

Caldwell, C., "Smoke gets in your eyes," *American Spectator,* **May 1992, p. 25.**

Comments that proving dangers to nonsmokers from environmental tobacco smoke has not been easy for anti-smoking activists. No established allergenic properties in tobacco smoke; no convincing evidence of the adverse effects of passive smoking; findings of several studies.

Carey, P. & L. Fraser, "Poor kids suffer when moms smoke," *Health,* **May/June 1992, p. 10.**

Reports on research by Fernando Martinez of the University of Arizona College of Medicine on the effects of second-hand smoke to children of mothers who smoke. Trend he found between middle class and lower-income.

Research

Holden, C., "Brand 'Z' less hazardous to health?" *Science,* **July 10, 1992, p. 160.**

Reports on a survey that found scientists were far more apt to villainize radon and environmental tobacco smoke when these were explicitly named than when presented with unnamed substances whose health effects were described identically.

Lesmes, G.R., "Passive smoking: The medical and economic issues," *American Journal of Medicine,* **July 15, 1992, p. 38S.**

Presents the opinion that since the 1970s, the dangers associated with passive (involuntary) smoking have been widely debated. What the research has produced; the Environmental Protective Agency and its report; the number of people that secondhand cigarette smoke kills per year.

Back Issues

Great Research on Current Issues Starts Right Here... Recent topics covered by The CQ Researcher are listed below. Before May 1991, reports were published under the name of Editorial Research Reports.

MAY 1991
School Choice
Racial Quotas
Animal Rights
U.S. and Japan

JUNE 1991
Children and Divorce
Teenage Suicide
Endangered Species
Europe 1992

JULY 1991
Teenagers and Abortion
Soviet Republics Rebel
Mexico's Emergence
Athletes and Drugs

AUGUST 1991
Sexual Harassment
Fetal Tissue Research
Oil Imports
The Palestinians

SEPTEMBER 1991
Police Brutality
Advertising Under Attack
Saving the Forests
Foster Care Crisis

OCTOBER 1991
Pay-Per-View TV
Youth Gangs
Gene Therapy
World Hunger

NOVEMBER 1991
Fast-Food Shake-Up
The Greening of Eastern Europe
Business' Role in Education
Cuba In Crisis

DECEMBER 1991
Retiree Health Benefits
Asian Americans
The Obscenity Debate
The Disabilities Act

JANUARY 1992
Term Limits
Oil Spills
Hunting Controversy
Alternative Medicine

FEBRUARY 1992
Threatened Coastlines
New Era in Asia
Assisted Suicide
Jobs in the '90s

MARCH 1992
Women and Sports
Underage Drinking
Garbage Crisis
Mafia Crackdown

APRIL 1992
Ozone Depletion
Welfare Reform
Politicians and Privacy
Illegal Immigration

MAY 1992
Native Americans
Jobs vs. Environment
Too Many Lawsuits?
Fairness in Salaries

JUNE 1992
Nuclear Proliferation
Food Irradiation
Lead Poisoning
Hard Times for Libraries

JULY 1992
Alternative Energy
Prescription Drug Prices
Alzheimer's Disease
Infant Mortality

AUGUST 1992
The Homeless
Work, Family and Stress
NATO's Changing Role
Marine Mammals vs. Fish

SEPTEMBER 1992
Domestic Partners
Violence in Schools
Public Broadcasting
Women in the Military

OCTOBER 1992
Depression
U.S. Auto Industry
Youth Apprenticeships
Hispanic Americans

NOVEMBER 1992
Physical Fitness
Privatization
Paying for College
U.S. Policy in Asia

Back issues are available for $4.00 (subscribers) or $7.00 (non-subscribers). Quantity discounts apply to orders over ten. To order, call Congressional Quarterly 1-800-432-2250.

Binders are available for $15.00. To order call 1-800-638-1710.

Future Topics

▶ *The CIA*

▶ *Eating Disorders*

▶ *Women and AIDS*

PUBLISHED BY CONGRESSIONAL QUARTERLY INC., IN CONJUNCTION WITH EBSCO PUBLISHING

The New CIA

Does the agency have a role in the post-cold war era?

T
HROUGH MORE THAN 40 YEARS OF U.S.-SOVIET
confrontation, the Central Intelligence Agency
warned American presidents that the cold war might
turn hot. But World War III never happened, and
now the agency is being criticized for failing to foresee the
speed with which communism would collapse in Eastern
Europe. This and other recent intelligence breakdowns have
given the CIA's critics more reasons to question the agency's
effectiveness. But while some observers see the agency's days
as numbered, others say the CIA is needed more than ever to
confront the growing threats of nuclear proliferation, narcotics
trafficking and terrorism. And some believe the CIA could
help halt the erosion of America's competitive edge by
ferreting out foreign business secrets for U.S. companies.

C_Q   **December 11, 1992 • Volume 2, No. 46 • 1073-1096**

Formerly Editorial Research Reports

December 11, 1992
Volume 2, No. 46

EDITOR
Sandra Stencel

MANAGING EDITOR
Thomas J. Colin

ASSOCIATE EDITOR
Richard L. Worsnop

STAFF WRITERS
Charles S. Clark
Mary H. Cooper
Rodman D. Griffin

PRODUCTION EDITOR
Sarah E. Merritt

EDITORIAL ASSISTANT
Michael M. Taylor

GRAPHICS
Jack Auldridge

PUBLISHED BY
Congressional Quarterly Inc.

CHAIRMAN
Andrew Barnes

VICE CHAIRMAN
Andrew P. Corty

EDITOR AND PUBLISHER
Neil Skene

EXECUTIVE EDITOR
Robert W. Merry

ASSOCIATE PUBLISHER
John J. Coyle

EDITOR, EBSCO PUBLISHING
Melissa Kummerer

The CQ Researcher (ISSN 1056-2036). Formerly Editorial Research Reports. Published weekly (48 times per year, not printed the first Friday of any month with five Fridays) by Congressional Quarterly Inc., 1414 22nd St., N.W., Washington, D.C. 20037. Rates are furnished upon request. Second-class postage paid at Washington, D.C. POSTMASTER: Send address changes to The CQ Researcher, 1414 22nd St., N.W., Washington, D.C. 20037.

The New CIA

BY RODMAN D. GRIFFIN

THE ISSUES

Several days before the Iraqi invasion of Kuwait on Aug. 2, 1990, executives of U.S. oil companies quietly began slipping out of Kuwait City. Other Americans living in the small Persian Gulf emirate sensed danger in the air, and several anxiously telephoned the U.S. Embassy. "No, no. You're just being silly," said one woman recalling an embassy officer's words.[1] The U.S. government assured its citizens in the region that there would be no Iraqi attack.

Within days, however, scores of American civilians were trapped as Iraqi tanks rolled into Kuwait City. Though satellite photography was capable of identifying Iraqi artillery units massed for the assault, the Central Intelligence Agency (CIA) failed to give sufficient warning of the imminent invasion, even after the savvy Western oilmen had packed their bags.

The Persian Gulf intelligence fiasco was the latest, but hardly the biggest, of the CIA's recent fumbles. Among other things, the agency failed to foresee the demise of communism. The CIA devoted year after year to assessing the military capabilities of the Soviet Union and the other Warsaw Pact nations — counting their tanks, troops, missiles and ships. But the agency was left virtually in the dark about the Soviet bloc's political, economic and societal decay, as well as the speed with which communism would collapse in Eastern Europe.

"For a quarter-century, they told the president everything there was to know about the Soviet Union, excepting the fact that it was collapsing. They missed that detail," noted Sen. Daniel Patrick Moynihan, D-N.Y., former vice chairman of the Senate Intelligence Committee.[2]

After the Soviet breakup, economists were amazed at the extent to which the CIA had overestimated the performance of the Soviet economy, leading many to speculate that the numbers were hyped to fuel the arms race. The agency's overall analysis in recent years has been "between abysmal and mediocre," says Allan Goodman, dean of Georgetown University's School of Foreign Service.

Many observers agree. Even supposed early successes — covert operations in Iran in 1953, Guatemala in 1954 and Chile in 1970 — are hardly the sort of accomplishments the world's leading democracy can crow about (see p. 1084). More recently, the ongoing revelations about Iran-contra and the CIA's dealings with the Luxembourg-based Bank of Credit and Commerce International, which has been linked to drug traffickers and Arab terrorists, have put the agency on the defensive.

America will probably never really know how well the CIA has performed — for in the spy business, as old hands say, those who know do not talk, and those who talk usually do not know. Little is known, for example, about secret information on Soviet missile technology purloined by agents. Broadcasting that information publicly would have put lives at stake.

So long as the cold war was on, intelligence budgets were sacred. Along with 11 related institutions in the U.S. espionage community — including the National Security Agency, the Defense Intelligence Agency and the supersecret National Reconnaissance Office — the CIA dined well on the flush national-security spending of the 1980s. (See story, p. 1079.) Intelligence budgets tripled over the decade to reach nearly $30 billion in 1992 — roughly the same amount the federal government spends on education and the environment. Until 1991, money for CIA operations and analyses continued to grow, years after Pentagon appropriations had peaked.

Like the behemoth automaker General Motors, which became obsessed with selling cars at all costs and forgot about quality, American intelligence has arguably grown complacent and narrow-minded in recent years. During his 1991 Senate confirmation hearings, Director of Central Intelligence (DCI) Robert M. Gates* depicted the agency's army of analysts as "close-minded, smug, arrogant" and prone to "flabby, complacent thinking and questionable assumptions."

If the CIA could once hide behind the veil of secrecy, it can't today. Officials say the agency must function more like a private company — watch the bottom line and be held accountable for its mistakes. "Our version of bankruptcy is irrelevancy," says Andrew Campbell, a

---

*During Gates' bruising confirmation hearings, senators questioned his role, as CIA deputy director, in the Iran-contra affair as well as his analysis of Soviet economic and military preparedness. A Bush appointee, Gates announced in November that he would step down after President-elect Bill Clinton takes office.

senior official in the CIA's Office of Strategic Direction. "In the private sector, companies are moving into niche markets. Here at the CIA we're moving into niche intelligence, and moving away from the mass Soviet target."

There is no question that the winds of global change are gusting through the CIA's sprawling wooded campus in Langley, Va., just outside Washington. Under fire on Capitol Hill, the CIA is in the throes of the biggest overhaul in its 45-year history. Under the 49-year-old Gates, the CIA has become more open to public scrutiny, restructured its bureaucracy to sharpen analysis and reduce redundancy and attempted to retool for the "new world order." A new CIA head, to be appointed after President-elect Bill Clinton takes office in January, undoubtedly will take those changes even further.

At issue is the fundamental question of what a post-cold war intelligence community should look like — and what the nation's spies and analysts should do now. The CIA's past challenges were far different than those it must encounter now: small states armed with weapons of mass destruction, virulent local conflicts over ethnic and nationalistic rivalries, drug trafficking and terrorism, even economic competition from longstanding allies.

For four decades, the U.S. intelligence community was obsessed with events in the tiny space within the Kremlin's walls. Tracking the Soviet threat consumed as much as two-thirds of the entire intelligence budget.* Today, the greater political threat is a long way from Moscow — in newly independent republics like Kazakhstan, where hundreds of former Soviet nuclear weapons are stored, in the streets of Medellín and Cali, Colombia, where

the drug cartels are based, and in the mosques of Iran, where the seeds of Islamic fundamentalism are sown.

While the "Red menace" may have faded, experts say these other, more subtle dangers are multiplying. No longer does U.S. intelligence have the luxury of concentrating on a single, nuclear-tipped enemy. "We literally need to remake the intelligence community to fit the changed world environment," says Sen. David L. Boren, D-Okla., chairman of the Senate Select Committee on Intelligence.

Robert M. Gates
Director of Central Intelligence

As budget-conscious policy-makers debate how to confront these new intelligence challenges, here are some of the major issues being discussed:

Now that the cold war has ended, does the United States really need the CIA?

While most observers agree that some intelligence-gathering capability is necessary, critics suggest that the CIA is ill-equipped for the tasks of the 1990s, when economic duels may well supplant military competition. Indeed, intelligence experts say the CIA is still laden with Kremlinologists and weapons bean-counters whose utility in the post-cold war era may be dubious. "Knowing the color of

underwear worn by generals in the KGB won't tell you much about the threat to transition in Russia today," quips Goodman at Georgetown.

Restructuring the CIA, which employs between 16,000 and 19,000 people, is no easy task. Like most federal bureaucracies, it has an entrenched power structure.

The CIA's cold war infrastructure, combined with challenges of the new world order, raises anew a question often posed by Sen. Moynihan: Without the Soviet threat, why not just abolish the CIA and let the State Department take over? The CIA is "the quintessential product of the cold war," and now that the war is over, he says, the agency belongs to the past. In 1991, Moynihan introduced legislation that would have all but abolished the agency.

Although Moynihan's radical proposal garnered little support among lawmakers, Vincent Cannistraro, former head of CIA counterterrorism operations, says it is a good idea. "Academia and think tanks have at least an equal record in forecasting significant trends and developments in the Soviet Union," he says. "Some have done better, despite the lack of access to sensitive intelligence data." Cannistraro believes that the State Department could take over political and economic data collection while the Pentagon handled military intelligence and counterterrorism.

Others contend that such measures are extreme. "I disagree with those people who say, 'The cold war's over, so let's disband CIA,'" counters former CIA head William E. Colby. "I've got a very simple answer to that. We disbanded intelligence after World War I and found we needed it; we disbanded it after World War II and found we needed it. Let's not do that again. That's absurd." [3]

Moreover, shifting responsibility for intelligence gathering to the State Department is problematic. For one thing, it would endanger the arm's-length re-

---

*In fiscal year 1993, only about a third of the intelligence community's resources — and less than 15 percent of the CIA's — will be devoted to the former Soviet Union.

lationship between those whose job is to provide objective information and those charged with making policy. "If the collection and analysis of intelligence is totally dominated and overseen by the policy-maker," argues Sen. Boren, "there will be too great a temptation for intelligence to 'serve' or to 'sell' policy rather than to 'inform' policy." [4]

For all the faults its critics cite, the CIA still serves a valuable function, most experts believe. There is no "*glasnost* dividend" for intelligence, warns George Carver, a fellow at the Center for Strategic and International Studies and a former CIA official. "As America's current defense capabilities decrease, more, not less, intelligence will be needed."

Richard M. Helms, director of central intelligence under Presidents Lyndon B. Johnson and Richard M. Nixon, agrees. "With the fall of communism, the intelligence job of the CIA has increased about tenfold," he says. "You have all these countries in the Soviet Union's land space with no clear control over the Soviet Union's weapons. You have all these people with know-how trying to sell themselves to countries that want to beat up on their neighbors. You can't discover their abilities or their plans by technical means, so you have to use spies." [5]

At the same time, there is a consensus even within the CIA that the intelligence community must cut back certain operations. "Moynihan's bill was a wake-up call to the agency," says Goodman. "There is no question it must do better work using less money."

"During the cold war, the CIA in-

creased its focus on all types of problems, not just the Soviet Union," he adds. "The problem is the agency spread itself too thin. The CIA should focus on areas where it has a comparative intelligence advantage — such as terrorism, nuclear-arms control and narcotics trafficking."

Ultimately, a narrower focus may mean that the CIA will not be able to cover the globe with the same vigor that it did in the past. Then again, it may not need to. "Previously, if there was a coup in Botswana, it was important to know if Moscow backed it," says a former CIA political analyst, who requested anonymity. "Now, who cares? It's no longer a threat to our national security."

Should the CIA get involved in industrial espionage to help U.S. companies compete in the global marketplace?

As the military threat has receded, the belief that American security rests in economic strength has grown. Many on Capitol Hill and in business and intelligence circles think eco-

The Central Intelligence Agency's sprawling campus is located in Langley, Va., just outside Washington, D.C.

nomic intelligence-gathering is the answer to the CIA's woes — a new mission to justify its $3.2 billion budget. The notion is that the agency should help halt the erosion of America's competitive edge by blocking the theft of U.S. trade secrets and even ferreting out foreign business secrets for U.S. companies. (*See "At Issue," p. 1089.*)

"I think [economics] is a primary area of intelligence in the '90s," says Stansfield Turner, who headed the CIA under Jimmy Carter. "I take the position that if we spy for military security, why shouldn't we spy for economic security?" [6]

The signs of a new mercantilist cold war are everywhere. Intelligence officials learned in 1990, for instance, that Indonesia was about to award a $100 million contract to the Japanese electronics company NEC to modernize its creaky phone system. Authorities say AT&T's European subsidiary had a more competitive bid and that Tokyo may have used its $2.1 billion in annual aid to Jakarta to sway the decision. After President Bush raised the matter with Indonesian President Suharto, the contract was split between NEC and AT&T.

Some observers note that other countries are getting more aggressive at gathering economic intelligence — even crossing the line into industrial espionage. Earlier this year, the FBI revised its list of the top national security threats posed by foreign operatives. The first item was acquisition of sensitive technologies, and the second was collection of U.S. "indus-

Paying the Bill for U.S. Intelligence

The Central Intelligence Agency only spends 10 percent of the $30 billion U.S. intelligence budget. The ultra-secret National Reconnaissance Office, which builds imagery satellites costing up to $1 billion each, gets more than $6 billion.

Intelligence Budgets (Estimates in millions of dollars)

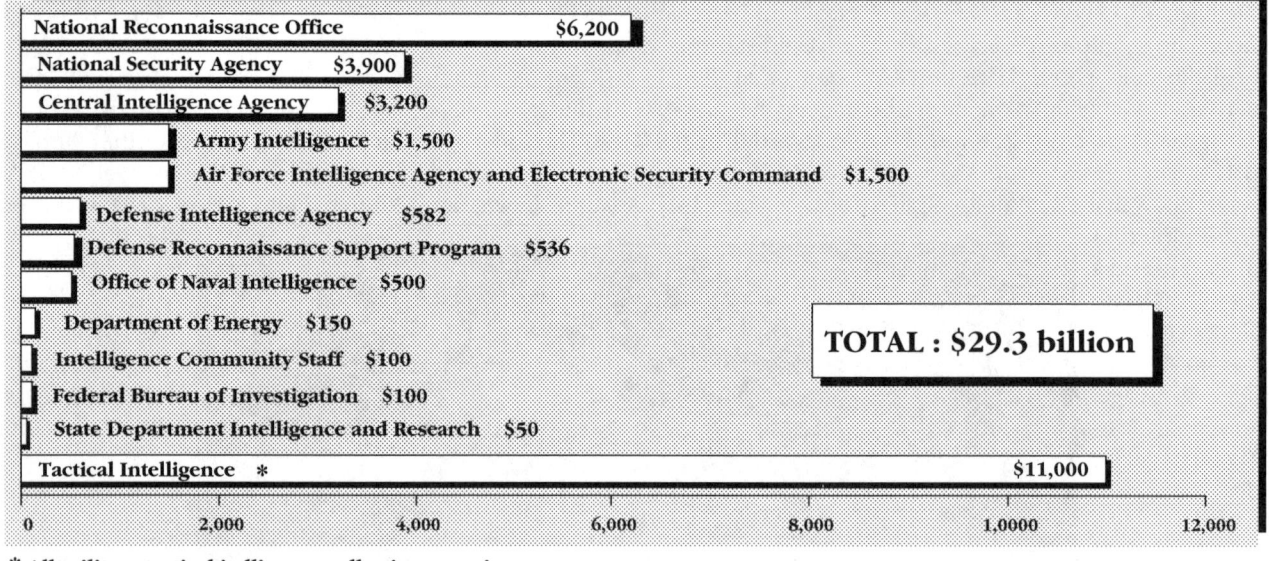

National Reconnaissance Office	$6,200
National Security Agency	$3,900
Central Intelligence Agency	$3,200
Army Intelligence	$1,500
Air Force Intelligence Agency and Electronic Security Command	$1,500
Defense Intelligence Agency	$582
Defense Reconnaissance Support Program	$536
Office of Naval Intelligence	$500
Department of Energy	$150
Intelligence Community Staff	$100
Federal Bureau of Investigation	$100
State Department Intelligence and Research	$50
Tactical Intelligence *	$11,000

TOTAL : $29.3 billion

* All military tactical itelligence collection agencies.

Source: Federation of American Scientists, fiscal 1992 estimates

---

trial proprietary economic information and technology."

The Soviet Union was particularly aggressive at this, and U.S. officials say the Russian intelligence service, the SVR, appears to be continuing the practice. Just since the beginning of this year, officials say, Soviet defectors helped break up two rings of former KGB agents apparently engaged in industrial espionage. In one case, Italy dismantled a ring of 20 spies; in the other, a defector in Belgium provided information that led to agents in four European nations.[7]

"Other countries practice industrial espionage, and so should we," argues Sam Halpern, a retired 30-year CIA veteran with extensive operations experience in the Far East and Latin America. "In fact, we've always done it. In the past, intelligence pro-

vided American industry with information on Soviet helicopters that couldn't have been gotten any other way. I subscribe to the view that countries do not have friends, they have interests."

Few people advocate sending CIA agents out to steal secrets from Mitsubishi or Siemens, the German manufacturing conglomerate. But between that extreme and doing nothing, many business executives see a broad middle ground where intelligence on business and technology, much of which the CIA sucks up from open sources, such as newspapers, trade journals and computer data bases, could be shared.

"The one thing that is unobjectionable and clearly needed is for the CIA to provide better assessments of other countries' competitive conditions," says Jerry Jasinowski, presi-

dent of the National Association of Manufacturers.

For their part, CIA officials say they are acutely aware of the increasing importance of international economic competition. But, deeply fearful of starting a slippery slide toward industrial espionage, the agency thus far has drawn a line: It will focus more on providing information to government officials making economic policy or conducting trade negotiations, but generally won't channel intelligence to companies or industries. As intelligence officers, they may be willing to die for America, but not for General Motors.

"We know that foreign intelligence services plant moles in our high-tech companies," Gates said during his confirmation hearings last fall. "We know that they rifle briefcases of our

Continued on p. 1080

Spy vs. Spy: Overkill in the U.S. Intelligence Community

"I do not believe in a big agency," former CIA Director Allen Dulles (1953-61) once said. "If this thing gets to be a great big octopus, it will not function well." Alas, critics say that is exactly what the intelligence community has become, tripping over its own tentacles.

"Not only is there considerable redundancy ... but more importantly, there is little meaningful centralized direction or coordination," said the House Intelligence Committee's report on fiscal 1992 spending.†

When most Americans think of "intelligence," they think of the CIA. But in terms of money and manpower, the CIA is a bit player. More than 85 percent of the nation's annual $30 billion intelligence budget goes to an array of low-profile agencies whose marching orders come from the Pentagon, not CIA headquarters in Langley, Va.

An estimated $6 billion goes to the ultra-secret National Reconnaissance Office — so secret that until three months ago the Pentagon wouldn't acknowledge it existed — which operates imagery satellites. The National Security Agency (NSA), based at Fort Meade, Md., employs more than 30,000 people, protecting U.S. communications and intercepting foreign messages. The Defense Intelligence Agency (DIA), headquartered in Maryland at Bolling Air Force Base, just outside Washington, is the Pentagon's growing analytical arm, and the four armed services each have their own intelligence commands. On top of all that, the State, Treasury and Energy departments and the FBI all operate smaller intelligence offices.

Experts say the problems of inefficiency and redundancy stem from the very structure of the intelligence bureaucracy. The director of central intelligence (DCI) wears two hats. In addition to heading the CIA, he is responsible for coordinating the budgets and policies of the entire intelligence network. But he does not control the budgets of military intelligence agencies or the careers of those who run them. Since they now dwarf the CIA, some insiders view the secretary of Defense as the real intelligence heavyweight.

In practice, experts say, the perennial split between the military and civilian agencies is the problem. The agencies, particularly those organized under the Department of Defense, are free to compete for budget allocations and free, up to a point, to determine their own priorities. "It just doesn't work," says Vincent Cannistraro, a veteran CIA official who retired in 1990. "And that is the crux of the real problem facing the U.S. intelligence community."††

Until earlier this year, a little-known group called the National Foreign Intelligence Council, chaired by the CIA director in his role as DCI, attempted to coordinate intelligence policy. But the council was disbanded. The reason: It lacked real power.

The generals who spend the money "literally believe it doesn't make any sense to take orders" from the civilians at the CIA, says retired Air Force Gen. Daniel Graham, a CIA veteran and former DIA chief.‡ At the same time, many CIA analysts view their DIA counterparts as a cut below par — less educated and less rigorous in their political analysis, one of the main functions of both agencies.

As a result, most observers say the relationship has degenerated into internecine warfare. A cease-fire "would require a kind of cooperation ... for which there's absolutely no precedent," says retired Army Gen. William Odom, a former NSA head. The standoffishness may have reached a nadir during Operation Desert Shield, when the CIA did not send a requested representative to the Pentagon's wartime Joint Intelligence Center until months after Iraq's invasion of Kuwait. And when he went, he was considered a "liaison" officer, not a member of the command group.

Lawmakers pressing for reforms were encouraged in June 1991 when Army Gen. H. Norman Schwarzkopf, who commanded Allied troops in the gulf war, vented his frustrations before the Senate Armed Services Committee. "There were so many disagreements within the intelligence community ... so many disclaimers," Schwarzkopf said, "that by the time you got done reading many of the intelligence estimates you received, no matter what happened, they would have been right. And that's not helpful to the guy in the field. It really isn't."

In 1991, Defense Secretary Dick Cheney ordered major restructuring of the Pentagon's intelligence operations, giving DIA more authority over the military services and outlining steps "to eliminate unnecessary duplication." At the CIA, officials have also moved to reduce redundancy and improve cooperation with other intelligence agencies. In both cases, however, critics contend the "baby steps" taken so far won't tame the sprawling octopus.

Turf battles have already begun. Some insiders say Pentagon officials hope to expand the military's global spy network to report on political as well as military intelligence. "Two separate empires have been built up over the years — civilian intelligence and military intelligence," says Sen. David L. Boren, D-Okla., chairman of the Senate Select Intelligence Committee. "Two separate empires with a lot of duplication and overlap. We just can't afford it any more."

---

† Quoted in *Government Executive,* March 1992, p. 13.

†† Quoted in *Newsweek,* May 27, 1991, p. 19.

‡ Quoted in *Rolling Stone,* June 27, 1991, p. 30.

Continued from p. 1078

businessmen who travel in their countries. We know that they collect information on what we're doing, and I think that the CIA and FBI working together should have a very aggressive program against it." But, he added, "There is a lot of concern about doing industrial espionage, if you will, and I frankly don't think that U.S. intelligence should be engaged in that." [8]

"Businesses spend a lot on their own espionage," adds Goodman, "probably more than the entire intelligence community. They believe it is important. Let them pay for that belief, not the American taxpayer."

Moreover, passing information into the private sector, officials say, would anger allies in other countries, expose intelligence sources and raise a welter of legal questions for officers deciding which industries or companies to assist. If the CIA has information useful to, say, the computer industry, who decides which companies get that information? If the CIA helps computer companies, what does it say to aircraft manufacturers wanting help? Indeed, who can tell what is and isn't an American company in these days of multinational corporations?.

Before the CIA delves deeper into the minefield of industrial espionage, such questions will have to be answered. The debate is as much about public policy as about the craft of intelligence. Under the Clinton administration, with its commitment to a greater government role in industrial development, pressure to do more will undoubtedly continue to mount.

Has the U.S. come to rely too heavily on satellite and electronic surveillance at the expense of human intelligence collected in the field?

If economics is one buzzword in the intelligence community today, the other is "HumInt" — shorthand for human intelligence, or information gained from case officers and agents in the field. Billion-dollar spy satellites are fine for revealing what's happening in a given place at a given time, but a human source can tell you where to look or listen, what to look for and, ideally, what to expect. With no reliable human "assets" in Iraq, U.S. intelligence agencies were slow to realize that Saddam Hussein's troop movements on the Kuwaiti border were not a bluff.

During the late 1970s, then-CIA Director Stansfield Turner fired many seasoned field operators in favor of "national technical means" — satellites and signals interception — to monitor the Communist threat. Throughout the 1980s, photo reconnaissance, radar-imaging satellites and listening-post satellites were bought as fast as they could be built, costing U.S. taxpayers billions.

Over the past decade, these extraordinarily sophisticated machines have produced a torrent of raw data. Yet the data-collecting ability of our spy technology far outstrips the capacity of humans to analyze it intelligently. Thus, much of the data has been either tossed out or collects dust on computer tapes. "In the Gulf, the real issue was not if we had the intelligence, but whether we had the capacity to use it all," noted Gary Foster, deputy director for CIA planning and coordination. [9]

Many experts believe the high-tech approach was justified when the Soviet Union and Warsaw Pact countries, with their tightly closed borders, were seen as the primary threat to Western security. Today, however, they say such dependence on technology has left the U.S. vulnerable. Eye-in-the-sky satellites and spy planes helped track Soviet missiles, but they cannot penetrate Muammar el-Qadaffi's head or Japan's Ministry of International Trade and Industry, no matter how sharp their lenses. For that, the experts say, you need double agents, go-betweens, eavesdroppers, false passports, blackmailers, frontier crossings, wads of cash in secret bank accounts — the whole bag of dirty tricks.

Obviously, sophisticated spy technology still has its place in the U.S. security arsenal, but experts say without an imminent threat from a nuclear superpower, minute-by-minute monitoring by satellites is no longer essential. In most cases, arms-control agreements can be verified by less costly, on-site inspections.

Three years ago, with the strong support of Sen. Boren, the CIA began an ambitious campaign to recruit and train more spies. (See story, p. 1090.) One reason for the renewed interest in HumInt, beyond the reduced need for satellite arms-control verification, is economics. Jeffrey T. Richelson, author of several books on military intelligence, estimates that it can cost as much as $1 billion to develop an imaging satellite, and another billion to build, launch and operate one. By comparison, spies are a bargain.

"In the end, it is clear that the intelligence community will need both technical and human intelligence," says Michael Nacht, dean of the School of Public Policy at the University of Maryland. "With budgets shrinking, finding a balance will require some tough policy choices." Already CIA officials have made clear that staff reductions at headquarters could top 20 percent, costing thousands their jobs. ■

BACKGROUND

The Glory Days

The reason Washington was caught by surprise at Pearl Harbor, according to Harry S Truman, was that nobody had drawn then-President Franklin D. Roosevelt's attention to intercepted Japanese cables or to the

Continued on p. 1082

Chronology

1940s-1950s *Fearing the uncontrolled expansion of communism, the United States sets up a peacetime intelligence framework to influence politics abroad.*

July 26, 1947
Congress passes the National Security Act, which among other things creates the Central Intelligence Agency.

August 1953
The CIA's Operation Ajax succeeds in overthrowing Iran's nationalist leader, Mohammed Mossadegh, returning the pro-U.S. Shah Mohammed Reza Pahlavi to power.

June 1954
The CIA orchestrates the overthrow of Guatemala's democratically elected president, Jacobo Arbenz.

———•———

1960s *As Cold War tensions rise, the United States and Soviet Union expand spy networks.*

Aug. 25, 1960
The ultra-secret National Reconnaissance Office is established after an American U-2 spy plane is shot down over the Soviet Union.

April 1961
The CIA-backed Bay of Pigs invasion of Cuba turns into a fiasco, marking one of the most embarrassing episodes in U.S. intelligence history.

Aug. 1, 1961
The Defense Intelligence Agency is established as the analytical arm of the Department of Defense.

Oct. 28, 1962
The Cuban Missile Crisis, the most serious Cold War confrontation, ends after President John F. Kennedy im-

poses a naval blockade of Cuba and threatens war unless Soviet missiles are removed.

———•———

1970s *Under increasing public scrutiny, the CIA shifts focus from human sources to satellites and electronic surveillance to keep track of the Soviet threat.*

September 1973
CIA-backed operations by the Chilean military against the government of Salvador Allende end with Allende's death and the overthrow of his government.

May 19, 1976
The Senate Select Committee on Intelligence is created to oversee intelligence activities; the House organizes the Permanent Select Committee on Intelligence a year later. The two oversight committees are established following revelations of assassination plots and bungled CIA covert operations, aired during the Church committee investigations.

———•———

1980s *CIA covert operations enjoy a resurgence during wars in Angola, Afghanistan and Nicaragua, but the agency in general suffers from damaging revelations of illegal activity.*

1982
The CIA funnels $29 million in covert military aid to the fledgling contra rebels in Nicaragua. At year's end, the House unanimously approves the Boland Amendment barring covert aid to overthrow the Sandinistas.

April 1984
The CIA mines Nicaraguan harbors in accelerating the covert war against the Sandinistas.

July 1987
The Iran-contra hearings on Capitol Hill implicate the CIA — and Director William J. Casey — in illegal efforts to fund Nicaragua's contras.

February 1989
The Soviet Union announces withdrawal of last remaining troops from Afghanistan, after protracted conflict with Afghan rebels backed by CIA.

Nov. 9, 1989
The Berlin Wall is razed, signaling the end of the cold war.

———•———

1990s *The end of the cold war and doubts about the accuracy of CIA analysis raise fundamental questions about the agency's mission, structure and budget.*

Aug. 2, 1990
Iraq invades Kuwait; U.S. intelligence community fails to give adequate warning.

Nov. 5, 1991
Robert M. Gates is confirmed as director of central intelligence after intense congressional hearings.

Nov. 15, 1991
President Bush issues National Security Directive 29, calling for "a top-to-bottom examination of the mission, role and priorities of the intelligence community."

Feb. 5, 1992
Sen. David L. Boren, D-Okla., and Rep. Dave McCurdy, D-Okla., announce separate plans to restructure the U.S. intelligence community.

Continued from p. 1080

mountains of scrap iron the Japanese were buying. "If we had had some central repository for information," he concluded, "somebody to look at it, fit all the pieces together, and report it, there never would have been a Pearl Harbor."[10]

Before the end of World War II, there was a movement to create a peacetime U.S. intelligence agency, not unlike the British Secret Intelligence Services (SIS, also known as MI-6). William "Wild Bill" Donovan, a Wall Street lawyer and World War I hero, led the charge, declaring, "In the age of bullies, we cannot afford to be a sissy."[11]

In November 1944, Donovan sent Roosevelt a long memorandum describing the sort of agency he thought was needed; it was much like the Office of Strategic Services (OSS), the wartime intelligence agency that Donovan had founded. Roosevelt agreed, a sign that he intended to use more than charm in dealing with Stalin, and he drafted an executive order to establish a "general intelligence service."[12]

But Donovan's plan was not without opponents. The Army's intelligence branch, G-2, was against it. The Office of Naval Intelligence was against it. The FBI's J. Edgar Hoover was against it.[13] The first secretary of Defense, James Forrestal, was against it. But by erecting the Iron Curtain, threatening Turkey and the Balkans and fighting the Marshall Plan, Josef Stalin canceled them all out.

Indeed, the early history of the CIA makes it clear that without The Cause — fighting the communist menace — Congress probably would never have approved the agency. The bureaucratic rationale emerged from fears of OSS officials that the United States was too dependent on British intelligence, that the Soviet Union was seeking control over Eastern Europe and that adequate information was needed to counterbalance Soviet expansion.

"The company," as the CIA is known to insiders, was established by the National Security Act of 1947, the cornerstone of U.S. defense structure. Among other things, the act created the National Security Council, which oversees the CIA, and the director of central intelligence.

From this early structure has evolved the present American intelligence community — of which the CIA is the linchpin and over which the DCI presides as the president's primary adviser on foreign intelligence. Basically, the CIA's work can be broken down into three general categories: intelligence-gathering and analysis, counterintelligence and political intervention in other countries.* Though interconnected, the three missions have flourished or languished depending on the preferences of the administration in power and on the temperature of the cold war at the time.

"Cowboys and Choirboys"

From the "company's" earliest days, there was always tension between case officers in the field and analysts in Washington, referred to by old OSS hands as "cowboys and choirboys." Before the 1970s, when the CIA was last overhauled, there was no question who had the power. "The cloak-and-dagger guys in operations ran the show," notes Michael Nacht. They were the ones with the cash — and the cachet.

In 1954, a commission appointed by President Dwight D. Eisenhower formulated an official position to justify cold war intelligence activities already under way. "It is now clear," the commission said, "that we are facing an implacable enemy whose avowed objective is world domination by whatever means and at whatever cost. There are no rules in such a game.... No one

---

*The FBI has primary responsibility for counterintelligence *within* the United States.

should be permitted to stand in the way of the prompt, efficient and secure accomplishment of this mission."[14]

Spying was indeed a dirty business. The operations of the CIA and other agencies were often seen as immoral, unconstitutional and criminal. But they were also deemed necessary by policymakers. Many of the CIA's activities — including assassination plots and coup attempts against democratically elected governments — would have made the public uneasy, so they had to be shrouded in secrecy.

Moreover, the agency has always felt a special allegiance to the president. Although the CIA was created by Congress, and is funded annually by congressional appropriations, generations of CIA chiefs have enjoyed privileged entree to the Oval Office. Early on, the agency developed a reputation for organizing complex information into comprehensible statements for senior policy-makers. It also displayed an impressive ability to mount operations and analytical studies quickly. In 1967, for example, agency analysts predicted Israel would win the Arab-Israeli Six Day War within two weeks, without U.S. assistance. At the time, the Israeli government and many in Congress claimed that Israel might lose without U.S. intervention.

Covert Action

Since the agency often operated at the president's behest, the executive branch became a kind of front for covert actions. Often misunderstood, "covert action" denotes an array of subtle and not-so-subtle ways in which the U.S. government interferes in the affairs of other countries, from nurturing the noncommunist left in Europe to secret attempts to overthrow unfriendly governments to actual paramilitary operations in the Third World. In many cases, the actions are designed not to be entirely secret but merely to distance the U.S. government from direct responsibility.

Continued on p. 1084

America's Top Spymasters

The onset of the Cold War convinced President Harry S Truman that his government needed to bring back a spy agency like the war-era Office of Strategic Services (OSS). So in 1947, the CIA was born. The agency, and its predecessor, have had an array of colorful — and sometimes controversial — spy chiefs who left a lasting imprint on the agency. They include:

William Donovan, OSS, 1942-45. "Wild Bill" gave the intelligence agency its enduring stamp: Eastern Establishment, dashing and glamorous. America's most celebrated spymaster, he founded the OSS and inspired the CIA. Beyond his reputation for derring-do, Medal of Honor winner Donovan organized covert efforts in five war theaters that were especially effective in running underground operations, breaking codes and providing tactical intelligence to the military.

Allen Dulles, CIA, 1953-61. His brother was secretary of State, and he had the complete trust and backing of President Eisenhower. Dulles oversaw the heyday of the CIA's covert acts, including the toppling of the Iranian government in 1953 and the Guatemalan government in 1954. He was also in charge during the CIA's most embarrassing failure: the Bay of Pigs fiasco in Cuba in 1961.

John McCone, CIA, 1961-65. The first director to see the future of technology, McCone improved the agency's analysis — and that helped him play a pivotal role in the Cuban missile crisis in 1962. But on his watch the CIA plotted the assassination of at least two world leaders — Cuba's Fidel Castro and Patrice Lumumba in the Congo — and carried out illegal surveillance of more than 10,000 Americans.

Richard Helms, CIA, 1966-73. The first agency professional to become director, Helms was the model of the well-informed, professional manager of agent networks and case officers. "There will be no Bay of Pigs or U-2s under Helms," he promised. Helms oversaw the CIA's destabilization campaign against Chilean President Salvador Allende in the early 1970s. He is also remembered for resisting attempts by the Nixon White House to involve CIA in the Watergate cover-up.

William E. Colby, CIA, 1973-76. Colby took the helm of the CIA in the midst of Watergate. During his tenure, the agency's illegal domestic surveillance was revealed, triggering the beginning of congressional oversight and greater public scrutiny of the CIA.

Stansfield Turner, CIA, 1977-81. Like his boss, President Jimmy Carter, Adm. Turner possessed the naval officer's view of the world, in which systems and facilities are most important. Turner accelerated the shift from human spies to spy satellites and electronic eavesdropping. But in the process of reining in the agency's covert operations, Turner fired a number of seasoned professionals and left the agency staff fractured and demoralized.

William Casey, CIA, 1981-87. Probably the most controversial spy chief, Casey is credited with rebuilding the agency and reinvigorating its covert operations. However, he personally helped lead the Reagan administration into the Iran-contra debacle. Most experts feel Casey's efforts to circumvent the nation's laws seriously damaged the agency's credibility.

Donovan

Dulles

McCone

Helms

Colby

Turner

Casey

Continued from p. 1082

Covert operations not only freed the CIA to conduct its mission unfettered but also served to shield the intelligence establishment from congressional and media inquiries. Such scrutiny might have prevented it from launching disastrous operations like the 1961 Bay of Pigs invasion of Cuba or Operation Phoenix in Vietnam, in which some 20,000 suspected Vietcong supporters were reportedly murdered by South Vietnamese forces.[15]

For decades, the CIA conducted interventions worldwide, subverting Soviet-backed governments, arming insurgences and spreading "black" propaganda, or disinformation.[16] Often these actions produced the intended results — but also harmful consequences. The "victorious" coup in Iran that expelled President Mohammed Mossadegh brought back the pro-U.S. shah, Mohammed Reza Pahlavi, whose repressive regime eventually yielded to the Ayatollah Ruhollah Khomeini. The U.S.-backed coup that overthrew Socialist President Salvador Allende in Chile left harsh military rule under Augusto Pinochet. And the 1954 coup that overthrew Guatemala's democratically elected government of Jacobo Arbenz resulted in several decades of cruel dictatorship and unrest. A quarter of a century later, an American official reportedly observed: "What we'd give to have an Arbenz now."[17]

Attempts at Reform

In the mid-1970s, widespread rumors about failed assassinations and bungled covert operations prompted Congress to set up ad hoc committees to investigate the CIA's performance. The committees, chaired by Sen. Frank Church, D-Idaho, and Rep. Otis G. Pike, D-N.Y., produced reports in 1976 that portrayed the intelligence community as "dangerous, often incompetent, and unaccountable to the American people" but "utterly responsive to the directions of the president."[18] Throughout the hearings, skeletons tumbled from the closet: bizarre plots to murder foreign leaders, mind-control experiments on unwitting human guinea pigs, miles of CIA files kept on Americans in violation of the agency's charter.

The Church committee reported that it had discovered at least eight separate plots against Cuban leader Fidel Castro, including a poisoned wet suit for scuba diving and a Mafia-aided effort to poison his food.[19]

CIA misadventures, however, were not limited to operations in foreign countries. The agency had infiltrated American religious groups, college campuses and news agencies. And it had opened so much first-class mail that it had 1.5 million Americans' names in its computers.

Following the embarrassing revelations, Congress in 1976 tried to put the agency on a shorter leash. New House and Senate "watchdog" intelligence committees were established to review the CIA budget and covert-action plans. At the same time, Director Stansfield Turner, appointed by President Jimmy Carter, drastically cut back on covert action, accelerating the shift to spy satellites and electronic eavesdropping.

Owing to the CIA's link to the president, its mission, to some degree, has ebbed and flowed with each administration. During the 1980s, President Ronald Reagan's former campaign manager, William J. Casey, became CIA director and began rebuilding the human-intelligence network. But Casey's penchant for secrecy — sometimes only he knew the full scope of CIA operations — plunged the agency into disrepute. The situation was epitomized by the Iran-contra debacle, in which the agency was implicated in the illegal diversion of money from arms sales to Iran to fund the Reagan administration's covert war against Nicaragua.

With Casey as DCI, the CIA cowboys were back in the saddle. Covert operations, which ate up about half of the agency's budget in the 1950s, had been reduced to about 4 percent in the 1970s; under Reagan (who authorized CIA-backed operations in Afghanistan, Nicaragua and Angola) they shot up to about 20 percent.[20]

What is most distressing to policy-makers — and many CIA officials — is that Casey took the CIA outside the law. To avoid congressional oversight, Casey and his covert operators ran off-the-books operations with millions of dollars extracted from kings, dictators and arms dealers, then lied about it when questioned by Congress.

According to *The Houston Post* and other papers, the CIA had extensive ties with financial institutions known for laundering money for drug traffickers and unscrupulous arms dealers. More than 20 savings and loan institutions and at least two banks had agency connections. The shady operations revealed too familiar ghosts of the old CIA. Even today, as the agency pledges reform, there is fresh evidence that officials withheld key information in a criminal case involving more than $5 billion in loans to Iraq by the Atlanta branch of the Italian-owned Banca Nazionale del Lavoro. "It's very frustrating," says Sen. Boren. He raises the possibility of a broad investigation of the CIA's role by joint panels — including Congress' Intelligence, Judiciary and Banking committees.[21]

Successes and Failures

Even the analytical side of the shop, which has grown considerably in stature since the 1970s and now does most of the agency's work, has come under intense fire from policy-makers. "I have grave misgivings about our intelligence [analysis]," said Sen. Ernest F. Hollings, D-S.C. "We've flunked Iran. We have flunked Angola ... Ethiopia ... Iraq, Kuwait. We have flunked ... the fall of the [Berlin] wall."[22]

Continued on p. 1086

Spying on the Environment

Thanks to the cold war, the CIA possesses perhaps the world's most comprehensive collection of information on the Earth's oil reserves, exploding population, ozone layer and water supply. But the trove has been largely ignored — or kept secret. Now scientists say we should use existing environmental data from spy satellites to measure the Earth's diminishing grasslands, forests and food resources.

Civilian scientists over the years have lofted a few specialized satellites for monitoring the environment and are planning to launch more. But the nation's fleet of spy satellites is already quite large, and its vast archive of data promises historical information unavailable by other means.

"There's a possibility we'll come up with something really fantastic," says Allen M. Solomon, an ecologist at Michigan Technological University. "For example, a photographic record of North Atlantic ice formation over 50 years." But he cautions that little of major importance might turn up, adding that the only way to find out is to search.

The push for scientific access to this secretive realm began more than two years ago in Congress when Sen. Al Gore, D.-Tenn., chairman of the Senate Science, Technology and Space Subcommittee, gained a preliminary release of secret spy data from the Navy. The vice president-elect had read that environmental scientists were unable to tap Navy data on polar ice thickness and sought to bring the two sides together. Momentum built slowly in private groups like the Council on Foreign Relations but eventually gathered speed in the Bush administration.

Last May, President Bush signed a directive that cleared the way for environmentalists to use the nation's spy gear and records. A group of private and government scientists is now being formed to review secret information and help officials determine how broadly to share it. "We're spending a lot of money on these satellites," cautions John E. Pike, director of space policy for the Federation of American Scientists. "They need to be looking for creative ways to make this more widely useful for the country." †

The science community in general is shifting its focus from traditional bombs and arms-control issues to global warming and other environmental concerns. In one sign of the times, Dr. Sidney Drell, deputy director of the Stanford Linear Accelerator Center at Stanford University, added his signature to those of more than 750 scientists who subscribed to a 1990 appeal, organized by the Union of Concerned Scientists, to prevent global warming.

For more than a year, scientists have quietly debated how reconnaissance could aid ecological research. One clear limit of spy satellites is their narrow field of view, which has often been likened to seeing the world through a soda straw. In contrast, satellites built to monitor the environment tend to have broader horizons. "From a climatological standpoint, spy satellites don't have that much to offer, simply because the resolution is too good," explains Pike.

One solution, says a former CIA analyst, would be to sample a wide region periodically. "It's like having thermometers scattered throughout the forest," he says. On the plus side, orbiting spy craft have unusual power. Radar satellites can see through clouds and all kinds of obstructions, in theory giving ecologists a rich harvest of new data. In 1981, an experimental radar system aboard a space shuttle unexpectedly penetrated up to 16 feet into the dry sands of the Sahara, revealing traces of ancient sub-Saharan rivers that had carved out valleys as broad as those of the present Nile.

Dr. Ferris Webster, an oceanographer at the University of Delaware, who is chairman of the National Academy of Sciences' Committee on Geophysical and Environmental Data, says a major problem in predicting the usefulness of reconnaissance information is that scientists have been in the dark about what is available. "Even the catalogs are classified," he notes. Many scientists caution that spy data might prove to be less revealing than hoped.

Even so, the search may be worthwhile. Pike estimates that over the decades the nation has probably spent $125 billion on its spy satellite operations and that it makes sense to examine the data more closely. "If you've invested $125 billion, and can get a billion dollars' worth of environmental data for a small additional investment, then it's certainly worth doing," he says. "There's so much stuff there that you're bound to find something useful."

Tools of the Trade

Satellites: Spy satellites whose powerful telescopes and cameras can read license plates from orbits hundreds of miles high also record snowfall data with possible clues to global temperature changes. Others use radar to peer through clouds, darkness and foliage, possibly helping ecologists gain new insights into the fate of the world's forests.

Aircraft: Spy planes take air measurements as well as photographs to track military activity. These records might reveal levels of methane and carbon dioxide, which have been implicated in global warming, and levels of chloroflurocarbons, which damage the Earth's protective ozone layer.

Ships: Navy vessels track changes in currents, temperature, salinity and chemistry in the world's oceans to support submarine warfare. The records may offer information about both ocean pollution and climate change.

---

† *The New York Times*, Nov. 3, 1992.

Continued from p. 1084

Hollings was probably guilty of colorful exaggeration. To be fair, there is an equally long list of arguable successes, from accelerating the Soviet collapse in Afghanistan (where the U.S. provided weapons to Afghan rebels) to the verification of arms-control treaties to the valuable insights gained from Soviet defectors, such as senior KGB officer Oleg Gordievsky.[23]

Nevertheless, there is no disputing that the CIA's directorate of intelligence — the "white" or non-operational branch of the agency — has lost much of its luster as a haven for dispassionate and scholarly expertise. At a minimum, the agency has often been wrong. The CIA estimated the Soviet gross national product at between 50 and 60 percent of America's — but it was about half that.[24] Analysis of military expenditures wasn't much sharper. Throughout the 1960s and '70s, the CIA estimated Soviet military spending at 6 percent of

GNP; in the 1980s, under political pressure, it upped its estimate to 12 percent. It turns out to have been twice that. Elsewhere, the intelligence elite dramatically misread the course of events in Iran, Lebanon and China at the time of Tiananmen Square.

Although CIA analysts were often inaccurate, bureaucratic arrangements made their judgments virtually unchallengeable: Since 1950, the U.S. government relied upon CIA analysis to guide its most important decisions. "By bureaucratic fiat, no other source of intelligence analysis could claim to be as authoritative as the CIA," explains Angelo Codevilla, a senior research fellow at the Hoover Institution.[25]

"Frankly, the reporting of intelligence has been extremely politicized," says Maryland's Nacht. "In the Casey period, any kind of study showing the Soviet Union was an economic basket case would have been shelved. It didn't comport with the overarching view of a communist threat." ∎

ing of an enemy's intentions.

"Among these challenges, perhaps the most dangerous and most urgent now is the proliferation in nearly two dozen countries of weapons of mass destruction," Gates told the Dallas World Affairs Council last month.

The intelligence community already is a voracious collector of economic information. The CIA, which has a big staff of economists and more Ph.D. holders than any other government agency, has long produced forecasts of world oil production and pricing, and studies of such topics as robotics. And while its analyses have been criticized at times, some have been right on target; for instance, the CIA accurately predicted in the mid-1970s that Europe's Airbus consortium would grow to claim about 20 percent of the commercial airliner market.[26]

Though it has received less attention, a new CIA group began working on environmental issues in 1989. CIA officials say the intelligence community could do more to help monitor international compliance with environmental agreements or treaties, and to track oil spills and deforestation. (See story, p. 1085.)

Fundamental changes in mission, however, don't come easy. "It's not an on-and-off switch," says George Kolt, director of the CIA's Office of Slavic and Eurasian Analysis, formerly the Office of Soviet Analysis. "You can't say to someone, 'You do research on Uzbekistan because people are interested in it,' then tomorrow say, 'Go do research in Latvia.' You have to train people. You can't switch people out of the blue."[27]

Indeed, one of the main criticisms of the CIA's proposed makeover is that it lacks the in-house expertise to confront post-cold war problems. As a former agency analyst puts it: "The CIA was established to find out everything it could about a closed society: Where were its factories? How much electricity did it generate? Now, the cold war is over, yet we still have

CURRENT SITUATION

After the Cold War

Despite misgivings about the CIA's dark history, most experts aren't quite ready to write off the agency. "It's still a dangerous and uncertain world," says Nacht. "We need specific information that only organizations like the CIA can provide, such as on Pakistani engineers doing sensitive nuclear research for Syria, Iran or Brazil."

Russia and the other former Soviet republics, which continue to control the world's second-largest nuclear arsenal, are reeling deeper into chaos. The Middle East remains as divided as ever. Terrorism and the drug trade have killed more Americans than have Soviet missiles, and aggressive economic competitors threaten to bury American businesses more effectively than Nikita S. Khrushechev ever dreamed.

The big issue, of course, concerns how policy-makers — particularly those in the Clinton administration — will define national security in the post-cold war era. And that's still not clear. For its part, the CIA has been scurrying to recast its mission, turning its sights on nuclear proliferation, narcotics trafficking, terrorism and, to a lesser degree, economic intelligence.

By all accounts, a major priority of the new intelligence community is its emphasis on human-source intelligence. With a smaller American military force positioned around the world, earlier warnings of hostile intentions will be essential. While satellite photographs and other technical data can reveal military movements before an attack, they cannot provide early warn-a huge cold war infrastructure."

Despite the hoopla, critics are quick to remind that nuclear proliferation, drug trafficking and terrorism aren't exactly new. Muammar el-Qaddafi has been coveting nuclear weapons since the 1970s and supporting terrorism for even longer. The intelligence community has been closely monitoring these security threats for decades. The billion-dollar question is: Does the CIA's new mission justify its $3.2 billion budget — or the intelligence community's $30 billion budget? Clearly not, says Georgetown's Allan Goodman. "The overall budget ought to go down from $30 billion to $20 billion within the next six to 18 months," he says.

Restructuring Plan

Just as many private companies have downsized to stay productive and competitive, so must the intelligence community. To meet the challenges of a changing intelligence environment, the agency over the last four years has reportedly cut its Soviet foreign policy staff by two-thirds and its weapons-analysis staff by 25 percent. It also established the Counterterrorist Center in 1986, the Counternarcotics Center in 1989 and the Non-Proliferation Center in 1991.

In November 1991, President Bush called for "a top-to-bottom examination of the mission, role and priorities of the intelligence community." Bush's order, known as National Security Directive No. 29, requested that some 20 federal departments and agencies project their intelligence requirements until the year 2005.

Based on that information, the CIA last April initiated a plan to restructure the agency. Among other things, according to Gates, changes have been implemented to "improve coordination [between] bureaucracies, to reduce duplication of effort, to enhance independence of our analysis ... and

to strengthen accountability." [28] Gates has also announced plans to declassify large numbers of CIA files, make CIA officials available to Congress and the media and publish more of the agency's assessments.

CIA officials say there is widespread support for restructuring within the agency, particularly among employees who do a lot of the actual analysis and operations. "But you can't fix the problem simply by restructuring, by moving the boxes around," admits the CIA's Andrew Campbell. "You have to change the approach. We are looking at the core government agencies involved in intelligence, and asking, 'What is the value-added to the taxpayer?' We have to enhance productivity."

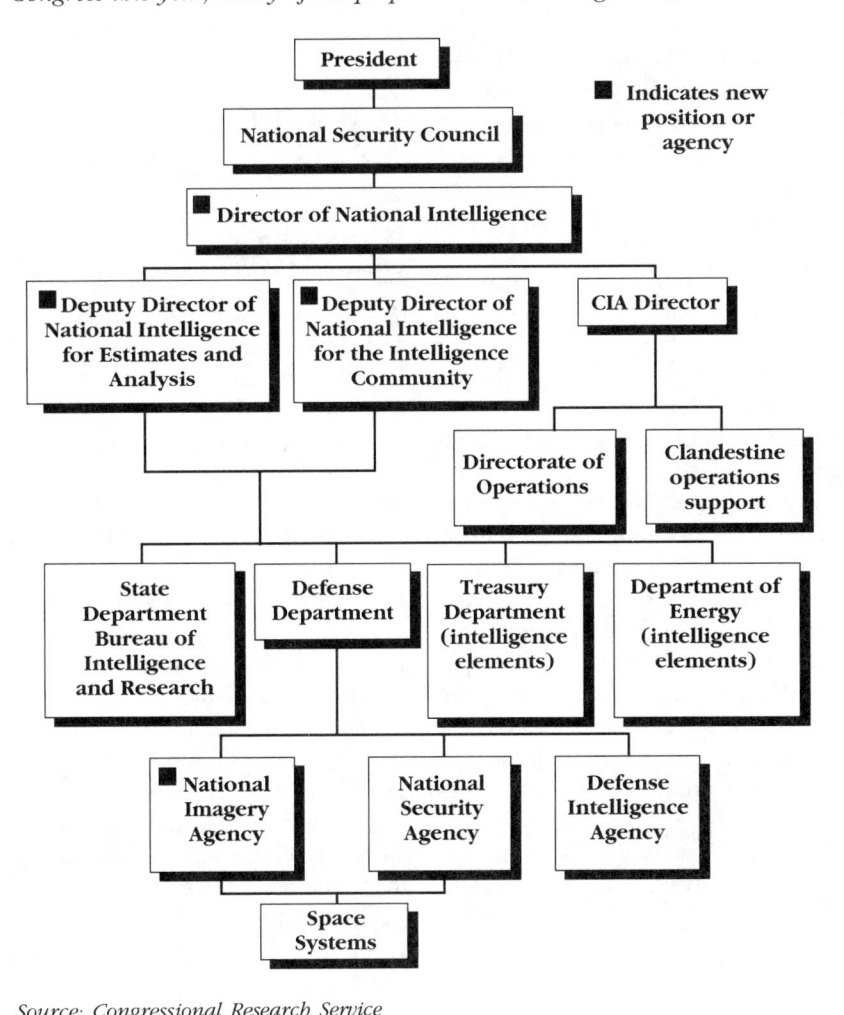

Revamping the Spy Agencies

A director of national intelligence would oversee all intelligence operations under sweeping reorganization plans proposed in February 1992 by Sen. David L. Boren, D-Okla., and Rep. Dave McCurdy, D-Okla., chairmen of the Senate and House Intelligence Committees. While the measures failed to pass Congress this year, many of the proposals are still being debated.

Source: Congressional Research Service

Whereas three years ago intelligence information was collected in the field and digested by regional specialists insulated from other departments of the agency, now there is a multidisciplinary approach, says Campbell. For example, in addition to there being an entire office dedicated to proliferation issues, there are branches within regional divisions with experts on nuclear technology. While the CIA once operated like a 1950s-era factory, with each division doing its own task, it now increasingly incorporates a "systems approach," the organizational structure currently in vogue in the business world. More than at any time in the past, insiders say, the operations and analytical shops are working in tandem.

Drastic Changes Sought

Nevertheless, many lawmakers believe that more drastic changes are necessary. Major legislative initiatives to restructure the intelligence community were introduced on Feb. 5, 1992, in the Senate by Sen. Boren and in the House by Rep. Dave McCurdy, D-Okla.* While the measures failed to pass Congress this year, many of their central themes are still being debated. Among the potential changes:

• A new director of national intelligence to oversee all intelligence operations. Unlike the DCI, whose responsibilities have developed haphazardly, the new intelligence chief would have broad statutory powers, a voice on the National Security Council and authority over spending now in Pentagon hands. The DCI "has become a captive of the CIA, as opposed to being a coordinator of intelligence from all the community," says McCurdy.

---

*The two bills, S 2198 and HR 4165, were slightly different. Since Boren's term as Senate Intelligence Committee chairman expires in January, and McCurdy may get a Cabinet post in the Clinton administration, it is unclear whether either bill will resurface next session. The new chairman of the Senate Intelligence Committee will be Sen. Dennis DeConcini, D-Ariz.

• A new National Intelligence Center to take over the CIA's directorate of intelligence as well as manage the intelligence analysts now working at the Pentagon, the State Department and other government departments.
• A smaller CIA. Some lawmakers say Congress should "strip down" the CIA, as Boren puts it, and restrict the agency to clandestine operations.
• Consolidation of satellite intelligence-collection efforts by the rest of the intelligence community under a deputy director with authority over military and civilian agencies. This deputy's domain would include a new National Imagery Agency — responsible for all satellite and airborne photography — and the existing National Security Agency, which intercepts communications around the world.

"The Boren/McCurdy legislation was a solid first step," says Georgetown's Goodman. "We need a new legal charter that takes us out of the cold war and into a new world order."

Critics charge that such changes, while building another large layer of bureaucracy, will not necessarily produce better intelligence or even cost-savings. They contend such reorganization would stifle competitive analysis and penalize the military, which already has been trying hard to eliminate duplication. "By putting analysis in one shop, you lose expert opinion in other groups," says retired CIA veteran Sam Halpern. "You need more competitive analysis, not less" ■

OUTLOOK

A New CIA

Many Americans loved the "bad" old CIA, loved the blood-pounding macho combination of danger and honor and deceit that went with its territory. They wanted the CIA, even in its most devious, covert operations, to be good at what it did. "People have been brainwashed for years with novels and movies that have glorified the business and romanticized the intelligence community and the CIA," says Victor Marchetti, a former high-ranking CIA official.[29] As long as the Cold War was on, it seemed, America was willing to forgive, or at least look the other way.

The Iran-contra debacle and the spate of other failures have changed that attitude, perhaps forever. "The CIA is like the dog that has bitten too many people," comments a former CIA analyst. "It has lost its credibility."

Other critics say that the CIA's directorate of operations, which runs covert actions, is becoming less relevant. The reason is twofold: the winding down of Soviet-U.S. competition in the Third World and the impossibility of keeping operations secret in the age of CNN. "Covert action should be used as an instrument of absolute last resort, rather than one of the early options considered," argues Goodman. "The world is more porous; we are operating in a goldfish bowl."

At the same time, today's complex world may require more intelligence manpower than during the Cold War's bipolar competition. In fact, most experts agree the United States needs more clandestine agents abroad to better track political trends. There is consensus that more resources should be devoted to recruiting economists and Third World specialists, particularly those with expertise in languages and cultures of the Middle East and Asia.

"In the future, I suspect we will pay less attention to the former Soviet Union and more to the potential military revival of allies — Japan and Germany," says Nacht. "We need the

Continued on p. 1090

At Issue:

Should the CIA get involved in economic espionage?

STANSFIELD TURNER

Former director of central intelligence, 1977-81
FROM *AN ARTICLE IN FOREIGN AFFAIRS*, FALL 1991.

*i*f the objective of collecting economic intelligence is to buttress national economic strength, then that requires making our businesses more competitive in the global marketplace. How can we do this with information acquired secretly abroad? Economic intelligence can range from the broad trends that foreign businesses are pursuing, all the way to what individual foreign competitors are bidding against U.S. corporations on specific contracts overseas.

Some argue that when it comes to specific data such as competitive bids the government should not become a partner of business and distort the free enterprise system. The United States, however, would have no compunction about stealing military secrets to help it manufacture better weapons.

If economic strength should now be recognized as a vital component of national security, parallel with military power, why should America be concerned about stealing and employing economic secrets? But if the government provides economic intelligence to specific American corporations, how does Washington decide which ones should benefit? What about a corporation that operates in the United States and provides jobs for Americans but is foreign-owned?

There are problems galore, but these are for the Commerce Department to handle on a case-by-case basis. One way to help, when there is no other, is to make information public. That may aid U.S. corporations less than some would like, but it also can lessen an advantage foreign corporations have over American firms.

While there are arguments over how far the U.S. government should go toward providing intelligence data to specific U.S. corporations, there is no question that friendly foreign countries make use of their intelligence services against U.S. businesses. Most everyone would agree that U.S. intelligence agencies should work closely with the American business community to prevent the loss of proprietary information to such foreign-government sponsored espionage. All of this says, then, that in an age of increasing attention to economic strength, there needs to be a more symbiotic relationship between the worlds of intelligence and business.

ROBERT M. GATES

Director of central intelligence
FROM A SPEECH DELIVERED BEFORE THE ECONOMIC CLUB OF DETROIT, APRIL 13, 1992.

*e*conomics is far from a new issue for the intelligence community. Contrary to the common perception, even in our earliest days we did not spend all of our time and energy working [on] Soviet throw-weights or the pecking order of the Chinese Communist Party. Early on, we recognized the importance that economic trends and events could have on national security interests.

Long before I became an intelligence analyst, the community had experts looking at everything from the stability of major foreign currencies to water resources in the Middle East....We had — and continue to have — recognized authorities on balance of payments of foreign countries, advanced technology developments, the inner workings of regional economic groupings, and many other economic issues....

In this post-Cold War period, I see three broad tasks for the intelligence community with respect to economic issues. The first task is to support U.S. policy-makers in the executive and legislative branches as they set this country's economic policy course....The second general economic intelligence task of the community is to monitor trends in technology that could affect national security.... The third and final general task is to undertake such counterintelligence measures as may be necessary to protect our economy from those who do not play by the rules. This is a task our intelligence professionals are uniquely equipped to handle. We've been doing it for a long time.

As for the role of the CIA and the intelligence community in the world of industrial or commercial espionage, I would like to state clearly that the U.S. intelligence community does not, should not, and will not engage in industrial espionage. This is not a comment I make lightly. This is an issue that I have looked at for a number of years and from a number of different perspectives. I have serious concerns about the ethical, legal, and sources-and-methods questions surrounding the issue of industrial espionage.

Plainly put, it is the role of U.S. business to size up their foreign competitors' trade secrets, marketing strategies and bid proposals. Some years ago, one of our clandestine service officers overseas said to me: "You know, I'm prepared to give my life for my country but not for a company." That case officer was absolutely right.

Recruiting the Next Generation of Spies

In the old days, "a WASP from Yale [was] considered the ideal spy for the old-boy network of the CIA," reporter Douglas Waller writes in *Newsweek*. † The agency was chock full of East Coast intellectuals whose Establishment ties, rightly or wrongly, implied patriotism. The preferred training for employment at "the company" was expertise in Soviet affairs.

Now, according to Waller, recruiters are looking for a different résumé. Skilled linguists, along with scientists and MBAs "who can read a spreadsheet," are part of the new generation of covert operatives the CIA needs in the post-Cold War era.

"In the past, there were tons of people monitoring Soviet weaponry," says Michael Nacht, dean of the University of Maryland's School of Public Policy. "We need less people who know the dimensions of an SS-18 silo, and more who speak Farsi and understand weapons proliferation. Basically we need a more diversified portfolio."

In addition, the traditional cover for spies — a U.S. embassy job — has become increasingly transparent: Foreign governments can spot many spooks simply by cross-checking State Department directories. Thus, the agency is promoting its network of non-official covers (NOCs), often native-language speakers who operate far from embassies and CIA stations. The agency also is reportedly hiring mid-level business managers and placing them undercover in multinational corporations around the world. "These are guys who will never set foot in [CIA headquarters in] Langley," one source told *Newsweek*. "They're trained remotely and buried in the multinationals."

"Since 1989," Waller writes, "Congress has secretly added several hundred million dollars to the CIA's Operations Directorate, which runs the agency's covert operations." During the Cold War, high-tech intelligence gathering helped "penetrate the Soviet monolith and gauge its war-making potential. But today's threats are more varied and require more eyes on the ground. CIA satellites can photograph the outside of a Third World nuclear facility. But to confirm that uranium is [being] enriched inside, it helps to have an agent who can scoop up earth samples around the building to be examined for traces of uranium hexafluoride."

If the past is any indicator, expanding the spy network won't be easy. Even some insiders say Langley has become just another bureaucracy. Its political analysis has been compared unfavorably with that of major newspapers, and its failure to provide early intelligence from the Persian Gulf underscored the agency's inability to recruit qualified Arabists.

Over the past 45 years, intelligence experts note "an alarming decline" in college graduates who have studied different languages and cultures. One recent study found that of CIA officers in Mexico, only 20 percent spoke Spanish.†† "I'm not surprised," notes Sam Halpern, a retired CIA official. "In order to wage the covert war against Nicaragua, the CIA had to pull older officers out of retirement because there weren't enough Spanish speakers on staff."

Part of the problem, experts say, is that since the 1970s many of the country's best and brightest had come to doubt the ethics of a CIA career. "On many campuses," says Nacht, "it was [not politically correct] to apply for a CIA job in the wake of the Vietnam War or during the covert war in Central America." Now, the agency is again welcome on many college campuses, and CIA recruiters say both the number and caliber of applicants are up.

To develop a new intelligence community talent pool, the recently passed National Security Education Act set up an endowment fund of $150 million to provide greater opportunities for study abroad and language- and area-studies programs in American universities.

Spy movies notwithstanding, the bulk of espionage is not the stuff of dark alleys, but plowing through stacks of data, photographs and interviews to glean a larger truth. The model for intelligence agents in the post-Cold War era may be less James Bond than Sherlock Holmes. That is because "by the end of the next decade, 80 percent of what a policy-maker wants to know will be available overtly," predicts Theodore Shackley, a former senior CIA official.

"The important person in the intelligence business is no longer going to be the spymaster," adds David Whipple, a former CIA station chief, "but the analyst" — the expert able to sift and make sense of an avalanche of information freely available in the global village of the 21st century.‡

---

† Douglas Waller, "The CIA's Next Generation," *Newsweek*, Feb. 17, 1992, p. 27.

†† Cited in Angelo Codevilla, "The CIA's Identity Crisis," *The American Enterprise*, January/February 1992, p. 31.

‡ Quoted in *The Wall Street Journal*, Nov. 6, 1991.

Continued from p. 1088
capability to monitor what Mitsubishi Heavy Industries and Daimler Benz are doing. Look how much equipment the Iraqis got from German companies. As it turns out, intelligence on that was

pretty good, but in the future we'll need to know more."

"If the intelligence community fails to make [necessary] changes," writes Sen. Boren in *Foreign Affairs*, "it will become an expensive and irrelevant di-

nosaur just when America most needs information and insight into the complex new challenges that it faces." [30]

Still, reorganization and language training will not give the intelligence agencies a program that can compare with the grand, global, cloak-and-dagger mission of the cold war. They are taking on new missions, without the consensus that existed before. Proponents are calling them essential, while detractors say they are make-work — "organizational maintenance," as Sen. Moynihan puts it.

"In many ways the situation today is similar to 1947, when the CIA was first created," says Adm. Bobby Ray Inman, former deputy director of central intelligence. "The essence of intelligence wasn't yet us vs. them, but was driven by challenges of the moment: How do you locate scarce resources or how do you govern a liberated country? You needed encyclopedic knowledge about the world because you didn't know where the next challenge would come from."

Finding a Different Mission

Either way, it is difficult to imagine how analysts or covert operators can get as excited about the environmental impact of Brazil's shrinking rain forest or the dumping of toxic waste in Eastern Europe as they did about the life-and-death struggle between East and West.

But senior agency officials insist that the CIA will have no problem finding a mission. "If ever there was a non-problem, this is it," said John L. Helgerson, the CIA's deputy director for intelligence. "So many people are asking us so many things — on China, on Yugoslavia, on North Korea, proliferation — it's a growth industry at the moment like no other. We could put everyone in the agency in proliferation and narcotics, and we still wouldn't solve the problem."[31]

Exactly what direction the CIA will take depends mightily on who President-elect Clinton chooses to guide its future. The names most frequently discussed for the post are Rep. McCurdy; James R. Woolsey Jr., former Navy under secretary during the Carter administration and an arms-control negotiator for the Bush administration; Gen. William E. Odom, a former head of the National Security Agency; and Morton I. Abramowitz, president of the Carnegie Endowment for International Peace and formerly the State Department's top intelligence officer. "These men are not insiders, but they are not outsiders either," says a Senate Intelligence Committee staffer. "Any of them would send a message to the agency that it won't be business as usual."

Whoever Clinton selects, the next DCI will face an onerous task. Even short of a total overhaul, the director will be expected to make spending cuts beyond what has been proposed thus far. And experts say he or she must have the clout to work closely with Congress and still implement structural changes without alienating career officials in the military and civilian intelligence communities.

"Ultimately, the biggest challenge is whether the CIA can do what no other intelligence service in the world has done — operate openly in a democratic society," says Goodman. "For more than 40 years, the U.S. intelligence community operated without openness, but that way is no longer tenable." ■

Notes

[1] Quoted in *USA Today*, May 1991, p. 10. *USA Today* is a magazine published by the Society for the Advancement of Education.

[2] Quoted in *National Journal*, Sept. 21, 1991, p. 2271.

[3] *Ibid.*, p. 2272.

[4] David L. Boren, "The Intelligence Community: How Crucial?" *Foreign Affairs*, summer 1992, p. 54.

[5] Quoted in *The Washington Monthly*, March 1992, p. 20.

[6] Stansfield Turner, "Intelligence for a New World Order," *Foreign Affairs*, fall, 1991, p. 152.

[7] See *The Wall Street Journal*, Aug. 4, 1992.

[8] Quoted in *The New York Times*, Feb. 4, 1992.

[9] Quoted in the *Los Angeles Times*, May 28, 1991.

[10] Quoted in *The Washington Monthly*, March 1992, p. 19.

[11] Quoted in John Ranelagh, *The Agency: The Rise and Decline of the CIA* (1990), p. 701.

[12] See Thomas Powers, *The Man Who Kept the Secrets* (1979), p. 31.

[13] The principal opponent to Donovan's plan was J. Edgar Hoover. Early in 1945, he personally handed copies of Donovan's memo to the *Chicago Tribune*, sparking a Washington controversy about an "American Gestapo" that effectively killed Donovan's initial proposal.

[14] Cited in *The Nation*, June 8, 1992, p. 778. The 1949 Central Intelligence Agency Act says the CIA can spend its budget "without regard to the provisions of law and regulations relating to the expenditure of government funds." For background, see Charles D. Ameringer, *U.S. Foreign Intelligence* (1990).

[15] At a 1971 congressional hearing, William E. Colby, who supervised Operation Phoenix, testified that most of those killed were combat deaths and not victims of South Vietnamese assassination plots. See Ranelagh, *op. cit.*, p. 440.

[16] The CIA recently funded rebel attempts to overthrow Soviet-backed leaders in Angola, Nicaragua, and Afghanistan. The agency was also closely associated with plotters who assassinated Raphael Trujillo in the Dominican Republic, Ngo Dinh Diem in Vietnam and Gen. Rene Schneider in Chile. For background, see Philip Agee, *Inside the Company: CIA Diary* (1975) and Ranelagh, *op. cit.*, p. 336.

[17] Ranelagh, *op. cit.*, pp. 190-269.

[18] Russ W. Baker, "CIA Out of Control," *Utne Reader*, January/February 1992, p. 80.

[19] Powers, *op. cit.*, p. 186.

[20] Budget figures cited by former CIA Director William E. Colby in *The Washington Monthly*, March 1992, p. 21.

[21] *USA Today*, Oct. 30, 1992.

[22] Quoted in *Newsweek*, Oct. 14, 1991, p. 32.

[23] Gordievsky provided information on Soviet agents scattered throughout the West, as well as on policy objectives of the Soviet Politburo. See Ranelagh, *op. cit.*, p. 701.

[24] *U.S. News & World Report*, June 3, 1991, p. 27.

[25] See Angelo Codevilla, "The CIA's Identity Crisis," *The American Enterprise*, January/February 1992, p. 34.

[26] *The Wall Street Journal*, Aug. 4, 1992.

[27] Quoted in *The New York Times*, Feb. 4, 1992.

[28] From speech before the Dallas World Affairs Council, Nov. 10, 1992.

[29] Quoted in *Utne Reader*, January/February 1992, p. 84.

[30] Boren, *op. cit.*, p. 51.

[31] Quoted in *The New York Times*, Feb. 4, 1992.

Bibliography

Selected Sources Used

Books

Ameringer, Charles D., *U.S. Foreign Intelligence: The Secret Side of American History*, Lexington Books, 1990.

This general text on foreign intelligence provides useful background on the roots of the CIA. It also contains a very informative section on covert action, including a chapter on former CIA Director William J. Casey.

Lowenthal, Mark M., *U.S. Intelligence: Evolution and Anatomy*, Praeger Publishers, 1984.

This primer on the U.S. intelligence community is particularly useful in understanding how secret intelligence decisions are made and what roles the various bodies within the intelligence community play. The author, a national defense specialist with the Congressional Research Service, offers an unbiased perspective.

Powers, Thomas, *The Man Who Kept the Secrets: Richard Helms and the CIA*, Simon & Schuster, 1979.

Powers, a Pulitzer Prize-winning journalist, offers one of the more compelling accounts of how the CIA operates, including extensive footnotes and references. Although the book is principally concerned with the career of former CIA Director Richard Helms, the insights are not limited to his person or his tenure as CIA chief.

Ranelagh, John, *The Agency: The Rise and Decline of the CIA*, Cambridge Publishing Ltd., 1986.

Perhaps the most thorough and readable account of the CIA's history, this detailed book focuses not only on the personalities who have made and carried out the policies of the CIA but also on how these policies have affected the course of U.S. history. This well-documented work is recommended by both critics and supporters of the agency.

Articles

Boren, David L., "The Intelligence Community: How Crucial?" *Foreign Affairs*, summer 1992, pp. 50-62.

Sen. Boren, chairman of the Senate Select Intelligence Committee (until January), makes a cogent argument for why the intelligence community needs to be restructured and proposes ways to do it. One of his central themes is to create a new director of national intelligence to oversee the CIA and the other military intelligence agencies.

Braden, Tom, "The Spies Who Came in From the Cold War," *The Washington Monthly*, March 1992, pp. 18-23.

Among other things, this interesting article by a former CIA official offers quotes from former CIA directors Richard Helms and William Colby, as well as Clark Clifford and others, expressing their views of the future CIA.

Carver, George A, "Intelligence in the Age of Glasnost," *Foreign Affairs*, summer 1990, pp.147-166.

Written before the Soviet Union's collapse, this thoughtful article nonetheless highlights some of the central issues for the intelligence community in the post-cold war era.

Cordevilla, Angelo, "The CIA's Identity Crisis: How Central is Central Intelligence?" *The American Enterprise*, January/February 1992, pp. 29-37.

An intelligence expert with extensive experience in the U.S. government takes a critical look at the past performance of the CIA and the prospects for reform.

May, Ernest R., "Intelligence: Backing into the Future," *Foreign Affairs*, summer 1992, pp. 63-72.

May, a well-known historian at Harvard, argues that the Boren proposal to revamp the CIA (outlined in the same issue of *Foreign Affairs*) looks backward, addressing the problems of the cold war-era rather than those of the "new world order."

Reports and Studies

Best, Richard A., Intelligence Reorganization Proposals, *Congressional Research Service Issue Brief*, updated Oct. 1, 1992.

This CRS document summarizes the main legislative efforts to restructure the intelligence community. It also briefly outlines the intelligence challenges that the CIA faces in the future.

***Senate Select Committee on Intelligence*, testimony concerning the Intelligence Reorganization Act of 1992, Feb. 20 and March 12, 1992.**

The testimony of military and intelligence experts regarding the legislation to restructure the intelligence community is an excellent source on how the CIA functions within the intelligence bureaucracy.

***Soviet Economy: Assessment of How Well the CIA Has Estimated the Size of the Economy*, U.S. General Accounting Office, September 1991.**

This report, conducted at the request of Sen. Daniel Patrick Moynihan, examines the much-discussed issue of whether the CIA blundered in its attempts to gauge the size and performance of the Soviet economy.

The Next Step

Additional Articles from Current Periodicals from EBSCO Publishing's Database

Books & reading

"Book notes," *Journal of Peace Research,* February 1992, p. 122.

Reviews the book "Escape From the CIA," by Ronald Kessler.

Alan, R., "The Angleton angle," *New Leader,* July 1, 1992, p. 13.

Reviews the book "Cold Warrior," by Tom Mangold and Jeff Goldberg. Studies the internal workings of the CIA, with a biography of the organization's master spy hunter, James Jesus Angleton.

Appleton, T.H., "Book reviews: Social sciences," *Library Journal,* Oct. 1, 1991, p. 122.

Reviews the book "Honorable Treachery: A History of U.S. Intelligence, Espionage, and Covert Action from the American Revolution to the CIA," by G.J.A. O'Toole.

De Toledano, R., "The intelligence gap," *National Review,* Aug. 3, 1992, p. 40.

Reviews the books "The Spy Who Saved the World: How A Soviet Colonel Changed the Course of the Cold War," by Jerrold L. Schechter and Peter S. Deriabin, "The Old Boys: The American Elite and the Origins of the CIA," by Burton Hersh, and "Informing Statecraft: Intelligence for a New Century," by Angelo Codevilla.

Kaganoff, P. & S. Steinberg, "Forecasts: Paperbacks," *Publishers Weekly,* April 20, 1992, p. 51.

Reviews the book "Cocaine Politics: Drugs, Armies, and the CIA in Central America," by Peter Dale Scott and Jonathan Marshall.

Corrupt practices

Hitchens, C., "Unlawful, unelected, and unchecked," *Harper's Magazine,* October 1991, p. 59.

Examines how the Central Intelligence Agency (CIA) subverts the government at home. Evasion in regard to the Bank of Credit and Commerce International (BCCI) scandal; Iran-contra affair; delay in the release of the hostages in Iran until after the 1980 election; found homes and jobs for Nazis and Nazi collaborators; financed experiments with LSD on unwitting civilians; annual budget.

Magner, D.K., "At Rochester Institute, a spectrum of opinions on links with the CIA," *The Chronicle of Higher Education,* July 10, 1991, p. A1.*

Details recent controversy concerning the relationship between the Rochester Institute of Technology and the Central Intelligence Agency which surfaced when RIT's president decided to take a sabbatical at the agency, and has spilled out into a stranger-than-fiction saga. No clear communication; CIA activities on campus; speculations on the appropriateness of CIA-university links; projects at RIT; M. Richard Rose's sabbatical.

McCoy, A.W., "The CIA connection," *Progressive,* July 1991, p. 20.

Suggests that during the long years of the cold war, American diplomats and CIA agents have been involved in narcotics traffic. Covert alliances, covering up for drug-lord allies and active engagement; examples of Afghanistan and Pakistan; denial by CIA.

Debates & issues

"CIA and openness," *Vital Speeches,* May 1, 1992, p. 430.

Presents a speech by director of the central intelligence, Robert M. Gates, "CIA and Openness," delivered to the Oklahoma Press Association in Oklahoma City, Oklahoma on Feb. 21, 1992, dealing with the CIA's relations with the people of the United States.

"Glasnost a la Gates," *Bulletin of the Atomic Scientists,* July/August 1992, p. 6.

Suggests that the CIA is not making much headway into making more information public, as was promised by CIA Director Robert M. Gates at his confirmation last fall.

"Spurn cloaked suitors, corporate America," *Business Week,* Oct. 14, 1991, p. 166.

Editorial. Present the opinion that with the meltdown of the Soviet Communist Party and the Soviet Union itself, the CIA is casting about for a new mission to justify its $3.2 billion budget. The CIA's track record in economic analysis is not encouraging; suggestions that the CIA spy for U.S. companies are troubling; policymakers should be skeptical about making economic intelligence a big new CIA account.

"We're looking for a few good spies," *Harper's Magazine,* May 1991, p. 27.

Presents a brochure about the Clandestine Service distributed by recruiters for the Central Intelligence Agency at job fairs and on college campuses.

Baker, R.W., "CIA out of control," *Utne Reader,* January/February 1992, p. 78.

Reprints an article from the *Village Voice* which claims that with the cold war over the intelligence community is seeking new bogeymen. Budget of over $35 billion per year; lessons of the Iran-contra scandal; counter-terrorism, the drug war and crisis management as growth areas for spymasters; growing role of the military in covert action. INSETS: Why it matters that George Bush is an ex-CIA director; CIA drug ties thwart our war on drugs.

Barry, J. & T. Morganthau, "Remaking the CIA," *Newsweek,* May 27, 1991, p. 18.

Considers the new challenge facing the U.S. Central Intelligence Agency (CIA) since the change in directors. Redefining its methods and mission; critical period now under director-designate Robert M. Gates; question about the goals and mission of major U.S. intelligence agencies; CIA's changing task; turf battles with the Pentagon.

Borrus, A., C. Hoots, et al., "Should the CIA start spying for corporate America?" *Business Week,* Oct. 14, 1991, p. 96.

Examines why many nations see economic intelligence-gathering — from tracking technology trends to passing foreign business secrets to domestic companies — as key to their economic survival. The CIA has always employed a legion of economists to analyze business and financial trends; nominee Robert M. Gates hopes to ferret out foreign spies in U.S. corporations.

Braden, T., "The spies who came in from the cold war," *Washington Monthly,* March 1992, p. 18.

Argues that since the Central Intelligence Agency's (CIA) obsession, the Communist menace, has ceased to exist maybe the CIA should cease to exist. The early history of the CIA; bungled attempts to assassinate foreign leaders; some observations on the future of the CIA by Clark Clifford, Richard Helms and William Colby.

Chua-Eoan, H.G., J. Peterzell, et al., "New trench coats?" *Time,* April 23, 1990, p. 40.

Reports that although the cold war may be over, intelligence agencies are still fighting for bigger budgets as they redeploy forces and shift priorities. Actions by the CIA; actions by the KGB; changes made; the practice of deception. INSET: Dieter: A former spy's story.

Fenyvesi, C., "Opening the gates," *U.S. News & World Report,* May 4, 1992, p. 24.

Reports that sentiment is growing on Capitol Hill for disclosing the total amount that the United States spends annually to collect, evaluate and disseminate intelligence data.

Garfield, B., "After this ad, CIA should take pitches undercover," *Advertising Age,* Nov. 4, 1991, p. 54.

Opinion. The Central Intelligence Agency (CIA) wants to determine your aptitude for employment by using an advertisement that assumes its target audience has no idea what the CIA is all about. Details; comments; more.

McCurdy, D., "Why spy?" *New Republic,* April 1, 1991, p. 18.

Argues that the United States continues to need an intelligence system of the highest possible quality. Flaws in the arguments of those who say we can now afford to shut down the Central Intelligence Agency.

Raskin, M., "Let's terminate the CIA," *Nation,* June 8, 1992, p. 776.

States that now that the cold war is over, it is time for a far-reaching public debate on the future role of the intelligence agencies. Central Intelligence Agency (CIA), the National Security Agency, and related agencies; opinion that they should be dismantled or transformed; senators still think of the intelligence community in terms of the cold war model; the CIA's failure to predict and analyze the likely consequences of a Soviet collapse; much more.

Sciolino, E., "Soviet upheaval injects urgency in U.S. debate over intelligence," *New York Times,* Sept. 2, 1991, p. 1.

Discusses the debate over the role of the American intelligence services, which has been heightened by the dissolution of the Soviet Union and the purge of the KGB. Congress has been forcing the Central Intelligence Agency (CIA) and the military intelligence agencies to rethink some of their priorities — and even their budgets — to adjust to the declining Soviet military threat.

Waller, D., "The CIA's next generation," *Newsweek,* Feb. 17, 1992, p. 27.

Reports that America is looking for a new breed of spy to serve in the Central Intelligence Agency (CIA). Skilled linguists, along with business executives and scientists, represent the new type of operatives the CIA is sending out.

Weiner, T., "Rewiring the CIA for a post-cold-war world," *Rolling Stone,* June 27, 1991, p. 29.

Comments on the need for reform of the U.S. Central Intelligence Agency (CIA) now that the cold war has ended. President Bush's choice of Robert Gates to succeed William Webster as the director of Central Intelligence; closed door hearings on reorganizing American intelligence by the Senate Select Intelligence Committee; debate over efficiency; recent failures of the CIA to accurately predict world events; details.

Wines. M., "A nomination sets off battle on CIA role,"

New York Times, **July 14, 1991, p. 1.**

Declares that beyond the charges and denials involving the Iran-contra affair, the struggle over Robert M. Gates's nomination as Director of Central Intelligence is a battle over the course of the nation's 50-year-old espionage establishment.

Wines, M., "CIA in search of a role," *New York Times,* **May 9, 1991, p. A1.**

Analyzes the role of the Central Intelligence Agency. CIA chief William H. Webster's retirement; improved image of the agency; stronger controls; public trust restored; changes needed due to end of cold war.

Government policy

"Sen. Daniel Patrick Moynihan," *U.S. News & World Report,* **Feb. 4, 1991, p. 19.**

Comments on the "End of the Cold War Act of 1991" proposal of New York's Sen. Daniel Patrick Moynihan, which would abolish the Central Intelligence Agency and put all intelligence operations under the secretary of State's control.

"Senate panel approves intelligence bill," *Congressional Quarterly Weekly Report,* **July 4, 1992, p. 1980.**

Details the Senate Select Intelligence Committee's approval of the fiscal 1993 intelligence authorization bill (HR 5095) on July 1, 1992, which would put into law many of the organizational changes for the intelligence community announced in April by Central Intelligence Agency (CIA) Director Robert M. Gates. Details.

Merry, R.W., "Tugging on the leash of U.S. spymasters," *Congressional Quarterly Weekly Report,* **Feb. 23, 1991, p. 506.**

Opinion. Announces that the Central Intelligence Agency (CIA) seems to be coming under increased congressional scrutiny these days, and suggests that perhaps that is good. Possible trap for CIA officials; Sen. David L. Boren; restructuring the espionage operations to diminish CIA's clout; Rep. Dave McCurdy; historical context; mid-1970's revelations; fostering mutual trust and good faith.

Towell, P., "Gates rejects legislative call, sets administrative changes," *Congressional Quarterly Weekly Report,* **April 4, 1992, p. 893.**

Covers CIA Director Robert M. Gates' rejection of congressional proposals for legislation to reorganize U.S. intelligence agencies and his announcement on April 1, 1992 of a series of administrative changes in the gathering, analysis and coordination of intelligence operations. The Gates-appointed task forces that recommended organizational changes; changes in the operation of the CIA (Central Intelligence Agency); details. INSET: CIA stays put — for now.

History

"America's top spy chiefs," *U.S. News & World Report,* **June 3, 1991, p. 26.**

Profiles five of the directors of the Central Intelligence Agency who were among the most colorful in that position. William Donovan (OSS-1942-45): America's greatest spy master. Allen Dulles (1953-61): the cold warrior. John McCone (1961-65): upgrading the agency's analysis. Richard M. Helms (1966-73): first agency professional to become boss. William J. Casey (1981-87): rebuilt a demoralized agency and reinvigorated its covert operations.

"Loving the bad old CIA," *Esquire,* **September 1991, p. 53.**

Explores the attitudes of Americans toward the CIA since World War II. Norman Mailer's view; the effects of Vietnam and the Iran-contra investigation; the nomination of Robert M. Gates as director.

International aspects

Deming, A., J. Whitmore, et al., "Have rebels, will travel," *Newsweek,* **March 25, 1991, p. 43.**

Traces the Central Intelligence Agency's involvement in training a force of Libyan commandos for covert operations in Libya. How the operation began in the late 1980s, with French- and U.S.-backed troops loyal to Chad's President Hissene Habre; U.S. plan to recruit disgruntled Libyan POWs, train them as commandos and send them back into Libya in an attempt to overthrow Muammar el-Qaddafi; how the CIA's commandos aren't welcome anymore; Kenya's role.

Kwitny, J., "The CIA's secret armies in Europe," *Nation,* **April 6, 1992, p. 444.**

Offers a look at the CIA's secret armies and new evidence of political manipulations that have surfaced due to the interest in these secret armies. Efforts of the CIA to disband the secret armies; Lt. Col. Bernard Legrand, head of the Belgian stay-behind force; CIA says everything about the armies is still classified; discoveries of well-armed guerilla organizations linked to the CIA; more.

Post, T., D. Waller, et al., "The CIA on the stump," *Newsweek,* **Oct. 21, 1991, p. 46.**

Offers a look at how a U.S. covert operation in Nicaragua put a free election at risk. In the eight months before the Feb. 25 presidential vote in Managua, the Central Intelligence Agency (CIA) ran a covert operation that paid about $600,000 to Miami-based contra political leaders to return to Nicaragua. Campaign of Violeta Chamorro who won; Sandinista candidate, President Daniel Ortega; U.S.-backed rebellion in Nicaragua; Nicaraguan Exile Relocation Program (NERP).

Back Issues

Great Research on Current Issues Starts Right Here... Recent topics covered by The CQ Researcher are listed below. Before May 1991, reports were published under the name of Editorial Research Reports.

JUNE 1991
Children and Divorce
Teenage Suicide
Endangered Species
Europe 1992

JULY 1991
Teenagers and Abortion
Soviet Republics Rebel
Mexico's Emergence
Athletes and Drugs

AUGUST 1991
Sexual Harassment
Fetal Tissue Research
Oil Imports
The Palestinians

SEPTEMBER 1991
Police Brutality
Advertising Under Attack
Saving the Forests
Foster Care Crisis

OCTOBER 1991
Pay-Per-View TV
Youth Gangs
Gene Therapy
World Hunger

Back issues are available for $4.00 (subscribers) or $7.00 (non-subscribers). Quantity discounts apply to orders over ten. To order, call Congressional Quarterly 1-800-432-2250.

Binders are available for $15.00. To order call 1-800-638-1710.

NOVEMBER 1991
Fast-Food Shake-Up
The Greening of Eastern Europe
Business' Role in Education
Cuba In Crisis

DECEMBER 1991
Retiree Health Benefits
Asian Americans
The Obscenity Debate
The Disabilities Act

JANUARY 1992
Term Limits
Oil Spills
Hunting Controversy
Alternative Medicine

FEBRUARY 1992
Threatened Coastlines
New Era in Asia
Assisted Suicide
Jobs in the '90s

MARCH 1992
Women and Sports
Underage Drinking
Garbage Crisis
Mafia Crackdown

APRIL 1992
Ozone Depletion
Welfare Reform
Politicians and Privacy
Illegal Immigration

MAY 1992
Native Americans
Jobs vs. Environment
Too Many Lawsuits?
Fairness in Salaries

JUNE 1992
Nuclear Proliferation
Food Irradiation
Lead Poisoning
Hard Times for Libraries

JULY 1992
Alternative Energy
Prescription Drug Prices
Alzheimer's Disease
Infant Mortality

AUGUST 1992
The Homeless
Work, Family and Stress
NATO's Changing Role
Marine Mammals vs. Fish

SEPTEMBER 1992
Domestic Partners
Violence in Schools
Public Broadcasting
Women in the Military

OCTOBER 1992
Depression
U.S. Auto Industry
Youth Apprenticeships
Hispanic Americans

NOVEMBER 1992
Physical Fitness
Privatization
Paying for College
U.S. Policy in Asia

DECEMBER 1992
Crackdown on Smoking

Future Topics

▶ *Eating Disorders*

▶ *Women and AIDS*

▶ *Hate Crimes*

THE CQ Researcher

PUBLISHED BY CONGRESSIONAL QUARTERLY INC., IN CONJUNCTION WITH EBSCO PUBLISHING

Eating Disorders

Is there too much pressure on women to be slim?

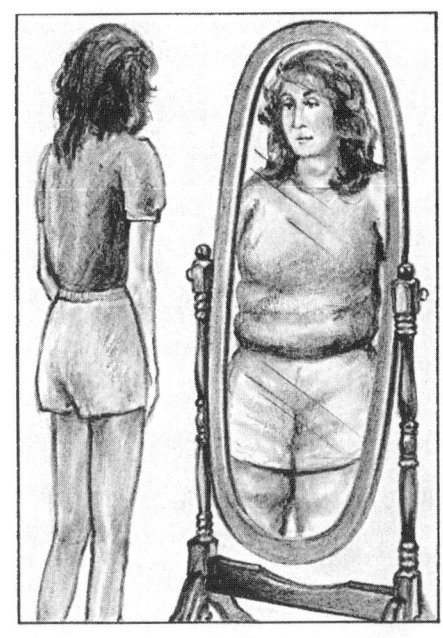

OR MILLIONS OF AMERICANS HELD HOSTAGE BY the pervasive emphasis on being slender, losing weight becomes an obsession that takes over their lives. These "dieters" usually develop one of the two main eating disorders — anorexia nervosa, characterized by self-starvation, or bulimia nervosa, marked by alternating phases of bingeing and purging. Although both disorders can cause serious physical damage — and even death — they are essentially psychological ailments. In the United States and elsewhere, about 90 percent of eating disorder sufferers are female. Psychiatrists and feminists cite numerous social pressures that make women strive for unrealistically svelte, fashion-model figures. The eating disorder problem would ease, these critics say, if society became more tolerant of a broad range of body shapes.

C_Q **December 18, 1992 • Volume 2, No. 47 • 1097-1120**

Formerly Editorial Research Reports

COVER ART: BARBARA SASSA-DANIELS

THE CQ Researcher

December 18, 1992
Volume 2, No. 47

EDITOR
Sandra Stencel

MANAGING EDITOR
Thomas J. Colin

ASSOCIATE EDITOR
Richard L. Worsnop

STAFF WRITERS
Charles S. Clark
Mary H. Cooper
Rodman D. Griffin

PRODUCTION EDITOR
Sarah E. Merritt

EDITORIAL ASSISTANT
Michael M. Taylor

GRAPHICS
Jack Auldridge

PUBLISHED BY
Congressional Quarterly Inc.

CHAIRMAN
Andrew Barnes

VICE CHAIRMAN
Andrew P. Corty

EDITOR AND PUBLISHER
Neil Skene

EXECUTIVE EDITOR
Robert W. Merry

ASSOCIATE PUBLISHER
John J. Coyle

EDITOR, EBSCO PUBLISHING
Melissa Kummerer

The CQ Researcher (ISSN 1056-2036). Formerly Editorial Research Reports. Published weekly (48 times per year, not printed the first Friday of any month with five Fridays) by Congressional Quarterly Inc., 1414 22nd St., N.W., Washington, D.C. 20037. Rates are furnished upon request. Second-class postage paid at Washington, D.C. POSTMASTER: Send address changes to The CQ Researcher, 1414 22nd St., N.W., Washington, D.C. 20037.

Eating Disorders

BY RICHARD L. WORSNOP

THE ISSUES

When her widowed mother decided to remarry several years ago, Dawn Ries of Naperville, Ill., resolved to lose weight for the wedding. To reach her goal, she did what millions of others have done in similar circumstances: She went on a crash diet.

Ries drastically limited her food intake, often ceasing to eat altogether, and the pounds came off quickly.* Avoidance of food soon became an ingrained habit. Before Ries realized what was happening, she was exhibiting tell-tale signs of anorexia nervosa, an eating disorder characterized by deliberate self-starvation.

"I stopped eating in front of my family," she says. "I basically would eat by myself in the bathroom." Her husband and four children were at a loss about what to do. Eventually, Ries was persuaded to seek professional help. But things got worse before they got better. Only after two hospitalizations and one suicide attempt did psychotherapy put her firmly on the path to recovery.

"I was very much in denial," says Ries. "I thought if I just corrected my eating habits, everything would be all right. Well, it didn't work out that way. The psychological issues turned out to be much more important than the physical issues."

Ries discovered that her disorder stemmed from feelings of anger, fed largely by her failure to accept her father's death years earlier. While she now regards herself as "fully recovered," she recognizes that "some of the problems in my life still haven't been

---

*Ries estimates she lost 30-35 pounds, even though she "was never heavy to start with."

solved, which means I need to keep looking at alternatives to stay healthy."

Ries' experience is far from unusual. According to the National Association of Anorexia Nervosa and Associated Disorders (ANAD), in Highland Park, Ill., some 8 million Americans suffer from eating disorders, chiefly anorexia, bulimia nervosa (alternating phases of bingeing and purging) and compulsive overeating. "Among these," says ANAD, "an estimated 3-6 percent of the serious cases will die — a far higher death rate than for any other mental illness."[1] Up to 90 percent of all eating-disorder sufferers are believed to be women.

Millions more people are at risk of developing full-blown eating disorders. The National Association to Advance Fat Acceptance (NAAFA) estimates that 38 million Americans are heavier than insurance industry height-weight "norms." (See table, p. 1112.) Society tends to view distinctly overweight people as unattractive and lacking inner discipline. Consequently, they often are discriminated against socially and in the job market. Such prob-

lems make overweight Americans especially susceptible to the lure of diet programs promising quick, long-lasting results. More ominously, these difficulties may help create the feelings of worthlessness and guilt often associated with chronic eating disorders (see p. 1108).

While the three main eating disorders share certain similarities, they vary in their causes, incidence and age of onset. Anorexia typically appears in early adolescence among girls who are high achievers academically but suffer from low self-esteem. Such girls sometimes have trouble accepting menstruation as a natural part of their development into mature women. They may also be uncomfortable with changes in their appearance, notably the enlargement of breasts and hips, regarding them as signs of incipient obesity.

When this happens, anorexia often follows. The young woman typically reduces her food consumption to less than 600 calories a day, resulting in the rapid loss of 25 percent or more of her body weight. This drastic fasting may be accompanied by self-induced vomiting, use of laxatives or diuretics and, sometimes, excessive exercise to produce even greater weight reduction.

Though the anorexic's emaciated body alarms her family and friends, she herself is convinced "she's regaining control over her life," psychiatrist Russell Marx has noted. She "feels relieved because weight loss reverses maturity. Menstruation stops. She becomes like a child again — physically, at least."[2]

Bulimia may arise from anorexia — studies show that at least half of all bulimics have practiced self-starvation — but it nonetheless constitutes a separate disorder. Bulimia is most often diagnosed in high school or college students who are extroverted, impulsive and sexually active. Bulimia's hallmarks are the distinc-

'Too Rich or Too Thin' — Too Much

Nearly everyone has heard the line, or some variant, yet no one seems quite sure who said it first. Some insist the svelte Duchess of Windsor coined the phrase, others credit Gloria Vanderbilt. Authorship aside, the thought itself expresses a feeling that is widely shared: "You can never be too rich or too thin."

Several companies well-tuned to popular culture have worked the message into advertising campaigns — but usually not for long. Under pressure from the National Association of Anorexia Nervosa and Associated Disor-

ders (ANAD), in Highland Park, Ill., five companies — Chanel, Hershey Foods, Revlon, Steve's Ice Cream and Women's Workout World — have voluntarily pulled the offending ads.

ANAD contends that the phrase conveys a sentiment that contributes to the spread of eating disorders. "The fact that statements like this can be used by major advertisers indicates that recognition of the danger of eating disorders is still in a pioneering state," says ANAD.

tive binge-purge eating pattern and an awareness that such behavior is abnormal. As a result, bulimics binge in secret, consuming great quantities of high-calorie, easily digested food such as ice cream. Vomiting or using laxatives or diuretics then follows.

Anorexics are easily recognized, since their emaciated bodies make them look seriously ill — as indeed they are. Bulimics, on the other hand, often escape detection because their weight gains and losses stay within a restricted range. A bulimic's weight may fluctuate 10 to 15 percent above or below the ideal level for her height, but it rarely falls 25 percent below that level — as in severe anorexia.

It is not uncommon for someone with anorexia to exhibit one or more bulimic behaviors as well. Sufferers of "bulimarexia," as this combination of disorders is known, have the severe weight loss of anorexia and practice the purging of bulimia.

Compulsive overeating, a third common eating disorder, is the one people find easiest to understand, or so they think. They assume that eating excessive amounts of fattening food is the main cause of obesity, especially among adolescents. Indeed, research does show that overeating problems tend to be self-reinforcing. According to Dr. Laurel M. Mellin, director of the Center for Adolescent

Obesity at the University of California-San Francisco, seriously overweight teenagers are "often caught in a downward spiral of inactivity, overeating, social isolation, depression, low self-esteem and weight gain."[3]

Mellin and other specialists point out, however, that compulsive overeating is far from the sole cause of adolescent obesity — and perhaps not even the principal one. Genetic factors may also play a significant role, although their contribution is not well understood. Moreover, studies suggest many obese adolescents consume no more calories than their non-obese peers. "The primary distinction between the eating behaviors of the obese and the non-obese is the frequency of eating," said Mellin, "with the obese more likely to skip meals and to eat less frequently."[4]

Although the news media and professional journals have devoted considerable attention to eating disorders in recent years, much remains to be discovered about their causes and treatment. Here are some of the key questions being asked about these increasingly common afflictions.

Do cultural pressures on women contribute to eating disorders?

Because celebrities have been involved in several well-publicized eating disorder cases (see p. 1110), it is often assumed that the disorders main-

ly afflict wealthy and privileged white women. A 1990 survey of about 200 patients treated in the eating disorders program of Children's Hospital at Stanford University indicated that female sufferers indeed outnumber males, by more than 10 to 1. But about 25 percent of the patients were poor or lower middle class, and 22 percent were Hispanic or Asian. Only blacks were clearly underrepresented, accounting for less than 1 percent of the patients surveyed.

The fact that eating disorders span the social spectrum suggests the great majority of American women are culturally conditioned to strive for a slender figure. Advertising, television, films and the fashion industry relentlessly drive home the message. Women who don't naturally fit the mold often respond by dieting, or even surgery.

The cultural conditioning begins at an early age. "We know that dieting is rampant in the fourth and fifth grades," says Vivian Meehan, president and founder of ANAD. "Children shouldn't have to be confronted with dieting and slimness at their age."

In a survey published last summer, Dr. Timothy Brewerton of the Medical University of South Carolina distributed questionnaires to more than 3,100 fifth-grade through eighth-grade students. More than 40 percent of the respondents felt they were too fat even though it was estimated that less than

"Barbie" has been blamed for popularizing unrealistic ideas about the female figure.

20 percent of the children actually were overweight. And 42.6 percent of the girls surveyed and 19.7 percent of the boys said they had dieted to lose weight. *(See poll results, p. 1109.)*

Popular icons like Mattel's Barbie doll are blamed by some for giving young girls unrealistic ideas about the female figure. If Barbie's vital statistics were extrapolated to an actual woman with a 36-inch bust, she would have a minuscule 18-inch waist and 33-inch hips. "Barbie is part of the message that it's better to be thin than not to be thin," says Dr. O. Wayne Wooley, co-director of the University of Cincinnati Medical School's eating disorders clinic. "But it's only one thing. If you took all the Barbies away, the very same message would be delivered in other ways."

And the message seems to be getting through. For instance, a 1989 study of British fashion models from 1967 to 1987 showed bodies were becoming more tubular as bust and hip dimensions shrank and height and waist measurements grew.[5]

A 1980 study of *Playboy* magazine centerfold models and Miss America contestants, covering the years 1959-1978, reached similar conclusions. The study's authors compared the "ideal" female bodies displayed in *Playboy* and at the Miss America Pageant with the average body size of U.S. women. They found that the average weights of *Playboy* centerfolds and Miss America contestants declined during the period in question. At the same time, the average weight of American women was increasing, according to the insurance industry's Society of Actuaries.[6]

The 1980 study was recently updated by researchers from American University in Washington, D.C. Spanning the years 1979-1988, the new study found the weight of *Playboy* centerfolds and Miss America contestants to have stabilized at 13 to 19 percent below the expected weight for women in comparable age groups.[7]

A possible explanation for the leveling off is that further weight reduction "would be … dangerously unhealthy," the AU researchers surmised. The American Psychiatric Association defines body weights of 15 percent or more below expected levels as one of the criteria for anorexia nervosa. "Thus a majority of these 'ideals' of our society may be classified as having one of the major symptoms of an eating disorder," the researchers wrote.

Beauty queens, of course, are not the only women susceptible to overconcern with weight. According to Patricia Fallon, a clinical pathologist in Seattle, "the 'superwoman syndrome,' which suggests that women can 'have it all' if they simply work hard enough," may also contribute to eating disorders.[8] A woman who chooses to be a full time housewife and mother draws little criticism or notice if she develops a matronly figure. But if family financial need forces the woman into the white-collar work force, she is expected to look slim.

"Although the reasons for this are unclear," eating-disorder experts David M. Garner and Susan C. Wooley wrote, "one argument holds that as women have moved into previously male-dominated activities, the 'traditional' female body shape has developed negative connotations while the masculine shape has come to symbolize self-discipline and competency."[9]

Author Naomi Wolf contends that efforts to conform to preconceived notions of physical appearance are self-defeating. In her 1991 book, *The Beauty Myth: How Images of Beauty Are Used Against Women,* Wolf argues that working women soon learn that hiring and promotion depend on adherence to a "professional beauty qualification" (PBQ). By making physical appearance a condition of advancement, she says, the male-dominated business power structure keeps women in a subordinate role despite the anti-discrimination provisions of federal and state equal employment opportunity laws.

Male and female anchors on television news programs illustrate how PBQ operates in practice, according to Wolf. Males on TV, she writes, are expected to project a "professional image." Females, on the other hand, are supposed to radiate "professional elegance." The double standard, Wolf says, "is a constant reminder that men are worth more and need not try as hard."[10]

New "Happy to Be Me" doll offers "a more realistic model of the female anatomy."

Are female athletes more likely than other women to develop eating disorders?

Women in what Naomi Wolf calls the "display professions" — fashion models, actresses, dancers, and so on — are thought to be at particular risk of developing eating disorders because thinness is virtually a job requirement. Women athletes also are vulnerable, especially in swimming, gymnastics and distance running, where a lean frame can give an athlete a competitive advantage.

In fact, eating problems are apparently widespread among U.S. women athletes. In August 1989, for example, the *Austin Statesman-American* reported that 10 percent of the female athletes at the University of Texas had eating disorders. Another 20 to 30 percent, the paper said, citing university records as well as interviews with athletes, administrators and medical officials, showed signs of such disorders. "If we knew for a fact that 10 percent of our athletes had spinal meningitis or AIDS, we'd be scared to death," said Randa Ryan, director of the Performance Team, an organization that offers nutrition and health counseling to University of Texas athletes. "Well, eating disorders are similar, life-threatening illnesses."[11]

Past and present sufferers include some of the biggest names in women's sports. Tennis player Zina Garrison recently disclosed that she has had bulimia since 1983. "It's something a lot of women and a lot of girls have a problem with," she said, "and a lot of them are afraid to talk about it."[12] Other women sports stars who have acknowledged being bulimic include gymnasts Nadia Comeneci, Cathy Rigby and Kathy Johnson.

A 1990 survey by the National Col-

legiate Athletic Association (NCAA) hinted at the breadth of the eating disorder problem in U.S. college sports. *(See poll results, p. 1103.)* Senior sports officials at all 803 NCAA member institutions received a one-page questionnaire asking whether any student athletes had experienced bulimia or anorexia in the previous two years. Of the 491 responding institutions, 313 said at least one such disorder had been noted. Women athletes accounted for 810 of the 872

Tennis player Zina Garrison recently disclosed that she has suffered from bulimia for 10 years.

reported cases. Moreover, at least one eating disorder case was reported in 15 of the 17 women's sports and 11 of the 20 men's sports covered in the study.[13]

Randy Dick, the NCAA's assistant director of sports sciences, cautions that the 1990 survey should be taken "with a couple of grains of salt." He notes that the questionnaires were filled out by athletic personnel "who are not necessarily experts in diagnosing eating disorders." All the NCAA tried to do, he

says, was to "get an idea of what the perception is of eating disorders on campus. I think the survey results suggest that no sport is exempt from the problem."

If weight loss were the only consequence of bulimic behavior among female athletes, there would be little cause for concern. However, research indicates that disordered eating, when combined with strenuous exercise, leads to physical damage that often is only partially reversible. *(See story, p. 1104.)*

As the problem has become more familiar to specialists, it has acquired a distinctive name: the female athlete triad. The triad consists of (1) *eating disorders,* including bulimia, anorexia nervosa, fasting, exclusion of certain foods or food groups from the diet and the use of laxatives and other weight-reduction aids; (2) *secondary amenorrhea,** or irregular menstruation, which means missing several consecutive periods; and (3) *premature osteoporosis,* or bone demineralization, which can lead to stress fractures.

In 1984, studies by medical research teams headed by Barbara L. Drinkwater of the Pacific Medical Center in Seattle and Christopher E. Cann of the University of California-San Francisco found significantly reduced bone density in female runners with amenorrhea.[14] The finding ran counter to the expectations of the medical community, because weight-bearing exercise was assumed to increase bone density.

Follow-up studies of the women in the Drinkwater group showed that those who reduced their exercising by 10 percent and gained at least 4 pounds

---

*Primary amenorrhea, also called delayed menarche, refers to the absence of menstruation as late as age 16.

resumed menstruation without any medical intervention. In addition, bone mass slowly increased. Subsequent research indicated, however, that bone density never returned to the levels found in women athletes who menstruate regularly. "The clear message," wrote sports medicine columnists Carol L. Otis and Roger Goldingay, "is that cessation of menstrual periods due to EAA [exercise-associated amenorrhea] leads to irreversible bone loss." [15]

According to Drinkwater, many female athletes actually welcome the onset of amenorrhea because "they do not want to have menstrual periods, which they find inconvenient and uncomfortable." [16] In fact, delayed menarche works to the female athlete's advantage, says Professor Anne B. Loucks, who teaches graduate courses in endocrinology and exercise physiology at Ohio University. That's because the long bones of the arms and legs continue to grow until menarche, with the result that "later-maturing girls may choose to participate in athletics because they can excel in it. At the same time, earlier-maturing girls may be socialized away from athletics." [17]

Do female athletes develop eating disorders before or after they decide to take up sports? Randy Dick calls that "the million-dollar question." Some experts feel bulimics and anorexics are drawn to sports because vigorous physical exercise is an effective method of weight control. Others believe abnormal eating patterns emerge only in response to the athlete's quest for a competitive edge through weight loss. In gymnastics, the U.S. Olympic Committee has noted, "Leanness creates an image which can enhance the athlete's score from judges." [18]

The committee went on to observe, however, that eating disorders generally impair athletic performance. "Vomiting, fluid restriction, laxative abuse and diuretics all contribute to dehydration," it stated in a position paper. "The continued rapid weight loss that results from starvation or semistarvation causes muscle fatigue, decreased coordination and poor judgment. This is not what makes a *winning* athlete!" [19]

Eating Disorders in Intercollegiate Women's Sports

Senior women administrators at 313 institutions reported 810 cases of bulimia or anorexia in 15 of 17 college athletic programs for women. Of 108 schools with gymnastics programs, 52 schools reported at least one eating-disorder case in the last two years.*

Sport	Sponsoring Schools	Schools Reporting Eating Disorders	% Sponsoring Schools Reporting Eating Disorders
Gymnastics	108	52	48%
Cross Country	642	146	23%
Swimming (only)	395	83	21%
Track (running events only)	537	111	21%
Basketball	762	101	13%
Soccer	293	37	13%
Field Hockey	219	27	12%
Volleyball	716	84	12%
Lacrosse	119	13	11%
Softball	556	53	10%
Skiing	39	3	8%
Tennis	694	58	8%
Golf	143	10	7%
Diving (only)	395	22	6%
Track (field events only)	537	10	2%
Fencing	49	0	0
Rifle	54	0	0

Prevalence by Sex

(313 schools - 872 reports)

Females
810 reports
93%

Males
62 reports
7%

*In the same survey, there were 62 reports (7 percent) of eating disorders among men in college athletic programs.

Source: National Collegiate Athletic Association/Athletic Training magazine, Summer 1991

How Eating Disorders Affect Health

Weight loss achieved by anorexics and bulimics is invariably attained at substantial cost to their health. The self-induced vomiting of bulimia, for example, is harmful because stomach acid burns other parts of the digestive tract. According to Harvard Medical School psychiatrists Harrison G. Pope Jr. and James I. Hudson, "Bulimic vomiters suffer vastly more acid burns than ordinary people, and research has shown that patients who suffer longstanding heartburn have a higher risk of developing cancer of the esophagus." †

Stomach acid is strong enough to corrode tooth enamel. As a result, dentists are often the first health professionals to recognize bulimia. Undoing the damage may cost thousands of dollars for capping and other dental repair work.

Meanwhile, chronic loss of stomach acid through vomiting causes the bulimic's blood and tissues to become more alkaline. This condition, in turn, may trigger pounding headaches and endanger the kidneys by making the urinary system more susceptible to recurrent infections. Frequent vomiting also depletes the body's store of electrolytes, essential minerals whose loss can weaken bones and make the heart beat irregularly.

Bulimics who take laxatives to purge unwanted food also court severe consequences. While laxatives move food through the intestines before it can be absorbed, they also expel vitally needed electrolytes and nutrients. Over time, laxative abuse causes intestines to lose the ability to contract — and, in extreme cases, even the ability to absorb protein.

Like bulimics, anorexics may experience chemical imbalances stemming from lack of sufficient minerals and nutrients. Moreover, the anorexic may suffer dehydration due to reduced fluid intake coupled with excessive fluid elimination. Constipation often follows.

Once an anorexic's weight drops below a critical level, the developmental changes of puberty shift into reverse. Anorexia brings regression to a prepubertal stage of development, signaling the victim's inability to cope with the stresses and demands of adolescence. This regression manifests itself in the suspension of menstruation, breast development and sexual interest.

---

†Harrison G. Pope Jr. and James I. Hudson, *New Hope for Binge Eaters* (1984), p. 26.

Does dieting damage one's health more than improve it?

It is an article of faith among most people that thin is better. Medical journals and the news media have warned for years that overweight people risk developing high blood pressure and other health conditions.

The concerns aroused by the media fed a growing popular appetite for information on dieting and exercise. In this connection, the 1980 study that tracked the changing measurements of *Playboy* centerfolds and Miss America contestants (*see p. 1106*) also tabulated the number of diet, exercise and diet-exercise articles appearing in six leading women's magazines — *Good Housekeeping, Harpers Bazaar, Ladies Home Journal, McCalls, Vogue* and *Woman's Day.* The study found a more or less steady increase in the number of such articles, as did the 1992 American University survey that updated the 1980 findings. The more recent survey found, in addition, that exercise articles now outnumber diet articles in the six magazines.*

Though popular faith in dieting remains strong, many health professionals claim that the resulting weight loss seldom endures. "Short-term [weight] losses are usually trivial, and long-term losses lead to inevitable relapse," asserts eating-disorder expert David Garner. He adds that "the health risks associated with obesity (the primary rationalization for treatment) have been grossly exaggerated and, in fact, dieting (the supposed cure for obesity) may be more dangerous than obesity itself." [20]

Dr. William Bennett, a former editor of the *Harvard Health Letter,* reached the same conclusion. "I am unaware of any weight-loss regimen based on diet-

---

*Between them, the two studies covered the years 1959-1988.

---

ing that has been shown to produce *and maintain* significant weight loss in a majority of people attempting it," he declared in a 1982 speech. "Moreover, the theory does not really take account of the complexities of human metabolism or behavior. The body and brain are treated as passive components of a chemical machine, and that is simply an unrealistic assumption." [21] In addition, recent research suggests genetics may be more influential in determining whether a person becomes obese than simple overeating is.

One of the most damaging outgrowths of the dieting myth, in Bennett's view, is the stigmatization — even by health professionals — of obese people who reduce their food intake as instructed yet fail to shed much weight. "As a result," he says, "fat people come to be seen not only as *patients* but as *bad* patients." [22]

Actually, said psychiatrist Hilde Bruch, a pioneer in the eating disorder field, the women who pursue thinness at all costs are the ones deserving of censure. "There is a great deal of talk about the weakness and self-indulgence of people who eat 'too much,'" she wrote. "Very little is said about the selfishness and self-indulgence involved in a life which makes one's appearance the center of all values, and subordinates all other considerations to it."[23]

One reason why obese people often have trouble losing weight is that sharp reduction of calorie intake may activate the body's starvation reflex, which essentially tries to prevent weight loss. Starvation lowers the body's metabolic rate so that fewer calories are needed. As a result of these adaptive changes in metabolism, the dieter may reach a frustrating plateau at which little or no weight is lost. Metabolic changes can also create problems for successful dieters, for as soon as they resume "normal" eating they often incur rapid weight gain — sometimes putting on more pounds than they lost.

For ANAD's Meehan, the most disturbing aspect of diet programs is that they may trigger an eating disorder. "Everybody I have ever heard of who has an eating disorder first went on some kind of a diet," she says. That does not mean every dieter will develop such disorders, "but for some people, diets do lead to problem behaviors regarding food."

The best way to treat people intent on losing weight, Meehan says, is to help them "look at why they need the [abnormal] food behaviors to get through life, and to make them see that they can develop coping mechanisms to help them deal with their problem."

It is estimated that only 5 to 10 percent of dieters succeed in maintaining substantial weight loss over an extended period. Nutritionists and psychiatrists are not certain how this minority wins its dieting battles. Garner, however, says he knows of "people who keep their weight down by maintaining a stance that is not dissimilar to anorexia

nervosa. That is, they're preoccupied with food and are obsessive about controlling their dietary intake."

Not surprisingly, non-prescription "diet pills" play a key role in the eating disorders debate. Doctors say the majority of patients they treat for anorexia or bulimia habitually misuse appetite suppressants, diuretics, laxatives and drugs like ipecac that induce vomiting. Large doses of laxatives and diuretics can deplete the body's reserves of electrolytes, such as sodium and potassium, sometimes triggering cardiac failure.

Diet pills containing phenylpropanolamine (PPA) are of particular concern. PPA, a mild stimulant that is chemically related to adrenalin, is found not only in appetite suppressants but also in some cold remedies as well. Meehan and others contend that products containing PPA have helped bring on hallucinations, hypertension, mental problems and even cerebral hemorrhages.

Dr. John P. Morgan, an adjunct professor of pharmacology at City University of New York's Medical School, sharply disagrees, branding PPA opponents' arguments as "ideological." The substance, he says, "is significantly less of a stimulant than caffeine." He contends that appetite suppressants containing PPA "have a modest but real effect. I think these aids could be used most effectively by those who are trying to maintain a weight loss."[24]

Ultimately, experts say, the big question is not about diet pills but whether some overweight people might be better off without dieting at all. Garner and Susan Wooley concede that "certain types of cancer appear to be more common with obesity," citing cervical, gall-bladder and post menopausal breast cancer in women and colon and prostate cancer in men. On the other hand, they say, "obesity appears to protect against [some] specific cancer types," including lung, stomach, colon and premenopausal breast cancer in women and lung and stomach cancer in men.[25] ∎

BACKGROUND

Evolving Standards

The taut, lean body so prized by fashion designers, the mass media and contemporary women has not always excited such desirability. Indeed, for much of recorded history plumpness was preferable. A rotund figure proclaimed, in effect, that a woman was affluent and well fed — important considerations in periods when famines were not uncommon.

Social historians say three types of women have been idealized in the West since about 1400. The first was the reproductive woman, characterized by a protruding belly. Throughout the Middle Ages, the ability to bear children was especially important to

high-born women, since producing an heir was the chief prerequisite for marital happiness. Nudes painted in the 15th and 16th centuries often look pregnant, and women's clothes of the period called attention to the abdomen. Fashion historian Anne Hollander wrote in *Seeing Through Clothes* (1978) that "in the erotic imagination of Europe, it was apparently impossible until the late 17th century to have too big a belly."

In the 17th century, the status of women began to shift. Upper-class families started limiting the number of children they produced, and a sense of emotional distancing crept into family life. But by 1700 parents were again exhibiting tenderness toward their children. A revised notion of feminine beauty accompanied the return to nurturing. The belly, symbol of fertility, lost its attractiveness, and prominent breasts, hips and buttocks became the ideals.

The 18th century brought another milestone: Women began to diet. Before then, the threat of famine made going hungry by choice seem absurd, but by the 1800s the English nobility, at least, had a secure food supply. Pallor became the rage, and women willingly submitted to food deprivation, enemas and purging to achieve it. Wire bodices pinched in waists and pushed up breasts, while bustles made buttocks look freakishly distended. Some women even had their lower ribs removed in the pursuit of a modish "hourglass" figure.

As the 19th century ended, women took up bicycling, roller skating, tennis and other sports. At the same time, changes in clothing styles — exemplified by the Gibson Girl look — gave them more freedom of movement. The arrival of motion pictures early in the 20th century enabled the entire nation to track the evolution of women's fashions and body configuration. Movies soon became the main trend-setter in feminine beauty as well as the leading source of mass entertainment.

The birth-control movement and women's suffrage — the two developments that contributed most to women's emancipation at the beginning of the century — had become firmly rooted by the 1920s. The '20s also saw the introduction of the slender silhouette, which in turn gave rise to the legendary flapper. "By 1926, the line [in women's clothing] from shoulder to hip was supposed to be straight, in spite of nature, and the general effect was supposed to be pencil-thin," recalled social historian Frederick Lewis Allen. "That double ambition caused anguish to many a matron; for the style of the middle and late 1920s was remarkably unkind to all but the unnaturally slender." [26] No wonder, then, that "the ladies were reducing as never before." [27]

In the 1940s and '50s, full-figured females came to the fore, popularized by movie stars like Ava Gardner, Jane Russell and Marilyn Monroe. But the vogue for buxomness was short-lived. The lean, almost emaciated female physique returned in the mid-1960s. Ironically, while the decade saw militant feminism emerge, it also ushered in a fashion image of prepubescence verging on androgyny.

The personification of this startling new look was a 5-foot-6-inch, 92-pound British teenager named Leslie Hornby, better-known as Twiggy. For a time, Twiggy reigned as the world's leading model. She "is of such a meager constitution that other models stare at her," *Vogue* noted in its first Twiggy photo layout. "Her legs look as though she has not had enough milk as a baby and her face has that expression one feels Londoners wore in the blitz." [28] But Twiggy insisted she ate "like a horse."

The Gibson Girl, a creation of magazine illustrator Charles Dana Gibson, was a slender young woman usually depicted in a shirtwaist blouse and ankle-length skirt.

Understanding Disorders

Though eating disorders doubtless have existed for many centuries,

---

Symptoms of Anorexia Nervosa

- Deliberate self-starvation with weight loss
- Intense, persistent fear of gaining weight
- Continuous dieting
- Denial of hunger
- Compulsive exercise
- Excessive facial/body hair
- Distorted body image
- Abnormal weight loss
- Sensitivity to cold
- Absent or irregular menstruation
- Hair loss

---

they were slow to be recognized, let alone understood. The first identification of anorexia in medical literature is usually credited to Richard Morton, an English physician who in 1689 described cases of "nervous consumption" in his *Phthisologia: or a Treatise on Consumption*. The symptoms were similar to those now ascribed to anorexia nervosa.[29]

Anorexia was finally identified as a distinct clinical entity in the 1870s by Ernest C. Lasègue, a French physician and professor of medicine, and Sir William Gull, an English physician. Lasègue saw anorexia as a "peripheral" disorder, while Gull insisted it was "probably rather central than peripheral." They agreed, however, that anorexia was a psychological disease, not an organic one. Later researchers tried to demonstrate that anorexia stemmed from disruption of the endocrine system, but by the 1940s the Gull-Lasègue theory of the disorder's psychological origins was generally accepted.

As more is learned about anorexia nervosa, researchers are increasingly hesitant to rule out any theory about its causes. "Anorexia is not a static condition," Hilde Bruch cautioned. "The ambition to 'explain' such a complex

Continued on p. 1108

Chronology

17th Century
For the first time, medical science takes formal notice of the class of ailments now identified as eating disorders.

1689
Richard Morton, an English physician, describes cases of "nervous consumption" in his book *Phthisologia: or a Treatise on Consumption.*

19th Century
The body of knowledge about eating disorders expands as the pace of life quickens, and women's clothing and body styles begin to change.

1873
Sir William Gull, an English physician, coins the term "anorexia nervosa" and speculates that it is a "central" rather than a "peripheral" disorder.

1900s
Bulimia, the eating disorder that most resembles anorexia nervosa, receives formal recognition in medical literature.

1903
Pierre M.F. Janet, a French neurologist, describes a woman's compulsive eating behavior in his book *Les Obsessions et la Psychasthènie.*

1960s
Women's body styles revert to the gaunt, mannish silhouette fashionable in the 1920s.

1962
Marilyn Monroe, the movie star most closely identified with the full-figured feminine look popular in films of the 1940s and '50s, dies at age 36.

1967
Twiggy, a 92-pound British teenager, becomes the world's most famous fashion model.

1969
The National Association to Aid Fat Americans (now called the National Association to Advance Fat Acceptance) is founded.

1970s-1980s
Increasing media attention to eating disorders reveals they are more widespread and hazardous than previously thought.

1976
Vivian Meehan, a professional nurse, founds Anorexia and Associated Disorders (now called the National Association of Anorexia and Associated Disorders).

February 1982
Pop singer Karen Carpenter, 32, dies of a heart attack after a two-year battle with anorexia nervosa.

Oct. 17, 1988
Hershey Foods Corp. informs ANAD that it will discontinue its ad campaign based on the slogan "You can never be too rich or too thin." ANAD had asked Hershey to cancel the campaign.

August 1989
The *Austin Statesman-American* reports that one of every 10 female athletes at the University of Texas suffers from an eating disorder. Another 20 to 30 percent, the paper says, show signs of such disorders.

1990s
Public understanding of eating disorders grows as the extent of such ailments among celebrities and athletes is publicized.

March 1990
The National Collegiate Athletic Association (NCAA) begins a survey of its 803 member institutions that finds eating disorders exist in most men's and women's college sports.

Nov. 15, 1990
Television talk-show star Oprah Winfrey tells viewers the name of the liquid-diet plan that helped her to lose 67 pounds in four months. Within hours after the Winfrey show, the company that devised the diet plan reports receiving more than 200,000 telephone inquiries about it.

May 29-June 2, 1991
The NCAA holds a symposium on "Nutrition and Eating Disorders in College Athletics" in connection with the American College of Sports Medicine's annual meeting.

June 18-19, 1992
The American College of Sports Medicine holds a conference in Washington on "The Female Athletic Triad" — three interrelated disorders that affect women athletes with eating difficulties.

August 1992
Tennis star Zina Garrison discloses that she has suffered from bulimia since 1983.

November 1992
Oprah Winfrey, who began regaining weight not long after her 1990 diet, is reported to weigh more than 200 pounds.

Symptoms of Bulimia Nervosa

- Preoccupation with food
- Binge eating, usually in secret
- Vomiting after bingeing
- Abuse of laxatives, diuretics, diet pills or emetics
- Compulsive exercising
- Swollen salivary glands
- Broken blood vessels in eyes

Continued from p. 1106

picture with one psychodynamic formulation has resulted in imposing stereotyped explanations on a condition that defies such a simplistic approach."

Bulimia was first described in modern medical terms in 1903 by French neurologist Pierre M. F. Janet, who described a woman's compulsive eating in *Les Obsessions et la Psychasthènie*. The first contemporary American account of binge eating was not offered until 1959, by Dr. Albert Stunkard, and it involved obesity — Stunkard's specialty.

Only in 1980, in the third edition of the American Psychiatric Association's widely used reference work, *Diagnostic and Statistical Manual of Mental Disorders* (*DSM-III*), did precise criteria for bulimia come into general usage. Bulimia, according to *DSM-III*, is characterized by "episodic binge eating accompanied by an awareness that the eating pattern is abnormal."

Once the principal eating disorders were identified, researchers began searching for their origins — a quest that continues. "An eating-disorder problem almost never exists in isolation," says Meehan. "Some other factor is usually intertwined with it, either in the person's perception or in reality." For instance, "people don't engage in abnormal eating behaviors without the expectation of being rewarded. The reward for being thin is that you constantly get complimented."

There can be other compensations

as well. For instance, two Australian researchers wrote that "the sufferer is able to avoid making decisions and can reduce the challenges made on her. If the challenges are sexual, the woman may use her emaciation, or her obesity, to avoid them, claiming that her distorted body shape would repel rather than attract men." [30]

An eating disorder can also reward the victim by making her the star of her immediate family circle. "The woman becomes the center of concern and induces the family to make expressions of love and go to great lengths to 'look after her.' In this way, she may be able to manipulate the family and obtains satisfaction from her behavior." [31]

Role of Depression, Sexual Abuse

Despite the rewards that eating disorders may bring to sufferers, some experts believe anorexia and bulimia may go hand in hand with depression. Drs. J. Raymond DePaulo Jr. and Keith Russell Ablow, psychiatrists specializing in mood disorders, write that "Depression can cause some people to become anorexic." On the other hand, they acknowledge that "anorexia can produce its own fatigue, inability to concentrate and moodiness. It may be difficult to determine whether these symptoms are coming from an underlying depression or from the eating disorder and subsequent state of starvation." [32]

Bulimia presents fewer problems of diagnosis, according to DePaulo and Ablow. They report that "most bulimics are not in a state of starvation when they come for treatment, and compared with anorexic patients their underlying mood is more easily assessed. When depression is found to play a role and is treated, bulimics often feel less urge to binge and purge." [33]

Increasingly in recent years, researchers have sought to establish whether childhood sexual abuse triggers eating disorders. Wayne Wooley says "women with eating disorders

seem to have sexual abuse in their history more often than those who don't have the disorders. Sexual abuse also shows up in the history of persons given to such abnormal behavior as self-mutilation or kleptomania — or, I would guess, alcoholism and drug abuse. Sexual abuse is one of the things that destroys people's self-esteem, so that later on they're more vulnerable to these ailments."

Psychiatrists Harrison G. Pope Jr. and James I. Hudson, of Harvard Medical School, are skeptical. They contend that patients with anorexia or bulimia report a level of sexual abuse "somewhat lower than that reported in the general population." This led them to conclude that "childhood sexual abuse is almost certainly a widespread phenomenon in our society, and it may have lasting deleterious effects. However, at the present state of the evidence, these effects do not appear to include the development of eating disorders." [34]

Other researchers suggest that the tensions generated in dysfunctional families spark eating disorders. In such households, the mother-daughter relationship may be key. According to Dr. Kathleen A. Pike of Columbia University's College of Physicians and Surgeons, "the mothers of daughters with disordered eating [behavior] perceive their daughters as significantly less attractive than the daughters perceive themselves. Interestingly, with regard to both weight and appearance, these mothers tend to be less critical of themselves than they are of their daughters." [35]

Many additional factors have been proposed as contributors to eating difficulties. Studies of twins, for example, suggest that genes may transmit chronic eating problems. Other suspects include living in a social climate of exceedingly high performance expectations, whether at home, school or work; drug and alcohol abuse among other members of the immediate family; metabolic disturbances; lack of physical conditioning; and even excessive television viewing. ∎

Treatment Debate

Just as eating disorders appear to have multiple causes, they also seem to call for a variety of treatments. "The consensus approach is the shotgun approach," says ANAD founder Meehan. "We use multidisciplinary treatment methods because nobody has identified any single therapy that will cure everybody."

Dr. Jeffrey Jonas of the Upjohn Co. agrees, adding that treatment "should also include family members, since many of the behaviors seen in families of patients who abuse alcohol and other drugs are seen in families of patients with eating disorders."[36]

Psychotherapy, also called talk therapy, is the most common way of combating eating disorders. Cognitive therapy, a form of talk therapy, is recommended when the disorder is thought to stem from feelings of low self-esteem. The goal of cognitive therapy is to alter the patient's negative mental habits and pessimistic outlook.

Psychoanalytic therapy, which originated with Sigmund Freud and others, seeks to uncover the unconscious childhood conflicts believed to underlie the patient's symptoms. According to Freud, the mental struggle to keep conflicts repressed eventually surfaces as symptoms of psychological disorder. Exposing the true source of the anger, Freudians say, enables the patient to find relief.

It was through psychoanalytic therapy that Dawn Ries of Naperville, Ill., traced her eating disorder to unresolved anger over her father's death many years earlier. Ries, who is now office administrator for ANAD, says treatment should begin as early as possible. If an eating-disorder victim puts off seeking help, she says, "the behavior becomes so ingrained that it's extremely hard to give up." Also, she warns, habitual food abusers risk incurring permanent physical damage. "I have very good friends who are long-term eating-disorder victims," she says, "and their bodies are in such bad shape that you wonder how much hope is left for them."

Ries credits her support group as a key to her treatment. "Being in a support group was a *must* in my recovery," she says. "I worked mostly with professional therapists, but I really needed the contact with other people who were going through the same thing." Today, Ries leads a support group in Naperville.

To some extent, summer camps specializing in weight-loss programs for children borrow the support-group principle. But professional opinion is divided over the effectiveness of the camp approach. "There may be some value in trying to increase exercise and improve the health habits of children attending such camps," says David Garner. However, he questions the

---

When Children Want to Diet

More than 40 percent of the 3,100 5th-8th graders surveyed recently in South Carolina showed concern about their weight. More than 30 percent said they had tried dieting or exercising, while a small number had tried more extreme ways of losing weight (See graph below).

Do you want to lose weight now?

Total	Females	Males
42%	55%	28.5%

Have you ever thought you looked fat to other people?

Total	Females	Males
41.4%	54.4%	27.8%

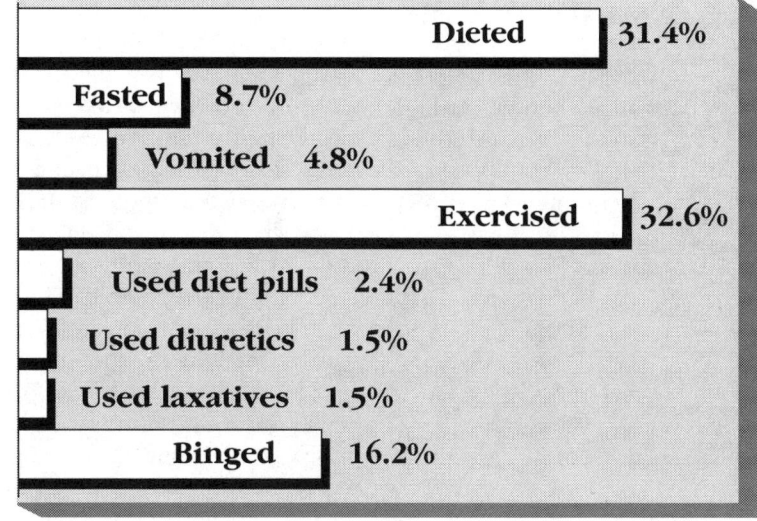

Dieted 31.4%
Fasted 8.7%
Vomited 4.8%
Exercised 32.6%
Used diet pills 2.4%
Used diuretics 1.5%
Used laxatives 1.5%
Binged 16.2%

Source: Medical University of South Carolina, Chicago Tribune (Aug. 15, 1992)

long-term results, noting that the camps can achieve short-term loss "simply by withholding food from kids and controlling their environment in ways that you can't do with adults."

Wayne Wooley calls weight-loss camps "harmful" to children and "mainly for parents who are ashamed of their kids. If there was a sure-fire way to lose weight, we'd all know about it." If follow-up surveys were conducted, he adds, "you'd find that the kids gained the weight back."

As with some other psychological problems, drug therapy also plays a part in combating eating disorders. Hudson and Pope note that tricyclic antidepressants and monoamine oxidase inhibitors, widely prescribed medications for depression sufferers, can "substantially reduce the frequency of eating binges and purging behaviors in bulimic patients." [37] They cite another study providing "sound scientific evidence" that fluoxetine, an antidepressant marketed under the trade name Prozac, "is effective in the short-term treatment of bulimia nervosa." [38]

When talk-show star Oprah Winfrey told viewers of her plan to go on a liquid diet, it was big news to supermarket tabloids. Winfrey eventually regained the weight she lost.

Troubled Celebrities

Many Americans choose to lose weight the old-fashioned way — by drastically curbing their food intake. Television talk-show hostess Oprah Winfrey did it before millions of her devoted fans.

Winfrey, who has often discussed her weight problem on her show, told *Ms.* magazine in 1986 that she first turned to food for solace after a botched permanent left her completely but temporarily bald. By the mid-1980s, her weight was hovering between 180 and 190 pounds. (Winfrey stands 5-foot-7.) She openly despaired of wearing the size 10 designer jeans hanging in her closet.

On one of her shows in July 1988, however, Winfrey dramatically announced, "I'm tired of this being a problem! I'm going to settle it." For the next four months, transfixed viewers watched her shed 67 pounds on a liquid-diet regimen. On Nov. 15, Winfrey strode triumphantly onto the studio set in her size 10 jeans and credited her newly trim figure to Optifast, a weight-loss program devised by Sandoz Nutrition Corp. of Minneapolis. Within hours after the show, Sandoz reported receiving more than 200,000 phone inquiries.*

The aftermath of Winfrey's apparent victory over demon food was surely disheartening for her and her fans — but not at all surprising to eating-disorder specialists. Within months, the pounds began creeping back. "I'll never diet again," she told viewers in November 1990. She now reportedly weighs over 200 pounds.

In recent weeks, though, Winfrey has touted author Geneen Roth, whose book, *When Food Is Love,* links compulsive overeating to deep-seated emotional turmoil. According to Roth, lasting weight reduction can be achieved, without dieting, by understanding the source of one's emotional turmoil. Perhaps taking a cue from Roth, Winfrey has offered fresh insights

Reuters

Diana, the Princess of Wales, is said to suffer from bulimia, caused in part by the stress of her highly public marriage to Prince Charles. The royal couple, shown here in 1981, recently separated.

into the origin of her food problems. On Nov. 4, she attributed her bouts of compulsive overeating to being raped by a cousin and sexually molested by an uncle during childhood.

Other female celebrities also have experienced serious food disorders. Pop singer Karen Carpenter died at 32 of a heart attack in 1982 after a two-year battle with anorexia. Actress Jane Fonda has discussed her struggle with bulimia from ages 12 to 35. The roster of recovered celebrity bulimics also includes singer Judy Collins, actresses Lynn Redgrave and Ally Sheedy and comedienne Joan Rivers.

The biggest celebrity bulimic of all, if two recent books are to be believed, may be Diana, the Princess of

*Optifast and other liquid diets like HMR and Medifast are aimed at people who are at least 30 percent or 50 pounds overweight. In a typical six-month program, dieters consume only a carbohydrate-and-protein powder mixed with liquids, lowering daily intake to 400 to 800 calories. Medical supervision of this and all diets is strongly recommended.

Men With Eating Disorders

Eating disorders occur 10 times more often among females than males. However, anorexics and bulimics of both sexes display roughly the same symptoms. Anorexic males, for example, often are compulsive exercisers, spending hours each day jogging, swimming or doing push-ups and other calisthenics. Why these men pursue thinness so relentlessly is something of a mystery, since most male adolescents aspire to be muscular rather than slender.

According to Randa Ryan, director of the Performance Team, an organization that offers health counseling to athletes at the University of Texas, men are not as emotionally attached to their bodies as women are "because men have not defined themselves through their body image nearly as much."

The situation may be changing "a little," says Ryan. "But in the past, at least, there were very few male athletes who would doubt that they were okay just because they didn't weigh this amount, or wear this size of pants, or whatever. That has not been true of women, who are bombarded with weight consciousness from the time they're born."[†]

In a 1990 survey of its 803 member institutions, the National Collegiate Athletic Association (NCAA) identified wrestling as the men's sport with the greatest number of reported eating disorder cases. That's because wrestling was the only men's sport surveyed in which a defined weight had to be met prior to competition. "[I]f a wrestler does not make weight," noted Randy Dick, the NCAA's assistant director of sports sciences, "he does not wrestle."[††]

To make their weight class, wrestlers will bake in a sauna while wearing a rubber sweat suit, drastically cut their intake of food and fluids and resort to vomiting, laxatives and diuretics.

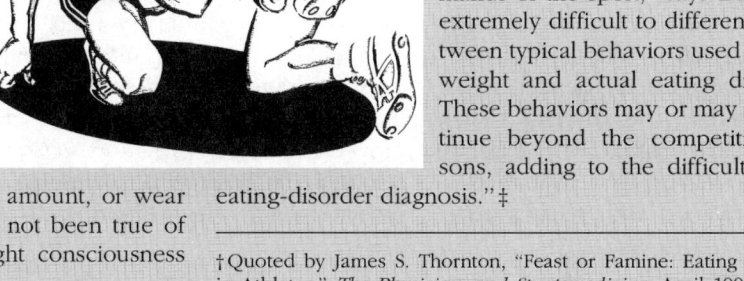

In the absence of further research, neither Dick or Steen is prepared to brand such behavior as irrefutable evidence of disordered eating. "[B]ecause of the unique weight demands of the sport," says Dick, "it is extremely difficult to differentiate between typical behaviors used to make weight and actual eating disorders. These behaviors may or may not continue beyond the competitive seasons, adding to the difficulty of an eating-disorder diagnosis."[‡]

[†] Quoted by James S. Thornton, "Feast or Famine: Eating Disorders in Athletes," *The Physician and Sportsmedicine,* April 1990, p. 119.

[††] Randall W. Dick, "Eating Disorders in NCAA Athletic Programs," *Athletic Training,* summer 1991, p. 139.

[‡] *Ibid.*

Wales. Both Andrew Morton (*Diana: the True Story*) and Lady Colin Campbell (*Diana in Private*) claim that the princess suffers from bulimia. No comments on the assertions have come from Diana herself or other members of the British royal family.

Still another recent book, Naomi Wolf's *The Beauty Myth,* advances the provocative thesis that anorexia and bulimia are not so much psychological disorders as problems ultimately caused by men who insist that women adhere to ideal standards of beauty. In this way, Wolf says, men perpetuate the subordination of women, especially in academia and the workplace. "The anorexic woman, like the anti-Semitic Jew and the self-hating black,

fits in," writes Wolf. "She is politically castrate, with exactly enough energy to do her schoolwork, neatly and completely, and to run around the indoor track in eternal circles. She has no energy to get angry or get organized, to chase sex, to yell through a bull horn asking ... for women's studies programs."[39]

Anorexia is on the rise, Wolf argues, "because it works." That is, the disorder protects its victims "from street harassment and sexual coercion; construction workers leave walking skeletons alone. Having no fat means having no breasts, thighs, hips, or ass, which for once means not having asked for it."[40] ∎

OUTLOOK

Cost of Treatment

When eating-disorder specialists look to the future, they see more needs than ways of meeting them. Obtaining additional treatment facilities ranks high on the wish list. Janis Walker, a licensed social worker and therapist at Johns Hopkins Hospital's eating and weight disorders clinic in Baltimore, says there's an urgent need for residential treatment centers "for people who have had eating disorders for a long time and haven't been able to attend school or go to work."

In a residential setting, says Walker, patients "can spend part of the day learning about coping mechanisms, shopping and selecting the right kinds of food. They can learn how to do all that while also going to school part time or working part time. And it's a lot less expensive than having to be in a hospital."

Dawn Ries agrees that more residential facilities would help, but because outpatient treatment of eating disorders is long-term, she adds, "it's also very costly." Moreover, the chances of locating enough money to cover those costs seem extremely remote at present. "Since health insurance companies aren't providing adequate coverage for treatment of eating disorders," she says, "it becomes almost impossible to afford new residential facilities."

"Insurance coverage is such a morass that it drives us all crazy," Meehan says. "Many of us feel we spend more time dealing with insurance issues than we do with patient care."

The basic problem, she says, is that "most insurance companies refuse to allow any kind of medical coverage for an eating disorder. And they also think we should be able to take care of eating-disorder problems in a few days to a couple of weeks."

The health-insurance industry defends its approach, which is to provide benefits for treatment of eating disorders under the mental health portion of group policies. Donald B. White, media relations manager for the Health Insurance Association of America, points out that payments for psychiatric care are now the fastest-growing segment of overall health-insurance benefits.

Even so, says White, the current trend within the industry is to "provide higher limits for mental health care coverage but also make greater use of provider networks and employee-assistance programs." Counselors in such programs attempt to detect mental health problems in

their early stages, when they are easier and less costly to treat. When outside care becomes necessary, the counselors steer employees to "cost-effective" treatment providers.

Improving the self-image of overweight people offers one way of holding down the cost of eating-disorders treatment. If such people could learn to accept their obesity, they presumably would be less tempted to try crash diets.

In Garner's opinion, "the stigmatization of obese people is one of the least publicized and most important civil rights issues today. We're spending a lot of time trying to treat people who are obese and not enough time attending to their civil rights and learning to tolerate a diversity of body shapes."

Ultimately, says Garner, "we should give people who are large the same kind of legislative protection enjoyed by other minorities. When I spoke on this topic eight or nine years ago, peo-

Continued on p. 1114

How Much Should You Weigh?

Height-weight "norms" are widely used by the insurance industry. According to the National Association to Advance Fat Acceptance, more than 38 million Americans exceed the standards for "normal" weight.

Height		Men Small Frame	Medium Frame	Large Frame	Height		Women Small Frame	Medium Frame	Large Frame
5	2	128-134	131-141	138-150	4	10	102-111	109-121	118-131
5	3	130-136	133-143	140-153	4	11	103-113	111-123	120-134
5	4	132-138	135-145	142-156	5	0	104-115	113-126	122-137
5	5	134-140	137-148	144-160	5	1	106-118	115-129	125-140
5	6	136-142	139-151	146-164	5	2	108-121	118-132	128-143
5	7	138-145	142-154	149-168	5	3	111-124	121-135	131-147
5	8	140-148	145-157	152-172	5	4	114-127	124-138	134-151
5	9	142-151	148-160	155-176	5	5	117-130	127-141	137-155
5	10	144-154	151-163	158-180	5	6	120-133	130-144	140-159
5	11	146-157	154-166	161-184	5	7	123-136	133-147	143-163
6	0	149-160	157-170	164-188	5	8	126-139	136-150	146-167
6	1	152-164	160-174	168-192	5	9	129-142	139-153	149-170
6	2	155-168	164-178	172-197	5	10	132-145	142-156	152-173
6	3	158-172	167-182	176-202	5	11	135-148	145-159	155-176
6	4	162-176	171-187	181-207	6	0	138-151	148-162	158-179

Source: MetLife Insurance Company

At Issue:

Are American women hampered by a cultural edict to be beautiful?

NAOMI WOLF

FROM *THE BEAUTY MYTH*, WILLIAM MORROW AND CO., 1991.

during the past decade, women breached the power structure; meanwhile, eating disorders rose exponentially and cosmetic surgery became the fastest-growing medical specialty. During the past five years, consumer spending doubled, pornography became the main media category, ahead of legitimate films and records combined and 33,000 American women told researchers that they would rather lose 10 to 15 pounds than achieve any other goal. More women have more money and power ... than we have ever had before; but in terms of how we feel about ourselves physically, we may actually be worse off than our unliberated grandmothers. Recent research consistently shows that inside the majority of the West's controlled, attractive, successful working women, there is a secret "underlife" poisoning our freedom; infused with notions of beauty, it is a dark vein of self-hatred, physical obsessions, terror of aging and dread of lost control.

It is no accident that so many potentially powerful women feel this way. We are in the midst of a violent backlash against feminism that uses images of female beauty as a political weapon against women's advancement: the beauty myth. It is the modern version of a social reflex that has been in force since the Industrial Revolution. As women released themselves from the feminine mystique of domesticity, the beauty myth took over its lost ground, expanding as it waned to carry on its work of social control.

The contemporary backlash is so violent because the ideology of beauty is the last one remaining of the old feminine ideologies that still has the power to control those women whom second wave feminism would have otherwise made relatively uncontrollable: It has grown stronger to take over the work of social coercion that myths about motherhood, domesticity, chastity and passivity no longer can manage. It is seeking right now to undo psychologically and covertly all the good things that feminism did for women materially and overtly....

The beauty myth of the present is more insidious than any mystique of femininity yet: A century ago, Nora slammed the door of the doll's house; a generation ago, women turned their backs on the consumer heaven of the isolated multiapplianced home; but where women are trapped today, there is no door to slam. The contemporary ravages of the beauty backlash are destroying women physically and depleting us psychologically. If we are to free ourselves from the dead weight that has once again been made out of femaleness, it is not ballots or lobbyists or placards that women will need first; it is a new way to see.

MARY G. GOTSCHALL

A freelance writer living in Virginia
FROM *NATIONAL REVIEW*, JULY 8, 1991.

ultimately, Miss Wolf ascribes all of modern women's social ills to the beauty myth, including the rise in rape, mental illness and sexual abuse of children during the last decade. In so doing, she falls into the trap of oversimplification.

Women's stature in modern society is the product of a confluence of factors, and the "beauty myth" is merely one of them. One must also weigh such factors as the force of tradition, our evolution from a "hunter-gatherer" society, the legal and political system, institutional pressures, religion, portrayals of beautiful women in Western art, biological and physiological functions and innate sex differences. The list goes on and on.

Beyond that, I would argue that much of what Miss Wolf criticizes in our culture springs from basic animal drives. Among many species, one sex uses decoration to entice the other to mate.... Women's pursuit of beauty serves a similar reproductive agenda....

There is also scientific evidence indicating that there are cognitive differences between men and women, which in turn manifest themselves in different styles of communication and behavior... From an early age, boys are object-oriented and girls are person-oriented; from these different orientations flow correspondingly different behavior. And ornamentation maybe be one such difference. Women take pleasure in adornment.

Women have free will, contrary to Miss Wolf's assertion, and they are not forced to buy beauty products. They choose to do so. If this were not so, fashion and the beauty industry would not thrive. The capitalist system is driven by the bottom line and not by politics.

The central flaw of *The Beauty Myth* is its extremism. It lacks moderation, balance, judiciousness. Miss Wolf goes overboard, hammering away at her central theme with the same fanaticism that she ascribes to women hooked on diet fads. *The Beauty Myth* shades into caricature — even paranoia — when she writes that, because of the pursuit of pulchritude, "life-fearing neuroses are everywhere."

Indeed, the book projects many of Miss Wolf's own psychological hang-ups onto all of womankind. In the section on eating disorders, for example, she admits that she was an anorexic when she was 13 years old, and one of her best friends died of anorexia. Presumably, her views on women's eating disorders have been shaped by these personal experiences.

Where to Get More Information on Eating Disorders

American Anorexia/Bulimia Association Inc., 418 E. 76th St., New York, N.Y. 10021, (212) 734-1114. AABA functions as an information and referral service for anorexics, bulimics and members of their immediate families.

American College of Sport Medicine, P.O. Box 1440, Indianapolis, Ind. 46206-1440, (317) 637-9200. This professional organization has devoted increasing attention in recent years to eating disorders among female athletes.

Massachusetts General Hospital, Eating Disorders Unit-ACC 625, 15 Parkman St., Boston, Mass. 02114, (617) 726-2724. Offers counseling, informational materials and referrals.

Michael Reese Hospital and Medical Center, Department of Psychology, Eating Disorders Project, Lakeshore Dr. at 31st St., Chicago, Ill. 60616, (312) 791-3878. Offers counseling, informational materials and referrals.

National Association of Anorexia Nervosa and Associated Disorders, Box 7, Highland Park, Ill. 60035, (708) 831-3438. ANAD, the oldest U.S. organization of its kind, sponsors support groups.

National Association to Advance Fat Acceptance, P.O. Box 188620, Sacremento, Calif. 95818, (916) 443-0303. NAAFA is a self-help group that attempts to improve the quality of life, self-esteem and legal protection of overweight people.

National Collegiate Athletic Association, 6201 College Blvd., Overland Park, Kan. 66211, (913) 339-1906. The NCAA now tracks eating disorders among athletes attending its 803 member colleges and universities.

Overeaters Anonymous, P.O. Box 92870, Los Angeles, Calif. 90009, (213) 618-8835. Modeled after Alcoholics Anonymous, this group uses a similar 12-step program to combat the disease of compulsive overeating.

UCLA Neuropsychiatric Institute, Eating Disorders Clinic, 760 Westwood Plaza, Los Angeles, Calif. 90024, (213) 825-0478. Offers counseling, informational materials and referrals.

Weight Watchers International, 500 N. Broadway, Jericho, N.Y. 11753-2196, (516) 949-0400. A commercial organization for overweight people, Weight Watchers gives its members a balanced, low-calorie diet to follow. Because of New Year's Day dieting resolutions, January is the group's peak enrollment month.

them to purchase two seats. The NAAFA picketers chanted, "We deserve to fly the skies/ Regardless of our shape or size!"

Though people with weight problems may someday win greater social acceptance, eating-disorder experts doubt society's overwhelming preference for slenderness will change in the foreseeable future. Wayne Wooley, for one, feels "pretty pessimistic" about any anti-dieting movement catching on. "The body-shape standard is thinner now than it ever has been, except in the 1920s," he says.

One possible harbinger of change could be the growing popularity of bodybuilding among women. "The woman who looks powerful, like a well-developed, young male adolescent — that's considered a beautiful female body now," says Wooley, adding, "as long as the additional weight is muscle." ∎

Notes

[1] National Association of Anorexia Nervosa and Associated Disorders, "When an Image Becomes an Obsession, It's Time to Take a Closer Look!" (brochure).

[2] Russell Marx, *It's Not Your Fault: Overcoming Anorexia and Bulimia Through Biopsychiatry* (1991), p. 35.

[3] Testimony at a hearing of the U.S. House Select Committee on Children, Youth and Families, San Francisco, July 31, 1987.

[4] *Ibid.*

[5] A. Morris, *et al.*, "The Changing Shape of Female Fashion Models," *International Journal of Eating Disorders,* 8(5), 1989, pp. 593-596.

[6] David M. Garner, *et al.*, "Cultural Expectations of Thinness in Women," *Psychological Reports,* 47, 1980, pp. 483-491.

[7] Claire V. Wiseman, *et al.*, "Cultural Expectations of Thinness in Women: An Update," *International Journal of Eating Disorders,* Vol. 11, No. 1, 1992, pp. 85-89.

[8] Prepared testimony before a hearing of the House Select Committee on Children, Youth

Continued from p. 1112
ple thought I was from another planet. Now they think I'm only from another state. So we're making some progress."

Indeed, overweight people have begun to challenge discriminatory business practices directed at them. Last May, for example, Southwest Airlines was the target of protests staged in five cities by the National Association to Advance Fat Acceptance (NAAFA).[41] The protesters contended the airline had refused to allow them to board, had them ejected from planes or forced

Exotic Eating Disorders

When it comes to exotic eating habits, there's a custom in the rural South that puts anorexia and bulimia to shame. It's called pica, and studies conducted in the 1970s by Dennis A. Frate, a University of Mississippi medical anthropologist, found it was practiced by one of every four adult black women in Holmes County, Miss.: They regularly consumed dirt. The freshly dug earth often was baked and flavored with salt and vinegar before being eaten.

"It's a cultural tradition that is practiced almost exclusively by women and young children," says Frate. "It's one of the few customs that survived the cultural change as slaves were brought from West Africa to the United States." †

No less an authority than the American Psychiatric Association's *Diagnostic and Statistical Manual of Mental Disorders* describes pica as a persistent craving for "nonnutritive substances" like dirt, chalk or ashes. Dirt-eating usually is harmless if done in moderation. However, the same cannot be said about eating baking soda or laundry starch, both of which have a soil-like consistency. Baking soda, for instance, is high in sodium, which contributes to high blood pressure.

Starch-eaters, who may go through one or more boxes of starch a day, also are at risk. They sometimes appear to have mumps or tumors because of a swelling of their parotid salivary glands, which are situated just below and in front of the ears.

† Quoted in the *Los Angeles Times*, April 3, 1989.

and Families, San Francisco, July 31, 1987.

[9] David M. Garner and Susan C. Wooley, "Confronting the Failure of Behavioral and Dietary Treatments for Obesity," *Clinical Psychology Review*, Vol. 11, 1991, p. 731. With her husband, O. Wayne Wooley, Susan Wooley is co-director of the University of Cincinnati Medical School's eating disorders clinic.

[10] Naomi Wolf, *The Beauty Myth: How Images of Beauty Are Used Against Women* (1991), pp. 48-49.

[11] Quoted by Craig Neff in *Sports Illustrated*, Aug. 14, 1989.

[12] Quoted in *The Washington Post*, Aug. 17, 1992.

[13] Randall W. Dick, "Eating Disorders in NCAA Athletic Programs," *Athletic Training*, summer 1991, pp. 137-140. *Athletic Training* is the quarterly journal of the National Athletic Trainers' Association.

[14] Barbara L. Drinkwater, *et al.*, "Bone Mineral Content of Amenorrheic and Eumenorrheic Athletes," *The New England Journal of Medicine*, Aug. 2, 1984, pp. 277-281; and Christopher E. Cann, *et al.*, "Decreased Spinal Mineral Content in Amenorrheic Women," *The Journal of the American Medical Association*, Feb. 3, 1984, pp. 626-629.

[15] Carol L. Otis and Roger Goldingay, "A Crucial Period," *Shape*, March 1992, p. 50. *Shape* magazine focuses on women's nutrition and fitness issues.

[16] Barbara L. Drinkwater, "Amenorrhea, Body Weight and Osteoporosis," in Kelly D. Brownell, *et al.*, eds., *Eating, Body Weight and Performance in Athletes: Disorders of Modern Society* (1992), p. 245.

[17] Anne B. Loucks, "Effects of Exercise Training on the Menstrual Cycle: Existence and Mechanisms," *Medicine and Science in Sports and Exercise*, Vol. 22, No. 3, p. 276.

[18] U.S. Olympic Committee, "Sports Nutrition: Eating Disorders," 1987, p. 1.

[19] *Ibid.*, p. 4.

[20] Testimony before hearings held by the House Subcommittee on Regulation, Business Opportunities and Energy, March 26, 1990.

[21] Address before the 1982 convention of the National Association to Advance Fat Acceptance, Columbus, Ohio.

[22] *Ibid.*

[23] Hilde Bruch, Eating Disorders: Obesity, Anorexia Nervosa and the Person Within (1973), p. 198.

[24] Quoted by Amanda Loudin in "Dieting to Death," *Pharmacy Update*, Nov. 19, 1990.

[25] Garner and Wooley, *op. cit.*, p. 753.

[26] Frederick Lewis Allen, *I Remember Distinctly: A Family Album of the American People, 1918-1941* (1947), p. 56.

[27] *Ibid.*, p. 59.

[28] Quoted in Nicholas Drake, ed., *The Sixties: A Decade in Vogue* (1988).

[29] Hilde Bruch, *op. cit.*, p. 211.

[30] Suzanne Abraham and Derek Llewellyn-Jones, *Eating Disorders: The Facts* (1987), p. 45.

[31] *Ibid.*

[32] J. Raymond DePaulo Jr., and Keith Russell Ablow, *How to Cope With Depression: A Complete Guide for You and Your Family* (1989), p. 58.

[33] *Ibid.*, p. 59.

[34] Harrison G. Pope Jr. and James I. Hudson, "Childhood Sexual Abuse and Bulimia Nervosa: Is There an Association?" *Newsletter* of the American Anorexia/Bulimia Association, fall 1992, p. 6.

[35] Kathleen M. Pike, "Mothers, Daughters and Disordered Eating," *Newsletter* of the American Anorexia/Bulimia Association, fall 1992, p. 7.

[36] Jeffrey Jonas, "An Examination of Eating Disorders and Addictions: Is There an Association?" *Newsletter* of the American Anorexia/Bulimia Association, fall 1992, p. 3.

[37] James I. Hudson and Harrison G. Pope Jr., "Update on the Use of Fluoxetine in the Treatment of Bulimia Nervosa," *Newsletter* of the American Anorexia/Bulimia Association Inc., fall 1992, p. 1. For background, see "Depression," The CQ Researcher, Oct. 9, 1992, pp. 857-880.

[38] Fluoxetine-Bulimia Collaborative Study Group, "Fluoxetine in the Treatment of Bulimia Nervosa: A Multicenter, Placebo-controlled, Double-blind Trial," *The Archives of General Psychiatry*, Vol. 49, 1992, pp. 139-147.

[39] Wolf, *op. cit.*, p. 199.

[40] *Ibid.*, pp. 198-199.

[41] NAAFA was founded in 1969 by Bill Fabrey, a New York man who was upset about the discrimination his overweight wife had to face.

Bibliography

Selected Sources Used

Books

Abraham, Suzanne, and Derek Llewellyn-Jones, *Eating Disorders: The Facts*, Oxford University Press, 1987.

Abraham and Llewellyn-Jones, faculty members of the obstetrics and gynecology department at Australia's Sydney University, set forth the basic facts about why eating disorders occur and how they can be controlled. They include numerous case histories.

Lemberg, Raymond, ed., *Controlling Eating Disorders With Facts, Advice and Resources,* Oryz Press, 1992.

The contributors to this book discuss various approaches to eating-disorder therapy. For instance, Drs. Marie C. Shafe and James M. Parsons favor a holistic model, "based on the belief that eating disorders are caused by multiple factors."

Marx, Russell, *It's Not Your Fault: Overcoming Anorexia and Bulimia Through Biopsychiatry*, Random House, 1991.

Marx analyzes the origins of various eating disorders. The potential anorexic, he notes, "lacks the inner strength to handle loss, rejection or change. She has aged, but she has not grown up. She has spent so much emotional energy pleasing others that she has none left to invest in understanding her own feelings.

Wolf, Naomi, *The Beauty Myth: How Images of Beauty Are Used Against Women,* Morrow, 1991.

In Wolf's view, eating disorders are just one manifestation of the male power structure's ongoing effort to keep women in a subordinate position by insisting they meet exacting standards of physical appearance.

Articles

Loudin, Amanda, "Dieting to Death," *Pharmacy Update*, Nov. 19, 1990.

Loudin takes a highly critical look at the effects of nonprescription drugs commonly used by teenage girls intent on losing weight.

Must, Aviva, *et al.*, "Long-Term Morbidity and Mortality of Overweight Adolescents," *The New England Journal of Medicine*, Nov. 5, 1992.

Must and five colleagues report that overweight teenagers are more likely than thin youngsters of the same age to develop such problems as heart disease, colon cancer, arthritis or gout by age 70.

Wiseman, Claire V., *et al.*, "Cultural Expectations of Thinness in Women: An Update," *International Journal of Eating Disorders*, Vol. 11, No. 1, 1992.

Wiseman and three colleagues at American University in Washington update earlier studies on the body measurements of *Playboy* centerfolds and Miss America contestants and the number of diet and exercise articles published by six leading women's magazines.

Reports and Studies

American College of Sports Medicine, *The Female Athlete Triad: Disordered Eating, Amenorrhea and Osteoporosis*, 1992.

This is a collection of papers submitted by participants in a June 1992 conference in Washington, D.C. All deal with various physical problems experienced by woman athletes with eating disorders.

Health Insurance Association of America, *The Evolution of Mental health Benefits,* June 1991.

HIAA, a Washington-based trade organization, sets forth the industry's rationale for the mental-health portion of group policies — the part that provides benefits for eating disorders, if these are covered at all.

Subcommittee on Regulation, Business Opportunities and Energy, U.S. House Committee on Small Business, *Deception and Fraud in the Diet Industry, Part I and Part II* (published proceedings of hearings held March 26 and May 7, 1990.

Critics of the multibillion-dollar U.S. diet industry assail what they regard as flagrant abuses in a largely unregulated field. Representatives of companies that make various diet products insist their firms are ethical and meet a demonstrated public need.

U.S. House Select Committee on Children, Youth and Families, *Eating Disorders: The Impact on Children and Families* (published proceedings of hearing held in San Francisco, July 31, 1987).

More than a dozen experts testify on the origins and treatment of eating disorders in young people, often supplementing their oral comments with prepared statements and other written material.

The Next Step

Additional Articles from Current Periodicals from EBSCO Publishing's Database

Books & reading

Frenzel, E.G., "Reviews," *Psychology of Women Quarterly*, March 1992, p. 137.

Reviews the book "Anorexia and Bulimia: Anatomy of a Social Epidemic," by Richard A. Gordon.

McCulley, L., "Book review: Junior high up," *School Library Journal*, May 1992, p. 146.

Reviews the book "Eating Disorders," by Don Nardo.

McCulley, L., "Book review: Junior high up," *School Library Journal*, May 1992, p. 144.

Reviews the book "When Food's a Foe: How to Confront and Conquer Eating Disorders," by Nancy Kolodny.

McCulley, L., "Book review: Junior high up," *School Library Journal*, November 1991, p. 141.

Reviews the book "Coping with Eating Disorders," by Barbara Moe.

McCulley, L., "Book review: Junior high up," *School Library Journal*, October 1991, p. 156.

Reviews the book "Straight Talk About Eating Disorders," by Michael Maloney and Rachel Kranz.

Royal, P., "Book review: Adult books for young adults," *School Library Journal*, October 1991, p. 166.

Reviews the book "It's Not Your Fault: Overcoming Anorexia and Bulimia through Biopsychiatry," by Russell Marx.

White, L.K., "Book review: Junior high up," *School Library Journal*, May 1992, p. 149.

Reviews the book "Hope and Recovery: A Mother-Daughter Story about Anorexia Nervosa, Bulimia, and Manic Depression," by Emma Lou Thayne and Becky Thayne Markosian.

Celebrities

"Di's private battle," *People*, Aug. 3, 1992, p. 60.

Offers a look at the Princess of Wales's battle with bulimia. Presents various royal watchers' views of how and when Diana, 31, developed the disease, and how she's dealt with it.

Eftimiades, M., M. Rosen, et al., "Eating disorders: A Hollywood history," *People*, Feb. 17, 1992, p. 96.

Offers a look at some Hollywood celebrities who have overcome eating disorders. Includes Sally Field, 45, Jane Fonda, 54, and Ally Sheedy, 29. Diseases; common eating habits; role models. INSET: Causes, signals — and hope for the victims (of eating disorders).

Sporkin, E., J. Wagner, et al., "A terrible hunger," *People*, Feb. 17, 1992, p. 92.

Covers the story of actress Tracey Gold, 22, of ABC's sitcom "Growing Pains." Gold is suffering from anorexia, having dropped to 90 lbs. on her 5'3', frame. Discusses her battle with the disease and the reactions of family, friends and co-workers.

Psychological aspects

"Like mother, like daughter," *Muscle & Fitness*, April 1992, p. 26.

States that many teenage girls with eating disorders can attribute them to mothers who also have eating disorders and the pressure from them to be thin. Modeling mothers' behavior; learned their eating patterns; treatment.

"My sister's anorexia, and me," *Seventeen*, August 1992, p. 126.

Describes how the author dealt with a sister who had anorexia. How their relationship deteriorated, but later, after her treatment, improved. What he learned from the ordeal.

"Parent talk shapes teens' body image," *Tufts University Diet & Nutrition Letter*, February 1992, p. 7.

Reports that teenage girls who feel their parents always lecture them rather than talk to them sensitively are more prone to have eating disorders, such as anorexia nervosa and bulimia. It was the same for students who felt their parents didn't take their problems seriously or were not willing to take the time to talk to them; number of female high-schoolers with typical eating disorder characteristics; the importance of a supportive family environment.

"Portrait of a binge eater," *Psychology Today*, March/April 1992, p. 15.

Offers a look at eating disorders and how they have changed. Anorexia nervosa and binge eating; why it is due for an overhaul; why people binge eat; following binges with purges; no way to tell a binge eater by body weight.

Agras, W.S., E. Rossiter, et al., "Pharmacologic and cognitive-behavioral treatment for bulimia nervosa: A controlled comparison," *American Journal of Psychiatry*, January 1992, p. 82.

Presents a study examining the relative effectiveness of desipramine, cognitive-behavioral therapy and their combination in the treatment of bulimia nervosa, together with the effects of withdrawing medication after two different lengths of treatment. Method; results; conclusions; details.

Anastasiades, P., M.J. Cooper, et al., "Selective processing of eating-, shape-, and weight-related words in persons with bulimia nervosa," *Journal of Abnormal Psychology*, May 1992, p. 352.

Presents a study using the Stroop color-naming task to investigate selective information processing in people with bulimia nervosa. Comparison between 36 patients with bulimia nervosa and age-matched female controls; method; results; discussion.

Baumeister, R.F. & T.F. Heatherton, "Binge eating as escape from self-awareness," *Psychological Bulletin*, July 1991, p. 86.

Proposes that binge eating is motivated by a desire to escape from self-awareness. Binge eaters suffer from high standards and expectations, especially an acute sensitivity to the difficult demands of others. Definitions and scope of coverage; review of relevant evidence; discussion.

Blouin, A., J. Blouin, et al., "Seasonal patterns of bulimia nervosa," *American Journal of Psychiatry*, January 1992, p. 73.

Discusses whether a seasonal pattern to symptoms of bulimia nervosa could be identified. Method; results; conclusions; details.

Frank, E.S., "Shame and guilt in eating disorders," *American Journal of Orthopsychiatry*, April 1991, p. 303.

Presents a study of 94 college students who supported the hypothesis that women with eating disorders experience more shame and guilt in relation to eating than do either normal or depressed women, and that such shame and guilt differentiate the eating disorders from other psychopathology. Method; results; discussion.

Grissett, N.I. & N.K. Norvell, "Perceived social support, social skills, and quality of relationships in bulimic women," *Journal of Consulting & Clinical Psychology*, April 1992, p. 293.

Presents a study exploring specific aspects of the bulimic's social network and interpersonal relationships as well as individual difference variables that might mediate her ability to obtain support or perceive this as adequate. The impaired relationship between bulimics and their environment; factors in the onset and perpetuation of bulimia; method; results; discussion.

Hudson, J. & H.G. Pope, "Is childhood sexual abuse a risk factor for bulimia nervosa?" *American Journal of Psychiatry*, April 1992, p. 455.

Reviews scientific literature bearing on bulimia nervosa in order to assess whether childhood sexual abuse is a risk factor for the development of the condition. Controlled retrospective studies comparing the prevalence of childhood sexual abuse among bulimic and control groups; studies of the prevalence of childhood sexual abuse in the general population; current evidence does not support sexual abuse as a risk factor for bulimia nervosa.

Jones, K.H. & K.L. Nagel, "Sociological factors in the development of eating disorders," *Adolescence*, spring 1992, p. 107.

Reviews the sociocultural, socioeconomic and sex-related factors that contribute to the development of eating disorders. Sex-role stereotyping; sex-role orientation; race characteristics; conclusion.

Larson, B.J., "Relationship of family communication patterns to eating disorder inventory scores," *Journal of the American Dietetic Association*, September 1991, p. 1065.

Attempts to identify risk factors for the development of the psychological and behavior traits associated with eating disorders. Methods; results; discussion; recommendations.

Melby, C.L., J.P. Sciacca, et al., "Body mass index and perceived weight status in young adults," *Journal of Community Health*, June 1991, p. 159.

Discusses the relationship between perception of overweight and the eating disorders anorexia nervosa and bulimia and presents a study of self-reported height and weight for 1,123 university students. Comparison of self-reported height and weight and actual height and weight; gender differences in weight perceptions of study participants; Body Mass Index (BMI); method; results; discussion.

Smith, J.M., "Hypophosphataemia, delerium and cardiac arrhythmia in anorexia nervosa," *Journal of the American Medical Association*, Jan. 1, 1992, p. 37.

Discusses the occurrence of hypophosphataemia in anorexia nervosa and suggests that it may be a factor in contributing to cardiac arrhythmia, which is a potentially fatal complication. Presents results of a retrospective study of adolescent girls or young women ages 14 to 31.

Talan, J., "Mothers and eating disorders," *American Health*, March 1992, p. 119.

Reports that a mother's behavior can influence her daughter's development of a serious eating disorder, according to psychologists at Yale University. Families with histories of dieting problems; mothers critical of daughters' appearance; bulimia and anorexia may be influenced by chemical imbalances.

Warsen, J., "Bulimia and light," *American Health,* January/February 1992, p. 40.

Contends that there may be a connection between seasonal affective disorder (SAD) and bulimia. Role of the brain chemical serotonin; tips for people with seasonal bulimic tendencies.

Wise, D., "Fat and fiction," *Mademoiselle,* January 1992, p. 42.

Discusses a University of Michigan study into the behavior of women with severe eating disorders. The study found that women with anorexia nervosa and bulimia engage in pathological daydreaming and other dissociative behavior, deluding themselves into thinking that they are obese.

Research

Bell, B., S. Reed, et al., "The weight-control urge that can kill," *People,* Aug. 3, 1992, p. 64.

Presents the stories of three ordinary women who were afflicted with bulimia. Tells how they have worked to conquer the disease. INSET: A debilitating obsession that doesn't spare celebs (famous previous bulimics); an expert confronts the complex challenges of bulimia nervosa (excerpts of interview with Dr. Katherine Halmi).

Christopher, F. & C. S. Johnston, "Multivariate analysis of the eating disorders inventory," *Journal of the American Dietetic Association,* May 1992, p. 605.

Discusses the results of a multivariate analysis of the Eating Disorders Inventory (EDI) by examining basic statistical assumptions. EDI commonly used to trace individuals with conditions of anorexia nervosa or bulimia; methods; results; conclusions and applications; more.

Comer, J., "Eating disorders," *Parents,* April 1992, p. 240.

Discusses two common eating disorders, anorexia nervosa and bulimia, and how they affect young people. Looks at the health risks of the disorders and where to get help. Summarizes common characteristics of sufferers.

Dunkin, A. & D. Dunn, "When thinness becomes illness," *Business Week,* Aug. 3, 1992, p. 74.

Discusses how about 11 million women and 1 million men in the United States suffer from one of two conditions that physicians classify as eating disorders. Unnatural slimness can seriously harm physical and mental health. Bulimia nervosa; anorexia nervosa; influenced by slender people on television; problem profile and danger signs; where to get aid.

Irwin, C., L. Mellin, et al., "Prevalence of disordered eating in girls: A survey of middle-class children," *Journal of the American Dietetic Association,* July 1992, p. 851.

Discusses a survey of middle-class children in which the prevalence of disordered eating habits in girls was studied. Methods; subjects and data collection; data analyses and results; discussion and implications; more.

McDonald, K., "Research notes: Scientists link high levels of chemical vasopressin to bulimia nervosa," *Chronicle of Higher Education,* April 15, 1992, p. A8.

Considers an article in *Journal of Clinical Endocrinology and Metabolism,* which states scientists have identified a chemical that is found in abnormally high levels in the brains of women with bulimia nervosa, an eating disorder that affects from 2 to 5 percent of adolescent and young women. Research by Mark A. Demitrack (University of Michigan) and colleagues (National Institute of Mental Health); chemical vasopressin in the cerebrospinal fluid.

Rader, W.C., "Adolescents and eating disorders," *Addiction & Recovery,* January/February 1992, p. 23.

Offers a look at teenage eating disorders. Statistics; obsession with weight loss; dangerous practices; the counselor's role; bulimia; details; concluding thought.

Therapy

Erickson, D., "Brain, food," *Scientific American,* November 1991, p. 90.

Reports that drugs based on neuropeptides may soon treat eating disorders. Reasons why obesity is now being examined as a treatable biochemical imbalance; some of the brain chemicals that control eating; attempts of scientists to predict eating disorder tendencies.

Farley, D., "Eating disorders require medical attention," *FDA Consumer,* March 1992, p. 27.

Focuses on the behavior and treatment of the eating disorders bulimia and anorexia nervosa. The life-threatening nature of these disorders; estimates on the incidence of these disorders from the National Center for Health Statistics (NCHS); symptoms; Jane Fonda and bulimia; Karen Carpenter and anorexia; studies of anti-depressants for the treatment of eating disorders; addresses and phone numbers for more information.

Hill, L., "Fairy tales: Visions for problem resolution in eating disorders," *Journal of Counseling & Development,* May/June 1992, p. 584.

Introduces a framework that uses fairy tales as a vision-to-action treatment alternative for psychological dysfunctions focusing on eating disorders. The treatment model; conclusion.

Back Issues

Great Research on Current Issues Starts Right Here... Recent topics covered by The CQ Researcher are listed below. Before May 1991, reports were published under the name of Editorial Research Reports.

JUNE 1991
Children and Divorce
Teenage Suicide
Endangered Species
Europe 1992

JULY 1991
Teenagers and Abortion
Soviet Republics Rebel
Mexico's Emergence
Athletes and Drugs

AUGUST 1991
Sexual Harassment
Fetal Tissue Research
Oil Imports
The Palestinians

SEPTEMBER 1991
Police Brutality
Advertising Under Attack
Saving the Forests
Foster Care Crisis

OCTOBER 1991
Pay-Per-View TV
Youth Gangs
Gene Therapy
World Hunger

NOVEMBER 1991
Fast-Food Shake-Up
The Greening of Eastern Europe
Business' Role in Education
Cuba In Crisis

DECEMBER 1991
Retiree Health Benefits
Asian Americans
The Obscenity Debate
The Disabilities Act

JANUARY 1992
Term Limits
Oil Spills
Hunting Controversy
Alternative Medicine

FEBRUARY 1992
Threatened Coastlines
New Era in Asia
Assisted Suicide
Jobs in the '90s

MARCH 1992
Women and Sports
Underage Drinking
Garbage Crisis
Mafia Crackdown

APRIL 1992
Ozone Depletion
Welfare Reform
Politicians and Privacy
Illegal Immigration

MAY 1992
Native Americans
Jobs vs. Environment
Too Many Lawsuits?
Fairness in Salaries

JUNE 1992
Nuclear Proliferation
Food Irradiation
Lead Poisoning
Hard Times for Libraries

JULY 1992
Alternative Energy
Prescription Drug Prices
Alzheimer's Disease
Infant Mortality

AUGUST 1992
The Homeless
Work, Family and Stress
NATO's Changing Role
Marine Mammals vs. Fish

SEPTEMBER 1992
Domestic Partners
Violence in Schools
Public Broadcasting
Women in the Military

OCTOBER 1992
Depression
U.S. Auto Industry
Youth Apprenticeships
Hispanic Americans

NOVEMBER 1992
Physical Fitness
Privatization
Paying for College
U.S. Policy in Asia

DECEMBER 1992
Crackdown on Smoking
The New CIA

Future Topics

▶ *Women and AIDS*

▶ *Hate Crimes*

▶ *Child Sexual Abuse*

THE CQ Researcher

PUBLISHED BY CONGRESSIONAL QUARTERLY INC., IN CONJUNCTION WITH EBSCO PUBLISHING

Women and AIDS

Are women becoming the main victims of AIDS?

S INCE ITS MYSTERIOUS APPEARANCE 11 YEARS ago, the virus that causes AIDS has infected more than 11 million people around the world — and 2 million victims have already died. In sub-Saharan Africa, where the disease probably originated, acquired immune deficiency syndrome was spread mainly through heterosexual contact, affecting men and women in equal proportions. In the United States, most victims initially were male homosexuals. Now, women constitute the fastest-growing category of U.S. AIDS sufferers. Yet because earlier research and treatment focused on adult males, the virus in women frequently goes unrecognized until it's too late for treatment. The rapid spread of AIDS among women and children means that many more Americans than previously thought are at risk of contracting the virus.

C Q | **December 25, 1992 • Volume 2, No. 48 • 1121-1144**

Formerly Editorial Research Reports

WOMEN AND AIDS

COVER: ELIZABETH GLASER (TOP PHOTO) BY JUDY LAWNE; MARY FISHER BY R. MICHAEL JENKINS

CQ Researcher

December 25, 1992
Volume 2, No. 48

EDITOR
Sandra Stencel

MANAGING EDITOR
Thomas J. Colin

ASSOCIATE EDITOR
Richard L. Worsnop

STAFF WRITERS
Charles S. Clark
Mary H. Cooper
Rodman D. Griffin

PRODUCTION EDITOR
Sarah E. Merritt

EDITORIAL ASSISTANT
Michael M. Taylor

GRAPHICS
Jack Auldridge

PUBLISHED BY
Congressional Quarterly Inc.

CHAIRMAN
Andrew Barnes

VICE CHAIRMAN
Andrew P. Corty

EDITOR AND PUBLISHER
Neil Skene

EXECUTIVE EDITOR
Robert W. Merry

ASSOCIATE PUBLISHER
John J. Coyle

EDITOR, EBSCO PUBLISHING
Melissa Kummerer

The CQ Researcher (ISSN 1056-2036). Formerly Editorial Research Reports. Published weekly (48 times per year, not printed the first Friday of any month with five Fridays) by Congressional Quarterly Inc., 1414 22nd St., N.W., Washington, D.C. 20037. Rates are furnished upon request. Second-class postage paid at Washington, D.C. POSTMASTER: Send address changes to The CQ Researcher, 1414 22nd St., N.W., Washington, D.C. 20037.

Women and AIDS

By Mary H. Cooper

The Issues

There was an air of electric expectancy at the Democratic National Convention last July as Elizabeth Glaser stepped to the podium. Eleven years into the AIDS epidemic, it was the first time a national political party had given such visible attention to the problem of AIDS. Elizabeth Glaser has the AIDS virus.

Glaser stunned the raucous convention hall into silence with her harrowing account of contracting the human immunodeficiency virus (HIV) through a transfusion of tainted blood following the birth of her daughter Ariel in 1981. She told how she unknowingly passed the virus on to her nursing infant and then, three years later, to a son, Jake, who contracted HIV before birth.

It was not until 1986, a year after Ariel developed full-blown AIDS, that Glaser learned what had happened. Ariel died in 1988 at age 7, and shortly afterwards Glaser and two friends founded the Pediatric AIDS Foundation to fund research and increase public awareness of the disease. *(See story, p. 1130.)*

A month after Glaser's dramatic appearance in New York,* Mary D. Fisher, the daughter of a prominent Republican fund-raiser, evoked similar emotions as she told her party's convention in Houston how she learned she was HIV-positive. The divorced mother of two uninfected sons, Fisher learned from a blood test that she had contracted the virus from her former husband.

At a time when many Americans still identify AIDS as a disease of gay men, Elizabeth Glaser and Mary Fisher represent the new faces of the spreading

---

*Robert Hattoy, who has AIDS, also addressed the Democratic National Convention.

epidemic. During the first seven months of 1992, the World Health Organization (WHO) estimates, 1 million adults contracted HIV, almost half of them women. In the United States alone, women accounted for 25,947 cases, or 11 percent of all AIDS cases reported through September. But AIDS is claiming women faster than men today: During 1991, the number of women with AIDS increased by 14.4 percent, compared with a 4.8 percent increase among men. And WHO warns that by the turn of the century more than half the world's new AIDS cases will be women.

The growing incidence of AIDS among American women does not surprise scientists who study the global course of the disease. "Worldwide, this is mainly a heterosexually transmitted disease, so women are clearly at risk," says Jonathan M. Mann, a professor of epidemiology and international health at Harvard University's School of Public Health. Mann, who was the founding director of WHO's Global Program on AIDS, says international health statis-

tics prove his point.

About 10 million to 12 million adults and 1 million children have contracted HIV since the beginning of the AIDS pandemic, so called by WHO because AIDS affects virtually every region of the globe. Yet the true dimensions of HIV infection are unknown. Unlike most viral diseases, which produce symptoms shortly after entering the body, HIV can remain latent for many years before its damage to the body's immune system makes the victim increasingly vulnerable to "opportunistic diseases," such as pneumonia and cancer, that manifest full-blown AIDS. More than 2 million of the 11 million to 13 million infected people have developed AIDS, and most of them have already died.

In the United States, the first cases of AIDS were officially diagnosed on June 5, 1981, in five young homosexual men. Eight years later, in September 1989, the total number of diagnosed AIDS cases in the United States reached 100,000. After that, it took just over two years for that number to double, reaching 200,000 cases in November 1991. By the end of 1992, more than 230,000 AIDS cases had been reported in the United States. Of these, about 152,000 have died.

A decade ago, men probably accounted for two-thirds of the adults infected with HIV, WHO reports. The proportion was even higher in the United States, Europe and parts of Latin America, where homosexual transmission, primarily by anal intercourse, was the main way the virus spread. The second most frequent route of transmission early in the pandemic was needle-sharing among users of injection drugs such as heroin. Because HIV is present in the blood, the virus can contaminate needles and syringes and infect any person who uses them without carefully cleaning them after each injection. Most injection drug users are

The Rapid Spread of AIDS

AIDS has been spreading more rapidly in the latter stages of the epidemic. From 1981 to 1989, the first 100,000 cases in the United States were reported to the Centers for Disease Control. From September 1989 through November 1991, a second 100,000 cases were reported.

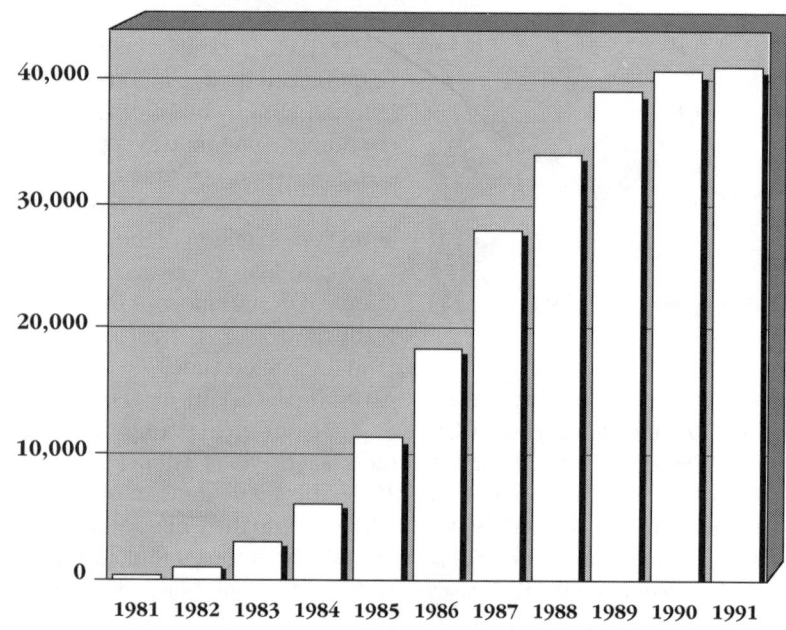

**Annual AIDS cases by year of report
United States, 1981-1991**

Source: Centers for Disease Control and Prevention, "Morbidity and Mortality Weekly Report," Jan. 17, 1992

men, further skewing the incidence of HIV infection among adult males early in the pandemic.

But heterosexual transmission of HIV, which occurs when an infected person infects a sex partner during intercourse, steadily increased in frequency over the decade. It is now clear that women are more vulnerable than men to HIV infection through heterosexual contact for two reasons. First, because most HIV-positive people currently are men, women are more likely than men to encounter an infected sex partner. Secondly, women are biologi-

cally more susceptible than men to infection through heterosexual intercourse because the virus enters the body more easily through mucosal tissues, such as the lining of the vagina, than through skin.

In the United States, gay men continue to get AIDS more than any other group, accounting for 58 percent of new cases reported. Injection drug users account for an additional 23 percent. Women, who account for 11 percent of U.S. AIDS victims today, are the fastest-growing group of AIDS cases.

In some areas, WHO's dire predictions about increasing AIDS cases among women are already close at hand: In Newark, N.J., fully 35 percent of the AIDS sufferers today are women, and a much larger percentage of HIV-positive people are assumed to be women, according to Marion Banzhaf, coordinator of the New Jersey Women and AIDS Network. "We're already seeing here [in Newark] the prediction that by the year 2000 the number of men and women around the world infected with HIV will be equal."

The sudden onslaught of HIV disease among women has left many sufferers without adequate care. Because health-care providers often fail to recognize the risk of HIV outside the gay community, symptoms of infection that are identified readily in men pass untreated in women at early stages of the disease. That's the stage when treatment with AZT and ddI, the two chief anti-HIV drugs, are most effective at delaying the course toward full-blown AIDS. Therefore, the disease generally progresses further in women before diagnosis. As a result, women die faster of AIDS than men. The average time between an AIDS diagnosis and death in women is less than 10 months, compared with just over a year in men.

As more women contract HIV, so too do more children. That's because most HIV-positive women are of childbearing age and because the virus can pass from mother to fetus before birth. About one infant in three who is born to an HIV-positive mother will also be infected. In the United States, an estimated 20,000 children are currently infected with the virus, and each year as many as 2,000 babies are born HIV-positive.

Although Elizabeth Glaser and Mary Fisher represent two new faces of HIV infection in the United States, they are far from typical. White, affluent women are only a small percentage of HIV-positive women. Most are black or Hispanic, and fully half are injection drug users.

Mann says the prevalence of HIV among these women in the United States is part of a global pattern. "Women and children are the two groups that are most discriminated against around the world," he says. "Once one understands that the major condition that fuels the spread of the virus is discrimination against people who are marginalized or stigmatized or out of the mainstream, the increased vulnerability and risk to women becomes straightforward."

In the United States, federal research and treatment efforts in the fight against AIDS are beginning to respond to demands for greater recognition of the disease's spread among women. The federal Centers for Disease Control and Prevention (CDC), which tracks epidemics, recently added three conditions to the list of 23 that it uses to define the onset of AIDS *(see p. 1132)*. The change, due to take effect Jan. 1, is expected to greatly increase the number of confirmed AIDS cases among women and make it easier for them to obtain treatment and disability benefits.

The increasing number of AIDS cases among women has overwhelmed the public health services they require. To help meet their needs, support groups have sprung up around the country to help HIV-positive women, especially the drug users and impoverished who make up the majority of infected women. Their services include directing infected women to clinical drug trials and treatment facilities, finding housing for evicted women and their children and helping victims obtain disability benefits from the Social Security Administration.

Prevention, of course, is the ultimate goal in the fight against AIDS. But it is also the most elusive because it entails changing personal behavior. *(See story, p. 1135.)* Most educational programs focus on the need to use condoms to prevent the spread of HIV, but women find this

problematical because men dislike using them.

"When we talk about teaching women to negotiate condom use, we're really going to the heart of some of the most basic levels of sexism in our society," says Kathleen Stoll, director of the National Resource Center on Women and AIDS, a project of the Center for Women Policy Studies in Washington. She and other activists call for more research on an anti-HIV virucide that a woman could use on her own.

There is much about the AIDS virus, especially as it affects women, that remains unknown. What is clear is that there is great demand for increased AIDS prevention and treatment services. "People's attitudes change slowly without really powerful leadership," says Glaser. "Not until people's lives are directly affected, and it's too late, do they start to pay attention. That's the tragedy of the human condition."

Is a heterosexual woman who does not use injection drugs at high risk of contracting HIV?

In theory, when Mary Fisher addressed the Republican National Convention Aug. 19, she embodied the Republican Party platform's AIDS prevention techniques of "marital fidelity, abstinence and a drug-free lifestyle." But, the 44-year-old divorced mother of two young sons told the shocked audience, her former husband had infected her with HIV.

"If you believe you are safe, you are at risk," Fisher said. "If you do not see this killer stalking your children, look again. There is no family or community, no race or religion, no place left in America that is safe. Until we genuinely embrace this message, we are a nation at risk."

Fisher's personal story certainly confirms her warning. But while women are the fastest-growing group with HIV, some American women are far more vulnerable than others.

The overall statistics are indeed

alarming: The percentage of U.S. women with AIDS has almost doubled, from 6 percent in 1982 to 11 percent today. AIDS among women rose an astounding 37 percent last year alone, bringing the number of cases to more than 24,000. The CDC reports that over half of all women with AIDS have used injection drugs and probably contracted the virus when infected blood entered their bodies from dirty needles.

Even among non-drug users, the risk of contracting HIV is much higher among some heterosexual adults than others. Those with multiple sex partners, those who are monogamous but whose partners are at risk and those who receive blood transfusions are more vulnerable to infection, according to a recent study by the Center for AIDS Prevention Studies. People with multiple sex partners tend to be black or white (compared with Hispanic) men, unmarried, highly educated and young, the study found.[1]

Perhaps the best-known example of this profile is Earvin "Magic" Johnson, the former professional basketball player who announced in 1991 that he had contracted HIV, probably through multiple sexual encounters.

Women and low-income adults, the study found, are most likely to have "risky" sexual partners — people who inject drugs and have multiple partners. About 71 percent of these individuals — mainly women — with risky partners reported not using condoms. "The overrepresentation of women among respondents with risky partners who were not using condoms may reflect relationships in which women feel powerless to . . . insist on protective actions that would prevent HIV transmission," the study concluded.[2]

Activists who work with HIV-positive women confirm these epidemiological data and say that prevention counseling that emphasizes condom use is often ineffective, and can even backfire. "I can give a woman a condom and then have her husband come

Trends in Reported AIDS Cases

The second 100,000 cases of AIDS reflected a drop in cases caused by homo-sexual/bisexual contact and a rise in cases caused by injection drug use and heterosexual contact (top graph); a rise in the number of females infected (middle graph); and a rise in blacks and Hispanics affected (bottom graph).

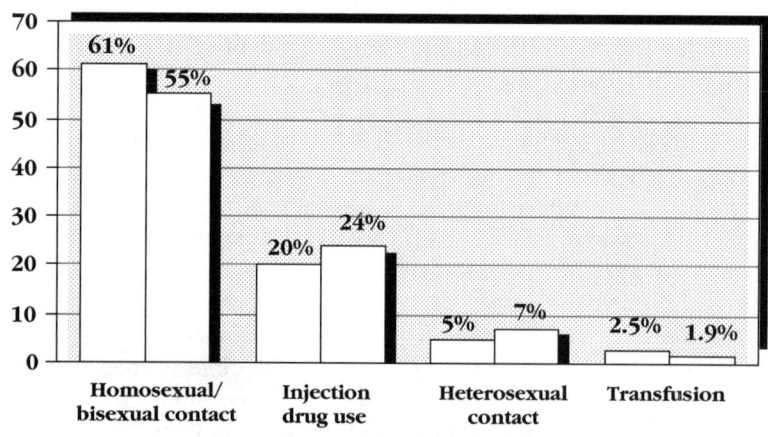

By risk category (adults)

Homosexual/bisexual contact: 61%, 55%
Injection drug use: 20%, 24%
Heterosexual contact: 5%, 7%
Transfusion: 2.5%, 1.9%

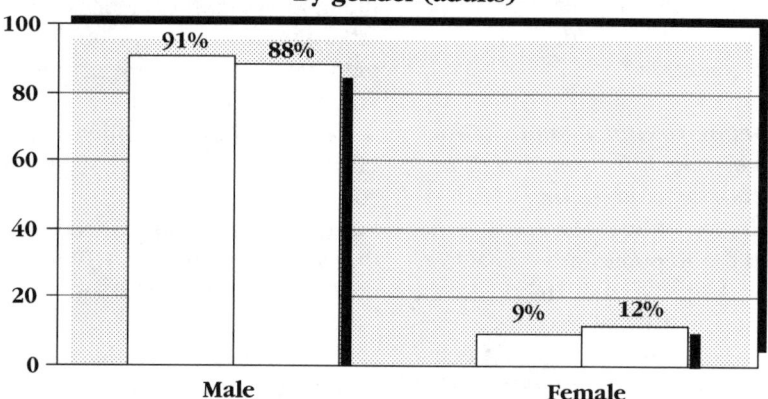

By gender (adults)

Male: 91%, 88%
Female: 9%, 12%

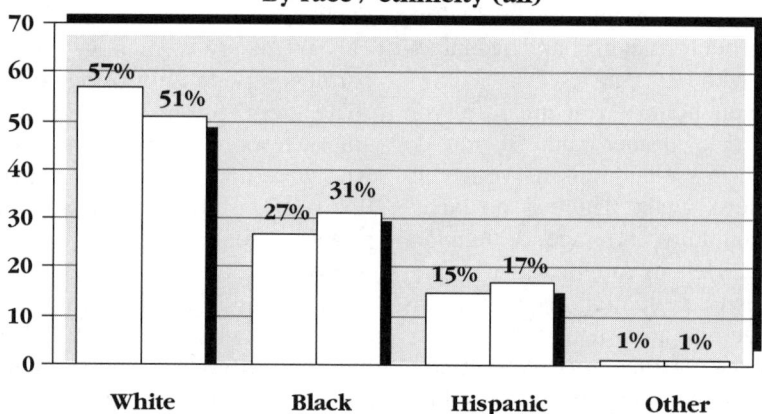

By race / ethnicity (all)

White: 57%, 51%
Black: 27%, 31%
Hispanic: 15%, 17%
Other: 1%, 1%

Source: Centers for Disease Control and Prevention, "HIV/AIDS Prevention Fact Book, 1992"

back here the next day with her," says Catherine Maier, who directs the San Francisco AIDS Fund's Women and Children's Services Program. "She has two black eyes. He tells me to stay out of their business and yells, 'I'm not go-ing to wear one of those damned things, and you can't make me.' "

Maier also confirms that heterosex-ual transmission of HIV has increased among the women she serves in the seven-year-old program — the oldest in the country helping HIV-positive women — because the social and economic problems they face often make it hard to pin down the source of HIV infection.

"We see many women who have had transfusions because of violent crimes committed against them or following a difficult childbirth, who are also injection drug users and may have a partner who is a drug user," she says.

For the vast majority of women who have never used injection drugs or re-ceived blood transfusions, virtually the only risk of contracting HIV is through heterosexual contact. But preventing exposure to the virus from a sex part-ner is far from easy for many women. Because the average AIDS latency peri-od — the time between infection and the onset of recognizable disease symptoms — is about 10 years, a wom-an with no other risk factors must have been in a mutually monogamous rela-tionship for at least a decade to be safe from HIV.

But even after a decade of monoga-my, a woman can't be sure about her sexual partner. "We call this the Mary Fisher syndrome — when you do everything exactly by the book and can still be infected," says Olga Grinstead, a clinical psychologist at the Cen-ter for AIDS Prevention Studies in San Francisco.

"What we're finding is that women of all different ethnicities and all differ-ent ages and varieties, married women and single women, are at risk for the AIDS virus."

Does attention to HIV in women and children detract from efforts to prevent and treat the disease among gay men, the main victims of AIDS?

The overwhelming consensus among scientists and activists is that HIV is spreading among women and children much faster than funding for research, treatment and support services to meet their needs. Because HIV is growing fastest among women, and probably will continue to do so for some time, funding for women's programs is unlikely to be adequate in the foreseeable future, especially at a time of concern over federal budget deficits.

But organizations representing gay men have balked at efforts to channel funds toward research on AIDS in other population groups, especially children, who account for only 4,000 of the nation's 230,000 AIDS patients. They became increasingly critical after the Los Angeles-based Pediatric AIDS Foundation successfully lobbied Congress to require the National Institutes of Health (NIH) to spend $22 million for pediatric research in 1991. To fulfill the lawmakers' mandate, NIH took $11 million out of existing programs testing AIDS drugs for adults.

Today, NIH budgets $44 million to support 24 separate sites for pediatric AIDS research and $75 million to fund research for adult AIDS victims at 35 sites. "Adult sites have lots of patients but no money," says Mark Harrington, an activist with the Treatment Action group in New York City. "Pediatrics have tons of money but no patients."[3]

Glaser defends her organization's efforts to get increased funding to combat pediatric AIDS, saying she never intended to have NIH plunder budgets for other AIDS programs. Indeed, Glaser says, funding disputes among various groups representing AIDS victims hurt them all in the end and only play into the hands of those who want to cut the federal budget

even at the expense of programs to help fight AIDS.

"I've always thought that competition for funding was part of the divide-and-conquer theory, that if you can get all the pieces of the AIDS war fighting against each other, feeling that they have to compete, then we don't have to move ahead for any of them," she says.

When her daughter fell ill with AIDS, Glaser explains, there was no research being done on pediatric AIDS, and drugs that were available to slow the onset of symptoms in adults, such as AZT, were not even administered to children. This lack prompted her to set up the foundation.

"Traditionally and historically, women and children are not paid attention to unless they find a way to have their voices be heard," Glaser says. "So it is important that as activists, as women, as

mothers, we keep this issue on the front burner but know that it's part of an overall effort." ∎

BACKGROUND

 **A Global Epidemic**

When the AIDS epidemic first emerged in Kenya during the 1970s, it was spread primarily through sexual contact, infecting women and men in roughly equal numbers. No one knows for sure where the virus came from. Current speculation places its origin in the rain forests of central Africa and points to man himself as its cause.

According to this view, HIV was probably confined to isolated popula-

---

How Men and Women Get AIDS

Homosexual contact accounted for 136,912 cases, or 65 percent, of the AIDS among adolescent and adult men in the United States through September 1992, while injection drug use caused 41,631 cases. Among women, injection drug use was the leading cause of AIDS, affecting 50 percent of all adult and adolescent females (12,844 cases), followed by 9,238 cases, or 36 percent, caused by heterosexual contact.

Male Exposure Category

Men who have sex with men	136,912 (65%)
Injection drug use	41,631 (20%)
Men who have sex with men and inject drugs	15,203 (7%)
Hemophilia/coagulation disorder	1,910 (1%)
Heterosexual contact	5,983 (3%)
Receipt of blood transfusion, blood component or tissue	2,956 (1%)
Other/undetermined	7,553 (4%)

Female Exposure Category

Injection drug use	12,844 (50%)
Hemophilia/coagulation disorder	43 (less than 1%)
Heterosexual contract	9,238 (36%)
Receipt of blood transfusion blood component or tissue	1,877 (7%)
Other/undetermined	1,945 (7%)

Source: Centers for Disease Control and Prevention, "HIV/AIDS Surveillance," October 1992

tions of chimpanzees or even humans and entered the global population as outsiders penetrated the wilderness. "Unknown viruses are coming out of the equatorial wildernesses of the earth and discovering the human race," writes Richard Preston. "It seems to be happening as a result of the destruction of tropical habitats. You might call AIDS the revenge of the rain forest."[4]

The nature of the AIDS virus made it an ideal candidate for the pandemic it then unleashed. For one thing, the virus has a long latency period, allowing it to go unnoticed in an infected human, who can unwittingly spread it to many others. Another characteristic that favors the virus' survival is its route of transmission. Like other sexually transmitted agents, HIV passes from one host to another through sexual contact, an aspect of personal behavior over which public health authorities have virtually no control.

The ability of HIV to mutate also favors its spread. Because the outer protein coat of the virus can change rapidly, it can evade attempts by the body's immunological system to identify and destroy it. A similar ability has been observed among influenza virus strains, which mutate so quickly that new vaccines must be developed each year to help defend against infection.

A dozen years after AIDS was first recognized, the AIDS virus remains a mystery to scientists. Unable to uncover the mechanism by which HIV breaks down the body's immune system, leaving it open to "opportunistic diseases," researchers offer little hope of discovering a vaccine to prevent infection in the near future. Drugs that treat HIV infections prolong life by slowing the virus' destruction of the immune system. AIDS remains, however, a fatal disease.

The global spread of AIDS demonstrates the virus' extraordinary ability to survive. From central Africa, the disease spread quickly to other parts of sub-Saharan Africa. In much of the affected region, men from rural villages often travel to far cities for work. There

they become infected and in turn spread the disease into the countryside when they return home. About half the 1 million people in the world who contracted HIV in the first six months of 1992 live in sub-Saharan Africa.

AIDS initially spread quickly in North America and Europe through homosexual contact, primarily anal intercourse, which causes lesions in the skin and mucosa through which the virus readily enters the body. Exchanges of blood through the use of dirty needles also spread HIV among injection-drug users on both continents. Although AIDS came later to much of Latin America and the Caribbean, today the disease is spreading faster there than in other parts of the Western Hemisphere.

The epidemic has only recently spread significantly in Asia. As in Africa, parts of Asia have seen an explosion of HIV infection from heterosexual contact. In India and especially Thailand, which has the region's leading sex trade, men who are infected by prostitutes often give the disease to their wives, who in turn can infect children during pregnancy.

In addition, a recent surge in heroin use has compounded the region's HIV incidence. The problem has been traced to increasing heroin exports from Burma, which have fueled an outbreak of AIDS in southern China along the route that smugglers follow to Pacific ports.

The 'Invisible Epidemic'

For years before media reports began drawing public attention to the problem of women and AIDS, the virus spread silently among women in what has been called the "invisible epidemic."

The first "official" case of AIDS in a woman was reported to the CDC in Atlanta in 1981, the same year that the disease was first described in gay men.

But many more women are thought to have had the disease at that time. In her recent book on women and AIDS, Gena Corea describes numerous reports by clergy members and social workers of women drug users and prison inmates who died of undiagnosed illnesses throughout the early 1980s, years of sparse media coverage of AIDS that focused almost exclusively on gay men.[5]

Government interest in AIDS was also narrowly focused. It was not until the first reports of death from AIDS among infants and recipients of transfusions in 1982 that Congress appropriated funds for AIDS research: a $2.6 million addition to the CDC budget. Early research into the causes and treatment of AIDS focused exclusively on men.

In 1985, media attention to the epidemic heightened with the AIDS death of actor Rock Hudson and the compelling saga of Ryan White, the HIV-positive hemophiliac from Indiana who had been barred from his high school. Widespread fear of AIDS sparked a campaign to inform the public that HIV could not be transmitted through such everyday contact as hugging, touching or eating from utensils used by infected individuals.

But still there was little mention of women's vulnerability to the virus through heterosexual contact. The first serious attention given to HIV-positive women was as transmitters of the virus to their children during pregnancy. (See story, p. 1133.)

The appearance in 1986 of crack, a cheap and potent form of cocaine, in American inner cities marked a grim turning point in the AIDS epidemic among women. "Dealers sell crack to young men, mostly men of color, and then the young men offer it to young women because it is a hypersexual drug," explains Maier of the San Francisco AIDS Fund. "Then the young women get hooked and have unprotected sex around the clock

Continued on p. 1130

Chronology

1980s
The human immunodeficiency virus (HIV), thought to have originated in central Africa in the 1970s, infects some 10 million people worldwide; about 2 million victims will die in the first full decade of the AIDS epidemic.

June 5, 1981
A mysterious immune-system disorder is discovered in five young homosexual men and reported to the U.S. Centers for Disease Control (CDC). Cases presenting similar symptoms are reported in central Africa and other parts of the world. The same year, the first case of AIDS in an American woman is reported.

July 1982
U.S. health officials name the new disease acquired immune deficiency syndrome, or AIDS. The first cases among hemophiliacs are reported.

January 1983
The first confirmed cases of AIDS contracted from sexual partners are reported in two American women, expanding the known population at risk for AIDS to heterosexuals.

March 1983
U.S. blood banks begin to ask people who are at risk of AIDS infection to refrain from donating blood.

May 1983
Dr. Luc Montagnier and his colleagues at the Pasteur Institute in Paris report that they have isolated the virus that causes AIDS.

April 1984
Dr. Robert Gallo announces that his team at the U.S. National Cancer Institute has discovered a test to uncover the AIDS virus in blood.

September 1984
AIDS is reported for the first time in Thailand, where the HIV infection rate will later become among the highest in the world, due mainly to the country's unbridled sex industry.

March 1985
The first test to detect HIV infection gains approval in the United States. Screening for HIV in the nation's blood supply begins this year to prevent transmission via blood transfusions.

October 1985
Hollywood film star Rock Hudson dies of AIDS.

March 1987
The U.S. Food and Drug Administration approves experimental use in adults of Zidovudine, or AZT, the first drug shown to combat HIV.

August 1989
Eight years into the epidemic, the number of AIDS cases in the United States reaches 100,000.

---•---

1990s
The spread of AIDS accelerates to women and other groups that have gone unrecognized as being at risk for HIV infection. The World Health Organization predicts that by the end of the second decade of the AIDS epidemic as many as 18 million people will have contracted AIDS and that more than half the new cases will be in women.

April 1990
Ryan White, an 18-year-old hemophiliac, dies from AIDS, triggering support in Congress for legislation to funnel money to cities with high levels of the disease.

Sept. 10, 1990
The National Institutes of Health (NIH) creates the Office of Research on Women's Health in response to growing criticism over the lack of adequate research into women's health conditions and the exclusion of women from clinical studies.

October 1991
Basketball star Earvin "Magic" Johnson announces he is infected with the AIDS virus. The FDA approves ddI, a second drug to combat AIDS.

February 1991
The NIH issues a new policy requiring the inclusion of women and minorities in clinical research.

April 1991
Dr. Bernadine Healy becomes the first female director of NIH, an event that women's advocates hope will spur greater research into diseases that affect women, including AIDS. She announces the Women's Health Initiative, calling for a $500 million, 10-year study on breast cancer, osteoporosis and heart disease.

November 1991
The total number of AIDS cases reported to the CDC reaches 200,000, having doubled in just over two years.

June 1992
The FDA approves another drug, DDC, to combat AIDS.

The Legacy of Elizabeth Glaser

Elizabeth Glaser became infected with HIV in August 1981, when she received a transfusion of tainted blood following the birth of her daughter Ariel. In 1985, a year after Glaser had given birth to a son, Jake, Ariel mysteriously fell ill. When doctors finally examined the family, Glaser, Ariel and Jake all tested HIV-positive. Only Glaser's husband, actor Paul Michael Glaser, tested negative. Ariel, who had been infected by breast milk, died in August 1988 at age 7.

As Elizabeth Glaser learned, infection with HIV can be a double tragedy for women. Because many years may pass before AIDS symptoms appear, infected women who are pregnant often unknowingly spread the virus to their babies. An estimated 30 percent of all infants born to HIV-positive women are infected, having been exposed to the virus during fetal development. An unknown percentage of infants may also be infected from breast milk.

One of the most difficult aspects of her daughter's illness, Glaser recalls, was the utter lack of drug treatment for children with AIDS. "Most people didn't even know that kids got AIDS," she says. "Funding for research and clinical trials was very low. Drugs weren't available for children when they should have been. There was terrible discrimination."

Glaser found a positive outlet for her frustration and grief by establishing the Pediatric AIDS Foundation with two friends, Susan DeLaurentis and Susie Zeegen. The foundation's goal is educating the public about the incidence and treatment of HIV in children and increasing federal and private support for pediatric AIDS research. The foundation has distributed about $10 million in research funds in the past four years and successfully lobbied the NIH to fund pediatric AIDS research.

Thanks largely to the foundation's efforts, infected children can now participate in a number of clinical drug trials, and the two approved AIDS drugs for adults, AZT

Judy Lawne

and ddI, are now also available for pediatric use. The foundation has been so successful that some observers say that pediatric AIDS — which accounts for less than 2 percent of total AIDS cases — takes too much of the available research budget (*see p. 1127*).

Glaser counters this criticism by calling for more funding for all types of AIDS research. As evidence that more pediatric research is still needed, she cites the lack of a vaccine trial anywhere in the country that is open to children, while vaccine trials for adults have been running for three years. "People don't want to start testing drugs in children," she explains. "But when you have a life-threatening disease, and the child will die without treatment in two years, you have to become flexible."

In memory of Glaser's daughter, the Pediatric AIDS Foundation recently launched the Ariel Project, which is aimed at preventing the transmission of HIV from an infected mother to her newborn. "If we can do that, no new kids would be born with HIV," Glaser explains. Expected to cost $3-4 million a year over at least three years, the research project will collect data from physicians across the country, aided by funds from the Magic Johnson Foundation.

Unlike most AIDS research efforts, which receive funding, guidance and oversight from federal agencies, the Ariel Project is being run entirely by the Pediatric AIDS Foundation. Only when the data are collected will the project involve the NIH. "At this point, we prefer to coordinate it ourselves because we can move faster," Glaser explains. "Being part of a family that's infected and having lost a child and having another child who's infected, I feel we don't have any time to waste. We know that unfortunately and painfully first hand. That is a large focus of the foundation — to do things in a different way and make sure that they happen faster."

Continued from p. 1128
with multiple partners." Making matters worse, both men and women inject heroin to come down off the crack, so they can also contract HIV

through needle sharing.

Although injection drug use is recognized as the most common route of HIV transmission among women, the link between AIDS in women

and drug abuse still is not a widely recognized issue. "People don't talk about it because it's happening in the projects, and it's seen as another minority problem," Maier says.

HIV Infections Around the World

Since the AIDS pandemic began in 1981, an estimated 10-12 million people have been infected with the human immunodeficiency virus. The vast majority of the cases are in Africa, equally divided among men and women. In the United States, the AIDS virus mainly affects men, though the number of women becoming infected is increasing.

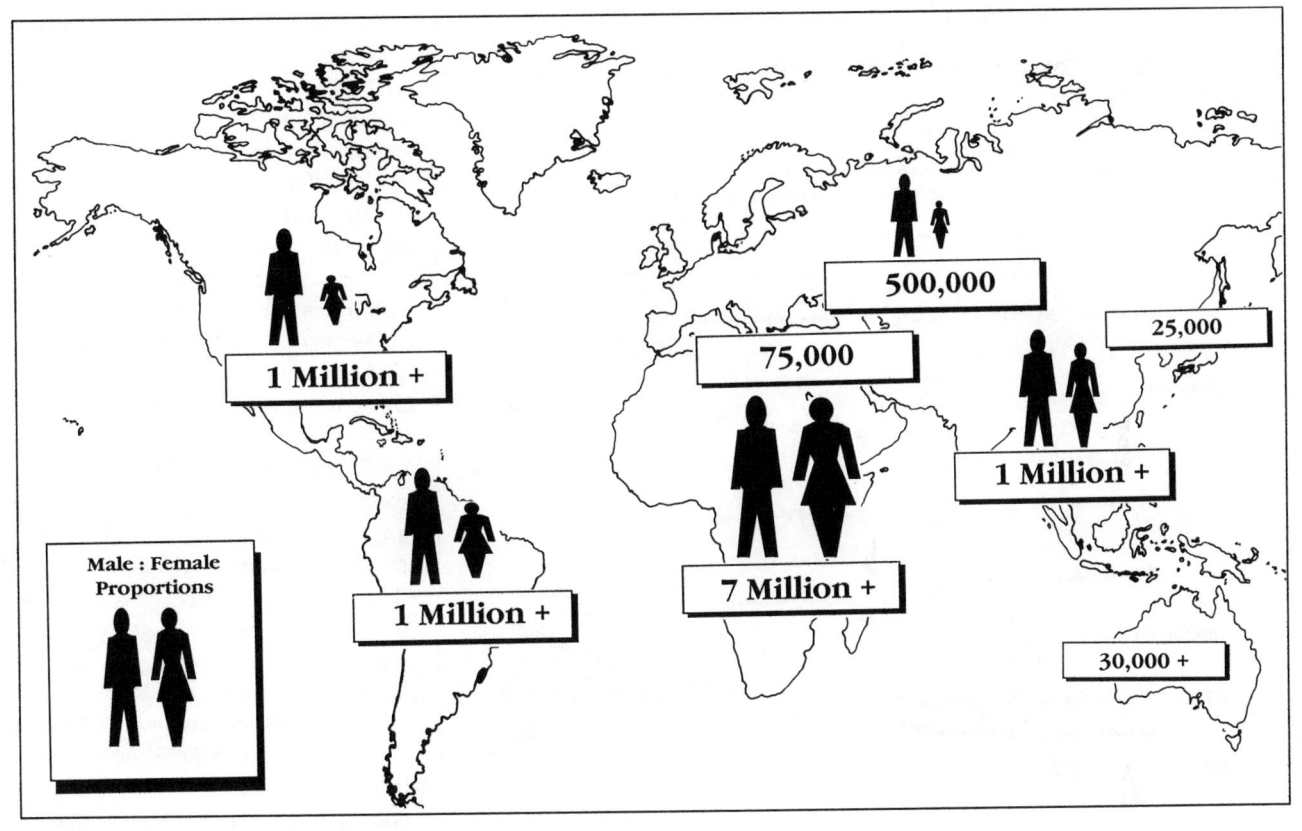

500,000

25,000

75,000

1 Million +

Male : Female
Proportions

1 Million +

7 Million +

1 Million +

30,000 +

Source: United Nations World Health Organization

Women's Participation in Clinical Trials

In 1987, the National Institute of Allergy and Infectious Diseases (NIAID) set up the AIDS Clinical Trials Group to coordinate federally funded testing of drugs to combat HIV. It was not until 1989, however, that women of childbearing age — the vast majority of HIV-positive women — were allowed to participate in these trials, which often offered the only way victims of the disease could obtain treatment.

The situation did not improve dramatically even after the restrictions were lifted. "Only 6 percent of the participants in all experimental trials done by the federal government in the AIDS Clinical Trial Group system have been women," says Marion Banzhaf of the New Jersey Women and AIDS Network. "Half of them were in one big trial to evaluate whether or not the dosage of AZT could be lowered. That means that only 3 percent of the women participants have been in trials to treat opportunistic infections."

Exclusion from clinical trials means that HIV-positive women are less likely to receive drugs such as AZT and ddI, which suppress the virus' destruction of the immune system and thus prolong the latency period before full-blown AIDS develops. Ignorance of the extent of HIV among women also leads health-care providers to ignore early signs of infection in women and thus delay treatment. As a result, women tend to be diagnosed with HIV much later than men, if at all. As many as 20 percent of the patients at the Newark Women's AIDS Clinic have died without a timely AIDS diagnosis, Banzhaf says.

Symptoms in Women

Because research into the natural history, or course, of HIV has focused on men, there is little informa-

Leading Causes of Death Among Women

Among women age 25-44, the death rate from AIDS and the HIV virus has been rising steadily since 1983, while other leading causes of death remain unchanged.

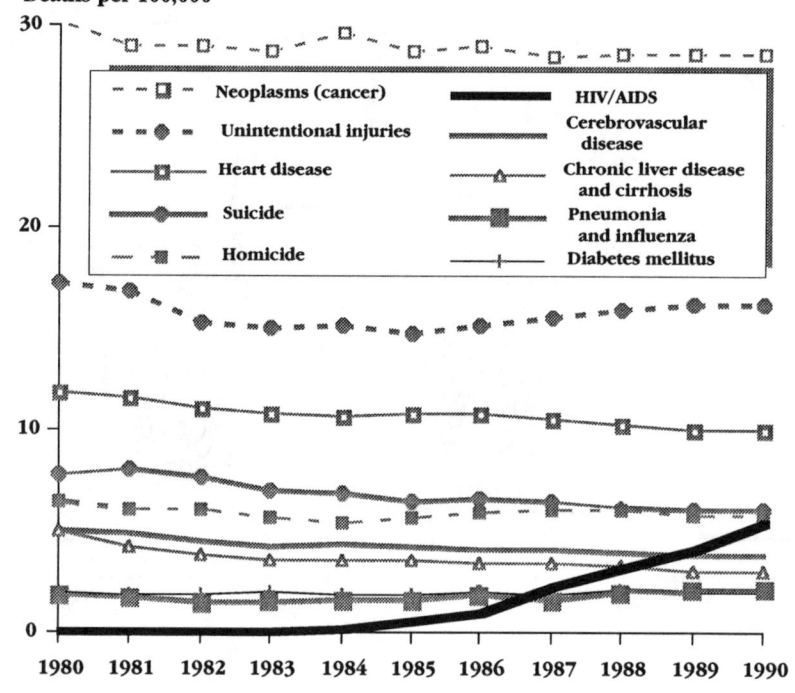

Leading Causes of Death Among Women 25-44
Deaths per 100,000

Legend:
- Neoplasms (cancer)
- Unintentional injuries
- Heart disease
- Suicide
- Homicide
- HIV/AIDS
- Cerebrovascular disease
- Chronic liver disease and cirrhosis
- Pneumonia and influenza
- Diabetes mellitus

Source: Centers for Disease Control and Prevention

mon infections more frequently than usual. This stage of the disease is sometimes called AIDS-Related Complex (ARC). Full-blown AIDS is said to occur when any of a number of more serious conditions occur. The CDC lists 23 so-called "opportunistic infections" whose presence in an HIV-positive individual indicates a diagnosis of AIDS.* Most of the 23 conditions that signal the onset of AIDS affect women as well as men, though some are much less common in women, such as Kaposi's sarcoma, a rare cancer that produces purplish splotches on the skin.

As of Jan. 1, 1993, the list of conditions that signal the onset of AIDS will include three additional diseases — invasive cervical cancer, pulmonary tuberculosis and recurrent pneumonia — that arise exclusively or frequently among women, as well as a lowering of CD4 cells, the protective immune system cells that HIV destroys. Levels of CD4 cells in the blood of 200 per cubic millimeter, or one-fifth the level of a healthy person, would prompt an AIDS diagnosis.

Before HIV-positive women actually come down with AIDS, they often suffer from numerous conditions that are not considered as AIDS-defining. These include endocarditis (inflammation of the

tion on how the virus behaves in women. Studies in men suggest that the latency period between infection and the onset of symptoms, for example, averages about 10 years, though some adults get AIDS after a much briefer period, while others have remained without symptoms for several years more than the average.

"The problem is, it's really hard to know when the infection actually occurred," says psychologist Olga Grinstead. "The other complicating factor is that women are often diagnosed very late in the disease, so it's even harder to determine the latency period in women."

Existing research data do suggest some difference in latency among different age groups. "It is known that AIDS comes more quickly in older people, and that most infants don't live very long," says Banzhaf. "But frankly, the NIH still hasn't even started a natural history study for women who have HIV, so we don't know how long the average latency period is in women."

People don't die directly of AIDS; rather, during the latency period the AIDS virus destroys the body's immune system, which protects it from many diseases. As a result, infected individuals often succumb to com-

*The 23 "opportunistic infections" that indicate a diagnosis of full-blown AIDS are: candidiasis of the bronchi, trachea or lungs; esophageal candidiasis; disseminated or extrapulmonary coccidioidomycosis; extrapulmonary cryptococcosis; chronic intestinal cryptosporidiosis of more than one month's duration; cytomegalovirus disease (other than the liver, spleen or nodes); cytomegalovirus retinitis with loss of vision; HIV encephalopathy; herpes simplex with chronic ulcer(s) of more than one month's duration, or bronchitis, pneumonitis or esophagitis; disseminated or extrapulmonary histoplasmosis; chronic intestinal isosporiasis of more than one month's duration; Kaposi's sarcoma; Burkitt's lymphoma; immunoblastic lymphoma; primary lymphoma in the brain; disseminated or extrapulmonary *Mycobacterium avium* complex or *M. kansasii*; disseminated or extrapulmonary *Mycobacterium tuberculosis*; disseminated or extrapulmonary *Mycobacterium* of other or unidentified species; *Pneumocystis carinii* pneumonia; progressive multifocal leukoencephalopathy; recurrent salmonella septicemia; toxoplasmosis of the brain; wasting syndrome due to HIV.

Common Illnesses of Women With HIV

Women infected with HIV often suffer more intense and more frequent gynecologic illnesses than non-infected women. Although relatively few cases of HIV infection are determined as a result of treatment for these conditions, AIDS activists urge physicians to consider any recurrent and drug-resistant gynecologic illness a red flag and to ask the patient if she has been tested for HIV.[†] Among the most common gynecologic illnesses associated with HIV infection are the following:

Sexually Transmitted Diseases (STDs): Genital herpes, chancroid, genital warts and syphilis cause ulcers, or sores, in the genital area that make it easier for the AIDS virus to enter the body. At the same time, these conditions also may be harder to treat in women already infected with HIV.

Pelvic Inflammatory Disease (PID): Comprising several inflammatory disorders of the upper genital tract in women, PID seems to occur more often and more severely in HIV-positive individuals than uninfected women, often requiring prolonged hospitalization and repeated surgery to treat abscesses.

Candidiasis: A common vaginal yeast infection that usually can be controlled with over-the-counter drugs in women without HIV, candidiasis can be crippling and drug-resistant in HIV-positive women, whose infection often spreads to the mouth, a condition called oral thrush. New or frequent recurrence of candidiasis is the most common clinical manifestation of HIV infection in women.

Cervical Dysplasia and Human Papilloma Virus (HPV): Pap smears, the commonly administered tests for cervical cancer, often show signs of dysplasia caused by infection with HPV in HIV-infected women. Two strains of HPV are thought to be the cause of most cervical cancers.

Finally, pregnancy presents special complications for women with HIV. Although there is no evidence that pregnancy changes the course of HIV disease in the United States, studies of women in Africa suggest that HIV-positive women are more likely than uninfected women to die in childbirth or suffer other complications. Some drugs used to treat HIV, such as zidovudine, may be toxic to the fetus.[††] About a third of all infants born to HIV-infected women contract the disease during fetal development, and an unknown percentage of infants may become infected while nursing.

[†] See "Me First! Medical Manifestations of HIV in Women," a pamphlet published by the New Jersey Women and AIDS Network.

[††] See Jeffrey Laurence, "Severe Manifestations of Common Disorders in Women," *The AIDS Reader*, September/October 1991, pp. 147-148.

---

heart lining); pulmonary tuberculosis; idiopathic thrombocytopenic purpura (low blood platelet count and bruising of unknown origin); kidney failure; and bacterial infections, including pneumonia, bronchitis, sinusitis and sepsis (bacterial blood infection).

Although research data are scarce on the course of the disease in women, several conditions are known to commonly affect women with full-blown AIDS.[6] The major conditions are:

• *Esophageal Candidiasis*: Caused by the same yeast infection that affects the mouth and the vagina, esophageal candidiasis frequently is the first AIDS-defining illness to appear in HIV-positive women and one of the most common opportunistic infections over the course of AIDS in women. The infection often begins in the mouth as oral thrush before spreading to the esophagus. It causes vomiting, weight loss and pain when swallowing. Prevention and treatment of vaginal yeast infections may help prevent this disease as well.

• *Wasting Syndrome*: This is the second most common AIDS-defining illness in women, and one that women are more than twice as likely to contract and die of as men. Symptoms include weight loss from a variety of causes, from infection to side effects of drugs taken to treat HIV. Treatment of wasting includes appetite stimulants and tube feeding.

"There is very little we've figured out to do with wasting syndrome," says Marion Banzhaf. "It has to do with the digestive system and the ability to retain nutrients, so conceivably treatment has to start when the patient is healthier to begin with to build up her diet and strength."

• *Invasive Cervical Cancer*: Due to be added to the list of AIDS-defining illnesses in January, cervical cancer is the most life-threatening gynecological condition that occurs more frequently in HIV-positive women than in uninfected women. Evidence suggests that HIV works with the human papilloma virus to accelerate the course of cervical cancer.

• *Pneumocystis carinii Pneumonia (PCP)*: This lung infection is the AIDS-defining opportunistic infection that is most often seen first in both men and women. Patients suffer from shortness of breath, dry cough and fever. Infection can be prevented in the vast majority of cases with sulfa drugs or sulfa alternatives.

• *Bacterial Pneumonia*: Recurrent pneumonia caused by a number of different bacteria affects about 10 percent of all AIDS patients. It is especially common — yet undiagnosed

— among HIV-positive women and injection drug users of both sexes. Pregnant women are especially vulnerable to bacterial pneumonia and may be even more susceptible if infected with the AIDS virus. Symptoms include chest pain, wet cough and fever. Some forms of the disease are easily treated with oral antibiotics, while others can lead to fatal complications. Pneumococcal and influenza vaccines and immunoglobulin therapy may be effective preventive measures in HIV-infected people with low CD4 cell counts.

• *Mycobacterium avium-intracellulare Complex (MAC)*: This life-threatening AIDS-defining illness tends to occur late in the course of AIDS, when CD4 cell counts plummet. It is caused by a combination of fungal and bacterial organisms that produce fever, diarrhea, anemia, weight loss and diseases of the liver, lungs, intestines, adrenal glands and bone marrow. MAC is easily confused with other complications of AIDS in women, such as severe anemia, liver damage and wasting from other causes. Clarithromycin and rifbutin may offer some hope to patients with this hard-to-treat condition.

• *Tuberculosis (TB)*: TB has reemerged as a major killer of HIV-infected people. Pulmonary TB, localized in the lungs, is easily spread when an infected person coughs or sneezes. An AIDS-defining form of the disease, disseminated, or widespread TB, affects the central nervous system, liver, reproductive organs, lymph nodes, adrenal glands, heart and skin, but is not highly contagious. Symptoms of both forms include fever, cough and chest pain.

Unlike many other opportunistic infections, TB can infect HIV-positive individuals with relatively high CD4 cell counts. TB is especially common in urban areas and in poorly ventilated environments, such as homeless shelters, substandard housing, prisons and hospitals, where many HIV-positive women are found. Most

forms of TB respond readily to antibiotics, but successful treatment often requires multiple doses administered regularly over long periods of time, often a year or more.* Such a regimen often proves hard to follow for injection drug users and impoverished women — the majority of HIV-positive women.

A final gender difference in the course of AIDS is the time of survival

---

*Failure to complete drug treatment for an initial episode of TB can result in resistance to later drug therapy. As the disease has spread among the poor, minority populations, injection drug users and people with HIV, multiple drug-resistant strains of TB have erupted in some urban areas, especially in New York and Florida. These virulent forms of TB are becoming an increasingly common cause of death among AIDS victims, including women.

---

from diagnosis of AIDS until death. Women in general die much sooner after an AIDS diagnosis than men. According to one study, men lived for an average 374 days, women for only 298 days, a 20 percent difference.[7] But no physiological reason has been found for women's accelerated decline from AIDS, researchers insist. Rather, HIV-infected women tend more often than men with the disease to be black or Hispanic, poor, injection drugs users and without access to health care. "Women die faster when they have little or no access to testing or when they do not receive the same standard treatment and care as men do upon entry into the health-care system," concludes a report in *World*, a California newsletter for women with HIV.[8] ∎

CURRENT SITUATION

Need for Education

A cure for AIDS or even a vaccine against infection both seem unlikely to become available for years. That means the only way to prevent the spread of AIDS is by changing personal behavior. To guard against sexually transmitted HIV, adolescents and adults can abstain from intercourse, maintain a mutually monogamous sexual relationship or use latex condoms — the only ones impermeable to the HIV virus — when engaging in sexual relations with partners whose HIV status is unknown. Where drug treatment is unavailable or ineffective, injection drug users can reduce their risk of AIDS by using clean needles.

These protective steps have been the centerpiece of AIDS education programs for more than a decade. There is some evidence that the message has had some effect. Thanks to

school programs across the country, the high number of teenagers engaging in risky sex is dropping, the CDC announced on Nov. 19. The proportion of students in grades 9 through 12 who said they had had sexual intercourse fell slightly from 1989 to 1992, the agency reported. Fewer reported having had two or more sexual partners, and almost half said they used condoms. Nonetheless, the incidence of AIDS among teenagers, while still low, increased by 77 percent, to 9,000 cases, over the last two years, according to a congressional study that called for more federal efforts to prevent the spread of AIDS among teens.[9]

But the message about protection is falling on deaf ears among other vulnerable members of the population. Almost a third of gay men surveyed in smaller U.S. cities reported engaging in unprotected anal intercourse with multiple partners, placing them at high risk for HIV infection, according to one study.[10] The findings suggest that educational efforts aimed at homosexual men are not reaching populations outside big cities like San Francisco and

How Women Can Protect Themselves from AIDS

Women can get AIDS by sharing intravenous needles with a person who is infected with the AIDS virus, by having intimate sexual contact with an infected person and by coming in contact with HIV-contaminated blood. The National Women's Health Network suggests that women take the following steps to protect themselves from getting AIDS:

• Always use both a condom and the spermicide nonoxynol 9 when having sexual intercourse. The spermicide is sold in contraceptive foams, jellies and creams and kills the AIDS virus on contact.

• Use a latex condom for vaginal and oral sex. The AIDS virus cannot penetrate a latex condom when it is properly used and does not break.

• Never have anal intercourse. Condoms are more likely to break, and the delicate rectal tissue is more likely to tear, increasing the risk of infection.

• Don't allow your sex partner's semen, urine, feces or blood to enter your body unless you know he is not infected. There are very few cases of woman-to-woman transmission. Because it is unknown whether vaginal secretions may contain HIV, some lesbians use latex barriers during oral sex and menstrual periods.

• Do not use intravenous drugs. If you do, never use a needle someone else has used.

• Ask each sex partner questions about past sexual history and drug use. People who have used intravenous drugs or had a sexually transmitted disease are at higher risk of carrying the AIDS virus.

• Take every precaution against this deadly disease. Your life is much too precious to risk.

Source: The National Women's Health Network, "AIDS: What Every Woman Needs to Know"

New York, where the epidemic has been concentrated.

Heterosexual adults, whose rate of HIV contagion is rising faster today than among other groups at risk, also have been slow to heed warnings of the dangers of heterosexual transmission. Almost a third of the 10,630 heterosexuals responding to a national survey of AIDS risk behaviors said they had placed themselves at risk for the disease in the last five years.[11] Risky behaviors include having had sex with two or more partners in the past five years, using injection drugs or having had sex with a "risky partner," one who engaged in the same activities, was HIV-positive, had had a transfusion between 1978 and 1985 or was a hemophiliac who had not been tested for HIV.

If AIDS education is to affect personal behavior, says Elizabeth Glaser, more leadership is needed from Washington. "One person that [we've] needed to hear talk about it is the president of the United States. Short of that or short of the surgeon general being on the airwaves talking about it all the time, it's going to be a very slow process."

Federal Efforts

Federal agencies are reacting, if belatedly, to the rising incidence of AIDS in women. Activists welcomed the CDC's addition of three conditions prevalent among women to its list of opportunistic infections that trigger a diagnosis of AIDS. The change, which followed intense lobbying by women's advocacy groups, is expected to increase the number of AIDS cases reported to the CDC by some 160,000, many of them women. It goes into effect Jan. 1.

Meanwhile, activists are still pressing for further expansion of the list to more accurately reflect the extent of HIV infection among women. One change many are seeking is the inclusion of cervical dysplasia, rather than invasive cervical cancer, which is being added to the list. "Invasive cervical cancer is the last stage of cervical cancer and is treatable only by hysterectomy," says Marion Banzhaf. "No one should have to get invasive cervical cancer. The only people who get it are women who have not had any care."

The revised AIDS definition is expected to help more HIV-infected women gain access to health care in time to receive life-prolonging treatment. "They will have better access to services because providers will be more aware of and attuned to the particular symptomology of women and therefore will pick them up more readily," says Joanna Omi, executive director for HIV at the Health and Human Services Planning Council in New York City. Her organization and planning councils in other urban areas hard hit by HIV help funnel federal money provided under the Ryan White Care Act* to local AIDS programs.

But the new CDC definition will have little immediate effect on the ability of infected women to obtain help from the Social Security Administration. The agency has its own criteria for determining when an HIV-infected person becomes eligible for disability benefits, including ac-

---

*The 1990 Ryan White Care Act, named for the Indiana student whose battle with the disease drew national attention, provides emergency funding to cities where the AIDS epidemic is especially severe.

cess to Medicaid, the health-care program for the poor.

Disability benefits are critical for gaining access to costly medical care for many AIDS sufferers who are unable to work and thus lack access to employer-provided health insurance. But because the Social Security Administration does not recognize several disabling HIV-related conditions in women, many never receive benefits. "Often, by the time a woman is included in the criteria and her Social Security goes through, she's dead," says Catherine Maier.

A year ago, Social Security officials revised their definition of HIV-related illnesses to make it easier for women and children to qualify. But activists say the agency still excludes many women who are effectively disabled by their illness, especially those who have recurrent candidiasis, which is not on the agency's list of AIDS-defining conditions. "I've had women come in with candidiasis that has spread outside the vagina all over their stomach and down their legs to the knees," Maier says. "We're talking about HIV-related yeast infections that do not respond to treatment, that never go away, that make a women's life miserable and break up their families. If the CDC would include this illness, the Social Security Administration couldn't ignore it."

Activists' pressure did prompt the Food and Drug Administration (FDA) to streamline the lengthy drug-testing process in order to rush promising new products to people with HIV. In October, the FDA approved expanded use of d4T, or stavudine, an experimental drug for patients who can't tolerate AZT or ddI, the only approved drugs to delay the onset of AIDS symptoms. In November, the agency also approved the sale of atovaquone (sold under the brand name Mepron) to treat *pneumocystis carinii* pneumonia, one of the most common opportunistic infections in women with AIDS.

Access to Clinical Trials

While lauding the FDA's efforts, activists are pressing the agency to help women gain access to drugs and preventive measures more quickly. The FDA could, for example, more strictly enforce a rule that drug companies conduct reproductive toxicity research on drugs being studied for HIV treatment. If no toxic effects were found, Banzhaf says, the companies would have no excuse for excluding women of reproductive age from clinical trials that could provide treatment for infected women.

Even though most clinical trials have lifted restrictions on non-pregnant women, they still are not readily accessible to many infected women who could benefit from them. "What is beginning to happen is that women are told they should have a gynecologic evaluation, but that they'll have to come back next week and go down the hall and around the corner to the other wing for that," says Kathleen Stoll, director of the National Resource Center on Women and AIDS. "When you're dealing with low-income women who have a hard time finding transportation or locating child care, that doesn't work. They need to have the gynecological evaluation happen on site at the time of the other medical evaluations."

Improving access of women to clinical trials is especially pressing if they are to participate in tests of several new agents approved in recent weeks. Just this month, the National Institute of Allergy and Infectious Diseases expanded clinical tests of two AIDS vaccines to include 320 uninfected men and women at five test sites around the country. The two genetically engineered vaccines are aimed at preventing infection.

The NIH also approved national trials of a new therapeutic vaccine, gp 160, designed to prevent the development of AIDS in people with HIV. The formal approval followed a controversial end run by Congress in

October around the agency's normal scientific-evaluation procedures. The lawmakers added $20 million for testing the vaccine to the Defense Department appropriation bill, following an intense lobbying effort by MicroGeneSys Inc., the Connecticut-based producer of the vaccine.

Another step forward was recently taken by the CDC. Although it will not yield meaningful data for several years, the center has finally undertaken a study of the natural history of HIV in women, similar to a larger study of infected male non-injection drug users the agency began in 1985. It is hoped that the new study, which is expected to begin enrolling 2,500 women in 1993, will reveal new information on gender-specific aspects of the disease.

Bush Administration's Record

AIDS activists have harsh words for the Republican administrations of Ronald Reagan and George Bush, which have occupied the White House since the AIDS epidemic began in 1981. With his vocal support of "family values," President Reagan was accused of ignoring AIDS because it was perceived to be a disease of homosexuals, whose behavior many Reagan supporters condemned as anti-family, as well as perverse and voluntary.

President Bush also has come under fire for allegedly spending too little money and attention on the victims of the disease, whose numbers have doubled since he came to office. Hundreds of activists loudly condemned Bush's record on AIDS spending at demonstrations outside the White House last fall, and Magic Johnson, whom Bush had appointed to the bipartisan National Commission on AIDS, resigned to protest what he called the administration's poor record on AIDS funding.

Bush defended his record on AIDS and the special plight of infected

Continued on p. 1138

At Issue:

Should AIDS-prevention programs for teenagers focus exclusively on sexual abstinence?

DR. WILLIAM ARCHER

Deputy Assistant Secretary for Population Affairs in the Department of Health an Human Services during the Bush administration
***WRITTEN FOR** THE CQ RESEARCHER, DECEMBER 1992.*

*a*dolescents should not be having sex. That's not a moral statement. It's a public health statement. It is our only hope of stopping the current epidemic of sexually transmitted diseases, including AIDS.

Our studies have shown that half of all adolescents have tried sex by age 17. Of those teenagers, 17 percent will have four or more partners before high school graduation.

One in 10 teenagers who experiment with sex at least once will end up pregnant as an adolescent. One in three will acquire a sexually transmitted disease. Not only AIDS, but Hepatitis B, which is deadly; chlamydia, which causes infertility; and human papilloma virus, which leads to cancer.

There is, literally, no way of making sex safe. Condoms break, condoms slip, condoms can legally be sold even if three out of every thousand leak water. Condoms only make sex *safer*. Kids are killing themselves with sex. Why? It's not because they can't help themselves. Kids have had the same hormones rushing through their veins since the days of Samson and Delilah. And though some of them have always given in, they haven't been sleeping around this way until very recently.

They are growing up in an eroticized culture. Sex is everywhere — in the movies, on television, in clothing ads. The whole culture is screaming at them, like Nike, "Just Do It!" Someone has to tell them "Don't." Now, some people will say that if you want to be relevant in kids' lives, you've got to stay current with their culture — they're going to have sex, so give them condoms. I'm saying that when the culture is killing them, then we've got to be counter-cultural.

You might ask, "Why is it the government's business to reduce sex among teenagers?" Even if you and I agree that teenagers shouldn't be having sex — and almost anyone would agree that 12 years old is too young — why should the government interfere in this kind of personal choice?

Because AIDS, chlamydia, human papilloma virus and pregnancy are epidemic among teenagers. And even when used properly, condoms have a proven 18 percent failure rate for teenagers for pregnancy, a 17 percent failure rate in preventing AIDS transmission and a 100 percent failure rate in preventing chlamydia over an extended period of time. There is no way to stop this epidemic except to tell kids that no matter what the kids in movies, in rock groups and in the commercials are doing, they shouldn't have sex.

KAREN HEIN

Associate professor at the Albert Einstein College of Medicine and director of the Adolescent AIDS Program at the Montefiore Medical Center (New York City)
FROM *ISSUES IN SCIENCE AND TECHNOLOGY,* SPRING 1991.

*t*eenagers should be informed about the need to reconsider patterns of sexual behavior. But talking is not enough; adolescents must learn skills related to contraception and to preventing the propagation of sexually transmitted diseases. They must have ready access to condoms. And they should be informed about the availability of voluntary HIV-antibody testing, but only if age-specific programs exist for . . . care of those who are HIV-positive.

Programs for teenagers must work toward these ends while recognizing that a primary goal of adolescence is to develop the kind of sexual attitudes and experiences that shape healthy adult relationships. In our efforts to inform adolescents about HIV/AIDS, we must be careful not to produce a generation of young people who are afraid of intimacy.

Teenagers, just beginning to deal with their own sexuality, are often uncomfortable discussing these subjects with adults. And for some the risks may be great; adolescents who acknowledge same-sex experiences or identify themselves as gay may be cast out of their school or home and become isolated from their peers. But it is impossible to learn safe behavior without talking about risky behavior. Therefore, it is critical that those who would work with teenagers in prevention programs be able to put them at ease, dealing with uncomfortable topics comfortably and providing the most current information in a way teenagers can understand. Unfortunately, it is often true that the adults given responsibility for teaching them — parents, teachers, health-care workers, and people in agencies serving youth — are ill-prepared for the task. . . .

Effective education programs also require appropriate education materials. But federal regulations, which apply to recipients of federal funds, can make creation of such tools difficult. By calling for a special review of AIDS materials to ensure that the language and content is understandable to the general public and not offensive, these regulations are burdensome, time-consuming, and counterproductive. A basic tenet of effective health education is that the language and content be culturally specific and understandable to the target group. If teenagers are to learn about HIV transmission, it must be in terms they understand — that is, explicit.

AIDS and the Law

Since the AIDS epidemic broke out a decade ago, public health authorities have had trouble convincing people that the AIDS virus cannot be transmitted in the same way as influenza or the common cold. Fearful parents have withheld their children from schools attended by a single HIV carrier, and untold numbers of adults have lost their jobs — all because the true risk of HIV infection is not understood.

HIV-positive individuals have filed numerous lawsuits against employers, landlords and others for discrimination. But the number of these suits may fall following enactment last summer of the Americans with Disabilities Act, which prohibits discrimination against all handicapped workers, including those with AIDS. The law requires employers to make "reasonable accommodations" to help disabled workers keep their jobs. In the case of AIDS, that may mean allowing infected workers to keep flexible schedules and take extra time off.†

But people with HIV suffered a potentially crippling legal setback in October, when the U.S. Supreme Court refused to consider a case involving an AIDS patient who lost his health insurance after he revealed that he was infected with the virus. John McGann had worked for the H&H Music Co. in Houston for five years when he learned in 1987 that he had AIDS. After he told his employer and began filing claims for medical care, the company changed health plans. Under the new plan, lifetime benefits for AIDS-related care were capped at $5,000, down from the $1 million provided under the old plan.

McGann, who has since died, sued his employer for discrimination under the 1974 Employee Retirement Income Security Act (ERISA). But he lost because the courts have consistently refused to include health benefits among the workers' rights protected under ERISA. The Supreme Court's refusal to hear the case leaves unresolved the problem of health coverage for victims of this costly and deadly disease.

The legal ramifications of AIDS involve more than protecting infected individuals. They also require HIV-positive people to take special responsibility for their behavior. Because AIDS is a fatal disease, support has grown in recent years for new laws that make the transmission of HIV a crime.

In November, Salvadore Gamberella, 28, an unemployed welder, became the first person to be convicted under Louisiana's five-year-old criminal AIDS law. Under the statute, prosecutors do not have to prove intent to harm the victim but only that the accused knew he was HIV-positive and failed to tell the victim. According to his former girlfriend, Gamberella did not tell her he was HIV-positive before infecting her through sexual contact.††

Twenty-five states now have laws like Louisiana's to deal specifically with AIDS cases. But special laws aren't always necessary to obtain a conviction on criminal charges related to HIV transmission. Also in November, another 28-year-old HIV carrier, Alberto Gonzalez, was sentenced in Oregon to more than nine years in prison following his conviction for attempted murder for knowingly exposing a 15-year-old girl to the AIDS virus. The conviction came under existing criminal statutes. The victim, who testified that she had had unprotected sex with Gonzalez, tested negative for HIV. Two other sex partners of the convicted man tested positive, however, and one has died.

People who infect their sex partners with HIV may be sued for their actions even after the partners' death from AIDS. In November, a New York state judge ruled that the parents of a man who died of AIDS can sue their son's sex partner for allegedly giving him the disease while concealing his own HIV status. This is one of the first cases in which an HIV-positive individual has been accused of spreading the AIDS virus under a wrongful-death law that allows survivors to sue for damages.‡

---

† See Elizabeth Kastor, "When Someone at Work Has AIDS," *The Washington Post*, Nov. 24, 1992.

†† See Adam Nossiter, "Man Is the First Convicted in Louisiana for Putting Partner at Risk of HIV," *The New York Times*, Nov. 28, 1992.

‡ See Wade Lambert and Junda Woo, "Suit Over AIDS Victim's Death Is Allowed," *The Wall Street Journal*, Nov. 18, 1992.

Continued from p. 1136
women during the presidential election campaign by pointing to the creation during his administration of a new Office of Research in Women's Health at NIH to ensure that women's health needs are addressed in research conducted or supported by the agency. He then appointed Mary Fish-er to take Johnson's place on the AIDS commission. Bush also cited his record budget request for $4.9 billion for AIDS programs in the current fiscal year, a claim many AIDS activists dismissed as misleading because, they said, it includes money spent for Medicaid and other programs serving sufferers of diseases other than AIDS. ■

OUTLOOK

Women at Risk

Just as AIDS was considered a gay men's disease during the first decade of the pandemic, it may well become a woman's disease in its second decade. "Assuming that the new cohorts of gay men maintain the safer sex practices of their elders, and that women continue to have a greater biological vulnerability to HIV than men, by the year 2000 more than half of all newly infected adults may be women," reported M.H. Merson, director of the World Health Organization's Global Program on AIDS. "This will also mean even more children born with HIV infection, as well as millions of youngsters escaping infection but becoming AIDS orphans on their mothers' death." [12]

In the United States as well, the proportion of women among new AIDS victims is expected to continue rising. Most worrisome to health officials are sexually active teenage girls, who may find it difficult to get their partners to use condoms. Teenagers are also vulnerable to contagion related to drug use. "Many young people are in danger of being infected because of the crack epidemic," says Maier, who predicts that because crack is a hypersexual drug "the correlation between crack and AIDS is going to explode."

Women who become infected with HIV as teenagers are unlikely to present symptoms until they are well into their 20s, the prime childbearing years. As a result, the number of infected children born each year in the United States is also expected to grow dramatically from the estimated 2,000 of today.

Hopes Pinned on New Administration

Unless an effective vaccine, virucide or other "magic bullet" to eliminate AIDS is found soon — a possibility few researchers expect before the turn of the century — the demand for prevention programs, research and treatment of HIV-infected men, women and children will greatly increase in coming years. President-elect Bill Clinton is being called upon to increase funding for all HIV-related services.

"Clinton has clearly stated that he will be more forthcoming than the past administration on this issue," says Glaser. "My sense is that this is a man of his word and that he is much more concerned about the problem of AIDS and more aware that we are not doing what we need to do."

Near the top of activists' list of policy changes is AIDS education. "During the last four years, the CDC was not allowed to talk about sex or use the word 'condom' in their educational efforts," Glaser says. "The Clinton administration will not only remove those restraints, but it is my understanding that they will demand we talk straight with the kids."

AIDS activists generally support Clinton's campaign promise to reorganize the various federal agencies involved in AIDS research and treatment under a single coordinator. Glaser also advocates the creation of a new position for director of AIDS research, a function now covered by the director of NIAID, Dr. Anthony Fauci. "We need someone whose sole mandate is AIDS," Glaser says, "someone who is not also an institute director."

Beyond the calls for more research and services for HIV-infected Americans, many women's advocates say the AIDS epidemic challenges men and women to find ways to express intimacy that pose fewer risks of infection to themselves and their partners. "When women get together and talk about safer sex, they often come up with creative ideas," says Marion Banzhaf. "It may mean changing your concept of what sex means from just intercourse to the intimate exchange of sexual pleasure between two people who care about each other. We talk about the use of 'outercourse,' providing concrete ideas for women to suggest different sexual things that can satisfy their partner and themselves while still not putting them at risk.

Banzhaf and other women's health advocates emphasize the need to develop a virucide, such as an antiviral cream or foam, against HIV infection.

With such a product, women and teenagers could protect themselves without even informing, much less getting cooperation from, their partners, as they must with condom use.

While supporting research into all potential weapons in the fight against HIV, many activists identify equality between the sexes as the ultimate defense against the virus. "If we can just change things so that men and women have equal rights in society," says Harvard's Jonathan Mann, "we will have the key to eliminating the pandemic. Then if a woman thinks her husband is infected and she doesn't want to sleep with him, she can say no without suffering physical, legal or economic death." ∎

Notes

[1] Joseph A. Catania *et. al.*, "Prevalence of AIDS-Related Risk Factors and Condom Use in the United States," *Science*, Nov. 13, 1992, pp. 1104-1105.

[2] *Ibid.*, p. 1105.

[3] Quoted by Malcolm Gladwell, "Pediatric AIDS Studies at Adults' Expense," *The Washington Post*, Oct. 5, 1992, p. A1.

[4] Richard Preston, "Crisis in the Hot Zone," *The New Yorker*, Oct. 26, 1992, p. 62.

[5] Gena Corea, *The Invisible Epidemic: The Story of Women and AIDS* (1992).

[6] Information on AIDS-defining diseases comes from Scott Wilson and Brenda Lein, "HIV Disease in Women," *Treatment Issues* (a newsletter of experimental AIDS therapies published by the Gay Men's Health Crisis in New York City), pp. 1-6.

[7] See Jeannette R. Ickovics and Judith Rodin, "Women and AIDS in the United States: Epidemiology, Natural History, and Mediating Mechanisms," *Health Psychology*, No. 1, pp. 6-7.

[8] "Women and the Amsterdam Conference," *WORLD* (Women Organized to Respond to Life-threatening Diseases), November 1992, p. 4.

[9] The House Select Committee on Children, Youth and Families issued its findings April 12, 1992.

[10] Jeffrey A. Kelly, "Acquired Immonodeficiency Syndrome — Human Immodeficiency Virus Risk Behavior Among Gay Men in Small Cities," *Archives of Internal Medicine*, November 1992.

[11] Catania *et. al.*, *op. cit.*, pp. 1101-1106.

[12] Merson presented his report, "Longitudinal Trends in the Epidemic," on July 20, 1992, to the Eighth International Conference on AIDS, held in Amsterdam.

Bibliography

Selected Sources Used

Books

Corea, Gena, *The Invisible Epidemic: The Story of Women and AIDS*, HarperCollins, 1992.

Long considered a gay man's disease, AIDS actually was observed in women from the start of the epidemic in the United States. The author offers proof that women with AIDS have been largely ignored in the diagnosis, research, treatment and provision of social services.

Fumento, Michael, *The Myth of Heterosexual AIDS*, Basic Books, 1990.

The controversial theory detailed in this book is that the vast majority of heterosexual Americans run a much smaller risk of contracting the AIDS virus than they are led to believe. Regardless of this notion's validity, the book shows how media coverage shapes public perceptions of the scope of the disease.

Mann, Jonathan, Daniel J.M. Tarantola and Thomas W. Netter, eds., *AIDS in the World*, Harvard University Press, 1992.

This detailed analysis of the spread of AIDS throughout the world identifies a common denominator among the many factors that favor the spread of this resilient virus: discrimination against the poor, and against women in particular.

Articles

Armstrong, Jill, "Socioeconomic Implications of AIDS in Developing Countries," *Finance & Development*, December 1991.

The AIDS epidemic has profoundly undermined social conditions in much of sub-Saharan Africa, where it apparently first appeared. In some areas, the rate of infection has reached 10 percent of the population, and AIDS deaths among children have wiped out gains made in pediatric health over recent decades. Deaths among adults are leaving more children orphans and the elderly without their sole source of support.

Foreman, Christopher H., Jr., "The Fast Track: Federal Agencies and the Political Demand for AIDS Drugs," *The Brookings Review*, spring 1991.

The Food and Drug Administration (FDA) traditionally has tried to protect the public from toxic new drugs by requiring extensive — and time-consuming — research into new products. The AIDS epidemic has spurred changes to speed up that process. Although changes have been made since this article appeared, it provides useful information on the drug-approval process.

Michaels, D., and C. Levine, "Estimates of the Number of Motherless Youth Orphaned by AIDS in the United States," *Journal of the American Medical Association*, Dec. 23-30, 1992, pp. 3456-3461.

A new study projects that by 2000 the number of children under 18 who will have lost their mothers to AIDS since the start of the epidemic could reach 125,000. As a result, the United States could face a "social catastrophe."

"Sex in the Age of AIDS," *Mirabella*, July and August 1992.

This two-part story begins with a conversation between Marcelle Clements, a novelist and essayist, and seven single women who talk about ways they are changing their behavior to protect themselves from HIV infection. The second article features the advice of an AIDS researcher and a feminist on steps women should take to ward off the virus.

"Teens and AIDS," *Newsweek*, Aug. 3, 1992.

This cover story describes the impact HIV infection is having among one of the most vulnerable groups at risk for AIDS. Already struggling with issues of sexuality and peer pressure, teenagers need an unusual degree of self-assertiveness to protect themselves from infection.

Reports and Studies

Center for Women Policy Studies, *The Guide to Resources on Women and AIDS*, September 1991.

This directory of more than 300 local organizations that provide services to women affected by HIV also includes a lengthy analysis of the course and treatment of AIDS in women and the impact of policy decisions on access by infected women to treatment and disability benefits.

Centers for Disease Control, *HIV/AIDS Prevention Fact Book 1992*, March 1992.

The CDC plays a pivotal role in efforts to prevent HIV infection and reduce the incidence of illness and death from the virus. Almost a third of the center's $1.5 billion budget now goes to HIV programs.

New York City Task Force on Women & AIDS, *Policy Document*, Oct. 10, 1991.

A group of doctors, nurses, social workers and others involved in helping women with HIV in one of the country's hardest-hit areas outlines AIDS issues from prevention to treatment and the need for social services that affect women with the virus. The proposals focus on the needs of special groups, including victims of abuse, pregnant women and the homeless.

The Next Step

Additional Articles from Current Periodicals from EBSCO Publishing's Database

Epidemiology

"AIDS in women — United States," *Journal of the American Medical Association,* **Jan. 2, 1991, p. 23.**

Provides statistics on the increasing number of women with the acquired immunodeficiency syndrome (AIDS) in the United States. Includes an editorial note from the Centers for Disease Control.

"Infection rate soaring for women," *USA Today,* **October 1991, p. 2.**

Observes that AIDS is infecting females at a higher rate than males. Projected statistics for females with AIDS by the year 2000; information on AIDS and women as reported in *Reproductive Health Quarterly*; tips on prevention.

"Research notes: Review highlights women's prospects of getting AIDS," *The Chronicle of Higher Education,* **Dec. 18, 1991, p. A9.**

Considers an article in *Health Psychology* which states women are 12 times as likely as men to be infected with the AIDS virus during heterosexual intercourse and they die 20 percent sooner than men when they contract the disease. Research by Judith Rodin and Jeannette Ickovics (Yale University); focusing on women's responses to treatment for AIDS; key findings of the research report.

"Study concludes women less likely to pass AIDS virus to men," *Jet,* **May 4, 1992, p. 32.**

Summarizes a report by the European Center for the Epidemiological monitoring of AIDS in France. It finds that men with the AIDS virus are nearly twice as likely to infect their female partners as the reverse.

"Women with AIDS," *American Journal of Medicine,* **March 1992, p. 3.**

Reports on a study that presents a comprehensive and alarming picture with regard to the prevalence and risk factors for development of AIDS in women in the United States. How women were infected; women are much more likely to be infected by men than vice versa; the need for more public education.

"Young women, at growing risk for AIDS, ignoring prevention advice," *Single Parent,* **January/February 1991, p. 41.**

Focuses on adolescent women and the increased risk of AIDS to them. Focus on inner-city youth; surprising findings; teens not modifying their behavior.

Brown, P., "Southern Europe's women face greater AIDS risk." *New Scientist,* **April 11, 1992, p. 7.**

Highlights the first Europe-wide report on AIDS and HIV since 1988. Shows Southern European women face a greater risk of contracting AIDS; reasons for the high level of infection in these countries; report prepared by WHO-EC Collaborating Centre on AIDS.

Byron, P., "Feds to study women with HIV," *Ms.,* **July/August 1991, p. 95.**

Reports that the first large-scale study of women infected with HIV will focus on pregnant women of color. The National Institute of Allergy and Infectious Diseases is sponsoring the study. ACTG protocol 076; criticism from AIDS activists; an obscure federal requirement that the father of the fetus must give his approval for the woman to participate.

Capell, F.J., D.J. Vugia, et al., "Distribution of HIV Type 1 infection in childbearing women in California," *American Journal of Public Health,* **February 1992, p. 254.**

Reports that the incidence of acquired immunodeficiency syndrome (AIDS) is increasing among California heterosexuals and children. Results of a study that assesses human immunodeficiency virus (HIV)-1 infection in childbearing women; methods; discussion.

Carpenter, C. & K.H. Mayer, "Women and AIDS," *Scientific American,* **March 1992, p. 118.**

Reports that although most of the Americans living with acquired immune deficiency syndrome (AIDS) and the virus that causes it are male, the epidemic is rapidly spreading among women. States that as is the case with several other sexually transmitted diseases, women are more susceptible to acquiring human immunodeficiency virus (HIV) from an infected male partner than the other way around.

Gillespie, M.A., "HIV: The global crisis," *Ms.,* **January/February 1991, p. 17.**

Examines the impact of the human immunodeficiency virus (HIV) and acquired immune deficiency syndrome (AIDS) on poor Third World Women, particularly those in sub-Saharan Africa. Statistics; male behavior and social attitudes that put women and children at risk; prostitution, rape, poverty; women's poor reproductive health; pregnancy and HIV; future outlook. INSET: How HIV spreads.

Lamp, G., "AIDS ad campaign aimed at rural America, teens and women," *Farm Journal,* **May 1992, p. 43.**

Reports on the new "America Responds to AIDS" ad campaign being aimed at small-town America, women, and sexually active young people. Comments on escalating magnitude of AIDS epidemic; criticisms of new ad campaign.

Lever, J. & P. Schwartz, "How often do men get AIDS from women?" *Glamour,* **January 1992, p. 24.**

Summarizes a study by University of California researchers on AIDS transmission from women to men. It shows that less than 2 percent of the men studied were infected by women.

Nelson, S., "Talking smart, acting stupid about AIDS," *Glamour,* **February 1992, p. 174.**

Looks at how even smart women are making foolish choices when it comes to AIDS prevention. Discusses reasons for the poor choices and what women must do to protect themselves from AIDS. INSETS: Can you ever stop using condoms? (after HIV exposure); who uses condoms, who doesn't? (survey results).

Shariff, S., "The hidden toll," *Maclean's,* **May 13, 1991, p. 56.**

Examines the reasons why more Canadian and U.S. women are becoming victims of AIDS. Alarming increase in the U.S.; possibility that the human immunodeficiency virus (HIV) triggers different symptoms in women than in men; expert's comments; support groups organized around the needs of homosexual men rather than the needs of women; transmission to unborn children; heterosexual contact; drug use.

Turvett, B., "Women and AIDS: The new danger," *McCall's,* **June 1992, p. 40.**

Looks at the risks heterosexual women face in contracting HIV, the AIDS virus. How most women get AIDS; assessing a partner's risk of having AIDS; how men become infected with AIDS; safety measures. INSET: Your chance of being infected.

Personal narratives

Aborn, S., "Love and sorrow," *Ladies' Home Journal,* **June 1992, p. 118.**

Presents excerpts from letters of *Ladies' Home Journal* readers whose own lives, or those of spouses, parents, children or other close relatives have been touched by AIDS. INSET: What every woman must know about AIDS.

Hilts, P.J., "Woman with AIDS seizes stage, asking Bush to help ease stigma," *The New York Times,* **Aug. 4, 1991, p. 1.**

Discusses a letter sent to President Bush by Belinda Mason, a former reporter from a local Kentucky newspaper who is dying of AIDS, as a plea for the president to use his influence to keep people with AIDS from being stigmatized.

How she acquired AIDS; refuses to be bitter; life isn't fair.

Pregnancy & motherhood

"Dan Quayle, the lawyers and the AIDS babies," *Forbes,* **Oct. 28, 1991, p. 194.**

Commentary. Presents the view of Peter Huber concerning a report in the *New Scientist* over the controversial trial of an AIDS vaccine for pregnant women, which is in limbo due to vaccine makers' fears of being sued if any of the babies born to women in the trial suffer from birth defects. No sane insurer is going to mess with vaccines for HIV-positive pregnant women; The American Bar Association's attempt to involve Vice President Dan Quayle; liability; the trek to Congress for help.

"HIV testing and pregnancy: In search of a national policy," *American Journal of Medicine,* **Oct. 1991, p. 1.**

Discusses the issue of HIV testing of pregnant women and newborns in the United States. Working group established by a consortium consisting of the Johns Hopkins School of Hygiene and Public Health and the Johns Hopkins Hospital; statistics on AIDS cases in American women; vertical transmission; mandatory testing; directive counseling for those women who are HIV positive and pregnant or considering a pregnancy; recommendation for voluntary rather than mandatory testing.

Abrams, E.J. & M.C. Heagarty, "Caring for HIV-infected women and children," *New England Journal of Medicine,* **March 26, 1992, p. 887.**

Editorial. Comments on an article by Sperling, *et al,* in the March 26, 1992 issue of *The New England Journal of Medicine,* that describes a survey of a small number of women who took zidovudine during some part of pregnancy. Hope of improved therapy for HIV-infected women and children; more.

Aldhous, P., "Blazing an ethical trail," *Nature,* **Sept. 5, 1991, p. 4.**

Discusses a clinical trial that plans to examine whether the AIDS drug zidovudine (AZT) can reduce the transmission of human immunodeficiency virus (HIV) from pregnant women to their fetuses. Study has broken new ethical ground; intense debate between pediatricians and AIDS researchers; National Institute of Allergy and Infectious Diseases (NIAID) coordinated the study.

Navarro, M., "Women with AIDS virus: Hard choices on motherhood," *The New York Times,* **July 23, 1991, p. A1.**

Comments on the heartwrenching choice that must be made by pregnant women infected with the HIV virus, which causes AIDS. Beyond the immediate risk, having a child poses other difficult questions: Who would care for the child if the mother falls ill or dies? Could the mother cope if the child gets sick or dies? Would the pregnancy make the mother sicker or shorten her life?

Sperling, R. S., P. Stratton, et al., "A survey of zidovudine use in pregnant women with human immunodeficiency virus infection," *New England Journal of Medicine,* March 26, 1992, p. 857.

Looks at the safety and toxicity of zidovudine treatment for pregnant women and their fetuses. Information reported by pediatricians and obstetricians at the AIDS Clinical Trials Units; methods; results; conclusion; duration of maternal zidovudine therapy and associated anemia in newborns; adverse outcomes in the cases of newborns whose mothers received zidovudine during pregnancy.

Teltsch, K., "Helping AIDS mothers on custody of children," *The New York Times,* Aug. 27, 1991, p. B1.

Discusses the project of the Montefiore Hospital's division of Legal and Ethical Issues. The project was founded to deal with the complicated and slow-moving legal system and laws that make it difficult for mothers to designate guardianship before their deaths without giving up custody of their children while they are alive. It is widely regarded as a leader in working with women with AIDS.

Wheeler, D.L., "Research notes: AIDS drug AZT is said not to harm pregnant women or fetuses," *The Chronicle of Higher Education,* April 1, 1992, p. A11.

Considers an article in *The New England Journal of Medicine* which found the drug most frequently used to treat AIDS does not appear to harm pregnant women or their fetuses. Research by Rhoda S. Sperling (Mount Sinai Medical Center) with colleagues from 10 other academic medical centers; National Institute of Child Health and Human Development; study of women receiving zidovudine, or AZT, during pregnancy; comments on the research; details of the infants.

Research

"Safer sex," *Health & Fitness Magazine,* January 1992, p. 14.

Advises women to stay aware and avoid AIDS. Testing; how long it takes for results; no risk; high risk; low risk; HIV groups and helplines.

Bruno, K., "AIDS update," *American Health,* June 1992, p. 10.

Reports on news related to AIDS and HIV. Centers for Disease Control (CDC) launched an AIDS education campaign targeted at teenagers, women and rural Americans; team of Japanese and American researchers have developed experimental drug for Kaposi's sarcoma; volunteers needed for a two-year nationwide clinical trial of AZT, and experimental drugs didanosine (DDI) and dideoxycytidine (DDC); more.

Forney, M. A., J. A. Inciardi, et al., "Exchanging sex for crack-cocaine: A comparison of women from rural and urban communities," *Journal of Community Health,* April 1992, p. 73.

Reports the findings of a comparative study of 60 female crack-cocaine users to determine their drug using and sexual practices and their knowledge about AIDS and HIV transmission. Differences in rates of syphilis and HIV infection between rural and urban areas; study methods; study of women in rural southeast Georgia and Miami, Fla.

Gregory, D. & V. Starr, "Black women and aids," *Essence,* April 1992, p. 36.

Observes that 60 percent of women of color do not believe they are at risk for contracting HIV. Statistics from a poll on the subject; why such lack of knowledge could be fatal; overview of HIV-related symptoms that are specific to women; proposed steps to better inform black women about AIDS.

Lever, J. & P. Schwartz, "Signs of AIDS in women," *Glamour,* January 1992, p. 24.

Reports that the Centers for Disease Control (CDC) is expanding its current definition of AIDS to include a sharp decline in immune system cells in women. The checklist currently has 23 symptoms.

Remez, L., "Concern over AIDS changed sexual behavior among one third of unmarried U.S. women," *Family Planning Perspectives,* September/October 1991, p. 234.

Declares that nearly one-third of sexually experienced, unmarried American women have changed their sexual behavior in response to the threat of AIDS; the most common change is limiting their number of sexual partners to one man. Addition of AIDS module to Cycle IV; low risk for married women; misinformation varied greatly by race and income; questions asked to the respondents; details.

Wiener, L.S., "Women and human immunodeficiency virus: A historical and personal psychosocial perspective," *Social Work,* September 1991, p. 375.

Details how little attention has been paid in clinical practice, research or public discussion to women in the AIDS epidemic. The portrayal in the media of how the disease affects men and their families; sexism, racism and classism; women as caregivers; confronting stigmatization; the potential risk faced by an estimated 500,000 intravenous drug-using women in the United States.

Back Issues

Great Research on Current Issues Starts Right Here... Recent topics covered by The CQ Researcher are listed below. Before May 1991, reports were published under the name of Editorial Research Reports.

JUNE 1991
Children and Divorce
Teenage Suicide
Endangered Species
Europe 1992

JULY 1991
Teenagers and Abortion
Soviet Republics Rebel
Mexico's Emergence
Athletes and Drugs

AUGUST 1991
Sexual Harassment
Fetal Tissue Research
Oil Imports
The Palestinians

SEPTEMBER 1991
Police Brutality
Advertising Under Attack
Saving the Forests
Foster Care Crisis

OCTOBER 1991
Pay-Per-View TV
Youth Gangs
Gene Therapy
World Hunger

NOVEMBER 1991
Fast-Food Shake-Up
The Greening of Eastern Europe
Business' Role in Education
Cuba In Crisis

DECEMBER 1991
Retiree Health Benefits
Asian Americans
The Obscenity Debate
The Disabilities Act

JANUARY 1992
Term Limits
Oil Spills
Hunting Controversy
Alternative Medicine

FEBRUARY 1992
Threatened Coastlines
New Era in Asia
Assisted Suicide
Jobs in the '90s

MARCH 1992
Women and Sports
Underage Drinking
Garbage Crisis
Mafia Crackdown

APRIL 1992
Ozone Depletion
Welfare Reform
Politicians and Privacy
Illegal Immigration

MAY 1992
Native Americans
Jobs vs. Environment
Too Many Lawsuits?
Fairness in Salaries

JUNE 1992
Nuclear Proliferation
Food Irradiation
Lead Poisoning
Hard Times for Libraries

JULY 1992
Alternative Energy
Prescription Drug Prices
Alzheimer's Disease
Infant Mortality

AUGUST 1992
The Homeless
Work, Family and Stress
NATO's Changing Role
Marine Mammals vs. Fish

SEPTEMBER 1992
Domestic Partners
Violence in Schools
Public Broadcasting
Women in the Military

OCTOBER 1992
Depression
U.S. Auto Industry
Youth Apprenticeships
Hispanic Americans

NOVEMBER 1992
Physical Fitness
Privatization
Paying for College
U.S. Policy in Asia

DECEMBER 1992
Crackdown on Smoking
The New CIA
Eating Disorders

Back issues are available for $4.00 (subscribers) or $7.00 (non-subscribers). Quantity discounts apply to orders over ten. To order, call Congressional Quarterly 1-800-432-2250.

Binders are available for $15.00. To order call 1-800-638-1710.

Future Topics

▶ *Hate Crimes*

▶ *Child Sexual Abuse*

▶ *Nuclear Fusion*

The CQ Researcher

Subject-Title Index

January 1991-December 1992

NOTE: Weekly CQ Researcher reports are indexed by title under boldface subject headings. Titles are followed by the date of the report and the number of the first page. Page numbers followed by asterisks refer to sidebars or the "At Issue" pro/con feature. Issues dated before May 10, 1991 were published under the name of Editorial Research Reports.